Neal

Best to

Oxford American Dictionary

Success in

Cost Accounting

Oxford American Dictionary

EUGENE EHRLICH
STUART BERG FLEXNER · GORTON CARRUTH
JOYCE M. HAWKINS

AVON
PUBLISHERS OF BARD, CAMELOT AND DISCUS BOOKS

AVON BOOKS
A division of
The Hearst Corporation
959 Eighth Avenue
New York, New York 10019

Copyright © 1980 by Oxford University Press, Inc.
Based on THE OXFORD PAPERBACK DICTIONARY
Copyright © 1979 Oxford University Press
Published by arrangement with Oxford University Press, Inc.
Library of Congress Catalog Card Number: 80-16510
ISBN: 0-380-51052-9

First Avon Printing, October, 1980

AVON TRADEMARK REG. U.S. PAT. OFF. AND IN
OTHER COUNTRIES, MARCA REGISTRADA, HECHO EN
U.S.A.

Printed in the U.S.A.

Preface

This new member of the Oxford family of dictionaries has been prepared especially for those who need a compact, up-to-date guide to American English. It contains words and phrases likely to be met in reading and everyday life, including a number of slang, informal, and technical words and phrases. Names of states of the United States are included, as well as state capitals, terms used to designate the people of each state, and names of the provinces of Canada. Names of the countries of the world, including those not yet well known, are also given, as are names of the capital cities and the terms used to designate the people of each country.

We take this opportunity to express our gratitude to members of the Oxford Dictionary Department of the Oxford University Press for assistance of various kinds, particularly to Dr. John B. Sykes, Editor of the *Concise Oxford Dictionary*, Sixth Edition, and to Dr. Robert Burchfield, Chief Editor of the Oxford English dictionaries. We are grateful as well to members of the staff of Oxford University Press in New York, most particularly to Marjorie Mueller, Janice Lorimer, and Cecelia Carollo, for help in all stages of our work.

We wish also to express our gratitude to the many members of The Hudson Group dictionary staff who worked on the *Oxford American Dictionary*. In particular we wish to thank senior staff members: Ernest S. Hildebrand, Jr., Margaret Huffman, Felice Levy, Lawrence T. Lorimer, and Gloria Solomon; associate staff members: Pamela Dupuis, Mary Egner, Richard Ehrlich, Raymond V. Hand, Jr., Joan Lizzio, David H. Scott, and Katherine G. Scott; and assistant staff members: Lee Jayne Ackerman, Christopher Carruth, Hayden Carruth, Cynthia Crippen, Peggy Daly, Patricia Farewell, Sandi Frank, Mary Mattimore, Sheila McCaffrey, and Mary Racette.

Pleasantville, New York   E.E., S.B.F., G.C., and J.M.H.
June 1980

Introduction

Spelling

Some words have two or more acceptable spellings in common use, but few variant spellings are given in this dictionary. The aim is not to dictate the use of a particular spelling but to offer a standard form to those who seek one. When two spellings are equally common, the preferred one is given first.

Many spellings commonly used in Canada, such as *centre, cheque, colour,* and *programme,* are not included in this dictionary.

Syllabication

Entry words of more than one syllable are shown with syllables separated by a center dot:

fac·sim·i·le

The center dots show the possible division of a word in writing, typing, or printing. Entry words that are normally hyphenated do not have a center dot where the hyphen occurs. A stress mark appears in place of a center dot after a stressed syllable in a word listed within an entry when its pronunciation clearly resembles that of the word at the head of that entry:

ice′skat·er *n.*

Word Forms

Plurals of nouns, comparatives in *-er* and superlatives in *-est* of adjectives and adverbs, and inflected forms of verbs are given when they are irregular or when there might be uncertainty about the spelling. Where only two verb forms are given:

ad·mit (ad-mit) *v.* **(ad·mit·ted, ad·mit·ting)**

the first form is both the past tense (he *admitted* it) and the past participle (it was *admitted*). When three forms are given:

come (kum) *v.* **(came, come, com·ing)**
freeze (freez) *v.* **(froze, fro·zen, freez·ing)**

the first is the past tense (he *came;* it *froze*) and the second is the past participle (he had *come;* it had *frozen*).

For certain inflected verb forms, such as *traveled* and *traveling,* some newspapers, journals, and books will use *travelled* and *travelling.* Such variant spellings are not given here.

When an entry word, such as **la·bel** (lay-bĕl) *n.,* occurs unchanged as a second part of speech, such as **label** *v.,* the word is given the second or subsequent times without pronunciation or stress.

Symbols

The symbol ▷ introduces usage notes, comments on the meanings of words that are often confused (such as *gourmand* and *gourmet*), grammatical points (such as whether *data* and *media* are singular or plural), and information about the origins of words and phrases (such as *fifth column* and *sour grapes*). The symbol ▷ is also used to indicate that an entry is to be treated as a foreign word:

ibid. *abbr.* ibidem, = in the same book or passage
etc. ▷ Latin.

The symbol ☐ introduces phrases employing the entry word (such as *gain ground* and *gain time* after the definition of *gain*).

Usage Labels

Certain entries in this dictionary carry usage labels. One of these labels, *contemptuous,* indicates that use of the entry word implies contempt. Where an entry word (or one of its meanings) is labeled *informal,* the word (or the word in one of its meanings) is used in everyday speech but should not be used when speaking or writing formally.

slea·zy (slee-zee) *adj.* **(-zi·er, -zi·est)** *(informal)*
dirty and slovenly.

The label *old use* indicates that the entry word (or one of its meanings) is no longer appropriate in current speech or writing. The label *slang* indicates that the entry word (or one of its meanings) is to be avoided except in extremely informal circumstances.

Proprietary Names

Entries known to be trademarks or proprietary names are so designated in this dictionary. The presence or absence of such designations should not be regarded as affecting the validity of any trademark or proprietary name.

Pronunciation

Pronunciation is shown in parentheses just after the entry word. Syllables are separated by hyphens in pronunciations, and syllables spoken with the most stress are shown in boldface type:

cease·less (sees-lis) *adj.*
cloak-and-dag·ger (klohk-ăn-dag-ĕr)

Only one pronunciation is generally given. When two pronunciations are equally common, the preferred one is given first:

ha·rass (hă-rass, har-ăs) *v.*

Only the stress is shown for a word listed within an entry when its pronunciation closely resembles that of the word at the head of the entry. In such cases syllables are separated by center dots, and the stressed syllable is followed by a stress mark:

com′pe·tent·ly *adv.*

Words of one syllable are shown unstressed:

vie (vɪ)

Pronunciation Key

a	*as in*	act, bat, marry	ng	*as in*	bring, singer, thank
ă	*as in*	ago, suitable, metal	o	*as in*	odd, box, hot
ah	*as in*	father, calm	ŏ	*as in*	official, lemon, ardor
ahr	*as in*	arm, cart, bar	oh	*as in*	oat, bone, sew
air	*as in*	air, dare, scary	ohr	*as in*	board, four, hoarse, adore
aw	*as in*	all, walk, saw	oi	*as in*	oil, join, toy
ay	*as in*	age, came, say	oo	*as in*	ooze, soon, too, rule
b	*as in*	boy, habit, rib	oor	*as in*	poor, tour, sure
ch	*as in*	chin, teacher, beach	or	*as in*	bored, for, horse, adorn
d	*as in*	dog, ladder, head	ow	*as in*	out, mouse, now
e	*as in*	egg, bed, merry	p	*as in*	pin, caper, cap
ĕ	*as in*	taken, nickel, lawyer	r	*as in*	red, carry, near
ee	*as in*	eat, meat, see, key	s	*as in*	sit, lesson, nice, cellar
eer	*as in*	ear, beer, tier	sh	*as in*	she, ashen, rush
f	*as in*	fat, effort, puff	t	*as in*	top, butter, hit
g	*as in*	get, wagon, big	th	*as in*	thin, method, path
h	*as in*	hat, ahead	th	*as in*	this, mother, breathe
hw	*as in*	wheat, nowhere	u	*as in*	up, cut, come
i	*as in*	if, give, mirror	ŭ	*as in*	suppose, circus, feature
ĭ	*as in*	pencil, credible	ur	*as in*	her, fir, burn, hurry
ɪ	*as in*	ice, bite, fire, spy	uu	*as in*	book, full, woman
j	*as in*	jam, magic, edge	v	*as in*	van, river, give
k	*as in*	king, token, back	w	*as in*	will, awoke, quick
l	*as in*	leg, alley, tell	y	*as in*	yes, you
m	*as in*	me, common, him	z	*as in*	zebra, lazy, tease
n	*as in*	no, manner, tan	zh	*as in*	vision, pleasure

Abbreviations

For the reader's convenience, few abbreviations are used in this dictionary. The following abbreviations are used throughout:

abbr.	abbreviation	*n. fem.*	feminine noun
adj.	adjective	*n. pl.*	plural noun
adv.	adverb	*n. sing.*	singular noun
comb. form	combining form	*pl.*	plural
conj.	conjunction	*poss.*	possessive
fem.	feminine	*pr.*	pronounced
interj.	interjection	*prep.*	preposition
n.	noun	*v.*	verb

Abbreviations in general use (such as ft., R.C.Ch., and etc.) are defined in the dictionary itself.

Publisher's Note
From OED to OAD

To trace the ancestry of this latest Oxford dictionary, one must go back to a little town in southeast Scotland where James Murray was born on February 7, 1837. The son and grandson of tailors, he worked first as a schoolteacher and bank clerk before going on to become one of the greatest lexicographers of all time, the chief editor of the most famous of all dictionaries.

Murray demonstrated a remarkable mind from his earliest days, including an extraordinary capacity for learning languages. He knew the English alphabet by the age of eighteen months, and by the time he was seven he had begun, by comparing various editions of the Bible, to learn Greek, Latin, Hebrew, and Chinese. His insatiable hunger for knowledge led him to lifetime interests in geology and botany, and he identified, classified, and analyzed similarities and differences in rocks and plants with passionate exactitude. He simply never stopped learning, as he described in a letter to his son:

> I employed all my leisure time . . . in learning everything that I could, learning as far as I could something about everything that I did not know, while also trying to learn everything that could be known about some things. . . .

Murray became a schoolteacher in 1854, when he was seventeen. From 1870 until 1885 he taught at Mill Hill School, near London. During this time he gained a reputation as a natural scientist and also became a leading scholar of philology, publishing pioneering papers on English dialects and on comparative and historical philology. He received an honorary LL.D from Edinburgh in 1874, entitling him to wear a cap and gown, which became his daily dress for the rest of his life. He also received honorary degrees from Cape Town, Dublin, and numerous other universities, including Oxford.

In 1857 the English Philological Society had come to a decision that was to prove fateful for Murray. The Society decided that all existing English dictionaries were incomplete and deficient and that the entire English language from Anglo-Saxon times onward must be reexamined. Using volunteer readers, the Society then plunged headlong into an erratic, often frenetic, twenty-two-year period of scouring ancient manuscripts as well as books and other publications from all periods. It amassed a somewhat disorganized collection of 4x6 inch slips, weighing almost two tons, on each of which were recorded one word and a citation. In time the Society, realizing that it was better suited to collecting material than to organizing and editing a dictionary, initiated negotiations with the Oxford University Press to take over the ever expanding, ever more complex project.

In 1878 Murray became president of the Philological Society and the following year, with much trepidation, signed a contract for the Society with the Delegates of the Oxford University Press to compile and edit a dictionary, then called *A New English Dictionary on Historical Principles.* The agreement was for a four-volume, 6400-page work to be completed in ten years, in 1889. It had been estimated that the editorial costs would be £6500. Murray soon came to regard the vast treasure of slips collected over the twenty-two-year period as only the nucleus of the work to come. He first had a Scriptorium build for him to work in and to house the citation files and then set about recruiting some 1300 readers throughout the English-speaking world to search out new words and citations systematically. Francis March, then one of America's leading philologists and historical grammarians, was chosen to direct the American readers. Other Americans, such as Fitzedward Hall, who had spent sixteen years teaching Sanskrit and English in India before moving to London and taking a professorship at King's College, were also major contributors. Thus, almost from the start, American sources have been included in the Oxford citation files, and American scholars have contributed their experience and knowledge.

Murray's dedication to the Dictionary was equaled only by his desire for perfection. He often labored eighty to ninety hours a week, initially with only a handful of helpers, which included members of his family. Before long more than a thousand citation slips were arriving daily at the Scriptorium. Moreover, he sent out each day between thirty and forty of his own handwritten letters to contributors and specialists, asking for specific citations, verification, advice, and additional research. He wrote many letters of encouragement and thanks to contributors, inquiring about their health and, eventually, as various sections of the Dictionary began to appear, apologizing to some for not including all their citations in the published work. This taxing correspondence was in addition to his own research on each entry of the Dictionary, the writing of definitions and, later, the editing, proofreading, and rewriting of the typeset galleys. The last was no small task, as his have the reputation of being the most heavily corrected proofs ever known. Some of the corrections derived from the citations and additional research that continued to pour in after entries were completed, but many others from Murray's insistence that not until he saw material in print could he determine the correct order of the definitions and the best choice of citations.

In 1884 the first 352 pages of the Dictionary, **A-Ant,** were published: half the number of years scheduled for the entire work had yielded the first half of the letter **A.** The Delegates of the Press felt deep concern over the slow progress and made their concern known to Murray. It was agreed that the work might be speeded by appointing additional editors and moving the Dictionary staff to the vicinity of the Press. In 1885, therefore, Murray relinquished his teaching position at Mill Hill School and moved, with his family and his files, to Oxford.

In Murray's garden at Sunnyside, on Banbury Road in Oxford, a new Scriptorium was built; it had to be sunk rather deep in the ground in order to preserve his next-door neighbor's view. The University provided Murray with a staff of eight assistants and asked him to finish the project at the rate of 704 pages a year. In

1887 Henry Bradley was appointed as a second editor with his own staff of assistants. Although **Anta-Battening** was published in 1885, **Battenlie-Bozzom** in 1887, and the final section of **B** in 1888, the actual rate of accomplishment at Oxford did not increase noticeably. The first nine years had produced only the first volume of a work that was ultimately to consist of twelve volumes.

The years of hard work went on. By the last half of the 1890s, the almost yearly crises and recriminations over the time spent on the Dictionary came to an end. By then it was realized that it was not Murray and his staff who were causing the delay but the complexities and perversities of the English language.

William Craigie, a Scotsman like Murray, joined the Dictionary team in 1897 and worked under Murray for four years before becoming a full editor and assuming responsibility for the letter **Q**. In 1914 C. T. Onions, who had been an assistant since 1895, became a full editor, and his article on **super-** and its compounds, rivaling Bradley's 23-page article on **set** and proclaimed a masterpiece, was to be the longest article in the Dictionary. Murray recognized the brilliance of Bradley and Craigie and accepted the two men, yet he was never convinced that anyone else had his complete dedication to the work or his knack of writing definitions. With eighteen assistants, Bradley, Craigie, Onions, and Murray together completed anywhere from fifteen to fifty final pages a month. Murray usually produced two or three times as many pages as the others, whose time was limited by teaching and other editing tasks.

In 1897 the Vice-Chancellor of Oxford, marking the completion of Volume III (dedicated to Queen Victoria), gave a dinner in honor of Murray, and at this time several University officials expressed the widespread conviction that, although the project would always be a drain on Oxford's finances, it was already a national asset. Murray, perhaps incautiously warming to their enthusiasm, predicted that the Dictionary would be completed by 1908, which proved to be just twenty years short of the mark. But the Dictionary was already developing into much more than a national asset of England. Around the world each new installment was eagerly awaited by scholars and word lovers. The parts already issued were becoming the final authority on the English language in law courts, government bureaus, scholarly debates, newspaper offices, and publishing houses.

Murray was knighted in 1908. In 1908, too, while watching Murray ride his tricycle through the streets of Oxford, the famous physician Sir William Osler told a friend: "The University pays me my salary to keep that old man alive till his 80th birthday in 1917 when the Dictionary will be finished." Indeed, Murray was now promising that the Dictionary would be finished on his eightieth birthday, and some of his visitors and correspondents had taken to wishing him well with "May you live to see Zymotic" (the last word in the Dictionary actually turned out to be **Zyxt**).

Murray did not live to see the dictionary completed. Having spent the last thirty-six years of his life on the project, he died after finishing **Trink-Turndown** in July 1915, two years short of his eightieth birthday. Much still remained to be done by Bradley, Craigie, and Onions, but Murray died knowing that the work would be completed and that it could never be—and would never need to be—done again.

The Oxford English Dictionary, as it was eventually named, was finished in 1928. H. L. Mencken had written that spies at Oxford told him the University would celebrate with "boxing matches between the dons . . . and a series of medieval drinking bouts," but the project had taken so long and already become so famous that only a modest celebration was held. The completed work, bound in twelve large volumes, contained 15,487 pages defining every known meaning of 414,825 words with 1,827,306 supporting and illustrative quotations from Anglo-Saxon times into the twentieth century. The historical record of every meaning, change of meaning, use, spelling, and grammatical form was given for each entry from its first appearance in the written language. The 178 miles of typeset material were completed seventy years after the Dictionary's inception and forty-four years after the first part of **A** had been published. No dictionary in any language has approached it in thoroughness, authority, and wealth of linguistic information. It was considered by many to be the greatest scholarly achievement of all time—and it still is.

When the final twelve-volume set was published, Oxford announced that a Supplement was in progress. That first Supplement, edited by Craigie and Onions, was published in 1933. *The Compact Edition of the Oxford English Dictionary,* which first appeared in 1971, comprises the twelve volumes plus this 1933 Supplement, reproduced micrographically in two volumes and boxed with a magnifying glass. The 1933 Supplement made it clear that constant growth and change in the living English language call for periodic publication of new supplements. Work continues today on "the longest running serial" in the English-speaking world. Under the direction of Dr. Robert Burchfield, the present Oxford dictionary staff of twenty editors and ten researchers—still using readers and advisors from around the world in special subject areas—is at work on a new Supplement.

Burchfield, like Murray before him, is "the man who came to dinner" at Oxford and never left. A New Zealander, he arrived at Oxford as a Rhodes scholar, stayed on to lecture on the English language, and was led into lexicography by C. T. Onions. He became editor of *A Supplement to the Oxford English Dictionary* and Chief Editor of the Oxford English dictionaries in 1971. Following in Murray's footsteps in more ways than one, in 1957 Burchfield thought that the new Supplement would be a one-volume project requiring seven years to complete. Volume I, **A-G,** of this new Supplement was published in 1972 and Volume II, **H-N,** in 1976. In 1980, he and his staff are editing and reading proofs for Volume III, **O-Scz.** His Supplement is growing into four volumes.

Long before the original twelve-volume *OED* was completed, Oxford lexicographers began to compile shorter dictionaries based on it and using its resources and methods. It was the Fowlers who set the pattern for these shorter Oxford dictionaries. The brothers' association with the Press began shortly after the turn of the century, when they undertook a four-volume translation of the second-century Greek satirist Lucian. Their translation was so meticulous and tasteful that the *New York Times* came to the conclusion that they were women. They were, in fact, grave, modest, and hardworking brothers, Henry W. born in 1858 and Frank G., twelve years his junior. After graduating from Oxford, Henry spent seventeen years as a schoolteacher before deciding to work as a journalist in London. He later left London to join Frank in Guernsey, an island in the English Channel, where the brothers built granite cottages and began their translation of Lucian.

In 1906 the Fowler brothers published *The King's English*, offering a set of marvelously inflexible rules to be followed and setting forth common blunders and "literary blemishes" to be avoided. Henry described it as "a sort of English composition manual from the negative point of view." The book had an added benefit: it provided the answer to Oxford's question of who would compile a "short dictionary" from the as yet only 70 percent completed *OED*. The reclusive Fowlers never met Murray, they did not visit Oxford, and no one from Oxford went to Guernsey. They finished the *Concise Oxford Dictionary* in 1911, the work having taken just five years—as they said it would.

When World War I broke out, fifty-seven-year-old Henry and forty-five-year-old Frank decided they were needed at the front. Lying about their ages, they enlisted in the British army and were dismayed when they were assigned to menial work rather than battle duty. Henry was discharged in 1916—fit and hearty—but Frank died of consumption in 1918 while still in the service. Henry returned to Guernsey and finished another dictionary based on the *OED*, *The Pocket Oxford Dictionary*, one size smaller than the *Concise*, which had been begun by Frank in 1911. It was published in 1924 and bore the names of both Henry and Frank Fowler. At the same time Henry continued writing the extraordinary *Modern English Usage*, which he had begun in 1911, a book in which every major hazard of English usage was pointed out for the edification and delight of writers for generations to come. In 1926, its first year of publication, it was reprinted four times in England, and sold over 50,000 copies in the United States. Fowler said he wrote it with "a cheerful attitude of infallibility." His now-famous warnings about vogue words and genteelisms are classic and, like most of the book's basic content, valid today.

The Fowlers were the first to use the *OED* to compile small Oxford dictionaries, and many other dictionaries have followed. All such Oxford dictionaries rely, of course, on the authority, standards, and scholarship created by the *OED* and maintained in its Supplements. The *Oxford American Dictionary (OAD)* differs from the others in that it is the first to use American lexicographers and editors. Although American and British English share a vast vocabulary, each has its own words, phrases, meanings, spellings, pronunciations, and forms. It was obvious, therefore, that an American staff was needed for the *Oxford American Dictionary*. With the help and advice of the Oxford dictionary staff in England, Oxford University Press in New York assembled an American staff under Eugene Ehrlich, Stuart Berg Flexner, and Gorton Carruth. Ehrlich is a member of the Department of English and Comparative Literature, Columbia University, and an authority on American usage. Flexner is a distinguished lexicographer and author, and Carruth is a well-known editor of reference books. All entries were chosen, compiled, spelled, syllabicated, and given pronunciation by this American staff, which worked closely with Joyce Hawkins, a member of the Oxford dictionary staff in England and editor of the *Oxford Paperback Dictionary*, which formed the basis of the present work. John Sykes, editor of the Sixth

Edition of the *Concise Oxford Dictionary,* and Robert Burchfield also gave generously of their experience and advice. The *Oxford American Dictionary* is thus true to the American language as well as to the Oxford dictionary tradition and standards. It is worth pointing out that the American editors followed the Fowlers' example in completing their manuscript on time and, to a degree, they have emulated Fowler's "cheerful attitude of infallibility" in matters of usage. They also were true to Murray's tradition in that they compiled a dictionary somewhat longer than originally planned.

Like the shorter Oxford dictionaries in England, this *Oxford American Dictionary* is not intended to be comprehensive or to be a substitute for an encyclopedia or larger dictionary. It has been compiled for everyday use in home, school, office, and library. It emphasizes concise and precise definitions presented in a straightforward way. It does not use synonyms to define words unless they help distinguish shades of meaning. It supplies the most common current meanings, spellings, and pronunciations. All spellings and pronunciations are American unless otherwise labeled. As a special feature, a new pronunciation system is employed that is simpler and easier to use than systems used in previous American dictionaries. It enables readers, no matter what their regional speech patterns, to pronounce words without difficulty.

Another feature of this dictionary is that it makes a particular point of indicating correct American usage. For speakers and writers, therefore, who want a dictionary that distinguishes between good and bad English, the *Oxford American Dictionary* sets high, somewhat conservative standards in usage. Many sample sentences are provided that serve as guides to usage while illuminating meanings. Usage labels and more than six hundred usage notes indicate the linguistic and social appropriateness of various words and phrases. (See, for example, the entries for *data, hopefully,* and *loan.*) These usage labels and notes reflect analysis of the current language tempered by linguistic experience and sensibility. For these reasons, Oxford University Press is confident the *OAD,* compiled by Americans for Americans and for students of the American language all over the world, will supply the precise information most needed by the user.

Oxford American Dictionary

A

A, a (ay) (*pl.* **As, A's, a's**) 1. the first letter of the alphabet. 2. *A*, a grade rating for excellent school work. □**A one, A1,** (*informal*) in perfect condition; first-rate. **from A to Z,** from beginning to end.
a *adj.* (called the *indefinite article*) 1. one person or thing but not any specific one, *I need a knife.* 2. per, *we pay $150 a week; twice a day.* ▷ See **an.**
a·back (ă-bak) *adv.* **taken aback,** disconcerted.
ab·a·cus (ab-ă-kŭs) *n.* (*pl.* **-cus·es, -ci,** *pr.* -sī) a frame containing parallel rods with beads that slide up and down, used for counting.
a·ban·don (ă-ban-dŏn) *v.* 1. to go away from (a person or thing or place) without intending to return; *abandon ship,* leave a sinking ship. 2. to give up, to cease work on, *abandon hope; abandon the attempt.* 3. to yield completely to an emotion or impulse, *abandoned himself to despair.* **abandon** *n.* careless freedom of manner. **a·ban'don·ment** *n.*
a·ban·doned (ă-ban-dŏnd) *adj.* (of behavior) showing abandon, lacking restraint, depraved.
a·base (ă-bays) *v.* (**a·based, a·bas·ing**) to humiliate, to degrade. **a·base'ment** *n.*
a·bash (ă-bash) *v.* to embarrass, to confound.
a·bashed (ă-basht) *adj.* embarrassed or ashamed. **a·bash'ed·ly** *adv.*
a·bate (ă-bayt) *v.* (**a·bat·ed, a·bat·ing**) 1. to make or become less. 2. (legal) to end, *abate the nuisance.* 3. to die down, reduce, *the storm abated.* **a·bate'ment** *n.*
ab·at·toir (ab-ă-twahr) *n.* a slaughterhouse.
ab·bess (ab-ĕs) *n.* a woman who is head of an abbey of nuns.
ab·bey (ab-ee) *n.* (*pl.* **-beys**) 1. a building occupied by monks or nuns living as a community. 2. the community itself. 3. the church of an abbey.
ab·bot (ab-ŏt) *n.* a man who is head of an abbey of monks.
abbr., abbrev. *abbr.* 1. abbreviated. 2. abbreviation.
ab·bre·vi·ate (ă-bree-vi-ayt) *v.* (**ab·bre·vi·at·ed, ab·bre·vi·at·ing**) to shorten (especially a word or title).
ab·bre·vi·a·tion (ă-bree-vi-ay-shŏn) *n.* 1. abbreviating, being abbreviated. 2. a shortened form of a word or title.
ABC (ay-bee-see) *n.* (*pl.* **ABC's, ABCs**) 1. the alphabet. 2. *ABC's, ABCs,* the elementary facts of a subject, *the ABC's of carpentry.*
ab·di·cate (ab-dĭ-kayt) *v.* (**ab·di·cat·ed, ab·di·cat·ing**) to resign from a throne or other high office. **ab·di·ca·tion** (ab-dĭ-kay-shŏn) *n.*
ab·do·men (ab-dŏ-měn) *n.* 1. the part of the body below the chest and diaphragm, containing most of the digestive organs. 2. the hindmost section of the body of an insect, spider, or crustacean, *head, thorax, and abdomen.* **ab·dom·i·nal** (ab-dom-ĭ-năl) *adj.* **ab·dom'i·nal·ly** *adv.*
ab·duct (ab-dukt) *v.* to carry off (a person) illegally by force or fraud. **ab·duc·tion** (ab-duk-shŏn) *n.* **ab·duc'tor** *n.*
Ab·er·deen Angus (ab-ĕr-deen ang-gŭs) a Scottish breed of black hornless cattle.
ab·er·rant (ă-ber-ănt) *adj.* deviating from what is normal or from a standard. **ab·er·rance** (ă-ber-ăns) *n.* **ab·er·ran·cy** (ă-ber-ăn-see) *n.*
ab·er·ra·tion (ab-ĕ-ray-shŏn) *n.* 1. a deviation from what is normal. 2. a mental or moral lapse. 3. a distortion, as of an image produced through an imperfect lens.
a·bet (ă-bet) *v.* (**a·bet·ted, a·bet·ting**) to encourage or assist in committing an offense. **a·bet'tor** *n.* **a·bet'ter** *n.* **a·bet'ment** *n.*
a·bey·ance (ă-bay-ăns) *n.* **in abeyance,** (of a right or rule or problem etc.) suspended for a time.
ab·hor (ab-hohr) *v.* (**ab·horred, ab·hor·ring**) to detest.
ab·hor·rent (ab-hohr-ĕnt) *adj.* detestable. **ab·hor'rence** *n.*
a·bide (ă-bīd) *v.* (**a·bode** *pr.* ă-bohd, or **a·bid·ed, a·bid·ing**) 1. (*old use*) to remain, to dwell. 2. to bear, to endure, *can't abide complainers.* □**abide by,** to act in accordance with; *abide by a promise,* keep it; *abide by the consequences,* accept them.
a·bid·ing (ă-bī-ding) *adj.* long-lasting, permanent. **a·bid'ing·ly** *adv.*
Ab·i·djan (ab-i-jahn) the capital of the Ivory Coast.
a·bil·i·ty (ă-bil-i-tee) *n.* (*pl.* **-ties**) 1. the quality that makes an action or process possible, the capacity or power to do something. 2. cleverness, talent.
ab·ject (ab-jekt, ab-jekt) *adj.* 1. wretched, without resources, *abject poverty.* 2. lacking all pride, *an abject coward.* 3. very humble, *an abject apology.* **ab·ject'ly** *adv.* **ab·ject'ness** *n.* **ab·jec·tion** (ab-jek-shŏn) *n.*
ab·jure (ab-joor) *v.* (**ab·jured, ab·jur·ing**) to renounce under oath. **ab·ju·ra·tion** (ab-jŭ-ray-shŏn) *n.* ▷Do not confuse *abjure* with *adjure.*
abl. *abbr.* ablative.
ab·la·tive (ab-lă-tiv) *adj.* of the case in Latin and other languages denoting direction from a place, also time and source, agent, or instrument. **ablative** *n.* 1. the ablative case. 2. a word in this case.
a·blaze (ă-blayz) *adj.* blazing.
a·ble (ay-běl) *adj.* (**a·bler, a·blest**) 1. having the ability to do something. 2. having great ability, competent. **ab'ly** *adv.*
a·ble-bod·ied (ay-běl-bod-eed) *adj.* fit and strong.

ab·lu·tions (ă-bloo-shŏnz) *n. pl.* washing. □**perform one's ablutions,** wash oneself.

ABM *abbr.* antiballistic missile.

ab·ne·gate (ab-nĕ-gayt) *v.* (**ab·ne·gat·ed, ab·ne·gat·ing**) 1. to deny oneself (something). 2. to renounce (a right or belief).

ab·ne·ga·tion (ab-nĕ-gay-shŏn) *n.* rejection or renunciation, especially of a belief, right, or responsibility.

ab·nor·mal (ab-nor-măl) *adj.* different from what is normal. **ab·nor'mal·ly** *adv.* **ab·nor·mal·i·ty** (ab-nor-mal-i-tee) *n.*

a·board (ă-bohrd) *adv. & prep.* on or into a ship, aircraft, or train.

a·bode¹ *see* **abide.**

a·bode² (ă-bohd) *n.* a dwelling place.

a·bol·ish (ă-bol-ish) *v.* to put an end to, *abolish slavery.* **ab·o·li·tion** (ab-ŏ-lish-on) *n.* **ab·o·li·tion·ism** (ab-ŏ-lish-ŏ-niz-ĕm) *n.* a movement against slavery.

ab·o·li·tion·ist (ab-ŏ-lish-ŏ-nist) *n.* (sometimes **Abolitionist**) a person who advocates abolition, especially of slavery of blacks in the U.S. in the 19th century.

A-bomb (ay-bom) *n.* an atomic bomb.

a·bom·i·na·ble (ă-bom-ĭ-nă-bĕl) *adj.* 1. detestable, loathsome. 2. very bad or unpleasant, *abominable weather.* □**Abominable Snowman,** a large manlike or bearlike animal said to exist in the Himalayas, a yeti.

a·bom·i·nate (ă-bom-ĭ-nayt) *v.* (**a·bom·i·nat·ed, a·bom·i·nat·ing**) to detest, to loathe.

a·bom·i·na·tion (ă-bom-ĭ-nay-shŏn) *n.* 1. loathing. 2. something loathed.

ab·o·rig·i·nal (ab-ŏ-rij-ĭ-năl) *adj.* existing in a land from earliest times or from before the arrival of colonists, *aboriginal inhabitants* or *plants.* **aboriginal** *n.* an aboriginal inhabitant, especially (*Aboriginal*) of Australia.

ab·o·rig·i·ne (ab-ŏ-rij-ĭ-nee) *n.* one of the earliest known inhabitants of a continent or country.

a·bort (ă-bort) *v.* 1. to cause abortion of. 2. to induce abortion in. 3. to suffer abortion. 4. to end or cause to end prematurely and unsuccessfully.

a·bor·tion (ă-bor-shŏn) *n.* 1. the expulsion (either spontaneous or induced) of a fetus from the womb before it is able to survive, especially in the first twenty-eight weeks of pregnancy. 2. the fetus so aborted. 3. an immature or incomplete idea etc.

a·bor·tion·ist (ă-bor-shŏ-nist) *n.* a person who induces abortions.

a·bor·tive (ă-bor-tiv) *adj.* 1. producing abortion. 2. unsuccessful, *an abortive attempt.* **a·bor'tive·ly** *adv.* **a·bor'tive·ness** *n.*

a·bound (ă-bownd) *v.* 1. to be plentiful, *fish abound in the river.* 2. to have in great quantities, *the river abounds in fish.*

a·bout (ă-bowt) *adv. & prep.* 1. all around, *look about you.* 2. somewhere near, not far off, *he's somewhere about.* 3. here and there in (a place), *papers were lying about or about the room.* 4. on the move, in circulation, *will soon be about again.* 5. approximately, *about $10.* 6. in connection with, on the matter or subject of, *what is he talking about?* 7. so as to face in the opposite direction, *put the ship about.* □**be about to,** to be on the point or verge of doing something.

a·bout-face (ă-bowt-fays) *n.* a complete reversal of previous actions or opinions.

a·bove (ă-buv) *adv.* 1. at or to a higher point. 2. earlier in a book or article, *mentioned above.* **above** *prep.* 1. over, higher than, more than. 2. upstream from. 3. beyond the level or reach of, *she is above suspicion.* 4. more important than, *this above all.*

a·bove·board (ă-buv-bohrd) *adj. & adv.* without deception or concealment, done honorably.

ab·ra·ca·dab·ra (ab-ră-kă-dab-ră) *n.* 1. a supposedly magic formula or spell. 2. gibberish.

a·brade (ă-brayd) *v.* (**a·brad·ed, a·brad·ing**) to scrape or wear away by rubbing. **a·bra·sion** (ă-bray-zhŏn) *n.*

a·bra·sive (ă-bray-sĭv) *adj.* 1. causing abrasion. 2. harsh, causing angry feelings, *an abrasive personality.* **abrasive** *n.* a substance used for grinding or polishing surfaces. **a·bra'sive·ly** *adv.* **a·bra'sive·ness** *n.*

a·breast (ă-brest) *adv.* 1. side by side and facing the same way. 2. keeping up, not behind, *keep abreast of modern developments.*

a·bridge (ă-brij) *v.* (**a·bridged, a·bridg·ing**) to shorten by using fewer words, *an abridged version of the novel.* **a·bridg'ment** *n.*

a·broad (ă-brawd) *adv.* 1. away from one's own country. 2. far and wide, everywhere, *scattered the seeds abroad.* 3. out and about, *the rumor has been abroad for many days.*

ab·ro·gate (ab-rŏ-gayt) *v.* (**ab·ro·gat·ed, ab·ro·gat·ing**) to cancel or repeal, *abrogate a law.* **ab·ro·ga·tion** (ab-rŏ-gay-shŏn) *n.* ▷Do not confuse *abrogate* with *arrogate.*

a·brupt (ă-brupt) *adj.* 1. sudden, *come to an abrupt stop.* 2. disconnected, not smooth, *short abrupt sentences.* 3. curt. 4. (of a slope) very steep. **a·brupt'ly** *adv.* **a·brupt'ness** *n.*

ab·scess (ab-ses) *n.* a collection of pus formed in the body. **ab'scessed** *adj.*

ab·scis·sa (ab-sis-ă) *n.* (*pl.* **-scis·sas, -scis·sae,** *pr.* **-sis-ee**) 1. the part of a line between a fixed point on it and the ordinate drawn to it from any other point. 2. a coordinate measured parallel to the *x*-axis (horizontal axis).

ab·scond (ab-skond) *v.* to go away secretly, especially after wrongdoing. **ab·scond'er** *n.*

ab·sence (ab-sĕns) *n.* 1. being away, the period of this. 2. lack, nonexistence, *in the absence of proof.* 3. inattention, *absence of mind.*

ab·sent (ab-sĕnt) *adj.* 1. not present, *absent from school.* 2. nonexistent, lacking. 3. with one's mind on other things, *stared in an absent way.* **absent** (ab-sent) *v.* to stay away, *absented himself from the meeting.* **ab'sent·ly** *adv.*

ab·sen·tee (ab-sĕn-tee) *n.* a person who is absent from work etc. □**absentee ballot,** a ballot cast by mail by a voter away from his or her usual voting place. **absentee landlord,** one who seldom visits the premises he lets.

ab·sen·tee·ism (ab-sĕn-tee-iz-ĕm) *n.* frequent absence from work or school.

ab·sent-mind·ed (ab-sĕnt-mɪn-did) *adj.* with one's mind on other things, forgetful.

ab·sinthe, ab·sinth (ab-sinth) *n.* a green liqueur made from brandy with wormwood and other herbs.

ab·so·lute (ab-sŏ-loot) *adj.* 1. complete, *absolute silence.* 2. unrestricted, *absolute power.* 3. independent, not relative, *there is no absolute standard for beauty.* 4. (*informal*) utter, out-and-out, *it's an absolute shame.* □**absolute pitch,** ability to recognize or reproduce the pitch of notes in music;

the pitch of a note defined scientifically in terms of vibrations per second.
ab·so·lute·ly (ab-sŏ-loot-lee) *adv.* 1. completely. 2. without restrictions, unconditionally. 3. actually, *it absolutely exploded.* 4. *(informal)* quite so, yes.
ab·so·lu·tion (ab-sŏ-loo-shŏn) *n.* a priest's formal declaration of the forgiveness of penitents' sins.
ab·so·lut·ism (ab-sŏ-loo-tiz-ĕm) *n.* the principle of absolute government, despotism. **ab'so·lut·ist** *n.*
ab·solve (ab-zolv) *v.* **(ab·solved, ab·solv·ing)** 1. to clear of blame or guilt. 2. to give absolution to (a person). 3. to free from an obligation.
ab·sorb (ab-sorb) *v.* 1. to take in, to combine or merge into itself or oneself, *absorb fluid, food, knowledge; the large firm absorbed the smaller ones,* gained control of them and incorporated them into its operations. 2. to bear the brunt of, to reduce the effect of, *buffers absorbed most of the shock.* 3. to occupy or hold the attention or interest of, *his work absorbs him completely; an absorbing book.* **ab·sorb'er** *n.* **ab·sorp·tion** (ab-sorp-shŏn) *n.* **ab·sorp·tive** (ab-sorp-tiv) *adj.* **ab·sorb'ing** *adj.* **ab·sorb'ing·ly** *adv.* ▷Do not confuse *absorb* with *adsorb.*
ab·sorb·a·ble (ab-sor-bă-bĕl) *adj.* able to be absorbed.
ab·sorb·ent (ab-sor-bĕnt) *adj.* able to absorb moisture etc., *absorbent cotton.* **ab·sorb'en·cy** *n.* ▷Do not confuse *absorbent* with *adsorbent.*
ab·stain (ab-stayn) *v.* 1. to keep oneself from some action or indulgence, especially from drinking alcohol. 2. to refrain from using one's vote. **ab·stain'er** *n.* **ab·sten·tion** (ab-sten-shŏn) *n.*
ab·ste·mi·ous (ab-stee-mi-ŭs) *adj.* sparing in one's taking of food and drink, not self-indulgent. ▷An *abstemious* person does not *abstain* entirely. **ab·ste'mi·ous·ly** *adv.* **ab·ste'mi·ous·ness** *n.*
ab·sti·nence (ab-stĭ-nĕns) *n.* abstaining, especially from food or alcohol. **ab'sti·nent** *adj.*
ab·stract (ab-strakt) *adj.* 1. having no material existence. 2. theoretical rather than practical. **abstract** *n.* 1. an abstract quality or idea. 2. a summary. 3. an example of abstract art. **abstract** (ab-strakt) *v.* 1. to take out, to separate, to remove. 2. to make a written summary. **ab·stract'ly** *adv.* **ab·stract'ness** *n.* **ab·stract'er** *n.* ▢**abstract art,** art that does not represent things pictorially but expresses the artist's ideas or sensations. **abstract expressionism,** a form of abstract art in which paint is applied by spontaneous or random action of the artist. **in the abstract,** regarded theoretically, *he favors economy in the abstract but refuses to economize.*
ab·stract·ed (ab-strak-tid) *adj.* with one's mind on other things, not paying attention. **ab·stract'ed·ly** *adv.* **ab·stract'ed·ness** *n.*
ab·strac·tion (ab-strak-shŏn) *n.* 1. abstracting, removing. 2. an abstract idea. 3. abstractedness. 4. an example of abstract art.
ab·struse (ab-stroos) *adj.* hard to understand, profound. **ab·struse'ly** *adv.* **ab·struse'ness** *n.*
ab·surd (ab-surd) *adj.* 1. not in accordance with common sense, very unsuitable. 2. ridiculous, foolish. **ab·surd'ly** *adv.* **ab·surd'i·ty** *n.* (*pl.* -ties).
A·bu Dha·bi (ah-boo dah-bee) the capital of the federation of United Arab Emirates.

a·bun·dance (ă-bun-dăns) *n.* a quantity that is more than enough, plenty.
a·bun·dant (ă-bun-dănt) *adj.* 1. more than enough, plentiful. 2. having plenty of something, rich, *a land abundant in minerals.* **a·bun'dant·ly** *adv.*
a·buse (ă-byoos) *n.* 1. a misuse. 2. an unjust or corrupt practice. 3. abusive words, insults. **abuse** (ă-byooz) *v.* **(a·bused, a·bus·ing)** 1. to make a bad or wrong use of, *abuse one's authority.* 2. to treat badly. 3. to attack in words, to utter insults or to about.
a·bu·sive (ă-byoo-siv) *adj.* insulting, criticizing harshly or angrily. **a·bu'sive·ly** *adv.* **a·bu'sive·ness** *n.*
a·but (ă-but) *v.* **(a·but·ted, a·but·ting)** to have a common boundary, to end or lean against, *their land abuts on ours.*
a·but·ment (ă-but-mĕnt) *n.* a support from which an arch or vault etc. springs, and which receives the lateral thrust.
a·bys·mal (ă-biz-măl) *adj.* 1. extreme, *abysmal ignorance.* 2. *(informal)* extremely bad, *their taste is abysmal.* **a·bys'mal·ly** *adv.*
a·byss (ă-bis) *n.* a hole so deep that it appears bottomless.
Ac *symbol* actinium.
AC, A.C., ac, a.c. *abbr.* alternating current.
A/C, a/c, ac *abbr.* 1. account. 2. account current.
a·ca·cia (ă-kay-shă) *n.* 1. a tree or shrub from which gum arabic is obtained. 2. a related tree (the false acacia or locust tree) grown for ornament.
acad. *abbr.* 1. academic. 2. academy.
ac·a·dem·ic (ak-ă-dem-ik) *adj.* 1. of a school, college, or university. 2. scholarly as opposed to technical or practical, *academic subjects.* 3. of theoretical interest only, with no practical application. **academic** *n.* an academic person. **ac·a·dem'i·cal·ly** *adv.*
a·cad·e·mi·cian (ă-kad-ĕ-mish-ăn) *n.* a member of an academy.
a·cad·e·my (ă-kad-ĕ-mee) *n.* (*pl.* -mies) 1. a school, especially for specialized training. 2. *Academy,* a society of scholars or artists.
a·can·thus (ă-kan-thŭs) *n.* 1. a herbaceous plant with large prickly leaves. 2. a decoration resembling such leaves, in Greek architecture.
a cap·pel·la (ah kă-pel-ă) (of choral music) unaccompanied. ▷Italian, = in church style.
acc. *abbr.* 1. account. 2. accusative.
ac·cede (ak-seed) *v.* **(ac·ced·ed, ac·ced·ing)** 1. to take office, to become monarch, *she acceded to the throne twenty-six years ago.* 2. to agree to what is proposed, *please accede to our request.* ▷Do not confuse *accede* with *exceed.*
ac·cel·er·ate (ak-sel-ĕ-rayt) *v.* **(ac·cel·er·at·ed, ac·cel·er·at·ing)** 1. to cause to move faster or happen earlier, to increase the speed of a motor vehicle. 2. to become faster, to move or happen more quickly. **ac·cel·er·a·tion** (ak-sel-ĕ-ray-shŏn) *n.*
ac·cel·er·a·tor (ak-sel-ĕ-ray-tŏr) *n.* 1. a device for increasing speed, a pedal controlling the throttle in a motor vehicle. 2. an apparatus using electric and magnetic fields to give high velocities to free electrons or other atomic particles.
ac·cent (ak-sent) *n.* 1. emphasis on a syllable or word. 2. a mark indicating such emphasis or the quality of a vowel sound. 3. a national, local, or individual way of pronouncing words. 4. the emphasis given to something, *the accent is on qual-*

ity. **accent** (ak-sent, ak-sent) *v.* 1. to pronounce with an accent. 2. to emphasize. **ac·cen·tu·al** (ak-sen-choo-ăl) *adj.*

ac·cen·tu·ate (ak-sen-choo-ayt) *v.* (**ac·cen·tu·at·ed, ac·cen·tu·at·ing**) to emphasize. **ac·cen·tu·a·tion** (ak-sen-choo-ay-shŏn) *n.*

ac·cept (ak-sept) *v.* 1. to take (a thing offered) willingly, to say yes to an offer or invitation. 2. to undertake (a responsibility); *we accept liability for the accident,* agree that we are legally responsible. 3. to treat as welcome, *they were never really accepted by their neighbors.* 4. to be willing to agree to, *we accept the proposed changes.* 5. to take as true, *we do not accept your conclusions.* **ac·cep'tor** *n.* ▷Do not confuse *accept* with *except.*

ac·cept·a·ble (ak-sep-tă-běl) *adj.* 1. worth accepting. 2. tolerable, *an acceptable risk.* **ac·cept'a·bly** *adv.* **ac·cept·a·bil·i·ty** (ak-sep-tă-bil-i-tee) *n.*

ac·cept·ance (ak-sep-tăns) *n.* 1. the act of accepting. 2. an agreement to pay a bill, a bill so accepted.

ac·cess (ak-ses) *n.* 1. a way in, a means of approaching or entering, *the window provided easy access.* 2. the right or opportunity of reaching or using, *students need access to books.* 3. an attack of emotion, *an access of tears.* ▷Do not confuse *access* with *excess.*

ac·ces·si·ble (ak-ses-ĭ-běl) *adj.* able to be reached or used. **ac·ces'si·bly** *adv.* **ac·ces·si·bil·i·ty** (ak-ses-ĭ-bil-i-tee) *n.*

ac·ces·sion (ak-sesh-ŏn) *n.* 1. reaching a rank or position, *the monarch's accession to the throne.* 2. an addition, being added, *recent museum accessions.*

ac·ces·so·ry (ak-ses-ŏ-ree) *adj.* additional, extra. **accessory** *n.* 1. a thing that is extra, useful, or decorative but not essential, a minor fitting or attachment. 2. a person who helps another in a crime.

ac·ci·dent (ak-si-děnt) *n.* 1. an unexpected or undesirable event, especially one causing injury or damage. 2. chance, fortune, *we met by accident.*

ac·ci·den·tal (ak-si-den-tăl) *adj.* happening by accident. **accidental** *n.* a sign attached to a single note in music, showing temporary departure from the key signature. **ac·ci·den'tal·ly** *adv.*

ac·claim (ă-klaym) *v.* to welcome with shouts of approval, to applaud enthusiastically. **acclaim** *n.* a shout of welcome, applause. **ac·cla·ma·tion** (ak-lă-may-shŏn) *n.* ▷Do not confuse *acclamation* with *acclimation.*

ac·cli·mate (ak-lĭ-mayt, ă-klɪ-mit) *v.* (**ac·cli·mat·ed, ac·cli·mat·ing**) to get used to a new climate or new conditions. **ac·cli·ma·tion** (ak-lĭ-may-shŏn) *n.* ▷Do not confuse *acclimation* with *acclamation.*

ac·cli·ma·tize (ă-klɪ-mă-tɪz) *v.* (**ac·cli·ma·tized, ac·cli·ma·tiz·ing**) to acclimate. **ac·cli·ma·ti·za·tion** (ă-klɪ-mă-ti-zay-shŏn) *n.*

ac·co·lade (ak-ŏ-layd) *n.* 1. a ceremonial tap on the shoulder with the flat of a sword, given to mark the conferring of knighthood. 2. praise, approval.

ac·com·mo·date (ă-kom-ŏ-dayt) *v.* (**ac·com·mo·dat·ed, ac·com·mo·dat·ing**) 1. to provide or supply. 2. to provide lodging or room for. 3. to adapt, to make harmonize, *I will accommodate my plans to yours.*

ac·com·mo·dat·ing (ă-kom-ŏ-day-ting) *adj.* willing to do as one is asked.

ac·com·mo·da·tion (ă-kom-ŏ-day-shŏn) *n.* 1. the process of accommodating or adapting. 2. *accommodations,* lodgings, living premises.

ac·com·pa·ni·ment (ă-kum-pă-ni-měnt) *n.* 1. an accompanying thing. 2. an instrumental part supporting a solo instrument, a voice, or a choir.

ac·com·pa·nist (ă-kum-pă-nist) *n.* a person who plays a musical accompaniment.

ac·com·pa·ny (ă-kum-pă-nee) *v.* (**ac·com·pa·nied, ac·com·pa·ny·ing**) 1. to go with, to travel with as a companion or helper. 2. to be present with, *the fever was accompanied by delirium.* 3. to provide in addition. 4. to play a musical accompaniment to.

ac·com·plice (ă-kom-plis) *n.* a partner in wrongdoing.

ac·com·plish (ă-kom-plish) *v.* to succeed in doing, to fulfill. **ac·com'plish·er** *n.*

ac·com·plished (ă-kom-plisht) *adj.* skilled, having many accomplishments.

ac·com·plish·ment (ă-kom-plish-měnt) *n.* 1. accomplishing. 2. skill in a social or domestic art.

ac·cord (ă-kord) *n.* consent, agreement. **accord** *v.* 1. to be in harmony or consistent. 2. to give or grant, *he was accorded this privilege.* **ac·cord'ant** *adj.* □of one's own accord, without being asked or compelled. **with one accord,** all agreeing.

ac·cord·ance (ă-kor-dăns) *n.* agreement, conformity.

ac·cord·ing (ă-kor-ding) *adv.* **according as,** in proportion as, in a manner that depends on, *was praised or blamed according as her work was good or bad.* **according to,** as stated by or in, *according to the Bible;* in a manner consistent with or in proportion to, *grouped according to size.*

ac·cord·ing·ly (ă-kor-ding-lee) *adv.* 1. according to what is known or stated, *find out the facts and act accordingly.* 2. therefore.

ac·cor·di·on (ă-kor-di-ŏn) *n.* a portable musical instrument with bellows, keys, and metal reeds. **accordion** *adj.* folding like a bellows.

ac·cor·di·on·ist (ă-kor-di-ŏ-nist) *n.* a person who plays the accordion.

ac·cost (ă-kawst) *v.* 1. to approach and speak to. 2. (of a prostitute) to solicit.

ac·count (ă-kownt) *n.* 1. a statement of money paid or owed for goods or services. 2. a credit arrangement with a bank or business firm. 3. importance, *that is of no account.* 4. a description, a report. **account** *v.* to regard as, *a person is accounted innocent until proved guilty.* □**account book,** a book for keeping accounts in. **account executive,** a person in a business who is responsible for overseeing a client's account. **account for,** to give a reckoning of (money received); to explain the cause of; to be the explanation of. **account payable,** (in bookkeeping) a liability to a creditor. **account receivable,** (in bookkeeping) a claim against a debtor. **by all accounts,** according to what everyone says. **give a good account of oneself,** to perform well. **keep accounts,** to keep a systematic record of money spent and received. **on account,** as an interim payment, *here is $10 on account;* debited to be paid for later, *bought it on account.* **on account of,** because of. **on no account,** under no circumstances, never. **on one's own account,** for one's own purposes and at one's own risk. **take into account,** to make allowances for.

ac·count·a·ble (ă-kown-tă-běl) *adj.* 1. obliged to give a reckoning or explanation for one's actions etc., responsible. 2. able to be explained. **ac·count·a·bil·i·ty** (ă-kown-tă-bil-i-tee) *n.*

ac·count·ant (ă-kown-tănt) *n.* a person whose profession is to audit and maintain business accounts and to file tax returns. **ac·count'an·cy** *n.*

ac·count·ing (ă-kown-ting) *n.* the process of keeping and verifying accounts.

ac·cou·tre·ments (ă-koo-trĕ-mĕnts) *n. pl.* equipment, a soldier's outfit other than weapons and clothes.

Ac·cra (ă-krah) the capital of Ghana.

ac·cred·it (ă-kred-it) *v.* 1. to gain sanction or belief for. 2. to provide with credentials, as an ambassador. 3. to certify as meeting specific requirements. 4. to attribute, to credit. **ac·cred·i·ta·tion** (ă-kred-i-tay-shŏn) *n.*

ac·cred·it·ed (ă-kred-i-tid) *adj.* 1. officially recognized, *the school is fully accredited.* 2. generally accepted or believed. 3. certified as being of a prescribed quality.

ac·crete (ă-kreet) *v.* (**ac·cret·ed, ac·cret·ing**) 1. to grow by addition of foreign material or by natural growth. 2. to grow together, into one.

ac·cre·tion (ă-kree-shŏn) *n.* 1. a growth or increase by means of gradual additions. 2. the growing of separate things into one.

ac·crue (ă-kroo) *v.* (**ac·crued, ac·cru·ing**) to come as a natural increase or advantage, to accumulate, *interest accrues on a savings account.* **ac·cru'al** *n.*

ac·cul·tur·a·tion (ă-kul-chŭ-ray-shŏn) *n.* process of adapting to a different culture.

ac·cu·mu·late (ă-kyoo-myŭ-layt) *v.* (**ac·cu·mu·lat·ed, ac·cu·mu·lat·ing**) 1. to acquire an increasing quantity of. 2. to increase in quantity or amount. **ac·cu'mu·la·tor** *n.* **ac·cu·mu·la·tion** (ă-kyoo-myŭ-lay-shŏn) *n.*

ac·cu·rate (ak-yŭ-rit) *adj.* 1. free from error, conforming exactly to a standard or to truth. 2. careful and exact, showing precision, *an accurate mind.* **ac'cu·rate·ly** *adv.* **ac'cu·ra·cy** *n.* **ac'cu·rate·ness** *n.*

ac·curs·ed (ă-kur-sid) *adj.* 1. under a curse. 2. (*informal*) detestable, hateful.

ac·cu·sa·tion (ak-yŭ-zay-shŏn) *n.* 1. accusing, being accused. 2. a statement accusing a person of a fault, crime, or wrongdoing.

ac·cu·sa·tive (ă-kyoo-ză-tiv) *adj.* of the case denoting the object of a verb or preposition. **accusative** *n.* 1. the accusative or objective case. 2. a word in this case, as *him* in *we saw him.*

ac·cuse (ă-kyooz) *v.* (**ac·cused, ac·cus·ing**) to state that one lays blame for a fault, crime, or wrongdoing etc. upon (a named person). **ac·cus'er** *n.* **ac·cus'ing·ly** *adv.* □**the accused,** the person accused in a criminal court case.

ac·cus·tom (ă-kus-tŏm) *v.* to make or become used to.

ac·cus·tomed (ă-kus-tŏmd) *adj.* usual, customary, *in his accustomed seat.*

ace (ays) *n.* 1. a playing card with one pip. 2. a fighter pilot who has shot down five or more enemy planes, a person who excels at something. 3. a tennis serve that one's opponent cannot return. **ace** *v.* (**aced, ac·ing**) to score an ace. □**have an ace up one's sleeve,** to have something effective kept secretly in reserve. **play one's ace,** to use one's best resource. **within an ace of,** on the verge of, *was within an ace of collapse.*

ac·er·bate (as-ĕr-bayt) *v.* (**ac·er·bat·ed**) **ac·**

er·bat·ing) 1. to make sour or bitter. 2. to make angry.

a·cer·bi·ty (ă-sur-bi-tee) *n.* sharpness of speech or manner. **a·cerb'** *adj.*

ac·e·tate (as-ĕ-tayt) *n.* 1. a compound derived from acetic acid. 2. a fabric made from cellulose acetate.

a·ce·tic (ă-see-tik) *adj.* of vinegar. □**acetic acid,** the acid that gives vinegar its characteristic taste and smell.

ac·e·tone (as-ĕ-tohn) *n.* a colorless liquid used as a solvent.

a·cet·y·lene (ă-set-i-leen) *n.* a gas that burns with a bright flame, used in cutting and welding metal.

a·ce·tyl·sal·i·cyl·ic (ă-see-tĭl-sal-ĭ-sil-ik) **acid** aspirin.

ache (ayk) *v.* (**ached, ach·ing**) 1. to suffer a dull continuous physical or mental pain. 2. to yearn. **ache** *n.* a dull continuous pain. **ach·y** (ay-kee) *adj.* (**ach·i·er, ach·i·est**).

a·chiev·a·ble (ă-chee-vă-bĕl) *adj.* able to be achieved.

a·chieve (ă-cheev) *v.* (**a·chieved, a·chiev·ing**) to accomplish, to gain or reach by effort, *we achieved success at last.* **a·chieve'ment** *n.*

A·chil·les (ă-kil-eez) **heel** a weak or vulnerable point. ▷ Named after a hero in Greek legend who was invulnerable except in his heel.

Achilles (ă-kil-eez) **tendon** a tendon in the heel by which calf muscles extend the foot.

ac·id (as-id) *adj.* 1. sharp tasting, sour. 2. looking or sounding bitter, *acid remarks.* **acid** *n.* 1. a sour substance. 2. any of a class of substances containing hydrogen that can be replaced by a metal to form a salt. 3. (*slang*) the drug LSD. **ac'id·ly** *adv.* □**acid test,** a severe or conclusive test. ▷ Acid is applied to a metal to test whether it is gold or not.

ac·id·head (as-id-hed) *n.* (*slang*) a user of LSD.

a·cid·ic (ă-sid-ik) *adj.* of or like an acid.

a·cid·i·fy (ă-sid-ĭ-fī) *v.* (**a·cid·i·fied, a·cid·i·fy·ing**) to make or become acid.

a·cid·i·ty (ă-sid-i-tee) *n.* 1. being acid. 2. an over-acid condition of the stomach.

ac·i·do·sis (as-i-doh-sis) *n.* an over-acid condition of the blood or body tissues.

a·cid·u·lat·ed (ă-sij-ŭ-lay-tid) *adj.* made slightly acid.

a·cid·u·lous (ă-sij-ŭ-lŭs) *adj.* 1. acidulated. 2. somewhat sarcastic.

ack-ack (ak-ak) *n.* antiaircraft guns or gunfire.

ac·knowl·edge (ak-nol-ij) *v.* (**ac·knowl·edged, ac·knowl·edg·ing**) 1. to admit that something is true or valid. 2. to report that one has received something, *acknowledge her letter.* 3. to express thanks for, *acknowledge his services to the town.* 4. to indicate that one has noticed or recognized, *acknowledged my presence with a smile.* **ac·knowl'edg·ment** *n.*

ac·me (ak-mee) *n.* the highest point, the peak of perfection.

ac·ne (ak-nee) *n.* inflammation of the oil glands of the skin, producing pimples.

ac·o·lyte (ak-ŏ-līt) *n.* a person who assists a priest in certain church services.

ac·o·nite (ak-ŏ-nīt) *n.* a perennial plant of the buttercup family, with a poisonous root.

a·corn (ay-korn) *n.* the nut of the oak tree.

a·cous·tic (ă-koo-stik) *adj.* of sound or the sense of hearing, of acoustics. **a·cous'ti·cal** *adj.* **a·cous'ti·cal·ly** *adv.*

a·cous·tics (ă-koo-stiks) *n. pl.* the properties of

sound, the qualities of a hall etc. that make it good or bad for carrying sound.

ac·quaint (ă-kwaynt) v. to make aware or familiar, *acquaint him with the facts.* □**be acquainted with,** to know slightly.

ac·quaint·ance (ă-kwayn-tăns) n. 1. being acquainted. 2. a person one knows slightly. **ac·quain'tance·ship** n.

ac·qui·esce (ak-wi-es) v. (**ac·qui·esced, ac·qui·esc·ing**) to agree without protest, to assent. □**acquiesce in,** to accept as an arrangement. **ac·qui·es·cent** (ak-wi-es-ĕnt) adj. acquiescing. **ac·qui·es'cence** n.

ac·quire (ă-kwɪr) v. (**ac·quired, ac·quir·ing**) to gain possession of. **ac·quire'ment** n. □**acquired taste,** a liking gained through experience.

ac·qui·si·tion (ak-wi-zish-ŏn) n. 1. acquiring. 2. something acquired.

ac·quis·i·tive (ă-kwiz-i-tiv) adj. eager to acquire things. **ac·quis'i·tive·ly** adv. **ac·quis'i·tive·ness** n.

ac·quit (ă-kwit) v. (**ac·quit·ted, ac·quit·ting**) to declare (a person) to be not guilty of the crime etc. with which he was charged. □**acquit oneself,** to conduct oneself, to perform, *he acquitted himself well in the test.*

ac·quit·tal (ă-kwit-ăl) n. a judgment that a person is not guilty of the crime with which he was charged.

a·cre (ay-kĕr) n. 1. a measure of land, 4840 sq. yds. 2. a stretch of land, *broad acres.*

a·cre·age (ay-kĕ-rij) n. 1. the total number of acres. 2. a large land holding.

ac·rid (ak-rid) adj. 1. having a bitter smell or taste. 2. bitter in temper or manner. **ac'rid·ness** n. **a·crid·i·ty** (ă-krid-i-tee) n.

ac·ri·mo·ny (ak-rĭ-moh-nee) n. bitterness of manner or words. **ac·ri·mo·ni·ous** (ak-rĭ-moh-ni-ŭs) adj. **ac·ri·mo'ni·ous·ly** adv.

ac·ro·bat (ak-rŏ-bat) n. a performer of spectacular gymnastic feats. **ac·ro·bat·ic** (ak-rŏ-bat-ik) adj. **ac·ro·bat'i·cal·ly** adv.

ac·ro·bat·ics (ak-rŏ-bat-iks) n. 1. the doing of acrobatic feats, *acrobatics is fun to watch.* 2. these feats.

ac·ro·nym (ak-rŏ-nim) n. a word formed from the initial letters of other words, as *NATO, radar.*

ac·ro·pho·bi·a (ak-rŏ-foh-bi-ă) n. an abnormal fear of being at a great height.

a·crop·o·lis (ă-krop-ŏ-lis) n. the citadel or upper fortified part of an ancient Greek city. □**the Acropolis,** that of Athens.

a·cross (ă-kraws) adv. & prep. 1. from one side of a thing to the other. 2. to or on the other side of. 3. so as to be understood or accepted, *got his points across to the audience.* 4. so as to form a cross or intersect, *laid across each other.* ▷The word *acrost* does not exist in good English.

a·cross-the-board (ă-kraws-thĕ-bohrd) adj. 1. (of a racing bet) wagering in equal amounts to win, place, and show. 2. applying to all members or groups, *an across-the-board cost-of-living increase.*

a·cros·tic (ă-kraw-stik) n. a word puzzle or poem in which the first or last letters of each line form a word or words. **acrostic** adj. **a·cros'ti·cal·ly** adv.

a·cryl·ic (ă-kril-ik) adj. of a synthetic material made from an organic acid. **acrylic** n. an acrylic fiber, plastic, or resin.

act (akt) n. 1. something done. 2. the process of

doing something, *caught in the act.* 3. a decree, statute, or law. 4. one of the main divisions of a play. 5. one of a series of short performances in a program, *a circus act.* 6. *(informal)* a pose or pretense, *put on an act.* **act** v. 1. to perform actions, to behave, *you acted wisely.* 2. to do what is required, to function, *act as umpire.* 3. to have an effect on, *acid acts on metal.* 4. to portray by actions, to perform a part in a play etc. □**act of God,** the operation of uncontrollable natural forces. **Acts of the Apostles,** a book of the New Testament relating the early history of the Christian Church and dealing largely with the lives and work of the Apostles Peter and Paul, traditionally ascribed to St. Luke. **act the fool,** to behave in a ridiculous manner. **act up,** to misbehave, to function improperly, (of an illness) to recur.

ACTH abbr. adrenocorticotrophic hormone.

act·ing (ak-ting) adj. serving temporarily, especially as a substitute, *the acting president of the group.*

ac·tin·i·um (ak-tin-i-ŭm) n. a radioactive metallic chemical element.

ac·tion (ak-shŏn) n. 1. the process of doing something, the exertion of energy or influence, *go into action; the action of acid on metal,* the way it affects metal. 2. a thing done, *generous actions.* 3. a series of events in a story or play, *the action is set in Spain.* 4. a way or manner of moving or functioning, the mechanism of an instrument. 5. a lawsuit. 6. a battle, *killed in action.* 7. *actions,* conduct. □**action painting,** abstract painting using spontaneous techniques of applying paint to the canvas, as dribbling or splattering. **out of action,** not working. **take action,** to do something in response to what has happened.

ac·tion·a·ble (ak-shŏ-nă-bĕl) adj. giving cause for a lawsuit.

ac·ti·vate (ak-tĭ-vayt) v. (**ac·ti·vat·ed, ac·ti·vat·ing**) 1. to make active. 2. to treat (charcoal etc.) so as to improve adsorptive properties. 3. to aerate (sewage) to hasten decomposition. 4. to call (a military unit etc.) to active duty. **ac'ti·va·tor** n. **ac·ti·va·tion** (ak-tĭ-vay-shŏn) n. ▷Note the differences between *activate* and *actuate.*

ac·tive (ak-tiv) adj. 1. moving about, characterized by energetic action. 2. taking part in activities. 3. functioning, in operation; *an active volcano,* one that erupts occasionally. 4. having an effect, *the active ingredients.* **active** n. the form of a verb used when the subject of the sentence is the doer of the action, as *saw* in *we saw him.* **ac'tive·ly** adv. **ac'tive·ness** n. □**active service,** full-time service in the armed forces.

ac·tiv·ist (ak-tĭ-vist) n. a person who follows a policy of vigorous action, especially in politics. **ac·tiv·i·ty** (ak-tiv-i-tee) n. (pl. **-ties**) 1. being active, the exertion of energy. 2. energetic action, being busy. 3. actions, occupations, *outdoor activities.*

ac·tor (ak-tŏr) n. a performer in a stage play, a film, etc. **ac·tress** (ak-tris) n. fem.

ac·tu·al (ak-choo-ăl) adj. existing in fact, real, current. **ac'tu·al·ly** adv.

ac·tu·al·i·ty (ak-choo-al-i-tee) n. (pl. **-ties**) reality.

ac·tu·al·ize (ak-choo-ă-lɪz) v. (**ac·tu·al·ized, ac·tu·al·iz·ing**) to realize in action. **ac·tu·al·i·za·tion** (ak-choo-ă-li-zay-shŏn) n.

ac·tu·ar·y (ak-choo-er-ee) *n.* (*pl.* **-ar·ies**) an expert in statistics who calculates insurance rates and premiums. **ac·tu·ar·i·al** (ak-choo-air-i-ăl) *adj.*

ac·tu·ate (ak-choo-ayt) *v.* (**ac·tu·at·ed, ac·tu·at·ing**) 1. to activate (a movement or process). 2. to be a motive for (a person's actions). **ac′tu·a·tor** *n.* **ac·tu·a·tion** (ak-choo-ay-shŏn) *n.* ▷Note the differences between *actuate* and *activate.*

a·cu·i·ty (ă-kyoo-i-tee) *n.* (*pl.* **-ties**) perception, keenness of perception.

a·cu·men (ă-kyoo-měn) *n.* sharpness of mind, shrewdness.

ac·u·punc·ture (ak-yŭ-pungk-chŭr) *n.* pricking the tissues of the body with fine needles to relieve pain or as a local anesthetic. **ac·u·punc·tur·ist** (ak-yŭ-pungk-chŭ-rist) *n.* a practitioner of acupuncture.

a·cute (ă-kyoot) *adj.* 1. sharp, pointed. 2. very perceptive, having a sharp mind. 3. sharp or severe in its effect, *acute pain; an acute shortage.* 4. (of an illness) coming sharply to a crisis of severity, *acute appendicitis.* **a·cute′ly** *adv.* **a·cute′ness** *n.* □**acute accent**, a mark over a vowel, as over *e* in *café.* **acute angle**, an angle of less than 90°.

ad (ad) *n.* *(informal)* an advertisement.

A.D. *abbr.* of the Christian era. ▷From the Latin *anno domini,* = in the year of Our Lord.

ad·age (ad-ij) *n.* an old familiar saying, a proverb.

a·da·gio (ă-dah-joh) *adj. & adv.* (as a musical direction) in slow time. **adagio** *n.* a musical movement in slow time.

Ad·am (ad-ăm) (in the Old Testament) the first man; *I don't know him from Adam,* do not recognize him or know what he looks like. □**Adam's apple,** the projection of cartilage at the front of the neck, especially in men.

ad·a·mant (ad-ă-mănt) *adj.* unyielding to requests, quite firm. **ad′a·mant·ly** *adv.*

Ad·ams (ad-ămz), **John** (1735–1826) the second president of the U.S. 1797–1801.

Ad·ams (ad-ămz), **John Quin·cy** (1767–1848) the sixth president of the U.S. 1825–29.

a·dapt (ă-dapt) *v.* to make or become suitable for a new use or situation. **a·dap′tive** *adj.* **ad·ap·ta·tion** (ad-ăp-tay-shŏn) *n.* ▷Do not confuse *adapt* with *adopt.*

a·dapt·a·ble (ă-dap-tă-běl) *adj.* 1. able to be adapted. 2. able to adapt oneself. **a·dapt·a·bil·i·ty** (ă-dap-tă-bil-i-tee) *n.*

a·dapt·er, a·dap·tor (ă-dap-těr) *n.* a device that connects pieces of equipment that were not originally designed to be connected.

add (ad) *v.* 1. to join (one thing to another) as an increase or supplement; *this adds to the expense,* increases it. 2. to put numbers or amounts together to get a total. 3. to make a further remark. **add′er** *n.* □**add up,** to find the total of; *(informal)* to seem consistent or reasonable, *his story doesn't add up.* **add up to,** to yield as a total; *(informal)* to result in, to be equivalent to.

ad·dend (ad-end) *n.* a number to be added to another.

ad·den·dum (ă-den-dŭm) *n.* (*pl.* **-da,** *pr.* -dă) additional matter at the end of a book or other document, *the paper has three addenda.*

ad·der (ad-ěr) *n.* 1. a small poisonous snake, the European viper. 2. any of several harmless North American snakes.

ad·dict (ad-ikt) *n.* a person who is addicted to something, especially to drugs. **addict** (ă-dikt) *v.* 1. to be or cause to be dependent on a drug. 2. to be or cause to be a devotee, to do or use something habitually. **ad·dic·tion** (ă-dik-shŏn) *n.*

ad·dict·ed (ă-dik-tid) *adj.* 1. doing or using something as a habit or compulsively. 2. devoted to something as a hobby or interest. **ad·dic·tive** (ă-dik-tiv) *adj.* causing addiction.

Ad·dis Ab·a·ba (ad-is ab-ă-bă) the capital of Ethiopia.

ad·di·tion (ă-dish-ŏn) *n.* 1. adding, being added. 2. a thing added to something else. □**in addition,** as an extra thing or circumstance. **ad·di·tion·al** (ă-dish-ŏ-năl) *adj.* added, extra. **ad·di′tion·al·ly** *adv.*

ad·di·tive (ad-i-tiv) *adj.* involving addition. **additive** *n.* a substance added in small amounts for a special purpose.

ad·dle (ad-ěl) *v.* (**ad·dled, ad·dling**) 1. to become rotten, *addled eggs.* 2. to muddle or confuse, *addle one's brains.*

ad·dress (ad-res, ă-dres) *n.* 1. the place where a person lives, particulars of where mail should be delivered to a person or firm. 2. (ă-dres) a speech delivered to an audience. **address** (ă-dres) *v.* 1. to write directions for delivery on (an envelope or package). 2. to make a speech to. 3. to direct a remark or written statement to. 4. to use a particular word or words in speaking or writing to, *how to address a bishop.* 5. to apply (oneself) to a task or problem. 6. to take aim at (the ball) in golf. □**forms of address,** words (as *Mr., Sir, Your Majesty*) used in addressing a person.

ad·dress·ee (ad-re-see) *n.* a person to whom a letter etc. is addressed.

ad·duce (ă-doos) *v.* (**ad·duced, ad·duc·ing**) to offer as an example, reason, or proof.

-ade *suffix* used to form nouns meaning act, action, as in *blockade;* product, especially a sweet drink, as in *orangeade.*

A·den (ah-děn) the capital of the Democratic Republic of Yemen.

ad·e·noids (ad-ě-noidz) *n. pl.* enlarged spongy tissue between the back of the nose and the throat, often hindering breathing. **ad·e·noi·dal** (ad-ě-noi-dăl) *adj.*

ad·ept (ă-dept) *adj.* very skillful. **adept** (ad-ept) *n.* a person who is very skillful, an *adept* at billiards. **a·dept′ly** *adv.* **a·dept′ness** *n.*

ad·e·quate (ad-ě-kwit) *adj.* 1. sufficient, satisfactory. 2. passable but not outstandingly good. **ad′e·quate·ly** *adv.* **ad·e·qua·cy** (ad-ě-kwă-see) *n.*

ad·here (ad-heer) *v.* (**ad·hered, ad·her·ing**) 1. to stick when glued or by suction or as if by these. 2. to remain faithful, to continue to give one's support (to a person or cause). 3. to keep to and not alter, *we adhered to our plan.*

ad·her·ent (ad-heer-ěnt) *adj.* sticking, adhering. **adherent** *n.* a supporter of a party or doctrine. **ad·her′ence** *n.*

ad·he·sion (ad-hee-zhŏn) *n.* 1. adhering. 2. the growing together of normally separate tissues of the body as a result of inflammation or injury, tissue growing in this way.

ad·he·sive (ad-hee-siv) *adj.* causing things to adhere, sticky. **adhesive** *n.* an adhesive substance. **ad·he′sive·ness** *n.* □**adhesive tape,** a strip of cloth, paper, or transparent material coated with adhesive, used for covering wounds, fastening packages, etc.

ad hoc (ad hŏk) for a specific purpose, *an ad hoc committee.* ▷Latin, = for this.

a·dieu (ă-dyoo) *interj.* & *n.* (*pl.* **-dieus, -dieux,** *pr.* ă-dyooz) goodby.

ad in·fi·ni·tum (ad in-fi-nī-tŭm) without limit, forever. ▷Latin, = to infinity.

ad·i·os (ad-i-ohs) *interj.* goodby.

ad·i·pose (ad-i-pohs) *adj.* of animal fat, fatty. **ad·i·pos·i·ty** (ad-i-pos-i-tee) *n.*

adj. *abbr.* 1. adjective. 2. adjutant.

ad·ja·cent (ă-jay-sĕnt) *adj.* lying near, adjoining.

ad·jec·tive (aj-ik-tiv) *n.* a word added to a noun to describe a quality or modify a meaning, as *old, tall, Swedish, my, this.* **ad·jec·ti·val** (aj-ik-tĭ-văl) *adj.* **ad·jec·ti'val·ly** *adv.*

ad·join (ă-join) *v.* to be next or nearest to. ▷Do not confuse *adjoin* with *adjourn.*

ad·join·ing (ă-joi-ning) *adj.* 1. touching or joining at a point or line. 2. connected by a shared door or doorway, *adjoining rooms.*

ad·journ (ă-jurn) *v.* 1. to postpone, to break off temporarily. 2. to break off and go elsewhere, *let's adjourn to the bar.* **ad·journ'ment** *n.* ▷Do not confuse *adjourn* with *adjoin.*

ad·judge (ă-juj) *v.* (**ad·judged, ad·judg·ing**) 1. to decide or award judicially, *he was adjudged to be guilty.* 2. to act as judge. 3. to deem to be.

ad·ju·di·cate (ă-joo-di-kayt) *v.* (**ad·ju·di·cat·ed, ad·ju·di·cat·ing**) 1. to act as judge in a court, tribunal, or competition. 2. to judge and pronounce a decision upon, to settle judicially.

ad·junct (aj-ungkt) *n.* something or someone added or attached but subordinate. **adjunct** *adj.* serving in this manner, *an adjunct professor.*

ad·jure (ă-joor) *v.* (**ad·jured, ad·jur·ing**) to command or urge solemnly, *I adjure you to tell the truth.* **ad·ju·ra·tion** (aj-ŭ-ray-shŏn) *n.* ▷Do not confuse *adjure* with *abjure.*

ad·just (ă-just) *v.* 1. to arrange, to put into the proper position. 2. to alter by a small amount so as to fit or be right for use, *the brakes need adjusting.* 3. to be able to be adjusted. 4. to adapt or adapt oneself to new circumstances, *had difficulty in adjusting to college.* 5. to assess (loss or damages). **ad·just'er** *n.* **ad·jus'tor** *n.* **ad·just'ment** *n.*

ad·just·a·ble (ă-jus-tă-bĕl) *adj.* able to be adjusted.

ad·ju·tant (aj-ŭ-tănt) *n.* an army officer assisting a superior officer with administrative work.

ad lib (ad lib) (*informal*) words, gestures, etc. spoken impromptu. ▷From the Latin *ad libitum,* according to pleasure.

ad-lib *v.* (**ad-libbed, ad-lib·bing**) (*informal*) to speak impromptu, to improvise remarks or actions. **ad-lib** *adj.* (*informal*) said or done impromptu, *his remarks were entirely ad-lib.*

adm. *abbr.* 1. administrative. 2. administration.

Adm. *abbr.* Admiral.

ad·man (ad-man) *n.* (*pl.* **ad·men,** *pr.* ad-men) (*slang*) a person who writes, solicits, or places advertisements to earn his livelihood.

ad·min·is·ter (ad-min-i-stĕr) *v.* 1. to manage the business affairs of, to be an administrator. 2. to give or hand out formally, to provide, *administer justice; administer the oath of office,* hear the person swear it officially. ▷See the note under **minister.**

ad·min·is·trate (ad-min-i-strayt) *v.* (**ad·min·is·trat·ed, ad·min·is·trat·ing**) to act as administrator of. ▷Careful writers prefer *administer.*

ad·min·is·tra·tion (ad-min-i-stray-shŏn) *n.* 1. administering. 2. the management of public or business affairs. 3. a governing group under a president, governor, etc., its period of office.

ad·min·is·tra·tive (ad-min-i-stray-tiv) *adj.* of or involving administration. **ad·min'is·tra·tive·ly** *adv.*

ad·min·is·tra·tor (ad-min-i-stray-tŏr) *n.* 1. a person responsible for administration, one who has a talent for this. 2. a person appointed to administer an estate.

ad·mi·ra·ble (ad-mĭ-ră-bĕl) *adj.* worthy of admiration, excellent. **ad'mi·ra·bly** *adv.*

ad·mi·ral (ad-mĭ-răl) *n.* a naval officer of high rank, commander of a fleet or squadron; *fleet admiral, admiral, vice admiral, rear admiral,* the four grades of such officers.

ad·mi·ral·ty (ad-mĭ-răl-tee) *n.* 1. the office and jurisdiction of an admiral. 2. a court of law dealing with maritime matters. **admiralty** *adj.* of or dealing with admiralty law.

ad·mire (ad-mɪr) *v.* (**ad·mired, ad·mir·ing**) 1. to regard with pleasure or satisfaction, to think highly of. 2. to express admiration of. **ad·mir'er** *n.* **ad·mir'ing·ly** *adv.* **ad·mi·ra·tion** (ad-mĭ-ray-shŏn) *n.*

ad·mis·si·ble (ad-mis-i-bĕl) *adj.* capable of being admitted or allowed. **ad·mis'si·bly** *adv.* **ad·mis·si·bil·i·ty** (ad-mis-ĭ-bil-i-tee) *n.*

ad·mis·sion (ad-mish-ŏn) *n.* 1. admitting, being admitted. 2. a statement admitting something, a confession, *an admission of guilt.* 3. acknowledgment of a fact, granting of an argument. 4. a fee paid to enter a place.

ad·mit (ad-mit) *v.* (**ad·mit·ted, ad·mit·ting**) 1. to allow to enter. 2. to accept into a school as a pupil, into a hospital as a patient, etc. 3. to accept as true or valid. 4. to state reluctantly, *we admit that the task is difficult.* 5. to leave room for, *the plan does not admit of improvement.* **ad·mit'tance** *n.*

ad·mit·ted·ly (ad-mit-id-lee) *adv.* as an acknowledged fact.

ad·mix·ture (ad-miks-chŭr) *n.* 1. something added as an ingredient. 2. a mixture.

ad·mon·ish (ad-mon-ish) *v.* 1. to advise or urge seriously. 2. to reprove mildly but firmly. **ad·mon·i·to·ry** (ad-mŏ-tohr-ee) *adj.* **ad·mo·ni·tion** (ad-mŏ-nish-ŏn) *n.*

ad nau·se·am (ad naw-zi-ŭm) to a sickening extent. ▷Latin.

a·do (ă-doo) *n.* fuss, trouble, excitement.

a·do·be (ă-doh-bee) *n.* 1. sun-dried clay used for building etc. 2. a house made of such clay bricks.

ad·o·les·cent (ad-ŏ-les-ĕnt) *adj.* between childhood and maturity. **adolescent** *n.* an adolescent person. **ad·o·les'cence** *n.*

A·do·nis (ă-don-is) *n.* a handsome young man. ▷Named after a beautiful youth in mythology, loved by Venus.

a·dopt (ă-dopt) *v.* 1. to take into one's family as a relation, especially as one's child with legal guardianship. 2. to take and use as one's own, *adopted this name or custom.* 3. to approve or accept (a report or financial accounts). **a·dop·tion** (ă-dop-shŏn) *n.* ▷Do not confuse *adopt* with *adapt.*

a·dop·tive (ă-dŏp-tiv) *adj.* related to adoption, *adoptive parents.*

a·dor·a·ble (ă-dohr-ă-bĕl) *adj.* 1. very lovable. 2. *(informal)* delightful. **a·dor'a·bly** *adv.*

a·dore (ă-dohr) *v.* (**a·dored, a·dor·ing**) 1. to love deeply. 2. to worship as divine. 3. *(informal)* to like very much. **a·dor'er** *n.* **ad·o·ra·tion** (ad-ŏ-ray-shŏn) *n.*

a·dorn (ă-dorn) *v.* 1. to decorate with ornaments. 2. to be an ornament to. **a·dorn'ment** *n.*

a·dre·nal (ă-dree-năl) *adj.* close to the kidneys. **adrenal** *n.* one of the **adrenal glands,** ductless glands on top of the kidneys, secreting adrenaline.

a·dren·a·line (ă-dren-ă-lin) *n.* a hormone that stimulates the nervous system, secreted by a part of the adrenal glands or prepared synthetically.

a·dre·no·cor·ti·co·trop·ic (ă-dree-noh-kor-tĭ-koh-trop-ik) **hormone** *n.* a hormone (ACTH) of the pituitary gland that stimulates the adrenal cortex.

A·dri·at·ic (ay-dri-at-ik) *adj.* of the Adriatic Sea, between Italy and Yugoslavia. **Adriatic** *n.* the Adriatic Sea.

a·drift (ă-drift) *adj. & adv.* 1. drifting. 2. *(informal)* without purpose or guidance.

a·droit (ă-droit) *adj.* skillful, ingenious. **a·droit'ly** *adv.* **a·droit'ness** *n.*

ad·sorb (ad-sorb) *v.* to hold molecules of a gas or liquid to the surface of a (usually) solid material. **ad·sorp·tive** (ad-sorp-tiv) *adj.* **ad·sorp·tion** (ad-sorp-shŏn) *n.* ▷ Do not confuse *adsorb* with *absorb.*

ad·sor·bent (ad-sor-bĕnt) *adj.* producing adsorption. **adsorbent** *n.* an adsorbent substance. ▷ Do not confuse *adsorbent* with *absorbent.*

ad·u·la·tion (aj-ŭ-lay-shŏn) *n.* excessive flattery. **ad·u·la·to·ry** (aj-ŭ-lă-tohr-ee) *adj.*

a·dult (ă-dult) *adj.* grown to full size or strength, mature. **adult** *n.* an adult person. **a·dult'hood** *n.*

a·dul·ter·ant (ă-dul-tĕ-rănt) *n.* a substance added in adulterating something.

a·dul·ter·ate (ă-dul-tĕ-rayt) *v.* (**a·dul·ter·ated, a·dul·ter·at·ing**) to make impure or poorer in quality by adding another substance, especially an inferior one. **a·dul·ter·a·tion** (ă-dul-tĕ-ray-shŏn) *n.*

a·dul·ter·er (ă-dul-tĕ-rĕr) *n.* a person who commits adultery. **a·dul·ter·ess** (ă-dul-tĕ-ris) *n. fem.*

a·dul·ter·y (ă-dul-tĕ-ree) *n.* the act of voluntary sexual intercourse by a married person with someone other than his or her own spouse. **a·dul'ter·ous** *adj.*

adv. *abbr.* 1. adverb. 2. advertisement.

ad va·lo·rem (ad va-lohr-ĕm) (of taxes) in proportion to estimated value of goods. ▷ Latin.

ad·vance (ad-vans) *v.* (**ad·vanced, ad·vanc·ing**) 1. to move or put forward, to make progress. 2. to help the progress of, *advance someone's interests.* 3. to bring forward or make, *advance a suggestion.* 4. to bring (an event) to an earlier date. 5. to lend (money), to pay before a due date, *advance her a month's salary.* 6. to promote in rank. **advance** *n.* 1. a forward movement, progress. 2. an increase in price or amount. 3. a loan, payment beforehand. 4. *advances,* attempts to establish a friendly relationship. **advance** *adj.* going before others, done or provided in advance, *the advance party.* **ad·vance'ment** *n.* □in advance, ahead in place or time, *she paid well in advance.*

ad·vanced (ad-vanst) *adj.* 1. far on in progress or in life, *an advanced age.* 2. not elementary, *advanced studies.* 3. (of ideas etc.) new and not yet generally accepted.

ad·van·tage (ad-van-tij) *n.* 1. a favorable condition or circumstance. 2. benefit, profit; *the treaty is to their advantage,* benefits them; *turn it to your advantage,* use it profitably. 3. the next point won after deuce in tennis. □take advantage of, to make use of; to exploit. **to advantage,** making a good effect, *the painting shows to advantage here.* ▷Do not confuse *advantage* with *vantage.*

ad·van·ta·geous (ad-văn-tay-jŭs) *adj.* profitable, beneficial. **ad·van·ta'geous·ly** *adv.*

Ad·vent (ad-vent) *n.* 1. the coming of Christ. 2. the season (with four Sundays) before Christmas Day. 3. *advent,* the arrival of an important person, event, or development.

ad·ven·ti·tious (ad-ven-tish-ŭs) *adj.* 1. accidental, casual. 2. occurring in an unusual position, sporadic. **ad·ven·ti'tious·ly** *adv.* **ad·ven·ti'tious·ness** *n.*

ad·ven·ture (ad-ven-chŭr) *n.* 1. an exciting or dangerous experience. 2. willingness to take risks, *the spirit of adventure.* **ad·ven'tur·ous** *adj.* **ad·ven'tur·ous·ly** *adv.* **ad·ven'ture·some** *adj.*

ad·ven·tur·er (ad-ven-chŭ-rĕr) *n.* 1. a person who seeks adventures. 2. a person who is ready to make gains for himself by risky or unscrupulous methods. **ad·ven·tur·ess** (ad-ven-chŭ-ris) *n. fem.*

ad·verb (ad-vurb) *n.* a word that qualifies a verb, adjective, or other adverb and indicates how, when, or where, as *gently, fully, soon.* **ad·ver·bi·al** (ad-vur-bi-ăl) *adj.* **ad·ver'bi·al·ly** *adv.*

ad·ver·sar·y (ad-vĕr-ser-ee) *n.* (*pl.* **-sar·ies**) an opponent, an enemy.

ad·verse (ad-vurs) *adj.* 1. unfavorable, *an adverse report.* 2. bringing misfortune or harm, *the drug has no adverse effects.* **ad·verse'ly** *adv.* ▷Do not confuse *adverse* with *averse.*

ad·ver·si·ty (ad-vur-si-tee) *n.* (*pl.* **-ties**) misfortune, trouble.

ad·ver·tise (ad-vĕr-tız) *v.* (**ad·ver·tised, ad·ver·tis·ing**) 1. to make generally or publicly known, *advertise a meeting.* 2. to call public attention to in order to encourage people to buy or use something, *advertise soap.* 3. to issue a public notice seeking to buy or obtain something, *advertise for a secretary.* **ad'ver·tis·er** *n.*

ad·ver·tise·ment (ad-vĕr-tız-mĕnt, -vur-tis-) *n.* 1. the process of advertising. 2. a public notice or broadcast announcing or advertising something.

ad·ver·tis·ing (ad-vĕr-tı-zing) *n.* 1. the process by which something is advertised. 2. advertisements. 3. the business that prepares and disseminates advertisements.

ad·vice (ad-vıs) *n.* 1. an opinion given about what to do or how to behave. 2. a piece of information, *we received advice that the goods had been shipped.* ▷Do not confuse *advice* with *advise.*

ad·vis·a·ble (ad-vı-ză-bĕl) *adj.* worth recommending as a course of action. **ad·vis·a·bil·i·ty** (ad-vı-ză-bil-i-tee) *n.*

ad·vise (ad-vız) *v.* (**ad·vised, ad·vis·ing**) 1. to give advice to, to recommend. 2. to inform, to notify. **ad·vis'er** *n.* **ad·vi'sor** *n.* ▷Do not confuse *advise* with *advice.*

ad·vised (ad-vızd) *adj.* deliberate, considered. **ad·vis·ed·ly** (ad-vı-zid-lee) *adv.*

ad·vi·so·ry (ad-vı-zŏ-ree) *adj.* giving advice, hav-

ing the power to advise, *an advisory committee.*
ad·vo·ca·cy (ad-vŏ-kă-see) *n.* 1. the advocating of a policy etc. 2. the function of an advocate.
ad·vo·cate (ad-vŏ-kayt) *v.* (**ad·vo·cat·ed, ad·vo·cat·ing**) to recommend, to be in favor of, *I advocate caution.* **advocate** (ad-vŏ-kit) *n.* 1. a person who advocates a policy, *an advocate of reform.* 2. a person who pleads on behalf of another. **ad·vo·ca·tion** (ad-vŏ-kay-shŏn) *n.*
advt. *abbr.* advertisement.
adz, adze (adz) *n.* a kind of ax with a blade at right angles to the handle, used for trimming or shaping wood.
Ae·ge·an (i-jee-ăn) *adj.* of the Aegean Sea, between Greece and Turkey. **Aegean** *n.* the Aegean Sea.
ae·gis (ee-jis) *n.* protection, sponsorship, *under the aegis of the Humane Society.*
ae·o·li·an (i-oh-li-ăn) **harp** a stringed instrument producing musical sounds as the wind passes across it.
ae·on *see* eon.
aer·ate (air-ayt) *v.* (**aer·at·ed, aer·at·ing**) 1. to expose to the chemical action of air. 2. to supply (the blood) with oxygen by respiration. 3. to add carbon dioxide to (a liquid) under pressure. **aer′a·tor** *n.* **aer·a·tion** (air-ay-shŏn) *n.*
aer·i·al (air-i-ăl) *adj.* 1. of or like air. 2. existing in the air, suspended overhead, *an aerial railway.* 3. by or from aircraft, *aerial bombardment.* **aerial** *n.* an antenna.
aer·i·al·ist (air-i-ă-list) *n.* a performer on a high wire or trapeze.
aer·ie (air-ee) *n.* 1. the nest of a bird that builds high up, especially of an eagle or other bird of prey. 2. a residence perched high on a mountain.
aer·o·bat·ics (air-ŏ-bat-iks) *n.* 1. spectacular feats of flying aircraft, especially for display, *the aerobatics were breathtaking.* 2. the performance of such feats, *aerobatics is not for me.* **aer·o·bat′ic** *adj.*
aer·o·dy·nam·ics (air-oh-dı-nam-iks) *n.* interaction between airflow and the movement of solid bodies (as aircraft, bullets) through air. **aer·o·dy·nam′ic** *adj.* **aer·o·dy·nam′i·cal·ly** *adv.*
aer·o·naut (air-ŏ-nawt) *n.* the navigator or pilot of a balloon or other lighter-than-air craft.
aer·o·nau·tics (air-ŏ-naw-tiks) *n.* the scientific study of the flight of aircraft. **aer·o·nau′tic** *adj.* **aer·o·nau′ti·cal** *adj.*
aer·o·plane (air-ŏ-playn) *n.* (chiefly *British*) an airplane.
aer·o·sol (air-ŏ-sohl) *n.* a substance sealed in a container under pressure, with a device for releasing it as a fine spray.
aer·o·space (air-ŏ-spays) *n.* 1. Earth's atmosphere and space beyond it. 2. the technology of aviation in this region. **aerospace** *adj.* concerned with missiles, satellites, vehicles, etc. for operation in aerospace, *aerospace industry.*
aes·thete (es-theet) *n.* a person who has or claims to have great understanding and appreciation of what is beautiful, especially in the arts.
aes·thet·ic (es-thet-ik) *adj.* 1. belonging to the appreciation of beauty, *the aesthetic standards of the times.* 2. having or showing such appreciation. 3. artistic, tasteful. **aes·thet′i·cal·ly** *adv.*
aes·thet·ics (es-thet-iks) *n.* a branch of philosophy dealing with the principles of beauty in art.
AF *abbr.* 1. Air Force. 2. audio frequency.

a·far (ă-fahr) *adv.* far off, far away.
AFB *abbr.* Air Force Base.
af·fa·ble (af-ă-bĕl) *adj.* polite and friendly. **af′fa·bly** *adv.* **af·fa·bil·i·ty** (af-ă-bil-i-tee) *n.*
af·fair (ă-fair) *n.* 1. a thing done or to be done, a matter, a concern. 2. public or private business, *current affairs; put your affairs in order.* 3. *(informal)* an event, a thing, *this camera is a complicated affair.* 4. a temporary romantic or sexual relationship.
af·fect (ă-fekt) *v.* 1. to pretend to have or feel or be, *she affected ignorance.* 2. to like and make a display of using or wearing, *he affects velvet jackets.* 3. to produce an effect on, (of a disease) to attack or infect, *his lungs are affected.* ▷The words *affect* and *effect* have totally different meanings and should not be confused.
af·fec·ta·tion (af-ek-tay-shŏn) *n.* behavior that is put on for display and is not natural or genuine, pretense. ▷Do not confuse *affectation* with *affection.*
af·fect·ed (ă-fek-tid) *adj.* 1. full of affectation. 2. pretended. 3. impaired, as by disease, *the affected organs.* **af·fect′ed·ly** *adv.*
af·fect·ing (ă-fek-ting) *adj.* having an effect upon one's emotions, *an affecting appeal.* **af·fect′ing·ly** *adv.*
af·fec·tion (ă-fek-shŏn) *n.* 1. love, a liking. 2. a disease or diseased condition. ▷Do not confuse *affection* with *affectation.*
af·fec·tion·ate (ă-fek-shŏ-nit) *adj.* showing affection, loving. **af·fec′tion·ate·ly** *adv.*
af·fi·ance (ă-fı-ăns) *v.* (**af·fi·anced, af·fi·anc·ing**) to engage to be married, to betroth.
af·fi·da·vit (af-i-day-vit) *n.* a written statement for use as legal evidence, sworn on oath to be true.
af·fil·i·ate (ă-fil-i-ayt) *v.* (**af·fil·i·at·ed, af·fil·i·at·ing**) to connect as a subordinate member or branch, *the club is affiliated with a national society.* **affiliate** (ă-fil-i-it) *n.* a person, group, business, etc. that is affiliated. **af·fil·i·a·tion** (ă-fil-i-ay-shŏn) *n.*
af·fin·i·ty (ă-fin-i-tee) *n.* (*pl.* **-ties**) 1. a relationship (especially by marriage) other than a blood relationship. 2. a similarity, close resemblance or connection, *affinities between different languages.* 3. a strong natural liking or attraction. 4. the tendency of certain substances to combine with others.
af·firm (ă-furm) *v.* 1. to assert, to state as a fact. 2. to uphold (a judgment). 3. to declare by affirmation.
af·fir·ma·tion (af-ĕr-may-shŏn) *n.* 1. affirming. 2. a solemn declaration made instead of an oath by a person who has conscientious objections to swearing an oath or who has no religion.
af·firm·a·tive (ă-fur-mă-tiv) *adj.* affirming, agreeing; *an affirmative reply,* answering "yes." **affirmative** *n.* an affirmative word or statement, *the answer is in the affirmative.* **af·firm′a·tive·ly** *adv.*
af·fix¹ (ă-fiks) *v.* 1. to stick on, to attach. 2. to add in writing, *affix your signature.*
af·fix² (af-iks) *n.* 1. appendage, addition. 2. a prefix or suffix.
af·flict (ă-flikt) *v.* to distress physically or mentally; *he is afflicted with rheumatism,* suffers from it. **af·flic′tive** *adj.*
af·flic·tion (ă-flik-shŏn) *n.* 1. pain, distress, misery. 2. something that causes this.
af·flu·ent (af-loo-ĕnt) *adj.* rich; *the affluent society,*

in which most people are relatively wealthy. **af′flu·ent·ly** *adv.* **af′flu·ence** *n.*

af·ford (ă-fohrd) *v.* 1. to have enough money, means, or time for a specified purpose, *we can afford to pay fifty dollars.* 2. to be in a position to do something, *we can afford to be critical.* 3. to provide, *her diary affords no information.*

af·for·est·a·tion (ă-for-i-stay-shŏn) *n.* planting with trees to form a forest.

af·fray (ă-fray) *n.* a breach of the peace by fighting or rioting in public.

af·fright (ă-frīt) *v.* *(old use)* to frighten.

af·front (ă-frunt) *v.* to insult deliberately, to offend or embarrass. **affront** *n.* a deliberate insult or show of disrespect.

Af·ghan (af-gan) *n.* 1. a native of Afghanistan. 2. the language spoken there, Pushtu. 3. *afghan,* a blanket or shawl of knitted or crocheted wool. □**Afghan hound,** a dog of a breed with long silky hair.

Af·ghan·i·stan (af-gan-i-stan) a country in southwest Asia.

a·fi·cio·na·do (ă-fish-yŏ-nah-doh) *n.* (*pl.* -dos) a devotee of a particular sport or pastime, especially bullfighting.

a·field (ă-feeld) *adv.* 1. far away from home, to or at a distance. 2. astray.

a·fire (ă-frr) *adj. & adv.* on fire.

a·flame (ă-flaym) *adj. & adv.* in flames, burning.

AFL-CIO *abbr.* American Federation of Labor and Congress of Industrial Organizations.

a·float (ă-floht) *adj. & adv.* 1. floating. 2. at sea, on board ship, *enjoying life afloat.* 3. flooded.

a·flut·ter (ă-flut-ĕr) *adj.* in a flutter.

a·foot (ă-fuut) *adj. & adv.* 1. on foot. 2. progressing, in operation, being planned, *there's a scheme afoot to raise taxes.*

a·fore·men·tioned (ă-fohr-men-shŏnd) *adj.* mentioned previously or earlier.

a·fore·said (ă-fohr-sed) *adj.* mentioned previously.

a·fore·thought (ă-fohr-thawt) *adj.* premeditated, planned in advance, *with malice aforethought.*

a·for·ti·o·ri (ay for-shi-ohr-ee) with stronger reason. ▷ Latin.

a·foul (ă-fowl) *adv.* tangled. □**fall** *or* **run afoul of,** to come into conflict with.

Afr. *abbr.* 1. Africa. 2. African.

a·fraid (ă-frayd) *adj.* 1. alarmed, frightened, anxious about consequences. 2. politely regretful, *I'm afraid there's none left.*

A-frame (ay-fraym) *n.* a building (usually a house) with a roof pitched so steeply that its shape seen from the front or back resembles the letter A.

a·fresh (ă-fresh) *adv.* anew, beginning again.

Af·ri·ca (af-ri-kă) a continent south of the Mediterranean Sea between the Atlantic and Indian Oceans.

Af·ri·can (af-ri-kăn) *adj.* of Africa or its people or languages. **African** *n.* a native of Africa, especially a dark-skinned person. □**African violet,** an East African plant with purple, pink, or white flowers, grown as a house plant.

Af·ri·kaans (af-ri-kahns) *n.* a language developed from Dutch, used in South Africa.

Af·ro (af-roh) *adj.* of African or Afro-American culture. **Afro** *n.* a bushy Afro hairstyle.

Afro- *prefix* African; *Afro-American,* of Africa and America, especially of American blacks.

aft (aft) *adv.* in, near, or toward the stern of a ship or the tail of an aircraft.

af·ter (af-tĕr) *prep.* 1. behind in place or order. 2. at a later time than. 3. in pursuit or search of, *run after him.* 4. about, concerning, *look after your own affairs.* 5. in imitation of, *painted after the manner of Picasso; named after a person,* given this person's Christian name in honor of him. **after** *adv.* 1. behind, *Jill came tumbling after.* 2. later, *twenty years after.* **after** *conj.* at or in a time later than, *they came after I left.* **after** *adj.* 1. later, following, *in after years.* 2. nearer the stern in a boat, *the after cabins.*

af·ter·birth (af-tĕr-burth) *n.* the placenta and fetal membrane discharged from the womb after childbirth.

af·ter·burn·er (af-tĕr-bur-nĕr) *n.* 1. a device for increasing jet-engine thrust by burning extra fuel through use of hot exhaust gases. 2. a device for burning undesirable exhaust fumes.

af·ter·care (af-tĕr-kair) *n.* further care or treatment of a patient after discharge from a hospital.

af·ter·deck (af-tĕr-dek) *n.* the back part of the deck of a ship.

af·ter·ef·fect (af-tĕr-i-fekt) *n.* an effect that arises or persists after its cause has gone.

af·ter·glow (af-tĕr-gloh) *n.* 1. a glow in the west after sunset. 2. a pleasant remembrance.

af·ter·life (af-tĕr-līf) *n.* life after death.

af·ter·math (af-tĕr-math) *n.* consequences, aftereffects, *the aftermath of war.*

af·ter·noon (af-tĕr-noon) *n.* the time from noon to about 6 P.M. or sunset (if this is earlier).

af·ter·shave (af-tĕr-shayv) *n.* a lotion for use after shaving.

af·ter·taste (af-tĕr-tayst) *n.* a taste remaining or recurring after eating or drinking something.

af·ter·thought (af-tĕr-thawt) *n.* something thought of or added later.

af·ter·ward (af-tĕr-wărd), **af·ter·wards** (af-tĕr-wărdz) *adv.* at a later time.

Ag *symbol* silver.

A.G. *abbr.* Adjutant General.

a·gain (ă-gen) *adv.* 1. another time, once more, *try again.* 2. as before, to or in the original place or condition, *you'll soon be well again.* 3. furthermore, besides. 4. on the other hand, *I might, and again I might not.*

a·gainst (ă-genst) *prep.* 1. in opposition to; *his age is against him,* is a disadvantage to him. 2. in contrast to, *against a dark background.* 3. in preparation for, as defense from, *settlers built a fort against Indian raids.* 4. opposite, so as to cancel or lessen, *advances to be charged against royalties.* 5. into collision or contact with, *lean against the wall.*

A·ga Kahn (ah-gă kahn) the spiritual leader of Ismaili Muslims.

a·gape (ă-gayp) *adj.* gaping, open-mouthed.

a·gar (ah-găr) *n.* a gelatinous substance obtained from various seaweeds and used as a laxative and as a solidifying agent in culture media for bacteria etc.

ag·ate (ag-it) *n.* a very hard stone with patches or concentric bands of color.

a·ga·ve (ă-gah-vee) *n.* a tropical plant of which some species are ornamental, and some yield fiber for making rope etc. and are the source of such beverages as pulque.

age (ayj) *n.* 1. the length of time a person has lived or a thing has existed. 2. the later part of life, old age. 3. a historical period, a time with special characteristics or events, *the Elizabethan*

Age; the atomic age. **4.** *(informal)* a very long time, *it was ages before he came.* **age** *v.* **(aged, a·ging** or **age·ing) 1.** to grow old, to show signs of age. **2.** to become mature, *heavy wines age slowly.* **3.** to cause to become old, *worry aged him rapidly.* **4.** to allow to mature. □**act your age!,** *(informal)* behave more sensibly. **age group,** people who are all of approximately the same age. **age limit,** an age fixed as a limit for people taking part in an activity. **age of consent,** the age at which a person's consent is legally valid. **of age,** having reached the age at which one has an adult's legal rights and obligations. **under age,** not yet of age.

-age *suffix* used to form nouns meaning aggregate or number of, as in *acreage;* function or condition, as in *bondage;* action, as in *breakage;* place, abode, as in *orphanage;* product of action, as in *wreckage.*

aged (ayjd) *adj.* **1.** of the age of, *aged ten.* **2.** (*pr.* ay-jid) very old, *an aged man.*

age·ism (ay-jiz-ĕm) *n.* discrimination against the elderly or middle aged.

age·less (ayj-lis) *adj.* not growing or appearing old.

a·gen·cy (ay-jĕn-see) *n.* (*pl.* **-cies) 1.** the business or place of business of an agent, *a travel agency.* **2.** the means of action through which something is done.

a·gen·da (ă-jen-dă) *n.* (*pl.* **-das) 1.** a program of items of business to be dealt with at a meeting. **2.** a list of things to be done, appointments, etc.

a·gent (ay-jĕnt) *n.* **1.** a person who does something or instigates some activity. **2.** one who acts on behalf of another, *write to our agents in Rome.* **3.** something that produces an effect or change, *yeast is the active agent.* **4.** a secret agent (*see* **secret**).

a·gent pro·vo·ca·teur (a-zhahn prŏ-vok-ă-tur) (*pl.* **a·gents pro·vo·ca·teurs,** *pr.* a-zhahn prŏ-vok-ă-tur) a person employed to detect suspected offenders by tempting them to do something illegal openly.

age-old (ayj-ohld) *adj.* having existed for a very long time.

ag·er·a·tum (aj-ĕ-ray-tŭm) *n.* a low-growing daisylike plant with soft blue or white flowers.

ag·glom·er·ate (ă-glom-ĕ-rayt) *v.* **(ag·glom·er·at·ed, ag·glom·er·at·ing)** to collect or become collected into a mass. **agglomerate** (ă-glom-ĕ-rit) *n.* something composed of clustered fragments. **ag·glom·er·a·tion** (ă-glom-ĕ-ray-shŏn) *n.*

ag·glu·ti·na·tion (ă-gloo-tĭ-nay-shŏn) *n.* sticking or fusing together.

ag·gran·dize (ă-gran-dīz) *v.* **(ag·gran·dized, ag·gran·diz·ing) 1.** to increase the power, rank, wealth, etc., of. **2.** to exaggerate. **ag·gran·dize·ment** (ă-gran-diz-mĕnt) *n.*

ag·gra·vate (ag-ră-vayt) *v.* **(ag·gra·vat·ed, ag·gra·vat·ing) 1.** to make worse or more serious. **2.** *(informal)* to annoy. **ag·gra·va·tion** (ag-ră-vay-shŏn) *n.* ▷Careful writers and speakers do not use *aggravate* in its second sense. Problems are *aggravated.* People are *irritated* or *annoyed.*

ag·gre·gate¹ (ag-rĕ-git) *adj.* combined, total, *the aggregate amount.* **aggregate** *n.* **1.** a total, a mass or amount brought together; *in the aggregate,* as a whole, collectively. **2.** hard substances (sand, gravel, broken stone, etc.) mixed with cement to make concrete.

ag·gre·gate² (ag-rĕ-gayt) *v.* **(ag·gre·gat·ed,**

ag·gre·gat·ing) to collect or form into an aggregate, to unite. **ag·gre·ga·tion** (ag-rĕ-gay-shŏn) *n.*

ag·gres·sion (ă-gresh-ŏn) *n.* **1.** the act of making an unprovoked attack. **2.** a hostile action, hostile behavior.

ag·gres·sive (ă-gres-iv) *adj.* **1.** apt to make attacks, showing aggression. **2.** self-assertive, forceful, *an aggressive salesman.* **ag·gres'sive·ly** *adv.* **ag·gres'sive·ness** *n.*

ag·gres·sor (ă-gres-ŏr) *n.* a person or country that attacks first or begins hostilities.

ag·grieve (ă-greev) *v.* **(ag·grieved, ag·griev·ing) 1.** to grieve, to distress. **2.** to oppress, to treat unfairly.

a·ghast (ă-gast) *adj.* filled with consternation.

ag·ile (aj-īl) *adj.* nimble, quick-moving. **ag'ile·ly** *adv.* **a·gil·i·ty** (ă-jil-i-tee) *n.*

ag·i·tate (aj-i-tayt) *v.* **(ag·i·tat·ed, ag·i·tat·ing) 1.** to shake or move briskly. **2.** to disturb, to cause anxiety to. **3.** to stir up public interest or concern. **ag'i·ta·tor** *n.* **ag·i·ta·tion** (aj-i-tay-shŏn) *n.*

ag·it·prop (aj-it-prop) *n.* **1.** the system of Russian Communist propaganda. **2.** this propaganda.

a·gleam (ă-gleem) *adj.* gleaming.

a·glit·ter (ă-glit-ĕr) *adj.* glittering, sparkling.

a·glow (ă-gloh) *adj.* glowing.

ag·nos·tic (ag-nos-tik) *n.* a person who believes that nothing can be known about the existence of God or of anything except material things. **agnostic** *adj.* of an agnostic. **ag·nos·ti·cism** (ag-nos-ti-siz-ĕm) *n.*

a·go (ă-goh) *adv.* in the past.

a·gog (ă-gog) *adj.* eager, expectant.

a-go-go (ă-goh-goh) *see* **go-go.**

ag·o·nize (ag-ŏ-nız) *v.* **(ag·o·nized, ag·o·niz·ing) 1.** to cause agony, to pain greatly; *agonized shrieks,* expressing agony. **2.** to suffer agony, to worry intensely, *agonizing over his mistakes.* **ag'o·niz·ing·ly** *adv.*

ag·o·ny (ag-ŏ-nee) *n.* (*pl.* **-nies**) extreme mental or physical suffering.

ag·o·ra·pho·bi·a (ag-ŏ-ră-foh-bi-ă) *n.* an abnormal fear of crossing open spaces.

ag·o·ra·pho·bic (ag-ŏ-ră-foh-bik) *n.* a person who suffers from agoraphobia.

agr. *abbr.* **1.** agricultural. **2.** agriculture.

a·grar·i·an (ă-grair-i-ăn) *adj.* of landed property or cultivated land.

a·grar·i·an·ism (ă-grair-i-ă-niz-ĕm) *n.* a movement advocating redistribution of landed property.

a·gree (ă-gree) *v.* **(a·greed, a·gree·ing) 1.** to consent, to say that one is willing, *I will agree to that.* **2.** to hold or reach a similar opinion, *I agree with you.* **3.** to get on well together. **4.** to be consistent, to harmonize, *your story agrees with what I've heard already.* **5.** to suit a person's health or digestion, *cucumbers don't agree with me.* **6.** to correspond in grammatical case, number, gender, or person, *the pronoun "she" agrees with the noun "woman"; "he" agrees with "man."* □**agree to disagree,** to agree to cease trying to convince one another.

a·gree·a·ble (ă-gree-ă-bĕl) *adj.* **1.** pleasing, giving pleasure, *an agreeable voice.* **2.** willing to agree, *we'll go if you are agreeable.* **a·gree'a·bly** *adv.* **a·gree'a·ble·ness** *n.*

a·gree·ment (ă-gree-mĕnt) *n.* **1.** agreeing. **2.** harmony in opinion or feeling. **3.** an arrangement agreed upon between people, a document stating such an arrangement.

ag·ri·cul·ture (ag-rĭ-kul-chŭr) *n.* the science or practice of cultivating land on a large scale, farming. **ag·ri·cul·tur·al** (ag-rĭ-kul-chŭ-răl) *adj.* **ag·ri·cul'tur·al·ly** *adv.* **ag·ri·cul'tur·ist** *n.* **ag·ri·cul'tur·al·ist** *n.*

a·gron·o·my (ă-gron-ŏ-mee) *n.* the science of soil management and crop production. **a·gron'o·mist** *n.*

a·ground (ă-grownd) *adj. & adv.* upon or touching the bottom in shallow water, *the ship ran aground.*

a·gue (ay-gyoo) *n.* 1. malarial fever. 2. a shivering fit.

ah (ah) *interj.* an exclamation of surprise, pity, admiration, etc.

a·ha (ah-hah) *interj.* an exclamation of surprise, triumph, or mockery.

a·head (ă-hed) *adv.* farther forward in space or time; *plan ahead,* plan for the future; *full speed ahead!,* go forward at full speed. ☐**ahead of,** farther advanced than; surpassing, more than.

a·hem (ă-hem) *interj.* the noise made when clearing one's throat, used to call attention or express doubt.

a·hoy (ă-hoi) *interj.* a cry used by seamen to call attention.

aid (ayd) *v.* to help. **aid** *n.* 1. help. 2. something that helps, *a hearing aid.*

AID *abbr.* Agency for International Development.

aide (ayd) *n.* 1. an aide-de-camp. 2. an assistant.

aide-de-camp (ayd-dĕ-kamp) *n.* (*pl.* **aides-de-camp,** *pr.* aydz-dĕ-kamp) a naval or military officer acting as an assistant to a senior officer.

ai·grette (ay-gret) *n.* 1. an ornamental tuft of upright plumes, especially from the long white tail feathers of an egret. 2. a spray of gems etc.

ail (ayl) *v.* to make ill or uneasy, *what ails him?*

ai·lan·thus (ay-lan-thŭs) *n.* a tree with pointed pinnate leaflets and a disagreeable odor.

ai·le·ron (ay-lĕ-ron) *n.* a hinged flap on an airplane wing, used to control balance.

ail·ing (ay-ling) *adj.* unwell, in poor condition.

ail·ment (ayl-mĕnt) *n.* a bodily disorder, a slight illness.

aim (aym) *v.* 1. to point or send toward a target, to direct (a blow, missile, remark, etc.) toward a specified object or goal. 2. to attempt, to try, *we aim to please.* **aim** *n.* 1. the act of aiming a weapon or missile at a target; *take aim,* aim a weapon. 2. purpose, intention; *what is his aim?,* what does he want to achieve?

aim·less (aym-lis) *adj.* without a purpose. **aim'less·ly** *adv.* **aim'less·ness** *n.*

ain't (aynt) = am not, is not, are not, has not, have not. ▷This word is avoided in standard speech except in humorous use, as in *she ain't what she used to be.*

Ai·nu (ɪ-noo) *n.* (*pl.* **-nus, -nu**) 1. a Caucasoid people in Japan and the U.S.S.R. with hairy bodies. 2. a member of this people. 3. their language.

air (air) *n.* 1. the mixture of gases surrounding Earth and breathed by all land animals and plants. 2. Earth's atmosphere, open space in this. 3. Earth's atmosphere as the place where aircraft operate. 4. a light wind. 5. an impression given, *an air of mystery.* 6. an impressive manner, *he does things with such an air.* 7. a melody, a tune. **air** *v.* 1. to expose to the air, to ventilate (a room etc.) so as to cool or freshen it. 2. to put (clothes etc.) into a warm place to finish drying. 3. to express

publicly, *air one's opinions.* ☐**by air,** in or by aircraft. **in the air,** current, exerting an influence, *dissatisfaction is in the air;* uncertain, *these plans are still in the air.* **on the air,** broadcast or broadcasting by radio or television. **put on airs,** to behave in an affected haughty manner.

air bag a safety device that fills with air to protect automobile passengers in a collision.

air·borne (air-bohrn) *adj.* 1. transported by the air, *airborne pollen.* 2. in flight after taking off, *no smoking until the plane is airborne.* 3. transported by aircraft, *airborne troops.*

air brake 1. a brake worked by air pressure. 2. a movable flap used to reduce the speed of an aircraft.

air·brush (air-brush) *n.* a fine spray for paint used in commercial art and for retouching photographs.

air cavalry airborne troops.

air-con·di·tioned (air-kŏn-dish-ŏnd) *adj.* having the air in a room or building etc. brought to the required humidity and temperature.

air conditioning a system controlling humidity and temperature.

air·craft (air-kraft) *n.* 1. a machine or structure capable of flight in the air and regarded as a vehicle or carrier. 2. such craft collectively, including airplanes, gliders, and helicopters. ☐**aircraft carrier,** a ship that carries and acts as a base for airplanes.

air·crew (air-kroo) *n.* the crew of an aircraft.

air·drop (air-drop) *n.* dropping material or personnel by parachute from an aircraft.

Aire·dale (air-dayl) *n.* a large rough-coated terrier.

air·field (air-feeld) *n.* an area of open level ground equipped with hangars and runways for aircraft.

air·foil (air-foil) *n.* any or all of the lift-producing surfaces of an aircraft, as wings, ailerons, fins, etc.

air force the branch of the armed forces that uses aircraft in fighting.

air·frame (air-fraym) *n.* the body of an aircraft as distinct from its engine(s).

air·freight (air-frayt) *n.* freight carried by aircraft.

air·gun (air-gun) *n.* a gun in which compressed air propels the missile.

air·ing (air-ing) *n.* 1. exposing to air or to a drying heat. 2. clothes being aired.

air lane a regular route of travel for aircraft.

air·less (air-lis) *adj.* 1. stuffy. 2. without a breeze, calm and still. **air'less·ness** *n.*

air·lift (air-lift) *n.* large-scale transport of troops or supplies by aircraft, especially in an emergency. **airlift** *v.* to transport in this way.

air·line (air-lɪn) *n.* a regular service of air transport for public use, a company providing this.

air·lin·er (air-lɪ-nĕr) *n.* a large passenger airplane.

air·lock (air-lok) *n.* 1. a stoppage of the flow in a pump or pipe, caused by an air bubble. 2. a compartment with an airtight door at each end, providing access to a pressurized chamber.

air·mail (air-mayl) *n.* mail carried by aircraft.

air·man (air-măn) *n.* (*pl.* **-men,** *pr.* -mĕn) 1. an enlisted man in the U.S. air force below the rank of sergeant. 2. an aviator.

air mass a large block of air with uniform temperature and humidity across a horizontal section.

air mattress an inflatable pad used as a mattress.

air-mile (air-mɪl) *n.* 6076 feet or 1852 kilometers.

air·mind·ed (air-mɪn-did) *adj.* interested in aviation.

air·mo·bile (air-moh-bɪl) *adj.* (used especially of

military troops and equipment) able to be transported by air.

air·plane (air-playn) *n.* a mechanically driven heavier-than-air aircraft with wings.

air pocket a local condition of the atmosphere, as a down current or sudden change of wind velocity, that causes aircraft to lose altitude suddenly.

air police air force police.

air·port (air-port) *n.* an airfield with facilities for passengers and goods.

air raid an attack by aircraft.

air·ship (air-ship) *n.* an aircraft that is lighter than air.

air·sick (air-sik) *adj.* nauseated because of the motion of an aircraft.

air·space (air-spays) *n.* 1. space containing air. 2. air lying over a particular territory and considered subject to its jurisdiction. 3. the space above a building.

air·speed (air-speed) *n.* speed of aircraft in relation to the air, as distinct from ground speed.

air·strip (air-strip) *n.* a strip of ground prepared for aircraft to land and take off.

air·tight (air-tɪt) *adj.* not allowing air to enter or escape.

air-to-air (air-tŏ-air) *adj.* released from one aircraft and directed toward another.

air travel travel by aircraft.

air·wave (air-wayv) *n.* the medium for transmission of radio and television signals.

air·way (air-way) *n.* 1. a ventilating passage in a mine. 2. an air lane.

air·wor·thy (air-wur-*thee*) *adj.* (of an aircraft) fit to fly. **air'wor·thi·ness** *n.*

air·y (air-ee) *adj.* **(air·i·er, air·i·est)** 1. well-ventilated. 2. light as air. 3. careless and lighthearted, *an airy manner.* **air'i·ly** *adv.* **air'i·ness** *n.*

aisle (ɪl) *n.* 1. a side part of a church. 2. a passage between sections of seats.

a·jar (ă-jahr) *adj. & adv.* slightly open.

AK *abbr.* Alaska.

AKC *abbr.* American Kennel Club.

a·kim·bo (ă-kim-boh) *adv.* with hands on hips and elbows pointed outward.

a·kin (ă-kin) *adj.* related, similar, *a feeling akin to envy.*

Al *symbol* aluminum.

-al[1] *suffix* used to form adjectives, as in *central, tropical.*

-al[2] *suffix* used to form nouns, as in *rival, arrival.*

Ala. *abbr.* Alabama.

Al·a·bam·a (al-ă-bam-ă) a state of the U.S. **Al·a·bam'i·an** *adj. & n.* **Al·a·bam'an** *adj. & n.*

al·a·bas·ter (al-ă-bas-tĕr) *n.* a translucent, usually white, form of gypsum, often carved into ornaments.

à la carte (al ă kahrt) (of a restaurant meal) ordered as separate items from a menu, with a separate price for each item on the menu (as opposed to a fixed price for an entire meal).

a·lac·ri·ty (ă-lak-ri-tee) *n.* prompt and eager readiness.

à la king (al ă king) prepared in a cream sauce with green pepper, pimento, etc.

à la mode (al ă mohd) 1. in the fashion, fashionable. 2. (of pie, etc.) served with ice cream on top. 3. (of beef) braised.

a·larm (ă-lahrm) *n.* 1. a warning sound or signal, an apparatus giving this. 2. an alarm clock. 3. fear caused by expectation of danger. **alarm** *v.* to arouse to a sense of danger, to frighten.

☐**alarm clock,** a clock with a device that rings or buzzes at a set time.

a·larm·ist (ă-lahr-mist) *n.* a person who raises unnecessary or excessive alarm.

a·las (ă-las) *interj.* an exclamation of sorrow.

Alas. *abbr.* Alaska.

A·las·ka (ă-las-kă) a state of the U.S. **A·las'kan** *adj. & n.* ☐**baked Alaska,** a baked dessert containing ice cream between sponge cake and meringue covering.

alb (alb) *n.* a white robe reaching to the feet, worn by some Christian priests at church ceremonies.

al·ba·core (al-bă-kohr) *n.* a large species of fish of the east and west coasts of North America, allied to tuna.

Al·ba·ni·a (al-bay-ni-ă) a country between Greece and Yugoslavia. **Al·ba'ni·an** *adj. & n.*

Al·ba·ny (awl-bă-nee) the capital of New York.

al·ba·tross (al-bă-traws) *n.* a long-winged seabird related to the petrel.

al·be·it (awl-bee-it) *conj.* though.

Al·ber·ta (al-bur-tă) a province of Canada.

al·bi·no (al-bɪ-noh) *n.* (*pl.* **-nos**) a person or animal with no coloring pigment in the skin and hair (which are white) and the eyes (which are pink). **al·bi·nism (al-bĭ-niz-ĕm)** *n.*

al·bum (al-bŭm) *n.* 1. a book in which a collection of autographs, photographs, postage stamps, etc. can be kept. 2. a set of phonograph records, a holder for these. 3. a long-playing record with several items by the same performer(s).

al·bu·men (al-byoo-mĕn) *n.* 1. white of egg. 2. albumin.

al·bu·min (al-byoo-mĭn) *n.* any of a class of water-soluble proteins, including the main constituent of white of egg.

al·bu·mi·nous (al-byoo-mĭ-nŭs) *adj.* of or like albumin.

al·che·my (al-kĕ-mee) *n.* a medieval form of chemistry, the chief aim of which was to discover how to turn ordinary metals into gold. **al'che·mist** *n.*

al·co·hol (al-kŏ-hawl) *n.* 1. a colorless inflammable liquid, the intoxicant present in wine, beer, whiskey, etc. 2. any liquor containing this. 3. a chemical compound of this type.

al·co·hol·ic (al-kŏ-hol-ik) *adj.* 1. of or containing alcohol. 2. caused by drinking alcohol. **alcoholic** *n.* a person suffering from alcoholism.

al·co·hol·ism (al-kŏ-haw-liz-ĕm) *n.* a diseased condition caused by continual heavy drinking of alcohol.

al·cove (al-kohv) *n.* 1. a recess in a wall, a hollowed-out part or space. 2. a recess forming an extension of a room.

al·der (awl-dĕr) *n.* a tree of the birch family, usually growing in marshy places.

al·der·man (awl-dĕr-măn) *n.* (*pl.* **-men,** *pr.* -mĕn) a member of the municipal governing body in some U.S. towns and cities.

ale (ayl) *n.* liquor made from an infusion of malt by fermentation, flavored with hops etc., similar to but stronger and more bitter than beer.

ale·house (ayl-hows) *n.* a place in which ale is retailed and served.

a·lert (ă-lurt) *adj.* watchful, observant. **alert** *n.* 1. a state of watchfulness or readiness. 2. a warning of danger, notice to stand ready. 3. the period during which an alert is in effect. **alert** *v.* 1. to make alert. 2. to warn of danger. **a·lert'ly** *adv.*

a·lert·ness (ă-lurt-nis) *n.* on the alert, on the lookout, watchful.

ale·wife (ayl-wɪf) n. (pl. **-wives,** pr. -wɪvz) a fish of North American Atlantic waters, allied to the herring.

al·ex·an·drine (al-ig-zan-drin) n. a line of six iambic feet, or twelve syllables, the French heroic verse. **alexandrine** adj. of or in alexandrines.

al·fal·fa (al-fal-fã) n. a leguminous plant with clover-like leaves and bluish-purple flowers, used for fodder.

al·fres·co (al-fres-koh) adj. & adv. in the open air, lunched alfresco; an alfresco lunch.

alg. abbr. algebra.

al·ga (al-gã) n. (pl. **al·gae,** pr. al-jee) a water plant with no true stems or leaves.

al·ge·bra (al-jě-brã) n. a branch of mathematics in which letters and symbols are used to represent quantities. **al·ge·bra·ic** (al-jě-bray-ik) adj. **al·ge·bra'i·cal·ly** adv.

Al·ge·ri·a (al-jeer-i-ã) a country in North Africa. **Al·ge'ri·an** adj. & n.

Al·giers (al-jeerz) the capital of Algeria.

Al·gon·quin (al-gong-kin) n. (pl. **-quins, -quin**) 1. one of a group of languages spoken by North American Indians. 2. a member of a group of Algonquin-speaking tribes.

al·go·rithm (al-gŏ-rith-ěm) n. a process or rules for calculating something, especially by machine.

a·li·as (ay-li-ǎs) n. (pl. **-as·es**) a false name, an assumed name, Brown had several aliases. **alias** adv. also called, John Brown, alias Peter Harrison, alias James Finch.

al·i·bi (al-i-bɪ) n. (pl. **-bis**) 1. evidence that an accused person was elsewhere when the crime was committed. 2. (informal) an excuse, an answer to an accusation. **alibi** v. (**al·i·bied, al·i·bi·ing**) to provide or offer an alibi for. ▷Careful writers avoid use of alibi when only an excuse is intended.

al·ien (ayl-yěn) n. a person who is not a citizen of the country in which he is living. **alien** adj. 1. foreign, not one's own, unfamiliar, alien customs. 2. of a different nature, contrary, cruelty is alien to her nature.

al·ien·ate (ayl-yě-nayt) v. (**al·ien·at·ed, al·ien·at·ing**) to cause to become unfriendly or hostile. **al·ien·a·tion** (ayl-yě-nay-shŏn) n.

a·light¹ (ă-lɪt) v. (**a·light·ed, a·lit,** pr. ă-lit, **a·light·ing**) 1. to get down from a horse or a vehicle. 2. to descend and settle, the bird alighted on a branch.

a·light² adj. 1. on fire. 2. lit up.

a·lign (ă-lɪn) v. 1. to place in line, to bring into line. 2. to join as an ally, they aligned themselves with the Liberals. **a·lign'ment** n. ☐**out of alignment,** not in line.

a·like (ă-lɪk) adj. & adv. like one another, in the same way.

al·i·men·ta·ry (al-ĭ-men-tă-ree) adj. nourishing, performing functions of nutrition, providing maintenance. ☐**alimentary canal,** the tubular passage through which food passes from mouth to anus in the process of being digested and absorbed by the body.

al·i·mo·ny (al-ĭ-moh-nee) n. an allowance payable by one spouse to the other for support pending or after a legal separation or divorce.

A-line (ay-lɪn) adj. (of a garment) having a narrow waist or shoulders and a somewhat flared skirt.

a·live (ă-lɪv) adj. 1. living. 2. alert, he is alive to the possible dangers. 3. active, lively, alert. 4. full of living or moving things, the river was alive with fish. ☐**look alive!,** hurry, get busy, be alert.

al·ka·li (al-kă-lɪ) n. (pl. **-lis, -lies**) one of a class of substances (as caustic soda, potash, and ammonia) that neutralize and are neutralized by acids, and form caustic or corrosive solutions in water. **al·ka·line** (al-kă-lɪn) adj. **al·ka·lin·i·ty** (al-kă-lin-i-tee) n.

al·ka·loid (al-kă-loid) n. any of a large group of nitrogenous organic substances of vegetable origin having basic or alkaline properties, many of which (as morphine, strychnine, cocaine) are being used as drugs.

all (awl) adj. the whole amount or number or extent of, waited all day; beyond all doubt, beyond any doubt whatever. **all** n. all men, the whole, every one, everything. **all** pronoun all persons concerned, everything, all are agreed; all is lost. **all** adv. entirely, quite, dressed all in white; an all-powerful dictator; ran all the faster, even faster. ☐**all but,** very little short of, it's all but impossible. **all clear,** a signal that a danger is over. **all for,** (informal) much in favor of. **all in,** (informal) exhausted. **all in all,** all things considered; as a whole. **all one to,** all the same to; a matter of indifference to. **all out,** using all possible strength, energy, or speed. **all over,** in or on all parts of, clothes were scattered all over the room; that's Jones all over, that is what one would expect of him. **all set,** (informal) ready to start. **all there,** (informal) mentally alert. **all the same,** in spite of this; making no difference. **be all eyes** or **ears,** to be watching or listening intently. **on all fours,** crawling on hands and knees. **not all there,** (informal) mentally deficient.

Al·lah (al-ă) the Muslim name of God.

all-American (awl-ă-mer-i-kăn) adj. typically American, chosen as best in any U.S. sport. **all-American** n. an all-American player.

all-around (awl-ă-rownd) = **all-round.**

al·lay (ă-lay) v. (**al·layed, al·lay·ing**) to calm, to put at rest, to allay suspicion.

al·le·ga·tion (al-ě-gay-shŏn) n. a statement made without proof.

al·lege (ă-lej) v. (**al·leged, al·leg·ing**) to declare (especially to those doubting one's truthfulness) without being able to prove, alleging that he was innocent; the alleged culprit, the person said to be the culprit.

al·leg·ed·ly (ă-lej-id-lee) adv. according to allegation.

Al·le·ghe·nies (al-ě-gay-neez) n. pl. the Allegheny Mountains, part of the Appalachians.

al·le·giance (ă-lee-jăns) n. loyalty owed to one's country, loyalty to or support of a person or cause.

al·le·go·ry (al-ě-gohr-ee) n. (pl. **-ries**) a story or description in which the characters and events symbolize some deeper underlying meaning. **al·le·gor·ic** (al-ě-gor-ik) adj. **al·le·gor'i·cal** adj. **al·le·gor'i·cal·ly** adv.

al·le·gro (ă-leg-roh) adv. (in music) fast and lively. **allegro** n. (pl. **-gros**) a passage to be played in this way.

al·le·lu·ia (al-ě-loo-yă) interj. & n. = **hallelujah.**

al·ler·gen (al-ěr-jen) n. a substance causing an allergic reaction. **al·ler·gen·ic** (al-ěr-jen-ik) adj.

al·ler·gic (ă-lur-jik) adj. 1. having an allergy. 2. caused by an allergy, an allergic reaction. 3. (informal) having a strong dislike, allergic to hard work.

al·ler·gist (al-ěr-jist) n. a specialist in treating allergies.

al·ler·gy (al-ěr-jee) n. (pl. **-ler·gies**) a condition producing an unfavorable reaction to certain foods, pollens, etc.

al·le·vi·ate (ă-lee-vi-ayt) v. (**al·le·vi·at·ed, al·le·vi·at·ing**) to lessen, to make less severe, *to alleviate pain.* **al·le·vi·a·tion** (ă-lee-vi-ay-shŏn) n.

al·ley (al-ee) n. (pl. **-leys**) 1. a narrow passage or street between or behind houses or other buildings. 2. a long enclosure for games such as bowling. ☐**alley cat**, a homeless city cat. ▷Do not confuse *alley* with *ally.*

al·ley·way (al-ee-way) n. a narrow passageway.

al·li·ance (ă-lɪ-ăns) n. a union or association formed for mutual benefit, especially of countries by treaty or families by marriage.

al·lied (ă-lɪd) adj. 1. of forces or countries in alliance. 2. of the same general kind, similar, *bronchitis and allied illnesses.*

al·li·ga·tor (al-ĭ-gay-tŏr) n. a reptile of the crocodile family, found especially in the rivers of tropical America and China. ☐**alligator pear**, avocado.

al·lit·er·ate (ă-lit-ĕ-rayt) v. (**al·lit·er·at·ed, al·lit·er·at·ing**) to use words that begin with the same letter or sound.

al·lit·er·a·tion (ă-lit-ĕ-ray-shŏn) n. the occurrence of the same letter or sound at the beginning of several words in succession, *sing a song of sixpence.* **al·lit·er·a·tive** (ă-lit-ĕ-rā-tiv) adj.

al·lo·cate (al-ŏ-kayt) v. (**al·lo·cat·ed, al·lo·cat·ing**) to allot. **al'lo·ca·tor** n. **al·lo·ca·tion** (al-ŏ-kay-shŏn) n.

al·lot (ă-lot) v. (**al·lot·ted, al·lot·ting**) to distribute officially, to give as a share of things available or tasks to be done.

al·lot·ment (ă-lot-mĕnt) n. 1. allotting. 2. a share allotted.

al·low (ă-low) v. 1. to permit; *dogs are not allowed in the park*, may not enter. 2. to permit to have, to give a limited quantity or sum, *the court allowed her $20,000 damages.* 3. to add or deduct in estimating, *allow ten percent for inflation; allow for shrinkage*, provide for this when estimating. 4. to agree that something is true or acceptable, to admit, *he allowed he had been absent without a good reason; the insurance company allowed the claim.* ▷Careful writers use *allow* in the sense of "raise no objection." They use *permit* in the sense of "grant permission" or "grant consent."

al·low·a·ble (ă-low-ă-bĕl) adj. able to be allowed. **al·low'a·bly** adv.

al·low·ance (ă-low-ăns) n. 1. allowing. 2. an amount or sum allowed. ☐**make allowances for**, to be lenient toward; to be an excuse for.

al·loy (al-oi) n. 1. a metal formed of a mixture of metals or of metal and another substance. 2. an inferior metal mixed with one of greater value. **alloy** (ă-loi) v. 1. to mix with metal(s) of lower value. 2. to weaken or spoil by adding something that reduces value or pleasure.

all right (awl rɪt) 1. as desired, satisfactorily. 2. in good condition, safe and sound. 3. yes, I consent.

all-round (awl-rownd) adj. general, not specialized; *a good all-round athlete*, good at various sports.

All Saints' Day (awl saynts day) a Christian feast observed November 1 in honor of all the saints.

All Souls' Day (awl sohlz day) a day of prayer observed on November 2 for the souls of departed Christians.

all·spice (awl-spɪs) n. spice made from berries combining the flavors of cinnamon, nutmeg, and cloves.

all-star (awl-stahr) adj. with or featuring star performers.

all-time (awl-tɪm) adj. unsurpassed, *an all-time record.*

al·lude (ă-lood) v. (**al·lud·ed, al·lud·ing**) to refer casually or indirectly in speaking or writing, *she alluded once again to my indecisiveness.* ▷See the note under **allusion.**

al·lure (ă-loor) v. (**al·lured, al·lur·ing**) to entice, to attract. **allure** n. attractiveness. **al·lure'ment** n.

al·lur·ing (ă-loor-ing) adj. attractive, charming.

al·lu·sion (ă-loo-zhŏn) n. 1. a passing or indirect reference to (something). 2. a reference to (something). ▷Careful writers use *allusion* only when they do not name the thing to which they *allude.* When they do name it, they use *reference.*

al·lu·sive (ă-loo-siv) adj. containing allusions. **al·lu'sive·ly** adv. **al·lu'sive·ness** n.

al·lu·vi·al (ă-loo-vi-ăl) adj. made of soil and sand left by rivers or floods.

al·lu·vi·um (ă-loo-vi-ŭm) n. (pl. **-viums, -vi·a,** pr. -vi-ă) an alluvial deposit.

al·ly (al-ɪ) n. (pl. **-lies**) 1. a country in alliance with another. 2. a person who cooperates with another in some project. **ally** (ă-lɪ) v. (**al·lied, al·ly·ing**) to form an alliance. ☐**the Allies**, the U.S., France, Great Britain, Russia, etc., united against the Central Powers in World War I and against the Axis Powers in World War II. ▷Do not confuse *ally* with *alley.*

-ally suffix used to form adverbs from adjectives, as in *finally, centrally.*

al·ma ma·ter (al-mă mah-tĕr) a title used in reference to one's university, college, or school.

al·ma·nac (awl-mă-nak) n. 1. an annual publication containing a calendar with times of sunrise and sunset, astronomical data, and other information. 2. a yearbook of sport, theater, etc. ▷The older spelling *almanack* is seen in some publications, as in *Poor Richard's Almanack.*

al·might·y (awl-mɪ-tee) adj. 1. all-powerful; *the Almighty*, God. 2. (informal) very great, *an almighty nuisance.*

al·mond (ah-mŏnd, am-ŏnd) n. 1. the kernel of the fruit of a tree related to the peach. 2. this tree. ☐**almond paste**, edible paste made from ground almonds.

al·mond-eyed (ah-mŏnd-ɪd, am-ŏnd-) adj. having eyes that appear to narrow and slant upward at the outer corners.

al·mo·ner (al-mŏ-nĕr, ah-) n. an official distributor of alms, as for a monastery or royal person.

al·most (awl-mohst) adv. all but, as the nearest thing to.

alms (ahmz) n. pl. money and gifts given to the poor.

al·oe (al-oh) n. 1. a plant with thick sharp-pointed leaves and bitter juice. 2. (often *aloes*) this juice, used in medicine.

a·loft (ă-lawft) adv. high up, up in the air, in the upper parts of a ship's rigging.

a·lo·ha (ă-loh-hah) interj. greetings, farewell.

a·lone (ă-lohn) adj. not with others, without the company or help of others or other things. **alone** adv. only, exclusively, *you alone can help me.*

a·long (ă-lawng) adv. 1. through part or the whole of a thing's length. 2. in company with oneself, in addition, *brought my sister along; I'll be along*

soon, will come and join you. **3.** onward, into a more advanced state, *push it along; it is coming along nicely.* **along** *prep.* close to or parallel with the length of something, *arranged along the wall.* ☐**all along,** all the time, from the beginning.
a·long·side (ă-lawng-sɪd) *adv.* close to the side of a ship, pier, or wharf. **alongside** *prep.* beside. ▷Do not use *of* after *alongside. Her car stands alongside ours.*
a·loof (ă-loof) *adv.* apart; *keep or hold aloof from,* deliberately take no part in. **aloof** *adj.* unconcerned, cool and remote in character, not friendly. **a·loof′ly** *adv.* **a·loof′ness** *n.*
a·loud (ă-lowd) *adj.* in a voice loud enough to be heard, not silently or in a whisper.
alp (alp) *n.* a high mountain. ☐**the Alps,** high mountains in Switzerland and adjacent countries.
al·pa·ca (al-pak-ă) *n.* **1.** a kind of llama with long woolly hair. **2.** a fabric made from this hair, with or without other fibers.
al·pha (al-fă) *n.* **1.** the first letter of the Greek alphabet (Aα). **2.** *Alpha,* the chief star in a constellation.
al·pha·bet (al-fă-bet) *n.* **1.** the letters used in writing a language. **2.** a list of these in a set order. **3.** symbols or signs indicating letters but not written, *the Morse alphabet.*
al·pha·bet·i·cal (al-fă-bet-i-kăl) *adj.* in the order of the letters of the alphabet. **al·pha·bet′i·cal·ly** *adv.*
al·pha·bet·ize (al-fă-bĕ-tɪz) *v.* (**al·pha·bet·ized, al·pha·bet·iz·ing**) to arrange in alphabetical order.
al·pha·nu·mer·ic (al-fă-noo-mer-ik) *adj.* containing both alphabetical and numerical symbols (used in computer technology etc.).
alpha particle the first of three types of radiation emitted by radioactive substances, consisting of positively charged particles.
alpha ray an alpha particle, originally regarded as a ray.
alpha rhythm the most common type of wave-form exhibited by the adult cerebral cortex, averaging eight to twelve smooth oscillations a second in adults at rest.
alpha wave alpha rhythm.
al·pine (al-pɪn) *adj.* **1.** of high mountains, growing on these. **2.** *Alpine,* of the Alps. **alpine** *n.* a plant suited to mountain regions.
al·ready (awl-red-ee) *adv.* **1.** before this time, *had already gone.* **2.** as early as this, *is he back already?* ▷Do not confuse *already* with *all ready,* as in *they were all ready* (prepared) *to go.*
al·right (awl-rɪt) *adv.* an incorrect form of *all right.*
al·so (awl-soh) *adv.* in addition, besides.
al·so-ran (awl-soh-ran) *n.* **1.** a horse or dog not among the first three to finish in a race. **2.** a person who fails to win a race, contest, etc.
alt. *abbr.* altitude.
al·tar (awl-tăr) *n.* **1.** the table on which bread and wine are consecrated in the Communion service. **2.** any structure on which offerings are made to a god.
al·tar·piece (awl-tăr-pees) *n.* a painting or sculpture above the back of an altar.
al·ter (awl-tĕr) *v.* to make or become different, to change in character, position, etc.; *alter a garment,* resew it in a different style or size. **al′ter·a·ble** *adj.* **al′ter·a·bly** *adv.* **al·ter·a·tion** (awl-tĕ-ray-shŏn) *n.*
al·ter·ca·tion (awl-tĕr-kay-shŏn) *n.* a noisy dispute or quarrel.

al·ter e·go (awl-tĕr ee-goh) one's other self, an intimate friend.
al·ter·nate¹ (awl-tĕr-nit) *adj.* happening or following in turns, first one and then the other; *on alternate days,* every second day. **al′ter·nate·ly** *adv.* ▷Do not confuse *alternate* with *alternative.*
al·ter·nate² (awl-tĕr-nayt) *v.* (**al·ter·nat·ed, al·ter·nat·ing**) **1.** to arrange, perform, or occur alternately. **2.** to consist of alternate things. **al·ter·na·tion** (awl-tĕr-nay-shŏn) *n.* ☐**alternating current,** electric current that reverses its direction at regular intervals.
al·ter·nate³ (awl-tĕr-nit) *n.* a deputy or substitute. ▷Do not confuse *alternate* with *alternative.*
al·ter·na·tive (awl-tur-nă-tiv) *adj.* available in place of something else. **alternative** *n.* one of two or more possibilities. **al·ter′na·tive·ly** *adv.* ▷Do not confuse *alternative* with *alternate.*
al·ter·na·tor (awl-tĕr-nay-tŏr) *n.* an electric generator producing alternating current.
al·though, **al·tho** (awl-*th*oh) *conj.* even though, in spite of the fact that. ▷Careful writers do not use *altho.*
al·tim·e·ter (al-tim-ĕ-tĕr) *n.* an instrument used especially in aircraft for showing altitude above sea level.
al·ti·tude (al-ti-tood) *n.* **1.** the height above sea level. **2.** the distance of a star etc. above the horizon, measured as an angle.
al·to (al-toh) *n.* (*pl.* **-tos**) **1.** the lowest female singing voice. **2.** a contralto. **3.** a singer with such a voice, a part written for it. **4.** a musical instrument with the second highest pitch in its group, *alto saxophone.*
al·to·geth·er (awl-tŏ-ge*th*-ĕr) *adv.* **1.** entirely, totally. **2.** on the whole. ☐**in the altogether,** (*informal*) nude. ▷Do not confuse *altogether* with *all together,* as in *we were all together* (reunited) *again.*
al·tru·ism (al-troo-iz-ĕm) *n.* unselfishness. **al·tru·is·tic** (al-troo-is-tik) *adj.* **al·tru·is′ti·cal·ly** *adv.*
al·tru·ist (al-troo-ist) *n.* an unselfish person.
al·um (al-ŭm) *n.* a white mineral salt used in medicine and in dyeing.
al·u·min·i·um (al-yŭ-min-i-ŭm) *n.* (*British*) aluminum.
a·lu·mi·nize (ă-loo-mĭ-nɪz) *v.* (**a·lu·mi·niz·ing**) to coat with aluminum.
a·lu·mi·num (ă-loo-mĭ-nŭm) *n.* a lightweight silvery metal used either pure or as an alloy for making utensils or fittings where lightness is an advantage.
a·lum·na (ă-lum-nă) *n.* (*pl.* **-nae,** *pr.* -nee) a female former student of a school or college.
a·lum·nus (ă-lum-nŭs) *n.* (*pl.* **-ni,** *pr.* -nɪ) a male former student of a school or college.
al·ways (awl-wayz) *adv.* **1.** at all times, on all occasions, forever. **2.** whatever the circumstances, at any time, *you can always change your plans.* **3.** repeatedly, *he is always complaining.*
am (am) *see* **be.**
Am *symbol* americium.
AM *abbr.* amplitude modulation.
a.m. *abbr.* ante meridiem.
A.M. *abbr.* **1.** ante meridiem. **2.** Master of Arts.
A.M.A. *abbr.* American Medical Association.
a·mah (ah-mah) *n.* a nursemaid.
a·mal·gam (ă-mal-găm) *n.* **1.** an alloy of mercury and another metal. **2.** any soft pliable mixture.
a·mal·ga·mate (ă-mal-gă-mayt) *v.* (**a·mal·ga·**

mat·ed, a·mal·ga·mat·ing) to mix, to combine. a·mal·ga·ma·tion (ă-mal-gă-may-shŏn) n.

a·man·u·en·sis (ă-man-yoo-en-sis) n. (pl. -ses, pr. -seez) a person who writes from dictation or copies manuscripts, a literary assistant.

am·a·ranth (am-ă-ranth) n. 1. an imaginary unfading flower. 2. pigweed, tumbleweed, etc. 3. a purple color.

am·a·ryl·lis (am-ă-ril-is) n. a lilylike plant growing from a bulb.

a·mass (ă-mas) v. to heap up, to collect, amassed a large fortune.

am·a·teur (am-ă-tĕr, -chĕr) n. a person who does something as a pastime rather than as a profession. am'a·teur·ism n.

am·a·teur·ish (am-ă-tur-ish, -choor-) adj. inexpert, lacking professional skill. am·a·teur' ish·ly adv. am·a·teur'ish·ness n.

am·a·to·ry (am-ă-tohr-ee) adj. of or involving a lover, lovemaking, or expressions of love.

a·maze (ă-mayz) v. (a·mazed, a·maz·ing) to overwhelm with wonder. a·maz'ing·ly adv. a·maze'ment n.

am·a·zon (am-ă-zon) n. a tall and strong or athletic woman. am·a·zo·ni·an (am-ă-zoh-ni-ăn) adj. ▷The Amazons were a race of female warriors in Greek mythology.

am·bas·sa·dor (am-bas-ă-dŏr) n. 1. a diplomat sent by one country as a permanent representative or on a special mission to another. 2. an official messenger. am·bas·sa·do·ri·al (am-bas-ă-dohr-i-ăl) adj.

am·ber (am-bĕr) n. 1. a hardened clear yellowish-brown resin used for making ornaments. 2. a yellow traffic light shown as a cautionary signal alone or between red (= stop) and green (= go). amber adj. 1. made of amber. 2. colored like amber.

am·ber·gris (am-bĕr-gris) n. a waxlike substance found floating in tropical seas and present in the intestines of sperm whales, used as a fixative in perfumes.

am·bi·dex·trous (am-bi-dek-strŭs) adj. able to use either hand equally well. am·bi·dex' trous·ly adv.

am·bi·ence, am·bi·ance (am-bi-ĕns) n. environment, surroundings.

am·bi·ent (am-bi-ĕnt) adj. surrounding.

am·big·u·ous (am-big-yoo-ŭs) adj. 1. having two or more possible meanings. 2. doubtful, uncertain. am·big'u·ous·ly adv. am·bi·gu·i·ty (am-bi-gyoo-ĭ-tee) n. ▷Do not confuse ambiguous with ambivalent.

am·bi·tion (am-bish-ŏn) n. 1. a strong desire to achieve something. 2. the object of this.

am·bi·tious (am-bish-ŭs) adj. full of ambition. am·bi'tious·ly adv.

am·biv·a·lent (am-biv-ă-lĕnt) adj. with mixed feelings toward a certain object or situation. am· biv'a·lent·ly adv. am·biv'a·lence n. ▷Do not confuse ambivalent with ambiguous.

am·ble (am-bĕl) v. (am·bled, am·bling) to walk at a slow easy pace. amble n. a slow easy pace.

am·bro·sia (am-broh-zhă) n. something delicious. am·bro'sial adj.

am·bu·lance (am-byŭ-lăns) n. a vehicle equipped to carry sick or injured people.

am·bu·la·to·ry (am-byŭ-lă-tohr-ee) adj. able to walk about.

am·bus·cade (am-bŭ-skayd) n. an ambush. am·buscade v. (am·bus·cad·ed, am·bus·cad·ing) to ambush.

am·bush (am-buush) n. 1. the placing of troops etc. in a concealed position to make a surprise attack on an enemy or a victim who has approached. 2. such an attack. ambush v. to lie in wait for, to attack from an ambush.

a·mel·io·rate (ă-meel-yŏ-rayt) v. (a·mel·io· rat·ed, a·mel·io·rat·ing) to make or become better. a·mel·io·ra·tion (ă-meel-yŏ-ray-shŏn) n.

a·men (ah-men) interj. an expression of assent.

a·me·na·ble (ă-mee-nă-bĕl, ă-men-ă-) adj. 1. answerable, subject to some authority or rule. 2. willing to be guided or controlled by some influence, she is not amenable to discipline.

a·mend (ă-mend) v. to correct an error in, to make minor alterations in, they amended the agreement. (▷Do not confuse amend with emend.) □make amends, to compensate or make up for something, brought a gift to make amends for his lateness.

a·mend·ment (ă-mend-mĕnt) n. 1. the process of amending something. 2. an addition to or correction of a document, bill, or law.

a·men·i·ty (ă-men-ĭ-tee, ă-mee-nĭ-) n. (pl. -ties) n. 1. the pleasantness of a place or circumstance. 2. a feature of a place etc. that makes life there easy or pleasant. 3. amenities, conventions observed in polite social intercourse.

Amer. abbr. 1. America. 2. American.

A·mer·i·ca (ă-mer-i-kă) 1. a continent of the western hemisphere (also called the Americas) consisting of the two great land masses, North America and South America, joined by the narrow isthmus of Central America. 2. the U.S.

A·mer·i·can (ă-mer-i-kăn) adj. 1. of the continent of America. 2. of the U.S. American n. 1. a native of America. 2. a citizen of the U.S. 3. (also American English) the English language as spoken in the U.S. □American Indian, see Indian. American Legion, an organization of veterans of U.S. wars, founded in 1919. American plan, the system of charging for a hotel room and service with inclusion of meals. American Revolution, the war between the thirteen American colonies and Great Britain (1775–1783) in which the colonies gained their independence.

A·mer·i·ca·na (ă-mer-i-kan-ă) n. pl. books, memorabilia, etc. relating to America, especially to U.S. history.

A·mer·i·can·ism (ă-mer-i-kă-niz-ĕm) n. a custom, belief, trait, phrase, etc. originating in the United States or peculiar to it.

A·mer·i·can·ize (ă-mer-i-kă-nīz) v. (A·mer· i·can·ized, A·mer·i·can·iz·ing) 1. to make or become American in character. 2. to naturalize as an American. A·mer·i·can·i·za·tion (ă-mer-i-kă-ni-zay-shŏn) n.

am·er·i·ci·um (am-ĕ-rish-i-ŭm) n. a metallic radioactive element.

Am·er·ind (am-ĕ-rind) n. an American Indian or Eskimo.

am·e·thyst (am-ĕ-thist) n. a precious stone, purple or violet quartz.

a·mi·a·ble (ay-mi-ă-bĕl) adj. feeling and inspiring friendliness, good-tempered. a'mi·a·bly adv. a·mi·a·bil·i·ty (ay-mi-ă-bil-i-tee) n.

am·i·ca·ble (am-i-kă-bĕl) adj. friendly. am'i·ca·bly adv.

a·mid (ă-mid), a·midst (ă-midst) prep. in the middle of, during, amid shouts of dismay. ▷Most writers and speakers prefer to use amid.

a·mid·ships (ă-mid-ships) *adv.* in the middle of a ship.

a·mi·no (ă-mee-noh) **acid** an organic acid found in proteins.

a·miss (ă-mis) *adj.* wrong, out of order, *something is amiss.* **amiss** *adv.* wrongly, faultily; *don't take his criticism amiss,* don't be offended by it.

am·i·ty (am-ĭ-tee) *n.* friendship, friendly relations.

Am·man (ah-mahn) the capital of Jordan.

am·me·ter (am-mee-tĕr) *n.* an instrument that measures electric current, usually in amperes.

am·mo (am-oh) *n. (informal)* ammunition.

am·mo·nia (ă-mohn-yă) *n.* 1. a colorless gas of nitrogen and hydrogen with a strong smell. 2. (also *ammonia water*) a solution of this in water.

am·mu·ni·tion (am-yŭ-nish-ŏn) *n.* 1. projectiles (bullets, shells, grenades, etc.) and their propellants. 2. facts and reasoning used to prove a point in an argument.

am·ne·sia (am-nee-zhă) *n.* loss of memory. **am·ne·si·ac** (am-nee-zhi-ak) *adj.* **am·nes·ic** (am-nee-sik) *adj.*

am·nes·ty (am-nĕ-stee) *n.* (*pl.* **-ties**) a general pardon, especially for offenses against a country. **amnesty** *v.* (**am·nes·tied, am·nes·ty·ing**) to give an amnesty to.

am·ni·o·cen·te·sis (am-ni-oh-sen-tee-sis) *n.* sampling of amniotic fluid by insertion of a hollow needle into the womb.

am·ni·on (am-ni-on) *n.* a membrane enclosing the embryo or fetus.

am·ni·ot·ic (am-ni-ot-ik) **fluid** the fluid surrounding the embryo or fetus.

a·moe·ba (ă-mee-bă) *n.* (*pl.* **-bas, -bae,** *pr.* -bee) a microscopic organism consisting of a single cell that changes shape constantly. **a·moe'bic** *adj.*

a·mok (ă-muk) *adv.* on the rampage in murderous frenzy, *to run amok.*

a·mong (ă-mung), **a·mongst** (ă-mungst) *prep.* 1. in an assembly of, surrounded by, *a single flower grew among the corn.* 2. in the number of, *this is reckoned among his best works.* 3. within the limits of, between; *quarreled among themselves,* with one another. ▷Do not use *amongst.* Also see the note under **between.**

a·mon·til·la·do (ă-mon-ti-lah-doh) *n.* a medium dry sherry of a matured type.

a·mor·al (ay-mor-ăl) *adj.* not based on moral standards, neither moral nor immoral. **a·mor'al·ly** *adv.*

am·o·rous (am-ŏ-rŭs) *adj.* of, showing, or readily feeling sexual love. **am'o·rous·ly** *adv.* **am'o·rous·ness** *n.*

a·mor·phous (ă-mor-fŭs) *adj.* having no definite shape or form.

am·or·tize (am-ŏr-tɪz) *v.* (**am·or·tized, am·or·tiz·ing**) 1. to pay off (a debt or mortgage) by periodic payments. 2. to write off the initial cost of (an asset) gradually. **am·or·ti·za·tion** (am-ŏr-tĭ-zay-shŏn) *n.*

a·mount (ă-mownt) *n.* 1. the total of anything. 2. a quantity, *a small amount of salt.* **amount** *v.* 1. to add up to. 2. to be equivalent to. ▷*Amount* refers to bulk, mass, or aggregate. It is correct to say or write *an amount of money* and *a number of coins.*

a·mour (ă-moor) *n.* a love affair, especially an illicit one.

amp (amp) *n. (informal)* an ampere.

am·per·age (am-pĕ-rij) *n.* the strength of electric current measured in amperes.

am·pere (am-peer) *n.* a unit for measuring electric current.

am·per·sand (am-pĕr-sand) *n.* the sign & (= and).

am·phet·a·mine (am-fet-ă-meen) *n.* a drug used as a stimulant or to relieve congestion.

am·phib·i·an (am-fib-i-ăn) *n.* 1. an animal able to live both on land and in water (as a frog). 2. an aircraft that can take off from and land on both land and water. 3. a vehicle that can move on both land and water.

am·phib·i·ous (am-fib-i-ŭs) *adj.* 1. living or operating both on land and in water. 2. involving both sea and land forces, *amphibious attack.*

am·phi·the·a·ter (am-f ĭ-thee-ă-tĕr) *n.* 1. an oval or circular building with tiers of seats surrounding an open central arena. (▷This is not the same as a Greek or Roman *theater,* which is semicircular.) 2. a large room with raised tiers of seats around a central stage for viewing performances, demonstrations, and the like.

am·pho·ra (am-fŏ-ră) *n.* (*pl.* **-rae,** *pr.* -ree, **-ras**) a Greek or Roman two-handled vase.

am·ple (am-pĕl) *adj.* (**-pler, -plest**) 1. plentiful, quite enough, *ample evidence.* 2. large, of generous proportions. **am'ply** *adv.*

am·pli·fi·er (am-plĭ-fɪ-ĕr) *n.* a device that increases electric voltage, current, or power, or the loudness of sounds.

am·pli·fy (am-plĭ-fɪ) *v.* (**am·pli·fied, am·pli·fy·ing**) 1. to increase the strength of, *to amplify sound.* 2. to make fuller, to add details to, *please amplify your statement.* **am·pli·fi·ca·tion** (am-plĭ-fi-kay-shŏn) *n.*

am·pli·tude (am-pli-tood) *n.* 1. breadth. 2. largeness, abundance. □**amplitude modulation,** variations in the amplitude of carrier waves used in radio transmission.

am·pule (am-pyool), **am·poule** (am-pool) *n.* a small sealed container holding a liquid, especially for hypodermic injection.

am·pu·tate (am-pyŭ-tayt) *v.* (**am·pu·ta·ted, am·pu·tat·ing**) to cut off by surgical operation. **am·pu·ta·tion** (am-pyŭ-tay-shŏn) *n.*

am·pu·tee (am-pyŭ-tee) *n.* a person who has had a limb amputated.

Am·ster·dam (am-stĕr-dam) the capital of the Netherlands.

amt. *abbr.* amount.

Am·trak (am-trak) *n.* a system of railroads in the U.S.

a·muck = amok.

am·u·let (am-yŭ-lit) *n.* a thing worn as a charm against evil.

a·muse (ă-myooz) *v.* (**a·mused, a·mus·ing**) 1. to cause to laugh or smile. 2. to make time pass pleasantly for. **a·muse'ment** *n.*

AMVETS (am-vets) *n.* an organization of U.S. veterans of World War II and the Korean War.

an (an) *adj.* (called the *indefinite article*) the form of *a* used before vowel sounds other than "u" (*pr.* yoo), *an egg, an hour* (but *a unit*).

an- *prefix* without, not, as in *anarchy, anhydrous.*

-an *suffix* used to form adjectives or nouns, especially from names of places, systems, zoological classes, and founders, as in *American, republican.*

a·nach·ro·nism (ă-nak-rŏ-niz-ĕm) *n.* 1. a mistake in placing something into a particular historical period. 2. the thing wrongly placed. 3. a person, custom, or idea regarded as out of date. **a·nach·ro·nis·tic** (ă-nak-rŏ-nis-tik) *adj.*

an·a·con·da (an-ă-kon-dă) *n.* a large Southern American snake that crushes its prey.

a·nae·mi·a = anemia.

an·aer·o·bic (an-ă-roh-bik) *adj.* living and reproducing in the absence of atmospheric oxygen.

an·aes·the·sia = anesthesia.

an·aes·thet·ic = anesthetic.

a·naes·the·tist = anesthetist.

a·naes·the·tize = anesthetize.

an·a·gram (an-ă-gram) *n.* a word or phrase formed from the rearranged letters of another (*carthorse* is an anagram of *orchestra*).

a·nal (ay-năl) *adj.* 1. of the anus. 2. of infantile psychosexual development that is centered on the anus.

anal. *abbr.* 1. analogous. 2. analogy. 3. analysis. 4. analytic.

an·al·ge·si·a (an-ăl-jee-zi-ă) *n.* loss of ability to feel pain while still conscious.

an·al·ge·sic (an-ăl-jee-zik) *adj.* relieving pain. analgesic *n.* a drug that relieves pain.

an·a·log (an-ă-lawg) **computer** a computer using physical quantities (voltage, weight, etc.) to represent numbers.

a·nal·o·gous (ă-nal-ă-gŭs) *adj.* similar in certain respects. a·nal'o·gous·ly *adv.*

an·a·logue, an·a·log (an-ă-lawg) *n.* an analogous word or thing.

a·nal·o·gy (ă-nal-ă-jee) *n.* (*pl.* -gies) a partial likeness between two things that are compared, *the analogy between the human heart and a pump.*

an·a·log·i·cal (an-ă-loj-i-kăl) *adj.* an·a·log'i·cal·ly *adv.*

a·nal·y·sis (ă-nal-ĭ-sis) *n.* (*pl.* -ses, *pr.* -seez) 1. analyzing. 2. a statement of the result of this. 3. psychoanalysis.

an·a·lyst (an-ă-list) *n.* 1. a person who is skilled in analysis of chemical substances etc. 2. a psychoanalyst.

an·a·lyt·ic (an-ă-lit-ik), an·a·lyt·i·cal (an-ă-lit-ĭ-kal) *adj.* of or using analysis. an·a·lyt'i·cal·ly *adv.*

an·a·lyze (an-ă-lɪz) *v.* (an·a·lyzed, an·a·lyz·ing) 1. to separate (a substance etc.) into its parts in order to identify it or study its structure. 2. to examine and interpret, *tried to analyze the causes of their failure.* 3. to psychoanalyze.

an·a·pest (an-ă-pest) *n.* a metrical foot of three syllables, the first two short and the last long. an·a·pes·tic (an-ă-pes-tik) *adj.*

an·ar·chist (an-ăr-kist) *n.* a person who believes that government and laws are undesirable and should be abolished. an'ar·chism *n.* an·ar·chist·ic (an-ăr-kis-tik) *adj.*

an·ar·chy (an-ăr-kee) *n.* 1. the absence of government or control, resulting in lawlessness. 2. disorder, confusion. an·ar·chic (an-ahr-kik) *adj.* an·ar'chi·cal *adj.*

an·as·tig·mat·ic (an-as-tig-mat-ik) *adj.* free from astigmatism.

anat. *abbr.* anatomy.

a·nath·e·ma (ă-nath-ĕ-mă) *n.* 1. a formal curse of the Church, excommunicating someone or condemning something as evil. 2. a detested person or thing, *blood sports are anathema to him.*

a·nath·e·ma·tize (ă-nath-ĕ-mă-tɪz) *v.* (a·nath·e·ma·tized, a·nath·e·ma·tiz·ing) to curse.

a·nat·o·my (ă-nat-ŏ-mee) *n.* 1. the scientific study of bodily structures. 2. the bodily structure of an animal or plant. an·a·tom·i·cal (an-ă-tom-i-kăl) *adj.* an·a·tom'i·cal·ly *adv.*

-ance *suffix* used to form nouns meaning quality, as in *arrogance, relevance;* action, as in *assistance, penance.*

an·ces·tor (an-ses-tŏr) *n.* any of the persons from whom a person is descended, especially those more remote than grandparents. an·ces·tral (an-ses-trăl) *adj.*

an·ces·try (an-ses-tree) *n.* (*pl.* -tries) a line of ancestors.

an·chor (ang-kŏr) *n.* 1. a heavy metal structure or other object used to moor a ship to the sea bottom or a balloon etc. to the ground; *at anchor,* moored by an anchor. 2. anything that gives stability or security. anchor *v.* 1. to lower an anchor, to make secure with an anchor. 2. to fix firmly. □anchor man, a strong member of a sports team who plays a vital part (as at the back of a tug-of-war team or as a last runner in a relay race); a broadcaster who introduces and comments on and coordinates the reports etc. of others. anchor person, a man or woman who plays the role of anchor man.

an·chor·age (ang-kŏ-rij) *n.* 1. a place where ships may anchor safely. 2. the charge for this.

an·cho·rite (ang-kŏ-rɪt) *n.* a hermit.

an·cho·vy (an-choh-vee) *n.* (*pl.* -vies) a small rich-flavored fish of the herring family.

an·cient (ayn-chĕnt) *adj.* belonging to times long past. □ancient history, history of the period before the end of the Western Roman Empire in 476 A.D. the ancients, people who lived in ancient times.

an·cil·lar·y (an-sĭ-ler-ee) *adj.* helping in a subsidiary way, *ancillary services.*

-ancy *suffix* used to form nouns meaning quality, as in *constancy, relevancy;* state, as in *expectancy, infancy.*

and (and) *conj.* 1. together with. 2. then again, repeatedly or increasingly, *gets better and better; miles and miles,* very many miles. 3. added to, *two and two make four.* 4. to, *go and buy one.* 5. with this consequence, *move and I shoot.* □and/or, together with or as an alternative, either one or both. ▷Careful writers do not use *and/or.*

an·dan·te (ahn-dahn-tay) *adv.* (of music) in moderately slow time. andante *n.* a passage to be played in this way.

An·de·an (an-dee-ăn) *adj.* of the Andes, a range of mountains in western South America.

and·i·ron (and-ɪ-ĕrn) *n.* an iron support (usually one of a pair) for holding logs in a fireplace.

and/or *see* and.

An·dor·ra (an-dor-ă) *n.* a small country in the Pyrenees. An·dor'ran *adj. & n.*

Andorra la Vel·la (lă vel-ă) the capital of Andorra.

an·dro·gen (an-drŏ-jĕn) *n.* a male sex hormone or other substance capable of developing and maintaining certain male sexual characteristics.

an·droid (an-droid) *n.* a robot with human form.

an·ec·dote (an-ik-doht) *n.* a short amusing or interesting story about a real person or event. an·ec·dot·al (an-ik-doh-tăl) *adj.* ▷Do not confuse *anecdote* with *antidote.*

a·ne·mi·a (ă-nee-mi-ă) *n.* lack of red corpuscles or of their hemoglobin in blood.

a·ne·mic (ă-nee-mik) *adj.* 1. suffering from anemia. 2. pale, weak in color. 3. lacking vigor or positive characteristics. a·ne'mi·cal·ly *adv.*

an·e·mom·e·ter (an-ĕ-mom-ĕ-tĕr) *n.* an instrument for measuring the force of wind.

a·nem·o·ne (ă-nem-ŏ-nee) *n.* a plant related to the buttercup, with white, red, or purple flowers.

an·e·roid (an-ĕ-roid) **barometer** a barometer that measures air pressure by the action of air on the lid of a box containing a vacuum, not by the height of a fluid column.

an·es·the·sia (an-is-thee-zhă) *n.* 1. loss of sensation. 2. insensibility, especially to pain, induced by certain drugs.

an·es·the·si·ol·o·gist (an-is-thee-zi-ol-ŏ-jist) *n.* a specialist in anesthesiology.

an·es·the·si·ol·o·gy (an-is-thee-zi-ol-ŏ-jee) *n.* the branch of medicine dealing with anesthesia.

an·es·thet·ic (an-is-thet-ik) *n.* a substance that produces loss of sensation and of ability to feel pain. **anesthetic** *adj.* having this effect.

an·es·the·tist (ă-nes-thĕ-tist) *n.* a person trained to administer anesthetics.

an·es·the·tize (ă-nes-thĕ-tız) *v.* **(an·es·the·tized, an·es·the·tiz·ing)** to administer an anesthetic to (a person etc.).

an·eu·rysm (an-yŭ-riz-ĕm) *n.* a localized dilation of an artery caused by weakening of its wall.

a·new (ă-noo, ă-nyoo) *adv.* again, in a new or different way.

an·gel (ayn-jĕl) *n.* 1. an attendant or messenger of God, usually shown in pictures as a being in human form with wings and dressed in long white robes. 2. a very beautiful or kind person. 3. a financial backer, especially of a theatrical production. □ **angel dust,** *(informal)* a white crystalline powder used as an anesthetic by veterinarians and as a narcotic by some people, in whom it can cause apathy and social estrangement.

an·gel·fish (ayn-jĕl-fish) *n.* (*pl.* **-fish·es, -fish)** a fish with winglike fins.

an·gel·food (ayn-jĕl-food) **cake** a light, white sponge cake.

an·gel·ic (an-jel-ik) *adj.* of or like an angel. **an·gel'i·cal·ly** *adv.*

an·gel·i·ca (an-jel-i-kă) *n.* a fragrant plant used in cookery and medicine.

an·ge·lus (an-jĕ-lŭs) *n.* (in the Roman Catholic Church) 1. a prayer to the Virgin Mary commemorating the Incarnation, said at morning, noon, and sunset. 2. a bell rung as a signal for this.

an·ger (ang-gĕr) *n.* extreme displeasure. **anger** *v.* to make angry.

an·gi·na (an-jɪ-nă) *n.* a spasmodic gripping sensation of pain. □**angina pectoris** (pek-tŏ-ris), a sharp pain in the chest, accompanied by a sense of suffocation, caused by an insufficient blood supply to the heart.

an·gle¹ (ang-gĕl) *n.* 1. the space or figure formed between two lines or surfaces that meet. 2. a sharp projecting corner. 3. a point of view, *written from the sportsman's angle.* **angle** *v.* **(an·gled, an·gling)** 1. to move or place in a slanting position. 2. to present (news etc.) from a particular point of view.

an·gle² *v.* **(an·gled, an·gling)** 1. to fish with hook and bait. 2. to try to obtain by hinting, *angling for an invitation.* **an'gler** *n.*

an·gle·worm (ang-gĕl-wurm) *n.* an earthworm used as bait.

An·gli·can (ang-gli-kăn) *adj.* of the Church of England. **Anglican** *n.* a member of this Church. **An'gli·can·ism** *n.*

an·gli·cize (ang-gli-sız) *v.* **(an·gli·cized, an·gli·ciz·ing)** to make English in form or character. **an·gli·ci·za·tion** (ang-glĭ-si-zay-shŏn) *n.*

An·glo (ang-gloh) *n.* (*pl.* **-glos)** *(slang)* an English-speaking white American.

Anglo- *prefix* English, British; *an Anglo-French agreement,* between Britain and France.

An·glo·phile (ang-glŏ-fɪl) *n.* a person who admires England or English things.

An·glo·phobe (ang-glŏ-fohb) *n.* a person who hates England or the English.

An·glo-Sax·on (ang-gloh-sak-sŏn) *n.* 1. an English person of the period before the Norman Conquest. 2. the English language of this period, also called *Old English.* 3. a person of English descent. **Anglo-Saxon** *adj.* of the Anglo-Saxons or their language.

An·go·la (ang-goh-lă) a country on the west coast of Africa. **An·go'lan** *adj.* & *n.*

an·go·ra (ang-gohr-ă) *n.* 1. a yarn or fabric made from the hair of angora goats or rabbits. 2. a long-haired variety of cat, goat, or rabbit.

an·gos·tu·ra (ang-gŏs-toor-ă) *n.* the bitter bark of a South American tree.

an·gry (ang-gree) *adj.* **(-gri·er, -gri·est)** 1. feeling or showing anger. 2. inflamed, *an angry sore.* **an'gri·ly** *adv.*

angst (ahngst) *n.* anxiety, remorse.

ang·strom (ang-strŏm) *n.* a unit of length used in measuring wavelengths and equal to one ten-billionth of a meter.

an·guish (ang-gwish) *n.* severe physical or mental pain.

an·guished (ang-gwisht) *adj.* feeling anguish.

an·gu·lar (ang-gyŭ-lăr) *adj.* 1. having angles or sharp corners. 2. lacking plumpness or smoothness. 3. measured by angle, *the angular distance.* **an·gu·lar·i·ty** (ang-gyŭ-lar-i-tee) *n.*

An·gus *n.* = **Aberdeen Angus.**

an·hy·drous (an-hɪ-drŭs) *adj.* without water, especially the water of crystallization.

an·i·line (an-ĭ-lin) *n.* an oily liquid obtained from nitrobenzene, used in the manufacture of dyes and plastics.

an·i·mad·ver·sion (an-ĭ-mad-vur-zhŏn) *n.* criticism.

an·i·mal (an-ĭ-măl) *n.* 1. a living thing that can feel and move voluntarily. 2. such a being other than a human being. 3. a four-footed animal as distinguished from a bird, fish, reptile, or insect. 4. a brutish person. **animal** *adj.* of or from or relating to animal life.

an·i·mal·cule (an-ĭ-mal-kyool) *n.* a microscopic animal.

an·i·mal·ism (an-ĭ-mă-liz-ĕm) *n.* 1. animal activity, sensualism. 2. the doctrine that men are mere animals.

an·i·mate (an-ĭ-mayt) *v.* **(an·i·mat·ed, an·i·mat·ing)** 1. to give life or movement to, to make lively, *her presence animated the meeting.* 2. to motivate, *he was animated by loyalty.* 3. to produce as an animated cartoon. **an'i·mat·ed** *adj.* **an'i·ma·tor** *n.* □**animated cartoon,** a film made by photographing a series of drawings, giving an illusion of movement.

an·i·ma·tion (an-ĭ-may-shŏn) *n.* 1. animating. 2. liveliness. 3. an animated cartoon or the techniques producing it.

an·i·mos·i·ty (an-ĭ-mos-i-tee) *n.* (*pl.* **-ties)** a spirit of hostility.

an·i·mus (an-ĭ-mŭs) *n.* animosity shown in speech or action.

an·i·on (an-ɪ-ŏn) *n.* an ion with a negative charge. **an·i·on·ic** (an-ɪ-on-ik) *adj.*

an·ise (an-is) *n.* a plant with aromatic fruits and licorice-flavored seeds.

an·i·seed (an-ī-seed) *n.* the seed of the plant anise, used for flavoring.

an·i·sette (an-i-set) *n.* a colorless sweet liqueur flavored with aniseed.

An·ka·ra (ang-kă-ră) the capital of Turkey.

ankh (angk) *n.* a key-like cross used in ancient Egypt as a symbol of life.

an·kle (ang-kĕl) *n.* 1. the joint connecting the foot with the leg. 2. the slender part between this and the calf.

an·kle·bone (ang-kĕl-bohn) *n.* the talus, the uppermost row of bones of the tarsus.

an·klet (ang-klit) *n.* 1. an ornamental chain or band worn around the ankle. 2. a short sock reaching to slightly above the ankle.

ann. *abbr.* 1. annual. 2. annuity.

an·nals (an-ălz) *n. pl.* a history of events year by year, historical records. **an·nal·ist** (an-ă-list) *n.*

An·nap·o·lis (ă-nap-ŏ-lis) the capital of Maryland.

an·neal (ă-neel) *v.* to toughen (glass or metals) by heating and then cooling, to temper.

an·nex (ă-neks) *v.* 1. to add or join to a larger thing. 2. to take possession of, *to annex territory.* **annex** (an-eks) *n.* a building attached to a larger one or forming a subordinate part of a main building. **an·nex·a·tion** (an-ek-say-shŏn) *n.*

an·ni·hi·late (ă-nī-ĭ-layt) *v.* **(an·ni·hi·lat·ed, an·ni·hi·lat·ing)** to destroy completely. **an·ni·hi·la·tor** *n.* **an·ni·hi·la·tion** (ă-nī-ĭ-lay-shŏn) *n.*

an·ni·ver·sa·ry (an-ī-vur-să-ree) *n.* (*pl.* **-ries**) the yearly return of the date of an event, a celebration of this.

an·no Do·mi·ni (an-oh dom-ī-nī) in the year of Our Lord (usually shortened to A.D.).

an·no·tate (an-oh-tayt) *v.* **(an·no·tat·ed, an·no·tat·ing)** to add notes of explanation to, *an annotated edition.* **an'no·ta·tor** *n.* **an·no·ta·tion** (an-oh-tay-shŏn) *n.*

an·nounce (ă-nowns) *v.* **(an·nounced, an·nounc·ing)** 1. to make known publicly or to an audience. 2. to make known the presence or arrival of. **an·nounce'ment** *n.*

an·nounc·er (ă-nown-sĕr) *n.* a person who announces something, especially one who introduces programs or reads news items over radio or television.

an·noy (ă-noi) *v.* 1. to cause slight anger to. 2. to be troublesome to, to harass. **an·noy'ance** *n.* **an·noyed'** *adj.* **an·noy'ing** *adj.* **an·noy'ing·ly** *adv.*

an·nu·al (an-yoo-ăl) *adj.* 1. coming or happening once every year, *her annual visit.* 2. of one year, reckoned by the year, *her annual income.* 3. lasting only one year or season, *annual plants.* **annual** *n.* 1. a plant that lives for one year or one season. 2. a book or periodical published in yearly issues. **an'nu·al·ly** *adv.* ☐**annual ring,** a ring in the cross section of a tree, fish, etc. from one year's growth.

an·nu·i·tant (ă-noo-i-tănt) *n.* a person who receives an annuity.

an·nu·i·ty (ă-noo-i-tee) *n.* (*pl.* **-ties**) a fixed annual allowance, especially one provided by a form of investment.

an·nul (ă-nul) *v.* **(an·nulled, an·nul·ling)** to make null and void, to destroy the validity of, *the marriage was annulled.* **an·nul'ment** *n.*

an·nu·lar (an-yŭ-lăr) *adj.* ringlike.

an·nun·ci·ate (ă-nun-si-ayt) *v.* **(an·nun·ci·at·ed, an·nun·ci·at·ing)** to announce. **an·nun·ci·a·tor** (ă-nun-si-ay-tŏr) *n.* **an·nun·ci·a·to·ry** (ă-nun-si-ă-tohr-ee) *adj.*

an·nun·ci·a·tion (ă-nun-si-ay-shŏn) *n.* 1. the act of announcing. 2. *Annunciation,* the announcement by the angel Gabriel to the Virgin Mary that she was to be the mother of Christ, the festival commemorating this.

an·ode (an-ohd) *n.* the electrode by which current enters a device. **an·od·ic** (an-od-ik) *adj.*

an·o·dize (an-ŏ-dız) *v.* **(an·o·dized, an·o·diz·ing)** to coat (metal) with a protective layer by electrolysis. **an·od·i·za·tion** (an-oh-di-zay-shŏn) *n.*

an·o·dyne (an-ŏ-dın) *n.* 1. a drug that relieves pain. 2. anything that relieves pain or distress.

a·noint (ă-noint) *v.* 1. to apply ointment or oil to, especially as a sign of consecration. 2. to smear or rub with grease. **a·noint·ment** (ă-noint-mĕnt) *n.*

a·nom·a·ly (ă-nom-ă-lee) *n.* (*pl.* **-lies**) something that deviates from the general rule or the usual type, an irregularity or inconsistency. **a·nom'a·lous** *adj.*

a·non (ă-non) *adv. (old use)* soon, presently, *I will say more of this anon.*

anon. *abbr.* by an anonymous author.

an·o·nym·i·ty (an-ŏ-nim-ĭ-tee) *n.* being anonymous.

a·non·y·mous (ă-non-ĭ-mŭs) *adj.* 1. with a name that is not known or not made public, *an anonymous donor.* 2. written or given by such a person, *an anonymous gift; an anonymous letter,* one that is not signed. **a·non'y·mous·ly** *adv.*

a·noph·e·les (ă-nof-ĕ-leez) *n.* a mosquito that carries malaria.

an·o·rec·tic (an-ŏ-rek-tik) *adj.* suffering from anorexia.

an·o·rex·i·a (an-ŏ-rek-si-ă) *n.* loss of appetite for food. ☐**anorexia nervosa,** a psychological condition causing chronic absence of appetite for food.

an·oth·er (ă-nuth-ĕr) *adj.* 1. additional, one more; *he is another Solomon,* one like him. 2. different, *use another pipe, this one leaks.* 3. some or any other, *will not do another man's work.* **another** *pronoun* another or a different person or thing.

an·swer (an-sĕr) *n.* 1. something said or written or needed or done to deal with a question, accusation, or problem. 2. the correct solution to a problem. **answer** *v.* 1. to make an answer to, to say, write, or do something in return; *answer the door,* go to it in response to a signal; *he answers to the name of Thomas,* is so called. 2. to suffice or be suitable for, *this will answer the purpose.* 3. to take responsibility for, to vouch for, *I will answer for his honesty; they must answer for their crimes,* must justify them or pay the penalty. 4. to correspond, *this bag answers to the description of the stolen one.* **an'swer·er** *n.* ☐**answer back,** to answer a rebuke impertinently. **answering service,** a business that receives telephone calls for its clients.

an·swer·a·ble (an-sĕ-ră-bĕl) *adj.* 1. able to be answered. 2. having to account for something.

ant (ant) *n.* a very small insect of which there are many species, all of which form and live in highly organized groups. ☐**ant lion,** an insect that traps ants.

ant. *abbr.* 1. antenna. 2. antonym.

Ant. *abbr.* Antarctica.

-ant¹ *suffix* used to form adjectives meaning existence of action, as in *repentant.*

-ant² *suffix* used to form nouns meaning agent, as in *assistant.*

ant·ac·id (ant-as-id) *n.* a substance that prevents or corrects acidity.

an·tag·o·nism (an-tag-ŏ-niz-ĕm) *n.* active opposition, hostility. **an·tag'o·nist** *n.*

an·tag·o·nis·tic (an-tag-ŏ-nis-tik) *adj.* showing or feeling antagonism. **an·tag·o·nis'ti·cal·ly** *adv.*

an·tag·o·nize (an-tag-ŏ-nɪz) *v.* **(an·tag·o· nized, an·tag·o·niz·ing)** to arouse antagonism in.

Ant·arc·tic (ant-ahrk-tik) *adj.* of the regions around the South Pole. **Antarctic** *n.* 1. these regions. 2. the Antarctic Ocean. □**Antarctic Circle,** the line of latitude 66° 30' S. ▷Be sure to pronounce the two "k" sounds in *Antarctic.*

Ant·arc·ti·ca (ant-ahrk-ti-kă) the continent mainly within the Antarctic Circle. ▷Be sure to pronounce the two "k" sounds in *Antarctica.*

an·te (an-tee) *n.* 1. a stake put up by each poker player before he sees his hand. 2. *(slang)* the cost or price. **ante** *v.* **(an·ted** or **an·teed, an·te· ing)** to put up an ante, to pay up. □**ante up,** to ante.

ante- *prefix* before. ▷Do not confuse *ante-* with *anti-.*

ant·eat·er (ant-ee-tĕr) *n.* a tropical American mammal feeding chiefly on ants and termites.

an·te·bel·lum (an-ti-bel-ŭm) *adj.* before the war, of the southern U.S. before the Civil War.

an·te·ced·ent (an-ti-see-dĕnt) *n.* 1. a preceding thing or circumstance, *the war and its antecedents; I know nothing of his antecedents,* of his ancestry or past life. 2. a noun, clause, or sentence to which a following pronoun refers (in *the book that I have,* book is the antecedent of *that*). **antecedent** *adj.* previous.

an·te·cham·ber (an-ti-chaym-bĕr) *n.* an anteroom.

an·te·date (an-ti-dayt) *v.* **(an·te·dat·ed, an· te·dat·ing)** 1. to put an earlier date on (a document) than that on which it was issued. 2. to precede in time, to be earlier.

an·te·di·lu·vi·an (an-ti-di-loo-vi-ăn) *adj.* 1. of the time before the Flood. 2. *(informal)* utterly out of date.

an·te·lope (an-tĕ-lohp) *n.* a swift-running animal resembling a deer, found especially in Africa.

an·te me·ri·di·em (an-ti mĕ-rid-i-ĕm) between midnight and noon. ▷Latin.

an·ten·na (an-ten-ă) *n.* (*pl.* **-ten·nae,** *pr.* -ten-ee, **-ten·nas**) 1. one of a pair of flexible sensitive projections on the heads of insects, crustaceans, etc., a feeler. 2. wire(s) or rod(s) used to transmit or receive radio waves, an aerial.

an·te·pe·nul·ti·mate (an-ti-pi-nul-tĭ-mit) *adj.* last but two.

an·te·ri·or (an-teer-i-ŏr) *adj.* coming before in position or time.

an·te·room (an-ti-room) *n.* a room leading to a more important one.

an·them (an-thĕm) *n.* 1. a short musical composition to be sung in religious services, often with words taken from the Bible. 2. a song of praise or gladness.

an·ther (an-thĕr) *n.* the part of a flower's stamen that contains pollen.

ant·hill (ant-hil) *n.* a mound over an ants' nest.

an·thol·o·gist (an-thol-ŏ-jist) *n.* a person who compiles an anthology.

an·thol·o·gize (an-thol-ŏ-jɪz) *v.* **(an·thol·o· gized, an·thol·o·giz·ing)** to include in an anthology.

an·thol·o·gy (an-thol-ŏ-jee) *n.* a collection of passages from literature, especially poems.

an·thra·cite (an-thră-sɪt) *n.* a hard form of coal that burns with little flame or smoke.

an·thrax (an-thraks) *n.* a disease of sheep and cattle that can be transmitted to people.

anthrop. *abbr.* anthropology.

an·thro·poid (an-thrŏ-poid) *adj.* manlike in form.

anthropoid *n.* an anthropoid ape such as a gorilla or chimpanzee.

an·thro·pol·o·gist (an-thrŏ-pol-ŏ-jist) *n.* an expert in anthropology.

an·thro·pol·o·gy (an-thrŏ-pol-ŏ-jee) *n.* the scientific study of mankind, especially of its origins, development, customs, and beliefs. **an·thro·po· log·i·cal** (an-thrŏ-pŏ-loj-i-kăl) *adj.* **an·thro· po·log'i·cal·ly** *adv.*

an·thro·po·mor·phic (an-thrŏ-pŏ-mor-fik) *adj.* attributing human form or personality to a god or animal or object. **an·thro·po·mor'phism** *n.*

an·ti (an-tɪ, -tee) *n.* (*pl.* **-tis**) a person who opposes a certain policy etc. **anti** *prep.* *(informal)* opposed to.

anti- *prefix* against, opposed to, as in *antislavery;* preventing, counteracting, as in *antiperspirant.* ▷Do not confuse *anti-* with *ante-.*

an·ti·air·craft (an-ti-air-kraft) *adj.* used against enemy aircraft.

an·ti-A·mer·i·can (an-ti-ă-mer-i-kăn) *adj.* 1. opposed to U.S. policy or interests. 2. hating Americans.

an·ti·bac·te·ri·al (an-ti-bak-teer-i-ăl) *adj.* stopping the growth of bacteria.

an·ti·bal·lis·tic (an-ti-bă-lis-tik) **missile** a defensive missile designed to intercept and destroy an attacking ballistic missile.

an·ti·bi·ot·ic (an-ti-bɪ-ot-ik) *n.* a substance capable of destroying or preventing the growth of bacteria.

an·ti·bod·y (an-ti-bod-ee) *n.* a protein formed in the blood in reaction to certain substances which it then attacks and destroys.

an·tic (an-tik) *n.* (usually **antics**) 1. absurd movements intended to cause amusement. 2. odd or foolish behavior.

an·ti·can·cer (an-ti-kan-sĕr) *adj.* stopping the growth of cancer cells.

an·ti·cath·o·lic (an-ti-kath-ŏ-lik) *adj.* opposed to the doctrine and influence of the Roman Catholic Church. **anti-Ca·thol·i·cism** (an-ti-kă-thol-ĭ-siz-ĕm) *n.*

An·ti·christ (an-ti-krɪst) *n.* a great enemy or opponent of Christ and his teachings.

an·tic·i·pate (an-tis-ĭ-payt) *v.* **(an·tic·i·pat· ed, an·tic·i·pat·ing)** 1. to deal with before the proper time; *be sure not to anticipate the check,* do not spend it before receiving it. 2. to take action before someone else has had time to do so, *others may have anticipated Columbus in the discovery of America.* 3. to notice what needs doing and take action in advance; *anticipate someone's needs,* provide for them in advance; *the boxer anticipated the blow,* saw it coming and blocked it. 4. to expect, *we anticipate that it will rain.* (▷Many people regard this use as unacceptable, but it is very common.) **an·tic·i·pa·tion** (an-tis-ĭ-pay-shŏn) *n.*

an·tic·i·pa·to·ry (an-tis-ĭ-pă-tohr-ee) *adj.* showing anticipation.

an·ti·cler·i·cal (an-ti-kler-i-kăl) *adj.* opposed to the influence of clergy or to the existence of an organized clerical hierarchy.

an·ti·cli·max (an-ti-klĭ-maks) *n.* a disappointing ending or outcome of events where a climax was expected. **an·ti·cli·mac·tic** (an-ti-klĭ-mak-tic) *adj.*

an·ti·cline (an-ti-klīn) *n.* an archlike fold in a bed of rock. **an·ti·cli·nal** (an-ti-klĭ-năl) *adj.*

an·ti·co·ag·u·lant (an-ti-koh-ag-yŭ-lănt) *adj.* retarding or preventing the clotting of blood. **anticoagulant** *n.* an anticoagulant substance.

an·ti·co·lo·ni·al (an-ti-kŏ-loh-ni-ăl) *adj.* opposed to the practice of maintaining overseas colonies. **an·ti·co·lo'ni·al·ism** *n.*

an·ti·com·mu·nism (an-ti-kom-yŭ-niz-ĕm) *n.* opposition to communism. **an·ti·com'mu·nist** *n.* **an·ti·com·mu·nis·tic** (an-ti-kom-yu-nis-tik) *adj.*

an·ti·cy·clone (an-ti-sɪ-klohn) *n.* an area in which atmospheric pressure is high, producing fine settled weather, with an outward flow of air. **an·ti·cy·clon·ic** (an-ti-sɪ-klon-ik) *adj.*

an·ti·de·pres·sant (an-ti-di-pres-ănt) *n.* a drug that counteracts mental depression. **an·ti·de·pres'sive** *adj.*

an·ti·dote (an-ti-doht) *n.* 1. a substance that counteracts the effects of a poison or a disease. 2. anything that counteracts unpleasant effects. ▷Do not confuse *antidote* with *anecdote.*

an·ti·es·tab·lish·ment (an-ti-es-tab-lish-mĕnt) *adj.* opposed to institutions of power in a society.

an·ti·fas·cist (an-ti-fash-ist) *adj.* opposed to fascism. **an·ti·fas'cism** *n.*

an·ti·fer·til·i·ty (an-ti-fĕr-til-i-tee) *n.* preventing or impeding conception.

an·ti·freeze (an-ti-freez) *n.* a substance added to water to lower its freezing point and therefore make it less likely to freeze.

an·ti·gen (an-ti-jĕn) *n.* a substance that stimulates production of an antibody when introduced into a living organism. **an·ti·gen·ic** (an-ti-jen-ik) *adj.* **an·ti·ge·nic·i·ty** (an-ti-jĕ-nis-i-tee) *n.*

an·ti·grav·i·ty (an-ti-grav-i-tee) *n.* a hypothetical force opposing gravity. **an·ti·grav·i·ta·tion·al** (an-ti-grav-i-tay-shŏ-năl) *adj.*

an·ti·he·ro (an-ti-heer-oh) *n.* a hero of an unconventional type in a novel etc.

an·ti·his·ta·mine (an-ti-his-tă-meen) *n.* a substance that counteracts the effects of histamine, used in treating allergies.

an·ti·hy·per·ten·sive (an-ti-hɪ-pĕr-ten-siv) *n.* a drug used to treat high blood pressure.

an·ti·im·pe·ri·al·ism (an-ti-im-peer-i-ă-liz-ĕm) *n.* opposed to imperialism. **an·ti·im·per'i·al·ist** *n.* **an·ti·im·per·i·al·is·tic** (an-ti-im-peer-i-ă-lis-tik) *adj.*

an·ti·knock (an-ti-nok) *adj.* preventing or reducing knocking in an internal combustion engine. **antiknock** *n.* a substance added to motor fuel to prevent or reduce knock.

an·ti·log·a·rithm (an-ti-law-gă-ri*th*-ĕm) *n.* a number to which a logarithm belongs.

an·ti·ma·cas·sar (an-ti-mă-kas-ăr) *n.* a covering on a chair back to protect it from hair grease or to serve as an ornament.

an·ti·mag·net·ic (an-ti-mag-net-ik) *adj.* resistant to magnetization, especially of watch movements.

an·ti·mat·ter (an-ti-mat-ĕr) *n.* hypothetical matter composed solely of antiparticles.

an·ti·mo·ny (an-ti-moh-nee) *n.* a brittle silvery metallic element used in alloys.

an·ti·nov·el (an-ti-nov-ĕl) *n.* a novel of unconventional or nontraditional type.

an·ti·par·ti·cle (an-ti-pahr-ti-kĕl) *n.* an elementary particle having the same mass as a given particle but an opposite electric charge or magnetic moment.

an·ti·pas·to (an-ti-pah-stoh) *n.* assorted appetizers such as smoked meats, fish, olives, etc.

an·tip·a·thy (an-tip-ă-thee) *n.* 1. a strong and settled dislike. 2. the object of this. **an·ti·pa·thet·ic** (an-ti-pă-thet-ik) *adj.*

an·ti·per·son·nel (an-ti-pur-sŏ-nel) *adj.* designed to kill or injure persons.

an·ti·per·spi·rant (an-ti-pur-spĕ-rănt) *n.* a substance used to reduce excessive underarm perspiration.

an·tiph·o·nal (an-tif-ŏ-nal) *adj.* sung alternately. **an·tiph'o·nal·ly** *adv.*

an·tip·o·des (an-tip-ŏ-deez) *n. pl.* places on opposite sides of Earth. **an·tip·o·de·an** (an-tip-ŏ-dee-ăn) *adj.* **an·ti·po·dal** (an-tip-ŏ-dăl) *adj.* □**the antipodes,** the region diametrically opposite Europe.

an·ti·pol·lu·tion (an-ti-pŏ-loo-shŏn) *adj.* against or preventing pollution.

an·ti·pope (an-ti-pohp) *n.* a pope in opposition to one who is held to be canonically chosen.

an·ti·pov·er·ty (an-ti-pov-ĕr-tee) *adj.* attempting to ameliorate or eliminate poverty.

an·ti·pro·ton (an-ti-proh-ton) *n.* an antiparticle of proton.

an·ti·quar·i·an (an-ti-kwair-i-ăn) *adj.* connected with the study of antiques or antiquity. **antiquarian** *n.* an antiquary. **an·ti·quar'i·an·ism** *n.*

an·ti·quar·y (an-tĭ-kwer-ee) *n.* one who studies or collects antiques or antiquities.

an·ti·quat·ed (an-tĭ-kway-tid) *adj.* old-fashioned, out of date.

an·tique (an-teek) *adj.* belonging to the distant past, in the style of past times. **antique** *n.* an antique object, especially furniture or a decorative object of a kind sought by collectors. **antique** *v.* (**an·tiqued,** **an·ti·quing**) to make (furniture etc.) appear antique by artificial means.

an·tiq·ui·ty (an-tik-wi-tee) *n. (pl.* **-ties**) 1. ancient times, especially before the Middle Ages; *it is of great antiquity,* it is very old. 2. an object dating from ancient times, *Greek and Roman antiquities.*

an·ti-Se·mit·ic (an-ti-sĕ-mit-ik) *adj.* hostile to Jews. **an·ti-Sem·ite** (an-ti-sem-ɪt) *n.* **an·ti-Sem·i·tism** (an-ti-sem-ĭ-tiz-ĕm) *n.*

an·ti·sep·tic (an-ti-sep-tik) *adj.* 1. killing or preventing the growth of bacteria etc. that cause things to become septic. 2. thoroughly clean and free from germs. **antiseptic** *n.* a substance with an antiseptic effect. **an·ti·sep'ti·cal·ly** *adv.*

an·ti·se·rum (an-ti-seer-ŭm) *n.* (*pl.* **-se·rums,** **-se·ra,** *pr.* -seer-ă) a serum containing antibodies.

an·ti·slav·er·y (an-ti-slay-vĕ-ree) *adj.* opposed to slavery.

an·ti·so·cial (an-ti-soh-shăl) *adj.* 1. opposed or hostile to the social institutions and laws of an organized community. 2. unsociable, withdrawing oneself from others. **an·ti·so'cial·ly** *adv.*

an·ti·stat·ic (an-ti-stat-ik) *adj.* counteracting the effects of static electricity.
an·ti·sub·ma·rine (an-ti-sub-mă-reen) *adj.* used against submarines.
an·ti·tank (an-ti-tangk) *adj.* used against tanks in war.
an·tith·e·sis (an-tith-ĕ-sis) *n.* (*pl.* **-ses,** *pr.* **-seez**) 1. the direct opposite of something, opposition or contrast, *slavery is the antithesis of freedom.* 2. contrast of ideas emphasized by choice of words or by their arrangement. **an·ti·thet·ic** (an-tĭ-thet-ik) *adj.* **an·ti·thet′i·cal** *adj.* **an·ti·thet′i·cal·ly** *adv.*
an·ti·tox·in (an-ti-tok-sin) *n.* a substance that neutralizes a toxin and prevents it from having a harmful effect. **an·ti·tox′ic** *adj.*
an·ti·trust (an-ti-trust) *adj.* opposed to or intended to regulate trusts and monopolies.
an·ti·ven·in (an-ti-ven-in) *n.* an antitoxin, especially against snake poison.
an·ti·viv·i·sec·tion·ist (an-ti-viv-ĭ-sek-shŏ-nist) *n.* a person who is opposed to making experiments on live animals.
ant·ler (ant-lĕr) *n.* a branched horn, one of a pair of these on a stag or other deer. **ant′lered** *adj.*
an·to·nym (an-tŏ-nim) *n.* a word that is opposite in meaning to another.
A (ay) **number one** *see* **A.**
a·nus (ay-nŭs) *n.* the opening at the end of the alimentary canal, through which waste matter passes out of the body.
an·vil (an-vil) *n.* a block of iron on which a blacksmith hammers metal into shape.
anx·i·e·ty (ang-zɪ-ĕ-tee) *n.* 1. the state of being anxious. 2. something causing this.
anx·ious (angk-shŭs) *adj.* 1. troubled and uneasy in mind. 2. causing worry, filled with such feeling, *an anxious moment.* 3. eager, *anxious to please.* **anx′ious·ly** *adv.* ▷ Careful writers do not use *anxious* in its third sense. They would write *eager to please.*
an·y (en-ee) *adj.* 1. one or some (but no matter which) from three or more or from a quantity. 2. every, whichever you choose, *any fool knows that.* 3. in a significant amount, *did not stay any length of time.* **any** *pronoun* any person, thing, or amount, *can't find any of them; we haven't any.* **any** *adv.* at all, in some degree, *isn't any better.* □**not having any,** *(informal)* unwilling to take part in something or to agree with what is said.
an·y·bod·y (en-i-bod-ee) *n. & pronoun* 1. any person. 2. a person of importance, *is he anybody?* □**anybody's guess,** something no one can be sure about.
an·y·how (en-i-how) *adv.* 1. in any way. 2. nevertheless, in any case.
an·y·more (en-i-mohr) *adv.* (in negative and interrogative constructions) now, henceforth. ▷ Do not confuse *anymore* with *any more. I do not see him anymore. Any more would be too many.*
an·y·one (en-i-wun) *n. & pronoun* anybody. ▷ Write *any one* only when you mean a particular person or thing or idea etc. *Here are four. Please choose any one of them.*
an·y·place (en-i-plays) *adv.* anywhere. ▷ Careful writers use *anywhere.*
an·y·thing (en-i-thing) *n. & pronoun* any thing, *anything will do; as easy as anything,* very easy. □**anything but,** far from being, *it's anything but cheap.* **like anything,** with great intensity.

an·y·time (en-i-tɪm) *adv.* at any time.
an·y·way (en-i-way) *adv.* in any way, in any case. ▷ *Anyways* is incorrect.
an·y·where (en-i-hwair) *adv.* in or to any place. ▷ *Anywheres* is incorrect.
An·zac (an-zak) *n.* 1. a member of the Australian and New Zealand Army Corps. (▷ The name is formed from the initial letters of the Corps.) 2. an Australian or a New Zealander.
A-O.K., **A-OK** (ay-oh-kay) *adj. & adv. (informal)* perfectly all right, excellent.
A one (ay wun) *see* **A.**
a·or·ta (ay-or-tă) *n.* (*pl.* **-tas, -tae,** *pr.* **-tee**) the great artery through which blood is carried from the left side of the heart.
A.P. *abbr.* Associated Press.
a·pace (ă-pays) *adv.* swiftly, *work proceeded apace.*
a·pache (ă-pash) *n.* a violent street ruffian in Paris, a member of the Parisian underworld. □**apache dance,** a violent dance for two persons.
A·pach·e (ă-pach-ee) *n.* a member of a tribe of North American Indians inhabiting the southwestern part of the U.S.
a·part (ă-pahrt) *adv.* 1. aside, separately in place or time, to or at a distance; *cannot tell them apart,* cannot distinguish one from the other. 2. into pieces, *it came apart.* □**apart from,** independently of, other than, *has no books apart from these.*
a·part·heid (ă-pahrt-hayt) *n.* a policy of racial segregation in the Republic of South Africa.
a·part·ment (ă-pahrt-mĕnt) *n.* a suite of rooms for dwelling in. □**apartment house** *or* **building,** a building divided into individual dwelling units.
ap·a·thy (ap-ă-thee) *n.* lack of interest or concern. **ap·a·thet·ic** (ap-ă-thet-ik) *adj.* **ap·a·thet′i·cal·ly** *adv.*
ape (ayp) *n.* 1. a tailless monkey (gorilla, chimpanzee, orangutan, gibbon). 2. *(slang)* a large uncouth man. **ape** *v.* **(aped, ap·ing)** to imitate, to mimic.
ape-man (ayp-man) *n.* (*pl.* **-men,** *pr.* **-men**) a member of an extinct genus of apelike men.
Ap·en·nines (ap-ĕ-ninz) *n. pl.* a mountain range in Italy.
a·per·çu (ap-ĕr-syoo) *n.* 1. a summary exposition. 2. an insight. ▷ French.
a·per·i·tif (ă-per-i-teef) *n.* an alcoholic drink taken as an appetizer.
ap·er·ture (ap-ĕr-chŭr) *n.* an opening, especially one that admits light.
a·pex (ay-peks) *n.* the tip or highest point, the pointed end, *the apex of a triangle.*
aph·a·nite (af-ă-nɪt) *n.* a close-grained igneous rock. **aph·a·nit·ic** (af-ă-nit-ik) *adj.*
a·pha·sia (ă-fay-zhă) *n.* partial or total loss of speech, or loss of understanding of language, resulting from brain damage. **a·pha·sic** (ă-fay-zik) *adj.*
a·phe·li·on (ă-fee-li-ŏn) *n.* (*pl.* **-lia,** *pr.* **-li-ă**) the point of a planet's or a comet's orbit farthest from the sun.
a·phid (ay-fid, af-id) *n.* a plant louse that sucks the juice of plants.
a·phis (ay-fis, af-is) *n.* (*pl.* **-i-des,** *pr.* af-i-deez) an aphid.
aph·o·rism (af-ŏ-riz-ĕm) *n.* a short wise saying, a maxim.
aph·ro·dis·i·ac (af-rŏ-diz-i-ak) *adj.* arousing sexual desire. **aphrodisiac** *n.* an aphrodisiac substance.
A·pi·a (ah-pee-ah) the capital of Western Samoa.
a·pi·ar·y (ay-pi-er-ee) *n.* a place with a number

of hives where bees are kept. **a·pi·a·rist** (ay-pi-ă-rist) *n.*

ap·i·cal (ap-i-kăl) *adj.* 1. belonging to an apex. 2. placed at the tip. 3. articulated with the tip of the tongue. **a′pi·cal·ly** *adj.*

a·piece (ă-pees) *adv.* for or by each one of a group, *cost a penny apiece.*

a·plomb (ă-plom) *n.* dignity and confidence.

A.P.O. *abbr.* Army Post Office.

a·poc·a·lypse (ă-pok-ă-lips) *n.* 1. a cataclysmic event, the end of the world. 2. *Apocalypse,* the *Revelation* (of St. John the Divine), the book in the New Testament containing a prophetic description of the end of the world. **a·poc·a·lyp·tic** (ă-pok-ă-lip-tik) *adj.* prophesying great and dramatic events like those described in the Apocalypse. **a·poc·a·lyp′ti·cal·ly** *adv.*

A·poc·ry·pha (ă-pok-rĭ-fă) *n.* 1. those books of the Old Testament that were not accepted by Jews as part of the Hebrew Scriptures and were excluded from the Protestant Bible at the Reformation. 2. *apocrypha,* any writings of dubious authenticity.

a·poc·ry·phal (ă-pok-rĭ-făl) *adj.* 1. untrue, invented, *an apocryphal account of his travels.* 2. *Apocryphal,* of the Apocrypha. **a·poc′ry·phal·ly** *adv.*

a·po·cyn·thi·on (ap-ŏ-sin-thi-ŏn) *n.* apolune.

ap·o·gee (ap-ŏ-jee) *n.* 1. the point in the orbit of the moon or any planet when it is at its farthest point from Earth. 2. the highest or most distant point, a climax. **a·po·ge·an** (ap-ŏ-jee-ăn) *adj.*

a·po·lit·i·cal (ay-pŏ-lit-i-kăl) *adj.* unconcerned with or detached from politics. **a·po·lit′i·cal·ly** *adv.*

A·pol·lo (ă-pol-oh) *n.* (*pl.* **-los**) a young man of great physical beauty. ▷ Apollo was the sun god in Greek mythology.

a·pol·o·get·ic (ă-pol-ŏ-jet-ik) *adj.* making an apology. **a·pol·o·get′i·cal·ly** *adv.*

ap·o·lo·gi·a (ap-ŏ-loh-ji-ă) *n.* a defense or justification of conduct or opinions.

a·pol·o·gist (ă-pol-ŏ-jist) *n.* a person who explains or defends a doctrine by reasoned argument.

a·pol·o·gize (ă-pol-ŏ-jɪz) *v.* (**a·pol·o·gized,** **a·pol·o·giz·ing**) to make an apology.

a·pol·o·gy (ă-pol-ŏ-jee) *n.* 1. a statement of regret for having done wrong or hurt someone's feelings. 2. an explanation or defense of one's beliefs. 3. a poor or scanty specimen, *this feeble apology for a meal.*

ap·o·lune (ap-ŏ-loon) *n.* the point in a body's orbit about the moon where it is farthest from the moon's center.

ap·o·plec·tic (ap-ŏ-plek-tik) *adj.* 1. of apoplexy. 2. suffering from apoplexy. 3. *(informal)* liable to fits of rage in which the face becomes very red. **ap·o·plec′ti·cal·ly** *adv.*

ap·o·plex·y (ap-ŏ-plek-see) *n.* sudden inability to feel and move, caused by blockage or rupture of an artery in the brain.

a·pos·ta·sy (ă-pos-tă-see) *n.* (*pl.* **-sies**) renunciation of one's religion, principles, political party, etc. **a·pos·tate** (ă-pos-tayt) *adj.* & *n.*

a pos·te·ri·o·ri (ay pos-teer-i-ohr-ɪ) (of reasoning) from effects to causes. ▷ Latin, = from what comes after.

a·pos·tle (ă-pos-ĕl) *n.* 1. *Apostle,* any of the twelve men sent forth by Jesus to preach the Gospel. 2. a leader or teacher of a new faith or movement.

ap·os·tol·ic (ap-ŏ-stol-ik) *adj.* 1. of the Apostles

or their teaching. 2. of the pope as successor to St. Peter. ☐**apostolic succession,** transmission of spiritual authority from the Apostles through successive popes and other bishops.

a·pos·tro·phe (ă-pos-trŏ-fee) *n.* the sign ' used to show that letters or numbers have been omitted (as in *can't* = cannot; *'05* = 1905), or showing the possessive case (the *boy's* book, the *boys'* books), or the plurals of letters (there are two *l's* in *bell*).

a·poth·e·car·y (ă-poth-ĕ-ker-ee) *n.* (*pl.* **-car·ies**) *(old use)* a druggist, pharmacist. ☐**apothecaries' weight,** a system of units formerly used by pharmacists.

ap·o·thegm (ap-ŏ-them) *n.* a terse or pithy saying.

a·poth·e·o·sis (ă-poth-i-oh-sis) *n.* (*pl.* **-ses,** *pr.* -seez) deification, deified ideal.

app. *abbr.* 1. apparent. 2. apparently. 3. appendix.

Ap·pa·la·chi·ans (ap-ă-lay-chi-ănz) *n. pl.* the Appalachian Mountains, in eastern North America.

ap·pall (ă-pawl) *v.* (**ap·palled, ap·pall·ing**) to fill with horror or dismay, to shock deeply.

ap·pall·ing (ă-paw-ling) *adj. (informal)* shocking, unpleasant.

Ap·pa·loo·sa (ap-ă-loo-să) *n.* a horse of a western American breed with dark spots on a light background.

ap·pa·nage (ap-ă-nij) *n.* 1. provision for the younger children of kings etc. 2. a perquisite. 3. a natural accompaniment or attribute.

ap·pa·ra·tus (ap-ă-rat-ŭs, -ray-tŭs) *n.* (*pl.* **-tus, -tus·es**) 1. the equipment used for doing something, the instruments etc. used in scientific experiments. 2. the equipment (as parallel bars) used in gymnastics. 3. a group of bodily organs by which some natural process is carried out, *the digestive apparatus.*

ap·par·el (ă-par-ĕl) *n.* clothing.

ap·par·ent (ă-par-ĕnt) *adj.* 1. clearly seen or understood; *it became apparent,* became obvious. 2. seeming but not real, *his reluctance was only apparent.* **ap·par′ent·ly** *adv.* ☐**heir apparent,** *see* **heir.**

ap·pa·ri·tion (ap-ă-rish-ŏn) *n.* 1. an appearance, something that appears, especially something remarkable or unexpected. 2. a ghost.

ap·peal (ă-peel) *v.* 1. to make an earnest request, *appealed for contributions.* 2. to ask a person or go to a recognized authority for an opinion or for confirmation of what one says, *appealed to the umpire.* 3. to take a question to a higher court for rehearing and a new decision. 4. to offer attraction, to seem pleasing, *cruises don't appeal to me.* **appeal** *n.* 1. the act of appealing. 2. attraction, pleasantness. 3. a request for public donations to a cause. **ap·peal′ing·ly** *adv.* ☐**snob appeal,** appeal to people's snobbish feelings.

ap·pear (ă-peer) *v.* 1. to be or become visible. 2. to present oneself, especially formally or publicly, *the actress is appearing in a new play this season.* 3. to act as counsel in a law court, *I appear for the defendant.* 4. to be published, *the story appeared in the newspapers.* 5. to give a certain impression, *you appear to have forgotten.*

ap·pear·ance (ă-peer-ăns) *n.* 1. appearing. 2. an outward sign, what something appears to be, *has an appearance of prosperity; judging by appearances,* by outward looks. ☐**keep up appearances,** to keep an outward show of prosperity or good behavior. **make an appearance,** appear; arrive. **put in an appearance,** to be present, especially for only a short time. **to all appear-ances,** so far as can be seen, *he was to all appear-ances dead.*

ap·pease (ă-peez) *v.* (**ap·peased, ap·peas-ing**) to make calm or quiet by making conces-sions or demands. **ap·peas'a·ble** *adj.* **ap·pease'ment** *n.*

ap·pel·lant (ă-pel-ănt) *n.* a person making an ap-peal to a higher court.

ap·pel·late (ă-pel-it) *adj.* having legal authority to hear appeals and reverse decisions. □**appellate court,** a court with such authority.

ap·pel·la·tion (ap-ĕ-lay-shŏn) *n.* 1. naming. 2. a name or title.

ap·pend (ă-pend) *v.* 1. to attach. 2. to add at the end, *append one's signature.*

ap·pend·age (ă-pen-dij) *n.* a thing added to or forming a natural part of something larger or more important.

ap·pen·dec·to·my (ap-ĕn-dek-tŏ-mee) *n.* (*pl.* **-to·mies**) surgical removal of the appendix of the intestine.

ap·pen·di·ci·tis (ă-pen-dĭ-sɪ-tis) *n.* inflammation of the appendix of the intestine.

ap·pen·dix (ă-pen-diks) *n.* (*pl.* **-dix·es, -di-ces,** *pr.* -di-seez) 1. a section with supplementary information at the end of a book or document. 2. a small blind tube of tissue attached to the intestine.

ap·per·tain (ap-ĕr-tayn) *v.* 1. to belong. 2. to be relevant, *the facts appertaining to his dismissal.*

ap·pe·tite (ap-ĕ-tɪt) *n.* 1. physical desire, especially for food. 2. a desire or liking, *an appetite for power.*

ap·pe·tiz·er (ap-ĕ-tɪ-zĕr) *n.* something eaten be-fore a meal to stimulate the appetite.

ap·pe·tiz·ing (ap-ĕ-tɪ-zing) *adj.* stimulating the appetite, *an appetizing smell.* **ap'pe·tiz·ing·ly** *adv.*

appl. *abbr.* applied.

ap·plaud (ă-plawd) *v.* 1. to show approval of (a thing) by clapping one's hands. 2. to praise, *we applaud your decision.*

ap·plause (ă-plawz) *n.* 1. handclapping by people applauding. 2. warm approval.

ap·ple (ap-ĕl) *n.* 1. a round fruit with firm juicy flesh. 2. the tree bearing this fruit. □**apple of one's eye,** a cherished person or thing. **apple pie order,** perfect order.

ap·ple·jack (ap-ĕl-jak) *n.* liquor distilled from cider, apple brandy.

ap·ple·sauce (ap-ĕl-saws) *n.* 1. apples (usually sweetened) stewed and passed through a sieve. 2. *(slang)* nonsense.

ap·pli·ance (ă-plɪ-ăns) *n.* a device, an instrument.

ap·pli·ca·ble (ap-lĭ-kă-bĕl) *adj.* able to be applied, appropriate. **ap·pli·ca·bil·i·ty** (ap-lĭ-kă-bil-i-tee) *n.*

ap·pli·cant (ap-lĭ-kănt) *n.* a person who applies, especially for a job. **ap'pli·can·cy** *n.*

ap·pli·ca·tion (ap-lĭ-kay-shŏn) *n.* 1. applying something, putting one thing on another, *ointment for external application only.* 2. the thing applied. 3. making a formal request, *the request itself, his application was refused.* 4. bringing a rule into use, putting something to practical use. 5. the ability to apply oneself.

ap·pli·ca·tor (ap-lĭ-kay-tŏr) *n.* a device for apply-ing something.

ap·plied (ă-plɪd) *adj.* put to practical use. □**applied science, applied mathematics,** etc., these subjects used in a practical way (as

in engineering), not merely theoretical.

ap·pli·qué (ap-lĭ-kay) *n.* a piece of material cut out and sewn or fixed ornamentally to another. **appliqué** *v.* (**ap·pli·quéd, ap·pli·qué·ing**) to ornament with appliqué.

ap·ply (ă-plɪ) *v.* (**ap·plied, ap·ply·ing**) 1. to put (one thing) into contact with another, to spread on a surface. 2. to bring into use or action, *apply economic sanctions; apply common sense to the problem,* use it to solve a problem; *this name was applied to them,* was used in describing or refer-ring to them. 3. to put into effect, to be relevant, *the rules must be applied in every case; what I said does not apply to you.* 4. to make a formal request, *to apply for a job.* □**apply oneself,** to give one's attention and energy to a task. **apply the brakes,** to cause them to act on the wheels.

ap·point (ă-point) *v.* 1. to fix or decide by authority, *they appointed a time for the next meeting.* 2. to choose (a person) for a job, to set up by choosing members, *appoint a committee.* □**well-ap-pointed,** well equipped or furnished.

ap·poin·tee (ă-poin-tee) *n.* the person appointed.

ap·point·ive (ă-poin-tiv) *adj.* subject to or relating to appointment, *many people in government hold appointive positions.*

ap·point·ment (ă-point-mĕnt) *n.* 1. an arrange-ment to meet or visit at a particular time. 2. appointing a person to a job. 3. the job or position itself. 4. *appointments,* equipment, furniture.

ap·por·tion (ă-pohr-shŏn) *v.* to divide into shares, to allot. **ap·por'tion·ment** *n.*

ap·po·site (ap-ŏ-zit) *adj.* (of a remark) appropriate for a purpose or occasion. **ap'po·site·ly** *adv.* **ap'po·site·ness** *n.*

ap·po·si·tion (ap-ŏ-zish-ŏn) *n.* 1. placing side by side. 2. a grammatical relationship in which a word or phrase is placed with another that it de-scribes; in "I admire Lincoln, the man," *the man* is in apposition to *Lincoln.*

ap·pos·i·tive (ă-poz-ĭ-tiv) *n.* a word or phrase in apposition. **appositive** *adj.* used in apposition.

ap·praise (ă-prayz) *v.* (**ap·praised, ap·prais-ing**) to estimate the value or quality of. **ap·prais'al** *n.* **ap·prais'er** *n.* ▷Do not confuse *appraise* with *apprise.*

ap·pre·cia·ble (ă-pree-shă-bĕl) *adj.* able to be seen or felt, considerable, *an appreciable change in tem-perature.* **ap·pre'cia·bly** *adv.*

ap·pre·ci·ate (ă-pree-shi-ayt) *v.* (**ap·pre·ci-at·ed, ap·pre·ci·at·ing**) 1. to value greatly, to be grateful for. 2. to enjoy intelligently, *to ap-preciate good poetry.* 3. to understand, *we appreci-ate their reluctance to give details.* 4. to increase in value, *the investments have appreciated greatly.*

ap·pre·ci·a·tion (ă-pree-shi-ay-shŏn) *n.*

ap·pre·cia·tive (ă-pree-shă-tiv) *adj.* feeling or showing appreciation. **ap·pre'cia·tive·ly** *adv.*

ap·pre·hend (ap-ri-hend) *v.* 1. to seize, to arrest. 2. to grasp the meaning of, to understand, to be-come aware of. 3. to expect with fear or anxiety.

ap·pre·hen·sion (ap-ri-hen-shŏn) *n.* 1. a feeling of fear about a possible danger or difficulty. 2. understanding. 3. arrest.

ap·pre·hen·sive (ap-ri-hen-siv) *adj.* feeling appre-hension, anxious. **ap·pre·hen'sive·ly** *adv.* **ap·pre·hen'sive·ness** *n.*

ap·pren·tice (ă-pren-tis) *n.* 1. a person learning a craft from a skilled worker (and, formerly, bound to an employer by legal agreement). 2. a novice. **apprentice** *v.* (**ap·pren·ticed,**

ap·pren·tic·ing) to bind or set (a person) to work as an apprentice.

ap·prise (ă-prīz) v. **(ap·prised, ap·pris·ing)** to inform. ▷Do not confuse *apprise* with *appraise*.

ap·proach (ă-prohch) v. 1. to come near or nearer in space or time, *winter is approaching.* 2. to set about doing or taking preliminary steps, *approach the problem in a practical way.* 3. to go to with a request or offer, *approach your bank for a loan.* 4. to be similar to, *his liking for it approaches infatuation.* **approach** n. 1. approaching, *watched their approach.* 2. a way of reaching a place. 3. the final part of an aircraft's flight before landing. 4. a method of doing or tackling something. 5. an effort to establish an agreement or friendly relations. 6. an approximation, *his nearest approach to a smile.*

ap·proach·a·ble (ă-proh-chă-bĕl) adj. able to be approached; *he is very approachable,* is friendly and easy to talk with. **ap·proach·a·bil·i·ty** (ă-proh-chă-bil-i-tee) n.

ap·pro·ba·tion (ap-rŏ-bay-shŏn) n. approval.

ap·pro·pri·ate (ă-proh-pree-it) adj. suitable, proper. **appropriate** (ă-proh-pree-ayt) v. **(ap·pro·pri·at·ed, ap·pro·pri·at·ing)** 1. to take and use as one's own. 2. to set aside for a special purpose, *$500 was appropriated for contingencies.* **ap·pro·pri·ate·ly** adv. **ap·pro·pri·ate·ness** n. **ap·pro·pri·a·tor** n. **ap·pro·pri·a·tion** (ă-proh-pree-ay-shŏn) n.

ap·prov·al (ă-proo-văl) n. feeling, showing, or saying that one considers something to be good or acceptable. ☐**on approval,** (of goods) taken by a customer for examination without obligation to buy unless satisfied.

ap·prove (ă-proov) v. **(ap·proved, ap·prov·ing)** 1. to say or feel that a thing is good or suitable. 2. to sanction, to agree to, *the expenditure has been approved.* **ap·prov·ing·ly** adv.

approx. abbr. 1. approximate. 2. approximately.

ap·prox·i·mate (ă-prok-sĭ-mit) adj. almost exact or correct but not completely so. **approximate** (ă-prok-sĭ-mayt) v. **(ap·prox·i·mat·ed, ap·prox·i·mat·ing)** to be or make similar, especially in quality, number, etc. **ap·prox·i·mate·ly** (ă-prok-sĭ-mit-lee) adv. **ap·prox·i·ma·tion** (ă-prok-sĭ-may-shŏn) n.

ap·pur·te·nance (ă-pur-tĕ-năns) n. 1. a minor piece of property, or a right or privilege that goes with a more important one. 2. an adjunct. **ap·pur'te·nant** adj.

Apr. abbr. April.

a·près-ski (ă-pray-skee) adj. of or suitable for the period after skiing, especially at a resort. **après-ski** n. this period.

ap·ri·cot (ap-ri-kot, ay-pri-) n. 1. a juicy oval fruit with a pit, related to the plum and peach and orange-pink when ripe. 2. this color.

A·pril (ay-prĭl) the fourth month of the year. ☐**April fool,** a person who is hoaxed on **April Fool's Day,** April 1, a day traditional for playing mild hoaxes.

a pri·o·ri (ay pri-ohr-ı) 1. reasoning from cause to effect, deductively. 2. presumptively, without investigation. 3. (of knowledge) existing in the mind independently of experience. ▷Latin, = from what is before.

a·pron (ay-prŏn) n. 1. a garment worn over the front part of the body to protect the wearer's clothes. 2. a similar garment worn as part of official dress by a bishop or freemason. 3. anything resembling such a garment in shape or function. 4. a hard-surfaced area on an airfield, where aircraft are maneuvered or loaded and unloaded. ☐**tied to mother's apron strings,** excessively dependent on or dominated by her.

ap·ro·pos (ap-rŏ-poh) adv. appropriately, to the point. **apropos** adj. suitable or relevant to what is being said or done. ☐**apropos of,** concerning, with reference to, *apropos of elections, who is to be our candidate?*

apse (aps) n. a recess, usually with an arched or domed roof, especially in a church.

apt (apt) adj. 1. suitable, appropriate, *an apt quotation.* 2. having a certain tendency, likely, *he is apt to be careless.* 3. quick at learning, *an apt pupil.* **apt'ly** adv. **apt'ness** n.

apt. abbr. apartment.

ap·ti·tude (ap-ti-tood) n. a natural ability or skill.

aq·ua (ak-wă) n. 1. water. 2. the color aquamarine.

aq·ua·cade (ak-wă-kayd) n. an entertainment by swimmers and divers, usually in time to music.

Aq·ua·lung (ak-wă-lung) n. (trademark) a diver's portable breathing apparatus, consisting of cylinders of compressed air connected to a face mask. **aq'ua·lung·er** n.

aq·ua·ma·rine (ak-wă-mă-reen) n. 1. a bluish-green beryl. 2. its color.

aq·ua·naut (ak-wă-nawt) n. an underwater explorer or swimmer, especially one who lives in an underwater installation for an extended time.

aq·ua·plane (ak-wă-playn) n. a board on which a person stands to be towed by a speedboat. **aquaplane** v. **(aq·ua·planed, aq·ua·plan·ing)** 1. to ride on such a board. 2. (of a car or car's wheel) to glide or skid uncontrollably on the wet surface of a road.

aq·ua re·gi·a (ak-wă ree-ji-ă) a mixture of concentrated nitric and hydrochloric acids, able to dissolve gold and platinum, which are not attacked by the unmixed acids.

a·quar·i·um (ă-kwair-i-ŭm) n. (pl. **a·quar·i·ums, a·quar·i·a,** pr. ă-kwair-i-ă) 1. an artificial pond or tank for keeping living fish and water animals and plants. 2. a building containing such ponds or tanks.

A·quar·i·us (ă-kwair-i-ŭs) a sign of the zodiac, the Water Bearer. **A·quar'i·an** adj. & n.

a·quat·ic (ă-kwat-ik, ă-kwot-ik) adj. 1. growing or living in or near water, *aquatic plants.* 2. taking place in or on water; *aquatic sports,* rowing, swimming, etc.

aq·ua·tint (ak-wă-tint) n. a kind of etching.

aq·ua·vit (ah-kwă-veet) n. a colorless or yellowish alcoholic spirit distilled from potatoes or other starch-containing plant, schnapps.

aq·ua vi·tae (ak-wă vɪ-tee) 1. brandy or other alcoholic spirit. 2. an alchemist's term for alcohol.

aq·ue·duct (ak-wĕ-dukt) n. an artificial channel carrying water across country, especially one built like a bridge above low ground. ▷There is only one "a" in *aqueduct.*

a·que·ous (ay-kwi-ŭs) adj. 1. of water, watery. 2. (in geology) produced by the action of water. ☐**aqueous humor,** the transparent fluid between the lens of the eye and the cornea.

aq·ui·cul·ture (ak-wĭ-kul-chŭr) n. the cultivation of plants or breeding of animals in water, hydroponics.

aq·ui·line (ak-wĭ-lın) adj. hooked like an eagle's beak, *an aquiline nose.*

Ar symbol argon.

Ar. *abbr.* Arabic.

AR *abbr.* Arkansas.

-ar *suffix* used to form adjectives, as in *angular,* or nouns, as in *scholar.*

Ar·ab (ar-ăb) *n.* a member of a Semitic people originally inhabiting the Arabian peninsula and neighboring countries, now also other parts of the Middle East and North Africa. **Arab** *adj.* of Arabs.

ar·a·besque (ar-ă-besk) *n.* 1. an elaborate design with intertwined leaves, branches, and scrolls. 2. a ballet dancer's posture with the body bent forward horizontally and one leg extended backward in line with it.

A·ra·bi·a (ă-ray-bi-ă) a peninsula in the Middle East between the Red Sea and the Persian Gulf. **A·ra′bi·an** *adj.*

Ar·a·bic (ar-ă-bik) *adj.* of the Arabs or their language. **Arabic** *n.* the language of the Arabs. ☐**arabic numerals,** the symbols 1, 2, 3, 4, 5, etc.

ar·a·ble (ar-ă-bĕl) *adj.* suitable for plowing and for growing crops.

a·rach·nid (ă-rak-nid) *n.* a member of the class of animals including spiders, scorpions, and mites.

Ar·a·ma·ic (ar-ă-may-ik) *n.* a Semitic language spoken in Syria and Palestine in New Testament times.

A·rap·a·ho (ă-rap-ă-hoh) *n.* (*pl.* **-hos, -ho**) 1. a tribe of North American Indians of the Algonquin speech group, formerly living in Nebraska and Kansas, now in Wyoming and Oklahoma. 2. a member of this tribe. 3. their language.

ar·ba·lest (ahr-bă-list) *n.* a crossbow with a special mechanism for drawing it.

ar·bi·ter (ahr-bi-tĕr) *n.* 1. a person who has the power to decide what shall be done or accepted, one with entire control, *French designers are no longer the arbiters of fashion.* 2. an arbitrator.

ar·bi·trar·y (ahr-bĭ-trer-ee) *adj.* 1. based on random choice or impulse, *an arbitrary decision.* 2. despotic, unrestrained, *arbitrary powers.* **ar·bi·trar′i·ly** *adv.* **ar′bi·trar·i·ness** *n.*

ar·bi·trate (ahr-bĭ-trayt) *v.* (**ar·bi·trat·ed, ar·bi·trat·ing**) to act as an arbitrator.

ar·bi·tra·tion (ahr-bĭ-tray-shŏn) *n.* settlement of a dispute by an arbitrator.

ar·bi·tra·tor (ahr-bĭ-tray-tŏr) *n.* an impartial person chosen to settle a dispute between parties.

ar·bor (ahr-bŏr) *n.* a shady place among trees, often made in a garden with climbing plants growing over a framework.

ar·bo·re·al (ahr-bohr-i-ăl) *adj.* 1. of trees. 2. living in trees.

a·bo·re·tum (ă-bŏ-ree-tŭm) *n.* (*pl.* **-tums, -ta,** *pr.* -tă) a place where trees are grown for study and display.

ar·bor·vi·tae (ahr-bŏr-vɪ-tee) *n.* a coniferous evergreen shrub or tree.

ar·bu·tus (ahr-byoo-tŭs) *n.* an evergreen plant of the heather family with red berries.

arc (ahrk) *n.* 1. part of a curve. 2. anything shaped like this. 3. a luminous electric current passing across a gap between two terminals. **arc** *v.* (**arced, arc·ing**) to form an electric arc. ☐**arc lamp** or **light,** lighting using an electric arc. **arc welding,** welding by means of an electric arc.

ARC *abbr.* American Red Cross.

ar·cade (ahr-kayd) *n.* 1. a covered passage or area, usually with shops on both sides. 2. a series of arches supporting or along a wall.

ar·cane (ahr-kayn) *adj.* mysterious, secret.

arch[1] (ahrch) *n.* 1. a curved structure supporting the weight of what is above it or used ornamentally. 2. something shaped like this. 3. the curved under part of the foot. **arch** *v.* to form into an arch.

arch[2] *adj.* consciously or affectedly playful, *an arch smile.* **arch′ly** *adj.* **arch′ness** *n.*

arch. *abbr.* 1. archaic. 2. architect. 3. architecture.

ar·chae·ol·o·gist (ahr-ki-ol-ŏ-jist) *n.* an expert in archaeology.

ar·chae·ol·o·gy, ar·che·ol·o·gy (ahr-ki-ol-ŏ-jee) *n.* the scientific study of past human life and civilizations through material remains. **ar·chae·o·log·i·cal** (ahr-ki-ŏ-loj-i-kăl) *adj.*

ar·cha·ic (ahr-kay-ik) *adj.* 1. belonging to former or ancient times. 2. (of a word or expression) characteristic of the past and surviving in some special uses. **ar·cha′i·cal·ly** *adv.*

arch·an·gel (ahrk-ayn-jĕl) *n.* an angel of the highest rank.

arch·bish·op (ahrch-bish-ŏp) *n.* a bishop ranking above other bishops in an ecclesiastical province.

arch·dea·con (ahrch-dee-kŏn) *n.* a priest ranking next below a bishop, or a clergyman who assists a diocesan bishop.

arch·di·o·cese (ahrch-dɪ-ŏ-sis) *n.* an archbishop's diocese or district.

arch·duke (ahrch-dook) *n.* a prince of the former imperial house of Austria.

arch·en·e·my (ahrch-en-ĕ-mee) *n.* (*pl.* **-mies**) the chief enemy.

arch·er (ahr-chĕr) *n.* 1. a person who shoots with bow and arrows. 2. *the Archer,* a sign of the zodiac, Sagittarius.

arch·er·y (ahr-chĕ-ree) *n.* the sport of shooting with bows and arrows.

ar·che·type (ahr-ki-tɪp) *n.* an original model from which others are copied. **ar·che·typ·al** (ahr-ki-tɪ-păl) *adj.* **ar·che·typ·i·cal** (ahr-ki-tip-i-kăl) *adj.*

arch·fiend (ahrch-feend) *n.* Satan.

ar·chi·e·pis·co·pal (ahr-ki-i-pis-kŏ-păl) *adj.* of an archbishop.

ar·chi·man·drite (ahr-kɪ-man-drɪt) *n.* a superior of a monastery in the Orthodox Church, equivalent to an abbot in Western churches.

ar·chi·pel·a·go (ahr-kĭ-pel-ă-goh) *n.* (*pl.* **-gos**) a group of many islands, a sea containing such a group.

ar·chi·tect (ahr-ki-tekt) *n.* a person who designs buildings.

ar·chi·tec·ture (ahr-ki-tek-chŭr) *n.* 1. the art or science of designing buildings. 2. the design or style of a building or buildings. **ar·chi·tec·tur·al** (ahr-ki-tek-chŭ-răl) *adj.* **ar·chi·tec′tur·al·ly** *n.*

ar·chi·trave (ahr-ki-trayv) *n.* 1. the main beam of a structure, resting immediately on to more columns. 2. a molded frame around a doorway, window, or arch.

ar·chives (ahr-kɪvz) *n. pl.* 1. the records or historical documents of an institution or community. 2. a place where such records or documents are kept.

ar·chi·vist (ahr-kĭ-vist) *n.* a person trained to deal with archives.

ar·chon (ahr-kon) *n.* 1. one of the nine chief magistrates in ancient Athens. 2. a ruler or president.

arch·way (ahrch-way) *n.* a passageway under an arch.

Arc·tic (ahrk-tik) *adj.* 1. of the regions around the North Pole. 2. *arctic,* very cold, *the weather was arctic.* **Arctic** *n.* 1. the Arctic regions. 2. the Arctic Ocean. ☐**Arctic Circle,** the line of latitude 66° 30′ N. ▷Be sure to pronounce the two "k" sounds in *Arctic.*

-ard *suffix* used to form nouns, as in *standard, drunkard.*

ar·dent (ahr-děnt) *adj.* full of ardor, enthusiastic. **ar′dent·ly** *adv.*

ar·dor (ahr-dŏr) *n.* great warmth of feeling.

ar·du·ous (ahr-joo-ŭs) *adj.* needing much effort, laborious. **ar′du·ous·ly** *adv.* **ar′du·ous·ness** *n.*

are[1] (air) *n.* a unit of square measure, 100 sq. meters.

are[2] (ahr) *see* **be.**

ar·e·a (air-i-ă) *n.* 1. the extent or measurement of a surface. 2. a region, *desert areas of the world.* 3. a space set aside for special use, *picnic area.* 4. the field of an activity or subject, *in the area of finance.* ☐**area code,** a three-digit number identifying telephone areas in the U.S. and Canada, used in long distance calls.

ar·e·a·way (air-i-ă-way) *n.* a sunken court in front of a house basement.

a·re·na (ă-ree-nă) *n.* 1. the level area in the center of an amphitheater. 2. a sports stadium. 3. a sphere of action, *the political arena.*

aren't (ahrnt) = are not.

ar·gent (ahr-jěnt) *n.* silver. **argent** *adj.* silver colored.

Ar·gen·ti·na (ahr-jen-tee-nă) a country in South America.

ar·gen·tine (ahr-jěn-tın) *adj.* of silver, silvery.

Ar·gen·tine (ahr-jěn-tın) *n.* Argentina.

Ar·gen·tin·e·an (ahr-jěn-tin-i-ăn) *adj.* of Argentina. **Argentinean** *n.* a native or inhabitant of Argentina.

ar·gen·tite (ahr-jěn-tıt) *n.* silver sulfide, a dark gray silver.

ar·gon (ahr-gon) *n.* an inert gaseous element, forming about one percent of air, used in gas-filled electric light bulbs etc.

ar·go·sy (ahr-gŏ-see) *n.* (*pl.* **-sies**) a large vessel carrying rich merchandise.

ar·got (ahr-goh) *n.* the jargon or slang of a class or group, especially of criminals.

ar·gu·a·ble (ahr-gyoo-ă-běl) *adj.* open to doubt or dispute, not certain. **ar′gu·a·bly** *adv.*

ar·gue (ahr-gyoo) *v.* (**ar·gued, ar·gu·ing**) 1. to express disagreement, to exchange angry words. 2. to give reasons for or against something, to debate. 3. to persuade by talking, *argued him into going.* 4. to indicate, *their style of living argues that they are well off.*

ar·gu·ment (ahr-gyŭ-měnt) *n.* 1. a discussion involving disagreement, a quarrel. 2. a reason put forward. 3. a theme or chain of reasoning.

ar·gu·men·ta·tion (ahr-gyŭ-men-tay-shŏn) *n.* arguing.

ar·gu·men·ta·tive (ahr-gyŭ-men-tă-tiv) *adj.* fond of arguing. **ar·gu·men′ta·tive·ly** *adv.*

ar·gyle (ahr-gıl) *n.* 1. a diamond-shaped varicolored knitting pattern, especially for socks. 2. a sock with this pattern.

a·ri·a (ahr-i-ă) *n.* an operatic song for one voice.

ar·id (ar-id) *adj.* 1. dry, parched, having too little rainfall to support agriculture; *arid regions,* deserts etc. 2. dull, uninteresting, *an arid lecture or life.* **ar′id·ly** *adv.* **ar′id·ness** *n.* **a·rid·i·ty** (ă-rid-i-tee) *n.*

Ar·ies (air-eez) a sign of the zodiac, the Ram.

Ar·i·an (air-i-ăn) *adj.* & *n.*

a·right (ă-rıt) *adv.* rightly.

a·rise (ă-rız) *v.* (**a·rose, a·ris·en**) 1. (*old use*) to get up, to stand up, to rise from the dead. 2. to come into existence, to come to people's notice, *problems arose; this fear arises from ignorance,* comes as a result of it.

ar·is·toc·ra·cy (ar-i-stok-ră-see) *n.* 1. the hereditary upper classes of people in a country, the nobility. 2. a country ruled by these.

a·ris·to·crat (ă-ris-tŏ-krat) *n.* a member of the aristocracy.

a·ris·to·crat·ic (ă-ris-tŏ-krat-ik) *adj.* 1. of the aristocracy. 2. noble in style. **a·ris·to·crat′i·cal·ly** *adv.*

a·rith·me·tic (ă-rith-mě-tik) *n.* the science of numbers, calculating by means of numbers. **ar·ith·met·i·cal** (ar-ith-met-i-kal) *adj.* **ar·ith·met′i·cal·ly** *adv.*

Ariz. *abbr.* Arizona.

Ar·i·zo·na (ar-i-zoh-nă) a state of the U.S. **Ar·i·zo′nan** *adj.* & *n.*

ark (ahrk) *n.* Noah's boat or a model of this. ☐**the Ark of the Covenant,** the sacred chest in which the ancient Hebrews kept the tablets of the Law.

Ark. *abbr.* Arkansas.

Ar·kan·sas (ahr-kăn-saw) a state of the U.S. **Ar·kan·san** (ahr-kăn-zăn) *adj.* & *n.*

arm[1] (ahrm) *n.* 1. either of the two upper limbs of the human body, from the shoulder to the hand. 2. a sleeve. 3. something shaped like an arm or projecting from a main part, *an arm of the sea; the arms of a chair.* ☐**arm in arm,** (of people) with the arm of one linked in the arm of another. **at arm's length,** at the outside limit that the arm can reach; *keep people at arm's length,* avoid becoming too friendly with them. **in arms,** (of babies) too young to walk. **the long arm of the law,** the authority or power of the law.

arm[2] *v.* 1. to supply or fit with weapons; *armed with a big stick,* carrying this as a weapon; *the enemy is arming,* is preparing as if for war. 2. to make (a bomb etc.) ready to explode, *the device was not yet armed.* **arm** *n.* each of the branches of a country's military forces, *a strong air arm.* ☐**armed forces** or **services,** military forces. **armed neutrality,** remaining neutral but prepared to defend oneself against attack. **armed to the teeth,** fully or elaborately armed.

ar·ma·da (ahr-mah-dă) *n.* a fleet of warships. ☐**the Spanish Armada,** that sent by Spain against England in 1588.

ar·ma·dil·lo (ahr-mă-dil-oh) *n.* (*pl.* **-los**) a small burrowing animal of South America, with a body covered with a shell of bony plates.

Ar·ma·ged·don (ahr-mă-ged-ŏn) *n.* 1. (in the Bible) the scene of the final conflict between the forces of good and evil at the end of the world. 2. any decisive conflict.

ar·ma·ment (ahr-mă-měnt) *n.* 1. the weapons with which an army or a ship, aircraft, or fighting vehicle is equipped. 2. the process of equipping for war.

ar·ma·ture (ahr-mă-chŭr) *n.* the wire-wound core of a dynamo or electric motor.

arm·chair (ahrm-chair) *n.* a chair with raised sides or supports for the arms. ☐**armchair critic,** one who criticizes without having practical experience. **armchair traveler,** one who reads or hears about foreign lands rather than experiencing them through travel.

Ar·me·ni·a (ahr-mee-ni-ă) *n.* a republic of the U.S.S.R. bordering on Turkey. **Ar·me′ni·an** *adj. & n.*

arm·ful (ahrm-fuul) *n.* **1.** as much as the arm can hold. **2.** *(slang)* an attractive woman, one a man would like to hold in his arms.

arm·hole (ahrm-hohl) *n.* an opening in a garment through which the arm is inserted.

ar·mi·stice (ahr-mi-stis) *n.* an agreement during a war or battle to stop fighting for a time.

arm·less (ahrm-lis) *adj.* without arms.

arm·let (ahrm-lit) *n.* a band worn around the upper arm or sleeve.

ar·mor (ahr-mŏr) *n.* **1.** a protective covering for the body, formerly worn in fighting. **2.** metal plates covering a warship, tank, etc. to protect it against missiles. **3.** armored fighting vehicles collectively.

ar·mored (ahr-mŏrd) *adj.* **1.** covered or protected with armor, *an armored car.* **2.** equipped with such vehicles, *armored divisions.*

ar·mor·er (ahr-mŏ-rĕr) *n.* **1.** a maker of arms or armor. **2.** a person in charge of small arms.

ar·mo·ri·al (ahr-mohr-i-ăl) *adj.* of heraldic arms.

ar·mor·y (ahr-mŏ-ree) *n.* (*pl.* **-mor·ies**) a place where weapons are kept or made.

arm·pit (ahrm-pit) *n.* the hollow under the arm below the shoulder.

arm·rest (ahrm-rest) *n.* the arm of a chair.

arms (ahrmz) *n. pl.* **1.** weapons, *an arms depot.* **2.** a coat of arms (*see* **coat**). □**arms race,** competition among nations in accumulating weapons. **up in arms,** angry, protesting vigorously.

ar·my (ahr-mee) *n.* (*pl.* **-mies**) **1.** an organized force equipped for fighting on land. **2.** a vast group, *an army of locusts.* **3.** a body of people organized for a particular purpose, *an army of helpers.* □**army ant,** any of the tropical American ants that move in vast numbers.

ar·ni·ca (ahr-ni-kă) *n.* **1.** a composite plant, largely American, having yellow flowers. **2.** a tincture prepared from the root and flowers of this and used for bruises, sprains, etc.

a·ro·ma (ă-roh-mă) *n.* a smell, especially a pleasant one. **ar·o·mat·ic (**ar-ŏ-mat-ik) *adj.*

a·rose (ă-rohz) *see* **arise.**

a·round (ă-rownd) *adv. & prep.* **1.** enveloping, on every side, in every direction. **2.** about, here and there; *he's somewhere around,* close at hand; *we shopped around,* went from place to place. **3.** along the circuit or circumference of, *sail around the world, walk around the block.* **4.** *(informal)* about, approximately at, *be here around five o'clock.* □**around the clock,** continuously throughout day and night. ▷Careful writers and speakers use *about* instead of *around* in the fourth sense of *around.*

a·rouse (ă-rowz) *v.* (**a·roused, a·rous·ing**) **1.** to awaken. **2.** to incite, to stimulate into activity. **a·rous′al** *n.*

ar·peg·gi·o (ahr-pej-i-oh) *n.* (*pl.* **-gi·os**) the notes of a musical chord played in succession instead of simultaneously.

ar·raign (ă-rayn) *v.* **1.** to indict, to accuse. **2.** to call before a court to answer an indictment. **ar·raign′ment** *n.*

ar·range (ă-raynj) *v.* (**ar·ranged, ar·rang·ing**) **1.** to put into a certain order, to adjust;

arrange flowers, place them attractively, especially in a vase. **2.** to form plans, to settle the details of, to prepare, *arrange to be there; arrange a meeting.* **3.** to adapt (a musical composition) for voices or instruments other than those for which it was written. **ar·rang′er** *n.* **ar·range′ment** *n.*

ar·rant (ar-ănt) *adj.* downright, out-and-out, *this is arrant nonsense!*

ar·ray (ă-ray) *v.* **1.** to arrange in order, *arrayed his forces along the river.* **2.** to dress, especially splendidly, *arrayed in her party gown.* **array** *n.* an imposing series, a display, *a fine array of tools.*

ar·rears (ă-reerz) *n. pl.* **1.** money that is owing and ought to have been paid earlier, *the arrears of two months' rent must be paid.* **2.** work that should have been finished but it still waiting to be dealt with. □**in arrears,** behind in payment or work, not paid or done when it was due, *he is in arrears with his rent; the rent is in arrears.*

ar·rest (ă-rest) *v.* **1.** to stop or check (a process or movement); *arrest attention,* catch and hold it. **2.** to seize (a person) by authority of the law, to take into custody by the police. **arrest** *n.* **1.** stoppage. **2.** seizure, legal arresting of an offender. □**under arrest,** arrested by the police.

ar·ri·val (ă-ri-văl) *n.* **1.** arriving. **2.** a person or thing that has arrived.

ar·rive (ă-rɪv) *v.* (**ar·rived, ar·riv·ing**) **1.** to reach one's destination or a certain point on a journey; *arrive at an agreement,* reach it after discussion. **2.** to come at last, to make an appearance, *the great day arrived; the baby arrived on Tuesday,* was born. **3.** to be recognized as having achieved success in the world, *she has really arrived.*

ar·ro·gant (ar-ŏ-gănt) *adj.* proud and overbearing through an exaggerated feeling of one's superiority. **ar′ro·gant·ly** *adv.* **ar′ro·gance** *n.*

ar·ro·gate (ar-ŏ-gayt) *v.* (**ar·ro·gat·ed, ar·ro·gat·ing**) to claim (a thing) unduly, *he arrogated all important decisions to himself.* ▷Do not confuse *arrogate* with *abrogate.*

ar·row (ar-oh) *n.* **1.** a straight thin pointed shaft to be shot from a bow. **2.** a mark or sign shaped like a line with an outward-pointing V at the end, used to show direction or position, as a road sign or on a map.

ar·row·head (ar-oh-hed) *n.* **1.** the pointed tip of an arrow. **2.** a water plant with arrow-shaped leaves, growing in ponds and slow streams.

ar·row·root (ar-oh-root) *n.* an edible starch prepared from the root of a tropical American plant.

ar·roy·o (ă-roi-oh) *n.* (*pl.* **-os**) **1.** a deep gully cut by a usually dry stream. **2.** a brook or stream.

ar·se·nal (ahr-sĕ-năl) *n.* a place where weapons and ammunition are stored or manufactured.

ar·se·nic (ahr-sĕ-nik) *n.* **1.** a brittle steel-gray poisonous chemical element. **2.** a violently poisonous white compound of this. **ar·sen·i·cal (**ahr-sen-i-kăl) *adj.*

ar·son (ahr-sŏn) *n.* the act of setting fire to a house or other property intentionally and unlawfully, either from malice or to claim insurance money. **ar·son·ist (ahr-**sŏn-ist) *n.* a person guilty of arson.

art[1] (ahrt) *n.* **1.** the production of something beautiful, skill or ability in such work. **2.** works such as paintings or sculptures produced by skill. **3.** any practical skill, a knack, *the art of sailing.* □**art film,** a motion picture produced as a form of artistic expression rather than as mere entertainment. **art gallery,** a gallery where paintings or pieces of sculpture etc. are displayed. **Art Nouveau**

(ahrt noo-voh), a decorative style (about 1880 to about 1910) using flowing curves and naturalistic motifs.

art² *(old use)* the present tense of **be**, used with *thou*.

art. *abbr.* article.

-art *suffix* used to form nouns, as in *braggart*.

ar·te·ri·ole (ahr-teer-i-ohl) *n.* a small artery.

ar·te·ri·o·scle·ro·sis (ahr-teer-i-oh-sklĕ-roh-sis) *n.* a condition in which the walls of arteries become thicker and less elastic, so that blood circulation is hindered.

ar·te·ry (ahr-tĕ-ree) *n.* (*pl.* **-ries**) 1. any of the tubes carrying blood away from the heart to all parts of the body. 2. an important transport route. **ar·te·ri·al** (ahr-teer-i-ăl) *adj.* □**arterial road,** an important main road.

ar·te·sian (ahr-tee-zhăn) **well** a well that is bored vertically into a place where a constant supply of water will rise to the earth's surface with little or no pumping.

art·ful (ahrt-fŭl) *adj.* crafty, cunningly clever at getting what one wants. **art′ful·ly** *adv.* **art′ful·ness** *n.*

ar·thri·tis (ahr-thrı-tis) *n.* a condition causing inflammation, pain, and stiffness in the joints. **ar·thrit·ic** (ahr-thrit-ik) *adj.*

ar·thro·pod (ahr-thrŏ-pod) *n.* one of the Arthropoda, the largest animal phylum, comprising insects, arachnids, myriapods, crustaceans, and trilobites, and characterized by jointed limbs and a hard jointed external skeleton.

Ar·thur (ahr-thŭr), **Ches·ter Al·an** (1830–86) the twenty-first president of the U.S. 1881–85.

ar·ti·choke (ahr-ti-chohk) *n.* a plant related to the daisies, with a flower consisting of thick leaflike scales, used as a vegetable. □**Jerusalem artichoke,** a kind of sunflower with tubers that are used as a vegetable. ▷The name is taken from the Italian word *girasole* (= sunflower), which was altered to *Jerusalem*.

ar·ti·cle (ahr-ti-kĕl) *n.* 1. a particular or separate thing; *articles of clothing, toilet articles,* things of the kind named. 2. a piece of writing, complete in itself, in a newspaper or periodical, *an article on immigration*. 3. a separate clause or item in an agreement. 4. a word (as *a, an,* and *the*) used before a noun to identify what it refers to. □**the definite article,** "the"; **the indefinite article,** "a" or "an."

ar·tic·u·lar (ahr-tik-yŭ-lăr) *adj.* of the joints of the body.

ar·tic·u·late (ahr-tik-yŭ-lit) *adj.* 1. spoken clearly, in words. 2. able to express ideas clearly. **articulate** (ahr-tik-yŭ-layt) *v.* **(ar·tic·u·lat·ed, ar·tic·u·lat·ing)** to say distinctly. **ar·tic′u·late·ly** *adv.* **ar·tic′u·late·ness** *n.* **ar·tic·u·la·tion** (ahr-tik-yŭ-lay-shŏn) *n.*

ar·ti·fact (ahr-tĭ-fakt) *n.* a manmade object, a simple prehistoric tool or weapon.

ar·ti·fice (ahr-tĭ-fis) *n.* trickery, a clever trick intended to mislead someone.

ar·tif·i·cer (ahr-tif-i-sĕr) *n.* 1. a skilled or artistic manual workman, a craftsman. 2. an inventor.

ar·ti·fi·cial (ahr-tĭ-fish-ăl) *adj.* not originating naturally, made by human skill in imitation of something natural, *artificial flowers; an artificial smile,* forced or pretended. **ar·ti·fi′cial·ly** *adv.* **ar·ti·fi·ci·al·i·ty** (ahr-tĭ-fish-i-al-i-tee) *n.* □**artificial insemination,** injection of semen into the uterus by artificial means. **artificial respiration,**

forcing air into and out of the lungs to start natural breathing or stimulate it when it has failed.

ar·til·ler·y (ahr-til-ĕ-ree) *n.* 1. large guns used in fighting on land. 2. the branch of an army that uses these. **ar·til′ler·y·man** *n.*

ar·ti·san (ahr-ti-zăn) *n.* a skilled manual workman in industry or trade.

ar·tist (ahr-tist) *n.* 1. a person who produces works of art, especially paintings. 2. a person who does something with exceptional skill. 3. a professional entertainer.

ar·tiste (ahr-teest) *n.* a professional entertainer.

ar·tis·tic (ahr-tis-tik) *adj.* 1. showing or done with skill and good taste, *an artistic display of flowers.* 2. of art or artists; *the artistic temperament,* impulsive and eccentric behavior thought to be characteristic of artists. **ar·tis′ti·cal·ly** *adv.*

ar·tis·try (ahr-ti-stree) *n.* artistic skill.

art·less (ahrt-lis) *adj.* free from artfulness, simple and natural. **art′less·ly** *adv.* **art′less·ness** *n.*

arts (ahrts) *n. pl.* subjects (as languages, literature, history, etc.) in which sympathetic understanding plays a great part, as opposed to sciences, in which exact measurements and calculations are used. □**arts and crafts,** decorative design and handicraft.

art·sy (ahrt-see) *adj.* *(contemptuous)* arty.

art·sy-craft·sy (ahrt-see-kraft-see) *adj.* *(contemptuous)* affecting artistry or craftsmanship or an interest in arts and crafts but without talent or taste.

art·y (ahr-tee) *adj.* **(art·i·er, art·i·est)** *(informal)* with an exaggerated and often affected display of artistic style or interests. **art′i·ness** *n.* **art′i·ly** *adv.*

ar·um (air-ŭm) *n.* a plant with a flower consisting of a single petallike part surrounding a central spike.

A.R.V. *abbr.* American Revised Version (of the Bible).

-ary *suffix* used to form adjectives, as in *budgetary,* or nouns, as in *dictionary.*.

Ar·y·an (air-i-ăn) *adj.* 1. of the parent language of the Indo-European family. 2. of European race, Nordic, (in Nazi Germany) of non-Jewish extraction. **Aryan** *n.* 1. the Aryan language. 2. an Aryan person.

as (az) *adv.* 1. in the same degree, equally; *I thought as much,* I thought so. 2. similarly, like. 3. in the character of, *which actor will appear as Hamlet?* **as** *conj.* 1. at the same time that, *they came as I left.* 2. because, for the reason that, *as he refuses, we can do nothing.* 3. in the way in which, *do as I do.* **as** *relative pronoun* that, who, which, *I had the same trouble as you; he was a foreigner, as I knew from his accent.* **as** *prep.* like, in the function of, *she acted as a friend.* □**as for,** with regard to, *as for you, I despise you.* **as if,** as it would be if, *he said it as if he meant it.* **as it was,** in the actual circumstances. **as it were,** as if it were actually so, *he became, as it were, a man without a country.* **as of,** at the date mentioned, *that was the position as of last Monday.* **as soon,** as willingly, *I'd just as soon go by train.* **as soon as,** at the moment that, when. **as though,** as if. **as to,** with regard to, *as to your plan, I reject it.* **as well,** in addition, too; desirable, *it might be as well to go; desirably, we might as well go.* **as well as,** in addition to. **as yet,** up to this time, *the land is as yet undeveloped.* **as you were!,** return to the previous position.

As *symbol* arsenic.

A.S. *abbr.* Anglo-Saxon.

as·a·fet·i·da (as-ă-fet-i-dă) *n.* a resinous plant gum with a strong smell of garlic, used in medicine.

as·bes·tos (as-bes-tŏs) *n.* a soft fibrous mineral, made into fireproof material or used for heat insulation.

as·bes·to·sis (as-bes-toh-sis) *n.* a lung disease caused by inhaling asbestos particles.

as·cend (ă-send) *v.* to go or come up. □**ascend the throne,** to become king or queen.

as·cend·an·cy (ă-sen-dăn-see) *n.* the state of being dominant; **gain ascendancy,** win control.

as·cend·ant (ă-sen-dănt) *adj.* ascending, rising. □**in the ascendant,** rising in power or influence.

as·cen·sion (ă-sen-shŏn) *n.* ascent. **Ascension Day,** the Thursday on which this is commemorated, the fortieth day after Easter. □**the Ascension,** the ascent of Christ into heaven, witnessed by the Apostles.

as·cent (ă-sent) *n.* 1. ascending. 2. a way up, an upward slope or path.

as·cer·tain (as-ĕr-tayn) *v.* to find out by making inquiries.

as·cer·tain·a·ble (as-ĕr-tay-nă-bĕl) *adj.* able to be ascertained.

as·cet·ic (ă-set-ik) *adj.* self-denying, not allowing oneself pleasures and luxuries. **ascetic** *n.* a person who leads a severely simple life without ordinary pleasures, often for religious reasons. **as·cet'i·cal·ly** *adv.* **as·cet·i·cism** (ă-set-i-siz-ĕm) *n.*

a·scor·bic (ă-skor-bik) **acid** vitamin C, found especially in citrus fruits and in certain vegetables.

as·cot (as-kot) *n.* a broad scarflike tie looped under the chin.

as·crib·a·ble (ă-skrı-bă-bĕl) *adj.* able to be ascribed.

as·cribe (ă-skrıb) *v.* (**as·cribed, as·crib·ing**) to attribute. **as·crip·tion** (ă-skrip-shŏn) *n.*

a·sep·tic (ay-sep-tik) *adj.* free from bacteria that cause something to become septic, surgically clean. **a·sep'ti·cal·ly** *adv.*

a·sex·u·al (ay-sek-shoo-ăl) *adj.* without sex or sex organs. **a·sex'u·al·ly** *adv.*

ash[1] (ash) *n.* 1. a tree with silver-gray bark and close-grained wood. 2. this wood.

ash[2] *n.* 1. the powder that remains after something has burned. 2. *ashes,* the remains of a body after cremation. □**ash can,** a container for ashes and refuse. **Ash Wednesday,** the first day of Lent.

a·shamed (ă-shaymd) *adj.* feeling shame. **a·sham·ed·ly** (ă-shay-mid-lee) *adv.*

ash·en (ash-ĕn) *adj.* 1. of ashes. 2. pale as ashes.

ash·lar (ash-lăr) *n.* 1. hewn or squared stone. 2. masonry made of this.

a·shore (ă-shohr) *adv.* to or on shore.

ash·ram (ahsh-răm) *n.* a place of religious retreat in India.

ash·tray (ash-tray) *n.* a receptacle for tobacco ashes.

ash·y (ash-ee) *adj.* 1. ashen. 2. covered with ash.

A·sia (ay-zhă) the largest of the continents, extending from Europe to the Pacific Ocean. **A'sian** *adj.* & *n.* □**Asia Minor,** a peninsula of western Asia between the Mediterranean and the Black Sea, including most of Turkey.

A·si·at·ic (ay-zhi-at-ik) *adj.* of Asia. **Asiatic** *n.* an Asian. ▷*Asian* is the preferred word when used of people or their customs.

a·side (ă-sıd) *adv.* 1. to or on one side, away from the main part or group, *pull it aside; step aside.* 2. away from one's thoughts or from consideration. 3. in reserve, *put money aside for a holiday.* **aside** *n.* words spoken so that only certain people will hear. □**aside from,** apart from.

as·i·nine (as-i-nın) *adj.* silly, stupid. **as·i·nin·i·ty** (as-i-nin-i-tee) *n.*

ask (ask) *v.* 1. to call for an answer to or about, to address a question to. 2. to seek to obtain from another person, *ask a favor of him; asked ten dollars for the book; you can have it for the asking,* you have only to ask and it will be given to you. 3. to invite, *ask him to dinner.* □**ask for,** to ask to be given, or to see or speak to. **ask for it** or **ask for trouble,** to behave in such a way that trouble is likely. **asking price,** the price at which something is offered for sale.

a·skance (ă-skans) *adv.* with a side glance, with distrust or disapproval, *looked askance at the new plan.*

a·skew (ă-skyoo) *adj.* & *adv.* not straight or level.

a·slant (ă-slant) *adv.* obliquely.

a·sleep (ă-sleep) *adj.* & *adv.* 1. in or into a state of sleep, *fell asleep.* 2. numbed, *my foot is asleep.*

asp (asp) *n.* a small poisonous snake.

as·par·a·gus (ă-spar-ă-gŭs) *n.* 1. a plant whose young shoots are cooked and eaten as a vegetable. 2. these shoots.

as·pect (as-pekt) *n.* 1. the look or appearance of a person or thing, *the forest has a sinister aspect; this aspect of the problem,* this feature of it. 2. the direction a thing faces, a side facing this way, *the house has a southern aspect.* 3. (in astrology) the relative position of a star or group of stars, regarded as having influence on events.

as·pen (as-pĕn) *n.* a kind of poplar with leaves that move in the slightest wind.

as·per·i·ty (ă-sper-i-tee) *n.* harshness or severity, especially of manner.

as·per·sion (ă-sper-zhŏn) *n.* an insulting remark, a statement that attacks a person's reputation, *casting aspersions at his rivals.*

as·phalt (as-fawlt) *n.* 1. a black sticky substance like coal tar. 2. a mixture of this with gravel etc. used for paving. **asphalt** *v.* to surface with asphalt. **as·phal·tic** (as-fawl-tik) *adj.* □**asphalt jungle,** a part of a large city in which people feel threatened by violence and crime.

as·pho·del (as-fŏ-del) *n.* any of various hardy plants of the lily family.

as·phyx·i·a (as-fik-si-ă) *n.* a condition caused by lack of air in the lungs, suffocation.

as·phyx·i·ate (as-fik-si-ayt) *v.* (**as·phyx·i·at·ed, as·phyx·i·at·ing**) to suffocate. **as·phyx·i·a·tion** (as-fik-si-ay-shŏn) *n.*

as·pic (as-pik) *n.* a savory meat gelatin used for coating meats, eggs, etc.

as·pi·dis·tra (as-pi-dis-tră) *n.* a plant with broad tapering leaves, grown as a house plant.

as·pi·rant (ă-spır-ănt, as-pī-rănt) *n.* a person who aspires.

as·pi·rate (as-pī-rit) *n.* the sound of "h." **aspirate** (as-pī-rayt) *v.* (**as·pi·rat·ed, as·pi·rat·ing**) 1. to pronounce with an "h." 2. to draw out with an aspirator.

as·pi·ra·tion (as-pī-ray-shŏn) *n.* 1. aspirating. 2. aspiring. 3. a strong desire or ambition.

as·pi·ra·tor (as-pī-ray-tŏr) *n.* a device used to suck fluid from a cavity.

as·pire (ă-spır) *v.* (**as·pired, as·pir·ing**) to have a high ambition, *she aspires to the presidency.*

as·pi·rin (as-pĭ-rin) *n.* a drug used to relieve pain and reduce fever, a tablet of this.

ass[1] (as) *n.* 1. a donkey. 2. *(informal)* a stupid person. □**make an ass of oneself,** to behave stupidly so that one is embarrassed.

ass[2] *n. (vulgar)* 1. the buttocks. 2. the rectum.

as·sail (ă-sayl) *v.* to attack violently and persistently, *was assailed with questions.* **as·sail'a·ble** *adj.*

as·sail·ant (ă-say-lănt) *n.* an attacker.

as·sas·sin (ă-sas-in) *n.* a person, especially one hired by others, who assassinates another.

as·sas·si·nate (ă-sas-ĭ-nayt) *v.* (**as·sas·si·nat·ed, as·sas·si·nat·ing**) to kill (an important person) by violent means, usually from political or religious motives. **as·sas·si·na·tion** (ă-sas-ĭ-nay-shŏn) *n.*

as·sault (ă-sawlt) *n.* 1. a violent attack. 2. an unlawful personal attack on another person, even if only with menacing words. 3. rape. **assault** *v.* to make an assault upon. □**assault and battery,** an assault involving a blow or touch.

as·say (as-ay, ă-say) *n.* 1. testing of metals, especially those used for coin or bullion, for quality. 2. an analysis of an ore to determine its composition. **assay** (ă-say, as-ay) *v.* 1. to make an assay of. 2. to try, to put to a test. 3. to judge critically, to evaluate after examination or analysis. ▷Do not confuse *assay* with *essay.*

as·sem·blage (ă-sem-blij) *n.* 1. assembling. 2. an assembly. 3. things assembled. 4. a work of art made of unrelated things joined together.

as·sem·ble (ă-sem-bĕl) *v.* (**as·sem·bled, as·sem·bling**) 1. to bring or come together. 2. to fit or put together.

as·sem·bly (ă-sem-blee) *n.* (*pl.* **-blies**) 1. an assembling. 2. an assembled group, especially of people meeting for a specific purpose. 3. a gathering of a student body in an auditorium for a program. 4. parts of a machine etc. put together to form a unit. 5. a military call by bugle, drum, etc. for troops to make a formation. 6. a deliberative or legislative body, especially the lower house of the legislature in some states. □**assembly line,** a sequence of machines and workers through which parts of a product move to be assembled in successive stages.

as·sem·bly·man (ă-sem-bli-măn) *n.* (*pl.* **-men,** *pr.* -mĕn) a member of a legislative assembly.

as·sent (ă-sent) *v.* to consent, to express agreement. **assent** *n.* consent or sanction.

as·sert (ă-surt) *v.* 1. to declare as true, to state, *asserted his innocence.* 2. to use effectively or aggressively, *asserted his authority.* □**assert itself,** to become active, to make its effect felt. **assert oneself,** to take effective action, to use one's authority, to insist on one's rights.

as·ser·tion (ă-sur-shŏn) *n.* 1. asserting. 2. a statement that something is a fact.

as·ser·tive (ă-sur-tiv) *adj.* asserting oneself, self-assertive. **as·ser'tive·ly** *adv.* **as·ser'tive·ness** *n.*

as·sess (ă-ses) *v.* 1. to decide or fix the amount or value of. 2. to estimate the worth or quality or likelihood of. **as·sess'ment** *n.* **as·ses'sor** *n.*

as·set (as-et) *n.* 1. any property that has money value, especially property that can be used or sold to pay debts. 2. a useful or valuable quality or skill, a person regarded as useful.

as·sev·er·ate (ă-sev-ĕ-rayt) *v.* (**as·sev·er·at·ed, as·sev·er·at·ing**) to assert solemnly. **as·sev·er·a·tion** (ă-sev-ĕ-ray-shŏn) *n.*

as·sid·u·ous (ă-sij-oo-ŭs) *adj.* diligent and persevering. **as·sid'u·ous·ly** *adv.* **as·sid'u·ous·ness** *n.* **as·si·du·i·ty** (as-i-doo-i-tee) *n.*

as·sign (ă-sın) *v.* 1. to allot, *rooms were assigned to us.* 2. to appoint or designate to perform a task etc., *assign your best investigator to the job.* 3. to give as a task. 4. to ascribe, to regard as belonging to, *we cannot assign an exact date to these ruins.* 5. to transfer (property, rights, etc.) formally. **assign** *n.* a person to whom a property right is formally transferred.

as·sign·a·ble (ă-sı-nă-bĕl) *adj.* able to be assigned.

as·sig·na·tion (as-ig-nay-shŏn) *n.* 1. assigning. 2. an arrangement to meet, an appointment, especially a secret one between lovers.

as·sign·ment (ă-sın-mĕnt) *n.* 1. assigning, being assigned. 2. a thing or task that is assigned to a person etc., a share.

as·sim·i·late (ă-sim-ĭ-layt) *v.* (**as·sim·i·lat·ed, as·sim·i·lat·ing**) 1. to absorb into the body or into a group, system, or culture. 2. to become absorbed into something. 3. to absorb into the mind as knowledge. **as·sim·i·la·tion** (ă-sim-ĭ-lay-shŏn) *n.*

as·sist (ă-sist) *v.* to help. **assist** *n.* (in sports) a player's action in helping to put out an opponent, score a goal, etc. **as·sis'tance** *n.*

as·sis·tant (ă-sis-tănt) *n.* a person who assists, a helper. **assistant** *adj.* assisting, helping a senior and ranking next below that person, *the assistant manager.*

assn. *abbr.* association.

assoc. *abbr.* 1. associate. 2. association.

as·so·ci·ate (ă-soh-si-ayt, -shi-) *v.* (**as·so·ci·at·ed, as·so·ci·at·ing**) 1. to join or cause to join as a companion, colleague, or supporter. 2. to have frequent dealings, to be often in certain company, *he associates with dishonest people.* 3. to connect in one's mind, *we associate pyramids with Egypt.* **associate** (ă-soh-si-it, -shi-) *n.* 1. a partner, colleague, or companion. 2. one who has been admitted to a lower level of membership of an association without the status of a full member. **associate** *adj.* 1. associated. 2. having subordinate membership. □**associate degree,** a degree awarded by some colleges to those who complete two years' study.

as·so·ci·a·tion (ă-soh-si-ay-shŏn, -shi-) *n.* 1. associating, being associated, companionship. 2. a group of people organized for some common purpose, *the American Booksellers Association.* 3. a mental connection between ideas.

as·so·ci·a·tive (ă-soh-si-ay-tiv, -shi-) *adj.* involving, resulting from, or tending toward association.

as·so·nance (as-ŏ-năns) *n.* 1. resemblance of sound between two syllables. 2. rhyming of one word with another in the accented vowel and those that follow but not in consonants (as *sonnet, porridge*). **as·so·nant** *adj.*

as·sort (ă-sort) *v.* to arrange or distribute according to kind, class, etc.

as·sort·ed (ă-sor-tid) *adj.* of different sorts put together, *assorted chocolates.*

as·sort·ment (ă-sort-mĕnt) *n.* a collection composed of several sorts.

ASSR *abbr.* Autonomous Soviet Socialist Republic.

asst. *abbr.* assistant.

as·suage (ă-swayj) *v.* (**as·suaged, as·suag·**

ing) to soothe, to make less severe, to satisfy, *to assuage one's thirst.*
as·sume (ă-soom) *v.* **(as·sumed, as·sum·ing)** 1. to take as true or sure to happen before there is proof, *we assume that we shall win.* 2. to take on, to undertake, *she assumed the extra responsibility.* 3. to put on, *assumed a serious expression.* ▷Do not use *assume* to mean *presume.* Compare the first senses of these two words.
as·sum·ing (ă-soo-ming) *adj.* presumptuous.
as·sump·tion (ă-sump-shŏn) *n.* 1. assuming. 2. something taken for granted, something assumed but not proved; *on this assumption,* assuming this to be true or sure to happen. ▢**the Assumption,** the reception of the Virgin Mary in bodily form into heaven, the festival commemorating this (August 15).
as·sur·ance (ă-shoor-ăns) *n.* 1. a formal declaration or promise given to inspire confidence. 2. self-confidence.
as·sure (ă-shoor) *v.* **(as·sured, as·sur·ing)** 1. to declare confidently, to promise, *I assure you there is no danger.* 2. to cause to know for certain, *tried the door to assure himself that it was locked.* 3. to make certain, to ensure, *this will assure your success.* 4. to insure.
as·sured (ă-shoord) *adj.* 1. sure. 2. confident, *has an assured manner.*
as·sur·ed·ly (ă-shoor-id-lee) *adv.* certainly.
as·ta·tine (as-tă-teen) *n.* a radioactive element of short life that does not occur in nature but can be made artificially, the heaviest element of the halogen group.
as·ter (as-tĕr) *n.* a garden plant with daisylike flowers of various colors.
as·ter·isk (as-tĕ-risk) *n.* a star-shaped symbol * used in writing or printing to call attention to something, serve as a reference mark, or indicate that letters or words have been omitted. **asterisk** *v.* to mark with an asterisk.
a·stern (ă-sturn) *adv.* 1. in or at or toward the stern of a ship or the tail of an aircraft, behind. 2. backward, *full speed astern!*
as·ter·oid (as-tĕ-roid) *n.* any of the small planets revolving around the sun, especially between the orbits of Mars and Jupiter. **as·ter·oi·dal** (as-tĕ-roi-dăl) *adj.*
asth·ma (az-mă) *n.* a chronic, usually allergic, condition causing difficulty in breathing.
asth·mat·ic (az-mat-ik) *adj.* 1. of asthma. 2. suffering from asthma. **asthmatic** *n.* one who suffers from asthma. **asth·mat·i·cal·ly** *adv.*
a·stig·ma·tism (ă-stig-mă-tiz-ĕm) *n.* a defect in an eye or lens preventing proper focusing. **as·tig·mat·ic** (as-tig-mat-ik) *adj.* **as·tig·mat·i·cal·ly** *adv.*
a·stir (ă-stur) *adj. & adv.* in motion, moving.
as·ton·ish (ă-ston-ish) *v.* to surprise very greatly. **as·ton·ish·ment** *n.* **as·ton·ish·ing·ly** *adv.*
as·tound (ă-stownd) *v.* to shock with surprise. **as·tound·ing** *adj.* **as·tound·ing·ly** *adv.*
as·tra·khan (as-tră-kăn) *n.* the dark curly fleece of young lambs, cloth imitating this, karakul.
as·tral (as-trăl) *adj.* of or from the stars.
a·stray (ă-stray) *adj. & adv.* away from the right path. ▢**go astray,** to be led into error or wrongdoing; (of things) to be mislaid.
a·stride (ă-strid) *adv.* 1. with legs wide apart. 2. with one leg on either side of something. **astride** *prep.* astride of, extending across.
as·trin·gent (ă-strin-jĕnt) *adj.* 1. causing skin or

body tissue to contract. 2. harsh, severe. **as·tringent** *n.* an astringent substance. **as·trin'gen·cy** *n.*
astrol. *abbr.* 1. astrologer. 2. astrological. 3. astrology.
as·tro·labe (as-trŏ-layb) *n.* a medieval instrument for measuring altitudes of stars etc.
as·trol·o·ger (as-trol-ŏ-jĕr) *n.* a person who is skilled in astrology.
as·trol·o·gy (ă-strol-ŏ-jee) *n.* the study of the supposed influence of stars on human affairs. **as·tro·log·i·cal** (as-trŏ-loj-i-kăl) *adj.* **as·tro·log'i·cal·ly** *adv.*
astron. *abbr.* 1. astronomer. 2. astronomical. 3. astronomy.
as·tro·naut (as-trŏ-nawt) *n.* a person trained to travel in a spacecraft.
as·tro·nau·tics (as-trŏ-naw-tiks) *n.* the scientific study of space travel and its technology. **as·tro·nau'tic** *adj.* **as·tro·nau'ti·cal** *adj.* **as·tro·nau'ti·cal·ly** *adv.*
as·tron·o·mer (ă-stron-ŏ-mĕr) *n.* a scientist specializing in astronomy.
as·tro·nom·i·cal (as-trŏ-nom-i-kăl) *adj.* 1. of astronomy. 2. enormous in amount, *an astronomical sum of money.* **as·tro·nom'i·cal·ly** *adv.* ▢**astronomical unit,** a unit for measuring astronomical distances, equal to the mean distance of Earth from the sun (roughly 93 million miles).
as·tron·o·my (ă-stron-ŏ-mee) *n.* the scientific study of the stars and planets and their movements.
as·tro·phys·ics (as-troh-fiz-iks) *n.* the branch of physics that deals with the physical or chemical properties of planets, stars, etc. **as·tro·phys'i·cal·ly** *adv.* **as·tro·phys·i·cist** (as-troh-fiz-i-sist) *n.*
as·tute (ă-stoot) *adj.* shrewd, quick at seeing how to gain an advantage. **as·tute'ly** *adv.* **as·tute'ness** *n.*
A·sun·ci·ón (ah-suun-si-awn) the capital of Paraguay.
a·sun·der (ă-sun-dĕr) *adv.* apart, into pieces, *torn asunder.*
A.S.V. *abbr.* American Standard Version (of the Bible).
a·sy·lum (ă-si-lŭm) *n.* 1. refuge and safety, a place of refuge. 2. protection or refuge, especially for political refugees. 3. (in former times) a mental home or institution.
a·sym·met·ric (ay-si-met-rik), **a·sym·met·ri·cal** (ay-si-met-ri-kăl) *adj.* not symmetrical. **a·sym·met'ri·cal·ly** *adv.* **a·sym·me·try** (ay-sim-ĕ-tree) *n.*
at (at) *prep.* (expressing position or state) 1. of place or order or time of day, *at the top; arrived at midnight.* 2. of condition or occupation, *at ease; they are at dinner; at one's own risk,* undertaking a known risk and accepting its dangers or consequences. 3. of price or amount or age etc., *sold at three dollars each; left school at fifteen.* 4. of cause, *was annoyed at his failure.* 5. of direction toward, *aimed at the target.* ▢**at all,** in any way, to any extent, of any kind. **at home,** in one's home; relaxed and at ease; familiar with a subject; available to callers. **at it,** engaged in some activity, working. **at once,** immediately; simultaneously. **at that,** at that point; moreover, *lost in ten moves, and to a beginner at that.*
At *symbol* astatine.
at·a·vism (at-ă-viz-ĕm) *n.* 1. resemblance to re-

mote ancestors rather than parents. 2. reversion to an earlier type. **at·a·vis·tic** (at-ă-vis-tik) *adj.*
ate (ayt) *see* eat.
-ate[1] *suffix* used to form adjectives, as in *desolate, ornate.*
-ate[2] *suffix* used to form nouns meaning office, state, function, group, or product, as in *episcopate, magistrate, electorate, filtrate.*
-ate[3] *suffix* used to form nouns meaning a salt of an acid with a corresponding name ending in *-ic,* as in *chlorate, nitrate.*
-ate[4] *suffix* used to form verbs, as in *hyphenate, fascinate.*
at·el·ier (at-ĕl-yay) *n.* an artist's workshop, a studio.
a·the·ist (ay-thi-ist) *n.* a person who does not believe in the existence of a god or gods. **a'the·ism** *n.* **a·the·is·tic** (ay-thi-is-tik) *adj.*
ath·e·nae·um, ath·e·ne·um (ath-ĕ-nee-ŭm) *n.* 1. an institution for the promotion of learning. 2. a library or reading room. 3. *Athenaeum,* an institute of rhetoric and poetry, founded at Rome about 133 A.D. by the Emperor Hadrian.
Ath·ens (ath-ĕnz) the capital of Greece.
ath·er·o·scle·ro·sis (ath-ĕ-roh-sklĕ-roh-sis) *n.* (*pl.* -ro·ses, *pr.* -roh-seez) a form of arteriosclerosis with fatty degeneration. **ath·er·o·scle·rot·ic** (ath-ĕ-roh-sklĕ-rot-ik) *adj.*
ath·lete (ath-leet) *n.* a person who is trained or skilled in athletics. ☐**athlete's foot,** a form of ringworm affecting the feet.
ath·let·ic (ath-let-ik) *adj.* 1. of athletes. 2. physically strong and active, muscular in build. **ath·let'i·cal·ly** *adv.* ☐**athletic supporter,** a jockstrap.
ath·let·ics (ath-let-iks) *n. pl.* physical exercises and sports.
at-home (at-hohm) *n.* a reception for visitors between certain hours.
a·thwart (ă-thwort) *adv.* across from side to side, usually obliquely. **athwart** *prep.* across.
a·tilt (ă-tilt) *adj. & adv.* tilted and nearly falling.
Atl. *abbr.* Atlantic.
At·lan·ta (at-lan-tă) the capital of Georgia.
At·lan·tic (at-lan-tik) *adj.* of the Atlantic Ocean. ☐**Atlantic Ocean,** the ocean lying between the Americas on the west and Europe and Africa on the east.
at·las (at-lăs) *n.* a book of maps.
atm. *abbr.* atmosphere(s).
at·mos·phere (at-mŏs-feer) *n.* 1. the mixture of gases surrounding Earth or any star or planet. 2. the air in any place. 3. a psychological environment, a feeling or tone conveyed by something, *an atmosphere of peace and calm.* 4. a unit of pressure, equal to the pressure of the atmosphere at sea level. **at·mos·pher·ic** (at-mŏs-fer-ik) *adj.* **at·mos·pher'i·cal·ly** *adv.*
at·mos·pher·ics (at-mŏs-fer-iks) *n. pl.* electrical disturbances in the atmosphere, crackling sounds or other interference in radio receiving apparatus caused by these.
at·oll (at-awl) *n.* a ring-shaped coral reef enclosing a lagoon.
at·om (at-ŏm) *n.* 1. the smallest particle of a chemical element. 2. this as a source of atomic energy. 3. a very small quantity or thing, *there's not an atom of truth in it.* ☐**atom bomb,** an atomic bomb. **atom smasher,** a high-speed particle accelerator.
a·tom·ic (ă-tom-ik) *adj.* of an atom or atoms.

☐**atomic bomb,** a bomb that derives its destructive power from atomic energy. **atomic clock,** a clock using atomic vibrations as a standard of time. **atomic energy,** energy obtained as the result of nuclear fission. **atomic number,** the number of positive charges carried by the nucleus of an atom of a chemical element. **atomic pile,** a nuclear reactor. **atomic weight,** the ratio between the mass of one atom of an element or isotope and one-twelfth of the weight of an atom of the isotope carbon 12.
at·om·ize (at-ŏ-mɪz) *v.* (**at·om·ized, at·om·iz·ing**) to reduce to atoms or fine particles. **at·om·i·za·tion** (at-ŏ-mi-zay-shŏn) *n.*
at·om·iz·er (at-ŏ-mɪ-zĕr) *n.* a device for reducing liquids to a fine spray.
a·ton·al (ay-toh-năl) *adj.* (of music) not written in any particular key or scale system.
a·tone (ă-tohn) *v.* (**a·toned, a·ton·ing**) to make amends, to make up for some error or deficiency. **a·tone'ment** *n.* ☐**Day of Atonement,** *see* Yom Kippur. **the Atonement,** the expiation of man's sin by Christ.
a·top (ă-top) *adj. & adv.* at or on the top. **atop** *prep.* on the top of.
a·tri·um (ay-tri-ŭm) *n.* (*pl.* **a·tri·a,** *pr.* ay-tri-ă, **a·tri·ums**) 1. the central court of a Roman house. 2. either of the two upper cavities (*left* or *right atrium*) of the heart, into which the veins pour the blood.
a·tro·cious (ă-troh-shŭs) *adj.* 1. extremely wicked, brutal. 2. (*informal*) very bad or unpleasant, *atrocious weather.* **a·tro'cious·ly** *adv.*
a·troc·i·ty (ă-tros-i-tee) *n.* (*pl.* -ties) 1. wickedness, a wicked or cruel act. 2. a repellent thing.
at·ro·phy (at-rŏ-fee) *n.* wasting away through undernourishment or lack of use. **atrophy** *v.* (**at·ro·phied, at·ro·phy·ing**) to cause or suffer atrophy.
at·ro·pine (at-rŏ-peen) *n.* a white crystallike alkaloid prepared from the plant *Atropa belladonna* (deadly nightshade), used to dilate the pupil of the eye or to relieve pain.
att. *abbr.* 1. attached. 2. attention. 3. attorney.
at·ta·boy (at-ă-boi) *interj.* (*slang*) an exclamation of admiration or encouragement.
at·tach (ă-tach) *v.* 1. to fix to something else. 2. to join as a companion or member, to assign (a person) to a particular group. 3. to attribute, *we attach no importance to the matter.* 4. to be ascribed, to be attributable, *no blame attaches to the company.* 5. to make a legal attachment of (money or goods).
at·ta·ché (at-ă-shay) *n.* a person who is attached to the staff of an ambassador in some specific field of activity, *the military attaché.* ☐**attaché case,** a small rectangular briefcase with rigid sides.
at·tached (ă-tacht) *adj.* 1. fastened on. 2. bound by affection or loyalty, *she is very attached to her cousin.*
at·tach·ment (ă-tach-mĕnt) *n.* 1. attaching, being attached. 2. something attached, an extra part that fixes on. 3. affection, devotion. 4. legal seizure of property or of a debtor's earnings before they are paid to him in order to pay his debts.
at·tack (ă-tak) *v.* 1. to act violently against, to start a fight against (a person or country). 2. to criticize strongly. 3. to act harmfully on, *rust attacks metals.* 4. to begin vigorous work on. **attack** *n.* 1. a violent attempt to hurt, overcome, or defeat.

2. a piece of strong criticism. 3. a sudden onset of illness, *an attack of flu.* **at·tack′er** *n.*

at·tain (ă-tayn) *v.* to succeed in doing or getting.

at·tain·a·ble (ă-tay-nă-bĕl) *adj.* able to be attained.

at·tain·der (ă-tayn-dĕr) *n.* (in former times) the legal consequences of sentence of death or outlawry (forfeiture of estate, loss of civil rights).

at·tain·ment (ă-tayn-mĕnt) *n.* 1. attaining. 2. something attained, a personal achievement.

at·tar (at-ăr) *n.* a fragrant oil obtained from flowers, *attar of roses.*

at·tempt (ă-tempt) *v.* to make an effort to accomplish, *that's attempting the impossible.* **attempt** *n.* 1. an effort to accomplish something. 2. an attack, an effort to overcome or surpass something.

at·tend (ă-tend) *v.* 1. to apply one's mind, to give care and thought. 2. to take care of, to look after, *which doctor is attending you?* 3. to be present at, to go regularly to, *five hundred people attended the ceremony; to attend school.* 4. to accompany as an attendant. □**attend to,** to deal with, to take care of.

at·ten·dance (ă-ten-dăns) *n.* 1. attending. 2. the number of people present.

at·ten·dant (ă-ten-dănt) *n.* a person who is present as a companion or whose function is to provide service. **attendant** *adj.* accompanying.

at·ten·tion (ă-ten-shŏn) *n.* 1. applying one's mind to something, mental concentration. 2. awareness, *it attracts attention.* 3. consideration, looking after, care, *she shall have every attention.* 4. a soldier's erect attitude of readiness with feet together and arms stretched downward, *stand at attention.* 5. *attentions,* small acts of kindness, courtesy, or courtship. **attention** *interj.* an exclamation used to call people to take notice or to assume an attitude of attention.

at·ten·tive (ă-ten-tiv) *adj.* 1. paying attention, watchful. 2. devotedly showing consideration or courtesy to another person. **at·ten′tive·ly** *adv.* **at·ten′tive·ness** *n.*

at·ten·u·ate (ă-ten-yoo-ayt) *v.* (**at·ten·u·at·ed, at·ten·u·at·ing**) 1. to make slender or thin. 2. to make weaker, to reduce the force or value of. **at·ten·u·a·tion** (ă-ten-yoo-ay-shŏn) *n.*

at·test (ă-test) *v.* 1. to provide clear proof of. 2. to declare to be true or genuine. **at·tes·ta·tion** (a-tes-tay-shŏn) *n.*

at·tic (at-ik) *n.* the space or room immediately below the roof of certain buildings.

at·tire (ă-tɪr) *n.* clothes. **attire (at·tired, at·tir·ing)** *v.* to clothe.

at·ti·tude (at-i-tood) *n.* 1. a position of the body or its parts. 2. a way of thinking or behaving. 3. the position of an aircraft or spacecraft relative to wind, direction, etc.

at·ti·tu·di·nize (at-i-too-di-nɪz) *v.* (**at·ti·tu·di·nized, at·ti·tu·di·niz·ing**) to assume attitudes, to act or speak etc. affectedly.

attn. *abbr.* attention.

at·tor·ney (ă-tur-nee) *n.* (*pl.* **-neys**) a lawyer, especially one qualified to represent or act for persons in legal proceedings. □**attorney general,** the chief legal representative and adviser of a country, state, etc.

at·tract (ă-trakt) *v.* 1. to draw toward itself by unseen force, *a magnet attracts iron.* 2. to get the attention of. 3. to arouse the interest or pleasure of.

at·tract·ant (ă-trak-tănt) *n.* a substance that attracts things (especially insects).

at·trac·tion (ă-trak-shŏn) *n.* 1. attracting. 2. the ability to attract. 3. something that attracts by arousing interest or pleasure.

at·trac·tive (ă-trak-tiv) *adj.* able to attract, pleasing in appearance or effect. **at·trac′tive·ly** *adv.* **at·trac′tive·ness** *n.*

attrib. *abbr.* 1. attribute. 2. attributive.

at·trib·ut·a·ble (ă-trib-yŭ-tă-bĕl) *adj.* able to be attributed.

at·trib·ute (ă-trib-yoot) *v.* (**at·trib·ut·ed, at·trib·ut·ing**) to regard as belonging to or caused by or originated by; *this play is attributed to Shakespeare,* people say that he wrote it. **attribute** (at-ri-byoot) *n.* a quality that is characteristic of a person or thing, *kindness is one of his attributes.* **at·tri·bu·tion** (at-ri-byoo-shŏn) *n.*

at·trib·u·tive (ă-trib-yŭ-tiv) *adj.* expressing an attribute and placed before the word it describes, as *old* in *the old dog* (but not in *the dog is old*). **at·trib′u·tive·ly** *adv.*

at·tri·tion (ă-trish-ŏn) *n.* 1. wearing something away by rubbing. 2. a gradual wearing down of strength and morale by continuous harassment, *a war of attrition.* 3. a gradual reduction of personnel, especially through retirement, voluntary departures, etc.

at·tune (ă-toon) *v.* (**at·tuned, at·tun·ing**) 1. to bring into musical accord. 2. to adjust, to adapt.

atty. *abbr.* attorney.

a·typ·i·cal (ay-tip-i-kăl) *adj.* not typical.

Au *symbol* gold.

au·burn (aw-bŭrn) *adj.* (of hair) reddish brown.

au cou·rant (oh koo-rahnt) acquainted with what is going on, well informed, up-to-date.

auc·tion (awk-shŏn) *n.* a public sale in which articles are sold to the highest bidder. **auction** *v.* to sell by auction. □**auction bridge,** a form of bridge (*see* **bridge**).

auc·tion·eer (awk-shŏ-neer) *n.* a person who conducts an auction.

aud. *abbr.* 1. audit. 2. auditor.

au·da·cious (aw-day-shŭs) *adj.* bold, daring. **au·da′cious·ly** *adv.* **au·dac·i·ty** (aw-das-i-tee) *n.*

au·di·ble (aw-dĭ-bĕl) *adj.* loud enough to be heard. **au′di·bly** *adv.* **au·di·bil·i·ty** (aw-dĭ-bil-i-tee) *n.*

au·di·ence (aw-di-ĕns) *n.* 1. people who have gathered to hear or watch something. 2. people within hearing. 3. a formal interview with a ruler or other important person.

au·di·o (aw-di-oh) *n.* 1. audible sound reproduced mechanically. 2. its reproduction. **audio** *adj.* 1. of electronic equipment that reproduces sound. 2. of or used in the transmission and reception of sound in television.

audio frequency a frequency of between 15,000 and 20,000 cycles per second, audible to the normal human ear.

au·di·ol·o·gy (aw-di-ol-ŏ-jee) *n.* the science of hearing. **au·di·ol′o·gist** *n.* **au·di·o·log·i·cal** (aw-di-ŏ-loj-i-kăl) *adj.*

au·di·o·phile (aw-di-oh-fɪl) *n.* a devotee of high-fidelity sound reproduction.

au·di·o·vis·u·al (aw-di-oh-vizh-oo-ăl) *adj.* (of teaching aids etc.) using both sight and sound. **audiovisual** *n.* (usually **audiovisuals**) educational material such as filmstrips, recordings, etc.

au·dit (aw-dit) *n.* an official examination of accounts to see that they are in order. **audit** *v.* to make an audit of.

au·di·tion (aw-**dish**-ŏn) *n.* a trial to test the ability of a prospective performer. **audition** *v.* 1. to hold an audition. 2. to be tested in an audition.

au·di·tor (**aw**-di-tŏr) *n.* a person who makes an audit.

au·di·to·ri·um (aw-di-**tohr**-i-ŭm) *n.* the part of a building in which an audience sits, a building or hall used for public gatherings.

au·di·to·ry (**aw**-di-tohr-ee) *adj.* of hearing.

auf Wie·der·seh·en (owf vee-dĕr-zay-ĕn) until we meet again, goodby for now. ▷German.

Aug. *abbr.* August.

au·ger (**aw**-gĕr) *n.* a tool for boring holes in wood, like a gimlet but larger.

aught¹ (awt) *n.* (*old use*) anything, *for aught I know.*

aught² *n.* zero, cipher.

aug·ment (awg-**ment**) *v.* to add to, to increase.

aug·men·ta·tion (awg-men-**tay**-shŏn) *n.*

au grat·in (oh **grah**-tin, **grat**-in) cooked with a crisp crust of bread crumbs and grated cheese.

au·gur (**aw**-gŭr) *v.* to foretell, to be a sign of; *this augurs well for your future,* is a favorable sign. **augur** *n.* diviner, soothsayer. **au·gu·ry** (**aw**-gyŭ-ree) *n.* (*pl.* **-ries**).

au·gust (aw-**gust**) *adj.* majestic, imposing.

Au·gust (**aw**-gŭst) *n.* the eighth month of the year.

Au·gus·ta (aw-**gus**-tă) the capital of Maine.

au jus (oh *zh*oo) (of meat) served with the natural juices obtained during roasting. ▷French.

auk (awk) *n.* a northern seabird with small narrow wings.

auld lang syne (ohld lang zın) (*Scottish*) days of long ago.

aunt (ant) *n.* 1. a sister or sister-in-law of one's father or mother. 2. (*children's informal*) an unrelated woman friend, *Aunt Jane.*

aunt·ie (**an**-tee) *n.* (*informal*) an aunt.

au pair (oh **pair**) **girl** a young woman from overseas helping with housework and receiving board and lodging in return.

au·ra (or-ă) *n.* 1. the atmosphere surrounding a person or thing and thought to come from him or it, *an aura of happiness.* 2. a luminous radiation.

au·ral (or-ăl) *adj.* of the ear or sense of hearing. **au'ral·ly** *adv.* ▷Do not confuse *aural* with *oral.*

au·re·ate (or-i-it) *adj.* 1. golden, resplendent. 2. (of language) very elaborate, rhetorical.

au·re·ole (or-i-ohl) *n.* 1. a halo shown around the head of a martyr, saint, etc. in paintings. 2. a halo or ring around the sun or moon.

au re·voir (oh rĕ-**vwahr**) goodby. ▷French.

au·ri·cle (or-i-kĕl) *n.* 1. the external ear of animals, an earlike part. 2. a small appendage to the atrium of the heart.

au·ric·u·lar (aw-**rik**-yŭ-lăr) *adj.* 1. pertaining to or like the ear. 2. pertaining to the auricle of the heart.

au·rif·er·ous (aw-**rif**-ĕ-rŭs) *adj.* yielding gold.

au·ro·ra (aw-**rohr**-ă) *n.* bands of colored light appearing in the sky at night and probably caused by electrical radiation from the North and South magnetic poles, specifically the **aurora borealis** (also called the **Northern Lights**) in the northern hemisphere, or the **aurora australis** in the southern hemisphere.

AUS *abbr.* Army of the United States.

aus·pice (**aw**-spis) *n.* (*pl.* **aus·pic·es**, *pr.* aw-spi-siz, -seez) 1. a forecast or omen. 2. *auspices,* patronage, *under the auspices of.*

aus·pi·cious (aw-**spish**-ŭs) *adj.* showing signs that promise success. **aus·pi'cious·ly** *adv.*

Aus·sie (**aw**-see) *n.* (*informal*) an Australian.

aus·tere (aw-**steer**) *adj.* severely simple and plain, without ornament or comfort. **aus·tere'ly** *adv.*

aus·ter·i·ty (aw-**ster**-i-tee) *n.* (*pl.* **-ties**) being austere, an austere condition, *the austerities of life in wartime.*

Aus·tin (**aw**-stin) the capital of Texas.

aus·tral (**aw**-străl) *adj.* southern.

Aus·tral·ia (aw-**strayl**-yă) a continent and a country between the Pacific and Indian Oceans. **Aus·tral'ian** *adj. & n.*

Aus·tri·a (aw-**stri**-ă) a country in Europe. **Aus'tri·an** *adj. & n.*

Aus·tro·ne·sia (aw-stroh-**nee**-zhă) the islands of the central and south Pacific Ocean.

auth. *abbr.* 1. authentic. 2. author. 3. authority. 4. authorized.

au·then·tic (aw-**then**-tik) *adj.* genuine, known to be true. **au·then'ti·cal·ly** *adv.* **au·then·tic·i·ty** (aw-then-tis-i-tee) *n.*

au·then·ti·cate (aw-**then**-ti-kayt) *v.* (**au·then·ti·cat·ed, au·then·ti·cat·ing**) to prove the truth or authenticity of. **au·then·ti·ca·tion** (aw-then-ti-**kay**-shŏn) *n.*

au·thor (**aw**-thŏr) *n.* 1. the writer of a book or books etc. 2. the originator of a plan or policy. **au·thor·ess** (aw-thŏ-ris) *n. fem.* (*old use*) **au'thor·ship** *n.* ▷Do not use *author* as a verb.

au·thor·i·tar·i·an (ă-thor-i-**tair**-i-ăn) *adj.* favoring complete obedience to authority as opposed to individual freedom. **authoritarian** *n.* a supporter of such principles.

au·thor·i·ta·tive (ă-**thor**-i-tay-tiv) *adj.* having or using authority. **au·thor'i·ta·tive·ly** *adv.*

au·thor·i·ty (ă-**thor**-i-tee) *n.* (*pl.* **-ties**) 1. the power or right to give orders and make others obey, or to take specific action. 2. a person or group with such power. 3. a person with specialized knowledge, a book etc. that can supply reliable information, *she is an authority on spiders.*

au·thor·ize (aw-thŏ-rız) *v.* (**au·thor·ized, au·thor·iz·ing**) 1. to give authority to. 2. to give authority for, to sanction, *I authorized this payment.* **au·thor·i·za·tion** (aw-thŏ-ri-**zay**-shŏn) *n.*

☐ **Authorized Version** (also **King James Version**) the English translation of the Bible (1611) made by order of King James I.

au·tis·tic (aw-**tis**-tik) *adj.* having a form of mental illness that causes a person to withdraw into a private world of fantasy and be unable to communicate with others or respond to the real environment, *autistic children.* **au·tism** (aw-tiz-ĕm) *n.*

au·to (**aw**-toh) *n.* (*pl.* **-tos**) an automobile.

auto- *prefix* by oneself, as in *autocracy;* by itself, as in *automation.*

au·to·bahn (**aw**-tŏ-bahn) *n.* an express highway in Germany.

au·to·bi·og·ra·phy (aw-toh-bı-**og**-ră-fee) *n.* (*pl.* **-phies**) the story of a person's life written by that person. **au·to·bi·og'ra·pher** *n.* **au·to·bi·o·graph·i·cal** (aw-toh-bı-ŏ-**graf**-i-kăl) *adj.*

au·toc·ra·cy (aw-**tok**-ră-see) *n.* (*pl.* **-cies**) government by one person having unlimited authority.

au·to·crat (**aw**-tŏ-krat) *n.* a person with unlimited power, a dictatorial person. **au·to·crat'ic** *adj.* **au·to·crat'i·cal·ly** *adv.*

au·to·gi·ro, au·to·gy·ro (aw-tŏ-**jır**-oh) *n.* (*pl.* **-ros**) an early form of helicopter with a conventional propeller and rotating horizontal vanes to provide lift and permit slow steep descent.

au·to·graph (aw-tŏ-graf) *n.* 1. a person's signature. 2. a manuscript in an author's own handwriting. **autograph** *v.* to write one's name on or in, *the author will autograph copies of his book tomorrow.*

au·to·mate (aw-tŏ-mayt) *v.* **(au·to·mat·ed, au·to·mat·ing)** 1. to control or operate by automation. 2. to convert to automation, to introduce automatic equipment in a plant or process, *the factory has been fully automated.*

au·to·mat·ic (aw-tŏ-mat-ik) *adj.* 1. working of itself without direct human control, self-regulating. 2. firing repeatedly until pressure on the trigger is released, *an automatic pistol.* 3. done without thought, done from habit or routine, *made an automatic gesture of apology.* **automatic** *n.* an automatic machine or tool or, especially, a firearm.

au·to·ma·tion (aw-tŏ-may-shŏn) *n.* the use of automatic equipment to save mental and manual labor.

au·tom·a·ton (aw-tom-ă-tŏn) *n.* 1. a robot. 2. a person who seems to act mechanically and without thinking.

au·to·mo·bile (aw-tŏ-mŏ-beel, aw-tŏ-mŏ-beel) *n.* a car.

au·to·mo·tive (aw-tŏ-moh-tiv) *adj.* of or relating to motor vehicles.

au·to·nom·ic (aw-tŏ-nom-ik) *adj.* of that part of the nervous system (*autonomic* or *involuntary nervous system*) that functions more or less independently of the will.

au·ton·o·mous (aw-ton-ŏ-mŭs) *adj.* self-governing. **au·ton'o·my** *n.*

au·top·sy (aw-top-see) *n.* a postmortem.

au·to·stra·da (aw-toh-strah-dă) *n.* an express highway in Italy.

au·tumn (aw-tŭm) *n.* the season between summer and winter. **au·tum·nal** (aw-tum-năl) *adj.* **au·tum'nal·ly** *adv.* ☐**autumnal equinox,** *see* **equinox.**

aux. *abbr.* auxiliary.

aux·il·ia·ry (awg-zil-yă-ree) *adj.* giving help or support, functioning as a subsidiary, *auxiliary services; an auxiliary verb,* one used in forming parts of other verbs, as *have* in *I have finished.* **auxiliary** *n.* (*pl.* **-ia·ries**) 1. an auxiliary person, group, or device. 2. an auxiliary verb. 3. *auxiliaries,* auxiliary troops.

aux·in (awk-sin) *n.* a class of substances that regulate or modify the growth of plants.

av. *abbr.* 1. average. 2. avoirdupois.

A.V. *abbr.* Authorized Version (of the Bible).

a·vail (ă-vayl) *v.* to be of help or advantage, *nothing availed against the storm; he availed himself of the opportunity,* made use of it. **avail** *n.* effectiveness, advantage, *it was of no avail.*

a·vail·a·ble (ă-vay-lă-bĕl) *adj.* ready or able to be used, obtainable, at hand. **a·vail·a·bil·i·ty** (ă-vay-lă-bil-i-tee) *n.*

av·a·lanche (av-ă-lanch) *n.* 1. a mass of snow or rock pouring down a mountainside. 2. a great onrush, *an avalanche of letters.*

a·vant-garde (a-vahnt-gahrd) *adj.* using or favoring an ultramodern or experimental style, especially in art or literature. **avant-garde** *n.* an avant-garde group.

av·a·rice (av-ă-ris) *n.* greed for gain. **av·a·ri·cious** (av-ă-rish-ŭs) *adj.* **av·a·ri'cious·ly** *adv.*

a·vast (ă-vast) *interj.* (used by seamen) stop, cease.

av·a·tar (av-ă-tahr) *n.* (in Hindu doctrine) the descent to Earth and incarnation of a diety.

a·vaunt (ă-vawnt) *interj.* *(old use)* begone.

avdp. *abbr.* avoirdupois.

ave. *abbr.* avenue.

A·ve Ma·ri·a (ah-vay mă-ree-ă) = **Hail Mary.**

a·venge (ă-venj) *v.* **(a·venged, a·veng·ing)** to take vengeance for. **a·veng'er** *n.*

av·e·nue (av-ĕn-yoo) *n.* 1. a wide street. 2. a way of approaching or making progress, *other avenues to fame.*

a·ver (ă-vur) *v.* **(a·verred, a·ver·ring)** to assert, to affirm.

av·er·age (av-ĕ-rij) *n.* 1. the value arrived at by adding several quantities together and dividing he total by the number of quantities. 2. the standard or level regarded as usual. **average** *adj.* 1. found by making an average, *the average age of the pupils is fifteen.* 2. of the ordinary or usual standard, *people of average intelligence.* **average** *v.* **(av·er·aged, av·er·ag·ing)** 1. to calculate the average of. 2. to amount to or produce as an average, *the car averaged forty miles a gallon on the highway.*

a·ver·ment (ă-vur-mĕnt) *n.* a positive statement, an affirmation, especially with offer of proof.

a·verse (ă-vurs) *adj.* unwilling, disinclined, *he is averse to hard work.* ▷Do not confuse *adverse* with *averse.*

a·ver·sion (ă-vur-zhŏn) *n.* 1. a strong dislike. 2. something disliked.

a·vert (ă-vurt) *v.* 1. to turn away, *people averted their eyes.* 2. to prevent, to ward off, *managed to avert disaster.*

avg. *abbr.* average.

a·vi·an (ay-vi-ăn) *adj.* of birds.

a·vi·ar·y (ay-vi-er-ee) *n.* a large cage or building for keeping birds.

a·vi·a·tion (ay-vi-ay-shŏn) *n.* 1. the art of flying an aircraft. 2. aircraft design and manufacture.

a·vi·a·tor (ay-vi-ay-tŏr) *n.* an aircraft pilot. **a·vi·a·trix** (ay-vi-ay-triks) *n. fem.*

av·id (av-id) *adj.* eager, greedy. **av·id·ly** *adv.* **a·vid·i·ty** (ă-vid-i-tee) *n.*

a·vi·on·ics (ay-vi-on-iks) *n.* the application of electronics in aviation. **a·vi·on'ic** *adj.*

a·vi·ta·min·o·sis (ay-vı-tă-mi-noh-sis) *n.* (*pl.* **-ses,** *pr.* **-seez**) a condition resulting from deficiency of one or more vitamins. **a·vi·ta·min·ot·ic** (ay-vı-tă-mi-not-ik) *adj.*

av·o·ca·do (av-ŏ-kah-doh, ah-vŏ-) *n.* (*pl.* **-dos**) 1. the edible pear-shaped fruit of a tropical tree. 2. the tree itself.

av·o·ca·tion (av-ŏ-kay-shŏn) *n.* a minor occupation, a hobby.

av·o·cet (av-ŏ-set) *n.* a wading bird with a long upturned beak.

a·void (ă-void) *v.* 1. to keep oneself away from (something dangerous or undesirable). 2. to refrain from, *avoid making rash promises.* **a·void'ance** *n.*

a·void·a·ble (ă-voi-dă-bĕl) *adj.* able to be avoided.

av·oir·du·pois (av-ŏr-dŭ-poiz) *n.* 1. weight, heaviness, especially personal weight. 2. (also *avoirdupois weight*) a system of weights based on the pound of 16 ounces and the ounce of 16 drams.

a·vow (ă-vow) *v.* to admit, to declare openly. **a·vow'al** *n.* **a·vow'ed·ly** *adv.*

a·vun·cu·lar (ă-vung-kyŭ-lăr) *adj.* of or like a kindly uncle.

a·wait (ă-wayt) *v.* 1. to wait for, *I await your reply.*

2. to be waiting for, *a surprise awaits you.*

a·wake (ă-wayk) *v.* **(a·woke** or **a·waked, a·wak·ing)** to wake, to cease to sleep, to arouse from sleep. **awake** *adj.* 1. not yet asleep, no longer asleep. 2. alert, aware, *he is awake to the possible danger.*

a·wak·en (ă-way-kĕn) *v.* to awake. **a·wak′en·ing** *n.*

a·ward (ă-word, *rhymes with* afford) *v.* to give by official decision as a payment, penalty, or prize. **award** *n.* 1. a decision of this kind. 2. a thing awarded.

a·ware (ă-wair) *adj.* having knowledge or realization, *I am aware of this possibility.* **a·ware′ness** *n.*

a·wash (ă-wosh) *adj.* washed over by water or waves.

a·way (ă-way) *adv.* 1. to or at a distance. 2. out of existence, *the water has boiled away.* 3. constantly, persistently, *we worked away at it.* 4. from here, *six miles away.* 5. elsewhere. 6. aside, *turned customers away.* 7. at once, *right away.* **away** *adj.* 1. absent. 2. distant. 3. played on an opponent's field, *the Yankees play two home games and two away games this week.*

awe (aw) *n.* respect combined with fear or wonder. **awe** *v.* **(awed, aw·ing)** to fill with awe.

a·weigh (ă-way) *adv.* hanging just clear of the sea bottom, *anchors aweigh.*

awe·some (aw-sŏm) *adj.* causing awe.

awe·struck (aw-struk), **awe·strick·en** (aw-strik-ĕn) *adj.* suddenly filled with awe.

aw·ful (aw-fŭl) *adj.* 1. inspiring awe. 2. extremely bad or unpleasant, *an awful accident.* 3. *(informal),* extreme, very great, *that's an awful lot of money.* ▷Careful writers do not use *awful* in its third sense. They would write *that is a great deal of money.*

aw·ful·ly (aw-fŭ-lee) *adv. (informal)* 1. very. 2. very much. ▷Careful writers avoid *awfully.*

a·while (ă-hwɪl) *adv.* for a short time.

a·whirl (ă-hwurl) *adj.* revolving rapidly, whirling.

awk·ward (awk-wărd) *adj.* 1. difficult to handle, use, or deal with. 2. ungraceful, clumsy, having little skill. 3. inconvenient, *came at an awkward time.* 4. embarrassed, *feel awkward about it.* **awk′ward·ly** *adv.* **awk′ward·ness** *n.*

awl (awl) *n.* a small pointed tool for making holes, especially in leather or wood.

awn·ing (aw-ning) *n.* a rooflike shelter, as of canvas, erected as a protection against sun or rain.

a·woke (ă-wohk) *see* **awake.**

AWOL (ay-wawl) *n. (slang)* absent without leave.

A.W.O.L. *abbr.* absent without leave.

a·wry (ă-rɪ) *adv.* 1. twisted to one side. 2. amiss, *plans went awry.* **awry** *adj.* crooked, wrong.

ax, axe (aks) *n.* (*pl.* **ax·es,** *pr.* ak-siz) a chopping tool with an edge head parallel to the handle. **ax** *v.* **(axed, ax·ing)** to remove by abolishing or dismissing, *the project was axed.* □**get the ax,** *(slang)* to be dismissed from one's job. **have an ax to grind,** to have some personal interest involved and be eager to take care of it.

ax·i·al (ak-si-ăl) *adj.* forming or belonging to an axis. **ax′i·al·ly** *adv.*

ax·i·om (ak-si-ŏm) *n.* an accepted general truth or principle. **ax·i·o·mat·ic** (ak-si-ŏ-mat-ik) *adj.* **ax·i·o·mat′i·cal·ly** *adv.*

ax·is (ak-sis) *n.* (*pl.* **ax·es,** *pr.* ak-seez) 1. a line through the center of an object, around which it rotates when spinning. 2. the line dividing a regular figure symmetrically. 3. an imaginary line around which a plane figure can be thought of as rotating to generate a given solid body. 4. the main stem or shoot of a plant. 5. the second cervical vertebra, on which the head turns. 6. an alliance between two or more countries. □**the Axis,** an alliance between Germany and Italy, and later Japan, during World War II.

ax·le (ak-sĕl) *n.* the bar or rod on which a wheel or wheels turn.

ax·le·tree (ak-sĕl-tree) *n.* a bar under an animal-drawn vehicle, connecting the wheels.

a·yah (ah-yă) *n.* a Hindu nurse.

ay·a·tol·lah (ah-yă-toh-lă) *n.* a chief spiritual leader of Shiite Muslims.

aye, ay (ɪ) *adv.* yes. **aye** *n.* a vote in favor of a proposal. □**the ayes have it,** those in favor are in the majority, they have won the vote.

AZ *abbr.* Arizona.

a·zal·ea (ă-zayl-yă) *n.* a shrublike flowering plant.

Az·er·bai·jan (ah-zĕr-bɪ-jahn) a republic of the U.S.S.R. bordering on the Caspian Sea. **Az·er·bai·ja′ni** *n.* a native or inhabitant of Azerbaijan.

az·i·muth (az-ɪ-mŭth) *n.* 1. an arc of the heavens extending from the zenith to the horizon, which it cuts at right angles. 2. the arc of the horizon between the north point (in the southern hemisphere, the south point) of the horizon and the point where the vertical circle passing through a heavenly body cuts the horizon. 3. the angle of lateral deviation of a bomb or shell.

Az·tec (az-tek) *n.* a member of an Indian people of Mexico before the Spanish conquest. **Az′tec·an** *adj.*

az·ure (azh-ŭr) *adj. & n.* sky blue.

B

B, b (bee) (*pl.* **Bs, B's, b's**) 1. the second letter of the alphabet. 2. *B*, a grade rating for good school work.
B *symbol* boron.
b. *abbr.* (also **B.**) 1. bachelor. 2. bass. 3. bishop. 4. book. 5. born.
Ba *symbol* barium.
B.A. *abbr.* Bachelor of Arts.
baa (bah) *n.* the cry of a sheep or lamb. **baa** *v.* to make this cry.
Bab·bitt (bab-it) a materialistic complacent businessman. ▷Named after the principal character of a novel by Sinclair Lewis.
Babbitt metal a soft alloy of tin, copper, and antimony, used for machine bearings.
bab·ble (bab-ĕl) *v.* (**bab·bled, bab·bling**) 1. to chatter in a thoughtless or confused way. 2. to make a continuous murmuring sound, *a babbling brook.* **babble** *n.* babbling talk or sound. **bab′bler** *n.*
babe (bayb) *n.* 1. a baby. 2. *(slang)* a girl or woman.
ba·bel (bay-bĕl) *n.* a scene of confusion and uproar, a confused mixture of voices. ▷From the tower of Babel in the Old Testament, built by men in an attempt to reach heaven that resulted in God's confounding their languages.
ba·boon (ba-boon) *n.* a large African or Arabian monkey.
ba·bush·ka (bă-buush-kă) *n.* a kerchief tied under the chin.
ba·by (bay-bee) *n.* (*pl.* **-bies**) 1. a very young child or animal. 2. a babyish or timid person. 3. the youngest or the smallest, something small of its kind. 4. *(slang)* a person, *he's a tough baby.* 5. something that is one's creation or in one's care. **baby** *adj.* 1. of a baby. 2. small, small or the smallest of its kind, *a baby grand piano.* **baby** *v.* (**ba·bied, ba·by·ing**) to treat like a baby, to pamper. **ba′by·ish** *adj.* **ba′by·ish·ly** *adv.* **ba′by·hood** *n.* □**baby carriage,** a four-wheeled carriage for a baby, pushed by a person walking.
ba·by's-breath (bay-beez-breth) *n.* a plant with branching clusters of small fragrant white flowers.
ba·by-sit (bay-bee-sit) *v.* (**ba·by-sat, ba·by-sit·ting**) to act as or be a baby-sitter.
ba·by-sit·ter (bay-bee-sit-ĕr) *n.* a person looking after a child while its parents are out.
bac·ca·lau·re·ate (bak-ă-lor-i-it) *n.* 1. a bachelor's degree. 2. a sermon delivered at a college commencement.
bac·ca·rat (bah-kă-rah) *n.* a gambling card game played against a banker in which the winner is the person whose cards have a total value of nine.
bac·cha·nal (bah-kă-nahl) *adj.* of the Greek god Bacchus or his rites. **bacchanal** *n.* drunken revelry, a wild party.

bac·cha·na·lia (bak-ă-nayl-yă) *n.* 1. a festival held in honor of the Greek god Bacchus. 2. a drunken revel, an orgy. **bac·cha·na′li·an** *adj.*
bach·e·lor (bach-ĕ-lŏr) *n.* 1. an unmarried man, especially one who has never married. 2. *Bachelor,* a person who holds the standard four-year university or college degree below that of Master. **bach′e·lor·hood** *n.* □**Bachelor of Arts, Science,** etc., a college degree awarded after four years of study, a person who holds this degree.
bach·e·lor's-but·ton (bach-ĕ-lŏrz-but-ŏn) *n.* any of various flowers of round or buttonlike form, such as the cornflower.
ba·cil·lus (bă-sil-ŭs) *n.* (*pl.* **-cil·li,** *pr.* **-sil-ı**) a rodlike bacterium. **bac·il·lar·y** (bas-ı̆-ler-ee) *adj.*
back[1] (bak) *n.* 1. the rear surface of the human body from neck to hip; the corresponding part of an animal's body. 2. that part of a chair etc. against which a seated person's back rests. 3. the part or surface of an object that is less used or less important, the part farthest from the front. 4. the part of a garment covering the back. 5. a football player or position behind the front line. □**be on someone's back,** to be a burden or hindrance to him. **have one's back to the wall,** to be fighting for survival. **get a person's back up,** to offend or antagonize him. **put one's back into something,** to use maximum effort on it.
back[2] *adj.* 1. situated behind or farthest from the front, *the back teeth.* 2. remote or inferior, *back streets.* 3. of or for a past time, *back pay.* **back** *adv.* 1. at or toward the rear, away from the front or center. 2. in check, *hold it back.* 3. in or into a previous time or position or condition; *I'll be back at six,* I shall return then. 4. in return, *pay it back.* □**back number,** an old issue of a periodical; an out-of-date person or idea. **back of,** behind, at or in the rear. **back seat,** a seat at the back; *take a back seat,* to take a less prominent position. **back-seat driver,** a person without responsibility who is eager to give orders to one who has responsibility. ▷Careful writers avoid *back of* in the sense of *behind; walk behind me* not *in back of me.*
back[3] *v.* 1. to go or cause to go backward. 2. (of wind) to change gradually in a counterclockwise direction. 3. to give one's support to, to assist. 4. to give financial support to, *he is backing the new business.* 5. to lay a bet on. 6. to cover the back of, *the rug is backed with canvas.* **back′er** *n.* □**back down,** to give up a claim; to withdraw one's argument. **back out,** to withdraw from an agreement. **back up,** to give one's support to; *back up someone's story,* confirm what he says; (of water or traffic) to accumulate behind an obstruction; to reverse (a vehicle).
back·ache (bak-ayk) *n.* a pain in one's back.

back·bite (bak-bıt) *v.* (**back·bit, back·bit·ten, back·bit·ing**) to slander. **back′bit·er** *n.*

back·board (bak-bohrd) *n.* (in basketball) the board to which the basket is attached.

back·bone (bak-bohn) *n.* 1. the column of small bones down the center of the back, the spine. 2. strength of character.

back·date (bak-dayt) *v.* (**back·dat·ed, back·dat·ing**) to declare that (a thing) is to be regarded as valid from some date in the past, especially to write a previous date on (a check).

back·drop (bak-drop) *n.* a painted curtain hung at the back of a stage.

back·field (bak-feeld) *n.* (in football) 1. the backs. 2. the area in which these play.

back·fire (bak-fır) *v.* (**back·fired, back·fir·ing**) 1. to ignite or explode prematurely, especially in the cylinder of an internal combustion engine. 2. to produce an undesired effect, especially upon the originators, *their plan backfired.* **backfire** *n.* an explosion in the exhaust of an internal combustion engine.

back·gam·mon (bak-gam-ŏn) *n.* a game played on a double board with pieces and dice.

back·ground (bak-grownd) *n.* 1. the back part of a scene or picture, the setting for the chief objects or people; *he was kept in the background,* in an inconspicuous position; *background music,* used as an accompaniment to a play, movie, etc. 2. the conditions and events surrounding and influencing something; *a person's background,* his family life, education, experience, etc.

back·hand (bak-hand) *adj.* (of a stroke, blow, or catch) made with the back of the hand turned outward. **backhand** *n.* a backhand stroke or blow.

back·hand·ed (bak-han-did) *adj.* 1. backhand. 2. indirect. □**backhanded compliment,** one made with underlying sarcasm so that it is not a compliment at all.

back·ing (bak-ing) *n.* 1. help, support; *he has a large backing,* many supporters. 2. material used to cover a thing's back or to support it.

back·lash (bak-lash) *n.* 1. a sudden or violent recoil. 2. a violent and usually hostile reaction to some event. **back′lash·er** *n.*

back·less (bak-lis) *adj.* 1. without a back. 2. (of a dress) cut low at the back.

back·log (bak-log) *n.* 1. a large log at the back of a hearth or hearth fire. 2. an accumulation of unfilled orders for work. **backlog** *v.* (**back·logged, back·log·ging**) to accumulate a backlog.

back·pack (bak-pak) *n.* a knapsack usually mounted on a light frame. **backpack** *v.* to hike while carrying a backpack. **back′pack·er** *n.*

back·ped·al (bak-ped-ăl) *v.* (**back·ped·aled, back·ped·al·ing**) 1. to work a pedal backward. 2. to back down from an argument or policy.

back·rest (bak-rest) *n.* a rest for one's back.

back·side (bak-sıd) *n.* (*informal*) the buttocks.

back·slap·per (bak-slap-ĕr) *n.* a noisy, overly effusive person.

back·slap·ping (bak-slap-ing) *n.* a display of effusive cordiality.

back·slide (bak-slıd) *v.* (**back·slid, back·slid** or **back·slid·den, back·slid·ing**) to slip back from good behavior into bad. **back′slid·er** *n.*

back·space (bak-spays) *v.* (**back·spaced, back·spac·ing**) to cause a typewriter carriage to move one space back.

back·spin (bak-spin) *n.* a reverse spin imparted to a ball to slow it or make it roll or bounce in an opposite direction from its original course.

back·stage (bak-stayj) *adj. & adv.* 1. behind the stage of a theater, in the wings or dressing rooms. 2. relating to the inner workings of an institution. 3. secret, of private lives.

back·stairs (bak-stairz) *adj.* underhanded, secret.

back·stop (bak-stop) *n.* 1. a barrier to stop a ball from going too far out of the playing area. 2. (*informal*) the catcher in baseball. 3. (*informal*) a substitute or support in case of need. **backstop** *v.* (**back·stopped, back·stop·ping**) to act as a backstop.

back·stretch (bak-strech) *n.* the straight section of a racetrack opposite the homestretch.

back·stroke (bak-strohk) *n.* a swimming stroke in which the swimmer is lying on his back.

back·swept (bak-swept) *adj.* slanting toward the back.

back·track (bak-trak) *v.* 1. to go back the same way that one came. 2. to back down from an argument or policy.

back·up (bak-up) *n.* 1. a person who supports or acts as deputy for another. 2. a stoppage (as of traffic, plumbing, etc.). 3. a substitute mechanism or program ready in case the original fails.

back·ward[1] (bak-wărd) *adj.* 1. directed toward the back or the starting point. 2. having made less than normal progress, retarded. 3. diffident, not putting oneself forward. **back′ward·ness** *n.*

back·ward[2] (bak-wărd), **back·wards** (bak-wărdz) *adv.* 1. toward the back. 2. with the back foremost, in a reverse direction or order. 3. toward the past. □**backwards and forwards,** in each direction alternately. **know it backwards and forwards,** to know it thoroughly. **lean over backward(s),** to do one's utmost.

back·wash (bak-wosh) *n.* 1. the backward flow of water or air. 2. the aftereffects of an action or event.

back·wa·ter (bak-waw-tĕr) *n.* 1. a stretch of stagnant water joining a stream. 2. a place unaffected by progress or new ideas.

back·woods (bak-wuudz) *n.* remote and only partially settled forest land.

back·woods·man (bak-wuudz-măn) *n.* (*pl.* -men, *pr.* -mĕn) a settler in the backwoods.

ba·con (bay-kŏn) *n.* salted or smoked meat from the back or sides of a pig. □**bring home the bacon,** (*informal*) to earn a living.

bac·te·ri·cide (bak-teer-ı̆-sıd) *n.* a substance that destroys bacteria. **bac·te·ri·cid·al** (bak-teer-ı̆-sı-dăl) *adj.*

bac·te·ri·ol·o·gist (bak-teer-i-ol-ŏ-jist) *n.* an expert in bacteriology.

bac·te·ri·ol·o·gy (bak-teer-i-ol-ŏ-jee) *n.* the branch of medicine dealing with the study of bacteria. **bac·te·ri·o·log·ic** (bak-teer-i-ŏ-loj-ik) *adj.* **bac·te·ri·o·log′i·cal** *adj.* **bac·te·ri·ol′o·gist** *n.*

bac·te·ri·o·phage (bak-teer-i-ŏ-fayj) *n.* a virus capable of destroying bacteria. **bac·te·ri·o·phag·ic** (bak-teer-i-ŏ-faj-ik) *adj.*

bac·te·ri·um (bak-teer-i-ŭm) *n.* (*pl.* -te·ri·a, *pr.* -teer-i-ă) a microscopic organism. **bac·te′ri·al** *adj.*

bad (bad) *adj.* (**worse, worst**) 1. wicked, evil, naughty. 2. unpleasant. 3. serious, severe. 4. inferior, of poor quality, worthless, incorrect, defective, faulty; *a bad business,* an unfortunate affair. 5. hurtful, unsuitable, *candy is bad for the teeth.* 6. in ill health, diseased. 7. decayed, spoiled, *the meat went bad.* **bad** *adv. (informal)* badly, *you must want something bad enough to die for it.* (▷ Careful writers prefer *badly* in place of *bad* in such expressions.) **bad** *n.* that which is bad or unfortunate, *return good for bad.* **bad′ness** *n.* □**bad blood,** ill feeling, enmity. **bad debt,** one that will not be repaid. **bad language,** swearwords. **bad news,** unwelcome news; *(slang)* (of a person) disliked or untrustworthy, *he is bad news.* **be in a bad way,** to be ill or in trouble. **feel bad about,** *(informal)* to feel upset or guilty about. **in bad with,** *(informal)* regarded with disapproval by. **not bad,** *(informal)* quite good.

bad·dy (bad-ee) *n. (pl.* **-dies)** *(informal)* a villain, *the goodies and the baddies.*

bade *see* **bid².**

badge (baj) *n.* a thing worn to show one's rank, occupation, or membership in an organization.

bad·ger (baj-ĕr) *n.* any of various flesh-eating mammals that burrow in the ground. **badger** *v.* to pester, to torment. □**badger game,** a dishonest trick in which a person is lured into a compromising situation and then surprised and blackmailed.

ba·di·nage (bad-ĭ-nahzh) *n.* banter.

bad·lands (bad-landz) *n.* a barren eroded region. □**the Badlands,** a section of southwestern South Dakota and northwestern Nebraska.

bad·ly (bad-lee) *adv.* **(worse, worst)** 1. in a bad way, defectively. 2. to a serious extent, *badly hurt.* ▷ Do not say *I feel badly* if you are not well or are upset; say *I feel bad.* Also see the note for **bad.**

bad·min·ton (bad-min-tŏn) *n.* a game played with rackets and shuttlecocks across a high net.

bad-tem·pered (bad-tem-pĕrd) *adj.* having or showing bad temper.

Bae·de·ker (bay-dĕ-kĕr) *n.* a travel guidebook. ▷ Originally one of a series prepared by Karl Baedeker, a German publisher.

baf·fle (baf-ĕl) *v.* **(baf·fled, baf·fling)** 1. to puzzle, to perplex. 2. to frustrate, *baffled their attempts.* **baffle** *n.* a screen placed to hinder or control the passage of sound, light, or fluid. **baf′fle·ment** *n.*

bag (bag) *n.* 1. a container made of flexible material with an opening at the top, used for holding or carrying things. 2. this with its contents, the amount it contains. 3. something resembling a bag; *bags under the eyes,* folds of loose skin. 4. the amount of game shot by a sportsman. 5. *(slang, contemptuous)* a woman, *the old bag.* **bag** *v.* **(bagged, bag·ging)** 1. to put into a bag or bags. 2. to kill or capture, *bagged a pheasant.* 3. *(informal)* to take possession of, to stake a claim to. 4. to bulge or hang loosely. □**bag and baggage,** with all one's belongings. **be in the bag,** *(informal)* to be secured or won as one wished.

ba·gasse (bă-gas) *n.* the residue left after juice has been extracted from sugar cane or sugar beet.

bag·a·telle (bag-ă-tel) *n.* 1. a pinball game. 2. something small and unimportant.

ba·gel (bay-gĕl) *n.* a hard ring-shaped bread roll.

bag·ful (bag-fuul) *n. (pl.* **-fuls)** as much as a bag will hold.

bag·gage (bag-ij) *n.* 1. suitcases and bags etc. containing a person's belongings taken on a trip. 2. portable equipment. 3. *(old use)* an immoral or contemptible woman. □**baggage strap,** a strap

fastened around a suitcase for additional security.

bag·gy (bag-ee) *adj.* **(-gi·er, -gi·est)** hanging in loose folds. **bag′gi·ly** *adv.* **bag′gi·ness** *n.*

Bagh·dad (bag-dad) *n.* the capital of Iraq.

bag·man (bag-măn) *n. (pl.* **-men,** *pr.* -men) an agent who collects or distributes money for dishonest or illegal purposes.

bagn·io (bahn-yoh) *n.* a brothel.

bag·pipe (bag-pɪp) *n.* (frequently **bagpipes** *n. pl.*) a musical instrument with air stored in a bag and pressed out through pipes.

ba·guette (ba-get) *n.* a gem cut in a long rectangular shape.

Ba·ha·mas (bă-hah-măz) a group of islands in the West Indies.

Bah·rain (bah-rayn) a sheikdom consisting of a group of islands in the Persian Gulf.

bail¹ (bayl) *n.* 1. money or property pledged as security that a person accused of a crime will return, if he is released temporarily, to stand trial. 2. permission for a person's release on such security. **bail** *v.* to obtain or allow the release of (a person) on bail. **bail′a·ble** *adj.* □**bail bond,** money pledged as bail. **bail bondsman,** a person who makes his livelihood by supplying bail for others. **go bail,** to pledge money etc. as bail. **out on bail,** released after bail is pledged. ▷ Do not confuse *bail* with *bale.*

bail² *v.* to scoop (water) out of a boat etc. □**bail out** *(slang)* to relieve by financial help in an emergency; to jump from an airplane in flight; *(slang)* to leave a bad situation. ▷ Do not confuse *bail* with *bale.*

bail³ *n.* 1. the handle of a bucket. 2. a bar holding paper against the platen of a typewriter. ▷ Do not confuse *bail* with *bale.*

bai·ley (bay-lee) *n.* the outer wall of a castle, a courtyard enclosed by this.

bail·iff (bay-lif) *n.* 1. a minor officer of a U.S. court. 2. *(British)* a law officer who helps a sheriff, serving writs etc.

bail·i·wick (bay-lĭ-wik) *n.* 1. a district, the jurisdiction of a bailiff. 2. one's area of knowledge, skill, etc.

bails·man (baylz-măn) *n. (pl.* **-men,** *pr.* -mĕn) a person who goes bail for another.

bairn (bairn) *n. (Scottish)* a child.

bait (bayt) *n.* 1. food (real or sham) placed to attract prey, especially fish. 2. an enticement. **bait** *v.* 1. to place bait on or in, *bait the trap.* 2. to torment by jeering.

baize (bayz) *n.* a thick woolen usually green cloth, used for covering tables or doors.

bake (bayk) *v.* **(baked, bak·ing)** 1. to cook or be cooked by dry heat. 2. to expose to great heat, to harden or be hardened by heat. □**baking powder,** a powder used as a raising agent for cakes etc. **baking soda,** sodium bicarbonate, used in baking.

bak·er (bay-kĕr) *n.* one who bakes and sells bread, cake, etc.

baker's dozen thirteen.

bak·er·y (bay-kĕ-ree) *n. (pl.* **-er·ies)** a place where bread, cake, etc. are baked for sale.

bake·shop (bayk-shop) *n.* a bakery, a store where baked goods are sold.

bak·sheesh (bak-sheesh) *n. (pl.* **-sheesh)** a small gift of money, a tip.

bal. *abbr.* balance.

bal·a·lai·ka (bal-ă-lɪ-kă) *n.* a Russian stringed instrument played by plucking.

bal·ance (bal-ăns) *n*. 1. a weighing apparatus with two scales or pans hanging from a crossbar. 2. the regulating apparatus of a clock. 3. an even distribution of weight or amount, a steady position or state. 4. the difference between credits and debits. 5. money remaining after payment of a debt. **balance** *v*. 1. to consider by comparing, *balance one argument against another.* 2. to be or put or keep (a thing) in a state of balance. 3. to compare the debits and credits of (an account) and make the entry needed to equalize these, to have these equal. □**balance of payments,** the difference between the amount paid to foreign countries for imports and services and the amount received from them for exports etc. in a given period. **balance of power,** a condition in which no country or group is stronger than another. **balance of trade,** the difference in value between imports and exports. **balance sheet,** a written statement of assets and liabilities. **balance wheel,** a wheel that stabilizes or regulates the speed of a mechanism, especially of a clock or watch. **hang in the balance,** to be in a state where the outcome is still uncertain. **off balance,** in danger of falling. **on balance,** taking everything into consideration.

bal·brig·gan (bal-brig-ăn) *n*. 1. a knitted cotton cloth. 2. *balbriggans,* underclothes or pajamas of this material.

bal·co·ny (bal-kŏ-nee) *n*. (*pl*. **-nies**) 1. a platform with a rail or parapet, projecting outside an upper story of a building. 2. a gallery in a building. 3. an upper floor of seats in a theater. **bal′co·nied** *adj*.

bald (bawld) *adj*. 1. with the scalp wholly or partly hairless. 2. (of tires) with the tread worn away. 3. bare, without details, *bald facts.* **bald′ly** *adv*. **bald′ness** *n*. □**bald eagle,** an eagle with a white head and tail, also called "American eagle," a symbol of the U.S.

bal·der·dash (bawl-děr-dash) *n*. nonsense.

bald·ing (bawl-ding) *adj*. becoming bald.

bal·dric (bawl-drik) *n*. a belt for supporting a sword, bugle, etc., worn over the shoulder and across the body to the opposite hip.

bale (bayl) *n*. 1. a large bundle of straw etc. bound with cord or wire. 2. a large package of goods. **bale** *v*. (**baled, bal·ing**) to make into a bale. ▷Do not confuse *bale* with *bail.*

ba·leen (bă-leen) *n*. whalebone.

bale·ful (bayl-fŭl) *adj*. menacing, destructive, *a baleful influence.* **bale′ful·ly** *adv*.

Ba·li·nese (bal-ĭ-neez) *adj*. of Bali, a mountainous island of Indonesia. **Balinese** *n*. (*pl*. **-nese**) a native or inhabitant of Bali.

balk (bawk) *v*. 1. to thwart, to hinder, to discourage. 2. to refuse to proceed. 3. (in baseball) to commit a balk. **balk** *n*. (in baseball) an illegal pitching motion made while one or more runners are on base.

Bal·kan (bawl-kăn) *adj*. of the peninsula in southeast Europe bounded by the Adriatic, Aegean, and Black Seas, or of its people or countries. □**the Balkans,** the Balkan countries.

balk·y (baw-kee) *adj*. (**balk·i·er, balk·i·est**) reluctant, perverse.

ball[1] (bawl) *n*. 1. a solid or hollow sphere. 2. such a sphere used in games. 3. a game played with a ball, especially baseball. 4. a single delivery of the ball by the pitcher in baseball, a pitched baseball that is not in the strike zone or is not swung at by the batter. 5. material gathered or wound into a round mass, *a ball of string.* 6. a rounded part. **ball** *v*. 1. to form into a ball. 2. to form a lump or lumps. □**ball bearing,** a bearing using small steel balls; one of these balls. **ball boy, ball girl,** one who retrieves balls in a tennis match. **ball carrier,** (in football) a player who runs with the ball. **ball of fire,** a very lively spirited person. **ball of the foot,** the rounded part under the foot at the base of the big toe. **ball point pen,** a pen with a tiny ball as its writing point. **on the ball,** *(informal)* alert, competent. **start the ball rolling,** to start an activity.

ball[2] *n*. a social gathering for dancing, especially a formal one. □**have a ball,** *(slang)* to enjoy oneself.

bal·lad (bal-ăd) *n*. a simple song or poem, especially one telling a story.

bal·lad·eer (bal-ă-deer) *n*. a person who sings ballads.

bal·last (bal-ăst) *n*. heavy material placed in a ship's hold to improve its stability; *the ship is in ballast,* is laden with ballast only.

bal·le·ri·na (bal-ĕ-ree-nă) *n*. a female ballet dancer.

bal·let (ba-lay) *n*. 1. a form of dancing and mime to music, a performance of this. 2. a company of ballet dancers.

bal·lis·tic (bă-lis-tik) *adj*. of projectiles such as bullets and missiles. □**ballistic missile,** one that is powered and guided during at least the initial stage of its flight.

bal·lis·tics (bă-lis-tiks) *n*. the scientific study of firearms or of the motion or flight characteristics of projectiles.

bal·loon (bă-loon) *n*. a bag or envelope inflated with air or a lighter gas, intended to rise and float in the atmosphere or used as a children's toy. **balloon** *v*. 1. to swell out like a balloon. 2. to travel in a balloon. 3. to increase or grow rapidly. □**balloon tire,** a wide pneumatic tire.

bal·loon·ist (bă-loo-nist) *n*. a person who travels by balloon.

bal·lot (bal-ŏt) *n*. 1. a paper or token used in secret voting. 2. voting by means of such papers etc. **ballot** *v*. (**bal·lot·ed, bal·lot·ing**) to vote by ballot.

ball·point (bawl-point) *n*. (also **ballpoint pen**) a pen having a tiny ball as its writing point.

ball·room (bawl-room) *n*. a large room where dances are held.

bal·ly·hoo (bal-ee-hoo) *n*. (*pl*. **-hoos**) exaggerated or sensational advertising or publicity. **ballyhoo** *v*. (**bal·ly·hooed, bal·ly·hoo·ing**) to publicize by ballyhoo.

balm (bahm) *n*. 1. an ointment that soothes or heals. 2. a soothing influence. 3. a fragrant herb.

balm·y (bah-mee) *adj*. (**balm·i·er, balm·i·est**) 1. like balm, fragrant. 2. soft and warm, *balmy breezes.* **balm′i·ness** *n*.

ba·lo·ney (bă-loh-nee) *n*. 1. *(slang)* nonsense. 2. bologna.

bal·sa (bawl-să) *n*. a very lightweight wood (also **balsa wood**) from a tropical American tree.

bal·sam (bawl-săm) *n*. 1. a soothing oil. 2. a flowering plant. 3. a tree yielding balm. □**balsam fir,** a North American evergreen tree widely used as a Christmas tree.

Bal·tic (bawl-tik) *adj*. of the Baltic Sea, an almost landlocked sea of northeast Europe. **Baltic** *n*. the Baltic Sea.

bal·us·ter (bal-ŭ-stĕr) n. one of the short stone pillars in a balustrade.

bal·us·trade (bal-ŭ-strayd) n. a row of short posts or pillars supporting a rail or stone coping around a balcony or terrace.

Bam·a·ko (bam-ă-koh) the capital of Mali.

bam·boo (bam-boo) n. a giant tropical grass with hollow stems.

bam·boo·zle (bam-boo-zĕl) v. **(bam·boo·zled, bam·boo·zling)** (slang) to trick.

ban (ban) v. **(banned, ban·ning)** to forbid officially. **ban** n. an order that bans something.

ba·nal (bă-nal, bay-năl) adj. commonplace, uninteresting. **ba·nal·i·ty** (bă-nal-ĭ-tee) n. (pl. **-ties)**.

ba·nan·a (bă-nan-ă) n. 1. the finger-shaped fruit of a treelike tropical plant. 2. this plant. ☐**go bananas,** (slang) to go crazy.

band (band) n. 1. a narrow strip, hoop, or loop. 2. a range of values, wavelengths, etc. within a series. 3. a group of people, animals, or objects. 4. a set of people playing music together, especially on wind or percussion instruments. **band** v. 1. to put a band on or around, to tie or fasten with a band. 2. to form into a league, to unite for a common cause, they banded together. **band'ed** adj. ☐**band saw,** an endless saw running over pulleys.

band·age (ban-dij) n. a strip of material for binding up a wound. **bandage** v. **(band·aged, band·ag·ing)** to bind up with a bandage.

ban·dan·na, ban·dan·a (ban-dan-ă) n. a large colored handkerchief with yellow or white spots or other bright pattern.

band·box (band-boks) n. (pl. **-box·es)** a box for hats (originally for neckbands). **bandbox** adj. conspicuously neat and clean.

ban·dit (ban-dit) n. a robber, especially a member of a band of robbers.

ban·do·lier (ban-dŏ-leer) n. a shoulder belt with loops or pockets for cartridges.

band·stand (band-stand) n. a covered outdoor platform for a band or orchestra.

band·wag·on (band-wag-ŏn) n. 1. a wagon carrying musicians in a circus parade. 2. an imaginary vehicle thought of as carrying a thing that is heading for success. ☐**climb or jump on the bandwagon,** to seek to join this thing or follow its example.

ban·dy¹ (ban-dee) v. **(ban·died, ban·dy·ing)** to pass to and fro. the story was bandied about; bandy words, exchange remarks in quarreling.

bandy² adj. curving apart at the knees. **ban'di·ness** n.

bane (bayn) n. 1. a poison. 2. a cause of trouble, misery, or anxiety. **bane'ful** adj. **bane'ful·ly** adv.

bang¹ (bang) v. 1. to make a sudden loud noise like an explosion. 2. to strike or shut noisily. **bang** n. 1. the sudden loud noise of or like an explosion. 2. a sharp blow. **bang** adv. 1. with a bang, abruptly. 2. exactly, bang in the middle. ☐**with a bang,** very successfully, impressively.

bang² n. a short fringe of hair over the forehead.

Bang·kok (bang-kok) the capital of Thailand.

Ban·gla·desh (bang-glă-desh) a Muslim country in southeast Asia. **Ban·gla·desh·i** (bang-glă-desh-ee) adj. & n. (pl. **-desh·is)**.

ban·gle (bang-gĕl) n. 1. a bracelet of rigid material. 2. any loose-hanging ornament.

Ban·gui (bahn-gee) the capital of the Central African Republic.

bang-up (bang-up) adj. (slang) excellent.

ban·ish (ban-ish) v. 1. to condemn to exile. 2. to dismiss from one's presence or one's mind, banish care. **ban'ish·ment** n.

ban·is·ter (ban-i-stĕr) n. 1. one of the uprights supporting the handrail of a stair. 2. the handrail itself. 3. the uprights and the rail together.

ban·jo (ban-joh) n. (pl. **-jos)** a stringed instrument like a guitar with a round body. **ban'jo·ist** n.

Ban·jul (bahn-juul) the capital of Gambia.

bank¹ (bangk) n. 1. a slope, especially at the side of a river. 2. a raised mass of sand etc. in a river bed. 3. a long mass of cloud or snow or other soft substance. 4. a tier, row, or series. **bank** v. 1. to build or form a bank; bank the fire, heap on fuel, ashes, etc. so that it burns slowly. 2. to tilt or be tilted sideways in rounding a curve.

bank² n. 1. an establishment for keeping people's money etc. safe and paying it out on a customer's order. 2. the money held by the keeper of a gaming table or the banker of a game. 3. a place for storing a reserve supply, a blood bank. **bank** v. 1. to place or keep money in a bank. 2. to base one's hopes, we are banking on your success. ☐**bank holiday,** a day (other than Sunday) on which banks are officially closed, usually a public holiday.

bank·book (bangk-buuk) n. a book containing a customer's copy of his savings account transactions with a bank.

bank·er (bang-kĕr) n. 1. an expert in banking. 2. the keeper of a gaming bank or one who keeps accounts of money, chips, etc. in a game.

bank·ing (bang-king) n. the business of running a financial bank.

bank·note (bangk-noht) n. a small strip of paper issued by a bank to serve as currency, printed with the amount for which it is valid.

bank·roll (bangk-rohl) n. a roll of banknotes, ready money. **bankroll** v. to finance.

bank·rupt (bangk-rupt) n. a person who is unable to pay his debts in full and whose affairs are administered for the benefit of his creditors. **bankrupt** adj. 1. declared by a law court to be a bankrupt. 2. financially ruined and in debt. **bankrupt** v. to make bankrupt. **bank·rupt·cy** (bangk-rupt-see) n.

ban·ner (ban-ĕr) n. 1. a flag. 2. a strip of cloth bearing an emblem or slogan, hung up or carried on a crossbar or between two poles in a procession etc. **banner** adj. foremost, a banner year.

banns (banz) n. pl. a public announcement in church of a forthcoming marriage between two named people.

ban·quet (bang-kwit) n. an elaborate ceremonial public meal. **banquet** v. **(ban·quet·ed, ban·quet·ing)** to give or take part in a banquet.

ban·shee (ban-shee) n. a female spirit in Irish and Scottish folklore whose wail is said to foretell a death in a house.

ban·tam (ban-tăm) n. a small domestic fowl.

ban·tam·weight (ban-tăm-wayt) n. a boxer between featherweight and flyweight weighing up to 118 pounds.

ban·ter (ban-tĕr) n. good-humored teasing. **banter** v. to joke in a good-humored way.

Ban·tu (ban-too) n. (pl. **-tus, -tu)** one of a group of African peoples or their languages.

ban·yan (ban-yăn) n. an Indian fig tree with spreading branches from which roots grow downward to the ground and form new trunks.

ban·zai (bahn-zɪ) *interj.* a Japanese patriotic greeting or cheer. □**banzai attack,** a suicidal desperate attack or charge.

ba·o·bab (bay-oh-bab) *n.* an African tree, naturalized also in India and Ceylon, bearing large woody fruit with edible pulp known as "monkey-bread."

bap·tism (bap-tiz-ĕm) *n.* the Christian sacrament of sprinkling a person with water or immersing him in it to symbolize purification and admission to the Church. **bap·tis·mal** (bap-tiz-măl) *adj.* □**baptismal name,** a name given at baptism, a Christian name.

Bap·tist (bap-tist) *n.* a member of a Protestant denomination believing that baptism should be by immersion and performed at an age when the person is old enough to understand its meaning. □**the Baptist,** St. John, who baptized Jesus.

bap·tis·ter·y, bap·tis·try (bap-ti-stree) *n.* (*pl.* -**ter·ies, -tries**) a building or part of a church used for baptism.

bap·tize (bap-tɪz) *v.* (**bap·tized, bap·tiz·ing**) 1. to perform baptism on. 2. to christen, name, or nickname. 3. to initiate (a person) by ordeal.

bar[1] (bahr) *n.* 1. a long piece of solid material. 2. a narrow strip. 3. any barrier or obstacle, a sandbank. 4. one of the vertical lines dividing a piece of music into equal units, a section contained by these. 5. the railing in a law court behind which persons on trial are stationed. 6. *the bar,* the legal profession, lawyers. 7. a counter or room where alcohol is served. 8. a place where refreshments are served across a counter, *a sandwich bar.* 9. a shop counter selling a single type of commodity or service, *the department store's hat bar.* **bar** *v.* (**barred, bar·ring**) 1. to fasten with a bar or bars. 2. to keep in or out by this. 3. to obstruct, *barred the way.* 4. to prevent or prohibit. **bar** *prep.* except, *she was the best of all, bar none.* □**be called to the bar,** to become a lawyer. **behind bars,** in prison.

bar[2] *n.* a unit of pressure used in meteorology.

barb (bahrb) *n.* 1. the backward-pointing part of an arrow, fishhook, etc. that makes it difficult to withdraw this from what it has pierced. 2. a wounding remark.

Bar·ba·dos (bahr-bay-dohs) a country in the Caribbean. **Bar·ba·di·an** (bahr-bay-di-ăn) *adj.* & *n.*

bar·bar·i·an (bahr-bair-i-ăn) *n.* an uncivilized person. **barbarian** *adj.* of barbarians.

bar·bar·ic (bahr-bar-ik) *adj.* suitable for barbarians, rough and wild. **bar·bar'i·cal·ly** *adv.*

bar·bar·ism (bahr-bă-riz-ĕm) *n.* 1. savagery. 2. absence of culture. 3. ignorance. 4. a word or phrase not in accordance with the established standard of a language, use of this.

bar·bar·i·ty (bahr-bar-i-tee) *n.* (*pl.* -**ties**) savage cruelty, an instance of this.

bar·ba·rous (bahr-bă-rŭs) *adj.* uncivilized, cruel. **bar'ba·rous·ly** *adv.*

bar·be·cue (bahr-bĕ-kyoo) *n.* 1. a metal frame for grilling food above an open fire. 2. an open-air party at which food is cooked on this. 3. the food itself. **barbecue** *v.* (**bar·be·cued, bar·be·cu·ing**) 1. to cook on a barbecue. 2. to cook in barbecue sauce. □**barbecue sauce,** a highly seasoned sauce of vinegar, spices, etc.

barbed (bahrbd) *adj.* having a barb or barbs. □**barbed wire** (also **barb wire**), a wire with short sharp points at intervals.

bar·bell (bahr-bel) *n.* an iron bar with a heavy disk at each end, used in weight lifting.

bar·ber (bahr-bĕr) *n.* a men's hairdresser.

bar·ber·ry (bahr-ber-ee) *n.* (*pl.* -**ries**) 1. a shrub with spiny shoots and small yellow flowers. 2. its oblong red sharply acid berry.

bar·ber·shop (bahr-bĕr-shop) *n.* an establishment for giving haircuts, shaves, etc.

bar·bi·can (bahr-bĭ-kăn) *n.* the outer defense of a city or castle, especially a double tower over a gate or bridge.

bar·bi·tu·rate (bahr-bich-ŭ-rit) *n.* a kind of sedative drug.

bar·bi·tu·ric (bahr-bĭ-toor-ik) **acid** a white crystalline substance from which barbiturates are derived.

bar·ca·role, bar·ca·rolle (bahr-kă-rohl) *n.* a gondolier's song, a song in this style.

bard (bahrd) *n.* 1. a Celtic minstrel. 2. a poet. □**the Bard of Avon,** Shakespeare.

bare (bair) *adj.* & *adv.* (**bar·er, bar·est**) 1. without clothing or covering; *trees were bare,* leafless; *with one's bare hands,* without tools or weapons. 2. exposed, undisguised, *lay bare the truth.* 3. plain, without detail, *the bare facts.* 4. empty of stores, *cupboard was bare.* 5. only just sufficient, *the bare necessities of life.* **bare** *v.* (**bared, bar·ing**) to uncover, to reveal, *bared its teeth in a snarl.* **bare'ness** *n.*

bare·back (bair-bak) *adj.* & *adv.* on a horse without a saddle.

bare·faced (bair-fayst) *adj.* 1. with the face uncovered. 2. shameless, undisguised.

bare·foot (bair-fuut), **bare·foot·ed** (bair-fuut-id) *adj.* & *adv.* with bare feet.

bare·hand·ed (bair-han-did) *adj.* & *adv.* without tools or weapons.

bare·head·ed (bair-hed-id) *adj.* & *adv.* not wearing a hat.

bare·ly (bair-lee) *adv.* scarcely, only just.

bar·fly (bahr-flɪ) *n.* (*pl.* -**flies**) (*informal*) a person who frequents bars.

bar·gain (bahr-gin) *n.* 1. an agreement made with obligations on both or all sides. 2. something obtained as a result of this. 3. a thing bought cheaply. **bargain** *v.* 1. to discuss the terms of an agreement. 2. to be prepared for, to expect, *didn't bargain on his arriving so early; got more than she bargained for,* was unpleasantly surprised. □**into the bargain,** in addition to other things.

barge (bahrj) *n.* a large flat-bottomed boat for use on canals or rivers, especially for carrying goods. **barge** *v.* (**barged, barg·ing**) 1. to transport by barge. 2. to move clumsily or heavily. □**barge in,** to intrude.

barge·man (bahrj-măn) *n.* (*pl.* -**men,** *pr.* -mĕn) a man in charge of or working on a barge.

bar·i·tone (bar-i-tohn) *n.* 1. a male voice between tenor and bass. 2. a singer with such a voice, a part written for this.

bar·i·um (bar-i-ŭm) *n.* 1. a soft silvery-white metal. 2. a chemical substance swallowed or injected into the digestive tract when this is to be x-rayed.

bark[1] (bahrk) *n.* the outer layer of tree trunks and branches. **bark** *v.* 1. to peel bark from. 2. to scrape the skin off accidentally, *barked my shins.*

bark[2] *n.* the sharp harsh sound made by a dog or fox. **bark** *v.* 1. to make this sound. 2. to speak in a sharp commanding voice, *barked out orders.* □**bark up the wrong tree,** to direct one's effort or complaint in the wrong direction. **his bark is worse than his bite,** he speaks harshly but does not behave thus.

bark³ *n.* a three-masted ship.

bar·keep·er (bahr-kee-pĕr) *n.* a person who owns or tends a bar serving alcoholic drinks.

bark·er (bahr-kĕr) *n.* a person who stands at the entrance to a show shouting its merits to attract customers.

bar·ley (bahr-lee) *n.* a kind of cereal plant, its grain. □**barley water,** a drink made from pearl barley.

bar·maid (bahr-mayd) *n.* a female attendant at a bar serving alcohol.

bar·man (bahr-măn) *n.* (*pl.* **-men,** *pr.* -mĕn) a male attendant at a bar serving alcohol.

bar mitz·vah (bahr mits-vă) 1. a religious initiation ceremony for a Jewish boy aged thirteen. 2. the boy for whom such a ceremony is held.

barn (bahrn) *n.* a farm building for storing grain, hay, etc. and housing livestock. □**barn owl,** an owl that often breeds and roosts in barns and other buildings.

bar·na·cle (bahr-nă-kĕl) *n.* a kind of shellfish that attaches itself to objects under water.

barn·storm (bahrn-storm) *v.* to travel and present theatrical productions or make speeches in the countryside or in small towns.

barn·yard (bahrn-yahrd) *n.* a yard or fenced area.

bar·o·gram (bar-ŏ-gram) *n.* a record of variations in atmospheric pressure.

bar·o·graph (bar-ŏ-graf) *n.* a barometer with an apparatus for making a barogram. **bar·o·graph·ic** (bar-ŏ-graf-ik) *adj.*

ba·rom·e·ter (bă-rom-i-tĕr) *n.* an instrument measuring atmospheric pressure, used for forecasting the weather. **bar·o·met·ric** (bar-ŏ-met-rik) *adj.* **bar·o·met'ri·cal** *adj.*

bar·on (bar-ŏn) *n.* 1. a member of the lowest rank of the British peerage (called Lord _____), or of other nobility (called Baron _____). 2. a magnate; *a newspaper baron,* one controlling many newspapers.

bar·on·ess (bar-ŏ-nis) *n.* 1. the wife or widow of a baron. 2. a woman with a baronial title in her own right.

bar·on·et (bar-ŏ-nit, bar-ŏ-net) *n.* a British nobleman ranking below a baron but above a knight, having the title "Sir."

bar·on·et·cy (bar-ŏ-nit-see) *n.* (*pl.* **-cies**) the rank of a baronet.

ba·ro·ni·al (bă-roh-ni-ăl) *adj.* of or suitable for a baron.

bar·o·ny (bar-ŏ-nee) *n.* (*pl.* **-nies**) the rank or lands of a baron.

ba·roque (bă-rohk) *adj.* of the ornate architectural style of the 17th and 18th centuries. **baroque** *n.* this style or ornamentation.

ba·rouche (bă-roosh) *n.* a four-wheeled horse-drawn carriage with a seat in front for the driver, and seats inside for two couples facing each other.

bar·racks (bar-ăks) *n.* (*sing.* also as *pl.*) a large building or group of buildings for soldiers to live in.

bar·ra·cu·da (bar-ă-koo-dă) *n.* (*pl.* **-da, -das**) a voracious fish found in warm seas.

bar·rage (bă-rahzh) *n.* 1. an artificial barrier, especially one damming a river. 2. a heavy continuous bombardment by artillery. 3. a rapid fire of questions or comments.

bar·ra·try (bar-ă-tree) *n.* (*pl.* **-tries**) 1. the purchase or sale of ecclesiastical promotions or offices of state. 2. annoying persistence in or incitement to litigation. 3. fraud or criminal negligence by a ship's master or crew.

barred (bahrd) *see* **bar**¹.

bar·rel (bar-ĕl) *n.* 1. a large round container with flat ends. 2. the amount this contains. 3. a tubelike part, especially of a gun. **barrel** *v.* (**bar·reled, bar·rel·ing**) 1. to put into barrels. 2. *(slang)* to travel at a very high speed. □**barrel organ,** an instrument from which music is produced by turning a handle and so causing a pin-studded cylinder to act on keys. **barrel roll,** a maneuver by an airplane that makes a complete rotation about its longitudinal axis. **over a barrel,** *(informal)* in a helpless position.

bar·ren (bar-ĕn) *adj.* 1. not fertile enough to produce crops, *barren land.* 2. not producing fruit or seeds, *a barren tree.* 3. unable to have young ones. **barren** *n.* 1. barren land. 2. elevated plains on which grow small trees and shrubs but no timber. **bar'ren·ly** *adv.* **bar'ren·ness** *n.*

bar·rette (bă-ret) *n.* a bar-shaped clip for a woman's hair.

bar·ri·cade (bar-i-kayd) *n.* a barrier, especially one hastily erected as a defense. **barricade** *v.* (**bar·ri·cad·ed, bar·ri·cad·ing**) to block or defend with a barricade.

bar·ri·er (bar-i-ĕr) *n.* something that prevents or controls advance, access, or progress. □**barrier reef,** a coral reef with a channel between it and the land.

bar·ri·o (bahr-ioh) *n.* (*pl.* **-ri·os**) 1. a Hispanic quarter of a U.S. city. 2. a district of a town in a Hispanic country.

bar·ris·ter (bar-i-stĕr) *n.* (*British*) a lawyer entitled to represent clients in the higher law courts.

bar·room (bahr-room) *n.* a room in which alcoholic drinks are sold.

bar·row¹ (bar-oh) *n.* 1. a wheelbarrow. 2. a small cart with two wheels and shafts so it can be pulled or pushed by hand.

barrow² *n.* a prehistoric burial mound.

barrow³ *n.* a male hog.

Bart. *abbr.* Baronet.

bar·ten·der (bahr-ten-dĕr) *n.* a person who prepares and serves alcoholic drinks at a bar.

bar·ter (bahr-tĕr) *v.* to trade by exchanging goods etc. for other goods, not for money. **barter** *n.* trading by exchange.

bas·al (bay-săl, -zăl) *adj.* of or at the base. □**basal metabolism,** the minimum amount of energy needed by an organism at rest.

ba·salt (bă-sawlt) *n.* a kind of dark rock of volcanic origin. **ba·sal'tic** *adj.*

base (bays) *n.* 1. the lowest part of anything, the part on which it rests or is supported. 2. a basic or fundamental part, the main ingredient. 3. a starting point. 4. the headquarters of an expedition or other enterprise. 5. a place at which an expedition or force stores its supplies. 6. a substance into which other things are mixed, *some paints have an oil base.* 7. a cream or liquid applied to the skin as a foundation for makeup. 8. a substance (as an alkali) capable of combining with an acid to form a salt. 9. one of the four stations at the corners of a baseball diamond, especially the first three (excluding home plate). **base** *v.* (**based, bas·ing**) to use as a base or foundation or as evidence for a forecast. **base** *adj.* (**bas·er, bas·est**) 1. dishonorable, *base motives.* 2. of inferior value, *base metals.* 3. debased, not of acceptable quality, *base coins.* **base'ly** *adv.* **base'ness** *n.* □**base exchange,** a post exchange at an air force base. **base hit,** a hit ena-

bling the batter to reach first base safely. **base on balls** (*pl.* **bases on balls**), advancement of a batter to first base after four balls. **off base,** (*informal*) mistaken.
base·ball (bays-bawl) *n.* 1. a team game played with a bat and a ball on a field with four bases arranged in a diamond and in which runs are scored by hitting a ball, getting walks, etc. and circling the bases. 2. the ball used in this game.
base·board (bays-bohrd) *n.* a narrow board around the wall of a room, close to the floor.
base·born (bays-born) *adj.* 1. of illegitimate birth. 2. born of humble family. 3. contemptible.
base·less (bays-lis) *adj.* without foundation, *baseless rumors.*
base·line (bays-lin) *n.* 1. a known line used as a geometrical base in trigonometry. 2. the line at each end of a tennis court. 3. the line between successive bases in baseball.
base·ment (bays-měnt) *n.* the lowest story of a building, below ground level.
bash (bash) *v.* 1. to strike violently. 2. to attack with blows. **bash** *n.* 1. a violent blow or knock. 2. (*slang*) a party, a festive good time.
bash·ful (bash-fŭl) *adj.* shy and self-conscious. **bash′ful·ly** *adv.* **bash′ful·ness** *n.*
ba·sic (bay-sik) *adj.* 1. forming a base or starting point, fundamental, *basic principles.* 2. of a chemical base. **ba′si·cal·ly** *adv.*
bas·il (baz-ĭl, bay-zĭl) *n.* a sweet-smelling herb.
ba·sil·i·ca (bă-sil-i-kă) *n.* 1. a large oblong hall or church with two rows of columns and an apse at one end. 2. a church or cathedral granted ceremonial privileges.
bas·i·lisk (baz-ĭ-lisk) *n.* a mythical reptile said to cause death by its glance or breath.
ba·sin (bay-sin) *n.* 1. a round open dish for holding liquids or soft substances. 2. this with its contents, the amount it contains. 3. a washbasin. 4. a sunken place where water collects; *a river basin,* the area drained by a river. 5. an almost landlocked harbor, *a yacht basin.* **ba′sin·ful** *n.* (*pl.* **-fuls**).
ba·sis (bay-sis) *n.* (*pl.* **-ses,** *pr.* -seez) a foundation or support, a main principle.
bask (bask) *v.* 1. to expose oneself comfortably to a pleasant warmth. 2. to enjoy someone's approval.
bas·ket (bas-kit) *n.* 1. a container for holding or carrying things, made of interwoven flexible material. 2. this with its contents. **bas′ket·ful** *n.* (*pl.* **-fuls**). □**basket case,** (*slang*) a person whose four limbs have been amputated; a completely ineffectual person. **basket weave,** a weave of textiles that looks like the weave of a basket.
bas·ket·ball (bas-kit-bawl) *n.* 1. a game played on a court (*basketball court*) by two teams of five players each, in which points are scored by throwing a ball through a raised hoop. 2. the ball used in this.
bas·ket·work (bas-kit-wurk) *n.* 1. a structure of interwoven rushes, twigs, etc. 2. the art of making this.
bas mitz·vah (bahs mits-vă), **bat mitz·vah** (baht mits-vă) *n.* 1. a religious initiation ceremony for a Jewish girl aged thirteen. 2. the girl for whom such a ceremony is held.
Basque (bask) *n.* 1. a member of a people living in the western Pyrenees. 2. their language.
bas-re·lief (bah-ri-leef) *n.* a sculpture or carving in low relief.

bass[1] (bas) *n.* (*pl.* **bass**) a spiny-finned sport and food fish of the perch family.
bass[2] (bays) *adj.* deep-sounding, of the lowest pitch in music. **bass** (also **basso**) *n.* 1. the lowest male voice, a singer with such a voice. 2. a part written for this. 3. the lowest pitched member of a group of similar musical instruments.
bas·set (bas-it) *n.* (also **basset hound**) a dog of a short-legged breed with long ears.
bas·si·net (bas-ĭ-net) *n.* a hooded cradle for a baby.
bas·so (bas-oh) *n.* (*pl.* **bas·sos, bas·si,** *pr.* basee) a man with a bass voice. □**basso profundo,** an unusually deep bass voice, a singer with such a voice.
bas·soon (ba-soon) *n.* a deep-toned woodwind instrument. **bas·soon′ist** *n.*
bass·wood (bas-wuud) *n.* 1. the linden tree of North America. 2. its wood.
bast (bast) *n.* 1. the inner bark of the linden tree or basswood, cut into strips and coarsely woven, to make matting etc. 2. a similar fiber from palms used for ropes, brooms, etc. 3. any flexible or fibrous bark.
bas·tard (bas-tărd) *n.* 1. an illegitimate child. 2. (*vulgar slang*) an unpleasant or difficult person or thing. **bastard** *adj.* 1. of illegitimate birth. 2. not considered a genuine specimen of its kind. **bas′tard·ly** *adj.* **bas′tar·dy** *n.*
bas·tard·ize (bas-tăr-dīz) *v.* (**bas·tard·ized, bas·tard·iz·ing**) 1. to declare or make (a person) a bastard. 2. to lower in quality or value.
baste[1] (bayst) *v.* (**bast·ed, bast·ing**) 1. to moisten with fat during cooking. 2. to thrash.
baste[2] *v.* (**bast·ed, bast·ing**) to sew together temporarily with long loose stitches.
bas·ti·na·do (bas-tĭ-nay-doh) *n.* (*pl.* **-does**) a beating given on the soles of the feet. **bastinado** *v.* (**bas·ti·na·doed, bas·ti·na·do·ing**) to punish by this.
bas·tion (bas-chŏn) *n.* 1. a projecting part of a fortification. 2. a fortified place near hostile territory. 3. something serving as a stronghold, *a bastion of democracy.*
bat[1] (bat) *n.* 1. a heavy stick. 2. a shaped wooden implement for striking the ball in baseball etc. 3. a sharp blow. 4. (in baseball) a turn batting. **bat** *v.* (**bat·ted, bat·ting**) 1. to use a bat, to take one's turn at this. 2. to strike with a bat, to hit. □**at bat,** (baseball) batting.
bat[2] *n.* a flying mammal with a mouselike body. □**blind as a bat,** completely blind. **have bats in the belfry,** (*informal*) to be crazy or eccentric.
bat[3] *v.* (**bat·ted, bat·ting**) to flutter, *it batted its wings; didn't bat an eyelid,* did not show any surprise.
bat·boy (bat-boi) *n.* a boy or young man who assists baseball batters by taking care of their bats.
batch (bach) *n.* 1. a number of loaves or cakes baked at the same time. 2. a number of people or things dealt with as a group, *a batch of recruits.*
ba·teau (ba-toh) *n.* (*pl.* **-teaux**) a light river boat, especially the long, tapering, flat-bottomed boat used by French Canadians.
bat·ed (bay-tid) *adj.* lessened. □**with bated breath,** with breath held anxiously.
bath (bath) *n.* (*pl.* **baths,** *pr.* ba*thz,* baths) 1. washing of the whole body by immersing it in water. 2. water for this. 3. a bathtub. 4. a bathroom. 5. a liquid in which something is immersed,

its container. 6. *baths,* a building with rooms where baths may be taken.

bathe (bayth) *v.* **(bathed, bath·ing)** 1. to apply liquid to, to immerse in liquid. 2. to make wet or bright all over, *fields were bathed in sunlight.* 3. to swim for pleasure. **bath'er** *n.* ☐**bathing suit,** a garment worn for swimming.

bath·house (bath-hows) *n.* a building with dressing rooms for bathers.

ba·thos (bay-thos) *n.* 1. descent from something important to something trivial in speech or writing. 2. excessive pathos. **ba·thet·ic** (bă-thet-ik) *adj.*

bath·robe (bath-rohb) *n.* a loose garment, often of absorbent material and resembling a dressing gown, worn before and after a bath.

bath·room (bath-room) *n.* a room containing a bathtub or shower and usually a washbowl and toilet.

bath·tub (bath-tub) *n.* a large container for water, in which one sits to wash all over.

bath·y·scaphe (bath-ĭ-skayf), **bath·y·scape** (bath-ĭ-skayp) *n.* a vessel that can travel under water for deep-sea diving and exploration.

bath·y·sphere (bath-ĭ-sfeer) *n.* a spherical diving apparatus for deep-sea observation.

ba·tik (ba-teek) *n.* 1. a method of printing colored designs on textiles by waxing the parts not to be dyed. 2. a fabric treated in this way.

ba·tiste (ba-teest) *n.* a very soft fine woven fabric.

bat·man (bat-măn) *n.* (*pl.* **-men,** *pr.* -měn) *(British)* a soldier acting as an officer's orderly.

bat mitz·vah *see* **bas mitzvah.**

ba·ton (ba-ton) *n.* 1. a short thick stick, especially one serving as a symbol of authority, a truncheon. 2. a thin stick used by the conductor of an orchestra for beating time. 3. a short stick or tube carried in relay races.

Bat·on Rouge (bat-ŏn roozh) the capital of Louisiana.

ba·tra·chi·an (bă-tray-ki-ăn) *n.* a tailless amphibian, such as a frog or toad. **batrachian** *adj.*

bats·man (bats-măn) *n.* (*pl.* **-men,** *pr.* -měn) a player who is batting, especially in cricket.

bat·tal·ion (bă-tal-yŏn) *n.* 1. an army unit made up of several companies and forming part of a regiment. 2. *(informal)* a large organized body of people.

bat·ten[1] (bat-ĕn) *n.* a strip of wood or metal fastening or holding something in place. **batten** *v.* to fasten with battens; *batten down the hatches,* close them securely.

batten[2] *v.* 1. to make or become fat. 2. to thrive or prosper at the expense of others or so as to injure them, *politicians battening on graft.*

bat·ter (bat-ĕr) *v.* to hit hard and often; *battered babies, battered wives,* those subjected to repeated violence. **batter** *n.* 1. a beaten mixture of flour, eggs, and milk for cooking. 2. a player at bat in baseball. ☐**battering ram,** a beam formerly used in war to breach walls or gates.

bat·ter·y (bat-ě-ree) *n.* (*pl.* **-ter·ies**) 1. a group of big guns on land or on a warship. 2. an artillery unit of guns, men, and vehicles. 3. a set of similar or connected units or items, *a whole battery of telephones.* 4. an electric cell or group of cells supplying current. 5. unlawful blows or a menacing touch on a person or his clothes. 6. the pitcher and the catcher of a baseball team.

bat·ting (bat-ing) *n.* a cotton or wool in sheets, for quilting etc.

bat·tle (bat-ĕl) *n.* 1. a fight between large organized forces. 2. any contest, *a battle of wits.* 3. victory; *confidence is half the battle,* a help toward success. **battle** *v.* **(bat·tled, bat·tling)** to engage in battle, to struggle. ☐**battle cry,** a war cry, a slogan. **battle fatigue,** mental disorder due to stress in wartime combat.

bat·tle-ax (bat-ĕl-aks) *n.* 1. a heavy ax used as a weapon in ancient times. 2. *(informal)* a formidable aggressive woman.

bat·tle·field (bat-ĕl-feeld) *n.* a place where a battle is or was fought.

bat·tle·ground (bat-ĕl-grownd) *n.* a battlefield.

bat·tle·ment (bat-ĕl-měnt) *n.* a parapet with gaps at intervals, originally for firing from.

bat·tle·ship (bat-ĕl-ship) *n.* the most heavily armed and armored kind of warship.

bat·tle·wag·on (bat-ĕl-wag-ŏn) *n.* (*slang*) a battleship.

bat·ty (bat-ee) *adj.* **(-ti·er, -ti·est)** *(slang)* crazy. **bat'ti·ness** *n.*

bau·ble (baw-bĕl) *n.* a showy but valueless ornament or fancy article.

baux·ite (bawk-sıt) *n.* the claylike substance from which aluminum is obtained. **baux·it·ic** (bawk-sit-ik) *adj.*

bawd (bawd) *n.* a procuress.

bawd·y (baw-dee) *adj.* **(bawd·i·er, bawd·i·est)** humorous in a coarse or indecent way. **bawd'i·ly** *adv.* **bawd'i·ness** *n.*

bawl (bawl) *v.* to shout or cry loudly. **bawl** *n.* 1. a howl or shout. 2. loud weeping. ☐**bawl a person out,** *(informal)* to scold him severely.

bay[1] (bay) *n.* a kind of laurel with deep green leaves that are dried and used for seasoning. ☐**bay leaf,** this seasoning, used in soups, stews, etc.

bay[2] *n.* a part of the sea or of a large lake within a wide curve of the shore.

bay[3] *n.* a compartment or recess in a room, building, structure, or area, *a parking bay.* ☐**bay window,** a window projecting from the outside wall of a house; *(informal)* a man's large protruding stomach.

bay[4] *n.* the deep drawn-out cry of a large dog or of hounds in pursuit of a hunted animal. **bay** *v.* to make this sound. ☐**at bay,** forced to face attackers and showing defiance in a desperate situation. **hold at bay,** to ward off.

bay[5] *adj.* reddish-brown. **bay** *n.* a bay horse.

bay·ber·ry (bay-ber-ee) *n.* (*pl.* **-ries**) 1. a shrub of eastern North America, bearing small gray-green berries. 2. a West Indian tree, the leaves of which are used in making bay rum.

bay·o·net (bay-ŏ-nit) *n.* a daggerlike blade that can be fixed to the muzzle of a rifle and used in hand-to-hand fighting. **bayonet** *v.* **(bay·o·net·ed, bay·o·net·ing)** to stab with a bayonet.

bay·ou (bı-oo) *n.* (*pl.* **-ous**) a marshy inlet or stagnant creek.

bay rum a fragrant liquid made from bay leaves, used as an astringent.

ba·zaar (bă-zahr) *n.* 1. a series of shops or stalls, especially in an Oriental country. 2. a sale of goods to raise funds, especially for charity.

BB (bee-bee) *n.* a pellet shot for firing from an air rifle.

B.B.A. *abbr.* Bachelor of Business Administration.

B.B.B. *abbr.* Better Business Bureau.

B.B.C. *abbr.* British Broadcasting Corporation.

bbl. *abbr.* barrel.

B.C. *abbr.* 1. Before Christ. 2. British Columbia.

bd. *abbr.* 1. board. 2. bond. 3. bound.

B.D. *abbr.* Bachelor of Divinity.

bdl. *abbr.* bundle.

bdrm. *abbr.* bedroom.

be (bee) *v.* **(am, are, is; was, were; been; being)** 1. to exist, to occur, to live, to occupy a position. 2. to have a certain identity or quality or condition; *how much is it? what does it cost?* 3. to equal, to become, *he wants to be a pilot.* **be** *auxiliary verb,* used to form parts of other verbs, as in *it is rising; he was laughing; I am to inform you,* it is my duty to inform you. □**be-all and end-all,** the supreme purpose or essence. **be that as it may,** no matter what the facts about it may be. **have been,** to have visited, *I have been to Cairo.* **let it be,** do not disturb it, do not change it or act upon it. ▷Do not use *being as how* or *being that* in place of *because* or *as* in such expressions as *because he is here* and *as she was our principal speaker.*

Be *symbol* beryllium.

B.E. *abbr.* Board of Education.

beach (beech) *n.* the shore between high and low water mark, covered with sand or waterworn pebbles. **beach** *v.* to bring on shore from out of the water. □**beach buggy,** a car equipped with extra-large tires for beach use. **beach flea,** a small crustacean found on beaches.

beach·comb·er (beech-koh-měr) *n.* 1. a person who salvages stray articles along a beach. 2. a loafer who lives on what he can earn casually on a waterfront. **beach′comb·ing** *n.*

beach·head (beech-hed) *n.* a fortified position established on a beach by an invading army.

bea·con (bee-kŏn) *n.* 1. a signal fire on a hill. 2. a light used as a signal or warning. 3. a signal station such as a lighthouse. 4. a transmitter giving out a beam to direct aircraft. **beacon** *v.* 1. to give light to. 2. to guide. 3. to shine as a beacon.

bead (beed) *n.* 1. a small shaped piece of hard material pierced for threading with others on a string or wire, or for sewing on to fabric. 2. a drop or bubble of liquid on a surface. 3. *beads,* a necklace of beads, a rosary. **bead** *v.* to form into a bead. □**draw a bead on,** take aim at.

bead·ing (bee-ding) *n.* 1. a decoration of beads. 2. a molding or carving like a series of beads. 3. a strip of material with one side rounded, used as a trimming on edges of wood.

bea·dle (bee-děl) *n.* a parish officer appointed to serve as usher and to keep order in church.

bead·y (bee-dee) *adj.* **(bead·i·er, bead·i·est)** like beads; *beady eyes,* small and bright.

bea·gle (bee-gěl) *n.* a small hound used for hunting.

beak (beek) *n.* 1. a bird's horny projecting bill. 2. any similar projection. **beak′less** *adj.* **beak·like** (beek-lık) *adj.* **beaked** (beekt) *adj.*

bea·ker (bee-kěr) *n.* 1. a small open glass vessel with straight sides and a lip for pouring liquids, used in laboratories. 2. a large drinking cup, often with a wide mouth.

beam (beem) *n.* 1. a long piece of squared timber or other solid material, supported at both ends and carrying the weight of part of a building or other structure. 2. a ship's breadth at its widest part. 3. the crosspiece of a balance, from which the scales hang. 4. a ray or stream of light or other radiation, a radio signal used to direct the course of an aircraft. 5. a bright look, a radiant smile. **beam** *v.* 1. to send out light or other radiation. 2. to aim (radio waves, a radio or television broadcast, etc.) with directional antennas. 3. to

smile radiantly. □**broad in the beam,** *(informal)* wide at the hips.

bean[1] (been) *n.* 1. a plant bearing seeds in long pods. 2. its seed used as a vegetable. 3. a similar seed of coffee and other plants. □**bean curd,** a creamy white cake of soybean cheese used in Oriental cooking. **full of beans,** *(informal)* in high spirits; full of nonsense or petty lies.

bean[2] *v. (slang)* to hit on the head.

bean·ball (been-bawl) *n.* a baseball deliberately thrown by the pitcher at the batter's head.

bean·ie (bee-nee) *n.* a small close-fitting hat worn on the top of the head.

bean·pole (been-pohl) *n.* 1. a pole for supporting growing bean plants. 2. *(informal)* a tall thin person.

bear[1] (bair) *n.* 1. a large heavy animal with thick fur. 2. a rough ill-mannered person. 3. a speculator who sells shares etc. in expectation that prices will fall very soon. □**bear market,** (on the stock exchange) a situation in which stock prices are falling rapidly. **the Great Bear, the Little Bear,** constellations near the North Star.

bear[2] *v.* **(bore, borne, bear·ing;** see the note under **borne).** 1. to carry, to support; *bear oneself bravely,* to behave bravely. 2. to have or show a certain mark or characteristic, *he still bears the scar; bears an honored name,* has it as his own or a family name. 3. to have in one's heart or mind, *bear a grudge; I will bear it in mind,* will remember it. 4. to endure, to tolerate, *grin and bear it.* 5. to be fit for, *his words won't bear repeating.* 6. to produce, to give birth to, *she had borne him two sons.* 7. to turn, to diverge, *bear right when the road forks.* 8. to exert pressure, to thrust. □**bear down,** to press downward; to work harder. **bear down on,** to move rapidly or purposefully toward. **bear on,** to be relevant to, *matters bearing on public health.* **bear out,** to confirm. **bear up,** to be strong enough not to give way or despair. **bear with,** to tolerate patiently. **bear witness to,** to provide evidence of the truth of. **it was borne in upon him,** he was convinced.

bear·a·ble (bair-ă-běl) *adj.* able to be borne, endurable. **bear′a·bly** *adv.*

beard (beerd) *n.* 1. hair on and around a man's chin. 2. a similar hairy or bristly growth of hair on an animal or plant. **beard** *v.* to confront boldly; *beard the lion in his den,* confront and oppose someone in his own stronghold. **beard·ed** (beer-did) *adj.* **beard′less** *adj.*

bear·er (bair-ěr) *n.* 1. a person who carries or bears something; *this check is payable to the bearer,* to the person who presents it at a bank. 2. a person who helps to carry something, (as a coffin to the grave, a stretcher).

bear·ing (bair-ing) *n.* 1. deportment, behavior, *a military bearing.* 2. relationship, relevance, *it has no bearing on this problem.* 3. a compass direction; *get one's bearings,* find out where one is by recognizing landmarks etc. 4. a device reducing friction in a part of a machine where another part turns.

bear·skin (bair-skin) *n.* 1. the skin or fur of a bear. 2. a rug, coat, hat, etc. made from this.

beast (beest) *n.* 1. a large four-footed animal. 2. a cruel or disgusting person.

beast·ly (beest-lee) *adj.* **(-li·er, -li·est)** 1. like a beast or its ways. 2. abominable, very unpleasant. **beastly** *adv.* very unpleasantly, *it was beastly cold.* **beast′li·ness** *n.*

beat[1] (beet) *v.* **(beat, beat·en, beat·ing)** 1. to

hit repeatedly, especially with a stick; *we heard the drums beating,* being beaten. 2. to strike; *the sun beat down,* shone with great heat. 3. to shape or flatten by blows; *beat a path,* make it by trampling things down. 4. to mix vigorously to a frothy or smooth consistency, *beat the eggs.* 5. (of the heart) to expand and contract rhythmically. 6. to overcome, to do better than, to act or arrive before (another); *it beats me,* is too difficult for me. ☐**beat about the bush,** to discuss a subject without coming to the point. **beat a person down,** to cause a seller to lower the price he is asking. **beat a retreat,** to go away defeated. **beaten path** or **track,** a well-worn path, the expected or usual way. **beat it,** *(slang)* to go away. **beat off,** to drive off by fighting. **beat up,** to assault violently with the fists.

beat[2] *n.* 1. a regular repeated stroke, a sound of this. 2. a recurring emphasis marking rhythm in music or poetry, the strongly marked rhythm of popular music. 3. the appointed round of a policeman or newspaper reporter; the area covered by this. 4. a beatnik.

beat[3] *adj.* 1. tired. 2. relating to young people of the 1960's with unconventional dress and behavior as an expression of social philosophy, *the beat generation.*

beat·er (bee-tĕr) *n.* 1. an implement for beating things. 2. a person employed to drive game out of cover toward those waiting with guns to shoot it.

be·a·tif·ic (bee-ă-tif-ik) *adj.* showing great happiness, *a beatific smile.*

be·at·i·fi·ca·tion (bi-at-ĭ-fi-kay-shŏn) *n.* the pope's official statement that a dead person is among the blessed in heaven, the first step toward canonization.

be·at·i·fy (bi-at-ĭ-fı̄) *v.* (**be·at·i·fied, be·at·i·fy·ing**) to honor by beatification.

beat·ing (bee-ting) *n.* 1. punishment by being hit with a stick etc. 2. a defeat.

be·at·i·tude (bi-at-ĭ-tood) *n.* blessedness. ☐**the Beatitudes,** the declarations made by Jesus in the Sermon on the Mount, beginning "Blessed are. . . ."

beat·nik (beet-nik) *n.* a member of the beat generation (*see* **beat**[3]).

beau (boh) *n.* (*pl.* **beaus, beaux,** *pr.* bohz) 1. a fop or dandy. 2. a suitor or sweetheart.

Beau·fort (boh-fŏrt) **scale** a scale and description of wind velocity ranging from (calm) to (hurricane).

beau geste (boh *zh*est) (*pl.* **beaux gestes,** *pr.* boh *zh*est) a display of generous conduct.

beau i·deal (boh ı̄-deel) one's highest or ideal type of excellence or beauty.

Beau·jo·lais (boh-*zh*ŏ-lay) *n.* a red or white burgundy wine from Beaujolais, France.

beau monde (boh mond) fashionable society.

beaut (byoot) *n.* (*slang*) a beauty, a fine specimen, *when I make a mistake, it's a beaut.*

beau·te·ous (byoo-ti-ŭs) *adj.* (*old use*) beautiful. **beau'te·ous·ly** *adv.* **beau'te·ous·ness** *n.*

beau·ti·cian (byoo-tish-ăn) *n.* a person whose job is to give beautifying treatments to the face or body.

beau·ti·ful (byoo-ti-fŭl) *adj.* 1. having beauty, giving pleasure to the senses or the mind. 2. (*informal*) very satisfactory. **beau'ti·ful·ly** *adv.* ☐**beautiful people,** wealthy trendsetters, fashionable people.

beau·ti·fy (byoo-ti-fı̄) *v.* (**beau·ti·fied, beau·ti·fy·ing**) to make beautiful. **beau·ti·fi·ca·tion** (byoo-ti-fi-kay-shŏn) *n.* **beau'ti·fi·er** *n.*

beau·ty (byoo-tee) *n.* (*pl.* **-ties**) 1. a combination of qualities that give pleasure to the sight or other senses or to the mind. 2. a person or thing having this, a beautiful woman. 3. a fine specimen, *here's a beauty.* 4. a beautiful feature; *that's the beauty of it,* the point that gives satisfaction. ☐**beauty parlor** or **shop,** a beauty salon. **beauty queen,** a woman judged to be the most beautiful in a competition. **beauty salon,** an establishment for giving beautifying treatments to the face, body, etc. **beauty sleep,** sleep that is said to make or keep a person beautiful. **beauty spot,** a place with beautiful scenery; a birthmark or artificial patch on the face, said to heighten beauty.

beaux arts (bohz ahr) the fine arts.

bea·ver (bee-vĕr) *n.* 1. a soft-furred animal with strong teeth that lives both on land and in water. 2. its brown fur. 3. (*informal*) a hard worker.

be·calm (bi-kahm) *v.* to make (a sailing ship) unable to move because of lack of wind. **be·calmed'** *adj.*

be·came (bi-kaym) *see* **become.**

be·cause (bi-kawz) *conj.* for the reason that, *did it because I was asked.* **because** *adv.* by reason, on account, *because of his age.* ▷Do not say or write *the reason is because.* Also see the note under **due.**

bé·cha·mel (bay-shă-mel) **sauce** a rich white sauce of butter, flour, cream, and seasoning.

beck (bek) *n.* a beckoning gesture. ☐**at someone's beck and call,** always ready and waiting to obey his orders.

beck·on (bek-ŏn) *v.* 1. to signal or summon by a gesture. 2. to attract.

be·cloud (bi-klowd) *v.* 1. to cover with clouds. 2. to obscure.

be·come (bi-kum) *v.* (**be·came, be·come, be·com·ing**) 1. to come or grow to be, to begin to be, *she became a doctor; ask what has become of it,* ask what happened to it, or where it is. 2. to suit, to be becoming to.

be·com·ing (bi-kum-ing) *adj.* giving a pleasing appearance or effect, suitable. **be·com'ing·ly** *adv.*

bed (bed) *n.* 1. a thing to sleep or rest on, a piece of furniture with a mattress and coverings. 2. a mattress, *a feather bed.* 3. the use of a bed, being in bed, *a quick drink and then bed; go to bed,* retire there to sleep. 4. a flat base on which something rests, a foundation. 5. the bottom of the sea or river etc. 6. a layer, *a bed of clay.* 7. a garden plot for plants. **bed** *v.* (**bed·ded, bed·ding**) 1. to provide with a place to sleep, to put to bed. 2. to place or fix in a foundation, *the bricks are bedded in concrete.* 3. to plant in a garden bed, *he was bedding out seedlings.* ☐**no bed of roses,** not a pleasant or easy situation.

be·daub (bi-dawb) *v.* to smear or daub with paint, mud, etc.

be·daz·zle (bi-daz-ĕl) *v.* (**be·daz·zled, be·daz·zling**) 1. to dazzle completely. 2. to confuse (a person). **be·daz'zle·ment** *n.*

bed·bug (bed-bug) *n.* a bloodsucking insect infesting beds.

bed·ding (bed-ing) *n.* mattresses and bedclothes.

be·deck (bi-dek) *v.* to adorn.

be·dev·il (bi-dev-ĭl) *v.* (**be·dev·iled, be·dev·il·ing**) to torment diabolically, to plague. **be·dev'il·ment** *n.*

be·dew (bi-doo, -dyoo) *v.* to cover with drops of or like dew.

bed·fast (bed-fast) *adj.* bedridden.

bed·fel·low (bed-fel-oh) *n.* 1. a person who shares one's bed. 2. an associate; *politics makes strange bedfellows,* obliges unlikely people to associate together.

be·di·zen (bi-dɪ-zĕn) *v.* to deck out gaudily.

bed·lam (bed-lăm) *n.* 1. *(old use)* a mental institution. 2. a scene of uproar.

Bed·ou·in (bed-oo-in) *n.* (*pl.* **-ins, -in**) a member of an Arab people living in tents in the desert.

bed·pan (bed-pan) *n.* a pan for use as a toilet by a person confined to bed.

bed·post (bed-pohst) *n.* one of the upright supports of a bedstead.

be·drag·gled (bi-drag-ĕld) *adj.* hanging in a limp untidy way, especially when wet or when dirty and disordered.

bed·rid·den (bed-rid-ĕn) *n.* confined to bed through illness or weakness, especially permanently.

bed·rock (bed-rok) *n.* 1. solid rock beneath loose soil. 2. basic facts or principles.

bed·roll (bed-rohl) *n.* bedding rolled into a bundle.

bed·room (bed-room) *n.* a room for sleeping in.

bed·side (bed-sɪd) *n.* a position by a bed; *a bedside table,* one for placing by a bed. □**bedside manner,** the attitude of a doctor toward his patient.

bed·sore (bed-sohr) *n.* a sore developed by lying in bed for a long time.

bed·spread (bed-spred) *n.* a covering spread over a bed during the day.

bed·stead (bed-sted) *n.* a wooden or metal framework supporting the springs and mattress of a bed.

bed·time (bed-tɪm) *n.* a time for going to bed.

bee (bee) *n.* 1. a four-winged stinging insect that produces wax and honey after gathering nectar from flowers. 2. a neighborly gathering for work and socializing, as a *husking bee* (to husk corn) or *quilting bee* (to sew patchwork quilts). □**have a bee in one's bonnet,** to have a particular idea that occupies one's thoughts continually. **make a beeline for,** to go straight or rapidly toward. **spelling bee,** a competiton in spelling.

beech (beech) *n.* (*pl.* **beech·es** or **beech**) 1. a kind of tree with smooth bark and glossy leaves. 2. its wood. 3. (also *beechnut*) its small triangular nut. **beech'en** *adj.*

beef (beef) *n.* (*pl.* **beeves,** *pr.* beevz, for 2; **beefs** for 4) 1. the flesh of a steer, bull, or cow used as meat. 2. the animal itself. 3. muscular strength, brawn. 4. *(slang)* a complaint. **beef** *v. (slang)* to complain. □**beef tea,** the juice from stewed beef, for invalids. **beef up,** *(informal)* to strengthen.

beef·burg·er (beef-bur-gĕr) *n.* a hamburger.

beef·eat·er (beef-ee-tĕr) *n.* a guard in the Tower of London, or a member of the Yeomen of the Guard, wearing Tudor dress as uniform.

beef·steak (beef-stayk) *n.* a slice of beef for broiling or frying.

beef·y (bee-fee) *adj.* (**beef·i·er, beef·i·est**) having a solid muscular body. **beef'i·ness** *n.*

bee·hive (bee-hɪv) *n.* a hive.

bee·keep·er (bee-kee-pĕr) *n.* a person who raises bees. **bee'keep·ing** *n.*

been (bin) *see* **be.**

beer (beer) *n.* an alcoholic drink brewed from malt and hops.

beer·y (beer-ee) *adj.* (**beer·i·er, beer·i·est**) like beer, smelling of beer.

bees·wax (beez-waks) *n.* a yellowish substance secreted by bees, used for polishing wood.

beet (beet) *n.* a plant with a fleshy root used as a vegetable or for making sugar.

bee·tle¹ (bee-tĕl) *n.* an insect with four wings, the outer pair being hard.

beetle² *v.* (**bee·tled, bee·tling**) to overhang, to project. **beetle** *adj.* projecting. □**beetle browed,** with projecting brows; scowling, lowering.

be·fall (bi-fawl) *v.* (**be·fell, be·fall·en, be·fall·ing**) *(formal)* to happen, to happen to.

be·fit (bi-fit) *v.* (**be·fit·ted, be·fit·ting**) to be right and suitable for. **be·fit'ting·ly** *adv.*

be·fog (bi-fog) *v.* (**be·fogged, be·fog·ging**) 1. to envelop in fog. 2. to confuse, to obscure.

be·fore (bi-fohr) *adv., conj. & prep.* 1. at an earlier time, earlier than. 2. ahead, ahead of, in front of; *they sailed before the wind,* under its impulse, with the wind behind them; *appeared before the judge,* in his presence for judgment. 3. rather than, in preference to, *death before dishonor!* □**before Christ,** before the birth of Christ.

be·fore·hand (bi-fohr-hand) *adv.* in advance, in readiness.

be·foul (bi-fowl) *v.* to make foul or dirty.

be·friend (bi-frend) *v.* to act as a friend to, to be kind and helpful to.

be·fud·dle (bi-fud-ĕl) *v.* (**be·fud·dled, be·fud·dling**) 1. to stupefy with alcohol. 2. to confuse. **be·fud'dler** *n.* **be·fud'dle·ment** *n.*

beg (beg) *v.* (**begged, beg·ging**) 1. to ask for as charity or as a gift, to obtain a living in this way. 2. to request earnestly or humbly. 3. to ask for formally, *I beg your pardon; beg to differ,* take the liberty of disagreeing. 4. (of a dog) to sit up expectantly, as it has been trained, with forepaws off the ground. □**beg off,** to ask to be excused from doing something. **beg the question,** to use circular reasoning (*see* **circular** definition 3). **go begging,** (of things) to be available but unwanted.

be·get (bi-get) *v.* (**be·got, be·got·ten, be·get·ting**) 1. to be the father of. 2. to give rise to, *war begets misery and ruin.*

beg·gar (beg-ăr) *n.* a person who lives by begging, a very poor person. **beggar** *v.* 1. to reduce to poverty. 2. to make seem poor or inadequate; *the scenery beggars description,* is so magnificent that any description is inadequate. **beg'gar·y** *n.*

beg·gar·ly (beg-ăr-lee) *adj.* 1. poverty-stricken. 2. mean and insufficient, *a beggarly salary.*

be·gin (bi-gin) *v.* (**be·gan, be·gun, be·gin·ning**) 1. to perform the earliest or first part of some activity, to be the first to do something; *I can't begin to thank you,* cannot thank you enough. 2. to come into existence, to arise. 3. to have its first element or starting point. □**to begin with,** as the first thing.

be·gin·ner (bi-gin-ĕr) *n.* a person who is just beginning to learn a skill.

be·gin·ning (bi-gin-ing) *n.* 1. the first part. 2. the starting point, the source or origin.

be·gone (bi-gawn) *v.* (especially as a command) to go away immediately, *begone with you!*

be·go·nia (bi-gohn-yă) *n.* a garden plant with brightly colored leaves and flowers.

be·grime (bi-grɪm) *v.* (**be·grimed, be·grim·ing**) to make dirty.

be·grudge (bi-gruj) *v.* (**be·grudged, be·grudg·ing**) 1. to grudge. 2. to do, give, or concede reluctantly or with ill will or annoyance.

be·guile (bi-gɪl) *v.* **(be·guiled, be·guil·ing)** 1. to deceive. 2. to win the attention or interest of, to amuse. 3. to coax by flattery or cunning. **be·guile′ment** *n.*

be·guine (bi-geen) *n.* 1. a native dance of tropical America. 2. a ballroom dance based on this. 3. a kind of syncopated bolero dance rhythm.

be·gum (bee-gŭm) *n.* an Indian Muslim woman of high rank.

be·gun (bi-gun) *see* begin.

be·half (bi-haf) *n.* **on behalf of,** in aid of; as the representative of, *speaking on behalf of his client.*

be·have (bi-hayv) *v.* **(be·haved, be·hav·ing)** 1. to act, react, or function in some specified way. 2. to show good manners, *the child must learn to behave* or *to behave himself.*

be·hav·ior (bi-hayv-yŏr) *n.* a way of behaving, treatment of others, manners; *on one's best behavior,* taking care to behave well. **be·hav·ior·al** (bi-hayv-yŏ-răl) *adj.*

be·hav·ior·ism (bi-hayv-yŏ-riz-ĕm) *n.* a school of psychology holding that psychological understanding should be based only on observation of animal and human behavior and stressing the importance of environmental factors in determining this behavior.

be·head (bi-hed) *v.* to cut the head from, to execute (a person) in this way.

be·he·moth (bi-hee-mŏth) *n.* an enormous creature.

be·hest (bi-hest) *n.* 1. a command. 2. an earnest request.

be·hind (bi-hɪnd) *adv.* 1. in or to the rear; *he was lagging behind,* did not keep up with the others; *stayed behind,* stayed after others had left. 2. late, slow. **behind** *prep.* 1. in the rear of, on the farther side of; *put the past behind you,* recognize that it is over and done with. 2. causing or supporting; *ask what lies behind his refusal,* what causes it; *the man behind the project,* supporting or promoting it. 3. having made less progress than, *two students are far behind the rest of the class.* 4. later than, *we are behind schedule; behind time,* unpunctual. □**behind a person's back,** kept secret from him deceitfully. **behind the scenes,** backstage, hidden from public view or knowledge. **behind the times,** having out-of-date ideas or practices. ▷See the note at back[2].

be·hold (bi-hohld) *v.* **(be·held, be·hold·ing)** to see, to observe. **be·hold′er** *n.*

be·hold·en (bi-hohl-děn) *adj.* owing thanks, *we don't want to be beholden to anybody.*

be·hoove (bi-hoov) *v.* **(be·hooved, be·hoov·ing)** to be obligatory for, to befit.

beige (bayzh) *n.* a light fawn color.

Bei·jing (bay-jeeng) = Peking.

be·ing (bee-ing) *n.* 1. existence; *come into being,* begin to exist; *the greatest army in being,* in existence. 2. something that exists and has life, especially a person. □**the Supreme Being,** God.

Bei·rut (bay-root) the capital of Lebanon.

be·la·bor (bi-lay-bŏr) *v.* 1. to thrash, to beat repeatedly. 2. to discuss at unreasonable length.

be·lat·ed (bi-lay-tid) *adj.* coming very late or too late. **be·lat′ed·ly** *adv.*

be·lay (bi-lay) *v.* **(be·layed, be·lay·ing)** to coil (a running rope) around a cleat etc. to secure it. **belay** *interj.* (used by seamen) stop! □**belaying pin,** a fixed wooden or iron pin for belaying on.

belch (belch) *v.* 1. to send out wind from the stomach noisily through the mouth. 2. to send out from an opening or funnel, to gush, *the chimney was belching smoke; smoke belched out.* **belch** *n.* an act or sound of belching.

be·lea·guer (bi-lee-gěr) *v.* to besiege. **be·lea′guered** *adj.* **be·lea′guer·er** *n.*

Bel·fast (bel-fast) the capital of Northern Ireland.

bel·fry (bel-free) *n.* (*pl.* **-fries**) a bell tower, a space for bells in a tower.

Belg. *abbr.* Belgium.

Bel·gium (bel-jŭm) a country in Europe. **Bel·gian** (bel-jăn) *adj.* & *n.*

Bel·grade (bel-grayd) the capital of Yugoslavia.

be·lie (bi-lɪ) *v.* **(be·lied, be·ly·ing)** 1. to show to be false. 2. to fail to justify or fulfill. 3. to give a false impression of.

be·lief (bi-leef) *n.* 1. the feeling that something is real and true, trust, confidence. 2. something accepted as true, what one believes. 3. religion, something taught as part of this, *Christian beliefs.*

be·liev·a·ble (bi-lee-vă-běl) *adj.* able to be believed.

be·lieve (bi-leev) *v.* **(be·lieved, be·liev·ing)** 1. to accept as true or as speaking or conveying truth. 2. to have religious faith, to believe in God. 3. to think, to suppose, *I believe it's raining.* □**believe in,** to have faith in the existence of; to feel sure of the value or worth of.

be·liev·er (bi-lee-věr) *n.* a person who believes, one with religious faith.

be·lit·tle (bi-lit-ěl) *v.* **(be·lit·tled, be·lit·tling)** to imply that (a thing) is unimportant or of little value.

bell (bel) *n.* 1. a cup-shaped metal instrument that makes a ringing sound when struck. 2. the sound of this, especially as a signal; *one to eight bells,* the strokes of a ship's bell, indicating the half hours of each four-hour watch; *eight bells,* 12, 4, or 8 o'clock. 3. a bell-shaped thing. **bell** *v.* 1. to hang a bell on, *who will bell the cat?* 2. to widen out like a bell lip. □**bell jar,** a bell-shaped glass used to protect instruments or contain gases etc. in a laboratory.

bel·la·don·na (bel-ă-don-ă) *n.* 1. deadly nightshade. 2. dried parts of this, containing atropine and related alkaloids, used in medicine as a narcotic and to dilate the pupils of the eyes.

bell·bot·tom (bel-bot-ŏm) *adj.* widening from knee to ankle, *bell-bottom trousers.* □**bell-bottoms,** bell-bottom trousers.

bell·boy (bel-boi) *n.* a man employed by a hotel or club to carry luggage, run errands, etc.

belle (bel) *n.* a beautiful and charming woman.

belles-let·tres (bel-let-rě) 1. literary studies and writings. 2. these as a branch of literature. ▷French.

bell·hop (bel-hop) *n.* a bellboy.

bel·li·cose (bel-ĭ-kohs) *adj.* belligerent, eager to make war. **bel′li·cose·ly** *adv.* **bel′li·cose·ness** *n.* **bel·li·cos·i·ty** (bel-ĭ-kos-ĭ-tee) *n.*

bel·lig·er·ent (bi-lij-ě-rěnt) *adj.* 1. waging a war, *the belligerent nations.* 2. aggressive, showing eagerness to fight, *a belligerent reply.* **bel·lig′er·ent·ly** *adv.* **bel·lig′er·ence** *n.* **bel·lig′er·en·cy** *n.*

bel·low (bel-oh) *n.* 1. the loud deep sound made by a bull. 2. a deep shout. **bellow** *v.* to utter a bellow.

bel·lows (bel-ohz) *n. sing.* or *pl.* 1. an apparatus for driving air into or through something; *a pair* *of bellows,* two-handled bellows for blowing air into a fire. 2. a device or part that can be expanded or flattened in a series of folds.

bell·weth·er (bel-we*th*-ĕr) *n.* 1. the leading sheep of the flock, with a bell on its neck. 2. any leader.

bel·ly (bel-ee) *n.* (*pl.* **-lies**) 1. the abdomen. 2. the stomach. 3. a bulging or rounded part of something. **belly** *v.* (**bel·lied, bel·ly·ing**) to swell out, *the sails bellied out; wind bellied out the sails.* ◻**belly dance,** an oriental dance by a woman, with erotic movement of the belly; *(v.)* to perform this. **belly dancer,** one who performs a belly dance. **belly flop,** an awkward dive in which the body hits the water almost horizontally. **belly laugh,** a deep loud laugh.

bel·ly·ache (bel-ee-ayk) *n.* a pain in the abdomen or stomach. **bellyache** *v.* (**bel·ly·ached, bel·ly·ach·ing**) *(slang)* to complain.

bel·ly·but·ton (bel-ee-but-ŏn) *n.* (*informal*) the navel.

bel·ly·ful (bel-ee-fŭl) *n.* (*pl.* **-fuls**) (*informal*) as much as one wants or rather more.

be·long (bi-lawng) *v.* 1. to be rightly assigned as property or as a part, appendage, inhabitant, etc., *the house belongs to me; that lid belongs to this jar.* 2. to be a member, *we belong to the club.* 3. to have a rightful or usual place, *the pans belong in the kitchen.*

be·long·ings (bi-lawng-ingz) *n. pl.* personal possessions.

Be·lo·rus·sia (byel-oh-**rush**-ă) a republic in the western U.S.S.R. **Be·lo·rus′sian** *adj. & n.*

be·loved (bi-luvd) *adj.* dearly loved, *she was beloved by all.* **be·lov·ed** (bi-luv-id) *adj. & n.* darling, *my beloved wife; my beloved.*

be·low (bi-loh) *adv.* 1. at or to a lower position, downstream. 2. at the foot of a page, further on in a book or article, *see chapter six below.* 3. on Earth (as opposed to *above* = in heaven). 4. in hell. **below** *prep.* 1. lower in position, amount, rank, etc. than. 2. downstream from, *the bridge is below the ford.*

belt (belt) *n.* 1. a strip of cloth or leather worn around the waist. 2. a continuous moving strap passing over pulleys and so driving machinery, *a fan belt.* 3. a long narrow region or strip, *a belt of rain will move eastward.* 4. *(slang)* a heavy blow. 5. *(slang)* a drink of whiskey. **belt** *v.* 1. to put a belt around. 2. to attach with a belt. 3. to thrash with a belt, *(slang)* to hit with the hand. 4. *(slang)* to drink (whiskey). ◻**belt out,** *(slang)* to sing or play loudly, *belting out pop songs.* **hit below the belt,** to give an unfair blow, to fight unfairly. **under one's belt,** (*informal*) eaten; obtained or achieved.

belt·way (belt-way) *n.* a highway circling a city or metropolitan area.

be·lu·ga (bi-loo-gă) *n.* 1. a white sturgeon, valued as a source of caviar. 2. a white whale.

bel·ve·dere (bel-vĕ-deer) *n.* a raised turret, or a summerhouse, from which to view scenery.

be·mire (bi-mɪr) *v.* (**be·mired, be·mir·ing**) 1. to cover or stain with mud. 2. to cause to be stuck in mud.

be·moan (bi-mohn) *v.* to lament.

be·mused (bi-myoozd) *adj.* 1. bewildered. 2. lost in thought.

bench (bench) *n.* 1. a long seat for two or more persons. 2. *the bench,* the seat of a judge in a law court, the judge or judges hearing a case, a law court. 3. a long working table. 4. seating for team members not participating in a game, or waiting their turn at bat in baseball. ◻**bench mark,** a surveyor's mark put on a stone etc. to indicate a point of known height above sea level. **bench warrant,** one issued by a judge.

bend (bend) *v.* (**bent, bend·ing**) 1. to force out of straightness, to make curved or angular. 2. to become curved or angular. 3. to turn downward, to stoop. 4. to turn in a new direction, *they bent their steps homeward; bend your mind to this,* give it your attention. 5. to draw (a bow) taut. 6. to apply one's efforts, *bend to it.* 7. to yield or force to yield, *bend them to my will.* **bend** *n.* 1. a curve or turn. 2. a kind of knot used to fasten a rope. 3. *the bends,* caisson disease. ◻**bend the rules,** to interpret them loosely to suit oneself. **on bended knees,** kneeling in prayer or supplication.

bend·er (ben-dĕr) *n.* *(slang)* a spree.

be·neath (bi-neeth) *adv. & prep.* 1. below, under, underneath. 2. not worthy of, not befitting; *beneath contempt,* not even worth despising.

ben·e·dict (ben-ĕ-dikt) *n.* a newly married man, especially one who has long been a bachelor.

Ben·e·dic·tine (ben-ĕ-dik-tin) *n.* 1. a monk of the order founded by St. Benedict. 2. a liqueur originally made by monks of this order.

ben·e·dic·tion (ben-ĕ-dik-shŏn) *n.* a spoken blessing.

ben·e·fac·tion (ben-ĕ-fak-shŏn) *n.* 1. the act of doing good. 2. a charitable gift.

ben·e·fac·tor (ben-ĕ-fak-tŏr) *n.* a person who gives financial or other help. **ben·e·fac·tress** (ben-ĕ-fak-tris) *n. fem.*

ben·e·fice (ben-ĕ-fis) *n.* 1. a position that provides a clergyman with a livelihood. 2. the income from this.

ben·ef·i·cence (bĕ-nef-i-sĕns) *n.* an act of kindness.

ben·ef·i·cent (bĕ-nef-i-sĕnt) *adj.* doing good, showing active kindness.

ben·e·fi·cial (ben-ĕ-fish-ăl) *adj.* having a helpful or useful effect. **ben·e·fi′cial·ly** *adv.*

ben·e·fi·ci·ar·y (ben-ĕ-fish-i-er-ee) *n.* (*pl.* **-ar·ies**) a person who receives a benefit, one who is left a legacy under someone's will.

ben·e·fit (ben-ĕ-fit) *n.* 1. something helpful, favorable, or profitable. 2. an allowance of money etc. to which a person is entitled from an insurance policy, from government funds, or from his employment, *death benefits.* 3. a performance or game held in order to raise money for a particular player, *a benefit performance.* **benefit** *v.* (**ben·e·fit·ed, ben·e·fit·ing**) 1. to do good to. 2. to receive benefit. ◻**benefit of the doubt,** the assumption that a person is innocent (or right) rather than guilty (or wrong) when nothing can be fully proved either way.

Ben·e·lux (ben-ĕ-luks) Belgium, the Netherlands, and Luxembourg, considered as a group.

be·nev·o·lent (bĕ-nev-ŏ-lĕnt) *adj.* 1. wishing to do good to others, kindly and helpful. 2. charitable, *a benevolent association.* **be·nev′o·lent·ly** *adv.* **be·nev′o·lence** *n.*

Ben·gal (ben-gawl) a former province of northeast India, now divided into West Bengal (a state of India) and Bangladesh.

Ben·gal·i (ben-gaw-lee) *adj.* of Bengal or its people or language. **Bengali** *n.* (*pl.* **-gal·is**) a native or the language of Bengal.

be·night·ed (bi-nɪ-tid) *adj.* 1. overtaken by night.

2. in intellectual or moral darkness, ignorant.
be·nign (bi-nīn) *adj.* 1. kindly. 2. mild and gentle in its effect; *a benign tumor,* one that is not malignant. **be·nign'ly** *adv.*
be·nig·nant (bi-nig-nănt) *adj.* kindly.
Be·nin (be-neen) a country in West Africa, formerly Dahomey.
ben·i·son (ben-i-zŏn) *n.* (*old use*) a blessing.
ben·ny (ben-ee) *n.* (pl. **-nies**) (*slang*) an amphetamine tablet.
bent (bent) *see* **bend. bent** *n.* a natural skill or liking, *she has a bent for needlework.* □**bent on,** determined or seeking to do something, *bent on mischief.*
ben·ton·ite (ben-tŏ-nīt) *n.* a kind of clay used as an absorbent, filler, etc. **ben·ton·it·ic** (ben-tŏ-nit-ik) *adj.*
bent·wood (bent-wuud) *n.* wood that has been artificially bent into a permanent curve, used for making chairs etc. □**bentwood rocker,** a rocking chair made of this.
be·numb (bi-num) *v.* to make numb or torpid, to paralyze.
Ben·ze·drine (ben-zĕ-dreen) *n.* (*trademark*) an amphetamine.
ben·zene (ben-zeen) *n.* a colorless liquid obtained from petroleum and coal tar, used as a solvent, as fuel, and in the manufacture of plastics. □**benzene ring,** a ringlike hexagonal arrangement of the six carbon atoms in the benzene molecule.
ben·zine (ben-zeen) *n.* a colorless liquid mixture of hydrocarbons obtained from petroleum and used as a solvent in dry cleaning.
ben·zo·ate (ben-zoh-ayt) *n.* a salt or ester of benzoic acid.
ben·zo·ic (ben-zoh-ik) **acid** benzene carboxylic acid.
ben·zo·in (ben-zoh-in) *n.* (also **gum benzoin**) a fragrant resin obtained from various trees of Sumatra and Thailand, and used in perfumery, medicine, etc. **ben·zo·ic** (ben-zoh-ik) *adj.*
ben·zol (ben-zohl) *n.* benzene.
be·queath (bi-kweeth) *v.* to leave as a legacy.
be·quest (bi-kwest) *n.* a legacy.
be·rate (bi-rayt) *v.* (**be·rat·ed, be·rat·ing**) to scold.
Ber·ber (bur-bĕr) *n.* a member of a fair-skinned aboriginal people of North Africa.
be·reave (bi-reev) *v.* (**be·reaved, be·reav·ing**) to deprive, especially of a relative, by death; *the bereaved husband,* the man whose wife died. **be·reave'ment** *n.*
be·reft (bĕ-reft) *adj.* deprived; *bereft of reason,* driven mad.
be·ret (bĕ-ray) *n.* a round flat cap with no peak.
berg (burg) *n.* (*informal*) an iceberg.
ber·i·ber·i (ber-ee-ber-ee) *n.* a disease affecting the nervous system, caused by lack of thiamine (vitamin B_1).
berke·li·um (burk-li-ŭm) *n.* a metallic radioactive synthetic element.
Ber·lin (bĕr-lin) former capital of Germany, now divided into **East Berlin** and **West Berlin.**
Ber·mu·da (bĕr-myoo-dă) a group of islands in the West Atlantic. **Ber·mu'dan** *adj.* □**Bermuda shorts,** knee-length shorts. **Bermuda triangle,** an area of the Atlantic Ocean where ships and airplanes are said to have vanished mysteriously.
Berne, Bern (burn) the capital of Switzerland.

ber·ry (ber-ee) *n.* (*pl.* **-ries**) a small round juicy stoneless fruit.
ber·serk (bĕr-surk) *adj.* frenzied. □**go berserk,** to go into an uncontrollable and destructive rage.
berth (burth) *n.* 1. a bunk or sleeping place in a ship or train. 2. a place for a ship to swing at anchor or tie up at a wharf. 3. a job, employment. **berth** *v.* to moor at a berth. □**give a wide berth to,** to keep at a safe distance from.
ber·yl (ber-ĭl) *n.* a transparent usually green precious stone.
be·ryl·li·um (bĕ-ril-i-ŭm) *n.* a very light metallic element obtained from beryl.
be·seech (bi-seech) *v.* (**be·sought, be·seech·ing**) to implore.
be·seem (bi-seem) *v.* (*old use*) to be fitting or seemly.
be·set (bi-set) *v.* (**be·set, be·set·ting**) to hem in, to surround; *the temptations that beset people,* that face them on all sides.
be·set·ting (bi-set-ing) *adj.* habitually affecting or troubling a person.
be·side (bi-sīd) *prep.* 1. at the side of, close to. 2. compared with, *his work looks poor beside yours.* 3. wide of, having nothing to do with, *that's beside the point.* □**be beside oneself,** to be at the end of one's self-control, *he was beside himself with rage.* ▷Do not confuse *beside* with *besides.* Do not write *beside roast beef, they asked for shrimp cocktails;* write *besides* or *in addition to.*
be·sides (bi-sīdz) *prep.* in addition to, other than, *he has no income besides his pension.* **besides** *adv.* also, moreover, *besides, I have no desire to offend her.* ▷Do not confuse *besides* with *beside.*
be·siege (bi-seej) *v.* (**be·sieged, be·sieg·ing**) 1. to lay siege to. 2. to crowd around with requests or questions. **be·sieg'er** *n.*
be·smear (bi-smeer) *v.* to smear, to daub.
be·smirch (bi-smurch) *v.* to soil, to sully. **be·smirch'er** *n.* **be·smirch'ment** *n.*
be·som (bee-zŏm) *n.* a broom made by tying a bundle of twigs to a long handle.
be·sot·ted (bi-sot-id) *adj.* 1. mentally stupefied, especially from drink. 2. silly, foolish. 3. infatuated.
be·span·gle (bi-spang-gĕl) *v.* (**be·span·gled, be·span·gling**) to cover with spangles.
be·spat·ter (bi-spat-ĕr) *v.* 1. to spatter. 2. to slander.
be·speak (bi-speek) *v.* (**be·spoke, be·spok·en, be·speak·ing**) 1. to engage beforehand, to order. 2. to indicate, to be evidence of.
be·sprin·kle (bi-spring-kĕl) *v.* (**be·sprin·kled, be·sprin·kling**) to sprinkle.
best[1] (best) *adj.* of the most excellent kind. **best** *adv.* 1. in the best manner, to the greatest degree, *she was best suited for a career in law.* 2. most usefully; *we had best go,* would find it wisest to go. **best** *n.* 1. that which is best, the chief merit or advantage, *it brings out the best in us; dressed in his best,* in his best clothes. 2. victory in a fight or argument; *we got the best of it,* won; *the best of three games,* the winning of two out of three. □**as best one can,** as well as one is able under the circumstances. **at best,** taking the most hopeful view. **best man,** the bridegroom's chief attendant at a wedding. **best part of,** most of. **best seller,** a book that sells in very large numbers. **make the best of,** to be as contented as possible with; to do what one can with. **put one's best foot forward,** to work as hard as one can.

to the best of one's ability, using all one's ability. **to the best of one's knowledge**, as far as one knows. **with the best of them,** as well as anyone.

best² (best) *v.* to defeat, to outdo, to outwit.

bes·tial (bes-chăl) *adj.* of or like a beast, savage. **bes'tial·ly** *adv.* **bes·ti·al·i·ty** (bes-chi-al-i-tee) *n.*

bes·ti·ar·y (bes-chi-er-ee) *n.* (*pl.* **-ar·ies**). a medieval moralizing treatise on real or mythical beasts.

be·stir (bi-stur) *v.* (**be·stirred, be·stir·ring**) **bestir oneself,** to exert or rouse to action.

be·stow (bi-stoh) *v.* to present as a gift. **be·stow'al** *n.*

be·stride (bi-strɪd) *v.* (**be·strode, be·strid·den, be·strid·ing**) to get or sit upon with legs astride, to stand astride over.

bet (bet) *n.* 1. an agreement pledging something that will be forfeited if one's prediction of the outcome of some event proves to be wrong. 2. the money etc. pledged. 3. a person or thing considered likely to be successful in something; *your best bet is to call tomorrow,* this is your best course of action. 4. *(informal)* a prediction, *my bet is that he won't come.* **bet** *v.* (**bet, bet·ted, bet·ting**) 1. to make a bet, to pledge in a bet. 2. *(informal)* to predict, to think most likely.

bet. *abbr.* between.

be·ta (bay-tä) *n.* 1. the second letter of the Greek alphabet (B β). 2. the second star in a constellation and in other classifications. □**beta particles,** fast-moving electrons emitted by radioactive substances, originally regarded as rays. **beta rays,** beta particles in a stream.

be·take (bi-tayk) *v.* (**be·took, be·tak·en, be·tak·ing**) **betake oneself,** *(old use)* to go.

be·ta·tron (bay-tä-tron) *n.* an apparatus for accelerating electrons.

be·tel (bee-tĕl) *n.* 1. a shrubby East Indian pepper plant. 2. the leaf of this plant chewed by people of India etc. for its stimulating and narcotic effects. □**betel nut,** the areca nut around which the betel leaf is wrapped for chewing.

bête noire (bayt nwahr) (*pl.* **bêtes noires,** same *pr.*) a thing or person that one dislikes very much. ▷French.

beth·el (beth-ĕl) *n.* 1. a hallowed spot. 2. a seamen's church (ashore or floating).

be·think (bi-thingk) *v.* (**be·thought, be·think·ing**) **bethink oneself of,** *(old use)* remember.

Beth·le·hem (beth-lĕ-hem) a town near Jerusalem, the birthplace of Jesus Christ.

be·tide (bi-tɪd) *v.* (**be·tid·ed, be·tid·ing**) to happen to; *woe betide him,* trouble will come to him.

be·times (bi-tɪmz) *adv. (old use)* early; in good time.

be·to·ken (bi-toh-kĕn) *v.* to be a token or advance sign of. **be·to'ken·er** *n.*

be·tray (bi-tray) *v.* 1. to give up or reveal disloyally to an enemy. 2. to be disloyal to. 3. to show unintentionally. **be·tray'al** *n.* **be·tray'er** *n.*

be·troth (bi-trohth) *v.* to engage with a promise to marry. **be·troth'al** *n.*

bet·ter¹ (bet-ĕr) *adj.* 1. of a more excellent kind; *one's better feelings,* more charitable feelings, conscience. 2. partly or fully recovered from an illness. **better** *adv.* in a better manner, to a better degree, more usefully; *we had better go,* would find it wiser to go. **better** *n.* that which is better. **better** *v.* to improve, to do better than. □**better half,** *(slang)* one's wife or husband. **better**

oneself, to get a better social position or status. **better part,** more than half. **get the better of,** to overcome. **go one better,** to do better than someone else's effort. ▷Do not use *better than* to mean *more.* Write *more than a mile away* instead of *better than a mile away.*

better² = **bettor.**

bet·ter·ment (bet-ĕr-mĕnt) *n.* making or becoming better, *she did that for the betterment of society.*

bet·tor (bet-ĕr) *n.* a person who bets.

be·tween (bi-tween) *adv. & prep.* 1. in the space bounded by two or more points, lines, or objects. 2. intermediate to, especially in time or quantity or quality etc. 3. separating, *the difference between right and wrong.* 4. to and from, *the liner sails between Naples and Haifa.* 5. connecting, *the great love between them.* 6. shared by, *divide the money between them; this is between you and me* or *between us* or *between ourselves,* to be kept secret. (▷The phrases *between you and I* and *between you and she* are incorrect. Use *between you and me* and *between you and her.*) 7. taking one and rejecting the other, *choose between them.* ▷Use *between* for two persons or things or ideas, *among* for three or more.

be·twixt (bi-twikst) *adv. & prep.* between. □**betwixt and between,** midway between in character etc.

bev·el (bev-ĕl) *n.* 1. a sloping edge or surface. 2. a tool for making such slopes. **bevel** *v.* (**bev·eled, bev·el·ing**) to give a sloping edge to.

bev·er·age (bev-ĕ-rij) *n.* any drink.

bev·y (bev-ee) *n.* (*pl.* **bev·ies**) a company, a large group.

be·wail (bi-wayl) *v.* to wail over, to mourn for.

be·ware (bi-wair) *v.* to be on one's guard. ▷*Beware* never changes form. It occurs most often in the imperative, as in *beware his sharp tongue* and *beware of the dog.*

be·wil·der (bi-wil-dĕr) *v.* to puzzle, to confuse, *the questions bewildered him.* **be·wil'der·ment** *n.*

be·witch (bi-wich) *v.* 1. to put under a magic spell. 2. to delight very much.

bey (bay) *n.* 1. a former Turkish provincial governor. 2. a man's title of honor and respect in Turkey, equivalent to Mr.

be·yond (bi-yond) *adv. & prep.* 1. at or to the farther side of, farther on. 2. outside, outside the range of, *this is beyond repair; it is beyond me,* too difficult for me to do or to understand. 3. besides, except. □**beyond doubt,** quite certain, unquestionably. **to live beyond one's income,** to spend more than one earns.

bez·el (bez-ĕl) *n.* 1. the sloped edge of a chisel etc. 2. any of the oblique faces of a cut gem. 3. a groove holding a gem or watch crystal.

b.f. *abbr.* bold face.

B.F.A. *abbr.* Bachelor of Fine Arts.

bhang (bang) *n.* 1. Indian hemp. 2. its leaves etc. used as a narcotic and intoxicant.

Bhu·tan (boo-tahn) a country between India and Tibet. **Bhu·tan·ese** (boo-tă-neez) *adj. & n.* (*pl.* **Bhu·tan·ese**).

Bi *symbol* bismuth.

bi·a·ly (bi-ah-lee) *n.* **bia·ly·stock** (byah-li-stok) a flat onion-flavored bread roll.

bi·an·nu·al (bɪ-an-yoo-ăl) *adj.* appearing or happening twice a year. **bi·an'nu·al·ly** *adv.* ▷*Biannual* and *biannually* do not mean "every two years."

bi·as (bɪ-ăs) *n.* 1. an opinion or feeling or influence that strongly favors one side in an argument or ·one item in a group or series. 2. the slanting direction across threads of woven material; *skirt is cut on the bias,* cut with the threads running slantwise across the up-and-down line of the garment. **bias** *v.* (**bi·ased, bi·as·ing**) to give a bias to, to influence. **bias** *adv.* on the bias, diagonally.

bi·ath·lon (bɪ-ath-lon) *n.* an athletic contest in which competitors engage in skiing and shooting.

bib (bib) *n.* a cloth or plastic covering put under a young child's chin to protect the child's clothes. □**best bib and tucker,** best clothes.

Bib. *abbr.* Bible.

bi·be·lot (bee-bĕ-loh) *n.* (*pl.* **-lots,** *pr.* -lohz) a small curio or artistic trinket.

Bi·ble (bɪ-bĕl) *n.* 1. the Christian scriptures. 2. the Jewish scriptures. 3. a copy of either the Old or New Testament. 4. *bible,* a book regarded as authoritative.

bib·li·cal (bib-li-kăl) *adj.* of or in the Bible.

bib·li·og·ra·phy (bib-li-og-ră-fee) *n.* (*pl.* **-phies**) 1. a list of books or articles about a particular subject or by a particular author. 2. the study of the history of books. **bib·li·o·graph·ic** (bib-li-ŏ-graf-ik) *adj.* **bib·li·o·graph′i·cal** *adj.*

bib·li·o·phile (bib-li-ŏ-fɪl) *n.* a lover of books, a collector of books.

bib·u·lous (bib-yŭ-lŭs) *adj.* addicted to drinking alcoholic beverages.

bi·cam·er·al (bɪ-kam-ĕ-răl) *adj.* having two legislative chambers.

bi·car·bon·ate (bɪ-kahr-bŏ-nit) *n.* a kind of carbonate. □**bicarbonate of soda,** sodium bicarbonate, used as an antacid, in baking, etc.

bi·cen·te·na·ry (bɪ-sen-tĕ-ner-ee) *n.* (*pl.* **-ries**) a bicentennial.

bi·cen·ten·ni·al (bɪ-sen-ten-i-ăl) *n.* a two-hundredth anniversary. **bicentennial** *adj.*

bi·ceps (bɪ-seps) *n.* (*pl.* **-ceps·es, -ceps**) the large muscle at the front of the upper arm that bends the elbow.

bi·chlo·ride (bɪ-klohr-ɪd) *n.* a compound combining two chlorine atoms with an atom of another element or group.

bick·er (bik-ĕr) *v.* to quarrel constantly about unimportant things.

bi·con·cave (bɪ-kon-kayv) *adj.* (of a lens) concave on both sides. **bi·con·cav·i·ty** (bɪ-kon-kav-i-tee) *n.*

bi·con·vex (bɪ-kon-veks) *adj.* (of a lens) convex on both sides. **bi·con·vex·i·ty** (bɪ-kon-vek-si-tee) *n.*

bi·cus·pid (bɪ-kus-pid) *n.* a tooth with two cusps.

bi·cy·cle (bɪ-si-kĕl) *n.* a two-wheeled vehicle driven by pedals. **bicycle** *v.* (**bi·cy·cled, bi·cy·cling**) to ride on a bicycle. **bi′cy·clist** *n.* □**bicycle clip,** one of a pair of clips for securing the trousers at the ankles while cycling.

bid[1] (bid) *n.* 1. an offer of a price in order to buy something, especially at an auction. 2. a statement of the number of tricks a player proposes to win in a card game. 3. an effort to obtain something, *made a bid for popular support.* **bid** *v.* (**bid, bid·ding**) to make a bid. **bid′der** *n.*

bid[2] *v.* (**bid,** *old use* **bade,** *pr.* bad; **bid·den, bid·ding**) 1. to command, *do as you are bid* or *bidden.* 2. to say as a greeting or farewell, *bidding them good night; we bade them good night three times.*

bid·da·ble (bid-ă-bĕl) *adj.* 1. willing to obey. 2. capable of being bid (as in a bridge game).

bid·ding (bid-ing) *n.* a command. □**do a person's bidding,** to do what he or she commands.

bid·dy (bid-ee) *n.* (*pl.* **-dies**) 1. a chicken. 2. *(informal)* an unpleasant woman.

bide (bɪd) *v.* (**bid·ed, bid·ing**) to wait. □**bide one's time,** to wait for a good opportunity.

bi·det (bi-day) *n.* a low narrow washbasin that one can sit astride for washing the genital and anal regions.

bi·en·ni·al (bɪ-en-i-ăl) *adj.* 1. lasting or living for two years. 2. happening every second year. **biennial** *n.* a plant that lives for two years, flowering and dying in the second. **bi·en′ni·al·ly** *adv.* ▷ *Biennial* and *biennially* do not mean "happening twice a year."

bi·en·ni·um (bɪ-en-i-ŭm) *n.* (*pl.* **-en·ni·ums, -en·ni·a**) *pr.* -en-i-ă) a period of two years.

bier (beer) *n.* a movable stand on which a coffin or a dead body is placed before burial.

bi·fo·cal (bɪ-foh-kăl) *adj.* having two foci.

bi·fo·cals (bɪ-foh-kălz) *n. pl.* eyeglasses with each lens made in two sections, the upper part for looking at distant objects and the lower part for reading and other close work.

bi·fur·cate (bɪ-fūr-kayt) *v.* (**bi·fur·cat·ed, bi·fur·cat·ing**) to divide into two branches, to fork. **bi·fur·ca·tion** (bɪ-fūr-kay-shŏn) *n.*

big (big) *adj.* (**big·ger, big·gest**) 1. large in size or amount or intensity. 2. more grown up, elder, *my big sister.* 3. important, *the big match.* 4. boastful, pretentious, *big talk.* 5. *(slang)* generous, *that's big of you.* **big** *adv. (informal)* 1. on a large scale; *think big,* plan ambitiously. 2. successfully, *it went over big.* **big′ness** *n.* □**big bang theory,** the theory that the universe began with a great explosion. **Big Ben,** the great bell, clock, and tower of the Houses of Parliament in London. **Big Brother,** an all-powerful dictator, government, or establishment that exercises close supervision and control while pretending to be kindly. **big business,** firms doing business on a large scale. **big deal!** *(slang)* I am not impressed. **big game,** the larger animals hunted for sport. **big gun,** *(slang)* an important and powerful person. **big head,** *(slang)* a conceited person. **big money,** a large amount of money. **big mouth,** *(slang)* a person who talks too much. **big name,** a famous person. **big shot,** *(slang)* an important and powerful person. **big stick,** threat of force. **big toe,** the first and largest toe. **big top,** the main tent at a circus; a circus. **big wheel,** *(slang)* a bigwig. **have big ideas,** to be ambitious. **too big for one's britches,** *(slang)* conceited.

big·a·mist (big-ă-mist) *n.* a person guilty of bigamy.

big·a·my (big-ă-mee) *n.* the crime of going through a marriage ceremony while one's previous marriage is still valid. **big′a·mous** *adj.* **big′a·mous·ly** *adv.*

big·heart·ed (big-hahr-tid) *adj.* very kind, generous.

big·horn (big-horn) *n.* (*pl.* **-horn, -horns**) a wild Rocky Mountain sheep with large curved horns.

bight (bɪt) *n.* 1. a long inward curve in a coast, *the Great Australian Bight.* 2. the slack part of a loop of rope.

big-league (big-leeg) *adj.* important.

big·ot (big-ŏt) *n.* a person who holds a prejudice against a racial or religious group.

big·ot·ed (big-ŏ-tid) *adj.* narrow-minded and intolerant.

big·ot·ry (big-ŏ-tree) *n.* (*pl.* **-ries**) being a bigot or bigoted.

big-time (big-tɪm) *adj.* (*slang*) of the highest or most important level.

big·wig (big-wig) *n.* (*informal*) an important person.

bike (bɪk) *n.* (*informal*) a bicycle or motorcycle.

bike *v.* (**biked, bik·ing**) (*informal*) to travel on either of these.

bike·way (bɪk-way) *n.* a path made especially for use by bicyclists.

bi·ki·ni (bi-kee-nee) *n.* a woman's two-piece beach garment consisting of a very scanty bra and briefs. ▷Named after *Bikini,* an atoll in the West Pacific, where an atomic bomb was tested in 1946.

bi·lat·er·al (bɪ-lat-ĕ-räl) *adj.* of two sides, having two sides; *a bilateral agreement,* made between two persons or groups. **bi·lat′er·al·ly** *adv.*

bile (bɪl) *n.* a bitter yellowish liquid produced by the liver and stored in the gall bladder, aiding digestion of fats.

bilge (bilj) *n.* 1. a ship's bottom, inside and outside. 2. the water that collects there. 3. (*slang*) worthless ideas or talk.

bi·lin·gual (bɪ-ling-gwäl) *adj.* 1. written in two languages. 2. able to speak two languages.

bil·ious (bil-yŭs) *adj.* 1. of biliousness, suffering from this. 2. of a sickly yellowish color or shade, *a bilious green.*

bil·ious·ness (bil-yŭs-nis) *n.* a sickness assumed to be caused by too much bile.

bilk (bilk) *v.* to escape paying one's debts to, to defraud.

bill¹ (bil) *n.* 1. a written statement of charges for goods supplied or services rendered. 2. a poster or placard. 3. a program of entertainment. 4. the draft of a proposed law, to be discussed by a legislature. 4. a piece of paper money, *a ten-dollar bill.* 5. a certificate; *a clean bill of health,* a declaration that there is no disease or defect. **bill** *v.* 1. to announce in a bill or poster, *Olivier was billed to appear as Hamlet.* 2. to send a statement of charges to, *we will bill you for these goods.* □**bill of exchange,** a written order to pay a specified sum of money to a named person or to the bearer. **bill of fare,** a menu. **bill of lading,** a list giving details of a ship's cargo. **Bill of Rights,** the statement of people's freedoms and rights embodied in the first ten amendments to the U.S. Constitution. **bill of sale,** a certificate transferring the ownership of personal property from seller to buyer. **fill the bill,** to be or do what is required.

bill² *n.* a bird's beak. **bill** *v.* (of doves) to stroke each other with their bills. □**bill and coo,** to exchange caresses.

bill·board (bil-bohrd) *n.* a large outdoor board for advertisements.

billet¹ *n.* 1. a lodging for troops, especially in a private house. 2. an order requiring someone to provide such lodgings. **billet** *v.* (**bil·let·ed, bil·let·ing**) to place in a billet.

billet² *n.* 1. an unfinished metal bar. 2. a thick piece of firewood.

bil·let–doux (bil-ee-doo) *n.* (*pl.* **bil·lets-doux,** *pr.* bil-ee-dooz) a love letter.

bill·fold (bil-fohld) *n.* a wallet for paper money.

bil·liards (bil-yărdz) *n.* 1. a game played with cues and three balls on a cloth-covered table. 2. (also **pocket billiards**) the game of pool. □**billiard ball,** a ball used in playing billiards. **billiard ta-**

ble, the table on which billiards is played.

bil·lings·gate (bil-ingz-gayt) *n.* violent vulgar words of abuse. ▷From the abusive language of fish-sellers in Billingsgate market, London.

bil·lion (bil-yŏn) *adj. & n.* a thousand million. **bil′lionth** *adj. & n.*

bil·lion·aire (bil-yŏ-nair) *n.* a person who possesses a billion dollars or more, a person of very great wealth.

bil·low (bil-oh) *n.* a great wave. **billow** *v.* to rise or roll like waves, *smoke billowed forth.*

bil·ly¹ (bil-ee) *n.* (*pl.* **-lies**) (chiefly *British*) a tin can or enameled container with a lid, used by campers etc. as a kettle or cooking pot.

billy² *n.* (*pl.* **-lies**) a truncheon. □**billy club,** a stick carried by policemen.

billy goat a male goat.

bi·me·tal·lic (bɪ-mĕ-tal-ik) *adj.* of two metals.

bi·month·ly (bɪ-munth-lee) *adj. & adv.* 1. happening every second month. 2. happening twice a month. (▷Careful writers do not use *bimonthly* in this sense. They use *semimonthly.*)

bimonthly *n.* (*pl.* **-lies**) a periodical published every second month.

bin (bin) *n.* a large rigid container or enclosed space for storing coal, grain, flour, etc.

bi·na·ry (bɪ-nă-ree) *adj.* 1. of or involving two things or parts. 2. of the binary system. **binary** *n.* (*pl.* **-ries**) something composed of two things or parts. □**binary digit,** one of two digits (usually 0 and 1) used in a binary scale. **binary notation** or **scale** or **system,** a system of numbers using only the two digits 0 and 1. **binary star,** two stars that revolve around each other.

bin·au·ral (bɪ-nor-ăl) *adj.* 1. of, using, or for both ears. 2. recorded by two microphones and usually transmitted separately to the two ears.

bind (bɪnd) *v.* (**bound, bind·ing**) 1. to tie or fasten, to tie up. 2. to hold together, to unite, *they had been bound by ties of friendship.* 3. to encircle with a strip or band of material; *bind up the wound,* bandage it. 4. to cover the edge of (a thing) in order to strengthen it or as a decoration. 5. to fasten the pages of (a book) into a cover. 6. to stick together in a solid mass, *bind the mixture with egg yolk.* 7. to place under an obligation or a legal agreement; *he was bound over to keep the peace,* was ordered to do so by a judge. □**in a bind,** (*informal*) in a difficult situation.

bind·er (bɪn-dĕr) *n.* 1. a person or thing that binds. 2. a bookbinder. 3. a machine that binds harvested grain into sheaves or bales. 4. a cover for papers.

bind·er·y (bɪn-dĕ-ree) *n.* (*pl.* **-er·ies**) a workshop where books are bound.

bind·ing (bɪn-ding) *n.* 1. a fabric used for binding edges. 2. the strong covering holding the leaves of a book together. **binding** *adj.* making a legal obligation, *a binding agreement is needed.*

bind·weed (bɪnd-weed) *n.* convolvulus or other climbing plant.

binge (binj) *n.* (*slang*) a spree, eating and drinking and making merry.

bin·go (bing-goh) *n.* a gambling game played with cards on which numbered squares are covered as the numbers are called at random. **bingo** *interj.* an exclamation of discovery or victory.

bin·na·cle (bin-ă-kĕl) *n.* a nonmagnetic stand for a ship's compass.

bin·oc·u·lar (bi-nok-yŭ-lăr) *adj.* of, using, or for both eyes. **bin·oc′u·lar·ly** *adv.*

bin·oc·u·lars (bɪ-nok-yŭ-lärz) *n. pl.* an instrument with lenses for both eyes, making distant objects seem nearer.

bi·no·mi·al (bɪ-noh-mi-ăl) *n.* an algebraic expression that is a sum or difference of two terms. **binomial** *adj.*

bi·o·chem·ist (bɪ-oh-kem-ist) *n.* an expert in biochemistry.

bi·o·chem·is·try (bɪ-oh-kem-i-stree) *n.* the chemistry of living organisms. **bi·o·chem′i·cal** *adj.* & *n.*

bi·o·ci·dal (bɪ-ŏ-sɪ-dăl) *adj.* destructive to life.

bi·o·de·grad·a·ble (bɪ-oh-di-gray-dă-běl) *adj.* able to be broken down by bacteria in the environment, *some plastics are not biodegradable.* **bi·o·deg·ra·da·tion** (bɪ-oh-deg-ră-day-shŏn) *n.* **bi·o·de·grad·a·bil·i·ty** (bɪ-oh-de-gray-dă-bil-i-tee) *n.*

bi·o·feed·back (bɪ-oh-feed-bak) *n.* a method of controlling mental reactions and physical functions that normally are involuntary by use of electronic monitoring devices.

biog. *abbr.* 1. biographer. 2. biographical. 3. biography.

bi·o·ge·og·ra·phy (bɪ-oh-ji-og-ră-fee) *n.* the scientific study of the geographical distribution of animals and plants. **bi·o·ge·o·graph·ic** (bɪ-oh-jee-ŏ-graf-ik) *adj.* **bi·o·ge·o·graph′i·cal** *adj.* **bi·o·ge·og′raph·er** *n.*

bi·og·ra·pher (bɪ-og-ră-fĕr) *n.* a person who writes a biography.

bi·og·ra·phy (bɪ-og-ră-fee) *n.* (*pl.* **-phies**) the story of a person's life written by someone other than himself. **bi·o·graph·ic** (bɪ-ŏ-graf-ik) *adj.* **bi·o·graph′i·cal** *adj.*

biol. *abbr.* 1. biological. 2. biologist. 3. biology.

bi·ol·o·gist (bɪ-ol-ŏ-jist) *n.* an expert in biology.

bi·ol·o·gy (bɪ-ol-ŏ-jee) *n.* the scientific study of the life and structure of living things. **bi·o·log·i·cal** (bɪ-ŏ-loj-i-kăl) *adj.* **bi·o·log′i·cal·ly** *adv.* □**biological clock,** an innate mechanism controlling an organism's regularly recurring functions or behavior. **biological warfare,** the deliberate use of organisms to spread disease among an enemy.

bi·on·ic (bɪ-on-ik) *adj.* (of a person or his faculties) operated by electronic means, not naturally.

bi·on·ics (bɪ-on-iks) *n.* the study of mechanical systems that are designed to behave like living beings.

bi·o·phys·i·cist (bɪ-oh-fiz-i-sist) *n.* an expert in biophysics.

bi·o·phys·ics (bɪ-oh-fiz-iks) *n.* the branch of physics dealing with the way the laws of physics apply to living things. **bi·o·phys′i·cal** *adj.*

bi·op·sy (bɪ-op-see) *n.* (*pl.* **-sies**) an examination of tissue cut from a living body.

bi·o·rhythm (bɪ-oh-riᵗʰ-ĕm) *n.* any of the recurring cycles of high and low levels of activity alleged to occur in living things.

bi·o·sat·el·lite (bɪ-oh-sat-ĕ-lɪt) *n.* a space satellite designed to transport animals or plants for scientific study.

bi·o·sci·ence (bɪ-oh-sɪ-ĕns) *n.* any of the sciences that deal with living organisms, especially in outer space.

bi·o·sphere (bɪ-ŏ-sfeer) *n.* regions of Earth's crust and atmosphere occupied by living matter.

bi·o·te·lem·e·try (bɪ-oh-tĕ-lem-ĕ-tree) *n.* the detecting and measuring at a great distance of the biological functions of a living being. **bi·o·tel·e·met·ric** (bɪ-oh-tel-ĕ-met-rik) *adj.*

bi·ot·ic (bɪ-ot-ik) *adj.* of or relating to life or to living things.

bi·o·tin (bɪ-ŏ-tin) *n.* the crystalline vitamin in yeast etc., controlling growth.

bi·par·ti·san (bɪ-pahr-ti-zăn) *adj.* of or involving two political parties.

bi·par·tite (bɪ-pahr-tɪt) *adj.* having two parts, shared by or involving two groups.

bi·ped (bɪ-ped) *n.* a two-footed animal.

bi·plane (bɪ-playn) *n.* an old type of airplane with two sets of wings, one above the other.

bi·po·lar (bɪ-poh-lär) *adj.* having two poles or extremities. **bi·po·lar·i·ty** (bɪ-poh-lar-i-tee) *n.*

bi·ra·cial (bɪ-ray-shăl) *adj.* consisting of members from at least two races, such as blacks and whites.

birch (burch) *n.* 1. a deciduous tree with a smooth bark and slender branches. 2. its wood. 3. a bundle of birch twigs formerly used for flogging delinquents. **birch** *v.* to flog with a birch.

Birch·er (bur-chĕr) *n. (informal)* a member of the John Birch Society, an ultranationalistic U.S. organization. **Birch′ism** *n.* **Birch′ist, Birch′ite** *n.*

bird (burd) *n.* 1. a feathered animal with two wings and two legs. 2. *(informal)* a person, *he's a cunning old bird.* □**bird of paradise,** a New Guinea bird with brightly colored plumage. **bird watcher,** a person who studies the habits of birds in their natural surroundings. **get the bird,** *(slang)* to be hissed and booed, to be rejected. **strictly for the birds,** *(slang)* trivial, unimportant, to be regarded with contempt.

bird·bath (burd-bath) *n.* a basin in a garden etc. with water for birds to bathe in.

bird·brain (burd-brayn) *n.* a stupid or flighty person.

bird·er (bur-dĕr) *n.* a bird watcher.

bird·house (burd-hows) *n.* a box placed in a tree etc. for birds to nest in.

bird·ie (bur-dee) *n.* 1. *(informal)* a little bird. 2. a score of one stroke under par for a hole at golf.

bird·seed (burd-seed) *n.* seed used as food for birds.

bird's-eye (burdz-ɪ) *adj.* 1. seen from above. 2. marked with spots resembling a bird's eye, *bird's-eye maple.* □**bird's-eye view,** a general view from above.

bi·ret·ta (bɪ-ret-ă) *n.* a square cap worn by Roman Catholic and some Anglican clergymen.

birth (burth) *n.* 1. the emergence of young from the mother's body. 2. origin, parentage, *he is of noble birth.* □**birth certificate,** an official document giving such information as the date and place of a person's birth. **birth control,** the prevention of unwanted pregnancy. **give birth to,** to produce as young from the body; to conceive (ideas etc.).

birth·day (burth-day) *n.* an anniversary of the day of one's birth. □**birthday suit,** a state of nakedness as at birth.

birth·mark (burth-mahrk) *n.* an unusual colored mark on a person's skin at birth.

birth·place (burth-plays) *n.* a person's place of birth or origin.

birth·rate (burth-rayt) *n.* the number of births per thousand of population per year.

birth·right (burth-rɪt) *n.* a privilege or property to which a person has a right through being born into a particular family (especially as the eldest son) or country.

birth·stone (burth-stohn) *n.* a gemstone associated with the month of one's birth.

bis·cuit (bis-kit) *n.* 1. a small cake of shortened bread raised with baking powder or soda. 2. *(British)* a cracker or cookie. 3. light brown.

bi·sect (bɪ-sekt) *v.* to divide into two equal parts. **bi·sec'tion** *n.* **bi·sec'tor** *n.* ▷ *Bisect in two* is incorrect.

bi·sex·u·al (bɪ-sek-shoo-ăl) *adj.* 1. of two sexes. 2. having both male and female sexual organs in one individual. 3. sexually attracted by members of both sexes. **bi·sex·u·al'i·ty** *n.*

bish·op (bish-ŏp) *n.* 1. a clergyman of high rank with authority over the work of the Church in a city or district (his *diocese*). 2. a chess piece shaped like a miter.

bish·op·ric (bish-ŏp-rik) *n.* the office or diocese of a bishop.

Bis·marck (biz-mahrk) the capital of North Dakota.

bis·muth (biz-mŭth) *n.* 1. a grayish-white metallic element used in alloys. 2. a compound of this used in medicines.

bi·son (bɪ-sŏn) *n.* (*pl.* **bi·son**) a wild ox of North America (also called *buffalo*).

bisque (bisk) *n.* 1. a thick soup of puréed shellfish etc. 2. an unglazed white ceramic used for statuettes etc.

bis·tro (bis-troh) *n.* (*pl.* **-tros**) a small bar or restaurant in Europe, an imitation of this.

bit[1] (bit) *n.* 1. a small piece or quantity or portion of anything; *I'm a bit puzzled,* slightly puzzled; *it's a bit of a nuisance,* rather a nuisance; *it takes a bit of doing,* is quite difficult. 2. a short time, *wait a bit.* □**bit by bit,** gradually. **bit part,** a small part in a play or film. **bits and pieces,** odds and ends. **do one's bit,** to do one's due share.

bit[2] *n.* 1. a metal bar forming the mouthpiece of a bridle. 2. the part of a tool that cuts or grips when twisted, the boring part of a drill. □**take the bit between one's teeth,** to get out of control.

bit[3] *n.* (in computers etc.) a unit of information expressed as a choice between two possibilities.

bit[4] (bit) *see* **bite.**

bitch (bich) *n.* 1. a female dog, fox, or wolf. 2. *(slang)* a spiteful woman. 3. *(slang)* an unpleasant or difficult thing. **bitch** *v.* to speak spitefully, to complain. **bitch'y** *adj.* (**bitch·i·er,** **bitch·i·est**), **bitch'i·ness** *n.*

bite (bɪt) *v.* (**bit, bit·ten, bit·ing**) 1. to cut into or nip with the teeth; *this dog bites,* is in the habit of biting people. 2. (of an insect) to sting, (of a snake) to pierce with its fangs. 3. to accept bait, *the fish are biting.* 4. to grip or act effectively, *wheels can't bite on a slippery surface.* **bite** *n.* 1. an act of biting. 2. a wound made by this. 3. a mouthful cut off by biting. 4. food to eat, a small meal. 5. the taking of bait by a fish. 6. a firm grip or hold, *this drill has no bite.* 7. the way the teeth close in biting. **bit'er** *n.* □**bite a person's head off,** to reply angrily. **bite off more than one can chew,** to attempt more than one can manage. **bite the dust,** to fall wounded and die. **put the bite on,** *(slang)* to borrow or try to borrow money.

bit·ing (bɪ-ting) *adj.* 1. causing a smarting pain, *a biting wind.* 2. (of remarks) sharp and critical.

bit·ten (bit-ĕn) *see* **bite.**

bit·ter (bit-ĕr) *adj.* 1. tasting sharp, like quinine or hops. 2. unwelcome to the mind, causing sorrow. 3. showing, feeling, or caused by mental pain or resentment, *bitter remarks.* 4. piercingly cold, *a bitter wind.* **bit'ter·ly** *adv.* **bit'ter·ness** *n.* □**to the bitter end,** until all that is possible has been done.

bit·tern (bit-ĕrn) *n.* marsh bird related to the heron, especially the kind known for the male's booming note.

bit·ters (bit-ĕrz) *n. sing.* or *pl.* an alcoholic liquor flavored with bitter herbs to give a stimulating taste.

bit·ter·sweet (bit-ĕr-sweet) *n.* 1. a climbing plant with bright orange or red berries or seeds. 2. sweetness with a bitter aftertaste or element. **bittersweet** *adj.* with bitterness and sweetness mingled together; *a bittersweet love affair,* one ending unhappily.

bi·tu·men (bi-too-mĕn) *n.* a black sticky substance obtained from petroleum, used for covering roads etc. **bi·tu'mi·nous** *adj.* □**bituminous coal,** coal that burns with a smoky flame.

bi·va·lent (bɪ-vay-lĕnt) *adj.* having a valence of two.

bi·valve (bɪ-valv) *n.* a shellfish with a hinged double shell. **bivalve** *adj.*

biv·ou·ac (biv-oo-ak) *n.* a temporary camp, especially one without tents or other cover. **bivouac** *v.* (**biv·ou·acked, biv·ou·ack·ing**) to camp in a bivouac.

bi·week·ly (bɪ-week-lee) *adj. & adv.* 1. happening every second week. 2. happening twice a week. (▷Careful writers do not use *biweekly* in this sense. They do use *semiweekly.*) **biweekly** *n.* (*pl.* **-lies**) a periodical published every second week.

bi·year·ly (bɪ-yeer-lee) *adj. & adv.* biennial.

biz (biz) *n. (slang)* business.

bi·zarre (bi-zahr) *adj.* strikingly odd in appearance or effect.

Bk *symbol* berkelium.

bk. *abbr.* book.

bkgd. *abbr.* background.

bl. *abbr.* 1. bale. 2. barrel. 3. black. 4. blue.

blab (blab) *v.* (**blabbed, blab·bing**) to talk indiscreetly, to let out a secret.

black (blak) *adj.* 1. of the very darkest color, like coal or soot. 2. having a black skin. 3. (often *Black*) of a dark-skinned race, especially of African descent. 4. soiled with dirt. 5. dismal, sullen, hostile; *things look black,* not hopeful; *a black day,* disastrous. 6. evil, wicked. **black** *n.* 1. black color. 2. a black substance or material, black clothes. 3. the black men in chess etc., the player using these. 4. the credit side of an account; *in the black,* having a credit balance. 5. (often *Black*) a member of dark-skinned race, especially of African descent. **black** *v.* 1. to make black. 2. to polish with blacking. **black'ly** *adv.* **black'ness** *n.* □**black and blue,** discolored by bruises. **black art,** black magic. **black bass,** a North American freshwater game fish. **black belt,** a belt awarded as a symbol of proficiency in judo. **black box,** an electronic device in an aircraft that records information about its flight. **black coffee,** coffee without milk. **black comedy,** comedy presenting a tragic theme or situation in comic terms. **Black Death,** the plague that swept through Europe in the 14th century. **black eye,** an eye with the skin around it darkened by a bruise; a disgrace. **Black Friars,** Dominicans. **black hole,** a region in outer space from which no matter or radiation can escape. **black light,** invisible ultraviolet or infrared radiation. **black lung disease,** illness contracted by coal miners as a result of inhaling coal dust. **black magic,** magic involving the invocation of devils. **Black Maria,** (chiefly *British*) a secure van for taking prisoners to and from prison. **black mark,** a mark of disapproval placed against a person's name. **black market,** the illegal buying and selling of goods or currencies. **Black Mass,** a travesty of the Christian Mass said to be used in the cult of Satanism. **Black Muslim,** a member of an American black Muslim sect proposing separation of races. **black nationalist,** an advocate of the establishment of a separate black nation in the U.S. **black sheep,** a bad character in an otherwise well-behaved group. **black tie,** a man's black bow tie worn with a dinner jacket; men's semiformal evening wear. **black widow,** a poisonous spider, the female being black with a red hourglass mark on its abdomen. **black work,** moonlighting for extra nontaxable cash income. **in black and white,** recorded in writing or print.

black·ball (blak-bawl) *v.* to prevent a person from being elected as a member of a club by voting against him in a secret ballot.

black·ber·ry (blak-ber-ee) *n.* (*pl.* **-ries**) 1. the bramble. 2. its small dark berry.

black·ber·ry·ing (blak-ber-i-ing) *n.* picking blackberries.

black·bird (blak-burd) *n.* any bird of the family that includes grackles, redwings, etc.

black·board (blak-bohrd) *n.* a board, usually colored black, for writing on with chalk in front of a class in school etc.

black·en (blak-ĕn) *v.* 1. to make or become black. 2. to defame or harm the reputation of, *blackened his character.*

black-eyed Su·san (blak-ıd soo-zăn) a flower with light petals and a dark center.

Black·foot (blak-fuut) *n.* (*pl.* **-feet, -foot**) a member of a tribe of North American Indians.

black·guard (blag-ahrd) *n.* a scoundrel.

black·head (blak-hed) *n.* a small hard lump blocking a pore in the skin.

black·ing (blak-ing) *n.* a paste or liquid for blacking or polishing shoes, boots, etc.

black·ish (blak-ish) *adj.* rather black.

black·jack (blak-jak) *n.* 1. a flexible loaded club. 2. the pirates' black flag. 3. a card game, twenty-one.

black·list (blak-list) *n.* a list of persons under suspicion, liable to punishment or unfavorable treatment etc. **blacklist** *v.* to enter (a person's name) on a blacklist.

black·mail (blak-mayl) *v.* to demand payment or action from (a person) by threats, especially of revealing a discreditable secret. **blackmail** *n.* 1. the crime of demanding payment in this way. 2. the money itself. **black′mail·er** *n.*

black·out (blak-owt) *n.* 1. the extinguishing of all lights accidentally, as from an electric power failure. 2. the deliberate obscuring of all lights, as during an air raid. 3. a temporary loss of consciousness. 4. suppression of news to prevent information from reaching people.

black·smith (blak-smith) *n.* a smith who works in steel.

black·thorn (blak-thorn) *n.* 1. a thorny shrub bearing a blue-black plumlike fruit. 2. a walking stick made from this.

black·top (blak-top) *n.* a type of road surfacing. **blacktop** *v.* (**black·topped, black·top·ping**) to cover with blacktop.

blad·der (blad-ĕr) *n.* 1. a bag in which urine collects in human and animal bodies. 2. an inflatable bag resembling this.

blade (blayd) *n.* 1. the flattened cutting part of a knife, sword, chisel, etc. 2. the flat wide part of an oar, spade, propeller, etc. 3. a flat narrow leaf especially of grass and cereals. 4. a broad flattish bone, *shoulder blade.*

blah (blah) *n.* (*informal*) high-sounding nonsense. **blah** *adj.* (*slang*) unwell. □**have the blahs,** (*slang*) feel unwell or depressed.

blame (blaym) *v.* (**blamed, blam·ing**) to hold responsible and criticize for a fault; *I don't blame you,* I feel your action was justified. **blame** *n.* responsibility for a fault, criticism for doing something wrong. ▷Careful writers do not *blame* anything *on* anyone; they *blame* people *for,* as in they *blamed him for the mistake.*

blame·less (blaym-lis) *adj.* deserving no blame, innocent.

blame·wor·thy (blaym-wur-*thee*) *adj.* deserving blame. **blame′wor·thi·ness** *n.*

blanch (blanch) *v.* to make or become white or pale; *blanch the almonds,* peel them, especially by scalding them.

blanc·mange (blă-mahnj) *n.* a flavored gelatin-like pudding made with milk.

bland (bland) *adj.* 1. mild in flavor, *bland foods.* 2. gentle and casual in manner, not irritating or stimulating. **bland′ly** *adv.* **bland′ness** *n.*

blan·dish·ment (blan-dish-mĕnt) *n.* a flattering or coaxing speech or action.

blank (blangk) *adj.* 1. not written or printed on, unmarked; *a blank wall,* without ornament or opening, an insurmountable obstacle. 2. without interest or expression, without result; *look blank,* to appear puzzled. **blank** *n.* 1. a blank space or paper, an empty surface; *his mind was a blank,* he could not remember anything. 2. a blank cartridge. **blank** *v.* (*informal*) to keep (an opponent) from scoring in a game. **blank′ly** *adv.* **blank′ness** *n.* □**blank cartridge,** one that contains no bullet. **blank check,** one with the amount left blank, to be filled in by the payee; carte blanche. **blank verse,** verse written in lines of usually ten syllables, without rhyme.

blan·ket (blang-kit) *n.* a thick covering made of woolen or other fabric; *a blanket of fog,* a thick covering mass; *a blanket agreement,* an inclusive one, covering all cases. **blanket** *v.* (**blan·ket·ed, blan·ket·ing**) to cover with a blanket.

blare (blair) *n.* a harsh loud sound like that of a trumpet. **blare** *v.* (**blared, blar·ing**) to make such a sound.

blar·ney (blahr-nee) *n.* smooth talk that flatters and deceives people. □**Blarney Stone,** a stone at Blarney Castle in Ireland said to confer a cajoling tongue on whoever kisses it.

bla·sé (blah-zay) *adj.* bored or unimpressed by things because one has experienced or seen them so often.

blas·pheme (blas-feem) *v.* (**blas·phemed, blas·phem·ing**) to utter blasphemies. **blas·phe′mer** *n.*

blas·phe·my (blas-fĕ-mee) *n.* (*pl.* **-mies**) contemptuous or irreverent talk about God or things

considered sacred. **blas'phe·mous** *adj.*
blas'phe·mous·ly *adv.*
blast (blast) *n.* 1. a sudden strong rush of wind
or air, a wave of air from an explosion. 2. the
sound made by a wind instrument, whistle, car
horn, etc. 3. *(slang)* a riotous party. **blast** *v.* 1.
to blow up with explosives. 2. to cause to wither,
to blight, to destroy. □**at full blast**, at maximum
power. **blast furnace,** a furnace for smelting ore,
with compressed hot air driven in. **blast off,** to
be launched by firing of rockets.
blast·ed (blas-tid) *adj. (informal)* damned.
blast-off (blast-awf) *n.* the launching of a spacecraft.
bla·tant (blay-tant) *adj.* attracting attention in a
very obvious way; *a blatant lie,* very obvious and
unashamed. **bla'tant·ly** *adv.*
blath·er (bla*th*-ĕr) *n.* foolish talk. **blather** *v.* to
utter foolish talk.
blaze[1] (blayz) *n.* 1. a bright flame or fire. 2. a bright
light, a brightly colored display. 3. an outburst,
a blaze of anger. 4. *blazes,* hell, *go to blazes.* **blaze**
v. **(blazed, blaz·ing)** 1. to burn or shine brightly.
2. to have an outburst of intense feeling or anger.
□**like blazes,** very quickly, exceedingly.
blaze[2] *n.* 1. a white mark on an animal's face. 2.
a mark chipped in the bark of a tree to mark a
route. **blaze** *v.* **(blazed, blaz·ing)** to mark (a
tree or route) with blazes; *blaze a trail,* to pioneer
and show the way for others to follow.
blaze[3] *v.* **(blazed, blaz·ing)** to proclaim, *blazed
the news abroad.*
blaz·er (blay-zĕr) *n.* a loose-fitting jacket, often
in the colors or bearing the emblem of a school,
club, or team.
bla·zon (blay-zŏn) *n.* a heraldic shield, a coat of
arms. **blazon** *v.* 1. to describe or paint arms he-
raldically. 2. to inscribe with arms, names, etc.
in colors or ornamentally. 3. to proclaim.
bldg. *abbr.* building.
bleach (bleech) *v.* to whiten by sunlight or chemicals. **bleach** *n.* a bleaching substance.
bleach·ers (blee-chĕrz) *n. pl.* outdoor uncovered
plank seats for spectators at a sports event.
bleak (bleek) *adj.* cold and cheerless; *the future
looks bleak,* unpromising. **bleak'ly** *adv.*
bleak'ness *n.*
blear (bleer) *v.* to dim (the eyes) with tears etc.
blear·y (bleer-ee) *adj.* **(blear·i·er, blear·i·est)**
bleared.
bleary-eyed, *adj.* with eyes watery and blurred.
bleat (bleet) *n.* the cry of a sheep, goat, or calf.
bleat *v.* 1. to make this cry. 2. to speak or say
plaintively.
bleed (bleed) *v.* **(bled, bleed·ing)** 1. to leak blood
or other fluid; *some dyes bleed,* come out in water.
2. to draw blood or fluid from. 3. to extort money
from.
bleed·er (blee-dĕr) *n.* a person suffering from hemophilia.
bleed·ing (blee-ding) **heart** 1. a plant with drooping red or pink heart-shaped flowers. 2. *(informal)*
an excessively soft-hearted person.
bleep (bleep) *n.* a short high-pitched sound used
as a signal. **bleep** *v.* 1. to make this sound. 2.
to censor (a word or words) from a television
or radio program by use of this sound. **bleep'er** *n.*
blem·ish (blem-ish) *n.* 1. a flaw or defect that spoils
the perfection of something. 2. a pimple. **blemish**
v. to spoil with a blemish.
blench (blench) *v.* 1. to flinch. 2. to turn pale.

blend (blend) *v.* 1. to mix in order to get a certain
quality. 2. to mingle, to become a mixture. 3.
to have no sharp or unpleasant contrast, *the colors
blend well.* **blend** *n.* a mixture of different sorts,
a blend of tea. □**blended whiskey,** a blend of
several whiskeys or of whiskey and neutral spirits.
blend·er (blen-dĕr) *n.* a kitchen appliance for combining cooking ingredients.
bless (bles) *v.* 1. to call holy, to praise, *to bless
God.* 2. to call God's favor upon, *Christ blessed
the children; bless his heart!,* an exclamation of
affection; *bless my soul!,* an exclamation of surprise. 3. to make sacred or holy with the sign
of the cross. □**be blessed** (*pr.* blest) **with,** to
be fortunate in having, *be blessed with good health.*
bless·ed (bles-id) *adj.* 1. holy, sacred. 2. in paradise. □**the Blessed,** the dead who have been
beatified. **the Blessed Sacrament,** the Eucharist. **the Blessed Virgin,** Mary, mother of Jesus
Christ. **bless'ed·ness** *n.*
bless·ing (bles-ing) *n.* 1. God's favor, a prayer
for this. 2. a short prayer of thanks to God before
or after a meal. 3. something one is glad of. □**a
blessing in disguise,** something unwelcome
that turns out to have a good effect.
blew (bloo) *see* **blow**[1].
blight (blīt) *n.* 1. a disease that withers plants. 2.
a fungus or insect causing this disease. 3. a malignant influence. 4. an unsightly area. **blight** *v.* 1.
to affect with blight. 2. to spoil.
blimp (blimp) *n.* a small nonrigid airship.
blind (blīnd) *adj.* 1. without sight; *a blind curve,*
where road users cannot see what is approaching.
2. without foresight or understanding, without
adequate information, *blind obedience.* 3. concealed. 4. *(slang)* very drunk. **blind** *adv.* blindly.
blind *v.* 1. to make blind. 2. to take away the
power of judgment. **blind** *n.* 1. a window screen,
especially one on a roller. 2. a pretext. **blind'ly**
adv. **blind'ness** *n.* □**blind alley,** an alley that
is closed at one end; a job with no prospects of
advancement. **blind date,** a date between persons
who have not met before. **blind landing,** the landing of an aircraft by instruments only. **blind spot,**
a point on the eye that is insensitive to light; an
area where understanding is lacking; an area cut
off from a motorist's vision. **turn a blind eye,**
to pretend not to notice.
blind·er (blīn-dĕr) *n.* a device on a bridle to keep
a horse looking straight ahead instead of to the
side.
blind·fold (blīnd-fohld) *adj. & adv.* with the eyes
covered with a cloth to block one's sight.
blindfold *n.* a cloth used for this. **blindfold** *v.*
to cover the eyes with a cloth.
blind·man's (blīnd-mänz) **buff** a game in which
a blindfolded player tries to catch and identify
one of the others.
blink (blingk) *v.* 1. to open and shut the eyes rapidly.
2. to shine unsteadily. 3. to ignore, to refuse to
consider. **blink** *n.* 1. an act of blinking. 2. a quick
gleam. □**on the blink,** *(slang)* not in good operating condition.
blink·er (bling-kĕr) *n.* 1. a device for flashing light
signals, especially for warning motorists of a road
hazard. 2. a blinder.
blintz (blints) *n.* (*pl.* **blintz·es**) a thin pancake
folded around a fruit or cheese filling.
blip (blip) *n.* a spot of light on a radar screen.
bliss (blis) *n.* perfect happiness. **bliss'ful** *adj.*
bliss'ful·ly *adv.*

blis·ter (blis-tĕr) *n.* 1. a bubble-like swelling on the skin, filled with watery liquid. 2. a raised swelling, as on a painted surface. **blister** *v.* to cause a blister on, to be affected with blisters. □**blister pack**, a transparent package enclosing merchandise.

blithe (blɪth) *adj.* casual and carefree. **blithe′ly** *adv.* □**blithe spirit**, a cheerful and carefree person.

blith·er·ing (blith-ĕ-ring) *adj. (informal)* absolute, contemptible, *blithering idiot.*

blitz (blits) *n.* a sudden, violent attack, especially one employing aircraft. **blitz** *v.* to attack or damage in a blitz.

blitz·krieg (blits-kreeg) *n.* a violent military campaign intended to bring about a speedy victory.

bliz·zard (bliz-ärd) *n.* a storm with wind-driven snow.

blk. *abbr.* 1. black. 2. block. 3. bulk.

bloat (bloht) *v.* to make or become swollen with fat, gas, or liquid.

bloat·ed (bloh-tid) *adj.* swollen with vanity or self-importance; overstuffed with rich food.

blob (blob) *n.* a drop of liquid, a round mass or spot, a coagulated mass.

bloc (blok) *n.* a group of parties or countries that unite to support a particular interest. ▷Do not confuse *bloc* with *block.*

block (blok) *n.* 1. a solid piece of wood or stone or other hard substance. 2. a log of wood. 3. a large piece of wood for chopping or hammering on; *the block,* that on which condemned people were beheaded. 4. a case in which a pulley or pulleys are mounted. 5. the main part of a gasoline engine, consisting of the cylinders and valves. 6. a section of a city bounded by streets, *drive around the block.* 7. a large section of shares, seats, etc. as a unit. 8. an obstruction; *a mental block,* failure to understand etc. caused by emotional tension. **block** *v.* 1. to obstruct, to prevent the movement or use of. 2. (in football) to intercept (an opponent) with one's body. □**block and tackle**, a system of pulleys and ropes used for lifting. **block letters**, plain capital letters. **knock someone's block off**, *(slang)* clout his head. ▷Do not confuse *block* with *bloc.*

block·ade (blo-kayd) *n.* the blocking by military forces of access to a place in order to prevent the entry of goods etc. **blockade** *v.* (**block·ad·ed, block·ad·ing**) to set up a blockade of.

block·age (blok-ij) *n.* 1. something that blocks. 2. the state of being blocked.

block·bust·er (blok-bus-tĕr) *n.* 1. a bomb capable of destroying a city block. 2. a thing of great power.

block·bust·ing (blok-bus-ting) *n.* inducing people to sell their homes at a low price by warning of a change in the racial patterns of a neighborhood.

block·head (blok-hed) *n. (informal)* a stupid person.

block·house (blok-hows) *n.* 1. a strong wooden fort with loopholes for defendants to shoot from. 2. a reinforced concrete shelter.

bloke (blohk) *n. (British slang)* a man.

blond, blonde (blond) *adj.* fair-haired. **blond** *n.* a fair-haired man. **blonde** *n.* a fair-haired woman.

blood (blud) *n.* 1. the red oxygen–bearing liquid circulating in the bodies of animals. 2. bloodshed. 3. temper, courage; *his blood is up,* he is in a fighting mood; *there is bad blood between them,* hatred. 4. race, descent, parentage; *new blood,*

members admitted to a family or group; *a prince of the blood,* of royal descent; *they are my own blood,* relatives. **blood** *v.* to give a first taste of blood to (a hound), to initiate. □**blood bank**, a place where a supply of blood for transfusion is stored. **blood bath**, a massacre. **blood count**, the number of corpuscles in a specific volume of blood. **blood group**, a class or type of human blood. **blood poisoning**, the condition that results when the bloodstream is infected with harmful microorganisms that have entered the body, especially through a cut or wound. **blood pressure**, the pressure of blood within the arteries and veins; *some suffered from high blood pressure and others from low blood pressure,* abnormal conditions. **blood relative**, one related by blood, not by marriage. **blood sports**, sports involving killing. **blood sugar**, glucose in the blood, the quantity of this. **blood test**, an examination of a specimen of blood in a medical diagnosis. **blood type**, blood group. **blood vessel**, a vein, artery, or capillary carrying blood. **in cold blood**, *see* **cold**.

blood·cur·dling (blud-kurd-ling) *adj.* horrifying.

blood·ed (blud-id) *adj.* 1. of a specified kind of blood, as in *red-blooded, hot-blooded,* etc. 2. (of animals) of pure or nearly pure stock.

blood·hound (blud-hownd) *n.* a large keen-scented dog used in tracking.

blood·less (blud-lis) *adj.* 1. having no blood. 2. looking pale, drained of blood. 3. without bloodshed. 4. lacking energy.

blood·let·ting (blud-let-ing) *n.* 1. surgical removal of some of a patient's blood. 2. bloodshed.

blood·line (blud-lɪn) *n.* the line of descent from ancestors, pedigree.

blood·mo·bile (blud-mŏ-beel) *n.* a vehicle in which donors can give blood for storage in a blood bank.

blood-red (blud-red) *adj.* as red as blood.

blood·root (blud-root) *n.* a North American wildflower with a red root and red juice.

blood·shed (blud-shed) *n.* the killing or wounding of people.

blood·shot (blud-shot) *adj.* (of eyes) red from dilated veins.

blood·stained (blud-staynd) *adj.* 1. stained with blood. 2. disgraced by bloodshed.

blood·stone (blud-stohn) *n.* a green variety of chalcedony spotted or streaked with red.

blood·stream (blud-streem) *n.* the blood circulating in the body.

blood·suck·er (blud-suk-ĕr) *n.* 1. a creature that sucks blood. 2. a person who extorts money.

blood·thirst·y (blud-thur-stee) *adj.* eager for bloodshed.

blood·y (blud-ee) *adj.* (**blood·i·er, blood·i·est**) 1. blood-stained. 2. with much bloodshed, *a bloody battle.* 3. *(British vulgar)* damned, very great. **bloody** *adv. (British vulgar)* very, *bloody awful.* **bloody** *v.* (**blood·ied, blood·y·ing**) to stain with blood. **blood′i·ly** *adv.* **blood′i·ness** *n.* □**Bloody Mary**, a drink of vodka, tomato juice, and spices.

bloom (bloom) *n.* 1. a flower. 2. beauty, perfection, *in the bloom of youth.* 3. fine powder on fresh ripe grapes etc. **bloom** *v.* 1. to bear flowers, to be in bloom. 2. to be in full beauty and perfection. □**in bloom**, in flower.

bloom·ers (bloo-mĕrz) *n. pl.* 1. loose knee-length trousers worn as an outer garment by some women in the 19th century. 2. women's undergarments of this shape.

bloop·er (bloo-pĕr) *n*. 1. *(informal)* an embarrassing mistake, especially one spoken on radio or television. 2. *(slang)* a baseball hit high but not far beyond the infield.

blos·som (blos-ŏm) *n*. 1. a flower, especially of a fruit tree. 2. a mass of such flowers. **blossom** *v*. 1. to open into flowers. 2. to develop and flourish.

blot (blot) *n*. 1. a spot of ink etc. 2. something ugly, *a blot on the landscape*. 3. a fault, a disgraceful act or quality. **blot** *v*. **(blot·ted, blot·ting)** 1. to make a blot or blots on. 2. to dry with blotting paper, to soak up. □**blot out,** to cross out thickly; to obscure, *mist blotted out the view;* to destroy completely.

blotch (bloch) *n*. a large irregular mark. **blotch** *v*. to make an irregular patch of ink or color. **blotch'y** *adj*. **(blotch·i·er, blotch·i·est).**

blot·ter (blot-ĕr) *n*. 1. a sheet of blotting paper. 2. a book for recording events as they occur, especially arrests, *police blotter*.

blot·ting (blot-ing) **paper** absorbent paper for drying ink writing.

blot·to (blot-oh) *adj*. *(slang)* very drunk.

blouse (blows) *n*. 1 a shirtlike garment worn by women and children. 2 a waist-length coat forming part of a military uniform.

blow¹ (bloh) *v*. **(blew, blown, blow·ing)** 1. to move or flow as a current of air does. 2. to send out a current of air or breath, to move or propel by this; *blow one's nose,* clear it by breathing out through it; *blow the whistle,* sound it, alert the authorities to an instance of wrongdoing. 3. to shape (molten glass) by blowing into it. 4. to be moved or carried by air, *the door blew open.* 5. to puff and pant. 6. to melt with too strong an electric current, *a fuse has blown.* 7. to break with explosives. 8. *(slang)* to reveal; *the spy's cover was blown,* became known to the enemy. 9. *(slang)* to spend recklessly. **blow** *n*. 1. a blowing of air. 2. a storm. □**blow dry,** to use a hand-held dryer to style washed hair while drying it. **blow in,** *(informal)* to arrive casually or unexpectedly. **blow one's mind,** *(slang)* to astound; to indulge in hallucinations. **blow one's own trumpet,** to praise oneself. **blow one's top,** *(slang)* to show great anger. **blow over,** to die down. **blow up,** to inflate; to exaggerate; to make an enlargement of (a photograph etc.); to explode; to shatter by an explosion; to lose one's temper, to reprimand severely; to become a crisis, *this problem has blown up purely.*

blow² *n*. 1. a hard stroke with a hand or weapon. 2. a shock, a disaster.

blow-by-blow (bloh-bɪ-bloh) *adj*. telling all the details of an event in their order of occurrence, *a blow-by-blow account.*

blow·er (bloh-ĕr) *n*. a person or thing that blows.

blow·fly (bloh-flɪ) *n*. (*pl.* **-flies**) a fly that lays its eggs on meat.

blow·gun (bloh-gun) *n*. a tube for propelling arrows or darts by blowing.

blown (blohn) *see* **blow¹**.

blow·out (bloh-owt) *n*. a burst tire.

blow·pipe (bloh-pɪp) *n*. 1. a tube for heating a flame by blowing air or other gas into it. 2. a tube used in glass blowing.

blow·sy, blow·zy (blow-zee) *adj*. red-faced and coarse looking, slatternly.

blow·torch (bloh-torch) *n*. an apparatus for directing a very hot flame on a selected spot, used for heating or cutting metals.

blow·up (bloh-up) *n*. 1. an explosion. 2. an enlargement (of a photograph etc.). 3. an outburst of anger.

blow·y (bloh-ee) *adj*. **(blow·i·er, blow·i·est)** windy.

BLT *abbr*. bacon, lettuce, and tomato sandwich.

blub·ber¹ (blub-ĕr) *n*. whale fat.

blub·ber² *v*. to weep noisily.

blu·cher (bloo-kĕr) *n*. a strong leather half boot or high shoe.

blud·geon (bluj-ŏn) *n*. a short stick with a thickened end, used as a weapon. **bludgeon** *v*. 1. to strike with a bludgeon. 2. to compel forcefully.

blue (bloo) *adj*. **(blu·er, blu·est)** 1. of the color of the sky on a cloudless day. 2. unhappy, depressed. 3. indecent, obscene, *blue jokes.* **blue** *n*. 1. blue color. 2. a blue substance or material, blue clothes. 3. *the blue,* the clear sky. **blue** *v*. **(blued, blue·ing)** to make blue. **blue'ness** *n*. □**blue baby,** one with blueness of the skin from a heart defect. **blue cheese,** a cheese with veins of blue mold. **blue funk,** *(slang)* a state of terror or depression. **blue jay,** a common North American crested bird with a blue back. **blue jeans,** blue denim trousers with reinforced seams and seat. **blue law,** a puritanical law. **blue plate special,** a specially priced main course in a restaurant. **blue ribbon,** the highest prize, honor, or distinction. **blue whale,** a whalebone whale, the largest known living animal. **once in a blue moon,** very rarely. **out of the blue,** unexpectedly. **true blue,** faithful, loyal.

blue·bell (bloo-bel) *n*. a plant with blue bell-shaped flowers.

blue·ber·ry (bloo-ber-ee) *n*. (*pl.* **-ries**) 1. a shrub with edible blue berries. 2. its fruit.

blue·bird (bloo-burd) *n*. a North American songbird with a blue back and rosy breast.

blue·black (bloo-blak) *adj*. black with overtones of dark blue.

blue·blood (bloo-blud) *n*. a person of aristocratic birth.

blue·bon·net (bloo-bon-it) *n*. 1. a wildflower with blue blossoms common in the southwestern U.S. 2. a round flat blue woolen cap formerly worn by men in Scotland.

blue·book (bloo-buuk) *n*. 1. a book in which students write their examinations. 2. a directory of socially prominent people.

blue·bot·tle (bloo-bot-ĕl) *n*. a large fly with a bluish body.

blue-chip (bloo-chip) **stock** a stock that is a reliable investment, paying good dividends.

blue·col·lar (bloo-kol-ăr) **worker** a manual or industrial worker.

blue·fish (bloo-fish) *n*. (*pl.* **-fish·es, -fish**) a voracious game fish.

blue·gill (bloo-gil) *n*. an edible North American freshwater sunfish of bluish hue.

blue·grass (bloo-gras) *n*. 1. a bluish grass, especially of Kentucky. 2. a kind of country music.

blue·jack·et (bloo-jak-it) *n*. a seaman in the U.S. Navy.

blue·nose (bloo-nohz) *n*. a puritanical person.

blue·pen·cil (bloo-pen-sɪl) *v*. **(blue-pen·ciled, blue-pen·cil·ing)** to cross out with a blue pencil, to censor.

blue·point (bloo-point) *n*. an oyster.

blue·print (bloo-print) *n.* **1.** a blue photographic print of building plans. **2.** a detailed plan or scheme. **blueprint** *v.* to make a blueprint of.

blues (blooz) *n.* melancholy jazz melodies originating from black American rhythms and lyrics. □**the blues,** a state of depression.

blue·stock·ing (bloo-stok-ing) *n.* a woman with strong literary tastes and learning.

blu·et (bloo-it) *n.* a blue-flowered plant.

bluff¹ (bluf) *adj.* **1.** with a broad steep front, *a bluff headland.* **2.** abrupt, frank, and hearty in manner. **bluff** *n.* a bluff headland or cliff. **bluff′ness** *n.*

bluff² *v.* to deceive someone by making a pretense, especially of strength. **bluff** *n.* bluffing, a threat intended to get results without being carried out. **bluff′er** *n.*

blu·ing, blue·ing (bloo-ing) *n.* a laundry powder or liquid used to keep white fabrics from yellowing.

blu·ish (bloo-ish) *adj.* rather blue.

blun·der (blun-dĕr) *v.* **1.** to move clumsily and uncertainly. **2.** to make a blunder. **blunder** *n.* a mistake made especially through ignorance or carelessness. **blun′der·er** *n.*

blun·der·buss (blun-dĕr-bus) *n.* an old type of gun firing many balls at one shot.

blunt (blunt) *adj.* **1.** with no sharp edge or point, not sharp. **2.** speaking or expressed in plain terms, *a blunt refusal.* **blunt** *v.* to make or become blunt. **blunt′ly** *adv.* **blunt′ness** *n.*

blur (blur) *n.* **1.** a smear. **2.** a confused or indistinct appearance. **blur** *v.* **(blurred, blur·ring) 1.** to smear. **2.** to make or become indistinct. **blur′ry** *adj.*

blurb (blurb) *n.* a description of something praising it, as in advertising matter.

blurt (blurt) *v.* to utter abruptly or tactlessly, *blurted it out.*

blush (blush) *v.* to become red in the face from shame or embarrassment. **blush** *n.* such reddening of the face. **blush′er** *n.* □**at first blush,** on first glimpse or impression.

blus·ter (blus-tĕr) *v.* **1.** to be windy, to blow in gusts. **2.** to talk aggressively, especially with empty threats. **bluster** *n.* such talk. **blus′ter·y** *adj.*

blvd *abbr.* boulevard.

BM *abbr.* **1.** basal metabolism. **2.** bowel movement.

BMR *abbr.* basal metabolic rate.

bn *abbr.* battalion.

B.O. *abbr. (informal)* body odor.

bo·a (boh-ă) *n.* (*pl.* **bo·as) 1.** a large nonpoisonous South American snake that kills its prey by crushing it. **2.** a woman's fluffy scarf, usually feathered. □**boa constrictor,** a Brazilian species of boa.

boar (bohr) *n.* **1.** a male wild pig. **2.** an uncastrated domestic pig.

board (bohrd) *n.* **1.** a long thin flat piece of wood. **2.** a flat piece of wood or stiff material for a special purpose, as a diving board, a chessboard. **3.** thick stiff paper used for book covers. **4.** daily meals obtained in return for payment or for services, *room and board.* **5.** a committee. **board** *v.* **1.** to cover with boards. **2.** to go on board (a ship, train, etc.). **3.** to receive or provide with room and board for payment. □**board up,** to block with fixed boards. **go by the board,** to be ignored or rejected. **on board,** on or in a ship, train, etc.

board·er (bohr-dĕr) *n.* a person who boards with someone.

board·ing (bohr-ding) *n.* **1.** boards. **2.** material from which boards are cut, a structure or covering made of this.

board·ing·house (bohr-ding-hows) *n.* a house at which room and board may be obtained for payment.

boarding school *n.* a school in which pupils receive room and board.

board·room (bohrd-room) *n.* a room in which the meetings of the board of a company etc. are held.

board·walk (bohrd-wawk) *n.* a footway made of boards.

boast (bohst) *v.* **1.** to speak with great pride and try to impress people, especially about oneself. **2.** to possess as something to be proud of, *the town boasts a fine park.* **boast** *n.* **1.** a boastful statement. **2.** a thing boasted of. **boast′er** *n.*

boast·ful (bohst-fŭl) *adj.* boasting frequently, full of boasting. **boast′ful·ly** *adv.* **boast′ful·ness** *n.*

boat (boht) *n.* **1.** a vessel for traveling on water, the kind moved by oars or sails or an engine, a steamer; *a ship's boats,* lifeboats carried on board ship. **2.** a boat-shaped serving dish for sauce or gravy. □**boat drill,** practice in launching a ship's boats. **in the same boat,** suffering the same troubles.

boat·er (boh-tĕr) *n.* **1.** a person who rows a boat. **2.** a hard flat straw hat.

boat·house (boht-hows) *n.* a shed at the water's edge for housing boats.

boat·ing (boh-ting) *n.* going out in a boat for pleasure.

boat·man (boht-măn) *n.* (*pl.* **-men,** *pr.* -mĕn) a man who rows or sails or rents out boats.

boat·swain (boh-sŭn) *n.* a ship's petty officer in charge of rigging, boats, anchors, etc.

bob¹ (bob) *v.* **(bobbed, bob·bing) 1.** to make a jerky movement, to move quickly up and down. **2.** to appear unexpectedly. **bob** *n.* **1.** a bobbing movement. **2.** a fishing-line float.

bob² *v.* **(bobbed, bob·bing)** to cut (hair) short so that it hangs loosely. **bob** *n.* the style of bobbed hair.

bob³ *n.* (*pl.* **bob)** *(British slang)* a shilling, 5p.

bob·bin (bob-in) *n.* a small spool holding thread or wire in a machine.

bob·ble (bob-ĕl) *v.* **(bob·bled, bob·bling) 1.** to fumble (a ball). **2.** to blunder. **bobble** *n.* a fumble.

bob·by (bob-ee) *n.* (*pl.* **-bies)** *(British slang)* a policeman.

bobby pin *n.* a flat hairpin.

bobby sox *n.* short socks covering the ankle. □**bobby soxer,** an adolescent girl.

bob·cat (bob-kat) *n.* a North American short-tailed lynx.

bob·o·link (bob-ŏ-lingk) *n.* a North American songbird.

bob·sled (bob-sled) *n.* **1.** a racing sled with two pairs of runners, a brake, and a steering mechanism. **2.** a sled formed by two short sleds operating in tandem. **bobsled** *v.* **(bob·sled·ded, bob·sled·ding)** to operate a bobsled. **bob′sled·ding** *n.*

bob·tail (bob-tayl) *n.* **1.** a docked tail. **2.** a horse or dog with this.

bob·white (bob-hwɪt) *n.* a North American quail.

boc·cie (boch-ee) *n.* an Italian bowling game.

bock (bok) *n.* (also **bock beer**) strong dark-colored German beer, usually brewed for drinking in the spring months.

bode[1] (bohd) v. (**bod·ed, bod·ing**) to be a sign of, to promise, *it boded well* or *ill for their future.*

bode[2] (bohd) *see* **bide.**

bod·ice (bod-is) n. the upper part of a woman's dress, down to the waist.

bod·i·less (bod-i-lis) *adj.* having no body or material form.

bod·i·ly (bod-i-lee) *adj.* of the human body or physical nature. **bodily** *adv.* 1. in person, physically. 2. as a whole, *the bridge was moved bodily fifty yards downstream.*

bod·kin (bod-kin) n. a blunt thick needle with a large eye, for drawing tape etc. through a hem, a small pointed instrument for piercing cloth etc.

bod·y (bod-ee) n. (*pl.* **bod·ies**) 1. the structure of bones, flesh, etc. of man or an animal, living or dead. 2. a corpse, a carcass. 3. the trunk, the main part of a body apart from the head and limbs. 4. the main part of anything, *an auto body.* 5. (*informal*) a person, *she's a cheerful old body.* 6. a group or quantity of people, things, or matter, regarded as a unit. 7. a distinct piece of matter, an object in space. 8. thick texture, strong quality, *this fabric has more body; this wine has no body.* □**body blow,** a severe setback; a hit to the body, as in boxing. **body count,** (in the Vietnam War) the count of enemy soldiers killed in combat. **body English,** twisting of the body during a game as if to help the ball travel in the desired path. **body language,** positions and attitudes of the human body said to communicate feelings. **body odor,** the smell of the human body, especially when unpleasant. **body politic,** the nation or a similar organized system. **body stocking,** a woman's undergarment covering the trunk, legs, and arms. **in a body,** all together. **keep body and soul together,** to have just enough food etc. to remain alive.

bod·y·guard (bod-ee-gahrd) n. a person's escort or personal guard.

bod·y·work (bod-ee-wurk) n. 1. the body of an automobile. 2. the repair of this.

Boer (bohr) n. a South African of Dutch descent.

bog (bog) n. an area of ground that is permanently wet and spongy, formed of decayed plants etc.

bog v. (**bogged, bog·ging**) to be stuck fast in wet ground, to cause to be stuck and unable to make progress. **bog'gy** *adj.* (**bog·gi·er, bog·gi·est**).

bo·gey (buug-ee) n. (*pl.* **-geys**) 1. an evil spirit. 2. something that causes fear. 3. (*pr.* boh-gee) a score of one over par in playing one hole in golf.

bo·gey·man (buug-ee-man) n. (*pl.* **-men,** *pr.* -men) an imaginary man feared by children, especially in the dark.

bog·gle (bog-ĕl) v. (**bog·gled, bog·gling**) to hesitate in fright, to raise objections, *the mind boggles at the idea.*

Bo·go·tá (boh-gŏ-tah) the capital of Colombia.

bo·gus (boh-gŭs) *adj.* sham, counterfeit.

bo·gy (buug-ee, boh-gee) = **bogey.**

Bo·he·mi·a (boh-hee-mi-ă) a province of Czechoslovakia.

Bo·he·mi·an (boh-hee-mi-ăn) n. 1. a native or inhabitant of Bohemia. 2. (often *bohemian*) a socially unconventional person, especially an artist or writer, of free-and-easy habits, manners, and sometimes morals. **Bohemian** *adj.*

boil[1] (boil) n. an inflamed swelling under the skin, producing pus.

boil[2] v. 1. to bubble up and change into vapor

through being heated. 2. to heat (a liquid or its container) so that the liquid boils, to cook or wash or process thus, to be heated or cooked etc. thus. 3. to seethe like a boiling liquid, to be hot with anger. **boil** n. the boiling point. □**boil down,** to reduce or be reduced in quantity by boiling; (*informal*) to express or be expressed in fewer words. **boiling hot,** (*informal*) very hot. **boiling point,** the temperature at which a liquid boils; a state of great anger or excitement. **boil over,** to overflow when boiling.

boil·er (boi-lĕr) n. 1. a container in which water or other liquid is boiled. 2. a tank in which water is heated and stored until used. 3. a tank in a plant in which steam is made.

boil·er·mak·er (boi-lĕr-may-kĕr) n. 1. a person who builds or repairs boilers. 2. a serving of whiskey with a beer chaser.

Boi·se (boi-zee) the capital of Idaho.

bois·ter·ous (boi-stĕ-rŭs) *adj.* noisy and cheerful, *boisterous children.* **bois'ter·ous·ly** *adv.* **bois'ter·ous·ness** n.

bo·la (boh-lă) n. (*pl.* **-las**) a South American weapon consisting of balls connected by a strong cord (when thrown, it brings down quarry by entangling the limbs).

bold (bohld) *adj.* 1. confident and courageous. 2. without feelings of shame, impudent. 3. (of colors) strong and vivid. **bold'ly** *adv.* **bold'ness** n.

bold·face (bohld-fays) n. type or print with thick heavy lines. **bold'faced** *adj.*

bole (bohl) n. the trunk of a tree.

bo·le·ro (bŏ-lair-oh) n. (*pl.* **-ros**) 1. a Spanish dance, the music for this. 2. a woman's short jacket with no front fastening.

bol·i·var (bol-ĭ-văr) n. (*pl.* **bol·i·vars, bol·i·va·res,** *pr.* bol-ĭ-vahr-es) the unit of money in Venezuela.

Bo·liv·i·a (bŏ-liv-i-ă) a country in South America. **Bo·liv'i·an** *adj.* & n.

boll (bohl) n. a rounded seed vessel, as in flax or cotton. □**boll weevil,** a small destructive insect infesting cotton plants.

bo·lo (boh-loh) n. (*pl.* **-los**) a heavy knife used in the Philippines. □**bolo tie,** a necktie in the form of a thick string held together by a decorative clip.

bo·lo·gna (bŏ-loh-nee) n. a type of large meat sausage.

bo·lo·ney (bŏ-loh-nee) n. (*slang*) nonsense.

Bol·she·vik (bohl-shĕ-vik) n. (*pl.* **Bol·she·viks, Bol·she·vi·ki,** *pr.* bohl-shĕ-vik-ee) 1. a member of the revolutionary party that seized power in Russia in 1917. 2. a socialist revolutionary. **Bol·she·vism** (bohl-shĕ-viz-ĕm) n. **Bol'she·vist** *adj.* & n.

bol·ster (bohl-stĕr) n. a long cushion or pillow usually kept at the head of a bed. **bolster** v. to support, to prop, *bolster up confidence.*

bolt[1] (bohlt) n. 1. a sliding bar for fastening a door. 2. the sliding part of a rifle breech. 3. a strong metal pin for fastening things together. 4. a shaft of lightning. 5. a roll of fabric. 6. the act of bolting. **bolt** v. 1. to fasten with a bolt or bolts. 2. to run away, (of a horse) to run off out of control. 3. to gulp down (food) hastily. □**a bolt from the blue,** a complete (usually unwelcome) surprise. **bolt upright,** quite upright.

bolt[2] v. to sift (flour).

bo·lus (boh-lŭs) n. 1. a large pill. 2. a quantity of food at the moment of swallowing.

bomb (bom) *n.* 1. a container filled with explosive or incendiary material to be set off by impact or by a timing device. 2. *the bomb,* an atomic or hydrogen bomb, regarded as the supreme weapon. 3. *(football slang)* a long forward pass. **bomb** *v.* 1. to attack with bombs. 2. *(slang)* to fail.

bom·bard (bom-**bahrd**) *v.* 1. to attack with shells from big guns. 2. to send a stream of high-speed particles against. 3. to attack with questions or complaints. **bom·bard'ment** *n.*

bom·bar·dier (bom-băr-**deer**) *n.* the member of a bomber crew who aims and releases bombs.

bom·bast (bom-bast) *n.* pompous speech.

bom·bas·tic (bom-**bas**-tik) *adj.* speaking pompously.

bom·ba·zine (bom-bă-**zeen**) *n.* a twilled dress material of worsted with or without silk or cotton.

bombed (bomd) *adj. (slang)* drunk.

bomb·er (bom-ĕr) *n.* 1. an aircraft that carries and drops bombs. 2. a person who throws or plants bombs.

bomb·proof (bom-proof) *adj.* strong enough to resist the explosion of a bomb.

bomb·shell (bom-shel) *n.* 1. a bomb. 2. something that comes as a great surprise and shock.

bomb·sight (bom-sıt) *n.* a device in an aircraft for aiming bombs.

bo·na fide (boh-nă fıd) genuine, without fraud, *bona fide customers.*

bo·na fi·des (boh-nă fı-deez) honest intention, sincerity, *he proved his bona fides.* ▷This is not a plural form of *bona fide.* It is incorrect to say "his bona fides *were* questioned"; say "*was* questioned."

bo·nan·za (bŏ-nan-ză) *n.* a source of sudden great wealth or luck, a windfall.

bon ap·pé·tit (bon ap-ĕ-tee) (I wish you) a good appetite. ▷French.

bon·bon (bon-bon) *n.* a candy, usually with a creamy filling.

bond (bond) *n.* 1. something that binds, attaches, or restrains, as a rope. 2. something that unites people. 3. a binding agreement, a document containing this. 4. money deposited as a guarantee. 5. a document issued by a government or public company acknowledging that money has been lent to it and will be repaid, usually with interest. 6. writing paper of high quality. **bond** *v.* 1. to connect or unite with a bond. 2. to put into a warehouse until taxes are paid. 3. to insure a contract etc. by means of a financial bond.

bond·age (bon-dij) *n.* slavery, captivity.

bond·ed (bon-did) *adj.* stored in bond. □**bonded whiskey,** whiskey that has been aged in a bonded warehouse for at least four years before bottling.

bond·hold·er (bond-hohl-dĕr) *n.* a person who owns bonds issued by a government or company.

bond·man (bond-măn), **bonds·man** (bondz-măn) *n.* (*pl.* **-men,** *pr.* -mĕn) a serf or slave.

bonds·man (bondz-măn) *n.* (*pl.* **-men,** *pr.* -mĕn) a bailsman.

bond·wom·an (bond-wuum-ăn) *n.* (*pl.* **-wom·en,** *pr.* -wim-in) a woman in serfdom or slavery.

bone (bohn) *n.* 1. one of the hard parts that make up the skeleton of an animal's body. 2. a piece of bone with meat on it, as food. 3. the substance from which such parts are made, a similar hard substance. **bone** *v.* (**boned, bon·ing**) to remove the bones from. **bone'less** *adj.* □**bone china,** fine china made of clay mixed with bone ash.

bone fish, a large game fish with many small bones. **bone of contention,** the subject of a dispute. **bone weary,** utterly weary. **feel in one's bones,** to feel sure by intuition. **have a bone to pick,** to have something to argue or complain about. **make no bones about,** to raise no objection to, to speak frankly about. **wet to the bone,** completely wet.

bone-dry (bohn-drı) *adj.* quite dry.

bone·head (bohn-hed) *n. (slang)* a stupid person. **bone'head·ed** *adj.*

bone·meal (bohn-meel) *n.* crushed powdered bones used as a fertilizer.

bon·er (boh-nĕr) *n. (slang)* a blunder.

bon·fire (bon-fır) *n.* a large fire built in the open air to destroy rubbish or as a celebration.

bon·go (bong-goh) *n.* (*pl.* **-gos, -goes**) one of a pair of drums played with the fingers.

bon·ho·mie (bon-ŏ-mee) *n.* a genial manner.

bo·ni·to (bŏ-nee-toh) *n.* (*pl.* **-tos, -to**) a large mackerel-like fish.

bon·kers (bong-kĕrz) *adj. (British slang)* crazy.

bon mot (bon moh) (*pl.* **bons mots, bon mots,** *pr.* bon mohz) a witty saying.

Bonn (bon) the capital of West Germany.

bon·net (bon-it) *n.* a hat with strings that tie under the chin.

bon·ny (bon-ee) *adj.* (**-ni·er, -ni·est**) *(Scottish)* good-looking.

bon·sai (bon-sı) *n.* 1. a plant or tree grown in miniature form in a pot by artificially restricting its growth. 2. the method of cultivating this.

bo·nus (boh-nŭs) *n.* (*pl.* **-nus·es**) a payment or benefit in addition to what is usual or expected.

bon vi·vant (bon vee-vahnt) (*pl.* **bon vi·vants, bons vi·vants,** *pr.* bon vee-vahnts) a person who lives well and especially one who enjoys good food and drink.

bon voy·age (bon vwah-yahzh) (I wish you) a pleasant journey.

bon·y (boh-nee) *adj.* (**bon·i·er, bon·i·est**) 1. like bones. 2. having large or prominent bones, having bones with little flesh. 3. full of bones. **bon'i·ness** *n.*

bonze (bonz) *n.* a Japanese or Chinese Buddhist priest.

boo (boo) *interj.* 1. a sound made to show disapproval or contempt. 2. an exclamation used to startle someone. **boo** *v.* to show disapproval by shouting "boo."

boob (boob) *n. (slang)* a foolish person. □**boob tube,** *(slang)* a television set.

boo·by (boo-bee) *n.* (*pl.* **-bies**) a foolish person. □**booby hatch,** *(slang)* a mental institution. **booby prize,** a prize given as a joke to the competitor with the worst score. **booby trap,** a hidden trap rigged up for a practical joke; a hidden bomb placed so that it will explode when some apparently harmless object is touched or moved.

boo·by-trap (boo-bee-trap) *v.* (**boo·by-trapped, boo·by-trap·ping**) to place a booby trap in or on.

boo·dle (boo-dĕl) *n. (slang)* 1. money, especially for political bribery. 2. loot from a robbery.

book (buuk) *n.* 1. a series of written, printed, or plain sheets of paper fastened together at one edge and enclosed in a cover. 2. a literary work that would fill such a book or books if printed, *he is working on his book.* 3. *(informal)* a magazine. 4. a number of checks, stamps, tickets, matches, etc. fastened together in the shape of a book. 5.

one of the main divisions of a written work. 6. a libretto. 7. a record of bets made; *make book,* act as bookmaker. **book** *v.* 1. to enter in a book or list; *the police booked him for speeding,* recorded a charge against him. 2. to reserve (a seat or accommodation etc.). □**book club,** an organization that sells books to its members at a reduced price. **book learning,** knowledge gained from books without practical experience. **book match,** one of the matches of a matchbook. **book value,** value of a company's shares as entered in the company books, as opposed to *market value.* **bring to book,** to make (a person) answer for his conduct. **by the book,** in accordance with the correct procedure. **the Book** *or* **the Good Book,** the Bible. **throw the book at,** *see* **throw.**

book·case (buuk-kays) *n.* a piece of furniture with shelves for books.

book·end (buuk-end) *n.* one of a pair of usually ornamental props to keep a row of books upright.

book·ie (buuk-ee) *n. (informal)* a bookmaker.

book·ish (buuk-ish) *adj.* fond of reading.

book·keep·er (buuk-kee-pĕr) *n.* a person who keeps the accounts of a business etc.

book·keep·ing (buuk-kee-ping) *n.* the systematic recording of business transactions.

book·let (buuk-lit) *n.* a small thin usually paper-covered book.

book·mak·er (buuk-may-kĕr) *n.* a person whose business is taking bets. **book'mak·ing** *n.*

book·mark (buuk-mahrk) *n.* a strip of paper or other material placed between the pages of a book to mark a place.

book·mo·bile (buuk-mŏ-beel) *n.* a vehicle equipped as a traveling lending library.

book·plate (buuk-playt) *n.* a decorative label with the owner's name pasted in the front of a book.

book·sell·er (buuk-sel-ĕr) *n.* a person whose business is selling books.

book·shelf (buuk-shelf) *n.* a shelf for standing books on.

book·stall (buuk-stawl) *n.* a booth at which books are sold.

book·store (buuk-stohr) *n.* a shop where books are sold.

book·worm (buuk-wurm) *n.* 1. a grub or insect that eats holes in books. 2. a person who is very fond of reading.

boom[1] (boom) *v.* 1. to make a hollow deep resonant sound. 2. to have a period of prosperity or rapid economic growth. **boom** *n.* 1. a booming sound. 2. a period of growth, prosperity, or increasing value. □**boom town,** a town undergoing sudden rapid growth, as after the discovery of gold.

boom[2] *n.* 1. a long pole used to keep the bottom of a sail stretched. 2. a floating barrier across a body of water, often used to contain oil spills. 3. a long pole or crane carrying a microphone etc.

boom·er·ang (boo-mĕ-rang) *n.* 1. a curved wooden missile that can be thrown so that it returns to the thrower if it fails to hit anything, used by Australian aborigines. 2. something that causes unexpected harm to its originator. **boom·erang** *v.* to act as a boomerang.

boon[1] (boon) *n.* a benefit.

boon[2] *adj.* **boon companion,** a pleasant, sociable companion.

boon·docks (boon-doks) *n. pl. (slang)* rough or isolated country.

boon·dog·gle (boon-dog-ĕl) *n. (informal)* trivial or unnecessary work. **boon'dog·gler** *n.*

boor (boor) *n.* an ill-mannered person. **boor'ish** *adj.* **boor'ish·ly** *adv.* **boor'ish·ness** *n.*

boost (boost) *v.* 1. to push upward. 2. to increase the strength, value, or good reputation of, to promote. **boost** *n.* 1. an upward thrust. 2. *(slang)* an increase. **boost'er** *n.* □**booster rocket,** a rocket that powers the liftoff or early stage of a missile launching, and then may drop away.

boot[1] (boot) *n.* 1. a shoe or outer covering for the foot and ankle or leg. 2. *the boot, (slang)* dismissal from a job. **boot** *v.* 1. to kick. 2. *(slang)* to dismiss. □**boot camp,** a training base for recruits in the U.S. Navy or Marines.

boot[2] *v. (old use)* to profit. □**to boot,** in addition, besides.

boot·black (boot-blak) *n.* a person engaged in the business of polishing shoes.

boo·tee, boo·tie (boo-tee) *n.* a baby's knitted or crocheted boot.

booth (booth) *n.* 1. a small temporary shelter at a market or fair. 2. an enclosure for a public telephone. 3. a compartment in a large room, as for voting at elections. 4. a seating accommodation in a restaurant. 5. an enclosed stand or table where merchandise or food is displayed for sale.

boot·leg (boot-leg) *v.* **(boot·legged, boot·leg·ging)** to smuggle or sell (especially liquor) illegally. **bootleg** *n.* bootlegged liquor. **bootleg** *adj.* (of liquor etc.) smuggled or sold illegally.

boot·lick (boot-lik) *v. (slang)* to behave obsequiously, to fawn. **boot'lick·er** *n.*

boo·ty (boo-tee) *n. (pl.* -ties) loot.

booze (booz) *v.* **(boozed, booz·ing)** *(informal)* to drink alcohol, especially in large quantities. **booze** *n. (informal)* liquor; *on the booze,* boozing. **booz'er** *n.* **booz'y** *adj.*

bop[1] (bop) *v.* **(bopped, bop·ping)** *(slang)* to hit or strike. **bop** *n. (slang)* a blow.

bop[2] *n.* a kind of jazz music with complex harmony and highly syncopated rhythm. **bop'per** *n.*

bo·rate (bohr-ayt) *n.* salt of boric acid.

bo·rax (bohr-aks) *n.* a soluble white powder that is a compound of boron, used in making glass, enamels, and detergents.

Bor·deaux (bor-doh) *n.* a red or white wine from Bordeaux in France, a similar wine from elsewhere.

bor·del·lo (bor-del-oh) *n. (pl.* -los) a brothel.

bor·der (bor-dĕr) *n.* 1. an edge or boundary, the part near this. 2. the line dividing two countries, the area near this. 3. an edging. 4. a strip of ground around a garden or a part of it, *a perennial border.* **border** *v.* to put or be a border to. □**border on,** to be next to; to come close to, *it borders on the absurd.*

bor·der·land (bor-dĕr-land) *n.* the district near a boundary.

bor·der·line (bor-dĕr-lın) *n.* the line that marks a boundary. **borderline** *adj.* on the borderline between different groups or categories.

bore[1] (bohr) *see* **bear**[2].

bore[2] (bohr) *v.* **(bored, bor·ing)** 1. to make (a hole or well etc.) with a revolving tool or by digging out soil. 2. to pierce or penetrate in this way; *bore one's way,* get through by pushing. **bore** *n.* 1. the hollow inside of a gun barrel or engine cylinder. 2. a hole made by boring.

bore[3] *v.* **(bored, bor·ing)** to make (a person) feel tired or uninterested by being dull or tedious.

bore *n.* a boring person or thing. **bore'dom** *n.* **bored** *adj.* **bor'ing** *adj.*

bore[4] *n.* a tidal wave with a steep front that moves up some channels.

bo·re·al (bohr-i-ăl) *adj.* of the north or the Arctic or the north wind.

bo·ric (bohr-ik) *adj.* of boron. □**boric acid,** a substance derived from boron, used as a mild antiseptic.

born (born) *see* **bear**[2]. (▷See the note under **borne.**) **be born,** to be brought forth by birth; *born to suffer,* destined for this by birth; *their courage was born of despair,* originated from this. **born** *adj.* 1. having a certain order or status or place of birth, *first-born; well-born; foreign-born.* 2. having a certain natural quality or ability, *a born leader.* □**born-again Christian,** a person who, through a profound spiritual experience, claims to have received a new spiritual life. **in all one's born days,** (*informal*) in all one's lifetime. **not born yesterday,** experienced in people's ways and not easy to deceive.

borne (bohrn) *see* **bear**[2]. ▷The word *borne* is used as part of the verb *to bear* only when it comes before *by* or after *have, has,* or *had,* as in *children borne by Eve; she had borne him a son.* The word *born* is used in such statements as *a son was born.*

bo·ron (bohr-on) *n.* a chemical element that is very resistant to high temperatures, used in metal working and in nuclear reactors.

bor·ough (bur-oh) *n.* 1. an incorporated town or village. 2. one of the five administrative districts of the City of New York.

bor·row (bor-oh) *v.* 1. to get the temporary use of, on the understanding that the thing received is to be returned. 2. to use without being the inventor; *borrow their methods,* copy them. **bor'row·er** *n.* □**borrowed time,** an extension of one's life.

borscht (borsht), **borsch** (borsh) *n.* a Russian or Polish soup made from beets. □**borscht belt,** a resort area in the Catskill mountains of New York.

bor·zoi (bor-zoi) *n.* (also **Russian wolfhound**) a large hound with a narrow head and silky coat.

bosh (bosh) *interj.* & *n.* (*informal*) nonsense.

bo's'n = **boatswain.**

bo·som (buuz-ŏm) *n.* 1. a person's breast. 2. the part of a garment covering this. 3. the center or innermost part; *returned to the bosom of his family,* to a loving family circle. □**bosom friend,** one who is dear and close.

bo·som·y (buuz-ŏ-mee) *adj.* having large breasts.

boss[1] (baws) *n.* (*informal*) 1. a person who employs or controls or gives orders to workers. 2. a manager of a political organization. **boss** *v.* (*slang*) to be the boss of, to give orders to; *boss someone about,* to order him about.

boss[2] *n.* a round projecting knob or stud. **boss** *v.* to ornament with bosses.

boss·y (baw-see) *adj.* (**boss·i·er, boss·i·est**) fond of ordering people about, doing this continually. **boss'i·ly** *adv.* **boss'i·ness** *n.*

Bos·ton (baw-stŏn) the capital of Massachusetts.

bo·sun = **boatswain.**

bot. *abbr.* 1. botanical. 2. botanist. 3. botany. 4. bottle.

bo·tan·i·cal (bŏ-tan-i-kăl), **bo·tan·ic** (bŏ-tan-ik) *adj.* of botany. □**botanical garden,** a garden where plants and trees are grown for scientific study.

bot·a·nist (bot-ă-nist) *n.* an expert in botany.

bot·a·ny (bot-ă-nee) *n.* the scientific study of plants.

botch (boch) *v.* to spoil by poor or clumsy work. **botch** *n.* a piece of spoiled work.

both (bohth) *adj., adv.,* & *pron.* the two, not only the one.

both·er (bo*th*-ĕr) *v.* 1. to cause trouble or worry or annoyance to, to pester. 2. to take trouble, to feel concern. **bother** *n.* 1. worry, minor trouble. 2. something causing this.

both·er·a·tion (bo*th*-ĕ-ray-shŏn) *interj.* & *n.* (*informal*) bother.

both·er·some (bo*th*-ĕr-sŏm) *adj.* causing bother.

Bot·swa·na (bot-swah-nă) a country in East Africa.

bot·tle (bot-ĕl) *v.* (**bot·tled, bot·tling**) 1. to store in bottles. 2. to preserve in glass jars. □**bottle party,** a party to which each guest brings a bottle of liquor. **hit the bottle,** (*slang*) to be an alcoholic; to drink heavily.

bot·tle-fed (bot-ĕl-fed) *adj.* fed with milk from a bottle.

bot·tle·neck (bot-ĕl-nek) *n.* 1. a narrow stretch of road where traffic cannot flow freely. 2. anything similarly obstructing progress.

bot·tom (bot-ŏm) *n.* 1. the lowest part of anything, the part on which it rests, the lowest place; *the bottom fell out of the market,* trade fell dramatically. 2. the buttocks, the part of the body on which one sits. 3. the ground under a stretch of water. **bottom** *adj.* lowest in position or rank or degree. □**at bottom,** basically, really. **be at the bottom of,** to be the underlying cause or originator of. **bottom line,** the final figure in a financial statement, showing profit or loss; the final consequence. **bottom out,** to reach the lowest level before beginning to rise again. **from the bottom of one's heart,** with deep feeling, sincerely. **get to the bottom of,** to find out the cause or origin of. **hit bottom,** to reach the lowest state or level.

bot·tom·land (bot-ŏm-land) *n.* the rich soil of a river valley.

bot·tom·less (bot-ŏm-lis) *adj.* 1. without a bottom, extremely deep. 2. nude from the waist down. □**bottomless bar,** a place where entirely nude dancers entertain. **bottomless dancer,** one entirely nude.

bot·tom·most (bot-ŏm-mohst) *adj.* lowest.

bot·u·lism (boch-ŭ-liz-ĕm) *n.* a kind of food poisoning.

bou·clé (boo-klay) *n.* 1. yarn with one of its strands looped at intervals. 2. fabric made from this.

bou·doir (boo-dwahr) *n.* a woman's small private room or (*informal*) bedroom.

bouf·fant (boo-fahnt) *adj.* puffed out.

bou·gain·vil·lae·a (boo-găn-vil-i-ă) *n.* a tropical shrub with red or purple bracts.

bough (bow) *n.* a large branch coming from the trunk of a tree.

bought (bawt) *see* **buy.**

bouil·la·baisse (bool-yă-bays) *n.* a fish stew made with several different types of fish.

bouil·lon (buul-yon) *n.* broth.

boul·der (bohl-dĕr) *n.* a large stone rounded by water or weather.

boul·e·vard (buul-ĕ-vahrd) *n.* a wide street, often with trees on each side.

bounce (bowns) *v.* (**bounced, bounc·ing**) 1. to spring back when sent against something hard, to cause to do this. 2. *(informal)* (of a check) to be sent back by the bank as worthless. 3. to jump suddenly, to move in a lively manner. **bounce** *n.* 1. bouncing, the power of bouncing. 2. a lively manner.

bounc·er (bown-sĕr) *n.* 1. a ball that bounces, as a baseball hit to the infield. 2. a man employed to eject undesirable customers from a club etc.

bounc·ing (bown-sing) *adj.* big and healthy, boisterous, *a bouncing baby boy.*

bounc·y (bown-see) *adj.* **(bounc·i·er, bounc·i·est)** full of bounce.

bound[1] (bownd) *v.* to limit, to be the boundary of.

bound[2] *v.* to jump or spring, to run with jumping movements. **bound** *n.* a bounding movement.

bound[3] *adj.* going or heading toward, *bound for Spain; northbound traffic.*

bound[4] *v. see* **bind. bound** *adj.* obstructed or hindered by, *fog-bound.* □**bound to,** certain to. **bound up with,** closely associated with. **I'll be bound,** I feel certain.

bound·a·ry (bown-dă-ree) *n.* (*pl.* **-ries**) a line that marks a limit.

bound·en (bown-dĕn) *adj. (old use)* obligatory, *bounden duty.*

bound·less (bownd-lis) *adj.* without limits. **bound′less·ness** *n.*

bounds (bowndz) *n. pl.* limits. □**out of bounds,** outside the areas one is allowed to enter; (in sports) outside the playing area.

boun·te·ous (bown-ti-ŭs) *adj.* beneficent, plentiful, freely bestowed. **boun′te·ous·ly** *adv.*

boun·ti·ful (bown-ti-fŭl) *adj.* 1. giving generously. 2. abundant. **boun′ti·ful·ly** *adj.*

boun·ty (bown-tee) *n.* (*pl.* **-ties**) 1. generosity in giving. 2. a generous gift. 3. a reward or payment given as an inducement. □**bounty hunter,** one who hunts wild animals in order to collect a bounty.

bou·quet (boo-kay, boh-kay) *n.* 1. a bunch of flowers for carrying in the hand. 2. a compliment, praise. 3. the perfume of wine. □**bouquet garni** (*pr.* gahr-nee), a bundle of herbs used for flavoring.

bour·bon (bur-bŏn) *n.* whiskey made mainly from corn mash.

bour·geois (boor-zhwah) *n.* (*pl.* **-geois,** *pr.* -zhwah, -zhwahz) (often *contemptuous*) a member of the middle class, with its conventional ideas and tastes. **bourgeois** *adj.*

bour·geoi·sie (boor-zhwah-zee) *n.* (sometimes *contemptuous*) the bourgeois class.

bourse (boors) *n.* a money market, especially the Parisian stock exchange.

bout (bowt) *n.* 1. a period of exercise or work or illness. 2. a boxing contest.

bou·tique (boo-teek) *n.* a small shop selling clothes etc. of the latest fashion.

bou·ton·niere (boo-tŏ-neer) *n.* a flower or spray of flowers worn in the lapel buttonhole.

bo·vine (boh-vɪn) *adj.* 1. of or like an ox or cow. 2. dull and stupid.

bow[1] (boh) *n.* 1. a piece of wood or plastic curved by a tight string joining its ends, used as a weapon for shooting arrows. 2. a rod with horsehair stretched between its ends, used for playing the violin etc. 3. a knot made with a loop or loops, ribbon etc. tied in this way. □**bow tie,** a man's necktie tied into a bow.

bow[2] (bow) *v.* bending of the head or body in greeting, respect, agreement, etc. **bow** *v.* 1. to make a bow, to bend in greeting etc. 2. to bend downward under a weight. 3. to submit or give in, *must bow to the inevitable.* □**bow and scrape,** to behave in an obsequious way.

bow[3] (bow) *n.* 1. the front or forward end of a boat or ship. 2. the oarsman nearest the bow.

bowd·ler·ize (bohd-lĕ-rɪz) *v.* **(bowd·ler·ized, bowd·ler·iz·ing)** to censor words or scenes considered improper. ▷Named after T. *Bowdler,* who produced a censored version of Shakespeare's plays.

bow·el (bow-ĕl) *n.* 1. the intestine. 2. *bowels,* the intestines, the innermost parts. □**bowel movement,** evacuation of the bowels; feces.

bow·er (bow-ĕr) *n.* a leafy shelter.

bowl[1] (bohl) *n.* 1. a basin for holding food or liquid. 2. this with its contents, the amount it contains. 3. the hollow rounded part of a spoon, tobacco pipe, etc. 4. a stadium for football etc., *Rose Bowl.* **bowl′ful** *n.* (*pl.* **-fuls**).

bowl[2] *n.* a ball used in bowling, skittles, etc. **bowl** *v.* 1. to send rolling along the ground. 2. to play at bowling. 3. *bowls,* a game played on a bowling green by rolling heavy balls so that they stop near a target. □**bowl over,** to knock down; to overwhelm with surprise or emotion.

bow·leg (boh-leg) *n.* outward curvature or bowing of one or both legs. **bow·leg·ged** (boh-leg-id) *adj.*

bowl·er[1] (boh-lĕr) *n.* 1. a person who plays at bowls. 2. a person who bowls in bowling or cricket.

bowler[2] *n.* (also **bowler hat**) a hard felt hat with a rounded top, a derby hat.

bow·line (boh-lin, -lɪn) *n.* a simple but secure knot used by sailors.

bow·ling (boh-ling) *n.* a game played by rolling a bowling ball down a wooden alley to knock down as many as possible of a triangular group of ten pins. □**bowling alley,** a long enclosure for bowling. **bowling green,** a lawn for playing bowls.

bow·man (boh-măn) *n.* (*pl.* **-men,** *pr.* mĕn) an archer.

bow·sprit (boh-sprit) *n.* a spar running out from a ship's stem, to which the forestays are attached.

bow·string (boh-string) *n.* the string of a bow.

box[1] (boks) *n.* 1. a container with a flat base and usually a lid, for holding solids. 2. the amount it contains. 3. a boxlike receptacle, a money box, mailbox, etc. 4. a compartment, as with seats for several persons in a theater, for a horse in a stable or vehicle, for the jury or witnesses in a law court. 5. a small hut or shelter, *sentry box.* **box** *v.* to put into a box. □**box in** *or* **up,** to shut into a small space, preventing free movement. **box kite,** a kite with an open boxlike frame. **box number,** a number used to identify a box in a newspaper office to which letters to an advertiser may be sent. **box office,** an office from which tickets are sold at a theater etc. **box pleat,** an arrangement of parallel pleats folding in alternate directions. **box spring,** one of a set of vertical springs in a mattress.

box[2] *v.* to fight with the fists, to engage in boxing. **box** *n.* a slap with the open hand. □**box a person's ears,** to slap them.

box[3] *n.* 1. a small evergreen shrub. 2. its wood.

box·car (boks-kahr) *n.* an enclosed railroad freight car.

box·er[1] (bok-sĕr) *n.* a person who engages in boxing.

boxer[2] *n.* a dog of a short-haired breed with tan coat.

box·ing (bok-sing) *n.* the sport of fighting with the fists. ☐**boxing gloves,** a pair of padded leather mittens worn in boxing. **boxing ring,** a square area, marked off by ropes, for boxing matches.

boy (boi) *n.* 1. a male child. 2. a young man. 3. a young male employee, *an office boy.* 4. *(contemptuous)* a male servant. **boy** *interj.* an exclamation of surprise or joy. **boy'hood** *n.* ☐**boy scout,** a member of the Boy Scouts, an organization intended to develop character through outdoor activities.

boy·cott (boi-kot) *v.* to refuse to have anything to do with; *boycotted the goods,* refused to handle or buy them. **boycott** *n.* boycotting, treatment of this kind.

boy·friend (boi-frend) a woman's usual or preferred male companion.

boy·ish (boi-ish) *adj.* like a boy. **boy'ish·ly** *adv.* **boy'ish·ness** *n.*

boy·sen·ber·ry (boi-zĕn-ber-ee) *n.* (*pl.* **-ries**) 1. a hybrid of several species of bramble. 2. its blackberrylike fruit.

bp *abbr.* bishop.

B.P. *abbr.* 1. bills payable. 2. blood pressure.

BPOE *abbr.* Benevolent and Protective Order of Elks.

br. *abbr.* 1. branch. 2. brass. 3. brother. 4. brown.

Br. *abbr.* 1. Britain. 2. British.

bra (brah) *n.* a woman's undergarment worn to support the breasts, a brassiere.

brace (brays) *n.* 1. a device that clamps things together or holds and supports them in position. 2. a pair, *five brace of partridge.* 3. **braces,** *(British)* suspenders for trousers. **brace** *v.* (**braced, brac·ing**) to support, to give firmness to. **brac'er** *n.* ☐**brace oneself** *or* **brace up,** to steady oneself in order to meet a blow or shock.

brace·let (brays-lit) *n.* 1. an ornamental band worn on the arm. 2. *bracelets, (slang)* handcuffs.

bra·ce·ro (brah-sair-oh) *n.* (*pl.* **-ros**) a Mexican doing seasonal agricultural work in the U.S.

brac·ing (bray-sing) *adv.* invigorating, stimulating.

brack·en (brak-ĕn) *n.* a large fern that grows on wasteland, a mass of such ferns.

brack·et (brak-it) *n.* 1. a support projecting from an upright surface. 2. either of the marks used in pairs for enclosing words or figures, [ ] 3. a group bracketed together as similar or falling between certain limits, *an income bracket.* **bracket** *v.* (**brack·et·ed, brack·et·ing**) 1. to enclose or join by brackets. 2. to put together to imply connection or equality. 3. to place shots both short of the target and beyond it in order to find the range.

brack·ish (brak-ish) *adj.* slightly salty, *brackish water.*

bract (brakt) *n.* a leaflike part of a plant, often highly colored.

brad (brad) *n.* a thin flattish nail of the same thickness throughout.

brae (bray) *n. (Scottish)* a hillside.

brag (brag) *v.* (**bragged, brag·ging**) to boast.

brag·ga·do·ci·o (brag-ă-doh-shi-oh) *n.* (*pl.* **-ci·os**) empty boasting.

brag·gart (brag-ărt) *n.* a person who brags.

Brah·man, Brah·min (brah-măn) *n.* 1. a member of the highest or priestly caste among Hindus. 2. *(informal)* a highly cultured or intellectual aloof person. 3. a breed of cattle native to India and developed in the U.S.

Brah·man·ism, Brah·min·ism (brah-mă-niz-ĕm) *n.* the social and religious practices, especially the caste system, of orthodox Hindus and Brahmans.

braid (brayd) *n.* 1. a woven ornamental trimming. 2. an interlacing of three or more strands of hair. **braid** *v.* 1. to plait. 2. to trim with braid.

Braille (brayl) *n.* a system of representing letters etc. by raised dots that blind people can read by touch. **Braille, braille** *v.* (**Brailled, Brail·ing**) to represent in Braille. ▷Named after its inventor, Louis Braille.

brain (brayn) *n.* 1. the organ that is the center of the nervous system in animals, a mass of soft gray matter in the skull. 2. the mind or intellect, intelligence. **brain** *v.* 1. to kill by a heavy blow on the head. 2. to hit on the head. ☐**brain drain,** the loss of educated people by emigration. **brain trust,** the group of advisers called in by President Franklin Roosevelt; a group of experts advising a government. **brain wave,** an electrical impulse in the brain.

brain·child (brayn-chïld) *n.* a person's invention or plan.

brain·less (brayn-lis) *adj.* stupid.

brain·pow·er (brayn-pow-ĕr) *n.* mental ability.

brain·storm (brayn-storm) *n.* a sudden bright idea.

brainstorm *v.* to engage in a conference designed to produce bright ideas.

brain·wash (brayn-wosh) *v.* to force (a person) to reject old beliefs and accept new ones by subjecting him to great mental pressure. **brain'wash·ing** *n.*

brain·y (bray-nee) *adj.* (**brain·i·er, brain·i·est**) clever, intelligent.

braise (brayz) *v.* (**braised, brais·ing**) to cook slowly with very little liquid in a closed container.

brake[1] (brayk) *n.* a device for reducing the speed of something or stopping its motion. **brake** *v.* (**braked, brak·ing**) to slow down by means of this. ☐**brake drum,** a cylinder attached to a wheel, receiving the pressure of the brake shoe. **brake fluid,** the liquid used in a hydraulic brake. **brake shoe,** the part of a brake coming in contact with the wheel.

brake[2] *n.* a thicket.

brake[3] *n.* a kind of bracken.

brake·man (brayk-măn) *n.* (*pl.* **-men,** *pr.* **-mĕn**) a member of a train crew who acts as an assistant to a conductor.

bram·ble (bram-bĕl) *n.* a rough shrub with long prickly shoots, a blackberry bush.

bran (bran) *n.* coarse meal consisting of the ground inner husks of grain sifted out from flour.

branch (branch) *n.* 1. an armlike part of a tree. 2. a similar part of a river, road, railroad, etc. 3. a subdivision of a family or a group of languages or a subject. 4. a local store, library, office, etc. belonging to a larger organization. **branch** *v.* to send out branches, to divide into branches. ☐**branch off,** to leave a main route and take a minor one. **branch out,** to begin a new line of activity.

brand (brand) *n.* 1. a trademark, goods of a particular make. 2. a mark of identification made with a hot iron, the iron used for this. 3. a piece of burning or charred wood. **brand** *v.* 1. to mark with a hot iron, to label with a trademark. 2. to

give a bad name to, *he was branded as a trouble-maker.*
bran·dish (bran-dish) *v.* to wave (a thing) in display or threateningly.
brand-new (brand-noo, -nyoo) *adj.* completely new.
bran·dy (bran-dee) *n.* (*pl.* **-dies**) a strong liquor distilled from wine or from fermented fruit juice.
brandy *v.* (**bran·died, bran·dy·ing**) to flavor or preserve with brandy.
brash (brash) *adj.* 1. vulgarly self-assertive. 2. reckless. **brash'ly** *adv.* **brash'ness** *n.*
Bra·sil·ia (brah-zeel-yä) the capital of Brazil.
brass (bras) *n.* 1. a yellow alloy of copper and zinc. 2. a thing or things made of this. 3. the brass wind instruments of an orchestra. 4. a brass memorial tablet in a church. 5. *(informal)* impudence. 6. *(slang)* high-ranking officers or officials, *the top brass.* **brass** *adj.* made of brass. □**brass band,** a band playing brass and percussion instruments only. **brass hat,** *(slang)* an officer of high rank. **brass knuckles,** *see* **knuckle. get down to brass tacks,** to begin to consider the basic facts or practical details.
bras·se·rie (bras-ĕ-ree) *n.* an unpretentious restaurant, originally one that served beer with food.
bras·siere (bră-zeer) *n.* a bra.
brass·y (bras-ee) *adj.* (**brass·i·er, brass·i·est**) 1. like brass in appearance or sound. 2. bold and vulgar. **brass'i·ness** *n.*
brat (brat) *n.* *(contemptuous)* an obnoxious badly behaved child. **brat'ty** *adj.* **brat'ti·ness** *n.*
bra·va·do (bră-vah-doh) *n.* (*pl.* **-does, -dos**) a show of boldness.
brave (brayv) *adj.* (**brav·er, brav·est**) 1. able to face and endure danger or pain. 2. splendid. **brave** *n.* an American Indian warrior. **brave** *v.* (**braved, brav·ing**) to face and endure with bravery. **brave'ly** *adv.* **brav'er·y** *n.* (*pl.* **-er·ies**)
bra·vo (brah-voh) *interj.* well done! **bravo** *n.* (*pl.* **-vos**) a shout of "bravo."
bra·vu·ra (bră-vyoor-ă) *n.* 1. a brilliant performance, an attempt at this. 2. a passage of music requiring great skill and spirit in performance.
brawl (brawl) *n.* a noisy quarrel or fight. **brawl** *v.* to take part in a brawl. **brawl'er** *n.*
brawn (brawn) *n.* muscular strength.
brawn·y (braw-nee) *adj.* (**brawn·i·er, brawn·i·est**) strong and muscular.
bray (bray) *n.* the cry of a donkey, a sound like this. **bray** *v.* to make this cry or sound.
braze (brayz) *v.* (**brazed, braz·ing**) to solder with a hard solder that has a high melting point, as with an alloy of brass and zinc. **braze** *n.* a brazed joint.
bra·zen (bray-zĕn) *adj.* 1. made of brass, like brass. 2. shameless, impudent. □**brazen it out,** to behave, after doing wrong, as if one has nothing to be ashamed of. **bra'zen·ly** *adv.* **bra'zen·ness** *n.*
bra·zier[1] (bray-zhĕr) *n.* a basketlike stand for holding burning coals.
brazier[2] *n.* a brass worker.
Bra·zil (bră-zil) a country in South America. **Bra·zil·ian** (bră-zil-yăn) *adj & n.* □**Brazil nut,** a large three-sided nut.
Braz·za·ville (braz-ă-vil) the capital of Republic of Congo.
breach (breech) *n.* 1. the breaking or neglect of a rule or agreement etc. 2. an estrangement. 3. a broken place, a gap. **breach** *v.* to break through, to make a gap in. □**breach of the peace,** a

disturbance of the public peace by a brawl, riot, etc. **step into the breach,** to give help in a crisis.
bread (bred) *n.* 1. a food made of flour and liquid, usually leavened by yeast and baked. 2. *(slang)* money. **bread** *v.* to coat with bread crumbs for cooking. □**bread crumbs,** bread crumbled for use in cooking.
bread·bas·ket (bred-bas-kit) *n.* 1. a grain-producing region. 2. *(slang)* the stomach.
bread·board (bred-bohrd) *n.* 1. a board to knead or cut bread on. 2. a board for making a flat model of an electric circuit etc. **breadboard** *v.* to construct an experimental assembly of an electric circuit etc.
bread·ed (bred-id) *adj.* coated with bread crumbs.
bread·fruit (bred-froot) *n.* the fruit of a tropical tree, with white pulp like fresh bread.
bread line poor people waiting in line for charity food.
bread·stuff (bred-stuf) *n.* 1. grain for making bread. 2. bread.
breadth (bredth) *n.* width, broadness.
bread·win·ner (bred-win-ĕr) *n.* the member of a family who earns the money to support the others.
break (brayk) *v.* (**broke, bro·ken, break·ing**) 1. to fall into pieces, to cause to do this; *she broke her leg,* broke the bone in it. 2. to damage, to make or become unusable. 3. to fail to keep (a promise). 4. to stop for a time, to make or become discontinuous, *broke the silence; we broke for coffee; broke into a run,* began to run; *broke the strike,* forced it to end by means other than bargaining. 5. to make a way suddenly or violently, *he broke out of prison;* (in billiards) to open play by scattering the object balls from their triangular arrangement. 6. to emerge or appear suddenly. 7. to reveal (news etc.), to become known, *the story broke.* 8. to surpass, *broke the world record.* 9. to make or become weak, to overwhelm with grief etc., to destroy, *the scandal broke him.* 10. (of a voice) to change its even tone, either with emotion or (of a boy's voice) by becoming suddenly deeper at puberty. 11. (of waves) to fall in foam. 12. (of boxers) to come out of a clinch. **break** *n.* 1. breaking. 2. an escape, a sudden dash. 3. a gap, a broken place. 4. an interval, between periods of work or exercise. 5. (in billiards) the opening play. 6. *(informal)* a piece of luck; *a bad break,* bad luck. 7. a fair chance; *give him a break,* an opportunity. 8. an escape, *a prison break.* 9. (in harness racing) a horse's change from one type of step to another. □**break down,** to cease to function because of mechanical failure; (of a person's health) to collapse; to give way to emotion; to act upon chemically and reduce to constituent parts; to analyze, *break down the expenditure.* **break even,** to make gains and losses that balance exactly. **break fresh ground,** to deal with some aspect of a subject for the first time. **break in,** to force one's way into a building; to interrupt; to accustom to a new routine; to use (shoes etc.) until wearable, fully operable, etc. **breaking point,** the point at which a person or thing gives way under stress. **break in on,** to disturb, to interrupt. **break of day,** dawn. **break off,** to bring to an end; to stop speaking. **break one's neck,** to fracture or dislocate one's neck; *(informal)* to make a great effort, *we broke our necks to finish on time.* **break out,** to begin suddenly; to exclaim; to force one's way out; to de-

velop as a rash etc. **break service,** to win a game at tennis when one's opponent is serving. **break the bank,** to use up all the resources of a casino gambling table. **break the heart of,** to overwhelm with grief. **break the ice,** to overcome formality. **break up,** to bring or come to an end; to become weaker; to separate; to disband. **break wind,** to expel wind from the bowels or stomach. **break with,** to give up; to end one's friendship with.

break·a·ble (bray-kă-běl) *adj.* able to be broken.
break·age (bray-kij) *n.* 1. breaking. 2. something broken. 3. an amount allowed for expected breaking. 4. change or an amount less than 1¢, 5¢, or 10¢ kept by a vendor, a gambling house, etc. when only full or round figures are given.
break·a·way (brayk-ă-way) *adj.* 1. becoming separate or free. 2. that breaks or has broken away, *a breakaway group.*
break·down (brayk-down) *n.* 1. a mechanical failure. 2. a weakening. 3. a collapse of health or mental stability. 4. an analysis.
break·er (bray-kěr) *n.* 1. a heavy ocean wave that breaks on the coast. 2. a person wishing to transmit a message (in CB radio).
break·fast (brek-făst) *n.* the first meal of the day. **breakfast** *v.* to eat breakfast.
break·front (brayk-frunt) *adj.* having a center section that projects beyond those at either side. **breakfront** *n.* a breakfront cabinet.
break-in (brayk-in) *n.* a forcible entry, especially by a thief.
break·neck (brayk-nek) *adj.* dangerously fast, *at breakneck speed.*
break·through (brayk-throo) *n.* a major advance in knowledge.
break·up (brayk-up) *n.* breaking up, dissolution.
break·wa·ter (brayk-waw-těr) *n.* a wall built out into the sea to protect a harbor or coast against heavy waves.
bream (breem) *n.* a fish of the carp family.
breast (brest) *n.* 1. either of the two milk-producing organs on the upper front of a woman's body. 2. the upper front part of the human body or of a garment covering this. 3. the corresponding part in animals. **breast** *v.* to face and advance, *breasted the waves.* □**breast stroke,** a swimming stroke performed face downward, with sweeping movements of the arms.
breast·bone (brest-bohn) *n.* the bone down the center of the upper front of the body.
breast-feed (brest-feed) *v.* **(breast-fed, breast-feed·ing)** to feed (a baby) by allowing it to suck at the mother's breast.
breast·plate (brest-playt) *n.* a piece of armor covering the breast.
breast·work (brest-wurk) *n.* a temporary defense or parapet a few feet high.
breath (breth) *n.* 1. air drawn into and sent out of the lungs. 2. breathing in, *take six deep breaths.* 3. a gentle blowing, *a breath of wind.* 4. a whisper, a trace, *not a breath of scandal.* □**in the same breath,** immediately after saying something else. **out of breath,** panting after violent exercise. **save one's breath,** to refrain from useless discussion. **take one's breath away,** to make one breathless with surprise or delight. **under one's breath,** in a whisper.
breathe (breeth) *v.* **(breathed, breath·ing)** 1. to draw air into the lungs and send it out again, (of plants) to respire. 2. to take into or send out

of the lungs, *breathing cigar smoke.* 3. to utter; *don't breathe a word of it,* keep it secret. □**breathe again,** to feel relieved of fear or anxiety. **breathing room,** room to breathe; a pause for rest.
breath·er (bree-thěr) *n.* 1. a pause for rest. 2. a short period in the fresh air.
breath·less (breth-lis) *adj.* out of breath, panting. **breath'less·ly** *adv.* **breath'less·ness** *n.*
breath·tak·ing (breth-tay-king) *adj.* very exciting, spectacular.
brec·ci·a (brech-i-ă) *n.* a composite rock of angular fragments of stone etc. cemented together.
bred (bred) *see* **breed.**
breech (breech) *n.* 1. the back part of a gun barrel. 2. the back part of anything. □**breech birth,** a birth in which the baby's buttocks appear first.
breech·cloth (breech-klawth) *n.* a loincloth.
breech·es (brich-iz) *n. pl.* trousers reaching to just below the knee.
breed (breed) *v.* **(bred, breed·ing)** 1. to produce offspring. 2. to keep (animals) for the purpose of producing young. 3. to bring up. 4. to give rise to. **breed** *n.* a variety of animals etc. within a species, having similar appearance.
breed·er (bree-děr) *n.* a person who breeds animals. □**breeder reactor,** a nuclear reactor that produces more fissile material than it uses.
breed·ing (bree-ding) *n.* 1. the production of young from animals, propagation. 2. good manners resulting from training or background.
breeze (breez) *n.* a light wind. **breeze** *v.* **(breezed, breez·ing)** *(informal)* to move in a lively manner, *they breezed in.*
breeze·way (breez-way) *n.* a roofed open-sided passageway connecting two buildings.
breez·y (bree-zee) *adj.* **(breez·i·er, breez·i·est)** 1. exposed to wind. 2. pleasantly windy. 3. lively, jovial. **breez'i·ly** *adv.* **breez'i·ness** *n.*
Bren (bren) **gun** a lightweight machine gun.
breth·ren (breth-rěn) *n. pl. (old use)* brothers. □**the Brethren,** members of various German Protestant groups.
Bre·ton (bret-ŏn) *adj.* of Brittany or its people. **Breton** *n.* a native of Brittany.
breve (breev) *n.* a mark ˘ placed over a vowel to indicate that it is short.
bre·vi·ar·y (bree-vi-er-ee) *n.* (*pl.* **-ar·ies**) a book of prayers to be said daily by Roman Catholic priests.
brev·i·ty (brev-i-tee) *n.* (*pl.* **-ties**) shortness, briefness.
brew (broo) *v.* 1. to make (beer) by boiling and fermentation, to make (tea) by steeping. 2. to be under preparation in this way, *the tea is brewing.* 3. to bring about, to develop, *trouble is brewing.* **brew** *n.* 1. a liquid made by brewing. 2. an amount brewed. 3. *(informal)* a glass of beer.
brew·er (broo-ěr) *n.* a person whose trade is brewing beer.
brew·er·y (broo-ě-ree) *n.* (*pl.* **-er·ies**) a building in which beer is brewed.
bri·ar (brI-ăr) = **brier.**
brib·a·ble (brI-bă-běl) *adj.* able to be bribed.
bribe (brIb) *n.* something offered in order to influence a person illegally or improperly to act in favor of the giver. **bribe** *v.* **(bribed, brib·ing)** to persuade by a bribe. **brib'er·y** *n.* (*pl.* **-er·ies**) the act or practice of bribing.

bric-a-brac (brik-ă-brak) *n. pl.* odd items of furniture, ornaments, etc. of no great value.
brick (brik) *n.* 1. a block of baked or dried clay or other substance used to build walls. 2. a rectangular block of something. 3. *(slang)* a kindhearted person. **brick** *adj.* 1. built of brick. 2. brick-red. **brick** *v.* to block with brickwork.
brick·bat (brik-bat) *n.* 1. a piece of brick, especially one used as a missile. 2. *(informal)* a piece of harsh criticism, *she threw brickbats at me.*
brick·lay·er (brik-lay-ěr) *n.* a workman who builds with bricks. **brick′lay·ing** *n.*
brick-red (brik-red) *adj.* of the red color of bricks.
brick·work (brik-wurk) *n.* a structure made of bricks.
brid·al (bri-dăl) *adj.* of a bride or wedding.
bride (brid) *n.* a woman on her wedding day, a newly married woman.
bride·groom (brid-groom) *n.* a man on his wedding day, a newly married man.
brides·maid (bridz-mayd) *n.* a girl or unmarried woman attending the bride at a wedding.
bridge[1] (brij) *n.* 1. a structure providing a way across something or carrying a road or railroad etc. across. 2. the raised platform on a ship from which the captain and officers direct its course. 3. the bony upper part of the nose. 4. something that joins or connects or supports other parts. **bridge** *v.* (**bridged, bridg·ing**) to make or form a bridge over.
bridge[2] *n.* a card game developed from whist. □**auction bridge,** a variety of bridge in which the right to name the trumps and to play with the dummy goes, with each deal, to the player who makes the highest bid. **contract bridge,** the most common form of bridge, in which only the tricks the declarer has undertaken to make count toward the game.
bridge·head (brij-hed) *n.* a fortified area established in enemy territory, especially on the far side of a river.
Bridge·town (brij-town) the capital of Barbados.
bridge·work (brij-wurk) *n.* a partial denture supported by teeth on each side.
bri·dle (bri-děl) *n.* the part of a horse's harness that goes on its head. **bridle** *v.* (**bri·dled, bri·dling**) 1. to put a bridle on. 2. to restrain, to keep under control. 3. to draw one's head up in pride or scorn. □**bridle path,** a path suitable for horseback riding but not for vehicles.
Brie (bree) *n.* a kind of soft cheese.
brief[1] (breef) *adj.* 1. lasting only for a short time. 2. concise. 3. short in length. **brief′ly** *adv.*
brief[2] *n.* 1. a summary of the facts of a case, drawn up by an attorney. 2. a summary. 3. instructions and information given in advance. 4. *briefs,* very short close-fitting underpants. **brief** *v.* 1. to give a brief to. 2. to instruct or inform concisely in advance. □**hold no brief for,** not to be obliged to support.
brief·case (breef-kays) *n.* a flat case with a handle for carrying documents.
brief·ing (bree-fing) *n.* a presentation (to reporters, government officials, etc.) of the facts of an event or other matter.
bri·er[1] (bri-ěr) *n.* 1. a thorny or prickly plant with a woody stem. 2. a patch of such plants.
brier[2] *n.* a white heath of southern Europe, the root of which is used for making tobacco pipes.
brig[1] (brig) *n.* a two-masted sailing vessel.
brig[2] *n.* a ship's prison.

Brig. *abbr.* 1. brigade. 2. Brigadier.
bri·gade (bri-gayd) *n.* 1. an army unit forming part of a division. 2. a group of people organized for a particular purpose.
brig·a·dier (brig-ă-deer) **general** an officer ranking immediately above colonel and below major general in the U.S. Army, Air Force, and Marine Corps.
brig·and (brig-ănd) *n.* a member of a band of robbers.
brig·an·tine (brig-ăn-teen) *n.* a two-masted vessel with a square-rigged foremast and a fore-and-aft rigged mainmast.
bright (brit) *adj.* 1. giving out or reflecting much light, shining. 2. cheerful. 3. quick-witted, clever. **bright** *adv.* brightly. **bright′ly** *adv.* **bright′ness** *n.*
bright·en (bri-těn) *v.* to make or become brighter. **bright′en·er** *n.*
bril·liant (bril-yănt) *adj.* 1. very bright or sparkling. 2. very clever. **brilliant** *n.* a cut diamond with many facets. **bril′liant·ly** *adv.* **bril′liance** *n.* **bril′lian·cy** *n.*
bril·lian·tine (bril-yăn-teen) *n.* a substance used to make the hair glossy.
brim (brim) *n.* 1. the edge of a cup or hollow or channel. 2. the projecting edge of a hat. **brim** *v.* (**brimmed, brim·ming**) to fill or be full to the brim. **brim′less** *adj.*
brim·ful (brim-fuul) *adj.* full to the brim.
brim·stone (brim-stohn) *n.* sulfur.
brin·dled (brin-děld) *adj.* brown with streaks of other color, *the brindled cow.*
brine (brin) *n.* salt water.
bring (bring) *v.* (**brought, bring·ing**) 1. to cause to come, especially with oneself by carrying, leading, or attracting. (▷In this sense, the action of bringing is always in the direction of the writer or speaker: *bring it to me, take it to her.*) 2. to produce as profit or income. 3. to result in, to cause, *war brought famine.* 4. to put forward (charges etc.) in a law court, *they brought an action for libel.* 5. to cause to arrive at a particular state, *bring it to the boil.* **bring′er** *n.* □**bring about,** to cause to happen. **bring back,** to restore; to make one remember. **bring down,** to cause to fall, *bring down the house,* to get loud applause in a theater etc. **bring forward,** to call attention to (a matter). **bring in,** to initiate, to introduce; to produce as profit or income; to pronounce as a verdict in court. **bring into being,** to cause to exist. **bring off,** to do successfully. **bring on,** to cause to develop rapidly. **bring oneself to do something,** to cause oneself to do it in spite of reluctance. **bring out,** to cause to appear, to show clearly; to publish. **bring to bear,** to concentrate as an influence, *pressure was brought to bear on the dissenters.* **bring up,** to look after and train (growing children); to vomit; to cause to stop suddenly; to raise for consideration. **bring up the rear,** to come last in a line. ▷The form *brung* is incorrect.
brink (bringk) *n.* 1. the edge of a steep place or of a stretch of water. 2. the verge, the edge of something unknown or dangerous or exciting.
brink·man·ship (bringk-măn-ship) *n.* the art of pursuing a dangerous policy to the brink of war etc. before stopping.
brin·y (bri-nee) *adj.* (**brin·i·er, brin·i·est**) salty. **briny** *n.* *(informal)* the sea. **brin′i·ness** *n.*
bri·o (bree-oh) *n.* vivacity, vigor, dash. ▷Italian.

bri·oche (bree-osh) *n.* a small sweetened bread roll, circular in shape.

bri·quette (bri-ket) *n.* a block of compressed coal dust.

brisk (brisk) *adj.* active, lively, moving quickly. **brisk′ly** *adv.* **brisk′ness** *n.*

bris·ket (bris-kit) *n.* 1. the chest of an animal. 2. a cut of beef from the breast.

bris·ling (bris-ling) *n.* a small herring or sprat, processed like sardines.

bris·tle (bris-ĕl) *n.* 1. a short stiff hair. 2. one of the stiff pieces of hair or wire etc. in a brush. **bristle** *v.* **(bris·tled, bris·tling)** 1. (of an animal) to raise the bristles in anger or fear. 2. to show indignation. 3. to be thickly set with bristles. ▢**bristle with**, to be full of, *the plan bristled with difficulties.*

bris·tly (bris-lee) *adj.* **(-tli·er, -tli·est)** full of bristles.

Brit. *abbr.* 1. Britain. 2. British.

Brit·ain (brit-ĭn) (also **Great Britain**) England, Wales, and Scotland.

Bri·tan·ni·a (bri-tan-i-ă) the personification of Britain, shown as a woman with a shield, helmet, and trident. ▢**Britannia metal,** an alloy of tin with copper, antimony, and sometimes bismuth, used for tableware etc.

Bri·tan·nic (bri-tan-ik) *adj.* of Britain, *Her Britannic Majesty.*

britch·es (brich-iz) *n. pl. (informal)* a pair of breeches or trousers.

Brit·i·cism (brit-i-siz-ĕm) *n.* a word or an idiom used in Great Britain but not in the U.S. etc.

Brit·ish (brit-ish) *adj.* of Great Britain or its inhabitants. ▢**British Columbia,** a province of Canada. **British English,** the English language as spoken in England. **British Isles,** Britain and Ireland with the islands near their coasts. **British thermal unit,** the amount of heat needed to raise the temperature of a pound of water by one degree F. **the British,** British people.

Brit·ish·er (brit-i-shĕr) *n.* a native or inhabitant of Britain.

Brit·on (brit-ŏn) *n.* 1. a native or inhabitant of southern Britain before the Roman conquest. 2. a native or inhabitant of Great Britain or (formerly) the British Empire.

brit·tle (brit-ĕl) *adj.* **(-tler, -tlest)** hard but easily broken. **brit′tle·ly** *adv.* **brit′tle·ness** *n.*

bro. *abbr.* brother.

broach (brohch) *v.* 1. to make a hole in (a cask) and draw out liquid. 2. to begin a discussion of, *broached the topic.* ▷Do not confuse *broach* with *brooch.*

broad (brawd) *adj.* 1. large across, wide. 2. measuring from side to side, *50 feet broad.* 3. full and complete, *broad daylight; a broad hint,* strong and unmistakable; *a broad New England accent,* strongly regional. 4. in general terms, not detailed, *in broad outline,* without details. 5. rather coarse, *broad humor.* **broad** *n.* 1. the broad part. 2. *(slang)* a woman. **broad′ly** *adv.* **broad′ness** *n.* ▢**broad bean,** an edible bean with large flat seeds. **broad jump,** a track event of jumping as far as possible along the ground in one leap, usually from a running start. **broadly speaking,** speaking in a general way.

broad·band (brawd-band) *adj.* of or sensitive to a wide range of frequencies.

broad·cast (brawd-kast) *v.* **(broad·cast, broad·cast·ed** or **broad·cast, broad·cast·**

ing) 1. to send out by radio or television. 2. to speak or appear in a radio or television program. 3. to make generally known. 4. to sow (seed) by scattering. **broadcast** *n.* a broadcast program. **broadcast** *adv.* scattered freely. **broad′cast·er** *n.*

broad·cloth (brawd-klawth) *n.* a fine twilled woolen cloth or plainly woven cotton cloth (the name refers to quality rather than width).

broad·en (braw-dĕn) *v.* to make or become broad. **broad′en·ing** *adj.*

broad·loom (brawd-loom) *adj.* woven in broad widths.

broad-mind·ed (brawd-mɪn-did) *adj.* having tolerant views.

broad·side (brawd-sɪd) *n.* 1. the firing of all guns on one side of a ship. 2. a strong attack in words. 3. an advertisement, usually printed on a large sheet of paper. ▢**broadside on,** sideways on.

broad-spec·trum (brawd-spek-trŭm) *adj.* having a wide range.

broad·sword (brawd-sohrd) *n.* a broad-bladed cutting sword.

broad·tail (brawd-tayl) *n.* caracul fur.

Broad·way (brawd-way) *n.* 1. a street in New York City extending the length of Manhattan and famous for its stores and theaters. 2. *(informal)* the professional theater in New York City.

bro·cade (broh-kayd) *n.* a fabric woven with raised patterns. **bro·cad′ed** *adj.*

broc·co·li (brok-ŏ-lee) *n.* (*pl.* **-li**) a variety of cauliflower, whose green flower head is cooked as a vegetable.

bro·chette (broh-shet) *n.* a skewer used in cooking.

bro·chure (brŏ-shoor) *n.* a booklet or pamphlet containing information.

bro·gan (broh-găn) *n.* a heavy work shoe reaching to the ankle.

brogue (brohg) *n.* 1. a strong shoe with ornamental perforated bands. 2. a dialectal accent, especially Irish.

broil (broil) *v.* 1. to cook (meat) on a fire or gridiron. 2. to make or be very hot, especially from sunshine.

broil·er (broi-lĕr) *n.* 1. a young chicken suitable or specially reared for broiling or roasting. 2. a pan for broiling food.

broke (brohk) *see* **break. broke** *adj. (slang)* having spent all one's money, bankrupt.

bro·ken (broh-kĕn) *see* **break. bro′ken·ly** *adv.* ▢**broken English,** English spoken imperfectly by a foreigner. **broken home,** a family lacking one parent as a result of divorce or separation.

bro·ken·heart·ed (broh-kĕn-hahr-tid) *adj.* crushed by grief.

bro·ker (broh-kĕr) *n.* an agent who buys and sells things on behalf of others, a stockbroker.

bro·ker·age (broh-kĕ-rij) *n.* 1. a broker's fee or commission. 2. a broker's business. ▢**brokerage firm,** a company whose business is buying and selling on commission.

bro·mide (broh-mɪd) *n.* 1. a compound of bromine, used in medicine to calm the nerves. 2. a commonplace or soothing remark. **bro·mid·ic** (broh-mid-ik) *adj.*

bro·mine (broh-meen) *n.* a chemical element, compounds of which are used in medicine and photography.

bron·chi·al (brong-ki-ăl) *adj.* of the branched tubes into which the windpipe divides before entering the lungs.

bron·chi·tis (brong-kı-tis) *n.* inflammation of the mucous membrane inside the bronchial tubes.
bron·chit·ic (brong-kit-ik) *adj.*
bron·chus (brong-kŭs) *n.* (*pl.* **-chi,** *pr.* -kı) either of the two main divisions of the windpipe.
bron·co (brong-koh) *n.* (*pl.* **-cos**) a wild or half-tamed horse of western North America. □**bronco buster,** a cowboy who breaks in broncos.
bron·to·saur (bron-tŏ-sor) *n.* (*pl.* **-saurs**), **bron·to·sau·rus** (bron-tŏ-sor-ŭs) (*pl.* **-rus·es**) a herbivorous dinosaur from the Jurassic and Cretaceous periods, one of the largest terrestrial vertebrates.
Bronx (brongks) **cheer** (*informal*) a rude sound made with the mouth, a raspberry.
bronze (bronz) *n.* 1. a brown alloy of copper and tin. 2. a thing made of this, a bronze medal (awarded as third prize). 3. its color. **bronze** *adj.* made of bronze, bronze-colored. **bronze** *v.* **(bronzed, bronz·ing)** to make or become tanned by sun. □**Bronze Age,** the period when weapons and tools were made of bronze.
brooch (brohch) *n.* an ornamental hinged pin fastened with a clasp. ▷Do not confuse *brooch* with *broach.*
brood (brood) *n.* 1. the young birds or other animals produced at one hatching or birth. 2. (*informal*) a family of children. **brood** *v.* 1. to sit on eggs to hatch them. 2. to think long and deeply or resentfully. **brood'er** *n.* □**brood mare,** a mare kept for breeding.
brook[1] (bruuk) *n.* a small stream. □**brook trout,** a common speckled food and game fish found in cold waters of eastern North America.
brook[2] *v.* to tolerate, *he would brook no interference.*
broom (broom) *n.* 1. a shrub with yellow or white flowers. 2. a long-handled brush for sweeping with.
broom·stick (broom-stik) *n.* a broom handle.
Bros. *abbr.* Brothers.
broth (brawth) *n.* the water in which meat or fish has been boiled, soup made with this.
broth·el (broth-ĕl) *n.* a house where women work as prostitutes.
broth·er (bru*th*-ĕr) *n.* 1. a son of the same parents as another person. 2. a man who is a fellow member of a church or labor union or other association. 3. a monk who is not a priest; *Brother,* his title. **broth'er·ly** *adj.* **broth'er·li·ness** *n.*
broth·er·hood (bru*th*-ĕr-huud) *n.* 1. the relationship of brothers. 2. brotherliness, comradeship. 3. an association of men, its members.
broth·er-in-law (bru*th*-ĕr-in-law) *n.* (*pl.* **broth·ers-in-law**) the brother of one's husband or wife, the husband of one's sister.
brougham (brohm) *n.* 1. a one-horse four-wheeled closed carriage with an open seat in front for the driver. 2. a closed electrically driven carriage for four or five passengers. 3. a limousine with an open seat for the driver.
brought (brawt) see **bring.**
brou·ha·ha (broo-hah-hah) *n.* a commotion.
brow (brow) *n.* 1. an eyebrow. 2. the forehead. 3. a projecting or overhanging part, *the brow of the hill,* the ridge at the top.
brow·beat (brow-beet) *v.* **(brow·beat, brow·beat·en, brow·beat·ing)** to intimidate.
brown (brown) *adj.* 1. of a color between orange and black. 2. having skin of this color, sun-tanned. 3. (of bread) brown in color, especially through

being made with whole-wheat flour. **brown** *n.* 1. brown color. 2. brown clothes or material. **brown** *v.* to make or become brown. □**brown bagging,** bringing lunch to work from home; carrying wine or liquor into a restaurant or club. **browned off,** (*slang*) bored, fed up. **brown paper,** strong coarse paper for wrapping parcels etc. **brown sugar,** sugar that is only partly refined. **do it up brown,** (*slang*) to do it wonderfully well. **in a brown study,** deep in thought.
brown·ie (brow-nee) *n.* 1. a friendly goblin. 2. a chocolate cookie cake.
Brown·ie (brow-nee) *n.* a member of the junior branch of Girl Scouts at ages seven and eight. □**earn Brownie points,** to do good deeds.
brown·ish (brow-nish) *adj.* rather brown.
brown·out (brow-owt) *n.* a partial blackout, a cut in electric current.
brown·stone (brown-stohn) *n.* 1. a dark brown sandstone used in building. 2. a building made of this.
browse (browz) *v.* **(browsed, brows·ing)** 1. to feed as animals do, on leaves or grass etc. 2. to look through a book, or examine items for sale, in a casual leisurely way. **browse** *n.* browsing. **brows'er** *n.*
bru·in (broo-in) *n.* a personifying name for a bear.
bruise (brooz) *n.* an injury caused by a knock or by pressure that discolors the skin without breaking it. **bruise** *v.* **(bruised, bruis·ing)** 1. to cause a bruise or bruises on. 2. to show the effects of a knock etc.
bruis·er (broo-zĕr) *n.* a big muscular man.
bruit (broot) *v.* to spread a report about.
brunch (brunch) *n.* (*informal*) a single meal instead of breakfast and lunch.
bru·net (broo-net) *n.* a man with darkish hair or skin. **brunet** *adj.* having dark color.
bru·nette (broo-net) *n.* a woman with darkish hair or skin. **brunette** *adj.* having dark color.
brunt (brunt) *n.* the chief stress or strain, *bore the brunt of the attack.*
brush[1] (brush) *n.* 1. an implement with bristles of hair, wire, or nylon etc. set in a solid base. 2. a brushlike piece of carbon or metal for making a good electrical connection. 3. the bushy tail of a fox or other animal. 4. a short sharp encounter. 5. a brushing, *give it a brush.* **brush** *v.* 1. to use a brush on, to remove with a brush or by passing something lightly over the surface of. 2. to touch lightly in passing. □**brush aside,** to reject casually or curtly. **brush off,** to reject curtly, to snub. **brush up,** to study and revive one's former knowledge of. **brush-up** *n.*
brush[2] = **brushwood.**
brushed (brusht) *adj.* with raised nap, *brushed nylon.*
brush·less (brush-lis) *adj.* used without a brush.
brush-off (brush-awf) *n.* a curt rejection, a snub.
brush·wood (brush-wuud) *n.* 1. a thicket. 2. cut or broken twigs.
brush·work (brush-wurk) *n.* the style of the strokes made with a painter's brush.
brusque (brusk) *adj.* curt and offhand in manner. **brusque'ly** *adv.* **brusque'ness** *n.*
Brus·sels (brus-ĕlz) the capital of Belgium. □**Brussels sprouts,** the edible buds growing thickly on the stem of a kind of cabbage.
brut (broot) *adj.* (of wine) dry, not sweet.
bru·tal (broo-tăl) *adj.* very cruel, merciless. **bru'tal·ly** *adv.* **bru·tal·i·ty** (broo-tal-i-tee) *n.*

bru·tal·ize (broo-tă-lɪz) v. (**bru·tal·ized, bru· tal·iz·ing**) to make brutal.
brute (broot) n. 1. an animal other than man. 2. a brutal person. 3. (informal) an unpleasant or difficult person or thing. **brute** adj. 1. like an animal. 2. savage, cruel. 3. unreasoning. **bru′tish** adj. □**brute force,** unreasoning force.
B.S. abbr. 1. Bachelor of Science. 2. bill of sale.
B.S.A. abbr. Boy Scouts of America.
B.Sc. abbr. Bachelor of Science.
bskt. abbr. basket.
B.t.v. abbr. British thermal unit(s).
bu. abbr. bushel(s).
bub·ble (bub-ĕl) n. 1. a thin ball of liquid enclosing air or gas. 2. a small ball of air in a liquid or in a solidified liquid, such as glass. 3. a transparent domed cover. **bubble** v. (**bub·bled, bub·bling**) 1. to send up bubbles, to rise in bubbles, to make the sound of these. 2. to show great liveliness. □**bubble bath,** a bath in which water is made to foam by a perfumed liquid or crystals; this substance. **bubble gum,** a chewing gum that can be blown into large bubbles.
bub·bly (bub-lee) adj. (**-bli·er, -bli·est**) full of bubbles. **bubbly** n. (slang) champagne.
bu·bo (byoo-boh) n. (pl. **-boes**) an inflamed swelling in a gland, especially in the groin or armpit.
bu·bonic (byoo-bon-ik) **plague** an epidemic disease characterized by buboes and fever.
buc·ca·neer (buk-ă-neer) n. a pirate.
Bu·chan·an (byoo-kan-ăn), James (1791–1868) the fifteenth president of the U.S. 1857–61.
Bu·cha·rest (boo-kă-rest) the capital of Rumania.
buck[1] (buk) n. the male of a deer, hare, or rabbit. **buck** v. 1. (of a horse) to jump with the back arched. 2. (slang) to resist or oppose, bucking the system. □**buck fever,** nervousness of an inexperienced hunter at the first chance to shoot. **buck up,** (slang) to make or become more cheerful.
buck[2] n. a counter placed as a reminder before the person whose turn it is to deal at poker. □**pass the buck,** (slang) to shift responsibility (and possible blame) to someone else. **buck-passing** n. **buck-passer** n.
buck[3] n. (slang) a dollar. □**a fast buck,** easy money.
buck[4] n. a small vaulting horse for gymnastics.
buck·board (buk-bohrd) n. 1. a plank slung upon wheels. 2. a light vehicle with a body consisting of this.
buck·et (buk-it) n. 1. a round open container with a handle, used for holding or carrying liquids or substances that are in small pieces. 2. this with its contents, the amount it contains. **buck′et· ful** n. (pl. **-fuls**). □**bucket seat,** an automobile seat with a rounded back for one person.
buck·eye (buk-ɪ) n. 1. a tree of the horse chestnut family. 2. its shiny brown nut.
buck·le (buk-ĕl) n. a device, usually with a hinged tongue, through which a belt or strap is threaded to secure it. **buckle** v. (**buck·led, buck·ling**) 1. to fasten with a buckle. 2. to crumple under pressure, to cause to do this. □**buckle down to,** to set about doing. **buckle to,** to make a vigorous start on work.
buck·ler (buk-lĕr) n. a small round shield, usually held by a handle.
buck·ram (buk-răm) n. a stiffened cloth, especially that used for binding books.
buck·saw (buk-saw) n. a saw for cutting firewood, with its blade set across a wooden frame.

buck·shot (buk-shot) n. coarse shot.
buck·skin (buk-skin) n. leather made of buck's skin. **buckskin** adj.
buck·thorn (buk-thorn) n. a kind of thorny shrub.
buck·tooth (buk-tooth) n. (pl. **-teeth**, pr. -teeth) a projecting upper front tooth. **buck·toothed** adj.
buck·wheat (buk-hweet) n. 1. a plant with seeds that are used as feed or made into flour. 2. its seeds.
bu·col·ic (byoo-kol-ik) adj. characteristic of country life.
bud (bud) n. 1. a small knob that will develop into a branch, leaf cluster, or flower. 2. a flower or leaf not fully open; in bud, putting forth such buds. **bud** v. (**bud·ded, bud·ding**) 1. to be in bud. 2. to graft a bud on a plant.
Bu·da·pest (boo-dă-pest) the capital of Hungary.
Bud·dha (boo-dă) n. 1. the title (often treated as a name) of the Indian philosopher Gautama (5th century B.C.), and a series of teachers of Buddhism. 2. a statue or carving representing Gautama Buddha.
Bud·dhism (boo-diz-ĕm) n. an Asian religion based on the teachings of Buddha. **Bud′dhist** adj. & n.
bud·ding (bud-ing) adj. beginning to develop, a budding poet.
bud·dy (bud-ee) n. (pl. **-dies**) (informal) a friend.
buddy-buddy (bud-ee-bud-ee) adj. (informal) extremely friendly.
budge (buj) v. (**budged, budg·ing**) 1. to move slightly. 2. to cause to alter a position or opinion.
bud·ger·i·gar (buj-ĕ-ri-gahr) n. a kind of Australian parakeet, often kept as a cage bird.
bud·get (buj-it) n. 1. an estimate or plan of income and expenditure. 2. the amount allotted for a particular purpose. **budget** v. (**bud·get·ed, bud· get·ing**) to plan or allot in a budget.
bud·gie (buj-ee) n. (informal) a budgerigar.
Bue·nos Ai·res (bway-nŏs ɪr-ĕz) the capital of Argentina.
buff (buf) n. 1. strong velvety dull-yellow leather made from the hide of the buffalo or other animals. 2. the color of this. 3. the bare skin, stripped to the buff. 4. (informal) a devotee of an activity etc. **buff** adj. dull yellow. **buff** v. to polish with soft material.
buf·fa·lo (buf-ă-loh) n. (pl. **-loes, -los, -lo**) 1. a kind of ox found in Asia and South Africa. 2. the bison of North America. **buffalo** v. 1. (slang) to intimidate. 2. to confuse or mystify.
buff·er[1] (buf-ĕr) n. something that lessens the effect of an impact, a device for this purpose. **buffer** v. to act as a buffer to. □**buffer state,** a small country between two powerful ones, thought to reduce the chance of war between these. **buffer zone,** a neutral zone between two hostile powers.
buffer[2] n. a person or thing that buffs or polishes something.
buf·fet[1] (bŭ-fay) n. 1. a counter where food and drink may be bought and consumed. 2. provision of food where guests serve themselves, a buffet lunch. 3. a cabinet for holding china.
buf·fet[2] (buf-it) n. a blow, especially with the hand. **buffet** v. (**buf·fet·ed, buf·fet·ing**) 1. to slap or punch. 2. to struggle ahead or force one's way.
buf·foon (bŭ-foon) n. a person who plays the fool. **buf·foon′er·y** n.
bug (bug) n. 1. any small insect. 2. (slang) a microbe, especially one causing disease. 3. (slang)

a very small hidden microphone installed secretly. 4. *(slang)* a mechanical defect. 5. *(slang)* a devotee of an activity etc. **bug** *v.* **(bugged, bug·ging)** *(slang)* 1. to fit with a hidden microphone secretly so that conversations etc. can be overheard from a distance. 2. to annoy.

bug·a·boo (bug-ă-boo) *n.* (*pl.* **-boos**) a bugbear.

bug·bear (bug-bair) *n.* something feared or disliked.

bug-eyed (bug-ɪd) *adj.* *(slang)* with bulging eyes.

bug·gy (bug-ee) *n.* (*pl.* **-gies**) 1. a light horsedrawn carriage. 2. a small sturdy vehicle, *beach buggy.*

bu·gle[1] (byoo-gĕl) *n.* a brass instrument like a small trumpet, used for sounding military signals.

bu·gle[2] *n.* a creeping plant with small dark blue flowers.

bu·gler (byoo-glĕr) *n.* one who sounds a bugle.

build (bild) *v.* **(built, build·ing)** to construct by putting parts or material together. **build** *n.* bodily shape, *of slender build.* □**build on**, to rely on.

build up, to accumulate; to establish gradually; to fill in with buildings; to boost with praise or flattering publicity. **build-up** *n.*

build·er (bil-dĕr) *n.* a person who builds, one whose trade is building houses etc.

build·ing (bil-ding) *n.* 1. the constructing of houses etc. 2. a house or similar structure. □**building and loan,** an organization that accepts deposits and lends out money on mortgage to people wishing to buy or build houses.

built (bilt) *see* **build. built** *adj.* having a specified build, *sturdily built.*

built-in (bilt-in) *adj.* incorporated as part of a structure.

built-up (bilt-up) *adj.* filled in with buildings; *built-up area,* an urban area.

Bu·jum·bu·ra (boo-joom-boo-rah) the capital of Burundi.

bulb (bulb) *n.* 1. a thick rounded mass of scalelike leaves from which a stem grows up and roots grow down. 2. a plant grown from this. 3. a bulbshaped object. 4. an electric lamp, the glass part of this. **bul'bous** *adj.*

Bul·gar·i·a (buul-gair-i-ă) a country in Europe. **Bul·gar'i·an** *adj.* & *n.*

bulge (bulj) *n.* a rounded swelling, an outward curve. **bulge** *v.* **(bulged, bulg·ing)** to form a bulge, to cause to swell out.

bul·gur (buul-gŭr) *n.* a form of wheat processed by parboiling, cracking, and drying.

bulk (bulk) *n.* 1. size or magnitude, especially when great. 2. the greater part, the majority. 3. a large shape or body or person. **bulk** *v.* to increase the size or thickness of.

bulk·head (bulk-hed) *n.* an upright partition in a ship, aircraft, or vehicle.

bulk·y (bul-kee) *adj.* **(bulk·i·er, bulk·i·est)** taking up much space.

bull[1] (buul) *n.* 1. an uncastrated male of any animal of the bovine family. 2. the male of the whale, elephant, and other large animals. 3. a speculator who buys shares etc. in the hope that prices will rise and that he will be able to sell them at a higher price very soon. 5. the bull's-eye of a target. 6. *the Bull,* a sign of the zodiac, Taurus. **bull'ish** *adj.* □**bull pen,** (in baseball) the area where relief pitchers warm up.

bull[2] *n.* an official edict issued by the pope.

bull[3] *n.* *(slang)* an obviously absurd statement, lies, nonsense. □**bull session,** *(slang)* a spontaneous

discussion. **shoot the bull,** *(slang)* to make idle talk.

bull·dog (buul-dawg) *n.* a dog of a powerful breed with a short thick neck. **bulldog** *v.* **(bull·dogged, bull·dog·ging)** to throw a steer by grasping its horns and twisting its head.

bull·doze (buul-dohz) *v.* **(bull·dozed, bull·doz·ing)** 1. to clear with a bulldozer. 2. *(informal)* to force or intimidate, *he bulldozed them into accepting it.*

bull·doz·er (buul-doh-zĕr) *n.* a powerful tractor with a broad steel blade mounted in front, used for shifting earth or clearing ground.

bul·let (buul-it) *n.* a small round or conical missile used in a rifle or revolver.

bul·le·tin (buul-ĕ-tin) *n.* 1. a short official statement of news. 2. a periodical publication, a journal.

bul·let·proof (buul-it-proof) *adj.* capable of protecting from the full impact of a bullet, *some policemen wear bulletproof vests.*

bull·fight (buul-fɪt) *n.* the Spanish and Latin American spectacle in which a bull is baited and killed by a matador.

bull·finch (buul-finch) *n.* a songbird with a strong beak and a pinkish breast.

bull·frog (buul-frog) *n.* a large American frog with a loud bellow.

bull·head (buul-hed) *n.* a small big-headed fish.

bull·head·ed (buul-hed-id) *adj.* obstinate, impetuous, blundering.

bull·horn (buul-horn) *n.* an electrically powered megaphone.

bul·lion (buul-yŏn) *n.* gold or silver in bulk or bars, before coining or manufacture.

bull·ock (buul-ŏk) *n.* a bull after castration.

bull·ring (buul-ring) *n.* an arena for bullfights.

bull's-eye (buulz-ɪ) *n.* 1. the center of a target. 2. a shot that hits this. **bull's-eye!** *interj.* perfect, just the thing.

bull terrier a dog of a breed originally produced by crossing a bulldog and a terrier.

bul·ly (buul-ee) *n.* (*pl.* **-lies**) a person who uses his strength or power to hurt or frighten others. **bully** *v.* **(bul·lied, bul·ly·ing)** to behave as a bully toward, to intimidate. **bully** *adj.* *(slang)* excellent. □**bully for you,** *(informal)* bravo.

bully beef *n.* canned or pickled beef.

bul·rush (buul-rush) *n.* a kind of tall rush with a thick velvety head.

bul·wark (buul-wărk) *n.* 1. a wall of earth built as a defense. 2. something that acts as a protection or defense. 3. *bulwarks,* a ship's side above the level of the deck.

bum (bum) *n.* *(informal)* a tramp, a loafer. **bum** *v.* **(bummed, bum·ming)** *(informal)* 1. to wander, to loaf. 2. to beg. **bum** *adj.* *(informal)* worthless.

bum·ble (bum-bĕl) *v.* **(bum·bled, bum·bling)** to move or act in a blundering way.

bum·ble·bee (bum-bĕl-bee) *n.* a large bee with a loud hum.

bum·mer (bum-ĕr) *n.* *(slang)* 1. a mistake, a failure. 2. an unpleasant experience, especially with a drug.

bump (bump) *v.* 1. to knock with a dull-sounding blow, to hurt by this. 2. to travel with a jolting movement. **bump** *n.* 1. a bumping sound or knock or movement. 2. a raised mark left by a blow. 3. a swelling or lump on a surface. □**bump into,** *(informal)* to meet by chance. **bump off,** *(slang)* to kill.

bump·er[1] (bum-pĕr) *n.* 1. something unusually large or plentiful. 2. a large cup filled to the brim. **bumper** *adj.* unusually large or plentiful, *a bumper crop.*

bumper[2] *n.* a horizontal bar attached to the front or back of a motor vehicle to lessen the effect of a collision. □**bumper sticker,** a printed slogan, advertisement, etc. made to affix to an auto bumper.

bump·kin (bump-kin) *n.* a country person with awkward manners.

bump·tious (bump-shŭs) *adj.* conceited. **bump′tious·ly** *adv.* **bump′tious·ness** *n.*

bump·y (bum-pee) *adj.* (**bump·i·er, bump·i·est**) full of bumps, causing jolts. **bump′i·ness** *n.*

bun (bun) *n.* 1. a small bread roll, *hamburger bun.* 2. a small sweet roll, *hot cross bun.* 3. hair twisted into a bun shape at the back of the head.

bunch (bunch) *n.* 1. a cluster, *a bunch of grapes.* 2. a number of small similar things held or fastened together, *a bunch of keys.* **bunch** *v.* to come or bring together into a bunch or in folds.

bun·co, bun·ko (bung-koh) *n.* (*pl.* **-cos, -kos**) (*slang*) a swindle, especially one made by card-sharping or confidence tricks.

bun·combe (bung-kŭm) = **bunkum.**

bun·dle (bun-dĕl) *n.* 1. a collection of things loosely fastened or wrapped together, a set of sticks or rods tied together. 2. (*slang*) a large amount of money, *won a bundle.* **bundle** *v.* (**bun·dled, bun·dling**) 1. to make into a bundle. 2. to put away hastily and untidily, to push hurriedly, *bundled him into a taxi.* □**bundle up,** dress warmly.

bun·dling (bun-dling) *n.* an early American courtship custom of lying or sleeping together clothed.

bung (bung) *n.* a stopper for closing a hole in a barrel or jar. **bung** *v.* to close with a bung.

bun·ga·low (bung-gă-loh) *n.* a small one-story house.

bung·hole (bung-hohl) *n.* a hole in a cask closed with a bung.

bun·gle (bung-gĕl) *v.* (**bun·gled, bun·gling**) to spoil by lack of skill, to attempt clumsily and without success. **bungle** *n.* a bungled attempt. **bun′gler** *n.*

bun·ion (bun-yŏn) *n.* swelling at the base of the big toe with thickened skin.

bunk[1] (bungk) *n.* a built-in shelflike bed, as on a ship. □**bunk bed,** one of a pair of small single beds mounted one above the other as a unit.

bunk[2] *n.* (*slang*) bunkum.

bun·ker (bung-kĕr) *n.* 1. a container for fuel. 2. a sandy hollow forming a hazard on a golf course. 3. a reinforced underground shelter. **bunker** *v.* to put fuel into the bunkers of (a ship).

bun·kered (bung-kĕrd) *adj.* trapped in a bunker at golf.

bunk·house (bungk-hows) *n.* a dormitory for ranch hands, campers, etc.

bun·kum (bung-kŭm) *n.* nonsense.

bun·ny (bun-ee) *n.* (*pl.* **-nies**) (*informal*) a rabbit, *bunny rabbit.*

Bun·sen (bun-sĕn) **burner** a device for burning air with gas for heating substances used in chemical laboratories etc. ▷Named after R. W. Bunsen, a German chemist.

bunt (bunt) *v.* 1. to push with the head. 2. (in baseball) to tap the ball with the bat without swinging. **bunt** *n.* 1. a push given with the head. 2. (in

baseball) a light tap to the ball with the bat.

bunt·ing[1] (bun-ting) *n.* a bird related to the finches.

bunt·ing[2] *n.* 1. flags and streamers for decorating streets and buildings. 2. a loosely woven fabric used for making these.

bu·oy (boo-ee) *n.* an anchored floating object marking a navigable channel or showing the position of submerged rocks etc. **buoy** *v.* 1. to mark with a buoy or buoys. 2. to keep (a thing) afloat. 3. to encourage, to hearten, *buoy up.*

buoy·ant (boi-ănt) *adj.* 1. able to float. 2. lighthearted, cheerful. **buoy′ant·ly** *adv.* **buoy′an·cy** *n.*

bur (bur) *n.* = **burr.**

bur. *abbr.* bureau.

bur·ble (bur-bĕl) *v.* (**bur·bled, bur·bling**) to make a gentle murmuring sound, to babble.

bur·den (bur-dĕn) *n.* 1. something carried, a heavy load. 2. something difficult to support, *the heavy burden of taxation.* **burden** *v.* to load, to put a burden on. □**beast of burden,** an animal that carries packs on its back. **the burden of proof,** the obligation to prove what one says.

bur·den·some (bur-dĕn-sŏm) *adj.* troublesome, tiring.

bur·dock (bur-dok) *n.* a coarse weedy plant with prickly flower heads and dock-like leaves.

bu·reau (byoor-oh) *n.* (*pl.* **-reaus, -reaux,** *pr.* byoor-ohz) 1. a chest of drawers, often with a mirror above it. 2. an office or department, *a travel bureau; the Federal Bureau of Investigation.*

bu·reau·cra·cy (byuu-rok-ră-see) *n.* (*pl.* **-cies**) 1. government by administrative officials. 2. these officials. 3. excessive official routine.

bu·reau·crat (byoor-ŏ-krat) *n.* an official who works in a government office, one who applies the rules of his department without exercising much judgment.

bu·reau·crat·ic (byoor-ŏ-krat-ik) *adj.* 1. of bureaucracy. 2. of or like bureaucrats.

bu·rette, bu·ret (byuu-ret) *n.* a graduated glass tube with a tap, used for measuring small quantities of liquid run out of it.

burg (burg) *n.* (*informal*) a small town.

bur·gee (bur-jee) *n.* a small swallow-tailed pennant used by yachts etc. as a distinguishing flag.

bur·geon (bur-jŏn) *v.* to begin to grow rapidly.

bur·ger (bur-gĕr) *n.* (*informal*) a hamburger.

bur·gess (bur-jis) *n.* 1. (*old use*) a member of the lower house of the colonial legislature of Virginia or Maryland. 2. (*old use*) a member of the English Parliament representing a town, borough, or university.

burgh (burg) *n.* (*old use*) a borough in Scotland.

bur·gher (bur-gĕr) *n.* a middle-class townsman.

bur·glar (bur-glăr) *n.* a person who breaks into a building illegally, especially in order to steal. **bur′gla·ry** *n.*

bur·glar·ize (bur-glă-rīz) *v.* (**bur·glar·ized, bur·glar·iz·ing**) to rob, as a burglar.

bur·gle (bur-gĕl) *v.* (**bur·gled, bur·gling**) (*informal*) to burglarize.

bur·go·mas·ter (bur-gŏ-mas-tĕr) *n.* the mayor of a Dutch, Flemish, German, or Austrian town.

bur·gun·dy (bur-gŭn-dee) *n.* (*pl.* **-dies**) 1. a red or white wine from Burgundy in France, a similar wine from elsewhere. 2. dark purplish red.

bur·i·al (ber-i-ăl) *n.* 1. burying, being buried. 2. a buried body, *a prehistoric burial was found.*

burl (burl) *n.* 1. a knot in wool, cloth, or wood.

2. an overgrown knot in walnut etc. used in veneering.

bur·lap (bur-lap) *n.* a coarse canvas of jute, used for sacks.

bur·lesque (bŭr-lesk) *n.* 1. a mocking imitation. 2. vaudeville, frequently featuring striptease. **burlesque** *v.* (**bur·lesqued, bur·les·quing**) to mock by burlesque.

bur·ley (bur-lee) *n.* (*pl.* **-leys**) a light type of tobacco.

bur·ly (bur-lee) *adj.* (**-li·er, -li·est**) *adj.* with a strong heavy body, sturdy. **bur'li·ness** *n.*

Bur·ma (bur-mă) a country of southeast Asia.

Bur·mese (bŭr-meez) *adj. & n.* (*pl.* **-mese**).

burn¹ (burn) *v.* (**burned** or **burnt, burn·ing**) 1. to damage or hurt or destroy by fire or heat or the action of acid. 2. to be injured or damaged in this way. 3. to produce (a mark etc.) by heat or fire; *money burns holes in his pocket,* makes him eager to spend it. 4. to use as fuel. 5. to produce heat or light, to be alight. 6. to be able to be set on fire. 7. to feel or cause to feel hot; *my ears are burning,* they feel hot, jokingly supposed to be a sign that one is being talked about. 8. to make or become brown from heat or light. 9. to kill or be killed by burning, *she was burned at the stake.* 10. (*slang*) to be electrocuted in the electric chair. 11. (*slang*) to cause damage to, *he was burned in the stock market.* **burn** *n.* 1. a mark or sore made by burning. 2. the firing of a spacecraft's rocket. □**burn down,** to burn less vigorously as fuel fails; to destroy by burning. **burn one's bridges behind one,** to do something that makes retreat impossible. **burn the midnight oil,** to study far into the night. **burn up,** (*slang*) to make or become angry. **have money to burn,** to have so much that one does not need to take care of it.

burn² *n.* (*Scottish*) a brook.

burn·er (bur-nĕr) *n.* 1. the part of a stove or lamp from which the flame or heat issues. 2. a fuel-burning device, *a gas burner.* □**on the back burner,** of no urgency.

burn·ing (bur-ning) *see* **burn¹. burning** *adj.* 1. intense, *a burning desire.* 2. hotly discussed, vital, *a burning question.*

bur·nish (bur-nish) *v.* to polish by rubbing. **bur'nish·er** *n.* **bur'nish·ing** *adj.*

bur·noose, bur·nous (bŭr-noos) *n.* an Arab or Moorish hooded cloak.

burn·out (burn-owt) *n.* the end of the powered stage in a rocket's flight, when the propellant has been used up.

burnt (burnt) *see* **burn¹. burnt** *adj.* of a deep shade, *burnt sienna, burnt umber.*

burp (burp) *n.* a belch, a belching sound. **burp** *v.* 1. to belch. 2. to pat (a baby) on the back to bring up wind from the stomach. □**burp gun,** (*slang*) an automatic pistol.

burr (bur) *n.* 1. a whirring sound. 2. the strong pronunciation of *r,* a soft country accent, especially one using this. 3. a small drill. 4. a plant's seedcase or flower that clings to hair or clothing, the plant itself. **burr** *v.* to make a whirring sound.

bur·ro (bur-oh) *n.* (*pl.* **-ros**) a small donkey, especially one used as a pack animal.

bur·row (bur-oh) *n.* a hole or tunnel dug by a fox or rabbit etc. as a dwelling. **burrow** *v.* 1. to dig a burrow, to tunnel. 2. to form by tunneling. 3. to search deeply, to delve.

bur·sa (bur-să) *n.* (*pl.* **-sae,** *pr.* -see) a pouch between joints or between muscles or skin etc. and bones, for lessening friction. **bur'sal** *adj.*

bur·sar (bur-săr) *n.* a person who manages the finances and other business of a school or college.

bur·si·tis (bŭr-sɪ-tis) *n.* inflammation of a bursa.

burst (burst) *v.* (**burst, burst·ing**) 1. to force or be forced open, to fly violently apart because of pressure inside; *buds are bursting,* opening out. 2. to appear or come suddenly and forcefully, *burst into flame.* 3. to let out a violent expression of feeling, *burst into tears, burst out laughing; she burst into song,* suddenly began to sing. **burst** *n.* 1. a bursting, a split. 2. an explosion or outbreak, a series of shots, *a burst of gunfire, of applause.* 3. a brief violent effort, a spurt. ▷Do not confuse *burst* with *bust.*

burst·ing (bur-sting) *adj.* full to the breaking point, *sacks bursting with grain; bursting with energy,* full of it; *we are bursting to tell you,* very eager.

Bu·run·di (bŭ-run-dee) a country in East Africa. **Bu·run'di·an** *adj. & n.*

bur·y (ber-ee) *v.* (**bur·ied, bur·y·ing**) 1. to place (a dead body) in the earth or a tomb or the sea; *she has buried both parents this year,* lost them by death. 2. to put underground, to hide in earth etc., to cover up; *buried himself in the country,* went and lived where he would meet few people; *buried themselves in their books,* gave all their time and attention to reading. □**bury the hatchet,** to cease quarreling and become friendly.

bus (bus) *n.* (*pl.* **bus·ses, bus·es**) 1. a long-bodied passenger vehicle. 2. (*slang*) a motor vehicle. **bus** *v.* (**bussed** or **bused, bus·sing** or **bus·ing**) 1. to travel by bus. 2. to transport by bus, to take (children) to a distant school by bus in order to counteract racial segregation. □**bus lane,** a strip of road for use by buses only. **bus station,** a station at which a number of buses stop, with facilities for passengers etc. **bus stop,** the regular stopping place of a bus.

bus. *abbr.* business.

bus·boy (bus-boi) *n.* a waiter's assistant.

bus·by (buz-bee) *n.* (*pl.* **-bies**) a tall fur cap worn as part of certain full-dress military uniforms.

bush (buush) *n.* 1. a shrub. 2. a thick growth or clump. 3. wild, remote uncultivated land. □**bush league,** (in baseball) a minor league. **bush telegraph,** a way in which news is passed on unofficially.

bushed (buusht) *adj.* (*informal*) exhausted.

bush·el (buush-ĕl) *n.* a measure for grain and fruit (4 pecks or 32 quarts). □**hide one's light under a bushel,** to conceal one's abilities.

bush·ing (buush-ing) *n.* a metal lining for an axle hole etc.

bush·man (buush-măn) *n.* (*pl.* **-men,** *pr.* -mĕn) 1. a dweller in the Australian bush. 2. *Bushman,* a member or the language of an aboriginal tribe of South Africa.

bush·mas·ter (buush-mas-tĕr) *n.* a very large venomous viper of Central and South America.

bush·whack (buush-hwak) *v.* 1. to make one's way through woods by clearing away brush, branches, etc. 2. to ambush.

bush·whack·er (buush-hwak-ĕr) *n.* 1. (*old use*) a backwoodsman. 2. a person who ambushes.

bush·y (buush-ee) *adj.* (**bush·i·er, bush·i·est**) 1. covered with bushes. 2. growing thickly. **bush'i·ness** *n.*

busi·ness (biz-nis) *n.* 1. a task or duty, a thing one is concerned with. 2. one's usual occupation, a profession, a trade. 3. a thing needing to be dealt with, the agenda. 4. a difficult matter, *what a business!* 5. an affair, subject, or device. 6. buying and selling, trade. 7. a commercial firm, a store, factory, etc., *they own a grocery business.* □**business end,** *(informal)* the working end of a tool, weapon, etc., not the handle. **have no business to,** to have no right to (do something). **busi·ness·like** (biz-nis-lɪk) *adj.* practical, systematic.

busi·ness·man (biz-nis-man) *n.* (*pl.* **-men,** *pr.* -men) a man who is engaged in trade or commerce. **busi·ness·wom·an** (biz-nis-wuum-ăn) *n.* (*pl.* **-wom·en,** *pr.* -wim-in).

bus·kin (bus-kin) *n.* 1. a boot reaching to the calf or knee. 2. a thick-soled boot worn by actors in ancient Greek tragedy, to increase their height.

bus·man (bus-măn) *n.* (*pl.* **-men,** *pr.* -měn) the driver of a bus. □**busman's holiday,** leisure time spent doing something similar to one's usual work.

buss (bus) *n.* a kiss. **buss** *v.* to kiss.

bust[1] (bust) *n.* 1. a sculpture of the head, shoulders, and chest. 2. the bosom. 3. the measurement around a woman's body at the bosom.

bust[2] *v.* (**bust·ed** or **bust, bust·ing**) *(slang)* 1. to burst. 2. to break, smash. 3. to hit. 4. to demote, *busted to private.* 5. to arrest, *busted for possession of drugs.* 6. to bankrupt. **bust** *n.* *(slang)* 1. a failure. 2. a spree. 3. a hit or blow. 4. a demotion. 5. an arrest. 6. a business or economic depression. ▷Do not confuse *bust* with *burst.*

bust·ed (bus-tid) *adj.* *(slang)* 1. broken. 2. demoted. 3. arrested. 4. bankrupt.

bust·er (bus-tĕr) *n.* *(slang)* an insulting form of address to a man.

bus·tle[1] (bus-ĕl) *v.* (**bus·tled, bus·tling**) 1. to make a show of hurrying. 2. to cause to hurry. **bustle** *n.* excited activity.

bustle[2] *n.* padding used to puff out the top of a woman's skirt at the back.

bust-up (bust-up) *n.* *(slang)* a quarrel, especially between close friends.

bus·y (biz-ee) *adj.* (**bus·i·er, bus·i·est**) 1. working, occupied, having much to do; *get busy,* start doing things. 2. full of activity, *a busy day; the telephone line is busy,* is engaged. 3. (of a picture or design) too full of detail. **busy** *v.* (**bus· ied, bus·y·ing**) to keep busy, *busy oneself.* **bus′i·ly** *adv.* □**busy signal,** an intermittent tone made by a telephone when the number called is in use.

bus·y·bod·y (biz-ee-bod-ee) *n.* (*pl.* **-bod·ies**) a meddlesome person.

bus·y·work (biz-ee-wurk) *n.* work performed just to keep oneself occupied.

but (but) *adv.* only, no more than, *we can but try.* **but** *conj. & prep.* 1. however, on the other hand. 2. except, otherwise than, *there's no one here but me; I'd have drowned but for you,* if you had not helped me. **but** *n.* an objection, *ifs and buts; but me no buts,* do not raise objections. ▷Careful writers avoid *but what* and *but that* in such sentences as *I don't know but what* (or *that*) *I might go.* For this they would write *I believe I will go* or *I may go* or any of dozens of other good sentences.

bu·tane (byoo-tayn) *n.* an inflammable gas produced from petroleum, used as a fuel.

butch (buuch) *n.* a short haircut (of a man or boy).

butch·er (buuch-ĕr) *n.* 1. a person whose trade is to slaughter animals for food, one who cuts up

and sells animal flesh. 2. a person who has people killed needlessly or brutally. 3. *(slang)* an unskillful craftsman or artist. **butcher** *v.* 1. to slaughter and cut up animals for food. 2. to kill needlessly or brutally. 3. *(slang)* to work (wood, metal, etc.) badly. □**butcher block,** a wooden block on which a butcher cuts meat; a similar piece of wood used as a table or counter top.

butch·er·y (buuch-ĕ-ree) *n.* (*pl.* **-er·ies**) 1. a butcher's trade. 2. needless or brutal killing.

but·ler (but-lĕr) *n.* the chief manservant of a household.

butt[1] (but) *n.* a large cask or barrel.

butt[2] *n.* 1. the thicker end of a tool or weapon. 2. a short remnant, a stub. 3. *(slang)* a cigarette.

butt[3] (but) *n.* 1. the mound of earth behind the targets on a shooting range. 2. a person or thing that is frequently a target for ridicule or teasing.

butt *v.* 1. to push with the head like a ram or goat. 2. to meet or place edge to edge, *the strips should be butted against each other, not overlapping.* □**butt in,** to interrupt; to meddle.

butte (byoot) *n.* an isolated steep flat-topped hill.

but·ter (but-ĕr) *n.* 1. a fatty food substance made from cream by churning. 2. a similar substance made from other materials, *peanut butter.* **butter** *v.* to spread with butter, cement, etc. **but′ter·y** *adj.* □**butter bean,** the dried seed of white varieties of lima bean, used as a vegetable. **butter up,** *(informal)* to flatter.

but·ter·ball (but-ĕr-bawl) *n.* 1. butter rolled into a ball. 2. *(slang)* a fat person.

but·ter·cup (but-ĕr-kup) *n.* a wild plant with bright yellow cup-shaped flowers.

but·tered (but-ĕrd) *adj.* cooked or spread with butter.

but·ter·fat (but-ĕr-fat) *n.* the fat content of milk.

but·ter·fin·gers (but-ĕr-fing-gĕrz) *n.* a person inclined to drop things. **but′ter·fin·gered** *adj.*

but·ter·fly (but-ĕr-flɪ) *n.* (*pl.* **-flies**) 1. an insect with four often brightly colored wings and knobbed feelers. 2. a swimming stroke in which both arms are lifted at the same time. □**have butterflies in the stomach,** to feel nervous tremors.

but·ter·milk (but-ĕr-milk) *n.* the liquid left after butter has been churned from milk.

but·ter·nut (but-ĕr-nut) *n.* 1. the large oily nut of the North American white walnut tree. 2. this tree.

but·ter·scotch (but-ĕr-skoch) *n.* a toffee or flavoring made from brown sugar and butter.

but·tock (but-ŏk) *n.* either of the two fleshy rounded parts at the lower end of the back of the human or an animal body.

but·ton (but-ŏn) *n.* 1. a knob or disk sewn on a garment as a fastener or ornament. 2. a small rounded object, a knob pressed to operate an electric bell etc. 3. *(slang)* the chin. **button** *v.* (**but· toned, but·ton·ing**) to fasten with a button or buttons. □**button chrysanthemum,** one with many small round flower heads. **button mushroom,** a small unopened mushroom. **on the button,** *(informal)* precisely.

but·ton·down (but-ŏn-down) *adj.* 1. (of a shirt) having a collar fold that buttons. 2. *(slang)* conservative, conventional.

but·ton·hole (but-ŏn-hohl) *n.* a slit through which a button is passed to fasten clothing. **buttonhole** *v.* (**but·ton·holed, but·ton·hol·ing**) to accost and detain with conversation.

but·ton·hook (but-ŏn-huuk) *n.* a small hook for buttoning shoes or gloves.

but·tress (but-ris) *n.* 1. a support built against a wall. 2. a thing that supports or reinforces something. **buttress** *v.* to prop up.

bux·om (buk-sŏm) *adj.* 1. plump and healthy looking. 2. full-bosomed.

buy (bi) *v.* (**bought, buy·ing**) 1. to obtain in exchange for money or by some sacrifice. 2. to win over by bribery. 3. *(slang)* to believe, to accept the truth of, *only a fool would buy that excuse.* **buy** *n.* a purchase; *a good buy,* a useful purchase, a bargain. □**buy it,** *(slang)* to be killed or destroyed; to believe it. **buy off,** to get rid of by payment. **buy out,** to obtain full ownership by paying (another person) to give up his share. **buy up,** to buy all or as much as possible of. ▷The form *boughten* is incorrect.

buy·er (bi-ĕr) *n.* 1. a person who buys something. 2. an agent choosing and buying merchandise for a store. □**buyers' market,** a state of affairs when goods are plentiful and prices are low.

buzz (buz) *n.* 1. a vibrating humming sound. 2. *(slang)* a telephone call, *give me a buzz.* **buzz** *v.* 1. to make a buzz. 2. to be filled with a buzzing noise. 3. to go about quickly and busily. 4. to fly (an airplane) close to or low over. □**buzz off,** *(slang)* to go away. **buzz saw,** a circular saw. **have a buzz on,** *(slang)* to be intoxicated.

buz·zard (buz-ărd) *n.* a kind of hawk.

buzz·er (buz-ĕr) *n.* a device that produces a buzzing note as a signal.

buzz·word (buz-wurd) *n.* a catch word or slogan popular in politics, a profession, etc. and often lacking precise meaning.

B.V. *abbr.* Blessed Virgin.

B.V.D. *(trademark)* underwear.

bwa·na (bwah-nă) *n.* (in Africa) master, sir.

bx. *abbr.* box.

B.X. *abbr.* Base Exchange.

by (bi) *adv. & prep.* 1. near, beside, in reserve; *north by east,* between north and north-northeast. 2. along, via, past. 3. during, *came by night.* 4. through the agency or means of, (of an animal) having as its sire. 5. (of numbers or measurements) taking it together with, *multiply six by four; it measures ten feet by eight,* with eight feet as a second dimension. 6. not later than, *be here*

by noon. 7. according to, *judging by appearances; sold by the dozen,* a dozen at a time. 8. after, succeeding, *bit by bit.* 9. to the extent of, *missed it by inches.* 10. in respect of, *a tailor, Jones by name; pull it up by the roots.* 11. in the belief of, *swear by God.* □**by and by,** before long. **by and large,** on the whole, considering everything. **by oneself,** alone; without help.

bye (bi) *n.* the state of having no opponent for one round in a tournament and so advancing to the next as if having won.

bye-bye (bi-bi) *interj.* *(informal)* goodby.

by-e·lec·tion (bi-i-lek-shŏn) *n.* *(British)* an election held for a seat in the House of Commons as a consequence of the death or resignation of a member.

Bye·lo·rus·sia = Belorussia.

by·gone (bi-gawn) *adj.* belonging to the past.

by·gones (bi-gawnz) *n. pl.* things belonging to the past. □**let bygones be bygones,** forgive and forget past offenses.

by·law (bi-law) *n.* a law or regulation made by a local authority, club, etc.

by-line (bi-lin) *n.* the author's name given at the beginning or end of an article in a newspaper or magazine.

by·pass (bi-pas) *n.* 1. a road taking traffic around a congested area. 2. a secondary channel allowing something to flow when the main route is blocked. **bypass** *v.* 1. to avoid by means of a bypass. 2. to omit or ignore (procedures, regulations, etc.) in order to act quickly.

by·path (bi-path) *n.* (*pl.* **-paths,** *pr.* -pa*th*z, -paths) a secluded path.

by·play (bi-play) *n.* action, usually without speech, of minor characters in a play etc.

by·prod·uct (bi-prod-ŭkt) *n.* a substance produced during the making of something else.

by·road (bi-rohd) *n.* a minor road.

by·stand·er (bi-stan-dĕr) *n.* a person standing near but taking no part when something happens.

byte (bit) *n.* a group of binary digits in a computer.

by·way (bi-way) *n.* a byroad.

by·word (bi-wurd) *n.* 1. a person or thing spoken of as a notable example, *the firm became a byword for mismanagement.* 2. a familiar saying.

Byz·an·tine (biz-ăn-teen) *adj.* 1. of Byzantium or the eastern Roman Empire. 2. complicated, devious, underhand.

C

C, c (see) (*pl.* **Cs, C's, c's**) 1. the third letter of the alphabet. 2. *C,* a grade rating for average school work. 3. the Roman numeral symbol for 100.
C, c *abbr.* 1. cape. 2. carat. 3. Celsius. 4. cent. 5. centigrade. 6. centimeter. 7. circa. 8. copyright.
C *symbol* carbon.
Ca *symbol* calcium.
CA *abbr.* California.
cab (kab) *n.* 1. a taxi. 2. a compartment for the driver of a train, bus, or crane.
CAB, C.A.B. *abbr.* Civil Aeronautics Board.
ca·bal (kă-bal) *n.* 1. a secret plot. 2. the people engaged in it.
cab·a·la (kab-ă-lă) *n.* 1. a Jewish mystical interpretation of Scripture, based on finding hidden meanings in its letters and words. 2. any secret or occult matter or doctrine. **cab·a·lis′tic** *adj.*
ca·bal·le·ro (kab-ăl-yair-oh) *n.* 1. a Spanish gentleman. 2. *(Southwestern use)* a horseman, a woman's male escort or admirer.
ca·ba·na (kă-ban-ă) *n.* a shelter at a beach or swimming pool, used as a bathhouse.
cab·a·ret (kab-ă-ray) *n.* a restaurant or nightclub that provides entertainment while the guests are eating or drinking.
cab·bage (kab-ij) *n.* a vegetable with green or purple leaves, usually forming a round head.
cab·by, cab·bie (kab-ee) *n.* (*pl.* **-bies**) *(informal)* a cab driver.
ca·ber (kay-běr) *n.* a roughly trimmed tree trunk used in the Scottish sport of **tossing the caber.**
cab·in (kab-in) *n.* 1. a small dwelling or shelter, especially one of wood. 2. a compartment in a ship or aircraft. □**cabin boy,** a boy waiting on the officers or passengers on a ship. **cabin class,** the intermediate class of accommodation on a ship. **cabin cruiser,** a large motorboat with one or more cabins.
cab·i·net (kab-ĭ-nit) *n.* 1. a cupboard with drawers or shelves for storing or displaying articles, or containing a radio or television set. 2. the group of department heads or ministers chosen by a president or prime minister to advise on government policy.
cab·i·net·mak·er (kab-ĭ-nit-may-kĕr) *n.* a skilled woodworker who makes fine furniture.
cab·i·net·work (kab-ĭ-nit-wurk) *n.* things produced by a cabinetmaker.
ca·ble (kay-běl) *n.* 1. a thick rope of fiber or wire. 2. an anchor chain. 3. a set of insulated wires for carrying electricity or telegraph messages. 4. a cablegram. 5. a knitted pattern **(cable stitch)** looking like twisted rope. **cable** *v.* **(ca·bled, ca·bling)** to send a telegram to (a person) abroad, to transmit (money or information) in this way. □**cable car,** one of the cars in a cable rail system;

cars drawn by an endless cable by means of a stationary engine. **cable TV,** television programs transmitted to homes from a community antenna by a coaxial cable; this system.
ca·ble·gram (kay-běl-gram) *n.* a telegraph message transmitted by a submarine cable.
cab·o·chon (kab-ŏ-shon) *n.* a polished unfaceted gem usually circular or elliptical in shape. **cabochon** *adv.* in the shape of a cabochon.
ca·boo·dle (kă-boo-děl) *n.* *(slang)* **the whole caboodle,** the whole lot.
ca·boose (kă-boos) *n.* the rear car on a freight train, for use by the crew.
cab·ri·o·let (kab-ri-ŏ-lay) *n.* 1. a light two-wheeled hooded one-horse carriage. 2. an automobile resembling a convertible coupe.
cab·stand (kab-stand) *n.* a place where cabs are permitted to wait for hire.
ca·ca·o (kă-kay-oh) *n.* (*pl.* **-ca·os**) 1. a tropical tree producing a seed **(cacao bean)** from which cocoa and chocolate are made. 2. its seed.
cac·cia·to·re (kach-ă-tohr-ee) *adj.* prepared with tomatoes, olive oil, spices, etc. ▷Italian.
cache (kash) *n.* 1. a hiding place for treasure or provisions. 2. hidden treasure or provisions. **cache** *v.* **(cached, cach·ing)** to place in a cache.
ca·chet (ka-shay) *n.* 1. a distinguishing mark. 2. prestige.
cack·le (kak-ĕl) *n.* 1. the loud clucking noise a hen makes after laying. 2. a loud silly laugh. 3. noisy chatter. **cackle** *v.* **(cack·led, cack·ling)** 1. to give a cackle. 2. to chatter noisily. **cack′ler** *n.*
ca·coph·o·ny (kă-kof-ŏ-nee) *n.* (*pl.* **-nies**) a harsh discordant sound. **ca·coph′o·nous** *adj.*
cac·tus (kak-tŭs) *n.* (*pl.* **-ti,** *pr.* **-tı**) a plant from a hot dry climate, with a fleshy stem and usually prickles but no leaves.
cad (kad) *n.* a person who behaves dishonorably. **cad′dish** *adj.* **cad′dish·ly** *adv.* **cad′dish·ness** *n.*
ca·dav·er (kă-dav-ĕr) *n.* a corpse.
ca·dav·er·ous (kă-dav-ĕ-rŭs) *adj.* gaunt and pale. **ca·dav′er·ous·ly** *adv.*
cad·die, cad·dy (kad-ee) *n.* (*pl.* **-dies**) a person who carries clubs for a golfer during a game. **caddie, caddy** *v.* **(cad·died, cad·dy·ing)** to act as caddie.
cad·dis·fly (kad-is-flı) *n.* (*pl.* **-flies**) a four-winged insect living near water.
cad·dis·worm (kad-is-wurm) *n.* the larva of the caddisfly, used as bait by fishermen.
cad·dy (kad-ee) *n.* (*pl.* **-dies**) a small box for holding tea etc.
ca·dence (kay-děns) *n.* 1. rhythm in sound. 2. the rise and fall of the voice in speaking. 3. the end of a musical phrase. **ca′denced** *adj.*

ca·den·za (kă-den-ză) *n.* an elaborate passage, usually toward the end of a composition for a solo instrument or voice, showing off the performer's skill.

ca·det (kă-det) *n.* 1. a young person receiving elementary training for service in the armed forces or the police force. 2. a younger son or brother. **ca·dette'** *n. fem.* □**Cadette Scout,** a member of the Girl Scouts, aged twelve through fourteen.

cadge (kaj) *v.* **(cadged, cadg·ing)** to ask for as a gift, to go about begging. **cadg'er** *n.*

cad·mi·um (kad-mi-ŭm) *n.* a grayish chemical element that looks like tin and is used especially in plating.

ca·dre (kad-rĕ, -ree) *n.* a group forming a nucleus of trained personnel in industry or the armed forces that can be increased when necessary.

ca·du·ce·us (kă-doo-si-ŭs) *n.* (*pl.* **-ce·i,** *pr.* **-si-ı**) 1. the wand of the Roman god Mercury, with two serpents twined around it and having wings at the top. 2. a similar staff used as the symbol of the medical profession.

cae·cum = **cecum.**

Cae·sar (see-zăr) *n.* 1. a title of the Roman emperors. 2. any powerful ruler or autocrat.

Cae·sar·e·an (si-zair-i-ăn) *n.* *(informal)* a **Caesarean section,** a surgical operation by which a child is taken from the womb by cutting through the wall of the mother's abdomen and into the womb. ▷So called from the story that Julius Caesar was born in this way.

cae·su·ra, ce·su·ra (si-zhoor-ă) *n.* (*pl.* **-su·ras, -su·rae,** *pr.* **-**zhoor-ee) a pause in the middle of a metrical line.

CAF *abbr.* cost and freight.

ca·fé (ka-fay) *n.* 1. a shop that sells refreshments, a small restaurant. 2. a barroom. □**café au lait** (ka-fay oh **lay**) 1. coffee mixed with an equal quantity of scalded milk. 2. the brownish-cream color of this.

caf·e·te·ri·a (kaf-ĕ-teer-i-ă) *n.* a restaurant where customers serve themselves or are served from a counter.

caf·feine, caf·fein (ka-feen) *n.* a stimulant found especially in tea and coffee.

caf·tan (kaf-tăn) *n.* 1. a long coat-like garment worn by men in the Near East. 2. a woman's long loose dress.

cage (kayj) *n.* 1. a framework with wires or bars in which birds or animals are kept. 2. any similar structure, the enclosed platform in which people travel in an elevator or in the shaft of a mine. **cage** *v.* **(caged, cag·ing)** to put or keep in a cage. □**cage bird,** a bird of a kind usually kept in a cage.

cage·ling (kayj-ling) *n.* a caged bird.

ca·gey (kay-jee) *adj.* **(-gi·er, -gi·est)** *(informal)* cautious about giving information, secretive. **ca'gi·ly** *adv.* **ca'gi·ness** *n.*

ca·hoots (kă-hoots) *n. pl.* *(slang)* **in cahoots with,** in league with.

cai·man, cay·man (kay-măn) *n.* any of several tropical American reptiles resembling alligators and crocodiles.

Cain (kayn) *n.* 1. the first son of Adam and Eve and murderer of his brother Abel. 2. a murderer. □**raise Cain,** *see* **raise.**

cairn (kairn) *n.* a pyramid of rough stones set up as a landmark or a monument. □**cairn terrier,** a small shaggy short-legged terrier.

Cai·ro (kır-oh) the capital of Egypt.

cais·son (kay-son) *n.* 1. a watertight box or chamber inside which work can be carried out on underwater structures. 2. a wheeled vehicle for transporting artillery shells. □**caisson disease,** a disease caused by working under high atmospheric pressure.

cai·tiff (kay-tif) *n.* *(old use)* a despicable person. **caitiff** *adj.* despicable.

ca·jole (kă-johl) *v.* **(ca·joled, ca·jol·ing)** to coax. **ca·jol'er·y** *n.* **ca·jole'ment** *n.*

Ca·jun, Cai·jan (kay-jŭn) *n.* 1. a descendant of French Canadian immigrants in Louisiana. 2. the dialect spoken by Cajuns.

cake (kayk) *n.* 1. a baked sweet breadlike food. 2. a mixture cooked in a round flat shape, *fish cakes.* 3. a shaped or hardened mass, *a cake of soap.* **cake** *v.* **(caked, cak·ing)** 1. to harden into a compact mass. 2. to encrust with a hardened mass.

cake·walk (kayk-wawk) *n.* 1. a ballroom march originated by black Americans, with a cake as the prize for the dancer with the most intricate steps. 2. a popular dance developed from these steps.

cal. *abbr.* 1. calendar. 2. caliber. 3. calorie.

Cal. *abbr.* California.

cal·a·bash (kal-ă-bash) *n.* 1. any of various gourds, especially with a hard shell. 2. a container made from the shell of such a gourd.

cal·a·boose (kal-ă-boos) *n.* *(informal)* a prison.

ca·la·di·um (kă-lay-di-ŭm) *n.* any of various tropical American plants with ornamental leaves.

cal·a·mine (kal-ă-mın) *n.* a pink powder, chiefly zinc carbonate or oxide, used in skin lotions.

ca·lam·i·ty (kă-lam-i-tee) *n.* (*pl.* **-ties**) a disaster. **ca·lam'i·tous** *adj.* **ca·lam'i·tous·ly** *adv.*

calc. *abbr.* calculate.

cal·car·e·ous (kal-kar-i-ŭs) *adj.* of or containing calcium carbonate or limestone. **cal·car'e·ous·ness** *n.*

cal·ce·o·lar·i·a (kal-si-ŏ-lair-i-ă) *n.* a garden plant with a slipper-shaped flower.

cal·cic (kal-sik) *adj.* composed of or containing calcium or lime.

cal·cif·er·ous (kal-sif-ĕ-rŭs) *adj.* yielding or containing calcium carbonate.

cal·ci·fy (kal-sı-fı) *v.* **(cal·ci·fied, cal·ci·fy·ing)** to harden by a deposit of calcium salts. **cal·ci·fi·ca·tion** (kal-sı-fı-kay-shŏn) *n.*

cal·ci·mine (kal-sı-mın) *n.* a white or lightly colored liquid preparation containing zinc oxide, used on walls and ceilings. **calcimine** *v.* **(cal·ci·mined, cal·ci·min·ing)** to paint with calcimine.

cal·ci·um (kal-si-ŭm) *n.* a grayish-white chemical element present in bones and teeth and forming the basis of lime. □**calcium carbonate,** a chemical compound frequently occurring as limestone or chalk. **calcium hydroxide,** a powder of water and lime, used in mortar, plaster, etc.

cal·cu·la·ble (kal-kyŭ-lă-bĕl) *adj.* able to be calculated.

cal·cu·late (kal-kyŭ-layt) *v.* **(cal·cu·lat·ed, cal·cu·lat·ing)** 1. to find out by using mathematics, to count. 2. to plan deliberately, to intend. 3 *(informal)* to suppose, to believe. **cal·cu·la·tion** (kal-kyŭ-lay-shŏn) *n.* □**calculated risk,** a risk taken deliberately with full knowledge of the dangers.

cal·cu·lat·ing (kal-kyŭ-lay-ting) *adj.* shrewd, scheming. **cal'cu·lat·ing·ly** *adv.*

cal·cu·la·tor (kal-kyŭ-lay-tŏr) *n.* 1. a person who calculates. 2. a machine that performs arithmetical processes.

cal·cu·lus (kal-kyŭ-lŭs) *n.* (*pl.* **-li,** *pr.* -lɪ, **-lus·es**) 1. a stone formed in the body. 2. a branch of mathematics that deals with problems involving rates of variation.

cal·de·ra (kal-der-ă) *n.* (*pl.* **-ras**) a deep hole at the top of a volcano.

cal·dron = **cauldron.**

Cal·e·do·ni·an (kal-ĕ-doh-ni-ăn) *adj.* of Scotland.

cal·en·dar (kal-ĕn-dăr) *n.* 1. a chart showing the days, weeks, and months of a particular year. 2. a device displaying the date. 3. a list of dates or events of a particular kind, *the academic calendar.* 4. the system by which time is divided into fixed periods, *the Gregorian calendar.* ▷ Do not confuse *calendar* with *calender.*

cal·en·der (kal-ĕn-dĕr) *n.* a machine in which cloth or paper is pressed by rollers to glaze or smooth it. **calender** *v.* to press in a calender. ▷ Do not confuse *calender* with *calendar.*

cal·ends (kal-ĕndz) *n. pl.* the first day of the month in the Roman calendar.

ca·len·du·la (kă-len-jŭ-lă) *n.* a garden plant with large yellow or orange flowers.

calf[1] (kaf) *n.* (*pl.* **calves,** *pr.* kavz) 1. the young of cattle, also of the seal, whale, and certain other animals. 2. leather made from calfskin.

calf[2] *n.* (*pl.* **calves**) the fleshy back part of the leg below the knee.

calf·skin (kaf-skin) *n.* calf leather, used especially in bookbinding and shoemaking. **calfskin** *adj.* made of calfskin.

cal·i·ber, cal·i·bre (kal-ĭ-bĕr) *n.* 1. the diameter of the inside of a tube or gun barrel. 2. the diameter of a bullet or shell. 3. ability, importance, *we need a person of your caliber.*

cal·i·brate (kal-ĭ-brayt) *v.* (**cal·i·brat·ed, cal·i·brat·ing**) 1. to mark or correct units of measurement on a gauge. 2. to measure the caliber of. **cal'i·bra·tor** *n.* **cal·i·bra·tion** (kal-ĭ-bray-shŏn) *n.*

cal·i·co (kal-ĭ-koh) *n.* (*pl.* **-coes, -cos**) a kind of cotton cloth printed with a figured pattern. **calico** *adj.* made of calico. □**calico cat,** a cat with variously colored markings.

Calif. *abbr.* California.

Cal·i·for·nia (kal-ĭ-for-nyă) a state of the U.S. **Cal·i·for′nian** *adj.* & *n.* □**California poppy,** a small cultivated herb related to the poppy.

cal·i·for·ni·um (kal-ĭ-for-ni-ŭm) *n.* a synthetic radioactive element.

cal·i·per (kal-ĭ-pĕr) *n.* (usually **calipers**) a compass for measuring the diameter of tubes or of round objects.

ca·liph, ca·lif (kay-lif) *n.* the chief civil and religious ruler in some Muslim countries. **ca·liph·ate** (kay-li-fayt) *n.*

cal·is·then·ics (kal-is-then-iks) *n.* light gymnastic exercises. **cal·is·then′ic** *adj.*

calk = **caulk.**

call[1] (kawl) *n.* 1. a shout or cry. 2. the characteristic cry of a bird. 3. a signal on a bugle etc. 4. a short visit. 5. a summons, an invitation; *the call of the wild,* its attraction. 6. a demand, a claim, *I have many calls on my time.* 7. a need, an occasion, *there's no call for you to worry.* 8. an act of telephoning, a conversation on the telephone. 9. *(informal)* a ruling by a referee or umpire in a game.

call[2] *v.* 1. to shout or speak loudly in order to attract attention etc. 2. to utter a call. 3. to pay a short visit. 4. to name, to describe or address as, *I call that cheating; let's call it even.* 5. to rouse deliberately, to summon to get up. 6. to summon, *call the fire department.* 7. to command or invite, to urge as if by commanding, *call a strike; duty calls,* claims my attention. 8. to communicate with by telephone or radio. 9. (in sports) to rule that play is ended. **call'er** *n.* □**call a person's bluff,** to challenge him to carry out his threat. **call down,** to reprimand. **call for,** to demand, to require; to come and collect. **call girl,** a prostitute who accepts appointments by telephone. **call in,** to report by telephone; to seek advice or help from; to order the return of, to take out of circulation. **call it a day,** to decide that enough work has been done for one day, and stop working. **call number,** a code assigned to a book to establish its proper location on a library shelf. **call off,** to call away, *call off your dog;* to cancel, *the strike was called off.* **call of nature,** a need to go to the toilet. **call on,** to make a short visit to (a person); to appeal to, to request. **call out,** to summon to action; to order to come out on strike. **call sign,** a signal identifying a radio transmitter. **call the tune,** to control the proceedings. **call to mind,** to remember; to cause a person to remember. **call up,** to telephone to; to bring back to one's mind; *(informal)* to summon for military service. **on call,** available to be called out on duty. **within call,** near enough to be summoned by calling.

cal·la (kal-ă) **lily** a tropical plant with a white showy petallike part surrounding a yellow spike.

call·back (kawl-bak) *n.* a manufacturer's recall of a product to correct a defect.

call-board (kawl-bohrd) *n.* a board on which notices are displayed, especially backstage in a theater.

cal·lig·ra·phy (kă-lig-ră-fee) *n.* beautiful handwriting, the art of producing this. **cal·lig′ra·pher** *n.* **cal·lig·raph·ic** (kal-ĭ-graf-ik) *adj.*

call·ing (kaw-ling) *n.* 1. an occupation, a profession or trade. 2. a strong impulse toward one of these.

cal·li·o·pe (kă-lɪ-ŏ-pee) *n.* a musical instrument consisting of steam whistles and a keyboard.

cal·los·i·ty (kă-los-i-tee) *n.* (*pl.* **-ties**) 1. abnormal hardness of the skin. 2. a callus.

cal·lous (kal-ŭs) *adj.* 1. hardened, having calluses. 2. unsympathetic. **callous** *v.* to make or become unsympathetic. **cal′lous·ly** *adv.* **cal′lous·ness** *n.* ▷ Do not confuse *callous* with *callus.*

cal·loused (kal-ŭst) *adj.* hardened, having calluses.

cal·low (kal-oh) *adj.* immature and inexperienced. **cal′low·ly** *adv.* **cal′low·ness** *n.*

call-up (kawl-up) *n.* a summons for military service.

cal·lus (kal-ŭs) *n.* (*pl.* **-lus·es**) an area of thick hardened skin or tissue. **callus** *v.* (**cal·lused, cal·lus·ing**) to form a callus. ▷ Do not confuse *callus* with *callous.*

calm (kahm) *adj.* 1. quiet and still, not windy. 2. not excited or agitated. 3. casual and confident. **calm** *n.* a calm condition or period. **calm** *v.* to make or become calm. **calm′ly** *adv.* **calm′ness** *n.*

cal·o·mel (kal-ŏ-mel) *n.* a heavy white powder used as a laxative and fungicide.

ca·lor·ic (kă-lor-ik) *adj.* 1. of calories. 2. of heat.

cal·o·rie (kal-ŏ-ree) *n.* 1. a unit for measuring a

quantity of heat. 2. a unit for measuring the energy value of food.

cal·o·rif·ic (kal-ŏ-rif-ik) *adj.* of, producing heat.

cal·o·rim·e·ter (kal-ŏ-rim-ĕ-tĕr) *n.* a device for measuring heat. **cal·o·rim'e·try** *n.* **cal·o·ri·met·ric** (kal-ŏ-ri-met-rik) *adj.* **cal·o·ri·met'ri·cal·ly** *adv.*

cal·u·met (kal-yŭ-met) *n.* a long-stemmed ornamental pipe used by North American Indians for ceremonial purposes, especially as a symbol of peace or friendship (the *peace pipe*).

ca·lum·ni·ate (kă-lum-ni-ayt) *v.* **(ca·lum·ni·at·ed, ca·lum·ni·at·ing)** to slander. **ca·lum'ni·a·tor** *n.* **ca·lum·ni·a·tion** (kă-lum-ni-ay-shŏn) *n.*

cal·um·ny (kal-ŭm-nee) *n.* (*pl.* **-nies**) 1. slander. 2. a slanderous statement. **ca·lum·ni·ous** (kă-lum-ni-ŭs) *adj.* **ca·lum'ni·ous·ly** *adv.*

Cal·va·ry (kal-vă-ree) *n.* (*pl.* **-ries**) the place or a representation of the Crucifixion. ▷Do not confuse *Calvary* with *cavalry.*

calve (kav) *v.* **(calved, calv·ing)** to give birth to a calf.

calves *see* **calf.**

Cal·vin·ism (kal-vĭ-niz-ĕm) *n.* the teachings of John Calvin, a French Protestant religious reformer who lived in Switzerland (1509–64), and of his followers. **Cal'vin·ist** *n.* **Cal·vin·is·tic** (kal-vĭ-nis-tik) *adj.*

ca·lyp·so (kă-lip-soh) *n.* (*pl.* **-sos**) a West Indian song with a variable rhythm and topical usually improvised lyrics.

ca·lyx (kay-liks) *n.* (*pl.* **-lyx·es, -ly·ces,** *pr.* **-lĭseez**) a ring of leaves *(sepals)* enclosing an unopened flower bud.

cam (kam) *n.* a projecting part on a wheel or shaft, shaped or mounted so that its circular motion, as it turns, transmits an up-and-down or back-and-forth motion to another part.

ca·ma·ra·de·rie (kah-mă-rah-dĕ-ree) *n.* comradeship.

cam·ber (kam-bĕr) *n.* a slight arch or upward curve given to a surface, especially of a road. **camber** *v.* 1. to have a camber. 2. to give a camber to. **cam'bered** *adj.*

cam·bi·um (kam-bi-ŭm) *n.* (*pl.* **-bi·ums, -bi·a,** *pr.* -bi-ă) a layer of cells that provide the base for growth of woody tissue and bark. **cam'bi·al** *adj.*

Cam·bo·di·a (kam-boh-di-ă) the former name of Kampuchea. **Cam·bo'di·an** *adj. & n.*

Cam·bri·an (kaym-bri-ăn) *adj.* of the earliest geologic period of the Paleozoic era. **Cambrian** *n.* the Cambrian period.

cam·bric (kaym-brik) *n.* thin cotton or linen cloth.

came (kaym) *see* **come.**

cam·el (kam-ĕl) *n.* 1. a long-necked animal with either one or two humps on its back, used in desert countries for riding and for carrying goods. 2. a fawn color. □**camel hair** *or* **camel's hair,** fine soft hair used in artists' brushes; a fabric made of this.

ca·mel·lia, ca·me·lia (kă-meel-yă) *n.* 1. an evergreen flowering shrub from China and Japan. 2. its flower.

ca·mel·o·pard (kă-mel-ŏ-pahrd) *n.* (*old use*) a giraffe.

Cam·em·bert (kam-ĕm-bair) *n.* a soft rich cheese of the kind made in Normandy, France.

cam·e·o (kam-i-oh) *n.* (*pl.* **-e·os**) 1. a small piece of hard stone carved with a raised design, espe-

cially with two colored layers cut so that one serves as a background to the design. 2. something small but well executed, such as a short description or a minor part in a play.

cam·er·a (kam-ĕ-ră) *n.* an apparatus for taking photographs, moving pictures, or television pictures.

cam·er·a·man (kam-ĕ-ră-măn) *n.* (*pl.* **-men,** *pr.* -men) a person whose job is to operate a film camera or television camera.

Cam·e·roon, Cam·e·roun (kam-ĕ-roon) a country on the west coast of Africa. **Cam·e·roo'ni·an** *adj. & n.*

cam·i·sole (kam-i-sohl) *n.* a short sleeveless shirt worn by women as an undergarment.

cam·o·mile (kam-ŏ-meel) *n.* a sweet-smelling plant with daisy-like flowers, which are dried for use in medicine as a tonic.

cam·ou·flage (kam-ŏ-flahzh) *n.* 1. a method of disguising or concealing objects by coloring or covering them so that they look like part of their surroundings. 2. the concealment itself. **camouflage** *v.* **(cam·ou·flaged, cam·ou·flag·ing)** to conceal in this way.

camp¹ (kamp) *n.* 1. a place where people live temporarily in tents, huts, or similar shelters. 2. the occupants. 3. a group of people with the same ideals. **camp** *v.* 1. to make or live in a camp. 2. to live temporarily as if in a camp. □**camp bed,** a folding portable bed. **campfire girl,** a member of the Campfire Girls, an organization similar to the Girl Scouts. **camp follower,** a civilian follower of military troops, especially a prostitute. **camp out,** to sleep in a tent or in the open. **go camping,** to spend a holiday outdoors, sleeping in tents or in sleeping bags.

camp² *adj.* 1. effeminate, homosexual. 2. exaggerated in style, especially for humorous effect. **camp** *n.* such a style or manner. **camp'y** *adj.* **(camp·i·er, camp·i·est)** camp. **camp'i·ly** *adv.* **camp'i·ness** *n.* □**camp it up,** to behave or perform in a camp way.

cam·paign (kam-payn) *n.* 1. a series of military operations with a set purpose, usually in one area. 2. a similar series of planned activities, *an advertising campaign.* **campaign** *v.* to take part in a campaign. **cam·paign'er** *n.*

cam·pa·ni·le (kam-pă-nee-lee) *n.* (*pl.* **-ni·les, -ni·li,** *pr.* -nee-lee) a bell tower, especially a freestanding one.

cam·pa·nol·o·gy (kam-pă-nol-ŏ-jee) *n.* the study of bells and their casting, ringing, etc. **cam·pa·nol'o·gist** *n.*

cam·pan·u·la (kam-pan-yŭ-lă) *n.* a plant with bell-shaped usually blue or white flowers.

camp·er (kam-pĕr) *n.* 1. a person who camps. 2. a truck-like vehicle outfitted as living quarters for camping or long excursions.

camp·ground (kamp-grownd) *n.* a place for camping or for religious meetings.

cam·phor (kam-fŏr) *n.* a strong-smelling white substance used in medicine and mothballs and in making plastics. □**camphor tree,** a species of laurel found in Japan, China, etc., from which camphor may be extracted.

cam·phor·at·ed (kam-fŏ-ray-tid) *adj.* containing camphor.

cam·pi·on (kam-pi-ŏn) *n.* a wild plant with pink or white flowers.

camp·o·ree (kam-pŏ-ree) *n.* a camp gathering of Girl or Boy Scouts, usually from the same district.

camp·site (kamp-sıt) *n.* a campground.

camp·stool (kamp-stool) *n.* a lightweight folding stool.

cam·pus (kam-pŭs) *n.* (*pl.* **-pus·es**) the grounds of a university or college.

cam·shaft (kam-shaft) *n.* a shaft bearing cams.

can[1] (kan) *n.* 1. a metal or plastic container for liquids. 2. a sealed metal container in which food or drink is preserved. 3. either of these with its contents, the amount it contains. 4. *(slang)* a jail. 5. *(slang)* the buttocks. **can** *v.* **(canned, can·ning)** 1. to preserve in a sealed can. 2. *(slang)* to dismiss from a job. **can′ner** *n.* □**can opener,** a tool for opening cans. **in the can,** made into a motion picture or phonograph record and ready for release to the public. **tin can,** *(slang)* a naval destroyer.

can[2] *auxiliary verb* expressing ability or knowledge of how to do something *(he can play the violin)* or permission *(you can go;* ▷ *may is more formal)* or desire or liberty to act *(we cannot allow this).*

Can. *abbr.* Canada.

Can·a·da (kan-ă-dă) a country in North America. **Ca·na·di·an** (kă-nay-di-ăn) *adj. & n.* □**Canada goose,** a wild goose of North America. **Canadian bacon,** a round piece of bacon cut from a strip of pork loin.

Ca·na·di·an·ism (kă-nay-di-ă-niz-ĕm) *n.* a custom, belief, trait, phrase, etc., originating in Canada or peculiar to it.

ca·naille (kă-nayl) *n.* the rabble. ▷ French.

ca·nal (kă-nal) *n.* 1. a channel cut through land for navigation or irrigation. 2. a tubular passage through which food or air passes in a plant or animal body, *the alimentary canal.* □**Canal Zone,** the area around the Panama Canal formerly governed by the U.S.

ca·nal·boat (kă-nal-boht) *n.* a barge, either self-propelled or towed, for use in a canal.

ca·nal·ize (kă-nal-ız) *v.* (**ca·nal·ized, ca·nal·iz·ing**) to channel. **ca·nal·i·za·tion** (kă-nal-i-zay-shŏn) *n.*

can·a·pé (kan-ă-pee, -pay) *n.* a small piece of bread or toast spread with savory food.

ca·nard (kă-nahrd) *n.* a false or unfounded story.

ca·nar·y (kă-nair-ee) *n.* (*pl.* **-nar·ies**) 1. a small yellow songbird. 2. *(slang)* person acting as a police informer. **canary** *adj.* bright-yellow.

Canary Islands a group of islands off the northwest coast of Africa.

ca·nas·ta (kă-nas-tă) *n.* a card game played with two packs of fifty-two cards plus four jokers.

Can·ber·ra (kan-ber-ă) the capital of Australia.

canc. *abbr.* 1. cancel. 2. cancellation.

can·can (kan-kan) *n.* a lively stage dance involving high kicking, performed by women in long skirts and petticoats.

can·cel (kan-sĕl) *v.* (**can·celed, can·cel·ing**) 1. to say that (something already decided upon or arranged) will not be done or take place. 2. to order (a thing) to be discontinued. 3. to neutralize, *his absences canceled his excellent work.* 4. to cross out. 5. to mark (a stamp or ticket) in order to prevent further use. **can·cel·la·tion** (kan-sĕ-lay-shŏn) *n.* □**cancel out,** to counterbalance, to neutralize (each other).

can·cer (kan-sĕr) *n.* 1. a tumor, especially a malignant one. 2. a disease in which malignant growths form. 3. something evil that spreads destructively. 4. *Cancer,* a sign of the zodiac, the Crab. **can′cer·ous** *adj.*

can·de·la (kan-dee-lă) *n.* a unit used in measuring the intensity of light.

can·de·la·brum (kan-dĕ-lah-brŭm) *n.* (*pl.* **-bra,** *pr.* **-bră, -brums**) a large branched candlestick or holder for lights. ▷ *Candelabra* is also used as a singular but not by careful writers.

can·des·cent (kan-des-ĕnt) *adj.* glowing, incandescent. **can·des′cence** *n.*

can·did (kan-did) *adj.* frank, not hiding one's thoughts. **can′did·ly** *adv.* **can′did·ness** *n.* □**candid camera,** a small camera for taking informal pictures, especially without the subject's knowledge.

can·di·date (kan-di-dayt) *n.* 1. a person who seeks or is nominated for appointment to an office or position or membership. 2. a person taking an examination. **can·di·da·cy** (kan-di-dă-see) *n.*

can·died (kan-deed) *adj.* encrusted with sugar, preserved in sugar. □**candied fruit,** small pieces of fruit or peel of citrus fruits candied for eating or use in cooking.

can·dle (kan-dĕl) *n.* 1. a stick of wax with a wick through it, giving light when burning. 2. a candela. **candle** *v.* (**can·dled, can·dling**) to examine (especially eggs) for freshness by holding up to a light. **can′dler** *n.* □**cannot hold a candle to,** is very inferior to. **game is not worth the candle,** the result does not justify the trouble or cost.

can·dle·light (kan-dĕl-lıt) *n.* the light of a candle or candles.

Can·dle·mas (kan-dĕl-măs) *n.* the religious festival in honor of the presentation of the infant Jesus in the temple, when candles are blessed (February 2).

can·dle·pow·er (kan-dĕl-pow-ĕr) *n.* the intensity of light expressed in candles.

can·dle·stick (kan-dĕl-stik) *n.* a holder for one or more candles.

can·dle·wick (kan-dĕl-wik) *n.* a fabric with a raised tufted pattern worked in soft cotton yarn.

can·dor (kan-dŏr) *n.* candid speech, frankness.

C and W *abbr.* country and western music.

can·dy (kan-dee) *n.* (*pl.* **-dies**) 1. a sweet confection flavored with chocolate, peppermint, fruit, etc. 2. a small piece of this. **candy** *v.* (**can·died, can·dy·ing**) 1. to cook or coat with sugar or syrup. 2. to reduce to crystals. □**candy striper,** a volunteer hospital worker, usually a girl of high-school age. **candy stripes,** alternate stripes of white and color.

can·dy·tuft (kan-dee-tuft) *n.* a plant growing in tufts and having white, pink, or purple flowers.

cane (kayn) *n.* 1. a wooden stick or metal rod carried when walking, especially as added support. 2. the hollow jointed stem of tall reeds and grasses (as bamboo, sugar cane), the solid stem of slender palms (as Malacca). 3. the material of these used for making furniture etc. **cane** *v.* (**caned, can·ing**) 1. to punish by beating with a cane. 2. to weave cane into (a chair etc.). □**cane sugar,** sugar obtained from the juice of sugar cane.

cane·brake (kayn-brayk) *n.* a tract of land overgrown with canes.

ca·nine (kay-nın) *adj.* of dogs. **canine** *n.* (also **canine tooth**) a strong pointed tooth next to the incisors.

can·is·ter (kan-i-stĕr) *n.* 1. a metal box or other container. 2. a cylinder, filled with shot or tear gas, that bursts and releases its contents when fired from a gun or thrown.

can·ker (kang-kĕr) *n.* 1. a disease that destroys the wood of plants and trees. 2. a disease that causes ulcerous sores in animals. **can′ker·ous** *adj.* □**canker sore,** an ulcerous sore of the mouth and lips.

can·ker·worm (kang-kĕr-wurm) *n.* the caterpillar of a moth that destroys the leaves or buds of plants and trees.

can·na·bis (kan-ă-bis) *n.* 1. a hemp plant. 2. a preparation of this for smoking or chewing as an intoxicant drug, marijuana.

canned (kand) *see* **can**[1]. **canned** *adj.* 1. preserved in jars or cans, *canned fruit.* 2. *(slang)* recorded, *canned music.*

can·nel·lo·ni (kan-ĕ-loh-nee) *n. pl.* rolls of pasta containing meat and seasoning.

can·ner·y (kan-ĕ-ree) *n.* (*pl.* **-ner·ies**) a canning factory.

can·ni·bal (kan-i-băl) *n.* a person who eats human flesh, an animal that eats its own kind. **can′ni·bal·ism** *n.* **can·ni·bal·is·tic** (kan-i-bă-lis-tik) *adj.*

can·ni·bal·ize (kan-i-bă-lız) *v.* (**can·ni·bal·ized, can·ni·bal·iz·ing**) to dismantle (a machine etc.) in order to provide spare parts for others. **can·ni·bal·i·za·tion** (kan-i-bă-li-zay-shŏn) *n.*

can·non (kan-ŏn) *n.* 1. an old type of large heavy gun firing solid metal balls. 2. an automatic shell-firing gun used in aircraft. **cannon** *v.* to collide heavily with. □**cannon fodder,** men regarded merely as material to be expended in war. ▷Do not confuse *cannon* with *canon.*

can·non·ade (kan-ŏ-nayd) *n.* continuous gunfire. **cannonade** *v.* (**can·non·ad·ed, can·non·ad·ing**) 1. to fire continually. 2. to bombard with gunfire.

can·non·ball (kan-ŏn-bawl) *n.* a round heavy missile formerly fired from a cannon. **cannonball** *v.* *(slang)* to move very quickly.

can·non·eer (kan-ŏ-neer) *n.* a person who fires a cannon.

can·not (kan-ot, ka-not) = **can not.** □**cannot but,** cannot help (doing something), must. ▷Use *cannot* when indicating no special emphasis on *not, I cannot do this.* Use *can not* when indicating such emphasis, *I can accept an occasional absence but I can not accept repeated absences.*

can·nu·la (kan-yŭ-lă) *n.* (*pl.* **-las, -lae,** *pr.* -lee) a small tube inserted into the body to allow fluid to enter or escape.

can·ny (kan-ee) *adj.* (**-ni·er, -ni·est**) shrewd. **can′ni·ly** *adv.* **can′ni·ness** *n.*

ca·noe (kă-noo) *n.* a light narrow boat propelled by paddles. **canoe** *v.* (**ca·noed, ca·noe·ing**) to paddle or travel in a canoe. **ca·noe′ist** *n.*

can·on (kan-ŏn) *n.* 1. a general principle. 2. a set of writings accepted as genuinely by a particular author, sacred writings included in the Bible. 3. a clergyman who is one of a group with duties in a cathedral. □**canon law,** church law. ▷Do not confuse *canon* with *cannon.*

cañ·on = **canyon.**

ca·non·i·cal (kă-non-i-kăl) *adj.* 1. ordered by canon law. 2. included in the canon of Scripture. 3. standard, accepted. **ca·non′i·cal·ly** *adv.*

ca·non·i·cals (kă-non-i-kălz) *n. pl.* the canonical dress of clergy.

can·on·ize (kan-ŏ-nız) *v.* (**can·on·ized, can·on·iz·ing**) to declare officially to be a saint. **can·on·i·za·tion** (kan-ŏ-ni-zay-shŏn) *n.*

can·o·py (kan-ŏ-pee) *n.* (*pl.* **-pies**) 1. a hanging cover forming a shelter above a throne, bed, or person, etc. 2. any similar covering. 3. the part of a parachute that spreads in the air. **canopy** *v.* (**can·o·pied, can·o·py·ing**) to place a canopy over.

cant[1] (kant) *v.* to slope, to tilt. **cant** *n.* a tilted or sloping position.

cant[2] *n.* 1. insincere talk. 2. jargon. **cant** *v.* to indulge in insincere talk.

can't = **cannot.**

can·ta·bi·le (kahn-tah-bi-lay) *adj. & adv.* flowing and songlike. **cantabile** *n.* music of this kind. ▷Italian.

can·ta·loupe (kan-tă-lohp) *n.* a kind of melon.

can·tan·ker·ous (kan-tang-kĕ-rŭs) *adj.* bad-tempered. **can·tan′ker·ous·ly** *adv.* **can·tan′ker·ous·ness** *n.*

can·ta·ta (kăn-tah-tă) *n.* a musical composition for singers, like an oratorio but shorter.

can·teen (kan-teen) *n.* 1. a restaurant for the employees of a factory, office, etc. 2. a soldier's or camper's water flask. 3. a place of entertainment for soldiers etc.

can·ter (kan-tĕr) *n.* a gentle gallop. **canter** *v.* to gallop gently.

Can·ter·bur·y (kan-tĕr-ber-ee) **bell** a cultivated campanula with large flowers.

can·ti·cle (kan-ti-kĕl) *n.* a song or chant with words taken from the Bible, as the Magnificat and the Nunc Dimittis.

can·ti·le·ver (kan-tĭ-lev-ĕr) *n.* a projecting beam or girder supporting a balcony or similar structure.

can·to (kan-toh) *n.* (*pl.* **-tos**) a division of a long poem.

can·ton (kan-ton) *n.* a division of a country, especially of Switzerland. **can·ton·al** (kan-tŏ-năl) *adj.*

Can·ton·ese (kan-tŏ-neez) *n.* (*pl.* **-ese**) 1. a Chinese language spoken in southern China and in Hong Kong. 2. a native or inhabitant of Canton. **Cantonese** *adj.*

can·ton·ment (kan-ton-mĕnt) *n.* a temporary lodging assigned to troops.

can·tor (kan-tŏr) *n.* 1. the chief singer of the liturgy in a synagogue. 2. the leader or chief singer of a church choir.

can·vas (kan-văs) *n.* 1. strong coarse cloth used for making tents and sails etc. and by artists for painting on. 2. a piece of canvas for painting on, especially in oils, an oil painting. 3. the floor of a boxing ring. ▷Do not confuse *canvas* with *canvass.*

can·vas·back (kan-văs-bak) *n.* a North American duck.

can·vass (kan-văs) *v.* to visit in order to ask for votes, orders for goods etc., or opinions. **canvass** *n.* canvassing. **can′vass·er** *n.* ▷Do not confuse *canvass* with *canvas.*

can·yon (kan-yŏn) *n.* a deep gorge, usually with a river flowing through it.

cap (kap) *n.* 1. a soft covering for the head without a brim but often with a peak. 2. an academic headdress, a mortarboard. 3. a caplike cover or top. 4. a percussion cap. **cap** *v.* (**capped, cap·ping**) 1. to put a cap on, to cover the top or end of. 2. to excel, to outdo; *can you cap that!* it cannot be surpassed. □**cap and gown,** the mortarboard and cassock-like gown worn on ceremonial occasions at colleges and universities; the academic community. **cap pistol** or **cap gun,** a toy gun that uses percussion caps.

CAP abbr. Civil Air Patrol.

cap. abbr. 1. capital. 2. chapter.

ca·pa·ble (kay-pǎ-běl) adj. 1. competent. 2. having a certain ability or capacity, *quite capable of lying.* **ca′pa·bly** adv. **ca·pa·bil·i·ty** (kay-pǎ-bil-i-tee) n.

ca·pa·cious (kǎ-pay-shŭs) adj. roomy, able to hold much. **ca·pa′cious·ly** adv. **ca·pa′cious·ness** n.

ca·pac·i·tance (kǎ-pas-i-tǎns) n. 1. the ratio of a change in an electric charge to a corresponding change in potential. 2. the ability to store an electric charge. **ca·pac′i·tive** adj. **ca·pac′i·tive·ly** adv.

ca·pac·i·tate (kǎ-pas-i-tayt) v. (**ca·pac·i·tat·ed, ca·pac·i·tat·ing**) to make capable or legally competent.

ca·pac·i·tor (kǎ-pas-i-tŏr) n. a device storing a charge of electricity.

ca·pac·i·ty (kǎ-pas-i-tee) n. (pl. **-ties**) 1. the ability to contain or accommodate, the amount that can be contained; *full to capacity,* quite full. 2. ability, capability; *working at full capacity,* as intensively as possible. 3. a position or function, *signed it in his capacity as chairman.*

cap-a-pie (kap-ǎ-pee) adv. from head to foot.

ca·par·i·son (kǎ-par-i-sŏn) n. 1. horses' ornamental trappings. 2. ornate clothing. **caparison** v. 1. to cover with a caparison. 2. to clothe ornately.

cape[1] (kayp) n. 1. a cloak. 2. a very short similarly shaped part of a coat etc. covering the shoulders.

cape[2] n. a coastal promontory. ☐the **Cape,** the Cape of Good Hope; Cape Cod.

ca·per[1] (kay-per) v. to jump or run about playfully. **caper** n. 1. capering. 2. (slang) an illegal escapade, an activity.

caper[2] n. 1. a bramble-like shrub. 2. one of its buds, which are pickled for use in sauces etc., *caper sauce.*

cape·skin (kayp-skin) n. soft leather made from sheepskin. **capeskin** adj.

Cape (kayp) **Town** one of the two capital cities of South Africa.

Cape Verde (vurd) a country off the western coast of Africa.

cap·il·lar·i·ty (kap-ĭ-lar-i-tee) n. (pl. **-ties**) surface tension that causes a liquid in contact with a solid to rise or fall.

cap·il·lar·y (kap-ĭ-ler-ee) n. (pl. **-lar·ies**) one of the very fine branching blood vessels that connect veins and arteries. **capillary** adj. of or like a capillary, *capillary action.*

cap·i·tal (kap-i-tǎl) adj. 1. principal, most important; *capital city,* the chief city of a country or state. 2. (informal) excellent. 3. involving the death penalty, *a capital offense.* 4. very serious, fatal, *a capital error.* 5. (of letters) of the form and size used to begin a name or a sentence, *a capital A.* **capital** n. 1. a capital city. 2. a capital letter. 3. the head or top part of a pillar. 4. wealth or property that is used or invested to produce more wealth, the money with which a business etc. is started. **cap′i·tal·ly** adv. ☐**capital gain** or **capital loss,** profit, loss, from the sale of investments or property. **capital goods,** goods intended for use in producing other goods. **capital punishment,** the death penalty. **capital ship,** a warship of the largest and most powerful type. **capital stock,** the total number of shares issued

by a corporation; the total value of these shares. **capital sum,** a lump sum of money. **make capital of,** to use (a situation etc.) to one's advantage. ▷Do not confuse *capital* with *capitol.*

cap·i·tal·ism (kap-i-tǎ-liz-ěm) n. an economic system in which trade and industry are controlled by private owners.

cap·i·tal·ist (kap-i-tǎ-list) n. 1. one who has much capital invested, a rich person. 2. an adherent of capitalism. **cap·i·tal·is·tic** (kap-i-tǎ-lis-tik) adj.

cap·i·tal·ize (kap-i-tǎ-līz) v. (**cap·i·tal·ized, cap·i·tal·iz·ing**) 1. to write or print as a capital letter. 2. to convert into capital, to provide with capital. **cap·i·tal·i·za·tion** (kap-i-tǎ-li-zay-shŏn) n. ☐**capitalize on,** to profit by, to use (a thing) to one's advantage.

cap·i·ta·tion (kap-i-tay-shŏn) n. 1. the levying of a tax or fee of so much per head. 2. a poll tax.

cap·i·tol (kap-i-tŏl) n. the building in which a state or national legislature meets. ☐**the Capitol,** the building in Washington, D.C., in which the U.S. Congress meets. ▷Do not confuse *capitol* with *capital.*

ca·pit·u·late (kǎ-pich-ŭ-layt) v. (**ca·pit·u·lat·ed, ca·pit·u·lat·ing**) to surrender. **ca·pit·u·la·tion** (kǎ-pich-ŭ-lay-shŏn) n.

ca·pon (kay-pon) n. a domestic male chicken castrated and fattened for eating.

ca·pric·ci·o (kǎ-pree-chi-oh) n. (pl. **-ci·os**) a lively, usually short musical composition.

ca·price (kǎ-prees) n. 1. a whim. 2. a piece of music in a lively fanciful style.

ca·pri·cious (kǎ-prish-ŭs) adj. 1. guided by caprice, impulsive. 2. changeable, *a capricious breeze.* **ca·pri′cious·ly** adv. **ca·pri′cious·ness** n.

Cap·ri·corn (kap-rĭ-korn) n. a sign of the zodiac, the Goat.

cap·ri·ole (kap-ri-ohl) n. 1. a caper, as in dancing. 2. a horse's high leap with all four feet off the ground without advancing. **capriole** v. (**cap·ri·oled, cap·ri·ol·ing**) to perform a capriole.

caps (kaps) n. pl. (informal) capital letters.

cap·si·cum (kap-sĭ-kŭm) n. 1. a tropical plant with hot-tasting seeds. 2. its fruit.

cap·size (kap-sIz) v. (**cap·sized, cap·siz·ing**) to overturn, *a wave capsized the boat; the boat capsized.*

cap·stan (kap-stǎn) n. 1. a thick revolving post used to pull in a rope or cable that winds around it as it turns, as for raising a ship's anchor. 2. a revolving spindle on a tape recorder. ☐**capstan bar,** a pole used as a lever when turning a capstan manually.

cap·stone (kap-stohn) n. 1. the top and last stone to be placed in a structure. 2. the greatest achievement, *her recent book is the capstone to her career.*

cap·su·late (kap-sŭ-lit) adj. enclosed in a capsule.

cap·sule (kap-sŭl) n. 1. a seed case that splits open when ripe. 2. a small soluble case in which a dose of medicine is enclosed for swallowing. 3. a detachable compartment of a spacecraft, containing instruments or crew. **capsule** adj. concise, summarizing.

Capt. abbr. Captain.

cap·tain (kap-tin) n. 1. a person given authority over a group or team. 2. an army officer ranking below a major and above a lieutenant. 3. a naval officer ranking below a commodore or rear admiral and above a commander. 4. the person commanding a ship. **5.** the pilot of a civil aircraft. **captain** v. to act as captain of. **cap′tain·cy** n.

cap·tion (kap-shŏn) n. **1.** a short title or heading. **2.** a description or explanation printed with an illustration etc. **3.** words shown on a television or movie screen. **caption** v. to write a caption for.

cap·tious (kap-shŭs) adj. fond of finding fault or raising objections about trivial matters. **cap′tious·ly** adv. **cap′tious·ness** n.

cap·ti·vate (kap-ti-vayt) v. (**cap·ti·vat·ed, cap·ti·vat·ing**) to capture the fancy of, to charm. **cap′ti·va·tor** n. **cap·ti·va·tion** (kap-ti-vay-shŏn) n.

cap·tive (kap-tiv) adj. **1.** taken prisoner. **2.** kept as a prisoner, unable to escape. **captive** n. a captive person or animal. □**captive audience,** people who cannot get away easily and therefore cannot avoid being addressed.

cap·tiv·i·ty (kap-tiv-i-tee) n. the state of being held captive.

cap·tor (kap-tŏr) n. one who captures a person or animal.

cap·ture (kap-chŭr) v. (**cap·tured, cap·tur·ing**) **1.** to make a prisoner of. **2.** to take or obtain by force, trickery, attraction, or skill; capture a likeness, to see and reproduce it. **capture** n. **1.** capturing. **2.** a thing captured.

Cap·u·chin (kap-yŭ-chin) n. a friar of a branch of the Franciscan order.

car (kahr) n. **1.** an automobile. **2.** a railroad car of a specified type, dining car, Pullman car. **3.** the passenger compartment of a cable railway. □**car bed,** a child's bed used in the rear of a car. **car coat,** a short coat designed for automobile drivers. **car park,** an area for parking cars. **car pool,** a group of commuters organized to take turns at driving the group to work or to share the expense involved in this.

ca·ra·ba·o (kahr-ă-bah-oh) n. (pl. **-ba·os**) (in the Philippines) a water buffalo.

car·a·bi·neer, car·a·bi·nier (kar-ă-bĭ-neer) n. a soldier armed with a carbine.

Ca·ra·cas (kă-rah-kăs) the capital of Venezuela.

car·a·cole (kar-ă-kohl) n. a horseman's half wheel to the right or left, a succession of such turns to the right and left alternately. **caracole** v. (**car·a·coled, car·a·col·ing**) to execute a caracole.

ca·rafe (kă-raf) n. a glass bottle in which wine or water is served at the table.

car·a·mel (kar-ă-měl) n. **1.** burnt sugar used for coloring and flavoring food. **2.** a chewy candy tasting like this.

car·a·mel·ize (kar-ă-mě-lız) v. (**car·a·mel·ized, car·a·mel·iz·ing**) to turn or be turned into caramel. **car·a·mel·i·za·tion** (kar-ă-mě-li-zay-shŏn) n.

car·a·pace (kar-ă-pays) n. the shell on the back of a tortoise or crustacean.

car·at (kar-ăt) n. **1.** a unit of weight for precious stones, 200 milligrams. **2.** karat.

car·a·van (kar-ă-van) n. **1.** a company of people (such as merchants) traveling together across desert country. **2.** a line of vehicles traveling together.

car·a·van·sa·ry (kar-ă-van-să-ree) (pl. **-ries**), **car·a·van·se·rai** (kar-ă-van-sĕ-rı) (pl. **-rais, -ral**) n. an inn in the Near East with a courtyard where caravans rest at night.

car·a·vel, car·a·velle (kar-ă-vel) n. a small light fast sailing ship, chiefly Spanish or Portuguese, of the 15th to 17th centuries.

car·a·way (kar-ă-way) n. a plant with spicy seeds (**caraway seeds**) that are used for flavoring cakes etc.

car·bide (kahr-bıd) n. a compound of carbon, used in making acetylene gas.

car·bine (kahr-been) n. a short light automatic rifle.

car·bo·hy·drate (kahr-bŏ-hı-drayt) n. **1.** an organic compound, such as the sugars and starches, composed of carbon, oxygen, and hydrogen. **2.** carbohydrates, starchy foods, considered to be fattening.

car·bon (kahr-bŏn) n. **1.** a chemical element that is present in all living matter and occurs in its pure form as diamond and graphite. **2.** a rod of carbon in an arc lamp. **3.** carbon paper. **4.** a carbon copy. **car′bon·less** adj. □**carbon black,** a black coallike substance used in making pigment, rubber, etc. **carbon copy,** a copy made with carbon paper; an exact copy. **carbon dating,** a method of determining the age of prehistoric objects by measuring the decay of radio carbon in them. **carbon dioxide,** a colorless odorless gas formed by the burning of carbon breathed out by animals in respiration. **carbon 14,** a naturally radioactive carbon, used in carbon dating. **carbon monoxide,** a very poisonous gas formed when carbon burns incompletely, as in the exhaust of automobile engines. **carbon paper,** a thin paper coated with carbon, placed between sheets of writing paper for making copies of what is written or typed on the top sheet. **carbon tetrachloride,** a colorless liquid used as a solvent in dry cleaning etc. **carbon 12,** a carbon isotope used as the standard by which atomic weights are measured.

car·bo·na·ceous (kahr-bŏ-nay-shŭs) adj. **1.** of or like coal or charcoal. **2.** consisting of or containing carbon.

car·bon·ate (kahr-bŏ-nayt) n. a compound that releases carbon dioxide when mixed with acid. **carbonate** v. (**car·bon·at·ed, car·bon·at·ing**) **1.** to form into a carbonate. **2.** to charge with carbon dioxide gas. □**carbonated drink,** a drink made fizzy with carbon dioxide gas.

car·bon·if·er·ous (kahr-bŏ-nif-ĕ-rŭs) adj. **1.** producing or containing carbon or coal. **2.** Carboniferous, of the geologic period of the Paleozoic era before the Devonian and after the Permian. **carboniferous** n. the carboniferous period.

car·bon·ize (kahr-bŏ-nız) v. (**car·bon·ized, car·bon·iz·ing**) **1.** to convert (a substance that contains carbon) into carbon alone, as by heating or burning it. **2.** to coat with carbon. **car·bon·i·za·tion** (kahr-bŏ-ni-zay-shŏn) n.

Car·bo·run·dum (kahr-bŏ-run-dŭm) n. (trademark) a hard compound of carbon and silicon used for polishing and grinding things.

car·boy (kahr-boi) n. a large round bottle surrounded by a protecting framework, used for transporting liquids safely.

car·bun·cle (kahr-bung-kĕl) n. **1.** a severe abscess in the skin. **2.** a bright red gem cut in a knoblike shape.

car·bu·re·tor (kahr-bŭ-ray-tŏr) n. an apparatus for mixing fuel and air in an internal combustion engine.

car·bu·rize (kahr-bŭ-rız) v. (**car·bu·rized, car·bu·riz·ing**) to combine or inject (a metal) with carbon. **car·bu·ri·za′tion** n.

car·cass (kahr-kăs) n. **1.** the dead body of an animal, especially one prepared for cutting up as meat. 2. the bony part of the body of a bird before or after cooking.

car·cin·o·gen (kahr-sin-ŏ-jĕn) *n.* a cancer-producing substance. **car·ci·no·gen·ic** (kahr-si-nŏ-jen-ik) *adj.* **car·ci·no·ge·nic·i·ty** (kahr-si-noh-jĕ-nis-i-tee) *n.*

car·ci·no·ma (kahr-si-noh-mă) *n.* (*pl.* **-mas, -ma·ta,** *pr.* -mă-tă) a cancerous growth. **car·ci·no′ma·tous** *adj.*

card[1] (kahrd) *n.* 1. a small piece of stiff paper or thin cardboard, often printed, used to send messages, greetings, etc., or to record information such as a person's name or the title of a book and for use as an identification or in a card index. 2. a program of horse races. 3. a playing card. 4. an odd or amusing person. 5. *cards,* card playing, a card game. **card** *v.* 1. to write or list on cards. 2. to score in golf, *he carded a 78.* ☐**be in the cards,** to be likely or possible. **card catalog,** a library file with information of books entered on cards. **card file,** a file in which each item is entered on a separate card. **card game,** a game using playing cards. **play one's cards right,** to use good judgment in managing one's affairs. **put one's cards on the table,** to be frank about one's resources and intentions.

card[2] *n.* a wire brush or toothed instrument for cleaning or combing wool. **card** *v.* to clean or comb with this.

Card. *abbr.* Cardinal.

car·da·mom (kahr-dă-mŏm) *n.* a spice consisting of the seed capsules of various plants, used as a medicine, in curries, etc.

card·board (kahrd-bohrd) *n.* pasteboard, especially for making into boxes.

card-car·ry·ing (kahrd-kar-i-ing) *adj.* being a registered member of a political party etc.

car·di·ac (kahr-di-ak) *adj.* 1. of the heart. 2. of heart disease. ☐**cardiac failure,** a heart attack.

Car·diff (kahr-dif) the capital of Wales.

car·di·gan (kahr-dĭ-găn) *n.* a sweater or knitted jacket opening down the front.

car·di·nal (kahr-dĭ-năl) *adj.* 1. chief, most important, *the cardinal virtues.* 2. deep scarlet. **cardinal** *n.* 1. a member of the Sacred College of the Roman Catholic Church, which elects the pope. 2. an American songbird, the male of which is bright red. **car′di·nal·ly** *adv.* ☐**cardinal flower,** a North American plant bearing a spike of red flowers. **cardinal numbers,** the whole numbers, 1, 2, 3, etc. **cardinal points,** the four main points of the compass, north, east, south, and west.

car·di·nal·ate (kahr-dĭ-nă-layt) *n.* 1. the College of Cardinals. 2. the rank, position, term, etc. of a Roman Catholic cardinal.

car·di·o·gram (kahr-di-ŏ-gram) *n.* an electrocardiogram.

car·di·o·graph (kahr-di-ŏ-graf) *n.* an electrocardiograph. **car·di·o·graph·ic** (kahr-di-ŏ-grafik) *adj.* **car·di·og·ra·phy** (kahr-di-og-ră-fee) *n.*

car·di·ol·o·gist (kahr-di-ol-ŏ-jist) *n.* a specialist in cardiology.

car·di·ol·o·gy (kahr-di-ol-ŏ-jee) *n.* the branch of medicine dealing with the heart, its movement, function, and diseases.

car·di·o·pul·mo·nary (kahr-di-oh-pul-mŏ-ner-ee) *adj.* of or involving the lungs and heart.

car·di·o·vas·cu·lar (kahr-di-oh-vas-kyū-lăr) *adj.* of or involving the blood vessels and heart.

card·shark (kahrd-shahrk) *n.* (*informal*) a card-sharp.

card·sharp (kahrd-shahrp), **card·sharp·er**

(kahrd-shahr-pĕr) *n.* a person who makes a living by cheating others at cards.

care (kair) *n.* 1. serious attention and thought, *planned with care.* 2. caution to avoid damage or loss, *handle with care.* 3. protection, charge, supervision, *left the child in her sister's care.* 4. worry, anxiety, *freedom from care.* **care** *v.* (**cared, car·ing**) 1. to feel concern or interest. 2. to feel affection or liking. 3. to feel willing, *would you care to try one?* **car′ing·ly** *adv.* ☐**care for,** to have in one's care. **care of, c/o,** to the address of (someone who will deliver or forward things), *write to him care of his bank.* **take care,** to be cautious. **take care of,** to take charge of; to see to the safety or well-being of; to deal with.

CARE (kair) *n.* an organization for helping the needy abroad. ▷ Cooperative for American Relief Abroad.

ca·reen (kă-reen) *v.* 1. to tilt or keel (a boat etc.) over to one side. 2. to swerve.

ca·reer (kă-reer) *n.* 1. an occupation, a way of making a living, especially one with opportunities for advancement or promotion. 2. progress through life, the development and progress of a political party etc. 3. quick or violent forward movement; *stopped him in mid career,* as he was rushing. **career** *v.* to move swiftly or wildly. ☐**career diplomat,** one who follows diplomacy as a career. **career woman,** a woman who works permanently in a paid occupation.

care·free (kair-free) *adj.* lighthearted through being free from anxiety or responsibility. ▷ Do not confuse *carefree* and *careless.*

care·ful (kair-fŭl) *adj.* 1. giving serious attention and thought, painstaking, *a careful worker.* 2. done with care, *careful work.* 3. cautious, avoiding damage or loss. **care′ful·ly** *adv.* **care′ful·ness** *n.*

care·less (kair-lis) *adj.* not careful. **care′less·ly** *adv.* **care′less·ness** *n.* ▷ Do not confuse *careless* with *carefree.*

ca·ress (kă-res) *n.* a loving touch, a kiss. **caress** *v.* to touch lovingly, to kiss.

car·et (kar-it) *n.* an omission mark: ∧.

care·tak·er (kair-tay-kĕr) *n.* a person employed to look after a house or building. ☐**caretaker government,** one holding office temporarily until another can be elected.

care·worn (kair-wohrn) *adj.* showing signs of prolonged worry.

car·fare (kahr-fair) *n.* bus or streetcar fare.

car·go (kahr-goh) *n.* (*pl.* **-goes, -gos**) goods carried on a ship, aircraft, or other vehicle.

car·hop (kahr-hop) *n.* (*informal*) a person employed to serve patrons in their cars at a drive-in restaurant etc.

Car·ib·be·an (kar-ĭ-bee-ăn) *adj.* of the Caribbean Sea, a part of the Atlantic off Central America. **Caribbean** *n.* the Caribbean Sea.

car·i·bou (kar-ĭ-boo) *n.* (*pl.* **-bou, -bous**) a North American reindeer.

car·i·ca·ture (kar-ĭ-kă-chŭr) *n.* a picture or description or imitation of a person or thing that exaggerates certain characteristics, especially for comic effect. **caricature** *v.* (**car·i·ca·tured, car·i·ca·tur·ing**) to make a caricature of. **car′i·ca·tur·ist** *n.*

car·ies (kair-eez) *n.* (*pl.* **car·ies**) decay in bones or teeth, *dental caries.*

car·il·lon (kar-ĭ-lon) *n.* a set of bells sounded either from a keyboard or mechanically. **car·il·lon·neur** (kar-ĭ-lŏ-nur) *n.*

car·i·ous (kair-i-ŭs) *adj.* (especially of bones or teeth) decayed.

car·load (kahr-lohd) *n.* 1. a load that fills a car, especially a freight car. 2. a large quantity of anything.

Car·mel·ite (kahr-mĕ-lıt) *n.* a member of an order of friars or of a corresponding order of nuns. **Carmelite** *adj.*

car·min·a·tive (kahr-min-ă-tiv) *adj.* curing flatulence. **carminative** *n.* a carminative drug.

car·mine (kahr-mĭn) *adj.* & *n.* deep red.

car·nage (kahr-nij) *n.* the killing of many people.

car·nal (kahr-năl) *adj.* of the body or flesh, not spiritual, *carnal desires.* **car′nal·ly** *adv.* **car·nal·i·ty** (kahr-nal-i-tee) *n.*

car·na·tion (kahr-nay-shŏn) *n.* a cultivated double-flowered clove-scented pink.

car·nau·ba (kahr-naw-bă) *n.* 1. a Brazilian wax palm. 2. its yellowish wax.

car·nel·ian (kahr-neel-yăn) *n.* a reddish or white semiprecious stone.

car·ney = **carny.**

car·ni·val (kahr-nĭ-văl) *n.* 1. a traveling amusement show having sideshows, game booths, and rides. 2. festivities and public merrymaking during the last three days or last week before Lent.

Car·niv·o·ra (kahr-niv-ŏ-ră) *n.* an order of mammals, mostly carnivorous, including cats, dogs, and many other animals.

car·ni·vore (kahr-nĭ-vohr) *n.* a carnivorous animal.

car·niv·o·rous (kahr-niv-ŏ-rŭs) *adj.* feeding on flesh or other animal matter. **car·niv′o·rous·ly** *adv.* **car·niv′o·rous·ness** *n.*

car·ny (kahr-nee) *n.* (*pl.* **-nies**) (*slang*) 1. a carnival. 2. a person working for a carnival.

car·ol (kar-ŏl) *n.* a joyful song, especially a Christmas hymn. **carol** *v.* (**car·oled, car·ol·ing**) 1. to sing carols. 2. to sing joyfully. **car′ol·er** *n.*

Car·o·li·na (kar-ŏ-lı-nă) either of two states of the U.S., *North* and *South Carolina.*

car·om (kar-ŏm) *n.* 1. (in billiards) the hitting of two balls successively by a player's ball. 2. a rebound, as of a rubber ball off a wall. **carom** *v.* 1. to make a carom. 2. to strike and rebound off.

car·o·tene (kar-ŏ-teen) *n.* an orange or red substance that occurs in carrots, tomatoes, and many other vegetables, and is a source of vitamin A.

ca·rot·id (kă-rot-id) *n.* either of the **carotid arteries**, the two great arteries (one on either side of the neck) carrying blood to the head. **carotid** *adj.* of these arteries.

ca·rouse (kă-rowz) *v.* (**ca·roused, ca·rous·ing**) to drink and be merry. **ca·rous′er** *n.* **ca·rous′al** *n.*

car·ou·sel, car·rou·sel (kar-ŏ-sel) *n.* 1. a merry-go-round. 2. a conveyor or delivery system that rotates like a merry-go-round.

carp[1] (kahrp) *n.* (*pl.* **carp, carps**) an edible freshwater fish that lives in lakes and ponds.

carp[2] *v.* to keep finding fault, to raise petty objections.

car·pal (kahr-păl) *adj.* of the wrist joint. **carpal** *n.* any of the wrist bones.

car·pe di·em (kahr-pee dı-ĕm) enjoy today without thought of tomorrow. ▷Latin.

car·pel (kahr-pĕl) *n.* the pistil of a flower, the part in which the seeds develop.

car·pen·ter (kahr-pĕn-tĕr) *n.* a person who makes or repairs wooden objects and structures. **car-**

penter *v.* to work as a carpenter. **car′pen·try** *n.* ☐**carpenter ant**, one that nests and bores in decaying trees and dead wood.

car·pet (kahr-pit) *n.* 1. a thick textile covering for floors. 2. a thick layer underfoot, *a carpet of leaves.* **carpet** *v.* (**car·pet·ed, car·pet·ing**) to cover with a carpet. ☐**carpet slippers**, slippers with cloth uppers. **carpet sweeper**, a household device with revolving brushes for sweeping carpets. **on the carpet**, (*informal*) being reprimanded.

car·pet·bag (kahr-pit-bag) *n.* a traveling bag made of carpet fabric.

car·pet·bag·ger (kahr-pit-bag-ĕr) *n.* 1. a Northerner who went into the South after the Civil War to profit from Reconstruction. 2. a person who meddles in the politics of a locality with which he has no genuine connection.

car·pet·ing (kahr-pi-ting) *n.* material for carpets.

car·port (kahr-pohrt) *n.* an open-sided shelter for a car, projecting from the side of a house.

car·pus (kahr-pŭs) *n.* (*pl.* **-pi**, *pr.* **-pı**) 1. the set of bones (eight in humans) connecting the forearm to the hand. 2. the wrist.

car·ra·geen, car·ra·gheen (kar-ă-geen) *n.* an edible purple seaweed.

car·rel (kar-ĕl) *n.* a cubicle for a reader in a library.

car·riage (kar-ij) *n.* 1. a wheeled vehicle, usually horse drawn, for carrying passengers. 2. (*British*) a railroad car for passengers. 3. the carrying of goods from place to place, the cost of this. 4. a gun carriage. 5. a moving part carrying or holding something in a machine. 6. the posture of the body when walking. 7. a baby carriage. ☐**carriage trade**, an affluent clientele; trade with this.

car·ri·er (kar-i-ĕr) *n.* 1. a person or thing that carries something. 2. a person or company (*common carrier*) that transports goods or people for payment. 3. a support for luggage or a seat for a passenger on a bicycle etc. 4. a person or animal that transmits a disease to others without being affected by it himself. 5. an aircraft carrier. 6. (also **carrier wave**) a transmitted wave that carries a television or radio signal. ☐**carrier pigeon**, a homing pigeon used to carry messages tied to its leg or neck.

car·ri·on (kar-i-ŏn) *n.* dead and decaying flesh.

car·rot (kar-ŏt) *n.* 1. a plant with a tapering orange-colored root. 2. this root, used as a vegetable. 3. a means of enticing someone to do something; *the carrot and the stick*, bribes and threats. **car′rot·y** *adj.*

car·rot-top (kar-ŏt-top) *n.* (*informal*) a red-headed person.

car·rou·sel = **carousel.**

car·ry (kar-ee) *v.* (**car·ried, car·ry·ing**) 1. to take from one place to another. 2. to have on one's person, *he is carrying a gun.* 3. to conduct, to take, *wires carry electric current.* 4. to support the weight of, to bear; *she carries that department*, but for her ability it would collapse. 5. to involve, to entail, *the crime carries a life sentence.* 6. to extend; *don't carry modesty too far*, do not be too modest. 7. to win, to capture; *the motion was carried*, was approved. 8. (of a newspaper or broadcast) to contain, *the networks carried the story.* 9. to hold and move (the body) in a certain way, *she carries herself with dignity.* 10. to be transmitted clearly, *sound carries across water.*

carry *n.* (*pl.* **-ries**) 1. the distance traveled by a golf ball in flight. 2. a portage between rivers etc. 3. range (of a gun, sound, etc.). ☐**be carried away,** to be very excited. **carry all before one,** to be very successful. **carry conviction,** to sound convincing. **carry forward,** to transfer to a new page of accounts in bookkeeping. **carrying charge,** the interest on an unpaid balance of a charge or installment account. **carry off,** to cause the death of; to win (a prize); to deal with (a situation) successfully. **carry on,** to continue; to take part in (a conversation); to manage or conduct (a business etc.); *(informal)* to behave excitedly, to complain lengthily. **carry on with,** *(informal)* to have an affair with, to flirt with. **carry out,** to put into practice, to accomplish. **carry over,** to carry forward in bookkeeping. **carry weight,** to be influential or important.

car·ry·all (kar-ee-awl) *n.* a roomy bag or basketlike container.

car·ry·on (kar-ee-on) *n.* *(informal)* a bag or suitcase small enough to be kept within an airplane cabin during flight. **carry-on** *adj.*

car·ry·out (kar-ee-owt) *adj.* *(informal)* (of food) to be taken along by the customer for eating elsewhere.

car·sick (kahr-sik) *adj.* made sick or queasy by the motion of a car. **car′sick·ness** *n.*

Car·son (kahr-sŏn) *City* the capital of Nevada.

cart (kahrt) *n.* 1. a two-wheeled vehicle used for carrying loads, pulled by a horse etc. 2. a light vehicle with a shaft, pushed or drawn by hand. **cart** *v.* 1. to carry in a cart. 2. *(informal)* to carry laboriously, to lug; *carted his family off to Italy,* made them go with him. **cart′er** *n.* ☐**put the cart before the horse,** to put a thing first when it should logically come second.

cart·age (kahr-tij) *n.* 1. carting goods. 2. the cost of this.

carte blanche (kahrt blahnch) full power to act as one thinks best. ▷French.

car·tel (kahr-tel) *n.* a combination of business firms to control production, marketing, etc. and avoid competing with one another.

Car·ter (kahr-tĕr), **James Earl, Jr.** (1924–　) the thirty-ninth president of the U.S. 1977–

Car·te·sian (kahr-tee-zhǎn) *adj.* of the French scholar Descartes or his philosophy or mathematical methods.

Car·thu·sian (kahr-thoo-zhǎn) *n.* a member of an order of monks founded at La Grande Chartreuse near Grenoble, France.

car·ti·lage (kahr-tĭ-lij) *n.* 1. tough white flexible tissue attached to the bones of animals. 2. a structure made of this. **car·ti·lag·i·nous** (kahr-tĭ-laj-ĭ-nŭs) *adj.*

car·tog·ra·phy (kahr-tog-rǎ-fee) *n.* map drawing. **car·tog′ra·pher** *n.* **car·to·gra·phic** (kahr-tŏ-graf-ik) *adj.*

car·ton (kahr-tŏn) *n.* 1. a cardboard box or container. 2. the amount it contains.

car·toon (kahr-toon) *n.* 1. an amusing drawing in a newspaper etc., especially as a comment on public matters. 2. a sequence of these telling a comic or serial story. 3. an animated cartoon. **cartoon** *v.* to draw cartoons, to represent in a cartoon. **car·toon·ist** (kahr-too-nist) *n.* a person who draws cartoons.

car·tridge (kahr-trij) *n.* 1. a tube or case containing explosive for firearms or blasting, with bullet or shot if for a rifle etc. 2. a sealed case holding film, recording tape, etc. put into an apparatus and removed from it as a unit. 3. the detachable head of a pickup on a record player, holding the stylus.

cart·wheel (kahrt-hweel) *n.* a handspring in which the body turns with limbs spread like spokes of a wheel, balancing on each hand in turn.

carve (kahrv) *v.* **(carved, carv·ing)** 1. to form or produce or inscribe by cutting solid material. 2. to cut (cooked meat) into slices for eating. 3. to make by great effort, *carved out a career for himself.* **carv′er** *n.* ☐**carve up,** to divide into parts or shares.

carv·ing (kahr-ving) *n.* a carved object or design.

car·wash (kahr-wosh) *n.* an establishment where automobiles are washed.

car·y·at·id (kar-ee-at-id) *n.* a sculptured female figure used as a supporting pillar in a building.

ca·sa·ba (kǎ-sah-bǎ) *n.* a winter muskmelon with a yellow rind and sweet flesh.

Cas·a·no·va (kaz-ǎ-noh-vǎ) *n.* a man with a reputation for having many love affairs. ▷Named after an Italian adventurer (18th century).

cas·cade (kas-kayd) *n.* 1. a waterfall. 2. something falling or hanging like this. **cascade** *v.* **(cas·cad·ed, cas·cad·ing)** to fall as or like a cascade.

cas·car·a (kas-kar-ǎ) *n.* 1. the bark of a North American buckthorn, used as a purgative. 2. the tree itself.

case[1] (kays) *n.* 1. an instance or example of the occurrence of something, an actual state of affairs. 2. a condition of disease or injury, a person suffering from this, *two cases of measles.* 3. something being investigated by police etc., *a murder case.* 4. a lawsuit. 5. a set of facts or arguments supporting something, *she made a case for keeping her secretary.* 6. the form of a noun or pronoun that shows its relation to another word, as in *Mary's hat, 's* shows the possessive case. ☐**case history,** a record of the pertinent history of a patient etc. **case law,** law based on judicial decision in an earlier case or cases rather than on statute. **case study,** a study of a person or a condition based on collected information. **in any case,** whatever the facts are; whatever may happen. **in case,** lest something should happen; *in case of fire,* if there should be a fire.

case[2] *n.* 1. a container or protective covering. 2. this with its contents, the amount it contains. 3. a suitcase. **case** *v.* **(cased, cas·ing)** 1. to enclose in a case. 2. *(slang)* to examine, to look at closely; *case the joint,* examine (a house etc.) in planning a crime. **case shot,** a projectile consisting of small pellets in a metal container.

case·book (kays-buuk) *n.* 1. a record of legal or medical cases. 2. a collection of scholarly articles on a single subject.

case·bound (kays-bownd) *adj.* (of a book) in hard cover.

case·hard·en (kays-hahr-děn) *v.* 1. to harden the surface of (a metal). 2. to render callous.

ca·sein (kay-seen) *n.* a protein found in milk, the basis of cheese.

case·load (kays-lohd) *n.* the number of cases with which a doctor etc. is concerned in a period of time.

case·ment (kays-měnt) *n.* a window that opens on hinges like a door.

case·work (kays-wurk) *n.* social work that involves dealing with people who have problems. **case′work·er** *n.*

case·worm (kays-wurm) *n.* an insect larva, such

as a caddisworm, enclosed within a case it builds for protection.

cash (kash) *n.* 1. money in coin or notes. 2. immediate payment for goods, as opposed to installment payments etc. 3. *(informal)* money, wealth, *they're short of cash.* **cash** *v.* to give or get cash for, *cashed a check.* □**cash and carry,** a method of shopping in which goods are paid for in cash and taken away by the buyer himself. **cash crop,** a crop grown for selling. **cash discount,** a discount given in return for payment in cash. **cash flow,** the flow of cash into a business as goods etc. are sold. **cash in on,** to make a large profit from; to turn to one's advantage. **cash in one's chips,** *(slang)* to die. **cash on delivery,** payment to be made when goods are delivered, not at the time of purchase. **cash register,** a device used in stores, with a mechanism for recording and storing the money received for each purchase.

cash·a·ble (kash-ă-běl) *adj.* able to be cashed.

cash·ew (kash-oo) *n.* 1. the small edible nut of a tropical tree. 2. this tree.

cash·ier[1] (ka-sheer) *n.* a person employed to receive and pay out money in a bank or to receive payments in a shop etc. □**cashier's check,** a check issued by a bank, drawn on the bank's own funds and signed by a cashier.

cashier[2] *v.* to dismiss from service, especially with disgrace.

cash·mere (kazh-meer) *n.* 1. a very fine soft wool, especially that from the Kashmir goat. 2. fabric made from this.

cas·ing (kay-sing) *n.* 1. a protective covering or wrapping. 2. the material from which this is made.

ca·si·no (kă-see-noh) *n.* (*pl.* **-nos**) a public building or room for gambling and other amusements.

cask (kask) *n.* 1. a barrel, especially for alcoholic drinks. 2. its contents.

cas·ket (kas-kit) *n.* a coffin.

casque (kask) *n.* a medieval helmet with a nose guard.

Cas·san·dra (kă-san-dră) *n.* a person who prophesies disaster. ▷ Named after a prophetess in Greek legend who foretold evil events but was doomed never to be believed.

cas·sa·va (kă-sah-vă) *n.* a tropical plant with starchy roots from which tapioca is obtained.

cas·se·role (kas-ě-rohl) *n.* 1. a covered dish in which meat etc. is cooked and served. 2. food cooked in such a dish.

cas·sette (kă-set) *n.* a small sealed case containing a reel of film or magnetic tape. □**cassette player,** a machine for playing a cassette tape.

cas·sia (kash-ă) *n.* 1. a coarse kind of cinnamon bark, the tree it comes from. 2. a plant found in warm climates, a medicinal preparation from its leaves.

cas·sit·er·ite (kă-sit-ě-rıt) *n.* a mineral, tin dioxide, that is the source of tin.

cas·sock (kas-ŏk) *n.* a long garment worn by certain clergymen and members of church choirs.

cas·so·war·y (kas-ŏ-wer-ee) *n.* a large bird like an ostrich but smaller.

cast (kast) *v.* (**cast, cast·ing**) 1. to throw, *cast a net; cast a shadow,* cause there to be one. 2. to shed. 3. to turn or send in a particular direction; *cast your eye over this,* examine it. 4. to give (one's vote). 5. to make (an object) by pouring metal etc. into a mold and letting it harden. 6. to calcu-

late, *cast a horoscope.* 7. to select actors for a play etc., to assign a role to. **cast** *n.* 1. an act of casting. 2. something made by putting soft material into a mold to harden, a plaster cast (*see* **plaster**). 3. a set of actors cast for parts in a play. 4. a slight squint. □**cast about for,** to search or look for. **cast iron,** a hard alloy of iron made by casting in a mold. **cast off,** to release a ship from its moorings; to loop stitches off a needle in knitting.

cas·ta·nets (kas-tă-nets) *n. pl.* a pair of shell-shaped pieces of wood or ivory etc., struck together with the fingers especially as an accompaniment to a Spanish dance.

cast·a·way (kas-tă-way) *n.* a shipwrecked person.

caste (kast) *n.* 1. one of the hereditary Hindu social classes. 2. any exclusive social class. □**lose caste,** to lose rank or social status.

cas·tel·lat·ed (kas-tě-lay-tid) *adj.* having turrets or battlements like a castle.

cast·er (kas-těr) *n.* 1. a small container for sugar or salt, with a perforated top for sprinkling from. 2. one of the small swiveled wheels fixed to the legs of furniture so that it can be moved easily. 3. a person who casts.

cas·ti·gate (kas-tĭ-gayt) *v.* (**cas·ti·gat·ed, cas·ti·gat·ing**) to punish by blows or by criticizing severely. **cas'ti·ga·tor** *n.* **cas·ti·ga·tion** (kas-tĭ-gay-shŏn) *n.*

cast·ing (kas-ting) *n.* 1. a piece of metal or other material shaped by melting and pouring into a mold. 2. something that is thrown off. 3. the act or process of throwing something, especially a fishing line. 4. the choice of actors and actresses for roles in a play etc.

cast·i·ron (kast-ı-ŏrn) *adj.* 1. made of cast iron. 2. very strong.

cas·tle (kas-ěl) *n.* 1. a large fortified building or group of buildings. 2. a chess piece also called a rook. **castle** *v.* (**cas·tled, cas·tling**) in chess, to move the rook to next to the king and the king to the other side of the rook. □**castles in the air,** daydreams.

cast-offs (kast-awfs) *n. pl.* clothes that the owner will not wear again.

cas·tor = **caster.**

cas·tor (kas-tŏr) **oil** oil from the seeds of a tropical plant (**castor-oil plant**), used as a laxative and as a lubricant. □**castor bean,** the seed of the castor-oil plant.

cas·trate (kas-trayt) *v.* (**cas·trat·ed, cas·trat·ing**) to remove the testicles of, to geld. **cas·tra'tion** *n.*

ca·su·al (kazh-oo-ăl) *adj.* 1. happening by chance, *a casual encounter.* 2. made or done without forethought, not serious, *a casual remark.* 3. not methodical, *a casual inspection.* 4. informal, for informal occasions, *casual clothes.* 5. irregular, not permanent, *found some casual work; casual laborers,* doing such work. **ca'su·al·ly** *adv.* **ca'su·al·ness** *n.*

ca·su·ist·ry (kazh-oo-is-tree) *n.* (*pl.* **-ries**) 1. reasoning, especially by a theologian, to settle questions of conscience and conduct. 2. dishonest or insincere reasoning in these matters. **ca'su·ist** *n.* **ca·su·is·tic** (kazh-oo-is-tik) *adj.* **ca·su·is'ti·cal** *adj.*

ca·sus bel·li (kay-sŭs bel-ı) (*pl.* **ca·sus bel·li**) an act justifying or regarded as reason for war. ▷ Latin.

cat (kat) *n.* 1. a small furry domesticated animal

often kept as a pet. 2. a wild animal related to this; *the great cats,* lion, tiger, leopard, etc. 3. *(informal)* a spiteful or malicious woman. 4. the cat-o'-nine-tails. □**cat and mouse,** a children's game; the practice of taking slight action repeatedly against a weaker party. **cat burglar,** a burglar who enters by climbing a wall or drainpipe etc. **cat's cradle,** a game with string forming looped patterns between the fingers. **let the cat out of the bag,** to give away a secret.
CAT *abbr.* clear-air turbulence.
cat. *abbr.* catalog.
ca·tab·o·lism (kă-tab-ŏ-liz-ĕm) *n.* the phase of metabolism in which complex compounds break into simpler ones. **cat·a·bol·ic** (kat-ă-bol-ik) *adj.* **cat·a·bol'i·cal·ly** *adv.*
cat·a·clysm (kat-ă-kliz-ĕm) *n.* a violent upheaval or disaster. **cat·a·clys·mic** (kat-ă-kliz-mik) *adj.*
cat·a·comb (kat-ă-kohm) *n.* an underground gallery with side recesses for tombs. □**the Catacombs,** those made by Jews and early Christians in and near Rome.
cat·a·falque (kat-ă-falk) *n.* a decorated platform on which the coffin of a distinguished person stands during the funeral or while the remains are lying in state, or on which the coffin is drawn in procession.
cat·a·lep·sy (kat-ă-lep-see) *n.* a seizure in which a person becomes rigid and unconscious. **cat·a·lep·tic** (kat-ă-lep-tik) *adj.*
cat·a·log, cat·a·logue (kat-ă-log) *n.* a list of items, usually in systematic order and with a description of each. **catalog(ue)** *v.* (**cat·a·loged, cat·a·log·ing; cat·a·logued, cat·a·logu·ing**) to list in a catalog. **cat'a·log·er, cat'a·logu·er** *n.*
ca·tal·pa (kă-tal-pă) *n.* a tree with large simple leaves, native to North America, tropical America, Japan, and China.
cat·a·lyst (kat-ă-list) *n.* 1. a substance that aids or speeds up a chemical reaction while remaining unchanged itself. 2. a person or thing that precipitates a change. **ca·tal·y·sis** (kă-tal-ĭ-sis) *n.* (*pl.* **-ses,** *pr.* -seez).
cat·a·lyt·ic (kat-ă-lĭt-ik) *adj.* causing catalysis. **cat·a·lyt'i·cal·ly** *adv.*
cat·a·ma·ran (kat-ă-mă-ran) *n.* a boat with twin hulls.
cat·a·mount (kat-ă-mownt) *n. see* **mountain lion.**
cat·a·pult (kat-ă-pult) *n.* 1. a device with elastic for shooting small stones etc. 2. a device for launching a glider or an aircraft from the deck of a carrier. **catapult** *v.* 1. to hurl from a catapult, to fling forcibly. 2. to rush violently.
cat·a·ract (kat-ă-rakt) *n.* 1. a large waterfall. 2. a condition in which the lens of the eye becomes cloudy and obscures sight. 3. this opaque area.
ca·tarrh (kă-tahr) *n.* inflammation of a mucous membrane, especially of the nose and throat, accompanied by a watery discharge. **ca·tarrh'al** *adj.*
ca·tas·tro·phe (kă-tas-trŏ-fee) *n.* a sudden great disaster. **cat·a·stroph·ic** (kat-ă-strof-ik) *adj.* **cat·a·stroph'i·cal·ly** *adv.*
cat·a·ton·ic (kat-ă-ton-ik) *adj.* schizophrenic and with attacks of catalepsy.
Ca·taw·ba (kă-taw-bă) *n.* 1. a grape cultivated in the eastern U.S. 2. a white wine made from this grape.
cat·bird (kat-burd) *n.* a North American songbird whose call sounds like the mewing of a cat. □**in**

the catbird seat, *(informal)* in advantageous position.
cat·boat (kat-boht) *n.* a broad-beamed sailboat with the mast well forward and rigged with one sail.
cat·call (kat-kawl) *n.* a shrill whistle of disapproval. **catcall** *v.*
catch (kach) *v.* (**caught, catch·ing**) 1. to capture in a net or snare or after a chase. 2. to overtake, *I caught him at the finish line.* 3. to grasp something moving and hold it, *the tight end caught the pass.* 4. to come unexpectedly upon, to take by surprise, to detect. 5. to be in time for and get on (a train etc.). 6. *(informal)* to hear (a broadcast), to watch (a film). 7. to get briefly, *caught a glimpse of it; you have caught the likeness well,* seen and reproduced it in painting etc.; *try to catch his eye,* make him notice you. 8. to become or cause to become fixed or prevented from moving. 9. to hit, *the blow caught him on the nose.* 10. to begin to burn, *the sticks caught* or *caught fire.* 11. to become infected with, *caught a cold.* **catch** *n.* 1. the act of catching. 2. something caught or worth catching; *he's a good catch,* worth getting as a husband. 3. a concealed difficulty or disadvantage, *there must be a catch in it; a catch question,* one involving a catch. 4. a device for fastening something. □**catch basin,** a well at a sewer opening, intended to prevent undesired materials from entering the sewer. **catch hold of,** to seize in the hand(s); *he caught hold of himself just in time,* stopped himself from blundering. **catch it,** *(informal)* to be scolded or punished. **catch on,** *(informal)* to become popular; to understand what is meant. **catch phrase,** a phrase in frequent current use, a catchword. **catch up,** to come abreast with; to do work that is in arrears. **play catch-up,** to use tactics that may enable one to catch up with a competitor.
catch·all (kach-awl) *n.* a receptacle for a variety of objects.
catch-as-catch-can (kach-ăz-kach-kan) *n.* wrestling in which few or no holds are barred.
catch·er (kach-ĕr) *n.* 1. one who catches. 2. a baseball player who is stationed at home plate.
catch·ing (kach-ing) *adj.* infectious.
catch·ment (kach-mĕnt) *n.* that which is caught. □**catchment area,** an area from which rainfall drains into a river or reservoir.
catch·pen·ny (kach-pen-ee) *adj.* intended to sell quickly for little money.
catch-22 *n.* *(slang)* a dilemma from which the victim has no escape. ▷From the title of a novel, *Catch-22,* by Joseph Heller, 1961.
catch·word (kach-wurd) *n.* a memorable word or phrase that is often used, a slogan.
catch·y (kach-ee) *adj.* (**catch·i·er, catch·i·est**) 1. pleasant and easy to remember, *a catchy tune.* 2. tricky, involving a catch.
cat·e·chism (kat-ĕ-kiz-ĕm) *n.* 1. *the Catechism,* a summary of the principles of a religion in the form of questions and answers. 2. a series of questions and answers.
cat·e·chist (kat-ĕ-kist) *n.* a person who puts questions to another.
cat·e·chize (kat-ĕ-kız) *v.* (**cat·e·chized, cat·e·chiz·ing**) to put a series of questions to (a person).
cat·e·chu·men (kat-ĕ-kyoo-mĕn) *n.* a Christian convert under instruction before baptism.
cat·e·gor·i·cal (kat-ĕ-gor-i-kăl) *adj.* absolute, un-

conditional, *a categorical refusal.* **cat·e·gor′i·cal·ly** *adv.* □**categorical imperative,** an absolute and universally binding moral law.

cat·e·go·rize (kat-ĕ-gŏ-rīz) *v.* **(cat·e·go·rized, cat·e·go·riz·ing)** to place in a particular category. **cat·e·go·ri·za·tion** (kat-ĕ-gŏ-ri-zay-shŏn) *n.*

cat·e·go·ry (kat-ĕ-gohr-ee) *n.* (*pl.* **-ries**) a class of things.

cat·e·nar·y (kat-ĕ-ner-ee) *n.* (*pl.* **-nar·ies**) a curve formed by a uniform chain hanging freely from two points not in the same vertical line. **catenary** *adj.*

ca·ter (kay-tĕr) *v.* to provide what is needed or wanted, especially food or entertainment, *cater for 50 people; cater to people's interest in scandal,* pander to it.

cat·er·cor·ner (kat-ĕr-kor-nĕr) = **catty-cornered.**

ca·ter·er (kay-tĕr-ĕr) *n.* one whose trade is to supply meals etc.

cat·er·pil·lar (kat-ĕr-pil-ăr) *n.* the larva of a butterfly or moth. □**caterpillar tread,** a steel band passing around two wheels of a tractor or tank, enabling it to travel over very rough ground.

cat·er·waul (kat-er-wawl) *v.* to make a cat's howling cry. **caterwaul** *n.* such a cry.

cat·fish (kat-fish) *n.* (*pl.* **-fish, -fish·es**) a large usually freshwater fish with whiskerlike feelers around the mouth.

cat·gut (kat-gut) *n.* a fine strong cord made from the dried intestines of animals, used for the strings of musical instruments and for sewing up surgical incisions.

Cath. *abbr.* 1. (often **cath.**) cathedral. 2. Catholic.

ca·thar·sis (kă-thahr-sis) *n.* (*pl.* **-ses,** *pr.* -seez) 1. the act of ridding or cleansing. 2. the relief of the emotions gained through viewing the experiences of others, especially in a drama. 3. the relieving of a neurotic state by reenacting an earlier emotional experience.

ca·thar·tic (kă-thahr-tik) *adj.* producing catharsis. **cathartic** *n.* a laxative.

ca·the·dral (kă-thee-drăl) *n.* the principal church of a bishop's see. □**cathedral ceiling,** a high ceiling constructed of or imitating exposed beams.

Cath·er·ine (kath-ĕ-rin) **wheel** a rotating firework. ▷Named after St. Catherine, who was martyred on a spiked wheel.

cath·e·ter (kath-ĕ-tĕr) *n.* a tube that can be inserted into a body passage or cavity.

cath·e·ter·ize (kath-ĕ-tĕ-rīz) *v.* **(cath·e·ter·ized, cath·e·ter·iz·ing)** to insert a catheter into.

cath·ode (kath-ohd) *n.* the electrode by which current leaves a device. **ca·thod·ic** (kă-thod-ik) *adj.* □**cathode ray tube,** a vacuum tube, for example, a television picture tube, in which beams of electrons are directed against a fluorescent screen where they produce a luminous image.

cath·o·lic (kath-ŏ-lik) *adj.* universal, including many or most things, *his tastes are catholic.*

Cath·o·lic (kath-ŏ-lik) *adj.* 1. Roman Catholic. 2. of all Churches or Christians. **Catholic** *n.* a Roman Catholic. **Ca·thol·i·cism** (kă-thol-i-siz-ĕm) *n.*

cath·o·lic·i·ty (kath-ŏ-lis-i-tee) *n.* 1. the quality of being of wide interest or use. 2. broadmindedness. 3. *Catholicity,* Roman Catholicism.

cat·i·on (kat-ı-ŏn) *n.* an ion with a positive charge.

cat·kin (kat-kin) *n.* a spike of small soft flowers hanging from trees such as willow and hazel.

cat·like (kat-lık) *adj.* like a cat.

cat·nap (kat-nap) *n.* a short nap. **catnap** *v.* **(cat·napped, cat·nap·ping)** to have a catnap.

cat·nip (kat-nip) *n.* a plant with a strong smell that attracts cats.

cat-o'-nine-tails (kat-ŏ-nın-taylz) *n.* a whip with nine knotted lashes, formerly used for flogging people.

cat's-eyes (kats-ız) *n. pl.* 1. reflector studs marking the edge of a road etc. 2. gems reflecting light.

cat's-paw (kats-paw) *n.* a person who is used by another to do something risky.

cat·sup (kat-sŭp) = **ketchup.**

cat·tail (kat-tayl) *n.* a reedlike marsh plant with flowers in tall cylindrical spikes.

cat·tle (kat-ĕl) *n.* large ruminant animals with horns and cloven hoofs, bred for their milk or meat. **cat·tle·man** (kat-ĕl-măn) *n.* (*pl.* **-men,** *pr.* -mĕn). a breeder of cattle. □**cattle car,** a penlike railroad car for transporting livestock.

cat·ty (kat-ee) *adj.* **(-ti·er, -ti·est)** spiteful, speaking spitefully. **cat′ti·ly** *adv.* **cat′ti·ness** *n.*

cat·ty-cor·nered (kat-ee-kor-nĕrd) *adv.* diagonally.

CATV *abbr.* community antenna television.

cat·walk (kat-wawk) *n.* a raised narrow pathway.

Cau·ca·sian (kaw-kay-zhăn) *n.* member of the light-skinned division of humanity. **Caucasian** *adj.*

cau·cus (kaw-kŭs) *n.* (*pl.* **-cus·es**) a meeting of a small group of political party leaders to decide policy etc. **caucus** *v.* **(cau·cused, cau·cus·ing)** to meet for such purposes.

cau·dal (kaw-dăl) *adj.* of or at the tail. **cau′dal·ly** *adv.*

cau·dil·lo (kaw-deel-yoh) *n.* (*pl.* **-los**) a military dictator in a Spanish-speaking country.

caught (kawt) *see* **catch.**

caul (kawl) *n.* 1. a membrane enclosing a fetus in the womb. 2. part of this found on a child's head at birth, once thought to be a charm against drowning.

caul·dron (kawl-drŏn) *n.* a large deep pot for boiling things in.

cau·li·flow·er (kaw-lĭ-flow-ĕr) *n.* a cabbage with a large white flower head. □**cauliflower ear,** an ear thickened by repeated blows, as in boxing.

caulk (kawk) *v.* to make watertight by filling seams or joints with waterproof material, or by driving edges of plating together. **caulk′er** *n.*

caulk·ing (kaw-king) *n.* material used to caulk seams etc.

caus·al (kaw-zăl) *adj.* of or forming a cause. **caus′al·ly** *adv.* **cau·sal·i·ty** (kaw-zal-i-tee) *n.*

cau·sa·tion (kaw-zay-shŏn) *n.* 1. the causing or producing of an effect. 2. the relation of cause and effect.

cause (kawz) *n.* 1. a person or thing that makes something happen or produces an effect. 2. a reason, *there is no cause for anxiety.* 3. a purpose or aim for which efforts are made, a movement or charity; *a good cause,* one deserving support. 4. a lawsuit; *pleading his cause,* his case. **cause** *v.* **(caused, caus·ing)** to be the cause of, to produce, to make happen. **caus·a·tive** (kaw-ză-tiv) *adj.* □**cause cé·lè·bre** (kohz say-leb-rĕ) a celebrated lawsuit or other issue.

cause·way (kawz-way) *n.* a raised road across low or wet ground.

caus·tic (kaws-tik) *adj.* 1. able to burn or corrode things by chemical action. 2. sarcastic. **caustic** *n.* a caustic substance. **caus'ti·cal·ly** *adv.* **caus·tic·i·ty** (kaws-tis-i-tee) *n.* □**caustic soda,** sodium hydroxide.

cau·ter·ize (kaw-tĕ-rɪz) *v.* (**cau·ter·ized, cau·ter·iz·ing**) to burn the surface of (living tissue) with a caustic or a hot iron in order to destroy infection or stop bleeding. **cau·ter·i·za·tion** (kaw-tĕ-ri-zay-shŏn) *n.*

cau·tion (kaw-shŏn) *n.* 1. avoidance of rashness, attention to safety. 2. a warning against danger etc. 3. a warning and reprimand, *let him off with a caution.* 4. (*informal*) an amusing person or thing, *he is a caution.* **caution** *v.* 1. to warn. 2. to warn and reprimand.

cau·tion·ar·y (kaw-shŏ-ner-ee) *adj.* conveying a warning.

cau·tious (kaw-shŭs) *adj.* having or showing caution. **cau'tious·ly** *adv.* **cau'tious·ness** *n.*

cav. *abbr.* cavalry.

cav·al·cade (kav-ăl-kayd) *n.* a procession, especially of people on horseback or in cars etc.

cav·a·lier (kav-ă-leer) *n.* 1. *Cavalier,* a supporter of Charles I in the English Civil War. 2. (*humorous*) a man escorting a woman. **cavalier** *adj.* arrogant, offhand, *a cavalier attitude.*

cav·al·ry (kav-ăl-ree) *n.* (*pl.* **-ries**) troops who fight on horseback. **cav·al·ry·man** (kav-ăl-ree-măn) *n.* (*pl.* **-men,** *pr.* -mĕn) ▷Do not confuse *cavalry* with *Calvary.*

cave (kayv) *n.* a natural hollow in the side of a hill or cliff, or underground. **cave** *v.* (**caved, cav·ing**) **cave in,** to fall inward, to collapse; to cause to do this; to withdraw one's opposition.

ca·ve·at (kav-ee-at) *n.* a warning. □**caveat emp·tor** (kav-ee-at emp-tŏr), "let the buyer beware," the legal maxim that the buyer buys at his own risk. **caveat ven·di·tor** (kav-ee-at ven-di-tŏr) "let the seller beware," the legal maxim that the seller sells at his own risk.

cave-in (kayv-in) *n.* 1. the act of collapsing. 2. a site at which earth or a structure has fallen inward.

cave·man (kayv-man) *n.* (*pl.* **-men,** *pr.* -men) 1. a person of prehistoric times living in caves. 2. a man with a rough primitive manner toward women.

cav·ern (kav-ĕrn) *n.* a large cave. **cav'ern·ous** *adj.* **cav'ern·ous·ly** *adv.*

cav·i·ar (kav-i-ahr) *n.* the pickled roe of sturgeon or other large fish.

cav·il (kav-ĭl) *v.* (**cav·iled, cav·il·ing**) to raise petty objections. **cavil** *n.* a petty objection. **cav'il·er** *n.*

cav·i·ta·tion (kav-i-tay-shŏn) *n.* 1. successive formation and collapse of bubbles in liquids by mechanical forces, as from a ship's propeller. 2. a pocket formed by this action.

cav·i·ty (kav-i-tee) *n.* (*pl.* **-ties**) a hollow within a solid body.

ca·vort (kă-vort) *v.* to caper about excitedly.

ca·vy (kay-vee) *n.* (*pl.* **-vies**) a large South American rodent, especially a guinea pig.

caw (kaw) *n.* the harsh cry of a raven or crow. **caw** *v.* to make this sound.

cay (kay) *n.* a small low island or reef of sand, rocks, etc.

cay·enne (kɪ-en) **pepper** a hot red powdered pepper.

cay·man *see* **caiman.**

cay·use (kɪ-yoos) *n.* 1. an Indian pony. 2. (*humorous*) a horse of poor quality.

Cb *symbol* columbium.

CB *abbr.* 1. citizens' band. 2. construction battalion, Seabee.

CBC *abbr.* Canadian Broadcasting Corporation.

CBW *abbr.* chemical and biological warfare.

cc *abbr.* cubic centimeter(s).

CCC *abbr.* 1. Civilian Conservation Corps. 2. Commodity Credit Corporation.

CCTV *abbr.* closed-circuit television.

ccw *abbr.* counterclockwise.

cd *abbr.* cord.

Cd *symbol* cadmium.

CD *abbr.* 1. certificate of deposit. 2. Civil Defense.

Cdr. *abbr.* commander.

Ce *symbol* cerium.

C.E. *abbr.* 1. civil engineer. 2. Corps of Engineers.

cease (sees) *v.* (**ceased, ceas·ing**) to come or bring to an end, to stop. **cease** *n.* ceasing. □**without cease,** not ceasing.

cease-fire (sees-fɪr) *n.* 1. a signal to stop firing guns in war. 2. a truce.

cease·less (sees-lis) *adj.* not ceasing, going on continually. **cease'less·ly** *adv.* **cease'less·ness** *n.*

ce·cum (see-kŭm) *n.* (*pl.* **ce·ca,** *pr.* see-kă) a tube with one closed end in an animal body. **ce'cal** *adj.*

ce·dar (see-dăr) *n.* 1. an evergreen tree with hard sweet-smelling wood. 2. its wood. □**cedar chest,** a storage chest made of cedar for protecting woolen clothing etc. from insects and rot.

cede (seed) *v.* (**ced·ed, ced·ing**) to give up one's rights to or possession of, *they were compelled to cede certain territories.*

ce·dil·la (si-dil-ă) *n.* a mark written under *c* in certain languages to show that it is pronounced as *s,* as in *façade.*

ceil·ing (see-ling) *n.* 1. the undersurface of the top of a room. 2. the maximum altitude at which a particular aircraft can fly. 3. an upper limit or level, *wage ceilings.*

cel·an·dine (sel-ăn-dɪn) *n.* a small wild plant with yellow flowers.

cel·e·brate (sel-ĕ-brayt) *v.* (**cel·e·brat·ed, cel·e·brat·ing**) 1. to do something to show that a day or event is important, to honor with festivities, to make merry on such an occasion. 2. to officiate at (a religious ceremony). **cel'e·bra·tor** *n.* **cel·e·bra·tion** (sel-ĕ-bray-shŏn) *n.* **cel·e·brant** (sel-ĕ-brănt) *n.*

cel·e·brat·ed (sel-ĕ-bray-tid) *adj.* famous.

ce·leb·ri·ty (sĕ-leb-ri-tee) *n.* (*pl.* **-ties**) 1. a well-known person. 2. fame, being famous.

ce·ler·i·ty (sĕ-ler-i-tee) *n.* swiftness.

cel·er·y (sel-ĕ-ree) *n.* a garden plant with crisp juicy stems used in salads or as a vegetable.

ce·les·ta (sĕ-les-tă) *n.* a musical instrument like a piano, with metal plates struck with hammers, and played from a keyboard.

ce·les·tial (sĕ-les-chăl) *adj.* 1. of the sky; *celestial bodies,* stars etc. 2. of heaven, divine. **ce·les'tial·ly** *adv.* □**celestial equator,** the great circle of the celestial sphere, formed by a plane cutting through Earth's center at right angles to its axis. **celestial navigation,** navigation by reference to celestial bodies. **celestial sphere,** the imaginary sphere on which the heavenly bodies appear to lie, having its center at the center of Earth (or at the point where the observer stands) and an infinite radius.

cel·i·bate (sel-ĭ-bit) *adj.* remaining unmarried, especially for religious reasons. **celibate** *n.* such an unmarried person. **cel·i·ba·cy** (sel-ĭ-bă-see) *n.* the unmarried state.

cell (sel) *n.* 1. a very small room, as for a monk in a monastery or for confining a prisoner. 2. a compartment in a honeycomb. 3. a device for producing electric current by chemical action. 4. a microscopic unit of living matter, containing a nucleus. 5. a small group of people forming a center or nucleus of political activities.

cel·lar (sel-ăr) *n.* 1. an underground room used for storing things. 2. a room in which wine is stored, a stock of wine.

cel·lar·age (sel-ă-rij) *n.* 1. a fee for storage in a cellar. 2. cellar space.

cel·lar·et (sel-ă-ret) *n.* a case or sideboard for holding bottles of wine.

cell·block (sel-blok) *n.* a set of cells forming a section of a prison.

cel·list (chel-ist) *n.* a person who plays the cello.

cel·lo (chel-oh) *n.* (*pl.* **-los**) a violoncello, an instrument like a large violin, played by a seated player who sets it between his knees.

cel·lo·phane (sel-ŏ-fayn) *n.* (*formerly a trademark*) thin moisture-proof transparent material used for wrapping things.

cel·lu·lar (sel-yŭ-lăr) *adj.* 1. of cells, composed of cells. 2. woven with an open mesh, *cellular blankets.*

Cel·lu·loid (sel-yŭ-loid) *n.* (*trademark*) a plastic made from cellulose nitrate and camphor.

cel·lu·lose (sel-yŭ-lohs) *n.* an organic substance found in all plant tissues, used in making plastics. □**cellulose acetate**, acetic ester of cellulose, used to make rayon, lacquer, plastics, etc. **cellulose nitrate**, a constituent of smokeless gunpowders and of cordite, Celluloid, etc.

Cel·si·us (sel-si-ŭs) *adj.* centigrade. (▷Named after Anders Celsius, a Swedish astronomer (1701–44), who devised the centigrade scale.) □**Celsius scale**, the centigrade scale.

Celt (kelt, selt) *n.* a member of an ancient European people who settled in Britain before the coming of the Romans, or of their descendants especially in Ireland, Wales, Cornwall, and Scotland. **Celt'ic** *adj.* of the Celts.

cem·ba·lo (chem-bă-loh) *n.* (*pl.* **-li**, *pr.* -lee) a harpsichord.

ce·ment (si-ment) *n.* 1. a gray powder, made by burning lime and clay, that sets to a stonelike mass when mixed with water and is used for building. 2. any similar soft substance that sets firm. **cement** *v.* 1. to put cement on or in, to join with cement. 2. to unite firmly. **ce·men·ta·tion** (see-men-tay-shŏn) *n.* □**cement mixer**, a machine that mixes cement, sand, etc. with water in a turning drum.

ce·men·tum (si-men-tŭm) *n.* the bonelike tissue at the base of a tooth, covering the root.

cem·e·ter·y (sem-ĕ-ter-ee) *n.* (*pl.* **-ter·ies**) a burial ground other than a churchyard.

cen·o·bite (sen-ŏ-bɪt) *n.* a member of a monastic community. **cen·o·bit·ic** (sen-ŏ-bit-ik) *adj.* **cen·o·bit'i·cal** *adj.*

cen·o·taph (sen-ŏ-taf) *n.* a tomblike monument to persons buried elsewhere.

Ce·no·zo·ic (see-nŏ-zoh-ik) *adj.* of the geologic era following the Mesozoic and including the pres-

ent era, marked by the appearance of birds and mammals. **Cenozoic** *n.* the Cenozoic era.

cen·ser (sen-sĕr) *n.* a container in which incense is burned, swung on chains in a religious ceremony to disperse its fragrance. ▷Do not confuse *censer* with *censor* or *censure.*

cen·sor (sen-sŏr) *n.* a person authorized to examine letters, books, films, etc. and remove or ban anything regarded as harmful. **censor** *v.* to subject to such examination or removal. (▷Do not confuse *censor* with *censer* or *censure.*) **cen·so·ri·al** (sen-sohr-i-ăl) *adj.* **cen'sor·ship** *n.*

cen·so·ri·ous (sen-sohr-i-ŭs) *adj.* severely critical. **cen·so'ri·ous·ly** *adv.* **cen·so'ri·ous·ness** *n.*

cen·sure (sen-shŭr) *n.* strong criticism or condemnation. **censure** *v.* (**cen·sured**, **cen·sur·ing**) to blame and rebuke. (▷Do not confuse *censure* with *censor* or *censer.*) **cen'sur·er** *n.* **cen'sur·a·ble** *adj.*

cen·sus (sen-sŭs) *n.* (*pl.* **-sus·es**) an official count of the population and its characteristics, such as sex, family size, and occupation.

cent (sent) *n.* 1. one 100th of a dollar or of certain other metric units of currency, a coin of this value. 2. (*informal*) a very small amount of money, *I haven't a cent.*

cent. *abbr.* 1. centigrade. 2. central. 3. century.

cen·taur (sen-tor) *n.* (in Greek mythology) a creature with the head, trunk, and arms of a human joined to the body and legs of a horse.

cen·ta·vo (sen-tah-voh) *n.* (*pl.* **-vos**) one 100th of a peso or similar unit of currency in several Spanish American countries.

cen·te·nar·i·an (sen-tĕ-nair-i-ăn) *n.* a person who is one hundred years old or more.

cen·te·nar·y (sen-tĕ-ner-ee) *n.* (*pl.* **-nar·ies**) a centennial. **centenary** *adj.*

cen·ten·ni·al (sen-ten-i-ăl) *n.* a 100th anniversary. **centennial** *adj.*

cen·ter (sen-tĕr) *n.* 1. the middle point or part. 2. a point toward which interest is directed or from which administration etc. is organized. 3. a place where certain activities or facilities are concentrated, *a shopping center.* 4. a political party or group holding moderate opinions. 5. (in some sports) the player who puts the ball into play. **center** *v.* 1. to place in or at the center. 2. to concentrate at one point. 3. (in hockey) to hit the puck toward center ice, (in football) to put the ball into play. □**center of gravity**, the point about which all parts of a body exactly balance each other. **center punch**, a tool used to make shallow impressions in metalwork or wood to guide the placing of a drill bit. ▷Do not say or write *centers around*; something may center *on* or *in* or *at.*

cen·ter·board (sen-tĕr-bohrd) *n.* a plate lowered through a slot in the keel of a sailboat to increase stability.

cen·tered (sen-tĕrd) *n.* 1. having an exact midpoint. 2. located in the center.

cen·ter·fold (sen-tĕr-fohld) *n.* a pair of facing pages at the center of a magazine.

cen·ter·piece (sen-tĕr-pees) *n.* a flower arrangement or other ornament for the center of a table.

cen·tes·i·mal (sen-tes-ĭ-măl) *n.* reckoning, reckoned, by hundredths.

centi- *prefix* one hundredth, hundred.

cen·ti·grade (sen-tĭ-grayd) *adj.* of or using a temperature scale divided into 100 degrees, 0° being the freezing point and 100° the boiling point of water.

cen·ti·gram (sen-tĭ-gram) *n.* one 100th of a gram.

cen·ti·li·ter (sen-tĭ-lee-tĕr) *n.* one 100th of a liter.

cen·time (sahn-teem) *n.* one 100th of a franc or a similar unit of currency.

cen·ti·me·ter (sen-tĭ-mee-tĕr) *n.* one 100th of a meter, about 0.4 inch. □**centimeter-gram-second**, of the system of units of measurement based on the centimeter, gram, and second as units of length, mass, and time.

cen·ti·pede (sĕn-tĭ-peed) *n.* a small crawling creature with a long thin segmented body and many legs, one pair on each segment.

cen·tral (sen-trăl) *adj.* 1. of or at or forming the center. 2. chief, most important, *the central character in this novel.* **central** *n.* *(old use)* a telephone exchange through which many line connections are made. **cen'tral·ly** *adv.* **cen·tral·i·ty** (sen-tral-i-tee) *n.* □**Central African Republic**, a country in central Africa. **Central America**, *see* **America**. **central heating**, a system of heating a building from one source by circulating hot water or hot air in pipes or by linked radiators. **Central Intelligence Agency**, the U.S. agency responsible for coordinating government intelligence activities. **central nervous system**, the brain and the spinal cord.

cen·tral·ize (sen-tră-lĭz) *v.* **(cen·tral·ized, cen·tral·iz·ing)** to bring under the control of one central authority. **cen'tral·iz·er** *n.* **cen·tral·i·za·tion** (sen-tră-li-zay-shŏn) *n.*

cen·trif·u·gal (sen-trif-yŭ-găl) *adj.* 1. moving away from the center or axis. 2. using **centrifugal force**, a force that appears to cause a body that is traveling around a center to fly outward and off its circular path. **cen·trif'u·gal·ly** *adv.*

cen·tri·fuge (sen-trĭ-fyooj) *n.* a machine using centrifugal force to separate substances, such as milk and cream. **centrifuge** *v.* **(cen·tri·fuged, cen·tri·fug·ing)** to separate by a centrifuge.

cen·trip·e·tal (sen-trip-ĕ-tăl) *adj.* moving toward the center or axis. **cen·trip'e·tal·ly** *adv.*

cen·trist (sen-trist) *n.* a holder of moderate views, especially in politics.

cen·tu·ri·on (sen-toor-i-ŏn) *n.* an army officer in ancient Rome, commanding approximately one hundred men.

cen·tu·ry (sen-chŭ-ree) *n.* *(pl.* **-ries)** 1. a subdivision of a Roman legion, with approximately one hundred men. 2. a period of one hundred years, one of these periods reckoned from the birth of Christ. □**century note**, *(slang)* a hundred dollar bill. **century plant**, a plant (thought to flower once in one hundred years) which flowers once in five to twenty years and then dies.

CEO *abbr.* chief executive officer.

ce·phal·ic (sĕ-fal-ik) *adj.* of the head.

ce·ram·ic (sĕ-ram-ik) *adj.* of pottery or similar substances. **ceramic** *n.* a ceramic substance. **ce·ra·mist** (se-răm-ist) *n.* □**ceramic tile**, a glazed decorative tile of fired clay or similar material.

ce·ram·ics (sĕ-ram-iks) *n.* the art of making pottery, *ceramics is her hobby.*

ce·re·al (seer-i-ăl) *n.* 1. a grass, such as wheat, rye, oats, or rice, producing an edible grain. 2. its seed. 3. a breakfast food made from such grain. **cereal** *adj.*

cer·e·bel·lum (ser-ă-bel-ŭm) *n.* *(pl.* **-bel·lums, -bel·la,** *pr.* **-bel-ă)** the portion of the human brain that coordinates movements of the muscles.

cer·e·bral (ser-ĕ-brăl, sĕ-ree-) *adj.* 1. of the brain. 2. intellectual. **cer'e·bral·ly** *adv.* □**cerebral cortex**, the surface tissue of the cerebrum. **cerebral palsy**, *see* **spastic**.

cer·e·brate (ser-ĕ-brayt) *v.* **(cer·e·brat·ed, cer·e·brat·ing)** to think.

cer·e·brum (ser-ĕ-brŭm) *n.* *(pl.* **-brums, -bra,** *pr.* **-bră)** the portion of the human brain that acts as the center for conscious thought.

cere·cloth (seer-klawth) *n.* *(pl.* **-cloths,** *pr.* **-klawthz, -klawths)** waxed cloth, formerly used for wrapping the dead.

cere·ment (seer-mĕnt) *n.* (usually **cerements**) cerecloth.

cer·e·mo·ni·al (ser-ĕ-moh-ni-ăl) *adj.* of a ceremony, used in ceremonies, formal. (▷ Do not confuse *ceremonial* with *ceremonious*.) **ceremonial** *n.* 1. ceremony. 2. a system of rules for ceremonies. **cer·e·mo'ni·al·ly** *adv.*

cer·e·mo·ni·ous (ser-ĕ-moh-ni-ŭs) *adj.* full of ceremony, elaborately performed. (▷ Do not confuse *ceremonious* with *ceremonial*.) **cer·e·mo'ni·ous·ly** *adv.* **cer·e·mo'ni·ous·ness** *n.*

cer·e·mo·ny (ser-ĕ-moh-nee) *n.* *(pl.* **-nies)** 1. a set of formal acts, especially those used on religious or public occasions. 2. formal politeness.

ce·re·us (seer-i-ŭs) *n.* *(pl.* **-us·es)** any of several cacti native to the western U.S. and tropical America.

ce·rise (se-rees) *adj. & n.* light clear red.

ce·ri·um (seer-i-ŭm) *n.* an element resembling iron in color and luster.

cer·met (sur-met) *n.* an alloy of ceramic with metal.

cert. *abbr.* 1. certificate. 2. certification. 3. certified. 4. certify.

cer·tain (sur-tăn) *adj.* 1. having no doubt, convinced. 2. known without doubt. 3. able to be relied on to come or happen or be effective. 4. specific but not named or stated for various reasons. 5. small in amount but definitely there, *I feel a certain reluctance.* 6. existing but not well known, *a certain John Smith.* □**for certain**, without doubt, as a certainty. **make certain**, to make sure.

cer·tain·ly (sur-tăn-lee) *adv.* 1. without doubt. 2. yes.

cer·tain·ty (sur-tăn-tee) *n.* *(pl.* **-ties)** 1. being certain. 2. something that is certain; *his victory is a certainty,* he is certain to win.

certif. *abbr.* certificate.

cer·ti·fi·a·ble (sur-tĭ-fĭ-ă-bĕl) *adj.* able to be certified. **cer'ti·fi·a·bly** *adv.*

cer·tif·i·cate (sĕr-tif-ĭ-kit) *n.* an official written or printed statement giving certain facts. □**certificate of deposit**, an interest-bearing bank receipt for a specified amount of money.

cer·ti·fy (sur-tĭ-fĭ) *v.* **(cer·ti·fied, cer·ti·fy·ing)** to declare formally, to show on a certificate or other document. □**certified check**, a check guaranteed by the bank on which it is drawn. **certified milk**, milk produced in dairies operating under strict standards of cleanliness. **certified public accountant**, one who has passed state examinations and received a certificate of professional competence. **cer'ti·fi·er** *n.* **cer·ti·fi·ca·tion** (sur-tĭ-fĭ-kay-shŏn) *n.*

cer·ti·tude (sur-tĭ-tood) *n.* a feeling of certainty.

ce·ru·le·an (sĕ-roo-li-ăn) *adj. & n.* deep blue.

ce·ru·men (sĕ-roo-mĕn) *n.* yellow waxy secretion of the glands of the external ear.

cer·vi·cal (sur-vi-kăl) *adj.* 1. of the neck, *cervical vertebrae.* 2. of a cervix, of the cervix of the womb.

cer·vix (sur-viks) *n.* (*pl.* **-vix·es, -vi·ces,** *pr.* -vi-seez) 1. the neck. 2. a necklike structure, the neck of the womb.

ce·si·um (see-zi-ŭm) *n.* a soft silvery metal element.

ces·sa·tion (se-say-shŏn) *n.* ceasing.

ces·sion (sesh-ŏn) *n.* ceding, giving up.

cess·pool (ses-pool) *n.* a covered pit or tank where liquid waste or sewage is stored temporarily.

Cey·lon (si-lon) the former name of Sri Lanka.

cf. *abbr.* compare.

Cf *symbol* californium.

cg, cgm *abbr.* centigram(s).

CG *abbr.* Commanding General.

cgs *abbr.* centimeter-gram-second.

CH *abbr.* 1. clearinghouse. 2. courthouse. 3. customhouse.

ch. *abbr.* 1. chapter. 2. (in chess) check. 3. church.

Chab·lis (sha-blee) *n.* a white burgundy.

cha-cha (chah-chah) *n.* a ballroom dance with a Latin-American rhythm. **cha-cha** *v.* to dance this.

Chad (chad) a country in North Africa. **Chad'i·an** *adj.* & *n.*

chafe (chayf) *v.* (**chafed, chaf·ing**) 1. to warm by rubbing. 2. to make or become sore from rubbing. 3. to become irritated or impatient. ▷Do not confuse *chafe* with *chaff.*

chaf·er (chay-fĕr) *n.* a large slow-moving beetle, especially a cockchafer.

chaff (chaf) *n.* 1. wheat husks separated from the seed by threshing or winnowing. 2. hay or straw cut up as food for cattle. 3. good-humored teasing or joking. **chaff** *v.* to tease or joke in a good-humored way. ▷Do not confuse *chaff* with *chafe.*

chaf·fer (chaf-ĕr) *v.* (**chaf·fered, chaf·fer·ing**) to haggle. **chaffer** *n.* bargaining. **chaf'fer·er** *n.*

chaf·finch (chaf-inch) *n.* a common European finch.

chaf·ing (chay-fing) **dish** a pan or dish with a heater under it for cooking food or keeping it warm at the table.

cha·grin (shă-grin) *n.* a feeling of annoyance and embarrassment or disappointment.

cha·grined (shă-grind) *adj.* affected with chagrin.

chain (chayn) *n.* 1. a series of connected metal links, used for hauling or supporting weights or for restraining things or as an ornament. 2. a connected series or sequence, *chain of mountains, chain of events.* 3. a number of stores or hotels etc. owned by the same company. 4. a unit of length for measuring land, 66 feet. **chain** *v.* to make fast with a chain or chains. □**chain gang,** a gang of convicts chained together at work to prevent escape. **chain letter,** a letter of which the recipient is asked to make copies and send these to other people, who will be asked to do the same. **chain mail,** chain armor. **chain reaction,** a chemical or other change forming products that themselves cause more changes; a series of events each of which causes or influences the next. **chain saw,** a saw with teeth set on an endless chain. **chain smoker,** a person who smokes cigarettes continually. **chain stitch,** a looped stitch that looks like a chain, in crochet or embroidery. **chain store,** one of a series of similar stores owned by one firm.

chain-smoke (chayn-smohk) *v.* (**chain-smoked,**

chain-smok·ing) to smoke many cigarettes in succession often lighting one from the end of another.

chair (chair) *n.* 1. a movable seat, with a back, for one person. 2. a position of authority at a meeting, the chairmanship; *address your remarks to the chair,* to the chairman. 3. a professorship. 4. the electric chair. **chair** *v.* 1. to seat in a chair of honor. 2. to carry in triumph on the shoulders of a group. 3. to act as chairman of. □**chair lift,** a series of chairs suspended from an endless cable, for carrying people up a mountain.

chair·man (chair-măn) *n.* (*pl.* **-men,** *pr.* -mĕn) 1. a person who presides over a meeting or a committee. 2. the president of a board of directors. **chair'man·ship** *n.* **chair·wom·an** (chairwuum-ăn) *n.* (*pl.* **-wom·en,** *pr.* -wim-in).

chair·per·son (chair-pur-sŏn) *n.* any person chosen to preside over a meeting, organization, etc. ▷The word *chairman* may be used of persons of either sex, but *chairperson* is increasingly heard in this sense.

chaise (shayz) *n.* 1. a light open carriage for one or two persons. 2. a chaise longue.

chaise longue (shayz lawng) (*pl.* **chaise longues,** *pr.* shayz **lawngz**) a chair with a very long seat on which the sitter can stretch out his legs. ▷ This expression is frequently written incorrectly as *chaise lounge.*

chal·ced·o·ny (kal-sed-ŏ-nee) *n.* (*pl.* **-nies**) a precious or semiprecious stone, a type of quartz.

chal·co·py·rite (kal-kŏ-pı-rīt) *n.* copper-iron sulfide ore.

cha·let (sha-lay) *n.* (*pl.* **-lets,** *pr.* **-layz**) 1. a Swiss hut or cottage. 2. a small villa. 3. a small cottage in a resort area.

chal·ice (chal-is) *n.* a vessel like a large goblet for holding wine, one from which consecrated wine is drunk at the Eucharist.

chalk (chawk) *n.* 1. a white soft limestone used for burning into lime. 2. a piece of this or of similar substance, white or colored, used in crayons for drawing. **chalk** *v.* to write or draw or mark with chalk, to rub with chalk. **chalk'y** *adj.* □**chalk up,** to make a note of something; to achieve, *chalked up another victory.*

chalk·board (chawk-bohrd) *n.* a blackboard or other smooth surface that is written on with chalk.

chal·lenge (chal-ĕnj) *n.* 1. a call to try one's skill or strength against another. 2. a call or demand to respond, a sentry's call for a person to identify himself. 3. a formal objection, as to a member of a jury. 4. a difficult or demanding task. **challenge** *v.* (**chal·lenged, chal·leng·ing**) 1. to make a challenge. 2. to raise a formal objection to. 3. to question the truth or rightness of. **chal'leng·er** *n.*

chal·leng·ing (chal-ĕn-jing) *adj.* offering problems that test one's ability, stimulating.

cham·ber (chaym-bĕr) *n.* 1. a room, a bedroom. 2. the hall used for meetings of a legislature etc., the members of the group using it. 3. a chamber pot. 4. a cavity or compartment in the body of an animal or plant, or in machinery. 5. *chambers,* a set of rooms, a judge's room for hearing cases that do not need to be heard in court. **cham'bered** *adj.* □**chamber music,** music written for a small number of players, suitable for performance in a room or small hall. **Chamber of Commerce,** an association of businessmen etc. to promote local commercial inter-

ests. Chamber of Horrors, the room of criminals etc. in Madame Tussaud's waxworks; a place full of horrifying things. **chamber pot,** a receptacle for urine etc., used in the bedroom.

cham·ber·lain (chaym-bĕr-lin) *n.* an official who manages the household of a sovereign or a great noble.

cham·ber·maid (chaym-bĕr-mayd) *n.* a woman employed to clean and take care of bedrooms in a hotel.

cham·bray (sham-bray) *n.* gingham with a linen finish.

cha·me·le·on (kă-mee-li-ŏn) *n.* a small lizard that can change color according to its surroundings.

cham·fer (cham-fĕr) *v.* to bevel the edge or corner of. **chamfer** *n.* such a bevel.

cham·ois (sham-ee) *n.* (*pl.* **-ois,** *pr.* **sham-eez**) 1. a small wild antelope found in the mountains of Europe and Asia. 2. a piece of **chamois leather,** soft yellowish leather made from the skin of sheep, goats, and deer and used for washing and polishing things.

champ[1] (champ) *v.* 1. to munch noisily, to make a chewing action or noise. 2. to show impatience, *the athletes were champing at the bit.*

champ[2] *n.* (*informal*) a champion.

cham·pagne (sham-payn) *n.* 1. a sparkling white wine from Champagne in France or elsewhere. 2. its pale straw color.

cham·pi·on (cham-pi-ŏn) *n.* 1. a person or thing that has defeated all others in a competition. 2. a person who fights, argues, or speaks in support of another or of a cause. **champion** *adj.* excelling over all competitors. **champion** *v.* to support as a champion. **cham'pi·on·ship** *n.*

chance (chans) *n.* 1. the way things happen through no known cause or agency, luck, fate; *games of chance,* those decided by luck not skill. 2. a possibility, likelihood. 3. an opportunity, an occasion when success seems very probable. **chance** *v.* **(chanced, chanc·ing)** 1. to happen without plan or intention. 2. (*informal*) to risk, *let's chance it.* **chance** *adj.* coming or happening by chance, *a chance meeting.* □**by chance,** as it happens or happened, without being planned. **chance on,** to come upon or find by chance. **take a chance,** to take a risk, to act in the hope that a particular thing will (or will not) happen. **take chances,** to behave riskily. **take one's chances,** to trust to luck.

chan·cel (chan-sĕl) *n.* the part of a church near the altar, used by the clergy and choir.

chan·cel·ler·y (chan-sĕ-lĕ-ree) *n.* (*pl.* **-ler·ies**) 1. a chancellor's position, department, or official residence. 2. an office attached to an embassy or consulate. ▷Do not confuse *chancellery* with *chancery.*

chan·cel·lor (chan-sĕ-lŏr) *n.* 1. a government or law official of various kinds. 2. the chief minister of state in West Germany and in Austria. 3. the head of some universities. **chan'cel·lor·ship** *n.* □**Chancellor of the Exchequer,** the finance minister of the United Kingdom, who prepares the budget.

chan·cer·y (chan-sĕ-ree) *n.* (*pl.* **-cer·ies**) 1. a court of equity. 2. an administrative office of a diocese. ▷Do not confuse *chancery* with *chancellery.*

chan·cre (shang-kĕr) *n.* an ulcer caused by syphilis.

chanc·y (chan-see) *adj.* **(chanc·i·er, chanc·i·est)** (*informal*) risky, uncertain.

chan·de·lier (shan-dĕ-leer) *n.* an ornamental hanging fixture with supports for several lights.

chan·dler (chand-lĕr) *n.* a dealer in ropes, canvas, and other supplies for ships. **chan'dler·y** *n.*

change (chaynj) *v.* **(changed, chang·ing)** 1. to make or become different. 2. to pass from one form or phase into another. 3. to take or use another instead of. 4. to put fresh clothes or coverings etc. on; *change the baby,* put a fresh diaper on it. 5. to go from one to another, *change trains.* 6. to exchange; *can you change a $20 bill,* give small money in change, or give different currency for it. **change** *n.* 1. changing, alteration; *a change of the moon,* a fresh phase. 2. substitution of one thing for another, variety; *pack a change of clothes,* a fresh outfit in reserve. 3. a fresh occupation or surroundings. 4. money in small units. 5. money returned as the balance when the price is less than the amount offered in payment. **chang'er** *n.* **change'ful** *adj.* **change'less** *adj.* □**change hands,** to pass into another person's possession. **change of heart,** a great alteration in one's attitude or feelings. **change of life,** the menopause. **change over,** to change from one system or position to another. **change ringing,** ringing a peal of bells in a series of different sequences. **for a change,** for the sake of variety, to vary one's routine.

change·a·ble (chayn-jă-bĕl) *adj.* 1. able to be changed. 2. altering frequently, *changeable weather.*

change·ling (chaynj-ling) *n.* (*old use*) a child believed to have been substituted secretly for another.

change·o·ver (chaynj-oh-vĕr) *n.* a change from one system or situation to another.

chan·nel (chan-ĕl) *n.* 1. the sunken bed of a stream of water. 2. the navigable part of a waterway, deeper than the parts on either side. 3. a stretch of water, wider than a strait, connecting two seas; *swim the Channel,* the English Channel. 4. a passage along which a liquid may flow, a sunken course or line along which something can move. 5. any course by which news or information etc. can travel. 6. a band of broadcasting frequencies reserved for a particular station. **channel** *v.* **(chan·neled, chan·nel·ing)** 1. to form a channel or channels in. 2. to direct through a channel or desired route.

chant (chant) *n.* 1. a tune to which the words of psalms or other works with irregular rhythm are fitted by singing several syllables or words to the same note. 2. a monotonous song. 3. a rhythmic call or shout. **chant** *v.* 1. to sing, especially a chant. 2. to call or shout rhythmically. **chant'er** *n.*

chan·teuse (shan-tooz) *n.* a female singer of popular songs, especially in nightclubs.

chan·tey (shan-tee) *n.* (*pl.* **-teys**) a sailors' traditional song, especially one sung to their work.

chan·ti·cleer (chan-tĭ-kleer) *n.* a domestic rooster, used as a proper name in medieval fables.

Cha·nu·kah = Hanukkah.

cha·os (kay-os) *n.* great disorder or confusion. **cha·ot·ic** (kay-ot-ik) *adj.* **cha·ot'i·cal·ly** *adv.*

chap[1] (chap) *v.* **(chapped, chap·ping)** to split or crack (skin); (of skin) to become cracked. **chap** *n.* a crack in the skin.

chap[2] *n.* the lower jaw or half of the cheek, especially of a pig, as food.

chap[3] *n.* (*informal*) a man.

chap. *abbr.* 1. chaplain. 2. chapter.

chap·ar·ral (shap-ǎ-ral) *n.* dense tangled shrubs, especially those that grow in poor soil in the southwest U.S. and in Mexico. □**chaparral bird,** a roadrunner.

chap·book (chap-buuk) *n.* a small book of popular tales, ballads, poems or religious tracts, of the kind formerly sold by peddlers.

cha·peau (sha-poh) *n.* (*pl.* **-peaux, -peaus,** *pr.* **-pohz**) (*humorous*) a hat.

chap·el (chap-ĕl) *n.* 1. a place used for religious worship, other than a cathedral, synagogue, or parish church. 2. a service in this, *go to chapel.* 3. a place with a separate altar within a church or cathedral.

chap·er·on, chap·er·one (shap-ĕ-rohn) *n.* an older person in charge of young people on social occasions. **chaperon(e)** *v.* (**chap·er·oned, chap·er·on·ing**) to act as chaperon to. **chap'er·on·age** *n.*

chap·fall·en (chap-faw-lĕn) *adj.* with jaw hanging down, dejected.

chap·lain (chap-lin) *n.* a clergyman attached to a chapel in a private house or institution, or to a military unit. **chap'lain·cy** *n.* (*pl.* **-cies**).

chap·let (chap-lit) *n.* 1. a wreath for the head. 2. a short rosary.

chaps (chaps) *n. pl.* long leather leggings worn by cowboys.

chap·ter (chap-tĕr) *n.* 1. a division of a book, usually numbered. 2. a local branch of an organization. 3. the canons of a cathedral or members of a monastic order, a meeting of these. □**chapter and verse,** an exact reference to a passage or authority. **chapter house,** the building used for meetings of a cathedral chapter or of a college fraternity.

char (chahr) *v.* (**charred, char·ring**) to make or become black by burning.

char·a·banc (shar-ă-bang) *n.* an early form of bus with bench seats from side to side, used for outings.

char·ac·ter (kar-ik-tĕr) *n.* 1. all those qualities that make a person, group, or thing what he or it is and different from others. 2. a person's moral nature. 3. moral strength. 4. a person, especially a noticeable or eccentric one. 5. a person in a novel or play etc. 6. a letter, sign, or mark used in a system of writing or printing etc. 7. a physical characteristic of a plant or animal. 8. (*old use*) a description of a person's qualities, a reference. □**character actor** *or* **actress,** one who portrays people with distinctive personal traits. **in character,** appropriate to a person's general character. **out of character,** not appropriate to a person's usual character.

char·ac·ter·is·tic (kar-ik-tĕ-ris-tik) *adj.* forming part of the character of a person or thing, showing a distinctive feature. **characteristic** *n.* a characteristic feature. **char·ac·ter·is'ti·cal·ly** *adv.*

char·ac·ter·ize (kar-ik-tĕ-rız) *v.* (**char·ac·ter·ized, char·ac·ter·iz·ing**) 1. to describe the character of. 2. to be a characteristic of. **char·ac·ter·i·za·tion** (kar-ik-tĕr-ri-zay-shŏn) *n.*

char·ac·ter·less (kar-ik-tĕr-lis) *adj.* lacking any positive character.

cha·rade (shă-rayd) *n.* 1. a scene acted as a clue to the word to be guessed in the game of **charades.** 2. an absurd pretense.

char·broil (chahr-broil) *v.* to broil over charcoal.

char·coal (chahr-kohl) *n.* a black substance made by burning wood slowly in an oven with little air, used as a filtering material or as fuel or for drawing. □**charcoal gray,** very dark gray.

chard (chahrd) *n.* (also **Swiss chard**) a kind of beet lacking a large root but having edible leaves and stalks.

charge (chahrj) *n.* 1. the price asked for goods or services. 2. the quantity of material that an apparatus holds at one time, the amount of explosive needed for one explosion. 3. the electricity contained in a substance, energy stored chemically for conversion into electricity. 4. a task or duty, custody. 5. a person or thing entrusted. 6. formal instructions about one's duty or responsibility. 7. an accusation, especially of having committed a crime. 8. a rushing attack. **charge** *v.* (**charged, charg·ing**) 1. to ask as a price. 2. to record as a debt, *charge it to my account.* 3. to load or fill, to put a charge into. 4. to give an electric charge to, to store energy in. 5. to give as a task or duty, to entrust. 6. to accuse formally. 7. to rush forward in attack; *charge in,* to act impetuously. □**charge account,** a credit account at a store, permitting a customer to receive goods in advance of billing. **charge card, charge plate,** a small metal or plastic card, usually valid for only one store or chain. **in charge,** in command. **take charge,** to take control.

charge·a·ble (chahr-jă-bĕl) *adj.* able to be charged.

char·gé d'af·faires (shahr-zhay-dă-fair) (*pl.* **char·gés d'af·faires,** *pr.* shahr-zhayz-dă-fair) 1. an ambassador's deputy. 2. an envoy to a minor country. ▷French.

charg·er (chahr-jĕr) *n.* 1. one who or that which charges; *battery charger,* an apparatus that charges storage batteries. 2. a horse that can be ridden into battle.

char·i·ot (char-i-ŏt) *n.* a two-wheeled horse-drawn carriage used in ancient times in battle and in racing.

char·i·o·teer (char-i-ŏ-teer) *n.* the driver of a chariot.

cha·ris·ma (kă-riz-mă) *n.* the power to inspire devotion and enthusiasm.

char·is·mat·ic (kar-iz-mat-ik) *adj.* having charisma.

char·i·ta·ble (char-i-tă-bĕl) *adj.* 1. generous in giving to the needy. 2. of or belonging to charities, *charitable institutions.* 3. unwilling to think badly of people or acts. **char'i·ta·bly** *adv.* **char'i·ta·ble·ness** *n.*

char·i·ty (char-i-tee) *n.* (*pl.* **-ties**) 1. loving kindness toward others. 2. unwillingness to think badly of people or acts. 3. generosity in giving to the needy. 4. an institution or fund for helping the needy.

char·la·dy (chahr-lay-dee) *n.* (*pl.* **-dies**) a charwoman.

char·la·tan (shahr-lă-tăn) *n.* a person who falsely claims to be an expert, especially in medicine.

Charles·ton (chahrl-stŏn) *n.* 1. a fast dance employing side kicks from the knee, popular in the 1920s. 2. the capital of West Virginia.

char·ley (chahr-lee) **horse** (*informal*) a stiffness or cramping of the muscles, especially in the thigh, from overexertion or injury.

char·lock (chahr-lŏk) *n.* wild mustard, a weed with yellow flowers.

char·lotte russe (shahr-lŏt roos) a mold of custard or cream enclosed in sponge cake.

charm (chahrm) *n.* 1. attractiveness, the power of arousing love or admiration. 2. an act or object or words believed to have magic power. 3. a small ornament worn on a chain or bracelet, *a charm bracelet.* **charm** *v.* 1. to give pleasure to. 2. to influence by personal charm. 3. to influence as if by magic. **charm′er** *n.*

charm·ing (chahr-ming) *adj.* delightful.

char·nel (chahr-nĕl) **house** a place in which the bodies or bones of the dead are kept.

chart (chahrt) *n.* 1. a map designed for navigators on water or in the air. 2. an outline map for showing special information, *a weather chart.* 3. a diagram, graph, or table giving information in an orderly form, *a temperature chart.* **chart** *v.* to make a chart of, to map. □**the charts,** those listing the recordings that are currently most popular.

char·ter (chahr-tĕr) *n.* 1. a document from a ruler or government granting certain rights or defining the form of an institution. 2. the chartering of a ship, aircraft, or vehicle. **charter** *v.* 1. to grant a charter to, to found by charter. 2. to let or hire a ship, aircraft, or vehicle. **char′ter·er** *n.* □**charter flight,** a flight by chartered aircraft. **charter member,** an original member of a society, corporation, etc.

char·treuse (shahr-trooz) *n.* 1. a fragrant green or yellow liqueur. 2. its green color.

char·wom·an (chahr-wuum-ăn) *n.* (*pl.* **-wom·en,** *pr.* -wim-in) a woman employed to clean a house or other building.

char·y (chair-ee) *adj.* (**char·i·er, char·i·est**) 1. cautious, wary. 2. sparing; *chary of giving praise,* seldom praising people. **char′i·ly** *adv.*

chase¹ (chays) *v.* (**chased, chas·ing**) 1. to go quickly after in order to capture or overtake or drive away. 2. to hurry, *chasing after bargains.* 3. (*informal*) to try to attain. **chase** *n.* 1. chasing, pursuit. 2. hunting, especially as a sport. 3. a steeplechase. □**give chase,** to begin to pursue.

chase² *v.* (**chased, chas·ing**) to engrave or emboss (metal).

chas·er (chay-sĕr) *n.* 1. a horse for steeplechasing. 2. (*informal*) a drink taken after a drink of another kind, as beer (**beer chaser**) after whiskey.

chasm (kaz-ĕm) *n.* a deep opening or gap, especially in earth or rock.

chas·sis (shas-ee, chas-ee) *n.* (*pl.* **chas·sis,** *pr.* shas-eez, chas-eez) a frame, especially of a vehicle, on which other parts are mounted.

chaste (chayst) *adj.* (**chast·er, chast·est**) 1. virgin, celibate. 2. not having sexual intercourse except with the person to whom one is married. 3. simple in style, not ornate. **chaste′ly** *adv.* **chaste′ness** *n.*

chas·ten (chay-sĕn) *v.* 1. to discipline, to punish by inflicting suffering. 2. to subdue the pride of. **chas′ten·er** *n.*

chas·tise (chas-tɪz) *v.* (**chas·tised, chas·tis·ing**) to punish severely, especially by beating. **chas·tise′ment** *n.*

chas·ti·ty (chas-ti-tee) *n.* 1. being chaste, virginity, celibacy. 2. simplicity of style.

chas·u·ble (chaz-yŭ-bĕl) *n.* a loose garment worn over all other vestments by a priest celebrating Mass or Eucharist.

chat (chat) *n.* a friendly informal conversation. **chat** *v.* (**chat·ted, chat·ting**) to have a chat.

châ·teau (sha-toh) *n.* (*pl.* **-teaus, -teaux,** *pr.* -tohz) a castle or large country house in France.

chat·e·laine (shat-ĕ-layn) *n.* the mistress of a large house.

chat·tel (chat-ĕl) *n.* a movable possession (as opposed to a house or land).

chat·ter (chat-ĕr) *v.* 1. to talk or converse quickly and continually about unimportant matters. 2. to make sounds like this, as some birds and animals do. 3. to make a repeated clicking or rattling sound. **chatter** *n.* 1. chattering talk. 2. a chattering sound. **chat′ter·er** *n.* **chat·ter·box** (chat-ĕr-boks) *n.* a talkative person. **chat·ty** (chat-ee) *adj.* (**-ti·er, -ti·est**) 1. fond of chatting. 2. resembling chat, *a chatty letter.* **chat′ti·ly** *adv.* **chat′ti·ness** *n.*

chauf·feur (shoh-fur) *n.* a person employed to drive a car. **chauffeur** *v.* to drive as chauffeur.

chau·vin·ism (shoh-vĭ-niz-ĕm) *n.* exaggerated patriotism. **chau′vin·ist** *n.* **chau·vin·is·tic** (shoh-vĭ-nis-tik) *adj.* **chau·vin·is′ti·cal·ly** *adv.* □**male chauvinism,** some men's prejudiced belief in their superiority over women.

Ch.E. *abbr.* chemical engineer.

cheap (cheep) *adj.* 1. low in price, worth more than it cost; *cheap money,* available at a low rate of interest. 2. charging low prices, offering good value. 3. poor in quality, of low value. 4. showy but worthless, silly. **cheap** *adv.* cheaply, *we got it cheap.* **cheap′ly** *adv.* **cheap′ness** *n.*

cheap·en (chee-pĕn) *v.* to make or become cheap.

cheap·skate (cheep-skayt) *n.* (*informal*) a stingy person.

cheat (cheet) *v.* 1. to act dishonestly or unfairly in order to win some profit or advantage. 2. to trick, to deceive, to deprive by deceit. **cheat** *n.* 1. a person who cheats, an unfair player. 2. a deception. **cheat′er** *n.*

cheat·ers (cheet-ĕrz) *n.* (*slang*) eyeglasses.

check¹ (chek) *v.* 1. to stop or slow the motion of suddenly, to restrain. 2. to make a sudden stop. 3. to threaten (an opponent's king) at chess. 4. to test or examine in order to make sure that something is correct or in good condition; *check the items off,* mark them when you find they are correct. 5. to correspond when compared. 6. to deposit (a coat etc.) in a checkroom. 7. to receive (such an item) for safekeeping. **check** *n.* 1. a stopping or slowing of motion, a pause. 2. a loss of the scent in hunting. 3. exposure of a chess king to possible capture. 4. a restraint. 5. a control to secure accuracy. 6. a test or examination to check that something is correct or in good working order. 7. a receipt for something handed over. 8. a bill in a restaurant. 9. a written order to a bank to pay out money from an account. □**checks and balances,** a series of limitations placed on various branches of government to prevent any one from usurping the powers invested in another. **check in,** to register on arrival (at an airport, hotel, etc.). **checking account,** a bank account for drawing checks against deposits. **check on** *or* **out** *or* **up on,** to examine or investigate the correctness of. **check out,** to pay one's hotel bill in preparation for departure; to investigate. **check valve,** a valve that allows a flow in one direction only. **keep in check,** to keep under control.

check² *n.* a pattern of squares like a chessboard, or of crossing lines.

check·book (chek-buuk) *n.* a book of printed checks.

checked (chekt) *adj.* patterned in crossing lines

that form small squares, *a checked fabric.*
check·er[1] (chek-ĕr) *v.* 1. to mark with squares, especially of alternate colors. 2. to break the uniformity of, to variegate.
checker[2] *n.* 1. one who checks (items, people, etc.). 2. a playing piece in checkers.
check·er·board (chek-ĕr-bohrd) *n.* a board with sixty-four squares of two alternating colors for playing checkers.
check·ered (chek-ĕrd) *adj.* 1. marked or patterned like a checkerboard. 2. undergoing varied fortunes, *a checkered career.*
check·ers (chek-ĕrz) *n.* a game played by two persons on a checkerboard with twenty-four pieces.
check·list (chek-list) *n.* a complete list of items, used for checking.
check·mate (chek-mayt) *n.* 1. a situation in chess in which the capture of a king cannot be prevented. 2. a complete defeat. **checkmate** *v.* (**check·mat·ed, check·mat·ing**) 1. to put into checkmate in chess. 2. to defeat finally, to foil.
check·off (chek-awf) *n.* payment of union dues by withholding their amount from employees' paychecks.
check·out (chek-owt) *n.* checking out. □**checkout counter**, a place where goods are paid for in a supermarket.
check·point (chek-point) *n.* a place where documents, vehicles, etc. are checked or inspected.
check·room (chek-room) *n.* a room in a restaurant etc. where coats, hats, etc. are checked for safekeeping.
check·up (chek-up) *n.* a thorough examination, medical or other.
Ched·dar (ched-ăr) *n.* a firm cheese of a kind originally made at Cheddar, England.
cheek (cheek) *n.* 1. either side of the face below the eye. 2. *(slang)* a buttock. 3. *(informal)* impudent speech, outspoken arrogance. □**cheek by jowl,** close together, in close association.
cheek·bone (cheek-bohn) *n.* the bone just below the eye.
cheek·y (chee-kee) *adj.* (**cheek·i·er, cheek·i·est**) 1. *(informal)* showing outspoken lack of respect. 2. coquettish. **cheek'i·ly** *adv.* **cheek'i·ness** *n.*
cheep (cheep) *n.* a weak shrill cry like that made by a young bird. **cheep** *v.* to make such a cry.
cheer (cheer) *n.* 1. a shout of encouragement or applause, *give three cheers.* 2. cheerfulness. **cheer** *v.* 1. to utter a cheer, to encourage or applaud with cheers. 2. to comfort, to gladden. □**cheer up,** to make or become more cheerful.
cheer·ful (cheer-fŭl) *adj.* 1. happy, contented, in good spirits. 2. pleasantly bright, *cheerful colors.* **cheer'ful·ly** *adv.* **cheer'ful·ness** *n.*
cheer·i·o (cheer-i-oh) *interj.* (British informal) goodby.
cheer·lead·er (cheer-lee-dĕr) *n.* a person who leads organized cheering.
cheer·less (cheer-lis) *adj.* gloomy, dreary. **cheer'less·ly** *adv.* **cheer'less·ness** *n.*
cheer·y (cheer-ee) *adj.* (**cheer·i·er, cheer·i·est**) showing good spirits. **cheer'i·ly** *adv.* **cheer'i·ness** *n.*
cheese (cheez) *n.* 1. a food made from milk curds. 2. a shaped mass of this. □**cheese it, the cops,** *(slang)* let's get out of here, the police are coming.
cheese·burg·er (cheez-bur-gĕr) *n.* a hamburger with cheese on it.
cheese·cake (cheez-kayk) *n.* 1. a cake made with

cream cheese or cottage cheese. 2. *(slang)* a picture displaying a woman's shapely body.
cheese·cloth (cheez-klawth) *n.* thin loosely woven cotton fabric.
chees·y (chee-zee) *adj.* (**chees·i·er, chees·i·est**) 1. of or like cheese. 2. *(slang)* of inferior quality.
chee·tah (chee-tă) *n.* a kind of leopard that can be trained to hunt deer.
chef (shef) *n.* a professional cook, the chief cook in a restaurant etc.
chef-d'oeu·vre (shay-duuv-rĕ) *n.* (*pl.* **chefs-d'oeu·vre,** *pr.* shay-duuv-rĕ) a masterpiece.
che·la (kee-lă) *n.* 1. (in Buddhism) a novice qualifying for initiation. 2. the pupil of a guru.
chem. *abbr.* 1. chemical. 2. chemist. 3. chemistry.
chem·i·cal (kem-i-kăl) *adj.* 1. of chemistry. 2. produced by chemistry. **chemical** *n.* a substance obtained by or used in a chemical process. **chem'i·cal·ly** *adv.* □**chemical engineering,** engineering concerned with processes that involve chemical change and with the equipment needed for these. **chemical warfare,** warfare employing chemical substances other than explosives.
che·mise (shĕ-meez) *n.* 1. a loose-fitting undergarment formerly worn by women, hanging straight from the shoulders. 2. a dress of similar shape.
chem·ist (kem-ist) *n.* 1. a scientist skilled in chemistry. 2. (chiefly *British*) a person or firm dealing in medicinal drugs.
chem·is·try (kem-i-stree) *n.* (*pl.* **-tries**) 1. the scientific study of substances and their elements and of how they react when combined or in contact with one another. 2. chemical structure, properties, and reactions.
che·mo·ster·il·ant (kee-mŏ-ster-ĭ-lănt) *n.* a chemical that produces sterility, especially in insects, without causing a change in mating habits.
che·mo·ther·a·py (kee-mŏ-ther-ă-pee) *n.* treatment of disease, especially cancer, using chemical substances. **che·mo·ther·a·peu·tic** (kee-mŏ-ther-ă-pyoo-tik) *adj.* **che·mo·ther·a·peu'ti·cal** *adj.*
chem·ur·gy (kem-ur-jee) *n.* chemical and industrial use of organic raw materials. **chem·ur·gic** (ke-mur-jik) *adj.*
che·nille (shĕ-neel) *n.* a fabric with a long velvety pile, used for curtains, bedspreads, etc.
cher·ish (cher-ish) *v.* 1. to look after lovingly. 2. to be fond of. 3. to keep in one's heart, *we cherish hopes of his return.*
Cher·o·kee (cher-ŏ-kee) *n.* (*pl.* **-kees, -kee**) a member of an Iroquoian-speaking tribe of North American Indians.
che·root (shĕ-root) *n.* a cigar with both ends open. 2. *(slang)* a cheap cigar.
cher·ry (cher-ee) *n.* (*pl.* **-ries**) 1. a small soft round fruit with a stone. 2. a tree producing this or grown for its ornamental flowers. 3. the wood of this tree. 4. deep red. **cherry** *adj.* deep red. □**cherry bomb,** a round firecracker. **cherry brandy,** a liqueur of brandy in which cherries have been steeped. **cherry picker,** a crane used to hold men working high above the ground.
cher·ry·stone (cher-ee-stohn) *n.* 1. a small variety of clam. 2. the seed of a cherry.
chert (churt) *n.* a flintlike form of quartz. **chert'y** *adj.*
cher·ub (cher-ŭb) *n.* (*pl.* especially for definition 1 **cher·u·bim,** *pr.* cher-ŭ-bim, **cher·ubs**) 1. one of the angelic beings usually grouped with the

seraphim. 2. a representation (in art) of a chubby infant with wings. 3. an angelic child.
che·ru·bic (chĕ-roo-bik) *adj.* like a cherub, with a plump innocent face.
cher·vil (chur-vil) *n.* an herb used for flavoring.
chess (ches) *n.* a game played by two persons on a chessboard with thirty-two chessmen. □**chess piece**, a chessman.
chess·board (ches-bohrd) *n.* a board with sixty-four squares of two alternating colors for playing chess.
chess·man (ches-măn) *n.* (*pl.* **-men**, *pr.* -měn) one of the pieces used in playing chess.
chest (chest) *n.* 1. a large strong box for storing or shipping things in. 2. the upper front surface of the body, the part containing the heart and lungs. **chest'ed** *adj.* □**chest of drawers**, a piece of furniture with drawers for storing clothes etc. **get it off one's chest**, *(informal)* to reveal what one is anxious about.
ches·ter·field (ches-tĕr-feeld) *n.* a man's single-breasted topcoat with a velvet collar.
chest·nut (ches-nut) *n.* 1. a tree with hard brown nuts, those of the Spanish or sweet chestnut being edible. 2. the wood of this tree. 3. its nut. 4. deep reddish brown. 5. a horse of reddish-brown or yellowish-brown color. 6. an old joke or story. **chestnut** *adj.* deep reddish brown or (of horses) yellowish brown.
chest·y (ches-tee) *adj.* (**chest·i·er, chest·i·est**) 1. of the chest, *a chesty cough*. 2. *(informal)* having a large chest. **chest'i·ness** *n.*
chev·a·lier (shev-ă-leer) *n.* a member of certain orders of knighthood or other groups.
chev·i·ot (shev-i-ŏt) *n.* 1. a sheep of a breed with short thick wool originally raised in Cheviot Hills, on the border between England and Scotland. 2. a fabric made from its wool.
chev·ron (shev-rŏn) *n.* a bent line or stripe or bar, especially one worn on the sleeve to show rank.
chew (choo) *v.* to work or grind between the teeth, to make this movement. **chew** *n.* 1. the act of chewing. 2. something for chewing. **chew'er** *n.* **chew'a·ble** *adj.* □**chewing gum**, a sticky substance sweetened and flavored for prolonged chewing. **chew over**, *(informal)* to think over. **chew the fat** *or* **rag**, *(slang)* to chat.
chew·y (choo-ee) *adj.* (**chew·i·er, chew·i·est**) 1. suitable for chewing. 2. needing to be chewed, not soft.
Chey·enne (shı-en) *n.* (*pl.* **-ennes, -enne**) 1. a member of a tribe of North American Indians formerly of central Minnesota and North and South Dakota, now mainly in Montana and Oklahoma. 2. the capital of Wyoming.
chg. *abbr.* 1. change. 2. charge.
chi (kı) *n.* the twenty-second letter of the Greek alphabet (X χ).
Chi·an·ti (ki-ahn-tee) *n.* a dry Italian wine, usually red.
chi·a·ro·scu·ro (ki-ahr-ŏ-skoor-oh) *n.* (*pl.* **-ros**) treatment of light and shade in painting, especially when strongly contrasted.
chic (sheek) *adj.* stylish and elegant. **chic** *n.* stylishness and elegance.
chi·can·er·y (shi-kay-nĕ-ree) *n.* (*pl.* **-er·ies**) trickery used to gain an advantage.
Chi·ca·no (chi-kah-noh) *n.* (*pl.* **-nos**) a Mexican-American.
chi·chi (shee-shee) *adj. (informal)* 1. fussily ornamented, showy. 2. (of manner) affected.

chick (chik) *n.* 1. a young bird before or after hatching. 2. *(slang)* a young woman.
chick·a·dee (chik-ă-dee) *n.* any of small gray North American titmice.
Chick·a·saw (chik-ă-saw) *n.* (*pl.* **-saws, -saw**) a member of a tribe of Indians, formerly in Mississippi and Alabama, now in Oklahoma.
chick·en (chik-ĕn) *n.* 1. a young bird, especially of the domestic fowl. 2. the flesh of domestic fowl as food. 3. *(slang)* a game testing courage, *to play chicken.* **chicken** *adj. (slang)* afraid to do something, cowardly. **chicken** *v. (slang)* to chicken out. □**be no chicken**, *(slang)* to be no longer young. **chicken colonel**, *(slang)* a colonel, not a lieutenant colonel. **chicken feed**, food for poultry; *(informal)* something that is of little value; a petty sum of money. **chicken hawk**, any of various types of hawks said to prey on poultry. **chicken out**, *(slang)* to withdraw through cowardice. **chicken pox**, a disease, especially of children, with red spots on the skin. **chicken wire**, light wire netting with hexagonal mesh.
chick·en-heart·ed (chik-ĕn hahr-tid) *adj.* cowardly.
chick·en-liv·ered (chik-ĕn liv-ĕrd) *adj.* cowardly.
chick·pea (chik-pee) *n.* a dwarf pea with yellow seeds.
chick·weed (chik-weed) *n.* a weed with small white flowers.
chic·le (chik-ĕl) *n.* the milky juice of a tropical American tree, the main ingredient of chewing gum.
chic·o·ry (chik-ŏ-ree) *n.* (*pl.* **-ries**) a blue-flowered plant cultivated for its salad leaves and for its root, which is roasted, ground, and used with or instead of coffee.
chide (chıd) *v.* (**chid·ed** or **chid, chid·den, chid·ding**) *(old use)* to scold.
chief (cheef) *n.* 1. a leader or ruler. 2. a person with the highest authority. **chief** *adj.* 1. highest in rank or authority. 2. most important. **chief'ly** *adv.* □**Chief Executive**, the President of the U.S. **chief executive officer**, usually the president of a large corporation. **chief justice**, the judge presiding over a court with several judges, especially the Supreme Court. **chief of staff**, the senior officer in command of a general staff. **chief of state**, the formal head of a nation. **chief petty officer**, a noncommissioned naval officer above petty officer first class and below senior petty officer. **chief warrant officer**, a noncommissioned army officer above warrant officer and below second lieutenant.
chief·tain (cheef-tin) *n.* the chief of a tribe, clan, or other group.
chif·fon (shi-fon) *n.* 1. a thin almost transparent fabric of silk or nylon etc. 2. a very light textured pudding or pie made with beaten egg white, *lemon chiffon.*
chig·ger (chig-ĕr) *n.* the larva of a parasitic mite that causes severe itching.
chi·gnon (sheen-yon) *n.* a knot or roll of long hair, worn at the back of the head by women.
Chi·hua·hua (chi-wah-wah) *n.* a very small smooth-haired dog of a breed that originated in Mexico.
chil·blain (chil-blayn) *n.* a painful swelling on the hand, foot, or ear, caused by exposure to cold and by poor circulation.
child (chıld) *n.* (*pl.* **chil·dren**, *pr.* **chil**-drĕn) 1. a young human being below the age of puberty, a

boy or girl. 2. a son or daughter. □**child abuse,** mistreatment of a child either by beating or neglect. **children of Israel,** the Jewish people. **child's play,** something very easy to do. **with child,** (old use) pregnant.

child·bear·ing (chɪld-bair-ing) n. pregnancy and childbirth.

child·birth (chɪld-burth) n. the process of giving birth to a child.

child·hood (chɪld-huud) n. the condition or period of being a child.

child·ish (chɪl-dish) adj. like a child, unsuitable for a grown person. (▷Do not confuse *childish* with *childlike;* the word *childish* is often applied contemptuously, whereas *childlike* is not.) **child′ish·ly** adv. **child′ish·ness** n.

child·less (chɪld-lis) adj. having no children. **child′less·ness** n.

child·like (chɪld-lɪk) adj. having the good qualities of a child, simple and innocent. ▷See the note under *childish.*

Chil·e (chil-ee) a country in South America. **Chil′e·an** adj. & n.

chil·i, chil·e, chil·li (chil-ee) n. (pl. **chil·ies, chil·es, chil·lies**) the dried pod of capsicum, acrid and pungent, used to make cayenne pepper. □**chili con carne** (chil-ee kon kahr-nee), a Mexican stew of chili-flavored minced beef. **chili sauce,** a sauce made from tomatoes with chili and other spices.

chill (chil) n. 1. unpleasant coldness. 2. an illness with feverish shivering. 3. a feeling of discouragement. **chill** adj. chilly. **chill** v. 1. to make or become unpleasantly cold. 2. to preserve at a low temperature without freezing, *chilled desserts.*

chill·er (chil-ĕr) n. a frightening mystery story.

chil·ly (chil-ee) adj. (**chill·i·er, chill·i·est**) 1. rather cold, unpleasantly cold. 2. cold and unfriendly in manner. **chil′li·ness** n.

chime (chɪm) n. a tuned set of bells, a series of notes sounded by these. **chime** v. (**chimed, chim·ing**) 1. (of bells) to ring. 2. (of a clock) to show the hour by chiming. □**chime in,** to insert a remark when others are talking. **chime in with,** to agree or correspond with.

chi·me·ra (ki-meer-ă) n. (pl. **-ras**) 1. a grotesque monster. 2. a thing of mixed character or fanciful origin.

chim·ney (chim-nee) n. (pl. **-neys**) a structure carrying off smoke or gases from a fire. □**chimney corner,** a warm seat within an old-fashioned fireplace. **chimney piece,** a mantel or decoration over a fireplace. **chimney pot,** a pipe fitted to the top of a chimney. **chimney swallow, chimney swift,** a type of swift that occasionally nests in a chimney. **chimney sweep,** a person whose trade is to remove soot from inside chimneys.

chimp (chimp) n. (informal) a chimpanzee.

chim·pan·zee (chim-pan-zee) n. an African ape, smaller than a gorilla.

chin (chin) n. the front of the lower jaw. **chin** v. (**chinned, chin·ning**) (informal) to chat. □**chin whiskers,** a beard. **keep one's chin up,** to remain cheerful.

Chin. abbr. 1. China. 2. Chinese.

chi·na (chɪ-nă) n. 1. fine earthenware, porcelain. 2. articles made of this, *household china.*

Chi·na (chɪ-nă) a country in Asia.

Chi·na·man (chɪ-nă-măn) n. (pl. **-men,** pr. -mĕn) (informal) a Chinese man. (▷This word is consid-

ered offensive.) □**Chinaman's chance,** (slang) a very small chance or none at all.

Chi·na·town (chɪ-nă-town) n. a section of a city outside China in which the Chinese live as a group.

chinch (chinch) **bug** a type of insect that feeds on grains.

chin·chil·la (chin-chil-ă) n. 1. a small squirrellike South American animal. 2. its soft gray fur. 3. a heavy nubby woolen cloth.

chine (chɪn) n. an animal's backbone, a cut of meat containing part of this. **chine** v. (**chined, chin·ing**) to cut along and separate the backbone in (a cut of meat).

Chi·nese (chɪ-neez) adj. of China or its people or language. **Chinese** n. (pl. **Chinese**) 1. a native of China, a person of Chinese descent. 2. the language of China. □**Chinese checkers,** a game in which marbles are moved from hole to hole across a board. **Chinese lantern,** a collapsible paper lantern; a plant with an orange calyx resembling this.

chink¹ (chingk) n. a narrow opening or slit. **chink** v. to fill in chinks in a log cabin wall etc.

chink² n. a sound like glasses or coins being struck together. **chink** v. to make or cause to make this sound.

chi·no (chee-noh) n. (pl. **-nos**) 1. cotton twill cloth, usually khaki colored. 2. *chinos,* trousers made of chino.

Chi·nook (shi-nuuk) n. (pl. **-nooks, -nook**) 1. a member of a North American Indian tribe. 2. a warm moist wind blowing from the sea on the coasts of Washington and Oregon. 3. a warm dry wind from the Rocky Mountains. □**Chinook jargon,** a mixture of English, French, and Indian words, formerly used by traders and Indians from Oregon to Alaska.

chintz (chints) n. a cotton cloth with a printed pattern, usually glazed, used for curtains etc.

chintz·y (chint-see) adj. (**chintz·i·er, chintz·i·est**) (informal) cheap, gaudy.

chi·o·no·dox·a (kɪ-ŏ-nŏ-dok-să) n. a blue-flowered plant blooming in early spring.

chip (chip) n. 1. a thin piece cut or broken off something hard. 2. a fried shaving of potato. 3. wood split into strips for making baskets, a basket made of such strips. 4. a place from which a chip has been broken. 5. a counter used to represent money, especially in gambling. 6. a microchip. **chip** v. (**chipped, chip·ping**) to cut or break at the surface or edge, to shape or carve by doing this. □**a chip off the old block,** a child who is very like its father. **a chip on one's shoulder,** a feeling of bitterness or resentment. **chip in,** (informal) to interrupt with a remark when someone is speaking; to contribute money. **chipped beef,** dried beef that has been shredded or made into very small pieces. **chip shot,** a short slightly lofted golf stroke. **hand or cash in one's chips,** (slang) to die. **when the chips are down,** when matters reach the point of decision.

chip·board (chip-bohrd) n. thin material made of compressed wood chips and resin.

chip·munk (chip-mungk) n. a small striped squirrellike animal of North America.

Chip·pen·dale (chip-ĕn-dayl) n. an 18th-century style of English furniture, named after its designer.

chip·per (chip-ĕr) adj. lively.

Chip·pe·wa (chip-ĕ-wah) n. (pl. **-was, -wa**) a

member of the Ojibwa tribe of North America.

chi·rog·ra·phy (kɪ-rog-ră-fee) *n.* handwriting.

chi·rog′ra·pher *n.* **chi·ro·graph·ic** (kɪ-rŏ-graf-ik) *adj.* **chi·ro·graph′i·cal** *adj.*

chi·rop·o·dist (kɪ-rop-ŏ-dist) *n.* an expert in chiropody.

chi·rop·o·dy (kɪ-rop-ŏ-dee) *n.* the treatment of ailments of the feet.

chi·ro·prac·tic (kɪ-rŏ-prak-tik) *n.* manipulation of the spine and joints as a method of treating disease.

chi·ro·prac·tor (kɪ-rŏ-prak-tŏr) *n.* a practitioner of chiropractic.

chirp (churp) *n.* the short sharp note made by a small bird or a grasshopper. **chirp** *v.* to make this sound.

chir·rup (chir-ŭp) *n.* a series of chirps. **chirrup** *v.* **(chir·ruped, chir·rup·ing)** to make this sound.

chis·el (chiz-ĕl) *n.* a tool with a beveled edge for shaping wood, stone, or metal. **chisel** *v.* **(chis·eled, chis·el·ing)** 1. to cut or shape with a chisel. 2. *(slang)* to treat unfairly, to swindle. **chis′el·er** *n.*

chit[1] (chit) *n.* a young child, a small young woman, *only a chit of a girl.*

chit[2] *n.* 1. a short written note. 2. a note containing an order or statement of money owed.

chit·chat (chit-chat) *n.* chat, gossip.

chi·tin (kɪ-tin) *n.* an organic substance forming a part of the exoskeleton of arthropods. **chi′tin·ous** *adj.*

chit·ter·lings, chit·lings, chit·lins (chit-linz) *n. pl.* the small intestines of a pig, cooked as food.

chi·val·ric (shiv-ăl-rik) *adj.* 1. of or as of the ideal knight, gallant, courteous, honorable. 2. of or pertaining to chivalry.

chiv·al·ry (shiv-ăl-ree) *n.* courtesy and considerate behavior, especially toward weaker persons. **chiv′al·rous** *adj.* **chiv′al·rous·ly** *adv.* **chiv′al·rous·ness** *n.*

chive (chɪv) *n.* a small herb with onion-flavored leaves.

chlo·ral (klohr-ăl) **hydrate** a white powder used as an anesthetic and to induce sleep.

chlor·dane (klohr-dayn), **chlor·dan** (klohr-dan) *n.* a liquid insecticide.

chlo·ride (klohr-ɪd) *n.* a compound of chlorine and one other element.

chlo·rin·ate (klohr-ɪ-nayt) *v.* **(chlo·rin·at·ed, chlo·rin·at·ing)** to treat or sterilize with chlorine. **chlo′ri·na·tor** *n.* **chlo·ri·na·tion** (klohr-i-nay-shŏn) *n.*

chlo·rine (klohr-een) *n.* a chemical element used in sterilizing water and in industry.

chlo·ro·form (klohr-ŏ-form) *n.* a liquid that gives off vapor that causes unconsciousness when breathed. **chloroform** *v.* to make unconscious by this.

chlo·ro·phyll, chlo·ro·phyl (klohr-ŏ-fil) *n.* the green coloring matter in plants.

chm. *abbr.* chairman.

choc. *abbr.* chocolate.

chock (chok) *n.* a block or wedge used to prevent something from moving. **chock** *v.* to wedge with a chock or chocks.

chock·a·block (chok-ă-blok) *adj. & adv.* crammed or crowded together.

chock-full (chok-fuul) *adj.* stuffed, crammed.

choc·o·late (chaw-kŏ-lit) *n.* 1. a powder or solid block made from roasted cacao seeds. 2. a drink made with this. 3. a candy made of or covered with this. 4. dark brown color.

Choc·taw (chok-taw) *n.* (*pl.* **-taws, -taw**) 1. a member of a tribe of Indians formerly living in Mississippi and Alabama, now chiefly in Oklahoma. 2. the language of this tribe.

choice (chois) *n.* 1. choosing, the right of choosing; *I have no choice,* no alternative. 2. a variety from which to choose, *a wide choice of holidays.* 3. a person or thing chosen, *this is my choice.* **choice** *adj.* **(choic·er, choic·est)** of the best quality, *choice bananas.*

choir (kwɪr) *n.* 1. an organized band of singers, especially leading the singing in church. 2. the part of the church where these sit. □**choir loft,** the raised part of a church occupied by the choir.

choir·boy (kwɪr-boi) *n.* a boy who sings in a church choir.

choir·mas·ter (kwɪr-mas-tĕr) *n.* the director or trainer of a choir.

choke (chohk) *v.* **(choked, chok·ing)** 1. to cause to stop breathing by squeezing or blocking the windpipe or (of smoke etc.) by being unfit to breathe. 2. to be unable to breathe from such causes. 3. to make or become speechless from emotion. 4. to clog, to smother, *the garden is choked with weeds.* **choke** *n.* 1. choking, a choking sound. 2. a valve controlling the flow of air into a gasoline engine. □**choke off,** to silence or discourage, usually by snubbing. **choke up,** *(informal)* to become speechless because of emotion, to perform badly because of fear etc.

chok·er (choh-kĕr) *n.* 1. a high stiff collar, a clerical collar. 2. a close-fitting necklace.

chol·er (kol-ĕr) *n.* 1. one of the four cardinal humors, bile. 2. *(old use)* anger.

chol·er·a (kol-ĕ-ră) *n.* an infectious and often fatal disease causing severe diarrhea.

chol·er·ic (kol-ĕ-rik) *adj.* easily angered, often angry.

cho·les·ter·ol (kŏ-les-tĕ-rohl) *n.* a fatty substance found in animal tissues, thought to cause hardening of the arteries.

chomp (chomp) *v.* *(informal)* to chew, to bite.

chon·drite (kon-drɪt) *n.* a meteorite containing granules.

chon·drule (kon-drool) *n.* a granule of olivine found in a chondrite.

choose (chooz) *v.* **(chose, cho·sen, choos·ing)** 1. to select out of a greater number of things. 2. to decide, to prefer, to desire; *there is nothing to choose between them,* they are about equal. **choos′er** *n.*

choos·y, choos·ey (choo-zee) *adj.* **(choos·i·er, choos·i·est)** *(informal)* careful and cautious in choosing, hard to please.

chop (chop) *v.* **(chopped, chop·ping)** 1. to cut by a blow with an ax or knife. 2. to hit with a short downward stroke or blow. **chop** *n.* 1. a cutting stroke, especially with an ax. 2. a chopping blow. 3. a thick slice of meat, usually including a rib. □**chop up,** to chop into small pieces.

chop·house (chop-hows) *n.* (*pl.* **-hous·es,** *pr.* -how-ziz) a restaurant specializing in chops or steaks.

chop·per (chop-ĕr) *n.* 1. a chopping tool, a short ax. 2. *(slang)* a helicopter.

chop·py (chop-ee) *adj.* **(-pi·er, -pi·est)** 1. full of

short broken waves. 2. jerky, not smooth.
chop'pi·ly *adv.* **chop'pi·ness** *n.*
chops (chops) *n. pl.* the jaws of an animal.
chop·stick (chop-stik) *n.* one of a pair of sticks
used in China etc. to lift food to the mouth.
chop su·ey (chop soo-ee) a Chinese-American
dish of small pieces of meat fried with rice and
vegetables.
cho·ral (kohr-ăl) *adj.* written for a choir or chorus,
sung or spoken by these. **cho'ral·ly** *adv.*
☐**choral society,** a society for singing choral
music.
cho·rale (kŏ-ral) *n.* a choral composition, using
the words of a hymn.
chord¹ (kord) *n.* a combination of notes sounded
together in harmony.
chord² *n.* a straight line joining two points on a
curve.
chore (chohr) *n.* a routine task, a tedious task.
cho·re·a (kŏ-ree-ă) *n.* St. Vitus's dance (*see* **saint**).
cho·re·o·graph (kohr-i-ŏ-graf) *v.* to arrange the
dancing in a ballet, musical comedy, etc. **chor·
e·og·ra·pher** (kohr-i-og-ră-fĕr) *n.*
cho·re·og·ra·phy (kohr-i-og-ră-fee) *n.* the composition of ballets or stage dances. **cho·re·o·
graph·ic** (kohr-i-ŏ-graf-ik) *adj.* **cho·re·o·
graph'i·cal·ly** *adv.*
chor·is·ter (kor-i-stĕr) *n.* a member of a choir.
chor·tle (chor-tĕl) *n.* a loud gleeful chuckle.
chortle *v.* (**chor·tled, chor·tling**) to utter a
chortle.
cho·rus (kohr-ŭs) *n.* (*pl.* **-rus·es**) 1. a group of
singers. 2. a piece of music for these. 3. something
spoken or sung by many people together, *a chorus
of approval.* 4. the refrain or main part of a song.
5. a group of singing dancers in a musical comedy,
the chorus line. **chorus** *v.* (**cho·rused, cho·
rus·ing**) to sing or speak or say in chorus.
☐**chorus girl,** a female member of a chorus in
a musical comedy etc. **in chorus,** speaking or
singing all together.
chose (chohz), **cho·sen** (choh-zĕn) *see* **choose.**
chow¹ (chow) *n.* a long-haired dog of a Chinese
breed.
chow² *n.* (*informal*) food. ☐**chow line,** (*informal*)
a line of people waiting to be served food.
chow·chow (chow-chow) *n.* a relish of chopped
vegetables pickled in mustard.
chow·der (chow-dĕr) *n.* a thick soup of clams or
fish and vegetables, usually in a milk base.
chow mein (chow mayn) a Chinese-American
dish of fried noodles with shredded meat and
vegetables.
Christ (krıst) the title of Jesus (= "the anointed
one"), now treated as a name. **Christ'like** *adj.*
chris·ten (kris-ĕn) *v.* 1. to admit to the Christian
Church by baptism. 2. to give a name or nickname
to.
Chris·ten·dom (kris-ĕn-dŏm) *n.* all Christians,
Christian countries.
chris·ten·ing (kris-ĕ-ning) *n.* the ceremony of bap-
tizing or naming.
Chris·tian (kris-chăn) *adj.* 1. of the doctrines of
Christianity, believing in or based on these. 2.
of Christians. 3. showing the qualitites of a Christian, kindly, humane. **Christian** *n.* a person who
believes in Christianity. ☐**Christian Era,** time
reckoned from the birth of Christ. **Christian
name,** a name given at a christening, a person's
given name. **Christian Science,** a religious system claiming that health and healing can be

achieved through the mental effect of true Christian faith, without medical treatment. **Christian
Scientist,** one who believes in this system.
Chris·ti·an·i·ty (kris-chi-an-i-tee) *n.* 1. the reli-
gion based on the belief that Christ was the incar-
nate Son of God, and on his teachings. 2. being
a Christian.
Chris·tian·ize (kris-chă-nız) *v.* (**Chris·tian·
ized, Chris·tian·iz·ing**) to make or to become
Christian.
Chris·tie (kris-tee) *n.* (*pl.* **-ties**) (formerly
Christiania) a turn in skiing with skis parallel,
used for stopping short.
Christ·mas (kris-măs) *n.* the Christian festival (celebrated on December 25) commemorating
Christ's birth, the period about this time.
☐**Christmas Club,** a bank account for which
money is deposited regularly over a year's time,
the total amount being returned to the depositor
in time for Christmas. **Christmas Day,** December 25. **Christmas Eve,** December 24.
Christmas tree, an evergreen (or artificial) tree
decorated at Christmas.
Christ·mas·sy (kris-măs-ee) *adj.* looking festive,
typical of Christmas.
Christ·mas·tide (kris-măs-tıd) *n.* the Christmas
season.
chro·mat·ic (kroh-mat-ik) *adj.* of color, in colors.
chro·mat'i·cism *n.* ☐**chromatic scale,** (in
music) a scale that ascends or descends by semitones.
chro·ma·tog·ra·phy (kroh-mă-tog-ră-fee) *n.* (in
chemistry) separation of mixed substances by slow
passage through or over adsorbing material.
chro·ma·to·graph·ic (kroh-mă-tŏ-graf-ik)
chro·ma·to·graph'i·cal·ly *adv.*
chrome (krohm) *n.* 1. chromium or a chromium
alloy, used especially as plating. 2. yellow coloring
matter obtained from a compound of chromium,
chrome yellow.
chro·mi·um (kroh-mi-ŭm) *n.* a chemical element,
a hard metal used in making stainless steel and
for plating other metals, *chromium-plated.*
chro·mo (kroh-moh) *n.* (*pl.* **-mos**) a picture
printed in color by lithography.
chro·mo·some (kroh-mŏ-sohm) *n.* one of the tiny
threadlike structures in animal and plant cells,
carrying genes. **chro·mo·som·al** (kroh-mŏ-soh-
măl) *adj.*
chro·mo·sphere (kroh-mŏ-sfeer) *n.* the red gaseous envelope around a star. **chro·mo·spher·
ic** (kroh-mŏ-sfer-ik) *adj.*
chron. *abbr.* 1. chronological. 2. chronology.
chron·ic (kron-ik) *adj.* 1. (of a disease) affecting
a person for a long time. 2. having had an illness
or a habit for a long time, *a chronic invalid.*
chron'i·cal·ly *adv.*
chron·i·cle (kron-i-kĕl) *n.* 1. a record of events
in the order of their happening. 2. *Chronicles,*
two historical books of the Old Testament.
chronicle *v.* (**chron·i·cled, chron·i·cling**) to
record in a chronicle. **chron'i·cler** *n.*
chron·o·graph (kron-ŏ-graf) *n.* an instrument
that records time accurately. **chron·o·graph·
ic** (kron-ŏ-graf-ik) *adj.* **chro·nog·ra·phy** (krŏ-
nog-ră-fee) *n.*
chron·o·log·i·cal (kron-ŏ-loj-i-kăl) *adj.* arranged
in the order in which things occurred. **chron·
o·log'i·cal·ly** *adv.*
chro·nol·o·gy (krŏ-nol-ŏ-jee) *n.* (*pl.* **-gies**) the
arrangement of events in the order in which they

occurred, as in history or geology. **chro·nol'o·gist** *n.*

chro·nom·e·ter (krŏ-nom-i-tĕr) *n.* a time-measuring instrument with a special mechanism for keeping exact time.

chrys·a·lis (kris-ă-lis) *n.* (*pl.* **chrys·a·lis·es, chry·sal·i·des,** *pr.* kri-sal-i-deez) the stage in an insect's life when it forms a sheath inside which it changes from a grub to an adult insect, especially a butterfly or moth.

chry·san·the·mum (kri-san-thĕ-mŭm) *n.* a garden plant with bright flowers, blooming in autumn.

chub (chub) *n.* (*pl.* **chub, chubs**) a thick-bodied river fish.

chub·by (chub-ee) *adj.* (**-bi·er, -bi·est**) round and plump. **chub'bi·ness** *n.*

chuck¹ (chuk) *v.* *(informal)* 1. to throw carelessly or casually. 2. to give up, to resign. 3. to touch playfully under the chin. **chuck** *n.* a playful touch. □**chuck out,** *(informal)* to throw away; to expel (a troublesome person).

chuck² *n.* 1. the part of a lathe that grips the drill, the part of a drill that holds the bit. 2. a cut of beef including the neck and shoulder blade, *chuck steak.*

chuck³ *n.* *(slang)* food. □**chuck wagon,** a wagon equipped for cooking and serving meals to workers at a ranch, lumber camp, etc.

chuck·hole (chuk-hohl) *n.* a hole in a road.

chuck·le (chuk-ĕl) *n.* a quiet or half-suppressed laugh. **chuckle** *v.* (**chuck·led, chuck·ling**) to give a chuckle.

chug (chug) *v.* (**chugged, chug·ging**) to make a dull short repeated sound, like an engine running slowly. **chug** *n.* this sound.

chuk·ka (chuk-ă) *n.* (also **chukka boot**) an ankle-high leather boot, originally worn for polo.

chuk·ker (chuk-ĕr) *n.* a period of play in polo.

chum¹ (chum) *n.* *(informal)* a close friend. **chum** *v.* (**chummed, chum·ming**) to form a close friendship.

chum² *n.* chopped or ground bait dropped into a fishing ground to attract fish. **chum** *v.* (**chummed, chum·ming**) to fish with such bait.

chum·my (chum-ee) *adj.* (**-mi·er, -mi·est**) very friendly. **chum'mi·ly** *adv.* **chum'mi·ness** *n.*

chump (chump) *n.* 1. a heavy block of wood. 2. *(slang)* a foolish person.

chunk (chungk) *n.* 1. a thick piece of something. 2. a substantial amount.

chunk·y (chung-kee) *adj.* (**chunk·i·er, chunk·i·est**) 1. short and thick. 2. in chunks, containing chunks.

church (church) *n.* 1. a building for public Christian worship. 2. a religious service in this, *see you after church.* 3. *the Church,* the whole body of Christian believers, a particular group of these, *the Protestant Episcopal Church;* the clergy, the clerical profession; *he went into the Church,* became a clergyman.* □**Church of England,** the episcopal church of England, rejecting the pope's supremacy. **Church of Jesus Christ of Latter-day Saints,** the official name of the Mormon Church.

church·less (church-lis) *adj.* not associated with or not belonging to a church.

church·man (church-măn) *n.* (*pl.* **-men,** *pr.* mĕn) 1. a clergyman. 2. a member of a church.

church·war·den (church-wor-dĕn) *n.* a representative of a parish in certain churches who helps with the business of the church.

church·wom·an (church-wuum-ăn) *n.* (*pl.* **wom·en,** *pr.* -wim-in) a female member of a church or of the clergy.

church·yard (church-yahrd) *n.* the enclosed land around a church, often used for burials.

churl (churl) *n.* 1. a rude boorish person. 2. a peasant.

churl·ish (chur-lĭsh) *adj.* 1. ill-mannered or rude. 2. in a peasantlike fashion. **churl'ish·ly** *adv.* **churl'ish·ness** *n.*

churn (churn) *n.* 1. a machine in which milk is beaten to make butter. 2. a large can in which milk is carried from a farm. **churn** *v.* 1. to beat (milk) or make (butter) in a churn. 2. to stir or swirl violently; *the tank churned up the field,* broke up its surface. 3. to produce in quantity without regard for quality.

chute (shoot) *n.* 1. a sloping or vertical channel down which things can slide or be dropped. 2. *(informal)* a parachute.

chut·ney (chut-nee) *n.* a highly seasoned relish of fruit, vinegar, spices, etc.

chutz·pah (huut-spă) *n.* shameless audacity. ▷Yiddish.

C.I. *abbr.* cost and insurance.

CIA, C.I.A. *abbr.* Central Intelligence Agency.

Cia. *abbr.* (Spanish *Compañia*) Company.

ciao (chow) *interj.* *(informal)* 1. goodby. 2. hello.

ci·ca·da (si-kay-dă) *n.* (*pl.* **-das, -dae,** *pr.* -dee) a grasshopper-like insect that makes a shrill chirping sound.

cic·a·trix (sik-ă-triks) *n.* (*pl.* **cic·a·tri·ces,** *pr.* sik-ă-trī-seez) the scar left by a healed wound.

ci·ce·ro·ne (sis-ĕ-roh-nee) *n.* (*pl.* **-nes, -ni,** *pr.* -nee) a guide who understands and explains antiquities etc.

C.I.D. *abbr.* Criminal Investigation Department (of Scotland Yard).

ci·der (sI-dĕr) *n.* a drink made from apples that may be either fermented (**hard cider**) or unfermented (**sweet cider**).

Cie. *abbr.* (French *Compagnie*) Company.

ci·gar (si-gahr) *n.* a roll of tobacco leaves for smoking. □**cigar store,** a store in which tobacco, cigars, and smoking accessories are sold.

cig·a·rette (sig-ă-ret) *n.* a roll of cut tobacco or other substance enclosed in thin paper for smoking. □**cigarette paper,** thin white paper used to make cigarettes.

cig·a·ril·lo (sig-ă-ril-oh) *n.* (*pl.* **-los**) 1. a small cigar. 2. a cigarette made from cut tobacco wrapped in tobacco leaf rather than paper.

cil·i·um (sil-i-ŭm) *n.* (*pl.* **cil·i·a,** *pr.* sil-i-ă) 1. an eyelash, a delicate hair resembling that on a leaf, insect's wing, etc. 2. a hairlike vibrating organ used as an aid to movement by many lower animals living in water.

C. in C. *abbr.* Commander in Chief.

cinch (sinch) *n.* 1. a girth for a saddle or pack. 2. *(informal)* a certainty, an easy task. **cinch** *v.* 1. to fix a saddle securely. 2. to make secure, to make sure of.

cin·cho·na (sin-koh-nă) *n.* a South American tree or shrub with fragrant pink and white flowers.

cinc·ture (singk-chŭr) *n.* a girdle, belt, or border.

cin·der (sin-dĕr) *n.* 1. a small piece of partly burned coal or wood. 2. *cinders,* ashes. □**cinder block,** a concrete block made with cement and cinders. **cinder track,** a running track made with fire cinders.

Cin·der·el·la (sin-dĕ-rel-ă) *n.* a girl who achieves

sudden recognition or wealth. □**Cinderella story,** a story of sudden success, usually involving change from rags to riches.

cin·e·ma (sin-ĕ-mă) *n.* 1. a theater where motion pictures are shown. 2. films as an art form or an industry.

cin·e·ma·theque (sin-ĕ-mă-tek) *n.* a motion-picture theater where art or avant-garde films are shown.

cin·e·mat·o·graph·ic (sin-ĕ-mat-ŏ-graf-ik) *adj.* for taking or projecting motion pictures. **cin·e·mat·o·graph'i·cal·ly** *adv.*

cin·e·ma·tog·ra·phy (sin-ĕ-mă-tog-ră-fee) *n.* the art or technique of motion picture photography. **cin·e·ma·tog'ra·pher** *n.*

cin·é·ma vé·ri·té (sin-ĕ-mă ver-i-tay) a documentary style of film-making that uses realistic techniques. ▷French.

cin·e·rar·i·a (sin-ĕ-rair-i-ă) *n.* a plant with heart-shaped leaves and brightly colored flowers.

cin·e·rar·i·um (sin-ĕ-rair-i-ŭm) *n.* (*pl.* **-rar·i·a,** *pr.* -rair-i-ă) a place for holding a person's ashes after cremation. □**cinerary urn,** an urn for such ashes.

cin·na·bar (sin-ă-bahr) *n.* 1. a red form of mercuric sulfide that is used as a pigment. 2. vermilion.

cin·na·mon (sin-ă-mŏn) *n.* 1. spice made from the inner bark of a southeast Asian tree. 2. its color, yellowish brown. □**cinnamon toast,** buttered toast spread with cinnamon and sugar.

cinque·foil (singk-foil) *n.* a plant related to the rose family, having compound leaves of five leaflets each.

ci·pher (sɪ-fĕr) *n.* 1. the symbol 0, representing naught or zero. 2. any Arabic numeral. 3. a person or thing of no importance. 4. a set of letters or symbols used to represent others for secrecy, *it was written in cipher.* **cipher** *v.* 1. to write in cipher. 2. to solve by arithmetic.

circ. *abbr.* 1. circa. 2. circuit. 3. circulation. 4. circumference.

cir·ca (sur-kă) *prep.* about, *china from circa 1850.* ▷Latin.

cir·ca·di·an (sur-kay-di-ăn) *adj.* of physiological activity occurring approximately every twenty-four hours.

cir·cle (sur-kĕl) *n.* 1. a perfectly round plane figure. 2. the line enclosing it, every point on which is the same distance from the center. 3. something shaped like this, a ring. 4. curved rows of seats rising in tiers at a theater etc., above the lowest level. 5. a number of people bound together by similar interests, *in business circles.* **circle** *v.* (**cir·cled, cir·cling**) to move in a circle, to form a circle around. □**come full circle,** to pass through a series of events etc. and return to the starting point. **go around in circles,** to be fussily busy but making no progress.

cir·clet (sur-klit) *n.* a circular band worn as an ornament, especially around the head.

cir·cuit (sur-kit) *n.* 1. a line or route or distance around a place. 2. the journey of a judge within a particular district to hold court sessions, the district itself. 3. a scheduled sequence of events, *the American golf circuit, the lecture circuit.* 4. a closed path for an electric current. 5. an apparatus with conductors, vacuum tubes, etc. through which electric current passes. □**circuit breaker,** a device for interrupting an electric current. **cir·cuit court,** a court that meets at various places within one judicial district. **circuit riders,** (old

use) judges or ministers who made circuits through an area to hold trials, preach, etc.

cir·cu·i·tous (sŭr-kyoo-i-tŭs) *adj.* roundabout, indirect. **cir·cu'i·tous·ly** *adv.*

cir·cuit·ry (sur-ki-tree) *n.* (*pl.* **-ries**) circuits, the equipment forming these.

cir·cu·i·ty (sŭr-kyoo-i-tee) *n.* (*pl.* **-ties**) the quality of being circuitous.

cir·cu·lar (sur-kyŭ-lăr) *adj.* 1. shaped like a circle. 2. moving around a circle; *a circular tour,* one by a route that brings travelers back to the starting point. 3. (of reasoning) using as evidence for its conclusion the very thing that it is trying to prove. 4. addressed to a circle of people, *a circular letter.* **circular** *n.* a circular letter or advertising leaflet. □**circular saw,** a power saw having a toothed disk as cutting edge. **cir·cu·lar·i·ty** (sur-kyŭ-lar-i-tee) *n.*

cir·cu·lar·ize (sur-kyŭ-lă-rɪz) *v.* (**cir·cu·lar·ized, cir·cu·lar·iz·ing**) to send circulars to.

cir·cu·late (sur-kyŭ-layt) *v.* (**cir·cu·lat·ed, cir·cu·lat·ing**) 1. to go around continuously. 2. to pass from place to place. 3. to cause to move around, to send around, *we will circulate this letter.*

cir·cu·la·tion (sur-kyŭ-lay-shŏn) *n.* 1. circulating, being circulated. 2. the movement of blood through the body, pumped by the heart. 3. the number of copies sold or distributed, especially of a newspaper.

cir·cu·la·to·ry (sur-kyŭ-lă-tohr-ee) *adj.* of the circulation of blood. □**circulatory system,** the system, including organs and tissues, that circulated blood and lymph through the body.

cir·cum·am·bu·late (sur-kŭm-am-byŭ-layt) *v.* (**cir·cum·am·bu·lat·ed, cir·cum·am·bu·lat·ing**) to walk around or about. **cir·cum·am·bu·la·tion** (sur-kŭm-am-byŭ-lay-shŏn) *n.*

cir·cum·cise (sur-kŭm-sɪz) *v.* (**cir·cum·cised, cir·cum·siz·ing**) to cut off the foreskin of (a male person) as a religious rite or surgically. **cir·cum·ci·sion** (sur-kŭm-sizh-ŏn) *n.*

cir·cum·fer·ence (sŭr-kum-fĕ-rĕns) *n.* the boundary of a circle, the distance around this.

cir·cum·flex (sur-kŭm-fleks) *n.* a mark over a vowel, as over *e* in *fête.*

cir·cum·lo·cu·tion (sur-kŭm-loh-kyoo-shŏn) *n.* 1. use of many words where a few would do. 2. evasive talk.

cir·cum·lu·nar (sur-kŭm-loo-năr) *adj.* moving or situated around the moon.

cir·cum·nav·i·gate (sur-kŭm-nav-i-gayt) *v.* (**cir·cum·nav·i·gat·ed, cir·cum·nav·i·gat·ing**) to sail completely around. **cir·cum·nav·i·ga·tion** (sur-kŭm-nav-i-gay-shŏn) *n.*

cir·cum·scribe (sur-kŭm-skrɪb) *v.* (**cir·cum·scribed, cir·cum·scrib·ing**) 1. to draw a line around. 2. to mark the limits of, to restrict. **cir·cum·scrip·tion** (sur-kŭm-skrip-shŏn) *n.*

cir·cum·so·lar (sur-kŭm-soh-lăr) *adj.* situated near or moving around the sun.

cir·cum·spect (sur-kŭm-spekt) *adj.* cautious and watchful, wary. **cir·cum·spec·tion** (sur-kŭm-spek-shŏn) *n.*

cir·cum·stance (sur-kŭm-stans) *n.* 1. one of the conditions or facts connected with an event or person or action; *he was a victim of circumstances,* the conditions affecting him were beyond his control; *what are his circumstances?* what is his financial position?; *they live in reduced circumstances,* in poverty that contrasts with their former prosperity. 2. ceremony, *pomp and circumstance.* □in *or* **under the circumstances,** owing to or making allowances for them. **under no circumstances,** no matter what may happen.

cir·cum·stan·tial (sur-kŭm-stan-shăl) *adj.* 1. giving full details. 2. consisting of facts that strongly suggest something but do not provide direct proof, *circumstantial evidence.* **cir·cum·stan'tial·ly** *adv.*

cir·cum·vent (sur-kŭm-vent) *v.* to evade, to find a way around, *managed to circumvent the rules.* **cir·cum·ven·tion** (sur-kŭm-ven-shŏn) *n.*

cir·cus (sur-kŭs) *n.* (*pl.* **-cus·es**) 1. a traveling show with performing animals, acrobats, and clowns. 2. *(informal)* a scene of lively action; the people in such action. 3. *(informal)* a group of people performing in sports or a series of lectures etc., either together or in succession.

cirque (surk) *n.* a bowl-shaped hollow at the head of a valley or on a mountain slope.

cir·rho·sis (si-roh-sis) *n.* a chronic disease, especially of alcoholics, in which the liver hardens into many small projections. **cir·rhot·ic** (si-rot-ik) *adj.*

cir·ro·cu·mu·lus (sir-oh-kyoo-myŭ-lŭs) *n.* (*pl.* **-lus**) a cloud formed of small roundish fleecy clouds.

cir·ro·stra·tus (sir-oh-stray-tŭs) *n.* (*pl.* **-tus**) a thin high cloud of horizontal or inclined sheets.

cir·rus (sir-ŭs) *n.* (*pl.* **cir·rus**) a light wispy cloud, typically at great altitude.

cis·lu·nar (sis-loo-năr) *adj.* between Earth and the moon.

Cis·ter·cian (sis-tur-shăn) *n.* a member of a religious order that was founded as a branch of the Benedictines.

cis·tern (sis-tĕrn) *n.* a tank or other vessel for storing water.

cit. *abbr.* 1. citation. 2. cited. 3. citizen.

cit·a·del (sit-ă-del) *n.* a fortress overlooking a city.

ci·ta·tion (si-tay-shŏn) *n.* 1. a mention in an official dispatch, a recommendation for a decoration or honor. 2. an official summons, especially one to appear in court. 3. the act of citing or quoting, something cited or quoted.

cite (sīt) *v.* (**cit·ed, cit·ing**) to quote or mention as an example or to support an argument. ▷Do not confuse *cite* with *site.*

cit·i·fy (sit-i-fī) *v.* (**cit·i·fied, cit·i·fy·ing**) to make urban in behavior or appearance.

cit·i·zen (sit-i-zĕn) *n.* 1. an inhabitant of a city. 2. a person who has full rights in a country etc. by birth or by naturalization. **cit'i·zen·ship** *n.* □**citizen's band,** radio frequencies reserved by the federal government for communication between private citizens. **citizen's band radio,** a radio that operates at these frequencies.

cit·i·zen·ry (sit-i-zĕn-ree) *n.* (*pl.* **-ries**) the citizens of a nation or state as a group.

cit·ric (sit-rik) **acid** the acid in the juice of lemons, limes, etc.

cit·ron (sit-rŏn) *n.* 1. an oval fruit, larger, less acid, and thicker skinned than the lemon. 2. a tree bearing this fruit.

cit·ron·el·la (sit-rŏ-nel-ă) *n.* 1. a South Asian grass yielding a fragrant oil. 2. this oil, used in insect repellents and perfume.

cit·rus (sit-rŭs) *n.* (*pl.* **-rus·es**) any of a group of related trees including lemon, orange, and grapefruit; *citrus fruit,* fruit from such a tree.

cit·y (sit-ee) *n.* (*pl.* **cit·ies**) 1. a large and important

town. 2. *the City,* the oldest part of London, England, now a center of commerce and finance. □**city hall,** municipal offices; *you can't fight City Hall,* ordinarily people are powerless against a bureaucracy. **city manager,** an appointed official directing the administration of a city. **city state,** one of the small republics of ancient Greece; a small sovereign state consisting of an autonomous city and its dependencies.

civ. *abbr.* 1. civil. 2. civilian.

civ·et (siv-it) *n.* 1. a civet cat. 2. a musky substance obtained from its glands, used in making perfumes. □**civet cat,** a cat-like animal of Central Africa.

civ·ic (siv-ik) *adj.* of or proper to a city or town, of citizens or citizenship. □**civic center,** an area containing municipal offices and other public buildings.

civ·ics (siv-iks) *n.* the study of government and of the rights and duties of citizens.

civ·il (siv-il) *adj.* 1. belonging to citizens; *civil liberty,* liberty restricted only by those laws established for the good of the community. 2. of the general public, not the armed forces or organized religion; *civil aviation,* nonmilitary; *civil marriage,* with a civil ceremony not a religious one. 3. involving civil law not criminal law, *a civil dispute.* 4. polite and obliging. **civ'il·ly** *adv.* □**civil defense,** organized protection of the civil population against air raids or other hostile action. **civil disobedience,** refusal to obey laws, pay taxes, etc. as a means of influencing government. **civil engineering,** the designing and construction of roads, bridges, canals, etc. **civil law,** law dealing with the private rights of citizens, not with crime. **civil rights,** the rights, privileges, and protection given to citizens; *civil rights movement,* an organized movement to secure civil rights for blacks and other minorities in the U.S. **civil servant,** an employee of a government department other than the armed forces. **civil war,** war between groups of citizens of the same country.

ci·vil·ian (si-vil-yăn) *n.* a person not serving in the armed forces.

ci·vil·i·ty (si-vil-i-tee) *n.* (*pl.* **-ties**) politeness, an act of politeness.

civ·i·li·za·tion (siv-ĭ-li-zay-shŏn) *n.* 1. making or becoming civilized. 2. a stage in the evolution of organized society, a particular type of this, *ancient civilizations.* 3. civilized conditions or society, *spent months in the jungle, far from civilization.*

civ·i·lize (siv-ĭ-līz) *v.* (**civ·i·lized, civ·i·liz·ing**) 1. to cause to improve from a savage or primitive stage of human society to a more developed one. 2. to improve the behavior of.

civ·vies (siv-eez) *n. pl. (slang)* civilian clothes.

CJ *abbr.* Chief Justice.

ck. *abbr.* 1. cask. 2. check.

Cl *symbol* chlorine.

CL *abbr.* carload.

cl. *abbr.* centiliter(s).

clack (klak) *n.* 1. a short sharp sound like that made by plates struck together. 2. the noise of chatter. **clack** *v.* to make such a sound or noise.

clad¹ (klad) *v. see* **clothe. clad** *adj.* clothed, *warmly clad; iron-clad,* protected with iron, as though protected thus.

clad² *v.* (**clad, clad·ding**) to provide (metal etc.) with cladding.

clad·ding (klad-ing) *n.* a metal or other material

applied to the surface of another as a protective covering.

claim (klaym) v. 1. to demand as one's right or due; *the floods claimed many lives,* people died as a result. 2. to declare that something is true or has been achieved, to state without being able to prove. **claim** n. 1. a demand for something as one's right; *lay claim to (see* **lay**³). 2. the right to something, *a widow has a claim on her deceased husband's estate.* 3. a statement claiming that something is true, an assertion.

claim·ant (klay-mănt) n. a person who makes a claim, especially in law.

clair·voy·ance (klair-voi-ăns) n. the supposed power of seeing in the mind either future events or things that are happening or existing out of sight.

clair·voy·ant (klair-voi-ănt) n. a person said to have clairvoyance. **clairvoyant** adj.

clam (klam) n. a shellfish with a hinged shell. **clam** v. **(clammed, clam·ming)** to fish for clams. □**clam up,** *(slang)* to refuse to talk.

clam·bake (klam-bayk) n. 1. a party held outdoors at which clams and other shellfish are eaten. 2. a large noisy party.

clam·ber (klam-běr) v. to climb with some difficulty.

clam·my (klam-ee) adj. **(-mi·er, -mi·est)** unpleasantly moist and sticky. **clam'mi·ness** n.

clam·or (klam-ör) n. 1. a loud confused noise especially of shouting. 2. a loud protest or demand. **clamor** v. to make a loud protest or demand. **clam'or·ous** adj.

clamp (klamp) n. a device for holding things tightly, often with a screw. **clamp** v. to grip with a clamp, to fix firmly. □**clamp down on,** to become stricter about, to put a stop to.

clam·shell (klam-shel) n. 1. the shell of a clam. 2. a bucket for dredging.

clan (klan) n. 1. a group with a common ancestor, *the Scottish clans.* 2. a large family forming a close group.

clan·des·tine (klan-des-tin) adj. kept secret, done secretly. **clan·des'tine·ly** adv.

clang (klang) n. a loud ringing sound. **clang** v. to make a clang.

clang·or (klang-ör) n. a clanging noise.

clank (klangk) n. a metallic sound like that of metal striking metal. **clank** v. to make a clank.

clan·nish (klan-ish) adj. showing clan feeling, clinging together and excluding others. **clan'nish·ness** n.

clap (klap) n. 1. the sharp noise of thunder. 2. the sound of the palms of the hands being struck together, especially in applause. 3. a friendly slap, *gave him a clap on the shoulder.* **clap** v. **(clapped, clap·ping)** 1. to strike the palms loudly together, especially in applause. 2. to flap (wings) audibly. 3. to put or place quickly, *clapped him into jail.* □**clap eyes on,** *(informal)* to catch sight of.

clap·board (klab-örd) n. a long narrow board with one edge thicker than the other, used to form the outside walls of houses.

clap·per (klap-ěr) n. the tongue or striker of a bell.

clap·trap (klap-trap) n. talk or ideas used only to win applause.

claque (klak) n. 1. people hired to applaud at a theater. 2. a group of fawning admirers.

clar·et (klar-it) n. a dry red wine.

clar·i·fy (klar-ĭ-fı) v. **(clar·i·fied, clar·i·fy·ing)** 1. to make or become clear or easier to understand. 2. to remove impurities from (fats), as by

heating. **clar·i·fi·ca·tion** (klar-ĭ-fi-kay-shŏn) n.

clar·i·net (klar-ĭ-net) n. a woodwind instrument with finger holes and keys.

clar·i·net·ist (klar-ĭ-net-ist) n. a person who plays the clarinet.

clar·i·on (klar-i-ŏn) adj. loud, clear, and rousing, *a clarion call.*

clar·i·ty (klar-i-tee) n. clearness.

clash (klash) v. 1. to strike making a loud harsh sound like that of cymbals. 2. to conflict, to disagree. 3. to take place at the same time as something else. 4. (of colors) to produce an unpleasant visual effect by not being harmonious. **clash** n. 1. a sound of clashing. 2. a conflict, a disagreement. 3. a clashing of colors.

clasp (klasp) n. 1. a device for fastening things, with interlocking parts. 2. a grasp, a handshake. **clasp** v. 1. to fasten, to join with a clasp. 2. to grasp, to hold or embrace closely.

class (klas) n. 1. people or animals or things with some characteristics in common. 2. people of the same social or economic level, *the working class.* 3. a set of students taught together, a session when these are taught. 4. a division according to quality, *first class; tourist class.* 5. distinction, high quality, *a tennis player with class.* **class** v. to place in a class, to classify. □**class action,** a lawsuit undertaken on behalf of a group of individuals. **class consciousness,** the feeling of belonging to a particular social or economic class. **class struggle,** competition for economic and political power between classes of people, as between capitalists and workers. **in a class by itself,** much superior to everything else of its kind.

clas·sic (klas-ik) adj. 1. having a high quality that is recognized and unquestioned, *Hardy's classic novel.* 2. very typical, *a classic case of malnutrition.* 3. having qualities like those of classical art, simple and harmonious; *classic clothes,* plain and conventional in style. 4. famous through being long established; *the classic races,* the Kentucky Derby, the Wanamaker Mile, etc. **classic** n. 1. a classic author or work etc., *"David Copperfield" is a classic.* 2. a garment in classic style. 3. a classic sporting event. ▷Note the various definitions of *classic* and compare them with the definitions of *classical.*

clas·si·cal (klas-i-kăl) adj. 1. model or first class, especially in literature. 2. of ancient Greek and Roman art, literature, and culture; *a classical scholar,* an expert in these. 3. simple and harmonious in style. 4. traditional and standard in style, *classical music.* **clas'si·cal·ly** adv. ▷Do not confuse *classical* with *classic.*

clas·si·cism (klas-i-siz-ĕm) n. 1. classical style. 2. classical scholarship. **clas'si·cist** n. a classical scholar.

clas·sics (klas-iks) n. works of ancient Greek and Roman literature, study of these works.

clas·si·fi·a·ble (klas-i-fı-ă-běl) adj. able to be classified.

clas·si·fied (klas-i-fıd) adj. 1. (of advertisements) arranged according to subject matter. 2. (of information) designated as officially secret and available only to specified people. □**classifieds,** *(informal)* classified advertisements.

clas·si·fy (klas-i-fı) v. **(clas·si·fied, clas·si·fy·ing)** to arrange systematically in classes or groups, to put into a particular class. **clas·si·fi·ca·tion** (klas-i-fi-kay-shŏn) n.

class·less (klas-lis) adj. without distinctions of social class.

class·mate (klas-mayt) *n.* a present or past member of the same class (as in school).
class·room (klas-room) *n.* a room where a class of students is taught.
class·y (klas-ee) *adj.* (**class·i·er, class·i·est**) *(informal)* stylish, superior.
clas·tic (klas-tik) *adj.* composed of broken pieces of older rock. **clastic** *n.* rock of this type.
clat·ter (klat-ĕr) *n.* 1. a sound like that of plates rattled together. 2. noisy talk. **clatter** *v.* to make or cause to make a clatter.
clause (klawz) *n.* 1. a single part in a treaty, law, or contract. 2. a part of a compound or complex sentence, with its own verb and subject.
claus·tro·pho·bi·a (klaws-trŏ-foh-bi-ă) *n.* abnormal fear of being in an enclosed space. **claus·tro·pho′bic** *adj.* suffering from or causing claustrophobia.
clav·i·chord (klav-ĭ-kord) *n.* a musical instrument resembling an upright piano.
clav·i·cle (klav-i-kĕl) *n.* the collarbone.
clav·ier, klav·ier (klă-veer) *n.* an early musical instrument resembling a piano.
claw (klaw) *n.* 1. the pointed nail on an animal's or bird's foot, a foot with such nails. 2. the pincers of a shellfish, *a lobster claw.* 3. a device like a claw, used for grappling and holding. **claw** *v.* to grasp or scratch or pull with a claw or with the hands. □**claw hammer,** a hammer with a head divided at one end for pulling out nails.
clay (klay) *n.* stiff, sticky earth that becomes hard when baked, used for making bricks and pottery. **clay′ey** *adj.* □**clay pigeon,** a breakable disk thrown up as a target for shooting.
clean (kleen) *adj.* 1. free from dirt or impurities, not soiled. 2. not yet used, *a clean page.* 3. (of a nuclear bomb) producing relatively little fallout. 4. with nothing dishonorable in it, (of a driver's license) with no violations. 5. attentive to cleanliness, with clean habits. 6. without projections or roughness, smooth and even. 7. keeping to the rules, not unfair, *a clean fighter.* 8. free from indecency; *keep it clean,* do not tell improper jokes. **clean** *adv.* completely, entirely, *I clean forgot; the thief got clean away,* escaped without a trace. **clean** *v.* 1. to make or become clean. 2. to dryclean. 3. to remove the innards of before cooking, to gut, *clean the fish.* **clean′ness** *n.* □**clean out,** to clean the inside of; *(slang)* to use up all the supplies or money of. **clean room,** any enclosed laboratory etc. where the air is kept free of all contaminants. **clean up,** to make clean, to tidy things or oneself; to rid of crime and corruption; *(informal)* to make a gain or profit. **make a clean breast of it,** to confess fully. **make a clean sweep,** *see* **sweep.**
clean-cut (kleen-kut) *adj.* sharply outlined, *clean-cut features.*
clean·er (klee-nĕr) *n.* 1. a device or substance used for cleaning things. 2. a person employed to clean rooms.
clean·ers (klee-nĕrz) *n. pl.* a dry cleaning establishment. □**take a person to the cleaners,** *(slang)* to rob or defraud him; to win all his money.
clean·ly (kleen-lee) *adv.* in a clean way. **cleanly** (klen-lee) *adj.* having clean habits. **clean·li·ness** (klen-li-nis) *n.*
cleanse (klenz) *v.* (**cleansed, cleans·ing**) to make thoroughly clean. □**cleansing cream,** a lotion for cleansing the skin.
cleans·er (klen-zĕr) *n.* a cleansing substance, especially one containing an abrasive.

clean-shav·en (kleen-shay-vĕn) *adj.* with beard, mustache, and whiskers shaved off.
clean·up (kleen-up) *n.* 1. the process of cleaning. 2. the process of ridding a community of crime and corruption. □**cleanup hitter** *or* **batter,** the fourth batter in a baseball batting order.
clear (kleer) *adj.* 1. transparent, *clear glass; clear water,* not muddy or cloudy; *clear soup,* not thickened. 2. free from blemishes, *a clear complexion.* 3. free from guilt, *a clear conscience.* 4. easily seen or heard or understood, distinct. 5. evident, *a clear case of cheating.* 6. free from doubt, not confused. 7. free from obstruction or from something undesirable. 8. net, without deductions, complete, *a clear profit.* **clear** *adv.* 1. clearly. 2. completely. 3. apart, not in contact, *stand clear!* **clear** *v.* 1. to make or become clear. 2. to free (one's throat) of phlegm or huskiness by a slight cough. 3. to get past or over, especially without touching. 4. to get approval or authorization for; *clear goods through customs,* satisfy official requirements there. 5. to pass (a check) through a clearinghouse. 6. to make as net gain or profit; *we cleared our expenses,* made enough money to cover these. **clear** *n.* a clear space. **clear′ly** *adv.* **clear′ness** *n.* □**clear away,** to remove; to remove used crockery etc. after a meal. **clear off,** to get rid of; *(slang)* to go away. **clear out,** to empty, to depart in haste. **clear the decks,** to clear away hindrances and prepare for action. **clear up,** to become better or brighter; *clear up the mystery,* solve it. **in the clear,** free of suspicion or difficulty.
clear·ance (kleer-ăns) *n.* 1. clearing. 2. authorization, permission. 3. the space left clear when one object moves within or past another. □**clearance papers,** official papers certifying that a ship may enter or leave a port. **clearance sale,** a sale at low prices to dispose of a store's merchandise.
clear-cut (kleer-kut) *adj.* 1. very distinct. 2. not open to doubt.
clear·head·ed (kleer-hed-id) *adj.* alert, perceptive, thinking clearly.
clear·ing (kleer-ing) *n.* an open space from which trees have been cleared in a forest.
clear·ing·house (kleer-ing-hows) *n.* 1. an office at which banks exchange checks and settle balances. 2. an agency that collects and distributes information etc.
cleat (kleet) *n.* 1. a short piece of wood or metal with projecting ends around which a rope may be fastened. 2. a strip or other projecting piece fixed to a gangway etc. or to footwear to prevent slipping. 3. a wedge.
cleav·age (klee-vij) *n.* 1. a split, a division made by cleaving. 2. the hollow between full breasts, exposed by a low-cut garment.
cleave[1] (kleev) *v.* (*see* ▷ *below*) 1. to divide by chopping, to split or become split. 2. to make a way through. ▷ The past tense may be either *he cleaved* or *he clove* or *he cleft,* or *he has cloven* or *he has cleft* or *he has cleaved.* The adjectives *cleft* and *cleft* are used of different objects (*see* **cleft** and **cloven**).
cleave[2] *v.* (**cleaved** or *old use* **clave, cleav·ing**) to stick fast.
cleav·er (klee-vĕr) *n.* a butcher's chopper.
clef (klef) *n.* a symbol on a stave in a musical score, showing the pitch of the notes (treble, bass, etc.).
cleft (kleft) *v. see* **cleave. cleft** *adj.* split, partly divided; *a cleft chin,* with a V-shaped hollow. **cleft**

n. a split, a cleavage. ☐**cleft palate,** a defect in the roof of the mouth where two sides of the palate failed to join before birth.

clem·a·tis (klem-ă-tis, kli-mah-tis) *n.* a climbing plant, usually with white or purplish flowers.

clem·en·cy (klem-ĕn-see) *n.* (*pl.* -cies) 1. mildness, especially of weather. 2. mercy. **clem·ent** (klem-ĕnt) *adj.*

clench (klench) *v.* 1. to close (the teeth or fingers) tightly. 2. to grasp tightly. 3. to clinch. **clench** *n.* a clenching action, a clenched state.

clere·sto·ry (kleer-stohr-ee) *n.* (*pl.* -ries) 1. an upper row of windows in a large church, above the level of the roofs of the aisles. 2. a similar row of windows placed high in other buildings.

cler·gy (klur-jee) *n.* (*pl.* -gies, -gy) the people who have been ordained as priests, ministers, rabbis, etc.

cler·gy·man (klur-ji-măn) *n.* (*pl.* -men, *pr.* -mĕn) a member of the clergy.

cler·ic (kler-ik) *n.* a clergyman.

cler·i·cal (kler-i-kăl) *adj.* 1. of clerks; *a clerical error,* one made in copying or writing something out. 2. of the clergy; *clerical collar,* an upright white collar fastening at the back, worn by some clergy.

cler·i·cal·ism (kler-i-kă-liz-ĕm) *n.* clerical rule or influence.

cler·i·hew (kler-i-hyoo) *n.* a short witty verse in four lines of unequal length, rhyming in couplets, the first line usually containing the name of a famous person. ▷From its inventor Edmund Clerihew Bentley, English writer (1875–1956).

clerk (klurk) *n.* 1. a person employed to keep records or accounts etc. in an office. 2. an official who keeps the records of a court or council etc. **clerk** *v.* ☐**clerk of the works,** the superintendent of a construction project.

Cleve·land (kleev-lănd), **Gro·ver** (1837–1908) the twenty-second and twenty-fourth president of the U.S. 1885–89, 1893–97.

clev·er (klev-ĕr) *adj.* 1. quick at learning and understanding things, skillful; *he was too clever for us,* he outwitted us. 2. showing skill, *a clever plan.* **clev′er·ly** *adv.* **clev′er·ness** *n.*

clev·is (klev-is) *n.* a U-shaped piece of metal with holes at the ends through which a bolt or pin is run.

clew = **clue.**

cli·ché (klee-shay) *n.* a hackneyed phrase or idea. **cli·chéd′** *adj.*

click (klik) *n.* a short sharp sound like that of billiard balls colliding. **click** *v.* 1. to make or cause to make a click, to fasten with a click. 2. *(slang)* to be a success, to become understood.

cli·ent (kli-ĕnt) *n.* 1. a person using the services of a lawyer or architect or a professional person other than a doctor, or of a business. 2. a customer.

cli·en·tele (kli-ĕn-tel) *n.* clients, customers.

cliff (klif) *n.* a steep rock face, especially on a coast.

cliff·hang·er (klif-hang-ĕr) *n.* a story or contest full of suspense. **cliff′hang·ing** *adj.* full of suspense.

cli·mac·ter·ic (kli-mak-tĕ-rik) *n.* the period of life when physical powers begin to decline. ▷Do not confuse *climactic* with *climatic.*

cli·mate (kli-mit) *n.* 1. the regular weather conditions of an area. 2. an area with certain weather conditions, *living in a hot climate.* 3. a general attitude or feeling, an atmosphere, *a climate of* hostility. **cli·mat·ic** (kli-mat-ik) *adj.* (▷Do not confuse *climatic* with *climactic.*) **cli·mat′i·cal·ly** *adv.* ☐**climate control,** air conditioning.

cli·ma·tol·o·gy (kli-mă-tol-ŏ-jee) *n.* the study of climates. **cli·ma·to·log·i·cal** (kli-mă-tŏ-loj-i-kăl) *adj.* **cli·ma·to·log′i·cal·ly** *adv.* **cli·ma·tol′o·gist** *n.*

cli·max (kli-maks) *n.* 1. the event or point of greatest interest or intensity. 2. sexual orgasm. **climax** *v.* to reach or bring to a climax.

climb (klim) *v.* 1. to go up or over by effort. 2. to move upward, to go higher, *the plane climbed rapidly.* 3. to grow up a support, *this rose climbs.* **climb** *n.* an ascent made by climbing. ☐**climb down,** to go downward by effort; to retreat from a position taken up in argument.

climb·a·ble (klim-ă-bĕl) *adj.* able to be climbed.

climb·er (kli-mĕr) *n.* 1. one who climbs, a mountaineer. 2. a climbing plant.

clime (klim) *n.* (*poetic*) 1. a region. 2. climate.

clinch (klinch) *v.* 1. to fasten (a nail or rivet) by hammering the point sideways after it is driven through. 2. (in boxing) to move too close together for a full-arm blow. 3. to settle conclusively, *clinched the deal.* **clinch** *n.* 1. a clinching position in boxing. 2. *(informal)* an embrace, *a slow fade-out on the clinch.*

clinch·er (klin-chĕr) *n.* *(informal)* a remark, argument, or fact that settles a matter.

cling (kling) *v.* (**clung, cling·ing**) 1. to hold on tightly. 2. to become attached, to stick. 3. to remain close or in contact, to be emotionally attached or dependent, *the brothers and sisters still cling together.* 4. to refuse to abandon, *clinging to hopes of rescue.*

cling·stone (kling-stohn) *n.* a kind of peach in which the stone is difficult to separate from the flesh.

clin·ic (klin-ik) *n.* 1. a place or session at which specialized treatment or advice is given to visiting persons, *prenatal clinic.* 2. a medical training session with hospital patients as subjects.

clin·i·cal (klin-i-kăl) *adj.* 1. of a clinic. 2. of or used in the treatment of patients, *clinical thermometer.* 3. of or based on observed signs and symptoms, *clinical medicine.* 4. looking bare and hygienic. 5. unemotional, cool and detached. **clin′i·cal·ly** *adv.*

cli·ni·cian (kli-nish-ăn) *n.* a physician who treats patients, as opposed to one who conducts research.

clink¹ (klingk) *n.* a thin sharp sound like glasses striking together. **clink** *v.* to make or cause to make this sound.

clink² *n.* *(slang)* prison, *in the clink.*

clink·er (kling-kĕr) *n.* 1. rough stony material left after coal has burned, a piece of this. 2. *(slang)* a bad mistake.

clink·er-built (kling-kĕr-bilt) *adj.* (of a boat) made with the outside planks or plates overlapping downward.

clip¹ (klip) *n.* 1. a device for holding things tightly or together, *a paper clip.* 2. a magazine for a firearm. 3. an ornament fastened by a clip. **clip** *v.* (**clipped, clip·ping**) to fix or fasten with a clip.

clip² *v.* (**clipped, clip·ping**) 1. to cut or trim with shears or scissors. 2. to punch a small piece from (a ticket) to show that it has been used. 3. *(informal)* to hit sharply, *clipped him on the ear.* **clip** *n.* 1. clipping. 2. the wool cut from a sheep or flock at one shearing. 3. an extract from a film.

4. *(informal)* a sharp blow. **5.** a rapid pace, *going at quite a clip.* ☐**clip joint,** *(slang)* a bar or restaurant charging outrageously high prices.

clip·board (klip-bohrd) *n.* a board with a spring clip for holding papers, etc.

clip-on (klip-on) *adj.* attached by a clip.

clip·per (klip-ĕr) *n.* (also **clipper ship**) a fast sailing ship.

clip·pers (klip-ĕrz) *n. pl.* an instrument for clipping hair, grass, etc.

clip·ping (klip-ing) *n.* a piece clipped off or out, an item cut from a newspaper.

clip·sheet (klip-sheet) *n.* a sheet of paper printed on one side, in order to facilitate reprinting, that is circulated by an organization.

clique (kleek) *n.* a small exclusive group. (▷Often mispronounced to rhyme with *chick.*) **cli·quish** (klee-kĭsh) *adj.*

cli·to·ris (klit-ŏ-ris) *n.* a small erectile part of the female genitals, at the upper end of the vulva. **clit'o·ral** *adj.*

cloak (klohk) *n.* **1.** a loose sleeveless outdoor garment. **2.** something that conceals, *under the cloak of darkness.* **cloak** *v.* to cover or conceal.

cloak-and-dag·ger (klohk-än-dag-ĕr) *adj.* involving dramatic adventures in spying.

cloak·room (klohk-room) *n.* **1.** a room where outdoor clothes and packages etc. may be left. **2.** a checkroom.

clob·ber (klob-ĕr) *v.* *(slang)* to hit repeatedly, to give a beating to, to defeat; *clobbering the taxpayers,* hurting them by heavy taxation.

cloche (klohsh) *n.* a woman's close-fitting bell-shaped hat.

clock[1] (klok) *n.* **1.** an instrument (other than a watch) for measuring and showing the time. **2.** any measuring device with a dial or displayed figures, as a taximeter, an odometer. **clock** *v.* **1.** to time (a race or competitor). **2.** *(informal)* to achieve as a speed, *he clocked ten seconds for the hundred meters.* ☐**clock in,** to register one's arrival for work. **clock out,** to register one's departure from work. **clock watcher,** a person who is constantly alert for the time when he may legitimately stop working.

clock[2] *n.* an ornamental pattern on the side of a stocking or sock.

clock·wise (klok-wɪz) *adj. & adv.* moving in a curve from left to right, as seen from the center of the circle.

clock·work (klok-wurk) *n.* a mechanism with wheels and springs, like that of a clock. ☐**like clockwork,** with perfect regularity and precision.

clod (klod) *n.* **1.** a lump of earth or clay. **2.** a stupid unimaginative person.

clod·hop·per (klod-hop-ĕr) *n.* **1.** a rustic, an unsophisticated person. **2.** *clodhoppers, (informal)* large heavy shoes.

clog (klog) *n.* a wooden-soled shoe. **clog** *v.* **(clogged, clog·ging)** to block, to become blocked.

cloi·son·né (kloi-zŏ-nay) *n.* enamelwork in which the colors of the pattern are separated by wires.

clois·ter (kloi-stĕr) *n.* **1.** a covered walk along the side of a church or other building, looking out on a courtyard. **2.** a monastery or convent, life in this. **cloister** *v.* to seclude in a monastery or convent.

clois·tered (kloi-stĕrd) *adj.* sheltered, secluded.

clone (klohn) *n.* **1.** a group of plants produced from one original stock or seedling. **2.** an organism asexually produced from and genetically identical with one ancestor. **clone** *v.* **(cloned, clon·ing)** to grow or propagate as a clone.

clop (klop) *n.* the sound of a horse's hoof striking a hard surface, a similar sound. **clop** *v.* **(clopped, clop·ping).** to make this sound.

close[1] (klohs) *adj.* **1.** near in space or time. **2.** near in relationship, *a close relative.* **3.** affectionate, *a close friend.* **4.** nearly alike, *a close resemblance.* **5.** in which the competitors are nearly equal, *a close contest.* **6.** dense, compact, with only slight intervals, *a close texture.* **7.** detailed, leaving no gaps or weaknesses, concentrated, *close study.* **8.** secretive. **9.** stingy. **10.** stuffy, humid, without fresh air. **close** *adv.* closely, in a near position, *they live close by.* **close'ly** *adv.* **close'ness** *n.* ☐**at close quarters,** very close together. **close call,** *(informal)* a narrow escape from death or danger; (in sports) an umpire's decision in a play that is difficult to decide. **close shave,** a narrow escape from an accident etc.

close[2] (klohz) *v.* **(closed, clos·ing)** **1.** to shut. **2.** to be or declare to be not open to the public. **3.** to bring or come to an end; *the closing days of the year,* the last ones. **4.** to bring or come closer or into contact; *close ranks,* agree after initial disagreement. **5.** to come within striking distance, to grapple. **close** *n.* a conclusion, an end. ☐**closed book,** a subject one has ceased considering. **closed-circuit television,** that transmitted by wires, not waves, to a restricted number of receivers. **close down,** to shut completely, to cease working. **closed season,** a period during which it is illegal to take certain specified game or fish. **closed shop,** the system whereby membership in a labor union is a condition of employment in a certain establishment. **close in,** to approach from all sides so as to shut in or entrap. **close out,** to discontinue, terminate, or dispose of (merchandise, a business, etc.). **close with,** to accept (an offer), to accept the offer made by (a person).

close·fist·ed (klohs-fis-tid) *adj.* niggardly, stingy.

close·fit·ting (klohs-fit-ing) *adj.* tightly fitting, clinging to the body.

close-knit (klohs-nit) *adj.* bound together.

close·mouthed (klohs-mowthd) *adj.* reticent or secretive.

close·out (klohz-owt) *n.* a sale of goods at low prices when going out of business or discontinuing certain kinds of merchandise.

clos·et (kloz-it) *n.* **1.** a small storage room or cabinet. **2.** *(old use)* any small room. **closet** *v.* **(clos·et·ed, clos·et·ing)** to shut off (people) in a room, as for a conference. **closet** *adj.* secret. ☐**closet homosexual,** one whose homosexuality is kept secret. **come out of the closet,** to acknowledge one's homosexuality publicly.

close-up (klohs-up) *n.* a photograph giving a detailed view of something.

clos·ing (kloh-zing) *n.* the concluding details of a sale of property.

clo·sure (kloh-zhŭr) *n.* **1.** the act or process of closing, a closed condition. **2.** cloture.

clot (klot) *n.* a small thickened mass formed from blood or other liquid. **clot** *v.* **(clot·ted, clot·ting)** to form clots. ☐**clotted cream,** cream thickened by being scalded.

cloth (klawth) *n.* **1.** woven or felted material. **2.** a piece of this for a special purpose, a dishcloth, tablecloth, etc. **3.** clerical clothes, the clergy, *respect for the cloth.*

clothe (klohth) *v.* **(clothed** or **clad, cloth·ing)**

to put clothes upon, to provide with clothes.
clothes (klohz, kloh*thz*) *n. pl.* things worn to cover the body and limbs.
clothes·horse (klohz-hors) *n.* 1. a frame with bars over which clothes etc. are hung to dry. 2. a person much concerned with dressing fashionably.
clothes·line (klohz-lın) *n.* a rope or wire on which washed clothes are hung to dry.
clothes·pin (klohz-pin) *n.* a forked peg or clip for fastening wash to a clothesline.
cloth·ier (kloh*th*-yĕr) *n.* a manufacturer or seller of men's clothes.
cloth·ing (kloh-*th*ing) *n.* clothes, garments.
clo·ture (kloh-chŭr) *n.* decision of a legislature to take a vote without further debate.
cloud (klowd) *n.* 1. a visible mass of condensed watery vapor, floating in the sky. 2. a mass of smoke or mist etc. 3. a mass of things moving in the air, *a cloud of insects.* 4. a state of gloom or trouble, *casting a cloud over the festivities.* **cloud** *v.* 1. to cover or darken with clouds or gloom or trouble. 2. to become overcast or indistinct or gloomy. □**on cloud nine,** *(informal)* extremely happy. **under a cloud,** out of favor, under suspicion, in disgrace. **with one's head in the clouds,** daydreaming.
cloud·burst (klowd-burst) *n.* a sudden violent rainstorm.
cloud·less (klowd-lis) *adj.* free from clouds.
cloud·y (klow-dee) *adj.* (**cloud·i·er, cloud· i·est**) 1. covered with clouds. 2. not transparent, *a cloudy liquid.* **cloud′i·ness** *n.*
clout (klowt) *n. (informal)* 1. a blow. 2. power of effective action, *trade unions with clout.* **clout** *v. (informal)* to hit.
clove¹ (klohv) *see* **cleave¹.**
clove² *n.* one of the small bulbs making up a compound bulb, *a clove of garlic.*
clove³ *n.* the dried unopened flower bud of tropical myrtle, used as a spice.
clove hitch a knot used to secure a rope around a spar or pole.
clo·ven (kloh-vĕn) *see* **cleave¹.** □**cloven hoof,** one that is divided, like those of oxen or sheep or goats.
clo·ver (kloh-vĕr) *n.* a plant with three-lobed leaves, used for fodder. □**in clover,** in ease and luxury.
clo·ver·leaf (kloh-vĕr-leef) *n.* an intersection of roads in a pattern resembling a four-leaf clover.
clown (klown) *n.* 1. a performer, especially in a circus, who does comical tricks and actions. 2. a person who is always behaving comically. **clown** *v.* to perform as a clown, to behave comically. **clown′ish** *adj.* **clown′ish·ly** *adv.* **clown′ish·ness** *n.*
cloy (kloi) *v.* to sicken by glutting with sweetness or pleasure, *cloy the appetite.*
cloy·ing (kloi-ing) *adj.* sickeningly sweet.
club (klub) *n.* 1. a heavy stick with one end thicker than the other, used as a weapon. 2. the headed stick used to hit the ball in golf. 3. a playing card of the suit *(clubs)* marked with black clover leaves. 4. a society of people who organize to provide themselves with sport or entertainment etc., their buildings or premises, *the tennis club.* 5. an organization offering members certain benefits, *a book club.* **club** *v.* (**clubbed, club·bing**) 1. to strike with a club. 2. to unite for a common purpose, *we clubbed together to buy a boat.* □**club car,** a railroad car outfitted like a club, with

chairs, tables, etc. and usually serving food. **club chair,** a low-backed chair with solid sides. **club sandwich,** a three-decker sandwich. **club soda,** soda water. **club steak,** a steak cut from the rib end of the short loin.
club·foot (klub-fuut) *n.* a deformed foot. **club′foot·ed** *adj.*
club·house (klub-hows) *n.* (*pl.* **-hous·es,** *pr.* -how-ziz) the premises used by a club.
club·man (klub-măn) *n.* (*pl.* **-men,** *pr.* -mĕn) a man who is a member of one or more fashionable clubs.
club·wom·an (klub-wuum-ăn) *n.* (*pl.* **-wom· en,** *pr.* -wim-in) a woman who is an active member of civic and social organizations.
cluck (kluk) *n.* 1. the throaty cry of a hen. 2. *(slang)* a stupid person. **cluck** *v.* to utter a cluck.
clue (kloo) *n.* 1. a fact or idea that gives a guide to the solution of a problem. 2. a word or phrase indicating what is to be inserted in a crossword or other word puzzle. **clue** *v.* (**clued, clu·ing**) to provide with a clue. □**clue in,** *(informal)* to inform.
clue·less (kloo-lis) *adj.* without a clue.
clump (klump) *n.* 1. a cluster or mass. 2. a clumping sound. **clump** *v.* 1. to form a clump, to arrange in a clump. 2. to walk with a heavy tread.
clum·sy (klum-zee) *adj.* (**-si·er, -si·est**) 1. heavy and ungraceful in movement or shape. 2. large and difficult to handle or use, *a clumsy instrument.* 3. done without tact or skill, *a clumsy apology.* **clum′si·ly** *adv.* **clum′si·ness** *n.*
clung (klung) *see* **cling.**
clunk (klungk) *n.* a dull sound like thick metal objects striking together. **clunk** *v.* to make this sound.
clus·ter (klus-tĕr) *n.* a small close group. **cluster** *v.* to bring or come together in a cluster. □**cluster zoning,** zoning practices that permit construction of buildings in clusters, with open space around these clusters.
clutch¹ (kluch) *v.* to grasp tightly; *clutch at,* to try to grasp. **clutch** *n.* 1. a tight grasp, a clutching movement. 2. a device for connecting and disconnecting certain working parts in machinery. 3. *(informal)* a critical moment, especially in sports. □**clutch hitter,** a baseball batter who usually makes a safe hit in a clutch. **get into a person's clutches,** to come into his possession or under his relentless control.
clutch² *n.* 1. a set of eggs for hatching. 2. the chickens hatched from these.
clut·ter (klut-ĕr) *n.* 1. things lying about untidily. 2. a crowded untidy state. **clutter** *v.* to fill with clutter, to crowd untidily.
Clydes·dale (klıdz-dayl) *n.* a horse of a heavily built breed used for pulling things.
cm *abbr.* centimeter(s).
Cm *symbol* curium.
Cmdr. *abbr.* Commander.
CMSgt *abbr.* Chief Master Sergeant.
CNO *abbr.* Chief of Naval Operations.
CNS, cns *abbr.* central nervous system.
Co *symbol* cobalt.
Co. *abbr.* 1. Company. 2. County.
CO *abbr.* Colorado.
c/o *abbr.* care of (*see* **care.**)
co- *prefix* together with, jointly, as in *coauthor, coexistence.*
C.O. *abbr.* 1. Commanding Officer. 2. conscientious objector.

coach (kohch) *n.* 1. a large four-wheeled horse-drawn carriage. 2. a railroad car. 3. (also **motor coach**) a bus. 4. an instructor in sports. 5. a teacher giving private specialized instruction, *a voice coach.* **coach** *v.* to train or teach.

coach·man (kohch-măn) *n.* (*pl.* **-men,** *pr.* -měn) a driver of a coach or carriage.

co·ad·ju·tor (koh-aj-ŭ-tŏr) *n.* a helper or assistant, especially one assisting a bishop.

co·ag·u·lant (koh-ag-yŭ-lănt) *n.* a coagulating agent.

co·ag·u·late (koh-ag-yŭ-layt) *v.* (**co·ag·u·lat·ed, co·ag·u·lat·ing**) to change from liquid to semisolid, to clot. **co·ag·u·la·tion** (koh-ag-yŭ-lay-shŏn) *n.*

co·ag·u·lum (koh-ag-yŭ-lŭm) *n.* (*pl.* **-la,** *pr.* -lă, **-lums**) a coagulated mass, a clot.

coal (kohl) *n.* 1. a hard black mineral used for burning to supply heat. 2. a piece of this, one that is burning, *a live coal.* **coal** *v.* to load a supply of coal into a ship. □**carry coals to Newcastle,** to take a thing to a place where it is already plentiful. **coal gas,** mixed gases extracted from coal and used for lighting and heating. **coal mine,** a mine where coal is dug. **coal oil,** kerosene. **coal tar,** tar produced when gas is made from coal. **drag over** *or* **rake over the coals,** to criticize sharply.

co·a·lesce (koh-ă-les) *v.* (**co·a·lesced, co·a·lesc·ing**) to combine and form one whole. **co·a·les'cence** *n.*

coal·field (kohl-feeld) *n.* an area in which coal occurs naturally.

co·a·li·tion (koh-ă-lish-ŏn) *n.* 1. union. 2. a temporary union between political parties. **co·a·li'tion·ist** *n.*

coarse (kohrs) *adj.* (**coars·er, coars·est**) 1. composed of large particles, rough or loose in texture. 2. rough or crude in manner or behavior, not refined; *coarse language,* improper, vulgar. 3. inferior, common. **coarse'ly** *adv.* **coarse'ness** *n.*

coars·en (kohr-sĕn) *v.* to make or become coarse.

coast (kohst) *n.* the seashore and the land near it, its outline. **coast** *v.* 1. to sail along a coast. 2. to ride down a hill or slope without using power. □**Coast Guard,** a branch of the U.S. Department of Transportation that helps regulate navigation and acts as a sea rescue force. **coast guardsman** (*pl.* **-men**), a member of the Coast Guard. **the coast is clear,** there is no chance of being seen or hindered.

coast·al (kohs-tăl) *adj.* of or near the coast.

coast·er (kohs-tĕr) *n.* 1. a ship that trades between ports on the same coast. 2. a tray for a wine bottle, a small dish or mat for a drinking glass. □**coaster brake,** a bicycle brake engaged by back-pedaling.

coast·line (kohst-lɪn) *n.* the shape or outline of a coast, *a rugged coastline.*

coat (koht) *n.* 1. an outdoor garment with sleeves. 2. an animal's hair or fur covering its body. 3. a covering layer, *a coat of paint.* **coat** *v.* to cover with a layer. □**coat of arms,** a design on a shield, used as an emblem by a family or a city or an institution.

co·a·ti (koh-ah-tee) *n.* (*pl.* **-tis**) a South American animal with a long slender snout and a ringed tail.

coat·ing (koh-ting) *n.* 1. a covering layer. 2. material for coats.

co·au·thor (koh-aw-thŏr) *n.* an author who writes books etc. with one or more other authors. **coauthor** *v.* to write in this manner.

coax (kohks) *v.* 1. to persuade gently or gradually. 2. to obtain in this way, *coaxed a smile from her.*

coax. *abbr.* coaxial.

co·ax·i·al (koh-ak-si-ăl) *adj.* having a common axis. **co·ax'i·al·ly** *adv.* □**coaxial cable,** an electrical transmission line in which there are two concentric conductors separated by insulation.

cob (kob) *n.* 1. a corncob. 2. a male swan. 3. a sturdy short-legged horse for riding.

co·balt (koh-bawlt) *n.* 1. a chemical element, a hard white metal used in many alloys, and with radioactive forms used in medicine and industry. 2. coloring matter made from this, its deep-blue color.

cob·ble[1] (kob-ĕl) *n.* a cobblestone. **cobble** *v.* (**cob·bled, cob·bling**) to pave with cobblestones.

cobble[2] *v.* (**cob·bled, cob·bling**) 1. to put together or mend roughly. 2. to mend shoes.

cob·bler (kob-lĕr) *n.* 1. a shoe repairer. 2. an iced drink of wine, sugar, and lemon. 3. a deep-dish fruit pie with a thick crust.

cob·ble·stone (kob-ĕl-stohn) *n.* a rounded stone used in paving.

COBOL (koh-bohl) *n.* a computer programing language. ▷ *Common Business Oriented Language.*

co·bra (koh-bră) *n.* a poisonous snake of India and Africa that can rear up.

cob·web (kob-web) *n.* the fine network spun by a spider, a strand of this.

co·caine (koh-kayn) *n.* a drug used as a local anesthetic or as a stimulant.

coc·cus (kok-ŭs) *n.* (*pl.* **coc·ci,** *pr.* kok-sɪ) a bacterium roughly spherical in shape.

coc·cyx (kok-siks) *n.* (*pl.* **-cy·ges,** *pr.* -si-jeez, **-cyx·es**) the small bone at the lower end of the spinal column in man and some apes.

coch·i·neal (koch-ĭ-neel) *n.* bright red coloring matter made from the dried bodies of certain insects.

co·chle·a (koh-kli-ă, kok-li-ă) *n.* (*pl.* **-le·ae,** *pr.* -li-ee, **-le·as**) a spiral cavity forming part of the inner ear in most mammals. **co'chle·ar** *adj.*

cock[1] (kok) *n.* 1. a male bird, especially of the domestic fowl. 2. a tap or spout for controlling the flow of a liquid. 3. a lever in a gun, raised ready to be released by the trigger; *at half cock,* only half ready for something. **cock** *v.* to tilt or turn upward; *the dog cocked his ears,* raised them attentively; *cock an eye,* to glance knowingly. 2. to raise the cock of (a gun) ready for firing, to set (the shutter of a camera) ready for release. □**cock of the walk,** the most influential person.

cock[2] *n.* a cone-shaped pile of straw or hay. **cock** *v.* to pile in cocks.

cock·ade (ko-kayd) *n.* a rosette of ribbon worn on a hat as a badge.

cock-a-doo·dle doo (kok-ă-doo-dĕl doo) *interj.* the sound of a cock crowing.

cock-a-leek·ie (kok-ă-lee-kee) *n.* a Scottish soup of cock boiled with leeks.

cock-and-bull (kok-ăn-buul) **story** a foolish story that one should not believe.

cock·a·too (kok-ă-too) *n.* (*pl.* **-toos**) a crested parrot.

cock·a·trice (kok-ă-tris) *n.* a mythical cock with

a serpent's tail whose glance was supposed to be deadly.

cock·chaf·er (kok-chay-fĕr) *n.* a large flying beetle.

cock·crow (kok-kroh) *n.* dawn, when cocks begin to crow.

cocked (kokt) **hat** a triangular hat worn with some uniforms. ☐**knock into a cocked hat,** to defeat utterly.

cock·er·el (kok-ĕ-rĕl) *n.* a young domestic cock.

cock·er (kok-ĕr) **spaniel** a small spaniel with a dense curly coat and long ears.

cock·eye (kok-ı) *n.* a squinting eye.

cock·eyed (kok-ıd) *adj.* 1. having a squinting eye. 2. *(slang)* crazy or foolish; drunk.

cock·fight (kok-fıt) *n.* a fight in which cocks are pitted against each other.

cock·le (kok-ĕl) *n.* an edible shellfish. ☐**warm the cockles of one's heart,** to make one rejoice.

Cock·ney (kok-nee) *n.* (*pl.* **-neys**) 1. a native of the East End of London. 2. the dialect or accent of this area. **cockney** *adj.* of Cockneys or Cockney.

cock·pit (kok-pit) *n.* 1. a place made for cockfighting. 2. the compartment for the pilot and crew of an aircraft. 3. the driver's seat in a racing car.

cock·roach (kok-rohch) *n.* a beetle-like insect that infests kitchens.

cocks·comb (koks-kohm) *n.* 1. a plant with red or purple flowers that resemble the comb of a rooster. 2. a coxcomb.

cock·sure (kok-shoor) *adj.* 1. quite convinced, very positive. 2. overly confident of oneself.

cock·tail (kok-tayl) *n.* 1. a mixed alcoholic drink. 2. an appetizer containing shellfish or fruit, *shrimp* or *grapefruit cocktail.* ☐**cocktail lounge,** a barroom. **cocktail party,** an early evening party at which liquor and tidbits are served. **fruit cocktail,** small pieces of fruit served as an appetizer.

cock·y (kok-ee) *adj.* (**cock·i·er, cock·i·est**) conceited and arrogant. **cock'i·ly** *adv.* **cock'i·ness** *n.*

co·co (kok-koh) *n.* (*pl.* **-cos**) the coconut palm or its fruit.

co·coa (koh-koh) *n.* 1. powder made from crushed cacao seeds. 2. a drink made from this. ☐**cocoa butter,** a fatty substance made from cacao seeds and used in cosmetics etc.

co·co·nut (koh-kŏ-nut) *n.* 1. the large hard-shelled seed of a tropical palm tree (the **coconut palm**) containing a milky juice. 2. its edible white lining. ☐**coconut matting,** matting made from the tough fiber of the coconut's outer husk. **coconut oil,** the oil or fat obtained from coconuts and used in cooking and in making soaps, candles, etc.

co·coon (kŏ-koon) *n.* 1. the silky sheath around a chrysalis. 2. a protective wrapping. **cocoon** *v.* to protect by wrapping completely.

cod (kod) *n.* (*pl.* **cod**) a large sea fish used as food. ☐**cod-liver oil,** oil obtained from cod livers, rich in vitamins A and D.

COD *abbr.* cash on delivery.

co·da (koh-dă) *n.* the concluding passage of a piece of music, after the main part.

cod·dle (kod-ĕl) *v.* (**cod·dled, cod·dling**) 1. to cherish and protect carefully. 2. to cook (eggs) in water just below boiling point.

code (kohd) *n.* 1. a set of laws or rules, *a code of practice for advertisers.* 2. a prearranged word or set of words representing a message, used for se-

crecy. 3. a system of symbols used to send messages etc. by machine, *the Morse code.* **code** *v.* (**cod·ed, cod·ing**) to put into code.

co·deine (koh-deen) *n.* a white substance made from opium, used to relieve pain or induce sleep.

co·dex (koh-deks) *n.* (*pl.* **-di·ces,** *pr.* -di-seez) a manuscript volume, especially of ancient writings.

cod·fish (kod-fish) *n.* (*pl.* **-fish·es, -fish**) a cod.

codg·er (koj-ĕr) *n. (informal)* a fellow, especially an old strange one.

cod·i·cil (kod-i-sil) *n.* an appendix to a will.

cod·i·fy (kod-i-fı) *v.* (**co·di·fied, co·di·fy·ing**) to arrange (laws or rules) systematically into a code. **cod·i·fi·ca·tion** (kod-i-fi-kay-shŏn) *n.*

cod·ling (kod-ling) *n.* a small codfish.

co·ed (koh-ed, koh-ed) *adj. (informal)* coeducational. **coed** *n. (informal)* a girl or young woman at a coeducational school or college.

co·ed·u·ca·tion (koh-ej-ŭ-kay-shŏn) *n.* education of boys and girls in the same classes. **co·ed·u·ca'tion·al** *adj.*

co·ef·fi·cient (koh-i-fish-ĕnt) *n.* a multiplier, a mathematical factor.

coe·la·canth (see-lă-kanth) *n.* a kind of fish that is extinct except for one species.

coe·len·ter·ate (si-len-tĕ-rit) *n.* an invertebrate animal, such as a jellyfish or a hydra, with a large internal cavity and tentacles. **coelenterate** *adj.*

co·e·qual (koh-ee-kwăl) *adj.* equal. **coequal** *n.* a person who is the equal of another. **co·e'qual·ly** *adv.* **co·e·qual·i·ty** (koh-i-kwol-i-tee) *n.*

co·erce (koh-urs) *v.* (**co·erced, co·erc·ing**) to compel by threats or force. **co·er·cion** (koh-ur-shŏn) *n.*

co·er·cive (koh-ur-siv) *adj.* using coercion.

co·e·val (koh-ee-văl) *adj.* of the same period or age, contemporary.

co·ex·ist (koh-ig-zist) *v.* to exist together. ▷ See **coexistence.**

co·ex·ist·ence (koh-ig-zis-tĕns) *n.* coexisting; *peaceful coexistence,* tolerance of each other by countries with different political and social systems. **co·ex·is'tent** *adj.*

co·ex·ten·sive (koh-ik-sten-siv) *adj.* extending over the same space or time.

C of C *abbr.* Chamber of Commerce.

C. of E. *abbr.* Church of England.

co·fea·ture (koh-fee-chŭr) *n.* a short film shown as part of the program at a motion picture theater. **co·fea'tured** *adj.*

cof·fee (kaw-fee) *n.* 1. the beanlike seeds of a tropical shrub, roasted and ground for making a drink. 2. this drink. 3. light brown color. ☐**coffee break,** an interruption of work for light refreshments. **coffee cup,** a cup from which coffee is drunk. **coffee klatch,** an informal meeting whose primary purpose is conversation and at which coffee is served. **coffee shop,** an informal restaurant, especially at a hotel. **coffee table,** a small low table.

cof·fee·cake (kaw-fee-kayk) *n.* a sweet bread or cake intended to be served with coffee.

cof·fee·pot (kaw-fee-pot) *n.* a pot in which coffee is made or served.

cof·fer (kaw-fĕr) *n.* 1. a large strongbox for holding money and valuables. 2. *coffers,* funds, financial resources.

cof·fer·dam (kaw-fĕr-dam) *n.* a temporary watertight structure built or placed around an area of water that can then be pumped dry to allow building, work, etc. to be done within.

cof·fin (kaw-fin) *n.* a box in which a dead body is placed for burial or cremation.

cof·fin·nail (kaw-fin-nayl) *n.* 1. a nail used in a coffin. 2. *(slang)* a cigarette.

C of S *abbr.* Chief of Staff.

cog (kog) *n.* one of a series of teeth on the edge of a wheel, fitting into and pushing those on another wheel. □**cog railway,** a railway with a cogged track that engages cogged wheels on trains and enables these to climb steep grades.

cog. *abbr.* cognate.

co·gent (koh-jĕnt) *adj.* convincing, compelling belief, *a cogent argument.* **co'gent·ly** *adv.* **co'gen·cy** *n.*

cog·i·tate (koj-i-tayt) *v.* (**cog·i·tat·ed, cog·i·tat·ing**) to think deeply. **cog'i·ta·tive** *adj.* **cog·i·ta·tion** (koj-i-tay-shŏn) *n.*

cog·nac (kohn-yak) *n.* French brandy, that made in Cognac in western France.

cog·nate (kog-nayt) *adj.* having the same source or origin, (of things) related.

cog·ni·tion (kog-nish-ŏn) *n.* the act or process of perceiving or knowing. **cog·ni'tion·al** *adj.* **cog·ni·tive** (kog-ni-tiv) *adj.*

cog·ni·zant (kog-ni-zănt) *adj.* aware, having knowledge. **cog'ni·zance** *n.* **cog·ni·za·ble** (kog-ni-ză-bĕl) *adj.*

cog·no·men (kog-noh-mĕn) *n.* (*pl.* **-mens, -nom·i·na,** *pr.* -nom-ĭ-nă) 1. a last name. 2. a nickname.

co·gno·scen·ti (kon-yŏ-shen-tee) *n. pl.* connoisseurs.

cog·wheel (kog-hweel) *n.* a toothed wheel, a gearwheel.

co·hab·it (koh-hab-it) *v.* to live together as man and wife, especially when not married to each other. **co·hab·i·ta·tion** (koh-hab-i-tay-shŏn) *n.*

co·heir (koh-air) *n.* a person who inherits jointly with others.

co·here (koh-heer) *v.* (**co·hered, co·her·ing**) to stick together, to remain united in a mass, *the particles cohere.*

co·her·ent (koh-heer-ĕnt) *adj.* 1. cohering. 2. connected logically, not rambling in speech or in reasoning. **co·her'ent·ly** *adv.* **co·her'ence** *n.*

co·he·sion (koh-hee-zhŏn) *n.* cohering, a tendency to stick together. **co·he·sive** (koh-hee-siv) *adj.*

co·ho (koh-hoh) *n.* (*pl.* **-hos, -ho**) a small light-colored salmon.

co·hort (koh-hort) *n.* 1. a group of admirers or followers. 2. an associate, an accomplice.

coif (koif) *n.* a cap shaped like a hood.

coif·feur (kwah-fur) *n.* a male hairdresser. ▷French.

coif·feuse (kwah-foos) *n.* a female hairdresser. ▷French.

coif·fure (kwah-fyoor) *n.* a hairstyle.

coil (koil) *v.* to wind into rings or a spiral. **coil** *n.* 1. something coiled. 2. one ring or turn in this. 3. a length of wire wound in a spiral to conduct electric current.

coin (koin) *n.* metal money, a piece of this. **coin** *v.* 1. to make (coins) by stamping metal. 2. to invent (a word or phrase). 3. *(informal)* to make (money) easily or rapidly, *we coined money in that business.* **coin'er** *n.*

coin·age (koi-nij) *n.* 1. coining. 2. coins, the system of coins in use. 3. a coined word or phrase.

co·in·cide (koh-in-sɪd) *v.* (**co·in·cid·ed, co·in·cid·ing**) 1. to occur at the same time, *his holidays don't coincide with hers.* 2. to occupy the

same portion of space. 3. to agree; *our tastes coincide,* are the same.

co·in·ci·dence (koh-in-si-dĕns) *n.* 1. coinciding. 2. a remarkable occurrence of similar or corresponding events at the same time by chance.

co·in·ci·dent (koh-in-si-dĕnt) *adj.* coinciding. **co·in·ci·den·tal** (koh-in-si-den-tăl) *adj.* happening by coincidence. **co·in·ci·den'tal·ly** *adv.*

co·i·tus (koh-i-tŭs) *n.* sexual intercourse. **co'i·tal** *n.*

coke[1] (kohk) *n.* the solid substance left after coal gas and coal tar have been extracted from coal, used as fuel.

coke[2] *n. (slang)* cocaine.

COL *abbr.* cost of living.

col. *abbr.* 1. collected. 2. collector. 3. college. 4. colonial. 5. colony. 6. color 7. colored. 8. column.

Col. *abbr.* 1. Colombia. 2. Colonel. 3. Colorado. 4. Columbia.

co·la (koh-lă) *n.* a carbonated drink made with dried coco leaves and kola nut seeds.

COLA *n.* cost-of-*living* adjustment.

col·an·der (kul-ăn-dĕr, kol-) *n.* a bowl-shaped container with holes for straining water from foods after cooking or washing.

cold (kohld) *adj.* 1. at or having a low temperature, especially when compared with the human body. 2. not heated, having cooled after being heated or cooked, *cold meat.* 3. *(slang)* unconscious, *knocked him cold.* 4. without friendliness or affection or enthusiasm, *got a cold reception.* 5. (of colors) suggesting coldness. 6. (of the scent in hunting) faint because no longer fresh. 7. (in children's games) far from finding or guessing what is sought. **cold** *adv.* in a cold state. **cold** *n.* 1. lack of heat or warmth, low temperature. 2. an infectious illness causing sneezing etc. **cold'ly** *adv.* **cold'ness** *n.* □**cold comfort,** poor consolation. **cold cream,** ointment for cleansing and softening the skin. **cold cuts,** sliced cheeses and meats, usually for sandwiches. **cold duck,** a mixture of champagne and sparkling burgundy. **cold fish,** a person who seems to lack feelings. **cold frame,** an unheated frame for growing small plants. **cold front,** the zone between a mass of warm air and one of cooler air that is moving onward to replace it. **cold shoulder,** deliberate unfriendliness, *he gave me the cold shoulder.* **cold snap,** a sudden period of cold weather. **cold sore,** a blister or group of blisters on the mouth, caused by a virus. **cold steel,** a steel weapon such as a bayonet or sword. **cold storage,** storage in a refrigerated place; *in cold storage,* (of plans etc.) postponed but available when required. **cold sweat,** perspiration accompanying a slight chill. **cold turkey,** *(slang)* sudden withdrawal of narcotic drugs from an addict, without preparation. **cold type,** any of various printing techniques employing photographic reproduction of text prepared by means other than metallic typesetting. **cold war,** intense hostility between nations without actual fighting. **cold wave,** a sudden severe drop in temperature; a wave set in the hair by means of a chemical solution. **cold weld,** to bond together without the use of pressure or heat. **get cold feet,** to feel afraid or reluctant. **have a person cold,** *(informal)* to have him at one's mercy. **have something (down) cold,** to know something perfectly. **in cold blood,** without passion, deliberately and ruthlessly. **leave cold,** to fail to affect or impress, *their promises leave me*

cold. leave out in the cold, to ignore or neglect. **throw** *or* **pour cold water on,** to make discouraging remarks about.

cold·blood·ed (kohld-blud-id) *adj.* **1.** having a body temperature that varies with the temperature of the surroundings, as fish do. **2.** unfeeling, deliberately ruthless, *a coldblooded killer.*

cold·heart·ed (kohld-hahr-tid) *adj.* lacking in emotion, unsympathetic or unfeeling.

cold-shoul·der (kohld-shohl-děr) *v.* to treat with deliberate unfriendliness.

cole·slaw (kohl-slaw) *n.* shredded raw cabbage coated in dressing, as a salad.

co·le·us (koh-li-ŭs) *n.* a plant grown for its variegated leaves.

col·ic (kol-ik) *n.* severe abdominal pain. **col′ick·y** *adj.*

col·i·se·um, col·os·se·um (kol-ĭ-see-ŭm) *n.* an amphitheater or stadium used especially for sporting events.

co·li·tis (kŏ-lr-tis) *n.* inflammation of the lining of the colon.

coll. *abbr.* **1.** collect. **2.** collection. **3.** collector. **4.** college. **5.** collegiate. **6.** colloquial.

col·lab·o·rate (kŏ-lab-ŏ-rayt) *v.* **(col·lab·o· rat·ed, col·lab·o·rat·ing)** to work in partnership. **col·lab′o·ra·tor** *n.* **col·lab·o·ra·tion** (kŏ-lab-ŏ-ray-shŏn) *n.*

col·lage (kŏ-lahzh) *n.* an artistic composition made by fixing bits of paper, cloth, string, etc. to a surface.

col·la·gen (kol-ă-jĕn) *n.* a protein substance found in bone and tissue.

col·lapse (kŏ-laps) *v.* **(col·lapsed, col·laps· ing)** **1.** to fall down or in suddenly. **2.** to lose strength or force suddenly, *enemy resistance collapsed.* **3.** to fold or be foldable. **4.** to cause to collapse; *collapsing the lung,* surgically reducing the amount of air in it. **collapse** *n.* collapsing, a breakdown.

col·laps·i·ble (kŏ-lap-si-bĕl) *adj.* made so as to fold together compactly, *a collapsible canoe.*

col·lar (kol-ăr) *n.* **1.** an upright or turned-over band around the neck of a garment. **2.** a band of leather etc. put around the neck of an animal. **3.** a band, ring, or pipe holding part of a machine. **collar** *v.* **1.** to put a collar on. **2.** *(informal)* to seize, to take for oneself. **col′lar·less** *adj.* □**collar button,** a button that fastens the neckband of a shirt.

col·lar·bone (kol-ăr-bohn) *n.* the bone joining the breastbone and shoulder blade, the clavicle.

col·lard (kol-ărd) *n.* a type of kale. □**collard greens,** the young leaves of this plant.

collat. *abbr.* collateral.

col·late (kol-ayt) *v.* **(col·lat·ed, col·lat·ing)** **1.** to compare in detail. **2.** to collect and arrange systematically, *collate information.* **col′la·tor** *n.*

col·lat·er·al (kŏ-lat-ĕ-răl) *adj.* **1.** parallel. **2.** additional but subordinate, *collateral evidence.* **3.** descended from the same ancestor but by a different line, *a collateral branch of the family.* **collateral** *n.* a collateral security. **col·lat′er·al·ly** *adv.* □**collateral security,** an additional security pledged; security presented by a third party, or consisting of stocks, shares, property, etc. as opposed to a personal guarantee.

col·la·tion (kol-ay-shŏn) *n.* **1.** collating. **2.** a light meal, especially at an unusual time.

col·league (kol-eeg) *n.* a fellow official or worker, especially in a business or profession.

col·lect¹ (kol-ĕkt) *n.* a short prayer in certain churches, usually to be read on an appointed day.

col·lect² (kŏ-lekt) *v.* **1.** to bring or come together. **2.** to get from a number of people, to ask for (payment or contributions) from people. **3.** to seek and obtain specimens of, especially as a hobby or for study. **4.** to fetch, *collect the children from school.* **5.** to gather (one's thoughts) into systematic order or control; *collect oneself,* to regain control of oneself. **collect** *adj.* & *adv.* requiring the recipient to pay for, *a collect phone call; send this package collect.* **col·lect′i·ble, col·lect′a·ble** *adj.* **col·lect′or** *n.*

col·lect·ed (kŏ-lek-tid) *adj.* calm and self-controlled. **col·lect′ed·ly** *adv.* **col·lect′ed· ness** *n.*

col·lec·tion (kŏ-lek-shŏn) *n.* **1.** collecting. **2.** money collected for a charity etc., as at a church service. **3.** objects collected systematically. **4.** a heap of things that have come together.

col·lec·tive (kŏ-lek-tiv) *adj.* of a group taken as a whole, *our collective impression of the new plan.* **collective** *n.* a collective farm. **col·lec′tive· ly** *adv.* □**collective bargaining,** bargaining by an organized group of employees. **collective farm,** a farm or group of small holdings organized and run by its workers, usually under government control. **collective noun,** a noun that is singular in form but denotes more than one individual, as *army, cattle, committee, herd.* **collective ownership,** ownership of land etc. by all and for the benefit of all.

col·lec·tiv·ism (kŏ-lek-ti-viz-ĕm) *n.* the doctrin of government control of all production and distribution. **col·lec′tiv·ist** *n.*

col·lec·ti·vize (kŏ-lek-ti-viz) *v.* **(col·lec·ti· vized, col·lec·ti·viz·ing)** to bring from private into collective ownership. **col·lec·ti·vi·za·tion** (kŏ-lek-ti-vi-zay-shŏn) *n.*

col·lec·tor (kŏ-lek-tŏr) *n.* a person who collects things; *a collector's item,* a thing worth placing in a collection because of its beauty, value, or interest.

col·leen (ko-leen) *n.* **1.** *(Irish)* a girl. **2.** an Irish girl.

col·lege (kol-ij) *n.* **1.** an educational establishment for higher or professional education. **2.** an independent part of a university with its own teachers and students. **3.** a school, *she went to business college.* **4.** the buildings of any of these. **5.** an organized body of professional people with common purposes and privileges, *the College of Cardinals.*

col·le·gian (kŏ-lee-jăn) *n.* a college student.

col·le·giate (kŏ-lee-jit) *adj.* of or belonging to a college or college student.

col·lide (kŏ-lrd) *v.* **(col·lid·ed, col·lid·ing)** **1.** (of a moving object) to strike violently against something, to meet and strike. **2.** to have a conflict of interests or opinions.

col·lie (kol-ee) *n.* a dog with a long pointed muzzle and shaggy hair.

col·lier (kol-yĕr) *n.* (chiefly *British*) **1.** a coal miner. **2.** a ship that carries coal as its cargo.

col·lier·y (kol-yĕ-ree) *n.* (pl. **-lier·ies**) (chiefly *British*) a coal mine and its buildings.

col·li·mate (kol-i-mayt) *v.* **(col·li·mat·ed, col· li·mat·ing)** to make rays of light etc. parallel to each other.

col·li·sion (kŏ-lizh-ŏn) *n.* colliding, the striking

of one body against another. □**collision course,** a set course that is bound to end in a collision.

col·lo·ca·tion (kol-ŏ-**kay**-shŏn) *n.* placing together or side by side.

col·lo·di·on (kŏ-loh-di-ŏn) *n.* a mixture of ether, alcohol, and other substances that hardens when exposed to air, used to dress wounds and in the production of photographic film.

col·loid (kol-oid) *n.* a gluey substance. **col·loi·dal** (ko-loi-dăl) *adj.* **col·loi'dal·ly** *adv.*

colloq. *abbr.* 1. colloquial. 2. colloquialism. 3. colloquially.

col·lo·qui·al (kŏ-loh-kwi-ăl) *adj.* suitable for ordinary conversation but not for formal speech or writing, informal. **col·lo'qui·al·ly** *adv.*

col·lo·qui·al·ism (kŏ-loh-kwi-ă-liz-ĕm) *n.* a colloquial word or phrase.

col·lo·qui·um (kŏ-loh-kwi-ŭm) *n.* (*pl.* **-qui·ums, -qui·a,** *pr.* -kwi-ă) an informal seminar or conference.

col·lo·quy (kol-ŏ-kwee) *n.* (*pl.* **-quies**) (*formal*) a conversation.

col·lu·sion (kŏ-loo-zhŏn) *n.* agreement between two or more people for a deceitful or fraudulent purpose. **col·lu·sive** (kŏ-loo-siv) *adj.*

col·lu·vi·um (kŏ-loo-vi-ŭm) *n.* (*pl.* **-vi·a,** *pr.* -vi-ă, **-vi·ums**) fragments of broken rock that have gathered at the foot of a hill. **col·lu'vi·al** *adj.*

Colo. *abbr.* Colorado.

co·logne (kŏ-lohn) *n.* eau de Cologne or other lightly scented liquid, used to cool and scent the skin.

Co·lom·bi·a (kŏ-lum-bi-ă) a country in South America. **Co·lom'bi·an** *adj.* & *n.*

Co·lom·bo (kŏ-lum-boh) the capital of Sri Lanka.

co·lon[1] (koh-lŏn) *n.* (*pl.* **-lons, -la,** *pr.* -lă) the lower and greater part of the large intestine. **co·lon·ic** (kŏ-lon-ik) *adj.*

colon[2] *n.* the punctuation mark : used (1) to show that what follows is an example or list or summary of what precedes it, or a contrasting idea; (2) between numbers that are in proportion, as in 1:2 = 2:4; (3) after the salutation in business letters etc.

colo·nel (kur-nĕl) *n.* 1. an army officer commanding a regiment, ranking next below a brigadier general. 2. a lieutenant colonel.

co·lo·ni·al (kŏ-loh-ni-ăl) *adj.* of a colony or colonies. **colonial** *n.* an inhabitant of a colony.

co·lo·ni·al·ism (kŏ-loh-ni-ă-liz-em) *n.* the policy of acquiring or maintaining colonies. **co·lo'ni·al·ist** *adj.* & *n.*

col·o·nist (kol-ŏ-nist) *n.* a pioneer settler in a colony.

col·o·nize (kol-ŏ-nɪz) *v.* (**col·o·nized, col·o·niz·ing**) to establish a colony in. **col'o·niz·er** *n.* **col·o·ni·za·tion** (kol-ŏ-ni-zay-shŏn) *n.*

col·on·nade (kol-ŏ-nayd) *n.* a row of columns.

col·o·ny (kol-ŏ-nee) *n.* (*pl.* **-nies**) 1. an area of land settled or conquered by a distant nation and controlled by it, *the American Colonies.* 2. its inhabitants. 3. a group of colonists. 4. people' of one nationality or occupation etc. living in a particular area, the area itself, *the artists' colony.*

col·o·phon (kol-ŏ-fon) *n.* 1. an inscription at the end of a book or manuscript giving information about its production, including author, title, name of publisher, etc. 2. a publisher's emblem on the title page or cover of a book.

col·or (kul-ŏr) *n.* 1. the sensation produced by various rays of light of different wavelengths, a particular variety of this. 2. the use of all colors, not just black and white; *in color,* using all colors; *color film,* producing photographs that are in color. 3. ruddiness of complexion; *she has no color,* looks pale. 4. the pigmentation of the skin, especially if dark. 5. pigment, paint, or dye. 6. *colors,* the flag of a ship or regiment. **color** *v.* 1. to put color on, to paint or stain or dye. 2. to change color or blush. 3. to give a special color or bias to, *his political opinions color his writings.* □**color bar,** legal or social discrimination between white and nonwhite people. **color code,** a system in which colors are used as a help in sorting, classifying, etc. **color guard,** an honor guard for the colors of a regiment. **color line,** a color bar. **color scheme,** a systematic combination of colors. **give** *or* **lend color to,** to give an appearance of truth to. **in its true colors,** with its real characteristics revealed.

Col·o·rad·o (kol-ŏ-rad-oh) a state of the U.S. **Col·o·rad·an** (kol-ŏ-rad-ăn) *adj.* & *n.* □**Colorado potato beetle,** a beetle with black and yellow stripes that feeds on potato leaves.

col·or·ant (kul-ŏ-rănt) *n.* coloring matter.

col·or·a·tion (kul-ŏ-ray-shŏn) *n.* coloring.

col·o·ra·tu·ra (kul-ŏ-ră-toor-ă) *n.* 1. the use of trills, runs, and other ornamentation in vocal music. 2. a soprano who specializes in singing coloratura.

col·or·blind (kul-ŏr-blɪnd) *adj.* unable to perceive the difference between certain colors. **col'or·blind·ness** *n.*

col·ored (kul-ŏrd) *adj.* 1. having color. 2. wholly or partly of non-Caucasian descent. 3. *Colored,* (in South Africa) of mixed white and non-white descent. **colored** *n.* 1. a colored person. 2. *Colored,* (in South Africa) a person of mixed white and non-white descent. ▷Many people consider *colored* (= *black*) offensive.

col·or·fast (kul-ŏr-fast) *adj.* dyed so that the color does not run or fade. **col'or·fast·ness** *n.*

col·or·ful (kul-ŏr-fŭl) *adj.* 1. full of color. 2. with vivid details, *a colorful account of her journey.* **col'or·ful·ly** *adv.*

col·or·ing (kul-ŏ-ring) *n.* 1. the way in which something is colored. 2. a substance used to color things. □**coloring book,** a child's book containing outline drawings to be colored with crayons or paints.

col·or·less (kul-ŏr-lis) *adj.* 1. without color. 2. lacking interest, *a colorless account.*

col·os·sal (kŏ-los-ăl) *adj.* 1. immense. 2. (*informal*) remarkable, splendid. **co·los'sal·ly** *adv.*

Co·los·sians (kŏ-losh-ănz) *n.* a book of the New Testament, the epistle of St. Paul to the Church at Colossae.

co·los·sus (kŏ-los-ŭs) *n.* (*pl.* **-los·sus·es, -los·si,** *pr.* -los-ɪ) 1. an immense statue, *the Colossus of Rhodes.* 2. a person of immense importance and influence.

co·los·to·my (kŏ-los-tŏ-mee) *n.* (*pl.* **-mies**) an artificial opening through which the bowel can empty, made surgically by bringing part of the colon to the surface of the abdomen.

co·los·trum (kŏ-los-trŭm) *n.* the first milk secreted after giving birth.

colt (kohlt) *n.* a young male horse. **colt'ish** *adj.*

colts·foot (kohlts-fuut) *n.* (*pl.* **-foots**) a weed with yellow flowers, its leaf suggesting the print of a colt's foot.

Co·lum·bi·a (kŏ-lum-bi-ă) the capital of South Carolina.

Columbia, District of a district of the U.S. coextensive with the city of Washington, capital of the U.S.

col·um·bine (kol-ŭm-bɪn) n. a garden flower with slender pointed projections on its petals.

col·um·bi·um (kŏ-lum-bi-ŭm) n. a metallic element, formerly known as niobium.

Co·lum·bus (kŏ-lum-bŭs) the capital of Ohio.

col·umn (kol-ŭm) n. 1. a round pillar. 2. something shaped like this, *a column of smoke; the spinal column*, the backbone. 3. a vertical section of a page, *there are two columns on this page.* 4. a regular feature of a newspaper, usually devoted to a special subject. 5. a long narrow formation of troops or vehicles etc. **col·umn·ar** (kŏ-lum-năr) adj. **col·umned** (kol-ŭmd) adj.

col·umn·ist (kol-ŭm-nist) n. a journalist who regularly writes a column of comments.

com., comm. abbr. 1. command. 2. commander. 3. commerce. 4. commercial. 5. commission. 6. commissioner. 7. committee. 8. common. 9. commonwealth.

Com. abbr. 1. Commander. 2. Commission. 3. Commissioner. 4. Commodore.

co·ma (koh-mă) n. (pl. -mas) a state of deep unconsciousness.

Co·man·che (kŏ-man-chee) n. (pl. -ches, -che) a member of a tribe of North American Indians formerly inhabiting parts of Texas.

com·a·tose (koh-mă-tohs) adj. 1. in a coma. 2. drowsy.

comb (kohm) n. 1. a strip of bone or plastic etc. with teeth, used for tidying the hair or holding it in place. 2. something shaped or used like this, as for separating strands of wool or cotton. 3. the fleshy crest of a fowl. 4. a honeycomb. **comb** v. 1. to tidy or untangle with a comb. 2. to search thoroughly. □**comb out**, (informal) to get rid of (unwanted people or things) from a group; to untangle with a comb.

comb. abbr. combining.

com·bat (kom-bat) n. a fight or contest. **combat** (kŏm-bat) v. (**com·bat·ted, com·bat·ting**) to counter, *to combat the effects of alcohol.* □**combat fatigue,** a mental disorder due to stress in wartime combat.

com·bat·ant (kŏm-bat-ănt) n. one who is engaged in fighting.

com·bat·ive (kŏm-bat-iv) adj. fond of fighting.

comb·er (koh-měr) n. 1. a person who combs. 2. a long curling ocean wave.

comb. form abbr. combining form.

com·bi·na·tion (kom-bĭ-nay-shŏn) n. 1. combining, being combined. 2. a number of people or things that are combined. 3. a sequence of numbers or letters used in opening a combination lock. □**combination lock,** a lock that can be opened only by turning one or more dials into a particular series of positions, indicated by numbers or letters.

com·bine (kŏm-bɪn) v. (**com·bined, com·bin·ing**) to join or be joined into a group or set or mixture. **combine** (kom-bɪn) n. 1. a combination of people or firms acting together in business. 2. a combined reaping and threshing machine. □**combining form,** a form of a word used in combinations, such as *euro-* (= *European*) in *eurocommunism.*

comb·ings (koh-mingz) n. loose hair removed by a brush or comb.

com·bo (kom-boh) n. (pl. -bos) 1. a small band that plays dance or jazz music. 2. (informal) a combination.

com·bus·ti·ble (kŏm-bus-tĭ-běl) adj. capable of catching fire and burning, used for burning. **combustible** n. a combustible substance. **com·bus·ti·bil·i·ty** (kŏm-bus-tĭ-bil-i-tee) n. **com·bus·tive** (kŏm-bus-tiv) adj.

com·bus·tion (kŏm-bus-chŏn) n. the process of burning, a chemical process (accompanied by heat) in which substances combine with oxygen in air.

comdg. abbr. commanding.

comdr. abbr. commander.

comdt. abbr. commandant.

come (kum) v. (**came, come, com·ing**) 1. to move toward the speaker or a place or point. 2. (of an illness) to begin to develop. 3. to arrive, to reach a point or condition or result, *when winter comes; we came to a decision,* made one; *for several years to come,* in the future. 4. to take or occupy a specified position, *what comes next?* 5. to be available, *the dress comes in three sizes; he's as tough as they come,* no one is tougher. 6. to happen, *how did you come to lose it?* 7. to occur as a result, *that's what comes of being too confident.* 8. to be descended, *she comes from a rich family.* **come** interj. think again, don't be hasty, *come, come, it's not that bad!* □**come about,** to happen. **come across,** (informal) to find or meet unexpectedly. **come along,** to make progress, to thrive, *coming along nicely; come along!,* hurry up. **come between,** to disrupt the relationship between (two people); to prevent (a person) from having something, *nothing must come between him and his career.* **come by,** to obtain (a thing). **come clean,** (informal) to confess fully. **come down,** to collapse, to fall, to become lower; *come down in the world,* to lose one's former high social position; *come down in favor of,* to decide in favor of. **come down on,** to rebuke. **come forward,** to offer oneself for a task etc. **come from,** to have as one's birthplace or as a place of origin. **come in,** to take a specified position in a race or competition, *he came in third;* to become seasonable or fashionable; to be received as income; to begin one's radio transmission; to have a part to play, to serve a purpose, *it will come in useful; where do I come in?,* what is my role?, where is my advantage?. **come in for,** to get a share of. **come into,** to inherit, *he came into the legacy.* **come of age,** to reach adult status. **come off,** to become detached or separated, to be detachable; to fall from, *she came off her bicycle;* (of a series of performances) to end; to fare, to acquit oneself, *they came off well;* to be successful. **come off it!,** (informal) stop talking or behaving like that. **come on,** to make progress, to thrive; to come on to the stage, to appear in a filmed scene etc.; to find or meet unexpectedly; *come on!,* hurry up. **come on strong,** (informal) to behave in an overbearing or aggressive manner. **come out,** to go on strike; to emerge from an examination etc. with a specified result; to emerge from behind clouds, *the sun came out;* to become visible in a photograph, *the house has come out well;* to become known, *the truth came out;* to be published; to be solved; to declare one's opinions publicly, *came out in favor of the plan;* (of stains etc.) to be removed. **come out with,** to utter. **come over,** (informal) to affect, *what has come over* *you?* **come round** *or* **around,** to make a casual or informal visit; to recover from faintness or bad temper; to be converted to another person's opinion. **come to,** to amount to, to be equivalent to; to regain consciousness. **come to pass,** to happen. **come true,** to happen in the way that was prophesied or hoped. **come up,** to arise for discussion etc., to occur, *a problem has come up.* **come upon,** to find or meet unexpectedly. **come up to,** to equal, *it doesn't come up to our expectations.* **come up with,** to contribute (a suggestion etc.). **come what may,** whatever may happen.

come·back (kum-bak) *n.* 1. a return to one's former successful position. 2. *(slang)* a reply or retort.

Com·e·con (kom-ĕ-kon) *n.* an economic organization of eastern European countries. ▷From Council for Mutual Economic Assistance.

co·me·di·an (kŏ-mee-di-ăn) *n.* 1. an actor who plays comic parts. 2. a humorous entertainer. 3. a person who behaves humorously.

co·me·di·enne (kŏ-mee-di-en) *n.* a female comedian.

com·e·do (kom-i-doh) *n.* (*pl.* **com·e·dos, com·e·do·nes,** *pr.* kom-ĕ-doh-neez) a blackhead.

come·down (kum-down) *n.* 1. a fall from rank, dignity, or importance. 2. an anticlimax.

com·e·dy (kom-ĕ-dee) *n.* (*pl.* **-dies)** 1. a light amusing play, film, television production, etc. 2. the branch of drama that consists of such plays. 3. an amusing incident. 4. humor. **com·e·dic** (kŏ-mee-dik) *adj.*

come-hith·er (kum-hi*th*-ĕr) *adj.* enticing, flirtatious, *a come-hither look.*

come·ly (kum-lee) *adj.* **(-li·er, -li·est)** good-looking. **come′li·ness** *n.*

com·er (kum-ĕr) *n.* 1. one who comes, *the first comers; all comers,* anyone who comes or challenges or applies. 2. a beginner who seems likely to succeed.

co·mes·ti·bles (kŏ-mes-ti-bĕlz) *n. pl.* things to eat.

com·et (kom-it) *n.* a hazy object that moves around the sun, usually with a starlike center and a tail pointing away from the sun.

come·up·pance (kum-up-ăns) *n.* *(informal)* one's deserts for misbehavior etc.

com·fort (kum-fŏrt) *n.* 1. a state of ease and contentment. 2. relief of suffering or grief. 3. a person or thing that gives this. **comfort** *v.* to give comfort to. □**comfort station,** a public toilet.

com·fort·a·ble (kumf-tă-bĕl, kum-fŏr-tă-bĕl) *adj.* 1. giving ease and contentment. 2. not close or restricted, *won by a comfortable margin.* 3. feeling at ease, in a state of comfort. **com′fort·a·bly** *adv.*

com·fort·er (kum-fŏr-tĕr) *n.* 1. a person who comforts. 2. a blanket, coverlet.

com·fy (kum-fee) *adj.* **(-fi·er, -fi·est)** *(informal)* comfortable.

com·ic (kom-ik) *adj.* 1. causing amusement or laughter. 2. of comedy. **comic** *n.* 1. a comedian. 2. a comic book. **com′i·cal** *adj.* **com′i·cal·ly** *adv.* □**comic book,** a magazine consisting of comic strips. **comic strip,** a series of cartoons telling a story. **the comics,** a section containing comic strips in the newspapers etc.

com·ing (kum-ing) *see* **come. coming** *adj.* 1. approaching, next, *the coming week.* 2. likely to be important in the near future, *a coming thing.*

coming *n.* arriving, *comings and goings.*

com·i·ty (kom-i-tee) *n.* (*pl.* **-ties)** courtesy, especially between nations.

coml. *abbr.* commercial.

comm. *abbr.* 1. commission. 2. committee. 3. commonwealth.

com·ma (kom-ă) *n.* the punctuation mark , indicating a slight pause or break between parts of a sentence, separating words or figures in a list, etc.

com·mand (kŏ-mand) *n.* 1. a statement, given with authority, that some action must be performed. 2. the right to control others, authority; *she is in command,* has this authority. 3. the ability to use something, mastery, *has a command of languages.* 4. a body of troops; a major element of the organization of the U.S. Army, *Continental Command.* **command** *v.* 1. to give a command or order to. 2. to have authority over. 3. to have at one's disposal, *the conglomerate commands great resources.* 4. to deserve and get, *they command our respect.* 5. to look down over or dominate from a strategic position, *the tower commands the harbor; in a commanding position.* □**command module,** a space vehicle designed to carry a crew and its equipment. **command post,** the headquarters of a military force.

com·man·dant (kom-ăn-dant) *n.* the officer in command of a fort or other military establishment.

com·man·deer (kom-ăn-deer) *v.* 1. to seize for military purposes. 2. to seize for one's own purposes.

com·mand·er (kŏ-man-dĕr) *n.* 1. the person in command. 2. a naval officer ranking next below a captain. □**commander in chief** (*pl.* **commanders in chief),** the supreme commander. **Commander in Chief,** the president of the U.S. as commander in chief of U.S. armed forces.

com·mand·ment (kŏ-mand-mĕnt) *n.* a divine command, one of the ten laws given by God to Moses.

com·man·do (kŏ-man-doh) *n.* (*pl.* **-dos, -does)** a member of a military unit specially trained for making raids and assaults.

comme il faut (kum eel foh) proper, as it should be (especially of behavior etc.). ▷French.

com·mem·o·rate (kŏ-mem-ŏ-rayt) *v.* **(com·mem·o·rat·ed, com·mem·o·rat·ing)** 1. to keep in the memory by means of a celebration or ceremony. 2. to be a memorial to, *a plaque commemorates the victory.* **com·mem·o·ra·tive** (kŏ-mem-ŏ-ră-tiv) *adj.* **com·mem·o·ra·tion** (kŏ-mem-ŏ-ray-shŏn) *n.* □**commemorative issue,** an object, as a coin, produced to memorialize a person or event etc. **commemorative stamp,** a postage stamp issued to honor a person or event etc.

com·mence (kŏ-mens) *v.* **(com·menced, com·menc·ing)** to begin.

com·mence·ment (kŏ-mens-mĕnt) *n.* 1. a commencing, a beginning. 2. a formal ceremony of graduation.

com·mend (kŏ-mend) *v.* 1. to praise. 2. to recommend. 3. to entrust, to commit, *commending his soul to God.* **com·men·da·tion** (kom-ĕn-day-shŏn) *n.*

com·mend·a·ble (kŏ-men-dă-bĕl) *adj.* worthy of praise. **com·mend′a·bly** *adv.*

com·men·su·ra·ble (kŏ-men-sŭ-ră-bĕl) *adj.* able to be measured by the same standard.

com·men·su·rate (kŏ-men-sŭ-rit) *adj.* 1. of the same size or extent. 2. proportionate, *the salary is commensurate with the responsibilities.*

com·ment (kom-ent) *n.* an opinion given briefly about an event or in explanation or criticism. **comment** *v.* to utter or write comments.

com·men·tar·y (kom-ĕn-ter-ee) *n.* (*pl.* -tar·ies) 1. a series of descriptive comments on an event or performance. 2. a collection of explanatory comments, *a new commentary on the Bible.*

com·men·ta·tor (kom-ĕn-tay-tŏr) *n.* a person who broadcasts or writes a commentary.

com·merce (kom-ŭrs) *n.* all forms of trade and the services that assist trading, as banking and insurance.

com·mer·cial (kŏ-mur-shăl) *adj.* 1. of or engaged in commerce; *commercial vehicles,* those carrying goods or fare-paying passengers; *commercial art,* art used in advertising etc.; *produced on a commercial scale,* in amounts suitable for marketing widely. 2. financed by firms etc. whose advertisements are included, *commercial television.* 3. intended to produce profits rather than to be of artistic or scholarly merit. **commercial** *n.* a broadcast advertisement. **com·mer′cial·ly** *adv.*

com·mer·cial·ism (kŏ-mur-shă-liz-ĕm) *n.* commercial practices and attitudes.

com·mer·cial·ize (kŏ-mur-shă-līz) *v.* (**com·mer·cial·ized, com·mer·cial·iz·ing**) to make commercial, to alter in order to make profitable, *a very commercialized resort.* **com·mer·cial·i·za·tion** (kŏ-mur-shă-li-zay-shŏn) *n.*

Com·mie (kom-ee) *n.* (*slang*) a Communist.

com·min·gle (kŏ-ming-gĕl) *v.* (**com·min·gled, com·min·gling**) to mingle together.

com·mis·er·ate (kŏ-miz-ĕ-rayt) *v.* (**com·mis·er·at·ed, com·mis·er·at·ing**) to express pity for, to sympathize. **com·mis·er·a·tion** (kŏ-miz-ĕ-ray-shŏn) *n.*

com·mis·sar (kom-i-sahr) *n.* (formerly) the head of a government department of the U.S.S.R.

com·mis·sar·i·at (kom-i-sair-i-ăt) *n.* 1. (*formerly*) a government department of the U.S.S.R headed by a commissar. 2. a military department that supplies food to military personnel.

com·mis·sar·y (kom-i-ser-ee) *n.* (*pl.* -sar·ies) 1. a store where food and general supplies are sold, especially on a military base. 2. a dining area or cafeteria in a motion-picture studio, factory, etc.

com·mis·sion (kŏ-mish-ŏn) *n.* 1. the giving of authority to someone to perform a certain task or duty. 2. the task etc. given, *a commission to paint a portrait.* 3. the body of people to whom such authority is given. 4. a certificate conferring rank on an officer in the armed forces. 5. performance, committing, *the commission of a crime.* 6. payment to an agent for selling goods or services, often calculated in proportion to the amount sold; *selling goods on commission,* receiving such payment. **commission** *v.* 1. to give a commission to. 2. to place an order for, *commissioned a portrait.* □**commissioned officer,** an officer in the armed forces who holds a commission. **commission merchant,** one who acts as an agent for suppliers and buyers of merchandise, receiving commission on goods bought and sold. **in commission,** (of a warship etc.) manned and ready for service. **out of commission,** not in commission; not in working order.

com·mis·sion·er (kŏ-mish-ŏ-nĕr) *n.* 1. a member

of a commission, *a police commissioner.* 2. a person who has been given a commission.

com·mit (kŏ-mit) *v.* (**com·mit·ted, com·mit·ting**) 1. to do, to perform, *commit a crime.* 2. to entrust for safekeeping or treatment; *commit a prisoner for trial,* send him to prison pending trial; *commit a body to the earth,* bury it with a formal ceremony. 3. to pledge, to bind with an obligation; *she did not commit herself,* gave no definite statement or opinion. □**committed** *adj.* dedicated or pledged, especially to support a doctrine or cause. **commit to memory,** to memorize.

com·mit·ment (kŏ-mit-mĕnt) *n.* 1. committing. 2. the state of being involved in an obligation. 3. an obligation or pledge.

com·mit·tal (kŏ-mit-ăl) *n.* 1. committing to prison or other place of confinement. 2. committing a body at burial or cremation.

com·mit·ted (kŏ-mit-id) *adj.* dedicated or pledged, especially to support a doctrine or cause.

com·mit·tee (kŏ-mit-ee) *n.* a group of people appointed to attend to special business or to manage the business of a club etc. **com·mit′tee·man** *n.* **com·mit′tee·wom·an** *n.* □**committee of one,** an individual authorized to perform the functions of a committee.

com·mode (kŏ-mohd) *n.* 1. a chest of drawers. 2. a chamber pot mounted in a chair or box with a cover. 3. a covered washstand.

com·mo·di·ous (kŏ-moh-di-ŭs) *adj.* roomy.

com·mod·i·ty (kŏ-mod-i-tee) *n.* (*pl.* -ties) a useful thing, an article of trade, a product. □**commodity exchange,** a place where commodities are bought and sold.

com·mo·dore (kom-ŏ-dohr) *n.* 1. a naval officer ranking above a captain and below a rear admiral. 2. the commander of a squadron or other division of a fleet. 3. the president of a yacht club.

com·mon (kom-ŏn) *adj.* 1. of or affecting the whole community; *it was common knowledge,* was known to most people. 2. belonging to or shared by two or more people or things; *common ground,* something on which two or more people agree or in which they share an interest. 3. occurring frequently, familiar, *a common weed.* 4. without special distinction, ordinary, *the common pigeon.* 5. ill-bred, not refined in behavior or style. 6. *the Commons,* the House of Commons (*see* **house**[1]). **common** *n.* an area of unfenced grassland for all to use. **com′mon·ly** *adv.* **com′mon·ness** *n.* □**common carrier,** a company or person that transports goods or people for a fee. **common denominator,** a number into which each of the denominators of a given set of fractions divides evenly; the feature that members of a group have in common. **lowest** *or* **least common denominator,** the lowest common multiple of the denominators of several fractions, *6 is the lowest common denominator of ½ and ⅓.* **Common Era,** the Christian era. **common law,** unwritten law based on custom and usage and on former court decisions. **common man,** the average person. **Common Market,** the European Economic Community, an association of certain European countries with internal free trade, and common tariffs on their imports from countries outside the community. **common room,** (chiefly *British*) a room shared for social purposes by pupils or students or teachers of a school or college. **common sense,** normal good sense in practical matters, gained by experience of life not by special study. **common stock,** shares in a company that represent residual ownership in it and have no preference in regard to dividends. **common year,** a year having 365 days. **in common,** in joint use between two or more people or things, shared as a possession or characteristic or interest.

com·mon·er (kom-ŏ-nĕr) *n.* one of the common people, not a member of the nobility.

common-law (kom-ŏn-law) **marriage** a marriage recognized by common law, without an official ceremony, usually after a period of cohabitation.

com·mon·place (kom-ŏn-plays) *adj.* ordinary, usual; *a few commonplace remarks,* lacking originality. **commonplace** *n.* something commonplace, *air travel is now a commonplace.* □**commonplace book,** a journal in which one records significant observations, poetry, etc.

com·mon·sense (kom-ŏn-sens) *adj.* showing common sense.

com·mon·weal (kom-ŏn-weel) *n.* 1. the public good. 2. *(old use)* a commonwealth.

com·mon·wealth (kom-ŏn-welth) *n.* 1. an independent nation, state, or community. 2. a republic. 3. a federation of states, *the Commonwealth of Australia.* □**New Commonwealth,** those countries that have achieved self-government within the British Commonwealth since 1945. **the Commonwealth** (also **British Commonwealth**), an association of the United Kingdom and various independent states (formerly subject to Britain) and dependencies.

com·mo·tion (kŏ-moh-shŏn) *n.* uproar, fuss and disturbance.

com·mu·nal (kŏ-myoo-năl) *adj.* shared among members of a group or community, *a communal kitchen.* **com·mu′nal·ly** *adv.*

com·mune¹ (kom′-yoon) *n.* 1. a group of people, not all of one family, sharing living arrangements and goods. 2. a small district of local government in France and certain other European countries.

com·mune² (kŏ-myoon) *v.* (**com·muned, com·mun·ing**) to communicate mentally or spiritually; *communing with nature,* absorbed in feeling oneself in harmony with it.

com·mu·ni·ca·ble (kŏ-myoo-ni-kă-bĕl) *adj.* able to be communicated.

com·mu·ni·cant (kŏ-myoo-ni-kănt) *n.* a person who receives Holy Communion, one who does this regularly.

com·mu·ni·cate (kŏ-myoo-ni-kayt) *v.* (**com·mu·ni·cat·ed, com·mu·ni·cat·ing**) 1. to make known, *communicate the news to your friends.* 2. to transfer, to transmit, *communicated the disease to others.* 3. to pass news and information to and fro, to have social dealings with. 4. to succeed in conveying information, *young people cannot always communicate with older ones.* 5. to be connected, *the passage communicates with the hall and stairs.* **com·mu·ni·ca·bil·i·ty** (kŏ-myoo-ni-kă-bil-i-tee) *n.*

com·mu·ni·ca·tion (kŏ-myoo-ni-kay-shŏn) *n.* 1. communicating. 2. something that communicates information from one person to another, a letter or message. 3. a means of communicating, as a road, railroad, telegraph line, radio, or other link between places.

com·mu·ni·ca·tive (kŏ-myoo-ni-kă-tiv) *adj.* ready and willing to talk and give information.

com·mun·ion (kŏ-myoon-yŏn) *n.* 1. fellowship,

having ideas or beliefs in common; *churches in communion with one another,* those that accept each other's doctrines and sacraments. 2. social dealings between people. 3. a body of Christians belonging to the same denomination, *the Anglican communion.* 4. *Communion,* (also *Holy Communion*) the Christian sacrament in which bread and wine are consecrated and consumed, the Eucharist.

com·mu·ni·qué (kŏ-myoo-ni-kay) *n.* an official communication giving a report of a meeting or a battle etc.

com·mu·nism (kom-yŭ-niz-ĕm) *n.* 1. a social system in which property is owned by the community and each member works for the common benefit. 2. *Communism,* a political doctrine or movement seeking to overthrow capitalism and establish a form of communism, such a system established in the U.S.S.R. and elsewhere.

com·mu·nist (kom-yŭ-nist) *n.* 1. a supporter of communism. 2. *Communist,* a member of the **Communist Party,** a political party supporting Communism.

com·mu·nis·tic (kom-yŭ-nis-tik) *adj.* of or like communism.

com·mu·ni·ty (kŏ-myoo-ni-tee) *n.* (*pl.* **-ties**) 1. a body of people living in one place or district or country and considered as a whole. 2. a group with common interests or origins, *the Hispanic community.* 3. fellowship, being alike in some way, *community of interests.* □**community antenna television,** a system for transmitting television signals employing cable and a single large antenna. **community center,** a place providing social, recreational, and educational facilities for a neighborhood. **Community Chest,** a fund of voluntary contributions for use in a community. **community college,** a junior college usually financed by taxes and attended primarily by local residents. **community property,** property regarded by law as owned jointly and shared equally by husband and wife. **community sing,** a concert by a large gathering of people singing in chorus.

com·mu·ta·tion (kom-yŭ-tay-shŏn) *n.* commuting. □**commutation ticket,** a passenger ticket available at a reduced rate for a set number of trips over a specified route.

com·mu·ta·tor (kom-yŭ-tay-tŏr) *n.* a device used to reverse the direction of an electric current.

com·mute (kŏ-myoot) *v.* (**com·mut·ed, com·mut·ing**) 1. to exchange for something else; *commuted part of his pension for a lump sum,* chose to take a lump sum in exchange. 2. to change (a punishment) into something less severe. 3. to travel from a suburb by bus or train or car to and from one's daily work in a city. **commute** *n.* *(slang)* a trip made in commuting, *she has a long commute.*

com·mut·er (kŏ-myoo-ter) *n.* a person who commutes to and from work.

Com·o·ros (kom-ŏ-rohz) a group of islands off the east coast of Africa. **Com·o′ran** *adj. & n.*

comp. *abbr.* 1. comparative. 2. compilation. 3. compiled. 4. compiler. 5. complete. 6. composition. 7. compositor. 8. compound.

com·pact¹ (kom-pakt) *n.* an agreement, a contract.

com·pact² (kŏm-pakt) *adj.* 1. closely or neatly packed together. 2. concise. **compact** (kom-pakt) *n.* 1. a small container for face powder etc. 2. a compact car. **com·pact′ly** *adv.* **com·pact′ness** *n.* □**compact car,** a small automobile designed for economical operation.

com·pact·ed (kŏm-pak-tĭd) *adj.* joined or pressed firmly together, packed into a small space.

com·pac·tor (kŏm-pak-tŏr) *n.* a machine that compresses waste for easy disposal.

com·pan·ion (kŏm-pan-yŏn) *n.* 1. a person who accompanies another or who shares in his work, pleasures, misfortunes, etc. 2. a person employed to live with and accompany another. 3. one of two things that match or go together, *the companion volume will be published later.*

com·pan·ion·a·ble (kŏm-pan-yŏ-nă-bĕl) *adj.* friendly, sociable. **com·pan′ion·a·bly** *adv.*

com·pan·ion·ate (kŏ-pan-yŏ-nit) *adj.* 1. pertaining to companions. 2. blending pleasantly. ☐**companionate marriage,** a form of marriage in which husband and wife have none of the legal obligations of marriage and which provides for easy divorce.

com·pan·ion·ship (kŏm-pan-yŏn-ship) *n.* the state of being companions, the friendly feeling of being with another or others.

com·pan·ion·way (kŏm-pan-yŏn-way) *n.* a staircase from a ship's deck to the saloon or cabins.

com·pa·ny (kum-pă-nee) *n.* (*pl.* for definitions 4 & 5 **-nies**) 1. companionship, *travel with us for company.* 2. a number of people assembled, guests, *we're expecting company.* 3. the people with whom one spends one's time, *got into bad company.* 4. people working together or united for business purposes, a firm; *the ship's company,* the officers and crew. 5. a subdivision of a military battalion. ☐**company man,** an employee devoted to promoting the interests of the company for which he works; an employee despised by fellow employees because of his strong allegiance to the company. **keep a person company,** to accompany, especially for the sake of companionship. **keep company with,** *(old use)* to date steadily. **part company,** *see* **part.**

compar. *abbr.* comparative.

com·pa·ra·ble (kom-pă-ră-bĕl) *adj.* able or suitable to be compared, similar. **com′pa·ra·bly** *adv.* **com·pa·ra·bil·i·ty** (kom-pă-ră-bil-i-tee) *n.*

com·par·a·tive (kŏm-par-ă-tiv) *adj.* 1. involving comparison, *a comparative study of the output of two firms.* 2. estimated by comparison; *their comparative merits,* measured in relation to each other; *living in comparative comfort,* comfortably when compared against a previous standard or that of others. 3. of a grammatical form used in comparing, expressing "more," as *bigger, greater, worse.* **comparative** *n.* a comparative form of a word. **com·par′a·tive·ly** *adv.*

com·pare (kŏm-pair) *v.* (**com·pared, com·par·ing**) 1. to estimate the similarity between one thing and another. 2. to liken, to declare to be similar; *this film is not to be compared with his earlier ones,* is not as good as these. 3. to be worthy of comparison, *he cannot compare with Dickens as a novelist.* 4. to form the comparative and superlative of (an adjective or adverb). **compare** *n.* comparison, *beautiful beyond compare.* ☐**compare apples and oranges,** *(informal)* to compare two things, ideas, etc. that are too unlike to justify fair comparison. **compare notes,** to exchange ideas or conclusions. ▷Use *compare with* when putting things or people etc. side by side to point out their similarities and differences, *he compared democracies with totalitarian nations.* Use *compare to* when likening a thing etc. to another, *shall I compare thee to a summer's day?*

com·par·i·son (kŏm-par-i-sŏn) *n.* comparing. ☐**beyond comparison,** not comparable because one is so much better than the other(s).

com·part·ment (kŏm-pahrt-mĕnt) *n.* 1. one of the spaces into which a structure is divided, separated by partitions. 2. such a division of a railroad car, steamship, etc.

com·part·men·tal·ize (kum-pahrt-men-tă-līz) *v.* (**com·part·men·tal·ized, com·part·men·tal·iz·ing**) to divide into compartments or categories. **com·part·men·tal·i·za·tion** (kum-pahrt-men-tă-li-zay-shŏn) *n.*

com·pass (kum-păs) *n.* 1. a device with a needle that points to the magnetic north; *a radio compass,* a similar device for determining direction. 2. range, scope, *that was outside my compass.* 3. (often **compasses**) an instrument used for drawing circles, usually with two legs joined at one end. **compass** *v.* to encompass.

com·pas·sion (kŏm-pash-ŏn) *n.* a feeling of pity that makes one want to help or show mercy. **com·pas·sion·ate** (kŏm-pash-ŏ-nit) *adj.* **com·pas′sion·ate·ly** *adv.*

com·pat·i·ble (kŏm-pat-i-bĕl) *adj.* 1. capable of living together harmoniously. 2. able to exist or be used together, *at a speed compatible with safety.* **com·pat′i·bly** *adv.* **com·pat·i·bil·i·ty** (kŏm-pat-i-bil-i-tee) *n.*

com·pa·tri·ot (kŏm-pay-tri-ŏt) *n.* a person from the same country as another.

com·peer (kŏm-peer) *n.* 1. an equal, a peer. 2. a comrade.

com·pel (kŏm-pel) *v.* (**com·pelled, com·pel·ling**) 1. to use force or influence to cause (a person) to do something, to allow no choice of action. 2. to arouse irresistibly, *her courage compels admiration.* ▷A person *compelled to do something* is forced to act against his will. When he is *impelled to do something,* he is responding to an inner motive.

com·pen·di·ous (kŏm-pen-di-ŭs) *adj.* giving much information concisely.

com·pen·di·um (kŏm-pen-di-ŭm) *n.* (*pl.* **-di·ums, -di·a,** *pr.* -di-ă) a concise and comprehensive summary.

com·pen·sate (kŏm-pĕn-sayt) *v.* (**com·pen·sat·ed, com·pen·sat·ing**) 1. to make a suitable payment in return for (a loss or damage etc.). 2. to counterbalance, *our present success compensates for earlier failures.* **com·pen·sa·tion** (kom-pĕn-say-shŏn) *n.*

com·pen·sa·to·ry (kŏm-pen-să-tohr-ee) *adj.* compensating.

com·pete (kŏm-peet) *v.* (**com·pet·ed, com·pet·ing**) to take part in a competition.

com·pe·tence (kom-pĕ-tĕns) *n.* 1. sufficiency of means for living. 2. being competent. 3. legal capacity or eligibility. **com′pe·ten·cy** *n.*

com·pe·tent (kom-pĕ-tĕnt) *adj.* 1. having the ability or authority to do what is required. 2. adequate, satisfactory, *a competent knowledge of French.* **com′pe·tent·ly** *adv.*

com·pe·ti·tion (kom-pĕ-tish-ŏn) *n.* 1. a friendly contest in which people try to do better than their rivals. 2. competing, *competition for export markets.* 3. those competing with oneself, *we have strong foreign competition.*

com·pet·i·tive (kŏm-pet-i-tiv) *adj.* of or involving competition, *competitive sports; the competitive spirit,* enjoying competition; *a competitive examination,* one in which people compete for a prize; *at competitive prices,* at prices that compare favor-

ably with those of rivals. **com·pet′i·tive·ly** adv.
com·pet′i·tive·ness n.
com·pet·i·tor (kŏm-pet-i-tŏr) n. one who competes.
com·pile (kŏm-pɪl) v. (**com·piled, com·pil·ing**) 1. to collect and arrange (information) into a list or book. 2. to make up (a book etc.) in this way, compile a dictionary. **com·pil′er** n.
com·pi·la·tion (kom-pi-lay-shŏn) n.
com·pla·cent (kŏm-play-sĕnt) adj. self-satisfied. **com·pla′cent·ly** adv. **com·pla′cence** n. **com·pla′cen·cy** n. ▷Do not confuse complacent with complaisant.
com·plain (kŏm-playn) v. 1. to say that one is dissatisfied, to protest that something is wrong. 2. to state that one is suffering from a pain etc. **com·plain′er** n. **com·plain′ant** n.
com·plaint (kŏm-playnt) n. 1. a statement saying that one is dissatisfied, a protest. 2. a cause of dissatisfaction, a list of complaints. 3. an illness.
com·plai·sant (kŏm-play-sănt) adj. willing to do what pleases others. **com·plai′sance** n. ▷Do not confuse complaisant with complacent.
com·ple·ment (kom-plĕ-mĕnt) n. 1. that which makes a thing complete. 2. the number or quantity needed to fill something, the bus had its full complement of passengers. **complement** v. to make complete, to form a complement to, the hat complements the outfit. ▷Do not confuse complement with compliment.
com·ple·men·ta·ry (kom-plĕ-men-tă-ree) adj. completing, forming a complement. □**complementary colors**, two colors of light that when mixed have the appearance of white or gray (as blue and yellow). ▷Do not confuse complementary with complimentary.
com·plete (kŏm-pleet) adj. 1. having all its parts, not lacking anything. 2. finished, the work is now complete. 3. thorough, in every way, a complete stranger. **complete** v. (**com·plet·ed, com·plet·ing**) 1. to add what is lacking to (a thing) and make it complete. 2. to finish (a piece of work etc.). 3. to add what is required, complete the questionnaire. **com·plete′ly** adv. **com·plete′ness** n.
com·ple·tion (kŏm-plee-shŏn) n. completing, being completed.
com·plex (kŏm-pleks) adj. 1. made up of parts. 2. complicated. **complex** (kom-pleks) n. 1. a complex whole. 2. a connected group of feelings or ideas that influence a person's behavior or mental attitude, a persecution complex. 3. a set of buildings. □**complex sentence**, a sentence containing at least one subordinate clause. **com·plex·i·ty** (kŏm-plek-si-tee) n. (pl. -ties).
com·plex·ion (kŏm-plek-shŏn) n. 1. the color, texture, and appearance of the skin of the face. 2. the general character or nature of things; that puts a different complexion on the matter, makes it seem different. **com·plex′ioned** adj.
com·pli·ance (kŏm-plɪ-ăns) n. 1. action in accordance with a request, a command, etc. 2. a tendency to submit easily. □**in compliance with**, according to (a regulation, request, etc.). **com·pli′an·cy** n.
com·pli·ant (kŏm-plɪ-ănt) adj. complying, obedient. **com·pli′ant·ly** adv.
com·pli·cate (kom-plĭ-kayt) v. (**com·pli·cat·ed, com·pli·cat·ing**) to make complex or complicated.
com·pli·cat·ed (kom-plĭ-kay-tid) adj. made up of many parts, difficult to understand or use because

of this. **com′pli·cat·ed·ly** adv. **com′pli·cat·ed·ness** n.
com·pli·ca·tion (kom-plĭ-kay-shŏn) n. 1. complicating, being made complicated. 2. a complex combination of things. 3. something that complicates or adds difficulties. 4. an illness or condition that arises during the course of another and makes it worse.
com·plic·i·ty (kŏm-plis-i-tee) n. (pl. -ties) partnership or involvement in wrongdoing.
com·pli·ment (kom-plĭ-mĕnt) n. 1. an expression of praise or admiration either in words or by action. 2. compliments, formal greetings conveyed in a message. **compliment** (kom-plĭ-ment) v. to pay a compliment to, to congratulate. ▷Do not confuse compliment with complement.
com·pli·men·ta·ry (kom-plĭ-men-tă-ree) adj. 1. expressing a compliment. 2. given free of charge. ▷Do not confuse complimentary with complementary.
com·ply (kŏm-plɪ) v. (**com·plied, com·ply·ing**) to do as one is asked or ordered; comply with the rules, obey them.
com·po·nent (kŏm-poh-nĕnt) n. one of the parts of which a thing is composed. **component** adj. being a component.
com·port·ment (kŏm-pohrt-mĕnt) n. behavior, manner of bearing.
com·pose (kŏm-pohz) v. (**com·posed, com·pos·ing**) 1. to form, to make up, the group was composed of twenty students. 2. to create in music or literature. 3. to arrange into good order. 4. to make calm, to compose oneself.
com·posed (kŏm-pohzd) adj. calm, with one's feelings under control. **com·pos·ed·ly** (kŏm-poh-zid-lee) adv.
com·pos·er (kŏm-poh-zĕr) n. a person who composes music etc.
com·pos·ite (kŏm-poz-it) adj. made up of parts, composite photograph; composite material. **composite** n. 1. a composite thing. 2. a plant of which the apparently single flower consists of many flowers (as daisy, dandelion, etc.).
com·po·si·tion (kom-pŏ-zish-ŏn) n. 1. putting together into a whole, composing. 2. something composed, a piece of music or writing, a short essay written as a school exercise. 3. the parts of which something is made up, the composition of the soil. 4. the arrangement of parts of a picture. 5. a compound artificial substance.
com·pos·i·tor (kŏm-poz-i-tŏr) n. a person who sets up type for printing.
com·pos men·tis (kŏm-pŏs men-tis) in one's right mind, sane. ▷Latin.
com·post (kom-pohst) n. 1. a mixture of decaying substances used as a fertilizer. 2. a mixture usually of soil and other ingredients for growing seedlings, cuttings, etc. **compost** v. to treat with compost, to make into compost.
com·po·sure (kŏm-poh-zhŭr) n. calmness of mind or manner.
com·pote (kom-poht) n. fruit stewed with sugar.
com·pound[1] (kom-pownd) adj. made up of several parts or ingredients. **compound** n. a compound thing or substance. **compound** (kŏm-pownd) v. 1. to put together to form a whole, to combine. 2. to add to or increase. 3. to pay (interest) on interest as well as on principal. 4. to refrain from revealing (a crime), compounding a felony. □**compound-complex sentence**, a sentence having two or more independent and one or more subordinate clauses. **compound fracture**, one

in which the fractured bone has pierced the skin.
compound interest, interest paid on the original
capital and on the interest that has been added
to it. **compound sentence,** a sentence having
two or more independent clauses.
compound² (kom-pownd) *n.* a fenced-in enclosure, (in India, China, etc.) an enclosure in which
a house or factory stands, *the Kennedy compound.*
com·pre·hend (kom-pri-hend) *v.* 1. to grasp mentally, to understand. 2. to include. **com·pre·
hend'ing·ly** *adv.* **com·pre·hen·sion** (kom-
pri-hen-shŏn) *n.*
com·pre·hen·si·ble (kom-pri-hen-si-bĕl) *adj.*
able to be understood. **com·pre·hen'si·bly**
adv. **com·pre·hen·si·bil·i·ty** (kom-pri-hen-si-
bil-i-tee) *n.*
com·pre·hen·sive (kom-pri-hen-siv) *adj.* inclusive, including much or all. **com·pre·hen'
sive·ly** *adv.* **com·pre·hen'sive·ness** *n.*
com·press (kŏm-pres) *v.* to squeeze together, to
force into less space. **compress** (kom-pres) *n.*
a pad or cloth pressed on the body to stop bleeding or to cool inflammation etc. **com·pressed'**
adj. **com·pres·sion** (kŏm-presh-ŏn) *n.* **com·
pres'sor** *n.* ☐**compressed air,** air that undergoes compression, so that it exerts greater pressure
than the surrounding atmosphere.
com·pres·si·ble (kŏm-pres-i-bĕl) *adj.* able to be
compressed.
com·prise (kŏm-prīz) *v.* **(com·prised, com·
pris·ing)** 1. to include. 2. to consist of, *the apartment comprises three rooms.* 3. to form, to make
up. (▷The words *constitute* or *compose* are prefer-
able in this sense. It is incorrect to say or write
the apartment is comprised of three rooms.)
com·pro·mise (kom-prŏ-mīz) *n.* 1. making a settlement by each side giving up part of its demands.
2. a settlement made in this way. 3. something
that is halfway between opposite opinions or
courses of action etc. **compromise** *v.* **(com·
pro·mised, com·pro·mis·ing)** 1. to settle a
dispute by a compromise. 2. to expose to danger
or suspicion or scandal etc. by unwise action, *a
compromising situation.*
comp·trol·ler (kŏn-troh-lĕr) = **controller.**
com·pul·sion (kŏm-pul-shŏn) *n.* 1. compelling,
being compelled. 2. an irresistible urge.
com·pul·sive (kŏm-pul-siv) *adj.* 1. compelling. 2.
acting as if from compulsion, *a compulsive gambler.* **com·pul'sive·ly** *adv.*
com·pul·so·ry (kŏm-pul-sŏ-ree) *adj.* that must be
done, required by the rules etc. **com·pul'so·
ri·ly** *adv.*
com·punc·tion (kŏm-pungk-shŏn) *n.* the pricking
of conscience, a slight regret or scruple.
com·pute (kŏm-pyoot) *v.* **(com·put·ed, com·
put·ing)** to reckon mathematically, to calculate.
com·pu·ta·tion (kŏm-pyŭ-tay-shŏn) *n.*
com·put·er (kŏm-pyoo-tĕr) *n.* an electronic machine for making calculations, storing and analyzing information fed into it, and controlling machinery automatically.
com·put·er·ize (kŏm-pyoo-tĕ-rīz) *v.* **(com·
put·er·ized, com·put·er·iz·ing)** 1. to equip
with a computer or computers. 2. to produce or
perform by means of a computer. **com·put·er·
i·za·tion** (kŏm-pyoo-tĕ-ri-zay-shŏn) *n.*
com·rade (kom-rad) *n.* 1. a companion who shares
one's activities. 2. a fellow socialist or communist.
com'rade·ly *adv.* **com'rade·ship** *n.*
COMSAT (kom-sat) *n.* Communications Satellite
Corporation.

con¹ (kon) *v.* **(conned, con·ning)** *(informal)* to
persuade or swindle after winning a person's confidence. ☐**con game,** *(slang)* a confidence game.
con man, *(slang)* a confidence man.
con² *adv.* opposing, against. **con** *n.* that which opposes, as a body of evidence, a vote, etc. ☐**pro
and con,** *see* **pro².**
con³ *n.* *(slang)* a convict.
Con·a·kry (kon-ă-kree) the capital of Guinea.
con brio (kon bree-oh) *(of music)* spiritedly, with
vigor. ▷Italian.
con·cat·e·nate (kon-kat-ĕ-nayt) *v.* **(con·cat·
e·nat·ed, con·cat·e·nat·ing)** to link (ideas,
facts, etc.) together.
con·cat·e·na·tion (kon-kat-ĕ-nay-shŏn) *n.* a sequence or combination.
con·cave (kon-kayv) *adj.* curving like the surface
of a ball as seen from the inside. **con·cav·i·
ty** (kon-kav-i-tee) *n.*
con·ceal (kŏn-seel) *v.* to keep secret or hidden.
con·ceal'ment *n.*
con·cede (kŏn-seed) *v.* **(con·ced·ed, con·
ced·ing)** 1. to admit that something is true. 2.
to grant, to allow, to yield, *they conceded us the
right to cross their land.* 3. to admit defeat in (a
contest), especially before the official end, *our opponents conceded.*
con·ceit (kŏn-seet) *n.* too much pride in oneself.
con·ceit·ed (kŏn-see-tid) *adj.* being too proud of
oneself.
con·ceiv·a·ble (kŏn-see-vă-bĕl) *adj.* able to be
imagined or believed. **con·ceiv'a·bly** *adv.*
con·ceive (kŏn-seev) *v.* **(con·ceived, con·
ceiv·ing)** 1. to become pregnant. 2. to form (an
idea, plan, etc.) in the mind, to think.
con·cen·trate (kon-sĕn-trayt) *v.* **(con·cen·
trat·ed, con·cen·trat·ing)** 1. to employ all
one's thought or attention or effort on something.
2. to bring or come together in one place. 3. to
make less dilute. **concentrate** *n.* a concentrated
substance or solution. **con·cen·tra·tion** (kon-
sĕn-tray-shŏn) *n.* **concentration camp,** a
place where civilian political prisoners are brought
together and confined.
con·cen·trat·ed (kon-sĕn-tray-tid) *adj.* 1. (of a
solution etc.) having a large proportion of effective
elements, not dilute. 2. intense, *concentrated hatred.*
con·cen·tric (kŏn-sen-trik) *adj.* having the same
center, *concentric circles.*
con·cept (kon-sept) *n.* an idea, a general notion,
the concept of freedom. **con·cep·tu·al** (kŏn-sep-
choo-ăl) *adj.*
con·cep·tion (kŏn-sep-shŏn) *n.* 1. conceiving, being conceived. 2. an idea.
con·cep·tu·al·ize (kŏn-sep-choo-ă-līz) *v.* **(con·
cep·tu·al·ized, con·cep·tu·al·iz·ing)** to
form an idea of. **con·cep·tu·al·i·za·tion** (kŏn-
sep-choo-ă-li-zay-shŏn) *n.*
con·cern (kŏn-surn) *v.* 1. to be about, to have as
its subject, *the story concerns a group of spies.*
2. to be of importance to, to affect. 3. to take
up the time or attention of; *she concerned herself
about it,* gave it her care and attention. **concern**
n. 1. something of interest or importance, a responsibility; *it's no concern of mine,* I have nothing
to do with it. 2. worry, anxiety. 3. a business, a
firm, *a going concern.*
con·cerned (kŏn-surnd) *adj.* worried, anxious.
con·cern·ing (kŏn-sur-ning) *prep.* about, in regard
to.
con·cert (kon-sĕrt) *n.* 1. a musical entertainment.

2. agreement, cooperation. **concert** (kŏn-surt) *v.* to arrange by mutual agreement or coordination. ☐**at concert pitch,** in a state of unusually great efficiency or intensity. **in concert,** in combination, together.

con·cert·ed (kŏn-sur-tid) *adj.* arranged by mutual agreement, done in cooperation.

con·cer·ti·na (kon-sĕr-tee-nă) *n.* a portable musical instrument with hexagonal ends and bellows, played by pressing keys at each end.

con·cert·ize (kon-sĕr-tız) *v.* **(con·cert·ized, con·cert·iz·ing)** to perform in concerts.

con·cert·mas·ter (kon-sĕrt-mas-tĕr) *n.* the leading first violinist of a symphony orchestra.

con·cer·to (kŏn-cher-toh) *n.* (*pl.* **-tos**) a musical composition for one or more solo instruments and an orchestra.

con·ces·sion (kŏn-sesh-ŏn) *n.* **1.** conceding. **2.** something conceded. **3.** a right given by the owners of land to extract minerals etc. from it or to sell goods there, *an oil concession; a food concession.*

con·ces·sion·aire (kŏn-sesh-ŏ-nair) one who holds a concession. *n.*

conch (konch) *n.* the spiral shell of a kind of shellfish, sometimes used as a horn.

con·cierge (kon-syerzh) *n.* the doorkeeper and janitor of a building, especially in France.

con·cil·i·ate (kŏn-sil-i-ayt) *v.* **(con·cil·i·at·ed, con·cil·i·at·ing)** **1.** to overcome the anger or hostility of, to win the goodwill of. **2.** to reconcile (people who disagree). **con·cil·i·a·tion** (kŏn-sil-i-ay-shŏn) *n.* **con·cil'i·a·tor** *n.* **con·cil·i·a·to·ry** (kŏn-sil-i-ă-tohr-ee) *adj.*

con·cise (kŏn-sıs) *adj.* brief, giving much information in few words. **con·cise'ly** *adv.* **con·cise'ness** *n.*

con·clave (kon-klayv) *n.* a private meeting for discussing something, in *conclave.*

con·clude (kŏn-klood) *v.* **(con·clud·ed, con·clud·ing)** **1.** to bring or come to an end. **2.** to arrange, to settle finally, *they concluded a treaty.* **3.** to arrive at a belief or opinion by reasoning, *we concluded that they were correct.*

con·clu·sion (kŏn-kloo-zhŏn) *n.* **1.** ending, an end, *at the conclusion of his speech.* **2.** arrangement, settling, *conclusion of the treaty.* **3.** a belief or opinion based on reasoning. ☐**in conclusion,** lastly, to conclude.

con·clu·sive (kŏn-kloo-siv) *adj.* ending doubt, completely convincing, *conclusive evidence of his guilt.* **con·clu'sive·ly** *adv.* **con·clu'sive·ness** *n.*

con·coct (kŏn-kokt) *v.* **1.** to prepare by putting ingredients together. **2.** to invent, *concocted an excuse.* **con·coc·tion** (kŏn-kok-shŏn) *n.*

con·com·i·tant (kŏn-kom-i-tănt) *adj.* accompanying. **concomitant** *n.* an accompanying thing.

con·cord (kon-kord) *n.* agreement or harmony between people or things.

Con·cord (kong-kŏrd) the capital of New Hampshire.

con·cord·ance (kon-kor-dăns) *n.* **1.** an index of the important words used in a book or an author's writings, *a concordance to the Bible.* **2.** harmony, agreement.

con·cor·dant (kon-kor-dănt) *adj.* harmonious, in concord (with).

con·cor·dat (kon-kor-dat) *n.* an official agreement.

Con·cord (kong-kŏrd) **grape** a large purplish grape of the eastern U.S.

con·course (kon-kohrs) *n.* **1.** a crowd, a gathering. **2.** an open area through which people pass, as at a railroad station.

con·crete (kon-kreet, kon-kreet) *n.* a mixture of cement with sand and gravel, used for building and paving. **concrete** *adj.* **1.** existing in material form, able to be touched and felt. **2.** definite, positive, *concrete evidence.* **concrete** *v.* **(con·cret·ed, con·cret·ing)** **1.** to cover with or embed in concrete. **2.** to form into a solid mass, to solidify. ☐**concrete jungle,** a city considered as a place where people have to struggle for survival. **con·crete'ly** *adv.* **con·crete'ness** *n.*

con·cre·tion (kon-kree-shŏn) *n.* a hard solid mass.

con·cu·bine (kong-kyŭ-bın) *n.* **1.** a secondary wife in countries where polygamy is customary. **2.** a woman cohabitating with a man who is not her husband. **con·cu·bin·age** (kon-kyoo-bĭ-nij) *n.*

con·cu·pis·cence (kon-kyoo-pi-sĕns) *n.* intense sexual desire. **con·cu'pis·cent** *adj.*

con·cur (kŏn-kur) *v.* **(con·curred, con·cur·ring)** **1.** to agree in opinion. **2.** to happen together, to coincide.

con·cur·rence (kŏn-kur-ĕns) *n.* **1.** agreement, *concurrence of opinion.* **2.** simultaneous occurrence of events.

con·cur·rent (kŏn-kur-ĕnt) *adj.* existing or occurring at the same time. **con·cur'rent·ly** *adv.*

con·cuss (kŏn-kus) *v.* **1.** to subject to concussion. **2.** to shake violently.

con·cus·sion (kŏn-kush-ŏn) *n.* injury to the brain caused by a hard blow.

con·demn (kŏn-dem) *v.* **1.** to express strong disapproval of. **2.** to pronounce guilty, to convict. **3.** to sentence, *was condemned to death.* **4.** to destine to an unhappy fate. **5.** to declare unfit for use or uninhabitable, *condemned houses.* **con·dem·na·tion** (kon-dem-nay-shŏn) *n.* **con·dem·na·to·ry** (kon-dem-nă-tohr-ee) *adj.*

con·den·sate (kon-dĕn-sayt) *n.* a product of condensation.

con·dense (kŏn-dens) *v.* **(con·densed, con·dens·ing)** **1.** to make denser or more concentrated. **2.** to change or be changed from gas or vapor into liquid. **3.** to express in fewer words, *a condensed report on the meeting.* **con·den·sa·tion** (kon-den-say-shŏn) *n.* ☐**condensed milk,** milk made thick by evaporation and sweetened.

con·dens·er (kŏn-dens-ĕr) *n.* a capacitator.

con·de·scend (kon-di-send) *v.* to behave in a way that shows (pleasantly or unpleasantly) one's feeling of dignity or superiority. **con·de·scen·sion** (kon-di-sen-shŏn) *n.* **con·des·cend'ing·ly** *adv.*

con·dign (kŏn-dın) *adj.* (of punishment etc.) severe and well-deserved.

con·di·ment (kon-dĭ-mĕnt) *n.* a seasoning (such as salt or pepper) for food, a relish (such as ketchup or mustard).

con·di·tion (kŏn-dish-ŏn) *n.* **1.** the state in which a person or thing is with regard to characteristics and circumstances. **2.** a state of physical fitness or (of things) fitness for use, *get into condition; out of condition,* not fully fit. **3.** an abnormality, *she has a heart condition.* **4.** something required as part of an agreement. **5.** *conditions,* the facts or situations or surroundings that affect something, *working conditions are good.* **condition** *v.* **1.** to bring into a desired condition, to make physically fit, to put into a proper state for work or use. **2.** to have a strong effect on. **3.** to train, to accustom. **con·di'tion·er** *n.* ☐**conditioned reflex** *or* **response**, a reaction produced by training, not a natural one. **on condition that**, on the understanding that (a thing will be done).

con·di·tion·al (kŏn-dish-ŏ-năl) *adj.* not absolute, containing a condition or stipulation, *a conditional agreement.* **con·di'tion·al·ly** *adv.*

con·do (kon-doh) *n.* (*pl.* **-dos**) (*informal*) a condominium (definitions 1 and 2).

con·dole (kŏn-dohl) *v.* (**con·doled, con·dol·ing**) to express sympathy. **con·dol'ence** *n.*

con·do·min·i·um (kon-dŏ-min-i-ŭm) *n.* (*pl.* **-ums**) 1. a building in which apartments are individually owned. 2. one of these apartments. 3. joint control of a territory by two or more nations. 4. a territory so controlled.

con·done (kŏn-dohn) *v.* (**con·doned, con·don·ing**) to forgive or overlook (wrongdoing) without punishment. **con·do·na·tion** (kon-doh-nay-shŏn) *n.*

con·dor (kon-dor) *n.* either of two large vultures, one of South America and the other of western North America (the **California condor**).

con·duce (kŏn-doos) *v.* (**con·duced, con·duc·ing**) to help to cause or produce.

con·du·cive (kŏn-doo-siv) *adj.* helping to cause or produce, *an atmosphere that is conducive to work.*

con·duct (kŏn-dukt) *v.* 1. to lead or guide; *conducted tour*, one escorted by a guide. 2. to be the conductor of (a choir or orchestra or music). 3. to manage or direct (business or negotiations etc., or an experiment). 4. to have the property of allowing heat, light, sound, or electricity to pass along or through. **conduct** (kon-dukt) *n.* 1. a person's behavior. 2. managing or directing affairs; *the conduct of the war*, the way it is being conducted. ☐**conduct oneself**, to behave.

con·duct·ance (kŏn-duk-täns) *n.* the conducting power of a substance.

con·duc·tion (kŏn-duk-shŏn) *n.* transmission or conducting of heat or electricity etc.

con·duc·tive (kŏn-duk-tiv) *adj.* having the property of conducting. **con·duc·tiv·i·ty** (kon-duk-tiv-i-tee) *n.*

con·duc·tor (kŏn-duk-tŏr) *n.* 1. a person who directs the performance of an orchestra or choir etc. by gestures. 2. one who collects the fares in a bus or train. 3. a substance that conducts heat or electricity etc.

con·duit (kon-doo-it) *n.* 1. a pipe or channel for conveying liquids. 2. a tube protecting insulated electric wires.

cone (kohn) *n.* 1. a solid body that narrows to a point from a round flat base. 2. something shaped like this. 3. the dry fruit of certain evergreen trees, consisting of woody scales arranged in a shape suggesting a cone. 4. an ice cream cone.

cone·head (kohn-hed) *n.* (*slang*) an intellectual.

Con·es·to·ga (kon-i-stoh-gă) **wagon** *n.* a covered wagon (*see* **cover**).

co·ney (koh-nee) *n.* 1. rabbit skin or rabbit fur used in making clothes. 2. a rabbit or small similar animal.

conf. *abbr.* conference.

con·fab (kon-fab) *n.* (*informal*) an impromptu or informal conference.

con·fec·tion (kŏn-fek-shŏn) *n.* something made of various things, especially sweet ones, put together. 2. candy.

con·fec·tion·er (kŏn-fek-shŏ-nĕr) *n.* a maker or retailer of confectionery.

con·fec·tion·er·y (kŏn-fek-shŏ-ner-ee) *n.* (*pl.* **-er·ies**) 1. candies. 2. a confectioner's store.

con·fed·er·a·cy (kŏn-fed-ĕ-ră-see) *n.* (*pl.* **-cies**) 1. a union of people or states. 2. **the Confederacy**, the Confederate States of America, the league of southern states that seceded from the U.S. in 1860–1.

con·fed·er·ate (kŏn-fed-ĕ-rit) *adj.* allied, joined by agreement or treaty. **confederate** *n.* 1. a member of a confederacy. 2. an ally, an accomplice. ☐**the Confederate States of America**, *see* **confederacy**.

con·fed·er·at·ed (kŏn-fed-ĕ-ray-tid) *adj.* united by agreement or treaty.

con·fed·er·a·tion (kŏn-fed-ĕ-ray-shŏn) *n.* 1. joining in an alliance. 2. a confederated group of people or organizations or nations or states.

con·fer (kŏn-fur) *v.* (**con·ferred, con·fer·ring**) 1. to grant, to bestow. 2. to hold a conference or discussion.

con·fer·ee (kon-fĕ-ree) 1. a person at a conference. 2. a recipient (of a grant etc.).

con·fer·ence (kon-fĕ-rĕns) *n.* a meeting for discussion.

con·fer·ment (kŏn-fur-mĕnt) *n.* granting, bestowing.

con·fer·ra·ble (kŏn-fur-ră-bĕl) *adj.* able to be conferred.

con·fess (kŏn-fes) *v.* 1. to state formally that one has done wrong or has a weakness. 2. to state one's attitude or reaction reluctantly, *I must confess that I am puzzled.* 3. to declare one's sins formally, especially to a priest. 4. (of a priest) to hear the confession of.

con·fess·ed·ly (kŏn-fes-id-lee) *adv.* according to a person's own confession.

con·fes·sion (kŏn-fesh-ŏn) *n.* 1. confessing. 2. a thing confessed, a statement of one's wrongdoing. 3. a declaration of one's religious beliefs or one's principles, *a confession of faith.*

con·fes·sion·al (kŏn-fesh-ŏ-năl) *n.* an enclosed stall in a church, where a priest sits to hear confessions. **confessional** *adj.* of confession.

con·fes·sor (kŏn-fes-ŏr) *n.* 1. a priest who hears confessions and gives spiritual counsel. 2. a person who keeps to the Christian faith in the face of danger, *King Edward the Confessor.*

con·fet·ti (kŏn-fet-ee) *n.* bits of colored paper for throwing, as by wedding guests at the bride and bridegroom.

con·fi·dant (kon-fi-dant, kon-fi-**dant**) *n.* a person in whom one confides. ▷Do not confuse *confidant* with *confident.*

con·fi·dante (kon-fi-dant, kon-fi-**dant**) *n.* a female confidant.

con·fide (kŏn-frd) *v.* (**con·fid·ed, con·fid·ing**) 1. to tell confidentially; *confided in his friend*, told him things confidentially. 2. to entrust.

con·fi·dence (kon-fi-dĕns) *n.* 1. firm trust. 2. a feeling of certainty, self-reliance, boldness, *he lacks confidence.* 3. something told confidentially, *he has listened to many confidences.* ☐**confidence man**, one who defrauds people by means of a **confidence game**, a dishonest scheme, such as one in which a victim is persuaded to entrust his valuables to the confidence man, who gives a false impression of honesty. **in confidence**, as a secret. **in a person's confidence**, trusted with his secrets.

con·fi·dent (kon-fi-dĕnt) *adj.* feeling confidence, bold. **con′fi·dent·ly** *adv.* ▷Do not confuse *confident* with *confidant.*

con·fi·den·tial (kon-fi-den-shăl) *adj.* 1. spoken or written in confidence, to be kept secret. 2. entrusted with secrets, *a confidential secretary.* 3. confiding, *he spoke in a confidential tone.* **con· fi·den′tial·ly** *adv.* **con·fi·den·ti·al·i·ty** (kon-fi-den-shi-al-i-tee) *n.*

con·fig·u·ra·tion (kŏn-fig-yŭ-ray-shŏn) *n.* a method of arrangement, a shape or outline.

con·fine (kŏn-fɪn) *v.* **(con·fined, con·fin·ing)** 1. to keep or restrict within certain limits. 2. to keep shut up, *the prisoner is confined to his cell; confined to bed,* in bed because of illness. **con· fin′er** *n.*

con·fined (kŏn-fɪnd) *adj.* narrow, restricted, *a confined space.*

con·fine·ment (kŏn-fɪn-mĕnt) *n.* 1. confining, being confined. 2. the time during which a woman is giving birth to a baby.

con·fines (kon-fɪnz) *n. pl.* the limits or boundaries of an area.

con·firm (kŏn-furm) *v.* 1. to provide supporting evidence for the truth or correctness of, to prove. 2. to establish more firmly, *it confirmed his dislike of animals.* 3. to make definite or valid formally, *reservations made by telephone must be confirmed in writing.* 4. to administer the rite of confirmation to.

con·fir·ma·tion (kon-fɪr-may-shŏn) *n.* 1. confirming. 2. something that confirms. 3. a religious rite confirming a baptized person as a member of a Christian church. 4. a ceremony initiating a Jewish boy or girl into the Jewish faith.

con·fir·ma·to·ry (kŏn-fur-mă-tohr-ee) *adj.* confirming, *we found confirmatory evidence.*

con·firmed (kŏn-furmd) *adj.* firmly settled in some habit or condition, *a confirmed bachelor.*

con·fis·cate (kon-fi-skayt) *v.* **(con·fis·cat·ed, con·fis·cat·ing)** to take or seize by authority. **con·fis·ca·tion** (kon-fi-skay-shŏn) *n.* **con·fis· ca·to·ry** (kŏn-fis-kă-tohr-ee) *adj.*

con·fla·gra·tion (kon-flă-gray-shŏn) *n.* a great and destructive fire.

con·flict (kon-flikt) *n.* 1. a fight, a struggle. 2. disagreement between people with different ideas or beliefs. **conflict** (kŏn-flikt) *v.* to be in opposition or disagreement. □**conflict of interest,** a situation in which a person holding office has private business affairs that affect or are affected by his official activities.

con·flu·ence (kon-floo-ĕns) *n.* the place where two rivers unite. **con′flu·ent** *adj.*

con·fo·cal (kon-foh-kăl) *adj.* having the same focus or foci.

con·form (kŏn-form) *v.* 1. to act or be in accordance with, *conform to the rules.* 2. to keep to rules or general custom, *she refuses to conform.* **con·form·a·ble** (kŏn-for-mă-bĕl) *adj.* 1. similar to. 2. consistent with or adapted to (a thing).

con·for·ma·tion (kon-for-may-shŏn) *n.* 1. the way a thing is formed, its structure. 2. conforming.

con·form·ist (kŏn-for-mist) *n.* a person who readily conforms to established rules or standards etc.

con·form·i·ty (kŏn-for-mi-tee) *n.* (*pl.* **-ties**) conforming to established rules or standards etc. □**in conformity with,** in accordance with.

con·found (kon-fownd) *v.* 1. to astonish and perplex, to bewilder. 2. to confuse. 3. *(old use) to*

defeat, to overthrow. **confound (kon-fownd)** *interj.* an exclamation of annoyance, *confound it!*

con·found·ed (kon-fown-did) *adj.* (*informal*) damned, *a confounded nuisance.*

con·fra·ter·ni·ty (kon-fră-tur-ni-tee) *n.* (*pl.* **-ties**) a brotherhood or association with religious or charitable aims.

con·frere (kon-frair) *n.* a fellow member of a profession, scientific organization, etc.

con·front (kŏn-frunt) *v.* 1. to be or come face to face with, *the problems confronting us.* 2. to face boldly as an enemy or in defiance. 3. to bring face to face, *we confronted him with his accusers.* **con·fron·ta·tion** (kon-frŏn-tay-shŏn) *n.*

Con·fu·cian·ism (kŏn-fyoo-shă-niz-ĕm) *n.* the system of morality taught by Confucius, a Chinese philosopher (551?–479? B.C.). **Con·fu′cian** *adj.* & *n.*

con·fuse (kŏn-fyooz) *v.* **(con·fused, con·fus· ing)** 1. to throw into disorder, to mix up. 2. to throw the mind or feelings of (a person) into disorder, to destroy the composure of, *confuse him.* 3. to mix up in the mind, to fail to distinguish between. 4. to make unclear, *confuse the issue.* **con·fu·sion** (kŏn-fyoo-zhŏn) *n.*

con·fused (kŏn-fyoozd) *adj.* (of a person) not mentally sound. **con·fus·ed·ly** (kŏn-fyoo-zid-lee) *adv.*

con·fute (kŏn-fyoot) *v.* **(con·fut·ed, con·fut· ing)** to prove (a person or argument) to be wrong. **con·fu·ta·tion** (kon-fyuu-tay-shŏn) *n.*

Cong. *abbr.* 1. Congregational. 2. Congress. 3. Congressional.

con·ga (kong-gă) *n.* a dance in which people form a long winding line **(conga line).**

con·geal (kŏn-jeel) *v.* to become semisolid instead of liquid.

con·gen·ial (kŏn-jeen-yăl) *adj.* 1. pleasant because similar to oneself in character or tastes, *a congenial companion.* 2. suited or agreeable to oneself, *a congenial climate.* **con·gen′ial·ly** *adv.* **con· ge·ni·al·i·ty** (kŏn-jee-ni-al-i-tee) *n.*

con·gen·i·tal (kŏn-jen-i-tăl) *adj.* 1. existing since a person's birth, *a congenital deformity.* 2. born in a certain condition, *a congenital idiot.* **con· gen′i·tal·ly** *adv.* ▷Do not confuse *congenital* with *genetic.* A *congenital defect* is considered to be one that is not carried in the genes but results from conditions of birth.

con·ger (kong-gĕr) *n.* (also **conger eel**) a large sea eel.

con·ge·ries (kon-jeer-eez) *n.* a disorderly collection, a mass, a heap.

con·gest (kŏn-jest) *v.* 1. to fill. 2. to cause to accumulate excessively. **con·ges′tive** *adj.*

con·gest·ed (kŏn-jes-tid) *adj.* 1. too full, overcrowded. 2. (of an organ or tissue of the body) abnormally full of blood.

con·ges·tion (kŏn-jes-chŏn) *n.* a congested condition.

con·glom·er·ate (kŏn-glom-ĕ-rit) *adj.* gathered into a mass. **conglomerate** *n.* 1. a conglomerate mass. 2. a company formed by merging or acquiring several companies in different branches of industry. **conglomerate** (kŏn-glom-ĕ-rayt) *v.* **(con·glom·er·at·ed, con·glom·er·at·ing)** to collect into a coherent mass.

con·glom·er·a·tion (kŏn-glom-ĕ-ray-shŏn) *n.* a mass of different things put together.

Con·go (kong-goh) a country in West Africa.

con·grat·u·late (kŏn-grach-ŭ-layt) *v.* **(con·**

grat·u·lat·ed, con·grat·u·lat·ing) to praise and tell (a person) that one is pleased about his achievement or good fortune; *congratulating ourselves on our escape,* thinking ourselves fortunate, taking pleasure in it. **con·grat·u·la·tion** (kŏngrach-ŭ-lay-shŏn) *n.*

con·grat·u·la·to·ry (kŏn-grach-ŭ-lǎ-tohr-ee) *adj.* expressing congratulations.

con·gre·gate (kong-grĕ-gayt) *v.* **(con·gre·gat·ed, con·gre·gat·ing)** to flock together into a crowd.

con·gre·ga·tion (kong-grĕ-gay-shŏn) *n.* a group of people gathered together to take part in religious worship. **con·gre·ga'tion·al** *adj.*

Con·gre·ga·tion·al·ism (kong-grĕ-gay-shŏ-nǎliz-ĕm) *n.* a Protestant denomination in which each congregation governs itself.

con·gress (kong-gris) *n.* 1. a formal meeting of representatives, for discussion. 2. *Congress,* the lawmaking body of a country, especially of the U.S. **con·gres·sion·al** (kŏn-gresh-ŏ-nǎl) *adj.* **con·gress·man** (kong-gris-mǎn) *n.* (*pl.* **-men,** *pr.* **-mĕn**) a member of the U.S. House of Representatives.

con·gru·ence (kong-groo-ĕns) *n.* agreement, consistency. **con'gru·en·cy** *n.* **con'gru·ent** *adj.*

con·gru·ous (kong-groo-ŭs) *adj.* 1. agreeing, conformable. 2. fitting. **con·gru·i·ty** (kŏn-groo-itee) *n.*

con·ic (kon-ik) *adj.* of a cone. □**conic section,** a figure formed by intersection of a cone and a plane. **con·i·cal** (kon-i-kǎl) *adj.* cone-shaped. **con'i·cal·ly** *adv.*

co·ni·fer (kon-i-fĕr) *n.* a coniferous tree. **co·nif·er·ous** (kŏ-nif-ĕ-rŭs) *adj.* bearing cones. **conj.** *abbr.* 1. conjugation. 2. conjunction.

con·jec·tur·al (kŏn-jek-chŭ-rǎl) *adj.* based on conjecture.

con·jec·ture (kŏn-jek-chŭr) *v.* **(con·jec·tured, con·jec·tur·ing)** to guess. **conjecture** *n.* a guess.

con·join (kŏn-join) *v.* to join, to combine. **con·joint'** *adj.*

con·ju·gal (kon-jŭ-gǎl) *adj.* of marriage, of the relationship between husband and wife. □**conjugal love,** a sexual relationship within marriage.

con·ju·gate (kon-jŭ-gayt) *v.* **(con·ju·gat·ed, con·ju·gat·ing)** to give the different forms of (a verb), as *get, gets.* **conjugate** (kon-jŭ-git) *adj.* joined together, coupled. **con·ju·ga·tion** (konjŭ-gay-shŏn) *n.*

con·junct (kŏn-jungkt) *adj.* joined together, combined.

con·junc·tion (kŏn-jungk-shŏn) *n.* 1. a word that joins words or phrases or sentences, as *and, but.* 2. combination, union, *the four countries acted in conjunction.* 3. the occurrence of events etc. at the same time. 4. the apparent nearness of two or more heavenly bodies to each other, *these planets are in conjunction.*

con·junc·ti·va (kon-jungk-tɪ-vǎ) *n.* (*pl.* **-vas, -vae,** *pr.* -vee) the mucous membrane lining the inner eyelid and part of the eyeball.

con·junc·tive (kŏn-jungk-tiv) *adj.* 1. serving to join. 2. (in grammar) of the nature of a conjunction.

con·junc·ti·vi·tis (kŏn-jungk-ti-vɪ-tis) *n.* inflammation of the conjunctiva.

con·jure (kon-jŭr) *v.* **(con·jured, con·jur·ing)** 1. to perform tricks that appear to be magical,

especially by movements of the hands, *conjuring tricks.* 2. to summon (a spirit) to appear. 3. to produce as if from nothing, *managed to conjure up a meal.* 4. to produce in the mind, *mention of the Arctic conjures up visions of snow and ice.* **con·ju·ra·tion** (kon-jŭ-ray-shŏn) *n.* □**a name to conjure with,** a name of great importance. **conjuring man, conjure man** (in southern U.S. and West Indies) one who practices witchcraft. **con·jur·er, con·jur·or** (kon-jŭ-rĕr) *n.* a person who performs conjuring tricks.

conk (kongk) *v.* (*slang*) to hit on the head. □**conk out,** (*slang*) (of a machine) to break down, to fail; (of a person) to become exhausted and give up, to faint, to die.

Conn. *abbr.* Connecticut.

con·nect (kŏ-nekt) *v.* 1. to join or be joined. 2. (of a train etc.) to be timed to arrive so that passengers from one train etc. can catch another in which to continue their journey. 3. to be united in a relationship, *the families are connected by marriage.* 4. to think of (things or persons) as being associated with each other.

Con·nect·i·cut (kŏ-net-ĭ-kŭt) a state of the U.S. **con·nec·tion** (kŏ-nek-shŏn) *n.* 1. connecting, being connected. 2. a place where things connect, a connecting part. 3. a train etc. timed to connect with another, transfer between such trains. 4. a person connected by family or marriage. 5. (*slang*) a drug dealer. 6. *connections,* influential friends or associates, *political connections, legal connections,* etc.

con·nec·tive (kŏ-nek-tiv) *adj.* connecting, *connective tissue.* **connective** *n.* (in grammar) a conjunction.

con·nec·tor (kŏ-nek-tŏr) *n.* a thing that connects others.

con·ning (kon-ing) **tower** a raised structure on a submarine containing the periscope.

con·nip·tion (kŏ-nip-shŏn) *n.* (*informal*) a tantrum.

con·nive (kŏ-nɪv) *v.* **(con·nived, con·niv·ing)** to conspire. □**connive at,** to take no notice of (wrongdoing), thus seeming to consent to it. **con·niv·er** *n.* **con·niv'ance** *n.*

con·nois·seur (kon-ŏ-sur) *n.* a person with expert understanding of artistic and similar subjects.

con·no·ta·tion (kon-ŏ-tay-shŏn) *n.* the implied meaning of an expression in addition to its primary meaning. ▷ Do not confuse *connotation* with *denotation.*

con·no·ta·tive (kon-ŏ-tay-tiv) *adj.* connoting, suggesting.

con·note (kŏ-noht) *v.* **(con·not·ed, con·not·ing)** to imply in addition to the literal meaning. **con·nu·bi·al** (kŏ-noo-bi-ǎl) *adj.* of marriage, of the relationship between husband and wife.

con·quer (kong-kĕr) *v.* 1. to overcome in war, to win. 2. to overcome by effort; *they have conquered Everest,* climbed it successfully. **con'quer·or** *n.*

con·quest (kon-kwest) *n.* 1. conquering; *the Norman Conquest,* conquest of England by the Normans in 1066. 2. something got by conquering.

con·quis·ta·dor (kon-kwis-tǎ-dor) *n.* a conqueror, especially one of the Spanish conquerors of Mexico and Peru in the 16th century.

Con·rail (kon-rayl) *n.* (also **ConRail**) a system of railroads established under government guidelines in 1976. ▷ From *Con*(solidated) *Rail* (Corporation).

cons. *abbr.* 1. consolidated. 2. consonant.

con·san·guin·i·ty (kon-sang-**gwin**-i-tee) *n.* (*pl.* -**ties**) relationship by descent from the same ancestor. **con·san·guin·e·ous** (kon-sang-**gwin**-i-ŭs) *adj.*

con·science (kon-**shĕns**) *n.* **1.** a person's sense of what is right and wrong, especially in his own actions or motives. **2.** a feeling of remorse, *I have no conscience about leaving them.* □**conscience money,** money paid by a person who feels conscience-stricken, especially about having evaded payment previously. **on one's conscience,** causing one to feel guilty or remorseful. **con·science-strick·en** (kon-shĕns-**strik**-ĕn) *adj.* filled with remorse.

con·sci·en·tious (kon-shi-en-**shŭs**) *adj.* showing or done with careful attention. **con·sci·en'tious·ly** *adv.* **con·sci·en'tious·ness** *n.* □**conscientious objector,** one who refuses to serve in the armed forces in a war because he believes the war is morally wrong.

con·scious (kon-**shŭs**) *adj.* **1.** with one's mental faculties awake, aware of one's surroundings. **2.** aware, *he was conscious of his guilt.* **3.** realized by oneself, intentional, *spoke with conscious superiority; a conscious insult.* **con'scious·ly** *adv.* **con'scious·ness** *n.*

con·script (kŏn-**skript**) *v.* to summon for compulsory military service. **conscript** (kon-skript) *n.* a conscripted recruit. **con·scrip·tion** (kŏn-**skrip**-shŏn) *n.*

con·se·crate (kon-sĕ-krayt) *v.* (**con·se·crat·ed, con·se·crat·ing**) to make or declare sacred, to dedicate formally to the service or worship of God. **con·se·cra·tion** (kon-sĕ-**kray**-shŏn) *n.*

con·sec·u·tive (kŏn-**sek**-yŭ-tiv) *adj.* following continuously, in unbroken order. **con·sec'u·tive·ly** *adv.*

con·sen·sus (kŏn-sen-**sŭs**) *n.* (*pl.* -**sus·es**) general agreement in opinion. ▷It is incorrect to say or write *consensus of opinion.*

con·sent (kŏn-**sent**) *v.* to say that one is willing to do or allow what someone wishes. **consent** *n.* agreement to what someone wishes, permission. □**age of consent,** the age at which a girl's consent to sexual intercourse is valid in law.

con·se·quence (kon-sĕ-**kwĕns**) *n.* **1.** a result produced by some action or condition. **2.** importance, *a person of consequence; the matter is of no consequence,* it is not important. □**in consequence,** as a result. **suffer** *or* **take the consequences,** to accept whatever results from one's choice or action.

con·se·quent (kon-sĕ-**kwĕnt**) *adj.* following as a result.

con·se·quen·tial (kon-sĕ-**kwen**-shăl) *adj.* following as a result. **con·se·quen'tial·ly** *adv.*

con·se·quent·ly (kon-sĕ-**kwent**-lee) *adv.* as a result, therefore.

con·ser·van·cy (kŏn-sur-**văn**-see) *n.* (*pl.* -**cies**) **1.** a committee or organization concerned with preservation of historical or natural resources, *a nature conservancy.* **2.** official conservation (of forests etc.).

con·ser·va·tion (kon-sĕr-**vay**-shŏn) *n.* **1.** conserving, being conserved. **2.** preservation, especially of the natural environment.

con·ser·va·tion·ist (kon-sĕr-**vay**-shŏ-nist) *n.* a person who supports preservation of the natural environment.

con·ser·va·tism (kŏn-sur-**vă**-tiz-ĕm) *n.* a conserv-

ative attitude, conservative principles (general or political).

con·ser·va·tive (kŏn-sur-**vă**-tiv) *adj.* **1.** disliking or opposed to great or sudden change. **2.** moderate, avoiding extremes; *a conservative estimate,* a low one. **conservative** *n.* **1.** a conservative person. **2.** *Conservative,* a member of the U.S. or British **Conservative Party,** favoring private enterprise and freedom from government control. **con·ser'va·tive·ly** *adv.*

con·ser·va·to·ry (kŏn-sur-**vă**-tohr-ee) *n.* (*pl.* -**ries**) **1.** a greenhouse, especially one built against an outside wall of a house that has an opening into it. **2.** a school for training musicians and composers.

con·serve (kŏn-**surv**) *v.* to keep from harm, decay, or loss, for future use. **conserve** (kon-surv, kŏn-**surv**) *n.* (often **conserves**) jam, especially that made from fresh fruit and sugar.

con·sid·er (kŏn-**sid**-ĕr) *v.* **1.** to think about, especially in order to make a decision, to weigh the merits of; *it is my considered opinion,* arrived at after some thought. **2.** to make allowances for, *consider people's feelings.* **3.** to think to be, to suppose, *consider yourself lucky.* **con·sid'ered** *adj.* □**all things considered,** taking all the events or possibilities into account.

con·sid·er·a·ble (kŏn-sid-ĕ-**ră**-bĕl) *adj.* fairly great in amount or extent etc., *of considerable importance.* **con·sid'er·a·bly** *adv.*

con·sid·er·ate (kŏn-sid-ĕ-rit) *adj.* taking care not to inconvenience or hurt others. **con·sid'er·ate·ly** *adv.*

con·sid·er·a·tion (kŏn-sid-ĕ-**ray**-shŏn) *n.* **1.** careful thought. **2.** being considerate, kindness. **3.** a fact that must be kept in mind, *time is now an important consideration.* **4.** payment given as a reward, *he will do it for a consideration.* □**in consideration of,** in return for, on account of. **on no consideration,** no matter what the circumstances may be. **take into consideration,** to allow for. **under consideration,** being considered.

con·sid·er·ing (kŏn-sid-ĕ-**ring**) *prep.* taking into consideration, *she's very active, considering her age; you've done very well, considering,* if we take the circumstances into consideration.

con·sign (kŏn-**sɪn**) *v.* **1.** to hand over or deliver formally. **2.** to give into someone's care.

con·sign·ee (kon-sɪ-**nee**) *n.* a firm or person to whom goods etc. are consigned.

con·sign·ment (kŏn-**sɪn**-mĕnt) *n.* **1.** consigning. **2.** a batch of goods etc. consigned.

con·sign·or (kŏn-sɪ-**nŏr**) *n.* a person or firm that consigns goods etc. to another.

con·sist (kŏn-**sist**) *v.* **1. consist of,** to be made up of, *the apartment consists of three rooms.* **2. consist in,** to have as its basis or essential feature, *their happiness consists in hoping.*

con·sis·ten·cy (kŏn-sis-**tĕn**-see) *n.* (*pl.* -**cies**) **1.** the degree of thickness, firmness, or solidity especially of a liquid or soft mixture, *mix it to the consistency of heavy cream.* **2.** being consistent.

con·sis·tent (kŏn-sis-**tĕnt**) *adj.* **1.** conforming to a regular pattern or style, unchanging, *they have no consistent policy.* **2.** not contradictory, *these reforms are consistent with their general policies.* **con·sis'tent·ly** *adv.*

con·sis·to·ry (kŏn-sis-tŏ-**ree**) *n.* (*pl.* -**ries**) an ecclesiastical assembly, especially of the cardinals of the Roman Catholic Church.

consol. *abbr.* consolidated.

con·sol·a·ble (kŏn-soh-lă-bĕl) *adj.* able to be consoled.

con·so·la·tion (kon-sŏ-lay-shŏn) *n.* consoling, being consoled. ▢**consolation prize,** a prize given to a competitor who has just missed winning one of the main prizes.

con·sole[1] (kŏn-sohl) *v.* **(con·soled, con·sol·ing)** to comfort in time of sorrow or disappointment.

con·sole[2] (kon-sohl) *n.* 1. a frame containing the keyboards and stops etc. of an organ. 2. a panel holding the controls of electrical or other equipment. 3. a cabinet containing a radio or television set, designed to stand on the floor.

con·sol·i·date (kŏn-sol-i-dayt) *v.* **(con·sol·i·dat·ed, con·sol·i·dat·ing)** 1. to make or become secure and strong, *consolidating his position as leader.* 2. to combine or become combined, to merge. **con·sol·i·da·tion** (kŏn-sol-i-day-shŏn) *n.*

con·som·mé (kon-sŏ-may) *n.* a clear meat soup.

con·so·nance (kon-sŏ-năns) *n.* agreement, harmony.

con·so·nant (kon-sŏ-nănt) *n.* 1. a letter of the alphabet other than a vowel. 2. the speech sound it represents. **consonant** *adj.* consistent, harmonious, *actions that are consonant with his beliefs.*

con·sort (kon-sort) *n.* a husband or wife, especially of a monarch. **consort** (kŏn-sort) *v.* to associate, to keep company, *consorting with criminals.*

con·sor·ti·um (kŏn-sor-shi-ŭm) *n.* (*pl.* **-ti·a,** *pr.* -shi-ă) a combination of countries or companies or other groups acting together.

con·spic·u·ous (kŏn-spik-yoo-ŭs) *adj.* easily seen, attracting attention. **con·spic′u·ous·ly** *adv.* **con·spic′u·ous·ness** *n.*

con·spir·a·cy (kŏn-spir-ă-see) *n.* (*pl.* **-cies**) 1. conspiring. 2. a plan made by conspiring. ▢**conspiracy of silence,** an agreement to say nothing about a certain matter.

con·spir·a·tor (kŏn-spir-ă-tŏr) *n.* a person who conspires. **con·spir·a·to·ri·al** (kŏn-spir-ă-tohr-i-ăl) *adj.* **con·spir·a·to′ri·al·ly** *adv.*

con·spire (kŏn-spır) *v.* **(con·spired, con·spir·ing)** 1. to plan secretly with others, especially for some unlawful purpose. 2. (of events) to seem to combine, *events conspired to bring about his downfall.*

const. *abbr.* 1. constable. 2. constant. 3. constitution. 4. constitutional.

Const. *abbr.* 1. Constable. 2. Constitution.

con·sta·ble (kon-stă-bĕl) *n.* a policeman or policewoman in a small town.

con·stab·u·lar·y (kŏn-stab-yŭ-ler-ee) *n.* (*pl.* **-lar·ies**) a police force.

con·stan·cy (kon-stăn-see) *n.* 1. the quality of being constant and unchanging. 2. faithfulness.

con·stant (kon-stănt) *adj.* 1. happening or continuing all the time, happening repeatedly. 2. unchanging, faithful, *remained constant to his principles.* **constant** *n.* something that does not vary. **con′stant·ly** *adv.*

con·stel·la·tion (kon-stĕ-lay-shŏn) *n.* a group of fixed stars.

con·ster·na·tion (kon-stĕr-nay-shŏn) *n.* a great surprise and anxiety or dismay.

con·sti·pate (kon-sti-payt) *v.* **(con·sti·pat·ed, con·sti·pat·ing)** to cause constipation in. **con·sti·pa·tion** (kon-sti-pay-shŏn) *n.* difficulty in emptying the bowels.

con·stit·u·en·cy (kŏn-stich-oo-ĕn-see) *n.* (*pl.* **-cies**) 1. a body of voters who elect a representative to a legislature or other elected body. 2. the district and its residents represented thus.

con·stit·u·ent (kŏn-stich-oo-ĕnt) *adj.* forming part of a whole, *its constituent parts.* **constituent** *n.* 1. a constituent part. 2. a member of a constituency.

con·sti·tute (kon-sti-toot) *v.* **(con·sti·tut·ed, con·sti·tut·ing)** 1. to make up, to form, *twelve months constitute a year.* 2. to appoint, *they constituted him chief adviser.* 3. to establish or be, *this does not constitute a precedent.*

con·sti·tu·tion (kon-sti-too-shŏn) *n.* 1. constituting. 2. composition. 3. the set of principles according to which a country is organized; *the Constitution,* that of the U.S. 4. general condition and character, especially of a person's body, *she has a strong constitution.*

con·sti·tu·tion·al (kon-sti-too-shŏ-năl) *adj.* 1. of a country's constitution, established or permitted or limited by this, *a constitutional crisis; constitutional government.* 2. of or produced by a person's physical or mental constitution, *a constitutional weakness.* **constitutional** *n.* a walk taken for the sake of one's health. **con·sti·tu′tion·al·ly** *adv.* **con·sti·tu·tion·al·i·ty** (kon-sti-too-shŏ-nal-i-tee) *n.*

constr. *abbr.* construction.

con·strain (kŏn-strayn) *v.* to compel, to oblige.

con·straint (kŏn-straynt) *n.* 1. constraining or being constrained, compulsion. 2. a strained manner caused by holding back one's natural feelings.

con·strict (kŏn-strikt) *v.* to tighten by making narrower, to squeeze. **con·stric·tion** (kŏn-strik-shŏn) *n.* **con·stric′tor** *n.* **con·stric·tive** (kŏn-strik-tiv) *adj.*

con·struct (kŏn-strukt) *v.* to make by placing parts together, to build. **con·struc′tor** *n.*

con·struc·tion (kŏn-struk-shŏn) *n.* 1. constructing, being constructed. 2. something constructed. 3. two or more words put together to form a phrase or clause or sentence. 4. an interpretation, *put a bad construction on their refusal.* **con·struc′tion·al** *adj.* ▢**construction paper,** heavy, usually colored, paper.

con·struc·tion·ist (kŏn-struk-shŏ-nist) *n.* **strict constructionist,** a legal scholar who interprets the Constitution in the most narrowly limited sense.

con·struc·tive (kŏn-struk-tiv) *adj.* offering helpful suggestions, *they made constructive criticisms.* **con·struc′tive·ly** *adv.*

con·strue (kŏn-stroo) *v.* **(con·strued, con·stru·ing)** to interpret, to explain, *her words were construed as a refusal.*

con·sub·stan·ti·a·tion (kon-sŭb-stan-shi-ay-shŏn) *n.* a Lutheran doctrine that the body and blood of Christ exist together with bread and wine in the Eucharist.

con·sul (kon-sŭl) *n.* an official appointed to live in a foreign city in order to assist and protect his countrymen who live or visit there and to help commercial relations between the two countries. **con′sul·ar** *adj.*

con·sul·ate (kon-sŭ-lit) *n.* 1. the official premises of a consul. 2. a consul's position.

con·sult (kŏn-sult) *v.* 1. to seek information or advice from; *a consulting engineer,* one who acts as a consultant. 2. to confer, *they consulted with* *their fellow workers.* **con·sul·ta·tion** (kon-sŭl-tay-shŏn) *n.*

con·sul·tan·cy (kŏn-sul-tăn-see) *n.* the position or practice of a consultant.

con·sult·ant (kŏn-sul-tănt) *n.* a person qualified to give expert professional advice.

con·sul·ta·tive (kŏn-sul-tă-tiv) *adj.* for consultation, *a consultative committee.*

con·sume (kŏn-soom) *v.* (**con·sumed, con·sum·ing**) 1. to use up, *much time was consumed in waiting.* 2. to eat or drink up, especially in large quantities. 3. to destroy completely, *fire consumed the building.* **con·sum'a·ble** *adj.*

con·sum·er (kŏn-soo-měr) *n.* a person who buys or uses goods or services. □**consumer advocate,** a person who represents consumers' interests. **consumer goods,** those bought and used by individual consumers (not capital goods).

con·sum·er·ism (kŏn-soo-mě-riz-ěm) *n.* the protection of consumers' interests.

con·sum·ing (kŏn-soo-ming) *adj.* overwhelming, dominating, *a consuming ambition.*

con·sum·mate (kon-sŭ-mayt) *v.* (**con·sum·mat·ed, con·sum·mat·ing**) to accomplish, to make complete; *consummate a marriage,* complete it by sexual intercourse between the partners. **consummate** (kŏn-sum-it, kon-sŭ-mit) *adj.* supremely skilled, *a consummate artist.* **con·sum·ma·tion** (kon-sŭ-may-shŏn) *n.*

con·sump·tion (kŏn-sump-shŏn) *n.* 1. consuming, using up, destruction. 2. the amount consumed. 3. *(old use)* tuberculosis of the lungs.

con·sump·tive (kŏn-sump-tiv) *adj.* suffering from tuberculosis of the lungs. **consumptive** *n.* a consumptive person.

cont. *abbr.* 1. containing. 2. contents. 3. continent. 4. continental. 5. continue. 6. continued. 7. contract.

con·tact (kon-takt) *n.* 1. touching, coming together. 2. being in touch, communication. 3. a connection for the passage of electric current. 4. a person who has recently been near someone with a contagious disease and may carry infection. 5. an acquaintance who may be contacted when one needs information or help. **contact** *v.* to get into touch with (a person). □**contact lens,** a very small lens worn in contact with the eyeball. ▷Careful writers do not use *contact* as a verb. Instead of *contacting someone,* they *call* or *write* or *visit* him.

con·ta·gion (kŏn-tay-jŏn) *n.* 1. the spreading of disease by contact or close association. 2. a disease that is spread in this way.

con·ta·gious (kŏn-tay-jŭs) *adj.* 1. able to be spread by contact or close association, *a contagious disease.* 2. capable of spreading disease in this way, *all these children are now contagious.*

con·tain (kŏn-tayn) *v.* 1. to have within itself, *the atlas contains forty maps; whiskey contains alcohol.* 2. to consist of, to be equal to, *a gallon contains eight pints.* 3. to restrain, *try to contain your laughter.* 4. to keep within limits, *enemy troops were contained in the valley.*

con·tain·er (kŏn-tay-něr) *n.* 1. a box or bottle etc. designed to contain a substance or goods. 2. a large boxlike receptacle of standard design for transporting goods.

con·tain·er·ize (kŏn-tay-ně-rīz) *v.* (**con·tain·er·ized, con·tain·er·iz·ing**) to transport in containers, to convert to this method of transport-

ing goods. **con·tain·er·i·za·tion** (kŏn-tay-ně-ri-zay-shŏn) *n.*

con·tain·er·ship (cŏn-tay-něr-ship) *n.* a vessel carrying cargo in containers.

con·tain·ment (kŏn-tayn-měnt) *n.* the policy of preventing expansion of a hostile country or influence.

con·tam·i·nate (kŏn-tam-i-nayt) *v.* (**con·tam·i·nat·ed, con·tam·i·nat·ing**) to pollute. **con·tam·i·na·tion** (kŏn-tam-i-nay-shŏn) *n.*

cont'd. *abbr.* continued.

con·tem·plate (kon-těm-playt) *v.* (**con·tem·plat·ed, con·tem·plat·ing**) 1. to gaze at thoughtfully. 2. to consider. 3. to intend, to have in view as a possibility, *she is contemplating a visit to New York City.* 4. to meditate. **con·tem·pla·tion** (kon-těm-play-shŏn) *n.*

con·tem·pla·tive (kŏn-tem-plă-tiv) *adj.* thoughtful, fond of contemplation.

con·tem·po·ra·ne·ous (kŏn-tem-pŏ-ray-ni-ŭs) *adj.* (of events) belonging to the same period.

con·tem·po·rar·y (kŏn-tem-pŏ-rer-ee) *adj.* 1. belonging to the same period; *Dickens was contemporary with Thackeray,* lived at the same time. 2. up-to-date, *contemporary designs.* **contemporary** *n.* (*pl.* **-rar·ies**) 1. a person contemporary with another, *Hemingway and his contemporaries.* 2. one who is approximately the same age as another, *she is my contemporary.*

con·tempt (kŏn-tempt) *n.* 1. the process or feeling of despising something. 2. the condition of being despised; *fell into contempt,* became despised. 3. disrespect. □**contempt of court,** disobedience or disrespect toward a court of law or its processes.

con·tempt·i·ble (kŏn-temp-ti-běl) *adj.* deserving contempt. **con·tempt'i·bly** *adv.* **con·tempt·i·bil·i·ty** (kŏn-temp-ti-bil-i-tee) *n.*

con·temp·tu·ous (kŏn-temp-choo-ŭs) *adj.* feeling or showing contempt. **con·temp'tu·ous·ly** *adv.* **con·temp'tu·ous·ness** *n.*

con·tend (kŏn-tend) *v.* 1. to strive or fight or struggle, especially in competition or against difficulties. 2. to assert, to argue, *the defendant contends that he is innocent.* **con·tend'er** *n.*

con·tent[1] (kŏn-tent) *adj.* contented, satisfied with what one has. **content** *n.* being contented, satisfaction. **content** *v.* to make content, to satisfy. **con·tent'ment** *n.* □**to one's heart's content,** as much as one desires.

con·tent[2] (kŏn-tent) *n.* what is contained in something, *the contents of the barrel; butter has a high fat content,* contains much fat; *table of contents,* the list of chapter headings etc. showing the subject matter of a book.

con·tent·ed (kŏn-ten-tid) *adj.* happy with what one has, satisfied. **con·tent'ed·ly** *adv.* **con·tent'ed·ness** *n.*

con·ten·tion (kŏn-ten-shŏn) *n.* 1. contending, quarreling or arguing. 2. an assertion made in arguing.

con·ten·tious (kŏn-ten-shŭs) *adj.* 1. quarrelsome. 2. likely to cause contention. **con·ten'tious·ly** *adv.*

con·ter·mi·nous (kŏn-tur-mi-nŭs) *adj.* 1. having a common boundary (with). 2. occurring in the same time or space, or having the same meaning, as something else. **con·ter'mi·nous·ly** *adv.*

con·test (kon-test) *n.* 1. a struggle for superiority or victory. 2. a competition, a test of skill or ability etc. between rivals. **contest** (kŏn-test) v. 1. to compete for or in; *contest a seat at an election,* run for election. 2. to dispute, to challenge; *contest a statement,* try to show that it is wrong; *contest an election,* challenge the results; *contest a will,* try to prove that it is not valid.

con·test·ant (kŏn-tes-tănt) n. one who takes part in a contest, a competitor.

con·text (kon-tekst) n. 1. the words that come before and after a particular word or phrase and help to fix its meaning. 2. the circumstances in which an event occurs, *shortages were tolerated in the context of war.* □**in context,** with the surrounding words and therefore giving a correct impression of the meaning. **out of context,** without the surrounding words and therefore giving a false impression of the meaning.

con·tig·u·ous (kŏn-**tig**-yoo-ŭs) adj. adjoining, *Vermont is contiguous to Canada.* **con·tig′ u·ous·ly** adv. **con·ti·gu·i·ty** (kon-ti-gyoo-i-tee) n.

con·ti·nent[1] (kon-ti-nĕnt) n. one of the main land masses of Earth (Europe, Asia, Africa, North and South America, Australia, Antarctica); *the Continent,* the mainland of Europe as distinct from the British Isles.

continent[2] adj. 1. able to control the excretion of one's urine and feces. 2. abstaining from sexual activity. **con′ti·nence** n.

con·ti·nen·tal (kon-tĭ-nen-tăl) adj. 1. of a continent. 2. *Continental,* of the Continent. **con·tinental** n. 1. a native or inhabitant of a continent, especially Europe. 2. *Continental,* a soldier of the Continental Army. 3. *Continental,* a piece of paper currency issued by the Continental Congress and individual states. □**Continental Army,** the American revolutionary army. **Continental breakfast,** a light breakfast of coffee and rolls etc. **Continental Congress,** the two assemblies of envoys from the colonies (later states) that governed America from 1774 to 1789. **continental divide,** the dividing line between river systems that flow to opposite sides of a continent. **continental shelf,** a shallow slope around a continent, outside which the ocean bed descends deeply. **continental slope,** the drop from the continental shelf to the ocean basin. **not worth a Continental,** not worth anything.

con·tin·gen·cy (kŏn-**tin**-jĕn-se) n. (pl. **-cies**) 1. something unforeseen. 2. a possibility, something that may occur at a future date; *contingency plans,* plans made in case something happens.

con·tin·gent (kon-tin-jĕnt) adj. 1. happening by chance. 2. possible, liable to occur but not certain. 3. depending on something that may or may not happen, *an advantage that is contingent on the success of the expedition.* **contingent** n. 1. a body of troops or ships etc. contributed to form part of a force. 2. a group of people forming part of a gathering. **con′gent·ly** adv.

con·tin·u·al (kŏn-**tin**-yoo-ăl) adj. continuing over a long time without stopping or with only short breaks. **con·tin′u·al·ly** adv. ▷Do not confuse *continual* with *continuous.*

con·tin·u·ance (kŏn-tin-yoo-ăns) n. continuing.

con·tin·u·a·tion (kŏn-tin-yoo-ay-shŏn) n. 1. continuing, starting again after ceasing. 2. a part etc. by which something is continued, *the book is a continuation of her previous novel.*

con·tin·ue (kŏn-tin-yoo) v. (**con·tin·ued, con· tin·u·ing**) 1. to keep up (an action etc.), to do

something without ceasing, *continue̅ to eat; continue the struggle.* 2. to remain in a certain place or condition, *he will continue as manager.* 3. to go farther, *the road continues beyond the bridge.* 4. to begin again after stopping, *to be continued next week.*

con·ti·nu·i·ty (kon-ti-noo-i-tee) n. (pl. **-ties**) 1. being continuous. 2. the uninterrupted succession of things. 3. motion-picture scenario, dialog for a radio drama.

con·tin·u·ous (kŏn-**tin**-yoo-ŭs) adj. continuing, without a break. **con·tin′u·ous·ly** adv. ▷Do not confuse *continuous* with *continual.*

con·tin·u·um (kŏn-**tin**-yoo-ŭm) n. (pl. **-u·a,** pr. -yoo-ă) something that extends continuously.

con·tort (kŏn-tort) v. to force or twist out of its usual shape. **con·tor·tion** (kŏn-tor-shŏn) n.

con·tor·tion·ist (kŏn-tor-shŏ-nist) n. a performer who can twist his body into unusual postures.

con·tour (kon-toor) n. 1. an outline. 2. (also **contour line**) a line (on a map) joining the points that are the same height above sea level.

contr. abbr. 1. contract. 2. contraction. 3. contralto.

contra- prefix against.

con·tra·band (kon-tră-band) n. 1. smuggled goods. 2. smuggling.

con·tra·cep·tion (kon-tră-sep-shŏn) n. the prevention of pregnancy.

con·tra·cep·tive (kon-tră-**sep**-tiv) adj. preventing conception. **contraceptive** n. a contraceptive drug or device.

con·tract (kon-trakt) n. 1. a formal agreement between people or groups or countries. 2. a document setting out the terms of such an agreement. **contract** (kŏn-trakt) v. 1. to make or become smaller or shorter. 2. to arrange or undertake by contract, *they contracted to supply oil to the factory.* 3. to catch (an illness), to form or acquire (a habit, a debt, etc.). **con·trac·tion** (kŏn-trak-shŏn) n. **con·trac′tor** n. □**contract bridge,** a form of bridge in which only tricks bid and won count toward the game. **contract out,** to assign (a job or task) by contract.

con·trac·tile (kŏn-trak-tĭl) adj. capable of or producing contraction. **con·trac·til·i·ty** (kon-trak-til-i-tee) n.

con·trac·tu·al (kŏn-trak-choo-ăl) adj. of a contract.

con·tra·dict (kon-tră-dikt) v. 1. to state that (what is said) is untrue or that (a person) is wrong. 2. to state the opposite of, to be contrary to, *these rumors contradict previous ones.* **con·tra·dic· tion** (kon-tră-dik-shŏn) n. **con·tra·dic·to·ry** (kon-tră-dik-tŏ-ree) adj. □**a contradiction in terms,** a statement that contradicts itself.

con·tra·dis·tinc·tion (kon-tră-di-stingk-shŏn) n. distinction by contrast, *crossing the Atlantic by air takes a few hours, in contradistinction to the journey by sea.*

con·trail (kon-trayl) n. a trail of condensation left by an airplane or missile.

con·tra·in·di·cate (kon-tră-in-dĭ-kayt) v. (con· tra·in·di·cat·ed, con·tra·in·di·cat·ing) (in medicine etc.) to act as an indication against (use of a particular treatment etc.). **con·tra·in·di· ca·tion,** (kon-tră-in-dĭ-kay-shŏn) n.

con·tral·to (kŏn-tral-toh) n. (pl. **-tos, -ti,** pr. -tee) 1. the lowest female singing voice. 2. a singer with such a voice, a part written for it.

con·trap·tion (kŏn-trap-shŏn) n. *(informal)* an odd-looking gadget or machine.

con·tra·pun·tal (kon-tră-**pun**-tăl) *adj.* of or in counterpoint.

con·tra·ri·wise (kon-trer-ee-wɪz) *adv.* on the other hand, in the opposite way.

con·tra·ry (kon-trer-ee) *adj.* 1. opposite in nature, opposed, *the result was contrary to expectation.* 2. opposite in direction; *delayed by contrary winds,* by unfavorable ones. 3. (*pr.* kŏn-**trair**-ee) doing the opposite of what is expected or advised, willful. **contrary** *n.* (*pl.* **-ries**) the opposite. **contrary** *adv.* in opposition, against, *acting contrary to instructions.* **con'trar·i·ness** *n.* ☐**on the contrary,** in denial of what is just said and stating that the opposite is true. **to the contrary,** proving or indicating the opposite, *there is no evidence to the contrary.*

con·trast (kon-trast) *n.* 1. the act of contrasting. 2. a difference clearly seen when things are put together. 3. something showing such a difference. 4. the degree of difference between tones or colors. **contrast** (kŏn-trast) *v.* 1. to compare or oppose two things so as to show their differences. 2. to show a striking difference when compared.

con·tra·vene (kon-tră-veen) *v.* (**con·tra·vened, con·tra·ven·ing**) to act in opposition to, to conflict with, *contravening the law.* **con·tra·ven·tion** (kon-tră-ven-shŏn) *n.*

con·tre·temps (kon-trĕ-tahn) *n.* an unfortunate happening.

contrib. *abbr.* 1. contribution. 2. contributor.

con·trib·ute (kŏn-trib-yoot) *v.* (**con·trib·ut·ed, con·trib·ut·ing**) 1. to give jointly with others, especially to a common fund. 2. to supply for publication in a newspaper or magazine or book. 3. to help to bring about, *drink contributed to her ruin.* **con·trib'u·tor** *n.* **con·tri·bu·tion** (kon-tri-byoo-shŏn) *n.*

con·trib·u·tor·y (kŏn-trib-yŭ-tohr-ee) *adj.* 1. contributing to a result; *contributory negligence,* failure to have taken proper precautions against an accident in which one becomes involved. 2. involving contributions to a fund, *a contributory pension scheme.*

con·trite (kŏn-trɪt) *adj.* penitent, feeling guilty. **con·trite'ly** *adv.* **con·tri·tion** (kŏn-trish-ŏn) *n.*

con·triv·ance (kŏn-trɪ-văns) *n.* 1. contriving. 2. something contrived, a plan. 3. a mechanical device.

con·trive (kŏn-trɪv) *v.* (**con·trived, con·triv·ing**) to plan cleverly, to achieve in a clever or resourceful way, to manage. **con·triv'er** *n.*

con·trol (kŏn-trohl) *n.* 1. the power to give orders or to restrain something. 2. a means of restraining or regulating; *the controls of a vehicle,* the devices by which it is operated. 3. restraint, self-restraint. 4. a standard of comparison for checking the results of an experiment or industrial process. 5. a place where cars taking part in a road race must stop for inspection etc. 6. a personality said to direct the actions of a spiritualist medium. **control** *v.* (**con·trolled, con·trol·ling**) 1. to have control of, to regulate. 2. to restrain. ☐**control tower,** an airport tower from which air traffic is directed by radar and radio. **in control,** controlling. **out of control,** no longer able to be controlled. **under control,** controlled, in proper order.

con·trol·la·ble (kŏn-troh-lă-bĕl) *adj.* able to be controlled.

con·trol·ler (kŏn-troh-lĕr) *n.* the person in charge of finance in a company or other institution.

con·tro·ver·sial (kon-trŏ-vur-shăl) *adj.* causing controversy. **con·tro·ver'sial·ly** *adv.*

con·tro·ver·sy (kon-trŏ-vur-see) *n.* (*pl.* **-sies**) a prolonged argument or dispute.

con·tro·vert (kon-trŏ-vurt) *v.* to deny the truth of, to contradict.

con·tro·vert·i·ble (kon-trŏ-vur-ti-bĕl) *adj.* able to be denied or disproved.

con·tu·ma·cious (kon-tuu-may-shŭs) *adj.* insubordinate, disobedient. **con·tu·ma'cious·ly** *adv.* **con·tu·ma·cy** (kon-tuu-mă-see) *n.*

con·tu·me·li·ous (kon-tuu-mee-li-ŭs) *adj.* insolent, reproachful.

con·tu·me·ly (kon-tuu-mĕ-lee) *n.* (*pl.* **-lies**) 1. rudeness, insolence. 2. an insulting remark or act.

con·tuse (kŏn-tooz) *v.* (**con·tused, con·tus·ing**) to bruise.

con·tu·sion (kŏn-too-zhŏn) *n.* a bruise.

co·nun·drum (kŏ-nun-drŭm) *n.* a hard question, a riddle.

con·ur·ba·tion (kon-ŭr-bay-shŏn) *n.* a large urban area formed where towns have spread and merged.

con·va·lesce (kon-vă-les) *v.* (**con·va·lesced, con·va·lesc·ing**) to regain health after illness. **con·va·les'cence** *n.* **con·va·les'cent** *adj. & n.*

con·vec·tion (kŏn-vek-shŏn) *n.* the transmission of heat within a liquid or gas by movement of the heated parts. **con·vec'tion·al** *adj.* **con·vec'tive** *adj.* **con·vec'tor** *n.*

con·vene (kŏn-veen) *v.* (**con·vened, con·ven·ing**) to assemble, to cause to assemble. **con·ven'er** *n.*

con·ven·ience (kŏn-veen-yĕns) *n.* 1. the quality of being convenient. 2. something that is convenient. ☐**at your convenience,** whenever or however you find convenient; *at your earliest convenience,* as soon as you can. **convenience foods,** those that are convenient to use because they need little preparation.

con·ven·ient (kŏn-veen-yĕnt) *adj.* 1. easy to use or deal with, not troublesome. 2. easy access, *convenient to shopping.* **con·ven'ient·ly** *adv.*

con·vent (kon-vent) *n.* 1. a religious community of nuns. 2. a building in which they live. 3. a convent school, a school run by members of a convent. **con·ven·tu·al** (kŏn-ven-choo-ăl) *adj.*

con·ven·ti·cle (kŏn-ven-ti-kĕl) *n.* 1. a clandestine religious meeting, especially of nonconformists or dissenters. 2. a building used for this.

con·ven·tion (kŏn-ven-shŏn) *n.* 1. a formal assembly of an organization, especially a political party. 2. a formal agreement, especially between countries, *the Geneva Convention.* 3. an accepted custom.

con·ven·tion·al (kŏn-ven-shŏ-năl) *adj.* done according to conventions, conventional; *conventional weapons,* non-nuclear. **con·ven'tion·al·ly** *adv.*

con·ven·tion·al·i·ty (kŏn-ven-shŏ-nal-i-tee) *n.*

con·ven·tion·al·ize (kŏn-ven-shŏ-nă-lɪz) *v.* (**con·ven·tion·al·ized, con·ven·tion·al·iz·ing**) to bring into agreement with conventions, to make conventional.

con·ven·tion·eer (kŏn-ven-shŏ-neer) *n.* a person who attends a convention.

con·verge (kŏn-vurj) *v.* (**con·verged, con·verg·ing**) to come to or toward the same point. **con·ver'gence** *n.* **con·ver'gen·cy** *n.* **con·ver'gent** *adj.*

con·ver·sant (kŏn-vur-sănt) *adj.* **conversant with,** having a knowledge of.

con·ver·sa·tion (kon-věr-say-shŏn) *n.* informal talk between people. con·ver·sa'tion·al *adj.* con·ver·sa'tion·al·ly *adv.* □conversation piece, an item of bric-a-brac that attracts attention.

con·ver·sa·tion·al·ist (kon-věr-say-shŏ-nă-list) *n.* a person who is good at conversation.

con·verse¹ (kŏn-vurs) *v.* (con·versed, con·vers·ing) to hold a conversation.

converse² (kŏn-vurs, kon-vurs) *adj.* opposite, contrary. converse (kon-vurs) *n.* an idea or statement that is the opposite of another. con·verse'ly *adv.*

con·vert (kŏn-vurt) *v.* 1. to change from one form or use or character to another. 2. to be able to be changed, *the sofa converts into a bed.* 3. to cause (a person) to change his attitude or beliefs, *he was converted to Christianity.* 4. to score a point or points after touchdown in football. convert (kon-vurt) *n.* a person who is converted, especially to a religious faith. con·ver·sion (kŏn-vur-zhŏn) *n.*

con·vert·er (kŏn-vur-těr) *n.* 1. a device for converting a direct current of electricity to alternating current or vice versa. 2. a person who converts others.

con·vert·i·ble (kŏn-vur-tĭ-běl) *adj.* able to be converted, *a convertible sofa.* convertible *n.* 1. a car with a roof that can be folded down or removed. 2. a sofa that can become a bed. con·vert·i·bil·i·ty (kŏn-vur-tĭ-bil-i-tee) *n.*

con·vex (kon-veks) *adj.* curving like the surface of a ball as seen from the outside. con·vex'ly *adv.* con·vex'i·ty *n.*

con·vey (kŏn-vay) *v.* 1. to carry or transport or transmit. 2. to communicate as an idea or meaning. 3. to transfer (ownership of land etc.). con·vey'a·ble *adj.*

con·vey·ance (kŏn-vay-ăns) *n.* 1. conveying. 2. a means of transporting people, a vehicle. 3. a legal document that conveys land etc.

con·vey·anc·ing (kŏn-vay-ăn-sing) *n.* the practice of law associated with transferring the ownership of land etc.

con·vey·or (kŏn-vay-ŏr) *n.* 1. a person or thing that conveys. 2. (also conveyor belt) a continuous moving belt for conveying objects in a factory etc.

con·vict (kŏn-vikt) *v.* to prove or declare (a person) to be guilty of a crime. convict (kon-vikt) *n.* a convicted person who is in prison for his crime.

con·vic·tion (kŏn-vik-shŏn) *n.* 1. convicting. 2. being convicted. 3. a firm opinion or belief.

con·vince (kŏn-vins) *v.* (con·vinced, con·vinc·ing) to make (a person) feel certain that something is true, *I am convinced of his honesty* or *that he is honest.* con·vinc'ing *adj.* con·vinc'ing·ly *adv.*

con·viv·i·al (kŏn-viv-i-ăl) *adj.* sociable and lively. con·viv'i·al·ly *adv.* con·viv·i·al·i·ty (kŏn-viv-i-al-i-tee) *n.*

con·vo·ca·tion (kon-vŏ-kay-shŏn) *n.* 1. convoking. 2. an assembly convoked.

con·voke (kŏn-vohk) *v.* (con·voked, con·vok·ing) to summon (people) to assemble.

con·vo·lute (kon-vŏ-loot) *adj.* 1. rolled up together, coiled and twisted, 2. complicated.

con·vo·lut·ed (kon-vŏ-loo-tid) *adj.* convolute.

con·vo·lu·tion (kon-vŏ-loo-shŏn) *n.* a coil, a twist.

con·vol·vu·lus (kon-vol-vyŭ-lŭs) *n.* a twining plant with trumpet-shaped flowers.

con·voy (kon-voi, kŏn-voi) *v.* to escort and protect, especially with an armed force or warships. con·voy (kon-voi) *n.* a group of ships or vehicles traveling under escort or together.

con·vulse (kŏn-vuls) *v.* (con·vulsed, con·vuls·ing) 1. to cause violent movement in. 2. to cause to double up with laughter.

con·vul·sion (kŏn-vul-shŏn) *n.* 1. a violent movement of the body, especially one caused by muscles contracting involuntarily. 2. a violent upheaval.

con·vul·sive (kŏn-vul-siv) *adj.* like a convulsion, producing upheaval. con·vul'sive·ly *adv.*

co·ny (koh-nee) = coney.

coo (koo) *v.* to make a soft murmuring sound. coo *n.* a cooing sound.

cook (kuuk) *v.* 1. to prepare (food) for eating, by using heat. 2. to undergo this preparation, *lunch is cooking.* 3. *(informal)* to alter or falsify in order to produce a desired result, *cooked the books.* cook *n.* a person who cooks, especially as a job. □cook a person's goose, to ruin his chances. cooking apple, an apple suitable for cooking. cook up, *(informal)* to concoct; to invent, *cook up an excuse.* what's cooking?, *(informal)* what is happening or being planned?

cook·book (kuuk-buuk) *n.* a book of recipes and directions for cooking.

cook·er (kuuk-ěr) *n.* a pot for cooking food.

cook·er·y (kuuk-ě-ree) *n.* the art and practice of cooking.

cook·ie (kuuk-ee) *n.* 1. a small cake made from sweet stiff dough. 2. *(slang)* a person, *a smart cookie.* □cookie cutter, a metal or plastic mold used to shape cookie dough. cookie pusher, *(informal)* a trivial person. the way the cookie crumbles, *(informal)* how things turn out.

cook·out (kuuk-owt) *n.* a party at which cooking is done outdoors.

cook·ware (kuuk-wair) *n.* utensils used in cooking.

cool (kool) *adj.* 1. moderately cold, not hot or warm. 2. (of colors) suggesting coolness. 3. calm and unexcited. 4. not enthusiastic, *got a cool reception.* 5. casual and confident, *I admired his cool manner.* 6. full in amount, *cost me a cool thousand.* cool *n.* 1. coolness, something cool, *the cool of evening.* 2. *(slang)* calmness, composure, *keep your cool.* cool *v.* to make or become cool. cool·ly (kool-lee) *adv.* cool'ness *n.* □cooling tower, a tower for cooling hot water in an industrial process so that the water can be reused. cool it, *(slang)* to calm down. cool one's heels, to be kept waiting.

cool·ant (koo-lănt) *n.* a fluid used for cooling machinery etc.

cool·er (koo-lěr) *n.* a container that cools its contents or keeps them cool.

Cool·idge (koo-lij), (John) Cal·vin (1872–1933) the thirtieth president of the U.S. 1923–29.

coo·lie (koo-lee) *n.* an unskilled native laborer in the Far East.

coon·hound (koon-hownd) *n.* any of several different hounds used in hunting raccoons or other small animals.

coon·skin (koon-skin) *n.* a raccoon pelt.

coop (koop) *n.* a cage for poultry. coop *v.* to confine or shut in, *he is cooped up in his room.*

co-op (koh-op) *n.* *(informal)* a cooperative.

coop·er (koo-pěr) *n.* a person whose job is making and repairing barrels and tubs.

coop·er·age (koo-pě-rij) *n.* a factory where barrels and tubs are made.

co·op·er·ate (koh-op-ĕ-rayt) *v.* **(co·op·er· at·ed, co·op·er·at·ing)** to work in a helpful way with another or others. **co·op'er·a·tor** *n.* **co·op·er·a·tion** (koh-op-ĕ-ray-shŏn) *n.* **co·op·er·a·tive** (koh-op-ĕ-ră-tiv) *adj.* 1. of co-operation. 2. willing to cooperate. 3. owned and run jointly by its members with profits shared among them. **cooperative** *n.* 1. a farm or business organized on a cooperative basis. 2. an apartment house owned jointly by its tenants. **co· op'er·a·tive·ly** *adv.*

co·opt (koh-opt) *v.* 1. to appoint to become a member of a group by the invitation of its existing members. 2. to take over an idea etc. for one's own. **co·op·tion** (koh-op-shŏn) *n.*

co·or·di·nate (koh-or-dĭ-nit) *adj.* equal in importance. **coordinate** *n.* 1. a coordinate thing. 2. a system of magnitudes used to give the position of a point etc., as latitude and longitude. 3. *coordinates,* items of women's clothing that can be worn together harmoniously. **coordinate** (koh-or-dĭ-nayt) *v.* **(co·or·di·nat·ed, co·or· di·nat·ing)** to bring (parts etc.) into a proper relationship, to work or cause to work together efficiently. **co·or·di·na·tion** (koh-or-dĭ-nay-shŏn) *n.* **co·or·di·na·tor** (koh-or-dĭ-nay-tŏr) *n.* **co·or·di·nate·ly** (koh-or-dĭ-nit-lee) *adv.*

coot (koot) *n.* 1. a kind of water bird, especially one with a horny white plate on the forehead. 2. *(informal)* a stubborn or foolish man, *an old coot.*

coot·ie (koo-tee) *n.* a body louse.

cop (kop) *v.* **(copped, cop·ping)** *(slang)* to steal. **cop** *n.* *(slang)* a policeman. □**cop a plea,** *(slang)* to plead guilty to a crime carrying a lesser penalty than that imposed for the crime of which one is accused. **cop out,** *(slang)* to fail to do what one promised.

cop. *abbr.* copyright.

cope[1] (kohp) *v.* **(coped, cop·ing)** to manage successfully. □**cope with,** to deal successfully with.

cope[2] *n.* a long loose cloak worn by clergy in certain ceremonies and processions.

Co·pen·ha·gen (koh-pĕn-hay-gĕn) the capital of Denmark.

cop·i·er (kop-i-ĕr) *n.* 1. a copying machine. 2. a person who copies.

co·pi·lot (koh-pɪ-lŏt) *n.* a second pilot in an aircraft.

cop·ing (koh-ping) *n.* the top row of masonry (usually sloping) in a wall. □**coping saw,** a saw used for cutting wood into curves. **coping stone,** a stone used in a coping.

co·pi·ous (koh-pi-ŭs) *adj.* existing in large amounts, plentiful. **co'pi·ous·ly** *adv.* **co'pi· ous·ness** *n.*

cop-out (kop-owt) *n.* *(slang)* a failure to do what one promised.

cop·per[1] (kop-ĕr) *n.* 1. a reddish-brown metal. 2. a coin made of copper or a copper alloy. 3. a reddish-brown color. **copper** *adj.* 1. made of copper. 2. reddish brown. □**copper beech,** a beech tree with copper-colored leaves.

copper[2] *n.* *(slang)* a policeman.

cop·per·head (kop-ĕr-hed) *n.* a venomous snake of eastern U.S., so called from the reddish-brown color of its head.

cop·per·plate (kop-ĕr-playt) *n.* neat clear handwriting.

cop·pice (kop-is) *n.* a copse.

cop·ra (koh-pră) *n.* the dried kernels of a coconut, from which coconut oil is extracted.

copse (kops) *n.* a wood of small trees and undergrowth, grown for periodic cutting.

cop·ter (kop-tĕr) *n.* *(informal)* a helicopter.

cop·u·la (kop-yŭ-lă) *n.* (*pl.* -las, -lae, *pr.* -lee) a verb such as *be,* which links a subject and predicate. **cop·u·la·tive** (kop-yŭ-lay-tiv) *adj.*

cop·u·late (kop-yŭ-layt) *v.* **(cop·u·lat·ed, cop· u·lat·ing)** to unite sexually as in the act of mating. **cop·u·la·tion** (kop-yŭ-lay-shŏn) *n.*

cop·y (kop-ee) *n.* (*pl.* **cop·ies**) 1. a thing made to look like another. 2. one specimen of a book or document or newspaper. 3. material for printing; *the trial made good copy,* interesting material for newspaper reporting. **copy** *v.* **(cop·ied, cop· y·ing)** 1. to make a copy of. 2. to try to do the same as, to imitate. □**copy desk,** a desk at which newspaper editors edit news copy and write headlines.

cop·y·book (kop-ee-buuk) *n.* a book containing specimens for students to imitate.

cop·y·boy (kop-ee-boi) *n.* an office boy for a newspaper.

cop·y·cat (kop-ee-kat) *n.* *(slang)* a person who slavishly imitates another.

cop·y·ed·it (kop-ee-ed-it) *v.* to prepare manuscripts for printing by correcting errors, improving style, etc. **cop'y ed'i·tor** *n.*

cop·y·ist (kop-ee-ist) *n.* a person who makes copies of documents etc.

cop·y·read·er (kop-ee-ree-dĕr) *n.* a newspaper editor who edits articles before they are printed.

cop·y·right (kop-ee-rɪt) *n.* the sole legal right to print, publish, perform, film, or record a literary or artistic or musical work. **copyright** *adj.* (of material) protected by copyright. **copyright** *v.* to protect (material) by copyright.

cop·y·writ·er (kop-ee-rɪt-ĕr) *n.* one who writes advertisements.

co·quet (koh-ket) *v.* **(co·quet·ted, co·quet· ting)** to play the coquette, to flirt or dally with. **co·quet·ry** (koh-ki-tree) *n.* (*pl.* -ries).

co·quette (koh-ket) *n.* a woman who flirts. **co· quet'tish** *adj.*

cor. *abbr.* 1. corner. 2. cornet. 3. coroner. 4. corpus. 5. correct. 6. corrected. 7. correction. 8. correspondence. 9. correspondent. 10. corresponding.

cor·a·cle (kor-ă-kĕl) *n.* a small wickerwork boat covered with watertight material.

cor·al (kor-ăl) *n.* 1. a hard red, pink, or white substance built by tiny sea creatures; *coral reef,* one formed by coral. 2. reddish-pink color. **coral** *adj.* reddish pink. □**coral snake,** a poisonous snake of the American tropics.

cor·bel (kor-bĕl) *n.* a stone or timber projection from a wall, to support something. **cor'beled** *adj.*

cord (kord) *n.* 1. long thin flexible material made from twisted strands, a piece of this. 2. a similar structure in the body, *the spinal cord.* 3. corduroy material. 4. a measure of cut wood, especially firewood, 8 feet by 4 feet by 4 feet. **cord** *v.* to fasten with a cord.

cord·age (kor-dij) *n.* cords or ropes.

cord·ed (kor-did) *adj.* (of fabric) with raised ridges.

cor·dial (kor-jăl) *n.* a liquor sweetened with fruit etc. **cordial** *adj.* warm and friendly, *cordial greetings.* **cor'dial·ly** *adv.* **cor·dial·i·ty** (kor-jal-i-tee) *n.* (*pl.* -ties).

cor·dil·le·ra (kor-dil-yair-ă) *n.* 1. one of a series of parallel mountain ridges, especially the Andes and in Mexico and in Central America. 2. a chain of mountains, especially a principal range. **cor·dil·le'ran** *adj.*

cord·ite (kor-dīt) *n.* a smokeless explosive used as a propellant in bullets and shells.

cord·less (kord-lis) *adj.* (of an electric appliance) needing no electric cord.

cor·don (kor-dŏn) *n.* **1.** a ring of people or military posts etc. enclosing or guarding something. **2.** an ornamental cord or braid worn as a badge of honor. **cordon** *v.* to enclose with a cordon.

cor·don bleu (kor-don bluu) of the highest degree of excellence in cookery. ▷French.

cor·do·van (kor-dŏ-văn) *n.* a kind of fine leather.

cor·du·roy (kor-dŭ-roi) *n.* **1.** cotton cloth with velvety ridges. **2.** *corduroys,* trousers made of corduroy fabric.

core (kohr) *n.* **1.** the horny central part of certain fruits, containing the seeds. **2.** the central or most important part of something. **core** *v.* **(cored, cor·ing)** to remove the core from. **cor'er** *n.* □**core curriculum,** a program of study in which most or all subjects are treated in relation to a central theme. **to the core,** thoroughly, entirely.

CORE (kor) *n.* Congress Of Racial Equality.

co·re·spon·dent (koh-ri-spon-dĕnt) *n.* the person with whom the person proceeded against in a divorce suit (the *respondent*) is said to have committed adultery.

cor·gi (kor-gee) *n.* (*pl.* -gis) a dog of a small Welsh breed with a foxlike head.

co·ri·an·der (kohr-i-an-dĕr) *n.* a plant with seeds used for flavoring.

Co·rin·thi·an (kŏ-rin-thi-ăn) *adj.* **1.** of Corinth, a city of ancient Greece. **2.** of the Corinthian order, the most ornate of the five classical orders of architecture. **3.** *Corinthians,* either of two books of the New Testament, the epistles of St. Paul to the Church at Corinth.

cork (kork) *n.* **1.** a light tough substance, the thick outer bark of a kind of South European oak (the **cork oak**). **2.** a piece of this used as a float. **3.** a bottle stopper made of this or other material. **cork** *v.* to close or stop up with a cork.

corked (korkt) *adj.* **1.** (of wine) contaminated by a decayed cork. **2.** (of a bottle) unopened.

cork·er (kor-kĕr) *n.* (*slang*) an excellent person or thing.

cork·ing (kor-king) *adj. & adv.* (*informal*) excellent.

cork·screw (kork-skroo) *n.* **1.** a tool for extracting corks from bottles. **2.** a spiral thing.

cork·y (kork-ee) *adj.* **(cork·i·er, cork·i·est) 1.** corklike. **2.** (of wine) tasting of the cork, spoiled.

corm (korm) *n.* a rounded underground base of a stem, from the top of which buds sprout.

cor·mo·rant (kor-mŏ-rănt) *n.* a large black sea bird.

corn¹ (korn) *n.* **1.** a cereal plant with tall stalks bearing kernels on ears. **2.** the ear of this plant. **3.** kernels of this plant. **4.** (also **peppercorn**) a single grain of pepper. **5.** (*informal*) something corny. **corn** *v.* to preserve beef in brine or by a process that imitates this. □**corn bread,** bread made with cornmeal. **corn muffin,** a muffin made with cornmeal. **corn oil,** oil pressed from corn kernels, used in cooking, cosmetics, etc. **corn pone,** corn bread made without milk or eggs. **corn shock,** a bundle of cornstalks in an upright position. **corn silk,** the silky fibers lining the husk of an ear of corn. **corn snake,** a rat snake of North America. **corn snow,** grain-like snow produced by periods of thawing and freezing.

corn sugar, dextrose. **corn syrup,** sweet syrup made from corn. **corn whiskey, corn liquor,** whiskey distilled from corn.

corn² *n.* a small area of horny hardened skin on the foot.

corn·ball (korn-bawl) *adj.* (*slang*) corny. **cornball** *n.* (*slang*) a corny person.

corn·cob (korn-kob) *n.* the woody core of an ear of corn. □**corncob pipe,** a tobacco pipe made from a corncob.

corn·crib (korn-krib) *n.* a building with ventilated sides, used for storing ears of corn.

cor·ne·a (kor-nee-ă) *n.* the tough transparent outer covering of the eyeball. **cor'ne·al** *adj.*

corned (kornd) *adj.* preserved in brine or by a similar process, *corned beef.*

cor·ner (kor-nĕr) *n.* **1.** the angle or area where two lines or sides meet or where two streets join. **2.** a hidden or remote place. **3.** a virtual monopoly of a certain type of goods or services, enabling the holder to control the price, *a corner on copper.* **corner** *v.* **1.** to drive into a corner, to force into a position from which there is no escape. **2.** to obtain (all or most of something) for oneself, to establish a monopoly of, *corner copper.* **3.** to move around a corner, *the car had cornered too fast.*

cor·ner·stone (kor-nĕr-stohn) *n.* a basis, a vital foundation, *hard work is the cornerstone of success.*

cor·net (kor-net) *n.* a brass musical instrument like a small trumpet.

corn·fed (korn-fed) *adj.* fed on corn.

corn·flakes (korn-flayks) *n. pl.* a breakfast cereal of toasted flakes of corn.

corn·flow·er (korn-flow-ĕr) *n.* a plant that grows wild in cornfields (especially a blue-flowered kind), or is cultivated as a garden plant.

corn·husk (korn-husk) *n.* the outer covering of an ear of corn.

cor·nice (kor-nis) *n.* an ornamental molding around the wall of a room just below the ceiling.

corn·meal (korn-meel) *n.* meal made of ground corn.

corn·stalk (korn-stawk) *n.* a stalk of corn.

corn·starch (korn-stahrch) *n.* corn flour used as a thickening agent in gravies etc.

cor·nu·co·pi·a (kor-nyŭ-koh-pi-ă) *n.* a horn of plenty, a horn-shaped container overflowing with fruit and flowers.

corn·y (kor-nee) *adj.* **(corn·i·er, corn·i·est)** (*informal*) hackneyed, repeated so often that people are tired of it, overly sentimental.

co·rol·la (kŏ-rol-ă) *n.* a ring of petals forming the inner envelope of a flower.

cor·ol·lar·y (kor-ŏ-ler-ee) *n.* (*pl.* -lar·ies) a natural consequence or result, something that follows logically after something else is proved.

co·ro·na (kŏ-roh-nă) *n.* a small circle or glow of light around something.

cor·o·nar·y (kor-ŏ-ner-ee) *adj.* of the arteries supplying blood to the heart. **coronary** *n.* (*pl.* -nar·ies) **1.** a coronary artery. **2.** a heart attack, coronary thrombosis. □**coronary thrombosis,** blockage of a coronary artery by a clot of blood.

cor·o·na·tion (kor-ŏ-nay-shŏn) *n.* the ceremony of crowning a king or queen or consort.

cor·o·ner (kor-ŏ-nĕr) *n.* an officer who holds an inquest into the cause of a death thought to be from violence or unnatural causes.

cor·o·net (kor-ŏ-net) *n.* **1.** a small crown. **2.** a band of gold, jewels, etc. for the head.

corp. *abbr.* **1.** corporal. **2.** corporation.

cor·po·ral¹ (kor-pŏ-răl) *adj.* of the body.

□**corporal punishment,** punishment by whipping or beating.

corporal[2] *n.* a noncommissioned officer ranking just below sergeant.

cor·po·rate (kor-pŏ-rit) *adj.* 1. shared by members of a group, *corporate responsibility.* 2. united in one group, *a corporate body.* 3. forming or belonging to a corporation, *corporate officers.*

cor·po·ra·tion (kor-pŏ-ray-shŏn) *n.* 1. a group of people authorized to act as an individual, especially in business. 2. a group of people elected to govern a municipality. 3. *(informal)* a protruding abdomen.

cor·po·re·al (kor-pohr-i-ăl) *adj.* 1. bodily. 2. tangible. **cor·po're·al·ly** *adv.* **cor·po·re·al·i·ty** (kor-pohr-i-al-i-tee) *n.*

corps (kohr) *n.* (*pl.* **corps,** *pr.* kohrz) 1. a military force, an army unit, *the Army Medical Corps.* 2. a body of people engaged in a special activity, *the diplomatic corps.* ▷Note the pronunciation of *corps.*

corpse (korps) *n.* a dead body.

corps·man (kohr-măn) *n.* (*pl.* **-men,** *pr.* -měn) a member of the medical troops.

cor·pu·lent (kor-pyŭ-lěnt) *adj.* having a bulky body, fat. **cor'pu·lence** *n.*

cor·pus (kor-pŭs) *n.* (*pl.* **-po·ra,** *pr.* -pŏ-ră) 1. a body or collection of writings. 2. a structure of special character or function in an animal body.

□**corpus delicti** (di-lik-tɪ), the material evidence that a crime has been committed; the body of a murdered person.

Cor·pus Chris·ti (kor-pŭs kris-tee) a Christian festival in honor of the Eucharist, celebrated on the Thursday after Trinity Sunday. ▷Latin, = the body of Christ.

cor·pus·cle (kor-pŭ-sěl) *n.* one of the red or white cells in the blood. **cor·pus·cu·lar** (kor-pus-kyŭ-lăr) *adj.*

corr. *abbr.* 1. corrected. 2. correction. 3. correspond. 4. correspondence. 5. correspondent. 6. corresponding.

cor·ral (kŏ-ral) *n.* an enclosure for horses, cattle, etc. **corral** *v.* (**cor·ralled, cor·ral·ling**) to drive animals into a corral.

cor·rect (kŏ-rekt) *adj.* 1. true, accurate. 2. proper, in accordance with an approved way of behaving or working. **correct** *v.* 1. to make correct, to set right by altering or adjusting. 2. to mark the errors in. 3. to point out faults in (a person), to punish (a person or a fault). **cor·rect'ly** *adv.* **cor·rect'ness** *n.* **cor·rec'tor** *n.* **cor·rect'a·ble** *adj.*

cor·rec·tion (kŏ-rek-shŏn) *n.* 1. correcting, being corrected. 2. an alteration made to something that was incorrect. **cor·rec'tion·al** *adj.* □**correctional institution,** a prison or reformatory.

cor·rec·tive (kŏ-rek-tiv) *adj.* correcting what is bad or harmful. **corrective** *n.* something that corrects.

cor·re·late (kor-ě-layt) *v.* (**cor·re·lat·ed, cor·re·lat·ing**) 1. to compare or connect systematically. 2. to have a systematic connection. **cor·re·la·tion** (kor-ě-lay-shŏn) *n.*

cor·rel·a·tive (kŏ-rel-ă-tiv) *adj.* 1. analogous. 2. (in grammar) corresponding with each other and regularly used together, as *either* and *or.* **correlative** *n.* a correlative word or thing. **cor·rel'a·tive·ly** *adv.* **cor·rel·a·tiv·i·ty** (kŏ-rel-ă-tiv-i-tee) *n.*

cor·re·spond (kor-ě-spond) *v.* 1. to be in harmony or agreement, *this corresponds with what I've*

heard. 2. to be similar or equivalent, *a parliament that corresponds to our Congress.* 3. to write letters to each other, *we correspond regularly.* **cor·re·spond'ing·ly** *adv.*

cor·re·spond·ence (kor-ě-spon-děns) *n.* 1. corresponding, harmony. 2. communicating by writing letters, the letters themselves. □**correspondence course,** instruction by means of materials sent by mail. **correspondence school,** a school conducting correspondence courses.

cor·re·spond·ent (kor-ě-spon-děnt) *n.* 1. a person who writes letters. 2. a person who is employed to gather news and contribute reports to a newspaper or to a television or radio station. 3. a business or person having regular business relations with another at a distance. **correspondent** *adj.* corresponding.

cor·ri·dor (kor-i-dŏr) *n.* a narrow passage, especially one from which doors open into rooms or compartments.

cor·ri·gen·da (kor-i-jen-dă) *n.* *pl.* = errata (*see* **erratum**).

cor·ri·gi·ble (kor-i-jĭ-běl) *n.* capable of being corrected.

cor·rob·o·rate (kŏ-rob-ŏ-rayt) *v.* (**cor·rob·o·rat·ed, cor·rob·o·rat·ing**) to get or give supporting evidence. **cor·rob·o·ra·tion** (kŏ-rob-ŏ-ray-shŏn) *n.* **cor·rob·o·ra·tive** (kŏ-rob-ŏ-ră-tiv, -ŏ-ră-tiv) *adj.*

cor·rode (kŏ-rohd) *v.* (**cor·rod·ed, cor·rod·ing**) to destroy gradually by chemical action, *rust corrodes metal.* **cor·ro·sion** (kŏ-roh-zhŏn) *n.* **cor·ro'sive** *adj.*

cor·ru·gate (kor-ŭ-gayt) *v.* (**cor·ru·gat·ed, cor·ru·gat·ing**) to wrinkle, to mark with or bend into parallel folds or ridges. **cor·ru·ga·tion** (kor-ŭ-gay-shŏn) *n.*

cor·ru·gat·ed (kor-ŭ-gay-tid) *adj.* shaped into alternate ridges and grooves, *corrugated iron.*

cor·rupt (kŏ-rupt) *adj.* 1. dishonest, accepting bribes. 2. immoral, wicked. 3. decaying. **corrupt** *v.* 1. to cause to become dishonest or immoral, to persuade to accept bribes. 2. to spoil, to taint. **cor·rup'tion** *n.*

cor·rupt·i·ble (kŏ-rup-ti-běl) *adj.* able to be corrupted. **cor·rupt·i·bil·i·ty** (kŏ-rup-ti-bil-i-tee) *n.*

cor·sage (kor-sahzh) *n.* fresh flowers worn by a woman on the shoulder or wrist.

cor·sair (kor-sair) *n.* (*old use*) 1. a Mediterranean pirate, especially of Barbary. 2. a corsair's ship.

cor·set (kor-sit) *n.* a close-fitting undergarment worn to shape or support the body.

cor·tege (kor-tezh) *n.* a funeral procession.

cor·tex (kor-teks) *n.* (*pl.* **-ti·ces,** *pr.* -ti-seez) 1. the gray matter of the brain. 2. the outer part of the kidney or suprarenal gland. 3. the inner bark of a tree.

cor·ti·sone (kor-ti-sohn) *n.* a hormone produced by the adrenal glands or made synthetically.

cor·us·cate (kor-ŭ-skayt) *v.* (**cor·us·cat·ed, cor·us·cat·ing**) to sparkle. **cor·us·ca·tion** (kor-ŭ-skay-shŏn) *n.*

cor·vette (kor-vet) *n.* a small fast gunboat designed for escorting merchant ships.

co·ry·za (kŏ-rɪ-ză) *n.* an inflammation of the nasal mucous membrane and sinuses.

cos[1] (kos) *n.* a kind of lettuce with long leaves.

cos[2] *abbr.* cosine.

C.O.S. *abbr.* 1. cash on shipment. 2. Chief of Staff.

co·sig·na·to·ry (koh-sig-nă-tohr-ee) *n.* (*pl.* **-ries**)

a person signing jointly with another or others.
cosignatory *adj.* signing jointly with another or others.
co·sign·er (koh-sı-něr) *n.* a cosignatory, especially of a promissory note.
co·sine (koh-sın) *n.* (in a right-angled triangle) the ratio of the length of a side adjacent to one of the acute angles to the length of the hypotenuse.
cos·met·ic (koz-met-ik) *n.* a substance for beautifying the body, especially the face. **cosmetic** *adj.* for beautifying or improving the appearance, *cosmetic surgery.*
cos·me·tol·o·gist (koz-mě-tol-ŏ-jist) *n.* a beautician. **cos·me·tol'o·gy** *n.*
cos·mic (koz-mik) *adj.* of the universe. **cos'mi·cal·ly** *adv.* ☐**cosmic rays,** high-energy radiation that reaches Earth from outer space.
cos·mog·o·ny (koz-mog-ŏ-nee) *n.* (*pl.* **-nies**) a theory of the creation and evolution of the universe. **cos·mog'o·nist** *n.* **cos·mo·gon·ic** (koz-mŏ-gon-ik) *adj.*
cos·mol·o·gy (koz-mol-ŏ-jee) *n.* (*pl.* **-gies**) the study of philosophy of the universe as an ordered whole. **cos·mol'o·gist** *n.* **cos·mo·log·i·cal** (koz-mŏ-loj-i-kăl) *adj.*
cos·mo·naut (koz-mŏ-nawt) *n.* an astronaut, especially one from the Soviet Union.
cos·mop·o·lis (koz-mop-ŏ-lis) *n.* a cosmopolitan city.
cos·mo·pol·i·tan (koz-mŏ-pol-i-tăn) *adj.* 1. of or from many parts of the world, containing people from many countries, *a cosmopolitan crowd* or *city.* 2. free from national prejudices and at home in all parts of the world, *a cosmopolitan outlook.* **cosmopolitan** *n.* a cosmopolitan person.
cos·mop·o·lite (koz-mop-ŏ-lıt) *n.* a cosmopolitan.
cos·mos[1] (koz-mŏs) *n.* the universe.
cosmos[2] *n.* a garden plant with pink, white, or purple flowers.
co·spon·sor (koh-spon-sŏr) *n.* a person who sponsors legislation, an event, etc. with one or more sponsors.
Cos·sack (kos-ak) *n.* a member of a people of south Russia, famous as horsemen. **Cossack** *adj.*
cos·set (kos-it) *v.* (**cos·set·ed, cos·set·ing**) to pamper.
cost (kawst) *n.* 1. an amount given or required as payment. 2. an expenditure of time or labor, a loss suffered in achieving something, *succeeded at the cost of his life.* 3. *costs,* the expenses involved in having something settled in a law court. **cost** *v.* (**cost** [in definition 3 **cost·ed**], **cost·ing**) 1. to be obtainable at a certain price. 2. to require a certain effort or loss etc. 3. to estimate the cost involved. ☐**at all costs,** no matter what the risk or loss involved may be. **at cost,** at cost price.
cost accountant, one employed to supervise a firm's cost of doing business. **cost effective,** producing useful results in relation to cost. **cost of living,** the general level of prices.
co-star (koh-stahr) *n.* a stage or film star performing with another of equal importance. **co-star** (koh-stahr) *v.* (**co-starred, co-star·ring**) to perform or include as a co-star.
Cos·ta Ri·ca (kos-tă ree-kă) a country in Central America. **Cos'ta Ri'can** *adj.* & *n.*
cos·tive (kos-tiv) *adj.* constipated or causing constipation.
cost·ly (kawst-lee) *adj.* (**-li·er, -li·est**) costing much, expensive. **cost'li·ness** *n.*
cos·tume (kos-tyoom) *n.* a style of clothes belong-

ing to a particular place or period or group or suitable for a particular activity, *peasant costume; a skating costume; costume plays,* in which the actors wear historical costume. ☐**costume jewelry,** jewelry made of inexpensive materials.
co·sy = **cozy.**
cot (kot) *n.* a lightweight narrow bed of canvas stretched on a collapsible frame.
cote (koht) *n.* a shed, stall, or shelter, especially for birds and animals.
co·te·rie (koh-tě-ree) *n.* a select group of people.
co·ter·mi·nous (koh-tur-mı̆-nŭs) *adj.* conterminous.
co·til·lion (kŏ-til-yŏn) *n.* 1. a dance with an elaborate series of steps and figures. 2. a coming-out party, a formal ball.
co·to·ne·as·ter (kŏ-toh-ni-as-těr) *n.* a deciduous or evergreen shrub or small tree with white or pinkish flowers and usually red or orange berries.
cot·tage (kot-ij) *n.* a small simple house in the country. ☐**cottage cheese,** soft white cheese made from curds without pressing. **cottage industry,** one that can be carried on at home, as knitting and some kinds of weaving.
cot·ter (kot-ěr) pin a split pin that opens wide at one end, used as a fastener.
cot·ton (kot-ŏn) *n.* 1. a soft white substance around the seeds of the cotton plant. 2. the plant itself. 3. thread made from this. 4. fabric made from this thread. **cotton** *v.* **cotton to** (*informal*) to like. ☐**cotton gin,** a machine for separating cotton from its seeds. **cotton up to,** (*informal*) to make friendly advances to.
cot·ton·mouth (kot-ŏn-mowth) *n.* (*pl.* **-mouths,** *pr.* -mow*thz,* mowths) a venomous snake of southeastern U.S. living in low-lying swampy areas.
cot·ton·seed (kot-ŏn-seed) *n.* the seed of the cotton plant, oil and cattle fodder. ☐**cottonseed oil,** oil obtained from cottonseed.
cot·ton·tail (kot-ŏn-tayl) *n.* any of several North American rabbits with a white fluffy tail.
cot·ton·wood (kot-ŏn-wuud) *n.* any of various North American species of poplar, with seeds surrounded by cotton-like tufts.
cot·ton·y (kot-ŏ-nee) *adj.* like cotton.
cot·y·le·don (kot-ı̆-lee-dŏn) *n.* the first leaf growing from a seed.
couch (kowch) *n.* 1. a sofa or settee. 2. a bedlike structure on which a doctor's patient can lie for examination. **couch** *v.* to express in words of a certain kind, *the request was couched in polite terms.*
cou·gar (koo-gǎr) *n.* (*pl.* **-gars, -gar**) a mountain lion.
cough (kawf) *v.* to send out air or other matter from the lungs with a sudden sharp sound. **cough** *n.* 1. an act or sound of coughing. 2. an illness causing frequent coughing. ☐**cough drop,** a lozenge taken to relieve coughing. **cough up,** (*slang*) to give (money etc.) with some reluctance.
could (kuud) *auxiliary verb* used as the past tense of **can**[2]. **could,** feel inclined to, *I could jump for joy.* ☐**could be,** might be; *he could have been delayed,* this is possible.
could·n't (kuud-ěnt) = could not.
cou·lee (koo-lee) *n.* a deep ravine.
cou·lomb (koo-lom) *n.* the amount of electricity carried in one second by a current of one ampere.
coun·cil (kown-sıl) *n.* 1. an assembly of people to advise on or discuss or organize something. 2. an elected body organizing municipal affairs.

▷ Do not confuse *council* with *counsel.*

coun·cil·man (kown-sĭl-măn) *n.* (*pl.* **-men,** *pr.* -měn) a member of a town or city council. **coun· cil·wom·an** (kown-sĭl-wuum-ăn) *n.* (*pl.* **-wom· en,** *pr.* -wim-in)

coun·ci·lor (kown-sĭ-lŏr) *n.* a member of a council. ▷ Do not confuse *councilor* with *counselor.*

coun·sel (kown-sĕl) *n.* 1. advice, suggestions, *give counsel.* 2. (*pl.* **counsel**) an attorney or group of attorneys giving advice in a legal case. **coun· sel** *v.* (**coun·seled, coun·sel·ing**) to advise, to give advice to people professionally on social problems. ☐**keep one's own counsel,** to keep one's views or plans secret. **take counsel with,** to consult. ▷ Do not confuse *counsel* with *council.*

coun·se·lor (kown-sĕ-lŏr) *n.* an adviser. ▷ Do not confuse *counselor* with *councilor.*

count[1] (kownt) *v.* 1. to find the total of. 2. to say or name the numbers in order. 3. to include or be included in a reckoning, *six of us, counting the dog; this will count against him,* will be a disadvantage to his reputation. 4. to be important, to be worth reckoning; *fine words count for nothing,* are of no value. 5. to regard or consider, *I should count it an honor.* **count** *n.* 1. counting, a calculation. 2. a number reached by counting, a total. 3. a point being considered, one of the charges against an accused person, *he was found guilty on all counts.* ☐**count down,** to count numerals backward to zero, as in the procedure before launching a rocket. **count in,** to include in a reckoning. **count on,** to rely on; to expect confidently. **count one's chickens before they are hatched,** to assume that something will be successful before this is certain. **count out,** to count one by one from a stock; to exclude from a reckoning; (of a referee) to count up to ten seconds over (a boxer or wrestler who has been knocked or fallen to the canvas). **count up,** to find the sum of. **down for the count,** defeated in a boxing match by failing to rise within ten seconds after falling to the canvas. **take the count,** to be down for the count in boxing.

count[2] *n.* a European nobleman corresponding to a British earl.

count·a·ble (kown-tă-bĕl) *adj.* able to be counted.

count·down (kownt-down) *n.* a count in reverse order in the process of counting.

coun·te·nance (kown-tĕ-năns) *n.* 1. the expression of the face. 2. an appearance of approval, *lending countenance to their plan.* **countenance** *v.* (**coun·te·nanced, coun·te·nanc·ing**) to give approval to.

count·er[1] (kown-tĕr) *n.* 1. a table or other flat surface over which goods, food, etc. are sold or served or business is transacted with customers. 2. a small disk used for keeping count in table games. 3. a person or device that counts something.

counter[2] *adv.* in the opposite direction. **counter** *adj.* opposed. **counter** *v.* to hinder or defeat by an opposing action. **counter** *n.* a parry.

counter- *prefix* against, opposite, as in *counteract, counterpoint.*

coun·ter·act (kown-tĕr-akt) *v.* to reduce or prevent the effects of. **coun·ter·ac·tion** (kown-tĕr-ak-shŏn) *n.* **coun·ter·ac·tive** (kown-tĕr-ak-tiv) *adj.*

coun·ter·at·tack (kown-tĕr-ă-tak) *n.* an attack directed against an enemy who has already attacked or invaded. **counterattack** (kown-tĕr-ă-tak) *v.* to make a counterattack.

coun·ter·bal·ance (kown-tĕr-bal-ăns) *n.* a weight or influence that balances another. **counterbalance** (kown-tĕr-bal-ăns) *v.* (**coun·ter· bal·anced, coun·ter·bal·anc·ing**) to act as a counterbalance to.

coun·ter·check (kown-tĕr-chek) *n.* an obstruction checking movement or operating against another.

coun·ter·claim (kown-tĕr-klaym) *n.* a claim made in opposition to another claim.

coun·ter·clock·wise (kown-tĕr-klok-wiz) *adj.* & *adv.* in a curve from right to left, that is, opposite to the movement of clock hands.

coun·ter·cul·ture (kown-tĕr-kul-chŭr) *n.* a mode of life of persons who reject established social values and practices.

coun·ter·es·pi·o·nage (kown-tĕr-es-pi-ŏ-nahzh) *n.* action taken to uncover and counteract enemy spying.

coun·ter·feit (kown-tĕr-fit) *adj.* fake. **counterfeit** *n.* a fake. **counterfeit** *v.* to fake. **coun'ter·feit· er** *n.*

coun·ter·foil (kown-tĕr-foil) *n.* a detachable section of a check or receipt etc. kept by the sender as a record.

coun·ter·in·sur·gen·cy (kown-tĕr-in-sur-jĕn-see) *n.* (*pl.* **-cies**) action taken to combat insurgent activity. **coun·ter·in·sur'gent** *n.*

coun·ter·in·tel·li·gence (kown-tĕr-in-tel-i-jĕns) *n.* counterespionage.

coun·ter·man (kown-tĕr-man) *n.* (*pl.* **-men,** *pr.* -men) a person who serves food to customers at a lunch counter.

coun·ter·mand (kown-tĕr-mand) *v.* to cancel (a command or order).

coun·ter·mea·sure (kown-tĕr-mezh-ŭr) *n.* action taken to counteract a threat or danger etc.

coun·ter·of·fen·sive (kown-tĕr-ŏ-fen-siv) *n.* a large-scale counterattack.

coun·ter·pane (kown-tĕr-payn) *n.* a bedspread.

coun·ter·part (kown-tĕr-pahrt) *n.* a person or thing corresponding to another in position or use.

coun·ter·point (kown-tĕr-point) *n.* a method of combining melodies.

coun·ter·poise (kown-tĕr-poiz) *n.* a counterbalance. **counterpoise** *v.* (**coun·ter·poised, coun·ter·pois·ing**) to counterbalance.

coun·ter·pro·duc·tive (kown-tĕr-prŏ-duk-tiv) *adj.* having the opposite of the desired effect.

Coun·ter (kown-tĕr) **Reformation** the reformation in the Roman Catholic Church following on the Protestant Reformation.

coun·ter·rev·o·lu·tion (kown-tĕr-rev-ŏ-loo-shŏn) *n.* a revolution undertaken to reverse the effects of a previous revolution. **coun'ter·rev· o·lu'tion·ar·y** (*pl.* **-ar·ies**) *adj.* & *n.*

coun·ter·sign (kown-tĕr-sın) *n.* a password. **countersign** *v.* to add another signature to (a document) to give it authority.

coun·ter·sig·na·ture (kown-tĕr-sig-nă-chŭr) *n.* a confirming signature added to a document.

coun·ter·sink (kown-tĕr-singk) *v.* (**coun·ter· sank, coun·ter·sunk, coun·ter·sink·ing**) to enlarge the top of (a hole) so that the head of a screw or bolt will lie level with or below the surface, to sink (a screw etc.) in such a hole.

coun·ter·spy (kown-tĕr-spı) *n.* (*pl.* **-spies**) a person who conducts counterespionage.

coun·ter·ten·or (kown-tĕr-ten-ŏr) *n.* 1. an adult male singing voice above tenor. 2. a singer with such a voice, a part written for it.

coun·ter·vail (kown-tĕr-**vayl**) v. to counterbalance.

coun·ter·weight (kown-tĕr-wayt) n. a counterbalancing weight or influence.

coun·tess (kown-tis) n. 1. the wife or widow of a count or earl. 2. a woman holding the rank of a count or earl.

count·less (kownt-lis) adj. too many to be counted.

coun·tri·fied (kun-tri-fĭd) adj. having the characteristics of the country or country life.

coun·try (kun-tree) n. (pl. **-tries**) 1. a nation, the land it occupies. 2. land consisting of fields and woods with few houses or other buildings. 3. an area of land with certain features, hill country. □**country and western**, country music. **country club**, a suburban club for golf, tennis, other sports, social activities, etc. **country music**, simple music, originated in the southern U.S., based on folk and cowboy songs, spirituals, and gospel music. **cross country**, across fields, not keeping to main roads or to a direct road.

coun·try·man (kun-tri-măn) n. (pl. **-men**, pr. -mĕn) 1. a man living in the country, not in a town. 2. a man of one's own country, a compatriot. **coun'try·wom·an** n. (pl. **-wom·en**, pr. -wim-in).

coun·try·side (kun-tri-sĭd) n. land outside a settled area.

coun·ty (kown-tee) n. (pl. **-ties**) 1. one of the main areas into which a state is divided for purposes of local government. 2. the people of a county. □**county seat**, a town in which the business of the county is transacted.

coup (koo) n. (pl. **coups**, pr. kooz) a sudden action taken to obtain power or achieve a desired result.

coup de grâce (koo dĕ grahs) (pl. **coups de grâce**, pr. koo de grahs) 1. a finishing stroke. 2. a deathblow administered as an act of mercy to a dying person. ▷French.

coup d'état (koo day-tah) (pl. **coups d'état**, pr. koo day-tah) the sudden overthrowing of a government by force or by unconstitutional means. ▷French.

coupe (koop) n. a small closed two-door automobile.

cou·ple (kup-ĕl) n. 1. two people or things considered together. 2. a man and woman who are engaged or married. 3. partners in a dance. **couple** v. (**cou·pled, cou·pling**) 1. to fasten or link together, to join by coupling. 2. to join in marriage. 3. to copulate.

cou·plet (kup-lit) n. two successive lines of verse that rhyme and have the same meter.

cou·pling (kup-ling) n. a device for connecting two railroad cars or parts of machinery.

cou·pon (koo-pon) n. 1. a detachable ticket or part of a document etc. that entitles the holder to receive something or that can be used as an application form. 2. a certificate attached to a bond, showing the interest due. □**clip coupons**, to detach the coupons from bonds and collect the interest; (informal) to live without having to earn one's livelihood.

cour·age (kur-ij) n. the ability to control fear when facing danger or pain, bravery. □**have the courage of one's convictions**, to be brave enough to do what one feels to be right.

cou·ra·geous (kŏ-**ray**-jŭs) adj. having or showing courage. **cou·ra'geous·ly** adv.

cou·ri·er (kur-i-ĕr) n. a messenger carrying news or important papers.

course (kohrs) n. 1. an onward movement in space or time, in the ordinary course of events. 2. the direction taken or intended, the course of the river; the ship was off course. 3. a series of things one can do to achieve something, your best course is to start again. 4. a series of talks or lessons or treatments etc., an English composition course; a course of exercises. 5. an area of land on which golf is played, a stretch of land or water over which a race takes place. 6. a continuous layer of brick or stone etc. in a wall. 7. one of the parts of a meal, the first course was soup. **course** v. 1. to hunt (especially rabbits) with hounds that follow game by sight not by scent. 2. to follow a course. 3. to move or flow freely, blood coursed through his veins. □**in course of**, in the process of, the bridge is in course of construction. **in due course**, in the natural order. **in the course of**, during; in the course of time, after some time has passed. **of course**, without a doubt, as was to be expected.

court (kohrt) n. 1. a courtyard. 2. a yard surrounded by houses, opening off a street. 3. an enclosed area for certain games, as squash, tennis. 4. a sovereign's establishment with attendants, councilors, etc.; the Court of St. James's, the British sovereign's court. 5. a law court. **court** v. 1. to try to win the favor or support of. 2. to woo. 3. to behave as though trying to provoke something harmful, courting danger. □**out of court**, without a trial, we settled the case out of court. **pay court to**, to pay special attention to a person in order to win that person's favor or interest.

cour·te·ous (kur-ti-ŭs) adj. polite. **cour'te·ous·ly** adv.

cour·te·san (kohr-tĕ-zăn) n. (old use) a prostitute with wealthy or upper-class clients.

cour·te·sy (kur-tĕ-see) n. (pl. **-sies**) courteous behavior. □**by courtesy of**, by the permission or favor of.

court·house (kohrt-hows) n. (pl. **-hous·es**, pr. -how-ziz) a building housing county courts and county administrative offices.

cour·ti·er (kohr-ti-ĕr) n. (old use) one of a sovereign's companions at court.

court·ly (kohrt-lee) adj. (**-li·er, -li·est**) dignified and polite. **court'li·ness** n.

court-mar·tial (kohrt-mahr-shăl) n. (pl. **courts-mar·tial**) 1. a court for trying offenses against military law. 2. trial by such a court. **court-martial** v. (**court-mar·tialed, court-mar·tial·ing**) to try by a court-martial.

court·room (kohrt-room) n. a room in which law courts meet.

court·ship (kohrt-ship) n. courting, the period during which this takes place.

court·yard (kohrt-yahrd) n. a space enclosed by walls or buildings.

cous·in (kuz-in) n. a child of one's uncle or aunt (also called first cousin); second cousin, a child of one's parent's first cousin. **cous'in·ly** adv.

cou·ture (koo-toor) n. the design and making of fashionable clothes.

cou·tu·ri·er (koo-toor-ee-ay) n. a designer or maker of fashionable clothes. **cou·tu·ri·ère** (koo-toor-ee-êr) n. fem.

co·va·lence (koh-vay-lĕns) n. 1. a covalent bond, the electrons forming this. 2. the number of covalent bonds an atom can form. **co·va'lent** adj. **co·va'lent·ly** adv.

cove (kohv) *n.* a small bay.
cov·en (kuv-ĕn) *n.* an assembly of witches.
cov·e·nant (kuv-ĕ-nănt) *n.* a formal agreement, a contract. **covenant** *v.* to undertake by covenant.
cov·er (kuv-ĕr) *v.* 1. to place (a thing) over or in front of, to conceal or protect in this way. 2. to spread (a thing) over; *covered with shame,* obviously ashamed. 3. to lie or extend over, to occupy the surface of, *the factory covers a large area.* 4. to travel over (a distance), *we covered ten miles a day.* 5. to protect by dominating the approach to, to have within range of one's gun(s), to keep a gun aimed at. 6. to protect by providing insurance or a guaranty, *covering you against fire or theft.* 7. to amount to enough money to pay for, *$44 will cover the fare.* 8. to include, to deal with (a subject); *a covering letter,* an explanatory letter sent with a document or goods. 9. to investigate or report for a newspaper etc., *who is covering the conference?* **cover** *n.* 1. a thing that covers. 2. the binding of a book etc., either half of this. 3. a wrapper or envelope. 4. a place or area giving shelter or protection, *there was no cover.* 5. a supporting force etc. protecting another from attack, *fighter cover.* 6. a screen or pretense, *under cover of friendship.* □**cover a lot of ground,** *(informal)* to travel far; to deal with a variety of topics. **cover charge,** an extra charge per person in a restaurant or nightclub. **cover crop,** a crop grown for the protection or enrichment of the soil. **covered wagon,** a large horse-drawn wagon with an arched canvas top, used by American pioneers going west during the 19th century. **cover girl,** a beautiful young woman whose picture appears on the cover of a magazine. **cover up,** to conceal (a thing or fact). **under separate cover,** in a separate envelope or package.
cov·er·age (kuv-ĕ-rij) *n.* 1. the act or fact of covering. 2. the area or amount covered. 3. reporting of a news event. 4. insurance against loss or damage etc.
cov·er·all (kuv-ĕr-awl) *n.* a full-length protective outer garment.
cov·er·let (kuv-ĕr-lit) *n.* a bedspread.
cov·ert (kuv-ĕrt) *n.* 1. an area of thick undergrowth in which animals hide. 2. a bird's feather covering the base of another. **covert** (koh-vĕrt) *adj.* concealed, done secretly, *covert glances.* **cov′ert·ly** *adv.* **cov′ert·ness** *n.* □**covert cloth,** a twilled woolen cloth used for suits or coats.
cov·er-up (kuv-ĕr-up) *n.* concealment, especially of facts.
cov·et (kuv-it) *v.* to desire eagerly, especially something belonging to another person.
cov·et·ous (kuv-ĕ-tŭs) *adj.* coveting. **cov′et·ous·ly** *adv.* **cov′et·ous·ness** *n.*
cov·ey (kuv-ee) *n.* (*pl.* **-eys**) a brood or small flock of partridges or quail.
cow[1] (kow) *n.* the mature female of cattle or of certain other large animals (as elephant, whale, seal). □**cow pony,** a cowboy's horse.
cow[2] *v.* to subdue by frightening with threats or force.
cow·ard (kow-ărd) *n.* a person who lacks courage. **cow′ard·ly** *adj.* **cow′ard·li·ness** *n.*
cow·ard·ice (kow-ăr-dis) *n.* lack of courage.
cow·bird (kow-burd) *n.* any of various American blackbirds that lay their eggs in other birds' nests.
cow·boy (kow-boi) *n.* 1. a man in charge of grazing cattle in the western U.S. 2. *(informal)* a per-

son who drives an automobile recklessly. **cow′ girl** *n.*
cow·catcher (kow-kach-ĕr) *n.* a wedge-shaped steel frame fixed to the front of a locomotive, for clearing the tracks.
cow·er (kow-ĕr) *v.* to crouch or shrink back in fear.
cow·hand (kow-hand) *n.* a cowboy (definition 1).
cow·hide (kow-hɪd) *n.* 1. the skin of a cow. 2. a whip made from this.
cowl (kowl) *n.* 1. a monk's hood or hooded robe. 2. a hood-shaped covering, as on a chimney.
cow·lick (kow-lik) *n.* a projecting lock of hair.
cowl·ing (kow-ling) *n.* a removable metal cover over an engine.
cow·man (kow-măn) *n.* (*pl.* **-men**, *pr.* -mĕn) *(slang)* the owner of a cattle ranch.
co·work·er (koh-wur-kĕr) *n.* a fellow worker.
cow·poke (kow-pohk) *n.* *(informal)* a cowboy (definition 1).
cow·pox (kow-poks) *n.* a disease of cows of which the virus is used in vaccination against smallpox.
cow·punch·er (kow-pun-chĕr) *n.* *(informal)* a cowboy (definition 1).
cow·rie, cow·ry (kow-ree) *n.* 1. a small gastropod of the Indian Ocean. 2. its shell, used as money in Africa and South Asia.
cow·shed (kow-shed) *n.* a shed where cattle are kept when not at pasture.
cow·slip (kow-slip) *n.* a wild plant with small fragrant yellow flowers.
cox (koks) *n.* *(informal)* a coxswain. **cox** *v.* to act as coxswain of.
cox·comb (koks-kohm) *n.* a conceited showy person.
cox·swain (kok-sɪn) *n.* 1. a person who steers a racing shell. 2. a sailor in charge of a ship's boat.
coy (koi) *n.* pretending to be shy or embarrassed, bashful. **coy′ly** *adv.* **coy′ness** *n.*
coy·ote (kɪ-oht, kɪ-oh-tee) *n.* a North American prairie wolf.
coy·pu (koi-poo) *n.* a beaverlike water animal, originally from South America.
coz·en (kuz-ĕn) *v.* 1. to cheat, defraud, beguile. 2. to act deceitfully. **coz·en·age** (kuz-ĕ-nij) *n.*
co·zy (koh-zee) *adj.* (**-zi·er, -zi·est**) warm and comfortable. **cozy** *n.* (*pl.* **-zies**) cover placed over a teapot etc. to keep it hot. **co′zi·ly** *adv.* **co′zi·ness** *n.*
cp. *abbr.* compare.
C.P. *abbr.* 1. Command Post. 2. Communist Party.
C.P.A. *abbr.* Certified Public Accountant.
cpd. *abbr.* compound.
CPI *abbr.* consumer price index.
Cpl. *abbr.* corporal.
CPO, C.P.O. *abbr.* Chief Petty Officer.
cps *abbr.* cycles per second.
Cr *symbol* chromium.
cr. *abbr.* 1. credit. 2. creditor. 3. creek. 4. crown.
crab (krab) *n.* 1. a ten-footed shellfish. 2. its flesh as food. 3. *the Crab,* a sign of the zodiac, Cancer.
crab *v.* (**crabbed, crab·bing**) *(informal)* to find fault with, to grumble. □**crab apple,** a kind of small sour apple.
crab·bed (krab-id) *adj.* 1. bad-tempered. 2. (of handwriting) difficult to read or decipher.
crab·by (krab-ee) *adj.* (**-bi·er, -bi·est**) bad-tempered.
crab·grass (krab-gras) *n.* a coarse creeping grass infesting lawns.
crack (krak) *n.* 1. a sudden sharp explosive noise.

2. a sharp blow. 3. *(informal)* a wisecrack, a joke. 4. a chink. 5. a line of division where something is broken but has not come completely apart. **crack** *adj. (informal)* first-rate. **crack** *v.* 1. to make or cause to make a sudden sharp explosive sound; *cracked his head against the wall,* gave his head a sharp blow. 2. to tell (a joke). 3. to break with a sharp sound. 4. to break into (a safe etc.). 5. to find the solution to (a code or problem). 6. to break without coming completely apart. 7. (of a voice) to become suddenly harsh, especially with emotion. 8. to collapse under strain, to cease to resist. 9. to break down (heavy oils) in order to produce lighter ones. ☐**crack down on,** *(informal)* to take severe measures against (something illegal); to enforce (a rule) strictly. **crack of dawn,** daybreak. **crack up,** *(informal)* to have a physical or mental breakdown; to laugh boisterously; to damage (an automobile etc.); to be involved in an accident. **get cracking,** *(informal)* to get busy on work that is waiting to be done. **have a crack at,** *(informal)* to attempt.

crack·brained (krak-braynd) *adj. (slang)* crazy.

crack·down (krak-down) *n.* strict enforcement of rules, laws, etc.

cracked (krakt) *adj. (slang)* crazy.

crack·er (krak-ĕr) *n.* 1. a firework that explodes with a sharp crack. 2. a small paper toy made so as to explode harmlessly when the ends are pulled. 3. a thin dry biscuit. 4. *(contemptuous)* a poor rural white person, especially in Georgia *(a Georgia cracker)* or Florida.

crack·er·jack (krak-ĕr-jak) *adj. (informal)* first-rate. **crackerjack** *n. (informal)* a first-rate person or thing.

crack·le (krak-ĕl) *v.* (**crack·led, crack·ling**) to make or cause to make a series of slight cracking sounds. **crackle** *n.* these sounds.

crack·ling (krak-ling) *n.* crisp skin on roast pork.

crack·pot (krak-pot) *n. (slang)* a person with crazy or impractical ideas.

cra·dle (kray-dĕl) *n.* 1. a small bed for a baby, usually on rockers. 2. a place where something originates, *the cradle of civilization.* 3. a supporting framework or structure. **cradle** *v.* (**cra·dled, cra·dling**) to hold or support as if in a cradle. ☐**rob the cradle,** to date or marry a person much younger than oneself.

cra·dle·song (kray-dĕl-sawng) *n.* a lullaby.

craft (kraft) *n.* 1. an occupation in which skill is needed. 2. such a skill or technique. 3. cunning, deceit. 4. *(pl.* **craft**) a ship or boat or raft, an aircraft or spacecraft.

crafts·man (krafts-măn) *n. (pl.* **-men,** *pr.* -mĕn) a workman who is skilled in a craft. **crafts′man·ship** *n.*

craft·y (kraf-tee) *adj.* (**craft·i·er, craft·i·est**) cunning, using underhand methods. **craft′i·ly** *adv.* **craft′i·ness** *n.*

crag (krag) *n.* a steep or rugged rock. **crag′gy** *adj.* (-**gi·er, -gi·est**) **crag′gi·ness** *n.*

cram (kram) *v.* (**crammed, cram·ming**) 1. to force into too small a space so that the container is overfull. 2. to overfill in this way. 3. to study intensively at the last minute for an examination.

cramp (kramp) *n.* 1. sudden painful involuntary tightening of a muscle. 2. (also **cramps**) a sharp pain in the abdomen. **cramp** *v.* to keep within too narrow limits. ☐**cramp a person's style,** to prevent him from acting freely or showing his best abilities.

cramped (krampt) *adj.* 1. put or kept in too narrow a space, without room to move. 2. (of handwriting) small and with letters close together.

cram·pon (kram-pŏn) *n.* an iron plate with spikes, worn on boots for walking or climbing on ice.

cran·ber·ry (kran-ber-ee) *n.* (*pl.* **-ries**) 1. the small tart red berry of a kind of shrub, used for making jelly and sauce. 2. the shrub itself.

crane (krayn) *n.* 1. a large wading bird with long legs, neck, and bill. 2. an apparatus for moving heavy objects, usually by suspending them from a jib by ropes or chains. **crane** *v.* (**craned, cran·ing**) to stretch (one's neck) in order to see something. ☐**crane fly,** a flying insect with very long legs.

cra·ni·um (kray-ni-ŭm) *n.* (*pl.* **-ni·ums, -ni·a,** *pr.* -ni-ă) the bones enclosing the brain, the skull. **cra′ni·al** *adj.*

crank (krangk) *n.* 1. an L-shaped part for converting to-and-fro motion into circular motion. 2. *(informal)* an eccentric person. 3. *(informal)* a grouch. **crank** *v.* to cause to move by means of a crank. ☐**crank out,** *(informal)* to mass-produce.

crank·case (krangk-kays) *n.* the case enclosing a crankshaft.

crank·shaft (krangk-shaft) *n.* the shaft driven by the crank in an internal combustion engine.

crank·y (krang-kee) *adj.* (**crank·i·er, crank·i·est**) 1. grouchy, ill-tempered. 2. crotchety, eccentric. **crank′i·ness** *n.*

cran·ny (kran-ee) *n.* (*pl.* **-nies**) a crevice.

crap (krap) *n.* a losing throw of the dice in craps.

crape (krayp) *n.* 1. a band of black fabric or paper used as a sign of mourning. 2. crepe.

crap·pie (krap-ee) *n.* a small U.S. fish.

craps (kraps) *n.* a gambling game played with a pair of dice; *shooting craps,* playing this game.

crap·shoot·er (krap-shoo-tĕr) *n.* 1. a person who plays craps. 2. *(informal)* a person who takes risks.

crash[1] (krash) *n.* 1. a sudden violent noise like that of something breaking by impact. 2. a violent collision or fall. 3. financial collapse. **crash** *v.* 1. to make a crash, to move or go with a crash. 2. to cause (a vehicle or aircraft) to have a collision, to be involved in a crash. 3. *(informal)* to enter without permission, to gatecrash. 4. to collapse financially. **crash** *adj.* involving intense effort to achieve something rapidly, *a crash program.* ☐**crash dive,** a sudden dive by an aircraft or submarine, especially in an emergency. **crash helmet,** a padded helmet worn to protect the head in case of a crash. **crash landing,** an emergency landing by an aircraft etc.

crash[2] *n.* a coarse linen or cotton fabric for towels etc.

crash-dive (krash-dıv) *v.* (**crash-dived** or **crash-dove, crash-dived, crash-div·ing**) 1. (of a submarine) to dive at a steep angle. 2. to cause to make such a dive.

crash-land (krash-land) *v.* 1. to land (an aircraft) in an emergency, especially with damage to it. 2. to be landed in this way.

crass (kras) *adj.* 1. gross, *crass stupidity.* 2. very stupid. **crass′ly** *adv.* **crass′ness** *n.*

crate (krayt) *n.* 1. a packing case made of wooden slats. 2. *(slang)* an old aircraft or car. **crate** *v.* (**crat·ed, crat·ing**) to pack into a crate.

cra·ter (kray-tĕr) *n.* a bowl-shaped cavity or hollow.

cra·ton (kray-ton) *n.* a relatively rigid and stationary part of Earth's crust.

cra·vat (kră-vat) *n.* 1. a short scarf. 2. a necktie.
crave (krayv) *v.* (**craved, crav·ing**) 1. to long for, to have a strong desire. 2. to ask earnestly for, *crave mercy* or *for mercy.*
cra·ven (kray-věn) *adj.* cowardly. **craven** *n.* a coward.
crav·ing (kray-ving) *n.* a strong desire, a longing.
craw·fish (kraw-fish) *n.* (*pl.* **-fish, -fish·es**) a crayfish.
crawl (krawl) *v.* 1. to move as snakes or ants do, with the body close to the ground or other surface. 2. to move on hands and knees. 3. to move slowly or with difficulty. 4. (*informal*) to seek favor by behaving in a servile way, *he crawls before the boss.* 5. to be covered with crawling things, *it was crawling with ants.* 6. to feel as if covered with crawling things. **crawl** *n.* 1. a crawling movement. 2. a very slow pace, *at a crawl.* 3. a swimming stroke with an overarm movement of each arm alternately. **crawl′er** *n.* □**crawl space,** a shallow cellar.
cray·fish (kray-fish) *n.* (*pl.* **-fish, -fish·es**) a freshwater shellfish like a very small lobster.
cray·on (kray-on) *n.* a stick of colored wax or chalk or other material for drawing. **crayon** *v.* to draw or color with crayons.
craze (krayz) *n.* 1. great but often short-lived enthusiasm for something. 2. the object of this.
crazed (krayzd) *adj.* driven insane, *crazed with grief.*
cra·zy (kray-zee) *adj.* (**-zi·er, -zi·est**) 1. insane. 2. very foolish, not sensible, *this crazy plan.* **craz′i·ly** *adv.* **craz′i·ness** *n.* □**crazy quilt,** a quilt made from pieces of fabric of many colors, sizes, and shapes. **like crazy,** (*informal*) like mad, very much.
CRC *abbr.* Civil Rights Commission.
creak (kreek) *n.* a harsh squeak like that of an unoiled hinge. **creak** *v.* to make such a sound. **creak′y** *adj.* (**creak·i·er, creak·i·est**) **creak′i·ly** *adv.*
cream[1] (kreem) *n.* 1. the fatty part of milk. 2. its color, yellowish white. 3. a food containing or like cream, *ice cream.* 4. a soft creamlike substance, especially a cosmetic. 5. the best part of something, *the cream of society.* **cream** *adj.* cream-colored. **cream** *v.* 1. to remove the cream from; *creaming off the best parts,* removing them for some special purpose. 2. to make creamy; *cream the butter and sugar,* beat the mixture to a creamy consistency. 3. to apply a cream to. □**cream cheese,** soft rich cheese made from whole milk and cream. **cream of tartar,** a compound of potassium used in cookery.
cream[2] *v.* (*slang*) to defeat badly in a contest. □**cream off,** (*slang*) to anger.
cream·er (kree-měr) *n.* 1. a cream pitcher. 2. a substitute for cream, not made from milk.
cream·er·y (kree-mě-ree) *n.* (*pl.* **-er·ies**) a place where milk and milk products are processed or sold.
cream·y (kree-mee) *adj.* (**cream·i·er, cream·i·est**) 1. rich in cream. 2. like cream. **cream′i·ness** *n.*
crease (krees) *n.* 1. a line caused by crushing or folding or pressing. 2. a line marking the area in front of the goal cage in hockey. **crease** *v.* (**creased, creas·ing**) 1. to make a crease or creases in. 2. to develop creases.
cre·ate (kri-ayt) *v.* (**cre·at·ed, cre·at·ing**) 1. to bring into existence, to originate. 2. to give rise to, to produce by what one does, *create a good*

impression. 3. to portray a dramatic role for the first time, *Mary Martin created Nellie Forbush.*
cre·a·tion (kri-ay-shŏn) *n.* 1. the act of creating. 2. all created things. 3. *the Creation,* God's act of creating the universe.
cre·a·tive (kri-ay-tiv) *adj.* 1. having the power or ability to create things. 2. showing imagination and originality as well as routine skill, creative work. **cre·a′tive·ly** *adv.* **cre·a·tiv·i·ty** (kree-ay-tiv-i-tee) *n.*
cre·a·tor (kri-ay-tŏr) *n.* one who creates something; *the Creator,* God.
crea·ture (kree-chŭr) *n.* 1. a living being, especially an animal. 2. a person; *a poor creature,* someone who is pitied or despised. □**creature comforts,** things that make one's life comfortable, such as comfortable surroundings. **creature of habit,** a person who does things from force of habit.
crèche (kresh) *n.* a model of the manger at Bethlehem.
cre·dence (kree-děns) *n.* belief. ▷Do not confuse *credence* with *credibility.*
cre·den·tial (kri-den-shăl) *n.* 1. anything that constitutes a basis for trust. 2. *credentials,* letters in introduction, evidence of qualifications or authority (usually in written form).
cre·den·za (kri-den-ză) *n.* a sideboard.
cred·i·bil·i·ty (kred-i-bil-i-tee) *n.* the quality of being credible. □**credibility gap,** people's disinclination to trust official statements or the person(s) making these. ▷Do not confuse *credibility* with *credence.*
cred·i·ble (kred-i-běl) *adj.* able to be believed, convincing. **cred′i·bly** *adv.* ▷Do not confuse *credible* with *creditable.*
cred·it (kred-it) *n.* 1. belief that something is true. 2. honor given for some achievement or good quality, *shared the credit with his fellow workers.* 3. a source of honor, *a credit to the firm.* 4. a system of doing business by trusting that a person will pay at a later date for goods or services supplied to him; *buy on credit,* with an arrangement to pay later. 5. the power to buy in this way. 6. the amount of money in a person's bank account or entered in a ledger as paid to the holder. 7. recognition given to a student on completing a requirement for a degree. 8. *credits,* a list of acknowledgements of participants' contributions shown at the end of a film or television program, a performer's or writer's past achievements. **credit** *v.* 1. to believe. 2. to attribute; *credit Strauss with this waltz,* say that he wrote it. 3. to enter as credit in a ledger. □**credit card,** a card authorizing a person to buy on credit. **credit line,** authority to borrow money. **credit union,** a cooperative organization that makes small loans to its members at low interest rates.
cred·it·a·ble (kred-i-tă-běl) *adj.* deserving praise. **cred′it·a·bly** *adv.* ▷Do not confuse *creditable* with *credible.*
cred·i·tor (kred-i-tŏr) *n.* a person to whom money is owed.
cre·do (kree-doh, kray-doh) *n.* (*pl.* **-dos**) 1. a creed, especially the Apostles' Creed or the Nicene Creed. 2. a musical setting for any of these.
cred·u·lous (krej-ŭ-lŭs) *adj.* too ready to believe things. **cre·du·li·ty** (kri-doo-li-tee) *n.*
Cree (kree) *n.* (*pl.* **Crees, Cree**) 1. a member of an Indian tribe of central Canada and Montana. 2. the Algonquin language of this tribe.
creed (kreed) *n.* 1. *Creed,* a formal summary of Christian beliefs. 2. a set of beliefs or principles.

creek (kreek) *n.* a small stream, a tributary to a river. □**up the creek,** *(slang)* in difficulties.

Creek (kreek) *n.* a member of an Indian tribe formerly of Georgia, Alabama, and Florida, now mainly in Oklahoma.

creel (kreel) *n.* a fisherman's wicker basket for carrying fish.

creep (kreep) *v.* **(crept, creep·ing)** 1. to move with the body close to the ground. 2. to move timidly or slowly or stealthily, to come on gradually. 3. (of plants) to grow along the ground or other surface. 4. to feel as if covered with crawling things; *it will make your flesh creep,* have this effect by causing fear or dislike. **creep** *n.* 1. creeping. 2. *(slang)* a person one dislikes, one who seeks favor by behaving in a servile way. □**give a person the creeps,** *(informal)* to make his flesh creep. **make one's flesh creep,** to make one's skin seem to move in horror.

creep·er (kree-pĕr) *n.* 1. a person or thing that creeps. 2. a creeping plant.

creep·y (kree-pee) *adj.* **(creep·i·er, creep·i·est)** making one's flesh creep, feeling this sensation. **creep'i·ness** *n.*

cre·mate (kree-mayt) *v.* **(cre·mat·ed, cre·mat·ing)** to burn (a corpse) to ashes. **cre·ma·tion** (kri-may-shŏn) *n.*

cre·ma·to·ri·um (kree-mă-tohr-i-ŭm, krem-ă-) *n.* (*pl.* **-to·ri·ums, -to·ri·a,** *pr.* -tohr-i-ă) a place where corpses are cremated.

cre·ma·to·ry (kree-mă-tohr-ee, krem-ă-) *adj.* of or pertaining to cremation. **crematory** *n.* (*pl.* **-ries**) a crematorium.

crème de la crème (krem dĕ lah krem) the very best, elite. ▷French.

crème de menthe (krem dĕ **mahnt**) a green liqueur flavored with peppermint.

cren·el·at·ed (kren-ĕ-lay-tid) *adj.* having battlements. **cren·el·a·tion** (kren-ĕ-lay-shŏn) *n.*

Cre·ole (kree-ohl) *n.* 1. a descendant of European settlers in Louisiana or the West Indies or Central or South America. 2. the dialect spoken by these.

cre·o·sote (kree-ŏ-soht) *n.* 1. a thick brown oily liquid obtained from coal tar, used as a preservative for wood. 2. a colorless liquid obtained from wood tar, used as an antiseptic. **creosote** *v.* **(cre·o·sot·ed, cre·o·sot·ing)** to treat with creosote.

crepe, crêpe (krayp, krep) *n.* 1. fabric with a wrinkled surface. 2. rubber with a wrinkled texture, used for shoe soles. □**crepe paper,** thin crepe-like paper. **crêpe Su·zette** (krayp soo-zet, krep) (*pl.* **crêpes Su·zettes,** *pr.* krayp soo-zet, krep) a small sweet pancake served flambé.

crept (krept) *see* **creep.**

cre·pus·cu·lar (kri-pus-kyŭ-lăr) *adj.* of or like twilight.

cres., cresc. *abbr.* crescendo.

cre·scen·do (kri-shen-doh) *adj. & adv.* gradually becoming louder. **crescendo** *n.* (*pl.* **-dos**) a gradual increase in loudness.

cres·cent (kres-ĕnt) *n.* 1. a narrow curved shape tapering to a point at each end. 2. something shaped like this. 3. a curved street.

cress (kres) *n.* any of various plants with pungent leaves, used in salads.

crest (krest) *n.* 1. a tuft or fleshy outgrowth on a bird's or animal's head. 2. a plume on a helmet. 3. the top of a slope or hill, the white top of a large wave. 4. a design above the shield on a coat of arms, or used separately on a seal or notepaper

etc. **crest** *v.* to reach the crest, to reach the highest level before receding. **crest·ed** (kres-tid) *adj.*

crest·fall·en (krest-faw-lĕn) *adj.* downcast, disappointed at failure.

cre·ta·ceous (kri-tay-shŭs) *adj.* 1. of or like chalk. 2. *Cretaceous,* of the latest geologic period of the Mesozoic era. **Cretaceous** *n.* this period.

Cre·tan (kree-tăn) *adj.* of Crete, an island in the East Mediterranean.

cre·tin (kree-tin) *n.* a person suffering from cretinism. **cre·tin·ism** (kree-tĭ-niz-ĕm) *n.* an abnormality in which a person is deformed and mentally undeveloped through lack of thyroid hormone. **cre·tin·ous** (kree-tĭ-nŭs) *adj.* 1. of or involving cretinism. 2. *(informal)* very stupid.

cre·tonne (kri-ton) *n.* heavy cotton cloth with a printed pattern, used in curtains and upholstery.

cre·vasse (krĕ-vas) *n.* a deep open crack, especially in the ice of a glacier.

crev·ice (krev-is) *n.* a narrow opening or crack, especially in a rock or wall.

crew¹ (kroo) *see* **crow².**

crew² *n.* 1. the people working a ship or aircraft. 2. all these except the officers. 3. a group of people working together, *the camera crew.* 4. a gang. **crew** *v.* to act as crew. □**crew cut,** a closely cropped haircut for men and boys.

crew·el (kroo-ĕl) *n.* thin worsted yarn for tapestry and embroidery.

crew·el·work (kroo-ĕl-wurk) *n.* design in worsted on a linen or cotton ground.

crib (krib) *n.* 1.a wooden framework from which animals can pull out fodder. 2. a baby's bed. 3. something copied from another person's work. 4. a literal translation (for use by students) of something written in a foreign language. **crib** *v.* **(cribbed, crib·bing)** to copy unfairly or without acknowledgment. **crib'ber** *n.*

crib·bage (krib-ij) *n.* a card game in which the score is kept on a board. □**cribbage board,** a board with pegs and holes for scoring cribbage.

crick (krik) *n.* a painful stiffness in the neck or back. **crick** *v.* to cause a crick in.

crick·et¹ (krik-it) *n.* an outdoor summer game played with a ball, bats, and wickets, between two sides of eleven players. □**not cricket,** *(informal)* not fair play.

cricket² *n.* a brown grasshopper-like insect that makes a shrill chirping sound.

crick·et·er (krik-ĕ-tĕr) *n.* a cricket player.

cri·er (krɪ-ĕr) *n.* 1. one who cries. 2. *(old use)* a town crier (*see* **town**).

crime (krɪm) *n.* 1. a serious offense, one for which there is punishment by law. 2. such offenses, serious law-breaking, *the detection of crime.* 3. *(informal)* a shame, a senseless act, *it would be a crime to miss such a chance.*

Cri·me·an (krɪ-mee-ăn) *adj.* of the Crimea, a peninsula in the south of the U.S.S.R.

crim·i·nal (krim-i-năl) *n.* a person who is guilty of crime. **criminal** *adj.* 1. of or involving crime, *a criminal offense.* 2. concerned with crime and its punishment, *criminal law.* **crim'i·nal·ly** *adv.* **crim·i·nal·i·ty** (krim-i-nal-i-tee) *n.*

crim·i·nol·o·gist (krim-i-nol-ŏ-jist) *n.* an expert in criminology.

crim·i·nol·o·gy (krim-i-nol-ŏ-jee) *n.* the scientific study of crime.

crimp (krimp) *v.* 1. to press into small folds or ridges. 2. to hamper. **crimp** *n.* 1. crimping. 2.

a thing that has been crimped. □**put a crimp into a person's style,** *(informal)* to thwart or interfere with his actions.

crim·son (krim-zŏn) *adj. & n.* deep red.

cringe (krinj) *v.* **(cringed, cring·ing)** to shrink back in fear, to cower.

crin·kle (kring-kĕl) *v.* **(crin·kled, crin·kling)** to make or become wrinkled. **crinkle** *n.* a wrinkle, a crease. **crin'kly** *adj.* **(-kli·er, -kli·est).**

crin·o·line (krin-ŏ-lin) *n.* **1.** a stiffened petticoat formerly worn to make a long skirt stand out, a skirt shaped by this. **2.** the fabric of which such a petticoat is made.

crip·ple (krip-ĕl) *n.* a person who is permanently lame. **cripple** *v.* **(crip·pled, crip·pling) 1.** to make a cripple of. **2.** to disable, to weaken or damage seriously, *the business was crippled by lack of money.*

cri·sis (kri-sis) *n.* **(***pl.* **-ses,** *pr.* **-seez) 1.** a decisive time. **2.** a time of acute difficulty or danger. □**energy crisis,** a period of shortage or impending shortage of fuel that threatens normal operation of an industrial society.

crisp (krisp) *adj.* **1.** brittle, breaking with a snap, *crisp pastry.* **2.** slightly stiff, *a crisp $20 bill; crisp curls.* **3.** cold and bracing, *a crisp winter morning.* **4.** brisk and decisive, *a crisp manner.* **crisp** *v.* to make or become crisp. **crisp'ly** *adv.* **crisp' ness** *n.* □**burned to a crisp,** burned until it is crisp, badly burned.

crisp·y (kris-pee) *adj.* **(crisp·i·er, crisp·i·est)** crisp.

criss·cross (kris-kraws) *n.* a pattern of crossing lines. **crisscross** *adj.* with crossing lines. **crisscross** *v.* to mark or form or move in this pattern.

crit. *abbr.* **1.** critic. **2.** critical. **3.** criticism.

cri·te·ri·on (kri-teer-i-ŏn) *n.* **(***pl.* **-te·ri·a,** *pr.* **-teer-i-ă, -te·ri·ons)** a standard of judgment. ▷Do not use *criteria* as a singular noun. It is correct to write *the criteria were demanding.*

crit·ic (krit-ik) *n.* **1.** a person who finds fault with something. **2.** a person who forms and expresses judgments about books or art or musical works etc.

crit·i·cal (krit-i-kăl) *adj.* **1.** looking for faults. **2.** expressing criticism, *critical remarks.* **3.** of or at a crisis; *the critical moment,* one when there will be a decisive change; *the patient's condition is critical,* he is dangerously ill. **crit'i·cal·ly** *adv.* **crit· i·cal·i·ty** (krit-i-kal-i-tee) *n.*

crit·i·cism (krit-i-siz-ĕm) *n.* **1.** finding fault, a remark pointing out a fault. **2.** the work of a critic, judgments about books or art or music etc., *expert criticism.*

crit·i·cize (krit-i-siz) *v.* **(crit·i·cized, crit·i· ciz·ing) 1.** to find fault with. **2.** to examine critically, to express judgments about.

cri·tique (kri-teek) *n.* a critical essay or review. **critique** *v.* to discuss critically.

croak (krohk) *n.* a deep hoarse cry or sound, like that of a frog. **croak** *v.* **1.** to utter or speak with a croak. **2.** *(slang)* to die.

cro·chet (kroh-shay) *n.* a kind of handiwork in which thread is looped into a pattern of connected stitches by means of a hooked needle. **crochet** *v.* **(cro·cheted,** *pr.* kroh-shayd, **cro·chet·ing,** *pr.* kroh-shay-ing) to do this needlework, to make (an article) by this.

crock (krok) *n.* **1.** an earthenware pot or jar. **2.** a broken piece of this.

crocked (krokt) *adj. (slang)* drunk.

crock·er·y (krok-ĕ-ree) *n.* earthenware household articles, as plates, cups, pots.

croc·o·dile (krok-ŏ-dɪl) *n.* **1.** a large tropical reptile with a thick skin, long tail, and huge jaws. **2.** its skin, used to make bags, shoes, etc. □**crocodile tears,** insincere sorrow. ▷So called from the belief that the crocodile wept while devouring its victim.

cro·cus (kroh-kŭs) *n.* **(***pl.* **-cus·es)** a small plant growing from a corm, with yellow, purple, or white flowers.

Croe·sus (kree-sŭs) *n.* a very rich man. ▷The name of a king of Lydia famous for his riches.

crois·sant (krwah-sahn) *n.* a rich crescent-shaped bread roll.

crone (krohn) *n.* a withered old woman.

cro·ny (kroh-nee) *n.* **(***pl.* **-nies)** a close friend or companion.

crook (kruuk) *n.* **1.** a hooked stick or staff, that used by a shepherd. **2.** something bent or curved, *carried it in the crook of her arm.* **3.** *(informal)* a person who makes a living dishonestly. **crook** *v.* **(crooked,** *pr.* kruukt, **crook·ing)** to bend into the shape of a crook.

crook·ed (kruuk-id) *adj.* **1.** not straight or level, having curves or bends or twists. **2.** dishonest, not straightforward. **crook'ed·ly** *adv.* **crook' ed·ness** *n.*

croon (kroon) *v.* to sing softly and gently. **croon' er** *n.*

crop (krop) *n.* **1.** a batch of plants grown for their produce. **2.** the harvest from this. **3.** a group or quantity appearing or produced at one time, *this year's crop of students.* **4.** the bag-like part of a bird's throat in which food is broken up for digestion before passing into the stomach. **5.** the handle of a whip, one with a loop instead of a lash. **6.** a very short haircut. **crop** *v.* **(cropped, crop·ping) 1.** to cut or bite off, *sheep crop the grass closely.* **2.** to cut (hair) very short. □**crop up,** to occur unexpectedly.

crop-dust·ing (krop-dus-ting) *n.* the spraying of growing crops from an airplane with insecticide or fungicide. **crop dust·er** *n.*

crop·land (krop-land) *n.* land on which crops can be grown.

crop·per (krop-ĕr) *n.* **come a cropper,** *(informal)* to have a heavy fall or a bad failure.

cro·quet (kroh-kay) *n.* a game played on a lawn with wooden balls that are driven through hoops with mallets.

cro·quette (kroh-ket) *n.* a fried ball or roll of potato, meat, or fish, coated with crumbs.

cro·sier (kroh-zhĕr) *n.* a hooked staff carried by a bishop as a symbol of office.

cross (kraws) *n.* **1.** a mark made by drawing one line across another. **2.** an upright post with another piece of wood across it, used in ancient times for crucifixion; *the Cross,* that on which Christ died. **3.** a model of this as a Christian emblem, a monument in this form. **4.** an affliction, an annoying thing one has to bear. **5.** a cross-shaped emblem or medal, the *Distinguished Service Cross.* **6.** an animal or plant produced by crossbreeding. **7.** a mixture of two different things. **cross** *v.* **1.** to place crosswise; *a crossed telephone line,* an accidental connection. **2.** draw a line across, *cross the t's.* **3.** to make the sign of the Cross on or over; *cross oneself,* do this as a sign of religious awe or to call upon God for protection. **4.** to go or extend across. 5. to frustrate, to oppose the wishes or plans of. 6. to crossbreed (animals), to cross-fertilize (plants). **cross** *adj.* 1. passing from side to side; *cross winds*, blowing across one's direction of travel. 2. annoyed, showing bad temper. **cross'ly** *adv.* **cross·ness** *n.* ☐**at cross purposes**, misunderstanding or conflicting with each other. **cross a person's path**, to come across him. **cross hairs**, fine wires at the focus of an optical instrument for use in measurement. **cross in the mail**, (of letters between two people) to be in the mails at the same time. **cross off**, to cross out. **cross one's mind**, to come briefly into one's mind. **cross out**, to show that (a thing) is no longer valid by drawing a line through it. **cross section**, a representation of the internal structure of something that has been cut crossways; a representative sample. **cross swords**, to have a controversy, *cross swords with her.* **cross talk**, unwanted transfer of signals between radio or telephone etc. communication channels. **keep one's fingers crossed**, to hope that nothing unfortunate will happen, crooking one finger over another to bring good luck.

cross·bar (kraws-bahr) *n.* a horizontal bar.

cross·bones (kraws-bohnz) *n.* a representation of two crossed thighbones (*see* **skull**).

cross·bow (kraws-boh) *n.* a bow fixed across a wooden stock, with a groove for the arrow and a mechanism for drawing and releasing the string. **cross'bow·man** *n.* (*pl.* **-men,** *pr.* -měn).

cross·breed (kraws-breed) *v.* (**cross·bred, cross·breed·ing)** to produce by mating an animal with one of a different kind. **crossbreed** *n.* an animal produced in this way.

cross-check (kraws-chek) *v.* to check by an alternative method of verification.

cross-coun·try (kraws-kun-tree) *adj. & adv.* across fields, not keeping to main roads or to a direct road. **cross-country** (kraws-kun-tree) *n.* a cross-country sport, especially running or skiing.

cross·cur·rent (kraws-kur-ĕnt) *n.* 1. a current of water running across the main current. 2. a trend or current of opinion running against the prevailing one.

cross·cut (kraws-kut) *n.* a cut across the grain (of wood). ☐**crosscut saw**, a saw for making such cuts.

crosse (kraws) *n.* a netted racket used in lacrosse.

cross-ex·am·ine (kraws-ig-zam-in) *v.* (**cross-ex·am·ined, cross-ex·am·in·ing)** to question closely in order to test answers given to previous questions. **cross-ex·am·i·na·tion** (kraws-ig-zam-i-nay-shŏn) *n.*

cross-eye (kraws-ɪ) *n.* an eye that is turned permanently toward the nose. **cross'-eyed** *adj.*

cross-fer·ti·lize (kraws-fur-tǐ-lɪz) *v.* (**cross-fer·ti·lized, cross-fer·ti·liz·ing)** 1. to fertilize (a plant or animal) from one of a different kind. 2. to help by an interchange of ideas etc. **cross-fer·ti·li·za·tion** (kraws-fur-tǐ-li-zay-shŏn) *n.*

cross·fire (kraws-fir) *n.* the firing of guns from two or more points so that the lines of fire cross.

cross-grained (kraws-graynd) *adj.* (of wood) with the grain in crossing directions.

cross-hatch (kraws-hach) *v.* to shade with intersecting sets of parallel lines.

cross·ing (kraw-sing) *n.* 1. a journey across water, *we had a smooth crossing.* 2. a place where things cross. 3. a specially marked place for pedestrians to cross a road.

cross-leg·ged (kraws-leg-ĭd) *adj.* sitting with legs crossed.

cross·patch (kraws-pach) *n.* a bad-tempered person

cross·piece (kraws-pees) *n.* a crosswise part of a structure etc.

cross·ply (kraws-plɪ) *adj.* (of tires) having fabric layers with cords lying crosswise.

cross-pol·li·nate (kraws-pol-ĭ-nayt) *v.* (**cross-pol·li·nat·ed, cross-pol·li·nat·ing)** to pollinate (a plant) from another. **cross-pol·li·na·tion** (kraws-pol-ĭ-nay-shŏn) *n.*

cross-pur·pose (kraws-pur-pŏs) *n.* a contrary or conflicting purpose.

cross-ques·tion (kraws-kwes-chŏn) *v.* to cross-examine.

cross-ref·er·ence (kraws-ref-ĕ-rĕns) *n.* a note directing readers to another part of a book or index for further information.

cross·roads (kraws-rohdz) *n.* a place where two or more roads intersect.

cross·town (kraws-town) *adj.* (of a street, bus, etc.) going across a city.

cross·walk (kraws-wawk) *n.* a marked path for people to use in walking across a street.

cross·ways (kraws-wayz) *adv.* crosswise.

cross·wise (kraws-wɪz) *adj. & adv.* in the form of a cross, with one crossing another.

cross·word (kraws-wurd) **puzzle** a puzzle in which intersecting words, indicated by clues, have to be inserted into blank squares in a diagram.

crotch (kroch) *n.* 1. a place where things fork. 2. the part of the body or of a garment where the legs fork.

crotch·et·y (kroch-ĕ-tee) *adj.* peevish.

crouch (krowch) *v.* to lower the body with the limbs bent and close to it, to be in this position. **crouch** *n.* this position.

croup (kroop) *n.* a disease in which inflammation of the windpipe causes a hard cough and difficulty in breathing. **croup'y** *adj.*

crou·pi·er (kroo-pee-ay) *n.* a person who rakes in the money at a gambling table and pays out winnings.

crou·ton (kroo-ton) *n.* a small piece of fried or toasted bread served with soup etc.

crow[1] (kroh) *n.* a large black bird. ☐**as the crow flies**, in a straight line. **crow's nest**, a protected lookout platform high on the mast of a ship. **to eat crow**, (*informal*) to submit to humiliation.

crow[2] *v.* (**crowed** or [chiefly *British*] **crew, crow·ing)** 1. (of a rooster) to make a loud shrill cry. 2. to express gleeful triumph. **crow** *n.* a crowing cry or sound.

Crow (kroh) *n.* (*pl.* **Crows, Crow**) 1. a member of a tribe of Indians in western U.S. 2. their language.

crow·bar (kroh-bahr) *n.* a steel bar with a chiseled end, used as a lever.

crowd (krowd) *n.* a large group of people gathered together. **crowd** *v.* 1. to come together in a crowd. 2. to fill or occupy fully or cram with people or things. **crowd·ed** (krow-did) *adj.* ☐**crowd out**, to keep out by crowding.

crow·foot (kroh-fuut) *n.* (*pl.* **-foots**) a small wild plant of the buttercup family.

crown (krown) *n.* 1. an ornamental headdress worn by a king or queen. 2. the sovereign, his or her authority, *loyalty to the crown.* 3. *the Crown*, the supreme governing power in the United Kingdom.

4. a wreath worn on the head, especially as a symbol of victory. 5. a crown-shaped object or ornament. 6. the top part of something (as of the head or a hat or a tooth), the highest part of something arched, *the crown of the road.* **crown** *v.* 1. to place a crown on, as a symbol of royal power or victory; *the crowned heads of Europe,* kings and queens. 2. to form or cover or ornament the top part of. 3. to make a successful conclusion to, *our efforts were crowned with success; to crown it all,* completing one's good or bad fortune. 4. to put an artificial top on (a tooth) 5. *(slang)* to hit on the head. □**crown jewels,** a sovereign's crown, scepter, orb, etc. used at coronations. **crown prince** *or* **princess,** the heir to a throne.

crow's-foot (krohz-fuut) *n.* a wrinkle in the skin at the side of the eye.

cru·cial (kroo-shăl) *adj.* very important, deciding an important issue, *at the crucial moment.* **cru′cial·ly** *adv.*

cru·ci·ble (kroo-sĭ-bĕl) *n.* a pot in which metals are melted.

cru·ci·fix (kroo-sĭ-fiks) *n.* a model of the Cross or of Christ on the Cross.

cru·ci·fix·ion (kroo-sĭ-fik-shŏn) *n.* crucifying, being crucified; *the Crucifixion,* that of Christ.

cru·ci·form (kroo-sĭ-form) *adj.* cross-shaped.

cru·ci·fy (kroo-sĭ-fī) *v.* (**cru·ci·fied, cru·ci·fy·ing**) 1. to put to death by nailing or binding to a cross. 2. to cause extreme mental pain to.

crude (krood) *adj.* (**crud·er, crud·est**) 1. in a natural state, not refined, *crude oil.* 2. not well finished or worked out, rough, *a crude attempt.* 3. without good manners, vulgar. **crude** *n.* crude oil. **crude′ly** *adv.* **crude′ness** *n.* **crud′i·ty** *n.* □**crude oil,** unrefined petroleum.

cru·el (kroo-ĕl) *adj.* (**-ei·er, -el·est**) 1. feeling pleasure in another's suffering, 2. causing pain or suffering, *this cruel war.* **cruel′ly** *adv.* **cruel′ty** *n.* (*pl.* **-ties**).

cru·et (kroo-it) *n.* a small glass bottle for holding oil or vinegar for use at the table.

cruise (krooz) *v.* (**cruised, cruis·ing**) 1. to sail about for pleasure or on patrol. 2. (of a vehicle or aircraft) to travel at a moderate speed that is economical of fuel. 3. to drive at moderate speed, or at random when looking for passengers etc. **cruise** *n.* a cruising voyage. □**cruise missile,** a low-flying jet-powered radar-controlled guided missile. **cruise ship,** a passenger ship that takes passengers on cruise.

cruis·er (kroo-zĕr) *n.* 1. a fast warship, smaller than a battleship. 2. a cabin cruiser (*see* **cabin**). 3. a police patrol car.

crul·ler (krul-ĕr) *n.* a crisp doughnut, often in a twisted shape.

crumb (krum) *n.* a small fragment, especially of bread or other food. □**crumb bun,** a sweet bread roll topped with crumbs.

crum·ble (krum-bĕl) *v.* (**crum·bled, crum·bling**) to break or fall into small fragments. ▷Do not confuse *crumble* with *crumple.*

crum·bly (krum-blee) *adj.* (**-bli·er, -bli·est**) easily crumbled.

crum·my (krum-ee) *adj.* (**crum·mi·er, crum·mi·est**) *(slang)* 1. dirty, squalid. 2. inferior, worthless.

crum·pet (krum-pit) *n.* (*British*) a soft cake of yeast mixture, baked on a griddle and eaten toasted.

crum·ple (krum-pĕl) *v.* (**crum·pled, crum·pling**) 1. to crush or become crushed into creases. 2.

to collapse loosely. ▷Do not confuse *crumple* with *crumble.*

crunch (krunch) *v.* 1. to crush noisily with the teeth. 2. to walk or move with a sound of crushing, to make such a sound. **crunch** *n.* 1. crunching. 2. a crunching noise. 3. a decisive event. □**energy crunch,** an energy crisis (*see* **crisis**). **when it comes to the crunch,** *(informal)* when there is a showdown.

cru·sade (kroo-sayd) *n.* 1. (also **Crusade**) any of the military expeditions made by Europeans in the Middle Ages to recover the Holy Land from the Muslims. 2. a campaign against something believed to be bad. **crusade** *v.* (**cru·sad·ed, cru·sad·ing**) to take part in a crusade. **cru·sad′er** *n.*

crush (krush) *v.* 1. to press so as to break or injure or wrinkle, to squeeze tightly. 2. to pound into small fragments. 3. to become crushed. 4. to defeat or subdue completely, *a crushing defeat or reply.* **crush** *n.* 1. a crowd of people pressed together. 2. a drink made from crushed fruit. 3. *(informal)* an infatuation.

crush·a·ble (krush-ă-bĕl) *adj.* able to be crushed easily.

crust (krust) *n.* 1. the hard outer layer of something, especially bread. 2. the rocky outer portion of Earth.

crus·ta·cean (krus-tay-shăn) *n.* an animal that has a hard shell (as crab, lobster, shrimp).

crust·y (krus-tee) *adj.* (**crust·i·er, crust·i·est**) 1. having a crisp crust. 2. having a harsh manner. **crust′i·ness** *n.*

crutch (kruch) *n.* 1. a support for a lame person, usually fitting under the armpit. 2. any support.

crux (kruks) *n.* (*pl.* **crux·es**) the vital part of a problem.

cru·zei·ro (kroo-zair-oh) *n.* (*pl.* **-ros**) the unit of money in Brazil.

cry (krī) *n.* (*pl.* **cries**) 1. a loud wordless sound expressing pain, grief, joy, etc. 2. a shout. 3. the call of a bird or animal. 4. an appeal, a demand. 5. a battle cry. 6. a spell of weeping, *have a good cry.* **cry** *v.* (**cried, crying**) 1. to shed tears; *cry one's heart* or *eyes out,* to weep bitterly. 2. to call out loudly in words. 3. to appeal, to demand; *a crying shame,* one demanding attention. 4. (of an animal) to utter its cry. 5. to announce for sale by shouting, *crying their wares.* □**cry wolf,** to raise false alarms. **in full cry,** in hot pursuit.

cry·ba·by (krī-bay-bee) *n.* (*pl.* **-bies**) a person who weeps easily without good cause.

cry·o·gen·ic (krī-ŏ-jen-ik) *adj.* at very low temperatures. **cry·o·gen′i·cal·ly** *adv.*

cry·o·gen·ics (krī-ŏ-jen-iks) *n.* the branch of physics dealing with very low temperatures and their effects.

cry·o·sur·ger·y (krī-oh-sur-jĕ-ree) *n.* the surgical use of intense cold for anesthesia or therapy.

crypt (kript) *n.* a room below the main floor of a church, used as a burial place.

cryp·tic (krip-tik) *adj.* concealing its meaning in a puzzling way. **cryp′ti·cal·ly** *adv.*

cryp·to·gam (krip-tŏ-gam) *n.* a flowerless plant such as a fern, moss, or fungus.

cryp·to·gen·ic (krip-tŏ-jen-ik) *adj.* of mysterious origin.

cryp·to·gram (krip-tŏ-gram) *n.* something written in code.

cryp·tog·ra·phy (krip-tog-ră-fee) *n.* the art of writing in or solving codes. **cryp·tog′ra·pher** *n.*

cryst. *abbr.* 1. crystalline. 2. crystallized. 3. crystallography.

crys·tal (kris-tăl) *n.* 1. a clear transparent colorless mineral. 2. a piece of this. 3. very clear glass of high quality. 4. one of the pieces into which certain substances solidify, *crystals of ice.* ☐**crystal ball,** a globe of glass used in crystal gazing. **crystal clear,** obvious. **crystal gazing,** looking into a crystal ball in an attempt to see future events pictured there.

crys·tal·line (kris-tă-lin) *adj.* 1. like or containing crystals. 2. transparent, very clear.

crys·tal·lize (kris-tă-lız) *v.* (**crys·tal·lized, crys·tal·liz·ing**) 1. to form crystals. 2. (of ideas or plans) to become clear and definite in form.

crys·tal·li·za·tion (kris-tă-li-zay-shŏn) *n.*

crys·tal·log·ra·phy (kris-tă-log-ră-fee) *n.* the scientific study of the structure, classification, and properties of crystals. **crys·tal·log'ra·pher** *n.* **crys·tal·lo·graph·ic** (kris-tă-lŏ-graf-ik) *adj.*

Cs *symbol* cesium.

C/S *abbr.* cycles per second.

C.S. *abbr.* 1. Chief of Staff. 2. Christian Science. 3. Christian Scientist. 4. Civil Service. 5. Confederate States.

C.S.A. *abbr.* Confederate States of America.

C.S.T. *abbr.* Central Standard Time.

CT *abbr.* Connecticut.

ct. *abbr.* 1. carat. 2. cent. 3. certificate. 4. county. 5. court.

C.T. *abbr.* Central Time.

ctf. *abbr.* certificate.

ctg. *abbr.* cartage.

ctn. *abbr.* carton.

ctr. *abbr.* center.

cts. *abbr.* 1. centimes. 2. cents.

Cu *symbol* copper.

cu. *abbr.* 1. cubic. 2. cumulus.

cub (kub) *n.* the young of certain animals, such as fox, bear, lion; *a cub reporter,* an inexperienced reporter. ☐**Cub Scout,** a member of the junior division of the Boy Scouts.

Cu·ba (kyoo-bă) a country in the Caribbean. **Cu'ban** *adj. & n.* ☐**Cuba li·bre** (lee-brě), a drink combining rum and cola.

cub·by·hole (kub-ee-hohl) *n.* a small compartment.

cube (kyoob) *n.* 1. a solid body with six equal square sides. 2. a block shaped like this. 3. the product of a number multiplied by itself twice, *the cube of 3 is 27* (3 × 3 × 3 = 27). **cube** *v.* (**cubed, cub·ing**) 1. to cut (food) into small cubes. 2. to find the cube of (a number). 3. to make (meat) tender by scoring. ☐**cube root,** see **root** (definition 7). **cube steak,** a thin slice of cubed beef.

cu·bic (kyoo-bik) *adj.* of three dimensions; *one cubic centimeter,* the volume of a cube with sides one centimeter long (used as a unit of measurement for volume).

cu·bi·cal (kyoo-bi-kăl) *adj.* cube-shaped.

cu·bi·cle (kyoo-bi-kĕl) *n.* a small division of a large room, an enclosed space screened for privacy.

cub·ism (kyoo-biz-ĕm) *n.* a style of painting in which objects are represented as cubes and other geometrical shapes. **cub·ist** (kyoo-bist) *adj. & n.*

cu·bit (kyoo-bit) *n.* an ancient measure of length, approximately equal to the length of the forearm.

cuck·old (kuk-ōld) *n.* a man whose wife has committed adultery during their marriage. **cuckold** *v.* to make a cuckold of (a married man).

cuck·oo (koo-koo) *n.* (*pl.* **-oos**) a bird with a call

that is like its name, laying its eggs in the nests of other birds. **cuckoo** *adj.* (*slang)* crazy, foolish. ☐**cuckoo clock,** a clock that strikes the hours with a sound like a cuckoo's call.

cu·cum·ber (kyoo-kum-běr) *n.* 1. a long greenskinned fleshy fruit eaten as salad or pickled. 2. the plant producing this.

cud (kud) *n.* the food that cattle etc. bring back from the stomach into the mouth and chew again, *chewing the cud.*

cud·dle (kud-ĕl) *v.* (**cud·dled, cud·dling**) 1. to hold closely and lovingly in one's arms. 2. to nestle. **cuddle** *n.* an affectionate hug.

cud·dle·some (kud-ĕl-sŏm) *adj.* cuddly.

cud·dly (kud-lee) *adj.* (**-dli·er, -dli·est**) pleasant to cuddle.

cudg·el (kuj-ĕl) *n.* a short thick stick used as a weapon. **cudgel** *v.* (**-eled, -el·ing**) to beat with a cudgel. ☐**cudgel one's brains,** to think hard, to try to remember. **take up the cudgels for,** to defend vigorously.

cue¹ (kyoo) *n.* something said or done that serves as a signal for something else to be done, as for an actor to speak in a play. **cue** *v.* (**cued, cu·ing**) to give a cue to.

cue² *n.* a long rod for striking the ball (**cue ball**) in billiards and similar games.

cuff¹ (kuf) *n.* 1. a doubled strip of cloth forming a band around the end part of a sleeve, or a separate band worn similarly. 2. the part of a glove covering the wrist. ☐**cuff link,** one of a pair of fasteners for shirt cuffs, used instead of buttons. **off the cuff,** without rehearsal or preparation. **off-the-cuff** *adj.* produced in this way. **on the cuff,** (*slang)* on credit, to be paid for later.

cuff² *v.* to strike with the open hand. **cuff** *n.* a cuffing blow.

cui bo·no? (kwee boh-noh) who gains by this? ▷Do not use this Latin phrase to mean "what is the use?"

cui·sine (kwi-zeen) *n.* a style of cooking.

cuke (kyook) *n.* (*informal)* a cucumber.

cul·de·sac (kul-dĕ-sak) *n.* a street with an opening at one end only, a blind alley.

cu·li·nar·y (kul-i-ner-ee) *adj.* of a kitchen or cooking, *the culinary art.*

cull (kul) *v.* 1. to pick (flowers). 2. to select. 3. to pick out and kill (surplus animals from a flock). **cull** *n.* 1. culling. 2. a thing culled as surplus.

cul·mi·nate (kul-mi-nayt) *v.* (**cul·mi·nat·ed, cul·mi·nat·ing**) to reach its highest point or degree, *the argument culminated in a fight.* **cul·mi·na·tion** (kul-mi-nay-shŏn) *n.*

cu·lottes (koo-lots) *n. pl.* women's trousers styled to look like a skirt.

cul·pa·ble (kul-pă-bĕl) *adj.* deserving blame. **cul'pa·bly** *adv.* **cul·pa·bil·i·ty** (kul-pă-bil-i-tee) *n.*

cul·prit (kul-prit) *n.* a person who has committed a crime or offense.

cult (kult) *n.* 1. a system of religious worship. 2. devotion to or admiration of a person or thing; *the Elvis Presley cult,* his devoted group of admirers. **cult'ist** *n.*

cul·ti·vate (kul-ti-vayt) *v.* (**cul·ti·vat·ed, cul·ti·vat·ing**) 1. to prepare and use (land) for crops. 2. to produce (crops) by tending them. 3. to spend time and care in developing (a thing); *cultivate a person,* try to win his good will. **cul·ti·va·ble** (kul-ti-vă-bĕl) *adj.* **cul·ti·va·tion** (kul-ti-vay-shŏn) *n.*

cul·ti·va·tor (kul-ti-vay-tŏr) *n.* 1. an implement

or machine for breaking up soil for planting or for uprooting weeds. 2. one who cultivates.

cul·tur·al (kul-chŭ-răl) *adj.* of culture. **cul′tur·al·ly** *adv.*

cul·ture (kul-chŭr) *n.* 1. the appreciation and understanding of literature, arts, music, etc. 2. the customs and civilization of a particular people or group, *West Indian culture.* 3. improvement by care and training, *physical culture.* 4. the cultivating of plants, the rearing of bees, silkworms, etc. 5. a quantity of bacteria grown for study. **culture** *v.* (**cul·tured, cul·tur·ing**) to grow (bacteria) for study. □**culture shock,** the confusion experienced when introduced to a culture strikingly different from one's own.

cul·tured (kul-chŭrd) *adj.* educated to appreciate literature, arts, music, etc. □**cultured pearl,** a pearl formed by an oyster when a foreign body is inserted artificially into its shell.

cul·vert (kul-vĕrt) *n.* a drain that crosses under a road or railroad etc.

cum (kum) *prep.* with. □**cum dividend,** including a dividend that is about to be paid.

cum. *abbr.* cumulative.

cum·ber·some (kum-bĕr-sŏm) *adj.* clumsy to carry or wear or manage.

cum div. *abbr.* cum dividend.

cum·in (kum-in) *n.* a plant with fragrant seeds that are used for flavoring.

cum lau·de (kum low-dee) with academic distinction. ▷Latin.

cum·mer·bund (kum-ĕr-bund) *n.* a sash worn around the waist, especially in men's formal dress.

cu·mu·la·tive (kyoo-myŭ-lă-tiv) *adj.* increasing in amount by one addition after another. **cu′mu·la·tive·ly** *adv.*

cu·mu·lo·nim·bus (kyoo-myŭ-loh-nim-bŭs) *n.* a type of gray dense column-shaped cloud with spreading top.

cu·mu·lus (kyoo-myŭ-lŭs) *n.* (*pl.* **-lus**) a type of cloud formed in rounded masses heaped on each other.

cu·ne·i·form (kyoo-nee-ĭ-form) *adj.* wedge-shaped. **cuneiform** *n.* wedge-shaped writing found in ancient inscriptions of Assyria, Persia, etc.

cun·ner (kun-ĕr) *n.* a small food fish found off the New England coast.

cun·ning (kun-ing) *adj.* 1. skilled at deceiving people, crafty. 2. ingenious, *a cunning device.* 3. attractive, quaint. **cunning** *n.* craftiness. **cun′ning·ly** *adv.*

cup (kup) *n.* 1. a small open container for drinking from, usually bowl-shaped and with a handle, used with a saucer. 2. its contents, the amount it contains (used as a measure in cookery). 3. something shaped like a cup. 4. an ornamental goblet-shaped vessel awarded as a prize. **cup** *v.* (**cupped, cup·ping**) 1. to form into a cuplike shape, *cupped his hands.* 2. to hold as if in a cup, *with her chin cupped in her hands.* **cup′ful** *n.* (*pl.* **-fuls**). □**not my cup of tea,** (*informal*) not what I like, not what interests me. ▷Note the plural of *cupful.*

cup·bear·er (kup-bair-ĕr) *n.* one who serves wine, especially an attendant in a noble or royal household.

cup·board (kub-ărd) *n.* a recess or piece of furniture with a door, in which things may be stored.

cup·cake (kup-kayk) *n.* a small, usually iced, cake baked in a cuplike pan.

Cu·pid (kyoo-pid) the Roman god of love. **cupid** *n.* a picture or statue of a beautiful boy with wings and a bow and arrows.

cu·pid·i·ty (kyoo-pid-i-tee) *n.* greed for gain.

cu·po·la (kyoo-pŏ-lă) *n.* a small dome on a roof.

cu·prite (kyoo-prīt) *n.* red ore of copper.

cu·pro·nick·el (kyoo-prŏ-nik-ĕl) *n.* an alloy of copper and nickel containing up to forty percent nickel.

cur (kur) *n.* 1. a bad-tempered or worthless dog. 2. a contemptible person.

cur. *abbr.* 1. currency. 2. current.

cur·a·ble (kyoor-ă-bĕl) *adj.* able to be cured.

cu·ra·çao (kyoor-ă-soh) *n.* a liqueur flavored with peel of bitter oranges.

cu·ra·cy (kyoor-ă-see) *n.* (*pl.* **-cies**) the position of a curate.

cu·ra·re (kyuu-rahr-ee) *n.* a bitter extract of various South American plants, used by South American Indians as a poison on arrows.

cu·rate (kyoor-it) *n.* a clergyman who assists a vicar or rector.

cur·a·tive (kyoor-ă-tiv) *adj.* helping to cure illness. **curative** *n.* a substance that cures illness.

cu·ra·tor (kyuu-ray-tŏr) *n.* a person in charge of a museum or other collection.

curb (kurb) *n.* 1. something that restrains, *put a curb on spending.* 2. a raised edge of a paved street or other surface. **curb** *v.* to restrain. □**curb service,** service (by a bank, restaurant, etc.) provided to people in parked automobiles.

curb·ing (kur-bing) *n.* 1. the material out of which a curb (definition 2) is formed. 2. a curb.

curb·stone (kurb-stohn) *n.* a stone or group of stones used as curbing.

curd (kurd) *n.* (often **curds**) the thick soft substance formed when milk turns sour.

cur·dle (kur-dĕl) *v.* (**cur·dled, cur·dling**) to form or cause to form curds. □**curdle one's blood,** to fill one with horror.

cure (kyoor) *v.* (**cured, cur·ing**) 1. to restore to health. 2. to get rid of (a disease or troublesome condition). 3. to preserve (meat, fruit, tobacco, or skins) by salting, drying, etc. 4. to vulcanize (rubber). **cure** *n.* 1. curing, being cured, *cannot guarantee a cure.* 2. a substance or treatment that cures a disease, a remedy.

cu·ré (kyuu-ray) *n.* a parish priest in France and French-speaking areas.

cure-all (kyoor-awl) *n.* a remedy for all kinds of diseases or troubles, a panacea.

cu·ret·tage (kyoor-ĕ-tah*zh*) *n.* scraping surgically to remove tissue or growths.

cu·rette, cu·ret (kyuu-ret) *n.* a surgeon's small scraping instrument. **curette, curet** *v.* (**cu·ret·ted, cu·ret·ting**) to scrape with a curette.

cur·few (kur-fyoo) *n.* a signal or time after which people must remain indoors until the next day.

Cu·ri·a (kyoor-i-ă) *n.* the government departments of the Vatican.

cu·rie (kyoor-ee) *n.* a unit of radioactivity, corresponding to 37 billion disintegrations per second.

cu·ri·o (kyoor-i-oh) *n.* (*pl.* **-ri·os**) an object that is interesting because it is rare or unusual.

cu·ri·os·i·ty (kyoor-i-os-i-tee) *n.* (*pl.* **-ties**) 1. a desire to find out and know things. 2. something that is of interest because it is rare or unusual.

cu·ri·ous (kyoor-i-ŭs) *adj.* 1. eager to learn or know something. 2. strange, unusual. **cu′ri·ous·ly** *adv.*

cu·ri·um (kyoor-i-ŭm) *n.* an artificially made radioactive metallic element.

curl (kurl) *v.* 1. to bend, to coil into a spiral. 2.

to move in a spiral form, *smoke curled upward.*
curl *n.* 1. something curved inward or coiled.
2. a coiled lock of hair. 3. a curling movement.
□**curl up,** *(informal)* to lie or sit with the knees
drawn up comfortably.
curl·er (kur-lĕr) *n.* a device for curling the hair.
cur·lew (kur-loo) *n.* a wading bird with a long
slender curved bill.
curl·i·cue (kur-li-kyoo) *n.* a decorative curl or
twist.
curl·ing (kur-ling) *n.* a game played with large flat
round stones that are sent along ice toward a
mark.
curl·y (kur-lee) *adj.* **(curl·i·er, curl·i·est)** curling, full of curls.
cur·mudg·eon (kŭr-muj-ŏn) *n.* a bad-tempered
person.
cur·rant (kur-ănt) *n.* 1. the dried fruit of a small
seedless grape, used in cookery. 2. a small round
red, white, or black berry, the shrub that produces
it. ▷Do not confuse *currant* with *current.*
cur·ren·cy (kur-ĕn-see) *n.* (*pl.* **-cies**) 1. money
in actual use in a country. 2. the state of being
in general or general use; *the rumor gained currency,* became generally known and believed.
cur·rent (kur-ĕnt) *adj.* 1. belonging to the present
time, happening now, *current events.* 2. in general
circulation or use, *some words are no longer current.* **current** *n.* 1. water or air etc. moving in
a certain direction, a running stream. 2. the flow
of electricity through something or along a wire
or cable. **cur′rent·ly** *adv.* ▷Do not confuse
current with *currant.*
cur·ric·u·lum (kŭ-rĭk-yŭ-lŭm) *n.* (*pl.* **-la,** *pr.* **-lă**)
a course of study.
cur·ry[1] (kur-ee) *n.* (*pl.* **-ries**) 1. seasoning made
with hot-tasting spices. 2. a dish flavored with
this. **curry** *v.* **(cur·ried, cur·ry·ing)** to flavor
with curry. □**curry powder,** a hot-tasting blend
of powdered cumin, coriander, turmeric, and
other spices.
curry[2] *v.* **(cur·ried, cur·ry·ing)** to groom (a horse)
with a **currycomb,** a pad with rubber or plastic
projections. □**curry favor,** to win favor by flattery.
curse (kurs) *n.* 1. a call for evil to come upon a
person or thing. 2. the evil produced by this. 3.
a violent exclamation of anger. 4. something that
causes evil or harm. **curse** *v.* **(cursed, curs·
ing)** 1. to utter a curse against. 2. to exclaim
violently in anger. □**be cursed with,** to have
as a burden or source of harm.
curs·ed (kur-sid) *adj.* damnable.
cur·sive (kur-siv) *adj.* of a style of writing with
joined characters and rounded angles.
cur·so·ry (kur-sŏ-ree) *adj.* hasty and not thorough,
a cursory inspection. **cur′so·ri·ly** *adv.* **cur′so·
ri·ness** *n.*
curt (kurt) *adj.* noticeably or rudely brief. **curt′ly**
adv. **curt′ness** *n.*
cur·tail (kŭr-tayl) *v.* to cut short, to reduce. **cur·
tail′ment** *n.*
cur·tain (kur-tin) *n.* 1. a piece of cloth or other
material hung up as a screen, especially at a window or between the stage and auditorium of a
theater. 2. the fall of a stage curtain at the end
of an act or scene. 3. a curtain call. 4. *curtains,
(slang)* the end. **curtain** *v.* to provide or shut
off with a curtain or curtains. □**curtain call,**
applause calling for an actor etc. to take a bow
after the curtain has been lowered.

curt·sy (*pl.* **-sies**), **curt·sey** (*pl.* **-seys**) (kurt-
see) *n.* a movement of respect made by women
and girls, bending the knees and lowering the body
with one foot forward. **curtsy (curt·sied, curt·
sy·ing), curtsey (curt·seyed, curt·sey·ing)**
v. to make a curtsy.
cur·va·ceous (kŭr-vay-shŭs) *adj. (informal)* having a shapely figure.
cur·va·ture (kur-vă-chŭr) *n.* curving, a curved
form, *curvature of the spine.*
curve (kurv) *n.* 1. a line of which no part is straight.
2. a smooth continuous surface of which no part
is flat. 3. a curved form or thing. **curve** *v.*
(curved, curv·ing) to bend or shape so as to
form a curve.
cush·ion (kuush-ŏn) *n.* 1. a bag of cloth or other
fabric filled with soft material, used to make a
seat etc. more comfortable. 2. a soft pad or other
means of support or of protection against jarring. 3. the elastic border around a billiard table,
from which the balls rebound. **cushion** *v.* 1. to
furnish with a cushion or cushions. 2. to lessen
the impact of (a blow, or shock). 3. to protect
from the effects of something harmful.
cush·y (kuush-ee) *adj.* **(cush·i·er, cush·i·est)**
(informal) pleasant and easy, *a cushy job.*
cusp (kusp) *n.* a pointed end where two curves
meet, as the horn of a crescent moon.
cus·pid (kus-pid) *n.* a tooth narrowing to a single
point.
cus·pi·dor (kus-pi-dor) *n.* a spittoon.
cuss (kus) *v. (informal)* to curse. **cuss** *n. (informal)*
1. a curse. 2. a person, *an awkward cuss.*
cuss·ed (kus-id) *adj. (informal)* 1. cursed. 2.
awkward and stubborn. **cuss′ed·ness** *n.*
cus·tard (kus-tărd) *n.* 1. a dish or sauce made with
beaten eggs and milk. 2. a similar food frozen,
frozen custard.
cus·to·di·al (kus-toh-di-ăl) *adj.* of or involving
custody.
cus·to·di·an (kus-toh-di-ăn) *n.* 1. a guardian or
keeper, especially of a public building or a trust
fund. 2. a janitor.
cus·to·dy (kus-tŏ-dee) *n.* (*pl.* **-dies**) 1. the right
or duty of taking care of something, guardianship;
in safe custody, safely guarded. 2. imprisonment.
□**take into custody,** to arrest.
cus·tom (kus-tŏm) *n.* 1. a usual way of behaving
or of doing something. 2. the regular patronage
of a merchant or a business by customers.
cus·tom·ar·y (kus-tŏm-e-ree) *adj.* in accordance
with custom, usual. **cus′tom·ar·i·ly** *adv.*
cus·tom-built (kus-tŏm-bilt) *adj.* custom-made.
cus·tom·er (kus-tŏ-mĕr) *n.* 1. a person who buys
goods or services from a shop or business. 2. a
person one has to deal with, *an ugly customer.*
cus·tom·house (kus-tŏm-hows) *n.* (also **cus-
tomshouse**) a building for Customs officials.
cus·tom-made (kus-tŏm-mayd) *adj.* made according to a customer's order.
cus·toms (kus-tŏmz) *n.* 1. duty charged on goods
imported from other countries. 2. *Customs,* the
government department dealing with such duties
and the ships and vehicles that carry the goods.
3. the area at a port or airport where Customs
officials examine goods and baggage brought into
a country. □**customs union,** a group of countries that have arranged to charge the same
amount of duty on imported goods.
cut (kut) *v.* **(cut, cut·ting)** 1. to divide or wound
or detach with an edged instrument; *the knife*

won't cut, is blunt. **2.** to shape or make or shorten in this way. **3.** to be able to be cut, *cotton fabric cuts easily.* **4.** to have (a tooth) appear through the gum, *she is cutting her first tooth.* **5.** to cross, to intersect; *you can cut across the field*, go across it as a shorter way. **6.** to reduce by removing part, *cut taxes; two scenes were cut by the producer.* **7.** to switch off (electric power, an engine, etc.). **8.** to lift part of a pack of playing cards. **9.** to hit a ball with a chopping movement in handball etc. **10.** to stay away deliberately from, *cut the class.* **11.** to ignore (a person) deliberately. **12.** to dilute (whiskey for drinking). **cut** *n.* **1.** the act of cutting, a division or wound made by this. **2.** a stroke with a sword or whip or cane. **3.** a stroke made by cutting a ball in sports. **4.** a piece of meat cut from the carcass of an animal. **5.** the way a thing is cut, the style in which clothes are made by cutting. **6.** a cutting remark. **7.** a reduction, *a tax cut.* **8.** the cutting out of part of a play or film etc. **9.** *(slang)* a share of profits, commission, loot, etc. □**a cut above**, noticeably superior to. **cut a dashing figure**, to make a brilliant show in appearance and behavior. **cut and dried**, planned or prepared in advance. **cut back**, to reduce; to prune. **cut both ways**, to result in simultaneous advantages and disadvantages. **cut corners**, to eliminate all but the essentials, *the planning committee was forced to cut corners.* **cut down**, to reduce. **cut in**, to interrupt; to return too soon to one's own side of the road, obstructing the path of an overtaken vehicle; to give a share of the profits to; *(informal)* to interrupt a dancing couple and take one of them as one's own partner. **cut it out**, *(slang)* stop doing that. **cut no ice**, *(slang)* to have no influence or effect. **cut off**, to prevent from continuing; to keep from contact; *cut off without a penny*, to deprive (a person) of further financial support. **cut one's losses**, to abandon a scheme that causes loss, before one loses too much. **cut out**, to shape by cutting; to outdo (a rival); to deprive of an inheritance or portion; to cease or cause to cease functioning, *the engine cut out.* **cut out for**, having the qualities and abilities needed for. **cut the ground from under someone's feet**, to anticipate his arguments or plans and leave him with no foundation for these. **cut up**, to cut into pieces; *be very cut up*, to be greatly distressed; *(slang)* to criticize severely, to reprimand, *the foreman really cut me up*; to behave comically.

cu·ta·ne·ous (kyoo-tay-ni-ŭs) *adj.* of the skin.

cut·a·way (kut-ă-way) *adj.* having a portion cut away. **cutaway** *n.* **1.** a man's formal coat, with sides tapering toward the back. **2.** (in television and motion pictures) a change from one scene to another.

cut·back (kut-back) *n.* a reduction in a rate or amount.

cute (kyoot) *adj.* (**cut·er, cut·est**) *(informal)* **1.** sharp, clever, shrewd. **2.** artificial, straining to impress. **3.** attractive, pretty. **cute'ly** *adv.* **cute'ness** *n.*

cut·i·cle (kyoo-ti-kĕl) *n.* skin at the base of a fingernail or toenail.

cut·lass (kut-lăs) *n.* a short sword with a slightly curved blade.

cut·ler (kut-lĕr) *n.* one who makes or deals in cutlery.

cut·ler·y (kut-lĕ-ree) *n.* knives, forks, and spoons used in eating or serving food.

cut·let (kut-lit) *n.* **1.** a slice of veal etc. from the ribs or legs of the animal for breading and frying. **2.** ground meat cooked in the shape of a cutlet.

cut·off (kut-awf) *n.* **1.** a device or mechanism that stops something. **2.** a road used as a shortcut or bypass. **3.** *(informal)* a termination point, *the cutoff is May 15.* **4.** a shorter channel made when a stream cuts across a bend.

cut-rate (kut-rayt) *adj.* offered for sale at a reduced price.

cut·ter (kut-ĕr) *n.* **1.** a person or thing that cuts. **2.** a kind of small boat with one mast.

cut·throat (kut-throht) *n.* a person who cuts throats, a murderer. **cutthroat** *adj.* intense and merciless, *cutthroat competition.* □**cutthroat trout**, a North American trout with a reddish mark on both sides of the throat.

cut·ting (kut-ing) *v. see* **cut. cutting** *adj.* (of words) hurtful, *cutting remarks.* **cutting** *n.* **1.** the act of cutting. **2.** a piece cut from a plant for replanting to form a new plant.

cut·tle·fish (kut-ĕl-fish) *n.* (*pl.* **-fish·es, -fish**) a sea creature that sends out a black liquid when attacked.

cut·up (kut-up) *n.* *(informal)* a person who behaves comically.

cw *abbr.* clockwise.

CWO *abbr.* chief warrant officer.

c.w.o. *abbr.* cash with order.

cwt *abbr.* hundredweight.

-cy *suffix* used to form nouns meaning state, condition, or quality, as in *complacency;* rank or office, as in *papacy;* action or practice, as in *truancy.*

cy·an (si-an) *n.* a greenish-blue color. **cyan** *adj.* greenish blue.

cy·a·nide (si-ă-nɪd) *n.* a very poisonous chemical substance.

cy·a·no·sis (si-ă-noh-sis) *n.* a condition in which the skin appears blue, caused by lack of oxygen in the blood.

cy·ber·net·ics (si-bĕr-net-iks) *n.* the science of communication and control in animals (as by the nervous system) and in machines (as by computers).

cy·cla·mate (si-klă-mayt) *n.* a salt of calcium or sodium, used as an artificial sweetener.

cy·cla·men (si-klă-mĕn) *n.* a plant with pink, purple, or white flowers with petals that turn back.

cy·cla·zo·cine (si-klă-zoh-seen) *n.* a drug that stops the effects of heroin or morphine.

cy·cle (si-kĕl) *n.* **1.** a series of events or operations that repeat regularly in the same order, *the cycle of the seasons.* **2.** the time needed for one such series. **3.** one complete occurrence of a continuously recurring process such as electrical oscillation or alternation of electric current. **4.** a complete set or series, as of songs or poems. **5.** a bicycle or motorcycle. **cycle** *v.* (**cy·cled, cy·cling**) **1.** ride a bicycle. **2.** to cause a machine to go through one cycle. **3.** to move in cycles.

cy·clic (si-klik, sik-lik) *adj.* **1.** recurring in cycles or series. **2.** forming a cycle. **cy'cli·cal** *adj.* **cy'cli·cal·ly** *adv.*

cy·clist (si-klist) *n.* a person who rides a bicycle etc.

cy·clom·e·ter (si-klom-ĕ-tĕr) *n.* an instrument attached to a wheel of a bicycle etc. to measure distance traveled.

cy·clone (si-klohn) *n.* **1.** a wind rotating around

a calm central area. 2. a violent destructive form of this. **cy·clon·ic** (sɪ-klon-ik) *adj.*

cy·clo·tron (sɪ-klŏ-tron) *n.* an apparatus for accelerating charged particles by making them move spirally in a magnetic field.

cyg·net (sig-nit) *n.* a young swan.

cyl. *abbr.* cylinder.

cyl·in·der (sɪl-in-dĕr) *n.* 1. a solid or hollow object with straight sides and circular ends. 2. a machine part shaped like this, the chamber in which a piston moves in an engine. **cy·lin·dri·cal** (si-lin-dri-kăl) *adj.*

cym·bal (sim-băl) *n.* a percussion instrument consisting of a brass plate struck with another or with a stick.

cym·bal·ist (sim-bă-list) *n.* a person who plays the cymbals.

cyn·ic (sin-ik) *n.* a person who believes people's motives are bad or selfish and shows this by sneering at them. **cyn'i·cal** *adj.* **cyn'i·cal·ly** *adv.*

cyn·i·cism (sin-i-siz-ĕm) *n.* the attitude of a cynic.

cy·no·sure (sɪ-nŏ-shoor) *n.* a center of attraction or admiration.

cy·press (sɪ-pris) *n.* a coniferous evergreen tree with dark feathery leaves.

Cy·prus (sɪ-prŭs) a country in the East Mediterranean. **Cyp·ri·ot** (sip-ri-ŏt) *adj. & n.*

Cy·ril·lic (si-ril-ik) *adj.* of the alphabet used for Russian, Bulgarian, and other Slavonic languages.

cyst (sist) *n.* an abnormal sac formed in the body, containing fluid or semisolid matter. **cyst·ic** (sis-tik) *adj.* 1. of the bladder. 2. like a cyst.

cys·ti·tis (si-stɪ-tis) *n.* inflammation of the bladder.

cy·tol·o·gy (sɪ-tol-ŏ-jee) *n.* the scientific study of cells. **cy·tol'o·gist** *n.* **cy·to·log·ic** (sɪ-tŏ-loj-ik) *adj.* **cy·to·log'i·cal** *adj.*

cy·to·plasm (sɪ-tŏ-plaz-ĕm) *n.* the cellular substance surrounding the cell nucleus. **cy·to·plas·mic** (sɪ-tŏ-plaz-mik) *adj.*

CZ, C.Z. *abbr.* Canal Zone.

czar (zahr) *n.* 1. (often **Czar**) formerly, the emperor of Russia. 2. a person with great authority. **cza·ri·na** (zah-ree-nă) *n. fem.* **czar'ist** *adj. & n.*

czar·das (chahr-dahsh) *n.* a Hungarian dance with a slow start and a quick wild finish.

Czech (chek) *n.* 1. a native or the language of western Czechoslovakia. 2. a Czechoslovak. **Czech** *adj.* of, relating to, Czechoslovakia or its people or language.

Czech·o·slo·va·ki·a (chek-ŏ-slŏ-vah-ki-ă) a country in central Europe. **Czech·o·slo·vak** (chek-ŏ-sloh-vak) *adj. & n.* **Czech·o·slo·va'ki·an** *adj. & n.*

D

D, d (dee) (*pl.* **Ds, D's, d's**) 1. the fourth letter of the alphabet. 2. *D*, a grade rating for poor school work. 3. the Roman numeral symbol for 500.
D *symbol* deuterium.
d. *abbr.* 1. date. 2. daughter. 3. day. 4. deceased. 5. degree. 6. delete. 7. dialect. 8. dialectical. 9. diameter. 10. died. 11. dime. 12. dividend. 13. dose.
D. *abbr.* 1. Democrat. 2. dimension (as in *3D*). 3. Dutch.
D.A. *abbr.* 1. days after acceptance. 2. Department of Agriculture. 3. deposit account. 4. District Attorney.
dab (dab) *n.* 1. a light or feeble blow, a tap. 2. quick gentle pressure on a surface with something soft, *a dab with a sponge.* 3. a small amount of a soft substance applied to a surface. **dab** *v.* **(dabbed, dab·bing)** 1. to strike lightly or feebly. 2. to press quickly and lightly.
dab·ble (dab-ĕl) *v.* **(dab·bled, dab·bling)** 1. to wet by splashing or by dipping in and out of water. 2. to move the feet, hands, or bill lightly in water or mud. 3. to study or work at something casually not seriously, *she dabbles in photography.* **dab′bler** *n.*
Dac·ca (dak-ă) the capital of Bangladesh.
dace (days) *n.* (*pl.* **dac·es, dace**) a small freshwater fish related to the carp.
da·cha (dah-chă) *n.* a small country house in Russia.
dachs·hund (doks-huund) *n.* a small dog of a breed with a long body and very short legs.
Da·cron (day-kron) *n.* *(trademark)* a synthetic fabric that is wrinkle-resistant.
dac·tyl (dak-tĭl) *n.* a metrical foot consisting of one long syllable followed by two short syllables, for example, *prac*·ti·cal, *hap*·pi·ness. **dac·tyl·ic** (dak-til-ik) *adj.*
dad (dad) *n.* *(informal)* father.
Da·da (dah-dah) *n.* an international movement in art during the early 20th century rejecting conventions and intending to shock. **Da·da·ist** (dah-dah-ist) *n.* **Da′da·ism** *n.*
dad·dy (dad-ee) *n.* (*pl.* **-dies**) *(informal)* father.
dad·dy-long·legs (dad-ee-lawng-legz) *n.* a spider-like animal, usually having long thin legs.
da·do (day-doh) *n.* (*pl.* **-does, -dos**) the lower part of the wall of a room or corridor when it is colored or faced differently from the upper part.
daf·fo·dil (daf-ŏ-dil) *n.* a yellow flower with a trumpetlike central part, growing from a bulb.
daf·fy (daf-ee) *adj.* **(-fi·er, -fi·est)** *(informal)* silly, foolish, crazy. **daf′fi·ness** *n.*
dag·ger (dag-ĕr) *n.* a short pointed two-edged weapon used for stabbing. □**look daggers at,** to stare angrily at.

da·guerre·o·type (dă-gerr-ŏ-tɪp) *n.* 1. an early photographic process using a silver or silvered plate. 2. a photograph produced by this.
dahl·ia (dal-yă) *n.* a garden plant with large brightly colored flowers and tuberous roots.
Dail Eir·eann (doil air-ăn) the lower house of Parliament in the Republic of Ireland.
dai·ly (day-lee) *adj.* happening or appearing on every day (or every weekday). **daily** *adv.* once a day. **daily** *n.* (*pl.* **-lies**) a daily newspaper. □**daily bread,** one's livelihood. **daily double,** a racetrack bet in which the bettor must select the winners of two specified races in order to win his bet. **daily dozen,** a set of daily exercises.
dain·ty (dayn-tee) *adj.* **(-ti·er, -ti·est)** 1. small and pretty, delicate. 2. fastidious, especially about food. **dain′ti·ly** *adv.* **dain′ti·ness** *n.*
dai·qui·ri (dɪ-kĭ-ree) *n.* (*pl.* **-ris**) a cocktail of rum, lime juice, and sugar.
dair·y (dair-ee) *n.* (*pl.* **dair·ies**) 1. a room or building where milk and milk products are processed. 2. a shop where these are sold. **dair′y·ing** *n.* □**dairy farm,** a farm producing chiefly milk.
dair·y·maid (dair-ee-mayd) *n.* a woman who works in a dairy.
dair·y·man (dair-ee-măn) *n.* (*pl.* **-men,** *pr.* -měn) a dealer in milk etc.
da·is (day-is) *n.* a low platform, especially at one end of a hall.
dai·shi·ki = **dashiki.**
dai·sy (day-zee) *n.* (*pl.* **-sies**) a flower with many white rays surrounding a center. □**pushing up the daisies,** *(slang)* dead and buried.
Da·kar (dah-kahr) the capital of Senegal.
Da·ko·ta (dă-koh-tă) either of two states of the U.S., *North* and *South Dakota.*
Da·lai La·ma (dah-lı lah-mă) the chief lama of Tibet.
dale (dayl) *n.* a small valley.
dal·ly (dal-ee) *v.* **(dal·lied, dal·ly·ing)** 1. to idle, to dawdle. 2. to flirt. **dal·li·ance** (dal-i-ăns) *n.*
Dal·ma·tian (dal-may-shăn) *adj.* of Dalmatia, the central region of the coast of Yugoslavia. **Dalmatian** *n.* a large white dog with dark spots.
dam[1] (dam) *n.* a barrier built across a river etc. to hold back water and control its flow or form a reservoir. **dam** *v.* **(dammed, dam·ming)** 1. to hold back with a dam. 2. to obstruct (a flow).
dam[2] *n.* the mother of a four-footed animal.
dam·age (dam-ij) *n.* 1. something done or suffered that reduces the value or usefulness of the thing affected or spoils its appearance. 2. *(slang)* the cost or charge, *what's the damage?* 3. *damages,* money claimed or paid as compensation for an injury. **damage** *v.* **(dam·aged, dam·ag·ing)** to cause damage to. **dam′ag·ing** *adj.*
dam·a·scene (dam-ă-seen) *v.* **(dam·a·scened,**

dam·a·scen·ing) to ornament metal or steel with inlaid gold or silver or wavy patterns produced in welding.

Da·mas·cus (dă-mas-kŭs) the capital of Syria. □**Damascus steel,** an early type of wavy-patterned steel, formerly used for sword blades.

dam·ask (dam-ăsk) n. silk or linen material woven with a pattern that is visible on either side. □**damask rose,** an old sweet-scented variety of rose.

dame (daym) n. 1. (slang) a woman. 2. Dame, the title of a woman who has been awarded an order of knighthood in Great Britain (corresponding to the title of Sir for a knight).

damn (dam) v. 1. to condemn to eternal punishment in hell; I'll be damned, (informal) I am astonished; I'm damned if I know, (informal) I certainly do not know. 2. to condemn as a failure. 3. to swear at, to curse. **damn** interj. an exclamation of anger or annoyance; let's go, and damn the expense, never mind the expense. **damn** n. "damn" said as a curse. **damn** adj. & adv. (informal) damned.

dam·na·ble (dam-nă-běl) adj. hateful, annoying. **dam′na·bly** adv.

dam·na·tion (dam-nay-shŏn) n. being damned or condemned to hell. **damnation** interj. an exclamation of anger or annoyance.

damned (damd) adj. (informal) damnable. **damned** (informal) adv. damnably, extremely, it's damned hot. □**do one's damnedest,** (informal) to do one's very best.

Dam·o·cles (dam-ŏ-kleez) n. **sword of Damocles,** imminent danger. ▷From the story of Damocles, a Greek of the 4th century B.C. above whose head a sword was once hung by a hair while he ate.

damp (damp) n. 1. moisture in the air or on a surface or throughout something. 2. foul or explosive gas in a mine. **damp** adj. slightly or moderately wet. **damp** v. 1. to make damp. 2. to dampen. 3. to stop the vibration of (a string in music). **damp′ly** adv. **damp′ness** n. □**damp down,** to heap ashes on (a fire) to make it burn more slowly.

damp·en (dam-pěn) v. 1. to decrease in activity or vigor. 2. to become or to make damp.

damp·er (dam-pěr) n. 1. a movable metal plate that regulates the flow of air into the fire in a stove or furnace. 2. a person or thing that damps or discourages enthusiasm, cast a damper over the proceedings.

dam·sel (dam-zěl) n. (old use) a young woman.

dam·sel·fly (dam-zěl-fli) n. (pl. -flies) an insect like a dragonfly but with wings that fold while it rests.

dam·son (dam-zŏn) n. 1. a small purple plum. 2. the tree that bears it.

dan (dan) n. 1. a degree of proficiency in judo. 2. a person who reaches this.

dance (dans) v. (danced, danc·ing) 1. to move with rhythmical steps or movements, usually to music. 2. to perform in this way. 3. to move in a quick or lively way, to bob up and down. **dance** n. 1. a piece of dancing. 2. a piece of music for dancing to. 3. a social gathering for the purpose of dancing. **danc′er** n.

danc·ing (dan-sing) n. the act of dancing.

d. and c. abbr. dilation (of the cervix) and curettage (of the womb).

dan·de·li·on (dan-dě-lɪ-ŏn) n. a wild plant with bright-yellow flowers.

dan·der (dan-děr) n. (informal) fighting spirit; his dander is up, he is angry.

dan·di·fied (dan-di-fɪd) adj. like a dandy.

dan·dle (dan-děl) v. (dan·dled, dan·dling) to dance (a child) in one's arms or on one's knees.

dan·druff (dan-drŭf) n. flakes of dead skin on the scalp and hair.

dan·dy (dan-dee) n. (pl. -dies) 1. a man who pays excessive attention to the smartness of his appearance and clothes. 2. (informal) something exceptionally good. **dandy** adj. (-di·er, -di·est) (informal) very good of its kind.

dan·ger (dayn-jěr) n. 1. liability or exposure to harm or to death 2. a thing that causes this.

dan·ger·ous (dayn-jě-rŭs) adj. causing danger. **dan′ger·ous·ly** adv.

dan·gle (dang-gěl) v. (dan·gled, dan·gling) 1. to hang loosely. 2. to hold or carry (a thing) so that it swings loosely. 3. to hold out (hopes) to a person temptingly. □**dangling participle,** a participle lacking proper grammatical connection, as walking in walking down the street the church appears on the left.

Dan·iel (dan-yěl) n. 1. a Hebrew prophet who was delivered by God from the lion's den. 2. a book of the Old Testament bearing his name.

Dan·ish (day-nish) adj. of Denmark or its people or language. **Danish** n. the language of Denmark. □**Danish pastry,** a sweet yeast roll filled or topped with cheese, fruit, nuts, etc.

dank (dangk) adj. unpleasantly damp and cold.

dan·seur (dahn-sur) n. a male ballet dancer.

dan·seuse (dahn-suuz) n. a female ballet dancer.

dap·per (dap-ěr) adj. neat and smart in dress and appearance, a dapper little man. **dap′per·ly** adv. **dap′per·ness** n.

dap·ple (dap-ěl) v. (dap·pled, dap·pling) to mark with spots or patches of shade or a different color.

dap·ple-gray (dap-ěl-gray) adj. gray with darker markings.

DAR, D.A.R. abbr. Daughters of the American Revolution.

dare (dair) v. (dared, dar·ing) 1. to have the courage or impudence to do something, to be bold enough, he didn't dare go or dare to go. 2. to take the risk of, to face as a danger. 3. to challenge (a person) to do something risky. □**I dare say,** I am prepared to believe, it is very likely, I do not deny it. ▷Durst is no longer a correct past form of dare.

dare·dev·il (dair-dev-ĭl) n. a recklessly daring person.

Dar es Sa·laam (dahr es să-lahm) the capital of Tanzania.

dar·ing (dair-ing) n. boldness. **daring** adj. 1. bold, taking risks boldly. 2. boldly dramatic or unconventional. **dar′ing·ly** adv.

dark (dahrk) adj. 1. with little or no light. 2. (of color) of a deep shade closer to black than to white, dark gray; a dark suit. 3. (of people) having a brown or black skin, having dark hair. 4. gloomy, cheerless, dismal, the long dark years of the war. 5. secret, keep it dark. 6. mysterious, remote and unexplored, in darkest Africa. **dark** n. 1. absence of light. 2. a time of darkness, night or nightfall, out after dark. 3. a dark color. **dark′ly** adv. **dark′ness** n. □**Dark Ages,** the early part of the Middle Ages in Europe, when learning and culture were in decline. **dark horse,**

a competitor of whose abilities little is known before the contest. **dark meat,** flesh (of a fowl) that appears dark after cooking. **in the dark,** having no information about something.

dark·en (dahr-kĕn) v. to make or become dark or darker. □**darken a person's door,** pay him an unwelcome visit.

dark·ish (dahr-kish) adj. rather dark.

dark·room (dahrk-room) n. a room from which daylight is excluded so that photographs can be processed.

dar·ling (dahr-ling) n. 1. a dearly loved or lovable person or thing, a favorite. 2. (informal) something charming. **darling** adj. dearly loved, (informal) charming.

darn¹ (dahrn) v. to mend by weaving yarn across a hole. **darn** n. a place mended by darning. □**darning needle,** a long needle for darning; (informal) a dragonfly.

darn² interj. & adj. = damn, damned.

darned (dahrnd) adj. = **damned.**

dart (dahrt) n. 1. a small pointed missile. 2. a small metal-tipped object used in the game of darts. 3. a darting movement. 4. a tapering stitched tuck in a garment. 5. darts, an indoor game in which darts are thrown at a target. **dart** v. 1. to spring or move suddenly and rapidly in some direction. 2. to send out rapidly, darted an angry look at him.

dart·board (dahrt-bohrd) n. a circular board used as a target in the game of darts.

dart·er (dahrt-ĕr) n. 1. one who darts. 2. a perchlike freshwater fish.

Dar·von (dahr-von) n. (trademark) a drug used to relieve pain.

dash (dash) v. 1. to run rapidly, to rush. 2. to knock or drive over (a thing) with force against something, to shatter (a thing) in this way; our hopes were dashed, were destroyed. 3. to write hastily, dashed off a letter. **dash** n. 1. a short rapid run, a rush, made a dash for the door. 2. a small amount of liquid or flavoring added, a dash of soda. 3. a dashboard. 4. energy, vigor. 5. lively spirit or appearance, flair, charm. 6. the punctuation mark — used to show a break in sense. 7. the longer of the two signals used in Morse code.

dash·board (dash-bohrd) n. a panel below the windshield of a motor vehicle, carrying various instruments and controls.

da·shi·ki (dă-shee-kee) n. (pl. -kis) a loose-fitting brightly colored shirt.

dash·ing (dash-ing) adj. spirited, smartly dressed.

das·tard (das-tărd) n. a despicable coward. **das'tard·ly** adj.

da·ta (day-tă) n. pl. facts or information to be used as a basis for discussing or deciding something, or prepared for being processed by a computer etc. (▷ Data should not be used with a singular verb, as in the data is inconclusive; it is by origin a Latin plural (the singular is datum) and should be used with a plural verb, the data are inconclusive.) □**data bank,** a large collection of data stored for use or analysis, especially by a computer. **electronic data processing,** analysis and storage of data in a computer.

dat·a·ble (day-tă-bĕl) adj. able to be dated.

da·ta·ma·tion (day-tă-may-shŏn) n. data processing.

date¹ (dayt) n. 1. the day on which something happened or was written or is to happen etc., a state-

ment of this in terms of day, month, and year (or any of these). 2. the period to which something belongs, objects of prehistoric date. 3. an appointment to meet socially. 4. a person of the opposite sex with whom one has a social appointment. **date** v. (dat·ed, dat·ing) 1. to mark with a date. 2. to assign a date to. 3. to originate from a particular date, the custom dates from Victorian times. 4. to show up the age of, to show signs of becoming out of date, some fashions date quickly. 5. to make or have a social appointment with a member of the opposite sex, to have such appointments with the same person regularly. **dat·ed (day-tid)** adj. □**out of date,** see **out.** **to date,** so far, until now, here are our sales figures to date. **up to date,** see **up.**

date² n. the small, brown sweet edible fruit of the **date palm,** a palm tree of North Africa and southwest Asia.

date·less (dayt-lis) adj. 1. having no date. 2. not becoming out of date. 3. too old to assign a date to.

date·line (dayt-lɪn) n. 1. (also **international date·line**) a line from north to south roughly along the meridian 180° from Greenwich, England, east and west of which the date differs (east being one day earlier). 2. a statement of the place and date of origin at the beginning of a newspaper article.

da·tive (day-tiv) n. the grammatical case showing indirect object, such as him in "we gave him our blessings." **dative** adj.

da·tum (day-tŭm) n. see **data.**

daub (dawb) v. to cover or smear roughly with a soft substance, to paint clumsily. **daub** n. 1. a clumsily painted picture. 2. a smear.

daugh·ter (daw-tĕr) n. 1. a female child in relation to her parents. 2. a female descendant, daughters of Eve. **daugh'ter·ly** adj.

daughter-in-law (daw-tĕr-in-law) n. (pl. **daughters-in-law**) a son's wife.

daunt (dawnt) v. to make afraid or discouraged. **daunt·less (dawnt-lis)** adj. brave, not daunted. **daunt'less·ly** adv.

dau·phin (daw-fin) n. a king of France's eldest son.

dav·it (dav-it) n. a kind of small crane on board ship.

Da·vy Jones (day-vee johnz) the spirit of the sea, the evil spirit of the sea. □**Davy Jones's locker,** the bottom of the sea as the graveyard of those who are drowned or buried at sea.

daw·dle (daw-dĕl) v. (daw·dled, daw·dling) to walk slowly and idly, to take one's time. **daw'dler** n.

dawn (dawn) n. 1. the first light of day. 2. the beginning, the dawn of civilization. **dawn** v. 1. to begin to grow light. 2. to begin to appear; the truth dawned on him, became evident to him.

day (day) n. 1. the time during which the sun is above the horizon. 2. the time for one rotation of Earth, a period of twenty-four hours, especially from one midnight to the next. 3. the hours given to work, an eight-hour day. 4. a specified or appointed day, New Year's Day, inauguration day. 5. a period, time, or era, in Abraham Lincoln's day; in my young days, when I was young. 6. a period of success; colonialism has had its day, its successful period is over. 7. victory in a contest, win the day. □**day boy, day girl, day student,** a pupil attending a boarding school but living at home. **day by day,** daily. **day in day out,**

every day, unceasingly. **Day of Atonement,** Yom Kippur. **day school,** a private school that pupils attend during the day, not a boarding school.

day·bed (day-bed) *n.* a couch that can be converted to a bed.

day·book (day-buuk) *n.* 1. a diary. 2. a bookkeeper's journal for daily transactions.

day·break (day-brayk) *n.* dawn, the first light of day.

day·care (day-kair) **center** a place where young children are looked after while their mothers are at work.

day·dream (day-dreem) *n.* idle and pleasant thoughts. **daydream** *v.* to have daydreams. **day′dream·er** *n.*

day·light (day-lıt) *n.* 1. the light of day. 2. dawn. □**beat** *or* **scare the daylights out of someone,** beat him severely, scare him greatly. **daylight saving,** creation of longer evening daylight in summer by making clocks show a time that is later than standard time. **see daylight,** to begin to understand what was previously puzzling; to begin to approach the end of a task.

day·time (day-tım) *n.* the time of daylight.

daze (dayz) *v.* **(dazed, daz·ing)** to make (a person) feel stunned or bewildered. **daze** *n.* a dazed state.

daz·zle (daz-ĕl) *v.* **(daz·zled, daz·zling)** 1. to make (a person) unable to see clearly because of too much bright light. 2. to amaze and impress or confuse (a person) by a splendid display. **dazzle** *n.* dazzling, a bright confusing light.

dB *abbr.* decibel(s).

dbl *abbr.* double.

DC, D.C., dc, d.c. *abbr.* direct current.

D.C. *abbr.* District of Columbia.

DD *abbr.* 1. days after date. 2. demand draft. 3. dishonorable discharge. 4. Doctor of Divinity.

D-day (dee-day) *n.* 1. the date on which an important operation is planned to begin. 2. June 6, 1944, the day on which Allied forces invaded France.

D.D.S. *abbr.* 1. Doctor of Dental Science. 2. Doctor of Dental Surgery.

DDT *abbr.* a white chemical used as an insecticide.

DE *abbr.* 1. Delaware. 2. Department of Education.

dea·con (dee-kŏn) *n.* 1. a clergyman ranking below a priest in certain Christian denominations. 2. a layman attending to church business in certain Christian denominations.

dea·con·ess (dee-kŏ-nis) *n.* a woman with duties similar to those of a deacon.

de·ac·ti·vate (dee-ak-tĭ-vayt) *v.* **(de·ac·ti·vat·ed, de·ac·ti·vat·ing)** to make inactive. **de·ac′ti·va·tor** *n.* **de·ac·ti·va·tion** (dee-ak-tĭ-vay-shŏn) *n.*

dead (ded) *adj.* 1. no longer alive. 2. numb, without feeling. 3. no longer used, *a dead language.* 4. lifeless and without luster or resonance or warmth. 5. no longer active or functioning, *the microphone went dead.* 6. dull, without interest or movement or activity, *it's a dead place on Sundays.* 7. complete, abrupt, exact, *dead silence; a dead stop; dead center; he is a dead shot,* shoots very accurately. **dead** *adv.* completely, exactly, *dead drunk; dead level; dead ahead.* **dead** *n.* 1. an inactive or silent time, *the dead of night.* 2. *the dead,* those who are dead, as opposed to the *living.* □**dead as a doornail,** quite dead. **dead ball,** (*slang*) a baseball that is out of play during a game. **dead duck,** (*slang*) something or someone doomed to failure. **dead end,** the closed end of a road or passage, a blind alley; an impasse.

dead-end job, a job with no prospects. **dead heat,** a race in which two or more competitors finish exactly even. **dead issue,** a matter no longer being considered. **dead letter,** a letter that cannot be delivered and must be returned to the sender; a law or practice that is no longer observed. **dead man's handle,** a controlling device (on a train etc.) that disconnects the driving power if it is released. **dead reckoning,** calculating a ship's position by log and compass etc. when observations are impossible. (▷Note that this does not mean "a reckoning that is exactly right.") **Dead Sea,** an inland salt lake between Israel and Jordan. **dead set,** determined, *he's dead set against voting for you.* **dead weight,** a heavy inert weight.

dead·beat (ded-beet) *n.* 1. a person who never pays his or her share. 2. a destitute person.

dead·en (ded-ĕn) *v.* to deprive of or lose vitality, loudness, feeling, etc.

dead·fall (ded-fawl) *n.* a trap with a falling weight, used to kill animals.

dead·head (ded-hed) *n.* (*informal*) a useless or unenterprising person.

dead·line (ded-lın) *n.* a time limit.

dead·lock (ded-lok) *n.* a complete standstill or lack of progress, especially between two negotiating parties. **deadlock** *v.* to reach a deadlock, to cause to do this.

dead·ly (ded-lee) *adj.* **(-li·er, -li·est)** 1. causing or capable of causing fatal injury or death. 2. deathlike, *a deadly silence.* 3. (*informal*) very dreary. **deadly** *adv.* 1. as if dead, *deadly pale.* 2. extremely, *deadly serious.* **dead′li·ness** *n.* □**deadly nightshade,** a plant with poisonous black berries, belladonna. **deadly sin,** one of the **seven deadly sins,** those that result in damnation for a person's soul.

dead·pan (ded-pan) *adj.* (*informal*) with an expressionless face. **deadpan** *v.* **(dead·panned, dead·pan·ning)** (*informal*) to show no expression.

dead·wood (ded-wuud) *n.* 1. dead trees or branches. 2. a useless person or persons.

deaf (def) *adj.* 1. wholly or partly without the sense of hearing, unable to hear. 2. refusing to listen, *deaf to all advice; turned a deaf ear to our requests.* **deaf′ness** *n.* □**the deaf,** deaf people.

deaf·en (def-ĕn) *v.* **(deaf·ened, deaf·en·ing)** to make deaf or unable to hear by a very loud noise. **deaf′en·ing** *adj.*

deaf-mute (def-myoot) *n.* a person who is both deaf and unable to speak.

deal (deel) *v.* **(dealt,** *pr.* delt, **deal·ing)** 1. to distribute among several people, to distribute (cards) to players in a card game. 2. to give, to inflict, *dealt him a severe blow.* 3. to do business, to trade, *we deal at Smith's; they deal in imported gems.* **deal** *n.* 1. dealing, a player's turn to deal, a round of play after dealing. 2. a business transaction, *the deal fell through; it's a deal,* I agree to this. 3. treatment, *didn't get a fair deal.* **deal′er** *n.* □**a good deal, a great deal,** a large amount. **deal with,** to do business with; to take action about or to see what is needed by (a problem etc.); *deal with a subject,* discuss it in a book or speech etc.

deal·er·ship (dee-lĕr-ship) *n.* a sales agency for a specified brand of merchandise etc.

dean (deen) *n.* 1. an Anglican clergyman who is head of a cathedral chapter. 2. an official in certain universities, responsible for a college or its students, or having some administrative function. 3.

the senior or leading member of a group, *the dean of American letters.*
dear (deer) *adj.* 1. much loved, cherished. 2. esteemed; *Dear Sir,* a polite phrase beginning a letter. 3. costing more than it is worth, not cheap. **dear** *n.* a dear person. **dear** *adv.* dearly, at a high price. **dear** *interj.* an exclamation of surprise or distress. **dear′ly** *adv.* **dear′ness** *n.* □**Dear John letter,** a letter (originally to a soldier) from a man's wife or girlfriend announcing that she has deserted him. **dear me,** an expression of surprise, distress, sympathy, etc.
dear·ie (deer-ee) *n. (informal)* dear.
dearth (durth) *n.* a scarcity.
death (deth) *n.* 1. the process of dying, the end of life. 2. the state of being dead. 3. a cause of death, *drink was the death of him.* 4. the ending or destruction of something, *the death of our hopes.* □**at death's door,** close to death. **death certificate,** an official statement of the date, place, and cause of a person's death. **death march,** a forced trek on which many die from exhaustion. **death penalty,** punishment for a crime by being put to death. **death rate,** the number of deaths in one year for every 1000 persons. **death rattle,** the sound in a dying person's throat. **death's head,** a picture of a skull as a symbol of death. **put to death,** to kill, to execute. **to death,** extremely, to the utmost limit, *bored to death.* **to the death,** until one or the other is killed, *a fight to the death.*
death·bed (deth-bed) *n.* the bed on which a person is dying or dies.
death·blow (deth-bloh) *n.* a blow that causes death.
death·less (deth-lis) *adj.* immortal.
death·ly (deth-lee) *adj. & adv.* like death, *a deathly hush; deathly pale.*
death·trap (deth-trap) *n.* a dangerous place or structure.
death·watch (deth-woch) *n.* a vigil kept over the dying or dead. □**death watch beetle,** a beetle whose larva bores holes in old wood and makes a ticking sound.
deb (deb) *n. (informal)* debutante.
de·ba·cle (di-bah-kĕl) *n.* a sudden disastrous collapse.
de·bar (di-bahr) *v.* **(de·barred, de·bar·ring)** to exclude, to prohibit.
de·bark (di-bahrk) *v.* to disembark. **de·bar·ka·tion** (dee-bahr-kay-shŏn) *n.*
de·base (di-bays) *v.* **(de·based, de·bas·ing)** to lower in quality or value. **de·base′ment** *n.*
de·bat·a·ble (di-bay-tă-bĕl) *adj.* questionable, open to dispute. **de·bat′a·bly** *adv.*
de·bate (di-bayt) *n.* a formal discussion. **debate** *v.* **(de·bat·ed, de·bat·ing)** 1. to hold a debate about. 2. to discuss, to consider. **de·bat′er** *n.* □**debating society,** a group formed to practice debating.
de·bauch (di-bawch) *v.* to make dissolute, to lead into debauchery.
de·bauch·er·y (di-baw-chĕ-ree) *n.* *(pl.* **-er·ies)** indulgence in harmful or immoral pleasures.
de·ben·ture (di-ben-chŭr) *n.* a certificate or bond acknowledging a debt on which fixed interest is being paid.
de·bil·i·tate (di-bil-i-tayt) *v.* **(de·bil·i·tat·ed, de·bil·i·tat·ing)** to cause debility in.
de·bil·i·ty (di-bil-i-tee) *n.* *(pl.* **-ties)** feebleness, weakness.
deb·it (deb-it) *n.* an entry in a ledger or other ac-

counting record of a debt. **debit** *v.* **(deb·it·ed, deb·it·ing)** to enter as a debit in an account.
deb·o·nair (deb-ŏ-nair) *adj.* having a carefree self-confident manner.
de·bouch (di-boosh) *v.* to march out of a ravine, wood, etc. into an open area.
de·brief (dee-breef) *v. (informal)* to question (a person) after his completion of a mission.
de·bris (dĕ-bree) *n.* scattered broken pieces.
debt (det) *n.* something owed by one person to another. □**debt of honor,** a gambling debt. **in a person's debt,** under obligation to him. **in debt,** owing something. **out of debt,** having paid what one owes.
debt·or (det-ŏr) *n.* a person who owes money to another.
de·bug (dee-bug) *v.* **(de·bugged, de·bug·ging)** to free from bugs (= insects, faults and errors, or secret microphones).
de·bunk (di-bungk) *v. (informal)* to show up (a claim or theory) as exaggerated or false.
de·but (day-byoo) *n.* a first appearance on the stage, in society, etc. ▷Do not use *debut* as a verb.
deb·u·tante (deb-yuu-tahnt) *n.* a girl making her first appearance in society.
dec. *abbr.* 1. deceased. 2. decimeter. 3. declared. 4. declension. 5. declination. 6. decrease. 7. decrescendo.
Dec. *abbr.* December.
dec·ade (dek-ayd) *n.* a period of ten years.
dec·a·dent (dek-ă-dĕnt) *adj.* becoming less worthy, deteriorating in standard. **dec′a·dence** *n.*
de·caf·fein·at·ed (dee-kaf-ĕ-nay-tid) *adj.* with the caffeine removed or reduced.
dec·a·gon (dek-ă-gon) *n.* a geometric figure with ten sides. **de·cag·o·nal** (de-kag-ŏ-năl) *adj.*
dec·a·gram = dekagram.
dec·a·he·dron (dek-ă-hee-drŏn) *n.* *(pl.* **-drons, -dra,** *pr.* -dră) a solid body with ten sides.
de·cal (dee-kal) *n.* 1. a picture transferred from paper to china or other material. 2. the paper bearing this picture.
de·cal·co·ma·ni·a (di-kal-kŏ-may-ni-ă) *n.* decal.
dec·a·li·ter = dekaliter.
Dec·a·logue (dek-ă-log) *n.* the Ten Commandments.
dec·a·me·ter = dekameter.
de·camp (di-kamp) *v.* to go away suddenly or secretly.
de·cant (di-kant) *v.* to pour (liquid) gently from one container into another without disturbing the sediment. **de·can·ta·tion** (di-kan-tay-shŏn) *n.*
de·cant·er (di-kan-tĕr) *n.* a stoppered glass bottle into which wine etc. may be decanted before serving.
de·cap·i·tate (di-kap-ĭ-tayt) *v.* **(de·cap·i·tat·ed, de·cap·i·tat·ing)** to behead. **de·cap·i·ta·tion** (di-kap-ĭ-tay-shŏn) *n.*
dec·a·syl·la·ble (dek-ă-si-lab-ĕl) *n.* a verse of ten syllables. **dec·a·syl·lab′ic** *adj.*
de·cath·lon (di-kath-lon) *n.* an athletic contest in which each competitor takes part in ten events.
de·cay (di-kay) *v.* 1. to become rotten, to cause to rot. 2. to lose quality or strength. **decay** *n.* decaying, rot.
de·cease (di-sees) *n. (formal)* death. **decease** *v.* **(de·ceased, de·ceas·ing)** *(formal)* to die.
de·ceased (di-seest) *adj.* dead; *the deceased,* the person(s) who died recently.
de·ce·dent (di-see-dĕnt) *n. (formal)* a deceased person.

de·ceit (di-seet) *n.* deceiving, a deception.
de·ceit·ful (di-seet-fŭl) *adj.* deceiving people.
de·ceit'ful·ly *adv.* de·ceit'ful·ness *n.*
de·ceive (di-seev) *v.* (de·ceived, de·ceiv·ing) 1. to cause (a person) to believe something that is not true. 2. to be sexually unfaithful to. de·ceiv'er *n.*
de·cel·er·ate (dee-sel-ĕ-rayt) *v.* (de·cel·er·at·ed, de·cel·er·at·ing) to cause to slow down, to decrease one's speed. de·cel·er·a·tion (dee-sel-ĕ-ray-shŏn) *n.*
De·cem·ber (di-sem-bĕr) *n.* the twelfth month of the year.
de·cen·cy (dee-sĕn-see) *n.* (*pl.* -cies) 1. being decent. 2. propriety, conforming to respectable behavior.
de·cen·ni·al (di-sen-ee-ăl) *adj.* lasting or recurring every ten years. de·cen'ni·al·ly *adv.*
de·cent (dee-sĕnt) *adj.* 1. conforming to the accepted standards of what is proper, not immodest or obscene. 2. respectable, *ordinary decent people.* 3. (*informal*) quite good, *earns a decent salary.* 4. (*informal*) kind, generous, obliging. de'cent·ly *adv.*
de·cen·tral·ize (dee-sen-tră-lız) *v.* (de·cen·tral·ized, de·cen·tral·iz·ing) to divide and distribute (powers etc.) from a central authority to places or branches away from the center. de·cen·tral·i·za·tion (dee-sen-tră-li-zay-shŏn) *n.* the process of doing this.
de·cep·tion (di-sep-shŏn) *n.* 1. deceiving, being deceived. 2. something that deceives people.
de·cep·tive (di-sep-tiv) *adj.* deceiving, easily mistaken for something else. de·cep'tive·ly *adv.* de·cep'tive·ness *n.*
dec·i·bel (des-ĭ-bĕl) *n.* a unit for measuring the relative loudness of sound.
de·cide (di-sıd) *v.* (de·cid·ed, de·cid·ing) 1. to think about and make a choice or judgment, to come to a decision. 2. to settle by giving victory to one side, *this goal decided the game.* 3. to cause to reach a decision, *that decided me.* de·cid'er *n.*
de·cid·ed (di-sı-did) *adj.* 1. determined, unhesitating. 2. clear, definite, *a decided difference.* de·cid'ed·ly *adv.*
de·cid·u·ous (di-sij-oo-ŭs) *adj.* 1. (of a tree) shedding its leaves annually. 2. falling off or shed after a time, *a deer has deciduous antlers.*
dec·i·gram (des-ĭ-gram) *n.* one-tenth of a gram.
dec·i·li·ter (des-ĭ-lee-tĕr) *n.* one-tenth of a liter.
dec·i·mal (des-ĭ-măl) *adj.* reckoned in tens or tenths. decimal *n.* a decimal fraction. □decimal currency, currency in which each unit is ten or one hundred times the value of the one next below it. decimal fraction, a fraction whose denominator is a power of ten, expressed in figures after a dot (the decimal point), as 0.5 = 5/10, 0.52 = 52/100. decimal system, a system of weights and measures with each unit ten times that immediately below it.
dec·i·mal·ize (des-ĭ-mă-lız) *v.* (dec·i·mal·ized, dec·i·mal·iz·ing) 1. to express as a decimal. 2. to convert to a decimal system. dec·i·mal·i·za·tion (des-ĭ-mă-li-zay-shŏn) *n.*
dec·i·mate (des-ĭ-mayt) *v.* (dec·i·mat·ed, dec·i·mat·ing) to destroy one-tenth of, to destroy a large proportion of. dec·i·ma·tion (des-ĭ-may-shŏn) *n.*
dec·i·me·ter (des-ĭ-mee-tĕr) *n.* one-tenth of a meter.

de·ci·pher (di-sı-fĕr) *v.* to make out the meaning of (a coded message, bad handwriting, or something difficult to interpret). de·ci'pher·a·ble *adj.*
de·ci·sion (di-sizh-ŏn) *n.* 1. deciding, making a reasoned judgment about something. 2. the judgment itself. 3. the ability to form clear opinions and act on them.
de·ci·sive (di-sı-siv) *adj.* 1. settling something conclusively, *a decisive battle.* 2. showing decision and firmness, *a decisive manner.* de·ci'sive·ly *adv.* de·ci'sive·ness *n.*
deck[1] (dek) *n.* 1. any of the horizontal floors in a ship. 2. a similar floor or platform, especially one of two or more. 3. (also tape deck) the part of a tape recorder that holds the tapes and their controls. 4. (*slang*) the ground, the floor. deck *v.* (*slang*) to knock to the floor. □hit the deck, (*slang*) fall to the ground.
deck[2] *v.* to decorate, to dress up, *decked with flags; decked out in her finest clothes.*
deck·chair (dek-chair) *n.* a portable folding chair of canvas on a wood or metal frame.
deck·hand (dek-hand) *n.* a seaman who works on deck.
deck·le (dek-ĕl) edge a ragged edge like that on handmade paper. deck'le-edged' *adj.*
de·claim (di-klaym) *v.* to speak or say impressively or dramatically. dec·la·ma·tion (dek-lă-may-shŏn) *n.*
de·clar·a·tor·y (di-klar-ă-tohr-ee) *adj.* explanatory.
de·clare (di-klair) *v.* (de·clared, de·clar·ing) 1. to make known, to announce openly or formally or explicitly. 2. to state firmly, *he declares that he is innocent.* 3. to inform customs officials that one has (goods) on which duty may be payable. de·clar'er *n.* de·clar·a·tive (di-klar-ă-tiv) *adj.* dec·la·ra·tion (dek-lă-ray-shŏn) *n.* □declarative sentence, one that makes a statement. declare war, to announce that a state of war exists.
de·clas·si·fy (dee-klas-ĭ-fı) *v.* (de·clas·si·fied, de·clas·si·fy·ing) to cease to designate (information) as secret.
de·clen·sion (di-klen-shŏn) *n.* 1. declining, deterioration. 2. variation of the form of a noun etc. to give its cases, the class into which a noun etc. is put according to this variation.
de·cline (di-klın) *v.* (de·clined, de·clin·ing) 1. to refuse; *decline the invitation,* say politely that one cannot accept it. 2. to slope downward. 3. to decrease, to lose strength or vigor; *one's declining years,* old age. 4. to give the declensions of (a noun etc.). decline *n.* a gradual decrease or loss of strength. de·clin'a·ble *adj.* dec·li·na·tion (dek-lĭ-nay-shŏn) *n.* □in decline, decreasing.
de·cliv·i·ty (di-kliv-i-tee) *n.* (*pl.* -ties) a downward slope.
de·code (dee-kohd) *v.* (de·cod·ed, de·cod·ing) to put (a coded message) into plain language. de·cod'er *n.*
de·colle·tage (day-kol-tahzh) *n.* a low neckline.
dé·colle·té (day-kol-tay) *adj.* having a low neckline.
de·com·mis·sion (dee-kŏ-mish-ŏn) *v.* to remove (a ship etc.) from active service.
de·com·pose (dee-kŏm-pohz) *v.* (de·com·posed, de·com·pos·ing) 1. to separate (a substance etc.) into its parts. 2. to decay, to cause

to decay. **de·com·po·si·tion** (dee-kom-pŏ-zish-ŏn) *n.*

de·com·press (dee-kŏm-pres) *v.* to subject to decompression.

de·com·pres·sion (dee-kŏm-presh-ŏn) *n.* 1. release from compression. 2. the gradual and safe reduction of air pressure on a person who has been in compressed air. □**decompression chamber,** an enclosed space where this can be done.

de·con·gest·ant (dee-kŏn-jes-tănt) *n.* a medicinal substance that relieves nasal congestion.

de·con·tam·i·nate (dee-kŏn-tam-i-nayt) *v.* (**de·con·tam·i·nat·ed, de·con·tam·i·nat·ing**) to rid of radioactive or other contamination. **de·con·tam·i·na·tion** (dee-kŏn-tam-i-nay-shŏn) *n.*

de·con·trol (dee-kŏn-trohl) *v.* (**de·con·trolled, de·con·trol·ling**) to release from government control. **decontrol** *n.* decontrolling.

dé·cor (day-kor) *n.* the style of furnishings and decoration used in a room etc.

dec·o·rate (dek-ŏ-rayt) *v.* (**dec·or·at·ed, dec·or·at·ing**) 1. to make (a thing) look attractive or striking or festive with objects or details added for this purpose. 2. to put fresh paint or paper on the walls etc. of. 3. to confer a medal or other award upon.

dec·o·ra·tion (dek-ŏ-ray-shŏn) *n.* 1. decorating. 2. something that decorates. 3. a medal etc. awarded and worn as an honor. □**Decoration Day,** Memorial Day.

dec·o·ra·tive (dek-ŏ-ră-tiv) *adj.* ornamental, pleasing to look at.

dec·o·ra·tor (dek-ŏ-ray-tŏr) *n.* a person who decorates, especially one whose job is to select and apply paints, fabrics, furnishings, etc.

dec·o·rous (dek-ŏ-rŭs) *adj.* polite and well-behaved, decent. **dec'or·ous·ly** *adv.* **dec'or·ous·ness** *n.*

de·co·rum (di-kohr-ŭm) *n.* correctness and dignity of behavior.

de·cou·page (day-koo-pahzh) *n.* 1. the art of decorating a surface with paper cutouts. 2. work produced by this.

de·coy (dee-koi) *n.* 1. something used to lure an animal or person into a trap or situation of danger. 2. a wooden duck used to attract live ducks. **decoy** (di-koi) *v.* to lure by means of a decoy.

de·crease (di-krees) *v.* (**de·creased, de·creas·ing**) to make or become shorter or smaller or less. **decrease** (dee-krees) *n.* 1. decreasing. 2. the amount by which something decreases.

de·cree (di-kree) *n.* 1. an order given by a government or other authority and having the force of a law. 2. a judgment or decision of certain law courts. **decree** *v.* (**de·creed, de·cree·ing**) to order by decree. □**decree ni·si** (nɪ-sɪ), a provisional order for divorce, made absolute unless cause to the contrary is shown within a fixed period.

dec·re·ment (dek-rĕ-mĕnt) *n.* a decrease, the amount lost by decrease.

de·crep·it (di-krep-it) *adj.* made weak by old age or hard use, dilapidated. **de·crep·i·tude** (di-krep-i-tood) *n.*

de·cre·scen·do (day-krĕ-shen-doh) *adj. & adv.* (in music) decreasing in loudness. **decrescendo** *n.* (*pl.* **-dos**) a decrescendo passage.

de·crim·i·nal·ize (dee-krim-i-nă-lɪz) *v.* (**de·crim·i·nal·ized, de·crim·i·nal·iz·ing**) to remove criminal penalties from (an act). **de·crim·**

i·nal·i·za·tion (dee-krim-i-nă-li-zay-shŏn) *n.*

de·cry (di-krɪ) *v.* (**de·cried, de·cry·ing**) to disparage. ▷Do not confuse *decry* with *descry.*

ded·i·cate (ded-i-kayt) *v.* (**ded·i·cat·ed, ded·i·cat·ing**) 1. to devote to a sacred person or use, *the church is dedicated to St. Peter.* 2. to devote one's time and energy to a special purpose, *he was dedicated to science.* 3. (of an author etc.) to address (a book or piece of music etc.) to a person as a compliment, putting that person's name at the beginning. **ded'i·ca·tor** *n.* **ded·i·ca·tion** (ded-i-kay-shŏn) *n.*

ded·i·ca·to·ry (ded-i-kă-tohr-ee) *adj.* making a dedication, *a dedicatory inscription.*

de·duce (di-doos) *v.* (**de·duced, de·duc·ing**) to arrive at (knowledge) by reasoning, to draw as a conclusion. ▷Do not confuse *deduce* with *deduct.*

de·duc·i·ble (di-doo-si-bĕl) *adj.* able to be deduced. ▷Do not confuse *deducible* with *deductible.*

de·duct (di-dukt) *v.* to take away (an amount or quantity), to subtract. ▷Do not confuse *deduct* with *deduce.*

de·duct·i·ble (di-duk-ti-bĕl) *adj.* 1. able to be deducted. 2. allowable as an income tax deduction. ▷Do not confuse *deductible* with *deducible.*

de·duc·tion (di-duk-shŏn) *n.* 1. deducting, something that is deducted. 2. deducing, a conclusion reached by reasoning. 3. logical reasoning that something must be true because it is a particular case of a general law that is known to be true.

de·duc·tive (di-duk-tiv) *adj.* of or reasoning by deduction.

deed (deed) *n.* 1. something done, an act. 2. a written or printed legal agreement, especially one giving ownership or rights, bearing the giver's signature. **deed** *v.* to convey or transfer by legal deed.

dee·jay (dee-jay) *n.* (*informal*) a disc jockey.

deem (deem) *n.* (*formal*) to believe, to consider, to judge.

de·em·pha·size (dee-em-fă-sɪz) *v.* (**de·em·pha·sized, de·em·pha·siz·ing**) to remove or reduce the emphasis of. **de·em/pha·sis** *n.*

deep (deep) *adj.* 1. going or situated far down or back or in, *a deep cut; deep shelves; a deep sigh,* coming from far down. 2. intense, extreme, *a deep sleep; deep colors,* strong in tone. 3. low-pitched and resonant, not shrill, *a deep voice.* 4. absorbed, *deep in thought.* 5. heartfelt, *deep sympathy.* 6. difficult to understand, obscure, *that's too deep for me; he has deep thoughts.* **deep** *adv.* deeply, far down or in. **deep** *n.* a deep place; *the deep,* the sea. **deep'ly** *adv.* **deep'ness** *n.* □**deep space,** the far distant regions beyond Earth's atmosphere or those beyond the solar system. **go off the deep end,** (*informal*) to give way to emotion.

deep·en (dee-pĕn) *v.* to make or become deep or deeper.

deep-freeze (deep-freez) *v.* (**deep-freezed** or **deep-froze, deep-freezed** or **deep-fro·zen, deep-freez·ing**) to freeze (food) quickly for storage. **deep-freeze** *n.* (*informal*) a freezer.

deep-fry (deep-frɪ) *v.* (**deep-fried, deep-fry·ing**) to fry in fat deep enough to cover (the food).

deep-root·ed (deep-roo-tid) *adj.* deep-seated.

deep-sea (deep-see) *adj.* of the deeper parts of the ocean, *deep-sea fishing.*

deep-seat·ed (deep-see-tid) *adj.* firmly established, not superficial, *a deep-seated distrust.*

deep-set (deep-set) *adj.* set far in.

deep-six (deep-siks) *v. (slang)* to throw overboard, to destroy.

deer (deer) *n. (pl.* **deer**) a ruminant swift-footed animal, the male of which usually has antlers. □**deer fly,** a small bloodsucking fly.

deer·skin (deer-skin) *n.* the skin of a deer, leather made from this.

deer·stalk·er (deer-staw-kĕr) *n.* a soft cloth cap with one peak in front and another at the back.

de·es·ca·late (dee-es-kă-layt) *v.* **(de·es·ca·lat·ed, de·es·ca·lat·ing)** to reduce the level or intensity of. **de·es·ca·la·tion** (dee-es-kă-lay-shŏn) *n.*

def. *abbr.* 1. defective. 2. defendant. 3. defense. 4. deferred. 5. defined. 6. definite. 7. definition.

de·face (di-fays) *v.* **(de·faced, de·fac·ing)** to spoil or damage the surface of. **de·face′ment** *n.*

de fac·to (dee fak-toh) existing in fact (whether by right or not). ▷Latin.

de·fal·ca·tion (dee-fal-kay-shŏn) *n.* misappropriation of funds, a breach of trust concerning money.

de·fam·a·to·ry (di-fam-ă-tohr-ee) *adj.* defaming.

de·fame (di-faym) *v.* **(de·famed, de·fam·ing)** to attack the good reputation of, to speak ill of. **def·a·ma·tion** (def-ă-may-shŏn) *n.*

de·fault (di-fawlt) *v.* to fail to fulfill one's obligations. **default** *n.* failure to fulfill an obligation or to appear; *they won by default,* because the other side did not appear. **de·fault′er** *n.*

de·feat (di-feet) *v.* 1. to win a victory over. 2. to cause to fail, to frustrate, *this defeats our hopes for reform.* 3. to baffle, *the problem defeats me.* **defeat** *n.* 1. defeating others. 2. being defeated, a lost battle or contest.

de·feat·ist (di-fee-tist) *n.* a person who expects to be defeated or accepts defeat too easily. **de·feat′ism** *n.*

def·e·cate (def-ĕ-kayt) *v.* **(def·e·cat·ed, def·e·cat·ing)** to empty the bowels. **def·e·ca·tion** (def-ĕ-kay-shŏn) *n.*

de·fect (dee-fekt, di-fekt) *n.* a deficiency, an imperfection. **defect** (di-fekt) *v.* to desert one's country, to abandon one's allegiance to a cause. **de·fec′tor** *n.* **de·fec·tion** (di-fek-shŏn) *n.*

de·fec·tive (di-fek-tiv) *adj.* 1. having defects, imperfect, incomplete. 2. (of a person) mentally deficient. **de·fec′tive·ly** *adv.* **de·fec′tive·ness** *n.*

de·fend (di-fend) *v.* 1. to protect by warding off an attack. 2. to try to preserve; *the champion is defending his title,* trying to defeat one who challenges him. 3. to uphold by argument, to put forward a justification of. 4. to represent (the defendant) in a lawsuit. **de·fend′er** *n.*

de·fend·ant (di-fen-dănt) *n.* a person accused or sued in a lawsuit.

de·fense (di-fens) *n.* 1. defending from or resistance against attack. 2. something that defends or protects against attack. 3. a justification put forward in response to an accusation. 4. the defendant's case in a lawsuit, the lawyer(s) representing an accused person.

de·fense·less (di-fens-lĭs) *adj.* having no defense, unable to defend oneself.

de·fen·si·ble (di-fen-sĭ-bĕl) *adj.* able to be defended. **de·fen′si·bly** *adv.* **de·fen·si·bil·i·ty** (di-fen-sĭ-bil-i-tee) *n.*

de·fen·sive (di-fen-siv) *adj.* used or done for defense, protective. **de·fen′sive·ly** *adv.* □**on the defensive,** in an attitude of defense, ready to defend oneself against criticism).

de·fer[1] (di-fur) *v.* **(de·ferred, de·fer·ring)** 1. to put off to a later time, to postpone. 2. to grant (a person) a delay in being drafted. **de·fer·ment** (di-fur-mĕnt) *n.*

defer[2] *v.* **(de·ferred, de·fer·ring)** to give way to a person's wishes or judgment or authority, to yield.

def·er·ence (def-ĕ-rĕns) *n.* polite respect. □**in deference to,** out of respect for.

def·er·en·tial (def-ĕ-ren-shăl) *adj.* showing deference. **def·er·en′tial·ly** *adv.*

de·fi·ance (di-fı̄-ăns) *n.* defying, open disobedience, bold resistance.

de·fi·ant (di-fı̄-ănt) *adj.* showing defiance. **de·fi′ant·ly** *adv.*

de·fi·cien·cy (di-fish-ĕn-see) *n. (pl.* **-cies**) 1. being deficient. 2. a lack or shortage, the amount by which something falls short of what is required. □**deficiency disease,** a disease (rickets etc.) caused by lack of vitamins or other essential elements in food.

de·fi·cient (di-fish-ĕnt) *adj.* 1. not having enough, *deficient in vitamins; mentally deficient.* 2. insufficient or not present at all.

def·i·cit (def-ĭ-sit) *n.* 1. the amount by which a total falls short of what is required. 2. the excess of expenditure over income, or of liabilities over assets. □**deficit spending,** expenditure by the government of funds raised by borrowing not by taxation.

de·file[1] (di-fı̄l) *v.* **(de·filed, de·fil·ing)** to make dirty, to pollute. **de·file′ment** *n.*

defile[2] *n.* a narrow way or gorge through which troops must file. **defile** *v.* **(de·filed, de·fil·ing)** to march in file.

de·fin·a·ble (di-fı̄-nă-bĕl) *adj.* able to be defined.

de·fine (di-fı̄n) *v.* **(de·fined, de·fin·ing)** 1. to give a definition of (a word etc.). 2. to state or explain precisely, *customers' rights are defined by the law.* 3. to outline clearly, to mark out the boundary of. **de·fin′er** *n.*

def·i·nite (def-ĭ-nit) *adj.* 1. having exact limits. 2. clear and unmistakable, not vague, *I want a definite answer.* 3. certain, settled, *is it definite that we are to move?* (▷See the note under **definitive.**) **def′i·nite·ly** *adv.* □**definite article,** the word "the."

def·i·ni·tion (def-ĭ-nish-ŏn) *n.* 1. a statement of the precise meaning of a word or phrase, or of the nature of a thing. 2. making or being distinct, clearness of outline.

de·fin·i·tive (di-fin-i-tiv) *adj.* finally fixing or settling something, conclusive. ▷Do not confuse this word with **definite.** A *definite offer* is one that is clearly stated. A *definitive offer* is one that is in its final form and must be accepted or refused without trying to alter its terms. A *definitive edition* of a work is one which has authoritative status.

de·flate (di-flayt) *v.* **(de·flat·ed, de·flat·ing)** 1. to let out air or gas from (an inflated tire etc.). 2. to cause (a person) to lose confidence or self-esteem. 3. to counteract inflation in (a country's economy), as by reducing the amount of money in circulation. 4. to become deflated. **de·fla′tion** *n.* **de·fla·tion·ar·y** (di-flay-shŏ-ner-ee) *adj.*

de·flect (di-flekt) *v.* to turn or cause to turn aside. **de·flec′tion** *n.* **de·flec′tor** *n.*

de·fog (dee-fog) *v.* **(de·fogged, de·fog·ging)** to remove the fog from. **de·fog′ger** *n.*

de·fo·li·ant (dee-foh-li-ănt) *n.* a chemical substance that destroys foliage.

de·fo·li·ate (dee-foh-li-ayt) *v.* (**de·fo·li·at·ed, de·fo·li·at·ing**) to strip of leaves, to destroy foliage by chemical means. **de·fo·li·a·tion** (dee-foh-li-ay-shŏn) *n.*

de·for·est (dee-for-ist) *v.* to clear of forests. **de·for·es·ta·tion** (dee-for-i-stay-shŏn) *n.*

de·form (di-form) *v.* to spoil the form or appearance of, to put out of shape. **de·for·ma·tion** (dee-for-may-shŏn) *n.*

de·formed (di-formd) *adj.* badly or abnormally shaped.

de·form·i·ty (di-for-mi-tee) *n.* (*pl.* **-ties**) 1. being deformed. 2. a deformed part of the body.

de·fraud (di-frawd) *v.* to deprive by fraud.

de·fray (di-fray) *v.* to provide money to pay (costs or expenses). **de·fray'al** *n.*

de·frock (dee-frok) *v.* to unfrock.

de·frost (di-frawst) *v.* 1. to remove frost or ice from. 2. to unfreeze (frozen food), to thaw, *defrost the chicken; let the chicken defrost.* **de·frost'er** *n.*

deft (deft) *adj.* skillful, handling things neatly. **deft'ly** *adv.* **deft'ness** *n.*

de·funct (di-fungkt) *adj.* 1. dead. 2. no longer existing or used or functioning.

de·fuse (dee-fyooz) *v.* (**de·fused, de·fus·ing**) 1. to remove the fuse of, to make (an explosive) unable to explode. 2. to reduce the dangerous tension in (a situation).

de·fy (di-fı) *v.* (**de·fied, de·fy·ing**) 1. to resist openly, to refuse to obey. 2. to challenge (a person) to try and do something that one believes he cannot or will not do, *I defy you to prove this.* 3. to offer difficulties that cannot be overcome, *the door defied all attempts to open it.*

deg. *abbr.* degree(s).

de·gas (di-gas) *v.* (**de·gassed, de·gas·sing**) to remove gas from.

de·gauss (dee-gows) *v.* to demagnetize (a television receiver, ship, etc.).

de·gen·er·ate (di-jen-ĕ-rayt) *v.* (**de·gen·er·at·ed, de·gen·er·at·ing**) to become worse or lower in standard, to lose good qualities. **degenerate** (di-jen-ĕ-rit) *adj.* having degenerated. **degenerate** *n.* a degenerate person or animal. **de·gen·er·ac·y** (di-jen-ĕ-ră-see) *n.* **de·gen·er·a·tion** (di-jen-ĕ-ray-shŏn) *n.* **de·gen·er·a·tive** (di-jen-ĕ-ră-tiv) *adj.*

de·grade (di-grayd) *v.* (**de·grad·ed, de·grad·ing**) 1. to reduce to a lower rank or status. 2. to bring disgrace or contempt on. **deg·ra·da·tion** (deg-ră-day-shŏn) *n.* **de·grad·a·ble** *adj.*

de·grad·ing (di-gray-ding) *adj.* shaming, humiliating.

de·gree (di-gree) *n.* 1. a step or stage in an ascending or descending series. 2. a stage in intensity or amount, *a high degree of skill.* 3. an academic rank awarded to a person who has successfully completed a course of study or as an honor. 4. a unit of measurement for angles or arcs, indicated by the symbol °, as 45°. 5. a unit of measurement in a scale, as of temperatures, *water freezes at 32° F.* □**by degrees**, step by step, gradually.

de·horn (dee-horn) *v.* to remove the horns from (an animal).

de·hu·man·ize (dee-hyoo-mă-nız) *v.* (**de·hu·man·ized, de·hu·man·iz·ing**) to take away human qualities, to make impersonal or machine-like. **de·hu·man·i·za·tion** (dee-hyoo-mă-ni-zay-shŏn) *n.*

de·hu·mid·i·fy (dee-hyoo-mid-ı-fı) *v.* (**de·hu·mid·i·fied, de·hu·mid·i·fy·ing**) to remove moisture from (air etc.). **de·hu·mid'i·fi·er** *n.* **de·hu·mid·i·fi·ca·tion** (dee-hyoo-mid-ı-fi-kay-shŏn) *n.*

de·hy·drate (dee-hı-drayt) *v.* (**de·hy·drat·ed, de·hy·drat·ing**) 1. to remove the moisture content from. 2. to lose moisture. **de·hy·dra·tion** (dee-hı-dray-shŏn) *n.*

de·hy·dro·ge·nate (dee-hı-droj-ĕ-nayt) *v.* (**de·hy·dro·ge·nat·ed, de·hy·dro·gen·at·ing**) to remove hydrogen from (a compound). **de·hy·dro·ge·na·tion** (dee-hı-droj-ĕ-nay-shŏn) *n.*

de·ice (dee-ıs) *v.* (**de·iced, de·ic·ing**) to remove or prevent the formation of ice on (a windshield or other surface). **de·ic'er** *n.*

de·i·fy (dee-ı-fı) *v.* (**de·i·fied, de·i·fy·ing**) to make a god of, to treat as a god. **de·i·fi·ca·tion** (dee-ı-fi-kay-shŏn) *n.*

deign (dayn) *v.* to condescend, to be kind or gracious enough to do something, *she did not deign to reply.*

de·i·on·ize (dee-ı-ŏ-nız) *v.* (**de·i·on·ized, de·i·on·iz·ing**) to remove ions or ionic constituents (from water etc.). **de·i·on·i·za·tion** (dee-ı-ŏ-ni-zay-shŏn) *n.*

de·ism (dee-iz-ĕm) *n.* belief in the existence of a god without accepting revelation. **de'ist** *n.* **de·is·tic** (dee-is-tik) *adj.*

de·i·ty (dee-ı-tee) *n.* (*pl.* **-ties**) 1. a god or goddess, *Roman deities; the Deity,* God. 2. divinity.

dé·jà vu (day-zhah voo) a mistaken feeling of having experienced the present situation before. ▷French. Do not make the mistake of using *déjà vu* when describing a situation you have experienced before.

de·jec·ted (di-jek-tid) *adj.* in low spirits, depressed. **de·jec'ed·ly** *adv.*

de·jec·tion (di-jek-shŏn) *n.* lowness of spirits, depression.

de ju·re (dee joor-ee) rightful, by right. ▷Latin.

dek·a·gram (dek-ă-gram) *n.* ten grams, 0.353 ounce.

dek·a·li·ter (dek-ă-lee-tĕr) *n.* ten liters, 9.08 quarts (dry), 2.64 gallons (liquid).

dek·a·me·ter (dek-ă-mee-tĕr) *n.* ten meters, 32.81 feet.

del. *abbr.* 1. delegate. 2. delegation. 3. delete.

Del. *abbr.* Delaware.

Del·a·ware (del-ă-wair) 1. a state of the U.S. 2. a member or language of an Indian tribe, originally of the Delaware River Valley. **Del·a·war·e·an** (del-ă-wair-ee-ăn) *adj.* & *n.*

de·lay (di-lay) *v.* 1. to make or be late, to hinder. 2. to put off until later, to postpone. **delay** *n.* 1. delaying, being delayed. 2. the amount of time for which something is delayed, *a two-hour delay.*

de·lec·ta·ble (di-lek-tă-bĕl) *adj.* delightful, enjoyable.

de·lec·ta·tion (dee-lek-tay-shŏn) *n.* enjoyment, delight, *for your delectation.*

del·e·gate (del-ĕ-git, -gayt) *n.* a person who represents others and acts according to their instructions. **delegate** (del-ĕ-gayt) *v.* (**del·e·gat·ed, del·e·gat·ing**) to entrust (a task, power, or responsibility) to an agent.

del·e·ga·tion (del-ĕ-gay-shŏn) *n.* 1. delegating. 2. a body of delegates.

de·lete (di-leet) *v.* (**de·let·ed, de·let·ing**) to

strike out (something written or printed), *several words were deleted by the censor.* **de·le·tion** (di-lee-shŏn) *n.*

del·e·te·ri·ous (del-ĕ-teer-i-ŭs) *adj.* harmful to the body or mind.

delft (delft) *n.* a kind of glazed earthenware, usually decorated in blue.

delft·ware (delft-wair) *n.* delft.

Del·hi (del-ee) the capital of India.

del·i (del-ee) *n.* (*pl.* **-is**) *(informal)* delicatessen.

de·lib·er·ate (di-lib-ĕ-rit) *adj.* 1. done or said on purpose, intentional, *a deliberate insult.* 2. slow and careful, unhurried, *entered with deliberate steps.* **deliberate** (di-lib-ĕ-rayt) *v.* **(de·lib·er·at·ed, de·lib·er·at·ing)** to think over or discuss carefully before reaching a decision. **de·lib'er·ate·ly** *adv.* **de·lib'er·ate·ness** *n.*

de·lib·er·a·tion (di-lib-ĕ-ray-shŏn) *n.* 1. careful consideration or discussion. 2. careful slowness.

de·lib·er·a·tive (di-lib-ĕ-ray-tiv) *adj.* for the purpose of deliberating or discussing things, a *deliberative assembly.*

del·i·ca·cy (del-i-kä-see) *n.* (*pl.* **-cies**) 1. delicateness. 2. avoidance of what is immodest or offensive or hurtful to others. 3. a choice food.

del·i·cate (del-i-kit) *adj.* 1. fine in texture, soft, slender. 2. of exquisite quality or workmanship. 3. (of color or flavor) pleasant and not strong or intense. 4. easily injured, liable to illness, (of plants) unable to withstand cold. 5. requiring skill or careful handling, *a delicate operation; the situation is delicate.* 6. skillful and sensitive, *has a delicate touch.* 7. taking great care to avoid what is immodest or offensive or hurtful to others. **del'i·cate·ly** *adv.* **del'i·cate·ness** *n.*

del·i·ca·tes·sen (del-i-kä-tes-ĕn) *n.* 1. a store selling prepared delicacies such as salads, cooked meats, and smoked fish. 2. these foods.

de·li·cious (di-lish-ŭs) *adj.* delightful, especially to the senses of taste or smell. **de·li'cious·ly** *adv.*

de·light (di-lrt) *v.* 1. to please greatly. 2. to be greatly pleased, to feel great pleasure, *she delights in giving surprises.* **delight** *n.* 1. great pleasure. 2. something that causes this. **de·light'ed** *adj.* **de·light'ed·ly** *adv.*

de·light·ful (di-lrt-fŭl) *adj.* giving delight. **de·light'ful·ly** *adv.*

De·li·lah (di-lr-lä) *n.* a seductive and treacherous woman. ▷From a woman in the Bible who betrayed Samson to the Philistines.

de·lim·it (di-lim-it) *v.* to fix the limits or boundaries of. **de·lim·i·ta·tion** (di-lim-i-tay-shŏn) *n.*

de·lin·e·ate (di-lin-i-ayt) *v.* **(de·lin·e·at·ed, de·lin·e·at·ing)** to show by drawing or by describing. **de·lin·e·a·tion** (di-lin-i-ay-shŏn) *n.*

de·lin·quent (di-ling-kwĕnt) *adj.* committing an offense or failing to perform a duty. **delinquent** *n.* a delinquent person, especially a young offender against the law. **de·lin'quen·cy** *n.* (*pl.* **-cies**).

del·i·quesce (del-i-kwes) *v.* **(del·i·quesced, del·i·quesc·ing)** to become liquid, to melt. **del·i·ques'cent** *adj.*

de·lir·i·ous (di-leer-i-ŭs) *adj.* 1. affected with delirium, raving. 2. wildly excited. **de·lir'i·ous·ly** *adv.*

de·lir·i·um (di-leer-i-ŭm) *n.* (*pl.* **-lir·i·ums, -lir·i·a**, *pr.* -leer-i-ă) 1. a disordered state of mind, especially during feverish illness. 2. wild excitement or emotion. ☐**delirium tre·mens** (tree-mĕnz), a form of delirium with tremors and terrifying delusions, caused chiefly by heavy drinking.

de·liv·er (di-liv-ĕr) *v.* 1. to take (letters or goods etc.) to the addressee or purchaser. 2. to transfer, to hand over, to present. 3. to utter (a speech). 4. to aim or launch (a blow or attack), to pitch (a ball) in baseball etc. 5. to rescue, to save or set free. 6. to give birth to, to assist (a female) in giving birth. **de·liv'er·er** *n.*

de·liv·er·ance (di-liv-ĕ-răns) *n.* rescue, setting free.

de·liv·er·y (di-liv-ĕ-ree) *n.* (*pl.* **-er·ies**) 1. delivering, being delivered. 2. a periodical distribution of letters or goods etc. 3. the manner of delivering a speech, *her delivery was poor.* 4. the manner of pitching a ball, throwing a blow in a fight, etc. 5. a baseball pitch. 6. childbirth. ☐**delivery boy,** a boy who delivers goods ordered from a store.

dell (del) *n.* a small wooded hollow or valley.

de·louse (dee-lows) *v.* **(de·loused, de·lous·ing)** to rid of lice.

del·phin·i·um (del-fin-i-ŭm) *n.* a garden plant with tall spikes of flowers, usually blue.

del·ta (del-tă) *n.* 1. the fourth letter of the Greek alphabet (Δ δ). 2. a triangular patch of land accumulated at the mouth of a river between two or more of its branches, *the Mississippi Delta.* ☐**delta ray,** a ray consisting of low-velocity electrons knocked from an atom during collision with other particles. **delta wing aircraft,** an aircraft with swept-back wings that give it a triangular appearance.

de·lude (di-lood) *v.* **(de·lud·ed, de·lud·ing)** to deceive.

del·uge (del-yooj) *n.* 1. a great flood, a heavy fall of rain; *the Deluge,* the flood in Noah's time. 2. anything coming in a heavy rush, *a deluge of questions.* **deluge** *v.* **(de·luged, de·lug·ing)** to flood, to come down on like a deluge.

de·lu·sion (di-loo-zhŏn) *n.* 1. a false belief or opinion. 2. a persistent false belief that is a symptom or form of madness. **de·lu'sion·al** *adj.* ▷Do not confuse *delusion* with *illusion.*

de·lu·sive (di-loo-siv) *adj.* deceptive, raising vain hopes.

de·luxe (di-luks) *adj.* of very high quality, luxurious.

delve (delv) *v.* **(delved, delv·ing)** to search deeply for information.

Dem. *abbr.* 1. Democrat. 2. Democratic.

de·mag·net·ize (dee-mag-nĕ-tīz) *v.* **(de·mag·net·ized, de·mag·net·iz·ing)** to remove the magnetic properties of. **de·mag·ne·ti·za·tion** (dee-mag-nĕ-ti-zay-shŏn) *n.*

dem·a·gogue (dem-ă-gawg) *n.* a leader or agitator who wins support by appealing to people's feelings and prejudices rather than by reasoning. **dem·a·gogu·er·y** (dem-ă-gaw-gĕ-ree) *n.* **dem·a·go·gy** (dem-ă-goh-jee) *n.*

de·mand (di-mand) *n.* 1. a request made imperiously or as if one had a right. 2. a desire for goods or services by people who wish to buy or use these, *there's a great demand for typists.* 3. an urgent claim, *there are many demands on my time.* **demand** *v.* 1. to make a demand for. 2. to need, *the work demands great skill.* ☐**demand deposit,** a bank deposit that can be withdrawn without advance notice. **in demand,** sought after. **on demand,** as soon as the demand is made, *payable on demand.*

de·mand·ing (di-man-ding) *adj.* 1. making many

demands. 2. requiring much skill or effort, *a demanding job.*

de·mar·cate (di-mahr-kayt) *v.* **(de·mar·cat·ed, de·mar·cat·ing)** to mark the boundaries of. **de·mar·ca·tion** (di-mahr-kay-shŏn) *n.*

dé·marche (day-mahrsh) *n.* a step or proceeding in politics etc., especially one initiating fresh policy. ▷French.

de·mean (di-meen) *v.* to lower the dignity of, *I wouldn't demean myself to ask for it.*

de·mean·or (di-mee-nŏr) *n.* the way a person behaves.

de·ment·ed (di-men-tid) *adj.* driven mad, crazy. **de·ment′ed·ly** *adv.*

de·men·tia (di-men-shă) *n.* a mental illness in which there is loss of reasoning power. ☐**dementia prae·cox** (pree-koks), schizophrenia.

de·mer·it (dee-mer-it) *n.* 1. a fault, a defect. 2. a mark against a person's school record.

de·mesne (di-mayn) *n.* 1. a domain 2. a landed estate.

dem·i·god (dem-ee-god) *n.* 1. the offspring of a god and a mortal. 2. a person who seems to have godlike powers.

dem·i·john (dem-ee-jon) *n.* a bulging narrow-necked bottle holding three to ten gallons.

de·mil·i·tar·ize (dee-mil-i-tă-rɪz) *v.* **(de·mil·i·ta·rized, de·mil·i·ta·riz·ing)** to remove military forces, installations, etc. from. **de·mil·i·tar·i·za·tion** (dee-mil-i-tă-ri-zay-shŏn) *n.* ☐**demilitarized zone,** an area required (by treaty or agreement) to have no military forces or installations in it.

dem·i·mon·daine (dem-ee-mon-dayn) *n.* a woman of the demimonde.

dem·i·monde (dem-ee-mond) *n.* the world of women of doubtful reputation and social standing.

de·mise (di-mɪz) *n. (formal)* death.

dem·i·tasse (dem-ee-tas) *n.* 1. a small cup for after-dinner coffee. 2. its contents. ☐**demitasse spoon,** a small spoon for demitasse.

dem·o (dem-oh) *n.* (*pl.* **dem·os**) *(informal)* 1. a demonstration. 2. an item used for demonstration (as an automobile or radio).

de·mo·bi·lize (dee-moh-bĭ-lɪz) *v.* **(de·mo·bil·ized, de·mob·il·iz·ing)** 1. to release from military service. 2. to reduce or disband military forces. **de·mo·bi·li·za·tion** (dee-moh-bĭ-li-zay-shŏn) *n.*

de·moc·ra·cy (di-mok-ră-see) *n.* (*pl.* **-cies**) 1. government by the whole people of a country, especially through representatives whom they elect. 2. a country governed in this way.

dem·o·crat (dem-ŏ-krat) *n.* 1. a person who favors democracy. 2. *Democrat,* a member of the Democratic Party in the U.S.

dem·o·crat·ic (dem-ŏ-krat-ik) *adj.* 1. of or like or supporting democracy. 2. in accordance with the principle of equal rights for all, *a democratic decision.* 3. *Democratic,* of the Democratic Party. **dem·o·crat′i·cal·ly** *adv.*

de·moc·ra·tize (di-mok-ră-tɪz) *v.* **(de·moc·ra·tized, de·moc·ra·tiz·ing)** to make democratic. **de·moc·ra·ti·za·tion** (di-mok-ră-ti-zay-shŏn) *n.*

dé·mo·dé (day-mo-day) *adj.* out of fashion. ▷French.

de·mog·ra·phy (di-mog-ră-fee) *n.* the scientific study of population statistics relating to births, deaths, diseases, etc. **de·mog′ra·pher** *n.* **de·**

mo·graph·ic (dee-mŏ-graf-ik) *adj.* **de·mo·graph′ic·al·ly** *adv.*

de·mol·ish (di-mol-ish) *v.* 1. to pull or knock down (a building). 2. to destroy (a person's argument or theory etc.). 3. *(informal)* to eat up. **dem·o·li·tion** (dem-ŏ-lish-ŏn) *n.*

de·mon (dee-mŏn) *n.* 1. a devil or evil spirit. 2. a cruel or forceful person. **demon** *adj.* 1. like, of a demon. 2. *(informal)* energetic, forceful, skilled, *a demon worker.*

de·mon·e·tize (dee-mon-ĕ-tɪz) *v.* **(de·mon·e·tized, de·mon·e·tiz·ing)** to withdraw (coins or bills) from use as money. **de·mon·e·ti·za·tion** (dee-mon-ĕ-ti-zay-shŏn) *n.*

de·mo·ni·ac (dee-moh-ni-ak) *adj.* 1. of or like a demon. 2. possessed by an evil spirit. 3. fiercely energetic, frenzied.

de·mo·ni·a·cal (dee-mŏ-nɪ-ă-kăl) *adj.* of or like a demon.

de·mon·ic (di-mon-ik) *adj.* of or like a demon. **de·mon′i·cal** *adj.*

de·mon·ol·o·gy (dee-mŏ-nol-ŏ-jee) *n.* the study of demons, belief in demons.

de·mon·stra·ble (di-mon-stră-bĕl) *adj.* able to be shown or proved. **de·mon′stra·bly** *adv.*

dem·on·strate (dem-ŏn-strayt) *v.* **(dem·on·strat·ed, dem·on·strat·ing)** 1. to show evidence of, to prove. 2. to describe and explain by the help of specimens or examples; *demonstrate the machine to customers,* show them how it works. 3. to take part in a demonstration. **dem′on·stra·tor** *n.*

dem·on·stra·tion (dem-ŏn-stray-shŏn) *n.* 1. demonstrating. 2. a show of feeling. 3. an organized gathering or march to express the opinion of a group publicly. 4. a display of military force.

de·mon·stra·tive (di-mon-stră-tiv) *adj.* 1. showing or proving. 2. expressing one's feelings openly; *she is not a demonstrative child,* does not readily show affection openly. 3. (in grammar) indicating the person or thing referred to, as *this* in *"this is wrong; this hat is right for me."* **demonstrative** *n.* a demonstrative word. **de·mon′stra·tive·ly** *adv.* **de·mon′stra·tive·ness** *n.* ☐**demonstrative pronoun,** *see* **pronoun.**

de·mor·al·ize (di-mor-ă-lɪz) *v.* **(de·mor·a·lized, de·mor·a·liz·ing)** to weaken the morale of, to dishearten. **de·mor·al·i·za·tion** (di-mor-ă-li-zay-shŏn) *n.*

de·mote (di-moht) *v.* **(de·mot·ed, de·mot·ing)** to reduce to a lower rank or category. **de·mo·tion** (di-moh-shŏn) *n.*

de·mot·ic (di-mot-ik) *adj.* of ordinary people. **demotic** *n.* demotic language or style etc.

de·mul·cent (di-mul-sĕnt) *n.* a soothing medicine. **demulcent** *adj.* soothing.

de·mur (di-mur) *v.* **(de·murred, de·mur·ring)** to raise objections, *they demurred at working on Sundays.* **demur** *n.* an objection raised, *they went without demur.* **de·mur′ral** *n.* a demur.

de·mure (di-myoor) *adj.* quiet and serious or pretending to be so. **de·mure′ly** *adv.* **de·mure′ness** *n.*

de·mur·rage (di-mur-ij) *n.* 1. the amount payable to a shipowner by the person or company that leases his ship for failure to load or unload the ship within the time allowed. 2. a similar charge with respect to a truck or railroad. 3. such a delay.

den (den) *n.* 1. a wild animal's lair. 2. a place where people gather for some illegal activity, *a gambling den; a den of iniquity.* 3. a small room in which a person shuts himself away to work or relax.

Den. *abbr.* Denmark.

de·na·tion·al·ize (dee-nash-ŏ-nă-lɪz) *v.* (**de·na·tion·al·ized, de·na·tion·al·iz·ing**) to transfer (an industry) from national to private ownership. **de·na·tion·al·i·za·tion** (dee-nash-ŏ-nă-li-zay-shŏn) *n.*

de·na·tured (dee-nay-chŭrd) *adj.* having had its natural qualities changed; *denatured alcohol,* alcohol made unfit for drinking but remaining usable for other purposes.

den·drol·o·gy (den-drol-ŏ-jee) *n.* the scientific study of trees. **den·drol'o·gist** *n.* **den·dro·log·ic** (den-drŏ-loj-ik) *adj.* **den·dro·log'i·cal** *adj.*

den·gue (deng-gay) *n.* infectious tropical fever causing acute pains in the joints.

de·ni·a·ble (di-nɪ-ă-bĕl) *adj.* able to be denied.

de·ni·al (di-nɪ-ăl) *n.* 1. denying. 2. a statement that a thing is not true. 3. refusal of a request or wish.

de·nier (dĕ-neer) *n.* a unit of weight by which the fineness of silk, rayon, or nylon yarn is measured.

den·i·grate (den-i-grayt) *v.* (**den·i·grat·ed, den·i·grat·ing**) to blacken the reputation of, to sneer at. **den·i·gra·tion** (den-i-gray-shŏn) *n.*

den·im (den-im) *n.* 1. a strong twilled cotton fabric used for making clothes. 2. *denims,* trousers made of denim.

den·i·zen (den-i-zĕn) *n.* a person or plant living or often present in a particular place, *denizens of the jungle.*

Den·mark (den-mahrk) a country in northern Europe.

de·nom·i·nate (di-nom-i-nayt) *v.* (**de·nom·i·nat·ed, de·nom·i·nat·ing**) 1. to give a name to. 2. to describe (a person or thing) as.

de·nom·i·na·tion (di-nom-i-nay-shŏn) *n.* 1. a name or title. 2. a distinctively named church or religious sect, *Baptists and other Protestant denominations.* 3. a unit of measurement, a unit of money, *coins of small denomination.*

de·nom·i·na·tion·al (di-nom-i-nay-shŏ-năl) *adj.* of a particular religious denomination.

de·nom·i·na·tor (di-nom-i-nay-tŏr) *n.* the number written below the line in a fraction, for example, 4 in ¾, showing how many parts the whole is divided into. □**common denominator,** *see* **common.**

de·no·ta·tion (dee-noh-tay-shŏn) *n.* the explicit meaning of a word, as distinct from its *connotation.* ▷Do not confuse *denotation* with *connotation.*

de·note (di-noht) *v.* (**de·not·ed, de·not·ing**) to be the sign or symbol or name of, to indicate, *on highway signs* **H** *denotes a hospital.* **de·no·ta·tive** (dee-noh-tay-tiv) *adj.*

de·noue·ment, dé·noue·ment (day-noo-mahn) *n.* 1. the clearing up, at the end of a play or story, of the complications of the plot. 2. the outcome of a tangled sequence of events.

de·nounce (di-nowns) *v.* (**de·nounced, de·nounc·ing**) 1. to speak publicly against. 2. to give information against, *denounced him as a spy.* 3. to announce that one is ending (a treaty or agreement). **de·nounc'er** *n.* **de·nounce'ment** *n.*

dense (dens) *adj.* (**dens·er, dens·est**) 1. thick, not easy to see through, *dense fog.* 2. massed closely together, *dense crowds.* 3. stupid. **dense'ly** *adv.* **dense'ness** *n.*

den·si·tom·e·ter (den-si-tom-ĕ-tĕr) *n.* an instrument for measuring photographic density etc.

den·si·ty (den-si-tee) *n.* (*pl.* **-ties**) 1. a dense or concentrated condition, *the density of the fog.* 2. stupidity. 3. the ratio of mass to volume, *the density of water is 62.5 pounds per cubic foot.*

dent (dent) *n.* 1. a depression left by a blow or by pressure. 2. a noticeable reduction, *that purchase made a dent in my bank account.* **dent** *v.* 1. to make a dent in. 2. to become dented. ▷Do not confuse *dent* with *dint.*

dent. *abbr.* 1. dental. 2. dentist. 3. dentistry.

den·tal (den-tăl) *adj.* 1. of or for the teeth. 2. of dentistry, *a dental practice.* **den'tal·ly** *adv.* □**dental floss,** strong thread used for cleaning between the teeth. **dental hygiene,** the care and cleaning of the teeth.

den·tate (den-tayt) *adj.* toothed, with toothlike notches.

den·ti·frice (den-tĭ-fris) *n.* toothpaste or tooth powder.

den·tin (den-tin), **den·tine** (den-teen) *n.* a hard dense tissue forming the main part of teeth.

den·tist (den-tist) *n.* a person who is qualified to fill or extract teeth, fit artificial ones, etc.

den·tis·try (den-ti-stree) *n.* the work or profession of a dentist.

den·ti·tion (den-tish-ŏn) *n.* 1. teething. 2. the characteristic arrangement of teeth.

den·ture (den-chŭr) *n.* a set of artificial teeth.

de·nu·cle·ar·ize (dee-noo-klee-ă-rɪz) *v.* (**de·nu·cle·ar·ized, de·nu·cle·ar·iz·ing**) to remove nuclear arms from. **de·nu·cle·ar·i·za·tion** (dee-noo-klee-ă-ri-zay-shŏn) *n.*

de·nude (di-nood) *v.* (**de·nud·ed, de·nud·ing**) 1. to make naked or bare, to strip the cover from, *the trees were denuded of their leaves.* 2. to deprive, *creditors denuded him of every penny.* **de·nu·da·tion** (dee-noo-day-shŏn) *n.*

de·nun·ci·a·tion (di-nun-si-ay-shŏn) *n.* denouncing.

Den·ver (den-vĕr) the capital of Colorado.

de·ny (di-nɪ) *v.* (**de·nied, de·ny·ing**) 1. to say that (a thing) is not true or does not exist. 2. to disown, to refuse to acknowledge, *Peter denied Christ.* 3. to refuse to give what is asked for or needed, to prevent from having, *no one can deny you your rights.* □**deny oneself,** to restrict one's food or drink or pleasure.

de·o·dor·ant (dee-oh-dŏ-rănt) *n.* a substance that removes or conceals unwanted odors. **deodorant** *adj.* deodorizing.

de·o·dor·ize (dee-oh-dŏ-rɪz) *v.* (**de·o·dor·ized, de·o·dor·iz·ing**) to destroy the odor of. **de·o'dor·iz·er** *n.* **de·o·dor·i·za·tion** (dee-oh-dŏ-ri-zay-shŏn) *n.*

de·ox·i·dize (dee-ok-si-dɪz) *v.* (**de·ox·i·dized, de·ox·i·diz·ing**) to remove oxygen from. **de·ox'i·diz·er** *n.*

de·ox·y·ri·bo·nu·cle·ic (dee-ok-si-rɪ-boh-noo-klee-ik) **acid** *n.* a substance in the chromosomes of higher creatures, storing genetic information.

dep. *abbr.* 1. depart. 2. departed. 3. department. 4. departure. 5. deponent. 6. deposed. 7. deposit. 8. depot. 9. deputy.

de·part (di-pahrt) *v.* 1. to go away, to leave. 2. (of trains or buses) to start, to begin a journey. 3. to cease to follow a particular course, *departing from our normal procedure.*

de·part·ed (di-pahr-tid) *adj.* bygone, *departed glories; the departed,* the dead.

de·part·ment (di-pahrt-mĕnt) *n.* one of the units, each with a specialized function, into which a business, store, or organization is divided. ☐**department store,** a large store in which there are various departments, each dealing in a separate type of goods. **de·part·men·tal** (dee-pahrt-men-tăl) *adj.* of a department.

de·par·ture (di-pahr-chŭr) *n.* 1. departing, going away. 2. setting out on a new course of action or thought.

de·pend (di-pend) *v.* **depend on,** 1. to be controlled or determined by, *whether we can have a picnic depends on the weather.* 2. to be unable to do without, *she depends on my help.* 3. to trust confidently, to feel certain about, *you can depend on John to be there when he's needed.* ☐**depend upon it,** you can be quite certain.

de·pend·a·ble (di-pen-dă-běl) *adj.* able to be relied on. **de·pend'a·bly** *adv.* **de·pend·a·bil·i·ty** (di-pen-dă-bil-i-tee) *n.*

de·pend·ence (di-pen-děns) *n.* depending, being dependent.

de·pend·en·cy (di-pen-děn-see) *n.* (*pl.* **-cies**) a country that is controlled by another.

de·pend·ent (di-pen-děnt) *adj.* 1. depending, conditioned, *promotion is dependent on ability.* 2. needing the help of, unable to do without, *he is dependent on drugs.* 3. controlled by another, not independent, *our dependent territories.* **dependent** *n.* one who depends on another for support, *he has four dependents.*

de·per·son·al·ize (dee-pur-sŏ-nă-lɪz) *v.* (**de·per·son·al·ized, de·per·son·al·iz·ing**) to make impersonal.

de·pict (di-pikt) *v.* 1. to show in the form of a picture. 2. to describe in words. **de·pic·tion** (di-pik-shŏn) *n.*

de·pil·a·to·ry (di-pil-ă-tohr-ee) *n.* (*pl.* **-ries**) a substance that removes superfluous hair. **depilatory** *adj.* removing hair.

de·plane (dee-playn) *v.* (**de·planed, de·plan·ing**) to descend or remove from an airplane.

de·plete (di-pleet) *v.* (**de·plet·ed, de·plet·ing**) to use up large quantities of, to reduce in number or quantity. **de·ple·tion** (di-plee-shŏn) *n.* ☐**depletion allowance,** a tax reduction for industries that deplete their unrenewable resources in the course of doing business.

de·plor·a·ble (di-plohr-ă-běl) *adj.* 1. regrettable. 2. exceedingly bad, shocking. **de·plor'a·bly** *adv.*

de·plore (di-plohr) *v.* (**de·plored, de·plor·ing**) 1. to regret deeply, *we deplore her death.* 2. to find deplorable, *we deplore their incompetence.*

de·ploy (di-ploi) *v.* to spread out, to bring or come into action systematically, *deploying his troops or resources; the ships and aircraft deployed in battle.* **de·ploy'ment** *n.*

de·po·lar·ize (dee-poh-lă-rɪz) *v.* (**de·po·lar·ized, de·po·lar·iz·ing**) 1. to reduce or remove polarization from. 2. to move closer together in opinion after being far apart. **de·po·lar·i·za·tion** (dee-poh-lă-ri-zay-shŏn) *n.* **de·po'lar·i·zer** *n.*

de·pon·ent (di-poh-něnt) *n.* a person making a deposition under oath.

de·pop·u·late (dee-pop-yŭ-layt) *v.* (**de·pop·u·lat·ed, de·pop·u·lat·ing**) to reduce the population of. **de·pop·u·la·tion** (dee-pop-yŭ-lay-shŏn) *n.*

de·port (di-pohrt) *v.* to remove (an unwanted person) from a country. **de·por·ta·tion** (dee-pohr-tay-shŏn) *n.*

de·port·ment (di-pohrt-mĕnt) *n.* behavior, a person's way of conducting himself, *the child's deportment was unacceptable.*

de·pose (di-pohz) *v.* (**de·posed, de·pos·ing**) 1. to remove from power, *the queen was deposed.* 2. to testify or bear witness, especially on oath in court.

de·pos·it (di-poz-it) *n.* 1. a thing deposited for safekeeping. 2. a sum of money paid into a bank. 3. a sum paid as a guaranty or a first installment. 4. a layer of matter deposited or accumulated naturally, *new deposits of copper were found.* **deposit** *v.* 1. to lay or put down, *she deposited the books on the desk.* 2. to store or entrust for safekeeping, to pay (money) into a bank. 3. to pay as a guaranty or first installment. 4. to leave as a layer or covering of matter, *floods deposited mud on the land.* **de·pos'i·tor** *n.* ☐**on deposit,** deposited with a (bank, store, etc.) for safekeeping or as a first installment.

dep·o·si·tion (dep-ŏ-zish-ŏn) *n.* 1. deposing or being deposed from power. 2. a statement made on oath. 3. depositing.

de·pos·i·to·ry (di-poz-i-tohr-ee) *n.* (*pl.* **-ries**) a storehouse, a place for safekeeping of things, *the merchant left his receipts in the night depository.*

de·pot (dee-poh) *n.* 1. a storehouse, especially for military supplies. 2. a place for assembling military recruits and replacement troops. 3. a place where goods are deposited or from which goods, vehicles, etc. are dispatched. 4. a bus station or railroad station.

de·prave (di-prayv) *v.* (**de·praved, de·prav·ing**) to make morally bad, to corrupt. **dep·ra·va·tion** (dep-ră-vay-shŏn) *n.*

de·praved (di-prayvd) *adj.* 1. immoral, wicked, *a depraved character.* 2. made bad, perverted, *depraved tastes.*

de·prav·i·ty (di-prav-i-tee) *n.* (*pl.* **-ties**) moral corruption, wickedness.

dep·re·cate (dep-rĕ-kayt) *v.* (**dep·re·cat·ed, dep·re·cat·ing**) 1. to feel and express disapproval of. 2. to try to turn aside (praise or blame etc.) politely. **dep·re·ca·tion** (dep-rĕ-kay-shŏn) *n.* **dep·re·ca·to·ry** (dep-rĕ-kă-tohr-ee) *adj.* ▷Do not confuse *deprecate* with *depreciate.*

de·pre·ci·ate (di-pree-shi-ayt) *v.* (**de·pre·ci·at·ed, de·pre·ci·at·ing**) 1. to make or become lower in value. 2. to belittle, to disparage. **de·pre·ci·a·tion** (di-pree-shi-ay-shŏn) *n.* ▷Do not confuse *depreciate* with *deprecate.*

de·pre·ci·a·to·ry (di-pree-shi-ă-tohr-ee) *adj.* disparaging.

dep·re·da·tion (dep-rĕ-day-shŏn) *n.* plundering, destruction.

de·press (di-pres) *v.* 1. to make sad, to lower the spirits of. 2. to make less active; *bad news depresses the stock market,* values are reduced. 3. to press down, *depress the lever.* **de·pressed'** *adj.* **de·pres'sor** *n.*

de·pres·sant (di-pres-ănt) *n.* a substance that reduces the activity of the nervous system, a sedative. **depressant** *adj.* depressing.

de·pres·sion (di-presh-ŏn) *n.* 1. a state of excessive sadness or hopelessness, often with physical symptoms. 2. a long period of inactivity in business and trade, with widespread unemployment. 3. a lowering of atmospheric pressure, an area of low pressure that may bring rain. 4. a sunken place or hollow on a surface. 5. pressing down. □**the Depression, the Great Depression,** the business slump that began in 1929 and ended when World War II broke out.

de·pres·sive (di-pres-iv) *adj.* 1. depressing. 2. involving mental depression. **depressive** *n.* a person suffering from mental depression.

de·priv·al (di-prɪ-văl) *n.* depriving, being deprived.

dep·ri·va·tion (dep-ri-vay-shŏn) *n.* 1. deprival 2. a keenly felt loss.

de·prive (di-prɪv) *v.* (**de·prived, de·priv·ing**) to take a thing away from, to prevent from using or enjoying, *the prisoner had been deprived of food.* □**deprived child,** one who has been prevented from having a normal home life.

de·pro·gram (dee-proh-gram) *v.* (**de·pro·gramed, de·pro·gram·ing**) to restore (a person's thought processes) to normal through systematic reindoctrination. **de·pro′gram·er** *n.*

dept. *abbr.* 1. department. 2. deponent. 3. deputy.

depth (depth) *n.* 1. being deep. 2. the distance from the top down, or from the surface inward, or from front to back. 3. deep learning or thought or feeling. 4. intensity of color or darkness. 5. lowness of pitch in a voice or sound. 6. the deepest or most central part, *living in the depths of the forest.* □**depth charge,** a bomb that will explode under water, for use against submarines etc. **in depth,** with thorough and intensive investigations, *studied it in depth; defense in depth,* a system of defense employing successive areas of resistance. **out of** or **beyond one's depth,** in water that is too deep to stand in; attempting something that is beyond one's ability.

dep·u·ta·tion (dep-yŭ-tay-shŏn) *n.* a body of people appointed to go on a mission on behalf of others.

de·pute (di-pyoot) *v.* (**de·put·ed, de·put·ing**) 1. to delegate (a task) to a person. 2. to appoint (a person) to act as one's representative.

dep·u·tize (dep-yŭ-tɪz) *v.* (**de·pu·tized, de·pu·tiz·ing**) to appoint as deputy.

dep·u·ty (dep-yŭ-tee) *n.* (*pl.* **-ties**) 1. a person appointed to act as substitute for another. 2. a member of a legislature in certain countries, *the Chamber of Deputies.* □**deputy sheriff,** an acting sheriff.

der. *abbr.* 1. derivation. 2. derivative. 3. derived.

de·rail (dee-rayl) *v.* 1. to cause (a train) to leave the rails. 2. (of a train) to leave the rails. **de·rail′ment** *n.*

de·range (di-raynj) *v.* (**de·ranged, de·rang·ing**) 1. to throw into confusion, to disrupt. 2. to make insane. **de·range′ment** *n.*

der·by (dur-bee) *n.* (*pl.* **-bies**) 1. a horse race of particular prominence. 2. a contest of any kind open to all, *a roller derby.* 3. (also *derby hat*) a man's stiff felt hat. 4. *the Derby,* the annual horse race at Churchill Downs, Kentucky; the annual horse race at Epsom, near London, England.

der·e·lict (der-ĕ-likt) *adj.* abandoned, deserted and left to fall into ruin. **derelict** *n.* 1. a person who is abandoned by society or who does not fit into a normal social background. 2. an abandoned ship, car, plane, etc.

der·e·lic·tion (der-ĕ-lik-shŏn) *n.* 1. neglect of duty. 2. abandoning, being abandoned.

de·ride (di-rɪd) *v.* (**de·rid·ed, de·rid·ing**) to laugh at scornfully, to treat with scorn.

de ri·gueur (dĕ ree-gur) required by custom or etiquette, *evening dress is de rigueur.* ▷French.

de·ri·sion (di-rizh-ŏn) *n.* scorn, ridicule.

de·ri·sive (di-rɪ-siv) *adj.* scornful, showing derision, *derisive cheers.* **de·ri′sive·ly** *adv.*

de·ri·so·ry (di-rɪ-sŏ-ree) *adj.* 1. derisive. 2. deserving derision, too insignificant for serious consideration, *a derisory offer.*

deriv. *abbr.* 1. derivation. 2. derivative. 3. derived.

der·i·va·tion (der-ĭ-vay-shŏn) *n.* 1. deriving. 2. origin.

de·riv·a·tive (di-riv-ă-tiv) *adj.* derived from a source. **derivative** *n.* a thing that is derived from another.

de·rive (di-rɪv) *v.* (**de·rived, de·riv·ing**) 1. to obtain from a source, *he derived great pleasure from music; some English words are derived from Latin,* originate from Latin words. 2. to be descended, *some English words derive from Latin.* 3. to show or assert that something is derived from (a source).

der·mal (dur-măl) *adj.* of the skin.

der·ma·ti·tis (dur-mă-tɪ-tis) *n.* inflammation of the skin.

der·ma·tol·o·gist (dur-mă-tol-ŏ-jist) *n.* a specialist in dermatology.

der·ma·tol·o·gy (dur-mă-tol-ŏ-jee) *n.* the scientific study of the skin and its diseases.

der·mis (dur-mis) *n.* skin, the layer of tissue below the epidermis.

der·o·gate (der-ŏ-gayt) *v.* (**der·o·gat·ed, der·o·gat·ing**) to detract from, *your statement derogates my authority.* **der·o·ga·tion** (der-ŏ-gay-shŏn) *n.*

de·rog·a·to·ry (di-rog-ă-tohr-ee) *adj.* disparaging, contemptuous.

der·rick (der-ik) *n.* 1. a kind of crane with an arm pivoted to the base of a central post or to a floor. 2. a framework over an oil well or other drilled hole, holding the drilling machinery etc.

der·ri·ère (der-i-air) *n.* buttocks. ▷French.

der·ring-do (der-ing-doo) *n.* heroic courage or action.

der·rin·ger (der-in-jĕr) *n.* a small large-bore pistol. ▷From its American inventor, Henry Deringer.

der·ris (der-is) *n.* 1. an East Indian leguminous plant. 2. an insecticide made from its powdered root.

der·vish (dur-vish) *n.* a member of a Muslim religious order, vowed to poverty and chastity.

de·sal·i·nate (dee-sal-ĭ-nayt) *v.* (**de·sal·i·nat·ed, de·sal·i·nat·ing**) to desalt. **de·sal·i·na·tion** (dee-sal-ĭ-nay-shŏn) *n.*

de·sa·lin·ize (dee-sal-ĭ-nɪz) *v.* to desalt. **de·sal·i·ni·za·tion** (dee-sal-ĭ-ni-zay-shŏn) *n.*

de·salt (dee-sawlt) *v.* to remove salt from (especially seawater).

de·scale (dee-skayl) *v.* (**de·scaled, de·scal·ing**) to remove scale from (a kettle or boiler etc.).

des·cant (des-kant) *n.* a melody sung or played in accompaniment to the main melody.

de·scend (di-send) *v.* 1. to come or go down. 2. to slope downward. 3. to make a sudden attack or visit, *the whole family descended on us for Easter.* 4. to sink or stoop to unworthy behavior, *to lower oneself, they would never descend to cheating.* 5. to be passed down by inheritance, *the title descended to his son.*

de·scend·ant (di-sen-dănt) *n.* a person who is descended from another, *the descendants of John Adams include many famous Americans.*

de·scent (di-sent) *n.* 1. descending. 2. a way by

which one may descend. 3. a downward slope.
4. a sudden attack or invasion, *the Danes made descents upon the English coast.* 5. lineage, family origin, *they are of French descent.*

de·scribe (di-skrıb) v. (**de·scribed, de·scrib·ing**) 1. to set forth in words, to say what something is like. 2. to mark out or draw the outline of, to move in a certain pattern, *described a complete circle.* **des·crib'a·ble** *adj.*

de·scrip·tion (di-skrip-shŏn) *n.* 1. describing. 2. an account or picture in words. 3. a kind or class of thing, *there's no food of any description.*

de·scrip·tive (di-skrip-tiv) *adj.* giving a description.

de·scry (di-skrı) v. (**de·scried, de·scry·ing**) to catch sight of. ▷Do not confuse *descry* with *decry.*

des·e·crate (des-ĕ-krayt) v. (**des·e·crat·ed, des·e·crat·ing**) to treat (a sacred thing) with irreverence or disrespect. **des'e·cra·tor** *n.* **des·e·cra·tion** (des-ĕ-kray-shŏn) *n.*

de·seg·re·gate (dee-seg-rĕ-gayt) v. (**de·seg·re·gat·ed, de·seg·re·gat·ing**) to abolish racial segregation in (public places, schools, etc.). **de·seg·re·ga·tion** (dee-seg-rĕ-gay-shŏn) *n.*

de·sen·si·tize (dee-sen-si-tız) v. (**de·sen·si·tized, de·sen·si·tiz·ing**) to make less sensitive to a substance or influence. **de·sen'si·tiz·er** *n.* **de·sen·si·ti·za·tion** (dee-sen-si-ti-zay-shŏn) *n.*

des·ert[1] (dez-ĕrt) *n.* a dry barren often sand-covered area of land. **desert** *adj.* 1. barren and uncultivated. 2. uninhabited, *a desert island.* ▷Do not confuse *desert* with *dessert.*

de·sert[2] (di-zurt) v. 1. to abandon, to leave without intending to return, to forsake. 2. to leave service in the armed forces without permission. **de·sert'er** *n.* **de·ser·tion** (di-zur-shŏn) *n.*

de·serts (di-zurtz) *n. pl.* what one deserves (whether good or bad), *she agreed that she had received her deserts.* ▷Do not confuse *deserts* with *desserts.*

de·serve (di-zurv) v. (**de·served, de·serv·ing**) to be worthy of or entitled to (a thing) because of actions or qualities.

de·serv·ed·ly (di-zur-vid-lee) *adv.* according to what is deserved, justly.

de·serv·ing (di-zur-ving) *adj.* worthy, worth rewarding or supporting, *a deserving charity;* those who are deserving of our sympathy.

des·ic·cant (des-i-kănt) *adj.* capable of drying. **desiccant** *n.* a drying agent.

des·ic·cate (des-ic-kayt) v. (**des·ic·cat·ed, des·ic·cat·ing**) to dry out the moisture from, to dry (solid food) in order to preserve it. **des'ic·ca·tor** *n.* **des·ic·ca·tion** (des-i-kay-shŏn) *n.*

de·sid·er·a·tum (di-sid-ĕ-ray-tŭm) *n.* (*pl.* **-ta**, *pr.* -tă) something that is lacking but needed or desired.

de·sign (di-zın) *n.* 1. a drawing that shows how something is to be made. 2. the art of making such drawings. 3. the general form or arrangement of something, *the design of the building is good.* 4. a combination of lines or shapes to form a decoration. 5. a mental plan, a purpose. **design** v. 1. to prepare a drawing or design for (a thing). 2. to plan, to intend for a specific purpose, *the book is designed for students.* **de·sign'er** *n.* □**have designs on**, to plan to get possession of.

des·ig·nate (dez-ig-nayt) v. (**des·ig·nat·ed, des·ig·nat·ing**) 1. to mark or point out clearly, to specify, *the river was designated as the western*

boundary. 2. to describe as, to give a name or title to. 3. to appoint to a position, *designated Smith as his successor.* **designate** (dez-ig-nayt, -nit) *adj.* appointed to office but not yet installed, *the ambassador designate.* □**designated hitter**, the tenth player on a baseball team, whose only role is to bat (instead of the pitcher). **des·ig·na·tion** (dez-ig-nay-shŏn) *n.* 1. designating. 2. a name or title.

de·sign·ed·ly (di-zı-nid-lee) *adv.* intentionally.

de·sign·ing (di-zı-ning) *adj.* crafty, scheming.

de·sir·a·ble (di-zır-ă-bĕl) *adj.* 1. arousing desire, worth desiring, *a desirable waterfront house.* 2. advisable, worth doing, *it is desirable that you be present.* **de·sir'a·bly** *adv.* **de·sir·a·bil·i·ty** (di-zır-ă-bil-i-tee) *n.*

de·sire (di-zır) *n.* 1. a feeling that one would get pleasure or satisfaction by obtaining or possessing something. 2. an expressed wish, a request, *at the desire of the company president.* 3. an object of desire, *all your heart's desires.* 4. strong sexual urge. **desire** v. (**de·sired, de·sir·ing**) 1. to have a desire for. 2. to ask for. □**leave much to be desired**, to be unsatisfactory.

de·sir·ous (di-zır-ŭs) *adj.* having a desire, desiring.

de·sist (di-zist) v. to cease from an action etc.

desk (desk) *n.* 1. a piece of furniture with a flat top and often drawers, used when reading or writing etc. 2. a counter behind which sits a cashier or receptionist etc., *ask at the information desk.* 3. a section of a newspaper office dealing with specified topics. 4. a section of the Department of State, *the Far East desk.*

Des Moines (dĕ moin) the capital of Iowa.

des·o·late (des-ŏ-lit) *adj.* 1. solitary, lonely. 2. deserted, uninhabited, barren, dismal, *a desolate landscape.* 3. forlorn and unhappy. **desolate** (des-ŏ-layt) v._(**des·o·lat·ed, des·o·lat·ing**) 1. to depopulate. 2. to devastate. 3. to make (a person) wretched. **des·o·late·ly** (des-ŏ-lit-lee) *adv.*

des·o·la·tion (des-ŏ-lay-shŏn) *n.* 1. a desolate or barren condition. 2. loneliness. 3. grief, wretchedness.

des·pair (di-spair) *n.* 1. complete loss or lack of hope. 2. a thing that causes this, *that project was the despair of the office.* **despair** v. to lose all hope. **des·pair'ing** *adj.* **des·pair'ing·ly** *adv.*

des·patch (di-spach) *n. & v.* dispatch.

des·per·a·do (des-pĕ-rah-doh) *n.* (*pl.* -**does**) a reckless criminal.

des·per·ate (des-pĕ-rit) *adj.* 1. leaving little or no hope, extremely serious, *the situation is desperate.* 2. made reckless by despair or urgency, *a desperate criminal; they are desperate for food.* 3. done or used in a nearly hopeless situation, *a desperate remedy.* **des'per·ate·ly** *adv.*

des·per·a·tion (des-pĕ-ray-shŏn) *n.* 1. hopelessness. 2. being desperate, recklessness caused by despair.

des·pi·ca·ble (des-pi-kă-bĕl) *adj.* deserving to be despised, contemptible. **des'pi·ca·bly** *adv.*

de·spise (di-spız) v. (**de·spised, de·spis·ing**) to regard as inferior or worthless, to feel disrespect for.

de·spite (di-spıt) *prep.* in spite of.

de·spoil (di-spoil) v. to plunder, to rob (a place or person) of. **de·spoil'er** *n.* **de·spoil'ment** *n.*

de·spo·li·a·tion (di-spoh-li-ay-shŏn) *n.* plundering.

de·spond·ent (di-spon-dĕnt) *adj.* in low spirits, dejected. **des·pond′ent·ly** *adv.* **des·spond′en·cy** *n.*

des·pot (des-pŏt) *n.* a tyrant, a ruler who has unrestricted power.

des·pot·ic (di-spot-ik) *adj.* having unrestricted power. **des·pot′i·cal·ly** *adv.*

des·pot·ism (des-pŏ-tiz-ĕm) *n.* 1. tyranny, government by a despot. 2. a country ruled by a despot.

des·sert (di-zurt) *n.* the course of sweet food, fruit, cheese, or the like served at the end of a meal. □**dessert fork**, a medium-sized fork for eating cake etc. **dessert spoon**, a medium-sized spoon used in eating dessert. ▷Do not confuse *dessert* with *desert.*

des·ti·na·tion (des-ti-nay-shŏn) *n.* the place to which a person or thing is going.

des·tine (des-tin) *v.* **(des·tined, de·stin·ing)** to settle or determine the future of, to set apart for a purpose; *he was destined to become President,* this was his destiny.

des·ti·ny (des-ti-nee) *n.* (*pl.* **-nies**) 1. fate considered as a power. 2. that which happens to a person or thing, thought of as determined in advance by fate.

des·ti·tute (des-ti-toot) *adj.* 1. penniless, without the necessities of life. 2. lacking in something, *a landscape destitute of trees.*

des·ti·tu·tion (des-ti-too-shŏn) *n.* being destitute, extreme poverty.

de·stroy (di-stroi) *v.* 1. to pull or break down, to reduce to a useless form, to spoil completely. 2. to kill (an animal) deliberately, *the horse had to be destroyed.* 3. to put out of existence, *it destroyed our chances.*

de·stroy·er (di-stroi-ĕr) *n.* 1. a person or thing that destroys. 2. a fast warship designed to protect other ships. □**destroyer escort**, a warship smaller than a destroyer, used to aid destroyers in their missions.

de·struct (di-strukt) *v.* (informal) to bring about the deliberate destruction of (one's own rocket etc.). **destruct** *n.* (informal) the action of destructing. ▷ *Destruct* is preferred by military and rocketry staff, especially in the word *self-destruct.* Careful writers use the verb *destroy* and the noun *destruction* except when referring to rockets and military devices.

de·struct·i·ble (di-struk-tĭ-bĕl) *adj.* able to be destroyed. **de·struc·ti·bil·i·ty** (di-struk-tĭ-bil-i-tee) *n.*

de·struc·tion (di-struk-shŏn) *n.* 1. destroying, being destroyed, *the earthquake caused great destruction.* 2. a cause of destruction or ruin, *gambling was his destruction.*

de·struc·tive (di-struk-tiv) *adj.* 1. destroying, causing destruction. 2. frequently destroying things, *some children are very destructive.* **de·struc′tive·ly** *adv.*

de·sue·tude (des-wi-tood) *n.* 1. passing into disuse. 2. a state of disuse.

des·ul·to·ry (des-ŭl-tohr-ee) *adj.* going aimlessly from one subject to another, not systematic. **des′ul·to·ri·ly** *adv.* **des′ul·to·ri·ness** *n.*

det. *abbr.* 1. detached. 2. detachment. 3. detail.

de·tach (di-tach) *v.* to release or remove from something else or from a group.

de·tach·a·ble (di-tach-ă-bĕl) *adj.* able to be detached.

de·tached (di-tacht) *adj.* 1. (of a house) not joined

to another. 2. (of the mind or opinions) free from bias or emotion.

de·tach·ment (di-tach-mĕnt) *n.* 1. detaching, being detached. 2. freedom from bias or emotion, aloofness, lack of concern. 3. a group of troops or ships etc. detached from a larger group for a special duty.

de·tail (di-tayl, dee-tayl) *n.* 1. an individual item, a small or subordinate particular. 2. a number of such particulars, *the description is full of detail.* 3. the minor decoration in a building or picture etc., *look at the detail in the carvings.* 4. a small military detachment assigned to special duty. **detail** *v.* 1. to give particulars of, to describe fully. 2. to assign to special duty. □**go into details,** to explain things in detail. **in detail,** describing the individual parts or events etc. fully.

de·tailed (di-tayld, dee-tayld) *adj.* giving or showing many details.

de·tain (di-tayn) *v.* 1. to keep in confinement or under restraint. 2. to keep waiting, to cause delay to, to keep from proceeding.

de·tain·ee (di-tay-nee) *n.* a person who is detained by the authorities.

de·tect (di-tekt) *v.* 1. to discover the existence or presence of. 2. to find (a person) doing something bad or secret, *like a boy detected while robbing an orchard.* **de·tect′a·ble** *adj.*

de·tec·tion (di-tek-shŏn) *n.* 1. detecting, being detected. 2. the work of a detective.

de·tec·tive (di-tek-tiv) *n.* a person, especially a member of the police force, whose job is to investigate crimes. **detective** *adj.* concerned with or used for detection. □**detective story,** a story that tells of crime and the detection of criminals.

de·tec·tor (di-tek-tŏr) *n.* a device for detecting the presence of something, *a smoke detector; a lie detector.*

de·tent (di-tent) *n.* a catch that has to be released in order to allow machinery to operate.

dé·tente (day-tahnt) *n.* the easing of strained relations between countries.

de·ten·tion (di-ten-shŏn) *n.* 1. detaining, being detained. 2. being kept in custody. □**detention center,** an institution where those charged with crime are kept for a short time.

de·ter (di-tur) *v.* **(de·terred, de·ter·ring)** to discourage or prevent from doing something through fear or dislike of the consequences. **de·ter′ment** *n.*

de·ter·gent (di-tur-jĕnt) *n.* a cleansing substance, especially a synthetic substance other than soap. **detergent** *adj.* having a cleansing effect.

de·te·ri·o·rate (di-teer-i-ŏ-rayt) *v.* **(de·te·ri·o·rat·ed, de·te·ri·o·rat·ing)** to become worse. **de·te·ri·o·ra·tion** (di-teer-i-ŏ-ray-shŏn) *n.*

de·ter·mi·na·ble (di-tur-mi-nă-bĕl) *adj.* able to be settled or calculated, *its age is not determinable.* **de·ter′mi·na·bly** *adv.*

de·ter·mi·nant (di-tur-mi-nănt) *n.* a decisive factor.

de·ter·mi·nate (di-tur-mi-nit) *adj.* limited, of fixed and definite scope or nature.

de·ter·mi·na·tion (di-tur-mi-nay-shŏn) *n.* 1. firmness of purpose. 2. the process of deciding, determining, or calculating.

de·ter·mine (di-tur-min) *v.* **(de·ter·mined, de·ter·min·ing)** 1. to find out or calculate precisely, *we must determine the height of the mountain.*

175   **determined / devil**

2. to settle, to decide, *determine what is to be done.* 3. to be the decisive factor or influence on, *income should determine one's standard of living.* 4. to decide firmly, *she determined to become a doctor.* **de·ter·mined** (di-tur-mind) *adj.* showing determination, firm and resolute. **de·ter′mined·ly** *adv.*
de·ter·min·ism (di-tur-mi-niz-ĕm) *n.* a doctrine that human action is not free but determined by motives regarded as external force acting on the will. **de·ter′min·ist** *n.*
de·ter·rence (di-tur-ĕns) *n.* 1. the act of deterring. 2. the capacity to deter.
de·ter·rent (di-tur-ĕnt) *n.* a thing that deters, a nuclear weapon that deters countries from attacking the one who has it. **deterrent** *adj.* deterring.
de·test (di-test) *v.* to dislike intensely, to loathe. **de·test·a·tion** (dee-tes-tay-shŏn) *n.*
de·test·a·ble (di-tes-tă-běl) *adj.* intensely disliked, hateful. **de·test′a·bly** *adv.*
de·throne (dee-throhn) *v.* (**de·throned, de·thron·ing**) to remove from a throne, to depose. **de·throne′ment** *n.*
det·o·nate (det-ŏ-nayt) *v.* (**det·o·nat·ed, det·o·nat·ing**) to explode or cause to explode loudly. **det·o·na·tion** (det-ŏ-nay-shŏn) *n.*
det·o·na·tor (det-ŏ-nay-tŏr) *n.* a device that detonates an explosive.
de·tour (dee-toor, di-toor) *n.* a deviation from one's direct or intended course, an alternative route to avoid a section of road that is blocked or under repair, *make a detour.* **detour** *v.* to make a detour.
de·tox·i·fy (dee-tok-si-fɪ) *v.* (**de·tox·i·fied, de·tox·i·fy·ing**) to remove poison from. **de·tox·i·fi·ca·tion** (dee-tok-si-fi-kay-shŏn) *n.*
de·tract (di-trakt) *v.* to take away a part, to lessen (a quantity, value, etc.), *it will not detract from our pleasure.* **de·trac·tion** (di-trak-shŏn) *n.* ▷Do not confuse *detract* with *distract.*
de·trac·tor (di-trak-tŏr) *n.* a person who criticizes something unfavorably, *the plan has its detractors.*
det·ri·ment (det-ri-měnt) *n.* harm, damage, *worked long hours to the detriment of her health.*
det·ri·men·tal (det-ri-men-tăl) *adj.* causing harm, *smoking is detrimental to health.* **det·ri·men′tal·ly** *adv.*
de·tri·tus (di-trɪ-tis) *n.* 1. fragments (of gravel, sand, silt, etc.) caused by the rubbing away of a larger mass. 2. any waste.
de trop (dě troh) not wanted, unwelcome, in the way. ▷French.
deuce[1] (doos) *n.* 1. (in tennis) the score of forty all. 2. the two on dice or a playing card. 3. (slang) a two-dollar bill.
deuce[2] *n.* (in exclamations of surprise or annoyance) the Devil, *where the deuce is it?*
deu·te·ri·um (doo-teer-i-ŭm) *n.* a heavy form of hydrogen.
Deu·ter·on·o·my (doo-tě-ron-ŏ-mee) *n.* the fifth book of the Old Testament, containing a repetition of the law of Moses.
Deut·sche (doi-chě) **mark** the unit of money in West Germany.
dev. *abbr.* deviation.
de·val·ue (dee-val-yoo) *v.* (**de·val·ued, de·val·u·ing**) to reduce the value of (currency) in relation to other currencies or to gold. **de·val·u·a·tion** (dee-val-yoo-ay-shŏn) *n.*
dev·as·tate (dev-ă-stayt) *v.* (**dev·a·stat·ed, dev·a·stat·ing**) 1. to lay waste, to cause great

destruction to. 2. to overwhelm mentally, *she was devastated by the death of her son.* **dev·as·ta·tion** (dev-ă-stay-shŏn) *n.*
dev·as·tat·ing (dev-ă-stay-ting) *adj.* 1. causing destruction. 2. overwhelming, *a devastating handicap.*
de·vel·op (di-vel-ŏp) *v.* (**de·vel·oped, de·vel·op·ing**) 1. to make or become larger or fuller or more mature or organized. 2. to bring or come gradually into existence, *a storm developed.* 3. to begin to exhibit or suffer from, to acquire gradually, *develop measles; develop bad habits.* 4. to convert (land) to a new purpose so as to use its resources, to use (an area) for the building of houses or stores or factories etc. 5. to treat (a photographic film or plate etc.) so as to make the picture visible. □**developing country,** a poor or primitive country that is developing better economic and social conditions.
de·vel·op·er (di-vel-ŏ-pěr) *n.* 1. one who develops. 2. a person or firm that develops land, constructs new areas of buildings or houses etc. 3. a substance used for developing photographic film etc.
de·vel·op·ment (di-vel-ŏp-měnt) *n.* 1. developing, being developed. 2. something that has developed or been developed, *the latest developments in science; a housing development.* **de·vel·op·men·tal** (di-vel-ŏp-men-tăl) *adj.*
de·vi·ant (dee-vi-ănt) *adj.* deviating from what is accepted as normal or usual. **deviant** *n.* a person who deviates from accepted standards in his beliefs or behavior. **de′vi·ance** *n.* **de′vi·an·cy** *n.*
de·vi·ate (dee-vi-ayt) *v.* (**de·vi·at·ed, de·vi·at·ing**) to turn aside or diverge from a course of action, a rule, truth, etc. **deviate** (dee-vi-it) *n.* a deviant. **de·vi·a·tion** (dee-vi-ay-shŏn) *n.* □**standard deviation,** (in statistics) the quantity calculated to indicate the extent of deviation for a group as a whole.
de·vi·a·tion·ist (dee-vi-ay-shŏ-nist) *n.* 1. a political party member, especially a Communist, who deviates from his party's accepted doctrines or practices. **de·vi·a′tion·ism** *n.*
de·vice (di-vɪs) *n.* 1. a thing that is made or used for a particular purpose, *a device for opening cans.* 2. a plan or scheme for achieving something. 3. a design used as a decoration or emblem. □**leave a person to his own devices,** to leave him to do as he wishes without help or advice. ▷Do not confuse *device* with *devise.*
dev·il (dev-il) *n.* 1. the Devil, (in Jewish and Christian teaching) the supreme spirit of evil and enemy of God. 2. an evil spirit. 3. a wicked or cruel or annoying person. 4. a mischievous person or a person of great cleverness. 5. (informal) something difficult or hard to manage, *a devil of a task.* 6. (informal) a person, *poor devil; lucky devil.* 7. (informal) used in exclamations of surprise or annoyance, *where the devil is it?* **devil** *v.* (**dev·iled, dev·il·ing**) to prepare or cook with hot seasoning, *deviled crabs; deviled eggs.* **dev′il·ish** *adj.* **dev′il·ish·ly** *adv.* **dev′il·ish·ness** *n.* □**between the devil and the deep blue sea,** between equally harsh alternatives. **Devil's advocate,** one who tests a theory by putting forward possible objections to it. **devil's food cake,** rich chocolate cake. **like the devil,** with great energy, intensely. **play the devil with,** to cause severe

damage to. **the devil to pay,** trouble to be expected.

dev·il-may-care (dev-il-may-kair) *adj.* cheerful and reckless.

dev·il·ment (dev-il-mĕnt) *n.* mischief.

dev·il·try (dev-il-tree) *n.* (*pl.* **-tries**) 1. wickedness. 2. mischief.

de·vi·ous (dee-vi-ŭs) *adj.* 1. winding, roundabout. 2. not straightforward, underhand. **de′vi·ous·ly** *adv.* **de′vi·ous·ness** *n.*

de·vise (di-vɪz) *v.* (de·vised, de·vis·ing) to think out, to plan, to invent. ▷Do not confuse *devise* with *device.*

de·vi·tal·ize (dee-vɪ-tă-lɪz) *v.* (de·vi·tal·ized, de·vi·tal·iz·ing) to remove life or vitality from.

de·void (di-void) *adj.* lacking or free from something, *devoid of merit.*

de·volve (di-volv) *v.* (de·volved, de·volv·ing) to pass or be passed on to a deputy or successor, *this work will devolve on the new manager.* **dev·o·lu·tion** (dev-ŏ-loo-shŏn) *n.*

De·vo·ni·an (dĕ-voh-ni-ăn) *adj.* of the geologic period of the Paleozoic era before the Carboniferous and after the Silurian. **Devonian** *n.* the Devonian period.

de·vote (di-voht) *v.* (de·vot·ed, de·vot·ing) to give or use for a particular activity or purpose, *devoted himself* or *his time to sport; six pages are devoted to business news.*

de·vo·ted (di-voh-tid) *adj.* showing devotion, very loyal or loving. **de·vot′ed·ly** *adv.* **de·vot′ed·ness** *n.*

de·vo·tee (dev-ŏ-tee) *n.* a person who is devoted to something, an enthusiast, *golf devotees.*

de·vo·tion (di-voh-shŏn) *n.* 1. great love or loyalty, enthusiastic zeal. 2. religious worship. 3. *devotions,* prayers.

de·vo·tion·al (di-voh-shŏ-năl) *adj.* used in religious worship.

de·vour (di-vowr) *v.* 1. to eat hungrily or greedily. 2. to destroy completely, to consume, *fire devoured the forest.* 3. to take in greedily with the eyes or ears, *they devoured the story.* 4. to absorb the attention of, *she was devoured by curiosity.* **de·vour′er** *n.*

de·vout (di-vowt) *adj.* 1. earnestly religious. 2. earnest, sincere, *a devout supporter.* **de·vout′ly** *adv.* **de·vout′ness** *n.*

dew (doo, dyoo) *n.* 1. small drops of moisture that condense on cool surfaces during the night from water vapor in the air. 2. moisture in small drops on a surface. □**dew point,** the temperature at which dew forms.

DEW (doo) *n. d*istant *e*arly *w*arning. □**DEW line,** a line of radar stations, crossing North America north of the Arctic Circle, that give early warning of approaching enemy missiles or aircraft.

dew·ber·ry (doo-ber-ee) *n.* (*pl.* **-ries**) a bluish fruit like a blackberry.

dew·claw (doo-klaw) *n.* a small claw on the inner side of a dog's leg, not reaching the ground in walking.

dew·drop (doo-drop) *n.* a drop of dew.

Dew·ey (doo-ee) **decimal system** a decimal system for classifying books in libraries.

dew·lap (doo-lap) *n.* a fold of loose skin that hangs from the throat of cattle and other animals.

dew·y (doo-ee) *adj.* (dew·i·er, dew·i·est) wet with dew.

dew·y-eyed (doo-ee-ɪd) *adj.* innocently trusting or sentimental.

dex·ter·i·ty (dek-ster-i-tee) *n.* skill in handling things.

dex·ter·ous, dex·trous (dek-strŭs) *adj.* showing dexterity. **dex′ter·ous·ly, dex′trous·ly** *adv.*

dex·trin (dek-strin) *n.* a gummy substance formed from starch, used as an adhesive.

dex·trose (dek-strohs) *n.* a form of glucose.

dg *abbr.* decigram.

dhow (dow) *n.* a triangular-rigged Arab sailing vessel.

DI *abbr.* 1. Department of the Interior. 2. drill instructor.

dia. *abbr.* diameter.

di·a·be·tes (dɪ-ă-bee-tis, -teez) *n.* a disease in which sugar and starch are not properly absorbed by the body.

di·a·bet·ic (dɪ-ă-bet-ik) *adj.* of diabetes. **diabetic** *n.* a person suffering from diabetes.

di·a·bol·ic (dɪ-ă-bol-ik) *adj.* of the Devil.

di·a·bol·i·cal (dɪ-ă-bol-i-kăl) *adj.* 1. like a devil, very cruel or wicked. 2. fiendishly clever or cunning or annoying. **di·a·bol′i·cal·ly** *adv.*

di·ab·o·lism (dɪ-ab-ŏ-liz-ĕm) *n.* worship of the Devil.

di·a·crit·ic (dɪ-ă-krit-ik) *n.* a diacritical mark.

di·a·crit·ic·al (dɪ-ă-krit-ĭ-kăl) **mark** a sign (such as ˜) used to indicate that a letter has a particular sound, as *ă* and *ĕ.*

di·a·dem (dɪ-ă-dem) *n.* 1. a crown or headband worn as a sign of sovereignty. 2. royal authority or status, *the diadem has passed to the younger son.*

diag. *abbr.* 1. diagonal. 2. diagram.

di·ag·nose (dɪ-ăg-nohs) *v.* (di·ag·nosed, di·ag·nos·ing) to make a diagnosis of, *typhoid fever was diagnosed in six patients.*

di·ag·no·sis (dɪ-ăg-noh-sis) *n.* (*pl.* **-no·ses,** *pr.* -noh-seez) a statement of the nature of a disease or other condition made after observing its signs and symptoms.

di·ag·nos·tic (dɪ-ăg-nos-tik) *adj.* of or used in diagnosis, *diagnostic procedures.* **di·ag·nos·ti·cian** (dɪ-ăg-nos-tish-ăn) *n.* an expert in making diagnoses.

di·ag·o·nal (dɪ-ag-ŏ-năl) *adj.* slanting, crossing from corner to corner. **diagonal** *n.* a straight line joining two opposite corners. **di·ag′o·nal·ly** *adv.*

di·a·gram (dɪ-ă-gram) *n.* a drawing that shows the parts of something or how it works. **diagram** *v.* (di·a·gramed, di·a·gram·ing) to show by a diagram. **di·a·gram·mat·ic** (dɪ-ă-gră-mat-ik) *adj.* **di·a·gram·mat′i·cal** *adj.* **di·a·gram·mat′i·cal·ly** *adv.*

di·al (dɪ-ăl) *n.* 1. the face of a clock or watch. 2. a similar flat plate marked with a scale for the measurement of something and having a movable pointer that indicates the amount registered. 3. a plate or disk etc. on a radio or television set showing the wavelength or channel selected. 4. a movable disk with finger holes over a circle of numbers or letters, manipulated in order to connect one telephone with another. **dial** *v.* (di·aled, di·al·ing) 1. to select or regulate by means of a dial. 2. to make a telephone connection by using a dial. □**dial tone,** a steady humming sound given over the telephone to show that the caller may begin to dial.

dial. *abbr.* 1. dialect. 2. dialectal. 3. dialectic. 4. dialectical.

di·a·lect (dɪ-ă-lekt) *n.* the words and pronunciation that are used in a particular area and differ from what is regarded as standard in the language as a whole. **di·a·lec′tal** adj.

di·a·lec·tic (dɪ-ă-lek-tik) n. (also **dialectics**) investigation of truths in philosophy etc. by systematic reasoning, Marxian dialectic holds great interest for me. **di·a·lec′ti·cal** adj.

di·a·logue, di·a·log (dɪ-ă-lawg) n. 1. a conversation or discussion. 2. the words spoken by characters in a play or story.

di·al·y·sis (dɪ-al-ĭ-sis) n. (pl. **-ses,** pr. -seez) purification of the blood by causing it to flow through a suitable membrane which traps impurities.

di·a·lyze (dɪ-ă-lɪz) v. (**di·a·lyzed, di·a·lyz·ing**) to separate by dialysis.

diam. abbr. diameter.

di·am·e·ter (dɪ-am-ĕ-tĕr) n. 1. a straight line passing from side to side through the center of a circle or sphere. 2. the length of this.

di·a·met·ri·cal (dɪ-ă-met-ri-kăl), **di·a·met·ric** (dɪ-ă-met-rik) adj. of or along a diameter; the diametrical opposite, the exact opposite. **di·a·met′ri·cal·ly** adv.

dia·mond (dɪ-mŏnd) n. 1. a very hard brilliant precious stone of pure crystallized carbon. 2. a figure with four equal sides and with angles that are not right angles. 3. something shaped like this. 4. a playing card of the suit (diamonds) marked with red figures of this shape. **diamond** adj. made of or set with diamonds. □**diamond in the rough,** a person who is excellent but has rough manners. **diamond jubilee,** the sixtieth or seventy-fifth anniversary of a sovereign's accession or other event. **diamond wedding,** the sixtieth or seventy-fifth anniversary of a wedding.

dia·mond·back (dɪ-mŏnd-bak) **rattlesnake** any of various large poisonous rattlesnakes with diamond patterns on the back.

di·an·thus (dɪ-an-thŭs) n. (pl. **-thus·es**) a type of flowering plant including the pink and carnation.

di·a·pa·son (dɪ-ă-pay-zŏn) n. 1. the fixed standard of musical pitch, the range of sound of a voice or instrument. 2. a melody, especially one that swells grandly.

dia·per (dɪ-pĕr) n. a piece of toweling, absorbent paper, etc. worn by a baby to absorb or retain its excreta.

di·aph·a·nous (dɪ-af-ă-nŭs) adj. (of fabric) light, delicate, and almost transparent.

di·a·pho·re·sis (dɪ-ă-fŏ-ree-sis) n. excessive perspiration, especially if artificially produced. **di·a·pho·ret·ic** (dɪ-ă-fŏ-ret-ik) adj.

di·a·phragm (dɪ-ă-fram) n. 1. the midriff, the internal muscular partition that separates the chest from the abdomen and is used in breathing. 2. a vibrating disk in a microphone or telephone receiver etc. 3. a device for varying the aperture of a camera lens. 4. a thin contraceptive cap fitting over the neck of the womb.

di·a·rist (dɪ-ă-rist) n. a person who keeps a diary.

di·ar·rhea (dɪ-ă-ree-ă) n. a condition in which bowel movements are very frequent and loose.

di·a·ry (dɪ-ă-ree) n. (pl. **-ries**) 1. a daily record of events or thoughts. 2. a book for this or for noting engagements.

Di·as·po·ra (dɪ-as-pŏ-ră) n. the dispersion of the Jews after the end of the Babylonian captivity.

di·as·to·le (dɪ-as-tŏ-lee) n. dilation of the heart alternating rhythmically with systole to form the pulse. **di·a·stol·ic** (dɪ-ă-stol-ik) adj.

di·as·tro·phism (dɪ-as-trŏ-fiz-ĕm) n. the action of forces that deform the earth's crust and so produce continents, mountains, etc. **di·a·stroph·ic** (dɪ-ă-strof-ik) adj.

di·a·ther·my (dɪ-ă-thur-mee) n. (pl. **-mies**) a kind of medical heat treatment by means of high-frequency electric currents.

di·a·tom (dɪ-ă-tŏm) n. a microscopic one-celled alga with a stony cell wall, existing in sea and fresh water and often forming fossil deposits.

di·a·tom·ic (dɪ-ă-tom-ik) adj. 1. consisting of two atoms. 2. containing two replaceable atoms of hydrogen.

di·a·ton·ic (dɪ-ă-ton-ik) adj. (in music) using the notes of the major or minor scale only, not of the chromatic scale.

di·a·tribe (dɪ-ă-trɪb) n. a violent attack in words, abusive criticism.

dib·ble (dib-ĕl) v. (**dib·bled, dib·bling**) to prepare soil with a dibble. **dibble** n. a pointed instrument for making holes in the ground for bulbs etc.

dice (dɪs) n. pl. (sing. **die**) 1. small cubes marked on each side with one to six spots, used in games of chance. 2. a game played with these, dice is not my game. **dice** v. (**diced, dic·ing**) 1. (old use) to gamble using dice. 2. to cut into small cubes, dice the carrots. □**no dice,** (slang) no success.

dic·ey (dɪ-see) adj. (**dic·i·er, dic·i·est**) (slang) risky, unreliable.

di·chot·o·my (dɪ-kot-ŏ-mee) n. (pl. **-mies**) division into two parts or kinds. **di·chot′o·mous** adj.

dick (dik) n. (slang) a detective.

dick·ens (dik-inz) n. (in exclamations of surprise or annoyance) the deuce, the Devil, where the dickens is it?

dick·er (dik-ĕr) v. (informal) to bargain, to haggle.

dick·ey (dik-ee) **dick·eys, dick·y** (pl. **dick·ies**) (dik-ee) n. a man's detachable or false shirt front, a woman's detachable blouse front or collar.

di·cot·y·le·don (dɪ-kot-ĭ-lee-dŏn) n. a flowering plant with two cotyledons. **di·cot·y·le′don·ous** adj.

dict. abbr. 1. dictation. 2. dictionary.

Dic·ta·phone (dik-tă-fohn) n. (trademark) a machine that records and plays back dictation.

dic·tate (dik-tayt, dik-tayt) v. (**dic·tat·ed, dic·tat·ing**) 1. to say or read aloud (words) to be written down by a person or recorded by a machine. 2. to state or order with the force of authority, dictate terms to a defeated enemy. 3. to give orders officiously, I will not be dictated to. **dic·ta·tion** (dik-tay-shŏn) n.

dic·tates (dik-tayts) n. pl. authoritative commands, the dictates of conscience.

dic·ta·tor (dik-tay-tŏr, dik-tay-) n. 1. a ruler who has unrestricted authority, especially one who has taken control by force. 2. a person with supreme authority in any sphere, one who dictates what is to be done. 3. a domineering person. **dic·ta′tor·ship** n.

dic·ta·to·ri·al (dik-tă-tohr-i-ăl) adj. 1. of or like a dictator. 2. domineering. **dic·ta·to′ri·al·ly** adv.

dic·tion (dik-shŏn) n. a person's manner of uttering or pronouncing words.

dic·tion·ar·y (dik-shŏ-ner-ee) n. (pl. **-ar·ies**) a book that lists and explains the words of a language or the words and topics of a particular subject, usually in alphabetical order.

dic·tum (dik-tŭm) *n.* (*pl.* **-ta,** *pr.* -tă) **1.** a formal expression of opinion. **2.** a saying.

did (did) *see* **do.**

di·dac·tic (dɪ-dak-tik) *adj.* **1.** giving instruction. **2.** having the manner of one who is lecturing pupils. **di·dac'ti·cal·ly** *adv.*

did·dle (did-ĕl) *v.* (**did·dled, did·dling**) (*informal*) **1.** to waste time. **2.** to cheat or swindle, *I was diddled out of $200.*

did·n't (did-ĕnt) = did not.

di·do (dɪ-doh) *n.* (*pl.* **-dos, -does**) (*informal*) an antic, a prank.

die[1] (dɪ) *v.* (**died, dy·ing**) **1.** to cease to be alive. **2.** to cease to exist; *the laugh died on his lips,* ceased abruptly. **3.** to cease to function, to stop, *the engine sputtered and died.* **4.** (of a fire or flame) to go out. **5.** to become exhausted, *we were dying with laughter.* **6.** to feel an intense longing, *we are dying to go; dying for a cool drink.* □**die away,** to become fainter or weaker and then cease, *the noise died away.* **die back,** (of plants) to wither from the tip toward the root. **die down,** to become less loud or less violent, *the excitement died down.* **die off,** to die one by one. **die out,** to pass out of existence, *the custom has died out; the family has died out,* no members of it are still alive. **never say die,** keep up courage, do not give in.

die[2] *n.* (*pl.* **dice**) a marked cube used in games of chance (*see* **dice**). □**straight as a die,** quite straight; very honest. **the die is cast,** a step has been taken and its consequences must follow.

die[3] *n.* an engraved device that stamps a design on coins or medals etc., a device that stamps or cuts or molds material into a particular shape. □**die stamping,** stamping with a die that leaves an embossed design.

die-cast (dɪ-kast) *adj.* made by casting metal in a mold.

die·hard (dɪ-hahrd) *n.* a person who obstinately refuses to abandon old theories or policies, one who resists change.

diel·drin (deel-drin) *n.* an insecticide which does not dissolve in water.

di·e·lec·tric (dɪ-ɪ-lek-trik) *adj.* not conducting electricity. **dielectric** *n.* a medium or substance with dielectric properties.

di·er·e·sis (dɪ-er-ĕ-sis) *n.* (*pl.* **-ses,** *pr.* -seez) a mark ¨ placed over a vowel to show that it is sounded separately, as in *naïve.*

die·sel (dee-zĕl) *n.* a diesel engine, a vehicle driven by this. □**diesel engine,** an oil-burning engine in which ignition is produced by the heat of highly compressed air. **diesel oil,** the fuel for this.

die·sel-e·lec·tric (dee-zĕl-ee-lek-trik) *adj.* driven by electric current from a generator driven by a diesel engine, employing diesel oil as fuel.

di·et[1] (dɪ-ĕt) *n.* **1.** the sort of foods usually eaten by a person or animal or community. **2.** a selection of food to which a person is restricted. **diet** *v.* (**di·et·ed, di·et·ing**) to restrict oneself to a special diet, especially in order to control one's weight. **di'et·er** *n.*

diet[2] *n.* a congress, a parliamentary assembly in certain countries, for example, Japan.

di·e·tar·y (dɪ-ĕ-ter-ee) *adj.* of or involving diet, *the dietary rules of Hindus.*

di·e·tet·ic (dɪ-ĕ-tet-ik) *adj.* **1.** of diet and nutrition. **2.** specially prepared or processed for people who are dieting. **3.** *dietetics,* the scientific study of diet and nutrition.

di·e·ti·tian, di·e·ti·cian (dɪ-ĕ-tish-ăn) *n.* an expert in dietetics.

dif., diff. *abbr.* **1.** difference. **2.** different.

dif·fer (dif-ĕr) *v.* **1.** to be unlike, to be distinguishable from something else. **2.** to disagree in opinion.

dif·fer·ence (dif-ĕ-rĕns) *n.* **1.** the state of being different or unlike. **2.** the point in which things differ, the amount or degree of unlikeness. **3.** the quantity by which amounts differ, the remainder left after subtraction, *the difference between 8 and 5 is 3.* **4.** a disagreement in opinion, a quarrel. □**make all the difference,** to make a very important or vital difference. **settle one's differences,** to reach agreement after a quarrel.

dif·fer·ent (dif-ĕ-rĕnt) *adj.* **1.** unlike, of other nature or form or quality, *we are different from them in many respects.* **2.** separate, distinct, *several different people.* **3.** unusual, *try Finland for a different holiday.* **dif'fer·ent·ly** *adv.* ▷ *Different than* is sometimes correct, but *different from* is always correct.

dif·fer·en·tial (dif-ĕ-ren-shăl) *adj.* of or showing or depending on a difference. **differential** *n.* **1.** a difference in wages between industries, between different classes of workers, etc. **2.** a differential gear. □**differential calculus,** a method of calculating rates of change, maximum and minimum values, etc. **differential gear,** an arrangement of gears that allows the rear wheels of an automobile to revolve at different speeds in rounding corners.

dif·fer·en·ti·ate (dif-ĕ-ren-shi-ayt) *v.* (**dif·fer·en·ti·at·ed, dif·fer·en·ti·at·ing**) **1.** to be a difference between, to make different, *the features that differentiate one breed from another.* **2.** to recognize as different, to distinguish, to discriminate; *the pension scheme does not differentiate between male and female employees,* does not treat them differently. **3.** to develop differences, to become different. **dif·fer·en·ti·a·tion** (dif-ĕ-ren-shi-ay-shŏn) *n.*

dif·fi·cult (dif-ĭ-kult) *adj.* **1.** needing much effort or skill, not easy to do or practice. **2.** troublesome, perplexing, *these are difficult times.* **3.** not easy to please or satisfy, *a difficult person.*

dif·fi·cul·ty (dif-ĭ-kul-tee) *n.* (*pl.* **-ties**) **1.** being difficult. **2.** a difficult problem or thing, a hindrance to action. **3.** a difficult state of affairs, trouble; *in financial difficulties,* short of money. □**make difficulties,** to raise objections, to put obstacles in the way of progress. **with difficulty,** not easily.

dif·fi·dent (dif-ĭ-dĕnt) *adj.* lacking self-confidence, hesitating to put oneself or one's ideas forward. **dif'fi·dent·ly** *adv.* **dif'fi·dence** *n.*

dif·frac·tion (dĭ-frak-shŏn) *n.* the process of breaking up a beam of light into a series of dark and light bands or the colored bands of the spectrum.

dif·fuse (di-fyooz) *v.* (**dif·fused, dif·fus·ing**) *v.* **1.** to spread widely or thinly throughout something, *to diffuse knowledge or light or heat.* **2.** to mix (liquids or gases) slowly, to become intermingled, **diffuse** (di-fyoos) *adj.* **1.** spread out, diffused, not concentrated, *diffuse light.* **2.** wordy, not concise, *a diffuse style.* **dif·fus·er** (di-fyoo-zĕr) *n.* **dif·fu·sion** (di-fyoo-zhŏn) *n.* **dif·fuse·ly** (di-fyoos-lee) *adv.* **dif·fuse·ness** (di-fyoos-nis) *n.*

dig (dig) *v.* (**dug, dig·ging**) **1.** to break up and move ground with a tool or machine or claws etc., to make (a way or a hole) by doing this,

dig the ground; dig through the hill; dig a tunnel.
2. to obtain or remove by digging, *dig potatoes.*
3. to excavate archaeologically. **4.** to thrust, to plunge, *dig a knife into it.* **5.** to prod, to nudge, *dug him in the ribs.* **6.** *(slang)* to appreciate, to enjoy, to understand, *they don't dig pop music; do you dig?* **dig** *n.* **1.** an archaeological excavation. **2.** *(informal)* a thrust, a poke, *a dig in the ribs.* **3.** *(informal)* a cutting remark; *that was a dig at me,* a remark directed against me. □**dig in** *or* **into,** to mix (a substance) with the soil by digging; *(informal)* to begin eating or working energetically. **dig oneself in,** to dig a defensive trench or pit; to establish oneself securely. **dig one's heels in,** to become obstinate, to refuse to give way. **dig up,** *(informal)* to seek or discover by investigation, *dug up some useful information.*

di·gest (di-jest, dı-) *v.* **1.** to dissolve (food) in the stomach etc. so that it can be absorbed by the body; *this food digests easily,* is easily absorbed. **2.** to think over, to absorb into the mind, *digesting the information.* **digest** (dı-jest) *n.* **1.** a methodical summary. **2.** a periodical publication giving excerpts and summaries of news, writings, etc.

di·gest·i·ble (di-jes-tı̆-bĕl, dı-) *adj.* able to be digested. **di·gest·i·bil·i·ty** (di-jes-tı̆-bil-i-tee, dı-) *n.*

di·ges·tion (di-jes-chŏn, dı-) *n.* **1.** the process of digesting. **2.** the power of digesting food, *has a good digestion.*

di·ges·tive (di-ges-tiv, dı-) *adj.* **1.** of or aiding digestion. **2.** having the function of digesting food, *the digestive system.* **digestive** *n.* a substance promoting digestion.

dig·ger (dig-ĕr) *n.* **1.** one who digs. **2.** a mechanical excavator.

dig·it (dij-it) *n.* **1.** any numeral from 0 to 9, especially when forming part of a number. **2.** a finger or toe.

dig·it·al (dij-i-tăl) *adj.* of digits. **dig'i·tal·ly** *adv.* □**digital clock,** a clock that shows the time by displaying a row of figures. **digital computer,** a device that makes calculations etc. with data represented as a series of digits or other discrete forms.

dig·i·tal·is (dij-i-tal-is) *n.* a drug prepared from dried foxglove leaves, used as a heart stimulant.

dig·ni·fied (dig-nı̆-fıd) *adj.* having or showing dignity.

dig·ni·fy (dig-nı̆-fı) *v.* (**dig·ni·fied, dig·ni·fy·ing**) **1.** to give dignity to. **2.** to make (a thing) sound more important than it is.

dig·ni·tar·y (dig-nı̆-ter-ee) *n.* (*pl.* **-tar·ies**) a person holding a high rank or position, especially in the Church or in government.

dig·ni·ty (dig-ni-tee) *n.* (*pl.* **-ties**) **1.** a calm and serious manner or style, showing suitable formality or indicating that one deserves respect. **2.** worthiness, *the dignity of labor.* **3.** a high rank or position. □**beneath one's dignity,** not worthy enough for one to do. **stand on one's dignity,** to insist on being treated respectfully.

di·graph (dı-graf) *n.* a pair of letters expressing one sound, as *sh* or *ea.*

di·gress (di-gres) *v.* to depart from the main subject temporarily in speaking or writing. **di·gres'sive** *adj.* **di·gres·sion** (di-gresh-ŏn) *n.*

dike (dık) *n.* **1.** a long wall or embankment to keep back water and prevent flooding. **2.** a ditch for draining water from land.

dil. *abbr.* dilute.

di·lap·i·dat·ed (di-lap-i-day-tid) *adj.* falling to pieces, in a state of disrepair.

di·lap·i·da·tion (di-lap-i-day-shŏn) *n.* a state of disrepair, bringing or being brought into this state.

di·late (dı-layt, dı-layt) *v.* (**di·lat·ed, di·lat·ing**) **1.** to make or become wider or larger. **2.** to speak or write at length, *dilating upon his favorite topic.* **di'la·tor** *n.*

di·la·tion (dı-lay-shŏn) *n.* **1.** dilating. **2.** widening of the neck of the womb, as for surgical curettage.

dil·a·to·ry (dil-ă-tohr-ee) *adj.* slow in doing something, not prompt. **dil'a·to·ri·ly** *adv.* **dil'a·to·ri·ness** *n.*

di·lem·ma (di-lem-ă) *n.* a perplexing situation, especially one in which a choice has to be made between alternatives that are equally undesirable.

dil·et·tante (dil-ĕ-tahnt) *n.* a person who dabbles in a subject for his own enjoyment.

dil·i·gent (dil-i-jĕnt) *adj.* **1.** hard-working, putting care and effort into what one does. **2.** done with care and effort, *a diligent search.* **dil'i·gent·ly** *adv.* **dil'i·gence** *n.*

dill (dil) *n.* a yellow-flowered herb with spicy seeds used for flavoring pickles etc.

dil·ly (dil-ee) *n.* (*pl.* **-lies**) *(informal)* a remarkable or excellent person or thing.

dil·ly·dal·ly (dil-ee-dal-ee) *v.* (**dil·ly·dal·lied, dil·ly·dal·ly·ing**) *(informal)* to dawdle, to waste time by not making up one's mind.

dil·u·ent (dil-yoo-ĕnt) *n.* a diluting agent.

di·lute (di-loot, dı-) *v.* (**di·lut·ed, di·lut·ing**) **1.** to thin down, to make a liquid less concentrated by adding water or other liquid. **2.** to weaken or reduce the forcefulness of, to water down. **dilute** *adj.* diluted, *a dilute acid.* **di·lu·tion** (di-loo-shŏn, dı-) *n.*

dim (dim) *adj.* (**dim·mer, dim·mest**) **1.** faintly lit, luminous but not bright. **2.** indistinct, not clearly seen or heard or remembered. **3.** not seeing clearly, *eyes dim with tears.* **4.** *(informal)* stupid. **dim** *v.* (**dimmed, dim·ming**) to make or become dim. **dim'ly** *adv.* **dim'ness** *n.* □**take a dim view of,** *(informal)* to disapprove of; to feel gloomy about.

dim. *abbr.* **1.** dimension. **2.** diminished. **3.** diminuendo. **4.** diminutive.

dime (dım) *n.* a ten-cent coin of the U.S. □**dime store,** a five-and-ten-cent store.

di·men·sion (di-men-shŏn, dı-) *n.* **1.** a measurement such as length, breadth, thickness, area, etc. **2.** size; *of great dimensions,* very large. **3.** extent, scope, *gave the problem a new dimension.* **di·men'sion·al** *adj.* **di·men'sion·al·ly** *adv.*

di·min·ish (di-min-ish) *v.* to make or become smaller or less.

di·min·u·en·do (di-min-yoo-en-doh) *adj. & adv.* (in music) gradually becoming quieter.

dim·i·nu·tion (dim-ı̆-noo-shŏn) *n.* **1.** diminishing, being diminished. **2.** a decrease.

di·min·u·tive (di-min-yŭ-tiv) *adj.* very small. **diminutive** *n.* a word for a small specimen of something (as *booklet, duckling*), or an affectionate form of a name etc. (as *dearie, Johnnie*). **2.** a suffix such as *-let* or *-kin* or *-ling* indicating smallness or affection, as in *ringlet, bodkin, duckling.*

dim·i·ty (dim-i-tee) *n.* (*pl.* **-ties**) cotton fabric woven with checks or stripes of heavier thread.

dim·mer (dim-ĕr) *n.* a device for reducing the brightness of lights.

di·mor·phic (dı-mor-fik) *adj.* occurring in two distinct forms in the same species, individual, etc.

di·mor'phism *n.* the occurrence of two forms in this way.

dim·out (dim-owt) *n.* a reduction in night lighting to conserve energy or as a protection in wartime.

dim·ple (dim-pĕl) *n.* a small hollow or dent, especially a natural one on the skin of the cheek or chin. **dimple** *v.* (**dim·pled, dim·pling**) 1. to produce dimples in. 2. to show dimples.

dim·wit (dim-wit) *n.* *(informal)* a stupid person. **dim·wit·ted** (dim-wit-id) *adj.* *(informal)* stupid.

din (din) *n.* a loud resonant and annoying noise.

din *v.* (**dinned, din·ning**) 1. to make a din. 2. to force (information) into a person by continually repeating it, *din it into him.*

di·nar (di-nahr) *n.* the unit of money in Yugoslavia and various countries of the Middle East and North Africa.

dine (dɪn) *v.* (**dined, din·ing**) 1. to eat dinner. 2. to entertain with dinner, *we were wined and dined.* ☐**dining car,** a railroad car in which meals are served at tables. **dining room,** a room in which meals are eaten.

din·er (dɪ-nĕr) *n.* 1. a person who dines. 2. a dining car on a train. 3. an inexpensive restaurant with a long counter and booths, shaped like or built from a railroad car.

din·ette (dɪ-net) *n.* 1. a small room or part of a room used for meals. 2. a compact set of furniture for dining.

ding (ding) *n.* the sound a bell makes.

ding-a-ling (ding-ă-ling) *n.* *(informal)* a stupid person.

ding-dong (ding-dong) *n.* the sound of a clapper bell or alternate strokes of two bells. **ding-dong** *adj.* *(informal)* with vigorous and alternating action, *a ding-dong argument; a ding-dong struggle,* in which each contestant has the better of it alternately.

din·ghy (ding-ee) *n.* (*pl.* **-ghies**) a small open boat driven by oars or sails.

din·go (ding-goh) *n.* (*pl.* **-goes**) an Australian wild dog.

ding·us (ding-ŭs) *n.* (*pl.* **-us·es**) *(slang)* a gadget.

din·gy (din-jee) *adj.* (**-gi·er, -gi·est**) dirty looking, not fresh or cheerful. **din'gi·ness** *n.* **din'gi·ly** *adv.*

din·ky (ding-kee) *adj.* (**-ki·er, -ki·est**) *(informal)* small, insignificant.

din·ner (din-ĕr) *n.* 1. the chief meal of the day, whether at midday or in the evening. 2. a formal evening meal in honor of a person or event. ☐**dinner jacket,** a tuxedo.

din·ner·ware (din-ĕr-wair) *n.* china, glasses, etc. for use at the dinner table.

di·no·saur (dɪ-nŏ-sor) *n.* an extinct lizard-like creature often of enormous size.

dint (dint) *n.* **by dint of,** by means of. ▷Do not confuse *dint* with *dent.*

di·o·cese (dɪ-ŏ-sis) *n.* a district under the care of a bishop. **di·oc·e·san** (dɪ-os-i-săn) *adj.*

di·ode (dɪ-ohd) *n.* any two-element electronic device having only two terminals that allows current to flow in only one direction.

di·op·ter (dɪ-op-tĕr) *n.* a unit measuring the power of a lens to bring rays of light to a focus.

di·o·ra·ma (dɪ-ŏ-ram-ă) *n.* a small-scale representation of a scene with three-dimensional objects, viewed through a window.

di·ox·ide (dɪ-ok-sɪd) *n.* an oxide with two atoms of oxygen to one of a metal or other element.

dip (dip) *v.* (**dipped, dip·ping**) 1. to put or lower into liquid; *dip sheep,* wash them in a vermin-killing liquid; *dip fabrics,* dye them in liquid. 2. to go under water and emerge quickly. 3. to set, *the sun dipped below the horizon.* 4. to put a hand or ladle etc. into something in order to take something out; *dip into one's pocket* or *reserves,* take out money etc. and use it. 5. to lower for a moment, *dip the flag.* 6. to slope or extend downward, *the path dips down to the river.* 7. to read short passages here and there in a book, *I've dipped into his autobiography.* **dip** *n.* 1. the act of dipping. 2. a quick plunge, a swim. 3. a downward slope. 4. a liquid into which something is dipped, *sheep dip.* 5. a creamy mixture into which crackers, potato chips, etc. are dipped before eating.

diph·the·ri·a (dif-theer-i-ă) *n.* an acute infectious disease causing inflammation of a mucous membrane especially in the throat. ▷Note the spelling and pronunciation of *diphtheria.*

diph·thong (dif-thawng) *n.* a compound vowel sound produced by combining two simple ones, such as *oi* in *point, ou* in *loud.* ▷Note the spelling and pronunciation of *diphthong.*

dipl. *abbr.* 1. diplomat. 2. diplomatic.

dip·loid (dip-loid) *n.* an organism or cell with twice the usual number of chromosomes.

di·plo·ma (di-ploh-mă) *n.* a certificate awarded by a college etc. to a person who has successfully completed a course of study.

di·plo·ma·cy (di-ploh-mă-see) *n.* 1. the handling of international relations, skill in this. 2. tact.

dip·lo·mat (dip-lŏ-mat) *n.* 1. a member of the diplomatic service. 2. a tactful person.

dip·lo·mate (dip-lŏ-mayt) *n.* a holder of a diploma, especially a medical specialist.

dip·lo·mat·ic (dip-lo-mat-ik) *adj.* 1. of or engaged in diplomacy; *the diplomatic service,* the officials engaged in diplomacy on behalf of their country. 2. tactful, *a diplomatic person* or *reply.* **dip·lo·mat'i·cal·ly** *adv.* ☐**diplomatic immunity,** exemption from arrest, taxation, etc., granted to diplomatic staffs abroad.

dip·per (dip-ĕr) *n.* 1. a diving bird, especially the European water ouzel. 2. a ladle. ☐**Big Dipper,** a constellation of seven bright stars in Ursa Major resembling a water dipper. **Little Dipper,** a similar constellation in Ursa Minor.

dip·py (dip-ee) *adj.* (**-pi·er, -pi·est**) *(slang)* crazy, silly.

dip·so (dip-soh) *n.* (*pl.* **-sos**) *(slang)* a dipsomaniac.

dip·so·ma·ni·a (dip-sŏ-may-ni-ă) *n.* an uncontrollable craving for alcohol.

dip·so·ma·ni·ac (dip-sŏ-may-ni-ak) *n.* a person suffering from dipsomania.

dip·stick (dip-stik) *n.* a graduated rod for measuring the depth of a liquid.

dip·ter·ous (dip-tĕ-rŭs) *adj.* two-winged, having two winglike appendages. **dip'ter·an** *adj.*

dip·tych (dip-tik) *n.* a painting, especially an altarpiece, of two panels hinged together.

dir. *abbr.* director.

dire (dɪr) *adj.* (**dir·er, dir·est**) 1. dreadful, terrible, *in dire peril.* 2. ominous, predicting trouble, *dire warnings.* 3. extreme and urgent, *in dire need.*

di·rect (di-rekt) *adj.* 1. going in a straight line, not curved or crooked or roundabout, *the direct route.* 2. with nothing or no one in between, in an unbroken line, *in direct contact; direct taxes,* those charged on income, as distinct from those added to the price of goods or services. **3.** straightforward, frank, going straight to the point, *a direct way of speaking.* **4.** exact, complete, *the direct opposite.* **direct** *adv.* by a direct route, *traveled to Rome direct.* **direct** *v.* **1.** to tell or show how to do something or get somewhere, *can you direct me to the station?* **2.** to address (a letter or parcel etc.). **3.** to cause to have a specified direction or target, to utter (remarks) to a particular hearer, *direct our energies toward higher productivity; the remark was directed at me.* **4.** to control, to manage, *there was no one to direct the workmen; direct a play,* supervise the acting and staging of it. **5.** to command, to order, *directed his men to advance.* **di·rect′ness** *n.* ☐**direct current,** electric current flowing in one direction only. **direct election,** an election decided by general voters not by representatives. **direct mail,** advertisements, requests for contributions, catalogues, etc. mailed individually to many people. **direct object,** (in grammar) the word(s) that receive the action of the verb, as *milk* in *cats drink milk.*

di·rec·tion (di-rek-shŏn, dı-) *n.* **1.** directing, aiming, guiding, managing. **2.** the line along which something moves or faces, *in the direction of Cleveland.* **3.** *directions,* instructions. ☐**sense of direction,** a person's ability to get his bearings without guidance.

di·rec·tion·al (di-rek-shŏ-năl, dı-) *adj.* **1.** of or indicating direction. **2.** operating or sending radio signals in one direction only.

di·rec·tive (di-rek-tiv, dı-) *n.* a general instruction issued by someone in authority. **directive** *adj.* giving guidance.

di·rect·ly (di-rekt-lee, dı-) *adv.* **1.** in a direct line, in a direct manner. **2.** without delay. **3.** very soon.

di·rec·tor (di-rek-tŏr, dı-) *n.* **1.** a person who supervises or manages things, especially a member of the board managing a business company. **2.** a person who directs a film or play. **di·rec′tor·ship** *n.*

di·rec·tor·ate (di-rek-tŏ-rit, dı-) *n.* **1.** the office of director. **2.** a board of directors.

di·rec·to·ry (di-rek-tŏ-ree, dı-) *n.* (*pl.* **-ries**) a book containing a list of telephone subscribers, residents of a city, members of a profession, business firms, etc.

dire·ful (dır-fŭl) *adj.* dire (definitions 1 and 2).

dirge (durj) *n.* a slow mournful song, a lament for the dead.

di·ri·gi·ble (dir-i-jı̆-bĕl, di-rij-ı̆-) *n.* a steerable balloon or airship.

dirk (durk) *n.* a kind of dagger.

dirn·dl (durn-dĕl) *n.* a full skirt gathered into a tight waistband.

dirt (durt) *n.* **1.** unclean matter that soils something. **2.** earth, soil. **3.** anything worthless or not deserving respect. **4.** foul words or talk, scandal. ☐**dirt cheap,** *(slang)* very cheap. **dirt track,** a racetrack made of earth or rolled cinders etc. **do a person dirt,** *(slang)* to cause him trouble, to harm or injure him maliciously.

dirt·y (dur-tee) *adj.* (**dirt·i·er, dirt·i·est**) **1.** soiled, unclean; *a dirty job,* causing the doer to become dirty. **2.** (of a nuclear bomb) producing much fallout. **3.** not having clean habits. **4.** dishonorable, mean, unfair, *a dirty trick; a dirty fighter.* **5.** (of weather) rough and stormy. **6.** lewd, obscene, *dirty jokes.* **dirty** *v.* (**dirt·ied, dirt·y·ing**) to make or become dirty. ☐**dirty look,** a

disapproving look. **dirty word,** an obscene word; a word denoting something that is regarded as discreditable, *welfare became a dirty word.* **dirty work,** dishonorable dealings.

dis·a·bil·i·ty (dis-ă-bil-i-tee) *n.* (*pl.* **-ties**) something that disables or disqualifies a person, a physical incapacity caused by injury or disease etc.

dis·a·ble (dis-ay-bĕl) *v.* (**dis·a·bled, dis·a·bling**) to deprive of some ability, to make unfit or useless. **dis·a′ble·ment** *n.*

dis·a·bled (dis-ay-bĕld) *adj.* having a physical disability.

dis·a·buse (dis-ă-byooz) *v.* (**dis·a·bused, dis·a·bus·ing**) to disillusion, to free from a false idea, *he was soon disabused of this notion.*

dis·ad·van·tage (dis-ad-van-tij) *n.* **1.** an unfavorable condition or circumstance; *at a disadvantage,* in an unfavorable position. **2.** damage to one's interest or reputations; *to our disadvantage,* causing us loss or inconvenience etc. **disadvantage** *v.* (**dis·ad·van·taged, dis·ad·van·tag·ing**) to put at a disadvantage.

dis·ad·van·taged (dis-ad-van-tijd) *adj.* suffering from unfavorable conditions of life, *disadvantaged countries; the disadvantaged,* those suffering disadvantage.

dis·ad·van·ta·geous (dis-ad-văn-tay-jŭs) *adj.* causing disadvantage.

dis·af·fect·ed (dis-ă-fek-tid) *adj.* discontented, having lost one's feelings of loyalty. **dis·af·fec·tion** (dis-ă-fek-shŏn) *n.*

dis·a·gree (dis-ă-gree) *v.* (**dis·a·greed, dis·a·gree·ing**) **1.** to have a different opinion. **2.** to be unlike, to fail to correspond, *your statement disagrees with your brother's.* **3.** to quarrel. **4.** (of food or climate etc.) to have bad effects, *hot weather disagrees with him.* **dis·a·gree′ment** *n.*

dis·a·gree·a·ble (dis-ă-gree-ă-bĕl) *adj.* **1.** unpleasant. **2.** badtempered. **dis·a·gree′a·bly** *adv.* **dis·a·gree′a·ble·ness** *n.*

dis·al·low (dis-ă-low) *v.* to refuse to allow or accept as valid, *the judge disallowed the claim.*

dis·ap·pear (dis-ă-peer) *v.* to cease to be visible, to pass from sight or from existence, *the problem may disappear.* **dis·ap·pear′ance** *n.*

dis·ap·point (dis-ă-point) *v.* to fail to do or be equal to what was hoped or desired or expected by. **dis·ap·point′ment** *n.*

dis·ap·point·ed (dis-ă-poin-tid) *adj.* feeling disappointment, *we were disappointed at the failure or in him* or *with the gift.*

dis·ap·pro·ba·tion (dis-ap-rŏ-bay-shŏn) *n.* disapproval.

dis·ap·prove (dis-ă-proov) *v.* (**dis·ap·proved, dis·ap·prov·ing**) to have or express an unfavorable opinion. **dis·ap·prov′al** *n.*

dis·arm (dis-ahrm) *v.* **1.** to deprive of weapons or of the means of defense. **2.** to disband or reduce armed forces. **3.** to defuse (a bomb). **4.** to make it difficult for a person to feel anger or suspicion or doubt, *his friendliness disarmed their hostility.*

dis·ar·ma·ment (dis-ahr-mă-mĕnt) *n.* reduction of a country's armed forces or weapons of war.

dis·ar·range (dis-ă-raynj) *v.* (**dis·ar·ranged, dis·ar·rang·ing**) to put into disorder, to disorganize. **dis·ar·range′ment** *n.*

dis·ar·ray (dis-ă-ray) *n.* disorder. **disarray** *v.* to disarrange.

dis·as·sem·ble (dis-ă-sem-bĕl) *v.* (**dis·as·sem·bled, dis·as·sem·bling**) to take (a machine etc.) apart. ▷Do not confuse *disassemble* with *dissemble.*

dis·as·so·ci·ate (dis-ă-soh-si-ayt) *v.* (**dis·as·so·ci·at·ed, dis·as·so·ci·at·ing**) to remove from association, to cease associating with.

dis·as·ter (di-zas-těr) *n.* 1. a sudden great misfortune. 2. a complete failure, *the performance was a disaster.* **dis·as'trous** *adj.* **dis·as'trous·ly** *adv.* ☐**disaster area**, an area in which a major disaster (such as an earthquake) has recently occurred.

dis·a·vow (dis-ă-vow) *v.* to disclaim. **dis·a·vow'al** *n.*

dis·band (dis-band) *v.* to break up, to separate, *disbanded the choir; the troops disbanded.* **dis·band'ment** *n.*

dis·bar (dis-bahr) *v.* (**dis·barred, dis·bar·ring**) to expel from membership in the legal profession. **dis·bar'ment** *n.*

dis·be·lieve (dis-bi-leev) *v.* (**dis·be·lieved, dis·be·liev·ing**) to refuse or be unable to believe. **dis·be·liev'er** *n.* **dis·be·lief** (dis-bi-leef) *n.*

dis·bur·den (dis-bur-děn) *v.* to relieve of a burden.

dis·burse (dis-burs) *v.* (**dis·bursed, dis·burs·ing**) to pay out (money), *disbursing large amounts.* **dis·burse'ment** *n.* **dis·burs'a·ble** *adj.* ▷Do not confuse *disburse* with *disperse.*

disc (disk) *n.* 1. a disk. 2. a phonograph record. 3. a plate coated with magnetic material on which computer data are stored. ☐**disc jockey,** *(informal)* a person who conducts a broadcast program of records of popular music.

disc. *abbr.* 1. discount. 2. discovered.

dis·card (di-skahrd) *v.* to throw away, to put aside as useless or unwanted. **discard** (dis-kahrd) *n.* something discarded.

dis·cern (di-surn, -zurn) *v.* to perceive clearly with the mind or senses. **dis·cern'ment** *n.*

dis·cern·i·ble (di-sur-nĭ-běl, -zur-) *adj.* able to be discerned. **dis·cern'i·bly** *adv.*

dis·cern·ing (di-sur-ning, -zur-) *adj.* perceptive, showing good judgment. **dis·cern'ing·ly** *adv.*

dis·charge (dis-chahrj) *v.* (**dis·charged, dis·charg·ing**). 1. to give or send out, *the pipes discharge their contents into the river; the river discharges into the sea,* flows into it; *the wound is still discharging,* matter is coming out. 2. to give out an electric charge, to cause to do this. 3. to fire (a missile or gun). 4. to dismiss from employment. 5. to allow to leave, *the patient was discharged from the hospital.* 6. to pay (a debt), to perform or fulfill (a duty or contract). **discharge** (dis-chahrj) *n.* 1. discharging, being discharged. 2. something that is discharged, *the discharge from the wound.*

dis·ci·ple (di-sɪ-pěl) *n.* 1. *Disciple,* one of the original followers of Christ. 2. a person who follows the teachings of another whom he accepts as a leader.

dis·ci·pli·nar·i·an (dis-ĭ-plĭ-nair-i-ăn) *n.* one who enforces or believes in strict discipline.

dis·ci·pli·nar·y (dis-ĭ-plĭ-ner-ee) *adj.* of or for discipline.

dis·ci·pline (dis-ĭ-plin) *n.* 1. training that produces obedience, self-control, or a particular skill. 2. controlled behavior produced by such training. 3. punishment given to correct a person or enforce obedience. 4. a branch of instruction or learning, *an academic discipline.* **discipline** *v.* (**dis·ci·plined, dis·ci·plin·ing**) 1. to train to be obedient and orderly. 2. to punish.

dis·claim (dis-klaym) *v.* to disown; *they disclaim responsibility for the accident,* say that they are not responsible.

dis·claim·er (dis-klay-měr) *n.* a statement disclaiming something.

dis·close (dis-klohz) *v.* (**dis·closed, dis·clos·ing**) to expose to view, to reveal, to make known. **dis·clo·sure** (dis-kloh-zhŭr) *n.*

dis·co (dis-koh) *n.* (*pl.* **-cos**) *(informal)* a discothèque. **disco** *adj.* *(informal)* of or suitable for a discothèque, *disco music; disco dancing.*

dis·col·or (dis-kul-ŏr) *v.* 1. to spoil the color of, to stain. 2. to become changed in color. **dis·col·or·a·tion** (dis-kul-ŏ-ray-shŏn) *n.*

dis·com·bob·u·late (dis-kŏm-bob-yŭ-layt) *v.* (**dis·com·bob·u·lat·ed, dis·com·bob·u·lat·ing**) *(informal)* to disturb or confuse.

dis·com·fit (dis-kum-fit) *v.* (**dis·com·fit·ed, dis·com·fit·ing**) to disconcert. **dis·com·fi·ture** (dis-kum-fi-chŭr) *n.* ▷Do not confuse *discomfit* with *discomfort.*

dis·com·fort (dis-kum-fŏrt) *n.* 1. lack of comfort in body or mind. 2. something that causes this. **discomfort** *v.* ▷Do not confuse *discomfort* with *discomfit.*

dis·com·mode (dis-kŏ-mohd) *v.* (**dis·com·mod·ed, dis·com·mod·ing**) *(old use)* to put to inconvenience.

dis·com·pose (dis-kŏm-pohz) *v.* (**dis·com·posed, dis·com·pos·ing**) to disturb the composure of, to agitate. **dis·com·po·sure** (dis-kom-poh-zhŭr) *n.*

dis·con·cert (dis-kŏn-surt) *v.* to upset the self-possession of, to fluster.

dis·con·nect (dis-kŏ-nekt) *v.* to break the connection of, to put out of action by disconnecting certain parts. **dis·con·nec'tion** *n.*

dis·con·nect·ed (dis-kŏ-nek-tid) *adj.* lacking orderly connection between its parts, *a disconnected speech.* **dis·con·nect'ed·ly** *adv.*

dis·con·so·late (dis-kŏn-sŏ-lit) *adj.* 1. unhappy at the loss of something, disappointed. 2. inconsolable, hopelessly unhappy. **dis·con'so·late·ly** *adv.*

dis·con·tent (dis-kŏn-tent) *n.* dissatisfaction, lack of contentment.

dis·con·tent·ed (dis-kŏn-ten-tid) *adj.* not contented, feeling discontent. **dis·con·tent'ed·ly** *adv.*

dis·con·tin·ue (dis-kŏn-tin-yoo) *v.* (**dis·con·tin·ued, dis·con·tin·u·ing**) to put an end to, to come to an end. **dis·con·tin'u·ance** *n.*

dis·con·tin·u·ous (dis-kŏn-tin-yoo-ŭs) *adj.* not continuous. **dis·con·ti·nu·i·ty** (dis-kon-ti-noo-i-tee) *n.*

dis·cord (dis-kord) *n.* 1. disagreement, quarreling. 2. a combination of notes producing a harsh or unpleasant sound. **dis·cord·ant** (dis-kor-dănt) *adj.* **dis·cord'ant·ly** *adv.*

dis·co·thèque (dis-kŏ-tek) *n.* a nightclub or hall where amplified recorded music is played for dancing.

dis·count (dis-kownt) *n.* an amount of money taken off the full price or total. **discount** (dis-kownt) *v.* 1. to disregard partly or wholly, *we cannot discount this possibility.* 2. to purchase a promissory note etc. for less than its value will be when matured. 3. to sell at a reduced price. **dis·count'a·ble** *adj.* ☐**at a discount,** below the usual or nominal price. **discount store,** one selling goods regularly at less than the standard price.

dis·coun·te·nance (dis-kown-tĕ-năns) *v.* **(dis· coun·te·nanced, dis·coun·te·nanc·ing)** to refuse to countenance, to discourage or show disapproval of.

dis·count·er (dis-kown-tĕr) *n.* a merchant who sells regularly at less than the standard price.

dis·cour·age (dis-kur-ij) *v.* **(dis·cour·aged, dis·cour·ag·ing)** 1. to dishearten. 2. to dissuade. 3. to deter. **dis·cour'age·ment** *n.* **dis· cour'ag·ing·ly** *adv.*

dis·course (dis-kohrs) *n.* a speech or lecture, a written treatise on a subject. **discourse** (dis-kohrs) *v.* **(dis·coursed, dis·cours·ing)** to utter or write a discourse.

dis·cour·te·ous (dis-kur-ti-ŭs) *adj.* lacking courtesy, rude. **dis·cour'te·ous·ly** *adv.*

dis·cour·te·sy (dis-kur-tĕ-see) *n.* (*pl.* **-sies**) rudeness, an impolite or uncivil action.

dis·cov·er (dis-kuv-ĕr) *v.* 1. to obtain sight or knowledge of, especially by searching or other effort. 2. to be the first to do this, *Herschel discovered a new planet.* **dis·cov'er·er** *n.* **dis· cov'er·a·ble** *adj.*

dis·cov·er·y (dis-kuv-ĕ-ree) *n.* (*pl.* **-er·ies**) 1. discovering, being discovered. 2. something that is discovered.

dis·cred·it (dis-kred-it) *v.* 1. to damage the good reputation of. 2. to refuse to believe. 3. to cause to be disbelieved. **discredit** *n.* 1. damage to reputation. 2. something that causes this. 3. doubt, lack of credibility.

dis·cred·it·a·ble (dis-kred-i-tă-bĕl) *adj.* bringing discredit, shameful. **dis·cred'it·a·bly** *adv.*

dis·creet (dis-skreet) *adj.* 1. showing caution and good judgment in what one does, not giving away secrets, *a discreet reply.* 2. not showy or obtrusive, *discreet manners.* **dis·creet'ly** *adv.* ▷Do not confuse *discreet* with *discrete.*

dis·crep·an·cy (dis-skrep-ăn-see) *n.* (*pl.* **-cies**) difference, disagreement, failure to tally, *there were several discrepancies between the two accounts.* **dis·crep'ant** *adj.*

dis·crete (dis-screet) *adj.* discontinuous, individually distinct, *there were three discrete parts.* **dis· crete'ly** *adv.* **dis·crete'ness** *n.* ▷Do not confuse *discrete* with *discreet.*

dis·cre·tion (dis-skresh-ŏn) *n.* 1. being discreet in one's speech, keeping secrets. 2. good judgment, *he acted with discretion.* 3. freedom to act according to one's judgment, *the treasurer has full discretion.* ☐**at a person's discretion,** in accordance with his decision.

dis·cre·tion·ar·y (dis-skresh-ŏ-ner-ee) *adj.* done or used at a person's discretion, *discretionary powers.* ☐**discretionary income,** money beyond that needed for essentials, which can be spent as one pleases.

dis·crim·i·nate (di-skrim-ĭ-nayt) *v.* **(dis·crim· i·nat·ed, dis·crim·i·nat·ing)** 1. to have good taste or judgment. 2. to make a distinction, to give unfair treatment, especially because of prejudice, *they had discriminated against him.* **dis· crim'i·nat·ing** *adj.* **dis·crim'i·nat·ing·ly** *adv.* **dis·crim·i·na·tion** (di-skrim-ĭ-nay-shŏn) *n.*

dis·crim·i·na·to·ry (di-skrim-ĭ-nă-tohr-ee) *adj.* characterized by discrimination and bias.

dis·cur·sive (dis-kur-siv) *adj.* rambling from one subject to another. **dis·cur'sive·ly** *adv.* **dis· cur'sive·ness** *n.*

dis·cus (dis-kŭs) *n.* (*pl.* **dis·cus·es, dis·ci,** *pr.* **dis-ɪ**) a heavy disk thrown for distance by a **discus thrower** in a track-and-field competition.

dis·cuss (di-skus) *v.* to examine by means of argument, to talk or write about. **dis·cus·sion** (di-skush-ŏn) *n.*

dis·cus·sant (di-skus-ănt) *n.* *(formal)* a person who takes part in a discussion.

dis·dain (dis-dayn) *n.* scorn, contempt. **disdain** *v.* 1. to regard with disdain, to treat as unworthy of notice. 2. to refrain because of disdain, *she disdained to reply.* **dis·dain'ful** *adj.* **dis· dain'ful·ly** *adv.*

dis·ease (di-zeez) *n.* an unhealthy condition caused by infection or diet or conditions of life, or inherited.

dis·eased (di-zeezd) *adj.* affected with disease.

dis·em·bark (dis-ĕm-bahrk) *v.* to put or go ashore.

dis·em·bar·ka·tion (dis-em-bahr-kay-shŏn) *n.*

dis·em·bod·i·ed (dis-em-bod-eed) *adj.* (of the soul or spirit) freed from the body.

dis·em·bow·el (dis-em-bow-ĕl) *v.* **(dis·em· bow·eled, dis·em·bow·el·ing)** to take out the bowels of. **dis·em·bow'el·ment** *n.*

dis·en·chant (dis-en-chant) *v.* to free from enchantment, to disillusion, *they are disenchanted with the government.* **dis·en·chant'ment** *n.*

dis·en·cum·ber (dis-en-kum-bĕr) *v.* to free from encumbrance.

dis·en·fran·chise (dis-en-fran-chɪz) *v.* **(dis·en· fran·chised, dis·en·fran·chis·ing)** to disfranchise. **dis·en·fran'chise·ment** *n.*

dis·en·gage (dis-en-gayj) *v.* **(dis·en·gaged, dis·en·gag·ing)** to free from engagement, to detach. **dis·en·gage'ment** *n.*

dis·en·gaged (dis-en-gayjd) *adj.* not engaged in attending to another person or to business, free.

dis·en·tan·gle (dis-en-tang-gĕl) *v.* **(dis·en· tan·gled, dis·en·tan·gling)** to free from tangles or confusion, to extricate. **dis·en·tan'gle· ment** *n.*

dis·es·tab·lish (dis-e-stab-lish) *v.* to end the established state of, to deprive (a church) of its official connection with the state.

dis·es·tab·lish·ment (dis-e-stab-lish-mĕnt) *n.* separation of church and state. **dis·es·tab·lish· men·tar·i·an·ism** (dis-e-stab-lish-men-ter-i-ă-niz-ĕm) *n.* a policy favoring disestablishment.

dis·es·teem (dis-ĕ-steem) *n.* lack of esteem.

di·seur (dee-zur) *n.* a male performer who recites monologues. ▷French.

di·seuse (dee-zuuz) *n.* a female diseur. ▷French.

dis·fa·vor (dis-fay-vŏr) *n.* dislike, disapproval.

dis·fig·ure (dis-fig-yŭr) *v.* **(dis·fig·ured, dis· fig·ur·ing)** to spoil the appearance of. **dis· fig'ure·ment** *n.*

dis·fran·chise (dis-fran-chɪz) *v.* **(dis·fran· chised, dis·fran·chis·ing)** to deprive of the right to vote. **dis·fran'chise·ment** *n.*

dis·gorge (dis-gorj) *v.* **(dis·gorged, dis·gorg· ing)** 1. to throw out from the gorge or throat, *the whale swallowed Jonah and then disgorged him.* 2. to pour forth, *the river disgorges itself into the sea.*

dis·grace (dis-grays) *n.* 1. loss of favor or respect. 2. something that causes this. **disgrace** *v.* **(dis· graced, dis·grac·ing)** to bring disgrace upon, to humiliate. **dis·grace'ful** *adj.* **dis·grace' ful·ly** *adv.*

dis·grun·tled (dis-grun-tĕld) *adj.* discontented, resentful.

dis·guise (dis-gɪz) *v.* **(dis·guised, dis·guis·ing)** 1. to conceal the identity of. 2. to conceal; *there's no disguising the fact,* it cannot be concealed. **disguise** *n.* 1. something worn or used for dis-

guising. 2. disguising, a disguised condition.
▷ Do not confuse *disguise* with *guise*.

dis·gust (dis-gust) *n.* a strong feeling of dislike, finding a thing very unpleasant or against one's principles. **disgust** *v.* to cause disgust in. **dis·gust'ing·ly** *adv.* **dis·gust·ed** (dis-gus-tid) *adj.* feeling disgust. **dis·gust'ed·ly** *adv.*

dish (dish) *n.* 1. a shallow flat-bottomed container for holding or serving food; *wash the dishes,* wash all the utensils after use at a meal. 2. the amount a dish contains. 3. the food itself, a particular kind of food. 4. a shallow concave object. 5. *(slang)* an attractive woman or girl. **dish** *v.* 1. to serve (food) in a dish. 2. to make or become concave. □**dish out,** *(informal)* to distribute. **dish up,** to put food into dishes ready for serving; *(slang)* to serve up as facts etc., *dished up the usual excuses.*

dis·ha·bille (dis-ă-beel) *n.* state of being only partly or not carefully dressed.

dis·har·mo·ny (dis-hahr-mŏ-nee) *n.* (*pl.* -nies) lack of harmony. **dis·har·mo·ni·ous** (dis-hahr-moh-ni-ŭs) *adj.*

dish·cloth (dish-klawth) *n.* (*pl.* -cloths, *pr.* -klaw*th*z) a cloth for washing dishes.

dis·heart·en (dis-hahr-těn) *v.* to cause to lose hope or confidence. **dis·heart'en·ment** *n.*

dished (disht) *adj.* concave.

di·shev·eled (di-shev-ĕld) *adj.* ruffled and untidy. **di·shev'el·ment** *n.*

dis·hon·est (dis-on-ist) *adj.* not honest. **dis·hon'est·ly** *adv.* **dis·hon'est·y** *n.*

dis·hon·or (dis-on-ŏr) *n.* 1. loss of honor or respect, disgrace. 2. something that causes this. **dishonor** *v.* to bring dishonor upon, to disgrace. **dis·hon·or·able** (dis-on-ŏ-ră-běl) *adj.* not honorable, shameful. **dis·hon'or·a·bly** *adv.*

dish·wash·er (dish-wosh-ĕr) *n.* a machine for washing dishes etc. automatically, a person who washes dishes.

dish·wa·ter (dish-waw-těr) *n.* water in which dishes have been washed. □**dull as dishwater,** very dull.

dis·il·lu·sion (dis-i-loo-zhŏn) *v.* to set free from pleasant but mistaken beliefs. **disillusion** *n.* the state of being disillusioned. **dis·il·lu'sion·ment** *n.*

dis·in·cen·tive (dis-in-sen-tiv) *n.* something that discourages an action or effort.

dis·in·cli·na·tion (dis-in-kli-nay-shŏn) *n.* unwillingness, a slight dislike.

dis·in·cline (dis-in-klɪn) *v.* (**dis·in·clined, dis·in·clin·ing**) to make (a person) feel reluctant or unwilling to do something.

dis·in·fect (dis-in-fekt) *v.* to cleanse by destroying bacteria that may cause disease. **dis·in·fec'tion** *n.*

dis·in·fect·ant (dis-in-fek-tănt) *n.* a substance used for disinfecting things.

dis·in·gen·u·ous (dis-in-jen-yoo-ŭs) *adj.* insincere, not frank.

dis·in·her·it (dis-in-her-it) *v.* to deprive (a person) of an inheritance by making a will naming another or others as one's heir(s).

dis·in·te·grate (di-sin-tĕ-grayt) *v.* (**dis·in·te·grat·ed, dis·in·te·grat·ing**) to break or cause to break into small parts or pieces. **dis·in·te·gra·tion** (di-sin-tĕ-gray-shŏn) *n.*

dis·in·ter (dis-in-tur) *v.* (**dis·in·terred, dis·in·ter·ring**) to dig up (something buried), to unearth.

dis·in·ter·est·ed (dis-in-tĕ-res-tid) *adj.* 1. unbiased, not influenced by self-interest. 2. uninterested, uncaring. (▷ Careful writers regard the second use as unacceptable because it obscures a useful distinction between *disinterested* and *uninterested.*) **dis·in'ter·est·ed·ly** *adv.* **dis·in'ter·est·ed·ness** *n.*

dis·join (dis-join) *v.* to separate.

dis·joint (dis-joint) *v.* 1. to cut (a roasted fowl) apart at the joints. 2. to dislocate, to disturb. **dis·joint·ed** (dis-join-tid) *adj.* 1. (of talk) disconnected, incoherent. 2. (of a roasted fowl) cut apart at the joints.

disk (disk) *n.* 1. something shaped or looking like a thin circular plate, *the sun's disk.* 2. a layer of cartilage between vertebrae. 3. a disc. □**disk brake,** one in which a flat plate presses against a plate at the center of a wheel. **disk harrow,** a harrow with rows of sloping concave disks. **slipped disk,** a disk between vertebrae that has become displaced.

dis·like (dis-lɪk) *n.* a feeling of not liking something. **dislike** *v.* (**dis·liked, dis·lik·ing**) to feel dislike for.

dis·lo·cate (dis-loh-kayt) *v.* (**dis·lo·cat·ed, dis·lo·cat·ing**) 1. to put (a thing) out of place in relation to connecting parts, to displace (a bone) from its proper position in a joint. 2. to put out of order, to disrupt, *fog dislocated traffic.* **dis·lo·ca·tion** (dis-loh-kay-shŏn) *n.*

dis·lodge (dis-loj) *v.* (**dis·lodged, dis·lodg·ing**) to move or force from an established position.

dis·loy·al (dis-loi-ăl) *adj.* not loyal. **dis·loy'al·ly** *adv.* **dis·loy'al·ty** *n.* (*pl.* -ties).

dis·mal (diz-măl) *adj.* 1. causing or showing gloom, dreary. 2. feeble, *a dismal attempt at humor.* **dis'mal·ly** *adv.*

dis·man·tle (dis-man-těl) *v.* (**dis·man·tled, dis·man·tling**) to take away fittings or furnishings from, to take to pieces. **dis·man'tle·ment** *n.*

dis·may (dis-may) *n.* a feeling of surprise and discouragement. **dismay** *v.* to fill with dismay. **dis·may'ing·ly** *adv.*

dis·mem·ber (dis-mem-běr) *v.* 1. to remove the limbs of. 2. to divide into parts, to partition (a country etc.). **dis·mem'ber·ment** *n.*

dis·miss (dis-mis) *v.* 1. to send away from one's presence or employment. 2. to put out of one's thoughts, to mention or discuss only briefly. 3. to reject without further hearing, *the case was dismissed for lack of evidence.* **dis·miss'al** *n.* **dis·miss'i·ble** *adj.*

dis·mount (dis-mownt) *v.* 1. to get off or down from something on which one is riding. 2. to cause to fall off, to unseat.

dis·o·be·di·ent (dis-ŏ-bee-di-ěnt) *adj.* not obedient. **dis·o·be'di·ent·ly** *adv.* **dis·o·be'di·ence** *n.*

dis·o·bey (dis-ŏ-bay) *v.* to disregard others, to fail or refuse to obey.

dis·o·blige (dis-ŏ-blɪj) *v.* (**dis·o·bliged, dis·o·blig·ing**) to disregard the wishes or convenience of (a person).

dis·or·der (dis-or-děr) *n.* 1. lack of order, untidiness. 2. a disturbance of public order, a riot. 3. disturbance of the normal working of the body or mind, *a nervous disorder.* **disorder** *v.* to throw into disorder, to upset. **dis·or'der·ly** *adj.*

dis·or·gan·ize (dis-or-gă-nɪz) *v.* (**dis·or·gan·ized, dis·or·gan·iz·ing**) to throw into confusion, to upset the orderly system or arrangement of.

dis·or·gan·ized (dis-or-gă-nɪzd) *adj.* lacking organization or an orderly system.

dis·o·ri·ent (dis-ohr-i-ent) *v.* to confuse (a person) and make him lose his bearings.

dis·o·ri·en·tate (dis-ohr-i-ĕn-tayt) *v.* **(dis·o·ri·en·tat·ed, dis·o·ri·en·tat·ing)** to disorient. **dis·o·ri·en·ta·tion** (dis-ohr-i-ĕn-tay-shŏn) *n.*

dis·own (dis-ohn) *v.* to refuse to acknowledge as one's own, to reject all connection with.

dis·par·age (di-spar-ij) *v.* **(dis·par·aged, dis·par·ag·ing)** to speak of in a slighting way, to belittle. **dis·par′ag·ing·ly** *adv.* **dis·par′age·ment** *n.*

dis·pa·rate (dis-pă-rit) *adj.* different in kind. **dis′pa·rate·ly** *adv.*

dis·par·i·ty (di-spar-i-tee) *n.* (*pl.* **-ties**) inequality, difference.

dis·pas·sion (dis-pash-ŏn) *n.* freedom from emotion.

dis·pas·sion·ate (dis-pash-ŏ-nit) *adj.* free from emotion, calm, impartial. **dis·pas′sion·ate·ly** *adv.*

dis·patch (di-spach) *v.* 1. to send off to a destination or for a purpose. 2. to give the deathblow to, to kill. 3. to complete or dispose of quickly. **dispatch** *n.* 1. dispatching, being dispatched. 2. promptness, speed, *she acted with dispatch.* 3. an official message or report sent with speed. 4. a news report sent to a newspaper or news agency etc. **dis·patch′er** *n.* □**dispatch case,** a container for carrying official documents.

dis·pel (di-spel) *v.* **(dis·pelled, dis·pel·ling)** to drive away, to scatter, *wind dispelled the fog; how can we dispel their fears?*

dis·pen·sa·ble (di-spen-să-bĕl) *adj.* 1. not essential. 2. able to be dispensed, *a dispensable drug.*

dis·pen·sa·ry (di-spen-să-ree) *n.* (*pl.* **-ries**) a place where medicines are dispensed, *the hospital dispensary.*

dis·pen·sa·tion (dis-pĕn-say-shŏn) *n.* 1. dispensing, distributing. 2. ordering or management, especially of the world by divine authority, *by the merciful dispensation of Providence.* 3. exemption from a penalty or duty, *was granted a dispensation.*

dis·pense (di-spens) *v.* **(dis·pensed, dis·pens·ing)** 1. to distribute, to deal out; *dispense justice,* to administer it. 2. to prepare and give out (medicines etc.) according to prescriptions. □**dispense with,** to do without; to make unnecessary.

dis·pens·er (di-spen-sĕr) *n.* 1. a person who dispenses medicines. 2. a device that deals out a quantity of something, *a soap dispenser.*

dis·per·sant (di-spur-sănt) *n.* a substance that disperses something.

dis·perse (di-spurs) *v.* **(dis·persed, dis·pers·ing)** to scatter, to go or drive or send in different directions. **dis·per′sal** *n.* **dis·per·sion** (di-spur-zhŏn) *n.* ▷Do not confuse *disperse* with *disburse.*

dis·pir·it (di-spir-it) *v.* to make despondent, to depress. **dis·pir′it·ed** *adj.*

dis·place (dis-plays) *v.* **(dis·placed, dis·plac·ing)** 1. to shift from its place. 2. to take the place of, to oust, *weeds tend to displace other plants.* **dis·place′ment** *n.* □**displaced person,** a refugee.

dis·play (di-splay) *v.* 1. to show, to arrange (a thing) so that it can be seen. 2. (of birds and animals) to make a display (see definition 3 below). **display** *n.* 1. displaying, being displayed. 2. something displayed conspicuously. 3. a special pattern of behavior used by birds and animals as a means of communication.

dis·please (dis-pleez) *v.* **(dis·pleased, dis·pleas·ing)** to offend, to arouse the disapproval or anger of.

dis·pleas·ure (dis-plezh-ŭr) *n.* a displeased feeling, dissatisfaction.

dis·port (dis-spohrt) *v.* (*formal*) to play, to amuse oneself, *disporting themselves on the beach.*

dis·pos·a·ble (dis-spoh-ză-bĕl) *adj.* 1. able to be disposed of. 2. at one's disposal; *disposable income,* the amount left after taxes have been deducted. 3. designed to be thrown away after being used once, *disposable diapers.*

dis·pos·al (di-spoh-zăl) *n.* disposing of something. □**at one's disposal,** available for one's use.

dis·pose (di-spohz) *v.* **(dis·posed, dis·pos·ing)** 1. to place suitably or in order, *disposed the troops in two lines.* 2. to determine the course of events, *man proposes, God disposes.* 3. to make willing or ready to do something, to incline, *their friendliness disposed us to accept the invitation; we felt disposed to accept.* **dis·pos′er** *n.* □**be well disposed toward,** to be friendly toward, to favor. **dispose of,** to get rid of; to deal with.

dis·po·si·tion (dis-pŏ-zish-ŏn) *n.* 1. setting in order, arrangement, *the disposition of troops.* 2. a person's natural qualities of mind and character, *has a cheerful disposition.* 3. a natural tendency or inclination, *they show a disposition to change jobs frequently.*

dis·pos·sess (dis-pŏ-zes) *v.* to deprive (a person) of the possession of something. **dis·pos·ses′sion** *n.*

dis·pro·por·tion (dis-prŏ-pohr-shŏn) *n.* lack of proper proportion, being out of proportion. **dis·pro·por′tion·ate** *adj.* **dis·pro·por′tion·ate·ly** *adv.*

dis·prove (dis-proov) *v.* **(dis·proved, dis·prov·ing)** to show to be false or wrong. **dis·proof** (dis-proof) *n.*

dis·put·a·ble (dis-pyoo-tă-bĕl) *adj.* able to be disputed, questionable. **dis·put′a·bly** *adv.*

dis·pu·tant (dis-pyoo-tănt) *n.* a person engaged in a dispute.

dis·pu·ta·tion (dis-pyŭ-tay-shŏn) *n.* argument, debate.

dis·pu·ta·tious (dis-pyŭ-tay-shŭs) *adj.* fond of, or given to, argument.

dis·pute (dis-pyoot) *v.* **(dis·put·ed, dis·put·ing)** 1. to argue, to debate. 2. to quarrel. 3. to question the truth or validity of, *dispute a claim; the disputed territory,* that which is the subject of a dispute. **dispute** *n.* 1. an argument or debate. 2. a quarrel. **dis·put′er** *n.* □**in dispute,** being argued about.

dis·qual·i·fy (dis-kwol-ɪ-fɪ) *v.* **(dis·qual·i·fied, dis·qual·i·fy·ing)** 1. to debar from a competition because of an infringement of the rules, *that team was disqualified from the race.* 2. to make unsuitable or ineligible, *weak eyesight disqualifies him for military service.* **dis·qual·i·fi·ca·tion** (dis-kwol-ɪ-fi-kay-shŏn) *n.*

dis·qui·et (dis-kwɪ-ĕt) *n.* uneasiness, anxiety. **disquiet** *v.* to make uneasy or anxious.

dis·qui·et·ing (dis-kwɪ-ĕ-ting) *adj.* causing disquiet.

dis·qui·e·tude (dis-kwɪ-ĕ-tood) *n.* a state of uneasiness, anxiety.

dis·qui·si·tion (dis-kwi-zish-ŏn) *n.* a long elaborate spoken or written account of something.

dis·re·gard (dis-ri-gahrd) *v.* to pay no attention to, to treat as of no importance. **disregard** *n.* lack of attention to something, treating it as of no importance, *complete disregard for his own safety.*

dis·re·mem·ber (dis-ri-mem-bĕr) *v. (informal)* to fail to remember. ▷Careful writers and speakers use this word humorously if at all.

dis·re·pair (dis-ri-pair) *n.* a bad condition caused by lack of repairs, *in a state of disrepair.*

dis·rep·u·ta·ble (dis-rep-yŭ-tă-bĕl) *adj.* having a bad reputation, not respectable in character or appearance. **dis·rep′u·ta·bly** *adv.*

dis·re·pute (dis-ri-pyoot) *n.* lack of good repute, discredit, *fell into disrepute.*

dis·re·spect (dis-ri-spekt) *n.* lack of respect, rudeness. **dis·re·spect′ful** *adj.*

dis·robe (dis-rohb) *v.* **(dis·robed, dis·rob·ing)** to take off official or ceremonial robes, to undress.

dis·rupt (dis-rupt) *v.* to cause to break up, to throw into disorder, to interrupt the flow or continuity of, *party quarrels disrupted the coalition; floods disrupted traffic.* **dis·rup·tion** (dis-rup-shŏn) *n.*

dis·rup·tive (dis-rup-tiv) *adj.* causing disruption.

dis·sat·is·fac·tion (dis-sat-is-fak-shŏn) *n.* lack of satisfaction or of contentment.

dis·sat·is·fy (dis-sat-is-fī) *v.* **(dis·sat·is·fied, dis·sat·is·fy·ing)** to fail to satisfy, to make discontented. **dis·sat′is·fied** *adj.*

dis·sect (di-sekt) *v.* 1. to cut apart, especially in order to examine internal structure, *we dissected a worm.* 2. to examine (a theory etc.) part by part. **dis·sec′tor** *n.* **dis·sec·tion** (di-sek-shŏn) *n.* ▷Note the spelling and pronunciation of *dissect.*

dis·sem·ble (di-sem-bĕl) *v.* **(dis·sem·bled, dis·sem·bling)** to conceal (one's true feelings or motives), to pretend. ▷Do not confuse *dissemble* with *disassemble.*

dis·sem·i·nate (di-sem-ĭ-nayt) *v.* **(dis·sem·i·nat·ed, dis·sem·i·nat·ing)** to spread (ideas etc.) widely. **dis·sem·i·na·tion** (di-sem-ĭ-nay-shŏn) *n.*

dis·sen·sion (di-sen-shŏn) *n.* disagreement that gives rise to strife.

dis·sent (di-sent) *v.* to have or express a different opinion. **dissent** *n.* a difference in opinion.

dis·sent·er (di-sen-tĕr) *n.* 1. a person who dissents. 2. *Dissenter,* a member of a church that has separated itself from the Church of England.

dis·sen·tient (di-sen-shĕnt) *adj.* dissenting. **dissentient** *n.* a person who dissents.

dis·ser·ta·tion (dis-ĕr-tay-shŏn) *n.* 1. a spoken or written discourse. 2. a substantial treatise written as part of the requirements for a doctorate.

dis·serv·ice (dis-sur-vis) *n.* a harmful action done by a person who intended to help.

dis·sev·er (di-sev-ĕr) *v.* to sever, to divide.

dis·si·dent (dis-i-dĕnt) *adj.* disagreeing. **dissident** *n.* a person who disagrees, one who opposes the authorities. **dis′si·dence** *n.*

dis·sim·i·lar (dis-sim-ĭ-lăr) *adj.* unlike. **dis·sim·i·lar·i·ty** (di-sim-ĭ-lar-i-tee) *n.*

dis·sim·u·late (di-sim-yŭ-layt) *v.* **(dis·sim·u·lat·ed, dis·sim·u·lat·ing)** to dissemble. **dis·sim·u·la·tion** (di-sim-yŭ-lay-shŏn) *n.*

dis·si·pate (dis-ĭ-payt) *v.* **(dis·si·pat·ed, dis·si·pat·ing)** 1. to dispel, to disperse. 2. to squander or fritter away.

dis·si·pat·ed (dis-ĭ-pay-tid) *adj.* indulging one's vices, living a dissolute life.

dis·si·pa·tion (dis-ĭ-pay-shŏn) *n.* 1. dissipating. 2. dissipated practices.

dis·so·ci·ate (di-soh-shi-ayt, di-soh-si-) *v.* **(dis·so·ci·at·ed, dis·so·ci·at·ing)** to separate in one's thought, *it is difficult to dissociate the man from his work; dissociate oneself from a project,* to declare that one has no connection with it. **dis·so·ci·a·tion** (di-soh-shi-ay-shŏn, di-soh-si-) *n.*

dis·so·lute (dis-ŏ-loot) *adj.* lacking moral restraint or self-discipline. **dis′so·lute·ly** *adv.* **dis′so·lute·ness** *n.*

dis·so·lu·tion (dis-ŏ-loo-shŏn) *n.* the dissolving of an assembly or partnership.

dis·solve (di-zolv) *v.* **(dis·solved, dis·solv·ing)** 1. to make or become liquid, to disperse or cause to be dispersed in a liquid. 2. to cause to disappear, to disappear gradually. 3. to dismiss or disperse (an assembly, such as a parliament), to annul or put an end to (a partnership, such as a marriage). 4. to give way to emotion, *she dissolved into tears.*

dis·so·nant (dis-ŏ-nănt) *adj.* discordant. **dis′so·nance** *n.*

dis·suade (di-swayd) *v.* **(dis·suad·ed, dis·suad·ing)** to discourage or persuade against a course of action, *dissuaded her from going.* **dis·sua·sion** (di-sway-zhŏn) *n.*

dis·sua·sive (di-sway-siv) *adj.* dissuading.

dist. *abbr.* 1. distance. 2. distant. 3. district.

dis·taff (dis-taf) *n.* 1. a cleft stick holding wool etc. for spinning. 2. woman's work. **distaff** *adj.* female, maternal. □**on the distaff side,** on the mother's side of a family.

dis·tal (dis-tăl) *adj.* (in anatomy) away from the center of the body or from the point of attachment, *a distal bone.*

dis·tance (dis-tăns) *n.* 1. the length of space between one point and another. 2. a distant part, *in the distance.* 3. being distant, remoteness. **distance** *v.* to outdistance in a race. □**at a distance,** far off, not very near; *keep someone at a distance,* to avoid becoming too friendly. **keep one's distance,** to remain at a safe distance; to behave aloofly, to be not very friendly. **within walking distance,** near enough to be reached easily by walking.

dis·tant (dis-tănt) *adj.* 1. at a specified or considerable distance away, *three miles distant.* 2. remote, much apart in space or time or relationship etc., *the distant past; a distant cousin.* 3. not friendly, aloof. **dis′tant·ly** *adv.*

dis·taste (dis-tayst) *n.* dislike.

dis·taste·ful (dis-tayst-fŭl) *adj.* unpleasant, arousing distaste. **dis·taste′ful·ly** *adv.*

dis·tem·per (dis-tem-pĕr) *n.* a disease of dogs and certain other animals, with coughing and weakness.

dis·tend (di-stend) *v.* to swell or become swollen by pressure from within. **dis·ten·tion, dis·ten·sion** (di-sten-shŏn) *n.* **dis·ten·si·ble** (di-sten-sĭ-bĕl) *adj.*

dis·tich (dis-tik) *n.* a pair of lines of verse, a couplet.

dis·till (di-stil) *v.* 1. to treat by distillation, to make or produce or purify in this way. 2. to undergo distillation.

dis·til·late (dis-tĭ-lit) *n.* a product of the vapor produced during distillation.

dis·til·la·tion (dis-tĭ-lay-shŏn) *n.* 1. the process

of turning a substance to vapor by heat, cooling the vapor so that it condenses, and collecting the resulting liquid in order to purify it or separate its constituents or extract an essence. 2. something distilled.

dis·till·er (dis-stil-ĕr) *n.* a person who distills, one who makes alcoholic liquors by distillation.

dis·till·er·y (di-stil-ĕr-ee) *n.* (*pl.* **-er·ies**) a place where whiskey and other alcoholic liquors are produced.

dis·tinct (dis-stingkt) *adj.* 1. able to be perceived clearly by the senses or the mind, definite and unmistakable, *a distinct improvement.* 2. different in kind, separate, *his hobbies are quite distinct from his work.* **dis·tinct′ly** *adv.* **dis·tinct′ness** *n.* ▷See the note under **distinctive.**

dis·tinc·tion (dis-stingk-shŏn) *n.* 1. seeing or making a difference between things. 2. a difference seen or made. 3. a thing that differentiates one thing from another. 4. a mark of honor. 5. excellence, *a person of distinction.*

dis·tinc·tive (dis-stingk-tiv) *adj.* serving to distinguish a thing by making it different from others. **dis·tinc′tive·ly** *adv.* **dis·tinc′tive·ness** *n.* ▷Do not confuse *distinctive* with *distinct.* A *distinct* sign is one that can be seen clearly; a *distinctive* sign is one not commonly found elsewhere.

dis·tin·guish (di-sting-gwish) *v.* 1. to see or point out a difference between, to draw distinctions, *we must distinguish facts from rumors.* 2. to make different, to be a characteristic mark or property of, *speech distinguishes man from animals.* 3. to make out by listening or looking, *unable to distinguish distant objects.* 4. to make notable, to bring honor to, *he distinguished himself by his bravery.* **dis·tin′guish·a·ble** *adj.*

dis·tin·guished (di-sting-gwisht) *adj.* 1. showing excellence, *the Distinguished Service Cross.* 2. famous for great achievements. 3. having an air of distinction and dignity.

dis·tort (di-stort) *v.* 1. to pull or twist (a thing) out of its usual shape. 2. to misrepresent, to twist out of the truth. **dis·tor·tion** (di-stor-shŏn) *n.*

distr. *abbr.* 1. distribute. 2. distribution. 3. distributor.

dis·tract (di-strakt) *v.* to draw away the attention of, *distracted him from his work.* ▷Do not confuse *distract* with *detract.*

dis·tract·ed (di-strak-tid) *adj.* distraught.

dis·trac·tion (di-strak-shŏn) *n.* 1. something that distracts the attention and prevents concentration. 2. an amusement or entertainment. 3. mental upset or distress. □**to distraction,** almost to a state of madness.

dis·traught (di-strawt) *adj.* greatly upset, nearly crazy with grief or worry.

dis·tress (di-stres) *n.* 1. suffering caused by pain, worry, illness, or exhaustion. 2. the condition of being damaged or in danger and requiring help, *a ship in distress.* **distress** *v.* to cause distress to. **dis·tress′ful** *adj.*

dis·trib·ute (di-strib-yoot) *v.* (**dis·trib·ut·ed, dis·trib·ut·ing**) 1. to divide and give a share to each of a number, to deal out. 2. to spread or scatter, to place at different points, *distributed his forces.* **dis·tri·bu·tion** (dis-tri-byoo-shŏn) *n.*

dis·trib·u·tive (di-strib-yŭ-tiv) *adj.* 1. of or concerned with distribution. 2. (in grammar) referring to each individual in a group, not to the group itself, as *each, neither, every.* **dis·trib′u·tive·ly** *adv.*

dis·trib·u·tor (dis-trib-yŭ-tŏr) *n.* 1. a person who distributes things, an agent who markets goods. 2. a device for distributing current to the spark plugs in an engine.

dis·trict (dis-trikt) *n.* a part of a country, city, or county having a particular feature or regarded as a unit for a special purpose, *the Lake District; District of Columbia; a postal district.* □**district attorney,** the public prosecutor of a judicial district.

dis·trust (dis-trust) *n.* lack of trust, suspicion. **distrust** *v.* to feel distrust in. **dis·trust′ful** *adj.* **dis·trust′ful·ly** *adv.*

dis·turb (di-sturb) *v.* 1. to break the rest or quiet or calm of. 2. to cause to move from a settled position. **dis·turb′er** *n.*

dis·tur·bance (di-stur-bǎns) *n.* 1. disturbing, being disturbed. 2. a commotion, an outbreak of social or political disorder.

dis·turbed (di-sturbd) *adj.* emotionally or mentally unstable or abnormal.

dis·u·nite (dis-yoo-nɪt) *v.* (**dis·u·nit·ed, dis·u·nit·ing**) to separate, to divide.

dis·u·ni·ty (dis-yoo-ni-tee) *n.* (*pl.* **-ties**) lack of unity.

dis·use (dis-yoos) *n.* the state of not being used, *rusty from disuse.*

dis·used (dis-yoozd) *adj.* no longer used.

ditch (dich) *n.* a narrow trench to hold or carry off water or to serve as a boundary. **ditch** *v.* 1. to make or repair ditches. 2. to drive (a vehicle) into a ditch. 3. (*slang*) to make a forced landing on the sea. 4. (*slang*) to abandon, to discard, to leave in the lurch. □**dull as ditchwater,** very dull (same as *dull as dishwater*).

dith·er (dith-ĕr) *v.* 1. to tremble, to quiver. 2. to hesitate indecisively. **dither** *n.* a state of dithering, nervous excitement or fear, *all in a dither.*

dit·to (dit-oh) *n.* (*pl.* **-tos**) (used in lists to avoid repeating something) the same again. □**ditto marks,** inverted commas " representing the word "ditto."

dit·ty (dit-ee) *n.* (*pl.* **-ties**) a short simple song.

di·u·ret·ic (dy-yŭ-ret-ik) *adj.* causing more urine to be secreted. **diuretic** *n.* a diuretic substance.

di·ur·nal (dɪ-ur-nǎl) *adj.* 1. of the day, not nocturnal. 2. occupying one day.

div. *abbr.* 1. divided. 2. dividend. 3. division. 4. divisor. 5. divorced.

di·va (dee-vǎ) *n.* (*pl.* **di·vas, di·ve,** *pr.* dee-vay) a great woman singer, a prima donna.

di·va·lent (dɪ-vay-lĕnt) *adj.* having a valence of two.

di·van (di-van) *n.* a low couch without a raised back or ends, a bed resembling this.

dive (dɪv) *v.* (**dived** or **dove, dived, div·ing**) 1. to plunge head first into water. 2. (of an aircraft) to plunge steeply downward. 3. (of a submarine or diver) to go under water, *our submarine has dived many times.* 4. to go down or out of sight suddenly, to rush headlong, *dived into a foxhole.* 5. to plunge (into an activity etc.); *she dives right into her work,* begins to work promptly and with great concentration. **dive** *n.* 1. an act of diving. 2. a sharp downward movement or fall. 3. (*slang*) a disreputable place. □**diving board,** a board for diving from. **diving suit,** a watertight suit, usually with a helmet and air supply, for work under water. ▷Careful writers use *dived* rather than *dove* in the past tense.

dive-bomb (dɪv-bom) *v.* to drop bombs from a

diving aircraft. □**dive bomber,** an aircraft used for divebombing.

div·er (dɪ-vĕr) *n.* 1. one who dives. 2. a person who works underwater in a diving suit.

di·verge (di-vurj, dɪ-) *v.* (**di·verged, di·verg·ing**) 1. to go in different directions from a common point or from each other, to become farther apart. 2. to go aside from a path; *diverge from the truth,* depart from it; *our views diverge further from theirs each day.* **di·ver'gent** *adj.* **di·ver'gence** *n.*

di·vers (dɪ-vĕrz) *adj.* (*old use*) several, various.

di·verse (di-vurs, dɪ-) *adj.* of differing kinds. **di·verse'ly** *adv.*

di·ver·si·fy (di-vur-si-fɪ, dɪ-) *v.* (**di·ver·si·fied, di·ver·si·fy·ing**) to introduce variety into, to vary. **di·ver·si·fi·ca·tion** (di-vur-si-fi-kay-shŏn, dɪ-) *n.*

di·ver·sion (di-vur-zhŏn, dɪ-) *n.* 1. diverting something from its course. 2. diverting of attention; *create a diversion,* do something to divert attention. 3. a recreation, an entertainment. 4. an alternative route when a road is temporarily closed to traffic. **di·ver'sion·a·ry** *adj.*

di·ver·si·ty (di-vur-si-tee, dɪ-) *n.* (*pl.* **-ties**) variety.

di·vert (di-vurt, dɪ-) *v.* 1. to turn (a thing) from its course, *divert the stream; divert attention,* distract it; *divert traffic,* cause it to go by a different route. 2. to entertain or amuse with recreations.

di·ver·tic·u·li·tis (dɪ-vĕr-tik-yŭ-lɪ-tis) *n.* inflammation of a diverticulum.

di·ver·tic·u·lum (dɪ-vĕr-tik-yŭ-lŭm) *n.* (*pl.* **-la,** *pr.* -lă) a tubular branch of a cavity or passage in the body, especially in the colon.

di·vert·ing (di-vur-ting, dɪ-) *adj.* entertaining, amusing.

di·vest (di-vest) *v.* 1. to strip of clothes, *divested himself of his robes.* 2. to take away, to deprive, *divested him of his power.*

di·vide (di-vɪd) *v.* (**di·vid·ed, di·vid·ing**) 1. to separate into parts, to split or break up, *divide the money between you; the river divides into two channels.* 2. to separate from something else, *the Pyrenees divide France from Spain.* 3. to arrange in separate groups, to classify. 4. to cause to disagree, *this controversy divided the party.* 5. to find how many times one number contains another, *divide 12 by 3.* 6. to be able to be divided. **divide** *n.* a dividing line, a watershed.

div·i·dend (div-i-dend) *n.* 1. a number that is to be divided. 2. a share of profits paid to shareholders. 3. a benefit from an action; *his long training paid dividends,* produced benefits.

di·vid·er (di-vɪ-dĕr) *n.* something that divides; *a room divider,* a screen or piece of furniture to divide a room into two parts.

di·vid·ers (di-vɪ-dĕrz) *n.* (*pl.* **-ders**) an instrument for measuring and for dividing lines and angles, a compass.

div·i·na·tion (div-ɪ-nay-shŏn) *n.* divining, foretelling future events or discovering hidden knowledge.

di·vine (di-vɪn) *adj.* 1. of, from, or like God or a god. 2. (*informal*) excellent, very beautiful, *this divine weather.* **divine** *v.* (**di·vined, di·vin·ing**) to discover or learn about future events by what are alleged to be magical means, or by inspiration or guessing. **divine** *n.* a clergyman. **di·vine'ly** *adv.* **di·vine'ment** *n.* □**divining rod,** a forked stick or rod used in dowsing.

di·vin·er (di-vɪ-nĕr) *n.* a dowser.

di·vin·i·ty (di-vin-i-tee) *n.* (*pl.* **-ties**) 1. being divine. 2. a god. 3. the study of Christianity, *she attended divinity school.* 4. **the Divinity,** God.

di·vis·i·ble (di-viz-ɪ-bĕl) *adj.* able to be divided. **di·vis·i·bil·i·ty** (di-viz-ɪ-bil-i-tee) *n.*

di·vi·sion (di-vizh-ŏn) *n.* 1. dividing, being divided. 2. a dividing line, a partition. 3. one of the parts into which a thing is divided. 4. a major unit of an organization, *our export division.* **di·vi'sion·al** *adj.* □**division sign,** the sign ÷ (as in 12 ÷ 4) indicating that one quantity is to be divided by another.

di·vi·sive (di-vɪ-siv) *adj.* tending to cause disagreement among members of a group. **di·vi'sive·ly** *adv.* **di·vi'sive·ness** *n.*

di·vi·sor (di-vɪ-zŏr) *n.* a number by which another is to be divided.

di·vorce (di-vohrs) *n.* 1. the legal termination of a marriage. 2. the separation of things that were together. **divorce** *v.* (**di·vorced, di·vorc·ing**) 1. to end a marriage with (one's husband or wife) by divorce. 2. to separate, especially in thought or organization.

di·vor·cée, **di·vor·cee** (di-vohr-say) *n.* a divorced woman.

div·ot (div-ŏt) *n.* a piece of turf cut out by a club head in making a stroke in golf.

di·vulge (di-vulj) *v.* (**di·vulged, di·vulg·ing**) to reveal (information). **di·vul·ga·tion** (di-vul-gay-shŏn) *n.*

div·vy (div-ee) *v.* (**div·vied, div·vy·ing**) **divvy up,** (*informal*) to share, to divide up.

Dix·ie (dik-see) *n.* (*informal*) the southern states of the U.S.

Dix·ie·land (dik-see-land) *n.* 1. (*informal*) Dixie. 2. a kind of jazz with strong two-beat rhythm.

diz·zy (diz-ee) *adj.* (**-zi·er, -zi·est**) 1. giddy, feeling confused. 2. causing giddiness, *dizzy heights.* **diz'zi·ly** *adv.* **diz'zi·ness** *n.*

DJ *abbr.* disc jockey.

Dja·kar·ta = Jakarta.

Dji·bou·ti (jee-boo-tee) 1. a country in Africa. 2. its capital.

dk. *abbr.* 1. dark. 2. deck. 3. dock.

D. Lit. *abbr.* Doctor of Literature.

D. Litt. *abbr.* Doctor of Letters.

DM *abbr.* Deutsche mark.

D.M.D. *abbr.* Doctor of Dental Medicine.

DMZ *abbr.* demilitarized zone.

dn. *abbr.* down.

DNA *abbr.* deoxyribonucleic acid.

do[1] (doo) *v.* (**did, done, doing**) 1. to perform, to carry out, to fulfill or complete (a work, duty, etc.). 2. to produce, to make, *do five copies.* 3. to deal with, to set in order, to solve, *do a crossword; do the room,* clean or decorate it; *do the flowers,* arrange them; *they did us in for (did us out of) $20,* (*slang*) cheated us out of it. 4. to cover (a distance) in traveling. 5. to visit, to see the sights, *we did Rome last year.* 6. to undergo; *did time for robbery,* was in prison. 7. to provide food etc. for, *they do well by us here.* 8. to act or proceed, *do as you like.* 9. to fare, to get on, to achieve something; *they did well with it,* profited by it. 10. to be suitable or acceptable, to serve a purpose, *it doesn't do to worry; that will do!,* stop it. **do** *auxiliary verb* 1. used to indicate present or past tense, *what does he think? what did he think?* 2. used for emphasis, *I do like nuts.* 3. used to avoid repetition of a verb just used,

we work as hard as they do. **do** *n.* (*pl.* **do's**) 1. a statement of what should be done, *do's and dont's.* 2. (*informal*) an entertainment, a party. □**do away with,** to abolish, to get rid of. **do for,** (*informal*) to ruin, to destroy, to kill; to do housework for. **do in,** (*slang*) to ruin, to kill; (*informal*) to tire out. **do one's (own) thing,** to do as one pleases; to perform one's specialty. **do or die,** to make a supreme effort, disregarding danger. **do over,** to do again; to redecorate. **do right by,** to treat fairly, to do justice to; *the family did right by the meal,* ate it all. **do up,** to fasten, to wrap up. **do with,** to get on with; to tolerate; to need or want. **do without,** to manage without.
do² (doh) *n.* a name for the first note of the musical scale.
do. *abbr.* ditto.
D.O.A. *abbr.* dead on arrival.
do·a·ble (doo-ă-bĕl) *adj.* able to be done.
D.O.B. *abbr.* date of birth.
dob·bin (dob-in) *n.* a draft or farm horse.
Do·ber·man (doh-bĕr-măn) *n.* (also **Doberman pinscher**) a German hound with a smooth short dark coat.
doc (dok) *n.* (*informal*) **doctor.**
doc. *abbr.* document.
doc·ile (dos-il) *adj.* willing to obey. **doc'ile·ly** *adv.* **doc·il·i·ty** (do-sil-i-tee) *n.*
dock¹ (dok) *n.* a weed with broad leaves.
dock² *v.* 1. to cut short (an animal's tail). 2. to reduce or take away part of (wages, supplies, etc.).
dock³ *n.* 1. an artificially enclosed body of water where ships are admitted for loading, unloading, or repair. 2. a platform at which freight cars, trucks, etc. are unloaded. **dock** *v.* 1. to bring or come into dock. 2. to join (two or more spacecraft) together in space, to become joined thus.
dock⁴ *n.* an enclosure for the prisoner in a criminal court.
dock·age (dok-ij) *n.* use of a ship's dock, the charge for this.
dock·et (dok-it) *n.* 1. a document or label listing goods delivered or the contents of a package, or recording payment of customs dues etc. 2. a list of matters to be dealt with, especially by a legislature or law court. **docket** *v.* (**dock·et·ed, dock·et·ing**) to enter on a docket, to label with a docket.
dock·work·er (dok-wur-kĕr) *n.* a worker in a dockyard.
dock·yard (dok-yahrd) *n.* an area with docks and equipment for building and repairing ships.
doc·tor (dok-tŏr) *n.* 1. a person who is qualified to be a practitioner of medicine, a physician. 2. a person who holds a doctorate, *Doctor of Philosophy.* **doctor** *v.* 1. to treat medically. 2. to patch up (machinery etc.). 3. to tamper with or falsify, *doctored the evidence.* **doc'tor·al** *adj.* □**doctor's degree,** a doctorate.
doc·tor·ate (dok-tŏ-rit) *n.* the highest degree at a university, entitling the holder to the title of "doctor."
doc·tri·naire (dok-tri-nair) *adj.* applying theories or principles without regard for practical considerations, *doctrinaire socialism.* **doctrinaire** *n.* a person who does this.
doc·trine (dok-trin) *n.* a principle or set of principles and beliefs held by a religious or political or other group. **doc'trin·al** *adj.*
doc·u·ment (dok-yŭ-mĕnt) *n.* a paper giving information or evidence about something.

document *v.* to prove or provide with documents; *she documented her report,* supported its statements by many references to evidence. **doc·u·men·ta·tion** (dok-yŭ-mĕn-tay-shŏn) *n.*
doc·u·men·ta·ry (dok-yŭ-men-tă-ree) *adj.* 1. consisting of documents, *documentary evidence.* 2. giving a factual dramatized report of a subject or activity. **documentary** *n.* (*pl.* **-ries**) a documentary film or television program.
DOD *abbr.* Department of Defense.
dod·der (dod-ĕr) *v.* to tremble or totter because of age or frailty. **dod'der·er** *n.* **dod'der·y** *adj.*
dodge (doj) *v.* (**dodged, dodg·ing**) 1. to move quickly to one side, to change position or direction in order to avoid something. 2. to evade by cunning or trickery, *dodged military service.* **dodge** *n.* 1. a quick movement to avoid something. 2. (*informal*) a clever trick, an ingenious way of doing something. **dodg'er** *n.*
do·do (doh-doh) *n.* (*pl.* **-dos, -does**) 1. a large bird that formerly lived in Mauritius but has long been extinct. 2. a stupid or hopelessly old-fashioned person.
doe (doh) *n.* the female of the deer, reindeer, rabbit, or hare.
DOE *abbr.* Department of Energy.
do·er (doo-ĕr) *n.* a person who does something, one who takes action rather than thinking or talking about things.
does (duz) third person singular present tense of **do¹.**
doe·skin (doh-skin) *n.* 1. the skin of a doe. 2. a soft leather made from this skin.
does·n't (duz-ĕnt) = does not.
doff (dof) *v.* to take off (one's hat etc.).
dog (dawg) *n.* 1. a four-legged carnivorous animal, commonly kept as a pet or trained for use in hunting etc. 2. the male of this or of the wolf or fox. 3. (*informal*) a person, *lucky dog.* 4. a mechanical device for gripping things. 5. a despicable person, *the dirty dog.* **dog** *v.* (**dogged,** *pr.* dawgd, **dog·ging**) to follow closely or persistently, *dogged his footsteps.* **dog'like** *adj.* □**dog paddle,** a simple swimming stroke with short quick movements of the arms and legs. **dog's life,** a life of misery. **Dog Star,** the star Sirius. **go to the dogs,** (*slang*) to become worthless, to be ruined. **not a dog's chance,** not the slightest chance. **put on the dog,** (*informal*) to show off. ▷Note that the past form *dogged* is pronounced differently from the adjective *dogged.*
dog·bane (dawg-bayn) *n.* an herb with milky juice and a bitter root.
dog·cart (dawg-kahrt) *n.* 1. a horse-drawn cart with two transverse seats back to back. 2. a cart drawn by a dog.
dog·catch·er (dawg-kach-ĕr) *n.* a public officer who rounds up stray dogs or cats.
doge (dozh) *n.* the former chief magistrate of Venice.
dog·ear (dawg-eer) *v.* to bend down the corners of the pages of (a book). **dog-eared** *adj.*
dog-eat-dog (dawg-eet-dawg) *n.* ruthless competition.
dog·fight (dawg-fit) *n.* 1. a fight between dogs. 2. (*informal*) a battle between (usually two) fighter aircraft.
dog·fish (dawg-fish) *n.* (*pl.* **-fish·es, -fish**) a kind of small shark found in coastal waters.
dog·ged (daw-gid) *adj.* determined, not giving up easily. **dog'ged·ly** *adv.* ▷Note that the adjective

dogged is pronounced differently from the past form *dogged.*

dog·ger·el (daw-gĕ-rĕl) *n.* bad verse.

dog·gie, dog·gy (daw-gee) *n.* (*pl.* **dog·gies**) *(informal)* a dog. □**doggie** (or **doggy**) **bag,** a small bag provided by a restaurant for taking home uneaten food.

dog·gone (dawg-gawn) *adj. (informal)* pesky or annoying. □**doggone it,** *(informal)* damn it.

dog·house (dawg-hows) *n.* (*pl.* **-hous·es,** *pr.* -how-ziz) a dog's kennel. □**in the doghouse,** *(slang)* in disgrace.

do·gie (doh-gee) *n. (Western use)* a stray motherless calf.

dog·leg (dawg-leg) *n.* something bent at a sharp angle, especially a path or road.

dog·ma (dawg-mä) *n.* (*pl.* **-ma·ta,** *pr.* -mä-tä, **-mas**) a doctrine or doctrines put forward by some authority, especially a Church, to be accepted as true without question.

dog·ma·tic (dawg-mat-ik) *adj.* 1. of or like dogma. 2. putting forward statements in a firm authoritative way. **dog·mat'i·cal·ly** *adv.*

dog·ma·tism (dawg-mä-tiz-ĕm) *n.* being dogmatic.

dog·ma·tize (dawg-mä-tız) *v.* (**dog·ma·tized, dog·ma·tiz·ing**) to make dogmatic statements.

do-good·er (doo-guud-ĕr) *n.* a well-meaning but unrealistic reformer or philanthropist.

dog-tired (dawg-tırd) *adj.* tired out.

dog·tooth (dawg-tooth) *n.* a canine tooth. □**dogtooth violet,** a North American spring-flowering plant with yellow flowers having reddish spots.

dog·trot (dawg-trot) *n.* an easy steady trot like a dog's. **dogtrot** *v.* (**dog·trot·ted, dog·trot·ting**) to run this way.

dog·watch (dawg-woch) *n.* one of the two-hour watches on a ship (4–6 or 6–8 P.M.).

dog·wood (dawg-wuud) *n.* an American tree with small white or pink flowers and with bright red berries in the autumn.

Do·ha (doh-hah) the capital of Qatar.

doi·ly (doi-lee) *n.* (*pl.* **-lies**) a small ornamental mat placed under a dish or under cake etc. on a dish.

do·ings (doo-ingz) *n. pl.* things done or being done.

do-it-your·self (doo-it-yoor-self) *adj.* for use by an amateur. **do-it-yourself, do-it-yourself'er** *n.*

dol. *abbr.* dollar(s).

dol·drums (dohl-drümz) *n. pl.* 1. the ocean regions near the equator where there is little or no wind. 2. a period of inactivity. □**in the doldrums,** in low spirits.

dole (dohl) *v.* (**doled, dol·ing**) to distribute sparingly, *dole it out.* **dole** *n. (informal)* a payment by a government to persons who are unable to find employment; *on the dole, (British)* receiving this.

dole·ful (dohl-fŭl) *adj.* mournful, sad. **dole'ful·ly** *adv.*

doll (dol) *n.* 1. a small model of a human figure, especially as a child's toy. 2. a pretty but empty-headed young woman. 3. *(slang)* a young woman, a lovable person. **doll** *v.* **doll up,** to dress smartly, *dolled herself up.*

dol·lar (dol-ăr) *n.* the unit of money in the U.S. and certain other countries. □**dollars and cents,** judged only in terms of the money involved.

dol·lop (dol-ŏp) *n.* a mass or quantity, a shapeless lump of something soft.

dol·ly (dol-ee) *n.* (*pl.* **-lies**) 1. *(informal)* a doll. 2. a movable platform for a heavy object.

dol·man (dohl-măn) **sleeve** a loose sleeve cut in one piece with the body of a garment.

dol·men (dohl-mĕn) *n.* a prehistoric structure with a large flat stone laid on upright ones.

do·lo·mite (doh-lŏ-mıt) *n.* a mineral or rock of calcium magnesium carbonate.

Do·lo·mites (doh-lŏ-mıts) *n. pl.* a rocky mountain range in north Italy.

do·lor·ous (doh-lŏ-rŭs) *adj.* mournful. **do'lor·ous·ly** *adv.* **do'lor·ous·ness** *n.*

dol·phin (dol-fin) *n.* 1. a sea animal like a porpoise but larger and with a beaklike snout. 2. either of two large fishes found in tropical waters and used as food.

dolt (dohlt) *n.* a stupid person.

dom. *abbr.* 1. domestic. 2. dominion.

-dom *suffix* used to form nouns with the meaning of rank, condition, or domain, as in *earldom, freedom, kingdom,* or group, as in *officialdom.*

do·main (doh-mayn) *n.* 1. a district or area under someone's control. 2. a field of thought or activity, *the domain of science.*

dome (dohm) *n.* 1. a rounded roof with a circular base. 2. something shaped like this.

domed (dohmd) *adj.* having a dome, shaped like a dome.

Domes·day (doomz-day) **Book** a record of the ownership of lands in England made in 1086 by order of William the Conqueror.

do·mes·tic (dŏ-mes-tik) *adj.* 1. of the home or household or family affairs. 2. of one's own country, not foreign or international, *domestic flights.* 3. (of animals) kept by man, not wild. **domestic** *n.* a servant in a household. **do·mes'ti·cal·ly** *adv.* □**domestic science,** the study of household management.

do·mes·ti·cate (dŏ-mes-ti-kayt) *v.* (**do·mes·ti·cat·ed, do·mes·ti·cat·ing**) 1. to become fond of home and its duties. 2. to tame (animals), to bring (animals) under control. **do·mes'ti·cat·ed** *adj.* **do·mes·ti·ca·tion** (dŏ-mes-ti-kay-shŏn) *n.*

do·mes·tic·i·ty (doh-mes-tis-i-tee) *n.* being domestic, domestic or home life.

dom·i·cile (dom-ı-sıl) *n.* a person's place of residence. **domicile** *v.* (**dom·i·ciled, dom·i·cil·ing**) to establish or settle in a place.

dom·i·ciled (dom-ı-sıld) *adj.* dwelling in a place.

dom·i·cil·i·ar·y (dom-ı-sil-i-er-ee) *adj.* of a dwelling place.

dom·i·nant (dom-i-nănt) *adj.* dominating. **dom'i·nance** *n.*

dom·i·nate (dom-i-nayt) *v.* (**dom·i·nat·ed, dom·i·nat·ing**) 1. to have a commanding influence over. 2. to be the most influential or conspicuous person or thing. 3. (of a high place) to tower over, *the mountain dominates the whole valley.* **dom·i·na·tion** (dom-i-nay-shŏn) *n.*

dom·i·neer (dom-i-neer) *v.* to behave in a forceful way, making others obey.

Dom·i·ni·ca (doh-mi-ni-că) an island country in the West Indies.

Do·min·i·can[1] (dŏ-min-i-kăn) *n.* a member of an order of friars founded by St. Dominic, or of a corresponding order of nuns. **Dominican** *adj.* of this order.

Dominican² *adj.* of the **Dominican Republic,** a country in the West Indies. **Dominican** *n.* a native or inhabitant of this country.

do·min·ion (dŏ-**min**-yŏn) *n.* 1. authority to rule, control. 2. territory controlled by a ruler or government, a domain.

Do·min·ion (dŏ-**min**-yŏn) **Day** July 1, a Canadian holiday celebrating establishment of the Dominion of Canada on July 1, 1867.

dom·i·no (dom-i-noh) *n.* (*pl.* **-noes**) one of the small oblong pieces marked with up to six pips on each half, used in the game of **dominoes.** ☐**domino effect,** an effect compared to a row of dominoes falling, when a political or other event in one place seems to cause similar events elsewhere.

don¹ (don) *v.* (**donned, don·ning**) to put on.

don² *n.* a head or fellow or tutor of an English college, especially at Oxford or Cambridge.

Don (don) *n.* a Spanish title put before a man's Christian name. ☐**Don Juan** (wahn), a man who has many love affairs.

Do·ña (doh-nyä) *n.* a woman's title equivalent to *Don.*

do·nate (doh-nayt, doh-**nayt**) *v.* (**do·nat·ed, do·nat·ing**) to give as a donation.

do·na·tion (doh-**nay**-shŏn) *n.* a gift of money etc. to a fund or institution.

done (dun) *see* **do. done** *adj.* cooked sufficiently. **done** *interj.* (in reply to an offer) I accept. ☐**done for,** doomed, ruined, dying. **done in,** (*informal*) very tired. **done to a turn,** cooked perfectly. **done with,** finished with; *it's over and done with,* ended. **it isn't done,** it is socially unacceptable.

don·key (dong-kee, dung-) *n.* (*pl.* **-keys**) an animal of the horse family, with long ears. ☐**donkey engine,** a small auxiliary engine. **donkey work,** drudgery, the laborious part of a job.

don·nish (don-ish) *adj.* like a college don, pedantic.

don·ny·brook (don-ee-bruuk) *n.* a wild fight, a free-for-all.

do·nor (doh-nŏr) *n.* 1. a person who gives or donates something. 2. one who provides blood for transfusion or semen for insemination or tissue for transplantation.

don't (dohnt) = do not. **dont** *n.* (*informal*) a prohibition, *do's and dont's.*

do·nut (doh-nut) *n.* a doughnut.

doo·dad (doo-dad) *n.* (*informal*) a gadget, a trivial ornament.

doo·dle (doo-dĕl) *v.* (**doo·dled, doo·dling**) to scribble while thinking about something else. **doodle** *n.* a drawing or marks made by doodling. **doo·dler** (dood-lĕr) *n.*

doom (doom) *n.* a grim fate, death or ruin. **doom** *v.* to destine to a grim fate.

dooms·day (doomz-day) *n.* the day of the Last Judgment, the end of the world.

door (dohr) *n.* 1. a hinged, sliding, or revolving barrier that closes an entrance or exit. 2. a doorway; *they live three doors away,* three houses away. 3. a means of obtaining or approaching something; *closed the door to any agreement,* made it impossible.

door·bell (dohr-bel) *n.* a bell inside a house, rung from the outside by visitors as a signal.

door·jamb (dohr-jam) *n.* one of two upright posts framing a door.

door·keep·er (dohr-kee-pĕr) *n.* a doorman.

door·knob (dohr-nob) *n.* a knob for turning to release the latch of a door.

door·man (dohr-man) *n.* (*pl.* **-men,** *pr.* -men) a person on duty at the entrance to a hotel or large building.

door·mat (dohr-mat) *n.* 1. a mat placed at a door, for wiping dirt from shoes. 2. a person who meekly allows himself to be bullied.

door·plate (dohr-playt) *n.* a small plate on the door to a house or apartment identifying its occupant.

door·step (dohr-step) *n.* a step leading to a door. ☐**on one's doorstep,** very near.

door·stop (dohr-stop) *n.* a device for keeping a door open or preventing it from striking a wall when it opens.

door-to-door (dohr-tŏ-dohr) *adj.* (of selling etc.) done at each house in turn.

door·way (dohr-way) *n.* an opening filled by a door.

door·yard (dohr-yahrd) *n.* a yard in front of a door or house.

do·pa (doh-pä) *n.* an amino acid used in treating Parkinson's disease.

dop·ant (doh-pănt) *n.* a substance added to a semiconductor to change its electrical properties.

dope (dohp) *n.* 1. a thick liquid used as a lubricant etc. 2. (*informal*) a medicine or drug, a narcotic, a drug given to a greyhound or racehorse to affect its performance. 3. a varnish used to protect the cloth on model airplanes. 4. (*slang*) information. 5. (*slang*) a stupid person. **dope** *v.* (**doped, dop·ing**) 1. to treat with dope. 2. to give a narcotic or stimulant to. ☐**dope out** (*informal*) to work out (a puzzle etc.).

dope·ster (dohp-stĕr) *n.* a person who tries to predict the outcome of a sports event, political election, etc.

dop·ey (doh-pee) *adj.* (**dop·i·er, dop·i·est**) (*slang*) 1. half asleep, stupefied by a drug. 2. stupid. **dop'i·ness** *n.*

Dor·ic (dor-ik) *adj.* of the *Doric order,* the simplest of the five classical orders of architecture.

dorm (dorm) *n.* (*informal*) a dormitory.

dor·mant (dor-mănt) *adj.* 1. sleeping, lying inactive as if in sleep. 2. (of plants) alive but not actively growing. 3. temporarily inactive, *a dormant volcano.* **dor'man·cy** *n.*

dor·mer (dor-mĕr) *n.* (also **dormer window**) an upright window under a small gable built out from a sloping roof.

dor·mi·to·ry (dor-mi-tohr-ee) *n.* (*pl.* **-ries**) a room with a number of beds, especially in a school or institution.

dor·mouse (dor-mows) *n.* (*pl.* **-mice,** *pr.* -mɪs) a mouselike animal that hibernates in winter.

dor·sal (dor-sål) *adj.* of or on the back of an animal or plant, *a dorsal fin.* **dor'sal·ly** *adv.*

do·ry (dohr-ee) *n.* (*pl.* **-ries**) a small flat-bottomed fishing boat.

dos·age (doh-sij) *n.* 1. the giving of medicine in doses. 2. the size of a dose.

dose (dohs) *n.* 1. an amount of medicine to be taken at one time. 2. an amount of radiation received by a person or thing. 3. (*informal*) an amount of flattery or punishment etc. **dose** *v.* (**dosed, dos·ing**) to give a dose or doses of medicine to.

do·sim·e·ter (doh-sim-i-tĕr) *n.* a device used to measure and record the amount of radiation absorbed. **do·sim'e·try** *n.*

dos·si·er (dos-i-ay, dos-i-ay) *n.* a set of documents containing information about a person or event.
dot (dot) *n.* 1. a small round mark, a point. 2. the shorter of the two signals used in the Morse code. **dot** *v.* (**dot·ted, dot·ting**) 1. to mark with a dot or dots, to place a dot over a letter. 2. to scatter here and there, *dot them about; the sea was dotted with ships.* ☐**dotted line,** a line of dots showing where a signature etc. is to be entered on a document. **dot the i's and cross the t's,** to be minutely accurate and explicit about details. **on the dot,** exactly on time.
DOT *abbr.* Department of Transportation.
dot·age (doh-tij) *n.* a state of weakness of mind caused by old age, *in his dotage.*
dot·ard (doh-tärd) *n.* a person who is in his dotage.
dote (doht) *v.* (**doted, dot·ing**) to show great fondness, *a doting husband; she dotes on her grandchildren.*
doth (duth) *v.* (*old use*) = does.
dot·tle (dot-ĕl) *n.* unburned tobacco left in a pipe.
dot·ty (dot-ee) *adj.* (**dot·ti·er, dot·ti·est**) (*informal*) feebleminded, eccentric, silly. **dot'ti·ness** *n.*
Dou·ay (doo-ay) **Bible** (also **Douay Version**) the English translation of the Latin Vulgate Bible used in the Roman Catholic Church.
dou·ble (dub-ĕl) *adj.* 1. consisting of two things or parts that form a pair. 2. twice as much or as many; *a double whiskey,* twice the standard portion. 3. designed for two persons or things, *a double bed.* 4. combining two things or qualities, *it has a double meaning.* 5. (of flowers) having more than one circle of petals. **double** *adv.* 1. twice the amount or quantity, *it costs double what it cost last year.* 2. in twos; *see double,* to see two things where there is only one. **double** *n.* 1. a double quantity or thing. 2. a person or thing that looks very like another. 3. (in baseball) a hit that enables a batter to reach second base. 4. a hotel room for two people. 5. *doubles,* a game between two pairs of players. **double** *v.* (**doubled, dou·bling**) 1. to make or become twice as much or twice as many. 2. to bend or fold in two. 3. to turn sharply back from a course, *the fox doubled back on its tracks.* 4. to be the double of (a person). 5. to increase the value of a contract in bridge. 6. (in baseball) to make a double. **doubly** *adv.* ☐**double agent,** one who spies for two rival countries. **double bass,** the lowest-pitched instrument of the violin family. **double bed,** a bed for two people. **double boiler,** a saucepan with a detachable upper compartment in which food is cooked slowly by water boiling in the lower. **double bond,** a pair of bonds between two atoms. **double chin,** a chin with a fold of loose flesh below it. **double dagger,** a printing mark ‡ used for footnotes or cross-references. **double date,** (*informal*) a date of two couples going out together. **double-date** *v.* (**double-dated, double-dating**) (*informal*) to date in this way. **double-digit inflation,** an inflation rate of 10 percent to 99 percent. **double dip,** two scoops of ice cream on a cone. **double dipper,** (*slang*) a retired soldier, airman, etc. who is employed by the U.S. government while also drawing a government pension. **double entry,** a system of bookkeeping in which each transaction is entered as a debit in one account and a credit in another. **double exposure,** accidentally or deliberately repeated exposure of film etc. **double**

feature, a motion picture program featuring two full-length films. **double figures,** any number from 10 to 99 inclusive. **double glazing,** two layers of glass in a window, with an air space between them. **double header,** two games of baseball etc. played on the same day between the same teams. **double helix,** a pair of parallel helices with a common axis, especially in the structure of the DNA molecule. **double indemnity,** provision for payment of twice face value of a life insurance policy in case of accidental death of the insured person. **double jeopardy,** subjection of a person to a second trial when he has already been acquitted on the same charge. **double knit,** a jersey-like fabric knitted as two thicknesses interlocked. **double negative,** incorrect use of two or more negative words in the same sentence, with the effect of canceling the intended meaning, as in *they cannot do no more.* **double or nothing,** a gamble (with dice etc.) deciding whether a person must pay twice what he owes or nothing at all. **double play,** a baseball play resulting in two put-outs. **double pneumonia,** pneumonia of both lungs. **double standard,** a moral code, criterion, etc. applied more strictly to one group than another, for example, permitting more social freedom to men than to women. **double star,** two stars actually or apparently close together. **double take,** a delayed reaction to a situation etc., coming immediately after one's first reaction. **double time,** payment of an employee at twice the normal rate; (in marching) taking approximately 180 steps a minute. **double up,** to bend into a stooping or curled up position; to share living or sleeping quarters. **on the double,** quickly, without wasting time; (in military use) running.
dou·ble-bar·reled (dub-ĕl-bar-ĕld) *adj.* (of a gun) having two barrels.
dou·ble-breast·ed (dub-ĕl-bres-tid) *adj.* (of a coat) having fronts that overlap to fasten across the breast.
dou·ble-check (dub-ĕl-chek) *v.* to verify twice or in two ways.
dou·ble-cross (dub-ĕl-kraws) *v.* to deceive or cheat a person with whom one pretends to be collaborating. **dou'ble-cross'er** *n.*
dou·ble-deal·ing (dub-ĕl-dee-ling) *n.* deceit, especially in business. **dou'ble-deal'er** *n.*
dou·ble-deck·er (dub-ĕl-dek-ĕr) *n.* 1. a bus with two decks. 2. a sandwich with two layers of filling.
dou·ble-edged (dub-ĕl-ejd) *adj.* 1. having two cutting edges. 2. damaging to the user as well as his opponent, *a double-edged question.*
dou·ble en·ten·dre (dub-ĕl ahn-tahn-drĕ) a phrase with two meanings, one of which is usually indecent.
dou·ble-joint·ed (dub-ĕl-join-tid) *adj.* having very flexible joints that allow the fingers, arms, or legs to bend in unusual ways.
dou·ble-park (dub-ĕl-pahrk) *v.* to park a car (illegally) alongside one already parked at the side of a street.
dou·ble-quick (dub-ĕl-kwik) *adj. & adv.* very quick, quickly.
dou·ble-space (dub-ĕl-spays) *v.* (**dou·ble-spaced, dou·ble-spac·ing**) to type (copy) leaving one line of space between lines.
dou·blet (dub-lit) *n.* 1. a man's close-fitting jacket with or without sleeves. 2. a pair, one of a pair.

dou·ble-talk (dub-ĕl-tawk) *n.* 1. talk that appears to have meaning but does not. 2. phrasing that is deliberately evasive or ambiguous.

dou·bloon (du-bloon) *n.* a former Spanish gold coin.

doubt (dowt) *n.* 1. a feeling of uncertainty about something, an undecided state of mind. 2. a feeling of disbelief. 3. an uncertain state of affairs. **doubt** *v.* 1. to feel uncertain or undecided about. 2. to hesitate to believe. **doubt'er** *n.* **doubt'a·ble** *adj.* ▢**doubting Thomas,** a person who (like St. Thomas) refuses to believe something until it has been fully proved. **no doubt,** certainly. **without doubt** *or* **without a doubt,** certainly.

doubt·ful (dowt-fŭl) *adj.* 1. feeling doubt. 2. causing doubt; *a doubtful ally,* unreliable; *a doubtful reputation,* not a good one. **doubt'ful·ly** *adv.*

doubt·less (dowt-lis) *adv.* no doubt. **doubtless** *adj.* with no doubt or uncertainty.

douche (doosh) *n.* 1. a jet of liquid applied to a part of the body to cleanse it or for medical purposes. 2. a device for applying this. **douche** *v.* **(douched, douch·ing)** to treat with a douche, to use a douche.

dough (doh) *n.* 1. a thick mixture of flour etc. and liquid, to be baked as bread, cake, or pastry. 2. *(slang)* money. **dough'y** *adj.* **(dough·i·er, dough·i·est).**

dough·boy (doh-boi) *n.* *(informal)* an American infantry soldier of World War I.

dough·nut (doh-nut) *n.* a small sweetened fried cake of dough.

dough·ty (dow-tee) *adj.* **(-ti·er, -ti·est)** valiant or stout-hearted.

Doug·las (dug-lis) fir a very tall fir of North America important in lumbering. ▷Named for David Douglas, a Scottish botanist in America.

dour (door, dowr) *adj.* stern, severe, gloomy looking. **dour'ly** *adv.* **dour'ness** *n.*

douse (dows) *v.* **(doused, dous·ing)** 1. to put into water, to throw water over. 2. to extinguish, *douse the light.* ▷Do not confuse *douse* with *dowse.*

dove¹ (duv) *n.* 1. a kind of bird with short legs, a small head, and a thick body, which makes a cooing sound. 2. a person who favors a policy of peace and negotiation rather than violence. **dov'ish** *adj.*

dove² (dohv) *see* **dive.**

dove·cote (duv-koht) *n.* a shelter for domesticated pigeons.

Do·ver (doh-vĕr) the capital of Delaware.

dove·tail (duv-tayl) *n.* a wedge-shaped joint interlocking two pieces of wood. **dovetail** *v.* 1. to join by such a joint. 2. to fit closely together, to combine neatly, *my plans dovetailed with hers.*

dow·a·ger (dow-ă-jĕr) *n.* 1. a woman who holds a title or property from her dead husband, *the dowager duchess.* 2. a dignified elderly woman.

dow·dy (dow-dee) *adj.* **(-di·er, -di·est)** 1. (of clothes) unattractively dull, not stylish. 2. dressed in dowdy clothes. **dow'di·ly** *adv.* **dow'di·ness** *n.*

dow·el (dow-ĕl) *n.* a headless wooden or metal pin for holding two pieces of wood or stone together by fitting into a corresponding hole in each. **dowel** *v.* **(dow·eled, dow·el·ing)** to fasten with a dowel.

dow·el·ing (dow-ĕ-ling) *n.* round rods for cutting into dowels.

dow·er (dow-ĕr) *n.* 1. a widow's share of her hus-

band's estate. 2. *(old use)* a dowry. **dower** *v.* to give a dower or dowry to.

dow·itch·er (dow-ich-ĕr) *n.* a shorebird similar to a snipe and having a long bill.

down¹ (down) *n.* an area of open rolling land.

down² (down) *n.* very fine soft furry feathers or short hairs.

down³ *adv.* 1. from an upright position to a horizontal one, *fell down.* 2. to or in or at a lower place or level or condition, to a smaller size, farther south; *they are two goals down,* are losing by this amount; *I'm $5 down in the game so far,* have lost this amount; *I'm down to my last penny,* have only this left. 3. so as to be less active, *quiet down.* 4. incapacitated by illness, *is down with flu.* 5. away from a central place, *he is down from headquarters.* 6. from an earlier to a later time, *down to the present day.* 7. in writing, *note it down; he is down to speak,* is listed in the program. 8. to the source or the place where something is, *track it down.* 9. as a payment at the time of purchase, *paid $100 down.* **down** *prep.* 1. downward along or through or into, along; from top to bottom of. 2. at a lower part of, *Cincinnati is farther down the river.* **down** *adj.* 1. directed downward, *a down draft.* 2. dejected. 3. completed, *nine down and one to go.* **down** *v.* 1. to knock or bring down. 2. to swallow. 3. to defeat. **down** *n.* 1. misfortune, *ups and downs.* 2. one of four consecutive plays in football in which a team seeks to advance at least ten yards. 3. a low point, a falling period. ▢**down and out,** completely destitute. **down at the heels,** shabby. **Down East,** in or into New England, especially the state of Maine. **down in the mouth,** looking unhappy. **down on,** disapproving or hostile toward, *she is down on smoking.* **down on one's luck,** suffering misfortune. **down payment,** a partial payment made at the time of purchase. **down under,** in Australia or other countries of the antipodes. **down wind,** in the direction toward which the wind is blowing. **down with,** may (a person or party etc.) be overthrown.

down-and-out·er (down-ăn-ow-tĕr) *n.* *(informal)* a destitute person.

down·beat (down-beet) *n.* (in music) an accented beat, the downward stroke of a conductor's baton to indicate the first beat of a measure. **downbeat** *adj.* *(informal)* depressing, gloomy.

down·cast (down-kast) *adj.* 1. looking downward, *downcast eyes.* 2. (of a person) dejected.

down·er (dow-nĕr) *n.* *(slang)* 1. a depressant, such as a barbiturate. 2. a depressing person or event.

down·fall (down-fawl) *n.* a fall from prosperity or power, something that causes this.

down·grade (down-grayd) *v.* **(down·grad·ed, down·grad·ing)** to reduce to a lower grade or rank. **downgrade** *n.* a downward incline or slope. ▢**on the downgrade,** falling from wealth, power, etc.

down·heart·ed (down-hahr-tid) *adj.* in low spirits.

down·hill (down-hil) *adj.* in a downward direction, on a downward slope. **downhill** *adj.* going or sloping downward. ▢**go downhill,** to deteriorate.

down·home (down-hohm) *adj.* *(informal)* 1. of or as in the southern U.S. 2. friendly, sociable. 3. homemade.

Down·ing (dow-ning) Street 1. a street in London containing the official residences of the British Prime Minister and other members of the government. 2. *(informal)* the British government.

down·pour (down-pohr) *n.* a great fall of rain.

down·range (down-raynj) *adj. & adv.* (of a missile) away from the launch pad and toward the target.

down·right (down-rıt) *adj.* 1. frank, straightforward. 2. thorough, complete, *a downright lie.* **downright** *adv.* thoroughly, *felt downright scared.*

down·shift (down-shift) *v.* to shift an automobile into a lower gear. **downshift** *n.* the act of shifting into a lower gear.

Down's (downz) syndrome Mongolism.

down·stage (down-stayj) *adj. & adv.* at or toward the front of a theater stage.

down·stairs (down-stairz) *adv.* down the stairs, to or on a lower floor. **downstairs** *adj.* situated downstairs.

down·stream (down-streem) *adj. & adv.* in the direction in which a stream or river flows.

down·stroke (down-strohk) *n.* a stroke executed in a downward direction.

down·swing (down-swing) *n.* 1. a swing downward. 2. a downturn, a decline.

down-to-earth (down-too-urth) *adj.* sensible and practical.

down·town (down-town) *adj. & adv.* of or in the business section of a town.

down·trod·den (down-trod-ĕn) *adj.* trampled underfoot, oppressed.

down·turn (down-turn) *n.* a decline in activity or prosperity.

down·ward (down-wărd) *adj.* toward what is lower or less important or later, *a downward movement.* **downward** *adv.* (also **downwards)** toward what is lower etc., *moved downward.*

down·y (dow-nee) *adj.* **(down·i·er, down·i·est)** like or covered with soft down. □**downy mildew,** a fungus disease of plants. **downy woodpecker,** a small black and white woodpecker of North America.

dow·ry (dow-ree) *n.* (*pl.* **-ries)** property or money brought by a bride to her husband.

dowse (dowz) *v.* **(dowsed, dows·ing)** to search for underground water or minerals by using a Y-shaped stick or rod. **dows'er** *n.* a person who does this. ▷Do not confuse *dowse* with *douse.*

dox·ol·o·gy (dok-sol-ŏ-jee) *n.* (*pl.* **-gies)** a set form of words praising God.

doz. *abbr.* dozen(s).

doze (dohz) *v.* **(dozed, doz·ing)** to sleep lightly; *dozed off,* fell into a doze. **doze** *n.* a short light sleep.

doz·en (duz-ĕn) *n.* a set of twelve, *pack them in dozens; dozens of things,* very many.

DP *abbr.* displaced person.

D.P. *abbr.* 1. data processing. 2. displaced person. 3. double play.

dpt. *abbr.* 1. department. 2. deponent.

DR *abbr.* dining room.

dr. *abbr.* 1. debit. 2. debtor. 3. drachma(s). 4. dram(s). 5. drawer. 6. drum.

Dr. *abbr.* 1. Doctor. 2. Drive.

drab¹ (drab) *adj.* **(drab·ber, drab·best)** 1. dull, uninteresting. 2. a dull grayish-brown color. **drab** *n.* drab color. **drab'ly** *adv.* **drab'ness** *n.*

drab² *n.* 1. a slovenly woman. 2. *(old use)* a female prostitute.

drach·ma (drak-mă) *n.* (*pl.* **-mas, -mae,** *pr.* **-mee)** the unit of money in Greece.

Dra·co·ni·an (dray-koh-ni-ăn) *adj.* very harsh, *Draconian laws.* ▷Named after Draco, who is said to have established severe laws in ancient Athens.

draft (draft) *n.* 1. a rough preliminary written version, *a draft of a speech.* 2. a written order for the payment of money by a bank, the drawing of money by this. 3. conscription. 4. drawing (of a load, a vehicle, etc.). 5. a drink, the amount drunk in one swallow. 6. the amount of air taken in one breath. 7. a current of air. 8. a device for controlling air to a stove or furnace. 9. the depth of water displaced by a loaded ship. **draft** *v.* 1. to prepare a written draft of. 2. to select for a special duty, *he was drafted to the Paris branch.* 3. to conscript. **draft** *adj.* 1. in preliminary form, *a draft report.* 2. used for pulling or carrying loads, *a draft animal.* 3. drawn from a barrel, *draft beer.* □**draft board,** officials who select people for a military draft.

draft·ee (draf-tee) *n.* a person who has been drafted into the armed forces.

drafts·man (drafts-măn) *n.* (*pl.* **-men,** *pr.* **-mĕn)** a person employed to make drawings, plans, or sketches.

draft·y (draf-tee) *adj.* **(draft·i·er, draft·i·est)** subject to currents of air. **draft'i·ness** *n.*

drag (drag) *v.* **(dragged, drag·ging)** 1. to pull along with effort or difficulty. 2. to trail or allow to trail along the ground, to move slowly and with effort. 3. to search the bottom of water with grapnels, nets, etc., *drag the river.* 4. to continue slowly in a dull manner, *the speeches dragged on.* 5. to puff on a cigarette etc., *dragged at his pipe.* **drag** *n.* 1. something that is made for pulling along the ground, for example, a heavy harrow, a dragnet. 2. something that slows progress, something boring. 3. *(slang)* women's clothes worn by men, *he went to the party in drag.* 4. *(informal)* a puff on a cigarette etc. □**drag in,** to bring in (a subject) unnecessarily or in an artificial way. **drag one's feet** *or* **heels,** to be deliberately slow or reluctant. **drag out,** to prolong unnecessarily. **drag race,** a race between cars to see which can accelerate fastest from a standstill. **drag strip,** a straight short paved strip for drag races. ▷*Dragged* is the correct past form of *drag. Drug* is not.

drag·net (drag-net) *n.* 1. a net drawn through a river to trap fish. 2. a systematic search by police to capture a criminal.

drag·on (drag-ŏn) *n.* an imaginary reptile usually with wings, able to breathe out fire.

drag·on·fly (drag-ŏn-flı) *n.* (*pl.* **-flies)** a long-bodied insect with wings that spread while it is resting.

dra·goon (dra-goon) *v.* to force into doing something. **dragoon** *n.* a cavalryman.

drain (drayn) *v.* 1. to draw off (liquid) by means of channels or pipes etc. 2. to flow or trickle away. 3. to dry or become dried when liquid flows away. 4. to deprive gradually of (strength or resources). 5. to drink, to empty (a glass etc.) by drinking its contents. **drain** *n.* 1. a channel or pipe through which liquid or sewage is carried away. 2. something that drains one's strength or resources. **drain'er** *n.* □**down the drain,** *(informal)* lost, wasted.

drain·age (dray-nij) *n.* 1. draining. 2. a system of drains. 3. what is drained off.

drain·board (drayn-bohrd) *n.* a sloping surface beside a sink, on which washed dishes are put to drain.

drain·pipe (drayn-pıp) *n.* a pipe used in a system of drains.

drake (drayk) *n.* a male duck.

dram (dram) *n.* 1. a small amount of anything. 2.

a small drink of liquor. 3. one-eighth of an ounce, apothecaries' weight. 4. one-sixteenth of an ounce, avoirdupois weight.

dra·ma (drah-mă, dram-ă) *n.* 1. a play for acting on the stage or for broadcasting. 2. plays as a branch of literature, their composition and performance. 3. a dramatic series of events, *the drama continued inside the consulate.* 4. dramatic quality, *the drama of the situation.*

Dram·a·mine (dram-ă-meen) *n. (trademark)* an antihistamine used to counteract motion sickness.

dra·mat·ic (dră-mat-ik) *adj.* 1. of drama. 2. exciting, impressive, *a dramatic change.* **dra·mat′i·cal·ly** *adv.*

dra·mat·ics (dră-mat-iks) *n. pl.* 1. the performance of plays. 2. exaggerated behavior, *she tired of his dramatics.*

dra·ma·tist (dram-ă-tist, dram-ă-) *n.* a writer of dramas.

dra·ma·tize (drah-mă-tiz, dram-ă-) *v.* **(dra·ma·tized, dra·ma·tiz·ing)** 1. to make (a story etc.) into a play. 2. to make things seem dramatic. **dra·ma·ti·za·tion** (drah-mă-ti-za-shŏn, dram-ă-) *n.*

drank (drangk) *see* **drink.**

drape (drayp) *v.* **(draped, drap·ing)** 1. to cover loosely or decorate with cloth etc. 2. to arrange loosely or in graceful folds.

dra·per·y (dray-pĕ-ree) *n.* (*pl.* **-per·ies**) 1. fabric arranged in loose folds. 2. *draperies,* heavy curtains.

drapes (drayps) *n. (informal)* draperies.

dras·tic (dras-tik) *adj.* having a strong or violent effect. **dras′ti·cal·ly** *adv.*

drat (drat) *interj. (informal)* curse.

drat·ted (drat-id) *adj. (informal)* cursed.

draught (draft) *n.* 1. the drawing of beer etc. from its container, *beer on draught.* 2. a drink, the amount drunk in one swallow. 3. *draughts, (British)* checkers.

draw (draw) *v.* **(drew, drawn, draw·ing)** 1. to pull; *draw a bow,* pull back its string; *draw the curtains,* pull them across the window. 2. to attract, *draw attention.* 3. to take in, *draw breath; the chimney draws well,* has a good draft; *he drew at his pipe,* sucked in smoke from it. 4. to take out, *drew the cork; draw water; draw $25,* withdraw it from one's account; *draw a salary,* receive it from one's employer; *draw blood,* cause blood to flow; *draw on one's imagination,* use it as a source. 5. to draw lots, to obtain in a lottery, *drew for partners; drew the winner.* 6. to get information from, *tried to draw him out about his plans.* 7. to finish a contest with neither side winning. 8. to require (a certain depth of water) in which to float, *the ship draws ten feet.* 9. to produce a picture or diagram by making marks on a surface. 10. to formulate, *draw a conclusion.* 11. to write out (a check) for cashing. 12. to make one's way, *draw near; the train drew in,* entered a station and stopped. 13. to flatten or shape (metal) by hammering etc. **draw** *n.* 1. the act of drawing; *quick on the draw,* quick at drawing a gun. 2. a person or thing that attracts customers, *a box-office draw.* 3. the drawing of lots. 4. a drawn game. □**draw a blank,** to get no response or result. **draw in one's horns,** to become less aggressive or less ambitious. **draw near,** to approach. **draw on,** to remove money from (one's bank account), to take advantage of (someone's good will). **draw oneself up,** to make oneself stiffly erect. **draw out,** to prolong (a dis-

cussion etc.); to encourage (a person) to talk. **draw the line at,** to refuse to do or tolerate. **draw up,** to come to a halt; to compose (a contract etc.).

draw·back (draw-bak) *n.* a disadvantage; *the drawback to the plan was its cost,* its disadvantageous aspect.

draw·bridge (draw-brij) *n.* a bridge over a moat, hinged at one end so that it can be drawn up.

draw·er (draw-ĕr *for definition* 1, drawr *for definition* 2) *n.* 1. a person who draws something, one who draws (writes out) a check. 2. a boxlike compartment without a lid, which can be slid horizontally in and out of a piece of furniture.

draw·ers (drawrz) *n. pl.* underpants.

draw·ing (draw-ing) *n.* a picture etc. drawn but not colored. □**drawing board,** a flat board on which paper is stretched while a drawing is made; *back to the drawing board,* we must begin planning all over again. **drawing card,** an entertainer or athlete or show etc. attracting a large audience. **drawing room,** a room for receiving guests in, a sitting room.

drawl (drawl) *v.* to speak lazily or with drawn-out vowel sounds. **drawl** *n.* a drawling manner of speaking.

drawn (drawn) *see* **draw. drawn** *adj.* (of a person's features) looking strained from tiredness or worry. □**drawn butter,** butter melted and clarified, often with herbs.

draw·string (draw-string) *n.* a string that can be pulled to tighten an opening.

dray (dray) *n.* a strong low flat cart for heavy loads. **dray·man** (dray-măn) *n.* (*pl.* **-men,** *pr.* -mĕn).

dray·age (dray-ij) *n.* 1. hauling by dray, trucking. 2. the charge for this.

dread (dred) *n.* great fear. **dread** *v.* to fear greatly. **dread** *adj. (old use)* dreaded, awe-inspiring.

dread·ful (dred-fŭl) *adj.* 1. causing dread. 2. troublesome, boring, very bad, *dreadful weather.* **dread′ful·ly** *adv.*

dread·nought (dred-nawt) *n.* a heavily armed battleship.

dream (dreem) *n.* 1. a series of pictures or events in a sleeping person's mind. 2. the state of mind of one dreaming or daydreaming, *goes around in a dream.* 3. an ambition, an ideal. 4. a beautiful person or thing. **dream** *v.* **(dreamed** or **dreamt,** *pr.* dremt, **dream·ing)** 1. to have a dream or dreams while sleeping. 2. to have an ambition, *dreamed of being champion.* 3. to think of as a possibility, *never dreamed it would happen; wouldn't dream of allowing it,* will certainly not allow it. **dream′er** *n.* **dream′less** *adj.* **dream′like** *adj.* □**dream up,** to imagine, to invent.

dream·land (dreem-land) *n.* 1. an ideal or imaginary land. 2. sleep.

dream·world (dreem-wurld) *n.* a world of fantasy.

dream·y (dree-mee) *adj.* **(dream·i·er, dream·i·est)** 1. daydreaming. 2. *(informal)* wonderful. **dream′i·ly** *adv.* **dream′i·ness** *n.*

drear (dreer) *adj. (old use)* dreary.

drear·y (dreer-ee) *adj.* **(drear·i·er, drear·i·est)** dull, boring, (of places, etc.) gloomy. **drear′i·ly** *adv.* **drear′i·ness** *n.*

dredge[1] (drej) *n.* an apparatus for scooping earth etc. from the bottom of a body of water. **dredge** *v.* **(dredged, dredg·ing)** to bring up or clean out with a dredge. **dredger** (drej-ĕr) *n.* a dredge, a boat equipped with a dredge.

dredge[2] *v.* **(dredged, dredg·ing)** to sprinkle with flour or sugar etc. **dredg·er** (drej-ẽr) *n.* a container with a perforated lid, used for sprinkling things.

dregs (dregz) *n. pl.* 1. bits of worthless matter that sink to the bottom of a liquid. 2. the worst and useless part, *the dregs of society.*

drench (drench) *v.* to make thoroughly wet.

Dres·den (drez-dẽn) **china** fine china made at Meissen, near Dresden, in Germany.

dress (dres) *n.* 1. clothing, especially the visible part of it. 2. a woman's or girl's garment with a waist and skirt. **dress** *v.* 1. to put clothes upon, to put on one's clothes, to provide clothes for; *she dresses well,* chooses and wears good clothes. 2. to put on evening dress, *they dress for dinner.* 3. to decorate; *dress a shop window,* arrange goods in it. 4. to put a dressing on (a wound etc.). 5. to groom and arrange (hair). 6. to finish or treat the surface of, *to dress leather.* 7. to prepare (poultry, crab, etc.) for cooking or eating. 8. to arrange (soldiers) into a straight line. **dress** *adj.* requiring formal dress, suitable for a formal occasion. ☐**dress circle,** the section of a concert hall or theater, usually the mezzanine, where evening dress was formerly required. **dress down,** to reprimand severely. **dress rehearsal,** a rehearsal in full costume. **dress shirt,** a shirt suitable for wearing with evening dress. **dress up,** to put on special clothes; to make (a thing) look more interesting.

dres·sage (dres-ij) *n.* the exhibition of a horse to show its obedience and deportment.

dress·er[1] (dres-ẽr) *n.* one who dresses a person or thing.

dress·er[2] *n.* a chest of drawers with a mirror.

dress·ing (dres-ing) *n.* 1. a sauce or stuffing for food. 2. manure etc. spread over the land. 3. a bandage, ointment, etc. for a wound. ☐**dressing gown,** a loose gown worn when one is not fully dressed. **dressing room,** a room for dressing or changing one's clothes. **dressing table,** a table with a mirror, for use while dressing.

dress·ing-down (dres-ing-down) *n.* a scolding.

dress·mak·er (dress-may-kẽr) *n.* a woman who makes women's clothes.

dress·mak·ing (dress-may-king) *n.* making women's clothes.

dress·y (dres-ee) *adj.* (**dress·i·er, dress·i·est**) 1. wearing stylish clothes. 2. (of clothes) elegant, elaborate.

drew (droo) *see* **draw.**

drib·ble (drib-ẽl) *v.* (**drib·bled, drib·bling**) 1. to allow saliva to flow from the mouth. 2. to flow or allow to flow in drops. 3. to move the ball forward in basketball with rapid continuous bounces. **dribble** *n.* a dribbling flow. **drib′bler** *n.*

drib·let (drib-lit) *n.* a small amount; *in driblets,* a little at a time.

dribs and drabs (dribz ăn drabz) small amounts.

dried (drīd) *see* **dry. dried** *adj.* (of foods) preserved by drying, *dried apricots.*

dri·er (drī-ẽr) *n.* 1. a substance added to paint etc. to make it dry quickly. 2. a dryer.

drift (drift) *v.* 1. to be carried by or as if by a current of water or air. 2. to move casually or aimlessly. 3. to be piled into drifts by wind, *the snow had drifted.* 4. to cause to drift. **drift** *n.* 1. a drifting movement. 2. a mass of snow or sand piled up by wind. 3. deviation from a set course. 4. the general tendency or meaning of a speech etc., *we couldn't get her drift.*

drift·age (drif-tij) *n.* drifting or the results of drifting, deviation from course.

drift·er (drif-tẽr) *n.* an aimless person.

drift·wood (drift-wuud) *n.* wood floating on the sea or washed ashore by it.

drill[1] (dril) *n.* 1. a pointed tool or a machine used for boring holes or sinking wells. 2. training in military exercises. 3. thorough training by practical exercises, usually with much repetition. 4. a single exercise designed to train, *a fire drill.* **drill** *v.* 1. to use a drill, to make (a hole) with a drill. 2. to train or be trained by means of drill. ☐**drill instructor,** a member of the U.S. Marine Crops who drills recruits. **drill press,** a drilling machine used primarily on metals.

drill[2] *n.* 1. a furrow. 2. a machine for making or sowing seed in furrows. 3. a row of seeds sown in this way. **drill** *v.* to plant in drills.

drill[3] *n.* strong twilled linen or cotton cloth.

drill·mas·ter (dril-mas-tẽr) *n.* a teacher who uses repetitious exercises to train his students.

dri·ly (drī-lee) *adv.* in a dry way.

drink (dringk) *v.* (**drank, drunk, drink·ing**) 1. to swallow (liquid), *we have drunk milk all our lives.* 2. (of plants, the soil, etc.) to take in or absorb liquid. 3. to take alcoholic liquors, especially in excess; *drank himself to death,* caused his death by drinking. 4. to pledge good wishes to by drinking, *drank his health.* **drink** *n.* 1. liquid for drinking. 2. alcoholic liquors. 3. a portion of liquid for drinking. 4. *(slang)* the sea. **drink′er** *n.* **drink′a·ble** *adj.* ☐**drink in,** to listen to with delight or eagerness. ▷Do not confuse *drank* (past) with *drunk* (past participle).

drip (drip) *v.* (**dripped, drip·ping**) to fall or let fall in drops. **drip** *n.* 1. liquid falling in drops, one of these drops. 2. the sound of this. 3. *(slang)* a weak or dull person. ☐**drip grind,** coffee that has been ground fine for use with a filter pot. **dripping wet,** very wet.

drip-dry (drip-drī) *v.* (**drip-dried, drip-dry·ing**) to dry easily when hung up wet, without wringing or ironing. **drip-dry** *adj.* made of fabric that will drip-dry.

drip·pings (drip-ingz) *n. pl.* fat and juices that have dripped from roast meat.

drive (drīv) *v.* (**drove, driv·en, driv·ing**) 1. to urge or send in some direction by blows, threats, violence, etc. 2. to push, send, or carry along. 3. to strike and propel (a ball etc.) forcibly. 4. to force to penetrate, *drove a stake into the ground;* *drove a tunnel through the hill,* dug it. 5. to operate (a vehicle or locomotive) and direct its course. 6. to travel or convey in a private vehicle, *we drive to work; he drove me to the station.* 7. (of steam or other power) to keep (machinery) going. 8. to cause, to compel, *was driven by hunger to steal; he drives himself too hard,* overworks; *drove him mad,* forced him into this state. 9. to rush, to move or be moved rapidly, *driving rain.* **drive** *n.* 1. a journey in a vehicle. 2. a stroke made by driving in baseball, golf, etc. 3. the transmission of power to machinery, *front-wheel drive; right-hand drive,* having the steering wheel on the right of the vehicle. 4. energy, persistence, a psychological urge. 5. an organized effort to achieve something, *a sales drive.* 6. a road, especially a scenic one. 7. a driveway. ☐**drive a hard bargain,** to conclude one without making concessions. **drive at,** to intend to convey as a meaning, *what was he driving at?* **drive-in** *adj.* (of a theater, bank, etc.) able to be used without getting out of one's car. **drive shaft,** a shaft that transmits motive power from the engine to the wheels of a motor vehicle. **drive wheel,** a wheel that transmits motive power in machinery.

driv·el (driv-ĕl) *n.* silly talk, nonsense. **drivel** *v.* (driv·eled, driv·el·ing) to talk or write drivel. **driv'el·er** *n.*

driv·er (drĭv-vĕr) *n.* 1. a person who drives a vehicle. 2. a golf club used to send the ball a long distance, especially from the tee.

drive·way (drĭv-way) *n.* a private road leading to a house or garage.

driz·zle (driz-ĕl) *n.* very fine rain. **drizzle** *v.* (driz·zled, driz·zling) to rain in very fine drops. **driz'zly** *adj.*

drogue (drohg) *n.* (also **drogue chute**) a funnel-shaped piece of fabric used as a windsock, brake, target, etc.

droll (drohl) *adj.* amusing in an odd way. **droll'ly** *adv.*

droll·er·y (droh-lĕ-ree) *n.* quaint humor.

drom·e·dar·y (drom-ĕ-der-ee) *n.* (*pl.* **-dar·ies**) a light one-humped camel bred for riding.

drone (drohn) *n.* 1. a male honeybee. 2. an idler. 3. a deep humming sound. 4. a remotely controlled airplane. **drone** *v.* (droned, dron·ing) 1. to make a deep humming sound. 2. to speak or utter monotonously.

drool (drool) *v.* 1. to water at the mouth, to dribble. 2. to show gushing appreciation.

droop (droop) *v.* to bend or hang downward through tiredness or weakness. **droop** *n.* a drooping attitude. **droop'y** *adj.* (droop·i·er, droop·i·est).

drop (drop) *n.* 1. a small rounded or pear-shaped mass of liquid. 2. something shaped like this, such as a candy. 3. a very small quantity. 4. the act of dropping. 5. a fall, *a drop in prices.* 6. a steep or vertical descent, the distance of this, *a drop of ten feet from the window.* 7. the length of a hanging curtain. 8. a thing that drops or is dropped, a trapdoor withdrawn from under the feet of a person executed by hanging. 9. *drops,* liquid medicine to be measured by drops. **drop** *v.* (dropped, drop·ping) 1. to fall by force of gravity from not being held, to allow to fall. 2. to sink from exhaustion; *feel ready to drop,* very tired. 3. to form a steep or vertical descent, *the cliff drops sharply to the sea.* 4. to lower, to become lower or weaker, *drop the hem; prices dropped; drop one's voice.* 5. to allow oneself to move to a position farther back, *dropped behind the others.* 6. to utter or send casually, *drop a hint; drop me a note.* 7. to omit, to fail to pronounce or insert, *drop one's h's.* 8. to set down (a passenger or parcel etc.). 9. to fell with an ax, blow, or bullet. 10. to give up, to reject, to cease to associate with, *dropped the habit; has dropped his friends; drop the subject,* cease talking about it. 11. to lose money in gambling etc. **drop'per** *n.* □**drop back,** to fall behind, go to the rear. **drop behind,** to fail to keep pace (with). **drop by** or **drop in,** to pay a casual visit. **drop off,** to fall asleep, to decline. **drop out,** to cease to participate.

drop·kick (drop-kik) *n.* a kick made by dropping a football to the ground and kicking it as it rebounds.

drop·let (drop-lit) *n.* a small drop.

drop·out (drop-owt) *n.* a person who drops out

from a course of study or from conventional society.

drop·per (drop-ĕr) *n.* a device for administering liquid in drops, *eye dropper, medicine dropper.*

drop·pings (drop-ingz) *n. pl.* the dung of animals.

drop·sy (drop-see) *n.* a disease in which watery fluid collects in the body. **drop'si·cal** *adj.*

dross (draws) *n.* 1. scum on molten metal. 2. impurities, rubbish.

drought (drowt), **drouth** (drowth) *n.* continuous dry weather. ▷Careful writers and speakers do not use *drouth.*

drove (drohv) *v. see* **drive. drove** *n.* 1. a moving herd or flock. 2. a large crowd, *droves of people.*

drov·er (droh-vĕr) *n.* a person who herds cattle or sheep to market or pasture.

drown (drown) *v.* (drowned, drown·ing) 1. to kill or be killed by suffocating in water or other liquid. 2. to flood, to drench. 3. to deaden (grief etc.) with drink, *drown one's sorrows.* 4. to overpower (a sound) with greater loudness, *the music drowned out the speech.* ▷ *Drownded* is incorrect.

drowse (drowz) *v.* (drowsed, drows·ing) to be half asleep. **drowse** *n.* this state.

drow·sy (drow-zee) *adj.* (-si·er, -si·est) half asleep. **drow'si·ly** *adv.* **drow'si·ness** *n.*

drub (drub) *v.* (drubbed, drub·bing) 1. to thrash. 2. to defeat thoroughly.

drub·bing (drub-ing) *n.* a beating, a severe defeat.

drudge (druj) *n.* a person who does dull or laborious or menial work. **drudge** *v.* (drudged, drudg·ing) to do such work. **drudg'er·y** *n.*

drug (drug) *n.* 1. a substance used in medicine. 2. a substance that acts on the nervous system, such as a narcotic or stimulant, especially one causing addiction. **drug** *v.* (drugged, drug·ging) 1. to add a drug to (food or drink). 2. to give drugs to, to stupefy. □**drug on the market,** something that is plentiful but not in demand.

drug·gist (drug-ist) *n.* a dispenser of prescription drugs etc. in a drugstore.

drug·store (drug-stor) *n.* a store that sells prescription drugs and usually a variety of merchandise.

Dru·id (droo-id) *n.* a priest or member of an ancient Celtic religion. **Dru'id·ism** *n.*

drum (drum) *n.* 1. a percussion instrument consisting of a parchment or skin stretched tightly across a round frame. 2. the sound of this being struck, a similar sound. 3. a cylindrical structure or object or container. 4. the eardrum. **drum** *v.* (drummed, drum·ming) 1. to play a drum or drums. 2. to make a drumming sound, to tap or thump continuously or rhythmically. 3. to drive (facts etc.) into a person's mind by constant repetition. □**drum brake,** one in which curved pads on a vehicle press against the inner cylindrical part of a wheel. **drum major,** the leader of a marching band. **drum majorette,** a female drum major. **drum out,** to dismiss in disgrace. **drum up,** to obtain through vigorous effort, *drum up support.*

drum·beat (drum-beet) *n.* the sound of a drum.

drum·head (drum-hed) *n.* the stretched parchment or skin of a drum.

drum·lin (drum-lin) *n.* a long oval mound formed of glacial drift.

drum·mer (drum-ĕr) *n.* 1. a person who plays a drum or drums. 2. *(old use)* a traveling salesman.

drum·stick (drum-stik) *n.* 1. a stick for beating a drum. 2. the lower part of a cooked fowl's leg.

drunk (drungk) *v. see* **drink. drunk** *adj.* excited

or stupefied with alcoholic drink; *drunk with success,* made greatly excited by it. **drunk** *n.* 1. a drunken person. 2. *(slang)* a bout of drinking, *he went on a drunk.* ▷See the note under **drunken.**

drunk·ard (drung-kărd) *n.* a person who is often drunk.

drunk·en (drung-kĕn) *adj.* 1. intoxicated, frequently in this condition. 2. happening during or because of drunkenness, *a drunken brawl.* **drunk'en·ly** *adv.* **drunk'en·ness** *n.* ▷ *Drunken* is used before a noun (as in *a drunken man*), whereas *drunk* is usually used after a verb, (as in *he is drunk, she feels drunk*).

drupe (droop) *n.* a fruit with juicy flesh around a stone with a kernel, as a peach.

dry (drı) *adj.* (**dri·er, dri·est**) 1. without water or moisture; *a dry country,* with little rainfall; *dry land,* not under water; *dry shampoo,* for use without water; *a dry cough,* without phlegm; *dry wall,* built without mortar or cement; *the cows are dry,* not producing milk. 2. eaten without butter etc., *dry bread.* 3. thirsty. 4. (of wine) not sweet. 5. uninteresting, *a dry book.* 6. expressed with pretended seriousness, *dry humor.* 7. not allowing the sale of liquor, *a dry county.* **dry** *v.* (**dried, dry·ing**) 1. to make or become dry. 2. to preserve (food) by removing its moisture. **dry** *n.* a person who opposes the sale and use of alcoholic beverages. **dri'ly, dry'ly** *adv.* **dry'ness** *n.* ☐**dry cell,** a cell in which the electrolyte is absorbed in a solid and cannot be spilled. **dry dock,** a dock that can be emptied of water, used for repairing ships. **dry goods,** clothing, textiles, and related articles of trade. **dry ice,** solid carbon dioxide, used as a refrigerant. **dry measure,** a measure of capacity for grain and other dry things. **dry rot,** decay of wood that is not well ventilated; the fungi that cause this; any moral or social decay. **dry run,** *(informal)* a practice exercise. **dry up,** to become depleted, *the money dried up; (informal)* to cease talking.

dry·ad (drı-ăd) *n.* a wood nymph.

dry-clean (drı-kleen) *v.* to clean (clothes etc.) by a solvent that evaporates very quickly, not by water.

dry·er (drı-er) *n.* any of various devices to dry laundry, hair, etc.

dry-fly (drı-flı) *adj.* (in fishing) using an artificial fly that floats.

dry·wall (drı-wawl) *n.* plasterboard, construction using plasterboard in place of plaster.

DSC *abbr.* 1. Distinguished Service Cross. 2. Doctor of Surgical Chiropody.

DSM *abbr.* Distinguished Service Medal.

DSO *abbr.* Distinguished Service Order.

DST *abbr.* 1. daylight-saving time. 2. Doctor of Sacred Theology.

D.T.'s, d.t.'s *abbr.* delirium tremens.

Du. *abbr.* Dutch.

du·al (doo-ăl) *adj.* composed of two parts, double. **du'al·ism** *n.* **du·al·i·ty** (doo-al-i-tee) *n.* ☐**dual control,** two linked sets of controls, enabling either of two persons to operate an aircraft or automobile. ▷Do not confuse *dual* with *duel.*

du·al-pur·pose (doo-ăl-pur-pŏs) *adj.* suitable for two purposes.

dub¹ (dub) *v.* (**dubbed, dub·bing**) 1. to make (a person) a knight by touching him on the shoulder with a sword. 2. to give a nickname to.

dub² *v.* (**dubbed, dub·bing**) to replace or add to

the soundtrack of (a film), especially in a different language.

dub·bin (dub-in) *n.* thick grease for softening and waterproofing leather.

du·bi·e·ty (doo-bı-ĕ-tee) *n.* (*pl.* **-ties**) 1. a feeling of doubt. 2. a doubtful matter.

du·bi·ous (doo-bi-ŭs) *adj.* doubtful. **du'bi·ous· ly** *adv.* **du'bi·ous·ness** *n.*

Dub·lin (dub-lin) the capital of the Republic of Ireland.

du·cal (doo-kăl) *adj.* of or like a duke.

duc·at (duk-ăt) *n.* 1. a gold coin formerly used in most European countries. 2. *(slang)* a ticket to an entertainment, sports event, etc.

duch·ess (duch-is) *n.* 1. a duke's wife or widow. 2. a woman whose rank is equal to that of a duke.

duch·y (duch-ee) *n.* (*pl.* **duch·ies**) the territory of a duke or duchess.

duck¹ (duk) *n.* 1. a swimming bird of various kinds. 2. the female of this. 3. its flesh as food. 4. a ducking movement. **duck** *v.* 1. to dip the head under water and emerge, to push (a person) under water. 2. to bob down, especially to avoid being seen or hit. 3. to dodge, to avoid (a task etc.).

duck² *n.* 1. strong linen or cotton cloth. 2. *ducks,* trousers made of this.

duck·bill (duk-bil) *n.* a platypus.

duck·boards (duk-bohrdz) *n. pl.* boards forming a narrow path across a trench or over mud.

duck·ling (duk-ling) *n.* a young duck.

duck·pin (duk-pin) *n.* 1. a short squat bowling pin. 2. *duckpins,* a bowling game using duckpins.

duck·weed (duk-weed) *n.* a plant that forms on the surface of ponds etc.

duck·y (duk-ee) *adj.* (**duck·i·er, duck·i·est**) *(informal)* excellent.

duct (dukt) *n.* 1. a tube or channel for conveying liquid, gas, air, cable, etc. 2. a tube in the body through which fluid passes, *tear ducts.* **duct** *v.* to convey through a duct. **duct'less** *adj.* ☐**ductless gland,** a gland that pours its secretion directly into the blood, not through a duct.

duc·tile (duk-til) *adj.* (of metal) able to be drawn out into thin strands.

dud (dud) *n.* *(informal)* something that is useless or counterfeit or that fails to work.

dude (dood) *n.* 1. a dandy. 2. *(slang)* a tough, a man. ☐**dude ranch,** a ranch used as a vacation resort.

dudg·eon (duj-ŏn) *n.* resentment, indignation, *in high dudgeon.*

duds (dudz) *n. pl. (slang)* clothes.

due (doo, dyoo) *adj.* 1. owed as a debt or obligation. 2. payable immediately, *it has become due.* 3. that ought to be given to a person, rightful, adequate, *with due respect.* 4. scheduled to do something or to arrive, *he is due to speak tonight; the train is due at 7:30.* 5. caused by. (▷See the note below.) **due** *adv.* exactly, *sailed due east.* **due** *n.* 1. a person's right, what is owed to him; *give the Devil his due,* give a disliked person credit for one of his good qualities or actions. 2. *dues, n. pl.* a fee, *club dues;* what one owes, *pay one's dues.* ☐**due process (of law),** the fair application of law in U.S. courts so that no person's rights are denied. **in due course,** in the natural sequence at the appropriate time. ▷The phrase *due to* is often wrongly used. Careful writers use *because of,* not *due to,* in such expressions as *play was delayed due to rain. Due to* should be used after a linking verb, as in *the delay was due to rain; her success was due to hard work,* not *she succeeded due to hard work.*

du·el (doo-ĕl) *n.* 1. a fight with weapons between two persons. 2. a contest between two persons or sides. **duel** *v.* (**du·eled, du·el·ing**) to fight a duel. **du′el·ist** *n.* ▷Do not confuse *duel* with *dual.*

du·en·de (doo-en-day) *n.* 1. an evil spirit. 2. inspiration. ▷Spanish.

du·en·na (doo-en-ă) *n.* an older woman acting as chaperon, especially in Spanish families.

du·et (doo-et) *n.* a musical composition for two performers.

duf·fel (duf-ĕl) *n.* a heavy woolen cloth with a thick nap. □**duffel bag,** a cylindrical canvas bag closed by a drawstring. **duffel coat,** a hooded overcoat made of duffel, fastened with toggles.

duf·fer (duf-ĕr) *n.* an inefficient or incompetent person, especially a poor golfer.

dug[1] (dug) *see* **dig.**

dug[2] *n.* an udder, a teat.

dug·out (dug-owt) *n.* 1. an underground shelter. 2. (also **dugout canoe**) a canoe made by hollowing a tree trunk.

duke (dook, dyook) *n.* 1. a nobleman of the highest rank. 2. the male ruler of a duchy or of certain small states.

duke·dom (dook-dŏm, dyook-) *n.* the position or lands of a duke.

dul·cet (dul-sit) *adj.* sounding sweet.

dul·ci·mer (dul-si-mĕr) *n.* a musical instrument with strings struck by two hammers.

dull (dul) *adj.* 1. not bright or clear. 2. slow in understanding, stupid. 3. not sharp, (of pain) not felt sharply, (of sound) not resonant. 4. not interesting or exciting, boring. **dull** *v.* to make or become dull. **dull′ly** *adv.* **dull′ness** *n.*

dull·ard (dul-ărd) *n.* a mentally dull person.

du·ly (doo-lee, dyoo-) *adv.* in a correct or suitable way.

du·ma (doo-mă) *n.* (*formerly*) a Russian council of state.

dumb (dum) *adj.* 1. unable to speak. 2. temporarily silent; *was struck dumb,* speechless from surprise etc. 3. stupid. **dumb′ly** *adv.* **dumb′ness** *n.* □**dumb show,** gestures without words. ▷Most people consider *dumb* offensive in referring to those who are unable to speak. The better word is *mute.*

dumb·bell (dum-bel) *n.* 1. a short bar with a weight at each end, lifted to exercise the muscles. 2. (*slang*) a stupid person.

dumb·found (dum-fownd) *v.* to astonish, to strike dumb with surprise.

dumb·wait·er (dum-way-tĕr) *n.* a small elevator for conveying food etc.

dum·dum (dum-dum) *n.* (also **dumdum bullet**) a soft-nosed bullet that expands on impact.

dum·my (dum-ee) *n.* (*pl.* **-mies**) 1. a sham article. 2. a model of the human figure, used to display clothes. 3. a ventriloquist's doll. 4. (in card games) a player whose cards are placed upward on the table and played by his partner. **dummy** *adj.* sham. □**dummy up,** (*slang*) to refuse to talk.

dump (dump) *v.* 1. to deposit as rubbish. 2. to put down carelessly. 3. to get rid of (something unwanted). 4. to market goods (especially abroad) at a lower price than is normally charged in order to secure a commercial advantage. **dump** *n.* 1. a rubbish heap, a place where rubbish may be

deposited. 2. a temporary store, *an ammunition dump.* 3. (*informal*) a dull or unattractive place. □**dump truck,** a truck whose body can be tilted to tip out its contents.

dump·ling (dump-ling) *n.* a ball of dough cooked with meat etc. or prepared with fruit inside it.

dumps (dumps) *n. pl.* (*informal*) low spirits, *in the dumps.*

dump·ster (dump-stĕr) *n.* a very large trash container.

dump·y (dum-pee) *adj.* (**dump·i·er, dump·i·est**) short and fat. **dump′i·ness** *n.*

dun[1] (dun) *adj. & n.* grayish brown.

dun[2] *v.* (**dunned, dun·ning**) to ask persistently for payment of a debt.

dunce (duns) *n.* a person who is slow at learning.

dun·der·head (dun-dĕr-hed) *n.* a dunce.

dune (doon) *n.* a sand dune (*see* **sand**). □**dune buggy,** a beach buggy (*see* **beach**).

dung (dung) *n.* animal excrement.

dun·ga·ree (dung-gă-ree) *n.* 1. blue denim. 2. *dungarees,* blue denims.

dun·geon (dun-jŏn) *n.* a strong underground cell for prisoners.

dung·hill (dung-hil) *n.* a heap of dung or refuse in a barnyard.

dunk (dungk) *v.* to dip into liquid.

du·o (doo-oh) *n.* (*pl.* **-os**) a pair of performers.

du·o·dec·i·mal (doo-ŏ-des-i-măl) *adj.* based on 12, reckoning by twelves.

du·o·de·num (doo-ŏ-dee-nŭm) *n.* the first part of the small intestine, immediately below the stomach. **du·o·de′nal** *adj.*

dup. *abbr.* 1. duplex. 2. duplicate.

dupe (doop) *n.* a person who is deceived or tricked. **dupe** *v.* (**duped, dup·ing**) to deceive, to trick.

du·plex (doo-pleks) *adj.* 1. having two parts. 2. (of an apartment) on two floors. **duplex** *n.* a duplex apartment.

du·pli·cate (doo-pli-kit) *n.* 1. one of two or more things that are exactly alike. 2. an exact copy. **duplicate** *adj.* exactly like another thing, being a duplicate. **duplicate** (doo-pli-kayt) *v.* (**du·pli·cat·ed, du·pli·cat·ing**) 1. to make or be an exact copy of something. 2. to repeat or do something twice. **du·pli·ca·tion** (doo-pli-kay-shŏn) *n.* □**duplicate bridge,** a bridge game in which identical hands are dealt at two or more tables at the same time. **in duplicate,** in two identical copies, *prepare this in duplicate.*

du·pli·ca·tor (doo-pli-kay-tŏr) *n.* a machine for copying documents.

du·plic·i·ty (doo-plis-i-tee) *n.* (*pl.* **-ties**) double-dealing, deceitfulness.

du·ra·ble (door-ă-bĕl, dyoor-) *adj.* likely to last, not wearing out or decaying quickly. **du′ra·bly** *adv.* **du·ra·bil·i·ty** (door-ă-bil-i-tee, dyoor-) *n.* □**durable goods,** manufactured products that can be used over a long period of time. **durable press,** (of a fabric) so processed that it has few wrinkles after being laundered or after prolonged use.

du·rance (door-ăns, dyoor-) *n.* (*old use*) imprisonment, *in durance vile.*

du·ra·tion (duu-ray-shŏn, dyuu-) *n.* the time during which a thing continues.

du·ress (duu-res, dyuu-) *n.* the use of force or threats to procure something.

dur·ing (door-ing, dyoo-) *prep.* throughout or at a point in the continuance of.

durst (durst) *see* **dare.**

du·rum (door-ŭm) *n.* a species of wheat with hard seeds, used chiefly for pasta.

dusk (dusk) *n.* the darker stage of twilight.

dusk·y (dus-kee) *adj.* (**dusk·i·er, dusk·i·est**) 1. shadowy, dim. 2. dark colored. **dusk'i·ness** *n.*

dust (dust) *n.* fine particles of earth or other matter. **dust** *v.* 1. to sprinkle with dust or powder. 2. to clear of dust by wiping, to clear furniture etc. of dust. □**dust bowl,** an area stripped of vegetation by drought and erosion. **dust cover, dust jacket,** a paper jacket on a book. **dust devil,** a small whirlwind made visible by dust it carries. **dust storm,** a severe dust-filled windstorm during a period of drought. **throw dust in (a person's) eyes,** to prevent him from seeing the truth.

dust·er (dus-tĕr) *n.* 1. a cloth or brush for dusting furniture etc. 2. a smocklike garment, a housecoat. 3. *(slang)* a baseball pitch intentionally thrown close to a batter's head.

dust·pan (dust-pan) *n.* a pan into which dust is brushed from a floor.

dust·y (dus-tee) *adj.* (**dust·i·er, dust·i·est**) 1. like dust, full of dust, covered with dust. 2. (of a color) grayish, *dusty pink.* **dust'i·ness** *n.* □**dusty miller,** a common plant with white dust on its leaves and flowers.

Dutch (duch) *adj.* of the Netherlands or its people or language. **Dutch** *n.* 1. the Dutch language. 2. *the Dutch,* Dutch people. **Dutch'man** *n.* **Dutch'wom·an** *n. fem.* □**Dutch courage,** that obtained by drinking whiskey. **Dutch door,** a door with upper and lower halves that can be opened independently. **Dutch elm disease,** a disease of elm trees, caused by a fungus, first found in the Netherlands. **Dutch oven,** a covered dish for cooking meat etc. slowly. **Dutch treat,** an outing at which each person pays his own expenses. **Dutch uncle,** *(informal)* a severe and candid critic. **go Dutch,** to share expenses on an outing. **in Dutch,** *(slang)* in trouble. **talk like a Dutch uncle,** *(informal)* to lecture a person severely but candidly.

du·te·ous (doo-ti-ŭs) *adj.* *(old use)* dutiful, obedient.

du·ti·a·ble (doo-ti-ă-bĕl) *adj.* on which customs or other duties must be paid.

du·ti·ful (doo-ti-fŭl) *adj.* doing one's duty, showing due obedience. **du'ti·ful·ly** *adv.* **du'ti·ful·ness** *n.*

du·ty (doo-tee) *n.* (*pl.* **-ties**) 1. a moral or legal obligation. 2. a task that must be done, action required from a particular person, *household duties; the duties of a postman.* 3. a tax charged on certain goods or on imports. □**do duty as** *or* **for,** to serve as (something else). **in duty bound,** obliged by duty. **on** *or* **off duty,** actually engaged or not engaged in one's regular work.

D.V. *abbr.* 1. God willing (Latin *deo volente*). 2. Douay Version (of the Bible).

D.V.M. *abbr.* Doctor of Veterinary Medicine.

dwarf (dworf) *n.* (*pl.* **dwarfs, dwarves,** *pr.* dworvz) a person, animal, or plant much below the usual size. **dwarf** *adj.* of a kind that is very small in size. **dwarf** *v.* 1. to stunt. 2. to make seem small by contrast or distance. **dwarf'ish** *adj.*

dwell (dwel) *v.* (**dwelt** or **dwelled, dwell·ing**) 1. to live as an inhabitant. 2. to think or speak or write lengthily about, *dwell on a subject.* **dwell'er** *n.*

dwell·ing (dwel-ing) *n.* a house etc. to live in.

dwin·dle (dwin-dĕl) *v.* (**dwin·dled, dwin·dling**) to become gradually less or smaller.

dwt. *abbr.* pennyweight(s).

DX (dee-eks) *n.* *(slang)* distance, especially in short-wave radio reception. □**DXer,** *(slang)* a long-distance radio hobbyist. **DXing,** *(slang)* the hobby of long-distance radio transmission and reception.

Dy *symbol* dysprosium.

dyb·buk (dib-ŭk) *n.* (*pl.* **dyb·buks, dyb·bu·kim,** *pr.* di-buuk-im) (in Jewish folklore) the evil spirit of a dead person that enters and controls a living person's body.

dye (dı) *v.* (**dyed, dye·ing**) 1. to color, especially by dipping in a liquid. 2. to be able to be dyed, *this fabric dyes well.* **dye** *n.* 1. a substance used for dyeing. 2. a color given by dyeing. **dy'er** *n.* □**dyed-in-the-wool,** unchangeable, *a dyed-in-the-wool Democrat,* one who never will vote for any other party.

dye·stuff (dı-stuf) *n.* material used as or producing a dye.

dy·ing (dı-ing) *see* **die¹.**

dyke = **dike.**

dy·nam·ic (dı-nam-ik) *adj.* 1. of force producing motion (as opposed to *static*). 2. (of a person) energetic, having force of character. **dy·nam'i·cal·ly** *adv.*

dy·nam·ics (dı-nam-iks) *n.* 1. *(sing.)* a branch of physics that deals with matter in motion. 2. *(pl.)* the forces operating in any complex matter, *the dynamics of presidential politics.*

dy·na·mite (dı-nă-mıt) *n.* 1. a powerful explosive made of nitroglycerine. 2. something likely to cause violent or dangerous reactions, *the frontier question is dynamite.* 3. *(informal)* great vitality or effectiveness. **dynamite** *v.* (**dy·na·mit·ed, dy·na·mit·ing**) to blow up with dynamite.

dy·na·mo (dı-nă-moh) *n.* (*pl.* **-mos**) a small compact generator producing electric current. □**human dynamo,** a dynamic person.

dy·na·mom·e·ter (dı-nă-mom-ĕ-tĕr) *n.* an instrument for measuring energy expended by some force.

dy·nas·ty (dı-nă-stee) *n.* (*pl.* **-ties**) a line of hereditary rulers. **dy·nas·tic** (dı-nas-tik) *adj.*

dys·en·ter·y (dis-ĕn-ter-ee) *n.* a disease with inflammation of the intestines, causing severe diarrhea.

dys·func·tion (dis-fungk-shŏn) *n.* failure to function normally.

dys·lex·i·a (dis-lek-si-ă) *n.* abnormal difficulty in reading and spelling, caused by a brain condition. **dys·lex'ic** *adj.* & *n.* ▷ *Dyslectic* is incorrect.

dys·pep·si·a (dis-pep-si-ă) *n.* indigestion.

dys·pep·tic (dis-pep-tik) *adj.* suffering from dyspepsia or the resultant irritability.

dys·pro·si·um (dis-proh-zi-ŭm) *n.* a highly magnetic chemical element.

dys·tro·phy (dis-trŏ-fee) *n.* a condition causing progressive weakening of the muscles, *muscular dystrophy.*

dz. *abbr.* dozen(s).

E

E, e (ee) (*pl.* **Es, E's, e's**) the fifth letter of the alphabet.
e *symbol* a constant having the approximate value 2.718, used as the base of the natural system of logarithms.
e. *abbr.* 1. east, eastern. 2. electron. 3. energy. 4. error.
E. *abbr.* 1. Earth. 2. East, Eastern. 3. Engineering. 4. English.
ea. *abbr.* each.
each (eech) *adj.* every one of two or more, *each child.* **each** *pronoun* each person or thing, *each of them.* **each** *adv.* apiece, *tickets are five dollars each.* □**each other**, showing mutual or reciprocal action between two or more persons or things; *they looked at each other.* ▷ *Each* requires a singular construction as in *each person has that privilege,* except when it refers to a plural noun or pronoun, as in *they each have that privilege.*
ea·ger (ee-gĕr) *adj.* full of strong desire, enthusiastic. **ea'ger·ly** *adv.* **ea'ger·ness** *n.* □**eager beaver**, *(informal)* an excessively diligent person. ▷ See the note under **anxious.**
ea·gle (ee-gĕl) *n.* 1. a large bird of prey. 2. a score of two strokes under par for a hole at golf. □**eagle eye**, very sharp eyesight, keen watchfulness.
ea·gle-eyed (ee-gĕl-ıd) *adj.* keen-sighted, observant.
ea·glet (ee-glit) *n.* a young eagle.
-ean *suffix* used to form adjectives and nouns, especially from names of people and places, as in *herculean, protean, European.*
ear¹ (eer) *n.* 1. the organ of hearing in man and certain animals, the external part of this. 2. the ability to distinguish sounds accurately; *has an ear for music,* enjoys it. 3. listening, attention; *lend an ear,* listen; *have a person's ear,* to have his favorable attention. 4. an ear-shaped thing. □**be all ears**, to listen attentively. **have one's ear to the ground**, to be alert to rumors or trends of opinion. **up to the ears**, *(informal)* deeply involved or occupied in something.
ear² *n.* the seed-bearing part of corn.
ear·ache (eer-ayk) *n.* pain in the eardrum.
ear·drum (eer-drum) *n.* a membrane inside the ear that vibrates when sound waves strike it.
ear·flaps (eer-flaps) *n. pl.* parts of a cap that can be turned down to cover the ears.
ear·ful (eer-fuul) *n.* (*pl.* **-fuls**) *(informal)* 1. a large amount of talk. 2. a strong reprimand.
earl (url) *n.* a British nobleman ranking between marquis and viscount.
ear·laps (eer-laps) *n. pl.* earflaps.
earl·dom (url-dŏm) *n.* the position or lands of an earl.

ear·lobe (eer-lohb) *n.* the lower fleshy part of the ear.
ear·ly (ur-lee) *adj.* & *adv.* (**ear·li·er, ear·li·est**) 1. before the usual or expected time. 2. not far on in a period of time or a development or a series, *his early years.* **ear'li·ness** *n.* □**early bird**, a person who gets up early or arrives early. **early on**, at an early stage.
ear·mark (eer-mahrk) *n.* a distinguishing mark. **earmark** *v.* 1. to put a distinguishing mark on. 2. to set aside for a particular purpose.
ear·muffs (eer-mufs) *n. pl.* a pair of ear coverings worn for protection against the cold.
earn (urn) *v.* 1. to get or deserve as a reward for one's work or merit. 2. (of money lent or invested) to gain as interest. □**earned income**, income derived from paid employment. **earned run**, (in baseball) a run scored without help from the opposing team.
ear·nest¹ (ur-nist) *adj.* showing serious feeling or intentions. **ear'nest·ly** *adv.* **ear'nest·ness** *n.* □**in earnest**, seriously, not jokingly; with determination, intensively.
earnest² *n.* 1. (also **earnest money**) a payment from a buyer to a seller to confirm an agreement. 2. something given as a pledge.
earn·ings (ur-ningz) *n. pl.* money earned.
ear·phone (eer-fohn) *n.* a radio receiver that fits into or over the ear.
ear·plug (eer-plug) *n.* a plug that is inserted in the ear to keep out noise or water.
ear·ring (eer-ring) *n.* an ornament worn on the earlobe.
ear·shot (eer-shot) *n.* range of hearing, *within earshot.*
ear·split·ting (eer-split-ing) *adj.* piercingly loud.
earth (urth) *n.* 1. *Earth,* the planet on which we live, the world in which we live. 2. its surface, dry land, the ground, *it fell to earth.* 3. soil. 4. an oxide with little taste or smell. □**earth science**, any of the sciences that study the history, composition, or processes of the earth. **on earth**, in existence, in this world (as distinct from a future life); *why on earth,* why ever; *look or feel like nothing on earth,* feel very unwell. **run a thing to earth**, to find it after a long search.
earth·bound (urth-bownd) *adj.* attached to the earth, moving toward Earth.
earth·en (ur-thĕn) *adj.* 1. made of earth. 2. made of baked clay.
earth·en·ware (ur-thĕn-wair, -thĕn-) *n.* pottery made of coarse baked clay.
earth·ling (urth-ling) *n.* an inhabitant of Earth.
earth·ly (urth-lee) *adj.* (**-li·er, -li·est**) of the living world, of man's life in it. **earth'li·ness** *n.* □**no earthly use**, *(informal)* no use at all. ▷ Use *earthly* when describing the human condition, as

in *our earthly existence prepares for heaven.* Use *earthy* when likening something to soil or describing something that is coarse, as in *his earthy language shocked all of them.*

earth·quake (urth-kwayk) *n.* a violent natural movement of a part of Earth's crust.

earth·shak·ing (urth-shay-king) *adj.* having a violent effect on established arrangements, beliefs, etc.

earth·ward (urth-wărd) *adj.* headed toward the earth. **earthward, earthwards** (urth-wărdz) *adv.* toward the earth.

earth·work (urth-wurk) *n.* an artificial bank of earth.

earth·worm (urth-wurm) *n.* a long worm that burrows in the soil.

earth·y (ur-thee) *adj.* (**earth·i·er, earth·i·est**) 1. like earth or soil. 2. gross, coarse, *earthy humor.* ▷See the note under **earthly.**

ear·wax (eer-waks) *n.* the waxy material found in the ear.

ear·wig (eer-wig) *n.* a small insect with pincers at the end of its body (formerly thought to enter man's head through the ear).

ease (eez) *n.* 1. freedom from pain or trouble or anxiety. 2. relief from pain. 3. absence of painful effort, *did it with ease.* **ease** *v.* (**eased, eas·ing**) 1. to relieve from pain or anxiety. 2. to make less tight or forceful or burdensome. 3. to move gently or gradually, *ease it in.* 4. to slacken, to reduce in severity or pressure etc., *it will ease off* or *up.* □**at ease,** free from anxiety, in comfort; standing relaxed with feet apart; a military order to stand in this way. **at one's ease,** relaxed, not feeling awkward or embarrassed.

ea·sel (ee-zĕl) *n.* a wooden frame to support a painting or a blackboard etc.

east (eest) *n.* 1. the point on the horizon where the sun rises, the direction in which this point lies. 2. the eastern part of something. 3. *the East,* the part of the world lying east of Europe, the Communist countries of eastern Europe, the eastern part of the U.S. **east** *adj. & adv.* toward or in the east; *an east wind,* blowing from the east; *look east.* □**East Asia,** the region comprising China, Japan, Korea, and the Asiatic part of the U.S.S.R. **East Germany,** the German Democratic Republic. **East Indies,** the islands of the Pacific and Indian oceans southeast of Asia.

East·er (ee-stĕr) *n.* the Christian festival (celebrated on **Easter Sunday,** a Sunday in March or April) commemorating Christ's resurrection. □**Easter bonnet,** a woman's hat worn especially for Easter. **Easter bunny,** a rabbit said to bring gifts to children at Easter. **Easter egg,** a chocolate artificial egg or decorated egg given as a gift at Easter. **Easter lily,** a plant with large white flowers used to decorate churches etc. at Easter. **Easter parade,** a procession on Easter Sunday to display fashionable clothes.

east·er·ly (ee-stĕr-lee) *adj.* in, from, or toward the east; *an easterly wind,* blowing from the east (approximately). **easterly** *n.* an easterly wind.

east·ern (ee-stĕrn) *adj.* (also **Eastern**) of or in the east. **East'ern·er** *n.* □**Eastern Church,** the Orthodox Church. **Eastern Hemisphere,** the half of the world that includes Europe, Asia, Africa, and Australia.

east·ward (eest-wărd) *adj.* toward the east, in the east. **eastward, eastwards** (eest-wărdz) *adv.* toward the east.

eas·y (ee-zee) *adj.* (**eas·i·er, eas·i·est**) 1. not difficult, done or obtained without great effort. 2. free from pain, trouble, or anxiety, *with an easy mind; easy manners,* relaxed and pleasant; *in easy circumstances,* with enough money to live comfortably. **easy** *adv.* in an easy way, with ease. **eas'i·ness** *n.* **eas'i·ly** *adv.* □**easy chair,** a large comfortable chair. **easy does it,** be careful; go slowly. **easy on the eye,** *(informal)* pleasant to look at. **Easy Street,** *(informal)* a state of affluence. **go easy on,** to be lenient with, *go easy on him;* to use with restraint, *go easy on starches.* **go easy with,** to be careful with (a person). **rest easy,** do not worry. **stand easy,** stand at ease. **take it easy,** to proceed comfortably or carefully; to rest or relax.

eas·y·go·ing (ee-zee-goh-ing) *adj.* not strict, placid and tolerant.

eat (eet) *v.* (**ate, eat·en, eat·ing**) 1. to take food into the mouth and swallow it for nourishment, to chew and swallow. 2. to have a meal, *when do we eat?* 3. to destroy gradually, to consume, *acids eat into metals; the car ate up the miles,* covered the distance rapidly. **eats** *n. pl. (slang)* food. **eat'er** *n.* □**eating apple,** an apple suitable for eating raw, as opposed to one grown primarily for cooking. **eat one's heart out,** to suffer greatly with vexation or longing. **eat one's words,** to be obliged to withdraw what one has said. **what's eating you?,** *(slang)* why are you annoyed?

eat·a·ble (ee-tă-bĕl) *adj.* fit to be eaten (because of its condition).

eat·a·bles (ee-tă-bĕlz) *n. pl.* food.

eat·er·y (ee-tĕ-ree) *n.* (*pl.* **-er·ies**) *(slang)* an inexpensive restaurant.

eau de Co·logne (oh de kŏ-lohn) a delicate toilet water originally made at Cologne, Germany.

eaves (eevz) *n. pl.* the overhanging edge of a roof.

eaves·drop (eevz-drop) *v.* (**eaves·dropped, eaves·drop·ping**) to listen secretly to a private conversation. **eaves'drop·per** *n.*

ebb (eb) *n.* 1. the outward movement of the tide, away from land. 2. a condition of lowness or decline. **ebb** *v.* 1. (of tides) to flow away from land. 2. to become lower, to weaken, *his strength ebbed.*

eb·on·ite (eb-ŏ-nıt) *n. see* **vulcanite.**

eb·on·y (eb-ŏ-nee) *n.* (*pl.* **-on·ies**) the hard black wood of a tropical tree (the **ebony tree**). **ebony** *adj.* black as ebony.

e·bul·lient (i-bul-yĕnt, -buul-) *adj.* exuberant, bubbling over with high spirits. **e·bul'lience** *n.* **eb·ul·li·tion** (eb-ŭ-lish-ŏn) *n.*

E.C. *abbr.* European Community (the Common Market nations).

ec·cen·tric (ik-sen-trik) *adj.* 1. unconventional in appearance or behavior. 2. (of circles) not concentric, (of orbits) not circular, (of a pivot) not placed centrally. **eccentric** *n.* an eccentric person. **ec·cen'tri·cal·ly** *adv.* **ec·cen·tric·i·ty** (ek-sen-tris-i-tee) *n.*

Eccl., Eccles. *abbr.* Ecclesiastes.

Ec·cle·si·as·tes (i-klee-zi-as-teez) *n.* a book of the Old Testament traditionally ascribed to Solomon and written in his name.

ec·cle·si·as·tic (i-klee-zi-as-tik) *n.* a clergyman.

ec·cle·si·as·ti·cal (i-klee-zi-as-ti-kăl) *adj.* of the church or the clergy. **ec·cle·si·as'ti·cal·ly** *adv.*

ECG *abbr.* electrocardiogram.

ech·e·lon (esh-ĕ-lon) *n.* 1. a staggered formation

of troops or aircraft etc. 2. a level of rank or authority, *the upper echelons of government*.
ech·o (ek-oh) *n.* (*pl.* **-oes**) 1. repetition of sound by the reflection of sound waves, a secondary sound produced in this way. 2. a close imitation or imitator. **echo** *v.* (**ech·oed, echo·ing**) 1. to repeat (sound) by echo, to resound. 2. to repeat or imitate.
ech·o·lo·ca·tion (ek-oh-loh-kay-shŏn) *n.* the location of objects by reflected sound.
é·clair (ay-klair) *n.* a finger-shaped pastry with cream filling.
é·clat (ay-klah) *n.* 1. conspicuous success. 2. general applause, acclaim. 3. elaborate display.
ec·lec·tic (i-klek-tik) *adj.* choosing or accepting from various sources. **eclectic** *n.* a person who borrows freely from various sources in forming opinion, taste, etc. **ec·lec'ti·cism** *n.*
e·clipse (i-klips) *n.* 1. the blocking of light from one heavenly body by another. 2. a loss of brilliance or power or reputation. **eclipse** *v.* (**e·clipsed, e·clips·ing**) 1. to cause an eclipse of. 2. to outshine, to throw into obscurity.
e·clip·tic (i-klip-tik) *n.* the sun's apparent path among stars during the year.
ec·logue (ek-lawg) *n.* a short pastoral poem, especially one in dialogue form.
E.C.M. *abbr.* European Common Market.
e·co·cide (ee-kŏ-sɪd, ek-ŏ-) *n.* the destruction of the human environment, especially through contamination by manmade waste.
ecol. *abbr.* 1. ecological. 2. ecology.
e·col·o·gy (i-kol-ŏ-jee) *n.* 1. the scientific study of living things in relation to each other and to their environment. 2. this relationship. (▷Note that *ecology* does not mean *environment*.) **ec·o·log·ic** (ee-kŏ-loj-ik, ek-ŏ-) *adj.* **ec·o·log'i·cal** *adj.* **ec·o·log'i·cal·ly** *adv.*
econ. *abbr.* 1. economic. 2. economics. 3. economy.
e·con·o·met·rics (ee-kon-ŏ-met-riks) *n.* the branch of economics concerned with the application of mathematical economics by use of statistics. **e·con·o·met'ric** *adj.* **e·con·o·met·ri'cian** *n.*
e·co·nom·ic (ee-kŏ-nom-ik, ek-ŏ-) *adj.* 1. of economics, *the government's economic policies*. 2. of one's own finances, *concerned with her economic well-being*. ▷Do not confuse *economic* with *economical, she was an expert in economic geography*.
e·co·nom·i·cal (ee-kŏ-nom-i-kăl, ek-ŏ-) *adj.* thrifty, avoiding waste. **e·co·nom'i·cal·ly** *adv.* ▷Do not confuse *economical* with *economic, she is an economical person*.
e·co·nom·ics (ee-kŏ-nom-iks, ek-ŏ-) *n.* 1. (*sing.*) the science concerned with the production and consumption or use of goods and services. 2. (*pl.*) the financial aspects of something, *the economics of farming*.
e·con·o·mist (i-kon-ŏ-mist) *n.* an expert in economics.
e·con·o·mize (i-kon-ŏ-mɪz) *v.* (**e·con·o·mized, e·con·o·miz·ing**) to be economical, to use or spend less than before, *economize on fuel*.
e·con·o·my (i-kon-ŏ-mee) *n.* (*pl.* **-mies**) 1. being economical, *practice economy*. 2. an instance of this, a saving, *make economies*. 3. a community's system of using its resources to produce wealth; *an agricultural economy*, one in which agriculture is the chief industry. 4. the state of a country's prosperity, *its economy lagged*. **economy** *adj.*

economical; *the large economy size, so large as to be economically advantageous to the customer*.
e·co·sys·tem (ee-koh-sis-tĕm, ek-oh-) *n.* all the organisms living in a place (small or large) as an interdependent and separate unit.
ec·ru (ek-roo) *n.* light fawn color.
ec·sta·sy (ek-stă-see) *n.* (*pl.* **-sies**) a feeling of intense delight. **ec·stat·ic** (ek-stat-ik) *adj.* **ec·stat'i·cal·ly** *adv.*
ec·to·plasm (ek-tŏ-plaz-ĕm) *n.* a substance supposed to be exuded from a spiritualist medium during a trance.
Ecua. *abbr.* Ecuador.
Ec·ua·dor (ek-wă-dor) a country in South America. **Ec·ua·dor'e·an, Ec·ua·dor'i·an** *adj. & n.*
ec·u·men·i·cal (ek-yuu-men-i-kăl) *adj.* 1. of the whole Christian church, not only of separate sects. 2. seeking worldwide Christian unity, *the ecumenical movement*. **ec·u·men'i·cal·ly** *adv.* **ec·u·me·nic·i·ty** (ek-yuu-mĕ-nis-i-tee) *n.*
ec·ze·ma (ek-sĕ-mă, eg-zĕ-) *n.* a skin disease causing scaly itching patches.
ED *abbr.* Department of Education.
ed. *abbr.* 1. edited. 2. edition. 3. editor. 4. education.
-ed[1] *suffix* used to form the past tenses and past participles of verbs, as in *wanted, granted, snowed*.
-ed[2] *suffix* used to form adjectives, as in *moneyed, talented, wooded*.
E·dam (ee-dăm) *n.* a round Dutch cheese, usually with a red rind.
ed·dy (ed-ee) *n.* (*pl.* **-dies**) a swirling patch of water or air or fog etc. **eddy** *v.* (**ed·died, ed·dy·ing**) to swirl in eddies.
e·del·weiss (ay-dĕl-vɪs) *n.* an alpine plant with white flowers and woolly leaves.
e·de·ma (i-dee-mă) *n.* the abnormal retention of fluid in body cavities or tissues.
E·den (ee-dĕn) the place where Adam and Eve lived at their creation. **Eden** *n.* a delightful place.
edge (ej) *n.* 1. the sharpened side of a blade. 2. its sharpness, *has lost its edge*. 3. the line where two surfaces meet at an angle. 4. a rim, the narrow surface of a thin or flat object, *the pages have gilt edges*. 5. the outer limit or boundary of an area, *the edge of the forest*. **edge** *v.* (**edged, edg·ing**) 1. to supply with a border, to form the border of. 2. to move gradually, *edging toward the door*. □**be on edge**, to be tense and irritable. **have the edge on**, (*informal*) to have an advantage over. **set a person's teeth on edge**, to upset his nerves by causing an unpleasant sensation. **take the edge off**, to dull or soften; *take the edge off one's appetite*, to make one's hunger less acute.
edge·wise (ej-wɪz), **edge·ways** (ej-wayz) *adv.* with the edge forward or outward. □**get a word in edgewise**, to manage to break into a lengthy monologue.
edg·ing (ej-ing) *n.* something placed around an edge to define or strengthen or decorate it.
edg·y (ej-ee) *adj.* (**edg·i·er, edg·i·est**) with nerves on edge, irritable.
ed·i·ble (ed-ĭ-bĕl) *adj.* fit or safe to be eaten (because of its nature). **ed·i·bil·i·ty** (ed-ĭ-bil-i-tee) *n.*
e·dict (ee-dikt) *n.* an order proclaimed by an authority.
ed·i·fice (ed-ĭ-fis) *n.* a large building.
ed·i·fy (ed-ĭ-fɪ) *v.* (**ed·i·fied, ed·i·fy·ing**) to be an uplifting influence on the mind of (a person). **ed·i·fi·ca·tion** (ed-ĭ-fi-kay-shŏn) *n.*

Ed·in·burgh (ed-in-bur-oh) the capital of Scotland.

ed·it (ed-it) v. 1. to act as editor of (a newspaper etc.). 2. to prepare (written material) for publication. 3. to prepare (a film or recording) by selecting individual sections and arranging them in sequence.

e·di·tion (i-dish-ŏn) n. 1. the form in which something is published, *a pocket edition*. 2. the number of copies of a book or newspaper printed from one set of type.

ed·i·tor (ed-i-tŏr) n. 1. a person who is responsible for the content and writing of a newspaper etc. or a section of this, *our financial editor*. 2. one who edits written material for publication. 3. one who edits film or recording tape. **ed'i·tor·ship** n.

ed·i·to·ri·al (ed-i-tohr-i-ăl) adj. of an editor, *editorial work.* **editorial** n. a newspaper or magazine article giving the editor's comments on current affairs, a similar statement by a radio or television station. **ed·i·to'ri·al·ly** adv.

ed·i·to·ri·al·ize (ed-i-tohr-i-ă-lız) v. (**ed·i·to·ri·al·ized, ed·i·to·ri·al·iz·ing**) 1. to write an editorial. 2. to express one's opinion when facts (and not opinions) are appropriate. **ed·i'to/ri·al·iz·er** n. **ed·i·to·ri·al·i·za·tion** (ed-i-tohr-i-ă-li-zay-shŏn) n.

EDP abbr. electronic data processing.

EDT, E.D.T. abbr. Eastern daylight time.

educ. abbr. 1. education. 2. educational.

ed·u·ca·ble (ej-ŭ-kă-běl) adj. able to be educated.

ed·u·cate (ej-ŭ-kayt) v. (**ed·u·cat·ed, ed·u·cat·ing**) to train the mind and abilities of, to provide education for. **ed'u·ca·tor** n.

ed·u·ca·tion (ej-ŭ-kay-shŏn) n. systematic training and instruction designed to impart knowledge and develop skill. **ed·u·ca'tion·al** adj. □**educational television**, television programing designed to promote learning.

e·duce (i-doos) v. (**e·duced, e·duc·ing**) 1. to bring out or develop, to elicit (from a person). 2. to infer (from information).

Ed·ward·i·an (ed-wor-di-ăn) adj. of the time of King Edward VII's reign in Britain (1901–10). **Edwardian** n. a person of this time.

E.E. abbr. Electrical Engineer(ing).

EEC abbr. European Economic Community.

EEG abbr. electroencephalogram.

eel (eel) n. a snakelike fish.

e'er (air) adv. (*old use*) ever.

ee·rie (eer-ee) adj. (**ee·ri·er, ee·ri·est**) causing a feeling of mystery and fear. **ee'ri·ness** n. **ee'ri·ly** adv.

ef·face (i-fays) v. (**ef·faced, ef·fac·ing**) to rub out, to obliterate. **ef·face'a·ble** adj. **ef·face'ment** n. □**efface oneself**, to make oneself inconspicuous.

ef·fect (i-fekt) n. 1. a change produced by an action or cause, a result; *have an effect*, to produce such a change. 2. an impression produced on a spectator or hearer etc., *special lighting gave the effect of moonlight; did it only for effect*, in order to impress people. 3. a state of being operative, *the law came into effect last week.* 4. *effects*, property, *her personal effects;* sounds and lighting etc. provided to accompany a broadcast or film, *special effects.* **effect** v. to bring about, to accomplish, *effect one's purpose; effect a cure; effect a settlement*, reach an agreement. (▷The words *effect* and *affect* have totally different meanings and should not be confused.) □**in effect**, in fact, really, *it is, in effect, a refusal.* **take effect**, to produce its effect(s); to become operative. **to that effect**, with that implication, *words to that effect.*

ef·fec·tive (i-fek-tiv) adj. 1. producing an effect, powerful in its effect. 2. making a striking impression. 3. actual, existing; *the effective membership*, the real (not nominal) number of members. 4. operative, *the law is effective after April 1.* **ef·fec'tive·ly** adv. **ef·fec'tive·ness** n. ▷Careful writers note a subtle difference between *effective* and *effectual.* A law that is *effective* (operative) becomes *effectual* (answers its purpose) only when it is enforced.

ef·fec·tu·al (i-fek-choo-ăl) adj. answering its purpose, sufficient to produce an effect. **ef·fec'tu·al·ly** adv. ▷See the note under **effective**.

ef·fec·tu·ate (i-fek-choo-ayt) v. (**ef·fec·tu·at·ed, ef·fec·tu·at·ing**) to cause to happen.

ef·fem·i·nate (i-fem-ĭ-nit) adj. unmanly, having qualities associated with women. **ef·fem'i·nate·ly** adv. **ef·fem·i·na·cy** (i-fem-ĭ-nă-see) n. (pl. **-cies**) ▷Do not use *effeminate* to describe women or girls.

ef·fen·di (i-fen-dee) n. 1. a person of education or standing in an eastern Mediterranean or Arab country. 2. a title of respect or courtesy formerly used in Turkey.

ef·fer·ent (ef-ě-rěnt) adj. (in physiology) conducting outward from an organ. **efferent** n. an efferent duct or nerve.

ef·fer·vesce (ef-ěr-ves) v. (**ef·fer·vesced, ef·fer·vesc·ing**) to give off small bubbles of gas. **ef·fer·ves'cence** n. **ef·fer·ves'cent** adj. **ef·fer·ves'cent·ly** adv.

ef·fete (i-feet) adj. having lost its vitality. **ef·fete'ness** n.

ef·fi·ca·cious (ef-ĭ-kay-shŭs) adj. producing the desired result. **ef·fi·ca·cy** (ef-ĭ-kă-see) n.

ef·fi·cient (i-fish-ěnt) adj. acting effectively, producing results with little waste of effort. **ef·fi'cient·ly** adv. **ef·fi'cien·cy** n.

ef·fi·gy (ef-i-jee) n. (pl. **-gies**) a sculpture or model of a person.

ef·flo·resce (ef-lŏ-res) v. (**ef·flo·resced, ef·flo·resc·ing**) to burst out into flower. **ef·flo·res'cence** n. **ef·flo·res'cent** adj.

ef·flu·ence (ef-loo-ěns) n. 1. the process of flowing out, especially of sewage. 2. an effluent.

ef·flu·ent (ef-loo-ěnt) adj. flowing out. **effluent** n. something that flows out, especially sewage.

ef·flu·vi·um (i-floo-vi-ŭm) n. an unpleasant or harmful gas.

ef·fort (ef-ŏrt) n. 1. the use of physical or mental energy to achieve something. 2. the energy exerted, *it was quite an effort to give up smoking.* 3. something produced by this, *this painting is a good effort.*

ef·fort·less (ef-ŏrt-lis) adj. done without effort. **ef'fort·less·ly** adv.

ef·fron·ter·y (i-frun-tě-ree) n. (pl. **-ter·ies**) shameless insolence.

ef·ful·gence (i-ful-jěns) n. radiance. **ef·ful'gent** adj.

ef·fu·sion (i-fyoo-zhŏn) n. 1. a pouring forth. 2. an unrestrained outpouring of thought or feeling.

ef·fu·sive (i-fyoo-siv) adj. expressing emotions in an unrestrained way. **ef·fu'sive·ly** adv. **ef·fu'sive·ness** n.

eft (eft) n. a newt.

E.F.T. abbr. electronic funds transfer.

Eg. abbr. 1. Egypt. 2. Egyptian.

e.g. *abbr.* for example. ▷From the Latin *exempli gratia.*

e·gad (i-gad, ee-gad) *interj. (old use)* by God.

e·gal·i·tar·i·an (i-gal-i-tair-i-ăn) *adj.* holding the principle of equal rights for all persons. **egalitarian** *n.* a person who holds this principle. **e·gal·i·tar′i·an·ism** *n.*

egg[1] (eg) *n.* 1. a reproductive cell produced by the female of birds, fish, reptiles, etc. 2. the hard-shelled egg of a domestic hen, used as food. □**bad egg,** *(informal)* a worthless or dishonest person. **egg cell,** the female reproductive cell. **egg cream,** a carbonated chocolate drink, formerly made with egg and cream. **egg cup,** a small cup for holding a boiled egg. **egg foo young,** an omelet-like Chinese-American dish filled with a meat and vegetable mixture. **egg roll,** a Chinese or Chinese-American dish made of egg dough wrapped around minced vegetables or meat or seafood and fried. **egg timer,** a device for timing the cooking of a boiled egg. **good egg,** *(informal)* a friendly helpful person.

egg[2] *v.* to urge a person to do something, *egging him on.*

egg-beat·er (eg-bee-tĕr) *n.* 1. a hand-operated device for whipping eggs, cream, etc. 2. *(slang)* a helicopter.

egg·head (eg-hed) *n. (informal)* an intellectual person.

egg·nog (eg-nog) *n.* a drink of whipped eggs, milk or cream, sugar, and usually liquor.

egg·plant (eg-plant) *n.* 1. a plant with deep-purple fruit used as a vegetable. 2. its fruit.

egg·shell (eg-shel) *n.* the shell of an egg. **eggshell** *adj.* 1. (of china) very fragile. 2. yellowish white.

e·gis = aegis.

eg·lan·tine (eg-lăn-tin) *n.* sweetbrier.

e·go (ee-goh, eg-oh) *n. (pl.* **-gos)** 1. the self. 2. self-esteem, conceit. 3. the part of the psyche that is concerned with the outside world. □**ego ideal,** the conscious idealization of oneself. **ego trip,** *(informal)* an activity undertaken with the sole purpose of indulging in one's own interests or in self-expression.

e·go·cen·tric (ee-goh-sen-trik, eg-oh-) *adj.* self-centered.

e·go·ism (ee-goh-iz-ĕm, eg-oh-) *n.* self-centeredness. **e′go·ist** *n.* **e·go·is·tic** (ee-goh-is-tik, eg-oh-) *adj.* **e·go·is′ti·cal** *adj.* **e·go·is′ti·cal·ly** *adv.*

e·go·tism (ee-gŏ-tiz-ĕm, eg-ŏ-) *n.* the practice of talking too much about oneself, conceit. **e′go·tist** *n.* **e·go·tis·tic** (ee-gŏ-tis-tik, eg-ŏ-) *adj.* **e·go·tis′ti·cal** *adj.* **e·go·tis′ti·cal·ly** *adv.*

e·gre·gious (i-gree-jŭs) *adj.* outstandingly bad, *egregious folly.* **e·gre′gious·ly** *adv.* **e·gre′gious·ness** *n.*

e·gress (ee-gres) *n.* an exit.

e·gret (ee-grit) *n.* a kind of heron with beautiful long tail feathers.

E·gypt (ee-jipt) a country in northeast Africa. **E·gyp·tian** (i-jip-shŏn) *adj.* & *n.*

E·gyp·tol·o·gist (ee-jip-tol-ŏ-jist) *n.* an expert in Egyptology.

E·gyp·tol·o·gy (ee-jip-tol-ŏ-jee) *n.* the study of Egyptian antiquities.

eh (ay) *interj. (informal)* an exclamation of doubt or inquiry or surprise.

EHF *abbr.* extremely high frequency.

ei·der (I-dĕr) *n.* (also **eider duck**) a large northern duck.

ei·der·down (I-dĕr-down) *n.* 1. the small soft feathers from the breast of the female eider. 2. a quilt stuffed with eiderdown or similar material. **eiderdown** *adj.* stuffed with eiderdown for warmth, *an eiderdown jacket.*

ei·det·ic (I-det-ĭk) **image** a mental image that is unusually vivid and detailed, as if actually visible.

ei·do·lon (I-doh-lŏn) *n.* (*pl.* **-lons, -la,** *pr.* -lă) 1. a specter, a phantom. 2. an idealized image.

eight (ayt) *adj.* & *n.* 1. one more than seven, (8, VIII). 2. anything having eight members or units, such as *an eight-track tape.* □**behind the eight ball,** *(slang)* out of luck, in deep trouble. **eight ball,** a billiard ball bearing the number 8.

eight·een (ay-teen) *adj.* & *n.* one more than seventeen (18, XVIII). **eight·eenth** (ay-teenth) *adj.* & *n.*

eighth (ayth) *adj.* & *n.* 1. next after seventh. 2. one of eight equal parts of a thing. **eighth′ly** *adv.* □**eighth note,** a musical note having one-eighth the count of a whole note.

eight·ies (ay-teez) *n. pl.* the numbers or years or degrees of temperature from 80 to 89.

eight-track (ayt-trak) *n. (informal)* a magnetic tape cartridge having eight parallel tracks for recording on.

eight·y (ay-tee) *adj.* & *n.* eight times ten (80, LXXX). **eight·i·eth** (ay-ti-ith) *adj.* & *n.*

ein·stein·i·um (In-stI-ni-ŭm) *n.* a radioactive chemical element.

Eir·e (air-ĕ) a former name of the Republic of Ireland.

Ei·sen·how·er (I-zĕn-how-ĕr), **Dwight Da·vid** (1890–1969) the thirty-fourth president of the U.S. 1953–56.

eis·tedd·fod (I-steth-vod) *n.* an annual Welsh gathering of poets and musicians for competitions.

ei·ther (ee-thĕr) *adj.* & *pron.* 1. one or the other of two, *either of you can go.* 2. each of two, *there are fields on either side of the river.* **either** *adv.* & *conj.* 1. as one alternative, *he is either mad or drunk.* 2. likewise, *any more than the other, the new lid doesn't fit either.* ▷Use a singular verb for the pronoun *either, he said that either is acceptable.*

e·jac·u·late (i-jak-yŭ-layt) *v.* (**e·jac·u·lat·ed, e·jac·u·lat·ing**) 1. to say suddenly and briefly. 2. to eject fluid (especially semen) from the body. **e·jac·u·la·tion** (i-jak-yŭ-lay-shŏn) *n.* **e·jac·u·la·to·ry** (i-jak-yŭ-lă-tohr-ee) *adj.*

e·ject (i-jekt) *v.* 1. to thrust or send out forcefully, *the gun ejects spent cartridges.* 2. to expel, to compel to leave. **e·jec′tor** *n.* **e·jec·tion** (i-jek-shŏn) *n.* □**ejection seat,** a seat that can eject the occupant out of an aircraft in an emergency so that he can descend by parachute.

eke (eek) *v.* (**eked, ek·ing**) **eke out** 1. to supplement, *eke out oil by burning wood.* 2. to make (a living) laboriously, *eke out a living.*

EKG *abbr.* electrocardiogram.

e·kis·tics (i-kis-tiks) *n.* the study of human settlements and their development. **e·kis′tic** *adj.*

el (el) *n.* an elevated railroad in a city.

el. *abbr.* elevation.

e·lab·o·rate (i-lab-ŏ-rit) *adj.* with many parts or details, complicated, *an elaborate pattern.* **elaborate** (i-lab-ŏ-rayt) *v.* (**e·lab·o·rat·ed, e·lab·o·rat·ing**) to work out or describe in detail. **e·lab′o·rate·ly** *adv.* **e·lab′o·rate·ness** *n.* **e·lab·o·ra·tion** (i-lab-ŏ-ray-shŏn) *n.*

é·lan (ay-lahn) *n.* 1. vivacity. 2. an impetuous rush.

e·land (ee-lănd) *n.* (*pl.* **-lands, -land**) a large African antelope with spirally twisted horns.

e·lapse (i-laps) *v.* (**e·lapsed, e·laps·ing**) (of time) to pass away, *hours have elapsed.* ▷ Do not confuse *elapse* with *lapse; days elapse* but *licenses lapse.*

e·las·tic (i-las-tik) *adj.* 1. going back to its original length or shape after being stretched or squeezed. 2. adaptable, not rigid, *the rules are somewhat elastic.* **elastic** *n.* cord or material made elastic by interweaving strands of rubber etc. **e·las·tic·i·ty** (i-las-tis-i-tee) *n.*

e·las·to·mer (i-las-tŏ-měr) *n.* a natural or synthetic rubber or a rubberlike plastic.

e·late (i-layt) *v.* (**e·lat·ed, e·lat·ing**) to make happy or proud. **e·lat·ed** (i-layt-ĕd) *adj.* feeling very pleased or proud. **e·la'tion** *n.*

el·bow (el-boh) *n.* 1. the joint between the forearm and upper arm, its outer part. 2. the part of a sleeve covering this. 3. a sharp bend in a pipe etc. **elbow** *v.* to thrust with one's elbow. ☐**elbow grease,** vigorous polishing; hard work. **el·bow·room** (el-boh-room) *n.* plenty of room to work or move.

eld·er[1] (el-děr) *adj.* older, *elder sister.* **elder** *n.* 1. an older person, *respect your elders.* 2. an official in certain churches. ☐**elder statesman,** an elderly influential person whose advice is valued because of his or her years of experience. ▷ Use *elder* and *eldest* for people, *older* and *oldest* for things or people.

el·der[2] *n.* a tree with white flowers and dark berries. **el·der·ber·ry** (el-děr-ber-ee) *n.* (*pl.* **-ries**) the berry of the elder tree.

eld·er·ly (el-děr-lee) *adj.* rather old, past middle age.

eld·est (el-dist) *adj.* oldest, first-born, *eldest son.* ▷ See the note under *elder.*

el·do·ra·do (el-dŏ-rah-doh) *n.* (*pl.* **-dos**) an imaginary land of riches.

elec., elect. *abbr.* 1. electric. 2. electrical. 3. electrician. 4. electricity.

e·lect (i-lekt) *v.* 1. to choose by vote, *elect a chairperson.* 2. to choose as a course, to decide, *he elected to become a lawyer.* **elect** *adj.* chosen; *the president-elect,* chosen but not yet in office. **elect** *n.* (*pl.* **elect**) a worthy or chosen person or persons, *they were considered the elect.*

e·lec·tion (i-lek-shŏn) *n.* 1. choosing or being chosen, especially by vote. 2. the process of electing representatives etc.

e·lec·tion·eer (i-lek-shŏ-neer) *v.* to work to promote a candidate or party in an election. **e·lec·tion·eer'ing** *n.*

e·lec·tive (i-lek-tiv) *adj.* 1. having the power to elect, *an elective assembly.* 2. chosen or filled by election, *an elective office.* **elective** *n.* a freely chosen course of study in a school.

e·lec·tor (i-lek-tŏr) *n.* one who has the right to vote in an election. **e·lec'tor·al** *adj.* ☐**Electoral College,** the body of electors, chosen by popular vote in each state, who elect the U.S. president and vice president.

e·lec·tor·ate (i-lek-tŏ-rit) *n.* the whole body of voters.

e·lec·tric (i-lek-trik) *adj.* 1. of or producing electricity. 2. worked by electricity. 3. causing sudden excitement, *the news had an electric effect.* ☐**electric chair,** a chair in which criminals are executed by electrocution. **electric eel,** an eellike fish able to give an electric shock. **electric eye,**

a photoelectric cell activating something when the beam of light it emits is broken. **electric guitar,** a guitar with a built-in microphone that transmits sound to an amplifier. **electric shock,** the effect of a sudden discharge of electricity through the body of a person or animal, stimulating the nerves and contracting the muscles.

e·lec·tri·cal (i-lek-tri-kăl) *adj.* 1. of or concerned with electricity, *electrical engineering.* 2. causing sudden excitement. **e·lec'tri·cal·ly** *adv.* ☐**electrical storm,** a thunderstorm.

e·lec·tri·cian (i-lek-trish-ăn) *n.* a person whose job is dealing with electricity and electrical equipment.

e·lec·tric·i·ty (i-lek-tris-i-tee) *n.* 1. a form of energy occurring in certain particles (electrons and protons) and hence in larger bodies, since they contain these. 2. a supply of electric current for lighting, heating, etc.

e·lec·tri·fy (i-lek-tri-fı) *v.* (**e·lec·tri·fied, e·lec·tri·fy·ing**) 1. to charge with electricity. 2. to convert (a railroad, farm, etc.) to the use of electric power. 3. to startle or excite suddenly.

e·lec·tri·fi·ca·tion (i-lek-trī-fi-kay-shŏn) *n.*

e·lec·tro·car·di·o·gram (i-lek-troh-kahr-di-ŏ-gram) *n.* the pattern traced by an electrocardiograph.

e·lec·tro·car·di·o·graph (i-lek-troh-kahr-di-ŏ-graf) *n.* a device that detects and records electric activity in the muscles of the heart. **e·lec·tro·car·di·o·graph·ic** (i-lek-troh-kahr-di-ŏ-graf-ik) *adj.* **e·lec·tro·car·di·og·ra·phy** (i-lek-troh-kahr-di-og-ră-fee) *n.*

e·lec·tro·chem·is·try (i-lek-troh-kem-i-stree) *n.* the branch of chemistry dealing with electricity as it applies to chemistry. **e·lec·tro·chem'i·cal** *adj.* **e·lec·tro·chem'i·cal·ly** *adv.*

e·lec·tro·cute (i-lek-trŏ-kyoot) *v.* (**e·lec·tro·cut·ed, e·lec·tro·cut·ing**) to kill by electricity. **e·lec·tro·cu·tion** (i-lek-troŏ-kyoo-shŏn) *n.*

e·lec·trode (i-lek-trohd) *n.* a solid conductor through which electricity enters or leaves a vacuum tube etc.

e·lec·tro·de·pos·it (i-lek-troh-di-poz-it) *v.* to deposit by electrolysis. **e·lec·tro·dep·o·si·tion** (i-lek-troh-dep-ŏ-zish-ŏn) *n.*

e·lec·tro·dy·nam·ics (i-lek-troh-dı-nam-iks) *n.* the branch of physics dealing with electrical currents. **e·lec·tro·dy·nam'ic** *adj.*

e·lec·tro·en·ceph·a·lo·gram (i-lek-troh-en-sef-ă-lŏ-gram) *n.* the pattern traced by an electroencephalograph.

e·lec·tro·en·ceph·a·lo·graph (i-lek-troh-en-sef-ă-lŏ-graf) *n.* a device that detects and records the electrical activity of the brain. **e·lec·tro·en·ceph·a·lo·graph·ic** (i-lek-troh-en-sef-ă-lŏ-graf-ik) *adj.* **e·lec·tro·en·ceph·a·log·ra·phy** (i-lek-troh-en-sef-ă-log-ră-fee) *n.*

e·lec·tro·form (i-lek-trŏ-form) *v.* to form in a mold by electrodeposition.

e·lec·tro·hy·drau·lic (i-lek-troh-hı-draw-lik) *adj.* of the interaction of electric and hydraulic mechanisms. **e·lec·tro·hy·drau'li·cal·ly** *adv.*

e·lec·trol·y·sis (i-lek-trol-i-sis) *n.* 1. chemical decomposition by electric current. 2. the breaking up of tumors, hair roots, etc. by electric current.

e·lec·tro·lyte (i-lek-trŏ-līt) *n.* a solution that conducts electric current, especially in an electric cell or battery. **e·lec·tro·lyt·ic** (i-lek-trŏ-lit-ik) *adj.*

e·lec·tro·mag·net (i-lek-troh-mag-nit) *n.* a magnet consisting of a metal core magnetized by a

coil, carrying electric current, wound around it.
e·lec·tro·mag·net·ic (i-lek-troh-mag-net-ik) *adj.*
having both electrical and magnetic properties.
e·lec·tro·mag·net'i·cal·ly *adv.* **e·lec·tro·**
mag·net·ism (i-lek-troh-mag-ně-tiz-ěm) *n.*
☐**electromagnetic radiation,** radiation consisting of electromagnetic waves, including visible
light, radio waves, gamma rays, etc. **electromag-**
netic wave, a wave resulting from acceleration
of an electric charge and propagated by periodic
disturbances in an electromagnetic field.
e·lec·tro·mo·tive (i-lek-trŏ-moh-tiv) *adj.* producing electric current. ☐**electromotive force,**
the energy derived as a result of the difference
in potential between the terminals of an electric
circuit.
e·lec·tron (i-lek-tron) *n.* a particle of matter with
a negative electric charge. ☐**electron micro-**
scope, a very high-powered microscope that uses
beams of electrons instead of rays of light. **elec-**
tron tube, a sealed container within which electrons are made to conduct current between at
least one pair of electrodes.
e·lec·tron·ic (i-lek-tron-ik) *adj.* 1. produced or
worked by a flow of electrons in a vacuum, gas,
or certain solids. 2. of or concerned with electronics, *an electronic engineer.* **e·lec·tron'i·cal·**
ly *adv.* ☐**electronic music,** electronically produced sounds taped and arranged to form a musical
composition. **electronic surveillance,** the gathering of information through use of wiretaps or
other electronic devices.
e·lec·tron·ics (i-lek-tron-iks) *n.* 1. *(sing.)* the development and application of electronic devices,
as in transistors, computers. 2. *(pl.)* electronic circuits.
e·lec·tro·pho·re·sis (i-lek-troh-fŏ-ree-sis) *n.* (*pl.*
-ses) the movement of colloidal particles in a
fluid under the influence of an electric field.
e·lec·tro·pho·ret·ic (i-lek-troh-fŏ-ret-ik) *adj.*
e·lec·tro·plate (i-lek-trŏ-playt) *v.* (**e·lec·tro·**
plat·ed, e·lec·tro·plat·ing) to coat with a thin
layer of silver etc. by electrolysis. **electroplate**
n. objects plated in this way.
e·lec·tro·shock (i-lek-troh-shok) **therapy** medical treatment for mental illness by means of electric shocks.
e·lec·tro·stat·ics (i-lek-troh-stat-iks) *n.* a branch
of physics dealing with static electricity.
e·lec·tro·type (i-lek-trŏ-tɪp) *n.* a copy formed by
electrolytic deposition of copper on a mold, especially for printing.
el·ee·mos·y·nar·y (el-ě-mos-ĭ-ner-ee) *adj.* of or
dependent on charity, charitable.
el·e·gant (el-ě-gănt) *adj.* tasteful, refined, and dignified in appearance or style. **el'e·gant·ly** *adv.*
el'e·gance *n.*
el·e·gy (el-ě-jee) *n.* a sorrowful or serious poem.
el·e·gi·ac (el-ě-jɪ-ăk) *adj.* ▷Do not confuse
elegy with *eulogy.*
elem. *abbr.* 1. element. 2. elementary. 3. elements.
el·e·ment (el-ě-měnt) *n.* 1. one of the parts that
make up a whole. 2. one of about one hundred
substances that cannot be split up by chemical
means into simpler substances. 3. an environment
that is suitable or satisfying; *water is a fish's element,* its natural habitat; *he is in his element when
organizing things,* this comes naturally to him.
4. a trace, *there's an element of truth in the story.*
5. the wire that gives out heat in an electric heater,
cooker, etc. 6. *elements,* atmospheric agencies or

forces, such as wind, rain, etc., *exposed to the
elements;* the basic or elementary principles of a
subject; the bread and wine used in Communion.
el·e·men·tal (el-ě-men-tăl) *adj.*
el·e·men·ta·ry (el-ě-men-tă-ree) *adj.* dealing with
the simplest facts of a subject. ☐**elementary
particle,** one of several subatomic particles not
known to be composed of simpler particles.
elementary school, a school in which elementary subjects are taught, comprising the first six
or eight grades.
el·e·phant (el-ě-fănt) *n.* a very large land animal
with a trunk and long curved ivory tusks.
el·e·phan·ti·a·sis (el-ě-făn-tɪ-ă-sis) *n.* a tropical
disease in which the legs etc. become grossly enlarged and the skin thickens.
el·e·phan·tine (el-ě-fan-tin) *adj.* 1. of or like elephants. 2. very large or clumsy.
el·e·vate (el-ě-vayt) *v.* (**el·e·vat·ed, el·e·vat·
ing**) 1. to raise to a higher place or position, to
lift up. 2. to raise to a higher moral or intellectual
level.
el·e·va·tion (el-ě-vay-shŏn) *n.* 1. elevating, being
elevated. 2. the altitude of a place. 3. a piece of
rising ground, a hill. 4. the angle that the direction
of something (as a gun) makes with the horizontal.
5. a plan or drawing showing one side of a structure, *a south elevation of the house.*
el·e·va·tor (el-ě-vay-tŏr) *n.* 1. an apparatus for
transporting people or goods from one floor of
a building to another. 2. a building for storing
grain, equipped with machinery for lifting and
discharging grain. 3. a movable part of an airplane, used to control altitude.
el·ev·en (i-lev-ěn) *adj. & n.* 1. one more than ten
(11, XI). 2. a team of eleven players at football.
el·ev·enth (i-lev-ěnth) *adj. & n.* 1. next after tenth.
2. one of eleven equal parts of a thing. ☐**at the
eleventh hour,** at the latest possible time for
doing something.
elf (elf) *n.* (*pl.* **elves,** *pr.* elvz) an imaginary small
being with magic powers. **elf'in** *adj.* **elf'ish** *adj.*
el·hi (el-hɪ) *adj.* of elementary and high school.
e·lic·it (i-lis-it) *v.* to draw out (information, a response, etc.). ▷Do not confuse *elicit* with *illicit.*
e·lide (i-lɪd) *v.* (**e·lid·ed, e·lid·ing**) to omit (a
vowel, consonant, or syllable) in pronouncing.
el·i·gi·ble (el-i-jǐ-běl) *adj.* 1. qualified to be chosen
for a position or allowed a privilege etc., *he is
eligible for a pension.* 2. regarded as suitable or
desirable, especially for marriage, *eligible young
men.* **eligible** *n.* an eligible person. **el·ig·i·bil·
i·ty** (el-i-jǐ-bil-i-tee) *n.*
e·lim·i·nate (i-lim-ĭ-nayt) *v.* (**e·lim·i·nat·ed, e·
lim·i·nat·ing**) 1. to get rid of (something that
is not wanted), *eliminate errors.* 2. to exclude from
a further stage of a competition etc. through defeat, *was eliminated in the fourth round.* **e·lim'i·
na·tor** *n.* **e·lim·i·na·tion** (i-lim-ĭ-nay-shŏn) *n.*
e·li·sion (i-lizh-ŏn) *n.* omission of part of a word
in pronouncing it (as in *I'm* = I am).
e·lite (i-leet, ay-) *n.* 1. a group of people regarded
as superior in some way and therefore favored.
2. a size of letters in typewriting (twelve per inch).
elite *adj.* having elite characteristics, *elite club,
elite type.*
e·lit·ist (i-lee-tist, ay-) *adj.* 1. advocating the selecting and treating of certain people as an elite. 2.
regarding oneself as elite. **elitist** *n.* an elitist person. **e·lit'ism** *n.*
e·lix·ir (i-lik-sɪr) *n.* 1. a fragrant liquid used as a

medicine or flavoring. 2. a remedy believed to cure all ills.

E·liz·a·be·than (i-liz-ă-bee-thăn) *adj.* of the time of Queen Elizabeth I's reign in England (1558–1603). **Elizabethan** *n.* a person of this time.

elk (elk) *n.* a large deer of northern Europe and Asia.

ell (el) *n.* a wing of a building at right angles to the main part.

el·lipse (i-lips) *n.* a regular oval that can be divided into four identical quarters.

el·lip·sis (i-lip-sis) *n.* (*pl.* **-ses**, *pr.* -seez) 1. omission of words needed to complete a meaning or a grammatical construction. 2. the mark . . . showing an intentional omission.

el·lip·soid (i-lip-soid) *n.* a solid of which all plane sections through one axis are ellipses and all other plane sections are ellipses or circles. **el·lip·soi·dal** (i-lip-soi-dăl) *adj.*

el·lip·ti·cal (i-lip-ti-kăl), **el·lip·tic** (i-lip-tik) *adj.* 1. shaped like an ellipse. 2. containing an ellipsis, having omissions. **el·lip'ti·cal·ly** *adv.*

elm (elm) *n.* 1. a deciduous tree with rough serrated leaves. 2. its wood.

el·o·cu·tion (el-ŏ-kyoo-shŏn) *n.* a person's style of speaking, the art of speaking expressively. **el·o·cu'tion·ist** *n.*

e·lon·gate (i-lawng-gayt) *v.* (**e·lon·gat·ed**, **e·lon·gat·ing**) to lengthen, to prolong. **e·lon·ga·tion** (i-lawng-gay-shŏn) *n.*

e·lope (i-lohp) *v.* (**e·loped**, **e·lop·ing**) to run away secretly with a lover, especially in order to get married. **e·lope'ment** *n.*

el·o·quence (el-ŏ-kwĕns) *n.* fluent and powerful speaking.

el·o·quent (el-ŏ-kwĕnt) *adj.* speaking fluently and powerfully. **el'o·quent·ly** *adv.*

El Sal·va·dor (el sal-vă-dor) a country in Central America.

else (els) *adj.* other, *someone else.* **else** *adv.* otherwise, if not, *run or else you'll be late.*

else·where (els-hwair) *adv.* somewhere else.

e·lu·ci·date (i-loo-si-dayt) *v.* (**e·lu·ci·dat·ed**, **e·lu·ci·dat·ing**) to throw light on (a problem), to make clear. **e·lu·ci·da·tion** (i-loo-si-day-shŏn) *n.*

e·lude (i-lood) *v.* (**e·lud·ed**, **e·lud·ing**) 1. to escape from, to avoid, *eluded his pursuers.* 2. to escape a person's understanding or memory etc., *the answer eludes me.* **e·lu·sion** (i-loo-zhŏn) *n.*

e·lu·sive (i-loo-siv) *adj.* 1. eluding, escaping. 2. eluding a person's understanding or memory. **e·lu'sive·ly** *adv.* **e·lu'sive·ness** *n.* ▷Do not confuse *elusive* with *illusive.*

el·ver (el-vĕr) *n.* a young eel.

elves *see* **elf.**

E·ly·si·um (i-lizh-i-ŭm) *n.* 1. (in Greek mythology) the abode of the blessed after death. 2. a place or state of ideal happiness. **E·ly'sian** *adj.* □**Elysian fields,** Elysium.

em (em) *n.* a unit for measuring the amount of printed matter in a line, equal to the space occupied by M.

EM *abbr.* 1. enlisted man. 2. enlisted men.

'em (ĕm) *pronoun* (*informal*) = them, *I love 'em.*

e·ma·ci·ate (i-may-shi-ayt) *v.* (**e·ma·ci·at·ed**, **e·ma·ci·at·ing**) to make thin and feeble as by disease or malnutrition. **e·ma·ci·a·tion** (i-may-shi-ay-shŏn) *n.*

em·a·nate (em-ă-nayt) *v.* (**em·a·nat·ed**, **em·**

a·nat·ing) to issue or originate from a source, *pleasant smells emanated from the kitchen.* **em·a·na·tion** (em-ă-nay-shŏn) *n.*

e·man·ci·pate (i-man-si-payt) *v.* (**e·man·ci·pat·ed**, **e·man·ci·pat·ing**) to liberate, to set free from slavery or some form of restraint. **e·man'ci·pa·tor** *n.* **e·man·ci·pa·tion** (i-man-si-pay-shŏn) *n.* □**Emancipation Proclamation,** the proclamation issued by President Lincoln, effective January 1, 1863, giving freedom to slaves in states still in conflict with the Union. **The Great Emancipator,** Abraham Lincoln.

e·mas·cu·late (i-mas-kyŭ-layt) *v.* (**e·mas·cu·lat·ed**, **e·mas·cu·lat·ing**) 1. to deprive of force; *an emasculated law,* one made weak by alterations to it. 2. to castrate. **e·mas·cu·la·tion** (i-mas-kyŭ-lay-shŏn) *n.*

em·balm (em-bahm) *v.* to preserve (a corpse) from decay by using spices or chemicals. **em·balm'er** *n.*

em·bank·ment (em-bangk-mĕnt) *n.* a long mound of earth or a stone structure to keep a river from spreading or to carry a road or railroad.

em·bar·go (em-bahr-goh) *n.* (*pl.* **-goes**) an order forbidding commerce or other activity. **embargo** *v.* to impose an embargo on (a product, a nation).

em·bark (em-bahrk) *v.* 1. to put or go on board ship at the start of a journey. 2. to begin an undertaking, *they embarked on a program of expansion.* **em·bar·ka·tion** (em-bahr-kay-shŏn) *n.* embarking on a ship.

em·bar·rass (em-bar-ăs) *v.* to make (a person) feel awkward or ashamed. **em·bar'rass·ment** *n.* **em·bar'rass·ing·ly** *adv.*

em·bas·sy (em-bă-see) *n.* 1. an ambassador and his staff. 2. his official headquarters. 3. a deputation sent on a mission to a foreign government.

em·bat·tled (em-bat-ĕld) *adj.* 1. prepared for battle, *embattled troops.* 2. fortified against attack.

em·bed (em-bed) *v.* (**em·bed·ded**, **em·bed·ding**) to fix firmly in a surrounding mass.

em·bel·lish (em-bel-ish) *v.* 1. to ornament. 2. to improve (a story etc.) by adding details that are entertaining but invented. **em·bel'lish·ment** *n.*

em·ber (em-bĕr) *n.* 1. a small piece of live coal or wood in a dying fire. 2. *embers,* the smoldering remains of a dying fire.

em·bez·zle (em-bez-ĕl) *v.* (**em·bez·zled**, **em·bez·zling**) to take fraudulently for one's own use (money or property placed in one's care). **em·bez'zler** *n.* **em·bez'zle·ment** *n.*

em·bit·ter (em-bit-ĕr) *v.* to arouse bitter feelings in.

em·bla·zon (em-blay-zŏn) *v.* to ornament with heraldic or other devices.

em·blem (em-blĕm) *n.* a symbol, a device that represents something, *the crown is the emblem of kingship.* **em·blem·at·ic** (em-blĕ-mat-ik) *adj.* serving as an emblem, symbolic. **em·blem·at'i·cal** *adj.* **em·blem·at'i·cal·ly** *adv.*

em·bod·y (em-bod-ee) *v.* (**em·bod·ied**, **em·bod·y·ing**) 1. to express principles or ideas in a visible form, *the house embodied her idea of a home.* 2. to incorporate, to include, *parts of the old treaty are embodied in the new one.* **em·bod'i·ment** *n.*

em·bold·en (em-bohl-dĕn) *v.* to make bold, to encourage.

em·bo·lism (em-bŏ-liz-ĕm) *n.* obstruction of an

artery or vein by an **em·bo·lus** (em-bŏ-lus), a clot of blood, an air bubble, etc. **em·bol·ic** (em-bol-ik) *adj.*

em·bon·point (ahm-bohn-**pwan**) *n.* plumpness (of a person). ▷French.

em·boss (em-baws) *v.* to decorate with a raised design.

em·bou·chure (am-bŭ-**shoor**) *n.* 1. the mouthpiece of a wind instrument. 2. the way in which the lips are applied to this. 3. the mouth of a river. 4. the opening out of a valley into flat land.

em·brace (em-brays) *v.* (**em·braced, em·brac·ing**) 1. to hold closely and affectionately in one's arms. 2. to accept eagerly, *embraced the opportunity.* 3. to adopt (a religion etc.). 4. to include, *their religion embraces many ideas.* **embrace** *n.* the act of embracing, a hug.

em·bra·sure (em-bray-zhŭr) *n.* 1. an opening in a wall for a door or window, with splayed sides. 2. a similar opening for a gun, widening toward the outside.

em·bro·cate (em-brŏ-kayt) *v.* (**em·bro·cat·ed, em·bro·cat·ing**) to apply an embrocation to.

em·bro·ca·tion (em-brŏ-kay-shŏn) *n.* a liquid used for rubbing on the body to relieve muscular pain etc.

em·broi·der (em-broi-dĕr) *v.* 1. to ornament with needlework. 2. to embellish (a story).

em·broi·der·y (em-broi-dĕ-ree) *n.* (*pl.* **-der·ies**) embroidering, embroidered material.

em·broil (em-broil) *v.* to involve in an argument or quarrel etc. **em·broil'ment** *n.*

em·bry·o (em-bri-oh) *n.* (*pl.* **-bry·os**) 1. an animal in the early stage of its development, before birth or emergence from an egg (used of a child in the first eight weeks of its development in the womb). 2. a rudimentary plant contained in a seed. 3. something in its very early stages. □**in embryo**, existing but undeveloped.

em·bry·ol·o·gy (em-bri-ol-ŏ-jee) *n.* the branch of science dealing with the development of embryos. **em·bry·ol'o·gist** *n.* **em·bry·o·log·ic** (em-bri-ŏ-loj-ik) *adj.* **em·bry·o·log'i·cal** *adj.*

em·bry·on·ic (em-bri-on-ik) *adj.* existing in embryo.

em·cee (em-see) *n.* (*informal*) master of ceremonies (▷from the abbreviation *m*aster of *c*eremonies.) **emcee** *v.* (*informal*) to serve as master of ceremonies.

e·mend (i-mend) *v.* to alter (something written) in order to remove errors. **e·men·da·tion** (ee-men-day-shŏn) *n.* ▷ Do not confuse *emend* with *amend.*

em·er·ald (em-ĕ-răld) *n.* 1. a bright-green precious stone. 2. its color. **emerald** *adj.* bright green. □**Emerald Isle**, Ireland.

e·merge (i-murj) *v.* (**e·merged, e·merg·ing**) 1. to come up or out into view. 2. (of facts or ideas) to be revealed by investigation, to become obvious. **e·mer'gence** *n.* **e·mer'gent** *adj.*

e·mer·gen·cy (i-mur-jĕn-see) *n.* (*pl.* **-cies**) a serious happening or situation needing prompt action. □**emergency room**, an area in a hospital for receiving and treating victims of accidents, sudden illnesses, etc.

e·mer·i·tus (i-mer-i-tŭs) *adj.* retired and holding an honorary title, as *professor emeritus.*

em·er·y (em-ĕ-ree) *n.* coarse abrasive used for polishing metal or wood etc. □**emery board.** a

small stiff strip of wood or cardboard coated with emery, used for filing the nails. **emery cloth,** cloth coated with emery.

e·met·ic (i-met-ik) *n.* medicine used to cause vomiting.

emf, EMF *abbr.* electromotive force.

em·i·grant (em-ĭ-grănt) *n.* one who emigrates.

em·i·grate (em-ĭ-grayt) *v.* (**em·i·grat·ed, em·i·grat·ing**) to leave one country and go to settle in another, *they emigrated from Germany.* **em·i·gra·tion** (em-ĭ-gray-shŏn) *n.* ▷Do not confuse *emigrate* with *immigrate.*

é·mi·gré (em-ĭ-gray) *n.* a person who emigrates, especially for political reasons.

em·i·nence (em-ĭ-nĕns) *n.* 1. the state of being famous or distinguished, *a surgeon of great eminence.* 2. a piece of rising ground. 3. a cardinal's title, *His Eminence.* □**éminence grise** (ay-mee-nahns greez), a confidential advisor, especially one who exercises power unofficially. (▷French.)

em·i·nent (em-ĭ-nĕnt) *adj.* 1. famous, distinguished. 2. conspicuous, outstanding, *a man of eminent goodness.* **em'i·nent·ly** *adv.* □**eminent domain,** the authority of a government to take private property for public use, with compensation to the owner. ▷Do not confuse *eminent* with *imminent.*

e·mir (ĕ-meer) *n.* the title of various Muslim rulers.

e·mir·ate (em-ĭ-rit) *n.* the territory of an emir.

em·is·sar·y (em-i-ser-ee) *n.* (*pl.* **-sar·ies**) a person sent to conduct negotiations.

e·mit (i-mit) *v.* (**e·mit·ted, e·mit·ting**) 1. to send out (light, heat, fumes, lava, etc.). 2. to utter, *she emitted a shriek.* **e·mit'ter** *n.* **e·mis·sion** (i-mish-ŏn) *n.*

Em·my (em-ee) *n.* (*pl.* **-mies**) (in television) an annual award for excellence.

e·mol·li·ent (i-mol-yĕnt) *adj.* softening or soothing the skin. **emollient** *n.* an emollient substance.

e·mol·u·ment (i-mol-yŭ-mĕnt) *n.* a fee received, a salary.

e·mote (i-moht) *v.* (**e·mot·ed, e·mot·ing**) to act emotionally.

e·mo·tion (i-moh-shŏn) *n.* an intense mental feeling, as love or hate.

e·mo·tion·al (i-moh-shŏ-năl) *adj.* 1. of emotions. 2. showing emotion excessively. **e·mo'tion·al·ly** *adv.*

e·mo·tive (i-moh-tiv) *adj.* rousing emotion.

Emp. *abbr.* 1. emperor. 2. empire. 3. empress.

em·pan·el (em-pan-ĕl) *v.* (**em·pan·eled, em·pan·el·ing**) to impanel.

em·pa·thy (em-pă-thee) *n.* the ability to identify oneself mentally with a person or thing and so understand his feelings or its meaning. **em·path·ic** (em-path-ik) *adj.* ▷Do not confuse *empathy* with *sympathy.*

em·pen·nage (ahm-pĕ-nahzh) *n.* the rear of an airplane, especially the stabilizing surfaces at the tail.

em·per·or (em-pĕ-rŏr) *n.* the male ruler of an empire.

em·pha·sis (em-fă-sis) *n.* (*pl.* **-ses**, *pr.* -seez) 1. special importance given to something, prominence, *the emphasis is on quality.* 2. vigor of expression or feeling or action, *nodded his head with emphasis.* 3. stress laid on part of a word or on a phrase etc. or on a note or notes in music.

em·pha·size (em-fă-sɪz) *v.* (**em·pha·sized, em·pha·siz·ing**) to lay emphasis on.

em·phat·ic (em-fat-ik) *adj.* using or showing emphasis, expressing oneself with emphasis. em·phat′i·cal·ly *adv.*

em·phy·se·ma (em-fi-see-mă) *n.* a condition in which the air cells in the lungs become dilated and lose their elasticity, causing difficulty in breathing.

em·pire (em-pɪr) *n.* 1. a group of countries ruled by a single supreme authority. 2. supreme political power. 3. a large commercial organization controlled by one person or group. ☐empire build-ing, the process of deliberately acquiring extra territory or authority etc.

em·pir·i·cal (em-pir-i-kal), em·pir·ic (em-pir-ik) *adj.* (of knowledge) based on observation or experiment, not on theory. em·pir′i·cal·ly *adv.* em·pir·i·cism (em-pir-i-siz-ĕm) *n.* 1. empirical method or procedure. 2. the doctrine that knowledge is obtainable only by direct experience through the physical senses. em·pir′i·cist *n.*

em·place·ment (em-plays-mĕnt) *n.* a place or platform for a gun or battery of guns.

em·ploy (em-ploi) *v.* 1. to give work to, to use the services of. 2. to make use of, *how do you employ your spare time?* employ *n.* employment. ☐in the employ of, employed by.

em·ploy·a·ble (em-ploi-ă-bĕl) *adj.* able to be em-ployed.

em·ploy·ee (em-ploi-ee) *n.* a person who works for another in return for wages.

em·ploy·er (em-ploi-ĕr) *n.* a person or firm that employs people.

em·ploy·ment (em-ploi-mĕnt) *n.* 1. employing. 2. the state of being employed. 3. work done as an occupation or to earn a livelihood.

em·po·ri·um (em-pohr-i-ŭm) *n.* (*pl.* -po·ri·ums, -po·ri·a, *pr.* -pohr-i-ă) 1. a center of com-merce. 2. a large retail store.

em·pow·er (em-pow-ĕr) *v.* to give power or author-ity to, *police are empowered to arrest people.*

em·press (em-pris) *n.* 1. the female ruler of an empire. 2. the wife or widow of an emperor.

emp·ties (emp-teez) *n. pl.* emptied boxes or bottles or trucks etc.

emp·ty (emp-tee) *adj.* (emp·ti·er, emp·ti·est) 1. containing nothing, *empty boxes; empty trucks,* not loaded. 2. without an occupant, *an empty chair; empty streets,* without people or traffic. 3. without effectiveness, *empty promises.* 4. lacking good sense or intelligence, *an empty head.* 5. (*informal*) hungry, *feel rather empty.* empty *v.* (emp·tied, emp·ty·ing) 1. to make or become empty. 2. to transfer the contents of one thing into another; *the Danube empties into the Black Sea,* flows into it. emp′ti·ly *adv.* emp′ti·ness *n.* ☐empty calorie, one that has no nutritive value. empty nesters, (*informal*) a middle-aged or elderly couple whose grown children live apart from them.

emp·ty-hand·ed (emp-tee-han-did) *adj.* bringing or taking away nothing.

emp·ty-head·ed (emp-tee-hed-id) *adj.* lacking good sense or intelligence.

em·py·re·an (em-pī-ree-ăn) *n.* 1. the highest heaven, as the sphere of fire in ancient cosmology or the abode of God. 2. the visible heavens. empyrean *adj.* of the heavens.

e·mu (ee-myoo) *n.* a large Australian bird resem-bling an ostrich.

em·u·late (em-yŭ-layt) *v.* (em·u·lat·ed, em·u·lat·ing) to try to do as well as or better than.

em′u·la·tor *n.* em·u·la·tion (em-yŭ-lay-shŏn) *n.*

e·mul·si·fy (i-mul-sī-fɪ) *v.* (e·mul·si·fied, e·mul·si·fy·ing) to convert or be converted into an emulsion. e·mul′si·fi·er *n.* e·mul′si·fi·able *adj.* e·mul·si·fi·ca·tion (i-mul-sī-fi-kay-shŏn) *n.*

e·mul·sion (i-mul-shŏn) *n.* 1. a creamy liquid in which particles of oil or fat are evenly distributed. 2. a medicine or paint in this form. 3. the light-sensitive coating on photographic film, a mixture of silver compound in gelatine. e·mul·sive (i-mul-siv) *adj.*

en- *prefix* used to form verbs meaning in or into, as in *enshroud;* to put in or on, as in *engage;* to cause to be, as in *enfranchise.*

-en[1] *suffix* used to form adjectives from nouns meaning consisting of or like, as in *wooden.*

-en[2] *suffix* used to form verbs from adjectives mean-ing becoming or causing to be, as in *toughen;* and to form verbs from nouns meaning causing or coming to have, as in *lengthen.*

en·a·ble (en-ay-bĕl) *v.* (en·a·bled, en·a·bling) to give the means or authority to do something.

en·act (en-akt) *v.* 1. to decree, to make into a law. 2. to perform, to act (a play, a part in a play). en·act′ment *n.*

e·nam·el (i-nam-ĕl) *n.* 1. a glasslike substance used for coating metal or pottery. 2. paint that dries hard and glossy. 3. the hard outer covering of teeth. enamel *v.* (e·nam·eled, e·nam·el·ing) to coat or decorate with enamel.

e·nam·el·ware (e-nam-ĕl-wair) *n.* enamel-coated metal utensils.

en·am·or (i-nam-ŏr) *v.* to inspire to love. en·am·ored (i-nam-ŏrd) *adj.* fond, *he was enamored of the sound of his own voice.*

en bloc (en blok) in a block, all at the same time. ▷French.

enc., encl. *abbr.* 1. enclosed. 2. enclosure.

en·camp (en-kamp) *v.* to settle in a camp.

en·camp·ment (en-kamp-mĕnt) *n.* a camp.

en·cap·su·late (en-kap-sŭ-layt) *v.* (en·cap·su·lat·ed, en·cap·su·lat·ing) 1. to enclose in a capsule. 2. to summarize. en·cap·su·la·tion (en-kap-sŭ-lay-shŏn) *n.*

en·case (en-kays) *v.* (en·cased, en·cas·ing) to enclose in a case.

-ence *suffix* used to form nouns, as in *congruence, decadence, reference.*

en·ceinte (ahn-sant) *adj.* (of a woman) pregnant. ▷French.

en·ceph·a·li·tis (en-sef-ă-lɪ-tis) *n.* inflammation of the brain.

en·ceph·a·lo·my·e·li·tis (en-sef-ă-loh-mɪ-ĕ-lɪ-tis) *n.* inflammation affecting the brain and the spinal cord.

en·ceph·a·lon (en-sef-ă-lon) *n.* (*pl.* -la, *pr.* -lă) the brain.

en·chain (en-chayn) *v.* 1. to chain up 2. to hold fast.

en·chant (en-chant) *v.* 1. to put under a magic spell. 2. to fill with intense delight. en·chant′ment *n.* en·chant′er *n.* a person who enchants, a magician. en·chant·ress (en-chant-ris) *n.* a female enchanter, a sorceress.

en·chi·la·da (en-chi-lah-dă) *n.* a meat-filled tor-tilla served with chili sauce.

en·ci·pher (en-sɪ-fĕr) *v.* to write (a message etc.) in cipher. en·ci′pher·ment *n.*

en·cir·cle (en-sur-kĕl) *v.* (en·cir·cled, en·cir·

cling) to surround. **en·cir'cle·ment** *n.*
en·clave (en-klayv) *n.* a small territory wholly
within the boundaries of another.
en·close (en-klohz) *v.* (**en·closed, en·clos·
ing**) 1. to put a wall or fence etc. around, to
shut in on all sides. 2. to shut up in a receptacle,
to put into an envelope along with a letter or
into a parcel along with the contents.
en·clo·sure (en-kloh-zhŭr) *n.* 1. enclosing. 2. an
enclosed area. 3. something enclosed with a letter
etc.
en·code (en-kohd) *v.* (**en·cod·ed, en·cod·
ing**) to put into code. **en·cod'er** *n.*
en·co·mi·um (en-koh-mi-ŭm) *n.* high praise given
in speech or writing.
en·com·pass (en-kum-păs) *v.* 1. to surround, to
encircle. 2. to contain, *her book encompasses all
her ideas.*
en·core (ahng-kohr) *interj.* a call for repetition of
a performance. **encore** *n.* 1. this call. 2. the item
performed in response to it. **encore** *v.* (**en·
cored, en·cor·ing**) to call for such a repetition.
en·coun·ter (en-kown-tĕr) *v.* 1. to meet, especially
by chance or unexpectedly. 2. to find oneself
faced with, *encounter difficulties.* 3. to meet in
battle. **encounter** *n.* 1. a sudden or unexpected
meeting. 2. a battle. ☐**encounter group,** a group
that meets under the guidance of a psychologist
to work toward improved emotional adjustment through confrontation among the members.
en·cour·age (en-kur-ij) *v.* (**en·cour·aged, en·
cour·ag·ing**) 1. to give hope or confidence to.
2. to urge, *encouraged him to try.* 3. to stimulate,
to help to develop, *to encourage exports.* **en·
cour'age·ment** *n.*
en·croach (en-krohch) *v.* 1. to intrude upon someone's territory or rights or time. 2. to advance
beyond the original or proper limits, *the sea en-
croached gradually upon the land.* **en·
croach'ment** *n.*
en·crust (en-krust) *v.* 1. to cover with or to form
a crust of hard material. 2. to ornament with a
layer of jewels etc. **en·crus·ta·tion** (en-krus-
tay-shŏn) *n.*
en·cum·ber (en-kum-bĕr) *v.* to be a burden to,
to hamper. **en·cum·brance** (en-kum-brăns) *n.*
something that encumbers.
ency., encyc. *abbr.* encyclopedia.
-ency *suffix* used to form nouns meaning quality,
as in *efficiency, fluency,* or state, as in *presidency.*
en·cyc·li·cal (en-sik-li-kăl) *n.* a pope's letter to
all the bishops of the church. **encyclical** *adj.*
intended for extensive circulation.
en·cy·clo·pe·di·a (en-sɪ-klŏ-pee-di-ă) *n.* a book
or set of books giving information about all
branches of knowledge or about one subject intensively, and usually arranged alphabetically.
en·cy·clo·pe·dic (en-sɪ-klŏ-pee-dik) *adj.* giving
or possessing information about many subjects
or intensively about one subject.
en·cyst (en-sist) *v.* to enclose or become enclosed
in a cyst. **en·cyst'ment** *n.*
end (end) *n.* 1. the extreme limit of something. 2.
the part or surface forming this; *to the ends of
the earth,* to its farthest points; *no problem at
my end,* in my share of the work. 3. *the end,
(informal)* the limit of what one can endure. 4.
the finish or conclusion of something, the latter
or final part. 5. destruction, downfall, death. 6.
a purpose or aim, *to gain his own ends.* 7. (in
football) one of two players at the ends of the

line of scrimmage. **end** *v.* 1. to bring to an end,
to put an end to. 2. to come to an end, to reach
a certain place or state eventually, *ended up
laughing.* ☐**end it all,** *(informal)* to commit suicide. **end man,** one of two performers in a minstrel show standing at the ends of a line of min-
strels and carrying on comic dialogue with the
interlocutor. **end on,** with the end facing one
or adjoining the end of the next object. **end prod·
uct,** the final product of a manufacturing process.
end run, a play in football in which the ball
carrier runs around one end of the line of scrimmage and then toward the goal line. **end table,**
a small table, usually placed alongside an end of
a couch or beside a chair. **keep one's end up,**
to do one's part in spite of difficulties. **make
(both) ends meet,** to keep one's expenditure
within one's income. **put an end to,** to abolish
or stop or destroy.
en·dan·ger (en-dayn-jĕr) *v.* to cause danger to.
en·dan'gered ☐**endangered species,** a
species facing possible extinction.
en·dear (en-deer) *v.* to cause to be loved, *endeared
herself to us all.* **en·dear'ing** *adj.* inspiring affection. **en·dear'ing·ly** *adv.*
en·dear·ment (en-deer-mĕnt) *n.* a word or words
expressing love.
en·deav·or (en-dev-ŏr) *v.* to attempt, to try.
endeavor *n.* an attempt.
en·dem·ic (en-dem-ik) *adj.* commonly found in
a particular country or district or group of people,
the disease is endemic in Africa. ▷ See the note
under **epidemic.**
end·ing (en-ding) *n.* the final part.
en·dive (en-dɪv) *n.* 1. a curly-leaved plant used
in salad. 2. the young chicory plant with broad
fleshy leaves used in salad.
end·less (end-lis) *adj.* without end, never stopping,
endless patience. **end'less·ly** *adv.* ☐**endless
belt,** one with the ends joined so that it forms
a continuous strip for use in machinery etc.
end·most (end-mohst) *adj.* nearest the end.
en·do·crine (en-dŏ-krin) *adj.* (of a gland) pouring
its secretions straight into the blood, not through
a duct. **endocrine** *n.* an endocrine gland, its secretion.
en·do·cri·nol·o·gist (en-dŏ-kri-nol-ŏ-jist) *n.* an
expert in endocrinology.
en·do·cri·nol·o·gy (en-dŏ-kri-nol-ŏ-jee) *n.* the
branch of science dealing with the endocrine
glands and their secretions.
en·dog·e·nous (en-doj-ĕ-nŭs) *adj.* growing or
originating from within. **en·dog'e·nous·ly**
adv.
en·dorse (en-dors) *v.* (**en·dorsed, en·dors·
ing**) 1. to sign or add a comment on (a document),
to sign the back of (a check) in order to obtain
the money indicated. 2. to confirm (a statement),
to declare one's approval of. **en·dors'er** *n.* **en·
dorse'ment** *n.* **en·dors'a·ble** *adj.*
en·do·scope (en-dŏ-skohp) *n.* a tubular instrument for viewing internal parts of the body. **en·
dos·co·py** (en-dos-kŏ-pee) *n.* **en·do·scop·
ic** (en-dŏ-skop-ik) *adj.*
en·do·ther·mic (en-doh-thur-mik), **en·do·
ther·mal** (en-doh-thur-măl) *adj.* occurring or
formed with the absorption of heat.
en·dow (en-dow) *v.* 1. to provide with a permanent
income, *endow a school.* 2. to provide with a power
or ability or quality, *was endowed with great talents.*

en·dow·ment (en-dow-mĕnt) n. 1. endowing. 2. an endowed income. 3. a natural ability. ☐**endowment policy,** a form of life insurance in which a fixed sum is paid to the insured person on a specified date or to his estate if he dies before this date.

en·drin (en-drin) n. an insecticide.

en·due (en-doo) v. (**en·dued, en·du·ing**) to furnish with (powers, qualities, etc.).

en·dur·able (en-door-ă-bĕl) adj. able to be endured.

en·dur·ance (en-door-ăns) n. ability to withstand pain or hardship or prolonged use or strain.

en·dure (en-door) v. (**en·dured, en·dur·ing**) 1. to experience pain or hardship or difficulties, to bear patiently. 2. to tolerate. 3. to remain in existence, to last.

en·dur·o (en-door-oh) n. (pl. -os) a race for motorcycles etc. in which the winner is the one who has traveled the greatest distance in a fixed period of time.

end·ways (end-wayz), **end·wise** (end-wiz) adv. 1. with the end toward the viewer. 2. on end, end to end, lengthwise.

ENE abbr. east-northeast.

en·e·ma (en-ĕ-mă) n. 1. the insertion of liquid into the rectum through the anus by means of a syringe, for medical purposes. 2. this liquid.

en·e·my (en-ĕ-mee) n. (pl. -mies) 1. one who is hostile toward another and seeks to harm the other. 2. a member of a hostile army or nation etc., an opposing military force, ship, aircraft, etc.

en·er·get·ic (en-ĕr-jet-ik) adj. full of energy, done with energy. **en·er·get'i·cal·ly** adv.

en·er·gize (en-ĕr-jiz) v. (**en·er·gized, en·er·giz·ing**) 1. to give energy to. 2. to cause electricity to flow to. ▷Do not confuse energize with enervate.

en·er·giz·er (en-ĕr-ji-zĕr) n. 1. that which energizes. 2. an antidepressant drug.

en·er·gy (en-ĕr-jee) n. (pl. -gies) 1. the capacity for vigorous activity. 2. the ability of matter or radiation to do work either because of its motion (kinetic energy), or because of its mass (released in nuclear fission etc.), or because of its electric charge etc. 3. fuel and other resources used for the operation of machinery etc., the energy crisis.

en·er·vate (en-ĕr-vayt) v. (**en·er·vat·ed, en·er·vat·ing**) to cause to lose vitality. I hate an enervating climate. **en·er·va·tion** (en-ĕr-vay-shŏn) n. ▷Do not confuse enervate with energize.

en·fant ter·ri·ble (ahn-fahn te-ree-blĕ) a person whose behavior is embarrassing or indiscreet or irresponsible. ▷French.

en·fee·ble (en-fee-bĕl) v. (**en·fee·bled, en·fee·bling**) to make feeble. **en·fee'ble·ment** n.

en·fi·lade (en-fi-layd) n. 1. gunfire sweeping a line of troops from end to end. 2. a line of troops subject to such fire. **enfilade** v. to sweep with fire in this way.

en·fold (en-fohld) v. 1. to wrap up. 2. to clasp.

en·force (en-fohrs) v. (**en·forced, en·forc·ing**) to compel obedience to, to impose by force or compulsion, the law was firmly enforced. **en·forc'er** n. **en·force'ment** n.

en·force·a·ble (en-fohr-să-bĕl) adj. able to be enforced.

en·fran·chise (en-fran-chiz) v. (**en·fran·chised, en·fran·chis·ing**) 1. to admit to citizenship, especially to the right to vote. 2. to release (a

slave etc.) from bondage. **en·fran·chise·ment** (en-fran-chiz-mĕnt) n.

eng. abbr. 1. engine. 2. engineer. 3. engineering. 4. engraved.

Eng. abbr. 1. England. 2. English.

en·gage (en-gayj) v. (**en·gaged, en·gag·ing**) 1. to take into one's employment, engage a typist. 2. to promise, to pledge. 3. to occupy the attention of, engaged her in conversation. 4. to occupy oneself, he engages in politics. 5. to begin a battle against, engaged the enemy troops. 6. to interlock (parts of a gear) so that it transmits power, to become interlocked in this way.

en·gaged (en-gayjd) adj. 1. having promised to marry, an engaged couple. 2. occupied or reserved by a person, occupied with business etc., I'm afraid the hall is engaged for that night.

en·gage·ment (en-gayj-mĕnt) n. 1. engaging something, being engaged. 2. an appointment made with another person. 3. a battle.

en·gag·ing (en-gay-jing) adj. attractive, charming. **en·gag'ing·ly** adv.

en·gen·der (en-jen-dĕr) v. to give rise to.

en·gine (en-jin) n. 1. a mechanical contrivance consisting of several parts working together, especially as a source of power. 2. a railroad locomotive. 3. a fire engine.

en·gi·neer (en-ji-neer) n. a person who is skilled in a branch of engineering. 2. one who is in charge of machines and engines, as on a ship. 3. one who plans or organizes something, a manager. **engineer** v. 1. to construct or control as an engineer. 2. to contrive or bring about, she engineered a meeting between them.

en·gi·neer·ing (en-ji-neer-ing) n. the application of scientific knowledge for the control and use of power, as in works of public utility such as the building of roads and bridges (civil engineering), machines (mechanical engineering), electrical apparatus (electrical engineering), etc.

Eng·land (ing-glănd) the country forming the southern part of Great Britain.

Eng·lish (ing-glish) adj. of England or its people or the language that originated in England. **English** n. 1. the English language, used in Britain, Canada, and many areas now or once under British jurisdiction. 2. the English, English people. **Eng'lish·man** n. **Eng'lish·wom·an** n. ☐**English Channel,** an arm of the Atlantic Ocean between England and France. **English horn,** an oboe-like woodwind instrument, lower in pitch than a regular oboe. **English muffin,** a small round bread, eaten toasted and buttered. **English sparrow,** a small hardy bird native to Europe but naturalized in many parts of the world.

engr. abbr. 1. engineer. 2. engraved. 3. engraving.

en·graft (en-graft) v. to insert as a graft, in propagation.

en·gram (en-gram) n. a supposed permanent change in the brain that would account for the existence of memory.

en·grave (en-grayv) v. (**en·graved, en·grav·ing**) 1. to cut or carve (a design) into a hard surface, to ornament with a design in this way. 2. to fix deeply in the mind or memory. **en·grav'er** n.

en·grav·ing (en-gray-ving) n. a print made from an engraved metal plate.

en·gross (en-grohs) v. to occupy fully by absorbing

the attention, *an engrossing book; he was engrossed in his book.*

en·gulf (en-gulf) *v.* to surround or cause to disappear by flowing around or over, to swamp.

en·hance (en-hans) *v.* **(en·hanced, en·hanc·ing)** to increase the attractiveness or other qualities of. **en·hance′ment** *n.*

e·nig·ma (ĕ-nig-mä) *n.* (*pl.* **-mas**) something very difficult to understand.

en·ig·mat·ic (en-ig-mat-ik) *adj.* mysterious and puzzling. **en′ig·mat′i·cal·ly** *adv.*

en·jamb·ment (en-jam-mĕnt) *n.* (in poetry) continuation of a sentence beyond the end of a line, couplet, or stanza.

en·join (en-join) *v.* 1. to order, to command. 2. (in law) to prohibit, to restrain by an injunction.

en·joy (en-joi) *v.* 1. to get pleasure from. 2. to have as an advantage or benefit, *to enjoy good health.* **en′joy′ment** *n.* □**enjoy oneself,** to experience pleasure from what one is doing.

en·joy·a·ble (en-joi-ă-bĕl) *adj.* giving enjoyment, pleasant. **en·joy′a·bly** *adv.*

enl. *abbr.* 1. enlarge. 2. enlarged. 3. enlisted.

en·large (en-lahrj) *v.* **(en·larged, en·larg·ing)** 1. to make or become larger. 2. to reproduce (a photograph) on a larger scale. 3. to say more about something, *enlarge upon this matter.*

en·large·ment (en-lahrj-mĕnt) *n.* 1. enlarging, being enlarged. 2. something enlarged, a photograph printed larger than its negative.

en·larg·er (en-lahr-jĕr) *n.* an apparatus for making photographic enlargements.

en·light·en (en-lɪ-tĕn) *v.* to give knowledge to, to inform. **en·light′en·ment** *n.* □**the Enlightenment,** a movement in 18th century European philosophy placing much emphasis on reason and individualism.

en·light·ened (en-lɪ-tĕnd) *adj.* freed from ignorance or prejudice, *in these enlightened days.*

en·list (en-list) *v.* 1. to take into or join the armed forces, *enlist as a soldier.* 2. to secure as a means of help or support, *enlisted their sympathy.* **en·list′ment** *n.* **en·list·ee** (en-lis-tee) *n.* □**enlisted man, woman,** a member of the U.S. armed forces without the rank of commissioned or warrant officer.

en·liv·en (en-lɪ-vĕn) *v.* to make more lively. **en·liv′en·ment** *n.*

en masse (ahn mas) all together. ▷French.

en·mesh (en-mesh) *v.* to entangle as if in a net.

en·mi·ty (en-mi-tee) *n.* (*pl.* **-ties**) hostility between enemies.

en·no·ble (en-noh-bĕl) *v.* **(en·no·bled, en·no·bling)** 1. to make (a person) a noble. 2. to make (a thing) noble or more dignified. **en·no′ble·ment** *n.*

en·nui (ahn-wee) *n.* boredom.

e·nor·mi·ty (i-nor-mi-tee) *n.* (*pl.* **-ties**) 1. great wickedness, *the enormity of this crime.* 2. a serious crime, *these enormities.* 3. enormous size, hugeness, *the enormity of their task.* ▷Careful writers do not use this word in the last meaning. They use *enormousness.*

e·nor·mous (i-nor-mŭs) *adj.* very large, huge. **e·nor′mous·ly** *adv.* **e·nor′mous·ness** *n.*

e·nough (i-nuf) *adj., adv., & pronoun* as much or as many as necessary.

en·plane (en-playn) *v.* **(en·planed, en·plan·ing)** to board an airplane.

en·quire (en-kwɪr) *v.* **(en·quired, en·quir·ing)** to inquire. **en·quir·y** (en-kwɪr-ee) *n.* an inquiry.

en·rage (en-rayj) *v.* **(en·raged, en·rag·ing)** to make furious.

en·rap·ture (en-rap-chŭr) *v.* **(en·rap·tured, en·rap·tur·ing)** to fill with intense delight.

en·rich (en-rich) *v.* 1. to make richer. 2. to improve the quality of by adding things, *this food is enriched with vitamins.* **en·rich′ment** *n.*

en·robe (en-rohb) *v.* to put a robe on.

en·roll (en-rohl) *v.* **(en·rolled, en·roll·ing)** 1. to become a member of a society, institution, etc. 2. to admit as a member. **en·roll′ment** *n.*

en route (ahn root, en) on the way, *met him en route from Chicago to Montreal.*

Ens. *abbr.* ensign.

en·sconce (en-skons) *v.* **(en·sconced, en·sconc·ing)** to establish securely or comfortably.

en·sem·ble (ahn-sahm-bĕl) *n.* 1. a thing viewed as a whole. 2. a group of musicians who perform together. 3. a woman's outfit of harmonizing items.

en·shrine (en-shrɪn) *v.* **(en·shrined, en·shrin·ing)** 1. to enclose in a shrine. 2. to serve as a shrine for.

en·shroud (en-shrowd) *v.* to cover completely.

en·sign (en-sin) *n.* 1. a military or naval flag, a special form of the national flag flown by ships. 2. a commissioned naval officer of the lowest rank.

en·si·lage (en-sĭ-lij) *n.* 1. silage. 2. storing fodder to produce silage.

en·sile (en-sɪl) *v.* **(en·siled, en·sil·ing)** 1. to preserve (fodder) in a silo. 2. to make (fodder) into silage.

en·slave (en-slayv) *v.* **(en·slaved, en·slav·ing)** to make a slave of. **en·slave′ment** *n.*

en·snare (en-snair) *v.* **(en·snared, en·snar·ing)** to entrap.

en·sue (en-soo) *v.* **(en·sued, en·su·ing)** to happen afterward or as a result; *a quarrel ensued.*

en·sure (en-shoor) *v.* **(en·sured, en·sur·ing)** to make safe or certain, to secure, *good food will ensure good health.* ▷Do not use this word to mean "to provide with financial insurance."

en·tail (en-tayl) *v.* 1. to make necessary, to involve, *these plans entail great expense.* 2. to leave (land) to a line of heirs so that none of them can give it away or sell it. **en·tail′ment** *n.*

en·tan·gle (en-tang-gĕl) *v.* **(en·tan·gled, en·tan·gling)** 1. to tangle. 2. to entwine in something that it is difficult to escape from. 3. to involve in something complicated. **en·tan′gle·ment** *n.*

en·tente (ahn-tahnt) *n.* a friendly understanding between countries.

en·ter (en-tĕr) *v.* 1. to go or come in or into. 2. to come on stage. 3. to penetrate, *the bullet entered his leg.* 4. to become a member of, *he entered the Navy.* 5. to put (a name, details, etc.) on a list or in a book. 6. to register as a competitor, *she entered the presidential race.* 7. to record formally, to present for consideration, *entered a plea of not guilty; entered a protest.* □**enter into,** to take part in (a conversation, an agreement, etc.); to form part of (calculations, plans, etc.). **enter on,** to begin (a process, stage of work, etc.).

en·ter·i·tis (en-tĕ-rɪ-tis) *n.* inflammation of the intestines.

en·ter·prise (en-tĕr-prɪz) *n.* 1. an undertaking, especially a bold or difficult one. 2. initiative, *she* shows true enterprise. 3. business activity, *private enterprise.*

en·ter·pris·ing (en-tĕr-prɪ-zing) *adj.* full of initiative.

en·ter·tain (en-tĕr-tayn) *v.* 1. to amuse, to occupy agreeably. 2. to receive (a person) with hospitality, *they entertained me at lunch.* 3. to have in the mind, *entertain doubts.* 4. to consider favorably, *refused to entertain the idea.*

en·ter·tain·er (en-tĕr-tay-nĕr) *n.* a person who performs in entertainments, especially as an occupation.

en·ter·tain·ment (en-tĕr-tayn-mĕnt) *n.* 1. entertaining, being entertained. 2. amusement. 3. something performed to amuse or interest an audience.

en·thrall (en-thrawl) *v.* to hold spellbound.

en·throne (en-throhn) *v.* **(en·throned, en·thron·ing)** to place on a throne, especially with ceremony. **en·throne'ment** *n.*

en·thuse (en-thooz) *v.* **(en·thused, en·thus·ing)** *(informal)* 1. to show enthusiasm. 2. to fill with enthusiasm. ▷Careful writers do not *enthuse.* They *become enthusiastic* and *show enthusiasm* and *are filled with enthusiasm.*

en·thu·si·asm (en-thoo-zi-az-ĕm) *n.* 1. a feeling of eager liking for or interest in something. 2. the object of this, *one of my enthusiasms.*

en·thu·si·ast (en-thoo-zi-ast) *n.* one who is full of enthusiasm for something, *a sports enthusiast.*

en·thu·si·as·tic (en-thoo-zi-as-tik) *adj.* full of enthusiasm. **en·thu·si·as'ti·cal·ly** *adv.*

en·tice (en-tɪs) *v.* **(en·ticed, en·tic·ing)** to attract or persuade by offering something pleasant. **en·tice'ment** *n.*

en·tire (en-tɪr) *adj.* whole, complete. **en·tire'ly** *adv.*

en·tire·ty (en-tɪr-tee) *n.* (*pl.* **-ties**) completeness, the total; *in its entirety,* in its complete form.

en·ti·tle (en-tɪ-tĕl) *v.* **(en·ti·tled, en·ti·tling)** 1. to give a title to (a book etc.). 2. to give a right, *the ticket entitles you to a seat.* **en·ti·tle·ment** *n.*

en·ti·ty (en-ti-tee) *n.* (*pl.* **-ties**) something that exists as a separate thing.

entom., entomol. *abbr.* 1. entomological. 2. entomology.

en·tomb (en-toom) *v.* to place in a tomb, to bury.

en·to·mol·o·gist (en-tŏ-mol-ŏ-jist) *n.* an expert in entomology.

en·to·mol·o·gy (en-tŏ-mol-ŏ-jee) *n.* the scientific study of insects. **en·to·mo·log·i·cal** (en-tŏ-mŏ-log-i-kăl) *adj.* ▷Do not confuse *entomology* with *etymology.*

en·tou·rage (ahn-tuu-rahzh) *n.* the people accompanying an important person.

en·tr'acte (ahn-trakt) *n.* 1. the interval between acts of a theatrical production. 2. entertainment, such as music or dancing, during this interval.

en·trails (en-traylz) *n. pl.* the intestines.

en·train (en-trayn) *v.* to put on or board a train.

en·trance¹ (en-trăns) *n.* 1. entering. 2. a door or passage by which one enters. 3. the right of admission, the fee charged for this.

en·trance² (en-trans) *v.* **(en·tranced, en·tranc·ing)** to fill with intense delight.

en·trant (en-trănt) *n.* one who enters, especially as a competitor.

en·trap (en-trap) *v.* 1. to catch, as in a trap. 2. to lure into difficulty or danger. **en·trap'ment** *n.*

en·treat (en-treet) *v.* to request earnestly or emotionally. **en·treat'y** *n.* (*pl.* **-treat·ies**).

en·tree, en·trée (ahn-tray) *n.* 1. the right or privilege of admission. 2. the main course of a meal. 3. a dish served between the fish and meat courses of a meal.

en·trench (en-trench) *v.* to establish firmly in a well-defended position; *entrenched ideas,* firmly fixed in the mind.

en·trench·ment (en-trench-mĕnt) *n.* 1. entrenching, being entrenched. 2. a trench made for defense.

en·tre·pre·neur (ahn-trĕ-prĕ-nur) *n.* a person who organizes and manages a commercial undertaking, especially one involving commercial risk. **en·tre·pre·neur·i·al** (ahn-trĕ-prĕ-nur-i-ăl) *adj.*

en·tro·py (en-trŏ-pi) *n.* a measure of the disorder of the molecules in substances etc. that are mixed or in contact with each other, indicating the amount of energy that (although it still exists) is not available for use because it has become more evenly distributed instead of being concentrated.

en·trust (en-trust) *v.* to give as a responsibility, to place (a person or thing) in a person's care, *being reluctant to entrust them with political power.*

en·try (en-tree) *n.* 1. entering. 2. a place of entrance; *entry-level job,* one at the lowest level of an employment category. 3. an item entered in a list, diary, etc. 4. a person or thing entered in a race or competition; *entry list,* a formal list of those entered.

en·twine (en-twin) *v.* **(en·twined, en·twin·ing)** to twine around, to interweave.

e·nu·mer·ate (i-noo-mĕ-rayt) *v.* **(e·nu·mer·at·ed, e·nu·mer·at·ing)** to count, to mention (items) one by one. **e·nu·mer·a·tion** (i-noo-mĕ-ray-shŏn) *n.*

e·nun·ci·ate (i-nun-si-ayt) *v.* **(e·nun·ci·at·ed, e·nun·ci·at·ing)** 1. to pronounce (words). 2. to state clearly. **e·nun·ci·a·tion** (i-nun-si-ay-shŏn) *n.*

en·u·re·sis (en-yŭ-ree-sis) *n.* involuntary urination, bed-wetting.

env. *abbr.* envelope.

en·vel·op (en-vel-ŏp) *v.* **(en·vel·oped, en·vel·op·ing)** to wrap up, to cover on all sides, *the hill was enveloped in mist.* **en·vel'op·ment** *n.*

en·ve·lope (en-vĕ-lohp) *n.* a wrapper or covering, especially a folded and gummed cover for a letter.

en·vi·a·ble (en-vi-ă-bĕl) *adj.* desirable enough to arouse envy, *an enviable achievement.* **en'vi·a·bly** *adv.* ▷Do not confuse *enviable* with *envious.*

en·vi·ous (en-vi-ŭs) *adj.* full of envy, *an envious person.* **en'vi·ous·ly** *adv.* **en'vi·ous·ness** *n.* ▷Do not confuse *envious* with *enviable.*

en·vi·ron·ment (en-vɪr-ŏn-mĕnt) *n.* surroundings, especially those affecting people's lives. **en·vi·ron·men·tal** (en-vɪr-ŏn-men-tăl) *adj.*

en·vi·ron·men·tal·ist (en-vɪr-ŏn-men-tăl-ist) *n.* a person who seeks to protect or improve the environment.

en·vi·rons (en-vɪr-ŏnz) *n. pl.* the surrounding districts, especially around a town.

en·vis·age (en-viz-ij) *v.* **(en·vis·aged, en·vis·ag·ing)** 1. to visualize, to imagine. 2. to foresee, *changes are envisaged.*

en·vi·sion (en-vizh-ŏn) *v.* to picture in the mind, especially a future occurrence.

en·voy (en-voi) *n.* 1. a diplomatic minister ranking below an ambassador. 2. a messenger or representative on a diplomatic mission.

en·vy (en-vee) *n.* (*pl.* **-vies**) 1. a feeling of discontent aroused by someone else's possession of things one would like to have oneself. 2. the object of this, *his car is the envy of the neighborhood.*

envy *v.* (**en·vied, en·vy·ing**) to feel envy of.

en·zyme (en-zīm) *n.* 1. a protein formed in living cells and assisting chemical processes (as in digestion). 2. a similar substance produced synthetically for use in chemical processes, household detergents, etc. **en·zy·mat·ic** (en-zī-mat-ik) *adj.*

E·o·cene (ee-ō-seen) *adj.* of the geologic epoch of the Tertiary period before the Oligocene and after the Paleocene. **Eocene** *n.* the Eocene epoch.

E·o·li·an = **Aeolian.**

e.o.m. *abbr.* end of month.

e·on (ee-ŏn) *n.* an immense time.

-eous *suffix* used to form adjectives meaning of the nature of, as in *vitreous, aqueous.*

EPA *abbr.* Environmental Protection Agency.

ep·au·let, ep·au·lette (ep-ŭ-let) *n.* an ornamental shoulder piece worn on uniforms.

é·pée (ay-pay) *n.* a sharp-pointed dueling sword, blunted for use in fencing.

e·pergne (i-purn) *n.* a centerpiece (especially in branched form) holding flowers or fruit.

e·phed·rine (i-fed-rin) *n.* a stimulant drug used to relieve asthma, hay fever, etc.

e·phem·er·al (i-fem-ĕ-răl) *adj.* lasting only a very short time.

E·phe·sians (i-fee-zhăns) *n.* a book of the New Testament ascribed to St. Paul, the epistle to the church at Ephesus.

ep·ic (ep-ik) *n.* 1. a long poem or other literary work telling of heroic deeds or history. 2. a book or film resembling this. 3. a subject fit to be told in an epic. **epic** *adj.* of or like an epic, on a grand scale. **ep′i·cal** *adj.* ▷ Do not confuse *epical* with *epochal.*

ep·i·cen·ter (ep-i-sen-tĕr) *n.* the point at which an earthquake reaches Earth's surface. **ep·i·cen·tral** (ep-i-sen-trăl) *adj.*

ep·i·cure (ep-i-kyoor) *n.* a person who enjoys well-prepared food and drink.

ep·i·cu·re·an (ep-i-kyoor-i-ăn) *n.* a person devoted to sensuous pleasures and luxuries. **epicurean** *adj.* of or suitable for an epicurean.

ep·i·dem·ic (ep-i-dem-ik) *n.* an outbreak of a disease etc. spreading rapidly through a community. **epidemic** *adj.* spreading in this way. ▷ Do not confuse *epidemic* with *endemic. Yellow fever was endemic in parts of South America. The last American epidemic of this disease occurred in New Orleans in 1905.*

ep·i·der·mis (ep-i-dur-mis) *n.* the outer layer of the skin. **ep·i·der′mal** *adj.*

ep·i·glot·tis (ep-i-glot-is) *n.* (*pl.* **-tis·es**) the flap of cartilage at the root of the tongue, which moves during swallowing to cover the glottis and prevents food from entering the windpipe.

ep·i·gram (ep-i-gram) *n.* a short witty saying.

e·pig·ra·phy (i-pig-ră-fee) *n.* the study of inscriptions, especially those on ancient stones, coins, etc. **ep·i·graph** (ep-ī-graf) *n.* such an inscription.

ep·i·lep·sy (ep-i-lep-see) *n.* a disorder of the nervous system causing mild or severe convulsions, sometimes with loss of consciousness. **ep·i·lep·tic** (ep-i-lep-tik) *adj. & n.*

ep·i·logue, ep·i·log (ep-i-lawg) *n.* a short concluding section in a literary work.

ep·i·neph·rine (ep-i-nef-rin) *n.* adrenalin.

E·piph·a·ny (i-pif-ă-nee) *n.* (*pl.* **-nies**) 1. the Christian festival commemorating the showing of

Jesus to the Magi, celebrated on January 6. 2. *epiphany,* an appearance of a superhuman being.

e·pis·co·pa·cy (i-pis-kŏ-pă-see) *n.* (*pl.* **-pa·cies**) 1. government of the church by bishops. 2. episcopate.

e·pis·co·pal (i-pis-kŏ-păl) *adj.* of a bishop or bishops, governed by bishops.

E·pis·co·pa·lian (i-pis-kŏ-payl-yăn) *adj.* of the Episcopal Church. **Episcopalian** *n.* a member of the Episcopal Church.

e·pis·co·pate (i-pis-kŏ-pit) *n.* 1. the office, position, or tenure of a bishop. 2. *the episcopate,* the bishops as a group.

ep·i·si·ot·o·my (i-pee-zi-ot-ŏ-mee) *n.* (*pl.* **-mies**) a cut made at the opening of the vagina during childbirth, to facilitate delivery of the baby.

ep·i·sode (ep-i-sohd, -zohd) *n.* 1. an incident or event forming one part of a sequence. 2. an incident in a story, one part of a serial. **ep·i·sod·ic** (ep-i-sod-ik, -zod-) *adj.*

e·pis·te·mol·o·gy (i-pis-tĕ-mol-ŏ-jee) *n.* (*pl.* **-gies**) a philosophic theory of the method or basis of human knowledge. **e·pis·te·mol′o·gist** *n.* **e·pis·te·mo·log·i·cal** (i-pis-tŏ-mŏ-loj-i-kăl) *adj.*

e·pis·tle (i-pis-ĕl) *n.* 1. a letter. 2. *Epistle,* any of the letters in the New Testament, written by the Apostles. **e·pis·to·lar·y** (i-pis-tŏ-ler-ee) *adj.* of or contained in letters.

ep·i·taph (ep-i-taf) *n.* words inscribed on a tomb or describing a dead person. ▷ Do not confuse *epitaph* with *epithet.*

ep·i·tha·la·mi·on (ep-i-thă-lay-mi-ŏn) (*pl.* **-mi·a,** *pr.* -mi-ă), **ep·i·tha·la·mi·um** (ep-i-thă-lay-mi-ŭm) (*pl.* **-mi·ums**) *n.* a song or poem in celebration of a wedding.

ep·i·the·li·um (ep-i-thee-li-ŭm) *n.* (*pl.* **-li·ums, -li·a,** *pr.* -li-ă) tissue forming the outer layer of a body surface, or the lining of a cavity that opens to a body surface. **ep·i·the′li·al** *adj.*

ep·i·thet (ep-i-thet) *n.* 1. a descriptive word or phrase, such as *the Great* in *Alfred the Great.* 2. a contemptuous word or phrase, *most of the epithets were deleted.* ▷ Do not confuse *epithet* with *epitaph.*

e·pit·o·me (i-pit-ŏ-mee) *n.* something that shows on a small scale the qualities of something much larger, a person who embodies a quality, *she is the epitome of kindness.* ▷ This word does not mean "the best." One can also be the *epitome of mediocrity,* the embodiment of it.

e·pit·o·mize (i-pit-ŏ-mīz) *v.* (**e·pit·o·mized, e·pit·o·miz·ing**) to be or to form the epitome of.

e plu·ri·bus u·num (ee ploor-i-bŭs yoo-nŭm) one out of many. ▷ Latin, the motto of the United States.

ep·och (ep-ŏk) *n.* 1. a particular period of history. 2. a division of a period of geologic time. **ep′och·al** *adj.* ▷ Do not confuse *epochal* with *epical.*

ep·och-mak·ing (ep-ŏk-may-king) *adj.* very important or remarkable, marking the beginning of a new epoch.

e·pon·y·mous (ĕ-pon-ĭ-mŭs) *adj.* of an eponym. **ep·o·nym** (ep-ŏ-nim) *n.* a person whose name is taken for a people, place, institution, etc., as A. J. Tasman (Dutch navigator) for *Tasmania,* Caesar for *Caesarean section.*

ep·ox·y (e-pok-see) *n.* (*pl.* **-ox·ies**) a synthetic thermosetting resin, used in adhesives and coatings. **epoxy** v. (**ep·ox·ied**, **ep·oxy·ing**) to glue with epoxy.

ep·si·lon (ep-si-lon) n. the fifth letter of the Greek alphabet (E, ε).

Ep·som (ep-sŏm) **salts** magnesium sulfate, used as a laxative.

eq. abbr. 1. equal. 2. equation. 3. equivalent.

eq·ua·ble (ek-wă-běl) adj. 1. even, unvarying; an equable climate, free from extremes of heat and cold. 2. even-tempered. **eq′ua·bly** adv. **eq·ua·bil·i·ty** (ek-wă-bil-i-tee) n. ▷Do not confuse equable with equitable.

e·qual (ee-kwăl) adj. 1. the same in size, amount, value, etc. 2. having the same rights or status. 3. having enough strength or courage or ability etc., he was equal to the task. **equal** n. a person or thing that is equal to another. **equal** v. (**e·qualed, e·qual·ing**) 1. to be equal to. 2. to produce or achieve something to match, no one has equaled her score. **e′qual·ly** adv. □**equal sign**, the symbol =, which indicates equality in a mathematical equation. **equal time**, the policy whereby a television or radio station provides broadcast time fairly for all candidates in an election.

e·qual·i·tar·i·an (i-kwol-i-tair-i-ăn) adj. egalitarian.

e·qual·i·ty (i-kwol-i-tee) n. (pl. **-ties**) being equal.

e·qual·ize (ee-kwă-lız) v. (**e·qual·ized, e·qual·iz·ing**) 1. to make or become equal. 2. to make uniform. **e·qual·i·za·tion** (ee-kwă-li-zay-shŏn) n.

e·qual·iz·er (ee-kwă-lı-zěr) n. 1. a thing that equalizes something. 2. (slang) a gun.

e·qua·nim·i·ty (ee-kwă-nim-i-tee) n. calmness of mind or temper.

e·quate (i-kwayt) v. (**e·quat·ed, e·quat·ing**) to consider to be equal or equivalent, can we equate those two crimes?

e·qua·tion (i-kway-zhŏn) n. 1. a mathematical statement that two expressions (connected by the sign =) are equal. 2. making equal.

e·qua·tor (i-kway-tŏr) n. an imaginary line around Earth at an equal distance from the North and South Poles.

e·qua·tor·i·al (ee-kwă-tohr-i-ăl, ek-wa-) adj. of or near the equator. □**Equatorial Guinea**, a country on the west coast of Africa.

eq·uer·ry (ek-wě-ree) n. (pl. **-ries**) an officer of the British royal household, attending members of the royal family.

e·ques·tri·an (i-kwes-tri-ăn) adj. of horse riding; an equestrian statue, a statue of a person on a horse. **equestrian** n. a person who is skilled in horsemanship.

e·ques·tri·enne (i-kwes-tri-en) n. a woman who is skilled in horsemanship.

e·qui·dis·tant (ee-kwi-dis-tănt) adj. at an equal distance.

e·qui·lat·er·al (ee-kwi-lat-ě-răl) adj. having all sides equal.

e·qui·lib·ri·um (ee-kwi-lib-ri-ŭm) n. a state of balance.

e·quine (ee-kwın) adj. of or like a horse.

e·qui·nox (ee-kwi-noks) n. the time of year when day and night are of equal length; autumnal equinox, that of September 22nd; vernal equinox, that of March 21st. **e·qui·noc·tial** (ee-kwi-nok-shăl) adj.

e·quip (i-kwip) v. (**e·quipped, e·quip·ping**) to supply with what is needed.

equip. abbr. equipment.

e·qui·page (ek-wĭ-pij) n. a carriage and horses with attendants.

e·quip·ment (i-kwip-měnt) n. 1. equipping. 2. the outfit, tools, and other things needed for a particular job or expedition etc.

e·qui·poise (ee-kwi-poiz) n. 1. equilibrium. 2. a counterbalance.

eq·ui·ta·ble (ek-wi-tă-běl) adj. fair and just. **eq′ui·ta·bly** adv. ▷Do not confuse equitable with equable.

eq·ui·ta·tion (ek-wi-tay-shŏn) n. riding on horseback, horsemanship.

eq·ui·ty (ek-wi-tee) n. (pl. **-ties**) 1. fairness, impartiality. 2. Equity, the actors' union. 3. equities, stocks not bearing fixed interest, common stocks.

equiv. abbr. equivalent.

e·quiv·a·lent (i-kwiv-ă-lěnt) adj. equal in value, importance, meaning, etc. **equivalent** n. an equivalent thing or amount or word. **e·quiv′a·lence** n.

e·quiv·o·cal (i-kwiv-ŏ-kăl) adj. 1. able to be interpreted in two ways, ambiguous. 2. questionable, suspicious, an equivocal character. **e·quiv′o·cal·ly** adv.

e·quiv·o·cate (i-kwiv-ŏ-kayt) v. (**e·quiv·o·cat·ed, e·quiv·o·cat·ing**) to use ambiguous words in order to conceal the truth, to avoid committing oneself. **e·quiv·o·ca·tion** (i-kwiv-ŏ-kay-shŏn) n.

Er symbol erbium.

-er[1] suffix used to form the comparative degree of adjectives and adverbs of one syllable, as in weaker, faster, and of some adjectives and adverbs of two or more syllables, as in narrower.

-er[2] suffix used to form nouns indicating occupation, as in astronomer; agent, as in maker; instrument, as in computer; person living in a place, as in Easterner.

e·ra (eer-ă, er-ă) n. 1. a period of history; the Christian era, the period reckoned from the birth of Christ. 2. a major division of geologic time, containing periods.

ERA abbr. Equal Rights Amendment.

e·rad·i·cate (i-rad-ĭ-kayt) v. (**e·rad·i·cat·ed, e·rad·i·cat·ing**) to get rid of, to remove all traces of. **e·rad·i·ca·tion** (i-rad-ĭ-kay-shŏn) n. **e·rad·i·ca·ble** (i-rad-ĭ-kă-běl) adj.

e·rase (i-rays) v. (**e·rased, e·ras·ing**) to rub or scrape out (marks, writing, etc.), to wipe out a recorded signal from (magnetic tape).

e·ras·er (i-ray-sěr) n. a thing that erases marks etc., a piece of rubber or other substance for rubbing out marks or writing.

e·ra·sure (i-ray-shŭr) n. 1. erasing. 2. a word etc. that has been erased.

er·bi·um (ur-bi-ŭm) n. a rare-earth chemical element.

ere (air) conj. & prep. (old use) before.

e·rect (i-rekt) adj. 1. standing on end, upright, vertical. 2. (of a part of the body) enlarged and rigid from excitement. **erect** v. to set up, to build. **e·rec′tor** n.

e·rec·tile (i-rek-tĭl) adj. (of parts of the body) able to become enlarged and rigid from excitement.

e·rec·tion (i-rek-shŏn) n. 1. erecting, being erected. 2. something erected, a building. 3. swelling and hardening (of a part of the body) in sexual excitement.

ere·long (air-lawng) adv. (old use) before long.

erg (urg) n. (in physics) a unit of work or energy.

er·go (ur-goh) adv. therefore.

er·gos·ter·ol (ur-gos-tĕ-rohl) *n.* a steroid present in ergot and yeast, a source of vitamin D.

er·got (ur-gŏt) *n.* a fungus affecting rye and other cereals, dried for use in medicine.

Er·ie (eer-ee) *n.* a member of an Indian tribe formerly of the Lake Erie region.

Er·in (er-in) (in poetry) Ireland.

er·mine (ur-min) *n.* (*pl.* -mines, -mine) 1. an animal of the weasel family, with brown fur that turns white in winter. 2. this white fur.

e·rode (i-rohd) *v.* (e·rod·ed, e·rod·ing) to wear away gradually, especially by rubbing or corroding.

e·rog·e·nous (i-roj-ĕ-nŭs) *adj.* arousing sexual desire, particularly sensitive to sexual stimulation.

E·ros (eer-os) *n.* 1. sexual love. 2. the Greek god of love, Cupid.

e·ro·sion (i-roh-zhŏn) *n.* 1. eroding, being eroded. 2. the natural processes by which the surface of Earth is worn away.

e·ro·sive (i-roh-siv) *adj.* causing erosion. **e·ro′sive·ness** *n.*

e·rot·ic (i-rot-ik) *adj.* of sexual love, arousing sexual desire. **e·rot′i·cal·ly** *adv.*

e·rot·i·ca (i-rot-i-kă) *n. pl.* erotic literature or art.

err (ur) *v.* (erred, err·ing) 1. to make a mistake, to be incorrect. 2. to sin.

er·rand (er-ănd) *n.* 1. a short journey on which a person goes or is sent to carry a message or deliver goods etc. 2. the purpose of a journey. ☐**errand of mercy,** a journey to bring help or relieve distress etc.

er·rant (er-ănt) *adj.* 1. misbehaving. 2. traveling in search of adventure, *a knight errant.*

er·ra·tic (i-rat-ik) *adj.* irregular or uneven in movement, quality, habit, etc. **er·rat′i·cal·ly** *adv.*

er·ra·tum (i-rah-tŭm) *n.* (*pl.* -ta, *pr.* -tă) 1. an error in printing or writing. 2. errata, errors shown in a list attached to a book etc.

erron. *abbr.* 1. erroneous. 2. erroneously.

er·ro·ne·ous (i-roh-ni-ŭs) *adj.* mistaken, incorrect. **er·ro′ne·ous·ly** *adv.*

er·ror (er-ŏr) *n.* 1. a mistake. 2. the condition of being wrong in opinion or conduct. 3. the amount of inaccuracy in a calculation or a measuring device, *an error of 2%.* 4. a baseball misplay that allows a runner to advance or that allows a player to be safe who should have been out. **er′ror·less** *adj.*

er·satz (er-zahts) *adj.* serving as a substitute, especially of inferior kind. **ersatz** *n.* an inferior substitute, *when coffee beans were unavailable, the Germans brewed ersatz.*

erst (urst) *adv.* (*old use*) formerly.

erst·while (urst-hwɪl) *adj.* & *adv.* former, formerly.

e·ruct (i-rukt) *v.* 1. to belch. 2. to discharge or emit with violence, as a volcano. **e·ruc·ta·tion** (i-ruk-tay-shŏn) *n.*

er·u·dite (er-yŭ-drt) *adj.* having or showing great learning. **er·u·di·tion** (er-yŭ-dish-ŏn) *n.*

e·rupt (i-rupt) *v.* 1. to break out suddenly and violently. 2. (of a volcano) to shoot forth lava etc., (of a geyser) to spurt water. 3. to form spots or patches on the skin. **e·rup·tive** (i-rup-tiv) *adj.*

e·rup·tion (i-rup-shŏn) *n.* ▷Do not confuse *eruption* with *irruption.*

-ery *suffix* used to form nouns meaning class of persons or things, as in *greenery;* condition, as in *slavery;* place or occupation, as in *brewery.*

er·y·sip·e·las (er-ĭ-sip-ĕ-lăs) *n.* inflammation of the skin, caused by a type of bacterium.

er·y·the·ma (er-ĭ-thee-mă) *n.* superficial redness of the skin in patches.

e·ryth·ro·cyte (e-rith-rŏ-sɪt) *n.* one of the red blood cells.

Es *symbol* einsteinium.

es·ca·late (es-kă-layt) *v.* (es·ca·lat·ed, es·ca·lat·ing) to increase or cause to increase in intensity or extent. **es·ca·la·tion** (es-kă-lay-shŏn) *n.*

es·ca·la·tor (es-kă-lay-tŏr) *n.* a staircase with an endless line of steps moving up or down. ☐**escalator clause,** a clause in a contract providing for automatic increases or decreases in wages, prices, benefits, etc. under specified conditions.

es·cal·lop, es·cal·op (e-skol-ŏp, e-skal-) *v.* to bake (food) in a sauce, usually topped with crumbs. **escallop** *n.* a scallop.

es·ca·pade (es-kă-payd) *n.* an act of reckless or mischievous conduct.

es·cape (e-skayp) *v.* (es·caped, es·cap·ing) 1. to get oneself free from confinement or control. 2. (of liquid or gas etc.) to get out of a container, to leak. 3. to succeed in avoiding (capture, punishment, etc.). 4. to be forgotten or unnoticed by; *his name escapes me,* I have forgotten it. 5. (of words, a sigh, etc.) to be uttered unintentionally. **escape** *n.* 1. the act of escaping, the fact of having escaped. 2. a means of escaping. 3. a temporary distraction or relief from reality or worry. **es·cap′er** *n.* ☐**escape clause,** a clause releasing a person etc. from a contract under specified conditions. **escape hatch,** a means of emergency exit from a ship etc. **escape velocity,** the minimum velocity needed for one body to escape from the gravitational pull of another.

es·cap·ee (e-skay-pee) *n.* a person who has escaped from prison or other confinement.

es·cape·ment (es-skayp-mĕnt) *n.* a mechanism regulating the movement of a watch or clock etc., a movable catch engaging the projections of a toothed wheel.

es·cap·ist (e-skay-pist) *n.* a person who likes to escape from the realities of life by absorbing his mind in entertainment or fantasy. **es·cap′ism** *n.* this tendency. **escapist** *adj.* having or catering to this tendency, *escapist literature.*

es·ca·role (es-kă-rohl) *n.* a variety of endive with wide frilled leaves, used in salads.

es·carp·ment (es-skahrp-mĕnt) *n.* a steep slope at the edge of a plateau.

-escence *suffix* used to form nouns meaning process, condition, or continuing state as in *convalescence,* corresponding to adjectives ending in *-escent.*

-escent *suffix* used to form adjectives meaning beginning to be or do, as in *pubescent, luminescent.*

es·chew (es-choo) *v.* to avoid or abstain from (certain kinds of action or food etc.).

es·cort (es-kort) *n.* 1. one or more persons or ships etc. accompanying a person or thing to give protection or as an honor. 2. a person accompanying a member of the opposite sex socially. **escort** (e-skort) *v.* to act as escort to.

es·cri·toire (es-kree-twahr) *n.* a writing desk with drawers.

es·crow (es-kroh) *n.* 1. a bond to do something, kept in a third person's custody until some condition has been fulfilled. 2. money or goods kept.

es·cu·do (e-skoo-doh) *n.* (*pl.* -dos) the unit of money in Portugal.

es·cutch·eon (e-skuch-ŏn) *n.* a shield or emblem bearing a coat of arms. ☐**a blot on one's escutcheon,** a stain on one's reputation.

ESE *abbr.* east-southeast.

-ese *suffix* used to form adjectives and nouns from names of foreign countries and cities, meaning an inhabitant or language of these, as in *Japanese Viennese,* or from nouns or names of writers meaning the style of writing characteristic of these, as in *officialese, Carlylese.*

Es·ki·mo (es-kĭ-moh) *n.* (*pl.* **-mos, -mo**) 1. a member of a people living near the Arctic coast of North America and eastern Siberia. 2. their language. ☐**Eskimo dog,** a breed of powerful dog with long hair, used by the Eskimos as a sled dog.

e·soph·a·gus (i-sof-ă-gŭs) *n.* (*pl.* **-gi,** *pr.* -jɪ) the tube leading from the mouth to the stomach, the gullet. **e·soph·a·ge·al** (i-sof-ă-jee-ăl) *adj.*

es·o·ter·ic (es-ŏ-ter-ik) *adj.* intended only for people with special knowledge or interest.

ESP *abbr.* extrasensory perception.

esp. *abbr.* especially.

es·pa·drille (es-pă-dril) *n.* a canvas shoe with a sole of rubber or twisted fiber.

es·pal·ier (e-spal-yĕr) *n.* a trellis or framework on which fruit trees or ornamental shrubs are trained, a tree etc. trained on this.

es·par·to (e-spahr-toh) *n.* (*pl.* **-tos**) (also **esparto grass**) a kind of grass of Spain and North Africa, used in making paper, shoes, etc.

es·pe·cial (e-spesh-ăl) *adj.* 1. special, outstanding, *of especial interest.* 2. belonging chiefly to one person or thing, *for your especial benefit.*

es·pe·cial·ly (e-spesh-ă-lee) *adv.* chiefly, more than in other cases.

Es·pe·ran·to (es-pĕ-rahn-toh) *n.* an artificial language designed in 1887 for use by people of all nations.

es·pi·o·nage (es-pi-ŏ-nahzh) *n.* spying or using spies to obtain secret information.

es·pla·nade (es-plă-nahd) *n.* a level area of ground where people may walk or ride for pleasure.

es·pouse (e-spowz) *v.* (**es·poused, es·pous·ing**) 1. to give support to (a cause). 2. to marry, to give (a woman) in marriage. **es·pou'sal** *n.*

es·pres·so (e-spres-oh) *n.* (*pl.* **-sos**) coffee made by forcing steam through powdered coffee beans. ▷This word is not pronounced *express-oh.*

es·prit de corps (es-pree de kor) loyalty and devotion uniting the members of a group.

Esq. *abbr.* Esquire.

Es·quire (es-kwɪr) *n.* a courtesy title (in formal use) placed after a man's surname where no title is used before his name.

-ess *suffix* used to form nouns meaning female, as in *lioness, actress.*

es·say (es-ay) *n.* 1. a short literary composition in prose. 2. an attempt. **essay** (e-say) *v.* (**es·sayed, es·say·ing**) to attempt. **es'say·ist** *n.* a writer of essays. ▷Do not confuse *essay* with *assay.*

es·sence (es-ĕns) *n.* 1. all that makes a thing what it is, its nature. 2. an indispensable quality or element. 3. an extract of something, containing all its important qualities in concentrated form. 4. a liquid perfume.

es·sen·tial (i-sen-shăl) *adj.* 1. indispensable. 2. of or constituting a thing's essence; *its essential quali-*

ties, those that make it what it is. **es·sen'tial·ly** *adv.* ☐**essential oil,** an oil that is like an essence, with the characteristic smell of the plant from which it is extracted. **the essentials,** indispensable elements of things.

EST *abbr.* Eastern Standard Time.

est. *abbr.* 1. establish. 2. established. 3. estate. 4. estuary.

-est[1] *suffix* used to form superlatives of adjectives and adverbs, as in *widest, fastest.*

-est[2] *suffix* (*old use*) used to form the second person singular of verbs, as in *knowest, goest.*

estab. *abbr.* established.

es·tab·lish (e-stab-lish) *v.* 1. to set up (a business or government etc.) on a permanent basis. 2. to settle (a person or oneself) in a place or position. 3. to cause people to accept (a custom or belief etc.). 4. to show to be true, to prove, *established his innocence.* ☐**established church** or **religion,** one that is made officially a country's national church or religion.

es·tab·lish·ment (e-stab-lish-mĕnt) *n.* 1. establishing, being established. 2. an organized body of people maintained for a purpose, a household or staff of servants etc. 3. a business firm or public institution, its members or employees or premises. ☐**the Establishment,** people who are established in positions of power and authority, exercising influence in the background of public life or other activity and generally resisting changes.

es·tate (e-stayt) *n.* 1. landed property. 2. all that a person owns, especially that left at his death. ☐**estate tax,** a tax levied on property after the owner's death, before transfer to the heirs.

es·teem (e-steem) *v.* 1. to think highly of. 2. to consider or regard, *I should esteem it an honor.* **esteem** *n.* favorable opinion, respect.

es·ter (es-tĕr) *n.* a chemical compound formed when an acid and an alcohol interact in a certain way.

Es·ther (es-tĕr) *n.* a book of the Old Testament containing the story of Esther, an Israelite queen of Persia who saved her people.

es·thete = aesthete.

es·thet·ic = aesthetic.

es·tim·a·ble (es-tĭ-mă-bĕl) *adj.* worthy of esteem.

es·ti·mate (es-tĭ-mit) *n.* 1. a judgment of a thing's approximate value or amount etc. 2. a contractor's statement of the sum for which he will undertake specified work. 3. a judgment of character or qualities. **estimate** (es-tĭ-mayt) *v.* (**es·ti·mat·ed, es·ti·mat·ing**) to form an estimate of. **es'ti·ma·tor** *n.*

es·ti·ma·tion (es-tĭ-may-shŏn) *n.* 1. estimating. 2. judgment of a person's or thing's worth.

Es·to·ni·a (e-stoh-ni-ă) a republic of the U.S.S.R., bordering on the Baltic Sea. **Es·to'ni·an** *adj. & n.*

es·trange (e-straynj) *v.* (**es·tranged, es·trang·ing**) to cause (people formerly friendly or loving) to become unfriendly or indifferent. **es·trange'ment** *n.*

es·tro·gen (es-trŏ-jĕn) *n.* a sex hormone or other substance capable of developing and maintaining female characteristics of the body. **es·tro·gen·ic** (es-trŏ-jen-ik) *adj.*

es·trus (es-trŭs) *n.* periodic sexual heat of animals, rut.

es·tu·ar·y (es-choo-er-ee) *n.* (*pl.* **-ar·ies**) the mouth of a large river where its flow is affected by ebb and flow of tides.

E.T. *abbr.* Eastern Time.

e·ta (ay-tă) *n.* the seventh letter of the Greek alphabet (H, η).

ETA *abbr.* estimated time of arrival.

é·ta·gère (ay-tă-z/air) *n.* a vertical series of open shelves, supported by legs at the corners, for ornaments.

et al. *abbr.* and others. ▷From the Latin *et alii* (= and other people), *et alia* (= and other things). Remember the period after *al.*

etc. *abbr.* = **et cetera** (et set-ĕ-ră), and other similar things, and the rest. **et cet·er·as** (et set-ĕ-răz) *n. pl. (informal)* the usual extras, sundries. ▷Do not say *and et cetera.* The Latin word *et* means *and.*

etch (ech) *v.* 1. to make (a pattern or picture) by engraving a metal plate with acids or corrosive substances, especially so that copies can be printed from this. 2. to impress deeply, *the scene is etched on my mind.* **etch′er** *n.*

etch·ing (ech-ing) *n.* a copy printed from an etched plate.

ETD *abbr.* estimated time of departure.

e·ter·nal (i-tur-năl) *adj.* 1. existing always without beginning or end. 2. unchanging, not affected by time. 3. *(informal)* ceaseless, too frequent, *these eternal arguments.* **e·ter′nal·ly** *adv.* □**eternal triangle**, two men and a woman or two women and a man, with problems resulting from conflict of sexual attractions. **the Eternal City**, Rome. **e·ter·ni·ty** (i-tur-ni-tee) *n.* (*pl.* -**ties**) 1. infinite time, past or future. 2. the endless period of life after death. 3. *(informal)* a very long time.

-eth[1] *suffix (old use)* used to form the third person singular present of verbs, as in *knoweth, goeth.*

-eth[2] *suffix* used to form ordinal numbers after *-ty,* as in *twentieth.*

eth·ane (eth-ayn) *n.* a colorless odorless gas used as a fuel, refrigerant, etc.

eth·a·nol (eth-ă-nohl) *n.* ethyl alcohol.

e·ther (ee-thĕr) *n.* 1. the clear sky, the upper regions beyond the clouds. 2. a kind of substance formerly thought to fill all space and act as a medium for transmission of radio waves etc. 3. a colorless liquid produced by the action of acids on alcohol, used as an anesthetic and as a solvent.

e·the·re·al (i-theer-i-ăl) *adj.* 1. light and delicate, especially in appearance. 2. of heaven, heavenly. **e·the′re·al·ly** *adv.* **e·the′re·al·ness** *n.* **e·the·re·al·i·ty** (i-theer-ri-al-i-tee) *n.*

eth·i·cal (eth-i-kăl) *adj.* 1. of ethics. 2. morally correct, honorable. 3. (of medicines) not advertised to the general public and usually available only on a doctor's prescription. **eth′i·cal·ly** *adv.*

eth·ics (eth-iks) *n.* 1. moral philosophy (*see* **moral**). 2. *ethics,* moral principles; *medical ethics,* those observed by the medical profession.

E·thi·o·pi·a (ee-thi-oh-pi-ă) a country of northeast Africa. **E·thi·o′pi·an** *adj. & n.*

E·thi·o·pic (ee-thi-oh-pik) *n.* an ancient Semitic language surviving in the Christian Church of Ethiopia. **Ethiopic** *adj.* of this language.

eth·nic (eth-nik) *adj.* 1. of a racial group. 2. (of clothes etc.) resembling the peasant clothes etc. of primitive peoples. **ethnic** *n.* a member of an ethnic group. **eth′ni·cal·ly** *adv.* □**ethnic group,** people who share distinctive cultural characteristics originating from a common national, linguistic, or racial heritage.

eth·nic·i·ty (eth-nis-i-tee) *n.* ethnic background, trait, etc.

ethnol. *abbr.* 1. ethnological. 2. ethnology.

eth·nol·o·gist (eth-nol-ŏ-jist) *n.* an expert in ethnology.

eth·nol·o·gy (eth-nol-ŏ-jee) *n.* the scientific study of human races and their characteristics. **eth·no·log·ic** (eth-nŏ-loj-ik) *adj.* **eth·no·log′i·cal** *adj.*

e·thol·o·gist (ee-thol-ŏ-jist) *n.* an expert in ethology.

e·thol·o·gy (ee-thol-ŏ-jee) *n.* 1. the study of character formation. 2. the study of animal behavior. **e·tho·log·i·cal** (ee-thŏ-loj-i-kăl) *adj.*

e·thos (ee-thos) *n.* the characteristic spirit and beliefs of a community, person, or literary work.

eth·yl (eth-il) *n.* a hydrocarbon, present in alcohol and ether. **e·thyl·ic** (ĕ-thil-ik) *adj.* □**ethyl alcohol,** an inflammable volatile liquid produced by the fermentation of sugars by yeast, used in intoxicating beverages and as a fuel and solvent.

eth·yl·ene (eth-ĭ-leen) *n.* an inflammable gas, used as an anesthetic and to improve the color of citrus fruits.

e·ti·o·late (ee-ti-o-layt) *v.* (**e·ti·o·lat·ed, e·ti·o·lat·ing**) to make (a plant) pale through lack of light. **e·ti·o·la·tion** (ee-ti-ŏ-lay-shŏn) *n.*

e·ti·ol·o·gy (ee-ti-ol-ŏ-jee) *n.* 1. the study of causes. 2. the assignment of cause, especially in disease. **e·ti·o·log·ic** (ee-ti-ŏ-loj-ik) *adj.* **e·ti·o·log′ic·al** *adj.*

et·i·quette (et-ĭ-kit) *n.* the rules of correct behavior in society or among the members of a profession.

E·tru·ri·a (i-troor-i-ă) an ancient country in what is now Italy, where the Etruscan civilization flourished.

E·trus·can (i-trus-kăn) *n.* a member or the language of the earliest historical inhabitants of Etruria. **Etruscan** *adj.*

et seq. *abbr.* (*pl.* **et seqq.**) and what follows. ▷From the Latin *et sequentia.*

-ette *suffix* used to form nouns meaning small one, as in *kitchenette;* imitation, as in *leatherette;* or female, as in *usherette.*

e·tude (ay-tood) *n.* a short musical composition.

ETV *abbr.* educational television.

ety. *abbr.* 1. etymological. 2. etymology.

et·y·mol·o·gist (et-ĭ-mol-ŏ-jist) *n.* an expert in etymology.

et·y·mol·o·gy (et-ĭ-mol-ŏ-jee) *n.* (*pl.* -**gies**) 1. an account of the origin and development of a word and its meaning. 2. the study of words and their origins. **et·y·mo·log′i·cal** *adj.* ▷Do not confuse *etymology* with *entomology.*

Eu *symbol* europium.

eu·ca·lyp·tus (yoo-kă-lip-tŭs) *n.* (*pl.* -**ti,** *pr.* -tʏ, -**tus·es**) 1. a kind of evergreen tree. 2. a strong-smelling oil obtained from its leaves.

Eu·char·ist (yoo-kă-rist) *n.* 1. the Christian sacrament of Holy Communion, in which bread and wine are consecrated and consumed. 2. the consecrated elements, especially the bread. **Eu·char·is·tic** (yoo-kă-ris-tik) *adj.*

eu·chre (yoo-kĕr) *n.* a card game played with a pack of thirty-two cards. **euchre** *v.* (**eu·chred, eu·chring**) to outwit.

Eu·clid·e·an (yoo-klid-i-ăn) *adj.* of Euclid, a mathematician of Alexandria *c.*300 B.C.

eu·gen·ics (yoo-jen-iks) *n.* the study of improving the human species by improvement of inherited qualities. **eu·gen′ic** *adj.* **eu·gen′i·cal·ly** *adv.* **eu·gen·i·cist** (yoo-jen-i-sist) *n.*

eu·lo·gis·tic (yoo-lŏ-jis-tik) *adj.* eulogizing.

eu·lo·gize (yoo-lŏ-jɪz) v. (**eu·lo·gized, eu·lo·giz·ing**) to write or utter a eulogy of.

eu·lo·gy (yoo-lŏ-jee) n. (pl. **-gies**) a speech or piece of writing in praise of a person or thing. ▷Do not confuse eulogy with elegy.

eu·nuch (yoo-nŭk) n. a castrated man, especially one employed in a harem.

eu·phe·mism (yoo-fĕ-miz-ĕm) n. a mild or roundabout expression substituted for one considered improper or too harsh or blunt (pass away is a euphemism for die). **eu·phe·mis·tic** (yoo-fĕ-mis-tik) adj. **eu·phe·mis'ti·cal·ly** adv.

eu·pho·ni·um (yoo-foh-ni-ŭm) n. a large brass wind instrument, a tenor tuba.

eu·pho·ny (yoo-fŏ-nee) n. (pl. **-nies**) pleasantness of sounds, especially in words. **eu·pho·ni·ous** (yoo-foh-ni-ŭs) adj.

eu·pho·ri·a (yoo-fohr-i-ă) n. a feeling of general well-being. **eu·phor'ic** adj.

Eur. abbr. 1. Europe. 2. European.

Eur·a·sia (yoo-ray-zha) Europe and Asia.

Eur·a·sian (yoo-ray-zhăn) adj. 1. of Europe and Asia. 2. of mixed European and Asian parentage. **Eurasian** n. a Eurasian person.

eu·re·ka (yuu-ree-kă) interj. I have found it, an exclamation of triumph at a discovery. ▷Said to have been uttered by the Greek mathematician Archimedes (3rd century B.C.) on realizing that the volume of an object can be calculated by the amount of water it displaces.

Euro- prefix Europe, European, as in Eurobond, Eurodollar.

Eu·ro·bond (yoor-oh-bond) n. a bond issued in dollar denominations by a U.S. corporation but sold outside the U.S., especially in Europe.

Eu·ro·com·mu·nism (yoor-oh-kom-yŭ-niz-ĕm) n. a form of Communism in European countries seeking independence from the Soviet Communist Party. **Eu·ro·com'mun·ist** n.

Eu·ro·dol·lar (yoor-oh-dol-ăr) n. a dollar held in a bank outside the U.S., usually in Europe.

Eu·rope (yoor-ŏp) a continent extending from Asia to the Atlantic Ocean. **Eu·ro·pe·an** (yoor-ŏ-pee-ăn) adj. & n. □**European Economic Community,** see **Common Market. European plan,** a hotel rate covering room and service but not meals.

eu·ro·pi·um (yuu-roh-pi-ŭm) n. a chemical element.

Eu·sta·chian (yoo-stay-shăn) **tube** the passage between the middle ear and the pharynx.

eu·tha·na·sia (yoo-thă-nay-zhă) n. the bringing about of a gentle and easy death for a person suffering from a painful incurable disease.

eu·troph·ic (yoo-troh-fik) adj. (of a pond etc.) rich in nutrients and hence having excessive plant growth, which kills animal life by depriving it of oxygen. **eu·tro·phi·ca·tion** (yoo-trŏ-fi-kay-shŏn) n. **eu·tro·phy** (yoo-trŏ-fee) n.

EVA abbr. extravehicular activity.

e·vac·u·ate (i-vak-yoo-ayt) v. (**e·vac·u·at·ed, e·vac·u·at·ing**) 1. to send (people) away from a place considered dangerous, to remove the occupants of (a place). 2. to empty (a vessel) of air etc. 3. to empty the contents of (the bowel or other organ). **e·vac·u·a·tion** (i-vak-yoo-ay-shŏn) n.

e·vac·u·ee (i-vak-yoo-ee) n. an evacuated person.

e·vade (i-vayd) v. (**e·vad·ed, e·vad·ing**) to avoid (a person or thing) by cleverness or trickery; evade the question, to avoid giving a direct answer to it.

e·val·u·ate (i-val-yoo-ayt) v. (**e·val·u·at·ed, e·val·u·at·ing**) to find out or state the value of, to assess. **e·val·u·a·tion** (i-val-yoo-ay-shŏn) n.

ev·a·nes·cent (ev-ă-nes-ĕnt) adj. (of an impression etc.) fading quickly. **ev·a·nes'cence** n.

e·van·gel·i·cal (ee-van-jel-i-kăl) adj. 1. according to the teaching of the gospel or the Christian religion. 2. (also Evangelical), of a Protestant group believing that salvation is achieved by faith in atonement through Christ. **e·van·gel'i·cal·ly** adv.

e·van·gel·ism (i-van-jĕ-liz-ĕm) n. preaching or spreading of the gospel. **e·van·gel·is·tic** (i-van-jĕ-lis-tik) adj. **e·van·gel·is'ti·cal·ly** adv.

e·van·ge·list (i-van-jĕ-list) n. 1. any of the authors of the four Gospels (Matthew, Mark, Luke, John). 2. a person who preaches the gospel.

e·van·gel·ize (i-van-jĕ-lɪz) v. (**e·van·gel·ized, e·van·gel·iz·ing**) to preach or spread the gospel to, to win over to Christianity. **e·van·gel·i·za·tion** (i-van-jĕ-li-zay-shŏn) n.

evap. abbr. evaporate.

e·vap·o·rate (i-vap-ŏ-rayt) v. (**e·vap·o·rat·ed, e·vap·o·rat·ing**) 1. to turn or be turned into vapor. 2. to lose or cause to lose moisture in this way. 3. to cease to exist, their enthusiasm evaporated. **e·vap'o·ra·tor** n. **e·vap'o·ra·tive** adj. **e·vap·o·ra·tion** (i-vap-ŏ-ray-shŏn) n. □**evaporated milk,** unsweetened milk thickened by partial evaporation and canned.

e·vap·o·rite (i-vap-ŏ-rɪt) n. a sedimentary rock formed by evaporation of seawater.

e·va·sion (i-vay-zhŏn) n. 1. evading. 2. an evasive answer or excuse.

e·va·sive (i-vay-siv) adj. evading, not frank or straightforward. **e·va'sive·ly** adv. **e·va'sive·ness** n.

eve (eev) n. 1. the evening or day before a festival, Christmas Eve. 2. the time just before an event, on the eve of an election. 3. (old use) evening. ▷Note that eve may refer to any period just before an event, but evening refers only to one time of day.

Eve (in the Bible) the first woman.

e·ven¹ (ee-vĕn) adj. 1. level, free from irregularities, smooth. 2. uniform in quality. 3. (of temper) calm, not easily upset. 4. equally balanced or matched. 5. equal in number or amount. 6. (of a number) exactly divisible by two. 7. (of money or time or quantity) exact, not involving fractions, an even dozen. **even** v. to make or become even. **e'ven·ly** adv. **e'ven·ness** n. □**be** or **get even with,** to have one's revenge on. **even chance,** when success is as likely as failure. **even money,** equal odds on both sides in a bet. **even up,** to make or become equal.

even² adv. 1. (used to emphasize a comparison) to a greater degree, ran even faster. 2. (used to suggest that something mentioned is unlikely or is an extreme case or should be compared with what might have happened etc.) does he even suspect the danger?; even a child could understand that; he didn't even try to avoid it (let alone succeed). □**even now,** in addition to previously; at this very moment. **even so,** although that is the case.

e·ven·hand·ed (ee-vĕn-han-did) adj. fair, impartial.

eve·ning (eev-ning) n. the part of the day between afternoon and bedtime. □**evening dress,** the kind of clothing usually worn for formal occasions in the evening. **evening gown,** a woman's long formal dress. **evening paper,** a newspaper published at about or later than midday. **evening primrose,** a plant with pale yellow flowers that open in the evening. **evening star,** a planet (especially Venus) when conspicuous in the west after sunset. ▷See the note under **eve.**

e·ven·song (ee-věn-sawng) *n.* 1. vespers in the Roman Catholic Church. 2. the service of evening prayer in the Church of England.

e·vent (i-vent) *n.* 1. something that happens, especially something important. 2. the fact of a thing happening; *in the event of his death,* if he dies. 3. an item in a sports program. □**at all events, in any event,** in any case. **in the event that,** if it happens that.

e·vent·ful (i-vent-fŭl) *adj.* full of incidents.

e·ven·tide (ee-věn-tĭd) *n.* *(old use)* evening.

e·ven·tu·al (i-ven-choo-ăl) *adj.* coming at last, ultimate, *his eventual success.* **e·ven'tu·al·ly** *adv.*

e·ven·tu·al·i·ty (i-ven-choo-al-i-tee) *n.* (*pl.* -ties) a possible event.

e·ven·tu·ate, (i-ven-choo-ayt) *v.* (**e·ven·tu·at·ed, e·ven·tu·at·ing**) to result, to be the outcome.

ev·er (ev-ěr) *adv.* 1. at all times, always, *ever hopeful.* 2. at any time, *the best thing I ever did.* 3. (used for emphasis) in any possible way, *why ever didn't you say so?* □**did you ever?,** *(informal)* an exclamation of surprise, = did you ever see or hear the like? **ever and ever,** always. **ever so,** *(informal)* very; very much, *it's ever so easy.*

ev·er·bloom·ing (ev-ěr-bloo-ming) *adj.* producing flowers during most of the growing season.

ev·er·glade (ev-ěr-glayd) *n.* 1. a marshy tract of land. 2. *Everglades,* a large partly forested everglade in southern Florida.

ev·er·green (ev-ěr-green) *adj.* (of a tree or shrub) having green leaves throughout the year. **evergreen** *n.* an evergreen tree or shrub.

ev·er·last·ing (ev-ěr-las-ting) *adj.* 1. lasting forever. 2. lasting a long time. 3. lasting too long, repeated too often, *his everlasting complaints.* 4. (of flowers) keeping shape and color when dried. **ev·er·last'ing·ly** *adv.*

ev·er·more (ev-ěr-mohr) *adv.* forever, always.

eve·ry (ev-ree) *adj.* 1. each single one without exception, *enjoyed every minute.* 2. each in a series, *went visiting every fourth day.* 3. all possible, *she will be given every care.* □**every other day** or **week** etc., with one between each two selected. ▷See the note under **everyone.**

eve·ry·bod·y (ev-ree-bod-ee) *pronoun* every person.

eve·ry·day (ev-ree-day) *adj.* 1. worn or used on ordinary days. 2. usual, commonplace.

Eve·ry·man (ev-ree-man) *n.* the ordinary or typical person, the "man in the street."

eve·ry·one (ev-ree-wun) *pronoun* everybody. ▷Do not confuse everyone with *every one* = each one. *He bought everyone a drink. I saw every one of them.*

eve·ry·thing (ev-ree-thing) *pronoun* 1. all things, all. 2. the most important thing, *speed is everything.* □**have everything,** *(informal)* to possess every advantage or attraction.

eve·ry·where (ev-ree-hwair) *adv.* in every place.

evg. *abbr.* evening.

e·vict (i-vikt) *v.* to expel (a tenant) by legal process. **e·vic·tion** (i-vik-shŏn) *n.*

ev·i·dence (ev-i-děns) *n.* 1. anything that establishes a fact or gives reason for believing something. 2. statements made or objects produced

in a law court as proof or to support a case. **evidence** *v.* (**ev·i·denced, ev·i·denc·ing**) to indicate, to be evidence of. □**be in evidence,** to be conspicuous.

ev·i·dent (ev-i-děnt) *adj.* obvious to the eye or mind. **ev'i·dent·ly** *adv.*

ev·i·den·tial (ev-i-den-shăl) *adj.* of or based on or providing evidence.

e·vil (ee-vĭl) *adj.* 1. morally bad, wicked. 2. harmful, intending to do harm. 3. very unpleasant or troublesome, *an evil temper.* **evil** *n.* an evil thing, sin, harm, **e'vil·ly** *adv.* **e'vil·ness** *n.* □**the evil eye,** a gaze or stare superstitiously believed to cause harm.

e·vil-mind·ed (ee-vĭl-mɪn-did) *adj.* having evil ideas, thoughts, plans, etc.

e·vince (i-vins) *v.* (**e·vinced, e·vinc·ing**) to indicate, to show that one has (a quality).

e·vis·cer·ate (i-vis-ĕ-rayt) *v.* (**e·vis·cer·at·ed, e·vis·cer·at·ing**) 1. to take out the intestines of. 2. to empty (a thing) of its vital contents.

e·vis·cer·a·tion (i-vis-ĕ-ray-shŏn) *n.*

e·voc·a·tive (i-vok-ă-tiv) *adj.* tending to evoke.

e·voke (i-vohk) *v.* (**e·voked, e·vok·ing**) to call up or produce or inspire (memories, feelings, a response, etc.). **ev·o·ca·tion** (ev-ŏ-kay-shŏn) *n.*

ev·o·lu·tion (ev-ŏ-loo-shŏn) *n.* 1. the process by which something develops gradually into a different form. 2. the origination of living things by development from earlier forms, not by special creation. **ev·o·lu'tion·ar·y** *adj.* **ev·o·lu'tion·ist** *n.*

e·volve (i-volv) *v.* (**e·volved, e·volv·ing**) 1. to develop or work out gradually, *evolve a plan.* 2. to develop or modify by evolution, *during the period when plants first evolved.* **e·volve'ment** *n.*

EW *abbr.* enlisted woman or women.

ewe (yoo) *n.* a female sheep.

ew·er (yoo-ěr) *n.* a wide-mouthed pitcher for holding water.

ex¹ (eks) *prep.* 1. out of, from. 2. without, excluding. □**ex dividend,** not including a dividend that is about to be paid.

ex² *n.* *(informal)* a former husband or wife.

ex. *abbr.* 1. examination. 2. examined. 3. example. 4. except. 5. exception. 6. exchange. 7. excursion. 8. executed. 9. executive. 10. express. 11. extra.

Ex. *abbr.* Exodus.

ex- *prefix* former, as in *ex-president, ex-convict,* outside, out of, as in *exodus.*

ex·ac·er·bate (ig-zas-ěr-bayt) *v.* (**ex·ac·er·bat·ed, ex·ac·er·bat·ing**) to make (pain, disease, anger, etc.) worse. **ex·ac·er·ba·tion** (ig-zas-ěr-bay-shŏn) *n.*

ex·act (ig-zakt) *adj.* 1. correct in every detail, free from error. 2. giving all details, *gave me exact instructions.* 3. capable of being precise, *the exact sciences.* **exact** *v.* to insist on and obtain, *exacted payment* or *obedience.* **ex·act'ness** *n.* **ex·ac·tion** (ig-zak-shŏn) *n.*

ex·act·ing (ig-zak-ting) *adj.* making great demands, requiring or insisting on great effort, *an exacting task* or *teacher.*

ex·ac·ti·tude (ig-zak-ti-tood) *n.* exactness.

ex·act·ly (ig-zakt-lee) *adv.* 1. in an exact manner. 2. (said in agreement) quite so, as you say. □**not exactly,** *(informal)* by no means, *didn't exactly enjoy it.*

ex·ag·ger·ate (ig-zag-ĕ-rayt) *v.* (**ex·ag·ger·at·ed, ex·ag·ger·at·ing**) to make (a thing) seem larger or better or smaller or worse than it really is; *with exaggerated courtesy,* with excessive courtesy. **ex·ag'ger·a·tor** *n.* **ex·ag·ger·at·ed·ly** (ig-zaj-ĕ-ray-tid-lee) *adv.* **ex·ag·ger·a·tion** (ig-zaj-ĕ-ray-shŏn) *n.*

ex·alt (ig-zawlt) *v.* 1. to raise (a person) in rank or power of dignity. 2. to praise highly.

ex·al·ta·tion (eg-zawl-tay-shŏn) *n.* 1. exalting, being exalted. 2. elation, spiritual delight. ▷Do not confuse *exaltation* with *exultation.*

ex·am (ig-zam) *n. (informal)* an examination.

ex·am·i·na·tion (ig-zam-ĭ-nay-shŏn) *n.* 1. examining, being examined or looked at. 2. the testing of knowledge or ability by oral or written questions or by exercises. 3. a formal questioning of a witness or an accused person in a court of law.

ex·am·ine (ig-zam-in) *v.* **(ex·am·ined, ex·am·in·ing)** 1. to look at in order to learn about or from, to look at closely. 2. to subject to questions or exercises etc. in order to test knowledge or ability. 3. to question formally in order to get information. **ex·am'i·ner** *n.*

ex·am·i·nee (ig-zam-ĭ-nee) *n.* a person being tested in an examination.

ex·am·ple (ig-zam-pĕl) *n.* 1. a fact that illustrates a general rule, a thing that shows the quality or characteristics of others in the same group or of the same kind. 2. something (especially conduct) that is worthy of imitation, *her courage is an example to us all.* □**for example,** by way of illustrating a general rule. **make an example of,** to punish as a warning to others. **set an example,** to behave in a way that is worthy of imitation.

ex·as·per·ate (ig-zas-pĕ-rayt) *v.* **(ex·as·per·at·ed, ex·as·per·at·ing)** to annoy greatly. **ex·as·per·a·tion** (ig-zas-pĕ-ray-shŏn) *n.*

exc. *abbr.* 1. excellent. 2. except. 3. exception. 4. excursion.

ex ca·the·dra (eks kă-thee-dră, kath-ĕ-dră) given by an authoritative person, especially the pope, as an infallible judgment.

ex·ca·vate (eks-kă-vayt) *v.* **(ex·ca·vat·ed, ex·ca·vat·ing)** 1. to make (a hole or channel) by digging, to dig out (soil). 2. to reveal or extract by digging. **ex'ca·va·tor** *n.* **ex·ca·va·tion** (eks-kă-vay-shŏn) *n.*

ex·ceed (ik-seed) *v.* 1. to be greater than. 2. to go beyond the limit of, to do more than is warranted by, *exceeded his authority.* ▷Do not confuse *exceed* with *accede.*

ex·ceed·ing·ly (ik-see-ding-lee) *adv.* very, extremely.

ex·cel (ik-sel) *v.* **(ex·celled, ex·cel·ling)** 1. to be better than. 2. to be very good at something. □**excel oneself,** to do better than one has ever done before.

ex·cel·lence (ek-sĕ-lĕns) *n.* very great merit or quality.

Ex·cel·len·cy (ek-sĕ-lĕn-see) *n.* (*pl.* **-cies**) the title of high officials such as ambassadors and governors.

ex·cel·lent (ek-sĕ-lĕnt) *adj.* extremely good. **ex'cel·lent·ly** *adv.*

ex·cel·si·or (ik-sel-si-ŏr) *interj.* (as a motto etc.) higher.

ex·cept (ik-sept) *prep.* not including, *they all left except me.* **except** *v.* to exclude from a statement or calculation etc. ▷Do not confuse *except* with *accept.*

ex·cept·ing (ik-sep-ting) *prep.* except.

ex·cep·tion (ik-sep-shŏn) *n.* 1. excepting, being excepted. 2. a thing that does not follow the general rule. □**take exception to,** to object to. **the exception proves the rule,** the excepting of some cases proves that the rule exists, or that it applies to all other cases. **with the exception of,** except.

ex·cep·tion·a·ble (ik-sep-shŏ-nă-bĕl) *adj.* open to objection.

ex·cep·tion·al (ik-sep-shŏ-năl) *adj.* 1. forming an exception, very unusual. 2. outstandingly good. **ex·cep'tion·al·ly** *adv.*

ex·cerpt (ek-surpt) *n.* an extract from a book or film or piece of music etc. **excerpt** (ik-surpt) *v.* to select excerpts from.

ex·cess (ik-ses, ek-ses) *n.* 1. the exceeding of due limits. 2. an amount by which one number or quantity etc. exceeds another. 3. *excesses,* immoderation in eating or drinking. □**excess baggage,** the amount that is over the weight for free carriage. **excess-profits tax,** a tax levied on business profits that are in excess of the average profits of a standard period. **in excess of,** more than. ▷Do not confuse *excess* with *access.*

ex·ces·sive (ik-ses-iv) *adj.* greater than what is normal or necessary, too much. **ex·ces'sive·ly** *adv.*

exch. *abbr.* 1. exchange. 2. exchequer.

ex·change (iks-chaynj) *v.* **(ex·changed, ex·chang·ing)** 1. to give or receive (one thing) in place of another. 2. to give to and receive from another person; *they exchanged glances,* looked at each other. **exchange** *n.* 1. exchanging (goods, prisoners, words, blows, etc.). 2. the exchanging of money for its equivalent in another currency, the relation in value between the money of two or more countries. 3. a place where merchants or stockbrokers etc. assemble to do business, *a stock exchange.* 4. the central telephone office of a district, where connections are made between lines concerned in calls.

ex·change·a·ble (iks-chayn-jă-bĕl) *adj.* able to be exchanged.

ex·cheq·uer (eks-chek-ĕr) *n.* a national treasury.

ex·cise¹ (ek-sɪz, -sɪs) *n.* duty or tax (also **excise tax**) levied on certain goods and licenses etc.

ex·cise² (ik-sɪz) *v.* **(ex·cised, ex·cis·ing)** to remove by cutting out or away, *excise tissue from the body; excise a passage from a book.* **ex·ci·sion** (ik-sizh-ŏn) *n.*

ex·cit·a·ble (ik-sɪ-tă-bĕl) *adj.* (of a person) easily excited. **ex·cit·a·bil·i·ty** (ik-sɪ-tă-bil-i-tee) *n.*

ex·cite (ik-sɪt) *v.* **(ex·cit·ed, ex·cit·ing)** 1. to rouse the feelings of, to cause (a person) to feel strongly, to make eager. 2. to cause (a feeling or reaction), *it excited curiosity.* 3. to produce activity in (a nerve or organ of the body etc.). **ex·ci·ta·tion** (eks-sɪ-tay-shŏn) *n.*

ex·cit·ed (ik-sɪ-tid) *adj.* feeling or showing excitement. **ex·cit'ed·ly** *adv.*

ex·cite·ment (ik-sɪt-mĕnt) *n.* 1. a state of great emotion, especially that caused by something pleasant. 2. something causing this.

ex·cit·ing (ik-sɪ-ting) *adj.* causing great interest or eagerness. **ex·cit'ing·ly** *adv.*

ex·claim (ik-sklaym) *v.* to cry out or utter suddenly from pain, pleasure, surprise, etc.

ex·cla·ma·tion (ek-sklă-may-shŏn) *n.* 1. exclaiming. 2. a word or words etc. exclaimed. □**exclamation point** *or* **mark,** the punctuation mark ! placed after an exclamation.

ex·clam·a·to·ry (ik-sklam-ă-tohr-ee) *adj.* of or containing or being an exclamation.

ex·clude (ik-sklood) *v.* (**ex·clud·ed, ex·clud· ing**) 1. to keep out (a person or thing) from a place or group or privilege etc. 2. to omit, to ignore as irrelevant, *do not exclude this possibility.* 3. to make impossible, to prevent. **ex·clu·sion** (ik-skloo-*zhŏn*) *n.*

ex·clu·sive (ik-skloo-siv) *adj.* 1. not admitting something else; *the schemes are mutually exclusive,* if you accept one you must reject the other. 2. (of groups or societies) admitting only certain carefully selected people to membership. 3. (of shops or their goods) catering only to the wealthy, expensive. 4. (of terms etc.) excluding all but what is specified. 5. (of an article in a newspaper or goods in a shop) not published or obtainable elsewhere. 6. done or held etc. so as to exclude everything else, *his exclusive occupation; we have the exclusive rights,* not shared with others. **exclusive** *adv.* not counting, *twenty men exclusive of our own.* **ex·clu′sive·ly** *adv.* **ex·clu′ sive·ness** *n.*

ex·com·mu·ni·cate (eks-kŏ-myoo-nĭ-kayt) *v.* (**ex·com·mu·ni·cat·ed, ex·com·mu·ni· cat·ing**) to cut off (a person) from participation in a religion, especially in its sacraments. **ex· com·mu·ni·ca·tion** (eks-kŏ-myoo-nĭ-kay-shŏn) *n.*

ex·co·ri·ate (ik-skohr-i-ayt) *v.* (**ex·co·ri·at·ed, ex·co·ri·at·ing**) 1. to remove part of the skin by abrasion, to strip or peel off (skin). 2. to denounce, to reproach harshly.

ex·cre·ment (ek-skrĕ-mĕnt) *n.* feces. **ex·cre· men·tal** (eks-krĕ-men-tăl) *adj.*

ex·cres·cence (ik-skres-ĕns) *n.* 1. an outgrowth, especially an abnormal one, on an animal body or a plant. 2. an ugly or disfiguring addition, as to a building. **ex·cres′cent** *adj.*

ex·cre·ta (ik-skree-tă) *n. pl.* waste matter expelled from the body, especially feces.

ex·crete (ik-skreet) *v.* (**ex·cret·ed, ex·cret· ing**) to separate and expel (waste matter) from the body or tissues. **ex·cre·tion** (ik-skree-shŏn) *n.*

ex·cre·to·ry (ek-skrĕ-tohr-ee) *adj.* of or used in excretion.

ex·cru·ci·at·ing (iks-kroo-shi-ay-ting) *adj.* intensely painful. **ex·cru′ci·at·ing·ly** *adv.*

ex·cul·pate (eks-kul-payt) *v.* (**ex·cul·pat·ed, ex·cul·pat·ing**) to free (a person) from blame, to clear of a charge of wrongdoing. **ex·cul·pa· tion** (eks-kul-pay-shŏn) *n.*

ex·cur·sion (ik-skur-*zhŏn*) *n.* 1. a short journey or ramble (returning afterward to the starting point). 2. a pleasure trip made by a number of people. **ex·cur′sion·ist** *n.*

ex·cur·sive (ik-skur-siv) *adj.* rambling in writing or speech.

ex·cus·a·ble (ik-skyoo-ză-bĕl) *adj.* able to be excused. **ex′cus·a·bly** *adv.*

ex·cuse (ik-skyooz) *v.* (**ex·cused, ex·cus· ing**) 1. to overlook or pardon (a slight offense or a person committing it) because of circumstances or some other reason. 2. (of a thing or circumstance) to justify a fault or error, *nothing can excuse such rudeness.* 3. to release from an obligation or duty, to grant exemption to. **excuse** (iks-kyoos) *n.* a reason put forward as a ground for excusing a fault etc. □**excuse me,** a polite apology for interrupting or disagreeing etc. **excuse oneself,** to ask permission or apologize for leaving.

ex div. *abbr.* ex dividend (*see* **ex**[1]).

exec. *abbr.* 1. executive. 2. executor.

ex·e·cra·ble (ek-sĕ-kră-bĕl) *adj.* abominable. **ex′e·cra·bly** *adv.*

ex·e·crate (ek-sĕ-krayt) *v.* (**ex·e·crat·ed, ex· e·crat·ing**) to detest greatly, to utter curses upon. **ex·e·cra·tion** (ek-sĕ-kray-shŏn) *n.*

ex·e·cute (ek-sĕ-kyoot) *v.* (**ex·e·cut·ed, ex· e·cut·ing**) 1. to carry out (an order), to put (a plan etc.) into effect. 2. to perform (an action or maneuver). 3. to produce (a work of art). 4. to make legally valid, as by signing, *execute a will.* 5. to inflict capital punishment on.

ex·e·cu·tion (ek-sĕ-kyoo-shŏn) *n.* 1. the carrying out or performance of something. 2. skill in playing sports, music, etc. 3. executing a condemned person.

ex·e·cu·tion·er (ek-sĕ-kyoo-shŏ-nĕr) *n.* a person who executes a condemned person.

ex·ec·u·tive (ig-zek-yŭ-tiv) *n.* a person or group that has administrative or managerial powers in a business or other organization, or with authority to put the laws or agreements etc. of a government into effect. **executive** *adj.* having the powers to execute plans or to put laws or agreements etc. into effect.

ex·ec·u·tor (ig-zek-yŭ-tŏr) *n.* a person appointed by a testator to carry out the terms of his or her will.

ex·ec·u·trix (ig-zek-yŭ-triks) *n.* a woman executor.

ex·e·ge·sis (ek-sĕ-jee-sis) *n.* (*pl.* **-ses,** *pr.* **-seez**) critical exposition or interpretation, especially of Scripture.

ex·em·plar (ig-zem-plăr) *n.* 1. a worthy model or pattern. 2. a typical example.

ex·em·pla·ry (ig-zem-plă-ree) *adj.* serving as an example; *exemplary conduct,* very good, an example to others; *exemplary damages,* very high damages, serving as a warning.

ex·em·pli·fy (ig-zem-plĭ-fı) *v.* (**ex·em·pli·fied, ex·em·pli·fy·ing**) to serve as an example of, *her life exemplifies devotion.* **ex·em·pli·fi·ca· tion** (ig-zem-plĭ-fi-kay-shŏn) *n.*

ex·empt (ig-zempt) *adj.* not liable, free from an obligation or payment etc. that is required of others or in other cases. **exempt** *v.* to make exempt. **ex·emp·tion** (ig-zemp-shŏn) *n.*

ex·er·cise (ek-sĕr-sız) *n.* 1. the using or application of mental powers of one's rights. 2. activity requiring physical exertion, done for the sake of health. 3. an activity or task designed for bodily or mental training; *military exercises,* a series of movements or operations designed for the training of troops. 4. an act of worship, *religious exercises.* **exercise** *v.* (**ex·er·cised, ex·er·cis·ing**) 1. to use or employ (mental powers, rights, etc.). 2. to take or cause to take exercise, to train by means of exercises. 3. to perplex, to worry. □**exercise book,** a book for writing in, especially by students. ▷Do not confuse *exercise* with *exorcise.*

ex·er·cis·er (ek-sĕr-sı-zĕr) *n.* a machine that assists a person in doing physical exercises.

ex·ert (ig-zurt) *v.* to bring (a quality or influence etc.) into use, *exert all one's strength.* □**exert oneself,** to make an effort.

ex·er·tion (ig-zur-shŏn) *n.* 1. exerting, being exerted. 2. a great effort.

ex·e·unt (ek-si-ŭnt) *v.* (*stage direction*) they leave the stage.

ex·hale (eks-hayl) *v.* (**ex·haled, ex·hal·ing**) to

breathe out. **ex·ha·la·tion** (eks-hă-lay-shŏn) *n.*
ex·haust (ig-zawst) *v.* 1. to use up completely. 2.
to make empty, to draw out all the contents of,
exhaust a well. 3. to tire out, *exhaust oneself.* 4.
to find out or say all there is to say about (a
subject); *exhaust the possibilities,* to try them all
in turn. **exhaust** *n.* 1. the expulsion or exit of
waste gases from an engine etc. 2. these gases.
3. the device through which they are sent out.
ex·haus·tion (ig-zaws-chŏn) *n.* 1. exhausting
something, being exhausted. 2. total loss of
strength.
ex·haus·tive (ig-zaws-tiv) *adj.* thorough, trying all
possibilities, *we made an exhaustive search.* **ex·
haus'tive·ly** *adv.* ▷Do not confuse *exhaustive*
with *exhausted* or *exhausting.*
ex·hib·it (ig-zib-it) *v.* to display, to present for the
public to see. **exhibit** *n.* a thing or collection of
things exhibited. **ex·hib'i·tor** *n.*
ex·hi·bi·tion (ek-sĭ-bish-ŏn) *n.* 1. exhibiting, being
exhibited. 2. a display or show, *an exhibition of
temper.* 3. a public display of works of art or
industrial products etc. or of a skilled performance. □**make an exhibition of oneself,** to
behave so that one appears ridiculous.
ex·hi·bi·tion·ism (ek-sĭ-bish-ŏ-niz-ĕm) *n.* a tendency toward exhibitionist behavior.
ex·hi·bi·tion·ist (ek-sĭ-bish-ŏ-nist) *n.* a person
who behaves in a way designed to attract attention
to himself. **exhibitionist** *adj.*
ex·hil·a·rate (ig-zil-ă-rayt) *v.* (**ex·hil·a·rat·
ed, ex·hil·a·rat·ing**) to make very happy or
lively. **ex·hil·a·ra·tion** (ig-zil-ă-ray-shŏn) *n.*
ex·hort (ig-zort) *v.* to urge or advise earnestly.
ex·hor·ta·tion (eg-zor-tay-shŏn) *n.*
ex·hume (ig-zoom, -zyoom) *v.* (**ex·humed, ex·
hum·ing**) to dig up (something buried, especially a corpse). **ex·hu·ma·tion** (egz-yoo-may-
shŏn) *n.*
ex·i·gen·cy (ek-si-jĕn-see) *n.* (*pl.* **-cies**) 1. an urgent need, *the exigencies of the situation.* 2. an
emergency.
ex·i·gent (ek-si-jĕnt) *adj.* 1. urgent. 2. exacting,
requiring much. **ex'i·gent·ly** *adv.*
ex·ig·u·ous (ig-zig-yoo-ŭs) *adj.* very small, scanty.
ex·ig·u·i·ty (eg-zĭ-gyoo-i-tee) *n.*
ex·ile (eg-zıl) *n.* 1. being sent away from one's
country as a punishment. 2. long absence from
one's country or home. 3. an exiled person. **exile**
v. (**ex·iled, ex·il·ing**) to send (a person) into
exile.
ex·ist (ig-zist) *v.* 1. to have place as part of what
is real, *do fairies exist?* 2. to have actual being
under specified conditions, to occur or be found.
3. continue living, *we cannot exist without food.*
ex·ist·ence (ig-zis-tĕns) *n.* 1. the state of existing,
occurrence, presence. 2. continuance in life or being, *the struggle for existence.*
ex·is·tent (ig-zis-tĕnt) *adj.* existing, actual, current.
ex·is·ten·tial·ism (eg-zis-ten-shă-liz-ĕm) *n.* a
philosophical theory emphasizing that man is responsible for his own actions and free to choose
his development and destiny. **ex·is·ten'tial·
ist** *adj. & n.*
ex·it (eg-zit, ek-sit) *v.* 1. *(stage direction)* he or she
leaves the stage. 2. to go out. **exit** *n.* 1. an actor's
or performer's departure from the stage. 2. the
act of going away or out, departure from a place
or position etc. 3. a passage or door to go out

by. □**exit visa,** permission to leave a country.
ex·o·bi·ol·o·gy (ek-soh-bı-ol-ŏ-jee) *n.* the study
of life outside Earth. **ex·o·bi·ol'o·gist** *n.* **ex·
o·bi·o·log·i·cal** (ek-soh-bı-ŏ-loj-i-kăl) *adj.*
ex·o·crine (ek-sŏ-krin) **gland** a gland that pours
out its secretions through a duct.
Exod. *abbr.* Exodus.
ex·o·dus (ek-sŏ-dŭs) *n.* 1. a departure of many
people. 2. *Exodus,* the second book of the Old
Testament, telling of the exodus of the Israelites
from Egypt.
ex of·fi·ci·o (eks ŏ-fish-i-oh) because of one's
official position, *the director is an ex officio member of this committee* or *is a member ex officio.*
▷Latin.
ex·og·e·nous (ek-soj-ĕ-nŭs) *adj.* growing or originating externally.
ex·on·er·ate (ig-zon-ĕ-rayt) *v.* (**ex·on·er·at·
ed, ex·on·er·at·ing**) to free from blame, to declare (a person) to be blameless. **ex·on·er·
a·tion** (ig-zon-ĕ-ray-shŏn) *n.*
exor. *abbr.* executor.
ex·or·bi·tant (ig-zor-bi-tănt) *adj.* (of a price or
demand) much too great.
ex·or·cise (ek-sŏr-sız) *v.* (**ex·or·cised, ex·
or·cis·ing**) 1. to drive out (an evil spirit) by
prayer. 2. to free (a person or place) of evil spirits.
ex·or·cism (ek-sor-siz-ĕm) *n.* **ex'or·cist** *n.*
▷Do not confuse *exorcise* with *exercise.*
ex·or·di·um (ig-zor-di-ŭm) *n.* (*pl.* **-di·ums,
-di·a,** *pr.* -di-ă) the beginning or introductory
part, especially of a discourse or treatise.
ex·o·skel·e·ton (ek-soh-skel-ĕ-tŏn) *n.* an external
bony or leathery covering of an animal, such as
the shell of a lobster.
ex·o·sphere (ek-sŏ-sfeer) *n.* the outermost layer
of Earth's atmosphere. **ex·o·spher·ic** (ek-sŏ-
sfer-ik) *adj.*
ex·o·ther·mic (ek-soh-thur-mik) *adj.* **ex·o·ther·
mal** (ek-soh-thur-măl) *adj.* liberating, as opposed
to absorbing, heat.
ex·ot·ic (ig-zot-ik) *adj.* 1. (of plants, words, or
fashions) introduced from abroad, not native. 2.
striking and attractive through being colorful or
unusual. **ex·ot'i·cal·ly** *adv.* **ex·ot·i·cism** (ig-
zot-ĭ-siz-ĕm) *n.* □**exotic dancer,** a striptease
dancer.
exp. *abbr.* 1. expenses. 2. experimental. 3. expired.
4. exponential. 5. export. 6. exportation. 7.
exported. 8. exporter. 9. express.
ex·pand (ik-spand) *v.* 1. to make or become larger,
to increase in bulk or importance. 2. to unfold
or spread out. 3. to give a fuller account of, to
write out in full (what is condensed or abbreviated). 4. to become genial, to throw off one's reserve. **ex·pand'er** *n.*
ex·panse (ik-spans) *n.* a wide area or extent of
open land or space, etc.
ex·pan·sion (ik-span-shŏn) *n.* expanding, increase,
extension.
ex·pan·sion·ism (ik-span-shŏ-niz-ĕm) *n.* a policy
or theory of expansion, especially of territory. **ex·
pan·sion·ist** *adj. & n.*
ex·pan·sive (ik-span-siv) *adj.* 1. able or tending
to expand. 2. (of a person or his manner) genial,
communicating thoughts and feelings readily. **ex·
pan'sive·ly** *adv.* **ex·pan'sive·ness** *n.*
ex par·te (eks pahr-tee) 1. on, or in the interests
of, one side only in a legal dispute. 2. made or
said thus, *an ex parte opinion.* ▷Latin.

ex·pa·ti·ate (ik-spay-shi-ayt) *v.* **(ex·pa·ti·at·ed, ex·pa·ti·at·ing)** to speak or write about (a subject) at great length or in detail. **ex·pa·ti·a·tion** (ik-spay-shi-ay-shŏn) *n.*

ex·pa·tri·ate (eks-pay-tri-ayt) *v.* **(ex·pa·tri·at·ed, ex·pa·tri·at·ing)** to banish, to withdraw (oneself) from one's native country and live abroad. **expatriate** (eks-pay-tri-it) *adj.* expatriated, living abroad. **expatriate** (eks-pay-tri-it) *n.* an expatriate person. **ex·pa·tri·a·tion** (eks-pay-tri-ay-shŏn) *n.*

ex·pect (ik-spekt) *v.* 1. to think or believe that (a thing) will happen or come, or that (a person) will come. 2. to wish for and be confident that one will receive, to consider necessary, *he expects obedience.* 3. to think, to suppose. □**be expecting,** *(informal)* to be pregnant. **expecting a baby,** pregnant.

ex·pect·an·cy (ik-spekt-ăn-see) *n.* a state of expectation. □**life expectancy,** the average period that persons of a certain age are expected to live.

ex·pect·ant (ik-spek-tănt) *adj.* filled with expectation. **ex·pect′ant·ly** *adv.* □**expectant mother,** a woman who is pregnant.

ex·pec·ta·tion (ek-spek-tay-shŏn) *n.* 1. expecting, looking forward with hope or pleasure. 2. a thing that is expected to happen. 3. the probability that a thing will happen. 4. *expectations,* prospects.

ex·pec·to·rant (ik-spek-tŏ-rănt) *n.* a medicine that causes a person to expectorate.

ex·pec·to·rate (ik-spek-tŏ-rayt) *v.* **(ex·pec·to·rat·ed, ex·pec·to·rat·ing)** to cough and spit out phlegm from the throat or lungs, to spit. **ex·pec·to·ra·tion** (ik-spek-tŏ-ray-shŏn) *n.*

ex·pe·di·ent (ik-spee-di-ĕnt) *adj.* 1. suitable for a particular purpose. 2. advantageous rather than right or just. (▷Do not confuse *expedient* with *expeditious.*) **expedient** *n.* a means of achieving something, a means to an end. **ex·pe′di·ent·ly** *adv.* **ex·pe′di·ence** *n.* **ex·pe′di·en·cy** *n.*

ex·pe·dite (ek-spĕ-dīt) *v.* **(ex·pe·dit·ed, ex·pe·dit·ing)** to help or hurry the progress of (business etc.), to perform (business) quickly. **ex′pe·dit·er** *n.*

ex·pe·di·tion (ek-spĕ-dish-ŏn) *n.* 1. a journey or voyage for a particular purpose. 2. the people or ships etc. making this. 3. promptness, speed, *solved it with expedition.*

ex·pe·di·tion·ar·y (ek-spĕ-dish-ŏ-ner-ee) *adj.* of or used in an expedition, *an expeditionary force.*

ex·pe·di·tious (ek-spĕ-dish-ŭs) *adj.* acting or done speedily and efficiently. **ex·pe·di′tious·ly** *adv.* ▷Do not confuse *expeditious* with *expedient.*

ex·pel (ik-spel) *v.* **(ex·pelled, ex·pel·ling)** 1. to force or send or drive out. 2. to compel (a person) to leave a school or country etc.

ex·pend (ik-spend) *v.* to spend (money, time, care, etc.), to use up.

ex·pend·a·ble (ik-spen-dă-běl) *adj.* 1. able to be expended. 2. not worth preserving, suitable for sacrificing in order to gain an objective.

ex·pend·i·ture (ik-spen-di-chŭr) *n.* 1. spending of money etc. 2. the amount expended.

ex·pense (ik-spens) *n.* 1. the cost or price of an activity. 2. a cause of spending money, *the car was a great expense.* 3. *expenses,* the amount spent in doing something, reimbursement for this. □**at the expense of,** so as to cause loss or damage to, *succeeded but at the expense of his health; had a good laugh at my expense,* by making fun of

me. **expense account,** a record of an employee's expenses to be paid by his employer.

ex·pen·sive (ik-spen-siv) *adj.* involving great expenditure, costing or charging more than the average. **ex·pen′sive·ly** *adv.* **ex·pen′sive·ness** *n.*

ex·pe·ri·ence (ik-speer-i-ĕns) *n.* 1. actual observation of facts or events, activity or practice in doing something. 2. skill or knowledge gained in this way. 3. an event or activity that gives one experience. **experience** *v.* **(ex·pe·ri·enced, ex·pe·ri·enc·ing)** to observe or share in (an event etc.) personally, to be affected by (a feeling).

ex·pe·ri·enced (ik-speer-i-ĕnst) *adj.* having knowledge or skill gained from much experience.

ex·pe·ri·en·tial (ik-speer-i-en-shăl) *adj.* of experience.

ex·per·i·ment (ik-sper-i-mĕnt) *n.* a test or trial carried out to see how something works or to find out what happens or to demonstrate a known fact. **experiment** (ik-sper-i-ment) *v.* to conduct an experiment. **ex·per′i·ment·er** *n.* **ex·per·i·men·ta·tion** (ik-sper-i-men-tay-shŏn) *n.*

ex·per·i·men·tal (ik-sper-i-men-tăl) *adj.* 1. of or used in or based on experiments. 2. still being tested. **ex·per·i·men′tal·ly** *adv.*

ex·pert (ek-spurt) *adj.* a person with great knowledge or skill in a particular thing. **expert** *adj.* having or showing great knowledge or skill. **ex·pert·ly** (eks-purt-lee) *adv.*

ex·pert·ise (ek-spĕr-teez) *n.* expert knowledge or skill.

ex·pi·ate (ek-spi-ayt) *v.* **(ex·pi·at·ed, ex·pi·at·ing)** to make amends for (wrongdoing). **ex·pi·a·tion** (ek-spi-ay-shŏn) *n.*

ex·pi·a·to·ry (ek-spi-ă-tohr-ee) *adj.* serving to make amends for (wrongdoing).

ex·pire (ik-spīr) *v.* **(ex·pired, ex·pir·ing)** 1. to breathe out (air). 2. to breathe one's last, to die. 3. to come to the end of its period of validity, *this license has expired.* **ex·pi·ra·tion** (ek-spī-ray-shŏn) *n.*

ex·plain (ik-splayn) *v.* 1. to make plain or clear, to show the meaning of. 2. to account for, *that explains his absence.* **ex·plain′a·ble** *adj.* **ex·plain′a·bly** *adv.* □**explain away,** to show why a fault etc. should not be blamed. **explain oneself,** to make one's meaning clear; to give an account of one's motives or conduct.

ex·pla·na·tion (ek-splă-nay-shŏn) *n.* 1. explaining. 2. a statement or fact that explains something.

ex·plan·a·to·ry (ik-splan-ă-tohr-ee) *adj.* serving or intended to explain something.

ex·ple·tive (ek-splĕ-tiv) *adj.* a violent or meaningless exclamation, an oath.

ex·pli·ca·ble (ek-splī-kă-běl) *adj.* able to be explained.

ex·pli·cate (ek-splī-kayt) *v.* **(ex·pli·cat·ed, ex·pli·cat·ing)** to make clear, to explain (a literary work etc.).

ex·plic·it (ik-splis-it) *adj.* stating something in exact terms, not merely implying things. **ex·plic′it·ly** *adv.* **ex·plic′it·ness** *n.*

ex·plode (ik-splohd) *v.* **(ex·plod·ed, ex·plod·ing)** 1. to expand suddenly with a loud noise because of the release of internal energy, to cause (a bomb etc.) to do this. 2. (of feelings) to burst out, (of a person) to show sudden violent emotion, *exploded with laughter.* 3. (of a population or a supply of goods etc.) to increase suddenly or rapidly. 4. to destroy (a theory) by showing it to

be false. □**exploded diagram,** one showing the parts of a structure in their relative positions but slightly separated from each other.
ex·ploit (ek-sploit) *n.* a bold or notable deed.
exploit (ik-sploit) *v.* 1. to work or develop (mines and other natural resources). 2. to take full advantage of, to use (workers, colonial possessions, etc.) for one's own advantage and without regard for theirs. **ex·ploi·ta·tion** (ek-sploi-tay-shŏn) *n.*
ex·plor·a·to·ry (ik-splohr-ă-tohr-ee) *adj.* for the purpose of exploring.
ex·plore (ik-splohr) *v.* **(ex·plored, ex·plor·ing)** 1. to travel into or through (a country etc.) in order to learn about it. 2. to examine by touch. 3. to examine or investigate (a problem, possibilities, etc.). **ex·plo·ra·tion** (ek-splŏ-ray-shŏn) *n.*
ex·plor·er (ik-splohr-ĕr) *n.* a person who explores unknown regions.
ex·plo·sion (ik-sploh-zhŏn) *n.* 1. exploding, being exploded, a loud noise caused by this. 2. a sudden outburst of anger, laughter, etc. 3. a sudden great increase, *the population explosion.*
ex·plo·sive (ik-sploh-siv) *adj.* 1. able to explode, tending to explode. 2. likely to cause violent and dangerous reactions, dangerously tense, *an explosive situation.* **explosive** *n.* an explosive substance.
ex·po (ek-spoh) *n.* (*pl.* **-pos**) (*informal*) an exposition (definition 2).
ex·po·nent (ik-spoh-nĕnt) *n.* 1. a person who sets out the facts or interprets something. 2. one who favors a particular theory or policy. 3. (in mathematics) a symbol indicating what power of a factor is to be taken, usually written at the upper right of the factor symbol. **ex·po·nen·tial** (ek-spŏ-nen-shăl) *adj.* **ex·po·nen'tial·ly** *adv.* □**exponential growth,** increasingly rapid growth.
ex·port (ik-spohrt, ek-spohrt) *v.* to send (goods etc.) to another country for sale. **export** (ek-spohrt) *n.* 1. exporting. 2. a thing exported. **ex·port'er** *n.* **ex·por·ta·tion** (ek-spohr-tay-shŏn) *n.*
ex·port·a·ble (ik-spohr-tă-bĕl) *adj.* able to be exported.
ex·pose (ik-spohz) *v.* **(ex·posed, ex·pos·ing)** 1. to leave (a person or thing) uncovered or unprotected, especially from the weather. 2. to subject to a risk etc. 3. to allow light to reach (photographic film or plate). 4. to make visible, to reveal. 5. to make known or reveal (a crime, fraud, impostor, etc.), to reveal the wrongdoings of (a person). □**expose oneself,** to expose one's body indecently.
ex·po·sé (ek-spoh-zay) *n.* public revelation of a scandal.
ex·posed (ik-spohzd) *adj.* (of a place) not sheltered.
ex·po·si·tion (ek-spŏ-zish-ŏn) *n.* 1. expounding, an explanatory account of a plan or theory etc. 2. a large public exhibition.
ex·pos·i·tor (ik-spoz-i-tŏr) *n.* a person who explains or expounds.
ex·pos·i·tor·y (ik-spoz-i-tohr-ee) *adj.* serving to clarify, expound, etc.; *expository writing,* exposition.
ex post fac·to (eks pohst fak-toh) acting or applying retrospectively. ▷ Latin.
ex·pos·tu·late (ik-spos-chŭ-layt) *v.* **(ex·pos·tu·lat·ed, ex·pos·tu·lat·ing)** to make a friendly protest, to reason or argue with a person.

ex·pos·tu·la·tion (ik-spos-chŭ-lay-shŏn) *n.*
ex·po·sure (ik-spoh-zhŭr) *n.* 1. exposing or being exposed to air or cold or danger etc.; *died of exposure,* from the effects of being exposed to cold. 2. the exposing of photographic film or plate to the light, the length of time for which this is done. 3. a section of film exposed as a unit. □**exposure meter,** a device measuring light and indicating the length of time needed for a photographic exposure.
ex·pound (ik-spownd) *v.* to set forth or explain in detail. **ex·pound'er** *n.*
ex·press (ik-spres) *adj.* 1. definitely stated, not merely implied. 2. going or sent quickly, designed for high speed, (of a train or elevator etc.) traveling rapidly to its destination with few or no intermediate stops. 3. (of a letter or parcel) delivered quickly by a special messenger or service. **express** *adv.* at high speed, by express service. **express** *n.* an express train. **express** *v.* 1. to make known (feelings or qualities). 2. to put (thought etc.) into words. 3. to represent by means of symbols, as in mathematics. 4. to press or squeeze out. 5. to send by express service. □**express oneself,** to communicate one's thoughts or feelings.
ex·press·i·ble (ik-spres-ĭ-bĕl) *adj.* able to be expressed.
ex·pres·sion (ik-spresh-ŏn) *n.* 1. expressing, being expressed. 2. a word or phrase. 3. a look that expresses one's feelings. 4. a manner of speaking or playing music in a way that shows feeling for the meaning. 5. a collection of mathematical symbols expressing a quantity.
ex·pres·sion·ism (ik-spresh-ŏ-niz-ĕm) *n.* a style of painting, drama, or music seeking to express the artist's or writer's emotional experience rather than represent the physical world realistically. **ex·pres·sion·ist** *n.* **ex·pres·sion·is·tic** (ik-spresh-ŏ-nis-tik) *adj.*
ex·pres·sion·less (ik-spresh-ŏn-lis) *adj.* without positive expression, not revealing one's thoughts or feelings, *an expressionless face.*
ex·pres·sive (ik-spres-iv) *adj.* 1. serving to express, *a tone expressive of contempt.* 2. full of expression, *an expressive voice.* **ex·pres·sive·ly** *adv.* **ex·pres'sive·ness** *n.*
ex·press·ly (ik-spres-lee) *adv.* 1. explicitly. 2. for a particular purpose.
ex·press·way (ik-spres-way) *n.* a limited-access highway for high-speed travel.
ex·pro·pri·ate (eks-proh-pri-ayt) *v.* **(ex·pro·pri·at·ed, ex·pro·pri·at·ing)** 1. to take away (property) by official action without an owner's approval. 2. to take and use (another's work, idea, etc.) as one's own. **ex·pro·pri·a·tion** (eks-proh-pri-ay-shŏn) *n.*
expt. *abbr.* experiment.
ex·pul·sion (ik-spul-shŏn) *n.* expelling, being expelled.
ex·pul·sive (ik-spul-siv) *adj.* expelling.
ex·punge (ik-spunj) *v.* **(ex·punged, ex·pung·ing)** to wipe out or rub out, to delete.
ex·pur·gate (ek-spŭr-gayt) *v.* **(ex·pur·gat·ed, ex·pur·gat·ing)** to remove objectionable matter from (a book etc.), to remove (such matter). **ex'pur·ga·tor** *n.* **ex·pur·ga·tion** (eks-spŭr-gay-shŏn) *n.*
expwy. *abbr.* expressway.
ex·qui·site (eks-kwiz-it, ik-skwiz-) *adj.* 1. having

special beauty. 2. having excellent discrimination, *exquisite taste in dress.* 3. acute, keenly felt, *exquisite pain.* **ex'qui•site•ly** *adv.*

ex•ser•vice•man (eks-sur-vis-man) *n.* (*pl.* **-men,** *pr.* -men) a male former member of the armed services.

ex•ser•vice•wom•an (eks-sur-vis-wuum-ăn) *n.* (*pl.* -wom•en, *pr.* -wim-in) a female former member of the armed services.

ext. *abbr.* 1. extension. 2. exterior. 3. external. 4. extinct. 5. extra. 6. extract.

ex•tant (ek-stănt) *adj.* still existing. ▷Do not confuse *extant* with *extent.*

ex•tem•po•ra•ne•ous (ik-stem-pŏ-ray-ni-ŭs) *adj.* unrehearsed, offhand. **ex•tem•po•ra'ne•ous•ly** *adv.*

ex•tem•po•re (ik-stem-pŏ-ree) *adj. & adv.* spoken or done without preparation, impromptu.

ex•tem•po•rize (ik-stem-pŏ-rīz) *v.* **(ex•tem•po•rized, ex•tem•po•riz•ing)** to speak or produce extempore. **ex•tem•po•ri•za•tion** (ik-stem-pŏ-ri-zay-shŏn) *n.*

ex•tend (ik-stend) *v.* 1. to make longer in space or time. 2. to stretch out (a hand or foot or limb etc.). 3. to reach, to be continuous over an area or from one point to another, *our land extends to the river.* 4. to enlarge, to increase the scope of. 5. to offer or grant, *extend a welcome.* 6. (of a task) to stretch the ability of (a person) fully. **ex'tend'er** *n.* ☐**extended family,** a family•in-cluding all relatives living near.

ex•tend•a•ble, ex•tend•i•ble (ik-sten-di-bĕl) *adj.* able to be extended.

ex•ten•si•ble (ik-sten-si-bĕl) *adj.* extendable.

ex•ten•sion (ik-sten-shŏn) *n.* 1. extending, being extended. 2. extent, range. 3. an addition or continuance, a section extended from the main part. 4. an additional period. 5. a subsidiary telephone distant from the main one, its number. 6. instruction by a university or college away from the institution proper, *extension courses.*

ex•ten•sive (ik-sten-siv) *adj.* 1. large in area, *extensive gardens.* 2. wide-ranging, large in scope, *extensive knowledge.* **ex•ten'sive•ly** *adv.* **ex•ten'sive•ness** *n.*

ex•tent (ik-stent) *n.* 1. the space over which a thing extends. 2. the range or scope of something, *the full extent of his power.* 3. a large area, *an extent of pasture.* ▷Do not confuse *extent* with *extant.*

ex•ten•u•ate (ik-sten-yoo-ayt) *v.* **(ex•ten•u•at•ed, ex•ten•u•at•ing)** to make (a person's guilt or offense) seem less great by providing a partial excuse, *extenuating circumstances.* **ex•ten•u•a•tion** (ik-sten-yoo-ay-shŏn) *n.*

ex•te•ri•or (ik-steer-i-ŏr) *adj.* on or coming from the outside. **exterior** *n.* an exterior surface or part or appearance.

ex•ter•mi•nate (ik-stur-mĭ-nayt) *v.* **(ex•ter•mi•nat•ed, ex•ter•mi•nat•ing)** to get rid of by destroying all members or examples of (a race, disease, etc.). **ex•ter'mi•na•tor** *n.* **ex•ter•mi•na•tion** (ik-stur-mi-nay-shŏn) *n.*

ex•tern (ek-sturn) *n.* a person having some association with an institution but not living in it, as a nonresident physician.

ex•ter•nal (ik-stur-năl) *adj.* 1. of or on the outside or visible part of something. 2. of or on the outside of the body, *for external use only.* 3. coming or obtained from an independent source, *external influences.* 4. belonging to the world outside a

person or people, not in the mind. **external** *n.* the outside or visible part. **ex•ter'nal•ly** *adv.*

ex•tinct (ik-stingkt) *adj.* 1. no longer burning, (of a volcano) no longer active. 2. no longer existing in living form, *extinct animals.*

ex•tinc•tion (ik-stingk-shŏn) *n.* 1. extinguishing, being extinguished. 2. making or becoming extinct.

ex•tin•guish (ik-sting-gwish) *v.* 1. to put out (a light or fire or flame). 2. to end the existence of (hope, passion, etc.). **ex•tin'guish•a•ble** *adj.* **ex•tin•guish•er** (ik-sting-gwi-shĕr) *n.* a device for discharging liquid chemicals or foam to extinguish a fire.

ex•tir•pate (ek-stĭr-payt) *v.* **(ex•tir•pat•ed, ex•tir•pat•ing)** to root out and destroy completely. **ex•tir•pa'tion** *n.*

ex•tol (ik-stohl) *v.* **(ex•tolled, ex•tol•ling)** to praise enthusiastically.

ex•tort (ik-stort) *v.* to obtain by force or threats or intimidation etc.

ex•tor•tion (ik-stor-shŏn) *n.* extorting (especially money). **ex•tor'tion•er** *n.* **ex•tor'tion•ist** *n.*

ex•tor•tion•ate (ik-stor-shŏ-nit) *adj.* excessively high in price, (of demands) excessive. **ex•tor'tion•ate•ly** *adv.*

ex•tra (ek-stră) *adj.* additional, more than is usual or expected. **extra** *adv.* more than usually, *extra strong.* **extra** *n.* 1. an extra thing, something additional. 2. a thing for which an additional charge is made. 3. a special issue of a newspaper etc. 4. a person engaged temporarily for a minor part or to form one of a crowd in a motion picture.

extra- *prefix* situated outside or not coming within the scope of, as in *extralegal.*

ex•tract (ik-strakt) *v.* 1. to take out by force or effort (something firmly fixed). 2. to obtain (money, information, etc.) from someone unwilling to give it. 3. to obtain (juice) by suction or pressure, to obtain (a substance) as an extract. 4. to obtain (information from a book etc.), to take or copy passages from (a book). 5. to derive (pleasure etc.) from. **extract** (ek-strakt) *n.* 1. a substance separated from another by dissolving it or by other treatment. 2. a concentrated substance prepared from another. 3. a passage from a book, play, film, or music. **ex•tract'a•ble** *adj.* **ex•tract'or** *n.*

ex•trac•tion (ik-strak-shŏn) *n.* 1. extracting. 2. descent, lineage, *he is of Polish extraction.*

ex•tra•cur•ric•u•lar (ek-stră-kŭ-rik-yŭ-lăr) *adj.* not coming within the curriculum, as school activities or sports.

ex•tra•dit•a•ble (ek-stră-dī-tă-bĕl) *adj.* liable to extradition, (of a crime) warranting extradition.

ex•tra•dite (ek-stră-dīt) *v.* **(ex•tra•dit•ed, ex•tra•dit•ing)** 1. to hand over (a person accused or convicted of a crime) to the country where the crime was committed. 2. to obtain (such a person) for trial or punishment. **ex•tra•di•tion** (ek-stră-dish-ŏn) *n.*

ex•tra•ga•lac•tic (ek-stră-gă-lak-tik) *adj.* outside the Milky Way.

ex•tra•le•gal (ek-stră-lee-găl) *adj.* beyond legal authority, not regulated by law.

ex•tra•mar•i•tal (ek-stră-mar-i-tăl) *adj.* of sexual relationships outside marriage.

ex•tra•mu•ral (ek-stră-myoor-ăl) *adj.* (of university teaching, studies, or sports) away from the campus.

ex·tra·ne·ous (ik-stray-ni-ŭs) *adj*. 1. of external origin. 2. not belonging to the matter or subject in hand. **ex·tra′ne·ous·ly** *adv*. **ex·tra′ne·ous·ness** *n*.

ex·traor·di·nary (ik-stror-dĭ-ner-ee) *adj*. 1. very unusual or remarkable. 2. beyond what is usual or ordinary, *an extraordinary general meeting*. **ex·traor·di·nar′i·ly** *adv*.

ex·trap·o·late (ik-strap-ŏ-layt) *v*. (**ex·trap·o·lat·ed**, **ex·trap·o·lat·ing**) to make an estimate of (something unknown and outside the range of one's data) on the basis of available data. **ex·trap·o·la·tion** (ik-strap-ŏ-lay-shŏn) *n*.

ex·tra·sen·so·ry (ek-stră-sen-sŏ-ree) *adj*. (of perception) achieved by some means other than the five senses.

ex·tra·ter·res·tri·al (ek-stră-tĕ-res-tri-ăl) *adj*. of or from outside Earth or its atmosphere.

ex·tra·ter·ri·to·ri·al (ek-stră-ter-i-tohr-i-ăl) *adj*. 1. located outside of territorial boundaries. 2. free from jurisdiction of the territory in which one resides, as diplomats etc. **ex·tra·ter·ri·to′ri·al·ly** *adv*.

ex·tra·u·ter·ine (ek-stră-yoo-tĕ-rin) *adj*. developing outside the uterus.

ex·trav·a·gant (ik-strav-ă-gănt) *adj*. 1. spending much more than is necessary. 2. (of prices) excessively high. 3. (of ideas or praise or behavior etc.) going beyond what is reasonable, not properly controlled. **ex·trav′a·gant·ly** *adv*. **ex·trav′a·gance** *n*.

ex·trav·a·gan·za (ik-strav-ă-gan-ză) *n*. 1. a fanciful composition in music. 2. a lavish spectacular film or theatrical production.

ex·tra·ve·hic·u·lar (ek-stră-vee-hik-yŭ-lăr) *adj*. outside a vehicle, especially a spacecraft. ☐**extravehicular activity**, work performed outside a spacecraft in flight.

ex·tra·vert = extrovert.

ex·treme (ik-streem) *adj*. 1. very great or intense, *extreme cold*. 2. at the end(s), furthest, farthest or outermost, *the extreme edge*. 3. going to great lengths in actions or views, not moderate. **extreme** *n*. 1. either end of anything. 2. an extreme degree or act or condition. **ex·treme′ly** *adv*. ☐**extremely high frequency**, any radio frequency in the range between 30,000 and 300,000 megahertz. **extreme unction**, *(formerly)* in the Roman Catholic Church, the anointing of a dying person by a priest. **go to extremes**, to take an extreme course of action. **in the extreme**, to an extreme degree.

ex·trem·ism (ik-stree-miz-ĕm) *n*. advocacy of extreme views, especially in politics. **ex·tre′mist** *n*.

ex·trem·i·ty (ik-strem-i-tee) *n*. (*pl*. -ties) 1. an extreme point, the end of something. 2. an extreme degree of feeling or need or danger etc. 3. *extremities*, the hands and feet.

ex·tri·ca·ble (ek-stri-kă-bĕl) *adj*. able to be extricated.

ex·tri·cate (ek-stri-kayt) *v*. (**ex·tri·cat·ed**, **ex·tri·cat·ing**) to disentangle or release from an entanglement or difficulty etc. **ex·tri·ca·tion** (ek-stri-kay-shŏn) *n*.

ex·trin·sic (ek-strin-sik) *adj*. 1. originating from outside, external. 2. not belonging to the basic nature of a person or thing. **ex·trin′si·cal·ly** *adv*. ▷Do not confuse *extrinsic* with *intrinsic*.

ex·tro·vert (ek-strŏ-vurt) *n*. a person more interested in the people and things around him than

in his own thoughts and feelings, a lively sociable person. **extrovert** *adj*. extroverted. **ex·tro·ver·sion** (ek-strŏ-vur-zhŏn) *n*.

ex·tro·vert·ed (ek-strŏ-vur-tid) *adj*. having the characteristics of an extrovert.

ex·trude (ik-strood) *v*. (**ex·trud·ed**, **ex·trud·ing**) 1. to thrust or squeeze out. 2. to shape (metal or plastic etc.) by forcing through a die. **ex·trud′er** *n*. **ex·tru·sion** (ik-stroo-zhŏn) *n*.

ex·tru·sive (ik-stroo-siv) *adj*. forced out (as molten matter) through Earth's crust.

ex·u·ber·ant (ig-zoo-bĕ-rănt) *adj*. 1. full of high spirits, very lively. 2. growing profusely, *plants with exuberant foliage*. **ex·u′ber·ant·ly** *adv*. **ex·u′ber·ance** *n*.

ex·ude (ig-zood) *v*. (**ex·ud·ed**, **ex·ud·ing**) 1. to ooze out, to give off like sweat or a smell. 2. to show (pleasure, confidence etc.) freely. **ex·u·date** (eks-yŭ-dayt) *n*. a substance that has been exuded. **ex·u·da·tion** (eks-yŭ-day-shŏn) *n*.

ex·ult (ig-zult) *v*. to rejoice greatly. **ex·ul·ta·tion** (eg-zül-tay-shŏn) *n*. ▷Do not confuse *exultation* with *exaltation*.

ex·ult·ant (ig-zul-tănt) *adj*. exulting. **ex·ult′ant·ly** *adv*.

ex·urb (ek-surb) *n*. a prosperous area beyond the suburbs. **ex·ur·bi·a** (ek-sur-bi-ă) *n*.

ex·ur·ban·ite (ek-sur-bă-nıt) *n*. a person who lives in an exurb.

-ey *suffix* used to form adjectives from nouns ending in *y*, as in *clayey*.

eye (ı) *n*. 1. the organ of sight in man and animals. 2. the iris of this, *blue eyes*. 3. the part of the face around it, *gave him a black eye*. 4. the power of seeing, observation, *sharp eyes*. 5. a thing like an eye, the spot on a peacock's tail, the leaf bud of a potato. 6. the hole in a needle, through which thread is passed. 7. a relatively calm spot at the center of a storm. **eye** *v*. (**eyed**, **eye·ing**) to look at, to watch. ☐**an eye for an eye**, retaliation in the same form as the injury done. **cast** *or* **run an eye over**, to examine quickly. **eye drops**, drops used to soothe the eyes. **eye shadow**, a cosmetic applied to the upper eyelid. **in the eyes of**, in the opinion or judgment of. **keep an eye on**, to watch carefully, to take care of. **keep one's eyes open** *or* **peeled**, to watch carefully, to be observant. **make eyes at**, to gaze at flirtatiously. **see eye to eye**, to be in full agreement with a person. **with an eye to**, with the aim or intention of. **with one's eyes open**, with full awareness.

eye·ball (ı-bawl) *n*. the ball of the eye, within the lids. ☐**eyeball to eyeball**, *(informal)* confronting a person closely. **up to the eyeballs**, *(informal)*, deeply involved or occupied in something.

eye-bank (ı-bangk) *n*. a depository for corneas from the recently dead for transplanting into the eyes of those who need them.

eye·brow (ı-brow) *n*. the fringe of hair growing on the ridge above the eye socket.

eye-catcher (ı-kach-ĕr) *n*. *(informal)* something that attracts attention because of its appearance. **eye·drop·per** (ı-drop-ĕr) *n*. a dropper for administering medicine to the eye.

eye·ful (ı-fuul) *n*. (*pl*. -fuls) 1. something thrown or blown into one's eye, *got an eyeful of sand*. 2. *(informal)* a thorough look, *having an eyeful*. 3. *(informal)* a remarkable or attractive sight, especially a desirable woman.

eye·glass (ɪ-glas) *n.* 1. a lens for correcting or assisting defective sight. 2. *eyeglasses,* a pair of these held in position by a frame.

eye·lash (ɪ-lash) *n.* one of the fringe of hairs on the edge of each eyelid.

eye·less (ɪ-lis) *adj.* having no eyes.

eye·let (ɪ-lit) *n.* 1. a small hole through which a rope or cord etc. is passed. 2. a metal ring strengthening this.

eye·lid (ɪ-lid) *n.* either of the two folds of skin that can be moved together to cover the eyeball.

eye·lin·er (ɪ-lɪ-nĕr) *n.* a cosmetic applied as a line around the eye.

eye-o·pen·er (ɪ-oh-pĕ-nĕr) *n.* an enlightening or surprising circumstance.

eye·piece (ɪ-pees) *n.* the lens or lenses to which the eye is applied at the end of a telescope or microscope etc.

eye·sight (ɪ-sɪt) *n.* 1. the ability to see. 2. range of vision, *within eyesight.*

eye·sore (ɪ-sohr) *n.* a thing that is ugly to look at.

eye·strain (ɪ-strayn) *n.* weariness of the eyes from excessive or incorrect use.

eye·tooth (ɪ-tooth) *n.* (*pl.* -**teeth**) a canine tooth in the upper jaw, under the eye.

eye·wash (ɪ-wosh) *n.* 1. a lotion for the eye. 2. *(slang)* talk or behavior intended to create a misleadingly good impression.

eye·wit·ness (ɪ-wit-nis) *n.* a person who actually saw an accident or crime etc. take place.

ey·rie = **aerie.**

E·ze·ki·el (ĕ-zee-ki-ĕl) *n.* 1. a Hebrew prophet of the 6th century B.C. 2. a book of the Old Testament containing his prophecies.

Ez·ra (ez-rä) *n.* 1. a Hebrew scribe and priest of the 5th century B.C. 2. a book of the Old Testament dealing with the return of the Israelites from Babylon and the rebuilding of the Temple.

F

F, f (ef) (*pl.* **Fs, F's, f's**) 1. the sixth letter of the alphabet. 2. *F*, a grade rating for failing school work.
f *symbol* focal length.
F *abbr.* 1. Fahrenheit. 2. French.
F *symbol* fluorine.
f. *abbr.* 1. false. 2. family. 3. female. 4. forte². 5. frequency.
fa (fah) *n.* (a name for) the fourth note of a scale in music.
FAA *abbr.* Federal Aviation Agency.
Fa·bi·an (fay-bi-ăn) *adj.* of the principles of or of the Fabian Society itself. (▷ The Fabian Society was organized in England in 1884 to promote socialist principles.) **Fabian** *n.* a member of or sympathizer with the Fabian Society. **Fa'bi·an·ism** *n.*
fa·ble (fay-běl) *n.* 1. a short story not based on fact, often with animals as characters and conveying a moral. 2. these stories or legends collectively. 3. untrue statements, *sort out fact from fable.*
fa·bled (fay-běld) *adj.* told of in fables, legendary.
fab·ric (fab-rik) *n.* 1. cloth, woven or knitted or felted material. 2. a plastic resembling this. 3. the framework or structure of something, *the fabric of modern society.*
fab·ri·cate (fab-ri-kayt) *v.* (**fab·ri·cat·ed, fab·ri·cat·ing**) 1. to construct, to manufacture. 2. to invent (a story), to forge (a document). **fab'ri·ca·tor** *n.* **fab·ri·ca·tion** (fab-ri-kay-shŏn) *n.*
fab·u·lous (fab-yŭ-lŭs) *adj.* 1. told of in fables. 2. incredibly great, *fabulous wealth.* 3. *(informal)* wonderful, marvelous. **fab'u·lous·ly** *adv.*
fac. *abbr.* 1. facsimile. 2. factor. 3. factory. 4. faculty.
fa·cade (fă-sahd) *n.* 1. the principal face or the front of a building. 2. an outward appearance, especially a deceptive one.
face (fays) *n.* 1. the front part of the head from forehead to chin. 2. the expression shown by its features, *a cheerful face; make a face,* make a grimace. 3. the outward show or aspect of something, *put a good face on things.* 4. the front or facade or right side of something, the dial of a clock, the distinctive side of a playing card. 5. the end of a coal mine or quarry in which digging is (or was) going on. 6. the striking surface of a golf club etc., the working surface of a tool. 7. the working surface of a printing type or plate.
face *v.* (**faced, fac·ing**) 1. to have or turn the face toward (a certain direction). 2. to be opposite to. 3. to meet confidently or defiantly, to accept and be prepared to deal with (unpleasant facts or problems). 4. to meet (an opponent) in a contest. 5. to present itself, *the problem that faces us.* 6. to cover (a surface) with a layer of different material, to put a facing on (a garment etc.).

□**face the music,** to face unpleasant consequences bravely. **face up to,** to face (a difficulty etc.) resolutely. **face value,** the value printed or stamped on money; *take a thing at its face value,* assume that it is genuinely what it seems to be. **have the face,** to be impudent enough. **in the face of,** despite. **lose face,** to suffer loss of prestige through a humiliation. **on the face of it,** judging by appearances. **put a good face on it,** to make an outward show of cheerful acceptance of something. **save face,** prevent (a person) from losing prestige. **to one's face,** openly in one's presence.
face·cloth (fays-klawth) *n.* a cloth for washing one's face.
face·less (fays-lis) *adj.* 1. without a face. 2. without identity. 3. purposely not identifiable. **face'less·ness** *n.*
face·lift (fays-lift) *n.* (also **face lifting**) 1. plastic surgery on the face to improve its appearance. 2. *(informal)* an alteration etc. that improves the appearance, as of a building.
face-off (fays-awf) *n.* (in ice hockey) the dropping of the puck between two opposing players by the referee to initiate play.
face·sav·ing (fays-say-ving) *adj.* protecting one's status or dignity, *a facesaving gesture.*
fac·et (fas-it) *n.* 1. one of the many sides of a cut stone or jewel. 2. one aspect of a situation or problem.
fa·ce·tious (fă-see-shŭs) *adj.* intended or intending to be amusing. **fa·ce'tious·ly** *adv.* **fa·ce'tious·ness** *n.*
face-to-face (fays-too-fays) *adv.* 1. in someone's presence. 2. confronting a person or danger etc.
fa·cial (fay-shăl) *adj.* of the face. **facial** *n.* a beauty treatment for the face.
fac·ile (fas-il) *adj.* 1. easily done. 2. (of a person) able to do something easily, *a facile speaker.* 3. achieved easily but without attention to quality, superficial, *a facile solution.*
fa·cil·i·tate (fă-sil-i-tayt) *v.* (**fa·cil·i·tat·ed, fa·cil·i·tat·ing**) to make easy, to lessen the difficulty of. **fa·cil·i·ta·tion** (fă-sil-i-tay-shŏn) *n.*
fa·cil·i·ty (fă-sil-i-tee) *n.* (*pl.* **-ties**) 1. the quality of being easy, absence of difficulty. 2. ease in doing something, *reads music with great facility.* 3. an aid, equipment, structure, etc. that makes it easy to do something, *you shall have every facility; sports facilities.* ▷ Do not confuse *facility* with *faculty.*
fac·ing (fay-sing) *n.* 1. an outer layer covering a surface. 2. a layer of material covering part of a garment etc. for contrast or to strengthen it.
fac·sim·i·le (fak-sim-ĭ-lee) *n.* 1. a reproduction of a document or book or painting etc. 2. a system of producing this by radio or telephone trans-

mission of signals from scanning the original.
fact (fakt) *n.* 1. something known to have happened
or to be true or to exist. 2. a thing asserted to
be true as a basis for reasoning, *his facts are disputed.* □**after the fact,** after something has occurred or become known. **facts of life,** *(informal)*
knowledge of human sexual functions. **in fact,**
in reality.
fac·tion (fak-shŏn) *n.* a small united group within
a larger one, especially in politics. **fac′tion·al**
adj. **fac′tion·al·ism** *n.*
fac·tious (fak-shŭs) *adj.* 1. having factions. 2. creating dissension. ▷Do not confuse *factious* with
fractious.
fac·ti·tious (fak-tish-ŭs) *adj.* artificial. **fac·ti′**
tious·ly *adv.*
fac·tor (fak-tŏr) *n.* 1. a circumstance or influence
that contributes to a result; *safety factor,* the margin of security against risks. 2. one of the numbers
or mathematical expressions by which a larger
number etc. can be divided exactly, *2, 3, 4, and
6 are factors of 12.* 3. a person or company that
finances the accounts of businesses. **factor** *v.* 1.
to separate into mathematical factors. 2. to finance
(business accounts).
fac·to·ri·al (fak-tohr-i-ăl) *n.* the product of a positive integer and all its lesser positive integers.
factorial *adj.* of a factor or a factorial.
fac·to·ry (fak-tŏ-ree) *n.* (*pl.* **-ries**) a building or
buildings in which goods are manufactured.
□**factory ship,** a fishing vessel that processes
its catch while at sea.
fac·to·tum (fak-toh-tŭm) *n.* a servant or assistant
doing all kinds of work.
fac·tu·al (fak-choo-ăl) *adj.* based on or containing
facts. **fac′tu·al·ly** *adv.*
fac·u·la (fak-yŭ-lă) *n.* (*pl.* **-lae,** *pr.* -lee) a bright
spot or streak on the sun.
fac·ul·ty (fak-ŭl-tee) *n.* (*pl.* **-ties**) 1. any of the
powers of the body or mind, *the faculty of sight;
he has lost his faculties.* 2. a particular kind of
ability, *a faculty for learning languages.* 3. a department teaching a particular subject in a university or college, *the faculty of law.* 4. the entire
teaching and administrative staff of a university
etc. ▷Do not confuse *faculty* with *facility.*
fad (fad) *n.* a person's particular like or dislike,
a craze. **fad′dish** *adj.* **fad′dish·ly** *adv.* **fad′**
dist *n.*
fade (fayd) *v.* (**fad·ed, fad·ing**) 1. to lose or cause
to lose color, freshness, or vigor. 2. to disappear
gradually, to become indistinct. 3. to cause (the
sound or picture in radio, film, etc.) to decrease
(*fade out*) or increase (*fade in*) gradually.
fade-in (fayd-in), **fade-out** (fayd-out) *n.* the
fading in or out of the sound or picture in radio,
film, etc.
FAdm *abbr.* Fleet Admiral.
fae·ces = feces.
fag (fag) *v.* (**fagged, fag·ging**) (of work) to make
tired. □**fag end,** an inferior or worthless remnant. **fagged out,** tired out.
fag·ot (fag-ŏt) *n.* a bundle of sticks or twigs bound
together.
fag·ot·ing (fag-ŏ-ting) *n.* embroidery in which
threads are fastened together like fagots.
Fah., Fahr. *abbr.* Fahrenheit.
Fahr·en·heit (far-ĕn-hıt) *adj.* of or using a temperature scale (**Fahrenheit scale**) with 32° being
the freezing point and 212° the boiling point of
water.

fa·ïence, fa·ience (fay-ahns, fı-) *n.* brilliantly
glazed earthenware or porcelain.
fail (fayl) *v.* 1. to be unsuccessful in what is attempted. 2. to be or become insufficient, (of crops)
to produce a very poor harvest. 3. to become weak
or ineffective, to cease functioning, *the engine
failed.* 4. to neglect or forget or be unable to do
something, *he failed to appear.* 5. to disappoint
the hopes of. 6. to become bankrupt. 7. to grade
(a candidate) as not having passed an examina-
tion. **fail** *n.* failure in an examination. □**fail safe,**
(of equipment) to revert to a danger-free condition
in the event of a breakdown or other failure. **without fail,** for certain, whatever happens.
failed (fayld) *adj.* unsuccessful, *a failed author.*
fail·ing (fay-ling) *n.* a weakness or fault, *a human
failing.* **failing** *prep.* if (a thing) does not happen,
if (a person) is not available.
faille (fıl) *n.* a closely woven silk, rayon, or cotton
fabric.
fail-safe (fayl-sayf) **device** one that ensures a safe
condition in the event of a breakdown or other
failure in equipment.
fail·ure (fayl-yŭr) *n.* 1. failing, nonperformance of
something, lack of success. 2. the ceasing of mechanism or power or a part of the body etc. to function, *heart failure.* 3. becoming bankrupt. 4. an
unsuccessful person or thing or attempt.
fain (fayn) *adj.* *(old use)* willing. **fain** *adv.* *(old use)*
willingly.
faint (faynt) *adj.* 1. not clearly perceived by the
senses, indistinct, not intense in color or sound
or smell. 2. weak, vague, *a faint hope.* 3. timid,
feeble. 4. about to lose consciousness. **faint** *v.*
to lose consciousness temporarily through failure
in the supply of blood to the brain. **faint** *n.*
an act or state of fainting. **faint′ly** *adv.* **faint′**
ness *n.*
faint·heart·ed (faynt-hahr-tid) *adj.* timid. **faint′**
heart·ed·ly *adv.*
fair[1] (fair) *n.* 1. a periodical gathering for the sale
of goods, often with shows and entertainments.
2. an exhibition of commercial or industrial goods.
3. an exhibition of agricultural produce, farm animals, etc.
fair[2] *adj.* 1. (of the hair or skin) light in color, (of
a person) having fair hair. 2. *(old use)* beautiful.
3. (of weather) fine, (of winds) favorable. 4. just,
unbiased, in accordance with the rules. 5. of moderate quality or amount. **fair** *adv.* in a fair manner.
fair′ness *n.* □**fair and square,** straightforwardly, aboveboard; exactly. **fair copy,** a neat
copy of a corrected document. **fair enough!,**
(informal) I agree to your conditions. **fair play,**
equal opportunities and treatment for all. **fair
shake,** *(slang)* an equal chance (to get a job etc.).
in a fair way to, at the stage where something
is likely, *he's in a fair way to succeed.* **in all fairness,** legitimately. **the fair sex,** women.
fair·ground (fair-grownd) *n.* a site for fairs, horse
races, etc.
fair-haired (fair-haird) *adj.* having fair hair. □**fair-
haired boy,** *(slang)* a boy or man favored by
his superiors.
fair·ing (fair-ing) *n.* a structure added to the exterior of a ship or aircraft etc. to streamline it.
fair·ly (fair-lee) *adv.* 1. in a fair manner. 2. moderately, *fairly difficult.* 3. actually, *fairly jumped
for joy.*
fair-spo·ken (fair-spoh-kĕn) *adj.* polite.
fair-trade (fair-trayd) *v.* (**fair-trad·ed, fair-trad·**

ing) to sell (merchandise) at a price set by the manufacturer.

fair·way (fair-way) *n.* **1.** the part of a golf course between tee and green, kept free of rough grass. **2.** an unobstructed passage, especially a navigable channel.

fair·y (fair-ee) *n.* (*pl.* **fair·ies**) an imaginary small being supposed to have magical powers. ☐**fairy godmother,** a benefactress who provides a sudden unexpected gift. **fairy story, fairy tale,** a tale about fairies or magic; an incredible story; a falsehood. **fair·y·land** (fair-ee-land) *n.* **1.** the world of fairies. **2.** a very beautiful place.

fait ac·com·pli (fayt ă-kom-plee) (*pl.* **faits ac·com·plis,** *pr.* fayts ă-kom-plee) a thing that is already done and not reversible. ▷French.

faith (fayth) *n.* **1.** reliance or trust in a person or thing. **2.** belief in religious doctrine. **3.** a system of religious belief, *the Christian faith.* **4.** loyalty, sincerity. ☐**break faith,** to break one's promise or loyalty. **faith cure,** something that heals a person because he believes that it will do so. **faith healer,** a person who practices **faith healing,** healing by prayer, not by medical skill. **in good faith,** with honest intention.

faith·ful (fayth-fŭl) *adj.* **1.** loyal, trustworthy, conscientious. **2.** true to the facts, accurate. **3.** *the faithful,* true believers (especially Muslims), loyal supporters. **faith′ful·ly** *adv.* **faith′ful·ness** *n.*

faith·less (fayth-lis) *adj.* **1.** lacking religious faith. **2.** false to promises, disloyal. **faith′less·ly** *adv.* **faith′less·ness** *n.*

fake (fayk) *n.* **1.** something that looks genuine but is not, a forgery. **2.** a person who tries to deceive others by pretending to be something that he is not. **fake** *adj.* faked, not genuine. **fake** *v.* **(faked, fak·ing) 1.** to make (a thing) that looks genuine, in order to deceive people. **2.** to pretend, *he faked illness.* **fak′er** *n.* ▷Do not confuse *faker* with *fakir.*

fa·kir (fă-keer, fay-kĭr) *n.* a Muslim or Hindu religious beggar regarded as a holy man. ▷Do not confuse *fakir* with *faker.*

fal·chion (fawl-chŏn) *n.* a broad curved convex-edged sword.

fal·con (fawl-kŏn) *n.* a small long-winged hawk. **fal·con·ry** (fawl-kŏn-ree) *n.* the breeding and training of hawks.

fall (fawl) *v.* **(fell, fall·en, fall·ing) 1.** to come or go down freely, as by force of weight or loss of balance or becoming detached. **2.** to come as if by falling, *silence fell.* **3.** to lose one's position or office, *fell from power.* **4.** to hang down. **5.** to decrease in amount or number or intensity, *prices fell; her spirits fell,* she became depressed. **6.** to slope downward. **7.** (of the face) to show dismay. **8.** to die in battle. **9.** (of a fortress or city) to be captured. **10.** to take a specified direction or place, *his glance fell on me.* **11.** to come by chance or be assigned as what one must have or do, *the job falls to you.* **12.** to happen to come, *fell into bad company.* **13.** to pass into a specified state, to become, *fall in love; fell asleep.* **14.** to occur, to have as a date, *Easter fell early.* **fall** *n.* **1.** the act of falling. **2.** giving way to temptation; *the Fall (of man),* Adam's sin and its results. **3.** the amount by which something falls. **4.** autumn. **5.** a throw in a wrestling match. **6.** (also *falls*) a waterfall. **7.** a woman's hairpiece. ☐**fall back,** to retreat. **fall back on,** to turn to for help when

something else has failed. **fall down on,** to fail in. **fall flat,** to fail to produce a result, to fail to produce the desired result. **fall for,** (*informal*) to fall in love with; to be taken in by (a deception). **fall foul of,** to collide with; to get into trouble with. **fall from grace,** to backslide or sin. **fall guy,** (*slang*) an easy victim; a scapegoat. **fall in,** to take one's place in a military formation, to cause (troops) to do this; (of a building) to collapse inward. **falling out,** a quarrel. **falling sickness,** (*old use*) epilepsy. **falling star,** a meteor. **fall into line,** to conform to a certain course of action. **fall in with,** to meet by chance; to agree to. **fall line,** a transition area between an upland and a lowland. **fall off,** to decrease in size or number or quality. **fall out,** to quarrel; to happen; to leave one's place in a military formation, to cause (troops) to do this. **fall over oneself,** to be very awkward; to be very hasty or eager. **fall short,** to be insufficient or inadequate. **fall short of,** to fail to obtain or reach. **fall through,** (of a plan) to fail, to come to nothing. **fall to,** to begin working or fighting or eating.

fal·la·cious (fă-lay-shŭs) *adj.* containing a fallacy. **fal·la·cy** (fal-ă-see) *n.* (*pl.* **-cies**) **1.** a false or mistaken belief. **2.** false reasoning.

fal·li·ble (fal-ĭ-bĕl) *adj.* liable to make mistakes. **fal·li·bil·i·ty** (fal-ĭ-bil-i-tee) *n.*

Fal·lo·pi·an tube (fă-loh-pi-ăn) *n.* either of the two tubes carrying egg cells from the ovaries to the womb.

fall·out (fawl-owt) *n.* **1.** airborne radioactive debris from a nuclear explosion. **2.** side effects.

fal·low[1] (fal-oh) *adj.* (of land) plowed but left unplanted in order to restore its fertility.

fallow[2] *adj.* pale yellowish brown. ☐**fallow deer,** a kind of small deer, spotted white in summer.

false (fawls) *adj.* **(fals·er, fals·est) 1.** wrong, incorrect. **2.** deceitful, lying, unfaithful. **3.** not genuine, sham, artificial, *false teeth.* **4.** improperly so called; *the false acacia,* not really an acacia tree. **false′ly** *adv.* **false′ness** *n.* ☐**false alarm,** an alarm raised without genuine cause. **false pretenses,** acts intended to deceive.

false·hood (fawls-huud) *n.* **1.** an untrue statement, a lie. **2.** telling lies.

fal·set·to (fawl-set-oh) *n.* (*pl.* **-tos**) a high-pitched voice above one's natural range, especially when used by male singers. **falsetto** *adv.* in a falsetto voice.

fal·sies (fawl-seez) *n. pl.* (*slang*) a padded bra, pads worn inside a bra.

fal·si·fy (fawl-sĭ-f/) *v.* **(fal·si·fied, fal·si·fy·ing) 1.** to alter (a document) fraudulently. **2.** to misrepresent (facts). **fal·si·fi·ca·tion** (fawl-sĭ-fĭ-kay-shŏn) *n.*

fal·si·ty (fawl-sĭ-tee) *n.* (*pl.* **-ties**) **1.** falseness. **2.** a falsehood, an error.

falt·boat (fahlt-boht) *n.* (also **foldboat**) a small boat with a collapsible frame.

falt·er (fawl-tĕr) *v.* **1.** to go or function unsteadily. **2.** to become weaker, to begin to give way, *his courage faltered.* **3.** to speak or utter hesitatingly, to stammer. **fal′ter·ing·ly** *adv.*

fame (faym) *n.* **1.** the condition of being known to many people. **2.** a good reputation. **famed** (faymd) *adj.* famous.

fa·mil·ial (fă-mil-yăl) *adj.* of or occurring in members of a family.

fa·mil·iar (fă-mil-yăr) *adj.* **1.** well known, often seen or experienced, *a familiar sight.* **2.** having a good knowledge (of a thing), well acquainted (with a person). 3. lacking formality, friendly and informal, *addressed him in familiar terms.* 4. too informal, assuming a greater degree of informality or friendship than is proper. **fa·mil′iar·ly** *adv.* **fa·mil·i·ar·i·ty** (fă-mil-i-ar-i-tee) *n.*

fa·mil·iar·ize (fă-mil-yă-rɪz) *v.* (**fa·mil·iar·ized, fa·mil·iar·iz·ing**) 1. to make well acquainted (with a person or thing). 2. to make well known. **fa·mil·iar·i·za·tion** (fă-mil-yă-ri-zay-shŏn) *n.*

fam·i·ly (fam-ĭ-lee) *n.* (*pl.* **-lies**) 1. parents and their children. 2. a person's children, *they have a large family.* 3. a set of relatives. 4. all the descendants of a common ancestor, *their line of descent.* 5. a group of things that are alike in some way. 6. a group of related plants or animals, *lions belong to the cat family.* ☐**family circle,** a group of close relatives. **family man,** one who is fond of home life with his family. **family planning,** birth control. **family tree,** a diagram showing how people in a family are related. **in the** (*or* **a**) **family way,** (informal) pregnant.

fam·ine (fam-in) *n.* extreme scarcity (especially of food) in a region.

fam·ish (fam-ish) *v.* to suffer from extreme hunger.

fa·mous (fay-mŭs) *adj.* known to very many people.

fa·mous·ly (fay-mŭs-lee) *adv.* extremely well, *getting on famously.*

fan[1] (fan) *n.* a device waved in the hand or operated mechanically to create a current of air. **fan** *v.* (**fanned, fan·ning**) 1. to drive a current of air upon, with or as if with a fan. 2. to stimulate (flames etc.) in this way. 3. to spread from a central point, *troops fanned out.* ☐**fan belt,** a belt driving the fan that cools the radiator of a motor vehicle.

fan[2] *n.* an enthusiastic admirer or supporter. (▷ Originally short for *fanatic.*) ☐**fan club,** an organized group of a person's admirers. **fan mail,** letters from fans to the person they admire.

fa·nat·ic (fă-nat-ik) *n.* a person filled with excessive enthusiasm or zeal for something. **fanatic** *adj.* **fa·nat′i·cal** *adj.* **fa·nat′i·cal·ly** *adv.*

fa·nat·i·cism (fă-nat-i-siz-ĕm) *n.* excessive enthusiasm.

fan·ci·er (fan-si-ĕr) *n.* 1. a person with special knowledge of and love for something, *a dog fancier.* 2. one whose hobby is breeding animals or growing plants.

fan·ci·ful (fan-si-fŭl) *adj.* 1. (of people) using the imagination freely, imagining things. 2. existing only in the imagination. 3. (of things) designed in a quaint or imaginative style. **fan′ci·ful·ly** *adv.*

fan·cy (fan-see) *n.* (*pl.* **-cies**) 1. a liking, *she took a fancy to the child.* 2. the power of imagining things, especially of an unreal or fantastic sort. 3. an unreasoning desire for something. 4. something imagined, an unfounded idea or belief. **fancy** *adj.* (**-ci·er, -ci·est**) 1. ornamental, not plain, elaborate. 2. based on imagination not fact. **fancy** *v.* (**fan·cied, fan·cy·ing**) 1. to imagine. 2. to be inclined to believe or suppose. 3. (informal) to take a fancy to, to like, to find (a person) attractive. ☐**fancy dress,** a costume worn for a party etc. at which the guests dress to represent animals, characters of history or fiction, etc. **fancy oneself,** (informal) to be rather conceited, to admire oneself. **fancy prices,** exces-

sively high prices. **take a fancy to,** to develop a liking for. **take a person's fancy,** to become liked by him.

fan·cy-free (fan-see-free) *adj.* not in love.

fan·cy·work (fan-see-wurk) *n.* decorative needlework.

fan·dan·go (fan-dang-goh) *n.* (*pl.* **-gos**) a lively Spanish dance for two people, music for this.

fan·fare (fan-fair) *n.* a short showy or ceremonious sounding of trumpets.

fang (fang) *n.* 1. a long sharp tooth, especially of dogs and wolves. 2. a snake's tooth with which it injects venom.

fan·jet (fan-jet) *n.* 1. a jet engine equipped with an exhausting fan. 2. an airplane having fanjets.

fan·light (fan-lɪt) *n.* a semicircular window above a door, a small window above another window or a door.

fan·ny (fan-ee) *n.* (*pl.* **-nies**) *(slang)* the buttocks.

fan·tail (fan-tayl) *n.* 1. a kind of pigeon with a semicircular tail. 2. the part of the stern of a ship extending aft from the last perpendicular.

fan·ta·sia (fan-tay-zhǎ) *n.* a fanciful musical or other composition of free form.

fan·ta·size (fan-tă-sɪz) *v.* (**fan·ta·sized, fan·ta·siz·ing**) to imagine in fantasy, to daydream.

fan·tas·tic (fan-tas-tik) *adj.* 1. absurdly fanciful. 2. designed in a very imaginative style. 3. (informal) very remarkable, excellent. **fan·tas′ti·cal** *adj.* **fan·tas′ti·cal·ly** *adv.*

fan·ta·sy (fan-tă-see, -zee) *n.* (*pl.* **-sies**) 1. imagination, especially when producing very fanciful ideas. 2. a wild or fantastic product of the imagination, a daydream. 3. a fanciful design, a fantasia.

FAO *abbr.* Food and Agricultural Organization.

far (fahr) *adv.* (**far·ther** or **fur·ther, far·thest** or **fur·thest**) at or to or by a great distance. **far** *adj.* distant, remote. ☐**a far cry from,** greatly different from. **as far as,** right to, *as far as my home;* to whatever extent, *as far as I am concerned.* **by far,** by a great amount. **far and away,** by far. **far and wide,** over a large area. **far be it from me,** I would certainly not. **Far East,** China, Japan, and other countries of east and southeast Asia. **Far West,** the part of the United States that lies west of the Great Plains. **go far,** to achieve a great deal. **so far,** to such an extent or distance, until now. **so far so good,** progress has been good.

far·ad (far-ăd) *n.* a unit of electrical capacitance, such that one coulomb of charge causes a difference of one volt in potential.

far·a·way (fahr-ă-way) *adj.* 1. distant. 2. dreamy, *faraway eyes.*

farce (fahrs) *n.* 1. a light comedy. 2. this kind of drama. 3. absurd and useless proceedings, a pretense. **far′ci·cal** *adj.*

fare (fair) *n.* 1. the price charged for a passenger to travel. 2. a passenger who pays a fare, especially for a hired vehicle. 3. food provided. **fare** *v.* (**fared, far·ing**) to have good or bad treatment, to progress, *how did they fare?*

fare·well (fair-wel) *interj.* goodby. **farewell** *n.* leave-taking. **farewell** *adj.*

far·fetched (fahr-fecht) *adj.* strained, not obvious, *a farfetched example.*

far·flung (fahr-flung) *adj.* widely extended.

fa·ri·na (fă-ree-nă) *n.* flour or meal used as a breakfast cereal.

far·i·na·ceous (far-ĭ-nay-shŭs) *adj.* 1. mealy in texture. 2. containing flour or meal. 3. starchy.

farm (fahrm) *n.* 1. an area of land and its buildings, owned or rented by one management, used for raising crops or livestock. 2. a farmhouse. 3. a body of water used for raising fish etc. **farm** *v.* 1. to grow crops or raise livestock. 2. to use (land) for this purpose. □**farm out,** to assign (work) to be done by others.

farm·er (fahr-měr) *n.* a person who owns or manages a farm. □**farmer cheese,** a pressed whole milk cheese.

farm·hand (fahrm-hand) *n.* a person who works on a farm.

farm·house (fahrm-hows) *n.* the farmer's house on a farm.

farm·ing (fahr-ming) *n.* operating a farm, agriculture.

farm·land (fahrm-land) *n.* land capable of being cultivated.

farm·yard (fahrm-yahrd) *n.* the enclosed area around farm buildings.

far·o (fair-oh) *n.* a card game in which bets are placed on the order of appearance of cards.

far·off (fahr-awf) *adj.* remote.

far-out (fahr-owt) *adj. (slang)* excellent.

far·ra·go (fă-rah-goh) *n.* (*pl.* **-gos**) a hodgepodge.

far·ri·er (far-i-ěr) *n.* a blacksmith.

far·row (far-oh) *v.* (of a sow) to give birth to young pigs. **farrow** *n.* 1. farrowing. 2. a litter of young pigs.

far·see·ing (fahr-see-ing) *adj.* prescient, prudent.

far·sight·ed (fahr-sɪ-tid) *adj.* 1. able to see distant objects more clearly than close ones. 2. farseeing. **far'sight'ed·ness** *n.*

far·ther (fahr-*th*ěr) *adj. & adv.* at or to a greater distance, more remote. ▷Careful writers use *farther* and *farthest* where the meaning of "actual distance" is involved. *She lived farther from my house than you did. You were never further from my thoughts. She lived farthest away. You were furthest from my thoughts.*

far·ther·most (fahr-*th*ěr-mohst) *adj.* farthest.

far·thest (fahr-*th*ist) *adj. & adv.* at or to the greatest distance, most remote. ▷See the note under **farther.**

far·thing (fahr-*th*ing) *n.* 1. a former British coin worth one quarter of a penny. 2. a coin of little value.

far·thin·gale (fahr-*th*ing-gayl) *n.* a hooped framework used in the 16th century for extending a woman's skirt.

fas·ces (fas-eez) *n.* a bundle of rods with an ax, carried by certain officials of ancient Rome as an emblem of authority.

fas·ci·cle (fas-i-kěl) *n.* one section of a book that is published in installments. **fas·cic·u·lar** (fă-sik-yŭ-lăr) *adj.*

fas·ci·nate (fas-ĭ-nayt) *v.* (**fas·ci·nat·ed, fas·ci·nat·ing**) 1. to attract and hold the interest of, to charm greatly. 2. to deprive (a victim) of the power of escape by a fixed look, as a snake does. **fas'ci·na·tor** *n.* **fas·ci·na·tion** (fas-ĭ-nay-shŏn) *n.*

fas·ci·nat·ing (fas-ĭ-nayt-ing) *adj.* having great attraction or charm.

fas·cism (fash-iz-ěm) *n.* a system of extreme rightwing dictatorial government. **fas'cist** *n.* **fas·cis·tic** (fa-shis-tik) *adj.*

fash·ion (fash-ŏn) *n.* 1. a manner or way of doing something, *continue in this fashion.* 2. the popular style of dress, customs, etc. at a given time. **fashion** *v.* to make into a particular form or shape.

□**after** *or* **in a fashion,** to some extent but not very satisfactorily. **in fashion,** fashionable. **out of fashion,** not fashionable.

fash·ion·a·ble (fash-ŏ-nă-běl) *adj.* 1. in or adopting a style that is currently popular. 2. frequented or used by stylish people, *a fashionable hotel.* **fash'ion·a·bly** *adv.*

fast¹ (fast) *adj.* 1. moving or done quickly. 2. producing or allowing quick movement, *a fast road.* 3. (of a clock etc.) showing a time ahead of the correct one. 4. (of a person) spending too much time and energy on pleasure, immoral. 5. (of photographic film) very sensitive to light, (of a lens) having a large aperture, allowing a short exposure to be used. 6. firmly fixed or attached. 7. (of colors or dyes) unlikely to fade or run. **fast** *adv.* 1. quickly. 2. firmly, tightly, securely, *stuck fast; fast asleep.* □**fast foods,** dishes that are quickly prepared and quickly served, such as hamburgers, fried chicken, etc. **fast worker,** one who makes rapid progress, especially in furthering his own interests. **play fast and loose,** to ignore one's obligations, to act deceitfully.

fast² *v.* to go without food or without certain kinds of food, especially as a religious duty. **fast** *n.* fasting, a day or season appointed for this.

fast·back (fast-bak) *n.* a car with a long sloping back, the back itself.

fas·ten (fas-ěn) *v.* 1. to fix firmly, to tie or join together. 2. to fix (one's glance or attention) intently. 3. to become fastened, *the door fastens with a latch.* □**fasten off,** to tie or secure the end (of a thread etc.). **fasten on,** to lay hold of; to single out for attack; to seize as a pretext.

fas·ten·er (fas-ě-něr), **fas·ten·ing** (fas-ě-ning) *n.* a device used for fastening something.

fas·tid·i·ous (fa-stid-i-ŭs) *adj.* 1. selecting carefully, choosing only what is good. 2. easily disgusted. **fas·tid'i·ous·ly** *adv.* **fas·tid'i·ous·ness** *n.*

fast·ness (fast-nis) *n.* 1. the state of being fast or firm, *color fastness.* 2. a stronghold, a fortress.

fast-talk (fast-tawk) *v.* to persuade by rapid or deceitful talk.

fat (fat) *n.* 1. a whitish or yellowish substance, insoluble in water, found in animal bodies and certain seeds. 2. this substance prepared for use in cooking. **fat** *adj.* (**fat·ter, fat·test**) 1. containing much fat, covered with fat. 2. excessively plump. 3. (of an animal) made plump for slaughter. 4. thick, *a fat book.* 5. fertile, *fat lands.* 6. richly rewarding, *a nice fat job.* **fat'ness** *n.* □**a fat chance,** *(informal)* none, no chance at all. **fat cat,** *(slang)* a wealthy person. **fat farm,** *(slang)* a resort for people who wish to lose weight. **live off the fat of the land,** to have the best of everything, especially without having to work for it. **the fat is in the fire,** something has happened that will cause an explosion of anger or other undesirable reaction.

fa·tal (fay-tăl) *adj.* 1. causing or ending in death. 2. causing disaster, *a fatal mistake.* 3. fateful, *the fatal day.* **fa'tal·ly** *adv.*

fa·tal·ist (fay-tă-list) *n.* a person who accepts and submits to what happens, regarding it as inevitable. **fa'tal·is·tic** (fay-tă-lis-tik) *adj.*

fa·tal·i·ty (fay-tal-i-tee) *n.* (*pl.* **-ties**) death caused by accident or in war etc.

fat·back (fat-bak) *n.* a strip of fat, from the upper part of a side of pork, cured by drying and salting.

fate (fayt) *n.* 1. a power thought to control all events and impossible to resist. 2. a person's destiny.
fat·ed (fay-tid) *adj.* destined by fate, doomed.
fate·ful (fayt-fŭl) *adj.* bringing or producing great and usually unpleasant events, *the fateful decision.* **fate′ful·ly** *adv.*
fath. *abbr.* fathom.
fat·head (fat-hed) *n. (informal)* a stupid person. **fat′head·ed** *adj.*
fa·ther (fah-*th*ĕr) *n.* 1. a male parent. 2. a male ancestor, *land of our fathers.* 3. the founder or originator of something. 4. *Father,* God, the First Person of the Trinity. 5. the title of certain priests, especially those belonging to religious orders. **father** *v.* 1. to beget, to be the father of. 2. to found or originate (an idea or plan etc.). **fa′ther·ly** *adj.*
fa′ther·hood *n.* ☐**Father Christmas,** (*British*) Santa Claus. **father figure,** an older man who is respected and trusted by others like a father.
Father's Day, a day (usually the third Sunday in June) on which special tribute is paid to fathers.
Father Time, the personification of time, shown as an old man with a scythe and an hourglass.
fa·ther-in-law (fah-*th*ĕr-in-law) *n.* (*pl.* **fa·thers-in-law**) the father of one's wife or husband.
fa·ther·land (fah-*th*ĕr-land) *n.* one's native country.
fa·ther·less (fah-*th*ĕr-lis) *adj.* without a living father, without a known father.
fath·om (fa*th*-ŏm) *n.* (*pl.* **-oms, -om**) a measure of six ft. used in stating the depth of water.
fathom *v.* 1. to measure the depth of. 2. to get to the bottom of, to understand. **fath′om·a·ble** *adj.* **fath′om·a·bly** *adv.*
fath·om·less (fa*th*-ŏm-lis) *adj.* too deep to fathom, too complicated to understand.
fa·tigue (fă-teeg) *n.* 1. tiredness resulting from hard work or exercise. 2. weakness in metals etc. caused by repeated stress. 3. (also **fatigue duty**) any of the nonmilitary duties of soldiers, such as cleaning and dishwashing. 4. *fatigues, (informal)* informal military dress. **fatigue** *v.* (**fa·tigued, fa·tigu·ing**) to cause fatigue to.
fat·ted (fat-id) *adj.* (of animals) fattened as food, *the fatted calf.*
fat·ten (fat-ĕn) *v.* to make or become fat.
fat·ty (fat-ee) *adj.* (**fat·ti·er, fat·ti·est**) like fat, containing fat. **fatty** *n.* (*pl.* **-ties**) (*informal*) a fat person. ☐**fatty acid,** any member of a series of acids derived from or occurring in animal or vegetable fats.
fat·u·ous (fach-oo-ŭs) *adj.* foolish, silly. **fat′u·ous·ly** *adv.* **fat′u·ous·ness** *n.* **fa·tu·i·ty** (fă-too-i-tee) *n.* (*pl.* **-ties**).
fau·bourg (foh-boor) *n.* a suburb of a French city.
fau·cet (faw-sit) *n.* a device for allowing water to come from a kitchen or lavatory pipe in a controllable flow.
fault (fawlt) *n.* 1. a defect or imperfection. 2. an offense, something wrongly done. 3. the responsibility for something wrong. 4. a break in the continuity of layers of rock, caused by movement of Earth's crust. 5. an incorrect serve in tennis etc.
fault *v.* 1. to find fault with, to declare to be faulty. 2. to make imperfect. ☐**at fault,** responsible for a mistake or shortcoming. **double fault,** two consecutive faults in tennis etc. **find fault with,** to seek and find mistakes in, to complain about. **to a fault,** excessively, *generous to a fault.*
fault·find·ing (fawlt-fɪn-ding) *n.* the act of com-

plaining or criticizing, especially in a petty way. **fault′find·er** *n.*
fault·less (fawlt-lis) *adj.* without fault. **fault′less·ly** *adv.*
fault·y (fawl-tee) *adj.* (**fault·i·er, fault·i·est**) having a fault or faults, imperfect. **fault′i·ly** *adv.* **fault′i·ness** *n.*
faun (fawn) *n.* one of a class of gods of the woods and fields in ancient mythology, with the legs and horns of a goat. **faun′like** *adj.* ▷Do not confuse *faun* with *fawn.*
fau·na (faw-nă) *n.* (*pl.* **-nas, -nae,** *pr.* -nee) the animals of an area or period of time.
Fauve (fohv) *n.* a member of a group of early 20th-century French artists whose works employ bright contrasting colors. **Fauv′ism** *n.* **Fauv′ist** *n.*
faux pas (foh pah) (*pl.* **faux pas,** *pr.* foh pahz) an embarrassing blunder. ▷French.
fa·vor (fay-vŏr) *n.* 1. liking, goodwill, approval. 2. an act that is kindly or helpful beyond what is due or usual. 3. support or preference given to one person or group at the expense of another. 4. an ornament or badge etc. worn to show that one supports a certain political or other party. 5. a small decorative object provided at a party. 6. *favors,* consent to sexual relations. **favor** *v.* 1. to regard or treat with favor. 2. to be in favor of. 3. to oblige, *favor us with a song.* 4. (of events or circumstances) to make possible or easy, to be advantageous to. 5. to resemble (one parent etc.), *the boy favors his father.* ☐**be in** or **out of favor,** to have or not have a person's goodwill. **in favor of,** in support of, in sympathy with; to the advantage of, *the exchange rate is in our favor;* (of checks) made out to a person or his account.
fa·vor·a·ble (fay-vŏ-ră-bĕl) *adj.* 1. giving or showing approval. 2. pleasing, satisfactory, *made a favorable impression.* 3. helpful, advantageous, *favorable winds.* **fa′vor·a·bly** *adv.*
fa·vor·ite (fay-vŏ-rit) *adj.* liked or preferred above others. **favorite** *n.* 1. a favored person or thing. 2. a competitor generally expected to win. ☐**favorite son,** a person preferred as a presidential candidate by delegates from his own state.
fa·vor·it·ism (fay-vŏ-ri-tiz-ĕm) *n.* unfair favoring of one person or group at the expense of another.
fawn[1] (fawn) *n.* 1. a fallow deer in its first year. 2. light yellowish brown. **fawn** *adj.* light yellowish brown. ▷Do not confuse *fawn* with *faun.*
fawn[2] *v.* 1. (of a dog etc.) to try to win affection or attention by crouching close to a person and licking him. 2. to try to win favor by obsequious behavior.
faze (fayz) *v.* (**fazed, faz·ing**) to disconcert.
fb. *abbr.* fullback.
FBI, F.B.I. *abbr.* Federal Bureau of Investigation.
FCC *abbr.* Federal Communications Commission.
fcp. *abbr.* foolscap.
fcy. *abbr.* fancy.
FD *abbr.* 1. fire department. 2. focal distance.
FDA *abbr.* Food and Drug Administration.
FDIC *abbr.* Federal Deposit Insurance Corporation.
Fe *symbol* iron.
fe·al·ty (fee-ăl-tee) *n.* (*pl.* **-ties**) loyalty, *oath of fealty.*
fear (feer) *n.* 1. an unpleasant emotion caused by the nearness of danger or expectation of pain etc. 2. the reverence or awe felt for God. **fear** *v.* 1. to feel fear of, to be afraid. 2. to reverence (God). 3. to have an uneasy feeling, to be politely regret-

ful, *I fear there's none left.* □**for fear of,** because of the risk of. **put the fear of God into,** to terrify. **without fear or favor,** impartially. **fear·ful** (feer-fŭl) *adj.* 1. feeling fear. 2. terrible, awful. 3. *(informal)* extreme, very great. **fear′ful·ly** *adv.* **fear·less** (feer-lis) *adj.* feeling no fear. **fear′less·ly** *adv.* **fear′less·ness** *n.* **fear·some** (feer-sŏm) *adj.* frightening or alarming in appearance, very great, *a fearsome task.* **fea·si·ble** (fee-zĭ-bĕl) *adj.* 1. able to be done, possible, suitable. 2. likely, plausible, *a feasible explanation.* **fea′si·bly** *adv.* **fea·si·bil·i·ty** (fee-zĭ-bil-i-tee) *n.* (*pl.* **-ties**) □**feasibility study,** a study undertaken to decide whether a proposed course of action is suitable. **feast** (feest) *n.* 1. a large elaborate meal. 2. a religious festival of rejoicing. **feast** *v.* 1. to eat heartily. 2. to give a feast to. 3. to give pleasure to, *feasting his eyes on the display.* □**feast or famine,** being characterized by ups and downs, *life is feast or famine for some actors.* **feat** (feet) *n.* a remarkable action or achievement. **feath·er** (feth-ĕr) *n.* 1. one of the structures that grow from a bird's skin and cover its body, consisting of a central shaft with a fringe of fine strands on each side. 2. long silky hair on a dog's or horse's legs. **feather** *v.* 1. to cover or fit with feathers. 2. to turn (an oar) so that the blade passes through the air edgeways. 3. to make (propeller blades) rotate in such a way as to lessen the resistance of the air or water. **feath′ered** *adj.* **feath′er·less** *adj.* □**a feather in one's cap,** an achievement one can be proud of. **feather bed,** a mattress stuffed with feathers. **feather duster,** a dusting brush made of feathers. **feather one's nest,** to enrich oneself when an opportunity occurs. **feath·er·bed·ding** (feth-ĕr-bed-ing) *n.* the requiring of an employer to hire more workers than are actually needed. □**featherbed contract,** a union contract that includes featherbedding. **feath·er·brain** (feth-ĕr-brayn) *n.* a silly person. **feath′er·brained** *adj.* **feath·er·edge** (feth-ĕr-ej) *n.* a fine edge of a wedge-shaped board etc. **feath·er·stitch** (feth-ĕr-stich) *n.* an ornamental stitch in embroidery or knitting, producing a featherlike pattern. **feath·er·weight** (feth-ĕr-wayt) *n.* 1. a boxer between bantamweight and lightweight weighing up to 126 pounds. 2. a very lightweight thing or person. 3. a person of little or no influence. **feath·er·y** (feth-ĕ-ree) *adj.* 1. light and soft, like feathers. 2. covered with feathers. **fea·ture** (fee-chŭr) *n.* 1. one of the named parts of the face (as the mouth, nose, eyes) that together make up its appearance. 2. a distinctive or noticeable quality of a thing. 3. a prominent article in a newspaper etc. 4. a long film (**feature film**) forming the main item in a film program. **feature** *v.* (**fea·tured, fea·tur·ing**) 1. to give special prominence to. 2. to be a feature of or in. **fea·ture·less** (fee-chŭr-lis) *adj.* without distinctive features. **feaze** (feez, fayz) *v.* (**feazed, feaz·ing**) to faze. **Feb.** *abbr.* February. **feb·ri·fuge** (feb-rĭ-fyooj) *n.* a cooling drink or medicine to reduce fever. **febrifuge** *adj.* serving to reduce fever. **fe·brile** (fee-brĭl, feb-rĭl) *adj.* feverish.

Feb·ru·ar·y (feb-roo-er-ee) *n.* (*pl.* **-ar·ies**) the second month of the year. **fe·ces** (fee-seez) *n.* waste matter discharged from the bowels. **fe·cal** (fee-kăl) *adj.* **feck·less** (fek-lis) *adj.* feeble and incompetent, irresponsible. **feck′less·ness** *n.* **fe·cund** (fee-kŭnd, fek-ŭnd) *adj.* fertile. **fe·cun·di·ty** (fi-kun-di-tee) *n.* **fe·cun·date** (fee-kŭn-dayt, fek-ŭn-) *v.* (**fe·cun·dat·ed, fe·cun·dat·ing**) to make fruitful. **fe·cun·da·tion** (fee-kŭn-day-shŏn, fek-ŭn-) *n.* **fed**[1] (fed) *v. see* **feed.** □**fed up,** *(slang)* discontented, displeased. **fed**[2] *n.* *(slang)* a federal law enforcement officer. **fed.** *abbr.* 1. federal. 2. federated. 3. federation. **fed·a·yeen** (fed-ă-yeen) *n. pl.* Palestinian guerrillas, operating especially against Israel. **fed·er·al** (fed-ĕ-răl) *adj.* 1. of a system of government in which several states unite under a central authority but remain independent in internal affairs. 2. belonging to this group as a whole (not to its separate parts), *federal laws.* 3. of an association of units that are largely independent. **fed′er·al·ly** *adv.* □**Federal Bureau of Investigation,** a section of the U.S. Department of Justice, responsible for investigating violations of federal law and safeguarding national security. **federal district,** a region used as the seat of a federal government. **fed·er·al·ism** (fed-ĕ-ră-liz-ĕm) *n.* 1. the federal principle of government. 2. *Federalism,* advocacy of a federal system, the principles of Federalists. **fed·er·al·ist** (fed-ĕ-ră-list) *n.* 1. a person who supports federalism. 2. *Federalist,* (in U.S. history) a member of the Federalist Party, which advocated a strong central government and adoption of the constitution. **fed·er·al·is·tic** (fed-ĕ-ră-lis-tik) *adj.* **fed·er·al·ize** (fed-ĕ-ră-lız) *v.* (**fed·er·al·ized, fed·er·al·iz·ing**) 1. to unite (states etc.) in a federal organization. 2. to put (militia etc.) under the control of a federal government. **fed·er·ate** (fed-ĕ-rayt) *v.* (**fed·er·at·ed, fed·er·at·ing**) 1. to unite on a federal basis. 2. to band together for a common object. **fed·er·a·tion** (fed-ĕ-ray-shŏn) *n.* 1. federating. 2. a federated society or group of states. **fedn.** *abbr.* federation. **fe·do·ra** (fi-dohr-ă) *n.* a low soft felt hat with the crown creased lengthways. **fee** (fee) *n.* 1. a sum payable to an official or a professional person for advice or services. 2. a sum payable for membership in a society, use of a laboratory or other facility, etc. **fee·ble** (fee-bĕl) *adj.* (**-bler, -blest**) weak, without strength or force or effectiveness. **fee′bly** *adv.* **fee′ble·ness** *n.* **fee·ble·mind·ed** (fee-bĕl-mın-did) *adj.* mentally deficient. **fee′ble·mind′ed·ness** *n.* **feed** (feed) *v.* (**fed, feed·ing**) 1. to give food to, to put food into the mouth of. 2. to give as food to animals, *feed oats to horses.* 3. (of animals) to take food. 4. to serve as food for, to nourish, 5. to supply, to pass a supply of material to. 6. to send passes to (a player) in basketball, hockey, etc. 7. to pass (information), especially to an informant or the press. **feed** *n.* 1. *(informal)* a big meal. 2. food for animals. 3. a pipe or channel etc. by which material is carried to a machine, the material itself. □**feed on,** to consume as food, to be nourished or sustained by.

feed·back (feed-bak) n. 1. return of part of the output of a system to its source, especially so as to modify the output. 2. the return of information about a product etc. to its supplier.

feed·er (fee-dĕr) n. 1. (of plants and animals) one that takes in food in a certain way, *a heavy feeder*. 2. a hopper or feeding apparatus in a machine. 3. a branch railroad line, airline, canal, etc. linking outlying areas with a central line or service.

feed·lot (feed-lot) n. a tract of land on which animals are fed before slaughter.

feed·stock (feed-stok) n. metal bars etc. fed into a cutting or shaping machine.

feed·stuff (feed-stuf) n. food for farm animals.

feel (feel) v. (**felt, feel·ing**) 1. to explore or perceive by touch. 2. to be conscious of, to be aware of being, *feel a pain; feel happy*. 3. to be affected by, *feels the loss deeply*. 4. to give a certain sensation or impression, *the water feels warm*. 5. to have a vague conviction or impression of something. 6. to have as an opinion, to consider, *we felt it was necessary to do this.* **feel** n. 1. the sense of touch. 2. the act of feeling. 3. the sensation produced by something touched, *silk has a soft feel*. □**feel for a person,** to sympathize with him. **feel free,** *(informal)* an expression of permission. **feel like,** to be in the mood for. **feel one's way,** to find one's way by feeling about; to proceed cautiously. **feel up to,** to feel capable of doing (work etc.). ▷It is incorrect to say or write *feel badly*. See the notes under **badly** and **good.**

feel·er (fee-lĕr) n. 1. a long slender part or organ in certain animals, used for testing things by touch. 2. a cautious proposal or suggestion put forward to test people's reactions. □**feeler gauge,** a gauge with many thin blades that can be inserted to measure gaps.

feel·ing (fee-ling) n. 1. the power and capacity to feel, *had lost all feeling in his legs*. 2. mental or physical awareness, emotion. 3. an idea or belief not wholly based on reason, *had a feeling of security*. 4. readiness to feel sympathy, *showed no feeling for the sufferings of others*. 5. opinion, attitude, *the feeling of the meeting was against it.* 6. *feelings,* the emotional side of a person's nature (contrasted with the intellect), sympathies, opinions, *we have strong feelings on this matter.* **feeling** adj. sensitive, sympathetic. **feel'ing·ly** adv. □**bad feelings,** ill will. **good feelings,** friendliness.

feet (feet) *see* **foot.**

feign (fayn) v. to pretend.

feint (faynt) n. a slight attack or movement made in one place to divert attention from the main attack coming elsewhere. **feint** v. to make a feint.

feld·spar (feld-spahr) n. a white or reddish mineral containing aluminum and other silicates.

fe·lic·i·tate (fi-lis-i-tayt) v. (**fe·lic·i·tat·ed, fe·lic·i·tat·ing**) to congratulate. **fe·lic·i·ta·tion** (fi-lis-i-tay-shŏn) n.

fe·lic·i·tous (fi-lis-i-tŭs) adj. (of words or remarks) well chosen, apt. **fe·lic'i·tous·ly** adv.

fe·lic·i·ty (fi-lis-i-tee) n. (pl. **-ties**) 1. being happy, great happiness. 2. a pleasing manner or style, *expressed himself with great felicity.*

fe·line (fee-lın) adj. of cats, catlike. **feline** n. an animal of the cat family.

fell[1] (fel) adj. (in poetry) ruthless, cruel, destructive. □**at one fell swoop,** in a single deadly action.

fell[2] v. 1. to strike down by a blow. 2. to cut (a

tree) down. 3. to stitch down (the edge of a seam) so that it lies flat.

fell[3] *see* **fall.**

fel·lah (fel-ă) n. (pl. **fel·lahs, fel·la·hin, fel·la·heen,** pr. fel-ă-heen) an Egyptian peasant.

fel·low (fel-oh) n. 1. one who is associated with another, a comrade. 2. a thing of the same class or kind, the other of a pair. 3. a member of a learned society. 4. a graduate student who is paid a stipend, sometimes in exchange for performing some academic duty. 5. *(informal)* a man or boy. □**fellow traveler,** one who sympathizes with the aims of the Communist Party but is not a member of it.

fel·low·man (fel-oh-man) n. (pl. **-men,** pr. **-men**) a kindred human being.

fel·low·ship (fel-oh-ship) n. 1. friendly association with others, companionship. 2. a number of people associated together, a society, membership of this. 3. the position of a college or university fellow.

fel·on (fel-ŏn) n. a person who has committed a felony.

fel·o·ny (fel-ŏ-nee) n. (pl. **-nies**) a crime regarded by the law as serious, usually involving violence.

felt[1] (felt) n. a kind of cloth made by matting and pressing fibers. **felt** v. 1. to make or become matted together like felt. 2. to cover with felt.

felt[2] *see* **feel.**

fem. abbr. 1. female. 2. feminine.

fe·male (fee-mayl) adj. 1. of the sex that can bear offspring or produce eggs. 2. (of plants) fruit-bearing, having a pistil and no stamens. **female** n. a female animal or plant.

fem·i·nine (fem-ĭ-nin) adj. 1. of or like or suitable for women, having the qualities or appearance considered characteristic of a woman. 2. having the grammatical form suitable for the names of females or for words corresponding to these, *"lioness" is the feminine noun corresponding to "lion."* **feminine** n. a feminine word or gender. **fem·i·nin·i·ty** (fem-ĭ-nin-i-tee) n. the quality of being feminine.

fem·i·nist (fem-ĭ-nist) n. a supporter of women's claims to be given rights, opportunities, and treatment equal to those of men. **fem'i·nism** n.

femme fa·tale (fem fä-tal) a dangerously attractive woman. ▷French.

fem·o·ral (fem-ŏ-răl) adj. of or near the femur.

fe·mur (fee-mŭr) n. (pl. **fe·murs, fem·o·ra,** pr. fem-ŏ-ră) the thighbone, extending from the pelvis to the knee.

fen (fen) n. a low-lying marshy or flooded tract of land.

fence (fens) n. 1. a structure of rails, stakes, wire, etc. put around a property, field, or garden to mark a boundary or keep animals from straying. 2. a person who knowingly buys and resells stolen goods. **fence** v. (**fenced, fenc·ing**) 1. to surround with a fence. 2. to act as a fence for (stolen goods). 3. to engage in fencing. □**fence in,** surround. **fence off,** to close off by fencing. **sit on the fence,** to avoid giving definite support to either side in a contest or dispute.

fenc·er (fen-sĕr) n. a person who engages in the sport of fencing.

fenc·ing (fen-sing) n. 1. fences, a length of fence. 2. the sport of fighting with foils or other kinds of swords.

fend (fend) v. **fend for,** to provide a livelihood for, to look after. **fend off,** to ward off.

fend·er (fen-dĕr) *n.* 1. the part of an automobile body immediately above each wheel. 2. a low frame bordering a fireplace, to keep falling coals etc. from rolling into the room. 3. a pad or a bundle of rope hung over a vessel's side to prevent damage when alongside a wharf or another vessel.

fen·es·tra·tion (fen-ĕ-stray-shŏn) *n.* 1. the arrangement of windows in a building. 2. a surgical operation in which an opening is made in the labyrinth of the ear to improve hearing.

Fe·ni·an (fee-ni-ăn) *n.* a member of a 19th-century society of Irish people in the U.S. and Ireland who advocated overthrow of British government in Ireland.

fen·nel (fen-ĕl) *n.* a fragrant yellow-flowered herb used for flavoring.

FEPC *abbr.* Fair Employment Practices Commission.

fe·ral (feer-ăl, fer-ăl) *adj.* 1. wild, untamed. 2. in a wild state after escape from captivity.

fer-de-lance (fer-dĕ-lans) *n.* a large poisonous snake of tropical South America.

fer·ment (fĕr-ment) *v.* 1. to undergo fermentation, to cause fermentation in. 2. to seethe with excitement or agitation. **ferment** (fur-ment) *n.* 1. fermentation. 2. something that causes this. 3. a state of seething excitement or agitation. ▷Do not confuse *ferment* with *foment.*

fer·men·ta·tion (fur-men-tay-shŏn) *n.* a chemical change caused by the action of an organic substance such as yeast, involving effervescence and the production of heat, as when sugar is converted into alcohol.

fer·mi·um (fur-mi-ŭm) *n.* a radioactive chemical element.

fern (furn) *n.* a kind of flowerless plant with feathery green leaves.

fern·er·y (fur-nĕ-ree) *n.* (*pl.* **-er·ies**) 1. a place where ferns are grown. 2. a collection of ferns.

fe·ro·cious (fĕ-roh-shŭs) *adj.* fierce, savage. **fe·ro′cious·ly** *adv.* **fe·ro′cious·ness** *n.* **fe·roc·i·ty** (fĕ-ros-i-tee) *n.*

fer·ret (fer-it) *n.* a small animal of the weasel family kept for driving rabbits from burrows, killing rats, etc. **ferret** *v.* (**fer·ret·ed, fer·ret·ing**) to search, to rummage. ☐**ferret out,** to discover by searching or rummaging.

fer·ric (fer-ik) *adj.* of iron. ☐**ferric oxide,** an iron oxide, used as a pigment and for polishing.

Fer·ris (fer-is) **wheel** a giant revolving vertical wheel with passenger cars on its rim, used at amusement parks.

fer·ro·con·crete (fer-oh-kon-kreet, -kong-) *n.* reinforced concrete.

fer·ro·mag·net·ic (fer-oh-mag-net-ik) *adj.* relating to substances that are easily magnetized. **fer·ro·mag·net·ism** (fer-oh-mag-nĕ-tiz-ĕm) *n.*

fer·rous (fer-ŭs) *adj.* containing iron, *ferrous and nonferrous metals.*

fer·rule (fer-ŭl) *n.* a metal ring or cap strengthening the end of a stick or tube.

fer·ry (fer-ee) *v.* (**fer·ried, fer·ry·ing**) 1. to convey (people or things) in a boat etc. across a stretch of water. 2. to transport from one place to another, especially as a regular service. **ferry** *n.* (*pl.* **-ries**) 1. a boat etc. used for ferrying. 2. the place where it operates. 3. the service it provides.

fer·ry·boat (fer-ee-boht) *n.* a boat for ferrying people or things.

fer·tile (fur-til) *adj.* 1. (of soil) rich in the materials needed to support vegetation. 2. (of plants) able to produce fruit, (of animals) able or likely to conceive or beget young. 3. (of seeds or eggs) capable of developing into a new plant or animal, fertilized. 4. (of the mind) able to produce ideas, inventive. **fer·til·i·ty** (fĕr-til-i-tee) *n.*

fer·til·ize (fur-tĭ-lız) *v.* (**fer·til·ized, fer·til·iz·ing**) 1. to make (soil etc.) fertile or productive. 2. to introduce pollen or sperm into (a plant or egg or female animal) so that it develops seed or young. **fer·til·i·za·tion** (fur-tĭ-li-zay-shŏn) *n.*

fer·til·iz·er (fur-tĭ-lız-ĕr) *n.* material (natural or artificial) added to soil to make it more fertile.

fer·ule (fer-ŭl) *n.* a rod or a stick used for punishing children.

fer·vent (fur-vĕnt) *adj.* showing warmth of feeling. **fer′vent·ly** *adv.* **fer′ven·cy** *n.*

fer·vid (fur-vid) *adj.* fervent. **fer′vid·ly** *adv.*

fer·vor (fur-vŏr) *n.* warmth and intensity of feeling, zeal.

fes·cue (fes-kyoo) *n.* a kind of grass used as pasture and fodder.

fes·tal (fes-tăl) *adj.* of a festival.

fes·ter (fes-tĕr) *v.* 1. to make or become septic and filled with pus. 2. to cause continuing resentment. **fester** *n.* a pus-filled sore.

fes·ti·val (fes-tĭ-văl) *n.* 1. a day or time of religious or other celebration. 2. a series of performances of music, drama, films, etc. given periodically, *the Shakespeare Festival.*

fes·tive (fes-tiv) *adj.* of or suitable for a festival. **fes′tive·ly** *adv.*

fes·tiv·i·ty (fes-tiv-i-tee) *n.* (*pl.* **-ties**) a festive occasion or celebration.

fes·toon (fes-toon) *n.* a chain of flowers, leaves, ribbons, etc. hung in a curve or loop as a decoration. **festoon** *v.* to decorate with hanging ornaments.

Fest·schrift (fest-shrift) *n.* (*pl.* **-schrift·en,** *pr.* -shrif-tĕn, **-schrifts**) a collection of articles, essays, etc., presented to a scholar to honor an occasion in his life.

fe·tal (fee-tăl) *adj.* of or relating to a fetus. ☐**fetal position,** resting like the fetus in the womb, with body curved and legs bent and pulled close to the chest.

fetch (fech) *v.* 1. to go for and bring back, *fetch a doctor.* 2. (of goods) to sell for a price, *your books won't fetch much.*

fetch·ing (fech-ing) *adj.* attractive. **fetch′ing·ly** *adv.*

fete, fête (fayt, fet) *n.* 1. a festival. 2. an outdoor entertainment or sale, usually to raise funds for a cause or charity. **fete** *v.* (**fet·ed, fet·ing**) to entertain (a person) in celebration of some achievement etc.

fe·ti·cide (fee-ti-sıd) *n.* destroying a fetus, causing an abortion.

fet·id (fet-id) *adj.* stinking.

fet·ish (fet-ish) *n.* 1. an object worshipped by primitive peoples who believe it to have magical powers or to be inhabited by a spirit. 2. anything to which foolishly excessive respect or devotion is given. 3. an object arousing erotic feeling.

fet·ish·ism (fet-i-shiz-ĕm) *n.* 1. belief in or use of fetishes. 2. blind devotion to fetishes or their use. **fet′ish·ist** *n.* **fet·ish·is·tic** (fet-i-shis-tik) *adj.*

fet·lock (fet-lok) *n.* the part of a horse's leg above and behind the hoof.

fet·or (fee-tŏr) *n.* a stench.
fet·ter (fet-ĕr) *n.* a chain or shackle for a prisoner's ankles. **fetter** *v.* 1. to put into fetters. 2. to impede or restrict.
fet·tle (fet-ĕl) *n.* condition, trim, *in fine fettle*.
fet·tu·ci·ni (fet-ŭ-chee-nee) *n.* a pasta in thin narrow strips.
fe·tus (fee-tŭs) *n.* (*pl.* **-tus·es**) a developed embryo in the womb, a human embryo more than eight weeks after conception.
feud (fyood) *n.* a lasting hostility between people or groups. **feud** *v.* to carry on a feud.
feu·dal (fyoo-dăl) *adj.* of or according to the **feudal system**, a method of holding land (during the Middle Ages in Europe) by giving one's services to the owner. **feu′dal·ism** *n.* **feu·dal·ist·ic** (fyoo-dă-lis-tik) *adj.*
fe·ver (fee-vĕr) *n.* 1. an abnormally high body temperature. 2. a disease characterized by this. 3. a state of nervous excitement or agitation. ☐**at fever pitch**, at a high level of excitement.
fe·vered (fee-vĕrd) *adj.* affected with fever.
fe·ver·ish (fee-vĕ-rish) *adj.* 1. having a fever, caused or accompanied by a fever. 2. restless with excitement or agitation. **fe′ver·ish·ly** *adv.* **fe′ver·ish·ness** *n.*
few (fyoo) *adj., n. & pron.* not many, a small number. (▷See the note under **less.**) **few′ness** *n.* ☐**a few**, some, not none. **quite a few**, *(informal)* a fairly large number. **the few**, the minority, select people.
fey (fay) *adj.* 1. showing unnaturally high spirits, playful, mischievous. 2. having a strange otherworldly charm. **fey′ness** *n.*
fez (fez) *n.* (*pl.* **fez·zes**) a man's high flat-topped red cap with a tassel, worn by Muslims in certain countries.
ff. *abbr.* 1. folios. 2. following pages. 3. fortissimo.
FHA *abbr.* Federal Housing Administration.
fi·an·cé, fi·an·cée (fee-ahn-say) *n.* a man *(fiancé)* or woman *(fiancée)* to whom one is engaged to be married.
fi·as·co (fee-as-koh) *n.* (*pl.* **-cos, -coes**) a complete and ludicrous failure in something attempted.
fi·at (fee-ăt, fı-) *n.* an order or decree. ☐**fiat money**, paper money made legal by government decree but not backed by silver or gold.
fib (fib) *n.* an unimportant lie. **fib** *v.* (**fibbed, fibbing**) to tell a fib. **fib′ber** *n.*
fi·ber (fı-bĕr) *n.* 1. one of the thin strands of which animal and vegetable tissue or a textile substance is made, a threadlike piece of glass. 2. a substance consisting of fibers. 3. strength of character, *moral fiber*. ☐**fiber optics**, a technique of transmitting images through glass etc. fibers by repeated internal reflection.
fi·ber·board (fı-bĕr-bohrd) *n.* board made of compressed fibers.
fi·ber·fill (fı-bĕr-fil) *n.* synthetic fibers used as filling for cushions, pillows, etc.
fi·ber·glass (fı-bĕr-glas) *n.* a textile fabric made from glass fibers, a plastic containing glass fibers.
fi·bril (fı-brıl, fib-ril) *n.* a small fiber.
fi·bril·la·tion (fı-brı-lay-shŏn, fib-rı-) *n.* rapid quivering of muscle fibers, especially in the heart.
fi·brin (fı-brin) *n.* an insoluble protein formed in blood clotting.
fi·brin·o·gen (fı-brin-ŏ-jĕn) *n.* a substance that yields fibrin.
fi·broid (fı-broid) *adj.* consisting of fibrous tissue.

fibroid *n.* a benign fibroid tumor in the womb.
fi·bro·sis (fı-broh-sis) *n.* development of excessive fibrous tissue.
fi·brous (fı-brŭs) *adj.* like fibers, made of fibers.
fib·u·la (fib-yŭ-lă) *n.* (*pl.* **-lae,** *pr.* **-lee, -las**) the bone on the outer side of the lower part of the leg.
F.I.C.A. *abbr.* Federal Insurance Contributions Act.
fiche (feesh) *n.* microfiche.
fich·u (fish-oo) *n.* a woman's small triangular scarf of lace or muslin draped around the neck and over the shoulders.
fick·le (fik-ĕl) *adj.* often changing, not constant or loyal. **fick′le·ness** *n.*
fic·tion (fik-shŏn) *n.* 1. a product of the imagination. 2. an invented story. 3. a class of literature consisting of books containing such stories. **fic′tion·al** *adj.* of novels and short stories. **fic′tion·al·ly** *adv.* ▷See the note under **fictitious.**
fic·tion·al·ize (fik-shŏ-nă-lız) *v.* (**fic·tion·al·ized, fic·tion·al·iz·ing**) 1. to make (a true story) into a fictional narrative. 2. to make (a film or play) into a novel.
fic·ti·tious (fik-tish-ŭs) *adj.* imagined, not real, not genuine, *gave a fictitious account of his movements*. ▷ *Fictitious* is used to describe untruths where we expect truths, *fictional* to describe literary invention.
fic·tive (fik-tiv) *adj.* creating or created by imagination, not genuine.
fid·dle (fid-ĕl) *n.* *(informal)* a violin. **fiddle** *v.* (**fid·dled, fid·dling**) 1. *(informal)* to play the fiddle. 2. to fidget with something, to handle a thing aimlessly. 3. *(slang)* to cheat or swindle; *he fiddled with the accounts*, falsified them. **fid′dler** *n.* ☐**fiddler crab**, a small crab, the male of which has one large claw held in position like a violinist's arm.
fid·dle·sticks (fid-ĕl-stiks) *interj.* nonsense.
fi·del·i·ty (fi-del-i-tee, fı-) *n.* (*pl.* **-ties**) 1. faithfulness, loyalty, 2. accuracy, truthfulness. 3. the quality or precision of reproduction of sound.
fid·get (fij-it) *v.* 1. to make small restless movements. 2. to be uneasy, to make (a person) uneasy, to worry. **fidget** *n.* 1. a person who fidgets. 2. *fidgets*, fidgeting movements.
fidg·et·y (fij-ĕ-tee) *adj.* inclined to fidget.
fi·do (fı-doh) *n.* (*pl.* **-dos**) a coin with a minting error. ▷From *f*reak *i*rregular *d*efect *o*ddity.
fi·du·ci·ar·y (fı-doo-shi-er-ee) *n.* (*pl.* **-ar·ies**) a trustee. **fiduciary** *adj.* of the relationship of a fiduciary and his or her client (the *principal*).
fie (fı) *interj.* an expression of disapproval or pretense of outraged propriety.
fief (feef) *n.* 1. a feudal estate. 2. a person's sphere of operation or control. **fief′dom** *n.*
field (feeld) *n.* 1. a piece of open ground, especially one used for pasture or cultivation. 2. an area of land rich in some natural product, a coal field or gas field or oil field. 3. a battlefield. 4. a sports ground, the playing area marked out on this. 5. the space within which an electric or magnetic or gravitational influence etc. can be felt, the force of that influence. 6. the area that can be seen or observed, *one's field of vision*. 7. the range of a subject or activity or interest, *an expert in the field of music*. 8. the scene or area of fieldwork, *field archaeology*. 9. all the competitors in an outdoor contest or sport, all except the one(s) specified. **field** *v.* 1. to act as a fielder in baseball. 2.

to stop and return (the ball) in baseball. 3. to put (a football team or other team) into the field. 4. to deal successfully with (a series of questions). ☐**field day,** a day of much activity, especially of brilliant and exciting events. **field event,** any track-and-field event other than a race, as jumping and shot put. **field glasses,** binoculars for outdoor use. **field goal,** a three-point score made in football by kicking the ball over the bar between the opponent's goal posts; a two-point score made in basketball while the ball is in play. **field gun,** a cannon set on wheels. **field hockey,** a game played on turf by two teams of eleven players using hockey sticks and a small hard ball. **field house,** a building housing an athletic field and storage facilities for athletic equipment. **field marshal,** an army officer of the highest rank, as in the British army. **field mouse,** the type of mouse found in open country. **field officer,** an army officer of the rank of colonel, lieutenant colonel, or major. **field of honor,** the scene of a duel. **field of view,** the expanse visible through an optical instrument. **field of vision,** the area that the eyes can see in a single look. **field trial,** a competition of sporting dogs conducted in the field. **field trip,** an educational trip by a group of students to a site away from their school building, a trip by a scholar to an archaeological, geological, etc. site to gather data.

field·er (feel-dĕr) *n.* a baseball player (other than pitcher or catcher) playing in the infield or outfield.

field·piece (feeld-pees) *n.* a field gun.

field·stone (feeld-stohn) *n.* stone found in fields and used in building.

field·work (feeld-wurk) *n.* practical work done outside libraries and laboratories, as by scientists and by social workers who visit people in their homes. **field′work·er** *n.*

fiend (feend) *n.* 1. an evil spirit. 2. a very wicked or cruel person, one who causes mischief or annoyance. 3. a devotee or addict, *a fresh-air fiend.* **fiend′ish** *adj.* **fiend′ish·ly** *adv.*

fierce (feers) *adj.* 1. violent in temper or manner or action, not gentle. 2. eager, intense, *fierce loyalty.* 3. unpleasantly strong or extreme, *fierce heat.* **fierce′ly** *adv.* **fierce′ness** *n.*

fi·er·y (fɪ-ĕ-ree) *adj.* (**fi·er·i·er, fi·er·i·est**) 1. consisting of fire, flaming. 2. looking like fire, bright red. 3. intensely hot, producing a burning sensation. 4. intense, passionate, *a fiery speech; fiery temper.* **fi′er·i·ness** *n.*

fi·es·ta (fee-es-tă) *n.* a religious festival in Spanish-speaking countries.

fife (fɪf) *n.* a kind of small shrill flute used with a drum in military music.

FIFO (fɪ-foh) *n.* (in accounting) *first in, first out.*

fif·teen (fif-teen) *adj. & n.* one more than fourteen (15, XV). **fif′teenth′** *adj. & n.*

fifth (fifth) *adj. & n.* 1. next after fourth. 2. one of five equal parts of a thing. 3. a fifth part of a gallon, a bottle (of liquor) holding this amount. 4. *the Fifth,* (*informal*) the Fifth Amendment; *the distraught witness took the Fifth,* remained silent. **fifth′ly** *adv.* ☐**Fifth Amendment,** the Constitutional amendment stating that no individual is required to testify against himself in a criminal case. **fifth column,** an organized body working for the enemy within a country at war. (▷ General Mola, leading four columns of troops toward Madrid in the Spanish Civil War, declared that he had a fifth column inside the city.) **fifth columnist,** a member of such a group. **fifth wheel,** a superfluous person or thing.

fif·ties (fif-teez) *n. pl.* the numbers or years or degrees of temperature from fifty to fifty-nine. **fif·ty** (fif-tee) *adj. & n.* (*pl.* **-ties**) five times ten (50, L). **fif′ti·eth** *adj. & n.*

fif·ty-fif·ty (fif-tee-fif-tee) *adj. & adv.* shared or sharing equally between two; *we went fifty-fifty,* we shared the cost; *a fifty-fifty chance,* an equal chance of winning or losing or surviving etc.

fig (fig) *n.* 1. a broad-leaved tree bearing a soft pear-shaped fruit. 2. this fruit. 3. a valueless thing, *I don't give a fig for conventions.* ☐**fig leaf,** a device used in statuary for concealing something thought to be indecent, especially the genitals.

fig. *abbr.* 1. figurative. 2. figuratively. 3. figure.

fight (fɪt) *v.* (**fought, fight·ing**) 1. to struggle against (a person or country) in physical combat or in war. 2. to carry on (a battle). 3. to struggle or contend in any way, to strive to obtain or accomplish something. 4. to strive to overcome or destroy, *they fought the fire.* 5. to make one's way by fighting or effort. **fight** *n.* 1. fighting, a battle. 2. a struggle or contest or conflict of any kind. 3. a boxing match. ☐**fight back,** to show resistance. **fighting chance,** a chance of succeeding provided that one makes a great effort. **fight it out,** to settle something by fighting or arguing until one side wins. **fight off,** to drive away by fighting. **show fight,** to show readiness to fight.

fight·er (fɪ-tĕr) *n.* 1. a person who fights. 2. one who does not yield without a struggle. 3. a fast military aircraft designed for attacking other aircraft.

fig·ment (fig-mĕnt) *n.* a thing that does not exist except in the imagination.

fig·u·ra·tive (fig-yŭ-ră-tiv) *adj.* using or containing a figure of speech, metaphorical, not literal. **fig′ur·a·tive·ly** *adv.* in a figurative way. ▷See the note under **literal.**

fig·ure (fig-yŭr) *n.* 1. the written symbol of a number. 2. a diagram. 3. a decorative pattern, a pattern traced in dancing or skating. 4. a representation of a person or animal in drawing, painting, sculpture, etc. 5. a person as seen or studied, *saw a figure leaning against the door; the most terrible figure in our history.* 6. external form or shape, bodily shape, *has a good figure.* 7. a geometrical shape enclosed by lines or surfaces. 8. *figures,* arithmetic, calculating, *she is good at figures.* **figure** *v.* (**fig·ured, fig·ur·ing**) 1. to represent in a diagram or picture. 2. to picture mentally, to imagine. 3. to form part of a plan etc., to appear or be mentioned, *he figures in all books on the subject.* ☐**figure of fun,** a person who looks ridiculous. **figure of speech,** a word or phrase used for vivid or dramatic effect and not literally. **figure on,** (*informal*) to count on, to expect. **figure out,** (*informal*) to work out by arithmetic; to interpret, to understand.

fig·ured (fig-yŭrd) *adj.* ornamented, decorated; *figured silk,* with designs woven into it.

fig·ure·head (fig-yŭr-hed) *n.* 1. a carved image at the prow of a ship. 2. a person at the head of an organization etc. but without real power.

fig·ur·ine (fig-yŭ-reen) *n.* a statuette.

Fi·ji (fee-jee) a country in the South Pacific. **Fi·ji·an** (fi-jee-ăn) *adj. & n.*

fil·a·ment (fil-ă-mĕnt) *n.* 1. a threadlike strand. 2. a fine wire in a light bulb etc. giving off light (and heat) when heated by the current.

fi·lar (fɪ-lär) *adj.* of or relating to a thread.

fil·bert (fĭl-bĕrt) *n.* the nut of a cultivated hazel.

filch (fĭlch) *v.* to pilfer, to steal (something of small value).

file¹ (fɪl) *n.* a steel tool with a roughened surface for shaping or smoothing things. **file** *v.* **(filed, fil·ing)** to shape or smooth with a file.

file² *n.* 1. a holder or cover or box etc. for keeping papers together and to arrange them for reference purposes. 2. its contents. 3. a line of people or things one behind the other; *in single file,* one at a time. **file** *v.* **(filed, fil·ing)** 1. to place in a file. 2. to place on record, *file an application.* 3. to march in file, *they filed out.*

fi·let mi·gnon (fi-lay min-yon) (*pl.* **fi·lets mi·gnons,** *pr.* fi-lay min-yonz) a small, choice filet of beef cut from the thick part of a beef tenderloin.

fil·i·al (fĭl-i-ăl) *adj.* of or due from a son or daughter, *filial duty.*

fil·i·bus·ter (fĭl-ĭ-bus-tĕr) *n.* the use of delaying tactics by a legislator to delay or prevent a vote on a bill, a long speech or other tactic used for this purpose. **filibuster** *v.* to delay things in this way. **fil·i·bus·ter·er** (fĭl-ĭ-bus-tĕ-rĕr) *n.*

fil·i·gree (fĭl-ĭ-gree) *n.* ornamental lacelike work in metal. **fil'i·greed** *adj.*

fil·ing (fɪ-ling) *n.* a particle rubbed off by a file.

Fil·i·pi·no (fĭl-ĭ-pee-noh) *n.* (*pl.* **-nos**) a native of the Philippine Islands. **Filipino** *adj.*

fill (fĭl) *v.* 1. to make or become full, to occupy the whole of. 2. to block up (a hole or cavity). 3. to spread over or through, *smoke began to fill the room.* 4. to hold (a position), to appoint a person to (a vacant post). 5. to occupy (vacant time). **fill** *n.* 1. enough to fill something. 2. enough to satisfy a person's appetite or desire. □**filled milk,** skim milk with a substitute for butterfat. **fill in,** to complete by writing or drawing inside an outline; to complete (an unfinished document etc.); (*informal*) to inform (a person) more fully; to act as a substitute. **fill out,** to enlarge, to become enlarged or plumper. **fill the bill,** to be suitable for what is required. **fill up,** to fill completely, to fill the gas tank of a car.

fill·er (fĭl-ĕr) *n.* an object or material used to fill a cavity or to increase the bulk of something.

fil·let (fĭl-it) *n.* 1. a boneless slice or cut of meat or fish. 2. a strip of ribbon etc. worn around the head. **fillet** *v.* to remove the bones from (fish etc.).

fill·ing (fĭl-ing) *n.* 1. material used to fill a tooth cavity. 2. material put into a container to absorb impact, between layers of bread to form a sandwich, etc. □**filling station,** a gas station.

fil·lip (fĭl-ĭp) *n.* 1. a quick smart blow or stroke given with a fingertip. 2. something that tends to excite interest or enthusiasm. **fillip** *v.* **(fil·liped, fil·lip·ing)** to strike with a fingernail in order to compel attention, obedience to a command, etc.

Fill·more (fĭl-mohr), **Mil·lard** (1800–74) the thirteenth president of the U.S. 1850–53.

fil·ly (fĭl-ee) *n.* (*pl.* **-lies**) a young female horse.

film (fĭlm) *n.* 1. a thin coating or covering layer. 2. a rolled strip or sheet coated with light-sensitive material used for taking photographs or making a motion picture, a single roll of this. 3. a motion picture. **film** *v.* 1. to cover or become covered with a thin coating or covering layer. 2. to make a film of (a story etc.). □**film star,** a star actor or actress in films.

film·go·er (fĭlm-goh-ĕr) *n.* a person who patronizes motion-picture theaters.

film·og·ra·phy (fĭl-mog-ră-fee) *n.* (*pl.* **-phies**) a list of films on a particular theme or by a particular director, producer, actor, or actress.

film·strip (fĭlm-strip) *n.* a series of transparencies for still projection, especially in teaching.

film·y (fĭl-mee) *adj.* **(film·i·er, film·i·est)** thin and almost transparent.

fil·ter (fĭl-tĕr) *n.* 1. a device or substance for holding back the impurities in a liquid or gas passed through it. 2. a screen for preventing light of certain wavelengths from passing through. 3. a device for suppressing electrical or sound waves of frequencies other than the ones required. 4. (*informal*) a filter tip. **filter** *v.* 1. to pass or cause to pass through a filter, to remove impurities in this way. 2. to come or make a way in or out gradually, *news filtered out; people filtered into the hall.* 3. to screen (information) in order to remove objectionable items etc. **fil'ter·a·ble** *adj.* **fil·tra·ble** (fĭl-tră-bĕl) *adj.* □**filter bed,** a tank or reservoir containing a layer of sand etc. for filtering large quantities of liquid. **filter paper,** porous paper for filtering liquids. **filter tip,** a cigarette with a filter at the mouth end to purify the smoke. **fil'ter-tipped** *adj.*

filth (fĭlth) *n.* 1. disgusting dirt. 2. obscenity.

filth·y (fĭl-thee) *adj.* **(filth·i·er, filth·i·est)** 1. disgustingly dirty. 2. obscene. **filth·i·ly** *adv.* **filth·i·ness** *n.*

fil·trate (fĭl-trayt) *v.* **(fil·trat·ed, fil·trat·ing)** to filter. **fil·tra·tion** (fĭl-tray-shŏn) *n.*

fin (fĭn) *n.* 1. a thin flat projection from the body of a fish etc., used by the animal for propelling and steering itself in the water. 2. an underwater swimmer's rubber flipper. 3. a small projection shaped like a fish's fin, to improve the stability of an aircraft, rocket, etc. **finned** *adj.*

fin. *abbr.* 1. finance. 2. financial. 3. finish.

Fin. *abbr.* 1. Finland. 2. Finnish.

fi·na·gle (fi-nay-gĕl) *v.* **(fi·na·gled, fi·na·gling)** (*informal*) to behave or obtain dishonestly. **fi·na'gler** *n.*

fi·nal (fɪ-năl) *adj.* 1. at the end, coming last. 2. putting an end to doubt or discussion or argument. **final** *n.* 1. the edition of a newspaper published latest in the day. 2. *finals,* the last examinations in a course or competition, the last event in an athletic competition. **fi'nal·ly** *adv.*

fi·na·le (fi-nal-ee) *n.* the final section of a musical composition or a drama or any activity.

fi·nal·ist (fɪ-nă-list) *n.* a person who competes in the finals of an athletic competition.

fi·nal·i·ty (fɪ-nal-i-tee) *n.* (*pl.* **-ties**) the quality of being final.

fi·nal·ize (fɪ-nă-lɪz) *v.* **(fi·nal·ized, fi·nal·iz·ing)** 1. to bring to an end. 2. to put into its final form. **fi·na·li·za·tion** (fɪ-nă-li-zay-shŏn) *n.* ▷Careful writers do not use *finalization* or *finalize.*

fi·nance (fi-nans, fɪ-nans) *n.* 1. the management of money. 2. money as support for an undertaking. 3. *finances,* the money resources of a country or company or person. **finance** *v.* **(fi·nanced, fi·nanc·ing)** to provide the money for. □**finance company,** a company that is mainly concerned with lending money for retail purchases.

fi·nan·cial (fi-nan-shăl, fɪ-) *adj.* of finance. **fi·nan'cial·ly** *adv.* ▷See the note under **monetary.**

fin·an·cier (fin-ăn-seer, fı-năn-) *n.* a person who is engaged in financing businesses etc. on a large scale.

finch (finch) *n.* any of a number of related birds, most of which have short stubby bills.

find (fınd) *v.* (**found, find·ing**) 1. to discover by search or effort or inquiry or by chance. 2. to become aware of, to discover (a fact). 3. to arrive at naturally, *water finds its own level.* 4. to succeed in obtaining, *can't find time to do it.* 5. to supply, to provide, *who will find the money for the expedition?* 6. (of a jury etc.) to decide and declare, *found him innocent; found for the plaintiff.* **find** *n.* 1. the finding of something. 2. a thing found, especially something useful or pleasing. □**find favor,** to be acceptable. **find oneself,** to discover one's natural powers or one's vocation. **find one's feet,** to become able to stand or walk; to develop one's powers and become able to act independently. **find out,** to get information about; to detect (a person) who has done wrong; to discover (a deception or fraud).

find·er (fın-děr) *n.* 1. one who finds something. 2. the viewfinder of a camera. 3. a small telescope attached to a larger one to locate an object for observation. □**finder's fee,** money paid to an agent for discovering a commercial opportunity and bringing buyer and seller together.

fin de siè·cle (fan dĕ sye-klĕ) the end of a century, especially the 19th century. ▷French.

find·ings (fın-dingz) *n. pl.* the conclusions reached by means of an inquiry.

fine[1] (fın) *n.* a sum of money fixed as a penalty for an offense. **fine** *v.* (**fined, fin·ing**) to punish by a fine.

fine[2] *adj.* (**fin·er, fin·est**) 1. of high quality. 2. excellent, of great merit. 3. (of weather) bright and clear, free from rain and fog etc. 4. of slender thread or thickness, small-sized, consisting of small particles. 5. requiring very skillful workmanship. 6. difficult to perceive, *making fine distinctions.* 7. complimentary especially in an insincere way, *said fine things about them.* 8. in good health, comfortable, *I'm fine, thank you.* **fine** *adv.* 1. finely. 2. *(informal)* very well, *that will suit me fine.* **fine** *v.* (**fined, fin·ing**) to make or become finer or thinner or less coarse. **fine'ly** *adv.* **fine'ness** *n.* □**fine arts** those appealing to the sense of beauty, especially painting, sculpture, and architecture. **not to put too fine a point on it,** to express it bluntly.

fine-drawn (fın-drawn) *adj.* 1. subtle. 2. extremely thin.

fin·er·y (fı-nĕ-ree) *n.* (*pl.* **-er·ies**) fine clothes or decorations.

fines herbes (feenz airb) mixed herbs used to flavor cooking. ▷French.

fine·spun (fın-spun) *adj.* 1. refined, delicately detailed. 2. excessively detailed.

fi·nesse (fi-nes) *n.* 1. delicate manipulation. 2. tact and cleverness in dealing with a situation. 3. (in bridge) taking a trick with a card that is not the highest and might lose to an opponent's card. **finesse** *v.* (**fi·nessed, fi·ness·ing**) 1. to use finesse. 2. (in bridge) to attempt a finesse.

fine-tooth (fın-tooth) **comb,** a comb with narrow close-set teeth; *go through something with a fine-tooth comb,* to examine it closely and thoroughly.

fin·fish (fın-fish) *n.* *(informal)* a true fish, not a shell fish.

fin·ger (fing-gĕr) *n.* 1. one of the five parts extending from each hand, or one of these other than the thumb. 2. the part of a glove that fits over a finger. 3. a fingerlike object. 4. *(slang)* the breadth of a finger (about three-quarters of an inch) as a measure of liquor in a glass. **finger** *v.* 1. to touch or feel with the fingers. 2. to play (a musical instrument) with the fingers. 3. *(slang)* to identify as a criminal suspect or a target for assassination. □**finger bowl,** a small bowl for rinsing one's fingers at the table. **finger mark,** a mark left on a surface by a finger. **finger paint,** paint formulated for applying with the fingers. **finger painting,** a painting made with the fingers; the technique of painting in this way. **finger wave,** a small wave set in the hair by fingers. **have a finger in the pie,** to be actively involved in a project.

fin·ger·board (fing-gĕr-bohrd) *n.* the part of the neck of a violin etc. where strings are pressed by fingers.

fin·ger·ing (fing-gĕ-ring) *n.* 1. a method of using the fingers in playing a musical instrument or in typing. 2. an indication of this in a musical score, usually by numbers.

fin·ger·ling (fing-gĕr-ling) *n.* a young fish smaller than a man's finger.

fin·ger·nail (fing-gĕr-nayl) *n.* the nail at the tip of the finger.

fin·ger·print (fing-gĕr-print) *n.* an impression of the ridges of the skin on the pad of a finger, especially as a means of identification. **fingerprint** *v.* to take such an impression of.

fin·ger·tip (fing-gĕr-tip) *n.* the tip of a finger. □**have at one's fingertips,** to be thoroughly familiar with (a thing or fact).

fin·i·al (fin-i-ăl) *n.* an ornament finishing off the apex of a roof, pediment, lamp, etc.

fin·ick·y (fin-ı-kee) *adj.* being fastidious, giving or requiring extreme care about details.

fi·nis (fin-is) *n.* the end or conclusion, especially of a book or film.

fin·ish (fin-ish) *v.* 1. to bring or come to an end, to complete. 2. to reach the end of a task or race etc. 3. to consume or get through all of, *finish the pie.* 4. to put the final touches to, to complete the manufacture of (woodwork, cloth, etc.) by surface treatment. **finish** *n.* 1. the last stage of something. 2. the point at which a race etc. ends. 3. the state of being finished or perfect. 4. the method or texture or material used for finishing woodwork etc. □**finishing school,** a private school preparing girls for life in fashionable society. **finish off,** to kill. **finish with,** to complete one's use of; to end one's association with.

fi·nite (fı-nıt) *adj.* limited, not infinite.

fink (fingk) *n.* *(slang)* 1. a despicable person. 2. an informer.

Fin·land (fin-lănd) a country of northeast Europe.

Finn (fin) *n.* a native or inhabitant of Finland.

fin·nan had·die (fin-ăn had-ee) haddock cured with smoke of green wood or of turf or peat.

Finn·ish (fin-ish) *adj.* of the Finns or their language. **Finnish** *n.* the language of the Finns.

FIO *abbr.* free in and out.

fiord = **fjord.**

fir (fur) *n.* 1. (also **fir tree**) a kind of evergreen cone-bearing tree with needlelike leaves on its shoots. 2. its wood.

fire (fır) *n.* 1. combustion producing light and heat. 2. destructive burning, *insured against fire.* 3.

burning fuel in a fireplace or furnace etc., an electric or gas fire. 4. angry or excited feeling, enthusiasm. 5. the firing of guns, *hold your fire.* **fire** *v.* **(fired, fir·ing)** 1. to set fire to. 2. to catch fire. 3. to supply (a furnace etc.) with fuel. 4. to bake (pottery or bricks). 5. to excite, to stimulate, *fired them with enthusiasm.* 6. to send a bullet or shell from a gun, to detonate. 7. (of a firearm) to discharge its missile. 8. to dismiss (an employee) from a job. **fir′er** *n.* □**catch fire,** to begin to burn; *(informal)* to develop or show enthusiasm. **fire alarm,** a bell or other device giving warning of fire. **fire ant,** a stinging ant that feeds on both animal and vegetable substances. **fire away,** *(informal)* to begin, to go ahead. **fire department,** an organized body of people trained and employed to extinguish fires. **fire dog,** a Dalmatian. **fire drill,** a rehearsal of the procedure to be used in case of fire. **fire eater,** a circus performer who appears to eat fire; a person who is fond of fighting or quarreling; *(slang)* a fireman. **fire engine,** a vehicle fitted with equipment used for fighting fires. **fire escape,** a special staircase or apparatus by which people may escape from a burning building etc. in case of fire. **fire extinguisher,** an apparatus used for putting out a fire. **fire fighter,** a person who works at putting out forest fires; *(informal)* a fireman. **fire irons,** a poker, tongs, and shovel for tending a domestic fire. **fire screen,** a protective screen placed in front of an open fireplace. **fire station,** the headquarters of the fire department. **fire storm,** a high wind or storm following fire caused by bombs. **fire tower,** a tower from which a watch for fires can be kept. **fire truck,** = **fire engine.** **firing line,** the front line in a battle, from which troops fire at the enemy; a position in the forefront of an activity. **firing squad,** a group ordered to fire a salute during a military funeral, or to shoot a condemned person. **on fire,** burning. **under fire,** under attack; under criticism.

fire·arm (fɪr-ahrm) *n.* a rifle, gun, pistol, or revolver.

fire·ball (fɪr-bawl) *n.* 1. a large meteor. 2. a ball of flame from a nuclear explosion, lightning, etc. 3. a highly energetic person.

fire·base (fɪr-bays) *n.* an artillery base, especially one quickly set up to support an infantry attack.

fire·boat (fɪr-boht) *n.* a ship furnished with fire-fighting equipment.

fire·bomb (fɪr-bom) *n.* an incendiary bomb. **firebomb** *v.* to bombard with or place a firebomb. **fire′bomb·er** *n.*

fire·box (fɪr-boks) *n.* 1. the fuel chamber of a steam boiler. 2. a box with an alarm or telephone for notifying the fire station about a fire.

fire·brand (fɪr-brand) *n.* a person who stirs up trouble.

fire·break (fɪr-brayk) *n.* a ditch or clearing to prevent a forest fire from spreading.

fire·brick (fɪr-brik) *n.* a brick made of fireclay.

fire·bug (fɪr-bug) *n.* *(informal)* a pyromaniac, an arsonist.

fire·clay (fɪr-klay) *n.* clay that resists great heat, used in firebricks and furnaces.

fire·crack·er (fɪr-krak-ĕr) *n.* a paper cylinder filled with an explosive and having a fuse, used as a noisemaker.

fire·damp (fɪr-damp) *n.* the miners' name for methane, which is explosive when mixed in certain proportions with air.

fire·dog (fɪr-dawg) *n.* an andiron.

fire·fly (fɪr-flɪ) *n.* (*pl.* **-flies**) a kind of beetle that gives off a phosphorescent light.

fire·house (fɪr-hows) *n.* a building housing equipment and personnel for fighting fires.

fire·light (fɪr-lɪt) *n.* the light from a fire in a fireplace.

fire·man (fɪr-măn) *n.* (*pl.* **-men,** *pr.* -měn) 1. a member of a fire department. 2. one whose job is to tend a furnace etc.

fire·place (fɪr-plays) *n.* 1. an open recess for a domestic fire, at the base of a chimney. 2. the surrounding structure.

fire·plug (fɪr-plug) *n.* *(informal)* a fire hydrant.

fire·pow·er (fɪr-pow-ĕr) *n.* the ability (of a military unit) to inflict destruction.

fire·proof (fɪr-proof) *adj.* 1. that does not catch fire. 2. that does not break when heated, *fireproof dishes.*

fire·re·sist·ant (fɪr-rĕ-zis-tănt) *adj.* capable of resisting, though not entirely preventing, destruction by fire.

fire·side (fɪr-sɪd) *n.* the part of a room near a fireplace, this as the center of one's home. **fire·side** *adj.* informal and friendly. □**fireside chat,** an informal discussion.

fire·trap (fɪr-trap) *n.* a building poorly protected against fire and without proper exits in case of fire.

fire·wa·ter (fɪr-waw-tĕr) *n.* *(slang)* whiskey.

fire·wood (fɪr-wuud) *n.* wood for use as fuel.

fire·work (fɪr-wurk) *n.* 1. a device containing chemicals that burn or explode with spectacular effect, used at celebrations. 2. *fireworks,* a display of fireworks; an outburst of anger.

firm[1] (furm) *n.* a partnership for carrying on a professional practice or a business, a commercial establishment.

firm[2] *adj.* 1. not yielding when pressed, hard, solid. 2. steady, not shaking. 3. securely based. 4. established, not easily changed or influenced, *a firm belief; a firm offer,* one that is not liable to be canceled. **firm** *adv.* firmly, *stand firm.* **firm** *v.* to make or become firm or compact, to fix firmly. **firm′ly** *adv.* **firm′ness** *n.*

fir·ma·ment (fur-mă-měnt) *n.* the sky with its clouds and stars.

first (furst) *adj.* coming before all others in time or order or importance. **first** *n.* something that is first, the first day of a month, the first occurrence or achievement of something. **first** *adv.* 1. before all others. 2. before another event or time; *must finish this work first,* before doing something else. 3. for the first time, *when did you first see him?* 4. in preference, *will see him dead first.* □**at first,** at the beginning. **at first hand,** obtained directly, from the original source. **first aid,** treatment given to an injured person before a doctor comes. **first base,** the first of the bases that must be reached to score a run in baseball; the portion of the field near this base; *get to first base,* to achieve the first step toward an objective. **first baseman,** the baseball player stationed at first base. **first blood,** the first success in a contest. **first class,** the best quality; the best accommodation in a boat or train or aircraft etc.; (of mail) the category that is most expensive and is intended to be delivered quickly and be given special treatment in handling. **first cousin,** *see* **cousin. first fruits,** the first of a season's agricultural products, offered to God; the first results of work etc. **first**

gear, the lowest forward gear in a motor vehicle. **first lady** (also **First Lady**), the wife of the president of the U.S. **first lieutenant,** *see* **lieutenant. first mate,** a ship's officer ranking just below the captain. **first name,** a personal or Christian name. **first night,** the first public performance of a play etc. **first offender,** a person convicted of a crime or guilty of an offense for the first time. **first officer,** the mate on a merchant ship. **first person,** *see* **person. first sergeant,** a noncommissioned officer acting as an administrative aide to the commander of a military company; a U.S. Army rank just below a command sergeant major; a U.S. Marine Corps rank below a sergeant major. **first string,** *(informal)* (in sports) the best players of a team. **first thing,** *(informal)* before anything else, *shall do it first thing.* **first violin,** one of the group of violinists in an orchestral group playing the leading part of two or more parts. **first violinist,** the first violin in a chamber music group.

first·born (furst-born) *adj.* & *n.* eldest, the eldest child.

first·hand (furst-hand) *adj.* & *adv.* obtained directly from the original source.

first·ling (furst-ling) *n.* the first result of anything, the firstborn in a season.

first·ly (furst-lee) *adv.* first, as a first consideration.

first·rate (furst-rayt) *adj.* & *adv.* of the best class, excellent; *(informal)* very well.

firth (furth) *n.* an estuary or a narrow inlet of the sea in Scotland.

fis·cal (fis-kăl) *adj.* of public revenue. **fis'cal·ly** *adv.* ☐**fiscal year,** the financial year of a business, government, etc., established without regard for the calendar year.

fish (fish) *n.* (*pl.* **fish·es, fish**) 1. a cold-blooded animal living wholly in water. 2. its flesh as food. 3. *(informal)* a person, *an odd fish.* 4. *the Fish* or *Fishes,* a sign of the zodiac, Pisces. **fish** *v.* 1. to try to catch fish; *fish the river,* try to catch fish from it. 2. to search for something in or under water or by reaching into something. 3. *(informal)* to bring out or up in this way, *fished out his keys.* 4. to try to obtain by hinting or indirect questioning, *fishing for information.* ☐**fish and chips,** fried fish fillets and French fried potatoes. **fish cake,** a small cake of shredded fish and mashed potato. **fish ladder,** a system of pools enabling fish to swim around or over a dam. **fish meal,** ground dried fish used as a fertilizer. **fish out of water,** a person who is out of his element. **fish story,** *(informal)* an exaggerated story, a lie. **have other fish to fry,** to have more important business to attend to. ▷Use the plural form *fishes* especially when you mean two or more species or kinds.

fish·bowl (fish-bohl) *n.* a glass bowl for keeping fish in.

fish·er (fish-ĕr) *n.* 1. a man who lives by fishing. 2. a large type of weasel found in North America.

fish·er·man (fish-ĕr-măn) *n.* (*pl.* **-men,** *pr.* -mĕn) 1. a man who earns a living by fishing. 2. one who goes fishing as a sport.

fish·er·y (fish-ĕ-ree) *n.* (*pl.* **-er·ies**) 1. part of the sea where fishing is carried on. 2. the business of fishing.

fish·hook (fish-huuk) *n.* a hook used for catching fish.

fish·ing (fish-ing) *n.* trying to catch fish. ☐**fishing ground,** an area used for fishing. **fishing rod,** a long rod to which a line is attached, used for fishing. **fishing tackle,** equipment used in fishing.

fish·net (fish-net) *n.* an open-meshed fabric.

fish·wife (fish-wīf) *n.* 1. a woman selling fish. 2. a crude woman.

fish·y (fish-ee) *adj.* **(fish·i·er, fish·i·est)** 1. like fish, smelling or tasting of fish. 2. *(informal)* causing disbelief or suspicion, *a fishy story.* **fish'i·ness** *n.*

fis·sile (fis-īl) *adj.* 1. tending to split. 2. capable of undergoing nuclear fission.

fis·sion (fish-ŏn) *n.* 1. splitting of the nucleus of certain atoms, with release of energy. 2. splitting or division of biological cells as a method of reproduction.

fis·sion·a·ble (fish-ŏ-nă-bĕl) *adj.* capable of undergoing nuclear fission.

fis·sure (fish-ŭr) *n.* a cleft made by splitting or separation of parts.

fist (fist) *n.* the hand when tightly closed, with the fingers bent into the palm. **fist'ed** *adj.*

fist·ful (fist-fŭl) *n.* (*pl.* **-fuls**) 1. a handful. 2. *(informal)* a person who is difficult to control, a troublesome task.

fist·i·cuffs (fis-tĭ-kufs) *n.* fighting with the fists.

fis·tu·la (fis-chŭ-lă) *n.* (*pl.* **-las, -lae,** *pr.* -lee) 1. a long pipelike ulcer. 2. an abnormal or surgically made passage in the body. 3. a natural pipe or spout in whales, insects, etc.

fit¹ (fit) *n.* 1. a brief spell of an illness or its symptoms, *a fit of coughing.* 2. a sudden violent seizure of epilepsy, apoplexy, etc., with convulsions or loss of consciousness. 3. an attack of strong feeling, *a fit of rage.* 4. a short period of certain feeling or activity, an impulse, *a fit of energy.* ☐**by fits and starts,** in short bursts of activity, not steadily or regularly. **throw a fit,** *(informal)* to express anger.

fit² (fit-ter, fit-test) *adj.* 1. suitable or well adapted for something, good enough. 2. right and proper, fitting. 3. feeling in a suitable condition to do something; *worked till they were fit to drop,* ready to drop from exhaustion. 4. in good athletic condition or health, *fit as a fiddle.* **fit** *v.* **(fit·ted, fit·ting)** 1. to be the right shape and size for something. 2. to put clothing on (a person) and adjust it to the right shape and size. 3. to put into place, *fit a lock on the door.* 4. to make or be suitable or competent, *his training fitted him for the position.* **fit** *n.* the way a thing fits, *the coat is a good fit.* **fit'ly** *adv.* **fit'ness** *n.* ☐**fit in,** to make room or time etc. for; to be or cause to be harmonious or in a suitable relationship. **fit out** *or* **up,** to supply or equip. **see** *or* **think fit,** to decide or choose to do something, especially when this is unwise or without good reason.

fit·ful (fit-fŭl) *adj.* occurring in short periods, not regularly or steadily. **fit'ful·ly** *adv.*

fit·ter (fit-ĕr) *n.* 1. a person who supervises the fitting of clothes etc. 2. a mechanic who fits together and adjusts the parts of machinery.

fit·ting (fit-ing) *adj.* proper, right, suitable. **fitting** *n.* 1. the trying on of clothing that has been altered or specially made. 2. a mechanical part or equipment. **fit'ting·ly** *adv.*

five (fīv) *adj.* & *n.* one more than four (5, V). ☐**five-and-ten-cent store, five-and-dime (store),** a store that sells a wide variety of inexpensive merchandise, formerly costing between five and ten cents. **give me five,** *(slang)* shake my hand.

five·fold (fīv-fohld) *adj.* & *adv.* 1. five times as

much or as many. 2. consisting of five parts.
fi·ver (fī-vĕr) *n.* *(slang)* a five-dollar bill.
five-star (fīv-stahr) *adj.* of the highest class. □**five-star general,** a general of the army.
fix (fīks) *v.* 1. to fasten firmly. 2. to implant (facts or ideas) firmly in the mind or memory. 3. to direct (the eyes or attention) steadily toward something. 4. to establish, to specify, *fixed a time for the meeting; how are you fixed for cash,* what is your situation as regards money? 5. to treat (a photographic image or a color etc.) with a substance that prevents it from fading or changing color. 6. to repair 7. *(slang)* to deal with, to get even with. 8. *(slang)* to use bribery or deception or improper influence on, to arrange (the result of a race etc.) fraudulently. **fix** *n.* 1. an awkward situation, a dilemma, *be in a fix.* 2. the finding of the position of a ship or aircraft etc. by taking bearings, the position found. 3. *(slang)* an addict's dose of a narcotic drug. □**fixed star,** an ordinary star, one that (unlike the sun and planets) is so far from Earth that it seems to have no motion of its own. **fix up,** to arrange; to organize; to provide for, *fixed him up with a job.*
fix·ate (fik-sayt) *v.* (**fix·at·ed, fix·at·ing**) 1. to direct one's gaze on. 2. to become emotionally arrested at an immature stage and therefore develop an abnormal attachment to certain persons or things. 3. to cause (a person) to undergo this process.
fix·a·tion (fik-say-shŏn) *n.* 1. fixing, being fixed. 2. an abnormal emotional attachment to a person or thing. 3. concentration on one idea, an obsession.
fix·a·tive (fik-să-tiv) *n.* 1. a substance for keeping things in position. 2. a substance for fixing colors etc., or for preventing perfumes from evaporating too quickly.
fixed (fikst) *adj.* firmly fastened or stationary, not to be changed or moved, *a fixed amount.*
fix·ed·ly (fik-sid-lee) *adv.* in a fixed way.
fix·er (fik-sĕr) *n.* 1. a person or thing that fixes something. 2. a substance for fixing photographic images. 3. *(slang)* a person who illegally arranges the results of a race etc. or attempts to bribe officials etc.
fix·ings (fik-singz) *n. pl.* the vegetables, puddings, etc. that accompany a main dish, *turkey with all the fixings.*
fix·i·ty (fik-si-tee) *n.* (*pl.* **-ties**) a fixed state, stability, permanence.
fix·ture (fiks-chŭr) *n.* 1. a thing that is fixed in position. 2. a person or thing that is firmly established and unlikely to leave. 3. a date appointed for a match or race etc., the match or race itself.
fizz (fiz) *v.* to make a hissing or spluttering sound, as when gas escapes in bubbles from a liquid. **fizz** *n.* 1. this sound. 2. a bubbling drink, *gin fizz.* **fiz′zy** *adj.* **fiz′zi·ness** *n.*
fiz·zle (fiz-ĕl) *v.* (**fiz·zled, fiz·zling**) 1. to make a feeble fizzing sound. 2. to fizzle out. **fizzle** *n.* 1. the sound of fizzling. 2. (of an effort) a failure. □**fizzle out,** to end feebly or unsuccessfully.
fjord (fyohrd) *n.* a long narrow inlet from the sea between high cliffs, as in Norway.
FL *abbr.* Florida.
fl. *abbr.* 1. floor. 2. flourished. 3. fluid.
Fla. *abbr.* Florida.
flab (flab) *n.* *(informal)* fat, flabbiness.
flab·ber·gast (flab-ĕr-gast) *v.* to overwhelm with astonishment.

flab·by (flab-ee) *adj.* (**flab·bi·er, flab·bi·est**) fat and limp, not firm. **flab′bi·ly** *adv.* **flab′bi·ness** *n.*
flac·cid (flak-sid) *adj.* hanging loose or wrinkled, not firm. **flac′cid·ly** *adv.* **flac·cid·i·ty** (flak-sid-i-tee) *n.* ▷Note the pronunciation of these words.
flack (flak) *n.* *(slang)* a press agent.
fla·con (flak-ŏn) *n.* a small bottle with a stopper.
flag[1] (flag) *n.* 1. a piece of cloth attached by one edge to a staff or rope and used as the distinctive symbol of a country etc. or as a signal. 2. an oblong device used as a signal that a taxi is for hire. 3. a small paper device resembling a flag. **flag** *v.* (**flagged, flag·ging**) 1. to mark out with flags. 2. to signal with or as if with a flag; *flagged the vehicle down,* signaled to it to stop. □**Flag Day,** June 14, the anniversary of the adoption of the Stars and Stripes in 1777. **flag of convenience,** a foreign flag of the nationality under which a ship is registered to avoid taxation or certain regulations.
flag[2] *v.* (**flagged, flag·ging**) 1. to hang down limply, to droop. 2. to lose vigor, to become weak, *interest flagged.*
flag[3] *n.* a flagstone. **flag** *v.* (**flagged, flag·ging**) to pave with flagstones.
flag·el·late (flaj-ě-layt) *v.* (**flag·el·lat·ed, flag·el·lat·ing**) to whip. **flag·el·la·tion** (flaj-ě-lay-shŏn) *n.*
fla·gel·lum (flă-jel-ŭm) *n.* (*pl.* **-gel·la,** *pr.* -jel-ă, **-gel·lums**) a lashlike appendage of protozoa, bacteria, etc.
flag·eo·let (flaj-ě-let) *n.* a small flute blown at the end, like a recorder but with thumb holes.
fla·gi·tious (flă-jish-ŭs) *adj.* deeply criminal, utterly villainous.
flag·man (flag-măn) *n.* (*pl.* **-men,** *pr.* -měn) a person who is employed to signal with a flag or light, as on a railroad or at a highway construction site.
flag·on (flag-ŏn) *n.* a vessel with a handle, lip, and lid for serving wine at the table.
flag·pole (flag-pohl) *n.* a pole on which a flag is displayed.
fla·grant (flay-grănt) *adj.* (of an offense or error or an offender) very bad and obvious. **fla′grant·ly** *adv.* **fla′gran·cy** *n.*
flag·ship (flag-ship) *n.* a ship that carries an admiral and flies his flag.
flag·staff (flag-staf) *n.* a flagpole.
flag·stone (flag-stohn) *n.* a flat slab of rock used for paving.
flail (flayl) *n.* an old-fashioned tool for threshing grain, consisting of a strong stick hinged on a long handle. **flail** *v.* 1. to beat with or as if with a flail. 2. to wave or swing about wildly.
flair (flair) *n.* a natural ability to do something well or to select and recognize what is good or useful etc. ▷Do not confuse *flair* with *flare.*
flak (flak) *n.* 1. shells fired by antiaircraft guns. 2. *(informal)* verbal abuse. □**flak jacket,** a heavy protective jacket, reinforced with metal.
flake (flayk) *n.* 1. a light fleecy piece of snow. 2. a small thin leaflike piece of something. **flake** *v.* (**flaked, flak·ing**) to come off in flakes. **flak′y** *adj.* (**flak·i·er, flak·i·est**) 1. of or like flakes. 2. *(slang)* strange, eccentric, *a flaky sense of humor.* □**flake out,** *(informal)* to faint or fall asleep from exhaustion.
flam·bé (flahm-bay) *adj.* (of food) covered with

liquor (usually brandy) and ignited before serving.

flam·beau (flam-boh) *n.* (*pl.* **-beaux**, *pr.* **-bohz**, **-beaus**) a flaming torch.

flam·boy·ant (flam-boi-ănt) *adj.* 1. colored or decorated in a very showy way. 2. (of people) having a very showy appearance or manner. **flam· boy′ant·ly** *adv.* **flam·boy′ance** *n.* **flam·boy′ an·cy** *n.*

flame (flaym) *n.* 1. the visible portion of a fire. 2. bright red. 3. passion, especially of love. 4. *(informal)* a sweetheart; *old flame,* a former sweetheart. **flame** *v.* (**flamed, flam·ing**) 1. to burn with flames, to send out flames. 2. to become bright red, *his face flamed with anger.*

fla·men·co (flă-meng-koh) *n.* (*pl.* **-cos**) a Spanish gypsy style of song or dance. ☐**flamenco dancer,** an entertainer who performs this dance.

flame·out (flaym-owt) *n.* loss of power in a jet engine through extinction of the flame in the combustion chamber.

flame·proof (flaym-proof) *adj.* not easily set on fire.

flame·throw·er (flaym-throh-ĕr) *n.* a weapon that projects a flame.

fla·min·go (flă-ming-goh) *n.* (*pl.* **-gos, -goes**) a long-legged wading bird with a long neck and pinkish feathers.

flam·ma·ble (flam-ă-bĕl) *adj.* able to be set on fire. **flam·ma·bil·i·ty** (flam-ă-bil-i-tee) *n.* ▷See the note under **inflammable.**

flan (flan) *n.* a custard dessert.

flange (flanj) *n.* a projecting rim or edge.

flank (flangk) *n.* 1. the fleshy part of the side of the body between the last rib and the hip. 2. the side of an animal or thing. 3. the right or left side of a body of troops etc. **flank** *v.* to place or be situated at the side of. ☐**flank steak,** a slice of meat from an animal's flank.

flank·er (flang-kĕr) *n.* 1. a thing or person that flanks. 2. (in football) a player on the offense who lines up far to the left or right of the end position and serves as a pass receiver.

flan·nel (flan-ĕl) *n.* 1. a kind of loosely woven woolen fabric. 2. *flannels,* trousers made of flannel or similar fabric.

flan·nel·ette (flan-ĕ-let) *n.* cotton fabric made to look and feel like flannel.

flap (flap) *v.* (**flapped, flap·ping**) 1. to sway or be swayed up and down or from side to side, to wave about. 2. to give a light blow with something flat, *flapped at a fly.* **flap** *n.* 1. the action or sound of flapping. 2. a light blow with something flat. 3. a broad hanging piece hinged or attached at one side, a hinged or sliding section on an aircraft wing etc. used to control lift. 2. *(slang)* a state of agitation, *the robbery caused a great flap.*

flap·jack (flap-jak) *n.* a pancake.

flap·pa·ble (flap-ă-bĕl) *adj.* (*informal*) excitable.

flap·per (flap-ĕr) *n.* 1. a broad fin or flipper. 2. a young woman of the 1920's, especially one having bold manners and dressing unconventionally.

flare (flair) *v.* (**flared, flar·ing**) 1. to blaze with a sudden irregular flame. 2. to burst into sudden activity or anger, *tempers flared.* 3. to widen gradually outward. **flare** *n.* 1. a sudden outburst of flame. 2. a device producing a flaring light as a signal or for illumination. 3. a flared shape, a gradual widening. ☐**flare up,** to become suddenly angry. ▷Do not confuse *flare* with *flair.*

flash (flash) *v.* 1. to give out a sudden bright light. 2. to come suddenly into view or into the mind,

the idea flashed upon me. 3. to move rapidly, *the train flashed past.* 4. to cause to shine briefly. 5. to signal with a light or lights. 6. to send (news etc.) by radio or telegraph. 7. *(slang)* to expose oneself in an indecent way. **flash** *n.* 1. a sudden burst of flame or light. 2. a very brief time, *in a flash.* 3. a brief news item sent out by radio etc. 4. a device producing a brief bright light in photography. 5. *(slang)* an act of indecent exposure. **flash** *adj.* sudden and brief, *a flash flood.* **flash′er** *n.* ☐**flash card,** any of a group of cards with words, numbers, or pictures shown briefly to pupils by a teacher during a drill. **flash in the pan,** something that makes a showy start and then fails. (▷Originally an explosion of gunpowder in the pan (the part that held the powder) of an old gun without actually firing the charge.) **flash point,** the temperature at which vapor from oil etc. will ignite; the point at which anger is ready to break out.

flash·back (flash-bak) *n.* the changing of the scene in a story or film to a scene at an earlier time.

flash·bulb (flash-bulb) *n.* an electric bulb that briefly emits a dazzling light when ignited, for taking photographs.

flash·cube (flash-kyoob) *n.* a small cube containing four flashbulbs for use in taking four successive photographs.

flash·gun (flash-gun) *n.* a device that simultaneously discharges a flashbulb and operates a camera shutter.

flash·ing (flash-ing) *n.* a strip of metal to prevent water entering at a joint in roofing etc.

flash·light (flash-lrt) *n.* a hand-held electric torch powered by a battery.

flash·tube (flash-toob) *n.* a gas-filled flashbulb that can be used again and again.

flash·y (flash-ee) *adj.* (**flash·i·er, flash·i·est**) showy, gaudy. **flash′i·ly** *adv.* **flash′i·ness** *n.*

flask (flask) *n.* 1. a narrow-necked bottle. 2. a vacuum flask.

flat (flat) *adj.* (**flat·ter, flat·test**) 1. horizontal, level. 2. spread out, lying at full length. 3. smooth and even, with a broad level surface and little depth, *a flat cap.* 4. absolute, unqualified, *a flat refusal.* 5. dull, monotonous. 6. (of drink) having lost its effervescence. 7. (in music) below the correct pitch; *D flat* etc., a half step lower than the corresponding note or key of natural pitch. 8. (of paint, surfaces, etc.) not reflecting light, not glossy. 9. deflated, *a flat tire.* **flat** *adv.* 1. in a flat manner. 2. *(informal)* completely, *I am flat broke.* 3. *(informal)* exactly, *in ten seconds flat.* 4. below the correct pitch in music, *he was singing flat.* **flat** *n.* 1. a flat thing or part, level ground. 2. an apartment. 3. (in music) a note that is a half step lower than the corresponding one of natural pitch, the sign indicating this. 4. a flat tire. 5. (often *flats*) an area of level or low ground, *the Bonneville Salt Flats.* **flat** *v.* (**flat·ted, flat· ting**) to make or become flat. **flat′ly** *adv.* **flat′ness** *n.* ☐**fall flat,** to fail to win applause or appreciation. **fall flat on one's face,** *(informal)* to fail ignominiously. **flat feet,** feet with less than the normal arch beneath. **flat out,** at top speed; using all one's strength or resources. **flat race,** a race over level ground, as distinct from a hurdle race or steeplechase. **flat rate,** a rate that is the same in all cases, not proportional. **flat tire,** one that is deflated because of a puncture etc.

flat·bed (flat-bed) *n.* a truck or trailer having a bed or platform without raised sides, ends, or top.

flat·boat (flat-boht) *n.* a boat with a flat bottom for transport in shallow water.

flat·car (flat-kahr) *n.* a railroad freight car without raised sides, ends, or top.

flat·fish (flat-fish) *n.* (*pl.* **-fish·es, -fish**) a type of fish with a flattened body and both eyes on the upper side, as sole, flounder, etc.

flat·foot (flat-fuut) *n.* 1. (*pl.* **-foots**) *(slang)* a policeman. 2. (*pl.* **-feet**) the condition of flat feet (*see* **flat**).

flat·foot·ed (flat-fuut-id) *adj.* 1. having flat feet. 2. *(informal)* unprepared, *he was caught flat-footed.*

Flat·head (flat-hed) *n.* a member of one of several Indian tribes of the American northwest coast thought to practice head flattening.

flat·i·ron (flat-ı-örn) *n.* a heavy iron heated by external means.

flat·land (flat-land) *n.* level land.

flat·ten (flat-ěn) *v.* to make or become flat.

flat·ter (flat-ěr) *v.* 1. to compliment (a person) excessively or insincerely, especially in order to win favor. 2. to gratify by honoring, *we were flattered to receive an invitation.* 3. to represent (a person or thing) favorably in a portrait etc. so that good looks are exaggerated. **flat'ter·er** *n.* □**flatter oneself,** to please or delude oneself with a belief.

flat·ter·y (flat-ě-ree) *n.* (*pl.* **-ter·ies**) 1. flattering. 2. excessive or insincere compliments.

flat·top (flat-top) *n.* *(informal)* an aircraft carrier.

flat·u·lent (flach-ŭ-lěnt) *adj.* causing or suffering from the formation of gas in the digestive tract. **flat'u·lence** *n.*

fla·tus (flay-tŭs) *n.* gas in or from the stomach or bowels.

flat·ware (flat-wair) *n.* flat tableware, domestic cutlery.

flat·work (flat-wurk) *n.* laundered articles that can be ironed flat by a machine.

flat·worm (flat-wurm) *n.* a type of worm with a flattened body.

flaunt (flawnt) *v.* 1. to display proudly or ostentatiously. 2. (of a flag etc.) to wave proudly. ▷Do not confuse *flaunt* with *flout.* We *flaunt our ignorance if we flout established grammatical principles.*

flau·tist (flaw-tist, flow-) *n.* a flute player.

fla·vor (flay-vŏr) *n.* 1. a distinctive taste. 2. a special quality or characteristic, *the story has a romantic flavor.* **flavor** *v.* to give a flavor to, to season. **fla'vor·ful** *adj.* **fla'vor·less** *adj.* **fla'vor·some** *adj.*

fla·vor·ing (flay-vŏ-ring) *n.* a substance used to give flavor to food.

flaw (flaw) *n.* an imperfection, a blemish. **flaw** *v.* to spoil with a flaw.

flaw·less (flaw-lis) *adj.* without a flaw. **flaw'less·ly** *adv.* **flaw'less·ness** *n.*

flax (flaks) *n.* 1. a blue-flowered plant cultivated for the textile fiber obtained from its stem and for its seeds (linseed). 2. its fiber.

flax·en (flak-sěn) *adj.* 1. made of flax. 2. pale yellow in color like dressed flax, *flaxen hair.*

flay (flay) *v.* 1. to strip off the skin or hide of. 2. to criticize severely.

flea (flee) *n.* a small wingless jumping insect that feeds on human and animal blood. □**flea market,** a street market.

flea·bag (flee-bag) *n.* *(slang)* 1. a cheap hotel or rooming house. 2. a worthless racehorse.

flea·bane (flee-bayn) *n.* one of various plants of the daisy family supposed to drive away fleas.

flea-bit·ten (flee-bit-ěn) *adj.* 1. bitten by fleas. 2. *(informal)* showing wear or heavy use. 3. seedy, disreputable.

fleck (flek) *n.* 1. a very small patch of color. 2. a small particle, a speck.

flecked (flekt) *adj.* marked with flecks.

fled (fled) *see* **flee.**

fledged (flejd) *adj.* 1. (of young birds) with fully grown wing feathers, able to fly. 2. mature, trained and experienced, *a full-fledged engineer.*

fledg·ling (flej-ling) *n.* 1. a young bird that has just grown the feathers necessary to fly. 2. a young inexperienced person.

flee (flee) *v.* (**fled, flee·ing**) 1. to run or hurry away. 2. to run away from, *fled the country.* 3. to pass away swiftly, to vanish, *all hope had fled.*

fleece (flees) *n.* 1. the woolly hair of a sheep or similar animal. 2. a soft fabric used for linings etc. **fleece** *v.* (**fleeced, fleec·ing**) *(informal)* to defraud, to rob by trickery. **fleec'y** *adj.*

fleer (fleer) *v.* to laugh impudently or mockingly, to jeer.

fleet[1] (fleet) *n.* 1. the naval force of a country, a number of warships under one commander. 2. a number of ships or aircraft or buses etc. moving or working under one command or ownership. □**fleet admiral,** the highest ranking officer in the U.S. Navy.

fleet[2] *adj.* moving swiftly, nimble. **fleet'ly** *adv.* **fleet'ness** *n.*

fleet·ing (flee-ting) *adj.* passing quickly, brief, *a fleeting glimpse.*

Flem. *abbr.* Flemish.

Flem·ish (flem-ish) *adj.* of Flanders or its people or language. **Flemish** *n.* 1. the Flemish language. 2. *the Flemish,* Flemish people.

flesh (flesh) *n.* 1. the soft substance of an animal body, consisting of muscle and fat. 2. this tissue of animal bodies (excluding fish and sometimes fowl) as food. 3. the body as opposed to the mind or soul. 4. the pulpy part of fruits and vegetables. □**flesh and blood,** human nature, people with their emotions and weaknesses; *one's own flesh and blood,* relatives, descendants. **flesh fly,** a fly that lays its eggs in flesh. **flesh out,** to make or become substantial. **flesh wound,** a wound that does not reach a bone or vital organ. **in the flesh,** in bodily form, in person.

flesh·ly (flesh-lee) *adj.* 1. of the flesh or body. 2. lascivious, sensual. 3. mortal, worldly, not spiritual. ▷Do not confuse *fleshly* with *fleshy.*

flesh·pot (flesh-pot) *n.* a place offering licentious high living and luxuries.

flesh·y (flesh-ee) *adj.* (**flesh·i·er, flesh·i·est**) 1. of or like flesh. 2. having much flesh, plump, (of plants or fruits etc.) pulpy. **flesh'i·ness** *n.* ▷Do not confuse *fleshy* with *fleshly.*

fleur-de-lis (flur-dě-lee) *n.* (*pl.* **fleurs-de-lis,** *pr.* flur-dě-leez) a design of three petallike parts used in heraldry.

flew (floo) *see* **fly**[2].

flex (fleks) *v.* to bend (a joint or limb), to move (a muscle) so that it bends a joint. □**flex one's muscles,** *(informal)* to show off one's strength or physique.

flex·i·ble (flek-sı̆-běl) *adj.* 1. able to bend easily

without breaking. 2. adaptable, able to be changed to suit circumstances. **flex'i·bly** *adv.* **flex·i·bil·i·ty** (flek-sĭ-bil-i-tee) *n.*

flex·time (fleks-tɪm), **flex·i·time** (flek-sĭ-tɪm) *(trademark) n.* a system of flexible working hours.

flex·ure (flek-shŭr) *n.* a curvature, a bend.

flib·ber·ti·gib·bet (flib-ĕr-ti-jib-it) *n.* a flighty, frivolous, or restless person.

flick[1] (flik) *n.* a quick light blow or stroke, as with a whip. **flick** *v.* to strike or remove with a quick light blow, to make a flicking movement.

flick[2] *n. (informal)* a movie. □ **the flicks**, the movies.

flick·er[1] (flik-ĕr) *v.* 1. to burn or shine unsteadily. 2. (of hope etc.) to occur briefly, to be at the point of disappearing. 3. to quiver, to move quickly to and fro. **flicker** *n.* a flickering movement or light, a brief occurrence of hope etc.

flicker[2] *n.* a large North American woodpecker with a spotted breast and brown back.

flied (flīd) *see* **fly**[2] definition 11.

fli·er (flĭr-ĕr) *n.* 1. a bird etc. that flies. 2. an animal or vehicle that moves very fast. 3. an aviator. 4. *(informal)* a speculation, a business risk; *take a flier*, to risk money on a speculation. 5. a handbill.

flight[1] (flīt) *n.* 1. the process of flying, the movement or path of a thing through the air. 2. a journey made by air, transport in an aircraft making a particular journey, *there are three flights a day to Rome.* 3. a flock of birds or insects. 4. a number of aircraft regarded as a unit. 5. a series of stairs in a straight line or between two landings. 6. a swift passage (of time). 7. an effort that is beyond the ordinary, *a flight of the imagination.* □ **flight bag**, a small bag for carrying by air travelers. **flight deck**, the cockpit of a large aircraft. **flight feather**, one of the large feathers that enable a bird to fly. **flight path**, the planned course of an aircraft or spacecraft. **top flight**, taking a leading place, excellent of its kind.

flight[2] *n.* fleeing, running or going away. □ **put to flight**, to cause to flee. **take flight** *or* **take to flight**, to flee.

flight·less (flīt-lis) *adj.* (of birds, as penguins) nonflying.

flight·test (flīt-test) *v.* to test (an aircraft, rocket, etc.) by flight.

flight·y (flĭr-tee) *adj.* (**flight·i·er, flight·i·est**) without a serious purpose or interest, frivolous. **flight'i·ness** *n.*

flim·flam (flim-flam) *n. (informal)* a trick or deception. **flimflam** *v. (informal)* to cheat, to deceive.

flim·sy (flim-zee) *adj.* (**flim·si·er, flim·si·est**) 1. light and thin, of loose structure, fragile. 2. unconvincing, *a flimsy excuse.* **flim'si·ly** *adv.* **flim'si·ness** *n.*

flinch (flinch) *v.* 1. to draw back in fear, to wince. 2. to shrink from one's duty etc.

fling (fling) *v.* (**flung, fling·ing**) 1. to throw violently or angrily or hurriedly; *fling caution to the winds,* act rashly. 2. to put or send suddenly or forcefully, *flung him into prison.* 3. to rush, to go angrily or violently, *she flung out of the room.* **fling** *n.* 1. the act or movement of flinging. 2. a kind of vigorous dance, *the Highland fling.* 3. a brief period of indulgence in pleasure, *have one's fling.* □ **take a fling at,** *(informal)* to make an attempt at.

flint (flint) *n.* 1. a very hard kind of stone that can produce sparks when struck against steel. 2. a piece of this. 3. a piece of hard alloy used in

a cigarette lighter etc. to produce a spark. □ **flint glass,** pure lustrous glass, originally made with ground flint.

flint·lock (flint-lok) *n.* 1. the lock of a gun discharged by a spark from flint. 2. a gun of this kind.

flint·y (flin-tee) *adj.* (**flint·i·er, flint·i·est**) like flint, very hard.

flip[1] (flip) *v.* (**flipped, flip·ping**) 1. to flick. 2. to toss (a thing) with a sharp movement so that it turns over in the air. 3. *(informal)* to experience a sudden strong emotion. **flip** *n.* the action of flipping something. □ **flip one's lid,** *(slang)* to show great anger, to lose self-control; *he flipped his lid over her,* became infatuated. **flip side,** *(informal)* the less important side of a phonograph record.

flip[2] *n.* a cocktail containing sugar and egg.

flip[3] *adj.* (**flip·per, flip·pest**) *(informal)* flippant. **flip·pant** (flip-ănt) *adj.* not showing proper seriousness. **flip'pant·ly** *adv.* **flip'pan·cy** *n.*

flip·per (flip-ĕr) *n.* 1. a limb of certain sea animals (as seals, turtles, penguins), used in swimming. 2. one of a pair of large flat rubber attachments worn on the feet for swimming and deep-sea diving.

flirt (flurt) *v.* 1. to court a person playfully or without serious intentions. 2. to toy, *flirted with the idea; flirting with death,* taking great risks. **flirt** *n.* a person who flirts. **flir·ta·tion** (flur-tay-shŏn) *n.*

flir·ta·tious (flur-tay-shŭs) *adj.* flirting, fond of flirting. **flir·ta'tious·ly** *adv.*

flit (flit) *v.* (**flit·ted, flit·ting**) to fly or move lightly and quickly.

flitch (flich) *n.* a side of bacon.

fliv·ver (fliv-ĕr) *n. (informal)* a small cheap automobile.

float (floht) *v.* 1. to rest or drift on the surface of a liquid without sinking, to be held up freely in air or gas. 2. to cause to do this. 3. to move lightly or casually. 4. to have or allow (currency) to have a variable rate of exchange. 5. to obtain (a loan) or issue (stocks or bonds) in order to finance an enterprise. **float** *n.* 1. a thing designed to float on liquid, a cork used on a fishing line to show when the bait has been taken, one of the corks supporting the edge of a fishing net. 2. a floating device to control the flow of water, gasoline, etc. 3. a structure to enable an aircraft to float on water. 4. a platform on wheels carrying a display in a parade. 5. the available supply of a company's common stock. 6. a drink made of ice cream and soda. □ **floating rib,** one of the ribs not joined to the breastbone.

float·er (floh-tĕr) *n.* 1. something that floats. 2. an office worker who is able to replace other workers when they are absent. 3. *(informal)* a person who goes aimlessly from one activity to another.

floc (flok) *n.* a fine mass formed by suspended particles in a precipitate etc.

floc·cu·late (flok-yŭ-layt) *v.* (**floc·cu·lat·ed, floc·cu·lat·ing**) to form (suspended particles) or be formed into tuftlike masses. **floc'cu·lant** *n.*

flock[1] (flok) *n.* 1. a number of sheep, goats, or birds kept together or feeding or traveling together. 2. a large number of people, *a flock of visitors.* 3. a number of people in someone's charge, a Christian congregation. **flock** *v.* to gather or go in a flock.

flock[2] *n.* 1. a tuft of wool or cotton etc. 2. wool

or cotton waste used for stuffing mattresses etc.
3. powdered wool or felt applied to paper, cloth, etc. to produce a pattern or texture.

floe (floh) *n.* a sheet of floating ice.

flog (flog) *v.* (**flogged, flog·ging**) to beat severely with a rod or whip, as a punishment. **flog'ger** *n.* **flog'ging** *n.*

flood (flud) *n.* 1. the coming of a great quantity of water over a place that is usually dry, the water itself; *the Flood,* that described in the Bible. 2. a great outpouring or outburst, *a flood of abuse.* 3. the inflow of the tide. **flood** *v.* 1. to cover or fill with a flood, to overflow. 2. (of a river etc.) to become flooded. 3. to come in great quantities, *letters flooded in.* □**be flooded out,** to be forced to leave because of a flood. **flood tide,** the advancing tide.

flood·gate (flud-gayt) *n.* a gate that can be opened or closed to control the flow of water, especially the lower gate of a lock.

flood·light (flud-lit) *n.* a lamp used for producing a broad bright beam of light to light up a stage or building etc. **floodlight** *v.* (**flood·lit, flood·light·ing**) to illuminate with this.

flood·plain (flud-playn) *n.* a plain that is subject to flooding.

flood·wa·ter (flud-waw-tĕr) *n.* the water of a flood.

floor (flohr) *n.* 1. the lower surface of a room, the part on which one stands. 2. the bottom of the sea or of a cave etc. 3. (in legislative assemblies) the part of the assembly hall where members sit. 4. a minimum level for wages or prices. 5. a story of a building, all the rooms having a continuous floor. **floor** *v.* 1. to put a floor into (a building). 2. to knock down (a person) in a fight. 3. *(informal)* to baffle, to overwhelm (a person) with a problem or argument. □**floor leader,** a legislator who is chosen by a political party to direct its activities on the floor of a legislative body. **floor manager,** a person at a political convention who leads support for his candidate for nomination. **floor show,** an entertainment presented on the floor of a nightclub etc. **have the floor,** to have the right to speak in a debate.

floor·board (flohr-bohrd) *n.* 1. one of the boards forming the floor of a room. 2. the floor of a motor vehicle etc.

floor·shift (flohr-shift) *n.* a manually operated gearshift located on the floor of an automobile.

floor·walk·er (flohr-waw-kĕr) *n.* *(old use)* a department store sales supervisor.

floo·zy, floo·zie (floo-zee) *n.* (*pl.* **-zies**) *(slang)* a disreputable woman.

flop (flop) *v.* (**flopped, flop·ping**) 1. to hang or sway heavily and loosely. 2. to fall down clumsily. 3. *(slang)* to be a failure. **flop** *n.* 1. a flopping movement or sound. 2. *(slang)* a failure. **flop** *adv.* with a flop.

flop·house (flop-hows) *n.* (*pl.* **-hous·es,** *pr.* -how-ziz) *(slang)* a low-grade rooming house or hotel.

flop·o·ver (flop-oh-vĕr) *n.* continuous vertical movement of a television picture.

flop·py (flop-ee) *adj.* (**flop·pi·er, flop·pi·est**) hanging heavily and loosely. **flop'pi·ness** *n.*

flo·ra (flohr-ă) *n.* (*pl.* **flo·ras, flo·rae,** *pr.* flohr-ee) the plants of an area or period of time.

flo·ral (flohr-ăl) *adj.* of flowers.

Flor·en·tine (flor-ĕn-teen) *adj.* of Florence, a city of north Italy.

flo·res·cence (floh-res-ĕns) *n.* a flowering time or state of being in bloom. **flo·res'cent** *adj.*

flo·ret (flohr-it) *n.* 1. a small flower. 2. one of the

small flowers making up a composite flower.

flo·ri·bun·da (flohr-ĭ-bun-dă) *n.* a rose or other plant bearing dense clusters of flowers.

flo·ri·cul·ture (flohr-ĭ-kul-chŭr) *n.* the cultivation of flowers.

flor·id (flor-id) *adj.* 1. elaborate and ornate. 2. (of the complexion) ruddy.

Flor·i·da (flor-i-dă) a state of the U.S. **Flo·rid·i·an** (flŏ-rid-i-ăn), **Flor'i·dan** *adj.* & *n.* □**Florida room,** a sunny sitting room (in a house) with windows on three sides.

flor·in (flor-in) *n.* 1. a Dutch coin. 2. a former British coin worth two shillings.

flo·rist (flor-ist) *n.* a person whose business is the selling or growing of flowers.

floss (flaws) *n.* 1. a mass of silky fibers. 2. silk thread with little or no twist, used in embroidery. 3. dental floss. **floss'y** *adj.* (**floss·i·er, floss·i·est**).

flo·ta·tion (floh-tay-shŏn) *n.* floating, especially the sale of bonds in the launching of a commercial venture. □**flotation collar,** a device to keep a space capsule afloat after splashdown.

flo·til·la (floh-til-ă) *n.* 1. a small fleet. 2. a fleet of boats or small ships.

flot·sam (flot-săm) *n.* wreckage found floating. □**flotsam and jetsam,** odds and ends; vagrants, tramps, etc.

flounce[1] (flowns) *v.* (**flounced, flounc·ing**) to go in an impatient annoyed manner, *flounced out of the room.* **flounce** *n.* a flouncing movement.

flounce[2] *n.* a deep frill of material sewn by its upper edge to a skirt etc.

flounced (flownst) *adj.* trimmed with a flounce.

floun·der[1] (flown-dĕr) *n.* a small edible flatfish.

flounder[2] *v.* 1. to move clumsily and with difficulty as in mud. 2. to make mistakes or become confused when trying to do something.

flour (flowr) *n.* fine meal or powder made from grain, used in cooking. **flour** *v.* to cover or sprinkle with flour.

flour·ish (flur-ish) *v.* 1. to thrive in growth or development. 2. to prosper, to be successful. 3. (of famous people) to be alive and active at a certain time, *Beethoven flourished in the early 19th century.* 4. to wave (a thing) dramatically. **flourish** *n.* 1. a dramatic sweeping gesture. 2. a flowing ornamental curve in writing etc. 3. a fanfare.

flout (flowt) *v.* to disobey openly and scornfully. ▷See the note under **flaunt.**

flow (floh) *v.* 1. to glide along as a stream, to move freely like a liquid or gas. 2. to proceed steadily and continuously, *keep the traffic flowing.* 3. (of talk or literary style) to proceed smoothly and evenly. 4. to hang loosely, (of a line or curve) to be smoothly continuous. 5. to gush forth, (of the tide) to come in, to rise. 6. to come (from a source), to be the result. **flow** *n.* 1. a flowing movement or mass. 2. the amount that flows. 3. an outpouring, a copious supply. 4. the inward movement of the tide, toward the land, *ebb and flow.*

flow·chart (floh-chahrt) *n.* a diagram of the movement of things or persons in a complex activity.

flow·er (flow-ĕr) *n.* 1. the part of a plant from which seed or fruit develops. 2. a blossom and its stem for use as a decoration etc. 3. a plant that is noticeable or cultivated for its fine flowers. 4. the best part of something. **flower** *v.* (of a plant) to produce flowers. □**flower girl,** a very young girl who precedes the bride in a wedding procession and carries flowers. **flower head,** a

cluster of florets. **in flower,** with the flowers out.
flow·ered (flow-ĕrd) *adj.* ornamented with flowers.
flow·er·pot (flow-ĕr-pot) *n.* a pot in which a plant may be grown.
flow·er·y (flow-ĕ-ree) *adj.* 1. full of flowers. 2. (of language) full of ornamental phrases.
flown (flohn) *see* **fly²**.
fl. oz. *abbr.* fluid ounce(s).
flu (floo) *n.* influenza.
flub (flub) *v.* **(flubbed, flub·bing)** *(informal)* to botch or bungle. **flub** *n.* *(informal)* a thing badly or clumsily done.
fluc·tu·ate (fluk-choo-ayt) *v.* **(fluc·tu·at·ed, fluc·tu·at·ing)** (of levels, prices, etc.) to vary irregularly, to rise and fall. **fluc·tu·a·tion** (fluk-choo-ay-shŏn) *n.*
flue (floo) *n.* 1. a smoke duct in a chimney. 2. a channel for conveying heat.
flu·ent (floo-ĕnt) *adj.* 1. (of a person) able to speak smoothly and readily, *fluent in three languages.* 2. (of speech) coming smoothly and readily. **flu'ent·ly** *adv.* **flu'en·cy** *n.*
fluff (fluf) *n.* 1. a light soft downy substance. 2. *(slang)* a bungled attempt, a mistake in speaking. **fluff** *v.* 1. to shake into a soft mass. 2. *(slang)* to bungle.
fluff·y (fluf-ee) *adj.* **(fluff·i·er, fluff·i·est)** having or covered with a soft mass of fur or fibers. **fluff'i·ness** *n.*
flu·id (floo-id) *n.* a substance that is able to flow freely as liquids and gases do. **fluid** *adj.* 1. able to flow freely, not solid or rigid. 2. (of a situation) not stable. **flu·id·i·ty** (floo-id-i-tee) *n.* ☐**fluid dram,** one-eighth of a fluid ounce. **fluid drive,** an automobile transmission employing liquid to transmit power. **fluid ounce,** one-sixteenth of a pint.
flu·id·ics (floo-id-iks) *n.* the technique of using small interacting flows and fluid jets for amplification, switching, etc.
fluke¹ (flook) *n.* an accidental stroke of good luck. **fluk'y** *adj.* **(fluk·i·er, fluk·i·est).**
fluke² *n.* 1. the broad triangular flat end of each arm of an anchor. 2. the barbed head of a harpoon etc. 3. one of the lobes of a whale's tail.
fluke³ 1. a kind of flatfish, especially the flounder. 2. a flatworm found as a parasite in sheep's liver.
flume (floom) *n.* 1. a ravine with a stream. 2. an artificial channel conveying water.
flum·mox (flum-ŏks) *v.* (chiefly *British slang*) to baffle.
flung (flung) *see* **fling.**
flunk (flungk) *v.* *(informal)* to fail, especially in an examination.
flun·ky (*pl.* **-kies**), **flun·key** (*pl.* **-keys**) (flung-kee) *n.* 1. *(British)* a male servant wearing livery. 2. *(contemptuous)* a person who performs menial duties.
fluo·resce (fluu-res, floo-ŏ-) *v.* **(fluo·resced, fluo·resc·ing)** to exhibit fluorescence.
fluo·res·cent (fluu-res-ĕnt, floo-ŏ-) *adj.* (of substances) taking in radiations and sending them out in the form of light, (of lamps) containing such a substance, (of a screen) coated with this. **fluo·res'cence** *n.* ☐**fluorescent lamp,** a tubular lamp in which phosphor on the inside of the tube is made to fluoresce by ultraviolet radiation.
fluo·ri·date (floor-i-dayt, flohr-) *v.* **(fluo·ri·dat·ed, fluo·ri·dat·ing)** to add or apply a fluoride to.

fluo·ri·da·tion (floor-i-day-shŏn, flohr-) *n.* the addition of traces of fluoride to drinking water to prevent or reduce tooth decay.
fluo·ride (floor-id, flohr-) *n.* a compound of fluorine and one other element.
fluo·ri·nate (floor-i-nayt, flohr-) *v.* **(flu·o·ri·nat·ed, flu·o·ri·nat·ing)** to introduce fluorine into (a compound).
fluo·rine (floor-een, flohr-) *n.* a chemical element, a pale yellow corrosive gas.
fluo·ro·car·bon (floor-oh-kahr-bŏn, flohr-) *n.* a synthetic compound of carbon and fluorine, used as a lubricant.
fluor·o·scope (floor-ŏ-skohp, flohr-) *n.* an instrument with a fluorescent screen, used to show x-ray effects. **fluor·o·scop·ic** (floor-ŏ-skop-ik) *adj.* **fluo·ros·co·pist** (floo-ros-kŏ-pist) *n.* **fluo·ros'co·py** *n.*
flur·ry (flur-ee) *n.* (*pl.* **-ries**) 1. a short sudden rush of wind or rain or snow. 2. a commotion. 3. a state of nervous agitation. **flurry** *v.* **(flur·ried, flur·ry·ing)** 1. to fluster 2. to come down as a flurry.
flush¹ (flush) *v.* 1. to become red in the face because of a rush of blood to the skin. 2. to cause (the face) to redden in this way. 3. to fill with pride, *flushed with success.* 4. to cleanse (a drain or lavatory etc.) with a flow of water, to dispose of in this way. **flush** *n.* 1. flushing of the face, a blush. 2. excitement caused by emotion, *the first flush of victory.* 3. a rush of water. **flush** *adj.* 1. level, in the same plane, without projections, *doors that are flush with the walls.* 2. *(informal)* well supplied with money.
flush² *n.* (in poker) a hand of cards all of one suit. ☐**royal flush,** a straight flush headed by an ace. **straight flush,** a flush that is a straight sequence.
flush³ *v.* to cause (a bird) to fly up and away, to drive out.
flus·ter (flus-tĕr) *v.* to make nervous and confused. **fluster** *n.* a flustered state.
flute (floot) *n.* 1. a wind instrument consisting of a long pipe with holes stopped by fingers or keys and a mouth hole near one end. 2. an ornamental groove. **flute** *v.* **(flut·ed, flut·ing)** to make ornamental grooves in. **flut'ed** *adj.*
flut·ing (floo-ting) *n.* ornamental grooves.
flut·ist (floo-tist) *n.* a flute player.
flut·ter (flut-ĕr) *v.* 1. to move the wings hurriedly in flying or trying to fly. 2. to wave or flap quickly and irregularly, (of the heart) to beat feebly and irregularly. **flutter** *n.* 1. a fluttering movement or beat. 2. a state of nervous excitement. 3. a stir, a sensation. 4. rapid variation in the pitch or loudness of reproduced sound. **flut'ter·y** *adj.*
flux (fluks) *n.* 1. a continuous succession of changes, *in a state of flux.* 2. flowing, flowing out.
fly¹ (flr) *n.* (*pl.* **flies**) 1. a two-winged insect. 2. a natural or artificial fly used as bait in fishing. ☐**fly casting,** the fishing technique of angling with the fly as a lure. **fly fishing,** fishing with flies as bait. **fly in the ointment,** one small thing that spoils enjoyment. **like flies,** in large numbers, *dying like flies.* **there are no flies on him,** *(slang)* he is very astute.
fly² *v.* **(flew, flown, fly·ing)** 1. to move through the air by means of wings as a bird does. 2. to travel through the air or through space. 3. to travel in an aircraft. 4. to direct or control the flight of (an aircraft etc.), to transport in an aircraft. 5. to raise (a flag) so that it waves, (of a

flag) to wave in the air. 6. to make (a kite) rise and stay aloft. 7. to go or move quickly, to rush along, (of time) to pass quickly. 8. to be scattered violently, *sparks flew in all directions.* 9. to become angry etc. quickly, *flew into a rage.* 10. to flee from, *must fly the country.* 11. (in baseball) to hit a fly ball. (▷ *Flied* is the past tense and past participle of *fly* in this sense; *he flied out; she has flied out.*) **fly** *n.* (*pl.* **flies**) 1. flying. 2. a flap of material on a garment to contain or cover a fastening, a flap at the entrance of a tent. 3. a speed-regulating device in clockwork or machinery. 4. (in baseball) a fly ball. □**fly at,** to attack violently, either physically or with words. **fly ball,** a baseball batted high in the air. **fly high,** to behave very ambitiously. **fly in the face of,** to disregard or disobey openly. **fly off the handle,** (*informal*) to become uncontrollably angry. **fly the coop,** (*informal*) to escape. **go fly a kite,** (*informal*) go away. **on the fly,** while in motion in the air, without stopping. **send flying,** to knock (a person or thing) violently aside.

fly·blown (flr-blohn) *adj.* (of meat etc.) tainted, especially by flies' eggs.

fly·by (flr-br) *n.* (*pl.* **-bys**) the close approach of an aircraft or spacecraft to a specific point without touching down.

fly-by-night (flr-br-nrt) *adj.* unscrupulous (in business). **fly-by-night** *n.* a business or person that is unscrupulous.

fly·catch·er (flr-kach-er) *n.* a bird that catches insects in the air.

fly·er = flier.

fly·ing (flr-ing) *adj.* able to fly. □**flying boat,** a seaplane with a boatlike fuselage. **flying buttress,** a buttress that springs from a separate structure, usually forming an arch with the wall it supports. **flying colors,** great success, *she passed the test with flying colors.* **flying fish,** a tropical fish with winglike fins, able to rise into the air. **flying leap,** a forward leap made while moving swiftly. **flying saucer,** an unidentified saucer-shaped object reported as seen in the sky. **flying start,** a vigorous start giving one an initial advantage. **flying tackle,** a tackle in football in which a player leaps at the ball-carrier.

fly·leaf (flr-leef) *n.* (*pl.* **-leaves,** *pr.* -leevz) a blank leaf at the beginning or end of a book etc.

fly·pa·per (flr-pay-pĕr) *n.* sticky paper for catching or poisoning flies.

fly·speck (flr-spek) *n.* 1. the mark left by the excrement of a fly. 2. a very tiny thing.

fly·way (flr-way) *n.* a migration route of birds.

fly·weight (flr-wayt) *n.* a boxer of the lightest weight class in boxing, weighing up to 112 pounds.

fly·wheel (flr-hweel) *n.* a heavy wheel revolving on a shaft to regulate machinery.

Fm *symbol* fermium.

FM *abbr.* 1. Field Marshal. 2. frequency modulation.

fm. *abbr.* fathom(s).

fn. *abbr.* footnote.

f num·ber a number indicating the ratio of the focal length and the diameter of a camera lens.

FO *abbr.* field officer.

fo. *abbr.* folio.

foal (fohl) *n.* the young of a horse or of a related animal. **foal** *v.* to give birth to a foal. □**in foal,** (of a mare) pregnant.

foam (fohm) *n.* 1. a collection of small bubbles formed in or on a liquid. 2. the froth of saliva or perspiration. 3. rubber or plastic in a light spongy form. 4. a frothy fire-extinguishing material used especially to fight airfield fires. **foam** *v.* to form or send out foam. **foam'y** *adj.* □**foam rubber,** light spongy rubber formed with air bubbles for use in cushions, mattresses, etc.

fob[1] (fob) *n.* an ornament worn hanging from a watch chain etc.

fob[2] *v.* (**fobbed, fob·bing**) **fob off,** to palm (a thing) off, to get (a person) to accept something of little or no value instead of what he is seeking.

F.O.B., f.o.b. *abbr.* free on board.

fo·cal (foh-kăl) *adj.* of or at a focus. □**focal length,** the distance between a lens or mirror and its focal point. **focal plane,** a plane through a focal point perpendicular to the axis of a lens or mirror. **focal point,** the point of focus; a center of action or interest.

fo·ci see focus.

fo'c's'le = forecastle.

fo·cus (foh-kŭs) *n.* (*pl.* **-cus·es, -ci,** *pr.* -sı) 1. the point at which rays meet or from which they appear to proceed. 2. the point or distance at which an object is most clearly seen by the eye or through a lens. 3. an adjustment on a lens to produce a clear image at varying distances. 4. a center of activity or interest etc. **focus** *v.* (**fo·cused, fo·cus·ing**) 1. to adjust the focus of (a lens or the eye). 2. to bring into focus. 3. to concentrate or be concentrated or directed (on a center etc.). □**in** *or* **out of focus,** seen or not seen sharply by the eye or a lens.

fod·der (fod-ĕr) *n.* dried food, hay, etc. for horses and farm animals.

foe (foh) *n.* an enemy.

F.O.E. *abbr.* Fraternal Order of Eagles.

fog (fog) *n.* 1. a thick mist that is difficult to see through. 2. cloudiness on a photographic negative etc., obscuring the image. **fog** *v.* (**fogged, fog·ging**) 1. to cover or become covered with fog or condensed vapor, *a fogged lens.* 2. to bewilder, to perplex.

fog·gy (fog-ee) *adj.* (**fog·gi·er, fog·gi·est**) 1. full of fog. 2. made opaque by condensed vapor etc., clouded. 3. obscure, vague, *only a foggy idea.* **fog'gi·ness** *n.* □**not the foggiest,** (*informal*) no idea at all.

fog·horn (fog-horn) *n.* 1. a sounding instrument for warning ships in fog. 2. (*informal*) a loud voice.

fo·gy (*pl.* **-gies,** *pr.* -geez), **fo·gey** (*pl.* **-geys,** *pr.* -geez) (foh-gee) *n.* a person with old-fashioned ideas, *an old fogy.*

foi·ble (foi-bĕl) *n.* a harmless peculiarity in a person's character.

foil[1] (foil) *n.* 1. metal hammered or rolled into a thin sheet, *tin foil.* 2. a person or thing that contrasts strongly with another and therefore makes the other's qualities more obvious.

foil[2] *v.* to frustrate, to thwart.

foil[3] *n.* a long thin sword with a blunt point, used in fencing.

foist (foist) *v.* to cause a person to accept (something inferior or unwelcome or undeserved), *the job was foisted on us.*

fol. *abbr.* 1. folio. 2. followed. 3. following.

fold[1] (fohld) *v.* 1. to bend or turn (a flexible thing) so that one part lies on another, to close or flatten by pressing parts together. 2. to become folded, to be able to be folded. 3. to clasp (the arms etc.) about, to hold (a person or thing) close to one's breast. 4. to envelop. 5. to blend (an ingredient)

in cooking by spooning one part over another.
6. to collapse, to cease to function, *the business had folded.* **fold** *n.* 1. a folded part, a hollow between two thicknesses. 2. a line made by folding. 3. a hollow among hills or mountains. □**fold one's arms,** to place them together or entwined across one's chest. **fold one's hands,** to clasp or place them together.

fold² *n.* 1. an enclosure for sheep. 2. an established body of people with the same beliefs or aims, the members of a religion. □**return to the fold,** to rejoin such a group.

fold·a·way (fohl-dă-way) *adj.* adapted to be folded away when not in use, *a foldaway cot.*

fold·boat (fohld-boht) *n.* a faltboat.

fold·er (fohl-děr) *n.* 1. a folding cover for loose papers. 2. a folded leaflet.

foi·de·rol (fol-dě-rol) *n.* a trifle, nonsense.

fold·out (fohld-owt) *n.* a large page that can be unfolded from a book, magazine, etc.

fo·li·age (foh-li-ij) *n.* the leaves of a tree or plant.

fo·li·at·ed (foh-li-ay-tid) *adj.* 1. split or arranged in leaves. 2. decorated with foils, as an arch etc.

fo·lic (foh-lik, fol-ik) **acid** a vitamin of the B group, deficiency of which causes anemia.

fo·li·o (foh-li-oh) *n.* (*pl.* **-li·os**) 1. a large sheet of paper folded once, making two leaves of a book. 2. a book made of such sheets, the largest-sized volume. 3. the page number of a printed book.

folk (fohk) *n.* 1. people in general. 2. the people of a certain group or nation etc., *country folk.* 3. one's relatives. □**folk dance, folk song** etc., a dance, song, etc., in the traditional style of a country. **folk mass,** a liturgical mass with folk music. **folk rock,** a style of music combining elements of rock-'n'-roll and folk music. **folk singer,** a person who sings folk songs.

folk·lore (fohk-lohr) *n.* the traditional beliefs and tales etc. of a community. **folk'lor·ist** *n.*

folk·sy (fohk-see) *adj.* (**folk·si·er, folk·si·est**) 1. simple in manner. 2. friendly, sociable.

folk·ways (fohk-wayz) *n.* traditional behavior common to a people.

foll. *abbr.* following.

fol·li·cle (fol-i-kěl) *n.* a very small sac or cavity in the body, especially one containing a hair root.

fol·low (fol-oh) *v.* 1. to go or come after. 2. to go along (a path or road etc.). 3. to provide with a sequel or successor. 4. to take as a guide or leader or example; *follow the fashion,* conform to it. 5. to grasp the meaning of, to understand. 6. to take an interest in the progress of (events, a team, etc.). 7. to happen as a result, to result from. 8. to be necessarily true in consequence of something else. □**follow one's nose,** to be guided by instinct. **follow on the heels of,** to come or occur immediately after. **follow suit,** to play a card of the suit led; to follow a person's example. **follow through,** to carry a stroke through to the fullest possible extent after striking a golf ball, baseball, etc.; to see (a project) through to completion. **follow up,** to add a further action or blow etc. to a previous one; to perform further work or investigation etc. upon.

fol·low·er (fol-oh-ěr) *n.* 1. one who follows. 2. a person who believes in or supports a religion or teacher or cause etc.

fol·low·ing (fol-oh-ing) *n.* a body of believers or supporters. **following** *adj.* now to be mentioned, *answer the following questions.* **following** *prep.*

as a sequel to, *following the fall of the dollar, prices rose sharply.* □**the following,** that which now is to be mentioned.

fol·low-up (fol-oh-up) *n.* an action performed after another to investigate or complete the earlier one.

fol·ly (fol-ee) *n.* (*pl.* **-lies**) foolishness, a foolish act; *Seward's folly,* the purchase of Alaska (considered a foolish act when arranged by Secretary of State William H. Seward in 1867).

fo·ment (foh-ment) *v.* 1. to arouse or stimulate (trouble, discontent, etc.). 2. to apply warm liquid etc. to (an area of the body). **fo·men·ta·tion** (foh-men-tay-shŏn) *n.* ▷Do not confuse *foment* with *ferment.*

fond (fond) *adj.* 1. affectionate, loving. 2. over-affectionate, doting. 3. (of hopes) cherished but unlikely to be fulfilled. **fond'ly** *adv.* **fond'ness** *n.* □**fond of,** having a liking for; much inclined to.

fon·dant (fon-dănt) *n.* a creamy sugar mixture used as a basis for candies.

fon·dle (fon-děl) *v.* (**fon·dled, fon·dling**) to touch or stroke lovingly.

fon·due (fon-doo) *n.* a dish of flavored melted cheese.

font¹ (font) *n.* a basin or vessel (often of carved stone) in a church, to hold water for baptism.

font² *n.* a set of printing type of one style and size.

fon·ta·nel, fon·ta·nelle (fon-tă-nel) *n.* a space under the skin on the top of an infant's head where the bones of the skull have not yet grown together.

fon·ti·na (fon-tee-nă) *n.* a type of Italian cheese made from ewe's milk.

food (food) *n.* 1. any substance that can be taken into the body of an animal or plant to maintain its life and growth. 2. a solid substance of this kind, *food and drink.* □**food chain,** a series of organisms dependent on one another for supply of food. **food for thought,** something that needs thinking about. **food poisoning,** illness caused by bacteria or toxins in food. **food processor,** a kitchen appliance for preparing foods by grinding, shredding, etc. **food stamps,** stamps distributed by the federal government that are used to purchase food. **food value,** the nourishing power of a food.

food·stuff (food-stuf) *n.* a substance used as food.

fool (fool) *n.* 1. a person who acts unwisely, one who lacks good sense or judgment. 2. a jester or clown during the Middle Ages. **fool** *v.* 1. to behave in a joking or teasing way. 2. to play about idly. 3. to trick or deceive (a person). □**fool around,** to spend one's time aimlessly; to flirt. **fool's errand,** a useless errand. **fool's gold,** iron pyrites, sometimes mistaken for gold. **fool's paradise,** happiness that is based on an illusion. **fool with,** to meddle with; to play aimlessly with. **make a fool of,** to make (a person) look foolish; to trick or deceive.

fool·er·y (foo-lě-ree) *n.* foolish acts or behavior.

fool·har·dy (fool-hahr-dee) *adj.* (**-di·er, -di·est**) rash, delighting in taking unnecessary risks. **fool'har·di·ness** *n.*

fool·ish (foo-lish) *adj.* 1. lacking in good sense or judgment. 2. (of actions) unwise. 3. ridiculous, *felt foolish.* **fool'ish·ly** *adv.* **fool'ish·ness** *n.*

fool·proof (fool-proof) *adj.* 1. (of rules or instructions) plain and simple and unable to be misinterpreted. 2. (of machinery) very simple to operate.

fools·cap (foolz-kap) *n.* a large size of writing paper. ▷So called from the use of a *fool's cap* (a jester's cap with bells) as a watermark.

foot (fuut) *n.* (*pl.* **feet,** *pr.* feet) 1. the end part of the leg below the ankle. 2. a similar part in animals, used in moving or for attaching the animal to things. 3. the lower end of a table or bed etc., the end opposite the head. 4. the part of a stocking covering the foot. 5. a person's step or tread or pace of movement, *fleet of foot.* 6. a lower usually projecting part of something (as of a table leg), the part of a sewing machine that is lowered on to the material to hold it steady. 7. the lowest part of something that has height or length, the bottom of a hill, ladder, page, list, etc. 8. a measure of length, = 12 inches (30.48 cm). 9. a unit of rhythm in a line of poetry, containing a stressed syllable, as each of the four divisions in *Jack/ and Jill/went up/the hill.* **foot** *v.* 1. to walk, not ride, *shall have to foot it.* 2. (*informal*) to pay (a bill). □**feet of clay,** a great weakness in a person or thing that is honored. **foot soldier,** an infantryman. **have a foot in both camps,** to be a member of each of two opposing factions. **have one foot in the grave,** to be nearing death or very old. **my foot!,** (*informal*) an exclamation of scornful contradiction. **on foot,** walking not riding. **to one's feet,** to a standing position. ▷It is incorrect to say *he is six foot tall.* Say *six feet tall.*

foot·age (fuut-ij) *n.* a length measured in feet, especially of exposed movie film.

foot-and-mouth (fuut-ăn-mowth) **disease** a contagious disease of cattle etc., causing ulceration of the mouth and feet.

foot·ball (fuut-bawl) *n.* 1. an elliptical inflated leather ball. 2. a game played with a football on a rectangular field between teams of eleven men each. 3. (in most countries of the world) soccer. 4. any of several other related games, as Rugby football, Canadian football, Australian football. 5. (*slang*) a difficult problem for which no one is eager to take responsibility, *the high cost of medical care is a political football.*

foot·board (fuut-bohrd) *n.* 1. a platform used to stand on. 2. an upright board fitted across the lower end of a bed.

foot·bridge (fuut-brij) *n.* a bridge for pedestrians, not for traffic.

foot-can·dle (fuut-kan-dĕl) *n.* a unit of illumination equal to that of one candela at a distance of one foot.

foot·er (fuut-ĕr) *n.* (*informal*) a person or thing of a specified height or length, used in combination, *a six-footer; an eight-footer.*

foot·fall (fuut-fawl) *n.* the sound of a footstep.

foot·hill (fuut-hil) *n.* one of the low hills near the bottom of a mountain or range.

foot·hold (fuut-hohld) *n.* 1. a place just wide enough for a foot to be placed on when climbing etc. 2. a small but secure position gained in a business etc.

foot·ing (fuut-ing) *n.* 1. a placing of the feet, a foothold; *lost his footing,* slipped. 2. a building foundation. 3. a status, conditions, *they were on a friendly footing; put the army on a war footing.*

foot·less (fuut-lis) *adj.* 1. having no feet. 2. lacking substance or basis.

foot·lights (fuut-lɪts) *n.* *pl.* a row of lights along the front of a stage floor.

foot·lock·er (fuut-lok-ĕr) *n.* a small trunk for personal belongings, especially for a soldier to keep at the foot of his bed.

foot·loose (fuut-loos) *adj.* independent, free to act or to travel as one pleases. □**footloose and fancy free,** entirely unattached.

foot·man (fuut-măn) *n.* (*pl.* **-men,** *pr.* -měn) a manservant (usually in livery) who admits visitors, waits at table, etc.

foot·note (fuut-noht) *n.* a note printed at the bottom of a page.

foot·pad (fuut-pad) *n.* (*old use*) an unmounted highwayman.

foot·path (fuut-path) *n.* a path for pedestrians.

foot·pound (fuut-pownd) *n.* the quantity of energy that will raise a weight of one pound to a height of one foot.

foot·print (fuut-print) *n.* an impression left by a foot or shoe.

foot·race (fuut-rays) *n.* a race between persons on foot.

foot·rest (fuut-rest) *n.* a support or platform to rest the feet on.

foot·sore (fuut-sohr) *adj.* having feet that are sore from walking.

foot·step (fuut-step) *n.* a step taken in walking, the sound of this. □**follow in someone's footsteps,** to do as an earlier person did.

foot·stool (fuut-stool) *n.* a stool for resting the feet on when sitting.

foot·wear (fuut-wair) *n.* shoes and stockings.

foot·work (fuut-wurk) *n.* the manner of moving or using the feet in boxing, football, etc.

fop (fop) *n.* a dandy. **fop′per·y** *n.* (*pl.* **-per·ies**) **fop′pish** *adj.*

for (for) *prep.* 1. in place of. 2. as the price or penalty of, *was fined for speeding.* 3. in defense or support or favor of. 4. with a view to, in order to find or obtain, *went for a walk; looking for a job.* 5. with regard to, in respect of, *ready for dinner.* 6. in the direction of, *set out for home.* 7. intended to be received by or belong to, *bought shoes for the children.* 8. so as to happen at a stated time, *an appointment for two o'clock.* 9. because of, on account of, *famous for its cider.* 10. to the extent or duration of, *walked for two miles; it will last for years.* **for** *conj.* because, *they hesitated, for they were afraid.* □**be in for it,** (*slang*) to be about to meet with punishment or trouble.

for. *abbr.* 1. foreign. 2. forester. 3. forestry.

for·age (for-ij) *n.* 1. food for horses and cattle. 2. foraging. **forage** *v.* (**for·aged, for·ag·ing**) to go searching, to rummage.

for·ay (for-ay) *n.* a sudden attack or raid, especially to obtain something.

for·bade (fŏr-bad, -bayd) *see* **forbid.**

for·bear[1] (for-bair) *v.* (**for·bore, for·borne, for·bear·ing**) to refrain, to refrain from, *could not forbear criticizing* or *from criticizing; forbore to mention it.*

for·bear[2] *n.* = **forebear.**

for·bear·ance (for-bair-ăns) *n.* patience, tolerance.

for·bear·ing (for-bair-ing) *adj.* & *n.* being patient or tolerant.

for·bid (fŏr-bid) *v.* (**for·bade, for·bid·den, for·bid·ding**) 1. to order (a person) not to do something or not to enter, *forbid him to go; forbid him the house.* 2. to refuse to allow, *forbid the marriage; he is forbidden wine,* not allowed to drink it.

for·bid·ding (for-bid-ing) *adj.* looking unfriendly or uninviting, stern.

force (fohrs) *n.* 1. strength, power, intense effort. 2. (in scientific use) a measurable influence tending to cause movement of a body, its intensity. 3. a body of troops or police. 4. a body of people organized or available for a purpose, *the labor force.* 5. compulsion. 6. effectiveness, legal validity, *the new rules come into force next week.* **force** *v.* (**forced, forc·ing**) 1. to use force in order to get or do something, to compel, to oblige. 2. to exert force on, to break open by force, *forced the lock.* 3. to strain to the utmost, to overstrain. 4. to impose, to inflict; *force an invitation on a person,* insist that he come. 5. to cause or produce by effort, *forced a smile.* 6. to cause (plants etc.) to reach maturity earlier than is normal. ☐**force a person's hand,** to compel him to take action. **forced landing,** an emergency landing of an aircraft. **forced march,** a lengthy march requiring special effort by troops etc. **force the issue,** to make an immediate decision necessary. **force the pace,** to adopt a high speed in a race etc. and so tire out others who are taking part. **in force,** in operation, valid.

force-feed (fohrs-feed) *v.* to feed (a prisoner, etc.) against his will.

force·ful (fohrs-fŭl) *adj.* powerful and vigorous, effective. **force'ful·ly** *adv.* **force'ful·ness** *n.*

force·meat (fohrs-meet) *n.* finely chopped meat seasoned and used as stuffing.

for·ceps (for-seps) *n.* (*pl.* **-ceps**) pincers or tongs used by dentists, surgeons, etc. for gripping things.

for·ci·ble (fohr-sĭ-bĕl) *adj.* done by force, forceful. **for'ci'bly** *adv.*

ford (fohrd) *n.* a shallow place where a river may be crossed by wading or riding or driving through. **ford** *v.* to cross in this way.

Ford (fohrd), **Ger·ald R.** (1913–) the thirty-eighth president of the U.S. 1974–76.

ford·a·ble (fohr-dă-bĕl) *adj.* able to be forded.

fore¹ (fohr) *adj.* situated in front. **fore** *adv.* in or at or toward the front. **fore** *n.* the fore part. ☐**to the fore,** in front, conspicuous.

fore² *interj.* a cry to warn a person who may be hit by a golf ball about to be played.

fore-and-aft (fohr-ănd-aft) *adj.* lengthwise in a ship.

fore·arm¹ (fohr-ahrm) *n.* the arm from elbow to wrist or fingertips.

fore·arm² (for-ahrm) *v.* to arm or prepare in advance against possible danger etc.

fore·bear (fohr-bair) *n.* an ancestor.

fore·bode (fohr-bohd) *v.* (**fore·bod·ed, fore·bod·ing**) to be an advance sign or token of (trouble).

fore·bod·ing (fohr-boh-ding) *n.* a feeling that trouble is coming.

fore·cast (fohr-kast) *v.* (**fore·cast** or **fore·cast·ed, fore·cast·ing**) to tell in advance (what is likely to happen). **forecast** *n.* a statement that forecasts something. **fore'cast·er** *n.*

fore·cas·tle (fohk-sĕl) *n.* the forward part of certain ships, where formerly the crew had their accommodation.

fore·close (fohr-klohz) *v.* (**fore·closed, fore·clos·ing**) 1. (of a firm etc. that has lent money

on mortgage) to take possession of property when the loan is not duly repaid, *the bank decided to foreclose* or *decided to foreclose the mortgage.* 2. to bar from a privilege. **fore·clo·sure** (fohr-kloh-zhŭr) *n.*

fore·court (fohr-kohrt) *n.* 1. an enclosed space in front of a building, an outer court. 2. (in tennis) the part of the court between the service line and the net.

fore·doom (fohr-doom) *v.* to doom or condemn beforehand.

fore·fa·ther (fohr-fah-thĕr) *n.* an ancestor.

fore·fin·ger (fohr-fing-gĕr) *n.* the finger next to the thumb.

fore·foot (fohr-fuut) *n.* (*pl.* **-feet**) an animal's front foot.

fore·front (fohr-frunt) *n.* the very front.

fore·gath·er = **forgather.**

fore·go·ing (fohr-goh-ing) *adj.* preceding, previously mentioned.

fore·gone (fohr-gawn) **conclusion** a result that can be foreseen easily and with certainty.

fore·ground (fohr-grownd) *n.* 1. the part of a scene or picture that is nearest to an observer. 2. the most conspicuous position.

fore·hand (fohr-hand) *adj.* 1. (of a stroke in tennis etc.) played with the palm of the hand turned forward. 2. on the side on which this stroke is made. **forehand** *n.* a forehand stroke.

fore·head (for-id, -hed) *n.* the part of the face above the eyes.

for·eign (for-in) *adj.* 1. of or in or from another country, not of one's own country. 2. dealing with or involving other countries, *foreign affairs.* 3. not belonging naturally, *jealousy is foreign to her nature.* 4. coming from outside, *a foreign body in the eye.* ☐**foreign exchange,** the currency of other countries; dealings in these currencies. **Foreign Legion,** see **legion. foreign minister,** the head of a government department dealing with foreign affairs.

for·eign·er (for-ĭ-nĕr) *n.* a person who was born in or comes from another country.

fore·knowl·edge (fohr-nol-ij) *n.* knowledge of something before it occurs.

fore·la·dy (fohr-lay-dee) *n.* (*pl.* **-dies**) a forewoman.

fore·land (fohr-land) *n.* a cape or promontory.

fore·leg (fohr-leg) *n.* an animal's front leg.

fore·limb (fohr-lim) *n.* a foreleg.

fore·lock (fohr-lok) *n.* a lock of hair just above the forehead.

fore·man (fohr-măn) *n.* (*pl.* **-men,** *pr.* -mĕn) 1. a workman whose job is to superintend other workmen. 2. a man acting as president and spokesman of a jury.

fore·mast (fohr-mast) *n.* the forward lower mast of a ship.

fore·most (fohr-mohst) *adj.* 1. most advanced in position or rank. 2. most important. **foremost** *adv.* in the foremost position etc.

fore·name (fohr-naym) *n.* a person's first name.

fore·named (fohr-naymd) *adj.* named or mentioned before.

fore·noon (fohr-noon) *n.* the day until noon, morning.

fo·ren·sic (fŏ-ren-sik) *adj.* 1. of or used in law courts. 2. of or involving **forensic medicine,** the medical knowledge needed in legal matters or police investigations (as in a poisoning case).

fo·ren·sics (fŏ-ren-siks) *n.* the art or practice of

formal debate and argument; *indulged in forensics,* argued at great length and with oratorical display.
fore·or·dain (fohr-or-dayn) *v.* to destine beforehand, *it was foreordained by God.*
fore·part (fohr-pahrt) *n.* a previous or early part.
fore·sail (fohr-sayl) *n.* 1. the lowest square sail in a square-rigged vessel. 2. the triangular sail before the mast in a fore-and-aft rigged vessel.
fore·see (fohr-see) *v.* (**fore·saw, fore·seen, for·see·ing**) to be aware of or realize (a thing) beforehand.
fore·see·a·ble (fohr-see-ă-běl) *adj.* able to be foreseen; *the foreseeable future,* the period during which the course of events can be predicted. **fore·see'a·bly** *adv.*
fore·shad·ow (fohr-shad-oh) *v.* to be a sign of (something that is to come).
fore·sheet (fohr-sheet) *n.* the inner part of the bows of an open boat.
fore·shore (fohr-shohr) *n.* the shore between highwater mark and low-water mark, or between water and land that is cultivated or built on.
fore·short·en (fohr-shohr-těn) *v.* to represent (an object, when drawing it) with shortening of certain lines to give an effect of distance, to cause such an effect in.
fore·sight (fohr-sɪt) *n.* the ability to foresee and prepare for future needs. **fore'sight·ed** *adj.* **fore'sight·ed·ness** *n.*
fore·skin (fohr-skin) *n.* the loose skin at the end of the penis.
for·est (for-ist) *n.* trees and undergrowth covering a large area. □**forest fire,** a large fire burning in a forest. **forest ranger,** a person caring for or supervising a forest.
fore·stall (fohr-stawl) *v.* to prevent or foil (a person or his plans) by taking action first.
for·est·a·tion (for-i-stay-shŏn) *n.* the planting of a forest.
for·est·ed (for-i-stid) *adj.* covered in forest.
for·est·er (for-i-stěr) *n.* an officer in charge of a forest or of growing timber.
for·est·land (for-ist-land) *n.* land that is covered by a forest.
for·es·try (for-i-stree) *n.* the science or practice of planting and caring for forests.
fore·taste (fohr-tayst) *n.* an experience of something in advance of what is to come. **foretaste** *v.* (**fore·tast·ed, fore·tast·ing**) to have a foretaste of.
fore·tell (fohr-tel) *v.* (**fore·told, fore·tell·ing**) to forecast, to prophesy.
fore·thought (fohr-thawt) *n.* careful thought and planning for the future.
fore·to·ken (fohr-toh-kěn) *v.* to portend, to indicate beforehand.
fore·top (fohr-top) *n.* 1. the top of a ship's foremast. 2. a platform on this.
for·ev·er (for-ev-ěr) *adv.* for all time, incessantly.
for·ev·er·more (for-ev-ěr-mohr) *adv.* forever.
fore·warn (fohr-worn) *v.* to warn beforehand.
fore·wing (for-weeng) *n.* either of the two front wings of a four-winged insect.
fore·wom·an (fohr-wuum-ăn) *n.* (*pl.* **-wom·en,** *pr.* -wim-in) 1. a woman whose job is to superintend other workers. 2. a woman acting as president and spokesman of a jury.
fore·word (fohr-wurd) *n.* introductory remarks at the beginning of a book, usually written by someone other than the author of the book.
for·feit (for-fit) *n.* something that has to be paid

or given up as a penalty. **forfeit** *adj.* paid or given up in this way. **forfeit** *v.* to pay or give up as a forfeit.
for·fei·ture (for-fi-chŭr) *n.* forfeiting.
for·fend (for-fend) *v.* (old use) to avert, to keep off, *may heaven forfend!*
for·gath·er (for-gath-ěr) *v.* to assemble.
forge¹ (forj) *v.* (**forged, forg·ing**) to make one's way forward by effort, *forged ahead.*
forge² *n.* 1. a workshop with a fire and an anvil where metals are heated and shaped, especially one used by a smith for shoeing horses and working iron. 2. a furnace or hearth for melting or refining metal, the workshop containing it. **forge** *v.* (**forged, forg·ing**) 1. to shape by heating in fire and hammering. 2. to make an imitation or copy of (a thing) in order to pass it off fraudulently as real. **forg'er** *n.*
for·ger·y (for-jě-ree) *n.* (*pl.* **-ger·ies**) 1. forging, imitating fraudulently. 2. something forged.
for·get (fŏr-get) *v.* (**for·got, for·got·ten, for·get·ting**) 1. to lose remembrance of (a thing or duty etc.). 2. to put out of one's mind, to stop thinking about, *decided to forget our quarrels.* □**forget oneself,** to behave without suitable dignity.
for·get·ful (fŏr-get-fŭl) *adj.* tending to forget things. **for·get'ful·ness** *n.* **for·get'ful·ly** *adv.*
for·get-me-not (fŏr-get-mee-not) *n.* a plant with small blue flowers.
forg·ing (for-jing) *n.* a piece of metal that has been forged.
for·give (fŏr-giv) *v.* (**for·gave, for·giv·en, for·giv·ing**) to cease to feel angry or bitter toward (a person) or about (an offense). **for·give'ness** *n.* **for·giv'a·ble** *adj.* **for·giv'a·bly** *adv.*
for·giv·ing (fŏr-giv-ing) *adj.* inclined to or showing forgiveness.
for·go (for-goh) *v.* (**for·went, for·gone, for·go·ing**) to give up, to go without.
for·int (for-int) *n.* the unit of money in Hungary.
fork (fork) *n.* 1. a pronged instrument used in eating or cooking. 2. a pronged agricultural implement used for digging or lifting things. 3. a thing shaped like this. 4. a place where something separates into two or more parts or branches. 5. a branch or tributary (of a river, road, etc.). **fork** *v.* 1. to lift or dig with a fork. 2. (of an object or road etc.) to form a fork by separating into two branches. 3. (of a person) to follow one of these branches, *fork left.* □**fork out, fork over, fork up,** (slang) to pay out money, hand over.
forked (forkt) *adj.* having a fork or forking branches.
fork·lift (fork-lift) *n.* (also **forklift truck**) a vehicle with a forklike mechanical device for lifting and moving heavy objects.
for·lorn (for-lorn) *adj.* left alone and unhappy. **for·lorn'ly** *adv.* □**forlorn hope,** the only faint hope left.
form (form) *n.* 1. the shape of something, its outward or visible appearance. 2. its structure. 3. a person or animal as it can be seen or touched. 4. the way in which a thing exists, *ice is a form of water.* 5. a fixed or usual method of doing something, a formality, a set of words in a ritual etc. 6. a document with blank spaces that are to be filled in with information. 7. (of a horse or athlete) condition of health and training; *is in good form,* performing well, (of a person) in good spirits. 8. details of previous performances, *study the form*

before betting. **form** *v.* 1. to shape, to mold, to produce or construct. 2. to bring into existence, to constitute, *form a committee.* 3. to take shape, to become solid, *icicles formed.* 4. to develop in the mind, *formed a plan; formed a habit,* developed it. 5. to arrange in a certain formation. □**form letter,** a standardized letter to deal with frequently occurring matters.
for·mal (for-măl) *adj.* 1. conforming to accepted rules or customs, showing or requiring formality, *a formal greeting* or *party.* 2. outward, *only a formal resemblance.* 3. regular or geometrical in design, *formal gardens.* **formal** *n.* 1. a formal dance. 2. a formal gown. **for'mal·ly** *adv.* □**formal dress,** men's and women's evening clothes.
form·al·de·hyde (for-mal-dĕ-hīd) *n.* a colorless gas used in solution as a preservative and disinfectant.
for·mal·ism (for-mă-liz-ĕm) *n.* strict observance of form, excessive regularity or symmetry.
for·mal·i·ty (for-mal-i-tee) *n.* (*pl.* **-ties**) 1. strict observance of rules and conventions. 2. a formal act, something required by law or custom, *legal formalities; it's just a formality,* is done only to comply with a rule.
for·mal·ize (for-mă-līz) *v.* (**for·mal·ized, for·mal·iz·ing**) to make formal or official. **for·mal·iz·a·tion** (for-mă-li-zay-shŏn) *n.*
for·mat (for-mat) *n.* the shape and size of a book etc.
for·ma·tion (for-may-shŏn) *n.* 1. forming, being formed. 2. a thing formed. 3. a particular arrangement or order.
form·a·tive (for-mă-tiv) *adj.* forming something; *during a child's formative years,* while its character is being formed.
for·mer (for-mĕr) *adj.* 1. of an earlier period, *in former times.* 2. mentioned before another; *the former,* the one mentioned first of two. ▷When referring to the first of three or more, say *the first,* not *the former.*
for·mer·ly (for-mĕr-lee) *adv.* in former times.
form·fit·ting (form-fit-ing) *adj.* fitting snugly; *a formfitting gown,* one that fits the curves of the figure closely.
For·mi·ca (for-mī-kă) *n.* (trademark) a hard heat-resistant plastic used on surfaces.
for·mic (for-mik) **acid** a colorless acid contained in fluid emitted by ants.
for·mi·da·ble (for-mi-dă-bĕl) *adj.* 1. inspiring fear or awe. 2. difficult to do or overcome, *a formidable task.* **for'mi·da·bly** *adv.* ▷It is incorrect to accent these words as formidable and formidably.
form·less (form-lis) *adj.* without distinct or regular form.
for·mu·la (for-myŭ-lă) *n.* (*pl.* **-las, -lae,** *pr.* **-lee**) 1. a fixed series of words, especially one used on social or ceremonial occasions. 2. a list of ingredients for making something; *diplomats seeking a formula,* a set of statements that can be agreed on, as in order to produce a peace treaty. 3. a set of chemical symbols showing the constituents of a substance. 4. a mathematical rule or statement expressed in algebraic symbols. 5. the classification of a racing car, especially by its engine capacity.
for·mu·late (for-myŭ-layt) *v.* (**for·mu·lated, for·mu·lat·ing**) 1. to reduce to or express in a formula. 2. to state clearly and exactly. 3. to make

according to a formula. **for·mu·la·tion** (for-myŭ-lay-shŏn) *n.*
for·ni·cate (for-nĭ-kayt) *v.* (**for·ni·cat·ed, for·ni·cat·ing**) (of unmarried people) to have sexual intercourse voluntarily. **for'ni·ca·tor** *n.* **for·ni·ca·tion** (for-nĭ-kay-shŏn) *n.*
for·sake (for-sayk) *v.* (**for·sook, for·sak·en, for·sak·ing**) 1. to give up, to renounce, *forsaking their former way of life.* 2. to withdraw one's help or friendship or companionship from, *forsook his wife and children.*
for·sooth (for-sooth) *adv.* (old use) truly, no doubt.
for·swear (for-swair) *v.* (**for·swore, for·sworn, for·swear·ing**) 1. to give up, renounce, *he forswore tobacco.* 2. to deny or renounce under oath. □**forswear oneself,** to swear falsely, commit perjury.
for·syth·i·a (for-sith-i-ă) *n.* a shrub with bright yellow flowers, blooming in spring.
fort (fort) *n.* a fortified building or position.
forte[1] (fort) *n.* a person's strong point.
for·te[2] (for-tay) *adv.* (in music) loudly.
forth (fohrth) *adv.* 1. onward, forward, *from this day forth.* □**and so forth,** and so on. **back and forth,** to and fro.
forth·com·ing (fohrth-**kum**-ing) *adj.* 1. about to come forth or appear; *forthcoming events,* things about to take place. 2. made available when needed, *money was not forthcoming.* 3. *(informal)* willing to give information, *the girl was not very forthcoming.*
forth·right (fohrth-rīt) *adj.* frank, outspoken.
forth'right·ly *adv.* **forth'right·ness** *n.*
forth·with (fohrth-with) *adv.* immediately.
for·ties (for-teez) *n. pl.* the numbers or years or degrees of temperature from forty to forty-nine.
for·ti·eth (for-ti-ith) *see* **forty.**
for·ti·fi·ca·tion (for-tĭ-fi-kay-shŏn) *n.* 1. fortifying. 2. a wall or building constructed to defend a place.
for·ti·fy (for-tĭ-fī) *v.* (**for·ti·fied, for·ti·fy·ing**) 1. to strengthen (a place) against attack, especially by constructing fortifications. 2. to strengthen (a person) mentally or morally, to increase the vigor of. 3. to increase the food value of (bread etc.) by adding vitamins, to strengthen (wine) by adding alcohol.
for·tis·si·mo (for-tis-i-moh) *adj. & adv.* (in music) very loud.
for·ti·tude (for-ti-tood) *n.* courage in bearing pain or trouble.
fort·night (fort-nīt) *n.* a period of two weeks.
fort'night·ly *adj. & adv.* happening or appearing once a fortnight.
for·tress (for-tris) *n.* a fortified building or town.
for·tu·i·tous (for-too-i-tŭs) *adj.* happening by chance. **for·tu'i·tous·ly** *adv.* **for·tu'i·tous·ness** *n.* ▷Do not confuse *fortuitous* with *fortunate.* A *fortuitous meeting* may be *unfortunate* as often as it is *fortunate.*
for·tu·i·ty (for-too-i-tee) *n.* (*pl.* **-ties**) fortuitousness, a chance occurrence.
for·tu·nate (for-chŭ-nit) *adv.* having or bringing or brought by good fortune. **for'tu·nate·ly** *adv.* ▷See the note under *fortuitous.*
for·tune (for-chŭn) *n.* 1. the events that chance brings to a person or undertaking. 2. chance as a power in the affairs of mankind. 3. a person's destiny. 4. prosperity, success, *seek one's fortune.* 5. a great amount of wealth, *left him a fortune.*

☐**fortune hunter,** a person seeking a rich spouse.
tell fortunes, to be a fortuneteller.

for·tune·tell·er (for-chŭn-tel-ĕr) *n.* a person who claims to foretell future events in people's lives.

for·ty (for-tee) *adj. & n. (pl.* **-ties)** four times ten (40, XL). **fortieth** *adj. & n.* ☐**forty winks,** a nap.

for·ty-five (for-tee-fɪv) *n.* a .45 caliber gun, or a 45 rpm record.

for·ty-nin·er (for-tee-nɪ-nĕr) *n.* a person who went to California in the gold rush of 1849.

fo·rum (fohr-ŭm) *n. (pl.* **fo·rums, fo·ra,** *pr.* fohr-ă) a place or meeting where a public discussion is held.

for·ward (for-wărd) *adj.* 1. directed or moving toward the front, situated in the front. 2. of or relating to the future, *forward thinking.* 3. having made more than the normal progress. 4. too bold in one's manner, presumptuous. **forward** *n.* an attacking player who is positioned near the desired goal in hockey or basketball, his position. **forward** *adv.* toward the front or future, in advance, ahead. **forward** *v.* 1. to send on (a letter etc.) to a new address. 2. to send or dispatch (goods) to a customer. 3. to help to advance (a person's interests). **for'ward·ness** *n.* ☐**forwarding address,** an address to which mail should be forwarded.

for·ward·er (for-wăr-dĕr) *n.* a person or agent that forwards things, especially one handling freight or sending goods to their destination.

for·wards (for-wărdz) *adv.* forward.

fos·sil (fos-ĭl) *n.* 1. the remains or traces of a prehistoric animal or plant once buried in earth and now hardened like rock. 2. *(informal)* a person who is out of date and unable to accept new ideas. **fossil** *adj.* 1. of or as a fossil. 2. (of fuel, as coal) formed in the geological past and dug out of the earth.

fos·sil·ize (fos-ĭ-lɪz) *v.* **(fos·sil·ized, fos·sil·iz·ing)** to turn or be turned into a fossil. **fos·sil·i·za·tion** (fos-ĭ-li-zay-shŏn) *n.*

fos·ter (faw-stĕr) *v.* 1. to promote the growth or development of. 2. to take care of and bring up (a child that is not one's own). ☐**foster child,** a child fostered in this way. **foster father, foster mother, foster parent,** one who fosters a child. **foster home,** a family home in which a foster child is brought up.

fos·ter·ling (faw-stĕr-ling) *n.* a foster child.

fought (fawt) *see* **fight.**

foul (fowl) *adj.* 1. causing disgust, having an offensive smell or taste. 2. morally offensive, evil. 3. (of language) disgusting, obscene. 4. (of weather) rough, stormy. 5. clogged, choked, overgrown with barnacles etc. 6. in collision or entangled. 7. unfair, against the rules of a game, *a foul blow.* **foul** *n.* a foul stroke or blow etc., breaking the rules of a game, *committed a foul.* **foul** *v.* 1. to make or become foul. 2. to entangle or collide with, to obstruct. 3. to commit a foul in a game. **foul'ly** *adv.* ☐**foul ball,** (in baseball) a ball hit outside the foul lines. **foul line,** (in baseball) one of two lines extending from home plate at right angles to the end of the outfield, marking the boundary of the playing field; (in basketball) one of two lines on the court at which players stand to take foul shots. **foul play,** a violent crime, especially murder. **foul shot,** (in basketball) a throw at the basket without interference by oppos-

ing players, awarded as a penalty against them. **foul up,** to make or become foul; to confuse or bungle.

fou·lard (foo-lahrd) *n.* a kind of silky material used for ties etc.

foul·ing (fow-ling) *n.* an incrustation, especially on a ship's bottom.

foul·mouthed (fowl-mow*th*d, -mowtht) *adj.* using foul language.

foul-up (fowl-up) *n. (slang)* confusion resulting from incompetence or mechanical breakdown.

found[1] (fownd) *see* **find.** ☐**found object,** a manufactured or natural object regarded as having artistic or decorative value.

found[2] *v.* **(found·ed, found·ing)** 1. to establish, to originate, to provide money for starting (an institution etc.). 2. to base or construct, *a novel that is founded on fact.* **found'er** *n.* ☐**Founding Fathers,** the American colonial leaders who founded the U.S.

found[3] *v.* **(found·ed, found·ing)** 1. to melt and mold (metal), to fuse (materials for glass). 2. to make (an object) in this way. **found'er** *n.*

foun·da·tion (fown-day-shŏn) *n.* 1. the founding of an institution etc. 2. the institution itself, a fund of money established for a charitable purpose. 3. the strong base from which a building is built up. 4. a cosmetic applied to the skin as the first layer of makeup. 5. the underlying principle or idea etc. on which something is based. ☐**foundation garment,** a woman's supporting undergarment, as a corset.

found·er[1] (fown-dĕr) *n. see* **found**[2]**, found**[3]**.**

founder[2] *v.* 1. to stumble or fall. 2. (of a ship) to fill with water and sink. 3. to fail completely, *the plan foundered.*

found·ling (fownd-ling) *n.* a deserted child of unknown parents.

found·ry (fown-dree) *n. (pl.* **-ries)** a factory or workshop where metal or glass is founded (*see* **found**[3]).

fount (fownt) *n.* a fountain, a source.

foun·tain (fown-tĭn) *n.* 1. a spring of water, especially a jet of water made to spout artificially as an ornament. 2. a structure providing a supply of drinking water in a public place. ☐**fountain pen,** a pen containing a reservoir of ink.

foun·tain·head (fown-tĭn-hed) *n.* an original source.

four (fohr) *adj. & n.* one more than three (4, IV). ☐**Four Hundred,** the most exclusive social set, originally that of New York. (▷From the period about 1890 when this set comprised about four hundred people.) **four-letter word,** a short word referring to sexual or excretory functions and regarded as obscene. **four o'clock,** a plant native to tropical America, with flowers opening about 4 P.M.

four·flush·er (fohr-flush-ĕr) *n. (informal)* a bluffer, a humbug.

four·fold (fohr-fohld) *adj. & n.* 1. four times as much or as many. 2. consisting of four parts.

Four-H (fohr-aych) **Club,** (also **4-H Club)** an organization sponsored by the U.S. Department of Agriculture to instruct young people in citizenship (improving *h*ead, *h*eart, *h*ands, and *h*ealth). **4-H'er** *n.* a member of the Four-H Club.

four-in-hand (fohr-in-hand) *n.* a necktie tied in a slipknot with long ends hanging and overlapping.

four·pen·ny (fohr-pen-ee) nail a nail one and one-half or one and three-eighths inches long.

four·post·er (fohr-poh-stĕr) *n.* a bed with four posts to support a canopy.

four·score (fohr-skohr) *adj.* eighty.

four·some (fohr-sŏm) *n.* 1. a company of four people. 2. a golf match between two pairs.

four·square (fohr-skwair) *adj.* solidly based, steady. **foursquare** *adv.* squarely; *they are four-square behind you,* support you completely.

four·teen (fohr-teen) *adj. & n.* one more than thirteen (14, XIV). **four'teenth'** *adj. & n.*

fourth (fohrth) *adj.* next after third. **fourth** *n.* 1. something that is fourth. 2. one of four equal parts of a thing. **fourth'ly** *adv.* □**fourth class,** a class of mail consisting of merchandise or certain printed matter and sent at lowest rate. **fourth dimension,** time viewed as a lengthlike quantity. **fourth estate,** the press. **the Fourth,** July 4, Independence Day.

four-wheel (fohr-hweel) *adj.* applied to all four wheels of a vehicle, *four-wheel drive.*

fowl (fowl) *n.* (*pl.* **fowl, fowls**) 1. kind of bird often kept at houses and farms to supply eggs and flesh for food. 2. the flesh of birds as food, *fish, flesh, and fowl.*

fowl·er (fow-ler) *n.* a person who goes fowling.

fowl·ing (fow-ling) *n.* catching or shooting or snaring wildfowl.

fox (foks) *n.* (*pl.* **fox·es**) 1. a wild animal of the dog family with a pointed snout and reddish fur and a bushy tail. 2. its fur. 3. a crafty person. 4. *(slang)* a sexy woman. **fox** *v.* to deceive or puzzle by acting craftily.

foxed (fokst) *adj.* (of things) discolored by brown spots caused by dampness.

fox·fire (foks-fir) *n.* phosphorescence from decaying wood.

fox·glove (foks-gluv) *n.* a tall plant with purple or white flowers like glove fingers.

fox·hole (foks-hohl) *n.* a small pit dug by soldiers as shelter against enemy fire.

fox·hound (foks-hownd) *n.* a kind of hound bred and trained to hunt foxes.

fox terrier a kind of short-haired terrier.

fox trot a ballroom dance with slow and quick steps, music for this.

fox-trot (foks-trot) *v.* (**fox-trot·ted, fox-trot·ting**) to dance a fox trot.

fox·y (fok-see) *adj.* (**fox·i·er, fox·i·est**) 1. reddish brown. 2. crafty. 3. looking like a fox. 4. *(slang)* (of a woman) pretty, sexy.

foy·er (foi-ĕr) *n.* an entrance hall or lobby.

fp. *abbr.* 1. foolscap. 2. foot-pound. 3. freezing point.

FPC *abbr.* 1. Federal Power Commission. 2. fish protein concentrate.

FPM, fpm *abbr.* feet per minute.

FPO *abbr.* 1. field post office. 2. fleet post office.

FPS, fps *abbr.* feet per second.

Fr *symbol* francium.

fr. *abbr.* 1. fragment. 2. franc. 3. from.

Fr. *abbr.* 1. Father. 2. franc. 3. France. 4. French. 5. Friar. 6. Friday.

fra·cas (fray-kăs) *n.* (*pl.* **-cas·es**) a noisy quarrel or disturbance.

frac·tion (frak-shŏn) *n.* 1. a number that is not a whole number, as $\frac{1}{3}$, $\frac{7}{8}$. 2. a very small part or piece or amount; *at a fraction of the original price,* very much reduced in price.

frac·tion·al (frak-shŏ-năl) *adj.* 1. of a fraction. 2. very small, *a fractional difference.* **frac'tion·al·ly** *adv.*

frac·tious (frak-shŭs) *adj.* irritable, peevish. **frac'tious·ly** *adv.* **frac'tious·ness** *n.* ▷Do not confuse *fractious* with *factious.*

frac·ture (frak-chŭr) *n.* breaking or breakage, especially of a bone. **fracture** *v.* (**frac·tured, frac·tur·ing**) to cause a fracture in, to suffer a fracture.

frag (frag) *v.* (**fragged, frag·ging**) *(slang)* to attack (especially an unpopular superior officer) with a hand grenade.

frag·ile (fraj-Il) *adj.* 1. easily damaged or broken. 2. of delicate constitution, not strong. **frag'ile·ly** *adv.* **fra·gil·i·ty** (fră-jil-i-tee) *n.*

frag·ment (frag-mĕnt) *n.* 1. a piece broken off something. 2. an isolated part, *a fragment of the conversation.* **fragment** (frag-ment, frag-ment) *v.* to break or be broken into fragments. **frag·men·ta·tion** (frag-men-tay-shŏn) *n.* □**fragmentation bomb,** a bomb designed to break into small fragments on exploding.

frag·men·tar·y (frag-mĕn-ter-ee) *adj.* consisting of fragments.

fra·grance (fray-grăns) *n.* 1. being fragrant. 2. something fragrant, perfume.

fra·grant (fray-grănt) *adj.* having a pleasant smell. **fra'grant·ly** *adv.*

frail (frayl) *adj.* not strong, physically weak.

frail·ty (frayl-tee) *n.* (*pl.* **-ties**) 1. being frail, weakness. 2. moral weakness, liability to yield to temptation.

frame (fraym) *n.* 1. a rigid structure forming a support for other parts of a building, vehicle, piece of furniture, etc. 2. an open case or a border in which a picture, door, pane of glass, pair of eyeglasses, etc. may be set. 3. the human or an animal body with reference to its size, *a small frame.* 4. a single exposure on a strip of movie film. 5. (in bowling) one of ten rounds in a game. 6. a boxlike structure used for protecting plants from the cold. **frame** *v.* (**framed, fram·ing**) 1. to put or form a frame around. 2. to construct. 3. to compose, to compress in words, *frame a treaty* or *a question.* 4. *(slang)* to arrange false evidence against, so that an innocent person appears to be guilty. □**frame house,** a house of wooden framework covered with boards etc. **frame of mind,** a temporary state of mind. **frame of reference,** a set of principles or standards by which ideas and behavior etc. are evaluated.

frame-up (fraym-up) *n.* *(slang)* the arrangement of false evidence against an innocent person.

frame·work (fraym-wurk) *n.* 1. the supporting frame of a building or other construction. 2. the basic structure (of an idea, treaty, etc.).

franc (frangk) *n.* the unit of money in France, Belgium, Switzerland, and certain other countries.

France (frans) a country in western Europe.

fran·chise (fran-chız) *n.* 1. the right to vote at public elections. 2. authorization to sell a company's goods or services in a particular area. **franchise** *v.* (**fran·chised, fran·chis·ing**) to grant a franchise to (a person or company). **fran'chis·er** *n.* one who grants a franchise.

fran·chis·ee (fran-chı-zee) *n.* one who receives or has a franchise.

Fran·cis·can (fran-sis-kăn) *n.* a member of an order of friars founded by St. Francis of Assisi, or of a corresponding order of nuns.

fran·ci·um (fran-si-ŭm) *n.* a radioactive chemical element.

fran·gi·ble (fran-jĭ-bĕl) *adj.* breakable, fragile.

frank¹ (frangk) *adj.* showing one's thoughts and feelings unmistakably. **frank'ly** *adv.* **frank' ness** *n.*

frank² *v.* to send (mail) free, *members of Congress have franking privileges.* **frank** *n.* a mark on mail that enables it to be sent free.

Frank·en·stein (frang-kĕn-stɪn) (also **Frankenstein's monster**) a thing that becomes formidable to the person who has created it. ▷From a character in and the title of a novel (1818) by Mary W. Shelley. Dr. Frankenstein created the monster that turned on him.

Frank·fort (frangk-fŏrt) the capital of Kentucky.

frank·furt·er (frangk-fūr-tĕr) *n.* a highly seasoned smoked sausage, a hot dog. ▷Originally made at Frankfurt in Germany.

frank·in·cense (frang-kin-sens) *n.* a kind of sweet-smelling gum burned as incense.

fran·tic (fran-tik) *adj.* wildly excited or agitated by anxiety etc., frenzied. **fran'ti·cal·ly** *adv.*

frap·pé (fra-pay), **frappe** (frap) *n.* 1. a milk shake. 2. a frozen fruit-flavored dessert. 3. a liqueur served with shaved ice.

fra·ter·nal (fră-tur-năl) *adj.* of a brother or brothers. **fra·ter'nal·ly** *adv.* ▢**fraternal twins**, twins developed from separate ova.

fra·ter·ni·ty (fră-tur-ni-tee) *n.* (*pl.* -**ties**) 1. a society of college men. 2. a group of people with common interests. 3. brotherhood, brotherly feeling.

frat·er·nize (frat-ĕr-nɪz) *v.* (**frat·er·nized, frat·er·niz·ing**) to associate with others in a friendly way. **frat·er·ni·za·tion** (frat-ĕr-ni-zay-shŏn) *n.*

frat·ri·cide (frat-ri-sɪd) *n.* 1. the act of killing of one's brother or sister. 2. a person who commits this crime. 3. the crime itself. **frat·ri·cid·al** (frat-ri-sɪ-dăl) *adj.*

Frau (frow) *n.* (*pl.* **Frau·en**, *pr.* frow-ĕn) the title of a German married woman, = Mrs.

fraud (frawd) *n.* 1. criminal deception, a dishonest trick. 2. a person (or thing) that is not what he (it) seems or pretends to be.

fraud·u·lent (fraw-jŭ-lĕnt) *adj.* acting with fraud, obtained by fraud. **fraud'u·lent·ly** *adv.* **fraud'u·lence** *n.*

fraught (frawt) *adj.* filled, involving, *fraught with danger.*

Fräu·lein (frow-lɪn) *n.* the title of a German unmarried woman, = Miss.

fray¹ (fray) *n.* a fight, a conflict, *ready for the fray.*

fray² *v.* 1. to make worn so that there are loose threads, especially at the edge. 2. to strain or upset (nerves or temper). 3. to become frayed.

fraz·zle (fraz-ĕl) *v.* (**fraz·zled, fraz·zling**) to wear down or exhaust. **frazzle** *n.* a completely exhausted state, *worn to a frazzle.*

FRB *abbr.* Federal Reserve Board.

freak (freek) *n.* 1. a person or thing that is abnormal in form. 2. something very unusual or irregular, *the storm was a freak.* 3. (*slang*) one who freaks out, a drug addict. **freak'y** *adj.* (**freak·i·er, feak·i·est**) ▢**freak out**, (*slang*) to have hallucinations from narcotic drugs, to have a strong emotional experience. **freak show,** a sideshow at a carnival, displaying freaks.

freak·ish (free-kish) *adj.* like a freak. **freak'ish·ly** *adv.* **freak'ish·ness** *n.*

freak·out (freek-owt) *n.* (*slang*) a period of insanity or hallucination.

freck·le (frek-ĕl) *n.* a light brown spot on the skin.

freckle *v.* (**freck·led, freck·ling**) to become or cause to become spotted with freckles.

free (free) *adj.* (**fre·er, fre·est**) 1. (of a person) not a slave, not in the power of another or others, having social and political liberty. 2. (of a country or its citizens or institutions) not controlled by a foreign or despotic government, having representative government, having private rights that are respected. 3. not fixed or held down, able to move without hindrance. 4. unrestricted, not controlled by rules. 5. without, not subject to or affected by (an influence etc.), *free from blame; the harbor is free of ice.* 6. without payment, costing nothing to the receiver. 7. (of a place or time) not occupied, not being used, (of a person) without appointments or things to do. 8. coming or given or giving readily, *he is very free with his advice.*

free *v.* (**freed, free·ing**) 1. to make free, to set at liberty. 2. to relieve, to rid or ease, *freed him from suspicion.* 3. to clear, to disengage or disentangle. **free·ly** *adv.* ▢**for free,** (*slang*) without payment. **free and easy,** informal. **free enterprise,** freedom of private business to operate without government control. **free fall,** the unrestricted fall of a body toward Earth under the force of gravity. **free flight,** flight of an aircraft or rocket without power or control. **free hand,** the right of taking what action one chooses. **free kick,** a kick allowed to be taken in soccer without interference from opponents, as a penalty against them. **free love,** *see* free-lance. **free love,** sexual intercourse irrespective of marriage. **free lunch,** light food formerly served free with the purchase of alcoholic beverages in a bar or saloon. **free on board,** without charge for delivery (of goods) to a ship or railroad or truck etc. **free port,** one open to all traders alike. **free ride,** something for nothing. **free speech,** the right to express opinions of any kind. **free trade,** trade left to its natural course without customs duties to restrict imports. **free university,** an informal organization of college students and teachers offering unconventional courses and methods. **free verse,** verse without metrical pattern or fixed or predictable rhythm. **free will,** the power of choosing one's own course of action. **free world,** the noncommunist countries' name for themselves.

free·bie, free·bee (free-bee) *n.* (*slang*) something given away without charge.

free·board (free-bohrd) *n.* the part of a ship's side between the line of flotation and the deck level.

free·boot·er (free-boo-tĕr) *n.* a pirate, a piratical adventurer.

free·born (free-born) *adj.* born a free man, not a slave.

free·dom (free-dŏm) *n.* 1. the condition of being free, independence. 2. frankness, outspokenness. 3. exemption from a defeat or duty etc. 4. unrestricted use, *has the freedom of the house.*

free-for-all (free-fŏr-awl) *n.* a fight or discussion in which anyone present may join.

free·hand (free-hand) *adj.* (of a drawing) done without ruler or compasses etc.

free·hold (free-hohld) *n.* the holding of land or a house etc. in absolute ownership for life. **free'hold·er** *n.*

free-lance (free-lans) *v.* (**free-lanced, free-lanc·ing**) to work as a free lance. ▢**free lance,** a person who works as a commercial artist or writer etc. for a fee rather than for a salary.

free·load (free-lohd) v. (slang) to eat, drink, be entertained, etc. at others' expense. **free′load·er** n.
free·man (free-măn) n. (pl. **-men**, pr. **-měn**) a person who has civil and political freedom, a citizen.
free·mar·tin (free-mahr-tin) n. a calf that is incapable of propagation.
Free·ma·son (free-may-sŏn) n. a member of an international fraternity (called the Free and Accepted Masons) for mutual help and fellowship, with elaborate secret rituals.
Free·ma·son·ry (free-may-sŏn-ree) n. 1. the system and institutions of Freemasons. 2. freemasonry, sympathy and mutual help between people of similar interests.
free·si·a (free-zhi-ă) n. a fragrant flowering plant growing from a bulb.
free·stand·ing (free-stan-ding) adj. not supported by a framework.
free·stone (free-stohn) n. 1. a fine-grained sandstone or limestone that can be cut easily. 2. a kind of fruit, especially a kind of peach with stone loose when the fruit is ripe.
free·style (free-stıl) adj. 1. (of swimming races and other sports) in which any style may be used. 2. (of wrestling) with few restrictions on the holds permitted.
free·think·er (free-thing-kěr) n. a person who rejects authority in religious belief, a rationalist. **free′think·ing** adj. & n.
Free·town (free-town) the capital of Sierra Leone.
free·way (free-way) n. a limited access highway, an expressway.
free·wheel (free-hweel) v. 1. to live irresponsibly, to act heedlessly. 2. to ride a bicycle without pedaling.
free·will (free-will) adj. voluntary.
freeze (freez) v. (**froze**, **fro·zen**, **freez·ing**) 1. to be so cold that water turns to ice, it was freezing last night. 2. to change or be changed from a liquid to a solid by extreme cold, to become full of ice or covered in ice. 3. to become very cold or rigid from cold, to chill by cold or fear etc. 4. to preserve (food) by refrigeration to below freezing point. 5. to make (credits or assets) unable to be realized. 6. to hold (prices, wages, etc.) at a fixed level. 7. to arrest the action or movement of. 8. to become unable to move because of shock or fright, the deer froze at the sound; the actor froze on seeing the audience. **freeze** n. 1. a period of freezing weather. 2. the freezing of prices, wages, etc. □**freeze out**, (slang) to exclude from business or social dealings. **freeze over**, (of a pond etc.) to become covered with ice. **freeze up**, to obstruct by the formation of ice. **freezing point**, the temperature at which a liquid freezes.
freeze-dry (freez-drı) v. (**freeze-dried**, **freeze-dry·ing**) to freeze and dry by evaporation of ice in a vacuum. **freeze′-dried′** adj.
freez·er (free-zěr) n. a refrigerated container or compartment for preserving and storing perishable goods by freezing them and keeping them at a very low temperature.
freight (frayt) n. 1. the shipment of goods in containers. 2. the goods shipped, cargo. 3. the charge for this. 4. (usually freight train) a train that carries only goods. **freight** v. to load (a ship) with cargo, to send or carry as cargo.
freight·er (fray-těr) n. a ship carrying mainly freight.
French (french) adj. of France or its people or language. **French** n. 1. the French language. 2. the

French, French people. 3. (informal) bad language, excuse my French. **French′man** n.
French′wom·an n. □**French cuff**, a shirt cuff of double thickness, fastened with a cuff link. **French door**, a door with glass panels along its full length. **French dressing**, salad dressing of oil and vinegar and seasonings. **French fries**, **French fried potatoes**, potatoes cut into thin strips and then fried in deep fat. **French fry**, to fry (food) in deep fat. **French horn**, a brass wind instrument with a long tube coiled in a circle. **French toast**, sliced bread dipped in egg and milk batter and lightly fried. **take French leave**, to absent oneself without permission.
fre·net·ic (frě-net-ik) adj. frantic, frenzied. **fre·net′i·cal·ly** adv.
fren·zied (fren-zeed) adj. in a state of frenzy, wildly excited or agitated. **fren′zied·ly** adv.
fren·zy (fren-zee) n. (pl. **-zies**) violent excitement or agitation.
Fre·on (free-on) n. (trademark) a fluorocarbon used as a refrigerant etc.
freq. abbr. 1. frequency. 2. frequent. 3. frequently.
fre·quen·cy (free-kwěn-see) n. (pl. **-cies**) 1. the state of being frequent, frequent occurrence. 2. the rate of the occurrence or repetition of something. 3. the number of cycles per second of a carrier wave, a band or group of similar frequencies. □**frequency modulation**, transmission of signals by modulating the frequency of the radio wave.
frequent[1] (free-kwěnt) adj. happening or appearing often. **fre′quent·ly** adv.
fre·quent[2] (fri-kwent) v. to go frequently to, to be often in (a place). **fre·quent′er** n.
fres·co (fres-koh) n. (pl. **-coes**) a picture painted on a wall or ceiling before the plaster is dry.
fresh (fresh) adj. 1. newly made or produced or gathered etc., not stale. 2. newly arrived. 3. new or different, not previously known or used. 4. (of food) not preserved by salting or pickling or canning or freezing etc. 5. not salty, not bitter. 6. (of air or weather) cool, refreshing, (of wind) moderately strong. 7. bright and pure in color, not dull or faded. 8. not weary, feeling vigorous. 9. (informal) presumptuous, forward. **fresh′ly** adv. **fresh′ness** n.
fresh·en (fresh-ěn) v. to make or become fresh.
fresh·et (fresh-it) n. 1. a rush of fresh water flowing into the sea. 2. an overflow of a river from heavy rain or melted snow.
fresh·man (fresh-măn) n. (pl. **-men**, pr. **-měn**) a first-year student at a high school or college.
fresh·wa·ter (fresh-waw-těr) adj. of fresh (not salty) water, not of the sea, freshwater fish.
fret[1] (fret) v. (**fret·ted**, **fret·ting**) 1. to make or become unhappy, to worry. 2. to wear away by gnawing or rubbing. **fret** n. a state of unhappiness or worry, vexation.
fret[2] n. a bar or ridge on the fingerboard of a guitar, banjo, etc.
fret[3] n. an example of fretwork.
fret·ful (fret-fŭl) adj. constantly worrying or irritable. **fret′ful·ly** adv. **fret′ful·ness** n.
fret·saw (fret-saw) n. a very narrow saw used for cutting thin wood in ornamental patterns.
fret·ted (fret-id) adj. (of a ceiling etc.) decorated with carved or embossed work.
fret·work (fret-wurk) n. carved work in decorative patterns, especially in wood cut with a fretsaw.
Freud·i·an (froi-di-ăn) adj. of Sigmund Freud, an

Austrian physician (1856–1939), the founder of psychoanalysis, or his theories. □**Freudian slip,** an unintentional error that seems to reveal subconscious feelings.

Fri. *abbr.* Friday.

fri·a·ble (frɪ-ă-bĕl) *adj.* easily crumbled.

fri·ar (frɪ-ăr) *n.* a man who is a member of certain Roman Catholic religious orders that combine monastic life with work in the outside world.

fri·ar·y (frɪ-ă-ree) *n.* (*pl.* **-ar·ies**) a monastery of friars.

fric·as·see (frik-ă-see) *n.* a dish of stewed or fried pieces of meat served in a thick sauce. **fricassee** *v.* (**fric·as·seed, fric·as·see·ing**) to make a fricassee of.

fric·tion (frik-shŏn) *n.* 1. the rubbing of one thing against another. 2. the resistance of one surface to another that moves over it. 3. conflict between people with different ideas or personalities. **fric'tion·al** *adj.* □**friction tape,** a strong cloth adhesive tape, used especially to insulate electrical conductors.

Fri·day (frɪ-day) the day of the week following Thursday.

fried (frɪd) *see* **fry**[1].

friend (frend) *n.* 1. a person with whom one is on terms of mutual affection and respect. 2. a helpful thing or quality, *darkness was our friend.* 3. a helper or sympathizer; *friends of the library,* people who regularly contribute money toward its upkeep. 4. *Friend,* a member of the Society of Friends, a Quaker. **friend'ship** *n.* □**make friends with,** to become a friend of.

friend·less (frend-lĕs) *adj.* without a friend.

friend·ly (frend-lee) *adj.* (**-li·er, -li·est**) 1. like a friend, kindly. 2. (of things) favorable, helpful. **friend'li·ness** *n.*

Frie·sian (free-zhăn) *n. see* **Holstein.**

frieze (freez) *n.* a band of sculpture or decoration around the top of a wall or building.

frig·ate (frig-it) *n.* a small fast naval escort vessel or a small destroyer. □**frigate bird,** a large swift brown seabird of tropical regions, with a habit of cruising near other species and snatching food from them.

fright (frɪt) *n.* 1. sudden great fear. 2. a ridiculous looking person or thing.

fright·en (frɪ-tĕn) *v.* 1. to cause fright to. 2. to feel fright, *he doesn't frighten easily.* 3. to drive or compel by fright, *frightened them into concealing it.* **fright'en·ing·ly** *adv.* □**be frightened of,** to be afraid of.

fright·ful (frɪt-fŭl) *adj.* 1. causing horror. 2. ugly. 3. *(slang)* very great, extreme, extremely bad, *a frightful expense; frightful weather.* **fright'ful·ly** *adv.* **fright'ful·ness** *n.*

frig·id (frij-id) *adj.* 1. intensely cold. 2. very cold and formal in manner. 3. (of a woman) unresponsive sexually. **frig'id·ly** *adv.* **fri·gid·i·ty** (frĭ-jid-i-tee) *n.* □**frigid zone,** a region lying within either polar circle.

frill (fril) *n.* 1. a gathered or pleated strip of trimming attached at one edge. 2. an unnecessary extra, *simple accommodations with no frills.* **frilled** *adj.* **frill'y** *adj.* (**frill·i·er, frill·i·est**).

fringe (frinj) *n.* 1. an ornamental edging of hanging threads or cords etc. 2. something resembling this. 3. the edge of an area or a group etc. **fringe** *v.* (**fringed, fring·ing**) 1. to decorate with a fringe. 2. to form a fringe to. □**fringe area,** an area in which television reception is unsatisfactory be-

cause of great distance from the station etc. **fringe benefit,** a benefit that is provided for an employee in addition to wages or salary.

frip·per·y (frip-ĕ-ree) *n.* (*pl.* **-per·ries**) showy unnecessary finery or ornaments.

Fris·bee (friz-bee) *n. (trademark)* a concave plastic disk thrown in the air as a game.

frisk (frisk) *v.* 1. to leap or skip playfully. 2. to pass one's hands over (a person) in order to search for concealed weapons etc.

frisk·y (fris-kee) *adj.* (**frisk·i·er, frisk·i·est**) lively, playful. **frisk'i·ness** *n.*

frit·ter[1] (frit-ĕr) *n.* a small fried or sautéed cake of batter containing sliced fruit or meat etc.

fritter[2] *v.* to waste little by little, especially on trivial things, *fritter away one's time* or *money.*

fritz (frits) *n.* **on the fritz,** *(slang)* out of order, *my telephone is on the fritz.*

friv·o·lous (friv-ŏ-lŭs) *adj.* lacking a serious purpose, pleasure-loving. **friv'o·lous·ly** *adv.* **fri·vol·i·ty** (fri-vol-i-tee) *n.* (*pl.* **-ties**).

friz, frizz (friz) *v.* to curl into a wiry mass. **frizz** *n.* a frizzed condition, frizzed hair. **friz'zy** *adj.* (**friz·zi·er, friz·zi·est**) **friz'zi·ness** *n.*

friz·zle (friz-ĕl) *v.* (**friz·zled, friz·zling**) to friz.

fro (froh) *adv. see* **to.**

frock (frok) *n.* a woman's or girl's dress. □**frock coat,** a man's long-skirted coat not cut away in front.

frog (frog) *n.* 1. a small cold-blooded jumping animal living both in water and on land. 2. a fastener consisting of a button and an ornamentally looped cord. □**frog kick,** (in swimming) a kick in which the legs are bent at the knees, then thrust down forcefully. **have a frog in one's throat,** to be unable to speak except hoarsely.

frog·man (frog-man) *n.* (*pl.* **-men,** *pr.* -men) a swimmer equipped with a rubber suit, flippers, etc., and an oxygen supply for underwater swimming and working.

frol·ic (frol-ik) *v.* (**frol·icked, frol·ick·ing**) to play about in a lively cheerful way. **frolic** *n.* lively cheerful playing or entertainment. **frol'ic·some** *adj.*

from (frum, from) *prep.* expressing separation or origin, 1. indicating the place or time or limit that is the starting point, *traveled from Chicago; from ten o'clock.* 2. indicating source or origin, *took water from the well.* 3. indicating separation, prevention, escape, etc., *was released from prison; cannot refrain from laughing.* 4. indicating difference or discrimination, *can't tell red from green.* 5. indicating cause or agent or means, *died from starvation.* 6. indicating material used in a process, *wine is made from grapes.* □**from day to day,** daily; *we live from day to day,* do not plan our future. **from time to time,** at intervals of time; *she finds work from time to time,* occasionally.

frond (frond) *n.* a leaflike part of a fern or other flowerless plant or of a palm tree.

front (frunt) *n.* 1. the foremost or most important side or surface. 2. the part normally nearer or toward the spectator or line of motion, *the front of a bus.* 3. the area where fighting is taking place in a war, the foremost line of an army etc. 4. outward appearance or show, something serving as a cover for secret activities. 5. the forward edge of an advancing mass of cold or warm air. 6. the part of a garment covering the front of the body. **front** *adj.* of the front, situated in front.

front v. 1. to face, to have the front toward, *fronting the sea* or *fronting on the sea*. 2. *(slang)* to serve as a front or cover for secret activities. □**front man**, *(slang)* a person acting as a front for secret activities. **front office**, the main office; the executive officers or policy makers of an organization. **front runner**, the contestant who seems most likely to succeed. **in front**, at the front of something. **put up a good front**, *(informal)* to conceal one's real feelings.

front·age (frun-tij) n. 1. the front of a building. 2. the land along its front. 3. land bordering something, *a thousand feet of ocean frontage.*

fron·tal (frun-tăl) *adj.* of or on the front; *full frontal nudity*, that of a completely naked person seen from the front. **fron'tal·ly** *adv.*

fron·tier (frun-teer) n. 1. the land border of a country. 2. the edge of settled territory, facing the wilderness. 3. the limit of what is known in a subject, *the frontiers of science.* **fron·tiers' man** n.

fron·tis·piece (frun-tis-pees) n. an illustration placed opposite the title page of a book.

frost (frawst) n. 1. a weather condition with temperature below the freezing point of water. 2. a white powder-like coating of frozen vapor produced by this. **frost** v. 1. to cover with frost or frosting. 2. to make (glass) opaque by roughening the surface. □**frost heave**, the rise of soil or buckling of pavement resulting from freezing of moisture in the soil beneath.

frost·bite (frawst-bɪt) n. an injury to the tissue of the body from freezing.

frost·bit·ten (frawst-bit-ĕn) *adj.* affected with frostbite.

frost·ing (fraw-sting) n. sugar icing for cakes.

frost·y (fraw-stee) *adj.* (**frost·i·er, frost·i·est**) 1. cold with frost. 2. very cold and unfriendly in manner. **frost'i·ly** *adv.* **frost'i·ness** n.

froth (frawth) n. foam. **froth** v. to cause froth in, to foam. **froth'y** *adj.* (**froth·i·er, froth·i·est**) **froth'i·ness** n.

frot·tage (fro-tahzh) n. 1. an abnormal desire for contact between clothed bodies of oneself and another. 2. the technique or process of taking a rubbing from an uneven surface to form the basis of a work of art.

frot·teur (fro-tur) n. a person who practices frottage.

frou·frou (froo-froo) n. rustling, especially of dresses.

frown (frown) v. 1. to wrinkle one's brow in thought or disapproval. 2. to be disapproving, *they frown on gambling.* **frown** n. a frowning movement or look.

frow·sy (frow-zee) *adj.* (**frow·si·er, frow·si·est**) 1. ill-smelling or musty. 2. unkempt, slovenly.

froze (frohz) *see* **freeze.**

fro·zen (froh-zĕn) v. *see* **freeze. frozen** *adj.* 1. changed from a liquid to a solid because of extreme cold. 2. covered with ice. 3. very cold, rigid with cold. 4. (of food) preserved by refrigeration to below freezing point. 5. motionless, unable to move because of shock or fright, *frozen with fear.* □**frozen assets**, property, securities, etc. that cannot be converted into money (because of government action, law suits, etc.). **frozen custard,** a chilled confection made with skim milk, similar to ice cream. **frozen stiff,** *(informal)* solidly frozen, extremely cold. **frozen tight,** (of a mechanical joint etc.) locked into position and unable to operate.

FRS *abbr.* Federal Reserve System.

frt. *abbr.* freight.

fruc·ti·fy (fruk-tĭ-fɪ, fruuk-) v. (**fruc·ti·fied, fruc·ti·fy·ing**) 1. to bear fruit. 2. to make fruitful or productive.

fruc·tose (fruk-tohs, fruuk-) n. a form of sugar found in fruits and honey.

fru·gal (froo-găl) *adj.* 1. careful and economical. 2. scanty, costing little, *a frugal meal.* **fru'gal·ly** *adv.* **fru·gal·i·ty** (froo-gal-i-tee) n. (*pl.* **-ties**).

fruit (froot) n. (*pl.* **fruits, fruit**) 1. the seed-containing part of a plant. 2. this used as food. 3. any plant product used as food, *the fruits of the earth.* 4. the product or rewarding outcome of labor. **fruit** v. 1. (of a plant) to produce fruit. 2. to cause or allow (a plant) to produce fruit. □**fruit fly,** any of several flies whose larvae feed on fruit. **fruit salad,** various fruits cut up and mixed.

fruit·cake (froot-kayk) n. a spiced cake containing raisins, nuts, preserved fruits, etc.

fruit·ed (froo-tid) *adj.* covered with fruit.

fruit·er·er (froo-tĕ-rĕr) n. a dealer in fruit.

fruit·ful (froot-fŭl) *adj.* 1. producing much fruit. 2. producing good results. **fruit'ful·ly** *adv.* **fruit'ful·ness** n.

fru·i·tion (froo-ish-ŏn) n. the fulfillment of hopes, results attained by work, *our plans never come to fruition.* ▷This word does not mean "fruiting" or "becoming fruitful."

fruit·less (froot-lis) *adj.* producing little or no result. **fruit'less·ly** *adv.* **fruit'less·ness** n.

fruit·y (froo-tee) *adj.* (**fruit·i·er, fruit·i·est**) like fruit in smell or taste.

frump (frump) n. a dowdily dressed woman. **frump'y** *adj.* (**frump·i·er, frump·i·est**) **frump'ish** *adj.*

frus·trate (frus-trayt) v. (**frus·trat·ed, frus·trat·ing**) to prevent (a person) from achieving what he intends, to make (efforts) useless. **frus'trat·ing·ly** *adv.* **frus·tra·tion** (frus-tray-shŏn) n.

frus·tum (frus-tŭm) n. (*pl.* **-tums, -ta,** *pr.* -tă) the remainder of a cone or pyramid whose upper past has been cut off by a plane parallel to the base, a part intercepted between two planes.

frwy. *abbr.* freeway.

fry[1] (frɪ) v. (**fried, fry·ing**) to cook or be cooked in boiling fat. **fry** n. (*pl.* **fries**) 1. a party at which fried food is cooked and eaten, *we went to a fish fry.* 2. a portion of fried food. 3. *fries,* French fried potatoes. □**frying pan,** a shallow pan used in frying. **out of the frying pan and into the fire,** from a bad situation to a worse one.

fry[2] n. (*pl.* **fry**) young or newly hatched fishes. □**small fry,** children; people of little importance.

fry·er (frɪ-ĕr) n. 1. a deep pot used for deep-frying. 2. a young chicken suitable for frying.

FSLIC *abbr.* Federal Savings and Loan Insurance Corporation.

f-stop (ef-stop) n. a camera lens aperture setting indicated by an f number.

ft. *abbr.* 1. foot. 2. feet.

FTC *abbr.* Federal Trade Commission.

ft-lb *abbr.* foot-pound(s).

fuch·sia (fyoo-shă) n. 1. an ornamental shrub with red or purple or white drooping flowers. 2. a purplish-pink color.

fud·dle (fud-ĕl) v. (**fud·dled, fud·dling**) to stupefy, especially with alcoholic drink. **fuddle** n. a confused state of mind.

fud·dy-dud·dy (fud-ee-dud-ee) n. (**-dud·dies**) (informal) a person who is out of date and unable to accept new ideas.

fudge¹ (fuj) n. 1. a soft candy made of milk, sugar, and butter, especially chocolate fudge. 2. nonsense (often used as an interjection).

fudge² v. (**fudged, fudg·ing**) to deal with or put together in a makeshift or dishonest way, to fake.

fu·el (fyoo-ĕl) n. 1. material burned as a source of warmth or light or energy, or used as a source of nuclear energy. 2. something that increases anger or other strong feelings. **fuel** v. (**fu·eled, fu·el·ing**) to supply with fuel. ☐**fuel cell**, a device producing electricity directly from chemical reaction. **fuel injection**, direct introduction of fuel under pressure into the combustion unit of an internal combustion engine.

fu·gi·tive (fyoo-ji-tiv) n. a person who is fleeing or escaping from something. **fugitive** adj. 1. fleeing, escaping. 2. transient.

fugue (fyoog) n. a musical composition in which one or more themes are introduced and then repeated in a complex pattern.

füh·rer, fueh·rer (fyoor-ĕr) n. a leader, especially a tyrannical one.

-ful¹ suffix used to form adjectives meaning full of, as in beautiful; suggesting, as in direful; accustomed to, as in forgetful.

-ful² suffix used to form nouns meaning the amount needed to fill, as in spoonful, handful.

ful·crum (fuul-krŭm, ful-) n. (pl. **-crums, -cra,** pr. -kră) the point on which a lever turns.

ful·fill (fuul-fil) v. 1. to accomplish, to carry out (a task). 2. to do what is required by (a treaty etc.), to satisfy the requirements of. 3. to make (a prophecy) come true. **ful·fill′ment** n. ☐**fulfill oneself** or **be fulfilled,** (of persons) to develop and use one's abilities etc. fully.

full¹ (fuul) adj. (**full·er, full·est**) 1. holding or having as much as the limits will allow. 2. having much or many, crowded, showing, full of vitality. 3. completely occupied with thinking of, full of himself; full of the news, unable to keep from talking about it. 4. fed to satisfaction, ate till he was full. 5. copious, give full details. 6. complete, reaching the usual or specified extent or limit etc., in full bloom; waited a full hour. 7. plump, rounded, a full figure. 8. (of clothes) fitting loosely, made with much material hanging in folds. 9. (of a tone) deep and mellow. **full** adv. 1. completely. 2. exactly, hit him full on the nose. **full** n. 1. whole. 2. the point or state of greatest fullness. **ful′ly** adv. **full′ness** n. ☐**full board,** provision of bed and all meals at a hotel etc. **full dress,** formal clothes, especially evening clothes. **full face,** with all the face toward the spectator. **full gainer,** a dive in which the diver initially faces forward for takeoff and then executes a backward somersault and finishes by entering the water feet first, facing away from the diving board. **full moon,** the moon with its whole disk illuminated; the time when this occurs. **full speed ahead!,** an order to move or work with maximum speed. **full stop,** the punctuation mark . used at the end of a sentence or abbreviation, a period; come to a full stop, cease completely, be unable to pro-

ceed. **full tilt** or **full speed,** with all one's energies, went at it full tilt; at full tilt, at full speed. **full time,** the whole of a working day or week. **in full,** with nothing omitted; for the whole amount, paid in full. **in full view,** wholly visible. **in the fullness of time,** at the proper or destined time. **to the full,** thoroughly, completely.

full² v. 1. to treat or beat (cloth) to clean and thicken it. 2. to clean and thicken (cloth etc.) in this way.

full·back (fuul-bak) n. (in football) the running back, who lines up behind the quarterback.

full-blood·ed (fuul-blud-id) adj. 1. of unmixed ancestry, a full-blooded Indian. 2. vigorous, hearty, sensual.

full-blown (fuul-blohn) adj. fully developed, a full-blown scandal.

full-bod·ied (fuul-bod-eed) adj. of full flavor, fully mature, a full-bodied wine.

full·er (fuul-ĕr) n. a person who cleans and thickens freshly woven cloth. ☐**fuller's earth,** a type of clay used for this process.

full-fash·ioned (fuul-fash-ŏnd) adj. knitted to the body's shape, as a sweater or stockings.

full-fledged (fuul-flejd) adj. 1. (of a bird) having full plumage. 2. having full status, a full-fledged member.

full-grown (fuul-grohn) adj. having reached maturity.

full-length (fuul-length) adj. not shortened or abbreviated.

full-time (fuul-tɪm) adj. for or during the whole of the working day or week.

full-tim·er (fuul-tɪ-mĕr) n. (informal) a person employed to work a full working week.

ful·mar (fuul-măr) n. an Arctic seabird related to the petrels.

ful·mi·nate (ful-mĭ-nayt) v. (**ful·mi·nat·ed, ful·mi·nat·ing**) to protest loudly and bitterly. **ful·mi·na·tion** (ful-mĭ-nay-shŏn) n.

ful·some (fuul-sŏm) adj. cloying, excessive, disgusting; fulsome praise, exaggerated flattery. ▷This word does not mean copious or plentiful.

fu·ma·role (fyoo-mă-rohl) n. a crevice in or near a volcano, through which come hot gases. **fu·ma·rol·ic** (fyoo-mă-rol-ik) adj.

fum·ble (fum-bĕl) v. (**fum·bled, fum·bling**) 1. to touch or handle something awkwardly; the quarterback fumbled, dropped the football. 2. to grope about. **fumble** n. a bungling attempt; there was a fumble on the play, the football was dropped.

fume (fyoom) n. strong-smelling smoke or gas or vapor. **fume** v. (**fumed, fum·ing**) 1. to treat with chemical fumes. 2. to emit fumes. 3. to seethe with anger.

fu·mi·gant (fyoo-mĭ-gănt) n. any substance used in fumigation.

fu·mi·gate (fyoo-mĭ-gayt) v. (**fu·mi·gat·ed, fu·mi·gat·ing**) to disinfect by means of fumes. **fu·mi·ga·tion** (fyoo-mĭ-gay-shŏn) n.

fun (fun) n. 1. light-hearted amusement. 2. a source of this. ☐**like fun,** (informal) certainly not. **make fun of,** to cause people to laugh at (a person or thing) by making it appear ridiculous.

func·tion (fungk-shŏn) n. 1. the special activity or purpose of a person or thing. 2. an important social or official ceremony. **function** v. to perform a function, to be in action. **func′tion·less** n.

func·tion·al (fungk-shŏ-năl) adj. 1. of a function or functions. 2. designed to perform a particular function without being decorative or luxurious. **func'tion·al·ly** adv.

func·tion·ar·y (fungk-shŏ-ner-ee) n. (pl. **-aries**) an official.

fund (fund) n. 1. a supply of money, especially that available for a particular purpose. 2. an available stock or supply, a fund of jokes. **fund** v. to provide with money.

fun·da·men·tal (fun-dă-men-tăl) adj. 1. of the basis or foundation of a subject etc., serving as a starting point. 2. very important, essential. 3. fundamentals n. pl. fundamental facts or principles. **fun·da·men'tal·ly** adv.

fun·da·men·tal·ism (fun-dă-men-tă-liz-ĕm) n. 1. strict maintenance of traditional orthodox religious beliefs (especially Protestant) such as the literal truth of the Bible. **fun·da·men'tal·ist** adj. & n.

fu·ner·al (fyoo-nĕ-răl) n. 1. the ceremony of burying or cremating the dead. 2. (slang) a person's unpleasant responsibility or concern, it's your funeral. **funeral** adj. of a funeral. □**funeral director,** an undertaker. **funeral home, funeral parlor,** an undertaker's establishment.

fu·ner·ar·y (fyoo-nĕ-rer-ee) adj. of or used for burial or a funeral.

fu·ne·re·al (fyoo-neer-i-ăl) adj. suitable for a funeral, dismal, dark.

fun·gi·cide (fun-ji-sɪd) n. a fungus-destroying substance. **fun·gi·cid·al** (fun-ji-sɪ-dăl) adj.

fun·go (fun-goh) n. (pl. **-goes**) (in baseball) a fly ball hit by a batter who has thrown the ball into the air for hitting. □**fungo bat,** a long narrow bat for this.

fun·gus (fung-gŭs) n. (pl. **fun·gi,** pr. **fun-jɪ, fun·gus·es**) any of those plants without leaves, flowers, or green coloring matter, growing on other plants or on decaying matter and including mushrooms, toadstools, and molds. **fun·gal** (fung-găl) adj. **fung'oid** adj. **fung'ous** adj. ▷Do not confuse fungus (noun) with fungous (adjective).

fu·nic·u·lar (fyoo-nik-yŭ-lăr) n. a cable railway with ascending and descending cars counterbalancing each other.

funk (fungk) n. (informal) 1. fear, panic. 2. dejection. □**in a funk,** in a bad mood.

funk·y (fung-kee) adj. (**funk·i·er, funk·i·est**) (slang) 1. (of jazz etc.) uncomplicated, emotional. 2. having a strong smell. 3. unconventional.

fun·nel (fun-ĕl) n. 1. a tube or pipe wide at the top and narrow at the bottom, for pouring liquids or powders etc. into small openings. 2. a metal chimney on a steam engine or ship. **funnel** v. (**fun·neled, fun·nel·ing**) to move through a funnel or a narrowing space.

fun·nies (fun-eez) n. pl. (informal) comic strips. **fun·ny** (fun-ee) adj. (**fun·ni·er, fun·ni·est**) 1. causing amusement. 2. puzzling, hard to account for. 3. (informal) insane or odd. **fun'ni·ly** adv. □**funny bone,** part of the elbow over which a very sensitive nerve passes. **funny business,** trickery. **funny papers,** (informal) comic strips.

fur (fur) n. 1. the short fine soft hair covering the bodies of certain animals. 2. animal skin with the fur on it, especially when used for making or trimming clothes etc. 3. fabric imitating this. 4. a coat or cape etc. of real or imitation fur. 5. a fur-like coating. **fur** v. (**fur·red, fur·ring**) to cover with fur.

fur. abbr. furlong(s).

fur·be·low (fur-bĕ-loh) n. showy trimmings, frills and furbelows.

fur·bish (fur-bish) v. to polish, to clean or renovate.

fu·ri·ous (fyoor-i-ŭs) adj. 1. full of anger. 2. violent, intense, a furious pace. **fu'ri·ous·ly** adv.

furl (furl) v. (**furled, furl·ing**) to roll up and fasten (a sail, flag, or umbrella).

fur·long (fur-lawng) n. one-eighth of a mile, 220 yards.

fur·lough (fur-loh) n. leave of absence, especially one granted to a soldier, went on furlough. **furlough** v. to grant a furlough to.

fur·nace (fur-nis) n. 1. a closed fireplace for heating water or air to warm a building etc. 2. an enclosed space for heating minerals or metals etc. or for making glass.

fur·nish (fur-nish) v. 1. to equip (a room or house etc.) with furniture. 2. to provide or supply.

fur·nish·ings (fur-ni-shingz) n. pl. the furniture and fixtures in a room or house.

fur·ni·ture (fur-ni-chŭr) n. the movable articles (such as tables, chairs, beds, etc.) needed in a room or house etc.

fu·ror (fyoor-or) n. 1. an outburst of enthusiasm. 2. an uproar. 3. a popular craze.

fur·ri·er (fur-i-ĕr) n. a person who deals in furs or who makes fur clothes.

fur·ring (fur-ing) n. 1. the fixing of strips of wood or metal to a ceiling or wall in preparation for level mounting of a new ceiling or wall. 2. strips used for this purpose.

fur·row (fur-oh) n. 1. a long cut in the ground made by a plow or other implement. 2. a groove resembling this, a deep wrinkle in the skin. **furrow** v. to make furrows in.

fur·ry (fur-ee) adj. (**fur·ri·er, fur·ri·est**) 1. like fur. 2. covered with fur.

fur·ther (fur-thĕr) adj. & adv. to a greater extent, more, shall inquire further; made further inquiries. (▷See the note under **farther**.) **further** v. to help the progress of, further someone's interests.

fur·ther·ance (fur-thĕ-răns) n. the furthering of someone's interests etc.

fur·ther·more (fur-thĕr-mohr) adv. in addition, moreover.

fur·ther·most (fur-thĕr-mohst) adj.

fur·thest (fur-thist) adj. & adv. to the greatest extent, they advanced our thinking furthest; she was furthest advanced. ▷See the note under **farther**.

fur·tive (fur-tiv) adj. sly, stealthy. **fur'tive·ly** adv. **fur'tive·ness** n.

fu·ry (fyoor-ee) n. (pl. **-ries**) 1. wild anger, rage. 2. violence of weather etc., the storm's fury. 3. a violently angry person, especially a woman. 4. the Furies, snake-haired goddesses in Greek mythology, sent from the underworld to punish crime. □**like fury,** (informal) intensely, furiously.

furze (furz) n. a wild evergreen shrub with yellow flowers and sharp thorns common in Europe.

fuse[1] (fyooz) v. (**fused, fus·ing**) to blend or amalgamate (metals, living bones, institutions, etc.) into a whole.

fuse[2] n. (in an electric circuit) a short length of wire designed to melt and thus break the circuit if the current exceeds a safe level. **fuse** v. to fit (a circuit or appliance) with a fuse. □**fuse box,** a metal box containing the fuses of an electrical system.

fuse[3] n. a length of easily burned material for igniting a bomb or an explosive charge. **fuse** v. to fit a fuse to.

fu·se·lage (fyoo-sĕ-lah*zh*) *n.* the body of an airplane.

fu·si·ble (fyoo-zi-bĕl) *adj.* able to be fused. (See **fuse**[1].)

fu·sil·lade (fyoo-sĭ-layd) *n.* 1. a simultaneous or continuous firing of guns. 2. a great outburst of questions, criticism, etc.

fu·sion (fyoo-*zh*ŏn) *n.* 1. fusing, the blending or uniting of different things into a whole. 2. the union of atomic nuclei to form a heavier nucleus, usually with release of energy.

fuss (fus) *n.* 1. unnecessary excitement or activity. 2. a display of worry about something unimportant. 3. a vigorous protest or dispute. **fuss** *v.* to make a fuss. ☐**make a fuss,** to complain vigorously. **make a fuss of** *or* **over,** to treat (a person) with a great display of attention or affection.

fuss·bud·get (fus-buj-it) *n.* *(informal)* a person who continually finds fault in trivial matters.

fus·sy (fus-ee) *adj.* **(fus·si·er, fus·si·est)** 1. often fussing. 2. fastidious. 3. full of unnecessary detail or decoration. **fus′si·ness** *n.* **fus′si·ly** *adv.*

fus·tian (fus-chăn) *n.* 1. a thick, twilled cotton cloth with a short nap, usually dyed in dark dull colors. 2. pompous language, bombast. **fustian** *adj.* 1. made of fustian. 2. bombastic.

fus·ty (fus-tee) *adj.* **(fus·ti·er, fus·ti·est)** 1. stale-smelling, stuffy. 2. old-fashioned in ideas etc. **fus′ti·ness** *n.*

fut. *abbr.* future.

fu·tile (fyoo-tĭl) *adj.* producing no result, useless. **fu·til·i·ty** (fyoo-til-i-tee) *n.*

fu·ture (fyoo-chŭr) *adj.* belonging to the time coming after the present. **future** *n.* future time or events or condition; *there's no future in it,* no prospect of success or advancement. ☐**future life,** existence after death. **future shock,** bewilderment and demoralization caused by swift social and technological change (▷coined by Alvin Toffler, American author). **in future,** from this time onward.

fu·tur·ism (fyoo-chŭ-riz-ĕm) *n.* a movement in art, literature, music, etc., with violent departure from traditional forms so as to express movement and growth. **fu′tur·ist** *n.*

fu·tur·is·tic (fyoo-chŭ-ris-tik) *adj.* looking suitable for the distant future, not traditional.

fu·tu·ri·ty (fyoo-toor-i-tee) *n.* (*pl.* **-ties**) future time.

fuze = **fuse**[3].

fuzz (fuz) *n.* 1. fluff, something fluffy or frizzy. 2. *(slang)* the police.

fuz·zy (fuz-ee) *adj.* **(fuz·zi·er, fuz·zi·est)** 1. like fuzz, covered with fuzz. 2. frizzy. 3. blurred, indistinct. **fuz′zi·ly** *adv.* **fuz′zi·ness** *n.*

fwd. *abbr.* forward.

FY *abbr.* fiscal year.

-fy *suffix* used to form verbs meaning make, as in *satisfy;* produce, as in *stupefy;* cause, as in *solidify.*

FYI *abbr.* for your information.

G

G, g (jee) (*pl.* **Gs, G's, g's**) 1. the seventh letter of the alphabet. 2. *(slang)* grand (= $1000). 3. a symbol indicating that a film is recommended for general audiences.

g *abbr.* 1. game. 2. gauge. 3. gender. 4. general. 5. generally. 6. gold. 7. good. 8. grain(s). 9. gram(s). 10. gravity.

G. *abbr.* German.

ga *abbr.* gauge.

Ga *symbol* gallium.

GA *abbr.* 1. general assembly. 2. general average. 3. general of the army. 4. Georgia.

Ga. *abbr.* Georgia.

gab (gab) *n.* *(informal)* chatter. □**have the gift of gab,** to be good at talking.

gab·ar·dine (gab-är-deen) *n.* a strong fabric woven in a twill pattern.

gab·ble (gab-ĕl) *v.* (**gab·bled, gab·bling**) to talk quickly and indistinctly. **gabble** *n.* gabbled talk. **gab′bler** *n.*

gab·bro (gab-roh) *n.* (*pl.* **-bros**) a dark granular igneous rock.

gab·by (gab-ee) *adj.* (**gab·bi·er, gab·bi·est**) talkative.

gab·fest (gab-fest) *n.* *(slang)* an informal get-together for prolonged conversation.

ga·ble (gay-bĕl) *n.* the triangular upper part of an outside wall, between sloping roofs. **ga′bled** *adj.*

Ga·bon (ga-bon) a country on the west coast of Africa. **Ga·bon·ese** (gab-ŏ-neez) *adj.* & *n.* (*pl.* **-ese**).

Ga·bo·ro·ne (gab-ŏ-roh-nĕ) the capital of Botswana.

gad[1] (gad) *v.* (**gad·ded, gad·ding**) to be a gadabout.

gad[2] *n.* 1. a stick for driving cattle. 2. a sharp tool used to break up rock, coal, etc. **gad** *v.* (**gad·ded, gad·ding**) to split up or loosen with a mining gad.

Gad (gad) *interj.* an exclamation of surprise (a euphemism for "God").

gad·a·bout (gad-ă-bowt) *n.* a person who goes about constantly in search of pleasure.

gad·fly (gad-flɪ) *n.* (*pl.* **-flies**) 1. a fly that bites horses and cattle. 2. a person who annoys others, especially by criticizing.

gadg·et (gaj-it) *n.* a small mechanical device or tool. **gadg′et·ry** *n.*

gadg·e·teer (gaj-ĕ-teer) *n.* a person who invents small devices.

gad·o·lin·i·um (gad-ŏ-lin-i-ŭm) *n.* a metallic chemical element.

Gael (gayl) *n.* a Scottish or Irish Celt.

Gael. *abbr.* Gaelic.

Gael·ic (gay-lik) *adj.* of Gaels. **Gaelic** *n.* their language, comprising Scottish Gaelic, Irish, and Manx.

gaff (gaf) *n.* a stick with an iron hook for landing large fish caught with rod and line. **gaff** *v.* to seize with a gaff, *gaffing a salmon.*

gaffe (gaf) *n.* a blunder.

gaf·fer (gaf-ĕr) *n.* *(informal)* an elderly man.

gag (gag) *n.* 1. something put into a person's mouth or tied across it to prevent him from speaking or crying out. 2. any action or order that prevents freedom of speech or of writing. 3. a joke or funny story, especially as part of a comedian's act. **gag** *v.* (**gagged, gag·ging**) 1. to put a gag into or over a person's mouth. 2. to prevent freedom of speech or of writing, *we cannot gag the press.* 3. to tell jokes or gags. 4. to retch or choke.

ga·ga (gah-gah) *adj.* *(slang)* crazy, *he went gaga.* □**gaga over,** *(slang)* crazy about, infatuated with.

gage[1] (gayj) *n.* a symbol of a challenge to fight, such as a glove or cap thrown on the ground.

gage[2] = **gauge.**

gag·gle (gag-ĕl) *n.* 1. a flock of geese. 2. a group of talkative people.

gai·e·ty (gay-ĕ-tee) *n.* (*pl.* **-ties**) 1. cheerfulness, a happy and light-hearted manner. 2. merrymaking.

gai·ly (gay-lee) *adv.* 1. in a cheerful light-hearted manner. 2. in bright colors.

gain (gayn) *v.* 1. to obtain, especially something desirable. 2. to make a profit. 3. to acquire gradually, to build up for oneself, *gained strength after illness.* 4. (of a clock etc.) to become ahead of the correct time. 5. to get nearer in racing or pursuit, *our horse was gaining on the favorite.* 6. to reach a desired place, *gained the shore.* **gain** *n.* 1. an increase in wealth or possessions. 2. an improvement, an increase in amount or power.

gain′er *n.* 1. a person or thing that gains. 2. *see* **full gainer** and **half gainer.** □**gain ground,** to make progress. **gain time,** to improve one's chances by arranging or accepting a delay.

gain·ful (gayn-fŭl) *adj.* profitable. **gain′ful·ly** *adv.*

gain·say (gayn-say) *v.* (**gain·said, gain·say·ing**) *(formal)* to deny or contradict, *there's no gainsaying it.* **gain′say·er** *n.*

gait (gayt) *n.* 1. a manner of walking or running. 2. any of the forward movements of a horse, such as trotting or cantering. **gait′ed** *adj.*

gai·ter (gay-tĕr) *n.* a covering of cloth or leather for the ankle and lower leg.

gal (gal) *n.* *(informal)* a girl or woman.

gal. *abbr.* gallon(s).

ga·la (gay-lă, gal-ă) *n.* a festive occasion, a fête. **gala** *adj.*

ga·lac·tic (gă-lak-tik) *adj.* 1. of a galaxy or galaxies. 2. of the Galaxy or Milky Way.

ga·lac·tose (gă-lak-tohs) *n.* a sugar obtained from lactose.

gal·an·tine (gal-ăn-teen) *n.* white meat boned and spiced and cooked in the form of a roll, served cold in aspic.

Ga·la·tians (gă-lay-shănz) *n.* a book of the New Testament, the epistle of St. Paul to the Church at Galatia.

gal·ax·y (gal-ăk-see) *n.* (*pl.* **-ax·ies**) 1. any of the large independent systems of stars existing in space; *the Galaxy*, that containing Earth (the Milky Way). 2. a brilliant company of beautiful or famous people.

gale (gayl) *n.* 1. a very strong wind; *gale-force winds*, winds with a speed of 35 to 50 m.p.h. 2. a noisy outburst, *gales of laughter*.

ga·le·na (gă-lee-nă) *n.* the commonest lead ore, lead sulfide.

gall[1] (gawl) *n.* 1. bile. 2. bitterness of feeling. 3. *(slang)* impudence.

gall[2] *n.* a sore spot on the skin of an animal, especially a horse, caused by rubbing. **gall** *v.* to rub and make sore.

gall[3] *n.* an abnormal growth produced by an insect, fungus, or bacterium on a plant.

gal·lant (gal-ănt) *adj.* 1. brave, chivalrous. 2. fine, stately, *our gallant ship*. **gallant** (gă-lănt) *n.* a fashionable or courteous young man. **gal'lant·ly** *adv.* **gal'lant·ry** *n.* (*pl.* **-ries**).

gall·blad·der (gawl-blad-ĕr) *n.* a pear-shaped organ attached to the liver, storing and releasing bile.

gal·le·on (gal-i-ŏn) *n.* a large Spanish sailing ship used in the 15th–17th centuries.

gal·ler·y (gal-ĕ-ree) *n.* (*pl.* **-ler·ies**) 1. a room or building for showing works of art. 2. the highest balcony in a theater, the people occupying this. 3. the spectators at a sporting event, especially a golf or tennis match. 4. a raised covered platform or passage along the wall of a building. 5. a long room or passage, especially one used for a special purpose, *a shooting gallery*. 6. an underground passageway, as in a mine. **gal'ler·ied** *adj.* ☐**play to the gallery**, to try to win favor by appealing to the taste of the general public.

gal·ley (gal-ee) *n.* (*pl.* **-leys**) 1. a long low medieval ship propelled by sails and oars. 2. an ancient Greek or Roman warship propelled by oars. 3. the kitchen in a ship or aircraft. 4. an oblong tray for holding type for printing. 5. a galley proof. ☐**galley proof**, a printed proof made from type set in a galley.

Gal·lic (gal-ik) *adj.* 1. of ancient Gaul. 2. of France, typically French, *Gallic wit.*

gal·li·mau·fry (gal-ĭ-maw-free) *n.* (*pl.* **-fries**) a medley or jumble.

gall·ing (gaw-ling) *adj.* vexing, humiliating.

gal·li·nule (gal-ĭ-nool) *n.* a small water bird with elongated webless toes.

gal·li·um (gal-i-ŭm) *n.* a soft bluish-white metallic element.

gal·li·vant (gal-ĭ-vant) *v. (informal)* to gad about.

gal·lon (gal-ŏn) *n.* a measure for liquids, = 4 quarts (3.785 liters). ☐**imperial gallon**, a British gallon (4.546 liters).

gal·lop (gal-ŏp) *n.* 1. a horse's fastest pace, with all four feet off the ground simultaneously in each stride. 2. a ride at this pace. **gallop** *v.* (**gal·loped**, **gal·lop·ing**) 1. to go at a gallop, to cause a horse to do this. 2. to go very fast, to rush; *galloping inflation*, getting worse rapidly. **gal'lop·er** *n.*

gal·lows (gal-ohz) *n.* (*pl.* **-lows**) 1. a framework with a suspended noose for the hanging of crimi-

nals. 2. *the gallows*, execution by hanging, *he went to the gallows.*

gall·stone (gawl-stohn) *n.* a small hard mass that sometimes forms in the gallbladder.

Gal·lup (gal-ŭp) **poll** a sampling of public opinion, made by questioning representative people and used especially to forecast how people will vote in an election. ▷Named after George Gallup (1901–   ), an American statistician.

gal·lus·es (gal-ŭ-siz) *n. pl. (informal)* a pair of suspenders.

ga·lore (gă-lohr) *adv.* in plenty, *whiskey galore.*

ga·losh (gă-losh) *n.* (*pl.* **-losh·es**) one of a pair of overshoes, usually rubber.

ga·lumph (gă-lumf) *v. (informal)* 1. to prance in triumph. 2. to move noisily or clumsily.

galv. *abbr.* galvanized.

gal·van·ic (gal-van-ik) *adj.* 1. producing an electric current by chemical action, *a galvanic cell.* 2. stimulating people into sudden activity. **gal·van'i·cal·ly** *adv.* **gal·van·ism** (gal-vă-niz-ĕm) *n.*

gal·va·nize (gal-vă-nız) *v.* (**gal·va·nized**, **gal·va·niz·ing**) 1. to stimulate into sudden activity. 2. to coat (iron) with zinc in order to protect it from rust, *galvanized iron.* **gal·va·ni·za·tion** (gal-vă-ni-zay-shŏn) *n.*

gal·va·nom·e·ter (gal-vă-nom-ĕ-tĕr) *n.* an instrument for detecting and measuring small electric currents. **gal·va·no·met·ric** (gal-vă-nŏ-met-rik) *adj.*

gam (gam) *n. (slang)* a leg.

Gam·bi·a (gam-bi-ă) a country in West Africa, also called *the Gambia.* **Gam'bi·an** *adj.* & *n.*

gam·bit (gam-bit) *n.* 1. an opening move in chess in which a player deliberately sacrifices a pawn or other piece in order to gain a favorable position. 2. an action or statement intended to secure some advantage.

gam·ble (gam-bĕl) *v.* (**gam·bled**, **gam·bling**) 1. to play games of chance for money. 2. to stake or risk money etc. in the hope of great gain; *gambled his fortune away*, lost it by gambling. 3. to stake one's hopes; *gambled on its being a fine day*, made plans in the hope of this. **gamble** *n.* 1. gambling. 2. a risky attempt or undertaking. **gam'bler** *n.* ▷Do not confuse *gamble* with *gambol.*

gam·bol (gam-bŏl) *v.* (**gam·boled**, **gam·bol·ing**) to jump or skip about in play. **gambol** *n.* a gamboling movement. ▷Do not confuse *gambol* with *gamble.*

gam·brel (gam-brĕl) **roof** a roof with two slopes (a lower steeper slope and an upper flatter one) on each side (of the house, barn, etc.).

game[1] (gaym) *n.* 1. a form of play or sport, especially one with rules. 2. a single section forming a scoring unit in some games (as in tennis or bridge). 3. a scheme or plan, a trick, *so that's his little game!* 4. wild animals or birds hunted for sport or food. 5. their flesh as food. 6. *(informal)* a person's occupation, *he's in the advertising game.* 7. *games*, athletics or sports, a sporting contest, *the Olympic Games.* **game** *v.* (**gamed**, **gam·ing**) to gamble for money stakes. **game** *adj.* (**gam·er**, **gam·est**) 1. brave. 2. having spirit or energy, *are you game for a lark?* **game'ly** *adv.* **game'ness** *n.* ☐**fair game**, an object that may fairly be attacked, *if you strike first, you're fair game.* **game fish**, an edible fish providing its captor with sport. **game law**, a law

regulating the killing and preservation of game.
game plan, a design for a course of action. **game point,** the state in a game, especially tennis or handball, when one side needs only one more point to win. **game theory,** the mathematical analysis of conflicts in war, economics, games of skill, etc. **give the game away,** to reveal a secret or scheme. **make game of,** to make fun of, to ridicule. **the game is up,** the secret or deception is revealed.

game² *adj.* lame, *a game leg.*
game·cock (gaym-kok) *n.* a male fowl of the kind formerly bred for cockfighting.
game·keep·er (gaym-kee-pĕr) *n.* a person employed to protect and breed game animals.
games·man (gaymz-măn) *n.* (*pl.* -men, *pr.* -mĕn) a person who practices gamesmanship.
games·man·ship (gaymz-măn-ship) *n.* the art of winning contests by upsetting the confidence of one's opponent.
game·some (gaym-sŏm) *adj.* merry, playful.
game·ster (gaym-stĕr) *n.* an habitual gambler.
gam·ete (gam-eet) *n.* a sexual cell capable of fusing with another in reproduction.
gam·in (gam-in) *n.* 1. a street urchin. 2. a child who looks or behaves like this.
gam·ine (gam-een) *n.* 1. a girl gamin. 2. a small mischievous-looking young woman.
gam·ma (gam-ă) *n.* the third letter of the Greek alphabet (Γ γ). □**gamma globulin,** a component of blood plasma containing antibodies used to treat measles, infectious hepatitis, etc. **gamma ray,** an x-ray of very short wavelength emitted by radioactive substances.
gam·mon (gam-ŏn) *n.* 1. cured or smoked ham. 2. the bottom piece of a side of bacon, including a hind leg.
gam·ut (gam-ŭt) *n.* 1. the whole series or range or scope of anything; *the whole gamut of emotion,* from greatest joy to deepest despair. 2. the whole range of musical notes used in medieval or modern music.
gam·y (gay-mee) *adj.* (gam·i·er, gam·i·est) 1. having the flavor or scent of game kept till it is slightly decomposed. 2. scandalous, sensational. 3. spirited. **gam'i·ness** *n.*
gan·der (gan-dĕr) *n.* 1. a male goose. 2. *(slang)* a look, a glance, *let's take a gander.*
gang (gang) *n.* 1. a number of workmen working together, *a road gang.* 2. a band of people going about together or working together, especially for some criminal purpose. **gang** *v.* to combine in a gang; *they ganged up on him,* combined against him.
gang·land (gang-land) *n.* the world of criminals and organized crime.
gan·gling (gang-gling) *adj.* tall, thin, and awkward looking.
gan·gli·on (gang-gli-ŏn) *n.* (*pl.* -gli·a, *pr.* -gli-ă) 1. a group of nerve cells from which nerve fibers radiate. 2. a cyst on a tendon sheath. 3. a center of activity. **gan·gli·on·ic** (gang-gli-on-ik) *adj.*
gang·plank (gang-plangk) *n.* a movable plank used as a bridge for walking into or out of a boat.
gan·grene (gang-green) *n.* death and decay of body tissue, usually caused by blockage of the blood supply to that part. **gan·gre·nous** (gang-grĕ-nŭs) *adj.*
gang·ster (gang-stĕr) *n.* a member of a gang of violent criminals.
gang·way (gang-way) *n.* 1. a passageway through a crowd at a stadium etc. 2. a temporary passage-

way at a construction site. 3. a movable bridge from a ship to the land, the opening in a ship's side into which this fits. **gangway (gang-way)** *interj.* make way!
gan·net (gan-it) *n.* a large seabird.
gant·let (gant-lit) = **gauntlet.**
gan·try (gan-tree) *n.* (*pl.* -tries) 1. a light bridgelike overhead framework for supporting a traveling crane, railroad signals over several tracks, etc. 2. a movable platform used to prepare large rockets for launching.
GAO *abbr.* General Accounting Office.
gaol (jayl) *(British)* = **jail.**
gap (gap) *n.* 1. a break or opening in something continuous, such as a hedge or fence or wall, or between hills. 2. an unfilled space or interval, *a gap between programs.* 3. something lacking, *a gap in one's education.* 4. a wide difference in ideas.
gape (gayp) *v.* (**gaped, gap·ing**) 1. to open the mouth wide. 2. to stare with open mouth, in surprise or wonder. 3. to open or be open wide, *a gaping chasm.* **gape** *n.* an open-mouthed stare.
gar (gahr) *n.* (also **gar·fish**) a fish with a long body and large teeth.
gar. *abbr.* garage.
ga·rage (gă-rahzh, -rahj) *n.* 1. a building in which to keep a motor vehicle or vehicles. 2. a commercial establishment where motor vehicles are repaired and serviced. **garage** *v.* (**ga·raged, ga·rag·ing**) to put or keep in a garage. □**garage sale,** a sale of used objects, held in or just outside a family's garage.
garb (gahrb) *n.* clothing, especially of a distinctive kind, *a man in clerical garb.* **garb** *v.* to clothe.
gar·bage (gahr-bij) *n.* 1. food waste. 2. any rubbish or trash. 3. *(informal)* anything that is useless or unnecessary.
gar·ban·zo (gahr-ban-zoh) *n.* (*pl.* -zos) (also **garbanzo bean**) a chickpea.
gar·ble (gahr-bĕl) *v.* (**gar·bled, gar·bling**) to give a confused account of, so that a message or story is distorted or misunderstood.
gar·çon (gahr-sohn) *n.* (*pl.* -çons, *pr.* -sohnz, -sohn) a waiter in a French restaurant, hotel, etc. ▷French.
gar·den (gahr-dĕn) *n.* 1. a piece of cultivated ground, especially near a house. 2. (often *gardens*) ornamental public grounds. 3. a large public hall for sports events etc., *Boston Garden.* **garden** *v.* to tend a garden. □**Garden of Eden,** the place where Adam and Eve lived before the Fall. **garden party,** a party held on a lawn or in a garden or park. **garden variety,** *(informal)* average or ordinary. **lead down the garden path,** to entice, to mislead deliberately.
gar·den·er (gahr-dĕ-nĕr) *n.* a person who tends a garden, either as a job or as a hobby.
gar·de·nia (gahr-deen-yă) *n.* 1. a tree or shrub with large fragrant white or yellow flowers. 2. its flower.
Gar·field (gahr-feeld), **James A.** (1831–81) the twentieth president of the U.S. 1881.
gar·fish (gahr-fish) = **gar.**
gar·gan·tu·an (gahr-gan-choo-ăn) *adj.* gigantic.
gar·gle (gahr-gĕl) *v.* (**gar·gled, gar·gling**) to wash or rinse the inside of the throat with liquid held there by air breathed out from the lungs. **gargle** *n.* a liquid used for this.
gar·goyle (gahr-goil) *n.* a grotesque carved face or figure, especially one used as a rainspout carrying water clear of a wall.

gar·ish (gair-ish) *adj.* excessively bright, gaudy, overdecorated.

gar·land (gahr-lănd) *n.* a wreath of flowers etc. worn or hung as a decoration. **garland** *v.* to deck with a garland or garlands.

gar·lic (gahr-lik) *n.* 1. an onionlike plant. 2. its bulbous root which has a strong taste and smell, used for flavoring. **gar′lick·y** *adj.*

gar·ment (gahr-mĕnt) *n.* an article of clothing. ▢**the Garment Center,** an area of New York City in which clothes are manufactured and sold at wholesale.

gar·ner (gahr-nĕr) *v.* 1. to store up. 2. to acquire or earn.

gar·net (gahr-nit) *n.* a semiprecious stone of deep transparent red.

gar·nish (gahr-nish) *v.* to decorate (especially food for the table). **garnish** *n.* something used for garnishing.

gar·nish·ee (gahr-ni-shee) *v.* (**gar·nish·eed, gar·nish·ee·ing**) 1. to serve (a person) with a garnishment. 2. to take (money or property) by legal authority.

gar·nish·ment (gahr-nish-mĕnt) *n.* 1. a legal warning served to a person holding the property of a debtor, ordering him to give it to the creditor. 2. a garnish.

gar·ni·ture (gahr-ni-chŭr) *n.* adornment or trimmings, especially of a dish of food.

gar·ret (gar-it) *n.* an attic, especially a poor one.

gar·ri·son (gar-i-sŏn) *n.* 1. troops stationed in a town or fort to defend it; *a garrison town,* one that has a permanent garrison. 2. the building or fort they occupy. **garrison** *v.* 1. to place a garrison in. 2. to occupy and defend, *troops garrisoned the town.*

gar·rote, ga·rotte (ga-rot) *n.* 1. a Spanish method of capital punishment by strangulation with a metal collar. 2. the apparatus used for this. 3. a cord or wire used to strangle a victim. **garrote** *v.* (**gar·rot·ed, gar·rot·ing**) to execute or strangle with a garrote.

gar·ru·lous (gar-ŭ-lŭs) *adj.* talkative. **gar′ru·lous·ly** *adv.* **gar′ru·lous·ness** *n.* **gar·ru·li·ty** (gă-roo-li-tee) *n.*

gar·ter (gahr-tĕr) *n.* a band especially of elastic worn around the leg to keep a stocking up. ▢**garter snake,** a small striped snake of North America.

gas (gas) *n.* (*pl.* **gas·es**) 1. a substance that does not become liquid or solid at ordinary temperatures, that diffuses readily, and that tends to distribute itself evenly throughout any enclosure. 2. one of the gases or mixtures of gases used for lighting, heating, or cooking; *gas stove,* an appliance using gas as fuel. 3. poisonous gas used to disable an enemy in war, dangerous gas occurring naturally in a coal mine. 4. nitrous oxide or other gas used as an anesthetic. 5. *(slang)* empty talk. 6. *(informal)* gasoline. 7. *(informal,* also *gas pedal)* the accelerator pedal in a motor vehicle; *step on the gas,* hurry up. **gas** *v.* (**gassed, gas·sing**) 1. to expose to gas, to poison or overcome by gas. 2. *(informal)* to talk idly for a long time. ▢**gas chamber,** a room that can be filled with poisonous gas to kill animals or people. **gas guzzler,** *(slang)* a car that uses a great deal of gasoline in operation. **gas mask,** a protective device worn over the face to protect the wearer against poisonous gas. **gas meter,** an apparatus registering the amount of heating gas consumed. **gas station,** a place that sells gasoline and performs minor

services on cars and other vehicles. **gas tank,** a container for storing heating gas.

gas·bag (gas-bag) *n.* *(informal)* a person who talks too much.

gas·e·ous (gas-i-ŭs) *adj.* of or like a gas.

gas-fired (gas-fIrd) *adj.* heated by burning gas.

gash (gash) *n.* a long deep slash or cut or wound. **gash** *v.* to make a gash in.

gas·i·fy (gas-i-fI) *v.* (**gas·i·fied, gas·i·fy·ing**) to change or become changed into gas.

gas·ket (gas-kit) *n.* a flat sheet or ring of rubber or other soft material used for sealing a joint between metal surfaces to prevent gas or steam or liquid from entering or escaping. ▢**blow a gasket,** *(slang)* to become extremely angry.

gas·light (gas-lIt) *n.* light given by a jet of burning gas.

gas·o·hol (gas-ŏ-hawl) *n.* a mixture of a small amount of alcohol with a large amount of gasoline, used as vehicular fuel.

gas·o·line (gas-ŏ-leen) *n.* a liquid distilled from petroleum, used mainly as a fuel for motor vehicles.

gasp (gasp) *v.* 1. to struggle for breath with the mouth open. 2. to draw in the breath sharply in astonishment etc. 3. to speak in a breathless way. **gasp** *n.* a breath drawn in sharply; *was at his last gasp,* was exhausted or at the point of death.

gas·sy (gas-ee) *adj.* (**-si·er, -si·est**) 1. of or like a gas. 2. talkative.

gas·tric (gas-trik) *adj.* of the stomach. ▢**gastric juice,** thin colorless acid fluid secreted by the stomach glands to aid in digestion.

gas·tri·tis (gas-trI-tis) *n.* inflammation of the stomach.

gas·tro·en·ter·i·tis (gas-troh-en-tĕ-rI-tis) *n.* inflammation of the stomach and intestines.

gas·tro·en·ter·ol·o·gy (gas-troh-en-tĕ-rol-ŏ-jee) *n.* the branch of medicine dealing with the structure and diseases of the digestive organs. **gas·tro·en·ter·ol′o·gist** *n.*

gas·tro·in·tes·ti·nal (gas-troh-in-tes-tI-năl) *adj.* of the stomach and intestines.

gas·tron·o·my (ga-stron-ŏ-mee) *n.* the art or science of good eating and drinking. **gas·tro·nom·ic** (gas-trŏ-nom-ik) *adj.* **gas·tro·nom′i·cal** *adj.*

gas·tro·pod (gas-trŏ-pod) *n.* a mollusk of the class to which snails belong, usually having a coiled shell.

gas·works (gas-wurks) *n.* a place where gas for lighting and heating is manufactured. ▢

gate (gayt) *n.* 1. a movable barrier serving as a door in a wall or fence, or regulating the passage of water etc. 2. the opening it covers. 3. a means of entrance or exit. 4. the number of spectators entering to see a football match etc., the amount of money taken in.

-gate *suffix* used to form words with the meaning of government scandal, as in *Koreagate* etc. ▷From *Watergate.* (*See* the entry for this.)

gate·crash (gayt-krash) *v.* *(informal)* to go to a private party etc. without being invited. **gate′crash·er** *n.*

gate·fold (gayt-fohld) *n.* a section in a magazine or book that folds out.

gate·house (gayt-hows) *n.* (*pl.* **-hous·es,** *pr.* -how-ziz) a house built at the side of or over a gate.

gate·keep·er (gayt-kee-pĕr) *n.* a person who guards a gate.

gate-leg (gayt-leg) **table** a table having legs that

can be moved back to allow the top to fold down.
gate·post (gayt-pohst) *n.* a post on which a gate is hung or against which it shuts.
gate·way (gayt-way) *n.* 1. an opening or structure framing a gate. 2. any means of entrance or exit, *the gateway to success.*
gath·er (ga*th*-ĕr) *v.* 1. to bring or come together. 2. to collect, to obtain gradually. 3. to collect as harvest, to pluck. 4. to increase gradually, *gather speed.* 5. to understand or conclude, *I gather your proposal was accepted.* 6. to draw parts together; *his brow was gathered in thought,* was wrinkled. 7. to pull fabric into gathers; *a gathered skirt,* made with gathers at the waist.
gath·er·ing (ga*th*-ĕ-ring) *n.* 1. an assembly of people. 2. bringing or coming together.
gath·ers (ga*th*-ĕrz) *n. pl.* a series of folds or tucks in a garment or cloth.
gauche (gohsh) *adj.* lacking in ease and grace of manner, awkward and tactless.
gau·che·rie (goh-shĕ-ree) *n.* gauche manners, a gauche action.
gau·cho (gow-choh) *n.* (*pl.* **-chos**) a cowboy from the South American pampas.
gaud (gawd) *n.* a gaudy ornament.
gaud·y (gaw-dee) *adj.* (**gaud·i·er, gaud·i·est**) showy or bright in a tasteless way. **gaud'i·ly** *adv.* **gaud'i·ness** *n.*
gauge (gayj) *n.* 1. a standard measure of contents, fineness of textile, thickness of sheet metal, or diameter of bullets. 2. the distance between pairs of rails or between opposite wheels. 3. an instrument used for measuring, marked with regular divisions or units of measurement. **gauge** *v.* (**gauged, gaug·ing**) 1. to measure exactly. 2. to estimate, to form a judgment of.
gaunt (gawnt) *adj.* 1. lean and haggard. 2. grim or desolate looking. **gaunt'ness** *n.*
gaunt·let[1] (gawnt-lit) *n.* 1. a glove with a wide cuff covering the wrist. 2. the cuff itself. 3. a glove with metal plates worn by soldiers in the Middle Ages. ☐**throw down the gauntlet,** to challenge someone to a fight.
gauntlet[2] *n.* two rows of men armed with clubs, paddles, etc. to strike a man forced to run between them. ☐**run the gauntlet,** to undergo this punishment; to face an ordeal in which gunfire, blows, criticism, etc. come from all sides at once.
gauss (gows) *n.* (*pl.* **gauss**) a unit of magnetic induction.
gauze (gawz) *n.* 1. thin transparent woven material of silk or cotton etc. 2. fine wire mesh. **gauz'y** *adj.*
ga·vage (gă-vahz*h*) *n.* forced feeding.
gave (gayv) *see* **give.**
gav·el (gav-ĕl) *n.* a hammer used by a judge or an auctioneer or a chairman etc. to call for attention or order etc.
ga·votte (ga-vot) *n.* a lively old French dance, the music for it.
gawk (gawk) *v.* to stare stupidly.
gawk·y (gaw-kee) *adj.* (**gawk·i·er, gawk·i·est**) awkward and ungainly. **gawk'i·ness** *n.*
gay (gay) *adj.* (**gay·er, gay·est**) 1. light-hearted and cheerful, happy and full of fun. 2. bright colored, dressed or decorated in bright colors. 3. *(informal)* homosexual, of homosexuals. **gay** *n.* *(informal)* a homosexual.
gaze (gayz) *v.* (**gazed, gaz·ing**) to look long and steadily. **gaze** *n.* a long steady look. **gaz'er** *n.*
ga·ze·bo (gă-zee-boh) *n.* (*pl.* **-bos**) a structure,

such as a summerhouse, with a fine wide view.
ga·zelle (gă-zel) *n.* (*pl.* **-zelles, -zelle**) a small graceful Asian or African antelope.
ga·zette (gă-zet) *n.* a newspaper or official journal.
gaz·et·teer (gaz-ĕ-teer) *n.* a dictionary or index of place names.
gaz·pa·cho (gahz-pah-choh) *n.* Spanish cold vegetable soup.
G.B. *abbr.* Great Britain.
GCA *abbr.* ground-controlled approach.
gd *abbr.* 1. good. 2. guard.
Gd *symbol* gadolinium.
G.D.R. *abbr.* German Democratic Republic.
gds *abbr.* goods.
Ge *symbol* germanium.
ge·an·ti·cline (jee-an-ti-klın) *n.* a great upward fold of Earth's crust. **ge·an·ti·cli·nal** (jee-an-ti-klı-năl) *n.*
gear (geer) *n.* 1. equipment, *hunting gear.* 2. *(informal)* clothes, *teenage gear.* 3. apparatus, appliances, *aircraft's landing gear.* 4. a set of toothed wheels working together in a machine, especially those in a motor vehicle that transmit the power of the engine to the axle, *an idler gear.* **gear** *v.* 1. to put (machinery) in gear. 2. to provide with or connect by gears. 3. to adjust or adapt; *a factory geared to the export trade,* organized for this specifically; *they geared up for the new season's production,* got everything ready for it. ☐**in gear,** with gear mechanism engaged. **out of gear,** with it disengaged.
gear·box (geer-boks) *n.* the box or case enclosing the gears of a car, motorcycle, bicycle, etc.
gear·shift (geer-shift) *n.* a device used to engage or change gears.
gear·wheel (geer-hweel) *n.* one of the toothed wheels working together in a machine.
geck·o (gek-oh) *n.* (*pl.* **geck·os, geck·oes**) a house lizard of warm climates, able to climb walls by the adhesive pads on its toes.
gee (jee) *interj.* **gee whiz** a mild exclamation of surprise, enthusiasm, etc.
geese (gees) *see* **goose.**
gee·zer (gee-zĕr) *n.* *(slang)* a person, an old man.
ge·fil·te (gĕ-fil-tĕ) **fish** a Jewish food of balls of boneless fish mixed with eggs, matzo, etc.
Gei·ger (gı-gĕr) **counter** a device for detecting and measuring radioactivity.
gei·sha (gay-shă, gee-) *n.* a Japanese hostess trained to entertain men by dancing and singing.
gel (jel) *n.* a jelly-like substance. **gel** *v.* (**gelled, gel·ling**) to set as a gel.
gel·a·tin, gel·a·tine (jel-ă-tin) *n.* a clear tasteless substance made by boiling the bones, skins, and connective tissue of animals, used in foods, medicine, and photographic film.
ge·lat·i·nous (jĕ-lat-ı-nŭs) *adj.* of or like gelatine, jelly-like.
geld (geld) *v.* (**geld·ed** or **gelt, geld·ing**) to castrate.
geld·ing (gel-ding) *n.* a gelded animal, especially a horse.
gel·id (jel-id) *adj.* icy, chilly. **gel'id·ly** *adv.*
gel·ig·nite (jel-ig-nıt) *n.* an explosive containing nitroglycerine.
gem (jem) *n.* 1. a precious stone, especially when cut and polished. 2. something valued because of its excellence or beauty; *the gem of the collection,* the most prized item.
gem·i·nate (jem-ı-nit) *adj.* combined in pairs.
gem·i·na·tion (jem-ı-nay-shŏn) *n.*

Gem·i·ni (jem-ĭ-nɪ, -nee) *n.* a sign of the zodiac, the Twins. **Gem·i·ni·an** (jem-ĭ-nɪ-ăn, -nee-) *adj. & n.*

gem·ol·o·gy (je-mol-ŏ-jee) *n.* the science of gems. **gem·ol·o·gist** *n.*

gem·stone (jem-stohn) *n.* a precious stone that can be cut and polished and used as a jewel.

ge·müt·lich (gĕ-moot-lik) *adj.* cheerful, genial.

gen. *abbr.* 1. gender. 2. general. 3. genitive. 4. genus.

Gen. *abbr.* 1. General. 2. Genesis.

gen·darme (zhahn-dahrm) *n.* a soldier, mounted or on foot, employed in police duties, especially in France.

gen·dar·me·rie (zhahn-dahr-mĕ-ree) *n.* a force of gendarmes.

gen·der (jen-dĕr) *n.* 1. the class in which a noun or pronoun is placed in grammatical grouping (in English, these are masculine, feminine, and neuter). 2. *(informal)* a person's sex.

gene (jeen) *n.* a chemical unit that carries hereditary characteristics from parent to child. **gen·ic** (jen-ik) *adj.*

ge·ne·al·o·gy (jee-ni-ol-ŏ-jee, -al-) *n.* (*pl.* **-gies**) 1. a record of one's descent from one's ancestors, especially in the form of a table. 2. the science or study of family descent. **ge·ne·al'o·gist** *n.* **ge·ne·a·log·i·cal** (jee-ni-ă-loj-i-kăl) *adj.* **ge·ne·a·log'i·cal·ly** *adv.*

gen·er·a (jen-ĕ-ră) *see* **genus.**

gen·er·al (jen-ĕ-răl) *adj.* 1. of or affecting all or nearly all, not partial or local or particular. 2. involving various kinds, not specialized, *a general education.* 3. involving only main features, not detailed or specific, *spoke only in general terms.* **general** *n.* an officer of the highest rank in the U.S. Marine Corps or of next-to-highest rank in the U.S. Army or Air Force. □**General Assembly,** the most important deliberative body of the United Nations; a legislative assembly in some states of the U.S. **general delivery,** a postal service whereby mail is delivered to a specific post office and held there for pickup by an addressee. **general election,** an election of officials at the local, state, or national level held at specified intervals. **general knowledge,** knowledge of a wide variety of subjects. **general meeting,** one open to all members. **general of the air force,** the highest ranking officer in the U.S. Air Force. **general of the army,** an officer of the highest rank in the U.S. Army. **general post office,** the chief post office in a town. **general practitioner,** a doctor who treats cases of all kinds. **general staff,** officers assisting a military commander at headquarters. **general store,** a retail store, especially in rural areas, that carries a wide range of goods but is not divided into departments. **in general,** as a general rule, usually; for the most part.

gen·er·al·is·si·mo (jen-ĕ-ră-lis-ĭ-moh) *n.* a commander of combined military, naval, and air forces in some countries.

gen·er·al·i·ty (jen-ĕ-ral-i-tee) *n.* (*pl.* **-ties**) 1. the quality of being general. 2. a general statement lacking precise details.

gen·er·al·ize (jen-ĕ-ră-lɪz) *v.* (**gen·er·al·ized, gen·er·al·iz·ing**) 1. to draw a general conclusion from particular instances. 2. to speak in general terms, to use generalities. 3. to bring into general use. **gen·er·al·i·za·tion** (jen-ĕ-ră-li-zay-shŏn) *n.*

gen·er·al·ly (jen-ĕ-ră-lee) *adv.* 1. usually, as a general rule. 2. widely, for the most part, *the plan was generally welcomed.* 3. in a general sense, without regard to details, *speaking generally.*

gen·er·al·ship (jen-ĕ-răl-ship) *n.* 1. the office of a general. 2. strategy and military skill. 3. skillful management, tact, diplomacy.

gen·er·ate (jen-ĕ-rayt) *v.* (**gen·er·at·ed, gen·er·at·ing**) to bring into existence, to produce. **gen·er·a·tive** (jen-ĕ-ray-tiv) *adj.*

gen·er·a·tion (jen-ĕ-ray-shŏn) *n.* 1. generating, being generated. 2. a single stage in the descent of a family; *three generations,* children, parents, and grandparents. 3. all persons born about the same time and therefore of the same age, *my generation; first-generation Americans,* Americans whose parents were of some other nationality. 4. the average period (regarded as about thirty years) in which children grow up and become parents. □**generation gap,** lack of understanding between people of different generations.

gen·er·a·tor (jen-ĕ-ray-tŏr) *n.* 1. a person or thing that generates; *she was known as a generator of fresh ideas,* an innovator. 2. a machine for converting mechanical energy to electricity. 3. an apparatus for producing gases, steam, etc.

ge·ne·ric (jĕ-ner-ik) *adj.* of a whole genus or group. **ge·ner'i·cal·ly** *adv.* □**generic drug,** a drug not protected by a registered trademark.

gen·er·ous (jen-ĕ-rŭs) *adj.* 1. giving or ready to give freely, free from meanness or prejudice. 2. given freely, plentiful, *a generous gift; a generous portion.* **gen'er·ous·ly** *adv.* **gen'er·ous·ness** *n.* **gen·er·os·i·ty** (jen-ĕ-ros-i-tee) *n.* (*pl.* **-ties**)

gen·e·sis (jen-ĕ-sis) *n.* (*pl.* **-ses,** *pr.* -seez) 1. a beginning or origin. 2. *Genesis,* the first book of the Old Testament, telling of the creation of the world.

ge·net·ic (jĕ-net-ik) *adj.* 1. of or relating to genetics. 2. of or relating to genes. 3. inherited, *a genetic defect.* **ge·net'i·cal·ly** *adv.* □**genetic code,** the system of storage of genetic information in chromosomes.

ge·net·ics (jĕ-net-iks) *n.* the scientific study of heredity.

ge·nial (jeen-yăl) *adj.* 1. kindly, pleasant, and cheerful. 2. mild, pleasantly warm, *a genial climate.* **ge'nial·ly** *adv.* **ge·ni·al·i·ty** (jee-ni-al-i-tee) *n.*

-genic *suffix* used to form adjectives meaning producing, as in *carcinogenic;* well suited to, as in *photogenic.*

ge·nie (jee-nee) *n.* (in Arabian tales) a spirit or goblin with strange powers.

genit. *abbr.* genitive.

gen·i·tal (jen-i-tăl) *adj.* of animal reproduction or reproductive organs. **gen'i·tal·ly** *adv.*

gen·i·ta·lia (jen-i-tayl-yă) *n. pl.* the genitals.

gen·i·tals (jen-i-tălz) *n. pl.* the external sex organs of people and animals.

gen·i·tive (jen-i-tiv) *adj.* of the grammatical case showing source or possession in certain languages, corresponding to the possessive case or to the use of a phrase beginning with *of* or *from* in English. **genitive** *n.* the possessive case, a word in this case.

gen·i·to·u·ri·nar·y (jen-i-toh-yoor-i-ner-ee) *adj.* of the genital and urinary organs and functions.

gen·ius (jeen-yŭs) *n.* (*pl.* **-ius·es**) 1. exceptionally great mental ability, any great natural ability. 2.

a person possessing this. 3. a guardian spirit, *one's good or evil genius.*

genl. *abbr.* general.

gen·o·cide (jen-ŏ-sɪd) *n.* deliberate extermination of a race of people.

gen·o·type (jen-ŏ-tɪp) *n.* 1. the genetic constitution of an individual or organism. 2. a group or class having a particular genetic constitution in common. **gen·o·typ·ic** (jen-ŏ-tip-ik) *adj.*

-genous *suffix* used to form adjectives meaning produced, as in *indigenous.*

gen·re (zhahn-rĕ) *n.* a particular kind or style of art or literature.

gens (jenz) *n.* (*pl.* **gen·tes,** *pr.* jen-teez) 1. (in Greek and Roman antiquity) a group of families with supposed common origin, sharing a name and religious rites, a clan. 2. (in biology) a group of related organisms. 3. line of descent through the father.

gent (jent) *n. (slang)* a man, a gentleman.

gen·teel (jen-teel) *adj.* affectedly polite and refined. **gen·teel'ly** *adv.*

gen·tian (jen-shăn) *n.* a plant usually with deep blue bell-like flowers.

gen·tile (jen-tɪl) *n.* (often *Gentile*) 1. anyone who is not Jewish. 2. (among Mormons) one who is not a Mormon. **gentile, Gentile** *adj.* of such persons.

gen·til·i·ty (jen-til-i-tee) *n.* good manners and elegance.

gen·tle (jen-tĕl) *adj.* (-tler, -tlest) 1. mild, moderate, not rough or severe, *a gentle breeze.* 2. of good family, *is of gentle birth.* **gentle** *v.* (**gen·tled, gen·tling**) 1. to make gentle or calm, to tame. 2. to coax. **gent'ly** *adv.* **gen'tle·ness** *n.*

gen·tle·folk (jen-tĕl-fohk) *n.* people of good family.

gen·tle·man (jen-tĕl-măn) *n.* (*pl.* **-men,** *pr.* -mĕn) 1. a man of honorable and kindly behavior. 2. a man of good social position 3. (in polite use) a man. **gen'tle·man·ly** *adv.* □**gentleman's agreement,** one that is regarded as binding in honor but not enforceable by law.

gen·tle·wom·an (jen-tĕl-wuum-ăn) *n.* (*pl.* -women, *pr.* -wim-in) *(old use)* a lady.

gen·tri·fi·ca·tion (jen-tri-fĭ-kay-shŏn) *n.* a movement of middle-class families into an urban area causing property values to increase and having the secondary effect of driving out poorer families.

gen·try (jen-tree) *n.* 1. people of prominent family, aristocracy. 2. *(British)* people next below the nobility in position and birth.

gen·u·flect (jen-yuu-flekt) *v.* to bend the knee and lower the body, especially in worship. **gen·u·flec·tion** (jen-yuu-flek-shŏn) *n.*

gen·u·ine (jen-yoo-in) *adj.* really what it is said to be, *genuine pearls; with genuine pleasure.* **gen'u·ine·ly** *adv.* **gen'u·ine·ness** *n.*

ge·nus (jee-nŭs) *n.* (*pl.* **gen·er·a,** *pr.* jen-ĕ-ră) 1. a group of animals or plants with common characteristics, usually containing several species. 2. *(informal)* a kind or sort.

ge·o·cen·tric (jee-oh-sen-trik) *adj.* considered as or representing Earth as a center. **ge·o·cen'tri·cal·ly** *adv.*

ge·o·chem·ist (jee-oh-kem-ist) *n.* an expert in geochemistry.

ge·o·chem·is·try (jee-oh-kem-i-stree) *n.* the chemistry of the earth. **ge·o·chem'i·cal** *adj.*

ge·o·chro·nol·o·gy (jee-oh-krŏ-nol-ŏ-jee) *n.* the

measurement of geological time, the ordering of geological events. **ge·o·chro·no·log·ic** *adj.* (jee-oh-kron-ŏ-loj-ik) **ge·o·chro·no·log'i·cal** *adj.*

ge·ode (jee-ohd) *n.* a rock containing a cavity lined with crystals or other mineral matter.

ge·o·des·ic (jee-ŏ-des-ik) *n.* (also **geodesic line**) the shortest line between points on a curved surface. □**geodesic dome,** a light domelike structure consisting of flat polygonal pieces, fitted together to form a rough hemisphere.

ge·od·e·sy (jee-od-ĕ-see) *n.* the branch of mathematics dealing with the shape and area of Earth or large portions of it. **ge·od'e·sist** *n.*

ge·o·det·ic (jee-ŏ-det-ik) *adj.* 1. of or relating to geodesy. 2. geodesic.

geog. *abbr.* 1. geographer. 2. geographic. 3. geographical. 4. geography.

ge·og·ra·pher (jee-og-ră-fĕr) *n.* an expert in geography.

ge·og·ra·phy (jee-og-ră-fee) *n.* 1. the scientific study of Earth's surface and its physical features, climate, products, and population. 2. the physical features and arrangement of a place. **ge·o·graph·ic** (jee-ŏ-graf-ik) *adj.* **ge·o·graph'i·cal** *adj.* **ge·o·graph'i·cal·ly** *adv.*

geol. *abbr.* 1. geologic. 2. geological. 3. geologist. 4. geology.

ge·ol·o·gist (jee-ol-ŏ-jist) *n.* an expert in geology.

ge·ol·o·gy (jee-ol-ŏ-jee) *n.* 1. the scientific study of Earth's crust and its strata. 2. the features and strata of Earth's crust. **ge·o·log·i·cal** (jee-ŏ-loj-i-kăl) *adj.* **ge·o·log'i·cal·ly** *adv.*

geom. *abbr.* 1. geometric. 2. geometrical. 3. geometry.

ge·o·mag·net·ic (jee-oh-mag-net-ik) *adj.* of or relating to Earth's magnetic properties. **ge·o·mag·ne·tism** (jee-oh-mag-nĕ-tiz-ĕm) *n.*

ge·om·e·try (jee-om-ĕ-tree) *n.* the branch of mathematics dealing with the properties and relations of lines, angles, surfaces, and solids. **ge·o·met·ric** (jee-ŏ-met-rik), **ge·o·met·ri·cal** (jee-ŏ-met-ri-kăl) *adj.* **ge·o·met'ri·cal·ly** *adv.* □**geometric progression,** progression with a constant ratio between successive quantities, as 1:3:9:27:81.

ge·o·mor·phol·o·gy (jee-ŏ-mor-fol-ŏ-jee) *n.* the study of the physical features of Earth's surface and their relation to its geological structures.

ge·o·phys·i·cist (jee-oh-fiz-i-sist) *n.* an expert in geophysics.

ge·o·phys·ics (jee-oh-fiz-iks) *n.* the branch of physics dealing with the physical properties of Earth, including meteorology, seismology, etc. **ge·o·phys'i·cal** *adj.*

ge·o·pol·i·tics (jee-oh-pol-i-tiks) *n.* the politics of a country as determined by its geographical features. **ge·o·po·lit·i·cal** (jee-oh-pŏ-lit-i-kăl) *adj.*

George·town (jorj-town) the capital of Guyana.

geor·gette (jor-jet) *n.* a thin silk or other crêpe dress material.

Geor·gia (jor-jă) 1. a state of the U.S. 2. a republic in the U.S.S.R., bordering on the Black Sea. **Geor'gian** *adj.* & *n.*

ge·o·sta·tion·ar·y (jee-oh-stay-shŏ-ner-ee) *adj.* (of an artificial satellite of Earth) moving so as to remain always above the same point on Earth's surface.

ge·o·ther·mal (jee-oh-thur-măl) *adj.* of or relat-

ing to Earth's internal heat. **ge·o·ther′mic** *adj.*
ger. *abbr.* gerund.
Ger. *abbr.* 1. German. 2. Germany.
ge·ra·ni·um (jĕ-ray-ni-ŭm) *n.* a garden plant with red, pink, or white flowers.
ger·bil (jur-bĭl) *n.* a desert rodent with long hind legs for leaping.
ger·i·a·tri·cian (jer-i-ă-trish-ăn), **ger·i·a·trist** (jer-i-at-rist) *n.* an expert in geriatrics.
ger·i·at·rics (jer-i-at-riks) *n.* the branch of medicine dealing with the diseases and care of old people. **ger·i·at′ric** *adj.*
germ (jurm) *n.* 1. a portion of a living organism capable of becoming a new organism, the embryo of a seed, *wheat germ.* 2. a beginning or basis from which something may develop, *the germ of an idea.* 3. a microorganism, especially one capable of causing disease. □**germ cell,** a cell (in the body of an organism) that is specialized for reproductive purposes. **germ plasm,** the nuclear part of a germ cell by which hereditary characteristics are transmitted. **germ warfare,** warfare using germs to spread disease.
Ger·man (jur-măn) *adj.* of Germany or its people or language. **German** *n.* 1. a native of Germany. 2. the language of Germany. □**German measles,** a contagious disease like mild measles. **German shepherd,** a breed of dog often used in police work and as a guide for blind people.
ger·mane (jĕr-mayn) *adj.* relevant.
Ger·man·ic (jĕr-man-ik) *adj.* having German characteristics.
ger·ma·ni·um (jĕr-may-ni-ŭm) *n.* a brittle grayish-white semimetallic element.
Ger·man·y (jur-mă-nee) a country in Europe, divided between the Federal Republic of Germany (= West Germany) and the German Democratic Republic (= East Germany).
ger·mi·cide (jur-mi-sĭd) *n.* a substance that kills germs or microorganisms. **ger·mi·cid·al** (jur-mi-sɪ-dăl) *adj.*
ger·mi·nate (jur-mĭ-nayt) *v.* (**ger·mi·nat·ed, ger·mi·nat·ing**) 1. to begin to develop and grow, to put forth shoots. 2. to cause to do this. **ger·mi·na·tion** (jur-mĭ-nay-shŏn) *n.*
ger·on·tol·o·gist (jer-ŏn-tol-ŏ-jist) *n.* an expert in gerontology.
ger·on·tol·o·gy (jer-ŏn-tol-ŏ-jee) *n.* the scientific study of the process of aging and of old people's special problems. **ge·ron·to·log·ic** (jĕ-ron-tŏ-loj-ik) *adj.* **ge·ron·to·log′i·cal** *adj.*
ger·ry·man·der (jer-i-man-dĕr) *v.* to arrange the boundaries of constituencies so as to give unfair advantages to one party or class in an election. ▷ Named after Governor Gerry of Massachusetts, who rearranged boundaries for this purpose in 1812.
ger·und (jer-ŭnd) *n.* a verbal noun ending in -*ing,* as *scolding* in *what is the use of my scolding him?*
Ge·sta·po (gĕ-stah-poh) *n.* the German secret police of the Nazi regime.
ges·ta·tion (je-stay-shŏn) *n.* 1. the process of carrying or being carried in the womb. 2. the time of this, from conception until birth.
ges·tic·u·late (je-stik-yŭ-layt) *v.* (**ges·tic·u·lat·ed, ges·tic·u·lat·ing**) to make expressive movements of the hands and arms. **ges·tic·u·la·tion** (je-stik-yŭ-lay-shŏn) *n.*
ges·ture (jes-chŭr) *n.* 1. an expressive movement of any part of the body. 2. something done to

convey one's intentions or attitude, *a gesture of friendship.* **gesture** *v.* (**ges·tured, ges·tur·ing**) to make a gesture.
ge·sund·heit (gĕ-zuunt-hīt) *interj.* an expression wishing good health to a person who sneezes. ▷ German.
get (get) *v.* (**got, got·ten, get·ting**) 1. to come into possession of, to obtain or receive. 2. to obtain radio transmissions from, to reach by telephone. 3. to fetch, to bring (a person, thing, etc.), to contract (an illness); *Bill got his, (slang)* was killed; *she got religion, (slang)* suddenly became very religious. 5. to capture, to catch; *I'll get him for that,* catch and kill or injure him; *the bullet got him in the leg,* struck him. 6. *(informal)* to understand, *I don't get your meaning.* 7. to prepare (a meal). 8. to bring or come into a certain condition, *get your hair cut; got wet.* 9. to move in a particular direction, to succeed in coming or going or bringing, *get off the grass; we got from here to Newark in an hour.* 10. to succeed in bringing or persuading, *got a message to her; got her to agree.* **get** *n.* the offspring of an animal, especially of a male animal. □**get across,** to make one's meaning clear. **get ahead,** to become successful. **get along,** to manage, to make progress. **get along with,** to be friendly or live harmoniously with. **get around,** to influence in one's favor, to coax; to evade (a law or rule) without actually breaking it. **get around to,** to find time for. **get at,** to reach; to mean, to imply. **get away,** to escape; *get away with something,* do it and yet escape blame or punishment or misfortune. **get back at,** *(informal)* to gain revenge. **get back to,** *(informal)* to return to a task, person, etc. **get by,** *(informal)* to pass, to be accepted; to manage to survive. **get down,** to climb down; to swallow (a thing); to record in writing; to cause depression in (a person), *gets him down.* **get down to,** to begin working on. **get going,** *(informal)* to begin moving or operating, to begin to be in progress. **get in,** to arrive. **get it,** *(informal)* to be punished or criticized; to understand a joke, puzzle, etc. **get it over (with),** to finish an unpleasant task or responsibility. **get off,** *(informal)* to begin a journey; to be acquitted; to escape with little or no punishment; to obtain an acquittal for, *a clever lawyer got him off.* **get on,** to make progress; to get along, *(informal)* to get along with; *(informal)* to advance in age; *he is getting on,* is elderly. **get out,** to leave, to give up a job etc. **get out of,** to avoid. **get over,** to overcome (a difficulty); to recover from (an illness or shock etc.). **get there,** to reach one's goal. **get through,** to finish or use up. **get through to,** *(informal)* to make (a person) understand; to make contact by telephone. **get to,** *(informal)* to be allowed to, *I get to go home tomorrow; (informal)* to bribe or threaten, *if the gang gets to him, he'll refuse to testify.* **get together,** to meet, to assemble. **get up,** to stand after sitting or kneeling etc., to get out of bed or from one's chair etc.; to organize, especially on short notice. **have got to,** *(informal)* must, *you have got to see him.*
get·a·way (get-ă-way) *n.* an escape after committing a crime; *the getaway car,* the car used in this.
get-to·geth·er (get-tŏ-geth-ĕr) *n. (informal)* a social gathering.
get·up (get-up) *n. (informal)* an outfit or costume.

gew·gaw (gyoo-gaw) *n.* a showy but valueless ornament or fancy article.

gey·ser (gɪ-zĕr) *n.* a natural spring that intermittently shoots out a column of hot water or steam.

Gha·na (gah-nă) a country in West Africa. **Gha·na·ian** (gah-ni-ăn) *adj.* & *n.*

ghast·ly (gast-lee) *adj.* 1. causing horror or fear, *a ghastly accident.* 2. *(informal)* very unpleasant, very bad, *a ghastly mistake.* 3. pale, ghostlike. **ghast'li·ness** *n.*

ghat (gawt) *n.* (in India) 1. a flight of steps down to a river, a landing place. 2. a mountain pass; *Eastern* and *Western ghats,* mountains along the east and west coasts of south India.

gher·kin (gur-kin) *n.* a small cucumber used for pickling.

ghet·to (get-oh) *n.* (*pl.* **-tos, -toes**) 1. a part of a European city in which all Jews were required to live. 2. a part of a city or region in which members of a minority group live as a result of social or economic discrimination.

ghost (gohst) *n.* 1. a person's spirit appearing after his death. 2. something very slight; *he hasn't a ghost of a chance,* he has no chance at all. 3. a duplicated image in a defective telescope or a television picture. **ghost** *v. (informal)* to ghostwrite. **ghost'ly** *adv.* **ghost'li·ness** *n.* □**ghost town,** a town abandoned by all or most of its former inhabitants. **give up the ghost,** to die.

ghost·write (gohst-rɪt) *v.* (**ghost·wrote, ghost·writ·ten, ghost·writ·ing**) to write (a book, article, or speech) for another person to take credit for the work. **ghost'writ·er** *n.*

ghoul (gool) *n.* 1. a spirit that robs graves and devours the corpses. 2. a person who enjoys gruesome things. **ghoul'ish** *adj.* **ghoul'ish·ly** *adv.*

GHQ *abbr.* general headquarters.

GI (jee-ɪ) *n.* (*pl.* **GI's, GIs**) an enlisted person in the U.S. Army. **GI** *adj.* of or relating to the U.S. armed forces or their enlisted personnel. □**GI bill,** a program of educational stipends for former members of the U.S. armed forces.

G.I. *abbr.* 1. gastrointestinal. 2. general issue. 3. government issue.

gi·ant (jɪ-ănt) *n.* 1. (in fairy tales) a man of very great height and size. 2. a man, animal, or plant that is much larger than the usual size. (*See* **panda.**) 3. a person of outstanding ability or influence. **giant** *adj.* of a kind that is very large in size.

gi·ant·ess (jɪ-ăn-tis) *n.* a female giant.

gib·ber (jĭb-ĕr) *v.* to make unintelligible or meaningless sounds, especially when shocked or terrified.

gib·ber·ish (jĭb-ĕ-rish) *n.* unintelligible talk or sounds, nonsense.

gib·bet (jĭb-it) *n.* (**gib·bet·ed, gib·bet·ing**) a gallows, especially an upright post with an arm from which a criminal is hanged. **gibbet** *v.* 1. to hang. 2. to expose to scorn and ridicule.

gib·bon (gib-ŏn) *n.* a long-armed ape of southeast Asia.

gibe (jɪb) *v.* (**gibed, gib·ing**) to jeer. **gibe** *n.* a jeering remark. ▷Do not confuse *gibe* with *jibe* or with *jive.*

gib·lets (jĭb-lits) *n. pl.* the edible parts of the inside of a bird, taken out before it is cooked.

Gib·son (gib-sŏn) *n.* a dry martini with a small onion.

gid·dy (gid-ee) *adj.* (**gid·di·er, gid·di·est**) 1. having the feeling that everything is spinning around. 2. causing this feeling, *giddy heights.* 3. frivolous, flighty. **gid'di·ly** *adv.* **gid'di·ness** *n.*

gift (gift) *n.* 1. a thing given or received without payment. 2. a natural ability, *has a gift for languages.* 3. an easy task. □**gift certificate,** a voucher (given as a gift) for money to buy something in a particular store. **gift of tongues,** glossolalia. **look a gift horse in the mouth,** to accept something ungratefully, examining it for faults.

gift·ed (gif-tid) *adj.* having great natural ability.

gift·wrap (gift-rap) *v.* (**gift-wrapped, gift-wrap·ping**) to wrap attractively as a gift.

gig¹ (gig) *n.* a light two-wheeled horse-drawn carriage.

gig² *n. (informal)* an engagement to play jazz etc., especially for a single performance.

gig³ *n.* a spear used for catching fish.

gig⁴ *n. (slang)* a military demerit or reprimand.

gi·gan·tic (jɪ-gan-tik) *adj.* very large. **gi·gan'ti·cal·ly** *adv.*

gig·gle (gig-ĕl) *v.* (**gig·gled, gig·gling**) to laugh in a silly or nervous way. **giggle** *n.* this kind of laugh. **gig'gly** *adj.*

gig·o·lo (zhig-ŏ-loh, jig-) *n.* (*pl.* **-los**) a man who is paid by a woman to be her escort or lover.

Gi·la (hee-lă) **monster** a large poisonous lizard of the southwestern United States.

gild¹ (gild) *v.* (**gild·ed** or **gilt, gild·ing**) to cover with a thin layer of gold or gold paint. □**gild the lily,** to spoil something already beautiful by trying to improve it.

gild² = **guild.**

gill¹ (jil) *n.* a quarter of a pint, four fluid ounces.

gill² (gil) *n.* 1. the organ with which a fish breathes in water. 2. the vertical plates on the under side of a mushroom cap. □**green around** or **about the gills,** looking sickly.

gilt¹ (gilt) *adj.* gilded, gold colored. **gilt** *n.* a substance used for gilding.

gilt² *n.* a young sow.

gilt-edged (gilt-ejd) *adj.* (of investments) considered to be very safe.

gim·bals (jim-bălz, jim-) *n. pl.* a contrivance of rings and pivots for keeping instruments horizontal in a moving ship etc.

gim·crack (jim-krak) *adj.* showy, worthless, and flimsy, *gimcrack ornaments.*

gim·let (gim-lit) *n.* 1. a small tool with a screwlike tip for boring holes. 2. a cocktail of gin and lime juice.

gim·mick (gim-ik) *n.* 1. *(slang)* a gadget. 2. *(informal)* a trick, device, or mannerism used for attracting notice or publicity, or for making an entertainer etc. easily recognized and remembered. **gim'mick·y** *adj.*

gim·mick·ry (gim-i-kree) *n.* the use of tricky devices.

gimp (gimp) *n. (slang)* 1. a limp. 2. a cripple. **gimp'y** *adj.*

gin¹ (jin) *n.* 1. a trap or snare for catching animals. 2. a cotton gin (*see* **cotton**). **gin** *v.* (**ginned, gin·ning**) to treat (cotton) in a gin.

gin² *n.* a colorless alcoholic liquor flavored with juniper berries. □**gin mill,** *(slang)* a bar. **gin rummy,** a form of rummy for two players. **gin sling,** a sweetened drink of gin and fruit juice etc.

gin·ger (jin-jĕr) *n.* 1. the hot-tasting root of a tropical plant. 2. this plant. 3. liveliness. 4. a light reddish yellow. **ginger** *v.* to make more lively,

ginger things up. **ginger** *adj.* ginger colored.
☐**ginger ale, ginger beer,** ginger-flavored fizzy drinks.

gin·ger·bread (jin-jĕr-bred) *n.* 1. a ginger-flavored cake. 2. elaborate ornamentation, especially on buildings.

gin·ger·ly (jin-jĕr-lee) *adj.* cautious. **gingerly** *adv.* cautiously.

gin·ger·snap (jin-jĕr-snap) *n.* a brittle cookie flavored with ginger and molasses.

ging·ham (ging-ăm) *n.* a cotton fabric often with a striped or checked pattern.

gin·gi·vi·tis (jin-jĭ-vɪ-tis) *n.* inflammation of the gums.

gink·go (ging-koh) *n.* (*pl.* **-goes**) a tree with fan-shaped leaves and yellow flowers, originally from China and Japan.

gin·seng (jin-seng) *n.* the root of a medicinal plant found in East Asia and North America.

gip·sy = gypsy.

gi·raffe (ji-raf) *n.* a long-necked African animal.

gird (gurd) *v.* (**gird·ed** or **girt, gird·ing**) to encircle or attach with a belt or band, *he girded on his sword.* ☐**gird up one's loins,** to prepare for an effort.

gird·er (gur-dĕr) *n.* a metal beam supporting part of a building or a bridge.

gir·dle (gur-dĕl) *n.* 1. a belt or cord worn around the waist. 2. an elastic corset. 3. a connected ring of bones in the body, *the pelvic girdle.* **girdle** *v.* (**gir·dled, gir·dling**) to surround.

girl (gurl) *n.* 1. a female child. 2. a young woman. 3. *(informal)* a woman of any age, a woman assistant or employee. (▷Considered offensive by many people in this definition.) 4. a man's girlfriend. **girl'hood** *n.* ☐**girl Friday,** a female assistant doing general duties in an office. (*See* **man.**) **Girl Scout,** a member of an organization of girls for developing character through participation in activities, especially those related to outdoor life.

girl·friend (gurl-frend) *n.* a female friend, especially a usual companion.

girl·ie (gur-lee) *n.* (*slang*) a girl. ☐**girlie magazines,** magazines containing erotic pictures of young women.

girl·ish (gur-lish) *adj.* like a girl. **girl'ish·ly** *adv.* **girl'ish'ness** *n.*

girt (gurt) *see* **gird.**

girth (gurth) *n.* 1. the distance around a thing. 2. a band passing under a horse's belly, holding the saddle in place.

gis·mo = gizmo.

gist (jist) *n.* the essential points or general sense of anything.

give (giv) *v.* (**gave, giv·en, giv·ing**) 1. to cause another person to receive or have (especially something in one's possession or at one's disposal), to supply; *give me Florida for holidays,* I prefer it. 2. to deliver (a message). 3. to utter, *gave a laugh.* 4. to pledge, *give one's word.* 5. to make over in exchange or payment; *I don't give a damn,* don't care at all. 6. to make or perform (an action or effort), to affect (another person or thing) with this, *gave him a scolding; gave the door a kick; I was given to understand,* was told. 7. to provide (a meal or party) as host. 8. to perform or present (a play etc.) in public. 9. to yield as a product or result. 10. to be the source of. 11. to permit a view of or access to, *the window gives on the street.* 12. to be flexible, to yield when pressed

or pulled; *woolen fabric gives,* it stretches slightly. 13. *(informal)* to be happening, *what gives?* **give** *n.* springiness, elasticity. ☐**give away,** to give as a present; to hand over (the bride) to the groom at a wedding; to reveal (a secret etc.) unintentionally. **give back,** to return (a thing). **give in,** to hand in (a document etc.); to acknowledge that one is defeated. **give it to a person,** *(informal)* to reprimand or punish him. **give off,** to produce and emit, *gasoline gives off fumes.* **give or take,** *(informal)* add or subtract (an amount) in estimating. **give out,** to distribute; to announce; to emit, *chimney was giving out smoke;* to become exhausted or used up. **give over,** to devote, *afternoons are given over to sports;* to entrust, *gave over management of the business to his partner.* **give up,** to cease doing something; to part with; to surrender; to abandon hope; to declare (a person) to be incurable or (a problem) to be too difficult for oneself to solve; *he was given up for dead,* was assumed to be dead. **give way,** to yield, to allow other traffic to go first; to collapse.

give·a·ble (giv-ă-bĕl) *adj.* able to be given.

give-and-take (giv-ăn-tayk) *n.* *(informal)* an exchange of talk and ideas, willingness on both sides to make concessions.

give·a·way (giv-ă-way) *n.* 1. a betrayal or unintentional disclosure. 2. something given away free, often to promote sales. 3. a radio or television show during which prizes are given.

giv·en (giv-in) *v.* *see* **give. given** *adj.* 1. specified or stated, *all the people in a given area.* 2. having a certain tendency, *he is given to swearing.* ☐**given name,** a first name (given in addition to a family name).

giv·er (giv-ĕr) *n.* a person who gives.

giz·mo (giz-moh) *n.* *(slang)* a gadget or device.

giz·zard (giz-ărd) *n.* a bird's second stomach, in which food is ground.

Gk. *abbr.* Greek.

gla·brous (glay-brŭs) *adj.* free from hair or down, smooth-skinned.

gla·cé (gla-say) *adj.* iced with sugar, preserved in sugar, *glacé fruits.*

gla·cial (glay-shăl) *adj.* 1. icy. 2. of or from glaciers or other ice, *glacial deposits.* **gla'cial·ly** *adv.*

gla·ci·ate (glay-shi-ayt) *v.* (**gla·ci·at·ed, gla·ci·at·ing**) to cover or become covered with glaciers or ice sheets. **gla·ci·a·tion** (glay-shi-ay-shŏn) *n.*

gla·cier (glay-shĕr) *n.* a river of ice moving very slowly.

gla·ci·ol·o·gist (glay-shi-ol-ŏ-jist) *n.* an expert in glaciology.

gla·ci·ol·o·gy (glay-shi-ol-ŏ-jee) *n.* the scientific study of the geological action of ice.

glad¹ (glad) *adj.* (**glad·der, glad·dest**) 1. pleased, expressing joy. 2. giving joy, *the glad news.* **glad'ly** *adv.* **glad'ness** *n.* ☐**be glad of,** to be grateful for. **glad eye,** *(slang)* an inviting look toward a member of the opposite sex. **glad hand,** *(informal)* a hearty welcome, especially when insincere. **glad rags,** *(informal)* dressy clothes.

glad² (glad) *n.* *(informal)* a gladiolus.

glad·den (glad-ĕn) *v.* to make glad.

glade (glayd) *n.* an open space in a forest.

glad-hand·er (glad-han-dĕr) *n.* *(informal)* a person who greets others in a hearty way, especially when insincere.

glad·i·a·tor (glad-i-ay-tŏr) *n.* 1. a man trained to fight at public shows in ancient Rome. 2. a person engaged in battle or controversy. **glad·i·a·to· ri·al** (glad-i-ă-tohr-i-ăl) *adj.*

glad·i·o·lus (glad-i-oh-lŭs) *n.* (*pl.* **-li,** *pr.* -lı) a garden plant with spikes of brightly colored flowers.

glad·some (glad-sŏm) *adj.* happy, cheerful.

glam·or·ize (glam-ŏ-rız) *v.* (**glam·or·ized, glam·or·iz·ing**) to make glamorous or romantic.

glam·our, glam·or (glam-ŏr) *n.* 1. magic, enchantment. 2. alluring beauty. 3. attractive and exciting qualities that arouse envy. **glam'or·ous** *adj.*

glance (glans) *v.* (**glanced, glanc·ing**) 1. to look briefly. 2. to strike at an angle and glide off (an object), *a glancing blow; the ball glanced off his bat.* **glance** *n.* a brief look. □**at a glance,** immediately upon looking, *I could tell at a glance he was drunk.*

gland (gland) *n.* an organ that secretes substances that are to be used by the body or expelled from it.

glan·ders (glan-dĕrz) *n.* 1. a contagious disease of horses with swellings below the jaw and a mucous discharge from the nostrils. 2. this disease communicated to man or to other animals.

glan·du·lar (glan-jŭ-lär) *adj.* of or like a gland. □**glandular fever,** a feverish illness in which certain glands are swollen.

glans (glanz) *n.* (*pl.* **glan·des,** *pr.* glan-deez) the conical part forming the end of the penis or clitoris.

glare (glair) *v.* (**glared, glar·ing**) 1. to shine with an unpleasant dazzling light. 2. to stare angrily or fiercely. **glare** *n.* 1. a strong unpleasant light; *the glare of publicity,* intense publicity. 2. an angry or fierce stare.

glar·ing (glair-ing) *adj.* 1. bright and dazzling. 2. very obvious, *a glaring error.* **glar'ing·ly** *adv.*

glass (glas) *n.* 1. a hard brittle substance (as used in windows), usually transparent. 2. an object made of this, such as a mirror. 3. a glass container for drinking from, its contents. 4. a lens or combination of lenses designed to improve vision, magnify, etc. 5. *glasses, (informal)* eyeglasses. 6. objects made of glass, glassware. 7. a barometer. **glass** *v.* to fit or enclose with glass. □**glass eye,** an artificial eye made of glass etc. **glass wool,** a mass of glass fibers resembling wool and used for insulation and in air filters.

glass·blow·ing (glas-bloh-ing) *n.* the process of shaping semimolten glass by blowing air into it through a tube. **glass'blow·er** *n.*

glass·ware (glas-wair) *n.* objects made of glass.

glass·y (glas-ee) *adj.* (**glass·i·er, glass·i·est**) 1. like glass in appearance. 2. with a dull expressionless stare, *glassy-eyed.* **glass'i·ly** *adv.* **glass'i· ness** *n.*

glau·co·ma (glow-koh-mă) *n.* a condition caused by increased pressure of the fluid within the eyeball, causing weakening or loss of sight.

glaze (glayz) *v.* (**glazed, glaz·ing**) 1. to fit or cover with glass. 2. to coat with a glossy surface. 3. to become glassy. **glaze** *n.* 1. a shiny surface or coating, especially on pottery. 2. the substance forming this.

gla·zier (glay-zhĕr) *n.* a person whose trade is to fit glass in windows etc.

gleam (gleem) *n.* 1. a beam or ray of soft light, especially one that comes and goes. 2. a brief show of some quality, *a gleam of hope.* **gleam** *v.* to send out gleams.

glean (gleen) *v.* 1. to pick up grain left by harvesters.

2. to gather scraps of information. **glean'er** *n.* **glean'ings** *n. pl.*

glee (glee) *n.* 1. lively or triumphant joy. 2. a part song, especially for male voices. □**glee club,** a type of choral group.

glee·ful (glee-fŭl) *adj.* full of glee. **glee'ful· ly** *adv.*

glen (glen) *n.* a narrow valley.

glib (glib) *adj.* (**glib·ber, glib·best**) ready with words but insincere or superficial, *a glib tongue; a glib excuse.* **glib'ly** *adv.* **glib'ness** *n.*

glide (glıd) *v.* (**glid·ed, glid·ing**) 1. to move along smoothly. 2. to fly in a glider or in an aircraft without engine power. **glide** *n.* a gliding movement. □**glide path,** an aircraft's line of descent to land.

glid·er (glı-dĕr) *n.* an aircraft without an engine.

glid·ing (glı-ding) *n.* the sport of flying in gliders.

glim·mer (glim-ĕr) *n.* a faint gleam. **glimmer** *v.* to gleam faintly.

glimpse (glimps) *n.* a brief view. **glimpse** *v.* (**glimpsed, glimps·ing**) to catch a glimpse of.

glint (glint) *n.* a very brief flash of light. **glint** *v.* to send out a glint.

glis·san·do (gli-sahn-doh) *adj. & adv.* (in music) performed with a gliding effect. **glissando** *n.* (*pl.* **-di,** *pr.* -dee, -dos) a glissando passage.

glis·ten (glis-ĕn) *v.* to shine like something wet or polished. **glisten** *n.* a glistening shine.

glis·ter (glis-tĕr) *v.* (*old use)* to sparkle or glitter, *all that glisters is not gold.*

glitch (glich) *n.* (*slang)* a sudden irregularity or malfunction of equipment or of a plan or scheme.

glit·ter (glit-ĕr) *v.* to sparkle. **glitter** *n.* a sparkle.

gloam·ing (gloh-ming) *n.* the evening twilight.

gloat (gloht) *v.* to be full of greedy or malicious delight.

glob (glob) *n.* 1. a large rounded lump of something. 2. a small drop, a globule.

glob·al (gloh-băl) *adj.* of the whole world, worldwide. **glob'al·ly** *adv.*

globe (glohb) *n.* 1. an object shaped like a ball, especially one with a map of Earth on it. 2. the world.

globe-trot·ter (glohb-trot-ĕr) *n.* a person who tours the world, spending little time in each country visited. **globe'-trot·ting** *adj. & n.*

glob·u·lar (glob-yŭ-lär) *adj.* shaped like a globe.

glob·ule (glob-yool) *n.* a small rounded drop.

glob·u·lin (glob-yŭ-lin) *n.* a kind of protein found in animal and plant tissue.

glock·en·spiel (glok-ĕn-shpeel) *n.* a musical instrument consisting of tuned steel bars fixed in a frame and struck by two hammers.

gloom (gloom) *n.* 1. semi-darkness. 2. a feeling of sadness and depression. **gloom** *v.* to look sullen, to be sad and depressed.

gloom·y (gloo-mee) *adj.* (**gloom·i·er, gloom· i·est**) 1. almost dark, unlighted. 2. depressed, sullen. 3. dismal, depressing. **gloom'i·ly** *adv.* **gloom'i·ness** *n.*

glop (glop) *n.* (*slang)* a liquid or thick sticky substance, especially unattractive food.

glo·ri·fy (glohr-i-fı) *v.* (**glo·ri·fied, glo·ri·fy· ing**) 1. to praise highly. 2. to worship. 3. to make something seem more splendid than it is, *their patio is only a glorified backyard.* **glo·ri·fi·ca· tion** (glohr-i-fi-kay-shŏn) *n.*

glo·ri·ous (glohr-i-ŭs) *adj.* 1. possessing or bringing glory. 2. splendid, *a glorious view; a glorious muddle,* very great. **glo'ri·ous·ly** *adv.*

glo·ry (glohr-ee) *n.* (*pl.* **-ries**) 1. fame and honor won by great deeds. 2. adoration and praise in worship, *glory to God.* 3. beauty, magnificence, *the glory of a sunset.* 4. a thing deserving praise and honor. **glory** *v.* (**glo·ried, glo·ry·ing**) to rejoice or pride oneself, *glorying in their success.*

gloss[1] (glos) *n.* the shine on a smooth surface. **gloss** *v.* to make glossy. ☐**gloss over**, to cover up (a mistake or fault).

gloss[2] *n.* (in literary texts) an explanatory comment, an interpretation. **gloss** *v.* 1. to write glosses. 2. to read a different sense into.

glos·sa·ry (glos-ă-ree) *n.* (*pl.* **-ries**) a list of technical or special words with their definitions.

glos·so·la·li·a (glos-ŏ-**lay**-li-ă) *n.* the power of speaking in unknown languages as claimed by religious groups in ecstatic worship or as miraculously conferred on early Christians, also called *gift of tongues.*

gloss·y (glos-ee) *adj.* (**gloss·i·ier, gloss·i·est**) shiny; *glossy photograph,* one printed on glossy paper. **gloss′i·ly** *adv.* **gloss′i·ness** *n.*

glot·tis (glot-is) *n.* (*pl.* **glot·tis·es, glot·ti·des,** *pr.* glot-i-deez) the opening at the upper end of the windpipe and between the vocal chords, affecting the modulation of the voice by contracting or dilating. **glot′tal** *adj.* ☐**glottal stop,** the sound produced by the sudden opening or shutting of the glottis.

glove (gluv) *n.* a covering for the hand, usually with separate divisions for each finger and the thumb. **gloved** (gluvd) *adj.* ☐**fit like a glove,** to fit exactly. **with the gloves off,** arguing in earnest, striving mercilessly.

glov·er (gluv-ĕr) *n.* a person whose trade is the making of gloves.

glow (gloh) *v.* 1. to send out light and heat without flame. 2. to have a warm or flushed look, color, or feeling; *a glowing account,* very enthusiastic or favorable. **glow** *v.* a glowing state, look, or feeling.

glow·er (glow-ĕr) *v.* to scowl, to stare angrily.

glow·worm (gloh-wurm) *n.* a kind of beetle that can give out a greenish light.

glox·in·i·a (glok-**sin**-i-ă) *n.* a tropical plant with bell-shaped flowers.

glu·cose (gloo-kohs) *n.* 1. a form of sugar found in fruit juice. 2. a thick syrup made from cornstarch and used commercially in candy making, treating tobacco, etc.

glue (gloo) *n.* a sticky substance used for joining things. **glue** *v.* (**glued, glu·ing**) 1. to fasten with glue. 2. to attach or hold closely, *his ear was glued to the keyhole.* **glu·ey** (gloo-ee) *adj.*

glum (glum) *adj.* (**glum·mer, glum·mest**) sad and gloomy. **glum′ly** *adv.* **glum′ness** *n.*

glut (glut) *v.* (**glut·ted, glut·ting**) 1. to supply with much more than is needed, *glut the market.* 2. to satisfy fully with food, *glut oneself or one's appetite.* **glue** *n.* an excessive supply, *a glut of apples.*

glu·ten (gloo-tĕn) *n.* a sticky protein substance that remains when starch is washed out of flour. ☐**gluten bread,** bread that contains much gluten and little starch.

glu·ti·nous (gloo-tĭ-nŭs) *adj.* gluelike, sticky.

glut·ton (glut-ŏn) *n.* 1. a person who eats far too much. 2. a person with a great desire or capacity for something; *a glutton for punishment,* one who enjoys arduous tasks. **glut′ton·ous** *adj.* **glut′ton·y** *n.*

glyc·er·in, glyc·er·ine (glis-ĕ-rin) *n.* a thick sweet colorless liquid used in ointments and medicines and in the manufacture of explosives.

glyc·er·ol (glis-ĕ-rohl) *n.* glycerin.

gly·co·gen (glɪ-kŏ-jĕn) *n.* a white powder serving to store carbohydrates in animal tissues and yielding glucose on hydrolysis.

GM *abbr.* 1. general manager. 2. grand marshal. 3. grand master. 4. guided missile.

gm. *abbr.* gram(s).

G-man (jee-man) *n.* (*pl.* **G-men,** *pr.* jee-men) (*slang*) a special agent of the Federal Bureau of Investigation.

Gmc. *abbr.* Germanic.

GMT *abbr.* Greenwich Mean Time.

gnarl (nahrl) *n.* a knot on a tree.

gnarled (nahrld) *adj.* (of a tree or hands) covered with knobby lumps, twisted and misshapen.

gnash (nash) *v.* 1. to grind (one's teeth). 2. (of teeth) to strike together.

gnat (nat) *n.* a small biting fly.

gnaw (naw) *v.* to bite persistently at something hard; *a gnawing pain,* hurting continuously.

gneiss (nɪs) *n.* a coarse-grained rock of quartz, feldspar, and mica.

gnome (nohm) *n.* a kind of dwarf in fairy tales, living underground and guarding the treasures of the earth. ☐**Gnomes of Zurich,** (*informal*) important Swiss international financiers with secret influence.

GNP *abbr.* gross national product.

gnu (noo) *n.* (*pl.* **gnus, gnu**) an oxlike antelope with curved horns.

go[1] (goh) *v.* (**went, gone, go·ing**) 1. to begin to move, to be moving, to pass from one point to another; *we must go at one o'clock,* must leave; *go shopping,* go out for this purpose. 2. to extend or lead from one place to another, *the highway goes to New York City.* 3. to be in a specified state, *they went hungry.* 4. to be functioning, *that clock doesn't go.* 5. to make a specified movement or sound, *the gun went bang.* 6. (of time) to pass, (of a distance) to be traversed or accomplished, *ten miles to go.* 7. to be allowable or acceptable, *anything goes; what he says, goes,* has final authority; *that goes without saying,* is too obvious to need to be mentioned. 8. to belong in some place or position, *plates go on the shelf.* 9. to be on the average, *it is cheap as things go these days.* 10. (of a story or tune etc.) to have a certain wording or content, *I forget how the chorus goes.* 11. to pass into a certain condition, *the fruit went bad.* 12. to make progress, to fare, *all went well; make the party go,* to make it lively and successful. 13. to be sold, *it's going cheap.* 14. (of money or supplies) to be spent or used up. 15. to be given up, dismissed, abolished, or lost, *some luxuries must go; my sight is going,* is becoming weaker. 16. to fail, to give way, to die. 17. to carry an action to a certain point; *that's going too far,* beyond the limits of what is reasonable or polite; *will go to fifty dollars for it,* will pay as much as that. 18. to be able to be put, *your clothes won't go into that suitcase; 3 goes into 12 four times.* 19. to be given or allotted, *his estate went to his nephew.* 20. to contribute, to serve, *it all goes to prove what I said.* **go** *n.* (*informal*) 1. energy, *full of go.* 2. a success; *make a go of it,* make it succeed. 3. (*pl.* **goes,** *pr.* gohz) a turn or try, *have a go; had three goes.* **go** *adj.* (*informal*) functioning properly; *all systems are go,* everything is ready. □**go about it**, to do a task, *he went about it in the wrong way.* **go ahead**, to proceed immediately. **go a long way**, to go far; to last long or buy much; to have a great effect toward achieving something. **go along with**, to agree with. **go around**, to be enough for everyone; to behave; *he goes around grumbling,* he grumbles to everyone he meets. **go back on**, to fail to keep a promise or agreement. **go by**, to be guided or directed by. **go by the boards**, to be rejected. **go down**, (of a ship) to sink; (of the sun) to appear to descend toward the horizon, to set; to be written down; to be swallowed; be received or accepted, *the suggestion went down very well.* **go far**, to achieve much; to contribute greatly toward something; to be worth much, *his income doesn't go very far these days.* **go for**, *(informal)* to like, to prefer, to choose; *(slang)* to attack. **go in for**, to engage in (an activity). **go into**, to investigate (a problem) or explain (a circumstance), *he told me about himself but didn't go into his illness;* to enter (a profession or trade). **go it alone**, to take action by oneself without assistance. **go off**, to explode; to cease functioning, *every night at ten the lights go off;* to fall asleep; to proceed, *the party went off well.* **go on**, to begin functioning, *at dusk the lights go on automatically;* to continue; to talk lengthily. **go on!**, *(informal)* do not expect me to believe that. **go out**, to go to social functions; to be broadcast, *the program goes out live;* to be extinguished; to cease to be fashionable; to walk out on strike; to lose consciousness; *my heart went out to him,* I sympathized with him. **go out with**, to have as a social companion of the opposite sex. **go places**, *(informal)* to become successful; *go places (and do things),* to go out to have a good time. **go to a person's head**, (of alcohol) to make him slightly drunk; (of success etc.) to make him conceited. **go to bat for**, *(informal)* to support, defend, or substitute for. **go under**, (of a business venture) to fail; *(informal)* to lose consciousness, especially from general anesthesia. **go up**, to rise in price; to explode; to burn rapidly. **go with**, to match, to harmonize with. **go without**, to put up with the lack of something. **no go**, *(informal)* useless, impossible. **on the go**, in constant motion, active.

go² *n.* a Japanese board game.
goad (gohd) *n.* 1. a pointed stick for prodding cattle to move onward. 2. something stimulating a person to activity. **goad** *v.* to act as a stimulus to, *goaded her into answering back.*
go-a·head (goh-ă-hed) *n.* a signal to proceed immediately.
goal (gohl) *n.* 1. a structure or area into which players try to send a ball in certain games. 2. a point scored in this way. 3. an objective. □**goal line**, (in football) the line across which a team must carry the ball for a score. **goal line stand**, (in football) defense of the goal at the goal line. **goal post**, (in football) one of a pair of vertical posts supporting a horizontal crossbar over which a football must be kicked for scoring a field goal or a point after touchdown.
goal·ie (goh-lee) *n.* *(informal)* a goalkeeper.
goal·keep·er (gohl-kee-pĕr) *n.* a player whose chief task is to keep the ball or puck out of the goal. **goal'keep·ing** *n.*
goat (goht) *n.* 1. a small horned animal kept for its milk. 2. a related wild animal, *mountain goat.*

3. *the Goat,* a sign of the zodiac, Capricorn. □**get someone's goat**, *(slang)* to annoy him.
goat·ee (goh-tee) *n.* a short pointed beard.
goat·herd (goht-hurd) *n.* a person who looks after a herd of goats.
goat·skin (goht-skin) *n.* 1. the skin of a goat. 2. a garment or bottle made of this.
gob¹ (gob) *n.* 1. a clot of a soft moist substance. 2. gobs, *(informal)* much, *gobs of whipped cream; gobs of money.*
gob² *n.* *(slang)* a sailor.
gob·ble (gob-ĕl) *v.* (**gob·bled, gob·bling**) 1. to eat quickly and greedily. 2. to make a throaty sound like a turkey. **gobble** *n.* a turkey-like sound.
gob·ble·dy·gook, gob·ble·de·gook (gob-ĕl-di-guuk) *n.* *(slang)* pompous and evasive language used by officials.
gob·bler (gob-lĕr) *n.* a male turkey.
go-be·tween (goh-bi-tween) *n.* a person who acts as a messenger or negotiator.
gob·let (gob-lit) *n.* a drinking glass with a stem and a foot.
gob·lin (gob-lin) *n.* a mischievous ugly elf.
go-cart (goh-kahrt) *n.* 1. a four-wheeled carriage for a small child to ride in, a stroller. 2. a kart.
god (god) *n.* 1. *God,* the creator and ruler of the universe in Christian, Jewish, and Muslim teaching. 2. a superhuman being regarded and worshipped as having power over nature and human affairs, *Mars was the Roman god of war.* 3. an image of a god, an idol. 4. a person or thing that is greatly admired or adored, *money is his god.* □**God forbid**, I wish that this may not happen. **God knows**, this is something we cannot hope to know; I call God to witness. **God willing**, if circumstances allow it. **good God!, my God!, oh God!, ye gods!**, exclamations of surprise or pain.
god·child (god-chīld) *n.* (*pl.* -chil·dren, *pr.* -children) a child in relation to its godparent(s).
god·daugh·ter (god-daw-tĕr) *n.* a female godchild.
god·dess (god-is) *n.* a female god.
god·fa·ther (god-fah-thĕr) *n.* 1. a male godparent. 2. a powerful Mafia leader.
God-fear·ing (god-feer-ing) *adj.* sincerely religious.
God·for·sak·en (god-fŏr-say-kĕn) *adj.* wretched, dismal.
God·head (god-hed) *n.* 1. being God, the divine nature. 2. God.
god·hood (god-huud) *n.* the state of being a god, divinity.
god·less (god-lis) *adj.* not having belief in God, wicked. **god'less·ly** *adv.* **god'less·ness** *n.*
god·like (god-līk) *adj.* like God or a god.
god·ly (god-lee) *adj.* (**god·li·er, god·li·est**) sincerely religious. **god'li·ness** *n.*
god·moth·er (god-muth-ĕr) *n.* a female godparent.
god·par·ent (god-pair-ĕnt) *n.* 1. a person who undertakes, when a child is baptized, to see that it is brought up in the faith. 2. a person who undertakes to act as sponsor or guardian of a child.
god·send (god-send) *n.* a piece of unexpected good fortune.
god·son (god-sun) *n.* a male godchild.
God·speed (god-speed) *n.* an expression of good wishes to a person starting a journey.
go·er (goh-ĕr) *n.* a person or thing that goes, as in *churchgoer,* a person who goes to church regularly.

go·fer (goh-fĕr) *n.* *(informal)* a person who runs errands for another.

go-get·ter (goh-get-ĕr) *n.* *(informal)* a person who is successful by being aggressive and energetic.

gog·gle (gog-ĕl) *v.* (**gog·gled, gog·gling**) to stare with wide-open eyes. **gog'gle-eyed** *adj.*

gog·gles (gog-ĕlz) *n. pl.* eyeglasses with side shields for protecting the eyes from wind, dust, water, etc.

go-go (goh-goh) *adj.* *(informal)* very active, energetic. □**go-go dancer,** a performer of lively erotic dancing at nightclubs etc.

go·ing (goh-ing) *v.* *see* **go¹. going** *n.* 1. moving away, departing, *comings and goings.* 2. the state of the ground for walking or riding on, *rough going.* 3. rate of progress, *it was good going to get there by noon.* **going** *adj.* 1. moving away, departing, working; *he has everything going for him,* all is operating in his favor. 2. current; *the going rate,* the current price. 3. active and prosperous, *a going concern.* □**be going to do something,** to be about to do it, to be likely to do it. **get going,** hurry up. **while the going is good,** while conditions are favorable.

go·ing-o·ver (goh-ing-oh-vĕr) *n.* 1. *(informal)* an inspection or overhaul. 2. *(slang)* a thrashing.

go·ings-on (goh-ingz-on) *n. pl.* surprising behavior or events.

goi·ter (goi-tĕr) *n.* an enlarged thyroid gland, often showing as a swelling in the neck. **goi·trous** (goi-trŭs) *adj.*

gold (gohld) *n.* 1. a yellow metallic element of very high value. 2. coins or other articles made of gold. 3. its color. 4. a gold medal (awarded as first prize). 5. something very good or precious. **gold** *adj.* made of gold, colored like gold. □**gold digger,** a woman who uses her attractions to obtain money from men. **gold dust,** gold found naturally in fine particles. **gold leaf,** gold beaten into a very thin sheet. **gold mine,** a place where gold is mined; a source of great wealth, *the shop was a little gold mine.* **gold plate,** tableware made of gold; material plated with gold. **gold reserve,** gold held by a central bank to guarantee the value of a country's currency. **gold rush,** a rush to a newly discovered goldfield. **gold standard,** a system by which the value of money is based on that of gold. **gold star,** an emblem indicating that a member of a family, organization, etc. has died in military service in war; *gold star mother* or *father,* one whose son or daughter has died thus.

gold·beat·er (gohld-bee-tĕr) *n.* a person who beats gold out into gold leaf.

gold·brick (gohld-brik) *n.* 1. something that looks valuable on the surface but is sham beneath. 2. *(slang)* a person who shirks work. **goldbrick** *v.* *(slang)* to shirk work.

gold·en (gohl-dĕn) *adj.* 1. made of gold. 2. colored like gold. 3. precious, excellent, *a golden opportunity.* □**golden age,** a time of great prosperity and achievement. **golden ager,** *(informal)* an old person. **golden anniversary,** the celebration of the fiftieth year of a marriage etc. **golden boy** *or* **girl,** a popular or successful person. **Golden Gate,** a channel of water in California between San Francisco Bay and the Pacific, spanned by a suspension bridge; this bridge. **golden hamster,** a tawny species of hamster, popular as a pet and used as a laboratory animal. **golden handshake,** a generous cash payment given by

a firm to one of its executives as compensation for being dismissed or for being forced to retire. **golden mean,** neither too much nor too little. **golden retriever,** a retriever dog with a thick golden coat. **golden rule,** a basic principle of action. **golden wedding,** the fiftieth anniversary of a wedding.

gold·en·rod (gohl-dĕn-rod) *n.* a plant with spikes of yellow flowers, blooming in late summer.

gold·field (gohld-feeld) *n.* an area where gold is found as a mineral.

gold·finch (gohld-finch) *n.* a songbird with a band of yellow across each wing.

gold·fish (gohld-fish) *n.* (*pl.* **-fish, -fish·es**) a small orange Chinese carp kept in a bowl or pond.

gold-plat·ed (gohld-play-tid) *adj.* coated with gold.

gold·smith (gohld-smith) *n.* a person whose trade is making articles in gold.

golf (golf) *n.* a game in which a small hard ball is struck with clubs toward and into a series of holes. **golf** *v.* to play golf. **golf'er** *n.* □**golf bag,** a bag used to carry golf clubs and ball. **golf ball,** a ball used in golf. **golf cart,** a light cart to carry golf clubs during a game. **golf club,** a club used in golf; an association for playing golf, its premises. **golf course, golf links,** an area of land on which golf is played.

gol·ly (gol-ee) *interj.* *(informal)* an exclamation of surprise.

go·losh = **galosh.**

-gon *suffix* used to form nouns meaning a specified number of angles, as in *hexagon.*

go·nad (goh-nad) *n.* an animal organ, as the testis or ovary, producing gametes. **go·nad·al** (goh-nad-ăl) *adj.*

gon·do·la (gon-dŏ-lă) *n.* 1. a boat with high pointed ends, used on the canals in Venice. 2. a basketlike structure suspended beneath a balloon, for carrying passengers etc. 3. a flat open railroad freight car with low sides.

gon·do·lier (gon-dŏ-leer) *n.* a man who propels a gondola by means of a pole.

gone (gawn) *v.* *see* **go¹. gone** *adj.* 1. departed, past. 2. dead. 3. used up. 4. *(slang)* pregnant, *she is six months gone.* □**gone on,** *(slang)* infatuated with.

gon·er (gaw-ner) *n.* *(slang)* a person or thing that is dead, ruined, or doomed.

gon·fa·lon (gon-fă-lŏn) *n.* a banner, often with streamers, hung from a crossbar.

gong (gawng) *n.* 1. a round metal plate that resounds when struck, especially one used as a signal for meals. 2. a similar device used electrically.

gon·o·coc·cus (gon-ŏ-kok-ŭs) *n.* (*pl.* **-coc·ci,** *pr.* **-kok-sɪ**) the microorganism causing gonorrhea. **gon·o·coc·cal** (gon-ŏ-kok-ăl) *adj.* **gon·o·coc·cic** (gon-ŏ-kok-sik) *adj.*

go-no-go (goh-noh-goh) *n.* (in a missile launch etc.) the point in a countdown at which a decision must be made to abort or proceed.

gon·or·rhe·a (gon-ŏ-ree-ă) *n.* a venereal disease causing a thick discharge from the sexual organs.

goo (goo) *n.* *(slang)* 1. sticky wet material. 2. sickly sentiment.

goo·ber (goo-bĕr) *n.* (chiefly *Southern U.S.*) a peanut.

good (guud) *adj.* (**bet·ter, best**) 1. having the right or desirable properties, satisfactory, *good food.* 2. right, proper, expedient. 3. morally correct, virtuous, kindly. 4. (of a child) well-behaved. 5. gratifying, enjoyable, beneficial, *have a good*

time; good morning, good evening, forms of greeting or farewell. **6.** efficient, suitable, competent, *a good driver; good at chess.* **7.** thorough, considerable, *a good beating.* **8.** not less than, full, *walked a good ten miles.* **9.** used in exclamations, *good God!* **good** *adv. (informal)* entirely; *good and angry,* very angry. **good** *n.* **1.** that which is morally right; *up to no good,* doing something mischievous or criminal. **2.** profit, benefit, *it will do him good; five dollars to the good,* having made this profit. □**as good as,** practically, almost, *the war is as good as over.* **for good,** permanently. **good behavior,** conduct that is legally correct. **Good Book,** the Bible. **good cheer,** hope and trust; having a very good time. **Good Conduct Medal,** a U.S. army medal given to enlisted men who have served with merit. **good for,** beneficial to; able to pay or undertake; *he is good for one hundred dollars, for a ten-mile walk; good for you!,* well done! **Good Friday,** the Friday before Easter, commemorating the Crucifixion. **good humor,** a cheerful mood or disposition, amiability. **good nature,** a kindly disposition, willingness to humor others. **good night!,** an exclamation of surprise or exasperation. **good offices,** influence deriving from one's position or power to reconcile; mediation. **Good Samaritan,** a genuinely charitable person who goes out of his way to help others. **in good time,** with no risk of being late; *all in good time,* in due course but without haste. **make good,** see **make. to the good,** as a balance on the right side; something extra.
▷It is incorrect to say *the machine works good* or *I am doing pretty good.* It is also incorrect to say *I feel good* when speaking of one's health. Say *I feel well.*

good·by, good·bye (guud-bı) *interj.* farewell, an expression used when parting or at the end of a telephone call. **goodby, goodbye** *n.* a farewell.
good-for-noth·ing (guud-fŏr-nuth-ing) *adj.* worthless. **good-for-nothing** *n.* a worthless person.
good-heart·ed (guud-hahr-tid) *adj.* kindly, willing to please.
good-hu·mored (guud-hyoo-mŏrd) *adj.* of a cheerful disposition.
good·ish (guud-ish) *adj.* fairly good.
good-look·ing (guud-luuk-ing) *adj.* having a pleasant appearance.
good·ly (guud-lee) *adj.* (-li·er, -li·est) rather large or great, *it's a goodly way from the station; a goodly amount of money.*
good-na·tured (guud-nay-chŭrd) *adj.* having or showing a kind disposition.
good·ness (guud-nis) *n.* **1.** the quality of being good. **2.** the good element of something; *the goodness is in the gravy,* this is the most nourishing part. **3.** used instead of "God" in exclamations, *goodness knows; for goodness' sake; thank goodness.* □**have the goodness to,** to be kind enough to (do something).
goods (guudz) *n. pl.* **1.** movable property. **2.** articles of trade, *leather goods.* □**the goods,** *(informal)* the genuine article, the real thing; *deliver the goods,* to produce what one has promised; *have the goods on a person,* to have evidence of his guilt.
good-tem·pered (guud-tem-perd) *adj.* having or showing good temper.
good·will (guud-wil) *n.* **1.** a friendly feeling. **2.** the

good relationship of a business to its customers, considered as an asset that can be sold.
good·y (guud-ee) *n. (pl.* **good·ies) 1.** *(informal)* something good or attractive, especially to eat. **2.** *(slang)* a person of good character, *the goodies and the baddies.* **goody** *adj.* smugly virtuous.
goody *interj.* an exclamation of delight.
good·y-good·y (guud-ee-guud-ee) *adj.* smugly virtuous. **goody-goody** *n. (pl.* **-good·ies)** a goody-goody person.
goo·ey (goo-ee) *adj.* **1.** wet and sticky. **2.** sickly and sentimental.
goof (goof) *n. (slang)* **1.** a stupid person. **2.** a mistake. **goof** *v.* **goof off,** *(slang)* to loaf or kill time.
goof·ball (goof-bawl) *n. (slang)* **1.** a pill containing a barbiturate or other drug. **2.** a very stupid or silly person.
goof-off (goof-awf) *n. (slang)* a person who goofs off.
goof·y (goo-fee) *adj* (**goof·i·er, goof·i·est)** *(slang)* stupid. **goof'i·ness** *n.*
gook (guuk) *n. (slang)* grimy sticky wet material.
goon (goon) *n. (slang)* **1.** a hired thug. **2.** a dull or stupid person.
goose (goos) *n. (pl.* **geese,** *pr.* gees) **1.** a web-footed bird larger than a duck. **2.** its flesh as food. **3.** *(informal)* a stupid person. □**goose pimples,** rough bristling skin caused by cold or fear. **goose step,** a way of marching without bending the knees.
goose·ber·ry (goos-ber-ee) *n. (pl.* **-ries) 1.** a thorny shrub. **2.** its edible berry.
goose·flesh (goos-flesh) *n.* goose pimples.
GOP *abbr.* Grand Old Party, the U.S. Republican party.
go·pher (goh-fĕr) *n.* a short-tailed burrowing rodent of North America having external cheek pouches.
Gor·di·an (gor-di-ăn) *adj.* **cut the Gordian knot,** to solve a problem forcefully or by some unexpected means. ▷An intricate knot was tied by Gordius, king of ancient Phrygia; it was eventually cut, rather than untied, by Alexander the Great.
gore¹ (gohr) *n.* thickened blood from a cut or wound.
gore² *n.* a triangular or tapering section of a skirt or a sail etc. **gored** *adj.*
gore³ *v.* (gored, gor·ing) to pierce with a horn or tusk.
gorge (gorj) *n.* a narrow steep-sided valley. **gorge** *v.* (gorged, gorg·ing) **1.** to eat greedily; *gorge oneself,* stuff oneself with food. **2.** to fill full, to choke up. □**make a person's gorge rise,** to sicken or disgust him.
gor·geous (gor-jŭs) *adj.* **1.** richly colored, magnificent. **2.** *(informal)* very pleasant, beautiful. **gor'geous·ly** *adv.* **gor'geous·ness** *n.*
gor·gon (gor-gŏn) *n.* a terrifying woman. ▷Named after the Gorgons in Greek mythology, three snake-haired sisters whose looks turned to stone anyone who saw them.
Gor·gon·zo·la (gor-gŏn-zoh-lă) *n.* a rich strong blue-veined cheese from Gorgonzola in north Italy or elsewhere.
go·ril·la (gŏ-ril-ă) *n.* a large powerful African ape.
gor·mand·ize (gor-măn-dız) *v.* (**gor·mand·ized, gor·mand·iz·ing)** to eat greedily. **gor'mand·iz·er** *n.*
gorse (gors) = **furze.**

gor·y (gohr-ee) *adj.* (**gor·i·er, gor·i·est**) 1. covered with blood. 2. involving bloodshed, *a gory battle.*

gosh (gosh) *interj.* an exclamation of surprise.

gos·hawk (gos-hawk) *n.* a large long-tailed hawk of North America and northern Europe.

gos·ling (goz-ling) *n.* a young goose.

gos·pel (gos-pĕl) *n.* 1. the teachings of Christ recorded in the first four books of the New Testament. 2. *Gospel,* any of these books. 3. a thing one may safely believe, *you can take it as gospel.* 4. a set of principles that one believes in. **gospel** *adj.* of the gospel, evangelical.

gos·sa·mer (gos-ă-mĕr) *n.* 1. a fine filmy piece of cobweb made by small spiders. 2. any flimsy delicate material.

gos·sip (gos-ip) *n.* 1. casual talk, especially about other people's affairs. 2. a person who is fond of gossiping. **gossip** *v.* (**gos·siped, gos·sip·ing**) to engage in or spread gossip. **gos′sip·y** *adj.* □**gossip column,** a section of a newspaper containing tidbits of information about people or social incidents.

got (got) *see* **get.**

Goth (goth) *n.* a member of a Germanic tribe that invaded the Roman Empire in the 3rd–5th centuries.

Goth. *abbr.* Gothic.

Goth·ic (goth-ik) *adj.* of the style of architecture common in western Europe in the 12th-16th centuries, with pointed arches and rich stone carvings. **Gothic** *n.* this style. □**Gothic novel,** a kind of English novel with sensational or horrifying events, popular in the 18th-19th centuries; a contemporary romance set in a remote place or time and featuring gloom, mystery, etc.

got·ten (got-ĕn) *see* **get.**

Gou·da (goo-dă) *n.* a flat round Dutch cheese.

gouge (gowj) *n.* a chisel with a concave blade, used for cutting grooves. **gouge** *v.* (**gouged, goug·ing**) 1. to cut out with a gouge. 2. to scoop or force out; *gouge out his eye,* force it out with one's thumb.

gou·lash (goo-lahsh) *n.* a stew of meat and vegetables, seasoned with paprika.

gourd (goord, gord) *n.* 1. the hard-skinned fleshy fruit of a climbing plant. 2. this plant. 3. a bowl or container made from the dried hollowed-out rind of this fruit.

gour·mand (goor-mahnd) *n.* a lover of food, a glutton. ▷This word is often applied to a person contemptuously, whereas *gourmet* is not.

gour·met (goor-may) *n.* a connoisseur of good food and drink. ▷See the note under **gourmand.**

gout (gowt) *n.* a disease causing inflammation of the joints, especially the toes, knees, and fingers. **gout′y** *adj.*

gov. *abbr.* 1. government. 2. governor.

gov·ern (guv-ĕrn) *v.* 1. to rule with authority, to conduct the affairs of a country or an organization. 2. to keep under control, *to govern one's temper.* 3. to influence or direct, *be governed by the experts' advice.*

gov·ern·ance (guv-ĕr-năns) *n.* governing, control.

gov·ern·ess (guv-ĕr-nis) *n.* a woman employed to teach children in a private household.

gov·ern·ment (guv-ĕrn-mĕnt) *n.* 1. governing, the system or method of governing. 2. the group or organization governing a country. 3. the government as an agent; *a government grant,* given from federal funds. **gov·ern·men·tal** (guv-ĕrn-men-

tăl) *adj.* □**government issue,** equipment issued, especially to soldiers, by the federal government. **government surplus,** unused equipment sold to the public by the federal government.

gov·er·nor (guv-ĕr-nŏr) *n.* 1. a person who governs a state or province, especially one of the states of the U.S. 2. the head or member of the governing body of an institution, *board of governors.* 3. a mechanism that automatically controls speed or the intake of gas or water etc. in a machine.

govt. *abbr.* government.

gown (gown) *n.* 1. a loose flowing garment, especially a woman's long dress. 2. a loose outer garment that is the official robe of judges etc.

gowned (gownd) *adj.* wearing a gown.

G.P. *abbr.* general practitioner.

GPO *abbr.* 1. general post office. 2. Government Printing Office.

GQ *abbr.* general quarters.

gr. *abbr.* 1. grade. 2. grain(s). 3. gram(s). 4. grammar. 5. gravity. 6. gross. 7. group. 8. great.

Gr. *abbr.* 1. Grecian. 2. Greece. 3. Greek.

grab (grab) *v.* (**grabbed, grab·bing**) 1. to grasp suddenly. 2. to take something greedily. 3. to operate harshly or jerkily, *the brakes are grabbing.* 4. *(slang)* to make an impression on someone; *how does that music grab you?,* do you like it? **grab** *n.* 1. a sudden clutch or an attempt to seize. 2. a mechanical device for gripping things and lifting them. □**up for grabs,** *(slang)* available for anyone to take.

gra·ben (grah-bĕn) *n.* a depression of the earth's surface between faults.

grace (grays) *n.* 1. the quality of being attractive, especially in movement, manner, or design. 2. elegance of manner; *he had the grace to apologize,* realized that this was right and proper, and did it. 3. favor, goodwill. 4. a delay or postponement granted as a favor, not as a right, *give him a week's grace.* 5. God's loving mercy toward mankind. 6. a short prayer of thanks before or after a meal. 7. *Grace,* the title used in speaking of or to a duke, duchess, or archbishop, *his Grace, her Grace, their Graces.* **grace** *v.* (**graced, grac·ing**) to confer honor or dignity on, to be an ornament to. □**be in a person's good graces,** to have his favor and approval. **days of grace,** the time allowed by law or custom after the day on which a payment is officially due. **grace note,** a music note that is not essential to the harmony but is added as an embellishment. **with good grace,** willingly or as if willingly.

grace·ful (grays-fŭl) *adj.* having or showing grace. **grace′ful·ly** *adv.* **grace′ful·ness** *n.*

grace·less (grays-lis) *adj.* 1. inelegant. 2. ungracious.

gra·cious (gray-shŭs) *adj.* 1. kind and pleasant in manner, especially to subordinates. 2. showing divine grace, merciful. 3. showing qualities associated with good taste and breeding, *gracious living.* **gracious!** *interj.* an exclamation of surprise, *good gracious! gracious me!* **gra′cious·ly** *adv.* **gra′cious·ness** *n.*

grack·le (grak-ĕl) *n.* the North American blackbird.

grad. *abbr.* 1. gradient. 2. graduate. 3. graduated.

gra·da·tion (gray-day-shŏn) *n.* a process of gradual change, a stage in such a process, *the gradation of color between blue and green.*

grade (grayd) *n.* 1. a step or stage or degree in some rank, quality, or value, *Grade A milk.* 2.

a class of people or things of the same rank or quality etc. 3. the mark given to a student for his standard of work. 4. gradient, slope. **grade** *v.* (**grad·ed, grad·ing**) 1. to arrange in grades. 2. to give a grade (to a student). 3. to adjust the gradient of (a road). □**grade crossing,** a place where a railroad and a road (or two railroads) cross each other at the same level. **grade school,** an elementary school. **make the grade,** to reach the desired standard.

grad·er (gray-dĕr) *n.* a machine that reduces earth to easy gradients, as in road building.

gra·di·ent (gray-di-ĕnt) *n.* 1. the amount of slope in a road or railroad; *the road has a gradient of one in ten,* it rises one foot in every ten feet of its length. 2. a sloping road or railroad.

grad·u·al (graj-oo-ăl) *adj.* taking place by degrees, not sudden or steep. **grad′u·al·ly** *adv.*

grad·u·al·ism (graj-oo-ă-liz-ĕm) *n.* the policy of accomplishing goals gradually rather than by sudden change.

grad·u·ate (graj-oo-ayt) *v.* (**grad·u·at·ed, grad·u·at·ing**) 1. to award or be awarded a degree or certificate showing successful completion of a course of study. 2. to divide into graded sections. 3. to mark into regular divisions or units of measurement, *the beaker was graduated.* **graduate** (graj-oo-it) *n.* a person who has completed a course of study, especially a college or university course. **graduate** *adj.* □**graduate school,** the division of a university that offers courses of study for those who have received the bachelor's degree. **graduate student,** one who studies in such a school. ▷It is incorrect to say *she graduated college.* Say *she graduated from* or *she was graduated from college.*

grad·u·a·tion (graj-oo-ay-shŏn) *n.* 1. graduating, being graduated. 2. the ceremony in which a person is awarded a degree or certificate. 3. a mark of measurement.

graf·fi·to (gră-fee-toh) *n.* (*pl.* **-ti,** *pr.* -tee) words or a drawing scratched or scribbled on a wall. ▷It is incorrect to use *graffiti* as a singular.

graft[1] (graft) *n.* 1. a shoot from one tree fixed into a cut in another to form a new growth. 2. a piece of living tissue transplanted surgically to replace diseased or damaged tissue. **graft** *v.* 1. to put a graft in or on. 2. to join (one thing) inseparably to another.

graft[2] *n.* 1. obtaining some advantage in business or politics by bribery or unfair influence or other shady means. 2. a bribe or bribery used in this way. 3. the advantage gained by it. **graft** *v.* to gain advantage in business or politics through shady means. **graft′er** *n.*

gra·ham (gray-ăm) *adj.* made from unsifted wholewheat flour.

Grail (grayl) *n.* **Holy Grail,** the cup or the platter used (according to legend) by Christ at the Last Supper and in which Joseph of Arimathea received drops of Christ's blood at the Crucifixion, sought in prolonged quests by knights in the Middle Ages.

grain (grayn) *n.* 1. a small hard seed of a food plant such as wheat or rice. 2. the gathered seeds of such plants. 3. the plants themselves. 4. a small hard particle, *a grain of sand.* 5. a unit of weight, about sixty-five milligrams. 6. the smallest possible amount, *he hasn't a grain of sense.* 7. the texture produced by the particles in flesh, stone, etc., or in photographic prints. 8. the pattern of lines made by fibers in wood or by layers in rock or coal etc. □**against the grain,** cutting or lying across a natural layer; contrary to one's natural inclinations. **grain alcohol,** ethyl alcohol.

grain·field (grayn-feeld) *n.* a field of grain.

grain·y (gray-nee) *adj.* (**grain·i·er, grain·i·est**) like grains in form or appearance or texture. **grain′i·ness** *n.*

gram (gram) *n.* a unit of weight in the metric system, one-thousandth part of a kilogram.

gram. *abbr.* 1. grammar. 2. grammarian. 3. grammatical.

-gram *suffix* used to form nouns meaning something written or pictured, as in *telegram, diagram.*

gram·mar (gram-ăr) *n.* 1. the study of words and of the rules for their formation and their relationships to each other in sentences. 2. the rules themselves. 3. a book about these. 4. speech or writing judged as good or bad according to these rules, *his grammar is appalling.* **gram·mar·i·an** (gră-mair-i-ăn) *n.* □**grammar school,** an elementary school.

gram·mat·i·cal (gră-mat-i-kăl) *adj.* in accordance with the rules of grammar. **gram·mat′i·cal·ly** *adv.*

gram·o·phone (gram-ŏ-fohn) *n.* a phonograph.

gram·pus (gram-pŭs) *n.* (*pl.* **-pus·es**) a large sea animal of the dolphin family.

gran·a·ry (gray-nă-ree) *n.* (*pl.* **-ries**) a storehouse for grain.

grand (grand) *adj.* 1. splendid, magnificent. 2. of the highest rank, *the Grand Duke Alexis.* 3. dignified, imposing, *she puts on a grand manner.* 4. *(informal)* very enjoyable or satisfactory, *we had a grand time.* 5. including everything, final, *the grand total.* **grand** *n.* 1. a grand piano. 2. *(slang)* a thousand dollars, *five grand.* **grand′ly** *adv.* **grand′ness** *n.* □**Grand Canyon,** a gorge one mile deep through which the Colorado River flows in Arizona. **grand jury,** a jury convened to indict an accused person if the evidence warrants it. **grand master,** the head of a military order of knighthood, or of Freemasons, etc. **grand opera,** opera in which everything is sung and there are no spoken parts. **grand piano,** a large full-toned piano with horizontal strings. **Grand Prix** (grahn-pree) any of several important international auto racing events over a road course. **grand slam,** (in bridge) *see* **slam;** (in tennis, golf, etc.) the winning of all of a group of championships; (in baseball) a home run with runners on all bases.

gran·dad (gran-dad) *n.* *(informal)* 1. grandfather. 2. an elderly man.

grand·child (grand-chıld) *n.* (*pl.* **-chil·dren,** *pr.* -chil-drĕn) the child of one's son or daughter.

grand·daugh·ter (gran-daw-tĕr) *n.* the daughter of one's son or daughter.

grande dame (grahnd dahm) *n.* a dignified lady of high rank. ▷French.

gran·dee (gran-dee) *n.* a person of high rank.

gran·deur (gran-jĕr) *n.* splendor, magnificence, grandness.

grand·fa·ther (gran-fah-thĕr) *n.* the father of one's father or mother. □**grandfather clock,** a clock in a tall wooden case, worked by weights.

gran·dil·o·quent (gran-dil-ŏ-kwĕnt) *adj.* using pompous language. **gran·dil′o·quent·ly** *adv.* **gran·dil′o·quence** *n.*

gran·di·ose (gran-di-ohs) *adj.* 1. imposing, planned on a large scale. 2. trying to be grand, pompous. **gran·di·os·i·ty** (gran-di-os-i-tee) *n.*

grand·ma (gran-mah) n. (informal) grandmother.

grand·moth·er (gran-muth-ĕr) n. the mother of one's father or mother.

grand·pa (gran-pah) n. (informal) grandfather.

grand·par·ent (gran-pair-ĕnt) n. one's parent's parent.

grand·sire (gran-sīr) n. (old use) grandfather.

grand·son (gran-sun) n. the son of one's son or daughter.

grand·stand (grand-stand) n. the principal roofed building with rows of seats for spectators at races and sporting events. □**grandstand play,** a play made by an athlete to impress the spectators; any action taken more for appearances than for substance.

grange (graynj) n. 1. a farm. 2. the Grange, a U.S. farmers' association founded in 1867; one of its local branches.

gran·ite (gran-it) n. a hard gray stone used for building.

gran·ite·ware (gran-it-wair) n. 1. a kind of speckled enameled ironware. 2. speckled pottery imitating the appearance of granite.

gran·ny (gran-ee) n. (pl. -nies) (informal) grandmother. □**granny glasses,** a pair of eyeglasses with round lenses and a thin wire frame. **granny knot,** a square knot with the threads crossed the wrong way and therefore likely to slip.

gra·no·la (gră-noh-lă) n. a dry breakfast food consisting of a mixture of grains, nuts, fruit, etc.

grant (grant) v. 1. to give or allow; grant a request, permit what is requested. 2. to admit or agree that something is true, I grant that your offer is generous. **grant** n. something granted, especially a sum of money. **grant′er** n. **grant·ee** (grantee) n. □**take for granted,** to assume that (a thing) is true or sure to happen; to be so used to having (a thing etc.) that one no longer appreciates it.

Grant (grant), **U·lys·ses S.** (1822–85) the eighteenth president of the U.S. 1869–77.

grant-in-aid (grant-in-ayd) n. (pl. **grants-in-aid**) a sum granted to a person to finance his university studies, or to an institution to finance research etc.

grants·man·ship (grants-măn-ship) n. (informal) the art of gaining grants-in-aid.

gran·u·lar (gran-yŭ-lăr) adj. like grains or granules. **gran·u·lar·i·ty** (gran-yŭ-lar-i-tee) n.

gran·u·late (gran-yŭ-layt) v. (**gran·u·lat·ed,** **gran·u·lat·ing**) 1. to form into grains or granules, granulated sugar. 2. to make rough and grainy on the surface. **gran·u·la·tion** (gran-yŭ-lay-shŏn) n.

gran·ule (gran-yool) n. a small grain.

grape (grayp) n. a green or purple berry growing in clusters on vines, used for making wine. □**grape hyacinth,** a small hyacinth-like plant with clusters of rounded usually blue flowers.

grape·fruit (grayp-froot) n. a large round yellow citrus fruit with a juicy acid pulp.

grape·shot (grayp-shot) n. (old use) small iron balls that scattered when fired from a cannon.

grape·vine (grayp-vīn) n. 1. the kind of vine on which grapes grow. 2. a way by which news is passed on unofficially, heard it on the grapevine.

graph (graf) n. a diagram consisting of a line or lines showing the relationship between two sets of quantities. **graph** v. to draw a graph of. □**graph paper,** paper ruled into small squares, used for plotting graphs.

-graph suffix used to form nouns meaning something written, drawn, or recorded, as in photograph, seismograph.

graph·ic (graf-ik) adj. 1. of drawing or painting or lettering or engraving, the graphic arts; a graphic artist. 2. giving a vivid description, a graphic account of the fight. □**graphic arts,** reproductive arts of engraving, etching, woodcut, lithography, etc.

graph·i·cal·ly (graf-i-klee) adv. in a graphic way.

graph·ics (graf-iks) n. 1. (sing.) the use of diagrams in calculation or in design. 2. (pl.) lettering and drawings, the graphics are by John James.

graph·ite (graf-īt) n. a soft black form of carbon used in lubrication, as a moderator in nuclear reactors, and in lead pencils.

graph·ol·o·gist (gra-fol-ŏ-jist) n. an expert in graphology.

graph·ol·o·gy (gra-fol-ŏ-jee) n. the scientific study of handwriting, especially as a guide to the writer's character. **graph·o·log·i·cal** (graf-ŏ-loj-i-kăl) adj.

grap·nel (grap-nĕl) n. 1. a small anchor with three or more flukes, used for boats and balloons. 2. a hooked grappling instrument used in dragging the bed of a lake or river.

grap·ple (grap-ĕl) v. (**grap·pled, grap·pling**) 1. to seize or hold firmly. 2. to struggle at close quarters; grapple with a problem, try to deal with it. □**grappling hook,** a grapnel (definition 2).

grasp (grasp) v. 1. to seize and hold firmly, especially with one's hands or arms. 2. to understand, he couldn't grasp what we meant. **grasp** n. 1. a firm hold or grip; within his grasp, close enough for him to grasp or obtain it. 2. a mental hold, understanding, a thorough grasp of his subject. □**grasp at,** to snatch at.

grasp·ing (gras-ping) adj. greedy for money or possessions.

grass (gras) n. 1. any of a group of common wild low-growing plants with green blades and stalks that are eaten by animals. 2. any species of this plant (in botanical use including cereal plants, reeds, and bamboos). 3. ground covered with grass, lawn, or pasture; put animals out to grass, put them to graze. 4. (slang) marijuana. □**grass roots,** the fundamental level or source; ordinary people, the rank and file of a political party or other group. **grass snake,** a small harmless snake. **grass widow,** a woman who is divorced from or lives apart from her husband.

grass·hop·per (gras-hop-ĕr) n. any of a number of insects with long back legs adapted for jumping.

grass·land (gras-land) n. a wide area covered in grass and with few trees.

grass·y (gras-ee) adj. (**grass·i·er, grass·i·est**) like grass, covered with grass.

grate[1] (grayt) n. 1. a metal framework that keeps fuel in a fireplace. 2. the recess where fire burns.

grate[2] v. (**grat·ed, grat·ing**) 1. to shred into small pieces by rubbing against a jagged surface. 2. to make a harsh noise by rubbing, to sound harshly, a grating laugh. 3. to have an unpleasant irritating effect. **grat·ing·ly** adv.

grate·ful (grayt-fŭl) adj. feeling or showing that one values a kindness or benefit received. **grate·ful·ly** adv.

grat·er (gray-tĕr) n. a device with a jagged surface for grating food.

grat·i·cule (grat-ĭ-kyool) n. 1. a network of lines on paper representing meridians and parallels for maps and charts. 2. fine lines incorporated in a telescope or other optical instrument as a measuring scale or as an aid in locating objects.

grat·i·fy (grat-ĭ-fī) v. (**grat·i·fied, grat·i·fy·ing**) to give pleasure to, to satisfy (wishes etc.). **grat·i·fi·ca·tion** (grat-ĭ-fĭ-kay-shŏn) n.

grat·ing (gray-ting) n. a screen of spaced metal bars placed across an opening.

gra·tis (grat-is) adj. & adv. free of charge, you can have the leaflet gratis.

grat·i·tude (grat-ĭ-tood) n. being grateful.

gra·tu·i·tous (gră-too-ĭ-tŭs) adj. 1. given or done without payment. 2. given or done without good reason, a gratuitous insult. **gra·tu'i·tous·ly** adv.

gra·tu·i·ty (gră-too-ĭ-tee) n. money given in recognition of services rendered, a tip.

grau·pel (grow-pĕl) n. snow pellets or soft hail.

gra·va·men (gră-vay-mĕn) n. (pl. **-va·mens, -vam·i·na,** pr. -vam-ĭ-nă) the essence, or the worst part, of an accusation or charge (especially in a court of law).

grave¹ (grayv) n. 1. a hole dug in the ground to bury a corpse. 2. the place where a corpse is buried. 3. the grave, death, being dead, gone to the grave.

grave² adj. (**grav·er, grav·est**) 1. serious, causing great anxiety, grave news. 2. solemn, not smiling. **grave'ly** adv. **grave'ness** n. □**grave** (pr. grayv, grahv) **accent,** a backward-sloping mark over a vowel, as in à la carte.

grav·el (grav-ĕl) n. coarse sand with small stones, as used for roads and paths. **gravel** v. (**grav·eled, grav·el·ing**) to cover with gravel.

grav·el·ly (grav-ĕ-lee) adj. 1. like gravel. 2. rough sounding, a gravelly voice.

grav·en (gray-vĕn) adj. carved, a graven image; graven on my memory, firmly fixed in it.

grave·stone (grayv-stohn) n. a stone monument over a grave.

grave·yard (grayv-yahrd) n. a burial ground. □**graveyard shift,** a work shift beginning at midnight; the workers on this shift.

grav·id (grav-id) adj. pregnant.

gra·vim·e·ter (gră-vim-ĕ-tĕr) n. an instrument measuring the difference in the force of gravity between two places.

grav·i·met·ric (grav-ĭ-met-rik) adj. of or relating to the measurement of weight.

grav·i·tate (grav-ĭ-tayt) v. (**grav·i·tat·ed, grav·i·tat·ing**) to move or be attracted toward.

grav·i·ta·tion (grav-ĭ-tay-shŏn) n. 1. gravitating. 2. the force of gravity. **grav·i·ta'tion·al** adj. **grav·i·ta'tion·al·ly** adv. **grav·i·ta·tive** (grav-ĭ-tay-tiv) adj.

grav·i·ty (grav-ĭ-tee) n. (pl. **-ties**) 1. the force that attracts bodies toward the center of Earth. 2. seriousness, the gravity of the situation. 3. solemnity. □**center of gravity,** the central point in an object about which its mass is evenly balanced. **gravity feed,** a supply system in which a substance falls from a higher level to a lower one by force of gravity rather than by mechanical means. **specific gravity,** see **specific.**

gra·vure (gră-vyoor) n. 1. a photomechanical printing process. 2. a printing process from engraved plates.

gra·vy (gray-vee) n. (pl. **-vies**) 1. juice that comes out of meat while it is cooking. 2. sauce made from this. 3. (slang) money or profit easily or unexpectedly acquired. □**gravy train,** (slang) a source of easy money.

gray (gray) adj. 1. of the color between black and white, colored like ashes or lead; he is going gray, his hair is losing its color; a gray day, without sun. 2. intermediate in character; a gray area, that part of a matter where there are no exact rules about right and wrong etc. **gray** n. 1. gray color. 2. a gray substance or material. 3. a gray horse. **gray** v. to make or become gray. **gray'ness** n. □**gray birch,** a tree of northeastern North America with grayish-white bark. **gray cells,** (humorous) brain or intelligence. **Gray Friars,** Franciscan friars. **gray matter,** the material of the brain and spinal cord; (informal) brain or intelligence. **gray power,** the political pressure of organized old or retired persons.

gray·beard (gray-beerd) n. an old man.

gray·head·ed (gray-hed-ĕd) adj. with gray hair.

gray·ish (gray-ish) adj. rather gray.

gray·ling (gray-ling) n. a silver-gray freshwater fish.

graze¹ (grayz) v. (**grazed, graz·ing**) 1. to eat growing grass, cattle grazing in the fields. 2. to put (animals) into a field to eat the grass. **graz'er** n.

graze² v. (**grazed, graz·ing**) 1. to touch or scrape lightly in passing. 2. to scrape the skin from.

Gr. Br. abbr. Great Britain.

grease (grees) n. 1. animal fat melted soft. 2. any thick semisolid oily substance; axle grease, grease used to lubricate axles. **grease** (greez, grees) v. (**greased, greas·ing**) to put grease on or in. □**grease a person's palm,** (slang) to bribe him. **grease gun,** a device for forcing grease into the parts of a machine. **grease monkey,** (slang) a mechanic who lubricates machines. **grease pencil,** a crayon-like pencil used for marking glossy surfaces. **like greased lightning,** (slang) very fast.

grease·paint (grees-paynt) n. makeup used by actors and other performers.

greas·y (gree-see,-zee) adj. (**greas·i·er, greas·i·est**) 1. covered with grease. 2. containing much grease. 3. slippery. 4. oily in manner. **greas'i·ly** adv. **greas'i·ness** n.

great (grayt) adj. 1. much above average in size or amount or intensity. 2. larger than others of similar kind, the great auk. 3. of remarkable ability or character, important, one of the great painters; Peter the Great; the great, great people; the greatest, (slang) a very remarkable person or thing. 4. elaborate, intense, told in great detail. 5. doing something frequently or intensively or very well, a great reader. 6. (informal) very enjoyable or satisfactory, we had a great time. 7. of a family relationship that is one generation removed in ancestry or descent, as great-grandfather, great-niece; great-great-grandfather, great-grandfather's father. **great'ly** adv. **great'ness** n. □**great ape,** a gorilla or chimpanzee or other manlike ape. **great blue heron,** a large American bird with blue-gray feathers. **Great Britain,** England, Wales, and Scotland. **great circle,** a circle on the surface of a sphere, whose plane passes through the center of the sphere. **Great Depression,** the period of economic troubles of the 1930's. **great divide,** the continental divide or separation of watersheds; the distance between life and death. **great guns!,** see **gun. great horned owl,** a large North American bird with head feathers resembling horns. **Great Lakes,** a series of five large lakes along the boundary between Canada and the U.S. **Great Plains,** the region of valleys and plains in central North America. **Great Powers,** important countries with international influence. **Great Salt Lake,** a shallow strongly saline lake in Utah. **Great Scott!,** an exclamation of surprise. **Great Seal of the U.S.,** the official seal affixed to important state papers. **great toe,** the big toe. **Great War,** World War I. **Great White Father,** the American Indian name for the U.S. president. **great white heron,** a large white bird of Florida, resembling the egret. **great white shark,** the large shark that is most feared for its attacks on human beings. **Great White Way,** the Broadway theater area of New York City.

great·coat (grayt-koht) *n.* a heavy overcoat.

great·heart·ed (grayt-hahr-tid) *adj.* having a noble or generous mind.

grebe (greeb) *n.* (*pl.* **grebes, grebe**) a diving bird.

Gre·cian (gree-shăn) *adj.* Greek.

Greece (grees) a country in southeast Europe.

greed (greed) *n.* an excessive desire for food or wealth.

greed·y (gree-dee) *adj.* (**greed·i·er, greed·i·est**) 1. showing greed. 2. very eager or keen for something. **greed'i·ly** *adv.* **greed'i·ness** *n.*

Greek (greek) *adj.* of Greece or its people or language. **Greek** *n.* 1. a member of the people living in ancient or modern Greece. 2. their language. ☐**Greek Church,** the Greek Orthodox Church (*see* **orthodox**). **it's Greek to me,** I cannot understand its meaning.

green (green) *adj.* 1. of the color between blue and yellow, the color of growing grass. 2. covered with grass or with growing leaves. 3. unripe, not seasoned; *wood is green,* not yet dry enough to burn well. 4. immature, inexperienced, easily deceived. 5. pale and sickly looking; *green with envy,* very jealous. **green** *n.* 1. green color. 2. a green substance or material. 3. a green light. 4. a piece of grassy public land, *the village green.* 5. a grassy area, *a putting green.* 6. **greens,** (*informal*) green vegetables. **green'ly** *adv.* **green'ness** *n.* ☐**green bean,** a string bean. **green belt,** an area of open land around a town, where the amount of building is restricted. **green-eyed monster,** jealousy. **green light,** a signal to proceed on a road; (*informal*) permission to go ahead with a project. **green manure,** growing plants plowed into the soil as fertilizer. **green pepper,** the unripe fruit of the sweet or red pepper, used as a vegetable. **green salad,** a salad consisting of leafy vegetables. **greens fee,** a fee paid to play golf. **green tea,** tea made from leaves that are steam dried, not fermented. **green thumb,** (*informal*) skill in making plants grow.

green·back (green-bak) *n.* a U.S. dollar.

green·er·y (gree-nĕ-ree) *n.* green foliage or growing plants.

green·finch (green-finch) *n.* a European finch with green and yellow feathers.

green·gage (green-gayj) *n.* a round plum with a greenish skin.

green·gro·cer (green-groh-sĕr) *n.* (*British*) a shopkeeper selling vegetables and fruit. **green'gro·cer·y** *n.* (*pl.* **-cer·ies**).

green·horn (green-horn) *n.* an inexperienced person.

green·house (green-hows) *n.* (*pl.* **-hous·es,** *pr.* -how-ziz) a building with glass sides and roof, for raising plants.

green·ish (gree-nish) *adj.* rather green.

Green·land (green-länd) a very large island in the Arctic Ocean, a possession of Denmark.

green·room (green-room) *n.* a room in a theater, for the use of actors when they are not on stage.

greens·keep·er (greenz-kee-pĕr), **green·keep·er** (green-kee-pĕr) *n.* the keeper of a golf course.

green·stick (green-stik) **fracture** a kind of bone fracture in which the bone is partly broken and partly bent.

green·sward (green-sword) *n.* a grassy turf.

Green·wich (gren-ich) a suburb of London, the former site of the Royal Observatory. ☐**Greenwich mean time,** time on the line of longitude that passes through Greenwich, used as a basis for calculating time throughout the world. **Greenwich Village,** an area of New York City known for its night life and for the famous writers and artists who have lived there.

green·wood (green-wuud) *n.* woodlands in summer.

greet (greet) *v.* 1. to address politely on meeting or arrival. 2. to receive with a certain reaction, *the news was greeted with dismay.* 3. to present itself to one's sight or hearing, *the sight that greeted our eyes.* **greet'er** *n.*

greet·ing (gree-ting) *n.* 1. words or gestures used to greet a person. 2. expressions of goodwill, *birthday greetings.* ☐**greeting card,** a printed card sent as a greeting, usually for a special occasion.

gre·gar·i·ous (grĕ-gair-i-ŭs) *adj.* 1. living in flocks or communities. 2. fond of company. **gre·gar'i·ous·ly** *adv.* **gre·gar'i·ous·ness** *n.*

Gre·go·ri·an (grĕ-gohr-i-ăn) *adj.* of or relating to Pope Gregory I or Pope Gregory XIII. ☐**Gregorian calendar,** the calendar introduced by Pope Gregory XIII in 1582 and still in general use. **Gregorian chant,** plainsong ritual music named for Pope Gregory I.

grem·lin (grem-lin) *n.* (*slang*) a mischievous spirit said to cause mishaps to machinery.

Gre·na·da (grĕ-nah-dă) an island country in the West Indies.

gre·nade (grĕ-nayd) *n.* a small bomb thrown by hand or fired from a rifle.

gren·a·dier (gren-ă-deer) *n.* a member of a British or European infantry regiment that was formerly armed with grenades.

gren·a·dine (gren-ă-deen) *n.* a French cordial syrup of pomegranates.

grew (groo) *see* **grow.**

grey = **gray.**

grey·hound (gray-hownd) *n.* a slender smooth-haired dog noted for its swiftness, used primarily in racing.

grid (grid) *n.* 1. a grating. 2. a network of squares on maps, numbered for reference. 3. any network of lines, an arrangement of electric-power cables or gas-supply lines for distributing current or gas over a large area. 4. a network of wires in a storage battery or vacuum tube. 5. a gridiron.

grid·dle (grid-ĕl) *n.* a flat pan or metal surface for cooking over heat. ☐**griddle cake,** a thin flat cake of batter cooked on a griddle, a pancake.

grid·i·ron (grid-ı-ŏrn) *n.* 1. a framework of metal bars for cooking on. 2. a field on which football is played, with parallel lines marking the area of play.

grid·lock (grid-lok) *n.* an urban traffic jam caused by continuous lines of intersecting traffic.

grief (greef) n. 1. deep sorrow. 2. something causing this. ☐**come to grief**, to meet with disaster, to fail, to fall.

grief-strick·en (greef-strik-ĕn) adj. overcome by grief.

griev·ance (gree-văns) n. a real or imagined cause of complaint. ☐**grievance committee**, a committee that presents complaints, especially of a labor union.

grieve (greev) v. (**grieved, griev·ing**) 1. to cause grief to. 2. to feel grief.

griev·ous (gree-vŭs) adj. 1. causing grief. 2. serious; *grievous bodily harm*, serious injury. **griev′ous·ly** adv.

grif·fin (grif-ĭn) n. a creature in Greek mythology, with an eagle's head and wings on a lion's body.

grif·fon (grif-ŏn) n. one of a breed of terrier-like dogs with coarse hair.

grill (gril) n. 1. a metal grid, a grating. 2. a grating or griddle for cooking on. 3. a device on a stove for radiating heat downward, a broiler. 4. meat, fish, or vegetables broiled or griddle fried. 5. (also **grillroom**) a restaurant featuring broiled or fried foods. **grill** v. 1. to broil or fry on a griddle. 2. to expose to great heat. 3. to question closely and severely. ▷Do not confuse *grill* with *grille*.

grille (gril) n. a grating, especially in a door or window. ▷Do not confuse *grille* with *grill*.

grill·work (gril-wurk) n. something made to look like or serve as a grille.

grilse (grils) n. (*pl.* **grils·es, grilse**) a young male salmon returning from the sea to fresh water to spawn for the first time.

grim (grim) adj. (**grim·mer, grim·mest**) 1. stern or severe in appearance. 2. severe, unrelenting, merciless, *held on like grim death.* 3. without cheerfulness, unattractive, *a grim prospect.* **grim′ly** adv. **grim′ness** n.

gri·mace (grim-ăs) n. a contortion of the face expressing pain or disgust, or intended to cause amusement. **grimace** v. (**gri·maced, gri·mac·ing**) to make a grimace.

grime (grim) n. dirt or soot ingrained in a surface or in the skin. **grime** v. (**grimed, grim·ing**) to blacken with grime. **grim′y** adj. (**grim·i·er, grim·i·est**).

grin (grin) v. (**grinned, grin·ning**) 1. to smile broadly, showing the teeth; *grin and bear it,* endure something without complaining. 2. to express by a grin, *he grinned his approval.* **grin** n. a broad smile.

grind (grīnd) v. (**ground, grind·ing**) 1. to crush or be crushed into grains or powder. 2. to produce in this way. 3. to sharpen or smooth by friction. 4. to oppress or crush by cruelty. 5. to rub harshly together, *grind one's teeth; the bus ground to a halt,* stopped laboriously with a grating sound. 6. to work (a thing) by turning a handle; *grind out a tune on the barrel organ,* produce it in this way. 7. (*informal*) to study hard, *grinding away at his algebra.* **grind** n. 1. the act of grinding. 2. the size of ground particles, *a coarse grind.* 3. hard monotonous work. 4. (*slang*) a student who does little else but study.

grind·er (grīn-dĕr) n. 1. a person or thing that grinds. 2. a molar tooth. 3. a large sandwich made on a long roll split lengthwise.

grind·stone (grīnd-stohn) n. a thick revolving disk used for sharpening or grinding things. ☐**keep one's nose to the grindstone**, to work hard without rest.

gri·ot (gree-ŏt) n. an African tribal poet, musician, and oral historian.

grip (grip) v. (**gripped, grip·ping**) 1. to take a firm hold of. 2. to hold a person's attention, *a gripping story.* **grip** n. 1. a firm grasp or hold. 2. the power of gripping, a way of grasping or holding. 3. understanding, mental hold or control, *has a good grip of his subject.* 4. the part of a tool or machine etc. that grips things. 5. the part (of a weapon or device) designed to be held. 6. (*informal*) a suitcase or traveling bag. ☐**come to grips with**, to begin to cope with, to deal with (a problem) firmly. **get a grip on oneself**, to regain one's self-control. **lose one's grip**, to become less competent than one was formerly.

gripe (grip) v. (**griped, grip·ing**) 1. to cause or suffer pain in the bowels. 2. (*informal*) to complain. **gripe** n. (*informal*) a complaint.

grippe (grip) n. influenza.

gris-gris (gree-gree) n. (*pl.* **gris-gris**) an African charm or fetish.

gris·ly (griz-lee) adj. (**-li·er, -li·est**) causing fear or horror or disgust, *all the grisly details.*

grist (grist) n. grain to be ground or already ground; *everything is grist to his mill,* he makes use of everything.

gris·tle (gris-ĕl) n. tough flexible tissue of animal bodies, especially in meat. **grist′ly** adj.

grist·mill (grist-mil) n. a mill that grinds grain, especially to the individual customer's order.

grit (grit) n. 1. particles of stone or sand. 2. courage and endurance. **grit** v. (**grit·ted, grit·ting**) 1. to make a slightly grating sound. 2. to clench; *grit one's teeth,* to keep the jaws tightly together, especially when enduring pain or trouble. 3. to spread grit on. **grit′ty** adj. **grit′ti·ness** n.

grits (grits) n. coarsely ground grain, especially corn.

griz·zled (griz-ĕld) adj. gray, gray haired.

griz·zly (griz-lee) adj. gray, gray haired. ☐**grizzly bear**, a large bear of North America.

gro. abbr. gross.

groan (grohn) v. 1. to make a long deep sound expressing pain or grief or disapproval. 2. to make a deep creaking noise resembling this. **groan** n. the sound made in groaning.

groats (grohts) n. pl. crushed grain, especially oats.

gro·cer (groh-sĕr) n. a shopkeeper who sells foods and household supplies.

gro·cer·y (groh-sĕr-ee) n. (*pl.* **-cer·ies**) 1. (also **grocery store**) a grocer's store. 2. groceries, goods sold by a grocer. 3. *groceries,* (*slang*) food; *he brings home the groceries,* provides the money needed to feed his family.

grog (grog) n. 1. liquor (especially rum) mixed with water. 2. alcoholic drink.

grog·gy (grog-ee) adj. (**-gi·er, -gi·est**) weak and unsteady, especially after illness. **grog′gi·ly** adv. **grog′gi·ness** n.

groin (groin) n. 1. the fold where each thigh joins the trunk. 2. this area of the body, where the genitals are situated. 3. the curved edge where two vaults meet in a roof.

grom·met (grom-it) n. a reinforced eyelet in cloth etc. to receive a cord or fastener etc.

groom (groom) n. 1. a person employed to look after horses. 2. a bridegroom. **groom** v. 1. to clean and brush (an animal). 2. to make neat and clean. 3. to prepare (a person) for a career or position.

groom·ing (groo-ming) *n.* personal cleanliness and neatness, *good grooming.*

groove (groov) *n.* 1. a long narrow channel in the surface of hard material. 2. a spiral cut on a phonograph record for the needle or stylus. 3. a way of living that has become a habit. **groove** *v.* **(grooved, groov·ing)** 1. to make grooves in. 2. *(slang)* to enjoy, to approve of. □**in the groove,** *(slang)* in top form.

groov·y (groo-vee) *adj.* **(groov·i·er, groov·i·est)** *(slang)* excellent, admired.

grope (grohp) *v.* **(groped, grop·ing)** 1. to feel about as one does in the dark, to seek by feeling. 2. to search mentally with some uncertainty, *groping for an answer.*

gros·beak (grohs-beek) *n.* any of various finches with large thick beaks.

gro·schen (groh-shĕn) *n.* (*pl.* **-schen**) a small coin of Germany or Austria.

gros·grain (groh-grayn) *n.* corded fabric of silky thread, used for ribbons etc.

gross (grohs) *adj.* 1. thick, large-bodied; *a gross fellow,* repulsively fat; *gross vegetation,* growing thickly. 2. not refined, vulgar, *gross manners.* 3. glaringly obvious, outrageous, *gross negligence.* 4. total, whole, without deductions; *gross income,* income before tax etc. is deducted. 5. *(slang)* disgusting. **gross** *n.* (*pl.* **gross**) twelve dozen (144) items; *ten gross,* 1440. **gross** *v.* to earn or make as a total income or profit prior to deducting expenses. **gross'ly** *adv.* **gross'ness** *n.* □**gross national product,** the total value of goods produced and services provided in a country in one year. **gross out,** *(slang)* to disgust, to repel.

gro·tesque (groh-tesk) *adj.* very odd or unnatural, fantastically ugly or absurd. **grotesque** *n.* a comically distorted figure, a design using fantastic human, animal, and plant forms. **gro·tesque'ly** *adv.* **gro·tesque'ness** *n.*

grot·to (grot-oh) *n.* (*pl.* **-toes, -tos**) a picturesque cave.

grouch (growch) *v.* *(informal)* to grumble. **grouch** *n.* *(informal)* 1. a grumble. 2. a grumbler. **grouch'er** *n.* **grouch'y** *adj.*

ground[1] (grownd) *n.* 1. the solid surface of the earth, especially contrasted with the air surrounding it. 2. an area or position or distance on the earth's surface, *gain or lose ground.* 3. a foundation or reason for a theory or action, *there are no grounds for suspicion.* 4. soil, earth, *marshy ground.* 5. an area used for a particular purpose, *burial ground.* 6. the underlying part, a surface worked on in embroidery or painting. **ground** *v.* 1. to run aground. 2. to prevent (an aircraft or airman) from flying, *all aircraft were grounded because of the fog.* 3. to teach thoroughly, to give good basic training to. 4. to base on, *is grounded on or in fact.* □**get off the ground,** to rise in the air; to make a successful start. **give ground,** to retreat, to yield. **ground ball,** (in baseball) a batted ball that rolls or bounces along the ground. **ground cloth,** a groundsheet. **ground cover,** low-growing plants used in place of grass or to control erosion. **ground crew,** workers, mechanics, etc. who service and maintain aircraft on the ground. **ground floor,** the floor at ground level in a building; *get in on the ground floor,* to be one of the first to have the advantage of sharing in a promising business. **ground ivy,** a creeping plant with bluish-purple flowers. **ground plan,** a plan of a building at ground level; an outline

or general design of a scheme. **ground rule,** a basic principle of a situation; a rule arising from the nature of the playing field or the location of spectators. **ground squirrel,** a kind of squirrel that burrows instead of living in trees. **ground zero,** the point on the ground under an exploding bomb. **run into the ground,** to explain at unreasonable length, to overdo.

ground[2] *v. see* **grind. ground** *adj.* **ground glass,** glass made nontransparent by grinding.

ground·er (grown-dĕr) *n.* (in baseball) a ground ball, *see* **grind.**

ground·hog (grownd-hawg) *n.* a woodchuck. □**groundhog day,** February 2, when the groundhog is supposed to come out of his hole at the end of hibernation. ▷If he sees his shadow, there are supposed to be six more weeks of winter weather.

ground·ing (grown-ding) *n.* thorough teaching, basic training, *a good grounding in arithmetic.*

ground·less (grownd-lis) *adj.* without basis, without good reason, *your fears are groundless.* **ground'less·ly** *adv.*

ground·mass (grownd-mas) *n.* a base of hard rock embedded with prominent crystals.

ground·nut (grownd-nut) *n.* 1. the edible tuber or underground nut of a plant, such as the peanut. 2. such a plant.

grounds (growndz) *n. pl.* 1. an area of enclosed land belonging to a large house or an institution. 2. solid particles that sink to the bottom of a liquid, *coffee grounds.*

ground·sheet (grownd-sheet) *n.* a waterproof sheet for spreading on the ground.

grounds·keep·er (growndz-kee-pĕr) *n.* a person who takes care of the grounds of an estate, a playing field, etc.

ground·swell (grownd-swel) *n.* 1. heavy slow-moving waves caused by a distant or recent storm. 2. a sudden spontaneous growth of enthusiasm and popular support, as for a political candidate.

ground·wa·ter (grownd-waw-tĕr) *n.* water lying below the earth's surface in springs and in pores of rock.

ground·work (grownd-wurk) *n.* preliminary or basic work.

group (groop) *n.* 1. a number of persons or things gathered, placed, or classed together, or working together for some purpose. 2. a number of commercial companies under one owner. 3. a trio, quartet, etc., especially of pop or jazz performers. **group** *v.* **(grouped, group·ing)** to form or gather into a group or groups. □**group practice,** a medical practice in which several doctors are associated. **group therapy,** psychological therapy in which patients with a similar condition are brought together to assist one another under the supervision of a therapist.

group·er (groo-pĕr) *n.* a salt-water fish used as food.

group·ie (groo-pee) *n.* *(slang)* a girl who follows touring pop groups.

grouse[1] (grows) *n.* (*pl.* **grouse**) 1. a game bird with feathered feet. 2. its flesh as food.

grouse[2] *v.* **(groused, grous·ing)** *(informal)* to complain. **grouse** *n.* *(informal)* a complaint. **grous'er** *n.*

grout (growt) *n.* thin mortar used to fill narrow cavities such as joints between stones or wall tiles. **grout** *v.* to fill with grout.

grove (grohv) *n.* a group of trees, a small wood.

grov·el (gruv-ĕl) *v.* (**grov·eled, grov·el·ing**) 1. to lie or crawl with the face downward in a show of humility or fear. 2. to humble oneself.

grow (groh) *v.* (**grew, grown, grow·ing**) 1. to increase in size or quantity, to become greater. 2. to develop; *the seeds are growing,* putting out shoots. 3. to be capable of developing as a plant, to flourish, *rice grows in warm climates.* 4. to become gradually, *he grew rich.* 5. to cause or allow to grow, to produce by cultivation, *grow a beard; grow roses.* 6. to become firmly established or more acceptable, *it's a habit that grows on you.* □**growing pains,** neuralgic pain in children's legs, usually caused by tiredness; problems arising because a project or development is in its early stages. **grow out of,** (of a growing child) to become too large to wear (certain clothes); to become too mature for, *grew out of his childish habits;* to have as a source, to arise or develop from. **grow up,** to develop, to become adult or mature.

grow·a·ble (groh-ă-bĕl) *adj.* able to be grown.

grow·er (groh-ĕr) *n.* 1. a person who grows plants, fruit, or vegetables commercially. 2. a plant that grows in a certain way, *a rapid grower.*

growl (growl) *v.* 1. to make a low threatening sound. 2. to speak or say in a growling manner, to grumble. **growl** *n.* a growling sound. **growl'er** *n.*

grown (grohn) *v. see* **grow. grown** *adj.* 1. fully developed, adult, *a grown man.* 2. covered with a growth, *a wall grown over with ivy.*

grown·up (grohn-up) *n.* an adult person. **grown-up** *adj.*

growth (growth) *n.* 1. the process of growing, development. 2. the cultivation of produce. 3. something that grows or has grown, *a thick growth of weeds.* 4. an abnormal formation of tissue in the body, a tumor. □**growth industry,** one developing faster than most others. **growth stocks,** common-stock investments thought likely to increase in value rather than yield high income.

grub (grub) *n.* 1. the thick-bodied wormlike larva of certain insects. 2. *(slang)* food. **grub.** *v.* (**grubbed, grub·bing**) 1. to dig the surface of the soil. 2. to clear away roots by digging, to dig up by the roots. 3. to search laboriously, to rummage.

grub·by (grub-ee) *adj.* (**grub·bi·er, grub·bi·est**) 1. infested with grubs. 2. dirty, unwashed. **grub'bi·ly** *adv.* **grub'bi·ness** *n.*

grub·stake (grub-stayk) *n.* supplies or money advanced (originally to a mining prospector) with the agreement that the profits will be shared with the lender.

grudge (gruj) *v.* (**grudged, grudg·ing**) to resent having to give or allow something; *I don't grudge him his success,* I admit that he deserves it. **grudge** *n.* a feeling of resentment or ill will. **grudg'ing** *adj.* **grudg'ing·ly** *adv.*

gru·el (groo-ĕl) *n.* a thin porridge made by boiling oatmeal in milk or water.

gru·el·ing (groo-ĕ-ling) *adj.* extremely tiring, exhausting.

grue·some (groo-sŏm) *adj.* filling one with horror or disgust, revolting, *the gruesome details of the murder.*

gruff (gruf) *adj.* 1. (of the voice) low and harsh, hoarse. 2. having a gruff voice. 3. surly in manner. **gruff'ly** *adj.* **gruff'ness** *n.*

grum·ble (grum-bĕl) *v.* (**grum·bled, grum·bling**) 1. to complain in a bad-tempered way. 2. to rumble, *thunder was grumbling in the dis-* *tance.* **grumble** *n.* 1. a complaint, especially a bad-tempered one. 2. a rumble.

grum·bler (grum-blĕr) *n.* a person who grumbles constantly.

grum·py (grum-pee) *adj.* (**grump·i·er, grump·i·est**) bad-tempered. **grump'i·ly** *adv.* **grump'i·ness** *n.*

grun·gy (grun-jee) *adj.* (**-gi·er, -gi·est**) *(slang)* unkempt, ugly.

grun·ion (grun-yŏn) *n.* a small California sea fish that comes ashore to spawn.

grunt (grunt) *v.* 1. to make the gruff snorting sound characteristic of a pig. 2. to speak or utter with such a sound, *he grunted a reply.* 3. to grumble. **grunt** *n.* 1. a grunting sound. 2. *(slang)* an infantryman.

gru·yère (groo-yair) *n.* a pale firm cheese with small cavities, made originally in Gruyère, Switzerland.

gr. wt. *abbr.* gross weight.

gryph·on = **griffin.**

GSA *abbr.* 1. General Services Administration. 2. Girl Scouts of America.

G-string (jee-string) *n.* 1. a string on a musical instrument, tuned to the note G. 2. a very brief covering for the genitals, especially that used in a burlesque show.

G-suit (jee-soot) *n.* a close-fitting inflatable suit worn by airmen or astronauts flying at high speed to prevent blood from draining away from the head and causing blackouts (G = gravity).

gt. *abbr.* great.

GT *abbr.* gross ton.

Gt. Br., Gt. Brit. *abbr.* Great Britain.

gtd. *abbr.* guaranteed.

gua·ca·mo·le (gwah-kă-moh-lee) *n.* a Mexican sauce of mashed avocado, hot peppers, etc.

gua·nine (gwah-neen) *n.* a white base obtained from guano and found as a constituent of DNA.

gua·no (gwah-noh) *n.* 1. dung of seabirds, used as fertilizer. 2. an artificial fertilizer, especially that made from fish.

guar·an·tee (gar-ăn-tee) *n.* 1. a formal promise to do what has been agreed, or that a thing is of specified quality and durability, with penalties for failure. 2. = guaranty (definitions 1 and 2). 3. a guarantor. **guarantee** *v.* (**guar·an·teed, guar·an·tee·ing**) 1. to give or be a guarantee for; *guarantee his debts,* undertake to pay them if he does not. 2. to promise, to state with certainty.

guar·an·tor (gar-ăn-tor) *n.* a person who gives a guarantee.

guar·an·ty (gar-ăn-tee) *n.* (*pl.* **-ties**) 1. a formal promise given by one person to another that he will be responsible for something to be done, or for a debt to be paid, by a third person. 2. something offered or accepted as security. 3. a guarantor. 4. giving security. **guaranty** *v.* (**guar·an·tied, guar·an·ty·ing**) to guarantee.

guard (gahrd) *v.* 1. to watch over and protect, to keep safe. 2. to watch over and supervise or prevent escape. 3. to keep in check, to restrain; *guard your tongue,* do not be outspoken or indiscreet. 4. to take precautions, *guard against errors.* **guard** *n.* 1. a state of watchfulness or alertness for possible danger. 2. a defensive attitude in boxing, fencing, etc. 3. a protector, a sentry. 4. a body of soldiers or others guarding a place or a person, serving as escort, or forming a separate part of an army. 5. a protecting part or device. □**guard**

duty, standing as sentry; guarding military prisoners. **guard of honor,** a ceremonial guard for a special occasion such as a military funeral. **off guard,** unprepared against attack or surprise. **on one's guard,** alert for possible danger etc. **stand guard,** to guard, to act as a protector or sentry.

guard·ed (gahr-did) *adj.* cautious, discreet, *a guarded statement.*

guard·house (gahrd-hows) *n.* (*pl.* **-hous·es,** *pr.* -how-ziz) a building for the accommodation of a military guard or for keeping prisoners under guard.

guard·i·an (gahr-di-ăn) *n.* 1. one who guards or protects. 2. a person who undertakes legal responsibility for someone who is incapable of managing his own affairs, such as an orphaned child. **guard'ian·ship** *n.* ☐**guardian angel,** an angel thought of as watching over a person or place.

guard·room (gahrd-room) *n.* a room for keeping prisoners under guard or for the use of a military guard on duty.

guards·man (gahrdz-măn) *n.* a member of a unit of guards.

Gua·te·ma·la (gwah-tĕ-mah-lă) 1. a country in Central America. 2. its capital city. **Gua·te·ma'lan** *adj.* & *n.*

gua·va (gwah-vă) *n.* 1. a tropical American tree. 2. its edible orange-colored acid fruit.

gu·ber·na·to·ri·al (goo-bĕr-nă-tohr-i-ăl) *adj.* of a governor or of the office of governor.

Guern·sey (gurn-zee) *n.* (*pl.* **-seys**) one of a breed of dairy cattle known for its rich milk.

guer·ril·la (gŭ-ril-ă) *n.* a person who takes part in **guerrilla warfare,** fighting or harassment by small groups acting independently.

guess (ges) *v.* 1. to form an opinion or make a statement or give an answer without calculating or measuring and without definite knowledge. 2. to think something likely. 3. *(informal)* to suppose, *I guess we ought to be going.* **guess** *n.* an opinion formed by guessing. **guess'er** *n.* ☐**keep a person guessing,** *(informal)* to keep him uncertain of one's feelings or future actions etc.

guess·ti·mate (ges-tĭ-mit) *n.* *(informal)* an estimate based on guesswork and reasoning. **guesstimate** (ges-tĭ-mayt) *v.* (**guess·ti·mat·ed, guess·ti·mat·ing**) *(informal)* to form a guesstimate.

guess·work (ges-wurk) *n.* the process of guessing, an example of this.

guest (gest) *n.* 1. a person staying or eating at another's house or visiting him by invitation. 2. a person staying at a hotel. 3. a visiting performer taking part in an entertainment, *a guest artist.* ☐**guest of honor,** the most honored guest at a party. **guest room,** a bedroom kept for the use of guests.

guest·house (gest-hows) *n.* (*pl.* **hous·es,** *pr.* -how-ziz) 1. a separate house for guests on an estate. 2. a small, informal hotel.

guff (guf) *n.* *(slang)* empty talk, nonsense.

guf·faw (gu-faw) *n.* a coarse noisy laugh. **guffaw** *v.* to give a guffaw.

gui·dance (gı-dans) *n.* 1. guiding, being guided. 2. advising or advice, especially on educational and vocational matters. ☐**guidance system,** a computer and associated devices for keeping a missile, spacecraft, etc. on course.

guide (gıd) *n.* 1. a person who shows others the way. 2. one employed to point out interesting sights on a journey or visit. 3. an adviser, a person

or thing that directs or influences one's behavior. 4. a book of information about a place or a subject, *a guide to Italy.* 5. a thing that marks a position, guides the eye, or steers moving parts. **guide** *v.* (**guid·ed, guid·ing**) to act as guide to. ☐**guide dog,** a dog trained to guide a blind person. **guided missile,** a missile that is under remote control or directed by equipment within itself. **guide rail,** a track for a window or sliding door. **guide rope,** a rope trailed along the ground by a balloon or small airship; a rope attached to the load of a crane to guide it. **guide word,** a word at the head of a page of a reference book indicating either the first or the last word on the page.

guide·book (gıd-buuk) *n.* a book of information about a place, for travelers or visitors.

guide·line (gıd-lın) *n.* a statement of principle giving practical guidance.

gui·don (gı-dŏn) *n.* a small flag or pennant used as a military unit's standard.

guild (gild) *n.* a society of people with similar interests and aims, one of the associations of craftsmen or merchants in the Middle Ages.

guil·der (gil-dĕr) *n.* a unit of money of the Netherlands, a florin.

guild·hall (gild-hawl) *n.* a hall built or used as a meeting place by a guild.

guile (gıl) *n.* treacherous cunning, craftiness. **guile'ful** *adj.* **guile'less** *adj.* **guile'less·ness** *n.*

guil·lo·tine (gil-ŏ-teen, gee-ŏ-) *n.* 1. a machine with a heavy blade sliding down in grooves, used for beheading criminals in France. 2. a machine with a long blade for cutting paper or metal. **guillotine** (gil-ŏ-teen, gee-ŏ-) *v.* (**guil·lo·tined, guil·lo·tin·ing**) to execute with a guillotine.

guilt (gilt) *n.* 1. the fact of having committed some offense. 2. a feeling that one is to blame for something.

guilt·less (gilt-lis) *adj.* without guilt, innocent.

guilt·y (gil-tee) *adj.* (**guilt·i·er, guilt·i·est**) 1. having done wrong. 2. feeling or showing guilt. **guilt'i·ly** *adv.* **guilt'i·ness** *n.*

guin·ea (gin-ee) *n.* a former British gold coin worth 21 shillings (£1.05).

Guin·ea (gin-ee) a country in West Africa. **Guin'e·an** *adj.* & *n.*

Gui·nea-Bis·sau (gin-ee-bi-soh) a country in West Africa bordering Guinea.

guinea (gin-ee) **fowl** a domestic fowl of the pheasant family, with gray feathers spotted with white.

guinea hen a female guinea fowl.

guinea pig 1. a short-eared animal like a large rat, kept as a pet or for biological experiments. 2. a person or thing used as a subject for experiment.

guise (gız) *n.* an outward manner or appearance put on in order to conceal the truth, a pretense, *they exploited him under the guise of friendship.* ▷ Do not confuse *guise* with *disguise.*

gui·tar (gi-tahr) *n.* a stringed musical instrument played by plucking with the fingers or with a plectrum; **electric guitar,** one with a built-in microphone.

gui·tar·ist (gi-tahr-ist) *n.* a person who plays the guitar.

gulch (gulch) *n.* a small ravine.

gulf (gulf) *n.* 1. an area of sea (larger than a bay) that is partly surrounded by land. 2. a deep chasm or canyon. 3. a wide difference in opinions or outlook. ☐**Gulf Stream,** a warm ocean current that flows from the Gulf of Mexico to Europe.

gull¹ (gul) *n.* a large seabird with long wings.

gull² *n.* (old use) a dupe. **gull** *v.* (old use) to deceive, to cheat.

Gul·lah (gul-ă) 1. one of a group of descendants of slaves from West Africa, inhabiting the Atlantic coastal region of the southeastern U.S. 2. the English-African dialect of these people.

gul·let (gul-it) *n.* 1. the passage by which food goes from the mouth to the stomach. 2. the throat.

gul·li·ble (gul-ĭ-bĕl) *adj.* easily deceived. **gul·li·bil·i·ty** (gul-ĭ-bil-i-tee) *n.*

gul·ly (gul-ee) *n.* (*pl.* **-lies**) a narrow channel cut in the soil by flowing water.

gulp (gulp) *v.* 1. to swallow (food or drink) hastily or greedily. 2. to suppress something by swallowing hard, *he gulped back his rage.* 3. to make a gulping movement, to choke or gasp, *gulping for breath.* **gulp** *n.* 1. the act of gulping. 2. a large mouthful of liquid.

gum¹ (gum) *n.* the firm flesh in which the teeth are rooted. **gum** *v.* **(gummed, gum·ming)** *(informal)* to chew without teeth.

gum² *n.* 1. a sticky substance exuded by some trees and shrubs, used for sticking things together. 2. chewing gum. 3. a gum tree. **gum** *v.* **(gummed, gum·ming)** to smear or cover with gum, to stick together with gum, to become gummy. □**gum arabic,** gum exuded by some kinds of acacia, used in making candies and glue. **gum tree,** a tree that exudes gum, a eucalyptus. **gum up,** *(informal)* to cause confusion or delay in, to spoil; *gum up the works,* to interfere with the smooth running of something.

gum³ *n.* (*slang,* in oaths) God, *by gum!*

gum·bo (gum-boh) *n.* (*pl.* **-bos**) 1. the okra plant or its pods. 2. soup thickened with these pods. 3. thick mud.

gum·boil (gum-boil) *n.* a small abscess on the gum.

gum·drop (gum-drop) *n.* a candy made of gelatin or gum arabic and coated with sugar.

gum·my (gum-ee) *adj.* **(gum·mi·er, gum·mi·est)** sticky with gum. **gum'mi·ness** *n.*

gump·tion (gump-shŏn) *n.* *(informal)* common sense and initiative.

gum·shoe (gum-shoo) *n.* *(slang)* a detective.

gun (gun) *n.* 1. any kind of firearm that sends shells or bullets from a metal tube. 2. a starting pistol. 3. a device that forces out a substance through a tube, *a grease gun.* 4. *(slang)* a gunman, *a hired gun.* **gun** *v.* **(gunned, gun·ning)** 1. to shoot with a gun, *gunned him down.* 2. to accelerate (an engine) briskly. □**be gunning for,** to have as one's target for attack, to seek to destroy. **big gun,** *see* **big. great guns,** *(informal)* vigorously, intensively, *blowing* or *going great guns.* **gun carriage,** a. wheeled structure on which a gun is mounted for transport. **gun metal,** dull bluish-gray, like the color of metal formerly used for guns. **gun moll,** *(slang)* a gangster's mistress; a woman criminal with a gun. **gun runner,** a person engaged in **gun running,** extensive smuggling of guns and ammunition into a country.

gun·boat (gun-boht) *n.* a small armed vessel with heavy guns. □**gunboat diplomacy,** diplomacy backed by threat of force.

gun·cot·ton (gun-kot-ŏn) *n.* an explosive made of acid-soaked cotton.

gun·fight (gun-fīt) *n.* a fight with guns. **gun'fight·er** *n.*

gun·fire (gun-fīr) *n.* the firing of guns.

gung ho (gung hoh) *(informal)* enthusiastic, eager.

gunk (gungk) *n.* unpleasantly viscous or slimy material.

gun·lock (gun-lok) *n.* the mechanism by which the charge of a gun is exploded.

gun·man (gun-măn) *n.* (*pl.* **-men,** *pr.* -mĕn) a man armed with a gun.

gun·nel = **gunwale.**

gun·ner (gun-ĕr) *n.* a soldier or member of an aircraft crew who operates a gun, *tail gunner.*

gun·ner·y (gun-ĕ-ree) *n.* the science of constructing and operating large guns. □**gunnery sergeant,** a noncommissioned officer in the U.S. marines, next in rank below a first sergeant.

gun·ny (gun-ee) *n.* (*pl.* **-nies**) a coarse material made from jute or hemp.

gun·ny·sack (gun-ee-sak) *n.* a sack made of gunny.

gun·point (gun-point) *n.* **at gunpoint,** under threat of being shot by a gun held ready.

gun·pow·der (gun-pow-dĕr) *n.* an explosive of saltpeter, sulfur, and charcoal.

gun·shot (gun-shot) *n.* 1. a shot fired from a gun. 2. the range of a gun, *within gunshot.*

gun-shy (gun-shī) *adj.* afraid of the sound of a gunshot.

gun·sling·er (gun-sling-ĕr) *n.* *(informal)* a gunman.

gun·smith (gun-smith) *n.* a person whose trade is making and repairing small firearms.

gun·wale (gun-ĕl) *n.* the upper edge of a small ship's or boat's side.

gup·py (gup-ee) *n.* (*pl.* **-pies**) a small tropical fish frequently kept in aquariums.

gur·gle (gur-gĕl) *n.* a low bubbling sound. **gurgle** *v.* **(gur·gled, gur·gling)** to make this sound.

Gur·kha (goor-kă) *n.* a member of a Hindu people in Nepal, known for their ability as soldiers.

gu·ru (goo-roo) *n.* (*pl.* **-rus**) 1. a Hindu spiritual teacher or head of a religious sect. 2. an influential or revered teacher.

gush (gush) *v.* 1. to flow or pour out suddenly or in great quantities. 2. to talk with extravagant enthusiasm or emotion, especially in an affected manner. **gush** *n.* 1. a sudden or great outflow. 2. an outpouring of feeling, effusiveness. **gush'y** *adj.* **(gush·i·er, gush·i·est).**

gush·er (gush-ĕr) *n.* 1. an effusive person. 2. an oil well from which oil flows strongly without needing to be pumped.

gus·set (gus-it) *n.* a triangular or diamond-shaped piece of cloth inserted in a garment to strengthen or enlarge it.

gus·set·ed (gus-i-tid) *adj.* fitted with a gusset.

gus·sy (gus-ee) *v.* **(gus·sied, gus·sy·ing)** *(slang)* to dress elegantly, to decorate, *gussy up.*

gust (gust) *n.* 1. a sudden rush of wind. 2. a burst of rain or smoke or sound. **gust** *v.* to blow in gusts. **gust'y** *adj.* **gust'i·ly** *adv.*

gus·ta·to·ry (gus-tă-tohr-ee) *adj.* of the sense of taste.

gus·to (gus-toh) *n.* zest, great enjoyment in doing something.

gut (gut) *n.* 1. the lower part of the alimentary canal, the intestine. 2. a thread made from the intestines of animals, used surgically and for violin and racket strings. 3. *guts,* (informal) the internal organs of the abdomen; the internal parts of anything, *the guts of the machine.* 4. *guts,* (slang) strength or vitality, courage. **gut** *adj.* 1. fundamental, basic, *a gut issue.* 2. instinctive, *a gut reaction.* **gut** *v.* **(gut·ted, gut·ting)** 1. to remove the guts from (a fish). 2. to remove or destroy the internal fittings or parts of (a building), *the factory was gutted by fire.* □**gut course,** *(slang)* a college course requiring little or no work. **gut shot,** a gunshot that wounds game in the stomach. **hate a person's guts,** *(slang)* to hate him intensely. **work one's guts out,** *(informal)* to work extremely hard.

gut·buck·et (gut-buk-it) *n.* a style of jazz, enthusiastically played.

gut·less (gut-lis) *adj. (informal)* lacking courage and determination.

guts·y (gut-see) *adj. (slang)* courageous.

gut·ta·per·cha (gut-ă-pur-chă) *n.* a tough rubberlike substance made from the juice of various Malayan trees.

gut·ter (gut-ĕr) *n.* 1. a shallow trough under the eaves of a building, or a channel at the side of a street, for carrying off rain water. 2. a slum environment. **gutter** *v.* (of a candle) to burn unsteadily so that melted wax flows freely down the sides.

gut·ter·snipe (gut-ĕr-snɪp) *n.* a dirty badly dressed child, a street urchin.

gut·tur·al (gut-ŭ-răl) *adj.* 1. throaty, harsh sounding, *a guttural voice.* 2. pronounced in the throat. **guttural** *n.* a guttural letter. **gut'tur·al·ly** *adv.*

gut·ty (gut-ee) = **gutsy.**

guy[1] (gɪ) *n.* a rope or cable used to keep something steady or secured, *guy wires.* **guy** *v.* **(guyed, guy·ing)** to secure with ropes or cables.

guy[2] *n. (informal)* a man.

Guy·a·na (gɪ-an-ă) a country in South America. **Guy·an·ese** (gɪ-ă-neez) *adj. & n. (pl. -ese).*

guz·zle (guz-ĕl) *v.* **(guz·zled, guz·zling)** to eat or drink greedily. **guz'zler** *n.*

gym (jim) *n. (informal)* 1. a gymnasium. 2. a physical education class. □**gym shoes,** rubber-soled shoes worn in a gymnasium. **gym suit,** clothing, usually brief, worn for a gym class.

gym·kha·na (jim-kah-nă) *n.* a public sports competition, especially one that tests skill in driving a car or in gymnastics.

gym·na·si·um (jim-nay-zi-ŭm) *n. (pl. -si·ums, -si·a,* pr. -zi-ă) a room designed for physical training and gymnastics.

gym·nast (jim-năst) *n.* an expert performer of gymnastics.

gym·nas·tic (jim-nas-tik) *adj.* of gymnastics. **gym·nas·tics** (jim-nas-tiks) *n. pl.* exercises performed to develop the muscles or demonstrate agility; *mental gymnastics,* mental agility, elaborate reasoning. **gymnastics** *n. sing.* gymnastics as a subject of study or practice.

gym·no·sperm (jim-nŏ-spurm) *n.* a plant having its seeds unprotected by seed vessels.

gyn. *abbr.* gynecology.

gyn·e·col·o·gist (gɪ-nĕ-kol-ŏ-jist) *n.* a specialist in gynecology.

gy·ne·col·o·gy (gɪ-nĕ-kol-ŏ-jee) *n.* the scientific study of the female reproductive system and its diseases. **gyn·e·co·log·i·cal** (gɪ-nĕ-kŏ-loj-i-kăl) *n.*

gyp (jip) *v.* **(gypped, gyp·ping)** *(informal)* to cheat, swindle, defraud. **gyp** *n. (informal)* 1. a swindle. 2. a cheater, swindler.

gyp·soph·i·la (jip-sof-ĭ-lă) *n.* a garden plant with many small white or pink flowers, such as baby's-breath.

gyp·sum (jip-sŭm) *n.* a chalklike substance from which plaster of Paris is made, also used as a fertilizer.

gyp·sy (jip-see) *n. (pl. -sies)* 1. a member of a nomadic people, now mainly in Europe and the U.S. 2. their language, Romany. 3. *(informal)* a person who lives like a gypsy. □**gypsy moth,** a moth whose larva is very destructive to trees.

gy·rate (jɪ-rayt) *v.* **(gy·rat·ed, gy·rat·ing)** to move around in circles or spirals, to revolve. **gy·ra·tion** (jɪ-ray-shŏn) *n.*

gyr·fal·con (jur-fal-kŏn) *n.* the largest of all falcons, living in Arctic America and Europe, with plumage in white, gray, and black phases.

gy·ro (jɪ-roh) *n. (pl. -ros) (informal)* 1. a gyroscope. 2. a gyrocompass.

gy·ro·com·pass (jɪ-roh-kum-păs) *n.* a navigation compass using a gyroscope and so not affected by Earth's rotation.

gy·ro·plane (jɪ-rŏ-playn) *n.* a form of aircraft, such as a helicopter, deriving its lift mainly from freely rotating overhead vanes.

gy·ro·scope (jɪ-rŏ-skohp) *n.* a device consisting of a heavy wheel which, when spinning fast, keeps the direction of its axis unchanged, used in navigation instruments in ships and in spacecraft etc. **gy·ro·scop·ic** (jɪ-rŏ-skop-ik) *adj.*

H

H, h (aych) *n.* (*pl.* **Hs, H's, h's**) the eighth letter of the alphabet.

H *abbr. (slang)* heroin.

H *symbol* 1. henry. 2. hydrogen.

h. *abbr.* 1. hard. 2. hardness. 3. height. 4. high. 5. (in baseball) hit(s). 6. hour(s).

ha (hah) *interj.* an exclamation of triumph or surprise.

Ha *symbol* hahnium.

ha. *abbr.* hectare(s).

ha·ba·ne·ra (hah-bă-**nair**-ă) *n.* a Cuban dance in slow time, music for this.

ha·be·as cor·pus (hay-bi-ăs kor-pŭs) an order requiring a person to be brought before a judge or into court, especially in order to investigate the right of the authorities to keep him imprisoned. ▷Latin, = you must have the body.

hab·er·dash·er (hab-ĕr-dash-ĕr) *n.* a shopkeeper dealing in small items of men's clothing, such as shirts, hats, and neckties.

hab·er·dash·er·y (hab-ĕr-dash-ĕ-ree) *n.* (*pl.* **-er·ies**) a haberdasher's shop or goods.

ha·bil·i·ment (hă-bil-ĭ-mĕnt) *n.* 1. (usually **habiliments**) dress suited to any office or occasion. 2. *(old use)* equipment, attire for a particular profession, way of life, etc.

hab·it (hab-it) *n.* 1. a settled way of behaving, something done frequently and almost without thinking. 2. something that is hard to give up, especially an addiction to narcotics. 3. the long dress worn by a monk or nun. 4. a woman's riding dress.

hab·it·a·ble (hab-i-tă-bĕl) *adj.* suitable for living in. **hab·it·a·ble·ness** *n.* **hab·it·a·bly** *adv.* **ha·bit·a·bil·i·ty** (hab-i-tă-bil-i-tee) *n.*

hab·it·ant (hab-i-tănt) *n.* 1. an inhabitant. 2. a descendant of the early French settlers in Canada and Louisiana.

hab·i·tat (hab-i-tat) *n.* the natural environment of an animal or plant.

hab·i·ta·tion (hab-i-tay-shŏn) *n.* 1. a place to live in. 2. inhabiting, being inhabited.

hab·it-form·ing (hab-it-for-ming) *adj.* causing addiction.

ha·bit·u·al (hă-bich-oo-ăl) *adj.* 1. done constantly, like or resulting from a habit. 2. regular, usual, *in his habitual place*. 3. doing something as a habit, *a habitual smoker*. **ha·bit'u·al·ly** *adv.* **ha·bit'u·al·ness** *n.*

ha·bit·u·ate (hă-bich-oo-ayt) *v.* (**ha·bit·u·at·ed, ha·bit·u·at·ing**) to accustom. **ha·bit·u·a·tion** (hă-bich-oo-ay-shŏn) *n.*

ha·bit·u·é (hă-bich-oo-ay) *n.* one who visits a place frequently or lives there.

ha·ci·en·da (hah-si-en-dă) *n.* (*pl.* **-das**) 1. (in Spanish America) a large estate. 2. the main house on a ranch or estate.

hack¹ (hak) *v.* 1. to cut or chop roughly. 2. to

cough harshly. **hack** *n.* 1. a cut or slash or notch made with a sharp implement. 2. a tool used in hacking. 3. a cough. **hack'er** *n.* □**hack it,** *(slang)* to deal with a situation appropriately, *he couldn't hack it at school.*

hack² *n.* 1. a horse for ordinary riding, one that may be hired. 2. a person paid to do hard and uninteresting work, especially as a writer. 3. *(informal)* a cab or carriage for hire, a taxicab or its driver. **hack** *adj.* 1. hired, *a hack writer.* 2. commonplace, hackneyed, *a hack novel.* **hack** *v. (informal)* to drive a cab or carriage.

hack·ie (hak-ee) *n. (informal)* hackman.

hack·ing (hak-ing) *adj.* (of a cough) short, dry, and frequent.

hack·le (hak-ĕl) *n.* one of the long feathers on the neck of a domestic rooster and other birds. □**with his hackles up,** (of a person) angry and ready to fight.

hack·man (hak-măn) *n.* (*pl.* **-men,** *pr.* -mĕn) the driver of a taxicab or carriage.

hack·ney (hak-nee) *n.* (*pl.* **-neys**) 1. a vehicle for hire, especially a taxi that carries people or goods. 2. a horse for ordinary riding.

hack·neyed (hak-need) *adj.* (of a saying etc.) having lost its original impact through long overuse.

hack·saw (hak-saw) *n.* a saw for cutting metal, with a short blade in a frame.

hack·work (hak-wurk) *n.* literary work written to order, usually according to a prescribed formula.

had (had) *see* have.

had·dock (had-ŏk) *n.* (*pl.* **-docks, -dock**) a saltwater fish like cod but smaller, used for food.

Ha·des (hay-deez) *n.* 1. (in Greek mythology) the underworld, the place where the spirits of the dead go. 2. hell.

had·n't (had-ĕnt) = had not.

haf·ni·um (haf-ni-ŭm) *n.* a gray metallic chemical element resembling and usually accompanying zirconium.

haft (haft) *n.* the handle of a knife or dagger or cutting tool.

hag (hag) *n.* an ugly old woman.

Hag·ga·dah (hă-gah-dă) *n.* the book recited at Seder in the Jewish festival of Passover.

hag·gard (hag-ărd) *adj.* looking exhausted and ugly from prolonged worry or illness or lack of sleep.

hag·gis (hag-is) *n.* A Scottish dish made from sheep's heart, lungs, and liver.

hag·gle (hag-ĕl) *v.* (**hag·gled, hag·gling**) to argue about price or terms when settling a bargain. **hag'gler** *n.*

ha·gi·og·ra·phy (hag-i-og-ră-fee) *n.* the writing of saints' lives. **hag·i·og'ra·pher** *n.*

Hague (hayg), **The** the seat of government of the Netherlands.

292

hah = ha.

ha-ha (hah-hah) *interj.* representing laughter.

hahn·i·um (hah-ni-ŭm) *n.* a newly discovered synthetic element.

hai·ku (hɪ-koo, hɪ-koo) *n.* (*pl.* **-ku**) a Japanese three-line poem of seventeen syllables, an English poem imitative of this form.

hail[1] (hayl) *v.* 1. to greet, to call to (a person or ship), to signal to (a taxi etc.) to stop and take one as a passenger; *within hailing distance,* close enough to do this. 2. to originate, to have come, *where does he hail from?* □**hail fellow well met,** very friendly toward strangers. **Hail Mary,** a prayer to the Virgin Mary beginning with these words.

hail[2] *n.* 1. pellets of frozen rain falling in a shower. 2. something coming in great numbers, *a hail of blows.* **hail** *v.* 1. to fall as hail in a shower, *it is hailing.* 2. to come or send down like hail. ▷Do not confuse *hail* with *hale.*

hail·stone (hayl-stohn) *n.* a pellet of hail.

hail·storm (hayl-storm) *n.* a storm of hail.

hair (hair) *n.* 1. one of the fine threadlike strands that grow from the skin of people and animals or on certain plants. 2. a mass of these, especially on the human head. **haired** *adj.* □**get in a person's hair,** to encumber or annoy him. **hair trigger,** a trigger that causes a gun to fire at the slightest pressure. **split hairs,** to make distinctions of meaning that are too small to be of any real importance.

hair·ball (hair-bawl) *n.* a ball of hair that collects in the intestines of an animal that licks its coat.

hair·brush (hair-brush) *n.* a brush for grooming the hair.

hair·cloth (hair-klawth) *n.* a stiff wiry upholstery fabric.

hair·cut (hair-kut) *n.* 1. shortening of the hair by cutting it. 2. the style in which it is cut.

hair·do (hair-doo) *n.* (*pl.* **-dos**) *(informal)* a particular way of styling or arranging a woman's hair.

hair·dress·er (hair-dres-ĕr) *n.* a person whose trade is to arrange and cut hair.

hair·less (hair-lis) *adj.* without hair, bald.

hair·line (hair-lɪn) *n.* 1. a very narrow line. 2. the edge of a person's hair around the face. □**hairline fracture,** a very narrow crack in a bone.

hair·piece (hair-pees) *n.* a quantity of false hair worn to increase the amount of a person's natural hair.

hair·pin (hair-pin) *n.* 1. a U-shaped pin for keeping the hair in place. 2. (also **hairpin curve** or **turn**) a very sharp doubling back of the road.

hair-rais·er (hair-ray-zĕr) *n.* a terrifying movie, story, experience, etc.

hair-rais·ing (hair-ray-zing) *adj.* terrifying, causing one's hair to stand on end.

hairs·breadth (hairz-bredth), **hair·breadth** (hair-bredth) *n.* a minute distance. **hairsbreadth** *adj.* □**hairsbreadth escape,** a very narrow escape.

hair·split·ter (hair-split-ĕr) *n.* a person who makes unnecessarily fine distinctions.

hair·spray (hair-spray) *n.* an aerosol spray used to keep the hair in place.

hair·spring (hair-spring) *n.* a fine spring regulating the balance wheel in a watch.

hair·style (hair-stɪl) *n.* the style in which hair is arranged. **hair'styl·ing** *n.*

hair·styl·ist (hair-stɪ-list) *n.* an expert in cutting and arranging hair.

hair-trig·ger (hair-trig-ĕr) *adj.* rapidly responsive to any stimulus, *a hair-trigger temper.*

hair·weav·ing (hair-wee-ving) *n.* the interweaving of natural hair and a nylon thread base, to cover a bald area.

hair·y (hair-ee) *adj.* (**hair·i·er, hair·i·est**) 1. having much hair. 2. *(slang)* hair-raising, difficult.

hair'i·ness *n.* □**hairy woodpecker,** a North American woodpecker with similar markings to but larger than the downy woodpecker.

Hai·ti (hay-tee) a country in the West Indies.

Hai·tian (hay-shăn) *adj.* & *n.*

haj·ji (haj-ee) *n.* (*pl.* **-jis**) a Muslim who has made a pilgrimage to Mecca.

hake (hayk) *n.* (*pl.* **hakes, hake**) a fish of the cod family, used as food.

hal·berd (hal-bĕrd) *n.* a combined spear and battle-ax.

hal·berd·ier (hal-bĕr-deer) *n.* a man armed with a halberd.

hal·cy·on (hal-si-ŏn) *adj.* calm and peaceful, happy and prosperous, *halcyon days.* ▷Named after a bird formerly believed to have the power of calming wind and waves while it nested on the sea.

hale[1] (hayl) *adj.* strong and healthy, *ʰale and hearty.* **hale'ness** *n.* ▷Do not confuse *hale* with *hail.*

hale[2] *v.* (**haled, hal·ing**) to bring as by dragging, *haled into court.*

half (haf) *n.* (*pl.* **halves,** *pr.* havz) one of two equal or corresponding parts into which a thing is divided. **half** *adj.* amounting to a half. **half** *adv.* to the extent of a half, partly, *half cooked; I'm half inclined to agree.* □**by half,** excessively, *too clever by half.* **by halves,** lacking thoroughness, *they never do things by halves.* **half a dozen,** six. **half and half,** being half of one thing and half of another, especially half milk and half cream. **half boot,** a boot reaching up to the calf of the leg. **half brother, sister,** a brother or sister with only one parent in common with the other. **half dollar,** a U.S. and a Canadian coin worth fifty cents. **half gainer,** a dive in which the diver initially faces forward for takeoff and then executes a half-backward somersault and finishes by entering the water headfirst, facing the diving board. **half hitch,** a knot used in fastening a rope. **half hour,** an interval of thirty minutes. **half measures,** a policy lacking thoroughness. **half nelson,** a hold in wrestling, with an arm under the opponent's arm and behind his neck. **half note,** a musical note having one half the count of a whole note. **half past,** thirty minutes past the hour. **half pint,** a half of a pint; *(informal)* a very short or small person. **half shell,** half of a mollusk shell, especially for serving seafood on. **half size,** any of the full figure sizes in women's clothes, indicated by the fraction one-half next to the size number. **half slip,** a woman's skirtlike undergarment. **half sole,** the sole of a boot or shoe from shank to toe. **half step,** a half interval in pitch between two whole tones. **half time,** the interval between the two halves of a game of football or hockey etc.

half·back (haf-bak) *n.* (in football) a player in the offensive backfield who often carries the ball.

half-baked (haf-baykt) *adj.* *(informal)* 1. not completely planned. 2. foolish.

half-breed (haf-breed) *n.* a person of mixed race.

half-caste (haf-kast) *n.* a person of mixed race.

half-cocked (haf-kokt) *adj.* 1. (of a gun) with the hammer in a half-ready position. 2. (of a person) only half ready; *go off half-cocked*, to begin without adequate preparation.

half·heart·ed (haf-hahr-tid) *adj.* lacking enthusiasm. **half′heart′ed·ly** *adv.* **half′heart′ed·ness** *n.*

half-life (haf-lɪf) *n.* the time it takes the radioactivity of a substance to fall to half its original value.

half-mast (haf-mast) *n.* a point about halfway up a mast, to which a flag is lowered as a mark of respect for a dead person.

half·pen·ny (hay-pĕ-nee) *n.* (*pl.* **half·pen·nies, half·pence,** *pr.* hay-pĕns) a British coin worth half a penny.

half-tim·bered (haf-tim-bĕrd) *adj.* (of a building) having a timbered frame with the spaces filled in by brick or plaster.

half·tone (haf-tohn) *n.* a black and white illustration in which light and dark shades are reproduced by means of small and large dots.

half-track (haf-trak) *n.* an armored vehicle having a propulsion system with wheels at the front and an endless driven belt at the back.

half-truth (haf-trooth) *n.* a statement conveying only part of the truth.

half·way (haf-way) *adj.* at a point between and equally distant from two others. **halfway** *adv.* partially. ☐**halfway house,** a special residence for former drug abusers, mental patients, prisoners, etc. where they are helped in adjusting to normal life.

half-wit (haf-wit) *n.* (*slang*) a mentally retarded or stupid person. **half′-wit′ted** *adj.*

hal·i·but (hal-ĭ-bŭt) *n.* (*pl.* **-but**) a large flatfish used for food.

Hal·i·fax (hal-ĭ-faks) the capital of Nova Scotia.

ha·lite (hal-ɪt) *n.* a rock salt.

hal·i·to·sis (hal-i-toh-sis) *n.* breath that smells unpleasant.

hall (hawl) *n.* 1. a large room or a building for meetings, meals, concerts, etc. 2. a corridor or passageway. 3. a space or passage into which the front entrance of a house etc. opens, a foyer or lobby. ☐**hall of fame,** a building with memorials of celebrated persons, *Baseball Hall of Fame.* **halls of learning, knowledge,** (*informal*) college or university settings for the instruction of students.

hal·le·lu·jah (hal-ĕ-loo-yă) *interj.* praise to the Lord. **hallelujah** *n.* a song of praise to God.

hall·mark (hawl-mahrk) *n.* 1. a mark, especially on articles of precious metal, to indicate their quality or purity. (▷Originally so marked at Goldsmith's Hall in England.) 2. a distinguishing characteristic, *the bombing bears the hallmark of recent guerrilla attacks.* **hall′marked** *adj.*

hal·low (hal-oh) *v.* to make holy, to honor as holy. **hal′lowed** *adj.*

Hal·low·een (hal-ŏ-ween) *n.* October 31, the eve of All Saints' Day.

hal·lu·ci·nate (hă-loo-sĭ-nayt) *v.* (**hal·lu·ci·nat·ed, hal·lu·ci·nat·ing**) to have or cause to have hallucinations. **hal·lu·ci·na·tive** (hă-loo-sĭ-nay-tiv) *adj.*

hal·lu·ci·na·tion (hă-loo-sĭ-nay-shŏn) *n.* 1. the illusion of seeing or hearing something when no such thing is present. 2. the thing seen or heard in this way.

hal·lu·ci·na·to·ry (hă-loo-sĭ-nă-tohr-ee) *adj.* of or causing hallucinations.

hal·lu·ci·no·gen (hă-loo-sĭ-nŏ-jĕn) *n.* a drug causing hallucinations. **hal·lu·ci·no·gen·ic** (hă-loo-sĭ-nŏ-jen-ik) *adj.*

hall·way (hawl-way) *n.* an entrance hall or corridor.

ha·lo (hay-loh) *n.* (*pl.* **-los, -loes**) 1. a disk or ring of light shown around the head of a sacred figure in paintings etc. 2. a disk of diffused light around a luminous body such as the sun or moon. **ha′loed** *adj.*

hal·o·gen (hal-ŏ-jĕn) *n.* any of the nonmetallic elements such as fluorine, chlorine, bromine, iodine, and astatine, which form halides by simple union with a metal. **hal·o·gen·oid** (hal-ŏ-jĕ-noid) *adj.* **ha·log·e·nous** (ha-loj-ĕ-nŭs) *adj.*

hal·o·gen·a·tion (hal-ŏ-jĕ-nay-shŏn) *n.* the introduction of a halogen atom into a molecule.

halt[1] (hawlt) *n.* a stop, an interruption, *work came to a halt.*

halt[2] *v.* 1. to falter in speech. 2. to walk hesitatingly. 3. to come or bring to a halt. **halt!** *interj.* a military order to stop. **halt** *adj.* (*old use*) lame, crippled.

hal·ter (hawl-tĕr) *n.* 1. a rope or leather strap put around a horse's head so that it may be led or fastened by this. 2. a style of dress top held up by a strap passing around the back of the neck, leaving the back and shoulders bare. 3. a rope with a noose for hanging a person. **halter** *v.* to put the halter on, to restrain, to hamper.

halt·ing (hawl-ting) *adj.* 1. walking slowly as if unsure of oneself. 2. spoken hesitantly, *a halting explanation.* **halt′ing·ly** *adv.*

hal·vah (hahl-vah) *n.* a sweet food of Turkish origin, made of sesame flour and honey.

halve (hav) *v.* (**halved, halv·ing**) 1. to divide or share equally between two. 2. to reduce by half.

halves (havz) *see* **half.**

hal·yard (hal-yărd) *n.* a rope for raising or lowering a sail or flag.

ham (ham) *n.* 1. the upper part of a pig's leg, dried and salted or smoked. 2. meat from this. 3. the back of the thigh, the thigh and buttock. 4. (*slang*) a poor actor or performer. 5. (*informal*) the operator of an amateur radio station, *a radio ham.* **ham** *v.* (**hammed, ham·ming**) (*slang*) to overact, to exaggerate one's actions deliberately, *hamming it up.* **ham′my** *adj.* (**-mi·er, -mi·est**).

ham·a·dry·ad (ham-ă-drɪ-ad) *n.* 1. (in Greek and Roman mythology) a nymph living and dying with the tree she inhabited. 2. the king cobra. 3. a large Arabian baboon held sacred in ancient Egypt.

ham·burg·er (ham-bur-gĕr) *n.* a flat round cake of ground beef served fried or broiled, often in a bread roll. ▷Named after Hamburg in Germany.

ham·let (ham-lit) *n.* a small village.

ham·mer (ham-ĕr) *n.* 1. a tool with a heavy metal head used for breaking things, driving nails in, etc. 2. something shaped or used like this, such as an auctioneer's mallet, part of the firing device in a gun, a lever striking the string in a piano. 3. a metal ball of about 15 pounds attached to a wire for throwing as an athletic contest. **hammer** *v.* to hit or beat with a hammer, to strike loudly. ☐**come under the hammer,** to be sold by auction. **hammer and sickle,** the symbols of manual workers and peasants used as the emblem of the U.S.S.R. **hammer and tongs,** fighting or arguing with great energy and noise. **hammer out,** to devise (a plan) with great effort.

ham·mer·head (ham-ĕr-hed) *n.* a shark with lateral extensions of the head bearing the eyes.

ham·mer·lock (ham-ĕr-lok) *n.* a hold in which a wrestler's arm is bent behind his back.

ham·mer·toe (ham-ĕr-toh) *n.* a toe that is permanently bent downward.

ham·mock (ham-ŏk) *n.* a hanging bed of canvas or rope mesh.

ham·per¹ (ham-pĕr) *n.* a basketwork container for clothes, food, etc.

hamper² *v.* to prevent the free movement or activity of, to hinder.

ham·ster (ham-stĕr) *n.* a small ratlike rodent with cheek pouches for carrying grain.

ham·string (ham-string) *n.* 1. one of the strong tendons at the back of the human knee. 2. the great tendon at the back of an animal's hock.

hamstring *v.* (ham·strung, ham·string·ing) 1. to cripple by cutting the hamstrings. 2. to cripple the activity or efficiency of.

hand (hand) *n.* 1. the end part of the arm below the wrist. 2. possession, control, care, *the child is in good hands.* 3. influence, activity, *many people had a hand in it.* 4. active help, *give him a hand.* 5. a pledge of marriage, *asked for her hand.* 6. a manual worker in a factory, on a farm, etc., a member of a ship's crew. 7. skill or style of workmanship, a person with reference to skill, *has a light hand with pastry; an old hand at this,* an experienced person. 8. style of handwriting. 9. a pointer on a clock, dial, etc. 10. side or direction, the right or left side, one of two contrasted sides in an argument etc., *on every hand; on the other hand.* 11. a unit of 4 inches used in measuring a horse's height. 12. the cards dealt to a player in a card game, one round of a card game. 13. *(informal)* applause, *got a big hand.* 14. done or operated or carried etc. by hand, *handsewn; hand brake; hand luggage.* **hand** *v.* 1. to give or pass with one's hand(s) or otherwise. 2. to help (a person) into a vehicle etc. □**at hand,** close by; about to happen. **by hand,** by a person (not a machine); delivered by a messenger; not through the mail. **hand and foot,** completely, *bound hand and foot;* assiduously, *waited on her hand and foot.* **hands down,** to transmit a decision (from the court). **hand in glove with,** working in close association with. **hand in hand,** holding each other's hand; closely associated, linked together. **hand it to a person,** *(informal)* to award praise to. **hand organ,** a barrel organ with a crank turned by hand. **hand over,** to put (a person or thing) into the custody or control of another person. **hand over fist,** *(informal)* with rapid progress, *making money hand over fist.* **hands down,** (of a victory won) easily, completely. **hands off!,** do not touch or interfere. **hands up!,** an order to raise both hands in surrender. **hand towel,** a small towel for wiping the hands after washing. **have one's hands full,** to be fully occupied. **hold a person's hand,** to give close guidance or moral support. **hold hands,** to be hand in hand with another person. **in hand,** in one's possession; in control. **live from hand to mouth,** to supply only one's immediate needs without provision for the future. **on hand,** available. **on one's hands,** resting on one as a responsibility. **out of hand,** out of control; without delay, *rejected it out of hand.* **out of one's hands,** out of one's control. **the upper hand,** the advantage. **to hand,** within reach.

hand·bag (hand-bag) *n.* a woman's bag to hold money and small personal articles.

hand·ball (hand-bawl) *n.* 1. a ball for hitting with the hand. 2. a game played with this ball in a walled court.

hand·bar·row (hand-bar-oh) *n.* a frame for loads etc. carried by two persons.

hand·bill (hand-bil) *n.* a printed notice circulated by hand.

hand·book (hand-buuk) *n.* a small book giving useful facts.

hand·breadth (hand-breth), **hand's·breadth** (handz-breth) *n.* the width of the average adult hand as a measure of distance, approximately four inches.

hand·car (hand-kahr) *n.* a small railroad car on four wheels operated by hand.

hand·cart (hand-kahrt) *n.* a cart drawn or pushed by hand.

hand·clap (hand-klap) *n.* a clapping of hands.

hand·clasp (hand-klasp) *n.* a handshake, a clasping of hands by two or more people to show friendship.

hand·craft (hand-kraft) *v.* to make by handicraft.

hand·cream (hand-kreem) *n.* a cream for softening the hands.

hand·cuff (hand-kuf) *n.* one of a pair of linked metal rings for securing a prisoner's wrists. **handcuff** *v.* to put handcuffs on (a prisoner).

hand·ed (han-did) *adj.* 1. using or made for use by one hand or the other, *left-handed.* 2. requiring or involving a particular number of people, *four-handed card game.*

hand·ful (hand-fuul) *n.* (*pl.* **-fuls**) 1. a quantity that fills the hand. 2. a small number of people or things. 3. *(informal)* a person who is difficult to control, a troublesome task.

hand·grip (hand-grip) *n.* 1. a friendly or hostile grasp, seizure of the hand. 2. a handle.

hand·gun (hand-gun) *n.* a gun held or fired with one hand.

hand·i·cap (han-di-kap) *n.* 1. a disadvantage imposed on a superior competitor in order to equalize chances. 2. a race or contest in which this is imposed. 3. the number of strokes by which a golfer normally exceeds par for the course. 4. anything that lessens one's chance of success or makes progress difficult. 5. a physical or mental disability. **handicap** *v.* (hand·i·capped, hand·i·cap·ping) to impose or be a handicap on.

hand·i·capped (han-dĭ-kapt) *adj.* suffering from a physical or mental disability.

hand·i·cap·per (han-di-kap-ĕr) *n.* 1. a person whose job is to predict winners in a horse race. 2. a racetrack official who assigns the weights that horses carry in a race.

hand·i·craft (han-di-kraft) *n.* work that needs both skill with the hands and artistic design, such as woodwork, needlework, pottery, etc. **hand'i·crafts·man** *n.* (*pl.* **-men**).

hand·i·ly (han-di-lee) *adv.* in a handy way, easily.

hand·i·work (han-di-wurk) *n.* 1. something done or made by the hands. 2. something done or made by a named person.

hand·ker·chief (hang-kĕr-chif) *n.* a small square of cloth for wiping the nose etc.

han·dle (han-dĕl) *n.* 1. the part of a thing by which it is to be held or carried or controlled. 2. *(slang)* one's name, *what's your handle?* **handle** *v.* (han·dled, han·dling) 1. to touch or feel or move with the hands. 2. to be able to be operated, *the car handles well.* 3. to manage, to deal with, *knows how to handle people.* 4. to deal in (goods). 5. *(informal)* to discuss or write about (a subject). □**fly off the handle,** see **fly²**.

han·dle·bar (han-dĕl-bahr) *n.* the steering bar of a bicycle etc., with a handle at each end.

☐**handlebar mustache,** a thick curving mustache shaped like this.

han·dler (hand-lĕr) *n.* a person who handles things, one in charge of a trained police dog etc.

hand·made (hand-mayd) *adj.* made by hand, the opposite of machine made.

hand·maid·en (hand-may-dĕn) *n.* a female servant.

hand-me-down (hand-mee-down) *n.* an article of secondhand clothing.

hand-off (hand-awf) *n.* a short lateral pass in football.

hand·out (hand-owt) *n. (informal)* 1. a prepared statement issued to the press. 2. something distributed free of charge.

hand·pick (hand-pik) *v.* to choose carefully. **hand'picked'** *adj.*

hand·rail (hand-rayl) *n.* a narrow rail for people to hold as a support when climbing stairs etc.

hand·saw (hand-saw) *n.* a saw held with one hand.

hand·set (hand-set) *n.* a telephone mouthpiece and earpiece as one unit.

hand·shake (hand-shayk) *n.* a grasping and shaking of a person's hand with one's own as a greeting.

hand·some (han-sŏm) *adj.* 1. good-looking. 2. generous, *a handsome present.* 3. (of a price or fortune etc.) very large. **hand'some·ly** *adv.* **hand'some·ness** *n.*

hand·spring (hand-spring) *n.* a somersault in which a person lands first on his hands, then on his feet.

hand·stand (hand-stand) *n.* balancing on one's hands with the feet in the air.

hand-to-hand (hand-tŏ-hand) **combat** a fight involving close personal contact between the combatants.

hand·wo·ven (hand-woh-vĕn) *adj.* produced on a hand-operated loom.

hand·writ·ing (hand-rı-ting) *n.* 1. writing done by hand with a pen or pencil. 2. a person's style of this.

hand·y (han-dee) *adj.* (**hand·i·er, hand·i·est**) 1. convenient to handle or use. 2. conveniently placed for being reached or used. 3. clever with one's hands. **hand'i·ly** *adv.* **hand'i·ness** *n.*

hand·y·man (han-di-man) *n.* (*pl.* **-men,** *pr.* -men) a person who does household repairs and odd jobs.

hang (hang) *v.* (**hung, hang·ing**) 1. to support or be supported from above so that the lower end is free. 2. to cause (a door or gate) to rest on hinges so that it swings freely back and forth, to be placed in this way. 3. to stick (wallpaper) to a wall. 4. to decorate with drapery or hanging ornaments. 5. (*past tense* **hanged**) to execute or kill by suspending from a rope that tightens around the neck, to be executed in this way. 6. to droop; *people hung over the gate,* leaned over it. 7. to remain in the air, *smoke hung over the area; the threat is hanging over him,* remains as something unpleasant. **hang** *n.* 1. the way something hangs. 2. (*informal*) a very small amount, *doesn't care a hang.* ☐**get the hang of,** (*informal*) to get the knack of. **hang around,** to loiter, not to disperse. **hang back,** to show reluctance to take action or to advance. **hang fire,** (of a gun) to be slow in going off; (of events) to be slow in developing. **hang glider,** a glider controlled and stabilized by movements of the operator suspended upright in it. **hang gliding,**

the sport of soaring through the air on a hang glider. **hang in (there),** (*slang*) to persist in spite of adversity. **hang on,** to hold tightly; to depend on, *much hangs on this decision;* to attend closely to, *they hung on his words;* to remain in office, to stick to one's duty etc.; (*slang*) to wait for a short time, *hang on a minute;* (*informal,* in telephoning) to hold the line. **hang out,** (*slang*) to frequent (a place), *hang out at that bar.* **hang together,** (of people) to help or support one another; (of statements) to fit well together, to be consistent. **hang up,** to end a telephone conversation by replacing the receiver; (*informal*) to cause delay or difficulty to. **not give a hang,** (*informal*) to not care at all.

han·gar (hang-ăr) *n.* a building for housing aircraft.

hang·dog (hang-dawg) *adj.* shamefaced.

hang·er (hang-ĕr) *n.* 1. a person who hangs things. 2. a loop or hook by which something is hung. 3. a shaped piece of wood, wire, or plastic for hanging a garment on.

hang·er-on (hang-ĕr-on) *n.* (*pl.* **hang·ers-on**) a person who attaches himself to another in the hope of personal gain.

hang·ing (hang-ing) *n.* 1. a drapery hung on walls. 2. an execution by hanging.

hang·man (hang-măn) *n.* (*pl.* **-men,** *pr.* -mĕn) a man whose job is to hang persons condemned to death.

hang·nail (hang-nayl) *n.* torn skin at the root of a fingernail.

hang·out (hang-owt) *n.* (*slang*) a place often visited by a person or group.

hang·o·ver (hang-oh-vĕr) *n.* 1. a severe headache or other unpleasant aftereffects from drinking too much alcohol. 2. something left from an earlier time.

hang-up (hang-up) *n.* (*slang*) a difficulty, an inhibition.

hank (hangk) *n.* a coil or length of wool or thread etc.

hank·er (hang-kĕr) *v.* to crave, to feel a longing. **hank'er·ing** *n.*

han·ky (hang-kee) *n.* (*pl.* **-kies**) (*informal*) a handkerchief.

han·ky-pan·ky (hang-kee-pang-kee) *n.* (*informal*) 1. trickery, dishonest dealing. 2. questionable or immoral behavior.

Ha·noi (ha-noi) the capital of Vietnam.

han·som (han-sŏm) *n.* a covered two-wheeled horse-drawn carriage, with the driver mounted behind.

Ha·nuk·kah, Cha·nu·kah (hah-nŭ-kă) *n.* the Jewish festival of lights, commemorating the victory over the Syrians in the 2nd century B.C.

hao·le (how-lee) *n.* a person who is not a member of the native race of Hawaii, especially a white person.

hap (hap) *n.* (*old use*) 1. chance, luck. 2. a chance occurrence.

hap·haz·ard (hap-haz-ărd) *adj.* done or chosen at random, without planning. **hap·haz'ard·ly** *adv.* **hap·haz'ard·ness** *n.*

hap·less (hap-lis) *adj.* unlucky.

hap·loid (hap-loid) *adj.* having a single set of unpaired chromosomes. **haploid** *n.* a haploid cell, an organism having this.

hap·pen (hap-ĕn) *v.* 1. to occur (by chance or otherwise). 2. to have the (good or bad) fortune to do something, *we happened to see him.* 3. to find by chance, *I happened on this book.* 4. to be the

fate or experience of, *what has happened to you?*
hap·pen·ing (hap-ĕ-ning) *n.* something that happens, an event.
hap·pen·stance (hap-ĕn-stans) *n.* *(informal)* a thing that happens by chance.
hap·py (hap-ee) *adj.* **(hap·pi·er, hap·pi·est)** 1. feeling or showing pleasure or contentment. 2. fortunate. 3. (of words or behavior) very suitable, pleasing. **hap′pi·ly** *adv.* **hap′pi·ness** *n.* □**happy medium,** something that achieves a satisfactory avoidance of extremes.
hap·py-go-luck·y (hap-ee-goh-luk-ee) *adj.* taking events cheerfully as they happen.
ha·ra-ki·ri (hahr-ă-keer-ee) *n.* suicide involving disembowelment, formerly practiced by Japanese army officers when in disgrace or under sentence of death.
ha·rangue (hă-rang) *n.* a lengthy speech, especially a pompous or bombastic one. **harangue** *v.* **(ha·rangued, ha·rangu·ing)** to make a harangue to. **ha·rangu′er** *n.*
har·ass (hă-ras, har-ăs) *v.* 1. to trouble and annoy continually. 2. to make repeated attacks on (an enemy). **ha·rass′ment** *n.*
har·assed (hă-rast, har-ăst) *adj.* tired and irritated by continual worry.
har·bin·ger (hahr-bin-jĕr) *n.* a person, event, or thing that announces the approach of another, a forerunner.
har·bor (hahr-bŏr) *n.* a place of shelter for ships. **harbor** *v.* 1. to give shelter to, to conceal (a criminal etc.). 2. to keep in one's mind, *harbor a grudge.*
hard (hahrd) *adj.* 1. firm, not yielding to pressure, not easily cut. 2. difficult to do or understand or answer. 3. causing unhappiness, difficult to bear. 4. severe, harsh, unsympathetic. 5. energetic, *a hard worker.* 6. (of weather) severe. 7. (of currency) not likely to drop suddenly in value. 8. (of drinks) strongly alcoholic. 9. (of water) containing mineral salts that prevent soap from lathering freely and cause a hard coating to form inside kettles, water tanks, etc. 10. (of colors or sounds) harsh to the eye or ear. 11. (of consonants) sounding sharp not soft, *the letter "g" is hard in "gun" and soft in "gin."* **hard** *adv.* 1. with great effort, intensively, *worked hard; it's raining hard.* 2. with difficulty, *hard-earned money.* 3. so as to be hard, *hard-baked.* **hard′ness** *n.* □**hard and fast,** (of a distinction made, a rule of behavior, etc.) strict. **hard and fast rules,** rules that cannot be altered to fit special cases. **hard bargaining,** making few concessions. **hard by,** close by. **hard cash,** coins and bills, not a check or a promise to pay later. **hard cider,** fermented cider. **hard coal,** anthracite. **hard copy,** a legible permanent record of matter stored in a computer etc. **hard core,** the stubborn unyielding nucleus of a group; *hard-core pornography,* explicitly sexual, in a prurient way. **hard court,** a tennis court with a hard surface. **hard drugs,** drugs that are likely to cause addiction. **hard hat,** protective headgear worn on construction sites; *(informal)* a construction worker. **hard labor,** compulsory labor by prisoners, with loss of privileges during the first few weeks of a sentence. **hard line,** an unyielding adherence to a firm policy. **hard of hearing,** slightly deaf. **hard palate,** the front part of the palate. **hard rock,** a form of rock-'n'-roll music characterized by a very loud and strong beat. **hard sauce,** a sauce of butter and sugar, often with brandy etc. added.

hard sell, aggressive salesmanship. **hard shoulder,** a strip of hardened land beside a highway for vehicles to leave the road in an emergency. **hard up,** *(informal)* short of money; *hard up for ideas,* short of these. **hard words,** words difficult to understand; angry talk.
hard·back (hahrd-bak) *adj.* & *n.* hardcover.
hard·ball (hahrd-bawl) *n.* a baseball. □**play hardball,** *(informal)* to act without restraint.
hard-bit·ten (hahrd-bit-ĕn) *adj.* unyielding in a fight.
hard·board (hahrd-bohrd) *n.* board made of compressed wood chips.
hard-boiled (hahrd-boild) *adj.* 1. (of eggs) boiled until the white and the yolk have become solid. 2. (of people) callous.
hard·bound (hahrd-bownd) *adj.* bound in stiff durable binding. **hardbound** *n.* a hardbound book.
hard·cov·er (hahrd-kuv-ĕr) *adj.* hardbound. **hardcover** *n.* a hardbound book.
hard·en (hahr-dĕn) *v.* 1. to make or become hard or hardy. 2. to make or become unyielding, *attitudes have hardened in the dispute.* **hard′en·er** *n.*
hard·hack (hahrd-hak) *n.* an American shrub related to roses, having rusty leaves with pink and white flowers.
hard·head·ed (hahrd-hed-id) *adj.* practical, not sentimental. **hard′head′ed·ly** *adv.* **hard′head′ed·ness** *n.*
hard·heart·ed (hahrd-hahr-tid) *adj.* unsympathetic. **hard′heart′ed·ly** *adv.* **hard′heart′ed·ness** *n.*
har·di·hood (hahr-di-huud) *n.* boldness, audacity.
Har·ding (hahr-deeng), **War·ren G.** (1865–1923) the twenty-ninth president of the U.S. 1921–23.
hard-lin·er (hahrd-lɪ-nĕr) *n.* a person unyielding in his adherence to a firm policy.
hard·ly (hahrd-lee) *adv.* 1. in a hard manner. 2. only with difficulty. 3. scarcely; *one can hardly expect it,* cannot reasonably expect it. ▷ It is incorrect to say *can't hardly.*
hard-nosed (hahrd-nohzd) *adj.* *(informal)* uncompromising.
hard·pan (hahrd-pan) *n.* firm subsoil of clay etc., hard unbroken ground.
hard-shell (hahrd-shel) *adj.* 1. having a hard shell. 2. rigid, uncompromising.
hard·ship (hahrd-ship) *n.* severe discomfort or lack of the necessities of life, a circumstance causing this.
hard·stand (hahrd-stand) *n.* an area adjacent to an airport runway with a hard surface for aircraft to stand on.
hard·tack (hahrd-tak) *n.* a saltless hard biscuit formerly used on naval ships.
hard·top (hahrd-top) *n.* an automobile with a metal roof and no center posts separating the windows.
hard·ware (hahrd-wair) *n.* 1. tools and household implements etc. 2. weapons, machinery. 3. the mechanical and electronic parts of a computer.
hard·wood (hahrd-wuud) *n.* the hard heavy wood obtained from deciduous trees, such as oak and teak.
hard·work·ing (hahrd-wur-king) *adj.* diligent.
har·dy (hahr-dee) *adj.* **(har·di·er, har·di·est)** 1. capable of enduring cold or difficult conditions. 2. (of plants) able to grow in the open air all year round. **har′di·ness** *n.* **har′di·ly** *adv.*
hare (hair) *n.* (*pl.* **hares, hare**) a field animal like a rabbit but larger.

hare·bell (hair-bel) *n.* a wild plant with blue bell-shaped flowers on a slender stalk.

hare·brained (hair-braynd) *adj.* wild and foolish, rash.

hare·lip (hair-lip) *n.* a deformed lip (usually the upper lip) with a vertical slit in it like that of a hare. **hare'lipped** *adj.*

ha·rem (hair-ĕm) *n.* 1. the women of a Muslim household. 2. their living quarters.

hark (hahrk) *v.* to listen. □**hark back,** to return to an earlier subject, to remember.

har·le·quin (hahr-lĕ-kwin, -kin) *n.* 1. (often **Harlequin**) a clownlike character in pantomime dressed in multicolored clothing. 2. a buffoon or clown. **harlequin** *adj.* multicolored.

har·lot (hahr-lŏt) *n. (old use)* a prostitute.

harm (hahrm) *n.* an injury, damage. **harm** *v.* to cause harm to.

harm·ful (hahrm-fŭl) *adj.* causing harm. **harm'ful·ly** *adv.*

harm·less (hahrm-lis) *adj.* 1. unlikely to cause harm. 2. inoffensive. **harm'less·ly** *adv.* **harm'less·ness** *n.*

har·mon·ic (hahr-mon-ik) *n.* 1. an overtone of a primary note played on an instrument. 2. *harmonics,* the science of the physical characteristics of musical sound. **harmonic** *adj.* relating to harmony, having a harmonious sound. **har·mon'i·cal·ly** *adv.*

har·mon·i·ca (hahr-mon-ĭ-kă) *n.* a small rectangular wind instrument played by passing it along the lips while blowing or sucking air.

har·mo·ni·ous (hahr-moh-ni-ŭs) *adj.* 1. sweet sounding, tuneful. 2. forming a pleasing or consistent whole. 3. free from disagreement or ill feeling. **har·mo'ni·ous·ly** *adv.* **har·mo'ni·ous·ness** *n.*

har·mo·ni·um (hahr-moh-ni-ŭm) *adj.* a musical instrument with a keyboard, in which notes are produced by air pumped through reeds, a reed organ.

har·mo·nize (hahr-mŏ-nīz) *v.* (**har·mo·nized, har·mo·niz·ing**) 1. to add notes to (a melody) to form chords. 2. to make or be harmonious. 3. to produce an agreeable artistic effect. **har'mo·niz·er** *n.* **har·mo·ni·za·tion** (hahr-mŏ-ni-zay-shŏn) *n.*

har·mo·ny (hahr-mŏ-nee) *n.* (*pl.* **-nies**) 1. the combination of musical notes to produce chords. 2. the study of chords and chord progressions. 3. a pleasant chord or progression of chords. 4. agreement, concord, *we were in perfect harmony with each other.*

har·ness (hahr-nis) *n.* 1. the straps and fittings by which a horse is controlled and fastened to a carriage, cart, etc. 2. fastenings resembling this (as for attaching a parachute to its wearer). **harness** *v.* 1. to put harness on (a horse), to attach by a harness. 2. to control and use (a river or other natural force) to produce electrical power etc. □**harness racing,** racing in which a horse pulls a two-wheeled vehicle and a driver. **in harness,** in the routine of daily work. **out of harness,** retired from work.

harp (hahrp) *n.* a musical instrument consisting of strings stretched on a roughly triangular frame, played by plucking with the fingers. **harp** *v.* to talk repeatedly and tiresomely about a subject, *is always harping on it.* **harp'er** *n.* **harp'ist** *n.*

har·poon (hahr-poon) *n.* a spearlike missile with

a rope attached, for killing whales etc. **harpoon** *v.* to spear with a harpoon. **har·poon'er** *n.*

harp·si·chord (hahrp-si-kord) *n.* a keyboard instrument in which the strings are plucked rather than struck as in a piano, used especially in the 16th-18th centuries.

har·py (hahr-pee) *n.* (*pl.* **-pies**) a grasping unscrupulous person. ▷Named after the Harpies, creatures in Greek mythology with a woman's head and body and a bird's wings and claws.

har·que·bus (hahr-kwĕ-bŭs) *n.* (*pl.* **-bus·es**) an early type of portable gun, supported on a tripod by a hook or on a forked rest. **har·que·bus·ier** (hahr-kwĕ-bŭ-seer) *n.*

har·ri·dan (har-i-dăn) *n.* a bad-tempered old woman.

har·ri·er[1] (har-i-ĕr) *n.* 1. a hound used for hunting hares. 2. a cross-country runner.

harrier[2] *n.* 1. a person or thing that harries. 2. a kind of falcon.

Har·ris·burg (har-ĭs-burg) the capital of Pennsylvania.

Har·ri·son (har-ĭ-sŏn), **Ben·ja·min** (1833–1901) the twenty-third president of the U.S. 1889–93. **Harrison, Wil·liam Hen·ry** (1773–1841) the ninth president of the U.S. 1841.

har·row (har-oh) *n.* a heavy frame with metal spikes or disks for breaking up clods, covering seeds, etc. **harrow** *v.* 1. to draw a harrow over (land). 2. to distress greatly.

har·row·ing (har-oh-ing) *adj.* distressing, tormenting, *a harrowing night in the emergency room.*

har·ry (har-ee) *v.* (**har·ried, har·ry·ing**) to harass.

harsh (hahrsh) *adj.* 1. rough and disagreeable, especially to the senses, *a harsh texture or voice.* 2. severe, cruel, *harsh treatment.* **harsh'ly** *adv.* **harsh'ness** *n.*

hart (hahrt) *n.* an adult male deer.

Hart·ford (hahrt-fŏrd) the capital of Connecticut.

harts·horn (hahrts-horn) *n.* a substance from horns of hart, formerly a chief source of ammonia.

har·um-scar·um (hair-ŭm-skair-ŭm) *adj. (informal)* wild and reckless. **harum-scarum** *n. (informal)* a wild and reckless person. **harum-scarum** *adv. (informal)* in a harum-scarum way.

har·vest (hahr-vist) *n.* 1. the gathering of a crop or crops, the season when this is done. 2. the season's yield of any natural product. 3. the product of any action. **harvest** *v.* to gather a crop, to reap. □**harvest moon,** the full moon nearest to the autumnal equinox (September 22 or 23).

har·ves·ter (hahr-vi-stĕr) *n.* 1. a person who gathers a crop. 2. a machine that gathers a crop.

has (haz) *see* have.

has-been (haz-bin) *n.* (*pl.* **has-beens**) *(informal)* a person or thing that is no longer as famous or successful as formerly.

ha·sen·pfef·fer (hah-sĕn-fef-ĕr) *n.* a stew of marinated rabbit meat.

hash[1] (hash) *n.* 1. a dish of cooked or preserved meat cut into small pieces and recooked. 2. a jumble, a mixture. **hash** *v.* to make (meat) into a hash. □**hash mark,** (in football) a mark between a sideline and the center of the field showing where the ball may be put into play; *(informal)* a service stripe on the uniform of an enlisted person in the armed services. **hash over,** *(informal)* to bring up again for discussion, especially when there is little hope of progress or resolution. **make**

a hash of, *(slang)* to make a mess of, to bungle.
settle a person's hash, *(informal)* to make an end of or subdue him.

hash[2] *n. (slang)* hashish.

hash·ish (hash-eesh) *n.* the top leaves and tender parts of hemp, dried for chewing or smoking as a narcotic.

has·n't (haz-ěnt) = has not.

hasp (hasp) *n.* a hinged metal strip with a slit in it that fits over a U-shaped staple through which a pin or padlock is then passed.

has·sle (has-ěl) *n. (informal)* a quarrel or struggle. **hassle** *v.* (**has·sled, has·sling**) *(informal)* 1. to quarrel. 2. to harass.

has·sock (has-ŏk) *n.* 1. a footstool or cushion for resting one's legs. 2. a cushion for kneeling (as in prayer).

hast (hast) *v. (old use)* the past tense of **have,** used with *thou.*

haste (hayst) *n.* urgency of movement or action, hurry. □**in haste,** quickly, hurriedly. **make haste,** to act quickly.

has·ten (hay-sěn) *v.* 1. to hurry. 2. to cause (a thing) to be done earlier or to happen earlier.

hast·y (hay-stee) *adj.* (**hast·i·er, hast·i·est**) 1. hurried, acting too quickly. 2. said or made or done too quickly. **hast'i·ly** *adv.* **hast'i·ness** *n.*

hat (hat) *n.* 1. a covering for the head, worn out of doors. 2. *(informal)* this thought of as symbolizing a person's position or job; *wear two hats,* to have two positions or jobs. □**keep it under your hat,** keep it secret. **pass the hat,** to collect contributions of money. **talk through one's hat,** to talk with scanty or incomplete knowledge of one's subject matter. **toss** *or* **throw one's hat into the ring,** to indicate one's intention of seeking election to office, promotion in employment, etc.

hat·band (hat-band) *n.* a band of ribbon etc. around a hat just above the brim.

hat·box (hat-boks) *n.* a round container for the storage or transportation of a hat.

hatch[1] (hach) *n.* 1. an opening in a door or floor or ceiling, an opening in a ship's deck. 2. a movable cover over any of these.

hatch[2] *v.* 1. (of a young bird or fish etc.) to emerge from an egg, (of an egg) to produce a young animal. 2. to cause (eggs) to produce young by incubating them. 3. to devise (a plot). **hatch** *n.* hatching, a hatched brood.

hatch[3] *v.* to mark with close parallel lines.

hatch·back (hach-bak) *n.* a car with a sloping back hinged at the top so that it can be opened, the back itself.

hatch·er·y (hach-ě-ree) *n.* (*pl.* **-er·ies**) a place for hatching eggs, especially of fish, *a trout hatchery.*

hatch·et (hach-it) *n.* a light short-handled ax. □**hatchet face,** a long sharp-featured face. **hatchet job,** *(informal)* a malicious verbal attack. **hatchet man,** *(informal)* one who commits murder for pay; a person employed to make unpopular decisions or to coerce, threaten, etc.

hatch·ing (hach-ing) *n.* the drawing or engraving of closely spaced parallel lines to produce shading.

hatch·way (hach-way) *n.* a hatch, or the passageway leading to or from the hatch.

hate (hayt) *v.* (**hat·ed, hat·ing**) 1. to dislike intensely, detest, be hostile to. 2. to be reluctant, *I hate to interrupt you.* **hate** *n.* 1. the feeling of

intense dislike or hostility. 2. *(informal)* the thing hated. **hat'er** *n.* □**hate letter,** a communication, frequently anonymous, expressing the sender's hostility toward the recipient.

hate·ful (hayt-fŭl) *adj.* arousing hatred. **hate'ful·ly** *adv.* **hate'ful·ness** *n.*

hat·ful (hat-fuul) *n.* (*pl.* **-fuls**) the amount a hat will hold.

hath (hath) *v. (old use)* has, *music hath charms to soothe the savage breast.*

hat·less (hat-lis) *adj.* not wearing a hat.

ha·tred (hay-trid) *n.* 1. the state of hating someone or something. 2. hate.

hat·ter (hat-ěr) *n.* a person whose trade is making, selling, or repairing hats.

haugh·ty (haw-tee) *adj.* (**-ti·er, -ti·est**) proud of oneself and looking down on other people. **haugh'ti·ly** *adv.* **haugh'ti·ness** *n.*

haul (hawl) *v.* 1. to pull or drag forcibly. 2. to carry by a truck etc. **haul** *n.* 1. hauling. 2. the amount gained as a result of effort, booty, *made a good haul.* 3. a distance to be traversed, *it's only a short haul from here.* **haul'er** *n.* □**over the long haul,** in the long run, considering the long term.

haul·age (haw-lij) *n.* the transport of goods, the charge for this.

haunch (hawnch) *n.* 1. the fleshy part of the buttock and thigh. 2. the leg and loin of deer etc. as food.

haunt (hawnt) *v.* 1. (of ghosts) to be frequently in (a place) with manifestations of their presence and influence. 2. to be persistently in (a place). 3. to linger in the mind of, *the memory haunts me.* **haunt** *n.* a place often visited by the person(s) named, *the inn is a favorite haunt of fishermen.* **haunt'er** *n.* **haunt'ing·ly** *adv.*

haunt·ed (hawn-tid) *adj.* frequented by a ghost or ghosts.

haut·boy, haut·bois (oh-boi) *n.* (*pl.* **-boys, -bois,** *pr.* -boiz) *(old use)* oboe.

haute cou·ture (oht koo-toor) high fashion, including the manufacturers and the products. ▷French.

haute cui·sine (oht kwee-zeen) elaborate (traditional French) cooking. ▷French.

haut·eur (oh-tur) *n.* haughtiness of manner.

Ha·van·a (hă-van-ă) the capital of Cuba. □**Havana (cigar),** a cigar made from Cuban tobacco or one resembling such a cigar,

have (hav) *v.* (**had, hav·ing**) 1. to be in possession of (a thing or quality), to possess in a certain relationship, *he has many enemies.* 2. to contain, *the house has six rooms.* 3. to experience, to undergo, *had a shock.* 4. to give birth to. 5. to put into a certain condition, *you had me worried; you have me there,* have we defeated or at a disadvantage. 6. *(slang)* to cheat or deceive, *we've been had.* 7. to have sexual intercourse with. 8. to engage in, to carry on, *had a talk with him; had breakfast,* ate it. 9. to allow, to tolerate, *won't have him bullied.* 10. to be under the obligation of, *we have to go now.* 11. to let (a feeling etc.) be present in the mind, *have no doubt.* 12. to show a quality, *have mercy on us.* 13. to receive, to accept, *we have news of her; will you have a cigarette?* 14. to cause a thing to be done, *have one's hair cut; have three copies made.* **have** auxiliary verb, used to form past tenses of verbs, *he has gone; we had expected it.* □**had better,** would find it wiser. **have at,** to attack. **have done with,** to be finished with. **have had it,**

(slang) to be unable or unwilling to tolerate more; to be near death, no longer usable, etc. **have it,** to have a sudden inspiration about a problem etc., *I have it!;* to win a decision in a vote, *the ayes have it.* **have it coming,** *(informal)* to deserve one's punishment or bad luck. **have it in for,** *(informal)* to show ill will toward (a person). **have it out,** to settle a problem by frank discussion. **have on,** to wear. **have over,** to invite someone to visit. **haves and have-nots,** rich and poor (people or nations). **have to do with,** to be connected with. **let someone have it,** to scold or punish.

ha·ven (hay-věn) *n.* a refuge.

have·n't (hav-ěnt) = have not.

ha·ver·sack (hav-ěr-sak) *n.* a strong bag carried on the back or over the shoulder.

hav·oc (hav-ŏk) *n.* widespread destruction, great disorder. □**cry havoc,** to alert to danger or disaster. **play havoc with,** to create havoc in.

haw¹ (haw) *n.* a hawthorn berry.

haw² *see* **hem².**

Ha·wai·i (hă-wɪ-ee) a state of the U.S. **Ha·wai′ ian** *adj. & n.*

hawk¹ (hawk) *n.* 1. a bird of prey. 2. a person who favors an aggressive policy.

hawk² *v.* to clear the throat noisily.

hawk³ *v.* to carry (goods) about for sale in the streets. **hawk′er** *n.*

hawk-eyed (hawk-ɪd) *adj.* keen-sighted.

hawk·ish (haw-kish) *adj.* favoring an aggressive policy.

haw·ser (haw-zěr) *n.* a heavy rope or cable for mooring or towing a ship.

haw·thorn (haw-thorn) *n.* a thorny tree or shrub with small red berries.

hay (hay) *n.* grass, clover, etc. mown and dried for fodder. **hay** *v.* to cut and dry and store (grass etc.) for use as fodder. □**hay fever,** an acute allergy to the pollen of certain plants, causing inflammation of mucous membranes of the eyes and nose. **hit the hay,** *(slang)* to go to bed. **make hay while the sun shines,** to seize opportunities before they disappear.

Hayes (hayz), **Ru·ther·ford B.** (1822–93) the nineteenth president of the U.S. 1877–81.

hay·fork (hay-fork) *n.* 1. a pitchfork. 2. a machine that turns over or loads hay.

hay·loft (hay-lawft) *n.* a part of a barn or a stable where hay is stored.

hay·mak·er (hay-may-kěr) *n.* *(informal)* a knock-out punch in a fight.

hay·mow (hay-mow) *n.* 1. hay stored in a barn. 2. the part of the barn in which it is stored.

hay·seed (hay-seed) *n.* 1. grass seed gleaned from hay. 2. *(slang)* a country bumpkin.

hay·stack (hay-stak) *n.* a regularly shaped pile of hay firmly packed for storing, with a pointed or ridged top.

hay·wire (hay-wɪr) *n.* *(informal)* badly disorganized, out of control.

haz·ard (haz-ărd) *n.* 1. risk, danger, a source of this. 2. an obstacle (such as a pond or bunker etc.) on a golf course. **hazard** *v.* to risk; *hazard a guess,* venture to make one.

haz·ard·ous (haz-ăr-důs) *adj.* risky. **haz′ard· ous·ly** *adv.*

haze¹ (hayz) *n.* 1. thin mist. 2. mental confusion or obscurity.

haze² *v.* (hazed, haz·ing) to harass and subject

to humiliation (college freshmen, fraternity initiates, etc.).

ha·zel (hay-zěl) *n.* 1. a bush with small edible nuts (hazel nuts). 2. a light brownish color.

ha·zy (hay-zee) *adj.* (-zi·er, -zi·est) 1. misty. 2. vague, indistinct. 3. feeling confused or uncertain. **ha′zi·ly** *adv.* **ha′zi·ness** *n.*

Hb *symbol* hemoglobin.

H-bomb (aych-bom) *n.* a hydrogen bomb.

hd. *abbr.* 1. hand. 2. head.

hdbk. *abbr.* handbook.

hdqrs. *abbr.* headquarters.

hdw., hdwe. *abbr.* hardware.

he (hee) *pronoun* 1. the male person or animal mentioned. 2. a person of unspecified sex, *he who hesitates is lost.* **he** *n.* a male animal; *a he-goat,* a male goat.

He *symbol* helium.

HE *abbr.* high explosive.

H.E. *abbr.* 1. high explosive. 2. His (or Her) Excellency. 3. His Eminence.

head (hed) *n.* 1. the part of the body containing the eyes, nose, mouth, and brain. 2. this as a measure of length, *the horse won by a head.* 3. the intellect, the imagination, the mind, *use your head.* 4. a mental ability or faculty, *has a good head for figures.* 5. an image or picture of a person's head; *heads,* the side of a coin on which a person's head appears. 6. a person, an individual person or animal, *crowned heads; it costs ten dollars a head.* 7. *(informal)* a headache, *did I have a head this morning!* 8. a number of animals, *twenty head of cattle.* 9. a thing like a head in form or position, such as the rounded end of a pin, the cutting or striking part of a tool etc., a rounded mass of leaves or petals etc. at the top of a stem, the flat surface of a barrel. 10. foam on top of beer etc. 11. the top of something long (such as a stair or mast) or of a list. 12. the top part of a boil or blister where it tends to break. 13. the upper end or part of a table (where the host sits) or lake (where a river enters) or bed (where a person's head rests) etc. 14. a body of water kept at a height (to work a water mill etc.), a confined body of steam for exerting pressure. 15. the leading part in a procession or army; *at the head,* in a position of command. 16. (in place names) a promontory, *Hilton Head.* 17. the chief person of a group or organization etc. 18. a headline. **head** *v.* 1. to be at the head or top of. 2. to strike (a ball) with one's head in soccer. 3. to move in a certain direction, *we headed south; heading for disaster.* **head** *adj.* 1. chief, leading, *he is the head spokesman for the cause.* 2. placed at the head or front. 3. coming or moving from the front, *head winds.* □**come to a head,** reach a crisis. **give him his head,** let him move or act freely. **go to a person's head,** (of alcohol) to make dizzy or slightly drunk; (of success) to make conceited. **head and shoulders (above),** clearly superior (to). **head cold,** a common cold generally characterized by nasal congestion. **head off,** to force to turn back or aside by getting in front of, *they headed him off at the pass.* **head over heels,** turning one's body upside down in a circular movement; very much, *he is head over heels in love with her.* **head start,** an advantage in a competition etc., *the child's early training gave him a head start in life.* **heads up,** quick to take advantage of opportunities; *heads up!,* be alert! **heads will roll,** some people will be punished or dismissed. **head wind,** a wind blowing from directly in front. **in one's head,** in one's mind, not written down. **keep one's head,** to remain calm in a crisis. **laugh one's head off,** to laugh uncontrollably. **lose one's head,** to act foolishly. **make heads or tails of,** to be able to understand. **out of one's head,** *(informal)* a usually temporary state of delirium or hysteria. **over one's head,** (of another's promotion etc.) when one has a prior or stronger claim; (of a book, speech, etc.) past one's ability to understand. **put heads together,** to pool ideas. **turn a person's head,** to make him vain.

head·ache (hed-ayk) *n.* 1. a pain in the head. 2. a problem causing worry.

head·band (hed-band) *n.* a band, usually ornamental, worn around the head.

head·board (hed-bohrd) *n.* an upright panel along the head of a bed.

head·cheese (hed-cheez) *n.* a seasoned loaf having as its base the head meat of a pig or calf.

head·dress (hed-dres) *n.* an ornamental covering or band worn on the head.

head·ed (hed-id) *adj.* 1. formed or grown into a head. 2. having a heading or head.

head·first (hed-furst) *adv.* 1. with the head in front of the rest of the body. 2. hastily, precipitately.

head·gear (hed-geer) *n.* a hat or cap.

head·hunt·er (hed-hun-tĕr) *n.* 1. a primitive tribesman who collects the heads of his enemies as trophies. 2. *(slang)* an employment agent or agency specializing in placement of managers and other skilled personnel. **head'hunt'ing** *n.*

head·ing (hed-ing) *n.* 1. a word or words put at the top of a section of printed or written matter as a title etc. 2. the compass direction in which a ship, aircraft, etc. is pointing or moving.

head·land (hed-land) *n.* a promontory.

head·less (hed-lis) *adj.* having no head.

head·light (hed-lıt) *n.* 1. a powerful light mounted on the front of a motor vehicle or railroad engine. 2. the beam from this.

head·line (hed-lın) *n.* a heading in a newspaper, especially the largest one at the top of the front page; *the news headlines,* a brief broadcast summary of news.

head·lock (hed-lok) *n.* a wrestling hold in which a contestant tightens his arm around an opponent's head.

head·long (hed-lawng) *adj.·& adv.* 1. falling or plunging with the head first. 2. in a hasty and rash way.

head·man (hed-man) *n.* (*pl.* **-men,** *pr.* -men) the highest ranking man in a tribe or *(informal)* business organization.

head·mas·ter (hed-mas-tĕr), **head·mis·tress** (hed-mis-tris) *n.* the director of a private school.

head·on (hed-on) *adj. & adv.* 1. with the head pointed directly toward something. 2. colliding head to head.

head·phone (hed-fohn) *n.* a radio or telephone receiver held over the ear(s) by a band fitting over the head.

head·piece (hed-pees) *n.* 1. a covering for the head. 2. an ornament at the beginning of the chapter of a book.

head·pin (hed-pin) *n.* the pin nearest the bowler as he faces the bowling alley, the number one pin.

head·quar·ters (hed-kwor-tĕrz) *n. pl.* the place from which a military or other organization is controlled. ▷This word can also be treated as singular.

head·rest (hed-rest) *n.* a head support, especially in motor vehicles.

head·room (hed-room) *n.* clearance above the head of a person or the top of a vehicle etc.

head·sail (hed-sayl) *n.* a sail set on or forward of the foremost mast of a vessel.

head·set (hed-set) *n.* a pair of earphones linked by a band that fits over the user's head.

head·stall (hed-stawl) *n.* the part of a bridle or halter that fits around the horse's head.

head·stand (hed-stand) *n.* the act of standing on one's head.

head·stone (hed-stohn) *n.* a stone set up at the head of a grave.

head·strong (hed-strong) *adj.* self-willed and obstinate.

head·wait·er (hed-way-tĕr) *n.* a supervisor of other waiters in a restaurant, often responsible for reservations.

head·wa·ters (hed-waw-tĕrz) *n. pl.* streams from the sources of a river.

head·way (hed-way) *n.* 1. progress, the rate of progress of a ship. 2. headroom. 3. the interval between successive buses etc. on a route.

head·word (hed-wurd) *n.* a word forming a heading, especially of a dictionary entry.

head·work (hed-wurk) *n.* mental work, conscious thinking.

head·y (hed-ee) *adj.* (**head·i·er, head·i·est**) 1. (of a person, thing, or action) impetuous, violent. 2. (of liquor or triumph etc.) apt to intoxicate. **head'i·ly** *adv.* **head'i·ness** *n.*

heal (heel) *v.* 1. (of sore or wounded parts) to form healthy flesh again, to unite after being cut or broken. 2. to cause to do this. 3. *(old use)* to cure, *healing the sick.* **heal'er** *n.*

health (helth) *n.* 1. the state of being well and free from illness, *was restored to health.* 2. the condition of the body, *ill health.* ☐**health foods,** foods thought to have health-giving qualities; natural unprocessed foods.

health·ful (helth-fŭl) *adj.* producing good health, beneficial. **health'ful·ly** *adv.* **health'ful·ness** *n.*

health·y (hel-thee) *adj.* (**health·i·er, health·i·est**) 1. having or showing or producing good health. 2. beneficial. 3. (of things) functioning well. **health'i·ly** *adv.* **health'i·ness** *n.*

heap (heep) *n.* 1. a number of things or mass of grains etc. lying on one another. 2. *heaps, (informal)* a great amount, plenty, *there's heaps of time.* 3. *(slang)* a car in poor condition. **heap** *v.* 1. to pile or become piled in a heap. 2. to load with large quantities, to give large quantities of, *heaped the plate with food; they heaped insults on him.*

hear (heer) *v.* (**heard, hear·ing**) 1. to perceive (sounds) with the ear. 2. to listen or pay attention to. 3. to listen to and try (a case) in a law court. 4. to receive information or a message or letter etc. **hear'er** *n.* ☐**hear a person out,** to listen to the whole of what he has to say. **hear of,** to have knowledge or information about, *we've never heard of this firm.* **will not hear of,** to refuse to allow, *won't hear of my paying for it.*

heard (hurd) *see* **hear.**

hear·ing (heer-ing) *n.* 1. the ability to hear; *within* *hearing distance,* near enough to be heard; *in my hearing,* in my presence, where I can hear. 2. an opportunity of being heard; a session before a judge prior to trial, *got a fair hearing.* ☐**hearing aid,** a small sound-amplifier worn by a deaf person to improve the hearing.

hark·en (hahr-kĕn) *v. (old use)* to listen.

hear·say (heer-say) *n.* things heard in rumors or gossip.

hearse (hurs) *n.* a vehicle for carrying the coffin at a funeral.

heart (hahrt) *n.* 1. the hollow muscular organ that keeps blood circulating in the body by contracting rhythmically. 2. the part of the body where this is, the bosom. 3. the center of a person's emotions or affections or inmost thoughts, *knew it in her heart.* 4. the ability to feel emotion, *a tender heart.* 5. courage, *take heart.* 6. enthusiasm, *his heart isn't in it.* 7. a beloved person, *dear heart.* 8. the innermost part of a thing, the close compact head of celery etc.; *the heart of the matter,* the vital part of it. 9. a symmetrical figure conventionally representing a heart. 10. a red figure shaped like this on playing cards, a playing card of the suit *(hearts)* marked with these. **heart'ed** *adj.* ☐**after one's own heart,** exactly to one's liking. **at heart,** basically. **by heart,** memorized thoroughly. **change of heart,** a change of feeling toward something. **have a heart!,** *(informal)* be considerate or sympathetic. **have the heart to,** to be hard-hearted enough to (do something). **heart attack** *or* **heart failure,** sudden failure of the heart to function normally. **heart-lung machine,** a pumping machine that enables these organs to be bypassed during a surgical operation by taking over their functions in blood circulation. **his heart is in the right place,** he has kindly intentions. **his heart was in his mouth,** he was violently alarmed. **set one's heart on,** to desire eagerly. **take to heart,** to be deeply troubled by; to consider seriously. **to one's heart's content,** as much as one wishes. **wear one's heart on one's sleeve,** to let one's feelings and emotions be obvious. **with all one's heart,** sincerely, with the greatest goodwill.

heart·ache (hahrt-ayk) *n.* mental pain, deep sorrow.

heart·beat (hahrt-beet) *n.* the beating of the heart.

heart·break (hahrt-brayk) *n.* overwhelming unhappiness. **heart'break·ing** *adj.* **heart'bro·ken** *adj.*

heart·burn (hahrt-burn) *n.* a burning sensation in the lower part of the chest.

heart·en (hahr-tĕn) *v.* to make (a person) feel encouraged.

heart·felt (hahrt-felt) *adj.* felt deeply or earnestly.

hearth (hahrth) *n.* 1. the floor of a fireplace, the area in front of this. 2. the fireside as the symbol of domestic comfort, *hearth and home.*

hearth·rug (hahrth-rug) *n.* a rug laid in front of a fireplace.

hearth·side (hahrth-sɪd) *n.* 1. the space around a fireplace. 2. a person's home.

hearth·stone (hahrth-stohn) *n.* 1. a flat stone forming a hearth. 2. a person's home.

heart·i·ly (hahr-ti-lee) *adv.* 1. in a hearty way. 2. very, *heartily sick of it.*

heart·land (hahrt-land) *n.* the central or most important part of an area.

heart·less (hahrt-lis) *adj.* not feeling pity or sympathy. **heart'less·ly** *adv.* **heart'less·ness** *n.*

heart·rend·ing (hahrt-ren-ding) *adj.* extremely distressing.

heart·sick (hahrt-sik) *adj.* extremely unhappy. **heart'sick·ness** *n.*

heart·strings (hahrt-stringz) *n. pl.* one's deepest feelings of love or pity.

heart·throb (hahrt-throb) *n.* 1. the beating of the heart. 2. *(slang)* the object of one's infatuation.

heart-to-heart (hahrt-tŏ-hahrt) *adj.* & *adv.* frank and personal, *a heart-to-heart talk; spoke heart-to-heart.*

heart·warm·ing (hahrt-wor-ming) *adj.* emotionally moving and encouraging.

heart·wood (hahrt-wuud) *n.* the dense inner part of a tree trunk, yielding the hardest timber.

heart·y (hahr-tee) *adj.* **(heart·i·er, heart·i·est)** 1. showing warmth of feeling, enthusiastic. 2. vigorous, strong, hale and hearty. 3. (of meals or appetites) large. **hearty** *n.* (*pl.* **heart·ies**) *(old use)* a hearty person. **heart'i·ness** *n.*

heat (heet) *n.* 1. a form of energy produced by movement of molecules, capable of transmission by conduction or convection or radiation. 2. the sensation produced by this, hotness. 3. hot weather. 4. a condition of sexual excitement and readiness for mating in female animals, *be in heat.* 5. an intense feeling, especially of anger; *take the heat out of a situation,* to reduce the anger or tension. 6. one of the preliminary contests of which winners take part in further contests or the final. 7. *(slang)* intense pressure, as of work, a police search, etc. **heat** *v.* to make or become hot or warm. **heat'less** *adj.* ☐**heat engine,** a machine producing motive power from heat. **heat exhaustion,** a state of physical exhaustion marked by dizziness, weakness, nausea, and sweating, resulting from excessive activity in a hot environment. **heat lightning,** lightning without audible thunder, seen close to the horizon on hot summer evenings. **heat pump,** a reversed heat engine using mechanical energy to transfer heat to a hotter place. **heat shield,** a device to protect from excessive heat, especially on spacecraft during reentry into Earth's atmosphere. **heat wave,** a period of very hot weather.

heat·ed (hee-tid) *adj.* (of a person or discussion) angry. **heat'ed·ly** *adv.*

heat·er (hee-tĕr) *n.* a stove or other device supplying heat.

heath (heeth) *n.* 1. *(British)* an area of flat uncultivated land with low shrubs. 2. a small shrubby plant of the heather kind.

hea·then (hee-thĕn) *n.* (*pl.* -thens, -then) 1. a person who is not a believer in any of the world's chief religions, especially one who is neither Christian, Jew, nor Muslim. 2. an unenlightened person, one regarded as lacking culture or moral principles. **hea'then·ish** *adj.* **hea'then·ism** *n.* **hea'then·dom** *n.*

heath·er (heth-ĕr) *n.* an evergreen plant or shrub with small purple or pinkish or white bell-shaped flowers.

heat·stroke (heet-strohk) *n.* a severe illness caused by too much exposure to heat.

heave (heev) *v.* **(heaved, heav·ing)** 1. to lift or haul (something heavy) with great effort. 2. to utter with effort, *heaved a sigh.* 3. *(informal)* to throw, *heave a brick at him.* 4. to rise and fall regularly like waves at sea. 5. to pant, to retch. **heave** *n.* 1. the act of heaving. 2. *heaves,* a disease of horses with labored breathing, *(slang)* an attack of vomiting. **heav′er** *n.* □**heave in sight,** (past tense **hove**) to come into view. **heave to,** (past tense **hove**) to bring (a ship) or come to a standstill with the ship's head to the wind.

heav·en (hev-ĕn) *n.* 1. the abode of God and of the righteous after death. 2. *Heaven,* God, Providence, the state of the soul's union with God. 3. a place or state of supreme bliss, something delightful. □**the heavens,** the sky as seen from Earth, in which the sun, moon, and stars appear.

heav·en·ly (hev-ĕn-lee) *adj.* 1. of heaven, divine. 2. of the heavens or sky; *heavenly bodies,* the sun and stars etc. 3. *(informal)* very pleasing.

heav·en-sent (hev-ĕn-sent) *adj.* providential, fortunate.

heav·en·ward (hev-ĕn-wărd) *adj. & adv.* toward heaven, *he sent his prayers heavenward.*

heav·y (hev-ee) *adj.* (**heav·i·er, heav·i·est**) 1. having great weight, difficult to lift or carry or move. 2. of more than average weight or amount or force, *heavy artillery; heavy rain.* 3. (of work) needing much physical effort. 4. severe, intense, *a heavy drinker; heavy drinking,* drinking much alcohol; *a heavy sleeper,* not easily awakened. 5. dense, *a heavy mist; heavy bread,* doughy from not having risen. 6. (of ground) clinging, difficult to travel over. 7. (of food) difficult to digest. 8. (of the sky) gloomy and full of clouds. 9. clumsy or ungraceful in appearance or effect or movement. 10. unhappy, *with a heavy heart.* 11. dull and tedious, serious in tone. 12. stern, *the heavy father.* **heavy** *n.* (*pl.* **heav·ies**) *(informal)* the villain in a play, story, etc. **heav′i·ly** *adv.* **heav′i·ness** *n.* □**heavy going,** progress made only with difficulty. **heavy industry,** industry producing metal, machines, etc. **heavy water,** deuterium oxide, a substance with the same chemical properties as water but greater density. **heavy with child,** in an advanced stage of pregnancy.

heav·y-du·ty (hev-ee-doo-tee) *adj.* intended to withstand hard use.

heav·y-hand·ed (hev-ee-han-did) *adj.* clumsy.

heav·y-heart·ed (hev-ee-hahr-tid) *adj.* sad.

heav·y·set (hev-ee-set) *adj.* having a solid and sturdy body.

heav·y·weight (hev-ee-wayt) *n.* 1. a person of more than average weight. 2. a boxer of the heaviest weight class in boxing, weighing over 175 pounds. 3. *(informal)* a person of great influence. **heavyweight** *adj.* having great weight or influence.

Heb. *abbr.* 1. Hebrew. 2. Hebrews.

He·bra·ism (hee-bray-iz-ĕm) *n.* 1. the Hebrew character or culture. 2. the Hebrew system of thought or religion. 3. a Hebrew idiom or expression, especially in the Greek of the Bible. **He′bra·ist** *n.* **He·bra·ic** (hi-bray-ik) *adj.*

He·brew (hee-broo) *n.* 1. a member of a Semitic people in ancient Palestine. 2. their language, a modern form of this used in Israel. 3. *Hebrews,* a book of the New Testament traditionally included among the letters of St. Paul but now usually held to be of other authorship. **Hebrew** *adj.* 1. of or in Hebrew. 2. of the Hebrews or the Jews.

heck (hek) *n.* *(informal,* in oaths) hell.

heck·le (hek-ĕl) *v.* (**heck·led, heck·ling**) to interrupt and harass (a public speaker) with aggressive questions and abuse. **heck′ler** *n.*

hec·tare (hek-tair) *n.* a unit of area, 10,000 square meters (2.471 acres).

hec·tic (hek-tik) *adj.* with feverish activity, *a hectic day.* **hec′ti·cal·ly** *adv.*

hec·to·gram (hek-tŏ-gram) *n.* one hundred grams (3.53 ounces).

hec·to·li·ter (hek-tŏ-lee-tĕr) *n.* one hundred liters (3.53 cubic feet; 2.84 bushels).

hec·to·me·ter (hek-tŏ-lee-tĕr) *n.* one hundred meters (109.36 yards).

hec·tor (hek-tŏr) *v.* to intimidate by bullying.

he'd (heed) = he had, he would.

hedge (hej) *n.* 1. a fence of closely planted bushes or shrubs. 2. a means of protecting oneself against possible loss, *bought diamonds as a hedge against inflation.* **hedge** *v.* (**hedged, hedg·ing**) 1. to surround or bound with a hedge. 2. to reduce the possible loss on (a bet) by another speculation. 3. to avoid giving a direct answer or commitment. **hedg′er** *n.* □**hedge sparrow,** a common European bird resembling a thrush.

hedge·hog (hej-hog) *n.* 1. a small European insect-eating animal with a piglike snout and a back covered with stiff spines, able to roll itself up into a prickly ball when attacked. 2. the porcupine.

hedge·hop (hej-hop) *v.* (**hedge·hopped, hedge·hop·ping**) to fly an airplane at an extremely low altitude following the contours of the land.

hedge·row (hej-roh) *n.* a row of bushes etc. forming a hedge.

he·do·nist (hee-dŏ-nist) *n.* a person who believes that pleasure is the chief good in life. **he′do·nism** *n.* **he·do·nis·tic** (hee-dŏ-nis-tik) *adj.*

hee·bie-jee·bies (hee-bee-jee-beez) *n. pl. (slang)* nervous anxiety or depression.

heed (heed) *v.* to pay attention to. **heed** *n.* careful attention, *take heed.* **heed′ful** *adj.* **heed′ful·ly** *adv.* **heed′ful·ness** *n.*

heed·less (heed-lis) *adj.* not taking heed. **heed′less·ly** *adv.* **heed′less·ness** *n.*

hee·haw (hee-haw) *n.* a donkey's bray. **hee·haw** *v.* to bray like a donkey.

heel[1] (heel) *n.* 1. the rounded back part of the human foot. 2. the part of a stocking etc. covering this. 3. a built-up part of a boot or shoe that supports a person's heel. 4. something like a heel in shape or position; *the heel of the hand,* the front part next to the wrist. 5. *(slang)* a dishonorable man. **heel** *v.* to repair the heels of (shoes etc.). □**at** *or* **on the heels of,** following closely after. **down at the heel,** (of a shoe) with the heel worn down by wear; (of a person) shabby. **take to one's heels,** to run away.

heel[2] *v.* to tilt (a ship) or become tilted to one side, *heeled over.*

heel·less (heel-lis) *adj.* (of shoes) with no built-up part under the heel.

heft (heft) *n.* weight. **heft** *v.* to lift, especially to judge weight.

heft·y (hef-tee) *adj.* (**heft·i·er, heft·i·est**) 1. (of a person) big and strong. 2. (of a thing) large and heavy, powerful.

he·gem·o·ny (hi-jem-ŏ-nee) *n.* (*pl.* **-nies**) dominance of leadership, especially by one nation over others.

He·gi·ra (hi-jɪ-ră, hej-ĕr-ă) *n.* 1. the flight of Muhammad from Mecca (A.D. 622), from which the Muslim era is reckoned. 2. *hegira,* a journey taken to escape danger.

heif·er (hef-ĕr) *n.* a young cow, especially one that has not given birth to a calf.

height (hīt) *n.* 1. measurement from base to top, the measurement of a person etc. from head to foot as he stands. 2. the distance (of an object or position) above ground or sea level. 3. a high place or area, *is afraid of heights.* 4. the highest degree of something, *dressed in the height of fashion; the height of the tourist season,* its most active time.

height·en (hī-těn) *v.* to make or become higher or more intense.

Heim·lich (hīm-lik) **maneuver** a first aid procedure in which the abdomen of a choking victim is pressed inward and upward by hand in order to assist in dislodging food or other obstruction from the esophagus. ▷Named after Dr. Henry J. Heimlich (1920–).

hei·nous (hay-nŭs) *adj.* very wicked, outrageous. **hei′nous·ly** *adv.* **hei′nous·ness** *n.*

heir (air) *n.* a person who inherits property or rank etc. from its former owner. □**heir apparent,** the legal heir (especially of a title or throne) whose claim cannot be set aside by the birth of a person with a stronger claim to inherit. **heir presumptive,** an heir whose claim may be set aside in this way.

heir·ess (air-is) *n.* a female heir, especially to great wealth.

heir·loom (air-loom) *n.* a possession that has been handed down in a family for several generations.

heist (hīst) *n. (slang)* a burglary or robbery.

held (held) *see* **hold¹**.

Hel·e·na (hel-ě-nă) the capital of Montana.

hel·i·cal (hel-ī-kăl) *adj.* like a helix.

hel·i·coid (hel-ī-koid), **hel·i·coid·al** (hel-i-koi-dăl) *adj.* arranged in or forming a spiral.

hel·i·cop·ter (hel-i-kop-těr) *n.* a kind of aircraft with horizontal revolving blades or rotors.

he·li·o·cen·tric (hee-li-oh-sen-trik) *adj.* as viewed from the center of the sun, taking the sun as center.

he·li·o·graph (hee-li-ŏ-graf) *n.* a signaling device using a movable mirror to reflect the sun's rays in flashes.

he·li·o·trope (hee-li-ŏ-trohp) *n.* 1. a plant with small sweet-smelling purple flowers. 2. a light purple color.

hel·i·pad (hel-ī-pad) *n.* a heliport, usually one that is privately owned.

hel·i·port (hel-ī-pohrt) *n.* an airport for helicopters.

he·li·um (hee-li-ŭm) *n.* a light colorless gaseous element.

he·lix (hee-liks) *n. (pl.* **hel·i·ces,** *pr.* hel-ī-seez, **he·lix·es**) a spiral with a diminishing circumference (like a corkscrew) or a constant circumference (like a watch spring).

hell (hel) *n.* 1. the place of punishment for the wicked after death, the abode of devils. 2. a place or state of supreme misery, something extremely unpleasant. 3. *(informal)* used in oaths, exclamations, comparisons, etc. to express anger or intensify a meaning or indicate something extreme, *what the hell does he want?; ran like hell; for the hell of it,* for amusement and without considering the consequence. □**beat** *or* **knock hell out of,** *(informal)* to pound heavily. **catch** *or* **get hell,** *(slang)* to receive a strong reprimand. **come hell or high water,** no matter what the obstacles. **hellbent for leather,** at full speed. **hell of a,** *(slang)* a very good or very bad (condition or situation etc.), *one hell of a baseball game; that's*

a hell of a way to dress to go to your grandmother's house.

he'll (heel) = he will.

hell·bent (hel-bent) *adj.* recklessly determined.

hell·cat (hel-kat) *n. (slang)* a spiteful or furious woman.

hel·le·bore (hel-ě-bohr) *n.* a poisonous plant with white or greenish flowers.

Hel·lene (hel-een) *n.* a native of modern Greece.

Hel·len·ic (he-len-ik) *adj.* of ancient or modern Greece.

Hel·len·ism (hel-ě-niz-ěm) *n.* 1. a Greek idiom or grammatical construction. 2. the Greek character or culture, especially in ancient times. **Hel′len·ist** *n.*

Hel·len·is·tic (hel-ě-nis-tik) *adj.* of the Greek language and culture of the fourth to first centuries B.C.

hell·fire (hel-fīr) *n.* the fire of hell.

hell·gram·mite (hel-gră-mīt) *n.* the aquatic larva of an American fly, much used as bait, especially for bass.

hell·hole (hel-hohl) *n.* 1. a very dirty uncomfortable place. 2. a place known for immoral or illegal practices.

hel·lion (hel-yŏn) *n. (informal)* a mischievous or troublesome person, especially a child.

hell·ish (hel-ish) *adj.* very unpleasant.

hel·lo (he-loh) *interj.* an exclamation used in greeting or to call attention or express surprise, generally the first word used in answering the telephone. **hello** *n. (pl.* **-los**) this word used as a greeting, *he gave her a great big hello.*

helm (helm) *n.* the tiller or wheel by which a ship's rudder is controlled. □**at the helm,** at the head of an organization etc., in control.

hel·met (hel-mit) *n.* a protective head covering worn by a policeman, fireman, diver, motorcyclist, etc.

helms·man (helmz-măn) *n. (pl.* **-men,** *pr.* -měn) a person who steers a ship by means of its helm.

hel·ot (hel-ŏt) *n.* a member of the class of serfs in ancient Sparta.

help (help) *v.* 1. to do part of another person's work for him. 2. to make it easier for (a person) to do something or for (a thing) to happen. 3. to do something for the benefit of (someone in need). 4. to prevent, to remedy, *it can't be helped; I couldn't help it,* I was unable to avoid taking a certain action. **help** *n.* 1. the action of helping or being helped. 2. a person or thing that helps. 3. a person or people employed for household or other duties; *good help is hard to find,* reliable household or other types of workers are scarce. **help′er** *n.* □**help oneself,** to serve oneself with (food) at a meal; to take without seeking assistance or permission. **help out,** to give help (especially in a crisis).

help·ful (help-fŭl) *adj.* giving help, useful. **help′ful·ly** *adv.* **help′ful·ness** *n.*

help·ing (help-ping) *n.* a portion of food given to one person at a meal.

help·less (help-lis) *adj.* 1. unable to manage without help, dependent on others. 2. incapable of action, indicating this, *helpless with laughter; gave him a helpless glance.* **help′less·ly** *adv.* **help′less·ness** *n.*

help·mate (help-mayt) *n.* a helper, a companion or partner who helps.

Hel·sin·ki (hel-sing-kee) the capital of Finland.

hel·ter·skel·ter (hel-těr-skel-těr) *adv.* in disorderly haste. **helter-skelter** *adj.* disorderly, haphazard.

helve (helv) *n.* the handle of a tool or weapon.

Hel·ve·tian (hel-vee-shăn) *n.* a Swiss. **Helvetian** *adj.* of or relating to the Swiss.

hem[1] (hem) *n.* the border of cloth where the edge is turned under and sewn or fixed down. **hem** *v.* (**hemmed, hem·ming**) 1. to turn and sew a hem on. 2. to surround and restrict the movement of, *hemmed in by enemy forces.* **hem·mer** *n.*

hem[2] *interj.* calling attention or expressing hesitation by a slight cough or clearing of the throat. **hem** *n.* the utterance of this. **hem** *v.* (**hemmed, hem·ming**) to utter the sound "hem," to clear the throat, to hesitate in speech. ☐**hem and haw,** to speak hesitantly.

he-man (hee-man) *n.* (*pl.* **-men,** *pr.* **-men**) a masterful or robust man.

he·ma·tite (hee-mă-tɪt) *n.* iron oxide, the principal ore of iron.

he·ma·tol·o·gy (hee-mă-tol-ŏ-jee) *n.* the scientific study of the blood and blood-forming organs. **he·ma·tol'o·gist** *n.* **hem·a·to·log·ic** (hem-ă-tŏ-loj-ik) *adj.* **hem·a·to·log'i·cal** *adj.*

heme (heem) *n.* a red compound containing iron and forming the nonprotein part of hemoglobin.

hem·i·sphere (hem-i-sfeer) *n.* 1. half a sphere. 2. either of the halves into which Earth is divided either by the equator (the **Northern** and **Southern hemispheres**) or by a line passing through the poles (the **Eastern hemisphere,** including Europe, Asia, and Africa; the **Western hemisphere,** the Americas). **hem·i·spher·i·cal** (hem-i-sfer-i-kăl) *adj.*

hem·i·stich (hem-i-stik) *n.* half a line of verse.

hem·line (hem-lɪn) *n.* the lower edge of a skirt or dress.

hem·lock (hem-lok) *n.* a poisonous plant with small white flowers.

he·mo·glo·bin (hee-mŏ-gloh-bin) *n.* the red oxygen-carrying substance in the blood.

he·mo·phil·i·a (hee-mŏ-fil-i-ă) *n.* a tendency (usually inherited) to bleed severely from even a slight injury, through failure of the blood to clot quickly.

he·mo·phil·i·ac (hee-mŏ-fil-i-ak) *n.* a person suffering from hemophilia.

hem·or·rhage (hem-ŏ-rij) *n.* bleeding, especially when extensive. **hemorrhage** *v.* (**hem·or·rhaged, hem·or·rhag·ing**) to bleed extensively.

hem·or·rhoids (hem-ŏ-roidz) *n. pl.* varicose veins at or near the anus.

he·mo·stat (hee-mŏ-stat) *n.* a chemical agent or a mechanical device used to reduce or stop bleeding during surgery.

hemp (hemp) *n.* 1. a plant from which coarse fibers are obtained for the manufacture of rope and cloth. 2. a narcotic drug made from this plant, such as hashish or marijuana. **hemp'en** *adj.*

hem·stitch (hem-stich) *v.* to decorate with a kind of drawn thread work.

hen (hen) *n.* a female bird, especially of the common domestic fowl. ☐**hen party,** *(informal)* a party of women only.

hen·bane (hen-bayn) *n.* a kind of poisonous plant.

hence (hens) *adv.* 1. *(old use)* from here. 2. from this time, *five years hence.* 3. for this reason.

hence·forth (hens-fohrth) *adv.* from now on.

hence·for·ward (hens-fohr-wărd) *adv.* from now on.

hench·man (hench-măn) *n.* (*pl.* **-men,** *pr.* **-měn**) a trusty supporter.

hen·na (hen-ă) *n.* 1. a reddish-brown dye used especially on the hair. 2. the tropical plant from which this is obtained.

hen·peck (hen-pek) *v.* *(informal)* to nag or harass (one's husband) in an attempt to domineer.

hen·ry (hen-ree) *n.* (*pl.* **-ries**) a unit of electrical inductance that gives an electromotive force of one volt in a closed circuit with a rate of change of current of one ampere per second.

hep (hep) *adj.* *(slang)* aware of the latest trends and styles. ☐**hepped up,** *(slang)* enthusiastic.

hep·a·rin (hep-ă-rin) *n.* a substance extracted from animal livers and used to prevent blood coagulation, especially in thrombosis.

he·pat·ic (hi-pat-ik) *adj.* of the liver.

he·pat·i·ca (hi-pat-i-kă) *n.* a plant of the buttercup family, having lobed leaves and delicate flowers.

hep·a·ti·tis (hep-ă-tɪ-tis) *n.* inflammation of the liver.

hep·cat (hep-kat) *n.* *(slang)* a hep person, a jazz or swing addict.

Hep·ple·white (hep-ĕl-hwɪt) *n.* a light and graceful style of furniture, named after George Hepplewhite, an 18th-century cabinetmaker.

hep·ta·gon (hep-tă-gon) *n.* a geometric figure with seven sides.

hep·tam·e·ter (hep-tam-ĕ-tĕr) *n.* a line of verse with seven metrical feet.

her (hur) *pronoun* 1. the objective case of **she,** *we saw her.* 2. *(informal)* = she, *it's her all right.* **her** *adj.* 1. of or belonging to her. 2. used in women's titles, *Her Majesty.* ▷It is incorrect to write *her's* (see the note under **its**).

her·ald (her-ăld) *n.* 1. an official in former times who made announcements and carried messages from a ruler. 2. a person or thing indicating the approach of something, *heralds of spring.* **herald** *v.* to proclaim the approach of.

he·ral·dic (hĕ-ral-dik) *adj.* of heralds or heraldry.

her·ald·ry (her-ăl-dree) *n.* the study of the coats of arms of old families.

herb (urb, hurb) *n.* 1. a soft-stemmed plant that dies down to ground after flowering. 2. a plant with leaves or seeds etc. that are used for food or in medicine or for flavoring. ☐**herb doctor,** a person who tries to cure people by using herbs.

her·ba·ceous (hur-bay-shŭs) *adj.* of or like herbs.

herb·age (ur-bij, hur-) *n.* 1. herbs collectively. 2. the succulent parts of herbs.

herb·al (ur-băl, hur-) *adj.* of herbs used in medicine or for flavoring. **herbal** *n.* a book with descriptions of these.

herb·al·ist (ur-bă-list, hur-) *n.* a dealer in medicinal herbs.

her·bar·i·um (hur-bair-i-ŭm, ur-) *n.* (*pl.* **-bar·i·ums, -bar·i·a,** *pr.* **-bair-i-ă**) 1. a systematically arranged collection of dried plants. 2. a book, case, or room containing this.

herb·i·cide (hur-bi-sɪd) *n.* a substance that is poisonous to plants, used to destroy unwanted vegetation. **her·bi·cid·al** (hur-bi-sɪ-dăl) *adj.*

her·bi·vore (hur-bi-vohr) *n.* a herbivorous animal.

her·biv·or·ous (hur-biv-ŏ-rŭs) *adj.* feeding on plants.

her·cu·le·an (hur-kyŭ-lee-ăn) *adj.* 1. as strong as Hercules, a hero in Greek mythology. 2. needing great strength or effort, *a herculean task.*

herd (hurd) *n.* 1. a number of cattle or other animals feeding or staying together. 2. a mob. **herd** *v.* 1. to gather or stay or drive as a group. 2. to tend (a herd of animals). ☐**herd instinct,** the

instinct to think and behave like the majority.
herds·man (hurdz-măn) *n.* (*pl.* **-men,** *pr.* -měn) a person who tends a herd of animals.
here (heer) *adv.* 1. in or at or to this place. 2. at this point in a process or a series of events. **here** *interj.* an exclamation calling an animal (= come here), calling attention to something (= here it is), or used as a reply (= I am here) in answer to a roll call. ☐**here and now,** immediately. **here and there,** in or to various places. **here goes,** I am about to begin. **here's to,** I drink to the health of. **neither here nor there,** of no importance or relevance.
here·a·bout (heer-ă-bowt) *adv.* somewhere near here.
here·af·ter (heer-af-tĕr) *adv.* in the future, from now on; *the hereafter,* the future, life after death.
here·by (heer-bɪ) *adv.* by this means, by this act or decree etc.
he·red·i·tar·y (hĕ-red-i-ter-ee) *adj.* 1. inherited, able to be passed or received from one generation to another, *hereditary characteristics.* 2. holding a position by inheritance, *hereditary ruler.*
he·red·i·ty (hĕ-red-i-tee) *n.* (*pl.* **-ties**) 1. inheritance of physical or mental characteristics from parents or ancestors. 2. the characteristics inherited in this way.
Her·e·ford (hur-fŏrd, her-ĕ-) *n.* one of a breed of red and white beef cattle.
here·in (heer-in) *adv.* in this matter, book, letter, etc.
here·of (heer-uv, -ov) *adv.* of this.
here·on (heer-on) *adv.* on this.
her·e·sy (her-ĕ-see) *n.* (*pl.* **-sies**) 1. a religious opinion that is contrary to the orthodox doctrine or accepted beliefs of a specific religion. 2. an opinion contrary to generally accepted beliefs in any field. 3. the holding of such an opinion.
her·e·tic (her-ĕ-tik) *n.* a person who holds a heresy or is guilty of heresy. **he·ret·i·cal** (hĕ-ret-i-kăl) *adj.*
here·to (heer-too) *adv.* to this document or subject.
here·to·fore (heer-tŏ-fohr) *adv.* before this time.
here·un·der (heer-un-dĕr) *adv.* under this.
here·up·on (heer-ŭ-pon) *adv.* after this, in consequence of this.
here·with (heer-with, -with) *adv.* with this, enclosed herewith.
her·i·ta·ble (her-i-tă-bĕl) *adj.* able to be inherited.
her·i·tage (her-i-tij) *n.* 1. property that may be or has been inherited. 2. values or traditions passed from earlier generations, *our democratic heritage.*
her·maph·ro·dite (hur-maf-rŏ-dɪt) *n.* an animal or plant that has both male and female sexual organs. **hermaphrodite** *adj.* combining the characteristics of both sexes. **her·maph·ro·dit·ic** (hur-maf-rŏ-dit-ik) *adj.*
her·met·ic (hur-met-ik) *adj.* 1. with an airtight closure, *hermetic sealing.* 2. protected from outside influences. **her·met′i·cal·ly** *adv.*
her·mit (hur-mit) *n.* a person who has withdrawn from human society and lives in solitude. ☐**hermit crab,** a crab that uses a castoff shell to protect its soft hinder parts.
her·mit·age (hur-mi-tij) *n.* a hermit's dwelling place.
her·ni·a (hur-ni-ă) *n.* (*pl.* **-ni·as, -ni·ae,** *pr.* -ni-ee) an abnormal condition in which a part or organ of the body protrudes through a wall of the cavity (especially the abdomen) that normally contains it, a rupture.

her·ni·ate (hur-nee-ayt) *v.* (**her·ni·at·ed, her·ni·at·ing**) to protrude through an abnormal opening in the body. **her·ni·a·tion** (hur-ni-ay-shŏn) *n.*
he·ro (heer-oh) *n.* (*pl.* **-roes**) 1. a man who is admired for his brave or noble deeds. 2. the chief male character in a story, play, or poem. ☐**hero sandwich,** a sandwich consisting of a long roll sliced lengthwise and filled with meat, cheese, onions, etc. **hero worship,** excessive devotion to an admired person.
he·ro·ic (hi-roh-ik) *adj.* having the characteristics of a hero, very brave. **he·ro′i·cal·ly** *adv.* ☐**heroic couplet,** two successive rhyming lines of iambic pentameters.
he·ro·ics (hi-roh-ɪks) *n. pl.* 1. brave actions. 2. overdramatic talk or behavior.
her·o·in (her-oh-in) *n.* a powerful sedative drug prepared from morphine, used chiefly by addicts.
her·o·ine (her-oh-in) *n.* 1. a woman who is admired for her brave or noble deeds. 2. the chief female character in a story, play, or poem.
her·o·ism (her-oh-iz-ĕm) *n.* heroic conduct.
her·on (her-ŏn) *n.* (*pl.* **-ons, -on**) a long-legged, long-necked wading bird living in marshy places.
her·pes (hur-peez) *n.* a virus disease causing blisters on the skin. ☐**herpes simplex,** a form of this, causing cold sores and other minor infections. **herpes zos·ter** (zos-tĕr), shingles, a painful disease involving the nervous system.
her·pe·tol·o·gist (hur-pĕ-tol-ŏ-jist) *n.* a specialist in herpetology.
her·pe·tol·o·gy (hur-pĕ-tol-ŏ-jee) *n.* a branch of zoology dealing with reptiles and amphibians. **her·pe·to·log·ic** (hur-pĕ-tŏ-loj-ik) *adj.* **her·pe·to·log′i·cal** *adj.*
Herr (her) *n.* (*pl.* **Her·ren,** *pr.* her-ĕn) the title of a German man, = Mr.
her·ring (her-ing) *n.* (*pl.* **-ring, -rings**) a North Atlantic fish much used for food.
her·ring·bone (her-ing-bohn) *n.* 1. a pattern consisting of a zigzag arrangement of lines. 2. cloth woven in a zigzag pattern.
hers (hurz) *possessive pronoun* of or belonging to her, the thing(s) belonging to her, *it is hers; hers are best.* ▷It is incorrect to write *her's* (see the note under **its**).
her·self (hĕr-self) *pronoun* the form of **her** used in reflexive constructions (as *she pleased herself*) and for emphasis (as *she herself told me*).
hertz (hurtz) *n.* (*pl.* **hertz**) a unit of frequency of electromagnetic waves, = one cycle per second.
he's (heez) = he is.
hes·i·tant (hez-i-tănt) *adj.* hesitating. **hes′i·tant·ly** *adv.* **hes′i·tan·cy** *n.*
hes·i·tate (hez-i-tayt) *v.* (**hes·i·tat·ed, hes·i·tat·ing**) 1. to be slow to speak or act or move because one feels uncertain or reluctant, to pause in doubt. 2. to be reluctant, to have moral doubts, *wouldn't hesitate to break the rules if it suited him.* **hes·i·ta·tion** (hez-i-tay-shŏn) *n.*
Hes·sian (hesh-ăn) *adj.* of Hesse in Germany. **Hessian** *n.* 1. a native or inhabitant of Hesse. 2. a mercenary used by the British army during the Revolutionary War.
het (het) *adj.* **het up,** (*slang*) excited, overwrought.
het·er·o·dox (het-ĕ-rŏ-doks) *adj.* not orthodox. **het′er·o·dox·y** *n.* (*pl.* **-dox·ies**).
het·er·o·ge·ne·ous (het-ĕ-rŏ-jee-ni-ŭs) *adj.* made up of people or things that are unlike each other. **het·er·o·ge′ne·ous·ly** *adv.* **het·er·o·ge′ne·ous·ness** *n.*

het·er·o·sex·u·al (het-ĕ-rŏ-sek-shoo-ăl) *adj.* feeling sexually attracted to people of the opposite sex, not homosexual. **heterosexual** *n.* a heterosexual person. **het·er·o·sex·u·al·i·ty** (het-ĕ-rŏ-sek-shoo-al-i-tee) *n.*

heu·ris·tic (hyuu-ris-tik) *adj.* 1. (of methods of teaching) encouraging students to discover information themselves. 2. (in solving problems by computer) proceeding by trial and error.

hew (hyoo) *v.* **(hewed, hewn, hew·ing)** to chop or cut with an ax or sword etc., to cut into shape. **hew'er** *n.*

hewn (hyoon) *adj.* made or shaped by hewing.

hex (heks) *n.* a magic spell, a curse. **hex** *v.* to put a hex on, to bewitch.

hex·a·gon (hek-să-gon) *n.* a geometric figure with six sides.

hex·ag·o·nal (hek-sag-ŏ-năl) *adj.* six-sided.

hex·a·he·dron (hek-să-hee-drŏn) *n.* (*pl.* **-drons, -dra,** *pr.* -dră) a solid figure with six faces. **hex·a·he'dral** *adj.*

hex·am·e·ter (hek-sam-ĕ-tĕr) *n.* a line of six metrical feet using dactyls and spondees.

hex·a·pod (hek-să-pod) *n.* an insect with six feet.

hey (hay) *interj.* an exclamation calling attention or expressing surprise or inquiry.

hey·day (hay-day) *n.* the time of greatest success or prosperity, *it was in its heyday.*

hf *abbr.* half.

Hf *symbol* hafnium.

HF *abbr.* high frequency.

hg *abbr.* hectogram(s).

Hg *symbol* mercury.

HG *abbr.* High German.

hgt. *abbr.* height.

hgwy. *abbr.* highway.

H.H. *abbr.* 1. His (or Her) Highness. 2. His Holiness.

hhd. *abbr.* hogshead.

hi (hī) *interj.* an exclamation calling attention or expressing greeting.

HI *abbr.* Hawaii.

H.I. *abbr.* Hawaiian Islands.

hi·a·tus (hī-ay-tŭs) *n.* (*pl.* **-tus·es, -tus**) a break or gap in a sequence or series.

hi·bach·i (hi-bah-chee) *n.* a small Japanese-style charcoal brazier, for cooking.

hi·ber·nate (hī-bĕr-nayt) *v.* **(hi·ber·nat·ed, hi·ber·nat·ing)** (of certain animals) to spend the winter in a state like deep sleep. **hi'ber·na·tor** *n.* **hi·ber·na·tion** (hī-bĕr-nay-shŏn) *n.*

hi·bis·cus (hī-bis-kŭs) *n.* a cultivated shrub or tree with trumpet-shaped flowers.

hic·cup (hik-up) *n.* a sudden stopping of the breath with a coughlike sound. **hiccup** *v.* **(hic·cuped, hic·cup·ing)** to make a hiccup.

hick (hik) *n.* (*informal, often contemptuous*) a rural person, a person of boorish manners.

hick·ey (hik-ee) *n.* (*pl.* **hick·eys**) 1. a gadget. 2. a pimple. 3. (*slang*) a red mark on the skin caused by a kiss.

hick·o·ry (hik-ŏ-ree) *n.* (*pl.* **-ries**) 1. an American tree related to the walnut. 2. its hard wood. □**hickory nut,** the nut or fruit of the hickory tree.

hid (hid), **hid·den** (hid-ĕn) *see* hide².

hi·dal·go (hi-dal-goh) *n.* (*pl.* **-gos**) a member of the lower nobility in Spain.

hide¹ (hīd) *n.* 1. an animal's skin (raw or dressed) as an article of commerce and manufacture. 2. (*informal*) the human skin; *save one's hide,* save ourself from punishment or danger.

hide² *v.* **(hid, hid·den, hid·ing)** 1. to put or keep out of sight, to prevent from being seen. 2. to keep secret. 3. to conceal oneself. **hid'er** *n.* □**hidden tax,** an indirect tax.

hide-and-seek (hīd-ăn-seek) *n.* a children's game in which some players conceal themselves and others try to find them.

hide·a·way (hīd-ă-way) *n.* (*informal*) a place of concealment.

hide·bound (hīd-bownd) *adj.* narrow-minded, refusing to abandon old customs and prejudices.

hid·e·ous (hid-i-ŭs) *adj.* very ugly, revolting to the senses or the mind. **hid'e·ous·ly** *adv.* **hid'e·ous·ness** *n.*

hide·out (hīd-owt) *n.* a safe place to hide, especially from law enforcement personnel.

hid·ing¹ (hī-ding) *n.* (*informal*) a thrashing.

hiding² *n.* the state of being or remaining hidden, *went into hiding.* □**hiding place,** a place where a person or thing is or could be hidden.

hie (hī) *v.* **(hied, hie·ing** or **hy·ing)** (*old use*) to go quickly.

hi·er·ar·chi·cal (hī-ĕ-rahr-ki-kăl) *adj.* of or arranged in a hierarchy.

hi·er·ar·chy (hī-ĕ-rahr-kee) *n.* (*pl.* **-chies**) 1. a system with grades of status or authority ranking one above another in a series. 2. the set of persons in such a system.

hi·er·o·glyph (hī-ĕ-rŏ-glif) *n.* 1. one of the pictures or symbols used in ancient Egypt and elsewhere to represent sounds or words or ideas. 2. a written symbol with a secret or cryptic meaning.

hi·er·o·glyph·ic (hī-ĕ-rŏ-glif-ik) *adj.* of or written in hieroglyphs.

hi·er·o·glyph·ics (hī-ĕ-rŏ-glif-iks) *n. pl.* hieroglyphs, hieroglyphic writing.

hi·er·o·phant (hī-ĕ-rŏ-fant) *n.* 1. a priest who initiated worshipers into secret religious rites in ancient Greece. 2. a person who expounds sacred mysteries. **hi·er·o·phant'ic** *adj.*

hi-fi (hī-fī) *adj.* (*informal*) reproducing sound with high fidelity (*see* high). **hi-fi** *n.* (*informal*) hi-fi equipment.

hig·gle·dy-pig·gle·dy (hig-ĕl-dee-pig-ĕl-dee) *adj. & adv.* completely mixed up, in utter disorder.

high (hī) *adj.* 1. extending far upward, extending above the normal or average level. 2. situated far above the ground or above sea level. 3. measuring a specified distance from base to top. 4. ranking above others in importance or quality; *the High Court,* the Supreme Court. 5. extreme, intense, greater than what is normal or average, *high temperatures; high prices; a high opinion,* very favorable. 6. (of time) fully reached, *high noon; it's high time we left.* 7. noble, virtuous, *high ideals.* 8. (of a sound or voice) shrill, not deep or low. 9. high gear. 10. (*slang*) intoxicated, under the influence of drugs. **high** *n.* 1. a high level or figure, *exports reached a new high.* 2. an area of high barometric pressure. **high** *adv.* 1. in or at or to a high level or position. 2. in or to a high degree; *feelings ran high,* were strong. □**high altar,** the chief altar of a church. **high and dry,** aground; stranded, isolated. **high and low,** everywhere, *hunted high and low.* **high and mighty,** arrogant. **high bar,** a raised bar fixed parallel to the floor for use in exercises and gymnastic competitions. **high beam,** a headlight with a long range. **High Church,** a group in the Anglican Church that stresses traditional liturgical practice and ceremony and the authority of the clergy. **high color,** a flushed complexion. **high command,** the highest authority or headquarters of a military force.

high explosive, explosive with a violently shattering effect. **high fashion,** high-class dressmaking; leading dressmakers collectively, or their products. **high fidelity,** reproduction of sound with the full range of audible frequencies and little distortion. **high finance,** dealing with large sums of money. **high flyer,** a person with great ambitions or with capacity for great achievements. **high frequency,** (in radio) 3 to 30 megahertz. **high gear,** the gear allowing a motor vehicle to run at its maximum speed. **High German,** a form of German originally spoken in the south, but now in literary and cultured use throughout Germany. **High Holy Day,** the Jewish New Year or the Day of Atonement. **high hurdles,** a series of ten barriers, each of which is 42 inches high and which must be jumped over by a person in a running race. **high jump,** an athletic competition involving jumping over a high horizontal bar. **high life** *or* **living,** a luxurious way of living. **High Mass,** a celebration of the Eucharist with incense, music, and the assistance of a deacon and subdeacon. **high noon,** the precise moment of twelve o'clock in the daytime. **high old time,** *(informal)* a most enjoyable time. **high priest,** the chief priest. **high school,** a secondary school. **high sea** *or* **seas,** the open seas, not under any country's jurisdiction. **high sign,** *(slang)* a warning or reassuring gesture. **high society,** the social class consisting of well-to-do and well-connected people. **high tea,** *(British)* an evening meal with tea and meat and other cooked food. **high tide,** the tide at its highest level; the time when this occurs. **high time,** the time just before becoming late; *(informal)* a pleasurable time. **high treason,** treason against one's country or ruler. **high water,** high tide. **high-water mark,** the level reached at high water; the highest point or value etc. recorded. **high wire,** a high tightrope.

high·ball (hɪ-bawl) *n.* a drink with whiskey or other liquor and soda etc. served in a tall glass. **highball** *v.* *(slang)* to go fast, to speed (usually referring to a train).

high·born (hɪ-born) *adj.* of noble birth.

high·boy (hɪ-boi) *n.* a tall chest of several drawers on legs.

high·bred (hɪ-bred) *adj.* of superior blood or heritage.

high·brow (hɪ-brow) *adj.* *(informal)* 1. very intellectual, cultured. 2. pretentious, smug. **highbrow** *n.* *(informal)* a highbrow person.

high·chair (hɪ-chair) *n.* an infant's chair with long legs and usually a tray, for use at meals.

high-class (hɪ-klas) *adj.* *(informal)* of high quality or social class.

high·er-up (hɪ-ër-up) *n.* *(informal)* a person of high or higher rank.

high·fa·lu·tin (hɪ-fă-loo-tin) *adj.* *(informal)* pompous.

high-flown (hɪ-flohn) *adj.* 1. having extravagant ways. 2. (of language) pompous.

high-grade (hɪ-grayd) *adj.* of high quality.

high-hand·ed (hɪ-han-did) *adj.* using authority arrogantly. **high'hand'ed·ly** *adv.* **high'hand' ed·ness** *n.*

high-hat (hɪ-hat) *v.* (**high-hat·ted, high-hat· ting**) *(informal)* to treat superciliously, to assume a superior attitude toward. **high-hat** *adj.*

high-keyed (hɪ-keed) *adj.* high-strung, tense.

high·land (hɪ-lănd) *adj.* 1. of or in highlands. 2. *Highland,* of the Scottish Highlands. ☐ **Highland**

fling, a vigorous Scottish folk dance. **high'land· er** *n.*

high·lands (hɪ-lăndz) *n. pl.* mountainous country; *the Highlands,* those of northern Scotland.

high-lev·el (hɪ-lev-ĕl) *adj.* (of negotiations) conducted by people of high rank.

high·light (hɪ-lɪt) *n.* 1. a light or bright area in a painting etc. 2. the brightest or most outstanding feature of something, *the highlight of the tour.* **highlight** *v.* to draw special attention to, to emphasize.

high·ly (hɪ-lee) *adv.* 1. in a high degree, extremely, *highly amusing; highly commended.* 2. very favorably, *thinks highly of her.*

high-mind·ed (hɪ-mɪn-did) *adj.* having high moral principles. **high'-mind'ed·ness** *n.*

high-muck-a-muck (hɪ-muk-ă-muk) *n.* *(slang)* an important person who is arrogant in manner.

high·ness (hɪ-nis) *n.* 1. the state of being high in rank or importance etc. 2. *Highness,* the title used in speaking of or to a prince or princess, *His* or *Her* or *Your Highness.*

high-oc·tane (hɪ-ok-tayn) *adj.* (of fuel used in internal combustion engines) having good antiknock properties and not detonating readily during the power stroke.

high-pitched (hɪ-picht) *adj.* (of a sound or voice) high.

high-pow·ered (hɪ-pow-ĕrd) *adj.* using great power or energy, forceful.

high-pres·sure (hɪ-presh-ür) *adj.* 1. having a pressure exceeding that of the atmosphere. 2. vigorous or urgent, especially in business matters, *a high-pressure salesman.* **high-pressure** *v.* (**-pres· sured, -pres·sur·ing**) to use high-pressure methods on.

high-rise (hɪ-rɪz) *adj.* (of a building) with many stories. **high-rise** *n.* such a building.

high·road (hɪ-rohd) *n.* 1. the main road. 2. an easy or direct course.

high-sound·ing (hɪ-sown-ding) *adj.* having an imposing or pompous sound.

high-speed (hɪ-speed) *adj.* operating at great speed.

high-spir·it·ed (hɪ-spir-ĭ-tid) *adj.* in high spirits, happy and lively.

high-strung (hɪ-strung) *adj.* very sensitive or nervous.

high·tail (hɪ-tayl) *v.* *(slang)* to move at high speed.

high-ten·sion (hɪ-ten-shŏn) *adj.* having or relating to high voltage, *high-tension wire.*

high-test (hɪ-test) *adj.* (of gasoline) having a low boiling point.

high-toned (hɪ-tohnd) *adj.* stylish, dignified, superior in manner.

high·way (hɪ-way) *n.* 1. a public road. 2. a main route by land or sea or air.

high·way·man (hɪ-way-măn) *n.* (*pl.* **-men,** *pr.* -měn) a man (usually on horseback) who robbed passing travelers in former times.

hi·jack, high·jack (hɪ-jak) *v.* to seize control of (a vehicle or aircraft in transit) in order to steal its goods or take its passengers hostage or force it to a new destination. **hijack** *n.* a hijacking. **hi'jack·er** *n.*

hike (hɪk) *n.* a long walk, especially a cross-country walk taken for pleasure. **hike** *v.* (**hiked, hik· ing**) 1. to go for a hike. 2. to walk laboriously. **hik'er** *n.*

hi·lar·i·ous (hi-lair-i-ŭs) *adj.* 1. extremely funny. 2. noisily merry. **hi·lar'i·ous·ly** *adv.* **hi·lar· i·ty** (hi-lar-i-tee) *n.*

hill (hil) *n.* 1. a natural elevation of the earth's surface, not as high as a mountain. 2. a slope in a road etc. 3. a heap or mound, *a hill of beans.*

hill·bil·ly (hil-bil-ee) *n.* (*pl.* **-lies**) (*informal,* often *contemptuous*) someone from a remote rural area in a southern state of the U.S.

hill·ock (hil-ŏk) *n.* a small hill, a mound.

hill·side (hil-sıd) *n.* the sloping side of a hill.

hill·top (hil-top) *n.* the summit of a hill.

hill·y (hil-ee) *adj.* (**hill·i·er, hill·i·est**) full of hills.

hilt (hilt) *n.* the handle of a sword or dagger etc. □**to the hilt,** completely, *he was in the plot to the hilt.*

him (him) *pronoun* 1. the objective case of **he,** *we saw him.* 2. (*informal*) = he, *it's him all right.*

Hi·ma·la·yas (him-ă-lay-ăz) *n. pl.* the Himalaya Mountains in Nepal and adjacent countries. **Him·a·la′yan** *adj.*

him·self (him-self) *pronoun* the form of **him** used in reflexive constructions (as *he cut himself*) and for emphasis (as *he himself had said it; told me himself*). □**be himself,** to behave in a normal manner without constraint; *he is not himself today,* is not in his normal good health or spirits. **by himself,** without companions; without help.

hind[1] (hınd) *n.* a female deer.

hind[2] *adj.* situated at the back, *hind legs.*

Hind. *abbr.* 1. Hindu. 2. Hindustan. 3. Hindustani.

hin·der[1] (hin-dĕr) *v.* to keep (a person or thing) back by delaying progress.

hind·er[2] (hın-dĕr) *adj.* hind[2], *the hinder part.*

Hin·di (hin-dee) *n.* 1. one of the official languages of India, a form of Hindustani. 2. a group of spoken languages of northern India.

hind·most (hınd-mohst) *adj.* farthest behind.

hind·quar·ters (hınd-kwor-tĕrz) *n. pl.* the hind legs and adjoining parts of a quadruped.

hin·drance (hin-drăns) *n.* 1. something that hinders. 2. hindering, being hindered, *went ahead without hindrance.*

hind·sight (hınd-sıt) *n.* wisdom about an event after it has occurred.

Hin·du (hin-doo) *n.* a person whose religion is Hinduism. **Hindu** *adj.* of the Hindus.

Hin·du·ism (hin-doo-iz-ĕm) *n.* a religion and philosophy native to India.

Hin·du·sta·ni (hin-duu-stah-nee) *n.* the language of much of northern India and Pakistan.

hinge (hinj) *n.* 1. a joint on which a lid, door, or gate etc. turns or swings. 2. a natural joint working similarly. 3. a small piece of gummed paper for fixing stamps in an album. **hinge** *v.* (**hinged, hing·ing**) 1. to attach or be attached by a hinge or hinges. 2. to depend on, *everything hinges on this meeting.*

hint (hint) *n.* 1. a slight indication, a suggestion made indirectly. 2. a small piece of practical information, *household hints.* **hint** *v.* to make a hint. □**hint at,** to refer indirectly to.

hin·ter·land (hin-tĕr-land) *n.* 1. a district lying behind a coast etc. or served by a particular port or center. 2. the back country, especially regions sparsely settled and hard to reach.

hip[1] (hip) *n.* 1. the projection formed by the pelvis and upper part of the thighbone on each side of the body; *hips,* the measurement around the body here. 2. the joint between the pelvis and the upper leg; *broken hip,* a fracture of one of the bones at this joint. □**hip boot,** a boot that covers the entire leg up to the hip. **hip flask,** a small flask for liquor etc., carried in the **hip pocket,** just behind the hip.

hip[2] *n.* the fruit (red when ripe) of a wild rose.

hip[3] *interj.* used in cheering, *hip, hip, hurray.*

hip[4] *adj.* (*slang*) well-informed, stylish.

hip·bone (hip-bohn) *n.* 1. the bone forming the hip socket. 2. the neck of the thighbone.

hip·hug·gers (hip-hug-ĕrz) *n. pl.* a pair of slacks secured to the body at the hips rather than at the waist.

hipped[1] (hipt) *adj.* having hips, especially of a certain kind, *narrow-hipped.*

hipped[2] *adj.* (*informal*) greatly interested, obsessed, *hipped on tennis.*

hip·pie (hip-ee) *n.* (*slang*) a young person who joins with others in adopting an unconventional style of dress etc., rejecting conventional ideas and organized society and often using (or thought to be using) hallucinogenic drugs.

hip·po (hip-oh) *n.* (*pl.* **-pos**) (*informal*) a hippopotamus.

Hip·po·crat·ic (hip-ŏ-krat-ik) *adj.* of Hippocrates, a Greek physician of the 5th century **B.C.** □**Hippocratic oath,** an oath taken by those beginning medical practice, to observe the code of professional behavior.

hip·po·drome (hip-ŏ-drohm) *n.* 1. (in ancient Greece and Rome) a course for chariot races etc. 2. a theater or arena for athletic events or circuses etc.

hip·po·pot·a·mus (hip-ŏ-pot-ă-mŭs) *n.* (*pl.* **-mus·es, -mi,** *pr.* -mı) a large African river animal with tusks, short legs, and thick dark skin.

hip·ster (hip-stĕr) *adj.* (*slang*) a person who is hip (see **hip**[4]).

hire (hır) *v.* (**hired, hir·ing**) to engage the services of (a person) or the use of (a thing) temporarily, for payment. **hire** *n.* hiring, payment for this. **hir′er** *n.*

hire·a·ble (hır-ă-bĕl) *adj.* able to be hired.

hire·ling (hır-ling) *n.* a person who serves for hire.

hir·sute (hur-soot) *adj.* hairy, shaggy. **hir′sute·ness** *n.*

his (hiz) *adj. & possessive pronoun* 1. of or belonging to him, the thing(s) belonging to him. 2. used in men's titles, *His Honor.*

His·pan·ic (hi-span-ik) *adj.* of Spain or Latin America. **Hispanic, His·pa·no** (hi-span-oh) *n.* a Spanish-speaking person in the U.S.

hiss (his) *n.* a sound like that of *s.* **hiss** *v.* 1. to make this sound. 2. to express disapproval in this way.

hist. *abbr.* 1. historian. 2. historical. 3. history.

his·ta·mine (his-tă-meen) *n.* a chemical compound in body tissues that is involved in many allergic reactions.

his·to·gram (his-tŏ-gram) *n.* a diagram in which columns represent frequencies of various ranges of values of a quantity.

his·tol·o·gist (hi-stol-ŏ-jist) *n.* a specialist in histology.

his·tol·o·gy (hi-stol-ŏ-jee) *n.* the scientific study of the minute structure of organic tissues.

his·tol·y·sis (hi-stol-ĭ-sis) *n.* the ⊗aking down of organic tissues.

his·to·ri·an (hi-stohr-i-ăn) *n.* an expert in history, a writer of history.

his·tor·ic (hi-stor-ik) *adj.* 1. famous or important in history. 2. momentous, that will make history, *this historic occasion.* ▷Do not confuse *historic* with *historical.*

his·tor·i·cal (hi-stor-i-kăl) *adj.* 1. belonging to or dealing with history or past events (as opposed to legend or prehistory), *historical novels.* 2. concerned with history, *a historical society.* **his·tor′i·cal·ly** *adv.* ▷Do not confuse *historical* with *historic.*

his·to·ri·og·ra·pher (hi-stohr-i-og-ră-fĕr) *n.* a writer of history, especially an official historian.

his·to·ri·og·ra·phy (hi-stohr-i-og-ră-fee) *n.* 1. the writing of history. 2. the study of the writing of history. **his·to·ri·og·ra′phic** *adj.*

his·to·ry (his-tŏ-ree) *n.* (*pl.* **-ries**) 1. a continuous methodical record of important or public events. 2. past events, those connected with a person or thing. 3. an interesting or eventful past, *the house has a history.* 4. the study of past events, especially of human affairs. □**make history,** to do something memorable, to be the first to do something.

his·tri·on·ic (his-tri-on-ik) *adj.* 1. of acting. 2. dramatic or theatrical in manner. **his·tri·on′i·cal·ly** *adv.*

his·tri·on·ics (his-tri-on-iks) *n. pl.* dramatic behavior intended to impress people.

hit (hit) *v.* (**hit, hit·ting**) 1. to strike with a blow or missile, to aim a blow etc., to come against (a thing) with force; *it hits you in the eye,* is very obvious. 2. to propel (a ball etc.) with a bat or club. 3. to have an effect on (a person), to cause to suffer. 4. to get at, to come to (a thing aimed at), to find (what is sought). 5. to reach, *can't hit the high notes; hit a snag,* encounter a difficulty. **hit** *n.* 1. a blow, a stroke. 2. a shot etc. that hits its target. 3. a success; *make a hit,* to win popularity. 4. (in baseball) a play in which a batter hits a ball and reaches base safely without an error being committed by a fielder. 5. a successful play or musical. 6. *(slang)* a murder, especially by a hired gunman. □**hit back,** to retaliate. **hit it off,** to get along well (with a person). **hit man,** *(slang)* a hired assassin. **hit on,** to discover suddenly or by chance. **hit parade,** a list or program of the most popular tunes. **hit the bottle,** *(slang)* to drink alcohol heavily. **hit the nail on the head,** to guess right, to express the truth exactly. **hit the road** *or* **trail,** *(slang)* to depart; to take up a wandering life.

hit-and-run (hit-ăn-run) *adj.* causing damage or injury and fleeing immediately. □**hit-and-run driver,** one who does this with a motor vehicle.

hit-and-run play, (in baseball) a play in which a baserunner runs for the next base as soon as the pitcher begins to pitch, and the batter swings at the pitched ball.

hitch (hich) *v.* 1. to move (a thing) with a slight jerk. 2. to fasten or be fastened with a loop or hook etc.; *hitch one's wagon to a star,* to set one's sights high, have high aspirations. 3. to hitchhike, to obtain (a ride) in this way. **hitch** *n.* 1. a slight jerk. 2. a noose or knot of various kinds. 3. a temporary stoppage, a snag. 4. *(slang)* a term of military service. □**get hitched,** *(slang)* to get married.

hitch·hike (hich-hīk) *v.* (**hitch·hiked, hitch·hik·ing**) to travel by signaling for free rides in passing vehicles. **hitch′hik·er** *n.*

hith·er (hith-ĕr) *adv.* to or toward this place. □**hither and yon,** hither and thither, to and fro, back and forth; in various directions.

hith·er·to (hith-ĕr-too) *adv.* until this time.

hit-or-miss (hit-ŏr-mis) *adj.* aimed or done carelessly.

hive (hīv) *n.* 1. a box or other container for bees to live in. 2. the bees living in this. **hive** *v.* (**hived, hiv·ing**) to gather or live in a hive.

hives (hīvz) *n. pl.* a skin eruption accompanied by itching and swelling.

H.M.O. *abbr.* health maintenance organization.

H.M.S. *abbr.* His (or Her) Majesty's Ship.

ho (hoh) *interj.* an exclamation of triumph or scorn, or calling attention; *land ho!,* used when land is first sighted from a ship.

Ho *symbol* holmium.

hoa·gie, hoa·gy (hoh-gee) *n.* (*pl.* **-gies**) *(northeastern U.S.)* a hero sandwich.

hoard (hohrd) *n.* a carefully saved and guarded store of money or food or treasured objects. **hoard** *v.* to save and store away. **hoard′er** *n.*

hoar·frost (hohr-frawst) *n.* a white frost.

hoarse (hohrs) *adj.* (**hoars·er, hoars·est**) 1. (of the voice) sounding rough, as if from a dry throat. 2. (of a person) having a hoarse voice. **hoarse′ly** *adv.* **hoarse′ness** *n.*

hoar·y (hohr-ee) *adj.* (**hoar·i·er, hoar·i·est**) 1. white or gray, *a hoary beard.* 2. with hoary hair, aged. 3. (of a joke etc.) old. **hoar′i·ness** *n.*

hoax (hohks) *n.* 1. a plot to trick or deceive. 2. the object used in the deception, a fake or fabrication. **hoax** *v.* to deceive by trickery. **hoax′er** *n.*

hob[1] (hob) *n.* a flat metal shelf at the side of a fireplace, where a kettle or pan etc. can be heated.

hob[2] *n.* a hobgoblin. □**to play** *or* **raise hob with,** *(informal)* to do harm or mischief to.

hob·ble (hob-ĕl) *v.* (**hob·bled, hob·bling**) 1. to walk lamely. 2. to fasten the legs of (a horse etc.) so as to limit but not entirely prevent movement. **hobble** *n.* a hobbling walk. □**hobble skirt,** a woman's skirt so narrow at the bottom that it restrains freedom of movement.

hob·ble·de·hoy (hob-ĕl-dee-hoi) *n.* a clumsy or awkward youth between boyhood and manhood.

hob·by (hob-ee) *n.* (*pl.* **-bies**) an occupation that a person does for pleasure, not as his main business. **hob′by·ist** *n.*

hob·by·horse (hob-ee-hors) *n.* 1. a rocking horse. 2. a stick with a horse's head, used as a toy. 3. a topic that a person is fond of discussing.

hob·gob·lin (hob-gob-lin) *n.* 1. a mischievous or evil spirit. 2. a bogey or bugbear.

hob·nail (hob-nayl) *n.* a heavy-headed nail for bootsoles. **hob′nailed** *adj.*

hob·nob (hob-nob) *v.* (**hob·nobbed, hob·nob·bing**) to spend time together in a friendly way.

ho·bo (hoh-boh) *n.* (*pl.* **-boes, -bos**) a migratory worker or tramp.

Hob·son's (hob-sŏnz) **choice** a situation in which one apparently has a choice but only one possibility is offered. ▷Thomas Hobson (17th century) of Cambridge, England, hired out horses and made people take the one nearest to the stable door.

hock[1] (hok) *n.* the middle joint of an animal's hind leg.

hock[2] *v.* *(slang)* to pawn. □**in hock,** in pawn; in prison; in debt.

hock·ey (hok-ee) *n.* 1. ice hockey (*see* **ice**). 2. field hockey (*see* **field**).

hock·shop (hok-shop) *n.* *(informal)* a pawnshop.

ho·cus-po·cus (hoh-kŭs-poh-kŭs) *n.* 1. a nonsense phrase used by conjurers. 2. trickery.

hod (hod) *n.* 1. a trough on a pole used by bricklayers for carrying mortar or bricks. 2. a cylindrical container for shoveling and holding coal. □**hod**

carrier, a worker who carries mortar etc. for a bricklayer or mason.

hodge·podge (hoj-poj) *n.* a mixture or medley.

Hodg·kin's (hoj-kinz) **disease** a disease characterized by the progressive enlargement and inflammation of the lymphoid tissues, especially the spleen.

hoe (hoh) *n.* a tool with a blade on a long handle, used for loosening soil or weeding. **hoe** *v.* **(hoed, hoe·ing)** to dig or scrape with a hoe.

hoe·cake (hoh-kayk) *n.* a thin cornmeal cake.

hoe·down (hoh-down) *n.* 1. a lively party featuring square dancing. 2. the music for square dancing.

hog (hog) *n.* 1. a mature domestic pig. 2. *(informal)* a greedy person. **hog** *v.* **(hogged, hog·ging)** *(slang)* to take more than one's fair share of, to hoard selfishly. **hog'gish** *adj.* □**eat** *or* **live high off the hog,** *(informal)* to live luxuriously or extravagantly. **go the whole hog,** *(slang)* to do something thoroughly.

ho·gan (hoh-găn) *n.* a Navaho Indian dwelling built of branches and covered with sod.

hog·back (hog-bak) *n.* a sharply crested ridge of a hill.

hog·nose (hog-nohz) **snake, hog·nosed** (hog-nohzd) **snake** one of several small harmless North American snakes having a flat snout.

hogs·head (hogz-hed) *n.* 1. a large barrel or cask. 2. a liquid or dry measure for various commodities, usually about 63 gallons.

hog·tie (hog-tɪ) *v.* **(hog·tied, hog·ty·ing)** 1. to secure by tying together an animal's feet or a person's hands and feet. 2. to hamper or frustrate.

hog·wash (hog-wosh) *n.* 1. swill for hogs. 2. *(informal)* nonsense.

hog·wild (hog-wɪld) *adj. (informal)* unrestrainedly enthusiastic or excited.

ho·hum (hoh-hum) *interj.* an expression of boredom.

hoi pol·loi (hoi pŏ-loi) *(contemptuous)* the common people, the masses.

hoist (hoist) *v.* to raise or haul up, to lift with ropes and pulleys etc. **hoist** *n.* 1. an apparatus for hoisting things. 2. a pull or haul up, *give it a hoist.*

hoi·ty-toi·ty (hoi-tee-toi-tee) *adj. (informal)* haughty.

hoke (hohk) *v.* **(hok·ed, hok·ing)** (also **hoke up,** *slang*) to treat in a falsely contrived way. **hoke** *n. (slang)* hokum.

ho·kum (hoh-kŭm) *n. (slang)* 1. nonsense. 2. stereotyped material, designed to appeal to the uncritical.

hold[1] (hohld) *v.* **(held, hold·ing)** 1. to take and keep in one's arms, hand(s), teeth, etc. 2. to keep in a particular position or condition, to grasp or keep so as to control, to detain in custody; *hold him to his promise,* insist that he keep it. 3. to be able to contain, *the bottle holds two pints.* 4. to have in one's possession or as something one has gained, *he holds the record for the high jump.* 5. to support, to bear the weight of. 6. to remain unbroken under strain, to continue, *the rope failed to hold; will the fine weather hold?* 7. to keep possession of (a place or position etc.) against attack. 8. to keep (a person's attention) by being interesting. 9. to have the position of, to occupy (a job etc.), *held the chairmanship.* 10. to cause to take place, to conduct, *hold a meeting or conversation.* 11. to restrain; *hold your tongue,* stop talking; *hold it, hold everything,* cease action or movement. 12. to believe, to consider, to assert. **hold** *n.* 1. the act or manner of holding something.

2. an opportunity or means of holding. 3. a means of exerting influence on a person. **holder** *n.* □**get hold of,** *(informal)* to acquire; to make contact with (a person). **get hold of oneself,** *(informal)* to establish control over oneself. **hold down,** to have (a job). **hold forth,** to speak lengthily. **hold good,** to remain valid. **hold off,** to wait, not to begin, *the rain held off.* **hold on,** to keep one's grasp of something; to refrain from hanging up (on the telephone); *(informal)* to wait. **hold one's ground,** to stand firm, to refuse to yield. **hold one's peace** *or* **tongue,** to keep silent. **hold out,** to offer (an inducement or hope); to last, *if supplies hold out.* **hold out for,** to refuse to accept anything other than. **hold out on,** *(informal)* to refuse the requests etc. of. **hold over,** to postpone; *holds the threat over him,* exerts influence on him by this threat. **hold the fort,** to act as a temporary substitute, to cope in an emergency. **hold the line,** to refrain from hanging up (on the telephone); to refuse to change one's position. **hold to,** to adhere to. **hold up,** to hinder; to stop by the use of threats or force for the purpose of robbery. **hold water,** (of reasoning) to be sound. **hold with,** *(informal)* to approve of, *we don't hold with bribery.* **no holds barred,** all methods are permitted. **take hold,** to grasp; to become established.

hold[2] *n.* a space below a ship's deck, where cargo is stored.

hold·ing (hohl-ding) *n.* 1. (often *holdings*) something held or owned, land held by an owner or tenant. 2. (in certain sports) hindering an opponent by illegal use of hands and arms. □**holding company,** one formed to hold the stock of other companies, which it then controls. **holding operation,** an expedient to prevent change. **holding pattern,** a circular route for aircraft temporarily prevented from landing.

hold·o·ver (hohld-oh-věr) *n.* something that remains from a previous period of time.

hold·up (hohld-up) *n.* 1. a stoppage or delay. 2. a robbery by armed robbers.

hole (hohl) *n.* 1. an empty place in a solid body or mass, a sunken place on a surface. 2. an animal's burrow. 3. *(informal)* a small or dark or wretched place. 4. *(slang)* an awkward situation. 5. a flaw or defect. 6. a hollow or cavity into which a ball etc. must be sent in various games. 7. a unit of play in golf, *we played nine holes.* 8. an opening through something. **hole** *v.* **(holed, hol·ing)** 1. to make a hole or holes in. 2. to put into a hole. **hol'ey** *adj.* □**hole in one,** (in golf) the hitting of the ball into the hole on one shot from the tee. **hole in the wall,** a small dingy establishment. **hole out,** (in golf) to get the ball into the hole. **hole up,** *(slang)* to hide oneself. **in holes,** worn so much that holes have formed.

hol·i·day (hol-i-day) *n.* 1. a day of festivity or recreation or commemoration of an event or person, when no work is done. 2. a day of special religious observance. 3. (chiefly *British*) a vacation. **holiday** *adj.* of or suitable for a holiday, joyful and carefree.

ho·li·er-than-thou (hoh-li-ěr-thǎn-thow) *adj.* self-righteous.

ho·li·ness (hoh-li-nis) *n.* being holy or sacred. □**His Holiness,** the title of the pope.

Hol·land (hol-ănd) the Netherlands.

hol·lan·daise (hol-ăn-dayz) **sauce** a creamy sauce containing butter, egg yolks, and vinegar.

hol·ler (hol-ĕr) v. (informal) to shout. **holler** n. (informal) a shout.

hol·low (hol-oh) adj. 1. empty inside, not solid. 2. sunken, hollow cheeks. 3. (of sound) echoing, as if from something hollow. 4. empty, worthless, a hollow triumph; a hollow laugh, cynical. **hollow** n. a hollow or sunken place, a hole, a valley. **hollow** adv. (informal) completely, beat them hollow. **hollow** v. to make or become hollow, hollow it out. **hol'low·ly** adv. **hol'low·ness** n.

hol·low·ware (hol-oh-wair) n. hollow articles of tableware, as bowls etc., especially those made of silver.

hol·ly (hol-ee) n. (pl. -lies) an evergreen shrub with prickly leaves and red berries.

hol·ly·hock (hol-ee-hok) n. a plant with large showy flowers on a tall stem.

hol·mi·um (hohl-mi-um) n. a rare-earth element.

hol·o·caust (hol-ŏ-kawst, hoh-lŏ-) n. large-scale destruction, especially by fire. ☐the Holocaust, the murder by the Nazis of over six million Jews.

Hol·o·cene (hol-ŏ-seen, hoh-lŏ-) adj. (in geology) recent, of the present geological period. **Holocene** n. the Holocene epoch.

hol·o·gram (hoh-lŏ-gram, hol-ŏ-) n. a three-dimensional photograph produced by a reflected laser beam.

hol·o·graph (hoh-lŏ-graf, hol-ŏ-) n. a document wholly written by the person named as its author. **hol·o·graph·ic** (hol-ŏ-graf-ik, hoh-lŏ-) adj. **hol·o·graph'i·cal** **hol·o·graph'i·cal·ly** adv.

ho·log·ra·phy (hŏ-log-ră-fee) n. the process or method of producing holograms.

Hol·stein (hohl-stɪn) n. (also Holstein-Frie·sian) one of a breed of large black-and-white dairy cattle originally from Friesland, a province of the Netherlands.

hol·ster (hohl-stĕr) n. a leather case for a pistol or revolver, fixed to a belt or saddle or under the arm.

ho·ly (hoh-le) adj. (ho·li·er, ho·li·est) 1. of God and therefore regarded with reverence, associated with God or religion, the Holy Bible. 2. consecrated, sacred, holy water. 3. devoted to the service of God, a holy man. ☐Holy City, a city held sacred by the adherents of a religion, especially Jerusalem; heaven. **Holy Communion,** see **Communion. Holy Father,** a title of the pope. **Holy Ghost,** the Holy Spirit. **Holy Grail,** see **Grail. Holy Land,** the western part of Palestine. **holy of holies,** a place or thing regarded as most sacred; the sacred inner chamber of a Jewish temple. **holy orders,** the Christian ministry; take holy orders, enter the ministry. **Holy See,** the position or diocese of the pope. **Holy Spirit,** the Third Person of the Trinity, God acting spiritually. **holy terror,** (informal) a troublesome child; a formidable person. **Holy Week,** the week before Easter Sunday. **Holy Writ,** the Bible.

ho·ly·stone (hoh-lee-stohn) n. a soft sandstone used for scouring decks. **holystone** v. (ho·ly·stoned, ho·ly·ston·ing) to scour with this.

hom·age (hom-ij, om-ij) n. 1. things said as a mark of respect, paid homage to his achievements. 2. a formal expression of loyalty to a ruler etc.

hom·burg (hom-burg) n. a man's soft felt hat with a narrow curled brim and a lengthwise dent in the crown.

home (hohm) n. 1. the place where one lives, especially with one's family. 2. one's native land, the district where one was born or where one has lived for a long time or to which one feels attached. 3. a house, homes for sale. 4. an institution where those needing care may live, an old people's home. 5. the natural environment of an animal or plant. 6. the place to be reached by a runner in a race or in certain games. 7. home plate. **home** adj. 1. of or connected with one's own home or country, done or produced there, home produce, home appliances. 2. played on one's own ground, a home game. **home** adv. 1. to or at one's home, go home; stay home, to stay at home. 2. to the point aimed at, the thrust went home; the criticism went home, made itself felt as true; drive a nail home, right in. **home** v. (homed, hom·ing) 1. (of a trained pigeon) to fly home. 2. to be guided to a target, to make for a particular destination. ☐at home, see at. **home away from home,** a place (other than home) where one feels comfortable and at home. **home economics,** the science of household management, including nutrition, child care, etc. **home free,** (slang) sure to win or gain success; safe. **home plate,** (in baseball) the base at which the batter stands and the last of the four that a base runner must touch in scoring a run. **home rule,** government of a country by its own citizens. **home run,** (in baseball) a hit that allows the batter to make a complete circuit of the bases and score a run. **home screen,** (informal) television.

home·bod·y (hohm-bod-ee) n. (pl. -bod·ies) a person who likes to stay at home.

home·bred (hohm-bred) adj. bred at home.

home·com·ing (hohm-kum-ing) n. 1. arrival at home. 2. a festive annual event usually held by a college or university for its alumni.

home-grown (hohm-grohn) adj. grown at home.

home·land (hohm-land) n. a person's native land.

home·less (hohm-lis) adj. lacking a place to live.

home·ly (hohm-lee) adj. (-li·er, -li·est) 1. simple and informal, not pretentious. 2. (of a person's appearance) plain, not beautiful. **home'li·ness** n.

home·made (hohm-mayd) adj. made at home.

home·mak·er (hohm-may-kĕr) n. a person who manages household affairs. **home'mak·ing** n.

ho·me·op·a·thy (hoh-mi-op-ă-thee) n. the treatment of disease by drugs, usually in minute doses, that in a healthy person would produce symptoms like those of the disease. **ho·me·o·path** (hohm-mi-ŏ-path) n. a person who is expert in homeopathy. **ho·me·o·path·ic** (hoh-mi-ŏ-path-ik) adj.

ho·me·o·sta·sis (hoh-mi-ŏ-stay-sis) n. maintenance of relatively stable conditions in a system (such as blood temperature in the body) by internal processes that counteract any departure from the normal. **ho·me·o·stat·ic** (hoh-mi-ŏ-stat-ik) adj.

ho·mer (hoh-mĕr) n. (in baseball) a home run.

Ho·mer·ic (hoh-mer-ik) adj. 1. of the writing or heroes of Homer, traditional author of Greek epic poems. 2. heroic, grand.

home·room (hohm-room) n. a schoolroom where a class meets daily to be checked for absences, receive special announcements, etc.

home·sick (hohm-sik) adj. feeling depressed through longing for one's home when one is away from it. **home'sick·ness** n.

home·spun (hohm-spun) adj. 1. made of yarn spun at home. 2. homely, unsophisticated. **homespun** n. homespun fabric.

home·stead (hohm-sted) n. a farmhouse or similar building with the land and buildings around it.

home·stead·er (hohm-sted-ĕr) *n.* a settler on a homestead, especially on a tract of 160 acres as granted by the Homestead Act of Congress in 1862.

home·stretch (hohm-strech) *n.* 1. the straight part of a racetrack between the final bend and the finish line. 2. the final part of a job.

home·town (hohm-town) *n.* the town of one's birth or early life or present fixed residence.

home·ward (hohm-wărd) *adj. & adv.* going toward home.

home·work (hohm-wurk) *n.* work to be done at home, especially lessons to be done by a schoolchild at home.

home·y (hoh-mee) *adj.* **(hom·i·er, hom·i·est)** homelike, homely.

hom·i·cide (hom-i-sɪd) *n.* the killing of one person by another. **hom·i·cid·al** (hom-i-sɪ-dăl) *adj.*

hom·i·ly (hom-i-lee) *n.* (*pl.* **-lies**) a sermon, a moralizing lecture.

hom·ing (hoh-ming) *adj.* returning home. ◻**homing pigeon**, a pigeon trained to fly home, bred for long-distance racing.

hom·i·ny (hom-ĭ-nee) *n.* hulled and dried kernels of corn from which the bran and germ have been removed. ◻**hominy grits**, ground hominy boiled with water or milk.

Ho·mo (hoh-moh) *n.* the genus of primates including man.

ho·mo·ge·ne·ous (hoh-mŏ-jee-ni-ŭs) *adj.* of the same kind as the others, formed of parts that are all of the same kind. **ho·mo·ge′ne·ous·ly** *adv.* **ho·mo·ge′ne·ous·ness** *n.* **ho·mo·ge·ne·i·ty** (hoh-moh-jĕ-nee-i-tee) *n.*

ho·mog·e·nize (hŏ-moj-ĕ-nɪz) *v.* **(ho·mog·e·nized, ho·mog·e·niz·ing)** to treat (milk) so that the particles of fat are broken down and the cream does not separate. **ho·mog′e·niz·er** *n.* **ho·mog·e·ni·za·tion** (hŏ-moj-ĕ-ni-zay-shŏn) *n.*

hom·o·graph (hom-ŏ-graf) *n.* a word spelled like another, but of different meaning or origin, such as *low* (= sound made by cattle), *low* (= not high or tall).

ho·mol·o·gous (hŏ-mol-ŏ-gŭs) *adj.* 1. having the same relation or relative position. 2. corresponding. 3. (of a limb or organ) similar to another in position and structure but not necessarily in function. **ho·mol·o·gy** (hŏ-mol-ŏ-jee) *n.* (*pl.* **-gies**) **hom·o·logue, hom·o·log** (hom-ŏ-lawg) *n.*

hom·o·nym (hom-ŏ-nim) *n.* a word of the same spelling or sound as another but with a different meaning, such as *grate* (= fireplace), *grate* (= to rub), *great* (= large).

hom·o·phone (hom-ŏ-fohn) *n.* a word with the same sound as another, such as *son, sun.*

Ho·mo sa·pi·ens (hoh-moh say-pi-ĕnz) man regarded as a species.

ho·mo·sex·u·al (hoh-mŏ-sek-shoo-ăl) *adj.* feeling sexually attracted only to people of the same sex as oneself. **homosexual** *n.* a homosexual person. **ho·mo·sex·u·al·i·ty** (hoh-mŏ-sek-shoo-al-i-tee) *n.*

Hon., hon. *abbr.* 1. Honorable. 2. Honorary.

hon·cho (hon-choh) *n.* (*pl.* **-chos**) *(informal)* a boss.

Hon·du·ras (hon-door-ăs) a country in Central America. **Hon·du′ran** *adj. & n.*

hone (hohn) *n.* a fine-grained stone used for sharpening razors and tools. **hone** *v.* **(honed, hon·ing)** to sharpen on this.

hon·est (on-ist) *adj.* 1. truthful, trustworthy. 2. (of an act or feeling) showing such qualities, *an honest opinion; an honest piece of work,* done conscientiously. 3. (of gain etc.) got by fair means; *earn an honest penny,* earn money fairly. ◻**honest injun,** *(informal)* truthfully, honestly. **honest to goodness,** *(informal)* real, straightforward.

hon·est·ly (on-ist-lee) *adv.* 1. in an honest way. 2. really, *that's all I know, honestly.*

hon·es·ty (on-i-stee) *n.* being honest.

hon·ey (hun-ee) *n.* (*pl.* **-eys**) 1. a sweet sticky yellowish substance made by bees from nectar. 2. its color. 3. sweetness, pleasantness, a sweet thing. 4. *(informal)* darling. ◻**honey locust,** a North American leguminous hardwood tree.

hon·ey·bee (hun-ee-bee) *n.* the common bee that lives in a hive.

hon·ey·bunch (hun-ee-bunch) *n.* *(informal)* darling.

hon·ey·comb (hun-ee-kohm) *n.* 1. a bees' wax structure of six-sided cells for holding honey and eggs. 2. a pattern or arrangement of six-sided sections. **honeycomb** *v.* to fill with holes or tunnels, *the rock was honeycombed with passages.*

hon·ey·dew (hun-ee-doo) *n.* a sweet sticky substance found on leaves and stems, excreted by aphids. ◻**honeydew melon,** a variety of melon with a pale smooth skin and sweet green flesh.

hon·ey·moon (hun-ee-moon) *n.* a holiday spent together by a newly married couple. **honeymoon** *v.* to take a honeymoon. ◻**honeymoon bridge,** a variety of bridge for two players.

hon·ey·suck·le (hun-ee-suk-ĕl) *n.* a climbing shrub with fragrant yellow and pink flowers.

honk (hongk) *n.* a loud harsh sound, the cry of the wild goose, the sound made by an old-style motor horn. **honk** *v.* to make a honk, to sound a car horn. **honk′er** *n.*

hon·ky-tonk (hong-kee-tongk) *n.* 1. *(informal)* a cheap or disreputable nightclub or dance hall. 2. a kind of ragtime music played on a piano, often with strings that give a tinny sound.

Hon·o·lu·lu (hon-ŏ-loo-loo) the capital of Hawaii.

hon·or (on-ŏr) *n.* 1. great respect, high public regard. 2. a mark of this, a privilege given or received. 3. a source of this, a person or thing that brings honor. 4. good personal character, a reputation for honesty and loyalty etc. 5. a title of respect given to certain judges or people of importance, *your Honor.* 6. (in certain card games) any of the cards of the highest value. 7. *honors,* a mark of academic recognition given to an outstanding student, a course of advanced study for outstanding students. **honor** *v.* 1. to feel honor for. 2. to confer honor on. 3. to acknowledge and pay (a check etc.). ◻**do the honors,** to perform the usual civilities to guests or visitors etc.

honor bound *or* **on one's honor,** under a moral obligation to do something. **on my honor,** I swear it.

hon·or·a·ble (on-ŏ-ră-bĕl) *adj.* 1. deserving honor. 2. possessing or showing honor. 3. *Honorable,* the courtesy title of certain high officials and judges. **hon′or·a·bly** *adv.*

hon·o·rar·i·um (on-ŏ-rair-i-ŭm) *n.* (*pl.* **-rar·i·ums, -rar·i·a,** *pr.* **-rair-i-ă**) a voluntary payment made for services where no fee is legally required.

hon·or·ar·y (on-ŏ-rer-ee) *adj.* 1. given as an honor, *an honorary degree.* 2. unpaid, *honorary treasurer.* **hon·or·ar·i·ly** (on-ŏ-rer-i-lee) *adv.*

hon·or·if·ic (on-ŏ-rif-ik) *adj.* implying respect.
honorific *n.* a mark of esteem, a title. **hon·or·**
if′i·cal·ly *adv.*
hooch (hooch) *n. (slang)* alcoholic liquor, especially
inferior or illicit whiskey.
hood[1] (huud) *n.* 1. a covering for the head and
neck, either as part of a garment or separate. 2.
a loose hoodlike garment forming part of academic dress. 3. something resembling a hood in
shape or use. 4. the hinged metal cover over an
automobile engine.
hood[2] *n. (slang)* a hoodlum.
-hood *suffix* used to form nouns and adjectives
meaning condition or quality or grouping, such
as *childhood, falsehood, sisterhood.*
hood·ed (huud-id) *adj.* 1. having a hood. 2. (of
animals) with a hoodlike part.
hood·lum (huud-lŭm) *n.* a thug or gangster.
hoo·doo (hoo-doo) *n.* 1. bad luck or something
that causes it. 2. voodoo. **hoodoo** *v.* to make
unlucky, to bewitch.
hood·wink (huud-wingk) *v.* to deceive.
hoo·ey (hoo-ee) *interj.* & *n. (slang)* nonsense.
hoof (huuf) *n.* (*pl.* **hoofs, hooves,** *pr.* huuvz)
the horny part of the foot of a horse and other
animals. **hoof** *v.* **hoof it,** *(slang)* to go on foot.
hoofed *adj.* □**hoof and mouth disease,** foot
and mouth disease (*see* **foot**). **on the hoof,** (of
cattle) live, not yet slaughtered.
hoof·er (huuf-ĕr) *n. (slang)* a professional dancer.
hook (huuk) *n.* 1. a bent or curved piece of metal
etc. for catching hold or for hanging things on.
2. something shaped like this; *Sandy Hook,* a projecting point of land on the coast of New Jersey.
3. a curved cutting tool, *reaping hook.* 4. (in golf)
a stroke that causes the ball to follow a hooked
path. 5. (in boxing) a short swinging blow with
the elbow bent. **hook** *v.* 1. to grasp or catch with
a hook, to fasten with a hook or hooks. 2. to
hit a ball in golf so that it takes a hooked path.
3. *(slang)* to obtain, to steal. □**by hook or by**
crook, by some means no matter what happens.
hook and eye, a small metal hook and loop
for fastening a dress etc. **hooked rug,** a rug made
by pulling woolen yarn through canvas with a
hook. **hook, line, and sinker,** *(informal)* entirely. **off the hook,** *(slang)* freed from difficulty.
hook·ah (huuk-ă) *n.* an Oriental pipe for smoking
with a long tube passing through a glass container
of water that cools the smoke as it is drawn
through.
hooked (huukt) *adj.* 1. hook-shaped, *a hooked nose.*
2. *(slang)* married. □**hooked on,** *(slang)* addicted to or captivated by.
hook·er (huuk-ĕr) *n. (slang)* a prostitute.
hook·up (huuk-up) *n. (informal)* a connection, especially an interconnection of broadcasting equipment for special transmissions.
hook·worm (huuk-wurm) *n.* a worm (the male of
which has hooklike spines) that can infest the
intestines of men and animals.
hook·y (huuk-ee) *n. (informal)* **play hooky,** to
play truant.
hoo·li·gan (hoo-lĭ-găn) *n. (informal)* a young ruffian. **hoo′li·gan·ism** *n.*
hoop (hoop) *n.* 1. a band of metal or wood etc.
forming part of a framework. 2. this used as a
child's toy for bowling along the ground, or swirling around the hips, or for circus riders and animals to jump through. **hoop** *v.* to bind or encircle
with hoops. **hoop′less** *adj.* □**be put through**

the hoops, to undergo a test or ordeal. **hoop**
skirt, a bell-shaped skirt supported by a framework of hoops. **hoop snake,** a mud snake native
to the southeastern U.S.
hoop·la (hoop-lah) *n. (informal)* 1. a commotion,
pretentious nonsense. 2. something spoken or
written that is intended to confuse people.
hoop·ster (hoop-stĕr) *n. (slang)* a basketball
player.
hoo·ray (huu-ray) = **hurray.**
hoose·gow (hoos-gow) *n. (slang)* a prison.
▷Mexican Spanish *jusga(d)o.*
Hoo·sier (hoo-zhĕr) *n.* a native or inhabitant of
Indiana.
hoot (hoot) *n.* 1. the cry of an owl. 2. the sound
made by a vehicle's horn or a steam whistle. 3.
a cry expressing scorn or disapproval. 4. *(infor-*
mal) laughter, a cause of this. **hoot** *v.* 1. to make
a hoot or hoots. 2. to receive or drive away with
scornful hoots. 3. to sound (a horn). **hoot′er**
n. □**doesn't care** *or* **give a hoot** *or* **two hoots,**
(slang) doesn't care at all.
hoot·en·an·ny (hoo-tĕ-nan-ee) *n.* (*pl.* **-nies**)
(informal) an informal social event featuring folk
music and singing.
Hoo·ver (hoov-ĕr), **Her·bert Clark** (1874–1964)
the thirty-first president of the U.S. 1929–33.
hop[1] (hop) *v.* 1. (of an animal) to spring from all
feet at once, (of a person) to jump, especially on
one foot. 2. to cross by hopping. 3. *(informal)*
to make a short quick trip. **hop** *n.* 1. a hopping
movement. 2. an informal dance. 3. a short flight
or one stage in a long-distance flight. □**hop in**
or **out,** *(informal)* to get into or out of quickly.
hopping mad, *(informal)* very angry.
hop[2] *n.* a plant cultivated for its cones (**hops**),
which are used for giving a bitter flavor to beer.
□**hop up,** *(slang)* to stimulate with a drug; to
add power to.
hope (hohp) *n.* 1. a feeling of expectation and desire
combined, a desire for certain events to happen.
2. a person or thing or circumstance that gives
cause for this. 3. what one hopes for. **hope** *v.*
(**hoped, hop·ing**) to feel hope, to expect and
desire, to feel fairly confident. □**hoping against**
hope, hoping for something that is barely possible.
hope·ful (hohp-fŭl) *adj.* 1. feeling hope. 2. causing
hope, seeming likely to be favorable or successful.
hopeful *n.* a person who hopes or seems likely
to succeed, *young hopefuls.* **hope′ful·ness** *n.*
hope·ful·ly (hohp-fŭ-lee) *adv.* 1. in a hopeful way.
2. it is to be hoped, *hopefully, we shall be there*
by one o'clock. ▷Many people regard the second
use as unacceptable.
hope·less (hohp-lis) *adj.* 1. feeling no hope. 2. admitting no hope, *a hopeless case.* 3. inadequate,
incompetent, *is hopeless at tennis.* **hope′less·**
ly *adv.* **hope′less·ness** *n.*
hop·head (hop-hed) *n. (slang)* a drug addict.
Ho·pi (hoh-pee) *n.* (*pl.* **-pis, -pi**) 1. a member of
an Arizona Indian tribe. 2. the language of this
tribe.
hop·per (hop-ĕr) *n.* 1. a person or animal that hops,
a hopping insect. 2. a funnel-shaped container
with an opening at the base through which contents can be discharged into a machine etc. 3.
a box into which copies of proposed bills are
dropped for consideration by a legislative body.
hop·sack·ing (hop-sak-ing) *n.* loosely woven
woolen fabric.

hop·scotch (hop-skoch) *n.* a children's game of hopping and jumping over marked squares to retrieve a stone tossed into these.

hor. *abbr.* 1. horizon. 2. horizontal.

ho·ra (hohr-ă) *n.* an Israeli dance.

horde (hohrd) *n.* a large group or crowd.

hore·hound (hohr-hownd) *n.* 1. an herb with woolly leaves and white flowers, producing a bitter juice. 2. a candy made with horehound extract.

ho·ri·zon (hŏ-rɪ-zŏn) *n.* 1. the line at which Earth and sky appear to meet. 2. the limit of a person's experience or knowledge or interests. □**on the horizon,** (of an event) about to happen, just becoming apparent.

hor·i·zon·tal (hor-i-zon-tăl) *adj.* parallel to the horizon, going across from left to right or right to left. **hor·i·zon'tal·ly** *adv.*

hor·mone (hor-mohn) *n.* a substance produced within the body of an animal or plant (or made synthetically) and carried by the blood or sap to an organ which it stimulates. **hor·mo·nal** (hor-moh-năl) *adj.*

horn (horn) *n.* 1. a hard pointed outgrowth on the heads of certain animals. 2. the hard smooth substance of which this consists. 3. a projection resembling a horn. 4. any of various wind instruments (originally made of horn) with a trumpet-shaped end. 5. a device for sounding a warning signal, especially the one on a motor vehicle. **horned** *adj.* **horn'less** *adj.* □**blow one's horn,** *(informal)* to brag. **draw in one's horns,** to restrain one's ambition or enthusiasm, to draw back.

horned toad, a small flat lizard with hornlike spines. **horn in,** *(informal)* to intrude, to interfere. **horn of plenty,** *see* **cornucopia. on the horns of a dilemma,** required to choose between two equally pleasant or unpleasant options.

horn·beam (horn-beem) *n.* a kind of tree or shrub with hard tough wood.

horn·bill (horn-bil) *n.* a tropical bird with a hornlike projection on its beak.

horn·blende (horn-blend) *n.* a black or green or dark brown mineral.

horn·book (horn-buuk) *n.* a paper containing the alphabet, Lord's prayer, etc. mounted on a wooden tablet with a handle, and protected by a thin plate of horn, formerly used as a school primer.

hor·net (hor-nit) *n.* a large kind of wasp inflicting a serious sting. □**stir up a hornets' nest,** to cause an outburst of angry feeling.

horn·pipe (horn-pɪp) *n.* a lively dance, usually for one person, traditionally associated with sailors.

horn-rimmed (horn-rimd) *adj.* (of eyeglasses) with frames made of a material like horn or tortoise shell.

horn·y (hor-nee) *adj.* (**horn·i·er,** **horn·i·est**) 1. of or like horn. 2. hardened and calloused, *horny hands.*

ho·rol·o·gy (hoh-rol-ŏ-jee) *n.* the study of measuring time or making clocks, watches, etc. **ho·rol'o·gist** *n.* **hor·o·log·i·cal** (hohr-ŏ-loj-i-kăl) *adj.*

hor·o·scope (hor-ŏ-skohp) *n.* 1. an astrologer's diagram showing the relative positions of the planets and stars at a particular time. 2. a forecast of future events, based on this.

hor·ren·dous (hŏ-ren-dŭs) *adj. (informal)* horrifying. **hor·ren'dous·ly** *adv.*

hor·ri·ble (hor-ĭ-běl) *adj.* 1. causing horror. 2.

(informal) unpleasant. **hor'ri·bly** *adv.* **hor'ri·ble·ness** *n.*

hor·rid (hor-id) *adj.* horrible. **hor'rid·ly** *adv.*

hor·rif·ic (haw-rif-ik) *adj.* horrifying.

hor·ri·fy (hor-ĭ-fɪ) *v.* (**hor·ri·fied, hor·ri·fy·ing**) to arouse horror in, to shock.

hor·ror (hor-ŏr) *n.* 1. a feeling of loathing and fear. 2. intense dislike or dismay. 3. a person or thing causing horror. □**horror movie,** one full of violence presented sensationally for entertainment.

hor·ror-struck (hor-ŏr-struk), **hor·ror-strick·en** (hor-ŏr-strik-ĕn) *adj.* horrified, shocked.

hors de com·bat (or dĕ kom-ba) out of the fight, disabled. ▷French.

hors d'oeu·vre (or durv) (*pl.* **hors d'oeu·vres,** *pr.* or durvz) food served as an appetizer before or at the start of a meal.

horse (hors) *n.* 1. a four-legged animal with a flowing mane and tail, used for riding on or to carry loads or pull wagons etc. 2. a frame on which something is supported, *a sawhorse.* 3. a vaulting horse (*see* **vault**[2]). 4. *(slang)* heroin. 5. *horses,* *(informal)* horsepower, *this engine has 250 horses.* **horse** *v.* (**horsed, hors·ing**) *(informal)* to indulge in horseplay, *horsing around.* □**hold your horses!** *(informal)* wait a minute; do not be impatient. **horse chestnut,** a large ornamental tree with upright conical clusters of white or pink or red flowers; its fruit. **horse latitudes,** the belt of calms at the northern edge of the northeast trade winds. **horse of another color,** a thing significantly different. **horse opera,** *(slang)* a play or motion picture etc. about the Wild West. **horse sense,** *(informal)* plain common sense. **horse trade, horse trading,** *(informal)* shrewd bargaining. **horse trader,** a person who trades in horses or bargains shrewdly. **on one's high horse,** behaving with pretentiousness or arrogance. **straight from the horse's mouth,** (of information) from a firsthand source.

horse·back (hors-bak) *n.* the back of a horse. □**on horseback,** mounted on a horse.

horse·feath·ers (hors-feth-ĕrz) *interj. & n. (slang)* nonsense.

horse·flesh (hors-flesh) *n.* 1. the flesh of horses, as food. 2. horses, *a good judge of horseflesh.*

horse·fly (hors-flɪ) *n.* (*pl.* **-flies**) a large insect troublesome to horses.

horse·hair (hors-hair) *n.* hair from a horse's mane or tail, used for padding furniture etc.

horse·hide (hors-hɪd) *n.* 1. the hide of a horse. 2. the leather made from the hide. 3. *(informal)* a baseball.

horse·laugh (hors-laf) *n.* a loud coarse laugh.

horse·man (hors-măn) *n.* (*pl.* **-men,** *pr.* -měn) a rider on horseback, especially a skilled one.

horse·man·ship (hors-măn-ship) *n.* the art and skill of riding on horseback.

horse·play (hors-play) *n.* boisterous play.

horse·pow·er (hors-pow-ĕr) *n.* a unit for measuring the power of an engine (550 foot-pounds per second).

horse·rad·ish (hors-rad-ish) *n.* a plant with a hot-tasting root, used to make a sauce.

horse·shoe (hors-shoo) *n.* 1. a U-shaped strip of metal nailed to a horse's hoof. 2. anything shaped like this. 3. *horseshoes,* a game in which horseshoes are thrown at a stake. □**horseshoe crab,** king crab.

horse·sho·er (hors-shoo-ĕr) *n.* a person who puts horseshoes on a horse.

horse·tail (hors-tayl) *n.* a rushlike plant with hollow jointed stems.

horse·whip (hors-hwip) *n.* a whip for horses.

horsewhip *v.* (**horse·whipped, horse·whip·ping**) to beat with a horsewhip.

horse·wom·an (hors-wuum-ăn) *n.* (*pl.* **-wom·en,** *pr.* -wim-in) a woman rider on horseback, especially a skilled one.

hor·sy, hors·ey (hor-see) *adj.* (**hors·i·er, hors·i·est**) 1. of or like a horse. 2. interested in horses and horse racing, showing this in one's dress and conversation etc.

hort. *abbr.* 1. horticultural. 2. horticulture.

hor·ta·tive (hor-tă-tiv), **hor·ta·to·ry** (hor-tătohr-ee) *adj.* tending or serving to exhort. **hor·ta·tion** (hor-tay-shŏn) *n.*

hor·ti·cul·ture (hor-tĭ-kul-chŭr) *n.* the art of garden cultivation. **hor·ti·cul·tur·al** (hor-tĭ-kulchŭ-răl) *adj.* **hor·ti·cul'tur·ist** *n.*

ho·san·na (hoh-zan-ă) *interj.* & *n.* (*pl.* **-nas**) a cry of adoration to God.

hose (hohz) *n.* (*pl.* **hose** for def. 1; **hos·es** for def. 2) 1. stockings or socks. 2. a flexible tube for transporting water or other liquids and gases.

hose *v.* (**hosed, hos·ing**) to water or spray with a hose, *hose the car down.*

ho·sier·y (hoh-zhĕ-ree) *n.* stockings and socks in general.

hosp. *abbr.* hospital.

hos·pice (hos-pis) *n.* 1. a lodging for travelers, especially one kept by a religious order. 2. a home for troubled, destitute, or sick people.

hos·pi·ta·ble (hos-pi-tă-běl) *adj.* giving and liking to give hospitality. **hos'pi·ta·bly** *adv.*

hos·pi·tal (hos-pi-tăl) *n.* an institution where people are treated and nursed when they are ill or injured.

hos·pi·tal·i·ty (hos-pi-tal-i-tee) *n.* (*pl.* **-ties**) friendly and generous reception and entertainment of guests.

hos·pi·tal·ize (hos-pi-tă-lız) *v.* (**hos·pi·tal·ized, hos·pi·tal·iz·ing**) to send or admit (a patient) to a hospital. **hos·pi·tal·i·za·tion** (hos-pi-tă-li-zay-shŏn) *n.* □ **hospitalization insurance,** insurance to cover the cost of care and treatment in a hospital.

host[1] (hohst) *n.* a large number of people or things.

host[2] *n.* 1. a person who receives and entertains another as his guest. 2. an organism on which another organism lives as a parasite. **host** *v.* (*informal*) to act as host to (a person) or at (an event). ▷ Careful writers do not use *host* as a verb.

Host (hohst) *n.* the bread consecrated in the Christian rite of Holy Communion.

hos·tage (hos-tij) *n.* a person held as security so that the holder's demands will be satisfied.

hos·tel (hos-tĕl) *n.* a lodging house for travelers, students, or other special groups. **hos'tel·er** *n.*

hos·tel·ry (hos-tĕl-ree) *n.* (*pl.* **-ries**) (*old use*) an inn.

host·ess (hohs-tis) *n.* 1. a woman who receives and entertains a person as her guest. 2. a woman employed to welcome people at a nightclub, restaurant, etc.

hos·tile (hos-tīl) *adj.* 1. of an enemy, *hostile aircraft.* 2. unfriendly, *a hostile glance; they are hostile toward reform,* are opposed to it. **hos'tile·ly** *adv.* □ **hostile witness,** one who has reason to be opposed to the party calling him.

hos·til·i·ties (ho-stil-i-teez) *n. pl.* acts of warfare.

hos·til·i·ty (ho-stil-i-tee) *n.* (*pl.* **-ties**) being hostile, enmity.

hot (hot) *adj.* (**hot·ter, hot·test**) 1. having great heat or high temperature, giving off heat, feeling heat. 2. producing a burning sensation to the taste. 3. eager, angry, excited, or excitable, *in hot pursuit; a hot temper.* 4. (of the scent in hunting) fresh and strong, (of news) fresh. 5. (*informal,* of a player) very skillful. 6. (of jazz etc.) strongly rhythmical and emotional. 7. (*slang*) radioactive. 8. (*slang,* of goods etc.) recently stolen and hence risky to handle. **hot** *adv.* hotly, in a hot state, *on steep hills, the car runs hot; coffee should always be served hot.* **hot'ly** *adv.* **hot'ness** *n.* □ **hot air,** (*slang*) excited or boastful talk. **hot cake,** a pancake. **hot cross bun,** a bun marked with a cross, prepared especially during Lent. **hot dog,** a hot frankfurter sandwiched in a roll of bread. **hot flash,** a flush, a rush of color or reddening of the face accompanied by perspiration and a sensation of extreme warmth, usually associated with the menopause. **hot line,** a direct line of communication, especially that between heads of governments in Washington and Moscow, and for emergency communications about potential drug and alcohol abuses, psychiatric patients, potential suicides, etc. **hot pepper,** a vegetable or condiment that has a hot taste. **hot plate,** a heated metal plate etc. for cooking food or keeping it hot. **hot potato,** (*informal*) a situation etc. likely to cause trouble to the person handling it. **hot rod,** (*slang*) a motor vehicle modified to have extra power and speed. **hot rodder,** (*slang*) a person who drives such a vehicle. **hot seat,** (*slang*) the position of someone who has difficult responsibilities or who is in trouble; the electric chair. **hot spring,** a hot water well. **hot stuff,** (*slang*) a person of high spirit or skill or passions; something high-powered. **hot tip,** secret information on a competitor sure to win a race or game, or on a good buy. **hot under the collar,** angry, resentful, or embarrassed. **hot war,** a war with active hostilities. **in hot water,** (*informal*) in trouble or disgrace. **make things hot for a person,** to make it uncomfortable for him, to persecute him. **sell like hot cakes,** to sell very readily.

hot·bed (hot-bed) *n.* 1. a bed of earth heated by fermenting manure. 2. a place favorable to the growth of something evil.

hot-blood·ed (hot-blud-id) *adj.* 1. ardent, passionate. 2. excitable.

hot·box (hot-boks) *n.* (in railroad cars) a metal bearing overheated by friction.

ho·tel (hoh-tel) *n.* a building where meals and rooms are provided for travelers. **ho·tel'keep·er** *n.*

hot·foot (hot-fuut) *adv.* in eager haste. **hotfoot** *n.* (*pl.* **-foots**) a practical joke in which a match is placed secretly between the sole and upper of someone's shoe and lighted. **hotfoot** *v.* (*informal*) to hurry eagerly, *hotfooting it.*

hot·head (hot-hed) *n.* an impetuous or excitable person. **hot'head'ed** *adj.* **hot'head'ed·ly** *adv.* **hot'head'ed·ness** *n.*

hot·house (hot-hows) *n.* a heated building made of glass, for growing plants in a warm temperature.

hot·shot (hot-shot) *n.* (*slang*) an aggressively successful person.

hot-tem·pered (hot-tem-pĕrd) *adj.* easily becoming very angry.

hot-wa·ter (hot-waw-tĕr) **bag** or **bottle** a small container to be filled with hot water for warmth in bed, to relieve pain, etc.

hound (hownd) *n.* 1. a dog used in hunting, a foxhound. 2. an enthusiast, especially one devoted to seeking something out, *an autograph hound.* **hound** *v.* 1. to harass or pursue, *hounded him out of society.* 2. *(informal)* to urge, to incite, *hound them on.* □ **hound's tooth, hound's-tooth check,** a woven check pattern giving a notched effect.

hour (owr) *n.* 1. a twenty-fourth part of a day and night, 60 minutes. 2. a time of day, a point of time, *always come at the same hour; seventeen hours,* this time on the 24-hour clock; *bus leaves on the hour,* when the clock indicates a whole number of hours from midnight. 3. a short period of time, the time for action, the present time, *the hour has come; question of the hour.* 4. (in the Roman Catholic Church) prayers to be said at one of the seven times of day appointed for prayer, *a book of hours.* 5. a period for a specified activity, *the lunch hour.* 6. *hours,* a fixed period for daily work, *office hours are nine to five; after hours.* □ **a late hour,** a time late at night. **credit hour,** one unit of academic credit representing one hour of instruction a week for an entire semester. **hour hand,** the hand showing the hour on the clock. **till all hours,** till very late.

hour·glass (owr-glas) *n.* a wasp-waisted glass container holding a quantity of fine sand that takes one hour to trickle through the small opening from the upper to the lower section.

hou·ri (hoor-ee) *n.* (*pl.* **-ris**) a young and beautiful woman of the Muslim paradise.

hour·ly (owr-lee) *adj.* 1. done or occurring once an hour, *an hourly bus service.* 2. continual, frequent, *lives in hourly dread of discovery.* **hourly** *adv.* every hour.

house (hows) *n.* (*pl.* **hous·es,** *pr.* **how-ziz**) 1. a building made for people (usually one family) to live in. 2. the people living in this house, a household. 3. a building used for a particular purpose, *the opera house.* 4. a residence hall at a school or college, the residents of this. 5. a legislative assembly, the building or chamber where it meets; *the House,* the U.S. House of Representatives. 6. a business firm, *a banking house.* 7. the audience of a theater, the theater itself, *a full house.* 8. a family or dynasty, *the House of Windsor.* 9. one of the twelve parts into which the heavens are divided in astrology. **house** (howz) *v.* (**housed, hous·ing**) 1. to provide accommodations for. 2. to store (goods etc.). 3. to encase in a housing. **house'less** *adj.* □ **house arrest,** detention in one's own house etc., not in prison. **house detective,** a detective employed by a hotel. **house of cards,** an insecure scheme. **House of Commons,** the assembly of elected representatives in the British parliament; the building where it meets. **house of correction,** a confined place for persons convicted of minor offenses. **house of detention,** a place for persons accused of a crime and awaiting trial. **house of God,** a church, a place of worship. **house of ill repute** *or* **ill fame,** *(old use)* a brothel. **House of Lords,** the assembly of members of the nobility and bishops in the British parliament; the building where it meets. **House of Representatives,** the lower legislative branch of the U.S. Congress, of many states, and of some other countries. **house organ,** a newspaper etc. published by a business or organization for its employees. **house party,** a number of guests staying at a house. **house plant,** a plant for growing indoors. **house spar-**

row, the English sparrow. **house trailer,** a trailer with living accommodations. **house wren,** an American wren that nests around houses. **like a house on fire,** fast, vigorously, excellently. **on the house,** at the owner's expense. **open house,** an event in which an institution is open for public viewing; a house party open to all friends and relatives. **play house,** to play at being a family in its home. **put one's house in order,** to make the necessary reforms. **set up house,** to begin to live in a separate dwelling.

house·boat (hows-boht) *n.* a bargelike boat fitted up as a dwelling.

house·bound (hows-bownd) *adj.* unable to leave one's house.

house·boy (hows-boi) *n.* a boy or a man as a servant in a house.

house·break (hows-brayk) *v.* (**house·broke, house·bro·ken, house·break·ing**) (of domestic animals) to train to be clean and behave well in the house. **house·bro·ken** (hows-broh-kĕn) *adj.*

house·break·er (hows-bray-kĕr) *n.* a burglar. **house'break·ing** *n.*

house·clean (hows-kleen) *v.* to clean a house and the furniture.

house·coat (hows-koht) *n.* a woman's long dresslike garment for informal wear in the house.

house·fly (hows-fli) *n.* (*pl.* **-flies**) a common fly found in houses.

house·ful (hows-fuul) *n.* (*pl.* **-fuls**) all that a house can hold.

house·guest (hows-gest) *n.* a person visiting with a household for one night or more.

house·hold (hows-hohld) *n.* 1. all the occupants of a house. 2. a home and its affairs. □ **household arts,** home economics. **household effects,** all the furnishings of a house; the belongings of a family. **household word,** a familiar saying or name.

house·hold·er (hows-hohl-dĕr) *n.* 1. a person owning or renting a house. 2. the head of a family or household.

house·keep·er (hows-kee-pĕr) *n.* a person employed to look after a household.

house·keep·ing (hows-kee-ping) *n.* the management of household affairs.

house·lights (hows-lits) *n. pl.* the lights in a theater auditorium.

house·maid (hows-mayd) *n.* a woman servant in a house, especially one who cleans rooms. □ **housemaid's knee,** inflammation of the kneecap, caused by kneeling to work.

house·man (hows-măn) *n.* (*pl.* **-men,** *pr.* **-men**) a houseboy.

house·moth·er (hows-muth-ĕr) *n.* a woman in charge of a residence for a group of people, especially a school or college dormitory or a fraternity or sorority house.

house-rais·ing (hows-ray-zing) *n.* a gathering of rural families for the purpose of building a house for a member of the community.

house-to-house (hows-tŏ-hows) *adj.* calling at each house in turn.

house·top (hows-top) *n.* the roof of a house.

house·train (hows-trayn) *v.* to housebreak.

house·wares (hows-wairz) *n. pl.* small household equipment.

house·warm·ing (hows-wor-ming) *n.* a party to celebrate the occupation of a new home.

house·wife (hows-wif) *n.* (*pl.* **-wives,** *pr.* **-wivz**) a woman managing a household. **house'wife·**

ly adj. **house′wif·er·y** n. **house′wife·li·ness** n. ▷From the old meaning of *wife* = "woman" (as in *fishwife*), not "married woman."

house·work (hows-wurk) n. the cleaning and cooking etc. done in housekeeping.

hous·ing (how-zing) n. 1. accommodations. 2. provision of accommodations for people. 3. a rigid casing enclosing machinery. □**housing development**, a number of houses in a residential area planned as a unit.

hove (hohv) *see* **heave.**

hov·el (huv-ĕl) n. a miserable dwelling.

hov·er (huv-ĕr) v. 1. (of a bird etc.) to remain in one place in the air. 2. to wait about, to linger, to wait close at hand.

Hov·er·craft (huv-ĕr-kraft) n. *(trademark)* a vehicle supported by air thrust downward against the surface (of the land or sea) just beneath it.

how (how) adv. 1. by what means, in what way? 2. to what extent or amount etc? 3. in what condition? **how** conj. the manner in which, *he knew how to bake a cake.* □**and how!** very much so. **how about?** what is your feeling about (this thing)?; would you like (this)? **how come?** *(informal)* why, how did it happen? **how do you do?**, a formal greeting. **how much?** what amount, what price? **the hows and whys,** *(informal)* a full explanation.

how·dah (how-dä) n. a seat for two or more persons, usually with a canopy, on an elephant's back.

how·dy (how-dee) *interj.* *(informal)* how do you do?

how·e′er (how-air) adv. & conj. however.

how·ev·er (how-ev-ĕr) adv. in whatever way, to whatever extent, *will not succeed, however hard he tries.* **however** conj. all the same, notwithstanding, nevertheless, *the corporation moved its headquarters to New York; however, most employees chose not to leave Connecticut.*

how·it·zer (how-it-sĕr) n. a short gun for firing shells at a high angle of elevation and low velocities.

howl (howl) n. 1. the long loud wailing cry of a dog etc. 2. a loud cry of amusement or pain or scorn. 3. a similar noise made by a strong wind or in an electrical amplifier. **howl** v. 1. to make a howl. 2. to weep loudly. 3. to utter with a howl. □**howl down,** to prevent (a speaker) from being heard by howling scorn at him. **howling success,** *(informal)* a very great success.

howl·er (how-lĕr) n. *(informal)* a foolish mistake.

how-to (how-too) adj. *(informal)* giving basic instruction in techniques, *a how-to book on insulating.*

hoy·den (hoi-dĕn) n. a girl who behaves boisterously. **hoy′den·ish** adj.

hp abbr. horsepower.

HQ abbr. headquarters.

hr(s). abbr. hour(s).

H.R. abbr. House of Representatives.

H.S. abbr. High School.

HST abbr. Hawaiian standard time.

HT abbr. high-tension.

ht. abbr. height.

Hts. abbr. Heights.

hua·ra·che (wä-rah-chee) n. a Mexican leather sandal with thongs.

hub (hub) n. 1. the central part of a wheel, from which spokes radiate. 2. a central point of activity, *the hub of the universe.*

hub·bub (hub-ub) n. a loud confused noise of voices.

hub·by (hub-ee) n. (pl. **-bies**) *(informal)* husband.

hub·cap (hub-kap) n. a metal covering over the center of a car wheel.

hu·bris (hyoo-bris) n. 1. an insolent pride or presumption. 2. (in Greek tragedy) arrogant pride toward the gods, leading to nemesis. **hu·bris·tic** (hyoo-bris-tik) adj.

huck·le·ber·ry (huk-ĕl-ber-ee) n. (pl. **-ries**) a blue or black fruit of a low berry-bearing shrub common in North America.

huck·ster (huk-stĕr) n. 1. a peddler. 2. a high-pressure salesman or advertiser. **huckster** v. to sell small articles for a living.

HUD (hud) n. Department of Housing and Urban Development.

hud·dle (hud-ĕl) v. (**hud·dled, hud·dling**) 1. to heap or crowd together into a small space. 2. to curl one's body closely, to nestle. **huddle** n. 1. a confused mass. 2. (in football) a gathering of a team to receive instructions for the next play. □**go into a huddle,** to hold a private conference.

hue[1] (hyoo) n. a color, a tint. **hued** (hyood) adj.

hue[2] n. **hue and cry,** a general outcry of alarm or demand or protest.

huff (huf) n. a fit of annoyance; *in a huff,* annoyed and offended. **huff** v. to blow; *huffing and puffing,* blowing or blustering.

huff·y (huf-ee) adj. (**huff·i·er, huff·i·est**) in a huff. **huff′i·ness** n.

hug (hug) v. (**hugged, hug·ging**) 1. to squeeze tightly in one's arms. 2. to keep close to, *the ship hugged the shore.* **hug** n. a strong clasp with the arms.

huge (hyooj) adj. extremely large, enormous. **huge′ly** adv. **huge′ness** n.

hug·ger-mug·ger (hug-ĕr-mug-ĕr) n. *(old use)* 1. confusion and disorder. 2. secrecy. **hugger-mugger** adj. *(old use)* 1. in disarray, confused. 2. in secret.

Hu·gue·not (hyoo-gĕ-not) n. a French Protestant of the 16th and 17th centuries.

huh (hu) *interj.* used as an expression of interrogation, contempt, etc.

hu·la (hoo-lä) n. (also **hula-hula**) a Hawaiian woman's dance with sinuous movements of the torso and arms. □**hula hoop,** a large hoop for spinning around the body with hula-like movements. **hula skirt,** a long grass Hawaiian skirt.

hulk (hulk) n. 1. the body of an old ship. 2. a large clumsy-looking person or thing.

hulk·ing (hul-king) adj. *(informal)* large, clumsy.

hull (hul) n. 1. the dry outer covering of a fruit or vegetable, as the pods of peas. 2. the cluster of leaves on a strawberry. 3. the basic frame of a ship or aircraft. **hull** v. to remove the hulls of (a vegetable etc.).

hul·la·ba·loo (hul-ä-bä-loo) n. (pl. **-loos**) an uproar.

hum (hum) v. (**hummed, hum·ming**) 1. to make a low steady continuous sound like that of a spinning object. 2. to sing with closed lips. 3. *(informal)* to be in a state of activity, *things started humming; make things hum.* **hum** n. a humming sound. **hum′mer** n.

hu·man (hyoo-män) adj. 1. of or consisting of the species to which men and women belong, *the human race.* 2. having the qualities that distinguish mankind, not divine or animal or mechanical. **human** n. a human being. □**human interest,**

something that appeals to personal emotions (in a newspaper story etc.). **human rights,** those held to be claimable by any living person, such as the right of free speech, the right to worship as one chooses, etc.

hu·mane (hyoo-mayn) *adj.* kindhearted, compassionate, merciful. **hu·mane′ly** *adv.* **hu·mane′ness** *n.* ▯**humane society,** an organized group concerned with the kind treatment of animals.

hu·man·ist (hyoo-mă-nist) *n.* 1. a person who is concerned with the study of mankind and human affairs (as opposed to theology or the physical sciences), or who seeks to promote human welfare. 2. a student (especially during the Renaissance) of Roman and Greek literature and antiquities. **hu′man·ism** *n.* **hu·man·is·tic** (hyoo-mă-nistik) *adj.*

hu·man·i·tar·i·an (hyoo-man-i-tair-i-ăn) *adj.* concerned with human welfare and the reduction of suffering. **humanitarian** *n.* a humanitarian person.

hu·man·i·ties (hyoo-man-i-teez) *n. pl.* arts subjects (especially study of the Greek and Latin classics) as opposed to the sciences.

hu·man·i·ty (hyoo-man-i-tee) *n.* (*pl.* -ties) 1. the human race, people. 2. being human. 3. being humane, kindheartedness.

hu·man·ize (hyoo-mă-nīz) *v.* **(hu·man·ized, hu·man·iz·ing)** 1. to make human, to give a human character to. 2. to make humane. **hu·man·i·za·tion** (hyoo-mă-ni-zay-shŏn) *n.*

hu·man·kind (hyoo-măn-kīnd) *n.* mankind.

hu·man·ly (hyoo-măn-lee) *adv.* 1. in a human way. 2. by human means, with human limitations, *as accurate as is humanly possible.*

hu·man·oid (hyoo-mă-noid) *adj.* having somewhat human characteristics. **humanoid** *n.* a humanoid robot.

hum·ble (hum-bĕl) *adj.* (-bler, -blest) 1. having or showing a modest estimate of one's own importance, not proud. 2. offered with such feelings, *humble apologies.* 3. of low social or political rank. 4. (of a thing) not large or elaborate, *a humble cottage.* **humble** *v.* **(hum·bled, hum·bling)** to make humble, to lower the rank or self-importance of. **hum′bly** *adv.* **hum′ble·ness** *n.* ▯**eat humble pie,** to make a humble apology. ▷From *umble pie,* that made with "umbles," the edible organs (heart, kidney, etc.) of deer.

hum·bug (hum-bug) *n.* 1. misleading behavior or talk that is intended to win support or sympathy. 2. a person who behaves or talks in this way. **humbug** *v.* **(hum·bugged, hum·bug·ging)** to delude, to behave like an impostor. **humbug** *interj.* nonsense.

hum·ding·er (hum-ding-ĕr) *n. (slang)* a remarkable person or thing.

hum·drum (hum-drum) *adj.* dull, commonplace, monotonous.

hu·mer·us (hyoo-mĕ-rŭs) *n.* the bone in the upper arm, from shoulder to elbow.

hu·mid (hyoo-mid) *adj.* (of the air or climate) damp. **hum′id·ly** *adv.* **hu·mid·i·ty** (hyoo-midi-tee) *n.*

hu·mid·i·fi·er (hyoo-mid-ĭ-fī-ĕr) *n.* a device for keeping the air moist in a room etc.

hu·mid·i·fy (hyoo-mid-ĭ-fī) *v.* **(hu·mid·i·fied, hu·mid·i·fy·ing)** to add moisture to (a room etc.). **hu·mid·i·fi·ca·tion** (hyoo-mid-ĭ-fi-kay-shŏn) *n.*

hu·mi·dor (hyoo-mi-dor) *n.* a box, room, etc. for storing and keeping cigars or tobacco moist.

hu·mil·i·ate (hyoo-mil-i-ayt) *v.* **(hu·mil·i·at·ed, hu·mil·i·at·ing)** to cause (a person) to feel disgraced. **hu·mil·i·a·tion** (hyoo-mil-i-ay-shŏn) *n.*

hu·mil·i·ty (hyoo-mil-i-tee) *n.* a humble condition or attitude of mind.

hum·ming·bird (hum-ing-burd) *n.* a small tropical bird that vibrates its wings rapidly, producing a humming sound.

hum·mock (hum-ŏk) *n.* a hump in the ground.

hu·mon·gous (hyoo-mong-gŭs) *adj. (slang)* huge, tremendous. ▷Loosely based on *huge* and *enormous.*

hu·mor (hyoo-mŏr) *n.* 1. the quality of being amusing. 2. the ability to perceive and enjoy amusement, *sense of humor.* 3. a state of mind, *in a good humor.* **humor** *v.* to keep (a person) contented by giving way to his wishes. **hu′mor·less** *adj.* **hu′mor·less·ly** *adv.* **hu′mor·less·ness** *n.*

hu·mor·esque (hyoo-mŏ-resk) *n.* a light and lively musical composition.

hu·mor·ist (hyoo-mŏ-rist) *n.* a writer or speaker who is noted for his humor.

hu·mor·ous (hyoo-mŏ-rŭs) *adj.* full of humor. **hu′mor·ous·ly** *adv.*

hump (hump) *n.* 1. a rounded projecting part. 2. a protuberance, especially on the back, as a deformity or (in the camel etc.) as a normal feature. **hump** *v.* 1. to form into a hump. 2. to exert oneself energetically. **humped** *adj.*

hump·back (hump-bak) *n.* a hunchback. ▯**humpback whale,** a whale with a dorsal fin forming a hump. **hump′backed** *adj.*

humph (humf) *interj.* & *n.* an inarticulate sound expressing doubt or dissatisfaction.

hu·mus (hyoo-mŭs) *n.* rich dark organic material, formed by the decay of dead leaves and plants etc. and essential to the fertility of soil.

Hun (hun) *n.* 1. a member of an Asiatic warlike nomad race who invaded and ravaged Europe in the 4th to 5th centuries. 2. an uncivilized vandal. **Hun′nish** *adj.* **Hun′nish·ness** *n.*

hunch (hunch) *v.* to bend into a hump. **hunch** *n.* 1. a hump, a hunk. 2. a feeling based on intuition.

hunch·back (hunch-bak) *n.* a person with a hump on his back. **hunch′-backed′** *adj.*

hun·dred (hun-drid) *adj.* & *n.* (*pl.* -dreds, -dred) ten times ten (100, C), *several hundred people; hundreds of people,* very many. **hun·dredth** (hundridth) *adj.* & *n.* ▯**hundred percent,** entirely, completely.

hun·dred·fold (hun-drid-fohld) *adj.* & *adv.* one hundred times as much or as many.

hun·dred·weight (hun-drid-wayt) *n.* 1. a measure of weight equaling 100 pounds *(short hundredweight).* 2. a measure of weight equaling 50 kilograms *(metric hundredweight).*

hung (hung) *see* **hang.** ▯**hung over,** *(slang)* having a hangover. **hung up on,** *(slang)* obsessed with.

Hung. *abbr.* 1. Hungarian. 2. Hungary.

Hun·ga·ry (hung-gă-ree) a country of central Europe. **Hun·gar·i·an** (hung-gair-i-ăn) *adj.* & *n.*

hun·ger (hung-gĕr) *n.* 1. need for food, the uneasy sensation felt when one has not eaten for some time. 2. a strong desire for something. **hun·ger** *v.* to feel hunger. ▯**hunger strike,** refusal of food, as a form of protest.

hun·gry (hung-gree) *adj.* **(-gri·er, -gri·est)** feeling hunger. **hun′gri·ly** *adv.*

hunk (hungk) *n. (informal)* a large or clumsy piece.

hun·ker (hung-kĕr) *v.* to squat.

hun·kers (hung-kĕrz) *n. pl.* the buttocks.

hunk·y-do·ry (hung-kee-dohr-ee) *adj. (slang)* excellent.

hunt (hunt) *v.* **1.** to pursue (wild animals) for food or sport. **2.** to pursue with hostility, to drive, *was hunted away.* **3.** to make a search, *hunted for it everywhere; hunt it out,* seek and find it. **hunt** *n.* **1.** hunting. **2.** an association of people for the purpose of hunting. □**hunt down,** to hunt (an animal etc.) until it is caught or killed; to hunt for and find. **hunting ground,** a place where people hunt; *happy hunting grounds,* life after death (especially as expected by the American Indians), a good place for hunting. **hunt up,** to search for and find.

hunt·er (hun-tĕr) *n.* **1.** one who hunts. **2.** a horse or dog used for hunting. □**hunter's moon,** the first full moon after the harvest moon.

hunt·ress (hun-tris) *n.* a woman who hunts.

hunts·man (hunts-măn) *n. (pl.* **-men,** *pr.* -mĕn) **1.** a man who hunts. **2.** a man in charge of a pack of hunting hounds.

hur·dle (hur-dĕl) *n.* **1.** a portable rectangular frame with bars, used for a temporary fence. **2.** an upright frame to be jumped over in a *hurdle race.* **3.** an obstacle or difficulty. **4.** *hurdles,* a hurdle race. **hurdle** *v.* **(hur·dled, hur·dling) 1.** to fence off etc. with hurdles. **2.** to leap over. **3.** to overcome (an obstacle). **hur′dler** *n.*

hur·dy-gur·dy (hur-dee-gur-dee) *n. (pl.* **-gur·dies) 1.** a musical instrument with a droning sound, played by turning a handle. **2.** *(informal)* a barrel organ.

hurl (hurl) *v.* **1.** to throw violently. **2.** to utter vehemently, *hurl insults.* **3.** *(informal)* to pitch a baseball. **hurl** *n.* a violent throw.

hurl·er (hur-lĕr) *n. (informal)* a baseball pitcher.

hurl·y-burl·y (hur-lee-bur-lee) *n. (pl.* **-bur·lies)** a rough bustle of activity.

Hu·ron (hyoor-ŏn) *n. (pl.* **-rons, -ron) 1.** a member of the Indian tribe living west of Lake Huron, originally from the St. Lawrence Valley. **2.** the language of this tribe.

hur·ray (hŭ-ray), **hur·rah** (hŭ-rah) *interj. & n.* an exclamation of joy or approval.

hur·ri·cane (hur-i-kayn) *n.* **1.** a storm with violent wind, especially a West Indian cyclone. **2.** a wind of 73 miles per hour or more. □**hurricane lamp,** a kerosene lamp or candlestick having a glass chimney, designed to resist high winds.

hur·ried (hur-eed) *adj.* done with great haste. **hur·ried·ly** (hur-id-lee) *adv.*

hur·ry (hur-ee) *n. (pl.* **-ries)** great haste, the need or desire for this. **hurry** *v.* **(hur·ried, hur·ry·ing)** to move or do something with eager haste or too quickly, to cause to move etc. in this way. □**hurry up,** *(informal)* make haste. **in a hurry,** hurrying; easily or willingly, *you won't beat that in a hurry; won't ask again in a hurry.*

hurt (hurt) *v.* **(hurt, hurt·ing) 1.** to cause pain or damage or injury to. **2.** to cause mental pain to, to distress. **3.** to cause or feel pain, *my leg hurts.* **hurt** *n.* an injury, harm.

hurt·ful (hurt-fŭl) *adj.* causing hurt.

hur·tle (hur-tĕl) *v.* **(hur·tled, hur·tling)** to move or hurl rapidly.

hus·band (huz-bănd) *n.* a married man in relation to his wife. **husband** *v.* to use economically, to try to save, *husband one's resources.*

hus·band·ry (huz-băn-dree) *n.* **1.** farming. **2.** the management of resources.

hush (hush) *v.* to make or become silent or quiet; *hush a thing up,* to prevent it from becoming generally known. **hush** *interj. & n.* silence. □**hush money,** money paid to prevent something discreditable from being revealed. **hush puppy,** quickly fried cornmeal bread; *Hush Puppies, (trademark)* light soft shoes.

hush-hush (hush-hush) *adj. (informal)* kept very secret.

husk (husk) *n.* the dry outer covering of certain seeds and fruits. **husk** *v.* to remove the husk(s) from. □**husking bee,** a gathering of families in farm areas to husk corn.

hus·ky¹ (hus-kee) *adj.* **(-ki·er, -ki·est) 1.** dry like husks. **2.** (of a person or his voice) dry in the throat, hoarse. **3.** big and strong, burly. **husk′i·ly** *adv.* **husk′i·ness** *n.*

husky² *n. (pl.* **-kies)** an Eskimo dog, used for pulling dogsleds.

Hus·sars (huu-zahrz) *n.* any of several European cavalry regiments.

hus·sy (hus-ee, huz-ee) *n. (pl.* **-sies) 1.** an immoral woman. **2.** an impertinent young woman.

hus·tings (hus-tingz) *n.* **1.** any place where political speeches are made during an election campaign. **2.** the travels of a political candidate while campaigning; *on the hustings,* campaigning in an election. ▷Originally a temporary platform from which candidates for the British parliament could address the electors.

hus·tle (hus-ĕl) *v.* **(hus·tled, hus·tling) 1.** to jostle, to push roughly. **2.** to hurry. **3.** to bustle (a person), to make (a person) act quickly and without time to consider things, *was hustled into a decision.* **4.** *(slang)* to earn a living by dishonest or questionable pursuits. **hustle** *n.* **1.** ambition, drive. **2.** an energetic popular dance. **3.** *(slang)* a game designed to defraud participants or those who gamble on it.

hus·tler (hus-lĕr) *n.* **1.** a person who hustles. **2.** *(slang)* a prostitute.

hut (hut) *n.* a small roughly made house or shelter.

hutch (huch) *n.* a boxlike pen for rabbits.

huz·zah (hu-zah) *interj. & n. (old use)* an expression of exultation, encouragement, or applause.

HV *abbr.* **1.** high velocity. **2.** high voltage.

hvy *abbr.* heavy.

hwy. *abbr.* highway.

hy·a·cinth (hɪ-ă-sinth) *n.* **1.** a plant with fragrant bell-shaped flowers, growing from a bulb. **2.** purplish blue.

hy·brid (hɪ-brid) *n.* **1.** an animal or plant that is the offspring of two different species or varieties. **2.** something made by combining two different elements. **hybrid** *adj.* produced in this way. **hy′brid·ism** *n.*

hy·brid·ize (hɪ-bri-dɪz) *v.* **(hy·brid·ized, hy·brid·iz·ing) 1.** to subject to crossbreeding. **2.** to produce hybrids, to interbreed. **hy′brid·iz·er** *n.* **hy·brid·i·za·tion** (hɪ-bri-di-zay-shŏn) *n.*

hy·dra (hɪ-dră) *n. (pl.* **-dras, -drae,** *pr.* -dree) **1.** a thing that is hard to get rid of. **2.** a freshwater polyp with tubular body and tentacles around the mouth. ▷Named after the *Hydra* in Greek mythology, a water snake with many heads that grew again if cut off.

hy·dra-head·ed (hɪ-dră-hed-id) *adj.* **1.** having

many divisions or facets. 2. producing many problems.

hy·dran·gea (hɪ-**drayn**-jä) n. a shrub with white, pink, or blue flowers growing in clusters.

hy·drant (hɪ-drănt) n. a pipe from a water main (especially in a street) with a nozzle to which a hose can be attached for fighting fires or cleaning streets etc.

hy·drate (hɪ-drayt) n. a chemical compound of water with another compound or element. **hydrate** v. (**hy·drat·ed, hy·drat·ing**) 1. to combine chemically with water. 2. to cause to absorb water. **hy·dra·tion** (hɪ-**dray**-shŏn) n.

hy·drau·lic (hɪ-**draw**-lik) adj. 1. operated by the movement of water, a hydraulic lift. 2. concerned with the use of water in this way, hydraulic engineer. 3. of water conveyed through pipes or channels. 4. hardening under water, hydraulic cement. **hy·drau'li·cal·ly** adv.

hy·drau·lics (hɪ-**draw**-liks) n. the science of the conveyance of liquids through pipes etc., especially as motive power.

hy·dro (hɪ-droh) adj. (informal) hydroelectric.

hy·dro·car·bon (hɪ-drŏ-**kahr**-bŏn) n. any of a class of compounds of hydrogen and carbon that are found in oil, coal, and natural gas.

hy·dro·ceph·a·lus (hɪ-drŏ-**sef**-ă-lŭs), **hy·dro·ceph·a·ly** (hɪ-drŏ-**sef**-ă-lee) n. a condition (especially of children) in which fluid accumulates on the brain, with resulting mental deficiency. **hy·dro·ce·phal·ic** (hɪ-droh-sĕ-**fal**-ik) adj.

hy·dro·chlo·ric (hɪ-drŏ-**klohr**-ik) **acid** a colorless corrosive acid containing hydrogen and chlorine.

hy·dro·cy·an·ic (hɪ-drŏ-sɪ-**an**-ik) **acid** a weak acid that is highly poisonous, prussic acid.

hy·dro·dy·nam·ic (hɪ-droh-dɪ-**nam**-ik) adj. of the force exerted by a moving liquid, especially water.

hy·dro·dy·nam·ics (hɪ-droh-dɪ-**nam**-iks) n. the scientific study of the force exerted by a moving liquid, especially water.

hy·dro·e·lec·tric (hɪ-droh-i-**lek**-trik) adj. using waterpower to produce electricity. **hy·dro·e·lec'tri·cal·ly** adv. **hy·dro·e·lec·tric·i·ty** (hɪ-droh-i-lek-**tris**-i-tee) n.

hy·dro·foil (hɪ-drŏ-foil) n. 1. a boat equipped with a structure designed to raise the hull out of the water when the boat is in motion, enabling it to travel fast and economically. 2. this structure.

hy·dro·gen (hɪ-drŏ-jĕn) n. a colorless odorless tasteless gaseous element, the lightest substance known, combining with oxygen to form water. □**hydrogen bomb**, an immensely powerful bomb releasing energy by fusion of hydrogen nuclei. **hydrogen peroxide,** a colorless liquid used in a dilute solution as a bleach and an antiseptic.

hy·dro·gen·ate (hɪ-**droj**-ĕ-nayt) v. (**hy·dro·gen·at·ed, hy·dro·gen·at·ing**) to charge or to cause to combine with hydrogen. **hy·dro·gen·a·tion** (hɪ-droj-ĕ-nay-shŏn) n.

hy·drog·ra·phy (hɪ-**drog**-ră-fee) n. the scientific study of seas and lakes and rivers and other surface waters of the earth. **hy·drog'ra·pher** n. **hy·dro·graph·ic** (hɪ-drŏ-**graf**-ik) adj.

hy·drol·o·gist (hɪ-**drol**-ŏ-jist) n. a specialist in hydrology.

hy·drol·o·gy (hɪ-**drol**-ŏ-jee) n. the scientific study of the distribution, circulation, and properties of the waters of the earth. **hy·dro·log·ic** (hɪ-drŏ-**loj**-ik) adj. **hy·dro·log'i·cal** adj.

hy·drol·y·sis (hɪ-**drol**-ĭ-sis) n. the decomposition of a substance by the chemical action of water.

hy·dro·lyt·ic (hɪ-drŏ-**lit**-ik) adj.

hy·drom·e·ter (hɪ-**drom**-ĕ-tĕr) n. an instrument that measures the specific gravity of liquids.

hy·dro·pho·bi·a (hɪ-drŏ-**foh**-bi-ă) n. 1. abnormal fear of water, especially as a symptom of rabies in man. 2. rabies.

hy·dro·phone (hɪ-drŏ-fohn) n. a device for listening under water.

hy·dro·plane (hɪ-drŏ-playn) n. a light fast motorboat designed to skim over the surface of water.

hy·dro·pon·ics (hɪ-drŏ-**pon**-iks) n. the art of growing plants without soil in water to which nutrients have been added. **hy·dro·pon'ic** adj.

hy·dro·sphere (hɪ-drŏ-sfeer) n. the waters on the surface of the earth.

hy·dro·stat·ic (hɪ-drŏ-**stat**-ik) adj. of the pressure and other characteristics of water or other liquid at rest.

hy·dro·stat·ics (hɪ-drŏ-**stat**-iks) n. the scientific study of the pressure and equilibrium of liquids at rest.

hy·dro·ther·a·py (hɪ-drŏ-**ther**-ă-pee) n. the use of water (internally and externally) in the treatment of disease and abnormal physical conditions.

hy·dro·ther·mal (hɪ-drŏ-**thur**-măl) adj. of the action of heated water on the earth's crust.

hy·drous (hɪ-drŭs) adj. (of substances) containing water.

hy·drox·ide (hɪ-**drok**-sɪd) n. a chemical compound of an element or a radical with hydroxyl.

hy·drox·yl (hɪ-**drok**-sil) n. a chemical radical containing hydrogen and oxygen.

hy·en·a (hɪ-ee-nă) n. a flesh-eating animal with a howl that sounds like wild laughter.

hy·giene (hɪ-jeen) n. the practice of cleanliness in order to maintain health and prevent disease.

hy·gien·ist (hɪ-jee-nist, -ji-en-ist) n.

hy·gi·en·ic (hɪ-ji-**en**-ik) adj. 1. according to the principles of hygiene. 2. clean and free from disease germs. **hy·gi·en'i·cal·ly** adv.

hy·grom·e·ter (hɪ-grom-ĕ-tĕr) n. an instrument that measures humidity. **hy·grom'e·try** n.

hy·ing (hɪ-ing) see **hie.**

hy·men (hɪ-mĕn) n. a membrane partly closing the external opening of the vagina of a virgin girl or woman.

hy·me·ne·al (hɪ-mĕ-nee-ăl) adj. nuptial.

hymn (him) n. a song of praise to God or a sacred being. □**hymn book,** a book of hymns.

hym·nal (him-năl) n. a hymn book.

hym·no·dy (him-nŏ-dee) n. 1. the singing or composing of hymns. 2. the hymns collectively. **hym'no·dist** n.

hyp. abbr. 1. hypotenuse. 2. hypothesis. 3. hypothetical.

hype (hɪp) n. (slang) misleading and exaggerated claims in advertising or publicity. **hype** v. (**hyped, hyp·ing**) (slang) to mislead by sensational publicity. □**hyped up,** (slang) stimulated by or as if by an injection of drugs.

hy·per·a·cid·i·ty (hɪ-pĕr-ă-**sid**-i-tee) n. excessive acidity. **hy·per·ac·id** (hɪ-pĕr-as-id) adj.

hy·per·ac·tive (hɪ-pĕr-ak-tive) adj. (especially of children) excessively or abnormally active. **hy·per·ac·tiv·i·ty** (hɪ-pĕr-ak-**tiv**-i-tee) n.

hy·per·bar·ic (hɪ-pĕr-**bar**-ik) adj. of or utilizing oxygen at high pressure.

hy·per·bo·la (hɪ-pur-bŏ-lă) *n.* (*pl.* **-lae,** *pr.* -lee) a plane curve of two equal infinite branches produced when a double cone is cut by a plane that makes a larger angle with the base than the side of the cone does. **hy·per·bol·ic** (hɪ-pĕr-bol-ik) *adj.*

hy·per·bo·le (hɪ-pur-bŏ-lee) *n.* an exaggerated statement that is not meant to be taken literally, as *a stack of work a mile high.* **hy·per·bol·i·cal** (hɪ-pĕr-bol-i-kăl) *adj.*

hy·per·bo·re·an (hɪ-pĕr-bohr-i-ăn) *n.* 1. an inhabitant of the extreme north of the earth. 2. *Hyperborean,* (in Greek mythology) a member of a race worshipping Apollo and living in the land of sunshine and plenty beyond the north wind.

hy·per·crit·i·cal (hɪ-pĕr-krit-i-kăl) *adj.* excessively critical. **hy·per·crit'i·cal·ly** *adv.*

hy·per·o·pi·a (hɪ-pĕr-oh-pi-ă) *n.* farsightedness. **hy·per·op·ic** (hɪ-pĕr-op-ik) *adj.*

hy·per·sen·si·tive (hɪ-pĕr-sen-si-tiv) *adj.* excessively sensitive. **hy·per·sen'si·tive·ness** *n.*

hy·per·sen·si·tiv·i·ty (hɪ-pĕr-sen-si-tiv-i-tee) *n.*

hy·per·son·ic (hɪ-pĕr-son-ik) *adj.* 1. relating to speeds more than about five times that of sound. 2. relating to sound frequencies above about a billion hertz. **hy·per·son'i·cal·ly** *adv.*

hy·per·ten·sion (hɪ-pĕr-ten-shŏn) *n.* 1. abnormally high blood pressure. 2. great emotional tension.

hy·per·ther·mi·a (hɪ-pĕr-thur-mi-ă) *n.* the condition of having a body temperature greatly above normal.

hy·per·thy·roid·ism (hɪ-pĕr-thɪ-roi-diz-ĕm) *n.* 1. increased activity of the thyroid gland. 2. the resulting condition of high metabolism in the body. **hy·per·thy'roid** *adj.*

hy·per·tro·phy (hɪ-pur-trŏ-fee) *n.* (*pl.* **-phies**) an enlargement (of an organ etc.) caused by excessive nutrition. **hy·per·tro·phic** (hɪ-pĕr-troh-fik) *adj.* **hypertrophy** *v.* (**hy·per·tro·phied, hy·per·tro·phy·ing**) to cause or suffer hypertrophy.

hy·per·ven·ti·la·tion (hɪ-pĕr-ven-tĭ-lay-shŏn) *n.* a condition of very rapid deep breathing resulting in a decrease of carbon dioxide in the blood.

hy·phen (hɪ-fĕn) *n.* the sign - used to join two words together (as in *house-raising*) or to divide a word into parts. **hyphen** *v.* to hyphenate.

hy·phen·ate (hɪ-fĕ-nayt) *v.* (**hy·phen·at·ed, hy·phen·at·ing**) to join or divide with a hyphen. **hy·phen·a·tion** (hɪ-fĕ-nay-shŏn) *n.*

hyp·no·sis (hip-noh-sis) *n.* 1. the sleeplike condition produced by hypnotism. 2. hypnotism.

hyp·not·ic (hip-not-ik) *adj.* 1. of or producing hypnosis or a similar condition. 2. (of a drug) producing sleep. **hypnotic** *n.* a hypnotic drug. **hyp·not'i·cal·ly** *adv.*

hyp·no·tism (hip-nŏ-tiz-ĕm) *n.* the production of a sleeplike condition in a person who is then very susceptible to suggestion and who acts only if told to do so.

hyp·no·tist (hip-nŏ-tist) *n.* a person who produces hypnotism in another.

hyp·no·tize (hip-nŏ-tɪz) *v.* (**hyp·no·tized, hyp·no·tiz·ing**) 1. to produce hypnosis in (a

person). 2. to fascinate, to dominate the mind or will of.

hy·po¹ (hɪ-poh) *n.* (*pl.* **-pos**) the fixing agent sodium thiosulphate used in photography.

hypo² *n.* (*pl.* **-pos**) (*informal*) a hypodermic.

hy·po·cen·ter (hɪ-pŏ-sen-tĕr) *n.* the point on the earth's surface directly below the center of a nuclear bomb explosion.

hy·po·chon·dri·a (hɪ-pŏ-kon-dri-ă) *n.* a mental condition in which a person constantly shows unnecessary anxiety about his health.

hy·po·chon·dri·ac (hɪ-pŏ-kon-dri-ak) *n.* a person who suffers from hypochondria.

hy·poc·ri·sy (hi-pok-rĭ-see) *n.* (*pl.* **-sies**) the simulation of virtue or goodness, insincerity.

hyp·o·crite (hip-ŏ-krit) *n.* a person who is guilty of hypocrisy. **hyp·o·crit·i·cal** (hip-ŏ-krit-i-kăl) *adj.* **hyp·o·crit'i·cal·ly** *adv.*

hy·po·der·mic (hɪ-pŏ-dur-mik) *adj.* 1. injected beneath the skin. 2. used for such injections. **hypodermic** *n.* a *hypodermic needle,* a syringe fitted with a hollow needle through which a liquid can be injected beneath the skin. **hy·po·der'mi·cal·ly** *adv.*

hy·po·gly·ce·mi·a (hɪ-poh-glɪ-see-mi-ă) *n.* an abnormally low level of glucose in the blood. **hy·po·gly·ce·mic** (hɪ-poh-glɪ-see-mik) *adj.*

hy·po·ten·sion (hɪ-pŏ-ten-shŏn) *n.* abnormally low blood pressure.

hy·pot·e·nuse (hɪ-pot-ĕ-noos) *n.* the side opposite the right angle in a right triangle.

hy·po·thal·a·mus (hɪ-pŏ-thal-ă-mŭs) *n.* the organ below the brain, controlling body temperature.

hy·poth·e·cate (hɪ-poth-ĕ-kayt) *v.* (**hy·poth·e·cat·ed, hy·poth·e·cat·ing**) to pledge, to mortgage. **hy·poth·e·ca·tion** (hɪ-poth-ĕ-kay-shŏn) *n.*

hy·po·ther·mi·a (hɪ-pŏ-thur-mi-ă) *n.* the condition of having a body temperature greatly below normal.

hy·poth·e·sis (hɪ-poth-ĕ-sis) *n.* (*pl.* **-ses,** *pr.* -seez) a supposition or conjecture put forward to account for certain facts and used as a basis for further investigation by which it may be proved or disproved.

hy·poth·e·size (hɪ-poth-ĕ-sɪz) *v.* (**hy·poth·e·sized, hy·poth·e·siz·ing**) 1. to frame a hypothesis. 2. to assume as hypothesis.

hy·po·thet·i·cal (hɪ-pŏ-thet-i-kăl) *adj.* of or based on a hypothesis, supposed but not necessarily true. **hy·po·thet'i·cal·ly** *adv.*

hy·po·thy·roid·ism (hɪ-poh-thɪ-roi-diz-ĕm) *n.* 1. a decreased activity of the thyroid gland. 2. the resulting condition of low metabolism in the body. **hy·po·thy'roid** *adj.*

hys·sop (his-ŏp) *n.* a bushy aromatic herb with small blue flowers, used medicinally.

hys·ter·ec·to·my (his-tĕ-rek-tŏ-mee) *n.* (*pl.* **-mies**) surgical removal of the uterus.

hys·te·ri·a (hi-ster-i-ă, -steer-) *n.* wild uncontrollable emotion or excitement.

hys·ter·i·cal (hi-ster-i-kăl) *adj.* caused by hysteria, suffering from this. **hys·ter'i·cal·ly** *adv.*

hys·ter·ics (hi-ster-iks) *n.* a hysterical outburst.

Hz *abbr.* hertz.

I

I, i (ī) (*pl.* **Is, I's, i's**) 1. the ninth letter of the alphabet. 2. the Roman numeral symbol for 1.
I (ī) *pronoun* the person who is speaking or writing and referring to himself.
I *abbr.* 1. independent. 2. interstate highway. 3. island(s). 4. isle(s).
I *symbol* iodine.
i. *abbr.* 1. interest. 2. intransitive. 3. island(s). 4. isle(s).
IA *abbr.* Iowa.
i·amb (ī-am, ī-amb), **i·am·bus** (ī-am-bŭs) *n.* a metrical foot consisting of one short followed by one long syllable, or of an unaccented followed by an accented syllable. **i·am'bic** *adj. & n.*
-ian *suffix* used to form adjectives that often are used as nouns, as in *Bostonian, Christian.*
I·be·ri·an (ī-beer-i-ăn) *adj.* of the peninsula in southwest Europe comprising Spain and Portugal.
i·bex (ī-beks) *n.* (*pl.* **i·bex·es, i·bex**) a mountain goat with long curving horns.
ibid. *abbr.* ibidem, = in the same book or passage etc. ▷Latin.
i·bis (ī-bis) *n.* (*pl.* **i·bis·es, i·bis**) a wading bird with a long curved bill, found in warm climates.
-ible *suffix* used to form adjectives with the same meanings as **-able**, as in *terrible, forcible.*
-ic¹ *suffix* used to form adjectives meaning having the form or character of, as in *scenic;* of or relating to, as in *Arabic;* in the manner of, as in *barbaric;* derived from or containing, as in *alcoholic;* dealing or associated with, as in *atomic;* characterized by, as in *tragic;* in a higher valence or degree of oxidation, as in *ferric.*
-ic² *suffix* used to form nouns meaning one having the nature or character of, as in *stoic;* one associated with or belonging to, as in *mechanic;* one that produces, as in *critic;* one affected by, as in *lunatic.*
-ical *suffix* used to form adjectives corresponding to nouns or adjectives ending in -ic, as in *classical, comical.*
ICBM *abbr.* intercontinental ballistic missile.
ICC *abbr.* Interstate Commerce Commission.
ice (īs) *n.* 1. frozen water, a brittle transparent solid. 2. a sheet of this. 3. (also **ices**) a refreshment made of flavored crushed ice. **ice** *v.* (**iced, ic·ing**) 1. to become covered with ice, *the pond iced over.* 2. to make very cold. 3. to decorate with icing. **iced** *adj.* □**Ice Age,** a period when much of the northern hemisphere was covered with glaciers. **ice bag,** an ice-filled rubber bag for medical use. **ice cap,** the permanent covering of ice in polar regions. **ice cream,** a sweet creamy frozen food. **ice cube,** a small block of ice made in a refrigerator. **ice field,** an extensive sheet of floating ice. **ice hockey,** a game resembling hockey,

played on ice between teams of skaters with a flat disk (a *puck*) instead of a ball. **ice milk,** ice cream made with greatly reduced butterfat. **ice pick,** an awl for chipping ice. **ice plant,** a plant with leaves that glisten as if with ice. **ice show,** an entertainment by skaters on ice. **ice skate,** a metal blade attached to the sole of a boot or shoe so that the wearer can glide over ice. **ice skater,** a person who uses ice skates. **ice storm,** a storm that leaves a coating of ice. **ice water,** water chilled by ice. **on thin ice,** in a risky situation.
Ice. *abbr.* 1. Iceland. 2. Icelandic.
ice·berg (īs-burg) *n.* a huge mass of ice floating in the sea with the greater part under water. □**iceberg lettuce,** a variety of lettuce with round crisp heads. **tip of the iceberg,** a small evident part of something much larger that lies concealed.
ice·boat (īs-boht) *n.* a boat mounted on runners for traveling on ice.
ice·bound (īs-bownd) *adj.* hemmed in by ice.
ice·box (īs-boks) *n.* 1. an insulated chest in which ice is put to preserve food. 2. (*informal*) a refrigerator.
ice·break·er (īs-bray-kĕr) *n.* 1. a boat with a reinforced bow for breaking a channel through ice. 2. a means of breaking through reserve or stiffness of manner.
ice-cold (īs-kohld) *adj.* as cold as ice.
ice-cream cone an edible sweet cone topped by at least one scoop of ice cream.
ice·house (īs-hows) *n.* (*old use*) a building for storing ice.
Ice·land (īs-lănd) an island country in the North Atlantic. **Ice'lan·der** *n.*
ice·lan·dic (īs-lan-dik) *adj.* of Iceland or its people or language. **Icelandic** *n.* the language of Iceland.
ice·man (īs-man) *n.* (*pl.* **-men,** *pr.* -men) a man who sells or delivers ice.
ice-skate (īs-skayt) *v.* (**ice-skat·ed, ice-skat·ing**) to skate on ice. **ice'skat·er** *n.*
i·chor (ī-kor) *n.* 1. a fluid said to flow like blood in the veins of the Greek Gods. 2. a thin fetid discharge from an ulcer or wound.
ich·thy·ol·o·gy (ik-thi-ol-ŏ-jee) *n.* the study of fishes. **ich·thy·ol'o·gist** *n.*
i·ci·cle (ī-si-kĕl) *n.* a pointed piece of ice hanging down, formed when dropping water freezes.
ic·ing (ī-sing) *n.* a mixture of sugar, butter or white of egg, and flavoring used to decorate cakes and cookies.
ICJ *abbr.* International Court of Justice.
ick·y (ik-ee) *adj.* (**ick·i·er, ick·i·est**) (*slang*) 1. sticky or gummy. 2. repulsive or repellent. 3. overly sentimental.

i·con (ɪ-kon) *n.* 1. an image or likeness. 2. (in the Eastern Church) a painting or mosaic of a sacred person, itself regarded as sacred.

i·con·o·clasm (ɪ-kon-ŏ-klaz-ĕm) *n.* the breaking of images.

i·con·o·clast (ɪ-kon-ŏ-klast) *n.* 1. a person who opposes the use of icons in worship. 2. a person who attacks cherished beliefs. **i·con·o·clas·tic** (ɪ-kon-ŏ-klas-tik) *adj.*

-ics *suffix* used to form nouns (variously considered plural or singular) meaning sciences and bodies of practical activity, facts, principles, etc., as in *acoustics, ethics, tactics.*

ic·tus (ik-tŭs) *n.* (*pl.* **-tus·es, -tus**) rhythmical or metrical stress.

ICU *abbr.* intensive care unit.

i·cy (ɪ-see) *adj.* (**i·ci·er, i·ci·est**) 1. very cold, as cold as ice, *icy winds.* 2. covered with ice, *icy roads.* 3. very cold and unfriendly in manner, *an icy voice.* **i′ci·ly** *adv.* **i′ci·ness** *n.*

id (id) *n.* the part of the psyche in which are the inherited instinctive impulses.

ID *abbr.* 1. Idaho. 2. identification. □**ID bracelet,** an identification bracelet. **ID card,** an identification card.

id. *abbr.* idem.

I'd (ɪd) = I had, I would.

i·da·ho (ɪ-dă-hoh) a state of the U.S.

i·de·a (ɪ-dee-ă) *n.* 1. a plan etc. formed in the mind by thinking. 2. a mental impression, *give him an idea of what is needed.* 3. an opinion, *tries to force his ideas on us.* 4. a vague belief or fancy, a feeling that something is likely, *I have an idea that we'll be late.* □**have no idea,** *(informal)* not to know; to be utterly incompetent. **the very ideal,** that is outrageous.

i·de·al (ɪ-dee-ăl, ɪ-deel) *adj.* satisfying one's idea of what is perfect, *ideal weather for sailing.* **ideal** *n.* a person or thing or idea that is regarded as perfect or as a standard for attainment or imitation, *the high ideals of the Christian religion.* **i·de′al·ly** *adv.*

i·de·al·ist (ɪ-dee-ă-list) *n.* a person who has high ideals and tries in an unrealistic way to achieve these. **i·de′al·ism** *n.* **i·de·al·is·tic** (ɪ-dee-ă-lis-tik) *adj.* **i·de·al·is′ti·cal·ly** *adv.*

i·de·al·ize (ɪ-dee-ă-lɪz) *v.* (**i·de·al·ized, i·de·al·iz·ing**) to regard or represent as perfect. **i·de·al·i·za·tion** (ɪ-dee-ă-li-zay-shŏn) *n.*

i·de·a·tion (ɪ-di-ay-shŏn) *n.* the formation of ideas. **i·de·a′tion·al** *adj.* **i·de·ate** (ɪ-di-ayt) *v.* (**i·de·at·ed, i·de·at·ing**).

i·dem (ɪ-dem) *pronoun* 1. the same author. 2. the same work. ▷Latin.

i·den·ti·cal (ɪ-den-ti-kăl) *adj.* 1. the same, *this is the identical place we stayed in last year.* 2. similar in every detail, exactly alike, *no two people have identical fingerprints.* **i·den′ti·cal·ly** *adv.* □**identical twins,** twins developed from a single fertilized ovum and therefore of the same sex and very similar in appearance.

i·den·ti·fi·a·ble (ɪ-den-tĭ-fɪ-ă-běl) *adj.* able to be identified.

i·den·ti·fy (ɪ-den-tĭ-fɪ) *v.* (**i·den·ti·fied, i·den·ti·fy·ing**) 1. to establish the identity of, to recognize as being a specified person or thing. 2. to consider to be identical, to equate, *one cannot identify riches with happiness.* 3. to associate very closely in feeling or interest, *he has identified himself with the progress of the firm.* 4. to regard oneself as sharing the characteristics or fortunes

of another person, *people like to identify with the characters in a film.* **i·den·ti·fi·ca·tion** (ɪ-den-tĭ-fi-kay-shŏn) *n.* □**identification bracelet,** a bracelet showing the owner's name etc. **identification card,** a card serving to identify the bearer.

i·den·ti·ty (ɪ-den-ti-tee) *n.* (*pl.* **-ties**) 1. the state of being identical, absolute sameness. 2. the condition of being a specified person or thing; *established his identity,* established who he was. □**identity crisis,** confusion in a person's mind, especially in adolescence, concerning his or her social role and true self.

id·e·o·gram (id-i-ŏ-gram) *n.* a symbol indicating the idea (not the sounds forming the name) of a thing, as numerals, Chinese characters, and symbols used in road signs.

i·de·o·log·i·cal (ɪ-di-ŏ-loj-i-kăl) *adj.* of or based on an ideology.

i·de·ol·o·gy (ɪ-di-ol-ŏ-jee) *n.* (*pl.* **-gies**) 1. the principal ideas or beliefs that characterize a particular class, group, or movement. 2. the ideas that form the basis of an economic or political theory etc., *Marxist ideology.*

ides (ɪdz) *n. pl.* in the ancient Roman calendar, the fifteenth of March, May, July, and October, the thirteenth of other months. □**ides of March,** the date (March 15) predicted for the assassination of Julius Caesar; an inauspicious day.

id est (id est) that is. ▷Latin.

id·i·o·cy (id-i-ŏ-see) *n.* (*pl.* **-cies**) 1. the state of being an idiot. 2. extreme stupidity. 3. stupid behavior, a stupid action.

id·i·om (id-i-ŏm) *n.* 1. a phrase that must be taken as a whole, usually having a meaning that is not clear from the meanings of the individual words, as *hang around* and *a change of heart.* 2. the use of particular words or of words in an order that is regarded as standard, *the idiom is "wash up the dishes" but not "wash up your hands."* 3. the language used by a people or group, *in the scientific idiom.* 4. a characteristic mode of expression in art or music etc.

id·i·o·mat·ic (id-i-ŏ-mat-ik) *adj.* 1. in accordance with idioms. 2. full of idioms. **id·i·o·mat′i·cal·ly** *adv.*

id·i·o·path·ic (id-i-ŏ-path-ik) *adj.* (of a disease) arising from an unknown cause or origin. **id·i·op·a·thy** (id-i-op-ă-thee) *n.*

id·i·o·syn·cra·sy (id-i-ŏ-sing-kră-see) *n.* (*pl.* **-sies**) a person's own attitude of mind or way of behaving etc. that is unlike that of others. **id·i·o·syn·crat·ic** (id-i-oh-sing-krat-ik) *adj.*

id·i·ot (id-i-ŏt) *n.* 1. a mentally deficient person who is permanently incapable of rational conduct. 2. *(informal)* a very stupid person. □**idiot card,** *(slang)* a card prompting a television performer. **id·i·ot·ic** (id-i-ot-ik) *adj.* very stupid. **id·i·ot′i·cal·ly** *adv.*

i·dle (ɪ-děl) *adj.* (**i·dler, i·dlest**) 1. doing no work, not employed, not active or in use. 2. (of time) spent doing nothing. 3. avoiding work, lazy, *an idle fellow.* 4. worthless, having no special purpose, *idle gossip; idle curiosity.* **idle** *v.* (**i·died, i·dling**). 1. to pass (time) without working, to be idle. 2. (of an engine) to run slowly in a neutral gear. **i′dly** *adv.* **i′dle·ness** *n.* **i′dler** *n.* □**idler gear,** an intermediate gear between two gears allowing them to rotate in the same direction.

i·dol (ɪ-dŏl) *n.* 1. an image of a god, used as an object of worship. 2. a person or thing that is

the object of intense admiration or devotion.
i·dol·a·ter (ı-dol-ă-tĕr) *n.* a person who worships
an idol or idols.
i·dol·a·try (ı-dol-ă-tree) *n.* (*pl.* -tries) 1. worship
of idols. 2. blind admiration or devotion. **i·dol'a·
trous** *adj.*
i·dol·ize (ı-dŏ-lız) *v.* (**i·dol·ized, i·dol·iz·ing**)
to feel excessive admiration or devotion to (a
person or thing). **i·dol·i·za·tion** (ı-dŏ-li-zay-
shŏn) *n.*
i·dyll (ı-dĭl) *n.* 1. a short description (usually in
verse) of a peaceful or romantic scene or incident,
especially in country life. 2. a scene or incident
of this kind.
i·dyl·lic (ı-dil-ik) *adj.* like an idyll, peaceful and
happy. **i·dyl'li·cal·ly** *adv.*
i.e. *abbr.* that is. ▷From the Latin *id est.*
-ier *suffix see* **-er**[1].
if (if) *conj.* 1. on condition that, *he'll do it only if
you pay him.* 2. in the event that, *if you are tired
we will rest.* 3. supposing or granting that, *even
if she said it she didn't mean it.* 4. even though,
I'll finish it, if it takes me all day. 5. whenever,
if they asked for food, it was brought. 6. whether,
see if you can turn the handle. (▷Careful writers
would use *whether* instead of *if.*) 7. (in exclamations of wish or surprise), *if only he would come!;
well, if it isn't Simon!* **if** *n.* a condition or supposition, *too many ifs about it.*
IF *abbr.* intermediate frequency.
if·fy (if-ee) *adj.* (**if·fi·er, if·fi·est**) (*informal*)
uncertain, doubtful.
ig·loo (ig-loo) *n.* (*pl.* -loos) a dome-shaped Eskimo
hut built of blocks of hard snow.
ig·ne·ous (ig-ni-ŭs) *adj.* (of rocks) formed by volcanic action.
ig·nite (ig-nıt) *v.* (**ig·nit·ed, ig·nit·ing**) 1. to set
fire to. 2. to catch fire.
ig·ni·tion (ig-nish-ŏn) *n.* 1. igniting, being ignited.
2. the mechanism providing the spark that ignites
the fuel in an internal combustion engine.
ig·no·ble (ig-noh-bĕl) *adj.* not noble in character
or aims or purpose. **ig·no'bly** *adv.*
ig·no·min·i·ous (ig-nŏ-min-i-ŭs) *adj.* bringing
contempt or disgrace, humiliating. **ig·no·min'i·
ous·ly** *adv.*
ig·no·min·y (ig-nŏ-min-ee) *n.* disgrace, humiliation.
ig·no·ra·mus (ig-nŏ-ray-mŭs) *n.* (*pl.* -mus·es)
an ignorant person.
ig·no·rant (ig-nŏ-rănt) *adj.* 1. lacking knowledge.
2. showing lack of knowledge. **ig'no·rant·ly**
adv. **ig'no·rance** *n.*
ig·nore (ig-nohr) *v.* (**ig·nored, ig·nor·ing**) 1. to
take no notice of, to disregard. 2. to refrain deliberately from acknowledging or greeting (a person).
i·gua·na (i-gwah-nă) *n.* a large tree-climbing lizard
of the West Indies and tropical America.
IHP *abbr.* indicated horsepower.
IHS *abbr.* Jesus. ▷From the first three letters of
the Greek word for Jesus, IHΣ.
i·kon = **icon.**
IL *abbr.* Illinois.
il·e·i·tis (il-i-ı-tŭs) *n.* inflammation of the ileum.
il·e·os·to·my (il-i-os-tŏ-mee) *n.* (*pl.* -mies) an
artificial opening through which the ileum can
empty, made surgically by bringing part of the
ileum to the surface of the abdomen.
il·e·um (il-i-ŭm) *n.* the lowest part of the small
intestine.

ILGWU *abbr.* International Ladies' Garment Workers' Union.
il·i·ac (il-i-ak) *adj.* of the flank or hipbone.
il·i·um (il-i-ŭm) *n.* the bone forming the upper part
of the pelvis.
ilk (ilk) *n.* (*informal*) kind, *others of that ilk.*
ill (il) *adj.* 1. physically or mentally unwell. 2. (of
health) unsound, not good. 3. harmful, *no ill effects.* 4. not favorable, *ill luck.* 5. hostile, unkind,
no ill feelings; ill humor, bad temper. **ill (worse,
worst)** *adv.* 1. badly, wrongly. 2. unfavorably.
3. imperfectly, scarcely, *ill provided for; can ill
afford to do this.* **ill** *n.* evil, harm, or injury. ☐**ill
at ease,** uncomfortable, embarrassed. **ill will,**
hostility, unkind feeling.
ill. *abbr.* 1. illustrated. 2. illustration. 3. illustrator.
Ill. *abbr.* Illinois.
I'll (ıl) = I shall, I will.
ill-ad·vised (il-ăd-vızd) *adj.* unwise. **ill-ad·vis·
ed·ly** (il-ăd-vı-zid-lee) *adv.*
ill-bred (il-bred) *adj.* having bad manners.
il·le·gal (i-lee-găl) *adj.* against the law. **il·le'gal·
ly** *adv.* **il·le·gal·i·ty** (il-ee-gal-i-tee) *n.*
il·leg·i·ble (i-lej-i-bĕl) *adj.* not able to be read,
not legible. **il·leg'i·bly** *adv.* **il·leg·i·bil·i·ty**
(i-lej-ı-bil-i-tee) *n.*
il·le·git·i·mate (il-i-jit-ı-mit) *adj.* 1. born of parents not married to each other. 2. contrary to
law or to rules. 3. (of a conclusion in an argument
etc.) not logical, wrongly inferred. **il·le·git'i·
mate·ly** *adv.* **il·le·git·i·ma·cy** (il-i-jit-ı-mă-
see) *n.*
ill-fat·ed (il-fay-tid) *adj.* unlucky.
ill-fa·vored (il-fay-vŏrd) *adj.* unattractive.
ill-got·ten (il-got-ĕn) *adj.* gained by evil or unlawful
means.
il·lic·it (i-lis-it) *adj.* unlawful, not allowed. **il·
lic'it·ly** *adj.* ▷Do not confuse *illicit* with *elicit.*
Il·li·nois (il-ı-noi) 1. a state of the U.S. 2. a tribe
of Indians that formerly lived in Illinois and
nearby regions.
il·lit·er·ate (i-lit-ĕ-rit) *adj.* unable to read and
write, showing lack of education. **illiterate** *n.* an
illiterate person. **il·lit·er·a·cy** (i-lit-ĕ-ră-see) *n.*
ill-man·nered (il-man-ĕrd) *adj.* having bad manners.
ill-na·tured (il-nay-chŭrd) *adj.* unkind.
ill·ness (il-nis) *n.* 1. the state of being ill in body
or mind. 2. a particular form of ill health.
il·log·i·cal (i-loj-i-kăl) *adj.* not logical, contrary
to logic. **il·log'i·cal·ly** *adv.* **il·log·i·cal·i·ty**
(i-loj-i-kal-i-tee) *n.*
ill-starred (il-stahrd) *adj.* unlucky.
ill-suit·ed (il-soo-tid) *adj.* inappropriate.
ill-tem·pered (il-tem-pĕrd) *adj.* peevish, irritable.
ill-timed (il-tımd) *adj.* done or occurring at an unfortunate time.
ill-treat (il-treet) *v.* to treat badly or cruelly. **ill'
-treat'ment** *n.*
il·lu·mi·nate (i-loo-mı-nayt) *v.* (**il·lu·mi·nat·ed,
il·lu·mi·nat·ing**) 1. to light up, to make bright.
2. to throw light on (a subject), to make understandable. 3. to decorate (a street or building etc.)
with lights. 4. to decorate (a manuscript) with
colored designs. **il·lu·mi·na·tion** (i-loo-mı-nay-
shŏn) *n.*
illus. *abbr.* 1. illustrated. 2. illustration. 3. illustrator.
ill-use (il-yooz) *v.* (**-used, -us·ing**) to treat badly.
ill-use (il-yoos) *n.* **ill-us·age** (il-yoo-sij) *n.* bad
treatment.

il·lu·sion (i-loo-zhŏn) n. 1. something that a person wrongly supposes to exist. 2. a false belief about the nature of something. ▷Do not confuse *illusion* with *allusion*.

il·lu·sion·ist (i-loo-zhŏ-nist) n. 1. a magician. 2. an artist who uses techniques (such as perspective drawing) to make a pictorial representation look realistic. il·lu′sion·ism n.

il·iu·sive (i-loo-siv) adj. deceptive, having the character of an illusion. ▷Do not confuse *illusive* with *elusive.*

il·lu·so·ry (i-loo-sŏ-ree) adj. based on illusion, not real.

illust. abbr. 1. illustrated. 2. illustration. 3. illustrator.

il·lus·trate (il-ŭ-strayt) v. (il·lus·trat·ed, il·lus·trat·ing) 1. to supply (a book or newspaper etc.) with drawings or pictures. 2. to make clear or explain by examples or pictures etc. 3. to serve as an example of. il′lus·tra·tor n.

il·lus·tra·tion (il-ŭ-stray-shŏn) n. 1. illustrating. 2. a drawing or picture in a book etc. 3. an example used to explain something.

il·lus·tra·tive (i-lus-trǎ-tiv) adj. serving as an illustration or example. il·lus′tra·tive·ly adv.

il·lus·tri·ous (i-lus-tri-ŭs) adj. famous and distinguished. il·lus′tri·ous·ly adv. il·lus′tri·ous·ness adj.

ILO abbr. International Labor Organization.

ILS abbr. instrument landing system.

I'm (Im) = I am.

im·age (im-ij) n. 1. a representation of the outward form of a person or thing, a statue. 2. the optical appearance of something produced in a mirror or through a lens etc. 3. something very like another in appearance, *he's the very image of his father.* 4. a mental picture. 5. the general impression of a person or firm or product etc. as perceived by the public. image v. (im·aged, im·ag·ing) 1. to make an image of, to portray. 2. to reflect, to mirror.

im·age·ry (im-ij-ree) n. (pl. -ries) 1. images. 2. the use of metaphorical language to produce pictures in the minds of readers or hearers.

i·mag·i·na·ble (i-maj-ĭ-nǎ-běl) adj. able to be imagined. i·mag′i·na·bly adv.

i·mag·i·nar·y (i-maj-ĭ-ner-ee) adj. existing only in the imagination, not real. ☐imaginary number, a number that is assumed to exist for a special purpose, as the square root of a negative quantity. imaginary part, the part of a complex number in which the imaginary unit is a factor. imaginary unit, the positive square root of minus one.

i·mag·i·na·tion (i-maj-ĭ-nay-shŏn) n. imagining, the ability to imagine creatively or to use this ability in a practical way (as in dealing with difficulties).

i·mag·i·na·tive (i-maj-ĭ-nǎ-tiv) adj. having or showing imagination. i·mag′i·na·tive·ly adv.

i·mag·ine (i-maj-in) v. (i·mag·ined, i·mag·in·ing) 1. to form a mental image of, to picture in one's mind. 2. to think or believe, to suppose, *don't imagine you'll get away with it.* 3. to guess, *can't imagine where it has gone.*

im·ag·ism (im-ă-jiz-ĕm) n. a movement in the early 20th century of American and British poets who, in revolt against romanticism, sought to achieve clarity of expression through the use of precise imagery. im′ag·ist adj. & n.

i·ma·go (i-may-goh) n. (pl. i·ma·goes, i·ma·gi·nes, pr. i-maj-ĭ-neez) 1. the final and perfect stage of an insect after all its metamorphoses. 2. an idealized mental image of a person, formed in childhood and retained in the unconscious.

i·ma·gi·nal (i-maj-ĭ-năl) adj.

i·mam (i-mahm) n. 1. the leader of prayers in a mosque. 2. Imam, the title of various Muslim spiritual leaders.

im·bal·ance (im-bal-ăns) n. lack of balance, disproportion.

im·be·cile (im-bě-sil) n. 1. a mentally deficient person, an adult whose intelligence is equal to that of an average five-year-old child. 2. a stupid person. imbecile, im·be·cil·ic (im-bě-sil-ik) adj. idiotic. im·be·cil·i·ty (im-bě-sil-i-tee) n.

im·bed (im-bed) v. (im·bed·ded, im·bed·ding) to embed.

im·bibe (im-brb) v. (im·bibed, im·bib·ing) 1. to drink. 2. to absorb (ideas etc.) into the mind. im·bib′er n. im·bi·bi·tion (im-bi-bish-ŏn) n. im·bi·bi′tion·al adj.

im·bri·ca·tion (im-brĭ-kay-shŏn) n. an arrangement that overlaps like tiles, as the scales of a fish. im·bri·cate (im-brĭ-kit) adj.

im·bro·glio (im-brohl-yoh) n. (pl. -glios) a confused situation, usually involving a disagreement.

im·brue (im-broo) v. (im·brued, im·bru·ing) to stain or saturate, especially with blood.

im·bue (im-byoo) v. (im·bued, im·bu·ing) to fill (a person) with certain feelings or qualities or opinions.

IMF abbr. International Monetary Fund.

imit. abbr. 1. imitation. 2. imitative.

im·i·ta·ble (im-i-tǎ-běl) adj. able to be imitated.

im·i·tate (im-i-tayt) v. (im·i·tat·ed, im·i·tat·ing) 1. to copy the behavior of, to take as an example that should be followed. 2. to mimic playfully or for entertainment. 3. to copy, to be like (something else). im′i·ta·tor n.

im·i·ta·tion (im-i-tay-shŏn) n. 1. imitating. 2. something produced by this, a copy. 3. the act of mimicking a person or thing for entertainment, *he does imitations.* imitation adj. showing resemblance to, not genuine; *imitation leather,* a material made to look like leather.

im·i·ta·tive (im-i-tay-tiv) adj. imitating. im′i·ta·tive·ly adv. im′i·ta·tive·ness n.

im·mac·u·late (im-mak-yŭ-lit) adj. 1. spotlessly clean. 2. free from moral blemish. 3. free from fault, right in every detail. im·mac′u·late·ly adv. im·mac′u·late·ness n. im·mac·u·la·cy (i-mak-yŭ-lă-see) n. ☐Immaculate Conception, the Roman Catholic doctrine that the Virgin Mary, from the moment of her conception by her mother, was and remained free from the taint of original sin.

im·ma·nent (im-ă-něnt) adj. 1. (of qualities) inherent. 2. (of God) permanently pervading the universe. im′ma·nence n. im′ma·nen·cy n. ▷Do not confuse *immanent* with *imminent* or *eminent.*

im·ma·te·ri·al (im-ă-teer-i-ăl) adj. 1. having no physical substance, *as immaterial as a ghost.* 2. of no importance or relevance, *it is now immaterial whether he goes or stays; some immaterial objections.* im·ma·te′ri·al·ly adv. im·ma·te·ri·al·i·ty (im-ă-teer-i-al-i-tee) n.

im·ma·ture (im-ă-toor, -tyoor, -choor) adj. not mature. im·ma·tur′i·ty n.

im·meas·ur·a·ble (i-mezh-ĕ-rǎ-běl) adj. not measurable, immense. im·meas′ur·a·bly adv.

im·me·di·ate (i-mee-di-it) adj. 1. occurring or

done at once, without delay. 2. nearest, next, with nothing between, *the immediate neighborhood; my immediate family.* **im·me′di·ate·ly** *adv. & conj.*

im·me·di·a·cy (i-mee-di-ă-see) *n.*

im·me·mo·ri·al (im-ĕ-mohr-i-ăl) *adj.* existing from before what can be remembered or found recorded, *from time immemorial.*

im·mense (i-mens) *adj.* exceedingly great. **im·mense′ly** *adv.* **im·men′si·ty** *n.*

im·merse (i-murs) *v.* (**im·mersed, im·mers·ing**) 1. to put completely into water or other liquid. 2. to absorb or involve deeply in thought or business etc.

im·mer·sion (i-mur-zhŏn) *n.* 1. immersing, being immersed. 2. baptism by putting the whole body into water. ☐**immersion heater,** an electric heating element designed to be placed in the liquid that is to be heated.

im·mi·grant (im-ĭ-grănt) *adj.* 1. immigrating. 2. of immigrants. **immigrant** *n.* a person who has immigrated.

im·mi·grate (im-ĭ-grayt) *v.* (**im·mi·grat·ed, im·mi·grat·ing**) to come into a foreign country as a permanent resident. **im·mi·gra·tion** (im-ĭ-gray-shŏn) *n.* ▷Do not confuse *immigrate* with *emigrate.*

im·mi·nent (im-ĭ-nĕnt) *adj.* (of events) about to occur, likely to occur at any moment. **im′mi·nent·ly** *adv.* **im′mi·nence** *n.* ▷Do not confuse *imminent* with *immanent* or *eminent.*

im·mis·ci·ble (i-mis-i-bĕl) *adj.* that cannot be mixed. **im·mis·ci·bil·i·ty** (i-mis-i-bil-i-tee) *n.*

im·mit·i·ga·ble (i-mit-ĭ-gă-bĕl) *adj.* that cannot be softened or lessened.

im·mo·bile (i-moh-bĭl) *adj.* 1. immovable. 2. not moving. **im·mo·bil·i·ty** (im-oh-bil-i-tee) *n.*

im·mo·bi·lize (i-moh-bĭ-lɪz) *v.* (**im·mo·bi·lized, im·mo·bi·liz·ing**) to make or keep immobile. **im·mo·bi·li·za·tion** (i-moh-bĭ-lɪ-zay-shŏn) *n.*

im·mod·er·ate (i-mod-ĕ-rit) *adj.* excessive, lacking moderation. **im·mod′er·ate·ly** *adv.* **im·mod·er·a·cy** (i-mod-ĕ-ră-see) *n.* **im·mod·er·a·tion** (i-mod-ĕ-ray-shŏn) *n.*

im·mod·est (i-mod-ist) *adj.* 1. lacking in modesty, indecent. 2. conceited. **im·mod′est·ly** *adv.* **im·mod′es·ty** *n.*

im·mo·late (im-ŏ-layt) *v.* (**im·mo·lat·ed, im·mo·lat·ing**) 1. to kill as a sacrifice, as by fire. 2. to sacrifice (one thing to another). **im·mo·la·tion** (im-ŏ-lay-shŏn) *n.*

im·mor·al (i-mor-ăl) *adj.* not conforming to the accepted rules of morality, morally wrong (especially in sexual matters). **im·mo′ral·ly** *adv.* **im·mo·ral·i·ty** (im-ŏ-ral-i-tee) *n.*

im·mor·tal (i-mor-tăl) *adj.* 1. living forever, not mortal. 2. famous for all time. **immortal** *n.* an immortal being or person. **im·mor′tal·ly** *adv.* **im·mor·tal·i·ty** (im-or-tal-i-tee) *n.*

im·mor·tal·ize (i-mor-tă-lɪz) *v.* (**im·mor·tal·ized, im·mor·tal·iz·ing**) to make immortal.

im·mo·tile (i-moh-tĭl) *adj.* without the ability to move. **im·mo·til·i·ty** (im-oh-til-i-tee) *n.*

im·mov·a·ble (i-moo-vă-bĕl) *adj.* 1. unable to be moved. 2. unyielding, not changing in one's purpose. **im·mov′a·bly** *adv.* **im·mov·a·bil·i·ty** (i-moo-vă-bil-i-tee) *n.*

im·mune (i-myoon) *adj.* having immunity, *immune from* or *against* or *to infection* etc.

im·mu·ni·ty (i-myoo-ni-tee) *n.* (*pl.* **-ties**) 1. the ability of an animal or plant to resist infection. 2. special exemption from a tax or duty or penalty;

granted immunity, pardoned in advance of testifying.

im·mu·nize (im-yŭ-nɪz) *v.* (**im·mu·nized, im·mu·niz·ing**) to make immune, especially against infection. **im·mu·ni·za·tion** (im-yŭ-ni-zay-shŏn) *n.*

im·mu·nol·o·gy (im-yŭ-nol-ŏ-jee) *n.* (*pl.* **-gies**) the study of resistance to infection in man and animals. **im·mu·nol′o·gist** *n.* **im·mu·no·log·ic** (im-yŭ-nŏ-loj-ik) *adj.* **im·mu·no·log′i·cal** *adj.*

im·mu·no·sup·pres·sive (im-yŭ-noh-sŭ-pres-iv) *adj.* suppressing the natural responses that produce immunity, as by drugs. **im·mu·no·sup·pres′sant** *n.* **im·mu·no·sup·pres′sion** *n.*

im·mure (i-myoor) *v.* (**im·mured, im·mur·ing**) to imprison, to shut in.

im·mu·ta·ble (i-myoo-tă-bĕl) *adj.* unchangeable. **im·mu′ta·bly** *adv.* **im·mu·ta·bil·i·ty** (i-myoo-tă-bil-i-tee) *n.*

imp (imp) *n.* 1. a small devil. 2. a mischievous child.

imp. *abbr.* 1. imperative. 2. imperfect. 3. imperial. 4. import. 5. important. 6. imported. 7. imprimatur.

im·pact (im-pakt) *n.* 1. a collision. 2. the force exerted when one body collides with another. 3. the force exerted by the influence of new ideas. **impact** (im-pakt) *v.* 1. to pack or drive or wedge firmly together. 2. to collide. **im·pac·tion** (im-pak-shŏn) *n.*

im·pact·ed (im-pak-tid) *adj.* (of a tooth) wedged in the jaw so that it cannot grow through the gum normally.

im·pair (im-pair) *v.* to damage, to cause weakening of, *impair one's health.* **im·pair′ment** *n.*

im·pa·la (im-pah-lă) *n.* (*pl.* **-pa·las, -pa·la**) a small antelope of southern Africa.

im·pale (im-payl) *v.* (**im·paled, im·pal·ing**) to fix or pierce by passing a sharp-pointed object into or through. **im·pale′ment** *n.*

im·pal·pa·ble (im-pal-pă-bĕl) *adj.* unable to be touched or felt. **im·pal′pa·bly** *adv.*

im·pan·el (im-pan-ĕl) *v.* (**im·pan·eled, im·pan·el·ing**) 1. to enter on a panel for jury duty. 2. to enroll (a jury) from the panel.

im·part (im-pahrt) *v.* 1. to give. 2. to reveal or make (information etc.) known.

im·par·tial (im-pahr-shăl) *adj.* not favoring one more than another. **im·par′tial·ly** *adv.* **im·par·tial·i·ty** (im-pahr-shi-al-i-tee) *n.*

im·pass·a·ble (im-pas-ă-bĕl) *adj.* (of roads or barriers) impossible to travel on or over.

im·passe (im-pas) *n.* a deadlock.

im·pas·si·ble (im-pas-ĭ-bĕl) *adj.* 1. incapable of feeling or emotion. 2. incapable of suffering injury. 3. incapable of being harmed. **im·pas′si·bly** *adv.* **im·pas·si·bil·i·ty** (im-pas-ĭ-bil-i-tee) *n.*

im·pas·sioned (im-pash-ŏnd) *adj.* full of deep feeling, *an impassioned appeal.*

im·pas·sive (im-pas-iv) *adj.* not feeling or showing emotion. **im·pas′sive·ly** *adv.* **im·pas′sive·ness** *n.* **im·pas·siv·i·ty** (im-pas-siv-i-tee) *n.*

im·pas·to (im-pah-stoh) *n.* (*pl.* **-tos**) 1. thick application of paint to a canvas, the paint so applied. 2. this style of painting.

im·pa·tiens (im-pay-shĕnz) *n.* any plant of the genus bearing this name, so called because its seed pods burst when barely touched.

im·pa·tient (im-pay-shĕnt) *adj.* 1. unable to wait patiently. 2. showing lack of patience, irritated,

got an impatient reply. 3. intolerant, impatient of delay. im·pa′tient·ly adv. im·pa′tience n.
im·peach (im-peech) v. 1. to charge a public official with misconduct in office before an appropriate tribunal. 2. to call in question, to discredit. im· peach′ment n. im·peach′a·ble adj.
im·pec·ca·ble (im-pek-ă-běl) adj. faultless. im· pec′ca·bly adv.
im·pe·cu·ni·ous (im-pě-kyoo-ni-ŭs) adj. having little or no money. im·pe·cu′ni·ous·ness n. im·pe·cu·ni·os·i·ty (im-pě-kyoo-ni-os-i-tee) n.
im·ped·ance (im-pee-dăns) n. the total resistance of an electric circuit to the flow of alternating current. ▷Do not confuse impedance with impediment.
im·pede (im-peed) v. (im·ped·ed, im·ped· ing) to hinder. im·ped′er n.
im·ped·i·ment (im-ped-ĭ-měnt) n. 1. a hindrance, an obstruction. 2. a defect that prevents something from functioning properly; has an impediment in his speech, has a lisp, stammer, etc. ▷Do not confuse impediment with impedance.
im·ped·i·men·ta (im-ped- ĭ-men-tă) n. pl. encumbrances, baggage.
im·pel (im-pel) v. (im·pelled, im·pel·ling) 1. to urge or drive to do something, curiosity impelled her to investigate. 2. to send or drive forward, to propel. ▷See the note under compel.
im·pel·ler (im-pel-ěr) n. 1. a person or thing that impels. 2. the rotary part of a machine.
im·pend (im-pend) v. 1. to be imminent. 2. to threaten or menace. 3. to hang or be suspended (over). im·pend′ing adj.
im·pen·e·tra·ble (im-pen-ě-tră-běl) adj. unable to be penetrated. im·pen′e·tra·bly adv. im· pen′e·tra·ble·ness n. im·pen·e·tra·bil·i· ty (im-pen-ě-tră-bil-i-tee) n.
im·pen·i·tent (im-pen-i-těnt) adj. not penitent, not repentant. im·pen′i·tent·ly adv. im·pen′i· tence n.
imper. abbr. imperative.
im·per·a·tive (im-per-ă-tiv) adj. 1. expressing a command. 2. essential, obligatory, further economies are imperative. imperative n. 1. a command, a form of a verb used in making commands (as come in come here!). 2. something essential or obligatory, survival is the first imperative. im· per′a·tive·ly adv.
im·per·cep·ti·ble (im-pěr-sep-tĭ-běl) adj. not perceptible, very slight or gradual and therefore difficult to see. im·per·cep′ti·bly adv. im·per· cep′ti·ble·ness n.
im·per·cep·tive (im-pěr-sep-tiv) adj. not perceptive. im·per·cep′tive·ness n.
im·per·cip·i·ent (im-pěr-sip-i-ěnt) adj. lacking in perception, imperceptive.
imperf. abbr. imperfect.
im·per·fect (im-pur-fikt) adj. 1. not fully formed or done, incomplete. 2. faulty. imperfect n. the imperfect tense. im·per′fect·ness n. im· per′fect·ly adv. □imperfect tense, a tense indicating action (usually in the past) going on but not completed, as he was running away.
im·per·fec·tion (im-pěr-fek-shǒn) n. 1. being imperfect. 2. a mark or fault or characteristic that prevents a thing from being perfect.
im·per·fo·rate (im-pur-fŏ-rit) adj. 1. not perforated, (in anatomy) lacking the normal opening. 2. without perforations, as a sheet of postage stamps.
im·pe·ri·al¹ (im-peer-i-ăl) adj. 1. of an empire or

emperor or empress. 2. majestic, imperious. 3. of superior quality or great size. im·pe′ri·al·ly adv.
imperial² n. a small pointed beard below the lower lip, as worn by Emperor Napoleon III.
im·pe·ri·al·ism (im-peer-i-ă-liz-ěm) n. belief in the desirability of acquiring colonies and dependencies. im·pe′ri·al·ist n. im·pe·ri·al·ist· ic (im-peer-i-ă-lis-tik) adj.
im·per·il (im-per-il) v. (im·per·iled, im·per· il·ing) to endanger. im·per′il·ment n.
im·pe·ri·ous (im-peer-i-ŭs) adj. commanding, bossy. im·pe′ri·ous·ly adv. im·pe′ri·ous· ness n.
im·per·ish·a·ble (im-per-i-shă-běl) adj. that cannot perish. im·per′ish·a·bly adv.
im·per·ma·nent (im-pur-mă-něnt) adj. not permanent. im·per′ma·nent·ly adv. im·per′ma· nence n. im·per′ma·nen·cy n.
im·per·me·a·ble (im-pur-mi-ă-běl) adj. not able to be penetrated, especially by liquid. im· per′me·a·bly adv. im·per·me·a·bil·i·ty (im-pur-mi-ă-bil-i-tee) n.
im·per·mis·si·ble (im-pěr-mis-ĭ-běl) adj. not permissible.
im·per·son·al (im-pur-sŏ-năl) adj. 1. not influenced by personal feeling, showing no emotion. 2. not referring to any particular person. 3. having no existence as a person, nature's impersonal forces. 4. (of verbs) used after "it" to make general statements such as "it is raining" or "it is hard to find one." im·per′son·al·ly adv. im·per· son·al·i·ty (im-pur-sŏ-nal-i-tee) n.
im·per·son·ate (im-pur-sŏ-nayt) v. (im·per· son·at·ed, im·per·son·at·ing) 1. to play the part of. 2. to pretend to be (another person) for entertainment or in fraud. im·per′son·a·tor n. im·per·son·a·tion (im-pur-sŏ-nay-shŏn) n.
im·per·ti·nent (im-pur-tĭ-něnt) adj. insolent, not showing proper respect. im·per′ti·nent·ly adv. im·per′ti·nence n.
im·per·turb·a·ble (im-pěr-tur-bă-běl) adj. not excitable, calm. im·per·turb′a·bly adv. im·per· turb·a·bil·i·ty (im-pěr-tur-bă-bil-i-tee) n.
im·per·vi·ous (im-pur-vi-ŭs) adj. 1. not able to be penetrated, impervious to water. 2. not influenced by, impervious to fear or argument. im· per′vi·ous·ly adv.
im·pe·ti·go (im-pě-tɪ-goh) n. a contagious skin disease causing spots that form yellowish crusts.
im·pet·u·ous (im-pech-oo-ŭs) adj. 1. moving quickly or violently, an impetuous dash. 2. acting or done on impulse. im·pet′u·ous·ly adv. im· pet·u·os·i·ty (im-pech-oo-os-i-tee) n.
im·pe·tus (im-pě-tŭs) n. (pl. -tus·es) 1. the force or energy with which a body moves. 2. a driving force, the treaty gave an impetus to trade.
im·pi·e·ty (im-pɪ-ě-tee) n. (pl. -ties) lack of reverence.
im·pinge (im-pinj) v. (im·pinged, im·ping· ing) 1. to make an impact. 2. to encroach. im· pinge′ment n.
im·pi·ous (im-pi-ŭs) adj. not reverent, wicked. im′pi·ous·ly adv. im′pi·ous·ness n.
im·pish (im-pish) adj. of or like an imp. imp′ish·ly adv. imp′ish·ness n.
im·plac·a·ble (im-plak-ă-běl) adj. not able to be placated, relentless. im·plac′a·bly adv. im· plac·a·bil·i·ty (im-plak-ă-bil-i-tee) n.
im·plant (im-plant) v. to plant, to insert or fix (ideas etc.) in the mind, to insert (tissue or other sub-

stance) in a living thing. **implant** (im-plant) *n.* something that is implanted. **im·plan·ta·tion** (im-plan-tay-shŏn) *n.*

im·plau·si·ble (im-plaw-zĭ-bĕl) *adj.* not plausible. **im·plau'si·bly** *adv.* **im·plau'si·ble·ness** *n.* **im·plau·si·bil·i·ty** (im-plaw-zĭ-bil-i-tee) *n.*

im·ple·ment (im-plĕ-mĕnt) *n.* a tool or instrument for working with. **implement** (im-plĕ-ment) *v.* to put into effect, *we implemented the plan.* **im·ple·men·ta·tion** (im-plĕ-mĕn-tay-shŏn) *n.*

im·pli·cate (im-plĭ-kayt) *v.* **(im·pli·cat·ed, im·pli·cat·ing)** to involve or show (a person) to be involved in a crime etc.

im·pli·ca·tion (im-plĭ-kay-shŏn) *n.* 1. implicating, being implicated. 2. implying, being implied. 3. something that is implied.

im·plic·it (im-plis-it) *adj.* 1. implied though not made explicit. 2. absolute, unquestioning, *expects implicit obedience.* **im·plic'it·ly** *adv.* **im·plic'it·ness** *n.*

im·plode (im-plohd) *v.* **(im·plod·ed, im·plod·ing)** to burst inward. **im·plo·sion** (im-ploh-zhŏn) *n.* **im·plo·sive** (im-ploh-siv) *adj.*

im·plore (im-plohr) *v.* **(im·plored, im·plor·ing)** to request earnestly, to entreat. **im·plor'ing·ly** *adv.*

im·ply (im-plɪ) *v.* **(im·plied, im·ply·ing)** 1. to suggest without stating directly, to hint. 2. to mean. 3. to involve necessarily, *the beauty of the carving implies a skilled craftsman.* ▷See the note under **infer.**

im·po·lite (im-pŏ-lɪt) *adj.* not polite. **im·po·lite'ly** *adv.*

im·pol·i·tic (im-pol-i-tik) *adj.* unwise, not expedient.

im·pon·der·a·ble (im-pon-dĕ-ră-bĕl) *adj.* not able to be estimated. **imponderable** *n.* a circumstance or factor difficult to estimate, *the construction schedule was carefully planned, but weather was the great imponderable.*

im·port (im-pohrt) *v.* 1. to bring in from another country or from an outside source. 2. to imply, to indicate, *his expression imported discontent.* **import** (im-pohrt) *n.* 1. something imported. 2. the act of importing, *the import of pianos from Japan.* 3. meaning, *what was the import of her words?* 4. importance, *a meeting of great import.* **im·por·ta·tion** (im-pohr-tay-shŏn) *n.*

im·por·tant (im-por-tănt) *adj.* 1. having or able to have a great effect. 2. (of a person) having great authority or influence. 3. pompous, *he has an important manner.* **im·por'tant·ly** *adv.* **im·por'tance** *n.*

im·port·er (im-pohr-tĕr) *n.* a person, company, etc., in the business of importing goods from another country.

im·por·tu·nate (im-por-chŭ-nit) *adj.* making persistent requests. **im·por'tu·nate·ly** *adv.* **im·por'tu·nate·ness** *n.*

im·por·tune (im-por-toon, -por-chŭn) *v.* **(im·por·tuned, im·por·tun·ing)** to make persistent requests. **im·por·tun·i·ty** (im-por-too-ni-tee) *n.*

im·pose (im-pohz) *v.* **(im·posed, im·pos·ing)** 1. to put (a tax or obligation etc.), *imposed heavy duties on tobacco.* 2. to inflict, *imposed a great strain on our resources.* 3. to force to be accepted, *imposed his ideas on the group.* 4. to take unfair advantage, *we don't want to impose on your hospitality.* **im·pos'er** *n.*

im·pos·ing (im-poh-zing) *adj.* impressive. **im·pos'ing·ly** *adv.*

im·po·si·tion (im-pŏ-zish-ŏn) *n.* 1. the act of imposing something. 2. something imposed, as a tax or duty. 3. a burden imposed unfairly.

im·pos·si·ble (im-pos-ĭ-bĕl) *adj.* 1. not possible, unable to be done or to exist. 2. unendurable, *an impossible person.* **im·pos'si·bly** *adv.* **im·pos·si·bil·i·ty** (im-pos-ĭ-bil-i-tee) *n.*

im·post¹ (im-pohst) *n.* a tax, duty, or tribute.

impost² *n.* the upper course of a pillar, bearing the arch.

im·pos·tor (im-pos-tŏr) *n.* a person who fraudulently pretends to be someone else.

im·pos·ture (im-pos-chŭr) *n.* a fraudulent deception.

im·po·tent (im-pŏ-tĕnt) *adj.* 1. powerless, unable to take action. 2. (of a man) unable to copulate or reach orgasm, unable to procreate. **im'po·tent·ly** *adv.* **im'po·tence** *n.* **im'po·ten·cy** *n.*

im·pound (im-pownd) *v.* to take (another person's property) into a pound or into legal custody, to confiscate. **im·pound'ment** *n.*

im·pov·er·ish (im-pov-ĕ-rish) *v.* 1. to cause to become poor. 2. to exhaust the natural strength or fertility of, *impoverished soil.* **im·pov'er·ish·ment** *n.*

im·prac·ti·ca·ble (im-prak-tĭ-kă-bĕl) *adj.* incapable of being put into practice. **im·prac·ti·ca·bil·i·ty** (im-prak-tĭ-kă-bil-i-tee) *n.*

im·prac·ti·cal (im-prak-tĭ-kăl) *adj.* not practical, unwise. **im·prac·ti·cal·i·ty** (im-prak-tĭ-kăl-i-tee) *n.*

im·pre·cate (im-prĕ-kayt) *v.* **(im·pre·cat·ed, im·pre·cat·ing)** to invoke (a curse or evil). **im·pre·ca·tion** (im-prĕ-kay-shŏn) *n.* **im'pre·ca·tor** *n.*

im·pre·cise (im-pri-sɪs) *adj.* not precise. **im·pre·cise'ly** *adv.* **im·pre·cise'ness** *n.* **im·pre·ci·sion** (im-pri-sizh-ŏn) *n.*

im·preg·na·ble (im-preg-nă-bĕl) *adj.* safe against attack, *an impregnable fortress.* **im·preg·na·bil·i·ty** (im-preg-nă-bil-i-tee) *n.* **im·preg'na·bly** *adv.*

im·preg·nate (im-preg-nayt) *v.* **(im·preg·nat·ed, im·preg·nat·ing)** 1. to introduce sperm or pollen into and fertilize (a female animal or plant). 2. to penetrate all parts of (a substance), to fill or saturate, *the water was impregnated with salts.* **im·preg·na·tion** (im-preg-nay-shŏn) *n.*

im·pre·sa·ri·o (im-prĕ-sahr-i-oh) *n.* (*pl.* **-ri·os**) the manager of an operatic or concert company.

im·press¹ (im-pres) *v.* 1. to make (a person) form a strong (usually favorable) opinion of something. 2. to fix firmly in the mind, *impressed on them the need for haste.* 3. to press a mark into, to stamp with a mark. **impress** (im-pres) *n.* a mark impressed on or into something.

impress² (im-pres) *v.* 1. to force into service in an army or navy. 2. to seize (goods etc.) for public service. **im·press'ment** *n.*

im·pres·sion (im-presh-ŏn) *n.* 1. an effect produced on the mind. 2. an uncertain idea or belief or remembrance. 3. an imitation of a person or sound, done for entertainment. 4. the impressing of a mark, an impressed mark. 5. a reprint of a book etc. made with few or no alterations to its contents. ☐**be under the impression,** to think (that something is a fact).

im·pres·sion·a·ble (im-presh-ŏ-nă-bĕl) *adj.* easily influenced.

im·pres·sion·ist (im-presh-ŏ-nist) *n.* one of the

painters of the late 19th century who adopted a style giving the general impression of a subject, especially by using the effects of light, without elaborate detail. **im·pres′sion·ism** *n.* **im·pres·sion·is·tic** (im-presh-ŏ-nis-tik) *adj.*

im·pres·sive (im-pres-iv) *adj.* making a strong impression, arousing admiration and approval. **im·pres′sive·ly** *adv.* **im·pres′sive·ness** *n.*

im·pri·ma·tur (im-pri-mah-tŭr, -may-) *n.* 1. official license to print, especially works sanctioned by the Roman Catholic Church. 2. permission, approval.

im·print (im-print) *n.* a mark made by pressing or stamping a surface; *the imprint of a foot*, a footprint. **imprint** (im-print) *v.* to impress or stamp a mark on. **im·print′er** *n.*

im·pris·on (im-priz-ŏn) *v.* 1. to put into prison. 2. to keep in confinement. **im·pris′on·ment** *n.*

im·prob·a·ble (im-prob-ă-bĕl) *adj.* not likely to be true or to happen. **im·prob′a·bly** *adv.* **im·prob·a·bil·i·ty** (im-prob-ă-bil-i-tee) *n.*

im·promp·tu (im-promp-too) *adj. & adv.* without preparation or rehearsal. **impromptu** *n.* a musical composition that gives the impression of being composed impromptu.

im·prop·er (im-prop-ĕr) *adj.* 1. wrong, incorrect, *made improper use of the blade.* 2. not conforming to the rules of social or lawful conduct. 3. indecent. **im·prop′er·ly** *adv.* **im·prop′er·ness** *n.* □**improper fraction,** one that is greater than unity, with the numerator greater than the denominator, as five-thirds (⅗).

im·pro·pri·e·ty (im-prŏ-prī-ĕ-tee) *n.* (*pl.* -ties) being improper, an improper act or remark etc.

im·prov·a·ble (im-proo-vă-bĕl) *adj.* able to be improved.

im·prove (im-proov) *v.* (**im·proved, im·prov·ing**) 1. to make or become better. 2. to make (land) more valuable, as by cultivating or building on it. 3. to make good use of. □**improve on,** to produce something better than.

im·prove·ment (im-proov-mĕnt) *n.* 1. improving, being improved. 2. an addition or alteration that improves something or adds to its value.

im·prov·i·dent (im-prov-i-dĕnt) *adj.* not providing for future needs, wasting one's resources. **im·prov′i·dent·ly** *adv.* **im·prov′i·dence** *n.*

im·pro·vise (im-prŏ-vīz) *v.* (**im·pro·vised, im·pro·vis·ing**) 1. to compose (a thing) impromptu. 2. to provide, in times of need, using whatever materials you can find, *improvised a bed from cushions and rugs.* **im′pro·vis·er** *n.* **im′pro·vi·sor** *n.* **im·prov·i·sa·tion** (im-prov-i-zay-shŏn) *n.* **im·prov′i·sa′tion·al** *adj.*

im·pru·dent (im-proo-dĕnt) *adj.* unwise, rash. **im·pru′dent·ly** *adv.* **im·pru′dence** *n.*

im·pu·dent (im-pyŭ-dĕnt) *adj.* impertinent, boldly showing lack of respect. **im′pu·dent·ly** *adv.* **im′pu·dence** *n.*

im·pugn (im-pyoon) *v.* to express doubts about the truth or honesty of, to try to discredit, *we do not impugn their motives.* **im·pugn′er** *n.*

im·pu·is·sance (im-pyoo-i-săns) *n.* impotence, weakness. **im·pu′is·sant** *adj.*

im·pulse (im-puls) *n.* 1. a push or thrust, impetus. 2. a stimulating force in a nerve, causing a muscle to react. 3. a sudden inclination to act, without thought for the consequences, *did it on impulse.* □**impulse buying,** buying of goods on impulse and not because of previous planning.

im·pul·sion (im-pul-shŏn) *n.* 1. an impelling push. 2. a mental impulse. 3. impetus.

im·pul·sive (im-pul-siv) *adj.* 1. (of a person) habitually acting on impulse. 2. (of an action) done on impulse. **im·pul′sive·ly** *adv.* **im·pul′sive·ness** *n.*

im·pu·ni·ty (im-pyoo-ni-tee) *n.* freedom from punishment or injury.

im·pure (im-pyoor) *adj.* not pure. **im·pure′ly** *adv.* **im·pur·i·ty** (im-pyoor-i-tee) *n.* (*pl.* -ties) 1. being impure. 2. a substance that makes another substance impure by being present in it.

im·pu·ta·tion (im-pyū-tay-shŏn) *n.* 1. imputing. 2. an accusation of wrongdoing.

im·pute (im-pyoot) *v.* (**im·put·ed, im·put·ing**) to attribute, to ascribe.

in (in) *prep.* expressing position or state. 1. of inclusion within the limits of space or time or circumstance or surroundings etc. 2. of quantity or proportion, *they are packed in tens.* 3. of form or arrangement, *hanging in folds.* 4. of activity or occupation or membership, *he is in the army.* 5. wearing as dress or color etc., *in a sweatshirt.* 6. of method or means of expression, *spoke in French.* 7. with the instrument or means of, *written in ink.* 8. of identity, *found a friend in Mary.* 9. under the influence of, *spoke in anger.* 10. with respect to, *lacking in courage.* 11. as the content of; *there's not much in it,* no great difference between the advantages or merits of various schemes or competitors etc. 12. after the time of, *back in ten minutes.* 13. (of a female animal) pregnant with, *in calf.* 14. into. 15. toward, *ran in all directions.* **in** *adv.* 1. expressing position bounded by certain limits, or to a point enclosed by these, *the window was open and the rain poured in.* 2. at home, *will you be in?* 3. on or toward the inside, *with the fur side in.* 4. in fashion or season or office, elected, in effective or favorable action, *my luck was in; the tide was in,* was high. 5. having arrived or been gathered or received, *train is in; harvest is in.* **in** *adj.* 1. internal, inside, inner. 2. (*informal*) fashionable, *it's the in thing to do.* **in** *n.* 1. a person with authority, *he is one of the ins in top management.* 2. influence, *the lawyer has an in at the courthouse.* □**be in for,** to be about to experience, *she's in for a surprise.* **be in on,** (*informal*) to be among those who know (a secret) or share in (discussions etc.). **in all,** in total number. **in box,** a desktop box or tray to hold documents or work that has been received but not yet dealt with. **in camera,** (of the hearing of evidence or lawsuits) in the judge's private room; in private or in secret. **ins and outs,** the details of an activity or procedure. **in that,** since, because. **in with,** on friendly terms with.

In *symbol* indium.

IN *abbr.* Indiana.

in. *abbr.* inch(es).

in-¹ *prefix* in, on, into, toward, within, as in *insight, incoming.*

in-² *prefix* not, as in *insane, inseparable;* the absence of, as in *insensitivity.*

in·a·bil·i·ty (in-ă-bil-i-tee) *n.* (*pl.* -ties) being unable.

in ab·sen·tia (in ab-sen-shă) in absence. ▷Latin.

in·ac·cept·a·ble (in-ak-sep-tă-bĕl) *adj.* not acceptable.

in·ac·ces·si·ble (in-ak-ses-ĭ-bĕl) *adj.* not accessible, unapproachable. **in·ac·ces·si·bil·i·ty** (in-ak-ses-ĭ-bil-i-tee) *n.*

in·ac·cu·rate (in-ak-yŭ-rit) *adj.* not accurate. **in·ac′cu·rate·ly** *adv.* **in·ac′cu·ra·cy** *n.*

in·ac·tion (in-ak-shŏn) *n.* lack of action, doing nothing.

in·ac·ti·vate (in-ak-tĭ-vayt) *v.* (**in·ac·ti·vat·ed, in·ac·ti·vat·ing**) to make inactive or inoperative. **in·ac·ti·va·tion** (in-ak-tĭ-vay-shŏn) *n.*

in·ac·tive (in-ak-tiv) *adj.* not active, showing no activity. **in·ac·tiv·i·ty** (in-ak-tiv-i-tee) *n.*

in·ad·e·quate (in-ad-ĕ-kwit) *adj.* 1. not adequate, insufficient. 2. not sufficiently able or competent, *felt inadequate.* **in·ad'e·quate·ly** *adv.* **in·ad'e·qua·cy** *n.* **in·ad'e·quate·ness** *n.*

in·ad·mis·si·ble (in-ad-mis-ĭ-bĕl) *n.* not allowable.

in·ad·ver·tent (in-ad-vur-tĕnt) *adj.* unintentional. **in·ad·ver'tent·ly** *adv.* **in·ad·ver'ten·ce** *n.* **in·ad·ver'ten·cy** *n.*

in·ad·vis·a·ble (in-ad-vɪ-ză-bĕl) *adj.* not advisable. **in·ad·vis'a·bly** *adv.* **in·ad·vis·a·bil· i·ty** (in-ad-vɪ-ză-bil-i-tee) *n.*

in·al·ien·a·ble (in-ayl-yĕ-nă-bĕl) *adj.* not able to be given away or taken away, *an inalienable right.* **in·al'ien·a·bly** *adv.* **in·al·ien·a·bil·i·ty** (in-ayl-yĕ-nă-bil-i-tee) *n.*

in·ane (i-nayn) *adj.* silly, lacking sense. **in·ane'ly** *adv.* **in·an·i·ty** (i-nan-i-tee) *n.*

in·an·i·mate (in-an-ĭ-mit) *adj.* 1. (of rocks and other objects) lifeless, (of plants) lacking animal life. 2. showing no sign of life. **in·an'i·mate· ly** *adv.* **in·an'i·mate·ness** *n.*

in·ap·pli·ca·ble (in-ap-lĭ-kă-bĕl) *adj.* not applicable. **in·ap'pli·ca·bly** *adv.*

in·ap·po·site (in-ap-ŏ-zit) *adj.* not suitable or pertinent, out of place.

in·ap·pre·ci·a·ble (in-ă-pree-shi-ă-bĕl) *adj.* imperceptible, not worth reckoning. **in·ap·pre'ci· a·bly** *adv.*

in·ap·pre·ci·a·tive (in-ă-pree-shi-ă-tiv) *adj.* failing to appreciate, not appreciative.

in·ap·proach·a·ble (in-ă-proh-chă-bĕl) *adj.* not able to be approached, not easy to approach.

in·ap·pro·pri·ate (in-ă-proh-pri-it) *adj.* unsuitable. **in·ap·pro'pri·ate·ly** *adv.* **in·ap· pro'pri·ate·ness** *n.*

in·ar·tic·u·late (in-ahr-tik-yŭ-lit) *adj.* 1. not expressed in words, *an inarticulate cry.* 2. unable to speak distinctly, *was inarticulate with rage.* 3. unable to express one's ideas clearly. **in·ar·tic'u· late·ly** *adv.* **in·ar·tic'u·late·ness** *n.*

in·ar·tis·tic (in-ahr-tis-tik) *adj.* not artistic. **in· ar·tis'ti·cal·ly** *adv.*

in·as·much (in-ăz-much) **as** since, because.

in·at·ten·tion (in-ă-ten-shŏn) *n.* lack of attention, neglect.

in·at·ten·tive (in-ă-ten-tiv) *adj.* not attentive, not paying attention.

in·au·di·ble (in-aw-dĭ-bĕl) *adj.* not audible, unable to be heard. **in·au'di·bly** *adv.* **in·au·di·bil· i·ty** (in-aw-dĭ-bil-i-tee) *n.*

in·au·gu·ral (in-aw-gyŭ-răl) *adj.* of or for an inauguration, *the inaugural ceremony.* **inaugural** *n.* 1. an inaugural speech, especially by a U.S. president. 2. a ceremony of inauguration.

in·au·gu·rate (in-aw-gyŭ-rayt) *v.* (**in·au·gu· rat·ed, in·au·gu·rat·ing**) 1. to admit (a person) to office with a ceremony. 2. to enter ceremonially upon (an undertaking), to open (a building or exhibition etc.) formally. 3. to be the beginning of, to introduce, *cable television service was inaugurated here last year.* **in·au'gu·ra·tor** *n.* **in· au·gu·ra·tion** (in-aw-gyŭ-ray-shŏn) *n.*

in·aus·pi·cious (in-aw-spish-ŭs) *adj.* not auspicious. **in·aus·pi'cious·ly** *adv.*

in·board (in-bohrd) *adj. & adv.* placed or attached inside or toward the center of a boat or aircraft.

in·born (in-born) *adj.* existing in a person or animal from birth, natural, *an inborn ability.*

in·bound (in-bownd) *adj.* (of ships, aircraft, etc.) inward bound.

in·bred (in-bred) *adj.* 1. produced by inbreeding. 2. inborn.

in·breed·ing (in-bree-ding) *n.* 1. breeding between closely related individuals. 2. *(informal)* restriction to a very limited range, as in selection of personnel. **in·breed** (in-breed) *v.* (**in·bred, in· breed·ing**).

inc. *abbr.* 1. incorporated. 2. increase.

Inc. *abbr.* Incorporated.

in·ca (ing-kă) *n.* a member of an American Indian people in Peru etc. before the Spanish conquest.

in·cal·cu·la·ble (in-kal-kyŭ-lă-bĕl) *adj.* unable to be calculated. **in·cal'cu·la·bly** *adv.* **in·cal'cu· la·ble·ness** *n.*

in·can·des·cent (in-kăn-des-ĕnt) *adj.* glowing with heat, shining. **in·can·des'cent·ly** *adv.* **in· can·des'cence** *n.* □**incandescent lamp,** an electric or other lamp in which a white-hot filament gives off light.

in·can·ta·tion (in-kan-tay-shŏn) *n.* words or sounds to be uttered as a magic spell, the uttering of these.

in·ca·pa·ble (in-kay-pă-bĕl) *adj.* not capable. **in· ca·pa·bil·i·ty** (in-kay-pă-bil-i-tee) *n.*

in·ca·pac·i·tate (in-kă-pas-i-tayt) *v.* (**in·ca· pac·i·tat·ed, in·ca·pac·i·tat·ing**) 1. to disable. 2. to make ineligible. **in·ca·pac·i·ta·tion** (in-kă-pas-i-tay-shŏn) *n.*

in·ca·pac·i·ty (in-kă-pas-i-tee) *n.* inability, lack of sufficient strength or power.

in·car·cer·ate (in-kahr-sĕ-rayt) *v.* (**in·car·cer· at·ed, in·car·cer·at·ing**) to imprison. **in·car· cer·a·tion** (in-kahr-sĕ-ray-shŏn) *n.*

in·car·na·dine (in-kahr-nă-dɪn) *adj.* crimson or flesh-colored. **incarnadine** *v.* (**in·car·na· dined, in·car·na·din·ing**) to dye crimson or the color of flesh.

in·car·nate (in-kahr-nit) *adj.* embodied, in human form, *a devil incarnate.*

in·car·na·tion (in-kahr-nay-shŏn) *n.* embodiment, especially in human form. □**the Incarnation,** the embodiment of God in human form as Christ.

in·case (in-kays) *v.* (**in·cased, in·cas·ing**) to encase.

in·cau·tious (in-kaw-shŭs) *adj.* not cautious, rash. **in·cau'tious·ly** *adv.*

in·cen·di·ar·y (in-sen-di-er-ee) *adj.* 1. (of a bomb etc.) designed to cause a fire, containing chemicals that ignite. 2. of arson, guilty of arson. 3. tending to stir up strife, inflammatory. **incendiary** *n.* (*pl.* **-ar·ies**) 1. an incendiary bomb etc. 2. an arsonist. 3. a person who stirs up strife.

in·cense[1] (in-sens) *n.* 1. a substance that produces a sweet smell when burning. 2. its smoke, used especially in religious ceremonies.

in·cense[2] (in-sens) *v.* (**in·censed, in·cens· ing**) to make angry.

in·cen·tive (in-sen-tiv) *n.* something that rouses or encourages a person to some action or effort. **incentive** *adj.* acting as an incentive.

in·cep·tion (in-sep-shŏn) *n.* the beginning of the existence of something. **in·cep'tive** *adj.*

in·cer·ti·tude (in-sur-ti-tood) *n.* uncertainty.

in·ces·sant (in-ses-ănt) *adj.* unceasing, continually repeated. **in·ces'sant·ly** *adv.*

in·cest (in-sest) *n.* sexual intercourse between people regarded as too closely related to marry each other. **in·ces·tu·ous** (in-ses-choo-ŭs) *adj.* **in·ces'tu·ous·ly** *adv.* **in·ces'tu·ous·ness** *n.*

inch (inch) *n.* **1.** a measure of length, one-twelfth (½₁₂) part of a foot (= 2.54 cm). **2.** an amount of rainfall that would cover a surface to a depth of one inch. **3.** a very small amount, *would not yield an inch.* **inch** *v.* to move slowly and gradually, *they inched forward.* ☐**every inch,** entirely, *looked every inch a soldier.* **within an inch of,** almost, close to. **within an inch of one's life,** almost to death.

in·cho·ate (in-koh-it) *adj.* **1.** just begun. **2.** undeveloped. **in·cho'ate·ly** *adv.*

inch·worm (inch-wurm) *n.* a caterpillar that moves by arching itself into loops.

in·ci·dence (in-si-děns) *n.* **1.** the rate at which something occurs or affects people or things, *studied the incidence of the disease.* **2.** the falling of something (as a ray of light) on a surface.

in·ci·dent (in-si-děnt) *n.* **1.** an event, especially a minor one. **2.** a hostile activity, *border incidents.* **3.** a public disturbance or accident, *the protest march took place without incident.* **4.** an event that attracts general attention. **incident** *adj.* **1.** liable to happen, accompanying something, *the risks incident to a pilot's career.* **2.** (of rays of light etc.) falling on a surface, *incident light.*

in·ci·den·tal (in-si-den-tăl) *adj.* **1.** occurring as a minor accompaniment, *incidental expenses.* **2.** liable to occur in consequence of or in connection with something, *the incidental hazards of exploration.* **3.** casual, occurring by chance. **incidental** *n.* (often *incidentals*) something incidental. ☐**incidental music,** music played as a background to the action of a play.

in·ci·den·tal·ly (in-si-den-tă-lee) *adv.* **1.** in an incidental way. **2.** as an unconnected comment, by the way.

in·cin·er·ate (in-sin-ĕ-rayt) *v.* **(in·cin·er·at·ed, in·cin·er·at·ing)** to reduce to ashes, to destroy by fire. **in·cin·er·a·tion** (in-sin-ĕ-ray-shŏn) *n.*

in·cin·er·a·tor (in-sin-ĕ-ray-tŏr) *n.* a furnace or enclosed device for burning trash.

in·cip·i·ent (in-sip-i-ěnt) *adj.* in its early stages, beginning, *incipient decay.* **in·cip'i·ence** *n.*

in·cise (in-sɪz) *v.* **(in·cised, in·cis·ing)** to make a cut in (a surface), to engrave by cutting.

in·ci·sion (in-siz*h*-ŏn) *n.* **1.** incising. **2.** a cut, especially one made surgically into the body.

in·ci·sive (in-sɪ-siv) *adj.* clear and decisive, *made incisive comments.* **in·ci'sive·ly** *adv.* **in·ci'sive·ness** *n.*

in·ci·sor (in-sɪ-zŏr) *n.* any of the sharp-edged front teeth in the upper and lower jaws.

in·cite (in-sɪt) *v.* **(in·cit·ed, in·cit·ing)** to urge on to action, to stir up. **in·cite'ment** *n.* **in·cit'er** *n.*

in·ci·vil·i·ty (in-sɪ-vil-i-tee) *n.* (*pl.* -ties) lack of civility, an impolite act or remark.

incl. *abbr.* **1.** inclosure. **2.** including. **3.** inclusive.

in·clem·ent (in-klem-ěnt) *adj.* (of weather) cold or wet or stormy. **in·clem'en·cy** *n.*

in·cli·na·tion (in-klĭ-nay-shŏn) *n.* **1.** a slope or slant, a leaning or bending movement. **2.** a tendency. **3.** a liking or preference; *against my inclination,* against my wish.

in·cline (in-klɪn) *v.* **(in·clined, in·clin·ing)** **1.** to lean, to slope. **2.** to bend (the head or body) forward. **3.** to have or cause a certain tendency, to

influence, *his manner inclines me to believe him.* **incline** (in-klɪn) *n.* a slope. **in·clin'a·ble** *adj.* ☐**be inclined,** to have a certain tendency or willingness, *the door is inclined to bang; I'm inclined to agree.*

in·close (in-klohz) *v.* **(in·closed, in·clos·ing)** to enclose.

in·clo·sure (in-kloh-zh*ŭr*) = **enclosure.**

in·clude (in-klood) *v.* **(in·clud·ed, in·clud·ing)** **1.** to have or regard or treat as part of a whole. **2.** to put into a certain category or list etc. **in·clu·sion** (in-kloo-zhŏn) *n.*

in·clu·sive (in-kloo-siv) *adj.* **1.** including what is mentioned, *the charge is $50 inclusive of service.* **2.** including much or everything. **inclusive** *adv.* including what is mentioned, *pages seven to twenty-six inclusive.* **in·clu'sive·ly** *adv.* **in·clu'sive·ness** *n.*

incog. *abbr.* incognito.

in·cog·ni·to (in-kog-ni-toh, -kog-nee-) *adj. & adv.* with one's identity kept secret, *she was traveling incognito.* **incognito** *n.* the identity assumed by one who is incognito.

in·co·her·ent (in-koh-heer-ĕnt) *adj.* rambling in speech or in reasoning. **in·co·her'ent·ly** *adv.* **in·co·her'ence** *n.*

in·com·bus·ti·ble (in-kŏm-bus-tĭ-běl) *adj.* not able to be burned by fire.

in·come (in-kum) *n.* money received during a certain period as wages or salary, interest on investments, etc. ☐**income tax,** tax payable on income.

in·com·ing (in-kum-ing) *adj.* **1.** coming in, *the incoming tide.* **2.** succeeding another person, *the incoming president.*

in·com·men·su·ra·ble (in-kŏ-men-sŭ-ră-běl, -shŭ-) *adj.* not capable of being measured, compared (with), or judged.

in·com·men·su·rate (in-kŏ-men-sŭ-rit, -shŭ-) *adj.* out of proportion, inadequate. **in·com·men'su·rate·ly** *adv.*

in·com·mode (in-kŏm-mohd) *v.* **(in·com·mod·ed, in·com·mod·ing)** to inconvenience.

in·com·mo·di·ous (in-kŏ-moh-di-ŭs) *adj.* not providing good accommodation, uncomfortable, especially through being too small.

in·com·mu·ni·ca·do (in-kŏ-myoo-ni-kah-doh) *adj.* not allowed to communicate with others, *the prisoner was held incommunicado.*

in·com·pa·ra·ble (in-kom-pă-ră-běl) *adj.* without an equal, beyond comparison. **in·com'pa·ra·bly** *adv.*

in·com·pat·i·ble (in-kŏm-pat-ĭ-běl) *adj.* **1.** not compatible. **2.** inconsistent; *the two statements are incompatible,* cannot both be true. **in·com·pat·i·bil·i·ty** (in-kŏm-pat-ĭ-bil-i-tee) *n.* **in·com·pat'i·bly** *adv.*

in·com·pe·tent (in-kom-pě-tĕnt) *adj.* **1.** not qualified or able (to do). **2.** not legally qualified. **incompetent** *n.* an incompetent person. **in·com'pe·tent·ly** *adv.* **in·com'pe·tence** *n.* **in·com'pe·ten·cy** *n.*

in·com·plete (in-kŏm-pleet) *adj.* not complete. **in·com·plete'ly** *adv.* **in·com·plete'ness** *n.*

in·com·pre·hen·si·ble (in-kom-pri-hen-sĭ-běl) *adj.* not able to be understood. **in·com·pre·hen'si·bly** *adv.* **in·com·pre·hen·si·bil·i·ty** (in-kom-pri-hen-sĭ-bil-i-tee) *n.*

in·con·ceiv·a·ble (in-kŏn-see-vă-běl) *adj.* **1.** unable to be imagined. **2.** (*informal*) impossible to believe. **in·con·ceiv'a·bly** *adv.*

in·con·clu·sive (in-kŏn-kloo-siv) *adj.* (of evidence

or an argument etc.) not fully convincing, not decisive. **in·con·clu'sive·ly** *adv.* **in·con· clu'sive·ness** *n.*

in·con·gru·ous (in-kong-groo-ŭs) *adj.* unsuitable, not harmonious. **in·con'gru·ous·ly** *adv.* **in· con·gru·i·ty** (in-kong-groo-i-tee) *n.*

in·con·se·quent (in-kon-sĕ-kwĕnt) *adj.* not following logically, irrelevant. **in·con'se·quent· ly** *adv.* **in·con'se·quence** *n.*

in·con·se·quen·tial (in-kon-sĕ-kwen-shăl) *adj.* 1. unimportant. 2. inconsequent. **in·con·se· quen'tial·ly** *adv.*

in·con·sid·er·a·ble (in-kŏn-sid-ĕ-ră-bĕl) *adj.* not worth considering, of small size or amount or value.

in·con·sid·er·ate (in-kŏn-sid-ĕ-rit) *adj.* not considerate toward other people. **in·con·sid'er· ate·ly** *adv.* **in·con·sid'er·ate·ness** *n.*

in·con·sis·tent (in-kŏn-sis-tĕnt) *adj.* not consistent. **in·con·sis'tent·ly** *adv.* **in·con·sis' ten·cy** *n.*

in·con·sol·a·ble (in-kŏn-soh-lă-bĕl) *adj.* not able to be consoled. **in·con·sol'a·bly** *adv.*

in·con·spic·u·ous (in-kŏn-spik-yoo-ŭs) *adj.* not conspicuous. **in·con·spic'u·ous·ly** *adv.* **in· con·spic'u·ous·ness** *n.*

in·con·stant (in-kon-stănt) *adj.* 1. fickle, changeable. 2. variable, irregular. **in·con'stant·ly** *adv.* **in·con'stan·cy** *n.*

in·con·test·a·ble (in-kŏn-tes-tă-bĕl) *adj.* indisputable. **in·con·test'a·bly** *adv.* **in·con·test· a·bil·i·ty** (in-kŏn-tes-tă-bil-i-tee) *n.*

in·con·ti·nent (in-kon-tĭ-nĕnt) *adv.* 1. unable to control the excretion of one's urine and feces. 2. lacking self-restraint in sexual desire. **in·con'ti· nence** *n.*

in·con·tro·ver·ti·ble (in-kon-trŏ-vur-tĭ-bĕl) *adj.* indisputable, undeniable. **in·con·tro·ver'ti· bly** *adv.*

in·con·ven·ience (in-kŏn-veen-yĕns) *n.* 1. being inconvenient. 2. a circumstance that is inconvenient. **inconvenience** *v.* **(in·con·ven·ienced, in·con·ven·ienc·ing)** to cause inconvenience or slight difficulty to.

in·con·ven·ient (in-kŏn-veen-yĕnt) *adj.* not convenient, not suiting one's needs or requirements, slightly troublesome. **in·con·ven'ient·ly** *adv.*

in·cor·po·rate (in-kor-pŏ-rayt) *v.* **(in·cor·po· rat·ed, in·cor·po·rat·ing)** 1. to include as a part, *your suggestions will be incorporated in the plan.* 2. to form into a legal corporation. **in·cor· po·ra·tion** (in-kor-pŏ-ray-shŏn) *n.* **in·cor'po· ra·tor** *n.*

in·cor·po·re·al (in-kor-pohr-i-ăl) *adj.* not composed of matter. **in·cor·po're·al·ly** *adv.*

in·cor·rect (in-kŏ-rekt) *adj.* 1. not in accordance with fact. 2. (of style etc.) improper, faulty. **in· cor·rect'ly** *adv.* **in·cor·rect'ness** *n.*

in·cor·ri·gi·ble (in-kor-i-jĭ-bĕl) *adj.* (of a person or his faults etc.) not able to be reformed or improved, *an incorrigible liar.* **in·cor'ri·gi·bly** *adv.* **in·cor·ri·gi·bil·i·ty** (in-kor-i-jĭ-bil-i-tee) *n.*

in·cor·rupt·i·ble (in-kŏ-rup-tĭ-bĕl) *adj.* 1. not liable to decay. 2. not able to be corrupted morally, as by bribes. **in·cor·rupt'i·bly** *adv.* **in·cor· rupt·i·bil·i·ty** (in-kŏ-rup-tĭ-bil-i-tee) *n.*

incr. *abbr.* 1. increase. 2. increased. 3. increasing.

in·crease (in-krees) *v.* **(in·creased, in·creasing)** to make or become greater in size or amount or intensity. **increase** (in-krees) *n.* 1. the process of increasing. 2. the amount by which something

increases. **in·creas'er** *n.* **in·creas'ing·ly** *adv.*

in·cred·i·ble (in-kred-ĭ-bĕl) *adj.* 1. unbelievable. 2. *(informal)* hard to believe, very surprising. **in· cred'i·bly** *adv.* **in·cred·i·bil·i·ty** (in-kred-ĭ- bil-i-tee) *n.* **in·cred'i·ble·ness** *n.* ▷ Do not confuse *incredible* with *incredulous.*

in·cred·u·lous (in-krej-ŭ-lŭs) *adj.* unbelieving, showing disbelief. **in·cred'u·lous·ly** *adv.* **in· cred·ul·i·ty** (in-krĕ-doo-li-tee) *n.* ▷ Do not confuse *incredulous* with *incredible.*

in·cre·ment (in-krĕ-mĕnt) *n.* an increase, an added amount, *he received a salary increment of twenty dollars a week.* **in·cre·men·tal** (in-krĕ-men-tăl) *adj.*

in·crim·i·nate (in-krim-ĭ-nayt) *v.* **(in·crim·i·nat· ed, in·crim·i·nat·ing)** to indicate as involved in wrongdoing, *his statement incriminated the guard.* **in·crim·i·na·tion** (in-krim-ĭ-nay- shŏn) *n.*

in·crim·i·na·to·ry (in-krim-ĭ-nă-tohr-ee) *adj.* causing incrimination.

in·crust (in-krust) = **encrust.**

in·crus·ta·tion (in-krus-tay-shŏn) *n.* 1. encrusting, being encrusted. 2. a crust or deposit formed on a surface.

in·cu·bate (in-kyŭ-bayt) *v.* **(in·cu·bat·ed, in· cu·bat·ing)** 1. to hatch (eggs) by the warmth of a bird's body as it sits on them or by artificial heat. 2. to cause (bacteria etc.) to develop in suitable conditions. **in'cu·ba·tive** *adj.*

in·cu·ba·tion (in-kyŭ-bay-shŏn) *n.* incubating; the *incubation period,* the time it takes for symptoms of a communicable disease to become apparent in a person who has been exposed to it.

in·cu·ba·tor (in-kyŭ-bay-tŏr) *n.* 1. an apparatus for hatching eggs by artificial warmth. 2. an apparatus in which babies born prematurely can be kept in a constant controlled heat and supplied with oxygen etc.

in·cu·bus (in-kyŭ-bŭs) *n.* (*pl.* **-bus·es, -bi,** -bī) 1. a spirit said to haunt or trouble people in their sleep. 2. a troublesome person or situation.

in·cul·cate (in-kul-kayt) *v.* **(in·cul·cat·ed, in· cul·cat·ing)** to implant (ideas or habits) by persistent urging, *desiring to inculcate obedience in the young.* **in·cul·ca·tion** (in-kul-kay-shŏn) *n.*

in·cul·pa·ble (in-kul-pă-bĕl) *adj.* blameless.

in·cul·pate (in-kul-payt) *v.* **(in·cul·pat·ed, in· cul·pat·ing)** to involve in a charge of wrongdoing, to incriminate.

in·cum·ben·cy (in-kum-bĕn-see) *n.* (*pl.* **-cies)** the office or tenure of an incumbent.

in·cum·bent (in-kum-bĕnt) *adj.* forming an obligation or duty, *it is incumbent on you to warn people of the danger.* **incumbent** *n.* a person who holds a particular office.

in·cum·ber (in-kum-bĕr) = **encumber.**

in·cu·nab·u·lum (in-kyuu-nab-yŭ-lŭm) *n.* (*pl.* **-la,** *pr.* -lă) a book printed at a very early date, especially before 1501.

in·cur (in-kur) *v.* **(in·curred, in·cur·ring)** to bring upon oneself, *incurred great expense of hatred.*

in·cur·a·ble (in-kyoor-ă-bĕl) *adj.* unable to be cured. **incurable** *n.* a person with an incurable disease. **in·cur'a·bly** *adv.*

in·cu·ri·ous (in-kyoor-i-ŭs) *adj.* feeling or showing no curiosity about something.

in·cur·sion (in-kur-zhŏn) *n.* a raid or brief invasion into someone else's territory etc.

in·cus (ing-kŭs) *n.* (*pl.* **in·cu·des,** *pr.* in-kyoo-

deez) the middle small anvil bone of the ear.
ind. *abbr.* 1. independent. 2. index. 3. indicative.
4. industrial. 5. industry.
Ind. *abbr.* 1. India. 2. Indian. 3. Indiana.
in·debt·ed (in-det-id) *adj.* owing money or gratitude. **in·debt′ed·ness** *n.*
in·de·cent (in-dee-sĕnt) *adj.* 1. offending against recognized standards of decency. 2. unseemly, *with indecent haste.* **in·de′cent·ly** *adv.* **in·de·cen·cy** (in-dee-sĕn-see) *n.* ☐**indecent exposure,** exposing one's genitals publicly with the intention of causing offense.
in·ci·pher·a·ble (in-di-sɪ-fĕ-ră-bĕl) *adj.* unable to be deciphered.
in·de·ci·sion (in-di-sizh-ŏn) *n.* inability to make up one's mind, hesitation.
in·de·ci·sive (in-di-sɪ-siv) *adj.* not decisive. **in·de·ci′sive·ly** *adv.* **in·de·ci′sive·ness** *n.*
in·de·clin·a·ble (in-di-klɪ-nă-bĕl) *adj.* without grammatical inflections.
in·dec·o·rous (in-dek-ŏ-rŭs) *adj.* improper, not in good taste. **in·dec′o·rous·ly** *adv.* **in·dec′o·rous·ness** *n.*
in·deed (in-deed) *adv.* 1. truly, really, *it was indeed remarkable.* 2. used to intensify a meaning, *very nice indeed.* 3. admittedly, *it is, indeed, his first attempt.* **indeed** *interj.* used to express irony or contempt or surprise etc.
indef. *abbr.* indefinite.
in·de·fat·i·ga·ble (in-di-fat-ɪ-gă-bĕl) *adj.* not becoming tired. **in·de·fat′i·ga·bly** *adv.*
in·de·fen·si·ble (in-di-fen-sɪ-bĕl) *adj.* unable to be defended, unable to be justified. **in·de·fen′si·bly** *adv.* **in·de·fen·si·bil·i·ty** (in-di-fen-sɪ-bil-i-tee) *n.*
in·de·fin·a·ble (in-di-fɪ-nă-bĕl) *adj.* unable to be defined or described clearly.
in·def·i·nite (in-def-ɪ-nit) *adj.* not clearly defined or stated or decided, vague. **in·def′i·nite·ness** *n.* ☐**indefinite article,** the word "a" or "an."
in·def·i·nite·ly (in-def-ɪ-nit-lee) *adv.* in an indefinite way, for an unlimited period.
in·del·i·ble (in-del-ɪ-bĕl) *adj.* 1. (of a mark or stain or feeling) unable to be removed or washed away. 2. (of a pencil etc.) making an indelible mark. **in·del′i·bly** *adv.*
in·del·i·cate (in-del-ɪ-kit) *adj.* 1. slightly indecent. 2. tactless. **in·del′i·cate·ly** *adv.* **in·del·i·ca·cy** (in-del-ɪ-kă-see) *n.*
in·dem·ni·fy (in-dem-nɪ-fɪ) *v.* (**in·dem·ni·fied, in·dem·ni·fy·ing**) 1. to protect or insure (a person) against penalties incurred by his actions etc. 2. to compensate (a person) for injury suffered.
in·dem·ni·ty (in-dem-ni-tee) *n.* (*pl.* **-ties**) 1. protection or insurance against penalties incurred by one's actions. 2. compensation for damage done.
in·dent (in-dent) *v.* 1. to make recesses or toothlike notches in; *an indented coastline,* one with deep recesses. 2. to start (a line of print or writing) farther from the margin than the others, *indent the first line of each paragraph.* **in·den′tion** *n.* **in·den·ta·tion** (in-den-tay-shŏn) *n.*
in·den·ture (in-den-chŭr) *n.* 1. a written contract or agreement. 2. *indentures,* an agreement binding an apprentice to work for a master. **indenture** *v.* (**in·den·tured, in·den·tur·ing**) to bind by indenture, especially as an apprentice.
in·de·pend·ence (in-di-pen-dĕns) *n.* being independent. ☐**Independence Day,** July 4, celebrated in the U.S. as the anniversary of the date

in 1776 when the American colonies formally declared themselves free and independent of Britain; a similar festival elsewhere.
in·de·pend·ent (in-di-pen-dĕnt) *adj.* 1. not dependent on or controlled by another person or thing, *he is now independent of his parents.* 2. not depending for its validity or operation on the thing(s) involved; *independent proof,* from another source. 3. self-governing. 4. free of commitment to a political party. 5. having or providing a sufficient income to make it unnecessary for the possessor to earn his living, *he has independent means.* 6. not influenced by others in one's ideas or conduct. 7. unwilling to be under an obligation to others. **independent** *n.* an independent person, especially a voter not committed to any political party. **in·de·pend′ent·ly** *adv.*
in-depth (in-depth) *adj.* thorough, very detailed, *an in-depth survey.*
in·de·scrib·a·ble (in-di-skrɪ-bă-bĕl) *adj.* unable to be described, too great or beautiful or bad etc. to be described. **in·de·scrib′a·bly** *adv.* **in·de·scrib·a·bil·i·ty** (in-di-skrɪ-bă-bil-i-tee) *n.*
in·de·struct·i·ble (in-di-struk-tɪ-bĕl) *adj.* unable to be destroyed. **in·de·struct′i·bly** *adv.* **in·de·struct′i·ble·ness** *n.* **in·de·struct·i·bil·i·ty** (in-di-struk-tɪ-bil-i-tee) *n.*
in·de·ter·mi·na·ble (in-di-tur-mɪ-nă-bĕl) *adj.* impossible to discover or decide. **in·de·ter′mi·na·bly** *adv.* ▷Do not confuse *indeterminable* with *indeterminate.*
in·de·ter·mi·nate (in-di-tur-mɪ-nit) *adj.* not fixed in extent or character etc., vague, left doubtful. **in·de·ter′mi·nate·ly** *adv.* **in·de·ter′mi·nate·ness** *n.* **in·de·ter·mi·na·cy** (in-di-tur-mɪ-nă-see) *n.* **in·de·ter·mi·na·tion** (in-di-tur-mɪ-nay-shŏn) *n.* ▷Do not confuse *indeterminate* with *indeterminable.*
in·dex (in-deks) *n.* (*pl.* **in·dex·es, in·di·ces,** *pr.* in-di-seez) 1. a list of names, titles, subjects, etc., especially an alphabetical list indicating where in a book etc. each can be found. 2. a figure indicating the relative level of prices or wages compared with that at a previous date. 3. (in printing) a hand-shaped symbol used to draw attention to a note etc. 4. an indication or sign of something, *her work is an index of her talent.* **index** *v.* 1. to make an index to (a book or collection of books etc.). 2. to enter in an index. 3. to increase (wages, pensions, etc.) according to increases in the cost of living. **in′dex·er** *n.* ☐**index finger,** the forefinger. **index of refraction,** the ratio of the velocity of light in two adjacent media.
In·di·a (in-di-ă) 1. a large peninsula of Asia south of the Himalayas, forming a subcontinent. 2. a country consisting of the greater part of this. ☐**India ink,** ink made with a black pigment (made orginally in China and Japan). **India paper,** a soft absorbent paper used for proofs of engravings; a thin tough opaque printing paper. **India rubber,** natural rubber made from the juice of tropical plants.
In·di·an (in-di-ăn) *adj.* of India or Indians. **Indian** *n.* 1. a native of India. 2. one of the original inhabitants of the continent of America (other than Eskimos) or their descendants, *American Indian.* ☐**Indian clubs,** a pair of wooden or metal bottle-shaped clubs for swinging to exercise the arms. **Indian corn,** a type of primitive corn with kernels of various colors. **Indian file,** single file. **Indian giver,** a person who gives something and then

takes it back. **Indian meal,** cornmeal. **Indian Ocean,** the ocean between India and Australia. **Indian paintbrush,** a plant common in Western America, with small flowers and bright-colored bracts. **Indian pipe,** a leafless plant with a single white flower, resembling a pipe. **Indian summer,** a period of dry sunny weather in late autumn; a period of tranquil enjoyment late in life. **Indian wrestling,** a contest in which two seated contestants each place a corresponding elbow on a table and, gripping hands with forearms up, attempt to force the other's hand down to the table.

In·di·an·a (in-di-an-ă) a state of the U.S. **In·di·an'i·an** adj. & n.

In·di·an·ap·o·lis (in-di-ă-nap-ŏ-lĭs) the capital of Indiana.

indic. abbr. indicative.

in·di·cate (in-dĭ-kayt) v. (**in·di·cat·ed, in·di·cat·ing**) 1. to point out, to make known. 2. to be a sign of, to show the presence of. 3. to show the need of, to require. 4. to state briefly. **in·di·ca·tion** (in-dĭ-kay-shŏn) n.

in·dic·a·tive (in-dik-ă-tiv) adj. 1. giving an indication, *the style is indicative of the author's origin.* 2. (of a form of a verb) used in making a statement, not in a command or wish etc., as *he said* or *he is coming.* **indicative** n. this form of a verb. **in·dic'a·tive·ly** adv.

in·di·ca·tor (in-dĭ-kay-tŏr) n. 1. a thing that indicates or points to something. 2. a meter or other device giving information about the functioning of a machine etc.

in·di·ci·a (in-dish-i-ă) n. pl. 1. identifying marks. 2. imprinted marks showing that postage has been paid.

in·dict (in-drt) v. to charge with a crime, especially by action of a grand jury. **in·dict'a·ble** adj. **in·dict'ment** n. ▷Do not confuse *indict* with *indite.*

in·dif·fer·ent (in-dif-ĕ-rĕnt) adj. 1. feeling or showing no interest or sympathy, unconcerned. 2. neither good nor bad. 3. not of good quality or ability, *he is an indifferent ballplayer.* **in·dif'fer·ent·ly** adv. **in·dif'fer·ence** n.

in·dig·e·nous (in-dij-ĕ-nŭs) adj. (of plants or animals or inhabitants) native.

in·di·gent (in-di-jĕnt) adj. needy, impoverished. **in'di·gence** n. **in'di·gent·ly** adv.

in·di·gest·i·ble (in-di-jes-tĭ-bĕl) adj. difficult or impossible to digest.

in·di·ges·tion (in-di-jes-chŏn) n. pain caused by difficulty in digesting food.

in·dig·nant (in-dig-nănt) adj. feeling or showing indignation. **in·dig'nant·ly** adv.

in·dig·na·tion (in-dig-nay-shŏn) n. anger aroused by something thought to be unjust or wicked etc.

in·dig·ni·ty (in-dig-ni-tee) n. (pl. **-ties**) 1. the quality of being humiliating. 2. treatment that makes a person feel undignified or humiliated.

in·di·go (in-dĭ-goh) n. (pl. **-gos, -goes**) a deep blue dye or color. □**indigo blue,** a color between blue and violet in the spectrum. **indigo bunting,** a brilliant blue songbird of the eastern U.S. **indigo snake,** a large harmless snake of tropical America.

in·di·rect (in-dĭ-rekt) adj. not direct. **in·di·rect'ly** adv. **in·di·rect'ness** n. **in·di·rec·tion** (in-dĭ-rek-shŏn) n. □**indirect object,** a person or thing affected by the action of a verb but not primarily acted on, as *him* in *give him the book.* **indirect tax,** a tax paid in the form of increased prices for goods etc., not on income or capital.

in·dis·cern·i·ble (in-di-sur-nĭ-bĕl, -zur-) adj. that cannot be discerned or distinguished from another.

in·dis·creet (in-di-skreet) adj. 1. not discreet, revealing secrets. 2. not cautious, unwise. **in·dis·creet'ly** adv.

in·dis·cre·tion (in-di-skresh-ŏn) n. an indiscreet action or statement.

in·dis·crim·i·nate (in-di-skrim-ĭ-nit) adj. showing no discrimination, doing or giving things without making a careful choice. **in·dis·crim'i·nate·ly** adv. **in·dis·crim'i·nate·ness** n.

in·dis·pen·sa·ble (in-di-spen-să-bĕl) adj. not able to be dispensed with, essential. **in·dis·pen'sa·bly** adv. **in·dis·pen·sa·bil·i·ty** (in-di-spen-să-bil-i-tee) n.

in·dis·posed (in-di-spohzd) adj. 1. slightly ill. 2. unwilling, *they seem indisposed to help us.*

in·dis·po·si·tion (in-dis-pŏ-zish-ŏn) n. 1. slight illness. 2. unwillingness.

in·dis·pu·ta·ble (in-di-spyoo-tă-bĕl) adj. not able to be disputed, undeniable. **in·dis·pu'ta·ble·ness** n. **in·dis·pu·ta·bil'i·ty** n. **in·dis·pu'ta·bly** adv.

in·dis·sol·u·ble (in-di-sol-yŭ-bĕl) adj. firm and lasting, not able to be dissolved or destroyed, *indissoluble bonds of friendship.* **in·dis·sol'u·bly** adv.

in·dis·tinct (in-di-stingkt) adj. not distinct. **in·dis·tinct'ly** adv. **in·dis·tinct'ness** n.

in·dis·tin·guish·a·ble (in-di-sting-gwi-shă-bĕl) adj. not distinguishable.

in·dite (in-drt) v. (**in·dit·ed, in·dit·ing**) to put into words, to compose (a poem, speech, etc.). ▷Do not confuse *indite* with *indict.*

in·di·um (in-di-ŭm) n. a rare silver-white soft metallic element occurring with zinc etc.

in·di·vid·u·al (in-dĭ-vij-oo-ăl) adj. 1. single, separate, *each individual strand.* 2. of or for one person, *baked in individual portions.* 3. characteristic of one particular person or thing, *has a very individual style.* **individual** n. 1. one person or plant or animal considered separately. 2. (*informal*) a person, *a most unpleasant individual.* **in·di·vid'u·al·ly** adv. **in·di·vid·u·al·i·ty** (in-dĭ-vij-oo-al-i-tee) n. ▷Careful writers do not use *individual* to mean "a person."

in·di·vid·u·al·ism (in-dĭ-vij-oo-ă-liz-ĕm) n. 1. self-centered feeling or conduct. 2. independence in thought and action. 3. a social theory advocating free and independent action of the individual.

in·di·vid·u·al·ist (in-dĭ-vij-oo-ă-list) n. a person who is very independent in thought or action. **in·di·vid·u·al·is·tic** (in-dĭ-vij-oo-ă-lis-tik) adj.

in·di·vid·u·al·ize (in-dĭ-vij-oo-ă-lɪz) v. (**in·di·vid·u·al·ized, in·di·vid·u·al·iz·ing**) 1. to give individual character to. 2. to specify. 3. to adapt to individual tastes or needs. **in·di·vid·u·al·i·za·tion** (in-dĭ-vij-oo-ă-li-zay-shŏn) n.

in·di·vid·u·ate (in-dĭ-vij-oo-ayt) v. (**in·di·vid·u·at·ed, in·di·vid·u·at·ing**) to individualize, to form into an individual. **in·di·vid·u·a·tion** (in-dĭ-vij-oo-ay-shŏn) n.

in·di·vis·i·ble (in-dĭ-viz-ĭ-bĕl) adj. not divisible. **in·di·vis'i·bly** adv. **in·di·vis·i·bil·i·ty** (in-dĭ-viz-ĭ-bil-i-tee) n.

In·do·chi·na (in-doh-chɪ-nă) a peninsula in southeast Asia. **In·do·chi·nese** (in-doh-chɪ-neez) adj. & n.

in·doc·tri·nate (in-dok-trĭ-nayt) v. (**in·doc·**

tri·nat·ed, in·doc·tri·nat·ing) to fill (a person's mind) with particular ideas or doctrines.

in·doc·tri·na·tion (in-dok-trī-nay-shŏn) *n.*

In·do-Eu·ro·pe·an (in-doh-yoor-ŏ-pee-ăn) *adj.* of the family of languages spoken over most of Europe and parts of Asia.

in·do·lent (in-dŏ-lĕnt) *adj.* lazy. **in'do·lent·ly** *adv.* **in'do·lence** *n.*

in·dom·i·ta·ble (in-dom-i-tă-bĕl) *adj.* having an unyielding spirit, stubbornly persistent when faced with difficulty or opposition. **in·dom'i·ta·bly** *adv.*

In·do·ne·sia (in-dŏ-nee-*zhă*) a country in southeast Asia. **In·do·ne'sian** *adj.* & *n.*

in·door (in-dohr) *adj.* situated or used or done inside a building, *indoor games; an indoor aerial.* **in·doors'** *adv.*

in·dorse (in-dors) *v.* **(in·dorsed, in·dors·ing)** to endorse.

in·drawn (in-drawn) *adj.* of a breath drawn into the lungs, *an indrawn gasp.*

in·du·bi·ta·ble (in-doo-bi-tă-bĕl) *adj.* that cannot reasonably be doubted. **in·du'bi·ta·bly** *adv.*

in·duce (in-doos) *v.* **(in·duced, in·duc·ing).** 1. to persuade. 2. to produce or cause. 3. to bring on by artificial means, *induce labor.* 4. to infer, to obtain by inductive reasoning. **in·duc'er** *n.*

in·duce·ment (in-doos-mĕnt) *n.* 1. inducing, being induced. 2. an attraction or incentive.

in·duct (in-dukt) *v.* 1. to install as an officer or member of a group. 2. to enroll into military service.

in·duct·ance (in-duk-tăns) *n.* the property of producing an electric current by induction, the measure of this.

in·duc·tee (in-duk-tee) *n.* a person inducted into military service.

in·duc·tion (in-duk-shŏn) *n.* 1. inducting. 2. inducing. 3. logical reasoning that a general law exists because particular cases that seem to be examples of it exist. 4. production of an electric or magnetic state in an object by bringing an electrified or magnetic object close to but not touching it. 5. drawing a fuel mixture into the cylinder(s) of an internal combustion engine. 6. production of an electric current in a circuit by varying the magnetic field.

in·duc·tive (in-duk-tiv) *adj.* 1. of or using induction, *inductive reasoning.* 2. of inductance. **in·duc'tive·ly** *adv.* **in·duc'tive·ness** *n.*

in·dulge (in-dulj) *v.* **(in·dulged, in·dulg·ing)** 1. to allow (a person) to have what he wishes. 2. to gratify (a wish). 3. to allow oneself something that gives pleasure, *he indulges in a cigar after lunch.* **in·dulg'er** *n.*

in·dul·gence (in-dul-jĕns) *n.* 1. indulging. 2. being indulgent. 3. something allowed as a pleasure or privilege. 4. (in the R. C. Ch.) remission of temporal punishment still due for sins after sacramental absolution.

in·dul·gent (in-dul-jent) *adj.* indulging a person's wishes too freely, kind and lenient. **in·dul'gent·ly** *adv.*

in·du·rate (in-dŭ-rayt) *v.* **(in·du·rat·ed, in·du·rat·ing)** 1. to make or become hard. 2. to make callous or unfeeling. 3. to accustom or become accustomed. **indurate** (in-dŭ-rit) *adj.* 1. hardened. 2. callous or unfeeling. **in·du·ra·tion** (in-dŭ-ray-shŏn) *n.* **in·du·ra·tive** (in-dŭ-ray-tiv) *adj.*

in·dus·tri·al (in-dus-tri-ăl) *adj.* 1. of or engaged

in industries, *industrial workers.* 2. for use in industries. 3. having many highly developed industries, *an industrial country.* **in·dus'tri·al·ly** *adv.*

☐ **industrial arts,** the technical arts of industry, especially as taught in school. **industrial park,** a land area zoned and planned and developed especially for industry and business. **Industrial Revolution,** the rapid development of industry by use of machines in the early 19th century.

in·dus·tri·al·ist (in-dus-tri-ă-list) *n.* a person who owns or is engaged in managing an industrial business.

in·dus·tri·al·ize (in-dus-tri-ă-līz) *v.* **(in·dus·tri·al·ized, in·dus·tri·al·iz·ing)** to become industrial, to develop industry. **in·dus·tri·al·i·za·tion** (in-dus-tri-ă-li-zay-shŏn) *n.*

in·dus·tri·ous (in-dus-tri-ŭs) *adj.* hard-working. **in·dus'tri·ous·ly** *adv.* **in·dus'tri·ous·ness** *n.*

in·dus·try (in-dŭ-stree) *n.* (*pl.* **-tries**) 1. the manufacture or production of goods. 2. a particular branch of this, any business activity, *the tourist industry.* 3. industrialists as a group. 4. the quality of being industrious.

in·dwell (in-dwel) *v.* **(in·dwelt, in·dwell·ing)** to be permanently present, as a spirit or principle.

in·e·bri·ate (i-nee-bri-ayt) *v.* **(in·e·bri·at·ed, in·e·bri·at·ing)** to make drunk. **inebriate** (i-nee-bri-it) *n.* a drunken person. **inebriate** *adj.*

in·e·bri·at·ed (i-nee-bri-ay-tid) *adj.* drunk.

in·e·bri·a·tion (i-nee-bri-ay-shŏn) *n.* drunkenness.

in·ed·i·ble (in-ed-ĭ-bĕl) *adj.* not edible (because of its nature).

in·ed·u·ca·ble (in-ej-ŭ-kă-bĕl) *adj.* incapable of being educated.

in·ef·fa·ble (in-ef-ă-bĕl) *adj.* too great to be described, *ineffable joy.* **in·ef'fa·bly** *adv.*

in·ef·face·a·ble (in-i-fay-să-bĕl) *adj.* that cannot be effaced.

in·ef·fec·tive (in-i-fek-tiv) *adj.* 1. not effective. 2. (of a person) inefficient. **in·ef·fec'tive·ly** *adv.*

in·ef·fec·tu·al (in-i-fek-choo-ăl) *adj.* not effectual. **in·ef·fec'tu·al·ly** *adv.*

in·ef·fi·ca·cious (in-ef-ĭ-kay-shŭs) *adj.* not producing the desired effect. **in·ef·fi·ca'cious·ly** *adv.*

in·ef·fi·ca·cy (in-ef-ĭ-kă-see) *n.* inability to produce the desired results.

in·ef·fi·cient (in-i-fish-ĕnt) *adj.* not efficient. **in·ef·fi'cient·ly** *adv.* **in·ef·fi·cien·cy** (in-i-fish-ĕn-see) *n.*

in·e·las·tic (in-i-las-tik) *adj.* 1. not elastic. 2. unadaptable, unyielding. **in·e·las·tic·i·ty** (in-i-las-tis-i-tee) *n.*

in·el·e·gant (in-el-ĕ-gănt) *adj.* not elegant. **in·el'e·gant·ly** *adv.* **in·el·e·gance** (in-el-ĕ-găns) *n.*

in·el·i·gi·ble (in-el-i-jĭ-bĕl) *adj.* not eligible, not fit or entitled to be chosen, as for office. **ineligible** *n.* an ineligible person. **in·el·i·gi·bil·i·ty** (in-el-i-jĭ-bil-i-tee) *n.*

in·e·luc·ta·ble (in-i-luk-tă-bĕl) *adj.* that cannot be avoided or overcome.

in·ept (in-ept) *adj.* 1. lacking ability or fitness for a task. 2. unsuitable, absurd. **in·ept'ly** *adv.* **in·ept'ness** *n.* **in·ep·ti·tude** (in-ep-ti-tood) *n.*

in·e·qual·i·ty (in-i-kwol-i-tee) *n.* (*pl.* **-ties**) lack of equality in size or standard or rank etc.

in·eq·ui·ta·ble (in-ek-wi-tă-bĕl) *adj.* unfair, unjust.

in·eq·ui·ty (in-ek-wi-tee) *n.* (*pl.* **-ties**) unfairness, bias.

in·e·rad·i·ca·ble (in-i-rad-i-kă-bĕl) *adj.* that cannot be rooted out.

in·er·rant (in-er-ănt) *adj.* not liable to err.

in·ert (i-nurt) *adj.* 1. (of matter) without power to move or act. 2. without active chemical or other properties, incapable of reacting, *an inert gas.* 3. not moving, slow to move or take action. **in·ert'ly** *adv.* **in·ert'ness** *n.*

in·er·tia (i-nur-shă) *n.* 1. inertness, slowness to take action. 2. the property of matter by which it remains in a state of rest or, if it is in motion, continues moving in a straight line, unless acted upon by an external force. **in·er'tial** *adj.* ☐**inertial guidance,** guidance of a missile or spacecraft or aircraft by automatic instruments that it carries.

in·es·cap·a·ble (in-e-skay-pă-bĕl) *adj.* unavoidable. **in·es·cap'a·bly** *adv.*

in·es·sen·tial (in-ĕ-sen-shăl) *adj.* not essential. **inessential** *n.* an inessential thing.

in·es·ti·ma·ble (in-es-tĭ-mă-bĕl) *adj.* too great or intense or precious etc. to be estimated. **in·es'ti·ma·bly** *adv.*

in·ev·i·ta·ble (in-ev-i-tă-bĕl) *adj.* 1. not able to be prevented, sure to happen or appear. 2. (*informal*) tiresomely familiar, *the tourist with his inevitable camera.* **in·ev'i·ta·bly** *adv.* **in·ev·i·ta·bil·i·ty** (in-ev-i-tă-bil-i-tee) *n.*

in·ex·act (in-ig-zakt) *adj.* not exact. **in·ex·act'ly** *adv.* **in·ex·ac·ti·tude** (in-ig-zak-ti-tood) *n.*

in·ex·cus·a·ble (in-ik-skyoo-ză-bĕl) *adj.* unable to be excused or justified. **in·ex·cus'a·bly** *adv.*

in·ex·haust·i·ble (in-ig-zaws-tĭ-bĕl) *adj.* 1. not able to be totally used up, available in unlimited quantity. 2. indefatigable. **in·ex·haust'i·bly** *adv.*

in·ex·o·ra·ble (in-ek-sŏ-ră-bĕl) *adj.* relentless, unable to be persuaded by request or entreaty. **in·ex'o·ra·bly** *adv.*

in·ex·pe·di·ent (in-ik-spee-di-ĕnt) *adj.* not expedient. **in·ex·pe·di·en·cy** (in-ik-spee-di-ĕn-see) *n.*

in·ex·pen·sive (in-ik-spen-siv) *adj.* not expensive, offering good value for the price. **in·ex·pen'sive·ly** *adv.*

in·ex·pe·ri·ence (in-ik-speer-i-ĕns) *n.* lack of experience. **in·ex·pe'ri·enced** *adj.*

in·ex·pert (in-ek-spurt, in-ik-spurt) *adj.* not expert, unskillful. **in·ex'pert·ly** *adv.*

in·ex·pi·a·ble (in-eks-pi-ă-bĕl) *adj.* (of an offense) that cannot be expiated, for which amends cannot be made.

in·ex·plic·a·able (in-ek-splĭ-kă-bĕl) *adj.* unable to be explained or accounted for. **in·ex'plic·a·bly** *adv.*

in·ex·press·i·ble (in-ik-spres-ĭ-bĕl) *adj.* that cannot be expressed in words. **in·ex·press'i·bly** *adv.*

in·ex·pres·sive (in-ik-spres-iv) *adj.* not expressive, without expression.

in·ex·tin·guish·a·ble (in-ik-sting-gwi-shă-bĕl) *adj.* not quenchable, indestructible.

in ex·tre·mis (in ik-stree-mis) 1. at the point of death. 2. in very great difficulties. ▷Latin.

in·ex·tri·ca·ble (in-eks-trĭ-kă-bĕl) *adj.* 1. unable to be extricated. 2. unable to be disentangled or sorted out. **in·ex'tri·ca·bly** *adv.*

inf. *abbr.* 1. infantry. 2. inferior. 3. infinitive. 4. information.

in·fal·li·ble (in-fal-ĭ-bĕl) *adj.* 1. incapable of making a mistake or being wrong. 2. never failing, *an infallible remedy.* **in·fal'li·bly** *adv.* **in·fal'li·ble·ness** *n.* **in·fal·li·bil·i·ty** (in-fal-ĭ-bil-i-tee) *n.*

in·fa·mous (in-fă-mŭs) *adj.* having or deserving a very bad reputation, detestable. **in'fa·mous·ly** *adv.*

in·fa·my (in-fă-mee) *n.* (*pl.* **-mies**) ill fame, notoriety caused by great evil.

in·fan·cy (in-făn-see) *n.* (*pl.* **-cies**) 1. early childhood, babyhood. 2. an early stage of development.

in·fant (in-fănt) *n.* a child during the earliest period of its life. **infant** *adj.* 1. of or for infants. 2. young and developing.

in·fan·ti·cide (in-fan-ti-sɪd) *n.* 1. murder of an infant soon after its birth. 2. a person guilty of this.

in·fan·tile (in-făn-tɪl) *adj.* 1. of infants or infancy. 2. very childish. ☐**infantile paralysis,** poliomyelitis.

in·fan·try (in-făn-tree) *n.* (*pl.* **-tries**) troops who fight on foot.

in·farct (in-fahrkt) *n.* an area of dead tissue caused by the blocking of blood circulation. **in·farc·tion** (in-fahrk-shŏn) *n.*

in·fat·u·ate (in-fach-oo-ayt) *v.* (**in·fat·u·at·ed, in·fat·u·at·ing**) to inspire with a temporary intense unreasoning love for a person or thing. **in·fat·u·a·tion** (in-fach-oo-ay-shŏn) *n.*

in·fea·si·ble (in-fee-zĭ-bĕl) *adj.* not able to be done easily, impracticable.

in·fect (in-fekt) *v.* 1. to affect or contaminate with a disease or with bacteria etc. that produce a diseased condition. 2. to affect with one's feeling, *we became infected with their enthusiasm.* **in·fec·tive** (in-fek-tiv) *adj.*

in·fec·tion (in-fek-shŏn) *n.* 1. infecting, being infected. 2. the spreading of disease, especially by air or water etc. 3. a disease that is spread in this way, a diseased condition.

in·fec·tious (in-fek-shŭs) *adj.* 1. (of a disease) able to spread by air or water etc. 2. infecting with disease. 3. quickly spreading to others, *his fear was infectious.* **in·fec'tious·ly** *adv.* **in·fec'tious·ness** *n.*

in·fe·lic·i·tous (in-fĕ-lis-i-tŭs) *adj.* unfortunate, inappropriate. **in·fe·lic·i·ty** (in-fĕ-lis-i-tee) *n.* (*pl.* **-ties**).

in·fer (in-fur) *v.* (**in·ferred, in·fer·ring**) 1. to reach an opinion from facts or reasoning. 2. to imply. (▷This use should be avoided because it conceals the distinction between *infer* and *imply.*) **in·fer·ence** (in-fĕ-rĕns) *n.* **in·fer·en·tial** (in-fĕ-ren-shăl) *adj.*

in·fe·ri·or (in-feer-i-ŏr) *adj.* low or lower in rank or importance or quality or ability. **inferior** *n.* a person who is inferior to another, especially in rank. **in·fe·ri·or·i·ty** (in-feer-i-or-i-tee) *n.* (*pl.* **-ties**) ☐**inferiority complex,** a strong and persistent feeling of inferiority; great lack of self-confidence.

in·fer·nal (in-fur-năl) *adj.* 1. of hell, *the infernal regions.* 2. (*informal*) detestable, tiresome, *an infernal nuisance.* **in·fer'nal·ly** *adv.*

in·fer·no (in-fur-noh) *n.* (*pl.* **-nos**) a place resembling hell, somewhere intensely hot, a raging fire.

in·fer·tile (in-fur-tɪl) *adj.* not fertile. **in·fer·til·i·ty** (in-fĕr-til-i-tee) *n.*

in·fest (in-fest) *v.* (of pets or vermin etc.) to be numerous and troublesome in (a place). **in·fes·ta·tion** (in-fes-tay-shŏn) *n.*

in·fi·del (in-fi-děl) *n.* 1. a person with no religious beliefs. 2. an unbeliever or a person not an adherent of a particular religion, as Christianity or Islam.

in·fi·del·i·ty (in-fi-del-i-tee) *n.* (*pl.* -ties) unfaithfulness.

in·field (in-feeld) *n.* 1. the part of a baseball field enclosed within the base lines. 2. the first, second, and third basemen and shortstop.

in·field·er (in-feel-děr) *n.* a person playing the infield.

in·fight·ing (in-fi-ting) *n.* 1. boxing with an opponent nearer than arm's length. 2. hidden conflict within an organization. **in'fight·er** *n.*

in·fil·trate (in-fil-trayt, in-fil-) *v.* (**in·fil·trat·ed, in·fil·trat·ing**) 1. to enter gradually and without being noticed, as settlers or spies. 2. to cause to do this. **in'fil·tra·tor** *n.* **in·fil·tra·tion** (in-fil-tray-shŏn) *n.*

infin. *abbr.* infinitive.

in·fi·nite (in-fi-nit) *adj.* 1. having no limit, endless. 2. too great or too many to be measured or counted. **in'fi·nite·ly** *adv.* **in'fi·nite·ness** *n.*

in·fin·i·tes·i·mal (in-fin-i-tes-i-măl) *adj.* extremely small. **in·fin·i·tes'i·mal·ly** *adv.*

in·fin·i·tive (in-fin-i-tiv) *n.* a form of a verb that does not indicate a particular tense or number or person, in English used with or without *to,* as *go* in *let him go* or *allow him to go.*

in·fin·i·tude (in-fin-i-tood) *n.* 1. being infinite. 2. infinity.

in·fin·i·ty (in-fin-i-tee) *n.* (*pl.* -ties) an infinite number or extent or time or space.

in·firm (in-furm) *adj.* physically weak, especially from old age or illness; *infirm of purpose,* not resolute, hesitant. **in·firm'ly** *adv.*

in·fir·ma·ry (in-fur-mă-ree) *n.* (*pl.* -ries) 1. a hospital. 2. a room or rooms for sick people in a school or other institution.

in·fir·mi·ty (in-fur-mi-tee) *n.* (*pl.* -ties) 1. being infirm. 2. a particular physical weakness.

infl. *abbr.* 1. influence. 2. influenced.

in fla·gran·te de·lic·to (in flă-gran-tee di-lik-toh) in the act of committing a crime, red-handed. ▷Latin.

in·flame (in-flaym) *v.* (**in·flamed, in·flam·ing**) 1. to provoke to strong feeling or emotion, to arouse anger in. 2. to cause inflammation in.

in·flam·ma·ble (in-flam-ă-běl) *adj.* able to be set on fire. ▷This word means the same as *flammable;* its opposite is *noninflammable.* Careful writers prefer *inflammable.*

in·flam·ma·tion (in-flă-may-shŏn) *n.* redness and heat and pain produced in the body, especially as a reaction to injury or infection.

in·flam·ma·to·ry (in-flam-ă-tohr-ee) *adj.* likely to arouse strong feeling or anger, *inflammatory speeches.*

in·flat·a·ble (in-flay-tă-běl) *adj.* able to be inflated.

in·flate (in-flayt) *v.* (**in·flat·ed, in·flat·ing**) to fill or become filled with air or gas and swell up, to increase artificially; *at an inflated price,* an excessively high price.

in·fla·tion (in-flay-shŏn) *n.* 1. inflating, being inflated. 2. a general increase of prices and fall in the purchasing value of money.

in·fla·tion·ar·y (in-flay-shŏ-ner-ee) *adj.* causing inflation.

in·fla·tion·ist (in-flay-shŏ-nist) *n.* a person who advocates inflationary monetary policies. **in·fla'tion·ism** *n.*

in·flect (in-flekt) *v.* 1. to change the pitch of (the voice) in speaking. 2. to change the ending or form of (a word) to show its grammatical relation or number etc., as *sing* changes to *sang* or *sung; child* changes to *children.*

in·flec·tion (in-flek-shŏn) *n.* 1. inflecting, bending. 2. modulation of voice, change in pitch or tone. 3. modification of a word to express a grammatical relationship. **in·flec'tion·al** *adj.*

in·flex·i·ble (in-flek-sĭ-běl) *adj.* 1. not flexible, unable to be bent. 2. not able to be altered, *an inflexible rule.* 3. refusing to alter one's demands etc., unyielding. **in·flex'i·bly** *adv.* **in·flex·i·bil·i·ty** (in-flek-sĭ-bil-i-tee) *n.*

in·flict (in-flikt) *v.* to cause (a blow or penalty etc.) to be suffered. **in·flic·tion** (in-flik-shŏn) *n.*

in·flight (in-flit) *adj.* (of food, movies, etc.) provided on a plane during a flight.

in·flo·res·cence (in-flŏ-res-ĕns) *n.* 1. the opening of blossoms. 2. the head of a flower. 3. the arrangement of the flowers of a plant in relation to the axis and to each other.

in·flow (in-floh) *n.* an inward flow, the amount that flows in, *a large inflow of cash.*

in·flu·ence (in-floo-ĕns) *n.* 1. the power to produce an effect, *the influence of the moon on the tides.* 2. the ability to affect someone's character or beliefs or actions. 3. a person or thing with this ability. **influence** *v.* (**in·flu·enced, in·flu·enc·ing**) to exert influence on.

in·flu·en·tial (in-floo-en-shăl) *adj.* having great influence.

in·flu·en·za (in-floo-en-ză) *n.* a virus disease causing fever, muscular pain, and inflammation of the respiratory system.

in·flux (in-fluks) *n.* an inflow, especially of people or things into a place.

in·fo (in-foh) *n.* (*slang*) information.

in·fold (in-fohld) *v.* to enfold.

in·form (in-form) *v.* 1. to give information to. 2. to reveal information to the police etc. about secret or criminal activities.

in·for·mal (in-for-măl) *adj.* not formal, without formality or ceremony. **in·for'mal·ly** *adv.* **in·for·mal·i·ty** (in-for-mal-i-tee) *n.* ▷In this dictionary, words and definitions marked *informal* are used in everyday speech but should not be used when speaking or writing formally.

in·for·mant (in-for-mănt) *n.* a person who gives information.

in·for·ma·tion (in-fŏr-may-shŏn) *n.* 1. facts told or heard or discovered. 2. facts fed into a computer etc. **in·for·ma'tion·al** *adj.* □**information industry,** commercial activity concerned with the collection, processing, distribution, etc. of information. **information retrieval,** the systematic recovery of data or information from the memory bank of a computer or from files etc.

in·form·a·tive (in-for-mă-tiv) *adj.* giving information.

in·formed (in-formd) *adj.* having good or sufficient knowledge of something, *informed opinion.*

in·form·er (in-for-měr) *n.* a person who reveals information to the police etc. about secret or criminal activities.

in·frac·tion (in-frak-shŏn) *n.* an infringement, a violation.

in·fra dig (in-fră dig) (*informal*) beneath one's dignity. ▷From the Latin *infra dignitatem.*

in·fra·red (in-fră-red) *adj.* 1. (of radiation) having a wavelength that is slightly longer than that of

visible light rays at the red end of the spectrum.
2. of or using this radiation.

in·fra·son·ic (in-fră-son-ik) *adj.* (of sound waves) with a pitch that is below the lower limit of normal human hearing.

in·fra·struc·ture (in-fră-struk-chŭr) *n.* the subordinate parts and installations etc. that form the basis of an enterprise.

in·fre·quent (in-free-kwĕnt) *adj.* not frequent. **in·fre′quent·ly** *adv.* **in·fre·quen·cy** (in-free-kwĕn-see) *n.*

in·fringe (in-frinj) *v.* **(in·fringed, in·fring·ing)** 1. to break or act against (a rule or agreement etc.), to violate. 2. to encroach, *do not infringe upon his rights.* **in·fringe′ment** *n.*

in·fu·ri·ate (in-fyoor-i-ayt) *v.* **(in·fu·ri·at·ed, in·fu·ri·at·ing)** to enrage. **in·fu′ri·at·ing·ly** *adv.*

in·fuse (in-fyooz) *v.* **(in·fused, in·fus·ing)** 1. to imbue, to instill, *infused them with courage; infused courage into them.* 2. to steep (tea or herbs etc.) in a liquid in order to make flavor or soluble constituents pass into the liquid, to allow (tea etc.) to undergo this process.

in·fu·si·ble (in-fyoo-zĭ-bĕl) *adj.* that cannot be fused or melted.

in·fu·sion (in-fyoo-zhŏn) *n.* 1. infusing, being infused. 2. a liquid made by infusing. 3. something added or introduced into a stock, *an infusion of new blood to improve the breed.*

-ing[1] *suffix* used to form the present participle of verbs, often used as adjectives, as in *charming, strapping.*

-ing[2] *suffix* used to form nouns meaning of a specific kind, as in *herring, gelding.*

-ing[3] *suffix* used to form nouns from verbs meaning action, as in *fighting;* an instance of action, as in *wedding;* the thing produced by action, as in *building, learning;* what is used for action, as in *binding, firm going;* material for, as in *fencing, clothing;* what is to undergo action, as in *darning, washing.*

in·gath·er·ing (in-gath-ĕ-ring) *n.* 1. a gathering in, as a harvest. 2. an assembly.

in·gen·ious (in-jeen-yŭs) *adj.* 1. clever at inventing new things or methods. 2. cleverly contrived, *an ingenious machine.* **in·gen′ious·ly** *adv.* ▷Do not confuse *ingenious* with *ingenuous.*

in·ge·nue, in·gé·nue (an-jĕ-noo, ahn-zhĕ-) *n.* (*pl.* **-nues**) an artless young woman, especially as a stage role.

in·ge·nu·i·ty (in-jĕ-noo-i-tee) *n.* cleverness, imagination, inventiveness.

in·gen·u·ous (in-jen-yoo-ŭs) *adj.* without artfulness, unsophisticated, *an ingenuous manner.* **in·gen′u·ous·ly** *adv.* **in·gen′u·ous·ness** *n.* ▷Do not confuse *ingenuous* with *ingenious.*

in·gest (in-jest) *v.* to take in as food. **in·ges·tion** (in-jes-chŏn) *n.*

in·gle·nook (ing-gĕl-nuuk) *n.* a nook forming a place for sitting beside a deeply recessed fireplace.

in·glo·ri·ous (in-glohr-i-ŭs) *adj.* 1. ignominious. 2. not bringing glory, obscure. **in·glo′ri·ous·ly** *adv.*

in·got (ing-gŏt) *n.* a brick-shaped piece of cast metal.

in·graft (in-graft) *v.* to engraft.

in·grain (in-grayn) *v.* 1. to firmly fix (habits or feelings or tendencies). 2. to work deeply into (a surface or texture). **in·grained′** *adj.*

in·grate (in-grayt) *n.* an ungrateful person.

in·gra·ti·ate (in-gray-shi-ayt) *v.* **(in·gra·ti·at·ed, in·gra·ti·a·ting)** to bring (oneself) into a person's favor, especially in order to gain an advantage.

in·grat·i·tude (in-grat-i-tood) *n.* lack of due gratitude.

in·gre·di·ent (in-gree-di-ĕnt) *n.* one of the parts or elements in a mixture or combination.

in·gress (in-gres) *n.* going in, the right to enter.

in·grown (in-grohn) *adj.* grown abnormally inward, especially into the flesh, *an ingrown toenail.*

in·gui·nal (ing-gwĭ-năl) *adj.* of the groin.

in·hab·it (in-hab-it) *v.* to live in (a place) as one's home or dwelling place.

in·hab·it·a·ble (in-hab-i-tă-bĕl) *adj.* able to be inhabited.

in·hab·i·tant (in-hab-i-tănt) *n.* one who inhabits a place.

in·hal·ant (in-hay-lănt) *n.* a medicinal substance to be inhaled.

in·ha·la·tor (in-hă-lay-tŏr) *n.* an apparatus for inhaling oxygen, medication, etc.

in·hale (in-hayl) *v.* **(in·haled, in·hal·ing)** 1. to breathe in, to draw into the lungs by breathing. 2. to take tobacco smoke into the lungs. **in·ha·la·tion** (in-hă-lay-shŏn) *n.*

in·hal·er (in-hay-lĕr) *n.* a device that produces or sends out a medicinal vapor to be inhaled.

in·har·mon·ic (in-hahr-mon-ik) *adj.* not harmonic, discordant.

in·har·mo·ni·ous (in-hahr-moh-ni-ŭs) *adj.* not harmonious, conflicting.

in·here (in-heer) *v.* **(in·hered, in·her·ing)** 1. (of qualities etc.) to exist or abide essentially or permanently. 2. (of rights etc.) to be invested in (a person etc.).

in·her·ent (in-her-ĕnt) *adj.* existing in something as a natural or permanent characteristic or quality. **in·her′ent·ly** *adv.*

in·her·it (in-her-it) *v.* 1. to receive (property or a title etc.) by legal right of succession or by a will etc. when its previous owner or holder has died. 2. to receive from a predecessor, *this government inherited many problems from the last one.* 3. to receive (a characteristic) from one's parents or ancestors. **in·her′i·tor** *n.* **in·her′it·a·ble** *adj.* ▷See the note under **congenital.**

in·her·i·tance (in-her-i-tăns) *n.* 1. inheriting. 2. a thing that is inherited. □**inheritance tax,** a tax on inherited property.

in·hib·it (in-hib-it) *v.* 1. to restrain, to prevent, *this substance inhibits the growth of moss.* 2. to hinder the impulses of (a person), to cause inhibitions. **in·hib′i·tor** *n.*

in·hi·bi·tion (in-i-bish-ŏn) *n.* 1. inhibiting, being inhibited. 2. repression of or resistance to an instinct or impulse or feeling.

in·hos·pi·ta·ble (in-hos-pi-tă-bĕl) *adj.* 1. not hospitable. 2. (of a place or climate) giving no shelter or no favorable conditions. **in·hos′pi·ta·bly** *adv.*

in-house (in-hows) *adj.* & *adv.* *(informal)* within an organization or using its own resources; *an in-house project,* not subcontracted.

in·hu·man (in-hyoo-măn) *adj.* brutal, lacking normal human qualities of kindness, pity, etc. (▷Do not confuse *inhuman* with *inhumane.*) **in·hu·man·i·ty** (in-hyoo-man-i-tee) *n.*

in·hu·mane (in-hyoo-mayn) *adj.* not humane. ▷Do not confuse *inhumane* with *inhuman.*

in·hume (in-hyoom) *v.* **(in·humed, in·hum·**

ing) to bury. **in·hu·ma·tion** (in-hyoo-may-shŏn) *n.*

in·im·i·cal (i-**nim**-i-kăl) *adj.* 1. hostile. 2. harmful. **in·im′i·cal·ly** *adv.*

in·im·i·ta·ble (i-**nim**-i-tă-bĕl) *adj.* impossible to imitate.

in·iq·ui·ty (i-**nik**-wi-tee) *n.* (*pl.* **-ties**) 1. great injustice. 2. wickedness, a wicked act. **in·iq′ui·tous** *adj.*

init. *abbr.* initial.

in·i·tial (i-**nish**-ăl) *adj.* of or belonging to the beginning, *the initial stages of the work.* **initial** *n.* the first letter of a word or name; *a person's initials,* those of his names, often used as a signature etc. **initial** *v.* (**in·i·tial·ed, in·i·tial·ing**) to sign or mark with initials. **in·i·tial·ly** (i-**nish**-ă-lee) *adv.* at first.

in·i·ti·ate (i-**nish**-i-ayt) *v.* (**in·i·ti·at·ed, in·i·ti·at·ing**) 1. to cause to begin, to start (a plan) working, *he initiated certain reforms.* 2. to admit (a person) into membership of a society etc., often with special ceremonies. 3. to give (a person) basic instruction or information about something that is new to him. **initiate** (i-**nish**-i-it) *n.* an initiated person. **in·i′ti·a·tor** *n.* **in·i·ti·a·tion** (i-nish-i-ay-shŏn) *n.*

in·i·ti·a·tive (i-**nish**-ă-tiv) *n.* 1. the first step in a process. 2. the power or right to begin something. 3. the ability to initiate things, enterprise, *he lacks initiative.* □**have the initiative,** to be in a position to control the course of events, as in a war. **on one's own initiative,** without being prompted by others. **take the initiative,** to be the first to take action.

in·i·ti·a·to·ry (i-nish-i-ă-tohr-ee) *adj.* 1. introductory, beginning. 2. tending to initiate.

in·ject (in-jekt) *v.* 1. to force or drive (a liquid etc.) into something, especially by means of a syringe. 2. to introduce a new element into, *inject some new ideas into the committee.* **in·jec′tor** *n.*

in·jec·tion (in-jek-shŏn) *n.* 1. injecting, an instance of this. 2. a liquid etc. that is injected.

in·ju·di·cious (in-joo-**dish**-ŭs) *adj.* showing lack of good judgment, unwise. **in·ju·di′cious·ly** *adv.*

in·junc·tion (in-jungk-shŏn) *n.* an order or command, especially an order from a law court stating that something must or must not be done.

in·jure (in-jŭr) *v.* (**in·jured, in·jur·ing**) to cause damage or harm or hurt to. **in′jur·er** *n.*

in·jured (in-jŭrd) *adj.* 1. damaged, harmed, hurt. 2. showing that one feels offended, *in an injured voice.* 3. wronged, *the injured party in a divorce.*

in·ju·ri·ous (in-joor-i-ŭs) *adj.* causing or likely to cause injury. **in·ju′ri·ous·ly** *adv.*

in·ju·ry (in-jŭ-ree) *n.* (*pl.* **-ries**) 1. damage, harm. 2. a particular form of this, *a leg injury.* 3. a wrong or unjust act.

in·jus·tice (in-jus-tis) *n.* 1. lack of justice. 2. an unjust action or treatment. □**do a person an injustice,** to make an unfair judgment about him.

ink (ingk) *n.* a colored liquid used in writing with a pen, a colored paste used in printing etc. and in ballpoint pens. **ink** *v.* to mark or cover with ink, to apply ink to; *ink these words out,* obliterate them with ink.

ink·blot (ingk-blot) *n.* a stain of spilled ink. □**inkblot test,** a Rorschach test; a similar test.

ink·horn (ingk-horn) *n.* a small vessel of horn formerly used for holding ink.

ink·ling (ing-kling) *n.* a hint, a slight knowledge or suspicion.

ink·stand (ingk-stand) *n.* a stand for one or more bottles of ink, often with a pen tray.

ink·well (ingk-wel) *n.* an ink bottle, especially one fitted into a hole in a desk or inkstand.

ink·y (**ing**-kee) *adj.* (**ink·i·er, ink·i·est**) 1. covered or stained with ink. 2. black like ink, *inky darkness.* **ink′i·ness** *n.*

in·laid (in-layd) *see* **inlay.**

in·land (in-lănd) *adj. & adv.* in or toward the interior of a country. **inland** *n.* the interior of a country.

in-law (in-law) *n.* (*pl.* **in-laws**) (*informal*) a relative by marriage.

in·lay (in-lay) *v.* (**in·laid, in·lay·ing**) to set (pieces of wood or metal etc.) into a surface so that they lie flush with it and form a design. **inlay** *n.* 1. inlaid material. 2. a design formed by this. 3. a dental filling shaped to fit a cavity.

in·let (in-let) *n.* 1. a strip of water extending into the land from a sea or lake, or between islands. 2. a way in, as for water into a tank, *the inlet pipe.*

in·mate (in-mayt) *n.* one of a number of inhabitants of a house or other building, especially a hospital or prison or other institution.

in me·mo·ri·am (in mĕ-mohr-i-ăm) in memory of a person who has died. ▷Latin.

in·most (in-mohst) *adj.* furthest inward.

inn (in) *n.* 1. a hotel, especially in the country. 2. a tavern or restaurant.

in·nards (in-ărdz) *n. pl.* (*informal*) 1. the stomach and bowels, entrails. 2. any inner parts.

in·nate (i-nayt) *adj.* inborn. **in·nate′ly** *adv.*

in·ner (in-ĕr) *adj.* nearer to the center or inside, interior, internal. □**inner city,** the central area of a city. **inner ear,** the internal part of the ear comprising the vestibule, semicircular canals, and cochlea. **inner tube,** a separate inflatable tube inside the cover of a pneumatic tire.

in·ner-di·rect·ed (in-ĕr-dĭ-rek-tid) *adj.* guided by personal standards rather than by external social pressure.

in·ner·most (in-ĕr-mohst) *adj.* furthest inward.

in·ner·sole (in-ĕr-sohl) *n.* insole.

in·ner·spring (in-ĕr-spring) *adj.* with springs inside. □**innerspring mattress,** a mattress having enclosed spiral springs supporting padding.

in·ner·vate (i-nur-vayt, in-ĕr-) *v.* (**in·ner·vat·ed, in·ner·vat·ing**) to connect (a muscle or organ) to the nervous system, to supply with nerve fiber. **in·ner·va·tion** (in-ĕr-vay-shŏn) *n.*

in·ning (in-ing) *n.* 1. a portion of a baseball game in which each team is at bat until it has three outs. 2. **innings,** (*informal*) a period during which a person has an opportunity to achieve something, *now I want my innings.*

inn·keep·er (in-kee-pĕr) *n.* a person who keeps an inn.

in·no·cence (in-ŏ-sĕns) *n.* 1. the state of being free from moral wrong, unacquainted with evil, not guilty of a crime. 2. guilelessness, naiveté.

in·no·cent (in-ŏ-sĕnt) *adj.* 1. not guilty of a particular crime etc. 2. free of all evil or wrongdoing, *as innocent as a newborn babe.* 3. harmless, not intended to be harmful, *innocent amusements; an innocent remark.* 4. foolishly trustful. **innocent** *n.* a person (especially a child) who is free of all evil or who is foolishly trustful. **in′no·cent·ly** *adv.*

in·noc·u·ous (i-nok-yoo-ŭs) *adj.* 1. not injurious, harmless. 2. insignificant and dull.

in·nom·i·nate (i-nom-ĭ-nit) *adj.* unnamed. □**in-**

nominate bone, the hipbone, a union of three bones, the ilium, ischium, and pubis.

in·no·vate (in-ŏ-vayt) *v.* **(in·no·vat·ed, in·no·vat·ing)** to introduce a new process or way of doing things. **in'no·va·tor** *n.* **in'no·va·tive** *adj.* **in·no·va·tion** (in-ŏ-vay-shŏn) *n.*

in·nu·en·do (in-yoo-en-doh) *n.* (*pl.* **-does**) an unpleasant insinuation.

in·nu·mer·a·ble (i-noo-mĕ-ră-bĕl) *adj.* too many to be counted.

in·oc·u·late (i-nok-yŭ-layt) *v.* **(in·oc·u·lat·ed, in·oc·u·lat·ing)** to treat (a person or animal) with vaccines or serums etc., especially in order to protect against a disease. **in·oc·u·la·tion** (i-nok-yŭ-lay-shŏn) *n.*

in·of·fen·sive (in-ŏ-fen-siv) *adj.* not offensive, harmless. **in·of·fen'sive·ly** *adv.*

in·op·er·a·ble (in-op-ĕ-ră-bĕl) *adj.* 1. unable to be cured by surgical operation. 2. not operable.

in·op·er·a·tive (in-op-ĕ-ră-tiv) *adj.* not functioning.

in·op·por·tune (in-op-ŏr-toon) *adj.* coming or happening at an unsuitable time. **in·op·por·tune'ly** *adv.*

in·or·di·nate (in-or-dĭ-nit) *adj.* excessive. **in·or'di·nate·ly** *adv.*

in·or·gan·ic (in-or-gan-ik) *adj.* of mineral origin, not organic. □**inorganic chemistry,** a branch of chemistry dealing with inorganic substances.

in·pa·tient (in-pay-shĕnt) *n.* a person who remains resident in a hospital while undergoing treatment.

in pet·to (in pet-oh) secretly, especially of cardinals appointed but not named as such. ▷Italian, = in the breast.

in·put (in-puut) *n.* 1. what is put in. 2. the place where energy or information etc. enters a system. **input** *v.* 1. to put in or into. 2. to supply (data, programs, etc., to a computer).

in·quest (in-kwest) *n.* a judicial investigation to establish facts, especially about a death that may not be the result of natural causes.

in·qui·e·tude (in-kwı̆-ĕ-tood) *n.* uneasiness of mind or body.

in·quire (in-kwır) *v.* **(in·quired, in·quir·ing)** to make an inquiry. **in·quir'er** *n.* **in·quir'ing·ly** *adv.* □**inquiring reporter,** a news reporter who questions passersby on the street to get their opinions on current events etc.

in·quir·y (in-kwır-ee, in-kwi-ree) *n.* (*pl.* **-quir·ies**) an investigation, especially an official one.

in·qui·si·tion (in-kwi-zish-ŏn) *n.* a detailed questioning or investigation. □**the Inquisition,** a tribunal established by the Roman Catholic Church in the Middle Ages, especially the very severe one in Spain, to discover and punish heretics.

in·quis·i·tive (in-kwiz-i-tiv) *adj.* 1. eagerly seeking knowledge. 2. prying. **in·quis'i·tive·ly** *adv.* **in·quis'i·tive·ness** *n.*

in·quis·i·tor (in-kwiz-i-tŏr) *n.* a person who questions another searchingly. **in·quis·i·tor·i·al** (in-kwiz-i-tohr-i-ăl) *adj.*

in re (in ree) in the matter of. ▷Latin.

INRI *abbr.* Jesus of Nazareth, King of the Jews. ▷Latin, *Iesus Nazarenus Rex Iudaeorum.*

in·road (in-rohd) *n.* a sudden attack or encroachment. □**make inroads into,** to use up large quantities of (resources etc.).

in·rush (in-rush) *n.* a rush in, a violent influx.

ins. *abbr.* 1. inches. 2. insurance.

in·sa·lu·bri·ous (in-să-loo-bri-ŭs) *adj.* (of a place or climate) unhealthy.

in·sane (in-sayn) *adj.* 1. not sane, mad. 2. ex-

tremely foolish. **in·sane'ly** *adv.* **in·san·i·ty** (in-san-i-tee) *n.*

in·sa·tia·ble (in-say-shă-bĕl) *adj.* unable to be satisfied, *an insatiable appetite.* **in·sa'tia·bly** *adv.*

in·sa·ti·ate (in-say-shi-it) *adj.* never satisfied.

in·scribe (in-skrıb) *v.* **(in·scribed, in·scrib·ing)** 1. to write or cut words etc. on (a surface), *inscribed their names on the stone; inscribed it with their names.* 2. to draw (one geometrical figure) within another so that certain points of their boundaries coincide.

in·scrip·tion (in-skrip-shŏn) *n.* words or names inscribed on a monument or coin or stone etc.

in·scru·ta·ble (in-skroo-tă-bĕl) *adj.* baffling, impossible to understand or interpret. **in·scru'ta·bly** *adv.*

in·seam (in-seem) *n.* the inner seam of a trouser leg etc.

in·sect (in-sekt) *n.* a small animal with six legs, no backbone, and a body divided into three parts (head, thorax, abdomen).

in·sec·ti·cide (in-sek-ti-sıd) *n.* a substance for killing insects. **in·sec·ti·cid·al** (in-sek-ti-sı-dăl) *adj.*

in·sec·tiv·o·rous (in-sek-tiv-ŏ-rŭs) *adj.* feeding on insects.

in·se·cure (in-sĕ-kyoor) *adj.* not secure or safe. **in·se·cure'ly** *adv.* **in·se·cur'i·ty** *n.* (*pl.* **-ties**).

in·sem·i·nate (in-sem-ı̆-nayt) *v.* **(in·sem·i·nat·ed, in·sem·i·nat·ing)** to insert semen into. **in·sem·i·na·tion** (in-sem-ı̆-nay-shŏn) *n.*

in·sen·sate (in-sen-sayt) *adj.* 1. without physical sensation. 2. without sensibility, unfeeling. 3. stupid, without sense. **in·sen'sate·ly** *adv.*

in·sen·si·ble (in-sen-sĭ-bĕl) *adj.* 1. unconscious. 2. without feeling, unaware, *seemed insensible of his danger.* 3. callous. 4. (of changes) imperceptible. **in·sen'si·bly** *adv.* **in·sen·si·bil·i·ty** (in-sen-sĭ-bil-i-tee) *n.* (*pl.* **-ties**).

in·sen·si·tive (in-sen-si-tiv) *adj.* not sensitive. **in·sen·si·tiv·i·ty** (in-sen-si-tiv-i-tee) *n.*

in·sen·ti·ent (in-sen-shi-ĕnt) *adj.* not sentient. **in·sen'ti·ence** *n.*

in·sep·a·ra·ble (in-sep-ă-ră-bĕl) *adj.* 1. unable to be separated. 2. liking to be constantly together, *inseparable companions.* **in·sep'a·ra·bly** *adv.* **in·sep·a·ra·bil·i·ty** (in-sep-ă-ră-bil-i-tee) *n.* **in·sep'a·ra·ble·ness** *n.*

in·sert (in-surt) *v.* to put (a thing) in or between or among. **insert** (in-surt) *n.* a thing inserted. **in·ser·tion** (in-sur-shŏn) *n.*

in·set (in-set) *v.* **(in·set, in·set·ting)** to set or place in, to decorate with an inset, *the crown was inset with jewels.* **inset** (in-set) *n.* something set into a larger thing.

in·shore (in-shohr) *adj. & adv.* near or nearer to the shore.

in·side (in-sıd) *n.* 1. the inner side of a surface or part. 2. a small group within an organization having authority and prestige and access to confidential information; *on the inside,* belonging to such a group. 3. *insides,* (*informal*) the organs in the abdomen, the stomach and intestines. **inside** (in-sıd) *adj.* on or coming from the inside; *inside information,* information that is not available to outsiders; *an inside job,* a crime committed or aided by someone living or working on the premises where it occurred. **inside** (in-sıd) *adv.* on or in or to the inside. **inside** (in-sıd) *prep.* on the inner side of, within; *inside an hour,* in less than an hour. □**inside left** *or* **right,** (in soccer) a player on the forward line near to the center on the left or right side; his position. **inside out,** with the inner surface turned to face the outside; *turn a place inside out,* to search it thoroughly; *know a subject inside out,* to know it thoroughly. **in·sid·er** (in-sɪ-dĕr) *n.* 1. an accepted member of a certain group. 2. a person who is made aware of a secret.

in·sid·i·ous (in-sid-i-ŭs) *adj.* spreading or developing or acting inconspicuously but with harmful effect, *an insidious rumor.* **in·sid′i·ous·ly** *adv.* **in·sid′i·ous·ness** *n.* ▷Do not confuse *insidious* with *invidious.*

in·sight (in-sɪt) *n.* 1. the ability to perceive and understand the true nature of something. 2. knowledge obtained by this. **in·sight·ful** (in-sɪt-fŭl) *adj.*

in·sig·ni·a (in-sig-ni-ä) *n. sing. & pl.* 1. the symbols of authority or office (as the crown and scepter of a king). 2. an identifying or distinguishing badge etc.

in·sig·nif·i·cant (in-sig-nif-i-kănt) *adj.* having little or no importance or value or influence. **in·sig·nif′i·cant·ly** *adv.* **in·sig·nif′i·cance** *n.*

in·sin·cere (in-sin-seer) *adj.* not sincere. **in·sin·cere′ly** *adv.* **in·sin·cer·i·ty** (in-sin-ser-i-tee) *n.*

in·sin·u·ate (in-sin-yoo-ayt) *v.* **(in·sin·u·at·ed, in·sin·u·at·ing)** 1. to insert gradually or craftily, *insinuate oneself into a person's good graces.* 2. to hint artfully or unpleasantly. **in·sin′u·at·ing** *adj.* **in·sin·u·a·tion** (in-sin-yoo-ay-shŏn) *n.*

in·sip·id (in-sip-id) *adj.* 1. lacking in flavor. 2. lacking in interest or liveliness. **in·sip′id·ly** *adv.* **in·sip·id·i·ty** (in-si-pid-i-tee) *n.*

in·sist (in-sist) *v.* 1. to declare emphatically. 2. to demand emphatically, *I insist on your being there.* **in·sist·ent** (in-sis-tĕnt) *adj.* 1. insisting, declaring or demanding emphatically. 2. forcing itself on one's attention, *the insistent throb of the engines.* **in·sist′ent·ly** *adv.* **in·sist′ence** *n.*

in si·tu (in sɪ-too) in its present or original place. ▷Latin.

in·so·far (in-soh-fahr) **as** to the extent that.

insol. *abbr.* insoluble.

in·so·la·tion (in-soh-lay-shŏn) *n.* solar radiation received, the amount of this per unit of horizontal surface.

in·sole (in-sohl) *n.* 1. the inner sole of a boot or shoe. 2. a loose piece of material laid in the bottom of a shoe for warmth or comfort.

in·so·lent (in-sŏ-lĕnt) *adj.* behaving insultingly, arrogant, contemptuous. **in′so·lent·ly** *adv.* **in′so·lence** *n.*

in·sol·u·ble (in-sol-yŭ-bĕl) *adj.* 1. unable to be dissolved. 2. unable to be solved, *an insoluble problem.* **in·sol′u·bly** *adv.* **in·sol·u·bil·i·ty** (in-sol-yŭ-bil-i-tee) *n.*

in·sol·vent (in-sol-vĕnt) *adj.* unable to pay one's debts. **in·sol·ven·cy** (in-sol-vĕn-see) *n.*

in·som·ni·a (in-som-ni-ä) *n.* habitual sleeplessness.

in·som·ni·ac (in-som-ni-ak) *n.* a person who suffers from insomnia.

in·so·much (in-soh-much) *adv.* to such an extent (that), inasmuch (as).

in·sou·ci·ant (in-soo-si-ănt) *adj.* carefree, unconcerned. **in·sou′ci·ance** *n.*

insp. *abbr.* 1. inspected. 2. inspector.

in·spect (in-spekt) *v.* 1. to examine (a thing) carefully and critically, especially looking for flaws.

2. to examine officially, to visit in order to make sure that certain rules and standards are being observed. **in·spec·tion** (in-spek-shŏn) *n.*

in·spec·tor (in-spek-tŏr) *n.* 1. a person whose job is to inspect things or supervise services etc. 2. (in some police departments) an officer above captain and below superintendent.

in·spi·ra·tion (in-spĭ-ray-shŏn) *n.* 1. inspiring. 2. an inspiring influence. 3. a sudden brilliant idea. **in·spi·ra′tion·al** *adv.*

in·spire (in-spɪr) *v.* **(in·spired, in·spir·ing)** 1. to stimulate (a person) to creative or other activity or to express certain ideas. 2. to fill with or instill a certain feeling, *he inspires confidence in us.* 3. to communicate ideas etc. by a divine agency, *the prophets were inspired by God.*

in·spir·it (in-spir-it) *v.* 1. to put life into, animate. 2. to encourage.

inst. *abbr.* 1. instant, = of the current month, *on the 6th inst.* 2. institute. 3. institution.

in·sta·bil·i·ty (in-stă-bil-i-tee) *n.* lack of stability.

in·stall (in-stawl) *v.* 1. to place (a person) in office, especially with ceremonies. 2. to set (apparatus) in position and ready for use. 3. to settle in a place, *he was comfortably installed in an armchair.*

in·stal·la·tion (in-stă-lay-shŏn) *n.* 1. installing, being installed. 2. apparatus etc. installed.

in·stall·ment (in-stawl-mĕnt) *n.* any of the parts in which something is presented or supplied, or a debt is paid, over a period of time. ☐**installment buying,** purchasing on the installment plan. **installment plan,** an arrangement for payment in installments.

in·stance (in-stăns) *n.* a case or example of something. **instance** *v.* **(in·stanced, in·stanc·ing)** to mention as an instance. ☐**in the first instance,** firstly.

in·stant (in-stănt) *adj.* 1. occurring immediately, *there was instant relief.* 2. (of food) designed to be prepared quickly and easily. **instant** *n.* 1. an exact point of time, the present moment, *come here this instant!* 2. a very short space of time, a moment, *not an instant too soon.* ☐**instant camera,** a camera that develops and prints a photograph almost instantly after an exposure is made. **instant replay,** the immediate reshowing of a short section of a television broadcast, usually a sports event.

in·stan·ta·ne·ous (in-stăn-tay-ni-ŭs) *adj.* occurring or done instantly, *death was instantaneous.* **in·stan·ta′ne·ous·ly** *adv.*

in·stan·ter (in-stan-tĕr) *adv.* (old use) immediately, at once.

in·stan·ti·ate (in-stan-shi-ayt) *v.* **(in·stan·ti·at·ed, in·stan·ti·at·ing)** to represent by an instance. **in·stan·ti·a·tion** (in-stan-shi-ay-shŏn) *n.*

in·stant·ly (in-stănt-lee) *adv.* immediately.

in·state (in-stayt) *v.* **(in·stat·ed, in·stat·ing)** to put in office, to install.

in·stead (in-sted) *adv.* as an alternative or substitute. ☐**instead of,** in place of.

in·step (in-step) *n.* 1. the upper surface of the foot between toes and ankle. 2. the part of a shoe etc. covering this.

in·sti·gate (in-stĭ-gayt) *v.* **(in·sti·gat·ed, in·sti·gat·ing)** to urge or incite, to bring about by persuasion, *instigated them to strike; instigated an inquiry.* **in′sti·ga·tor** *n.* **in·sti·ga·tion** (in-stĭ-gay-shŏn) *n.*

in·still (in-stil) *v.* to implant (ideas, feelings, etc.)

into a person's mind gradually. **in·still′ment** *n.*

in·stinct (in-stingkt) *n.* 1. an inborn impulse or tendency to perform certain acts or behave in certain ways. 2. a natural ability, *has an instinct for finding a good place.* **in·stinc·tu·al** (in-stingk-choo-ăl) *adj.*

in·stinc·tive (in-stingk-tiv) *adj.* prompted by instinct. **in·stinc′tive·ly** *adv.*

in·sti·tute (in-sti-toot) *n.* 1. a society or organization for promotion of a scientific or educational or social etc. activity. 2. the building used by this. **institute** *v.* **(in·sti·tut·ed, in·sti·tut·ing)** 1. to establish, to found. 2. to cause (an inquiry or a custom) to be started.

in·sti·tu·tion (in-sti-too-shŏn) *n.* 1. instituting, being instituted. 2. an institute, especially for a charitable or social activity. 3. an established law or custom or practice, *(informal)* a person who has become a familiar figure in some activity. **in·sti·tu·tion·al** (in-sti-too-shŏ-năl) *adj.* of or like an institution. **in·sti·tu′tion·al·ly** *adv.*

in·sti·tu·tion·al·ize (in-sti-too-shŏ-nă-līz) *v.* **(in·sti·tu·tion·al·ized, in·sti·tu·tion·al·iz·ing)** to place or keep (a person) in an institution that will provide the care he needs; *become institutionalized,* to be so used to living in an institution that one cannot live independently. **in·sti·tu·tion·al·i·za·tion** (in-sti-too-shŏ-nă-li-zay-shŏn) *n.*

instr. *abbr.* 1. instructor. 2. instrument.

in·struct (in-strukt) *v.* 1. to give (a person) instruction in a subject or skill. 2. to inform. 3. to give instructions to, to direct or command.

in·struc·tion (in-struk-shŏn) *n.* 1. the process of teaching. 2. knowledge or teaching imparted. 3. *instructions,* statements making known to a person what he is required to do, an order.

in·struc·tion·al (in-struk-shŏ-năl) *adj.* imparting knowledge.

in·struc·tive (in-struk-tiv) *adj.* giving or containing instruction, enlightening.

in·struc·tor (in-struk-tŏr) *n.* 1. a person who instructs, a teacher. 2. a college teacher who ranks below an assistant professor. **in·struc′tor·ship** *n.*

in·stru·ment (in-strŭ-mĕnt) *n.* 1. a tool or implement used for delicate or scientific work. 2. a measuring device giving information about the operation of an engine etc. or used in navigation. 3. a device designed for producing musical sounds, *musical instruments.* 4. a person used and controlled by another to perform an action, *was made the instrument of another's crime.* 5. a formal or legal document, *signed the instrument of abdication.* □**instrument landing** or **flying,** landing or navigating using only the instruments of the aircraft.

in·stru·men·tal (in-strŭ-men-tăl) *adj.* 1. serving as an instrument or means of doing something, *was instrumental in finding her a job.* 2. performed on musical instruments, *instrumental music.*

in·stru·men·tal·ist (in-strŭ-men-tă-list) *n.* a musician who plays a musical instrument (as distinct from one who is a singer).

in·stru·men·tal·i·ty (in-strŭ-men-tal-i-tee) *n.* (*pl.* **-ties**) a means or agency.

in·stru·men·ta·tion (in-strŭ-men-tay-shŏn) *n.* 1. the arrangement or composition of music for instruments. 2. the provision or use of mechanical or scientific instruments.

in·sub·or·di·nate (in-sŭ-bor-dĭ-nit) *adj.* disobe-dient, rebellious. **in·sub·or·di·na·tion** (in-sŭ-bor-dĭ-nay-shŏn) *n.*

in·sub·stan·tial (in-sŭb-stan-shăl) *adj.* 1. not existing in reality, imaginary. 2. not made of a strong or solid substance; *insubstantial evidence,* weak, not well-founded.

in·suf·fer·a·ble (in-suf-ĕ-ră-bĕl) *adj.* 1. unbearable. 2. unbearably conceited or arrogant. **in·suf′fer·a·bly** *adv.*

in·suf·fi·cient (in-sŭ-fish-ĕnt) *adj.* not sufficient. **in·suf·fi′cient·ly** *adv.* **in·suf·fi·cien·cy** (in-sŭ-fish-ĕn-see) *n.*

in·su·lar (in-sŭ-lăr) *adj.* 1. of or on an island. 2. of or like people who live on an island and are isolated from outside influences, narrow-minded, *insular prejudices.* **in·su·lar·i·ty** (in-sŭ-lar-i-tee) *n.*

in·su·late (in-sŭ-layt) *v.* **(in·su·lat·ed, in·su·lat·ing)** 1. to cover or protect (a thing) with a substance or device that prevents the passage of electricity or sound or the loss of heat; *insulating tape,* tape that prevents the passage of electricity. 2. to isolate (a person or place) from influences that might affect it. **in′su·lat·or** *n.* **in·su·la·tion** (in-sŭ-lay-shŏn) *n.*

in·su·lin (in-sŭ-lin) *n.* a hormone produced in the pancreas, controlling the absorption of sugar by the body. □**insulin shock,** bodily collapse caused by an overdose of insulin.

in·sult (in-sult) *v.* to speak or act in a way that hurts the feelings or pride of (a person) and rouses his anger. **insult** (in-sult) *n.* an insulting remark or action. **in·sult′ing·ly** *adv.*

in·su·per·a·ble (in-soo-pĕ-ră-bĕl) *adj.* unable to be overcome, *an insuperable difficulty.*

in·sup·port·a·ble (in-sŭ-pohr-tă-bĕl) *adj.* 1. unbearable. 2. unjustifiable.

in·sur·a·ble (in-shoor-ă-bĕl) *adj.* able to be insured against loss, injury, etc.

in·sur·ance (in-shoor-ăns) *n.* 1. a contract undertaking to provide compensation for loss or damage or injury etc., in return for a payment made in advance once or regularly. 2. the business of providing such contracts. 3. the amount payable to the company etc. providing the contract, a premium. 4. the amount payable by the company etc. in compensation. 5. anything done as a safeguard against loss or failure etc.

in·sure (in-shoor) *v.* **(in·sured, in·sur·ing)** 1. to protect by a contract of insurance. 2. to ensure.

in·sured (in-shoord) *n.* a person protected by insurance.

in·sur·er (in-shoor-ĕr) *n.* a company offering insurance.

in·sur·gent (in-sur-jĕnt) *adj.* rebellious, rising in revolt. **insurgent** *n.* a rebel. **in·sur′gence** *n.* **in·sur·gen·cy** (in-sur-jĕn-see) *n.*

in·sur·mount·a·ble (in-sŭr-mown-tă-bĕl) *adj.* unable to be surmounted, insuperable. **in·sur·mount′a·bly** *adv.*

in·sur·rec·tion (in-sŭ-rek-shŏn) *n.* rising in open resistance to established authority, rebellion. **in·sur·rec′tion·ist** *n.*

in·sus·cep·ti·ble (in-sŭ-sep-tĭ-bĕl) *adj.* not susceptible.

int. *abbr.* 1. interest. 2. interior. 3. internal. 4. international. 5. intransitive.

in·tact (in-takt) *adj.* undamaged, complete.

in·ta·glio (in-tal-yoh) *n.* (*pl.* **-glios**) a kind of carving in which the design is sunk below the surface.

in·take (in-tayk) *n.* 1. the process of taking some-

thing in, the place where liquid or air etc. is channeled into something. 2. the number or quantity of people or things etc. accepted or received, *a school's annual intake of pupils.*
in·tan·gi·ble (in-tan-jĭ-bĕl) *adj.* not tangible, not material. **intangible** *n.* something intangible. **in·tan'gi·bly** *adv.*
in·te·ger (in-tĕ-jĕr) *n.* a whole number such as 0, 3, 19, etc., not a fraction.
in·te·gral (in-tĕ-grăl) *adj.* 1. (of a part) constituent, necessary to the completeness of a whole, *Flatbush is an integral part of Brooklyn.* 2. complete, forming a whole, *an integral design.*
in·te·grate (in-tĕ-grayt) *v.* **(in·te·grat·ed, in·te·grat·ing)** 1. to combine or form (a part or parts) into a whole. 2. to bring or come into equal membership of a community. **in·te·gra·tion** (in-tĕ-gray-shŏn) *n.* ☐**integrated circuit,** a small piece of material holding a complex electronic circuit, designed to replace a conventional circuit of many components.
in·teg·ri·ty (in-teg-ri-tee) *n.* 1. honesty, incorruptibility. 2. wholeness, entirety. 3. soundness.
in·teg·u·ment (in-teg-yŭ-mĕnt) *n.* a skin, husk, rind, or other (usually natural) covering.
in·tel·lect (in-tĕ-lekt) *n.* 1. the mind's power of reasoning and acquiring knowledge (contrasted with feeling and instinct). 2. ability to use this power, *people of intellect.*
in·tel·lec·tu·al (in-tĕ-lek-choo-ăl) *adj.* 1. of the intellect. 2. needing use of the intellect, *an intellectual occupation.* 3. having a well-developed intellect and a taste for advanced knowledge. **intellectual** *n.* an intellectual person. **in·tel·lec'tu·al·ly** *adv.*
in·tel·lec·tu·al·ism (in-tĕ-lek-choo-ă-liz-ĕm) *n.* 1. use or exercise of the intellect only. 2. the doctrine that knowledge is wholly or mainly derived from pure reason.
in·tel·lec·tu·al·ize (in-tĕ-lek-choo-ă-lɪz) *v.* **(in·tel·lec·tu·al·ized, in·tel·lec·tu·al·iz·ing)** 1. to use the intellect. 2. to analyze (a situation or problem) without recognizing the emotional content. **in·tel·lec·tu·al·i·za·tion** (in-tĕ-lek-choo-ă-li-zay-shŏn) *n.*
in·tel·li·gence (in-tel-i-jĕns) *n.* 1. mental ability, the power of learning and understanding. 2. information, news, especially that of military value. 3. the people engaged in collecting this. ☐**intelligence quotient,** a number that shows how a person's intelligence compares with that of an average person of the same age.
in·tel·li·gent (in-tel-i-jĕnt) *adj.* having great mental ability. **in·tel'li·gent·ly** *adv.*
in·tel·li·gent·si·a (in-tel-i-jent-si-ă, -gent-) *n.* intellectual people regarded as a class.
in·tel·li·gi·ble (in-tel-i-jĭ-bĕl) *adj.* able to be understood. **in·tel'li·gi·bly** *adv.* **in·tel·li·gi·bil·i·ty** (in-tel-i-jĭ-bil-i-tee) *n.*
in·tem·per·ate (in-tem-pĕ-rit) *adj.* 1. drinking alcohol excessively. 2. (of person or conduct or speech) immoderate, unrestrained, violent. **in·tem'per·ance** *n.*
in·tend (in-tend) *v.* 1. to have in mind as what one wishes to do or achieve. 2. to plan that (a thing) shall be used or interpreted in a particular way, *we intended this room for you; the remark was intended as an insult.*
in·tend·ed (in-ten-did) *n.* (informal) fiancé(e).
in·tense (in-tens) *adj.* 1. strong in quality or degree, *intense heat.* 2. (of a person) emotional. **in·**

tense'ly *adv.* **in·ten·si·ty** (in-ten-si-tee) *n.* ▷Do not confuse *intense* with *intensive.*
in·ten·si·fy (in-ten-sĭ-fɪ) *v.* **(in·ten·si·fied, in·ten·si·fy·ing)** to make or become more intense. **in·ten·si·fi·ca·tion** (in-ten-sĭ-fĭ-kay-shŏn) *n.*
in·ten·sive (in-ten-siv) *adj.* 1. employing much effort, concentrated, *intensive study.* 2. (in grammar) expressing intensity or giving force to a word or phrase. **intensive** *n.* an intensive word or prefix, as *very* in *the very last one.* **in·ten'sive·ly** *adv.* **in·ten'sive·ness** *n.* ☐**intensive care,** constant surveillance of critically ill patients in a hospital. ▷Do not confuse *intensive* with *intense.*
in·tent (in-tent) *n.* intention, *with intent to kill.* **intent** *adj.* 1. intending, having one's mind fixed on some purpose, *intent on killing.* 2. with one's attention concentrated, *an intent gaze.* **in·tent'ly** *adv.* **in·tent'ness** *n.* ☐**for** or **to all intents and purposes,** practically, virtually.
in·ten·tion (in-ten-shŏn) *n.* what one intends to do or achieve, one's purpose.
in·ten·tion·al (in-ten-shŏ-năl) *adj.* done on purpose, intended, not accidental. **in·ten'tion·al·ly** *adv.*
in·ter (in-tur) *v.* **(in·terred, in·ter·ring)** to bury (a dead body) in the earth or in a tomb.
inter- *prefix* between, among, as in *inter-American,* between or among the countries of North and South America.
in·ter·act (in-tĕr-akt) *v.* to have an effect upon each other. **in·ter·ac·tion** (in-tĕr-ak-shŏn) *n.* **in·ter·ac'tive** *adj.*
in·ter a·li·a (in-tĕr ay-li-ă) among other things. ▷Latin.
in·ter·breed (in-tĕr-breed) *v.* **(in·ter·bred, in·ter·breed·ing)** to breed with each other, to crossbreed.
in·ter·ca·lar·y (in-tur-kă-ler-ee) *adj.* 1. inserted in the calendar to harmonize the calendar with the solar year, as February 29 in leap year. 2. interpolated, intervening.
in·ter·ca·late (in-tur-kă-layt) *v.* **(in·ter·ca·lat·ed, in·ter·ca·lat·ing)** 1. to insert (an intercalary day etc.). 2. to interpose or interpolate. **in·ter·ca·la·tion** (in-tur-kă-lay-shŏn) *n.*
in·ter·cede (in-tĕr-seed) *v.* **(in·ter·ced·ed, in·ter·ced·ing)** to intervene on behalf of another person or as a peacemaker.
in·ter·cel·lu·lar (in-tĕr-sel-yŭ-lăr) *adj.* located between or among cells.
in·ter·cept (in-tĕr-sept) *v.* 1. to stop or catch (a person or thing) between his or its starting point and destination. 2. (in mathematics) to mark off (space) between two points or lines or planes. **intercept** (in-tĕr-sept) *n.* 1. (in mathematics) the part of a line etc. between two points of intersection with other lines. 2. the interception of an enemy, especially enemy aircraft, missiles, etc. **in·ter·cep·tion** (in-tĕr-sep-shŏn) *n.*
in·ter·cep·tor (in-tĕr-sep-tŏr) *n.* a fighter plane or missile for intercepting enemy planes or missiles.
in·ter·ces·sion (in-tĕr-sesh-ŏn) *n.* interceding. **in·ter·ces'sor** *n.* one who intercedes. **in·ter·ces'sor·y** *adj.*
in·ter·change (in-tĕr-chaynj) *v.* **(in·ter·changed, in·ter·chang·ing)** 1. to put (each of two things) into the other's place. 2. to make an exchange of, to give and receive (one thing for another). 3. to alternate. **interchange** (in-tĕr-chaynj) *n.* 1. interchanging. 2. a road junction

designed so that streams of traffic do not intersect on the same level.

in·ter·change·a·ble (in-tĕr-**chayn**-jă-bĕl) *adj.* able to be interchanged.

in·ter·col·le·giate (in-tĕr-kŏ-**lee**-jit) *adj.* between different colleges or universities.

in·ter·com (**in**-tĕr-kom) *n. (informal)* an intercommunication system.

in·ter·com·mu·ni·cate (in-tĕr-kŏ-**myoo**-ni-kayt) *v.* (**in·ter·com·mu·ni·cat·ed, in·ter·com·mu·ni·cat·ing**) 1. to communicate with each other. 2. to have free passage to each other, as rooms etc. **in·ter·com·mu·ni·ca·tion** (in-tĕr-kŏ-myoo-ni-**kay**-shŏn) *n.* ☐**intercommunication system,** a system of internal communication by telephone or radio, etc. with equipment for sending and receiving messages at each station.

in·ter·con·nect (in-tĕr-kŏ-**nekt**) *v.* to connect with each other. **in·ter·con·nec·tion** (in-tĕr-kŏ-**nek**-shŏn) *n.*

in·ter·con·ti·nen·tal (in-tĕr-kon-ti-**nen**-tăl) *adj.* connecting or carried on between two continents, (of missiles) able to be fired from one continent to another.

in·ter·cos·tal (in-tĕr-**kos**-tăl) *adj.* between the ribs.

in·ter·course (**in**-tĕr-kohrs) *n.* 1. any dealings or communication between people or countries. 2. sexual intercourse, copulation.

in·ter·cul·tur·al (in-tĕr-**kul**-chŭ-răl) *adj.* occurring among or between or relating to different cultures.

in·ter·de·nom·i·na·tion·al (in-tĕr-di-nom-ĭ-**nay**-shŏ-năl) *adj.* relating to more than one religious denomination.

in·ter·de·part·men·tal (in-tĕr-dee-pahrt-**men**-tăl) *adj.* relating to more than one department.

in·ter·de·pend·ent (in-tĕr-di-**pen**-dĕnt) *adj.* dependent on each other. **in·ter·de·pend'ence** *n.*

in·ter·dict (in-tĕr-**dikt**) *v.* to prohibit or forbid authoritatively. **interdict** (**in**-tĕr-dikt) *n.* an authoritative prohibition. **in·ter·dic·tion** (in-tĕr-**dik**-shŏn) *n.*

in·ter·dis·ci·pli·na·ry (in-tĕr-dis-ĭ-**plĭ**-ner-ee) *adj.* concerning or combining more than one branch of learning.

in·ter·est (**in**-tĕ-rist, **in**-trist) *n.* 1. a feeling of curiosity or concern about something. 2. the quality of arousing such feeling, *the subject has no interest for me.* 3. a thing toward which one feels it, *music is one of his interests.* 4. advantage, benefit, *she looks after her own interests.* 5. a legal right to a share in something, a financial stake in a business etc. 6. money paid for the use of money lent; *return someone's kindness with interest,* give back more than one received. **interest** *v.* 1. to arouse the interest of. 2. to cause to take an interest in, *interested herself in welfare work.* ☐**interest group,** a group acting together from common interest or purpose. **in the interest of,** in behalf of, to the benefit of.

in·ter·est·ed (**in**-tĕ-ri-stid, **in**-tri-) *adj.* 1. feeling or showing interest or curiosity. 2. having a private interest in something, *interested parties.*

in·ter·est·ing (**in**-tĕ-ri-sting, **in**-tri-) *adj.* arousing interest.

in·ter·face (**in**-tĕr-fays) *n.* 1. a surface forming a common boundary between two regions. 2. a place, or piece of equipment, where interaction occurs between two systems, processes, etc.

in·ter·faith (in-tĕr-**fayth**) *adj.* between or among adherents of different religions.

in·ter·fere (in-tĕr-**feer**) *v.* (**in·ter·fered, in·ter·fer·ing**) 1. to take part in dealing with other people's affairs without right or invitation. 2. to obstruct wholly or partially.

in·ter·fer·ence (in-tĕr-**feer**-ĕns) *n.* 1. interfering. 2. the fading of received radio signals because of static or unwanted signals. 3. (in football) the blockers who run ahead of the ball carrier to keep tacklers away; illegal hindering of a pass receiver before he catches a pass.

in·ter·fer·om·e·ter (in-tĕr-f-**rom**-ĕ-tĕr) *n.* a device for making precise measurements by means of interference phenomena. **in·ter·fer·om'e·try** *n.*

in·ter·fer·on (in-tĕr-**feer**-on) *n.* a protein substance that prevents the development of a virus in living cells.

in·ter·fuse (in-tĕr-**fyooz**) *v.* (**in·ter·fused, in·ter·fus·ing**) 1. to intersperse. 2. to blend.

in·ter·ga·lac·tic (in-tĕr-gă-**lak**-tik) *adj.* of or in the space between galaxies.

in·ter·gen·er·a·tion·al (in-tĕr-jen-ĕ-**ray**-shŏ-năl) *adj.* occurring between generations.

in·ter·im (**in**-tĕ-rim) *n.* an intervening period of time, *in the interim.* **interim** *adj.* of or in such a period; *an interim report,* one made before the main report, showing what has happened so far.

in·te·ri·or (in-**teer**-i-ŏr) *adj.* nearer to the center, inner. **interior** *n.* 1. an interior part or region, the central or inland part of a country. 2. the inside of a building or room. ☐**interior decoration,** the art or profession of designing the layout and furnishings of the inside of buildings or rooms. **interior decorator,** a person engaged in interior decoration.

interj. *abbr.* interjection.

in·ter·ject (in-tĕr-**jekt**) *v.* to put in (a remark) when someone is speaking.

in·ter·jec·tion (in-tĕr-**jek**-shŏn) *n.* 1. interjecting. 2. an interjected remark. 3. an exclamation such as *oh!* or *good heavens!*

in·ter·lace (in-tĕr-**lays**) *v.* (**in·ter·laced, in·ter·lac·ing**) to weave or lace together.

in·ter·lard (in-tĕr-**lahrd**) *v.* to insert contrasting remarks here and there in (a speech etc.), *interlarded his speech with quotations.*

in·ter·leaf (**in**-tĕr-leef) *n.* (*pl.* **-leaves**, *pr.* -leevz) an extra blank leaf inserted between the leaves of a book.

in·ter·leave (in-tĕr-**leev**) *v.* (**in·ter·leaved, in·ter·leav·ing**) to insert blank leaves between the leaves of (a book).

in·ter·li·brar·y (in-tĕr-**lɪ**-brer-ee) *adj.* existing between libraries. ☐**interlibrary loan,** a system by which books belonging to one library may be borrowed at another.

in·ter·line¹ (in-tĕr-**lɪn**) *v.* (**in·ter·lined, in·ter·lin·ing**) to insert words between the lines of.

interline² (**in**-tĕr-lɪn-) *v.* to put an extra lining between the ordinary lining and the outer material (of a garment). **in'ter·lin'ing** *n.*

in·ter·lin·e·ar (in-tĕr-lin-i-ăr) *adj.* written or printed between the lines of a text.

in·ter·link (in-tĕr-**lingk**) *v.* to link together.

in·ter·lock (in-tĕr-**lok**) *v.* to fit into each other, especially so that parts engage.

in·ter·loc·u·tor (in-tĕr-**lok**-yŭ-tŏr) *n.* 1. a person who takes part in dialogue or conversation. 2. the center man in a minstrel show who acts as

announcer and exchanges jokes with the end men.
in·ter·loc·u·to·ry (in-tĕr-lok-yŭ-tohr-ee) *adj.* (of a decree etc.) given in the course of a legal action, before the final decision.
in·ter·lope (in-tĕr-lohp) *v.* (**in·ter·loped, in·ter·lop·ing**) to intrude or interfere in the affairs of another. **in·ter·lop·er** (in-tĕr-loh-pĕr) *n.*
in·ter·lude (in-tĕr-lood) *n.* 1. an interval between parts of a play etc. 2. something performed during this. 3. an intervening time or event etc. of a different kind from the main one.
in·ter·lu·nar (in-tĕr-loo-năr) *adj.* of or relating to the period of the lunar month when the moon is invisible.
in·ter·mar·ry (in-tĕr-mar-ee) *v.* (**in·ter·mar·ried, in·ter·mar·ry·ing**) 1. (of tribes or nations or families etc.) to become connected by marriage. 2. to marry within one's own family. **in·ter·mar·riage** (in-tĕr-mar-ij) *n.*
in·ter·me·di·ar·y (in-tĕr-mee-di-er-ee) *n.* (*pl.* **-ar·ies**) a mediator, a go-between. **intermediary** *adj.* 1. acting as an intermediary. 2. intermediate in position or form.
in·ter·me·di·ate (in-tĕr-mee-di-it) *adj.* coming between two things in time or place or order. **intermediate** *n.* 1. an intermediate thing. 2. an intermediary. ☐**intermediate school,** a middle school or junior high school, for the grades between elementary school and high school.
in·ter·ment (in-tur-mĕnt) *n.* burial. ▷Do not confuse **interment** with **internment**.
in·ter·mez·zo (in-tĕr-met-soh) *n.* (*pl.* **-zos**) a short musical composition to be played between acts of a play etc. or between sections of a larger work or independently.
in·ter·mi·na·ble (in-tur-mĭ-nă-bĕl) *adj.* endless, long and boring. **in·ter'mi·na·bly** *adv.*
in·ter·min·gle (in-tĕr-ming-gĕl) *v.* (**in·ter·min·gled, in·ter·min·gling**) to mingle.
in·ter·mis·sion (in-tĕr-mish-ŏn) *n.* an interval, a pause in work or action.
in·ter·mit (in-tĕr-mit) *v.* (**in·ter·mit·ted, in·ter·mit·ting**) 1. to suspend, to discontinue. 2. to stop for a time.
in·ter·mit·tent (in-tĕr-mit-ĕnt) *adj.* occurring at intervals, not continuous, *intermittent rain.* **in·ter·mit'tent·ly** *adv.*
in·ter·mix (in-tĕr-miks) *v.* to mix.
in·tern[1] (in-turn) *v.* to compel (an enemy alien or prisoner of war etc.) to live in a special area or camp.
in·tern[2], **in·terne** (in-turn) *n.* an advanced student or recent graduate undergoing supervised practical training, especially a medical school graduate acting as an assistant doctor in a hospital. **intern** *v.* to serve as an intern. **in'tern·ship** *n.*
in·ter·nal (in-tur-năl) *adj.* 1. of or in the inside of a thing. 2. belonging to a thing because of its nature or structure; *internal evidence,* evidence contained in the thing being discussed. 3. of or in the interior of the body, *internal organs.* 4. of the domestic affairs of a country. **in·ter'nal·ly** *adv.* ☐**internal-combustion engine,** an engine that produces power by burning fuel inside the engine itself rather than externally. **internal medicine,** the branch of medicine dealing with the diagnosis and nonsurgical treatment of disease. **internal revenue,** the revenue of a government derived from sources within the country.
in·ter·na·tion·al (in-tĕr-nash-ŏ-năl) *adj.* of or ex-

isting or agreed between two or more countries. **International** *n.* 1. one of several associations founded to promote socialist or communist action. 2. (often *international*) a labor union with locals in two or more countries. **in·ter·na'tion·al·ly** *adv.*
in·ter·na·tion·al·ism (in-tĕr-nash-ŏ-nă-liz-ĕm) *n.* the policy of cooperation among nations, especially in political and economic affairs. **in·ter·na'tion·al·ist** *n.*
in·ter·na·tion·al·ize (in-tĕr-nash-ŏ-nă-lız) *v.* (**in·ter·na·tion·al·ized, in·ter·na·tion·al·iz·ing**) to make international, especially to bring under the combined protection etc. of different nations. **in·ter·na·tion·al·i·za·tion** (in-tĕr-nash-ŏ-nă-lī-zay-shŏn) *n.*
in·ter·ne·cine (in-tĕr-nee-seen, -nes-een) *adj.* 1. mutually destructive. 2. of a struggle within a nation, organization, group, etc.
in·tern·ee (in-tur-nee) *n.* a person who is interned.
in·tern·ist (in-tur-nist) *n.* a specialist in internal medicine.
in·tern·ment (in-turn-mĕnt) *n.* interning, being interned. ☐**internment camp,** a place where internees are imprisoned. ▷Do not confuse **internment** with **interment.**
in·ter·nun·ci·o (in-tĕr-nun-shi-oh) *n.* (*pl.* **-cios**) the pope's ambassador when or where no nuncio is employed.
in·ter·of·fice (in-tĕr-aw-fis) *adj.* functioning or passing between the offices of an organization.
in·ter·per·son·al (in-tĕr-pur-sŏ-năl) *adj.* of the relations between persons. **in·ter·per'son·al·ly** *adv.*
in·ter·plan·e·tar·y (in-tĕr-plan-ĕ-ter-ee) *adj.* of or existing between planets.
in·ter·play (in-tĕr-play) *n.* interaction.
In·ter·pol (in-tĕr-pohl) *n. International* Criminal *Pol*ice Commission, an organization that coordinates investigations made by the police forces of member countries into crimes with an international basis.
in·ter·po·late (in-tur-pŏ-layt) *v.* (**in·ter·po·lat·ed, in·ter·po·lat·ing**) 1. to interject. 2. to insert (new material) misleadingly into a book etc. **in·ter·po·la·tion** (in-tur-pŏ-lay-shŏn) *n.*
in·ter·pose (in-tĕr-pohz) *v.* (**in·ter·posed, in·ter·pos·ing**) 1. to insert between, to interject. 2. to intervene. **in·ter·po·si·tion** (in-tĕr-pŏ-zish-ŏn) *n.*
in·ter·pret (in-tur-prit) *v.* 1. to explain the meaning of. 2. to understand in a specified way. 3. to act as interpreter. **in·ter·pre·ta·tion** (in-tur-prĕ-tay-shŏn) *n.* **in·ter'pre·tive** *adj.*
in·ter·pre·ta·tive (in-tur-prĕ-tay-tiv) *adj.* interpreting.
in·ter·pret·er (in-tur-prĕ-tĕr) *n.* a person whose job is to translate a speech etc. into another language, orally in the presence of the speaker.
in·ter·ra·cial (in-tĕr-ray-shăl) *adj.* for, of, among, or between races or people of different races.
in·ter·reg·num (in-tĕr-reg-nŭm) *n.* (*pl.* **-nums, -na,** *pr.* **-nă**) 1. a period between the rule of two successive rulers. 2. a break in continuity.
in·ter·re·late (in-tĕr-ri-layt) *v.* (**in·ter·re·lat·ed, in·ter·re·lat·ing**) to relate to each other. **in·ter·re·la'ted·ness** *n.* **in·ter·re·la'tion** *n.* **in·ter·re·la'tion·ship** *n.*
interrog. *abbr.* 1. interrogation. 2. interrogative.
in·ter·ro·gate (in-ter-ŏ-gayt) *v.* (**in·ter·ro·gat·ed, in·ter·ro·gat·ing**) to ask questions of,

especially closely or formally. **in·ter'ro·ga·tor** *n.* **in·ter·ro·ga·tion** (in-ter-ŏ-gay-shŏn) *n.*

in·ter·rog·a·tive (in-tĕ-rog-ă-tiv) *adj.* questioning, having the form of a question, *an interrogative tone.* **in·ter·rog'a·tive·ly** *adv.* □**interrogative pronoun,** *see* **pronoun.**

in·ter·rog·a·to·ry (in-tĕ-rog-ă-tohr-ee) *adj.* questioning. **interrogatory** *n.* a set of questions, (in law) one formally put to an accused person.

in·ter·rupt (in-tĕ-rupt) *v.* 1. to break the continuity of. 2. to break the flow of a speech etc. by inserting a remark. 3. to obstruct (a view etc.). **in·ter·rupt'er** *n.* **in·ter·rup'tive** *adj.* **in·ter·rup·tion** (in-tĕ-rup-shŏn) *n.*

in·ter·scho·las·tic (in-tĕr-skŏ-las-tik) *adj.* existing between schools.

in·ter·sect (in-tĕr-sekt) *v.* 1. to divide (a thing) by passing or lying across it. 2. (of lines or roads etc.) to cross each other.

in·ter·sec·tion (in-tĕr-sek-shŏn) *n.* a place where lines or roads etc. intersect.

in·ter·ses·sion (in-tĕr-sesh-ŏn) *n.* a school or college semester coming between spring and summer or between summer and fall semesters.

in·ter·sperse (in-tĕr-spurs) *v.* (**in·ter·spersed, in·ter·spers·ing**) to insert contrasting material here and there in (a thing). **in·ter·sper·sion** (in-tĕr-spur-zhŏn) *n.*

in·ter·state (in-tĕr-stayt) *adj.* existing or carried on between states. □**interstate highway,** a road of the highway system that links states of the U.S.

in·ter·stel·lar (in-tĕr-stel-ăr) *adj.* of or existing between stars.

in·ter·stice (in-tur-stis) *n.* (*pl.* **-stic·es,** *pr.* -stiseez, -siz) a small intervening space, a crevice. **in·ter·sti·tial** (in-tĕr-stish-ăl) *adj.*

in·ter·tid·al (in-tĕr-tɪ-dăl) *adj.* of or relating to the space between low and high tide marks.

in·ter·twine (in-tĕr-twɪn) *v.* (**in·ter·twined, in·ter·twin·ing**) to twine together, to entwine.

in·ter·ur·ban (in-tĕr-ur-băn) *adj.* between or connecting cities.

in·ter·val (in-tĕr-văl) *n.* 1. a time between two events or parts of an action. 2. a pause between two parts of a performance. 3. a space between two objects or points. 4. the difference in musical pitch between two notes. □**at intervals,** with some time or distance between, not continuous.

in·ter·vene (in-tĕr-veen) *v.* (**in·ter·vened, in·ter·ven·ing**) 1. to occur in the time between events, *in the intervening years.* 2. to cause hindrance by occurring, *we should have finished harvesting but a storm intervened.* 3. to enter a discussion or dispute etc. in order to change its course or resolve it. **in·ter·ven'er** *n.*

in·ter·ven·tion (in-tĕr-ven-shŏn) *n.* the act of intervening or interfering, especially in the affairs of nations. **in·ter·ven'tion·ism** *n.* **in·ter·ven'tion·ist** *n.*

in·ter·view (in-tĕr-vyoo) *n.* a formal meeting or conversation with a person, held in order to assess his or her merits as a candidate etc. or to obtain comments and information. **interview** *v.* to hold an interview with. **in'ter·view·er** *n.*

in·ter·vo·cal·ic (in-tĕr-voh-kal-ik) *adj.* (usually of a consonant) between two vowels.

in·ter·weave (in-tĕr-weev) *v.* (**in·ter·wove, in·ter·wo·ven, in·ter·weav·ing**) to weave (strands etc.) into one another, to become woven together. **in·ter·wo·ven** (in-tĕr-woh-vĕn) *adj.*

in·tes·tate (in-tes-tayt) *adj.* not having made a valid will before death occurs, *he died intestate.* **in·tes·ta·cy** (in-tes-tă-see) *n.*

in·tes·tine (in-tes-tin) *n.* the long tubular section of the alimentary canal, extending from the outlet of the stomach to the anus. **in·tes'tin·al** *adj.* □**intestinal flu,** a gastric disorder of unknown origin. **large intestine,** the broader and shorter part of the intestine, including the colon and rectum. **small intestine,** the narrower and longer part.

in·ti·mate¹ (in-tĭ-mit) *adj.* 1. having a close acquaintance or friendship with a person. 2. having a sexual relationship with a person, especially outside marriage. 3. private and personal. 4. (of knowledge) detailed and obtained by much study or experience. **intimate** *n.* an intimate friend. **in'ti·mate·ly** *adv.* **in·ti·ma·cy** (in-tĭ-mă-see) *n.*

in·ti·mate² (in-tĭ-mayt) *v.* (**in·ti·mat·ed, in·ti·mat·ing**) to make known, especially by hinting. **in·ti·ma·tion** (in-tĭ-may-shŏn) *n.*

in·tim·i·date (in-tim-i-dayt) *v.* (**in·tim·i·dat·ed, in·tim·i·dat·ing**) to subdue or influence by frightening with threats or force. **in·tim·i·da·tion** (in-tim-i-day-shŏn) *n.*

in·tinc·tion (in-tingk-shŏn) *n.* the dipping of the Eucharistic bread in the wine, to enable the communicant to receive both elements together.

intl. *abbr.* international.

in·to (in-too) *prep.* 1. to the inside of, to a point within, *went into the house; fell into the river; far into the night.* 2. to a particular state or condition or occupation, *got into trouble; grew into an adult; went into banking.* 3. (in mathematics) *4 into 20,* 4 divided by 20. 4. *(slang)* interested in, *my brother is into rock.*

in·tol·er·a·ble (in-tol-ĕ-ră-bĕl) *adj.* unbearable. **in·tol'er·a·bly** *adv.*

in·tol·er·ant (in-tol-ĕ-rănt) *adj.* not tolerant, unwilling to tolerate ideas or beliefs etc. that differ from one's own, *intolerant of opposition.* **in·tol'er·ant·ly** *adv.* **in·tol'er·ance** *n.*

in·to·na·tion (in-tŏ-nay-shŏn) *n.* 1. intoning. 2. the tone or pitch of the voice in speaking. 3. the quality of a musical sound, especially with regard to pitch; *the violinist's performance was marred by faulty intonation,* some notes were not on pitch.

in·tone (in-tohn) *v.* (**in·toned, in·ton·ing**) to recite in a chanting voice, especially on one note.

in to·to (in toh-toh) completely. ▷Latin.

in·tox·i·cant (in-tok-sĭ-kănt) *n.* something that intoxicates, especially an alcoholic beverage.

in·tox·i·cate (in-tok-sĭ-kayt) *v.* (**in·tox·i·cat·ed, in·tox·i·cat·ing**) 1. to make drunk. 2. to excite or exhilarate beyond self-control. **in·tox·i·ca·tion** (in-tok-sĭ-kay-shŏn) *n.*

intr. *abbr.* intransitive.

intra- *prefix* within, as in *intramural, intravenous.*

in·trac·ta·ble (in-trak-tă-bĕl) *adj.* unmanageable, hard to deal with or control, *an intractable difficulty; intractable children.* **in·trac·ta·bil·i·ty** (in-trak-tă-bil-i-tee) *n.*

in·tra·dos (in-tră-dos) *n.* (*pl.* **-dos, -dos·es**) the inside curve of an arch.

in·tra·mo·lec·u·lar (in-tră-mŏ-lek-yŭ-lăr) *adj.* occurring within a molecule. **in·tra·mo·lec'u·lar·ly** *adv.*

in·tra·mu·ral (in-tră-myoor-ăl) *adj.* occurring within an institution, especially a school, *an intramural contest.*

in·tra·mus·cu·lar (in-tră-mus-kyŭ-lăr) *adj.* into

a muscle, *intramuscular injections.* **in·tra·mus′cu·lar·ly** *adv.*

intrans. *abbr.* intransitive.

in·tran·si·gent (in-tran-si-jĕnt) *adj.* unwilling to compromise, stubborn. **intransigent** *n.* an intransigent person. **in·tran′si·gence** *n.*

in·tran·si·tive (in-tran-si-tiv) *adj.* (of a verb) used without being followed by a direct object, as *hear* in *we can hear* (but not in *we can hear you*). **in·tran′si·tive·ly** *adv.*

in·tra·state (in-tră-stayt) *adj.* existing within a state.

in·tra·u·ter·ine (in-tră-yoo-tĕ-rin) *adj.* within the uterus. □**intrauterine device,** a contraceptive that is inserted and left in the uterus.

in·tra·ve·nous (in-tră-vee-nŭs) *adj.* into a vein. **in·tra·ve′nous·ly** *adv.*

in·trench (in-trench) = **entrench.**

in·trep·id (in-trep-id) *adj.* fearless, brave. **in·trep′id·ly** *adv.* **in·trep·id·i·ty** (in-tre-pid-i-tee) *n.*

in·tri·cate (in-trĭ-kit) *adj.* very complicated. **in′tri·cate·ly** *adv.* **in·tri·ca·cy** (in-trĭ-kă-see) *n.*

in·trigue (in-treeg) *v.* **(in·trigued, in·tri·gu·ing)** 1. to plot with someone in an underhand way, to use secret influence. 2. to rouse the interest or curiosity of, *the subject intrigues me.* **intrigue** (in-treeg, in-treeg) *n.* 1. underhand plotting, an underhand plot. 2. a secret love affair. **in·trigu′ing·ly** *adv.*

in·trin·sic (in-trin-sik) *adj.* belonging to the basic nature of a person or thing; *the intrinsic value of a coin,* the value of the metal in it as opposed to its face value. **in·trin′si·cal·ly** *adv.* ▷Do not confuse *intrinsic* with *extrinsic.*

in·tro (in-troh) *n.* (*pl.* **intros**) (*informal*) an introduction.

intro., introd. *abbr.* 1. introduction. 2. introductory.

in·tro·duce (in-trŏ-doos) *v.* **(in·tro·duc·ed, in·tro·duc·ing)** 1. to make (a person) known by name to others. 2. to announce (a speaker or broadcast program etc.) to listeners or viewers. 3. to bring (a bill) before a legislature. 4. to cause (a person) to become acquainted with a subject. 5. to bring (a custom or idea etc.) into use or into a system. 6. to bring or put in, *introduce the needle into a vein.*

in·tro·duc·tion (in-trŏ-duk-shŏn) *n.* 1. introducing, being introduced. 2. the formal presentation of one person to another. 3. a short explanatory section at the beginning of a book or speech etc. 4. an introductory treatise. 5. a short preliminary section leading up to the main part of a musical composition.

in·tro·duc·to·ry (in-trŏ-duk-tŏ-ree) *adj.* introducing a person or subject.

in·troit (in-troh-it) *n.* 1. a psalm or antiphon sung while the priest approaches the altar to celebrate mass in the Roman Catholic Church. 2. a psalm or choral response sung at the beginning of a church service.

in·tro·mit (in-trŏ-mit) *v.* **(in·tro·mit·ted, in·tro·mit·ting)** to let in or admit (into), to insert. **in·tro·mit′tent** *adj.* **in·tro·mis·sion** (in-trŏ-mish-ŏn) *n.*

in·tro·spec·tion (in-trŏ-spek-shŏn) *n.* examination of one's own thoughts and feelings. **in·tro·spec′tive** *adj.* **in·tro·spec′tive·ly** *adv.*

in·tro·vert (in-trŏ-vurt) *n.* a person who is concerned more with his own thoughts and feelings than with the people and things around him, a shy person. **in′tro·vert·ed** *adj.* **in·tro·ver·sion** (in-trŏ-vur-zhŏn) *n.*

in·trude (in-trood) *v.* **(in·trud·ed, in·trud·ing)** to come or join in without being invited or wanted. **in·trud′er** *n.* **in·tru·sion** (in-troo-zhŏn) *n.*

in·tru·sive (in-troo-siv) *adj.* intruding. **in·tru′sive·ness** *n.*

in·tu·it (in-too-it) *v.* to know by intuition.

in·tu·i·tion (in-too-ish-ŏn) *n.* the power of knowing or understanding something immediately without reasoning or being taught.

in·tu·i·tive (in-too-ĭ-tiv) *adj.* of or possessing or based on intuition. **in·tu′i·tive·ly** *adv.*

in·tu·mesce (in-tŭ-mes) *v.* **(in·tu·mesced, in·tu·mesc·ing)** to swell up. **in·tu·mes′cence** *n.* **in·tu·mes′cent** *adj.*

in·un·date (in-ŭn-dayt, in-un-) *v.* **(in·un·dat·ed, in·un·dat·ing)** 1. to flood, to cover with water. 2. to overwhelm as if with a flood. **in·un·da·tion** (in-ŭn-day-shŏn) *n.*

in·ure (in-yoor, i-noor) *v.* **(in·ured, in·ur·ing)** to accustom, especially to something unpleasant.

in·urn (in-urn) *v.* to put (the ashes of a cremated body) in an urn.

in u·ter·o (in yoo-tĕr-oh) in the womb, before birth. ▷Latin.

inv. *abbr.* invoice.

in va·cu·o (in vak-yoo-oh) in a vacuum. ▷Latin.

in·vade (in-vayd) *v.* **(in·vad·ed, in·vad·ing)** 1. to enter (territory) with armed forces in order to attack or damage or occupy it. 2. to crowd into, *tourists invaded the city.* 3. to penetrate harmfully, *the disease had invaded all parts of the body.* **in·vad′er** *n.*

in·va·lid¹ (in-vă-lid) *n.* a person who is weakened by illness or injury, one who suffers from ill health for a long time. **invalid** *adj.* 1. weakened by illness or injury. 2. of or for invalids. **invalid** *v.* 1. to disable (a person) by illness or injury. 2. to remove from active service because of ill health or injury, *he was invalided out of the army.*

in·val·id² (in-val-id) *adj.* not valid. **in·val·id·i·ty** (in-vă-lid-i-tee) *n.*

in·val·i·date (in-val-ĭ-dayt) *v.* **(in·val·i·dat·ed, in·val·i·dat·ing)** to make invalid. **in·val·i·da·tion** (in-val-ĭ-day-shŏn) *n.*

in·val·u·a·ble (in-val-yoo-ă-bĕl) *adj.* having a value that is too great to be measured. **in·val′u·a·bly** *adv.* ▷Do not confuse *invaluable* with *valuable* or *valueless.*

in·var·i·a·ble (in-vair-i-ă-bĕl) *adj.* not variable, always the same. **in·var′i·a·bly** *adv.*

in·va·sion (in-vay-zhŏn) *n.* invading, being invaded.

in·va·sive (in-vay-siv) *adj.* invading; *an invasive plant,* one that spreads freely into areas where it is not wanted.

in·vec·tive (in-vek-tiv) *n.* a violent attack in words, abusive language.

in·veigh (in-vay) *v.* to attack violently or bitterly in words.

in·vei·gle (in-vay-gĕl) *v.* **(in·vei·gled, in·vei·gling)** to entice.

in·vent (in-vent) *v.* 1. to create by thought, to make or design (something that did not exist before). 2. to construct (a false or fictional story), *invented an excuse.* **in·ven′tor** *n.*

in·ven·tion (in-ven-shŏn) *n.* 1. inventing, being invented. 2. something invented.

in·ven·tive (in-ven-tiv) *adj.* able to invent things. **in·ven'tive·ness** *n.*

in·ven·to·ry (in-věn-tohr-ee) *n.* (*pl.* -ries) a detailed list of goods or property or supplies and materials in stock etc. **Inventory** *v.* (**in·ven·to·ried, in·ven·to·ry·ing**) to make an inventory of, to enter in an inventory.

in·verse (in-vurs, in-vurs) *adj.* reversed in position or order or relation; *in inverse proportion,* with the first quantity increasing in proportion as the other decreases, or vice versa. **inverse** *n.* 1. an inverse state. 2. a thing that is the exact opposite of another. **in·verse'ly** *adv.*

in·ver·sion (in-vur-zhŏn) *n.* 1. inverting, being inverted. 2. anything inverted. 3. an atmospheric condition in which hot polluted air is trapped near the ground by a layer of motionless cool air.

in·vert (in-vurt) *v.* to turn (a thing) upside down, to reverse the position or order or relationship etc. of. **in·vert'i·ble** *adj.*

in·ver·te·brate (in-vur-tě-brit, -brayt) *adj.* not having a backbone. **invertebrate** *n.* an invertebrate animal.

in·vest (in-vest) *v.* 1. to use (money) to buy securities or property etc. in order to earn interest or bring profit for the buyer. 2. to spend money or time or effort on something that will be useful, *invest in a freezer.* 3. to confer a rank or office or power upon (a person). 4. to endow with a quality. **in·ves'tor** *n.*

in·ves·ti·gate (in-ves-tĭ-gayt) *v.* (**in·ves·ti·gat·ed, in·ves·ti·gat·ing**) to make a careful study of (a thing) in order to discover the facts about it. **in·ves'ti·ga·tor** *n.* **in·ves'ti·ga·tive** *adj.* **in·ves·ti·ga·to·ry** (in-ves-tĭ-gă-tohr-ee) *adj.* **in·ves·ti·ga·tion** (in-ves-tĭ-gay-shŏn) *n.* ☐**investigative reporting** *or* **journalism,** reporting based on information obtained by systematic research into a subject that is of public interest.

in·ves·ti·ture (in-ves-tĭ-chŭr) *n.* the process of investing a person with rank or office etc., a ceremony at which the sovereign confers honors.

in·vest·ment (in-vest-měnt) *n.* 1. investing. 2. a sum of money invested. 3. something in which money or time or effort is invested.

in·vet·er·ate (in-vet-ĕ-rit) *adj.* 1. habitual, *an inveterate smoker.* 2. firmly established, *inveterate prejudices.* **in·vet·er·a·cy** (in-vet-ĕ-ră-see) *n.* **in·vet'er·ate·ly** *adv.*

in·vid·i·ous (in-vid-i-ŭs) *adj.* likely to cause resentment because of real or imagined injustice, *an invidious comparison.* **in·vid'i·ous·ly** *adv.* ▷Do not confuse *invidious* with *insidious.*

in·vig·or·ate (in-vig-ŏ-rayt) *v.* (**in·vig·or·at·ed, in·vig·or·at·ing**) to fill with vigor, to give strength or courage to.

in·vin·ci·ble (in-vin-sĭ-běl) *adj.* unconquerable. **in·vin'ci·bly** *adv.* **in·vin·ci·bil·i·ty** (in-vin-sĭ-bil-i-tee) *n.*

in·vi·o·la·ble (in-vı-ŏ-lă-běl) *adj.* not to be violated. **in·vi·o·la·bil·i·ty** (in-vı-ŏ-lă-bil-i-tee) *n.*

in·vi·o·late (in-vı-ŏ-lit) *adj.* 1. not violated. 2. not broken. 3. not profaned.

in·vis·i·ble (in-viz-i-běl) *adj.* not visible, unable to be seen. **in·vis'i·bly** *adv.* **in·vis·i·bil·i·ty** (in-viz-ĭ-bil-i-tee) *n.* ☐**invisible ink,** colorless ink for writing words etc. that cannot be seen until the paper is heated or treated in some way.

in·vi·ta·tion (in-vi-tay-shŏn) *n.* 1. the act of invit-

ing to come or to do. 2. a written or printed request for one's presence.

in·vi·ta·tion·al (in-vi-tay-shŏ-năl) *adj.* limited to those invited, *invitational tournament.*

in·vite (in-vrt) *v.* (**in·vit·ed, in·vit·ing**) 1. to ask (a person) in a friendly way to come to one's house or to a gathering etc. 2. to ask (a person) formally to do something. 3. to ask for (comments, suggestions, etc.). 4. to act so as to be likely to cause (a thing) unintentionally, *you're inviting disaster.* 5. to attract, to tempt. **invite** (in-vrt) *n.* (*slang*) an invitation.

in·vit·ing (in-vı-ting) *adj.* attracting one to do something pleasant and tempting.

in·vo·ca·tion (in-vŏ-kay-shŏn) *n.* invoking, calling upon God in prayer.

in·voice (in-vois) *n.* a list of goods sent or services performed, with prices and charges. **invoice** *v.* (**in·voiced, in·voic·ing**) 1. to make an invoice of (goods). 2. to send an invoice to (a person).

in·voke (in-vohk) *v.* (**in·voked, in·vok·ing**) 1. to call upon (God) in prayer. 2. to call for the help or protection of, *invoked the law.* 3. to summon up (a spirit) with words.

in·vo·lu·cre (in-vŏ-loo-kěr) *n.* 1. a whorl of bracts surrounding an inflorescence. 2. a covering.

in·vol·un·tar·y (in-vol-ŭn-ter-ee) *adj.* done without intention or without conscious effort of the will, *an involuntary movement* (as jumping when startled). **in·vol·un·tar·i·ly** (in-vol-ŭn-ter-ĭ-lee) *adv.*

in·vo·lute (in-vŏ-loot) *adj.* 1. curled spirally. 2. involved or intricate.

in·vo·lu·tion (in-vŏ-loo-shŏn) *n.* 1. an involving, entanglement. 2. intricacy. 3. a curling inward, or a part so curled. 4. the raising of a mathematical quantity to any power.

in·volve (in-volv) *v.* (**in·volved, in·volv·ing**) 1. to contain within itself, to make necessary as a condition or result, *the plan involves much expense.* 2. to include or affect in its operation, *the safety of the nation is involved.* 3. to bring (a person or thing) into difficulties, *it will involve us in much expense.* 4. to show (a person) to be concerned in a crime etc. 5. to take up all of one's attention. 6. to complicate (a matter). **in·volve'ment** *n.*

in·volved (in-volvd) *adj.* 1. complicated. 2. concerned in something.

in·vul·ner·a·ble (in-vul-ně-ră-běl) *adj.* not vulnerable. **in·vul·ner·a·bil·i·ty** (in-vul-ně-ră-bil-i-tee) *n.*

in·ward (in-wărd) *adj.* 1. situated on the inside. 2. going toward the inside. 3. in the mind or spirit, *inward happiness.* **in·ward, in·wards** (in-wărdz) *adv.* 1. toward the inside. 2. toward the mind or spirit, *he turned inward.*

in·ward·ly (in-wărd-lee) *adv.* 1. toward the inside. 2. in the mind or spirit, *inwardly occupied.*

i·o·dide (ı-ŏ-dıd) *n.* a compound of iodine with another element or radical.

i·o·dine (ı-ŏ-dın) *n.* a chemical element found in seawater and certain seaweeds, used in solution as an antiseptic.

i·o·dize (ı-ŏ-dız) *v.* (**i·o·dized, i·o·diz·ing**) to impregnate with iodine or a compound of it.

i·on (ı-on) *n.* one of the electrically charged particles in certain substances. **i·on·ic** (ı-on-ik) *adj.*

I·on·ic (ı-on-ik) *adj.* of the *Ionic order,* one of the five classical orders of architecture, characterized by columns with scroll-like ornamentation at the top.

i·on·ize (ī-ŏ-nīz) v. (**i·on·ized, i·on·iz·ing**) to convert or be converted into ions. **i'on·iz·er** n.

i'on·iz·a·ble adj. **i·on·i·za·tion** (ī-ŏ-nī-zay-shŏn) n.

i·on·o·sphere (ī-on-ŏ-sfeer) n. an ionized region of the upper atmosphere, able to reflect radio waves for transmission to another part of Earth. **i·on·o·spher·ic** (ī-on-ŏ-sfer-ik) adj.

IOOF abbr. Independent Order of Odd Fellows.

i·o·ta (ī-oh-tă) n. 1. the ninth letter of the Greek alphabet (Ī ι). 2. the smallest possible amount, a jot, it doesn't make an iota of difference.

IOU (ī-oh-yoo) n. (pl. **IOUs**) a signed paper acknowledging that one owes a sum of money to the holder (= I owe you).

i·o·wa (ī-ŏ-wă) a state of the U.S. **i'o·wan** adj. & n.

IP abbr. innings pitched.

IPA abbr. International Phonetic Alphabet.

ip·e·cac (ip-ĕ-kak) n. ipecacuanha, the dried root of a South American plant, used as an emetic or purgative.

IPS, ips abbr. inches per second.

ip·so fac·to (ip-soh fak-toh) by that very fact or act. ▷ Latin.

IQ abbr. intelligence quotient.

Ir symbol iridium.

IR abbr. 1. information retrieval. 2. internal revenue.

Ir. abbr. 1. Ireland. 2. Irish.

IRA abbr. individual retirement account.

I.R.A. abbr. Irish Republican Army.

I·ran (i-ran) a country in southwest Asia, formerly called Persia. **I·ra·ni·an** (i-ray-ni-ăn) adj. & n.

I·raq (i-rak) a country lying between Iran and Saudi Arabia. **I·raq·i** (i-rak-ee) adj. & n. (pl. **I·raq·is**).

i·ras·ci·ble (i-ras-ĭ-běl) adj. irritable, hot-tempered. **i·ras'ci·bly** adv. **i·ras·ci·bil·i·ty** (i-ras-ĭ-bil-i-tee) n.

i·rate (ī-rayt, ī-rayt) adj. angry, enraged. **i·rate'ly** adv.

IRBM abbr. intermediate range ballistic missile.

ire (īr) n. anger.

Ire·land (īr-lănd) an island west of Great Britain, divided into Northern Ireland (which forms part of the United Kingdom) and the Republic of Ireland.

i·ren·ic (ī-ren-ik) adj. tending toward or promoting peace.

ir·i·des·cent (ir-i-des-ĕnt) adj. showing rainbow-like colors, showing a change of color when its position is altered. **ir·i·des'cence** n.

i·rid·i·um (i-rid-i-ŭm) n. a white metallic brittle element of the platinum group, used especially in hard alloys.

i·ris (ī-ris) n. (pl. **i·ris·es, i·ri·des**, pr. ī-ri-deez, ir-i-) 1. the flat circular colored membrane in the eye, with a circular opening (the pupil) in the center. 2. a plant with sword-shaped leaves and showy flowers with large petals.

I·rish (ī-rish) adj. of Ireland or its people or language. **Irish** n. 1. the Celtic language of Ireland. 2. the Irish, people of Irish birth or descent. 3. (informal) bad temper; with his Irish up, angry. **I'rish·man** n. **I'rish·wom·an** n. (pl. **-wom·en**, pr. -wim-in) □**Irish coffee**, hot coffee and Irish whiskey, with sugar and whipped cream. **Irish setter**, one of a breed of bird dogs with a silky brownish red coat. **Irish stew**, a stew of meat, potatoes, and onions. **Irish tweed**, a kind of tweed used in making suits and coats. **Irish**

whiskey, a kind of whiskey distilled in Ireland, especially from malted barley.

irk (urk) v. to annoy, to be tiresome to. **irk·some** (urk-sŏm) adj. tiresome. **irk'some·ly** adv.

i·ron (ī-ŏrn) n. 1. a very common hard gray metal, capable of being magnetized. 2. a tool made of this, branding iron. 3. a golf club with an iron or steel head. 4. an implement with a flat base that is heated for smoothing cloth or clothes etc. 5. something thought to be as unyielding as iron, a constitution or will of iron. 6. irons, fetters, in irons. **iron** adj. 1. of iron. 2. very strong. 3. firm, unyielding, merciless, an iron will. **iron** v. to smooth (clothes etc.) with an iron; iron out the difficulties, deal with and remove them. □**Iron Age**, the period when weapons and tools were made of iron. **Iron Curtain**, an invisible barrier preventing the free passage of people and information between the U.S.S.R. (and countries under its influence) and the Western world. **ironing board**, a narrow flat strip of wood etc. on which clothes etc. are ironed. **iron lung**, a rigid case fitting over a patient's body, used for administering artificial respiration for a prolonged period by means of mechanical pumps. **iron out**, to remove (difficulties etc.). **iron pyrite**, a mineral that is a sulfide of iron, pyrite. **many irons in the fire**, many undertakings or resources.

i·ron·bound (ī-ŏrn-bownd) adj. 1. bound with iron. 2. (of a coast) rugged, rocky. 3. rigid, inflexible, unyielding.

i·ron·clad (ī-ŏrn-klad) adj. 1. covered with or protected by iron. 2. rigid, exacting.

i·ron·ic (ī-ron-ik), **i·ron·i·cal** (ī-ron-i-kăl) adj. using or expressing irony. **i·ron'i·cal·ly** adv.

i·ron·ing (ī-ŏr-ning) n. clothing etc. ironed or to be ironed.

i·ron·stone (ī-ŏrn-stohn) n. 1. hard iron ore. 2. a kind of hard white pottery.

i·ron·ware (ī-ŏrn-wair) n. light articles made of iron.

i·ron·weed (ī-ŏrn-weed) n. a North American weedy plant with tubular red or purple flowers.

i·ron·wood (ī-ŏrn-wuud) n. 1. a tree with very hard wood, especially the hornbeam. 2. its wood.

i·ron·work (ī-ŏrn-wurk) n. articles such as gratings, rails, railings, etc. made of iron. **i·ron·works** (ī-ŏrn-wurks) n. a place where iron is smelted or where heavy iron goods are made. **i'ron·work·er** n.

i·ro·ny (ī-rŏ-nee) n. (pl. **-nies**) 1. the expression of one's meaning by using words of the opposite meaning in order to make one's remarks forceful, as that will please him (used of something that will not please him at all). 2. (of an occurrence) the quality of being so unexpected or ill-timed that it appears to be deliberately perverse.

Ir·o·quois (ir-ŏ-kwoi, -kwoiz) n. (pl. **Ir·o·quois**) 1. any of several Indian tribes of a powerful confederacy formerly inhabiting New York state. 2. a member of these tribes. **Ir·o·quoi'an** adj. & n.

ir·ra·di·ate (i-ray-di-ayt) v. (**ir·ra·di·at·ed, ir·ra·di·at·ing**) to shine upon, to subject to radiation. **ir·ra·di·a·tion** (i-ray-di-ay-shŏn) n.

ir·ra·tion·al (i-rash-ŏ-năl) adj. 1. not rational, not guided by reasoning, illogical, irrational fears or behavior. 2. not capable of reasoning. **ir·ra'tion·al·ly** adv. **ir·ra·tion·al·i·ty** (i-rash-ŏ-nal-i-tee) n. □**irrational number**, a number not expressible by an ordinary finite proper or improper fraction.

ir·re·claim·a·ble (ir-i-klay-mă-běl) *adj.* not to be reclaimed or reformed.

ir·rec·on·cil·a·ble (i-rek-ŏn-sı-lă-běl) *adj.* unable to be reconciled. **ir'·rec·on·cil·a·bil·i·ty** (i-rek-ŏn-sı-lă-bil-i-tee) *n.*

ir·re·cov·er·a·ble (ir-i-kuv-ĕ-ră-běl) *adj.* unable to be recovered. **ir·re·cov'·er·a·bly** *adv.*

ir·re·deem·a·ble (ir-i-dee-mă-běl) *adj.* unable to be redeemed. **ir·re·deem'a·bly** *adv.*

ir·re·den·tism (ir-i-den-tiz-ĕm) *n.* a policy that seeks to recover a linguistically or historically related area from foreign rule. **ir·re·den'tist** *n.*

ir·re·duc·i·ble (ir-i-doo-sı-běl) *adj.* unable to be reduced, *an irreducible minimum.* **ir·re·duc'i·bly** *adv.*

ir·ref·ra·ga·ble (i-ref-ră-gă-běl) *adj.* indisputable, unanswerable.

ir·ref·u·ta·ble (i-ref-yŭ-tă-běl) *adj.* unable to be refuted. **ir·ref'u·ta·bly** *adv.*

irreg. *abbr.* 1. irregular. 2. irregularly.

ir·reg·u·lar (i-reg-yŭ-lăr) *adj.* 1. not regular, uneven, varying. 2. contrary to rules or to established custom. 3. (of troops) not belonging to the regular armed forces. **irregular** *n.* a member of an irregular military force. **ir·reg'u·lar·ly** *adv.* **ir·reg·u·lar·i·ty** (i-reg-yŭ-lar-i-tee) *n.*

ir·rel·e·vant (i-rel-ĕ-vănt) *adj.* not relevant. **ir·rel'e·vant·ly** *adv.* **ir·rel'e·vance** *n.*

ir·re·li·gious (ir-i-lij-ŭs) *adj.* not religious, irreverent. **ir·re·li'gious·ly** *adv.*

ir·re·me·di·a·ble (ir-i-mee-di-ă-běl) *adj.* that cannot be remedied.

ir·re·mov·a·ble (ir-i-moo-vă-běl) *adj.* unable to be moved.

ir·rep·a·ra·ble (i-rep-ă-ră-běl) *adj.* unable to be repaired or made good, *irreparable damage* or *loss.* **ir·rep'a·ra·bly** *adv.*

ir·re·place·a·ble (ir-i-play-să-běl) *adj.* unable to be replaced, being a loss that cannot be made good.

ir·re·press·i·ble (ir-i-pres-ı̆-běl) *adj.* unable to be repressed or restrained. **ir·re·press'i·bly** *adv.*

ir·re·proach·a·ble (ir-i-proh-chă-běl) *adj.* blameless, faultless. **ir·re·proach'a·bly** *adv.*

ir·re·sist·i·ble (ir-i-zis-tı̆-běl) *adj.* too strong or too convincing or delightful to be resisted. **ir·re·sist'i·bly** *adv.*

ir·res·o·lute (i-rez-ŏ-loot) *adj.* feeling or showing uncertainty, hesitating. **ir·res'o·lute·ly** *adv.* **ir·res·o·lu·tion** (i-rez-ŏ-loo-shŏn) *n.*

ir·re·spec·tive (ir-i-spek-tiv) *adj.* not taking something into account, *prizes are awarded to winners irrespective of nationality.*

ir·re·spon·si·ble (ir-i-spon-sı̆-běl) *adj.* not showing a proper sense of responsibility. **ir·re·spon'si·bly** *adv.* **ir·re·spon·si·bil·i·ty** (ir-i-spon-sı̆-bil-i-tee) *n.*

ir·re·triev·a·ble (ir-i-tree-vă-běl) *adj.* not retrievable. **ir·re·triev'a·bly** *adv.*

ir·rev·er·ent (i-rev-ĕ-rěnt) *adj.* not reverent, not respectful. **ir·rev'er·ent·ly** *adv.* **ir·rev'er·ence** *n.*

ir·re·vers·i·ble (ir-i-vur-sı̆-běl) *adj.* not reversible, unable to be altered or revoked. **ir·re·vers'i·bly** *adv.*

ir·rev·o·ca·ble (i-rev-ŏ-kă-běl) *adj.* unable to be revoked, final and unalterable. **ir·rev'o·ca·bly** *adv.*

ir·ri·gate (ir-ı̆-gayt) *v.* (**ir·ri·gat·ed, ir·ri·gat·ing**) 1. to supply (land or crops) with water by

means of streams, channels, pipes, etc. 2. to wash (a wound) with a constant flow of liquid. **ir·ri·ga·tion** (ir-ı̆-gay-shŏn) *n.*

ir·ri·ta·ble (ir-i-tă-běl) *adj.* easily annoyed, badtempered. **ir'ri·ta·bly** *adv.* **ir·ri·ta·bil·i·ty** (ir-i-tă-bil-i-tee) *n.*

ir·ri·tant (ir-i-tănt) *adj.* causing irritation. **irritant** *n.* something that causes irritation.

ir·ri·tate (ir-i-tayt) *v.* (**ir·ri·tat·ed, ir·ri·tat·ing**) 1. to annoy, to rouse impatience or slight anger in (a person). 2. to cause itching. **ir'ri·tat·ing·ly** *adv.* **ir·ri·ta·tion** (ir-i-tay-shŏn) *n.*

ir·rupt (i-rupt) *v.* 1. to invade, to enter forcibly or violently. 2. (of an animal population) to increase abruptly. **ir·rup'tive** (i-rup-tiv) *adj.* **ir·rup·tion** (ir-rup-shŏn) *n.* ▷Do not confuse *irruption* with *eruption.*

IRS *abbr.* Internal Revenue Service.

is (iz) *see* **be.**

Is., Isa. *abbr.* Isaiah.

is. *abbr.* 1. island. 2. isle.

I·sa·iah (ı-zay-ă) *n.* a book of the Old Testament containing the prophecies of Isaiah, a Hebrew prophet of the 8th century B.C.

ISBN *abbr.* International Standard Book Number.

is·chi·um (is-ki-ŭm) *n.* (*pl.* **-chi·a,** *pr.* -ki-ă) the curved bone forming the base of each half of the pelvis.

-ish *suffix* used to form adjectives meaning nationality, as in *British;* belonging to, of the nature of, as in *devilish.*

i·sin·glass (ı-zing-glas) *n.* 1. a semitransparent substance obtained from the viscera of certain fishes, especially the sturgeon, and used in making jellies, glue, etc. 2. mica.

isl. *abbr.* 1. island. 2. isle.

Is·lam (is-lahm, is-lahm) *n.* 1. the Muslim religion, based on the teaching of Muhammad. 2. the Muslim world. **Is·lam·ic** (is-lah-mik) *adj.*

Is·lam·a·bad (is-lah-mă-bahd) the capital of Pakistan.

is·land (ı-lănd) *n.* 1. a piece of land surrounded by water. 2. something resembling this because it is detached or isolated; *a traffic island,* a paved or raised area in the middle of a road, where people crossing may be safe from traffic.

is·land·er (ı-lăn-děr) *n.* an inhabitant of an island.

isle (ıl) *n.* an island.

is·let (ı-lit) *n.* a little island.

ism (iz-ĕm) *n.* (*informal*) any distinctive doctrine or practice.

-ism *suffix* used to form nouns meaning action, as in *baptism;* condition or conduct, as in *heroism;* a system or belief, as in *conservatism;* a peculiarity of language, as in *archaism;* a pathological condition, as in *Parkinsonism.*

is·n't (iz-ĕnt) = is not.

i·so·bar (ı-sŏ-bahr) *n.* a line, drawn on a map, connecting places that have the same atmospheric pressure. **i·so·bar·ic** (ı-sŏ-bar-ik) *adj.*

i·so·late (ı-sŏ-layt) *v.* (**i·so·lat·ed, i·so·lat·ing**) 1. to place apart or alone. 2. to separate (an infectious person) from others. 3. to separate (one substance etc.) from a compound. **i·so·la·tion** (ı-sŏ-lay-shŏn) *n.*

i·so·la·tion·ism (ı-sŏ-lay-shŏ-niz-ĕm) *n.* the policy of holding aloof from other countries or groups. **i·so·la'tion·ist** *n.*

i·so·mer (ı-sŏ-měr) *n.* one of two or more substances composed of molecules having the same atoms differently arranged and therefore different properties. **i·so·mer·ic** (ı-sŏ-mer-ik) *adj.* **i·som·er·ism** (ı-som-ĕ-riz-ĕm) *n.*

i·so·met·ric (ı-sŏ-met-rik) *adj.* 1. of equal measure or dimensions. 2. of isometrics. □**isometric exercise,** one of a system of physical exercises in which the muscles act against each other or against a fixed object.

i·so·met·rics (ı-sŏ-met-riks) *n.* isometric exercises.

i·so·prene (ı-sŏ-preen) *n.* a volatile hydrocarbon liquid used in making synthetic rubber.

i·sos·ce·les (ı-sos-ĕ-leez) *adj.* (of a triangle) having two sides equal.

i·so·therm (ı-sŏ-thurm) *n.* a line, drawn on a map, connecting places that have the same temperature. **i·so·therm'al** *adj.*

i·so·ton·ic (ı-sŏ-ton-ik) *adj.* 1. having the same osmotic pressure. 2. (of muscle action) taking place with normal contraction.

i·so·tope (ı-sŏ-tohp) *n.* one of two or more forms of a chemical element with different atomic weight and different nuclear properties but the same chemical properties. **i·so·top·ic** (ı-sŏ-top-ik) *adj.* **i·so·top'i·cal·ly** *adv.*

Isr. *abbr.* 1. Israel. 2. Israeli.

Is·ra·el (iz-ree-ĕl, -ray-) 1. a country in the Middle East at the eastern end of the Mediterranean Sea. 2. the Hebrew nation of Biblical times, said to descend from Jacob whom God called Israel.

Is·rael·i (iz-**ray**-lee) *n.* (*pl.* **-is**) a native or inhabitant of Israel. **Israeli** *adj.* of the state of Israel or its inhabitants.

Is·ra·el·ite (iz-ree-ĕ-lıt) *n.* a member of the ancient Hebrew nation.

is·sue (ish-oo) *n.* 1. an outgoing or outflow. 2. the issuing of things for use or for sale, the number or quantity issued. 3. one set of publications in a series issued regularly, *the May issue.* 4. a result, an outcome. 5. the point in question, an important topic for discussion, *what are the real issues?* 6. offspring, *died without male issue.* **issue** *v.* **(is·sued, is·su·ing)** 1. to come or go or flow out. 2. to supply or distribute for use, *campers were issued blankets.* 3. to put out for sale, to publish. 4. to send out, *issue orders.* 5. to result, to originate. **is'su·er** *n.* **is'su·ance** *n.* □**at issue,** being discussed or disputed or risked. **join** *or* **take issue,** to proceed to argue.

-ist *suffix* used to form personal nouns meaning action or production, as in *copyist;* specialization in a subject, as in *dentist;* adherence to a creed or system, as in *atheist;* ability to play a musical instrument, as in *pianist;* operation of a device, as in *balloonist.*

isth·mus (is-mŭs) *n.* (*pl.* **-mus·es**) a narrow strip of land connecting two masses of land that would otherwise be separated by water. **isth·mi·an** (is-mi-ăn) *adj.*

it (it) *pronoun* 1. the thing mentioned or being discussed. 2. the person in question, *who is it? It is I.* 3. used as the subject of a verb making a general statement about the weather (as *it is raining*) or about circumstances etc. (as *it is 35 miles to Boston*) or as an indefinite object *(run for it!).* 4. used as the subject or object of a verb, with reference to a following clause or phrase, as *it is seldom that he fails; I take it that you agree.* 5. *(informal)* exactly what is needed, *that's exactly it!* 6. *(slang)* the end, *he put the gun to my head and said, "This is it."* 7. (in children's games) the player

who has to catch others. ▷See the note under **its.**

It., Ital. *abbr.* 1. Italian. 2. Italy.

ital. *abbr.* 1. italic(s). 2. italicized.

I·tal·ian (i-tal-yăn) *adj.* of Italy or its people or language. **Italian** *n.* 1. a native of Italy. 2. the Italian language.

i·tal·ic (i-tal-ik) *adj.* 1. (of printed letters) sloping *like this.* 2. (of handwriting) compact and pointed like an early form of Italian handwriting. **italic** *n.* italics.

i·tal·i·cize (i-tal-ı-sız) *v.* **(i·tal·i·cized, i·tal·i·ciz·ing)** to print (words) in italics, usually for emphasis or distinction.

i·tal·ics (i-tal-iks) *n.* sloping printed letters *like these.*

It·a·ly (it-ă-lee) a country in southern Europe.

itch (ich) *n.* 1. an itching feeling in the skin. 2. a restless desire or longing. **itch** *v.* 1. to have or feel a tickling sensation in the skin, causing a desire to scratch the affected part. 2. to feel a restless desire or longing. **itch'y** *adj.* **(itch·i·er, itch·i·est)** **itch'i·ness** *n.* □**have an itching palm,** to be greedy for money.

-ite *suffix* used to form nouns meaning a resident or native, as in *Muscovite;* an adherent or follower, as in *Pre-Raphaelite;* a fossil or mineral, as in *anthracite;* a commercial product, as in *dynamite, vulcanite.*

i·tem (ı-tĕm) *n.* 1. a single thing in a list or number of things. 2. a single piece of news in a newspaper etc.

i·tem·ize (ı-tĕ-mız) *v.* **(i·tem·ized, i·tem·iz·ing)** to list, to state the individual items involved. **i·tem·i·za·tion** (ı-tĕ-mi-zay-shŏn) *n.*

it·er·ate (it-ĕ-rayt) *v.* **(it·er·at·ed, it·er·at·ing)** to repeat.

i·tin·er·ant (i-tin-ĕ-rănt) *adj.* traveling from place to place, *an itinerant preacher.* **itinerant** *n.* a person who wanders from place to place.

i·tin·er·ar·y (ı-tin-ĕ-rer-ee) *n.* (*pl.* **-ar·ies**) a route, a list of places to be visited on a trip.

it'll (it-ĕl) = it will.

its (its) *adj.* & *possessive pronoun* of or belonging to it. ▷Do not confuse *its* with *it's,* which has a different meaning (see the next entry). The word *its* is the possessive form of *it,* and, (like *hers, ours, theirs, yours*) has no apostrophe; correct usage is *wagged its tail* (not *it's*), *the dog is hers* (not *her's*), *these are ours* (not *our's*).

it's (its) = it is, it has, *it's very hot; it's broken all records.* ▷Do not confuse *it's* with *its.*

it·self (it-self) *pronoun* corresponding to *it,* used in the same ways as **himself.**

it·ty-bit·ty (it-ee-bit-ee), **it·sy-bit·sy** (it-see-bit-see) *adj. (informal)* tiny, insignificant.

ITV *abbr.* instructional television.

-ity *suffix* used to form nouns meaning quality or condition, as in *purity, authority,* or an instance or degree of this, as in *monstrosity, humidity.*

IUD *abbr.* intrauterine device.

IV *abbr.* intravenous. □**IV injection,** an intravenous injection.

I've (ıv) = I have.

-ive *suffix* used to form adjectives meaning tending to or having the nature of, as in *active, evasive,* and nouns, as in *captive, directive.*

i·vo·ry (ı-vŏ-ree) *n.* (*pl.* **-ries**) 1. the hard creamy white substance forming the tusks of elephants etc. 2. an object made of this. 3. creamy white color. **4.** *ivories, (slang)* piano keys, dice. **ivory** *adj.* creamy white. □**ivory tower,** a place or situation where people live secluded from the harsh realities of everyday life.

I·vo·ry (ı̄-vŏ-ree) **Coast** a country in West Africa.

i·vy (ı̄-vee) *n.* (*pl.* **i·vies**) a climbing evergreen shrub with shiny often five-pointed leaves. **i·vied** (ı̄-veed) *adj.* □**Ivy League,** an association of colleges in the northeastern U.S.

IWW *abbr.* Industrial Workers of the World.

ix·i·a (ik-si-ă) *n.* a plant of the iris family.

-ize *suffix* used to form verbs meaning to treat in a specified way, as in *monopolize;* to follow a specified practice, as in *gourmandize;* to bring or come into a specified state, as in *vaporize, Anglicize;* to treat or act according to the method of, as in *pasteurize;* to impregnate with or affect with or provide with, as in *oxidize, magnetize.*

J

J, j (jay) (*pl.* **Js, J's, j's**) the tenth letter of the alphabet.
J, j *abbr.* joule(s).
J. *abbr.* 1. (in cards) jack. 2. journal. 3. justice.
J. A. *abbr.* Judge Advocate.
jab (jab) *v.* (**jabbed, jab·bing**) 1. to poke roughly, to thrust (a thing) into. 2. (in boxing) to hit with a short quick punch. **jab** *n.* 1. a rough blow or thrust, especially with something pointed. 2. a short quick punch.
jab·ber (jab-ĕr) *v.* 1. to talk rapidly and unintelligibly. 2. to chatter like monkeys. **jabber** *n.* jabbering talk or sound. **jab'ber·er** *n.*
jab·ber·wock·y (jab-ĕr-wok-ee) *n.* (*pl.* **-wock·ies**) nonsensical writing or speech, especially for comic effect. ▷From the title of a poem by Lewis Carroll.
ja·bot (*zh*a-boh) *n.* ornamental frilling down the front of a shirt or blouse or dress.
jac·a·ran·da (jak-ă-ran-dă) *n.* a tropical American tree with trumpet-shaped blue flowers.
ja·cinth (jay-sinth) *n.* a reddish-orange gem, a variety of zircon.
jack (jak) *n.* 1. a portable device for raising heavy weights off the ground, especially one for raising the axle of a motor vehicle so that a tire may be changed. 2. a ship's flag (smaller than an ensign) flown at the bow of a ship to show its nationality. 3. a playing card ranking below a queen in card games. 4. a small white ball aimed at in lawn bowling. 5. a male donkey. 6. a socket that accepts a plug in an electrical circuit. 7. a small six-pointed metal object used in the children's game of jacks. 8. (*slang*) money. **jack** *v.* to raise with a jack. □**before you can say Jack Robinson,** very quickly or suddenly. **every man Jack,** every individual man. **Jack Frost,** frost personified. **jack of all trades,** a person who can do many different kinds of work.
jack·al (jak-ăl) *n.* a wild flesh-eating animal of Africa and Asia, related to the dog.
jack·a·napes (jak-ă-nayps) *n.* an impertinent or conceited person, especially a young man.
jack·ass (jak-as) *n.* 1. a male donkey. 2. (*informal*) a stupid or foolish person.
jack·boot (jak-boot) *n.* a large boot coming above the knee.
jack·daw (jak-daw) *n.* a European bird of the crow family.
jack·et (jak-it) *n.* 1. a short coat, usually reaching to the hips. 2. an outer covering; *book jacket,* a colored paper wrapper in which a bound book is issued. 3. the skin of a potato baked without being peeled, *baked in their jackets.* **jack'et·ed** *adj.*
jack·ham·mer (jak-ham-ĕr) *n.* a pneumatic hammer that breaks pavement, drills rock, etc.
jack-in-the-box (jak-in-*th*ĕ-boks) *n.* (*pl.* **-box·es**)

a toy figure that springs out of a box when the lid is lifted.
jack-in-the-pul·pit (jak-in-*th*ĕ-puul-pit) *n.* (*pl.* **-pul·pits**) a plant of eastern North America having an upright flower spike partly enclosed by a hoodlike spathe.
jack·knife (jak-nɪf) *n.* (*pl.* **-knives**) 1. a large pocket knife. 2. a dive in which the body is first bent double and then straightened. **jackknife** *v.* (**jack·knifed, jack·knif·ing**) (of a trailer truck) to fold one part against another as in an accident.
jack·leg (jak-leg) *adj.* (*slang*) 1. not trained for one's work, incompetent. 2. makeshift.
jack-o'-lan·tern (jak-ŏ-lan-tĕrn) *n.* a hollowed-out pumpkin lantern with a carved face.
jack·pot (jak-pot) *n.* the accumulated stakes in various games, increasing in value until won. □**hit the jackpot,** to have sudden great success or good fortune.
jack·rab·bit (jak-rab-it) *n.* a large hare of western North America with very long ears and legs.
jack·screw (jak-skroo) *n.* a device for lifting heavy loads, operated by turning a screw.
Jack·son (jak-sŏn) the capital of Mississippi.
Jackson, An·drew (1767–1845) the seventh president of the U.S. 1829–37.
jack·straw (jak-straw) *n.* 1. a thin splinter of wood or plastic used in the game of jackstraws. 2. *jackstraws,* a game in which a heap of jackstraws is to be removed one at a time without disturbing the others.
jack tar, Jack Tar (jak-tahr) (*informal*) a sailor.
Jac·o·be·an (jak-ŏ-bee-ăn) *adj.* of the reign of James I of England (1603–25).
Jac·o·bite (jak-ŏ-bɪt) *n.* a supporter of James II of England after his abdication (1688), or of his exiled heirs.
Ja·cob's (jay-kŏbz) **ladder** 1. a blue-flowered perennial plant with leaves giving a ladderlike appearance. 2. a rope ladder with wooden rungs for ascending a ship's rigging.
jac·quard (jak-ahrd) *n.* a fabric woven with an intricate figured pattern.
jade (jayd) *n.* 1. a hard, green, blue, or white stone from which ornaments are carved. 2. the green color of jade.
jad·ed (jay-did) *adj.* 1. feeling or looking tired and bored. 2. (of the appetite) dulled, lacking zest for food.
jade·ite (jay-dɪt) *n.* a rare form of jade.
Jaf·fa (jaf-ă) *n.* a large oval thick-skinned variety of orange, originally grown near the port of Jaffa in Israel.
jag¹ (jag) *n.* a sharp projection, as a point of rock.
jag² *n.* (*slang*) a drinking bout, a spree.
jag·ged (jag-id) *adj.* having an uneven edge or outline with sharp projections.
jag·uar (jag-wahr) *n.* a large fierce flesh-eating an-

imal of the cat family, found in tropical America.
jai a·lai (hī lī, hī ä-lī) a game in which players use a long curved basket strapped to the arm to catch a small hard ball and throw it against the wall.
jail (jayl) n. a public prison. **jail** v. to put in jail, to imprison. **jail′er, jail′or** n.
jail·bird (jayl-burd) n. a person who is or has been in prison.
jail·break (jayl-brayk) n. an escape from jail.
Jain (jīn) n. a member of an Indian sect **(Jainism)** with doctrines like those of Buddhism. **Jain** adj. of this sect.
Ja·kar·ta (jă-kahr-tă) the capital of Indonesia.
jal·ap (jal-ăp) n. 1. a purgative drug obtained especially from the tuberous roots of a Mexican climbing plant. 2. this plant.
ja·lop·y (jă-lop-ee) n. (pl. **-lop·ies**) a battered old car.
jal·ou·sie (jal-ŏ-see) n. a slatted shutter or blind designed to admit air and light but not rain.
jam¹ (jam) v. **(jammed, jam·ming)** 1. to squeeze or wedge into a space, to become wedged. 2. to make (part of a machine) immovable so that the machine will not work, to become unworkable in this way. 3. to crowd or block (an area) with people or things. 4. to thrust or apply forcibly, *jammed the brakes on.* 5. to cause interference to (a radio transmission), making it unintelligible. 6. to participate in a jam session. **jam** n. 1. a squeeze or crush or stoppage caused by jamming. 2. a crowded mass making movement difficult, *traffic jams.* 3. (informal) a difficult situation, *I'm in a jam.* □**jam session**, improvised playing by a group of jazz musicians.
jam² n. a sweet substance made by boiling fruit with sugar to a thick consistency.
Jam. abbr. Jamaica.
Ja·mai·ca (jă-may-kă) a country in the Caribbean Sea. **Ja·mai′can** adj. & n.
jamb (jam) n. the vertical side post of a doorway or window frame.
jam·bo·ree (jam-bŏ-ree) n. 1. a large party, a celebration. 2. a large rally of Boy Scouts.
James (jaymz) n. a book of the New Testament traditionally ascribed to James, one of the twelve Apostles.
jam-packed (jam-pakt) adj. (informal) packed full and tightly.
Jan. abbr. January.
jan·gle (jang-gĕl) n. a harsh metallic sound. **jangle** v. **(jan·gled, jan·gling)** 1. to make or cause to make this sound. 2. to cause irritation to (nerves etc.) by discord.
jan·i·tor (jan-i-tŏr) n. the caretaker of a building. **jan·i·tress** (jan-i-tris) n. fem. **jan·i·to·ri·al** (jan-i-tohr-i-ăl) adj.
Jan·u·ar·y (jan-yoo-er-ee) n. the first month of the year.
Jap. abbr. 1. Japan. 2. Japanese.
ja·pan (jă-pan) n. 1. a hard black varnish originating in Japan and used to produce a glossy finish. 2. work varnished and decorated in the Japanese style. **japan** v. **(ja·panned, ja·pan·ning)** to cover with japan.
Ja·pan (jă-pan) a country in eastern Asia. **Jap·a·nese** (jap-ă-neez) adj. & n. (pl. **-nese**) □**Japanese beetle**, a bronze and green beetle introduced from Japan into the U.S., where the larvae and adult insects are major plant pests.
jape (jayp) v. **(japed, jap·ing)** to joke or quip. **jape** n. a joke or quip.

ja·pon·i·ca (jă-pon-i-kă) n. an ornamental variety of quince, with red flowers.
jar¹ (jahr) n. 1. a cylindrical container made of glass or earthenware. 2. this with its contents, the amount it contains.
jar² v. **(jarred, jar·ring)** 1. to make a sound that has a discordant or painful effect. 2. (of an action etc.) to be out of harmony, to have a harsh or disagreeable effect. 3. to cause an unpleasant jolt or a sudden shock. **jar** n. a jarring movement or effect.
jar·di·niere (jahr-dī-neer) n. a large ornamental pot for holding indoor plants.
jar·gon (jahr-gŏn) n. words or expressions developed for use within a particular group, hard for outsiders to understand, *scientists' jargon.*
jas·mine (jaz-min) n. a shrub with yellow or white flowers.
jas·per (jas-pĕr) n. an opaque variety of quartz, usually red, yellow, or brown.
ja·to (jay-to) n. (pl. **-tos**) jet-assisted takeoff, auxiliary jet engine(s) to provide temporary extra thrust at takeoff.
jaun·dice (jawn-dis) n. a condition in which the skin becomes abnormally yellow as a result of excessive bile in the bloodstream.
jaun·diced (jawn-dist) adj. 1. discolored by jaundice. 2. filled with resentment or jealousy.
jaunt (jawnt) n. a short trip, especially one taken for pleasure.
jaun·ty (jawn-tee) adj. **(jaun·ti·er, jaun·ti·est)** 1. cheerful and self-confident in manner. 2. (of clothes) stylish and cheerful. **jaun′ti·ness** n. **jaun′ti·ly** adv.
Ja·va (jah-vă) an island of Indonesia. **java** n. (slang) coffee. **Jav·a·nese** (jah-vă-neez) adj. & n.
jav·e·lin (jav-ĕ-lin) n. 1. a light spear. 2. a wooden or metal shaft thrown for distance in track and field meets.
jaw (jaw) n. 1. either of the two bones that form the framework of the mouth and in which the teeth are set. 2. the lower of these, the part of the face covering it. 3. *jaws,* something resembling a pair of jaws, as the gripping part of a tool, *the jaws of a vise.* **jaw** v. (slang) to talk long and boringly, to gossip.
jaw·bone (jaw-bohn) n. either of the bones of the jaw. **jawbone** v. **(jaw·boned, jaw·bon·ing)** (slang) to attempt to persuade.
jaw·break·er (jaw-bray-kĕr) n. 1. a word that is very long or difficult to pronounce. 2. a very hard round candy.
jay (jay) n. any of several brightly colored chattering birds related to the crow.
jay·bird (jay-burd) n. a jay. □**naked as a jaybird,** (informal) completely naked.
Jay·cee (jay-see) n. a member of a junior chamber of commerce.
jay·vee (jay-vee) n. (informal) a member of a junior varsity team.
jay·walk (jay-wawk) v. to walk across a street without observing the traffic regulations. **jay′walk·er** n.
jazz (jaz) n. 1. a kind of music (originally native American) with strong rhythm and much syncopation, often improvised. 2. (slang) a matter, especially something regarded as pretentious or as nonsense, *talked of the honor of the firm and all that jazz.* **jazz** v. to play or arrange as jazz. □**jazz up,** to enliven, to brighten.
jazz·y (jaz-ee) adj. **(jazz·i·er, jazz·i·est)** 1. of

or like jazz. 2. *(slang)* flashy, showy, *a jazzy sports car.*

JCC *abbr.* Junior Chamber of Commerce.

J.C.S., JCS *abbr.* Joint Chiefs of Staff.

jct. *abbr.* junction.

JD *abbr.* 1. juvenile delinquency. 2. juvenile delinquent.

J.D. *abbr.* 1. Doctor of Jurisprudence (Latin, *Juris Doctor).* 2. Doctor of Laws (Latin, *Jurum Doctor).* 3. Justice Department. 4. juvenile delinquent.

JDL *abbr.* Jewish Defense League.

jea·lous (jel-ŭs) *adj.* 1. feeling or showing resentment toward a person whom one thinks of as a rival. 2. taking watchful care, *is very jealous of his own rights.* **jeal′ous·ly** *adv.* **jeal′ous·y** *n.* ▷Do not confuse *jealous* with *zealous.*

jeans (jeenz) *n. pl.* pants made of strong twilled cotton for informal wear.

jeep (jeep) *n.* 1. a small sturdy military motor vehicle with four-wheel drive. 2. *Jeep, (trademark)* a similar civilian passenger car.

jeer (jeer) *v.* to laugh or shout at rudely and scornfully. **jeer** *n.* a jeering remark or shout.

Jef·fer·son (jef-ĕr-sŏn) *City* the capital of Missouri.

Jefferson, Tho·mas (1743–1826) the third president of the U.S. 1801–09.

Je·ho·vah (jĕ-hoh-vă) the name of God in the Old Testament. ☐**Jehovah's Witnesses,** a Christian sect believing that the end of the world is near for all except its own adherents, and rejecting allegiance to any country.

je·june (ji-joon) *adj.* 1. meager, not nourishing. 2. insipid, unsatisfying to the mind. 3. childish.

je·ju·num (ji-joo-nŭm) *n.* the part of the small intestine between the duodenum and the ileum. **je·ju′nal** *adj.*

Jek·yll and Hyde (jek-ĭl ăn hɪd) a person having a dual personality, one good and the other evil. ▷From a story by Robert Louis Stevenson in which the hero could transform himself from the respectable Dr. Jekyll into the evil Mr. Hyde by means of a potion that he drank.

jell (jel) *v.* 1. to set as jelly. 2. to take definite form, *our ideas began to jell.*

jel·lied (jel-eed) *adj.* set in jelly, *jellied eels.*

jel·ly (jel-ee) *n. (pl.* **-lies)** 1. a soft solid food made of liquid set with gelatin or pectin, especially one made of strained fruit juice and sugar. 2. a substance of similar consistency, *petroleum jelly.* **jelly** *v.* (**jel·lied, jel·ly·ing**) = **jell** (definition 1). ☐**jelly roll,** a thin flat sponge cake spread with fruit jelly or jam and rolled up.

jel·ly·bean (jel-ee-been) *n.* a bean-shaped candy consisting of chewy filling and a hard sugar coating.

jel·ly·fish (jel-ee-fish) *n. (pl.* **-fish·es, -fish)** a sea animal with a jelly-like body and stinging tentacles.

jen·net (jen-it) *n.* 1. a small Spanish horse. 2. a female donkey.

jen·ny (jen-ee) *n. (pl.* **-nies)** a female donkey.

jeop·ard·ize (jep-ăr-dɪz) *v.* (**jeop·ard·ized, jeop·ard·iz·ing**) to endanger.

jeop·ard·y (jep-ăr-dee) *n. (pl.* **-ard·ies)** danger. **jeop′ard·ous** *adj.*

Jer. *abbr.* Jeremiah.

jer·bo·a (jĕr-boh-ă) *n.* a small ratlike animal of the North African desert, with long hind legs used for leaping.

jer·e·mi·ad (jer-ĕ-mɪ-ad) *n.* a long mournful lament about one's troubles. ▷Named after Jeremiah, a Hebrew prophet (7th–6th centuries B.C.) and the book of the Old Testament containing his account of the troubles of the Israelites.

Jer·e·mi·ah (jer-ĕ-mɪ-ă) *n.* the book of the Old Testament containing the prophecies of Jeremiah (see the previous entry).

jerk (jurk) *n.* 1. a sudden sharp movement, an abrupt pull or push or throw. 2. *(slang)* a stupid or insignificant person. **jerk** *v.* to pull or throw or stop with a jerk, to move with a jerk or in short uneven movements.

jer·kin (jur-kin) *n.* a sleeveless jacket.

jerk·wat·er (jurk-waw-tĕr) *adj. (informal)* rustic (town), slow (train), unimportant (person). **jerk·water** *n.*

jerk·y (jur-kee) *adj.* (**jerk·i·er, jerk·i·est**) making abrupt starts and stops, not moving or acting smoothly. **jerk′i·ly** *adv.* **jerk′i·ness** *n.*

jer·ry-built (jer-ee-bilt) *adj.* built badly and with poor materials.

jer·sey (jur-zee) *n. (pl.* **-seys)** 1. plain machine-knitted fabric used for making clothes. 2. a close-fitting knitted pullover with sleeves.

Jer·sey (jur-zee) *n. (pl.* **-seys)** one of a breed of light-brown dairy cattle.

Je·ru·sa·lem (jĕ-roo-să-lĕm) 1. the ancient capital of Judea; the holy city of the Jews, sacred also to Christians and Muslims. 2. the capital of modern Israel.

jess (jes) *n.* a short strap around the legs of a hawk used in falconry.

jes·sa·mine (jes-ă-min) *n.* = **jasmine.**

jest (jest) *n.* a joke. **jest** *v.* to make jokes. ☐**in jest,** in fun, not seriously.

jest·er (jes-tĕr) *n.* 1. a person who makes jokes. 2. a professional entertainer at a king's court in the Middle Ages.

Jes·u·it (jezh-oo-it) *n.* a member of the Society of Jesus, a Roman Catholic religious order.

Jes·us (jee-zŭs) the founder of the Christian religion.

jet[1] (jet) *n.* 1. a hard black mineral that can be polished, used as a gem. 2. its color, deep glossy black. **jet′-black′** *adj.*

jet[2] *n.* 1. a stream of water, gas, or flame etc. shot out from a small opening. 2. a spout or opening from which this comes, a burner on a gas stove. 3. a jet engine, a jet-propelled aircraft. **jet** *v.* (**jet·ted, jet·ting**) 1. to spurt in jets. 2. *(informal)* to travel or convey by jet-propelled aircraft. ☐**jet engine,** an engine using jet propulsion to give forward thrust. **jet lag,** delayed physical effects of tiredness etc. felt after a flight across time zones in a jet-propelled aircraft. **jet propulsion,** propulsion by engines that give forward thrust by sending out a high-speed jet of gases etc. at the back. **jet set,** wealthy people who make frequent air journeys between social or business events. **jet stream,** a narrow current of strong westerly winds in the upper troposphere.

jet·port (jet-pohrt) *n. (informal)* an airport designed for jet aircraft.

jet·sam (jet-săm) *n.* goods thrown overboard from a ship in distress to lighten it, especially those that are washed ashore. ▷Do not confuse *jetsam* with *flotsam.*

jet·ti·son (jet-i-sŏn) *v.* 1. to throw (goods) overboard, especially to lighten a ship in distress. 2. to discard (what is unwanted).

jet·ty (jet-ee) *n.* (*pl.* **-ties**) a structure extending into a body of water, used to protect a harbor or coast from the influence of currents or tides, or as a wharf.

jeu d'es·prit (z*h*uu des-pree) (*pl.* **jeux d'es·prit,** *pr.* z*h*uu des-pree) a piece of witty or humorous speech or writing. ▷French.

Jew (joo) *n.* a person of Jewish descent, or one whose religion is Judaism. ☐**jew's harp,** a musical instrument consisting of a small U-shaped metal frame held in the teeth while a springy metal strip joining its ends is twanged with a finger.

jew·el (joo-ĕl) *n.* 1. a precious stone. 2. an ornament for wearing, containing one or more precious stones. 3. a person or thing that is highly valued. **jewel** *v.* to adorn or furnish with jewels.

jew·eled (joo-ĕld) *adj.* ornamented or set with jewels.

jew·el·er (joo-ĕ-lĕr) *n.* a person who makes or deals in jewels or jewelry.

jew·el·ry (joo-ĕl-ree) *n.* jewels or similar ornaments to be worn.

jew·el·weed (joo-ĕl-weed) *n.* any of several plants having yellow flowers sometimes marked with reddish-brown spots.

Jew·ish (joo-ish) *adj.* of Jews.

Jew·ry (joo-ree) *n.* the Jewish people.

Jez·e·bel (jez-ĕ-bĕl) *n.* a shameless woman.

jg, j.g. *abbr.* junior grade.

jib (jib) *n.* 1. a triangular sail stretching forward from the mast. 2. the projecting arm of a crane. **jib** *v.* (**jibbed, jib·bing**) to refuse to proceed in some action; *jibbed at it,* showed unwillingness or dislike. ☐**the cut of a person's jib,** (*informal*) his general appearance.

jibe (j*i*b) *v.* (**jibed, jib·ing**) (*informal*) to fit or agree with, *your information jibes with mine.* ▷Do not confuse *jibe* with *gibe* or *jive.*

Jid·da (jid-ă) the administrative capital of Saudi Arabia.

jif·fy (jif-ee) *n.* (*informal*) a moment, *in a jiffy.*

jig (jig) *n.* 1. a lively jumping dance, the music for this. 2. a device for holding a piece of work and guiding the tools working on it. **jig** *v.* (**jigged, jig·ging**) 1. to dance a jig. 2. to move up and down rapidly and jerkily. ☐**the jig is up,** (*slang*) success is now impossible.

jig·ger (jig-ĕr) *n.* a measure of spirits etc., a glass holding this amount.

jig·gle (jig-ĕl) *v.* (**jig·gled, jig·gling**) to rock or jerk lightly. **jiggle** *n.* a jiggling movement. **jig'gly** *adj.*

jig·saw (jig-saw) *n.* 1. a thin machine saw that moves vertically and is used in cutting curved or irregular lines. 2. a **jigsaw puzzle,** a picture pasted on wood or cardboard and cut into irregular pieces which are then shuffled and reassembled for amusement.

ji·had (ji-hahd) *n.* 1. a Muslim holy war against unbelievers. 2. a campaign against a doctrine, policy, etc.

jilt (jilt) *v.* to drop or abandon (a person) after having courted or promised to marry him or her. **jilt** *n.* a person who jilts another. **jilt'er** *n.*

Jim Crow, jim crow (jim kroh) the segregating of or discriminating against blacks in the U.S. **Jim Crow·ism** (jim kroh-iz-ĕm).

jim-dan·dy (jim-dan-dee) *adj.* (*informal*) of excellent quality.

jim·my (jim-ee) *n.* (*pl.* **-mies**) a short crowbar with curved ends, used by burglars to pry open doors and windows etc. **jimmy** *v.* (**jim·mied, jim·my·ing**) to force open with a jimmy.

jim·son (jim-sŏn) **weed** a highly poisonous tall weed having large trumpet-shaped purple or white flowers.

jin·gle (jing-gĕl) *v.* (**jin·gled, jin·gling**) to make or cause to make a metallic ringing or clinking sound like that of small bells or of keys struck together. **jingle** *n.* 1. a jingling sound. 2. verse or words with simple catchy rhymes or repetitive sounds.

jin·go·ism (jing-goh-iz-ĕm) *n.* an aggressive attitude combining excessive patriotism and contempt for other countries. **jin'go·ist** *adj.* & *n.* **jin·go·is·tic** (jing-goh-is-tik) *adj.*

jink (jingk) *v.* to dodge by turning suddenly and sharply. ☐**high jinks,** noisy merrymaking, boisterous fun.

jinn (jin), **jin·ni** (ji-nee) *n.* (*pl.* **jinn**) (in Islamic mythology) a spirit lower than the angels, with supernatural power over men.

jin·rick·sha (jin-rik-shaw) *n.* = **rickshaw.**

jinx (jingks) *n.* a person or thing that is thought to bring bad luck.

jit·ney (jit-nee) *n.* (*pl.* **-neys**) a small bus or taxi carrying passengers at low rates.

jit·ter (jit-ĕr) *v.* (*informal*) to feel nervous, to behave nervously. **jit'ter·y** *adj.* ☐**the jitters,** (*informal*) extreme nervousness.

jit·ter·bug (jit-ĕr-bug) *n.* 1. a quick-tempo dance to swing music, popular in the 1940's. 2. a person addicted to this dance. **jitterbug** *v.* (**jit·ter·bugged, jit·ter·bug·ging**) to dance the jitterbug.

jiu·jit·su = **jujitsu.**

jive (j*i*v) *n.* (*slang*) 1. fast lively jazz music, dancing to this. 2. the jargon of jazz musicians and jazz fans. 3. unintelligible and foolish talk. **jive** *v.* (**jived, jiv·ing**) (*slang*) 1. to talk jive, especially if trying to deceive. 2. to perform or dance to jive music. ▷Do not confuse *jive* with *jibe* or *gibe.*

jnt. *abbr.* joint.

job (job) *n.* 1. a piece of work to be done. 2. (*slang*) a robbery or other criminal act. 3. something completed, a product of work, *did a good job.* 4. a paid position of employment, *got a job at the factory.* 5. something one has to do, a responsibility, *it's your job to lock the gates.* 6. (*informal*) a difficult task, *you'll have a job to move it.* **job** *v.* (**jobbed, job·bing**) 1. to do jobs, to hire out for a definite time or job, *we jobbed out the work.* 2. to act as a middleman, wholesaler, or jobber. ☐**job action,** an organized protest by employees forbidden by law to strike. **job bank,** a computerized data file to help place unemployed workers in suitable jobs. **job lot,** a collection of miscellaneous articles bought together.

Job (johb) *n.* the book of the Old Testament containing the story of Job, a Hebrew patriarch who suffered great misfortunes. ☐**Job's comforter,** a person who aggravates the distress of the person he is supposed to be comforting. **the patience of Job,** great patience, like that of Job in the face of tribulation.

job·ber (job-ĕr) *n.* 1. a businessman who purchases merchandise from a manufacturer and sells it to retailers. 2. a person who does odd jobs or works by the job, a pieceworker.

job·hold·er (job-hohl-dĕr) *n.* a person having a steady or regular job.

job·less (job-lis) *adj.* unemployed, out of work.
job′less·ness *n.*

jock (jok) *n.* *(slang)* an athlete.

jock·ey (jok-ee) *n.* (*pl.* **-eys**) a person who rides horses in horse races, especially a professional rider. **jockey** *v.* (**jock·eyed, jock·ey·ing**) to maneuver in order to gain an advantage, *jockeying for position; jockeyed him into doing it,* forced him by skillful or unfair methods.

jock·strap (jok-strap) *n.* a support or protective covering for the male genitals, worn while taking part in sports.

jo·cose (joh-kohs) *adj.* joking.

joc·u·lar (jok-yŭ-lăr) *adj.* joking, avoiding seriousness. **joc′u·lar·ly** *adv.* **joc·u·lar·i·ty** (jok-yŭ-lar-i-tee) *n.*

joc·und (jok-ŭnd) *adj.* merry, cheerful.

jodh·purs (jod-pŭrz) *n. pl.* riding breeches reaching to the ankle, fitting closely below the knee and loosely above it.

jog[1] (jog) *v.* (**jogged, jog·ging**) 1. to give a slight knock or push to, to shake with a push or jerk. 2. to rouse or stimulate, *jogged his memory.* 3. to move up and down with an unsteady movement. 4. (of a horse) to move at a jogtrot. 5. to run at a leisurely pace, as a form of exercise. **jog** *n.* 1. a slight shake or push, a nudge. 2. a slow walk or trot. **jog′ger** *n.*

jog[2] *n.* 1. a section of a line or surface that juts out or recedes. 2. a change of course or direction.

jog·gle (jog-ĕl) *v.* (**jog·gled, jog·gling**) to shake slightly, to move by slight jerks. **joggle** *n.* a joggling movement, a slight shake.

jog·trot (jog-trot) *n.* a slow regular trot.

john (jon) *n.* 1. *(slang)* a toilet. 2. *(slang)* a prostitute's client.

John (jon) *n.* 1. one of the twelve apostles and traditional author of the fourth Gospel, three Epistles, and the Book of Revelation. 2. the fourth Gospel.

John Bull (jon buul) a typical Englishman, Englishmen as a whole.

John Doe (jon doh) a name used in legal proceedings for a fictitious person or an unidentified one whose real name is unknown.

john·ny (jon-ee) *n.* (*pl.* **-nies**) *(slang)* a gown worn by hospital patients.

John·ny-come-late·ly (jon-ee-kum-layt-lee) *n.* (*pl.* **-late·lies**) *(informal)* a recently arrived person, an upstart.

John·ny-jump-up (jon-ee-jump-up) *n.* a small type of pansy, grown especially in rock gardens.

John·son (jon-sŏn), **An·drew** (1805–75) the seventeenth president of the U.S. 1865–69.

Johnson, Lyn·don Baines (1908–73) the thirty-sixth president of the U.S. 1963–69.

joie de vi·vre (zhwah dĕ vee-vrĕ) a feeling of great enjoyment of life. ▷French, = joy of living.

join (join) *v.* 1. to put together, to fasten or unite or connect. 2. to come together, to become united, *the Missouri joins the Mississippi near St. Louis,* meets and flows into it. 3. to take part with others in doing something, *joined in the chorus.* 4. to come into the company of, *join us for lunch.* 5. to become a member of, *joined the Navy.* □**join battle,** to begin fighting. **join forces,** to combine efforts. **join hands,** to clasp each other's hands; to work cooperatively. **join up,** to enlist in the armed forces.

join·er (joi-nĕr) *n.* 1. a person who makes doors, interior moldings, window sashes, and other woodwork that is lighter than a carpenter's products. 2. *(informal)* a person who readily joins clubs and organizations.

joint (joint) *n.* 1. a place where two things are joined. 2. a structure in an animal body by which bones are fitted together, especially where the structure allows movement of the bones in relation to each other, *knee joint; ball-and-socket joint.* 3. a place or device at which two parts of a structure are joined. 4. one of the parts into which a butcher divides a carcass, this cooked and served. 5. *(slang)* a place where people meet for gambling or drinking etc. 6. *(slang)* a marijuana cigarette. **joint** *adj.* 1. shared or held or done by two or more people together, *a joint account.* 2. sharing in an activity etc., *joint authors.* **joint** *v.* 1. to connect by a joint or joints. 2. to divide (a carcass) into joints. □**joint-stock company,** a business company with stock held jointly by a number of people who may independently sell or transfer their shares. **out of joint,** dislocated; in disorder, *the times are out of joint.*

joint·ly (joint-lee) *adv.* so as to be shared or done by two or more people together.

joist (joist) *n.* one of the parallel beams, extending from wall to wall, on which floor boards or ceiling laths are fixed.

joke (johk) *n.* 1. something said or done to cause laughter. 2. a ridiculous person or thing or circumstance. **joke** *v.* (**joked, jok·ing**) to make jokes. **jok′ing·ly** *adv.* □**it's no joke,** it is a serious matter.

jok·er (joh-kĕr) *n.* 1. a person who jokes. 2. *(slang)* a fellow. 3. an extra playing card used in certain card games as the highest trump. 4. a clause unobtrusively inserted in a bill or document and affecting its operation in a way not immediately apparent.

jol·li·fi·ca·tion (jol-ĭ-fĭ-kay-shŏn) *n.* merrymaking, festivity.

jol·li·ty (jol-i-tee) *n.* (*pl.* **-ties**) being jolly, merriment, merrymaking.

jol·ly (jol-ee) *adj.* (**jol·li·er, jol·li·est**) 1. full of high spirits, cheerful, merry. 2. cheerful because slightly drunk. 3. very pleasant, delightful. **jolly** *adv.* (chiefly British *informal*) very, *jolly good.* **jolly** *v.* (**jol·lied, jol·ly·ing**) *(informal)* to keep (a person) in a good humor, especially in order to win his cooperation, *jolly him along.* □**Jolly Roger,** the pirates' black flag with a white skull and crossbones.

jolt (johlt) *v.* 1. to shake or dislodge with a jerk. 2. to move along jerkily, as on a rough road. **jolt** *n.* 1. a jolting movement. 2. a surprise or shock. 3. *(slang)* a drink of whiskey.

jon·gleur (jong-glĕr) *n.* a wandering minstrel in medieval France and England. ▷French.

jon·quil (jong-kwil) *n.* a kind of narcissus with clusters of fragrant flowers.

Jor·dan (jor-dăn) 1. a river flowing south into the Dead Sea. 2. a country in the Middle East, bordering on the east of Israel. **Jor·da·ni·an** (jor-day-ni-ăn) *adj.* & *n.*

josh (josh) *v.* *(informal)* to joke or tease.

Josh. *abbr.* Joshua.

Josh·u·a (josh-oo-ă) *n.* the sixth book of the Old Testament, telling of the conquests of Joshua, the successor to Moses as leader of Israel.

Joshua tree a treelike plant of the southwestern U.S. having branches like outstretched arms.

joss (jos) *n.* a Chinese idol. □**joss stick,** a thin

stick that burns to give off a smell of incense.
jos·tle (jos-ĕl) v. (**jos·tled, jos·tling**) to push roughly, especially when in a crowd.
jot (jot) n. a very small amount, *not one jot or tittle.* **jot** v. (**jot·ted, jot·ting**) to write briefly or hastily, *jot it down.*
jot·tings (jot-ingz) n. pl. jotted notes.
joule (jool) n. a unit of energy.
jounce (jowns) v. (**jounced, jounc·ing**) to bump, bounce, or jolt. **jounce** n. a jouncing motion.
jour. abbr. journal.
jour·nal (jur-năl) n. 1. a daily record of news or events or business transactions. 2. a newspaper or periodical.
jour·nal·ese (jur-nă-leez) n. a style of language used in inferior newspaper and magazine writing, full of hackneyed or artificially elaborate phrases.
jour·nal·ist (jur-nă-list) n. a person employed in writing for a newspaper or magazine. **jour'nal·ism** n. **jour·nal·is·tic** (jur-nă-lis-tik) adj.
jour·ney (jur-nee) n. (pl. **-neys**) 1. a course of travel, a trip. 2. the distance traveled or the time required for this, *a day's* or *four days' journey.* **journey** v. (**jour·neyed, jour·ney·ing**) to make a journey.
jour·ney·man (jur-nee-măn) n. (pl. **-men**, pr. -měn) 1. a workman who has completed his apprenticeship and works for an employer. 2. a reliable workman.
joust (just, jowst) n. a formal combat or tilting match with lances between two mounted knights in armor. **joust** v. to participate in a joust.
Jove (johv) Jupiter, the king of the gods in Roman mythology. □**by Jove,** an exclamation of surprise.
jo·vi·al (joh-vi-ăl) adj. full of cheerful good humor. **jo'vi·al·ly** adv. **jo·vi·al·i·ty** (joh-vi-al-i-tee) n.
jowl[1] (jowl) n. the jaw or cheek.
jowl[2] n. loose skin on a person's or animal's lower jaw or throat. **jowl'y** adv.
joy (joi) n. 1. a deep emotion of pleasure, gladness. 2. a thing that causes delight.
joy·ful (joi-fůl) adj. full of joy. **joy'ful·ly** adv. **joy'ful·ness** n.
joy·less (joi-lis) adj. without joy.
joy·ous (joi-ŭs) adj. joyful. **joy'ous·ly** adv.
joy·ride (joi-rɪd) n. a reckless automobile ride taken for the pleasure of speed, danger, etc.
J.P. abbr. justice of the peace.
Jpn. abbr. 1. Japan. 2. Japanese.
Jr. abbr. Junior.
ju·bi·lant (joo-bĭ-lănt) adj. showing joy, rejoicing. **ju'bi·lant·ly** adv.
ju·bi·la·tion (joo-bĭ-lay-shŏn) n. rejoicing.
ju·bi·lee (joo-bĭ-lee) n. 1. a special anniversary, *silver* (25th) or *golden* (50th) or *diamond* (60th) *jubilee.* 2. a time of rejoicing.
Ju·da·ic (joo-day-ik), **Ju·da·ic·al** (joo-day-i-kăl) adj. of Judaism or Jews.
Ju·da·i·ca (joo-day-i-kă) n. things relating to Jews or their religion, especially books and artifacts relating to Jewish history and culture.
Ju·da·ism (joo-dee-iz-ĕm) n. the religion of the Jewish people, with belief in one God and based on the teachings of the Old Testament and the Talmud.
Ju·das (joo-dăs) n. a betrayer or traitor. (▷Named after Judas Iscariot, who betrayed Christ.) □**Judas tree,** a tree with purplish-pink flowers appearing in the spring before the leaves, supposed to be the tree on which Judas hanged himself.

Jude (jood) n. the last epistle of the new Testament, ascribed to Jude, one of the twelve Apostles.
Judg. abbr. Judges.
judge (juj) n. 1. a public officer elected or appointed to hear and try cases in a court of law. 2. a person appointed to decide who has won a contest. 3. a person who is able to give an authoritative opinion on the merits of something. 4. any of the leaders of Israel between the time of Joshua and that of the kings. **judge** v. (**judged, judg·ing**) 1. to try (a case) in a court. 2. to act as judge of (a contest etc.). 3. to form and give an opinion about. 4. to estimate, *judged the distance accurately.*
Judg·es (juj-iz) n. the seventh book of the Old Testament.
judg·ment (juj-měnt) n. 1. judging, being judged. 2. the decision of a judge etc. in a law court, *the judgment was in his favor.* 3. ability to judge wisely, good sense, *he lacks judgment.* 4. misfortune considered or jokingly said to be a punishment sent by God, *it's a judgment on you!* 5. an opinion, *in the judgment of most people.* □**Judgment Day** or **Day of Judgment,** the day of the **Last Judgment,** when, according to Christian belief, God will judge all mankind.
ju·di·ca·to·ry (joo-dĭ-kă-tohr-ee) adj. having to do with the administration of justice.
ju·di·ca·ture (joo-dĭ-kă-chŭr) n. 1. the administration of justice. 2. = **judiciary** (definition 2).
ju·di·cial (joo-dish-ăl) adj. 1. of law courts or the administration of justice. 2. of a judge or judgment, *a judicial decision.* 3. able to judge things wisely, *a judicial mind.* **ju·di'cial·ly** adv.
ju·di·ci·ar·y (joo-dish-i-er-ee) n. (pl. **-ar·ies**) 1. the judicial branch of government. 2. a system of courts of law and their judges. **judiciary** adj. of courts of law or judges or judicial decisions.
ju·di·cious (joo-dish-ŭs) adj. judging wisely, showing good sense, *a judicious action.* **ju·di'cious·ly** adv.
ju·do (joo-doh) n. a Japanese system of unarmed combat, based on jujitsu.
ju·do·ist (joo-doh-ist) n. a student of or an expert in judo.
jug (jug) n. 1. a vessel for holding and pouring liquids, with a handle and a shaped lip. 2. (slang) prison, *in the jug.* **jug'ful** n. (pl. **-fuls**).
jug·ger·naut (jug-ĕr-nawt) n. a large overwhelmingly powerful object or institution etc. (▷*Juggernaut* was the title of a Hindu god whose image was drawn in procession on a huge wheeled vehicle; devotees are said to have thrown themselves under its wheels.
jug·gle (jug-ĕl) v. (**jug·gled, jug·gling**) 1. to toss and catch a number of objects skillfully for entertainment, keeping one or more in the air at one time. 2. to manipulate skillfully when handling several objects. 3. to rearrange (facts or figures) in order to achieve something or to deceive people.
jug·gler (jug-lĕr) n. a person who juggles, an entertainer who performs juggling tricks.
jug·u·lar (jug-yŭ-lăr) n. a **jugular vein,** one of the great veins of the neck, carrying blood from the head. □**go for the jugular,** to attack with intent to kill or to defeat decisively.
juice (joos) n. 1. the fluid content of fruits or vegetables or meat. 2. fluid secreted by an organ of the body, *the digestive juices.* 3. (slang) electricity. 4. (slang) gasoline used in an engine etc. □**juice up,** (slang) to enliven.

juic·er (joo-sĕr) *n.* a machine that extracts juice from fruits or vegetables.

juic·y (joo-see) *adj.* (**juic·i·er, juic·i·est**) 1. full of juice. 2. *(informal)* interesting, especially because of its scandalous nature, *juicy stories.* **juic′i·ly** *adv.* **juic′i·ness** *n.*

ju·jit·su (joo-jit-soo) *n.* a Japanese system of self-defense in which special holds or maneuvers are used to turn an opponent's strength and weight against him.

ju·jube (joo-joob) *n.* 1. the fleshy edible fruit of a spiny tree. 2. a chewy fruit-flavored candy.

juke·box (jook-boks) *n.* a machine that automatically plays a selected record when a coin is inserted.

Jul. *abbr.* July.

ju·lep (joo-lip) *n.* 1. a tall drink of liquor, sugar, shaved ice and flavoring, especially mint. 2. a sweet syrupy drink, especially one containing medicine.

Ju·li·an (joo-li-ăn) **Calendar** the calendar introduced by Julius Caesar, since replaced by the Gregorian calendar.

ju·li·enne (joo-li-en) *adj.* (of vegetables or meats) cut into long thin strips. **julienne** *n.* a clear meat soup containing julienne vegetables.

Ju·ly (joo-lɪ) *n.* (*pl.* **-lies**) the seventh month of the year.

jum·ble (jum-bĕl) *v.* (**jum·bled, jum·bling**) to mix in a confused way. **jumble** *n.* articles jumbled together, a muddle.

jum·bo (jum-boh) *n.* (*pl.* **-bos**) something very large of its kind. **jumbo** *adj.* □**jumbo jet,** a very large jet aircraft able to carry several hundred passengers.

jump (jump) *v.* 1. to move up off the ground etc. by bending and then extending the legs or (of fish) by a movement of the tail. 2. to move suddenly with a jump or bound, to rise suddenly from a seat etc; *jump in,* to get quickly into a car etc. 3. to pass over by jumping, to use (a horse) for jumping. 4. to pass over (a thing) to a point beyond, to skip (part of a book etc.) in reading or studying. 5. to give a sudden movement from shock or excitement. 6. to rise suddenly in amount or price or value. 7. to leave (rails or a track) accidentally. 8. to pounce on, to attack suddenly. **jump** *n.* 1. a jumping movement. 2. a sudden movement caused by shock etc. 3. a sudden rise in amount or price or value. 4. a sudden change to a different condition or set of circumstances, a gap in a series etc. 5. an obstacle to be jumped over. □**have the jump on,** *(slang)* to have an advantage over. **jump at,** to accept eagerly. **jump bail,** to fail to come for trial when summoned after being released on bail. **jump ball,** (in basketball) a ball tossed up between two players by the referee to start or resume play. **jump down a person's throat,** to reprimand him severely. **jumping bean,** the seed of a Mexican plant that jumps owing to the movement of an enclosed larva. **jumping-off point** *or* **place,** a starting point. **jump on,** to reprimand or criticize a person or situation. **jump rope,** a children's game in which one jumps over a twirling rope; the rope used. **jump ship,** (of a seaman) to desert one's ship. **jump suit,** a one-piece garment for the whole body, like that worn by paratroops. **jump the gun,** to start or act before the permitted time. **jump to conclusions,** to reach them too hastily. **jump to it,** to make an energetic start.

jump up and down, to show great happiness, eagerness, etc., *they were jumping up and down for joy.* **one jump ahead,** one stage ahead of one's rival. **the jumps,** *(slang)* extreme nervousness.

jump·er¹ (jum-pĕr) *n.* a person or animal that jumps, *is a good jumper.*

jumper² *n.* 1. a dress without sleeves or collar, worn over a blouse or sweater. 2. a short wire used to make or break an electrical circuit. □**jumper cables,** cables for conveying current from one battery to recharge another.

jump-off (jump-awf) *n.* a deciding round between competitors with equal scores in a horse-riding contest.

jump·y (jum-pee) *adj.* (**jump·i·er, jump·i·est**) nervous.

jun. *abbr.* junior.

Jun. *abbr.* 1. June. 2. Junior.

junc. *abbr.* junction.

jun·co (jung-koh) *n.* (*pl.* **-cos, -coes**) a North American finch with a slate-gray body and white tail feathers.

junc·tion (jungk-shŏn) *n.* 1. a place where things join or cross. 2. a place where roads or railroad lines etc. meet and unite or cross.

junc·ture (jungk-chŭr) *n.* a point of time, a critical convergence of events.

June (joon) *n.* the sixth month of the year.

Ju·neau (joo-noh) the capital of Alaska.

jun·gle (jung-gĕl) *n.* 1. land overgrown with tangled vegetation, especially in the tropics. 2. a wild tangled mass. 3. a scene of struggle, *the black-board jungle* (in schools), *concrete jungle* (in cities).

jun·ior (joon-yŏr) *adj.* 1. younger in age (used to distinguish a son from a father with the same name). 2. lower in rank or authority, *junior faculty.* 3. for younger persons, *junior membership.* 4. of the next-to-last year in a high school or college. **junior** *n.* 1. a junior person; *he is my junior,* he is younger than I am. 2. a student in the junior year of high school or college. 3. *(informal)* the son in a family. □**junior college,** one offering courses for only the first two years of college studies. **junior high school,** a school generally including grades 7, 8, and 9. **junior size,** (of clothing) made for women of slight frame. **junior varsity,** an athletic team whose members do not qualify for the varsity.

ju·ni·per (joo-nĭ-pĕr) *n.* an evergreen shrub with prickly leaves and dark purplish berries.

junk¹ (jungk) *n.* 1. discarded material, trash. 2. *(informal)* anything regarded as useless or of little value, *all that junk in the trunk of the car.* 3. *(slang)* a narcotic drug, heroin. □**junk food,** food having low nutritional value and usually high in calories. **junk mail,** unsolicited advertising matter sent via the postal service. **junk shop,** a shop selling miscellaneous cheap secondhand goods.

junk² *n.* a kind of flat-bottomed ship with sails, used in the China seas.

junk·er (jung-kĕr) *n.* an old worn-out motor vehicle useful only for scrap metal.

Jun·ker (yuung-kĕr) *n.* (*old use*) a member of the militaristic Prussian aristocracy.

jun·ket (jung-kit) *n.* 1. a sweet custard-like dessert made of flavored milk curdled with rennet. 2. a trip taken by a public official at public expense. **junket** *v.* to make a trip at public expense.

junk·ie (jung-kee) *n.* *(slang)* a drug addict.

jun·ta (huun-tă, juun-) *n.* a group of people who combine to rule a country, especially having seized power after a revolution.

Ju·pi·ter (joo-pi-tĕr) 1. a planet in the solar system. 2. the supreme god in Roman mythology.

Ju·ras·sic (juu-ras-ik) *adj.* of the middle geologic period of the Mesozoic era, when dinosaurs and the earliest mammals existed. **Jurassic** *n.* the Jurassic period.

ju·rid·i·cal (juu-rid-i-kăl) *adj.* 1. of judicial proceedings. 2. relating to the law. **ju·rid'i·cal·ly** *adv.*

ju·ris·dic·tion (joor-is-dik-shŏn) *n.* 1. authority to interpret and apply the law. 2. official power exercised within a particular sphere of activity. 3. the extent or territory over which legal or other power extends. **ju·ris·dic'tion·al** *adj.*

ju·ris·pru·dence (joor-is-proo-dĕns) *n.* the study of law or of a particular part of law, *medical jurisprudence.*

ju·rist (joor-ist) *n.* a person skilled in the law, as an eminent judge or lawyer.

ju·ris·tic (juu-ris-tik) *adj.* 1. of a jurist or jurists. 2. legal, created by law.

ju·ror (joor-ŏr) *n.* a member of a jury.

ju·ry¹ (joor-ee) *n.* (*pl.* **-ries**) 1. a body of people sworn to give a verdict on a case presented to them in a court of law. 2. a body of people appointed to select the winner(s) in a competition. □**jury box,** an enclosure for the jury in a court of law. **ju·ry·man** (joor-ee-măn) *n.* (*pl.* **-men,** *pr.* -mĕn) **ju·ry·wom·an** (joor-ee-wuum-ăn) *n.* (*pl.* **-wom·en,** *pr.* -wim-in).

jury² *adj.* (in nautical use) temporarily replacing something broken or lost, *a jury mast; jury-rigged.*

just (just) *adj.* 1. giving proper consideration to the claims of everyone concerned. 2. deserved, right in amount etc., *a just reward.* **just** *adv.* 1. exactly, *just at that spot.* 2. barely, no more than, by only a short distance, *I just managed it; just below the knee.* 3. at this moment or only a little time ago, *he has just gone.* 4. (*informal*) simply, merely, *we are just good friends.* 5. really, certainly, *it's just splendid.* **just'ly** *adv.* **just'ness** *n.* □**just about,** (*informal*) almost exactly or completely. **just in case,** as a precaution. **just now,** at this moment; a little time ago. **just so,** exactly arranged, *she likes everything just so;* it is exactly as you say.

jus·tice (jus-tis) *n.* 1. just treatment, fairness. 2. legal proceedings, *a court of justice.* 3. a magistrate. 4. a judge, the title of a judge, *Mr. Justice Brandeis.* □**do justice to,** to show (a thing) to advantage; to show appreciation of. **justice of the peace,** a nonprofessional magistrate.

jus·ti·fi·a·ble (jus-tĭ-fī-ă-bĕl) *adj.* able to be justified. **just'ti·fi·a·bly** *adv.*

jus·ti·fy (jus-tĭ-fī) *v.* (**jus·ti·fied, jus·ti·fy·ing**) 1. to show (a person or statement or act etc.) to be right or just or reasonable. 2. to make free from blame or guilt. 3. to be a good or sufficient reason for, *increased production justifies an increase in wages.* 4. to adjust (a line of type in printing) so that it fills a space neatly. **jus·ti·fi·ca·tion** (jus-tĭ-fī-fī-kay-shŏn) *n.*

jut (jut) *v.* (**jut·ted, jut·ting**) to project, *it juts out.*

jute (joot) *n.* a fiber from the bark of certain tropical plants, used for making sacks, rope, etc.

juv. *abbr.* juvenile.

ju·ve·nile (joo-vĕ-nīl) *adj.* 1. youthful, childish. 2. for young people. **juvenile** *n.* a young person. □**juvenile delinquency,** illegal behavior by a young offender, below the age when he may be held legally responsible for his actions. **juvenile delinquent,** such an offender.

ju·ve·nil·i·a (joo-vĕ-nil-i-ă) *n. pl.* the works produced by an author or artist in his youth.

jux·ta·pose (juk-stă-pohz) *v.* (**jux·ta·posed, jux·ta·pos·ing**) to put (things) side by side. **jux·ta·po·si·tion** (juk-stă-pŏ-zish-ŏn) *n.*

JV *abbr.* junior varsity.

K

K, k (kay) (*pl.* **Ks, K's, k's**) the eleventh letter of the alphabet.

K *abbr.* 1. Kelvin. 2. kindergarten. 3. (in chess) king. 4. knight.

K *symbol* potassium.

k. *abbr.* 1. (in electricity) capacity. 2. karat(s). 3. kilogram(s). 4. (in chess) king. 5. kitchen.

Kaa·ba (kah-bă) *n.* a shrine at Mecca containing a sacred black stone.

ka·bob (kă-bob) = **kebob.**

ka·bu·ki (kă-boo-kee) *n.* a traditional popular Japanese drama with highly stylized song and dance, acted by males only.

Ka·bul (kah-bool) the capital of Afghanistan.

Kad·dish (kah-dish) *n.* (*pl.* **Kad·di·shim,** *pr.* kahdish-im) a Jewish prayer in praise of God, especially a form of this recited by mourners.

kaf·fee klatsch (kah-fay klahch) = **coffee klatsch.**

Kai·ser (kı-zĕr) *n.* the title of the German and Austrian emperors until 1918.

kale (kayl) *n.* a kind of cabbage with curly leaves that do not form a compact head.

ka·lei·do·scope (kă-lı-dŏ-skohp) *n.* a toy consisting of a tube containing small brightly colored fragments of glass etc. and mirrors that reflect these to form changing patterns. **ka·lei·do·scop·ic** (kă-lı-dŏ-skop-ik) *adj.*

ka·ma·ai·na (kah-mă-ı-nă) *n.* a person who has lived in Hawaii for many years.

kame (kaym) *n.* a short ridge of sand and gravel deposited from the water of a melted glacier.

ka·mi·ka·ze (kah-mı́-kah-zee) *n.* 1. a World War II Japanese aircraft laden with explosives and deliberately crashed by its pilot on its target. 2. its pilot.

Kam·pa·la (kahm-pah-lă) the capital of Uganda.

kam·pong (kam-pong) *n.* an enclosure or village in parts of southeast Asia where Malay is spoken.

Kam·pu·che·a (kam-poo-chi-ă) a country in Asia, formerly Cambodia.

kan·ga·roo (kang-gă-roo) *n.* (*pl.* **-roos, -roo**) an Australian animal that jumps along on its strong hind legs, the female having a pouch on the front of the body in which young are carried. □**kangaroo court,** a court formed illegally by a group of people (such as prisoners or strikers) to settle disputes among themselves.

Kans. *abbr.* Kansas.

Kan·sas (kan-zăs) a state of the U.S.

ka·o·lin, ka·o·line (kay-ŏ-lin) *n.* a fine white clay used in making porcelain and in medicine.

ka·pok (kay-pok) *n.* a substance resembling cotton, used for padding things.

kap·pa (kap-ă) *n.* the tenth letter of the Greek alphabet (K κ).

ka·put (kah-puut) *adj.* *(slang)* done for, ruined, out of order.

kar·a·kul (kar-ă-kŭl) *n.* 1. an Asian sheep whose young have dark curled fleece. 2. its fur.

kar·at (kar-ăt) *n.* a measure of the purity of gold, pure gold being 24 karats.

ka·ra·te (kă-rah-tee) *n.* a Japanese system of unarmed combat in which the hands and feet are used as weapons.

kar·ma (kahr-mă) *n.* 1. (in Buddhism and Hinduism) the sum of a person's actions in one of his successive existences, thought to decide his fate for the next. 2. fate, destiny. **kar′mic** *adj.*

karst (kahrst) *n.* a region with underground drainage and many cavities etc. caused by dissolution of rock. ▷From the name of such a region in Yugoslavia.

kart (kahrt) *n.* a miniature racing car with a lowslung skeleton body. **kart′ing** *n.*

ka·sha (kah-shă) *n.* buckwheat groats, a dish prepared from these.

Kat·man·du (kat-man-doo) the capital of Nepal.

ka·ty·did (kay-ti-did) *n.* any of several large green North American insects related to grasshoppers and crickets and producing a characteristic noise, from which they get their name.

kay·ak (kı-ak) *n.* 1. an Eskimo canoe with a sealskin covering closed around the waist of the occupant. 2. a small covered canoe resembling this.

kay·o (kay-oh) *n.* (*pl.* **kay·os**) *(slang)* a knockout. **kayo** *v.* (**kay·oed, kay·o·ing**) *(slang)* to knock out. ▷From the abbreviation *K.O.*

Ka·zak·stan (kah-zahk-stahn) a republic of the U.S.S.R. bordering on China and the Caspian Sea. **Ka·zak′** *n.* a native or inhabitant of Kazakstan.

ka·zoo (kă-zoo) *n.* (*pl.* **-zoos**) a toy musical instrument into which the player sings or hums.

kc *abbr.* kilocycle(s).

K.C. *abbr.* Knight(s) of Columbus.

kc/s *abbr.* kilocycle(s) per second.

ke·bob, ke·bab (kĕ-bob) *n.* a small piece of meat cooked on a skewer.

kedge (kej) *v.* (**kedged, kedg·ing**) 1. to move (a ship) by winding in a hawser attached to a small anchor. 2. to move in this way. **kedge** *n.* a small anchor for this purpose.

keel (keel) *n.* the timber or steel structure along the base of a ship, on which the ship's framework is built up. **keel** *v.* to become tilted, to overturn, to collapse, *keeled over.* □**on an even keel,** steady.

keel·haul (keel-hawl) *v.* to haul (a person) under the keel of a ship as punishment.

keen¹ (keen) *adj.* 1. sharp, having a sharp edge or point. 2. (of sound or light) acute, penetrating. 3. piercingly cold, *keen wind.* 4. intense, *keen* *interest; keen competition.* **5.** showing or feeling eagerness or desire, *a keen swimmer; is keen to go.* **6.** perceiving things very distinctly, *keen sight.* **7.** *(slang)* excellent. **keen′ly** *adv.* **keen′ness** *n.* ☐**keen on,** *(informal)* much attracted to.

keen² *n.* an Irish funeral song accompanied by wailing. **keen** *v.* to utter the keen, to utter in a wailing tone.

keep (keep) *v.* (**kept, keep·ing**) **1.** to remain or cause to remain in a specified state or position or condition, *she was kept in prison overnight.* **2.** to prevent or hold back from doing something, to detain, *what kept you?* **3.** to put aside for a future time. **4.** to pay proper respect to; *keep a promise,* not break it. **5.** to celebrate (a feast or ceremony). **6.** to guard or protect, to keep safe, *God bless you and keep you.* **7.** to continue to have, to have and not give away, *keep the change.* **8.** to provide with the necessities of life; *it keeps him in cigarettes,* provides him with money for these. **9.** to own and look after (animals) for one's use or enjoyment, *keep hens.* **10.** to manage, *keep shop.* **11.** to have (a commodity) regularly in stock or for sale. **12.** to make entries in (a diary or accounts etc.), to record in this way. **13.** to continue doing something, to do frequently or repeatedly, *the strap keeps breaking.* **14.** to continue in a specified direction, *keep straight on.* **15.** (of food) to remain in good condition; *the work or news will keep,* can be put aside until later. **keep** *n.* **1.** provision of the necessities of life, the food required for this, *she earns her keep.* **2.** the central tower or other strongly fortified structure in a castle. ☐**for keeps,** *(informal)* permanently. **keep a secret,** not tell it to others. **keep at,** to nag, *he keeps at me.* **keep down,** to keep low in amount or number, *it keeps the weeds down;* to eat and not vomit (food); to suppress, to repress. **keep early hours,** to go to bed early. **keep fit,** to be and remain healthy. **keep house,** to look after a house or a household. **keep on,** to continue doing something. **keep one's feet,** not fall. **keep one's head above water,** to keep out of debt. **keep the peace,** to obey the laws and refrain from causing trouble. **keep to oneself,** to keep (a thing) secret; to avoid meeting people. **keep under,** to repress. **keep up,** to progress at the same pace as others; to prevent from sinking or getting low; to continue to observe, *keep up old customs;* to continue, *kept up the attack all day;* to maintain in proper condition, *the cost of keeping up a large house;* to stay informed, *keep up on the news.* **keep up with the Joneses,** to strive to remain on terms of social or material equality with one's neighbors.

keep·er (kee-pĕr) *n.* a person who keeps or looks after something, the custodian of a museum or zoo etc.

keep·ing (kee-ping) *n.* **1.** custody, charge, *in my keeping.* **2.** harmony, conformity, *a style that is in keeping with his dignity.*

keep·sake (keep-sayk) *n.* a thing that is given or kept as a reminder of a person or event.

keg (keg) *n.* a small barrel.

keg·ler (keg-lĕr) *n.* *(informal)* a person who bowls.

kelp (kelp) *n.* a large brown seaweed.

Kelt (kelt) = **Celt.**

kel·vin (kel-vin) *n.* a degree (equivalent to the Celsius degree) of the **Kelvin scale** of temperature (with zero at absolute zero, −273.15°C).

ken (ken) *n.* the range of sight or knowledge, *beyond my ken.* **ken** *v.* (**kenned, ken·ning**) *(Scottish)* to know.

Ken·ne·dy (ken-ĕ-dee), **John Fitz·ger·ald** (1917–63) the thirty-fifth president of the U.S. 1961–63.

ken·nel (ken-ĕl) *n.* **1.** a shelter for a dog or dogs. **2.** (also *kennels*) an establishment for boarding or breeding dogs. **kennel** *v.* (**ken·neled, ken·nel·ing**) to put into a kennel.

ke·no (kee-noh) *n.* a gambling game resembling bingo.

Ken·tuck·y (ken-tuk-ee) a state of the U.S. **Ken·tuck′i·an** *adj. & n.* ☐**Kentucky bluegrass,** a grass found especially in Kentucky and Virginia, used as pasture and for hay. **Kentucky Derby,** *see* **derby.**

Ken·ya (keen-yă) a country in east Africa. **Ken′yan** *adj. & n.*

ke·pi (kay-pee) *n.* (*pl.* **ke·pis**) a French military cap with a visor.

kept (kept) *see* **keep.**

ker·a·tin (ker-ă-tin) *n.* a strong protein forming the basis of horns, claws, nails, feathers, hair, etc. **ke·ra·ti·nous** (ke-rat-ĭ-nŭs) *adj.*

ker·chief (kur-chif) *n.* a square scarf worn on the head.

kerf (kurf) *n.* a slit made by cutting, especially with a saw.

ker·nel (kur-nĕl) *n.* **1.** the softer (usually edible) part inside the shell of a nut or stone fruit. **2.** the part of a grain or seed within the husk. **3.** the central or important part of a subject or plan or problem etc.

ker·o·sene (ker-ŏ-seen) *n.* a fuel oil distilled from petroleum etc.

ketch (kech) *n.* a small sailing boat with two masts.

ketch·up (kech-ŭp) *n.* a thick sauce made from tomatoes and vinegar etc., used as a seasoning.

ket·tle (ket-ĕl) *n.* a metal container with a spout and handle, for boiling water in. ☐**a pretty kettle of fish,** an awkward state of affairs.

ket·tle·drum (ket-ĕl-drum) *n.* a percussion instrument consisting of a hollow shaped body over which a skin is stretched.

key¹ (kee) *n.* (*pl.* **keys**) **1.** a small piece of metal shaped so that it will move the bolt of a lock and so lock or unlock something. **2.** a similar instrument for winding a clock or tightening a spring etc. **3.** something that provides access or control or insight, *the key to the mystery; a key industry,* one that is important to other industries and to a country's economy. **4.** a set of answers to problems, a word or list of symbols for interpreting a code etc. **5.** a system of related notes in music, based on a particular note, *the key of C major.* **6.** the general tone or degree of intensity of something; *all in the same key,* monotonous in character. **7.** one of a set of levers to be pressed by the fingers in playing a musical instrument or operating a typewriter etc. **key** *v.* (**keyed, key·ing**) to link closely with something else, *the factory is keyed to the export trade.* **key** *adj.* central, all-important, *the key parts to the puzzle.* ☐**key club,** a private club to which each member has a personal door key. **keyed up,** stimulated, nervously tense. **key money,** payment demanded from an incoming tenant, nominally for the provision of the key to the premises. **key ring,** a ring on which keys are kept.

key² *n.* a low offshore island or reef, especially in the West Indies or off the coast of Florida. ☐**key lime,** a citrus fruit of the Florida keys. **key lime pie,** a meringue pie made with key limes.

key·board (kee-bohrd) *n.* the set of keys on a piano or typewriter etc.

key·hole (kee-hohl) *n.* the hole by which a key is put into a lock. ☐**keyhole saw,** a small-bladed saw for cutting holes etc.

key·note (kee-noht) *n.* 1. the note on which a key in music is based. 2. the prevailing tone or idea of a speech etc. ☐**keynote speech** *or* **address,** a speech, especially at a political convention, stating basic policies and principles.

key·punch (kee-punch) *n.* a machine for recording coded data by punching holes in cards for later processing by a computer. **keypunch** *v.* to punch with holes in this way. **key′punch·er** *n.*

key·stone (kee-stohn) *n.* 1. the central wedge-shaped stone at the summit of an arch, locking the others in position. 2. a central principle etc. on which all depends, *the keystone of her philosophy.*

key·word (kee-wurd) *n.* the key to a cipher etc.

kg. *abbr.* kilogram(s).

KGB *abbr.* the secret police of the U.S.S.R. since 1954.

kha·ki (kak-ee) *adj.* 1. dull brownish yellow. 2. made of khaki fabric. **khaki** *n.* (*pl.* -kis) 1. the color of khaki. 2. khaki cotton fabric used in the army for field uniforms. 3. such a uniform.

khan (kahn) *n.* 1. the title of rulers and officials in central Asia, Afghanistan, etc. 2. the supreme ruler of Turkish, Tartar, and Mongol tribes, and emperors of China, in the Middle Ages.

Khar·toum (kahr-toom) the capital of Sudan.

khe·dive ((kĕ-deev) *n.* the title of the viceroy of Egypt under Turkish government, 1867–1914.

kHz *abbr.* kilohertz.

KIA *abbr.* killed in action.

kib·ble (kib-ĕl) *v.* (**kib·bled, kib·bling**) to grind coarsely, to crush into small pieces. **kibble** *n.* the product of kibbling, especially dry pet food.

kib·butz (ki-buuts) *n.* (*pl.* **kib·but·zim,** *pr.* ki-buut-seem) a communal settlement in Israel.

kib·butz·nik (ki-buuts-nik) *n.* a member of a kibbutz.

kib·itz (kib-its) *v.* (*informal*) 1. to watch and comment on a game of cards. 2. to give advice that is not sought or appreciated. **kib′itz·er** *n.* (*informal*).

ki·bosh (kɪ-bosh) *n.* (*slang*) nonsense. ☐**put the kibosh on,** (*slang*) to put an end to.

kick (kik) *v.* 1. to strike or thrust or propel with the foot. 2. (in football) to score by kicking, *he kicked (for) the extra point.* 3. to treat contemptuously, *gets kicked around.* 4. (of a gun) to recoil when fired. 5. (*informal*) to complain. **kick** *n.* 1. an act of kicking, a blow from being kicked. 2. (*informal*) a thrill, a pleasurable effect, *get a kick out of it; did it for kicks.* 3. (*slang*) an interest or activity, *the health food kick.* 4. the recoil of a gun when it is fired. 5. (*informal*) a complaint, *I'm tired of their kicks.* **kick′er** *n.* ☐**alive and kicking,** (*informal*) fully active. **kick in,** (*slang*) to contribute. **kick off,** to start a football game by kicking the ball; (*informal*) to start (proceedings). **kick out,** (*informal*) to drive out forcibly; to dismiss. **kick over,** (*informal*) to start (an engine); (of an engine) to start. **kick over the traces,** *see* **trace².** **kick the bucket,** (*slang*) to

die. **kick the habit,** (*slang*) to give it up. **kick up,** (*informal*) to create (a fuss or noise). **kick up one's heels,** to show great energy or initiative. **kick upstairs,** to promote (a person) to a higher position, which is in fact less influential, in order to get rid of him.

kick·back (kik-bak) *n.* 1. a sharp reaction. 2. (*informal*) a payment for help in making a profit etc.

kick·off (kik-awf) *n.* 1. (in football) a kick made to start play. 2. (*informal*) the start of an activity, *kickoff of our campaign.*

kick·stand (kik-stand) *n.* a metal bar used to keep a two-wheeled vehicle upright when not in use.

kick·y (kik-ee) *adj.* (**kick·i·er, kick·i·est**) (*slang*) vivacious, charming, exciting.

kid (kid) *n.* 1. a young goat. 2. leather made from its skin. 3. (*slang*) a child. **kid** *v.* (**kid·ded, kid·ding**) 1. to give birth to a young goat. 2. (*informal*) to deceive (especially for fun), to tease. **kid′der** *n.* **kid′ding·ly** *adv.* ☐**kid gloves,** kidskin gloves. **kid-glove treatment,** tactfulness. **kid stuff,** (*informal*) something easy or childish.

kid·dy (kid-ee) *n.* (*pl.* -dies) (*informal*) a child.

kid·nap (kid-nap) *v.* (**kid·naped** or **kid·napped, kid·nap·ing** or **kid·nap·ping**) to carry off (a person) by force or fraud in order to obtain a ransom. **kid′nap·er, kid′nap·per** *n.*

kid·ney (kid-nee) *n.* (*pl.* -neys) 1. either of a pair of organs that remove waste products from the blood and secrete urine. 2. this as food. ☐**kidney bean,** an oval-shaped bean, especially one that is deep red. **kidney machine,** an apparatus that performs the functions of a kidney. **kidney stone,** a small hard mass that sometimes forms in the kidney.

kid·skin (kid-skin) *n.* the leather made from the skin of a young goat.

kiel·ba·sa (kil-bah-să) *n.* (*pl.* -ba·sas, -ba·sy, *pr.* -bah-see) a Polish sausage.

Ki·ga·li (kee-gah-lee) the capital of Rwanda.

kill (kil) *v.* 1. to cause the death of (a person), to destroy the vitality of (a plant etc.). 2. to put an end to (a feeling etc.); *kill a light* or *an engine,* switch it off. 3. to make (a color) seem insipid by contrast. 4. to spend (time) unprofitably while waiting for something. 5. (*slang*) to cause severe pain to, *my feet are killing me.* 6. (*slang*) to consume completely, *they killed a quart of Scotch.* **kill** *n.* 1. the act of killing. 2. the animal(s) killed by a hunter. **kill′er** *n.* ☐**in at the kill,** present at the time of victory. **kill off,** to get rid of by killing. **kill two birds with one stone,** to achieve two purposes with one action. **kill with kindness,** to harm with excessive kindness. **make a killing,** to have a great financial success.

kill·deer (kil-deer) *n.* a large American ring plover.

kill·joy (kil-joi) *n.* a person who spoils the enjoyment of others.

kiln (kil, kiln) *n.* an oven for hardening or drying things such as pottery or bricks or hops, or for burning lime.

ki·lo (kee-loh) *n.* (*pl.* **ki·los**) a kilogram.

kilo- *prefix* one thousand.

kil·o·cy·cle (kil-ŏ-sɪ-kĕl) *n.* 1. 1000 cycles as a unit of wave frequency. 2. (*informal*) kilohertz.

kil·o·gram (kil-ŏ-gram) *n.* the basic unit of mass in the International System of Units (2.205 lbs.).

kil·o·hertz (kil-ŏ-hurts) *n.* (*pl.* **-hertz**) a unit of frequency of electromagnetic waves, = 1000 cycles per second.

kil·o·li·ter (kil-ŏ-lee-tĕr) *n.* 1000 liters.

ki·lo·me·ter (ki-lom-ĕ-tĕr) *n.* a distance of 1000 meters (0.62 mile).

kil·o·ton (kil-ŏ-tun) *n.* 1. 1000 tons. 2. a unit of explosive power equivalent to 1000 tons of TNT.

ki·lo·volt (kil-ŏ-vohlt) *n.* 1000 volts.

kil·o·watt (kil-ŏ-wot) *n.* the power of 1000 watts.

kil·o·watt-hour (kil-ŏ-wot-owr) *n.* an amount of energy equal to one kilowatt operating for one hour.

kilt (kilt) *n.* a knee-length pleated skirt of tartan wool, worn as part of a Scottish Highland man's dress or by women and children.

kil·ter (kil-tĕr) *n.* (*informal*) good working order. □**out of kilter,** not working properly.

ki·mo·no (ki-moh-nŏ) *n.* (*pl.* **-nos**) 1. a long loose Japanese robe with wide sleeves, worn with a sash. 2. a dressing gown resembling this.

kin (kin) *n.* (*pl.* **kin**) a person's relative(s).

kind[1] (kınd) *n.* a class of similar things or animals, a type. □**a kind of,** something that belongs approximately to the class named, *he is a kind of stockbroker.* **in kind,** (of payment) in goods or natural produce, not in money; *repaid his insolence in kind,* by being insulting in return. **kind of,** (*informal*) slightly, *I felt kind of sorry for him.* **of a kind,** similar. ▷It is incorrect to say *these kind of cards.* Say *this kind* when you mean *one kind; these kinds,* when you mean *more than one kind.*

kind[2] *adj.* gentle and considerate in one's manner or conduct toward others. **kind′ness** *n.*

kin·der·gar·ten (kin-dĕr-gahr-tĕn) *n.* a school or class for very young children.

kin·der·gart·ner, kin·der·gar·ten·er (kin-dĕr-gahrt-nĕr) *n.* a child in kindergarten.

kind·heart·ed (kınd-hahr-tĭd) *adj.* having a kind heart, sympathetic to others.

kin·dle (kin-dĕl) *v.* (**kin·dled, kin·dling**) 1. to set on fire, to cause (a fire) to begin burning. 2. to arouse or stimulate, *kindled our hopes.* 3. to become kindled.

kin·dling (kin-dling) *n.* small pieces of wood for lighting fires.

kind·ly (kınd-lee) *adj.* (**kind·li·er, kind·li·est**) kind in character or manner or appearance. **kindly** *adv.* 1. in a kind way. 2. please, *kindly shut the door.* **kind′li·ness** *n.* □**not take kindly to,** to be displeased by.

kin·dred (kin-drid) *n.* a person's relative(s). **kindred** *adj.* 1. related. 2. of similar kind, *chemistry and kindred subjects.* □**a kindred spirit,** a person whose interests or tastes are similar to one's own.

kine (kın) *n. pl.* (*old use*) cows, cattle.

kin·e·mat·ics (kin-ĕ-mat-iks) *n.* the science of pure motion, considered abstractly without reference to force or mass. **kin·e·mat′ic** *adj.* **kin·e·mat′i·cal** *adj.* **kin·e·mat′i·cal·ly** *adv.*

kin·e·scope (kin-ĕ-skohp) *n.* 1. a television picture tube. 2. a motion picture made from a picture appearing on a kinescope.

ki·ne·sics (ki-nee-siks) *n.* the study of body movements (shrugs etc.) contributing to communication. **ki·ne′sic** *adj.*

kin·es·the·sia (kin-is-thee-zhă) *n.* the sensation of bodily position or of strain or movement of the muscles, tendons, etc. of one's body. **kin·es·thet·ic** (kin-is-thet-ik) *adj.*

ki·net·ic (ki-net-ik) *adj.* of or produced by movement, characterized by movement. □**kinetic art,** art that depends for its effect on the movement of some of its parts, as in air currents. **kinetic energy,** *see* **energy.**

kin·folk (kin-fohk), **kin·folks** (kin-fohks) *n. pl.* a person's relative(s).

king (king) *n.* 1. a man who is the supreme ruler of an independent country by right of succession to the throne. 2. a person or thing regarded as supreme in some way; *king of beasts, king penguin.* 3. a large species of animal, *king penguin.* 4. the piece in chess that has to be protected from capture. 5. a piece in checkers that has been crowned on reaching the opponent's end of the board. 6. a playing card bearing a picture of a king and ranking next above queen. 7. *Kings,* two historical books of the Old Testament covering the kingdom of Judah from the death of David to the destruction of the Temple. **king′less** *adj.* □**king crab,** a large marine crab having a horseshoe-shaped shell; any of several large edible crabs. **king's pawn, knight, bishop,** etc., that closest to the king's side of the chessboard at the start of the game.

king·bolt (king-bohlt) *n.* a main or large bolt.

king·dom (king-dŏm) *n.* 1. a country ruled by a king or queen. 2. the spiritual reign of God; *thy Kingdom come,* may the rule of God be established. 3. a division of the natural world, *the animal* or *vegetable kingdom.* □**kingdom come,** (*slang*) the next world.

king·fish·er (king-fish-ĕr) *n.* a small bird with bright bluish plumage that dives to catch fish.

King (king) **James** (jaymz) **Version** an Authorized Version of the Bible, used by Protestants, prepared during the reign of James I of England.

king·ly (king-lee) *adj.* (**king·li·er, king·li·est**) of or like or suitable for a king.

king·pin (king-pin) *n.* 1. a vertical bolt used as a pivot. 2. (in bowling) the head or middle pin. 3. an indispensable person or thing.

king·ship (king-ship) *n.* being a king, a king's position or reign.

king·size (king-sız) *adj.* (also **king′sized′**) extra large.

Kings·ton (king-stŏn) the capital of Jamaica.

kink (kingk) *n.* 1. a short twist in a wire or rope or hair etc. 2. a mental or moral peculiarity. **kink** *v.* to form or cause to form a kink or kinks.

kin·ka·jou (king-kă-joo) *n.* a carnivorous nocturnal animal of Central and South America, with a tail used for grasping branches etc.

kink·y (king-kee) *adj.* (**kink·i·er, kink·i·est**) 1. full of kinks. 2. (*slang*) bizarre, eccentric, perverted. **kink′i·ness** *n.*

Kin·sha·sa (kin-shah-sah) the capital of Zaire.

kin·ship (kin-ship) *n.* 1. a blood relationship. 2. similarity or alliance in character.

kins·man (kinz-măn) *n.* (*pl.* **-men,** *pr.* -měn) a blood relative, especially a male.

kins·wom·an (kinz-wuum-ăn) *n.* (*pl.* **-wom·en,** *pr.* -wim-in) a female blood relative.

ki·osk (kee-osk) *n.* a light structure in a public place for selling newspapers, refreshments, etc.

Ki·o·wa (kı-ŏ-wă) *n.* (*pl.* **-wa, -was**) 1. a member of a tribe of Plains Indians of the southwestern U.S. 2. the language of this tribe.

kip·per (kip-ĕr) *n.* a kippered herring. **kipper** *v.* to cure (fish) by splitting, cleaning, and drying it in the open air or in smoke.

Kir·ghi·zia (kir-gee-zhǎ) a republic of the U.S.S.R. bordering on China.

kirk (kurk) *n. (Scottish)* a church.

kirsch (keersh) *n.* a colorless brandy made from the juice of cherries.

kis·met (kiz-mit) *n.* destiny, fate.

kiss (kis) *n.* 1. a touch or caress given with the lips. 2. a small candy, especially of chocolate. **kiss** *v.* 1. to touch with the lips in affection or as a greeting or in reverence. 2. (of billiard balls etc.) to touch lightly. □**kiss of death,** an apparently friendly act causing ruin.

kiss·er (kis-ĕr) *n. (slang)* the mouth or face.

kit (kit) *n.* 1. the clothing and personal equipment of a soldier etc. or a traveler. 2. the equipment needed for a particular activity or situation, *a first-aid kit; a shaving kit.* 3. a set of parts sold together to be assembled, *in kit form.* □**the whole kit and caboodle,** *(informal)* everyone and everything, the whole lot.

kitch·en (kich-ĭn) *n.* a room in which meals are prepared. □**kitchen garden,** a garden for growing one's own fruit and vegetables. **kitchen police,** military personnel assigned to help the cooks; this work.

kitch·en·ette (kich-ĕ-net) *n.* a small room or an alcove used as a kitchen.

kitch·en·ware (kich-ĕn-wair) *n.* equipment used in the kitchen.

kite (kit) *n.* 1. a large bird of prey of the hawk family. 2. a toy consisting of a light covered framework, to be flown in a strong wind on the end of a long string. □**go fly a kite,** *(slang)* go away, leave.

kith (kith) *n.* **kith and kin,** kinfolk, one's friends and relatives.

kitsch (kich) *n.* pretentiousness and lack of good taste in art, art of this type.

kit·ten (kit-ĕn) *n.* the young of a cat or certain other small mammals. **kitten** *v.* to give birth to kittens. **kit'ten·ish** *adj.* □**have kittens,** *(slang)* to be very agitated or nervous.

kit·ty¹ (kit-ee) *n. (pl.* **-ties)** a cat, especially a kitten.

kitty² (kit-ee) *n. (pl.* **-ties)** 1. the pool of stakes to be played for in some card games. 2. a fund of money for communal use.

ki·wi (kee-wee) *n. (pl.* **-wis)** 1. a New Zealand bird that does not fly, with a long bill, rudimentary wings, and no tail. 2. *Kiwi, (informal)* a New Zealander.

K.J.V. *abbr.* King James Version.

KKK *abbr.* Ku Klux Klan.

klep·to·ma·ni·a (klep-tŏ-may-ni-ă) *n.* an uncontrollable tendency to steal things, with no desire to use or profit by them.

klep·to·ma·ni·ac (klep-tŏ-may-ni-ak) *n.* a person suffering from kleptomania.

klieg (kleeg) **light** (also **kleig light**) a powerful lamp used in a motion picture studio.

km., km *abbr.* kilometer(s).

kn *abbr.* knot(s).

knack (nak) *n.* 1. the ability to do something skillfully. 2. the habit of doing, *he has a knack for saying the wrong thing.*

knack·wurst = **knockwurst.**

knap·sack (nap-sak) *n.* a bag worn strapped on the back for carrying supplies and gear, used by soldiers on a march or by hikers.

knave (nayv) *n.* 1. *(old use)* a rogue. 2. a jack in a deck of playing cards. **knav'ish** *adj.* **knav'er·y** *n.*

knead (need) *v.* 1. to work (moist flour or clay) by pressing and stretching it with the hands. 2. to make (bread etc.) in this way. 3. to massage with kneading movements. **knead'er** *n.*

knee (nee) *n.* 1. the joint between the thigh and the lower part of the human leg, the corresponding joint in animals. 2. the part of a garment covering this. 3. the upper surface of the thigh of a sitting person, *sit on my knee.* 4. something shaped like a bent knee. **knee** *v.* **(kneed, knee·ing)** to touch or strike with the knee. □**fall on** *or* **to one's knees,** to kneel. **knee breeches,** breeches reaching to or just below the knee. **knee jerk,** an involuntary jerk of the leg when a tendon below the knee is struck.

knee·cap (nee-kap) *n.* the small bone covering the front of the knee joint.

knee-deep (nee-deep) *adj.* of or in sufficient depth to cover a person up to the knees; *knee-deep in work,* deeply occupied.

knee·hole (nee-hohl) *adj.* (of a desk) with space for the knees between pedestals fitted with drawers.

kneel (neel) *v.* **(kneit, kneel·ing)** to take or be in a position where the body is supported on the knees with the lower leg bent back, especially in prayer or reverence. **kneel'er** *n.*

knee-length (nee-lengkth) *adj.* reaching to the knees.

knell (nel) *n.* the sound of a bell tolled solemnly after a death or at a funeral.

knelt (nelt) *see* **kneel.**

knew (noo) *see* **know.**

knick·ers (nik-ĕrz) *n. pl.* (formerly **knick·er·bock·ers,** *pr.* nik-ĕr-bok-ĕrz) men's loose-fitting breeches gathered in at the knee.

knick·knack (nik-nak) *n.* a small ornamental article.

knife (nif) *n. (pl.* **knives,** *pr.* nivz) 1. a cutting instrument or weapon consisting of a sharp blade with a handle. 2. the cutting blade of a machine. **knife** *v.* **(knifed, knif·ing)** to cut or stab with a knife. □**go under the knife,** to have a surgical operation. **knife in the back,** to betray secretly. **on a knife edge,** in a situation involving extreme tension or anxiety about the outcome.

knight (nit) *n.* 1. a man of noble birth and military status in the Middle Ages. 2. *(British)* a man given a certain rank as an honor by the sovereign and addressed as "Sir." 3. a chess piece, usually with the form of a horse's head. **knight** *v.* to confer a knighthood on. **knight'ly** *adv.* □**knight errant,** a medieval knight wandering in search of chivalrous adventures; a person of chivalrous or quixotic spirit.

knight·hood (nit-huud) *n.* the rank of knight.

knish (knish) *n.* a dumpling of flaky dough filled with mashed potato, meat, etc. and baked or fried.

knit (nit) *v.* **(knit·ted,** or **knit, knit·ting)** 1. to make (a garment etc.) from yarn formed into interlocking loops either by long needles held in the hands or on a machine. 2. to form (yarn) into fabric etc. in this way. 3. to make a plain (not purl) stitch in knitting. 4. to unite or grow together, *the broken bones were knitting well; a well-knit frame,* compact bodily structure. **knit** *n.* a garment or fabric made by knitting. **knit'ter** *n.* □**double knit,** *see* **double. knit one's brow,** to frown.

knit·ting (nit-ing) *n.* work in the process of being knitted. □**knitting needle,** one of the long nee-

dles used for knitting by hand. **tend to one's knitting,** (*informal*) to look after one's responsibilities.
knit·wear (nit-wair) *n.* knitted garments.
knob (nob) *n.* 1. a rounded projecting part, especially one forming the handle of a door or drawer or for controlling a radio, television, etc. **knobbed** *adj.*
knob·by (nob-ee) *adj.* (**-bi·er, -bi·est**) with many small projecting lumps.
knock (nok) *v.* 1. to strike with an audible sharp blow. 2. to make a noise by striking something, as at a door to summon a person or gain admittance. 3. (of an engine) to make a thumping or rattling noise while running. 4. to drive or make by knocking, *knocked a hole in it.* 5. (*slang*) to say critical or insulting things about, *stop knocking the schools.* **knock** *n.* 1. an act or sound of knocking. 2. a sharp blow. 3. (in an engine) knocking. □**knock around** *or* **about,** to treat roughly; to wander aimlessly. **knock down,** to hit (a person) with one's fists until he falls; to dispose of (an article) at auction; to take apart (furniture, displays, etc.); (*slang*) to earn (money), *he knocks down $300 a week.* **knock knees,** an abnormal inward curving of the legs at the knees. **knock off,** (*informal*) to cease work; to deduct (an amount) from a price; (*informal*) to complete (a specified amount of work), *he knocked off a day's work in four hours;* (*slang*) to steal; (*slang*) to kill (a person). **knock out,** to make unconscious by hitting on the head; to disable (a boxer) in this way so that he is unable to rise or continue in a specified time; (*informal*) to exhaust or disable, *he felt knocked out after work.* **knock the spots off,** to be easily superior to.
knock·er (nok-ĕr) *n.* 1. a person who knocks. 2. a hinged metal flap for rapping against a door to summon a person.
knock·out (nok-owt) *n.* 1. a blow that knocks a boxer out. 2. a boxing match that ends when one contestant is knocked out. 3. (*slang*) an outstanding or irresistible person or thing. □**knockout drops,** liquid added to a drink to cause unconsciousness when swallowed.
knock·wurst (nok-wurst) *n.* a short thick seasoned sausage.
knoll (nohl) *n.* a small hill, a mound.
knot (not) *n.* 1. an intertwining of one or more pieces of thread or rope etc. to fasten them together. 2. a tangle. 3. a hard mass in something, especially on a tree trunk where a branch joins it. 4. a round cross-grained spot in timber where a branch joined. 5. a cluster of people or things. 6. a unit of speed used by ships at sea and by aircraft, = one nautical mile per hour. **knot** *v.* (**knot·ted, knot·ting**) 1. to tie or fasten with a knot; *my stomach knotted up,* gave me severe pain. 2. to entangle. 3. (*slang*) to tie the score in a game. □**tie in knots,** (*informal*) to make (a person) baffled or confused. **tie the knot,** (*informal*) to get married.
knot·hole (not-hohl) *n.* a hole in timber formed where a knot has fallen out.
knot·ty (not-ee) *adj.* (**knot·ti·er, knot·ti·est**) 1. full of knots. 2. puzzling, full of problems or difficulties. □**knotty pine,** pine timber used for interior paneling in which the knots are decorative.
knout (nowt) *n.* a flogging whip formerly used in Russia.
know (noh) *v.* (**knew, known, know·ing**) 1. to

have in one's mind or memory as a result of experience or learning or information. 2. to feel certain, *I know I left it here!* 3. to recognize (a person), to have had social contact with, to be familiar with (a place). 4. to recognize with certainty, *knows a bargain when she sees one.* 5. to understand and be able to use (a subject or language or skill), *she knows how to please people; knows better than to do that,* is too wise or well-mannered to do it. □**in the know,** (*informal*) having inside information. **know one's mind,** to know firmly what one wants or intends. **know the ropes,** *see* **rope.**
know·a·ble (noh-ă-bĕl) *adj.* able to be known.
know·how (noh-how) *n.* practical knowledge or skill in a particular activity.
know·ing (noh-ing) *adj.* showing knowledge or awareness, showing that one has inside information. **know'ing·ly** *adv.*
know-it-all (noh-it-awl) *n.* a person who behaves as if he knows everything.
knowl·edge (nol-ij) *n.* 1. knowing. 2. all that a person knows. 3. all that is known, an organized body of information.
knowl·edge·a·ble (nol-i-jă-bĕl) *adj.* well-informed.
knuck·le (nuk-ĕl) *n.* 1. a finger joint. 2. the knob at an animal's joint. **knuckle** *v.* (**knuck·led, knuck·ling**) to strike or press or rub with the knuckles. □**brass knuckles,** a metal device worn over the knuckles to protect them and increase the injury done by a blow. **knuckle down,** to begin to work earnestly. **knuckle under,** to yield, to submit.
knuck·le·bone (nuk-ĕl-bohn) *n.* a bone forming the knuckle.
knuck·le·dus·ter (nuk-ĕl-dus-tĕr) *n.* (*slang*) brass knuckles.
knuck·le·head (nuk-ĕl-hed) *n.* (*informal*) a stupid person. **knuck'le·head·ed** *adj.*
knurl (nurl) *n.* a small projecting knob or ridge to assist in gripping an object. **knurled** *adj.*
K.O., KO (kay-oh) *n.* (*pl.* K.O.'s, KO's) (*slang*) knockout. **K.O.** *v.* (*slang*) to knock out; **K.O.'d, KO'd,** knocked out.
ko·a·la (koh-ah-lă) *n.* (also **koala bear**) an Australian tree-climbing animal with thick gray fur and large ears, feeding on the leaves of the eucalyptus tree.
K. of C. *abbr.* Knights of Columbus.
kohl·ra·bi (kohl-rah-bee) *n.* (*pl.* **-bies**) a plant with an edible turnip-shaped stem.
ko·la (koh-lă) **nut** the seed of a West African tree, used as a condiment and in making soft drinks.
ko·lin·sky (kŏ-lin-skee) *n.* (*pl.* **-skies,** *pr.* **-skeez**) the fur of a Siberian mink.
kook (kook) *n.* (*slang*) a foolish or eccentric person. **kook'y** *adj.* (**kook·i·er, kook·i·est**) **kook'i·ness** *n.*
kook·a·bur·ra (kuuk-ă-bur-ă) *n.* an Australian bird of the kingfisher family whose cry sounds like wild laughter.
ko·peck, ko·pek (koh-pek) *n.* a Russian coin, one-hundredth part of a ruble.
Ko·ran (koh-rahn) *n.* the sacred book of the Muslims containing the revelations of Muhammad, written in Arabic.
Ko·re·a (kŏ-ree-ă) a country in Asia, divided between the Republic of Korea (= South Korea) and the Democratic People's Republic of Korea (= North Korea). **Ko·re'an** *adj.* & *n.*

ko·sher (koh-shĕr) *adj.* (of food etc.) conforming to the requirements of Jewish dietary laws.

ko·to (koh-toh) *n.* a Japanese musical instrument with thirteen long silk strings.

kow·tow (kow-tow, kow-tow) *v.* to behave with exaggerated respect toward a person. ▷The *kowtow* was a former Chinese custom of touching the ground with one's forehead as a sign of worship or submission.

KP *abbr.* kitchen police.

k.p.h. kph, K.P.H., KPH *abbr.* kilometer(s) per hour.

Kr *symbol* krypton.

kraal (krahl) *n.* (in South Africa) 1. a village of huts enclosed by a fence. 2. an enclosure for cattle or sheep.

kraut (krowt) *n.* (informal) sauerkraut.

krem·lin (krem-lin) *n.* 1. a citadel within a Russian town, especially that of Moscow. 2. *the Kremlin,* the government of the U.S.S.R.

Krem·lin·ol·o·gist (krem-li-nol-ŏ-jist) *n.* an expert in the study of the government and policies of the Soviet Union. **Krem·lin·ol'o·gy** *n.*

Krish·na (krish-nă) *n.* an incarnation of Vishnu, a popular Hindu diety.

kro·na (kroh-nă) *n.* the unit of money in Sweden (*pl.* **-nor,** *pr.* -nŏr) and Iceland (*pl.* **-nur,** *pr.* -nŭr).

kro·ne (kroh-nĕ) *n.* (*pl.* **-ner,** *pr.* -nĕr) the unit of money in Denmark and Norway.

Kru·ger·rand (kroo-gĕr-rand) *n.* a South African one-ounce gold coin bearing a portrait of President Kruger (1825–1904).

kryp·ton (krip-ton) *n.* a gaseous chemical element.

KS *abbr.* Kansas.

kt. *abbr.* 1. karat. 2. kiloton. 3. knot.

Kt. *abbr.* 1. Knight. 2. (in chess) knight.

Kua·la Lum·pur (kwah-lă luum-poor) the capital of Malaysia.

ku·dos (koo-dohz) *n.* (informal) honor and glory. ▷This word is always singular: *all the kudos she received has made her conceited.*

kud·zu (kuud-zoo) *n.* a rapid-growing Chinese and Japanese vine, now grown in the U.S. primarily to prevent soil erosion.

Ku Klux Klan (koo kluks klan) a secret society hostile to blacks, originally formed in the southern states after the Civil War.

ku·lak (koo-lahk) *n.* (in the U.S.S.R.) a peasant proprietor working for his own profit.

küm·mel (kim-ĕl) *n.* a sweet liqueur flavored with caraway seeds.

kum·quat (kum-kwot) *n.* a plum-sized fruit like an orange with a sweet rind and acid pulp.

kung fu (kung foo) a Chinese form of unarmed combat, similar to karate.

Kurd (kurd) *n.* a member of a pastoral people of Kurdistan, a mountainous region of east Turkey, north Iraq, and northwest Iran. **Kurd'ish** *adj. & n.*

Ku·wait (koo-wayt) 1. a country in the Middle East, bordering on the Persian Gulf. 2. its capital city. **Ku·wai·ti** (koo-way-tee) *adj. & n.* (*pl.* **-tis**).

kv, kV *abbr.* kilovolt(s).

kw, kW *abbr.* kilowatt(s).

kwash·i·or·kor (kwash-ee-or-kor) *n.* a tropical disease of children, caused by lack of protein in the diet.

kwh, kWh *abbr.* kilowatt-hour(s).

Ky., KY *abbr.* Kentucky.

ky·pho·sis (kı-foh-sis) *n.* an abnormal curvature of the spine, convex backward.

L

L, l (el) (*pl.* **Ls, L's, l's**) 1. the twelfth letter of the English alphabet. 2. Roman numeral symbol for 50.
l *abbr.* 1. lake. 2. left. 3. line 4. liter(s).
L (el) *n.* something shaped like the letter L.
L *abbr.* large.
l. *abbr.* 1. left. 2. length. 3. line. 4. lire. 5. liter(s).
L. *abbr.* 1. lake. 2. Latin. 3. left.
la (lah) *n.* a name for the sixth note of a scale in music.
La *symbol* lanthanum.
LA *abbr.* Louisiana.
La. *abbr.* Louisiana.
L.A. *abbr.* 1. Law Agent. 2. Los Angeles.
lab (lab) *n.* *(informal)* laboratory.
Lab. *abbr.* Labrador.
la·bel (lay-bĕl) *n.* 1. a slip of paper or cloth or metal etc. fixed on or beside an object and showing its nature, owner, name, destination, or other information about it. 2. a descriptive word or phrase classifying people etc. **label** *v.* **(la·beled, la·bel·ing)** 1. to attach a label to. 2. to describe or classify, *he was labeled a troublemaker.*
la·bi·a *see* **labium.**
la·bi·al (lay-bi-ăl) *adj.* of the lips.
la·bile (lay-bıl) *adj.* unstable, liable to displacement or change.
la·bi·um (lay-bi-ŭm) *n.* (*pl.* **la·bi·a,** *pr.* lay-bi-ă) a lip of the female genitals. □**labia ma·jo·ra** (mă-johr-ă), **mi·no·ra** (mı̆-nohr-ă), the fleshy outer folds, the inner folds.
la·bor (lay-bŏr) *n.* 1. physical or mental work, exertion. 2. a task; *a labor of Hercules,* a herculean task. 3. the pains or contractions of the uterus at childbirth. 4. workers, working people distinguished from management or considered as a political force. **labor** *v.* 1. to exert oneself, to work hard. 2. to have to make a great effort, to operate or progress only with difficulty, *the engine was laboring.* 3. to treat at great length or in excessive detail, *I will not labor the point.* □**Labor Day,** a public holiday in honor of working people, celebrated in the U.S. and Canada on the first Monday of September; a similar holiday in other countries, often celebrated on May 1. **labor union,** an organized association of employees of an industry or group of allied industries formed to protect and promote their common interests.
la·bored (lay-bŏrd) *adj.* showing signs of great effort, not spontaneous, forced.
la·bor·er (lay-bŏ-rĕr) *n.* a person employed to do unskilled manual work.
la·bor·in·ten·sive (lay-bŏr-in-ten-sı̆v) *adj.* (of an industry) needing to employ many people.
la·bo·ri·ous (lă-bohr-i-ŭs) *adj.* 1. needing much effort or perseverance. 2. hardworking. **la·bo'ri·ous·ly** *adv.*

la·bor·sav·ing (lay-bŏr-say-ving) *adj.* designed to reduce the amount of work or effort needed.
Lab·ra·dor (lab-ră-dor) a region of Canada.
Labrador *n.* (also **Labrador retriever**) a retriever dog of a breed with a smooth black or golden coat.
lab·ra·dor·ite (lab-ră-daw-rıt) *n.* a feldspar with several changing colors.
la·bur·num (lă-bur-nŭm) *n.* an ornamental tree with hanging clusters of yellow flowers.
lab·y·rinth (lab-ı̆-rinth) *n.* a complicated network of paths through which it is difficult to find one's way. **lab·y·rin·thine** (lab-ı̆-rin-thin) *adj.*
lac·co·lith (lak-ŏ-lith) *n.* a dome-shaped intrusion of igneous rock from beneath sedimentary rock.
lace (lays) *n.* 1. fabric or trimming made in an ornamental openwork design. 2. a cord or narrow leather strip threaded through holes or hooks for pulling opposite edges together and securing them. **lace** *v.* **(laced, lac·ing)** 1. to fasten with a lace or laces. 2. to pass (a cord) through, to intertwine. 3. to flavor or fortify (a drink) with liquor.
lac·er·ate (las-ĕ-rayt) *v.* **(lac·er·at·ed, lac·er·at·ing)** 1. to injure (flesh) by tearing. 2. to wound (feelings). **lac·er·a·tion** (las-ĕ-ray-shŏn) *n.*
lace·wing (lays-wing) *n.* an insect having delicately veined gauzelike wings.
lach·ry·mal (lak-rı̆-măl) *adj.* 1. of tears, secreting tears. 2. lacrimal (definition 1).
lach·ry·mose (lak-rı̆-mohs) *adj.* tearful.
lack (lak) *n.* the state or fact of not having something. **lack** *v.* to be without or not have (a thing) when it is needed; *they lack for nothing,* have plenty of everything.
lack·a·dai·si·cal (lak-ă-day-zi-kăl) *adj.* lacking vigor or determination, unenthusiastic. **lack·a·dai'si·cal·ly** *adv.*
lack·ey (lak-ee) *n.* (*pl.* **-eys**) 1. a person's servile follower. 2. a footman, a servant.
lack·ing (lak-ing) *adj.* 1. undesirably absent, *money was lacking.* 2. deficient, *he is lacking in courage.*
lack·lus·ter (lak-lus-tĕr) *adj.* (of the eye etc.) not bright, dull.
la·con·ic (lă-kon-ik) *adj.* terse, not talkative. **la·con'i·cal·ly** *adv.*
lac·quer (lak-ĕr) *n.* a hard glossy varnish. **lacquer** *v.* to coat with lacquer.
lac·ri·mal (lak-rı̆-măl) *adj.* 1. of the glands that produce tears. 2. lachrymal.
lac·ri·ma·tion (lak-rı̆-may-shŏn) *n.* a flow of tears.
la·crosse (lă-kraws) *n.* a game resembling hockey but with players using a netted crook (a *crosse*) to catch or carry or throw the ball.
lac·tate (lak-tayt) *v.* **(lac·tat·ed, lac·tat·ing)** to secrete milk.

lac·ta·tion (lak-tay-shŏn) *n.* the secreting of milk in breasts or udder, the period during which this occurs.

lac·tic (lak-tik) *adj.* of milk. □**lactic acid**, a colorless liquid formed in sour milk.

lac·tose (lak-tohs) *n.* sugar present in milk, less sweet than sucrose.

la·cu·na (lǎ-kyoo-nǎ) *n.* (*pl.* **-nae**, *pr.* **-nee**, **-nas**) a gap, a section missing from a book or argument etc.

lac·y (lay-see) *adj.* (**lac·i·er, lac·i·est**) like lace.

lad (lad) *n.* 1. a boy, a young fellow. 2. (*informal*) a fellow.

lad·der (lad-ĕr) *n.* 1. a set of crossbars (*rungs*) between two uprights of wood etc., used as a means of climbing up or down something. 2. a means or series of stages by which a person may advance in his career etc., *the political ladder.*

lad·die (lad-ee) *n.* a lad.

lad·en (lay-dĕn) *adj.* loaded with a cargo or burden.

la-di-da (lah-dee-dah) *adj.* (*informal*) affected.

lad·ing (lay-ding) *n.* cargo; *bill of lading* (*see* **bill**[1]).

la·dle (lay-dĕl) *n.* 1. a large spoon with a cup-shaped bowl and a long handle, for transferring liquids. 2. a vessel for transporting molten metal in a foundry. **ladle** *v.* (**la·dled, la·dling**) to transfer with a ladle. **la′dler** *n.*

la·dy (lay-dee) *n.* (*pl.* **-dies**) 1. a woman of good social position, a woman of polite and kindly behavior. 2. (in polite use) a woman. 3. (*old use*) a wife, *the colonel's lady.* 4. *Lady,* a title used for the wives or daughters of certain noblemen. 5. a woman with authority over a household etc., *the lady of the house.* 6. a woman to whom a man is chivalrously devoted. □**ladies' man,** a man who is fond of female society. **ladies' room,** a women's public lavatory. **lady beetle,** a ladybug. **lady of the evening,** a prostitute. **lady's slipper,** a wild or garden flower of the orchid family, with a bloom shaped like a slipper or pouch.

la·dy·bird (lay-dee-burd) *n.* a ladybug.

la·dy·bug (lay-dee-bug) *n.* a small flying beetle, usually reddish brown with black spots.

la·dy·fin·ger (lay-dee-fing-gĕr) *n.* a finger-shaped sponge cake.

la·dy-in-wait·ing (lay-dee-in-way-ting) *n.* (*pl.* **la·dies-in-wait·ing**) a lady attending a queen or princess.

la·dy·like (lay-dee-lɪk) *adj.* polite and suitable for a lady, *ladylike manners.*

la·dy·love (lay-dee-luv) *n.* a man's sweetheart.

la·dy·ship (lay-dee-ship) *n.* a title used in speaking to or about a woman of the rank of Lady, *Your Ladyship.*

la·e·trile (lay-ĕ-tril) *n.* a drug obtained from apricot or peach pits and claimed to cure cancer.

lag (lag) *v.* (**lagged, lag·ging**) to go too slowly, to fail to keep up with others. **lag** *n.* lagging, a delay.

la·ger (lah-gĕr) *n.* a kind of light beer.

lag·gard (lag-ărd) *n.* a person who lags behind. **laggard** *adj.* going too slowly. **lag′gard·ly** *adj. & adv.* **lag′gard·ness** *n.*

la·gniappe (lan-yap) *n.* a thing given as a bonus or gratuity. ▷Originally Louisiana French, derived from Spanish *la ñapa.*

la·goon (lǎ-goon) *n.* 1. a shallow saltwater lake separated from the sea by a sandbank or coral reef etc. 2. a small freshwater lake near a larger lake or river.

La·gos (lah-gohs, lay-) the capital of Nigeria.

laid (layd) *see* **lay**[3].

lain (layn) *see* **lie**[2].

lair (lair) *n.* 1. a sheltered place where a wild animal regularly sleeps or rests. 2. a person's hiding place.

laird (laird) *n.* (*Scottish*) a landowner.

lais·sez faire (les-ay fair) the policy of noninterference, especially the policy of government noninterference in economic affairs or business. ▷French, = let act.

la·i·ty (lay-i-tee) *n.* 1. the people of a church who are not clergy. 2. people not initiated into a particular discipline, *sociologists find it difficult to communicate with the laity.*

lake (layk) *n.* a large body of water entirely surrounded by land.

lal·ly·gag (lol-ee-gag) *v.* (**lal·ly·gagged, lal·ly·gag·ging**) (*informal*) to do nothing or pass time with aimless activity.

lam[1] (lam) *v.* (**lammed, lam·ming**) (*slang*) to hit hard, to thrash; *lammed into him,* attacked him physically or verbally.

lam[2] *v.* (**lammed, lam·ming**) (*slang*) to depart abruptly. □**on the lam,** (*slang*) fleeing from the police.

lam. *abbr.* laminated.

Lam. *abbr.* Lamentations.

la·ma (lah-mǎ) *n.* a priest in Lamaism. ▷Do not confuse *lama* with *llama.*

La·ma·ism (lah-mǎ-iz-ĕm) *n.* the form of Buddhism found in Tibet and Mongolia.

la·ma·ser·y (lah-mǎ-ser-ee) *n.* (*pl.* **-ser·ies**) a monastery of lamas.

La·maze (lǎ-mahz) **method** a method of preparing for natural childbirth in which the father helps the mother to relax and control her breathing.

lamb (lam) *n.* 1. a young sheep. 2. its flesh as food. 3. (*informal*) a gentle or endearing person. **lamb** *v.* to give birth to a lamb. □**Lamb of God,** in Christianity, a term applied to Jesus.

lam·baste (lam-bast) or **lam·bast** (lam-bayst) *v.* (**lam·bast·ed, lam·bast·ing**) (*informal*) to thrash or beat or reprimand severely.

lamb·da (lam-dǎ) *n.* the eleventh letter of the Greek alphabet (Λ λ).

lam·bent (lam-bĕnt) *adj.* 1. (of flame or light) playing on a surface without burning it, with soft radiance. 2. (of eyes, sky, etc.) softly radiant. 3. (of wit etc.) lightly brilliant. **lam′bent·ly** *adv.* **lam·ben·cy** (lam-bĕn-see) *n.*

lamb·skin (lam-skin) *n.* the skin of a lamb, either with its wool on (used in making clothing etc.) or as leather.

lambs·wool (lamz-wuul) *n.* soft fine wool used in making machine-knitted garments.

lame (laym) *adj.* 1. unable to walk normally because of an injury or defect, especially in a foot or leg. 2. (of an excuse or argument) weak, unconvincing. **lame** *v.* (**lamed, lam·ing**) to make lame. **lame′ly** *adv.* **lame′ness** *n.* □**lame duck,** an elected official after another has been elected to replace him and before the new person has taken office; any official in the last days of his term of office.

la·mé (la-may) *n.* a fabric in which gold or silver thread is interwoven.

lame·brain (laym-brayn) *n.* (*slang*) a stupid person.

la·ment (lǎ-ment) *n.* 1. a passionate expression of grief. 2. a song or poem expressing grief. **lament** *v.* to feel or express great sorrow or regret.

lam·en·ta·ble (lam-ĕn-tă-bĕl) *adj.* regrettable, deplorable. **lam'en·ta·bly** *adv.*

lam·en·ta·tion (lam-ĕn-tay-shŏn) *n.* 1. lamenting. 2. a lament, an expression of grief. 3. *Lamentations,* a poetical book of the Old Testament traditionally ascribed to Jeremiah.

la·ment·ed (lă-men-tid) *adj.* mourned for, *your late lamented father.*

la·mi·a (lay-mi-ă) *n.* an evil mythological being, half woman and half serpent.

lam·i·na (lam-ĭ-nă) *n.* (*pl.* **-nae,** *pr.* -nee, **-nas**) a thin scale, plate, layer, or flake of metal, bone, membrane, stratified rock, vegetable tissue, etc. **lam'i·nar** *adj.* **lam'i·nal** *adj.*

lam·i·nate (lam-ĭ-nayt) *v.* (**lam·i·nat·ed, lam·i·nat·ing**) 1. to form in or to make into thin layers. 2. to split into layers. **laminate** (lam-ĭ-nayt, -nit) *n.* a laminated material. **laminate** (lam-ĭ-nit) *adj.* having laminae. **lam·i·na·tion** (lam-ĭ-nay-shŏn) *n.*

lam·i·nat·ed (lam-ĭ-nay-tid) *adj.* made of layers joined one upon the other, *laminated plastic.*

lamp (lamp) *n.* 1. a device for giving light, either by the use of electricity or gas or by burning oil or alcohol. 2. a light bulb. 3. an electrical device producing radiation, *an infrared lamp.*

lamp·black (lamp-blak) *n.* a pigment made from soot.

lamp·light·er (lamp-lĭ-tĕr) *n.* 1. a person who lit gas street lamps. 2. a thin strip of wood or folded or twisted paper for lighting lamps.

lam·poon (lam-poon) *n.* a piece of writing that attacks a person with ridicule. **lampoon** *v.* to ridicule in a lampoon.

lamp·post (lamp-pohst) *n.* a tall post supporting a street light.

lam·prey (lam-pree) *n.* (*pl.* **-preys**) a small eellike water animal with a round mouth used as a sucker for attaching itself to things.

lamp·shade (lamp-shayd) *n.* a shade placed over a lamp to soften or screen its light.

la·nai (lă-nɪ) *n.* (*pl.* **-nais**) a veranda furnished as an outdoor living room.

lance (lans) *n.* a weapon used for spearing fish etc., consisting of a long wooden shaft with a pointed steel head, resembling that used by mounted knights or cavalry in the Middle Ages. **lance** *v.* (**lanced, lanc·ing**) to prick or cut open a wound, boil, etc. □**lance corporal,** an enlisted person in the U.S. Marine Corps ranking below a corporal and above a private first class.

lan·cer (lan-sĕr) *n.* a soldier of a certain cavalry regiment formerly armed with lances.

lan·cet (lan-sit) *n.* a pointed two-edged knife used by surgeons.

land (land) *n.* 1. the solid part of Earth's surface, the part not covered by water or sea. 2. the ground or soil as used for farming etc. 3. an expanse of country, *forest land.* 4. a country or state or nation, *land of the free and the brave; in the land of the living,* alive. 5. property consisting of land. **land** *v.* 1. to arrive or put on land from a ship. 2. to bring (an aircraft or its passengers etc.) down to the ground, to come down in this way. 3. to alight after a jump or fall. 4. to bring (a fish) to land, to win (a prize) or obtain (a position etc.), *landed an excellent job.* 5. to arrive or cause to arrive at a certain place or stage or position, *landed in jail; landed us all in a mess.* 6. to strike with a blow, *landed him one in the eye.* 7. to present with a problem etc., *landed us with the*

job of sorting it out. **land'less** *adj.* □**land bank,** a bank that supplies capital or credit for real estate transactions. **land grant,** a tract of public land appropriated by the government for building a highway, a state college, etc., *land-grant college.* **land mine,** an explosive mine laid in or on the ground. **land office,** a government office for transacting business relating to the sale and transfer of public lands. **land-office business,** (*informal*) a very active and flourishing business.

lan·dau (lan-dow) *n.* (*old use*) 1. a four-wheeled carriage having a two-part folding top. 2. an automobile with a top whose rear section was collapsible.

land·ed (lan-did) *adj.* 1. owning land, *landed gentry.* 2. consisting of land, *landed estates.*

land·er (lan-dĕr) *n.* a space vehicle built for landing on a celestial body.

land·fall (land-fawl) *n.* approach to land after a journey by sea or air.

land·fill (land-fil) *n.* a lowland built up with layers of trash and garbage alternating with layers of earth.

land·form (land-form) *n.* a natural feature of the surface of Earth.

land·hold·er (land-hohl-dĕr) *n.* an owner or tenant of land. **land'hold·ing** *adj. & n.*

land·ing (lan-ding) *n.* 1. the process of coming or bringing something to land or of alighting after a jump etc. 2. a place where people and goods may be landed from a boat etc. 3. a level area between flights or at the top of a flight of stairs. □**landing craft,** a naval vessel designed for putting ashore troops and equipment. **landing field,** a flat, smooth area where planes land and take off. **landing gear,** the undercarriage of an aircraft. **landing strip,** an airstrip.

land·la·dy (land-lay-dee) *n. fem.* (*pl.* **-dies**) the owner of an apartment building or other rental property.

land·locked (land-lokt) *adj.* almost or entirely surrounded by land.

land·lord (land-lord) *n.* the owner of an apartment building or other rental property.

land·lub·ber (land-lub-ĕr) *n.* (*informal*) a person who is not accustomed to the sea and seamanship.

land·mark (land-mahrk) *n.* 1. a conspicuous and easily recognized feature of a landscape. 2. an event that marks a stage or change in the history of something. 3. an historic building or location.

land·mass (land-mas) *n.* a large area of Earth's surface, such as a continent.

land·own·er (land-oh-nĕr) *n.* a person who owns land.

land-poor (land-poor) *adj.* needing money while owning unprofitable land.

land·scape (land-skayp) *n.* 1. the scenery of an inland area. 2. a picture of this. **landscape** *v.* (**land·scaped, land·scap·ing**) to lay out (an area) attractively, with natural features. □**landscape artist,** a painter or other artist whose specialty is landscapes. **landscape gardening,** the arrangement and planting of trees, shrubs, grass, etc. on a tract of land.

land·slide (land-slɪd) *n.* 1. the sliding down of a mass of land on a slope or mountain. 2. an overwhelming majority of votes for one side in an election.

lands·man[1] (landz-măn) *n.* (*pl.* **-men,** *pr.* -mĕn) a person who is not a sailor.

lands·man[2] (lahnts-măn) *n.* (*pl.* **-men,** *pr.*-mĕn) a person from the same town or country, a compatriot. ▷ Yiddish.

land·ward (land-wărd) *adj. & adv.* toward the land.

lane (layn) *n.* 1. a narrow road or track. 2. a narrow street or alley between buildings. 3. a strip of road for a single line of traffic, a strip of track or water for a runner or rower or swimmer in a race. 4. a route prescribed for or regularly followed by ships or aircraft, *shipping lanes.*

lang. *abbr.* language.

lan·guage (lang-gwij) *n.* 1. words and their use. 2. a system of words used in one or more countries. 3. a system of signs or symbols used for conveying information or in computer programs. 4. a particular style of wording. 5. the vocabulary of a particular group of people, *medical language.* ☐**language laboratory,** a room equipped with tape recorders etc. for learning a language by repeated practice.

lan·guid (lang-gwid) *adj.* lacking vigor or vitality. **lan′guid·ly** *adv.* **lan′guid·ness** *n.*

lan·guish (lang-gwish) *v.* 1. to lose or lack vitality. 2. to live under miserable conditions, to be neglected.

lan·guish·ing (lang-gwi-shing) *adj.* putting on a languid look in an attempt to win sympathy or affection.

lan·guor (lang-gŏr) *n.* 1. tiredness, listlessness, lack of vitality. 2. a languishing expression. 3. oppressive stillness of the air. **lan′guor·ous** *adj.* **lan′guor·ous·ly** *adv.*

lank (langk) *adj.* 1. tall and lean. 2. (of plants) long and limp, (of hair) straight and limp.

lank·y (lang-kee) *adj.* **(lank·i·er, lank·i·est)** ungracefully lean and long or tall. **lank′i·ness** *n.*

lan·o·lin (lan-ŏ-lin) *n.* fat extracted from sheep's wool and used as a basis for ointments.

Lan·sing (lan-sing) the capital of Michigan.

lan·ta·na (lan-tah-nă) *n.* a tropical shrublike plant with bright fragrant flowers.

lan·tern (lan-těrn) *n.* a transparent case for holding a light and shielding it against wind etc. outdoors.

lan·tern-jawed (lan-těrn-jawd) *adj.* having long thin jaws so that the face has a hollow look.

lan·tha·num (lan-thă-nŭm) *n.* a soft silvery metallic chemical element.

lan·yard (lan-yärd) *n.* 1. a short rope or line used on a ship to fasten something or secure it. 2. a cord worn around the neck or on the shoulder, to which a knife or whistle etc. may be attached.

La·os (lah-ohs) a country in southeast Asia. **La·o·tian** (lay-oh-shăn) *adj. & n.*

lap¹ (lap) *n.* 1. the flat area formed by the upper part of the thighs of a seated person. 2. the part of a dress etc. covering this. ☐**in a person's lap,** as his responsibility; *in the lap of the gods,* for fate to decide. **in the lap of luxury,** in great luxury. **lap robe,** a heavy blanket or fur robe used to keep the lap and legs warm, especially when sitting outdoors or while traveling.

lap² (lap) *n.* 1. an overlapping part, the amount of overlap. 2. a single circuit of something such as a racecourse. 3. one section of a journey, *the last lap.* **lap** *v.* **(lapped, lap·ping)** 1. to fold or wrap around. 2. to overlap. 3. to be one or more laps ahead of (another competitor) in a race. ☐**victory lap,** a ceremonial circuit of a racetrack or sports field etc. by the winner(s).

lap³ *v.* **(lapped, lap·ping)** 1. to take up (liquid) by movements of the tongue, as a cat does. 2.

to flow with ripples making a gentle splashing sound, *waves lapped the shore* or *against the shore.*

lap *n.* 1. the act of lapping, the amount taken up by it. 2. the sound of small waves on a beach. ☐**lap up,** to take in eagerly, *she lapped up art history.*

La Paz (lă pahz) the capital of Bolivia.

lap·board (lap-bohrd) *n.* a thin smooth board held on or above the lap and used as a table or desk.

lap·dog (lap-dawg) *n.* a small pet dog.

la·pel (lă-pel) *n.* a flap at the edge of each front of a coat etc., folded back to lie against its outer surface.

lap·i·dar·y (lap-i-der-ee) *adj.* of stones, engraved on stone.

lap·in (lap-in) *n.* rabbit fur, trimmed and dyed to look like more expensive skins.

lap·is laz·u·li (lap-is laz-uu-lee) a bright blue semiprecious stone.

Lap·land (lap-land) a region at the north of Scandinavia. **Lap′land·er** *n.* a native or inhabitant of Lapland.

Lapp (lap) *n.* 1. a Laplander. 2. the language of Lapland.

lapse (laps) *n.* 1. a slight error, especially one caused by forgetfulness or weakness or inattention. 2. backsliding, a decline into an inferior state. 3. the passage of a period of time, *after a lapse of six months.* 4. the termination of a privilege or legal right through disuse. **lapse** *v.* **(lapsed, laps·ing)** 1. to fail to maintain one's position or standard. 2. (of rights and privileges) to be lost or no longer valid because not used or claimed or renewed.

lap·wing (lap-wing) *n.* an Old World bird of the plover family.

lar·board (lahr-bohrd) *n. (old use)* = **port³.**

lar·ce·ny (lahr-sĕ-nee) *n.* (*pl.* **-nies**) theft of personal goods. **lar′ce·nous** *adj.*

larch (lahrch) *n.* a tall cone-bearing deciduous tree of the pine family.

lard (lahrd) *n.* a white greasy substance prepared from pig fat and used in cooking. **lard** *v.* 1. to place strips of fat bacon in or on (meat) before cooking, in order to prevent it from becoming dry while roasting. 2. to interlard.

lard·er (lahr-děr) *n.* a room or cupboard for storing food.

large (lahrj) *adj.* 1. of considerable size or extent. 2. of the larger kind, *the large intestine.* **large** *adv.* in a large way, on a large scale, *bulk* or *loom large.* ☐**at large,** free to roam about, not in confinement; in a general way, at random; as a whole, in general, *is popular with the country at large.*

large-heart·ed (lahrj-hahr-tid) *adj.* kindly.

large·ly (lahrj-lee) *adv.* to a great extent, *his success was largely due to luck.*

large-scale (lahrj-skayl) *adj.* 1. drawn to a large scale so that many details can be shown, *a large-scale map.* 2. extensive, involving large quantities etc., *large-scale operations.*

lar·gess, lar·gesse (lahr-zhes, -jes) *n.* money or gifts generously given.

lar·go (lahr-goh) *adj. & adv.* (of music) in slow time and dignified style.

lar·i·at (lar-i-ăt) *n.* a lasso, a rope used to catch or tether a horse etc.

lark¹ (lahrk) *n.* any of several small sandy-brown birds, especially the skylark.

lark² *n.* 1. a playful adventurous action. 2. an amusing incident. **lark** v. to play about lightheartedly.

lark·spur (lahrk-spur) n. a plant with spur-shaped blue or pink flowers.

lar·rup (lar-ŭp) v. (**lar·rupped, lar·rup·ping**) (informal) to thrash.

lar·va (lahr-vă) n. (pl. **-vae**, pr. -vee) an insect in the first stage of its life after coming out of the egg. **lar'val** adj.

lar·yn·gi·tis (lar-in-jɪ-tis) n. inflammation of the larynx.

lar·ynx (lar-ingks) n. (pl. **la·ryn·ges**, pr. lă-rin-jeez, **lar·ynx·es**) the part of the throat containing the vocal cords.

la·sa·gna (lă-zahn-yă) n. 1. pasta formed into ribbonlike strips. 2. a dish in which these are baked, usually with tomato sauce, cheese, and ground meat.

las·car (las-kăr) n. a seaman from the countries southeast of India.

las·civ·i·ous (lă-siv-i-ŭs) adj. lustful. **las·civ'i·ous·ly** adv. **las·civ'i·ous·ness** n.

la·ser (lay-zĕr) n. a device that generates an intense and highly concentrated beam of light, laser beams. ▷From light amplification by stimulated emission of radiation.

lash (lash) v. 1. to move in a whiplike movement, lashed its tail. 2. to strike with a whip, to beat or strike violently, rain lashed against the windows. 3. to attack violently in words. 4. to fasten or secure with cord etc., lashed them together. **lash** n. 1. a stroke with a whip etc. 2. the flexible part of a whip. 3. an eyelash. □**lash out**, to attack with blows or words.

lass (lass) n. (also **las·sie**, pr. las-ee) a girl, a young woman.

las·si·tude (las-i-tood) n. tiredness, listlessness.

las·so (las-oh) n. (pl. **-sos, -soes**) a rope with a running noose, used for catching cattle. **lasso** v. (**las·soed, las·so·ing**) to catch with a lasso.

last¹ (last) n. a block of wood or metal shaped like a foot, used in making and repairing shoes. □**to stick to one's last**, to stay with the work for which one is best fitted.

last² adj. & adv. 1. after all others in position or time, coming at the end. (▷See the note under **latter**.) 2. latest, most recent, most recently; last night, in the night that has just passed. 3. remaining as the only one(s) left, our last hope. 4. least likely or suitable, she is the last person I'd have chosen. **last** n. 1. a person or thing that is last. 2. the last performance of certain actions, breathe or look one's last. 3. the last mention or sight of something, shall never hear the last of it. □**at last** or **at long last**, in the end, after much delay. **last ditch**, a place of final desperate defense. **last hurrah**, a final unsuccessful effort to win in politics. **Last Judgment**, in Christian belief, the day when God will judge all men. **last straw**, a slight addition to one's difficulties that makes them unbearable. **Last Supper**, the meal eaten by Christ and his disciples on the eve of the Crucifixion. **last word**, the final statement in a dispute; a definitive statement; the latest fashion. **on one's** or **its last legs**, near death or the end of usefulness.

last³ v. 1. to continue for a period of time, to endure, the rain lasted all day. 2. to be sufficient for one's needs, enough food to last us for three days. □**last out**, to be strong enough or sufficient to last.

last·ing (las-ting) adj. able to last for a long time.

last·ly (last-lee) adv. in the last place, finally.

last-min·ute (last-min-it) adj. at the latest possible time when an event can be altered or influenced, a last-minute decision.

lat. abbr. latitude.

Lat. abbr. Latin.

lat·a·ki·a (lat-ă-kee-ă) n. a kind of Turkish tobacco chiefly used in mixtures.

latch (lach) n. 1. a small bar fastening a door or gate, lifted from its catch by a lever. 2. a spring lock that catches when the door is closed. **latch** v. to fasten or be fastened with a latch. □**latch on to**, (informal) to cling to; to get possession of; to take in as an idea.

latch·et (lach-it) n. (old use) a thong for fastening a shoe.

latch·key (lach-kee) n. the key of an outer door.

latch·string (lach-string) n. a string fastened to a latch and left hanging outside the door for use in raising the latch.

late (layt) adj. & adv. (**lat·er, lat·est**) 1. after the proper or usual time. 2. flowering or ripening late in the season. 3. far on in the day or night or a period of time or a series etc., in the late 1920s. 4. of recent date or time, the latest news. 5. no longer alive, no longer holding a certain position, the late president. **late'ness** n. □**late in the day**, at a late stage in the proceedings. **of late**, lately.

late·com·er (layt-kum-ĕr) n. a person who arrives late.

late·ly (layt-lee) adv. in recent times, not long ago.

la·tent (lay-tĕnt) adj. existing but not yet active or developed or visible. **la·ten·cy** (lay-tĕn-see) n.

lat·er·al (lat-ĕ-răl) adj. of or at or toward the side(s). **lateral** n. 1. a side part, member, or object, especially a lateral shoot or branch. 2. a short football pass thrown parallel to the goal line or in a direction somewhat backward from the passer. **lat'er·al·ly** adv.

la·tex (lay-teks) n. 1. a milky fluid exuded from the cut surfaces of certain plants, such as the rubber plant. 2. a synthetic product resembling this, used in paints and adhesives.

lath (lath, lath) n. a narrow thin strip of wood, used especially as a support for plaster etc.

lathe (layth) n. a machine for holding and turning pieces of wood or metal etc. against a tool that will shape them.

lath·er (lath-ĕr) n. 1. a froth produced by soap or detergent mixed with water. 2. frothy sweat, especially on horses. **lather** v. 1. to cover with lather. 2. to form a lather. □**in a lather**, (informal) excited or upset.

Lat·in (lat-in) n. the language of the ancient Romans. **Latin** adj. 1. of or in Latin. 2. of the countries or peoples (such as France, Spain, Portugal, Italy) using languages developed from Latin. □**Latin America**, the parts of Central and South America where Spanish or Portuguese is the main language. **Latin American**, a native of Latin America. **Latin Church**, the Roman Catholic Church.

Lat·in·A·mer·i·can (lat-in-ă-mer-i-kăn) adj. of Latin America.

La·ti·no (la-tee-noh) n. (pl. **-nos**) a Latin-American inhabitant of the U.S.

lat·i·tude (lat-i-tood) n. 1. the distance of a place from the equator, measured in degrees. 2. a region, especially with reference to temperature; high latitudes, regions near the North or South Pole; low *latitudes,* near the equator. **3.** freedom from restrictions in actions or opinions.

lat·i·tu·di·nar·i·an (lat-i-too-dǐ-nair-i-ăn) *n.* a person allowing latitude, especially in religion, one who regards the details of particular creeds and forms of worship as unimportant.

la·trine (lă-treen) *n.* a communal toilet, especially one in a camp or barracks etc.

lat·ter (lat-ĕr) *adj.* **1.** mentioned after another; *the latter,* the one mentioned second of two things. (▷When referring to the last of three or more, *the last,* not *the latter,* should be used.) **2.** nearer to the end, *the latter half of the year.*

lat·ter-day (lat-ĕr-day) *adj.* modern, recent. □ **Latter-day Saint,** a Mormon.

lat·ter·ly (lat-ĕr-lee) *adv.* of late, nowadays.

lat·tice (lat-is) *n.* **1.** a framework of crossed laths or bars with spaces between, used as a screen or fence etc. **2.** a structure resembling this. □**lattice window,** one made with a lattice.

lat·tice·work (lat-is-wurk) *n.* a lattice or work constructed of lattices.

Lat·vi·a (lat-vi-ă) a republic in the U.S.S.R., bordering on the Baltic Sea. **Lat′vi·an** *adj.* & *n.*

laud (lawd) *v.* *(formal)* to praise.

laud·a·ble (law-dă-běl) *adj.* praiseworthy, *a laudable donation.* **laud′a·bly** *adv.* ▷Do not confuse *laudable* with *laudatory.*

lau·da·num (law-dă-nŭm) *n.* opium prepared for use as a sedative.

laud·a·to·ry (law-dă-tohr-ee) *adj.* praising, *laudatory words.* ▷Do not confuse *laudatory* with *laudable.*

laugh (laf) *v.* **1.** to make the sounds and movements of the face and body that express lively amusement or amused scorn. **2.** to have these emotions. **3.** to utter or treat with a laugh; *laughed him out of it,* ridiculed him until he stopped a habit etc. **laugh** *n.* **1.** an act or manner of laughing. **2.** *(informal)* an amusing incident. **laugh′ing·ly** *adv.* □ **laugh at,** to make fun of, to ridicule; to look upon with amusement. **laugh in a person's face,** to show one's amused scorn for him openly.

laughing gas, nitrous oxide, which can cause involuntary laughter in a person who inhales it.

laugh it off, to get rid of embarrassment by making a joke about it. **laugh on the other side of one's face,** to change from amusement to dismay. **no laughing matter,** not a fit subject for laughter.

laugh·a·ble (laf-ă-běl) *adj.* causing people to laugh, ridiculous.

laugh·ing·stock (laf-ing-stok) *n.* a person or thing that is ridiculed.

laugh·ter (laf-tĕr) *n.* the action or sound of laughing.

launch[1] (lawnch) *v.* **1.** to send forth by hurling or thrusting, to send on its course, *launch a rocket.* **2.** to cause (a ship) to move or slide from land into the water. **3.** to put into action, *launch an attack* or *a business.* **4.** to enter boldly or freely into a course of action. **launch** *n.* the process of launching a ship or spacecraft. □ **launching pad** *or* **launch pad,** a concrete platform from which spacecraft are launched. **launch out** *or* **forth,** to start on an ambitious enterprise. **launch window,** the period of time during which a spacecraft must be launched to carry out a particular mission.

launch[2] *n.* a large motorboat.

launch·er (lawn-chĕr) *n.* **1.** a device that launches grenades from a rifle. **2.** a structure to hold a rocket during launching, a rocket releasing a satellite into orbit.

laun·der (lawn-dĕr) *v.* **1.** to wash and iron (clothes etc.). **2.** *(slang)* to conceal the source of (money received illegally) by sending it through foreign banks or through a legitimate business. **laun′der·er** *n.* **laun·dress** (lawn-dris) *n. fem.*

Laun·dro·mat (lawn-drŏ-mat) *n.* *(trademark)* an establishment fitted with washing machines to be used by customers for a fee.

laun·dry (lawn-dree) *n.* (*pl.* **-dries**) **1.** a place where clothes etc. are laundered, a business establishment that launders things for customers. **2.** a batch of clothes etc. for washing, these after washing. **laun·dry·man** (lawn-dree-măn) *n.* (*pl.* **-men,** *pr.* -měn) **laun·dry·wom·an** (lawn-dree-wuum-ăn) *n.* (*pl.* **-wom·en,** *pr.* -wim-in) □ **laundry list,** *(informal)* a list of miscellaneous articles.

lau·re·ate (lor-i-it) *n.* a person receiving highest honors; *a Nobel laureate,* a recipient of the Nobel Prize. **laureate** *adj.* □ **poet laureate,** the poet appointed to write poems for state occasions, *Robert Frost was poet laureate of Vermont.*

lau·rel (lor-ěl) *n.* an evergreen shrub with smooth glossy leaves. □ **look to one's laurels,** to beware of losing one's position of superiority. **rest on one's laurels,** to cease to strive for further successes. ▷From the ancient use of a branch or wreath of laurel as a token of victory.

la·va (lah-vă) *n.* flowing molten rock discharged from a volcano, the solid substance formed when this cools.

la·va·bo (lă-vay-boh) *n.* a stone basin used for ritual washing in a monastery.

lav·age (lă-vahzh) *n.* the process of washing out an organ of the body.

lav·a·liere (lav-ă-leer) *n.* a decorative pendant worn on a fine chain around the neck.

lav·a·to·ry (lav-ă-tohr-ee) *n.* (*pl.* **-ries**) a room having one or more toilets and wash basins.

lave (layv) *v.* (**laved, lav·ing**) *(old use)* to wash or bathe.

lav·en·der (lav-ĕn-dĕr) *n.* **1.** a shrub with fragrant purple flowers that are dried and used to scent linen etc. **2.** light purple. □ **lavender water,** a delicate perfume made from lavender.

lav·ish (lav-ish) *adj.* **1.** giving or producing something in large quantities. **2.** plentiful, *a lavish display.* **lavish** *v.* to bestow lavishly. **lav′ish·ly** *adv.* **lav′ish·ness** *n.*

law (law) *n.* **1.** a rule established among a community by authority or custom. **2.** a body of such rules. **3.** their controlling influence, their operation as providing a remedy against wrongs, *law and order.* **4.** the subject or study of such rules. **5.** *(informal)* the police. **6.** something that must be obeyed or believed, *his word was law.* **7.** a factual statement of what always happens in certain circumstances, as of regular natural occurrences, *the laws of nature; the law of gravity; Murphy's Law,* what can go wrong will go wrong. **8.** *the Law,* the commandments of God in Jewish and Christian belief, especially those given to Moses. □ **law of averages,** the proposition that the occurrence of one extreme will be matched by that of the other extreme so as to maintain the normal average. **law of the jungle,** a state of ruthless competition. **law unto oneself** *or* **itself,** a person or thing that does not behave in the customary fashion. **take the law into one's own hands,** to right a wrong oneself without legal sanction.

law·a·bid·ing (law-ă-bɪ-ding) *adj.* obeying the law.

law·break·er (law-bray-kĕr) *n.* a person who violates the law.

law·ful (law-fŭl) *adj.* permitted or recognized by law, *lawful business; his lawful wife.* **law'ful·ly** *adv.*

law·giv·er (law-giv-ĕr) *n.* a person who makes laws, especially a code of laws.

law·less (law-lis) *adj.* 1. (of a country) where laws do not exist or are not applied. 2. disregarding the law, uncontrolled, *lawless men.* **law'less·ness** *n.*

law·mak·er (law-may-kĕr) *n.* a legislator.

law·man (law-man) *n.* (*pl.* **-men,** *pr.* -men) (chiefly Western U.S.) a police officer, sheriff, etc.

lawn[1] (lawn) *n.* fine woven cotton or synthetic material.

lawn[2] *n.* an area of closely cut grass. ☐ **lawn bowling,** the game of bowls (*see* **bowls**). **lawn mower,** a machine with revolving blades for cutting the grass of lawns. **lawn tennis,** (*old use*) tennis, especially when played on grass courts.

law·ren·ci·um (law-ren-si-ŭm) *n.* an artificially produced radioactive metallic element.

law·suit (law-soot) *n.* the process of bringing a problem or claim etc. before a court of law for settlement.

law·yer (law-yĕr) *n.* a person who is trained and qualified in legal matters.

lax (laks) *adj.* slack, not strict or severe, *discipline was lax.* **lax'ly** *adv.* **lax·i·ty** (lak-sĭ-tee) *n.*

lax·a·tive (lak-să-tiv) *n.* a medicine that stimulates the bowels to empty. **laxative** *adj.* having this effect.

lay[1] (lay) *n.* (*old use*) a poem meant to be sung, a ballad.

lay[2] *adj.* 1. not ordained into the clergy. 2. not professionally qualified, especially in law or medicine; *lay opinion,* the opinion of nonprofessional people. ☐ **lay analyst,** a psychoanalyst lacking a medical degree.

lay[3] *v.* (**laid, laying**) 1. to place or put on a surface or in a certain position. 2. to place or arrange in a horizontal position, to put in place, *lay a carpet; lay the fire,* put logs etc. ready for lighting. 3. to place or assign, *lay emphasis on neatness; laid the blame on her.* 4. to formulate, to establish, *we laid our plans.* 5. to cause to be in a certain condition, *laid himself open to suspicion.* 6. to cause to subside, *laid the dust; laid the ghost,* made it cease being troublesome. 7. to present or put forward for consideration, *laid claim to it.* 8. (of a hen bird) to produce (an egg or eggs) from the body. 9. to stake as a wager, to bet. **lay** *n.* the way in which something lies. ☐ **lay about one,** to hit out on all sides. **lay aside,** to put away, to cease to use or practice or think of; to save (money etc.) for future needs. **lay away,** a purchase left by a customer at the store until paid for. **lay claim to,** to claim as one's right. **lay down,** to put on the ground etc.; to give up (office); to establish as a rule or instruction. **lay down the law,** to talk with authority and certainty. **lay figure,** a jointed model of the human body, used by artists. **lay hold of,** to grasp. **lay in,** to provide oneself with a stock of. **lay into,** (*slang*) to thrash; to reprimand harshly. **lay it on the line,** (*slang*) to offer without reserve; to

speak frankly. **lay it on thick** *or* **with a trowel,** (*slang*) to exaggerate greatly; to flatter a person excessively. **lay low,** to overthrow; to humble; to incapacitate by illness. **lay off,** to discharge (workers) temporarily owing to shortage of work; (*informal*) to cease, especially from causing trouble or annoyance. **lay on,** to inflict blows forcefully. **lay open,** to break the skin of (part of the body); to expose to criticism. **lay out,** to arrange according to a plan; to prepare (a body) for burial; to spend (money) for a purpose; to knock unconscious. **lay to rest,** to bury in a grave; to prove the falsity of (rumors, accusations, etc). **lay up,** to store or save; to cause (a person) to be confined to bed or unfit for work etc.; to put (a car etc.) out of service temporarily. **lay waste,** to destroy the crops and buildings etc. of (a district). ▷Do not confuse *lay* (= put down; past tense is *laid*) with *lie* (= recline; past tense is *lay*). Correct uses are as follows: *go and lie down; she went and lay down; please lay it on the floor; they laid it on the floor.* Incorrect use is *go and lay down.*

lay·a·way (lay-ă-way) *n.* 1. a system of reserving an item of merchandise by making a deposit of part of the purchase price. 2. an item reserved in this way.

lay·er (lay-ĕr) *n.* 1. a person etc. that lays something; *hen is a poor layer,* lays few eggs. 2. a thickness of material (often one of several) laid over a surface. **layer** *v.* to arrange in layers. ☐**layer cake,** cake consisting of layers with filling between.

lay·er·ing (lay-ĕ-ring) *n.* propagation of a shrub etc. by fastening one of its stems to the earth to take root while still attached to the parent plant.

lay·ette (lay-et) *n.* the clothes and bedding etc. prepared for a newborn baby.

lay·man (lay-măn) *n.* (*pl.* **-men,** *pr.* -mĕn) a person not ordained into the clergy or not professionally qualified (*see* **lay**[2]). **lay·wom·an** (lay-wuum-ăn) *n.* (*pl.* **-wom·en,** *pr.* -wim-in) **lay·per·son** (lay-pur-sŏn) *n.*

lay·off (lay-awf) *n.* a temporary discharge, the act of temporarily discharging employees.

lay·out (lay-owt) *n.* an arrangement of parts etc. according to a plan.

lay·o·ver (lay-oh-vĕr) *n.* a stopover.

laz·ar (laz-ăr) *n.* (*old use*) a poor and diseased person, especially a leper.

laze (layz) *v.* (**lazed, laz·ing**) (*informal*) to spend time idly or in idle relaxation. **laze** *n.* an act or period of lazing.

la·zy (lay-zee) *adj.* (**la·zi·er, la·zi·est**) 1. unwilling to work, doing little work. 2. showing or characterized by lack of energy, *a lazy yawn.* **la'zi·ly** *adv.* **la'zi·ness** *n.* ☐**lazy Susan,** a revolving tray set in the middle of a dining table so that all can help themselves without passing serving dishes.

lazy·bones (lay-zee-bohnz) *n.* (*informal*) a lazy person.

lb. *abbr.* pound weight. ▷From the Latin *libra.*

lbs. *abbr.* pounds weight.

l.c. *abbr.* lower case.

L.C. *abbr.* Library of Congress.

L/C, l/c *abbr.* letter of credit.

L.C.D. *abbr.* least common denominator.

LCDR *abbr.* lieutenant commander.

LCL *abbr.* less-than-carload lot.

L.C.M. *abbr.* least common multiple.

LCpl *abbr.* lance corporal.

LD *abbr.* lethal dose.

ld. *abbr.* load.

ldg. *abbr.* 1. landing. 2. loading.

L-do·pa (el-doh-pă) *n.* a drug used in treatment of Parkinson's disease.

lea (lee) *n.* *(old use)* a tract of open ground, especially grassland.

leach (leech) *v.* to make (liquid) percolate through soil or ore etc., to remove (soluble matter) in this way, *leach it out.*

lead[1] (leed) *v.* (**led, lead·ing**) 1. to cause to go with oneself, to guide, especially by going in front or by holding the hand or an attached rein etc. 2. to influence the actions or opinions of, *what led you to believe this?* 3. to be a route or means of access, *the door leads into a passage.* 4. to have as its result, *this led to confusion.* 5. to live or pass one's life, *was leading a double life.* 6. to be in first place or position in, to be ahead, *lead the world in electronics.* 7. to be the leader or head of, to control. 8. to make one's start with, *Ali led with his left.* 9. (in card games) to be the first player to play a card. **lead** *n.* 1. guidance given by going in front, an example. 2. a clue, *it gave us a lead.* 3. a leading place, leadership, the amount by which one competitor is in front, *take the lead; a lead of five points.* 4. an electrical conductor (usually a wire) conveying current from a source to a place of use. 5. a leash. 6. the act or right of playing one's card first in a card game, the card played. 7. the chief part in a play or other performance, one who takes this part, *play the lead.* **lead** *adj.* in the first or front position, *the lead car* (in a race), *the lead singer* (in a group). ☐**lead astray,** to lead into error or wrongdoing. **lead by the nose,** to control the actions of (a person) completely. **lead off,** to begin. **lead someone a merry chase** *or* **dance,** to cause someone much trouble, especially by making him search. **lead someone on,** to entice him, especially with false promises. **lead story** *or* **article,** the item of news given greatest prominence in a newspaper etc. **lead time,** the period between starting and finishing a production process. **lead up** (*or* **down**) **the garden path,** *see* **garden.** **lead up to,** to serve as an introduction to or preparation for; to direct the conversation toward (a subject).

lead[2] (led) *n.* 1. a heavy metallic element of dull grayish color. 2. a thin stick of graphite forming the writing substance in a pencil. 3. a lump of lead used in taking soundings in water. 4. (in printing) a metal strip used to give space between lines. 5. *(slang)* bullets, gunfire, *he went down in a hail of lead.* **lead** *v.* 1. to cover, weight, frame (panes of glass) with lead. 2. to add lead or lead compound to (gasoline etc.). **lead'ed** *adj.* ☐**lead poisoning,** acute or chronic poisoning caused by taking lead into the body.

lead·en (led-ĕn) *adj.* 1. made of lead. 2. heavy, slow as if weighted with lead. 3. lead colored, dark gray, *leaden skies.*

lead·er (lee-dĕr) *n.* 1. a person or thing that leads. 2. one who has the principal part in something, the head of a group etc. 3. one whose example is followed, *a leader of fashion.* 4. a short length of transparent line to which a fishing hook or lure is attached. 5. an item advertised at a special low price to attract customers to a store. **lead'er·less** *adj.*

lead·er·ship (lee-dĕr-ship) *n.* 1. being a leader. 2. ability to be a leader. 3. the leaders of a group.

lead·ing[1] (lee-ding) *adj. see* **lead**[1]. ☐**leading lady** *or* **man,** one taking the chief part in a play etc. **leading light,** a prominent member of a group. **leading question,** one that is worded so that it prompts a person to give the desired answer or to reveal more than he intends (▷not the same as a *searching question*).

lead·ing[2] (led-ing) *n.* a covering or framework of lead (metal).

lead·off (leed-awf) *n.* a beginning, the first. ☐**leadoff man,** (in baseball) the first player at bat in an inning or in a line-up.

leaf (leef) *n.* (*pl.* **leaves,** *pr.* leevz) 1. a flat organ (usually green) growing from the stem or branch of a plant or directly from the root. 2. a single thickness of the paper forming the pages of a book. 3. a very thin sheet of metal, *gold leaf.* 4. a hinged flap of a table, an extra section inserted to extend a table. **leaf** *v.* to turn over the leaves or pages of a book, *leafed through it.* ☐**in leaf,** the state of having leaves out. **leaf mold,** soil or compost consisting chiefly of decayed leaves. **take a leaf out of someone's book,** to follow his example.

leaf·age (lee-fij) *n.* foliage.

leaf·hop·per (leef-hop-ĕr) *n.* any of various leaping insects that suck plant juices and transmit diseases among plants.

leaf·less (leef-lis) *adj.* having no leaves.

leaf·let (leef-lit) *n.* 1. a small leaf or leaflike part of a plant. 2. a printed sheet of paper (sometimes folded but not stitched) giving information, especially for distribution free of charge.

leaf·stalk (leef-stawk) *n.* a petiole.

leaf·y (lee-fee) *adj.* (**leaf·i·er, leaf·i·est**) 1. covered in leaves. 2. consisting of leaves, *leafy vegetables.*

league[1] (leeg) *n.* 1. a group of people or countries that combine formally for a particular purpose. 2. a group of sports teams that compete against each other for a championship. 3. a class of contestants, *he is out of his league.* **league** *v.* (**leagued, lea·guing**) to form a league. ☐**in league with,** allied with, conspiring with. **not in the same league with,** much inferior to.

league[2] *n.* a measure of distance, usually about three miles.

leak (leek) *n.* 1. the process of leaking, a hole or crack etc. through which liquid or gas may accidentally get in or out. 2. the liquid or gas that passes through this. 3. a similar escape of an electric charge, the charge itself. 4. a disclosure of secret information. **leak** *v.* 1. (of liquid or gas etc.) to escape accidentally through an opening. 2. (of a container) to allow such an escape, to let out (liquid or gas). 3. to disclose, *leaked the news to a reporter.* 4. (of a secret) to become known improperly, *it leaked out.*

leak·age (lee-kij) *n.* 1. leaking. 2. a thing or amount that has leaked out.

leak·y (lee-kee) *adj.* (**leak·i·er, leak·i·est**) liable to leak.

lean[1] (leen) *adj.* 1. (of a person or animal) without much flesh. 2. (of meat) containing little or no fat. 3. scanty, *a lean harvest.* **lean** *n.* the lean part of meat. **lean'ness** *n.* ☐**lean years,** years of scarcity.

lean[2] *v.* (**leaned, lean·ing**) 1. to put or be in a sloping position. 2. to rest against or on something

for support. **3.** to rely or depend on for help.
□**lean on,** *(informal)* to seek to influence by intimidating.
lean·ing (lee-ning) *n.* a tendency or partiality, *has leanings toward socialism.*
lean-to (leen-too) *n.* **1.** a building with a sloping roof resting against the side of a larger building. **2.** a rough shed or hut.
leap (leep) *v.* (**leaped** or **leapt,** *pr.* lept, **leap·ing**) to jump vigorously. **leap** *n.* a vigorous jump. □**by leaps and bounds,** with very rapid progress. **leap year,** a year with an extra day (February 29).
leap·frog (leep-frog) *n.* a game in which each player in turn vaults with parted legs over another who is bending down. **leapfrog** *v.* (**leap·frogged, leap·frog·ging**) **1.** to perform this vault. **2.** to overtake alternately.
learn (lurn) *v.* (**learned, learn·ing**) **1.** to gain knowledge of or skill in a subject etc. by study or experience or by being taught; *learn it by heart,* memorize it thoroughly so that one can repeat it. **2.** to become aware by information or from observation. **3.** *(incorrect or humorous use)* to teach, *that'll learn you!* □**learn the ropes,** see **rope.**
learn·ed (lur-nid) *adj.* **1.** having much knowledge acquired by study, *learned men.* **2.** of or for learned people, *a learned society.* **learn'ed·ly** *adv.*
learn·er (lur-něr) *n.* a person who is learning a subject or skill. □**learner's permit,** a permit to drive a motor vehicle for the purpose of learning in order to qualify for a driver's license.
learn·ing (lur-ning) *n.* knowledge obtained by study.
lease (lees) *n.* a contract by which the owner of land or a building etc. allows another person to use it for a specified time, usually in return for payment. **lease** *v.* (**leased, leas·ing**) **1.** to grant the use of (a property) by lease. **2.** to obtain or hold (a property) by lease. □**a new lease on life,** a chance to continue living or to live more happily because of recovery from illness or anxiety, or (of things) to continue in use after repair.
lease·hold (lees-hohld) *n.* the holding of land or a house or apartment etc. by means of a lease. **lease'hold·er** *n.*
leash (leesh) *n.* a strap or cord etc. attached to the collar of a dog etc. and held to keep the animal under restraint, especially while walking it. **leash** *v.* to hold on a leash.
least (leest) *adj.* **1.** smallest in amount or degree. **2.** lowest in rank or importance. **least** *n.* the least amount or degree. **least** *adv.* in the least degree. □**at least,** not less than what is stated; anyway. **in the least,** at all; in the smallest degree. **least common denominator,** see **denominator. least common multiple,** the lowest positive whole number that is exactly divisible by each of two or more whole numbers. **to say the least of it,** putting the case moderately.
least·wise (leest-wiz) *adv.* *(informal)* at least.
leath·er (leth-ěr) *n.* **1.** material made from animal skins by tanning or a similar process. **2.** the leather part(s) of something. **leather** *adj.* made of leather. **leath'ern** *adj.*
leath·er·neck (leth-ěr-nek) *n.* *(slang)* a U.S. Marine. ▷From the leather neckband that was once part of a Marine uniform.
leath·er·y (leth-ě-ree) *adj.* as tough as leather.

leave¹ (leev) *v.* (**left, leav·ing**) **1.** to go away from, to go away finally or permanently. **2.** to cease to belong to (a group) or live at (a place), to cease working for an employer. **3.** to cause or allow to remain, to depart without taking, *left the door open; left my gloves in the bus; he leaves a wife and two children,* is survived by these. **4.** to give as a legacy. **5.** to allow to stay or proceed without interference, *leave the dog alone.* **6.** to refrain from consuming or dealing with, *left all the fat; let's leave the dishes.* **7.** to entrust or commit to another person; *was left with the problem,* had this as a burden; *leave it to me,* I will deal with it. **8.** to deposit for collection or transmission, *leave your coat in the hall; leave a message.* **9.** to abandon, to desert, *was left in the lurch.* □**leave off,** to cease. **leave out,** to omit, not include. ▷It is incorrect to say *leave me go.* Say *let me go.*
leave² *n.* **1.** permission. **2.** official permission to be absent from duty, the period for which this lasts; *on leave,* absent in this way. □**take leave of one's senses,** to go mad. **take one's leave,** to say farewell and go away.
leav·en (lev-ěn) *n.* **1.** a substance (such as yeast) that produces fermentation in dough. **2.** a quality or influence that lightens or enlivens something. **leaven** *v.* **1.** to add leaven to. **2.** to enliven.
leav·en·ing (lev-ě-ning) *n.* a leaven.
leaves (leevz) *see* **leaf.**
leave-tak·ing (leev-tay-king) *n.* a departure, taking one's leave.
leav·ings (lee-vingz) *n. pl.* what is left.
Leb·a·non (leb-ă-non) a country in the Middle East, at the eastern end of the Mediterranean Sea. **Leb·a·nese** (leb-ă-neez) *adj. & n.*
lech·er (lech-ěr) *n.* a man given to lechery.
lech·er·y (lech-ě-ree) *n.* unrestrained indulgence of sexual lust. **lech'er·ous** *adj.*
lec·i·thin (les-ĭ-thin) *n.* a complex fatty substance containing phosphorus and found in egg yolk.
lect. *abbr.* **1.** lecture. **2.** lecturer.
lec·tern (lek-těrn) *n.* a stand with a sloping top to hold a book or notes for a reader or speaker.
lec·tor (lek-tŏr) *n.* a reader of lessons in a church service.
lec·ture (lek-chŭr) *n.* **1.** a speech giving information about a subject to an audience or class. **2.** a long serious speech, especially one giving reproof or warning. **lecture** *v.* (**lec·tur·ed, lec·tur·ing**) **1.** to give a lecture or series of lectures. **2.** to talk to (a person) seriously or reprovingly. **lec'tur·er** *n.* **lec'ture·ship** *n.*
led (led) *see* **lead¹.**
LED (el-ee-dee) *n.* a semiconductor diode that responds to the application of voltage by giving off light. ▷From *light-emitting diode.*
le·der·ho·sen (lay-děr-hoh-zěn) *n.* leather shorts as worn by men in Bavaria etc.
ledge (lej) *n.* **1.** a narrow horizontal projection or shelf, especially on a building or a cliff. **2.** a reef in the sea.
ledg·er (lej-ěr) *n.* a book used by a business firm to record income and expenses.
lee (lee) *n.* shelter, the sheltered side or part of something. **lee** *adj.*
leech (leech) *n.* **1.** a small bloodsucking worm usually living in water. **2.** a person who drains the resources of another.
leek (leek) *n.* a plant related to the onion but with broader leaves and a cylindrical white bulb.

leer (leer) v. to look slyly or maliciously or lustfully. **leer** n. a leering look.
leer·y (leer-ee) adj. wary, suspicious.
lees (leez) n. pl. sediment that settles at the bottom of a quantity of wine etc.
lee·ward (lee-wărd, loo-) adj. situated on the side turned away from the wind. **leeward** n. the leeward side or region. **leeward** adv.
lee·way (lee-way) n. 1. a ship's sideways drift from its course. 2. a degree of freedom of action, these instructions give us plenty of leeway.
left[1] (left) see **leave**[1].
left[2] adj. & adv. on or toward the left-hand side. **left** n. 1. the left-hand side or region. 2. the left hand, a blow with this. 3. (in marching) the left foot. 4. the Left (also the left), political parties that favor radical or liberal causes. □**left hand,** the hand that in most people is less used, on the same side of the body as the heart.
left-hand (left-hand) adj. of or toward the side of a person's left hand or the corresponding side of a thing.
left-hand·ed (left-han-did) adj. 1. using the left hand usually, by preference. 2. (of a blow or tool) made with or operated by the left hand. 3. (of a screw) to be turned toward the left. 4. (of a compliment) ambiguous in meaning, backhanded.
left-hand·er (left-han-děr) n. a left-handed person or blow.
left·ist (lef-tist) n. a supporter of the Left in politics. **leftist** adj. of the left wing in politics etc.
left·over (left-oh-věr) n. something remaining when the rest is finished, especially food not finished at a meal.
left (left) **wing** see **wing** (definitions 6 and 7); those in a political party who favor or lean toward the left. **left-wing** adj. **left'-wing'er** n.
left·y (lef-tee) n. (pl. **left·ies**) (informal) a left-handed person.
leg (leg) n. 1. one of the projecting parts of an animal's body, on which it stands or moves. 2. this as food. 3. either of the two lower limbs of the human body, an artificial replacement of this. 4. the part of a garment covering this. 5. one of the projecting supports beneath a chair or other piece of furniture. 6. one branch of a forked object. 7. one section of a journey. **leg** v. (**legged, leg·ging) leg it,** (informal) to walk or run rapidly, to go on foot. □**give someone a leg up,** help him to mount or to get over an obstacle or difficulty. **has not a leg to stand on,** has no facts to support his argument.
leg. abbr. 1. legal. 2. legislation. 3. legislative. 4. legislature.
leg·a·cy (leg-ă-see) n. (pl. **-cies**) 1. money or an article left to someone in a will. 2. something handed down by a predecessor, a legacy of distrust.
le·gal (lee-găl) adj. 1. of or based on law; my legal adviser, a lawyer etc. 2. in accordance with the law, authorized or required by law. **le'gal·ly** adv.
le·gal·i·ty (lee-gal-i-tee) n. (pl. **-ties**) □**legal age,** the age at which a person assumes the legal responsibilities and rights of an adult, usually eighteen or twenty-one. **legal aid,** payment from public funds toward the cost of legal advice or proceedings. **legal holiday,** a holiday set by law. **legal tender,** currency that cannot legally be refused in payment of a debt.
le·gal·ism (lee-gă-liz-ěm) n. strict, literal, and often excessive adherence to the law. **le·gal·is·tic** (lee-gă-lis-tik) adj.

le·gal·ize (lee-gă-lız) v. (**le·gal·ized, le·gal·iz·ing**) to make legal. **le·gal·i·za·tion** (lee-gă-lĭ-zay-shŏn) n.
leg·ate (leg-it) n. a representative or ambassador, especially one representing the pope.
leg·a·tee (leg-ă-tee) n. a person who receives a legacy.
le·ga·tion (li-gay-shŏn) n. 1. a diplomatic minister and his staff. 2. his official residence or office.
le·ga·to (lĕ-gah-toh) adj. & adv. (in music) in a smooth even manner.
leg·end (lej-ĕnd) n. 1. a story (which may or may not be true) handed down from the past. 2. such stories collectively. 3. an inscription on a coin or medal. 4. wording on a map etc. explaining the symbols used.
leg·end·ar·y (lej-ĕn-der-ee) adj. 1. of or based on legends, described in a legend. 2. (informal) famous, often talked about.
leg·er·de·main (lej-ĕr-dĕ-mayn) n. sleight of hand, magic tricks.
leg·gings (leg-ingz) n. pl. protective outer coverings for the legs.
leg·gy (leg-ee) adj. (**-gi·er, -gi·est**) having noticeably long legs.
leg·horn (leg-horn) n. 1. fine plaited straw. 2. a hat made of this. 3. one of a small hardy breed of domestic fowl.
leg·i·ble (lej-ĭ-běl) adj. (of print or handwriting) clear enough to be deciphered, readable. **leg'i·bly** adv. **leg·i·bil·i·ty** (lej-ĭ-bil-i-tee) n.
le·gion (lee-jŏn) n. 1. a division of the ancient Roman army. 2. a vast group, a multitude; they are legion or their name is legion. **le·gion·ar·y** (lee-jŏ-ner-ee) adj. & n. □**American Legion,** an organization for former members of the U.S. armed forces. **Foreign Legion,** a body of foreign volunteers in an army, especially the French army.
le·gion·naire (lee-jŏ-nair) n. a member of a legion. □**legionnaires' disease,** a severe and often fatal sickness of uncertain cause, with a high temperature and acute nausea. ▷From an outbreak of the disease at an American Legion convention in 1976.
legis. abbr. 1. legislation. 2. legislative. 3. legislature.
leg·is·late (lej-is-layt) v. (**leg·is·lat·ed, leg·is·lat·ing**) to make laws.
leg·is·la·tion (lej-is-lay-shŏn) n. legislating, the laws themselves.
leg·is·la·tive (lej-is-lay-tiv) adj. making laws, a legislative assembly.
leg·is·la·tor (lej-is-lay-tŏr) n. a member of a legislative assembly.
leg·is·la·ture (lej-is-lay-chŭr) n. a country's or state's legislative assembly.
le·git (lĕ-jit) adj. (slang) legitimate. **legit** n. (slang) the legitimate theater.
le·git·i·mate (lĕ-jit-ĭ-mit) adj. 1. in accordance with the law or rules. 2. logical, justifiable, a legitimate reason for absence. 3. (of a child) born of parents who are married to each other. 4. (of drama or theater) including plays but excluding musical comedies, revues, motion pictures, etc. **le·git'i·mate·ly** adv. **le·git·i·ma·cy** (lĕ-jit-ĭ-mă-see) n.
le·git·i·mize (lĭ-jit-ĭ-mız) v. (**le·git·i·mized, le·git·i·miz·ing**) to make legitimate.
leg·less (leg-lis) adj. without legs.
leg·man (leg-man) n. (pl. **-men,** pr. **-men**) 1. a newspaperman assigned to gather news outside

379

the office. 2. a salesman or other businessman who works primarily away from his office.
leg·room (leg-room) *n.* space for a seated person to extend his or her legs.
leg·ume (leg-yoom) *n.* 1. a leguminous plant. 2. a pod of this, especially when edible.
le·gu·mi·nous (li-gyoo-mĭ-nŭs) *adj.* of the family of plants that bear their seeds in pods, such as peas and beans.
leg·work (leg-wurk) *n.* *(informal)* work that involves much walking about.
lei (lay) *n.* a garland of flowers worn around the neck.
lei·sure (lee-zhŭr, lezh-ŭr) *n.* time that is free from work, time in which one can do as one chooses. **leisure** *adj.* □**at leisure**, not occupied; in an unhurried way. **at one's leisure**, when one has time. **leisure suit**, a man's suit for informal wear, having a shirt-like jacket and generally worn with no necktie.
lei·sured (lee-zhŭrd, lezh-ŭrd) *adj.* having plenty of leisure.
lei·sure·ly (lee-zhŭr-lee, lezh-ŭr-) *adj. & adv.* without hurry.
leit·mo·tif, leit·mo·tiv (līt-moh-teef) *n.* a theme associated throughout a musical piece or literary work with some person, situation, or sentiment.
LEM (lem) *n.* *l*unar *e*xcursion *m*odule.
lem·ming (lem-ing) *n.* a small mouselike rodent of arctic regions, one species of which periodically migrates in large numbers and is said to run into the sea and drown.
lem·on (lem-ŏn) *n.* 1. an oval fruit with acid juice. 2. the tree that bears it. 3. its pale yellow color. 4. *(slang)* something disappointing or unsuccessful, *his automobile is a lemon.* **lem′on·y** *adj.* □**lemon drop**, a hard candy flavored with lemon.
lem·on·ade (lem-ŏ-nayd) *n.* a lemon-flavored soft drink.
le·mur (lee-mŭr) *n.* a monkey-like animal of Madagascar.
lend (lend) *v.* (**lent, lend·ing**) 1. to give or allow the use of (a thing) temporarily on the understanding that it or its equivalent will be returned. 2. to provide (money) temporarily in return for payment of interest. 3. to contribute as a temporary help or effect etc., *lend dignity to the occasion; lend a hand,* help; *lend an ear,* listen. 4. to be of use, to be suitable, *this garden lends itself to relaxation.* **lend′er** *n.* ▷See the note under **loan.**
lend-lease (lend-lees) *n.* an arrangement (1941) whereby the U.S. supplied equipment etc. to Great Britain and its allies, originally as a loan in return for the use of British-owned military bases.
length (lengkth) *n.* 1. measurement or extent from end to end, especially along a thing's greatest dimension. 2. the amount of time occupied by something, *the length of our vacation.* 3. the distance a thing extends used as a unit of measurement, the length of a horse or boat etc. as a measure of the lead in a race. 4. the degree of thoroughness in an action, *went to great lengths.* 5. a piece of cloth or other material from a larger piece, *a length of wire.* □**at length**, after a long time; taking a long time, in detail.
length·en (lengk-thĕn) *v.* to make or become longer.
length·wise (lengkth-wīz) *adj. & adv.* in the direction of the length of something.

length·y (lengk-thee) *adj.* (**length·i·er, length·i·est**) very long, long and boring. **length′i·ly** *adv.*
le·ni·ent (lee-ni-ĕnt) *adj.* merciful, not severe (especially in giving out punishment), mild. **le′ni·ent·ly** *adv.* **le′ni·ence** (leen-yĕns) *n.* **le·ni·en·cy** (lee-ni-ĕn-see) *n.*
len·i·tive (len-i-tiv) *adj.* soothing or alleviating pain.
len·i·ty (len-i-tee) *n.* mercifulness, an act of mercy.
lens (lenz) *n.* (*pl.* **lens·es**) 1. a piece of glass or glasslike substance with one or both sides curved, for use in optical instruments. 2. a combination of lenses used in photography etc. 3. the transparent part of the eye, behind the pupil.
lent (lent) *see* **lend.**
Lent (lent) *n.* the period from Ash Wednesday to Easter, of which the forty weekdays are observed as a time of fasting and penitence. **Lent′en** *adj.*
len·til (len-til) *n.* 1. a kind of bean plant. 2. its edible seed.
Le·o (lee-oh) *n.* a sign of the zodiac, the Lion.
le·o·nine (lee-ŏ-nɪn) *adj.* of or like a lion.
leop·ard (lep-ărd) *n.* a large African and South Asian flesh-eating animal of the cat family, having a yellowish coat with dark spots. **leop′ard·ess** *n. fem.*
le·o·tard (lee-ŏ-tahrd) *n.* a close-fitting one-piece garment worn by acrobats etc.
lep·er (lep-ĕr) *n.* 1. a person with leprosy. 2. a person who is shunned.
lep·re·chaun (lep-rĕ-kawn) *n.* (in Irish folklore) an elf resembling a little old man.
lep·ro·sy (lep-rŏ-see) *n.* an infectious disease affecting skin and nerves, resulting in mutilations and deformities. **lep′rous** *adj.*
les·bi·an (lez-bi-ăn) *n.* a homosexual woman. **les′bi·an·ism** *n.*
lese maj·es·ty, lèse ma·jes·té (leez maj-ĕ-stee) 1. an insult to a sovereign or ruler. 2. *(humorous)* presumptuous behavior.
le·sion (lee-zhŏn) *n.* a harmful change in the tissue of an organ of the body, caused by injury or disease.
Le·so·tho (lĕ-soh-toh) a country in central southern Africa.
less (les) *adj.* 1. not so much of, a smaller quantity of, *eat less meat.* 2. smaller in amount or degree etc., *of less importance.* **less** *adv.* to a smaller extent. **less** *n.* a smaller amount or quantity etc., *will not take less.* **less** *prep.* minus, deducting, *a year less three days; was paid one hundred dollars, less tax.* ▷The word *less* is used of things that are measured by amount (for example in *eat less butter; use less fuel*). Its use with things measured by number is regarded as incorrect (for example in *we need less workers;* correct usage is *fewer workers*).
-less *suffix* used to form adjectives meaning not having, as in *childless;* free from, as in *harmless;* unable to be, as in *tireless.*
les·see (le-see) *n.* a person who holds a property by lease.
less·en (les-ĕn) *v.* to make or become less.
less·er (les-ĕr) *adj.* not so great as the other, *the lesser evil.* ▷Do not confuse *lesser* with *lessor.*
les·son (les-ŏn) *n.* 1. a thing to be learned by a pupil. 2. an amount of teaching given at one time; *give lessons in a subject,* give systematic instruction in it. 3. an example or experience by which one can learn, *let this be a lesson to you!* 4. a passage

from the Bible read aloud during a church service.
les·sor (les-or) *n.* a person who leases a property
to another. ▷Do not confuse *lessor* with *lesser*.
lest (lest) *conj.* 1. in order that not, to avoid the
risk of, *lest we forget.* 2. that, *were afraid lest
we should be late.*
let¹ (let) *n.* 1. stoppage, *without let or hindrance.*
2. (in tennis etc.) an obstruction of the ball in
certain ways, requiring the ball to be served again.
let² *v.* (**let, let·ting**) 1. to allow to, not prevent
or forbid, *let me see it.* 2. to cause to, *let us know
what happens; let us hear from you.* 3. to allow
or cause to come or go or pass, *let the dog in;
let me through; let the rope down.* 4. to rent. 5.
used as an auxiliary verb in requests or commands
(let's try; let there be light), assumptions *(let AB
equal CD),* and challenges *(let him do his worst).*
□**let alone,** to refrain from interfering with or
doing; apart from, far less or more than, *too tired
to walk, let alone run.* **let be,** to refrain from
interfering with or doing. **let down,** to reduce
the level of activity; to fail to support or satisfy,
to disappoint; to lengthen (a garment) by adjusting the hem; *let one's hair down,* to abandon conventional restraint in one's behavior; *let him down
gently,* do not treat him too severely. **let fly,** to
shoot or send out violently; to hurl strong abuse.
let go, to set at liberty; to loose one's hold of;
to cease discussion of, to ignore; *let oneself go,*
to behave in an unrestrained way, to cease to take
trouble. **let in for,** to involve in (loss or difficulty).
let loose, to release. **let off,** to fire (a gun); to
cause (a bomb) to explode; to ignite (a firework);
to excuse from doing (duties etc.); to give little
or no punishment to. **let off steam,** to allow it
to escape; to do something that relieves one's pent-
up energy or feelings. **let on,** *(slang)* to pretend,
the impostor let on he was a company executive;
to reveal a secret, *don't let on that I am ill.* **let
out,** to release from restraint or obligation; to
make (a garment) looser by adjusting the seams.
let slip, to reveal a secret; to miss an opportunity.
let up, *(informal)* to become less intense, to relax
one's efforts. ▷See the note under **leave.**
-let *suffix* used to form nouns meaning small or
minor, as in *booklet, starlet.*
let·down (let-down) *n.* 1. a disappointment. 2. the
descent of an airplane, as when preparing for landing. 3. a slowdown or slackening.
le·thal (lee-thăl) *adj.* causing or able to cause death.
le'thal·ly *adv.* **le·thal·i·ty** (lee-thal-i-tee) *n.*
leth·ar·gy (leth-ăr-jee) *n.* extreme lack of energy
or vitality. **le·thar·gic** (lĕ-thahr-jik) *adj.* **le·
thar'gi·cal·ly** *adv.*
let's (lets) = let us.
Lett (let) *n.* 1. a member of a people living near
the Baltic Sea, mainly in Latvia. 2. the Lettish
language.
let·ter (let-ĕr) *n.* 1. a symbol representing a sound
used in speech. 2. a written message addressed
to one or more persons, usually sent by mail.
letter *v.* to inscribe letters on, to draw or inscribe
letters. **let'ter·er** *n.* □**letter bomb,** a terrorist
explosive device disguised as a letter sent by mail.
letter box, a mailbox. **letter carrier,** a mail carrier, a postman. **letter of the law,** its exact requirements (as opposed to its spirit or true purpose). **letters patent,** a written document from
a govenment granting some specific rights, as to
land or an invention, to a person. **man of letters,**
a scholar, a literary man. **to the letter,** paying
strict attention to every detail.

let·ter·head (let-ĕr-hed) *n.* a printed heading on
stationery, stationery with this.
let·ter·ing (let-ĕ-ring) *n.* 1. the act of marking
something with letters by printing, writing, etc.
2. the actual letters.
let·ter·per·fect (let-ĕr-pur-fikt) *adj.* perfect or correct in every detail.
let·ter·press (let-ĕr-pres) *n.* 1. printing from
raised type, not from plates, blocks, etc. 2. the
contents of an illustrated book other than the illustrations.
Let·tish (let-ish) *adj.* of the Letts or their language.
Lettish *n.* the language of the Letts.
let·tuce (let-is) *n.* a garden plant with broad crisp
leaves much used as salad.
let·up (let-up) *n.* a reduction in intensity, relaxation
of effort.
leu·ke·mia (loo-kee-mi-ă) *n.* a disease in which
the white corpuscles multiply uncontrollably in
the body tissues and usually in the blood. **leu·
ke'mic** *adj.*
leu·ko·cyte, leu·co·cyte (loo-kŏ-sıt) *n.* a white
or colorless corpuscle of blood also found in the
lymph etc., a white blood cell.
leu·kor·rhe·a, leu·cor·rhe·a (loo-kŏ-ree-ă) *n.*
an abnormal white discharge from the vagina.
Lev. *abbr.* Leviticus.
Le·vant (lĕ-vant) *n.* the countries and islands in
the eastern part of the Mediterranean Sea. **Le·
van·tine** (lev-ăn-tın) *adj.* & *n.*
lev·ee¹ (lev-ee) *n.* an assembly of visitors or guests,
especially at a formal reception.
levee² *n.* 1. an embankment against river floods.
2. a landing place by a river.
lev·el (lev-ĕl) *n.* 1. an imaginary line or plane joining points of equal height. 2. a measured height
or value etc., position on a scale, *the level of alcohol in the blood.* 3. relative position in rank or
class or authority, *decision at cabinet level.* 4. a
more or less flat surface or layer or area. 5. an
instrument for testing a horizontal line or plane.
level *adj.* 1. horizontal. 2. (of ground) flat, without hills or hollows. 3. on a level with, at the
same height or rank or position on a scale. 4.
steady, uniform, (of a voice) not changing in tone.
level *v.* (**lev·eled, lev·el·ing**) 1. to make or
become level or even or uniform; *level up or down,*
to bring up or down to a standard; *level out,* to
become level. 2. to knock down (buildings) to
the ground. 3. to aim (a gun or missile). 4. to
direct (an accusation or criticism) at a person.
lev'el·ly *adv.* **lev'el·er** *n.* **lev'el·ness** *n.* □**do
one's level best,** *(informal)* to make all possible
efforts. **find one's level,** to reach one's right
place in relation to others. **level with,** *(informal)*
to tell the truth to. **on the level,** *(informal)* with
no dishonesty or deception.
lev·el·head·ed (lev-ĕl-hed-id) *adj.* mentally well
balanced, sensible.
lev·er (lev-ĕr, lee-vĕr) *n.* 1. a bar or other device
pivoted on a fixed point (the *fulcrum*) in order
to lift something or force something open. 2. a
projecting handle used in the same way to operate
or control machinery etc. **lever** *v.* to use a lever,
to lift or move by this.
lev·er·age (lev-ĕ-rij) *n.* 1. the action or power of
a lever. 2. power, influence.
le·vi·a·than (li-vı-ă-thăn) *n.* something of enormous size and power. ▷Named after a sea monster in the Bible.
Le·vis (lee-vız) *n. pl. (trademark)* a type of usually
blue denim jeans.

lev·i·tate (lev-i-tayt) *v.* **(lev·i·tat·ed, lev·i·tat·ing)** to rise or cause to rise and float in the air in defiance of gravity. **lev·i·ta·tion** (lev-i-tay-shŏn) *n.*

Le·vit·i·cus (li-vit-ĭ-kŭs) *n.* the third book of the Old Testament containing details of the law and ritual of the Levites.

lev·i·ty (lev-i-tee) *n.* a humorous attitude, especially toward matters that should be treated with respect.

lev·y (lev-ee) *v.* **(lev·ied, lev·y·ing)** to impose or collect (a payment etc.) by authority or by force. **levy** *n.* (*pl.* **lev·ies**) 1. levying. 2. the payment levied.

lewd (lood) *adj.* indecent, treating sexual matters in a vulgar way. **lewd′ly** *adv.* **lewd′ness** *n.*

lex. *abbr.* lexicon.

lex·i·cal (lek-si-kăl) *adj.* 1. of the words of a language as distinguished from its grammatical structure. 2. of a lexicon. **lex′i·cal·ly** *adv.*

lex·i·cog·ra·phy (lek-si-kog-ră-fee) *n.* the process and principles of compiling a dictionary. **lex·i·cog′ra·pher** *n.* **lex·i·co·graph·ic** (lek-si-kŏ-graf-ik) *adj.* **lex·i·co·graph′i·cal** *adj.*

lex·i·con (lek-si-kon) *n.* 1. a dictionary of certain languages, especially Greek or Hebrew. 2. the special vocabulary of a person, a branch of knowledge, a profession, etc.

l.f. *abbr.* (in printing) lightface.

L.F. *abbr.* low frequency.

LG *abbr.* 1. liquefied gas. 2. Low German.

lg. *abbr.* 1. large. 2. long.

LGk. *abbr.* Late Greek.

LH *abbr.* 1. left hand. 2. lower half.

L.H.D. *abbr.* Doctor of Humane Letters.

Li *symbol* lithium.

li·a·bil·i·ty (lɪ-ă-bil-i-tee) *n.* (*pl.* **-ties**) 1. being liable. 2. (*informal*) a handicap, a disadvantage. 3. **liabilities**, debts, obligations.

li·a·ble (lɪ-ă-bĕl) *adj.* 1. held responsible by law, legally obliged to pay a tax or penalty etc. 2. able or likely to do or suffer something, *cliff is liable to crumble.*

li·ai·son (lee-ay-zon, lee-ă-) *n.* 1. communication and cooperation between units of an organization. 2. a person who acts as a link or go-between. 3. a secret or illicit relationship.

li·ar (lɪ-ăr) *n.* a person who tells lies.

lib (lib) *n.* (*informal*) liberation, *women's lib.* **lib′ber** *n.* (*informal*) a person who advocates liberation.

lib. *abbr.* 1. liberal. 2. librarian. 3. library.

li·ba·tion (lɪ-bay-shŏn) *n.* 1. the pouring of a drink such as wine as an offering to a god. 2. a drink offered to a god. 3. (*informal*) an alcoholic drink. **li·ba·tion·ar·y** (lɪ-bay-shŏ-ner-ee) *adj.*

li·bel (lɪ-bĕl) *n.* 1. a published false statement that damages a person's reputation. 2. the act of publishing it, *was charged with libel.* 3. (*informal*) a statement or anything that brings discredit on a person or thing, *the portrait is a libel on him.* **libel** *v.* **(li·beled, li·bel·ing)** to utter or publish a libel against. **li′bel·er** *n.* **li′bel·ist** *n.* **li′bel·ous** *adj.*

lib·er·al (lib-ĕ-răl) *adj.* 1. giving generously. 2. ample, given in large amounts. 3. not strict or literal, *a liberal interpretation of the rules.* 4. (of education) broadening the mind in a general way, not only training it in technical subjects. 5. tolerant, open-minded, especially in religion and politics. 6. favoring democratic reform and individual liberty, moderately progressive. **liberal** *n.* **lib′er·**

al·ly *adv.* **lib′er·al·ism** *n.* **lib·er·al·i·ty** (lib-ĕ-ral-i-tee) *n.* □**liberal arts,** studies in the humanities, mathematics, and the social and natural sciences as distinct from professional or technical subjects.

lib·er·al·ize (lib-ĕ-ră-lɪz) *v.* **(lib·er·al·ized, lib·er·al·iz·ing)** to make less strict. **lib·er·al·i·za·tion** (lib-ĕ-ră-li-zay-shŏn) *n.*

lib·er·ate (lib-ĕ-rayt) *v.* **(lib·er·at·ed, lib·er·at·ing)** to set free, especially from control by an authority that is considered to be oppressive. **lib′er·a·tor** *n.* **lib·er·a·tion** (lib-ĕ-ray-shŏn) *n.*

Li·ber·i·a (lɪ-beer-i-ă) a country on the coast of West Africa. **Li·ber′i·an** *adj.* & *n.*

lib·er·tar·i·an (lib-ĕr-tair-i-ăn) *n.* 1. a believer in free will as a doctrine. 2. an advocate of liberty.

lib·er·tine (lib-ĕr-teen) *n.* a person who lives an irresponsible and immoral life.

lib·er·ty (lib-ĕr-tee) *n.* (*pl.* **-ties**) 1. freedom from captivity, slavery, imprisonment, or despotic control by others. 2. the right or power to do as one chooses. 3. a right or privilege granted by authority. 4. the setting aside of convention, improper familiarity; *take the liberty of doing or to do something,* venture to do it. □**at liberty** (of a person) not imprisoned, free; allowed, *you are at liberty to leave;* not occupied or engaged. **take liberties,** to behave too familiarly toward a person; to interpret facts etc. too freely.

li·bid·i·nous (li-bid-ĭ-nŭs) *adj.* lustful.

li·bi·do (li-bee-doh) *n.* (*pl.* **-dos**) emotional energy or urge, especially that associated with sexual desire. **li·bid·i·nal** (li-bid-ĭ-năl) *adj.*

Li·bra (lee-bră) *n.* a sign of the zodiac, the Scales. **Li′bran** *adj.* & *n.*

li·brar·i·an (lɪ-brair-i-ăn) *n.* a person in charge of or assisting in a library. **li·brar′i·an·ship** *n.*

li·brar·y (lɪ-brer-ee) *n.* (*pl.* **-brar·ies**) 1. a collection of books for reading or borrowing. 2. a room or building where these are kept. 3. a similar collection of records, films, etc.

li·bret·to (li-bret-oh) *n.* (*pl.* **-tos**) the words of an opera or other long musical work.

Li·bre·ville (lee-brĕ-veel) the capital of Gabon.

Lib·y·a (lib-i-ă) a country in North Africa. **Lib′y·an** *adj.* & *n.*

lice *see* **louse.**

li·cense (lɪ-sĕns) *n.* 1. a permit from the government or other authority to own or do something or to carry on a certain trade. 2. permission. 3. disregard of rules or customs etc., lack of due restraint in behavior. 4. a writer's or artist's exaggeration, or disregard of rules etc., for the sake of effect, *poetic license.* **license** *v.* **(li·censed, li·cens·ing)** to grant a license to or for, to authorize, *licensed to sell alcoholic beverages.*

li·cen·see (lɪ-sĕn-see) *n.* a person who holds a license.

li·cen·ti·ate (lɪ-sen-shi-it) *n.* a person who holds a certificate showing that he is competent to practice a certain profession.

li·cen·tious (lɪ-sen-shŭs) *adj.* disregarding the rules of conduct, especially in sexual matters. **li·cen′tious·ness** *n.* **li·cen′tious·ly** *adv.*

li·chee = **litchi.**

li·chen (lɪ-kĕn) *n.* a dry-looking plant that grows on rocks, walls, tree trunks, etc., usually green or yellow or gray.

lic·it (lis-it) *adj.* lawful, not forbidden. **lic′it·ly** *adv.*

lick (lik) *v.* 1. to pass the tongue over, to take up or make clean by doing this. 2. (of waves or flame) to move like a tongue, to touch lightly. 3. *(slang)* to defeat. 4. *(slang)* to thrash. **lick** *n.* 1. an act of licking with the tongue. 2. a blow with a stick etc. 3. a salt lick. □**lick and a promise,** *(informal)* hasty performance of a task. **lick a person's boots,** to be servile toward him. **lick into shape,** to make presentable or efficient. **lick one's lips,** to show pleasure and eagerness or satisfaction. **lick one's wounds,** to remain in retirement trying to recover after a defeat.

lick·e·ty-split (lik-ĕ-tee-split) *adv.* *(informal)* at full speed, headlong.

lick·ing (lik-ing) *n.* *(slang)* 1. a defeat. 2. a thrashing.

lick·spit·tle (lik-spit-ĕl) *n.* a sycophant, a toady.

lic·o·rice (lik-ŏ-ris, -rish) *n.* 1. a black substance used in medicine and as a candy. 2. the plant from whose root it is obtained.

lid (lid) *n.* 1. a hinged or removable cover for a box or pot etc. 2. an eyelid. **lid'ded** *adj.* **lid'less** *adj.* □**keep the lid on,** to prevent a situation from getting out of control. **with the lid off,** with all the horrors etc. exposed to view.

lie[1] (lī) *n.* 1. a statement that the speaker knows to be untrue, *tell a lie.* 2. a thing that deceives, an imposture. **lie** *v.* (**lied, ly·ing**) 1. to tell a lie or lies. 2. to be deceptive. □**give the lie to,** to show that something is untrue. **lie detector,** an instrument that can detect changes in the pulse rate, respiration, etc. brought on by the tension caused by telling lies.

lie[2] *v.* (**lay, lain, ly·ing**) 1. to have or put one's body in a flat or resting position on a more or less horizontal surface. 2. (of a thing) to be at rest on a surface. 3. to be or be kept or remain in a specified state, *the road lies open; machinery lay idle; lie in ambush.* 4. to be situated, *the island lies near the coast.* 5. to exist or be found, *the remedy lies in education.* **lie** *n.* the way or position in which something lies. □**how the land lies,** what the situation is. **it lies with you,** it is your business or right. **lie down,** to have a brief rest in or on a bed etc. **lie low,** to conceal oneself or one's intentions. **take it lying down,** to accept an insult etc. without protest. ▷See the note under **lay**[3].

Liech·ten·stein (lik-tĕn-stīn) a country in Europe between Austria and Switzerland.

lied (leed) *n.* (*pl.* **lied·er,** *pr.* lee-dĕr) a German song or ballad.

lief (leef) *adv.* *(old use)* gladly, willingly.

liege (leej) *n.* 1. a vassal. 2. a ruler or feudal lord. **liege** *adj.* faithful, loyal.

lien (leen) *n.* the right to keep another person's property until a debt owed in respect of it (such as for repairing it) is paid.

lieu (loo) *n.* **in lieu,** instead, in place, *accepted a check in lieu of cash.*

lieut. *abbr.* lieutenant.

lieu·ten·ant (loo-ten-ănt) *n.* 1. a navy officer next below a lieutenant commander. 2. an officer ranking just below one specified, *lieutenant colonel, lieutenant commander, lieutenant general.* 3. a deputy, a chief assistant. **lieu·ten·an·cy** (loo-ten-ăn-see) *n.* □**first lieutenant,** an Air Force, Army, or Marine Corps officer next below a captain. **lieutenant governor,** an elected state official next below a governor, substituting for him in case of his absence, incapacity, or death. **lieutenant junior grade,** a Navy officer next below lieutenant. **second lieutenant,** an Air Force, Army, or Marine Corps officer next below a first lieutenant.

life (līf) *n.* (*pl.* **lives,** *pr.* līvz) 1. being alive, the ability to function and grow that distinguishes animals and plants (before their death) from rocks and synthetic substances. 2. living things, *plant life; is there life on Mars?* 3. a living form or model, *portrait is drawn from life.* 4. liveliness, interest, *full of life.* 5. the period for which a person or organism is or has been or will be alive; *life imprisonment* or *a life sentence,* a sentence of imprisonment for the rest of one's life. 6. *(informal)* a life sentence. 7. a person's or people's activities or fortunes or manner of existence, *in private life; village life.* 8. the business and pleasures and social activities of the world, *we do see life!* 9. a biography. 10. a period during which something exists or continues to function, *the battery has a life of two years.* □**a matter of life and death,** an event or decision etc. that could cause a person to die; something of vital importance. **for life,** for the rest of one's life. **for one's life** or **for dear life,** in order to escape death or as if to do this. **life belt,** a life preserver worn as a belt. **life buoy,** a device to keep a person afloat. **life cycle,** the series of forms into which a living thing changes until the first form appears again. **life jacket,** a life preserver worn as a jacket. **life preserver,** a belt, jacket, or other device of buoyant or inflatable material to support a person's body in the water. **life raft,** a raft used during emergencies at sea when people have to abandon ship. **life sciences,** biology and related subjects. **life-support system,** (in a spacecraft) equipment that provides an environment in which the crew can live. **not on your life,** *(informal)* most certainly not. **this life,** life on Earth (as opposed to an existence after death). **to the life,** exactly like the original.

life·blood (līf-blud) *n.* 1. a person's or animal's blood, necessary to his or its life. 2. an influence that gives vitality to something.

life·boat (līf-boht) *n.* 1. a small boat carried on a ship for use if the ship has to be abandoned at sea. 2. a boat specially constructed for going to the help of people in danger at sea along a coast.

life·guard (līf-gahrd) *n.* an expert swimmer employed to rescue bathers who are in danger of drowning.

life·less (līf-lis) *adj.* 1. without life, dead or never having had life. 2. unconscious. 3. lacking vitality. **life'less·ly** *adv.* **life'less·ness** *n.*

life·like (līf-līk) *adj.* exactly like a real person or other living thing.

life·line (līf-līn) *n.* 1. a rope etc. used in rescuing people, as one attached to a life belt. 2. a diver's signaling line. 3. a sole means of communication or transport.

life·long (līf-lawng) *adj.* continued all one's life.

lif·er (lī-fĕr) *n.* *(slang)* 1. a person sentenced to life imprisonment. 2. one who spends a career in military service.

life·sav·ing (līf-say-ving) *adj.* designed for or concerning the protection of human life. **life'sav·er** *n.*

life-size (līf-sīz), **life-sized** (līf-sīzd) *adj.* of the same size as the person or thing represented.

life·style (līf-stīl) *n.* *(informal)* a person's way of life.

life·time (līf-tīm) *n.* the duration of a person's life

or of a thing's existence; *the chance of a lifetime,* the best chance one will ever get.
life·work (lɪf-wurk) *n.* the major or total work of a person's life.
LIFO (lɪ-foh) *n.* a system for valuing inventories. ▷From *last* in *f*irst *o*ut.
lift (lift) *v.* 1. to raise to a higher level or position; *lift one's eyes,* look up. 2. to take up from the ground or from its resting place. 3. *(informal)* to steal, to copy from another source. 4. to go up, to rise, (of fog etc.) to disperse. 5. to remove or abolish (restrictions). **lift** *n.* 1. lifting, being lifted. 2. *(informal)* a ride as a passenger without payment. 3. a device for lifting a vehicle in a garage for repairs. 4. a ski lift or chair lift. 5. the upward pressure that air exerts on an aircraft in flight. 6. a feeling of elation, *the praise gave me a lift.* ☐**have one's face lifted,** to have an operation for removing wrinkles on the face by tightening the skin. **lift truck,** a small truck used to lift and carry loads.
lift·off (lift-awf) *n.* the vertical takeoff of a rocket or spacecraft.
lig·a·ment (lig-ă-měnt) *n.* the tough flexible tissue that holds bones together or keeps organs in place in the body.
li·gate (lɪ-gayt) *v.* **(li·gat·ed, li·gat·ing)** to tie with a ligature. **li·ga·tion** (lɪ-gay-shŏn) *n.*
lig·a·ture (lig-ă-chŭr) *n.* 1. a thing used in tying, especially in surgical operations. 2. a slur in music. 3. joined printed letters such as œ.
light¹ (lɪt) *n.* 1. the agent that stimulates the sense of sight, a kind of radiation. 2. the presence or amount or effect of this. 3. a source of light, especially an electric light, *leave the light on.* 4. a flame or spark, something used to produce this. 5. brightness, the bright parts of a picture etc. 6. enlightenment; *light dawned on him,* he began to understand. 7. the aspect of something, the way it appears to the mind, *sees the matter in a different light; did his best according to his lights.* 8. a window or opening to admit light. 9. a traffic light. **light** *adj.* 1. full of light, not in darkness. 2. pale, *light blue.* **light** *v.* **(light·ed** or **lit, light·ing)** 1. to set burning, to begin to burn. 2. to cause to give out light. 3. to provide with light, to guide with a light. 4. to brighten. **light′ness** *n.* ☐**bring** *or* **come to light,** to reveal or be revealed, to make or become known. **in the light of this,** with the help given by these facts. **light bulb,** a rounded glass container enclosing a filament that is made to glow by electricity. **light meter,** an exposure meter. **light show,** a display of changing colored lights for entertainment. **light up,** to make or become bright with light or color or animation; to begin to smoke a pipe or cigarette. **shed** *or* **throw light on,** to help to explain.
light² *adj.* 1. having little weight, not heavy, easy to lift or carry or move. 2. of less than average weight or amount or force, *light traffic; light artillery,* armed with lighter weapons than heavy artillery. 3. (of work) needing little physical effort. 4. not intense; *a light sleeper,* one easily awakened. 5. not dense, *light mist.* 6. (of food) easy to digest. 7. moving easily and quickly. 8. cheerful, free from worry, *with a light heart.* 9. not profound or serious, intended as entertainment, *light music.* **light** *adv.* lightly, with little load, *we travel light.* **light′ly** *adv.* **light′ness** *n.* ☐**light heavy·weight,** a boxer between middleweight and heavyweight weighing up to 175 pounds. **light**

industry, industry producing small or light articles. **light opera,** a play with music, operetta. **make light of,** to treat as unimportant; *made light of his injuries,* said they were not serious.
light³ *v.* **(lighted** or **lit, light·ing)** to find accidentally, to settle on, *we lighted on this book.* ☐**light into,** *(slang)* to attack. **light out,** *(slang)* to depart, *lit out for home.*
light·en¹ (lɪ-těn) *v.* 1. to shed light on. 2. to make or become brighter. 3. to produce lightning.
light·en² *v.* 1. to make or become lighter in weight. 2. to relieve or be relieved of care or worry.
light·er¹ (lɪ-těr) *n.* a device for lighting cigarettes and cigars.
lighter² *n.* a flat-bottomed boat used for loading and unloading ships that are not brought to a wharf or into a harbor, and for transporting goods in a harbor.
light·face (lɪt-fays) *n.* a printing type with thin light lines. **light′faced** *adj.*
light·fin·gered (lɪt-fing-gěrd) *adj.* apt to steal.
light·foot·ed (lɪt-fuut-id) *adj.* stepping or dancing nimbly or lightly.
light·head·ed (lɪt-hed-id) *adj.* feeling slightly faint, dizzy, delirious.
light·heart·ed (lɪt-hahr-tid) *adj.* 1. cheerful, without cares. 2. too casual, not treating a thing seriously. **light′heart′ed·ly** *adv.* **light′heart′ed·ness** *n.*
light·house (lɪt-hows) *n.* (*pl.* **-hous·es,** *pr.* -howziz) a tower or other structure containing a beacon light to warn or guide ships.
light·ing (lɪ-ting) *n.* equipment for providing light to a room or building or street etc., the light itself.
light·ning (lɪt-ning) *n.* a flash of bright light produced by natural electricity, between clouds or cloud and ground. **lightning** *adj.* very quick, *with lightning speed.* ☐**lightning bug,** a firefly. **lightning rod,** a metal rod or wire attached to an exposed part of a building etc. to divert lightning into the earth. **like lightning,** with very great speed.
light·proof (lɪt-proof) *adj.* not admitting light.
lights (lɪts) *n. pl.* the lungs of sheep, pigs, etc., used as food for animals.
light·ship (lɪt-ship) *n.* a moored or anchored ship with a beacon light, serving the same purpose as a lighthouse.
light·weight (lɪt-wayt) *n.* 1. a person of less than average weight. 2. a boxer between welterweight and featherweight weighing up to 135 pounds. 3. a person of little influence. **lightweight** *adj.* not having great weight or influence.
light-year (lɪt-yeer) *n.* the distance light travels in one year (about six trillion miles).
lig·ne·ous (lig-ni-ŭs) *adj.* woody.
lig·ni·fy (lig-nĭ-fɪ) *v.* **(lig·ni·fied, lig·ni·fy·ing)** to change into or turn to wood or woodlike material. **lig·ni·fi·ca·tion** (lig-nĭ-fɪ-kay-shŏn) *n.*
lig·nite (lig-nɪt) *n.* brown coal showing traces of plant structure.
lik·a·ble (lɪ-kă-běl) *adj.* pleasant, easy to like.
like¹ (lɪk) *adj.* 1. having some or all of the qualities or appearance etc. of, similar; *what is he like?, what sort of person is he?* 2. characteristic of, *it was like him to do that.* 3. in a suitable state or the right mood for something, *it looks like rain; we felt like a walk.* 4. such as, for example, *in subjects like music.* **like** *prep.* in the manner of, to the same degree as, *he swims like a fish.* **like**

conj. (informal) 1. in the same manner as, to the same degree as, *do it like I do.* (▷A careful person avoids this construction and uses instead *do it as I do* or *do it like me.*) 2. as if, *she doesn't act like she belongs here.* **like** *adv. (informal)* likely, *as like as not they'll refuse.* **like** *n.* one that is like another, a similar thing, *shall not see his like again; the likes of you,* people like you. □**and the like,** and similar things.

like² *v.* **(liked, lik·ing)** 1. to find pleasant or satisfactory. 2. to wish for, *would like to think it over.* **likes** *n. pl.* the things one likes or prefers. ▷It is incorrect to say *I'd like for you to do this.* Delete *for.*

-like *suffix* used to form adjectives meaning similar to, as in *flowerlike, ladylike.*

like·li·hood (lɪk-li-huud) *n.* being likely, probability.

like·ly (lɪk-lee) *adj.* **(like·li·er, like·li·est)** 1. such as may reasonably be expected to occur or be true etc., *rain is likely.* 2. seeming to be suitable, *the likeliest place.* 3. showing promise of being successful, *a likely lad.* **likely** *adv.* probably. **like'li·ness** *n.* □**not likely!,** *(informal)* this will certainly not be possible. ▷The use of *likely* as an adverb without *very, most,* or *more* (for example in *the rain will likely die out*) is incorrect.

like·mind·ed (lɪk-mɪn-did) *adj.* having the same tastes or opinions. **like'mind'ed·ness** *n.*

lik·en (lɪ-kĕn) *v.* to point out the resemblance of one thing to another, *likened the heart to a pump.*

like·ness (lɪk-nis) *n.* 1. being like, a resemblance. 2. a copy, portrait, or picture.

like·wise (lɪk-wɪz) *adv.* 1. moreover, also. 2. similarly, *do likewise.*

lik·ing (lɪ-king) *n.* 1. what one likes, one's taste, *is it to your liking?* 2. one's feeling that one likes something, *a liking for it.*

li·lac (lɪ-lăk) *n.* 1. a shrub with fragrant purplish or white flowers. 2. pale purple. **lilac** *adj.* of lilac color.

lil·li·pu·tian (lil-i-pyoo-shăn) *adj.* very small. **lilliputian** *n.* a very small person. ▷Named after the inhabitants of Lilliput, a country in Swift's *Gulliver's Travels,* who were only six inches tall.

lilt (lilt) *n.* a light pleasant rhythm, a song or tune having this. **lilt'ing** *adj.*

lil·y (lil-ee) *n.* (*pl.* **lil·ies**) 1. a plant grown from a bulb, with large white or reddish flowers. 2. a plant of this family. □**lily of the valley,** a spring flower with small fragrant white bell-shaped flowers. **lily pad,** a floating leaf of a water lily.

lil·y-liv·ered (lil-ee-liv-ĕrd) *adj. (slang)* cowardly.

lil·y-white (lil-ee-hwɪt) *adj.* 1. as white as a lily. 2. (of an organization etc.) prohibiting participation by blacks.

lim. *abbr.* limit.

Li·ma (lee-mă) the capital of Peru. □**lima** (lɪ-mă) **bean,** a bean plant bearing pods that contain flat white or pale green edible seeds; the seed.

limb (lim) *n.* 1. a projecting part of an animal body, used in movement or in grasping things, an arm or leg. 2. a main branch of a tree. □**out on a limb,** isolated, stranded; at a disadvantage because separated from others. **tear limb from limb,** to dismember completely with violence.

lim·ber (lim-bĕr) *adj.* flexible, supple, lithe. **limber** *v.* to make limber. □**limber up,** to exercise in preparation for athletic activity.

lim·bo¹ (lim-boh) *n.* (*pl.* **-bos**) 1. *Limbo,* in certain Christian teachings, the supposed abode of souls not admitted to heaven (as of a person not baptized) but not condemned to punishment. 2. an intermediate state or condition (as of a plan not yet accepted but not rejected), a condition of being neglected and forgotten.

limbo² *n.* (*pl.* **-bos**) a West Indian dance in which the dancer bends back and passes repeatedly under a gradually lowered horizontal bar.

Lim·burg·er (lim-bur-gĕr) *n.* a soft white cheese with a characteristic strong smell, originally made in Limburg, Belgium.

lime¹ (lɪm) *n.* a white substance (calcium oxide) used in making cement and mortar and as a fertilizer. **lime** *v.* **(limed, lim·ing)** to treat with lime.

lime² *n.* 1. a round fruit like a lemon but smaller and more acid. 2. (also **lime green**) its yellowish-green color.

lime·ade (lɪm-ayd) *n.* a drink made of lime juice, water, and a sweetener.

lime·kiln (lɪm-kiln) *n.* a furnace or kiln in which lime is made by heating limestone or shells.

lime·light (lɪm-lɪt) *n.* great publicity. ▷Named after the brilliant light, obtained by heating lime, formerly used to illuminate the stages of theaters.

lim·er·ick (lim-ĕ-rik) *n.* a type of humorous poem with five lines. ▷Named after Limerick, a town in Ireland.

lime·stone (lɪm-stohn) *n.* a kind of rock from which lime is obtained by heating.

lim·it (lim-it) *n.* 1. the point or line or level beyond which something does not continue. 2. the greatest amount allowed, *the speed limit.* 3. *(slang)* something that is as much as or more than one can tolerate, *she really is the limit!* **limit** *v.* to set or serve as a limit, to keep within limits. **lim'it·less** *adj.*

lim·i·ta·tion (lim-i-tay-shŏn) *n.* 1. limiting, being limited. 2. a lack of ability; *knows his limitations,* knows what he cannot achieve.

lim·it·ed (lim-i-tid) *adj.* 1. confined within limits. 2. restricted, scanty. □**limited war,** a war in which the belligerents do not seek total victory.

limn (lim) *v. (old use)* 1. to paint (a picture). 2. to depict, to portray.

lim·o (lim-oh) *n.* (*pl.* **lim·os**) *(informal)* a limousine.

lim·ou·sine (lim-ŏ-zeen) *n.* 1. a luxurious car, often driven by a chauffeur. 2. an airport bus.

limp¹ (limp) *v.* to walk or proceed lamely. **limp** *n.* a limping walk.

limp² *adj.* 1. not stiff or firm. 2. lacking strength or energy, wilting. **limp'ly** *adv.* **limp'ness** *n.*

lim·pet (lim-pit) *n.* a small shellfish that sticks tightly to rocks.

lim·pid (lim-pid) *adj.* (of liquids etc.) clear, transparent.

lin. *abbr.* 1. lineal. 2. linear.

lin·age (lɪ-nij) *n.* 1. the number of lines in printed matter. 2. payment according to this. ▷Do not confuse *linage* with *lineage.*

linch·pin (linch-pin) *n.* 1. a pin passed through the end of an axle to keep the wheel in position. 2. a person or thing that is vital to an organization or plan etc.

Lin·coln (ling-kŏn) the capital of Nebraska.

Lin·coln, A·bra·ham (1809–65) the sixteenth president of the U.S. 1861–65.

lin·den (lin-dĕn) *n.* a tree with smooth heart-shaped leaves and fragrant yellow flowers.

line¹ (lɪn) *n.* 1. a straight or curved continuous extent of length without breadth. 2. a long narrow mark on a surface. **3.** something resembling this, a band of color, a wrinkle or crease in the skin. **4.** an outline, the shape to which something is designed; *a proposal along these lines,* with these general features. **5.** a limit, a boundary. **6.** one of a set of military fieldworks or boundaries of an encampment. **7.** a row of people or things, a row of words on a page or in a poem; *an actor's lines,* the words of his part in a play. **8.** a series of people awaiting their turns for something. **9.** a brief letter, *drop me a line.* **10.** a series of ships or buses or aircraft etc. regularly traveling between certain places, the company running these, *Cunard Line.* **11.** a connected series, several generations of a family, *a line of kings.* **12.** a direction or course or track, *line of march.* **13.** a single track of rails in a railroad, one branch of a system, *the main line north.* **14.** a course of procedure or thought or conduct, *in the line of duty; don't take that line with me.* **15.** a department of activity, a type of business; *not my line,* not among my interests or skills. **16.** a class of goods, *a nice line of handbags.* **17.** a piece of cord used for a particular purpose, *fishing with rod and line.* **18.** a wire or cable used to connect electricity or telephones, connection by this, *the line is bad.* **19.** (in football) the center, guard, tackles, and ends together. **20.** *(slang)* an exaggerated story or a fabrication told to win sympathy or justify oneself, *gave us a line about his poor sick mother.* **line** *v.* **(lined, lin·ing) 1.** to mark with lines. **2.** to arrange in a line, *line them up.* ☐**come** *or* **bring into line,** to become or cause to become a straight line or row; to conform or cause to conform with others. **down the line,** wholly or completely. **draw the line,** *see* **draw. get a line on,** *(informal)* to discover information about. **hold that line,** (in football) do not let the opposing players break through the line. **hold the line,** *see* **hold. in line,** so as to form a straight line; waiting one's turn (to buy a ticket, etc.); in accordance with expectations or general practice, *it would be in line for you to give her a call.* **in line for,** likely to get (a promotion etc.). **in line with,** in accordance with. **line drawing,** a drawing done with pen or pencil or a pointed instrument, chiefly in lines and solid masses. **line drive,** (in baseball) a batted ball hit low and straight. **line of scrimmage,** on a football field, an imaginary line on each side of which the opposing players line up before a play. **line score,** a score of a baseball game that shows the hits, runs, and errors of each team. **on the line,** *(slang)* at great risk, in a dangerous spot; with money instead of credit. **out of line,** not in line; not in accordance with expectations or general practice; *his remarks were way out of line,* were inappropriate.

line² *v.* **(lined, lin·ing) 1.** to cover the inside surface of (a thing) with a layer of different material. **2.** to be the lining of. ☐**line one's pockets,** to make a lot of money, especially by underhand or dishonest methods.

lin·e·age (lin-ee-ij) *n.* ancestry, the line of descendants of an ancestor. ▷Do not confuse *lineage* with *linage.*

lin·e·al (lin-ee-ăl) *adj.* of or in a line, especially as a descendant.

lin·e·a·ments (lin-ee-ă-mĕnts) *n. pl.* distinguishing features, especially of the face.

lin·e·ar (lin-ee-ăr) *adj.* **1.** of a line, of length. **2.** arranged in a line.

line·back·er (lIn-bak-ĕr) *n.* a football player who is positioned just behind the line on defense.
line·man (lIn-măn) *n.* (*pl.* **-men,** *pr.* -mĕn) **1.** a person who works on power communication lines. **2.** one of the players on the forward line in a football game.
lin·en (lin-in) *n.* **1.** cloth made of flax. **2.** sheets, tablecloths, etc., which were formerly made of this, *bed linen; table linen.*
lin·er¹ (lI-nĕr) *n.* a ship or airplane traveling on a regular route.
liner² *n.* a removable lining.
lines·man (lInz-măn) *n.* (*pl.* **-men,** *pr.* -mĕn) an official assisting the referee in tennis, football, etc., especially in deciding whether or where a ball crosses a line.
line·up (lIn-up) *n.* **1.** persons or things lined up for identification or inspection. **2.** the members of a team participating in a game.
ling¹ (ling) *n.* a kind of heather.
ling² *n.* a sea fish of northern Europe, used (usually salted) as food.
ling. *abbr.* linguistics.
lin·ger (ling-gĕr) *v.* **1.** to stay a long time, especially as if reluctant to leave. **2.** to dawdle. **3.** to remain alive although becoming weaker.
lin·ge·rie (lahn-zhĕ-ree) *n.* women's underwear.
lin·go (ling-goh) *n.* (*pl.* **-goes)** *(informal)* a foreign language, jargon.
lin·gua fran·ca (ling-gwă frang-kă) *a* language used between the people of an area where several languages are spoken.
lin·gual (ling-gwăl) *adj.* **1.** of or formed by the tongue. **2.** of speech or languages.
lin·guist (ling-gwist) *n.* **1.** a student of linguistics. **2.** a person who knows foreign languages well.
lin·guis·tic (ling-gwis-tik) *adj.* of language or linguistics.
lin·guis·tics (ling-gwis-tiks) *n.* the scientific study of languages and their structure.
lin·i·ment (lin-ĭ-mĕnt) *n.* a liquid for rubbing on the body to relieve aches or bruises.
lin·ing (lI-ning) *n.* **1.** a layer of material used to line something, the material itself. **2.** the tissue covering the inner surface of an organ of the body.
link (lingk) *n.* **1.** one ring or loop of a chain. **2.** a cuff link. **3.** a connecting part, a person who is a connection between others. **link** *v.* to make or be a connection between; *link hands,* to hold the hand of a person on each side, as in a chain.
link·age (ling-kij) *n.* linking, a link.
links (lingks) *n. pl.* a golf course.
link·up (lingk-up) *n.* **1.** a meeting, connection, or contact. **2.** something functioning as a linking device or system.
lin·net (lin-it) *n.* a small Old World finch.
li·no·le·um (li-noh-li-ŭm) *n.* a kind of floor covering made by pressing a thick coating of powdered cork and linseed oil etc. on to a canvas backing. ☐**linoleum block,** a piece of linoleum mounted on a wood block into which a pattern etc. has been incised or carved for use in making prints.
Lin·o·type (lI-nŏ-tIp) *n. (trademark)* a machine that sets a line of type as a single strip of metal.
lin·seed (lin-seed) *n.* the seed of flax, pressed to form **linseed oil,** an oil used in paint and varnish.
lin·sey-wool·sey (lin-zee-wuul-zee) *n.* (*pl.* **-seys)** an inferior wool material woven on cotton warp.
lint (lint) *n.* **1.** fluff, tiny bits of thread or fiber. **2.** staple cotton fiber. **3.** (chiefly *British*) a soft material for dressing wounds.

lin·tel (lin-těl) *n.* a horizontal piece of timber or stone etc. over a door or other opening.

li·on (lɪ-ŏn) *n.* 1. a large powerful flesh-eating animal of the cat family. 2. *the Lion,* a sign of the zodiac, Leo. **li·on·ess** (lɪ-ŏ-nis) *n. fem.* □the **lion's share,** the largest or best part of something that is divided.

li·on·heart·ed (lɪ-ŏn-hahr-tid) *adj.* very brave.

li·on·ize (lɪ-ŏ-nɪz) *v.* **(li·on·ized, li·on·iz·ing)** to treat (a person) as a celebrity.

lip (lip) *n.* 1. either of the fleshy edges of the mouth opening. 2. *(slang)* impudence. 3. the edge of a cup or other hollow container or of an opening. 4. a projecting part of such an edge shaped for pouring. **lipped** *adj.* □keep a stiff upper lip, *see* **stiff. lip reading,** understanding what a person is saying by watching the movements of his lips, not by hearing. **lip sync,** synchronizing movement of lips with recorded sound. **pay lip service to,** to state that one approves of something but fail to support it by actions.

lip·stick (lip-stik) *n.* 1. a stick of cosmetic for coloring the lips. 2. this cosmetic.

liq. *abbr.* 1. liquid. 2. liquor.

liq·ue·fy (lik-wě-fɪ) *v.* **(liq·ue·fied, liq·ue·fy·ing)** to make or become liquid. **liq'ue·fi·er** *n.* **liq'ue·fi·a·ble** *adj.* **liq·ue·fac·tion** (lik-wě-fak-shŏn) *n.*

li·queur (li-kur) *n.* a strong sweet alcoholic liquor with fragrant flavoring.

liq·uid (lik-wid) *n.* a substance like water or oil that flows freely but is not a gas. **liquid** *adj.* 1. in the form of a liquid. 2. having the clearness of water. 3. (of sounds) flowing clearly and pleasantly, *a thrush's liquid notes.* 4. (of assets) easily converted into cash. **li·quid·i·ty** (li-kwid-i-tee) *n.* □liquid measure, a system for measuring the volume of liquids. **liquid oxygen,** a clear light-bluish liquid produced by compressing and cooling oxygen, used as an oxidizer in certain rocket fuels.

liq·ui·date (lik-wi-dayt) *v.* **(liq·ui·dat·ed, liq·ui·dat·ing)** 1. to pay or settle (a debt). 2. to close down (a business) and divide its assets among its creditors. 3. to get rid of, especially by killing. **liq'ui·da·tor** *n.* **liq·ui·da·tion** (lik-wi-day-shŏn) *n.* □go into liquidation, (of a business) to be closing or closed down with its assets divided, especially in bankruptcy.

liq·uid·ize (lik-wi-dɪz) *v.* **(liq·uid·ized, liq·uid·iz·ing)** to liquefy. **liq'uid·iz·er** *n.*

liq·uor (lik-ŏr) *n.* 1. alcoholic drink. 2. juice produced in cooking, liquid in which food has been boiled.

li·ra (leer-ä) *n.* (*pl.* **li·re,** *pr.* leer-ay, **li·ras)** the unit of money in Italy and Turkey.

Lis·bon (liz-bŏn) the capital of Portugal.

lisle (lɪl) *n.* a fine smooth cotton thread formerly used for stockings.

lisp (lisp) *n.* a speech defect in which *s* is pronounced like *th* (as in *thin*) and *z* like *th* (as in *they*). **lisp** *v.* 1. to speak or utter with a lisp. 2. to speak in a childish or affected manner.

lis·some, lis·som (lis-ŏm) *adj.* lithe, agile.

list[1] (list) *n.* a series of names, items, figures, etc. written or printed. **list** *v.* to make a list of, to enter (a name etc.) in a list. □enter the lists, to make or accept a challenge, especially in a controversy. **list price,** the published or advertised price of merchandise.

list[2] *v.* (of a ship) to lean over to one side. **list** *n.* a listing position, a tilt.

list[3] *v.* (*old use)* to listen.

lis·ten (lis-ěn) *v.* 1. to make an effort to hear something, to wait alertly in order to hear a sound. 2. to hear by doing this, to pay attention. 3. to allow oneself to be persuaded by a suggestion or request. □listen in, to overhear a conversation, especially by telephone.

lis·ten·er (lis-ě-něr) *n.* 1. a person who listens; a good listener, one who can be relied on to listen attentively or sympathetically. 2. a person listening to a radio broadcast.

list·less (list-lis) *adj.* without energy or vitality, showing no enthusiasm. **list'less·ly** *adv.* **list' less·ness** *n.*

lit (lit) *see* **light**[1], **light**[3].

lit. *abbr.* 1. liter(s). 2. literal. 3. literally. 4. literary. 5. literature.

lit·a·ny (lit-ă-nee) *n.* 1. a form of prayer consisting of a series of supplications to God and with set responses by the congregation. 2. a long monotonous recital, *a litany of complaints.*

li·tchi (lee-chee) *n.* (*pl.* -tchies) 1. (also **litchi nut)** a fruit consisting of a sweetish white pulp in a thin brown shell. 2. the tree (originally from China) that bears this.

li·ter (lee-těr) *n.* a unit of capacity in the metric system (about 1¾ pints) used for measuring liquids.

lit·er·a·cy (lit-ě-ră-see) *n.* the ability to read and write.

lit·er·al (lit-ě-răl) *adj.* 1. in accordance with the primary meaning of a word or the actual words of a phrase, as contrasted with a metaphorical or exaggerated meaning; *a literal translation,* keeping strictly to the words of the original. 2. (of a person) tending to interpret things in a literal way, unimaginative. **lit'er·al·ly** *adv.* **lit'er·al·ness** *n.* ▷The word *literally* is sometimes used mistakenly in statements that are clearly not to be taken literally, as in *he was literally glued to the TV set every night.*

lit·er·al·ism (lit-ě-ră-liz-ěm) *n.* 1. adherence to the exact meaning. 2. complete realism in art, literature, etc. **lit·er·al·is·tic** (lit-ě-ră-lis-tik) *adj.*

lit·er·ar·y (lit-ě-rer-ee) *adj.* of or concerned with literature.

lit·er·ate (lit-ě-rit) *adj.* able to read and write. **literate** *n.* a literate person.

lit·e·ra·ti (lit-ě-rah-tee) *n. pl.* men and women of letters (*see* **letter**).

lit·e·ra·tim (lit-ě-ray-tim) *adv.* letter for letter. ▷Latin.

lit·e·ra·ture (lit-ě-ră-chŭr) *n.* 1. writings that are valued for their beauty of form, especially novels and poetry and plays etc. as contrasted with technical books and journalism. 2. the writings of a country or a period or a particular subject. 3. *(informal)* printed pamphlets or leaflets etc., *some literature about bus tours.*

lith. *abbr.* 1. lithograph. 2. lithographic. 3. lithography.

lithe (lɪth) *adj.* flexible, supple, agile.

lithe·some (lɪth-sŏm) *adj.* flexible, supple.

lith·i·um (lith-i-ŭm) *n.* a soft silver-white metallic element, the lightest alkali metal.

lith·o (lith-oh) *n.* the lithographic process. **lith·o·graph** (lith-ŏ-graf) *n.* a picture etc. printed by lithography. **lithograph** *v.* 1. to print by lithography. 2. to write or engrave on stone. **li·thog·ra·pher** (li-thog-ră-fěr) *n.* **li·thog·ra·phy** (li-thog-ră-fee) *n.* a process of printing from a smooth surface (such as a metal

plate) treated so that ink will adhere to the design to be printed and not to the rest of the surface.
lith·o·graph·ic (lith-ŏ-graf-ik) *adj.*
li·thol·o·gy (li-thol-ŏ-jee) *n.* the scientific study of the nature and composition of stones and rocks.
lith·o·log·ic (lith-ŏ-loj-ik) *adj.*
lith·o·sphere (lith-ŏ-sfeer) *n.* the earth's crust.
Lith·u·a·ni·a (lith-oo-ay-ni-ă) a republic in the U.S.S.R., bordering on the Baltic Sea. **Lith·u·a′ni·an** *adj. & n.*
lit·i·gant (lit-ĭ-gănt) *n.* a person who is involved in a lawsuit, one who brings suit.
lit·i·gate (lit-ĭ-gayt) *v.* **(lit·i·gat·ed, lit·i·gat·ing)** 1. to go to law, to be a party to a lawsuit. 2. to contest (a point) at law.
lit·i·ga·tion (lit-ĭ-gay-shŏn) *n.* a lawsuit, the process of bringing a suit.
li·ti·gious (li-tij-ŭs) *adj.* 1. inclined to litigate, fond of going to law. 2. disputable at law, offering matter for a lawsuit. 3. of lawsuits. **li·ti′gious·ness** *n.*
lit·mus (lit-mŭs) *n.* a blue coloring matter that is turned red by acids and can be restored to blue by alkalis. □**litmus paper,** paper stained with this, used to tell whether a solution is acid or alkaline.
li·tre = **liter.**
Litt.D. *abbr.* 1. Doctor of Letters. 2. Doctor of Literature.
lit·ter (lit-ĕr) *n.* 1. odds and ends of trash left lying about. 2. straw etc. put down as bedding for animals. 3. the young animals brought forth at a birth. 4. a stretcher on which an ill or wounded person is carried. 5. a conveyance consisting of a couch on shafts, which can be carried by men or animals. **litter** *v.* 1. to make untidy by scattering odds and ends, to scatter as litter. 2. to give birth to (a litter of young). □**litter basket,** a container for deposit of waste paper etc.
lit·te·ra·teur (lit-ĕ-ră-tur) *n.* a literary man.
lit·ter·bug (lit-ĕr-bug) *n. (informal)* a person who carelessly leaves refuse on the street.
lit·tle (lit-ĕl) *adj.* **(-tier, -tlest)** 1. small in size or amount or intensity etc., not great or big or much. 2. smaller than others of the same kind, *little finger; Little Italy,* a small area having many Italians. 3. young, younger, *our little boy; his little sister.* 4. unimportant, *bothers me with every little detail.* **little** *n.* only a small amount, some but not much, a short time or distance. **little** *adv.* 1. to a small extent only, *little-known authors.* 2. not at all, *he little knows.* □**little by little,** gradually, by a small amount at a time. **Little Dipper,** *see* **dipper.** **little people,** the fairies; ordinary people without particular wealth or influence. **Little Rock,** the capital of Arkansas. **little slam,** *see* **slam. little theater,** a noncommercial and experimental drama group performing to small audiences. **little woman,** *(informal,* now sometimes considered derogatory) a man's wife. **make little of,** *see* **make. think little of,** to consider insignificant or contemptible.
lit·tle·neck (lit-ĕl-nek) *n.* (also **littleneck clam)** a young quahog clam.
lit·to·ral (lit-ŏ-răl) *adj.* of or on the shore. **littoral** *n.* the region lying along the shore.
lit·ur·gy (lit-ŭr-jee) *n.* (*pl.* **-gies**) a fixed form of public worship used in churches. **li·tur·gi·cal** (li-tur-ji-kăl) *adj.* **li·tur′gi·cal·ly** *adv.*
liv·a·ble (liv-ă-bĕl) *adj.* suitable for living; *felt that life wasn't livable,* was unbearable.
live¹ (lɪv) *adj.* 1. alive. 2. actual, not pretended, *a*

real live burglar. 3. glowing, burning, *a live coal.* 4. (of a shell or match) not yet exploded or used. 5. (of a wire or cable etc.) carrying electricity. 6. of interest or importance at the present time, *pollution is a live issue.* 7. (of a broadcast) transmitted while actually happening or being performed, not recorded or edited. □**a live wire,** *(informal)* a highly energetic forceful person. **live oak,** an evergreen oak of the southeastern U.S.
live² (lɪv) *v.* **(lived, liv·ing)** 1. to have life, to be or remain alive, (of things without life) to remain in existence. 2. to be kept alive, *living on fruit.* 3. to get a livelihood, *they lived on or off her earnings; live by one's wits,* to get money or food etc. by ingenious or dishonest methods. 4. to have one's dwelling place, *have lived in tents.* 5. to conduct one's life in a certain way, *lived like a hermit; lived a peaceful life; live a lie,* express it by one's life. 6. to enjoy life to the full, *I don't call that living.* □**live down,** to live in such a way that a past guilt or scandal etc. becomes forgotten. **live in** or **out,** (of an employee) to live on or off the premises, *the elevator man lives in.* **live it up,** *(informal)* to live in a lively extravagant way. **live together,** to live in the same house etc.; (of a man and woman not married to each other) to live as man and wife. **live up to,** to live or behave in accordance with, *didn't live up to his principles.* **live with,** to live together; to tolerate, *you'll have to learn to live with it.*
lived-in (livd-in) *adj.* inhabited, (of a room) used frequently.
live·li·hood (lɪv-lee-huud) *n.* a means of living, a way in which a person earns a living.
live·long (liv-lawng) *adj.* **the livelong day,** the whole length of the day.
live·ly (lɪv-lee) *adj.* **(live·li·er, live·li·est)** full of life or energy, vigorous and cheerful, full of action. **live′li·ness** *n.* □**look lively,** to move more quickly or energetically.
liv·en (lɪ-vĕn) *v.* to make or become lively, *liven it up; things livened up.*
liv·er (liv-ĕr) *n.* 1. a large organ in the abdomen, secreting bile. 2. the liver of certain animals, used as food. 3. dark reddish brown.
liv·er·ied (liv-ĕ-reed) *adj.* wearing a livery.
liv·er·ish (liv-ĕ-rish) *adj.* 1. resembling liver, especially in color. 2. irritable, glum.
liv·er·wort (liv-ĕr-wurt) *n.* any of numerous moss-like plants growing in damp places.
liv·er·wurst (liv-ĕr-wurst) *n.* a sausage made with a large amount of liver.
liv·er·y (liv-ĕ-ree) *n.* (*pl.* **-er·ies**) a distinctive uniform worn by male servants in a great household. □**livery stables,** stables where horses are kept for their owner in return for a fee, or where horses may be hired.
liv·er·y·man (liv-ĕ-ree-măn) *n.* (*pl.* **-men,** *pr.* liv-ĕ-ree-men) a keeper of or attendant in a livery stable.
lives *see* **life.**
live·stock (lɪv-stok) *n.* animals kept for use or profit, such as cattle or sheep etc. on a farm.
liv·id (liv-id) *adj.* 1. of the color of lead, bluish gray. 2. furiously angry.
liv·ing (liv-ing) *adj.* 1. alive. 2. (of a likeness) exact, true to life, *she's the living image of her mother.* 3. (of rock) not detached from the earth, (of water) always flowing. **living** *n.* 1. being alive. 2. a means of earning or providing enough food etc. to sustain life. 3. a manner of life, *their standard of living.* 4. *the living,* those now alive (as opposed to *the dead).* □**living room,** a room for general use

during the day. **living wage,** a wage on which it is possible to live. **within living memory,** within the memory of people who are still alive.

liz·ard (liz-ărd) *n.* a reptile with a rough or scaly hide, four legs, and a long tail.

Lk. *abbr.* Luke.

LL *abbr.* Late Latin.

ll. *abbr.* lines.

lla·ma (lah-mă) *n.* a South American animal related to the camel but with no hump, kept as a beast of burden and for its soft woolly hair. ▷Do not confuse *llama* with *lama*

lla·no (lah-noh) *n.* (*pl.* **-nos**) any of the treeless grassy plains of Latin America.

LL.B. *abbr.* Bachelor of Laws.

LL.D. *abbr.* Doctor of Laws.

LM *abbr.* lunar module.

LNG *abbr.* liquefied natural gas.

lo (loh) *interj. (old use)* see.

loach (lohch) *n.* a small edible freshwater fish of Europe and Asia.

load (lohd) *n.* 1. something carried. 2. the quantity that can be carried, as on a cart. 3. a unit of weight or measure for certain substances. 4. the amount of electric current supplied by a dynamo or generating station. 5. a burden of responsibility or worry or grief. 6. *(informal)* plenty, *loads of time.* **load** *v.* 1. to put a load in or on, to fill with goods or cargo etc., to receive a load. 2. to fill heavily. 3. to weight with something heavy. 4. to put ammunition into (a gun) or film into (a camera), to ready for use. 5. to add an extra charge to (an insurance premium etc.) for special reasons. □**get a load of this,** *(slang)* take notice. **loaded question,** one that is worded unfairly. **load shedding,** cutting off of the supply of electric current on certain lines when the demand is greater than the supply available. **load the dice,** to weight dice to give the owner of them unfair advantage; to take unfair advantage of; *the dice were loaded against him,* he did not have a fair chance.

load·ed (loh-did) *adj. (slang)* 1. very rich. 2. drunk.

load·er (loh-děr) *n.* a person or machine that loads things.

load·stone (lohd-stohn) *n.* an iron ore having magnetic properties.

loaf[1] (lohf) *n.* (*pl.* **loaves,** *pr.* lohvz) 1. a mass of bread shaped in one piece. 2. (also **meat loaf**) ground meat molded into a loaf pan and baked.

loaf[2] *v.* to spend time idly, to stand or saunter about. **loaf′er** *n.*

loaf·ers (loh-fĕrz) *n. pl.* leather shoes shaped like moccasins with flat heels.

loam (lohm) *n.* rich soil containing clay and sand and decayed vegetable matter. **loam′y** *adj.*

loan (lohn) *n.* 1. something lent, especially a sum of money. 2. lending, being lent; *on loan,* lent; *have the loan of,* borrow. **loan** *v.* to lend. ▷Many writers prefer *lend* over *loan* as a verb.

loan·word (lohn-wurd) *n.* a word adopted by one language from another.

loath (lohth, loh*th*) *adj.* unwilling, *was loath to depart.* □**nothing loath,** quite willing. ▷Do not confuse *loath* with *loathe.*

loathe (loh*th*) *v.* (**loathed, loath·ing**) to feel great hatred and disgust for. **loath′ing** *n.* ▷Do not confuse *loathe* with *loath.*

loath·some (loh*th*-sŏm) *adj.* arousing loathing, repulsive.

lob (lob) *v.* (**lobbed, lob·bing**) to send or strike (a ball) slowly or in a high arc in tennis etc. **lob** *n.* a lobbed ball in tennis etc.

lo·bar (loh-băr, -bahr) *adj.* of a lobe, especially of the lung, *lobar pneumonia.*

lob·by (lob-ee) *n.* (*pl.* **-bies**) 1. an entrance hall used as a waiting room. 2. a body of people engaged in lobbying for a particular cause. **lobby** *v.* (**lob·bied, lob·by·ing**) to seek to persuade (a legislator) to support one's cause. **lob′by·ist** *n.*

lobe (lohb) *n.* a rounded flattish part or projection (especially of an organ of the body), the lower soft part of the ear.

lobed (lohbd) *adj.* having lobes.

lo·bel·ia (loh-beel-yă) *n.* a low-growing garden plant with blue, red, white, or purple flowers.

lo·bot·o·my (loh-bot-ŏ-mee) *n.* (*pl.* **-mies**) an incision into the frontal lobe of the brain to relieve some cases of mental illness.

lob·ster (lob-stěr) *n.* (*pl.* **-sters, -ster**) 1. a large shellfish with eight legs and two long claws that turns scarlet after being boiled. 2. its flesh as food. □**lobster Newburg,** a dish consisting of pieces of cooked lobster in a rich cream sauce containing brandy or sherry. **lobster pot,** a slatted wooden box for trapping lobsters. **lobster thermidor,** a mixture of lobster meat, mushrooms, cream, egg yolks, and sherry cooked in the lobster shell.

lob·ule (lob-yool) *n.* a small lobe. **lob·u·lar** (lob-yŭ-lăr) *adj.*

lo·cal (loh-kăl) *adj.* 1. belonging to a particular place or a small area, *letters for local delivery; local bus,* of the neighborhood and not long-distance. 2. affecting a particular place, not general, *a local anesthetic.* **local** *n.* 1. an inhabitant of a particular district. 2. a bus, train, subway, etc. making all stops. 3. the local branch of a labor union, etc. **lo′cal·ly** *adv.* □**local call,** a telephone call to a nearby place. **local color,** details characteristic of a place or of the scene in which a novel etc. is set, added to make it seem more real. **local government,** the system of administration of a district or county etc. by the elected representatives of people who live there.

lo·cale (loh-kal) *n.* the scene or locality of operations or events.

lo·cal·i·ty (loh-kal-i-tee) *n.* (*pl.* **-ties**) a particular place, the site or neighborhood of something.

lo·cal·ize (loh-kă-lız) *v.* (**lo·cal·ized, lo·cal·iz·ing**) to make local not general, to confine within a particular area, *a localized infection.* **lo·cal·i·za·tion** (loh-kă-li-zay-shŏn) *n.*

lo·cate (loh-kayt) *v.* (**lo·cat·ed, lo·cat·ing**) 1. to discover the place where something is, *locate the electrical fault.* 2. to assign to or establish in a particular location; *the town hall is located in the city center,* is situated there. 3. *(informal)* to take up residence or business, *they located in Chicago.*

lo·ca·tion (loh-kay-shŏn) *n.* 1. the place where something is situated. 2. finding the location of, being found. □**on location,** (of a film) being filmed in a suitable environment instead of in a film studio.

loc. cit. *abbr.* in the passage already quoted. ▷Latin, = in the place cited.

loch (lok) *n. (Scottish)* a lake or an arm of the sea.

lock[1] (lok) *n.* 1. a portion of hair that hangs together. 2. *locks,* the hair of the head.

lock[2] *n.* 1. a device for fastening a door or lid etc.

into position when it is closed, with a bolt that needs a key or other device to work it; *under lock and key*, locked up. **2.** a wrestling hold that keeps an opponent's arm or leg etc. from moving. **3.** a mechanism for exploding the charge of a gun. **4.** a section of a canal or river where the water level changes, fitted with gates and sluices so that water can be let in or out to raise or lower boats from one level to another. **5.** a decompression chamber. **6.** the interlocking of parts. **lock** *v.* **1.** to fasten or be able to be fastened with a lock. **2.** to shut into a place that is fastened by a lock; *locked in* or *into the situation*, hindered by circumstances. **3.** to store away securely or inaccessibly, *his capital is locked up in land.* **4.** to bring or come into a rigidly fixed position, to jam. ☐**lock keeper**, a person in charge of a lock on a canal or river. **lock out**, to shut out by locking a door. **lock stitch**, a sewing machine stitch that locks threads firmly together. **lock, stock, and barrel**, completely, including everything.

lock·er (lok-ĕr) *n.* a small compartment where things can be stored safely, especially for an individual's use in a public place. ☐**locker room**, a room adjacent to a gymnasium etc., equipped with lockers.

lock·et (lok-it) *n.* a small ornamental case holding a portrait or lock of hair etc., worn on a chain around the neck.

lock·jaw (lok-jaw) *n.* a form of tetanus in which the jaws become rigidly closed.

lock·nut (lok-nut) *n.* a nut screwed down on another to keep it tight.

lock·out (lok-owt) *n.* an employer's procedure of refusing to allow workers to enter their place of work until certain conditions are agreed to.

lock·smith (lok-smith) *n.* a maker and mender of locks.

lock·step (lok-step) *n.* a way of marching in a very close single file.

lock·up (lok-up) *n.* (*informal*) a jail.

lo·co (loh-koh) *adj.* (*slang*) crazy.

lo·co·mo·tion (loh-kŏ-moh-shŏn) *n.* moving or the ability to move from place to place.

lo·co·mo·tive (loh-kŏ-moh-tiv) *n.* an engine for drawing a train along rails. **locomotive** *adj.* of locomotion, *locomotive power.*

lo·co·mo·tor (loh-kŏ-moh-tŏr) *adj.* of or affecting locomotion; *locomotor ataxia*, a disease affecting the coordination of bodily movements.

lo·co·weed (loh-koh-weed) *n.* a poisonous plant of the southwestern U.S. causing disease in livestock.

lo·cus (loh-kŭs) *n.* (*pl.* **-ci**, *pr.* -sī) **1.** the exact place of something. **2.** the line or curve etc. formed by all the points satisfying certain conditions. ☐**locus clas·si·cus** (klas-i-kŭs), the best-known or most authoritative passage on a subject.

lo·cust (loh-kŭst) *n.* **1.** a kind of grasshopper that migrates in swarms and eats all the vegetation of a district. **2.** the cicada. **3.** an American tree with thorny branches and white flowers.

lo·cu·tion (loh-kyoo-shŏn) *n.* a word or phrase.

lode (lohd) *n.* a vein of metal ore.

lo·den (loh-děn) *n.* a thick waterproof woolen cloth. ☐**loden green**, the dark green color in which this is often made.

lode·star (lohd-stahr) *n.* a star used as a guide in navigation, especially the North Star.

lode·stone = **loadstone.**

lodge (loj) *n.* **1.** a country house for use in certain seasons, *a hunting lodge.* **2.** the main building of a camp or resort. **3.** the members or meeting place of a branch of a society such as the Freemasons. **4.** a beaver's or otter's lair. **lodge** *v.* (**lodged, lodg·ing**) **1.** to provide with sleeping quarters or temporary accommodations. **2.** to live as a lodger. **3.** to deposit, to be or become embedded, *bullet lodged in his brain.* **4.** to present formally for attention, *lodged a complaint.* **lodg'ment** *n.*

lodg·er (loj-ĕr) *n.* a person living in another's house and paying for his accommodations.

lodg·ing (loj-ing) *n.* a place where one lodges.

lodg·ings (loj-ingz) *n. pl.* a room or rooms rented for living in.

lo·ess (loh-es, les, lus) *n.* a deposit of fertile yellowish-brown windblown dust. **lo·ess·i·al** (loh-ess-i-ăl, les-, lus-) *adj.*

loft (lawft) *n.* **1.** an upper floor of a factory or warehouse. **2.** a space under the roof of a house. **3.** a space under the roof of a stable or barn, used for storing hay etc. **4.** a gallery or upper level in a church or hall, *the organ loft.* **5.** a backward slope in the face of a golf club. **6.** a lofted stroke. **loft** *v.* to send (a ball) in a high arc.

loft·y (lawf-tee) *adj.* (**loft·i·er, loft·i·est**) **1.** (of things) very tall, towering. **2.** (of thoughts or aims etc.) noble. **3.** haughty, *a lofty manner.* **loft'i·ly** *adv.* **loft'i·ness** *n.*

log¹ (lawg) *n.* **1.** a length of tree trunk that has fallen or been cut down. **2.** a short piece of this, especially as firewood. **3.** a device for gauging a ship's speed. **4.** a detailed record of a ship's voyage or an aircraft's flight, any similar record. **log** *v.* (**logged, log·ging**) **1.** to cut trees down for lumber. **2.** to enter (facts) in a logbook. **3.** to achieve a certain speed or distance or number of hours worked etc., as recorded in a logbook or similar record, *the pilot had logged two hundred hours on jets.* ☐**log cabin**, a dwelling built of logs.

log² *n.* a logarithm, *log tables.*

lo·gan·ber·ry (loh-găn-ber-ee) *n.* (*pl.* **-ries**) a large dark red fruit resembling a blackberry.

log·a·rithm (law-gă-ri*th*-ĕm) *n.* a number showing the power to which a certain fixed number (the base) must be raised to yield a specified number (adding together the logarithms of the two numbers gives the logarithm of the two numbers' product). **log·a·rith·mic** (law-gă-ri*th*-mik) *adj.*

log·book (lawg-buuk) *n.* a book in which details of a voyage etc. or of the registration details of a motor vehicle are recorded.

loge (loh*zh*) *n.* a box in a theater etc. or the forward section of the lowest balcony.

log·ger·head (law-gĕr-hed) *n.* a large-headed turtle of Atlantic waters. ☐**at loggerheads**, disagreeing, arguing, or quarreling.

log·gia (loj-ă) *n.* an open-sided gallery or arcade, especially one looking on an open court or forming part of a house and facing a garden.

log·ic (loj-ik) *n.* **1.** the science of reasoning. **2.** a particular system or method of reasoning. **3.** a chain of reasoning regarded as good or bad. **4.** the ability to reason correctly.

log·i·cal (loj-i-kăl) *adj.* **1.** of or according to logic, correctly reasoned. **2.** (of an action etc.) in accordance with what seems reasonable or natural. **3.** capable of reasoning correctly. **log'i·cal·ly** *adv.* **log·i·cal·i·ty** (loj-i-kal-i-tee) *n.*

lo·gi·cian (loh-jish-ăn) *n.* an expert or specialist in logic.

lo·gis·tics (loh-jis-tiks) *n.* the organization of supplies and services etc. **lo·gis'tic** *adj.*

log·jam (lawg-jam) *n.* 1. an immovable mass of logs floating in a river. 2. any similar blockage or deadlock.

lo·go (loh-goh) *n.* (*pl.* -gos) = logotype.

log·o·type (law-gŏ-tīp) *n.* a symbol used by a corporation or business company etc. as its emblem.

log·roll·ing (lawg-roh-ling) *n.* 1. mutual help, especially to aid each other's political projects. 2. a sport in which contestants try to knock each other off floating logs.

lo·gy (loh-gee) *adj.* (lo·gi·er, lo·gi·est) lethargic, sluggish, dull.

-logy *suffix* used to form nouns meaning character of speech or language, as in *tautology;* subject of study, as in *mineralogy, theology.*

loid (loid) *v.* (*slang*) to force back the spring lock on (a door) by insertion of a piece of celluloid or plastic.

loin (loin) *n.* 1. the side and back of the body between the ribs and the hipbone. 2. a cut of meat that includes the vertebrae of this part.

loin·cloth (loin-klawth) *n.* a piece of cloth worn around the body at the hips, especially as the only garment.

loi·ter (loi-tĕr) *v.* to linger or stand about idly, to proceed slowly with frequent stops. **loi'ter·er** *n.* one who spends time this way.

loll (lol) *v.* 1. to lean lazily against something, to stand or sit or lie lazily. 2. to hang loosely, *tongue lolling out.*

lol·li·pop (lol-ee-pop) *n.* a large round usually flat candy on a small stick.

lol·ly·gag (lol-i-gag) *v.* (lol·ly·gagged, lol·ly·gag·ging) = lallygag.

Lo·mé (law-may) the capital of Togo.

Lond. *abbr.* London.

Lon·don (lun-dŏn) the capital of England and of the United Kingdom. **Lon'don·er** *n.* ☐London broil, a broiled flank steak served in thin slices.

lone (lohn) *adj.* solitary, without companions, *a lone horseman; play a lone hand,* to take action without the support of others; *lone wolf,* a person who prefers to do this or to be by himself.

lone·ly (lohn-lee) *adj.* (lone·li·er, lone·li·est) 1. solitary, without companions. 2. sad because one lacks friends or companions. 3. (of places) far from inhabited places, remote, not often frequented, *a lonely road.* **lone'li·ness** *n.* ☐lonely heart, a person who feels permanently lonely. **lonely hearts column,** a newspaper column of advice to those who ask for help with personal problems.

lon·er (loh-nĕr) *n.* (*informal*) a person who prefers not to associate with others.

lone·some (lohn-sŏm) *adj.* lonely, causing loneliness. **lone'some·ness** *n.*

long[1] (lawng) *adj.* 1. having great length in space or time. 2. having a certain length of duration, *two miles or two hours long.* 3. seeming to be longer than it really is, *ten long years.* 4. lasting, going far into the past or future, *a long memory; take the long view,* consider the later effects. 5. (*informal*) having much of a certain quality, *he's not long on tact.* 6. of elongated shape. 7. (of vowel sounds) having a pronunciation that is considered to last longer than that of a corresponding "short" vowel (the *a* in *cane* is long, in *can* it is short). **long** *n.* 1. a long time, *will you be gone for long?* 2. a long syllable or vowel, a mark indicating this. 3. a size in clothing. **long** *adv.* 1. for a long time, by a long time; *I shan't be long,* shall not take a long time. 2. throughout a specified time, *all day long; I am no longer a child,* am not one now or henceforth. ☐as *or* so long as, provided that, on condition that. before long, soon. in the long run, in the end, over a long period. long division, the process of dividing one number by another with all calculations written down. long face, a dismal expression. long in the tooth, rather old. long johns, (*informal*) underwear with long legs. long jump, an athletic competition of jumping as far as possible along the ground in one leap. long odds, very uneven odds in betting. long shot, an enterprise or wager with very slight chances for success. long suit, many playing cards of one suit in a hand; a thing at which one excels, *modesty is not his long suit.* long ton, *see* ton. the long and the short of it, all that need be said; the general effect or result.

long[2] *v.* to feel a longing.

long. *abbr.* longitude.

long·boat (lawng-boht) *n.* a sailing ship's largest boat.

long·bow (lawng-boh) *n.* a bow drawn by hand and shooting a long feathered arrow.

long-dis·tance (lawng-dis-tăns) *adj.* traveling or operating between distant places.

lon·gev·i·ty (lon-jev-i-tee) *n.* 1. long life. 2. length of life.

long·hair (lawng-hair) *n.* (*slang*) 1. an intellectual. 2. a lover of classical music. **long'haired** *adj.*

long·hand (lawng-hand) *n.* ordinary writing, contrasted with shorthand or typing or printing.

long·horn (lawng-horn) *n.* one of a breed of cattle with long horns.

long·ing (lawng-ing) *n.* an intense persistent wish. **long'ing·ly** *adv.*

long·ish (lawng-ish) *adj.* rather long.

lon·gi·tude (lon-ji-tood) *n.* the distance east or west (measured in degrees) from the meridian that runs from pole to pole through Greenwich, England.

lon·gi·tu·di·nal (lon-ji-too-dĭ-năl) *adj.* 1. of longitude. 2. of or in length, measured lengthwise. **lon·gi·tu'di·nal·ly** *adv.*

long-leg·ged (lawng-leg-id) *adj.* having long legs.

long-lived (lawng-lɪvd) *adv.* having a long life, lasting for a long time.

long-play·ing (lawng-play-ing) *adj.* of or relating to microgroove phonograph records that play at 33⅓ revolutions per minute.

long-range (lawng-raynj) *adj.* having a long range, relating to a period far into the future.

long·shore·man (lawng-shohr-măn) *n.* (*pl.* -men, *pr.* -mĕn) one who is employed in loading and unloading ships.

long·stand·ing (lawng-stan-ding) *adj.* having existed for a long time, *a longstanding grievance.*

long-suf·fer·ing (lawng-suf-ĕ-ring) *adj.* bearing provocation patiently.

long-term (lawng-turm) *adj.* of or for a long period.

long·time (lawng-tɪm) *adj.* having been for a long time.

long·ways (lawng-wayz), **long·wise** (lawng-wɪz) (*informal*) *adv.* lengthwise.

long-wind·ed (lawng-win-did) *adj.* talking or writing at tedious length.

loo·fah (loo-fǎ) *n.* the dried pod of a kind of gourd, used as a rough sponge.

look (luuk) *v.* 1. to use or direct one's eyes in order to see or search or examine. 2. to direct one's eyes or one's attention, to consider; *they look to her for help,* rely on her to provide it. 3. (of things) to face in a certain direction. 4. to have a certain appearance, to seem to be, *the fruit looks ripe; made him look foolish.* **look** *n.* 1. the act of looking, a gaze or glance. 2. an inspection or search, *take a look.* 3. appearance, *is blessed with good looks; wet-look paint; I don't like the look of this,* find it alarming. □**look after,** to take care of; to attend to. **look down on** *or* **look down one's nose at,** to regard with contempt. **look for,** to expect, to hope or be on the watch for. **look forward to,** to be waiting eagerly for an expected thing or event. **look here!,** an exclamation of protest. **look in,** to make a short visit. **looking glass,** a glass mirror. **look into,** to investigate. **look on,** to be a spectator. **look out,** to be vigilant. **look over,** to inspect. **look sharp,** be alert. **look to,** to attend to; to rely on. **look up,** to search for information about, *look up words in a dictionary;* to improve in prospects, *things are looking up;* to go to visit, *look us up.* **look up to,** to admire and respect as superior.

look·a·like (luuk-ǎ-lɪk) *n.* a person or thing closely resembling another.

look·out (luuk-owt) *n.* 1. looking out, a watch. 2. one who keeps watch. 3. a place from which observation is kept. 4. a person's own concern, *that's his lookout.*

look-see (luuk-see) *n. (informal)* a quick overall survey.

loom¹ (loom) *n.* an apparatus for weaving cloth.

loom² *v.* to come into view suddenly, to appear close at hand or with threatening aspect.

loon (loon) *n.* a diving bird with a loud wild cry.

loon·y (loo-nee) *n.* (*pl.* **loon·ies**) *(slang)* a lunatic. **loony** *adj. (slang)* crazy. □**loony bin,** *(slang)* a mental hospital.

loop (loop) *n.* 1. the shape produced by a curve that crosses itself. 2. any path or pattern shaped roughly like this. 3. a length of cord or wire etc. forming a curve, a curved piece of metal serving as a handle. 4. a complete circuit for electrical current. 5. a flying stunt in which an airplane does a vertical circle, turning upside down between climb and dive. 6. a film whose ends have been spliced together so that it will run continuously. 7. a contraceptive coil. **loop** *v.* 1. to form into a loop or loops. 2. to fasten or join with a loop or loops. 3. to enclose in a loop. □**the Loop,** the central part of Chicago, within a loop of elevated railroad tracks. ▷Do not confuse *loop* with *loupe.*

loop·hole (loop-hohl) *n.* 1. a narrow opening in the wall of a fort etc., for shooting or looking through or to admit light or air. 2. a way of evading a rule or contract etc., especially through an omission or inexact wording in its provisions.

loose (loos) *adj.* (**loos·er, loos·est**) 1. freed from bonds or restraint, (of an animal) not tethered or shut in; *a loose ball,* (in football etc.) not in any player's possession. 2. detached or detachable from its place, not rigidly fixed. 3. not fastened together, not held or packed or contained in something. 4. not organized strictly, *a loose confederation.* 5. slack, relaxed, not tense or tight, *loose skin; loose bowels,* with a tendency to diarrhea;

a loose tongue, indiscreet. 6. not compact, not dense in texture, arranged at wide intervals, *a loose weave.* 7. inexact, vague; *a loose translation,* approximate, not close to the original. 8. slack in moral principles or conduct, promiscuous, *loose women.* **loose** *adv.* loosely, *loose-fitting.* **loose** *v.* (**loosed, loos·ing**) 1. to release. 2. to untie or loosen. 3. to fire a gun or missile, *loose off a round of ammunition.* **loose'ly** *adv.* **loose'ness** *n.* □**at loose ends,** without definite occupation. **loose end,** a point that has not been settled. **on the loose,** having a spree; free, not confined.

loose-joint·ed (loos-join-tid) *adj.* having supple joints.

loose-leaf (loos-leef) *adj.* (of a notebook etc.) with each leaf separate and removable.

loose-limbed (loos-limd) *adj.* having supple limbs.

loos·en (loo-sěn) *v.* to make or become loose or looser. □**loosen a person's tongue,** to make him talk freely. **loosen up,** to relax, to limber up.

loose·strife (loos-strɪf) *n.* a kind of marsh plant.

loose-tongued (loos-tungd) *adj.* speaking freely or too freely.

loot (loot) *n.* 1. goods taken from an enemy or by theft. 2. *(informal)* a collection of gifts, awards, or purchased goods. **loot** *v.* 1. to plunder, to take as loot. 2. to rob or steal from stores or houses that are left unprotected after a violent event. **loot'er** *n.*

lop¹ (lop) *v.* (**lopped, lop·ping**) to cut away branches or twigs of, to cut off.

lop² *v.* (**lopped, lop·ping**) to hang limply.

lope (lohp) *v.* (**loped, lop·ing**) to run with a long bounding stride. **lope** *n.* a long bounding stride.

lop-eared (lop-eerd) *adj.* having drooping ears.

lop·sid·ed (lop-sɪ-did) *adj.* with one side lower or smaller or heavier than the other. **lop'sid'ed·ly** *adv.* **lop'sid'ed·ness** *n.*

loq. *abbr.* he or she speaks (with speaker's name added, as a stage direction or to inform the reader). ▷Latin *loquitur.*

lo·qua·cious (loh-kway-shǔs) *adj.* talkative. **lo·qua'cious·ly** *adv.* **lo·quac·i·ty** (loh-kwas-i-tee) *n.*

lor·an (loh-ran) *n.* a system of navigation using signal pulses from radio transmitters. ▷From *lo*(ng) *ra*(nge) *n*(avigation).

lord (lord) *n.* 1. a master or ruler or sovereign. 2. a nobleman; *live like a lord,* live sumptuously. 3. *the Lord,* God, the translation for several biblical words referring to the God of the Old Testament and to Christ. 4. the title or form of address to certain high officials in Britain, *the Lord Chief Justice.* 5. *the Lords,* the British House of Lords. **lord** *v.* to domineer, *lording it over the whole club.* □**lord of the manor,** (in the Middle Ages) the master from whom men held land and to whom they owed service. **Lord's day,** the sabbath or day of rest in Judaism and Christianity, observed by Jews and some Christians on Saturday and by the majority of Christians on Sunday. **Lord's Prayer,** the prayer taught by Christ to his disciples, beginning "Our Father." **Lord's Supper,** the Eucharist.

lord·ly (lord-lee) *adj.* (**lord·li·er, lord·li·est**) 1. haughty, imperious. 2. suitable for a lord, *a lordly mansion.*

lor·do·sis (lor-doh-sis) *n.* an abnormal forward curvature of the spine.

lord·ship (lord-ship) *n.* a title used in speaking to or about a man of the rank of Lord, *your lordship.*

lore (lohr) *n.* a body of traditions and knowledge on a subject or possessed by a class of people, *bird lore; gypsy lore.*

lor·gnette (lorn-yet) *n.* a pair of eyeglasses or opera glasses held to the eyes on a long handle.

lose (looz) *v.* **(lost, los·ing)** 1. to be deprived of, (as by death or accident). 2. to cease to have or maintain, *lose confidence; lose one's balance; car lost speed.* 3. to become unable to find, to miss from among one's possessions. 4. to fail to keep (a thing etc.) in sight or to follow (a piece of reasoning) mentally; *lose one's way,* to fail to find the right path etc. 5. to fail to obtain, *lost the contract.* 6. to get rid of, *lose weight; managed to lose our pursuers.* 7. to be defeated in a contest or lawsuit or argument etc. 8. to forfeit, *he lost his right of appeal by pleading guilty.* 9. to waste time or an opportunity, *lost twenty minutes because of a flat tire.* 10. to suffer loss, to be worse off, *we lost on the deal.* 11. to cause (a person) the loss of, *delay lost them the contract.* 12. (of a clock) to become slow; *it loses two minutes a day,* becomes this amount behind the correct time. **los'er** *n.* □**lose ground,** to be forced to retreat or give way. **lose heart,** to become discouraged. **lose one's heart,** to fall in love. **lose one's life,** to be killed. **lose out,** *(informal)* to be unsuccessful; to suffer loss. **losing battle,** one in which defeat seems certain.

loss (laws) *n.* 1. losing, being lost. 2. a person or thing lost. 3. money lost in a business transaction, the excess of outlay over returns. 4. a disadvantage or suffering caused by losing something; *it's no loss,* the loss does not matter. □**be at a loss,** to be puzzled, to be unable to know what to do or say. **loss leader,** a popular article sold at a loss to attract customers who may then buy other articles.

lost (lawst) *v.* *see* **lose. lost** *adj.* 1. strayed or separated from its owner, *a lost dog.* 2. engrossed, *lost in thought.* □**be lost on,** to fail to influence or draw the attention of, *our hints were lost on him.* **get lost!,** *(slang)* cease being annoying. **lost cause,** an undertaking that can no longer be successful.

loth = **loath.**

Lo·thar·i·o (loh-thair-i-oh) *n.* (*pl.* **-os**) a libertine.

lo·tion (loh-shŏn) *n.* a medicinal or cosmetic liquid applied to the skin.

lot·ter·y (lot-ĕ-ree) *n.* (*pl.* **-ter·ies**) 1. a system of raising money by selling numbered tickets and distributing prizes to the holders of numbers

drawn at random. 2. something whose outcome is thought to be governed by luck, *marriage is a lottery.*

lot·to (lot-oh) *n.* a game of chance resembling bingo.

lo·tus (loh-tŭs) *n.* (*pl.* **-tus·es**) 1. a kind of tropical water lily. 2. a mythical fruit represented as inducing a state of lazy and luxurious dreaminess. □**lotus position,** a cross-legged position in yoga, adopted for meditation.

loud (lowd) *adj.* 1. easily heard, producing much noise. 2. (of colors etc.) unpleasantly bright, gaudy. **loud** *adv.* loudly. **loud'ly** *adv.* **loud' ness** *n.*

loud·mouth (lowd-mowth) *n.* (*pl.* **-mouths,** *pr.* -mow*th*z) a person who talks loudly and annoyingly. **loud·mouthed** (lowd-mow*th*d, -mowtht) *adj.*

loud·speak·er (lowd-spee-kĕr) *n.* an apparatus (especially part of a radio) that converts electrical impulses into audible sound.

Lou·i·si·an·a (loo-ee-zi-an-ă) a state of the U.S.

lounge (lownj) *v.* **(lounged, loung·ing)** to loll, to sit or stand about idly. **lounge** *n.* 1. a waiting room at an airport etc., with seats for waiting passengers. 2. a public room (in a hotel etc.) for sitting in. **loung'er** *n.*

loupe (loop) *n.* a magnifying instrument consisting of a lens mounted on a frame, *jeweler's loupe.* ▷Do not confuse *loupe* with *loop.*

lour (lowr) = **lower²**.

louse (lows) *n.* (*pl.* **lice,** *pr.* lis) 1. a small insect that lives as a parasite on animals or plants. 2. (*pl.* **lous·es**) *(slang)* a contemptible person. □**louse up,** *(slang)* to make a mess of.

lous·y (low-zee) *adj.* **(lous·i·er, lous·i·est)** 1. infested with lice. 2. *(slang)* disgusting, very bad or ill, *I feel lousy.* 3. *(slang)* well provided, swarming, *he's lousy with money; lousy with tourists.* **lous'i·ly** *adv.* **lous'i·ness** *n.*

lout (lowt) *n.* a clumsy ill-mannered young man. **lout·ish** (low-tish) *adj.* like a lout.

lou·ver (loo-vĕr) *n.* one of a set of overlapping slats arranged to admit air but exclude light or rain. **lou'vered** *adj.*

lov·a·ble (luv-ă-bĕl) *adj.* easy to love.

lov·age (luv-ij) *n.* an herb with leaves that are used for flavoring soups and in salads.

love (luv) *n.* 1. warm liking or affection for a person, affectionate devotion; *there's no love lost between them,* they dislike each other. 2. sexual affection or passion, the relation between sweethearts. 3. God's benevolence toward mankind. 4. strong liking for a thing, *love of music.* 5. affectionate greetings, *send one's love.* 6. a loved person, a sweetheart, *(informal)* a familiar form of address. 7. (in games) no score, zero; *love all,* neither side has yet scored; *a love game,* in which the loser has not scored at all. **love** *v.* **(loved, lov·ing)** 1. to feel love for. 2. to like greatly, to take pleasure in having or doing something. □**for love,** because of affection; without receiving payment; *cannot get it for love or money,* by any means. **in love,** feeling love (especially romantic or sexual love) for another person. **love affair,** a romantic or sexual relationship between two people who are in love. **love apple,** *(old use)* the tomato. **love beads,** a long string of beads worn by members of both sexes to indicate freedom from traditional attitudes and customs. **love feast,** a meal in token of brotherly love among early Christians;

a modern religious service in imitation of this; any convivial gathering. **love-hate relationship,** an intense emotional response involving both love and hate. **love knot,** a kind of double knot with interlacing bows on each side, symbolizing true love. **love letter,** a letter between sweethearts and concerning their love. **love match,** a marriage made because the two people are in love with each other. **love seat,** an armchair or sofa for two persons. **love song,** a song expressing love. **love story,** a novel etc. of which the main theme is romantic love. **make love,** *see* **make.**

love·bird (luv-burd) *n.* a kind of parakeet that seems to show great affection for its mate.

love·less (luv-lis) *adj.* without love, *a loveless marriage.*

love·lorn (luv-lorn) *adj.* pining with love, forsaken by one's lover.

love·ly (luv-lee) *adj.* **(love·li·er, love·li·est)** 1. beautiful, attractive. 2. *(informal)* delightful, *having a lovely time.* **lovely** *n.* *(pl.* **-lies)** *(informal)* a pretty woman. **love'li·ness** *n.*

love·mak·ing (luv-may-king) *n.* 1. courtship. 2. sexual intercourse.

lov·er (luv-ĕr) *n.* 1. someone (especially a man) who is in love with another person, a suitor. 2. a person having an illicit love affair. 3. one who likes or enjoys something, *lover of music; music lovers.* ☐**lovers' lane,** a secluded road or place used by couples seeking privacy.

love·sick (luv-sik) *adj.* languishing because of love. **love'sick·ness** *n.*

lov·ing (luv-ing) *adj.* feeling or showing love. **lov'ing·ly** *adv.* ☐**loving cup,** a large drinking vessel with two or more handles, passed around at a banquet; a sports cup *(see* **cup** *n.,* definition 4).

low[1] (loh) *n.* the deep sound made by cattle, a moo. **low** *v.* to make this sound.

low[2] *adj.* 1. not high or tall, not extending far upward. 2. (of ground) not far above sea level, low in relation to surrounding land. 3. ranking below others in importance or quality. 4. ignoble, vulgar, *low cunning; keeps low company.* 5. less than what is normal in amount or intensity etc., *low prices; a low opinion,* unfavorable. 6. (of a sound or voice) deep, not shrill, having slow vibrations. 7. not loud, *spoke in a low voice.* 8. lacking in vigor, depressed. **low** *n.* 1. a low level or figure, *stock prices reached a new low.* 2. an area of low barometric pressure. **low** *adv.* 1. in or at or to a low level or position. 2. in or to a low degree. 3. in a low tone, (of sound) at a low pitch. **low'ness** *n.* ☐**low beam,** the short range of an automobile headlight. **Low Church,** that section of the Anglican Church that gives only a low place to ritual and the authority of bishops and clergy. **Low Countries,** the Netherlands, Belgium, and Luxembourg. **lowest common denominator,** *see* **denominator. lowest common multiple,** *see* **least. low frequency,** (in radio) thirty to three hundred kilohertz. **low gear,** the motor vehicle gear that produces the most power and least speed. **Low German,** the dialects of the German language that are not High German. **low profile,** deliberately restrained behavior to avoid being noticed. **low season,** the period when a resort etc. has relatively few visitors. **low tide,** the tide at its lowest level; the time when this occurs. **low water,** low tide.

low·boy (loh-boi) *n.* a chest with drawers and fairly short legs.

low·brow (loh-brow) *adj.* *(informal)* not intellectual or cultured. **lowbrow** *n.* *(informal)* a lowbrow person.

low-cal (loh-kal) *adj.* *(informal)* having very few calories.

low-class (loh-klas) *adj.* of low quality or social class.

low·down (loh-down) *adj.* dishonorable. **lowdown** (loh-down) *n.* *(slang)* the true facts, inside information.

low·er[1] (loh-ĕr) *adj.* 1. less high in place or position. 2. situated on less high land or to the south; *Lower Egypt,* the part nearest to the Nile Delta. 3. ranking below others; *the lower animals* or *plants,* those of relatively simple structure, not highly developed; *lower classes,* people of low social or cultural rank. **lower** *adv.* in or to a lower position etc. **lower** *v.* 1. to let or haul down. 2. to make or become lower, to reduce in amount or quantity etc.; *lower one's eyes,* to direct one's gaze downward. ☐**lower case,** letters (for printing type) that are not capitals. **lower house,** the more broadly representative (and usually larger) body in a bicameral legislature, as the U.S. House of Representatives (as distinct from the Senate).

low·er[2] (loh-ĕr) *v.* 1. to frown or scowl. 2. (of clouds or the sky etc.) to look dark and threatening.

low·er-class (loh-ĕr-klas) *adj.* relating to the lowest class in society.

low·er·class·man (loh-ĕr-klas-măn) *n.* *(pl.* **-men,** *pr.* -mĕn) a freshman or sophomore in a high school or college.

low·er·most (loh-ĕr-mohst) *adj.* below all else, the lowest.

low-key (loh-kee) *adj.* restrained.

low·land (loh-lănd) *n.* low-lying land. **lowland** *adj.* of or in lowland.

low·land·er (loh-lăn-dĕr) *n.* a native or inhabitant of lowlands, especially those of Scotland.

low·ly (loh-lee) *adj.* **(low·li·er, low·li·est)** of humble rank or condition. **low'li·ness** *n.*

low-pitched (loh-picht) *adj.* 1. (of sound) low. 2. (of a roof) not very steep.

low-rise (loh-rīz) *adj.* (of buildings) having few stories and no elevators.

low-ten·sion (loh-ten-shŏn) *adj.* having or operating at low voltage.

lox[1] (loks) *n.* smoked salmon.

lox[2], **LOX** *n.* liquid oxygen.

loy·al (loi-ăl) *adj.* steadfast in one's allegiance to a person or cause or to one's country. **loy'al·ly** *adv.* **loy·al·ty** (loi-ăl-tee) *n.* (*pl.* **-ties**).

loy·al·ist (loi-ă-list) *n.* 1. a person who is loyal, especially to the established government during a revolt. 2. *Loyalist,* a colonist loyal to the British government during the American Revolution.

loz·enge (loz-inj) *n.* 1. a four-sided diamond-shaped figure. 2. a small tablet of flavored sugar or medicine to be dissolved in the mouth.

LP *abbr.* (*pl.* LPs, LP's) a long-playing record.

L.P. *abbr.* low pressure.

LPG *abbr.* liquefied petroleum gas.

LPN *abbr.* licensed practical nurse.

Lr *symbol* lawrencium.

LR *abbr.* living room.

L.S. *abbr.* 1. left side. 2. letter signed. 3. the place of the seal (Latin *locus sigilli*).

LSD (el-es-dee) *n.* a powerful drug that produces

hallucinations (= *ly*sergic acid *d*iethylamide).
LSS *abbr.* life-support system.
lt. *abbr.* light.
Lt. *abbr.* lieutenant.
L.T. *abbr.* 1. long ton. 2. low-tension.
Lt. Col., LTC *abbr.* lieutenant colonel.
Lt. Comdr. *abbr.* lieutenant commander.
Ltd. *abbr.* Limited.
Lt. Gen., LTG *abbr.* lieutenant general.
ltr. *abbr.* letter.
Lu *symbol* lutetium.
Lu·an·da (loo-ahn-dă) the capital of Angola.
lu·au (loo-ow) *n.* (*pl.* **lu·aus**) a Hawaiian feast.
lub·ber (lub-ĕr) *n.* 1. a big clumsy person, especially a seaman. 2. a landlubber. **lub'ber·ly** *adv.*
lube (loob) *n.* (*informal)* lubricant.
lu·bri·cant (loo-brĭ-kănt) *n.* a lubricating substance.
lu·bri·cate (loo-brĭ-kayt) *v.* (**lu·bri·cat·ed, lu·bri·cat·ing**) to oil or grease (machinery etc.) so that it moves easily. **lu·bri·ca·tion** (loo-brĭ-kay-shŏn) *n.*
lu·bri·cious (loo-brish-ŭs) *adj.* 1. slippery, smooth, oily. 2. lewd, salacious. **lu·bric·i·ty** (loo-bris-i-tee) *n.*
lu·cent (loo-sĕnt) *adj.* 1. shining, luminous. 2. translucent.
lu·cid (loo-sid) *adj.* 1. clearly expressed, easy to understand. 2. sane; *lucid intervals,* periods of sanity between periods of insanity. **lu'cid·ly** *adv.* **lu'cid·ness** *n.* **lu·cid·i·ty** (loo-sid-i-tee) *n.*
Lu·ci·fer (loo-sĭ-fĕr) *n.* the chief rebel angel, Satan, before his fall.
Lu·cite (loo-sɪt) *n.* (*trademark)* a tough unsplinterable transparent acrylic thermoplastic, much lighter than glass.
luck (luk) *n.* 1. chance thought of as a force that brings either good or bad fortune. 2. the events etc. (either favorable or unfavorable to one's interests) that it brings. 3. good fortune, *it will bring you luck.* □**in luck,** having good fortune. **out of luck,** not in luck.
luck·y (luk-ee) *adj.* (**luck·i·er, luck·i·est**) having or bringing or resulting from good luck. **luck'i·ly** *adv.*
lu·cra·tive (loo-kră-tiv) *adj.* profitable, producing much money. **lu'cra·tive·ness** *n.* **lu'cra·tive·ly** *adv.*
lu·cre (loo-kĕr) *n.* (*contemptuous)* money, money-making as a motive for action. □**filthy lucre,** (*humorous)* money.
lu·cu·bra·tion (loo-kyuu-bray-shŏn) *n.* 1. studying hard, especially late at night. 2. a literary work, especially of pedantic or elaborate character.
lu·di·crous (loo-dĭ-krŭs) *adj.* absurd, ridiculous, laughable. **lu'di·crous·ly** *adv.* **lu'di·crous·ness** *n.*
luff (luf) *v.* to bring a ship's head nearer to the direction from which the wind is blowing. **luff** *n.* the side of a fore-and-aft sail next to the mast or stay.
lug¹ (lug) *v.* (**lugged, lug·ging**) to drag or carry with great effort.
lug² *n.* an earlike part or projection on an object, by which it may be carried or fixed in place etc. □**lug nut,** a heavy-duty nut for securing a wheel to a motor vehicle. **lug wrench,** a tool for tightening or removing a lug nut.
lug·gage (lug-ij) *n.* a traveler's baggage.

lu·gu·bri·ous (luu-goo-bri-ŭs) *adj.* dismal, mournful. **lu·gu'bri·ous·ly** *adv.* **lu·gu'bri·ous·ness** *n.*
lug·worm (lug-wurm) *n.* a large marine worm used as bait.
Luke (look) *n.* 1. one of the twelve apostles closely associated with St. Paul and author of the third Gospel and Acts of the Apostles. 2. the third Gospel.
luke·warm (look-worm) *adj.* 1. only slightly warm. 2. not enthusiastic, *got a lukewarm reception.*
lull (lul) *v.* 1. to soothe or send to sleep. 2. to calm (suspicions etc.). 3. (of a storm or noise) to lessen, to become quiet. **lull** *n.* a temporary period of quiet or inactivity.
lull·a·by (lul-ă-bɪ) *n.* (*pl.* **-bies**) a soothing song sung to put a child to sleep.
lum·ba·go (lum-bay-goh) *n.* rheumatic pain in the muscles of the lower back.
lum·bar (lum-băr, -bahr) *adj.* of or in the lower back.
lum·ber¹ (lum-bĕr) *n.* timber sawed into planks. **lumber** *v.* to cut lumber or saw it into planks. **lum'ber·man** *n.* □**lumber jacket,** a cold-weather hip-length jacket.
lumber² *v.* to move in a heavy clumsy way.
lum·ber·jack (lum-bĕr-jak) *n.* a person whose trade is the cutting or conveying or preparing of timber.
lum·ber·yard (lum-bĕr-yahrd) *n.* a place where lumber and various building materials are sold.
lu·mi·nar·y (loo-mĭ-ner-ee) *n.* (*pl.* **-nar·ies**) 1. a natural light-giving body, especially the sun or the moon. 2. a person having much intellectual, moral, or spiritual influence.
lu·mi·nes·cent (loo-mĭ-nes-ĕnt) *adj.* emitting light without being hot. **lu·mi·nes'cence** *n.*
lu·mi·nous (loo-mĭ-nŭs) *adj.* emitting light, glowing in the dark. **lu·mi·nos·i·ty** (loo-mĭ-nos-i-tee) *n.*
lum·mox (lum-ŏks) *n.* (*informal)* a clumsy or stupid person.
lump¹ (lump) *n.* 1. a hard or compact mass, usually one without a regular shape. 2. a protuberance or swelling. 3. (*informal)* a heavy dull or stupid person. 4. *lumps, (slang)* misfortunes or criticism or punishment. **lump** *v.* to put or consider together, to treat as alike, *lump them together.* □**lump in the throat,** a feeling of pressure there caused by emotion. **lump sugar,** sugar in small lumps or cubes. **lump sum,** a single payment covering a number of items or paid all at once, not in installments.
lump² *v.* **lump it,** (*informal)* to put up with something one dislikes.
lump·ish (lum-pish) *adj.* heavy and dull or stupid.
lump·y (lum-pee) *adj.* (**lump·i·er, lump·i·est**) full of lumps, covered in lumps. **lump'i·ness** *n.*
lu·na·cy (loo-nă-see) *n.* 1. insanity. 2. great folly.
lu·nar (loo-năr) *adj.* of the moon. □**lunar month,** the interval between new moons (about 29½ days); four weeks.
lu·na·tic (loo-nă-tik) *n.* an insane person, one who is extremely foolish or reckless. **lunatic** *adj.* insane, extremely foolish or reckless. □**lunatic asylum,** (*old use)* a mental hospital. **lunatic fringe,** a few eccentric or fanatical members of a political or other group.
lunch (lunch) *n.* a meal taken in the middle of the

day. **lunch** *v.* to eat lunch. ☐**lunch box,** a small metal or plastic case used by working people to carry sandwiches and other food for lunch to their jobs. **lunch break,** time given to employees for eating lunch. **lunch counter,** a restaurant with quick service of lunches. **out to lunch,** *(slang)* silly or distracted.

lunch·eon (lun-chŏn) *n.* *(formal)* lunch. ☐**luncheon meat,** any of several kinds of meat loaf sliced and served cold for sandwiches or salads.

lunch·eon·ette (lun-chŏ-net) *n.* an establishment selling light lunches.

lunch·room (lunch-room) *n.* a luncheonette, a cafeteria or room where food may be eaten, as in a school or place of work.

lunch·time (lunch-tɪm) *n.* the time when lunch is eaten.

lune (loon) *n.* a crescent-shaped figure formed on a sphere or plane by two arcs intersecting at two points.

lu·nette (loo-net) *n.* a crescent-shaped or semicircular object or opening or space.

lung (lung) *n.* either of the two breathing organs, in the chest of man and most vertebrates, that draw in air and bring it into contact with the blood. ☐**lung power,** power of voice.

lunge (lunj) *n.* a sudden forward movement of the body toward something, a thrust. **lunge** *v.* **(lunged, lung·ing)** to make a lunge.

lung·fish (lung-fish) *n.* (*pl.* **-fish·es, -fish**) a fish that has lungs as well as gills.

lunk·head (lungk-hed) *n.* *(slang)* a stupid or dull person.

lu·pine[1] (loo-pin) *n.* a garden plant with long tapering spikes of flowers, bearing seeds in pods.

lu·pine[2] (loo-pɪn) *adj.* of wolves, wolflike.

lu·pus (loo-pŭs) *n.* an ulcerous disease of the skin, especially tuberculosis of the skin. ☐**lupus er·y·the·ma·to·sus** (er-ĭ-thee-mă-toh-sŭs), a disease in which one's antibodies attack one's own cells, characterized by a masklike inflammation of the cheeks and nose.

lurch[1] (lurch) *n.* **leave in the lurch,** to abandon (a person etc.) so that he is left in an awkward situation.

lurch[2] *n.* an unsteady swaying movement to one side. **lurch** *v.* to make such a movement, to stagger.

lure (loor) *n.* 1. something that attracts or entices or allures. 2. its power of attracting. 3. a bait or decoy for wild animals or for fish, a device used to attract and recall a trained hawk. **lure** *v.* **(lured, lur·ing)** to entice, to attract by the promise of pleasure or gain.

lu·rid (loor-id) *adj.* 1. in glaring colors or combinations of color. 2. sensationally and shockingly vivid, *the lurid details.* **lu′rid·ly** *adv.* **lu′rid·ness** *n.*

lurk (lurk) *v.* 1. to lie hidden while waiting to attack. 2. to wait near a place furtively or unobtrusively. 3. to be latent or lingering, *a lurking sympathy for the rebels.*

Lu·sa·ka (loo-sah-kă) the capital of Zambia.

lus·cious (lush-ŭs) *adj.* 1. richly sweet in taste or smell. 2. voluptuously attractive, *a luscious blonde.* **lus′cious·ly** *adv.* **lus′cious·ness** *n.*

lush[1] (lush) *adj.* 1. (of grass etc.) growing thickly and strongly. 2. luxurious, *lush furnishings.* **lush′ly** *adv.* **lush′ness** *n.*

lush[2] *n.* *(slang)* a drunkard.

lust (lust) *n.* 1. intense sexual desire. 2. any intense desire for something, *lust for power.* **lust** *v.* to feel lust. **lust′ful** *adj.*

lus·ter (lus-tĕr) *n.* 1. the soft brightness of a smooth or shining surface. 2. glory, distinction, *add luster to the assembly.* 3. a kind of metallic glaze on pottery and porcelain. **lus′ter·less** *adj.* **lus·trous** (lus-trŭs) *adj.*

lus·tral (lus-trăl) *adj.* of or used in ceremonial purification.

lust·y (lus-tee) *adj.* **(lust·i·er, lust·i·est)** strong and vigorous, full of vitality. **lust′i·ly** *adv.* **lust′i·ness** *n.*

lute (loot) *n.* a guitarlike instrument with a pearshaped body, popular in the 14th–17th centuries.

lu·te·ti·um (loo-tee-shi-ŭm) *n.* a rare-earth metallic element.

Lu·ther·an (loo-thĕ-răn) *adj.* 1. of Martin Luther (1483–1546), leader of the Protestant Reformation in Germany, or his teachings. 2. of the Christian denomination bearing his name. **Lutheran** *n.* a member of a Lutheran church. **Lu′ther·an·ism** *n.*

Lux·em·bourg (luk-sĕm-burg) 1. a country in Europe between France and Germany. 2. its capital city.

lux·u·ri·ant (lug-zhoor-ee-ănt) *adj.* growing profusely. **lux·u′ri·ant·ly** *adv.* **lux·u′ri·ance** *n.* ▷Do not confuse *luxuriant* with *luxurious.*

lux·u·ri·ate (lug-zhoor-ee-ayt) *v.* **(lux·u·ri·at·ed, lux·u·ri·at·ing)** to feel great enjoyment, to enjoy as luxury, *luxuriating in the warm sun.*

lux·u·ri·ous (lug-zhoor-ee-ŭs) *adj.* supplied with luxuries, very comfortable. **lux·u′ri·ous·ly** *adv.* **lux·u′ri·ous·ness** *n.* ▷Do not confuse *luxurious* with *luxuriant.*

lux·u·ry (lug-zhŭ-ree) *n.* (*pl.* **-ries**) 1. surroundings and food, dress, etc. that are choice and costly; *a luxury apartment,* comfortable and expensive. 2. luxuriousness, self-indulgence. 3. something costly that is enjoyable but not essential.

lv. *abbr.* leave.

-ly[1] *suffix* used to form adjectives, especially from nouns, meaning having the qualities of, as in *kingly, motherly;* recurring at intervals of, as in *daily, hourly.*

-ly[2] *suffix* used to form adverbs from adjectives meaning in a (specified) manner, as in *boldly, nastily, pathetically;* to or from a (specified) point of view, as in *gradually, outwardly.*

ly·ce·um (lɪ-see-ŭm) *n.* a literary institution or lecture hall.

lye (lɪ) *n.* any strong alkaline solution, especially for washing.

ly·ing (lɪ-ing) *see* **lie**[1], **lie**[2].

ly·ing-in (lɪ-ing-in) *n.* (*pl.* **ly·ings-in, ly·ing-ins**) confinement at childbirth.

lymph (limf) *n.* a colorless fluid from tissues or organs of the body, containing white blood cells. **lym·phat·ic** (lim-fat-ik) *adj.* **lym·phoid** (limfoid) *adj.* ☐**lymph node,** a small mass of tissue where lymph is purified.

lynch (linch) *v.* (of a mob) to execute or punish violently, without a lawful trial.

lynx (lingks) *n.* (*pl.* **lynx·es, lynx**) a wild animal of the cat family with spotted fur, noted for its keen sight.

lynx-eyed (lingks-ɪd) *adj.* keen-sighted.

ly·on·naise (lɪ-ŏ-nayz) *adj.* cooked with onions.

lyre (lɪr) *n.* an ancient musical instrument with strings fixed in a U-shaped frame.

lyre·bird (lɪr-burd) *n.* an Australian bird, the male of which can spread its tail in the shape of a lyre.

lyr·ic (lir-ik) *adj.* of poetry that expresses the poet's thoughts and feelings. **lyric** *n.* 1. a lyric poem. 2. (also *lyrics*) the words of a song.

lyr·i·cal (lir-ĭ-kăl) *adj.* 1. lyric, using language suitable for this. 2. *(informal)* expressing oneself enthusiastically. **lyr'i·cal·ly** *adv.*

lyr·i·cist (lir-ĭ-sist) *n.* a person who writes lyrics, especially for popular songs.

ly·ser·gic (lɪ-sur-jik) **acid di·eth·yl·a·mide** (dɪ-eth-ĭl-ă-mɪd) = **LSD.**

ly·sin (lɪ-sin) *n.* an antibody that destroys bacterial cells.

LZ *abbr.* landing zone.

M

M, m (em) (*pl.* **Ms, M's, m's**) 1. the thirteenth letter of the alphabet. 2. the Roman numeral symbol for 1,000.

m *abbr.* 1. meter(s). 2. mile(s). 3. million(s).

M *abbr.* 1. Mach. 2. mass. 3. medium.

m. *abbr.* 1. male. 2. mark. 3. married. 4. masculine. 5. medium. 6. meter(s). 7. minim. 8. minute. 9. month. 10. moon.

M. *abbr.* 1. Majesty. 2. medicine. 3. Medieval. 4. Meridian. 5. Monday. 6. Monsieur. 7. mountain. 8. noon (Latin *meridies*).

ma (mah) *n.* *(informal)* mother.

MA *abbr.* 1. Massachusetts. 2. mental age.

M.A. *abbr.* Master of Arts.

ma'am (mam) *n.* *(informal)* (as a form of address) madam.

ma·ca·bre (mă-kah-brĕ, mă-kahb) *adj.* gruesome, suggesting death.

mac·ad·am (mă-kad-ăm) *n.* layers of broken stone used in road making, usually with hot tar or asphalt, each layer being rolled hard before the next is put down. **mac·ad'am·ized** *adj.* paved in this way.

ma·caque (mă-kahk) *n.* a monkey of Asia and North Africa.

mac·a·ro·ni (mak-ă-roh-nee) *n.* 1. pasta formed into long tubes. 2. *(old use)* an 18th-century dandy affecting continental manners and fashions.

mac·a·roon (mak-ă-roon) *n.* a cookie made with sugar, white of egg, and ground almonds or coconut.

ma·caw (mă-kaw) *n.* a brightly colored South and Central American parrot with a long tail.

mace[1] (mays) *n.* 1. a medieval weapon. 2. a ceremonial staff as the symbol of a public official's authority.

mace[2] *n.* a spice made from the dried outer covering of nutmeg.

Mace (mays) *n.* *(trademark)* a chemical sprayed in the face in order to subdue or disable by causing tears, dizziness, and nausea. **mace** *v.* **(maced, mac·ing)** to attack with Mace.

mac·é·doine (mas-ĕ-dwahn) *n.* a mixture of chopped fruits or vegetables, often served set in jelly.

mac·er·ate (mas-ĕ-rayt) *v.* **(mac·er·at·ed, mac·er·at·ing)** to make or become soft by steeping in a liquid. **mac·er·a·tion** (mas-ĕ-ray-shŏn) *n.*

Mach (mahk) *n.* **Mach number,** the ratio of the speed of a body to the speed of sound in the same medium; a body traveling at *Mach one* is traveling at the speed of sound, *Mach two* is twice this.

mach. *abbr.* 1. machine. 2. machinery. 3. machinist.

ma·chet·e (mă-shet-ee) *n.* a broad heavy knife used in Central America and the West Indies as a tool and weapon.

mach·i·a·vel·li·an (mak-i-ă-vel-i-ăn) *adj.* elaborately cunning or deceitful. ▷Named after Niccolo dei Machiavelli (1469–1527), an Italian statesman who advised the use of any means, however unscrupulous, that would strengthen a nation. **mach·i·a·vel'li·an·ism** *n.*

ma·chic·o·la·tion (mă-chik-ŏ-lay-shŏn) *n.* an opening in the floor of a parapet, used for dropping stones etc. on attackers. **ma·chic·o·late** (mă-chik-ŏ-layt) *v.* **(ma·chic·o·lat·ed, ma·chic·o·lat·ing)** to provide with machicolations.

mach·i·na·tions (mak-ĭ-nay-shŏnz) *n. pl.* clever scheming, things done by this.

ma·chine (mă-sheen) *n.* 1. an appara us for applying mechanical power, having several parts each with a definite function. 2. something operated by such apparatus, as a bicycle or aircraft. 3. a complex controlling system of an organization, *the political machine.* **machine** *v.* **(ma·chined, ma·chin·ing)** to make or produce or work on (a thing) with a machine. □**machine gun,** a mounted gun mechanically operated that can deliver a rapid and continuous fire of bullets. **machine language,** the signs, symbols, numbers, and letters used by a computer. **machine tool,** a mechanically operated tool.

ma·chine-gun (mă-sheen-gun) *v.* **(ma·chine-gunned, ma·chine-gun·ning)** to shoot at with a machine gun.

ma·chin·er·y (mă-shee-nĕ-ree) *n.* (*pl.* **-er·ies**) 1. machines. 2. mechanism. 3. an organized system for doing something.

ma·chin·ist (mă-shee-nist) *n.* a person who makes or works machinery, one who operates machine tools.

ma·chis·mo (mah-chiz-moh) *n.* the need to prove one's virility or courage by daring action.

ma·cho (mah-choh) *n.* (*pl.* **-chos**) a virile courageous man. **macho** *adj.* virile, manly.

mack·er·el (mak-ĕ-rĕl) *n.* (*pl.* **-el, -els**) an edible seafish. □**mackerel sky,** rows of small white fleecy clouds.

mack·i·naw (mak-ĭ-naw) *n.* 1. a heavy woolen cloth. 2. a warm belted coat of this.

mack·in·tosh (mak-in-tosh) *n.* 1. (chiefly *British*) a raincoat. 2. a waterproof material of rubber and cloth.

mac·ra·mé (mak-ră-may) *n.* 1. a fringe or trimming of knotted thread or cord. 2. the art of making this.

mac·ro·bi·ot·ic (mak-roh-bɪ-ot-ik) *adj.* of or relating to a diet of pure vegetable foods etc. intended to prolong life.

mac·ro·ce·phal·ic (mak-roh-sĕ-fal-ik) *adj.* having a long or large head. **mac·ro·ceph·a·lous** (mak-roh-sef-ă-lŭs) *adj.*

mac·ro·cosm (mak-rŏ-koz-ĕm) *n.* 1. the great

world, the universe. 2. any great whole. **mac·ro·cos·mic** (mak-rŏ-koz-mik) *adj.*

ma·cron (may-kron) *n.* the written or printed mark ¯ placed over a long or stressed vowel.

mac·ro·scop·ic (mak-rŏ-skop-ik), **mac·ro·scop·i·cal** (mak-rŏ-skop-i-kăl) *adj.* 1. visible to the naked eye. 2. regarded in terms of large units, *macroscopic economics.* **mac·ro·scop'i·cal·ly** *adv.*

mad (mad) *adj.* (**mad·der, mad·dest**) 1. having a disordered mind, not sane. 2. extremely foolish, *a mad scheme.* 3. wildly enthusiastic, *is mad about sports.* 4. *(informal)* very annoyed. 5. frenzied, *a mad scramble.* 6. (of an animal) suffering from rabies, *a mad dog.* **mad'ly** *adv.* **mad'ness** *n.* ☐**like mad,** with great haste or energy or enthusiasm.

Mad·a·gas·car (mad-ă-gas-kăr) an island off the southeast coast of Africa, part of the Malagasy Republic.

mad·am (mad-ăm) *n.* 1. a word used in speaking politely to a woman, or prefixed to the name of her office in formal address, *Madam Chairman.* 2. a woman in charge of a brothel.

Ma·dame (mă-dam) *n.* (*pl.* **Mes·dames,** *pr.* may-dam) the title of a French-speaking woman, = Mrs. or madam.

mad·cap (mad-kap) *n.* a wildly impulsive person. **madcap** *adj.* wildly impulsive.

mad·den (mad-ĕn) *v.* to make mad or angry, to irritate. **mad'den·ing** *adj.* **mad'den·ing·ly** *adv.*

mad·der (mad-ĕr) *n.* 1. an Old World plant with yellowish flowers. 2. a red dye prepared from its root or made synthetically.

mad·ding (mad-ing) *adj.* *(old use)* maddening. ☐**the madding crowd,** the frenzied crowd.

made (mayd) *see* **make.**

Ma·dei·ra (mă-deer-ă) *n.* a fortified white wine produced on the island of Madeira.

mad·e·leine (mad-ĕ-len) *n.* a small rich plain cake baked in a round tapering tin.

Ma·de·moi·selle (mad-ĕ-mŏ-zel) *n.* (*pl.* **Mes·de·moi·selles,** *pr.* may-dĕ-mŏ-zel) the title of a French-speaking girl or unmarried woman, = Miss or madam.

made-to-or·der (mayd-too-or-dĕr) *adj.* made according to specific instructions.

made-up (mayd-up) *adj.* 1. fabricated, concocted. 2. wearing makeup. 3. put together.

mad·house (mad-hows) *n.* *(informal)* 1. a mental hospital. 2. a scene of confused uproar.

Ma·di·na do Boe (mă-dee-nă dŏ boh) the capital of Guinea-Bissau.

Mad·i·son (mad-i-sŏn) the capital of Wisconsin.

Mad·i·son (mad-i-sŏn), **James** (1751–1836) the fourth president of the U.S. 1809–17.

mad·man (mad-măn) *n.* (*pl.* **-men,** *pr.* -mĕn) a man who is a lunatic.

Ma·don·na (mă-don-ă) *n.* 1. the Virgin Mary. 2. a picture or statue of the Virgin Mary. ☐**Madonna lily,** a tall lily with white flowers.

ma·dras (mad-răs, mă-dras) *n.* a light cotton fabric often with colored stripes.

Ma·drid (mă-drid) the capital of Spain.

mad·ri·gal (mad-rĭ-găl) *n.* a part song for voices, usually without instrumental accompaniment.

mad·wom·an (mad-wuum-ăn) *n.* (*pl.* **-wom·en,** *pr.* -wim-in) a woman who is a lunatic.

mael·strom (mayl-strŏm) *n.* 1. a great whirlpool. 2. an agitated or tumultuous state of affairs.

mae·nad (mee-nad) *n.* 1. a Bacchante, a priestess of Bacchus. 2. a riotous or frenzied woman.

maes·tro (mɪ-stroh) *n.* (*pl.* **maes·tros, maes·tri,** *pr.* mɪ-stree) 1. a great musical composer or teacher or conductor. 2. a master of any art.

Mae West (may west) *(slang)* an inflatable life jacket. ▷Named after an American film actress (1892–) noted for her large bust.

Ma·fi·a (mah-fi-ă) *n.* 1. a secret organization in Sicily, opposed to legal authority and engaged in crime. 2. a criminal organization involved in smuggling, racketeering, etc.

ma·fi·o·so (mah-fi-oh-soh) *n.* (*pl.* **-si,** *pr.* -see) a member of the Mafia.

mag. *abbr.* 1. magnesium. 2. magnetic. 3. magnetism. 4. magneto. 5. magnitude.

mag·a·zine (mag-ă-zeen) *n.* 1. a paper-covered illustrated periodical publication containing articles or stories etc. by a number of writers. 2. a store for arms and ammunition, or for explosives. 3. a chamber for holding cartridges to be fed into the breech of a gun. 4. a similar device in a camera or slide projector.

ma·gen·ta (mă-jen-tă) *adj. & n.* bright purplish red.

mag·got (mag-ŏt) *n.* a larva, especially of the bluebottle. **mag'got·y** *adj.*

Ma·gi (may-jɪ) *n. pl.* the three wise men from the East who brought offerings to the infant Christ at Bethlehem.

mag·ic (maj-ik) *n.* 1. the supposed art of controlling events or effects etc. by supernatural power. 2. superstitious practices based on belief in this. 3. a mysterious and enchanting quality, *the magic of a spring day.* 4. a type of entertainment such as sleight of hand. **magic** *adj.* of magic, used in producing magic, *magic words.* **mag'i·cal** *adj.* **mag'i·cal·ly** *adv.* ☐**magic carpet,** a mythical carpet able to transport a person on it to any place.

ma·gi·cian (mă-jish-ăn) *n.* 1. a person who is skilled in magic. 2. a conjurer.

mag·is·te·ri·al (maj-i-steer-i-ăl) *adj.* 1. of a magistrate. 2. having or showing authority, imperious. **mag·is·te'ri·al·ly** *adv.*

mag·is·tral (maj-i-străl) *adj.* 1. of a master or masters. 2. of a remedy devised by a physician for a particular case, not included in the pharmacopoeia.

mag·is·trate (maj-i-strayt) *n.* a minor judge, a civil officer who administers the law. **mag·is·tra·cy** (maj-i-stră-see) *n.*

mag·ma (mag-mă) *n.* 1. a crude pasty mixture of mineral or organic matter. 2. a semi-molten stratum under the solid crust of Earth, from which igneous rock is formed by cooling. **mag·ma·tic** (mag-mat-ik) *adj.*

Mag·na Char·ta (mag-nă kahr-tă) the charter establishing the English people's rights concerning personal and political liberty, obtained from King John in 1215.

mag·na cum lau·de (mag-nă kum law-dee) with great academic distinction. ▷Latin.

mag·nan·i·mous (mag-nan-ĭ-mŭs) *adj.* 1. noble and generous in one's conduct, not petty. 2. above revenge, forgiving. **mag·nan'i·mous·ly** *adv.* **mag·nan'i·mous·ness** *n.* **mag·na·nim·i·ty** (mag-nă-nim-i-tee) *n.*

mag·nate (mag-nayt) *n.* a wealthy and influential person, especially in business. ▷Do not confuse *magnate* with *magnet.*

mag·ne·sia (mag-nee-z*h*ǎ) *n.* a white powder that is a compound of magnesium, used as an antacid and mild laxative. **mag·ne'sian** *adj.*

mag·ne·si·um (mag-nee-zi-ŭm) *n.* a silvery white metal that burns with an intensely bright flame.

mag·net (mag-nit) *n.* 1. a piece of iron or steel etc. that can attract iron and that points north and south when suspended. 2. a person or thing that exerts a powerful attraction. ▷Do not confuse *magnet* with *magnate.*

mag·net·ic (mag-net-ik) *adj.* 1. having the properties of a magnet. 2. produced or acting by magnetism. 3. having the power to attract people, *a magnetic personality.* **mag·net'i·cal·ly** *adv.* ☐**magnetic compass,** one using a **magnetic needle** that points north and south. **magnetic core,** iron material that forms the center of an electromagnet, transformer, etc.; a small magnetized iron loop that stores bits of information, acting as one of the basic elements of a computer memory. **magnetic field,** the force field around a magnetic substance. **magnetic flux,** the total of all the lines of force in a magnetic field. **magnetic induction,** magnetizing a body by bringing it close to a magnetized body. **magnetic needle,** a rod that, when used in a compass, indicates the direction of north and south. **magnetic north pole,** the point indicated by a magnetic needle, close to the geographic North Pole but not identical with it. **magnetic pickup,** a phonograph pickup that converts the vibrations of the stylus into electric impulses through the use of a coil in a magnetic field. **magnetic pole,** either pole of a magnet. **magnetic recording,** the process of recording sounds or signals on a magnetic tape, disk, or cartridge. **magnetic storm,** a disturbance of Earth's magnetic field by charged particles from the sun etc. **magnetic tape,** a strip of plastic coated or impregnated with magnetic particles for use in the recording and reproduction of sound.

mag·net·ism (mag-ně-tiz-ĕm) *n.* 1. the properties and effects of magnetic substances. 2. the scientific study of these. 3. great charm and attraction, *personal magnetism.*

mag·net·ite (mag-ně-tɪt) *n.* a magnetic iron oxide.

mag·net·ize (mag-ně-tɪz) *v.* (**mag·net·ized, mag·net·iz·ing**) 1. to give magnetic properties to. 2. to attract as a magnet does. 3. to exert attraction on (a person or people). **mag'net·iz·er** *n.* **mag'ne·tiz·able** *adj.* **mag·net·i·za·tion** (mag-ně-ti-zay-shŏn) *n.*

mag·ne·to (mag-nee-toh) *n.* (*pl.* -tos) a small electric generator using permanent magnets, especially one used to produce electricity for the spark in the ignition system of an engine.

mag·ne·tom·e·ter (mag-ně-tom-ě-těr) *n.* an instrument measuring magnetic forces, especially terrestrial magnetism.

mag·ne·to·sphere (mag-nee-tŏ-sfeer) *n.* the region in which Earth's magnetic field is effective.

mag·ne·to·spher·ic (mag-nee-tŏ-sfer-ik) *adj.*

mag·ne·tron (mag-ně-tron) *n.* an electron tube for amplifying or generating microwaves, with the flow of electrons controlled by an external magnetic field.

mag·ni·fi·ca·tion (mag-nĭ-fĭ-kay-shŏn) *n.* 1. magnifying. 2. the amount by which a lens etc. magnifies things.

mag·nif·i·cent (mag-nif-ĭ-sĕnt) *adj.* 1. splendid in appearance etc. 2. excellent in quality. **mag·nif'i·cent·ly** *adv.* **mag·nif'i·cence** *n.*

mag·nif·i·co (mag-nif-ĭ-koh) *n.* (*pl.* -coes, -cos) 1. a Venetian magnate. 2. a grandee, a noble personage.

mag·ni·fy (mag-nĭ-fɪ) *v.* (**mag·ni·fied, mag·ni·fy·ing**) 1. to make (an object) appear larger than it really is, as a lens or microscope does. 2. to exaggerate. 3. *(old use)* to praise, *My soul doth magnify the Lord.* **mag'ni·fi·er** *n.* ☐**magnifying glass,** a lens (often mounted in a frame) that magnifies things.

mag·nil·o·quent (mag-nil-ŏ-kwĕnt) *adj.* 1. lofty in expression. 2. boastful. **mag·nil'o·quent·ly** *adv.* **mag'nil·o·quence** *n.*

mag·ni·tude (mag-ni-tood) *n.* 1. largeness, size. 2. importance. 2. the degree of brightness of a star. ☐**of the first magnitude,** very important.

mag·no·lia (mag-nohl-yǎ) *n.* a tree having large waxlike usually white or pale pink flowers.

mag·num (mag-nŭm) *n.* a bottle containing two quarts of wine or alcoholic liquor. ☐**magnum opus,** a great literary undertaking, a writer's or other artist's chief production. (▷Latin, = great work.)

mag·pie (mag-pɪ) *n.* 1. a noisy bird with black-and-white plumage. 2. a chatterer. 3. a person who collects objects at random.

Mag·yar (mag-yahr) *n.* 1. a member of a people originally from Finland and western Siberia, now predominant in Hungary. 2. their language. **Magyar** *adj.* of the Magyars or their language.

ma·ha·ra·ja, ma·ha·ra·jah (mah-hǎ-rah-jǎ) *n.* the former title of certain Indian princes.

ma·ha·ra·ni, ma·ha·ra·nee (mah-hǎ-rah-nee) *n.* a maharaja's wife or widow.

ma·ha·ri·shi (mah-hǎ-ree-shee) *n.* a Hindu man of great wisdom.

ma·hat·ma (mǎ-haht-mǎ) *n.* (in India etc.) a title of respect for a person regarded with reverence.

Ma·hi·can (mǎ-hee-kǎn) *n.* (*pl.* -can, -cans) a member of an Indian tribe located in the upper Hudson River valley.

mah·jong, mah·jong (mah-jawng) *n.* a Chinese game for four people, played with pieces called tiles.

ma·hog·a·ny (mǎ-hog-ǎ-nee) *n.* 1. a very hard reddish-brown wood much used for furniture. 2. the tropical tree that produces this. 3. the color of the wood.

ma·hout (mǎ-howt) *n.* an elephant driver.

maid (mayd) *n.* 1. *(old use)* a maiden, a girl. 2. a woman servant. ☐**maid of honor** (*pl.* **maids of honor**), the principal bridesmaid. **the Maid of Orleans,** Joan of Arc.

maid·en (may-děn) *n.* 1. *(old use)* a girl or young unmarried woman, a virgin. 2. a racehorse that has not yet won a race. **maiden** *adj.* 1. unmarried, *maiden aunt.* 2. first, *a maiden speech; maiden voyage.* **maid'en·ly** *adj. & adv.* **maid'en·hood** *n.* ☐**maiden name,** a woman's family name before she marries.

maid·en·hair (may-děn-hair) *n.* a fern with fine hairlike stalks and delicate foliage.

maid·en·head (may-děn-hed) *n.* 1. *(old use)* virginity. 2. the hymen.

maid-in-wait·ing (mayd-in-way-ting) *n.* (*pl.* **maids-in-wait·ing**) a young unmarried woman attending a queen or princess.

maid·ser·vant (mayd-sur-vǎnt) *n.* a female servant especially for indoor work.

mail[1] (mayl) *n.* 1. the official conveyance of letters etc. 2. the letters etc. conveyed. 3. a single collec-

tion or delivery of these. **mail** *v.* to put (a letter etc.) into a post office or mailbox for transmission. ☐**mailing list,** a list of people to whom advertising matter etc. is to be mailed. **mail order,** an order for goods to be sent by mail; *mail-order firm,* a firm doing business mainly by this system. **mail train,** a train carrying mail.
mail² ** *n.* body armor made of metal rings or chains. **mail *v.* to clothe with mail. **mailed** *adj.*
mail·bag (mayl-bag) *n.* a large bag for carrying mail.
mail·box (mayl-boks) *n.* 1. a public box for holding letters etc. to be transmitted. 2. a private box for holding letters etc. delivered by the mailman.
mail·lot (mah-yoh) *n.* (*pl.* **-lots,** *pr.* **-yohz**) 1. a woman's one-piece bathing suit. 2. a jersey. 3. a dancer's or gymnast's tights.
mail·man (mayl-man) *n.* (*pl.* **-men,** *pr.* -men) a man who delivers mail.
maim (maym) *v.* to wound or injure so that some part of the body is useless.
main (mayn) *adj.* principal, most important, greatest in size or extent. **main** *n.* the main pipe or channel or cable in a public system for conveying water, gas, etc. **main'ly** *adv.* ☐**in the main,** for the most part, on the whole. **main line,** the chief railroad line; the chief road or street; (*slang*) a principal vein, especially as the site of drug injection. **Main Line,** a fashionable residential area extending for approximately twenty miles west of Philadelphia and served by a railroad line.
Maine (mayn) a state of the U.S.
main·land (mayn-länd) *n.* a country or continent without its adjacent islands.
main·line (mayn-lın) *v.* (**main·lined, main· lin·ing**) (*slang*) to take illegal drugs through injection into a vein.
main·mast (mayn-mast, -măst) *n.* the principal mast of a sailing ship.
main·sail (mayn-sayl, -săl) *n.* the lowest sail on the mainmast in a square-rigged vessel, the sail set on the aft part of the mainmast in a fore-and-aft-rigged vessel.
main·spring (mayn-spring) *n.* 1. the principal spring of a watch or clock etc. 2. the chief force motivating the actions of a person or group.
main·stay (mayn-stay) *n.* 1. the strong cable that secures the mainmast. 2. the chief support.
main·stream (mayn-streem) *n.* the dominant trend of opinion or style etc.
main·tain (mayn-tayn) *v.* 1. to cause to continue, to keep in existence. 2. to keep in repair, *the house is well maintained.* 3. to support, to provide for, to bear the expenses of, *maintaining his son at college.* 4. to assert as true. **main·tain'a·ble** *adj.*
main·te·nance (mayn-tĕ-năns) *n.* 1. maintaining, being maintained. 2. keeping equipment etc. in repair; *maintenance man,* one employed to do this. 3. provision of the means to support life, an allowance of money for this.
mai tai (mı tı) a rum drink with lemon and pineapple juice on ice.
maî·tre d' (may-tĕr dee, may-trĕ) (*pl.* **maî·tres d',** *pr.* may-tĕrz dee, may-trĕz) (*informal*) = **maître d'hotel.**
maî·tre d'ho·tel (may-tĕr doh-tel, may-trĕ) (*pl.* **mai·tres d'ho·tel,** *pr.* may-tĕr doh-tel, may-trĕ) 1. a major-domo. 2. a head waiter. ▷French.
maize (mayz) *n.* 1. Indian corn. 2. (*British*) corn. 3. the yellow color of corn.

Maj. *abbr.* Major.
ma·jes·tic (mă-jes-tik) *adj.* stately and dignified, imposing. **ma·jes'ti·cal** *adj.* **ma·jes'ti·cal·ly** *adv.*
maj·es·ty (maj-ĕ-stee) *n.* (*pl.* **-ties**) 1. impressive stateliness. 2. sovereign power. 3. the title used in speaking of or to a sovereign or a sovereign's wife or widow, *His* or *Her* or *Your Majesty.*
Maj. Gen. *abbr.* Major General.
ma·jol·i·ca (mă-jol-ĭ-kă) *n.* 1. Renaissance Italian earthenware with colored ornamentation on opaque enamel. 2. a modern imitation of this.
ma·jor (may-jŏr) *adj.* 1. greater, very important, *major roads.* 2. (of a surgical operation) involving danger to the patient's life. 3. (in music) of or based on a scale that has a semitone next above the third and seventh notes and a whole tone elsewhere. **major** *n.* 1. an army officer below lieutenant colonel and above captain. 2. an officer in charge of a section of band instruments, *drum major.* 3. a course of study in which one is specializing. 4. *the majors,* (*informal*) the major leagues. **major** *v.* to specialize (in a certain subject) at a college or university. ☐**major general,** an army officer next below a lieutenant general. **major league,** either of the two highest ranking professional baseball leagues. **major leaguer,** a member of a major league baseball team. **major suit,** (in bridge) spades or hearts.
ma·jor-do·mo (may-jŏr-doh-moh) *n.* (*pl.* **-mos**) the head steward of a great household.
ma·jor·ette (may-jŏ-ret) *n.* a drum majorette (*see* **drum**).
ma·jor·i·ty (mă-jor-i-tee) *n.* (*pl.* **-ties**) 1. the greatest part of a group or class. 2. the number of votes for one party etc. above half of those cast. 3. (in law) legal age, *attained his majority.* ☐**majority rule,** the principle that no minority (especially an ethnic or religious one) should hold political power greatly disproportionate to its numbers. ▷A *majority* is distinguished from a *plurality* as follows: a majority is more than 50% of votes cast; a plurality is the margin of victory for the winner over his nearest rival.
ma·jus·cule (mă-jus-kyool) *n.* a large letter, capital, or uncial. **majuscule, ma·jus'cu·lar** *adj.* written in such letters.
make (mayk) *v.* (**made, mak·ing**) 1. to construct or create or prepare from parts or from other substances. 2. to draw up as a legal document or contract, *make a will.* 3. to establish (laws or rules or distinctions). 4. to arrange ready for use, *make the beds.* 5. to cause to exist, to produce, *make difficulties; make peace.* 6. to result in, to amount to, *two and two make four.* 7. to cause to be or become, *it made me happy; don't make a habit of it; make a day of it,* to carry on an activity etc. so that it fills a day. 8. to frame in the mind, *made a decision.* 9. to succeed in arriving at or achieving a position, *we made Las Vegas by midnight; she finally made the team.* 10. (*slang*) to catch (a train etc.). 11. to form, to serve for, to turn out to be, *this makes pleasant reading; she made him a good wife.* 12. to gain or acquire, *make a profit; make friends,* to become friends. 13. to consider to be, *what do you make the time?; see what you can make of her letter,* how to interpret it. 14. to cause or compel, *make him repeat it.* 15. to perform (an action etc.), *make an attempt; make war.* 16. to ensure the success of,

wine can make the meal; this made my day. **make** *n.* 1. making, the way a thing is made. 2. the origin of manufacture, *British make; our own make of shoes.* □**a made man,** one who has attained success in his life or career. **be made for,** to be ideally suited to. **be the making of,** to be the main factor in the success of. **have it made,** *(slang)* to be sure of success. **have the makings of,** to have the essential qualities for becoming, *she had the makings of a good manager.* **make believe,** to pretend. **make do,** to manage with something that is not really adequate or satisfactory. **make for,** to proceed toward, to try to reach; to tend to bring about, *it makes for domestic harmony.* **make fun of,** to ridicule. **make good,** to become successful or prosperous; *make good the loss,* pay compensation; *make good the damage,* repair it; *made good his escape,* succeeded in escaping. **make it,** to achieve what one wanted, to be successful. **make it up,** to become reconciled after a quarrel. **make it up to someone,** to compensate him. **make love,** to embrace and kiss in courtship; to have sexual intercourse. **make money,** to make a large profit. **make much or little of,** to treat as important or unimportant; *make much of a person,* to give him much flattering attention. **make off,** to go away hastily. **make off with,** to carry away, to steal. **make out,** to write out (a list etc.); to manage to see or read something, *made out a shadowy figure;* to understand the nature of, *I can't make him out;* to assert or claim or pretend to be, *made him out to be a fool; (informal)* to fare, *how did you make out?; (slang)* to pet erotically. **make over,** to transfer the ownership of; to convert for a new purpose. **make room,** to clear a space for something by moving another person or thing. **make time,** to contrive to find time to do something. **make up,** to form or constitute; to put together, to prepare (medicine etc.); to invent (a story etc.); to compensate (for a loss or mistake), *they made up for lost time;* to complete (an amount) by supplying what is lacking; to apply cosmetics to; to reconcile, *let's make up and be friends again; make up one's mind,* to decide. **make up to,** to court, to curry favor with. **make way,** to forge ahead, to progress, to open a way for someone or something. **on the make,** *(slang)* intent on gain; seeking a sexual partner.

make-be·lieve (mayk-bĕ-leev) *adj.* pretended. **make-believe** *n.* pretense.

mak·er (may-kĕr) *n.* one who makes something. □**our** *or* **your Maker,** God.

make·shift (mayk-shift) *n.* a temporary or improvised substitute. **makeshift** *adj.* serving as this.

make·up (mayk-up) *n.* 1. cosmetics applied to the skin, especially of the face. 2. the way something is made up, its composition or constituent parts. 3. a person's character and temperament.

make-work (mayk-wurk) *n.* busywork that prevents idleness on the part of workers but does not accomplish anything of value.

mak·ings (may-kingz) *n. pl.* the essential qualities for becoming.

Mal. *abbr.* 1. Malay. 2. Malayan.

mal- *prefix* badly, faulty, as in *maladjusted, malfeasance.*

Ma·la·bo (mă-lah-boh) the capital of Equatorial Guinea.

Ma·lac·ca (mă-lak-ă) *n.* (also **Malacca cane**) a brown walking stick made from the stem of a kind of palm tree.

mal·a·chite (mal-ă-kɪt) *n.* a green mineral that can be polished.

mal·a·dapt·ed (mal-ă-dap-tid) *adj.* ill suited to a particular environment or purpose or condition.

mal·ad·just·ed (mal-ă-jus-tid) *adj.* (of a person) not well-adjusted to his own circumstances. **mal·ad·just′ment** *n.*

mal·ad·min·is·ter (mal-ăd-min-i-stĕr) *v.* to administer (a business or public affairs) badly or improperly. **mal·ad·min·is·tra·tion** (mal-ăd-min-i-stray-shŏn) *n.*

mal·a·droit (mal-ă-droit) *adj.* bungling. **mal·a·droit′ly** *adv.* **mal·a·droit′ness** *n.*

mal·a·dy (mal-ă-dee) *n.* (*pl.* **-dies**) an illness, a disease.

Mal·a·gas·y (mal-ă-gas-ee) *n.* 1. the language of Madagascar. 2. a native or inhabitant of Madagascar. **Malagasy** *adj.* of Madagascar. □**Malagasy Republic,** a country, including Madagascar, in the Indian Ocean.

ma·laise (mă-layz) *n.* a feeling of illness or mental uneasiness.

mal·a·mute (mal-ă-myoot) *n.* an Eskimo dog.

mal·a·prop·ism (mal-ă-prop-iz-ĕm) *n.* a comical confusion of words, as in *it will percussion the blow* (for *cushion the blow*). ▷Named after Mrs. Malaprop in Sheridan's play *The Rivals,* who made mistakes of this kind.

mal·ap·ro·pos (mal-ap-rŏ-poh) *adj.* inappropriate. **malapropos** *adv.* inappropriately.

ma·lar·i·a (mă-lair-i-ă) *n.* a disease causing fever that recurs at intervals, transmitted by mosquitoes. **ma·lar′i·al** *adj.*

ma·lar·key (mă-lahr-kee) *n. (informal)* nonsense.

mal·a·thi·on (mal-ă-thɪ-on) *n.* an insecticide containing phosphorus.

Ma·la·wi (mah-lah-wee) a country in southeast Africa. **Ma·la′wi·an** *adj. & n.*

Ma·lay (may-lay, mă-lay) *adj.* of a people living in Malaysia and Indonesia. **Malay** *n.* 1. a member of this people. 2. their language.

Ma·lay·a (mă-lay-ă) a group of states forming part of Malaysia. **Ma·lay′an** *adj. & n.*

Malay Archipelago a group of islands in the Indian and Pacific oceans southeast of Asia.

Ma·lay·sia (mă-lay-zhă) a country in southeast Asia. **Ma·lay′sian** *adj. & n.*

mal·con·tent (mal-kŏn-tent) *n.* a person who is discontented and inclined to rebel.

mal de mer (mal dĕ mair) seasickness. ▷French.

Mal·dives (mal-dɪvz) a country consisting of a group of islands southwest of India, formerly the Maldive Islands. **Mal·div′i·an** *adj. & n.*

male (mayl) *adj.* 1. of the sex that can beget offspring by fertilizing egg cells produced by the female. 2. (of a plant) having flowers that contain pollen-bearing organs and not seeds. 3. of a man or men, *male voice choir.* 4. (of parts of machinery etc.) designed to fit into a corresponding female part, *a male screw.* **male** *n.* a male person or animal or plant. **male′ness** *n.*

Ma·lé (mah-lee) the capital of the Maldives.

mal·e·dic·tion (mal-ĕ-dik-shŏn) *n.* a curse.

mal·e·fac·tor (mal-ĕ-fak-tŏr) *n.* a wrongdoer. **mal·e·fac·tion** (mal-ĕ-fak-shŏn) *n.*

ma·lef·ic (mă-lef-ik) *adj.* (of magical arts etc.) harmful, baleful.

ma·lef·i·cent (mă-lef-i-sĕnt) *adj.* 1. hurtful. 2. criminal. **ma·lef'i·cence** *n.*

ma·lev·o·lent (mă-lev-ŏ-lĕnt) *adj.* wishing harm to others. **ma·lev'o·lent·ly** *adv.* **ma·lev'o·lence** *n.*

mal·fea·sance (mal-fee-zăns) *n.* an unlawful act, evildoing, especially official misconduct.

mal·for·ma·tion (mal-for-may-shŏn) *n.* faulty formation. **mal·formed'** *adj.*

mal·func·tion (mal-fungk-shŏn) *n.* faulty functioning. **malfunction** *v.* to function faultily.

Ma·li (mah-lee) a country in West Africa. **Ma'li·an** *adj. & n.*

mal·ice (mal-is) *n.* a desire to harm others or to tease.

ma·li·cious (mă-lish-ŭs) *adj.* feeling or showing or caused by malice. **ma·li'cious·ly** *adv.*

ma·lign (mă-lɪn) *adj.* 1. harmful, *a malign influence.* 2. showing malice. **malign** *v.* to say unpleasant and untrue things about, *maligning an innocent person.* **ma·lig·ni·ty** (mă-lig-ni-tee) *n.*

ma·lig·nant (mă-lig-nănt) *adj.* 1. (of a tumor) growing uncontrollably. 2. feeling or showing great ill will. **ma·lig'nant·ly** *adv.* **ma·lig·nan·cy** (mă-lig-năn-see) *n.*

ma·lin·ger (mă-ling-gĕr) *v.* to pretend to be ill in order to avoid work. **ma·lin'ger·er** *n.*

mall (mawl) *n.* 1. *(old use)* a sheltered walk. 2. a shopping center (*see* **shopping**). 3. a paved or grassy strip dividing a highway.

mal·lard (mal-ărd) *n.* (*pl.* **-lard, -lards**) a kind of wild duck, the male of which has a glossy green head.

mal·le·a·ble (mal-i-ă-bĕl) *adj.* 1. able to be hammered or pressed into shape. 2. easy to influence, adaptable. **mal'le·a·bly** *adv.* **mal·le·a·bil·i·ty** (mal-i-ă-bil-i-tee) *n.*

mal·let (mal-it) *n.* 1. a hammer, usually of wood. 2. a similarly shaped instrument with a long handle, for striking the ball in croquet or polo.

mal·le·us (mal-i-ŭs) *n.* (*pl.* **mal·le·i,** *pr.* mal-i-ɪ) a bone of the middle ear.

mal·low (mal-oh) *n.* a plant with hairy stems and leaves, bearing purple or pink or white flowers.

malm·sey (mahm-zee) *n.* a kind of strong sweet wine.

mal·nour·ished (mal-nur-isht) *adj.* poorly nourished.

mal·nu·tri·tion (mal-noo-trish-ŏn) *n.* insufficient nutrition.

mal·oc·clu·sion (mal-ŏ-kloo-zhŏn) *n.* faulty contact of upper and lower teeth in biting.

mal·o·dor·ous (mal-oh-dŏ-rŭs) *adj.* stinking. **mal·o'dor·ous·ly** *adv.* **mal·o'dor·ous·ness** *n.*

mal·prac·tice (mal-prak-tis) *n.* wrongdoing.

malt (mawlt) *n.* 1. grain (usually barley) that has been allowed to sprout and then dried, used for brewing or distilling or vinegar making. 2. *(informal)* malt liquors. **malt** *v.* to make or be made into malt. **malt'y** *adj.* □**malted milk,** a drink made from dried milk and malt.

Mal·ta (mawl-tă) a country in the Mediterranean Sea.

Mal·tese (mawl-teez) *n.* (*pl.* **-tese**) 1. the language of Malta. 2. a native or inhabitant of Malta. **Maltese** *adj.* of or relating to its people or their language. □**Maltese cat,** cat of a bluish-gray short-haired breed. **Maltese cross,** a cross with four equal arms broadening outward, often indented at the ends. **Maltese dog, Maltese ter-**

rier, a spaniel or terrier of a small breed.

Mal·thu·si·an (mal-thoo-zhăn) *n.* a supporter of the ideas of Malthus. ▷T. R. Malthus (1766–1835) was an English clergyman who argued, in an essay, that population increases faster than the means of subsistence and that its increase should be checked, mainly by sexual restraint. **Malthusian** *adj.* of Malthus. **Mal·thu'si·an·ism** *n.*

malt·ose (mawl-tohs) *n.* a sugar produced by the hydrolysis of starch.

mal·treat (mal-treet) *v.* to treat badly. **mal·treat'ment** *n.*

ma·ma (mah-mă, mă-mah) *n. (informal)* mother.

mam·ba (mahm-bah) *n.* a poisonous black or green South African snake.

mam·bo (mahm-boh) *n.* (*pl.* **-bos**) 1. a Latin American dance like the rhumba. 2. the music for it. **mambo** *v.* to dance the mambo.

mam·ma (mah-mă) *n. (informal)* mother.

mam·mal (mam-ăl) *n.* a member of the class of animals that suckle their young. **mam·ma·li·an** (mă-may-li-ăn) *adj.*

mam·ma·ry (mam-ă-ree) *adj.* of the breasts. □**mammary gland,** a milk-secreting gland.

mam·mo·graph (mam-ŏ-graf) *n.* an x-ray of the breast for the purpose of detecting cancer. **mam·mo·graph·y** (ma-mog-ră-fee) *n.*

mam·mon (mam-ŏn) *n.* (also **Mammon**) wealth personified, regarded as an evil influence.

mam·moth (mam-ŏth) *n.* a large extinct elephant with a hairy coat and curved tusks. **mammoth** *adj.* huge.

mam·my (mam-ee) *n.* (*pl.* **-mies**) 1. *(informal)* mother. 2. *(old use)* a black woman in charge of white children.

man (man) *n.* (*pl.* **men**) 1. a human being, distinguished from other animals by superior mental development, power of articulate speech, and upright posture. 2. mankind. 3. an adult male person. 4. an individual male person considered as an expert or one's assistant or opponent etc., *if you want a good teacher, he's your man.* 5. a type of unspecified sex, an individual, *every man for himself.* 6. a manly person; *is he man enough to do it?,* is he brave enough? 7. a male servant or employee or workman, *masters and men.* 8. an ordinary soldier etc., not an officer. 9. one of the set of small objects moved on a board in playing board games such as chess and checkers. 10. *the man* (*slang,* among blacks) white men, especially the police. **man** *v.* (**manned, man·ning**) to supply with men for service or to operate something, *man the pumps.* □**as one man,** in unison. **be one's own man,** to be independent. **man about town,** a man who spends much of his time in sophisticated social amusements. **man Friday,** a male assistant doing general duties in an office etc. (▷From *Man Friday,* a character in the novel *Robinson Crusoe* by Daniel DeFoe.) **man in the street,** an ordinary person, not an expert. **man of the house,** the male head of a household. **man of the world,** *see* **world. man on man,** (in sports) with one player directly responsible for guarding another one. **man to man,** with frankness, *let's speak man to man.* **to a man,** all without exception.

man. *abbr.* manual.

Man. *abbr.* Manitoba.

man·a·cle (man-ă-kĕl) *n.* one of a pair of fetters for the hands. **manacle** *v.* (**man·a·cled, man·a·cling**) to fetter with manacles.

man·age (man-ij) *v.* (**man·aged, man·ag·ing**) **1.** to have under effective control. **2.** to be the manager of (a business etc.). **3.** to succeed in doing or producing something (often with inadequate means), to be able to cope, *managed without help.* **4.** to contrive to persuade (a person) to do what one wants, by use of tact or flattery or other means. **man·age·a·ble** (man-i-jă-běl) *adj.* able to be managed. **man′age·a·bly** *adv.* **man′age·a·ble·ness** *n.* **man·age·a·bil·i·ty** (man-i-jă-bil-i-tee) *n.*

man·age·ment (man-ij-měnt) *n.* **1.** managing, being managed. **2.** the process of managing a business, people engaged in this.

man·ag·er (man-i-jěr) *n.* **1.** a person who is in charge of the affairs of a business etc. **2.** one who deals with the business affairs of a sports team or entertainer etc. **3.** one who manages household affairs in a certain way, *she is a good manager.* **man·a·ge·ri·al** (man-i-jeer-i-ăl) *adj.*

man·ag·ing (man-i-jing) *adj.* having executive control or authority, *managing editor.*

Ma·na·gua (mă-nah-gwă) the capital of Nicaragua.

Ma·na·ma (ma-na-mă) the capital of Bahrain.

ma·ña·na (mă-nyah-nă) *adv.* & *n.* tomorrow, as a symbol of easygoing procrastination in Spanish-speaking countries.

man·a·tee (man-ă-tee) *n.* a large aquatic herbivorous mammal, a sea cow.

Man·chu (man-choo) *n.* (*pl.* **-chus, -chu**) **1.** a member of the Tartar people forming the last Chinese imperial dynasty. **2.** their language. **Manchu** *adj.*

Man·chu·ri·a (man-choor-i-ă) *n.* a region in northeast China. **Man·chu′ri·an** *adj.* & *n.*

man·da·mus (man-day-mŭs) *n.* a judicial writ issued as a command to an inferior court, or ordering a person or corporation to perform a public or statutory duty.

man·da·rin (man-dă-rin) *n.* **1.** a high-ranking influential official. **2.** (also **mandarin orange**) a small flattened orange with a skin easy to peel. □mandarin collar, a high upright collar not quite meeting in front.

Man·da·rin (man-dă-rin) *n.* the standard language of China.

man·date (man-dayt) *n.* authority given to someone to perform a certain task or apply certain policies. **mandate** *v.* (**man·dat·ed, man·dat·ing**) to give by a mandate.

man·da·to·ry (man-dă-tohr-ee) *adj.* obligatory, compulsory.

man·di·ble (man-dĭ-běl) *adj.* **1.** a jaw. **2.** either of the parts of a bird's beak. **3.** the corresponding part in insects etc. **man·dib·u·lar** (man-dib-yŭ-lăr) *adj.*

man·do·lin (man-dŏ-lin, man-dŏ-lin) *n.* a musical instrument rather like a guitar, played with a plectrum.

man·do·lin·ist (man-dŏ-lin-ist) *n.* a person who plays the mandolin.

man·drag·o·ra (man-drag-ŏ-ră) *n.* the mandrake, especially as a narcotic.

man·drake (man-drayk) *n.* **1.** a poisonous plant with white or purple flowers and large yellow fruit. **2.** May apple (*see* **May**).

man·drel, man·dril (man-drěl) *n.* a shaft to which work is fixed while being turned, as in a lathe.

man·drill (man-dril) *n.* a large fierce baboon of western Africa.

mane (mayn) *n.* **1.** the long hair on a horse's or lion's neck. **2.** a person's long hair. **maned** *adj.*

man·eat·er (man-ee-těr) *n.* a cannibal, shark, tiger, etc. that eats human flesh. **man′-eat·ing** *adj.*

ma·nège, ma·nege (ma-ne*zh*) *n.* **1.** a riding school. **2.** the movements of a trained horse. **3.** horsemanship.

ma·nes, Ma·nes (may-neez, mah-nes) *n. pl.* **1.** the deified souls of departed ancestors. **2.** (as *n. sing.*) the spirit of a departed person as an object of reverence.

ma·neu·ver (mă-noo-věr) *v.* **1.** to move a thing's position or course etc. carefully, *maneuvered the car into the garage.* **2.** to perform maneuvers. **3.** to guide skillfully or craftily, *maneuvered the conversation toward money.* **maneuver** *n.* **1.** a planned and controlled movement of a vehicle or a body of troops etc. **2.** a skillful or crafty proceeding, a trick. **3.** *maneuvers,* the large-scale exercises of troops, warships, etc., *on maneuvers.* **ma·neu′ver·a·ble** *adj.* **ma·neu′ver·er** *n.* **ma·neu·ver·a·bil·i·ty** (mă-noo-vě-ră-bil-i-tee) *n.*

man·ful (man-fŭl) *adj.* brave, resolute. **man′ful·ly** *adv.*

man·ga·nese (mang-gă-neez) *n.* a hard brittle gray metal or its black oxide.

mange (maynj) *n.* a skin disease affecting hairy animals, caused by a parasite.

man·ger (mayn-jěr) *n.* a long open trough or box in a stable etc. for horses or cattle to eat from.

man·gle¹ (mang-gěl) *n.* a wringer. **mangle** *v.* (**man·gled, man·gling**) to press (clothes etc.) in a mangle.

mangle² *v.* (**man·gled, man·gling**) to damage by cutting or crushing roughly, to mutilate. **man′gler** *n.*

man·go (mang-goh) *n.* (*pl.* **-goes, -gos**) **1.** a tropical fruit with yellowish flesh. **2.** the tree that bears it.

man·grove (mang-grohv) *n.* a tropical tree or shrub growing in tidal areas and swamps, with many tangled roots above ground.

man·gy (mayn-jee) *adj.* (**man·gi·er, man·gi·est**) **1.** having mange. **2.** squalid, shabby.

man·han·dle (man-han-děl) *v.* (**man·han·dled, man·han·dling**) **1.** to move (a thing) by human effort alone. **2.** to treat roughly. **man′han·dler** *n.*

man·hat·tan (man-hat-ăn) *n.* (often *Manhattan*) a cocktail made of whiskey and sweet vermouth etc. ▷Named after Manhattan, a borough of New York City.

man·hole (man-hohl) *n.* an opening (usually with a cover) through which a person can enter a sewer or pipe or boiler etc. to inspect or repair it.

man·hood (man-huud) *n.* **1.** the state of being a man; *reach manhood,* become an adult male person. **2.** manly qualities, courage. **3.** the men of a country.

man-hour (man-owr) *n.* the amount of work that one person can do in one hour, considered as a unit.

man·hunt (man-hunt) *n.* an organized search for a person, especially a criminal.

ma·ni·a (may-ni-ă) *n.* **1.** violent madness. **2.** extreme enthusiasm for something, *a mania for sport.*

-mania *comb. form* meaning a special type of madness, as in *kleptomania;* eager pursuit, as in *bibliomania.*

ma·ni·ac (may-ni-ak) *n.* a person affected with mania.

ma·ni·a·cal (mă-nı-ă-kăl) *adj.* of or like a mania or a maniac. **ma·ni′a·cal·ly** *adv.*

man·ic (man-ik) *adj.* of or affected by mania.

man·ic-de·pres·sive (man-ik-di-pres-iv) *adj.* of a mental disorder with alternating bouts of excitement and depression. **manic-depressive** *n.* a person suffering from this disorder.

man·i·cure (man-ĭ-kyoor) *n.* cosmetic care and treatment of the hands and fingernails. **manicure** *v.* (**man·i·cured, man·i·cur·ing**) to apply such treatment to.

man·i·cur·ist (man-ĭ-kyoor-ist) *n.* a person whose job is to manicure people's hands.

man·i·fest (man-ĭ-fest) *adj.* clear and unmistakable. **manifest** *v.* **1.** to show (a thing) clearly, to give signs of, *the crowd manifested its approval by cheering.* **2.** to become apparent or visible, *no disease manifested itself.* **manifest** *n.* a list of cargo or passengers carried by a ship or aircraft etc. **man′i·fest·ly** *adv.* **man·i·fes·ta·tion** (man-ĭ-fe-stay-shŏn) *n.*

man·i·fes·to (man-ĭ-fes-toh) *n.* (*pl.* **-tos, -toes**) a public declaration of principles and policy.

man·i·fold (man-ĭ-fohld) *adj.* of many kinds, very varied. **manifold** *n.* **1.** a pipe or chamber (in a piece of mechanism) with several openings that connect with other parts. **2.** a copy, a facsimile. **manifold** *v.* to make several copies of.

man·i·kin, man·ni·kin (man-ĭ-kin) *n.* **1.** a little man, a dwarf. **2.** an artist's lay figure. **3.** an anatomical model of the body. **4.** a mannequin.

Ma·nil·a (mă-nil-ă) *n.* the administrative capital of the Philippines. □**Manila hemp,** a strong fiber of a Philippine tree. **Manila paper,** a brown wrapping paper made from Manila hemp. **Manila rope,** a rope made of Manila hemp.

man·i·oc (man-i-ok) *n.* **1.** cassava. **2.** flour made from this.

ma·nip·u·late (mă-nip-yŭ-layt) *v.* (**ma·nip·u·lat·ed, ma·nip·u·lat·ing**) **1.** to handle or manage or use (a thing) skillfully. **2.** to arrange or influence cleverly or craftily; *manipulate figures,* alter or adjust them to suit one's purposes. **ma·nip′u·la·tor** *n.* **ma·nip·u·la·tive** (mă-nip-yŭ-lă-tiv) *adj.* **ma·nip·u·la·tion** (mă-nip-yŭ-lay-shŏn) *n.*

Man·i·to·ba (man-i-toh-bă) a province of Canada.

man·i·tou (man-i-too) *n.* a good or evil spirit as an object of reverence among American Indians.

man·kind (man-kınd) *n.* human beings in general, the human race.

man·like (man-lık) *adj.* **1.** having the qualities of a man. **2.** (of a woman) mannish. **3.** (of an animal) resembling a human being.

man·ly (man-lee) *adj.* having the qualities expected of a man (as strength and courage), suitable for a man. **man′li·ness** *n.*

man·made (man-mayd) *adj.* made by man not by nature, synthetic.

man·na (man-ă) *n.* **1.** (in the Bible) a substance miraculously supplied as food to the Israelites in the wilderness after the exodus from Egypt. **2.** something unexpected and delightful.

manned (mand) *v. see* **man. manned** *adj.* (of a spacecraft etc.) carrying a human crew, *manned flights.*

man·ne·quin (man-ĕ-kin) *n.* **1.** a woman who models clothes. **2.** a dummy for displaying clothes in a shop.

man·ner (man-ĕr) *n.* **1.** the way a thing is done or happens. **2.** a person's bearing or way of behaving toward others. **3.** kind, sort; *all manner of things,* every kind of thing. **4.** a style in literature or art, *sketch in the manner of Rembrandt.* **5.** *manners,* social behavior, *good manners;* polite social behavior, *has no manners.* □**in a manner of speaking,** as one might say (used to qualify or weaken what one says).

man·nered (man-ĕrd) *adj.* **1.** having manners of a certain kind, *well-mannered.* **2.** full of mannerisms, *a mannered style.*

man·ner·ism (man-ĕ-riz-ĕm) *n.* a distinctive personal habit or way of doing something.

man·ner·ly (man-ĕr-lee) *adj.* polite. **man′ner·li·ness** *n.*

man·nish (man-ish) *adj.* having masculine characteristics, suitable for a man. **man′nish·ly** *adv.* **man′nish·ness** *n.*

man-of-war (man-ŏv-wor) *n.* (*pl.* **men-of-war**) *(old use)* an armed ship.

man·or (man-ŏr) *n.* a large country house or the landed estate belonging to it; *manor house,* this house. **ma·no·ri·al** (mă-nohr-i-ăl) *adj.*

man·pow·er (man-pow-ĕr) *n.* **1.** power supplied by human physical effort. **2.** the number of people working on a particular task or available for work or service.

man·qué (mahng-kay) *adj.* that might have been but is not, not fulfilled; *a Beethoven manqué,* an unsuccessful composer. ▷French.

man·sard (man-sahrd) *n.* (also **mansard roof**) a type of roof that has a steep lower part and a less steep upper part on all four sides of a building.

manse (mans) *n.* a Presbyterian minister's house and land, especially in Scotland.

man·ser·vant (man-sur-vănt) *n.* (*pl.* **men·ser·vants,** *pr.* men-sur-vănts) a male servant.

man·sion (man-shŏn) *n.* a large stately house.

man-sized (man-sızd) *adj.* (also **man-size**) **1.** of the size of a man. **2.** adequate for a man, *a man-sized sandwich.*

man·slaugh·ter (man-slaw-tĕr) *n.* the act of killing a person unlawfully but not intentionally, or by negligence.

man·sue·tude (man-swĕ-tood) *n.* *(old use)* meekness, docility, gentleness.

man·ta (man-tă) *n.* a shawl or cloak from the southwestern U.S. and Latin America. □**manta ray,** a very large ray (fish) with large flaps on each side of the head.

man·teau (man-toh) *n.* a loose cloak.

man·tel (man-tĕl) *n.* a structure of wood or marble etc. above and around a fireplace.

man·tel·piece (man-tĕl-pees) *n.* a shelf above a fireplace.

man·til·la (man-til-ă, -tee-ă) *n.* a lace scarf worn by Spanish women over the hair and shoulders.

man·tis (man-tis) *n.* (*pl.* **-tis·es, -tes,** *pr.* -teez) (also **praying mantis**) an insect resembling a grasshopper.

man·tis·sa (man-tis-ă) *n.* the decimal part of a logarithm.

man·tle (man-tĕl) *n.* **1.** a loose sleeveless cloak. **2.** something likened to this, a covering, *a mantle of secrecy.* **3.** a fragile gauzy cover fixed around the flame of a gas lamp, producing a strong light when heated. **4.** the geological region between the crust and core of Earth. **5.** a mantel. **mantle** *v.* (**man·tled, man·tling**) to envelop or cover as if with a mantle.

man·tle·rock (man-těl-rok) *n.* the layer of crumbled rock fragments, including soil, that covers Earth's solid rock.

man·tra (man-tră) *n.* a Hindu or Buddhist devotional incantation.

man·u·al (man-yoo-ăl) *adj.* 1. of the hands. 2. done or operated by hand, *manual labor; manual gearshift,* operated by the driver, not automatically. **manual** *n.* 1. a handbook. 2. an organ keyboard that is played with the hands, not with the feet. 3. a military exercise in handling the rifle. **man'u·al·ly** *adv.* ☐**manual alphabet,** a system of signs made with the hands, representing letters etc., for communication with deaf people. **manual training,** training in woodwork, metalwork, etc. **manuf.** *abbr.* 1. manufacture. 2. manufacturing.

man·u·fac·ture (man-yŭ-fak-chŭr) *v.* **(man·u·fac·tured, man·u·fac·tur·ing)** 1. to make or produce (goods) on a large scale by machinery. 2. to invent, *manufactured an excuse.* **manufacture** *n.* the process of manufacturing. **man·u·fac'tur·er** *n.*

man·u·mit (man-yŭ-mit) *v.* **(man·u·mit·ted, man·u·mit·ting)** to set (slaves) free. **man·u·mis·sion (man-yŭ-mish-ŏn)** *n.*

ma·nure (mă-noor) *n.* any substance such as dung or compost or artificial material used as a fertilizer; **manure** *v.* **(ma·nured, ma·nur·ing)** to apply manure to. ☐**green manure,** *see* **green.**

man·u·script (man-yŭ-skript) *n.* 1. something written by hand, not typed or printed. 2. an author's work as written or typed, not a printed book.

Manx (mangks) *adj.* of the Isle of Man. **Manx** *n.* 1. *the Manx,* Manx people. 2. their Celtic language. ☐**Manx cat,** a tailless variety of domestic cat.

man·y (men-ee) *adj.* **(more, most)** great in number, numerous; *many a time,* many times. **many** *pronoun* many persons or things, *many were lost.* **many** *n.* a large number of people or things, *the many.*

man·y-sid·ed (men-ee-sɪ-did) *adj.* having many sides, aspects, capabilities, interests, etc.

Mao·ism (mow-iz-ěm) *n.* the doctrines of Mao Zedong, a Chinese Communist statesman (1893–1976). **Mao'ist** *n.*

Mao·ri (mow-ree) *n.* (*pl.* **-ris**) a member of a brown aboriginal race in New Zealand. **Maori** *adj.*

map (map) *n.* a representation (usually on a plane surface) of Earth's surface or a part of it, or of the sky showing the positions of the stars etc. **map** *v.* **(mapped, map·ping)** 1. to make a map of. 2. to plan in detail, *map out one's time.* **map'per** *n.* ☐**put a thing on the map,** *(informal)* to make it become famous or important.

ma·ple (may-pěl) *n.* a kind of tree with broad leaves, grown for ornament or for its wood. ☐**maple sugar,** a sugar made by evaporating the sap of the maple. **maple syrup,** a syrup made by boiling down the sap of the maple.

Ma·pu·to (mă-poo-toh) the capital of Mozambique.

mar (mahr) *v.* **(marred, mar·ring)** to damage, to spoil.

mar. *abbr.* 1. maritime. 2. married.

Mar. *abbr.* March.

mar·a·bou (mar-ă-boo) *n.* (*pl.* **-bous, -bou**) 1. a large stork of Africa. 2. its down used as a trimming.

ma·ra·ca (mă-rah-kă) *n.* a hand-held club-like gourd containing beans, beads, etc., shaken in pairs as percussion instruments.

mar·a·schi·no (mar-ă-skee-noh, -shee-) *n.* (*pl.* **-nos**) 1. a strong sweet liqueur made from small black Dalmatian cherries. 2. (also **maraschino cherry**) a cherry cooked in syrup and flavored with maraschino.

mar·a·thon (mar-ă-thon) *n.* 1. a long-distance foot race, especially that of 26 miles 385 yards in the modern Olympic Games. (▷Named after Marathon in Greece, where an invading Persian army was defeated in 490 B.C.; a man who fought at the battle ran to Athens, announced the victory, and died.) 2. any very long race or other test of endurance.

ma·raud·ing (mă-raw-ding) *adj.* going about in search of plunder or prey. **ma·raud'er** *n.* one who does this.

mar·ble (mahr-běl) *n.* 1. a kind of limestone that can be polished, used in sculpture and building. 2. a piece of sculpture in marble, *the Elgin Marbles.* 3. a small ball made of glass or clay etc. used in games played by children. **marble** *adj.* like marble, hard and smooth and white or mottled.

mar·bled (mahr-běld) *adj.* 1. having a veined or mottled appearance. 2. (of meat) with alternating layers of lean and fat.

mar·bling (mahr-bling) *n.* 1. (in meat) the alternation of fat and lean. 2. a pattern resembling marble.

mar·ca·site (mahr-kă-sɪt) *n.* crystallized iron pyrites, a piece of this used as an ornament.

mar·cel (mahr-sel) *n.* a kind of deep wave in the hair. **marcel** *v.* **(mar·celled, mar·cel·ling)** to wave the hair in this manner.

march (mahrch) *v.* 1. to walk in a military manner with regular paces, to walk in an organized column. 2. to walk purposefully, *marched up to the manager.* 3. to cause to march or walk, *marched them up the hill; he was marched off.* 4. to progress steadily, *time marches on.* **march** *n.* 1. marching, the distance covered by marching troops etc.; *a protest march,* a demonstration taking the form of a parade. 2. progress, *the march of events.* 3. music suitable for marching to. **march'er** *n.* ☐**get one's marching orders,** to be told to go. **on the march,** marching, advancing.

March (mahrch) *n.* the third month of the year.

march·es (mahr-chiz) *n. pl.* *(old use)* border regions.

mar·chio·ness (mahr-shŏ-nis) *n.* 1. the wife or widow of a marquis. 2. a woman holding the rank of marquis in her own right.

Mar·di gras (mahr-dee grah) merrymaking on the Tuesday before Ash Wednesday.

mare¹ (mair) *n.* the female of a horse or related animal. ☐**mare's nest,** a discovery that is thought to be interesting but turns out to be false or worthless; a very complicated or confused situation; *his room is a mare's nest,* is very disorderly.

ma·re² (mahr-ay) *n.* (*pl.* **ma·ri·a,** *pr.* **mahr-i-ă**) a large flat dark area on the moon, once thought to be a sea. ☐**mare clau·sum (klow-soom),** a sea under the jurisdiction of a particular country. **mare li·be·rum (leeb-ě-ruum),** a sea open to all nations.

mar·ga·rine (mahr-jă-rin) *n.* a substance used like butter, made from animal or vegetable fats.

mar·gin (mahr-jin) *n.* 1. an edge or border of a

surface. 2. a blank space around printed or written matter on a page. 3. an amount over and above the essential minimum, *was defeated by a narrow margin; margin of safety.* 4. (in business) the difference between cost price and selling price, *profit margins.*

mar·gin·al (mahr-ji-näl) *adj.* 1. written in a margin, *marginal notes.* 2. of or at an edge. 3. very slight in amount, *its usefulness is marginal.* **mar′gin·al·ly** *adv.*

mar·gi·na·li·a (mahr-ji-nay-li-ă) *n. pl.* marginal notes.

mar·grave (mahr-grayv) *n.* the hereditary title of some princes of the Holy Roman Empire.

mar·gue·rite (mahr-gĕ-reet) *n.* a large daisy-like flower with a yellow center and white petals.

ma·ri·a·chi (mahr-i-ah-chee) *n.* 1. a strolling Mexican band. 2. a member of such a band. 3. its music.

mar·i·gold (mar-i-gohld) *n.* a garden plant with golden or bright yellow flowers.

ma·ri·jua·na (mar-i-wah-nă) *n.* the dried leaves, stems, and flowering tops of the hemp plant, used to make a hallucinogenic drug, especially in the form of cigarettes.

ma·rim·ba (mă-rim-bă) *n.* 1. a xylophone of African and Central American natives. 2. a modern orchestral instrument evolved from this.

ma·ri·na (mă-ree-nă) *n.* a harbor for yachts and pleasure boats.

mar·i·nade (mar-i-nayd, mar-i-nayd) *n.* a seasoned flavored liquid in which meat or fish is steeped before being cooked. **marinade** (mar-i-nayd) *v.* **(mar·i·nad·ed, mar·i·nad·ing)** to marinate.

mar·i·nate (mar-i-nayt) *v.* **(mar·i·nat·ed, mar·i·nat·ing)** to steep in a marinade.

ma·rine (mă-reen) *adj.* 1. of or living in the sea, *marine animals.* 2. of shipping, nautical, *marine insurance.* 3. for use at sea. **marine** *n.* 1. a country's shipping, *the merchant marine.* 2. a member of a body of troops trained to serve on land or sea. □**tell it to the marines,** *(informal)* I do not believe you. **U.S. Marine Corps, the Marines,** a branch of the U.S. Navy trained for land and sea operations.

mar·i·ner (mar-ĭ-nĕr) *n.* a sailor, a seaman.

mar·i·o·nette (mar-i-ŏ-net) *n.* a puppet worked by strings.

mar·i·tal (mar-i-tăl) *adj.* of marriage, of or between husband and wife. ▷Do not confuse *marital* with *martial.*

mar·i·time (mar-ĭ-tım) *adj.* 1. living or situated or found near the sea, *maritime provinces.* 2. of seafaring or shipping, *maritime law.*

mar·jo·ram (mahr-jŏ-răm) *n.* an herb with fragrant leaves, used in cooking.

mark¹ (mahrk) *n.* the unit of money in East Germany.

mark² *n.* 1. something that visibly breaks the uniformity of a surface, especially one that spoils its appearance. 2. a distinguishing feature or characteristic. 3. something that indicates the presence of a quality or feeling, *as a mark of respect.* 4. a symbol placed on a thing to indicate its origin or ownership or quality; *Mark I or II,* the first (or second) design of a machine or piece of equipment etc. 5. a written or printed symbol, *punctuation marks.* 6. a lasting impression, *poverty had left its mark.* 7. a unit awarded for the merit or quality of a piece of work or a performance, *got high marks; deserves a good mark for effort,*

deserves credit. 8. a target, a standard to be aimed at; *not feeling up to the mark,* not feeling well. 9. a line or object serving to indicate position. **mark** *v.* 1. to make a mark on. 2. to distinguish with a mark, to characterize. 3. to assign marks of merit to. 4. to notice, to watch carefully, *mark my words!* □**make one's mark,** to make a significant achievement, to become famous. **mark down,** to notice and remember the place etc. of; to reduce the price of. **mark off,** to separate by a boundary. **mark out,** to mark the boundaries of; to destine, to single out, *is marked out for promotion.* **mark time,** to move the feet rhythmically as if in marching but without advancing; to occupy time in routine work without making progress. **mark up,** to increase the price of. **off the mark,** off the point, irrelevant; having made a start. **on the mark,** ready to start; correct, *right on the mark.*

Mark (mahrk) *n.* 1. one of the twelve Apostles, companion of Peter and Paul, possibly the author of the second Gospel. 2. the second Gospel.

mark·down (mahrk-down) *n.* 1. a reduced price. 2. the amount of this reduction.

marked (mahrkt) *adj.* clearly noticeable, a marked improvement. **mark·ed·ly** (mahr-kid-lee) *adv.* □**a marked man,** one who is singled out as an object of vengeance.

mark·er (mahr-kĕr) *n.* 1. a person or tool that marks. 2. something that serves to mark a position. 3. *(slang)* an IOU.

mar·ket (mahr-kit) *n.* 1. a gathering for the sale of goods or livestock. 2. a space or building used for this. 3. the conditions or opportunity for buying or selling, *found a ready market.* 4. a place where goods may be sold, a particular class of buyers, *foreign markets; the teenage market.* 5. the stock market. **market** *v.* to offer for sale; *go marketing,* to go buying food etc. for domestic use. □**be in the market for,** to wish to buy. **market day,** the day on which a market is regularly held. **market research,** study of consumers' needs and preferences. **market town,** one where a market is held regularly. **market value,** the amount for which something can be sold, its current value. **on the market,** offered for sale.

mar·ket·a·ble (mahr-ki-tă-bĕl) *adj.* able or fit to be sold.

mar·ket·place (mahr-kit-plays) *n.* an open space where a market is held in a town.

mark·ing (mahr-king) *n.* 1. a mark or marks. 2. the coloring of an animal's skin or feathers or fur.

marks·man (mahrks-măn) *n.* (*pl.* -men, *pr.* -mĕn) a person who is a skilled shot. **marks′man·ship** *n.*

mark·up (mahrk-up) *n.* the amount a seller adds to the cost price of an article to determine the selling price.

mar·lin (mahr-lin) *n.* (*pl.* -lin, -lins) a large saltwater fish with a pointed snout.

mar·line·spike, mar·lin·spike (mahr-lin-spık) *n.* a pointed iron tool used to separate strands of rope or wire.

mar·ma·lade (mahr-mă-layd) *n.* a kind of jam made from citrus fruit, especially oranges.

mar·mo·re·al (mahr-mohr-i-ăl) *adj.* of or like marble.

mar·mo·set (mahr-mŏ-set) *n.* a small bushy-tailed monkey of tropical America.

mar·mot (mahr-mŏt) *n.* a small burrowing animal of the squirrel family.

ma·roon[1] (mă-roon) *n.* a brownish-red color. **maroon** *adj.* brownish red.

maroon[2] *v.* to abandon or isolate (a person), as on an island or in a deserted place.

mar·quee (mahr-kee) *n.* 1. a canopy over the entrance to a building. 2. a large tent used for a party or an exhibition etc.

mar·quess (mahr-kwĕs) = **marquis.**

mar·que·try (mahr-ki-tree) *n.* inlaid work in wood or ivory etc.

mar·quis (mahr-kwis, mahr-kee) *n.* a nobleman ranking between duke and earl or count.

mar·quise (mahr-keez) *n.* (*pl.* **quis·es,** *pr.* -keeziz) 1. (in European nobility) a marchioness. 2. a finger ring set with an oval pointed cluster of gems.

mar·qui·sette (mahr-ki-zet) *n.* a fine light net fabric used for curtains etc.

mar·riage (mar-ij) *n.* 1. the state in which a man and a woman are formally united for the purpose of living together (usually in order to procreate children) and with certain legal rights and obligations toward each other. 2. the act or ceremony of being married.

mar·riage·a·ble (mar-i-jă-bĕl) *adj.* old enough or fit for marriage.

mar·row (mar-oh) *n.* the soft fatty substance in the cavities of bones; *felt chilled to the marrow, right through.*

mar·row·bone (mar-oh-bohn) *n.* a bone containing edible marrow.

mar·ry (mar-ee) *v.* (**mar·ried, mar·ry·ing**) 1. to unite or give or take in marriage. 2. to take a husband or wife in marriage, *she never married.* 3. to unite, to put (things) together as a pair. **mar·ried** (mar-eed) *adj.*

Mars (mahrz) *n.* a planet in the solar system.

Mar·sa·la (mahr-sah-lă) *n.* a dark sweet fortified wine of a kind originally made in Sicily.

Mar·seil·laise (mahr-say-ez) *n.* the national anthem of France.

marsh (mahrsh) *n.* low-lying watery ground. **marsh'y** *adj.* □**marsh gas,** methane. **marsh marigold,** a golden-flowered plant growing in moist meadows etc.

mar·shal (mahr-shăl) *n.* 1. an officer of high or the highest rank, *Air Marshal; Field Marshal.* 2. an administrative officer of a federal court. 3. the head of a police or fire department. 4. an official with responsibility for arranging certain public events or ceremonies. **marshal** *v.* (**mar·shaled, mar·shal·ing**) 1. to arrange in proper order. 2. to cause to assemble. 3. to usher, *marshaled him into the governor's office.*

marsh·land (mahrsh-land) *n.* marshy land.

marsh·mal·low (mahrsh-mel-oh) *n.* a soft confection made from sugar, egg white, and gelatin.

mar·su·pi·al (mahr-soo-pi-ăl) *n.* an animal, such as the kangaroo, the female of which has a pouch in which its young are carried until they are fully developed. **marsupial** *adj.* of a marsupial.

mart (mahrt) *n.* a market.

mar·ten (mahr-tĕn) *n.* a weasel-like animal with thick soft fur.

mar·tial (mahr-shăl) *adj.* of war, warlike, *martial music.* **mar'tial·ly** *adv.* **mar'tial·ism** *n.* **mar'tial·ist** *n.* □**martial arts,** ways of fighting, especially without weapons. **martial law,** military rule imposed on a country temporarily in an emergency, suspending ordinary law. ▷ Do not confuse *martial* with *marital.*

Mar·tian (mahr-shăn) *adj.* of the planet Mars. **Martian** *n.* (in science fiction etc.) an inhabitant of Mars.

mar·tin (mahr-tĭn) *n.* a bird of the swallow family.

mar·ti·net (mahr-tĭ-net) *n.* a person who demands strict obedience.

mar·tin·gale (mahr-tĭn-gayl) *n.* 1. a strap or set of straps fastened to prevent a horse from rearing. 2. a rope for holding down a jib boom. 3. a gambling system of continually doubling the stakes in hope of an eventual win that must yield an overall profit.

mar·ti·ni (mahr-tee-nee) *n.* a cocktail of gin or vodka etc. and dry vermouth.

mar·tyr (mahr-tĭr) *n.* 1. a person who suffers death rather than give up religious faith. 2. one who undergoes death or great suffering in support of a belief or cause or principle. 3. one who suffers greatly; *is a martyr to rheumatism,* suffers constantly from this. **martyr** *v.* to put to death or torment as a martyr. **mar·tyr·dom** (mahr-tĭr-dŏm) *n.*

mar·vel (mahr-vĕl) *n.* a wonderful thing. **marvel** *v.* (**mar·veled, mar·vel·ing**) to be filled with wonder.

mar·vel·ous (mahr-vĕ-lŭs) *adj.* astonishing, excellent. **mar'vel·ous·ly** *adv.* **mar'vel·ous·ness** *n.*

Marx·ism (mahrk-siz-ĕm) *n.* the political and economic theory of Karl Marx, a German socialist writer (1818–83), on which Communism is based. **Marx'ist** *adj. & n.* **Marx'i·an** *adj. & n.*

Mar·y·land (mer-ĭ-lănd) a state of the U.S.

mar·zi·pan (mahr-zĭ-pan) *n.* a paste of ground almonds, egg whites, and sugar, made into small cakes or candies or used to coat large cakes.

masc. *abbr.* masculine.

mas·car·a (ma-skar-ă) *n.* a cosmetic for darkening the eyelashes.

mas·con (mas-kon) *n.* a concentration of dense matter below the moon's surface, with strong gravitational pull.

mas·cot (mas-kot) *n.* a person or thing believed to bring good luck.

mas·cu·line (mas-kyŭ-lin) *adj.* 1. of or like or suitable for men, having the qualities or appearance considered characteristic of a man. 2. having the grammatical form suitable for the names of males or for words corresponding to these, *"hero" is a masculine noun, "heroine" is the corresponding feminine noun.* **mas·cu·lin·i·ty** (mas-kyŭ-lin-i-tee) *n.*

ma·ser (may-zĕr) *n.* a device that amplifies or generates concentrated electromagnetic radiation, especially microwaves. ▷ From *microwave* amplification by *stimulated emission of radiation.*

Mas·e·ru (maz-ĕ-roo) the capital of Lesotho.

mash (mash) *n.* 1. grain or bran etc. cooked in water to form a soft mixture, used as animal food. 2. any soft mass or pulp made by crushing or mixing with water, milk, etc. 3. a mixture of malt and hot water used in brewing. **mash** *v.* to beat or crush into a soft mixture, *mashed potatoes.*

MASH (mash) *n.* a mobile army surgical hospital.

mash·er (mash-ĕr) *n.* (*slang*) a man who makes forcible advances to a woman.

mask (mask) *n.* 1. anything that disguises or conceals, especially a covering worn over the face (or part of it) as a disguise or for protection. 2. a carved or molded replica of a face, often grotesque. 3. a respirator worn over the face to filter air for breathing or to supply gas for inhaling. 4. the face or head, as of a fox. 5. a screen used in photography to exclude part of the image. 6. a masque. **mask** v. 1. to cover with a mask. 2. to disguise or screen or conceal, *mask one's feelings.* **mask'er** n.

mas·och·ist (mas-ŏ-kist) n. 1. a person who derives sexual excitement and satisfaction from his own pain or humiliation. 2. one who enjoys what seems to be painful or tiresome. **mas'och·ism** n. **mas·och·is·tic** (mas-ŏ-kis-tik) adj. **mas·och·is'ti·cal·ly** adv.

ma·son (may-sŏn) n. 1. a person who builds or works with stone. 2. *Mason,* a Freemason. □**Mason-Dixon line,** the boundary between Pennsylvania and Maryland, taken as the northern limit of slave-owning states before abolition of slavery in the U.S.

Ma·son·ic (mă-son-ik) adj. of Freemasons.

ma·son·ry (may-sŏn-ree) n. 1. mason's work, stonework. 2. *Masonry,* Freemasonry.

masque (mask) n. 1. a masquerade. 2. an amateur dramatic and musical entertainment, especially in the 16th and 17th centuries.

mas·quer·ade (mas-kĕ-rayd) n. 1. a masked ball. 2. a false show or pretense. **masquerade** v. (**mas·quer·ad·ed, mas·quer·ad·ing**) 1. to appear in disguise or costume. 2. to pretend to be what one is not, *masqueraded as a policeman.* **mas·quer·ad'er** n.

mass (mas) n. 1. a coherent unit of matter with no specific shape. 2. a large quantity or heap, an unbroken extent; *the garden was a mass of flowers,* was full of flowers. 3. (in technical usage) the quantity of matter a body contains (called *weight* in nontechnical usage). 4. *the masses,* the common people. **mass** v. to gather or assemble into a mass. **mass'less** adj. □**mass hysteria,** hysteria affecting many persons at the same time. **mass media,** the media (*see* **media**). **mass meeting,** one attended by a large number of people. **mass number,** the total number of protons and neutrons in the atomic nucleus. **mass production,** the manufacture in large numbers of identical articles by standardized processes.

Mass (mas) n. (especially in the Roman Catholic Church) 1. a celebration of the Eucharist. 2. the form of service used in this, a musical setting for the words of it.

Mass. *abbr.* Massachusetts.

Mas·sa·chu·setts (mas-ă-choo-sits) a state of the U.S.

mas·sa·cre (mas-ă-kĕr) n. slaughter of a large number of people or animals. **massacre** v. (**mas·sa·cred, mas·sa·cring**) to slaughter in large numbers.

mas·sage (ma-sahzh, -sahj) n. rubbing and kneading the body to lessen pain or stiffness. **massage** v. (**mas·saged, mas·sag·ing**) to treat in this way. **mas·sag'er** n. **mas·sag'ist** n. □**massage parlor,** an establishment for massage and prostitution.

mas·seur (mă-sur) n. a man who practices massage professionally.

mas·seuse (mă-soos, -sooz) n. a woman who practices massage professionally.

mas·sif (ma-seef) n. mountain heights forming a compact group.

mas·sive (mas-iv) adj. 1. large and heavy or solid. 2. unusually large. 3. substantial, *a massive improvement.* **mas'sive·ly** adv. **mas'sive·ness** n.

mass-pro·duce (mas-proh-doos) v. (**mass-pro·duced, mass-pro·duc·ing**) to manufacture by mass production (*see* **mass**).

mast[1] (mast) n. 1. a long upright pole that supports a ship's sails. 2. a tall pole from which a flag is flown. 3. a tall steel structure for the aerials of a radio or television transmitter. **mast'ed** adj. □**before the mast,** *(old use)* serving as an ordinary seaman (quartered in the forecastle).

mast[2] n. the fruit of beech, oak, chestnut, and other forest trees, used as food for pigs.

mas·tec·to·my (ma-stek-tŏ-mee) n. (*pl.* -mies) surgical removal of a breast.

mas·ter (mas-tĕr) n. 1. a man who has control of people or things. 2. the captain of a merchant ship. 3. the male head of a household. 4. the male owner of a dog etc. 5. an employer, *masters and men.* 6. a male teacher, a schoolmaster. 7. *Master,* the holder of a university degree awarded for study beyond the level of a bachelor's degree; *Master of Arts* or *Science,* a master's degree or its holder. 8. a respected teacher. 9. a person with very great skill, a great artist. 10. a chess player of proven ability at international level. 11. a document or film or record etc. from which a series of copies is made. 12. *Master,* a title prefixed to the name of a boy who is not old enough to be called *Mr.* **master** v. 1. to overcome, to bring under control. 2. to acquire knowledge or skill in. □**master chef,** the chief chef. **master chief petty officer,** a U.S. Navy petty officer of the highest rank. **master gunnery sergeant,** a U.S. Marine Corps noncommissioned officer. **master key,** a key that opens a number of locks, each also opened by a separate key. **master mariner,** the captain of a merchant ship. **master of ceremonies,** a person in charge of a social or other occasion, who introduces the events or performers. **master plan,** an overall plan, a guide for all actions to be taken. **master sergeant,** a noncommissioned officer of second highest rank in the U.S. Army, Air Force, or Marine Corps.

mas·ter·ful (mas-tĕr-fŭl) adj. 1. domineering. 2. very skillful. **mas'ter·ful·ly** adv.

mas·ter·ly (mas-tĕr-lee) adj. worthy of a master, very skillful.

mas·ter·mind (mas-tĕr-mɪnd) n. 1. a person with outstanding mental ability. 2. the person directing an enterprise. **mastermind** v. to plan and direct, *masterminded the whole scheme.*

mas·ter·piece (mas-tĕr-pees) n. 1. an outstanding piece of workmanship. 2. a person's best piece of work.

mas·ter·stroke (mas-tĕr-strohk) n. an outstandingly skillful act of policy etc.

mas·ter·work (mas-tĕr-wurk) n. a masterpiece.

mas·ter·y (mas-tĕ-ree) n. 1. complete control, supremacy. 2. thorough knowledge or skill, *his mastery of Arabic.*

mast·head (mast-hed) n. 1. the highest part of the mast, especially the lower mast as a place of observation or punishment. 2. the title etc. of a newspaper etc. at the head of the front page or editorial page.

mas·tic (mas-tik) n. 1. a gum or resin exuding from the bark of certain trees, used in making varnish. 2. a type of adhesive.

mas·ti·cate (mas-tĭ-kayt) v. (**mas·ti·cat·ed,**

mas·ti·cat·ing) to chew (food). **mas·ti·ca· tion** (mas-tĭ-kay-shŏn) n. **mas·ti·ca·to·ry** (mas-tĭ-kă-tohr-ee) adj.

mas·tiff (mas-tif) n. a large strong dog with drooping ears.

mas·to·don (mas-tŏ-don) n. a large extinct mammal, like an elephant. **mas·to·don·tic** (mas-tŏ-don-tik) adj.

mas·toid (mas-toid) n. 1. part of a bone behind the ear. 2. (informal) mastoiditis.

mas·toid·i·tis (mas-toi-dɪ-tis) n. inflammation of the mastoid.

mas·tur·bate (mas-tŭr-bayt) v. (**mas·tur·bat· ed, mas·tur·bat·ing)** to produce a sexual orgasm by stimulating the genitals by hand. **mas· tur·ba·tion** (mas-tŭr-bay-shŏn) n.

mat¹ (mat) n. 1. a piece of material used as a floor covering, a doormat. 2. a small pad or piece of material placed under an ornament or vase etc. or under a hot dish, to protect the surface on which it stands. 3. a thick pad for landing on in gymnastics etc. 4. a tangled mass, as of weeds or hair. **mat** v. (**mat·ted, mat·ting)** to make or become entangled to form a thick mass, matted hair.

mat² n. a cardboard framing a picture. **mat** v. (**mat·ted, mat·ting)** to provide with a mat.

mat³ adj. (also **matt, matte**) (of a color or surface etc.) having a dull finish, not shiny.

Mat·a·be·le (mat-ă-bee-lee) n. (pl. **-les, -le**) a member of a Bantu-speaking people of Zimbabwe.

mat·a·dor (mat-ă-dor) n. a performer whose task is to fight and kill the bull in a bullfight.

match¹ (mach) n. a short piece of wood (a matchstick) or pasteboard with a head made of material that bursts into flame when rubbed on a rough or specially prepared surface.

match² n. 1. a contest in a game or sport. 2. a person or animal with abilities equaling those of another whom he meets in contest, meet one's match; you are no match for him, not strong enough or skilled enough to defeat him. 3. a person or thing exactly like or corresponding to another. 4. a marriage; they made a match of it, married. 5. a person considered as a partner for marriage, especially with regard to rank or fortune. **match** v. 1. a place in competition, the teams were matched with or against each other. 2. to equal in ability or skill etc. 3. to be alike or correspond in color, quality, quantity, etc. 4. to find something similar to, I want to match this wool. 5. to put or bring together as corresponding, matching unemployed workers with available jobs. **match'er** n. □**match point,** the stage in a match when one side will win if it gains the next point; this point.

match·book (mach-buuk) n. a cardboard folder for holding matches.

match·box (mach-boks) n. a box for holding matches.

match·less (mach-lis) adj. unequaled. **match' less·ly** adv.

match·mak·er (mach-may-kĕr) n. 1. a person who is fond of scheming to bring about marriages, one who arranges marriages. 2. a person who arranges boxing matches and wrestling matches. **match'mak·ing** adj. & n.

match·wood (mach-wuud) n. 1. wood that splinters easily. 2. wood reduced to splinters.

mate¹ (mayt) n. 1. a partner in marriage. 2. one of a mated pair of birds or animals. 3. a fellow

member or sharer, teammate; roommate. 4. an officer on a merchant ship ranking next below the master. **mate** v. (**mat·ed, mat·ing)** 1. to put or come together as a pair or as corresponding. 2. to put (two birds or animals) together so that they can breed, to come together in order to breed.

mate² n. a checkmate.

ma·te·ri·al (mă-teer-i-ăl) n. 1. the substance or things from which something is or can be made or with which something is done, clay is used as material for bricks; materials to do the job; select those regarded as officer material, those with qualities that make them suitable to become officers. 2. cloth, fabric. 3. facts or information or events etc. to be used in composing something, gathering material for a book on poverty. **material** adj. 1. of matter, consisting of matter, of the physical (as opposed to spiritual) world, material things; had no thought of material gain. 2. of bodily comfort, our material well-being. 3. important, significant, at the material time; is this material to the issue? **ma·te'ri·al·ly** adv.

ma·te·ri·al·ism (mă-teer-i-ă-liz-ĕm) n. 1. belief that only the material world exists. 2. excessive concern with material possessions rather than spiritual or intellectual values. **ma·te'ri·al·ist** n. **ma·te·ri·al·is·tic** (mă-teer-i-ă-lis-tik) adj. **ma·te·ri·al·is'ti·cal·ly** adv.

ma·te·ri·al·ize (mă-teer-i-ă-lız) v. (**ma·te·ri· al·ized, ma·te·ri·al·iz·ing)** 1. to appear or become visible, the ghost didn't materialize; the boy failed to materialize, did not come. 2. to become a fact, to happen, if the threatened strike materializes. **ma·te·ri·al·i·za·tion** (mă-teer-i-ă-li-zay-shŏn) n.

ma·té·ri·el, ma·te·ri·el (mă-teer-i-el) n. materials and equipment in warfare.

ma·ter·nal (mă-tur-năl) adj. 1. of a mother, of motherhood. 2. motherly. 3. related through one's mother; maternal uncle, one's mother's brother. **ma·ter'nal·ly** adv.

ma·ter·ni·ty (mă-tur-ni-tee) n. motherhood. **maternity** adj. of or suitable or caring for women in pregnancy or childbirth, maternity dress; maternity ward.

math (math) n. (informal) mathematics.

math. abbr. 1. mathematical. 2. mathematician. 3. mathematics.

math·e·ma·ti·cian (math-ĕ-mă-tish-ăn) n. a person who is skilled in mathematics.

math·e·mat·ics (math-ĕ-mat-iks) n. 1. the science of number, quantity, and space. 2. the use of this science. **math·e·mat'i·cal** adj. **math·e·mat'i· cal·ly** adv.

mat·i·née, mat·i·nee (mat-ĭ-nay) n. an afternoon performance at a theater.

mat·ins (mat-inz) n. 1. (in the Church of England) morning prayer. 2. (in the Roman Catholic Church) prayers said between midnight and four A.M.

ma·tri·arch (may-tri-ahrk) n. a woman who is head of a family or tribe. **ma·tri·ar·chal** (may-tri-ahr-kăl) adj.

ma·tri·ar·chy (may-tri-ahr-kee) n. (pl. **-chies**) 1. a social organization in which the mother is head of the family and descent is through the female line. 2. a society in which women have most of the authority.

mat·ri·cide (mat-ri-sɪd) n. 1. a person who kills his mother. 2. the crime itself. **mat·ri·ci·dal** (mat-ri-sɪ-dăl) adj.

ma·tric·u·late (mă-trik-yŭ-layt) v. (**ma·tric·u·lat·ed, ma·tric·u·lat·ing**) to enroll or be enrolled as a student at a college or university. **ma·tric·u·la·tion** (mă-trik-yŭ-lay-shŏn) n.

mat·ri·mo·ny (mat-rĭ-moh-nee) n. marriage. **mat·ri·mo·ni·al** (mat-rĭ-moh-ni-ăl) adj. **mat·ri·mo'ni·al·ly** adv.

ma·trix (may-triks) n. (pl. **-trix·es, -tri·ces,** pr. -tri-seez) 1. a mold in which something is cast or shaped. 2. a place in which a thing is developed.

ma·trix·ing (may-trik-sing) n. an electronic process by which four-channel sound can be recorded in a two-channel form, to be played back by reconversion to four channels.

ma·tron (may-trŏn) n. 1. a married woman, especially one who is middle-aged or elderly and dignified. 2. a woman attendant in a prison. 3. the head nurse in a hospital or other institution. ⬜**matron of honor,** a married woman as the chief attendant of the bride at a wedding.

ma·tron·ly (may-trŏn-lee) adj. like or suitable for a dignified married woman. **ma'tron·li·ness** n.

matt, matte = mat³.

Matt. abbr. Matthew.

mat·ter (mat-ĕr) n. 1. that which occupies space in the visible world, as opposed to spirit or mind or qualities etc. 2. a particular substance or material, coloring matter. 3. a discharge from the body, pus. 4. material for thought or expression, the content of a book or speech as distinct from its form, subject matter. 5. things of a specified kind, reading matter. 6. a situation or business being considered, it's a serious matter; a matter for complaint. 7. a quantity, for a matter of forty years. **matter** v. to be of importance, it doesn't matter. ⬜**a matter of course,** an event etc. that follows naturally or is to be expected. **for that matter,** as far as that is concerned. **matter of fact,** something that is a fact not an opinion etc. **no matter,** it is of no importance. **the matter,** the thing that is amiss, the trouble or difficulty, what's the matter?

mat·ter-of-fact (mat-ĕr-ŏv-fakt) adj. strictly factual and not imaginative or emotional, down-to-earth. **mat'ter-of-fact'ly** adv. **mat'ter-of-fact'ness** n.

Mat·thew (math-yoo) n. 1. one of the twelve Apostles, traditionally but erroneously thought to be the author of the first Gospel, which was written after A.D. 70 and was based largely on St. Mark. 2. the first Gospel.

mat·ting (mat-ing) n. mats, material for making these.

mat·tock (mat-ŏk) n. a farm tool with the blade set at right angles to the handle, used for loosening soil and digging out roots.

mat·tress (mat-ris) n. a fabric or heavy cloth case filled with soft or firm or springy material, used on or as a bed.

mat·u·rate (mach-ŭ-rayt) v. (**mat·u·rat·ed, mat·u·rat·ing**) (of a boil etc.) to come to maturation.

mat·u·ra·tion (mach-ŭ-ray-shŏn) n. the process of maturing, ripening. **mat·u·ra'tion·al** adj. **ma·tur·a·tive** (mă-choor-ă-tiv) adj.

ma·ture (mă-toor, -choor) adj. 1. having reached full growth or development. 2. having or showing fully developed mental powers, capable of reasoning and acting sensibly. 3. (of wine) having reached a good stage of development. 4. (of a bill, bond, loan, etc.) due for payment. **mature**

v. (**ma·tured, ma·tur·ing**) to make or become mature. **ma·ture'ly** adv. **ma·tur'i·ty** n.

ma·tu·ti·nal (mă-too-ti-năl) adj. of or occurring in the morning.

mat·zo, mat·zoh (maht-sŏ, -soh) n. (pl. **mat·zos, mat·zoth,** pr. maht-soht) an unleavened bread for Passover.

maud·lin (mawd-lin) adj. sentimental in a silly or tearful way, especially from drunkenness. **maud'lin·ly** adv.

maul (mawl) v. to treat roughly, to injure by rough handling. **maul** n. a type of heavy hammer, commonly of wood, especially for driving piles.

maun·der (mawn-dĕr) v. to talk in a rambling way. **maun'der·er** n.

maun·dy (mawn-dee) n. (in the Roman Catholic Church) the ceremony of washing the feet of the poor on Maundy Thursday. ⬜**Maundy Thursday,** the Thursday before Easter, celebrated in commemoration of the Last Supper.

Mau·ri·ta·ni·a (mor-i-tay-ni-ă) a country in northwest Africa. **Mau·ri·ta'ni·an** adj. & n.

Mau·ri·tius (maw-rish-ŭs) a country in the southwest Indian Ocean. **Mau·ri'tian** adj. & n.

mau·so·le·um (maw-sŏ-lee-ŭm) n. a magnificent tomb. ▷Named after that erected at Halicarnassus in Asia Minor for King Mausolus in the 4th century B.C.

mauve (mohv) adj. & n. pale purple.

mav·er·ick (mav-ĕ-rik) n. 1. an unbranded calf or other young animal. 2. a person of unorthodox independence, one who dissents from the ideas and beliefs of an organized political or other group to which he belongs.

ma·vin (may-vin) n. (informal) a connoisseur, an expert. ▷Yiddish.

maw (maw) n. the jaws or mouth or stomach of a voracious animal.

mawk·ish (maw-kish) adj. sentimental in a sickly way. **mawk'ish·ly** adv. **mawk'ish·ness** n.

max. abbr. maximum.

max·i (mak-see) n. (pl. **max·is**) (informal) a coat or skirt reaching to the ankles.

maxi- comb. form very large or long, as in maxicoat.

max·il·la (mak-sil-ă) n. (pl. **max·il·lae,** pr. mak-sil-ee) the jawbone, especially the upper jaw in most vertebrates. **max·il·lar·y** (mak-si-ler-ee) adj. & n. (pl. **-lar·ies**).

max·im (mak-sim) n. a general truth or rule of conduct, such as "waste not, want not."

max·i·mal (mak-sĭ-măl) adj. greatest possible. **max'i·mal·ly** adv.

max·i·mize (mak-sĭ-mız) v. to increase to a maximum. **max·i·mi·za·tion** (mak-sĭ-mĭ-zay-shŏn) n.

max·i·mum (mak-sĭ-mŭm) n. (pl. **-mums, max·i·ma,** pr. mak-sĭ-mă) the greatest or greatest possible number or amount or intensity etc. **maximum** adj. greatest, greatest possible.

may (may) auxiliary verb (also **might**) expressing possibility (it may be true) or permission (you may go) or wish (long may she reign) or uncertainty (whoever it may be). ▷Do not confuse may with can. Careful writers and speakers avoid can in the sense of permission; you may sit with us is an invitation to do so, you can sit with us is a recognition that no one can prevent the act. (See the note under **might**.)

May (may) n. the fifth month of the year. ⬜**May apple,** a plant bearing yellow egg-shaped fruit in May; its fruit. **May Day,** May 1, a festival celebrated with dancing; an international holiday in honor of workers. **Queen of the May,** a girl crowned with flowers as queen of festivities on May Day.

Ma·ya (mah-yă) *n.* (*pl.* **-ya, -yas**) 1. a member of an Indian people living in Mexico until the 15th century A.D. 2. the language of this people. **Ma'yan** *adj.*

may·be (may-bee) *adv.* perhaps, possibly.

may·day (may-day) *n.* an international radio signal of distress. ▷Representing the pronunciation of French *m'aider* = help me.

may·flow·er (may-flow-ĕr) *n.* 1. any flower that blooms in May. 2. *Mayflower,* the ship that sailed from England in 1620 to bring the Pilgrims to America.

may·fly (may-flı) *n.* (*pl.* **-flies**) (also **May fly**) an insect with two or three long hairlike tails, living briefly in spring.

may·hem (may-hem) *n.* 1. the crime of maiming or mutilating a person so as to render him partly or wholly defenseless. 2. violent or damaging action.

may·n't (may-ĕnt) = may not.

may·o (may-oh) *n.* (*informal*) mayonnaise.

may·on·naise (may-ŏ-nayz) *n.* a creamy sauce made with egg yolks, oil, and vinegar or lemon juice.

may·or (may-ŏr) *n.* the head of a city or other municipality. **may'or·al** *adj.* **may'or·al·ty** *n.*

may·or·ess (may-ŏ-ris) *n.* 1. a mayor's wife, or other woman performing the mayor's ceremonial duties. 2. a woman mayor.

May·pole (may-pohl) *n.* a tall pole for dancing around on May Day, with ribbons attached to its top.

maze (mayz) *n.* 1. a complicated network of paths, a labyrinth. 2. a network of paths and hedges designed as a puzzle in which to try and find one's way. 3. a state of bewilderment. **maz'y** *adj.*

ma·zel (mah-zĕl) *n.* (*informal*) luck. □**mazel tov** (tawv), an expression of pleasure or congratulations among Jews. ▷Yiddish, = good luck.

ma·zur·ka (mă-zur-kă) *n.* a lively Polish dance in triple time, music for this.

MBA *abbr.* Master of Business Administration.

Mba·bane (ĕm-bah-bahn) the capital of Swaziland.

mc *abbr.* megacycle.

MC *abbr.* 1. Marine Corps. 2. Medical Corps. 3. Member of Congress.

M.C. *abbr.* 1. Master of Ceremonies. 2. Member of Congress.

Mc·Coy (mă-koi) *n.* (*informal*) the real thing, the genuine article, *this pearl's the real McCoy.*

Mc·Kin·ley (mă-kin-lee), **Wil·liam** (1843–1901) the twenty-fifth president of the U.S. 1897–1901.

MCPO *abbr.* master chief petty officer.

mc/s *abbr.* megacycle(s) per second.

Md *symbol* mendelevium.

MD *abbr.* 1. Maryland. 2. Middle Dutch.

Md. *abbr.* Maryland.

M.D. *abbr.* Doctor of Medicine.

mdnt. *abbr.* midnight.

mdse. *abbr.* merchandise.

MDT *abbr.* Mountain Daylight Time.

me (mee) *pronoun* 1. the objective case of I. (▷See the note under **between**.) 2. (*informal*) = I, *it's me.* ▷Only the most careful speaker says, "It is I" when this statement stands alone, but it would be incorrect to use *me* in the sentence "It is I who will have to pay."

ME *abbr.* 1. Maine. 2. Middle English.

Me. *abbr.* Maine.

M.E. *abbr.* 1. Mechanical Engineer. 2. Middle English. 3. Mining Engineer.

mead (meed) *n.* an alcoholic drink of fermented honey and water.

mead·ow (med-oh) *n.* a field of grass.

mead·ow·land (med-oh-land) *n.* meadow.

mead·ow·lark (med-oh-lahrk) *n.* an American songbird of open fields.

mead·ow·sweet (med-oh-sweet) *n.* a North American meadow plant with fragrant creamy-white flowers.

mea·ger (mee-gĕr) *adj.* scanty in amount. **mea'ger·ly** *adv.*

meal[1] (meel) *n.* 1. an occasion when food is eaten. 2. the food itself. □**make a meal of,** to consume as a meal. **meal ticket,** a ticket entitling one to a meal; (*informal*) a person or thing that provides one with food.

meal[2] *n.* coarsely ground grain.

meal·time (meel-tım) *n.* the usual time for a meal.

meal·y (mee-lee) *adj.* (**meal·i·er, meal·i·est**) 1. like or containing meal, dry and powdery. 2. mealymouthed.

meal·y·bug (mee-lee-bug) *n.* an insect infesting vines etc., whose body is covered with a white powdery secretion.

meal·y·mouthed (mee-lee-mowthd, -mowtht) *adj.* trying excessively to avoid offending people.

mean[1] (meen) *adj.* (of a point or quantity) equally far from two extremes, average. **mean** *n.* a middle point or condition or course etc. □**mean time** or **mean solar time,** the time based on a fictitious sun moving in the celestial equator at the mean rate of the real sun.

mean[2] *v.* (**meant, mean·ing**) 1. to have as one's purpose or intention. 2. to design or destine for a purpose; *it was meant for you,* you were intended to receive or hear it. 3. to intend to convey (a sense) or to indicate or refer to (a thing). 4. (of words) to have as an equivalent in the same or another language, *"maybe" means "perhaps."* 5. to entail, to involve, *it means catching the early train.* 6. to be likely or certain to result in, *this means war.* 7. to be of a specified importance, *the honor means a lot to me.* □**mean business,** (*informal*) to be ready to take action, not merely talk. **mean well,** to have good intentions. **what do you mean by it?,** can you justify such behavior?

mean[3] *adj.* 1. poor in quality, value, or appearance, low in rank; *he is no mean golfer,* he is a very good one. 2. unkind, small-minded, spiteful, *a mean trick.* 3. not generous, miserly. 4. vicious. **mean'ly** *adv.* **mean'ness** *n.*

me·an·der (mee-an-dĕr) *v.* 1. (of a stream) to follow a winding course, flowing slowly and gently. 2. to wander in a leisurely way. **meander** *n.* a winding course. **me·an'der·er** *n.*

mean·ing (mee-ning) *n.* what is meant. **meaning** *adj.* full of meaning, expressive, *gave him a meaning look; a well-meaning teacher,* one with good intentions. **mean'ing·less** *adj.* □**with meaning,** full of meaning, significantly.

mean·ing·ful (mee-ning-fŭl) *adj.* significant. **mean'ing·ful·ly** *adv.*

means (meenz) *n. sing.* that by which a result is brought about; *transported their goods by means of trucks,* by using trucks. **means** *n. pl.* resources, money or other wealth considered as a means of supporting oneself, *has private means.* □**by all means,** certainly. **by no means,** not nearly, *it is by no means certain.* **means test,** an inquiry to establish a person's neediness before financial help is given.

meant (ment) *see* **mean²**.

mean·time (meen-tɪm) *n.* an intervening period of time, *in the meantime.* **meantime** *adv.* meanwhile.

mean·while (meen-hwɪl) *adv.* 1. in the intervening period of time. 2. at the same time, while something else takes place. **meanwhile** *n.* meantime, *in the meanwhile.*

mean·y, mean·ie (mee-nee) *n.* (*pl.* **mean·ies**) (*informal*) a small-minded or miserly person.

meas. *abbr.* measure.

mea·sles (mee-zĕlz) *n.* an infectious disease producing small red spots on the whole body.

mea·sly (mee-zlee) *adj.* 1. affected with measles. 2. (*slang*) meager.

meas·ur·a·ble (mezh-ŭ-ră-bĕl) *adj.* able to be measured. **meas'ur·a·bly** *adv.*

meas·ure (mezh-ŭr) *n.* 1. the size or quantity of something, found by measuring. 2. extent or amount, *he is in some measure responsible; had a measure of success.* 3. a unit or standard or system used in measuring, *the meter is a measure of length.* 4. a device used in measuring, such as a container of standard size (*pint measure*) or a marked rod or tape. 5. the rhythm or meter of poetry, the time of a piece of music, a bar of music. 6. suitable action taken for a particular purpose, a law or proposed law, *measures to stop tax evasion.* **measure** *v.* (**meas·ured, meas·ur·ing**) 1. to find the size or quantity or extent of something by comparing it with a fixed unit or with an object of known size. 2. to be of a certain size, *it measures two feet by four.* 3. to mark or deal out a measured quantity, *measured out their rations.* 4. to estimate (a quality etc.) by comparing it with some standard. **meas'ur·er** *n.* □**beyond measure,** very great, very much, *kind* or *kindness beyond measure.* **for good measure,** in addition to what was needed; as a finishing touch. **made to measure,** made in accordance with measurements taken. **measure up to,** to reach the standard required by.

meas·ured (mezh-ŭrd) *adj.* 1. rhythmical, regular in movement, *measured tread.* 2. carefully considered, *in measured language.*

meas·ure·ment (mezh-ŭr-mĕnt) *n.* 1. measuring. 2. size etc. found by measuring and expressed in units.

meat (meet) *n.* animal flesh as food (usually excluding fish and poultry). **meat'less** *adj.* □**meat packing,** killing and butchering of animals for food.

meat·ball (meet-bawl) *n.* 1. chopped or ground meat shaped into a ball before cooking. 2. (*slang*) a clumsy person.

meat·head (meet-hed) *n.* (*slang*) a clumsy person.

meat·man (meet-man) *n.* (*pl.* -men, *pr.* -men) (*informal*) a butcher.

meat·y (mee-tee) *adj.* (**meat·i·er, meat·i·est**) 1. like meat. 2. full of meat, fleshy. 3. full of subject matter, *a meaty book.*

Mec·ca (mek-ă) 1. a city in Saudi Arabia, the birthplace of Muhammad and chief place of Muslim pilgrimage. 2. a place that a person or people with certain interests are eager to visit.

mech. *abbr.* 1. mechanical. 2. mechanics. 3. mechanism.

me·chan·ic (mĕ-kan-ik) *n.* a skilled workman who uses or repairs machines or tools.

me·chan·i·cal (mĕ-kan-i-kăl) *adj.* 1. of machines or mechanism. 2. worked or produced by machinery. 3. (of a person or action) like a machine, as if acting or done without conscious thought. 4. (of work) needing little or no thought. 5. of or belonging to the science of mechanics. **me·chan'i·cal·ly** *adv.* □**mechanical advantage,** the ratio of a machine's output of force to that supplied to it. **mechanical drawing,** drawing done with compasses etc. **mechanical engineer,** one who engages in mechanical engineering. **mechanical engineering,** engineering dealing with the design and development of machinery.

me·chan·ics (mĕ-kan-iks) *n. sing.* 1. the scientific study of motion and force, *mechanics is difficult to learn.* 2. the science of machinery. 3. *mechanics, n. pl.* the processes by which something is done or functions, *the mechanics of that process are too difficult for me.*

mech·an·ism (mek-ă-niz-ĕm) *n.* 1. the way a machine works. 2. the structure or parts of a machine. 3. the process by which something is done, *the mechanism of government.*

mech·a·nize (mek-ă-nɪz) *v.* (**mech·a·nized, mech·a·niz·ing**) to equip with machines, to use machines in or for; *a mechanized army unit,* one that is equipped with tanks and armored cars etc. **mech'a·ni·zer** *n.* **mech·a·ni·za·tion** (mek-ă-ni-zay-shŏn) *n.*

med. *abbr.* 1. medical. 2. medicine. 3. medieval. 4. medium.

M.Ed. *abbr.* Master of Education.

med·al (med-ăl) *n.* a small flat piece of metal, usually shaped like a coin, bearing a design and commemorating an event, saint, etc. or given as an award for an achievement. □**Medal of Honor,** the highest military award given by the U.S. Congress, for conspicuous gallantry above and beyond the call of duty.

med·al·ist (med-ă-list) *n.* one who wins a medal as a prize, *gold medalist.*

me·dal·lion (mĕ-dal-yŏn) *n.* 1. a large medal. 2. a large circular ornamental design, as on a carpet.

med·dle (med-ĕl) *v.* (**med·dled, med·dling**) 1. to interfere in people's affairs. 2. to tinker. **med'dler** *n.*

med·dle·some (med-ĕl-sŏm) *adj.* often meddling.

Mede (meed) *n.* one of the inhabitants of ancient Persia. □**the law of the Medes and Persians,** an unchanging law.

me·di·a (mee-di-ă) *n. pl. see* **medium.** □**the media,** newspapers and broadcasting, by which information is conveyed to the general public. ▷This word is the plural of *medium* and should have a plural verb: *the media are* (not *is*) *influential.* It is incorrect to refer to one of these services, such as television, as *a media* or *the media,* or to several of them as *medias.*

me·di·ae·val (mee-di-ee-văl) = **medieval.**

me·di·al (mee-di-ăl) *adj.* situated in the middle, intermediate between two extremes. **me'di·al·ly** *adv.*

me·di·an (mee-di-ăn) *adj.* medial. **median** *n.* a median point or line etc.

me·di·ate (mee-di-ayt) *v.* (**me·di·at·ed, me·di·at·ing**) 1. to act as negotiator or peacemaker

between the opposing sides in a dispute. 2. to bring about (a settlement) in this way. **me'di·a·tor** *n.* **me·di·a·tion** (mee-di-ay-shŏn) *n.*
med·ic (med-ik) *n. (informal)* 1. a doctor. 2. a medical student. 3. a medical corpsman.
Med·i·caid (med-ĭ-kayd) *n.* a joint federal and state health insurance program aiding those unable to pay for hospital and medical care.
med·i·cal (med-i-kăl) *adj.* of or involving the science of medicine, of this as distinct from surgery; *medical examination,* physical examination by a doctor to determine a person's state of health. **medical** *n. (informal)* a medical examination. **med'i·cal·ly** *adv.* □**medical examiner,** a coroner. **medical practitioner,** a physician or surgeon.
me·dic·a·ment (mĕ-dik-ă-ment, med-i-kă-) *n.* any medicine or ointment etc.
Med·i·care (med-ĭ-kair) *n.* a federal program of health insurance for those over sixty-five.
med·i·cate (med-ĭ-kayt) *v.* (**med·i·cat·ed, med·i·cat·ing**) to treat or impregnate with a medicinal substance, *medicated gauze.* **med·i·ca·tive** (med-ĭ-kay-tiv) *adj.* **med·i·ca·tion** (med-ĭ-kay-shŏn) *n.*
me·dic·i·nal (mĕ-dis-ĭ-năl) *adj.* of a medicine, having healing properties. **me·dic'i·nal·ly** *adv.*
med·i·cine (med-ĭ-sin) *n.* 1. the scientific study of the prevention and cure of diseases and disorders of the body. 2. this as distinct from surgery. 3. a substance used to treat a disease etc., especially one taken by mouth. □**a dose of one's own medicine,** treatment such as one is accustomed to giving others. **medicine ball,** a stuffed leather ball used in exercise. **medicine chest,** a wall cabinet in a bathroom. **medicine man,** a witch doctor. **take one's medicine,** to submit to punishment for one's wrongdoing.
med·i·co (med-ĭ-koh) *n.* (*pl.* **-cos**) *(informal)* a doctor or medical student.
me·di·eval (mi-dee-văl) *adj.* of the Middle Ages.
me·di·e·val·ist (mi-dee-văl-ist) *n.* a specialist in the study of the literature etc. of the Middle Ages.
me·di·o·cre (mee-di-oh-kĕr) *adj.* 1. of medium quality, neither good nor bad. 2. second-rate. (▷It is incorrect to say that something is *very mediocre,* just as we should not say that something is very average or very second-rate.) **me·di·oc·ri·ty** (mee-di-ok-rĭ-tee) *n.*
med·i·tate (med-i-tayt) *v.* (**med·i·tat·ed, med·i·tat·ing**) 1. to think deeply and quietly, to contemplate. 2. to plan in one's mind. **med·i·ta·tion** (med-i-tay-shŏn) *n.*
med·i·ta·tive (med-i-tay-tiv) *adj.* meditating, accompanied by meditation. **med'i·ta·tive·ly** *adv.*
Med·i·ter·ran·e·an (med-i-tĕ-ray-ni-ăn) *adj.* of or characteristic of the Mediterranean Sea or the regions bordering on it. **Mediterranean** *n.* the Mediterranean Sea. □**Mediterranean Sea,** a sea lying between Europe and North Africa.
me·di·um (mee-di-ŭm) *n.* (*pl.* **-di·a, -di·ums**) 1. a middle quality or degree of intensiveness etc.; *the happy medium,* avoidance of unpleasant extremes. 2. a substance or surroundings in which something exists or moves or is transmitted, *air is the medium through which sound travels.* 3. an environment. 4. a liquid (as oil or water) in which pigments are mixed for use in painting. 5. an agency or means by which something is done, *the use of television as a medium for advertis-*

ing. (▷See the entry for **media**.) 6. the material or form used by an artist or composer, *sculpture is his medium.* 7. (*pl.* **mediums**) a person who claims to be able to communicate with the spirits of the dead. **medium** *adj.* intermediate between two extremes or amounts, average, moderate.
me·di·um·is·tic (mee-di-ŭ-mis-tik) *adj.* of spiritualist mediums.
med·lar (med-lăr) *n.* 1. an Old World fruit like a small brown apple that is not edible until it begins to decay. 2. the tree that bears it.
med·ley (med-lee) *n.* (*pl.* **-leys**) 1. an assortment of things. 2. music combining passages from different sources. □**medley relay,** a relay race between teams in which each member runs a different distance or uses a different swimming stroke.
me·dul·la (mi-dul-ă) *n.* (*pl.* **-dul·las, -dul·lae,** *pr.* **-dul·ee**) the marrow of bone, the spinal marrow. □**medulla oblongata,** the hindmost section of the brain.
meek (meek) *adj.* quiet and obedient, making no protest. **meek'ly** *adv.* **meek'ness** *n.*
meer·schaum (meer-shŭm, -showm) *n.* a tobacco pipe with a bowl made from a white claylike substance.
meet¹ (meet) *adj. (old use)* suitable, proper. **meet'ly** *adv.* **meet'ness** *n.*
meet² *v.* (**met, meet·ing**) 1. to come face to face with, to come together (as socially or for discussion). 2. to come into contact, to touch. 3. to go to a place to be present at the arrival of, *I will meet your train.* 4. to make the acquaintance of, to be introduced. 5. to come together as opponents in a contest or battle. 6. to find oneself faced (with a thing), to experience or receive, *met with difficulties; met his death.* 7. to deal with (a problem), to satisfy (a demand etc.), to pay (the cost or what is owing). **meet** *n.* a meeting of people and hounds for a hunt, or of athletes etc. for a competition. □**meet a person halfway,** to respond readily to his suggestions; to make a compromise with him. **meet the eye** or **ear,** to be visible or audible; *there's more in it than meets the eye,* there are hidden qualities or complications; *meet a person's eye,* to look directly at the eyes of a person who is looking at one's own. **meet up with,** *(informal)* to meet (a person), to encounter (a thing).
meet·ing (mee-ting) *n.* 1. coming together. 2. an assembly of people for discussion etc. or (of Quakers) for worship. □**meeting house,** a place of worship, especially for Quakers. **meeting place,** a place appointed for a meeting.
meg. *abbr.* megohm.
mega- *prefix* large, as in *megalith;* one million, as in *megacycle.*
meg·a·cy·cle (meg-ă-sı-kĕl) *n.* 1. one million cycles as a unit of wave frequency. 2. *(informal)* megahertz.
meg·a·death (meg-ă-deth) *n.* the death of one million people (regarded as a unit in estimating the possible casualties in nuclear war).
meg·a·hertz (meg-ă-hurts) *n.* a unit of frequency of electromagnetic waves, = one million cycles per second.
meg·a·lith (meg-ă-lith) *n.* a huge stone used in the building of prehistoric monuments. **meg·a·lith·ic** (meg-ă-lith-ik) *adj.*
meg·a·lo·ma·ni·a (meg-ă-loh-may-ni-ă) *n.* 1. a form of madness in which a person has exagger-

ated ideas of his own importance etc. 2. an obsessive desire to do things on a grand scale. **meg·a·lo·ma·ni·ac** (meg-ă-loh-may-ni-ak) *n.*

meg·a·lop·o·lis (meg-ă-lop-ŏ-lis) *n.* 1. a very large city or its way of life. 2. the thickly populated area surrounding one or more cities.

meg·a·phone (meg-ă-fohn) *n.* a funnel-shaped device used for directing and amplifying a speaker's voice so that it can be heard at a distance.

meg·a·ton (meg-ă-tun) *n.* a unit of explosive power equal to that of one million tons of TNT.

meg·a·vi·ta·min (meg-ă-vI-tă-mĭn) *n.* an extraordinarily large dosage of any vitamin.

meg·a·volt (meg-ă-vohlt) *n.* one million volts.

meg·a·watt (meg-ă-wot) *n.* one million watts.

me·gil·lah (mĕ-gil-ă) *n. (slang)* an involved explanation or extremely lengthy account. ▷From Hebrew, *Megillah,* the Book of Esther in the Old Testament.

meg·ohm (meg-ohm) *n.* an electrical unit of resistance, = one million ohms.

mei·o·sis (mI-oh-sis) *n.* a process of division of diploid cell nuclei whereby the number of chromosomes is halved, to be combined with another half-set at fertilization. **mei·ot·ic** (mI-ot-ik) *adj.*

mel·a·mine (mel-ă-meen) *n.* a resilient kind of plastic.

mel·an·cho·li·a (mel-ăn-koh-li-ă) *n.* mental depression. **mel·an·chol·ic** (mel-ăn-kol-ik) *adj.* **mel·an·chol'i·cal·ly** *adv.*

mel·an·chol·y (mel-ăn-kol-ee) *n. (pl.* **-chol·ies**) 1. mental depression, thoughtful sadness. 2. an atmosphere of gloom. **melancholy** *adj.* sad, gloomy, depressing.

Mel·a·ne·sia (mel-ă-nee-*zh*ă) a group of South Pacific islands northeast of Australia. **Mel·a·ne'sian** *n.* 1. a native of Melanesia. 2. the language of Melanesia. **Mel·a·ne'sian** *adj.*

mé·lange (may-lahn*zh*) *n.* a mixture.

mel·a·nin (mel-ă-nin) *n.* dark pigment in skin and hair. **me·lan·ic** (mĕ-lan-ik) *adj. & n.*

mel·a·nism (mel-ă-niz-ĕm) *n.* darkness of color resulting from the abnormal development of dark pigment in the skin, hair, etc.

mel·a·no·ma (mel-ă-noh-mă) *n. (pl.* **-mas, -ma·ta,** *pr.* -mă-tă) a dark colored usually malignant tumor of the skin.

Mel·ba (mel-bă) **toast** thin crisp toast.

meld¹ (meld) *v.* (in some card games) to declare for a score. **meld** *n.* melding, a group of cards for melding.

meld² *v.* to merge, to blend, to combine.

me·lee (may-lay, may-lay) *n.* 1. a confused fight. 2. a muddle.

me·lio·rate (meel-yŏ-rayt) *v.* (**me·lio·rat·ed, me·lio·rat·ing**) to improve. **me·lio·ra·tive** (meel-yŏ-ray-tiv) *adj.* **me·lio·ra·tion** (meel-yŏ-ray-shŏn) *n.*

mel·lif·lu·ous (me-lif-loo-ŭs) *adj.* sweet sounding. **mel·lif'lu·ous·ly** *adv.* **mel·lif'lu·ous·ness** *n.*

mel·low (mel-oh) *adj.* 1. sweet and rich in flavor. 2. (of sound or color) soft and rich, free from harshness or sharp contrast. 3. made kindly and sympathetic by age or experience. 4. genial, jovial. **mellow** *v.* to make or become mellow. **mel'low·ly** *adv.* **mel'low·ness** *n.*

me·lo·de·on (mĕ-loh-di-ŏn) *n.* a small organ in which air is drawn through reeds.

me·lod·ic (mĕ-lod-ik) *adj.* of melody. **me·lod'i·cal·ly** *adv.*

me·lo·di·ous (mĕ-loh-di-ŭs) *adj.* full of melody.

me·lo'di·ous·ly *adv.* **me·lo'di·ous·ness** *n.*

mel·o·dra·ma (mel-ŏ-drah-mă) *n.* 1. a play full of suspense in real life resembling this. 2. a situation in real life resembling this. **mel·o·dra·mat·ic** (mel-oh-dră-mat-ik) *adj.* **mel·o·dra·mat'i·cal·ly** *adv.* **mel·o·dra·mat·ics** (mel-oh-dră-mat-iks) *n. pl.* melodramatic behavior.

mel·o·dy (mel-ŏ-dee) *n. (pl.* **-dies**) 1. sweet music, tunefulness. 2. a song or tune, *old Irish melodies.* 3. the main part in a piece of harmonized music.

mel·on (mel-ŏn) *n.* 1. the large sweet fruit of various gourds. 2. *(slang)* spoils or profits to be shared.

melt (melt) *v.* 1. to make into or become liquid by heat. 2. (of food) to be softened or dissolved easily, *it melts in the mouth.* 3. to make or become gentler through pity or love. 4. to dwindle or fade away, to pass slowly into something else, *one shade of color melted into another.* 5. (*informal,* of a person) to depart unobtrusively. **melt** *n.* 1. a melted metal etc. 2. the amount melted at one time. 3. the process of melting. □**melt down,** to melt (metal objects) in order to use the metal as raw material; (of metal objects) to be melted thus. **melting point,** the temperature at which a solid melts. **melting pot,** a place or situation where things are being mixed or reconstructed, *the United States was thought of as a melting pot for all the peoples of the world.*

melt·down (melt-down) *n.* a nuclear accident in which the reactor core could melt, the melting of nuclear fuel rods.

melt·wa·ter (melt-waw-tĕr) *n.* the water formed by melting snow and ice, especially from a glacier.

mem. *abbr.* 1. member. 2. memoir. 3. memorial.

mem·ber (mem-bĕr) *n.* 1. a person or thing that belongs to a particular group or society. 2. a part or organ of the body, especially a limb.

mem·ber·ship (mem-bĕr-ship) *n.* 1. being a member. 2. the total number of members.

mem·brane (mem-brayn) *n.* thin flexible skinlike tissue, especially that covering or lining organs or other structures in animals and plants. **mem·bra·nous** (mem-bră-nŭs) *adj.*

me·men·to (mĕ-men-toh) *n. (pl.* **-tos, -toes**) a souvenir.

mem·o (mem-oh) *n. (pl.* **mem·os**) *(informal)* a memorandum.

mem·oir (mem-wahr) *n.* a written account of events that one has lived through or of the life or character of a person whom one knew, *write one's memoirs.*

mem·o·ra·bil·i·a (mem-ŏ-ră-bil-i-ă) *n. pl.* memorable things.

mem·o·ra·ble (mem-ŏ-ră-bĕl) *adj.* worth remembering, easy to remember. **mem'o·ra·bly** *adv.* **mem'o·ra·ble·ness** *n.* **mem·o·ra·bil·i·ty** (mem-ŏ-ră-bil-i-tee) *n.*

mem·o·ran·dum (mem-ŏ-ran-düm) *n. (pl.* **-dums, -da,** pr. dä) 1. a note or record of events written as a reminder, for future use. 2. an informal written communication from one person to another in an office or organization.

me·mo·ri·al (mĕ-mohr-i-ăl) *n.* an object or institution or custom established in memory of an event or person. **memorial** *adj.* serving as a memorial. □**Memorial Day,** once May 30, commemorating those who died in active military service, now observed on the last Monday in May.

me·mo·ri·al·ize (mĕ-mohr-i-ă-lız) *v.* (**me·mo·ri·al·ized, me·mo·ri·al·iz·ing**) 1. to com-

memorate. 2. to address a memorial to.
mem·o·rize (mem-ŏ-rīz) v. (**mem·o·rized,
mem·o·riz·ing**) to learn (a thing) so as to know
it from memory. **mem'o·riz·er** n. **mem·o·ri·
za·tion** (mem-ŏ-ri-zay-shŏn) n.
mem·o·ry (mem-ŏ-ree) n. (pl. **-ries**) 1. the ability
to keep things in one's mind or to recall them
at will. 2. remembering, a thing remembered,
memories of childhood; of happy memory, remembered with pleasure. 3. the length of time over
which people's memory extends, *within living
memory.* □**from memory,** recalled into one's
mind without the aid of notes etc. **in memory
of,** in honor of a person or thing that is remembered with respect. **memory bank,** the part of
a computer in which data are stored for retrieval.
men (men) *see* **man.**
men·ace (men-is) n. 1. something that seems likely
to bring harm or danger, a threatening quality.
2. an annoying or troublesome person or thing.
menace v. (**men·aced, men·ac·ing**) to
threaten with harm or danger. **men'ac·ing·ly**
adv.
mé·nage (may-nahzh) n. a household. □**ménage
à trois** (a trwah), a household consisting of husband, wife, and the lover of one of these.
me·nag·er·ie (mĕ-naj-ĕ-ree) n. a collection of wild
or strange animals in captivity, for exhibition.
me·nar·che (mĕ-nahr-kee) n. the onset of first
menstruation.
mend (mend) v. 1. to make whole (something that
is damaged), to repair. 2. to make or become better; *mend one's manners,* improve them; *mend
matters,* to set right or improve the state of affairs.
mend n. a repaired place. **mend'er** n. □**on the
mend,** improving in health or condition.
men·da·cious (men-day-shŭs) *adj.* untruthful,
telling lies. **men·da'cious·ly** *adv.* **men·dac·
i·ty** (men-das-i-tee) n.
men·de·le·vi·um (men-dĕ-lee-vi-ŭm) n. an artificially produced chemical element.
men·di·cant (men-dī-kănt) *adj.* begging; *mendicant friars,* friars who depend on alms for a
living. **mendicant** n. a beggar, a mendicant friar.
men·di·can·cy (men-dī-kăn-see) n.
mend·ing (mend-ing) n. clothes to be mended.
men·folk (men-fohk), **men·folks** (men-fohks) n.
pl. (informal) men in general, the men of one's
family.
men·ha·den (men-hay-dĕn) n. (pl. **-den, -dens**)
a large herring from the east coast of North America.
men·hir (men-heer) n. a tall upright stone set up
in prehistoric times.
me·ni·al (mee-ni-ăl) *adj.* lowly, degrading, *menial
tasks.* **menial** n. *(contemptuous)* a servant, a person who does humble tasks. **me'ni·al·ly** *adv.*
me·nin·ges (mĕ-nin-jeez) n. pl. *(sing.* **me·ninx,**
pr. mee-ningks) the membranes that enclose the
brain and spinal cord. **me·nin·ge·al** (mĕ-nin-
ji-ăl) *adj.*
men·in·gi·tis (men-in-jɪ-tis) n. inflammation of
the meninges.
me·nis·cus (mĕ-nis-kŭs) n. (pl. **-nis·ci,** *pr.*
-nis-ɪ, **-nis·cus·es**) 1. a lens that is convex on
one side and concave on the other. 2. (in mathematics) a figure of crescent form. 3. (in physics)
a curved upper surface of liquid in a tube.
Men·non·ite (men-ŏ-nɪt) n. a member of a Protestant sect with evangelical beliefs.
men·o·pause (men-ŏ-pawz) n. the time of life dur-

ing which a woman finally ceases to menstruate.
men·o·pau·sal (men-ŏ-paw-zăl) *adj.*
me·nor·ah (mĕ-nohr-ă) n. a seven-branched cande-
labrum used in Jewish worship.
men·ses (men-seez) n. pl. the blood etc. discharged
in menstruation.
men·stru·al (men-stroo-ăl) *adj.* of or in menstruation.
men·stru·ate (men-stroo-ayt) v. (**men·stru·
at·ed, men·stru·at·ing**) to experience the discharge of blood from the uterus that normally
occurs in women between puberty and middle age
at approximately monthly intervals. **men·stru·
a·tion** (men-stroo-ay-shŏn) n.
men·sur·a·ble (men-shŭ-ră-bĕl) *adj.* measurable,
having fixed limits. **men·sur·a·bil·i·ty** (men-
shŭ-ră-bil-i-tee) n.
men·sur·a·tion (men-shŭ-ray-shŏn) n. 1. measuring. 2. mathematical rules for finding lengths,
areas, and volumes. **men·su·ral** (men-shŭ-răl)
adj. **men·su·ra·tive** (men-shŭ-ray-tiv) *adj.*
mens·wear (menz-wair) n. clothes for men.
men·tal (men-tăl) *adj.* 1. of the mind, existing in
or performed by the mind; *mental arithmetic,* calculations done without the aid of written figures.
2. *(informal)* suffering from a disorder of the
mind, mad, *a mental case.* **men'tal·ly** *adv.*
□**mental age,** the level of a person's mental development expressed as the age at which this level
is reached by an average person. **mental deficiency,** lack of normal intelligence through imperfect mental development. **mentally deficient,**
suffering from this. **mental home** *or* **hospital,**
an establishment for the care of patients suffering
from mental illness. **mental reservation,** *see*
reservation. **mental retardation,** mental deficiency.
men·tal·ist (men-tă-list) n. a mind reader.
men·tal·i·ty (men-tal-i-tee) n. (pl. **-ties**) a person's mental ability or characteristic attitude of
mind.
men·thol (men-thohl) n. a solid white substance
obtained from peppermint oil or made synthetically, used as a flavoring and to relieve pain.
men·tho·lat·ed (men-thŏ-lay-tid) *adj.* impregnated with menthol.
men·tion (men-shŏn) v. to speak or write about
briefly, to refer to by name. **mention** n. mentioning, being mentioned; *won honorable mention,* formal recognition of merit, especially of a candidate
or competitor just below those receiving prizes.
□**don't mention it,** a polite reply to thanks or
to an apology. **not to mention,** and as another
important thing.
men·tor (men-tor, -tŏr) n. a trusted adviser.
men·u (men-yoo) n. a list of dishes to be served
or available in a restaurant etc.
me·ow (mee-ow) = **mew.**
me·phit·ic (mĕ-fit-ik) *adj.* (of vapors etc.) smelling
unpleasant, poisonous.
mer. *abbr.* meridian.
mer·can·tile (mur-kăn-teel, -tɪl) *adj.* trading, of
trade or merchants.
mer·ce·nar·y (mur-sĕ-ner-ee) *adj.* 1. working
merely for money or other reward, grasping. 2.
(of professional soldiers) hired to serve a foreign
country. **mercenary** n. (pl. **-nar·ies**) a professional soldier serving a foreign country. **mer'ce·
nar·i·ness** n. **mer·ce·nar·i·ly** (mur-sĕ-nair-ĭ-
lee) *adv.*
mer·cer (mur-sĕr) n. *(old use)* a dealer in textiles,

especially silks and other costly materials. **mer′cer·y** n.

mer·cer·ized (mur-sĕ-rızd) adj. (of cotton fabric or thread) treated with a substance that gives greater strength and a slight gloss.

mer·chan·dise (mur-chăn-dız, -dıs) n. goods or commodities bought and sold, goods for sale. **merchandise** v. (**mer·chan·dised, mer· chan·dis·ing**) 1. to buy and sell, to trade. 2. to promote sales of (goods etc.). **mer′chan· dis·er** n.

mer·chant (mur-chănt) n. 1. a wholesale trader who buys and sells for profit. 2. a retail trader, a storekeeper. 3. (slang) a person who is fond of or proficient in a certain activity, speed mer- chant. □**merchant bank**, a bank dealing in com- mercial loans and the financing of businesses. **merchant marine**, shipping employed in com- merce. **merchant ship**, a ship carrying merchan- dise.

mer·chant·a·ble (mur-chăn-tă-bĕl) adj. salable, marketable.

mer·chant·man (mur-chănt-măn) n. (pl. -men, pr. -mĕn) a merchant ship.

mer·ci·ful (mur-si-fŭl) adj. 1. showing mercy. 2. giving relief from pain or suffering, a merciful death. **mer′ci·ful·ly** adv.

mer·ci·less (mur-si-lis) adj. showing no mercy. **mer′ci·less·ly** adv.

mer·cu·ri·al (mĕr-kyoor-i-ăl) adj. 1. having a lively temperament. 2. liable to sudden changes of mood. **mer·cu′ri·al·ly** adv. **mer·cu′ri·al· ness** n.

mer·cu·ric (mĕr-kyoor-ik) adj. of or containing mercury.

Mer·cu·ro·chrome (mĕr-kyoor-ŏ-krohm) n. (trademark) a mercuric compound used as an an- tiseptic solution.

mer·cu·ry (mur-kyŭ-ree) n. (pl. -ries) 1. a heavy silvery normally liquid metallic element, used in thermometers and barometers etc. 2. Mercury, a Roman god of eloquence, skill, thieving, etc., and messenger of the gods. 3. Mercury, a planet in the solar system.

mer·cy (mur-see) n. (pl. -cies) 1. refraining from inflicting punishment or pain on an offender or enemy etc. who is in one's power. 2. a disposition to behave in this way, a tyrant without mercy. 3. a merciful act, a thing to be thankful for, it's a mercy no one was killed. **mercy** interj. an excla- mation of surprise or fear, mercy on us! □**at the mercy of**, wholly in the power of; liable to danger or harm from. **mercy killing**, euthanasia.

mere (meer) adj. nothing more or better than what is specified, she is a mere child; mere words, words alone, without deeds; it's no mere theory, is not only a theory. **mere′ly** adv.

mer·est (meer-ĕst) adj. very small or insignificant, the merest trace of color.

mer·e·tri·cious (mer-ĕ-trish-ŭs) adj. showily at- tractive but cheap or insincere. **mer·e· tri′cious·ly** adv. **mer·e·tri′cious·ness** n.

mer·gan·ser (mĕr-gan-sĕr) n. a diving duck that feeds on fish.

merge (murj) v. (**merged, merg·ing**) 1. to unite or combine into a whole, the two companies merged or were merged. 2. to pass slowly into something else, to blend or become blended.

merg·er (mur-jĕr) n. the combining of two or more business organizations etc. into one.

me·rid·i·an (mĕ-rid-i-ăn) n. any of the great semi- circles on the globe, passing through a given place and the North and South Poles; the meridian of Greenwich, that passing through Greenwich, Eng- land, shown on maps as 0° longitude.

me·ringue (mĕ-rang) n. 1. a mixture of sugar and white of egg baked crisp. 2. a cake of this.

me·ri·no (mĕ-ree-noh) n. (pl. -nos) 1. a kind of sheep with fine soft wool. 2. a kind of fine soft woolen yarn or fabric.

mer·it (mer-it) n. 1. the quality of deserving to be praised, excellence. 2. a feature or quality that deserves praise; judge it on its merits, according to its own qualities. **merit** v. (**mer·i·ted, mer· i·ting**) to deserve.

mer·i·toc·ra·cy (mer-i-tok-ră-see) n. 1. govern- ment or control by people of high ability, selected by some form of competition. 2. these people.

mer·i·to·ri·ous (mer-i-tohr-i-ŭs) adj. having merit, deserving praise. **mer·i·to′ri·ous·ly** adv. **mer·i·to′ri·ous·ness** n.

mer·maid (mur-mayd) n. an imaginary sea crea- ture, a woman with a fish's tail in place of legs.

mer·man (mur-man) n. (pl. -men, pr. -men) an imaginary male sea creature similar to a mermaid.

mer·ri·ment (mer-i-mĕnt) n. being merry, hilarity, fun.

mer·ry (mer-ee) adj. (**mer·ri·er, mer·ri·est**) cheerful and lively, joyous. **mer′ri·ly** adv. □**make merry**, to hold lively festivities.

mer·ry-go-round (mer-ee-goh-rownd) n. 1. a ma- chine at amusement parks with a circular revolv- ing platform with models of horses or other ani- mals etc. for riding on while it revolves. 2. a busy series of occupations or events in social or business life.

mer·ry·mak·ing (mer-ee-may-king) n. lively fes- tivities. **mer′ry·mak·er** n.

me·sa (may-să) n. a high rocky plateau with steep sides.

més·al·li·ance (may-ză-lı-ăns, may-zal-i-ăns) n. a marriage with a person of inferior social posi- tion. ▷French.

mes·ca·line (mes-kă-lin) n. a hallucinogenic drug, made from the buttonlike tops of a Mexican cac- tus.

Mes·dames see **Madame**.

Mes·de·moi·selles see **Mademoiselle**.

mes·em·bry·an·the·mum (mĕ-zem-bri-an-thĕ- mŭm) n. a low-growing plant with pink, orange, or white daisy-like flowers opening at about noon.

mesh (mesh) n. 1. one of the spaces between threads in a net or sieve or wire screen etc. 2. network fabric. **mesh** v. 1. to catch in a net, to entangle. 2. to come together, to coordinate, to match. 3. (of a toothed wheel) to engage with another or others.

mesh·work (mesh-wurk) n. mesh or netted work.

mes·mer·ize (mez-mĕ-rız) v. (**mes·mer·ized, mes·mer·iz·ing**) to hypnotize, to dominate the attention or will of. **mes′mer·ism** n. **mes·mer· ic** (mez-mer-ik) adj.

mes·o·lith·ic (mez-ŏ-lith-ik) adj. of the Stone Age between paleolithic and neolithic.

me·son (mee-zon) n. an elementary particle inter- mediate in mass between a proton and an elec- tron.

mes·o·sphere (mez-ŏ-sfeer) n. a region of Earth's atmosphere from the top of the stratosphere to an altitude of about fifty miles. **mes·o·spher· ic** (mez-ŏ-sfer-ik) adj.

Mes·o·zo·ic (mez-ŏ-zoh-ik) adj. of the geologic

era before the Cenozoic and after the Paleozoic and marked by the appearance and eventual disappearance of dinosaurs. **Mesozoic** *n.* the Mesozoic era.

mes·quite (me-skeet) *n.* a North American tree bearing beanlike pods, found especially in Mexico and southwestern U.S.

mess (mes) *n.* 1. a dirty or untidy condition, an untidy collection of things, something spilled. 2. a difficult or confused situation, trouble. 3. any disagreeable substance or concoction, a domestic animal's excreta. 4. *(informal)* a person who looks untidy or dirty or slovenly. 5. (in the armed forces) a group who take meals together, the place where such meals are eaten, the meals themselves. **mess** *v.* 1. to make untidy or dirty. 2. to muddle or bungle (business etc.), *messed it up.* 3. *(informal)* to putter, *mess about* or *around.* 4. *(informal)* to meddle or tinker, *don't mess with the transistor.* 5. to take one's meals with a military or other group, *they mess together.* □**make a mess of,** to bungle.

mes·sage (mes-ij) *n.* 1. a spoken or written communication. 2. the inspired moral or social teaching of a prophet or writer etc., *a film with a message.* □**get the message,** *(informal)* to understand what is meant or implied.

mes·sen·ger (mes-ĕn-jĕr) *n.* the bearer of a message.

Mes·si·ah (mĕ-sɪ-ă) *n.* 1. the expected deliverer and ruler of the Jewish people, whose coming was prophesied in the Old Testament. 2. Christ, regarded by Christians as this. 3. *messiah,* any deliverer.

Mes·si·an·ic (mes-ee-an-ik) *adj.* of the Messiah. **messianic** *adj.* of a messiah.

Mes·sieurs *see* **Monsieur.**

mess·mate (mes-mayt) *n.* *(informal)* a person with whom one eats regularly in the same mess aboard ship.

Messrs. *see* **Mr.**

mes·sy (mes-ee) *adj.* (**mes·si·er, mes·si·est**) 1. untidy or dirty, slovenly. 2. causing a mess, *a messy task.* 3. complicated and difficult to deal with. **mes′si·ly** *adv.* **mes′si·ness** *n.*

mes·ti·zo (me-stee-zoh) *n.* (*pl.* **-zos, -zoes**) a person of mixed ancestry, especially the offspring of a Spaniard and an American Indian.

met (met) *see* **meet²**.

met. *abbr.* 1. meteorology. 2. metropolitan. □**the Met,** *(informal)* the Metropolitan Opera House in New York City.

me·tab·o·lism (mĕ-tab-ŏ-liz-ĕm) *n.* the process by which food is built up into living material or used to supply energy in a living organism. **met·a·bol·ic** (met-ă-bol-ik) *adj.*

me·tab·o·lize (mĕ-tab-ŏ-līz) *v.* (**me·tab·o·lized, me·tab·o·liz·ing**) to process (food) in metabolism.

met·a·car·pus (met-ă-kahr-pŭs) *n.* the part of the hand between the wrist and the fingers, the set of bones in this.

met·a·gal·ax·y (met-ă-gal-ăk-see) *n.* the entire universe, all the galaxies.

met·al (met-ăl) *n.* any of a class of mineral substances such as gold, silver, copper, iron, uranium, etc., or an alloy of any of these. **metal** *adj.* made of metal. ▷Do not confuse *metal* with *mettle.*

me·tal·lic (mĕ-tal-ik) *adj.* 1. of or like metal. 2. (of sound) like metals struck together, sharp and ringing. **me·tal′li·cal·ly** *adv.*

met·al·lif·er·ous (met-ă-lif-ĕ-rŭs) *adj.* containing metal.

met·al·loid (met-ă-loid) *n.* a nonmetal element that has the properties of a metal and a nonmetal. **metalloid** *adj.* having the form or appearance of metal.

met·al·lurg·ist (met-ă-lur-jist) *n.* an expert in metallurgy.

met·al·lur·gy (met-ă-lur-jee) *n.* the scientific study of the properties of metals and alloys, the art of working metals or of extracting them from their ores. **met·al·lur·gi·cal** (met-ă-lur-ji-kăl) *adj.* **met·al·lur′gi·cal·ly** *adv.*

met·al·ware (met-ăl-wair) *n.* household utensils made of metal.

met·al·work (met-ăl-wurk) *n.* 1. the process of shaping objects from metal. 2. these objects. **me′tal·work·er** *n.* **met′al·work·ing** *n.*

met·a·mor·phic (met-ă-mor-fik) *adj.* of or characterized by metamorphosis.

met·a·mor·phose (met-ă-mor-fohz) *v.* (**met·a·mor·phosed, met·a·mor·phos·ing**) to change or be changed in form or character.

met·a·mor·pho·sis (met-ă-mor-fŏ-sis) *n.* (*pl.* **-ses,** *pr,* -seez) a change of form or character.

met·a·phor (met-ă-for) *n.* the application of a word or phrase to something that it does not apply to literally, in order to indicate a comparison with the literal usage, as the *evening* of one's life, *food* for thought, *cut off one's nose to spite one's face.* □**mixed metaphor,** an unsuitable combination of metaphors, as in *the only thing this government will listen to is muscle.*

met·a·phor·i·cal (met-ă-for-i-kăl) *adj.* in a metaphor, not literal. **met·a·phor′i·cal·ly** *adv.*

met·a·phys·ics (met-ă-fiz-iks) *n.* a branch of philosophy that deals with the nature of existence and of truth and knowledge. **met·a·phys′i·cal** *adj.*

me·tas·ta·sis (mĕ-tas-tă-sis) *n.* (*pl.* **-ses,** *pr,* -seez) transference of a disease, tumor, etc., from one part or organ to another. **me·tas′ta·size** *v.* (**me·tas·ta·sized, me·tas·ta·siz·ing**) to pass from one part or organ of the body to another. **met·a·stat·ic** (met-ă-stat-ik) *adj.*

met·a·tar·sus (met-ă-tahr-sŭs) *n.* 1. the part of the foot between the ankle and toes. 2. the set of bones in this. **met·a·tar·sal** (met-ă-tahr-săl) *adj.*

me·tath·e·sis (mĕ-tath-ĕ-sis) *n.* (*pl.* **-ses,** *pr,* -seez) 1. the transposition of sounds or letters in a word. 2. chemical interchange of atoms or groups of atoms between two molecules. **met·a·thet·ic** (met-ă-thet-ik) *adj.* **met·a·thet′i·cal** *adj.*

met·a·thet·i·cize (mĕ-tath-ĕ-sɪz) *v.* (**me·tath·e·sized, me·tath·e·siz·ing**) 1. to transfer by metathesis. 2. to undergo metathesis.

mete (meet) *v.* (**met·ed, met·ing**) **mete out,** to distribute, *mete out punishment to wrongdoers.*

me·tem·psy·cho·sis (mĕ-tem-sɪ-koh-sis) *n.* (*pl.* **-ses,** *pr,* -seez) supposed transmigration of the soul of a human being or animal at death into a new body of the same or a different species.

me·te·or (mee-ti-ŏr) *n.* a bright moving body seen in the sky, formed by a small mass of matter from outer space that becomes luminous from compression of air as it enters Earth's atmosphere.

me·te·or·ic (mee-ti-or-ik) *adj.* 1. of meteors. 2. like a meteor in brilliance or sudden appearance, *a meteoric career.* **me·te·or′i·cal·ly** *adv.*

me·te·or·ite (mee-ti-ŏ-rɪt) *n.* a fallen meteor, a fragment of rock or metal reaching Earth's surface from outer space. **me·te·or·it·ic** (mee-ti-ŏ-rit-ik) *adj.*

me·te·or·oid (mee-ti-ŏ-roid) *n.* a body moving through space, of the same nature as those that become visible as meteors when they enter Earth's atmosphere. **me·te·or·oid·al** (mee-ti-ŏ-roi-dăl) *adj.*

meteorol. *abbr.* 1. meteorological. 2. meteorology.

me·te·or·ol·o·gy (mee-ti-ŏ-rol-ŏ-jee) *n.* the scientific study of atmospheric conditions, especially in order to forecast weather. **me·te·or·ol'o·gist** *n.* **me·te·or·o·log·i·cal** (mee-ti-ŏ-rŏ-loj-i-kăl) *adj.*

me·ter¹ (mee-tĕr) *n.* a device designed to measure and indicate the quantity of a substance supplied, or the distance traveled and fare payable, or the time that has elapsed, etc. **meter** *v.* (**me·tered, me·ter·ing**) 1. to measure by meter. 2. to use a postage meter in processing (mail). ☐**meter maid,** a woman employed to enforce parking regulations.

meter² *n.* 1. a unit of length in the metric system, about 39.4 inches. 2. rhythm in poetry, a particular form of this.

-meter *suffix* used to form nouns meaning a measuring instrument, as in *barometer;* a linear meter², as in *kilometer.*

me·ter-kil·o·gram-sec·ond (mee-tĕr-kil-ŏ-gram-sek-ŏnd) *adj.* relating to a system of measurement based on the meter as the unit of length, the kilogram as the unit of mass, and the second as the unit of time.

meth (meth) *n.* *(slang)* methadone.

meth·a·done (meth-ă-dohn), **meth·a·don** (meth-ă-don) *n.* a powerful synthetic drug used as a substitute for morphine or heroin.

meth·am·phet·a·mine (meth-am-fet-ă-meen) *n.* an amphetamine derivative with quicker and longer action, used as a stimulant.

meth·ane (meth-ayn) *n.* a colorless inflammable gas that occurs in coal mines and marshy areas.

meth·a·nol (meth-ă-nohl) *n.* methyl alcohol.

meth·a·qua·lone (meth-ă-kwah-lohn) *n.* a nonbarbiturate drug used as a sedative and to induce sleep.

me·thinks (mi-thingks) *v.* (past tense **me·thought,** *pr.* mi-thawt) *(old use)* it seems to me.

meth·od (meth-ŏd) *n.* 1. a procedure or way of doing something. 2. orderliness, *he's a man of method.*

me·thod·i·cal (mě-thod-i-kăl) *adj.* orderly, systematic. **me·thod'i·cal·ly** *adv.* **me·thod'i·cal·ness** *n.*

Meth·od·ist (meth-ŏ-dist) *n.* a member of a Protestant religious denomination originating in the 18th century and based on the teachings of John and Charles Wesley and their followers. **Meth·od·ism** *n.*

meth·od·ize (meth-ŏ-dɪz) *v.* (**meth·od·ized, meth·od·iz·ing**) to reduce to order, to arrange in an orderly manner.

meth·od·ol·o·gy (meth-ŏ-dol-ŏ-jee) *n.* (*pl.* **-gies**) the body of methods used in a particular branch of activity. **meth·od·o·log·i·cal** (meth-ŏ-dŏ-loj-ĭ-kăl) *adj.*

meth·yl (meth-ĭl) *n.* a chemical unit present in methane and in many organic compounds. ☐**methyl alcohol,** a colorless volatile inflammable liquid, the simplest alcohol.

me·tic·u·lous (mě-tik-yŭ-lŭs) *adj.* giving or showing great attention to detail, very careful and exact. **me·tic'u·lous·ly** *adv.* **me·tic'u·lous·ness** *n.*

mé·tier (may-tyay, may-tyay) *n.* 1. a person's trade, profession, or department of activity. 2. a person's forte. ▷French.

met·ric (met-rik) *adj.* 1. of or using the metric system. 2. of poetic meter. **met'ri·cal·ly** *adv.* ☐**go metric,** *(informal)* to adopt the metric system. **metric system,** a decimal system of weights and measures, using the meter, liter, and gram as units. **metric ton,** one thousand kilograms (2205 lbs.).

met·ri·cal (met-ri-kăl) *adj.* of or composed in rhythmic meter, not prose, *metrical psalms.* **met'ri·cal·ly** *adv.*

met·ri·cate (met-ri-kayt) *v.* (**met·ri·cat·ed, met·ri·cat·ing**) to change or adapt to the metric system of measurement. **met·ri·ca·tion** (met-ri-kay-shŏn) *n.*

met·ro (met-roh) *n.* (*pl.* **-ros**) *(informal)* a subway train.

me·trol·o·gy (me-trol-ŏ-jee) *n.* the science or system of weights and measures. **me·trol'o·gist** *n.* **met·ro·log·i·cal** (met-rŏ-loj-i-kăl) *adj.* **met·ro·log'i·cal·ly** *adv.*

met·ro·nome (met-rŏ-nohm) *n.* a device, often with an inverted pendulum, that sounds a click at a regular interval, used to indicate tempo while practicing music.

me·trop·o·lis (mě-trop-ŏ-lis) *n.* (*pl.* **-lis·es**) the chief city of a country or region.

met·ro·pol·i·tan (met-rŏ-pol-i-tăn) *adj.* of a metropolis. **metropolitan** *n.* the chief bishop in an ecclesiastical province.

met·tle (met-ĕl) *n.* courage or strength of character, *test his mettle.* ☐**on one's mettle,** determined to show one's courage or ability. ▷Do not confuse *mettle* with *metal.*

met·tle·some (met-ĕl-sŏm) *adj.* spirited, courageous.

MEV *abbr.* million electron volts.

mew (myoo) *n.* the characteristic cry of a cat. **mew** *v.* to make this sound.

mews (myooz) *n.* a set of what were formerly stables in a small street or square, now rebuilt or converted into dwellings or garages.

Mex. *abbr.* 1. Mexican. 2. Mexico.

Mex·i·co (mek-sĭ-koh) a country in Central America. **Mex'i·can** *adj. & n.* ☐**Mexico City,** its capital city.

mez·za·nine (mez-ă-neen) *n.* an extra story between the ground floor and the first floor, often in the form of a wide balcony.

mez·zo (met-soh) *adv.* (in music) moderately; *mezzo forte,* moderately loudly.

mez·zo-so·pran·o (met-zoh-sŏ-prah-noh) *n.* 1. a voice between soprano and contralto. 2. a singer with this voice. 3. a part written for it.

MF *abbr.* 1. medium frequency. 2. Middle French.

MFA *abbr.* Master of Fine Arts.

mfd. *abbr.* manufactured.

mfg. *abbr.* manufacturing.

mfr. *abbr.* 1. manufacture. 2. manufacturer.

mg *abbr.* milligram(s).

Mg *symbol* magnesium.

MG *abbr.* 1. machine gun. 2. major general. 3. military government.

mgr. *abbr.* 1. manager. 2. monseigneur. 3. monsignor.

mgt. *abbr.* management.

M.H. *abbr.* medal of honor.
mho (moh) *n.* a unit of electrical conductance.
▷From *ohm* reversed.
MHz *abbr.* megahertz.
mi (mee) *n.* a name for the third note of a scale in music.
MI *abbr.* 1. Michigan. 2. military intelligence.
mi. *abbr.* mile(s).
MIA *abbr.* missing in action.
Mi·am·i (mı-am-ee) *n.* (*pl.* -am·i, -am·is) a member of an Indian tribe originally from Indiana and Wisconsin.
mi·aow (mee-ow) = **mew.**
mi·as·ma (mı-az-mă, mee-) *n.* (*pl.* -ma·ta, *pr.* -mă-tă, -mas) unpleasant or unwholesome air. **mi·as′mic** *adj.* **mi·as′mal** *adj.* **mi·as·mat·ic** (mı-az-mat-ik, mee-) *adj.*
mi·ca (mı-kă) *n.* a mineral substance used as an electrical insulator.
mice (mıs) *see* **mouse.**
Mich. *abbr.* Michigan.
Mich·i·gan (mish-ı̆-găn) a state of the U.S.
Mick·ey Finn (mik-ee fin) *(slang)* a substance added to a drink to make the drinker unconscious.
Mic·mac (mik-mak) *n.* (*pl.* -mac, -macs) a member of an Indian tribe from eastern Canada.
micro- *prefix* small; one millionth of a unit, as in *microgram.*
mi·crobe (mı-krohb) *n.* a microorganism, especially one that causes disease or fermentation. **mi·cro·bi·al** (mı-kroh-bi-ăl) *adj.*
mi·cro·bi·ol·o·gist (mı-kroh-bı-ol-ŏ-jist) *n.* an expert in microbiology.
mi·cro·bi·ol·o·gy (mı-kroh-bı-ol-ŏ-jee) *n.* the scientific study of microorganisms. **mi·cro·bi·o·log·i·cal** (mı-kroh-bı-ŏ-loj-i-kăl) *adj.*
mi·cro·bus (mı-kroh-bus) *n.* (*informal*) a station wagon bus.
mi·cro·cap·sule (mı-kroh-kap-sŭl) *n.* a small capsule that releases its contents through breaking, dissolving, or melting.
mi·cro·chip (mı-kroh-chip) *n.* a small piece of silicon holding a complex electronic circuit.
mi·cro·cir·cuit (mı-kroh-sur-kit) *n.* an integrated circuit or other very small electronic circuit.
mi·cro·cli·mate (mı-kroh-klı-mit) *n.* the climate of a small area. **mi·cro·cli·ma·tol·o·gy** (mı-kroh-klı-mă-tol-ŏ-jee) *n.*
mi·cro·cop·y (mı-kroh-kop-ee) *n.* (*pl.* -cop·ies) a miniature scale reproduction of a photograph.
mi·cro·cosm (mı-krŏ-koz-ĕm) *n.* a world in miniature, something regarded as resembling something else on a very small scale.
mi·cro·dot (mı-krŏ-dot) *n.* a photograph of a document etc. reduced to the size of a dot.
mi·cro·e·lec·tron·ics (mı-kroh-i-lek-tron-iks) *n.* the design, manufacture, and use of microcircuits. **mi·cro·e·lec·tron′ic** *adj.*
mi·cro·en·cap·su·late (mı-kroh-in-kap-sŭ-layt) *v.* (mi·cro·en·cap·su·lat·ed, mi·cro·en·cap·su·la·ting) to encase (microcircuits and other microminiature components). **mi·cro·en·cap·su·la·tion** (mı-kroh-in-kap-sŭ-lay-shŏn) *n.*
mi·cro·fiche (mı-krŏ-feesh) *n.* (*pl.* -fiche, -fiches) a piece of microfilm in a form suitable for filing like an index card.
mi·cro·film (mı-krŏ-film) *n.* a length of film on which written or printed material is photographed in greatly reduced size. **microfilm** *v.* to photograph on this.

mi·cro·gram (mı-krŏ-gram) *n.* a unit of weight, = one millionth of a gram.
mi·cro·graph (mı-krŏ-graf) *n.* a photograph taken with a microscope.
mi·cro·groove (mı-krŏ-groov) *n.* 1. a very narrow groove. 2. a phonograph record with such grooves.
mi·cro·me·te·or·ite (mı-kroh-mee-ti-ŏ-rıt) *n.* a tiny meteorite. **mi·cro·me·te·or·ic** (mı-kroh-mee-ti-or-ik) *adj.*
mi·crom·e·ter (mı-krom-ĕ-tĕr) *n.* an instrument for measuring small objects or angular distances.
mi·cro·min·i·a·ture (mı-kroh-min-i-ă-chŭr) *adj.* of an extremely tiny size.
mi·cro·min·i·a·tur·i·za·tion (mı-kroh-min-i-ă-chŭ-ri-zay-shŏn) *n.* the making of electronic devices in a greatly reduced size.
mi·cron (mı-kron) *n.* a measure of length, = one millionth of a meter.
Mi·cro·ne·sia (mı-krŏ-nee-*zh*ă) a small Pacific island group east of the Philippines. **Mi·cro·ne′sian** *adj.* & *n.*
mi·cro·or·gan·ism (mı-kroh-or-gă-niz-ĕm, mı-kroh-or-) *n.* an organism that cannot be seen by the naked eye, as a bacterium or virus.
mi·cro·phone (mı-krŏ-fohn) *n.* an instrument for picking up sound waves for recording, amplifying, or broadcasting.
mi·cro·pho·to·graph (mı-krŏ-foh-tŏ-graf) *n.* a photograph reduced to very small size.
mi·cro·proc·es·sor (mı-kroh-pros-e-sŏr) *n.* a miniature computer, or a unit of this, consisting of one or more microchips. **mi·cro·proc′es·sing** *n.*
mi·cro·scope (mı-krŏ-skohp) *n.* an instrument with lenses that magnify objects or details too small to be seen by the naked eye. **mi·cros·co·py** (mı-kros-kŏ-pee) *n.*
mi·cro·scop·ic (mı-krŏ-skop-ik) *adj.* 1. of the microscope. 2. too small to be visible without the aid of a microscope. 3. extremely small. **mi·cro·scop′i·cal** *adj.* **mi·cro·scop′i·cal·ly** *adv.*
mi·cro·sec·ond (mı-kroh-sek-ŏnd) *n.* a unit of time, = one millionth of a second.
mi·cro·state (mı-kroh-stayt) *n.* (*informal*) a small country, usually recently independent.
mi·cro·sur·ger·y (mı-kroh-sur-jĕ-ree, mı-kroh-sur-) *n.* a surgical procedure done under a microscope. **mi·cro·sur·gi·cal** (mı-kroh-sur-ji-kăl) *adj.*
mi·cro·wave (mı-kroh-wayv) *n.* an electromagnetic wave of length between about 50 centimeters and 1 millimeter. □**microwave oven,** an oven that cooks with heat from microwave penetration of the food.
mid (mid) *adj.* in the middle of, middle, *in mid career; to mid-August.*
mid. *abbr.* middle.
mid·air (mid-air) *n.* a point in the air quite high off the ground; *a midair collision, between aircraft in flight.*
Mi·das (mı-dăs) *n.* **the Midas touch,** ability to make money in all one's activities. ▷Named after a legendary king in Asia Minor, whose touch turned all things to gold.
mid·day (mid-day) *n.* the middle of the day, noon.
mid·dle (mid-ĕl) *adj.* 1. at an equal distance from extremes or outer limits. 2. occurring halfway between beginning and end. 3. intermediate in rank or quality, moderate in size etc., *a man of middle height.* **middle** *n.* 1. a middle point, position, time,

area, or quality etc. 2. the waist. □**in the middle of,** during or halfway through (an activity etc.). **in the middle of nowhere,** (informal) in a very remote place. **middle age,** the period between youth and old age. **Middle Ages,** about 1000–1400 A.D. **Middle America,** the American working class. **middle C,** the note C that occurs near the middle of the piano keyboard. **middle class,** the class of society between the upper and working classes, including business and professional people. **middle ear,** the cavity of the central part of the ear behind the drum. **Middle East,** the area covered by countries from Egypt to Iran inclusive. **Middle English,** the English language between c.1150 and 1500 A.D. **middle school,** the middle grades of an independent school; a school for children aged about nine to thirteen years. **Middle West,** the region of the U.S. near the northern Mississippi.

mid·dle-aged (mid-ĕl-ayjd) adj. of middle age, approximately between forty-five and sixty-five.

mid·dle·brow (mid-ĕl-brow) adj. moderately intellectual. **middlebrow** n. a middlebrow person.

mid·dle·man (mid-ĕl-man) n. (pl. -men, pr. -men) any of the traders handling a commodity between producer and consumer.

mid·dle-of-the-road (mid-ĕl-ŏv-thĕ-rohd) adj. favoring a moderate policy, avoiding extremes.

mid·dle-sized (mid-ĕl-sīzd) adj. of medium size.

mid·dle·weight (mid-ĕl-wayt) n. a boxer between welterweight and light heavyweight weighing up to 160 pounds.

mid·dling (mid-ling) adj. & adv. moderately good, moderately well.

mid·dy (mid-ee) n. (pl. -dies) (informal) a midshipman. □**middy blouse,** a woman's or child's loose blouse with a collar as worn by sailors.

Mid·east (mid-eest) n. the Middle East.

midge (mij) n. a small biting gnatlike insect.

midg·et (mij-it) n. an extremely small person or thing. **midget** adj. extremely small.

mid·i (mid-ee) n. a woman's or girl's garment of medium length, between maxi and mini.

mid·land (mid-lănd) adj. of the middle part of a country. □**the Midlands,** the inland counties of central England.

mid·night (mid-nit) n. twelve o'clock at night, the time near this. □**midnight blue,** very dark blue. **midnight sun,** the sun visible at midnight during the summer in the polar regions.

mid·point (mid-point) n. a point in the middle of a journey, task, etc.

mid·riff (mid-rif) n. the front part of the body or of a garment just above the waist.

mid·sec·tion (mid-sek-shŏn) n. 1. (informal) the midriff. 2. the middle part.

mid·ship·man (mid-ship-măn) n. (pl. -men, pr. -men) a Navy or Coast Guard student officer.

midst (midst) n. the middle part. □**in the midst of,** among, surrounded by.

mid·stream (mid-streem) n. the middle of a stream. □**change horses in midstream,** to change one's plans etc. in the middle of a project.

mid·sum·mer (mid-sum-ĕr) n. the middle of the summer.

mid·term (mid-turm) n. 1. the middle of a term of public office or of school. 2. an examination in the middle of a school term.

mid·town (mid-town) n. the central area of a city.

mid·way (mid-way) adv. halfway between places. **midway** n. the carnival section of a fair.

mid·week (mid-week) n. the middle of the week.

Mid·west (mid-west) n. the Middle West.

mid·wife (mid-wīf) n. (pl. -wives, pr. -wīvz) a person trained to assist women in childbirth.

mid·wife·ry (mid-wī-fĕ-ree) n. the work of a midwife.

mid·win·ter (mid-win-tĕr) n. the middle of the winter.

mid·year (mid-yeer) n. 1. a point at the middle of the calendar or school year. 2. an examination taken at midyear.

mien (meen) n. a person's manner or bearing.

miff (mif) n. (informal) a petty quarrel, a huff. **miff** v. (informal) to put out of humor, to offend.

might¹ (mit) n. great strength or power, with all one's might. □**with might and main,** with all one's power and energy.

might² auxiliary verb used as the past tense of **may;** you might call at the baker's, I should like you to do so; you might have offered, ought to have offered. ▷Note that might in the second sense implies a missed responsibility: if you had thought about it, you might have offered.

might-have-been (mit-hav-bin) n. (pl. -beens) an event that might have happened but did not.

might·n't (mi-tĕnt) = might not.

might·y (mi-tee) adj. (might·i·er, might·i·est) 1. having or showing great strength or power. 2. very great in size. **mighty** adv. (informal) very, mighty fine. **might'i·ly** adv. **might'i·ness** n.

mi·gnon·ette (min-yŏ-net) n. an annual plant with fragrant grayish-green leaves.

mi·graine (mi-grayn) n. a severe form of headache that tends to recur.

mi·grant (mi-grănt) adj. migrating. **migrant** n. a migrant person or animal. □**migrant worker,** an agricultural laborer etc. who moves from one place to another in search of work.

mi·grate (mi-grayt) v. (mi·grat·ed, mi·grat·ing) 1. to leave one place and settle in another. 2. (of animals, birds) to go periodically from one place to another, living in each place for part of a year. **mi·gra·tion** (mi-gray-shŏn) n. **mi·gra'tion·al** adj.

mi·gra·to·ry (mi-gră-tohr-ee) adj. of or involving migration, migrating.

Mi·ka·do (mi-kah-doh) n. (pl. -dos) the emperor of Japan.

mike (mik) n. (informal) a microphone.

mil (mil) n. one-thousandth of an inch. ▷Do not confuse mil with mill. (See **mill².**)

mil. abbr. military.

mi·la·dy (mi-lay-dee) n. (pl. -dies) 1. a title used to or to an English noblewoman. 2. a fashionable woman.

milch (milch) adj. giving milk. □**milch cow,** a cow kept for its milk rather than for beef.

mild (mild) adj. 1. moderate in intensity or character or effect, not severe or harsh or drastic. 2. (of a person) gentle in manner. 3. not strongly flavored, not sharp or strong in taste. **mild'ly** adv. **mild'ness** n.

mil·dew (mil-doo) n. a minute fungus that forms a white coating on things exposed to moisture. **mildew** v. to become coated with mildew. **mil'dewed** adj.

mile (mil) n. 1. a measure of length, = 5280 feet (about 1.609 kilometers); nautical mile, a unit used in navigation, 6075 feet (1.852 kilometers). 2. (informal) a great distance, the two sides were miles apart. 3. a race extending over a distance of one mile.

mile·age (mi-lij) n. 1. distance measured in miles.

2. the number of miles a vehicle travels on one gallon of fuel. 3. traveling expenses at a fixed rate per mile. 4. *(informal)* benefit, *he gets a lot of mileage out of his family name.*

mile·post (mɪl-pohst) *n.* a post that shows the distance in the miles to a given place.

mil·er (mɪ-lĕr) *n.* a person who specializes in races that are one mile in length.

mile·stone (mɪl-stohn) *n.* 1. a stone set up beside a road to show the distance in miles to a given place. 2. a significant event or stage in life or history.

mi·lieu (meel-yuu) *n.* (*pl.* **-lieus, -lieux,** *pr.* -yuuz) environment, surroundings.

mil·i·tant (mil-i-tănt) *adj.* 1. prepared to take aggressive action in support of a cause. 2. involved in warfare or fighting. **militant** *n.* a militant person. **mil'i·tant·ly** *adv.* **mil·i·tan·cy** (mil-i-tăn-see) *n.*

mil·i·ta·rism (mil-i-tă-riz-ĕm) *n.* reliance on military strength and methods. **mil'i·tar·ist** *n.* **mil·i·tar·is·tic** (mil-i-tă-ris-tik) *adj.*

mil·i·ta·rize (mil-i-tă-rız) *v.* (**mil·i·ta·rized, mil·i·ta·riz·ing**) 1. to provide with armed forces. 2. to infuse with military spirit.

mil·i·tar·y (mil-i-ter-ee) *adj.* of soldiers or the army or all armed forces, *military service; the military,* armed forces as distinct from police or civilians. **mil·i·tar·i·ly** (mil-i-ter-ĭ-lee) *adv.* ☐**military band,** a combination of woodwind, brass, and percussion instruments. **military-industrial complex,** an unofficial combination in the U.S. of senior officers of the armed forces and companies supplying aircraft, guns, etc. **military police,** soldiers assigned to police work.

mil·i·tate (mil-i-tayt) *v.* (**mil·i·tat·ed, mil·i·tat·ing**) to serve as a strong influence, *several factors militated against the success of our plan.* ▷Do not confuse *militate* with *mitigate.*

mi·li·tia (mi-lish-ă) *n.* a military force, especially one consisting of civilians trained as soldiers and available to supplement the regular army in an emergency.

mi·li·tia·man (mi-lish-ă-măn) *n.* (*pl.* **-men,** *pr.* -mĕn) a person who serves in the militia.

milk (milk) *n.* 1. a white fluid secreted by female mammals as food for their young. 2. the milk of cows, used as food by human beings. 3. a milklike liquid, such as that in a coconut. **milk** *v.* 1. to draw milk from (a cow or goat etc.). 2. to extract juice from (a tree etc.). 3. to exploit or get money undeservedly from, *milking the welfare state.* ☐**milk and honey,** abundant means for gratifying one's material needs. **milk bar,** a bar for the sale of nonalcoholic drinks, especially those made from milk, and light refreshments. **milk chocolate,** chocolate (for eating) made with milk. **milk glass,** an opaque white glass. **milking machine,** an electric machine for milking several cows at the same time. **milking stool,** a stool used when milking animals. **milk of magnesia,** a milky white laxative or antacid. **milk punch,** an alcoholic drink with a milk base. **milk shake,** a drink made of milk and flavoring, mixed or shaken until frothy. **milk snake,** a harmless brightly colored kingsnake. **milk toast,** buttered toast served in warm milk with salt and pepper or with sugar. **milk tooth,** any of the first (temporary) teeth in young mammals.

milk·er (mil-kĕr) *n.* 1. a person who milks an animal. 2. an animal that gives milk, *that cow is a good milker.*

milk·maid (milk-mayd) *n.* a woman who milks cows.

milk·man (milk-man) *n.* (*pl.* **-men,** *pr.* -men) a man who delivers milk to customers' houses.

milk·sop (milk-sop) *n.* a boy or man who is weak or timid, a weakling.

milk·weed (milk-weed) *n.* any of several wild plants with milky juice.

milk-white (milk-hwɪt) *adj.* white like milk.

milk·y (mil-kee) *adj.* (**milk·i·er, milk·i·est**) 1. of or like milk. 2. made with milk, containing much milk. 3. (of a gem or liquid) cloudy, not clear. **milk'i·ness** *n.* ☐**Milky Way,** the broad faintly luminous band of stars encircling the sky, the Galaxy.

mill¹ (mil) *n.* 1. machinery for grinding grain, a building fitted with this. 2. any machine for grinding or crushing a solid substance into powder or pulp, *coffee mill.* 3. a machine or a building fitted with machinery for processing material of certain kinds, *cotton mill; paper mill; sawmill.* **mill** *v.* 1. to grind or crush in a mill. 2. to produce in a mill. 3. to produce regular markings on the edge of (a coin), *silver coins with a milled edge.* 4. to cut or shape (metal) with a rotating tool. 5. (of people or animals) to move around and around in a confused mass. ☐**go** *or* **put through the mill,** to undergo or subject to training or experience or suffering. **mill wheel,** the wheel that drives a water mill.

mill² *n.* one-tenth of a cent. ▷Do not confuse *mill* with *mil.*

mill·age (mil-ij) *n.* a tax rate expressed in mills.

mill·dam (mil-dam) *n.* a dam to make a millpond.

mil·len·ni·um (mi-len-i-ŭm) *n.* (*pl.* **-len·ni·ums, -len·ni·a,** *pr.* -len-i-ă) 1. a period of one thousand years. 2. the thousand-year reign of Christ on Earth prophesied in the Bible. 3. a period of great happiness and prosperity for everyone. **mil·len'ni·al** *adj.*

mill·er (mil-ĕr) *n.* a person who owns or runs a mill for grinding grain.

mil·let (mil-it) *n.* 1. a kind of cereal plant growing three to four feet high and producing a large crop of small seeds. 2. its seeds, used as food.

milli- *prefix* one-thousandth.

mil·li·am·pere (mil-i-am-peer) *n.* one-thousandth of an ampere.

mil·li·bar (mil-ĭ-bahr) *n.* one-thousandth of a bar as a unit of pressure in meteorology.

mil·li·gram (mil-ĭ-gram) *n.* one-thousandth of a gram.

mil·li·li·ter (mil-ĭ-lee-tĕr) *n.* one-thousandth of a liter.

mil·li·me·ter (mil-ĭ-mee-tĕr) *n.* one-thousandth of a meter (0.04 inch).

mil·li·ner (mil-ĭ-nĕr) *n.* a person who makes or sells women's hats.

mil·li·ner·y (mil-ĭ-ner-ee) *n.* milliner's work, women's hats sold in a shop.

mill·ing (mil-ing) *n.* the regular markings on the edge of a coin.

mil·lion (mil-yŏn) *adj. & n.* 1. one thousand thousand (1,000,000). 2. a million dollars or pounds etc. 3. an enormous number. **mil·lionth** (mil-yŏnth) *adj. & n.*

mil·lion·aire (mil-yŏ-nair) *n.* a person who possesses a million dollars, one who is extremely wealthy.

mil·li·pede (mil-ĭ-peed) *n.* a small crawling creature like a centipede but usually with two pairs of legs on each segment of its body.

mil·li·sec·ond (mil-i-sek-ŏnd) *n.* one-thousandth of a second.

mil·li·volt (mil-ĭ-vohlt) *n.* one-thousandth of a volt.

mil·li·watt (mil-i-wot) *n.* one-thousandth of a watt.

mill·pond (mil-pond) *n.* the water dammed in a stream for use in a water mill; *the sea was like a millpond,* very calm.

mill·race (mil-rays) *n.* the channel in which flows the water driving a mill.

mill·stone (mil-stohn) *n.* 1. one of a pair of circular stones between which grain is ground. 2. a heavy mental or emotional burden, *a millstone around one's neck.*

mill·work (mil-wurk) *n.* the woodwork produced in a sawmill.

mill·wright (mil-rıt) *n.* a person who builds mills or installs and maintains their equipment.

milque·toast (milk-tohst) *n.* an easily dominated timid man.

milt (milt) *n.* the roe of a male fish, fish sperm discharged into the water over the eggs laid by the female.

mime (mım) *n.* 1. acting with gestures and without words, a performance using this. 2. a performer in this. **mime** *v.* (**mimed, mim·ing**) to act with mime.

mim·e·o (mim-i-oh) *n. & v. (informal)* mimeograph.

mim·e·o·graph (mim-i-ŏ-graf) *n.* an apparatus for making copies from stencils of written pages. **mimeograph** *v.* to make copies on such an apparatus.

mi·me·sis (mi-mee-sis) *n.* imitation, mimicry; *many insects find protection in mimesis,* their close resemblance to other insects which are distasteful or harmful to predators.

mim·ic (mim-ik) *v.* (**mim·icked, mim·ick·ing**) 1. to copy the appearance or ways of (a person etc.) playfully or for entertainment. 2. to pretend to be, (of things) to resemble closely. **mimic** *n.* a person who is clever at mimicking others, especially for entertainment.

mim·ic·ry (mim-i-kree) *n.* (*pl.* **-ries**) mimicking, a thing that mimics another.

mi·mo·sa (mi-moh-să) *n.* any of several usually tropical trees or shrubs, especially the kind with clusters of small ball-shaped fragrant flowers.

min. *abbr.* 1. mineralogical. 2. mineralogy. 3. minim(s). 4. minimum. 5. mining. 6. minor. 7. minute(s).

min·a·ret (min-ă-ret) *n.* a tall slender tower on or beside a mosque, with a balcony from which a muezzin calls Muslims to prayer.

min·a·to·ry (min-ă-tor-ee) *adj.* threatening.

mince (mins) *v.* (**minced, minc·ing**) 1. to cut into small pieces with a knife or mincer. 2. to walk or speak in an affected way, trying to appear refined. □**mince pie,** a pie containing mincemeat. **not to mince matters** *or* **words,** to speak bluntly.

mince·meat (mins-meet) *n.* a mixture of currants, raisins, sugar, apples, candied peel, etc., used in pies. □**make mincemeat of,** to destroy utterly in argument.

minc·er (min-sĕr) *n.* a machine with revolving blades for mincing food.

mind (mınd) *n.* 1. the ability to be aware of things and to think and reason, originating in the brain. 2. a person's thoughts and attention, *keep your mind on the job.* 3. remembrance, *keep it in mind.* 4. opinion, *change one's mind; to my mind he's*

a genius. 5. a way of thinking and feeling, *state of mind.* 6. sanity, normal mental faculties; *in one's right mind,* sane; *out of one's mind,* insane or extremely agitated. 7. a person, as embodying mental qualities, *she is one of the best minds of our generation.* **mind** *v.* 1. to take care of, to attend to, *minding the baby* or *the shop.* 2. to feel annoyance or discomfort at, to object to, *she doesn't mind the cold; I shouldn't mind a cup of tea,* should like one. 3. to bear in mind, to give heed to or concern oneself about, *never mind the expense; mind you,* please take note. 4. to remember and take care, *mind you lock the door.* 5. to be careful about, *mind the step; mind how you carry that tray.* □**bear** *or* **keep in mind,** to keep in one's thoughts, to remember. **have a good** *or* **half a mind to,** to feel tempted or inclined to. **have a mind of one's own,** to be capable of forming opinions independently of others. **in mind,** in one's thoughts. **make up one's mind,** to decide; *made up her mind to work,* resolved to do so. **mind one's P's and Q's,** to be careful in one's speech or behavior. **mind over matter,** determination overcoming physical or other obstacles. **mind reader,** an entertainer who pretends to read people's thoughts. **mind's eye,** the faculty of imagination. **on one's mind,** constantly in one's thoughts, causing worry. **put a person in mind of,** to remind him of.

mind-bend·ing (mınd-ben-ding) *adj. (slang)* strongly influencing the mind.

mind-blow·ing (mınd-bloh-ing) *adj. (slang)* overwhelming or astounding, affecting one in the manner of a psychedelic drug.

mind·ed (mın-did) *adj.* 1. having a mind of a certain kind, *independent-minded.* 2. having certain interests, *politically minded; car-minded.* 3. inclined or disposed to do something, *if she's minded to help; could do it if he were so minded.*

mind-ex·pand·ing (mınd-ek-span-ding) *adj.* distorting one's perceptions inordinately, as by using psychedelic drugs.

mind·ful (mınd-fūl) *adj.* taking thought or care of something, *mindful of his public image.* **mind'ful·ly** *adv.* **mind'ful·ness** *n.*

mind·less (mınd-lis) *adj.* without a mind, without intelligence, 2. careless. **mind'less·ly** *adv.* **mind'less·ness** *n.*

mine[1] (mın) *possessive pronoun* the thing(s) belonging to me, *mine are missing.* **mine** *adj. (old use)* of or belonging to me, *mine enemies.* ▷The old adjective *mine* was used only before words beginning with vowel sounds.

mine[2] *n.* 1. an excavation in the earth for extracting metal or coal etc. 2. an abundant source of something, *a mine of information.* 3. a receptacle filled with explosive, placed in or on the ground (also called **land mine**), or in water, ready to explode when something strikes it or passes near it. **mine** *v.* (**mined, min·ing**) 1. to dig for minerals, to extract (metal or coal etc.) in this way. 2. to lay explosive mines in (an area). □**mine detector,** an instrument for detecting the presence of land mines.

mine·field (mın-feeld) *n.* an area where explosive mines have been laid.

mine·lay·er (mın-lay-ĕr) *n.* a ship or aircraft for laying mines.

min·er (mı-nĕr) *n.* a person who works in a mine.

min·er·al (min-ĕ-răl) *n.* 1. an inorganic substance that occurs naturally in the earth. 2. an ore or

other substance obtained by mining. **mineral** adj. of or containing minerals. ☐**mineral jelly,** a petroleum jelly used in stabilizing explosives. **mineral oil,** an oily colorless liquid distilled from petroleum. **mineral spring,** a spring of natural mineral waters. **mineral water,** water that is found naturally containing dissolved mineral salts or gases; a nonalcoholic usually fizzy drink.
min·er·al·o·gy (min-ĕ-ral-ŏ-jee) n. the scientific study of minerals. **min·er·al'o·gist** n. an expert in mineralogy. **min·er·al·og·i·cal** (min-ĕ-ră-loj-i-kăl) adj.
min·e·stro·ne (min-ĕ-stroh-nee) n. an Italian soup containing chopped mixed vegetables and pasta.
mine·sweep·er (mɪn-swee-pĕr) n. a ship for clearing away explosive mines laid in the sea.
mine·work·er (mɪn-wur-kĕr) n. a miner.
min·gle (ming-gĕl) v. (**min·gled, min·gling**) 1. to mix, to blend. 2. to go about among people etc., *mingled with the crowd.* **min'gler** n.
ming (ming) **tree** an artificially dwarfed tree grown in a container.
min·i (min-ee) n. *(informal)* a miniskirt.
mini- comb. form short, as in *miniskirt;* small, as in *minibus.*
min·i·a·ture (min-i-ă-chŭr) adj. very small, made or represented on a small scale. **miniature** n. 1. a very small and detailed portrait. 2. a small-scale copy or model of something. ☐**in miniature,** on a very small scale. **miniature camera,** one that produces small negatives.
min·i·a·tur·ist (min-i-ă-chŭ-rist) n. a person who paints miniatures.
min·i·a·tur·ize (min-i-ă-chŭ-rɪz) v. (**min·i·a·tur·ized, min·i·a·tur·iz·ing**) to design or construct (a thing) on a small scale. **min·i·a·tur·i·za·tion** (min-i-ă-chŭ-ri-zay-shŏn) n.
min·i·bike (min-ee-bɪk) n. a low-slung lightweight single-passenger motorcycle.
min·i·bus (min-ee-bus) n. a small vehicle like a bus with seats for only a few people.
min·i·com·put·er (min-ee-kŏm-pyoo-tĕr) n. a relatively inexpensive small computer.
min·im (min-im) n. 1. a half note in music (*see* half). 2. one-sixtieth of a fluid dram, about one drop.
min·i·mal (min-ɪ-măl) adj. very small, the least possible. **min'i·mal·ly** adv. ☐**minimal art,** a form of abstract art consisting primarily of geometric forms. **minimal artist,** one painting in this way.
min·i·mize (min-ɪ-mɪz) v. (**min·i·mized, min·i·miz·ing**) 1. to reduce to a minimum. 2. to estimate at the smallest possible amount, to represent at less than the true value or importance. **min'i·miz·er** n.
min·i·mum (min-i-mŭm) n. (pl. **-mums, -ma,** pr. -mă) the lowest or lowest possible number or amount or intensity etc. **minimum** adj. minimal.
min·ing (mɪ-ning) n. 1. the process of extracting minerals etc. from the earth. 2. the process of laying explosive mines.
min·ion (min-yŏn) n. *(contemptuous)* a subordinate assistant.
min·is·cule (min-ɪ-skyool) = **minuscule.**
min·i·se·ries (min-ee-seer-eez) n. a short series of television dramas, usually based on a single novel, biography, etc.
min·i·skirt (min-ee-skurt) n. a very short skirt ending at about the middle of the thighs.
min·i·state (min-ee-stayt) n. a small independent country.

min·is·ter (min-i-stĕr) n. 1. a person at the head of a government department or a main branch of this. 2. a diplomatic representative usually ranking below ambassador. 3. a clergyman, especially in Protestant sects. **minister** v. to attend to people's needs, *nurses ministered to the wounded.* **min·is·te·ri·al** (min-i-steer-i-ăl) adj. ▷Do not confuse *minister* with *administer.* Nurses do not administer to the wounded. Administrators administer their departments.
min·is·trant (min-i-strănt) n. a person who ministers.
min·is·tra·tion (min-i-stray-shŏn) n. giving aid or service, especially in religious matters.
min·is·try (min-i-stree) n. (pl. **-tries**) 1. the profession or functions of a clergyman or religious leader. 2. *the ministry,* clergymen as a group. 3. a government department headed by a minister, the building occupied by it. 4. a period of government under one premier, his body of ministers.
mink (mingk) n. 1. a small animal of the weasel family. 2. its highly valued fur. 3. a coat made of this.
Minn. abbr. Minnesota.
min·ne·sing·er (min-i-sing-ĕr) n. a German lyric poet and singer in the 12th to 14th centuries.
Min·ne·so·ta (min-ĕ-soh-tă) a state of the U.S. **Min·ne·so'tan** adj. & n.
min·now (min-oh) n. (pl. **-nows, -now**) a small freshwater fish.
Mi·no·an (mi-noh-ăn) adj. of the Bronze Age civilization of Crete (about 3000–1100 B.C.). **Minoan** n. a person of this civilization. ▷Named after Minos, a legendary king of Crete.
mi·nor (mɪ-nŏr) adj. 1. lesser, less important, *minor roads; a minor operation,* a surgical operation that does not involve danger to the patient's life. 2. (in music) of or based on a scale that has a semitone next above the second note. **minor** n. 1. a person under legal age. 2. a course of study in a field secondary to one's major. **minor** v. to take such a course of study.
mi·nor·i·ty (mi-nor-i-tee, mɪ-) n. (pl. **-ties**) 1. the smallest part of a group or class. 2. a small group differing from others. 3. (in law) the state of being under legal age, *during his minority.*
min·strel (min-strĕl) n. 1. a traveling singer and musician in the Middle Ages 2. a performer in a minstrel show. ☐**minstrel show,** a formerly popular entertainment in which white performers in black makeup sang and danced and told jokes.
mint¹ (mint) n. 1. a place authorized to make a country's coins. 2. a vast amount, *left him a mint of money.* **mint** v. to make (coins) by stamping metal. 2. to invent or coin (a word etc.). **mint'er** n. ☐**in mint condition,** fresh and unsoiled as if newly from the mint.
mint² n. 1. a plant with fragrant leaves that are used for flavoring sauces and drinks etc. 2. peppermint, a candy flavored with this. **mint'y** adj. ☐**mint julep,** a frosted drink of bourbon, ice, sugar, and mint.
mint·age (min-tij) n. 1. minting money. 2. the mark imprinted on a coin showing where it was minted.
min·u·end (min-yoo-end) n. a quantity or number from which another is to be subtracted.
min·u·et (min-yoo-et) n. a slow stately dance in triple time, music suitable for this.
mi·nus (mɪ-nŭs) prep. 1. reduced by the subtraction of, *seven minus three equals four* ($7 - 3 = 4$).

2. below zero, *temperatures of minus ten degrees Centigrade* (−10° C). 3. *(informal) without,* returned *minus his shoes.* **minus** *adj.* less than zero (= negative), less than the amount or number indicated, *a minus quantity; A−,* a grade slightly below A. **minus** *n.* 1. the sign −. 2. a disadvantage. □**minus sign,** the sign −.

mi·nus·cule (min-ŭ-skyool) *adj.* extremely small. **minuscule** *n.* a lower case letter.

min·ute[1] (min-it) *n.* 1. one-sixtieth of an hour. 2. a very short time, a moment. 3. an exact point of time. 4. one-sixtieth of a degree used in measuring angles. 5. *minutes,* an official record of the proceedings of an assembly or committee etc. made during a meeting. □**minute hand,** the long hand that marks the minutes on the face of a clock or watch. **minute steak,** a thin slice of steak that can be cooked quickly.

mi·nute[2] (mɪ-noot, -nyoot) *adj.* 1. extremely small. 2. very detailed and precise, *a minute examination.* **mi·nute′ly** *adv.* **mi·nute′ness** *n.*

Min·ute·man (min-it-man) *n.* (*pl.* **-men,** *pr.* -men) an American militiaman of the Revolutionary War period. ▷From the requirement to be ready to march at a minute's notice.

mi·nu·ti·ae (mi-noo-shi-ee) *n. pl.* (*sing.* **mi·nu·ti·a,** *pr.* mi-noo-shi-ă) very small details.

minx (mingks) *n.* a cheeky or mischievous girl.

Mi·o·cene (mɪ-ŏ-seen) *adj.* of the geologic epoch of the Tertiary period before the Pliocene and after the Oligocene. **Miocene** *n.* the Miocene epoch.

mir·a·cle (mir-ă-kĕl) *n.* 1. a remarkable and welcome event that seems impossible to explain by means of the known laws of nature and is therefore attributed to a supernatural agency. 2. a remarkable example or specimen, *it's a miracle of ingenuity.*

mi·rac·u·lous (mi-rak-yŭ-lŭs) *adj.* of or like a miracle, wonderful. **mi·rac′u·lous·ly** *adv.* **mi·rac′u·lous·ness** *n.*

mi·rage (mi-rah*z*h) *n.* an optical illusion caused by atmospheric conditions, especially making sheets of water seem to appear in a desert or on a hot road.

mire (mɪr) *n.* 1. swampy ground, bog. 2. mud or sticky dirt.

mir·ror (mir-ŏr) *n.* a piece of glass backed with silver so that reflections can be seen in it. **mirror** *v.* to reflect in or as if in a mirror. □**mirror image,** a reflection or copy in which the right and left sides of the original are reversed.

mirth (murth) *n.* merriment, laughter. **mirth′ful** *adj.* **mirth′ful·ly** *adv.* **mirth′ful·ness** *n.* **mirth′less** *adj.*

MIRV (murv) *n.* multiple independently targeted reentry vehicle (a type of missile carrying warheads separately aimed at various targets).

mis- *prefix* badly, wrongly.

mis·ad·ven·ture (mis-ad-ven-chŭr) *n.* a piece of bad luck.

mis·a·lign (mis-ă-lɪn) *v.* to align incorrectly. **mis·align·ment** (mis-ă-lɪn-mĕnt) *n.*

mis·al·li·ance (mis-ă-lɪ-ăns) *n.* an unsuitable alliance, especially an unsuitable marriage.

mis·al·lo·cate (mis-al-ŏ-kayt) *v.* to distribute in an improper or faulty manner. **mis·al·lo·ca·tion** (mis-al-ŏ-kay-shŏn) *n.*

mis·an·thro·py (mis-an-thrŏ-pee) *n.* dislike of people in general. **mis·an′thro·pist** *n.* **mis·an·thrope** (mis-ăn-throhp) *n.* **mis·an·thro·pic** (mis-ăn-throp-ik) *adj.*

mis·ap·ply (mis-ă-plɪ) *v.* (**mis·ap·plied, mis·ap·ply·ing**) to apply wrongly, especially funds. **mis·ap·pli·ca·tion** (mis-ap-lĭ-kay-shŏn) *n.*

mis·ap·pre·hend (mis-ap-ri-hend) *v.* to misunderstand. **mis·ap·pre·hen·sion** (mis-ap-ri-hen-shŏn) *n.*

mis·ap·pro·pri·ate (mis-ă-proh-pri-ayt) *v.* (**mis·ap·pro·pri·at·ed, mis·ap·pro·pri·at·ing**) to take dishonestly, especially for one's own use. **mis·ap·pro·pri·a·tion** (mis-ă-proh-pri-ay-shŏn) *n.*

mis·be·got·ten (mis-bi-got-ĕn) *adj.* contemptible. **mis·be·have** (mis-bi-hayv) *v.* (**mis·be·haved, mis·be·hav·ing**) to behave badly. **mis·be·ha·vior** (mis-bi-hayv-yŏr) *n.* to brand in a misleading or illegal manner.

mis·brand (mis-brand) *v.* to brand in a misleading or illegal manner.

misc. *abbr.* 1. miscellaneous. 2. miscellany.

mis·cal·cu·late (mis-kal-kyŭ-layt) *v.* (**mis·cal·cu·lat·ed, mis·cal·cu·lat·ing**) to calculate incorrectly. **mis·cal·cu·la·tion** (mis-kal-kyŭ-lay-shŏn) *n.*

mis·call (mis-kawl) *v.* to give a wrong or inappropriate name to.

mis·car·riage (mis-kar-ij, mis-kar-) *n.* 1. abortion occurring without being induced. 2. a mistake or failure to achieve the correct result, *a miscarriage of justice.* 3. the miscarrying of a letter or goods or of a scheme etc.

mis·car·ry (mis-kar-ee) *v.* (**mis·car·ried, mis·car·ry·ing**) 1. (of a pregnant woman) to have a miscarriage. 2. (of a scheme etc.) to go wrong, to fail. 3. (of a letter etc.) to fail to reach its destination.

mis·cast (mis-kast) *v.* (**mis·cast, mis·cast·ing**) to cast (an actor) in an unsuitable role.

mis·ce·ge·na·tion (mis-ĕ-jĕ-nay-shŏn, mi-sej-ĕ-) *n.* marriage or interbreeding of races, especially of whites with nonwhites.

mis·cel·la·ne·ous (mis-ĕ-lay-ni-ŭs) *adj.* 1. of various kinds, *miscellaneous items.* 2. of mixed compositon or character, *a miscellaneous collection.* **mis·cel·la′ne·ous·ly** *adv.* **mis·cel·la′ne·ous·ness** *n.*

mis·cel·la·ny (mis-ĕ-lay-nee) *n.* (*pl.* **-nies**) a collection of various items.

mis·chance (mis-chans) *n.* misfortune.

mis·chief (mis-chif) *n.* 1. conduct (especially of children) that is annoying or does slight damage but is not malicious. 2. a tendency to tease or cause annoyance playfully, *full of mischief.* 3. harm or damage, *did a lot of mischief.* □**do someone a mischief,** to injure him. **make mischief,** to cause discord or ill-feeling.

mis·chief-mak·er (mis-chif-may-kĕr) *n.* a person who makes mischief.

mis·chie·vous (mis-chĕ-vŭs) *adj.* (of a person) full of mischief, (of an action) brought about by mischief. **mis′chie·vous·ly** *adv.* **mis′chie·vous·ness** *n.* ▷Do not put an extra *i* after the *v* in any of these words.

mis·ci·ble (mis-ĭ-bĕl) *adj.* able to be mixed. **mis·ci·bil·i·ty** (mis-ĭ-bil-i-tee) *n.*

mis·com·mu·ni·cate (mis-kŏ-myoo-ni-kayt) *v.* (**mis·com·mu·ni·cat·ed, mis·com·mu·ni·cat·ing**) to communicate incorrectly. **mis·com·mu·ni·ca·tion** (mis-kŏ-myoo-ni-kay-shŏn) *n.*

mis·con·ceive (mis-kŏn-seev) *v.* (**mis·con·ceived, mis·con·ceiv·ing**) to misunderstand, to interpret incorrectly.

mis·con·cep·tion (mis-kŏn-sep-shŏn) *n.* a wrong interpretation.

mis·con·duct (mis-kon-dukt) *n.* 1. bad behavior. 2. adultery. 3. mismanagement.

mis·con·strue (mis-kŏn-stroo) *v.* (**mis·con·strued, mis·con·stru·ing**) to misinterpret. **mis·con·struc·tion** (mis-kŏn-struk-shŏn) *n.*

mis·cop·y (mis-kop-ee) *v.* (**mis·cop·ied, mis·cop·y·ing**) to copy incorrectly.

mis·count (mis-kownt) *v.* to count incorrectly. **miscount** *n.* an incorrect count.

mis·cre·ant (mis-kree-ănt) *n.* a wrongdoer, a villain.

mis·cue (mis-kyoo) *n.* a failure to strike a ball properly in billiards. **miscue** *v.* (**mis·cued, mis·cu·ing**) to make a miscue.

mis·date (mis-dayt) *v.* (**mis·dat·ed, mis·dat·ing**) to date (an event, a letter, etc.) wrongly.

mis·deal (mis-deel) *v.* (**mis·dealt, mis·deal·ing**) to make a mistake in dealing playing cards. **misdeal** *n.* an incorrect dealing.

mis·deed (mis-deed) *n.* a wrong or improper act, a crime.

mis·de·mean·or (mis-di-mee-nŏr) *n.* 1. a misdeed, wrongdoing. 2. an indictable offense less serious than a felony.

mis·di·rect (mis-di-rekt) *v.* to direct incorrectly. **mis·di·rec·tion** (mis-di-rek-shŏn) *n.*

mise-en-scène (meez-ahn-sen) 1. the scenery and properties of an acted play. 2. the surroundings of an event. ▷French.

mi·ser (mɪ-zĕr) *n.* a person who hoards money and spends as little as possible. **mi'ser·ly** *adj.* **mi'ser·li·ness** *n.*

mis·er·a·ble (miz-ĕ-ră-bĕl) *adj.* 1. full of misery, feeling very unhappy or uneasy or uncomfortable. 2. surly and discontented, disagreeable. 3. unpleasant, *miserable weather.* 4. wretchedly poor in quality or surroundings etc., *a miserable attempt; miserable slums.* **mis'er·a·bly** *adv.* **mis'er·a·ble·ness** *n.*

mis·er·y (miz-ĕ-ree) *n.* (*pl.* **-er·ies**) 1. a feeling of great unhappiness or discomfort. 2. something causing this. 3. (often *pl.*) (*informal*) a physical discomfort or pain, *I've got the miseries.*

mis·fea·sance (mis-fee-zăns) *n.* a transgression, especially the wrongful exercise of lawful authority.

mis·file (mis-fɪl) *v.* (**mis·filed, mis·fil·ing**) to file in the wrong place.

mis·fire (mis-fɪr) *v.* (**mis·fired, mis·fir·ing**) 1. (of a gun) to fail to go off correctly. 2. (of an engine etc.) to fail to start, to function incorrectly. 3. to fail to have the intended effect, *the joke misfired.* **misfire** *n.* a misfiring.

mis·fit (mis-fit, mis-fit) *n.* 1. a garment etc. that does not fit the person it was meant for. 2. a person who is not well suited to his work or to his environment.

mis·for·tune (mis-for-chŭn) *n.* bad luck, an unfortunate event.

mis·giv·ing (mis-giv-ing) *n.* a feeling of doubt or slight fear or mistrust.

mis·gov·ern (mis-guv-ĕrn) *v.* to govern badly. **mis·gov'ern·ment** *n.*

mis·guid·ed (mis-gɪ-did) *adj.* mistaken in one's opinions or actions, ill-judged. **mis·guid'ed·ly** *adv.*

mis·han·dle (mis-han-dĕl) *v.* (**mis·han·dled, mis·han·dling**) to deal with (a thing) badly or inefficiently.

mis·hap (mis-hap, mis-hap) *n.* an unlucky accident.

mis·hear (mis-heer) *v.* (**mis·heard, mis·hear·ing**) to hear incorrectly.

mish·mash (mish-mosh, -mash) *n.* a confused mixture.

mis·in·form (mis-in-form) *v.* to give wrong information to. **mis·in·for·ma·tion** (mis-in-fŏr-may-shŏn) *n.*

mis·in·ter·pret (mis-in-tur-prit) *v.* to interpret incorrectly. **mis·in·ter·pre·ta·tion** (mis-in-tur-prĕ-tay-shŏn) *n.*

mis·judge (mis-juj) *v.* (**mis·judged, mis·judg·ing**) to have a wrong opinion of, to estimate incorrectly. **mis·judg'ment** *n.*

mis·la·bel (mis-lay-bĕl) *v.* (**mis·la·beled, mis·la·bel·ing**) to label incorrectly or misleadingly.

mis·lay (mis-lay) *v.* (**mis·laid, mis·lay·ing**) to put (a thing) in a place and be unable to remember where it is, to lose temporarily.

mis·lead (mis-leed) *v.* (**mis·led, mis·lead·ing**) to cause (a person) to gain a wrong impression of something. **mis·lead'ing·ly** *adv.*

mis·man·age (mis-man-ij) *v.* (**mis·man·aged, mis·man·ag·ing**) to manage (affairs) badly or wrongly. **mis·man'age·ment** *n.*

mis·match (mis-mach) *v.* to match unsuitably or incorrectly. **mismatch** (mis-mach, mis-mach) *n.* a bad match.

mis·name (mis-naym) *v.* (**mis·named, mis·nam·ing**) to miscall.

mis·no·mer (mis-noh-mĕr) *n.* a name or description that is wrongly applied to something.

mi·sog·a·mist (mi-sog-ă-mist) *n.* a person who hates marriage. **mi·sog'a·my** *n.*

mi·sog·y·nist (mi-soj-i-nist) *n.* a person who hates women. **mi·sog'y·nous** *adj.* **mi·sog'y·ny** *n.*

mis·place (mis-plays) *v.* (**mis·placed, mis·plac·ing**) 1. to put (a thing) in the wrong place. 2. to place (one's confidence etc.) unwisely. 3. to use (words or action) in an unsuitable situation, *misplaced humor.*

mis·play (mis-play) *n.* a wrong or ineffective play in a game, contest, etc. **misplay** *v.* to play in a wrong or ineffective manner.

mis·print (mis-print, mis-print) *n.* an error in printing. **misprint** (mis-print) *v.* to print incorrectly.

mis·pri·sion (mis-prizh-ŏn) *n.* a wrong action or omission by a public official. □**misprision of felony,** the concealment of knowledge that a felony has taken place.

mis·pro·nounce (mis-prŏ-nowns) *v.* (**mis·pro·nounced, mis·pro·nounc·ing**) to pronounce wrongly. **mis·pro·nun·ci·a·tion** (mis-prŏ-nun-si-ay-shŏn) *n.*

mis·quote (mis-kwoht) *v.* (**mis·quot·ed, mis·quot·ing**) to quote incorrectly. **mis·quo·ta·tion** (mis-kwoh-tay-shŏn) *n.*

mis·read (mis-reed) *v.* (**mis·read, mis·read·ing**) to read or interpret incorrectly.

mis·rep·re·sent (mis-rep-ri-zent) *v.* to represent in a false or misleading way. **mis·rep·re·sen·ta·tion** (mis-rep-ri-zen-tay-shŏn) *n.*

mis·rule (mis-rool) *n.* bad government. **misrule** *v.* (**mis·ruled, mis·rul·ing**) to govern badly.

miss[1] (mis) *v.* 1. to fail to hit or reach or catch (an object). 2. to fail to see or hear or understand etc., *we missed the signpost; missed that remark.* 3. to fail to catch (a train etc.) or keep (an appointment) or meet (a person), to fail to seize (an opportunity). 4. to omit, to lack. 5. to notice the absence or loss of. 6. to feel regret at the absence or loss of; *old Smith won't be missed,* no one will feel regret at his absence or death. 7. to avoid, *go this way and you'll miss the traffic.* 8. (of an engine etc.) to misfire. **miss** *n.* 1. failure to hit or attain what is aimed at. 2. *(informal)* a miscarriage. □**a miss is as good as a mile**, a narrow margin (of escape, failure, etc.) is a margin nonetheless. **miss out**, to omit. **miss out on**, to fail to get benefit or enjoyment from. **miss the boat**, *(informal)* to lose an opportunity.

miss² *n.* 1. a girl or unmarried woman. 2. *Miss*, a title used of or to a girl or unmarried woman, *Miss Smith* (pl. *the Miss Smiths*); *Miss America, Miss New England,* the title of the winner of a beauty contest in the specified region etc. 3. one of a range of sizes of garments suitable for women of average build, *miss size 14; misses' dresses.*

Miss. *abbr.* Mississippi.

mis·sal (mis-ăl) *n.* a book containing the prayers used in the Mass of the Roman Catholic Church.

mis·send (mis-send) *v.* **(mis·sent, mis·send·ing)** to send incorrectly.

mis·shape (mis-shayp) *v.* **(mis·shap·en, mis·shap·ing)** to give a bad shape or form to.

mis·shap·en (mis-shay-pĕn) *adj.* badly shaped, distorted.

mis·sile (mis-īl) *n.* an object or weapon suitable for throwing or projecting at a target.

mis·sile·man (mis-īl-man) *n.* (*pl.* **-men,** *pr.* -men) a person who designs, builds, or launches guided missiles.

mis·sile·ry (mis-īl-ree) *n.* the construction and use of guided missiles.

miss·ing (mis-ing) *adj.* 1. lost, not in its place, *two pages are missing.* 2. not present, *he's always missing when there's work to be done.* 3. absent from home and with one's whereabouts unknown, *she's listed as a missing person.* 4. (of a soldier etc.) neither present after a battle nor known to have been killed, *he was reported as missing in action.* □**missing link**, a thing lacking to complete a series; a type of animal supposed to have existed between the anthropoid apes and the development of man.

mis·sion (mish-ŏn) *n.* 1. a body of envoys sent to a foreign country or to an international organization. 2. an establishment of missionaries. 3. an organization for spreading the Christian faith, a series of religious services etc. for this purpose. 4. the work or premises of a religious or other mission. 5. a person's vocation, *his mission in life.*

mis·sion·ar·y (mish-ŏ-ner-ee) *n.* a person who is sent to spread the Christian faith among members of a community. **missionary** *adj.* of or concerned with religious or similar missions; *I was impressed with her missionary zeal,* her enthusiasm and persistence.

mis·sion·er (mish-ŏ-nĕr) *n.* a missionary.

Mis·sis·sip·pi (mis-i-sip-ee) a state of the U.S.

Mis·sis·sip·pi·an (mis-i-sip-ee-ăn) *adj.* 1. of a Paleozoic period about 300 to 350 million years ago. 2. of the state of Mississippi. **Mississippian** *n.* a native or inhabitant of Mississippi.

mis·sive (mis-iv) *n.* a written message, a letter.

Mis·sou·ri (mi-zoor-i) a state of the U.S. **Mis·sour'i·an** *adj. & n.*

mis·spell (mis-spel) *v.* **(mis·spelled** *or* **mis·spelt, mis·spell·ing)** to spell incorrectly.

mis·spend (mis-spend) *v.* **(mis·spent, mis·spend·ing)** to spend badly or unwisely.

mis·state (mis-stayt) *v.* **(mis·stat·ed, mis·stat·ing)** to state wrongly. **mis·state'ment** *n.*

mis·step (mis-step) *n.* a wrong step or action.

mist (mist) *n.* 1. water vapor near the ground in

drops smaller than raindrops, clouding the atmosphere less thickly than fog does. 2. condensed vapor clouding a window etc. 3. something resembling mist in its form or effect. **mist** *v.* to cover or become covered with mist, *the windshield misted up.*

mis·tak·a·ble (mi-stay-kă-bĕl) *adj.* able to be mistaken for another person or thing.

mis·take (mi-stayk) *n.* an incorrect idea or opinion, something done incorrectly. **mistake** *v.* **(mis·took, mis·tak·en, mis·tak·ing)** 1. to misunderstand the meaning or intention of. 2. to choose or identify wrongly, *mistake one's vocation; she is often mistaken for her sister.* □**by mistake,** as the result of carelessness or forgetfulness etc.

mis·tak·en (mis-tay-kĕn) *adj.* 1. wrong in one's opinion, *you are mistaken.* 2. applied unwisely, *mistaken kindness.* **mis·tak'en·ly** *adv.*

mis·ter (mis-tĕr) *n. (informal)* a form of address to a man, used without his name. (*See* **Mr.**).

mis·time (mis-tɪm) *v.* **(mis·timed, mis·tim·ing)** to say or do (a thing) at a wrong time.

mis·tle·toe (mis-ĕl-toh) *n.* a plant with white berries that grows as a parasite on trees.

mis·tral (mis-trăl, mi-strahl) *n.* a cold north or northwest wind in the Mediterranean provinces of France etc.

mis·treat (mis-treet) *v.* to treat badly. **mis·treat'ment** *n.*

mis·tress (mis-tris) *n.* 1. a woman who is in a position of authority or control. 2. the female head of a household. 3. the female owner of a dog or other animal. 4. a female teacher. 5. a man's female lover with whom he has a continuing illicit sexual relationship.

mis·tri·al (mis-trɪ-ăl) *n.* a trial that is invalid because of procedural error.

mis·trust (mis-trust) *v.* to feel no trust in. **mistrust** *n.* lack of trust. **mis·trust'ful** *adj.* **mis·trust'ful·ly** *adv.* **mis·trust'ful·ness** *n.*

mist·y (mis-tee) *adj.* **(mist·i·er, mist·i·est)** 1. full of mist. 2. indistinct in form or idea etc. **mist'i·ly** *adv.* **mist'i·ness** *n.*

mis·un·der·stand (mis-un-dĕr-stand) *v.* **(mis·un·der·stood, mis·un·der·stand·ing)** to form an incorrect interpretation or opinion of.

mis·un·der·stand·ing (mis-un-dĕr-stan-ding) *n.* 1. a disagreement. 2. a misinterpretation.

mis·us·age (mis-yoo-sij) *n.* 1. bad treatment. 2. misuse, especially of words.

mis·use (mis-yooz) *v.* **(mis·used, mis·us·ing)** 1. to use wrongly or incorrectly. 2. to treat badly. **misuse** (mis-yoos) *n.* wrong or incorrect use.

mite (mɪt) *n.* 1. a very small spiderlike parasitic animal found in food, *cheese mites.* 2. a very small contribution, *offered a mite of comfort.* 3. a very small creature, a small child.

mi·ter (mɪ-tĕr) *n.* 1. the tall headdress worn by bishops as a symbol of office. 2. a joint or joining of two pieces of wood with their ends evenly tapered so that together they form a right angle. **miter** *v.* to join in a miter.

mit·i·gate (mit-ɪ-gayt) *v.* **(mit·i·gat·ed, mit·i·gat·ing)** to make less intense or serious or severe; *mitigating circumstances,* facts that partially excuse wrongdoing. **mit'i·ga·tor** *n.* **mit·i·ga·tive** (mit-ɪ-gay-tiv) *adj.* **mit·i·ga·to·ry** (mit-ɪ-gă-tohr-ee) *adj.* **mit·i·ga·tion** (mit-i-gay-shŏn) *n.* ▷ Do not confuse *mitigate* with *militate.*

mi·to·sis (mɪ-toh-sis) *n.* division of a cell or nucleus. **mi·tot·ic** (mɪ-tot-ik) *adj.*

mitt (mit) *n.* 1. a mitten. 2. *(informal)* a baseball glove, usually one worn by a catcher or first baseman. 3. *(slang)* a hand.

mit·ten (mit-ĕn) *n.* a kind of glove that leaves the fingers and thumb tip bare or that has no partition between the fingers.

mix (miks) *v.* 1. to put different things together so that the substances etc. are no longer distinct, to make or prepare (a thing) by doing this. 2. to be capable of being blended, *oil will not mix with water.* 3. to combine, to be able to be combined, *mix business with pleasure; drinking and driving don't mix.* 4. (of a person) to be sociable or harmonious. **mix** *n.* 1. a mixture. 2. a mixture prepared commercially from suitable ingredients for making something, *cake mix; concrete mix.* **mix′a·ble** *adj.* □**mix it up,** *(informal)* to fight.

mix up, to mix thoroughly; to confuse (things) in one's mind; to make (a person) feel confused; *be mixed up in a crime* etc., to be involved in it.

mixed (mikst) *adj.* 1. composed of various qualities or elements. 2. containing persons from various races or social classes. 3. for people of both sexes, *mixed swimming.* □**mixed bag,** an assortment of different things or people. **mixed blessing,** a thing that has advantages and also disadvantages. **mixed doubles,** a doubles game in tennis with a man and woman as partners on each side. **mixed farming,** farming of both crops and livestock. **mixed feelings,** a mixture of pleasure and dismay at the same event. **mixed grill,** a dish of various grilled meats and vegetables. **mixed marriage,** marriage between people of different race or religion. **mixed number,** a number containing an integer and a fraction.

mixed-up (mikst-up) *adj. (informal)* having problems of the emotions and behavior through not being well adjusted socially.

mix·er (mik-sĕr) *n.* 1. a device that mixes or blends things, *food mixers.* 2. a person who gets on in a certain way with others, *a good mixer.* 3. a gathering designed to help people become acquainted with one another.

mixt. *abbr.* mixture.

mix·ture (miks-chŭr) *n.* 1. mixing, being mixed. 2. something made by mixing, a combination of things or ingredients or qualities etc.

mix·up (miks-up) *n.* a confusion.

miz·zen (miz-en) *n.* the lowest fore-and-aft sail of a fully rigged ship.

miz·zen·mast (miz-ĕn-mast, -măst) *n.* 1. the aftmost mast in a vessel with two or three masts. 2. the third mast in a vessel with four or more masts.

Mk. *abbr.* mark.

mks *abbr.* meter-kilogram-second.

mktg *abbr.* marketing.

ml *abbr.* milliliter(s).

ML *abbr.* Medieval Latin.

Mlle. *abbr.* Mademoiselle.

Mlles. *abbr.* Mesdemoiselles.

mm *abbr.* millimeter(s).

MM. *abbr.* Messieurs.

Mme. *abbr.* Madame.

Mmes. *abbr.* Mesdames.

Mn *symbol* manganese.

MN *abbr.* Minnesota.

mne·mon·ic (ni-mon-ik) *adj.* aiding the memory.

mnemonic *n.* a verse or other aid to help one remember facts. **mne·mon′i·cal·ly** *adv.*

Mo *symbol* molybdenum.

MO *abbr.* Missouri.

mo. *abbr.* month(s).

Mo. *abbr.* 1. Missouri. 2. Monday.

M.O. *abbr.* 1. mail order. 2. medical officer. 3. method of operation (Latin, *modus operandi*). 4. money order.

moan (mohn) *n.* 1. a low mournful inarticulate sound, usually indicating pain or suffering. 2. a grumble. **moan** *v.* 1. to utter a moan, to say with a moan. 2. (of wind etc.) to make a sound like a moan. 3. to grumble. **moan′er** *n.*

moat (moht) *n.* a deep wide ditch surrounding a castle or house etc., usually filled with water. **moat·ed** (moh-tid) *adj.* surrounded by a moat.

mob (mob) *n.* 1. a large disorderly crowd of people. 2. *the mob,* the common people, the rabble. 3. *(slang)* a gang. **mob** *v.* (**mobbed, mob·bing**) to crowd around in great numbers either to attack or to admire. □**mob rule,** rule imposed and enforced by the mob.

mo·bile (moh-bīl) *adj.* 1. movable, not fixed, able to move or be moved easily and quickly; *mobile shop,* one accommodated in a vehicle so that it can be driven from place to place. 2. (of the features of the face) readily changing expression. **mobile** (moh-beel) *n.* a structure of metal or plastic or cardboard etc. that may be hung so that its parts move freely in currents of air. **mo·bil·i·ty** (moh-bil-i-tee) *n.* □**mobile home,** a large automotive vehicle or trailer equipped as a home.

mo·bi·lize (moh-bĭ-līz) *v.* (**mo·bi·lized, mo·bi·liz·ing**) 1. to assemble (troops) for service, to prepare for war or other emergency. 2. to assemble for a particular purpose, *they mobilized support from all parties.* **mo′bi·liz·er** *n.* **mo·bi·li·za·tion** (moh-bĭ-lĭ-zay-shŏn) *n.*

mob·ster (mob-stĕr) *n. (slang)* a gangster.

moc·ca·sin (mok-ă-sin) *n.* 1. a kind of soft leather shoe, stitched around the vamp. 2. a poisonous snake of the southeastern U.S.

mo·cha (moh-kă) *n.* a kind of coffee, flavoring made with this.

mock (mok) *v.* 1. to make fun of by imitating, to mimic. 2. to scoff or jeer, to defy contemptuously. **mock** *adj.* sham, imitation, *a mock battle.* □**mock orange,** a shrub with strongly scented white flowers. **mock turtle soup,** soup made from calf's head or other meat, to resemble turtle soup.

mock·er·y (mok-ĕ-ree) *n.* (*pl.* **-er·ies**) 1. ridicule, contempt. 2. a ridiculous or unsatisfactory imitation, a travesty.

mock·he·ro·ic (mok-hi-roh-ik) *adj.* burlesquing heroic style.

mock·ing·bird (mok-ing-burd) *n.* a bird that mimics the notes of other birds.

mock·up (mok-up) *n.* an experimental model showing the appearance of a proposed book, ship, etc.

mod (mod) *adj. (informal)* modern, bold and not traditional in style of dress. **mod** *n. (informal)* 1. a young person who adopts a mod style. 2. a modification.

mod. *abbr.* 1. moderate. 2. modern.

mode (mohd) *n.* 1. the way in which a thing is done. 2. the current fashion. 3. the value of a variable corresponding to its greatest frequency of occurrence. **mod·al** (moh-dăl) *adj.*

mod·el (mod-ĕl) *n.* 1. a three-dimensional reproduction of something, usually on a smaller scale. 2. a design or style of structure, as of a car, *this year's model.* 3. a garment by a well-known designer, a copy of this. 4. a person or thing regarded as excellent of its kind and worthy of imitation. 5. a person employed to pose for an artist. 6. a person employed to display clothes in a shop etc. by wearing them. **model** *adj.* excellent of its kind, exemplary; *a model child,* well behaved. **model** *v.* (**mod·eled, mod·el·ing**) 1. to make a model of (a thing) in clay or wax etc., to shape (clay etc.) into a model. 2. to design or plan (a thing) in accordance with a model, *the new method is modeled on the old one.* 3. to work as an artist's model or as a fashion model, to display (clothes) in this way.

mod·er·ate (mod-ĕ-rit) *adj.* 1. medium in amount or intensity or quality etc. 2. keeping or kept within reasonable limits, not extreme or excessive; *a moderate climate,* mild, not intensely hot or intensely cold. 3. not holding extremist views. **moderate** (mod-ĕ-rayt) *v.* (**mod·er·at·ed, mod·er·at·ing**) 1. to make or become moderate or less intense etc. 2. to preside at a meeting. **moderate** (mod-ĕ-rit) *n.* a person who holds moderate opinions, especially in politics. **mod·er·ate·ly** (mod-ĕ-rit-lee) *adv.* **mod·er·a·tion** (mod-ĕ-ray-shŏn) *n.* □in moderation, in moderate amounts.

mod·er·a·tor (mod-ĕ-ray-tŏr) *n.* 1. a person who presides at a meeting. 2. a Presbyterian minister presiding over a church court or assembly.

mod·ern (mod-ĕrn) *adj.* 1. of the present or recent times, *modern history.* 2. in current fashion, not antiquated. 3. (of artistic or literary forms) new and experimental, not following traditional styles. **modern** *n.* a person of modern times or with modern tastes or style. **mod'ern·ly** *adv.* **mod'ern·ness** *n.* **mod·ern·i·ty** (mŏ-dur-ni-tee) *n.* □**Modern English,** the English language from 1500 onward.

mod·ern·ism (mod-ĕr-niz-ĕm) *n.* modern views or methods.

mod·ern·ist (mod-ĕr-nist) *n.* a person who favors modernism. **mod·ern·is·tic** (mod-ĕr-nis-tik) *adj.*

mod·ern·ize (mod-ĕr-nız) *v.* (**mod·ern·ized, mod·ern·iz·ing**) to make modern, to adapt to modern ideas or tastes etc. **mod'ern·iz·er** *n.* **mod·ern·i·za·tion** (mod-ĕr-ni-zay-shŏn) *n.*

mod·est (mod-ist) *adj.* 1. not vain, not boasting about one's merits or achievements. 2. rather shy, not putting oneself forward. 3. moderate in size or amount etc., not showy or splendid in appearance. 4. (of a woman) showing regard for conventional decencies in dress or behavior. **mod'est·ly** *adv.* **mod'es·ty** *n.*

mod·i·cum (mod-ĭ-kŭm) *n.* a small amount.

modif. *abbr.* modification.

mod·i·fy (mod-ĭ-fı) *v.* (**mod·i·fied, mod·i·fy·ing**) 1. to make less severe or harsh or violent. 2. to make partial changes in, *some clauses in the agreement have been modified.* 3. (in grammar) to qualify by describing, *adjectives modify nouns.* **mod·i·fi·ca·tion** (mod-ĭ-fĭ-kay-shŏn) *n.* **mod·i·fi·er** (mod-ĭ-fı-ĕr) *n.*

mod·ish (moh-dish) *adj.* fashionable. **mod'ish·ly** *adv.* **mod'ish·ness** *n.*

mo·diste (moh-deest) *n.* (*old use*) a milliner, a dressmaker.

mod·u·lar (moj-ŭ-lăr) *adj.* constructed of standardized units.

mod·u·lar·ize (moj-ŭ-lă-rız) *v.* (**mod·u·lar·ized, mod·u·lar·iz·ing**) to construct of standardized units.

mod·u·late (moj-ŭ-layt) *v.* (**mod·u·lat·ed, mod·u·lat·ing**) 1. to adjust or regulate, to moderate. 2. to vary the tone or pitch of (one's voice). 3. to pass from one key to another in music. 4. to alter the amplitude or frequency or phase of (a carrier wave) so as to convey a particular signal. **mod'u·la·tor** *n.* **mod·u·la·to·ry** (moj-ŭ-lă-tohr-ee) *adj.* **mod·u·la·tion** (moj-ŭ-lay-shŏn) *n.*

mod·ule (moj-ool) *n.* 1. a unit or standard used in measuring. 2. a standardized part or an independent unit in furniture or buildings or a spacecraft etc.

mo·dus op·er·an·di (moh-dŭs op-ĕ-ran-dı) 1. a person's method of working. 2. the way a thing operates. ▷Latin, = way of operating.

mo·dus viv·en·di (moh-dŭs vi-ven-dı) an arrangement that enables parties who are in dispute to carry on instead of having their activities paralyzed until the dispute has been settled. ▷Latin, = way of living.

Mog·a·dish·u (mog-ă-dish-oo) the capital of Somalia.

mo·gul¹ (moh-gŭl) *n.* (*informal*) an important or influential person, *movie moguls.*

mogul² *n.* a bump on a ski run.

mo·hair (moh-hair) *n.* 1. the fine silky hair of the angora goat, or a mixture of it with wool or cotton. 2. yarn or fabric made from this.

Mo·ham·med·an (moh-ham-ĕ-dăn) = **Muhammadan.**

Mo·hawk (moh-hawk) *n.* (*pl.* **-hawk, -hawks**) a member or language of a tribe of Indians living in New York State.

Mo·he·gan (moh-hee-găn) (*pl.* **-gan, -gans**) **Mo·hi·can** (moh-hee-kăn) (*pl.* **-can, -cans**) *n.* 1. a member of an Indian tribe formerly living in Connecticut and Massachusetts. 2. a Mahican.

Mohs' scale (mohz) **scale** a scale of mineral hardness.

moi·e·ty (moi-ĕ-tee) *n.* (*pl.* **-ties**) approximately half of something.

moi·ré, moire (maw-ray, mwahr) *n.* fabric that looks like watered silk.

moist (moist) *adj.* slightly wet, damp. **moist'ly** *adv.* **moist'ness** *n.*

mois·ten (moi-sĕn) *v.* to make or become moist. **mois'ten·er** *n.*

mois·ture (mois-chŭr) *n.* water or other liquid diffused through a substance or present in the air as vapor or condensed on a surface.

mois·tur·ize (mois-chŭ-rız) *v.* (**mois·tur·ized, mois·tur·iz·ing**) to make (the skin) less dry by use of certain cosmetics. **mois'tur·iz·er** *n.*

mol. *abbr.* 1. molecular. 2. molecule.

mo·lar (moh-lăr) *n.* any of the teeth at the back of the mouth that have broad tops and are used for grinding food in chewing. **molar** *adj.* of these teeth.

mo·las·ses (mŏ-las-iz) *n.* a thick sticky dark liquid produced when sugar is refined.

mold¹ (mohld) *n.* soft fine loose earth that is rich in organic matter, *leaf mold.*

mold² *n.* 1. a hollow container into which a soft or liquid substance is poured to set or cool into a desired shape. 2. a pudding, gelatin dessert, etc. made in a mold. **mold** *v.* 1. to cause to have a certain shape, to produce by shaping. 2. to guide or control the development of, *mold a person's character.*

mold³ *n.* a fine furry growth of very small fungi forming on things that lie in moist warm air. **mold** *v.* to become moldy. **mold'y** *adj.* **mold'i·ness** *n.*

Mol·da·vi·a (mol-day-vee-ă) a republic of the U.S.S.R. bordering on Rumania. **Mol·da'vi·an** *adj. & n.*

mold·board (mohld-bohrd) *n.* a board in a plow that turns over the furrow slice.

mold·er[1] (mohl-dĕr) *v.* to decay into dust, to rot away.

molder[2] *n.* a person who molds or shapes things.

mold·ing (mohl-ding) *n.* 1. shaping in a mold. 2. a molded object, especially an ornamental strip of plaster or wood etc. decorating or outlining something.

mole[1] (mohl) *n.* a small permanent dark spot on the human skin.

mole[2] *n.* a structure built out into the sea as a breakwater or causeway.

mole[3] *n.* a small burrowing animal with dark velvety fur and very small eyes.

mole[4] *n.* a unit of molecular weight.

mol·e·cule (mol-ĕ-kyool) *n.* 1. the smallest unit (usually consisting of a group of atoms) into which a substance can be divided without a change in its chemical nature. 2. a small particle. **mo·lec·u·lar** (mŏ-lek-yŭ-lăr) *adj.*

mole·hill (mohl-hil) *n.* a small mound of earth thrown up by a burrowing mole. □**make a mountain out of a molehill**, to behave as if a small difficulty were a very great one.

mole·skin (mohl-skin) *n.* 1. the fur of the mole. 2. a fabric having a soft thick nap.

mo·lest (mŏ-lest) *v.* to annoy or pester a person in a hostile way or in a way that causes injury. **mol·lest'er** *n.* **mol·les·ta·tion** (moh-le-stay-shŏn) *n.*

moll (mol) *n. (informal)* a gangster's female companion.

mol·li·fy (mol-ĭ-fī) *v.* (**mol·li·fied, mol·li·fy·ing**) to soothe the anger of. **mol·li·fi·ca·tion** (mol-ĭ-fī-kay-shŏn) *n.*

mol·lusk, mol·lusc (mol-ŭsk) *n.* any of a group of animals that have soft bodies and hard shells (such as snails, oysters, mussels) or no shell (such as slugs, octopuses). **mol·lus·kan, mol·lus·can** (mŏ-lus-kăn) *adj.*

mol·ly (mol-ee) *n.* (*pl.* -**lies**) a freshwater aquarium fish whose young are born alive, not in the form of eggs.

mol·ly·cod·dle (mol-ee-kod-ĕl) *v.* (**mol·ly·cod·dled, mol·ly·cod·dling**) to coddle excessively, to pamper. **mollycoddle** *n.* a mollycoddled person.

Mo·lo·tov (mol-ŏ-tawf) **cocktail** a kind of incendiary bomb thrown by hand.

molt (mohlt) *v.* to shed feathers or skin, as of reptiles, birds, etc. **molt** *n.* 1. the process or act of molting. 2. the castoff covering. **molt'er** *n.*

mol·ten (mohl-tĕn) *adj.* melted, made liquid by very great heat.

Mo·luc·ca (mŏ-luk-ă) **Islands** a group of islands in Indonesia. **Mo·luc'can** *adj. & n.*

mo·ly (moh-lee) *n.* (*pl.* -**lies**) a mythical herb with white flowers and black root, endowed with magical properties.

mo·lyb·de·num (mŏ-lib-dĕ-nŭm) *n.* a silver white brittle metallic element.

mom (mom) *n. (informal)* mother. □**mom and pop store**, an independent retail business small enough to be run by two people, especially by a husband and wife.

mo·ment (moh-mĕnt) *n.* 1. a very brief portion of time. 2. an exact point of time; *he'll be here any moment*, at any time now, very soon. 3. importance, *these are matters of great moment.* □**at the moment**, now. **for the moment**, for now, temporarily. **in a moment**, instantly; very soon. **moment of truth**, a time of test or crisis (▷from a Spanish phrase referring to the final sword thrust in a bullfight).

mo·men·tar·y (moh-mĕn-ter-ee) *adj.* lasting only a moment. **mo·men·tar·i·ly** (moh-mĕn-ter-ĭ-lee) *adv.*

mo·men·tous (moh-men-tŭs) *adj.* of great importance. **mo·men'tous·ly** *adv.* **mo·men'tous·ness** *n.*

mo·men·tum (moh-men-tŭm) *n.* impetus gained by movement, *the sled gathered momentum as it went downhill; as the election wore on, the candidate lost momentum*, his popularity faded.

mom·my (mom-ee) *n.* (*pl.* -**mies**) *(informal)* mother.

Mon. *abbr.* Monday.

Mon·a·co (mon-ă-koh) 1. a country on the French Riviera. 2. its capital city.

mon·arch (mon-ărk) *n.* 1. a ruler with the title of king, queen, emperor, or empress. 2. (also **monarch butterfly**) a large orange and black butterfly. **mon·ar·chic** (mŏ-nahr-kik) *adj.* **mon·ar'chi·cal** *adj.*

mon·ar·chist (mon-ăr-kist) *n.* a person who favors government by a monarch or who supports a monarch against opponents of this system. **mon'ar·chism** *n.* **mon·ar·chist·ic** (mon-ăr-kis-tik) *adj.*

mon·ar·chy (mon-ăr-kee) *n.* (*pl.* -**chies**) 1. a form of government in which a monarch is the supreme ruler. 2. a country with this form of government.

mon·as·ter·y (mon-ă-ster-ee) *n.* (*pl.* -**ter·ies**) a building in which monks live as a secluded community under religious vows. **mon·as·ter·i·al** (mon-ă-steer-i-ăl) *adj.*

mo·nas·tic (mŏ-nas-tik) *adj.* of monks or monasteries. **mo·nas'ti·cal·ly** *adv.* **mo·nas·ti·cism** (mŏ-nas-ti-siz-ĕm) *n.*

mon·au·ral (mon-or-ăl) *adj.* monophonic. **mon·au'ral·ly** *adv.*

Mon·day (mun-day) *n.* the day of the week following Sunday.

mon·e·tar·ism (mon-ĕ-tă-riz-ĕm) *n.* the theory that governments create inflation by putting too much money into the economy. **mon'e·tar·ist** *n.* a person who supports this theory.

mon·e·tar·y (mon-ĕ-ter-ee) *adj.* 1. of a country's currency, *our monetary system.* 2. of or involving money, *its monetary value.* ▷Do not confuse *monetary* with *financial.* Monetary experts pay attention to the amount of currency in circulation. Financial experts are concerned with banking, business, or governmental transactions involving money.

mon·ey (mun-ee) *n.* 1. coin, portable pieces of stamped metal in use as a medium of exchange. 2. coins and banknotes. 3. (*pl.* **moneys** or **monies**) specific sums of currency. 4. an amount of money, wealth; *they've got plenty of money*, are wealthy; *there's money in it*, much profit can be made from it. □**get one's money's worth**, to get good value for one's money. **in the money**, *(informal)* winning money prizes; *(slang)* having plenty of money. **make money**, to make a profit; to become rich by doing this. **marry money**, to marry a rich person. **money box**, a closed box into which savings or contributions are dropped through a slit. **money of account**, a unit of money used in reckoning for which there may or may not be an equivalent coin or paper money. **money order,** a printed order for the payment of money, issued by a post office, bank, etc. for payment at any of its branches. **money supply,** the amount of currency, plus demand or checking account deposits, in public hands. ▷ Note that there is rarely a need for the plural form of *money* (see definition 3 above for one use of the plural form.)

mon·ey-back (mun-ee-bak) *adj.* (of a guarantee) promising to return a customer's money if he is not satisfied.

mon·ey·bags (mun-ee-bagz) *n.* *(slang)* a rich person.

mon·ey·chang·er (mun-ee-chayn-jĕr) *n.* a person whose business is to change money at a stated rate.

mon·eyed (mun-eed) *adj.* wealthy.

mon·ey-grub·ber (mun-ee-grub-ĕr) *n.* a person who is greedily intent on making money.

mon·ey·lend·er (mun-ee-len-dĕr) *n.* a person whose business it is to lend money on which the borrower will pay interest.

mon·ey·mak·er (mun-ee-may-kĕr) *n.* a person or business etc. that is successful in making a profit. **mon'ey·mak·ing** *adj.* & *n.*

Mon·gol (mong-gŏl) *adj.* Mongolian. **Mongol** *n.* a Mongolian person.

Mon·go·li·a (mong-goh-li-ă) a region north of China, including Inner Mongolia, controlled by China, and the Mongolian People's Republic. **Mon·go'li·an** *adj.* & *n.*

Mongolian (mong-goh-li-ăn) **People's Republic** a country in north central Asia.

mon·go·lism (mong-gŏ-liz-ĕm) *n.* an abnormal congenital condition in which a person suffers from mental deficiency and has a Mongoloid appearance.

Mon·go·loid (mong-gŏ-loid) *adj.* 1. resembling the Mongols in racial characteristics, having yellowish skin, a broad flat face, and straight black hair. 2. of or suffering from mongolism. **Mongoloid** *n.* 1. a Mongoloid person. 2. a person suffering from mongolism.

mon·goose (mong-goos) *n.* (*pl.* **-goos·es**) a weasel-like tropical animal that can attack and kill poisonous snakes.

mon·grel (mong-grĕl) *n.* 1. a dog of no definable type or breed. 2. an animal or plant of mixed breed. **mongrel** *adj.* of mixed origin or character.

mon·ick·er, mon·i·ker (mon-ĭ-kĕr) *n.* *(slang)* a person's name.

mon·ism (mon-iz-ĕm) *n.* the doctrine that only one ultimate principle or being exists. **mon'ist** *n.*

mo·nis·tic (mŏ-nis-tik) *adj.*

mo·ni·tion (moh-nish-ŏn) *n.* 1. a warning of danger. 2. a formal notice from a bishop or an ecclesiastical court admonishing someone to refrain from some offense.

mon·i·tor (mon-i-tŏr) *n.* 1. a pupil who is given special duties in a school. 2. a device used for observing or testing the operation of something. 3. a person who monitors broadcasts etc. 4. a television set used in a studio to check or select transmissions. **monitor** *v.* to keep watch over, to record or test or control the working of.

mon·i·to·ry (mon-i-tohr-ee) *adj.* serving as a warning, admonitory.

monk[1] (mungk) *n.* a member of a community of men living apart from the world under the rules of a religious order. □**monk's cloth,** a rough cotton cloth of basket weave.

monk[2] *n.* *(informal)* monkey.

mon·key (mung-kee) *n.* (*pl.* **-keys**) 1. an animal of a group closely related to man, especially one of the small long-tailed species. 2. a mischievous person. **monkey** *v.* (**mon·keyed, mon·key·ing**) to play about mischievously; *don't monkey with the switch,* do not tamper with it. □**monkey business,** *(slang)* mischief; underhand dealings. **monkey suit,** *(slang)* a uniform, a man's formal evening dress. **monkey wrench,** a wrench with adjustable jaws.

mon·key·shines (mung-kee-shĭnz) *n.* *pl.* *(slang)* mischief or tricks.

monk·ish (mung-kish) *adj.* of or like a monk. **monk'ish·ly** *adv.* **monk'ish·ness** *n.*

monks·hood (mungks-huud) *n.* a poisonous plant with blue hood-shaped flowers.

mon·o[1] (mon-oh) *adj.* monophonic. **mono** *n.* (*pl.* **mon·os**) 1. monophonic sound or recording. 2. a monophonic record.

mono[2] *n.* *(informal)* mononucleosis.

mono- *prefix* one, single, alone.

mon·o·chrome (mon-ŏ-krohm) *adj.* done in only one color, black and white. **mon·o·chro·mat·ic** (mon-oh-kroh-mat-ik) *adj.*

mon·o·cle (mon-ŏ-kĕl) *n.* an eyeglass for one eye only.

mon·o·cot·y·le·don (mon-ŏ-kot-ĭ-lee-dŏn) *n.* a flowering plant with a single cotyledon. **mon·o·cot·y·le'don·ous** *adj.*

mo·noc·u·lar (mŏ-nok-yŭ-lăr) *adj.* with one eye, using or intended for use with one eye.

mon·o·dy (mon-ŏ-dee) *n.* (*pl.* **-dies**) 1. an ode sung by a single actor in a Greek tragedy. 2. a poem in which a mourner bewails someone's death. **mon'o·dist** *n.* **mo·nod·ic** (mŏ-nod-ik) *adj.*

mon·o·fil·a·ment (mon-ŏ-fil-ă-mĕnt) *n.* a single untwisted synthetic filament.

mo·nog·a·my (mŏ-nog-ă-mee) *n.* the system of being married to only one person at a time. **mo·nog'a·mist** *n.* **mo·nog'a·mous** *adj.* **mon·o·gam·ic** (mon-ŏ-gam-ik) *adj.*

mon·o·gram (mon-ŏ-gram) *n.* two or more letters (especially a person's initials) combined in one design. **monogram** *v.* (**mon·o·grammed, mon·o·gram·ming**) to mark with a monogram. **mon'o·grammed** *adj.*

mon·o·graph (mon-ŏ-graf) *n.* a scholarly treatise on a single subject or on some aspect of a subject.

mon·o·lin·gual (mon-ŏ-ling-gwăl) *adj.* expressed in or knowing or using only one language.

mon·o·lith (mon-ŏ-lith) *n.* a large single upright block of stone.

mon·o·lith·ic (mon-ŏ-lith-ik) *adj.* 1. consisting of one or more monoliths. 2. like a monolith in being single and massive, *a monolithic organization.*

mon·o·logue, mon·o·log (mon-ŏ-lawg) *n.* a long speech by one performer or by one person in a group. **mon·o·log·ist** (mŏ-nol-ŏ-jist) *n.*

mon·o·ma·ni·a (mon-ŏ-may-ni-ă) *n.* an obsession with one idea or interest. **mon·o·ma'ni·ac** *n.*

mon·o·mer (mon-ŏ-mĕr) *n.* a chemical compound that can be polymerized.

mo·no·mi·al (moh-noh-mi-ăl) *n.* an algebraic expression consisting of one term. **monomial** *adj.*

mon·o·nu·cle·o·sis (mon-oh-noo-kli-oh-sis) *n.* an infectious disease with swelling of the lymph glands.

mon·o·phon·ic (mon-ŏ-fon-ik) *adj.* (of sound re-

production) using only one transmission channel.
mon·o·phon'i·cal·ly adv.

mon·o·plane (mon-ŏ-playn) n. a type of airplane with only one set of wings.

mo·nop·o·list (mŏ-nop-ŏ-list) n. a person who has a monopoly. **mo·nop·o·lis·tic** (mŏ-nop-ŏ-lis-tik) adj.

mo·nop·o·lize (mŏ-nop-ŏ-lız) v. (**mo·nop·o·lized, mo·nop·o·liz·ing**) to take exclusive control or use of; monopolize the conversation, give others no chance to join in. **mo·nop·o·li·za·tion** (mŏ-nop-ŏ-li-zay-shŏn) n.

mo·nop·o·ly (mŏ-nop-ŏ-lee) n. (pl. **-lies**) 1. exclusive possession of the trade in some commodity. 2. sole possession or control of anything. 3. Monopoly, (trademark) a board game in which squares represent properties which players buy with imitation money.

mon·o·rail (mon-ŏ-rayl) n. a railway in which the track consists of a single rail.

mon·o·so·di·um glu·ta·mate (mon-ŏ-soh-di-ŭm gloo-tă-mayt) a salt used to intensify flood flavors.

mon·o·syl·la·ble (mon-ŏ-sil-ă-běl) n. a word of one syllable. **mon·o·syl·lab·ic** (mon-ŏ-si-lab-ik) adj. **mon·o·syl·lab'i·cal·ly** adv.

mon·o·the·ism (mon-ŏ-thee-iz-ěm) n. the doctrine that there is only one God. **mon'o·the·ist** n. **mon·o·the·is·tic** (mon-ŏ-thee-is-tik) adj.

mon·o·tone (mon-ŏ-tohn) n. a level unchanging tone of voice in speaking or singing.

mo·not·o·nous (mŏ-not-ŏ-nŭs) adj. lacking in variety or variation, tiring or boring because of this. **mo·not'o·nous·ly** adv. **mo·not'o·ny** n.

mon·ox·ide (mŏ-nok-sıd) n. an oxide with one atom of oxygen.

Mon·roe (mŏn-roh), **James** (1758–1831) the fifth president of the U.S. 1817–25.

Mon·ro·vi·a (mŏn-roh-vi-ă) the capital of Liberia.

Mon·sei·gneur (mon-sen-yur) n. the title of an eminent French person, especially a prince, cardinal, archbishop, or bishop.

Mon·sieur (mŏ-syur) n. (pl. **Mes·sieurs**, pr. mes-ěrz, may-syur) the title of a Frenchman, = Mr. or sir.

Mon·si·gnor (mon-seen-yŏr) n. the title of certain Roman Catholic priests and officials.

mon·soon (mon-soon) n. 1. a seasonal wind blowing in South Asia, especially in the Indian Ocean. 2. the rainy season accompanying the southwest monsoon.

mon·ster (mon-stěr) n. 1. a large ugly or frightening imaginary creature. 2. an animal or plant that is very abnormal in form. 3. anything of huge size. 4. an extremely cruel or wicked person.

mon·strance (mon-străns) n. (in the Roman Catholic Church) a framed open or transparent holder in which the consecrated bread of the Eucharist is exposed for veneration.

mon·stros·i·ty (mon-stros-i-tee) n. (pl. **-ties**) a monstrous thing.

mon·strous (mon-strŭs) adj. 1. like a monster, huge. 2. outrageous, very wrong or absurd. **mon'strous·ly** adv. **mon'strous·ness** n.

Mont. abbr. Montana.

mon·tage (mon-tahzh) n. 1. the joining of a number of short disconnected shots (in a motion picture) to indicate passage of time, change of place, etc. 2. the process of making a composite picture by putting together pieces from other pictures or designs. 3. a picture produced in this way.

Mon·tan·a (mon-tan-ă) a state of the U.S. **Mon·tan'an** adj. & n.

Mon·tes·so·ri (mon-tě-sohr-ee) **method** a method of educating very young children by direction of their natural activities rather than by strict control.

Mon·te·vi·de·o (mon-tě-vi-day-oh) the capital of Uruguay.

Mont·gom·ery (mont-gum-ě-ree) the capital of Alabama.

month (munth) n. 1. any of the twelve portions into which a year is divided. 2. the period between the same dates in successive months. □**month of Sundays**, a very long time.

month·ly (munth-lee) adj. happening or published or payable etc. once a month. **monthly** adv. once a month. **monthly** n. a monthly magazine etc.

Mont·pel·ier (mont-peel-yěr) the capital of Vermont.

mon·u·ment (mon-yŭ-měnt) n. 1. anything (especially a structure) designed or serving to celebrate or commemorate a person or event etc. 2. a structure that is preserved because of its historical importance.

mon·u·men·tal (mon-yŭ-men-tăl) adj. 1. of or serving as a monument, monumental brasses in the church. 2. (of a literary work) massive and of permanent importance. 3. extremely great, a monumental achievement or blunder. **mon·u·men'tal·ly** adv.

moo (moo) n. the low deep sound made by a cow. **moo** v. to make this sound.

mooch (mooch) v. (slang) to obtain (money, cigarettes, etc.) by cadging. **mooch'er** n.

mood [1] (mood) n. 1. a temporary state of mind or spirits. 2. the feeling or tone conveyed by a literary or artistic work, the visual mood of a film. 3. a fit of bad temper or depression, he's in one of his moods.

mood [2] n. a grammatical form of a verb that shows whether it is a statement (he stopped) or a command (stop!) etc.

mood·y (moo-dee) adj. (**mood·i·er, mood·i·est**) gloomy, sullen, liable to become like this. **mood'i·ly** adv. **mood'i·ness** n.

moon (moon) n. 1. the natural satellite of Earth, made visible by light that it reflects from the sun. 2. this when it is visible, there's no moon tonight. 3. a natural satellite of any planet. 4. something regarded as unlikely to be attained, reach for the moon; promised us the moon, made very extravagant promises. **moon** v. to move or look or pass time dreamily or listlessly. □**once in a blue moon**, hardly ever.

moon·beam (moon-beem) n. a ray of moonlight.

moon·ie (moo-nee) n. (slang) a follower of the Rev. Sun Myung Moon, a Korean evangelist in the U.S.

moon·less (moon-lis) adj. without a moon, moonless nights.

moon·light (moon-lıt) n. light from the moon. **moonlight** v. (informal) to have two paid jobs, one during the day and the other in the evening. **moon'light·er** n.

moon·lit (moon-lit) adj. lit by the moon.

moon·rise (moon-rız) n. the rising of the moon, the time of this.

moon·scape (moon-skayp) n. 1. the scenery of the moon. 2. a picture of this.

moon·shine (moon-shın) n. 1. foolish ideas. 2.

moonlight. **3.** (informal) illegally distilled or smuggled whiskey.

moon·shot (moon-shot) n. the launching of a spacecraft or rocket traveling to the moon.

moon·stone (moon-stohn) n. a semiprecious stone with a pearly appearance.

moon·struck (moon-struk) adj. **1.** deranged in mind, supposedly because of the influence of the moon. **2.** romantic.

moon·walk (moon-wawk) n. a walk on the surface of the moon.

moon·y (moo-nee) adj. (**moon·ier, moon·i·est**) listless, dreamy.

moor[1] (moor) n. (British) a stretch of open uncultivated land with low shrubs.

moor[2] v. to secure (a boat or other floating thing) to a fixed object by means of cable(s).

Moor (moor) n. a member of a Muslim people living in northwest Africa. **Moor'ish** adj.

moor·ings (moor-ingz) n. pl. **1.** cables etc. by which something is moored. **2.** a place where a boat is moored.

moose (moos) n. (pl. **moose**). **1.** a large animal of North America belonging to the deer family. **2.** the European elk.

moot (moot) adj. debatable, undecided, that's a moot point. **moot** v. to raise (a question) for discussion. ☐**moot court,** a law students' court for trying hypothetical cases. ▷Do not confuse moot with mute.

mop (mop) n. **1.** a bundle of yarn or cloth etc. fastened at the end of a stick, used for cleaning floors. **2.** a small device of similar shape for various purposes, dish mop. **3.** (informal) a thick mass of hair. mop v. (**mopped, mop'ping**) to clean or wipe with a mop etc., to wipe away. ☐**mop up,** to wipe up with a mop etc.; to finish off a task; to clear (an area) of the remnants of enemy troops etc. after a victory.

mope (mohp) v. (**moped, mop·ing**) to be in low spirits and listless.

mo·ped (moh-ped) n. a motorized bicycle.

mop·pet (mop-it) n. a young child.

mo·quette (moh-ket) n. a material with raised loops or cut pile used for carpets and upholstery.

mo·raine (mŏ-rayn) n. a mass of debris carried down and deposited by a glacier.

mor·al (mor-ăl) adj. **1.** of or concerned with the goodness and badness of human character or with the principles of what is right and wrong in conduct, moral philosophy. **2.** virtuous. **3.** capable of understanding and living by the rules of morality. **4.** based on people's sense of what is right or just, not on legal rights and obligations, we had a moral obligation to help. **5.** psychological, mental not physical or concrete, moral courage; moral support, encouragement and approval. **moral** n. **1.** a moral lesson or principle. **2.** morals, a person's moral habits, especially sexual conduct. **mor'al·ly** adv. ☐**moral certainty,** a probability so great that no reasonable doubt is possible. **moral victory,** a triumph, although nothing concrete is obtained by it. ▷Do not confuse moral with morale.

mo·rale (mŏ-ral) n. the state of a person's or group's spirits and confidence. ▷Do not confuse morale with moral.

mor·al·ist (mor-ă-list) n. a person who expresses or teaches moral principles. **mor·al·is·tic** (mor-ă-lis-tik) adj. **mor·al·is'ti·cal·ly** adv.

mo·ral·i·ty (mŏ-ral-i-tee) n. (pl. **-ties**) **1.** moral principles or rules. **2.** a particular system of

morals, political morality. **3.** being moral, conforming to moral principles, goodness or rightness. ☐**morality play,** a kind of drama with abstract qualities as the main characters and teaching a moral lesson, popular in the 16th century.

mor·al·ize (mor-ă-lız) v. (**mor·al·ized, mor·al·iz·ing**) to talk or write about the principles of right and wrong and conduct etc. **mor'al·iz·er** n. **mor·al·i·za·tion** (mor-ă-li-zay-shŏn) n.

mo·rass (mŏ-ras) n. **1.** a marsh, a bog. **2.** an entanglement, something that confuses or impedes people.

mor·a·to·ri·um (mor-ă-tohr-iŭm) n. (pl. **-to·ri·ums, -to·ri·a,** pr. -tohr-i-ă) **1.** legal authorization to debtors to postpone payment. **2.** a temporary ban or suspension on some activity, asked for a moratorium on strikes.

mo·ray (mohr-ay) n. (also **moray eel**) a dangerous eel of tropical seas.

mor·bid (mor-bid) adj. **1.** (of the mind or ideas) unwholesome, preoccupied with gloomy or unpleasant things. **2.** caused by or indicating disease, unhealthy, a morbid growth. **mor'bid·ly** adv. **mor'bid·ness** n. **mor·bid'i·ty** n.

mor·dant (mor-dănt) adj. characterized by a biting sarcasm, his mordant wit. **mor'dant·ly** adv.

more (mohr) adj. greater in quantity or intensity etc. **more** n. a greater quantity or number. **more** adv. **1.** in a greater degree, was more frightened than hurt. **2.** again, once more. ☐**more or less,** in a greater or less degree; approximately.

mo·rel (mŏ-rel) n. a type of edible mushroom with a soft cap.

mo·rel·lo (mŏ-rel-oh) n. (pl. **-los**) a kind of sour dark cherry.

more·o·ver (mohr-oh-vĕr) adv. besides, in addition to what has already been said.

mo·res (mohr-ayz) n. pl. the customs or conventions regarded as essential to or characteristic of a community.

Mor·gan (mor-găn) n. one of a North American breed of light saddle and carriage horses descended from a stallion named Justin Morgan.

mor·ga·nat·ic (mor-gă-nat-ik) adj. (of a marriage) between a man of high rank and a woman of low rank who retains her former status, their children having no claim to the father's possessions or title.

morgue (morg) n. a mortuary.

mor·i·bund (mor-i-bund) adj. in a dying state; a moribund institution, no longer effective.

Mor·mon (mor-mŏn) n. a member of a religious organization (the Church of Jesus Christ of Latter-day Saints) founded in the U.S. in 1830. **Mor'mon·ism** n.

morn (morn) n. (poetical) morning.

morn·ing (mor-ning) n. **1.** the early part of the day, ending at noon or at the midday meal. **2.** sunrise, dawn, when morning broke. **3.** (informal, used as a greeting) = good morning. ☐**morning after,** (informal) a hangover. **morning dress,** formal dress for a man consisting of a tailcoat, striped trousers, and top hat. **morning glory,** a climbing plant with trumpet-shaped flowers that often close in the afternoons. **morning sickness,** nausea in the morning during early pregnancy. **morning star,** a bright star or planet (especially Venus) seen in the east before sunrise.

Mo·roc·co (mŏ-rok-oh) a country in North Africa.

morocco n. a fine flexible leather made (originally in Morocco) from goatskins, or an imitation

of this. **Mo·roc·can** (mŏ-rok-ăn) *adj. & n.*
mo·ron (mohr-on) *n.* 1. an adult with intelligence
equal to that of an average child of eight to twelve
years. 2. *(informal)* a very stupid person. **mo·**
ron·ic (mŏ-ron-ik) *adj.* **mo·ron'i·cal·ly** *adv.*
Mo·ro·ni (mŏ-roh-nee) the capital of the Comoro
Islands.
mo·rose (mŏ-rohs) *adj.* sullen, gloomy, and unsociable. **mo·rose'ly** *adv.* **mo·rose'ness** *n.*
mor·pheme (mor-feem) *n.* the smallest meaningful
grammatical unit of a language, such as *in, come,*
-ing, -or. **mor·phem·ic** (mor-fee-mik) *adj.*
mor·phi·a (mor-fi-ă) *n.* morphine.
mor·phine (mor-feen) *n.* a drug made from opium,
used for relieving pain.
mor·phol·o·gy (mor-fol-ŏ-jee) *n.* 1. the study of
the form of animals and plants. 2. the study of
the form of words, the system of forms in a language. **mor·phol·o·gist** (mor-fol-ŏ-jist) *n.*
mor·pho·log·i·cal (mor-fŏ-loj-i-kăl) *adj.*
mor·ris (mor-is) **dance** a traditional English folk
dance performed by men in costume with ribbons
and bells, *morris dancers.*
mor·row (mor-oh) *n. (old use)* the following day.
Morse (mors) **code** a code used in signaling in
which letters of the alphabet are represented by
various combinations of short and long sounds
or flashes of light (dots and dashes).
mor·sel (mor-sĕl) *n.* a small quantity, a small
amount or piece of food.
mor·tal (mor-tăl) *adj.* 1. subject to death. 2. causing
death, fatal, *a mortal wound.* 3. deadly, lasting
until death, *mortal enemies; in mortal combat.*
4. intense, *in mortal fear.* 5. *(slang)* without exception, *sold every mortal thing.* **mortal** *n.* a person
who is subject to death, a human being. **mor'tal·**
ly *adv.* □**mortal sin,** (in Roman Catholic teaching) sin that causes death of the soul or that is
fatal to salvation.
mor·tal·i·ty (mor-tal-i-tee) *n.* 1. being mortal, subject to death. 2. loss of life on a large scale.
□**mortality rate,** the death rate. **mortality ta-**
bles, tables showing the expectation of life of
people according to their age.
mor·tar[1] (mor-tăr) *n.* a mixture of lime or cement
with sand and water, for joining bricks or stones.
mortar *v.* to plaster or join (bricks etc.) with
mortar.
mortar[2] *n.* 1. a vessel of hard material in which
substances are pounded with a pestle. 2. a short
cannon for firing shells at a high angle.
mor·tar·board (mor-tăr-bohrd) *n.* a stiff square
cap worn as part of academic dress.
mort·gage (mor-gij) *v.* **(mort·gaged, mort·**
gag·ing) to give someone a claim on (property)
as security for payment of a debt or loan. **mort·**
gage *n.* 1. mortgaging. 2. an agreement giving
a claim of this kind. 3. the amount of money
borrowed or lent against the security of a property
in this way.
mort·ga·gee (mor-gă-jee) *n.* a firm (such as a
bank) or a person to whom property is mortgaged.
mort·ga·gor, mort·gag·er (mor-gă-jĕr) *n.* a person who mortgages his property.
mor·ti·cian (mor-tish-ăn) *n.* an undertaker.
mor·ti·fy (mor-tĭ-fi) *v.* **(mor·ti·fied, mor·ti·**
fy·ing) 1. to humiliate greatly. 2. to subdue by
discipline or self-denial. 3. (of flesh) to become
gangrenous. **mor'ti·fy·ing·ly** *adv.* **mor·ti·fi·**
ca·tion (mor-tĭ-fĭ-kay-shŏn) *n.*
mor·tise (mor-tis) *n.* a hole in one part of a framework into which the end of another part is inserted

so that the two fit together. **mortise** *v.* **(mor·**
tised, mor·tis·ing) to cut a mortise in, to join
with a mortise. □**mortise joint,** a joint made
by a mortise and tenon.
mor·tu·ar·y (mor-choo-er-ee) *n.* (*pl.* **-ar·ies**) a
place where dead bodies may be kept temporarily.
mos. *abbr.* months.
mo·sa·ic (moh-zay-ik) *n.* a pattern or picture made
by placing together small pieces of glass or stone
etc. of different colors.
Mo·sa·ic (moh-zay-ik) *adj.* of Moses or his teaching, *Mosaic Law.*
Mos·cow (mos-kow) the capital of the U.S.S.R.
mo·selle (moh-zel) *n.* a dry white wine from the
Moselle valley in Germany.
mo·sey (moh-zee) *v.* **(mo·seyed, mo·sey·**
ing) *(informal)* to walk in a leisurely or aimless
manner.
Mos·lem (moz-lĕm, mos-) *adj. & n.* = **Muslim.**
mosque (mosk) *n.* a Muslim place of worship.
mos·qui·to (mŏ-skee-toh) *n.* (*pl.* **-toes**) a kind
of gnat, the female of which bites and sucks blood
from people and animals. □**mosquito boat,** a
light motorized boat used chiefly to launch torpedoes. **mosquito net,** a net of fine mesh used to
keep out mosquitoes.
moss (maws) *n.* a small flowerless plant that forms
a dense growth on moist surfaces or in bogs; *a
rolling stone gathers no moss,* one who constantly
moves about or changes jobs will not grow rich.
moss·back (maws-bak) *n. (informal)* a very old-
fashioned conservative person.
moss·y (maw-see) *adj.* **(moss·i·er, moss·i·est)**
like moss, covered in moss. **moss'i·ness** *n.*
most (mohst) *adj.* greatest in quantity or intensity
etc. **most** *n.* the greatest quantity or number.
most *adv.* 1. in the greatest degree. 2. very, *a
most amusing book.* □**at most** or **at the most,**
not more than. **for the most part,** in most cases;
in most of its extent. **make the most of,** to use
to best advantage; to represent at its best or at
its worst. ▷It is incorrect to use *most* in place
of *almost.*
-most *suffix* used to form adjectives carrying a superlative meaning, as in *foremost, uppermost.*
most·ly (mohst-lee) *adv.* for the most part.
mot (moh) *n.* (*pl.* **mots,** *pr.* mohz) a witty saying.
□**mot juste** (*zh*oost) the expression that conveys
a desired shade of meaning with more precision
than any other. ▷French.
mote (moht) *n.* a particle of dust.
mo·tel (moh-tel) *n.* a roadside hotel or group of
furnished cabins providing accommodation for
motorists and their vehicles.
moth (mawth) *n.* 1. an insect resembling a butterfly
but usually flying at night. 2. (also **clothes
moth**) a small similar insect that lays its eggs
in cloth or fur fabrics on which its larvae feed.
moth·ball (mawth-bawl) *n.* a small ball of pungent
substance for keeping moths away from clothes.
□**in mothballs,** stored out of use for a considerable time. **mothball fleet,** naval vessels stored
for later use.
moth-eat·en (mawth-ee-tĕn) *adj.* 1. damaged by
moth larvae. 2. antiquated, decrepit.
moth·er (*muth*-ĕr) *n.* 1. a female parent. 2. a quality
or condition that gives rise to another, *necessity
is the mother of invention.* 3. a woman who is
head of a female religious community, *Mother
Superior.* 4. *(informal)* a title used in addressing
an old woman. 5. an apparatus generating
warmth, used for rearing chickens without a hen.

mother v. to look after in a motherly way.
moth'er·hood n. ☐**Mother Church,** a church from which others have sprung. **mother country,** a country in relation to its colonies. **Mother Hubbard,** a woman's loose shapeless dress. **mother lode,** a rich or important vein of metal ore. **Mother of God,** the Virgin Mary. **Mother's Day,** the second Sunday in May. **mother ship,** the ship in charge of a group of torpedo boats, submarines, etc. **mother tongue,** one's native language.
moth·er-in-law (mu*th*-ĕr-in-law) n. (pl. **moth·ers-in-law**) the mother of one's wife or husband.
moth·er·land (mu*th*-ĕr-land) n. one's native country.
moth·er·less (mu*th*-ĕr-lis) adj. without a living mother.
moth·er·ly (mu*th*-ĕr-lee) adj. like a mother, showing a mother's kindliness and tenderness. **moth'er·li·ness** n.
moth·er-of-pearl (mu*th*-ĕr-ŏv-purl) n. a pearly substance lining the shells of oysters and mussels etc.
mo·tif (moh-teef) n. 1. a recurring design or feature in a literary or artistic work. 2. a short melody or theme that recurs and is developed in a piece of music.
mo·tile (moh-tīl) adj. capable of motion. **mo·til·i·ty** (moh-til-i-tee) n.
mo·tion (moh-shŏn) n. 1. moving, change of position. 2. manner of movement. 3. change of posture, a particular movement, a gesture. 4. a formal proposal that is to be discussed and voted on at a meeting. **motion** v. to make a gesture directing a person to do something, *motioned him to sit beside her.* ☐**go through the motions,** to do something in a perfunctory or insincere manner. **in motion,** moving, not at rest; *set something in motion,* to start it working or operating. **motion picture,** a story or record of events recorded on film for showing to an audience. **motion sickness,** a feeling of queasiness experienced by a passenger in a moving vehicle or boat.
mo·tion·less (moh-shŏn-lis) adj. not moving. **mo'tion·less·ly** adv. **mo'tion·less·ness** n.
mo·ti·vate (moh-tī-vayt) v. (**mo·ti·vat·ed, mo·ti·vat·ing**) 1. to give a motive or incentive to, to be the motive of, *she was motivated by kindness.* 2. to stimulate the interest of, to inspire. **mo·ti·va·tion** (moh-tī-vay-shŏn) n.
mo·ti·vat·ed (moh-tī-vay-tid) adj. having a definite and positive desire to do things.
mo·tive (moh-tiv) n. that which induces a person to act in a certain way. **motive** adj. producing movement or action; *motive power,* that which drives machinery etc. **mo'tive·less** adj.
mot·ley (mot-lee) adj. 1. diversified in color. 2. of varied character, *a motley crew.*
mo·tor (moh-tŏr) n. a machine that supplies motive power for a vehicle or boat etc. or for another device with moving parts, an internal combustion engine. **motor** adj. 1. giving or producing motion; *motor nerves,* those that carry impulses from the brain etc. to the muscles. 2. driven by a motor, *motor vehicle.* 3. of or for motor vehicles, *motor parts.* **motor** v. to go or convey in a motorcar. ☐**motor court, hotel, inn, lodge,** a motel. **motor home,** a mobile home. **motor scooter,** a motorbike. **motor vehicle,** a vehicle with a motor engine, for use on ordinary roads.
mo·tor·bike (moh-tŏr-bık) n. a lightweight motorcycle.

mo·tor·boat (moh-tŏr-boht) n. a boat powered by an inboard or outboard motor engine.
mo·tor·cade (moh-tŏr-kayd) n. a procession or parade of motor vehicles.
mo·tor·car (moh-tŏr-kahr) n. an automobile.
mo·tor·cy·cle (moh-tŏr-sı-kĕl) n. a two-wheeled motor-driven road vehicle that cannot be driven by pedals. **motorcycle** v. (**mo·tor·cy·cled, mo·tor·cy·cling**) to drive or ride on a motorcycle. **mo'tor·cy·clist** n.
mo·tor·ist (moh-tŏ-rist) n. the driver of an automobile.
mo·tor·ize (moh-tŏ-rız) v. (**mo·tor·ized, mo·tor·iz·ing**) 1. to equip with a motor or motors. 2. to equip (troops) with motor vehicles. **mo·tor·i·za·tion** (moh-tŏ-ri-zay-shŏn) n.
mo·tor·man (moh-tŏr-măn) n. (pl. **men,** pr. -mĕn) a driver of a subway train, trolley car, etc.
mot·tle (mot-ĕl) v. (**mot·tled, mot·tling**) to mark or pattern with irregular patches of color.
mot·to (mot-oh) n. (pl. **-toes, -tos**) a short sentence or phrase adopted as a rule of conduct or as expressing the aims and ideals of a family or country or institution etc.
moue (moo) n. a pouting facial expression.
mound (mownd) n. a mass of piled-up earth or stones, a small hill; *pitcher's mound,* the elevated ground on which a baseball pitcher stands when pitching.
mount¹ (mownt) n. a mountain or hill, *Mount Everest.*
mount² v. 1. to ascend, to go upward, to rise to a higher level. 2. to get or put on to a horse etc. for riding, to provide with a horse for riding. 3. to increase in amount or total or intensity, *the death toll mounted.* 4. to put into place on a support, to fix in position for use or display or study. 5. to take action to bring into being; *mount an offensive,* to arrange and begin it. 6. to place on guard, *mount sentries around the palace; mount guard over it,* keep watch to protect it. **mount** n. 1. a horse for riding. 2. something on which a thing is mounted for support or display etc.
moun·tain (mown-tīn) n. 1. a mass of land that rises to a great height, especially of over one thousand feet. 2. a large heap or pile, a huge quantity. ☐**mountain ash,** a species of ash bearing red or orange berries and white flowers. **mountain chain,** a connected series of mountains. **mountain dew,** whiskey, especially when illicitly distilled. **mountain goat,** a white goatlike animal of the Rocky Mountains and north to Alaska. **mountain laurel,** a North American evergreen shrub with white flowers and glossy leaves. **mountain lion,** a puma. **mountain range,** a line of mountains connected by high ground.
moun·tain·eer (mown-tī-neer) n. a person who is skilled in mountain climbing.
moun·tain·eer·ing (mown-tī-neer-ing) n. the sport of climbing mountains.
moun·tain·ous (mown-tī-nŭs) adj. 1. full of mountains, *mountainous country.* 2. huge.
moun·tain·side (mown-tīn-sıd) n. the slope of a mountain below the summit.
moun·tain·top (mown-tīn-top) n. the summit of a mountain.
moun·te·bank (mown-tĕ-bangk) n. a swindler or charlatan.
mount·ed (mown-tid) adj. serving on horseback, *mounted police.*
Moun·tie (mown-tee) n. (*informal*) a member of the Royal Canadian Mounted Police.

mount·ing (mown-ting) *n.* a mount, setting, or support for something.

mourn (mohrn) *v.* to feel or express sorrow for a person who has died or regret for a thing that is lost or past.

mourn·er (mohr-nĕr) *n.* a person who mourns, one who attends a funeral.

mourn·ful (mohrn-fŭl) *adj.* sorrowful, showing grief. **mourn'ful·ly** *adv.* **mourn'ful·ness** *n.*

mourn·ing (mohr-ning) *n.* 1. black or dark clothes worn as a conventional sign of bereavement. 2. the period during which a death is mourned.

mouse (mows) *n.* (*pl.* **mice**) 1. a small rodent with a long thin tail. 2. a shy or timid person. 3. (*slang*) a black eye.

mouse-col·ored (mows-kul-ŏrd) *adj.* dull grayish-brown.

mous·er (mow-zĕr) *n.* a cat as a hunter of mice.

mouse·trap (mows-trap) *n.* 1. a trap for catching mice. 2. a stratagem for trapping or deceiving an unwary opponent. □**build a better mouse-trap,** to improve on an existing product.

mous·ing (mow-sing) *n.* hunting mice.

mous·sa·ka (moo-sah-kah) *n.* a Greek dish consisting of layers of ground lamb and eggplant, usually topped with cheese sauce.

mousse (moos) *n.* 1. a dish of cream or a similar substance flavored with fruit, chocolate, etc. 2. meat or fish purée mixed with cream etc. and shaped in a mold.

mousse·line (moos-leen) *n.* 1. muslin. 2. a kind of thin soft dress material.

mous·tache = mustache.

mous·y, mous·ey (mow-see) *adj.* 1. mouse-colored. 2. quiet and shy or timid. **mous'i·ness** *n.*

mouth (mowth) *n.* (*pl.* **mouths,** *pr.* mowth*z*) 1. the opening in the face through which food is taken in. 2. the opening of a bag, cave, cannon, trumpet, etc. 3. the place where a river enters the sea. **mouth** (mow*th*) *v.* 1. to form (words) with the lips without speaking them aloud. 2. to declaim pompously or with exaggerated distinctness. □**big mouth,** *see* **big. down in the mouth,** *see* **down. keep one's mouth shut,** (*slang*) to refrain from revealing a secret. **mouth organ,** a harmonica. **out of a person's own mouth,** by using his own words. **put one's money where one's mouth is,** (*informal*) to be ready to support one's opinions by action. **put words into a person's mouth,** to tell him what to say; to represent him as having said this. **take the words out of a person's mouth,** to say what he was about to say.

mouth·ful (mowth-fuul) *n.* (*pl.* **-fuls,** *pr.* -fuulz) 1. an amount that fills the mouth. 2. a small quantity of food etc. 3. a lengthy word or phrase, one that is difficult to utter. 4. (*slang*) an important statement, *you said a mouthful.*

mouth·piece (mowth-pees) *n.* 1. the part of a device or musical instrument etc. that is placed between or near the lips. 2. (*slang*) a person who speaks on behalf of another or others, a lawyer.

mouth·wash (mowth-wawsh) *n.* a liquid for cleansing the mouth.

mouth·wa·ter·ing (mowth-waw-tĕ-ring) *adj.* so appetizing as to cause saliva to flow.

mou·ton (moo-ton) *n.* 1. a sheepskin sheared and processed to resemble seal or beaver. 2. a coat made of this.

mov·a·ble (moo-vă-bĕl) *adv.* able to be moved.

□**movable feast,** a religious celebration that changes its date each year (such as Easter).

move (moov) *v.* (**moved, mov·ing**) 1. to change or cause to change in position or place or posture. 2. to be or cause to be in motion. 3. to change one's place or residence. 4. to cause (bowels) to empty, to be emptied thus. 5. to make progress, *the work moves slowly.* 6. to make a move at chess etc. 7. to provoke a reaction or emotion in, *moved her to laughter; felt very moved,* very affected with emotion. 8. to prompt or incline, to motivate, *what moved them to invite us?; he works as the spirit moves him,* only when he chooses. 9. to put forward formally for discussion and decision at a meeting. 10. to initiate some action, *unless the employers move quickly, there will be a strike.* 11. to live or be active in a particular group, *she moves in the best circles.* 12. (*slang*) to sell (merchandise).

move *n.* 1. the act or process of moving. 2. the moving of a piece in chess etc., a player's turn to do this, *it's your move.* 3. a calculated action done to achieve some purpose, *a move toward settling the dispute.* □**get a move on,** (*slang*) to hurry. **move in,** to take possession of a new dwelling place etc. **move out,** to give up possession of a dwelling place etc.; to leave a bivouac or fortified position to go into combat etc., *the regiment moved out at dawn.* **move over** *or* **up,** to alter position in order to make room for another. **on the move,** moving from one place to another; progressing.

move·a·ble = movable.

move·ment (moov-mĕnt) *n.* 1. moving, being moved. 2. action, activity, *watch every movement.* 3. the moving parts in a mechanism, especially of a clock or watch. 4. a series of combined actions by a group to achieve some purpose, the group itself, *the Women's Lib movement.* 5. a trend, *the movement toward more casual styles in fashion.* 6. market activity in some commodity; *the movement in stocks and bonds,* their rise and fall in price. 7. one of the principal divisions in a musical work. 8. emptying of the bowels, feces.

mov·er (moo-vĕr) *n.* 1. one who moves. 2. a person or company in the business of moving furniture etc. from one residence etc. to another. 3. (*slang*) a person who makes progress.

mov·ie (moo-vee) *n.* (*informal*) 1. a motion picture. 2. a motion-picture theater. 3. *the movies,* the motion-picture industry.

mov·ing (moo-ving) *adj.* affecting the emotions, *a very moving story.* □**moving picture,** a motion picture. **moving sidewalk,** a structure like a conveyor belt for carrying pedestrians. **moving van,** a truck used by furniture movers.

mow[1] (moh) *v.* (**mowed, mown, mow·ing**) to cut down (grass or grain etc.), to cut the grass etc. from, *mow the lawn.* □**mow down,** to kill or destroy at random or in great numbers.

mow[2] (mow) *n.* 1. a stack of hay or grain. 2. the place in the barn where mows are kept.

mow·er (moh-ĕr) *n.* a person or machine that mows.

Mo·zam·bique (moh-zam-beek) a country in southeastern Africa.

moz·za·rel·la (mot-să-rel-ă) *n.* a white mild unripened soft Italian cheese.

MP *abbr.* military policeman.

mp. *abbr.* melting point.

M.P. *abbr.* 1. Member of Parliament. 2. military policeman.

MPG, mpg *abbr.* miles per gallon.

mph, m.p.h. *abbr.* miles per hour.
Mr. (mis-tĕr) *n.* (*pl.* **Messrs.,** *pr.* mes-ĕrz) the title prefixed to a man's name or to the name of his office, *Mr. Jones; Mr. Chairman.*
Mrs. (mis-iz) *n.* (*pl.* **Mrs.**) the title prefixed to a married woman's name.
MS, ms *abbr.* manuscript.
Ms. (miz) *n.* the title prefixed to a woman's name without distinction of married or unmarried status.
msec. *abbr.* millisecond(s).
MSG *abbr.* monosodium glutamate.
msg. *abbr.* message.
Msgr. *abbr.* Monsignor.
MSgt. *abbr.* master sergeant.
M.S.L. *abbr.* mean sea level.
MSS, mss *abbr.* manuscripts.
MST *abbr.* Mountain Standard Time.
Mt. *abbr.* Mount.
mtg. *abbr.* 1. meeting. 2. mortgage.
mtge. *abbr.* mortgage.
mu (myoo) *n.* the twelfth letter of the Greek alphabet (M μ).
much (much) *adj.* existing in great quantity. **much** *n.* a great quantity. **much** *adv.* 1. in a great degree, *much to my surprise.* 2. approximately, *much the same.* □**I thought as much,** I thought so. **make much of,** *see* **make. much as,** even though, however much, *I can't go, much as I should like to.* **not much,** *(slang)* certainly not; *not much of a poet,* not a good one.
mu·ci·lage (myoo-sĭ-lij) *n.* a type of adhesive. **mu·ci·lag·i·nous** (myoo-sĭ-laj-ĭ-nŭs) *adj.*
muck (muk) *n.* 1. farmyard manure. 2. *(informal)* dirt, filth. 3. *(informal)* untidy things, a mess. **muck** *v.* to make dirty, to mess. □**muck about** *or* **around,** *(slang)* to mess about. **muck out,** to remove muck from, *mucking out the stable.* **muck up,** *(slang)* to spoil.
muck·rak·er (muk-ray-kĕr) *n.* 1. a person who looks for and exposes scandal. 2. a book that exposes scandal in government, business, etc.
muck·rak·ing (muk-ray-king) *n.* looking for and exposing scandal.
muck·y (muk-ee) *adj.* (**muck·i·er, muck·i·est**) covered with muck, dirty.
mu·cous (myoo-kŭs) *adj.* of or like mucus, covered with mucus. □**mucous membrane,** the moist skin lining the nose, mouth, throat, etc. ▷Do not confuse *mucous* (adjective) with *mucus* (noun).
mu·cus (myoo-kŭs) *n.* the moist sticky substance that lubricates and forms a protective covering on the inner surface of hollow organs of the body. ▷Do not confuse *mucus* (noun) with *mucous* (adjective).
mud (mud) *n.* wet soft earth. □**his name is mud,** *(informal)* he is in disgrace. **mud flat,** a stretch of muddy land left uncovered at low tide.
mud·dle (mud-ĕl) *v.*(**mud·dled, mud·dling**) 1. to bring into a state of confusion and disorder. 2. to confuse (a person) mentally. 3. to confuse or mistake (one thing for another). **muddle** *n.* a muddled condition, disorder. **mud'dler** *n.* □**muddle on** *or* **along,** to work in a haphazard way. **muddle through,** to succeed in the end in spite of one's inefficiency.
mud·dle·head·ed (mud-ĕl-hed-id) *adj.* liable to muddle things, mentally confused.
mud·dy (mud-ee) *adj.* (**mud·di·er, mud·di·est**) 1. like mud, full of mud. 2. (of color) not

clear or pure. 3. mentally confused or unclear. **muddy** *v.* (**mud·died, mud·dy·ing**) to make muddy. **mud'di·ness** *n.*
mud·guard (mud-gahrd) *n.* a flap behind the wheel of a vehicle to prevent mud etc. from being thrown up as it travels.
mud·pup·py (mud-pup-ee) *n.* (*pl.* **-pies**) a large salamander.
mud·room (mud-room) *n.* *(informal)* a room near a side door of a home in which damp outer clothing may be removed before entering another room of the house.
mud·sling·ing (mud-sling-ing) *n.* *(slang)* speaking evil of someone, trying to damage someone's reputation. **mud'sling·er** *n.*
Muen·ster (mun-stĕr, muun-) *n.* a mild white soft cheese.
mu·ez·zin (myoo-ez-in) *n.* a man who proclaims the hours of prayer for Muslims, usually from a minaret.
muff[1] (muf) *n.* a short tubelike covering of fur etc. into which both hands are thrust from opposite ends to keep them warm.
muff[2] *v.* *(informal)* to bungle or blunder, to miss (a catch) in a game. **muff** *n.* *(informal)* a failure to catch a ball.
muf·fin (muf-in) *n.* a light round cake, eaten toasted and buttered.
muf·fle (muf-ĕl) *v.* (**muf·fled, muf·fling**) 1. to wrap or cover for warmth or protection. 2. to wrap up or pad in order to deaden the sound of. 3. to deaden, to make less loud or less distinct, *fog muffled the sound.*
muf·fler (muf-lĕr) *n.* 1. a scarf worn around the neck for warmth. 2. something used to muffle sound, *an engine muffler.*
muf·ti (muf-tee) *n.* plain clothes worn by one who has the right to wear a uniform, *in mufti.*
mug (mug) *n.* 1. a large drinking vessel (usually with a handle) for use without a saucer. 2. its contents. 3. *(slang)* the face or mouth. 4. *(slang)* a person who is easily deceived. 5. *(slang)* a ruffian or thug. **mug** *v.* (**mugged, mug·ging**) 1. to assault, to rob with violence, especially in a public place. 2. *(slang)* to photograph (a person under arrest) for police records. 3. *(slang)* to make faces, especially before an audience or camera. **mug'ger** *n.* □**mug shot,** *(slang)* an identification photograph made by police.
mug·ging (mug-ing) *n.* an assault or robbery with violence, especially in a public place.
mug·gy (mug-ee) *adj.* (**mug·gi·er, mug·gi·est**) oppressively damp and warm, *a muggy day; muggy weather.* **mug'gi·ness** *n.*
mug·wump (mug-wump) *n.* 1. a person who stands aloof from party politics. 2. a person who avoids declaring support for either side in an election etc.
Mu·ham·mad (muu-ham-ăd) *n.* the founder of Islam.
Mu·ham·mad·an (muu-ham-ă-dăn) *n.* a Muslim. **Mu·ham'mad·an·ism** *n.*
muk·luk (muk-luk) *n.* an Eskimo boot made of the skin of the reindeer or seal.
mu·lat·to (mŭ-lat-oh) *n.* (*pl.* **-toes**) a person who has one white and one black parent.
mul·ber·ry (mul-ber-ee) *n.* (*pl.* **-ries**) 1. a purple or white fruit rather like a blackberry. 2. the tree that bears it. 3. dull purplish red.
mulch (mulch) *n.* a mixture of wet straw, grass, leaves, etc., spread on the ground to protect plants

or retain moisture. **mulch** v. to cover with a mulch.

mulct (mulkt) v. to take away money from (a person), as by a fine or taxation, or by dubious means.

mule[1] (myool) n. an animal that is the offspring of a horse and a donkey, known for its stubbornness. □**mule deer,** a deer with long ears found in western North America.

mule[2] n. a backless slipper.

mu·le·teer (myoo-lĕ-teer) n. a mule driver.

mu·li·eb·ri·ty (myoo-li-eb-ri-tee) n. womanhood, normal characteristics of a woman.

mul·ish (myoo-lish) adj. stubborn. **mul'ish·ly** adv. **mul'ish·ness** n.

mull[1] (mul) v. to heat (wine or beer etc.) with sugar and spices, as a drink.

mull[2] v. **mull over,** to think over, to ponder, mulled it over.

mul·lah (mul-ä) n. a Muslim who is learned in Islamic theology and sacred law.

mul·lein (mul-in) n. a biennial herb with downy leaves and tall spikes of yellow flowers.

mul·let (mul-it) n. a kind of fish used for food.

mul·li·gan (mul-i-găn) n. (also **mulligan stew**) (slang) a stew of odds and ends of meat, vegetables, etc.

mul·li·ga·taw·ny (mul-i-gă-taw-nee) n. a highly seasoned soup flavored like curry.

mul·lion (mul-yŏn) n. an upright strip between the panes of a tall window.

multi- prefix many.

mul·ti·cel·lu·lar (mul-ti-sel-yŭ-lăr) adj. having many cells.

mul·ti·col·ored (mul-ti-kul-ŏrd) adj. of many colors.

mul·ti·di·men·sion·al (mul-tee-di-men-shŏ-năl) adj. (of a problem, a personality, etc.) having many dimensions.

mul·ti·di·rec·tion·al (mul-tee-di-rek-shŏ-năl) adj. able to send or receive or to be sent or received in more than one direction, a multidirectional signal; a multidirectional antenna.

mul·ti·en·gined (mul-tee-en-jind) adj. having three or more engines.

mul·ti·fac·et·ed (mul-tee-fas-ĕ-tid) adj. having many facets, complex.

mul·ti·fam·i·ly (mul-tee-fam-ĭ-lee) adj. designed for several families, multifamily dwellings.

mul·ti·far·i·ous (mul-ti-fair-i-ŭs) adj. very varied, of many kinds, his multifarious duties. **mul·ti·far'i·ous·ly** adv. **mul·ti·far'i·ous·ness** n.

mul·ti·form (mul-ti-form) adj. having many forms, of many kinds. **mul·ti·for·mi·ty** (mul-ti-for-mi-tee) n.

mul·ti·lat·er·al (mul-ti-lat-ĕ-răl) adj. (of an agreement etc.) involving three or more parties.

mul·ti·lev·el (mul-tee-lev-ĕl) adj. having several levels, a multilevel apartment.

mul·ti·lin·gual (mul-ti-ling-gwăl) adj. in or using many languages. **mul·ti·lin'gual·ism** n.

mul·ti·me·di·a (mul-ti-mee-di-ä) adj. using several media; multimedia instruction, employing books, film, etc.; the candidate launched a multimedia campaign, used radio and television commercials and newspaper advertisements.

mul·ti·mil·lion·aire (mul-tee-mil-yŏ-nair) n. a person with a fortune of several millions.

mul·ti·na·tion·al (mul-ti-nash-ŏ-năl) adj. (of a business company) operating in several countries. **multinational** n. a multinational company.

mul·ti·ple (mul-tĭ-pĕl) adj. having several or many parts or elements or components. **multiple** n. a quantity that contains another (a factor) a number of times without remainder, is a multiple of. □**multiple choice,** a test question accompanied by several possible answers from which the correct answer or answers are to be selected. **multiple sclerosis,** a chronic progressive disease in which patches of tissue harden in the brain or spinal cord, causing partial or complete paralysis.

mul·ti·plex (mul-ti-pleks) adj. 1. having many parts or forms, consisting of many elements. 2. involving simultaneous transmission of several messages in a channel of communication.

mul·ti·pli·cand (mul-ti-pli-kand) n. a quantity to be multiplied by a multiplier.

mul·ti·pli·ca·tion (mul-ti-pli-kay-shŏn) n. multiplying, being multiplied. □**multiplication sign,** the sign × (as in 2 × 3) or · (as in 2a · 3b) indicating that one quantity is to be multiplied by another. **multiplication tables,** a series of lists showing the results when a number is multiplied by each number (especially 1 to 12) in turn.

mul·ti·plic·i·ty (mul-ti-plis-i-tee) n. a great variety.

mul·ti·pli·er (mul-tĭ-plɪ-ĕr) n. the number by which a quantity is multiplied.

mul·ti·ply (mul-tĭ-plɪ) v. (**mul·ti·plied, mul·ti·ply·ing**) 1. (in mathematics) to take a specified quantity a specified number of times and find the quantity produced, multiply 6 by 4 and get 24. 2. to make or become many; multiply examples, to produce large numbers of examples; rabbits multiply rapidly, they increase in number by breeding.

mul·ti·pur·pose (mul-ti-pur-pŏs) adj. serving more than one purpose, a multipurpose vehicle.

mul·ti·ra·cial (mul-ti-ray-shăl) adj. composed of people of many races, a multiracial society.

mul·ti·sense (mul-ti-sens) adj. (of words) having several meanings.

mul·ti·stage (mul-ti-stayj) adj. (of a rocket etc.) having several stages of operation; a multistage rocket, one that uses three or more engines in succession.

mul·ti·sto·ry (mul-ti-stoh-ree) adj. having several stories, multistory apartments.

mul·ti·tude (mul-ti-tood) n. a great number of things or people; the multitude, the common people.

mul·ti·tu·di·nous (mul-ti-too-dĭ-nŭs) adj. very numerous.

mul·ti·ver·si·ty (mul-ti-vur-si-tee) n. (pl. -ties) a large university with many campuses.

mul·ti·vi·ta·min (mul-ti-vɪ-tă-min) n. a tablet or liquid preparation combining several vitamins.

mum[1] (mum) adj. silent, keep mum; mum's the word, say nothing about this.

mum[2] n. (informal) a chrysanthemum.

mum·ble (mum-bĕl) v. (**mum·bled, mum·bling**) to speak or utter indistinctly. **mumble** n. indistinct speech. **mum'bler** n.

mum·ble·ty-peg (mum-bĕl-ti-peg) n. a children's game played with a pocketknife which is tossed point-first into the ground.

mum·bo jum·bo (mum-boh jum-boh) 1. meaningless ritual. 2. words or actions that are made deliberately obscure in order to mystify or confuse people.

mum·mer (mum-ĕr) n. an actor in a traditional mime. **mum'mer·y** n.

mum·mi·fy (mum-ĭ-fɪ) v. (**mum·mi·fied, mum·**

mi·fy·ing) to preserve (a corpse) by embalming it as in ancient Egypt. mum·mi·fi·ca·tion (mum-ĭ-fĭ-kay-shŏn) n.

mum·my¹ (mum-ee) n. (pl. -mies) 1. the body of a person or animal embalmed for burial so as to preserve it, especially in ancient Egypt. 2. a dried-up body preserved from decay by an accident of nature.

mummy² n. (pl. -mies) (informal) mother.

mumps (mumps) n. a virus disease that causes painful swellings in the neck.

mun., munic. abbr. municipal.

munch (munch) v. to chew steadily and vigorously.

mun·dane (mun-dayn, mun-dayn) adj. 1. dull, routine. 2. worldly, not spiritual. mun·dane'ly adv.

mu·nic·i·pal (myoo-nis-ĭ-păl) adj. of a town or city or its self-government.

mu·nic·i·pal·i·ty (myoo-nis-ĭ-pal-ĭ-tee) n. (pl. -ties) a self-governing town or district.

mu·nif·i·cent (myoo-nif-ĭ-sĕnt) adj. splendidly generous. mu·nif'i·cent·ly adv. mu·nif'i·cence n.

mu·ni·tions (myoo-nish-ŏnz) n. pl. military weapons and ammunition and equipment etc.

mu·ral (myoor-ăl) adj. of or on a wall. mural n. a wall painting, a fresco.

mur·der (mur-dĕr) n. 1. the intentional and unlawful killing of one person by another. 2. (informal) something very difficult or unpleasant or painful. murder v. 1. to kill (a person) unlawfully and intentionally. 2. (informal) to ruin by bad performance or pronunciation etc. mur'der·er n. mur·der·ess (mur-dĕ-ris) n. fem.

mur·der·ous (mur-dĕ-rŭs) adj. 1. involving murder, capable of or intent on murder. 2. very angry, suggesting murder, a murderous look. mur'der·ous·ly adv.

mu·ri·at·ic (myoor-i-at-ik) acid hydrochloric acid.

murk·y (murk-kee) adj. (murk·i·er, murk·i·est) 1. dark, gloomy. 2. (of liquid) muddy, full of sediment. 3. unclear, murky prose. murk'i·ness n.

mur·mur (mur-mŭr) n. 1. a low continuous sound. 2. a low abnormal sound made by the heart. 3. softly spoken words. 4. a subdued expression of feeling, murmurs of discontent. murmur v. to make a murmur, to speak or utter in a low voice. mur'mur·er n. mur'mur·ous adj.

mur·rain (mur-in) n. 1. an infectious disease in cattle. 2. (old use) a plague.

mus. abbr. 1. museum. 2. music. 3. musical. 4. musician.

mus·cat (mus-kat) n. a sweet grape.

Mus·cat (mus-kat) the capital of Oman.

mus·ca·tel (mus-kă-tel) n. a sweet dessert wine made from muscats.

mus·cle (mus-ĕl) n. 1. a band or bundle of fibrous tissue able to contract and relax and so produce movement in an animal body. 2. a part of the body made chiefly of such tissue. 3. muscular power. 4. strength, labor unions with plenty of muscle. muscle v. (mus·cled, mus·cling) muscle in, (slang) to force one's way. mus'cled adj.

mus·cle·bound (mus-ĕl-bownd) adj. with muscles stiff and inelastic through excessive exercise or training.

Mus·co·vite (mus-kŏ-vɪt) adj. of Moscow. Muscovite n. a native or inhabitant of Moscow.

mus·cu·lar (mus-kyŭ-lăr) adj. 1. of or affecting the muscles, muscular rheumatism. 2. having well-developed muscles. mus'cu·lar·ly adv. mus·cu·lar·i·ty (mus-kyŭ-lar-i-tee) n.

mus·cu·la·ture (mus-kyŭ-lă-chŭr) n. the muscular system of a body or organ.

muse (myooz) v. (mused, mus·ing) to ponder.

Muse (myooz) n. 1. one of the nine sister goddesses in Greek and Roman mythology, presiding over branches of learning and the arts. 2. a poet's inspiring goddess, a poet's genius.

mu·sette (myoo-zet) n. (also musette bag) a small knapsack.

mu·se·um (myoo-zee-ŭm) n. a building or room in which antiques or other objects of historical or scientific interest are collected and exhibited. □museum piece, a fine specimen suitable for a museum; (contemptuous) an antiquated person or thing.

mush¹ (mush) n. 1. soft pulp. 2. boiled corn meal. 3. (slang) feeble sentimentality.

mush² v. to journey across snow with a dog sled; (as a command to sled dogs) get moving! mush n. such a journey.

mush·room (mush-room) n. an edible fungus with a stem and domed cap, noted for its rapid growth. mushroom v. 1. to spring up rapidly in large numbers, fast-food restaurants mushroomed. 2. to rise and spread in the shape of a mushroom. □mushroom cloud, a cloud of mushroom shape, especially from a nuclear explosion.

mush·y (mush-ee) adj. (mush·i·er, mush·i·est) 1. as or like mush. 2. feebly sentimental. mush'i·ness n.

mu·sic (myoo-zik) n. 1. the art of arranging the sounds of voice(s) or instrument(s) or both in a pleasing sequence or combination. 2. the sound(s) or composition(s) produced, a written or printed score for this. 3. any pleasant sound or series of sounds, such as bird song. □face the music, see face. music box, a box with a mechanical device that produces music by means of a toothed cylinder that strikes a comb-like metal plate. music hall, a hall or theater used for variety entertainment.

mu·si·cal (myoo-zi-kăl) adj. 1. of music; musical instruments, devices producing music by means of tuned strings or membranes or air in pipes, or electronically. 2. fond of or skilled in music. 3. accompanied by music, set to music. musical n. a musical comedy, a motion picture film resembling this. mu'si·cal·ly adv. □musical chairs, a game in which players walk around chairs (one fewer than the number of players) until the music stops, when the one who finds no chair is eliminated and a chair is removed before the next round. musical comedy, a light play in which songs and dancing alternate with the dialogue.

mu·si·cale (myoo-zi-kal) n. a social entertainment featuring music.

mu·si·cian (myoo-zish-ăn) n. a person who is skilled at music, one whose profession is music. mu·si'cian·ship n. proficiency in performing music.

mu·si·col·o·gy (myoo-zi-kol-ŏ-jee) n. the study of music other than that directed to proficiency in performance or composition. mu·si·col'o·gist n. mu·si·co·log·i·cal (myoo-zi-kŏ-loj-i-kăl) adj. mu·si·co·log'i·cal·ly adv.

musk (musk) n. 1. a substance secreted by male musk deer or certain other animals, or produced artificially, used as the basis of perfumes. 2. a plant with a musky smell. ☐**musk deer**, a small hornless deer of central Asia. **musk gland**, the gland of the male musk deer which secretes musk. **musk ox**, a shaggy animal with curved horns native to Arctic America. **musk rose**, a rambling European rose with large white flowers that have a musky fragrance.

mus·keg (mus-keg) *n.* a level swamp or bog in northern North America.

mus·kel·lunge (mus-kĕ-lunj) *n.* (*pl.* **-lunge**) a large North American pike especially prevalent in the Great Lakes.

mus·ket (mus-kit) *n.* a large-caliber gun with a long barrel formerly used by infantry, now replaced by the rifle.

mus·ket·eer (mus-kĕ-teer) *n.* a soldier armed with a musket.

mus·ket·ry (mus-ki-tree) *n.* 1. the art of firing muskets. 2. muskets or those who fire them.

musk·mel·on (musk-mel-ŏn) *n.* any of several varieties of oblong or round fruits, as the cantaloupe.

musk·rat (musk-rat) *n.* a large ratlike water animal of North America, valued for its fur.

musk·y (mus-kee) *adj.* (**musk·i·er, musk·i·est**) smelling like musk. **musk'i·ness** *n.*

Mus·lim (muz-lim) *n.* a person who believes in the Islamic faith. **Muslim** *adj.* of Muslims or their faith.

mus·lin (muz-lin) *n.* a kind of thin cotton cloth.

muss (mus) *v.* (also **muss up**) (*informal*) to make untidy.

mus·sel (mus-ĕl) *n.* a kind of bivalve mollusk, the marine variety of which is edible.

Mus·sul·man (mus-ŭl-măn) *adj.* & *n.* (*pl.* **-mans**) (*old use*) Muslim.

must (must) *auxiliary verb* used to express necessity or obligation (*you must go*), certainty (*night must fall*), insistence (*I must repeat, all precautions were taken*). **must** *n.* (*informal*) a thing that should not be overlooked or missed, *the exhibition is a must.*

mus·tache (mŭ-stash, mus-tash) *n.* hair allowed to grow on a man's upper lip.

mus·tang (mus-tang) *n.* a wild horse of Mexico and California.

mus·tard (mus-tărd) *n.* 1. a plant with yellow flowers and with black or white sharp-tasting seeds in long pods. 2. these seeds ground and made into paste as a condiment. 3. darkish yellow color. **mustard** *adj.* darkish yellow. ☐**mustard gas**, a kind of poison gas that burns the skin.

mus·ter (mus-tĕr) *v.* 1. to assemble or cause to assemble. 2. to summon, *muster or muster up one's strength.* **muster** *n.* an assembly or gathering of people or things. ☐**muster out**, to discharge (military personnel) from service. **pass muster**, to be accepted as adequate.

must·n't (mus-ĕnt) = must not.

mus·ty (mus-tee) *adj.* (**mus·ti·er, mus·ti·est**) 1. stale, smelling or tasting moldy. 2. antiquated. **mus'ti·ly** *adv.* **mus'ti·ness** *n.*

mu·ta·ble (myoo-tă-bĕl) *adj.* liable to change, fickle. **mu·ta·bil·i·ty** (myoo-tă-bil-i-tee) *n.*

mu·tant (myoo-tănt) *n.* a living thing that differs basically from its parents as a result of genetic change. **mutant** *adj.* differing in this way.

mu·tate (myoo-tayt) *v.* (**mu·tat·ed, mu·tat·ing**) to undergo or cause to undergo mutation. **mu·ta·tive** (myoo-tă-tiv) *adj.*

mu·ta·tion (myoo-tay-shŏn) *n.* 1. change or altera-

tion in form. 2. a mutant. **mu·ta'tion·al** *adj.*

mu·ta·tis mu·tan·dis (moo-tah-tees moo-tahn-dees) when the necessary alteration of details has been made (in comparing things). ▷Latin.

mute (myoot) *adj.* 1. silent, refraining from speaking. 2. not having the power of speech, dumb. 3. not expressed in words, *in mute adoration.* **mute** *n.* 1. a person who is mute. 2. a device fitted to a musical instrument to deaden its sound. **mute** *v.* (**mut·ed, mut·ing**) to deaden or muffle the sound of. **mute'ly** *adv.* **mute'ness** *n.* ▷Do not confuse *mute* with *moot.*

mu·ti·late (myoo-tĭ-layt) *v.* (**mu·ti·lat·ed, mu·ti·lat·ing**) to injure or disfigure by cutting off an important part. **mu'ti·la·tor** *n.* **mu·ti·la·tion** (myoo-tĭ-lay-shŏn) *n.*

mu·ti·neer (myoo-tĭ-neer) *n.* a person who mutinies.

mu·ti·nous (myoo-tĭ-nŭs) *adj.* rebellious, ready to mutiny. **mu'ti·nous·ly** *adv.*

mu·ti·ny (myoo-tĭ-nee) *n.* (*pl.* **-nies**) open rebellion against authority, especially by members of the armed forces against their officers. **mutiny** *v.* (**mu·ti·nied, mu·ti·ny·ing**) to engage in mutiny.

mutt (mut) *n.* (*slang*) a mongrel dog.

mut·ter (mut-ĕr) *v.* 1. to speak or utter in a low unclear tone. 2. to utter subdued grumbles. **mutter** *n.* muttering, muttered words.

mut·ton (mut-ŏn) *n.* the flesh of sheep as food. **mut'ton·y** *adj.*

mut·ton·chops (mut-ŏn-chops) *n. pl.* side whiskers that are bushy and broad at the bottom, in the shape of a mutton chop.

mu·tu·al (myoo-choo-ăl) *adj.* 1. (of a feeling or action) felt or done by each toward the other, *mutual affection; mutual aid.* 2. having the same specified relationship to each other, *mutual enemies.* 3. common to two or more people, *our mutual friend.* **mu'tu·al·ly** *adv.* ☐**mutual fund**, an investment company that invests shareholders' pooled funds in various types of securities.

muu·muu (moo-moo) *n.* a loose brightly colored dress.

Mu·zak (myoo-zak) *n.* (*trademark*) piped music, recorded light music as a background.

muz·zle (muz-ĕl) *n.* 1. the projecting nose and jaws of certain animals (such as dogs). 2. the open end of a firearm. 3. a strap or wire etc. put over an animal's head to prevent it from biting or feeding. **muzzle** *v.* (**muz·zled, muz·zling**) 1. to put a muzzle on (an animal). 2. to silence, to prevent (a person or newspaper etc.) from expressing opinions freely.

muz·zle·load·er (muz-ĕl-loh-dĕr) *n.* a gun that is loaded through the muzzle.

mV *abbr.* millivolt(s).

MV *abbr.* megavolt(s).

Mv *symbol* mendelevium.

MVP *abbr.* (in baseball) most valuable player.

mW *abbr.* milliwatt(s).

MW *abbr.* megawatt(s).

my (mɪ) *adj.* 1. of or belonging to me. 2. used in forms of address (*my lord, my dear*), or exclamations of surprise etc. (*my God!*).

My·ce·nae·an (mɪ-sĕ-nee-ăn) *adj.* of a Bronze Age civilization of Greece, remains of which were found at Mycenae in the Peloponnese and elsewhere. **Mycenaean** *n.* 1. a member of this civilization. 2. its language.

my·col·o·gy (mɪ-kol-ŏ-jee) *n.* the study of fungi.

my·col′o·gist *n.* **my·co·log·i·cal** (mɪ-kŏ-loj-i-kăl) *adj.*

my·e·li·tis (mɪ-ĕ-lɪ-tis) *n.* inflammation of the spinal cord.

My·lar (mɪ-lahr) *n.* *(trademark)* polyester film used in recording tape, electrical insulation, etc.

my·na, my·nah (mɪ-nă) *n.* an Asian bird of the starling family.

my·o·pi·a (mɪ-oh-pi-ă) *n.* 1. inability to see clearly what is close. 2. *(informal)* lack of foresight. **my·op·ic** (mɪ-op-ik) *adj.* **my·op′i·cal·ly** *adv.*

my·ri·ad (mir-i-ăd) *n.* a vast number. **myriad** *adj.*

myr·mi·don (mur-mĭ-don) *n.* a henchman.

myrrh (mur) *n.* a kind of gum resin used in perfumes and medicine and incense.

myr·tle (mur-tĕl) *n.* an evergreen shrub with dark leaves and scented white flowers.

my·self (mɪ-self) *pronoun* corresponding to *I* and *me*, used in the same ways as *himself.*

mys·te·ri·ous (mi-steer-i-ŭs) *adj.* full of mystery, puzzling or obscure. **mys·te′ri·ous·ly** *adv.* **mys·te′ri·ous·ness** *n.*

mys·ter·y (mis-tĕ-ree) *n.* (*pl.* **-ter·ies**) 1. a matter that remains unexplained or secret. 2. the quality of being unexplained or obscure, *its origins are wrapped in mystery.* 3. the practice of making a secret of things. 4. a religious truth that is beyond human powers to understand. 5. a story or play that deals with a puzzling crime.

mys·tic (mis-tik) *adj.* 1. of hidden or symbolic meaning, especially in religion, *mystic ceremonies.* 2. inspiring a sense of mystery and awe. **mystic** *n.* a person who seeks to obtain union with God by spiritual contemplation and self-surrender. **mys·ti·cal** (mis-ti-kăl) *adj.* 1. of mystics or mysticism. 2. having spiritual meaning or value or symbolism. **mys′ti·cal·ly** *adv.*

mys·ti·cism (mis-ti-siz-ĕm) *n.* 1. mystical quality. 2. being a mystic.

mys·ti·fy (mis-tĭ-fɪ) *v.* (**mys·ti·fied, mys·ti·fy·ing**) to cause (a person) to feel puzzled. **mys·ti·fi·ca·tion** (mis-tĭ-fĭ-kay-shŏn) *n.*

mys·tique (mi-steek) *n.* an aura of mystery or mystical power.

myth (mith) *n.* 1. a traditional story containing ideas or beliefs about ancient times or about natural events (such as the four seasons). 2. such stories collectively, *in myth and legend.* 3. an imaginary person or thing. 4. an idea that forms part of the beliefs of a group or class but is not founded on fact. **myth′ic** *adj.*

myth. *abbr.* 1. mythological. 2. mythology.

myth·i·cal (mith-i-kăl) *adj.* 1. of myths, existing in myths. 2. imaginary, fancied.

my·thol·o·gy (mi-thol-ŏ-jee) *n.* (*pl.* **-gies**) 1. a body of myths, *Greek mythology.* 2. the study of myths. **my·thol′o·gist** *n.* **myth·o·log·i·cal** (mith-ŏ-loj-i-kăl) *adj.*

N

N, n (en) (*pl.* **Ns, N's n's**) the fourteenth letter of the English alphabet.

N *symbol* nitrogen.

n. *abbr.* 1. name. 2. net. 3. neuter. 4. nominative. 5. noon. 6. north. 7. northern. 8. note. 9. noun. 10. number.

N. *abbr.* 1. Navy. 2. noon. 3. (in chemistry) normal. 4. Norse. 5. north. 6. northern. 7. November.

-n *suffix see* **-en.**

Na *symbol* sodium.

N.A. *abbr.* 1. North America. 2. not applicable. 3. not available.

NAACP *abbr.* National Association for the Advancement of Colored People.

nab (nab) *v.* **(nabbed, nab·bing)** *(slang)* 1. to catch (a wrongdoer) in the act, to arrest. 2. to seize, to grab.

na·bob (nay-bob) *n.* 1. a Muslim official or governor under the Mogul empire. 2. *(old use)* a wealthy luxury-loving person, especially a European returned from India with a fortune.

na·celle (nă-sel) *n.* the outer casing of an airplane's engine.

na·cre (nay-kĕr) *n.* a shellfish that yields mother-of-pearl.

na·dir (nay-dĭr) *n.* the lowest point, the time of deepest depression.

nae (nay) *adj. & adv. (Scottish)* no.

nae·vus = **nevus.**

nag¹ (nag) *n. (informal)* a horse.

nag² *v.* **(nagged, nag·ging)** 1. to make scolding remarks to, to find fault continually. 2. (of pain or worry) to be felt persistently. **nag′ger** *n.*

nai·ad (nay-ad) *n.* (*pl.* **-ads, -a·des,** *pr.* -ă-deez) a water nymph.

na·ïf (nah-eef) = **naive.**

nail (nayl) *n.* 1. the layer of horny substance over the outer tip of a finger or toe. 2. a claw or talon. 3. a small metal spike driven in with a hammer to hold things together or as a peg or protection or ornament. **nail** *v.* 1. to fasten with a nail or nails. 2. *(informal)* to catch or arrest, *nailed the intruder.* 3. *(informal)* to hit or strike (a person). □**hit the nail on the head,** *see* **hit. nail down,** to establish clearly; to make (a person) agree to keep to a promise or arrangement etc. or declare his intentions definitely. **nail file, nail scissors,** those designed for shaping and trimming the nails. **nail polish,** a substance for giving a shiny tint to the nails.

nail·brush (nayl-brush) *n.* a brush for scrubbing one's nails.

nail·head (nayl-hed) *n.* an architectural ornament like the head of a nail.

nain·sook (nayn-suuk) *n.* a kind of fine soft cotton fabric, shiny on one side.

Nai·ro·bi (nɪ-roh-bee) the capital of Kenya.

na·ive, na·ïve (nah-eev) *adj.* showing a lack of experience or of informed judgment. **na·ive′ly** *adv.* **na·ive′ness** *n.*

na·ive·té, na·ïve·té (nah-eev-tay) *n.* 1. the state or quality of being naive. 2. a naive action.

na·ked (nay-kid) *adj.* 1. without clothes on, nude. 2. without the usual coverings or ornamentation etc.; *a naked sword,* without its sheath. 3. undisguised, *the naked truth.* **na′ked·ly** *adv.* **na′ked·ness** *n.* □**naked eye,** the eye unassisted by a telescope or microscope etc.

N.A.M. *abbr.* National Association of Manufacturers.

nam·by-pam·by (nam-bee-pam-bee) *adj.* lacking positive character, feeble, not manly. **namby-pamby** *n.* (*pl.* **-bies**) a person of this kind.

name (naym) *n.* 1. a word or words by which a person or animal or place or thing is known or indicated. 2. a reputation, *has got a bad name; made a name for himself,* became famous. 3. a famous person, *the film has some big names in it.* **name** *v.* **(named, nam·ing)** 1. to give a name to. 2. to state the name(s) of. 3. to nominate or appoint to an office etc. 4. to mention or specify; *name your price,* say what price you want; *name the day,* to arrange a date, especially of a woman fixing the date for her wedding. □**call a person names,** to speak abusively to him or about him. **have to one's name,** to possess. **in name only,** so called but not so in reality. **in the name of,** invoking or calling to witness, *in the name of God, what are you doing?;* by authority of, *open in the name of the law!;* under the designation or pretense of, *did it all in the name of friendship.* **name day,** the day of a saint after whom a person is named. **the name of the game,** *(informal)* the purpose or essence of an activity.

name·a·ble (nay-mă-bĕl) *adj.* able to be named.

name-drop·ping (naym-drop-ing) *n.* mention of famous people's names in order to impress others by implying that one is familiar with such people. **name′-drop·per** *n.*

name·less (naym-lis) *adj.* 1. having no name or no known name. 2. not mentioned by name, anonymous, *others who shall be nameless.* 3. too bad to be named, *nameless horrors.* **name′less·ly** *adv.*

name·ly (naym-lee) *adv.* that is to say, specifically.

name·plate (naym-playt) *n.* a plaque affixed with the name of the occupant.

name·sake (naym-sayk) *n.* a person or thing with the same name as another.

Na·mib·i·a (nă-mib-i-ă) a country in southwest Africa, formerly South West Africa.

nan·keen (nan-keen) *n.* a kind of cotton cloth, originally made in Nanking in China from naturally yellow cotton.

nan·ny (nan-ee) *n.* (*pl.* **-nies**) 1. (chiefly *British*) a child's nurse. 2. a nanny goat. □**nanny goat,** a female goat.

na·no·me·ter (nay-nŏ-mee-tĕr) *n.* a unit of measurement, one billionth of a meter.

na·no·sec·ond (na-nŏ-sek-ŏnd) *n.* a unit of time, one billionth of a second.

nap[1] (nap) *n.* a short sleep or doze, especially during the day. **nap** *v.* **(napped, nap·ping)** to have a nap. □**catch a person napping,** to catch a person off his guard.

nap[2] *n.* short raised fibers on the surface of cloth or leather. **nap'less** *adj.*

na·palm (nay-pahm) *n.* a jellylike gasoline substance used in incendiary bombs, flamethrowers, etc.

nape (nayp) *n.* the back part of the neck.

na·per·y (nay-pĕ-ree) *n.* (*old use*) household or table linen.

naph·tha (naf-thă) *n.* an inflammable oil obtained from coal or petroleum, used in making plastics.

naph·tha·lene (naf-thă-leen) *n.* a strong-smelling white substance obtained from coal tar, used in dyes and as a moth repellent.

nap·kin (nap-kin) *n.* a square piece of cloth or paper used at meals to protect one's clothes or for wiping one's lips or fingers.

na·po·le·on (nă-poh-li-ŏn) *n.* 1. a many-layered cream-filled pastry. 2. a French gold twenty-franc piece of Napoleon I.

Na·po·le·on·ic (nă-poh-li-on-ik) *adj.* of Napoleon (1769–1821), a French general, emperor of France 1804–15.

narc (nahrk) *n.* (*slang*) a government narcotics agent.

nar·cis·sism (nahr-si-siz-ĕm) *n.* a tendency to self-worship, excessive or erotic interest in one's own personal features. **nar'cis·sist** *n.*

nar·cis·sus (nahr-sis-ŭs) *n.* (*pl.* **-cis·sus, -cis·sus·es, -cis·si,** *pr.* -sis-ı, -sis-ee) any of a group of flowers including jonquils and daffodils, especially the kind with heavily scented single white flowers.

nar·co·sis (nahr-koh-sis) *n.* a state of sleep or drowsiness produced by drugs or by electricity.

nar·cot·ic (nahr-kot-ik) *adj.* causing sleep or drowsiness. **narcotic** *n.* a narcotic drug.

nar·co·tize (nahr-kŏ-tız) *v.* **(nar·co·tized, nar·co·tiz·ing)** 1. to induce a state of drowsiness, sleep, or unawareness in. 2. to treat with a narcotic.

nard (nahrd) *n.* 1. a fragrant balsam believed to have been used by the ancients. 2. the plant yielding this.

nark = narc.

Nar·ra·gan·sett (nar-ă-gan-sit) *n.* a member of an Indian tribe from Rhode Island.

nar·rate (nar-ayt, na-rayt) *v.* **(nar·rat·ed, nar·rat·ing)** to tell (a story), to give an account of, to utter or write a narrative. **nar'ra·tor** *n.* **nar·ra·tion** (na-ray-shŏn) *n.*

nar·ra·tive (nar-ă-tiv) *n.* a spoken or written account of something. **narrative** *adj.* in the form of a narrative.

nar·row (nar-oh) *adj.* 1. of small width in proportion to length. 2. having or allowing little space, *within narrow bounds.* 3. with little scope or variety, small, *a narrow circle of friends.* 4. with little margin, *a narrow escape; a narrow majority.* 5. narrow-minded. **narrow** *v.* to make or become

narrower. **nar'row·ly** *adv.* **nar'row·ness** *n.*

nar·row-mind·ed (nar-oh-mın-did) *adj.* rigid in one's views and sympathies, not tolerant. **nar'row-mind'ed·ly** *adv.* **nar'row-mind'ed·ness** *n.*

nar·rows (nar-ohz) *n.* a narrow passage in a body of water, a strait.

nar·thex (nahr-theks) *n.* the railed-off western porch in an early Christian church, used by women, penitents, etc.

nar·whal (nahr-wăl) *n.* an arctic animal related to the whale, the male of which has long spirally grooved tusk.

nar·y (nair-ee) *adj.* **nary a,** (*old use*) not a, not one.

NAS *abbr.* 1. National Academy of Sciences. 2. Naval Air Station.

NASA (nas-ă) *n.* National Aeronautics and Space Administration.

na·sal (nay-zăl) *adj.* 1. of the nose. 2. (of a voice or speech) sounding as if the breath came out through the nose. **nasal** *n.* 1. a nasal letter or sound. 2. a nosepiece on a helmet. **na'sal·ly** *adv.*

na·sal·ize (nay-ză-lız) *v.* **(na·sal·ized, na·sal·iz·ing)** 1. to speak with a twang described as speaking through the nose. 2. to make nasal. **na·sal·i·za·tion** (nay-ză-li-zay-shŏn) *n.*

nas·cent (nas-ĕnt, nay-sĕnt) *adj.* 1. in the act of being born, just beginning to be, not yet mature. 2. (of a chemical element) just being formed and therefore unusually reactive. **nas'cence** *n.*

Nash·ville (nash-vil) the capital of Tennessee.

Nas·sau (nas-aw) the capital of the Bahamas.

na·stur·tium (na-stur-shŭm) *n.* a trailing garden plant with bright orange or yellow or red flowers and round flat leaves.

nas·ty (nas-tee) *adj.* **(nas·ti·er, nas·ti·est)** 1. unpleasant. 2. unkind, spiteful. 3. difficult to deal with, *a nasty problem.* **nas'ti·ly** *adv.* **nas'ti·ness** *n.*

nat. *abbr.* 1. national. 2. native. 3. natural.

na·tal (nay-tăl) *adj.* of or from one's birth.

na·tal·i·ty (nay-tal-i-tee) *n.* the birthrate.

na·tes (nay-teez) *n. pl.* 1. the buttocks. 2. the anterior pair of optic lobes in the brain.

na·tion (nay-shŏn) *n.* a large community of people of mainly common descent, language, history, etc., usually inhabiting a particular territory and under one government.

na·tion·al (nash-ŏ-năl) *adj.* of a nation, common to a whole nation. **national** *n.* a citizen or subject of a particular country. **na'tion·al·ly** *adv.* □**national anthem,** a song of loyalty or patriotism adopted by a country. **national bank,** one chartered under the federal government. **national debt,** the total amount owed by a country to those who have lent money to it. **national forest,** a forest maintained by the federal government. **National Guard,** a U.S. military reserve force maintained by the states but available for federal use. **national monument,** a building, natural site, or structure designated in commemoration of a person, event, etc. and maintained by the federal government. **national park,** an area of historical, scientific, or scenic significance declared to be public property for the use and enjoyment of the people. **national seashore,** a seacoast recreational area maintained by the federal government.

na·tion·al·ism (nash-ŏ-nă-liz-ĕm) *n.* 1. patriotic feeling or principles or efforts. 2. a movement

favoring independence for a country that is controlled by or forms part of another.
na·tion·al·ist (nash-ŏ-nă-list) n. a supporter of nationalism.
na·tion·al·ist·ic (nash-ŏ-nă-lis-tik) adj.
na·tion·al·i·ty (nash-ŏ-nal-i-tee) n. (pl. -ties) the condition of belonging to a particular nation.
na·tion·al·ize (nash-ŏ-nă-lız) v. (na·tion·al·ized, na·tion·al·iz·ing) to convert (industries etc.) from private to government ownership. na·tion·al·i·za·tion (nash-ŏ-nă-li-zay-shŏn) n.
na·tion·wide (nay-shŏn-wıd) adj. extending over the whole of a nation.
na·tive (nay-tiv) adj. 1. belonging to a person or thing by nature, inborn, natural. 2. (of a person) belonging to a particular place by birth, (of a thing) belonging to a person because of his place of birth, one's native land or language. 3. grown or produced or originating in a specified place. 4. of the natives of a place. native n. 1. a person who was born in a specified place or country. 2. a local inhabitant of a place, as opposed to strangers, visitors, foreigners. 3. an animal or plant grown or originating in a specified place.
na·tiv·ism (nay-ti-viz-ĕm) n. the doctrine that innate ideas exist.
na·tiv·i·ty (nă-tiv-i-tee) n. (pl. -ties) 1. a person's birth with regard to its place or circumstances, especially the Nativity, that of Christ. 2. Nativity, a picture of a scene with Christ as a newborn infant. □Nativity play, a play dealing with the birth of Christ.
natl., nat'l. abbr. national.
NATO (nay-toh) n. North Atlantic Treaty Organization.
nat·ty (nat-ee) adj. (nat·ti·er, nat·ti·est) neat and trim, dapper. nat'ti·ly adv.
nat·u·ral (nach-ŭ-răl) adj. 1. of or existing in or produced by nature; a country's natural resources, its mineral deposits, forests, etc. 2. in accordance with the course of nature, normal, a natural death. 3. (of a person) having certain inborn qualities or abilities, a natural leader. 4. not looking artificial, not affected in manner etc. 5. not surprising, to be expected. 6. (in music, of a note) neither sharp nor flat, B natural. natural n. 1. a person or thing that seems to be naturally suited for something. 2. (in music) a natural note, the sign for this (♮). 3. pale fawn color. nat'u·ral·ly adv. nat'u·ral·ness n. □natural childbirth, a system of childbirth in which the mother has been taught to relax and so needs little or no anesthetic. natural gas, gas found in the earth's crust, not manufactured. natural history, the study of animal and vegetable life. natural science, see science. natural selection, survival of the organisms that are best adapted to their environment while the less well adapted ones die out.
nat·u·ral·ism (nach-ŭ-ră-liz-ĕm) n. realism in art and literature, drawing or painting or representing things as they are in nature. nat·u·ral·ist·ic (nach-ŭ-ră-lis-tik) adj.
nat·u·ral·ist (nach-ŭ-ră-list) n. an expert in natural history.
nat·u·ral·ize (nach-ŭ-ră-lız) v. (nat·u·ral·ized, nat·u·ral·iz·ing) 1. to admit (a person of foreign birth) to full citizenship of a country. 2. to adopt (a foreign word or custom) into the language or customs of a country. 3. to introduce and acclimatize (an animal or plant) into a country where it is not native. 4. to cause to appear natural;

daffodil bulbs suitable for naturalizing, suitable for planting so that they appear to be growing wild. nat·u·ral·i·za·tion (nach-ŭ-ră-li-zay-shŏn) n.
na·ture (nay-chŭr) n. 1. the world with all its features and living things, the physical power that produces these; Nature, this power personified. 2. a kind or sort or class, things of this nature; the request was in the nature of a command. 3. the complex of qualities and characteristics innate in a person or animal. 4. a thing's essential qualities, its characteristics. □back to nature, returning to what are regarded as the natural conditions of living before the spread of civilization. in a state of nature, in an uncultivated or undomesticated state; totally naked. nature study, (in schools) the practical study of plant and animal life. nature trail, a path through woods or countryside where interesting natural objects can be seen. nature walk, a walk through nature trails, often under the guidance of a leader who points out interesting objects of nature.
Nau·ga·hyde (naw-gă-hıd) n. (trademark) a vinyl material often used for upholstery.
naught (nawt) n. (old use) nothing.
naugh·ty (naw-tee) adj. (naugh·ti·er, naugh·ti·est) 1. behaving badly, disobedient. 2. improper, shocking or amusing people by mild indecency. naught'i·ly adv. naught'i·ness n.
Na·u·ru (nah-oo-roo) a country in the central Pacific, near the equator. Na·u'ru·an adj. & n.
nau·se·a (naw-zi-ă) n. a feeling of sickness or disgust.
nau·se·ate (naw-zi-ayt) v. (nau·se·at·ed, nau·se·at·ing) to affect with nausea. nau'se·at·ing·ly adv.
nau·seous (naw-shŭs, naw-zi-ŭs) adj. 1. causing nausea. 2. (informal) experiencing nausea. ▷Careful writers do not use nauseous in its second sense. Write we felt nauseated not we felt nauseous.
naut. abbr. nautical.
nautch (nawch) n. an Indian exhibition of dancing girls.
nau·ti·cal (naw-ti-kăl) adj. of sailors or seamanship. nau'ti·cal·ly adv. □nautical mile, see mile.
nau·ti·lus (naw-tĭ-lŭs) n. (pl. -lus·es, -li, pr. -lı) a deep sea mollusk with a spiral shell divided into many chambers by thin pearly walls. □paper nautilus, a small mollusk of which the female has a very thin shell and webbed sail-like arms.
nav. abbr. 1. naval. 2. navigable. 3. navigation.
Nav·a·ho, Nav·a·jo (nav-ă-hoh) n. (pl. -ho, -hos, -hoes) 1. a member of a large Indian tribe living in New Mexico and Arizona. 2. the language of these people.
na·val (nay-văl) adj. of a navy, of warships; a naval power, a country with a strong navy. □naval stores, cordage, tar, timber, and other materials much used in former times in building wooden sailing ships; rosin, tar, turpentine, and other products of the pine tree, used in manufacture of paint, roofing, lubricants, etc. ▷Do not confuse naval with navel.
nave (nayv) n. the body of a church apart from the chancel, aisles, and transepts.
na·vel (nay-věl) n. 1. the small hollow in the center of the abdomen where the umbilical cord was attached. 2. the central point of something. □navel orange, a large orange with a navel-

like formation at the top. ▷Do not confuse *navel* with *naval.*

nav·i·ga·ble (nav-ĭ-gă-běl) *adj.* 1. (of rivers or seas) suitable for ships to sail in. 2. (of a ship etc.) able to be steered and sailed. **nav'i·ga·bly** *adv.* **nav·i·ga·bil·i·ty** (nav-ĭ-gă-bil-i-tee) *n.*

nav·i·gate (nav-ĭ-gayt) *v.* (**nav·i·gat·ed, nav·i·gat·ing**) 1. to sail in or through (a sea or river etc.). 2. to direct the course of (a ship or aircraft or vehicle etc.). **nav'i·ga·tor** *n.* **nav·i·ga·tion** (nav-ĭ-gay-shŏn) *n.*

na·vy (nay-vee) *n.* 1. a country's warships. 2. the officers and men of these. 3. navy blue. **navy** *adj.* navy blue. ☐**navy bean,** a small white kidney bean for cooking. **navy blue,** very dark blue like that used in naval uniforms. **navy exchange,** a post exchange on a naval base. **navy yard,** a government shipyard for the construction and repair of naval ships.

nay (nay) *adv.* 1. no. 2. or rather, and even, and more than that. **nay** *n.* a negative vote.

Na·zi (naht-see) *n.* (*pl.* **Na·zis**) a member of the National Socialist party in Germany, brought to power by Hitler. **Nazi** *adj.* of the Nazis. **Na'zism** *n.*

Nb *symbol* niobium.

N.B. *abbr.* 1. New Brunswick. 2. note well. (Latin *nota bene*).

NBA, N.B.A. *abbr.* 1. National Basketball Association. 2. National Boxing Association.

NBC *abbr.* National Broadcasting Company.

N-bomb (en-bom) *n.* a neutron bomb.

NBS *abbr.* National Bureau of Standards.

NC, N.C. *abbr.* North Carolina.

NCO, N.C.O. *abbr.* noncommissioned officer.

n.d. *abbr.* no date.

Nd *symbol* neodymium.

ND, N.D. *abbr.* North Dakota.

N. Dak. *abbr.* North Dakota.

NDEA *abbr.* National Defense Education Act.

N'Dja·me·na (en-jah-mě-nă) the capital of Chad.

Ne *symbol* neon.

NE *abbr.* 1. Nebraska. 2. northeast. 3. northeastern.

N.E. *abbr.* 1. New England. 2. northeast. 3. northeastern.

NEA *abbr.* National Education Association.

Ne·an·der·thal (ni-an-děr-thawl) *adj.* 1. of an extinct type of mankind *(Neanderthal man)* living in prehistoric Europe. 2. *(slang)* uncouth; old-fashioned, *Neanderthal politics.* **Neanderthal** *n.* a Neanderthal person.

neap (neep) *n.* **neap tide,** the tide when there is the least rise and fall of water, halfway between spring tides.

Ne·a·pol·i·tan (nee-ă-pol-i-tăn) *adj.* of Naples. **Neapolitan** *n.* a native or inhabitant of Naples. ☐**Neapolitan ice cream,** ice cream made in layers of different colors and flavors.

near (neer) *adj.* 1. at or to or within a short distance or interval. 2. nearly, *as near as I can guess.* **near** *prep.* near to. **near** *adj.* 1. with only a short distance or interval between, *in the near future.* 2. closely related. 3. with little margin, *a near escape.* **near** *v.* to draw near. **near'ness** *n.* ☐**near beer,** a malt liquor containing less than one half percent alcohol. **Near East,** the Middle East. **near miss,** something that missed its objective only narrowly; not a direct hit but near enough to do damage. **near thing,** something achieved or missed by only a narrow margin; a narrow escape.

near·by (neer-bɪ) *adv.* not far off, *they live nearby.*

nearby *adj.* near in position, *a nearby house.*

near·ly (neer-lee) *adv.* 1. closely; *we are nearly related,* are closely related. 2. almost. ☐**not nearly,** nothing like, far from, *not nearly enough.*

near·sight·ed (neer-sɪ-tid) *adj.* shortsighted. **near'sight·ed·ly** *adv.* **near'sight·ed·ness** *n.*

neat (neet) *adj.* 1. simple and clean and orderly in appearance. 2. done or doing things in a precise and skillful way. 3. undiluted, *neat whiskey.* 4. *(slang)* great, wonderful. **neat'ly** *adv.* **neat'ness** *n.*

neat·en (nee-těn) *v.* to make or become neat.

neath (neeth) *prep. (poetic)* beneath.

neat's-foot (neets-fuut) **oil** a fatty oil made from cattle bones, used to dress leather.

neb (neb) *n. (Scottish)* 1. a beak or bill. 2. a nose, a snout. 3. a tip, spout, or point.

Neb., Nebr. *abbr.* Nebraska.

NEB *abbr.* New English Bible.

neb·bish (neb-ish) *n. (slang)* a submissive timid person.

Ne·bras·ka (ně-bras-kă) a state of the U.S. **Ne·bras'kan** *adj. & n.*

neb·u·la (neb-yŭ-lă) *n.* (*pl.* **-las, -lae,** *pr.* -lee) a bright or dark patch in the sky caused by distant stars or a cloud of dust or gas. **neb'u·lar** *adj.*

neb·u·lize (neb-yŭ-lɪz) *v.* (**neb·u·lized, neb·u·liz·ing**) to reduce to a fine spray. **neb'u·liz·er** *n.*

neb·u·los·i·ty (neb-yŭ-los-i-tee) *n.* (*pl.* **-ties**) 1. the state of being vague, hazy, or indistinct. 2. nebulous matter.

neb·u·lous (neb-yŭ-lŭs) *adj.* indistinct, having no definite form, *nebulous ideas.* **neb'u·lous·ly** *adv.*

nec·es·sar·i·ly (nes-ě-ser-ĭ-lee) *adv.* as a necessary result, inevitably.

nec·es·sar·y (nes-ě-ser-ee) *adj.* 1. essential in order to achieve something. 2. unavoidable, happening or existing by necessity, *the necessary consequence.* **necessary** *n.* (*pl.* **-ies**) something without which life cannot be maintained or is exceedingly harsh.

ne·ces·si·tate (ně-ses-i-tayt) *v.* (**ne·ces·si·tat·ed, ne·ces·si·tat·ing**) to make necessary, to involve as a condition or accompaniment or result.

ne·ces·si·tous (ně-ses-i-tus) *adj.* needy.

ne·ces·si·ty (ně-ses-i-tee) *n.* (*pl.* **-ties**) 1. the state or fact of being necessary, *the necessity of adequate food.* 2. a necessary thing. 3. the compelling power of circumstances. 4. a state of need or great poverty or hardship.

neck (nek) *n.* 1. the narrow part of the body connecting the head to the shoulders. 2. the part of a garment around this. 3. the length of a horse's head and neck as a measure of its lead in a race. 4. the flesh of an animal's neck as food. 5. a narrow part of anything (especially of a bottle or cavity), a narrow connecting part or channel. **neck** *v. (slang,* of couples) to kiss and caress each other lovingly. ☐**get it in the neck,** *(slang)* to suffer a reprimand or a severe blow. **neck and neck,** running level in a race. **risk** *or* **save one's neck,** to risk or save one's own life. **up to one's neck in,** *(informal)* very deeply involved in.

neck·band (nek-band) *n.* a strip of material around the neck of a garment.

neck·er·chief (nek-ěr-chif) *n.* a square of cloth worn around the neck.

neck·lace (nek-lis) *n.* an ornament of precious

stones or metal or beads etc. worn around the neck.

neck·line (nek-lɪn) *n.* the outline formed by the edge of a garment at or below the neck.

neck·tie (nek-tɪ) *n.* a strip of material worn around the neck, passing under the collar and knotted in front.

neck·wear (nek-wair) *n.* ties and other articles worn around the neck.

ne·crol·o·gy (nĕ-krol-ŏ-jee) *n.* (*pl.* **-gies**) 1. a list of persons recently dead. 2. an obituary.

nec·ro·man·cy (nek-rŏ-man-see) *n.* 1. the art of predicting events by allegedly communicating with the dead. 2. witchcraft. **nec′ro·man·cer** *n.*

ne·crop·o·lis (nĕ-krop-ŏ-lis) *n.* (*pl.* **-lis·es**) the cemetery of an ancient city.

ne·cro·sis (nĕ-kroh-sis) *n.* the death of a piece of tissue, especially of the bones. **ne·cro·tic** (nĕ-krot-ik) *adj.*

nec·tar (nek-tăr) *n.* 1. (in Greek mythology) the drink of the gods. 2. any delicious drink. 3. sweet fluid produced by plants and collected by bees for making honey.

nec·tar·ine (nek-tă-reen) *n.* a kind of peach that has a thin skin with no down and firm flesh.

nec·ta·ry (nek-tă-ree) *n.* the nectar-secreting part of a plant or flower.

nee, née (nay) *adj.* born (used in giving a married woman's maiden name, *Mrs. Jane Smith, née Jones*).

need (need) *n.* 1. circumstances in which a thing or course of action is required, *there is no need to worry.* 2. a situation of great difficulty or misfortune, *a friend in need.* 3. lack of necessaries, poverty. 4. a requirement, a thing necessary for life, *my needs are few.* **need** *v.* 1. to be in need of, to require. 2. to be under a necessity or obligation, *need you ask?* □**if need be,** if necessary.

need·ful (need-fŭl) *adj.* necessary.

nee·dle (nee-dĕl) *n.* 1. a small thin piece of polished steel with a point at one end and a hole for thread at the other, used in sewing. 2. something resembling this in shape or use, such as one of the long thin leaves of pine trees, a sharp pointed rock, an obelisk (*Cleopatra's needle*), the sharp hollow end of a hypodermic syringe. 3. a long thin piece of smooth metal or plastic etc. with one or both ends pointed, used in knitting by hand. 4. the pointer of a compass or gauge. **needle** *v.* (**nee·dled, nee·dling**) to annoy or provoke. □**needle in a haystack,** a thing so buried among others that search for it is hopeless.

nee·dle·craft (nee-dĕl-kraft) *n.* skill in needlework.

nee·dle·point (nee-dĕl-point) *n.* a kind of fine embroidery on canvas.

need·less (need-lis) *adj.* not needed, unnecessary. **need′less·ly** *adv.* **need′less·ness** *n.*

nee·dle·wom·an (nee-dĕl-wuum-ăn) *n.* (*pl.* **-wom·en,** *pr.* -wim-in) a woman with a certain skill in needlework, *a good needlewoman.*

nee·dle·work (nee-dĕl-wurk) *n.* sewing or embroidery.

need·n't (nee-dĕnt) = need not.

needs (needz) *adv.* of necessity; *must needs do it,* foolishly insists on doing it, cannot help doing it; *needs must do it,* must do it.

need·y (nee-dee) *adj.* (**need·i·er, need·i·est**) lacking the necessaries of life, extremely poor.

ne′er (nair) *adv.* (*old use*) never.

ne′er-do-well (nair-doo-wel) *n.* a good-for-nothing person.

ne·far·i·ous (ni-fair-i-ŭs) *adj.* wicked. **ne·far′i·ous·ly** *adv.* **ne·far′i·ous·ness** *n.*

neg. *abbr.* negative.

ne·gate (ni-gayt) *v.* (**ne·gat·ed, ne·gat·ing**) to nullify, to disprove. **ne·ga·tion** (ni-gay-shŏn) *n.*

neg·a·tive (neg-ă-tiv) *adj.* 1. expressing or implying denial or refusal or prohibition; *a negative reply,* saying "no." 2. not positive, lacking positive qualities or characteristics; *the result of the test was negative,* indicated that a specific substance etc. was not present. 3. (of a quantity) less than zero, minus. 4. in the direction opposite of that regarded as positive. 5. containing or producing the kind of electric charge carried by electrons; *negative terminal of a battery,* the one through which current enters an external circuit. 6. (of a photograph) having the lights and shades of the actual object or scene reversed, or its colors represented by complementary ones. **negative** *n.* 1. a negative statement or reply or word; *the answer is in the negative,* is "no." 2. a negative quality or quantity. 3. a negative photograph, from which positive pictures can be obtained. **negative** *v.* (**neg·a·tived, neg·a·tiv·ing**) 1. to veto. 2. to contradict (a statement). 3. to neutralize (an effect). **neg′a·tive·ly** *adv.* □**negative pole,** the south-seeking pole of a magnet. **negative sign,** the sign −.

neg·a·tiv·ism (neg-ă-ti-viz-ĕm) *n.* an attitude of confirmed skepticism, denial of accepted beliefs.

ne·glect (ni-glekt) *v.* 1. to pay no attention or not enough attention to. 2. to fail to take proper care of. 3. to omit to do something, as through carelessness or forgetfulness. **neglect** *n.* neglecting, being neglected. **ne·glect′ful** *adj.*

neg·li·gee (neg-li-zhay) *n.* a woman's light flimsy ornamental dressing gown.

neg·li·gence (neg-li-jĕns) *n.* lack of proper care or attention, carelessness. **neg′li·gent** *adj.* **neg′li·gent·ly** *adv.* ▷Do not confuse *negligent* with *negligible.*

neg·li·gi·ble (neg-li-jĕ-bĕl) *adj.* very small in amount etc. and not worth taking into account. ▷Do not confuse *negligible* with *negligent.*

ne·go·ti·a·ble (ni-goh-shi-ă-bĕl) *adj.* 1. able to be modified after discussion, *the salary is negotiable.* 2. (of a check etc.) able to be converted into cash or transferred to another person.

ne·go·ti·ate (ni-goh-shi-ayt) *v.* (**ne·go·ti·at·ed, ne·go·ti·at·ing**) 1. to try to reach an agreement or arrangement by discussion, to arrange in this way, *negotiated a treaty.* 2. to get or give money in exchange for (a check or bonds etc.). 3. to get over or through (an obstacle or difficulty) successfully. **ne·go′ti·a·tor** *n.* **ne·go·ti·a·tion** (ni-goh-shi-ay-shŏn) *n.*

neg·ri·tude (neg-ri-tood) *n.* 1. the quality of being a black. 2. affirmation of the value of black culture.

Ne·gro (nee-groh) *n.* (*pl.* **Ne·groes**) a member of the black-skinned race of mankind. **Negro** *adj.* of this race, black-skinned. **Ne·groid** (nee-groid) *adj. & n.* ▷These words are considered offensive by many people, who prefer the word *black.*

Ne·he·mi·ah (nee-ĕ-mɪ-ă) *n.* a historical book of the Old Testament telling of the rebuilding of the walls of Jerusalem.

neigh (nay) *n.* the long high-pitched cry of a horse.

neigh *v.* to make this cry.

neigh·bor (nay-bŏr) *n.* 1. a person who lives near or next to another. 2. a person to whom one should be friendly or kind. 3. a person or thing situated near or next to another, *Britain's nearest neighbor is France.* **neighbor** *v.* to join, to border on.

neigh·bor·hood (nay-bŏr-huud) *n.* 1. a district. 2. the people living in it. □**in the neighborhood of,** somewhere near, approximately, *in the neighborhood of five hundred dollars.*

neigh·bor·ing (nay-bŏ-ring) *adj.* living or situated near by.

neigh·bor·ly (nay-bŏr-lee) *adj.* kind and friendly, as one neighbor should be to another. **neigh'bor·li·ness** *n.*

nei·ther (nee-thĕr, nı-) *adj. & pronoun* not either, *neither of them likes it.* (▷Note the use of the singular verb; *neither of them like it* would be incorrect.) **neither** *adv. & conj.* 1. not either, *she neither knew nor cared.* 2. also not, *you don't know and neither do I.* 3. *(incorrect use)* either, *I don't know that neither.* □**be neither here nor there,** to be of no importance or relevance.

nel·son (nel-sŏn) *n.* a kind of hold in wrestling in which the arm is passed under the opponent's arm from behind and the hand applied to his neck.

nem·a·tode (nem-ă-tohd) *n.* a worm of slender unsegmented cylindrical shape. **nematode** *adj.*

nem·e·sis (nem-ĕ-sis) *n.* 1. retributive justice. 2. a downfall. 3. the agent of downfall, a victorious rival.

neo- *prefix* new, recent, a new form of.

ne·o·clas·sic (nee-oh-klas-ik) *adj.* of a revival of classical style or treatment in art, literature, music, etc. **ne·o·clas'si·cal** *adj.* **ne·o·clas·si·cism** (nee-oh-klas-i-siz-ĕm) *n.*

ne·o·co·lo·ni·al·ism (nee-oh-kŏ-loh-ni-ăl-iz-ĕm) *n.* the use of economic, political, or other means to obtain or retain influence over former colonies. **ne·o·co·lo'ni·al** *adj.* **ne·o·co·lo'ni·al·ist** *n.*

ne·o·dym·i·um (nee-oh-dim-i-ŭm) *n.* a rare-earth metallic element used to color glass.

ne·o·im·pres·sion·ism (nee-oh-im-presh-ŏ-niz-ĕm) *n.* a late 19th-century French art movement reintroducing the idea (rejected by impressionists) that a picture should be deliberately planned and composed. **ne·o·im·pres'sion·ist** *adj. & n.*

ne·o·lith·ic (nee-ŏ-lith-ik) *adj.* of the later Stone Age, when ground or polished stone weapons and implements prevailed.

ne·ol·o·gism (nee-ol-ŏ-jiz-ĕm), **ne·ol·o·gy** (nee-ol-ŏ-jee) *n.* 1. a newly coined word or phrase. 2. the coining or using of new words.

ne·on (nee-on) *n.* a kind of gas much used in illuminated signs because it glows orange-red when electricity is passed through it.

ne·o·na·tal (nee-oh-nay-tăl) *adj.* of or relating to a newborn child. **ne·o·na'tal·ly** *adv.* **ne·o·nate** (nee-ŏ-nayt) *n.*

ne·o·phyte (nee-ŏ-fıt) *n.* 1. a new convert, especially among primitive Christians or among Roman Catholics. 2. a novice in a religious order. 3. a beginner, a novice, a tyro.

ne·o·plasm (nee-ŏ-plaz-ĕm) *n.* a new growth of tissue in some part of the body, especially a tumor. **ne·o·plas·tic** (nee-oh-plas-tik) *adj.*

ne·o·prene (nee-ŏ-preen) *n.* a tough synthetic rubberlike substance.

Ne·pal (nĕ-pawl) a country northeast of India. **Ne·pa·lese** (nep-ă-leez) *adj. & n.* (*pl.* **-lese**).

ne·pen·the (ni-pen-thee) *n.* 1. a drug believed by the ancient Greeks to cause forgetfulness of grief. 2. anything causing a lack of awareness of pain and sorrow.

neph·ew (nef-yoo) *n.* one's brother's or sister's son.

neph·rite (nef-rıt) *n.* a form of jade, ranging in color from whitish to green.

ne·phrit·ic (nĕ-frit-ik) *adj.* 1. of or in the kidneys, renal. 2. of nephritis.

ne·phri·tis (nĕ-frı-tis) *n.* inflammation of the kidneys.

ne plus ul·tra (nee plus ul-tră) the furthest point attainable, the highest form of something. ▷Latin, = do not go beyond this point.

nep·o·tism (nep-ŏ-tiz-ĕm) *n.* favoritism shown to relatives in appointing them to jobs.

Nep·tune (nep-toon) *n.* 1. the Roman god of the sea. 2. a planet in the solar system. **Nep·tu·ni·an** (nep-too-ni-ăn) *adj.*

nep·tu·ni·um (nep-too-ni-ŭm) *n.* the element produced when uranium atoms absorb bombarding neutrons.

nerd (nurd) *n. (slang)* a gauche person.

Ne·re·id (neer-i-id) *n.* 1. a sea nymph of Greek mythology. 2. a long sea worm or centipede.

ne·rit·ic (nĕ-rit-ik) *adj.* of or relating to shallow water along the seacoast.

nerve (nurv) *n.* 1. any of the fibers or bundles of fibers carrying impulses of sensation or of movement between the brain or spinal cord and all parts of the body. 2. courage, coolness in danger, *lose one's nerve.* 3. *(informal)* impudent boldness, *had the nerve to ask for more.* 4. *nerves,* a condition in which a person suffers from mental stress and easily becomes anxious or upset, nervousness. **nerve** *v.* **(nerved, nerv·ing)** to give strength or vigor or courage to; *nerve oneself,* to brace oneself to face danger or suffering. □**get on a person's nerves,** to be irritating to him. **nerve cell,** a cell transmitting impulses in nerve tissue. **nerve center,** a group of closely connected ganglion cells; a center of control from which instructions are sent out. **nerve gas,** a poison gas that affects the nervous system.

nerve·less (nurv-lis) *adj.* 1. incapable of effort or movement, *the knife fell from his nerveless fingers.* 2. confident, not nervous. **nerve'less·ly** *adv.* **nerve'less·ness** *n.*

nerve-rack·ing (nurv-rak-ing) *adj.* inflicting great strain on the nerves.

nerv·ous (nur-vus) *adj.* 1. of the nerves or nervous system, *a nervous disorder.* 2. excitable, easily agitated, timid. 3. uneasy, *a nervous laugh.* **nerv'ous·ly** *adv.* **nerv'ous·ness** *n.* □**nervous breakdown,** loss of mental and emotional stability. **nervous system,** the system of nerves throughout the body.

nerv·y (nur-vee) *adj.* **(nerv·i·er, nerv·i·est)** 1. *(informal)* bold and presumptuous. 2. cool and confident. **nerv'i·ly** *adv.* **nerv'i·ness** *n.*

-ness *suffix* used to form nouns meaning a state or condition, as in *happiness;* an instance of this state or condition, as in *kindness.*

Nes·sel·rode (nes-ĕl-rohd) **pie** a pie containing a mixture of preserved fruits, nuts, etc.

nest (nest) *n.* 1. a structure or place in which a bird lays its eggs and shelters its young. 2. a place where certain creatures (such as mice or wasps) live, or produce and keep their young. 3. a snug place. 4. a secluded shelter or hiding place. 5. a set of similar articles designed to fit inside each other in a series, *a nest of tables.* **nest** *v.* to make or have a nest. □**nest egg,** a sum of money saved for future use.

nes·tle (nes-ĕl) v. (**nes·tled, nes·tling**) 1. to curl up or press oneself comfortably into a soft place. 2. to lie half-hidden or sheltered. **nes'tler** n.

nest·ling (nes-ling) n. a bird too young to leave the nest.

net¹ (net) n. 1. openwork material of thread or cord or wire etc. woven or joined at intervals. 2. a piece of this used for a particular purpose, as covering or protecting something, catching fish, dividing a tennis court, surrounding a goal space etc. **net** v. (**net·ted, net·ting**) 1. to make by forming threads into a net, to make netting. 2. to place nets in, to cover or confine with or as if with a net. 3. to catch in or as if in a net.

net² adj. 1. remaining when nothing more is to be taken away; *net profit,* profit after tax etc. has been deducted from the gross profit; *net weight,* weight of contents only, excluding wrappings. 2. (of an effect etc.) positive, excluding unimportant effects or those that cancel each other out, *the net result.* **net** v. (**net·ted, net·ting**) to obtain or yield as net profit. **net** n. a net amount, gain, or weight. **net'ta·ble** adj.

NET abbr. National Educational Television.

Neth. abbr. Netherlands.

neth·er (neth-ĕr) adj. lower, *the nether regions.* **neth'er·most** adj.

Neth·er·lands (neth-ĕr-lăndz), **the** (also **Holland**) a country in Europe. **Neth'er·land'er** n.

neth·er·world (neth-ĕr-wurld) n. the underworld, hell.

net·ting (net-ing) n. fabric of netted thread or cord or wire etc.

net·tle (net-ĕl) n. 1. a common wild plant with hairs on its leaves that sting and redden the skin when they are touched. 2. a plant resembling this. **nettle** v. (**net·tled, net·tling**) 1. to sting with nettles. 2. to irritate, to provoke, to annoy. **net'tler** n. □**nettle rash,** an eruption on the skin with red patches like those made by nettle stings.

net·tle·some (net-ĕl-sŏm) adj. causing irritation or annoyance.

net·work (net-wurk) n. 1. an arrangement or pattern with intersecting lines, *a network of railroads.* 2. a chain of interconnected people or operations, or broadcasting stations, *a spy network.*

neu·ral (noor-ăl) adj. of nerves.

neu·ral·gia (nuu-ral-jă) n. sharp intermittent pain along the course of a nerve, especially in the head or face. **neu·ral'gic** adj.

neu·ras·the·ni·a (noor-ăs-thee-ni-ă) n. a debility of nerves causing fatigue, listlessness, etc. **neu·ras·then·ic** (noor-ăs-then-ik) adj. & n.

neu·ri·tis (nuu-ry-tis) n. inflammation of a nerve or nerves. **neu·rit·ic** (nuu-rit-ik) adj.

neuro- comb. form nerve, nervous system, as in neurosurgeon.

neurol. abbr. neurology.

neu·rol·o·gist (nuu-rol-ŏ-jist) n. an expert in neurology.

neu·rol·o·gy (nuu-rol-ŏ-jee) n. the scientific study of nerve systems and their diseases. **neu·ro·log·i·cal** (noor-ŏ-loj-i-kăl) adj. **neu·ro·log'i·cal·ly** adv.

neu·ron (noor-on), **neu·rone** (noor-ohn) n. a nerve cell and its appendages.

neu·ro·sci·ence (noor-oh-sy-ĕns) n. a science that deals with the anatomy, physiology, and biochem-

istry of the entire nervous system as it relates to learning, memory, and behavior. **neu·ro·sci·en·tist** (noor-oh-sy-ĕn-tist) n.

neu·ro·sis (nuu-roh-sis) n. (pl. **-ses,** pr. -seez) a mental disorder producing depression or abnormal behavior, sometimes with physical symptoms but with no evidence of disease.

neu·ro·sur·geon (noor-oh-sur-jŏn) n. an expert in neurosurgery.

neu·ro·sur·ger·y (noor-oh-sur-jĕ-ree) n. surgery performed on the nervous system.

neu·rot·ic (nuu-rot-ik) adj. 1. of or caused by a neurosis. 2. (of a person) subject to abnormal anxieties or obsessive behavior. **neurotic** n. a neurotic person. **neu·rot'i·cal·ly** adv.

neut. abbr. neuter.

neu·ter (noo-tĕr) adj. 1. (of a noun) neither masculine nor feminine. 2. (of plants) without male or female parts. 3. (of insects) sexually undeveloped, sterile. **neuter** n. a neuter word or plant or insect, a castrated animal. **neuter** v. to castrate.

neu·tral (noo-trăl) adj. 1. not supporting or assisting either side in a dispute or conflict. 2. belonging to a country or person etc. that is neutral, *neutral ships.* 3. having no positive or distinctive characteristics, not definitely one thing or the other. 4. (of colors) not strong or positive, gray or fawn. 5. neither acid nor alkaline. 6. neither electrically positive nor negative. **neutral** n. 1. a neutral person or country, one who is a subject of a neutral country. 2. gray or fawn color. 3. neutral gear. **neu'tral·ly** adv. □**neutral gear,** a position of a gear mechanism in which the engine is disconnected from its driven parts.

neu·tral·ism (noo-tră-liz-ĕm) n. the policy of neutrality in international relations.

neu·tral·i·ty (noo-tral-i-tee) n. (pl. **-ties**) 1. the state of being neutral. 2. the policy or status of a nation that does not participate in a war.

neu·tral·ize (noo-tră-lyz) v. (**neu·tral·ized, neu·tral·iz·ing**) to make ineffective by means of an opposite force or effect. **neu·tra·li·za·tion** (noo-tră-li-zay-shŏn) n.

neu·tri·no (noo-tree-noh) n. (pl. **-nos**) an elementary particle with no electric charge and probably no mass, interacting only very slightly with matter.

neu·tron (noo-tron) n. a particle with no electric charge, present in the nuclei of all atoms except those of certain isotopes of hydrogen. □**neutron bomb,** a nuclear bomb that kills people by intense radiation but does little damage to buildings etc.

Nev. abbr. Nevada.

Ne·vad·a (nĕ-vad-ă) a state of the U.S. **Ne·va'dan** adj. & n.

nev·er (nev-ĕr) adv. 1. at no time, on no occasion; *never-ending, never-failing,* not ending or failing ever. 2. not at all, *never fear.* 3. (informal) surely not, *you never left the key in the lock!* 4. not, *never a care in the world.* □**never mind,** do not be troubled; do not trouble about, you may ignore, *never mind the bread;* I refuse to answer your question. **never-never land,** an imaginary place, a fantasyland. **well I never!,** an exclamation of surprise.

nev·er·more (nev-ĕr-mohr) adv. at no future time.

nev·er·the·less (nev-ĕr-thĕ-les) adv. & conj. in spite of this.

ne·vus (nee-vŭs) n. (pl. **-vi,** pr. -vy) a birthmark consisting of a mole or a red patch on the skin.

new (noo) adj. 1. not existing before, recently made

or invented or discovered or experienced. **2.** unfamiliar, unaccustomed, *it was new to me; I am new to the job.* **3.** recently changed or renewed, different, *the new chairman.* **new** *adv.* newly, recently, just, *newborn; new-laid.* **new′ness** *n.* □**new blood,** a recent arrival in an organization, expected to bring new ideas and revitalize the system. **New Brunswick,** a province of Canada. **New Deal,** the economic and administrative policies of Franklin D. Roosevelt in the 1930s, designed for economic recovery and social reform. **New Delhi,** the capital of India. **New England,** a group of six states in the northeast of the U.S. **New Englander,** a native or inhabitant of New England. **New Hampshire,** a state of the U.S. **New Jersey,** a state of the U.S. **New Jerseyite,** a native or inhabitant of New Jersey. **New Left,** a radical movement launched in the mid-1960s seeking social, political, and economic change. **new math,** *(informal)* mathematics based on the set theory. **New Mexico,** a state of the U.S. **new moon,** the moon when it is seen in the evening as a crescent; (on calendars) the precise moment when the moon is in conjunction with the sun and is invisible. **New South Wales,** a state of Australia. **New Testament,** *see* **testament.** **new wave,** a French cinematic movement of the late 1950s and 1960s that emphasized innovations in photography, story, and style. **New World,** the Americas. **new year,** the first few days of January. **New Year's Day,** January 1. **New Year's Eve,** December 31. **New York,** a state and city of the U.S. **New Yorker,** a native or inhabitant of New York. **New Zealand,** a country southeast of Australia. **New Zealander,** a native or inhabitant of New Zealand.

new·born (noo-born) *adj.* **1.** recently born. **2.** born anew. **newborn** *n.* (*pl.* **-born, -borns**) a newborn baby or animal.

new·com·er (noo-kum-ĕr) *n.* a person who has arrived recently.

new·el (noo-ĕl) *n.* **1.** (also **newel post**) a post that supports the handrail of a stair at the top or bottom of a staircase. **2.** the center pillar of a winding stair.

new·fan·gled (noo-fang-gĕld) *adj.* objectionably new in method or style.

new·found (noo-fownd) *adj.* recently discovered or disclosed.

New·found·land (noo-fŭnd-lănd) *n.* **1.** a province of Canada. **2.** a dog of a large breed with a thick dark coat. **New′found·land′er** *n.*

new·ish (noo-ish) *adj.* fairly new.

new·ly (noo-lee) *adv.* recently, freshly.

new·ly·wed (noo-lee-wed) *adj.* recently married. **newlywed** *n.* a recently married person.

news (nooz) *n.* **1.** information about recent events. **2.** a broadcast report of this. **3.** newsworthy information, *when man bites dog, that's news.* □**news vendor,** a newspaper seller.

news·boy (nooz-boi) *n.* a boy who delivers or sells newspapers.

news·cast (nooz-kast) *n.* a broadcast news report. **news′cast·er** *n.*

news·deal·er (nooz-dee-lĕr) *n.* a dealer in newspapers etc.

news·letter (nooz-let-ĕr) *n.* an informal printed report giving information that is of interest to members of a club etc.

news·mag·a·zine (nooz-mag-ă-zeen) *n.* a magazine providing a summary and analysis of the news, usually issued weekly or biweekly.

news·man (nooz-man) *n.* (*pl.* **-men,** *pr.* -men) **1.** a newsdealer. **2.** a journalist.

news·pa·per (nooz-pay-pĕr) *n.* **1.** a printed publication, usually issued daily or weekly, containing news reports, advertisements, articles on various subjects, etc. **2.** the sheets of paper forming this, *wrapped in newspaper.*

news·pa·per·man (nooz-pay-pĕr-man) *n.* (*pl.* **-men,** *pr.* -men) **1.** a journalist. **2.** the owner of a newspaper.

new·speak (noo-speek) *n.* vague and misleading language as used especially by government spokesmen trying to conceal truth and influence public opinion. ▷The artificial official language in George Orwell's *1984.*

news·print (nooz-print) *n.* the type of paper on which a newspaper is printed.

news·reel (nooz-reel) *n.* a film showing current items of news.

news·stand (nooz-stand) *n.* a stall for the sale of newspapers.

news·wor·thy (nooz-wur-*thee*) *adj.* important or interesting enough to be mentioned as news.

news·y (noo-zee) *adj.* (**news·i·er, news·i·est**) *(informal)* full of news. **news′i·ness** *n.*

newt (noot) *n.* a small lizardlike creature that can live in water or on land.

New Test. *abbr.* New Testament.

New·to·ni·an (noo-toh-ni-ăn) *adj.* of the theories etc. devised by the English scientist Sir Isaac Newton (1642–1727).

next (nekst) *adj.* **1.** lying or living or being nearest to something. **2.** coming nearest in order or time or sequence, soonest come to. **next** *adv.* in the next place or degree, on the next occasion. **next** *n.* the next person or thing. **next** *prep.* in or into the next place to, on the next occasion to, in the next degree to. □**next best,** second best. **next door,** in the next house or room. **next door to,** not far from, almost, *it's next door to impossible.* **next of kin,** one's closest relative. **next world,** life after death.

next-door (nekst-dohr) *adj.* living or situated next door.

nex·us (nek-sŭs) *n.* (*pl.* **-us·es, -us**) a connected group or series.

Nez Percé (nez purs) (*pl.* **Nez Percé, Nez Percés**) a member of an Indian tribe from Idaho, Washington, and Oregon.

Nfld. *abbr.* Newfoundland.

n.g. *abbr.* no good.

N.G. *abbr.* **1.** National Guard. **2.** no good.

NGk *abbr.* New Greek.

NH, N.H. *abbr.* New Hampshire.

Ni *symbol* nickel.

ni·a·cin (nɪ-ă-sin) *n.* nicotinic acid.

Ni·ag·a·ra (nɪ-ag-ă-ră) *n.* a cataract, torrent, or deluge, *a Niagara of lame excuses.*

Nia·mey (nyah-may) the capital of Niger.

nib (nib) *n.* the metal point of a pen.

nib·ble (nib-ĕl) *v.* (**nib·bled, nib·bling**) **1.** to take small quick or gentle bites. **2.** to eat in small amounts, *no nibbling between meals.* **3.** to show interest in an offer etc. but without being definite. **nibble** *n.* **1.** a small quick bite. **2.** a small amount of food. **nib′bler** *n.*

nib·lick (nib-lik) *n.* a golf iron with a large round heavy head, used especially for playing out of bunkers.

Nic·a·ra·gua (nik-ă-rah-gwă) a country in Central America. **Nic·a·ra′guan** *adj. & n.*

nice (nɪs) *adj.* (**nic·er, nic·est**) **1.** pleasant, satisfactory. 2. *(ironically)* difficult, bad, *this is a nice mess.* 3. needing precision and care, involving fine distinctions, *it's a nice point.* 4. fastidious. **nice′ly** *adv.* **nice′ness** *n.*

ni·ce·ty (nɪ-sĕ-tee) *n.* (*pl.* **-ties**) 1. precision. 2. a subtle distinction or detail. 3. (usually *niceties*) dainty or refined elegance.

niche (nich) *n.* 1. a shallow recess, especially in a wall. 2. a position in life or employment to which the holder is well suited, *has found his niche.*

nick (nik) *n.* a small cut or notch. **nick** *v.* to make a nick in. ☐**in the nick of time,** only just in time.

nick·el (nik-ĕl) *n.* 1. a hard silvery white metal much used in alloys. 2. a five-cent piece. ☐**nickel silver,** an alloy of nickel, zinc, and copper.

nick·el·o·de·on (nik-ĕ-loh-di-ŏn) *n.* 1. an early movie theater with an admission price of five cents. 2. a jukebox.

nick·name (nik-naym) *n.* a name given humorously to a person instead of or as well as his real name. **nickname** *v.* (**nick·named, nick·nam·ing**) to give a nickname to.

Nic·o·si·a (nik-ŏ-see-ă) the capital of Cyprus.

nic·o·tine (nik-ŏ-teen) *n.* a poisonous substance found in tobacco.

nic·o·tin·ic (nik-ŏ-tin-ik) *adj.* relating to nicotine. ☐**nicotinic acid,** a vitamin of the B group obtained from nicotine.

niece (nees) *n.* one's brother's or sister's daughter.

nif·ty (nif-tee) *adj.* (**-ti·er, -ti·est**) *(informal)* 1. spruce, smart, stylish. 2. excellent. 3. clever.

Ni·ger (nɪ-jĕr, nee-zhair) a country in central Africa. **Ni·ge·rois** (nee-zher-wah) *n.*

Ni·ge·ri·a (nɪ-jeer-i-ă) a country in West Africa. **Ni·ge′ri·an** *adj. & n.*

nig·gard (nig-ărd) *n.* a very stingy person. **nig′gard·ly** *adj.* **nig′gard·li·ness** *n.*

nig·gle (nig-ĕl) *v.* (**nig·gled, nig·gling**) to fuss over details, to find fault in a petty way. **nig′gler** *n.*

nig·gling (nig-ling) *adj.* 1. petty. 2. showing or demanding much attention to details. **nig′gling′ly** *adv.*

nigh (nɪ) *adj., adv., & prep.* *(old use)* near.

night (nɪt) *n.* 1. the dark hours between sunset and sunrise. 2. nightfall. 3. a specified or appointed night, an evening on which a performance or other activity occurs, *the first night of the play.* ☐**make a night of it,** to spend a night in festivity etc. **night and day,** at all times, without ceasing. **night blindness,** poor vision in twilight and the dark. **night crawler,** a large earthworm that comes out of the earth at night. **night light,** a faint light kept burning in a bedroom (as for a child or invalid) at night. **night owl,** *(informal)* a person active at night. **night school,** a school where instruction is provided in the evening for people who are at work during the day. **night shift,** a shift of workers employed during the night. **night table,** a small stand or table placed next to a bed. **night watchman,** a person keeping watch at night, especially in a building that is closed for business.

night·cap (nɪt-kap) *n.* 1. a soft cap formerly worn in bed. 2. a drink taken just before going to bed.

night·clothes (nɪt-klohz) *n. pl.* garments for wearing in bed.

night·club (nɪt-klub) *n.* an establishment open at night, providing meals and entertainment.

night·dress (nɪt-dres) *n.* a nightgown.

night·fall (nɪt-fawl) *n.* the coming of darkness at the end of the day.

night·gown (nɪt-gown) *n.* a woman's or girl's loose garment for sleeping in.

night·hawk (nɪt-hawk) *n.* 1. a night-flying bird similar to a whippoorwill. 2. *(informal)* a night owl.

night·ie (nɪ-tee) *n.* *(informal)* a nightgown.

night·in·gale (nɪ-ting-gayl) *n.* a small reddish-brown thrush, the male of which sings melodiously both by night and in the day.

night·jar (nɪt-jahr) *n.* an Old World night-flying bird with a harsh cry.

night·life (nɪt-lɪf) *n.* urban entertainment open at night, such as theaters, restaurants, and nightclubs.

night·long (nɪt-lawng) *adj. & adv.* throughout the night.

night·ly (nɪt-lee) *adj.* 1. happening or done or existing etc. in the night. 2. happening every night. **nightly** *adv.* every night.

night·mare (nɪt-mair) *n.* 1. a bad dream. 2. *(informal)* a terrifying or very unpleasant experience. **night′mar·ish** *adj.*

night·rid·er (nɪt-rɪ-dĕr) *n.* a member of a secret terrorist group riding at night and committing acts of violence.

night·shade (nɪt-shayd) *n.* any of several wild plants with poisonous berries.

night·shirt (nɪt-shurt) *n.* a boy's or man's long shirt for sleeping in.

night·stick (nɪt-stik) *n.* a short club carried by a policeman or policewoman.

night·time (nɪt-tɪm) *n.* night.

night·walk·er (nɪt-waw-kĕr) *n.* a person who is out and about at night for no good purpose.

NIH *abbr.* 1. National Institutes of Health. 2. not invented here.

ni·hil·ism (nɪ-ĭ-liz-ĕm) *n.* 1. a negative doctrine, the total rejection of current beliefs in religion or morals. 2. a form of skepticism that denies all existence. **ni′hil·ist** *n.* **ni·hil·ist·ic** (nɪ-ĭ-lis-tik) *adj.*

nil (nil) *n.* nothing.

nim·ble (nim-bĕl) *adj.* (**-bler, -blest**) 1. able to move quickly, agile. 2. (of the mind or wits) able to think quickly. **nim′bly** *adv.* **nim′ble·ness** *n.*

nim·bus (nim-bŭs) *n.* (*pl.* **-bi,** *pr.* **-bɪ, -bus·es**) 1. a bright cloud imagined as surrounding deities when they appear on earth. 2. a halo shown around the head of a sacred figure. 3. a rain cloud.

Nim·rod (nim-rod) *n.* a great hunter or sportsman. ▷Named after Nimrod in the Bible.

nin·com·poop (nin-kŏm-poop) *n.* a foolish person.

nine (nɪn) *adj. & n.* one more than eight (9, IX). ☐**dressed to the nines,** dressed very elaborately. **nine days' wonder,** something that attracts much attention at first but is soon forgotten.

nine·pins (nɪn-pinz) *n.* 1. a game played with nine objects to be knocked down by rolling a ball. 2. *ninepin,* one of these objects.

nine·teen (nɪn-teen) *adj. & n.* one more than eighteen (19, XIX). **nine′teenth′** *adj. & n.* ☐**talk nineteen to the dozen,** to talk continually.

nine·ty (nɪn-tee) *adj. & n.* (*pl.* **-ties**) 1. nine times ten (90, XC). 2. *nineties,* the numbers or years or degrees of temperature from 90 to 99. **nine′ti·eth** *adj. & n.*

nin·ny (nin-ee) *n.* (*pl.* **-nies**) a foolish person.

ninth (nɪnth) *adj. & n.* 1. next after eighth. 2. one of nine equal parts of a thing. **ninth′ly** *adv.*

ni·o·bi·um (nɪ-oh-bi-ŭm) *n.* a silvery metallic element, used in steel alloys.

nip¹ (nip) *v.* **(nipped, nip·ping)** 1. to pinch or squeeze sharply, to bite quickly with the front teeth. 2. to break off by doing this, *nip off the side shoots.* 3. to pain or harm with biting cold, *a nipping wind.* 4. *(informal)* to snatch away quickly, to steal. **nip** *n.* 1. a sharp pinch or squeeze or bite. 2. biting coldness, *a nip in the air.* □**nip and tuck,** neck and neck. **nip in the bud,** to destroy at an early stage of development.

nip² *n.* a small drink of liquor. **nip** *v.* **(nipped, nip·ping)** to take frequent nips.

nip·per (nip-ĕr) *n.* 1. *(slang)* a young boy or girl. 2. the great claw of a lobster or similar animal. 3. any person or thing that nips. 4. *nippers,* pincers or forceps for gripping things or breaking things off.

nip·ple (nip-ĕl) *n.* 1. a small projection in the center of a male or female mammal's breasts, containing (in females) the outlets of the milk-secreting organs. 2. the rubber mouthpiece of a nursing bottle. 3. a nipple-like projection. 4. a rubber teat.

Nip·pon (nip-on) Japan. **Nip·pon·ese** (nip-ŏ-neez) *adj. & n.*

nip·py (nip-ee) *adj.* **(-pi·er, -pi·est)** *(informal)* 1. nimble, quick. 2. bitingly cold. **nip′pi·ness** *n.*

nir·va·na (nir-vah-nă) *n.* (in Buddhist and Hindu teaching) the state of perfect bliss attained when the soul is freed from all suffering and absorbed into the supreme spirit.

Ni·sei (nee-say) *n.* (*pl.* **-sei, -seis)** a person of Japanese descent whose parents were immigrants from Japan.

ni·si (nɪ-sɪ) *adj.* subject to conditions as regards taking effect. (See **decree nisi.**) ▷Latin, = unless.

nit (nit) *n.* 1. the egg or young of a louse or other parasite. 2. *(slang)* a trivial detail.

ni·ter (nɪ-tĕr) *n.* saltpeter, potassium nitrate.

nit·pick (nit-pik) *v.* *(slang)* to find fault in a petty way. **nit′pick·er** *n.*

ni·trate (nɪ-trayt) *n.* 1. a salt or ester of nitric acid. 2. potassium or sodium nitrate used as a fertilizer. **nitrate** *v.* **(ni·trat·ed, ni·trat·ing)** to treat, combine, impregnate with nitric acid or a nitrate.

ni·tric (nɪ-trik) *adj.* of or containing nitrogen. □**nitric acid,** a colorless caustic highly corrosive acid. **nitric oxide,** a colorless gas.

ni·tri·fy (nɪ-trĭ-fɪ) *v.* **(ni·tri·fied, ni·tri·fy·ing)** 1. to impregnate with nitrogen. 2. to turn into nitrous or nitric acid. **ni·tri·fi·ca·tion** (nɪ-trĭ-fĭ-kay-shŏn) *n.*

ni·trite (nɪ-trɪt) *n.* a salt or ester of nitrous acid.

ni·tro·ben·zene (nɪ-troh-ben-zeen) *n.* a poisonous yellow oil used as a solvent and in making certain dyes.

ni·tro·cel·lu·lose (nɪ-troh-sel-yŭ-lohs) *n.* a cellulose nitrate used in lacquers etc. **ni·tro·cel·lu·los·ic** (nɪ-troh-sel-yŭ-loh-sik) *adj.*

ni·tro·gen (nɪ-trŏ-jĕn) *n.* a colorless odorless gas forming about four-fifths of the atmosphere. **ni·trog·e·nous** (nɪ-troj-ĕ-nŭs) *adj.* □**nitrogen cycle,** the continuous transfer of nitrogen in various forms from soil to plants to animals, and back by decay.

ni·tro·glyc·er·in, ni·tro·glyc·er·ine (nɪ-troh-glis-ĕ-rin) *n.* a powerful explosive made by adding glycerine to a mixture of nitric and sulfuric acids.

ni·trous (nɪ-trŭs) *adj.* of or containing nitrogen. □**nitrous acid,** an acid containing less oxygen than nitric acid. **nitrous oxide,** a

colorless gas used as an anesthetic, laughing gas.

nit·ty-grit·ty (nit-ee-grit-ee) *n.* (*pl.* **-ties)** *(slang)* the basic fact or reality of a matter.

nit·wit (nit-wit) *n.* *(informal)* a stupid or foolish person.

nix (niks) *n.* *(slang)* nothing. **nix** *v.* **(nixed, nix·ing)** *(slang)* to veto.

Nix·on (nik-sŏn), **Rich·ard Mil·hous** (mil-hows) (1913–) the thirty-seventh president of the U.S. 1969–74.

NJ, N.J. *abbr.* New Jersey.

n.l. *abbr.* it is not permitted. ▷From the Latin *non licet.*

NL *abbr.* New Latin.

NLRB *abbr.* National Labor Relations Board.

nm. *abbr.* nautical mile.

NM *abbr.* 1. New Mexico. 2. night message. 3. not marked.

N.M., N. Mex. *abbr.* New Mexico.

NNE *abbr.* north-northeast.

NNW *abbr.* north-northwest.

no (noh) *adj.* 1. not any. 2. not a, quite other than, *she is no fool.* **no** *adv.* 1. used as a denial or refusal of something. 2. not at all, no better than before. **no** *n.* (*pl.* **noes, nos)** a negative reply or vote, a person voting against something. □**no go,** *(informal)* the task is impossible, the situation is hopeless. **no man's land,** a space between the fronts of two opposing armies in war. **no one,** no person, nobody. **no way,** *(informal)* that (method etc.) is impossible.

No, Noh (noh) *n.* traditional Japanese drama with dance and song, evolved from Shinto rites.

No *symbol* nobelium.

No., no. *abbr.* number.

No·bel·ist (noh-bel-ist) *n.* a person who wins a Nobel prize.

no·be·li·um (noh-bee-li-ŭm) *n.* an artificially produced chemical element.

No·bel (noh-bel) **prize** any of the prizes awarded annually for outstanding achievements in the sciences, literature, economics, and the promotion of world peace, from the bequest of Alfred Nobel (1833–96), the Swedish inventor of dynamite.

no·bil·i·ty (noh-bil-i-tee) *n.* (*pl.* **-ties)** nobleness of mind or character or rank; *the nobility,* people of aristocratic birth or rank, titled people.

no·ble (noh-bĕl) *adj.* **(-bler, -blest)** 1. belonging to the aristocracy by birth or rank. 2. possessing excellent qualities, especially in one's character, free from pettiness or meanness. 3. imposing in appearance, a noble edifice. **noble** *n.* a nobleman or noblewoman. **no′bly** *adv.* **no′ble·ness** *n.*

no·ble·man (noh-bĕl-măn) (*pl.* **-men,** *pr.* -mĕn) **no·ble·wom·an** (noh-bĕl-wuum-ăn) (*pl.* **-wom·en,** *pr.* -wim-in) *n.* a member of the nobility.

no·blesse o·blige (noh-bles oh-bleezh) noble people must behave nobly, privilege entails responsibility. ▷French.

no·bod·y (noh-bod-ee) *pronoun* no person. **nobody** *n.* (*pl.* **-bod·ies)** a person of no importance or authority, *he's nobody or a nobody.* □**like nobody's business,** *(informal)* very much, intensively.

noc·tur·nal (nok-tur-năl), *adj.* 1. of or in the night. 2. active in the night, *nocturnal animals.* **noc·tur′nal·ly** *adv.*

noc·turne (nok-turn) *n.* a dreamy piece of music.

noc·u·ous (nok-yoo-ŭs) *adj.* noxious, harmful. **noc′u·ous·ly** *adv.*

nod (nod) *v.* **(nod·ded, nod·ding)** 1. to move the head down and up again quickly as a sign of agreement or casual greeting, to indicate (agreement etc.) in this way. 2. to let the head fall forward in drowsiness, to be drowsy. 3. (of plumes or flowers etc.) to bend downward and sway. **nod** *n.* a nodding movement in agreement or greeting; *give* or *get the nod,* to give or get agreement or a signal to proceed. □a **nodding acquaintance,** a slight acquaintance with a person or subject. **land of Nod,** sleep.

nod·dle (nod-ĕl) *n.* (informal) the head.

nod·dy (nod-ee) *n.* (pl. -dies) 1. a simpleton. 2. a tropical seabird resembling the tern.

node (nohd) *n.* 1. a knoblike swelling. 2. the point on the stem of a plant where a leaf or bud grows out. **nod'al** adj.

nod·ule (noj-ool) *n.* a small rounded lump, a small node. **nod·u·lar** (noj-ŭ-lăr) adj.

No·el (noh-el) *n.* (in carols) Christmas.

noes (nohz) *n. see* **no.**

no-fault (noh-fawlt) *n.* 1. a form of automobile insurance that is valid regardless of allocation of blame for an accident. 2. a type of divorce awarded without attaching blame to either party.

no-frills (noh-frilz) adj. with no luxuries or extras.

nog·gin (nog-in) *n.* 1. a small measure of alcohol, usually one-fourth pint. 2. a small mug. 3. (informal) the head.

no-good (noh-guud) adj. (informal) of very poor quality, worthless. **no-good** *n.* (informal) a worthless or undependable person.

Noh = No.

no-hit·ter (noh-hit-ĕr) *n.* a baseball game in which one team makes no hits.

no-how (noh-how) adv. in no way.

noise (noiz) *n.* a sound, especially one that is loud or harsh or confused or undesired. **noise** *v.* **(noised, nois·ing)** to make public; *noised it abroad,* made it generally known. **noise'less** adj. □**noise pollution,** disturbance of human activity by harmful levels of noise.

noise·mak·er (noiz-may-kĕr) *n.* a device for making loud noise at a festivity etc.

noi·some (noi-sŏm) adj. 1. harmful, noxious. 2. evil smelling. 3. objectionable, offensive. ▷This word is unrelated to *noise.*

nois·y (noi-zee) adj. **(nois·i·er, nois·i·est)** making much noise. **nois'i·ly** adv. **nois'i·ness** *n.*

no-knock (noh-nok) adj. **no-knock law,** a law permitting forcible entry by the police into one's home or business.

no-load (noh-lohd) *n.* (also **no-load fund**) a mutual fund with no sales charge.

no·lo con·ten·de·re (noh-loh kŏn-ten-dĕ-ree) a legal plea acknowledging validity of conviction but not guilt. ▷Latin, = I do not wish to contend. **nom.** abbr. nominal.

no·mad (noh-mad) *n.* 1. a member of a tribe that roams from place to place seeking pasture for its animals. 2. a wanderer. **no·mad·ic** (noh-mad-ik) adj.

nom de guerre (nom dĕ gair) a pseudonym, an assumed name under which a person fights, plays, writes, etc. ▷French, = war-name.

nom de plume (nom dĕ ploom) a writer's pseudonym. ▷The French words mean "pen name," but the expression is not used in French.

no·men·cla·ture (noh-měn-klay-chŭr) *n.* a system of names, such as those used in a particular science.

nom·i·nal (nom-ĭ-năl) adj. 1. in name only, *nominal ruler of that country.* 2. (of an amount or sum of money) very small but charged or paid as a token that payment is required, *a nominal fee.* **nom'i·nal·ly** adv. □**nominal value,** the face value of a coin etc.

nom·i·nate (nom-ĭ-nayt) *v.* **(nom·i·nat·ed, nom·i·nat·ing)** 1. to name as candidate for or future holder of an office. 2. to appoint to an office. **nom'i·na·tor** *n.* **nom·i·na·tion** (nom-ĭ-nay-shŏn) *n.*

nom·i·na·tive (nom-ĭ-nă-tiv) *n.* the form of a noun or pronoun used when it is the subject of a verb.

nom·i·nee (nom-ĭ-nee) *n.* a person who is nominated by another.

non- prefix not. ▷The number of words with this prefix is almost unlimited, and many of those whose meanings are obvious are not listed below.

non·age (non-ij) *n.* 1. the period of being under age. 2. any time of immaturity, an early stage.

non·a·ge·nar·i·an (non-ă-jĕ-nair-i-ăn) *n.* a person who is in his or her nineties.

non·ag·gres·sion (non-ă-gresh-ŏn) *n.* the avoidance of offensive action. □**nonaggression pact,** a treaty between nations agreeing not to take offensive action against each other.

non·al·co·hol·ic (non-al-kŏ-haw-lik) adj. containing no alcohol.

non·a·ligned (non-ă-lɪnd) adj. not in alliance with any bloc. **non·a·lign·ment** (non-ă-lɪn-měnt) *n.*

non·book (non-buuk) *n.* a book exploring a fad, current event, sensational subject, etc., with no literary or graphic merit.

nonce (nons) *n.* **for the nonce,** for the time being or present occasion. **nonce word,** a word coined for one occasion.

non·cha·lant (non-shă-lahnt) adj. not feeling or showing anxiety or excitement, calm and casual. **non·cha·lant'ly** adv. **non·cha·lance'** *n.*

non·com (non-kom) *n.* (informal) a noncommissioned officer.

non·com·bat·ant (non-kom-bă-tănt, -kŏm-bat-ănt) *n.* 1. a member of an army etc. whose duties do not involve fighting, as a doctor or chaplain. 2. a civilian during a war.

---

non·a·bra'sive adj.	**non·ad·just'a·ble** adj.	**non·be·liev'er** *n.*
non·ab'so·lute adj. & *n.*	**non·af·fil'i·at·ed** adj.	**non·bel·lig'er·ent** adj. & *n.*
non·ab·sorb'ent adj. & *n.*	**non·a·gree'ment** *n.*	**non·can'cer·ous** adj.
non·ac·a·dem'ic adj.	**non·an·a·lyt'ic** adj.	**non·can'di·date** *n.*
non·ac·cep'tance *n.*	**non·ap·pear'ance** *n.*	**non·car'bo·nat·ed** adj.
non·ac'id adj. & *n.*	**non·ap'pli·ca·ble** adj.	**non-Cath'o·lic** adj. & *n.*
non·ac'tive adj.	**non·ar·o·mat'ic** adj.	**non-Cau·ca'sian** adj. & *n.*
non·a·dap'tive adj.	**non-Ar'y·an** adj. & *n.*	**non·cel'lu·lar** adj.
non·ad·dict'ing adj.	**non·as·ser'tive** adj.	**non-Chris'tian** adj. & *n.*
non·ad·dic'tive adj.	**non·as·ser'tive·ly** adv.	**non·co·ag'u·lat·ing** adj.
non·ad·he'sive adj.	**non·ath·let'ic** adj.	**non·co·he'sive** adj.
non·ad·ja'cent adj.	**non·at·tend'ance** *n.*	**non·col·lect'i·ble** adj.

non·com·mis·sioned (non-kŏ-**mish**-ŏnd) *adj.* not holding a commission, *noncommissioned officers.*

non·com·mit·tal (non-kŏ-**mit**-ăl) *adj.* not committing oneself, not showing what one thinks or which side one supports.

non com·pos men·tis (non **kom**-pŏs **men**-tis) insane. ▷Latin.

non·con·duc·tor (non-kŏn-**duk**-tŏr) *n.* a substance that does not conduct heat or electricity.
non·con·duc'ting *adj.*

non·con·form·ist (non-kŏn-**for**-mist) *n.* 1. a person who does not conform to established principles. 2. *Nonconformist,* a member of certain Protestant sects that do not conform to the teaching or practices of the Church of England or other established churches.

non·con·form·i·ty (non-kŏn-**for**-mi-tee) *n.* failure to conform to a principle or rule or tradition etc.

non·con·trib·u·to·ry (non-kŏn-**trib**-yŭ-tohr-ee) *adj.* not involving the payment of contributions, *a noncontributory pension scheme.*

non·co·op·er·a·tion (non-koh-op-ĕ-**ray**-shŏn) *n.* 1. an unwillingness to work together for a common purpose. 2. refusal to cooperate with the government by engaging in civil disobedience.

non·cred·it (non-**kred**-it) *adj.* of or relating to a course of study that does not fulfill a requirement for a degree; *a noncredit course,* one not recognized by a school as a requirement for a degree.

non·dair·y (non-**dair**-ee) *adj.* containing no milk or dairy products. ☐**nondairy creamer,** = **creamer** (definition 2).

non·de·duct·i·ble (non-di-**duk**-tĭ-bĕl) *adj.* not able to be deducted, as from a bill or tax assessment. **nondeductible** *n.* a nondeductible item.

non·de·nom·i·na·tion·al (non-di-nom-i-**nay**-shŏ-năl) *adj.* not restricted to one religion or religious denomination.

non·de·pend·ence (non-di-**pen**-dĕns) *n.* the state of not being dependent on a drug after rehabilitation.

non·de·script (non-di-**skript**) *adj.* lacking in distinctive characteristics and therefore not easy to classify. **nondescript** *n.* a nondescript person or thing.

non·dis·crim·i·na·to·ry (non-di-skrim-ĭ-nă-tohr-ee) *adj.* making no distinction in favor of or against a person or thing based on prejudice.

non·di·vis·i·ble (non-di-**viz**-ĭ-bĕl) *adj.* unable to be divided evenly, as of a number or of certain rights of people.

non·drink·er (non-**dring**-kĕr) *n.* a person who does not drink alcoholic beverages.

none (nun) *pronoun* 1. not any. (▷This word may be followed by either a singular or a plural verb, *none of them is* (or *are*) *required.* Use a singular verb when you have a reason for thinking of *none* as a singular, as in *none of the work was ready on time.*) 2. no person(s), no one, *none can tell.* **none** *adv.* by no amount, not at all, *is none the worse for it.* ☐**none other,** no other person. **none too,** not very, not at all, *he's none too pleased.*

non·ed·u·ca·ble (non-ej-ŭ-kă-bĕl) *adj.* incapable of being educated, as certain types of people and those with certain levels of mental retardation.

non·en·ti·ty (non-en-ti-tee) *n.* (*pl.* **-ties**) a person or thing of no importance.

nones (nohnz) *n. pl.* 1. the 9th day by inclusive reckoning before the ides in the Roman calendar (7th day of March, May, July, and October, 5th of other months). 2. the 5th of the canonical hours of prayer, originally said at the 9th hour.

none·such (**nun**-such) *n.* a person or thing that is unrivaled, a paragon.

none·the·less (nun-thĕ-les) *adv.* nevertheless.

non·e·vent (non-i-vent) *n.* an event that was expected or intended to be important but proves to be disappointing.

non·ex·is·tent (non-ig-zis-tĕnt) *adj.* not existing.
non·ex·ist'ence *n.*

non·fat (non-fat) *adj.* containing no or very little animal fat; *nonfat milk,* milk with less animal fat than found in low-fat milk.

non·fer·rous (non-fer-ŭs) *adj.* of metals other than iron or steel.

non·fic·tion (non-fik-shŏn) *n.* a class of literature that includes books of all types other than fiction. **non·fic'tion·al** *adj.*

non·flam·ma·ble (non-flam-ă-bĕl) *adj.* unable to be set on fire. ▷See the note under **inflammable.**

non·he·ro (non-heer-oh) *n.* an antihero.

non·com·bus'ti·ble *adj. & n.*	**non·con·vert'i·ble** *adj.*	**non·ex·pend'a·ble** *adj.*
non·com·mer'cial *adj.*	**non·cor·rod'ing** *adj.*	**non·ex·plo'sive** *adj.*
non·com·mer'cial·ly *adv.*	**non·cor·ro'sive** *adj.*	**non·ex·port'a·ble** *adj.*
non·com·mu'ni·ca·ble *adj.*	**non·crit'i·cal** *adj.*	**non·fac'tu·al** *adj.*
non·com·mu'ni·ca·tive *adj.*	**non·de·liv'er·y** *n.*	**non·fil'ter·a·ble** *adj.*
non·com'mu·nist *adj. & n.*	**non·dem·o·crat'ic** *adj.*	**non·flex'i·ble** *adj.*
non·com·pet'i·tive *adj.*	**non·de·struc'tive** *adj.*	**non·flow'er·ing** *adj.*
non·com·pli'ance *n.*	**non·de·tach'a·ble** *adj.*	**non·ful·fill'ment** *n.*
non·com·ply'ing *adj.*	**non·dis·tinc'tive** *adj.*	**non·func'tion·al** *adj.*
non·con·cil'i·a·to·ry *adj.*	**non·dis·tinc'tive·ly** *adv.*	**non·gas'e·ous** *adj.*
non·con·clu'sive *adj.*	**non·dis·tinc'tive·ness** *n.*	**non·gov·ern·men'tal** *adj.*
non·con·clu'sive·ly *adv.*	**non·dis·tri·bu'tion** *n.*	**non·ha·bit'u·al** *adj.*
non·con·clu'sive·ness *n.*	**non·ed·u·ca'tion·al** *adj.*	**non·ha·bit'u·at·ing** *adj.*
non·con·cur'rence *n.*	**non·ef·fec'tive** *adj.*	**non·haz'ard·ous** *adj.*
non·con·duc'tive *adj.*	**non·ef·fer·ves'cent** *adj.*	**non·he·red'i·tar·y** *adj.*
non·con·flict'ing *adj.*	**non·e·las'tic** *adj.*	**non·hu'man** *adj.*
non·con·struc'tive *adj.*	**non·e·lec'tric** *adj.*	**non·i·den'ti·cal** *adj.*
non·con·struc'tive·ly *adv.*	**non·el'i·gi·ble** *adj.*	**non·i·de·o·log'i·cal** *adj.*
non·con·sump'tion *n.*	**non·e·mo'tion·al** *adj.*	**non·id·i·o·mat'ic** *adj.*
non·con·ta'gious *adj.*	**non·en·force'a·ble** *adj.*	**non·im·mu'ni·ty**
non·con·tro·ver'sial *adj.*	**non·en·force'ment** *n.*	(*pl.* **-ties**) *n.*
non·con·tro·ver'sial·ly *adv.*	**non·es·sen'tial** *adj.*	**non·im·por·ta'tion** *n.*
non·con·ven'tion·al *adj.*	**non·ex·change'a·ble** *adj.*	**non·in·clu'sive** *adj.*

non·in·ter·ven·tion (non-in-tĕr-ven-shŏn) *n.* the policy of not interfering in the affairs of others, particularly nations.

non·met·al (non-met-ăl) *n.* an element that is not a metal, such as carbon, sulfur, etc. **non·me·tal·lic** (non-mĕ-tal-ik) *adj.*

non·neg·a·tive (non-neg-ă-tiv) *adj.* expressing a quantity of zero or above.

non·ob·jec·tive (non-ŏb-jek-tĭv) *adj.* 1. not objective. 2. nonrepresentational. **non·ob·jec′tive·ly** *adv.* **non·ob·jec·tiv·i·ty** (non-ob-jek-tiv-i-tee) *n.*

non·pa·reil (non-pă-rel) *n.* a person having no equal. **nonpareil** *adj.* without equal.

non·par·ti·san (non-pahr-ti-zăn) *adj.* without regard to political party interests or policies.

non·per·son (non-pur-sŏn) *n.* a person regarded by the government as not existing or as never having existed, an unperson.

non·plussed (non-plust) *adj.* completely perplexed.

non·pre·scrip·tion (non-pri-skrip-shŏn) **drug** a drug sold legally without the requirement for a physician's order or prescription.

non·pro·fes·sion·al (non-prŏ-fesh-ŏ-năl) *adj.* not belonging to a profession. **nonprofessional** *n.*

non·prof·it (non-prof-it) *adj.* not established for the purpose of gain or making money. ☐**nonprofit corporation,** one in which the purpose is service to society rather than profit.

non·pro·lif·er·a·tion (non-proh-lif-ĕ-ray-shŏn) *n.* the process of curbing the rapid increase in numbers of something, especially nuclear weapons.

non·read·er (non-ree-dĕr) *n.* a person who does not read, especially a child who is slow in learning to read.

non·rep·re·sen·ta·tion·al (non-rep-ri-zen-tay-shŏ-năl) *adj.* not representing any actual or natural object, form, or scene, etc.

non·res·i·dent (non-rez-i-dĕnt) *adj.* living in a place for a short time only, residing elsewhere. **nonresident** *n.* a person who is nonresident.

non·re·sis·tance (non-ri-zis-tăns) *n.* the practice or policy of passively submitting to force or unjust authority. **non·re·sis′tant** *adj.*

non·re·stric·tive (non-ri-strik-tiv) *adj.* 1. (of a clause, etc.) describing the antecedent, but not limiting its meaning. 2. (of membership etc.) open to all.

non·re·turn·a·ble (non-ri-tur-nă-bĕl) *adj.* not able to be returned, as an item purchased from a store.

non·rig·id (non-rij-id) *adj.* 1. limp, flexible. 2. (of a type of airship) without supporting framework and held in shape only by the pressure of internal gas. **non·ri·gid·i·ty** (non-ri-jid-i-tee) *n.*

non·sal·a·ried (non-sal-ă-reed) *adj.* not paid a regular wage or salary for one's work, as an employee who is paid a commission or a consultant who receives a fee.

non·sched·uled (non-skej-oold) **airline** one operating without a regular timetable.

non·sec·tar·i·an (non-sek-tair-i-ăn) *adj.* not restricted to or not affiliated with any particular religion.

non·sense (non-sens) *n.* 1. words put together in a way that does not make sense. 2. absurd or foolish talk or ideas or behavior. **non·sen·si·cal** (non-sen-si-kăl) *adj.* not making sense, absurd, foolish. **non·sen′si·cal·ly** *adv.*

non seq. *abbr.* non sequitur.

non se·qui·tur (non sek-wi-tŭr) a conclusion that does not follow from the evidence given. ▷ Latin, = it does not follow.

non·sked (non-sked) *adj. (informal)* nonscheduled. **nonsked** *n. (informal)* a nonscheduled airline or cargo plane.

non·skid (non-skid) *adj.* (of tires) designed to prevent or reduce skidding.

non·smok·er (non-smoh-kĕr) *n.* 1. a person who does not smoke. 2. a train or airplane compartment where smoking is forbidden.

non·stand·ard (non-stan-dărd) *adj.* (of language) varying in usage from what is usually regarded as preferred or correct.

non·start·er (non-stahr-tĕr) *n.* 1. a person who does not assume the initiative to take action. 2.

---

non·in·crim′i·nat·ing *adj.*
non·in·de·pend′ent *adj.*
non·in·duc′tive *adj.*
non·in·dus′tri·al *adj.*
non·in·fec′tious *adj.*
non·in·for′ma·tive *adj.*
non·in·hab′it·a·ble *adj.*
non·in·her′it·a·ble *adj.*
non·in·sti·tu′tion·al *adj.*
non·in·ter·change′a·ble *adj.*
non·in·ter·sect′ing *adj.*
non·in·tox′i·cant *n.*
non·in·tox′i·cat·ing *adj.*
non·ir′ri·tant *n.*
non·ir′ri·tat·ing *adj.*
non·ju·di′cial *adj.*
non·ko′sher *adj.*
non·le′thal *adj.*
non·lin′e·ar *adj.*
non·lit′er·ar·y *adj.*
non·ma·lig′nant *adj.*
non·mar′ket·a·ble *adj.*
non·ma·te′ri·al *adj.*
non·mem′ber *n.*
non·mi′gra·to·ry *adj.*
non·mil′i·tar·y *adj.*

non·ne·go′ti·a·ble *adj.*
non·nu·tri′tious *adj.*
non·ob·ser′vance *n.*
non·oil′y *adj.*
non·op′er·a·ble *adj.*
non·or·gan′ic *adj.*
non·par′al·lel *adj.*
non·par·tic·i·pa′tion *n.*
non·pay′ing *adj.*
non·pay′ment *n.*
non·per·form′ance *n.*
non·per′ish·a·ble *adj.*
non·per′ma·nent *adj.*
non·phys′i·cal *adj.*
non·poi′son·ous *adj.*
non·po·lit′i·cal *adj.*
non·po′rous *adj.*
non·pos·ses′sive *adj.*
non·pos·ses′sive·ly *adv.*
non·pos·ses′sive·ness *n.*
non·pre′cious *adj.*
non·pre·dict′a·ble *adj.*
non·pre·scrip′tive *adj.*
non·pro·duc′er *n.*
non·pro·duc′tive *adj.*
non·pro·pri′e·ta·ry *adj.*

non·pun′ish·a·ble *adj.*
non·ra′cial *adj.*
non·ra·di·o·ac′tive *adj.*
non·re·al·is′tic *adj.*
non·re·cip′ro·cal *adj.*
non·rec·og·ni′tion *n.*
non·re·cov′er·a·ble *adj.*
non·re·cur′rent *adj.*
non·re·deem′a·ble *adj.*
non·re·fill′a·ble *adj.*
non·re·li′gious *adj.*
non·re·mov′a·ble *adj.*
non·re·mu′ner·a·tive *adj.*
non·rep·re·sen′ta·tive *adj.*
non·sci·en·tif′ic *adj.*
non·sea′son·al *adj.*
non·seg′re·gat·ed *adj.*
non·se·lec′tive *adj.*
non·sex′u·al *adj.*
non·shrink′a·ble *adj.*
non·skilled′ *adj.*
non·slip′ *adj.*
non·smok′ing *adj.*
non·so′cial *adj.*
non·spe′cial·ized *adj.*
non·stain′ing *adj.*

(of a race) a horse, racing car, etc. scratched at the last moment.

non·stick (non-stik) *adj.* (of frying pans etc.) coated with a substance that prevents food from sticking during cooking.

non·stop (non-stop) *adj.* 1. (of a train or plane etc.) not stopping at intermediate places. 2. not ceasing, *nonstop chatter*. **nonstop** *adv.* without stopping or pausing, *they laughed nonstop.*

non·sup·port (non-sŭ-pohrt) *n.* failure to support a legal dependent.

non·ten·ured (non-ten-yŭrd) *adj.* not holding a tenured position (*see* **tenured**).

non trop·po (non trop-oh) (in music) not too much.

non·un·ion (non-yoon-yŏn) *adj.* 1. not belonging to a labor union. 2. refusing to recognize a labor union or its policy. 3. not produced by members of a labor union.

non·us·er (non-yoo-zĕr) *n.* 1. a person who is not a consumer or user of a certain product. 2. a person who is not a habitual user of drugs.

non·vi·o·lence (non-vɪ-ŏ-lĕns) *n.* the policy of refraining from the use of violence to gain one's objectives. **non·vi′o·lent** *adj.*

non·vot·er (non-voh-tĕr) *n.* a person who is eligible to vote but does not.

non·white (non-hwɪt) *adj.* not belonging to the white race of mankind.

noo·dle (noo-dĕl) *n.* 1. a strip of dough made of flour and eggs, dried and used in soups etc. 2. (*informal*) the head.

nook (nuuk) *n.* a secluded place or corner, a recess.

noon (noon) *n.* twelve o'clock in the day, midday.

noon·day (noon-day) *n.* **noon·time (noon-tɪm)** *n.*

noose (noos) *n.* a loop of rope etc. with a knot that tightens when pulled.

no-par (noh-pahr) *adj.* having no face value.

nope (nohp) *interj.* (*informal*) no.

nor (nor) *adv. & conj.* and not.

Nor. *abbr.* 1. Norway. 2. Norwegian.

NORAD (nor-ad) *n. North American Air Defense Command.*

Nor·dic (nor-dik) *adj.* of the racial type found especially in Scandinavia, tall and blond with blue eyes.

Nor·folk (nor-fŏk) jacket a man's loose-belted jacket with box pleats.

norm (norm) *n.* 1. a standard or pattern or type considered to be representative of a group. 2. a standard amount of work etc. to be done or produced.

nor·mal (nor-măl) *adj.* 1. conforming to what is standard or usual. 2. free from mental or emotional disorders. **normal** *n.* 1. a normal person. 2. the usual state, level, value, etc. **nor′mal·ly** *adv.* **nor·mal·cy (nor-măl-see)** *n.* **nor·mal·i·ty (nor-mal-i-tee)** *n.* □**normal school,** (*old use*) a school for training teachers.

nor·mal·ize (nor-mă-lɪz) *v.* (**nor·mal·ized, nor·mal·iz·ing**) to make normal or conforming. **nor·mal·i·za·tion (nor-mă-li-zay-shŏn)** *n.*

Nor·man (nor-măn) *adj.* of the Normans. **Norman**

n. a member of the people of Normandy in northern France. □**Norman Conquest,** *see* **conquest.**

nor·ma·tive (nor-mă-tiv) *adj.* of or establishing a norm. **nor′ma·tive·ly** *adv.* **nor′ma·tive·ness** *n.*

Norse (nors) *adj.* of ancient Norway or Scandinavia. **Norse** *n.* the Norwegian language or the Scandinavian group of languages.

Norse·man (nors-măn) *n.* (*pl.* **-men,** *pr.* **-mĕn**) a native of ancient Scandinavia, especially of Norway.

north (north) *n.* 1. the point or direction to the left of a person facing east. 2. the northern part of something. **north** *adj. & adv.* toward or in the north; *a north wind,* blowing from the north. □**North America,** the northernmost continent of the Western Hemisphere. **North American,** of or relating to North America or an inhabitant of North America. **North Carolina,** a state of the U.S. **North Carolinian,** a native or inhabitant of North Carolina. **North Dakota,** a state of the U.S. **North Dakotan,** a native or inhabitant of North Dakota. **North Korea,** a country formed in 1948 by the division of Korea, situated in northeast Asia. **North Pole,** the northernmost point of Earth. **north pole,** (of a magnet) the pole that is attracted to the north. **North Star,** the pole star. **North Vietnam,** a former country of southeast Asia, now reunited with South Vietnam as *Vietnam.* **the North,** the northern part of the U.S., north of the Ohio River and the Mason-Dixon line; the Union side in the Civil War.

north·bound (north-bownd) *adj.* traveling northward.

north·east (north-eest) *n.* 1. the point or direction midway between north and east. 2. *Northeast,* the northeast region of the U.S. **northeast** *adj. & adv.* toward or in the northeast **north·east·ward (north-eest-wărd)** *adj. & adv.* **north·east′wards** *adv.* toward the northeast. **north·east·ern** *adj.* **north·east′er·ly** *adj. & adv.*

north·east·er (north-ee-stĕr) *n.* a northeast wind or storm.

north·er (nor-thĕr) *n.* a strong cold north wind blowing in autumn and winter over Texas, Florida, and the Gulf of Mexico.

north·er·ly (nor-thĕr-lee) *adj.* in or toward the north; *a northerly wind,* blowing from the north (approximately). **northerly** *n.* a northerly wind.

north·ern (nor-thĕrn) *adj.* of or in the north. □**Northern Hemisphere,** the half of Earth north of the equator. **Northern Ireland,** *see* **Ireland. northern lights,** the aurora borealis.

north·ern·er (nor-thĕr-nĕr) *n.* 1. a native or inhabitant of the northeast U.S. 2. a Union supporter in the Civil War.

north·ern·most (nor-thĕrn-mohst) *adj.* farthest north.

north·ward (north-wărd) *adj.* toward the north, in the north. **northward, northwards (north-wardz)** *adv.* toward the north.

north·west (north-west) *n.* 1. the point or direction midway between north and west. 2. *Northwest,*

non·stim′u·lat·ing *adj.*	**non·tax′a·ble** *adj.*	**non·ven′om·ous** *adj.*
non·stra·te′gic *adj.*	**non·tech′ni·cal** *adj.*	**non·ver′bal** *adj.*
non·strik′er *n.*	**non·think′ing** *adj.*	**non·vi′a·ble** *adj.*
non·strik′ing *adj.*	**non·tox′ic** *adj.*	**non·vir′u·lent** *adj.*
non·sur′gi·cal *adj.*	**non·trans′fer·a·ble** *adj.*	**non·vo′cal** *adj.*
non·sus·tain′ing *adj.*	**non·vas′cu·lar** *adj.*	**non·vo·ca′tion·al** *adj.*

the northwest region of the U.S. **northwest** adj. & adv. toward or in the northwest. **north·west·ward** (north-west-wărd) adj. & adv. **north·west'wards** adv. toward the northwest. **north·west'ern** adj. **north·west'er·ly** adj. & adv. ☐**Northwest Territories,** the part of Canada lying north of the 60th parallel.

Norw. abbr. 1. Norway. 2. Norwegian.

Nor·way (nor-way) a country in northern Europe.

Nor·we·gian (nor-wee-jăn) adj. of Norway or its people or language. **Norwegian** n. 1. a native or inhabitant of Norway. 2. the language of Norway.

Nos., nos. abbr. numbers.

nose (nohz) n. 1. the organ at the front of the head in man and animals, containing the nostrils and used for breathing and smelling. 2. a sense of smell. 3. the ability to detect things of a particular kind, has a nose for scandal. 4. the open end of a tube or piping etc. 5. the front end or projecting front part of something. **nose** v. **(nosed, nos·ing)** 1. to detect or search by using one's sense of smell. 2. to smell at, to rub with the nose, to push the nose against or into. 3. to push one's way cautiously ahead, the car nosed past the obstruction. ☐**by a nose,** by a very narrow margin. **keep one's nose clean,** to stay out of trouble. **nose cone,** the cone-shaped nose of a rocket or missile. **nose dive,** an airplane's steep downward plunge with the nose first; any sudden drop or plunge. **pay through the nose,** to pay an unfairly high price. **put someone's nose out of joint,** to make him envious because of another's success or promotion etc. **rub his nose in it,** to remind him humiliatingly of his error. **turn up one's nose at,** to reject or ignore contemptuously. **under a person's nose,** where he can or should see it clearly. **with one's nose in the air,** haughtily.

nose·bag (nohz-bag) n. a bag containing fodder, for hanging on a horse's head.

nose·band (nohz-band) n. the lower band of a bridle passing over the nose and attached to the cheek straps.

nose·bleed (nohz-bleed) n. bleeding from the nose.

nose-dive (nohz-dıv) v. **(nose-dived, nose-div·ing)** (of an airplane etc.) to plunge straight down.

nose·gay (nohz-gay) n. a small bunch of flowers.

nose·piece (nohz-pees) n. 1. the part of a helmet protecting the nose. 2. the bridge of a pair of eyeglasses.

nosh (nosh) n. (slang) food. **nosh** v. (slang) to snack. **nosh'er** n. (slang) a habitual snacker.

no-show (noh-shoh) n. (informal) a person who reserves a seat, especially on an airplane, but who does not use it or cancel it.

nos·tal·gia (no-stal-jă) n. sentimental memory of or longing for things of the past. **nos·tal'gic** adj. **nos·tal'gi·cal·ly** adv.

nos·tril (nos-trĭl) n. either of the two openings in the nose through which air is admitted.

nos·trum (nos-trŭm) n. a quack remedy.

nos·y, nos·ey (noh-zee) adj. **(nos·i·er, nos·i·est)** (informal) inquisitive. **nos'i·ly** adv. **nos'i·ness** n. ☐**Nosy** or **Nosey Parker,** (informal) an inquisitive person, a busybody.

not (not) adv. expressing a negative or denial or refusal. ☐**not at all,** a polite reply to thanks. **not half,** not nearly, not half enough; (informal) not at all, it's not half bad.

no·ta be·ne (noh-tă bee-nee, bay-nay) observe what follows, note well. ▷Latin.

no·ta·bil·i·ty (noh-tă-bil-i-tee) n. 1. being notable. 2. a notable person.

no·ta·ble (noh-tă-běl) adj. worthy of notice, remarkable, eminent. **notable** n. an eminent person.

no·ta·bly (noh-tă-blee) adv. remarkably, especially.

no·tar·i·al (noh-tair-i-ăl) adj. of a notary public.

no·ta·rize (noh-tă-rız) v. **(no·ta·rized, no·ta·riz·ing)** to attest as a notary.

no·ta·ry (noh-tă-ree) **public** (pl. **no·ta·ries public**) a person officially authorized to witness the signing of documents and to perform other formal transactions.

no·ta·tion (noh-tay-shŏn) n. a system of signs or symbols representing numbers, quantities, musical notes, etc.

notch (noch) n. 1. a V-shaped cut or indentation. 2. a narrow pass through mountains. 3. one of the levels in a graded system, everyone moved up a notch. **notch** v. 1. to make a notch or notches in. 2. to score, notched up another win. **notch'y** adj.

note (noht) n. 1. a brief record of something, written down to aid the memory. 2. a short or informal letter, a memorandum, a formal diplomatic communication. 3. a short comment on or explanation of a word or passage in a book etc. 4. a promise to pay money, a promissory note. 5. a tone of definite pitch made by a voice or instrument or engine etc. 6. a written sign representing the pitch and duration of a musical sound. 7. one of the keys on a piano etc. 8. a significant sound or indication of feelings etc., a note of optimism. 9. eminence, distinction, a family of note. 10. notice, attention; take note of what he says, pay attention to it. **note** v. **(not·ed, not·ing)** 1. to notice, to pay attention to. 2. to write down, noted it down.

note·book (noht-buuk) n. a book with blank pages on which to write memoranda etc.

not·ed (noh-tid) adj. famous, well-known. **not'ed·ly** adv.

note·pa·per (noht-pay-pěr) n. paper for writing letters on.

note·wor·thy (noht-wur-thee) adj. worthy of notice, remarkable.

noth·ing (nuth-ing) n. 1. no thing, not anything. 2. no amount, naught. 3. nonexistence, what does not exist. 4. a person or thing of no importance. **nothing** adv. not at all, in no way, it's nothing like as good. ☐**for nothing,** without payment, free; without a reward or result. **nothing doing,** (slang) a statement of refusal or failure.

noth·ing·ness (nuth-ing-nis) n. nonexistence, faded into nothingness.

no·tice (noh-tis) n. 1. news or information of what has happened or is about to happen; at short notice, with little time for preparation. 2. a formal announcement that one is to end an agreement or leave a job at a specified time, gave him a month's notice. 3. written or printed information or instructions displayed publicly. 4. attention, observation, it escaped my notice. 5. an account or review in a newspaper. **notice** v. **(no·ticed, no·tic·ing)** 1. to perceive, to become aware of, to take notice of. 2. to remark upon, to speak of. ☐**take notice,** to show signs of interest; take no notice of it, ignore it, take no action about it.

no·tice·a·ble (noh-ti-să-běl) *adj.* easily seen or noticed. **no'tice·a·bly** *adv.*

no·ti·fy (noh-tĭ-fɪ) *v.* (**no·ti·fied, no·ti·fy·ing**) 1. to inform. 2. to report, to make (a thing) known. **no·ti·fi·ca·tion** (noh-tĭ-f ĭ-kay-shŏn) *n.*

no·tion (noh-shŏn) *n.* 1. an idea or opinion, especially one that is vague or probably incorrect. 2. an understanding or intention, *has no notion of discipline.* 3. *notions,* small items used in sewing (such as spools of cotton, buttons).

no·tion·al (noh-shŏ-năl) *adj.* hypothetical, assumed to be correct or valid for a particular purpose, *an estimate based on notional figures.* **no'tion·al·ly** *adv.*

no·to·ri·ous (noh-tohr-i-ŭs) *adj.* well known, especially in an unfavorable way. **no·to'ri·ous·ly** *adv.* **no·to·ri·e·ty** (noh-tŏ-rɪ-ĕ-tee) *n.*

no-trump (noh-trump) *n.* (in bridge) a declaration or bid involving playing without a trump suit.

not·with·stand·ing (not-wɪth-stan-dĭng) *prep.* in spite of. **notwithstanding** *adv.* nevertheless. **notwithstanding** *conj.* although.

Nouak·chott (nwahk-shot) the capital of Mauritania.

nou·gat (noo-gaht) *n.* a chewy candy made of nuts, sugar or honey, and egg white.

nought = **naught**.

noun (nown) *n.* a word or phrase used as the name of a person or place or thing. □**common nouns,** words such as *man* or *dog* or *table* or *sport,* which are used of whole classes of people or things. **proper nouns,** words such as *John* and *Smith* and *London,* which name a particular person, place, or thing.

nour·ish (nur-ish) *v.* 1. to keep (a person or animal or plant) alive and well by means of food. 2. to foster or cherish (a feeling etc.). **nour'ish·ment** *n.*

nou·veau riche (noo-voh reesh) (*pl.* **nou·veaux riches,** *pr.* noo-voh reesh) (*contemptuous*) a person who has recently acquired wealth and is ostentatious. ▷French.

Nov. *abbr.* November.

no·va (noh-vă) *n.* (*pl.* **-vas, -vae,** *pr.* -vee) a star that suddenly becomes much brighter for a short time.

No·va Sco·tia (noh-vă skoh-shă) a province of Canada. **No'va Sco'tian** *adj. & n.*

nov·el (nov-ĕl) *n.* a book-length story. **novel** *adj.* of a new kind, *a novel experience.*

nov·el·ette (nov-ĕ-let) *n.* a short novel.

nov·el·ist (nov-ĕ-list) *n.* a writer of novels.

nov·el·ize (nov-ĕ-lɪz) *v.* (**nov·el·ized, nov·el·iz·ing**) to convert into a novel. **nov·el·i·za·tion** (nov-ĕ-li-zay-shŏn) *n.*

no·vel·la (noh-vel-ă) *n.* (*pl.* **-vel·las, -vel·lae,** *pr.* -vel-ee) a short novel or narrative.

nov·el·ty (nov-ĕl-tee) *n.* (*pl.* **-ties**) 1. the quality of being novel. 2. a novel thing or occurrence. 3. a small unusual object, especially one suitable for giving as a present, *a store selling novelties.*

No·vem·ber (noh-vem-běr) *n.* the eleventh month of the year.

no·ve·na (noh-vee-nă) *n.* (*pl.* **-nas, -nae,** *pr.* -nee) a Roman Catholic devotion consisting of special prayers or a service on nine successive days.

nov·ice (nov-is) *n.* 1. a person who is inexperienced in the work etc. that he is doing, a beginner. 2. one who has been accepted into a religious order but has not yet taken the final vows.

no·vi·ti·ate (noh-vish-i-it) *n.* the period of being a novice in a religious order.

No·vo·caine (noh-vŏ-kayn) *n.* (*trademark*) procaine.

now (now) *adv.* 1. at the time when or of which one is writing or speaking. 2. by this time. 3. immediately, *must go now.* 4. (with no reference to time, giving an explanation or comfort etc.) I beg or wonder or warn you or am telling you, *now why didn't I think of that?* **now** *conj.* as a consequence of the fact, simultaneously with it, *now that you have come, we'll start; I do remember, now you mention it.* **now** *n.* the present time, *they ought to be here by now.* **now** *adj.* (*slang*) 1. current or of the present, *the now people.* 2. stylishly new, *clothes with a now look.* □**for now,** until a later time, *goodbye for now.* **now and again** *or* **now and then,** occasionally.

NOW (now) *n.* 1. National Organization for Women. 2. (also *N.O.W.*) negotiable order of withdrawal for a checking account (a *NOW account*) that earns interest.

now·a·days (now-ă-dayz) *adv.* at the present time (contrasted with years ago).

no·way (noh-way) *adv.* (*informal*) in no way, to no degree, *she felt noway responsible for his errors.*

no·where (noh-hwair) *adv.* not anywhere. **nowhere** *n.* a place that is obscure or remote or unknown, etc. □**come from nowhere,** to be suddenly present. **get nowhere,** to make no progress. **in the middle of nowhere,** (*informal*) not near any towns etc. **nowhere near,** not nearly. ▷The word *nowheres* is incorrect.

no·wise (noh-wɪz) *adv.* in no way, not at all.

nox·ious (nok-shŭs) *adj.* unpleasant and harmful. **nox'ious·ly** *adv.* **nox'ious·ness** *n.*

noz·zle (noz-ĕl) *n.* the vent or spout of a hose etc. through which a stream of liquid or air is directed.

np *abbr.* 1. no pagination. 2. no place (of publication). 3. notary public.

Np *symbol* neptunium.

NP *abbr.* 1. no protest. 2. notary public. 3. noun phrase.

NRA *abbr.* 1. National Recovery Administration. 2. National Rifle Association of America.

NRC *abbr.* Nuclear Regulatory Commission.

NS *abbr.* 1. not specified. 2. nuclear ship.

N.S. *abbr.* Nova Scotia.

NSA *abbr.* National Security Agency.

NSC *abbr.* National Security Council.

NSF *abbr.* 1. National Science Foundation. 2. not sufficient funds.

NT *abbr.* New Testament.

nth (enth) *adj.* **to the nth degree,** to the utmost.

NTP *abbr.* normal temperature and pressure.

nt. wt. *abbr.* net weight.

nu (noo) *n.* the thirteenth letter of the Greek alphabet (N ν).

NU *abbr.* name unknown.

nu·ance (noo-ahns) *n.* a subtle difference in meaning, a shade of meaning.

nub (nub) *n.* 1. a small knob or lump. 2. the central point or core of a matter or problem.

nub·bin (nub-in) *n.* 1. a stunted or imperfect ear of corn. 2. anything small or stunted.

nub·by (nub-ee) *adj.* (**-bi·er, -bi·est**) full of small lumps, *nubby tweeds.*

nu·bile (noo-bil) *adj.* marriageable, physically attractive, *nubile young women.*

nu·cle·ar (noo-klee-ăr) *adj.* 1. of a nucleus. 2. of or using nuclear energy, *nuclear weapons; nuclear* *power.* □**nuclear energy,** energy that is released or absorbed during reactions taking place in the nuclei of atoms. **nuclear family,** father, mother, and children. **nuclear physics,** the branch of physics dealing with atomic nuclei and their reactions. ▷Do not pronounce *nuclear* noo-kyuu-lăr.

nu·cle·ate (noo-kli-ayt) *v.* **(nu·cle·at·ed, nu· cle·at·ing)** to form into a nucleus. **nu′cle·a· tor** *n.* **nu·cle·a·tion** (noo-kli-ay-shŏn) *n.*

nu·cle·ic (noo-klee-ik) **acid** any of a group of complex organic substances present in all living cells.

nu·cle·on (noo-kli-on) *n.* a proton or neutron, especially as a particle in an atomic nucleus. **nu· cle·on·ic** (noo-kli-on-ik) *adj.*

nu·cle·on·ics (noo-kli-on-iks) *n.* the branch of science and engineering that deals with the practical uses of nuclear energy.

nu·cle·us (noo-kli-ŭs) *n.* (*pl.* **-cle·i,** *pr.* -kli-ı, **-cle·us·es**) **1.** the central part or thing around which others are collected. **2.** something established that will receive additions, *this collection of books will form the nucleus of a new library.* **3.** the central positively charged portion of an atom. **4.** the dense central part of a plant or animal cell containing genetic material.

nu·clide (noo-klıd) *n.* a particular kind of atom defined by the composition of its nucleus. **nu· clid·ic** (noo-klid-ik) *adj.*

nude (nood) *adj.* not clothed, naked. **nude** *n.* a nude human figure in a painting etc. **nud·i·ty** (noo-dĭ-tee) *n.* □**in the nude,** not clothed, naked.

nudge (nuj) *v.* **(nudged, nudging) 1.** to poke (a person) gently with the elbow in order to draw his attention quietly. **2.** to push slightly or gradually. **nudge** *n.* this movement. **nudg′er** *n.*

nud·ist (noo-dist) *n.* a person who believes that going unclothed is good for the health. **nud′ism** *n.* □**nudist camp,** a settlement where people live unclothed.

nu·ga·to·ry (noo-gă-tohr-ee) *adj.* **1.** trifling, worthless, futile. **2.** inoperative, not valid.

nug·get (nug-it) *n.* **1.** a rough lump of gold or platinum as found in the earth. **2.** something small and valuable, *nuggets of information.*

nui·sance (noo-săns) *n.* a source of annoyance, an annoying person or thing. □**nuisance tax,** a tax collected in small amounts directly from a person or business. **nuisance value,** capacity to harass or frustrate.

Nu·ku·a·lo·fa (noo-koo-ă-law-fă) the capital of Tonga.

null (nul) *adj.* **1.** having no legal force, *declared the agreement null and void.* **2.** without effect on value, insignificant. **3.** amounting to nothing. **nul· li·ty** (nul-ĭ-tee) *n.*

nul·li·fy (nul-ĭ-fı) *v.* **(nul·li·fied, nul·li·fy·ing) 1.** to make (a thing) null. **2.** to cancel or neutralize the effect of. **nul·li·fi·ca·tion** (nul-ĭ-fı-kay-shŏn) *n.*

num. *abbr.* numeral.

Num., Numb. *abbr.* Numbers.

numb (num) *adj.* deprived of the power to feel or move, *numb with cold* or *shock.* **numb** *v.* to make numb. **numb′ly** *adv.* **numb′ness** *n.*

num·ber (num-bĕr) *n.* **1.** a symbol or word indicating how many, a numeral. **2.** a numeral identifying a person or thing (such as a telephone or a house in a street) by its position in a series. **3.** a single issue of a magazine. **4.** a song or piece of music etc., especially as an item in a theatrical perfor-

mance. **5.** *(informal)* an object (such as a garment or car) considered as an item. **6.** a total of people or things; *a number of,* some; *numbers of,* very many. **7.** the category "singular" or "plural" in grammar. **8.** *numbers,* arithmetic, *does numbers well.* **9.** *Numbers,* the fourth book of the Old Testament, a part of which contains the census of the Israelites. **number** *v.* **1.** to count, to find out how many. **2.** to amount to. **3.** to assign a number to (each in a series), to distinguish in this way. **4.** to include or regard as, *I number him among my friends.* □**by numbers,** following simple instructions identified by numbers. **do it by the numbers,** to follow a prescribed procedure. **have a person's number,** *(slang)* to understand him or his motives. **his days are numbered,** he has not long to live or to remain in his present position. **number one,** *(slang)* oneself, *always takes care of number one.* **the numbers game,** a lottery based on the occurrence of unpredictable numbers in the results of races etc. **without number,** innumerable.

▷See the note under **amount.**

num·ber·less (num-bĕr-lis) *adj.* innumerable.

numb·skull = numskull.

nu·mer·a·ble (noo-mĕ-ră-bĕl) *adj.* able to be numbered or counted.

nu·mer·al (noo-mĕ-răl) *n.* a symbol that represents a certain number, a figure. **numeral** *adj.* of or denoting a number or numbers.

nu·mer·ate (noo-mĕ-rayt) *v.* **(nu·mer·at·ed, nu·mer·at·ing)** to enumerate. **nu·mer·a·tion** (noo-mĕ-ray-shŏn) *n.*

nu·mer·a·tor (noo-mĕ-ray-tŏr) *n.* the number above the line in a fraction.

nu·mer·i·cal (noo-mer-i-kăl), **nu·mer·ic** (noo-mer-ik) *adj.* of a number or series of numbers, *placed in numerical order.* **nu·mer′i·cal·ly** *adv.*

nu·mer·ol·o·gy (noo-mĕ-rol-ŏ-jee) *n.* **1.** divination by numbers. **2.** the study of the occult meaning of numbers. **nu·mer·ol′o·gist** *n.*

nu·mer·ous (noo-mĕ-rŭs) *adj.* many, consisting of many items. **nu′mer·ous·ly** *adv.* **nu′mer·ous· ness** *n.*

numis. *abbr.* numismatic(s).

nu·mis·mat·ics (noo-miz-mat-iks) *n.* the scientific study of coins and similar objects, such as medals. **nu·mis·mat′ic** *adj.*

nu·mis·ma·tist (noo-miz-mă-tist) *n.* an expert in numismatics.

num·skull (num-skul) *n.* a stupid person.

nun (nun) *n.* a member of a community of women living apart from the world under the rules of a religious order.

nun·ci·o (nun-shi-oh) *n.* (*pl.* **-ci·os**) a diplomatic representative of the pope, accredited to a civil government.

nun·ner·y (nun-ĕ-ree) *n.* (*pl.* **-ner·ies**) a convent for nuns.

nup·tial (nup-shăl) *adj.* of marriage, of a wedding ceremony.

nup·tials (nup-shălz) *n. pl.* a wedding.

nurse (nurs) *n.* **1.** a person trained in caring for sick or injured or infirm people. **2.** a woman employed to take charge of young children. **nurse** *v.* **(nursed, nurs·ing) 1.** to work as a nurse, to look after in this way. **2.** to feed or be fed at the breast or udder. **3.** to hold carefully. **4.** to give special care to; *nurse a constituency,* try to keep its favor by continued attentions. □**nursing home,** a privately run hospital or home for invalids. **nursing mother,** one who is suckling an infant.

nurse·maid (nurs-mayd) *n.* a woman employed to take charge of young children.

nurs·er·y (nur-sĕ-ree) *n. (pl.* **-er·ies)** 1. a room set apart for young children. 2. a place where young plants are reared for transplanting and usually for selling. ☐**nursery rhyme,** a simple traditional song or story in rhyme for children. **nursery school,** a school for children below normal school age.

nurs·er·y·man (nur-sĕ-ri-măn) *n. (pl.* **-men,** *pr.* -mĕn) a person who owns or works in a plant nursery.

nurs·ling (nurs-ling) *n.* a baby or young animal that is being suckled.

nur·ture (nur-chŭr) *v.* **(nur·tured, nur·tur· ing)** 1. to nourish and rear. 2. to bring up, *a delicately nurtured girl.* **nurture** *n.* the process of nurturing.

nut (nut) *n.* 1. fruit consisting of a hard shell and an edible kernel. 2. this kernel. 3. *(slang)* the head. 4. *(slang)* an insane or eccentric person. 5. a small piece of metal with a hole in its center, designed for use with a bolt; *the nuts and bolts of something,* practical details.

nut·brown (nut-brown) *adj.* brown like a ripe hazelnut.

nut·crack·er (nut-krak-ĕr) *n.* a pair of pincers for cracking nuts.

nut·hatch (nut-hach) *n.* a small climbing bird that feeds on nuts and insects.

nut·meat (nut-meet) *n.* the kernel of a nut.

nut·meg (nut-meg) *n.* the hard fragrant seed of a tropical tree, ground or grated as spice.

nut·pick (nut-pik) *n.* a sharp table instrument for the removal of the kernel of a nut.

nu·tri·a (noo-tri-ă) *n.* the skin or fur of the coypu.

nu·tri·ent (noo-tri-ĕnt) *adj.* nourishing. **nutrient** *n.* a nourishing substance.

nu·tri·ment (noo-trĭ-mĕnt) *n.* nourishment.

nu·tri·tion (noo-trish-ŏn) *n.* nourishment. **nu· tri′tion·al** *adj.* **nu·tri′tion·ist** *n.*

nu·tri·tious (noo-trish-ŭs) *adj.* nourishing, efficient as food. **nu·tri′tious·ly** *adv.* **nu·tri′tious· ness** *n.*

nu·tri·tive (noo-trĭ-tiv) *adj.* nourishing. **nutritive** *n.* a nourishing substance.

nuts (nuts) *adj. (slang)* crazy; *nuts about,* very enthusiastic about. **nuts** *interj. (slang)* contemptuous emphatic refusal, *nuts to you.*

nut·shell (nut-shel) *n.* the hard outer shell of a nut. ☐**in a nutshell,** expressed in the briefest possible way.

nut·ting (nut-ing) *n.* gathering nuts, *go nutting.*

nut·ty (nut-ee) *adj.* **(-ti·er, -ti·est)** 1. full of nuts. 2. tasting like nuts. 3. *(slang)* crazy.

nuz·zle (nuz-ĕl) *v.* **(nuz·zled, nuz·zling)** to press or rub gently with the nose.

NV *abbr.* Nevada.

NW, N.W. *abbr.* 1. northwest. 2. northwestern.

NWT *abbr.* Northwest Territories.

NY, N.Y. *abbr.* New York.

NYC, N.Y.C. *abbr.* New York City.

ny·lon (nɪ-lon) *n.* 1. a synthetic fiber of great lightness and strength. 2. fabric made from this.

nymph (nimf) *n.* 1. (in mythology) a semidivine maiden living in the sea or woods etc. 2. a young insect that resembles its parents in form.

nym·pho·ma·ni·a (nim-fŏ-may-ni-ă) *n.* excessive and uncontrollable sexual desire in women.

nym·pho·ma·ni·ac (nim-fŏ-may-ni-ak) *n.* a woman suffering from nymphomania.

nys·tag·mus (ni-stag-mŭs) *n.* abnormal continual rapid involuntary movement of the eyeballs.

N.Z. *abbr.* New Zealand.

O

O, o (oh) (*pl.* **Os, O's, o's**) the fifteenth letter of the alphabet.

O *interj.* **1.** *(old use)* prefixed to a name, especially in a formally expressed wish or entreaty, *O God our help.* **2.** a natural exclamation of sudden feeling.

O *abbr.* **1.** ohm. **2.** Old.

O *symbol* **1.** oxygen. **2.** zero.

o. *abbr.* **1.** old. **2.** off. **3.** (in baseball) out(s).

O. *abbr.* **1.** ocean. **2.** October. **3.** Ohio.

o/a *abbr.* on or about.

oaf (ohf) *n.* (*pl.* **oafs**) an awkward lout. **oaf′ish** *adj.* **oaf′ish·ly** *adv.* **oaf′ish·ness** *n.*

oak (ohk) *n.* **1.** a deciduous forest tree with irregularly shaped leaves, bearing acorns. **2.** its wood. **oak·en** (oh-kĕn) *adj.* made of oak.

oa·kum (oh-kŭm) *n.* loose fiber obtained by picking old rope to pieces, used in caulking wooden ships.

oar (ohr) *n.* **1.** a pole with a flat blade at one end, used to propel a boat by its leverage against water. **2.** an oarsman, *he's a good oar.* □**put one's oar in,** to interfere.

oar·lock (ohr-lok) *n.* a device on the side of a boat serving as a fulcrum for an oar and keeping it in place.

oars·man (ohrz-măn) *n.* (*pl.* **-men,** *pr.* -mĕn) a rower.

oars·man·ship (ohrz-măn-ship) *n.* skill in rowing.

OAS *abbr.* Organization of American States.

o·a·sis (oh-ay-sis) *n.* (*pl.* **-ses,** *pr.* -seez) a fertile spot in a desert, with a spring or well of water.

oat (oht) *n.* **1.** a hardy cereal plant grown in cool climates for food (*oats* for horses, *oatmeal* for people). **2.** its grain. □**feel one's oats,** to be lively; to be self-important. **sow one's wild oats,** to lead a wild life while young, before settling down.

oat·cake (oht-kayk) *n.* a thin cake made of oatmeal.

oath (ohth) *n.* **1.** a solemn promise to do something or that something is true, appealing to God or a revered object as witness. **2.** casual use of the name of God etc. in anger or to give emphasis. □**on** *or* **under oath,** having made a solemn oath.

oat·meal (oht-meel) *n.* **1.** meal prepared from oats. **2.** a breakfast food cooked from this.

OAU *abbr.* Organization of African Unity.

OB *abbr.* obstetrics.

ob. *abbr.* **1.** he or she died (▷Latin *obiit*). **2.** incidentally (▷Latin *obiter*).

ob·bli·ga·to (ob-li-gah-toh) *n.* (*pl.* **-tos**) an important accompanying part in a musical composition.

ob·du·rate (ob-dŭ-rit) *adj.* stubborn and unyielding. **ob·du·ra·cy** (ob-dŭ-ră-see) *n.*

o·be·di·ent (oh-bee-di-ĕnt) *adj.* doing what one is told to do, willing to obey. **o·be′di·ent·ly** *adv.* **o·be′di·ence** *n.*

o·bei·sance (oh-bay-sĕns) *n.* a deep bow or curtsy. **o·bei′sant** *adj.*

ob·e·lisk (ob-ĕ-lisk) *n.* a tall pillar set up as a monument.

o·bese (oh-bees) *adj.* very fat. **o·be·si·ty** (oh-bee-si-tee) *n.*

o·bey (oh-bay) *v.* (**o·beyed, o·bey·ing**) to do what is commanded by (a person or law or instinct etc.), to be obedient,

ob·fus·cate (ob-fus-kayt, ob-fŭ-skayt) *v.* (**ob·fus·cat·ed, ob·fus·cat·ing**) **1.** to darken or obscure, confuse. **2.** to stupefy or bewilder. **ob·fus·ca·tion** (ob-fŭ-skay-shŏn) *n.*

o·bi (oh-bee) *n.* (*pl.* **o·bis,** *pr.* oh-beez) a bright broad sash worn with a kimono by Japanese women and children.

o·bit (oh-bit) *n.* *(informal)* obituary.

ob·i·ter dic·tum (ob-i-tĕr dik-tŭm) (*pl.* **dic·ta,** *pr.* **dik-tă**) **1.** a judge's expression of opinion uttered in arguing a point or giving judgment but not essential to his decision and therefore without binding authority. **2.** an incidental remark. ▷Latin, = thing said by the way.

o·bit·u·ar·y (oh-bich-oo-er-ee) *n.* (*pl.* **-ar·ies**) a notice of a person's death, especially in a newspaper, often with a short account of his life and achievements.

obj. *abbr.* **1.** object. **2.** objection. **3.** objective.

ob·ject (ob-jikt) *n.* **1.** something solid that can be seen or touched. **2.** a person or thing to which some action or feeling is directed, *an object of pity.* **3.** a purpose, an intention. **4.** (in grammar) a noun or its equivalent acted upon by a transitive verb or by a preposition (*him* is the object in *the dog bit him* and *against him*). **object** (ŏb-jekt) *v.* to say that one is not in favor of something, to protest. **ob·jec′tor** *n.* □**no object,** not forming an important or limiting factor; *expense is no object,* cost is not a consideration. **object lesson,** a striking practical illustration of some principle.

ob·jec·tion (ŏb-jek-shŏn) *n.* **1.** a feeling of disapproval or opposition, a statement of this. **2.** a reason for objecting, a drawback in a plan etc.

ob·jec·tion·a·ble (ŏb-jek-shŏ-nă-bĕl) *adj.* causing objections or disapproval, unpleasant. **ob·jec′tion·a·bly** *adv.*

ob·jec·tive (ŏb-jek-tiv) *adj.* **1.** having real existence outside a person's mind, not subjective. **2.** not influenced by personal feelings or opinions, *an objective account of the problem.* **3.** (in grammar) of the objective case. **objective** *n.* something one is trying to achieve or reach or capture. **ob·jec′tive·ly** *adv.* **ob·jec′tive·ness** *n.* **ob·jec·tiv·i·ty** (ob-jek-tiv-i-tee) *n.* □**objective case,** the form of a word used when it is the object of a verb or preposition.

459

ob·jet d'art (ob-z*h*ay dahr) (*pl.* **ob·jets d'art**, *pr.* ob-z*h*ay dahr) a small artistic object. ▷French.

ob·jet trou·vé (ob-z*h*ay troo-vay) *n.* (*pl.* **ob· jets trou·vés**, *pr.* ob-z*h*ay troo-vay) a found object (*see* **found¹**). ▷French.

ob·jur·gate (ob-jŭr-gayt) *v.* (**ob·jur·gat·ed, ob·jur·gat·ing**) to denounce, to scold. **ob·jur· ga·tion** (ob-jŭr-gay-shŏn) *n.*

obl. *abbr.* 1. oblique. 2. oblong.

ob·late (ob-layt) *adj.* (of a spheroid) flattened at the poles.

ob·la·tion (o-blay-shŏn) *n.* a religious offering, sacrifice, or donation.

ob·li·gate (ob-lǐ-gayt) *v.* (**ob·li·gat·ed, ob· li·gat·ing**) to bind (a person) legally or morally to do something.

ob·li·ga·tion (ob-lǐ-gay-shŏn) *n.* 1. being obliged to do something. 2. what one must do in order to comply with an agreement or law etc., one's duty. □**under an obligation**, owing gratitude to another person for some service or benefit.

ob·lig·a·to·ry (ŏ-blig-ă-tohr-ee) *adj.* required by law or rule or custom, compulsory not optional.

o·blige (ŏ-blɪj) *v.* (**o·bliged, o·blig·ing**) 1. to compel by law or agreement or custom or necessity. 2. to help or gratify by performing a small service, *oblige me with a loan.* **o·blig'er** *n.* □**be obliged to a person**, to be indebted to him for some service. **much obliged**, thank you.

o·blig·ing (ŏ-blɪ-jing) *adj.* courteous and helpful. **o·blig'ing·ly** *adv.*

ob·lique (ŏ-bleek) *adj.* 1. slanting. 2. expressed indirectly, not going straight to the point, *an oblique reply.* **ob·lique'ly** *adv.* **ob·lique'ness** *n.* □**oblique angle**, an acute or obtuse angle.

ob·lit·er·ate (ŏ-blit-ĕ-rayt) *v.* (**ob·lit·er·at· ed, ob·lit·er·at·ing**) to blot out, to destroy and leave no clear traces of. **ob·lit·er·a·tion** (ŏ-blit-ĕ-ray-shŏn) *n.*

ob·liv·i·on (ŏ-bliv-i-ŏn) *n.* 1. the state of being forgotten. 2. the state of being oblivious.

ob·liv·i·ous (ŏ-bliv-i-ŭs) *adj.* unaware or unconscious of something, *oblivious of* or *to her surroundings.* **ob·liv'i·ous·ly** *adv.* **ob·liv'i·ous· ness** *n.*

ob·long (ob-lawng) *n.* a rectangular shape that is longer than it is broad. **oblong** *adj.* having this shape.

ob·lo·quy (ob-lŏ-kwee) *n.* (*pl.* **-quies**) 1. verbal abuse or censure. 2. being generally spoken ill of.

ob·nox·ious (ŏb-nok-shŭs) *adj.* very unpleasant, objectionable. **ob·nox'ious·ly** *adv.* **ob·nox' ious·ness** *n.*

o·boe (oh-boh) *n.* a woodwind instrument of treble pitch.

o·bo·ist (oh-boh-ist) *n.* a person who plays the oboe.

obs. *abbr.* 1. observation. 2. observatory. 3. obsolete.

ob·scene (ob-seen) *adj.* indecent in a repulsive or very offensive way. **ob·scene'ly** *adv.*

ob·scen·i·ty (ob-sen-i-tee) *n.* (*pl.* **-ties**) 1. being obscene. 2. an obscene action or word etc.

ob·scu·rant·ism (ob-skyoor-ăn-tiz-ĕm) *n.* 1. opposition to inquiry, enlightenment, and reform. 2. deliberate avoidance of clarity or explanation. **ob·scu'rant·ist** *adj. & n.*

ob·scu·ra·tion (ob-skyŭ-ray-shŏn) *n.* making or being made obscure.

ob·scure (ŏb-skyoor) *adj.* (**-scur·er, -scur·est**) 1. dark, indistinct. 2. remote from people's observation. 3. not famous, *an obscure poet.* 4. not easily understood, not clearly expressed. **obscure** *v.* (**ob·scured, ob·scur·ing**) to make obscure, to conceal from view. **ob·scure'ly** *adv.* **ob·scur·i·ty** (ŏb-skyoor-i-tee) *n.*

ob·se·quies (ŏb-sĕ-kweez) *n. pl.* funeral rites, a funeral.

ob·se·qui·ous (ŏb-see-kwi-ŭs) *adj.* excessively or sickeningly respectful. **ob·se'qui·ous·ly** *adv.* **ob·se'qui·ous·ness** *n.*

ob·serv·a·ble (ŏb-zur-vă-bĕl) *adj.* able to be observed.

ob·serv·ance (ŏb-zur-văns) *n.* the keeping of a law or rule or custom etc., the keeping or celebrating of a religious festival or of a holiday.

ob·serv·ant (ŏb-zur-vănt) *adj.* 1. quick at noticing things. 2. attentive in observance, acute or diligent in taking notice. 3. careful in observing law or ritual, especially in religious matters. **ob· serv'ant·ly** *adv.*

ob·ser·va·tion (ob-zĕr-vay-shŏn) *n.* 1. observing, being observed. 2. a comment or remark. 3. the gathering and recording of data about the natural world for scientific analysis.

ob·serv·a·to·ry (ŏb-zur-vă-tohr-ee) *n.* (*pl.* **-ries**) a building designed and equipped for scientific observation of the stars or weather.

ob·serve (ŏb-zurv) *v.* (**ob·served, ob·serv· ing**) 1. to see and notice, to watch carefully. 2. to pay attention to (rules etc.). 3. to keep or celebrate, *not all countries observe New Year's Day.* 4. to remark. 5. to make scientific observations. **ob·serv'er** *n.*

ob·sess (ob-ses) *v.* to occupy the thoughts of (a person) continually.

ob·ses·sion (ob-sesh-ŏn) *n.* 1. obsessing, being obsessed. 2. a persistent idea that dominates a person's thoughts. **ob·ses'sion·al** *adj.*

ob·ses·sive (ob-ses-iv) *adj.* of or causing or showing obsession. **ob·ses'sive·ly** *adv.*

ob·sid·i·an (ob-sid-i-ăn) *n.* dark vitreous lava or volcanic rocklike glass.

obsolesc. *abbr.* obsolescent.

ob·so·les·cent (ob-sŏ-les-ĕnt) *adj.* becoming obsolete, going out of use or out of fashion. **ob· so·les'cence** *n.*

ob·so·lete (ob-sŏ-leet, ob-sŏ-leet) *adj.* no longer used, antiquated.

ob·sta·cle (ob-stă-kĕl) *n.* a thing that obstructs progress. □**obstacle course**, an athletic or a military training track in which artificial or natural obstacles have to be passed. **obstacle race**, a race over such a track.

obstet. *abbr.* obstetrics.

ob·ste·tri·cian (ob-stĕ-trish-ăn) *n.* a specialist in obstetrics.

ob·stet·rics (ŏb-stet-riks) *n.* the branch of medicine and surgery that deals with childbirth. **ob· stet'ric** *adj.* **ob·stet'ri·cal** *adj.*

ob·sti·nate (ob-stĭ-nit) *adj.* 1. keeping firmly to one's opinion or to one's chosen course of action, not easily persuaded. 2. not easily overcome, *an obstinate cold.* **ob'sti·nate·ly** *adv.* **ob·sti·na· cy** (ob-stĭ-nă-see) *n.*

ob·strep·er·ous (ob-strep-ĕ-rŭs) *adj.* noisy, unruly, *obstreperous children.* **ob·strep'er·ous· ly** *adv.* **ob·strep'er·ous·ness** *n.*

ob·struct (ŏb-strukt) *v.* 1. to prevent or hinder movement along (a path etc.) by means of an object or objects placed in it, *obstructing the high-*

way. 2. to prevent or hinder the movement or progress or activities of, *obstructing the police*. 3. to conceal from sight, *obstruct the view*. **ob·struc′tor, ob·struc′ter** *n.*
ob·struc·tion (ŏb-struk-shŏn) *n.* 1. obstructing, being obstructive. 2. a thing that obstructs. **ob·struc·tion·ist** (ŏb-struk-shŏ-nist) *n.* a person who seeks to obstruct plans or legislation etc. **ob·struc′tion·ism** *n.*
ob·struc·tive (ŏb-struk-tiv) *adj.* causing or intended to cause obstruction. **ob·struc′tive·ly** *adv.* **ob·struc′tive·ness** *n.*
ob·tain (ŏb-tayn) *v.* 1. to get, to come into possession of (a thing) by effort or as a gift. 2. to be established or in use as a rule or custom, *this custom still obtains in some districts*. **ob·tain′ment** *n.*
ob·tain·a·ble (ŏb-tay-nă-bĕl) *adj.* able to be obtained.
ob·trude (ŏb-trood) *v.* **(ob·trud·ed, ob·trud·ing)** 1. to force (oneself or one's ideas) on others. 2. to thrust or push out.
ob·tru·sive (ŏb-troo-siv) *adj.* obtruding oneself, unpleasantly noticeable. **ob·tru′sive·ly** *adv.* **ob·tru′sive·ness** *n.*
ob·tuse (ŏb-toos) *adj.* 1. of blunt shape, not sharp or pointed. 2. stupid, slow at understanding. **ob·tuse′ly** *adv.* **ob·tuse′ness** *n.* □**obtuse angle,** an angle of more than 90° but less than 180°.
obv. *abbr.* obverse.
ob·verse (ob-vurs) *n.* 1. the side of a coin or medal etc. that bears the head or the principal design. 2. a counterpart. **obverse** (ob-vurs, ob-vurs) *adj.* 1. turned toward the observer. 2. acting as a counterpart. 3. narrower at the base or the point of attachment than at the apex or top. **ob·verse′ly** *adv.*
ob·vi·ate (ob-vi-ayt) *v.* **(ob·vi·at·ed, ob·vi·at·ing)** to make unnecessary, *the bypass obviates the inconvenience of driving through the city*. **ob·vi·a·tion** (ob-vi-ay-shŏn) *n.*
ob·vi·ous (ob-vi-ŭs) *adj.* easy to see or recognize or understand. **ob′vious·ly** *adv.* **ob′vi·ous·ness** *n.*
oc·a·ri·na (ok-ă-ree-nă) *n.* a small egg-shaped terra cotta or metal wind instrument.
OCAS *abbr.* Organization of Central American States.
occ. *abbr.* occupation.
occas. *abbr.* 1. occasional. 2. occasionally.
oc·ca·sion (ŏ-kay-zhŏn) *n.* 1. the time at which a particular event takes place. 2. a special event, *this is quite an occasion*. 3. a suitable time for doing something, an opportunity. 4. a need or reason or cause, *had no occasion to speak French*. **occasion** *v.* to cause. □**on occasion,** when need arises, occasionally.
oc·ca·sion·al (ŏ-kay-zhŏ-năl) *adj.* 1. happening from time to time but not regularly or frequently, *occasional showers*. 2. used or meant for a special event, *occasional verses*. **oc·ca′sion·al·ly** *adv.* □**occasional table,** a small table for use as required.
Oc·ci·dent (ok-si-dĕnt) *n.* the West as opposed to the Orient.
oc·ci·den·tal (ok-si-den-tăl) *adj.* western. **Occidental** *n.* a native of the western world.
oc·clude (ŏ-klood) *v.* **(oc·clud·ed, oc·clud·ing)** 1. to stop up, close, obstruct. 2. (in chemistry) to absorb and retain (gases). 3. to meet with opposite surfaces together, as the teeth when the

jaws are closed. **oc·clu·sion** (ŏ-kloo-zhŏn) *n.* **oc·clu·sive** (ŏ-kloo-siv) *adj.*
oc·cult (ŏ-kult, ok-ult) *adj.* 1. secret, hidden except from those with more than ordinary knowledge. 2. involving the supernatural, *occult powers*. □**the occult,** the world of the supernatural, mystical, or magical.
oc·cult·ism (ŏ-kul-tiz-ĕm) *n.* belief in or study of the occult, practicing occult arts. **oc·cult′ist** *n.*
oc·cu·pant (ok-yŭ-pănt) *n.* a person occupying a place or dwelling or position. **oc·cu·pan·cy** (ok-yŭ-păn-see) *n.*
oc·cu·pa·tion (ok-yŭ-pay-shŏn) *n.* 1. occupying, being occupied. 2. taking or holding possession by force, especially of a defeated country or district. 3. an activity that keeps a person busy, one's employment.
oc·cu·pa·tion·al (ok-yŭ-pay-shŏ-năl) *adj.* of or caused by one's occupation. **oc·cu·pa′tion·al·ly** *adv.* □**occupational hazard,** a risk of accident or illness associated with a certain job. **occupational therapy,** creative activities designed to aid recovery from certain illnesses.
oc·cu·py (ok-yŭ-pɪ) *v.* **(oc·cu·pied, oc·cu·py·ing)** 1. to dwell in, to inhabit. 2. to take possession of and establish one's troops in (a country or strategic position etc.) in war. 3. to place oneself in (a building etc.) as a political or other demonstration. 4. to take up or fill (space or a position). 5. to hold as one's official position, *he occupies the post of manager*. 6. to keep (a person or his time) filled with activity. **oc′cu·pi·er** *n.*
oc·cur (ŏ-kur) *v.* **(oc·curred, oc·cur·ring)** 1. to come into being as an event or process. 2. to be found to exist in some place or conditions, *these plants occur in marshy areas*. 3. to come into a person's mind, *it did not occur to me to mention it.*
oc·cur·rence (ŏ-kur-ĕns) *n.* 1. occurring. 2. an incident or event.
OCD *abbr.* Office of Civil Defense.
o·cean (oh-shăn) *n.* the sea surrounding the continents of Earth, especially one of the five large named areas of this, *the Atlantic, Pacific, Indian, Arctic, and Antarctic Oceans.*
o·cean·ar·i·um (oh-shă-nair-i-ŭm) *n.* (*pl.* **-i·ums, -i·a,** *pr.* -i-ă) a large marine aquarium.
o·cean·front (oh-shŏn-frunt) *n.* an area that borders on the ocean.
o·cean·go·ing (oh-shŏn-goh-ing) *adj.* (of ships) made for crossing the sea, not for coastal or river journeys.
o·ce·an·ic (oh-shi-an-ik) *adj.* of the ocean.
o·cean·og·ra·pher (oh-shă-nog-ră-fĕr) *n.* an expert in oceanography.
o·cean·og·ra·phy (oh-shă-nog-ră-fee) *n.* the scientific study of the ocean. **o·cean·o·graph·ic** (oh-shă-nŏ-graf-ik) *adj.*
o·ce·lot (os-ĕ-lot, oh-sĕ-) *n.* 1. a leopardlike animal of Central and South America. 2. its fur.
o·cher, o·chre (oh-kĕr) *n.* 1. a yellow or brownish or reddish mineral consisting of clay and iron oxide, used as a pigment. 2. pale brownish yellow.
o′clock (ŏ-klok) *adv.* 1. = of the clock (used in specifying the hour), *six o'clock*. 2. according to a method for indicating relative position by imagining a clock dial with the observer at the center, "twelve o'clock" being directly ahead of or above him, *enemy aircraft approaching at two o'clock.*
OCS, O.C.S. *abbr.* Officer Candidate School.
oct. *abbr.* octavo.

Oct. *abbr.* October.

oc·ta·gon (ok-tă-gon) *n.* a geometric figure with eight sides.

oc·tag·o·nal (ok-tag-ŏ-năl) *adj.* having eight sides.

oc·ta·he·dron (ok-tă-hee-drŏn) *n.* (*pl.* **-drons, -dra,** *pr.* -drä) a solid figure with eight faces.

oc·tane (ok-tayn) *n.* a hydrocarbon compound occurring in motor fuel. □**high octane gasoline,** fuel having a high percentage of a certain form of octane and therefore good antiknock properties.

octane number, a measure of the antiknock properties of a gasoline in comparison with those of a fuel taken as standard.

oc·tave (ok-tiv) *n.* 1. a note that is eight degrees (counting inclusively) above or below a given note. 2. the interval between these notes. 3. the series of notes filling this.

oc·ta·vo (ok-tah-voh) *n.* (*pl.* **-vos**) the size of a book or page given by folding a sheet of standard size three times to form eight leaves.

oc·tet (ok-tet) *n.* a group of eight instruments or voices, a musical composition for these.

Oc·to·ber (ok-toh-bĕr) *n.* the tenth month of the year.

oc·to·ge·nar·i·an (ok-tŏ-jĕ-nair-i-ăn) *n.* a person who is in his or her eighties.

oc·to·pus (ok-tŏ-pŭs) *n.* (*pl.* **-pus·es, -pi,** *pr.* -pī) a sea mollusk with a soft body and eight long tentacles.

oc·to·roon (ok-tŏ-roon) *n.* an offspring of a quadroon and a white, a person of one-eighth black ancestry.

oc·to·syl·lab·ic (ok-toh-si-lab-ik) *adj.* having eight syllables. **octosyllabic** *n.* a verse or line having eight syllables.

oc·u·lar (ok-yŭ-lăr) *adj.* of or for or by the eyes, visual. **ocular** *n.* an eyepiece.

oc·u·list (ok-yŭ-list) *n.* 1. an ophthalmologist. 2. an optometrist.

OD (oh-dee) *n.* (*slang*) an overdose of a narcotic.

OD *v.* (**OD'd, OD'ing**) (*slang*) to take such an overdose.

OD, O.D. *abbr.* 1. officer of the day. 2. olive drab. 3. outside diameter. 4. overdraft. 5. overdrawn.

O.D. *abbr.* Doctor of Optometry.

odd (od) *adj.* 1. (of a number) not even, not exactly divisible by two. 2. designated by such a number. 3. belonging to a pair or set or series of which the other member(s) are lacking, *found an odd glove; several odd volumes; you're wearing odd socks,* two that do not form a pair. 4. exceeding a round number or amount, *keep the odd change; forty odd,* between 40 and 50. 5. not regular or habitual or fixed, *does odd jobs; at odd moments.* 6. unusual, strange, eccentric, *an odd sort of person.* **odd'ly** *adv.* **odd'ness** *n.* □**odd man out,** a person or thing differing in some way from others of a group.

odd·ball (od-bawl) *n.* (*slang*) an eccentric person.

odd-e·ven (od-ee-vĕn) *adj.* based on odd and even numbers, *we have not seen the last of the odd-even gasoline rationing.*

odd·i·ty (od-i-tee) *n.* (*pl.* **-ties**) 1. strangeness. 2. an unusual person or thing or event.

odd·ment (od-mĕnt) *n.* something left over, an isolated article.

odds (odz) *n. pl.* 1. the probability that a certain thing will happen, this expressed as a ratio, *the odds are five to one against throwing a six.* 2. the ratio between amounts staked by parties to a bet, *gave odds of three to one.* □**at odds with,** in

disagreement or conflict with. **by all odds,** certainly. **odds and ends,** oddments.

odds-on (odz-on) *adj.* 1. with success more likely than failure. 2. with betting odds in favor of its success, *the odds-on favorite.*

ode (ohd) *n.* a poem expressing noble feelings, often addressed to a person or celebrating an event.

o·di·ous (oh-di-ŭs) *adj.* hateful, detestable. **o'di·ous·ly** *adv.* **o'di·ous·ness** *n.* ▷ Do not confuse *odious* with *odorous.*

o·di·um (oh-di-ŭm) *n.* widespread hatred or disgust felt toward a person or his or her actions.

o·dom·e·ter (oh-dom-ĕ-tĕr) *n.* an instrument for measuring the distance traveled by a wheeled vehicle.

o·dor (oh-dŏr) *n.* a smell. **o'dor·less** *adj.*

o·dor·if·er·ous (oh-dŏ-rif-ĕ-rŭs) *adj.* diffusing a usually agreeable scent.

o·dor·ous (oh-dŏr-ŭs) *adj.* smelly. ▷ Do not confuse *odorous* with *odious.*

od·ys·sey (od-i-see) *n.* (*pl.* **-seys**) a long adventurous journey. ▷ Named after the *Odyssey,* a Greek epic poem telling of the wanderings of the hero Odysseus.

OE, O.E. *abbr.* Old English.

OECD *abbr.* Organization for Economic Cooperation and Development.

OED, O.E.D. *abbr.* Oxford English Dictionary.

oed·i·pal (ed-ĭ-păl, ee-dī-) *adj.* of or relating to the Oedipus complex.

Oed·i·pus (ed-ĭ-pŭs, ee-dī-) **complex** sexual feelings toward one's parents, involving attraction to the parent of the opposite sex (especially the mother) and jealousy of the other parent. ▷ Named after Oedipus in Greek legend, who in ignorance killed his father and married his mother.

oe·no·phile (ee-nŏ-fīl) *n.* a connoisseur of wines.

OEO *abbr.* Office of Economic Opportunity.

o'er (oh-ĕr) *adv.* & *prep.* (*poetical*) over.

oeu·vre (uu-vrĕ) *n.* (*pl.* **-vres,** *pr.* -vrĕ) the totality of the works of an author, painter, composer, etc.

of (uv, ov) *prep.* indicating relationships, 1. belonging to or originating from. 2. concerning, *told us of his travels.* 3. composed or made from, *built of brick; a farm of 100 acres.* 4. in regard to, with reference to, *never heard of it.* 5. for or involving or directed toward, *love of one's country.* 6. so as to bring separation or relief from, *cured him of smoking.* 7. during, *he visits of an evening.* 8. owing to, *he was proud of his son's accomplishments.* 9. connected to or associated with, *he's a friend of mine.* 10. named, called, or signified as, *the state of Oregon.* 11. before, *she called at five of seven.* 12. characterized or identified by, *he of the rose tattoo.* □**of itself,** by itself or in itself.

▷ It is incorrect to use *of* in place of *have* in such phrases as *could have been, might have seen.*

OF, O.F. *abbr.* Old French.

off (awf) *adv.* 1. away, at or to a distance, *rode off; is three miles or three years off.* 2. out of position, not touching or attached, separate, *take the lid off.* 3. disconnected, not functioning, no longer obtainable, canceled, *turn the gas off; the wedding is off; take the day off,* away from work. 4. to the end, completely, so as to be clear, *finish it off; sell them off.* 5. situated as regards money or supplies, *how are you off for cash?* **off** *prep.* 1. from, away from, not on, *fell off a ladder; off duty.* 2. abstaining from, not attracted by the time being, *is off his food* or *off smoking; off form* or *off his game,* not performing as well as usual. 3. leading from, not far from, *in a street off Grand Avenue.* 4. at sea a short distance from, *sank off Cape Horn.* 5. at the expense of, by the means provided by, *he lived off his capital.* **off** *adj.* 1. more distant or remote. 2. detached, disconnected, not on, *the radio is off.* 3. not functioning or continuing, *the engine is off.* 4. less or fewer, *business is off.* 5. inferior, below standard; *an off day,* a day when a person is not at his best. 6. wrong, incorrect, *the measurement is off.* 7. slight or remote, *an off chance.* 8. in a particular condition. **off** *v. (slang)* 1. to go away. 2. to kill, to murder. □**off and on,** now and then; wavering. **off chance,** a remote possibility. **off color,** not the right color; in bad taste. **off hour,** an unusual hour (for a specified activity). **off limits,** an area forbidden to a specified group. **off the wall,** *(slang)* bizarre, foolish. **off year,** a year in which there are no major elections; a year in which production falls or business slows down.

▷It is incorrect to write *off of* in place of *off* in such phrases as *off the bus, off the table.*

off. *abbr.* 1. office. 2. officer. 3. official.

of·fal (aw-făl) *n.* 1. the parts cut off as waste from a butchered animal. 2. refuse or waste in general.

off-beat (awf-beet) *adj.* 1. unconventional, unusual. 2. of the unaccented part of a musical bar.

off Broad·way (awf brawd-way) low-cost and usually experimental drama staged in New York City theaters outside the Broadway theater district.

of·fend (ŏ-fend) *v.* 1. to cause offense or displeasure to. 2. to do wrong, *offend against the law.* 3. to sin, to act immorally. **of·fend′er** *n.*

of·fense (ŏ-fens) *n.* 1. breaking of the law, an illegal act. 2. a feeling of annoyance or resentment, *give* or *take offense.*

of·fen·sive (ŏ-fen-siv) *adj.* 1. causing offense, insulting, *offensive remarks.* 2. disgusting, repulsive, *an offensive smell.* 3. used in attacking, aggressive, *offensive weapons.* **offensive** *n.* an aggressive action or campaign; *take the offensive,* to begin hostilities. **of·fen′sive·ly** *adv.* **of·fen′sive·ness** *n.*

of·fer (aw-fĕr) *v.* (**of·fered, of·fer·ing**) 1. to present (a thing) so that it may be accepted or rejected, or considered. 2. to state what one is willing to do or pay or give. 3. to show for sale. 4. to provide, to give opportunity, *the job offers prospects of promotion.* 5. to show an intention, *the dog didn't offer to bark.* 6. to present to a deity by way of sacrifice, to give in worship or devotion. **offer** *n.* 1. an expression of willingness to give or do or pay something. 2. an amount offered, *offers above $500.*

of·fer·ing (aw-fĕ-ring) *n.* 1. a gift or contribution etc. that is offered. 2. a presentation or gift as an act of religious worship.

of·fer·to·ry (aw-fĕr-tohr-ee) *n.* (*pl.* **-ries**) 1. the act of offering bread and wine for consecration at the Eucharist. 2. money collected in a religious service.

off·hand (awf-hand) *adj.* 1. without previous thought or preparation. 2. (of behavior etc.) casual or curt and unceremonious. **offhand** *adv.* in an offhand way. **off′hand·ed** *adj.* **off′hand·ed·ly** *adv.*

of·fice (aw-fis) *n.* 1. a room or building used as a place of business, especially for clerical and similar work or for a special department, *the exchange*

office. 2. the staff working there. 3. a branch of the U.S. government next in rank below a department, *the Office of Management and Budget.* 4. a position of authority or trust, the holding of an official position, *seek office; be in office,* hold such a position. 5. an authorized form of Christian worship, *the Office for the Dead.* 6. *offices,* a piece of kindness or a service, *through the good offices of his friends; the last offices,* ceremonial rites for the dead. □**office boy,** a youth employed to do minor jobs in a business office. **office hours,** the hours during which business is regularly conducted. **office seeker,** a candidate for public office. **office worker,** a clerk in a business office.

of·fice·hold·er (aw-fis-hohl-dĕr) *n.* a person holding a public office.

of·fic·er (aw-fi-sĕr) *n.* 1. a person holding a position of authority or trust, an official, *customs officers.* 2. a person who holds authority in any of the armed services (especially with a commission), merchant marine, or on a passenger ship. 3. a policeman. □**officer of the day,** the military officer responsible for the guard, inspection, and barracks on an assigned day. **officer of the guard,** the officer under the orders of the officer of the day who is directly responsible for the guard.

of·fi·cial (ŏ-fish-ăl) *adj.* 1. of an office or position of authority, *in his official capacity.* 2. suitable for or characteristic of officials and bureaucracy, *official red tape.* 3. properly authorized, *the news is official.* **official** *n.* a person holding office. **of·fi′cial·ly** *adv.* ▷Do not confuse *official* with *officious.*

of·fi·cial·dom (ŏ-fish-ăl-dŏm) *n.* those people holding public office or engaged in official duties.

of·fi·cial·ese (ŏ-fish-ă-leez) *n. (informal)* the jargon often used by officials, characterized by long words and complicated construction.

of·fi·cial·ism (ŏ-fish-ă-liz-ĕm) *n.* very strict adherence to official systems and routines.

of·fi·ci·ant (ŏ-fish-i-ănt) *n.* a person who performs a priestly office, performs a divine service, etc.

of·fi·ci·ate (ŏ-fish-i-ayt) *v.* (**of·fi·ci·at·ed, of·fi·ci·at·ing**) to act in an official capacity, to be in charge.

of·fi·cious (ŏ-fish-ŭs) *adj.* asserting one's authority, bossy. **of·fi′cious·ly** *adv.* **of·fi′cious·ness** *n.* ▷Do not confuse *officious* with *official.*

off·ing (aw-fing) *n.* **in the offing,** in view, not far away in distance or future time.

off·ish (aw-fish) *adj. (informal)* inclined to aloofness.

off-key (awf-kee) *adj.* 1. out of tune. 2. not quite appropriate or normal.

off-line (awf-lrn) *adj. & adv.* (of computer operations) not on-line, not directly connected to the central processor.

off·load (awf-lohd) *v. (informal)* to unload.

off-peak (awf-peek) *adj.* in or used at a time that is less popular or less busy, *off-peak electricity.*

off·print (awf-print) *n.* a separately produced reprint of part of a book or magazine.

off-put·ting (awf-puut-ing) *adj. (informal)* repellent, disconcerting.

off-sea·son (awf-see-zŏn) *n.* the time when business etc. is fairly slack.

off·set (awf-set) *n.* 1. an offshoot. 2. anything that balances or compensates for or neutralizes etc. something else. 3. a method of printing in which the ink is transferred to a rubber surface and from this to paper. 4. the sloping ledge of a wall where the thickness of the part above is diminished. 5. the bend made in a pipe to carry it past an obstacle. 6. a short distance measured perpendicularly from the main line of measurement in surveying. **off·set** (awf-set) *v.* **(off·set, off·set·ting)** 1. to counterbalance or compensate for. 2. (in printing) to make an offset. 3. to form an offset in (a wall).

off·shoot (awf-shoot) *n.* 1. a side shoot. 2. a subsidiary product.

off·shore (awf-shohr) *adj.* 1. (of wind) blowing from the land toward the sea. 2. at sea some distance from the shore. **offshore** *adv.* at a distance from the shore.

off·side (awf-sɪd) *adj. & adv.* (of a player or an action in sports) in a position where a play is forbidden by the rules.

off·spring (awf-spring) *n.* (*pl.* **-spring**) 1. the child or children of a particular person or persons. 2. the young of an animal.

off·stage (awf-stayj) *adj. & adv.* in the wings or behind the stage set of a theater, not seen by the audience.

off-the-record (awf-*thĕ*-rek-ŏrd) *adj.* unofficial, not for publication or quotation.

off-the-shelf (awf-*thĕ*-shelf) *adj.* (goods) at hand and ready to be sold.

off·track (awf-trak) *adj.* of a means of legal betting on horse races other than at the site of the races.

off-white (awf-hwɪt) *adj.* white with a gray or yellowish tinge.

oft (awft) *adv. (old use)* often.

of·ten (aw-fĕn) *adv.* 1. frequently, many times, at short intervals. 2. in many instances.

of·ten·times (aw-fĕn-tɪmz), **oft·times** (awf-tɪmz) *adv. (old use)* often.

o·gle (oh-gĕl) *v.* to eye flirtatiously.

o·gre (oh-gĕr) *n.* 1. a cruel or man-eating giant in fairy tales and legends. 2. a terrifying person. **o·gress** (oh-gris) *n. fem.*

oh (oh) *interj.* 1. an exclamation of surprise or delight or pain. 2. used for emphasis, *oh yes I will.*

OH *abbr.* Ohio.

O·hi·o (oh-hɪ-oh) a state of the U.S. **O·hi′o·an** *adj. & n.*

ohm (ohm) *n.* a unit of electrical resistance.

ohm·me·ter (ohm-mee-tĕr) *n.* an instrument for measuring ohms.

o·ho (oh-hoh) *interj.* an expression of surprise or exultation.

oil (oil) *n.* 1. a thick slippery liquid that will not dissolve in water. 2. petroleum. 3. a form of petroleum used as fuel; *oil heater, oil lamp, oil stove,* domestic appliances using oil as fuel. 4. oil color. 5. *(informal)* an oil painting. 6. *(slang)* flattery. **oil** *v.* to apply oil to, to lubricate or treat with oil; *oiled silk,* silk made waterproof by being treated with oil. **oil′er** *n.* □**oil color, paint,** paint made by mixing powdered pigment in oil. **oil field,** an area where oil is found in the ground or beneath the sea. **oil painting,** a picture painted in oil colors. **oil shale,** a shale that yields oil through distillation. **oil tanker,** a ship with tanks for transporting oil in bulk. **oil the wheels,** to make things go smoothly by tactful behavior or flattery etc. **oil well,** a well yielding mineral oil.

oil·can (oil-kan) *n.* a can with a long nozzle through which oil flows, used for oiling machinery.

oil·cloth (oil-klawth) *n.* strong fabric treated with oil and used to cover tables etc.

oil-fired (oil-fɪrd) *adj.* using oil as fuel.

oil·skin (oil-skin) *n.* 1. cloth waterproofed by treatment with oil. 2. (often *oilskins*) waterproof clothing made of this.

oil·y (oi-lee) *adj.* **(oil·i·er, oil·i·est)** 1. of or like oil, covered in oil, containing much oil. 2. unpleasantly smooth in manner, trying to win favor by flattery. **oil′i·ness** *n.*

oink (oingk) *n.* the sound made by a pig grunting. **oink** *v.* to make such a sound.

oint·ment (oint-mĕnt) *n.* a thick slippery paste rubbed on the skin to heal roughness or injuries or inflammation etc. or for cosmetic purposes.

O·jib·wa, O·jib·way (oh-jib-way) *n.* (*pl.* **-was, -wa** or **-ways, -way**) 1. a member of an Algonquian Indian tribe living near Lake Superior. 2. the language of this tribe.

OJT *abbr.* on-the-job training.

OK *abbr.* Oklahoma.

OK, O.K. (oh-kay) *adj. & adv. (informal)* all right, satisfactory. **OK, O.K.** *n.* (*pl.* **OK's, O.K.'s**) *(informal)* approval, agreement to a plan etc. **OK, O.K.** *v.* **(OK'd, OK'ing, O.K.'d, O.K.'ing)** *(informal)* to give one's approval or agreement to.

o·ka·pi (oh-kah-pee) *n.* (*pl.* **-pis, -pi**) an animal of central Africa, like a giraffe but with a shorter neck and a striped body.

o·kay = **OK, O.K.**

o·key-doke (oh-kee-dohk), **o·key-do·key** (-doh-kee) *adv. (slang)* OK.

Okla. *abbr.* Oklahoma.

O·kla·ho·ma (oh-klă-hoh-mă) a state of the U.S. **O·kla·ho′man** *adj. & n.* □**Oklahoma City,** the capital of Oklahoma.

o·kra (oh-kră) *n.* a tropical plant with seed pods that are used as a vegetable.

old (ohld) *adj.* 1. having lived or existed for a long time; *the old,* old people. 2. made long ago, used or established or known for a long time. 3. shabby from age or wear. 4. of a particular age, *ten years old, a ten-year-old.* 5. not recent or modern, *in the old days.* 6. former, original, *in its old place.* 7. skilled through long experience, *an old hand at negotiating.* 8. *(informal)* used for emphasis in friendly or casual mention, *good old Winnie; any old time.* **old′ness** *n.* □**of old,** of or in former times; *we know him of old,* since long ago. **old age,** the period of a person's life from about 65 to 70 onward. **old boy,** *(informal)* an elderly man, a man or male animal regarded affectionately. **old country,** mother country of colonists or immigrants. **Old Dominion,** the state of Virginia. **Old English,** the English language from the 5th to the 12th century. **Old French,** the French language from the 9th to the 16th century. **old girl,** (used in ways corresponding to *old boy*). **Old Glory,** the U.S. flag. **old goat,** a mean unpopular old man; an aging lecher. **old gold,** dull gold color. **old guard,** the original or past or conservative members of a group. **old hand,** a practiced workman, someone with a lot of experience. **old hat,** *(informal)* out-of-date, no longer in vogue; commonplace, trite. **Old High German,** the High German language prior to the 12th century. **old lady,** *(informal)* a mother or wife. **Old Low German,** the German lowland language before the 12th century. **old maid,** an elderly spinster; an old-maidish person. **old man,** *(informal)* one's employer or manager or husband or father. **old master,** a great painter of former times (especially 13th–17th centuries in Europe); a painting by such a painter. **Old Nick,** the Devil. **Old Testament,** *see* **testament. old wives' tale,** an old but foolish belief. **old woman,** a fussy or timid man; *(informal)* a wife. **Old World,** Europe, Asia, and Africa, as distinct from the Americas. **old year,** the year just ended or about to end. ▷See the note under **elder**[1].

old·en (ohl-děn) *adj. (old use)* old-time.

old-fash·ioned (ohld-fash-ŏnd) *adj.* in a fashion that is no longer in style, having the ways or tastes current in former times. □**Old Fashioned,** a cocktail made of water or soda water, whiskey, bitters, and sugar, and containing slices of citrus fruit.

old·ie (ohl-dee) *n. (informal)* an old person or thing.

old·ish (ohl-dish) *adj.* fairly old.

old-line (ohld-lɪn) *adj.* established, conservative. **old'-lin'er** *n.*

old-maid·ish (ohld-may-dish) *adj.* fussy and prim.

old·ster (ohld-stěr) *n.* an old person.

old-time (ohld-tɪm) *adj.* belonging to former times.

old-tim·er (ohld-tɪ-měr) *n. (informal)* a person with long experience or standing.

o·lé (oh-lay) *n.* a shout of approval or encouragement.

o·le·ag·i·nous (oh-li-aj-ĭ-nŭs) *adj.* like oil, containing or producing oil.

o·le·an·der (oh-li-an-děr) *n.* a poisonous evergreen shrub of warm climates, with red or white or pink flowers.

o·le·o (oh-li-oh) *n. (informal)* oleomargarine.

o·le·o·mar·ga·rine (oh-li-oh-mahr-jă-rin) *n.* margarine.

ol·fac·to·ry (ol-fak-tŏ-ree) *adj.* concerned with smelling, *olfactory organs.*

ol·i·garch (ol-ĭ-gahrk) *n.* a member of an oligarchy.

ol·i·gar·chy (ol-ĭ-gahr-kee) *n. (pl.* **-chies)** 1. a form of government in which power is in the hands of a few people. 2. these people. 3. a country governed in this way. **ol·i·gar·chic** (ol-ĭ-gahr-kik) *adj.* **ol·i·gar'chi·cal** *adj.*

Ol·i·go·cene (ol-ĭ-goh-seen) *adj.* of the middle geologic epoch of the Tertiary period. **Oligocene** *n.* the Oligocene epoch.

o·li·o (oh-li-oh) *n. (pl.* **o·li·os)** 1. a miscellaneous collection. 2. a stew of meats and vegetables.

ol·ive (ol-iv) *n.* 1. a small oval fruit with a hard stone and bitter pulp from which an oil *(olive oil)* is obtained. 2. the evergreen tree that bears it. 3. a greenish color. **olive** *adj.* greenish like an unripe olive or (of the complexion) yellowish brown. □**olive branch,** something done or offered to show one's desire to make peace. **olive drab,** the grayish olive color of U.S. Army uniforms.

ol·i·vine (ol-ĭ-veen) *n.* magnesium iron silicate, a mineral, usually olive green.

O·lym·pi·a (oh-lim-pee-ă) the capital of Washington.

O·lym·pi·an (oh-lim-pi-ăn) *adj.* (of manners etc.) majestic and imposing.

O·lym·pic (oh-lim-pik) *adj.* of the **Olympic Games,** athletic and other contests held every fourth year at Olympia in Greece in ancient times and revived since 1896 as international competitions, held each time in a different part of the world.

O·lym·pics (oh-lim-piks) *n. pl.* the Olympic Games.

om (awm) *n.* a word of fulfillment or affirmation, intoned as part of a mantra while meditating.

O·ma·ha (oh-mă-hah) *n. (pl.* **-has, -ha)** a member of an Indian tribe that migrated from the Ohio River Valley to northeastern Nebraska.

O·man (oh-mahn) a country in the Middle East. **O·ma·ni** (oh-mah-nee) *adj. & n. (pl.* **-is).**

OMB *abbr.* Office of Management and Budget.

om·buds·man (om-buudz-măn) *n. (pl.* **-men,** *pr.* -měn) an official appointed to investigate individuals' complaints about maladministration by public authorities.

o·me·ga (oh-mee-gă) *n.* the twenty-fourth (last) letter of the Greek alphabet (Ω ω).

om·e·let, om·e·lette (om-lit) *n.* a dish made of beaten eggs cooked in a frying pan, often served folded around a filling.

o·men (oh-měn) *n.* an event regarded as a prophetic sign.

om·i·cron (om-ĭ-kron) *n.* the fifteenth letter of the Greek alphabet (O o).

om·i·nous (om-ĭ-nŭs) *adj.* looking or seeming as if trouble is at hand, *an ominous silence.* **om'i·nous·ly** *adv.* **om'i·nous·ness** *n.*

o·mis·sion (oh-mish-ŏn) *n.* 1. omitting, being omitted. 2. something that has been omitted or not done.

o·mit (oh-mit) *v.* **(o·mit·ted, o·mit·ting)** 1. to leave out, not insert or include. 2. to leave not done, to neglect or fail to do.

om·ni·bus (om-nĭ-bŭs) *n.* 1. a bus. 2. a volume containing a number of books or stories. **omnibus** *adj.* serving several objects at once, comprising several items.

om·nip·o·tent (om-nip-ŏ-těnt) *adj.* having unlimited power or very great power. **om·nip'o·tent·ly** *adv.* **om·nip'o·tence** *n.* □**the Omnipotent,** God.

om·ni·pres·ent (om-nĭ-prez-ěnt) *adj.* present everywhere at the same time, widely or constantly met with. **om·ni·pres'ence** *n.*

om·nis·cient (om-nish-ěnt) *adj.* knowing everything, having very extensive knowledge. **om·nis'cient·ly** *adv.* **om·nis'cience** *n.*

om·ni·um-gath·er·um (om-ni-ŭm-gath-ĕ-rŭm) *n. (pl.* **-ums)** a miscellaneous assemblage of persons or things, a strange mixture.

om·niv·o·rous (om-niv-ŏ-rŭs) *adj.* 1. feeding on both plants and animal flesh. 2. *(humorous)* reading whatever comes one's way. **om·niv'o·rous·ly** *adv.* **om·niv'o·rous·ness** *n.*

on (on) *prep.* 1. supported by or attached to or covering, *sat on the floor; lives on her pension; got any money on you?,* are you carrying any with you? 2. using as a basis or ground or reason etc., *was arrested on suspicion; profits on sales.* 3. close to, in the direction of, *they live on the coast; the army advanced on Paris; on form or on his game,* performing at his usual high standard. 4. (of time) exactly at, during, *on the next day.* 5. in a certain manner or state, *on one's best behavior.* 6. concerning, engaged with, so as to affect, *a book on grammar; on holiday; is on the pill,* taking it; *the drinks are on me,* at my expense. 7. added to, *5¢ on the price of gasoline.* **on** *adv.* 1. so as to be supported by or attached to or covering something, *put the lid on.* 2. farther forward, toward something, *move on; from that day on; broadside on,* with that part forward. 3. with continued movement or action, *slept on.* 4. in operation or activity, (of a play etc.) being performed or broadcast, (of an actor etc.) performing on the stage, (of gas or water or electric current) running or available or activated, (of an event) due to take

place, not canceled, (of an employee) on duty.
on *adj.* 1. on a base in baseball. 2. turned on, *the radio is on.* ☐**be on,** *(informal)* to be willing to participate in something; to be practicable or acceptable, *the party is on; you're on!, (informal)* I accept your proposition or wager. **be on to a thing,** to notice it or realize its importance. **be** *or* **keep on at,** *(informal)* to nag. **on and off,** from time to time, not continually. **on and on,** continuing, continually. **on high,** in or to heaven or a high place. **on to,** to a position on *(see* **onto***)*.
once (wuns) *adv., conj.,* & *n.* 1. on one occasion only, one time or occurrence, *once is enough.* 2. at all, ever, as soon as, *once I can get this job done.* 3. formerly, *people who once lived here.* ☐**at once,** *see* **at. once and for all,** in a final manner, conclusively. **once in a while,** from time to time, not often. **once more,** an additional time. **once upon a time,** at some vague time in the past.
once-o·ver (wuns-oh-věr) *n. (informal)* a rapid inspection, *give it the once-over.*
on·com·ing (on-kum-ing) *adj.* approaching.
one (wun) *adj.* single, individual, forming a unity. **one** *n.* 1. the smallest whole number (1, I). 2. a single thing or person. 3. *(informal)* a joke, *do you know the one about the dog that could play poker?* 4. *(informal)* a blow, *belted him one.* **one** *pronoun* 1. a thing or person, *loved ones.* 2. any person, the speaker or writer as representing people in general, *one doesn't want to seem mean.* 3. a thing of the kind referred to, *the book is a good one.* ☐**one another,** each other. **one-armed bandit,** *(slang)* a slot machine operated by pulling down an armlike handle. **one day,** at some unspecified date. **one too many for,** such as to outwit or baffle (a person). **one-track mind,** a mind that can think of only one topic. **one up,** scoring one point more than an opponent; having an advantage. **one-way street,** a street in which traffic may move in one direction only. **one-way ticket,** a single ticket, not a return.
O·nei·da (oh-nɪ-dǎ) *n.* (*pl.* **-das, -da**) 1. a member of an Indian tribe that used to live in New York. 2. the language of this tribe.
one-lin·er (wun-lɪ-něr) *n.* a very brief joke or comical saying.
one-man (wun-man) *adj.* done or managed by one person, *a one-man job.*
one·ness (wun-nis) *n.* 1. being one, singleness. 2. unity, union, agreement, concord.
on·er·ous (on-ě-rǔs) *adj.* burdensome. **on'er·ous·ness** *n.*
one·self (wun-self) *pronoun* corresponding to **one** (*pronoun,* definition 2), used in the same ways as *himself.*
one-sid·ed (wun-sɪ-did) *adj.* (of opinions or judgments) unfair, prejudiced.
one·time (wun-tɪm) *adj.* former.
one-to-one (wun-tǒ-wun) *adj.* with correspondence of one member of one group to one of another.
one-up·man·ship (wun-up-măn-ship) *n. (informal)* the art of gaining and maintaining a psychological advantage over others.
on·go·ing (on-goh-ing) *adj.* continuing to exist or progress.
on·ion (un-yǒn) *n.* a vegetable with an edible rounded bulb that has a strong smell and strong flavor. **on'ion·y** *adj.* ☐**know one's onions,** *(slang)* to know one's subject or one's job thoroughly.

on·ion·skin (un-yǒn-skin) *n.* 1. the outermost or any outer coat of an onion. 2. thin smooth translucent paper.
on-line (on-lɪn) *adj.* & *adv.* operated directly by a computer, directly connected to the central processor.
on·look·er (on-luuk-ěr) *n.* a spectator.
on·ly (ohn-lee) *adj.* 1. being the one specimen or all the specimens of a class, sole. 2. most or best worth considering, *gliding is the only sport.* **only** *adv.* 1. without anything or anyone else, and that is all. 2. no longer ago than, *saw her only yesterday.* **only** *conj.* but then, *he makes good resolutions, only he never keeps them.* ☐**only too,** extremely, *we'll be only too pleased.*
on·o·mat·o·poe·ia (on-ǒ-mat-ǒ-pee-ă) *n.* formation of words that imitate or suggest what they stand for, as *cuckoo, plop, sizzle.* **on·o·mat·o·poe·ic** *adj.* **on·o·mat·o·poe'i·cal·ly** *adv.* **on·o·mat·o·po·et·ic** (on-ǒ-mat-ǒ-poh-et-ik) *adj.* **on·o·mat·o·po·et'i·cal·ly** *adv.*
On·on·da·ga (on-ǒn-dah-gǎ) *n.* (*pl.* **-gas, -ga**) 1. a member of a tribe of Indians of upper New York and Ontario. 2. the language of this tribe.
on·rush (on-rush) *n.* an onward rush.
on·set (on-set) *n.* 1. a beginning, *the onset of winter.* 2. an attack or assault.
on·shore (on-shohr) *adj.* (of wind) blowing from the sea toward the land.
on·slaught (on-slawt) *n.* a fierce attack.
Ont. *abbr.* Ontario.
On·tar·i·o (on-tair-i-oh) 1. a province of Canada. 2. one of the Great Lakes between Canada and the U.S.
on·to (on-too) *prep.* to a position on. ▷Note that *onto* cannot be used where *on* is an adverb, as in *we walked on to the hotel* (= continued walking until we reached it). *The cat jumped onto the chair* (= jumped from the floor to the seat of the chair). Many people prefer not to use *onto,* and write *on to* in all cases.
on·tog·e·ny (on-toj-ě-nee) *n.* the origin and development of an individual organism.
on·tol·o·gy (on-tol-ǒ-jee) *n.* the branch of metaphysics dealing with the nature of existence. **on·to·log·i·cal** (on-tǒ-loj-i-kǎl) *adj.*
o·nus (oh-nǔs) *n.* (*pl.* **o·nus·es**) the duty or responsibility of doing something; *the onus of proof rests with you,* you must prove what you say.
on·ward (on-wǎrd) *adj.* & *adv.* with an advancing motion, farther on.
on·wards (on-wǎrdz) *adv.* farther on.
on·yx (on-iks) *n.* a stone like marble with different colors in layers.
oo·dles (oo-dělz) *n. (informal)* a great quantity.
ooh (oo) *interj.* an exclamation of surprise or pleasure or pain.
o·o·lite (oh-ǒ-lɪt) *n.* a rock, especially limestone, made up of rounded grains. **o·o·lit·ic** (oh-ǒ-lit-ik) *adj.*
oomph (uumf) *n. (slang)* 1. attractiveness, especially sex appeal. 2. energy, enthusiasm.
ooze (ooz) *v.* (**oozed, ooz·ing**) 1. (of fluid) to trickle or flow out slowly. 2. (of a substance) to exude moisture. 3. to show (a feeling) freely, *ooze confidence.* **ooze** *n.* mud at the bottom of a river or sea. **ooz'y** *adj.* **ooz'i·ness** *n.*
op., Op. *abbr.* opus.
o·pac·i·ty (oh-pas-i-tee) *n.* being opaque.
o·pal (oh-pǎl) *n.* an iridescent quartzlike stone often used as a gem.

o·pal·es·cent (oh-pă-les-ĕnt) *adj.* iridescent like an opal. **o·pal·es'cence** *n.*

o·paque (oh-payk) *adj.* not clear, not transparent. **o·paque'ly** *adv.* **o·paque'ness** *n.*

op (op) **art** optical art, an abstract art form that causes or seeks to cause optical illusions. **op' art'ist** *n.*

op. cit. *abbr.* in the work already quoted. ▷ Latin *opere citato.*

ope (ohp) *v.* **(oped, op·ing)** *(old use)* to open.

OPEC (oh-pek) *n.* Organization of Petroleum Exporting Countries.

op-ed (op-ed) **page** the page in a newspaper opposite the editorial page, usually for signed articles written by contributors.

o·pen (oh-pĕn) *adj.* 1. not closed or blocked up or sealed or locked. 2. not covered or concealed or restricted; *an open championship,* for which anyone may enter. 3. admitting visitors or customers, *the shops are open.* 4. spread out, unfolded. 5. with wide spaces between solid parts, *open texture.* 6. frank, communicative, *was quite open about her reasons.* 7. not yet settled or decided. 8. available, *three courses are open to us.* 9. willing to receive, *we are open to offers.* **open** *n.* 1. *the open,* open space or country or air. 2. an open championship or competition. **open** *v.* 1. to make or become open or more open. 2. to begin or establish, to make a start, *open a business* or *a debate; to open fire,* to begin firing. 3. to declare ceremonially to be open to the public. **o'pen· ness** *n.* ☐in the open air, not inside a house or building. **open a person's eyes,** to make him see the truth or reality. **open classroom,** a classroom in which students are free to pursue their activities individually. **open-heart surgery,** surgery with the heart exposed and with blood circulating temporarily through a bypass. **open house,** hospitality to all comers. **open letter,** a letter of comment or protest nominally addressed to a person but sent to and printed in a newspaper. **open mind,** a mind that is unprejudiced or undecided. **open question,** a matter on which no final verdict has yet been made or on which none is possible. **open (faced) sandwich,** a slice of bread covered with a layer of meat or cheese etc. **open secret,** one known to so many people that it is no longer a secret. **open sesame,** *see* **sesame. open shop,** an establishment in which one can work without belonging to a labor union. **with open arms,** with an enthusiastic welcome.

o·pen-air (oh-pĕn-air) *adj.* taking place in the open air.

o·pen-and-shut (oh-pĕn-ăn-shut) *adj. (informal)* perfectly straightforward.

o·pen-end·ed (oh-pĕn-en-did) *adj.* with no fixed limit, *an open-ended contract.*

o·pen·er (oh-pĕ-nĕr) *n.* 1. a person or thing that opens something. 2. a device for opening cans or bottles. 3. *openers,* cards entitling the holder to open the betting in poker etc. ☐for openers, *(informal)* to begin with, for a start.

o·pen·hand·ed (oh-pĕn-han-did) *adj.* generous in giving. **o'pen·hand'ed·ly** *adv.* **o'pen· hand'ed·ness** *n.*

o·pen·ing (oh-pĕ-ning) *n.* 1. a space or gap, a place where something opens. 2. the beginning of something. 3. an opportunity.

o·pen·ly (oh-pĕn-lee) *adv.* without concealment, publicly, frankly.

o·pen-mind·ed (oh-pĕn-mɪn-did) *adj.* with an open mind, unprejudiced. **o'pen-mind'ed· ness** *n.*

o·pen·work (oh-pĕn-wurk) *n.* a pattern with spaces between threads or strips of metal etc. **o·pen·worked** (oh-pĕn-wurkt) *adj.*

op·er·a (op-ĕ-ră) *n.* 1. a play in which the words are sung to a musical accompaniment. 2. dramatic works of this kind. **opera** *n. pl. see* **opus.** ☐opera glasses, small binoculars for use at the opera or theater.

op·er·a·ble (op-ĕ-ră-bĕl) *adj.* 1. able to be operated. 2. able to be treated by surgical operation. **op'er·a·bly** *adv.* **op·er·a·bil·i·ty** (op-ĕ-ră-bil-i-tee) *n.*

op·er·ate (op-ĕ-rayt) *v.* **(op·er·at·ed, op·er· at·ing)** 1. to be in action, to produce an effect, *the new tax operates to our advantage.* 2. to control the functioning of, *he operates the crane.* 3. to perform a surgical or other operation on. ☐operating theater, a room for surgical operations.

op·er·at·ic (op-ĕ-rat-ik) *adj.* of or like opera.

op·er·a·tion (op-ĕ-ray-shŏn) *n.* 1. operating, being operated. 2. the way a thing works. 3. a piece of work, something to be done, *begin operations.* 4. strategic military activities in war or during maneuvers. 5. an act performed by a surgeon, on any part of the body, to take away or deal with a diseased or injured or deformed part. 6. (in mathematics) the subjection of a number or quantity or function to a process affecting its value or form, such as multiplication or division.

op·er·a·tion·al (op-ĕ-ray-shŏ-năl) *adj.* 1. of or engaged in or used in operations. 2. able to function, *is the system operational yet?*

op·er·a·tive (op-ĕ-ră-tiv) *adj.* 1. having an effect, working or functioning. 2. of surgical operations. **operative** *n.* a spy or secret agent. 2. an artisan or skilled workman who operates a machine. **op'er·a·tive·ly** *adv.*

op·er·a·tor (op-ĕ-ray-tŏr) *n.* 1. a person who operates a machine or engages in business or runs a business etc. 2. one who makes connections of lines at a telephone exchange. 3. *(slang)* one who earns a living through clever persuasion and speculation and the avoidance of restrictions and regulations.

op·er·et·ta (op-ĕ-ret-ă) *n.* a short or light opera.

oph·thal·mic (of-thal-mik) *adj.* of or for the eyes.

oph·thal·mol·o·gist (of-thal-mol-ŏ-jist) *n.* a specialist in ophthalmology.

oph·thal·mol·o·gy (of-thal-mol-ŏ-jee) *n.* the scientific study of the eye and its diseases.

oph·thal·mo·scope (of-thal-mŏ-skohp) *n.* an instrument for examining the retina and other parts of the eye.

o·pi·ate (oh-pi-it) *n.* 1. a sedative drug containing opium. 2. a thing that soothes the feelings or dulls activity.

o·pine (oh-pɪn) *v.* **(o·pined, o·pin·ing)** to express or hold the opinion (that).

o·pin·ion (ŏ-pin-yŏn) *n.* 1. a belief or judgment that is held firmly but without actual proof of its truth, a view held as probable. 2. what one thinks on a particular point, *public opinion.* 3. a judgment or comment given by an expert who is consulted. 4. an estimate, *have a low opinion of him.*

o·pin·ion·at·ed (ŏ-pin-yŏ-nay-tid) *adj.* having strong opinions and holding them obstinately.

o·pi·um (oh-pi-ŭm) *n.* a drug made from the juice of certain poppies, smoked or chewed as a stimulant or narcotic, and used in medicine as a sedative.

o·pos·sum (ŏ-pos-ŭm) *n.* a small furry American marsupial that lives in trees.

opp. *abbr.* 1. opposed. 2. opposite.

op·po·nent (ŏ-poh-nĕnt) *n.* a person or group opposing another in a contest or war.

op·por·tune (op-ŏr-toon) *adj.* 1. (of time) suitable or favorable for a purpose. 2. done or occurring at a favorable time. **op·por·tune·ly** *adv.*

op·por·tun·ist (op-ŏr-too-nist) *n.* one who grasps opportunities, often in an unprincipled way. **op·por·tun·ism** *n.* **op·por·tun·is·tic** (op-ŏr-too-nis-tik) *adj.*

op·por·tu·ni·ty (op-ŏr-too-ni-tee) *n.* (*pl.* **-ties**) a time or set of circumstances that are suitable for a particular purpose. □**opportunity knocks,** a favorable situation presents itself.

op·pose (ŏ-pohz) *v.* (**op·posed, op·pos·ing**) 1. to show resistance to, to argue or fight against. 2. to place opposite, to place or be in opposition to. 3. to represent (things) as contrasting. **op·pos·a·ble** *adj.* □**as opposed to,** in contrast with.

op·po·site (op-ŏ-zit) *adj.* 1. having a position on the other or farther side, facing. 2. of a contrary kind, as different as possible from; *the opposite sex,* men in relation to women or vice versa; *they traveled in opposite directions,* moving away from or toward each other. **opposite** *n.* an opposite thing or person. **opposite** *adv. & prep.* in an opposite place or position or direction to (a person or thing). **op′po·site·ly** *adv.* **op′po·site·ness** *n.* □**one's opposite number,** a person holding a similar position to oneself in another group or organization.

op·po·si·tion (op-ŏ-zish-ŏn) *n.* 1. resistance, being hostile or in conflict or disagreement. 2. the people who oppose a proposal etc., one's competitors or rivals; *the opposition,* a political party opposed to the one that is in office. 3. placing or being placed opposite, contrast.

op·press (ŏ-pres) *v.* 1. to govern harshly, to treat with continual cruelty or injustice. 2. to weigh down with cares or unhappiness. **op·pres′sor** *n.* **op·pres·sion** (ŏ-presh-ŏn) *n.*

op·pres·sive (ŏ-pres-iv) *adj.* 1. oppressing. 2. difficult to endure. 3. (of weather) sultry and tiring. **op′pres′sive·ly** *adv.* **op·pres′sive·ness** *n.*

op·pro·bri·ous (ŏ-proh-bri-ŭs) *adj.* (of words etc.) showing scorn or reproach, abusive. **op·pro′bri·ous·ly** *adv.*

op·pro·bri·um (ŏ-proh-bri-ŭm) *n.* 1. great disgrace brought by shameful conduct. 2. the cause of such disgrace.

opt (opt) *v.* to make a choice. □**opt out,** to choose not to participate.

opt. *abbr.* 1. optical. 2. optician. 3. optics. 4. optional.

op·ta·tive (op-tă-tiv) *adj.* expressing a desire or a wish.

op·tic (op-tik) *adj.* of the eye or the sense of sight. □**optic nerve,** the nerve of sight between the optic centers of the brain and the eye.

op·ti·cal (op-ti-kăl) *adj.* 1. of the sense of sight. 2. aiding sight; *optical instruments,* telescopes etc. **op′ti·cal·ly** *adv.* □**optical art,** op art. **optical illusion,** an involuntary mental misinterpretation of something seen, caused by its deceptive appearance. **optical scanner,** a photoelectric instrument that converts written or printed matter into machine-readable form.

op·ti·cian (op-tish-ăn) *n.* a maker or seller of eyeglasses and other optical equipment.

op·tics (op-tiks) *n.* the scientific study of sight and of light as its medium.

op·ti·mal (op-ti-măl) *adj.* optimum. **op′ti·mal·ly** *adv.*

op·ti·mism (op-ti-miz-ĕm) *n.* a tendency to take a hopeful view of things, or to expect that results will be good. **op′ti·mist** *n.*

op·ti·mis·tic (op-ti-mis-tik) *adj.* showing optimism, hopeful. **op·ti·mis′ti·cal·ly** *n.*

op·ti·mum (op-ti-mŭm) *n.* (*pl.* **-ma,** *pr.* -mă, **-mums**) the best or most favorable conditions or amount etc. **optimum** *adj.* best, most favorable.

op·tion (op-shŏn) *n.* 1. freedom to choose, *had no option but to go.* 2. a thing that is or may be chosen, *none of the options is satisfactory.* 3. the right to buy or sell something at a certain price within a limited time, *we have ten days' option on the house.* □**keep one's options open,** to avoid committing oneself, so that one still has a choice.

op·tion·al (op-shŏ-năl) *adj.* not compulsory. **op′tion·al·ly** *adv.*

op·tom·e·trist (op-tom-ĕ-trist) *n.* an expert in optometry.

op·tom·e·try (op-tom-ĕ-tree) *n.* the profession of testing the refractive power and visual range of the eye.

op·u·lent (op-yŭ-lĕnt) *adj.* 1. wealthy, rich. 2. abundant, luxuriant. **op′u·lent·ly** *adv.* **op′u·lence** *n.*

o·pus (oh-pŭs) *n.* (*pl.* **o·pus·es, o·pe·ra,** *pr.* oh-pĕ-ră) a musical composition numbered as one of a composer's works (usually in order of publication), *Beethoven opus 15.*

or (or) *conj.* 1. as an alternative, *are you coming or going?* 2. also known as, *hydrophobia or rabies.*

OR *abbr.* 1. operating room. 2. Oregon.

-or *suffix* used to form nouns meaning action or occupation, as in *escalator, inventor.*

or·a·cle (or-ă-kĕl) *n.* 1. a place where the ancient Greeks consulted one of their gods for advice or prophecy. 2. the reply given. 3. a person or thing regarded as able to give wise guidance. **o·rac·u·lar** (oh-rak-yŭ-lăr) *adj.*

or·al (ohr-ăl) *adj.* 1. spoken not written, *oral evidence.* 2. of the mouth, done or taken by mouth. **oral** *n.* (*informal*) a spoken (not written) examination. **or′al·ly** *adv.* □**oral contraceptive,** a contraceptive taken by mouth. **oral history,** a history recorded, usually on tape, through the spoken words of its participants. ▷See the note under **verbal.**

or·ange (or-inj) *n.* 1. a round juicy citrus fruit with reddish-yellow peel. 2. the evergreen tree that bears this fruit. 3. reddish yellow. **orange** *adj.* orange colored, reddish yellow. □**orange blossom,** white sweet-scented flowers of the orange tree, traditionally worn by brides. **orange stick,** a small thin stick (originally of wood from an orange tree) designed for manicuring the nails.

or·ange·ade (or-inj-ayd) *n.* an orange-flavored soft drink.

or·ange·ry (or-inj-ree) *n.* (*pl.* **-ries**) an enclosed place for growing orange trees in cool climates.

o·rang-u·tan, o·rang·ou·tan (oh-rang-ŭ-tan) *n.*

a large long-armed ape of Borneo and Sumatra.

o·rate (oh-rayt) v. (**o·rat·ed, o·rat·ing**) to make a speech, to speak pompously.

o·ra·tion (oh-ray-shŏn) n. a long speech, especially of a ceremonial kind.

or·a·tor (or-ă-tŏr) n. a person who makes public speeches, one who is good at public speaking.

or·a·to·ri·o (or-ă-tohr-i-oh) n. (pl. **-os**) a musical composition for solo voices, chorus, and orchestra, usually with a biblical theme.

or·a·to·ry[1] (or-ă-tohr-ee) n. 1. the art of public speaking. 2. eloquent speech. **or·a·tor·i·cal** (or-ă-tor-i-kăl) adj. **or·a·tor′i·cal·ly** adv.

oratory[2] n. (pl. **-ries**) a small chapel or place for private worship.

orb (orb) n. 1. a sphere or globe. 2. a heavenly body.

or·bit (or-bit) n. 1. the curved path of a planet or satellite or spacecraft etc. around another body; *in orbit,* moving in an orbit. 2. a sphere of influence, a range of action or experience. **orbit** v. to move in an orbit, to travel in an orbit around (a body).

or·bit·al (or-bi-tăl) adj. of an orbit, *orbital velocity.*

or·bit·er (or-bi-těr) n. a spacecraft or artificial satellite in orbit or designed to be in orbit.

orch. abbr. 1. orchestra. 2. orchestrated by.

or·chard (or-chărd) n. 1. a piece of land planted with fruit trees. 2. these trees. **or′chard·ist** n.

or·ches·tra (or-ki-stră) n. 1. a large body of people playing various musical instruments, including stringed and wind instruments. 2. the part of a theater where these sit *(orchestra pit).* 3. the seats on the main floor of a theater. **or·ches·tral** (or-kes-trăl) adj.

or·ches·trate (or-ki-strayt) v. (**or·ches·trat·ed, or·ches·trat·ing**) 1. to compose or arrange (music) for performance by an orchestra. 2. to coordinate (things) deliberately, *an orchestrated series of protests.* **or·ches·tra·tion** (or-ki-stray-shŏn) n.

or·chid (or-kid) n. 1. a kind of plant with showy often irregularly shaped flowers. 2. its flower.

or·chis (or-kis) n. an orchid, especially a wild one.

ord. abbr. 1. order. 2. ordinary. 3. ordnance.

or·dain (or-dayn) v. 1. to appoint ceremonially to the Christian ministry, *was ordained priest.* 2. (of God or fate) to destine, *providence ordained that they should meet.* 3. to appoint or decree authoritatively, *what the laws ordain.*

or·deal (or-deel) n. a difficult experience that tests a person's character or power of endurance.

or·der (or-děr) n. 1. the way in which things are placed in relation to one another. 2. a proper or customary sequence. 3. a condition in which every part or unit is in its right place or in a normal or efficient state, *in good working order; out of order.* 4. the condition brought about by good and firm government and obedience to the laws, *law and order.* 5. a system of rules or procedure. 6. a command, an instruction given with authority, *custody by order of the court.* 7. a request to supply goods, the goods themselves. 8. a written direction (especially to a bank or post office) to pay money, or giving authority to do something, *a postal money order.* 9. a rank or class in society, *the lower orders.* 10. a kind or sort or quality, *showed courage of the highest order.* 11. a monastic organization or institution, *the Franciscan Order.* 12. *orders* = holy orders (see below). 13. a company of people to which distinguished people are admitted as an honor or reward, the insignia worn by its members, *the Order of the Garter.* 14. a style of ancient Greek or Roman architecture distinguished by the type of column used, *there are five classical orders.* 15. a group of plants or animals classified as similar in many ways. 16. a serving of food as ordered in a restaurant, *an order of ham and eggs.* **order** v. 1. to put in order, to arrange methodically. 2. to issue a command, to command that something shall be done. 3. to give an order for (goods etc.), to tell a waiter to serve (certain food). □**holy orders,** see **holy. in order to** or **that,** with the intention that, with the purpose of. **in short order,** quickly. **made to order,** made according to the buyer's instructions. **on order,** (of goods) ordered but not yet received. **order about,** to keep on giving commands to. **order book,** a book in which a tradesman enters orders. **order form,** a form to be filled in by a customer ordering goods.

or·der·ly (or-děr-lee) adj. 1. well arranged, in good order, tidy. 2. methodical, *an orderly mind.* 3. obedient to discipline, well behaved, *an orderly crowd.* **orderly** n. 1. a soldier in attendance on an officer to assist him or take messages etc. 2. an attendant in a hospital. **or′der·li·ness** n. □**orderly room,** a room where business is conducted in a military barracks.

or·di·nal (or-dĭ-năl) n. any of the *ordinal numbers,* the numbers defining a thing's position in a series (such as *first, fifth, twentieth*).

or·di·nance (or-dĭ-nans) n. a rule made by authority, a decree. ▷Do not confuse *ordinance* with *ordnance.*

or·di·nar·y (or-dĭ-ner-ee) adj. usual, customary, not exceptional. **or′di·nar·i·ness** n. **or·di·nar·i·ly** (or-dĭ-ner-ĭ-lee) adv. □**in the ordinary way,** if the circumstances were not exceptional. **ordinary seaman,** one ranking lower than an able seaman.

or·di·nate (or-di-nit) n. the straight line from any point drawn parallel to one coordinate axis and meeting the other.

or·di·na·tion (or-dĭ-nay-shŏn) n. ordaining or being ordained as a clergyman.

ord·nance (ord-năns) n. 1. military supplies, especially weapons and their equipment and ammunition. 2. cannon, artillery. ▷Do not confuse *ordnance* with *ordinance.*

Or·do·vi·cian (or-dŏ-vish-ăn) adj. of the geologic period of the Paleozoic era before the Silurian and after the Cambrian. **Ordovician** n. the Ordovician period.

or·dure (or-jūr) n. excrement, dung.

ore (ohr) n. solid rock or mineral, found in the earth's crust, from which metal or other useful or valuable substances can be extracted, *iron ore.*

Oreg., Ore. abbr. Oregon.

o·reg·a·no (ŏ-reg-ă-noh) n. a dried wild marjoram used as a seasoning.

Or·e·gon (or-ĕ-gŏn) a state of the U.S. **Or·e·go′ni·an** adj. & n.

org. abbr. 1. organic. 2. organization. 3. organized.

or·gan (or-găn) n. 1. a musical instrument consisting of pipes that sound notes when air is forced through them, played by keys pressed with the fingers and pedals pressed with the feet. 2. a distinct part of an animal or plant body, adapted for a particular function, *digestive organs; organs of speech.* 3. a medium of communication (such as a newspaper) giving the views of a particular group. □**organ bank**, a supply of human body organs kept frozen for the purposes of transplant and research. **organ grinder**, a person who plays a barrel organ.

or·gan·dy, or·gan·die (or-găn-dee) *n.* a kind of fine translucent usually stiffened cotton fabric.

or·gan·ic (or-gan-ik) *adj.* 1. of or affecting an organ or organs of the body, *organic diseases.* 2. of or formed from living things, *organic matter.* 3. (of food etc.) produced without the use of artificial fertilizers or pesticides. 4. organized or arranged as a system of related parts, *the business forms an organic whole.* **or·gan′i·cal·ly** *adv.* □**organic chemistry**, chemistry of carbon compounds, which are present in all living matter and in substances derived from it.

or·gan·ism (or-gă-niz-ĕm) *n.* a living being, an individual animal or plant. **or·gan·is·mic** (or-gă-niz-mik) *adj.* **or·gan·is′mal** *adj.*

or·gan·ist (or-gă-nist) *n.* a person who plays the organ.

or·gan·i·za·tion (or-gă-ni-zay-shŏn) *n.* 1. organizing, being organized. 2. an organized body of people, an organized system. **or·gan·i·za′tion·al** *adj.* □**organization man**, a man who regards the needs of the company he serves as taking priority over his own needs and those of other people.

or·gan·ize (or-gă-nız) *v.* (**or·gan·ized, or·gan·iz·ing**) 1. to arrange in an orderly or systematic way. 2. to make arrangements for, *organize a picnic.* 3. to form (people) into an association for a common purpose. **or′gan·iz·er** *n.*

or·gan·za (or-gan-ză) *n.* thin stiff transparent fabric of silk or synthetic fiber.

or·gasm (or-gaz-ĕm) *n.* the climax of sexual excitement. **or·gasm·ic** (or-gaz-mik) *adj.* **or·gast·ic** (or-gas-tik) *adj.*

or·gi·as·tic (or-ji-as-tik) *adj.* of the nature of an orgy.

or·gy (or-jee) *n.* (*pl.* **-gies**) 1. a wild drunken party or revelry. 2. great indulgence in one or more activities, *an orgy of spending.*

o·ri·el (ohr-i-ĕl) *n.* a kind of projecting window in an upper story, usually supported on corbels.

o·ri·ent (ohr-i-ĕnt) *v.* 1. to place or determine the position of (a thing) with regard to the points of a compass. 2. to face or be directed (toward a certain direction). 3. to acquaint (a person) with a new environment, *orient the new students.* **o·ri·en·ta·tion** (ohr-i-ĕn-tay-shŏn) *n.* □**orient oneself**, to get one's bearings; to become accustomed to a new situation.

Orient *n.* the East, countries east of the Mediterranean, especially East Asia.

o·ri·en·tal (ohr-i-en-tăl) *adj.* of the Orient, of the eastern or Asian world or its civilization. **Oriental** *n.* a native of the Orient. □**oriental rug**, a highly prized rug or carpet made by hand in the Orient, usually in Asia, and which achieves the status of an antique after it is one hundred years old.

o·ri·en·tate (ohr-i-ĕn-tayt) *v.* (**o·ri·en·tat·ed, o·ri·en·tat·ing**) to orient. ▷Careful writers use *orient* rather than *orientate.*

or·i·en·teer·ing (ohr-i-en-teer-ing) *n.* the sport of finding one's way on foot across rough country by map and compass.

or·i·fice (or-ĭ-fis) *n.* the opening of a cavity etc.

orig. *abbr.* 1. origin. 2. original. 3. originally.

o·ri·ga·mi (or-ĭ-gah-mee) *n.* 1. the Japanese art of folding paper into intricate designs. 2. (*pl.* **-mis**) an object made in this way.

or·i·gin (or-ĭ-jin) *n.* 1. the point or source or cause from which a thing begins its existence. 2. a person's ancestry or parentage, *a man of humble origin.* 3. a fixed point from which coordinates are measured.

o·rig·i·nal (ŏ-rij-ĭ-năl) *adj.* 1. existing from the first, earliest. 2. being a thing from which a copy or translation has been made. 3. firsthand, not imitative, new in character or design. 4. thinking or acting for oneself, inventive, creative, *an original mind.* **original** *n.* 1. the first form of something. 2. the thing from which a copy may be made. **o·rig′i·nal·ly** *adv.* **o·rig·i·nal·i·ty** (ŏ-rij-ĭ-nal-i-tee) *n.* □**original sin**, the condition of wickedness thought to be common to all mankind since Adam's sin.

o·rig·i·nate (ŏ-rij-ĭ-nayt) *v.* (**o·rig·i·nat·ed, o·rig·i·nat·ing**) 1. to give origin to, to cause to begin. 2. to have origin, to begin, *the quarrel originated in rivalry; from what country did the custom originate?* **o·rig′i·na·tor** *n.* **o·rig·i·na·tion** (ŏ-rij-i-nay-shŏn) *n.*

o·ri·ole (ohr-i-ohl) *n.* 1. an Old World bird of which the male has black and yellow plumage. 2. any of various North American songbirds of which the male has bright yellow or orange and black plumage.

O·ri·on (oh-rı-ŏn) *n.* a brilliant constellation on the equator shaped as a hunter with a belt and a sword.

or·i·son (or-i-zŏn) *n.* (*old use*) a prayer.

Or·lon (or-lon) *n.* (*trademark*) a lightweight synthetic acrylic textile fiber.

or·mo·lu (or-mŏ-loo) *n.* 1. gilded bronze or a gold-colored alloy of copper, used in decorating furniture. 2. articles made of or decorated with this.

or·na·ment (or-nă-mĕnt) *n.* 1. a decorative object or detail. 2. decoration, adornment, *this is for use, not only for ornament.* 3. a person or thing that adds distinction, *he is an ornament to his profession.* **ornament** *v.* to decorate, to be an ornament to.

or·na·men·tal (or-nă-men-tăl) *adj.* serving as an ornament.

or·na·men·ta·tion (or-nă-men-tay-shŏn) *n.* an adornment, something that beautifies.

or·nate (or-nayt) *adj.* elaborately ornamented. **or·nate′ly** *adv.* **or·nate′ness** *n.*

or·ner·y (or-nĕ-ree) *adj.* (*informal*) cantankerous, coarse, unpleasant.

ornith. *abbr.* 1. ornithological. 2. ornithology.

or·ni·thol·o·gist (or-nĭ-thol-ŏ-jist) *n.* an expert in ornithology.

or·ni·thol·o·gy (or-nĭ-thol-ŏ-jee) *n.* the scientific study of birds. **or·ni·tho·log·i·cal** (or-nĭ-thŏ-loj-i-kăl) *adj.*

o·rog·e·ny (oh-roj-ĕ-nee) *n.* the process of the formation of mountains. **or·o·ge·nic** (or-ŏ-jen-ik) *adj.*

o·ro·tund (ohr-ŏ-tund) *adj.* with full voice, imposing, dignified, pompous. **o·ro·tun·di·ty** (ohr-ŏ-tun-di-tee) *n.* ▷Do not confuse *orotund* with *rotund.*

or·phan (or-făn) *n.* a child whose parents are dead. **orphan** *v.* to make (a child) an orphan.

or·phan·age (or-fă-nij) *n.* an institution where orphans are housed and cared for.

or·ris (or-is) *n.* a kind of iris that has a fragrant root (*orrisroot*) which is dried for use in perfumery and medicine.

or·tho·don·tia (or-thŏ-**don**-shă) *n.* orthodontics.

or·tho·don·tics (or-thŏ-**don**-tiks) *n.* the branch of dentistry dealing with the correction of irregularities in the teeth and jaws. **or·tho·don'tic** *adj.*

or·tho·don·tist (or-thŏ-**don**-tist) *n.* a specialist in orthodontics.

or·tho·dox (or-thŏ-doks) *adj.* of or holding correct or conventional or currently accepted beliefs, especially in religion; *orthodox Jews,* those who follow traditional observances strictly. **or'tho·dox·y** *n.* □**Orthodox Church,** the Eastern or Greek Church (recognizing the Patriarch of Constantinople as its head), and the national churches of Russia, Rumania, etc. in communion with it.

or·tho·e·py (or-thoh-ĕ-pee) *n.* the science of the proper pronunciation of words. **or·tho'e·pist** *n.*

or·thog·ra·phy (or-thog-ră-fee) *n.* 1. correct or conventional spelling. 2. a perspective projection used in maps or elevations. **or·tho·graph·ic** (or-thŏ-**graf**-ik) *adj.*

or·tho·pe·dics (or-thŏ-**pee**-diks) *n.* the branch of medicine dealing with the correction of deformities in bones or muscles. **or·tho·pe'dic** *adj.*

or·tho·pe·dist (or-thŏ-**pee**-dist) *n.* a specialist in orthopedics.

or·to·lan (or-tŏ-lăn) *n.* a small European bird frequenting gardens and esteemed as a table delicacy.

Os *symbol* osmium.

OS, O.S. *abbr.* ordinary seaman.

O·sage (oh-sayj) *n.* (*pl.* **-sages, -sage**) 1. a member of an Indian tribe formerly occupying territory in Ohio. 2. the language of this tribe.

Os·car (os-kăr) *n.* one of the statuettes awarded by the Academy of Motion Picture Arts and Sciences for excellence in motion pictures.

os·cil·late (os-ĭ-layt) *v.* (**os·cil·lat·ed, os·cil·lat·ing**) 1. to move to and fro like a pendulum. 2. to vary between extremes of opinion or condition etc. 3. to fluctuate between high and low values. **os'cil·la·tor** *n.* **os·cil·la·tion** (os-ĭ-lay-shŏn) *n.* **os·cil·la·to·ry** (os-ĭ-lă-tohr-ee) *adj.*

os·cil·lo·scope (ŏ-sil-ŏ-skohp) *n.* a device for viewing oscillations, usually on a fluorescent screen. **os·cil·lo·scop·ic** (ŏ-sil-ŏ-**skop**-ik) *adj.* **os·cil·lo·scop'i·cal·ly** *adv.*

os·cu·late (os-kyŭ-layt) *v.* (**os·cu·lat·ed, os·cu·lat·ing**) to kiss.

o·sier (oh-zhĕr) *n.* 1. a kind of willow with flexible twigs used in basketwork. 2. a twig from this.

Os·lo (oz-loh, os-) the capital of Norway.

os·mi·um (oz-mi-ŭm) *n.* a hard blue-white metal of the platinum group, the heaviest known metal.

os·mo·sis (oz-moh-sis, os-) *n.* diffusion of fluid through a porous partition into another fluid. **os·mot·ic** (oz-mot-ik, os-) *adj.*

os·prey (os-pree) *n.* (*pl.* **-preys**) a large bird preying on fish.

os·si·fy (os-ĭ-fı) *v.* (**os·si·fied, os·si·fy·ing**) 1. to change into bone, to make or become hard like bone. 2. to make or become rigid and unprogressive, *their ideas had ossified.* **os·si·fi·ca·tion** (os-ĭ-fĭ-kay-shŏn) *n.*

os·su·ar·y (osh-oo-er-ee) *n.* (*pl.* **-ar·ies**) a receptacle for the bones of the dead.

os·ten·si·ble (o-sten-sĭ-bĕl) *adj.* pretended, put forward as a reason etc. to conceal the real one, *their ostensible motive was trade.* **os·ten'si·bly** *adv.*

os·ten·ta·tion (os-ten-tay-shŏn) *n.* a showy display intended to impress people. **os·ten·ta'tious** *adj.* **os·ten·ta'tious·ly** *adv.*

os·te·o·path (os-ti-ŏ-path) *n.* a practitioner who treats certain diseases and abnormalities by manipulating bones and muscles. **os·te·o·path·ic** (os-ti-ŏ-**path**-ik) *adj.* **os·te·op·a·thy** (os-ti-op-ă-thee) *n.*

os·tra·cize (os-tră-sız) *v.* (**os·tra·cized, os·tra·ciz·ing**) to refuse to associate with, to cast out from a group or from society. **os·tra·cism** (os-tră-siz-ĕm) *n.*

os·trich (os-trich) *n.* 1. a swift-running African bird that cannot fly, said to bury its head in the sand when pursued, in the belief that it then cannot be seen. 2. a person who refuses to face facts.

OT *abbr.* 1. Old Testament. 2. overtime.

O.T. *abbr.* Old Testament.

OTB *abbr.* offtrack betting.

OTC *abbr.* over-the-counter.

oth·er (*uth*-ĕr) *adj.* 1. alternative, additional, being the remaining one or set of two or more, *has no other income; try the other shoe; my other friends.* 2. not the same, *wouldn't want her to be other than she is.* **other** *n.* & *pronoun* the other one, the other person or thing, *where are the others?* **other** *adv.* otherwise. □**other world,** the future life; some imagined world. **the other day** or **week** etc., a few days or weeks etc. ago.

oth·er·wise (*uth*-ĕr-wız) *adv.* 1. in a different way, *could not have done otherwise.* 2. in other respects, *is otherwise correct.* 3. if circumstances were different, or else, *write it down, otherwise you'll forget.* **otherwise** *adj.* in a different state, not as supposed, *the truth is quite otherwise.*

oth·er·world·ly (*uth*-ĕr-wurld-lee) *adv.* concerned with the future life or some imagined world to the neglect of the present or real one. **oth'er·world'li·ness** *n.*

o·ti·ose (oh-shi-ohs) *adj.* not required, serving no practical purpose.

o·to·lar·yn·gol·o·gist (oh-toh-lar-ing-gol-ŏ-jist) *n.* an expert in otolaryngology.

o·to·lar·yn·gol·o·gy (oh-toh-lar-ing-gol-ŏ-jee) *n.* the branch of medicine concerned with the ear, nose, and throat.

Ot·ta·wa¹ (ot-ă-wă) the capital of Canada.

Ottawa² *n.* (*pl.* **-was, -wa**) 1. a member of a tribe of Indians in Michigan and southern Ontario. 2. the language of this tribe.

ot·ter (ot-ĕr) *n.* a fish-eating water mammal with webbed feet, a flat tail, and thick brown fur.

ot·to·man (ot-ŏ-măn) *n.* (*pl.* **-mans**) 1. a long cushioned seat without back or arms. 2. an upholstered footstool. 3. a heavy fabric of silk with cotton or wool. 4. *Ottoman,* a Turk, especially a subject of the former Turkish empire (14th c.–1918). **Ottoman** *adj.* of Turkey, especially its former empire.

Oua·ga·dou·gou (wah-gă-doo-goo) the capital of Upper Volta.

ou·bli·ette (oo-blee-et) *n.* a secret dungeon with entrance only by a trapdoor at the top.

ouch (owch) *interj.* an exclamation of sudden pain or annoyance.

ought (awt) *auxiliary verb* expressing duty or rightness or advisability or strong probability. **oughtn't** = ought not.

Oui·ja (wee-jă, -jee) *n.* (*trademark*) a device consisting of a board on which words, letters of the alphabet, and various signs, numbers, and symbols are written, used with a movable pointer in an attempt to obtain messages in spiritualistic seances.

ounce (owns) *n.* 1. a unit of weight equal to one sixteenth of a pound (about 28 grams). 2. one twelfth of a pound (about 31 grams) in apothecaries' weight, also called a troy ounce. 3. a fluid ounce (*see* **fluid**).

our (owr) *adj.* of or belonging to us.

ours (owrz) *possessive pronoun* belonging to us, the thing(s) belonging to us, *ours was disqualified.* ▷It is incorrect to write *our's* (see the note under **its**).

our·selves (ahr-selvz, owr-) *pronoun* corresponding to *we* and *us,* used in the same ways as *himself.*

-ous *suffix* used to form adjectives meaning abounding in, characterized by, or of the nature of, as in *envious, mountainous.*

oust (owst) *v.* to drive out, to eject from office or a position or employment etc.

oust·er (ow-stĕr) *n.* an expulsion or ejection, a wrongful dispossession.

out (owt) *adv.* 1. away from or not in a place, not in its normal or usual state, not at home; *the tide is out,* is low. 2. not in effective or favorable action, no longer in fashion or in office, (in baseball etc.) having had one's batters or runners retired, (of workers) on strike, (of a light or fire etc.) no longer burning. 3. away from the center or inside, *the wall juts out.* 4. no longer visible, *paint it out.* 5. not possible, *skating is out until the ice thickens.* 6. unconscious. 7. into the open, into existence or hearing or view etc., visible, revealed, *the sun is out; the secret is out; the flowers are out,* opened, no longer in bud. 8. to or at an end, completely, *tired out; sold out.* 9. in a finished form, *type it out.* 10. (in radio conversations) transmission ends. **out** *adj.* 1. located away or at a distance, *an out island.* 2. (in baseball) not successful in reaching base. **out** *prep.* out of.

out *n.* 1. a way of escape. 2. a person or thing that is out. 3. a baseball play that retires a batter or base runner. **out** *interj.* get out. **out** *v.* to become known, *murder will out.* □**be on the outs with,** *(informal)* to be alienated from (another person). **be out to,** to be acting with the intention of, *is out to cause trouble.* **out box,** a box for documents, letters, etc. that have been dealt with and are to be taken elsewhere. **out of,** from within or among; beyond the range of; so as to be without a supply of; (of an animal) having as its dam. **out of bounds,** *see* **bounds. out of date,** no longer fashionable or current or valid, *this passport is out of date.* **out of doors,** in the open air. **out of the way,** no longer an obstacle; remote; unusual. **out of this world,** incredibly good, indescribable. **out of work,** having no work; unable to find paid employment. **out with,** let us eject or dismiss (a person). **out with it,** say what you are thinking.

out- *prefix* more than, so as to exceed, as in *outbid, outgrow, out-talk.*

out·age (ow-tij) *n.* a period during which a power supply is not operating.

out-and-out (owt-ăn-owt) *adj.* thorough, extreme.

out·back (owt-bak) *n. (Australian)* remote inland districts.

out·bal·ance (owt-bal-ăns) *v.* **(out·bal·anced, out·bal·anc·ing)** to outweigh.

out·bid (owt-bid) *v.* **(out·bid, out·bid·ding)** to bid higher than (another person).

out·board (owt-bohrd) *adj.* (of a motor) placed

or attached to the outside of the stern of a boat or near the end of an airplane wing.

out·bound (owt-bownd) *adj.* outward bound.

out·break (owt-brayk) *n.* a breaking out of anger or war or a disease etc.

out·build·ing (owt-bil-ding) *n.* a building (such as a shed or barn etc.) belonging to but separate from a house.

out·burst (owt-burst) *n.* a bursting out of anger or laughter etc.

out·cast (owt-kast) *n.* a person who has been driven out of a group or rejected by society.

out·class (owt-klas) *v.* to surpass greatly.

out·come (owt-kum) *n.* the result or effect of an event etc.

out·crop (owt-krop) *n.* 1. part of an underlying layer of rock that projects on the surface of the ground. 2. a breaking out.

out·cry (owt-krɪ) *n.* (*pl.* **-cries**) 1. a loud cry. 2. a strong protest.

out·dat·ed (owt-day-tid) *adj.* out of date.

out·dis·tance (owt-dis-tăns) *v.* **(out·dis·tanced, out·dis·tanc·ing)** to get far ahead of (a person) in a race etc.

out·do (owt-doo) *v.* **(out·did, out·done, out·do·ing)** to do better than (another person).

out·door (owt-dohr) *adj.* 1. of or for use in the open air. 2. enjoying open-air activities, *she's not an outdoor type.*

out·doors (owt-dohrz) *adv.* in or to the open air. □**the outdoors,** the world outside buildings, the open air.

out·doors·man (owt-dohrz-măn) *n.* (*pl.* **-men,** *pr.* -mĕn) a man who enjoys being in the open air.

out·draw (owt-draw) *v.* **(out·drew, out·drawn, out·draw·ing)** 1. to ready one's firearm for discharge faster than (one's competitor or opponent). 2. to attract more spectators than (another performer).

out·er (ow-tĕr) *adj.* farther from the center or from the inside, exterior, external. □**outer space,** the universe beyond Earth's atmosphere.

out·er·most (ow-tĕr-mohst) *adj.* farthest outward, most remote.

out·er·wear (ow-tĕr-wair) *n.* garments worn over other clothes.

out·face (owt-fays) *v.* **(out·faced, out·fac·ing)** to disconcert (a person) by one's defiant or confident manner.

out·field (owt-feeld) *n.* 1. the outer part of a baseball field. 2. the players (left fielder, center fielder and right fielder) who play the outfield. **out·field·er** *n.*

out·fight (owt-frt) *v.* **(out·fought, out·fight·ing)** to surpass in fighting.

out·fit (owt-fit) *n.* 1. complete equipment or a set of things for a purpose. 2. a set of clothes to be worn together. 3. *(informal)* an organization, a group of people regarded as a unit. **outfit** *v.* **(out·fit·ted, out·fit·ting)** to supply with equipment.

out·fit·ter (owt-fit-ĕr) *n.* a supplier of equipment or of men's clothing.

out·flank (owt-flangk) *v.* to get around the flank of (an enemy).

out·flow (owt-floh) *n.* an outward flow, the amount that flows out.

out·fox (owt-foks) *v.* to outwit.

out·go (owt-goh) *n.* (*pl.* **-goes**) an expenditure, the money paid out.

out·go·ing (owt-goh-ing) *adj.* 1. going out. 2. sociable and friendly.

out·grow (owt-groh) *v.* **(out·grew, out·grow, out·grow·ing)** 1. to grow faster than. 2. to grow out of (clothes or habits).

out·growth (owt-grohth) *n.* 1. something that grows out of another thing. 2. a natural development, an effect.

out·guess (owt-ges) *v.* to guess correctly what is intended by (another person).

out·gun (owt-gun) *v.* **(out·gunned, out·gun·ning)** to surpass in power of guns.

out·house (owt-hows) *n.* (*pl.* **-hous·es,** *pr.* -howziz) an outdoor toilet.

out·ing (ow-ting) *n.* a pleasure trip, an airing.

out·land·ish (owt-lan-dish) *adj.* looking or sounding strange or foreign. **out·land'ish·ly** *adv.* **out·land'ish·ness** *n.*

out·last (owt-last) *v.* to last longer than.

out·law (owt-law) *n.* 1. (in the Middle Ages) a person who was punished by being placed outside the protection of the law. 2. a person living as a fugitive. **outlaw** *v.* 1. to make (a person) an outlaw. 2. to declare to be illegal. **out'law·ry** *n.*

out·lay (owt-lay) *n.* what is spent on something.

out·let (owt-lit) *n.* 1. a way out for water or steam etc. 2. a means or occasion for giving vent to one's feelings or energies. 3. a market for goods. 4. a point in an electrical wiring system at which current may be drawn by inserting a plug.

out·line (owt-lɪn) *n.* 1. a line or lines showing the shape or boundary of something. 2. a statement or summary of the chief facts about something. 3. a sketch containing lines but no shading. **outline** *v.* **(out·lined, out·lin·ing)** to draw or describe in outline, to mark the outline of. ☐**in outline,** giving only an outline.

out·live (owt-liv) *v.* **(out·lived, out·liv·ing)** to live longer than.

out·look (owt-luuk) *n.* 1. a view on which one looks out, *a pleasant outlook over the lake.* 2. a person's mental attitude or way of looking at something. 3. future prospects.

out·ly·ing (owt-lɪ-ing) *adj.* situated far from a center, remote.

out·ma·neu·ver (owt-mă-noo-věr) *v.* to outdo in maneuvering.

out·mod·ed (owt-moh-did) *adj.* no longer fashionable.

out·most (owt-mohst) *adj.* 1. outermost. 2. uttermost.

out·num·ber (owt-num-běr) *v.* to exceed in number.

out-of-date (owt-ŏv-dayt) *adj.* no longer current, not valid, obsolete.

out-of-town·er (owt-ŏv-tow-něr) *n.* (*informal*) a visitor from another city or town.

out·pace (owt-pays) *v.* **(out·paced, out·pac·ing)** to go faster than.

out·pa·tient (owt-pay-shěnt) *n.* a person who visits a hospital for treatment but does not remain there.

out·per·form (owt-pěr-form) *v.* to perform better than.

out·play (owt-play) *v.* to surpass in playing.

out·point (owt-point) *v.* to score more points than.

out·post (owt-pohst) *n.* 1. a detachment of troops stationed at a distance from the main army. 2. any distant branch or settlement.

out·pour·ing (owt-pohr-ing) *n.* 1. what is poured out. 2. a spoken or written expression of emotion.

out·put (owt-puut) *n.* 1. the amount produced. 2. the electrical power produced by a machine. 3. the work done by a computer, especially the transmission of information from an internal computer unit to an external one or to an outside device. **output** *v.* **(out·put·ted** or **out·put, out·put·ting)** to produce as output.

out·rage (owt-rayj) *n.* 1. an act that shocks public opinion. 2. strong resentment (at). 3. an injury or insult. **outrage** *v.* **(out·raged, out·rag·ing)** 1. to commit an outrage against, to shock and anger greatly. 2. to rape.

out·ra·geous (owt-ray-jŭs) *adj.* greatly exceeding what is moderate or reasonable, shocking. **out·ra'geous·ly** *adv.* **out·ra'geous·ness** *n.*

out·rank (owt-rangk) *v.* to be of higher rank than.

ou·tré (oo-tray) *adj.* outside the bounds of what is usual or proper. ▷French.

out·reach (owt-reech) *v.* 1. to reach farther than, to surpass. 2. to stretch out (an arm etc.). ☐**outreach program,** a program run by a social or government agency or a church etc. to help people in a community.

out·rid·er (owt-rɪ-děr) *n.* a mounted attendant or a motorcyclist riding as guard with a carriage or procession.

out·rig·ger (owt-rig-ěr) *n.* 1. a beam or spar or structure projecting from the side of a ship for various purposes. 2. a strip of wood fixed parallel to a canoe by struts projecting from it, to give stability. 3. a boat with either of these.

out·right (owt-rɪt) *adv.* 1. completely, entirely, not gradually; *bought the house outright,* by a single payment. 2. openly, frankly, *told him outright.* **outright** *adj.* thorough, complete, *an outright fraud.* **out'right'ness** *n.*

out·run (owt-run) *v.* **(out·ran, out·run, out·run·ning)** 1. to run faster or farther than. 2. to go beyond (a specified point or limit). 3. to flee or escape from.

out·sell (owt-sel) *v.* **(out·sold, out·sell·ing)** to sell or be sold in greater quantities than.

out·set (owt-set) *n.* the beginning, *from the outset of his career.*

out·shine (owt-shɪn) *v.* **(out·shone, out·shin·ing)** to surpass in splendor or excellence, to shine more brightly than.

out·side (owt-sɪd, owt-sɪd) *n.* 1. the outer side of a surface or part. 2. the exterior, the utmost extent or limit, the space beyond. **outside** *adj.* 1. of or coming from the outside; *her outside interests,* interests other than work or household. 2. negligible, remote, *an outside chance.* 3. greatest possible, *the outside price.* 4. not belonging to some circle or institution. **outside** *adv.* on or at or to the outside. **outside** *prep.* 1. on the outer side of, at or to the outside of, other than, *has no interests outside his work; outside an hour,* for longer than this. 2. beyond the limits of. 3. with the exception of. ☐**at the outside,** (of amounts) at most. **outside of,** external to, not included in, beyond the limits of, other than, not in.

out·sid·er (owt-sɪ-děr) *n.* 1. a nonmember of a certain group or profession. 2. a horse or person thought to have no chance in a race or competition which he has been entered.

out·size (owt-sɪz), **out·sized** (owt-sɪzd) *adj.* much larger than average.

out·skirts (owt-skurts) *n. pl.* the outer districts or outlying parts, especially of a town.

out·smart (owt-smahrt) *v. (informal)* to outwit.

out·spo·ken (owt-spoh-kĕn) *adj.* speaking or spoken without reserve, very frank. **out·spo'ken·ness** *n.*

out·spread (owt-spred) *adj.* spread out.

out·stand·ing (owt-stan-ding) *adj.* 1. conspicuous. 2. exceptionally good. 3. not yet paid or settled, *some of his debts are still outstanding.* **out·stand'ing·ly** *adv.*

out·sta·tion (owt-stay-shŏn) *n.* a station at a distance from headquarters or from populous areas.

out·stay (owt-stay) *v.* to stay longer than.

out·stretched (owt-strecht) *adj.* stretched out.

out·strip (owt-strip) *v.* (**out·stripped, out·strip·ping**) 1. to outrun. 2. to surpass.

out·vote (owt-voht) *v.* (**out·vot·ed, out·vot·ing**) to defeat by a majority of votes.

out·ward (owt-wărd) *adj. & adv.* 1. situated on the outside. 2. going toward the outside. 3. in one's expression or actions etc. as distinct from in one's mind or spirit.

out·ward·ly (owt-wărd-lee) *adv.* on the outside.

out·wards (owt-wărdz) *adv.* toward the outside.

out·wear (owt-wair) *v.* (**out·wore, out·worn, out·wear·ing**) 1. to wear or endure longer than. 2. to wear out, to exhaust.

out·weigh (owt-way) *v.* to be greater in weight or importance or significance than.

out·wit (owt-wit) *v.* (**out·wit·ted, out·wit·ting**) to get the better of (a person) by one's cleverness or craftiness.

out·work (owt-wurk) *n.* an advanced or detached part of a fortification. **outwork** (owt-wurk) *v.* to work faster or harder than.

out·worn (owt-wohrn) *adj.* worn out, damaged by wear.

ou·zo (oo-zoh) *n.* a Greek liqueur flavored with aniseed.

o·va (oh-vă) *see* **ovum.**

o·val (oh-văl) *n.* a rounded symmetrical shape longer than it is broad. **oval** *adj.* having this shape. □**the Oval Office,** the White House office in which the U.S. President conducts official business.

o·va·ry (oh-vă-ree) *n.* (*pl.* **-ries**) 1. either of the two organs in which egg cells are produced in female animals. 2. part of the pistil in a plant, from which fruit is formed. **o·var·i·an** (oh-vair-i-ăn) *adj.*

o·vate (oh-vayt) *adj.* shaped like an egg as a solid or in outline, oval.

o·va·tion (oh-vay-shŏn) *n.* enthusiastic applause.

ov·en (uv-ĕn) *n.* an enclosed compartment in which things are cooked or heated.

ov·en·bird (uv-ĕn-burd) *n.* an American warbler that builds its dome-shaped nest on the forest floor.

ov·en·ware (uv-ĕn-wair) *n.* dishes for cooking and serving food.

o·ver (oh-vĕr) *adv.* 1. with movement outward and downward from the brink or from an upright position. 2. with movement from one side to the other or so that a different side is showing. 3. across a street or other space or distance, *is over here from England.* 4. so as to cover or touch a whole surface, *the lake froze over; brush it over.* 5. with transference or change from one hand or one side or one owner etc. to another, *went over to the enemy; hand it over; over to you,* I await your action. 6. (in radio conversation) it is your turn to transmit. 7. besides, in addition or excess. 8. with repetition, *ten times over.* 9. thoroughly, with detailed consideration, *think it over.* 10. at an end, *the battle is over.* **over** *adj.* 1. upper. 2. higher. 3. superior. 4. covering. 5. remaining. 6. ended. **over** *prep.* 1. in or to a position higher than. 2. above and across, so as to clear. 3. throughout the length or extent of, during, *over the years; stayed over the weekend.* 4. so as to visit or examine all parts, *looked over the house; went over the plan again.* 5. transmitted by, *heard it over the radio.* 6. while engaged with, *we can talk over dinner.* 7. concerning, *quarreled over money.* 8. more than, *it's over a mile away.* 9. in superiority or preference to, *their victory over Yale.* □**over and above,** besides. **over and over,** so that the same point comes uppermost repeatedly; repeated many times.

over- *prefix* above, as in *overlay;* too much, excessively, as in *overanxiety, overanxious.*

o·ver·a·bun·dance (oh-vĕr-ă-bun-dăns) *n.* an excess over what is desirable or suitable. **o'ver·a·bun'dant** *adj.*

o·ver·act (oh-vĕr-akt) *v.* to act one's part in an exaggerated manner.

o·ver·ac·tive (oh-vĕr-ak-tiv) *adj.* too active.

o·ver·age[1] (oh-vĕr-ayj) *adj.* of more than the normal age.

o·ver·age[2] (oh-vĕ-rij) *n.* a surplus of goods, especially a larger quantity of merchandise than has been recorded as having been shipped or stored.

o·ver·ag·gres·sive (oh-vĕr-ă-gres-iv) *adj.* too aggressive.

o·ver·all (oh-vĕr-awl) *adj.* 1. including everything, total. 2. taking all aspects into account. **overall** (oh-vĕr-awl) *adv.* in all parts, taken as a whole.

o·ver·alls (oh-vĕr-awlz) *n. pl.* a one-piece garment covering body and legs, worn as protective clothing.

o·ver·anx·ious (oh-vĕr-angk-shŭs) *adj.* too anxious.

o·ver·arm (oh-vĕr-ahrm) *adj.* 1. performed with the arm above the shoulder. 2. (in swimming) with the arm lifted out of the water and stretched forward beyond the head.

o·ver·awe (oh-vĕr-aw) *v.* (**o·ver·awed, o·ver·aw·ing**) to overcome with awe.

o·ver·bal·ance (oh-vĕr-bal-ăns) *v.* (**o·ver·bal·anced, o·ver·bal·anc·ing**) to lose balance and fall over, to cause to do this.

o·ver·bear (oh-vĕr-bair) *v.* (**o·ver·bore, o·ver·borne, o·ver·bear·ing**) 1. to bear down or upset by weight or force. 2. to put down or repress by power or authority. 3. to surpass in importance etc., to outweigh.

o·ver·bear·ing (oh-vĕr-bair-ing) *adj.* domineering. **o·ver·bear'ing·ly** *adv.*

o·ver·bid (oh-vĕr-bid) *v.* (**o·ver·bid·ding**) 1. to make a higher bid than. 2. (in bridge) to make a bid higher than the cards in one's hand justify.

o·ver·blown (oh-vĕr-blohn) *adj.* 1. excessively pompous or pretentious. 2. rather stout. 3. (of a flower etc.) too fully open, past its prime.

o·ver·board (oh-vĕr-bohrd) *adv.* from within a ship into the water. □**go overboard,** *(informal)* to be very enthusiastic. **throw overboard,** to abandon, to discard.

o·ver·bold (oh-vĕr-bohld) *adj.* more bold than is suitable, rash.

o·ver·book (oh-vĕr-**buuk**) *v.* to book too many passengers or visitors for (an aircraft flight or a hotel etc.).

o·ver·bur·den (oh-vĕr-bur-dĕn) *v.* to burden excessively.

o·ver·buy (oh-vĕr-**bɪ**) *v.* (**o·ver·bought, o·ver·buy·ing**) to buy more than is needed.

o·ver·care·ful (oh-vĕr-kair-fŭl) *adj.* excessively careful.

o·ver·cast (oh-vĕr-kast) *adj.* (of the sky) covered with cloud. **overcast** *v.* (**o·ver·cast, o·ver·cast·ing**) to stitch over (an edge) to prevent it from fraying.

o·ver·cau·tious (oh-vĕr-kaw-shŭs) *adj.* more cautious than the circumstances warrant.

o·ver·charge (oh-vĕr-**chahrj**) *v.* (**o·ver·charged, o·ver·charg·ing**) 1. to charge too high a price. 2. to fill too full. **overcharge** (oh-vĕr-chahrj) *n.* an excessive charge, usually of money.

o·ver·cloud (oh-vĕr-**klowd**) *v.* to make obscure, to cover as with clouds or gloominess etc.

o·ver·coat (oh-vĕr-koht) *n.* a warm outdoor coat.

o·ver·come (oh-vĕr-**kum**) *v.* (**o·ver·came, o·ver·come, o·ver·com·ing**) 1. to win a victory over, to succeed in subduing. 2. to be victorious. 3. to make helpless, to deprive of proper control of oneself, *overcome by gas fumes or by grief*. 4. to find a way of dealing with (a problem etc.).

o·ver·com·pen·sate (oh-vĕr-kom-pĕn-sayt) *v.* (**o·ver·com·pen·sat·ed, o·ver·com·pen·sat·ing**) to correct in an exaggerated manner a real or fancied character defect.

o·ver·con·fi·dent (oh-vĕr-kon-fi-dĕnt) *adj.* too confident. **o′ver·con′fi·dence** *n.*

o·ver·con·sci·en·tious (oh-vĕr-kon-shi-en-shŭs) *adj.* too painstaking and careful.

o·ver·cooked (oh-vĕr-**kuukt**) *adj.* cooked for an excessive length of time.

o·ver·crit·i·cal (oh-vĕr-krit-i-kăl) *adj.* too inclined to find fault.

o·ver·crowd (oh-vĕr-**krowd**) *v.* to crowd too many people into (a place or vehicle etc.).

o·ver·do (oh-vĕr-**doo**) *v.* (**o·ver·did, o·ver·done, o·ver·do·ing**) 1. to do (a thing) excessively. 2. to cook (food) too long. □**overdo it** *or* **things**, to work too hard; to exaggerate.

o·ver·dose (oh-vĕr-**dohs**) *n.* too large a dose of a drug etc.

o·ver·draft (oh-vĕr-draft) *n.* overdrawing of a bank account, the amount by which an account is overdrawn.

o·ver·draw (oh-vĕr-**draw**) *v.* (**o·ver·drew, o·ver·drawn, o·ver·draw·ing**) to draw more from (a bank account) than the amount credited; *be overdrawn,* to have done this.

o·ver·dress (oh-vĕr-**dres**) *v.* 1. to dress with too much display or formality, *she was overdressed for the party.* 2. to dress too warmly for the weather. **o·ver·dressed′** *adj.*

o·ver·drive (oh-vĕr-**drɪv**) *n.* mechanism providing an extra gear above the normal top gear in a vehicle.

o·ver·due (oh-vĕr-**doo**) *adj.* not paid or arrived etc. by the due or expected time.

o·ver·ea·ger (oh-vĕr-ee-gĕr) *adj.* unduly eager.

o·ver·eat (oh-vĕr-**eet**) *v.* (**o·ver·ate, o·ver·eat·en, o·ver·eat·ing**) to eat too much.

o·ver·ed·u·cat·ed (oh-vĕr-ej-ŭ-kay-tid) *adj.* educated too much for one's position.

o·ver·em·pha·sis (oh-vĕr-em-fă-sis) *n.* too much stress or importance.

o·ver·em·pha·size (oh-vĕr-em-fă-sɪz) *v.* (**o·ver·em·pha·sized, o·ver·em·pha·siz·ing**) 1. to put too much stress on (a word etc.). 2. to give too much prominence to (a fact or idea).

o·ver·es·ti·mate (oh-vĕr-es-ti-mayt) *v.* (**o·ver·es·ti·mat·ed, o·ver·es·ti·mat·ing**) to form too high an estimate of.

o·ver·ex·cite (oh-vĕr-ik-sɪt) *v.* (**o·ver·ex·cit·ed, o·ver·ex·cit·ing**) to excite excessively.

o·ver·ex·ert (oh-vĕr-ig-zurt) *v.* to exert too much.

o·ver·ex·pose (oh-vĕr-ik-spohz) *v.* (**o·ver·ex·posed, o·ver·ex·pos·ing**) to expose for too long. **o·ver·ex·po·sure** (oh-vĕr-ik-spoh-zhŭr) *n.*

o·ver·ex·tend (oh-vĕr-ik-stend) *v.* 1. to extend too much. 2. to commit (oneself) excessively in financial obligations.

o·ver·feed (oh-vĕr-**feed**) *v.* (**o·ver·fed, o·ver·feed·ing**) to feed too much.

o·ver·fill (oh-vĕr-fil) *v.* to fill too full or to overflowing.

o·ver·flow (oh-vĕr-**floh**) *v.* 1. to flow over (the edge or limits or banks etc.). 2. (of a crowd) to spread beyond the limits of (a room etc.). **overflow** (oh-vĕr-floh) *n.* 1. what overflows. 2. an outlet for excess liquid.

o·ver·fly (oh-vĕr-**flɪ**) *v.* (**o·ver·flew, o·ver·flown, o·ver·fly·ing**) to fly over (a place or territory). **o·ver·flight** (oh-vĕr-flɪt) *n.*

o·ver·fond (oh-vĕr-fond) *adj.* having too great an affection or liking.

o·ver·full (oh-vĕr-**fuul**) *adj.* overfilled, too full.

o·ver·gen·er·ous (oh-vĕr-jen-ĕ-rŭs) *adj.* excessively generous.

o·ver·glaze (oh-vĕr-**glayz**) *n.* a second glaze applied to pottery. **overglaze** *v.* (**o·ver·glazed, o·ver·glaz·ing**) to apply a glaze or overglaze to.

o·ver·graze (oh-vĕr-**grayz**) *v.* (**o·ver·grazed, o·ver·graz·ing**) to graze (land) to excess.

o·ver·grown (oh-vĕr-grohn) *adj.* 1. having grown too large. 2. covered with weeds etc.

o·ver·hand (oh-vĕr-hand) *adj. & adv.* = **overarm**.

o·ver·hang (oh-vĕr-**hang**) *v.* (**o·ver·hung, o·ver·hang·ing**) 1. to jut out over. 2. to impend, to hang threateningly over. **overhang** (oh-vĕr-hang) *n.* 1. an overhanging part, such as a projection or an upper part of a building beyond the lower part. 2. the extent of such a projection.

o·ver·hast·y (oh-vĕr-hay-stee) *adj.* unduly hasty. **o·ver·hast′i·ly** *adv.* **o·ver·hast′i·ness** *n.*

o·ver·haul (oh-vĕr-**hawl**) *v.* 1. to examine and make any necessary repairs or changes. 2. to overtake. **overhaul** (oh-vĕr-hawl) *n.* an examination and repair etc.

o·ver·head (oh-vĕr-hed) *adj. & adv.* above the level of one's head, in the sky. **overhead** *n.* the expenses involved in running a business. **overhead** *adj.* of or relating to business costs.

o·ver·hear (oh-vĕr-**heer**) *v.* (**o·ver·heard,** *pr.* **-hurd, o·ver·hear·ing,** *pr.* **-heer-ing**) to hear accidentally or without the speaker's knowledge or intention.

o·ver·heat (oh-vĕr-**heet**) *v.* to make or become too hot.

o·ver·in·dulge (oh-vĕr-in-**dulj**) *v.* (**o·ver·in·dulged, o·ver·in·dulg·ing**) 1. to gratify the wishes of (a person) excessively. 2. to consume or enjoy an excessive amount.

o·ver·in·dul·gence (oh-vĕr-in-**dul**-jĕns) *n.* 1. overindulging. 2. being overindulgent. 3. overconsumption, especially of food or drink. **o·ver·in·dul'gent** *adj.*

o·ver·in·sure (oh-vĕr-in-**shoor**) *v.* (**o·ver·in·sured, o·ver·in·sur·ing**) to insure for an excessive amount.

o·ver·joyed (oh-vĕr-**joid**) *adj.* filled with very great joy.

o·ver·kill (oh-vĕr-kil) *n.* a surplus of power above what is needed to defeat an opponent or destroy an enemy.

o·ver·land (oh-vĕr-land) *adj. & adv.* by land, not by sea.

o·ver·lap (oh-vĕr-lap) *v.* (**o·ver·lapped, o·ver·lap·ping**) 1. to extend beyond the edge of (a thing) and partly cover it. 2. to coincide partially, *our holidays overlap.* **overlap** *n.* overlapping, an overlapping part or amount.

o·ver·lay (oh-vĕr-lay) *v.* (**o·ver·laid, o·ver·lay·ing**) 1. to cover with a surface layer. 2. to lie on top of. **overlay** (oh-vĕr-lay) *n.* a thing laid over another, a coverlet.

o·ver·leaf (oh-vĕr-leef) *adv.* on the other side of a page of a book etc.

o·ver·lie (oh-vĕr-lɪ) *v.* (**o·ver·lay, o·ver·lain, o·ver·ly·ing**) 1. to lie on top of. 2. to smother (a child) in this way.

o·ver·load (oh-vĕr-lohd) *v.* to put too great a load on or into. **overload** (oh-vĕr-lohd) *n.* a load that is too great.

o·ver·long (oh-vĕr-lawng) *adj. & adv.* too long.

o·ver·look (oh-vĕr-luuk) *v.* 1. to have a view of or over (a place) from above. 2. to oversee. 3. to fail to observe or consider. 4. to take no notice of, to allow (an offense) to go unpunished. **overlook** (oh-vĕr-luuk) *n.* a high place from which one can view the scenery below.

o·ver·lord (oh-vĕr-lord) *n.* a supreme lord.

o·ver·ly (oh-vĕr-lee) *adv.* excessively.

o·ver·man (oh-vĕr-man) *v.* (**o·ver·manned, o·ver·man·ning**) to provide with too many people as workmen or crew etc.

o·ver·mas·ter (oh-vĕr-mas-tĕr) *v.* to master completely, to conquer.

o·ver·match (oh-vĕr-mach) *v.* 1. to be more than a match for. 2. to match with an opponent who is superior.

o·ver·mod·est (oh-vĕr-mod-ist) *adj.* excessively modest.

o·ver·much (oh-vĕr-much) *adv.* too much.

o·ver·night (oh-vĕr-nɪt) *adv.* 1. during the length of a night. 2. very suddenly or quickly. **overnight** (oh-vĕr-nɪt) *adj.* of or for or during a night, *an overnight stop in Rome.*

o·ver·op·ti·mism (oh-vĕr-op-tĭ-miz-ĕm) *n.* undue optimism. **o·ver·op·ti·mis·tic** (oh-vĕr-op-tĭ-mis-tik) *adj.*

o·ver·pass (oh-vĕr-pas) *n.* a road that crosses another by means of a bridge.

o·ver·pay (oh-vĕr-pay) *v.* (**o·ver·paid, o·ver·pay·ing**) to pay too highly.

o·ver·play (oh-vĕr-play) *v.* to play a theatrical role with exaggeration. □**overplay one's hand,** to take unjustified risks by overestimating one's strength.

o·ver·pop·u·lat·ed (oh-vĕr-pop-yŭ-lay-tid) *adj.* (of an area) having more people than can be supported by the resources. **o·ver·pop·u·la·tion** (oh-vĕr-pop-yŭ-lay-shŏn) *n.*

o·ver·pow·er (oh-vĕr-pow-ĕr) *v.* 1. to overcome by greater strength or numbers. 2. to be too intense for, to overwhelm.

o·ver·pow·er·ing (oh-vĕr-pow-ĕ-ring) *adj.* (of heat or feelings) extremely intense.

o·ver·praise (oh-vĕr-prayz) *v.* to praise too highly.

o·ver·price (oh-vĕr-prɪs) *v.* (**o·ver·priced, o·ver·pric·ing**) to price too highly.

o·ver·print (oh-vĕr-print) *v.* 1. to print (a photograph) darker than was intended. 2. to print too many copies of (a book etc.). 3. to print further matter on (an already printed surface, especially a postage stamp).

o·ver·pro·duce (oh-vĕr-prŏ-doos) *v.* (**o·ver·pro·duced, o·ver·pro·duc·ing**) to produce more of (a commodity) than is wanted.

o·ver·pro·duc·tion (oh-vĕr-prŏ-duk-shŏn) *n.* the producing of too much, an amount that has been produced in excess of demand.

o·ver·pro·tec·tive (oh-vĕr-prŏ-tek-tiv) *adj.* supplying more protection than is warranted.

o·ver·proud (oh-vĕr-prowd) *adj.* too proud.

o·ver·qual·i·fied (oh-vĕr-kwol-ĭ-fɪd) *adj.* with more experience or education than a job requires.

o·ver·rate (oh-vĕr-rayt) *v.* (**o·ver·rat·ed, o·ver·rat·ing**) 1. to have too high an opinion of. 2. to assess the taxes of (a place) too highly.

o·ver·reach (oh-vĕr-reech) *v.* **overreach oneself,** to fail through being too ambitious. **o·ver·reach'er** *n.*

o·ver·re·act (oh-vĕr-ri-akt) *v.* to respond more strongly than is justified.

o·ver·ride (oh-vĕr-rɪd) *v.* (**o·ver·rode, o·ver·rid·den, o·ver·rid·ing**) 1. to set aside (an order) by having, or behaving as if one had, superior authority. 2. to prevail over, *considerations of safety override all others.* 3. to intervene and cancel the operation of (an automatic mechanism).

o·ver·ripe (oh-vĕr-rɪp) *adj.* too ripe.

o·ver·rule (oh-vĕr-rool) *v.* (**o·ver·ruled, o·ver·rul·ing**) to set aside (a decision etc.) by using one's authority.

o·ver·run (oh-vĕr-run) *v.* (**o·ver·ran, o·ver·run, o·ver·run·ning**) 1. to spread over and occupy or injure, *the place is overrun with mice.* 2. to exceed (a limit or time allowed etc.), *the broadcast overran its allotted time.* 3. to defeat overwhelmingly. 4. to overflow. **overrun** (oh-vĕr-run) *n.* 1. an act or instance of overrunning, the extent of this. 2. costs exceeding preliminary estimates. 3. extra printed copies of a publication or of a part of its contents.

o·ver·seas (*adv.* oh-vĕr-seez; *adj.* oh-vĕr-seez) *adj. & adv.* across or beyond the sea, abroad.

o·ver·see (oh-vĕr-see) *v.* (**o·ver·saw, o·ver·seen, o·ver·see·ing**) to superintend. **o·ver·seer** (oh-vĕr-seer) *n.*

o·ver·sell (oh-vĕr-sel) *v.* (**o·ver·sold, o·ver·sell·ing**) 1. to sell more of (a thing) than one can deliver. 2. to exaggerate the merits of.

o·ver·sen·si·tive (oh-vĕr-sen-si-tiv) *adj.* unduly sensitive.

o·ver·sew (oh-vĕr-soh) *v.* (**o·ver·sewed, o·ver·sewn, o·ver·sew·ing**) to sew together (two edges) so that each stitch lies over the edges.

o·ver·sexed (oh-vĕr-sekst) *adj.* having unusually great sexual desires.

o·ver·shad·ow (oh-vĕr-shad-oh) *v.* 1. to cast a shadow over. 2. to make (a person or thing) seem unimportant in comparison.

o·ver·shoe (oh-vĕr-shoo) *n.* a shoe worn over an ordinary one as a protection against wet etc.

o·ver·shoot (oh-vĕr-shoot) *v.* (**o·ver·shot, o·ver·shoot·ing**) 1. to pass beyond (a target or limit etc.), *the plane overshot the runway when landing.* 2. to miss by shooting beyond.

o·ver·shot (oh-vĕr-shot) *adj.* 1. (of a water wheel) turned by water falling on it from above. 2. having the upper part extending beyond the lower, *an overshot jaw.*

o·ver·sight (oh-vĕr-sɪt) *n.* 1. supervision. 2. an unintentional omission or mistake.

o·ver·sim·pli·fy (oh-vĕr-sim-plĭ-fɪ) *v.* (**o·ver·sim·pli·fied, o·ver·sim·pli·fy·ing**) to misrepresent (a problem etc.) by stating it in terms that are too simple. **o·ver·sim·pli·fi·ca·tion** (oh-vĕr-sim-plĭ-f ĭ-kay-shŏn) *n.*

o·ver·size (oh-vĕr-sɪz), **o·ver·sized** (oh-vĕr-sɪzd) *adj.* of more than the usual size.

o·ver·sleep (oh-vĕr-sleep) *v.* (**o·ver·slept, o·ver·sleep·ing**) to sleep longer than one intended.

o·ver·spe·cial·ize (oh-vĕr-spesh-ă-lɪz) *v.* (**o·ver·spe·cial·ized, o·ver·spe·cial·iz·ing**) to concentrate too narrowly on one specialty. **o·ver·spe·cial·i·za·tion** (oh-vĕr-spesh-ă-li-zay-shŏn) *n.*

o·ver·spend (oh-vĕr-spend) *v.* (**o·ver·spent, o·ver·spend·ing**) to spend too much.

o·ver·spread (oh-vĕr-spred) *v.* to cover or occupy the surface of.

o·ver·staffed (oh-vĕr-staft) *adj.* having more than the necessary number of staff.

o·ver·state (oh-vĕr-stayt) *v.* (**o·ver·stat·ed, o·ver·stat·ing**) to exaggerate. **o·ver·state·ment** (oh-vĕr-stayt-mĕnt) *n.*

o·ver·stay (oh-vĕr-stay) *v.* to stay longer than; *overstay one's welcome,* to stay so long that one is no longer welcome.

o·ver·steer (oh-vĕr-steer) *v.* (of a car etc.) to have a tendency to turn more sharply than was intended.

o·ver·step (oh-vĕr-step) *v.* (**o·ver·stepped, o·ver·step·ping**) to go beyond (a limit).

o·ver·stim·u·late (oh-vĕr-stim-yŭ-layt) *v.* (**o·ver·stim·u·lat·ed, o·ver·stim·u·lat·ing**) to stimulate excessively.

o·ver·stock (oh-vĕr-stok) *v.* to stock beyond facilities or requirements. **overstock** (oh-vĕr-stok) *n.* a stock greater than that required.

o·ver·strict (oh-vĕr-strikt) *adj.* excessively strict.

o·ver·stuffed (oh-vĕr-stuft) *adj.* 1. (of cushions etc.) filled with much or too much stuffing. 2. (of furniture) made soft and comfortable by thick upholstery.

o·ver·sub·scribed (oh-vĕr-sŭb-skrɪbd) *adj.* with applications for an issue of shares etc. in excess of the number offered.

o·ver·sup·ply (oh-vĕr-sŭ-plɪ) *n.* (*pl.* -**plies**) a supply greater than that required.

o·vert (oh-vurt, oh-vurt) *adj.* done or shown openly, *overt hostility.* **o·vert′ly** *adv.*

o·ver·take (oh-vĕr-tayk) *v.* (**o·ver·took, o·ver·tak·en, o·ver·tak·ing**) 1. to come abreast with or level with. 2. to pass (a moving person or vehicle) by faster movement.

o·ver·tax (oh-vĕr-taks) *v.* 1. to levy excessive taxes on. 2. to put too heavy a burden or strain on.

o·ver-the-coun·ter (oh-vĕr-*th*ĕ-kown-tĕr) *adj.* 1. (of securities) not traded on a regular stock ex-

change. 2. (of drugs) purchasable without a doctor's prescription.

o·ver·throw (oh-vĕr-throh) *v.* (**o·ver·threw, o·ver·thrown, o·ver·throw·ing**) 1. to cause the downfall of, *overthrew the government.* 2. to throw over or past. 3. to upset or knock down. **overthrow** (oh-vĕr-throh) *n.* downfall, defeat.

o·ver·time (oh-vĕr-tɪm) *n.* 1. time worked beyond regular working hours. 2. payment for this. **o′ver·time** *adj. & adv.*

o·ver·tired (oh-vĕr-tɪrd) *adj.* fatigued to the point of exhaustion.

o·ver·tone (oh-vĕr-tohn) *n.* 1. an additional quality or implication, *overtones of malice in his comments.* 2. one of the higher tones adding fullness to a musical sound.

o·ver·top (oh-vĕr-top) *v.* (**o·ver·topped, o·ver·top·ping**) to be or become higher than, to surpass.

o·ver·trick (oh-vĕr-trik) *n.* a trick taken in excess of one's contract in the game of bridge.

o·ver·ture (oh-vĕr-chŭr) *n.* 1. an orchestral composition forming a prelude to an opera or ballet etc. 2. a composition resembling this. 3. *overtures,* a friendly approach showing willingness to begin negotiations, a formal proposal or offer.

o·ver·turn (oh-vĕr-turn) *v.* 1. to turn over, to cause to turn over. 2. to overthrow, to abolish or invalidate.

o·ver·use (oh-vĕr-yooz) *v.* (**o·ver·used, o·ver·us·ing**) to use excessively. **overuse** (oh-vĕr-yoos) *n.* too much use.

o·ver·val·ue (oh-vĕr-val-yoo) *v.* (**o·ver·val·ued, o·ver·val·u·ing**) to put too high a value on.

o·ver·view (oh-vĕr-vyoo) *n.* a general survey.

o·ver·ween·ing (oh-vĕr-wee-ning) *adj.* 1. arrogant, presumptuous. 2. excessive.

o·ver·weight (oh-vĕr-wayt) *adj.* weighing more than is normal or required or permissible.

o·ver·whelm (oh-vĕr-hwelm) *v.* 1. to bury or drown beneath a hugh mass. 2. to overcome completely, especially by force of numbers. 3. to make helpless with emotion.

o·ver·whelm·ing (oh-vĕr-hwel-ming) *adj.* irresistible through force of numbers or amount or influence etc.

o·ver·wind (oh-vĕr-wɪnd) *v.* (**o·ver·wound,** *pr.* -wownd, **o·ver·wind·ing**) to wind (a watch etc.) beyond the proper stopping point.

o·ver·work (oh-vĕr-wurk) *v.* 1. to work or cause to work so hard that one becomes exhausted. 2. to make excessive use of, *an overworked phrase.* **overwork** (oh-ver-wurk) *n.* excessive work causing exhaustion.

o·ver·wrought (oh-vĕr-rawt) *adj.* in a state of nervous agitation through overexcitement.

o·ver·zeal·ous (oh-vĕr-zel-ŭs) *adj.* too zealous.

o·vi·duct (oh-vi-dukt) *n.* one of a pair of canals through which the eggs pass from an ovary to the exterior.

o·vip·a·rous (oh-vip-ă-rŭs) *adj.* producing young by means of eggs expelled from the body before they are hatched. **o·vip′ar·ous·ly** *adv.* **o·vi·par·i·ty** (oh-vi-par-i-tee) *n.*

o·void (oh-void) *adj.* egg-shaped, oval. **ovoid** *n.* an ovoid shape or mass.

o·vu·late (ov-yŭ-layt) *v.* (**o·vu·lat·ed, o·vu·lat·ing**) to produce or discharge an ovum from an ovary. **o·vu·la·tion** (ov-yŭ-lay-shŏn) *n.*

o·vule (oh-vyool) *n.* 1. a small part in a plant's ovary that develops into a seed when fertilized. 2. an unfertilized ovum.

o·vum (oh-vŭm) *n.* (*pl.* **o·va,** *pr.* oh-vă) a female egg cell capable of developing into a new individual when fertilized by male sperm.

ow (ow) *interj.* an exclamation of surprise or pain.

owe (oh) *v.* (**owed, ow·ing**) 1. to be under an obligation to pay or repay (money etc.) in return for what one has received, to be in debt. 2. to have a duty to render, *owe allegiance to the flag.* 3. to feel (gratitude etc.) toward another in return for a service. 4. to have (a thing) as a result of the work or action of another person or cause, *we owe this discovery to Newton; he owes his success to luck.*

ow·ing (oh-ing) *adj.* owed and not yet paid. ☐**owing to,** caused by; because of.

owl (owl) *n.* a bird of prey with a large head, large eyes, and a hooked beak, usually flying at night.

owl·et (ow-lit) *n.* a small or young owl.

owl·ish (ow-lish) *adj.* like an owl. **owl′ish·ly** *adv.*

own[1] (ohn) *adj.* belonging to oneself or itself. ☐**get one's own back,** (*informal*) to have one's revenge. **hold one's own,** to succeed in holding one's position; not lose strength. **of one's own,** belonging to oneself exclusively. **on one's own,** alone; independently.

own[2] *v.* 1. to have as one's property, to possess. 2. to acknowledge that one is the author or possessor or father etc. of. 3. to confess, *she owns to having said it.* **own** *pronoun* the one or ones belonging to oneself. ☐**own up,** (*informal*) to confess, to admit that one is guilty.

own·er (oh-nĕr) *n.* a person who owns something as his property. **own′er·ship** *n.*

own·er·less (oh-nĕr-lis) *adj.* having no owner or no known owner.

ox (oks) *n.* (*pl.* **ox·en**) an adult castrated bull.

ox·al·ic (ok-sal-ik) **acid** a sour poisonous acid found in certain plants, used for cleaning and bleaching.

ox·blood (oks-blud) *n.* a deep dull red color.

ox·bow (oks-boh) *n.* 1. the U-shaped collar of an ox yoke. 2. a horseshoe bend in a river.

Ox·bridge (oks-brij) *n.* the universities of Oxford and Cambridge in England, as distinct from newer (*redbrick*) universities.

ox·eye (oks-ı) *n.* any of several daisy-like flowers with a large center from which petals radiate, *oxeye daisy.*

ox·ford (oks-fŏrd) *n.* a low shoe laced over the instep.

ox·i·dant (ok-si-dănt) *n.* an oxidizing agent.

ox·i·da·tion (ok-sĭ-day-shŏn) *n.* the process of combining or causing to combine with oxygen.

ox·ide (ok-sıd) *n.* a compound of oxygen and one other element.

ox·i·dize (ok-si-dız) *v.* (**ox·i·dized, ox·i·diz·ing**) 1. to combine or cause to combine with oxygen. 2. to coat with an oxide. 3. to make or become rusty. **ox′i·diz·er** *n.* **ox′i·diz·a·ble** *adj.*

ox·tail (oks-tayl) *n.* the tail of an ox, used to make soup or stew.

ox·y·a·cet·y·lene (ok-si-ă-set-ĭ-leen) *adj.* using a mixture of oxygen and acetylene, especially in the cutting and welding of metals.

ox·y·gen (ok-si-jĕn) *n.* a colorless odorless tasteless gas existing in air and combining with hydrogen to form water. ☐**oxygen tent,** a tentlike covering permitting an ill person to breathe air with increased oxygen content.

ox·y·gen·ate (ok-sĭ-jĕ-nayt) *v.* (**ox·y·gen·at·ed, ox·y·gen·at·ing**) to supply or treat or mix with oxygen. **ox·y·gen·a·tion** (ok-sĭ-jĕ-nay-shŏn) *n.*

ox·y·mo·ron (oks-i-moh-rŏn) *n.* (*pl.* **-mo·ra,** *pr.* -moh-ră) a figure of speech combining seemingly contradictory expressions, as *faith unfaithful kept him falsely true.*

ox·y·to·cin (ok-sĭ-toh-sin) *n.* a hormone controlling contractions of the womb, used in synthetic form to induce labor in childbirth.

oys·ter (oi-stĕr) *n.* a kind of shellfish used as food, some types of which produce pearls inside their shells. **oys′ter·ing** *n.* **oys′ter·man** *n.* ☐**oyster cracker,** a small salted cracker usually served with oyster stew or soup.

oz, oz. *abbr.* ounce(s). ☐**oz. ap.,** ounce apothecary's. **oz. av.,** ounce avoirdupois.

o·zone (oh-zohn) *n.* 1. a form of oxygen with a sharp smell. 2. (*humorous*) invigorating air at the seaside.

o·zo·no·sphere (oh-zoh-nŏ-sfeer) *n.* the atmospheric region about 25 miles above Earth, characterized by a high ozone content.

P

P, p (pee) (*pl.* **Ps, P's, p's**) the sixteenth letter of the alphabet.

p *abbr.* 1. participle. 2. pawn (in chess). 3. proton. 4. softly (in music, short for *piano*).

P *symbol* phosphorus.

p. *abbr.* 1. page. 2. participle. 3. past. 4. pawn (in chess). 5. pence. 6. penny. 7. per. 8. pint. 9. pitcher (in baseball). 10. population. 11. president. 12. pressure. 13. purl.

pa (pah) *n.* (*informal*) father.

Pa *symbol* protactinium.

PA *abbr.* Pennsylvania.

Pa. *abbr.* Pennsylvania.

p.a. *abbr.* per annum.

P.A. *abbr.* 1. power of attorney. 2. press agent. 3. public address. 4. purchasing agent.

pab·u·lum (**pab**-yŭ-lŭm) *n.* 1. a soft food. 2. food for thought.

Pac. *abbr.* Pacific.

pace¹ (pays) *n.* 1. a single step made in walking or running. 2. the distance passed in this. 3. a style of walking or running (especially of horses). 4. speed in walking or running. 5. the rate of progress in some activity. **pace** *v.* (**paced, pacing**) 1. to walk with a slow or regular pace. 2. to walk to and fro across (a room etc.). 3. to measure by pacing, *pace it out.* 4. to set the pace for (a runner etc.). □**keep pace,** to advance at an equal rate. **put a person through his paces,** to test his ability. **stand the pace,** to be able to keep up with others.

pa·ce² (pay-see) *prep.* although (a named person) may not agree. ▷ Latin, = with the permission of.

pace·mak·er (pays-may-kĕr) *n.* 1. a runner etc. who sets the pace for another. 2. an electrical device placed under the skin to stimulate contractions of the heart.

pac·er (pay-sĕr) *n.* 1. a pacing horse in harness racing. 2. a pacemaker.

pace·set·ter (pays-set-ĕr) *n.* a person who sets the standard for achievement.

pa·chin·ko (pă-**ching**-koh) *n.* the Japanese form of pinball.

pa·chu·co (pă-**choo**-koh) *n.* a member of a street gang. **pa·chu′ca** *n. fem.*

pach·y·derm (pak-i-durm) *n.* a thick-skinned animal, especially an elephant or rhinoceros.

pach·y·san·dra (pak-i-san-dră) *n.* a low-growing evergreen plant, used as ground cover.

pa·cif·ic (pă-**sif**-ik) *adj.* peaceful, making or loving peace. **pa·cif′i·cal·ly** *adv.*

Pa·cif·ic (pă-**sif**-ik) *adj.* of or characteristic of the Pacific Ocean or the regions bordering on it. **Pacific** *n.* the Pacific Ocean. □**Pacific Ocean,** the ocean lying between the Americas and Asia/Australia.

pac·i·fi·er (**pas**-ĭ-fī-ĕr) *n.* a person or thing that pacifies. 2. a rubber or plastic nipple, *we gave the baby its pacifier.*

pac·i·fist (**pas**-ĭ-fist) *n.* a person who totally opposes war, believing that disputes should be settled by peaceful means. **pac′i·fism** *n.* **pac·i·fis·tic** (pas-ĭ-fis-tik) *adj.*

pac·i·fy (**pas**-ĭ-fī) *v.* (**pac·i·fied, pac·i·fy·ing**) 1. to calm and make quiet. 2. to establish peace in. **pac·i·fi·ca·tion** (pas-ĭ-fi-kay-shŏn) *n.*

pack¹ (pak) *n.* 1. a collection of things wrapped or tied together for carrying. 2. a set of things packed for selling. 3. a complete set of playing cards (usually fifty-two). 4. a group of hounds or wolves etc. 5. a gang of people, an organized group of Cub Scouts or Brownies. 6. a large amount or collection, *a pack of lies.* 7. an absorbent material to be applied to the body or a wound. **pack** *v.* 1. to put (things) into a container for transport or storing or for marketing, to fill with things in this way. 2. to be able to be packed, *this dress packs easily.* 3. to cram or press or crowd together into, to fill (a space) in this way; *the hall was packed,* was very crowded. 4. to cover or protect (a thing) with something pressed tightly on or in or around it. **pack′er** *n.* □**pack a gun,** (*slang*) to carry a pistol or revolver. **pack a punch,** (*slang*) to be capable of delivering a powerful blow. **pack ice,** large crowded floating pieces of ice in the sea. **packing case,** a wooden case or framework for packing goods in. **pack it in,** (*slang*) to cease doing something; to eat in great amounts. **pack off,** to send (a person) away. **pack rat,** a large hoarding rodent; (*slang*) a hoarder of miscellaneous useless items. **pack up,** to put one's things together in readiness for departing or ceasing work. **send packing,** to dismiss abruptly.

pack² *v.* to select (a jury etc.) fraudulently so that its decision will be in one's favor; *the President tried to pack the court,* add justices favorable to his policies.

pack·age (pak-ij) *n.* 1. a parcel. 2. a box etc. in which goods are packed. 3. a package deal. **package** *v.* (**pack·aged, pack·ag·ing**) 1. to put together in a package. 2. to wrap or box, especially in an attractive way to improve sales. □**package deal,** a number of proposals offered or accepted as a whole. **package store,** a liquor store. **package vacation** *or* **tour,** one with set arrangements at an inclusive price.

pack·et (pak-it) *n.* 1. a small package. 2. a boat that carries mail and cargo following a regular schedule on a set route.

pack·horse (pak-hors) *n.* a horse for carrying packs.

pack·ing (pak-ing) *n.* 1. the work of a packer. 2.

a substance used to fill gaps in order to protect or cushion what is packed. 3. oil-absorbing material closing a joint or assisting in lubrication of a piston etc.

pack·ing·house (pak-ing-hows) *n.* (*pl.* **-hous·es,** *pr.* -how-ziz) 1. a slaughterhouse. 2. an establishment for canning or freezing fruits and vegetables for sale.

pack·sad·dle (pak-sad-ĕl) *n.* a saddle adapted for supporting packs and rider.

pack·thread (pak-thred) *n.* a stout thread for sewing or tying up packs.

pact (pakt) *n.* an agreement, a treaty.

pad[1] (pad) *n.* 1. a flat cushion, a piece of soft material used to protect against jarring or to add bulk or to hold or absorb fluid etc., or used for rubbing. 2. a padded protection for the leg and ankle in certain games. 3. a set of sheets of writing paper or drawing paper fastened together at one edge. 4. the soft fleshy underpart of the foot of certain animals. 5. a flat surface from which spacecraft are launched or helicopters take off. 6. (*slang*) a lodging. **pad** *v.* (**pad·ded, pad·ding**) 1. to put a pad or pads on or into. 2. to stuff. 3. to fill (a book or speech etc.) with unnecessary material in order to lengthen it. □**padded cell,** a room with padded walls in a mental hospital etc.

pad[2] *v.* (**pad·ded, pad·ding**) to walk, especially with a soft dull steady sound of steps.

pad·ding (pad-ing) *n.* material used to pad things.

pad·dle[1] (pad-ĕl) *n.* 1. a short oar with a broad blade, used without an oarlock. 2. an instrument shaped like this for beating, stirring, etc. 3. a table tennis racket. 4. one of the boards on a paddle wheel. **paddle** *v.* (**pad·dled, pad·dling**) 1. to propel by using a paddle or paddles. 2. to row gently. □**paddle one's own canoe,** to be independent. **paddle wheel,** a wheel with boards around its rim that drive a boat by pressing against the water as the wheel revolves.

paddle[2] *v.* (**pad·dled, pad·dling**) to dabble (the feet or hands) gently in water.

pad·dock (pad-ŏk) *n.* 1. a small field where horses are kept. 2. an enclosure at a racetrack where horses are saddled before a race.

pad·dy (pad-ee) *n.* (*pl.* **-dies**) a field where rice is grown.

paddy wagon (*slang*) a police van for prisoners.

pad·lock (pad-lok) *n.* a detachable lock with a U-shaped bar that fastens through the loop of a staple or ring. **padlock** *v.* to fasten with a padlock.

pa·dre (pah-dray) *n.* 1. the form of address for a priest in Spain, Latin America, Italy, etc. (= father). 2. (*informal*) a priest or other clergyman. 3. (*informal*) a chaplain in the armed forces.

pae·an (pee-ăn) *n.* a song of praise or triumph.

pa·el·la (pah-ay-lă, -ay-yă) *n.* a Spanish dish of rice, chicken, seafood, etc., cooked and served in a large shallow pan.

pa·gan (pay-găn) *adj.* heathen. **pagan** *n.* a heathen. **pa·gan·ism** *n.*

page[1] (payj) *n.* 1. a leaf in a book or newspaper etc. 2. one side of this. **page** *v.* (**paged, pag·ing**) 1. to number the pages of (a book). 2. to leaf through (a book).

page[2] *n.* a uniformed boy or man employed to go on errands, deliver messages, etc. **page** *v.* (**paged, pag·ing**) to summon (a person) by sending a page or by calling his name until he is found.

pag·eant (paj-ănt) *n.* a public show consisting of a procession of people in costume, or a perfor-

mance of a historical play. **pag'eant·ry** *n.*

page·boy (payj-boi) *n.* 1. a page (*see* **page**[2].) 2. a boy employed as a personal attendant of a person of rank.

pag·i·nate (paj-ĭ-nayt) *v.* (**pag·i·nat·ed, pag·i·nat·ing**) to number the pages (of a book).

pag·i·na·tion (paj-ĭ-nay-shŏn) *n.* the numbering or ordering of the pages of a book.

pa·go·da (pă-goh-dă) *n.* a Hindu temple shaped like a pyramid, or a Buddhist tower with several stories, in India and countries of the Far East.

paid (payd) *see* **pay. paid** *adj.* receiving money in exchange for goods or services, *a paid assistant; paid vacation,* during which normal wages continue to be paid.

pail (payl) *n.* a bucket. **pail·ful** (payl-fuul) *n.* (*pl.* **-fuls**).

pain (payn) *n.* 1. an unpleasant feeling caused by injury or disease of the body. 2. mental suffering. 3. (*old use*) punishment, *pains and penalties; on* or *under pain of death,* with the threat of this punishment. 4. *pains,* careful effort, trouble taken, *take pains with the work.* **pain** *v.* to cause pain to. □**a pain in the neck,** (*informal*) an annoying or tiresome person or thing.

pained (paynd) *adj.* distressed or annoyed, *a pained look.* ▷Do not confuse *pained* with *painful.*

pain·ful (payn-fŭl) *adj.* 1. causing pain, *a painful condition.* 2. (of a part of the body) suffering pain. 3. causing trouble or difficulty, laborious, *a painful performance.* **pain'ful·ly** *adv.* **pain'ful·ness** *n.* ▷Do not confuse *painful* with *pained.*

pain·kil·ler (payn-kil-ĕr) *n.* a medicine that lessens pain.

pain·less (payn-lis) *adj.* not causing pain. **pain'less·ly** *adv.* **pain'less·ness** *n.*

pains·tak·ing (paynz-tay-king) *adj.* careful, using or done with great care and effort.

paint (paynt) *n.* 1. coloring matter for applying in liquid form to a surface. 2. *paints,* a collection of tubes or cakes of paint. **paint** *v.* 1. to coat or decorate with paint. 2. to make a picture or portray by using paint(s). 3. to describe vividly; *he's not as black as he is painted,* not as bad as he is said to be. 4. to apply (liquid or cosmetic) to the skin; *paint one's face,* to use or apply makeup. □**paint the town red,** (*slang*) to go on a riotous spree.

paint·box (paynt-boks) *n.* a box holding dry paints for use by an artist.

paint·brush (paynt-brush) *n.* a brush for applying paint.

paint·er[1] (paynt-tĕr) *n.* a person who paints as an artist or as a housepainter.

painter[2] *n.* a rope attached to the bow of a boat for tying it up.

paint·ing (paynt-ting) *n.* 1. a painted picture. 2. the art or work of a painter, *she is studying painting.*

pair (pair) *n.* (*pl.* **pairs, pair**) 1. a set of two things or people, a couple. 2. an article consisting of two joined and corresponding parts, *a pair of scissors.* 3. an engaged or married couple. 4. two mated animals. 5. the other member of a pair, *can't find a pair to this sock.* 6. two legislators of opposing views who arrange mutually to be absent from a vote. **pair** *v.* 1. to arrange or be arranged in couples. 2. (of animals) to mate. 3. to partner (a person) with a member of the opposite sex. 4. to make a pair in a legislature. □**pair off,** to form into pairs. ▷Careful writers avoid *pair* as a plural form. They write *six pairs of gloves* not *six pair of gloves.*

pais·ley, Pais·ley (payz-lee) *adj.* having a pattern of tapering petal-shaped figures with much detail.

Pai·ute (pɪ-oot) *n.* (*pl.* **-utes, -ute**) 1. a member of an Indian tribe of the western U.S. 2. the language of this tribe.

pa·ja·mas (pă-jah-măz) *n. pl.* a loose jacket and pants for sleeping or lounging in; *pajama top,* the jacket of this. □**pajama party,** an overnight party for girls.

Pak·i·stan (pak-i-stan) a country in southern Asia. **Pak·i·sta·ni** (pak-i-stan-ee) *adj. & n.* (*pl.* **-nis**).

pal (pal) *n.* (*informal*) a friend. **pal** *v.* (**palled, pal·ling,** *pr.* pald, pal-ing) **pal around with,** (*informal*) to be friends with.

pal·ace (pal-is) *n.* 1. the official residence of a sovereign. 2. a splendid mansion. □**palace guard,** a police force or soldiers charged with the safety of the palace and its occupants; a group of aides who act to prevent the press etc. from gaining access to a ruler or president etc. **palace revolution,** overthrow of a ruler without civil war.

pal·a·din (pal-ă-din) *n.* 1. one of the Twelve Peers of Charlemagne's court, of whom the Count of Palatine was the chief. 2. a knight errant, a champion.

pal·an·quin (pal-ăn-keen) *n.* a covered litter for one in India and the East carried usually by four or six men.

pal·at·a·ble (pal-ă-tă-běl) *adj.* pleasant to the taste or to the mind.

pal·ate (pal-it) *n.* 1. the roof of the mouth. 2. the sense of taste, *pleasing to the palate.* ▷Do not confuse *palate* with *palette* or *pallet.*

pa·la·tial (pă-lay-shăl) *adj.* like a palace, spacious and splendid.

pa·lat·i·nate (pă-lat-ĭ-nayt) *n.* the territory under a palatine.

pal·a·tine (pal-ă-tɪn) *n.* (*old use*) a count having sovereign jurisdiction within his territory.

pa·lav·er (pă-lav-ěr) *n.* 1. long aimless talk, idle chatter. 2. (*old use*) a parley, especially with primitive peoples.

pale[1] (payl) *adj.* (**pal·er, pal·est**) 1. (of a person's face) having little color, lighter than normal. 2. (of color or light) faint, not bright or vivid. **pale** *v.* (**paled, pal·ing**) to turn pale. **pale'ly** *adv.* **pale'ness** *n.*

pale[2] *n.* 1. a stake forming part of a fence. 2. a boundary. **pale** *v.* (**paled, pal·ing**) to enclose with pales or stakes, to fence in. □**beyond the pale,** outside the bounds of acceptable behavior. **the Pale,** the part of Russia to which Jews were confined.

pale·face (payl-fays) *n.* a white person. ▷Said to be the American Indian term for a European.

Pa·le·o·cene (pay-li-ŏ-seen) *adj.* of the earliest geologic epoch of the Tertiary period. **Paleocene** *n.* the Paleocene epoch.

pa·le·og·ra·pher (pay-li-og-ră-fěr) *n.* an expert in paleography.

pa·le·og·ra·phy (pay-li-og-ră-fee) *n.* the study of ancient writing and inscriptions.

pa·le·o·lith·ic (pay-li-ŏ-lith-ik) *adj.* of the early part of the Stone Age.

pa·le·o·mag·ne·tism (pay-li-oh-mag-ně-tiz-ěm) *n.* 1. the magnetism remaining in rocks from past times. 2. the study of this magnetism. **pa·le·o·mag·net·ic** (pay-li-oh-mag-net-ik) *adj.* **pa·le·o·mag·net'i·cal·ly** *adv.*

paleon. *abbr.* paleontology.

pa·le·on·tol·o·gist (pay-li-on-tol-ŏ-jist) *n.* an expert in paleontology.

pa·le·on·tol·o·gy (pay-li-on-tol-ŏ-jee) *n.* the scientific study of life in the geological past.

Pa·le·o·zo·ic (pay-li-ŏ-zoh-ik) *adj.* of the geologic era following the Precambrian and containing the oldest forms of highly organized life (reptiles, seed-bearing plants, insects, etc.). **Paleozoic** *n.* the Paleozoic era.

Pal·es·tine (pal-ĕ-stɪn) the former name of a country at the eastern end of the Mediterranean Sea, now divided between Israel and Jordan. **Pal·es·tin·i·an** (pal-ĕ-stin-ee-ăn) *adj. & n.*

pal·ette (pal-it) *n.* a thin board, with a hole for the thumb by which it is held, on which an artist mixes colors when painting. □**palette knife,** an artist's knife for mixing or spreading paint. ▷Do not confuse *palette* with *palate* or *pallet.*

pal·frey (pawl-free) *n.* (*pl.* **-freys**) (*old use*) a saddle horse for ordinary riding, especially for ladies.

pal·imp·sest (pal-imp-sest) *n.* writing material or a manuscript from which the original writing has been partially or completely effaced to make room for a second writing.

pal·in·drome (pal-in-drohm) *n.* a word or phrase that reads the same backward as forward, as *rotator; nurses run; Madam I'm Adam.*

pal·ing (pay-ling) *n.* 1. fencing made of wooden posts or railings. 2. one of its uprights.

pal·i·sade (pal-i-sayd) *n.* 1. a fence of pointed stakes. 2. **palisades,** a line of high cliffs.

pall (pawl) *n.* 1. a cloth spread over a coffin. 2. something forming a dark heavy covering, *a pall of smoke.* **pall** *v.* to become uninteresting or boring, *the subject began to pall on us.*

pal·la·di·um (pă-lay-di-ŭm) *n.* a hard white metallic element.

pall·bear·er (pawl-bair-ěr) *n.* one of the people carrying or walking beside the coffin at a funeral.

pal·let[1] (pal-it) *n.* 1. a mattress stuffed with straw. 2. a hard narrow bed, a makeshift bed. ▷Do not confuse *pallet* with *palate* or *palette.*

pallet[2] *n.* a large tray or platform for carrying goods that are being lifted or in storage, especially one that can be raised by a forklift. ▷Do not confuse *pallet* with *palate* or *palette.*

pal·li·ate (pal-i-ayt) *v.* (**pal·li·at·ed, pal·li·at·ing**) to make less intense or less severe. **pal·li·a·tion** (pal-i-ay-shŏn) *n.*

pal·li·a·tive (pal-i-ă-tiv) *adj.* reducing the bad effects of something. **palliative** *n.* something that does this.

pal·lid (pal-id) *adj.* pale, especially from illness.

pal·lor (pal-ŏr) *n.* paleness.

palm[1] (pahm) *n.* 1. the inner surface of the hand between the wrist and the fingers. 2. the part of a glove that covers this. **palm** *v.* 1. to conceal in one's hand. 2. to get (a thing) accepted fraudulently; *palmed it off on them,* induced them to accept something false or inferior, or something they did not want.

palm[2] *n.* 1. a palm tree. 2. an imaginary award for success. □**palm oil,** the oil obtained from various palm trees. **Palm Sunday,** the Sunday before Easter, commemorating Christ's triumphal entry into Jerusalem when the people strewed leaves in his path. **palm tree,** a kind of tree growing in warm or tropical climates, with no branches and with large leaves growing in a mass at the top.

pal·mate (pal-mayt) *adj.* shaped like a hand with the fingers spread out.

palm·er (pah-měr) *n.* (*old use*) a pilgrim, especially one returning from the Holy Land with a palm branch or leaf as a symbol of his pilgrimage.

pal·met·to (pal-met-oh) *n.* (*pl.* -tos) a kind of small palm tree with fan-shaped leaves.

palm·ist (pahm-ist) *n.* a person skilled in palmistry.

palm·is·try (pah-mi-stree) *n.* the pretended art of telling a person's future or interpreting his character by examining the lines or creases etc. in the palm of his hand.

palm·y (pah-mee) *adj.* (**palm·i·er, palm·i·est**) 1. full of palms. 2. flourishing, *in their former palmy days.*

pal·o·mi·no (pal-ŏ-mee-noh) *n.* (*pl.* -nos) a golden or cream-colored horse with light-colored mane and tail.

pal·pa·ble (pal-pă-běl) *adj.* 1. able to be touched or felt. 2. easily perceived, obvious. **pal′pa·bly** *adv.* **pal·pa·bil·i·ty** (pal-pă-bil-i-tee) *n.*

pal·pate (pal-payt) *v.* (**pal·pat·ed, pal·pat·ing**) to examine by feeling with the hands, especially as part of a medical examination. **pal·pa·tion** (pal-pay-shŏn) *n.*

pal·pi·tate (pal-pi-tayt) *v.* (**pal·pi·tat·ed, pal·pi·tat·ing**) 1. to pulsate, to throb rapidly. 2. (of a person) to quiver with fear or excitement. **pal·pi·ta·tion** (pal-pi-tay-shŏn) *n.*

pal·sy (pawl-zee) *n.* (*pl.* -sies) paralysis, especially with involuntary tremors. **pal′sied** *adj.*

pal·sy-wal·sy (pal-zee-wal-zee) *adj.* (*informal*) very friendly.

pal·ter (pawl-těr) *v.* (**pal·tered, pal·ter·ing**) 1. to talk or act insincerely. 2. to haggle.

pal·try (pawl-tree) *adj.* (**pal·tri·er, pal·tri·est**) worthless, trivial, contemptible.

pam. *abbr.* pamphlet.

pam·pas (pam-păz) *n. pl.* vast grassy plains in South America.

pam·per (pam-pěr) *v.* to treat very indulgently.

pam·phlet (pam-flit) *n.* a leaflet or paper-covered booklet containing information or a treatise.

pan[1] (pan) *n.* 1. a metal or earthenware vessel with a flat base and often without a lid, used for cooking and other domestic purposes. 2. its contents. 3. any similar vessel. 4. the bowl of a pair of scales. 5. a natural or artificial depression in the land. 6. (*informal*) hardpan. **pan** *v.* (**panned, pan·ning**) 1. to wash (gravel) in a pan in search of gold. 2. (*informal*) to criticize severely. **pan·ful** (pan-fuul) *n.* (*pl.* -fuls) □**pan out,** (of circumstances or events) to turn out; to be successful in outcome.

pan[2] *v.* (**panned, pan·ning**) 1. to turn (a camera) horizontally to give a panoramic effect or follow a moving object. 2. (of a camera) to turn in this way.

Pan. *abbr.* Panama.

pan- *prefix* all-, of the whole of a continent or racial group etc., as in *pan-African, pan-American.*

pan·a·ce·a (pan-ă-see-ă) *n.* a remedy for all kinds of diseases or troubles.

pa·nache (pă-nash) *n.* a confident stylish manner.

pan·a·ma (pan-ă-mah) *n.* 1. (also **Panama hat**) a hat of fine pliant strawlike material. 2. a woven fabric used for jackets and skirts etc.

Pan·a·ma (pan-ă-mah) a country in Central America. **Pan·a·ma·ni·an** (pan-ă-may-ni-ăn) *adj. & n.* □**Panama Canal,** the canal extending from the Atlantic Ocean to the Pacific Ocean through

Panama. **Panama City,** the capital of Panama.

pan·a·tel·la (pan-ă-tel-ă) *n.* a thin cigar.

pan·cake (pan-kayk) *n.* 1. a thin round cake of batter fried on both sides, sometimes rolled up with filling. 2. makeup in the form of a flat cake. □**pancake landing,** a landing in which an aircraft descends vertically in a level position.

pan·chro·mat·ic (pan-kroh-mat-ik) *adj.* sensitive to all colors of the visible spectrum, *panchromatic film.*

pan·cre·as (pan-kree-ăs) *n.* a gland near the stomach discharging a digestive secretion into the duodenum and insulin into the blood. **pan·cre·at·ic** (pan-kree-at-ik) *adj.*

pan·da (pan-dă) *n.* 1. (also **giant panda**) a large rare bearlike black-and-white animal living in the mountains of southwest China. 2. (also **lesser panda**) a raccoon-like animal of India.

pan·dem·ic (pan-dem-ik) *adj.* (of a disease) occurring over a whole country or the whole world.

pan·de·mo·ni·um (pan-dě-moh-ni-ŭm) *n.* uproar.

pan·der (pan-děr) *v.* to gratify a person's weakness or vulgar tastes, *pandering to the public interest in scandal.* **pander** *n.* (also **panderer**) 1. a pimp. 2. a go-between in an illicit love affair.

P and L *abbr.* profit and loss.

Pan·do·ra's (pan-dohr-ăz) **box** (in Greek mythology) a box which, when opened, let loose all kinds of misfortunes upon mankind.

pan·dow·dy (pan-dow-dee) *n.* (*pl.* -dies) a deep-dish apple (and usually molasses) pie with a thick crust cover.

pane (payn) *n.* a single sheet of glass in a window or door.

pan·e·gy·ric (pan-ě-jir-ik) *n.* a speech or piece of writing praising a person or thing.

pan·el (pan-ěl) *n.* 1. a distinct usually rectangular section of a surface. 2. a strip of board or other material forming a separate section of a wall or door or cabinet etc., a section of the metal bodywork of a vehicle. 3. a strip of material set lengthwise in or on a garment. 4. a group of people assembled to discuss or decide something, *a panel discussion.* 5. a list of jurors, a jury. 6. the part of a vehicle supporting the controls, dials, etc., *instrument panel; control panel.* **panel** *v.* (**pan·eled, pan·el·ing**) to cover or decorate with panels. □**panel show,** a quiz or similar form of radio or television entertainment in which a panel of people take part. **panel truck,** a small fully enclosed truck.

pan·el·ing (pan-ě-ling) *n.* 1. a series of panels in a wall. 2. wood used for making panels.

pan·el·ist (pan-ě-list) *n.* a member of a panel.

pang (pang) *n.* a sudden sharp feeling of pain or a painful emotion, *pangs of jealousy.*

pan·han·dle (pan-han-děl) *v.* **pan·han·dled, pan·han·dling** (*informal*) to beg in the street. **panhandle** *n.* a long narrow strip of a larger territory, *the Texas Panhandle.* **pan′han·dler** *n.*

pan·ic (pan-ik) *n.* 1. sudden terror, wild infectious fear. 2. a sudden rush to sell or buy in the stock market etc. **panic** *v.* (**pan·icked, pan·ick·ing**) to affect or be affected with panic. **pan′ick·y** *adj.* □**panic button,** a button to be pressed as a signal etc. in an emergency.

pan·i·cle (pan-i-kěl) *n.* a loose-branching cluster of flowers.

pan·ic-strick·en (pan-ik-strik-ěn) *adj.* affected with panic.

pan·jan·drum (pan-jan-drŭm) *n.* 1. a mock title of an exalted personage. 2. a pompous official or pretender.

pan·nier (pan-yěr) *n.* a large basket, especially one of a pair carried on either side of a pack animal.

pan·o·ply (pan-ŏ-plee) *n.* (*pl.* **-plies**) a splendid array, *in full panoply.*

pan·o·ram·a (pan-ŏ-ram-ă) *n.* 1. a view of a wide area, a picture or photograph of this. 2. a view of a constantly changing scene or series of events.

pan·o·ram·ic (pan-ŏ-ram-ik) *adj.*

pan·sy (pan-zee) *n.* (*pl.* **-sies**) 1. a garden plant of the violet family, with broad flat rounded richly colored petals. 2. its flower.

pant (pant) *v.* 1. to breathe with short quick breaths. 2. to utter breathlessly. 3. to be extremely eager. **pant** *n.* a panting breath.

pan·ta·lets (pan-tă-lets) *n. pl. (old use)* women's long underwear with frills at the ankles.

pan·ta·loons (pan-tă-loonz) *n. pl. (old use)* men's trousers, especially close-fitting trousers worn in the 1800s.

pan·the·ism (pan-thee-iz-ĕm) *n.* the doctrine that God is everything and everything is God. **pan'the·ist** *n.* **pan·the·is·tic** (pan-thee-is-tik) *adj.*

pan·the·on (pan-thee-on) *n.* 1. a temple dedicated to all the gods, especially the circular one in Rome. 2. the deities of a people collectively. 3. a building in which the illustrious dead are buried or have memorials.

pan·ther (pan-thěr) *n.* 1. a large black leopard. 2. a cougar.

pan·ties (pan-teez) *n. pl. (informal)* underpants for women or children.

pan·to·mime (pan-tŏ-mım) *n.* 1. expressive movements of the face and body used to convey a story or meaning. 2. a show or performance done in pantomime. **pantomime** *v.* (**pan·to·mimed, pan·to·mim·ing**) to express a story or meaning by movements. **pan·to·mim·ic** (pan-tŏ-mim-ik) *adj.*

pan·try (pan-tree) *n.* (*pl.* **-tries**) a room in which food, china, glasses, etc. are kept.

pants (pants) *n. pl.* 1. trousers. 2. *(informal)* underpants.

pant·suit (pant-soot) *n.* (also **pants suit**) a woman's tailored suit of jacket and trousers.

pan·ty (pan-tee) **hose** women's hosiery, combining underpants and stockings.

pan·ty·waist (pan-tee-wayst) *n.* an effeminate person. **pantywaist** *adj.*

pan·zer (pan-zěr) *adj.* (of German troops) armored, *panzer divisions.*

pap (pap) *n.* 1. soft or semiliquid food suitable for infants or invalids. 2. mash, pulp. 3. undemanding reading matter.

pa·pa (pah-pă) *n. (informal)* father.

pa·pa·cy (pay-pă-see) *n.* the position or authority of the pope, the system of Church government by popes.

pa·pa·in (pă-pay-in) *n.* an enzyme from papaya trees, used to tenderize meat.

pa·pal (pay-păl) *adj.* of the pope or the papacy.

pa·paw (paw-paw) *n.* 1. the small fleshy many-seeded fruit of a central and southern North American tree. 2. this tree.

pa·pa·ya (pă-pah-yă) *n.* 1. the oblong orange edible fruit of a palmlike tropical American tree. 2. this tree, whose stem, leaves, and fruit contain papain.

pa·per (pay-pěr) *n.* 1. a substance manufactured in thin sheets from wood fiber, rags, etc., used for writing or printing or drawing on or for wrapping things. 2. a newspaper. 3. wallpaper. 4. a document; *a ship's papers*, documents establishing its identity etc. 5. an essay or dissertation, especially one read to a learned society. **paper** *v.* to cover (walls etc.) with wallpaper. □on **paper,** in writing; in theory, when judged from written or printed evidence, *the scheme looks good on paper.* **paper clip,** a piece of bent wire or plastic for holding a few sheets of paper together. **paper doll,** a paper drawing of a human figure that can be dressed in paper clothes. **paper money,** banknotes as distinct from coins. **paper over the cracks,** to seek to conceal flaws or disagreement. **paper the house,** to give away free tickets for a public performance in order to ensure a large audience. **paper tiger,** a person or thing that has a threatening appearance but can do no harm.

pa·per·back (pay-pěr-bak) *adj.* bound in a flexible paper binding, not in a stiff cover. **paperback** *n.* a book bound in this way.

pa·per·board (pay-pěr-bohrd) *n.* cardboard.

pa·per·boy (pay-pěr-boi) *n.* a boy who delivers newspapers. **pa·per·girl** (pay-pěr-gurl) *n.*

pa·per·hang·er (pay-pěr-hang-ěr) *n.* a person whose business is to cover walls with wallpaper. **pa'per·hang·ing** *n.*

pa·per·weight (pay-pěr-wayt) *n.* a small heavy object placed on top of loose papers to keep them in place.

pa·per·work (pay-pěr-wurk) *n.* routine clerical work and record keeping.

pa·per·y (pay-pě-ree) *adj.* like paper in texture and thickness.

pa·pier-mâ·ché (pay-pěr-mă-shay) *n.* molded paper pulp, used for making boxes or trays or ornaments etc.

pa·pil·la (pă-pil-ă) *n.* (*pl.* **-pil·lae,** *pr.* **-pil**-ee) a small projection in a part or organ of the body. **pap·il·lar·y** (pap-ĭ-ler-ee) *adj.*

pa·pil·lote (pah-pee-yoht) *n.* a paper decoration or cover for the end of the bone of a lamb chop etc. □en (ahn) **papillote,** (of fish etc.) baked within a wrapping of greased paper.

pa·pist (pay-pist) *n. (contemptuous)* a Roman Catholic.

pa·poose (pa-poos) *n.* a North American Indian baby.

pa·pri·ka (pa-pree-kă) *n.* a mild spice made of ground sweet red peppers.

Pap (pap) **test** (also **Pap smear**) a test for the early detection of uterine cancer. ▷The test was devised by George N. Papanicolaou (1883–1962), an American medical scientist.

Pap·u·a (pap-yoo-ă) **New Guinea** a country consisting of a group of islands between Asia and Australia.

pap·ule (pap-yool) *n.* a pimple. **pap·u·lar** (pap-yŭ-lăr) *adj.*

pa·py·rus (pă-pɪ-rŭs) *n.* (*pl.* **-rus·es, -ri,** *pr.* -rɪ) 1. a reedlike water plant with thick fibrous stems from which a kind of paper was made by the ancient Egyptians. 2. this paper. 3. a manuscript written on this.

par (pahr) *n.* 1. an average or normal amount or condition or degree etc., *was feeling below par.* 2. the face value of stocks and bonds etc.; *at par,* at face value. 3. (in golf) the number of strokes

set as a standard for a hole or course. □on a
par with, on an equal footing with.

par. abbr. 1. paragraph. 2. parallel. 3. parish.

par·a·ble (par-ă-bĕl) n. a story told to illustrate
a moral or spiritual truth.

pa·rab·o·la (pă-rab-ŏ-lă) n. a curve like the path
of an object thrown into the air and falling back
to earth. par·a·bol·ic (par-ă-bol-ik) adj.

par·a·chute (par-ă-shoot) n. an umbrella-shaped
device used to slow the descent of a person or
heavy object falling from a great height, especially
from a moving aircraft; parachute troops,
paratroops. parachute v. (par·a·chut·ed, par·
a·chut·ing) to descend by parachute, to drop
(supplies etc.) by parachute. par'a·chut·ist n.

pa·rade (pă-rayd) n. 1. a procession of people or
things, especially in a display or exhibition. 2. a
formal assembly of troops for inspection or roll
call etc. 3. an ostentatious display, makes a parade
of his virtues. parade v. (pa·rad·ed, pa·rad·
ing) 1. to march or walk with display. 2. to make
a display of, he paraded his knowledge before us.
□on parade, taking part in a parade.

par·a·digm (par-ă-dɪm) n. something serving as
an example or model of how things should be
done.

par·a·dise (par-ă-dɪs) n. 1. heaven. 2. Eden. par·
a·di·si·a·cal (par-ă-di-sɪ-ă-kăl), par·a·dis·i·
ac (par-ă-dis-i-ak) adj.

par·a·dox (par-ă-doks) n. a statement etc. that
seems to contradict itself or to conflict with common sense but which contains a truth (as "more
haste, less speed"). par·a·dox·i·cal (par-ă-dok-
si-kăl) adj. par·a·dox'i·cal·ly adv.

par·af·fin (par-ă-fin) n. a white waxy substance
obtained from petroleum and used for making
candles, sealing, and coating.

par·a·gon (par-ă-gon) n. a model of excellence,
an apparently perfect person or thing.

par·a·graph (par-ă-graf) n. one or more sentences
on a single theme, forming a distinct section of
a piece of writing and beginning on a new (usually
indented) line. paragraph v. to arrange in para-
graphs.

Par·a·guay (par-ă-gway) n. a country in South
America. Par·a·guay·an (par-ă-gway-ăn) adj.
& n.

par·a·keet (par-ă-keet) n. a kind of small parrot,
often with a long tail.

par·al·de·hyde (pă-ral-dĕ-hɪd) n. a substance
used as a sedative.

par·al·lax (par-ă-laks) n. an apparent difference
in the position or direction of an object when it
is viewed from two different points.

par·al·lel (par-ă-lel) adj. 1. (of lines or planes) continuously at the same distance from each other.
2. having this relationship, the road runs parallel
to (or with) the railroad. 3. similar, having features
that correspond, parallel situations. parallel n.
1. an imaginary line on Earth's surface or a corresponding line on a map parallel to and passing
through all points equidistant from the equator.
2. a person or situation etc. that is parallel to
another. 3. a comparison, drew a parallel between
the two situations. parallel v. (par·al·leled, par·
al·lel·ing) 1. to be parallel to. 2. to find or mention something parallel or corresponding, to compare. par'al·lel·ism n. □in parallel, (of electrical conductors etc.) arranged so as to join at
common points at each end. parallel bars, a pair

of parallel rails supported on posts for gymnastic
exercises.

par·al·lel·o·gram (par-ă-lel-ŏ-gram) n. a plane
four-sided figure with its opposite sides parallel
to each other.

pa·ral·y·sis (pă-ral-ĭ-sis) n. 1. loss of the power
of movement, caused by disease or injury to
nerves. 2. inability to move normally.
par·a·lyt·ic (par-ă-lit-ik) adj. affected with paralysis. paralytic n. a person affected with paralysis.

par·a·lyze (par-ă-lɪz) v. (par·a·lyzed, par·
a·lyz·ing) 1. to affect with paralysis, to make
unable to act or move normally. 2. to bring to
a standstill.

Par·a·mar·i·bo (par-ă-mar-ĭ-boh) the capital of
Surinam.

par·a·me·ci·um (par-ă-mee-si-ŭm) n. (pl. -ci·a,
pr. -si-ă) a slipper-shaped protozoan that uses cilia
to move.

par·a·med·i·cal (par-ă-med-i-kăl) adj. (of services etc.) supplementing and supporting medical
work. par·a·med'ic n.

pa·ram·e·ter (pă-ram-ĕ-tĕr) n. 1. a variable quantity or quality that restricts or gives a particular
form to the thing it characterizes, the parameters
studied were height and weight. 2. (informal) a
limit, we have the freedom to act within the parameters set by the Constitution. (▷Careful writers
avoid this use.) par·a·met·ric (par-ă-met-rik)
adj.

par·a·mil·i·tar·y (par-ă-mil-i-ter-ee) adj. organized like a military force but not a part of the
armed services.

par·a·mount (par-ă-mownt) adj. chief in importance, supreme.

par·a·mour (par-ă-moor) n. (old use) a married
person's illicit lover.

pa·rang (pah-rahng) n. a heavy Malayan sheath
knife.

par·a·noi·a (par-ă-noi-ă) n. 1. a mental disorder
in which a person has delusions of grandeur or
persecution etc. 2. an abnormal tendency to suspect and mistrust others.

par·a·noi·ac (par-ă-noi-ak) adj. & n. = paranoid.

par·a·noid (par-ă-noid) adj. of or like or suffering
from paranoia. paranoid n. a person suffering
from paranoia.

par·a·pet (par-ă-pit) n. 1. a low protective wall
along the edge of a balcony or roof or bridge
etc. 2. a defense of earth or stone to conceal and
protect troops.

par·a·pher·nal·ia (par-ă-fĕr-nayl-yă) n. numerous small possessions or pieces of equipment etc.

par·a·phrase (par-ă-frayz) v. (par·a·phrased,
par·a·phrasing) to express the meaning of (a
passage) in other words. paraphrase n. reword-
ing in this way, a reworded passage.

par·a·ple·gi·a (par-ă-plee-ji-ă) n. paralysis of the
legs and part or all of the trunk. par·a·ple'gic
adj. & n.

par·a·pro·fes·sion·al (par-ă-prŏ-fesh-ŏ-năl) n.
a person who works as assistant to a professional.

par·a·psy·chol·o·gy (par-ă-sɪ-kol-ŏ-jee) n. the
scientific study of mental perceptions (as those
occurring in clairvoyance and telepathy) that
seem to be outside normal mental abilities. par·
a·psy·chol'o·gist n.

par·a·site (par-ă-sɪt) n. 1. an animal or plant that
lives on or in another from which it draws its
nourishment. 2. a person who lives off another

or others and gives no useful return. **par·a·sit·ism** (par-ă-sı-tiz-ĕm) *n.* **par·a·sit·ic** (par-ă-sit-ik) *adj.*

par·a·si·tize (par-ă-si-tız) *v.* (**par·a·si·tized, par·a·si·tiz·ing**) to infest as a parasite.

par·a·si·tol·o·gy (par-ă-si-tol-ŏ-jee) *n.* the scientific study of parasites. **par·a·si·tol'o·gist** *n.*

par·a·sol (par-ă-sawl) *n.* a light umbrella used to give shade from the sun.

par·a·sym·pa·thet·ic (par-ă-sim-pă-thet-ik) *adj.* of the part of the nervous system that connects with nerve cells in or near viscera.

par·a·thi·on (par-ă-thı-ŏn) *n.* an extremely poisonous insecticide.

par·a·thy·roid (par-ă-thı-roid) *n.* (also **parathyroid gland**) the gland adjacent to the thyroid that secretes a hormone regulating calcium levels in the body.

par·a·troops (par-ă-troops) *n. pl.* troops trained to be dropped into battle by parachute. **par'a·troop·er** *n.* ▷ It is incorrect to use "a paratroop" to mean "a paratrooper."

par·a·ty·phoid (par-ă-tı-foid) *n.* (also **paratyphoid fever**) a kind of fever resembling typhoid but milder.

par·boil (**pahr**-boil) *v.* to boil (food) until it is partly cooked.

par·cel (**pahr**-sĕl) *n.* 1. a thing or things wrapped up for carrying or for sending by mail. 2. a piece of land. **parcel** *v.* (**par·celed, par·cel·ing**) to divide into portions, *parceled it out.* □**parcel post**, a postal service dealing with packages; the parcels handled by this service.

parch (pahrch) *v.* to make hot and dry or thirsty.

parch·ment (**pahrch**-mĕnt) *n.* □1. a heavy paperlike material made from animal skins. 2. a kind of paper resembling this.

pard (pahrd) *n.* 1. *(old use)* a leopard. 2. *(slang)* a partner or comrade.

par·don (**pahr**-dŏn) *n.* 1. forgiveness. 2. cancellation of a punishment incurred through a crime or conviction. 3. a kind of indulgence, as for a slight discourtesy or for failing to hear or understand, *I beg your pardon.* **pardon** *v.* (**par·doned, par·don·ing**) to forgive, to overlook (a slight discourtesy etc.) kindly.

par·don·a·ble (**pahr**-dŏ-nă-bĕl) *adj.* able to be pardoned. **par'don·a·bly** *adv.*

par·don·er (**pahr**-dŏ-nĕr) *n.* *(old use)* a person licensed to sell religious pardons or indulgences.

pare (pair) *v.* (**pared, par·ing**) 1. to trim by cutting away the edges of, to peel. 2. to reduce little by little, *pared down their expenses.*

par·e·gor·ic (par-ĕ-gor-ik) *n.* a camphorated tincture of opium, used to stop diarrhea.

paren. *abbr.* parenthesis.

par·ent (**pair**-ĕnt) *n.* 1. one who has procreated offspring, a father or mother. 2. an ancestor. 3. a person who has adopted a child. 4. an animal or plant from which others are derived. 5. a source from which other things are derived, *the parent company.* **par'ent·hood** *n.*

par·ent·age (**pair**-ĕn-tij) *n.* descent from parents, ancestry.

pa·ren·tal (pă-ren-tăl) *adj.* of parents.

pa·ren·the·sis (pă-ren-thĕ-sis) *n.* (*pl.* **-ses,** *pr.* -seez) 1. an additional word or phrase or sentence inserted in a passage that is grammatically complete without it, and usually marked off by dashes or commas or parentheses. 2. either of the pair

of curved marks (like these) used to mark off a parenthesis or to group some symbols in a mathematical expression.

par·en·thet·ic (par-ĕn-thet-ik) *adj.* 1. of or as a parenthesis. 2. interposed as an aside or digression. **par·en·thet'i·cal** *adj.* **par·en·thet'i·cal·ly** *adv.*

pa·re·sis (pă-ree-sis) *n.* partial paralysis, affecting muscular movement but not sensation. **pa·ret·ic** (pă-ret-ik) *adj. & n.*

par ex·cel·lence (pahr ek-sĕ-lahns) more than all others, in the highest degree. ▷French.

par·fait (pahr-fay) *n.* 1. a rich iced custard made of eggs and cream or ice cream. 2. layers of ice cream and fruit etc. served in a tall glass.

pa·ri·ah (pă-rı-ă) *n.* an outcast.

pa·ri·e·tal (pă-rı-ĕ-tăl) *adj.* 1. of the wall of the body or of any of its cavities; *the parietal bones,* those forming part of the sides and top of the skull. 2. of or relating to residence within a college; *parietal rules,* those governing the conduct of resident students.

par·i·mu·tu·el (par-i-**myoo**-choo-ĕl) *n.* a form of betting in which the losers' stakes (less a percentage for the track and taxes) are divided among the winners.

par·ing (pair-ing) *n.* a piece pared off, *apple parings.*

pa·ri pas·su (par-i pas-oo) with equal pace, simultaneously and equally. ▷Latin.

Par·is (par-is) the capital of France. **Pa·ris·ian** (pă-ree-zhăn) *adj. & n.*

par·ish (par-ish) *n.* 1. an area within a diocese, having its own church and clergyman. 2. (in Louisiana) a governmental unit equivalent to a county. 3. the people of a parish. □**parish register,** a book recording the baptisms, marriages, and burials that have taken place at a parish church.

pa·rish·ion·er (pă-rish-ŏ-nĕr) *n.* an inhabitant or member of a parish.

par·i·ty (par-i-tee) *n.* (*pl.* **-ties**) 1. equality, equal status or pay etc. 2. being valued at par.

park (pahrk) *n.* 1. a public garden or recreation ground. 2. a field or stadium for sporting events. **park** *v.* 1. to place and leave (a vehicle) temporarily. 2. *(informal)* to deposit temporarily, *park oneself,* to sit down. □**parking lot,** an outdoor area for parking vehicles. **parking meter,** a coin-operated meter in which fees are inserted for parking a vehicle beside it on the street. **parking ticket,** a notice of a fine imposed for parking a vehicle illegally.

par·ka (**pahr**-kă) *n.* 1. a fur jacket with hood attached, worn by Eskimos. 2. a jacket or coat shaped like this.

Park·in·son's (**pahr**-kin-sŏnz) **disease** a disease of the nervous system causing tremor and weakness of the muscles.

Parkinson's law any of several facts humorously formulated by C. Northcote Parkinson, especially "work expands so as to fill the time available for its completion."

park·way (**pahrk**-way) *n.* a wide high-speed landscaped highway.

parl. *abbr.* 1. parliament. 2. parliamentary.

par·lance (**pahr**-lăns) *n.* phraseology.

par·lay (**pahr**-lay) *v.* 1. to use (money won on a bet) as a further stake. 2. to increase in value by parlaying. **parlay** *n.* (*pl.* **-lays**) a bet so made, the act of parlaying. ▷Do not confuse *parlay* with *parley.*

par·ley (pahr-lee) *n.* (*pl.* **-leys**) a discussion or conference, especially between enemies or opponents to settle points in dispute. **parley** *v.* (**par·leyed, par·ley·ing**) to hold a parley. ▷Do not confuse *parley* with *parlay.*

par·lia·ment (pahr-lă-mĕnt) *n.* an assembly that makes the laws of certain countries; *Parliament,* that of the United Kingdom, consisting of the House of Commons and the House of Lords.

par·lia·men·tar·i·an (pahr-lă-men-tair-i-ăn) *n.* an expert in the rules of parliamentary procedure, especially one whose job is to make decisions about procedure in a meeting.

par·lia·men·ta·ry (pahr-lă-men-tă-ree) *adj.* of or involving a parliament, *parliamentary government.* ☐**parliamentary procedure,** formal rules for debate in an assembly, club, etc.

par·lor (pahr-lŏr) *n.* 1. *(old use)* the living room of a family in a private house. 2. a room or establishment for a particular kind of activity or business, *beauty parlor; milking parlor,* a place for milking cows. ☐**parlor car,** a luxuriously fitted railroad passenger car. **parlor game,** an indoor game.

par·lous (pahr-lŭs) *adj.* *(old use)* perilous. **parlous** *adv.* *(old use)* extremely.

Par·me·san (pahr-mĕ-zăn) *n.* a kind of hard cheese made at Parma, Italy, and elsewhere, usually grated before use.

par·mi·gia·na (pahr-mi-jah-nă) *adj.* cooked with sliced Parmesan cheese, *eggplant parmigiana.*

pa·ro·chi·al (pă-roh-ki-ăl) *adj.* 1. of a parish. 2. merely local, showing interest in a limited area only. **pa·ro·chi·al·ism** *n.* ☐**parochial school,** a school maintained by a church parish or religious body.

par·o·dy (par-ŏ-dee) *n.* (*pl.* **-dies**) 1. a comic imitation of a well-known person or literary work or style etc. 2. a grotesque imitation, a travesty. **parody** *v.* (**par·o·died, par·o·dy·ing**) to mimic humorously, to compose a parody of.

pa·role (pă-rohl) *n.* release of a convicted person from a prison before his sentence has expired, on condition of good behavior. **parole** *v.* (**pa·roled, pa·rol·ing**) to release on parole. **pa·rol·ee** (pă-roh-lee) *n.* ☐**parole violation,** breaching the terms of parole.

par·ox·ysm (par-ŏk-siz-ĕm) *n.* a spasm, a sudden attack or outburst of pain or rage or laughter etc. **par·ox·ys·mal** (par-ŏk-siz-măl) *adj.*

par·quet (pahr-kay) *n.* 1. flooring of wooden parquetry. 2. the main floor of a theater.

par·quet·ry (pahr-ki-tree) *n.* inlaid wood for a floor.

par·ra·keet = parakeet.

par·ri·cide (par-i-sıd) *n.* 1. the act of killing one's father, mother, or near relative. 2. a person who commits parricide. **par·ri·ci·dal** (par-i-sı-dăl) *adj.*

par·rot (par-ŏt) *n.* 1. a tropical bird with a short hooked bill and often with brightly colored plumage. 2. a person who repeats another's words or imitates his actions unintelligently. **parrot** *v.* to repeat (words etc.) mechanically; *parroted her,* repeated everything she said. ☐**parrot fever,** psittacosis.

par·ry (par-ee) *v.* (**par·ried, par·ry·ing**) 1. to ward off (an opponent's weapon or blow) by using one's own weapon etc. to block the thrust. 2. to evade (an awkward question) skillfully. **parry** *n.* (*pl.* **-ries**) an action of this kind.

parse (pahrs) *v.* (**parsed, pars·ing**) to explain the grammatical form and function of (a word or words in a sentence).

par·sec (pahr-sek) *n.* a unit of distance used in astronomy, about 3.26 light-years.

par·si·mo·ni·ous (pahr-sĭ-moh-ni-ŭs) *adj.* stingy, very sparing in the use of resources. **par·si·mo·ni·ous·ly** *adv.* **par·si·mo·ny** (pahr-sĭ-moh-nee) *n.*

pars·ley (pahrs-lee) *n.* a garden plant with crinkled green leaves used for seasoning and decorating food and in sauces. **pars'lied** *adj.*

pars·nip (pahrs-nip) *n.* 1. a plant with a large yellowish tapering root that is used as a vegetable. 2. this root.

par·son (pahr-sŏn) *n.* a Protestant minister.

par·son·age (pahr-sŏ-nij) *n.* a house provided by a church for its parson.

part (pahrt) *n.* 1. some but not all of a thing or number of things. 2. a division of a book or broadcast serial etc., especially as much as is issued at one time. 3. a region. 4. an integral element, *she's part of the family.* 5. a distinct portion of a human or animal body or of a plant. 6. a component of a machine or structure. 7. each of several equal portions of a whole; *a fourth part,* a quarter; *three parts,* three-quarters. 8. a portion allotted, a share of work etc. 9. the character assigned to an actor in a play etc., the words spoken by this character, a copy of these. 10. the melody or other line of music assigned to a particular voice or instrument. 11. a side in an agreement or in a dispute; *for* or *on my part,* as far as I am concerned. 12. a line where hair is combed away in different directions. **part** *adv.* in part, partly. **part** *v.* 1. to separate or divide, to cause to do this; *part one's hair,* to make a part in it. 2. *(informal)* to pay out (money), *he couldn't bear to part with a dollar* ☐**a man of parts,** one with many abilities. **in good part,** good-humoredly, without taking offense. **in part,** partly. **part and parcel of,** an essential part of. **part company,** to go different ways after being together; to cease to associate; to disagree, *on that subject you and I part company.* **parting shot,** a sharp remark made by a person as he departs (see **Parthian**). **part of speech,** one of the classes into which words are divided in grammar (noun, adjective, pronoun, verb, adverb, preposition, conjunction, interjection). **part owner,** one who shares the ownership of something with other people. **part song,** a song with three or more voice parts, often without accompaniment. **part time,** less than full time. **part with,** to give up possession of, to hand over.

part. *abbr.* 1. participial. 2. participle. 3. particular.

par·take (pahr-tayk) *v.* (**par·took, par·tak·en, par·tak·ing**) 1. to participate. 2. to take a part or portion, especially of food. **par·tak'er** *n.*

par·terre (pahr-tair) *n.* 1. the level space in a garden occupied by flower beds. 2. the part of the ground floor of an auditorium or theater that lies under a rear balcony.

par·the·no·gen·e·sis (pahr-thĕ-noh-jen-ĕ-sis) *n.* a process of reproduction without fertilization, especially in invertebrates and the lower plants. **par·the·no·ge·net·ic** (pahr-thĕ-noh-jĕ-net-ik) *adj.*

Par·thi·an (par-thi-an) *adj.* **Parthian shot,** a parting shot. ▷The horsemen of ancient Parthia were renowned for turning to shoot their arrows at the enemy while retreating.

par·tial (pahr-shăl) *adj.* 1. in part but not complete or total, *a partial eclipse.* 2. biased, unfair. **par′tial·ly** *adv.* ☐**be partial to,** to have a strong liking for.

par·ti·al·i·ty (pahr-shi-al-i-tee) *n.* 1. bias, favoritism. 2. a strong liking.

par·ti·ble (pahr-tĭ-běl) *adj.* that can or must be divided, *partible inheritance.*

par·tic·i·pate (pahr-tis-ĭ-payt) *v.* (**par·tic·i·pat·ed, par·tic·i·pat·ing**) to have a share, to take part in something. **par·tic′i·pant** *n.* **par·tic′i·pa·tor** *n.* **par·tic·i·pa·tion** (pahr-tis-ĭ-pay-shŏn) *n.*

par·tic·i·pa·to·ry (pahr-tis-ĭ-pă-tohr-ee) *adj.* sharing, taking a part in something.

par·ti·ci·ple (pahr-ti-sip-ĕl) *n.* a word formed from a verb (as *going, gone; burning, burned*) and used in compound verb forms (*she is going or has gone*) or as an adjective (*a going concern*). **par·ti·cip·i·al** (pahr-ti-sip-i-ăl) *adj.* ☐**past participle,** one that expresses completed action, as *burned, frightened, wasted.* **present participle,** one that expresses continuing action, as *burning, frightening, wasting.*

par·ti·cle (pahr-ti-kĕl) *n.* 1. a very small portion of matter, *a subatomic particle.* 2. the smallest possible amount, *he hasn't a particle of sense.* 3. a part of speech that connects or limits or shows the relation of other units, such as a conjunction, preposition, or article. ☐**particle board,** a board made of bonded wood chips.

par·ti·col·ored (pahr-ti-kul-ŏrd) *adj.* colored partly in one color and partly in another or others.

par·tic·u·lar (păr-tik-yŭ-lăr) *adj.* 1. relating to one person or thing as distinct from others, individual, *this particular tax is no worse than others.* 2. special, exceptional, *took particular trouble.* 3. selecting carefully, insisting on certain standards, *is very particular about what he eats.* **particular** *n.* a detail, a piece of information, *gave particulars of the stolen property.* **par·tic′u·lar·ly** *adv.* **par·tic·u·lar·i·ty** (păr-tik-yŭ-lar-i-tee) *n.* ☐**in particular,** particularly, especially, *we liked this one in particular;* specifically, *did nothing in particular.*

par·tic·u·lar·ize (păr-tik-yŭ-lă-rīz) *v.* (**par·tic·u·lar·ized, par·tic·u·lar·iz·ing**) to specify, to name specially or one by one.

par·tic·u·late (păr-tik-yŭ-lit) *adj.* (of matter) in the form of separate particles.

part·ing (pahr-ting) *n.* leave-taking.

par·ti·san (pahr-ti-zăn) *n.* 1. a strong and often uncritical supporter of a person or group or cause. 2. a guerrilla. **partisan** *adj.* characteristic of partisans. **par′ti·san·ship** *n.*

par·ti·tion (pahr-tish-ŏn) *n.* 1. division into parts. 2. a part formed in this way. 3. a structure that divides a room or space, a thin wall. **partition** *v.* 1. to divide into parts, to assign parts (of a task, territory, etc.) in this way. 2. to divide (a room etc.) by means of a partition.

par·ti·tive (pahr-ti-tiv) *adj.* (in grammar) denoting part of a collective whole. **partitive** *n.* 1. a word of this kind (as *some, any*). 2. the grammatical case employing a partitive.

part·ly (pahrt-lee) *adv.* to some extent but not completely or wholly.

part·ner (pahrt-nĕr) *n.* 1. one who shares with another or others in some activity, especially in a business firm where he shares risks and profits. 2. either of two people dancing together or playing tennis or cards etc. on the same side. 3. a husband or wife. **part′ner·ship** *n.*

par·took (pahr-tuuk) *see* **partake.**

par·tridge (pahr-trij) *n.* (*pl.* **-tridg·es, -tridge**) 1. a game bird with brown feathers and a plump body. 2. its flesh as food.

part-time (pahrt-tɪm) *adj.* for or during only part of the working day or week.

part-tim·er (pahrt-tɪ-měr) *n.* a person employed in part-time work.

par·tu·ri·tion (pahr-chŭ-rish-ŏn) *n.* the process of giving birth to young, childbirth.

part·way (pahrt-way) *adv.* (*informal*) partly, to some extent.

par·ty (pahr-tee) *n.* (*pl.* **-ties**) 1. a social gathering, usually of invited guests. 2. a number of people traveling or working together as a unit, *a search party.* 3. a group of people united in support of a cause or policy etc., especially a political group organized on a national basis to put forward its policies and candidates for office. 4. the person(s) forming one side in an agreement or dispute. 5. a person who participates in or knows of or supports an action or plan etc., *refused to be a party to the conspiracy.* 6. (*informal*) a person. **party** *v.* (**par·tied, par·ty·ing**) (*informal*) to give or to attend social gatherings. ☐**party line,** a shared telephone line; the set policy of a political party.

par·ve (pahr-vĕ) *adj.* (of food in the Jewish tradition) permitted to be eaten both with meat and with dairy products.

par·ve·nu (pahr-vĕ-noo) *n.* a person of obscure origin who has gained wealth or position, an upstart.

pas (pah) *n.* (*pl.* **pas,** *pr.* pah) a step in dancing. ☐**pas de deux** (pah dĕ duu), a ballet dance for two persons.

pas·chal (pas-kăl) *adj.* 1. of the Jewish Passover. 2. of Easter. ☐**paschal lamb,** the lamb slaughtered for the feast on the first night of Passover. **Paschal Lamb,** Jesus as the Lamb of God (*see* **lamb**).

pa·sha (pah-shă) *n.* a former Turkish title (placed after a name) for an official of high rank, *Glubb Pasha.*

pass (pas) *v.* (**passed, pass·ing**) 1. to go or proceed or move onward or past something. 2. to cause to move across or over or past. 3. to go from one person to another, to be transferred, *his title passed to his eldest son.* 4. to hand or transfer, (in football etc.) to throw the ball to another player of one's own side. 5. to discharge from the body as or with excreta. 6. to change from one state or condition into another. 7. to come to an end. 8. to happen, to be done or said, *we heard what passed between them.* 9. to occupy (time). 10. to circulate, to be accepted or currently known in a certain way. 11. to be tolerated or allowed. 12. to examine and declare satisfactory, to approve (a law etc.), especially by vote. 13. to achieve the required standard in performing (a test), to be accepted as satisfactory. 14. to go beyond. 15. to utter, to pronounce as a decision, *passed some remarks; pass judgment.* 16. (in cards) to refuse one's turn (as in bidding). **pass** *n.* 1. passing, especially of an examination or at cards. 2. a movement made with the hand(s) or something held. 3. a permit to go into or out of a place or to be absent from one's quarters. 4. a throw of the ball to another player of one's own side in football etc. 5. a gap in a mountain range, allowing access to the other side. 6. a critical state of affairs, *things have come to a pretty pass.* **pass′ er** *n.* □**bring to pass,** to cause to happen. **make a pass at,** to attempt but without much effort; *(informal)* to try to attract sexually. **pass away,** to cease; to die. **pass for,** be accepted as, *he passed for Lebanese.* **pass off,** to offer or dispose of (a thing) under false pretenses, *passed it off as his own;* to evade or dismiss (an awkward remark etc.) lightly. **pass out,** *(informal)* to faint. **pass over,** to disregard; to ignore the claims of (a person) to promotion etc. **pass the buck,** see **buck**[2]. **pass up,** *(informal)* to refuse to accept (an opportunity etc.). **pass water,** to urinate. **pass.** *abbr.* 1. passenger. 2. passive.

pass·a·ble (pas-ă-běl) *adj.* 1. able to be passed on traversed. 2. satisfactory, fairly good but not outstanding. **pass′a·bly** *adv.*

pas·sage (pas-ij) *n.* 1. the process of passing. 2. the right to pass through, right of conveyance as a passenger by sea or air, *book your passage.* 3. a journey by sea or air. 4. a way through, especially with walls on either side. 5. a tubelike structure through which air or secretions etc. pass in the body. 6. a particular section of a literary or musical work.

pas·sage·way (pas-ij-way) *n.* a passage giving a way through.

pass·book (pas-buuk) *n.* a book recording a customer's deposits and withdrawals from a bank account.

pas·sé (pa-say) *adj.* past its or his prime, no longer fashionable. ▷ French.

pas·sel (pas-ěl) *n.* *(informal)* a large group, *a passel of children.*

pas·sen·ger (pas-ěn-jěr) *n.* a person (other than the driver or pilot or member of crew etc.) traveling in a vehicle or ship or aircraft. □**passenger seat,** the seat beside the driver's seat in a car or truck. **passenger train,** a train for carrying passengers not goods.

pass·er·by (pas-ěr-bi) *n.* (*pl.* **-ers·by**) a person who happens to be going past a thing.

pas·sim (pas-im) *adv.* in many places in a book etc. ▷ Latin.

pass·ing (pas-ing) *adj.* not lasting long, casual, *a passing glance.* **passing** *n.* the end of something, a death.

pas·sion (pash-ŏn) *n.* 1. strong emotion. 2. an outburst of anger. 3. sexual love. 4. great enthusiasm for something, the object of this, *chess is his passion.* 5. *Passion,* the sufferings of Christ on the Cross, the account of this in the Gospels, a musical setting for this account. **pas′sion·less** *adj.* □**Passion Sunday,** the Sunday two weeks before Easter in the Christian calendar.

pas·sion·ate (pash-ŏ-nit) *adj.* 1. full of passion, showing or moved by strong emotion. 2. (of emotion) intense. **pas′sion·ate·ly** *adv.*

pas·sion·flow·er (pash-ŏn-flow-ěr) *n.* a climbing plant with flowers thought to resemble the crown of thorns and other things associated with the Passion of Christ.

pas·sion·fruit (pash-ŏn-froot) *n.* the edible fruit of some kinds of passionflower.

pas·sive (pas-iv) *adj.* 1. acted upon and not active. 2. not resisting, submissive. 3. lacking initiative or forceful qualities. 4. (of substances) inert, not active. **passive** *n.* the form of a verb used when

the subject of the sentence receives the action, such as *was seen* in *he was seen there.* **pas′sive·ly** *adv.* **pas′sive·ness** *n.* **pas·siv·i·ty** (pa-siv-ĭ-tee) *n.* □**passive resistance,** resistance by refusal to cooperate.

pass·key (pas-kee) *n.* 1. a key to a door or gate. 2. a master key.

Pass·o·ver (pas-oh-věr) *n.* a Jewish festival commemorating the liberation of the Jews from slavery in Egypt.

pass·port (pas-pohrt) *n.* 1. an official document issued by a government identifying the holder as one of its citizens and entitling him to travel abroad under its protection. 2. a thing that enables one to obtain something, *such ability is a passport to success.*

pass·word (pas-wurd) *n.* a selected word or phrase known only to one's own side, enabling sentries to distinguish friend from enemy.

past (past) *adj.* belonging to the time before the present, (of time) gone by. **past** *n.* 1. time that is gone by, *in the past.* 2. past events. 3. a person's past life or career, especially one that is discreditable, *a man with a past.* **past** *prep.* 1. beyond in time or place, *hurried past me.* 2. beyond the limits or power or range or stage of, *past belief; she's past caring what happens.* **past** *adv.* beyond in time or place, up to and farther, *drove past.* □**past master,** a thorough master in or of a subject, an expert. **would not put it past him,** *(informal)* regard him as morally capable of doing it.

pas·ta (pah-stă) *n.* 1. dried paste made with flour and produced in various shapes (such as macaroni, spaghetti). 2. a cooked dish made with this.

paste (payst) *n.* 1. a moist fairly stiff mixture, especially of a powdery substance and a liquid. 2. an adhesive. 3. an edible doughy substance, *almond paste.* 4. an easily spread preparation of ground meat or fish etc., *anchovy paste.* 5. a hard glasslike substance used in making imitation gems. **paste** *v.* (**past·ed, past·ing**) 1. to fasten with paste. 2. to coat with paste. 3. *(slang)* to beat or thrash.

paste·board (payst-bohrd) *n.* a kind of thin board made of layers of paper or wood fibers pasted together.

pas·tel (pa-stel) *n.* 1. a chalklike crayon. 2. a drawing made with this. 3. a light delicate shade of color. **pastel** *adj.* (of color) pale and subdued.

pas·tern (pas-těrn) *n.* the part of a horse's foot between fetlock and hoof.

pas·teur·ize (pas-chŭ-riz) *v.* (**pas·teur·ized, pas·teur·iz·ing**) to sterilize (milk etc.) partially by heating and then chilling it. **pas·teur·i·za·tion** (pas-chŭ-ri-zay-shŏn) *n.* ▷The method was devised by Louis Pasteur (1822–95), a French chemist.

pas·tiche (pa-steesh) *n.* a musical or other composition made up of selections from various sources.

pas·tille (pa-steel) *n.* a small flavored candy for sucking, a lozenge.

pas·time (pas-tim) *n.* something done to pass time pleasantly, a recreation.

pas·tor (pas-tŏr) *n.* a minister in charge of a church or congregation.

pas·to·ral (pas-tŏ-răl) *adj.* 1. of shepherds or country life, *a pastoral scene.* 2. of a pastor, concerned with spiritual guidance. **pastoral** *n.* a poem, picture, etc. dealing with country life.

pas·tor·ate (pas-tŏ-rit) *n.* 1. a pastor's official resi-

dence. 2. his term of office. 3. pastors as a unit.
pas·tra·mi (pă-**strah**-mee) *n.* a highly seasoned smoked beef.
pas·try (**pay**-stree) *n.* (*pl.* **-tries**) 1. dough made of flour, fat, and water, used for covering pies or holding filling. 2. food made with this. 3. a cake in which pastry is used.
pas·tur·age (**pas**-chŭ-rij) *n.* 1. pasture land. 2. the right to graze animals on this.
pas·ture (**pas**-chŭr) *n.* 1. land covered with grass and similar plants suitable for grazing cattle. 2. grass etc. on such land. **pasture** *v.* (**pas·tured, pas·tur·ing**) 1. to put (animals) to graze in a pasture. 2. (of animals) to graze.
past·y (**pay**-stee) *adj.* (**past·i·er, past·i·est**) 1. of or like paste. 2. unhealthily pale, *pasty-faced.*
pat¹ (pat) *v.* (**pat·ted, pat·ting**) 1. to tap gently with the open hand or with something flat. 2. to flatten or shape by doing this. **pat** *n.* 1. a patting movement. 2. the sound of this. 3. a small mass of butter or other soft substance. □**a pat on the back,** praise, congratulations.
pat² *adj. & adv.* known and ready for any occasion, *had any number of pat answers; had his answers pat.* □**stand pat,** to stick firmly to what one has said; (in poker) to draw no additional cards.
pat. *abbr.* 1. patent. 2. patented.
patch (pach) *n.* 1. a piece of material or metal etc. put over a hole to mend it. 2. a bandage or a pad placed over a wound etc. to protect it. 3. a large or irregular area on a surface, differing in color or texture etc. from the rest. 4. a piece of ground, especially for growing vegetables, *cabbage patch.* 5. a small area or volume of anything, *patches of fog.* **patch** *v.* 1. to put a patch or patches on. 2. to serve as a patch for. 3. to piece (things) together. □**patch pocket,** a pocket made by sewing a piece of cloth on the surface of a garment. **patch test,** a test for allergy made by applying to the skin patches containing allergenic substances. **patch up,** to repair with patches; to put together hastily or as a makeshift; to settle (a quarrel etc.).
patch·ou·li (pă-**choo**-lee) *n.* 1. a fragrant plant grown in the Far East. 2. perfume made from this.
patch·work (**pach**-wurk) *n.* 1. a kind of needlework in which assorted small pieces of cloth are joined edge to edge, often in a pattern; *patchwork quilt,* one made in this way. 2. anything made of assorted (also ill-assorted) pieces.
patch·y (**pach**-ee) *adj.* (**patch·i·er, patch·i·est**) 1. having patches, existing in patches, *patchy fog.* 2. uneven in quality. **patch'i·ly** *adv.* **patch'i·ness** *n.*
pate (payt) *n.* (*old use*) the head.
pa·té (pă-**tay**) *n.* a paste or spread of meat etc.
pa·tel·la (pă-**tel**-ă) *n.* (*pl.* **-tel·las, -tel·lae,** *pr.* **-tel**-ee) the kneecap.
pat·en (**pat**-ĕn) *n.* a metal plate on which bread is placed at the Eucharist.
pat·ent¹ (**pat**-ĕnt) *n.* 1. a document granting an inventor the sole right to make or use or sell an invention. 2. an invention or process protected in this way. **patent** *adj.* protected by a patent, *patent medicines.* **patent** *v.* to obtain or hold a patent. **pat'ent·ed** *adj.* □**patent leather,** leather with a glossy varnished surface. **patent office,** the government office from which patents are issued. **patent pending,** notice that a patent has been applied for but not yet received.

pat·ent² (**pay**-tĕnt) *adj.* obvious, unconcealed, *his patent dislike of the plan.*
pat·ent·ee (pat-ĕn-**tee**) *n.* a person who holds a patent.
pat·ent·ly (**pay**-tĕnt-lee) *adv.* obviously, *his suggestion was patently ridiculous.*
pa·ter·fa·mil·i·as (pay-tĕr-fă-**mil**-i-ăs) *n.* (*pl.* **-as·es**) (*informal*) the head of the family or household.
pa·ter·nal (pă-**tur**-năl) *adj.* 1. of a father, of fatherhood. 2. fatherly. 3. related through one's father; *paternal grandmother,* one's father's mother. **pa·ter'nal·ly** *adv.*
pa·ter·nal·ism (pă-**tur**-nă-liz-ĕm) *n.* the policy of governing or controlling people in a paternal way, providing for their needs but giving them no responsibility. **pa·ter·nal·is·tic** (pă-tur-nă-**lis**-tik) *adj.*
pa·ter·ni·ty (pă-**tur**-ni-tee) *n.* 1. fatherhood, being a father. 2. descent from a father. □**paternity test,** a test to determine from blood samples whether a man may be the father of a particular child.
pa·ter·nos·ter (pay-tĕr-**nos**-tĕr) *n.* the Lord's Prayer, especially in Latin.
path (path) *n.* (*pl.* **paths,** *pr.* pa*th*z) 1. a way by which people pass on foot, a track. 2. a line along which a person or thing moves. 3. a course of action.
path. *abbr.* 1. pathological. 2. pathology.
pa·thet·ic (pă-**thet**-ik) *adj.* 1. arousing pity or sadness. 2. miserably inadequate. **pa·thet'i·cal·ly** *adv.*
path·find·er (**path**-fīn-dĕr) *n.* an explorer.
path·o·gen (**path**-ŏ-jĕn) *n.* an agent (such as a bacterium or virus) causing disease. **path·o·gen·ic** (path-ŏ-**jen**-ik) *adj.*
pathol. *abbr.* 1. pathological. 2. pathology.
path·o·log·i·cal (path-ŏ-**loj**-i-kăl) *adj.* 1. of pathology. 2. of or caused by a physical or mental disorder, *a pathological liar.* **path·o·log'i·cal·ly** *adv.*
pa·thol·o·gist (pă-**thol**-ŏ-jist) *n.* an expert in pathology.
pa·thol·o·gy (pă-**thol**-ŏ-jee) *n.* 1. the scientific study of diseases of the body. 2. abnormal changes in body tissue, caused by disease.
pa·thos (**pay**-thos) *n.* a quality that arouses pity or sadness.
path·way (**path**-way) *n.* a path.
pa·tience (**pay**-shĕns) *n.* 1. calm endurance of hardship or annoyance or inconvenience or delay etc. 2. perseverance. 3. a card game (usually for one player) in which cards have to be brought into a particular arrangement. □**have no patience with,** to feel irritated by.
pa·tient (**pay**-shĕnt) *adj.* having or showing patience. **patient** *n.* a person receiving treatment by a doctor or dentist etc. **pa'tient·ly** *adv.*
pat·i·na (pat-**ī**-nă) *n.* 1. an attractive green incrustation on the surface of old bronze. 2. a gloss on the surface of woodwork, produced by age.
pa·ti·o (**pat**-i-oh) *n.* (*pl.* **-os**) 1. an inner courtyard, open to the sky, in a Spanish or Spanish-American house. 2. a paved area beside a house, used for outdoor meals or relaxation.
pat·ois (**pat**-wah) *n.* (*pl.* **pa·tois,** *pr.* pat-wahz) a dialect.
pat. pend. *abbr.* patent pending.
pa·tri·arch (**pay**-tri-ahrk) *n.* 1. the male head of a family or tribe; *the Patriarchs,* the men named

in the book of Genesis as the ancestors of mankind or of the tribes of Israel. 2. a bishop of high rank in certain churches. 3. a venerable old man. **pa·tri·ar·chy** (pay-tri-ahr-kee) *n.* **pa·tri·ar·chate** (pay-tri-ahr-kit) *n.* **pa·tri·ar·chal** (pay-tri-ahr-kăl) *adj.*

pa·tri·cian (pă-trish-ăn) *n.* a member of the aristocracy, especially in ancient Rome. **patrician** *adj.* aristocratic.

pat·ri·cide (pat-rĭ-sɪd) *n.* 1. the act of killing one's father. 2. a person who commits this crime. **pat·ri·cid·al** (pat-ri-sɪ-dăl) *adj.*

pat·ri·mo·ny (pat-rĭ-moh-nee) *n.* property inherited from one's father or ancestors, a heritage. **pat·ri·mo·ni·al** (pat-rĭ-moh-ni-ăl) *adj.*

pa·tri·ot (pay-tri-ŏt) *n.* a patriotic person. **pa·tri·ot·ic** (pay-tri-ot-ik) *adj.* loyally supporting one's country. **pa·tri·ot·i·cal·ly** *adv.* **pa·tri·ot·ism** (pay-tri-ŏ-tiz-ĕm) *n.*

pa·tris·tic (pă-tris-tik) *adj.* of the study of the early Christian writers or their works.

pa·trol (pă-trohl) *v.* **(pa·trolled, pa·trol·ling)** to walk or travel regularly through (an area or building) in order to see that all is secure and orderly. **patrol** *n.* 1. patrolling, *on patrol.* 2. the person(s) or ship(s) or aircraft whose job is to patrol an area. □**patrol wagon,** a police van for prisoners.

pa·trol·man (pă-trohl-măn) *n.* (*pl.* **-men,** *pr.* -měn) a policeman assigned to foot patrol.

pa·tron (pay-trŏn) *n.* 1. a person who gives encouragement or financial or other support to an activity or cause etc. 2. a regular customer of a shop or restaurant etc. **pa·tron·ess** (pay-trŏ-nis) *n. fem.* □**patron saint,** a saint regarded as giving special protection to a person or place or activity.

pa·tron·age (pay-trŏ-nij) *n.* 1. support given by a patron. 2. the right of appointing a person to a job in government.

pa·tron·ize (pay-trŏ-nɪz) *v.* **(pa·tron·ized, pa·tron·iz·ing)** 1. to act as a patron toward, to support or encourage. 2. to be a regular customer at (a store etc.). 3. to treat in a condescending way. **pa·tron·iz·ing** (pay-trŏ-nɪ-zing) *adj.* condescending. **pa'tron·iz·ing·ly** *adv.*

pat·ro·nym·ic (pat-rŏ-nim-ik) *n.* a name derived from the name of a father or ancestor.

pa·troon (pă-troon) *n.* (*old use*) the owner of a landed estate with rights to levy taxes and fees.

pat·sy (pat-see) *n.* (*pl.* **-sies**) (*slang*) a person who is ridiculed or deceived or victimized.

pat·ter¹ (pat-ĕr) *v.* 1. to make a series of light quick taps. 2. to run with short quick steps. **patter** *n.* a series of light quick tapping sounds.

patter² *n.* rapid and often glib or deceptive speech, such as that used by a magician, salesman, comedian, etc.

pat·tern (pat-ĕrn) *n.* 1. an arrangement of lines or shapes or colors, a decorative design. 2. a model or design or instructions according to which something is to be made. 3. an excellent example, a model. 4. the regular form or order in which actions or qualities etc. occur, *behavior patterns.* **pattern** *v.* 1. to model according to a pattern. 2. to decorate with a pattern.

pat·ty (pat-ee) *n.* (*pl.* **-ties**) 1. a round flattened piece of ground meat or other food, *hamburger patty; potato patty.* 2. a small pie.

pau·ci·ty (paw-si-tee) *n.* smallness of supply or quantity.

paunch (pawnch) *n.* 1. the belly. 2. a protruding abdomen. **paun'chy** *adj.*

pau·per (paw-pĕr) *n.* a very poor person. **pau'per·ism** *n.*

pau·per·ize (paw-pĕ-rɪz) *v.* **(pau·per·ized, pau·per·iz·ing)** to make a pauper of.

pause (pawz) *n.* a temporary stop in action or speech. **pause** *v.* **(paused, paus·ing)** to make a pause. □**give pause to,** to cause (a person) to hesitate.

pave (payv) *v.* **(paved, pav·ing)** to cover (a road or path etc.) with stones or concrete etc. to make a hard surface. **pav'ing** *n.* □**pave the way,** to prepare the way for changes etc. **paving stone,** a slab of stone for paving.

pave·ment (payv-mĕnt) *n.* a paved surface, a paved path for pedestrians at the side of a road.

pa·vil·ion (pă-vil-yŏn) *n.* 1. a light building or other structure used as a shelter, as in a park. 2. an ornamental building used for dances and concerts etc.

paw (paw) *n.* 1. the foot of an animal that has claws. 2. (*informal*) a person's hand. **paw** *v.* 1. to strike with a paw. 2. to scrape (the ground) with a hoof. 3. (*informal*) to touch awkwardly or rudely with the hands.

pawl (pawl) *n.* a lever with a catch that engages with the notches of a ratchet wheel.

pawn¹ (pawn) *n.* 1. a chessman of the smallest size and value. 2. a person whose actions are controlled by others.

pawn² *v.* to deposit (a thing) with a pawnbroker as security for money borrowed. **pawn** *n.* something deposited as a pledge. □**in pawn,** deposited as a pawn. **pawn ticket,** a receipt for a thing deposited with a pawnbroker.

pawn·brok·er (pawn-broh-kĕr) *n.* a person licensed to lend money on the security of personal property deposited with him.

Paw·nee (paw-nee) *n.* (*pl.* **-nees, -nee**) 1. a member of an Indian tribe from Kansas and Nebraska. 2. the language of this tribe.

pawn·shop (pawn-shop) *n.* a pawnbroker's place of business.

paw·paw = **papaw.**

pay (pay) *v.* **(paid, pay·ing)** 1. to give (money) in return for goods or services. 2. to give what is owed, to hand over the amount of (wages, a debt, ransom, etc.). 3. to bear the cost of something. 4. to be profitable or worthwhile. 5. to bestow or render or express, *pay attention; paid them a visit; paid them a compliment.* 6. to let out (a rope) by slackening it. **pay** *n.* 1. payment. 2. wages. 3. paid employment, *he is in the pay of the enemy.* **pay'er** *n.* □**pay as you go,** living within one's means, not relying on credit or borrowing, *a pay-as-you-go policy.* **pay for,** to suffer or be punished because of (a mistake etc.). **paying guest,** one who pays for his board and lodging. **pay its way,** to make enough profit to cover expenses. **pay off,** to pay in full and be free from (a debt) or discharge (an employee); to yield good results, *the risk paid off.* **pay one's way,** not get into debt. **pay phone,** a coin-operated telephone. **pay up,** to pay in full; to pay what is demanded.

pay·a·ble (pay-ă-běl) *adj.* that must or may be paid.

pay·check (pay-chek) *n.* wages or salary, a check paying this.

pay·ee (pay-ee) *n.* a person to whom money is paid or is to be paid.

pay·load (pay-lohd) *n.* 1. the part of an aircraft's load from which revenue is derived (passengers or cargo). **2.** the total weight of bombs or instruments carried by an aircraft or rocket etc.

pay·mas·ter (pay-mas-tĕr) *n.* an official who pays troops or workmen etc.

pay·ment (pay-mĕnt) *n.* **1.** paying. **2.** money given in return for goods or services. **3.** reward, compensation.

pay·off (pay-awf) *n. (slang)* **1.** payment. **2.** reward or retribution. **3.** a climax, especially of a joke or story.

pay·o·la (pay-oh-lă) *n.* **1.** a bribe offered to one who promotes a commercial product by dishonestly making use of his position or influence etc. **2.** bribery of this kind.

pay·roll (pay-rohl) *n.* a list of a firm's employees receiving regular pay.

Pb *symbol* lead.

PBB *n.* a toxic chemical. ▷From *poly*brominated *bi*phenyl.

PBS *abbr.* Public Broadcasting Service.

PBX *abbr.* private branch exchange (a private telephone system).

PCB *n.* a toxic chemical. ▷From *poly*chlorinated *bi*phenyl.

PCP *n.* a hallucinogenic drug. ▷From *phen*cylidine *pill.*

pct. *abbr.* percent.

Pd *symbol* palladium.

PD *abbr.* Police Department.

pd. *abbr.* paid.

P.D.Q. *abbr. (slang)* pretty damn quickly.

PDT *abbr.* Pacific Daylight Time.

PE *abbr.* **1.** physical education. **2.** printer's error. **3.** Professional Engineer. **4.** Protestant Episcopal.

pea (pee) *n. (pl.* **peas**) **1.** a climbing plant bearing seeds in pods. **2.** the seed of certain varieties of this, used as a vegetable. □**pea green,** bright green, like vegetable peas. **pea souper,** *(informal)* a thick yellowish fog.

peace (pees) *n.* **1.** a state of freedom from war, cessation of war. **2.** a treaty ending a war, *signed the peace.* **3.** freedom from civil disorder, *a breach of the peace.* **4.** quiet, calm; *peace of mind,* freedom from anxiety. **5.** a state of harmony between people, absence of strife. □**Peace Corps,** an organization of Americans who work in the developing countries. **peace offering,** something offered to show that one is willing to make peace. **peace officer,** a policeman. **peace pipe,** a tobacco pipe as a token of peace among North American Indians.

peace·a·ble (pee-să-bĕl) *adj.* **1.** not quarrelsome, desiring to be at peace with others. **2.** peaceful, without strife, *a peaceable settlement.* **peace'a·bly** *adv.*

peace·ful (pees-fŭl) *adj.* **1.** characterized by peace. **2.** belonging to a state of peace not of war, *peaceful uses of atomic energy.* **peace'ful·ly** *adv.* **peace'ful·ness** *n.*

peace·keep·ing (pees-kee-ping) *adj.* refraining from or preventing strife. **peace'keep·er** *n.*

peace·mak·er (pees-may-kĕr) *n.* a person who brings about peace.

peace·time (pees-tım) *n.* a period when a country is not at war.

peach (peech) *n.* **1.** a round juicy fruit with downy yellowish or reddish skin and a rough stone. **2.** the tree that bears this. **3.** *(slang)* a person or thing that is greatly admired, an attractive young woman. **4.** yellowish-pink color. **peach** *adj.* yellowish pink. **peach'y** *adj.* (**peach·i·er, peach·**

i·est) □**peach Melba,** a dish of ice cream and peaches with raspberry syrup.

pea·cock (pee-kok) *n.* a male bird with long tail feathers that can be spread upright like a fan. □**peacock blue,** brilliant blue like the feathers on a peacock's neck.

pea·hen (pee-hen) *n.* the female of a peacock.

pea jacket a sailor's short double-breasted overcoat of coarse woolen cloth.

peak (peek) *n.* **1.** a pointed top, especially of a mountain. **2.** the mountain itself. **3.** any shape or edge or part that tapers to form a point. **4.** a projecting part of the edge of a cap. **5.** the point of highest value or achievement or intensity etc., *at the peak of her career; peak hours,* the hours when traffic is heaviest or consumption of electric current etc. is at its highest. **peak** *v.* to reach a peak in value or intensity etc.

peak·ed (pee-kid) *adj.* having a drawn and sickly appearance.

peal (peel) *n.* **1.** the loud ringing of a bell or set of bells. **2.** a set of bells with different notes. **3.** a loud sustained sound of thunder or laughter. **peal** *v.* to sound or cause to sound in a peal.

pea·nut (pee-nut) *n.* **1.** a plant bearing pods that ripen underground, usually containing two edible seeds. **2.** this seed. **3.** *peanuts, (informal)* a trivial or contemptibly small amount of money. □**peanut brittle,** a hard caramel and peanut candy. **peanut butter,** a spread of ground roasted peanuts. **peanut gallery,** *(informal)* the rear section of a theater balcony. **peanut oil,** oil derived from peanuts.

pear (pair) *n.* **1.** a rounded fleshy fruit that tapers toward the stalk. **2.** the tree that bears this.

pearl (purl) *n.* **1.** a round usually white mass of a lustrous substance formed inside the shells of certain oysters, valued as a gem. **2.** an imitation of this. **3.** something resembling it in shape. **4.** something valued because of its excellence or beauty. □**cast pearls before swine,** to offer a good thing to someone who is incapable of appreciating it. **pearl barley,** barley grains ground small. **pearl diver,** one who dives or fishes for oysters containing pearls. **pearl gray,** a pale bluish gray.

pearled (purld) *adj.* formed into or covered with pearllike drops.

pearl·y (pur-lee) *adj.* (**pearl·i·er, pearl·i·est**) **1.** like pearls. **2.** with pearls. □**Pearly Gates,** *(informal)* the gates of heaven.

peas·ant (pez-ănt) *n.* (in some countries) a member of the class of farm laborers and small farmers.

peas·ant·ry (pez-ăn-tree) *n.* peasants.

pea·shoot·er (pee-shoo-tĕr) *n.* a toy tube from which peas or pellets are shot by blowing.

peat (peet) *n.* vegetable matter decomposed by the action of water in marshes etc. and partly carbonized, used in horticulture or cut in pieces as fuel. **peat'y** *adj.* □**peat moss,** moss that has formed peat, used to improve soil.

peb·ble (peb-ĕl) *n.* a small stone worn round and smooth by the action of water. **pebble** *v.* (**peb·bled, peb·bling**) **1.** to cover with pebbles. **2.** to give a textured surface to (leather or paper). **peb'bly** *adj.*

pe·can (pi-kahn) *n.* **1.** a smooth edible nut of a hickory tree. **2.** the tree bearing this nut.

pec·ca·dil·lo (pek-ă-dil-oh) *n.* (*pl.* **-loes, -los**) a trivial offense.

pec·ca·ry (pek-ă-ree) *n.* (*pl.* **-ries, -ry**) a wild pig of tropical America.

peck[1] (pek) *n.* 1. a dry measure, = 8 quarts or one-quarter of a bushel. 2. a lot, *a peck of trouble.*
peck[2] *v.* 1. to strike or nip or pick up with the beak. 2. to make (a hole) with the beak. 3. to kiss lightly and hastily. **peck** *n.* 1. a stroke or nip made with the beak. 2. a light hasty kiss. **peck′er** *n.* □**peck at,** to eat (food) lightly.
pecking order, a social hierarchy, originally as observed among domestic fowl.
pec·tin (pek-tin) *n.* a gelatinous substance found in ripe fruits etc., causing jams and jellies to set. **pec′tic** *adj.*
pec·to·ral (pek-tŏ-răl) *adj.* 1. of or in or on the chest or breast, *pectoral muscles.* 2. worn on the breast, *a pectoral cross.*
pec·u·la·tion (pek-yŭ-lay-shŏn) *n.* embezzlement.
pe·cu·liar (pi-kyool-yăr) *adj.* 1. strange, eccentric. 2. belonging exclusively to a particular person or place or time, *customs peculiar to the 18th century.* 3. particular, special, *a point of peculiar interest.*
pe·cu·li·ar·i·ty (pi-kyoo-li-ar-i-tee) *n.* (*pl.* -ties) 1. being peculiar. 2. a characteristic. 3. something unusual, an eccentricity.
pe·cul·iar·ly (pi-kyool-yăr-lee) *adv.* 1. in a peculiar way. 2. especially, *peculiarly annoying.*
pe·cu·ni·ar·y (pi-kyoo-ni-er-ee) *adj.* of or in money, *pecuniary aid.*
ped·a·gogue (ped-ă-gog) *n.* a person who teaches in a pedantic way.
ped·a·go·gy (ped-ă-goh-jee) *n.* teaching, the art of teaching. **ped·a·gog·ic** (ped-ă-goj-ik) *adj.* **ped·a·gog′i·cal** *adj.*
ped·al (ped-ăl) *n.* a lever operated by the foot in a motor vehicle or cycle or other machine, or in certain musical instruments. **pedal** *v.* (**ped·aled, ped·al·ing**) 1. to work the pedal(s) of. 2. to move or operate by means of pedals, to ride a bicycle. □**pedal pushers,** women's short slacks reaching below the knee. ▷ Do not confuse *pedal* with *peddle.*
ped·al·boat (ped-ăl-boht) *n.* a pleasure boat operated by pedals.
ped·ant (ped-ănt) *n.* a person who parades his learning or who insists unimaginatively on strict observance of formal rules and details in the presentation of knowledge. **ped′ant·ry** *n.* **pe·dan·tic** (pi-dan-tik) *adj.* **pe·dan′ti·cal·ly** *adv.*
ped·dle (ped-ĕl) *v.* (**ped·dled, ped·dling**) to sell (goods) as a peddler. ▷ Do not confuse *peddle* with *pedal.*
ped·dler (ped-lĕr) *n.* a person who goes from house to house selling small articles.
ped·er·ast (ped-ĕ-rast) *n.* a man who commits sodomy with a boy. **ped′er·as·ty** *n.*
ped·es·tal (ped-ĕ-stăl) *n.* a base supporting a column or pillar or statue etc. □**put a person on a pedestal,** to admire or respect him greatly or excessively.
pe·des·tri·an (pĕ-des-tri-ăn) *n.* a person who is walking, especially in a street. **pedestrian** *adj.* 1. of walking, of or for pedestrians. 2. unimaginative, dull. □**pedestrian crossing,** *see* **crossing** (definition 3).
pe·di·a·tri·cian (pee-di-ă-trish-ăn) *n.* a specialist in pediatrics.
pe·di·at·rics (pee-di-at-riks) *n.* the branch of medicine dealing with the diseases of children. **pe·di·at′ric** *adj.*
ped·i·cab (ped-ĭ-kab) *n.* a rickshaw pulled by a cyclist.

ped·i·cure (ped-ĭ-kyoor) *n.* care and treatment of the feet and toenails. **ped′i·cur·ist** *n.*
ped·i·gree (ped-ĭ-gree) *n.* a line or list of ancestors, especially of a distinguished kind. **pedigree** *adj.* (of animals) having a recorded line of descent that shows pure breeding, *pedigree cattle.*
ped·i·ment (ped-ĭ-mĕnt) *n.* a triangular gable crowning the front of a building of the classical Greek style.
ped·lar (ped-lăr) *n.* (*old use*) a peddler.
pe·dom·e·ter (pĕ-dom-ĕ-tĕr) *n.* a device that calculates the distance a person walks by counting the number of steps taken.
pe·dun·cle (pi-dung-kĕl) *n.* the stalk of a flower, fruit, or cluster, especially the main stalk bearing a solitary flower or subordinate stalk.
pee (pee) *v.* (**peed, pee·ing**) (*informal*) to urinate. **pee** *n.* (*informal*) 1. urination. 2. urine.
peek (peek) *v.* to peep or glance. **peek** *n.* a peep or glance.
peel (peel) *n.* the skin of certain fruits and vegetables. **peel** *v.* 1. to remove the peel of. 2. to strip away, to pull off (a skin or covering). 3. to be able to be peeled. 4. to come off in strips or layers, to lose skin or bark etc. in this way. □**peel off,** to veer away from a formation of which one formed a part.
peel·ing (pee-ling) *n.* a strip of skin peeled from potatoes etc.
peen (peen) *n.* the wedge-shaped or spherical end of the head of a hammer. **peen** *v.* 1. to hammer with this. 2. to treat with a stream of metal shot.
peep[1] (peep) *v.* 1. to look through a narrow opening. 2. to look quickly or surreptitiously or from a concealed place. 3. to come briefly or partially into view, to show slightly. **peep** *n.* a brief or surreptitious look. □**peeping Tom,** a man who furtively watches someone undressing or engaging in sexual activities. (▷ Named after the Coventry tailor in the story of Lady Godiva.) **peep show,** a small exhibition of pictures etc. viewed through a lens in a small opening.
peep[2] *n.* a weak high chirping sound like that made by young birds. **peep** *v.* to make this sound. □**didn't make a peep,** (*informal*) made no sound or complaint.
peep·hole (peep-hohl) *n.* a small hole to peep through.
peer[1] (peer) *v.* 1. to look searchingly or with difficulty. 2. to peep out.
peer[2] *n.* 1. one who is equal to another (or others) in rank or merit or quality etc. 2. a member of the peerage in Great Britain, a duke, marquis, earl, viscount, or baron, also called **peers of the realm,** with the right to sit in the House of Lords. □**has no peer,** is unequaled in merit, quality, etc. **peer group,** a group of people who are of equal status, similar occupation, etc.
peer·age (peer-ij) *n.* 1. peers, the nobility. 2. the rank of peer or peeress. 3. a book containing a list of peers.
peer·ess (peer-is) *n.* a female peer, a peer's wife.
peer·less (peer-lis) *adj.* without equal, superb.
peeve (peev) *n.* (*informal*) 1. a cause of annoyance, *my pet peeve.* 2. a mood of vexation, *in a peeve.* **peeve** *v.* (**peeved, peev·ing**) (*informal*) to annoy.
pee·vish (pee-vish) *adj.* irritable. **pee′vish·ly** *adv.* **pee′vish·ness** *n.*
pee·wee (pee-wee) *n.* (*informal*) an unusually small boy.

peg (peg) *n.* 1. a wooden or metal pin or bolt for fastening things together, hanging things on, holding a tent rope taut, or marking a position; *a peg on which to hang a sermon,* a suitable theme or pretext for it. 2. a wooden screw for tightening or loosening the strings of a violin. 3. *(slang)* a throw of a baseball. **peg** *v.* **(pegged, peg·ging)** 1. to fix or mark by means of a peg or pegs. 2. to keep (wages or prices) at a fixed amount. 3. *(slang)* to throw (a baseball). □**peg away,** to work diligently, to be persistent in doing something. **peg leg,** *(slang)* an artificial leg. **take a person down a peg,** to reduce his pride, to humble him.

peg·board (peg-bohrd) *n.* a board with holes and pegs.

P.E.I. *abbr.* Prince Edward Island.

peign·oir (payn-**wahr**) *n.* a woman's dressing gown.

pe·jo·ra·tive (pi-**jor**-ă-tiv) *adj.* disparaging, derogatory. **pe·jo′ra·tive·ly** *adv.*

peke (peek) *n.* *(informal)* a Pekingese dog.

Pe·king (pee-**king**) former spelling of Beijing, the capital of China.

Pe·king·ese (pee-kĭ-**neez**) *n.* (*pl.* **-ese**) a dog of a breed with short legs, flat face, and long silky hair.

pe·koe (pee-koh) *n.* a kind of black tea made from young leaves.

pel·age (pel-ij) *n.* the fur, hair, wool of a mammal.

pe·lag·ic (pě-**laj**-ik) *adj.* of, or performed on, the open sea.

pelf (pelf) *n.* *(contemptuous)* money, wealth.

pel·i·can (pel-ĭ-kăn) *n.* a large water bird of warm regions, with a pouch in its long bill for storing fish.

pel·la·gra (pě-**lag**-ră) *n.* a deficiency disease causing cracking of the skin, disorders of the nervous system, and diarrhea.

pel·let (pel-it) *n.* 1. a small rounded closely packed mass of a soft substance. 2. a small bullet or shot.

pell·mell (pel-mel) *adj. & adv.* in a hurrying disorderly manner, headlong.

pel·lu·cid (pě-**loo**-sid) *adj.* very clear.

pelt[1] (pelt) *n.* an animal skin, especially with the fur or hair still on it.

pelt[2] *v.* 1. to throw missiles at. 2. (of rain etc.) to come down fast.

pel·vis (pel-vis) *n.* the basin-shaped framework of bones at the lower end of the body. **pel′vic** *adj.*

pem·mi·can, pem·i·can (pem-ĭ-kăn) *n.* a North American Indian cake of dried and pounded meat mixed with melted fat.

pen[1] (pen) *n.* a small fenced enclosure especially for cattle, sheep, poultry, etc. **pen** *v.* **(penned, pen·ning)** to shut in or as if in a pen.

pen[2] *n.* a device with a metal point, rolling ball, felt tip, etc. for writing with ink. **pen** *v.* **(penned, pen·ning)** to write (a letter etc.). □**pen name,** an author's pseudonym. **pen pal,** a friend with whom a person corresponds without meeting.

pen[3] *n.* a female swan.

pen[4] *n.* *(slang)* a penitentiary.

pen. *abbr.* peninsula.

P.E.N. *abbr.* International Association of Poets, Playwrights, Editors, Essayists, and Novelists.

pe·nal (pee-năl) *adj.* of or involving punishment, especially according to law. □**penal code,** the body of laws concerned with punishment of criminals.

pe·nal·ize (pee-nă-lız) *v.* **(pe·nal·ized, pe·**

nal·iz·ing) 1. to inflict a penalty on. 2. to place at a serious disadvantage.

pen·al·ty (pen-ăl-tee) *n.* (*pl.* **-ties**) 1. a punishment for breaking a law or rule or contract. 2. a disadvantage or hardship brought on by some action or quality, *the penalties of fame.* 3. a disadvantage to which an athlete or team must submit for breaking a rule. □**penalty area,** an area in front of the goal on a soccer field in which a foul by the defenders involves the award of a penalty kick. **penalty box,** a place for penalized players in hockey. **penalty kick,** a free kick at goal awarded as a penalty in soccer.

pen·ance (pen-ăns) *n.* 1. an act performed as an expression of penitence. 2. (in the Roman Catholic and Orthodox Churches) a sacrament including confession, absolution, and an act of penitence imposed by a priest. □**do penance,** to perform an act of this kind.

pence (pens) *n. pl.* *(British)* a plural form of *penny,* used for a sum of money, *the fare has increased to 20 pence.* ▷This form is like the U.S. *20 cents,* which means coins totaling this amount, not 20 pennies. See **penny.**

pen·chant (pen-chănt, pahn-**shahn**) *n.* a liking or inclination, *has a penchant for Indian music.*

pen·cil (pen-sĭl) *n.* 1. an instrument for drawing or writing, consisting of a thin stick of graphite or colored chalk etc. enclosed in a cylinder of wood or fixed in a metal case. 2. something used or shaped like this. **pencil** *v.* **(pen·cil·ed, pen·cil·ing)** to write or draw or mark with a pencil. □**pencil box,** a container for pencils. **pencil in,** to enter (a suggested date or estimate etc.) provisionally.

pen·dant (pen-dănt) *n.* a hanging ornament, especially one attached to a chain worn around the neck.

pen·dent (pen-dĕnt) *adj.* hanging.

pend·ing (pen-ding) *adj.* 1. waiting to be decided or settled. 2. about to come into existence, *your pending promotion.* **pending** *prep.* 1. during, *pending these negotiations.* 2. until, *pending his return.*

pen·du·lous (pen-ju-lŭs) *adj.* hanging downward, hanging so as to swing freely.

pen·du·lum (pen-jŭ-lŭm) *n.* 1. a weight hung from a cord so that it can swing freely. 2. a rod with a weighted end that regulates the movement of a clock etc. □**swing of the pendulum,** the tendency for public opinion to favor an opposite policy or political party etc. after a time.

pe·ne·plain (pee-nĕ-playn) *n.* a region that is almost a plain, as a result of erosion.

pen·e·tra·ble (pen-ĕ-tră-běl) *adj.* able to be penetrated. **pen·e·tra·bil·i·ty** (pen-ĕ-tră-bil-i-tee) *n.*

pen·e·trate (pen-ĕ-trayt) *v.* **(pen·e·trat·ed, pen·e·trat·ing)** 1. to make a way into or through, to pierce. 2. to enter and permeate. 3. to see into or through, *our eyes could not penetrate the darkness.* 4. to discover or understand, *penetrated their secrets.* 5. to be absorbed by the mind, *my hint didn't penetrate.* **pen′e·tra·tor** *n.* **pen·e·tra·tion** (pen-ĕ-tray-shŏn) *n.*

pen·e·trat·ing (pen-ĕ-tray-ting) *adj.* 1. having or showing great insight. 2. (of a voice or sound) loud and carrying, piercing.

pen·e·tra·tive (pen-ĕ-tray-tiv) *adj.* able to penetrate, penetrating.

pen·guin (pen-gwin, peng-) *n.* a seabird of the Antarctic and nearby regions, with webbed feet and wings developed into flippers used for swimming.

pen·hold·er (pen-hohl-děr) n. a wooden or plastic rod holding a nib.

pen·i·cil·lin (pen-ĭ-sil-in) n. an antibiotic of the kind obtained from mold fungi.

pen·in·su·la (pĕ-nin-sŭ-lă) n. a piece of land that is almost surrounded by water or that projects far into the sea. **pen·in'su·lar** adj.

pe·nis (pee-nis) n. (pl. **-nis·es, -nes,** pr. -neez) the organ by which a male animal copulates and (in mammals) urinates.

pen·i·tent (pen-i-těnt) adj. feeling or showing regret that one has done wrong. **penitent** n. a penitent person. **pen'i·tent·ly** adv. **pen'i·tence** n.

pen·i·ten·tial (pen-i-ten-shăl) adj. of penitence or penance.

pen·i·ten·tia·ry (pen-i-ten-shă-ree) n. a prison for offenders convicted of serious crimes.

pen·knife (pen-nıf) n. (pl. **-knives,** pr. -nıvz) a small folding knife, usually carried in a person's pocket.

pen·light (pen-lıt) n. a small flashlight shaped like a fountain pen.

pen·man (pen-măn) n. (pl. **-men,** pr. -měn) an expert in penmanship.

pen·man·ship (pen-măn-ship) n. skill in writing with a pen, his penmanship is poor.

Penn., Penna. abbr. Pennsylvania.

pen·nant (pen-ănt) n. 1. a long tapering flag flown on a ship. 2. a flag as a symbol of achievement; they won the American League Pennant, won the championship. □**pennant race,** the competition between baseball teams in a league.

pen·ni·less (pen-i-lis) adj. having no money, very poor, destitute.

pen·non (pen-ŏn) n. 1. a nautical flag, especially a long narrow triangular or swallow-tailed one. 2. a long pointed streamer on a ship.

Penn·syl·va·ni·a (pen-sĭl-vay-ni-ă) a state of the U.S. **Penn·syl·va'ni·an** adj. & n.

pen·ny (pen-ee) n. (pl. **-nies**) 1. a U.S. coin worth one cent. 2. a British coin worth one-hundredth of a pound. (▷The British plural form 20 pennies means 20 individual coins, just as it does in the U.S. See the note under **pence.**) 3. a very small sum of money, won't cost you a penny. □**penny ante,** a poker game played for small stakes; (informal) a trivial matter. **penny arcade,** an amusement area having coin-operated machines and games. **penny loafers,** (informal) loafers that have leather slots in front in which a penny or other coin is placed. **penny wise and pound foolish,** careful in small matters but wasteful in large ones. **pretty penny,** (informal) a large amount of money.

pen·ny-pinch·ing (pen-ee-pin-ching) adj. niggardly. **penny-pinching** n. niggardliness.

pen·ny·roy·al (pen-ee-roi-ăl) n. a species of mint, containing a pungent oil.

pen·ny·weight (pen-ee-wayt) n. a measure of weight = 24 grains, one-twentieth of a troy ounce.

pe·nol·o·gy (pi-nol-ŏ-jee) n. the scientific study of crime, its punishment, and prison management. **pe·nol'o·gist** n.

pen·sion (pen-shŏn) n. 1. a periodic payment made by the government or a former employer to a person who is retired, disabled, or widowed. 2. (pr. pen-syohn) a boarding house in Europe. **pension** v. 1. to pay a pension to. 2. to dismiss or allow to retire with a pension, pensioned him off.

pen·sion·er (pen-shŏ-něr) n. a person who receives a pension.

pen·sive (pen-siv) adj. deep in thought, thoughtful and gloomy. **pen'sive·ly** adv. **pen'sive·ness** n.

pen·stock (pen-stok) n. 1. a sluice or floodgate. 2. a channel for conveying water to a water wheel.

pent (pent) adj. shut in a confined space, pent in or up.

pen·ta·cle (pen-tă-kěl) n. a pentagram or other figure used as a symbol, especially in magic.

pen·ta·gon (pen-tă-gon) n. a geometric figure with five sides. □**the Pentagon,** a five-sided building near Washington, D.C., headquarters of the U.S. Department of Defense and of the leaders of the armed forces; the department itself.

pen·tag·o·nal (pen-tag-ŏ-năl) adj. five-sided.

pen·ta·gram (pen-tă-gram) n. a five-pointed star.

pen·tam·e·ter (pen-tam-ĕ-těr) n. a line of verse with five metrical feet.

Pen·ta·teuch (pen-tă-took) n. the first five books of the Old Testament.

pen·tath·lon (pen-tath-lon) n. an athletic contest in which each competitor takes part in the five events it includes.

Pen·te·cost (pen-tĕ-kawst) n. 1. the Jewish harvest festival (Shabuoth), falling fifty days after the second day of Passover. 2. the Christian festival commemorating the descent of the Holy Spirit upon the Apostles, falling on the seventh Sunday (Whitsunday) after Easter.

Pen·te·cos·tal (pen-tĕ-kaw-stăl) n. a member of a highly evangelistic Christian church. **Pentecostal** adj. **Pen·te·cos'tal·ism** n.

pent·house (pent-hows) n. (pl. **-hous·es,** pr. -how-ziz) an apartment (usually with a terrace) on the roof of a tall building.

pent-up (pent-up) adj. 1. shut in. 2. kept from being expressed openly, pent-up anger.

pe·nul·ti·mate (pi-nul-tĭ-mit) adj. next to last.

pe·num·bra (pi-num-bră) n. (pl. **-brae,** pr. -bree, **-bras**) the partly shaded region around the shadow of an opaque body, especially around the total shadow of the moon or Earth in eclipse.

pe·nu·ri·ous (pĭ-noor-i-ŭs) adj. 1. stingy. 2. poverty-stricken.

pen·u·ry (pen-yŭ-ree) n. extreme poverty.

pe·on (pee-on) n. a day laborer in Spanish America. **pe·on·age** (pee-ŏ-nij) n.

pe·o·ny (pee-ŏ-nee) n. (pl. **-nies**) a garden plant with large round red or pink or white flowers.

peo·ple (pee-pěl) n. pl. 1. human beings in general. 2. the persons belonging to a place or forming a group, the subjects or citizens of a state. 3. ordinary persons, those who have no special rank or authority. 4. a person's parents or other relatives. **people** n. sing. the persons composing a community or tribe or race or nation, a warlike people; the English-speaking peoples were united during the war. **people** v. (**peo·pled, peo·pling**) to fill (a place) with people, to populate.

pep (pep) n. vigor, energy. **pep** v. (**pepped, pep·ping**) (informal) to fill with vigor, to enliven, pep it up. **pep'py** adj. □**pep pill,** a pill containing a stimulant drug. **pep talk,** a talk urging the hearer(s) to great effort or courage.

pep·per (pep-ěr) n. 1. a hot-tasting powder made from the dried berries of certain plants, used to season food. 2. a kind of capsicum grown as a vegetable, its fruit used unripe (green pepper) or ripe (red or yellow pepper); sweet pepper, one with

a relatively mild taste. **pepper** *v.* 1. to sprinkle with pepper. 2. to pelt with small missiles. 3. to sprinkle here and there, *a speech peppered with jokes.* □**pepper box,** a small container with a perforated lid for sprinkling pepper on food.
pepper mill, a device for grinding peppercorns.
pepper pot, a West Indian stew of meat, vegetables, etc.
pep·per-and-salt (pep-ĕr-ăn-sawlt) *adj.* woven with light and dark threads producing an effect of small dots.
pep·per·corn (pep-ĕr-korn) *n.* the dried black berry from which pepper is made.
pep·per·mint (pep-ĕr-mint) *n.* 1. a kind of mint grown for its strong fragrant oil, used in medicine, candies, etc. 2. the oil itself. 3. a candy flavored with this.
pep·per·y (pep-ĕ-ree) *adj.* 1. like pepper, containing much pepper. 2. sharp-tongued. 3. easily angered.
pep·sin (pep-sin) *n.* an enzyme contained in gastric juice, helping to digest food.
pep·tic (pep-tik) *adj.* of digestion. □**peptic ulcer,** an ulcer in the stomach or duodenum.
per (pur, *unstressed* pĕr) *prep.* 1. for each, *$2 per gallon.* 2. *(informal)* in accordance with, *as per instructions; as per usual, (informal)* as usual. 3. *(old use)* by means of, *per post.* □**per an·num** (an-ŭm), for each year. **per cap·i·ta** (kap-i-tă), for each person. **per di·em** (dee-ŭm), for each day. ▷Many writers avoid the use of *per* except in business expressions.
per. *abbr.* 1. period. 2. person.
Per. *abbr.* 1. Persia. 2. Persian.
per·ad·ven·ture (pĕr-ăd-ven-chŭr) *n. (old use)* uncertainty, chance, conjecture, doubt.
per·am·bu·late (pĕr-am-byŭ-layt) *v.* (**per·am·bu·lat·ed, per·am·bu·lat·ing**) 1. to walk through or over or around (an area), to travel through and inspect. 2. to walk about. **per·am·bu·la·tion** (pĕr-am-byŭ-lay-shŏn) *n.*
per·am·bu·la·tor (pĕr-am-byŭ-lay-tŏr) *n.* a baby carriage.
per an. *abbr.* per annum.
per·cale (pĕr-kayl) *n.* a closely woven cotton fabric.
per·ceive (pĕr-seev) *v.* (**per·ceived, per·ceiv·ing**) to become aware of, to see or notice.
per·cent (pĕr-sent) *n.* a percentage, one part in every hundred. **percent** *adj. & adv.* in every hundred.
per·cent·age (pĕr-sen-tij) *n.* 1. a rate or proportion expressed as a percent. 2. a proportion or part.
per·cen·tile (pĕr-sen-tıl) *n.* (in statistics) one of 99 values of a variable dividing a population into 100 equal groups in regard to the value of that variable.
per·cep·ti·ble (pĕr-sep-tĭ-bĕl) *adj.* able to be perceived. **per·cep'ti·bly** *adv.* **per·cep·ti·bil·i·ty** (pĕr-sep-tĭ-bil-i-tee) *n.*
per·cep·tion (pĕr-sep-shŏn) *n.* perceiving, the ability to perceive.
per·cep·tive (pĕr-sep-tiv) *adj.* having or showing insight and sensitive understanding. **per·cep'tive·ly** *adv.* **per·cep'tive·ness** *n.*
per·cep·tu·al (pĕr-sep-choo-ăl) *adj.* of or involving perception. **per·cep'tu·al·ly** *adv.*
perch¹ (purch) *n.* 1. a bird's resting place (such as a branch), a bar or rod provided for this purpose. 2. a high place or narrow ledge etc. on which

a person sits or positions himself. **perch** *v.* to rest or place on or as if on a perch.
perch² *n.* (*pl.* **perch**) an edible freshwater fish with spiny fins.
per·chance (pĕr-chans) *adv. (old use)* perhaps.
per·cip·i·ent (pĕr-sip-i-ĕnt) *adj.* perceiving, perceptive. **per·cip'i·ence** *n.*
per·co·late (pur-kŏ-layt) *v.* (**per·co·lat·ed, per·co·lat·ing**) 1. to filter or cause to filter, especially through small holes. 2. to prepare (coffee) in a percolator. **per·co·la·tion** (pur-kŏ-lay-shŏn) *n.*
per·co·la·tor (pur-kŏ-lay-tŏr) *n.* a pot in which coffee is made and served, in which boiling water is made to circulate repeatedly up a central tube and downward through ground coffee held in a perforated drum near the top.
per·cus·sion (pĕr-kush-ŏn) *n.* 1. the striking of one object against another. 2. the percussion instruments in an orchestra. **per·cus'sion·ist** *n.*
□**percussion cap,** a small metal device containing explosive powder that explodes when it is struck, used as a detonator. **percussion instrument,** a musical instrument (such as drum, cymbals, tambourine) played by striking.
per·di·tion (pĕr-dish-ŏn) *n.* eternal damnation.
per·dur·a·ble (pĕr-door-ă-bĕl) *adj.* very durable, permanent. **per·dur·a·bil·i·ty** (pĕr-door-ă-bil-i-tee) *n.*
per·e·gri·na·tion (per-ĕ-grĭ-nay-shŏn) *n.* traveling, a journey.
per·e·grine (per-ĕ-grin) *n.* (also **peregrine falcon**) a kind of falcon that can be trained to hunt and catch small animals and birds.
per·emp·to·ry (pĕ-remp-tŏ-ree) *adj.* imperious, insisting on obedience, *a peremptory order.* **per·emp·to·ri·ly** (pĕ-remp-tŏ-ri-lee) *adv.*
per·en·ni·al (pĕ-ren-i-ăl) *adj.* 1. lasting a long time or forever, constantly recurring, *a perennial problem.* 2. (of a plant) living for several years. **perennial** *n.* a perennial plant. **per·en'ni·al·ly** *adv.*
perf. *abbr.* 1. perfect. 2. perforated.
per·fect (pur-fikt) *adj.* 1. complete, having all its essential qualities. 2. faultless, excellent. 3. exact, precise, *a perfect circle.* 4. entire, total, *a perfect stranger.* **perfect** (pĕr-fekt) *v.* to make perfect.
perfect (pur-fikt) *n.* the perfect tense. □**perfect tense,** a tense indicating a completed action or event viewed in relation to the present or to a specified time. (See **tense.**)
per·fec·ta (pĕr-fek-tă) *n.* a system of betting in which the bettor must name the first and second horses or dogs to finish in a race.
per·fect·i·ble (pĕr-fek-tĭ-bĕl) *adj.* able to be perfected. **per·fect·i·bil·i·ty** (pĕr-fek-tĭ-bil-i-tee) *n.*
per·fec·tion (pĕr-fek-shŏn) *n.* 1. making or being perfect. 2. a person or thing considered perfect. □**to perfection,** perfectly.
per·fec·tion·ist (pĕr-fek-shŏ-nist) *n.* a person who is satisfied with nothing less than what he thinks is perfect. **per·fec'tion·ism** *n.*
per·fect·ly (pur-fikt-lee) *adv.* 1. in a perfect way. 2. completely, quite, *perfectly satisfied.*
per·fec·to (pĕr-fek-toh) *n.* (*pl.* **-tos**) a large thick cigar pointed at each end.
per·fid·i·ous (pĕr-fid-i-ŭs) *adj.* treacherous, disloyal. **per·fid'i·ous·ly** *adv.* **per·fi·dy** (pur-fi-dee) *n.* (*pl.* **-dies**).
per·fo·rate (pur-fŏ-rayt) *v.* 1. to make a hole or

holes through, to pierce with a row or rows of tiny holes so that part(s) can be torn off easily. **2.** to penetrate. **per·fo·ra·tion** (pur-fŏ-ray-shŏn) *n.*

per·force (pĕr-fohrs) *adv.* by force of circumstances, necessarily.

per·form (pĕr-form) *v.* **1.** to carry into effect, to accomplish, to do. **2.** to go through (a particular proceeding), to execute, *performed the ceremony.* **3.** to function, *the car performed well when tested.* **4.** to act in a play etc., to play an instrument or sing or do tricks before an audience. **per·form'er** *n.* ☐**performing arts,** those arts, such as drama etc., that require public performance.

per·for·mance (pĕr-for-măns) *n.* **1.** the process or manner of performing. **2.** a notable action or achievement. **3.** the performing of a play or other entertainment, *two performances a day.*

per·fume (pur-fyoom, pĕr-fyoom) *n.* **1.** a sweet smell. **2.** a fragrant liquid for giving a pleasant smell, especially to the body. **perfume** (pĕr-fyoom) *v.* **(per·fumed, per·fum·ing)** to give a sweet smell to, to apply perfume to.

per·fum·er·y (pĕr-fyoo-mĕ-ree) *n.* (*pl.* **-er·ies**) perfumes, the preparation of these.

per·func·to·ry (pĕr-fungk-tŏ-ree) *adj.* **1.** done as a duty or routine but without much care or interest. **2.** (of a person) acting in this way. **per·func'to·ri·ly** *adv.* **per·func'to·ri·ness** *n.*

per·go·la (pur-gŏ-lă) *n.* an arbor or covered walk formed of climbing plants trained over trellises.

perh. *abbr.* perhaps.

per·haps (pĕr-haps) *adv.* it may be, possibly.

per·i·car·di·um (per-ĭ-kahr-di-ŭm) *n.* (*pl.* **-di·a,** *pr.* -di-ă) the membranous sac enclosing the heart.

per·i·carp (per-ĭ-kahrp) *n.* a vessel containing seed formed from the wall of a ripened ovary or fruit.

per·i·gee (per-ĭ-jee) *n.* the point (in the orbit of the moon, a planet, or an artificial satellite) nearest to Earth.

per·i·he·li·on (per-ĭ-hee-li-ŏn) *n.* (*pl.* **-he·li·a,** *pr.* -hee-li-ă) the point (of a planet's or comet's orbit) nearest to the sun.

per·il (per-ĭl) *n.* serious danger.

per·il·ous (per-ĭ-lŭs) *adj.* full of risk, dangerous. **per'il·ous·ly** *adv.*

per·i·lune (per-ĭ-loon) *n.* the point in an object's orbit about the moon where it is closest to the moon's center.

pe·rim·e·ter (pĕ-rim-ĕ-tĕr) *n.* **1.** the outer edge or boundary of a closed geometric figure or of an area. **2.** the length of this.

per·i·ne·um (per-ĭ-nee-ŭm) *n.* (*pl.* **-ne·a,** *pr.* -nee-ă) the region of the body between the anus and the scrotum or vulva. **per·i·ne'al** *adj.*

pe·ri·od (peer-i-ŏd) *n.* **1.** a length or portion of time. **2.** a time with particular characteristics, *the colonial period.* **3.** the time allotted for a lesson in school. **4.** an occurrence of menstruation. **5.** a mark of punctuation . used at the end of a sentence, to indicate an abbreviation etc. **6.** the geologic time forming part of an era. **period** *adj.* (of furniture or dress or architecture) belonging to a past age.

pe·ri·od·ic (peer-i-od-ik) *adj.* occurring or appearing at intervals. ☐**periodic table,** a chart depicting the arrangement of elements in order of atomic numbers and in which elements of similar chemical properties appear at regular intervals.

pe·ri·od·i·cal (peer-i-od-i-kăl) *adj.* periodic.

periodical *n.* a magazine etc. published at regular intervals. **pe·ri·od'i·cal·ly** *adv.*

per·i·o·don·tal (per-i-ŏ-don-tăl) *adj.* of the tissues surrounding and supporting the teeth.

per·i·pa·tet·ic (per-i-pă-tet-ik) *adj.* going from place to place.

pe·riph·er·al (pĕ-rif-ĕ-răl) *adj.* **1.** of or on the periphery. **2.** of minor importance to something.

pe·riph·er·y (pĕ-rif-ĕ-ree) *n.* (*pl.* **-er·ies**) **1.** the boundary of a surface or area, the region immediately inside or beyond this. **2.** the fringes of a subject etc.

pe·riph·ra·sis (pĕ-rif-ră-sis) *n.* (*pl.* **-ses,** *pr.* -seez) a roundabout phrase or way of speaking, a circumlocution.

per·i·scope (per-ĭ-skohp) *n.* an apparatus with a tube and mirror(s) by which a person in a trench or submerged submarine or at the rear of a crowd etc. can see things that are otherwise out of sight.

per·ish (per-ish) *v.* **1.** to suffer destruction, to become extinct, to die a violent or untimely death. **2.** to distress or wither by cold or exposure.

per·ish·a·ble (per-i-shă-bĕl) *adj.* liable to decay or go bad in a short time.

per·ish·a·bles (per-i-shă-bĕlz) *n. pl.* perishable foods.

per·i·stal·sis (per-ĭ-stawl-sis) *n.* (*pl.* **-ses,** *pr.* -seez) the automatic muscular movement, consisting of successive wavelike contractions and relaxations, by which the contents of the alimentary canal etc. are propelled along it. **per·i·stal·tic** (per-ĭ-stawl-tik) *adj.*

per·i·style (per-ĭ-stɪl) *n.* **1.** a row of columns surrounding a temple, court, building, etc. **2.** the space so surrounded.

per·i·to·ne·um (per-ĭ-tŏ-nee-ŭm) *n.* the membrane lining the abdomen.

per·i·to·ni·tis (per-ĭ-tŏ-nɪ-tis) *n.* inflammation of the peritoneum.

per·i·wig (per-ĭ-wig) *n.* (*old use*) a wig.

per·i·win·kle[1] (per-i-wing-kĕl) *n.* an evergreen trailing plant with blue or white flowers. **periwinkle**[2] *n.* an edible small sea snail.

per·jure (pur-jŭr) *v.* **(per·jured, per·jur·ing) perjure oneself,** to make a perjured statement. **per'jur·er** *n.*

per·ju·ry (pur-jŭ-ree) *n.* (*pl.* **-ries**) the deliberate giving of false evidence while on oath, the evidence itself.

perk[1] (purk) *v.* to raise (the head etc.) briskly or jauntily. ☐**perk up,** to regain or cause to regain courage or confidence or vitality.

perk[2] *n.* (*informal*) a perquisite.

perk[3] *v.* (*informal*) to percolate (coffee), to bubble up in a percolator.

perk·y (pur-kee) *adj.* **(perk·i·er, perk·i·est)** lively and cheerful. **perk'i·ly** *adv.* **perk'i·ness** *n.*

per·lite (pur-lɪt) *n.* a volcanic rock, expandable by heating, used in insulating material, concrete, etc.

perm. *abbr.* permanent.

per·ma·frost (pur-mă-frawst) *n.* the permanently frozen subsoil in polar regions.

per·ma·nent (pur-mă-nĕnt) *adj.* lasting or meant to last indefinitely. **permanent** *n.* a permanent wave. **per'ma·nent·ly** *adv.* **per'ma·nence** *n.* **per·ma·nen·cy** (pur-mă-nĕn-see) *n.* ☐**permanent press,** (of a fabric) requiring little or no ironing because of its wrinkle-resistant quality. **permanent wave,** a long-lasting artificial wave in the hair.

per·me·a·ble (pur-mi-ă-běl) *adj.* able to be permeated by fluids etc. **per·me·a·bil·i·ty** (pur-mi-ă-bil-i-tee) *n.*

per·me·ate (pur-mi-ayt) *v.* to pass or flow or spread into every part of. **per·me·a·tion** (pur-mi-ay-shŏn) *n.*

Per·mi·an (per-mi-ăn) *adj.* of the latest geologic period of the Paleozoic era. **Permian** *n.* the Permian period.

per·mis·si·ble (pěr-mis-ĭ-běl) *adj.* such as may be permitted, allowable. **per·mis′si·bly** *adv.*

per·mis·sion (pěr-mish-ŏn) *n.* consent or authorization to do something.

per·mis·sive (pěr-mis-iv) *adj.* 1. giving permission. 2. tolerant, allowing much freedom in social conduct and sexual matters, or in raising children. **per·mis′sive·ness** *n.*

per·mit (pěr-mit) *v.* (**per·mit·ted, per·mit·ting**) 1. to give permission or consent, to authorize. 2. to give opportunity, to make possible, *weather permitting.* **permit** (pur-mit) *n.* a written order giving permission, especially for entry into a place. ▷See the note under **allow.**

per·mu·ta·tion (pur-myū-tay-shŏn) *n.* 1. variation of the order of a set of things. 2. any one of these arrangements.

per·mute (pěr-myoot) *v.* (**per·mut·ed, per·mut·ing**) to vary the order or arrangement of.

per·ni·cious (pěr-nish-ŭs) *adj.* having a very harmful effect. **per·ni′cious·ly** *adv.* □**pernicious anemia,** a severe progressive frequently fatal form of anemia.

per·o·ra·tion (per-ŏ-ray-shŏn) *n.* a lengthy speech, the last part of this.

per·ox·ide (pě-rok-sɪd) *n.* 1. a compound containing the maximum proportion of oxygen. 2. hydrogen peroxide (*see* **hydrogen**). **peroxide** *v.* (**per·ox·id·ed, per·ox·id·ing**) to bleach with hydrogen peroxide.

perp. *abbr.* perpendicular.

per·pen·dic·u·lar (pur-pěn-dik-yŭ-lăr) *adj.* 1. at a right angle (90°) to another line or surface. 2. upright, at right angles to the horizontal. 3. (of a cliff etc.) having a vertical face. 4. *Perpendicular,* of the style of English Gothic architecture in the 14th–15th centuries, with vertical tracery in large windows. **perpendicular** *n.* a perpendicular line or direction. **per·pen·dic′u·lar·ly** *adv.* **per·pen·dic·u·lar·i·ty** (pur-pěn-dik-yŭ-lar-i-tee) *n.*

per·pe·trate (pur-pě-trayt) *v.* (**per·pe·trat·ed, per·pe·trat·ing**) to commit (a crime or error), to be guilty of (a blunder etc.). **per·pe·tra·tion** (pur-pě-tray-shŏn) *n.* **per′pe·tra·tor** *n.*

per·pet·u·al (pěr-pech-oo-ăl) *adj.* 1. lasting for a long time, not ceasing. 2. (*informal*) frequent, often repeated, *this perpetual quarreling.* **per·pet′u·al·ly** *adv.* □**perpetual calendar,** one that can be used for any year or over a long period.

per·pet·u·ate (pěr-pech-oo-ayt) *v.* (**per·pet·u·at·ed, per·pet·u·at·ing**) to preserve from being forgotten or from going out of use, *his invention will perpetuate his memory.* **per·pet·u·a·tion** (pěr-pech-oo-ay-shŏn) *n.*

per·pe·tu·i·ty (pur-pě-too-i-tee) *n.* (*pl.* **-ties**) the state or quality of being perpetual. □**in perpetuity,** forever.

per·plex (pěr-pleks) *v.* 1. to bewilder, to puzzle. 2. to make more complicated.

per·plex·ed·ly (pěr-plek-sid-lee) *adv.* in a perplexed way.

per·plex·i·ty (pěr-plek-si-tee) *n.* (*pl.* **-ties**) bewilderment.

per·qui·site (pur-kwi-zit) *n.* a profit or allowance or privilege etc. given or looked upon as one's right in addition to wages or salary. ▷Do not confuse *perquisite* with *prerequisite.*

Pers. *abbr.* 1. Persia. 2. Persian.

per se (pěr say) by or in itself, intrinsically. ▷Latin.

per·se·cute (pur-sě-kyoot) *v.* (**per·se·cut·ed, per·se·cut·ing**) 1. to subject to constant hostility or cruel treatment, especially because of religious or political beliefs. 2. to harass. **per′se·cu·tor** *n.* **per·se·cu·tion** (pur-sě-kyoo-shŏn) *n.* □**persecution complex,** an insane delusion that one is being persecuted. ▷Do not confuse *persecute* with *prosecute.*

per·se·vere (pur-sě-veer) *v.* (**per·se·vered, per·se·ver·ing**) to continue steadfastly, especially in something that is difficult or tedious. **per·se·ver·ance** (pur-sě-veer-ăns) *n.*

Per·sia (pur-zhă) the ancient and now the alternative name of Iran.

Per·sian (pur-zhăn) *adj.* of Persia or its people or language. **Persian** *n.* 1. a native or inhabitant of Persia. 2. the language of Persia. 3. a Persian cat. □**Persian cat,** a cat of a breed that has long silky fur. **Persian lamb,** the silky tightly curled fur of lambs of a kind of Asian sheep.

per·si·flage (pur-sĭ-flahzh) *n.* banter.

per·sim·mon (pěr-sim-ŏn) *n.* 1. an American or East Asian tree bearing a red-orange edible plum-like fruit. 2. this fruit.

per·sist (pěr-sist) *v.* 1. to continue firmly or obstinately, *she persists in breaking the rules.* 2. to continue to exist, *the custom persists in some areas.* **per·sist′ent** *adj.* **per·sist′ent·ly** *adv.* **per·sist′ence** *n.* **per·sist′en·cy** *n.*

per·snick·et·y (pěr-snik-ě-tee) *adj.* (*informal*) fastidious, scrupulous.

per·son (pur-sŏn) *n.* 1. an individual human being. 2. the living body of a human being; *offenses against the person,* bodily attacks etc. 3. (in Christian doctrine) one of the three modes of being of the Godhead; *the three Persons of the Trinity,* the Father (*First Person*), the Son (*Second Person*), the Holy Spirit (*Third Person*). 4. (in grammar) any of the three classes of personal pronouns and verb forms, referring to the person speaking (*first person,* = I, me, we, us), or spoken to (*second person,* = thee, thou, you), or spoken of (*third person,* = he, him, she, her, it, they, them). □**in person,** physically present.

per·son·a·ble (pur-sŏ-nă-běl) *adj.* having a pleasing manner, good-looking.

per·son·age (pur-sŏ-nij) *n.* a person, especially one of importance or distinction.

per·son·al (pur-sŏ-năl) *adj.* 1. one's own or a particular person's own, *will give it my personal attention.* 2. of one's own or another's private life, *a personal matter.* 3. making remarks about a person's appearance or his private affairs, especially in a critical or hostile way, *let's not become personal.* 4. done or made etc. in person, *several personal appearances.* 5. of the body and clothing, *personal hygiene.* 6. existing as a person, *a personal God.* □**personal column** *or* **personals,** a column of private messages or advertisements in a newspaper. **personal effects,** articles belonging to a person, such as clothing. **personal pronoun,** *see* **pronoun.** ▷Do not confuse *personal* with *personnel.*

per·son·al·i·ty (pur-sŏ-nal-i-tee) *n.* (*pl.* **-ties**) 1. a person's own distinctive character. 2. a person with distinctive qualities, especially pleasing ones. 3. a celebrity. ☐**personality cult,** veneration of a famous or successful person, hero worship.

per·son·al·ize (pur-sŏ-nă-lɪz) v. (**per·son·al·ized, per·son·al·iz·ing**) to make personal, especially by marking as one's own property.

per·son·al·ly (pur-sŏ-nă-lee) adv. 1. in person, not through an agent, showed us around personally. 2. as a person, in a personal capacity, we don't know him personally. 3. in a personal manner, don't take it personally. 4. as regards oneself, personally, I like it.

per·so·na non gra·ta (pĕr-soh-nă non grah-tă) (pl. **per·so·nae non gra·tae**, pr. pĕr-soh-nee non grah-tee) a person not acceptable to certain others. ▷Latin.

per·son·ate (pur-sŏ-nayt) v. (**per·son·at·ed, per·son·at·ing**) to impersonate.

per·son·i·fy (pĕr-son-ĭ-fɪ) v. (**per·son·i·fied, per·son·i·fy·ing**) 1. to represent (an idea) in human form or (a thing) as having human characteristics, Justice is personified as a blindfolded woman holding a pair of scales. 2. to embody in one's life or behavior, he was meanness personified. **per·son·i·fi·ca·tion** (pĕr-son-ĭ-fĭ-kay-shŏn) n.

per·son·nel (pur-sŏ-nel) n. 1. the body of people employed in any work, staff. 2. the department (in a business firm etc.) dealing with employees and their problems and welfare. ▷Do not confuse personnel with personal.

per·spec·tive (pĕr-spek-tiv) n. 1. the art of drawing solid objects on a flat surface so as to give an impression of their relative position, size, solidity, etc. 2. the apparent relationship between visible objects as to position, distance, etc. 3. a view of a visible scene or of facts and events. 4. a mental picture of the relative importance of things. ☐**in perspective,** drawn according to the rules of perspective; with its relative importance understood.

per·spi·ca·cious (pur-spi-kay-shŭs) adj. having or showing great insight. **per·spi·ca'cious·ly** adv. **per·spi·cac·i·ty** (pur-spi-kas-i-tee) n. ▷Do not confuse perspicacious with perspicuous.

per·spic·u·ous (pĕr-spik-yoo-ŭs) adj. easily understood, clearly expressed. **per·spi·cu·i·ty** (pur-spi-kyoo-i-tee) n. ▷Do not confuse perspicuous with perspicacious.

per·spire (pĕr-spɪr) v. (**per·spired, per·spir·ing**) to sweat. **per·spi·ra·tion** (pur-spi-ray-shŏn) n.

per·suad·a·ble (pĕr-sway-dă-bĕl) adj. able to be persuaded.

per·suade (pĕr-swayd) v. (**per·suad·ed, per·suad·ing**) to cause (a person) to believe or do something by reasoning with him.

per·sua·sion (pĕr-sway-zhŏn) n. 1. persuading, being persuaded. 2. persuasiveness. 3. belief, especially religious belief, people of the same persuasion.

per·sua·sive (pĕr-sway-siv) adj. able or trying to persuade. **per·sua'sive·ly** adv. **per·sua'sive·ness** n.

pert (purt) adj. 1. cheeky. 2. lively. **pert'ly** adv. **pert'ness** n.

PERT (purt) n. program evaluation and review technique.

pert. abbr. pertaining.

per·tain (pĕr-tayn) v. 1. to be relevant, evidence pertaining to the case. 2. to belong as part, the responsibilities pertaining to high office.

per·ti·na·cious (pur-tĭ-nay-shŭs) adj. holding firmly to an opinion or course of action, persistent and determined. **per·ti·na'cious·ly** adv. **per·ti·nac·i·ty** (pur-tĭ-nas-i-tee) n.

per·ti·nent (pur-tĭ-nĕnt) adj. pertaining, relevant. **per'ti·nent·ly** adv. **per'ti·nence** n.

per·turb (pĕr-turb) v. to disturb greatly, to make anxious or uneasy. **per·tur·ba·tion** (pur-tŭr-bay-shŏn) n. **per·turb'a·ble** adj. **per·turb'ed·ly** adv. **per·turb·a·bil·i·ty** (pĕr-tur-bă-bil-i-tee) n.

Pe·ru (pĕ-roo) a country in South America. **Pe·ru·vi·an** (pĕ-roo-vi-ăn) adj. & n.

pe·ruke (pĕ-rook) n. (old use) a wig.

pe·ruse (pĕ-rooz) v. (**pe·rused, pe·rus·ing**) to read or examine (printed material), especially with great care. **pe·rus'al** n.

per·vade (pĕr-vayd) v. (**per·vad·ed, per·vad·ing**) to spread or be present throughout, to permeate, a pervading atmosphere of optimism. **per·va·sion** (pĕr-vay-zhŏn) n.

per·va·sive (pĕr-vay-siv) adj. pervading. **per·va'sive·ness** n.

per·verse (pĕr-vurs) adj. 1. obstinately doing something different from what is reasonable or required, intractable. 2. indicating or characterized by a tendency of this kind, a perverse satisfaction. **per·verse'ly** adv. **per·verse'ness** n. **per·ver·si·ty** (pĕr-vur-si-tee) n. (pl. -ties). ▷Do not confuse perverse with perverted.

per·ver·sion (pĕr-vur-zhŏn) n. 1. perverting, being perverted. 2. a perverted form of something. 3. a preference for a form of sexual activity that is considered abnormal or unacceptable.

per·vert (pĕr-vurt) v. 1. to turn (a thing) from its proper course or use, pervert the course of justice. 2. to lead astray from right behavior or beliefs, to corrupt. **pervert** (pur-vĕrt) n. a perverted person, one showing perversion of sexual instincts. ▷Do not confuse perverted with perverse.

pe·se·ta (pĕ-say-tă) n. the unit of money in Spain.

pes·ky (pes-kee) adj. (**pes·ki·er, pes·ki·est**) (informal) troublesome, annoying.

pe·so (pay-soh) n. (pl. -sos) the unit of money in many Latin-American countries, and in the Philippines.

pes·sa·ry (pes-ă-ree) n. (pl. -ries) a device placed in the vagina to prevent displacement of the womb or as a contraceptive.

pes·si·mism (pes-ĭ-miz-ĕm) n. a tendency to take a gloomy view of things or to expect that results will be bad. **pes'si·mist** n.

pes·si·mis·tic (pes-ĭ-mis-tik) adj. showing pessimism. **pes·si·mis'ti·cal·ly** adv.

pest (pest) n. 1. a troublesome or annoying person or thing. 2. an insect or animal that is destructive to cultivated plants or to stored food etc.

pes·ter (pes-tĕr) v. to make persistent requests, to annoy with frequent requests or questions.

pes·ti·cide (pes-tĭ-sɪd) n. a substance for destroying harmful insects etc.

pes·tif·er·ous (pe-stif-ĕ-rŭs) adj. troublesome.

pes·ti·lence (pes-tĭ-lĕns) n. a deadly epidemic disease.

pes·ti·lent (pes-tĭ-lĕnt) adj. harmful to life or to society.

pes·ti·len·tial (pes-tĭ-len-shăl) adj. troublesome, pernicious. **pes·ti·len'tial·ly** adv.

pes·tle (pes-ĕl) n. a club-shaped instrument for pounding substances in a mortar.

pet¹ (pet) n. 1. an animal that is tamed and treated

with affection, kept for companionship or amusement. **2.** a darling or favorite. **pet** *adj.* **1.** kept or treated as a pet, *pet lamb.* **2.** favorite; *pet aversion,* something one particularly dislikes. **pet** *v.* (**pet·ted, pet·ting**) **1.** to stroke gently with affection. **2.** *(informal)* to kiss and fondle. □**pet name,** a name (other than the real name) used affectionately.

pet² *n.* offense at being slighted; *he's in a pet,* sulking.

pet. *abbr.* petroleum.

pet·al (pet-ăl) *n.* one of the bright or delicately colored outer parts of a flower head.

pe·tard (pi-tahrd) *n.* *(old use)* a kind of small bombshell; *hoist with his own petard,* injured by his own devices against others.

pe·ter (pee-tĕr) *v.* **peter out,** to diminish gradually and cease to exist.

Pe·ter (pee-tĕr) *n.* **1.** one of the twelve Apostles. **2.** either of two books of the New Testament ascribed to him.

pet·i·ole (pet-i-ohl) *n.* a slender stalk joining leaf to stem.

pe·tit (pet-ee) *adj.* **petit bourgeois,** a member of the lower middle class. **petit four,** a small fancy cake. **petit jury,** a jury convened to hear civil or criminal cases at trial, as distinct from a *grand jury* (*see* **grand**). **petit larceny,** larceny involving property of small value. **petit mal,** a mild form of epilepsy without loss of consciousness. **petit point,** embroidery on canvas using small stitches.

pe·tite (pĕ-teet) *adj.* (of a woman) of small dainty build.

pe·ti·tion (pĕ-tish-ŏn) *n.* **1.** an earnest request. **2.** a formal document appealing to an authority for a right or benefit etc., especially one signed by a large number of people. **3.** a formal application made to a court of law for a writ or order etc. **petition** *v.* to make or address a petition to. **pe·ti'tion·er** *n.*

pet·rel (pet-rĕl) *n.* a kind of seabird that flies far from land.

pet·ri·fy (pet-rĭ-fɪ) *v.* (**pet·ri·fied, pet·ri·fy·ing**) **1.** to change or cause to change into a stony mass. **2.** to paralyze or stun with astonishment or fear etc. **pet·ri·fi·ca·tion** (pet-rĭ-fĭ-kay-shŏn) *n.*

pet·ro·chem·i·cal (pet-roh-kem-i-kăl) *n.* a chemical substance obtained from petroleum or natural gas. **pet·ro·chem·is·try** (pet-roh-kem-i-stree) *n.*

pet·ro·dol·lar (pet-rŏ-dol-ăr) *n.* a dollar earned by a country that exports petroleum (= oil).

pe·trog·ra·phy (pi-trog-ră-fee) *n.* the scientific description of the composition and formation of rocks. **pe·trog'ra·pher** *n.* **pet·ro·graph·ic** (pet-rŏ-graf-ik) *adj.* **pet·ro·graph'i·cal** *adj.*

pet·rol (pet-rŏl) *n.* *(British)* gasoline.

pet·ro·la·tum (pet-rŏ-lay-tŭm) *n.* petroleum jelly.

pe·tro·le·um (pĕ-troh-li-ŭm) *n.* a mineral oil found underground, refined for use as fuel (as, gasoline, kerosene) or for use in dry cleaning etc. □**petroleum jelly,** a greasy translucent substance obtained from petroleum, used as a lubricant etc.

pe·trol·o·gy (pi-trol-ŏ-jee) *n.* the scientific study of the origin, structure, etc. of rocks. **pe·trol'o·gist** *n.* **pet·ro·log·ic** (pet-rŏ-loj-ik) *adj.* **pet·ro·log'i·cal** *adj.* **pet·ro·log'i·cal·ly** *adv.*

pet·ti·coat (pet-i-koht) *n.* a woman's or girl's dress-length undergarment worn hanging from the shoulders or waist beneath a dress or skirt. □**petticoat government,** *(contemptuous)* dominance of women in the home or in politics.

pet·ti·fog (pet-i-fog) *v.* (**pet·ti·fogged, pet·ti·fog·ging**) **1.** to quibble. **2.** to engage in legal trickery. **pet'ti·fog·ger** *n.*

pet·ting (pet-ing) *n.* **1.** affectionate treatment. **2.** *(informal)* kissing and fondling.

pet·tish (pet-ish) *adj.* peevish, irritable or unreasonably impatient. **pet'tish·ly** *adv.* **pet'tish·ness** *n.*

pet·ty (pet-ee) *adj.* (**pet·ti·er, pet·ti·est**) **1.** unimportant, trivial, *petty details; petty jury* = petit jury (*see* **petit**); *petty larceny* = petit larceny (*see* **petit**). **2.** small-minded, *petty spite.* **pet'ti·ly** *adv.* **pet'ti·ness** *n.* □**petty cash,** a small amount of money kept by an office etc. for or from small payments. **petty officer,** a noncommissioned officer in the navy.

pet·u·lant (pech-ŭ-lănt) *adj.* peevish, unreasonably impatient. **pet'u·lant·ly** *adv.* **pet'u·lance** *n.*

pe·tu·nia (pĕ-too-nyă) *n.* a garden plant with funnel-shaped flowers in bright colors.

pew (pyoo) *n.* one of the long bench-like seats with a back and sides, usually fixed in rows, for the congregation in a church.

pe·wee (pee-wee) *n.* a phoebe.

pew·ter (pyoo-tĕr) *n.* **1.** a gray alloy of tin with lead or other metal, used for making mugs and dishes etc. **2.** articles made of this.

pe·yo·te (pay-oh-tee) *n.* **1.** a Mexican cactus. **2.** the hallucinogenic drug prepared from this plant.

pf. *abbr.* **1.** pfennig. **2.** preferred.

PFC *abbr.* private first class.

pfd. *abbr.* preferred.

pfen·nig (fen-ig) *n.* (*pl.* **pfen·nigs, pfen·ni·ge,** *pr.* fen-i-gĕ) a German coin worth one-hundredth of a mark.

PG *abbr.* **1.** parental guidance. **2.** postgraduate.

pg. *abbr.* page.

pH (pee-aych) *n.* a measure of the acidity or alkalinity of a solution.

pha·e·ton (fay-ĕ-tŏn) *n.* an old type of open horse-drawn carriage with four wheels.

phage (fayj) *n.* a bacteriophage.

pha·lanx (fay-langks, fal-angks) *n.* (*pl.* **pha·lanx·es, pha·lan·ges,** *pr.* fă-lan-jeez) a number of people forming a compact mass or banded together for a common purpose.

phal·a·rope (fal-ă-rohp) *n.* a small wading and swimming bird resembling the sandpiper.

phal·lic (fal-ik) *adj.* of or resembling a model of the penis (phallus) in erection, symbolizing generative power in nature, *phallic emblems.* **phal'lus** *n.* (*pl.* **phal·li,** *pr.* fal-ɪ, **phal·lus·es**).

phan·tasm (fan-taz-ĕm) *n.* a phantom.

phan·tas·ma·go·ri·a (fan-taz-mă-gohr-i-ă) *n.* a rapidly shifting scene of real or imagined figures.

phan·tom (fan-tŏm) *n.* **1.** a ghost, an apparition. **2.** something without reality, as seen in a dream or vision, *phantom ships.* **phan'tom·like** *adj.*

Phar·aoh (fair-oh) *n.* the title of the king of ancient Egypt.

Phar·i·see (far-ɪ-see) *n.* **1.** a member of an ancient Jewish sect that practiced strict observation of religious laws and is represented in the New Testament as making a show of sanctity and piety. **2.** *pharisee,* a hypocritical self-righteous person. **phar·i·sa·ic** (far-ɪ-say-ik) *adj.* **phar·i·sa'i·cal** *adj.* **phar·i·sa'i·cal·ly** *adv.*

pharm. *abbr.* 1. pharmaceutical. 2. pharmacist. 3. pharmacy.

phar·ma·ceu·ti·cal (fahr-mă-soo-ti-kăl), **phar·ma·ceu·tic** (fahr-mă-soo-tik) *adj.* of or engaged in pharmacy, of medicinal drugs. **pharmaceutical** *n.* a pharmaceutical product.

phar·ma·cist (fahr-mă-sist) *n.* a person engaged in pharmacy, a druggist.

phar·ma·col·o·gy (fahr-mă-kol-ŏ-jee) *n.* the scientific study of medicinal drugs and their effects on the body. **phar·ma·col·o·gist** *n.* **phar·ma·co·log·ic** (fahr-mă-kŏ-loj-ik) *adj.* **phar·ma·co·log'i·cal** *adj.*

phar·ma·co·poe·ia, **phar·ma·co·pe·ia** (fahr-mă-kŏ-pee-ă) *n.* 1. a book containing a list of medicinal drugs with directions for their use. 2. a stock of medicinal drugs.

phar·ma·cy (fahr-mă-see) *n.* (*pl.* **-cies**) 1. the preparation and dispensing of medicinal drugs. 2. a drugstore.

phar·os (fair-os) *n.* a lighthouse or beacon to guide ships at sea.

phar·yn·gi·tis (far-in-jɪ-tis) *n.* inflammation of the pharynx.

phar·ynx (far-ingks) *n.* (*pl.* **pha·ryn·ges**, *pr.* fă-rin-jeez, **phar·ynx·es**) the cavity at the back of the nose and throat. **pha·ryn·ge·al** (fă-rin-ji-ăl) *adj.*

phase (fayz) *n.* 1. a stage of change or development or of a recurring sequence of changes. 2. any of the forms in which the moon or a planet appears when part or all of its disk is seen illuminated (new moon, first quarter, full moon, last quarter). **phase** *v.* (**phased, phas·ing**) to carry out (a program etc.) in stages. □**phase in** *or* **out**, to bring gradually into or out of use.

Ph.D. *abbr.* Doctor of Philosophy.

pheas·ant (fez-ănt) *n.* 1. a long-tailed game bird with bright feathers. 2. its flesh as food.

phe·nac·e·tin (fĕ-nas-ĕ-tin) *n.* a medicinal drug used to reduce fever.

phe·no·bar·bi·tal (fee-noh-bahr-bĭ-tawl) *n.* a medicinal drug used to calm the nerves and induce sleep.

phe·nom (fi-nom) *n.* (*slang*) a phenomenal person.

phe·nom·e·nal (fi-nom-ĕ-năl) *adj.* extraordinary, remarkable. **phe·nom'e·nal·ly** *adv.*

phe·nom·e·non (fi-nom-ĕ-non) *n.* (*pl.* **-na**, *pr.* -nă) 1. a fact or occurrence or change perceived by any of the senses or by the mind, *snow is a common phenomenon in winter.* 2. a remarkable person or thing, a wonder.

phe·no·type (fee-nŏ-tɪp) *n.* the set of observable characteristics of an individual or group as determined by the genotype and the environment.

pher·o·mone (fer-ŏ-mohn) *n.* a substance secreted and released by an animal for detection and response by another of the same species. **pher·o·mo·nal** (fer-ŏ-moh-năl) *adj.*

phew (fyoo) *interj.* an exclamation of wonder or surprise or impatience or discomfort etc.

phi (fɪ) *n.* the twenty-first letter of the Greek alphabet (Φ φ). □**Phi Beta Kappa**, a national honor society and the oldest U.S. college fraternity, named from the initial letters of its Greek motto, = "philosophy the guide to life"; a member of this organization.

phi·al (fɪ-ăl) *n.* a vial.

phil., philol. *abbr.* 1. philological. 2. philology. 3. philosophical. 4. philosophy.

Phil. *abbr.* 1. Philharmonic. 2. Philippines.

Phil·a·del·phi·a (fil-ă-del-fi-ă) **lawyer** 1. a lawyer skilled in finding and manipulating subtleties of the law. 2. a person who delights in arguing petty points.

phi·lan·der (fi-lan-dĕr) *v.* to flirt, to engage in a love affair without serious intent. **phi·lan'der·er** *n.*

phil·an·throp·ic (fil-ăn-throp-ik) *adj.* 1. benevolent. 2. concerned with human welfare and the reduction of suffering. **phil·an·throp'i·cal·ly** *adv.*

phil·an·thro·pist (fi-lan-thrŏ-pist) *n.* a philanthropic person.

phi·lan·thro·py (fi-lan-thrŏ-pee) *n.* love of mankind, benevolence, philanthropic acts and principles.

phi·lat·e·ly (fi-lat-ĕ-lee) *n.* stamp collecting. **phi·lat'e·list** *n.* **phil·a·tel·ic** (fil-ă-tel-ik) *adj.*

Phi·le·mon (fi-lee-mŏn) *n.* a book of the New Testament, the epistle of St. Paul to a well-to-do Christian probably living at Colossae.

phil·har·mon·ic (fil-hahr-mon-ik, fil-ăr-) *adj.* (in names of symphony orchestras and music societies) devoted to music.

Phil·ip·pi·ans (fi-lip-ee-ănz) *n.* a book of the New Testament, the epistle of St. Paul to the Church at Philippi.

phi·lip·pic (fi-lip-ik) *n.* 1. a tirade. 2. *philippics,* a series of bitter verbal attacks.

Phil·ip·pine (fil-ĭ-peen) *adj.* of the Philippines, Filipino. **Philippines** *n. pl.* the Philippine Islands, a country consisting of a group of islands in the western Pacific.

Phil·is·tine (fil-i-steen) *n.* 1. a member of a people in ancient Palestine who were enemies of the Israelites. 2. *philistine,* an uncultured person, one whose interests are material and commonplace. **philistine** *adj.* having or showing uncultured tastes.

phil·o·den·dron (fil-ŏ-den-drŏn) *n.* (*pl.* **-drons**, **-dra**, *pr.* -dră) a tropical American climbing plant.

phi·lol·o·gy (fi-lol-ŏ-jee) *n.* the scientific study of languages and their development. **phi·lol'o·gist** *n.* **phil·o·log·i·cal** (fil-ŏ-loj-i-kăl) *adj.*

philos. *abbr.* 1. philosopher. 2. philosophy.

phi·los·o·pher (fi-los-ŏ-fĕr) *n.* 1. an expert in philosophy or in one of its branches. 2. one who expounds a particular philosophical system. 3. one who speaks or behaves philosophically.

phil·o·soph·ic (fil-ŏ-sof-ik), **phil·o·soph·i·cal** (fil-ŏ-sof-i-kăl) *adj.* 1. of philosophy. 2. calmly reasonable, bearing unavoidable misfortune unemotionally. **phil·o·soph'i·cal·ly** *adv.*

phi·los·o·phize (fi-los-ŏ-fɪz) *v.* (**phi·los·o·phized, phi·los·o·phiz·ing**) to reason like a philosopher, to moralize.

phi·los·o·phy (fi-los-ŏ-fee) *n.* (*pl.* **-phies**) 1. the search, by logical reasoning, for understanding of the basic truths and principles of the universe, life, and morals, and of human perception and understanding of these. 2. a system of ideas concerning this or a particular subject, a system of principles for the conduct of life. 3. the ideas or teaching of a particular philosopher. 4. advanced learning in general, *Doctor of Philosophy.* 5. calm endurance of misfortune etc.

phil·ter (fil-tĕr) *n.* a supposedly magic potion.

phle·bi·tis (flĕ-bɪ-tis) *n.* inflammation of the walls of a vein.

phle·bot·o·my (flĕ-bot-ŏ-mee) *n.* (*pl.* **-mies**) blood-letting as a medical operation.

phlegm (flem) *n.* thick mucus in the throat and bronchial passages, ejected by coughing.

phleg·mat·ic (fleg-mat-ik) *adj.* 1. not easily excited or agitated. 2. sluggish, apathetic. **phleg·mat'i·cal·ly** *adv.*

phlo·em (floh-ĕm) *n.* the soft tissue of plant stems.

phlox (floks) *n.* a plant with a cluster of reddish or purple or white flowers at the end of each stem.

Phnom Penh (nom pen, pĕ-nom) the capital of Kampuchea.

pho·bi·a (foh-bi-ă) *n.* a lasting abnormal fear or great dislike of something.

phoe·be (fee-bee) *n.* a small grayish-brown bird with a call resembling its name.

Phoe·ni·cian (fŏ-nee-shăn) *n.* 1. a member of an ancient Semitic people of the eastern Mediterranean. 2. their language. **Phoenician** *adj.* of the Phoenicians or their language.

phoe·nix (fee-niks) *n.* 1. a mythical bird of the Arabian desert, said to live for hundreds of years and then burn itself on a funeral pyre, rising from its ashes young again to live for another cycle. 2. *Phoenix,* the capital of Arizona.

phon. *abbr.* phonetics.

phone (fohn) *n.* a telephone. **phone** *v.* (**phoned, phon·ing**) to telephone. □**on the phone,** using the telephone. **over the phone,** by use of the telephone.

pho·neme (foh-neem) *n.* a unit of significant sound in a specified language, as *m* in *mute* and *b* in *bag*. **pho·ne·mic** (fŏ-nee-mik) *adj.*

phonet. *abbr.* phonetics.

pho·net·ic (fŏ-net-ik) *adj.* 1. representing each speech sound by a particular symbol that is always used for that sound; *the phonetic alphabet,* a set of symbols used in this way. 2. (of speech sounds) corresponding to pronunciation. **pho·net'i·cal·ly** *adv.*

pho·net·ics (fŏ-net-iks) *n.* the study of speech sounds. **pho·ne·ti·cian** (foh-nĕ-tish-ăn) *n.*

pho·ney = phony.

phon·ic (fon-ik) *adj.* of sound. **phon'i·cal·ly** *adv.*

phon·ics (fon-iks) *n.* 1. the study of sound. 2. the use of sound in teaching people to read.

pho·no·graph (foh-nŏ-graf) *n.* a record player. **pho·no·graph·ic** (foh-nŏ-graf-ik) *adj.* **pho·no·graph'i·cal·ly** *adv.*

pho·nol·o·gy (foh-nol-ŏ-jee) *n.* the study of sounds in a language. **pho·nol'o·gist** *n.* **pho·no·log·i·cal** (foh-nŏ-loj-i-kăl) *adj.*

pho·ny (foh-nee) *adj.* (**pho·ni·er, pho·ni·est**) *(slang)* sham, not genuine, insincere. **phony** *n.* (*pl.* **-nies**) *(slang)* a phony person or thing.

phoo·ey (foo-ee) *interj. (informal)* an exclamation of disgust.

phos·phate (fos-fayt) *n.* a salt or ester of phosphoric acid, an artificial fertilizer composed of or containing this. **phos·phat·ic** (fos-fat-ik) *adj.*

phos·phor (fos-fŏr) *n.* a synthetic fluorescent or phosphorescent substance.

phos·pho·resce (fos-fŏ-res) *v.* (**phos·pho·resced, phos·pho·resc·ing**) to be phosphorescent.

phos·pho·res·cent (fos-fŏ-res-ĕnt) *adj.* luminous, glowing with a faint light without burning or perceptible heat. **phos·pho·res'cent·ly** *adv.* **phos·pho·res'cence** *n.*

phos·phor·ic (fos-for-ik) *adj.* of or containing phosphorus. □**phosphoric acid,** a crystalline acid used in making fertilizers etc.

phos·pho·rus (fos-fŏ-rŭs) *n.* a chemical element existing in several forms, a yellowish waxlike form of it that appears luminous in the dark. **phos'pho·rous** *adj.* of or containing phosphorus. ▷Do not confuse the spelling of the noun with that of the adjective.

pho·to (foh-toh) *n.* (*pl.* **-tos**) *(informal)* a photograph. □**photo finish,** a very close finish of a race, photographed to enable the judge to decide the winner.

pho·to·cell (foh-toh-sel) *n.* a photoelectric cell.

pho·to·chem·i·cal (foh-toh-kem-i-kăl) *adj.* of or relating to the chemical effects of light.

pho·to·com·pose (foh-toh-kŏm-pohz) *v.* (**pho·to·com·posed, pho·to·com·pos·ing**) to set type by projecting photographic images of letters on sensitized paper or film. **pho·to·com·po·si·tion** (foh-toh-kom-pŏ-zish-ŏn) *n.*

pho·to·cop·i·er (foh-tŏ-kop-ee-ĕr) *n.* a machine for photocopying documents.

pho·to·cop·y (foh-tŏ-kop-ee) *n.* (*pl.* **-cop·ies**) a copy (of a document etc.) made by photographing the original. **photocopy** *v.* (**pho·to·cop·ied, pho·to·cop·y·ing**) to make a photocopy of.

pho·to·e·lec·tric (foh-toh-i-lek-trik) *adj.* of or using the electrical effects of light. □**photoelectric cell,** an electronic device that emits an electric current when light falls on it, used to measure light for photography, to count objects passing it, to cause a door to open when someone approaches it, etc.

pho·to·en·grave (foh-toh-en-grayv) *v.* (**pho·to·en·graved, pho·to·en·grav·ing**) to make a photoengraving of.

pho·to·en·grav·ing (foh-toh-en-gray-ving) *n.* 1. a process for reproducing a photograph on a metal plate for printing. 2. a print made by photoengraving. 3. a photoengraved plate.

pho·to·flash (foh-toh-flash) *n.* a flashbulb.

pho·tog (fŏ-tog) *n. (informal)* a photographer.

photog. *abbr.* 1. photographer. 2. photographic. 3. photography.

pho·to·gen·ic (foh-tŏ-jen-ik) *adj.* being a good subject for photography, coming out well in photographs.

pho·to·graph (foh-tŏ-graf) *n.* a picture formed by means of the chemical action of light or other radiation on a light-sensitive surface. **photograph** *v.* 1. to take a photograph of. 2. to come out in a certain way when photographed, *it photographs badly.*

pho·tog·ra·pher (fŏ-tog-ră-fĕr) *n.* a person who takes photographs.

pho·to·graph·ic (foh-tŏ-graf-ik) *adj.* 1. of or used on or produced by photography. 2. (of the memory) recalling accurately what was seen, as if by a process of photography. **pho·to·graph'i·cal·ly** *adv.*

pho·tog·ra·phy (fŏ-tog-ră-fee) *n.* the taking of photographs.

pho·to·gra·vure (foh-toh-gră-vyoor) *n.* 1. a picture produced from a photographic negative that has been transferred to a metal plate and etched in. 2. this process.

pho·to·jour·nal·ism (foh-toh-jur-nă-liz-ĕm) *n.* journalism in which photographs are intended to predominate. **pho·to·jour'nal·ist** *n.*

pho·to·li·thog·ra·phy (foh-toh-li-thog-ră-fee) *n.* lithography with plates made photographically.

pho·tom·e·ter (foh-tom-ĕ-tĕr) *n.* an instrument

for measuring light. **pho·tom′e·try** n. **pho·to·met·ric** (foh-tŏ-met-rik) adj.

pho·to·mi·cro·graph (foh-toh-mɪ-krŏ-graf) n. a photograph of an object that has been enlarged by a microscope. **photomicrograph** v. to take photomicrographs of. **pho·to·mi·cro·graph·ic** (foh-tŏ-mɪ-krŏ-graf-ik) adj. **pho·to·mi·crog·ra·phy** (foh-tŏ-mɪ-**krog**-ră-fee) n.

pho·to·mu·ral (foh-toh-**myoor**-ăl) n. a large photograph used as a mural or wall decoration.

pho·ton (foh-ton) n. a quantum of electromagnetic radiation energy, proportional to the frequency of radiation.

pho·to·play (foh-toh-play) n. (old use) a screenplay.

pho·to·sen·si·tive (foh-toh-sen-sī-tiv) adj. reacting chemically etc. to light. **pho·to·sen·si·ti·za·tion** (foh-tŏ-sen-sī-tī-**zay**-shŏn) n.

pho·to·sphere (foh-tŏ-sfeer) n. the luminous envelope of the sun or a star from which its light and heat radiate. **pho·to·spher·ic** (foh-tŏ-**sfer**-ik) adj.

Pho·to·stat (foh-tŏ-stat) n. (trademark) 1. a type of photocopier. 2. (also photostat) a copy made with this. **photostat** v. to photocopy with this machine. **pho·to·stat′ic** adj.

pho·to·syn·the·sis (foh-tŏ-sin-thĕ-sis) n. the process by which green plants use sunlight to convert carbon dioxide (taken from the air) and water into complex substances. **pho·to·syn·the·size** (foh-tŏ-sin-thĕ-sɪz) v. **pho·to·syn·the·tic** (foh-tŏ-sin-**thet**-ik) adj.

pho·to·vol·ta·ic (foh-toh-vol-tay-ik) adj. of or relating to the production of electric current at the junction of two substances exposed to light.

phr. abbr. phrase.

phrase (frayz) n. 1. a group of words forming a unit, especially as an idiom or a striking or clever way of saying something. 2. a group of words (usually without a finite verb) forming a unit within a sentence or clause, as in the garden. 3. the way something is worded, we didn't like his choice of phrase. 4. a short distinct passage forming a unit in a melody. **phrase** v. (**phrased, phras·ing**) 1. to express in words. 2. to divide (music) into phrases. **phras′ing** n. □**phrase book**, a book listing common phrases and their equivalents in a foreign language, for use by travelers.

phra·se·ol·o·gy (fray-zi-ol-ŏ-jee) n. wording, the way something is worded.

phre·net·ic = frenetic.

phren·ic (fren-ik) adj. of the diaphragm.

phre·nol·o·gy (fri-**nol**-ŏ-jee) n. the study of the external shape of a person's skull as a supposed indication of his character and abilities.

PHS abbr. Public Health Service.

phy·lac·ter·y (fi-**lak**-tĕ-ree) n. (pl. **-ter·ies**) a small leather box containing Hebrew texts on vellum, worn by Jews at morning weekday prayer to remind them to keep the Jewish religious law.

phy·log·e·ny (fi-**loj**-ĕ-nee) n. the evolution of an animal or plant type.

phy·lum (fr-lŭm) n. (pl. **-la**, pr. **-lă**) a major division of the animal or plant kingdom, containing species having the same general form.

phys. abbr. 1. physical. 2. physician. 3. physics.

phys·ic (fiz-ik) n. (informal) a laxative.

phys·i·cal (fiz-i-kăl) adj. 1. of the body, physical fitness. 2. of matter or the laws of nature (as opposed to moral or spiritual or imaginary things),

the physical world; a physical map, one showing mountains and rivers and other natural features. 3. of physics. **physical** n. (informal) a physical examination. **phys′i·cal·ly** adv. □**physical chemistry**, a branch of chemistry in which physics is used to study substances and their reactions. **physical education**, a course of study emphasizing sports, exercise, and hygiene. **physical examination**, a medical examination. **physical geography**, a branch of geography dealing with the natural features of Earth's surface (such as mountains, lakes, rivers). **physical science**, see **science. physical therapy**, physiotherapy.

phy·si·cian (fī-zish-ăn) n. a doctor, especially one who practices medicine (as distinct from surgery).

phys·i·cist (fiz-i-sist) n. an expert in physics.

phys·ics (fiz-iks) n. 1. the scientific study of the properties and interactions of matter and energy. 2. these properties and interactions.

phys·i·og·no·my (fiz-i-og-nŏ-mee) n. (pl. **-mies**) the features of a person's face.

phys·i·og·ra·phy (fiz-i-og-ră-fee) n. a description of nature, of natural phenomena, or of a class of objects. **phys·i·o·graph·ic** (fiz-i-ŏ-**graf**-ik) adj.

physiol. abbr. 1. physiologist. 2. physiology.

phys·i·o·log·ist (fiz-i-ol-ŏ-jist) n. an expert in physiology.

phys·i·ol·o·gy (fiz-i-ol-ŏ-jee) n. 1. the scientific study of the bodily functions of living organisms and their parts. 2. these functions. **phys·i·o·log·i·cal** (fiz-i-ŏ-loj-i-kăl) adj. **phys·i·o·log′ic** adj.

phys·i·o·ther·a·py (fiz-i-oh-ther-ă-pee) n. treatment of a disease or injury or deformity or weakness by massage, exercises, heat, etc. **phys·i·o·ther′a·pist** n.

phy·sique (fi-zeek) n. a person's physical build and muscular development, a man of powerful physique.

pi¹ (pɪ) n. (pl. **pis**, pr. pɪz) the sixteenth letter of the Greek alphabet (Π π). ▷ π is used as a symbol for the ratio of the circumference of a circle to its diameter (approximately 3.14159).

pi², **pie** (pɪ) v. (**pied, pi·ing**) to mix up (printing type).

pi·a·nis·si·mo (pi-ă-nis-ī-moh) adv. (in music) very softly.

pi·an·ist (pi-an-ist, pee-ă-nist) n. a person who plays the piano.

pi·an·o¹ (pi-an-oh) n. (pl. **-an·os**) a musical instrument in which metal strings are struck by hammers operated by pressing the keys of a keyboard. □**piano roll**, a roll of perforated paper used in operating a player piano. **piano wire**, a thin strong steel wire.

piano² (pi-ah-noh) adv. (in music) softly.

pi·an·o·for·te (pi-an-ŏ-fohr-tee) n. a piano.

pi·as·ter, pi·as·tre (pi-as-tĕr) n. a small coin of various Middle Eastern countries.

pi·az·za (pi-az-ă) n. (pl. **-az·zas**) 1. a porch. 2. a public square in an Italian town.

pi·broch (pee-brok) n. a series of variations on a theme, for bagpipes. ▷Note that this does not mean the bagpipes.

pi·ca (pɪ-kă) n. 1. a size of letters in typewriting (ten per inch). 2. a unit of type size = one-sixth inch.

pic·a·dor (pik-ă-dohr) n. a mounted man with a lance in bullfighting.

pic·a·resque (pik-ă-**resk**) adj. (of fiction) dealing

with the adventures of rogues, *a picaresque novel.*
pic·a·yune (pik-ă-yoon) *adj.* 1. trifling, petty. 2. mean, contemptible.
pic·ca·lil·li (pik-ă-lil-ee) *n.* a relish of pickled chopped vegetables, mustard, and hot spices.
pic·co·lo (pik-ŏ-loh) *n.* (*pl.* **-los**) a small flute, sounding an octave higher than the ordinary one.
pick[1] (pik) *n.* 1. a tool consisting of a curved iron bar with one or both ends pointed, mounted at right angles to its handle, used for breaking up hard ground, stones, etc. 2. a plectrum.
pick[2] *v.* 1. to use a pointed instrument or the fingers or beak etc. in order to make a hole in or remove bits from (a thing); *pick at one's food,* to eat it in small bits or without appetite. 2. to detach (a flower or fruit) from the plant bearing it. 3. to select carefully; *pick a winner,* choose a person or thing that will later prove to be successful. **pick** *n.* 1. picking. 2. selection; *have first pick,* have the right to choose first. 3. the best part; *pick of the bunch,* the best of the lot. **pick'er** *n.* □**pick a lock,** to use a piece of wire or a pointed tool to open it without a key. **pick and choose,** to select with excessive care. **pick a person's brains,** to extract ideas or information from him for one's own use. **pick a person's pocket,** to steal its contents while he is wearing the garment. **pick a quarrel,** to provoke one deliberately. **pick at,** to pick on; to eat without interest. **pick holes in,** to find fault with. **pick off,** to pluck off; to select and shoot or destroy one by one; *the pitcher turned quickly and picked him off,* put him out before he could return to the base. **pick on,** to single out, especially as a target for nagging or harassment. **pick out,** to take from among a number of things; to recognize; to distinguish from surrounding objects or areas; to play (a tune) by searching for the right notes. **pick over,** to select the best of. **pick up,** to lift or take up; to call for and take with one, to take aboard (passengers or freight etc.); (of police etc.) to catch, to find and take into custody; to get or acquire by chance or casually; to meet casually and become acquainted with; to succeed in seeing or hearing by means of a telescope, a radio, etc.; to recover health, to show an improvement; to recover speed; *pick up speed,* accelerate; *pick up the bill,* be the one who pays it. **pick up on,** (*slang*) to understand; to agree with.
pick-a-back (pik-ă-bak) = **piggyback.**
pick·a·nin·ny (pik-ă-nin-ee) *n.* (*pl.* **-nies**) (*contemptuous*) a black child.
pick·ax (pik-aks) *n.* pick (see **pick**[1], definition 1).
pick·er·el (pik-ĕ-rĕl) *n.* (*pl.* **-els, -el**) any of several small species of pike.
pick·er·el·weed (pik-ĕ-rĕl-weed) *n.* a North American flowering plant found in shallow fresh waters.
pick·et (pik-it) *n.* 1. a pointed stake set into the ground to form a palisade, secure a tent, tether an animal, etc. 2. an outpost of troops, a party of sentries. 3. a person or group of persons stationed by strikers outside their place of work to dissuade others from entering. **picket** *v.* (**pick·et·ed, pick·et·ing**) 1. to secure or enclose with a stake or stakes. 2. to station or act as a picket during a strike. □**picket line,** a group of pickets outside a building or other site.
pick·ings (pik-ingz) *n. pl.* 1. scraps of good food etc. remaining, gleanings. 2. odd gains or perquisites, profits from stealing.

pick·le (pik-ĕl) *n.* 1. food (especially a cucumber) preserved in vinegar or brine. 2. vinegar or brine used for this. 3. (*informal*) a plight, a mess. **pickle** *v.* (**pick·led, pick·ling**) to preserve in vinegar or brine.
pick·led (pik-ĕld) *adj.* (*slang*) drunk.
pick·lock (pik-lok) *n.* 1. a device used for picking locks. 2. a person who picks locks.
pick-me-up (pik-mee-up) *n.* a tonic to restore health or relieve depression.
pick·pock·et (pik-pok-it) *n.* a thief who picks pockets.
pick·up (pik-up) *n.* 1. the process of picking up. 2. an acquaintance met informally. 3. a small open truck. 4. the part carrying the stylus in a record player.
pick·y (pik-ee) *adj.* (**pick·i·er, pick·i·est**) excessively fastidious, *a picky eater.*
pic·nic (pik-nik) *n.* 1. an informal meal taken in the open air for pleasure, an excursion for this. 2. (*informal*) something very agreeable or easily done. **picnic** *v.* (**pic·nicked, pic·nick·ing**) to take part in a picnic. **pic'nick·er** *n.*
pi·co·sec·ond (pɪ-koh-sek-ŏnd) *n.* a unit of time, = one-trillionth of a second.
pi·cot (pee-koh) *n.* one of a series of small loops of twisted thread forming an ornamental edging.
pic·ric (pik-rik) **acid** a yellow substance used in dyeing and in explosives.
Pict (pikt) *n.* a member of an ancient people of northern Britain. **Pict'ish** *adj.*
pic·to·graph (pik-tŏ-graf) *n.* 1. a pictorial symbol. 2. a primitive record consisting of these. **pic·to·graph·ic** (pik-tŏ-graf-ik) *adj.*
pic·to·ri·al (pik-tohr-i-ăl) *adj.* 1. of or expressed in a picture or pictures. 2. illustrated by pictures. **pic·to'ri·al·ly** *adv.*
pic·ture (pik-chŭr) *n.* 1. a representation of a person or people or object(s) etc., made by painting, drawing, or photography, especially as a work of art. 2. a portrait. 3. something that looks beautiful, *the garden is a picture.* 4. a scene, the total impression produced on one's sight or mind. 5. a perfect example, *she is the picture of health.* 6. a motion picture. 7. the image on a television screen. **picture** *v.* (**pic·tured, pic·tur·ing**) 1. to represent in a picture. 2. to describe vividly. 3. to form a mental picture of, *picture to yourself a deserted beach.* □**in the picture,** (of a person) considered important, powerful, etc.; fully informed, *let me put you in the picture.* **out of the picture,** (of a person) no longer considered important, powerful, etc. **picture gallery,** a hall etc. containing a collection of pictures. **picture hat,** a woman's wide-brimmed highly decorated hat. **picture postcard,** a postcard with a picture on one side. **picture tube,** a cathode ray tube forming the screen of a television set. **picture window,** a large window facing an attractive view.
pic·tur·esque (pik-chŭ-resk) *adj.* 1. forming a striking and pleasant scene, *picturesque villages.* 2. (of words or a description) very expressive, vivid. **pic·tur·esque'ly** *adv.* **pic·tur·esque' ness** *n.*
pid·dle (pid-ĕl) *v.* (**pid·dled, pid·dling**) 1. to spend time idly, *piddle away the afternoon.* 2. (*informal*) to urinate.
pid·dling (pid-ling) *adj.* trivial, unimportant, *piddling problems.*
pidg·in (pij-in) *n.* a simplified form of English or

another language, containing elements of the local language(s) and used for communication (in parts of the Far East etc.) between people speaking different languages, *pidgin English.*

pie (pɪ) *n.* a baked dish of fruit or meat or fish etc. enclosed in or covered with pastry or other crust. □**pie in the sky,** a prospect (considered unrealistic) of future happiness.

pie·bald (pɪ-bawld) *adj.* (of a horse etc.) with irregular patches of white and black or other dark color. **piebald** *n.* a piebald horse.

piece (pees) *n.* 1. one of the distinct portions of which a thing is composed or into which it is divided or broken; *worked piece by piece,* one after another until all were done. 2. one of a set of things, *three-piece suite.* 3. something regarded as a unit, *a fine piece of work.* 4. a musical or literary or artistic composition. 5. a poem, speech, etc. learned by a child for recitation before adults. 6. a coin, *ten-cent piece.* 7. one of the set of small objects moved on a board in playing board games, a chessman other than a pawn. 8. a fixed unit of work; *payment by the piece, piece rates,* payment according to this (not by the hour). 9. a slice, as of bread or pie. **piece** *v.* **(pieced, piec·ing)** to make by joining or adding pieces together; *piece it together,* put parts together to form a whole. □**go to pieces,** (of a person) to lose one's strength or ability etc., to collapse. **in one piece,** not broken; *arrived in one piece,* without mishap. **of a piece,** of the same kind, consistent. **piece goods,** fabric cut and sold to the customer's order. **piece of cake,** *(informal)* something very easy or pleasant. **piece of one's mind,** reproach or scolding giving one's frank criticisms. **say one's piece,** to make a prepared statement; to give one's opinion.

pièce de ré·sis·tance (pyes dĕ ray-zees-tahns) (*pl.* **pièces de ré·sis·tance,** *pr.* pyes dĕ ray-zees-tahns) 1. the principal dish at a meal. 2. the most important or remarkable item. ▷French.

piece·meal (pees-meel) *adj. & adv.* done piece by piece, part at a time.

piece·work (pees-wurk) *n.* a type of work paid according to the quantity done, not by the time spent on it.

pied (pɪd) *adj.* parti-colored, *Pied Piper* (dressed in parti-colored clothing).

pi·ed-à-terre (pi-ed-ă-tair) *n.* (*pl.* **pi·eds-à-terre,** *pr.* pi-ed-ă-tair) a small place for use as temporary quarters when needed. ▷French.

pie-eyed (pɪ-ɪd) *adj. (slang)* drunk.

pie·plant (pɪ-plant) *n.* the rhubarb plant, used in pies.

pier (peer) *n.* 1. a structure built out into the sea to serve as a breakwater or dock or amusement area. 2. one of the pillars or similar structures supporting an arch or bridge. 3. solid masonry between windows etc.

pierce (peers) *v.* **(pierced, pierc·ing)** 1. to go into or through like a sharp-pointed instrument, to make a hole in (a thing) in this way. 2. to force one's way into or through.

Pierce (peers), **Frank·lin** (1804–69) the fourteenth president of the U.S. 1853–57.

pierc·ing (peer-sing) *adj.* (of cold or wind etc.) penetrating sharply, (of a voice or sound) shrilly audible.

Pierre (peer) the capital of South Dakota.

pi·e·ty (pɪ-ĕ-tee) *n.* (*pl.* **-ties**) piousness.

pi·e·zo·e·lec·tric (pi-ay-zoh-i-lek-trik) *adj.* becoming electrically polarized under pressure.

pif·fle (pif-ĕl) *n. (slang)* nonsense, worthless talk.

piffle *v.* **(pif·fled, pif·fling)** *(slang)* to talk nonsense.

pif·fling (pif-ling) *adj. (slang)* trivial, worthless.

pig (pig) *n.* 1. a domestic or wild animal with short legs, cloven hoofs, and a broad blunt snout. 2. *(informal)* a greedy, dirty, or unpleasant person. 3. *(slang, contemptuous)* a policeman. 4. an oblong mass of metal from a smelting furnace, pig iron. □**buy a pig in a poke,** to buy a thing without seeing it or knowing whether it will be satisfactory. **pig iron,** crude iron from a smelting furnace. **Pig Latin,** made-up jargon that systematically moves the initial consonants of words to the ends of the words and adds "ay," as *ademay* for *made, adsay* for *sad.*

pi·geon (pij-ŏn) *n.* 1. a bird of the dove family. 2. *(slang)* a victim of fraud or deception. □**pigeon breast,** a deformed chest in which the breastbone forms a protruding curve.

pi·geon·hole (pij-ŏn-hohl) *n.* 1. a small recess for a pigeon to nest in. 2. one of a set of small compartments in a desk or cabinet, used for holding papers or letters etc. **pigeonhole** *v.* **(pi·geon·holed, pi·geon·hol·ing)** 1. to put away for future consideration or indefinitely. 2. to classify mentally as belonging to a particular group or kind.

pi·geon-toed (pij-ŏn-tohd) *adj.* having the toes turned inward.

pig·gish (pig-ish) *adj.* like a pig, dirty or greedy.

pig·gy (pig-ee) *adj.* **(-gi·er, -gi·est)** like a pig; *piggy eyes,* small eyes like those of a pig. □**piggy bank,** a toy bank made in the shape of a pig.

pig·gy·back (pig-ee-bak) *adj. & adv.* carried on the shoulders and back or on the top of a larger object.

pig·head·ed (pig-hed-id) *adj.* obstinate, stubborn.

pig·let (pig-lit) *n.* a young pig.

pig·ment (pig-mĕnt) *n.* coloring matter. **pigment** *v.* to color (skin or other tissue) with natural pigment. **pig·men·ta·tion** (pig-mĕn-tay-shŏn) *n.*

pig·my = **pygmy.**

pig·pen (pig-pen) *n.* a pigsty.

pig·skin (pig-skin) *n.* 1. leather made from the skin of pigs. 2. *(informal)* a football.

pig·sty (pig-stɪ) *n.* (*pl.* **-sties**) 1. a partly covered pen for pigs. 2. a very dirty or untidy place.

pig·tail (pig-tayl) *n.* long hair worn hanging in a braid at the back of the head.

pike¹ (pɪk) *n.* a long wooden shaft with a pointed metal head. **pike** *v.* **(piked, pik·ing)** to stick, to wound or to kill with a pike.

pike² *n.* a large voracious freshwater fish with a long narrow snout.

pike³ *n.* a turnpike, a main road; *down the pike,* a long way off

pik·er (pɪ-kĕr) *n. (informal)* a person who does things in a timid way.

pi·laf (pi-lahf) *n.* an oriental dish of rice or wheat with meat and spices.

pi·las·ter (pi-las-tĕr) *n.* a rectangular column, especially an ornamental one that projects from a wall into which it is set.

pil·chard (pil-chărd) *n.* a small sea fish related to the herring.

pile¹ (pɪl) *n.* a heavy beam of metal or concrete or timber driven vertically into the ground as a foundation or support for a building or bridge. □**pile driver,** a machine for driving piles into the ground.

pile² *n.* 1. a number of things lying one upon another. 2. a funeral pyre. 3. *(informal)* a large quantity, *a pile of work.* 4. *(informal)* a large quantity of money, *made a pile.* **pile** *v.* **(piled, pil·ing)** 1. to heap or stack or load. 2. to crowd, *they all piled into one car.* □**pile it on,** *(slang)* to exaggerate. **pile up,** to accumulate; to run (a ship) on the rocks or aground; to cause (a vehicle) to crash.

pile³ *n.* cut or uncut loops on the surface of a fabric.

piles (pɪlz) *n. pl.* hemorrhoids.

pile·up (pɪl-up) *n.* a collision of several motor vehicles.

pil·fer (pil-fĕr) *v.* to steal small items or in small quantities. **pil′fer·er** *n.*

pil·fer·age (pil-fĕ-rij) *n.* loss caused by theft of goods during transit or storage.

pil·grim (pil-grim) *n.* a person who travels to a sacred or revered place as an act of religious devotion. □**Pilgrim Fathers,** the English Puritans who founded the colony of Plymouth, Massachusetts, in 1620.

pil·grim·age (pil-grĭ-mij) *n.* a pilgrim's journey, a journey made to a place as a mark of respect (as to a person's birthplace).

pil·ing (pɪ-ling) *n.* a support structure of piles.

pill¹ (pil) *n.* a small ball or flat round piece of medicinal substance for swallowing whole. □**bitter pill,** a humiliation. **the pill,** a contraceptive pill; *on the pill,* taking this regularly.

pill² *v.* (of fabric) to form tiny balls of fiber on the surface.

pil·lage (pil-ij) *v.* **(pil·laged, pil·lag·ing)** to plunder. **pillage** *n.* plunder. **pil′lag·er** *n.*

pil·lar (pil-ăr) *n.* 1. a vertical structure used as a support or ornament. 2. something resembling this in shape, *a pillar of rock.* 3. a person regarded as one of the chief supporters of something, *a pillar of the community.* □**from pillar to post,** from one place or situation to another.

pill·box (pil-boks) *n.* 1. a small round box for holding pills. 2. a hat shaped like this. 3. a small concrete shelter for a gun emplacement.

pil·lion (pil-yŏn) *n.* a saddle for a passenger seated behind the driver of a motorcycle.

pil·lo·ry (pil-ŏ-ree) *n.* (*pl.* **-ries**) a wooden framework with holes for the head and hands, into which offenders were formerly locked for exposure to public ridicule. **pillory** *v.* **(pil·lo·ried, pil·lo·ry·ing)** 1. to put into the pillory as a punishment. 2. to hold up to public ridicule or scorn.

pil·low (pil-oh) *n.* a cushion used (especially in bed) for supporting the head. **pillow** *v.* to rest or prop up on or as if on a pillow.

pil·low·case (pil-oh-kays) *n.* a cloth cover into which a pillow is placed for use.

pil·low·slip (pil-oh-slip) *n.* a pillowcase.

pi·lot (pɪ-lŏt) *n.* 1. a person who operates the flying controls of an aircraft. 2. a person qualified to take charge of ships entering or leaving a harbor or traveling through certain waters. 3. a guide. **pilot** *v.* **(pi·lot·ed, pi·lot·ing)** 1. to act as pilot of. 2. to guide. **pilot** *adj.* experimental, testing (on a small scale) how an idea etc. will work, *a pilot project.* □**pilot light,** a small jet of gas kept lit and lighting a larger burner when this is turned on; an electric indicator light.

pi·lot·age (pɪ-lŏ-tij) *n.* piloting, the charge for this.

pi·lot·fish (pɪ-lŏt-fish) *n.* (*pl.* **-fish·es, -fish**) a small fish said to act as pilot to food for a shark.

pi·lot·house (pɪ-lŏt-hows) *n.* (*pl.* **-hous·es,** *pr.* -how-ziz) an enclosed shelter for the ship's pilot and his equipment on the upper deck of a ship.

pi·lot·less (pɪ-lŏt-lis) *adj.* having no pilot.

pi·men·to (pi-men-toh) *n.* (*pl.* **-tos**) 1. allspice, the West Indian tree yielding this. 2. a sweet pepper.

pimp (pimp) *n.* a man who solicits clients for a prostitute or brothel. **pimp** *v.* to be a pimp.

pim·per·nel (pim-pĕr-nel) *n.* a wild plant with small scarlet or blue or white flowers that close in cloudy or wet weather.

pim·ple (pim-pĕl) *n.* a small inflamed spot on the skin.

pim·ply (pim-plee) *adj.* covered with pimples, especially on the face.

pin (pin) *n.* 1. a short thin stiff piece of metal with a sharp point and a round broadened head, used for fastening fabrics or papers etc. together or (with an ornamental head) as a decoration. 2. a peg of wood or metal used for various purposes. 3. a stick with a flag on it, placed in a hole on a golf course to mark its position. 4. a hairpin, bowling pin, rolling pin, or safety pin. 5. *pins, (informal)* legs, *quick on his pins.* **pin** *v.* **(pinned, pin·ning)** 1. to fasten with a pin or pins. 2. to transfix with a weapon or arrow etc. and hold fast, to restrict and make unable to move, *he was pinned under the wreckage.* 3. to attach or fix; *we pinned our hopes on you,* counted on you to succeed; *pinned the blame on her,* made her the scapegoat. □**pin curl,** a curl made in the hair while wet and held in place by a hairpin or clip. **pin down,** to establish clearly; to make (a person) agree to keep to a promise or arrangement etc. or declare his intentions definitely. **pin money,** money allowed to a woman or earned by her for private expenses; a trivial amount of money. **pins and needles,** a tingling sensation; *on pins and needles,* in a state of anxiety or suspense. **pin seal,** leather made from young seals.

pin·a·fore (pin-ă-fohr) *n.* 1. a woman's or girl's sleeveless dress closing at the back. 2. a full apron like this.

pin·ball (pin-bawl) *n.* a game played on a sloping board on which a ball is projected so that it strikes pins or targets or falls into a pocket. □**pinball machine,** a coin-operated machine for playing pinball.

pince-nez (pans-nay) *n.* (*pl.* **pince-nez,** *pr.* pans-nayz) a pair of glasses with a spring that clips on the nose and no sidepieces.

pin·cers (pin-sĕrz) *n. pl.* 1. a tool for gripping and pulling things, consisting of a pair of pivoted jaws with handles that are pressed together to close them. 2. a claw-like part of a lobster etc. □**pincer movement,** an attack in which forces converge from each side on an enemy position.

pinch (pinch) *v.* 1. to squeeze tightly or painfully between two surfaces, especially between finger and thumb; *look pinched with cold,* have a drawn appearance from feeling unpleasantly cold. 2. to shorten or remove by squeezing, *pinch out the tops of the plants.* 3. to stint, to be niggardly, *pinching and scrimping.* 4. *(slang)* to steal. 5. *(slang)* to arrest. **pinch** *n.* 1. pinching, squeezing. 2. stress or pressure of circumstances, *began to*

feel the pinch. **3.** as much as can be held between the tips of the thumb and forefinger. **pinch′er** *n.* □**in a pinch,** in time of difficulty or necessity.
pinch-hit (pinch-hit) *v.* (**pinch-hit, pinch-hit·ting**) **1.** to bat as a replacement for a scheduled baseball batter. **2.** *(informal)* to act as substitute. **pinch hit′ter** *n.*
pin·cush·ion (pin-kuush-ŏn) *n.* a small pad into which pins are stuck to keep them ready for use.
pine[1] (pin) *n.* **1.** an evergreen tree with needle-shaped leaves growing in clusters. **2.** its wood.
pine[2] *v.* (**pined, pin·ing**) **1.** to waste away through grief or yearning. **2.** to feel an intense longing.
pin·e·al (pin-i-ăl) *adj.* shaped like a pine cone. □**pineal body** *or* **gland,** an eyelike conical gland of unknown function located in the brain.
pine·ap·ple (pin-ap-ĕl) *n.* **1.** a large juicy tropical fruit with a tough prickly segmented skin. **2.** the plant that bears it.
pin·feath·er (pin-feth-ĕr) *n.* a developing feather that has just broken through the skin.
ping (ping) *n.* a short sharp ringing sound. **ping** *v.* **1.** to make or cause to make this sound. **2.** (of an engine) to make slight explosive sounds when running imperfectly.
Ping-Pong (ping-pong) *n.* *(trademark)* table tennis.
pin·head (pin-hed) *n.* **1.** the head of a pin. **2.** *(slang)* a stupid person. **pin′head·ed** *adj.* stupid.
pin·hole (pin-hohl) *n.* a hole made by or as if by a pin.
pin·ion[1] (pin-yŏn) *n.* a bird's wing, especially the outer segment. **pinion** *v.* **1.** to clip the wings of (a bird) to prevent it from flying. **2.** to restrain (a person) by holding or binding his arms or legs.
pinion[2] *n.* a small cogwheel that engages with a larger one or with a rack.
pink[1] (pingk) *n.* **1.** pale red color. **2.** a garden plant with fragrant white or pink or variegated flowers. **3.** the best or most nearly perfect condition, *the pink of perfection.* **pink** *adj.* **1.** of pale red color. **2.** *(slang)* mildly communist. **pink′ness** *n.* □**in the pink,** *(slang)* in very good health. **pink elephants,** *(informal)* hallucinations while drunk.
pink[2] *v.* **1.** to pierce slightly. **2.** to cut a zigzag edge on. □**pinking shears,** dressmaker's scissors with serrated blades for cutting a zigzag edge.
pink·eye (pingk-i) *n.* conjunctivitis.
pin·kie (ping-kee) *n.* *(informal)* the little finger of the hand. □**pinkie ring,** a ring worn on this finger.
pink·ish (ping-kish) *adj.* rather pink.
pin·nace (pin-is) *n.* a ship's small boat, usually motor-driven.
pin·na·cle (pin-ă-kĕl) *n.* **1.** a pointed ornament on a roof. **2.** a peak. **3.** the highest point, *the pinnacle of his fame.*
pin·nate (pin-ayt) *adj.* having like parts (leaves, tentacles, branches, etc.) arranged on each side of a common stalk or axis. **pin′nate·ly** *adv.*
pi·noch·le (pee-nok-ĕl) *n.* a card game played with a double pack of forty-eight cards, ace to nine only.
pi·ñon (pin-yŏn, peen-yohn) *n.* (*pl.* **pi·ñons, pi·ño·nes,** *pr.* pin-yoh-neez) **1.** a pine tree of the Rocky Mountain region, bearing nuts. **2.** its nut.
pin·point (pin-point) *n.* **1.** the point of a pin. **2.** something very small or sharp. **pinpoint** *adj.* showing or requiring care and precision, *pinpoint bombing; pinpoint accuracy.* **pinpoint** *v.* to locate or to identify precisely.

pin·prick (pin-prik) *n.* **1.** a small puncture. **2.** a small annoyance.
pin·set·ter (pin-set-ĕr) *n.* a machine at a bowling alley that clears and resets pins.
pin·stripe (pin-strip) *n.* **1.** a very narrow stripe in cloth. **2.** a suit made from such cloth. **pin′striped** *adj.*
pint (pint) *n.* **1.** a measure for liquids, = half a quart. **2.** this quantity of liquid, especially whiskey.
pin·to (pin-toh) *adj.* mottled, piebald. **pinto** *n.* (*pl.* **-tos**) a piebald horse. □**pinto bean,** a type of string bean with mottled beans.
pin-up (pin-up) *n.* *(informal)* **1.** a picture of an attractive person (often an attractive scantily clad woman) pinned up on a wall etc. **2.** such a person.
pin·wheel (pin-hweel) *n.* **1.** a toy resembling a windmill, with light vanes attached to a stick and able to turn when blown by the wind. **2.** a rotating firework.
pin·worm (pin-wurm) *n.* an intestinal parasitic worm in man.
pin·y (pi-nee) *adj.* like pine trees, *a piny smell.*
pin·yon = **piñon.**
pi·o·neer (pi-ŏ-neer) *n.* a person who is one of the first to enter or settle a new region or to investigate a new subject or method etc. **pioneer** *v.* to be a pioneer, to take part in (a course of action etc.) that leads the way for others to follow.
pi·o·ni·um (pi-oh-ni-ŭm) *n.* a quasi-atomic particle.
pi·ous (pi-ŭs) *adj.* **1.** devout in religion. **2.** ostentatiously virtuous. **pi′ous·ly** *adv.* **pi′ous·ness** *n.*
pip[1] (pip) *n.* **1.** one of the small seeds of an apple, pear, orange, etc. **2.** *(informal)* a wonderful thing or person, *a pip of an idea.*
pip[2] *n.* **1.** a spot on a domino or die or playing card. **2.** *(informal)* a signal on a radar screen.
pip[3] *n.* a disease of poultry and other birds. □**the pip,** *(slang)* a feeling of disgust or depression or bad temper.
pip[4] *n.* a short high-pitched sound, as a chirp or peep or one produced mechanically, *the six pips of the time signal.*
pipe (pip) *n.* **1.** a tube through which something can flow. **2.** a wind instrument consisting of a single tube, each of the tubes by which sound is produced in an organ; *the pipes,* bagpipes. **3.** a boatswain's whistle, its sounding. **4.** a narrow tube with a bowl at one end in which tobacco burns for smoking, the quantity of tobacco held by this. **5.** *pipes,* *(slang)* the human respiratory system; *Caruso had great pipes,* sang well and loudly. **pipe** *v.* (**piped, pip·ing**) **1.** to convey (water etc.) through pipes. **2.** *(informal)* to transmit (music or a broadcast program etc.) by wire or cable. **3.** to play (music) on a pipe, to lead or bring or summon by sounding a pipe etc. **4.** to utter in a shrill voice. **5.** to ornament (a dress etc.) with piping. □**pipe bomb,** a homemade bomb inside a metal pipe. **pipe clay,** a fine white clay used for tobacco pipes, for whitening leather etc. **pipe down,** *(informal)* to cease talking, to become less noisy or less insistent. **pipe dream,** an impractical hope or scheme. **pipe organ,** an organ using pipes as well as reeds. **pipe up,** *(informal)* to begin talking, to complain.
pipe·line (pip-lin) *n.* **1.** a pipe for conveying petroleum etc. **2.** a channel of supply or information. □**in the pipeline,** on the way, in the process of being prepared.

pip·er (pɪ-pěr) *n.* a person who plays on a pipe or bagpipes.

pi·pette, pi·pet (pɪ-pet) *n.* a slender tube used in a laboratory for transferring or measuring small quantities of liquids.

pip·ing (pɪ-ping) *n.* 1. pipes, a length of pipe. 2. a pipelike fold (often enclosing a cord) ornamenting edges or seams of clothing or upholstery. ☐**piping hot,** (of water or food) very hot.

pip·it (pip-it) *n.* a kind of small bird resembling a lark.

pip·kin (pip-kin) *n.* a small earthenware pot or pan.

pip·pin (pip-in) *n.* a kind of apple.

pip·squeak (pip-skweek) *n.* *(slang)* a small or unimportant but self-assertive person.

pi·quant (pee-kănt, -kahnt) *adj.* 1. pleasantly sharp in its taste or smell. 2. pleasantly stimulating or exciting to the mind. **pi′quant·ly** *adv.* **pi·quan·cy** (pee-kăn-see, -kahn-) *n.*

pique (peek) *v.* **(piqued, piqu·ing)** 1. to hurt the pride or self-respect of. 2. to stimulate, *their curiosity was piqued.* **pique** *n.* a feeling of hurt pride.

pi·qué (pi-kay) *n.* a firm fabric especially of cotton, with a lengthwise corded effect or *(waffle piqué)* a woven honeycomb pattern.

pi·quet (pi-ket) *n.* a card game for two players with a pack of thirty-two cards, ace to seven.

pi·ra·nha (pi-rahn-yă) *n.* a voracious South American freshwater fish.

pi·rate (pɪ-rit) *n.* 1. a person on a ship who unlawfully attacks and robs another ship at sea, or who makes a plundering raid on the shore. 2. the ship used for this. 3. one who infringes another's copyright or business rights, or who broadcasts without authorization, *a pirate radio station.* **pirate** *v.* **(pi·rat·ed, pi·rat·ing)** to reproduce (a book etc.) or trade (goods) without due authorization. **pi·rat·i·cal** (pɪ-rat-i-kăl) *adj.* **pi·ra·cy** (pɪ-ră-see) *n.*

pir·ou·ette (pir-oo-et) *n.* a spinning movement of the body while balanced on the point of the toe or the ball of the foot. **pirouette** *v.* **(pir·ou·et·ted, pir·ou·et·ting)** to perform a pirouette.

pis·ca·to·ri·al (pis-kă-tohr-i-ăl) *adj.* of fishing or fish.

Pis·ces (pɪ-seez) *n.* a sign of the zodiac, the Fishes. **Pis′ce·an** *adj. & n.*

pis·mire (pis-mɪr) *n.* *(old use)* an ant.

pis·ta·chi·o (pi-stash-i-oh) *n.* (*pl.* **-chi·os**) a kind of nut with an edible green kernel.

pis·til (pis-tĭl) *n.* the seed-producing part of a flower, comprising ovary, style, and stigma. **pis·til·late** (pis-tĭ-layt) *adj.*

pis·tol (pis-tŏl) *n.* a small gun. ☐**pistol grip,** a handle shaped and held like the butt of a pistol.

pis·tol-whip (pis-tŏl-hwip) *v.* **(pis·tol-whipped, pis·tol-whip·ping)** to beat (a person) with a pistol.

pis·ton (pis-tŏn) *n.* 1. a sliding disk or cylinder fitting closely inside a tube in which it moves up and down as part of an engine or pump. 2. the sliding valve in a trumpet or other brass wind instrument.

pit[1] (pit) *n.* 1. a hole in the ground, especially one from which material is dug out, *chalk pit.* 2. a depression in the skin or in any surface; *pit of the stomach,* the depression between the ribs below the breastbone. 3. a part of the floor of a commodity exchange assigned to special trading, *the wheat pit.* 4. a sunken area at the front of a theater

where musicians sit, *orchestra pit.* 5. a sunken area in a garage floor, giving access to the underside of motor vehicles. 6. a place (at a racetrack) at which racing cars are refueled etc. during a race. **pit** *v.* **(pit·ted, pit·ting)** 1. to make pits or depression in, to become marked with hollows, *pitted with craters.* 2. to match or set in competition, *was pitted against a strong fighter.* ☐**pit stop,** a stop during a race during which racing cars are refueled etc.; *(slang)* refreshment time, a stop for food, drink, etc. **pit viper,** a poisonous snake with a pit between eye and nostril. **the pits,** a mine, *he's spent his life in the pits; (slang)* the worst of anything, *his jokes are the pits.*

pit[2] *n.* the stone of a fruit, such as the peach.

pit-a-pat (pit-ă-pat) *n.* a quick tapping sound. **pit-a-pat** *adv.* with this sound.

pitch[1] (pich) *n.* a dark resinous tarry substance that sets hard, used for caulking seams of ships etc. **pitch** *v.* to coat with pitch. ☐**pitch black, pitch dark,** quite black, with no light at all. **pitch pine,** a kind of pine tree that yields much resin.

pitch[2] *v.* 1. to throw or fling. 2. to erect and fix (a tent or camp). 3. to set at a particular degree or slope or level, *pitched their hopes high.* 4. to fall heavily. 5. (in baseball) to throw (the ball) to the batter for hitting. 6. (of a ship or vehicle) to plunge up and down or forward and backward alternately. 7. *(slang)* to attempt to sell (a product or service) using persuasive talk or advertising. **pitch** *n.* 1. the act or process of pitching. 2. the steepness of a slope. 3. the intensity of a quality etc. 4. the degree of highness or lowness of a musical note or a voice. 5. a throw of the ball to the batter in baseball. 6. *(slang)* a salesman's persuasive talk; *made a big pitch,* worked hard at selling. ☐**pitched battle,** a battle fought by troops in prepared positions, not a skirmish. **pitch in,** *(informal)* to begin to work vigorously. **pitch into,** *(informal)* to attack or reprimand vigorously. **pitch out,** (in baseball) to pitch wide of the strike zone and beyond the batter's reach in order to enable the catcher to prevent a base runner from stealing a base. **pitch pipe,** a small pipe blown by mouth to set the pitch for singing or tuning. **pitch shot,** (in golf) a lofted approach shot with little run to the ball after landing on the green.

pitch·blende (pich-blend) *n.* a mineral ore (uranium oxide) that yields uranium and radium.

pitch·er[1] (pich-ĕr) *n.* the baseball player who throws the ball to the batter. ☐**pitcher's duel,** a low-scoring baseball game whose outcome depends on the skill of the two pitchers. **pitcher's mound,** the raised area in the infield between home plate and second base on which the pitcher stands for pitching.

pitch·er[2] *n.* a jug for holding and pouring liquids. ☐**little pitchers have big ears,** children are apt to overhear things. **pitcher plant,** a plant with pitcher-shaped leaves holding a secretion in which insects become trapped.

pitch·fork (pich-fork) *n.* a long-handled fork used for pitching hay. **pitchfork** *v.* to lift or move (a thing) with a pitchfork.

pitch·man (pich-măn) *n.* (*pl.* **-men,** *pr.* -měn) 1. a traveling salesperson dealing in patent medicines etc., a street vendor. 2. *(slang)* a high pressure salesperson.

pit·e·ous (pit-i-ŭs) *adj.* deserving or arousing pity. **pit′e·ous·ly** *adv.*

pit·fall (pit-fawl) *n.* an unsuspected danger or difficulty.

pith (pith) *n.* 1. the spongy tissue in the stems of certain plants. 2. the essential part, *the pith of the argument.*

pith·y (pith-ee) *adj.* (**pith·i·er, pith·i·est**) 1. like pith, containing much pith. 2. brief and full of meaning, *pithy comments.*

pit·i·a·ble (pit-i-ă-běl) *adj.* deserving or arousing pity or contempt. **pit'i·a·bly** *adv.*

pit·i·ful (pit-ĭ-fŭl) *adj.* pitiable. **pit'i·ful·ly** *adv.*

pit·i·less (pit-i-lis) *adj.* showing no pity. **pit'i·less·ly** *adv.*

pi·ton (pee-ton) *n.* a spike or peg with a hole through which a rope can be passed, driven into a rock or crack as a support in mountain climbing.

pit·tance (pit-ăns) *n.* 1. a very small allowance. 2. a very small amount.

pit·ted (pit-id) *adj.* 1. filled with pits, pockmarked. 2. (of fruit) with pits removed, *pitted cherries.*

pit·ter-pat·ter (pit-ěr-pat-ěr) *n.* a light tapping sound. **pitter-patter** *v.* to make such a sound.

pi·tu·i·tar·y (pi-too-i-ter-ee) *n.* (*pl.* **-tar·ies**) (also **pituitary gland**) a small ductless gland at the base of the brain, with important influence on growth and bodily functions.

pit·y (pit-ee) *n.* (*pl.* **pit·ies**) 1. a feeling of sorrow for another person's suffering. 2. a cause for regret, *what a pity.* **pity** *v.* (**pit·ied, pit·y·ing**) to feel pity for. ☐**take pity on,** to feel concern for and therefore help (a person who is in difficulty).

piv·ot (piv-ŏt) *n.* 1. a central point or shaft etc. on which something turns or swings. 2. a pivoting movement. **pivot** *v.* (**piv·ot·ed, piv·ot·ing**) to turn or place to turn on a pivot. **piv·ot·al** (piv-ŏ-tăl) *adj.*

pix·ie, pix·y (pik-see) *n.* a small supernatural being in fairy tales.

piz·za (peet-să) *n.* an Italian dish consisting of a layer of dough baked with a topping of tomato sauce, cheese, spices, etc. ☐**pizza parlor,** a pizzeria.

piz·zazz (pĭ-zaz) *n.* (*slang*) 1. flamboyant elegance. 2. vitality, zest, *lots of pizzazz.*

piz·ze·ri·a (peet-sě-ree-ă) *n.* a place where pizzas are made and sold.

piz·zi·ca·to (pit-sĭ-kah-toh) *adv.* plucking the string of a musical instrument (instead of using the bow).

pj's (pee-jayz) *n. pl.* (*informal*) pajamas.

pk. *abbr.* 1. pack. 2. park. 3. peak. 4. peck.

pkg. *abbr.* package.

pkt. *abbr.* 1. packet. 2. pocket.

pkwy. *abbr.* parkway.

pl. *abbr.* 1. place. 2. plate. 3. plural.

plac·ard (plak-ărd) *n.* a poster or other notice for displaying. **placard** *v.* to post placards on (a wall etc.).

pla·cate (play-kayt) *v.* (**pla·cat·ed, pla·cat·ing**) to pacify, to conciliate. **plac·a·to·ry** (plak-ă-tohr-ee) *adj.*

place (plays) *n.* 1. a particular part of space or of an area on a surface. 2. a particular town or district or building etc., *one of the places we visited.* 3. (in names) a short street, a square or the buildings around it. 4. a passage or part in a book etc., the part one has reached in reading, *lose one's place.* 5. a proper position for a thing, a position in a series, one's rank or position in a community, a duty appropriate to this, *not his place to give orders.* 6. a position of employment. 7. a space or seat or accommodation for a person, *save me a place on the train.* 8. one's home or dwelling. 9. (in dog or horse racing) the position of second to finish a race. 10. a step in the progression of an argument or statement, *in the first place, the dates are wrong.* 11. the position of a figure after a decimal point etc., *correct to three decimal places.* **place** *v.* (**placed, plac·ing**) 1. to put into a particular place or rank or position or order etc., to find a place for. 2. to locate, to identify in relation to circumstances etc., *I know his face but can't place him.* 3. to put or give, *placed an order with the firm.* 4. (of a horse in a race) to finish second. ☐**in place,** in the right position; suitable. **in place of,** instead of. **out of place,** in the wrong position or environment; unsuitable. **place mat,** a small mat on a dining table for one place setting. **place setting,** a set of dishes or cutlery for one person at a dining table.

pla·ce·bo (plă-see-boh) *n.* (*pl.* **-bos**) a harmless substance given as if it were medicine, to humor a patient or as a dummy pill etc. in a controlled experiment.

place·kick (plays-kik) *n.* a kick made in football when the ball is placed on the ground for that purpose. **placekick** *v.* to kick the ball in such a manner. **place'kick·er** *n.*

place·ment (plays-měnt) *n.* placing. ☐**placement office,** an agency at a college or school that helps students and graduates find jobs.

pla·cen·ta (plă-sen-tă) *n.* (*pl.* **-tas, -tae,** *pr.* -tee) an organ that develops in the womb during pregnancy and supplies the fetus with nourishment. **pla·cen'tal** *adj.*

plac·er (play-sěr) *n.* a deposit of sand, gravel, etc., in a stream bed containing valuable minerals in particles. ☐**placer mining,** removing the valuable minerals from a placer by washing.

plac·id (plas-id) *adj.* calm and peaceful, not easily made anxious or upset. **plac'id·ly** *adv.* **pla·cid·i·ty** (pla-sid-i-tee) *n.*

plack·et (plak-it) *n.* an opening in a woman's skirt to make it easy to put on and take off.

pla·gia·rize (play-jă-rız) *v.* (**pla·gia·rized, pla·gia·riz·ing**) to take and use (another person's ideas or writings or inventions) as one's own. **pla·gia·rism** (play-jă-riz-ěm) *n.* **pla'gia·rist** *n.*

plague (playg) *n.* 1. a deadly contagious disease, especially the bubonic plague in Europe between 1340 and 1700. 2. an infestation of a pest, *a plague of caterpillars.* 3. (*informal*) a nuisance. **plague** *v.* (**plagued, plagu·ing**) to annoy, to pester.

plaice (plays) *n.* (*pl.* **plaice**) a kind of flatfish used as food.

plaid (plad) *n.* 1. a long piece of woolen cloth, usually with a tartan or similar pattern, worn over the shoulder as part of Highland dress. 2. this pattern.

plain (playn) *adj.* 1. unmistakable, easy to see or hear or understand. 2. not elaborate or intricate or luxurious, *plain cooking; plain soda,* without flavoring etc. 3. straightforward, candid, *some plain speaking.* 4. ordinary, homely in manner, without affectation. 5. lacking beauty. **plain** *adv.* plainly, simply, *it's plain stupid.* **plain** *n.* a large area of level country. **plain'ly** *adv.* **plain'ness** *n.* ☐**plain stitch,** the ordinary stitch in knitting, producing a smooth surface toward the knitter.

plain·clothes (playn-klohz) *n.* civilian clothes as

distinct from uniform or official dress. □**plainclothesman,** a detective or other policeman who does not wear a uniform.
plains·man (playnz-măn) *n.* (*pl.* **-men,** *pr.* -měn) an inhabitant of a plain.
plain·song (playn-sawng) *n.* a medieval type of church music for voices singing in unison, without regular rhythm.
plain·spo·ken (playn-spoh-kĕn) *adj.* frank.
plaint (playnt) *n.* (*old use*) 1. a complaint. 2. a lamentation.
plain·tiff (playn-tif) *n.* the party that brings an action in a court of law (opposed to the *defendant*).
plain·tive (playn-tiv) *adj.* sounding sad. **plain'tive·ly** *adv.*
plait (playt, plat) *v.* to braid. **plait** *n.* 1. something plaited. 2. a pleat.
plan (plan) *n.* 1. a drawing showing the relative position and size of parts of a building etc. 2. a map of a town or district. 3. a method or way of proceeding thought out in advance; *it all went according to plan,* happened as planned. **plan** *v.* (**planned, plan·ning**) 1. to make a plan or design of. 2. to arrange a method etc. for, to make plans. **plan'ner** *n.* □**planned parenthood,** the practice of birth control in order to regulate the number and frequency of children.
plan·ar (play-năr) *adj.* of, relating to, in the form of a geometric plane.
plan·chette (plan-chet) *n.* a small board on casters with a vertical pencil said to trace marks on paper at spiritualist seances without conscious direction by hand.
plane¹ (playn) *n.* 1. a tall spreading tree with broad leaves, *the London plane.* 2. a sycamore.
plane² *n.* 1. a flat or level surface. 2. an imaginary surface of this kind. 3. a level of thought or existence or development, *on the same plane as a savage.* 4. an airplane. **plane** *adj.* lying in a plane, level, *a plane figure* or *surface.* □**plane angle,** an angle formed by two intersecting lines. **plane geometry,** geometry that deals with figures in one plane.
plane³ *n.* 1. a tool with a blade projecting from the base, used for smoothing the surface of wood by paring shavings from it. 2. a similar tool for smoothing metal. **plane** *v.* (**planed, plan·ing**) to smooth or pare with a plane.
plane·load (playn-lohd) *n.* a load of passengers or cargo that fills a plane to capacity.
plan·et (plan-it) *n.* one of the heavenly bodies moving around the sun. **plan·e·tar·y** (plan-ĕ-ter-ee) *adj.*
plan·e·tar·i·um (plan-ĕ-tair-i-ŭm) *n.* a room with a domed ceiling on which lights are projected to show the appearance of the stars and planets in the sky at any chosen place or time.
plan·e·tes·i·mal (plan-ĕ-tes-ĭ-măl) *n.* one of the vast number of minute bodies that, according to the *planetesimal hypothesis,* formed the planets by accretion in a cold state.
plan·e·toid (plan-ĕ-toid) *n.* an asteroid.
plan·e·tol·o·gy (plan-ĕ-tol-ŏ-jee) *n.* the branch of astronomy that deals with the planets. **plan·e·tol'o·gist** *n.*
plan·gent (plan-jĕnt) *adj.* (of sounds) 1. resonant, reverberating. 2. loud and mournful. **plan·gen·cy** (plan-jĕn-see) *n.*
plank (plangk) *n.* 1. a long flat piece of timber

several inches thick. 2. one of the basic principles of a political platform. **plank** *v.* 1. to lay with planks. 2. to cook and serve (fish etc.) on a board.
plank·ing (plang-king) *n.* a structure or floor of planks.
plank·ton (plangk-tŏn) *n.* the forms of organic life (chiefly microscopic) that drift or float in the sea or in fresh water. **plank·ton·ic** (plangk-ton-ik) *adj.*
planned (pland) *see* **plan.**
plan·ning (plan-ing) *n.* making plans, especially with reference to the controlled design of buildings and development of land, *town planning.*
plant (plant) *n.* 1. a living organism that makes its own food from inorganic substances and has neither the power of movement nor special organs of sensation and digestion. 2. a small plant (distinguished from a tree or shrub). 3. a factory or its machinery and equipment. 4. (*slang*) a person or thing deliberately placed for discovery by others, a hoax or trap. **plant** *v.* 1. to place in the ground or in soil for growing, to put plants or seeds into (ground or soil) for growing. 2. to fix or set or place in position, *planted his foot on the ladder; planted the idea in her mind.* 3. to station (a person) as a lookout or spy. 4. to conceal (stolen or incriminating articles) in a place where they will be discovered and mislead the discoverer, *planted the evidence.* □**plant food,** nourishment for plants. **plant kingdom,** the division of the natural world comprising all living things that are not animal. **plant louse,** a small insect that infests plants, especially the aphid. **plant pathology,** the branch of botany that deals with diseases of plants.
plan·tain¹ (plan-tin) *n.* a common wild plant with broad flat leaves, bearing seeds that are used as food for cage birds.
plantain² *n.* a tropical tree with fruit resembling the banana.
plan·tar (plan-tăr) *adj.* of the sole of the foot.
plan·ta·tion (plan-tay-shŏn) *n.* 1. a number of cultivated plants or trees, the area of land on which they grow. 2. an estate on which cotton or tobacco or tea etc. is cultivated.
plant·er (plan-tĕr) *n.* 1. a person who owns or manages a plantation, especially in a tropical or subtropical country. 2. a machine for planting things, *potato planter.* 3. a container for decorative plants. □**planter's punch,** an iced drink made from rum, lime, sugar, and water or soda.
plaque (plak) *n.* 1. a flat metal or porcelain plate fixed on a wall or on a piece of wood as an ornament or memorial. 2. film on teeth, where bacteria can live.
plash (plash) *v.* to splash. **plash** *n.* a splashing sound.
plas·ma (plaz-mă) *n.* 1. the colorless fluid part of blood, in which the corpuscles are suspended. 2. whey. 3. a kind of gas containing positively and negatively charged particles in approximately equal numbers. **plas·mat·ic** (plaz-mat-ik) *adj.*
plas·ter (plas-tĕr) *n.* 1. a soft mixture of lime, sand, and water etc. used for coating walls and ceilings. 2. plaster of Paris. 3. a medicinal preparation spread on cloth etc. for applying to the body. **plaster** *v.* 1. to cover (a wall etc.) with plaster or a similar substance. 2. to coat or daub to, to cover thickly. 3. to make smooth with a fixative etc., *his hair was plastered down.* **plas'ter·er** *n.*

☐**plaster cast,** a cast of a statue etc. made in plaster; plaster molded around a part of the body to keep it rigid. **plaster of Paris,** white paste made from gypsum, used for making molds or casts.

plas·ter·board (plas-tĕr-bohrd) n. paper-covered board with a core of gypsum and felt, used for making partitions etc.

plas·tered (plas-tĕrd) adj. (slang) drunk.

plas·tic (plas-tik) n. a synthetic resinous substance that can be given any permanent shape, as by molding it under pressure while heated. **plastic** adj. 1. made of plastic, plastic bag. 2. able to be shaped or molded, clay is a plastic substance. 3. giving form to clay or wax etc.; the plastic arts, those concerned with sculpture or ceramics etc. **plas·tic·i·ty** (plas-tis-i-tee) n. ☐**plastic explosive,** a putty-like explosive, capable of being molded by hand. **plastic surgeon,** a specialist in **plastic surgery,** the repairing or replacing of injured or defective external tissue.

plate (playt) n. 1. an almost flat usually circular utensil from which food is eaten or served, its contents. 2. a similar shallow vessel for the collection of money in church. 3. dishes and other domestic utensils made of gold or silver or other metal. 4. plated metal, objects made of this. 5. a flat thin sheet of metal or glass or other rigid material. 6. this coated with material sensitive to light or other radiation, for use in photography etc. 7. a flat piece of metal on which something is engraved. 8. a piece of metal, plastic, etc. in a printing press, which is inked and transfers an impression to the paper. 9. an illustration on special paper in a book. 10. a thin flat structure or formation in a plant or animal body. 11. a piece of plastic material molded to the shape of the gums or roof of the mouth for holding false teeth, (informal) a denture. 12. a flat piece of whitened rubber marking the station of the batter (home plate) in baseball. **plate** v. (plat·ed, plat·ing) 1. to cover with plates of metal. 2. to coat (metal) with a thin layer of silver or gold or tin. ☐**on one's plate,** (informal) for one to deal with or consider, he had too much on his plate. **plate glass,** glass of fine quality for shop windows etc. **plate rack,** a rack in which plates are kept or placed to drain.

pla·teau (pla-toh) n. 1. an area of fairly level high ground. 2. a state in which there is little variation following an increase, the firm's export trade reached a plateau.

plate·ful (playt-fuul) n. (pl. -fuls) 1. as much as a plate will hold. 2. (informal) a large amount of work etc. to deal with.

plat·en (plat-ĕn) n. 1. a plate in a printing press by which paper is pressed against type. 2. the corresponding part in a typewriter etc.

plat·form (plat-form) n. 1. a level surface raised above the surrounding ground or floor, especially one from which a speaker addresses an audience. 2. a raised area along the side of the rails at a railroad station, where passengers get on or off the trains. 3. the declared policy or program of a political party.

plat·ing (play-ting) n. a coating of gold, silver, etc.

plat·i·num (plat-ĭ-nŭm) n. a silver-white metallic element that does not tarnish. ☐**platinum blonde,** a woman with very light blonde hair.

plat·i·tude (plat-i-tood) n. a commonplace remark, especially one uttered solemnly as if it were new. **plat·i·tu·di·nous** (plat-i-too-dĭ-nŭs) adj.

pla·ton·ic (plă-ton-ik) adj. (often **Platonic**) of the ancient Greek philosopher Plato (4th century B.C.) or his doctrines. ☐**platonic love** or **friendship,** affection that does not involve sexual love.

pla·toon (plă-toon) n. a subdivision of a military company.

plat·ter (plat-ĕr) n. 1. a flat dish or plate, often of wood. 2. a large shallow dish or plate for serving food. 3. (informal) a phonograph record. ☐**on a platter,** (informal) available without the recipient having to make an effort.

plat·y (plat-ee) n. (pl. **plat·y, plat·ys, plat·ies**) a brightly colored freshwater fish often kept in aquariums.

plat·y·pus (plat-i-pŭs) n. (pl. **-pus·es, -pi,** pr. -pi) an Australian animal with a duck-like beak and a flat tail, which lays eggs but suckles its young.

plau·dits (plaw-dits) n. pl. a round of applause, an emphatic expression of approval.

plau·si·ble (plaw-zĭ-bĕl) adj. 1. (of a statement) seeming to be reasonable or probable but not proved. 2. (of a person) persuasive but deceptive. **plau'si·bly** adv. **plau·si·bil·i·ty** (plaw-zĭ-bil-i-tee) n.

play (play) v. 1. to occupy oneself in a game or other recreational activity. 2. to take part in (a game), play football. 3. to compete against (a player or team) in a game. 4. to occupy (a specified position) in a game. 5. to move (a piece) or put (a card) on the table or strike (a ball etc.) in a game. 6. to act in a drama etc., to act the part of; play the fool, to behave like one. 7. to perform (a part in a process). 8. to perform on (a musical instrument), to perform (a piece of music). 9. to cause (a record player or tape recorder etc.) to produce sound. 10. to move lightly or irregularly, to allow (light or water) to fall on something, (of a fountain or hose pipe) to discharge water. 11. to allow (a hooked fish) to exhaust itself by its pulling against the line. **play** n. 1. playing; a play on words, a pun. 2. a move or action in a game, a chess play; a football play. 3. activity, operation, other influences came into play. 4. a literary work written for performance on the stage, a similar work for broadcasting. 5. free movement, bolts should have half an inch of play. **play'a·ble** adj. ☐**in** or **out of play,** (of a ball) being used, or temporarily out of use according to the rules, in a game. **make a play for,** (informal) to try to win as a girlfriend or boyfriend. **play along,** to cooperate unenthusiastically. **play around,** to behave irresponsibly. **play at,** to perform in a trivial or halfhearted way. **play ball,** (informal) to cooperate. **play both ends against the middle,** to manipulate two opposing groups, taking advantage of both for personal gain. **play by ear,** to perform (music) without having seen a written score; to proceed step by step, going by one's instinct or by results. **play down,** to minimize the importance of. **played out,** exhausted, used up. **play for time,** to seek to gain time by delaying. **play games,** to act without serious intent. **play group,** a group of young children who play together regularly under supervision. **playing card,** one of a pack or set of fifty-two oblong pieces of pasteboard used to play a variety of games, marked on one side to show one of thirteen ranks in one of four suits. **playing field,** a field used for outdoor games. **play into someone's hands,** to do something that unwittingly gives him an advantage. **play off one person against another,** to oppose one person to another in order to serve one's own interests. **play on,** to affect and make use of (a person's sympathy etc.). **play one's cards right** *or* **well,** to make good use of one's opportunities. **play safe,** to act with caution. **play the field,** *(informal)* to avoid exclusive commitment to one person. **play the game,** to keep the rules; to behave honorably. **play the market,** to speculate in stocks etc. **play up to,** to try to win the favor of or encourage (a person) by flattery etc. **play with,** to toy with; *play with fire,* to treat frivolously something that could prove dangerous.

pla·ya (**plī**-ä) *n.* a desert basin that becomes a lake after a heavy rainfall.

play·act·ing (**play**-ak-ting) *n.* 1. the playing of a part in a play. 2. the act of pretending.

play·back (**play**-bak) *n.* 1. the playing back of sound. 2. a device for doing this. **playback** *v.* to play (what has recently been recorded) on a tape recorder etc.

play·bill (**play**-bil) *n.* a placard or program of a theatrical play.

play·book (**play**-buuk) *n.* a book containing diagramed football plays.

play·boy (**play**-boi) *n.* a pleasure-loving usually rich man.

play-by-play (**play**-bī-play) *n.* a detailed account, such as a broadcast of a sports event.

play·er (**play**-ĕr) *n.* 1. a person who takes part in a game. 2. a performer on a musical instrument. 3. an actor. □**player piano,** a piano fitted with apparatus that enables it to play automatically.

play·ful (**play**-fŭl) *adj.* 1. full of fun. 2. in a mood for play, not serious. **play'ful·ly** *adv.* **play'ful·ness** *n.*

play·go·er (**play**-goh-ĕr) *n.* a person who frequently attends theatrical plays.

play·ground (**play**-grownd) *n.* 1. a piece of ground for children to play on. 2. a favorite place for recreation.

play·house (**play**-hows) *n.* (*pl.* **-hous·es,** *pr.* -how-ziz) 1. a theater. 2. a small house that children play in.

play·let (**play**-lit) *n.* a short play.

play·mate (**play**-mayt) *n.* a child's companion in play.

play·off (**play**-awf) *n.* a match played to decide a draw or tie.

play·pen (**play**-pen) *n.* a portable enclosure for a young child to play in.

play·suit (**play**-soot) *n.* a garment for a young child to play in.

play·thing (**play**-thing) *n.* 1. a toy. 2. something treated as a thing to play with.

play·time (**play**-tīm) *n.* time assigned for children to play.

play·wright (**play**-rīt) *n.* a person who writes plays, a dramatist.

pla·za (**plaz**-ä, **plah**-zä) *n.* a public square or open space in a city or town.

plea (plee) *n.* 1. a formal statement (especially of "guilty" or "not guilty") made by or on behalf of a person charged in a court of law. 2. an appeal or entreaty, *a plea for mercy.* 3. an excuse, *on the plea of ill health.* □**plea bargaining,** the procedure whereby a defendant agrees to plead guilty in return for a light sentence or other leniency.

plead (pleed) *v.* (**plead·ed** or **pled, plead·ing**) 1. to put forward as a plea in a court of law. 2. to address a court of law as an advocate, to put forward (a case) in court. 3. to make an appeal or entreaty; *plead with a person,* to entreat him. 4. to put forward as an excuse, *pleaded a previous engagement.*

pleas·ant (**plez**-ănt) *adj.* 1. pleasing, giving pleasure to the mind or feelings or senses. 2. having an agreeable manner. **pleas'ant·ly** *adv.* **pleas'ant·ness** *n.*

pleas·ant·ry (**plez**-ăn-tree) *n.* (*pl.* **-ries**) 1. a courteous or friendly remark. 2. a humorous or playful remark or act.

please (pleez) *v.* (**pleased, pleas·ing**) 1. to give pleasure to, to make (a person etc.) feel satisfied or glad. 2. to be so kind as to, *please ring the bell.* 3. to think fit, to have the desire, *take what you please.* **please** *adv.* a polite phrase of request. □**if you please,** *(formal)* please; an ironical phrase, pointing out unreasonableness, *and so, if you please, we're to get nothing!* **please oneself,** to do as one chooses.

pleased (pleezd) *adj.* feeling or showing pleasure or satisfaction.

pleas·ur·a·ble (**plezh**-ŭ-ră-bĕl) *adj.* causing pleasure. **pleas'ur·a·bly** *adv.*

pleas·ure (**plezh**-ŭr) *n.* 1. a feeling of satisfaction or joy, enjoyment. 2. a source of pleasure, *it's a pleasure to talk to him.* 3. choice, desire, *at your pleasure.* **pleasure** *adj.* done or used for pleasure, *a pleasure trip.* □**with pleasure,** willingly, gladly.

pleat (pleet) *n.* a flat fold made by doubling cloth on itself. **pleat** *v.* to make a pleat or pleats in. **pleat·ed** (**plee**-tid) *adj.* having pleats, as a skirt.

plebe (pleeb) *n.* a member of the lowest (freshman) class at the U.S. Naval Academy or the U.S. Military Academy.

ple·be·ian (plĕ-**bee**-ăn) *adj.* 1. of the lower social classes. 2. uncultured, vulgar, *plebeian tastes.* **plebeian** *n.* a member of the lower classes.

pleb·i·scite (**pleb**-i-sīt) *n.* a referendum, a vote by all the people of a country etc. on an important public matter.

plebs (plebz) *n.* (*pl.* **ple·bes,** *pr.* plee-beez) 1. the common people of ancient Rome. 2. the common people.

plec·trum (**plek**-trŭm) *n.* (*pl.* **-tra,** *pr.* -trä, **-trums**) a small piece of metal or bone or ivory held or attached to a finger for plucking the strings of a musical instrument.

pledge (plej) *n.* 1. a solemn promise. 2. a thing deposited as security for payment of a debt or fulfillment of a contract etc., and liable to be forfeited in case of failure. 3. a token of something, *as a pledge of his devotion.* 4. a toast drunk to someone's health. 5. a provisional member of a fraternity or sorority. **pledge** *v.* (**pledged, pledg·ing**) 1. to promise or cause to promise solemnly. 2. to deposit (an article) as a pledge. 3. to drink to the health of. 4. to promise to join (a fraternity, sorority, etc.).

Pleis·to·cene (**plīs**-tŏ-seen) *adj.* of the earlier geologic epoch of the Quaternary period. **Pleistocene** *n.* the Pleistocene epoch.

ple·na·ry (**plee**-nă-ree) *adj.* 1. attended by all members, *a plenary session of the assembly.* 2. full, complete, a legislature with *plenary powers.*

plen·i·po·ten·ti·ar·y (plen-i-pŏ-**ten**-shi-er-ee) *n.* (*pl.* **-ar·ies**) an envoy with full powers to take action or make decisions etc. on behalf of the government he represents. **plenipotentiary** adj. having these powers.

plen·i·tude (plen-i-tood) n. abundance, a plenitude of flowers; trees in plenitude. ▷The word is plenitude not plentitude.

plen·te·ous (plen-ti-ŭs) adj. plentiful.

plen·ti·ful (plen-ti-fŭl) adj. in large quantities or numbers, abundant. **plen'ti·ful·ly** adv.

plen·ty (plen-tee) n. (pl. **-ties**) quite enough, as much as one could need or desire. **plenty** adv. (informal) quite, fully, it's plenty big enough.

ple·num (plee-nŭm) n. (pl. **-nums, -na,** pr. -nä) 1. a space filled with matter. 2. a full assembly.

ple·o·nasm (plee-ŏ-naz-ĕm) n. an expression in which a word is redundant, as in hear with one's ears.

pleth·o·ra (pleth-ŏ-rä) n. an overabundance.

pleu·ri·sy (ploor-ĭ-see) n. inflammation of the membrane (the pleura) lining the chest and surrounding the lungs.

Plex·i·glas (plek-si-glas) n. (trademark) plexiglass.

plex·i·glass (plek-si-glas) n. a transparent acrylic plastic, used in signs, windows, etc.

plex·us (plek-sŭs) n. (pl. **-us·es, -us**) 1. a network of nerves or blood vessels. 2. a network, a complication.

pli·a·ble (plɪ-ă-bĕl) adj. 1. bending easily, flexible. 2. easily influenced. **pli'a·bly** adv. **pli·a·bil·i·ty** (plɪ-ă-bil-i-tee) n.

pli·ant (plɪ-ănt) adj. pliable. **pli'ant·ly** adv. **pli·an·cy** (plɪ-ăn-see) n.

pli·ers (plɪ-ĕrz) n. pl. pincers having jaws with flat surfaces that can be brought together for gripping small objects or wire etc.

plight[1] (plɪt) n. a serious and difficult situation.

plight[2] v. (old use) to pledge. □**plight one's troth,** to say one's marriage vows; to be engaged to marry.

plinth (plinth) n. a block or slab forming the base of a column or a support for a vase etc.

Pli·o·cene (plɪ-ŏ-seen) adj. of the latest geologic epoch of the Tertiary period. **Pliocene** n. the Pliocene epoch.

PLO abbr. Palestine Liberation Organization.

plod (plod) v. (**plod·ded, plod·ding**) 1. to walk doggedly or laboriously, to trudge. 2. to work at a slow but steady rate. **plod** n. plodding. **plod'der** n. **plod'ding·ly** adv.

plop (plop) n. a sound like that of something dropping into water without a splash. **plop** v. (**plopped, plop·ping**) to cause to fall in this manner, plop an ice cube into this glass.

plot (plot) n. 1. a small measured piece of land, building plots. 2. the plan or story in a play or novel or film. 3. a conspiracy, a secret plan, Gunpowder Plot. **plot** v. (**plot·ted, plot·ting**) 1. to make a plan or map of. 2. to mark on a chart or diagram. 3. to plan secretly, to contrive a secret plan. **plot'ter** n.

plov·er (pluv-ĕr, ploh-vĕr) n. (pl. **-ers, -er**) a kind of wading bird.

plow (plow) n. 1. an implement for cutting furrows in soil, drawn by a tractor or by draft animals. 2. an implement resembling a plow, snowplow. **plow** v. 1. to turn up (earth) or cast out (roots etc.) with a plow, to cut (a furrow). 2. to clear snow from (a driveway etc.). 3. to make one's way laboriously, plowed through the mud or through a book. □**plow back,** to turn (growing grass etc.) into the soil to enrich it; to reinvest profits in the business that produced them. **plow'er** n. **plow'a·ble** adj.

plow·man (plow-măn) n. (pl. **-men,** pr. -měn) a man who guides a plow.

plow·share (plow-shair) n. the cutting blade of a plow.

ploy (ploi) n. a cunning maneuver to gain an advantage.

pluck (pluk) v. 1. to pick (a flower or fruit), to pull out (a hair or feather etc.). 2. to strip (a bird) of its feathers. 3. to pull at or twitch. 4. to sound (the string of a musical instrument) by pulling and then releasing it with the finger(s) or a plectrum. **pluck** n. 1. plucking, a pull. 2. courage, spirit. □**pluck up courage,** to summon up one's courage.

pluck·y (pluk-ee) adj. (**pluck·i·er, pluck·i·est**) showing pluck, brave. **pluck'i·ly** adv.

plug (plug) n. 1. something fitting into and stopping or filling a hole or cavity. 2. a device with metal pins that fit into an outlet to make an electrical connection. 3. a spark plug. 4. a cake of tobacco, a piece of this cut off for chewing. 5. (informal) a piece of favorable publicity for a commercial product. 6. an artificial fishing lure. 7. (slang) an old worn-out horse. **plug** v. (**plugged, plug·ging**) 1. to put a plug into, to stop with a plug. 2. (slang) to shoot (a person etc.). 3. (informal) to mention favorably, to seek to popularize (a song or product or policy etc.) by constant commendation. □**plug away,** to work diligently or persistently. **plug in,** to connect electrically by inserting a plug into a socket.

plum (plum) n. 1. a fleshy fruit with sweet pulp and a flattish pointed pit. 2. the tree that bears it. 3. (old use) a dried grape or raisin used in cooking; plum cake or pudding, containing such fruit. 4. reddish-purple color. 5. a good thing, the best of a collection, something considered good and desirable, the job was a real plum.

plum·age (ploo-mij) n. a bird's feathers.

plumb (plum) n. a piece of lead tied to the end of a cord, used for finding the depth of water or testing whether a wall etc. is vertical. **plumb** adj. exactly vertical, straight up and down. **plumb** adv. 1. exactly, plumb in the middle. 2. (informal) completely, plumb crazy. **plumb** v. 1. to measure or test with a plumb line. 2. to reach, plumbed the depths of the lake. 3. to get to the bottom of (a matter). □**plumb bob,** the weight attached to a plumb line. **plumb line,** a cord with a plumb attached.

plumb·er (plum-ĕr) n. a person whose job is to fit and repair plumbing. **plumb** v. to work as a plumber. □**plumber's helper,** a plumber's assistant; (informal) = **plunger** (definition 2).

plumb·ing (plum-ing) n. a system of water pipes, water tanks, drainpipes, etc. in a building.

plume (ploom) n. 1. a feather, especially a large one used for ornament. 2. an ornament of feathers or similar material. 3. something resembling this, a plume of smoke. **plume** v. (**plumed, plum·ing**) to preen, the bird plumed itself or its feathers.

plumed (ploomd) adj. ornamented with plumes.

plum·met (plum-it) n. a plumb or plumb bob. **plummet** v. (**plum·met·ed, plum·met·ing**) to fall or plunge steeply.

plump[1] (plump) adj. having a full rounded shape. **plump** v. to make or become plump, to plump a pillow. **plump'ness** n.

plump² *v.* to drop or plunge abruptly, *plumped down.* **plump** *adv.* with a sudden or heavy fall. □**plump for,** to choose or vote for wholeheartedly, to decide on.

plun·der (**plun**-dĕr) *v.* to rob (a place or person) forcibly or systematically, to steal or embezzle. **plunder** *n.* 1. the taking of goods or money etc. in this way. 2. the goods etc. acquired. **plun′ der·er** *n.*

plunge (plunj) *v.* (**plunged, plung·ing**) 1. to thrust or go forcefully into something. 2. to descend suddenly. 3. to jump or dive into water. 4. to enter or cause to enter a condition or set of circumstances, *plunged the world into war.* 5. (of a horse) to start forward violently, (of a ship) to thrust its bow down into the water, to pitch. 6. to gamble heavily or run deeply into debt. **plunge** *n.* plunging, a dive. □**take the plunge,** to take a bold decisive step.

plung·er (**plun**-jĕr) *n.* 1. the part of a mechanism that works with a plunging or thrusting movement. 2. a rubber cup on a handle for removing blockages by alternate thrusting and suction. 3. a reckless gambler, a speculator.

plunk (plungk) *v.* 1. (*informal*) to throw or place or drop down heavily. 2. to hit unexpectedly. 3. to pluck the strings of a harp, banjo, etc. **plunk** *n.* the sound or act of plunking. □**plunk down,** to drop heavily.

plu·per·fect (ploo-pur-fikt) *adj. & n.* = past perfect (*see* **tense**).

plu·ral (ploor-ăl) *n.* the form of a noun or verb used with reference to more than one person or thing, *the plural of "child" is "children."* **plural** *adj.* 1. of this form. 2. of more than one.

plu·ral·ism (ploor-ă-liz-ĕm) *n.* a form of society in which members of minority groups maintain independent traditions. **plu′ral·ist** *adj.* **plu·ral· ist·ic** (ploor-ă-lis-tik) *adj.*

plu·ral·i·ty (pluu-ral-i-tee) *n.* (*pl.* **-ties**) 1. the state of being plural. 2. the number of votes by which the total cast for the winner exceeds that of his nearest rival. ▷See the note under **majority.**

plu·ral·ize (ploor-ă-lız) *v.* (**plu·ral·ized, plu· ral·iz·ing**) to make or express as plural. **plu· ral·i·za·tion** (ploor-ă-li-zay-shŏn) *n.*

plus (plus) *prep.* 1. with the addition of. 2. above zero, *temperature between minus ten and plus ten degrees.* **plus** *n.* (*pl.* **plus·es**) 1. the sign +. 2. an advantage. **plus** *adj.* more than the quantity indicated; *B plus (B+),* a grade slightly above B. □**plus fours,** knickers once worn especially by golfers (▷so named because the length was increased by four inches to produce the overhang). **plus sign,** the sign + .

plush (plush) *n.* a kind of cloth with long soft nap, used in home furnishings. **plush** *adj.* 1. made of plush. 2. plushy.

plush·y (plush-ee) *adj.* (**plush·i·er, plush·i· est**) luxurious. **plush′i·ness** *n.*

Plu·to (ploo-toh) *n.* 1. a planet in the solar system. 2. the god of the underworld in Greek mythology.

plu·toc·ra·cy (ploo-tok-ră-see) *n.* (*pl.* **-cies**) 1. rule of the wealthy. 2. a nation ruled by the wealthy.

plu·to·crat (ploo-tŏ-krat) *n.* a person who is powerful because of his wealth. **plu·to·crat·ic** (ploo-tŏ-krat-ik) *adj.*

plu·ton (ploo-ton) *n.* a body of rock exposed after solidification at a great depth.

plu·to·ni·um (ploo-toh-ni-ŭm) *n.* a radioactive chemical element, used in nuclear weapons and reactors.

plu·vi·al (ploo-vi-ăl) *adj.* 1. of rain, rainy. 2. (in geology) caused by rain.

plu·vi·om·e·ter (ploo-vi-om-ĕ-tĕr) *n.* a rain gauge.

ply¹ (plı) *n.* (*pl.* **plies**) 1. a thickness or layer of wood or cloth etc. 2. a strand in yarn, *three-ply wool.*

ply² *v.* (**plied, ply·ing**) 1. to use or wield (a tool or weapon). 2. to work at, *ply one's trade.* 3. to work steadily. 4. to keep offering or supplying, *plied her with food* or *with questions.* 5. to go to and fro regularly, *the boat plies between the two harbors.*

Plym·outh (plim-ŭth) **Rock** 1. a medium-sized breed of domestic fowl of American origin. 2. a boulder on the coast at Plymouth, Massachusetts, said to be the landing place of the Pilgrim Fathers.

ply·wood (plı-wuud) *n.* strong thin board made by gluing layers with the grain crosswise.

Pm *symbol* promethium.

pm. *abbr.* premium.

p.m. *abbr. post meridiem.*

P.M. *abbr.* 1. paymaster. 2. postmaster. 3. *post meridiem.* 4. postmortem. 5. Prime Minister. 6. provost marshal.

pmk. *abbr.* postmark.

pmt. *abbr.* payment.

PN *abbr.* promissory note.

pneu·mat·ic (nuu-mat-ik) *adj.* filled with or operated by compressed air, *pneumatic tires; pneumatic drills.* **pneu·mat′i·cal·ly** *adv.*

pneu·mat·ics (nuu-mat-iks) *n.* the branch of physics that deals with the physical properties of gases.

pneu·mo·co·ni·o·sis (noo-moh-koh-ni-oh-sis) *n.* a lung disease caused by inhalation of dust etc.

pneu·mo·nia (nuu-mohn-yă) *n.* inflammation of one or both lungs.

Po *symbol* polonium.

P.O. *abbr.* 1. petty officer. 2. post office.

poach¹ (pohch) *v.* 1. to cook (an egg removed from its shell) in boiling water or in a poacher. 2. to cook (fish or fruit etc.) by simmering it in a small amount of liquid.

poach² *v.* 1. to take (game or fish) illegally from private land or water. 2. to trespass or encroach on something that properly belongs to another person. **poach′er¹** *n.* a person who poaches.

poach·er² (poh-chĕr) *n.* a pan with one or more cup-shaped containers in which eggs are placed for cooking over boiling water.

POB *abbr.* post office box.

POC *abbr.* port of call.

pock (pok) *n.* (also **pockmark**) 1. one of the spots that erupt on the skin in smallpox. 2. a scar left by this.

pock·et (pok-it) *n.* 1. a small baglike part sewn into or on a garment, for holding money or small articles. 2. one's resources of money; *beyond my pocket,* more than I can afford. 3. a pouchlike compartment in a suitcase or on a car door etc. 4. one of the pouches at the corners or sides of a pool table, into which balls are driven. 5. an isolated group or area, *small pockets of resistance.* **pocket** *adj.* of a size or shape suitable for carrying in a pocket, *pocket calculator.* **pocket** *v.* 1. to put into one's pocket. 2. to take for oneself (dishonestly or otherwise). 3. to send (a ball) into a pocket on a pool table. 4. to suppress or hide (one's feelings), *pocketing his pride.* □**in a person's pocket,** completely under his influence. **in pocket,** having gained in a transaction. **out of pocket,** having lost in a transaction. **out-of-pocket expenses,** cash expenses incurred while doing something. **pocket gopher,** = **gopher.** **pocket money,** money for small expenses. **pocket veto,** an indirect veto of a bill by a president or governor etc. who retains the bill unsigned until after adjournment of the legislature. **pocket watch,** a watch designed to be carried in a special pocket of a man's suit.

pock·et·book (pok-it-buuk) *n.* 1. a purse or handbag. 2. financial resources. 3. a paperback book, small enough to be carried in a pocket.

pock·et·ful (pok-it-fuul) *n.* (*pl.* **-fuls**) the amount that a pocket will hold.

pock·et·knife (pok-it-nif) *n.* (*pl.* **-knives,** *pr.* nɪvz) a knife with a folding blade or blades, for carrying in the pocket.

pock·marked (pok-mahrkt) *adj.* marked by scars or pits.

pod (pod) *n.* 1. a long seed vessel like that of a pea or bean. 2. a compartment suspended under an aircraft. **pod** *v.* (**pod·ded, pod·ding**) to bear or form pods.

POD *abbr.* 1. pay on delivery. 2. port of debarkation.

po·di·a·trist (pŏ-dɪ-ă-trist) *n.* an expert in podiatry.

po·di·a·try (pŏ-dɪ-ă-tree) *n.* the study and treatment of ailments of the human foot, as bunions, calluses, etc.

po·di·um (poh-di-ŭm) *n.* a pedestal or platform.

POE *abbr.* 1. port of embarkation. 2. port of entry.

po·em (poh-ĕm) *n.* a literary composition in verse, especially one expressing deep feeling or noble thought in an imaginative way.

po·e·sy (poh-ĕ-zee) *n.* (*pl.* **-sies**) (*old use*) the art of poetry.

po·et (poh-it) *n.* a writer of poems. **po·et·ess** (poh-i-tis) *n. fem.* ▷Many regard the word *poetess* as objectionable and prefer to use *poet* for women as well as for men.

po·et·as·ter (poh-it-as-tĕr) *n.* an inferior poet.

po·et·ic (poh-et-ik) *adj.* of or like poetry, of poets. □**poetic justice,** well-deserved punishment or reward.

po·et·i·cal (poh-et-i-kăl) *adj.* poetic, written in verse, *poetical works.* **po·et'i·cal·ly** *adv.*

po·et·ry (poh-i-tree) *n.* 1. poems, a poet's art or work. 2. a quality that pleases the mind as poetry does, *the poetry of motion.*

po·grom (pŏ-grom) *n.* an organized massacre, originally and especially of Jews in Russia.

poi (poi) *n.* a Hawaiian food made from the taro root.

poign·ant (poin-yănt) *adj.* arousing sympathy, deeply moving to the feelings, keenly felt, *poignant grief.* **poign'ant·ly** *adv.* **poign·an·cy** (poin-yăn-see) *n.*

poi·lu (pwah-loo) *n.* (*old use*) a French private soldier.

poin·ci·an·a (poin-si-an-ă) *n.* a tropical tree with bright red flowers.

poin·set·ti·a (poin-set-i-ă) *n.* a plant with large sometimes scarlet petallike leaves.

point (point) *n.* 1. the tapered or sharp end of something, the tip. 2. a projection, a promontory of land. 3. (in geometry) that which has position but not magnitude, such as the intersection of two lines. 4. a dot used as a punctuation mark,

a decimal point. 5. a particular place or spot, an exact moment, a stage or degree of progress or increase of temperature etc. 6. one of the directions marked on the compass, a corresponding direction toward the horizon. 7. a unit of measurement or value or scoring. 8. a separate item or detail, *we differ on several points.* 9. a distinctive feature or characteristic; *it has its points,* has certain useful features. 10. the essential thing, the thing under discussion, *come to the point.* 11. the important feature of a story or joke or remark. 12. effectiveness, purpose, value, *there's no point in wasting time.* **point** *v.* 1. to direct or aim (a finger or weapon etc.). 2. to be directed or aimed. 3. to direct attention, to indicate; *it all points to a conspiracy,* is evidence of one. 4. to sharpen. 5. to fill in the joints of (brickwork etc.) with mortar or cement. □**a case in point,** one that is relevant to what has just been said. **beside the point,** irrelevant. **make a point of,** to treat as important, to do something with ostentatious care. **on the point of,** on the very verge of (an action). **point of no return,** the point in a long journey at which one must continue onward because supplies are insufficient to enable one to return to the starting point; the point after which one cannot withdraw from an action. **point of view,** a way of looking at a matter. **point out,** to indicate, to draw attention to. **point up,** to emphasize. **stretch a point,** to exaggerate or misrepresent the fact. **to the point,** relevant, relevantly.

point·blank (point-blangk) *adj.* 1. (of a shot) aimed or fired at very close range. 2. (of a remark) direct, straightforward, *a pointblank refusal.* **pointblank** *adv.* in a pointblank manner, *refused pointblank.*

point·ed (poin-tid) *adj.* 1. tapering or sharpened to a point. 2. (of a remark or manner) clearly aimed at a particular person or thing, emphasized. **point'ed·ly** *adv.*

point·er (poin-tĕr) *n.* 1. a thing that points to something, a mark or rod that points to figures etc. on a dial or scale. 2. a rod used to point to things on a blackboard etc. 3. (*informal*) a brief piece of advice, *pointers on good grooming.* 4. a dog of a breed that on scenting game stands rigidly with muzzle pointing toward it.

poin·til·lism (pwan-tĭ-liz-ĕm) *n.* (in painting) a technique of producing light effects by crowding a surface with small spots of various colors, which are blended by the spectator's eye.

poin·til·list (pwan-tĭ-list) *n.* a painter who uses pointillism.

point·less (point-lis) *adj.* 1. without a point. 2. having no purpose or meaning. **point'less·ly** *adv.*

poise (poiz) *v.* (**poised, pois·ing**) 1. to balance or be balanced. 2. to hold suspended or supported. **poise** *n.* 1. balance, the way something is poised. 2. a dignified and self-assured manner.

poised (poizd) *adj.* having poise of manner.

poi·son (poi-zŏn) *n.* 1. a substance that can destroy the life or harm the health of a living animal or plant. 2. a harmful influence. **poison** *v.* 1. to give poison to, to kill with poison. 2. to put poison on or in. 3. to corrupt, to fill with prejudice, *poisoned their minds.* **poi'son·er** *n.* □**poison hemlock,** a poisonous herb of the carrot family. **poison ivy,** a climbing plant with shiny leaves that secrete an irritant oil. **poison oak,** a plant closely related to poison ivy and possessing similar properties. **poison pen,** a person who writes malicious or slanderous anonymous letters, *poison pen letters.*

poi·son·ous (poi-zŏ-nŭs) *adj.* 1. containing or having the effect of poison. 2. likely to corrupt people, *a poisonous influence.*

poke¹ (pohk) *v.* **(poked, pok·ing)** 1. to thrust with the end of a finger or a stick etc.; *poke the fire,* stir it with a poker. 2. to thrust or be thrust forward, to protrude. 3. to produce by poking, *poked a hole in it.* 4. to search, to pry, *poking about in the attic.* 5. to move slowly, to dawdle, *they were poking along to school as if they had all day.* 6. *(informal)* to punch (a person). **poke** *n.* poking, a thrust or nudge. □**poke fun at,** to ridicule. **poke one's nose into something,** to pry or intrude.

poke² *n. (informal)* a bag or sack, *buy a pig in a poke (see* **pig**).

pok·er¹ (poh-kĕr) *n.* a stiff metal rod for poking a fire.

poker² *n.* a card game in which players bet on whose hand of cards has the highest value. □**poker face,** a face that does not reveal thoughts or feelings; a person with such a face.

poke·weed (pohk-weed) *n.* a tall American plant with purple berries and white flowers.

pok·y (poh-kee) *adj.* **(pok·i·er, pok·i·est)** 1. slow to accomplish something or get somewhere. 2. small and cramped, *poky little rooms.* **poky, pok·ey** *n. (slang)* jail.

pol (pol) *n. (informal)* a politician.

pol. *abbr.* 1. political. 2. politics.

Pol. *abbr.* 1. Poland. 2. Polish.

Po·land (poh-lănd) a country in eastern Europe.

po·lar (poh-lăr) *adj.* 1. of or near the North Pole or South Pole. 2. of one of the poles of a magnet. 3. directly opposite in character or tendency. □**polar bear,** a white bear living in arctic regions.

Po·lar·is (pŏ-lair-is) *n.* the North Star.

po·lar·i·ty (poh-lar-i-tee) *n.* (*pl.* **-ties**) the possessing of negative and positive poles.

po·lar·ize (poh-lă-rız) *v.* **(po·lar·ized, po·lar·iz·ing)** 1. to confine similar vibrations of (light waves etc.) to a single direction or plane. 2. to give polarity to. 3. to set or become set at opposite extremes of opinion, *public opinion had polarized.* **po·lar·i·za·tion** (poh-lă-ri-zay-shŏn) *n.*

Po·lar·oid (poh-lă-roid) *n. (trademark)* 1. a material that polarizes the light passing through it, used in spectacle lenses etc. to protect the eyes from glare. 2. a kind of camera that develops and prints a photograph rapidly when an exposure is made.

pol·der (pohl-dĕr) *n.* a piece of low-lying land reclaimed from the sea or a river, especially in the Netherlands.

pole¹ (pohl) *n.* 1. a long slender rounded piece of wood or metal, especially one used as part of a supporting structure. 2. a unit of measurement = rod. **pole** *v.* **(poled, pol·ing)** to push along (a raft etc.) by using a pole. □**pole vault,** a vault over a high crossbar with the help of a pole held in the hands.

pole² *n.* 1. either extremity of Earth's or another body's axis, either of two points in the sky about which stars appear to rotate, the North Pole or South Pole. 2. each of the two points in a magnet that attract or repel magnetic bodies. 3. the positive or negative terminal of an electric cell or battery. 4. each of two opposed principles. □**be poles apart,** to differ greatly.

Pole (pohl) *n.* a Polish person.

pole·ax (pohl-aks) *n.* 1. a battle-ax with a long handle. 2. a butcher's implement for slaughtering cattle. **pole-ax** *v.* **(pole-axed, pole-ax·ing)** to strike down with or as if with a poleax.

pole·cat (pohl-kat) *n.* 1. a skunk. 2. *(slang)* a rascal.

po·lem·ic (pŏ-lem-ik) *n.* 1. a verbal attack on a belief or opinion. 2. *polemics,* the practice of argumentation. **polemic** *adj.* 1. controversial. 2. argumentative. **po·lem'i·cal** *adj.* **po·lem·i·cist** (pŏ-lem-ĭ-sist) *n.*

pole·star (pohl-stahr) *n.* a star in the Little Bear, near the North Pole in the sky, Polaris.

po·lice (pŏ-lees) *n.* 1. a civil force responsible for the keeping of public order, its members, *the police have been called.* 2. a force responsible for enforcing the regulations of an organization etc., *military police; campus police.* **police** *v.* **(po·liced, po·lic·ing)** to keep order in (a place) by means of police, to patrol. □**police action,** a military action taken without formal declaration of war when international peace or order is violated or threatened. **police car,** a special car for policemen to use while on duty. **police court,** a municipal court for trying persons accused of minor offenses or for referring to a higher court those accused of major offenses. **police dog,** a German shepherd or dog of another breed used to assist the police. **police officer,** a policeman or policewoman. **police power,** a nation's sovereign power to regulate the conduct of its citizens. **police state,** a country (usually a totalitarian state) in which political police supervise and control citizens' activities. **police station,** the office of a police force. **police wagon,** a van used by police for transporting prisoners.

po·lice·man (pŏ-lees-măn) *n.* (*pl.* **-men,** *pr.* -mĕn) a man who is a member of a police force.

po·lice·wom·an (pŏ-lees-wuum-ăn) *n.* (*pl.* -**wom·en,** *pr.* -wim-in) a woman member of a police force.

pol·i·cy¹ (pol-ĭ-see) *n.* (*pl.* **-cies**) the course or general plan of action adopted by a government or party or person.

policy² *n.* 1. a contract of insurance, the document containing this. 2. *(slang)* a gambling game in which bets are made on the occurrence of three numbers that are unpredictable, such as the last three digits in a parimutuel pool.

pol·i·cy·hold·er (pol-ĭ-see-hohl-dĕr) *n.* a person or firm for which an insurance policy is written.

po·li·o (poh-li-oh) *n.* poliomyelitis.

po·li·o·my·e·li·tis (poh-li-oh-mı-ĕ-lı-tis) *n.* an infectious disease caused by a virus, producing temporary or permanent paralysis.

pol·ish (pol-ish) *v.* 1. to make or become smooth and glossy by rubbing. 2. to make better by correcting or putting finishing touches. **polish** *n.* 1. smoothness and glossiness. 2. the process of polishing. 3. a substance for polishing a surface. 4. a high degree of elegance. **pol'ish·er** *n.* □**polish off,** to finish off.

Po·lish (poh-lish) *adj.* of Poland or its people or language. **Polish** *n.* 1. the language of Poland. 2. *the Polish,* the people of Poland.

pol·ished (pol-isht) *adj.* elegant, refined, perfected, *polished manners; a polished performance.*

polit. *abbr.* 1. political. 2. politics.

Po·lit·bu·ro (pol-it-byoor-oh) *n.* (*pl.* -ros) the principal committee of a Communist party.

po·lite (pŏ-līt) *adj.* (-lit·er, -lit·est) 1. having good manners, socially correct. 2. refined, *polite society.* **po·lite'ly** *adv.* **po·lite'ness** *n.*

pol·i·tic (pol-i-tik) *adj.* showing good judgment, prudent. ☐**the body politic,** *see* **body.**

po·lit·i·cal (pŏ-lit-i-kăl) *adj.* 1. of or engaged in politics. 2. of the way a country is governed, *its political system.* **po·lit'i·cal·ly** *adv.* ☐**political asylum,** refuge in foreign territory for refugees from political persecution. **political prisoner,** a person imprisoned for a political offense.

pol·i·ti·cian (pol-i-tish-ăn) *n.* a person who is engaged in politics.

po·lit·i·cize (pŏ-lit-i-sīz) *v.* (**po·lit·i·cized, po· lit·i·ciz·ing**) 1. to give political character to, *politicized the Department of Public Welfare.* 2. to engage in or talk politics.

pol·i·tick (pol-i-tik) *v.* *(informal)* to engage in or talk politics.

po·lit·i·co (pŏ-lit-i-koh) *n.* (*pl.* -cos) *(slang)* a politician.

pol·i·tics (pol-i-tiks) *n. sing.* 1. the science and art of governing a country. 2. political affairs or life. 3. maneuvering for power etc. within a group, *office politics.* **politics** *n. pl.* political principles or affairs or tactics.

pol·i·ty (pol-i-tee) *n.* (*pl.* -ties) 1. the form or process of civil government. 2. a nation or other politically organized society.

Polk (pohk), **James K.** (1795-1849) the eleventh president of the U.S. 1845-49.

pol·ka (pohl-kä) *n.* a lively dance for couples, of Bohemian origin. **polka** *v.* to dance the polka.

pol·ka (pohl-kä) **dots** round dots, evenly spaced to form a pattern on fabric.

poll (pohl) *n.* 1. voting at an election, the counting of votes, the number of votes recorded. 2. *polls,* the place where voting is held. 3. an estimate of public opinion made by questioning a representative sample of people. 4. *(old use)* the head. **poll** *v.* 1. to vote at an election. 2. (of a candidate) to receive as votes. 3. to interview in a poll. 4. to cut off the horns of (cattle) or the top of (a tree etc.). ☐**polling place,** a place where votes are recorded. **poll tax,** a tax levied on every person, formerly a prerequisite for voting in some states.

pol·lack (pol-ăk) *n.* (*pl.* -lack, -lacks) a sea fish related to the cod, used as food.

pol·lard (pol-ărd) *n.* 1. a tree that is polled so as to produce a close head of young branches. 2. an animal that has cast or lost its horns, an ox or sheep or goat of a hornless breed. **pollard** *v.* to make (a tree) into a pollard, *pollarded willows.*

polled (pohld) *adj.* made hornless.

pol·len (pol-ĕn) *n.* a fine powdery substance produced by the anthers of flowers, containing the fertilizing element. ☐**pollen count,** an index of the amount of pollen in the air, published as a warning to those who are allergic to pollen.

pol·li·nate (pol-ĭ-nayt) *v.* (**pol·li·nat·ed, pol· li·nat·ing**) to shed pollen on, to fertilize with pollen. **pol·li·na·tion** (pol-i-nay-shŏn) *n.*

pol·li·wog (pol-i-wog) *n.* a tadpole.

poll·ster (pohl-stĕr) *n.* a person who conducts opinion polls.

pol·lu·tant (pŏ-loo-tănt) *n.* a substance causing pollution.

pol·lute (pŏ-loot) *v.* (**pol·lut·ed, pol·lut·ing**) 1. to make dirty or impure, especially by adding harmful or offensive substances. 2. to corrupt, *polluting the mind.* **pol·lut'er** *n.* **pol·lu·tion** (pŏ-loo-shŏn) *n.*

po·lo (poh-loh) *n.* a game played by teams on horseback with long-handled mallets. ☐**polo coat,** a double-breasted coat, usually of camel's hair. **polo shirt,** a short-sleeved sport shirt.

pol·o·naise (pol-ŏ-nayz) *n.* a stately dance of Polish origin, music for this or in this style.

po·lo·ni·um (pŏ-loh-ni-ŭm) *n.* a radioactive metallic element.

pol·ter·geist (pohl-tĕr-gīst) *n.* a ghost or spirit that throws things about noisily.

pol·troon (pol-troon) *n.* *(old use)* a spiritless coward.

poly- *prefix* many, much, as in *polygamy.*

pol·y·an·dry (pol-i-an-dree) *n.* the system of having more than one husband at a time.

pol·y·chrome (pol-i-krohm) *adj.* painted or printed or decorated in many colors.

pol·y·clin·ic (pol-i-klin-ik) *n.* a hospital devoted to treatment of all diseases.

pol·y·crys·tal (pol-i-kris-tăl) *n.* a polycrystalline body.

pol·y·crys·tal·line (pol-i-kris-tă-lin) *adj.* consisting of several or many crystals with various orientations.

pol·y·es·ter (pol-i-es-tĕr, pol-i-es-tĕr) *n.* a polymerized substance, especially as a synthetic resin or fiber.

pol·y·eth·yl·ene (pol-i-eth-ĭ-leen) *n.* a polymer used for electrical insulation, packaging, etc.

po·lyg·a·my (pŏ-lig-ă-mee) *n.* the system of having more than one wife at a time. **po·lyg'a· mous** *adj.* **po·lyg'a·mist** *n.*

pol·y·glot (pol-i-glot) *adj.* knowing or using or written in several languages. **polyglot** *n.* a person who knows several languages.

pol·y·gon (pol-i-gon) *n.* a geometric figure with many (usually five or more) sides. **po·lyg·o· nal** (pŏ-lig-ŏ-năl) *adj.*

pol·y·graph (pol-i-graf) *n.* 1. a lie detector. 2. a writer of many or various works.

pol·y·he·dron (pol-i-hee-drŏn) *n.* a solid figure with many (usually seven or more) faces. **pol· y·he'dral** *adj.*

pol·y·math (pol-i-math) *n.* a person with knowledge of many subjects, a great scholar.

pol·y·mer (pol-ĭ-mĕr) *n.* a compound whose molecule is formed of a large number of simpler molecules of the same kind. **pol·y·mer·ic** (pol-ĭ-mer-ik) *adj.*

po·lym·er·ize (pŏ-lim-ĕ-rīz) *v.* (**po·lym·er· ized, po·lym·er·iz·ing**) to combine or become combined into a polymer. **po·lym·er·i·za·tion** (pŏ-lim-ĕ-ri-zay-shŏn) *n.*

Pol·y·ne·sia (pol-ĭ-nee-*zh*ă) a group of islands in the Pacific Ocean, including New Zealand, Hawaii, and Samoa. **Pol·y·ne'sian** *adj.* & *n.*

pol·y·no·mi·al (pol-ĭ-noh-mi-ăl) *n.* an algebraic expression of more than two terms. **polynomial** *adj.*

pol·yp (pol-ip) *n.* 1. a simple organism with a tube-shaped body, such as one of the organisms of which coral is composed. 2. an abnormal growth projecting from a mucous membrane, as in the nose.

pol·y·phon·ic (pol-i-fon-ik) *adj.* (of music) having two or more intertwined melodic lines. **po·ly· pho·ny** (pŏ-li-phŏ-nee) *n.*

pol·y·sty·rene (pol-i-stɪ-reen) *n.* a kind of hard plastic, a polymer of styrene.

pol·y·syl·lab·ic (pol-i-si-lab-ik) *adj.* having three or more syllables, *polysyllabic words.*

pol·y·syl·la·ble (pol-i-sil-ă-běl) *n.* a word of three or more syllables.

pol·y·tech·nic (pol-i-tek-nik) *n.* an institution giving instruction in many subjects, especially technical ones and industrial arts.

pol·y·the·ism (pol-i-thee-iz-ěm) *n.* belief in or worship of more than one god. **pol′y·the·ist** *n.* **pol·y·the·is·tic** (pol-i-thee-is-tik) *adj.*

pol·y·un·sat·u·rat·ed (pol-i-un-sach-ŭ-ray-tid) *adj.* of a kind of fat or oil that (unlike animal and dairy fats) is not associated with the formation of cholesterol in the blood.

pol·y·ur·e·thane (pol-i-yoor-ě-thayn) *n.* a kind of synthetic resin or plastic.

pol·y·vi·nyl (pol-i-vɪ-nǐl) *adj.* made from polymerized vinyl. □**polyvinyl chloride,** a plastic used for insulation, floor coverings, fabrics, etc.

po·made (pŏ-mayd, -mahd) *n.* a scented ointment for the hair. **pomade** *v.* (**po·mad·ed, po·mad·ing**) to apply pomade to.

po·man·der (poh-măn-děr, pŏm-an-děr) *n.* (also **pomander ball**) a ball of mixed sweet-smelling substances or a round container for this, used to perfume closets etc.

po·me·gran·ate (pom-ě-gran-it, pom-ě-gran-it) *n.* 1. a tropical fruit with tough rind and reddish pulp enclosing many seeds. 2. the tree that produces it.

Pom·er·a·ni·an (pom-ě-ray-ni-ăn) *n.* a dog of a small silky-haired breed.

pom·mel (pum-ěl) *n.* 1. a knob on the handle of a sword. 2. an upward projection at the front of a saddle. **pommel** *v.* (**pom·meled, pom·mel·ing**) to pummel.

pomp (pomp) *n.* a stately and splendid ceremonial.

pom·pa·dour (pom-pă-dohr) *n.* a hairstyle in which the hair is brushed up and back from the forehead.

pom·pa·no (pom-pă-noh) *n.* (*pl.* -**nos,** -**no**) a food fish from the West Indies and South America.

pom-pom (pom-pom) *n.* 1. a decorative tuft or ball on a cap or costume. 2. a type of dahlia or other flower with small tightly clustered petals.

pom·pon (pom-pon) *n.* a pom-pom.

pomp·ous (pom-pŭs) *adj.* full of ostentatious dignity and self-importance. **pomp′ous·ly** *adv.* **pom·pos·i·ty** (pom-pos-i-tee) *n.*

pon·cho (pon-choh) *n.* (*pl.* -**chos**) 1. a blanketlike piece of cloth with a slit in the center for the head, worn as a cloak. 2. a garment shaped like this.

pond (pond) *n.* a small area of still water.

pon·der (pon-děr) *v.* 1. to be deep in thought. 2. to think something over thoroughly.

pon·der·o·sa (pon-dě-roh-să) **pine** 1. a tall tree of western North America. 2. its wood.

pon·der·ous (pon-dě-rŭs) *adj.* 1. heavy, unwieldy. 2. laborious in style. **pon′der·ous·ly** *adv.*

pone (pohn) *n.* a fine light bread made with milk, eggs, etc.

pon·gee (pon-jee) *n.* a soft silk fabric, usually in its natural tan color.

pon·iard (pon-yărd) *n.* a dagger.

pon·tiff (pon-tif) *n.* 1. the Pope. 2. a bishop. 3. a high priest.

pon·tif·i·cal (pon-tif-i-kăl) *adj.* 1. of or relating to the Pope or pontiff. 2. pompously dogmatic. **pon·tif′i·cal·ly** *adv.* □**Pontifical Mass,** one

celebrated by a bishop in full vestments.

pon·tif·i·cate (pon-tif-i-kayt) *v.* (**pon·tif·i·cat·ed, pon·tif·i·cat·ing**) to speak in a pontifical way. **pontificate** (pon-tif-i-kit) *n.* the office of a pontiff.

pon·toon (pon-toon) *n.* 1. a kind of flat-bottomed boat. 2. one of a number of boats or hollow metal cylinders etc. used to support a temporary bridge. □**pontoon bridge,** a temporary bridge held in place by pontoons.

po·ny (poh-nee) *n.* (*pl.* -**nies**) 1. a horse of any small breed. 2. a crib for students. 3. a small serving of whiskey etc.

po·ny·tail (poh-nee-tayl) *n.* a woman's or girl's long hair drawn back and tied at the back of the head so that it hangs down.

pooch (pooch) *n.* (*slang*) a dog.

poo·dle (poo-děl) *n.* a dog with thick curly hair often clipped or shaved in a pattern.

pooh (poo) *interj.* an exclamation of impatience or contempt.

Pooh Bah (poo bah) a person who holds many offices at once. ▷From a character in W. S. Gilbert's *The Mikado.*

pooh-pooh (poo-poo) *v.* to dismiss (an idea etc.) scornfully.

pool¹ (pool) *n.* 1. a small area of still water, especially one that is naturally formed. 2. a shallow patch of water or other liquid lying on a surface, a puddle. 3. a swimming pool. 4. a deep place in a river.

pool² *n.* 1. a common fund, such as one containing the total stakes in a gambling venture. 2. a common supply of vehicles or commodities or services etc. for sharing among a number of people or firms. 3. a game resembling billiards but played on a pool table. **pool** *v.* to put into a common fund or supply, for sharing. □**pool hall** or **room,** a place for playing pool. **pool table,** a table with six pockets for playing pool.

poop¹ (poop) *n.* the stern of a ship, a raised deck at the stern.

poop² *n.* (*slang*) information.

poop³ *n.* (*slang*) feces, especially of animals or children. □**poop′er scoop′er,** a scoop designed for picking up feces from sidewalks and streets.

pooped (poopt) *adj.* (*slang*) (of a person) tired. □**poop out,** (*slang*) to become too tired to continue.

poor (poor) *adj.* 1. having little money or means; *the poor,* poor people. 2. deficient in something, *poor in minerals.* 3. scanty, inadequate, less good than is usual or expected, *a poor crop; he is a poor driver; poor soil,* not fertile; *a poor loser,* one who is resentful at losing. 4. lacking in spirit, despicable. 5. deserving pity or sympathy, unfortunate, *poor fellow!* **poor′ness** *n.* □**poor boy,** a hero sandwich. **poor laws,** those relating to support of paupers.

poor·house (poor-hows) *n.* (*pl.* -**hous·es,** *pr.* -how-ziz) a public institution for paupers.

poor·ly (poor-lee) *adv.* in a poor way, badly. **poorly** *adj.* unwell, *feeling poorly.* ▷Careful speakers say *feeling poor.*

poor-mouth (poor-mowth) *v.* (*informal*) to complain about one's poverty, using it as an excuse.

pop¹ (pop) *n.* 1. a small sharp explosive sound. 2. a carbonated drink, *soda pop.* **pop** *v.* (**popped, pop·ping**) 1. to make or cause to make a pop. 2. to cause to burst with a pop, to heat (corn) until it bursts open. 3. to put quickly or suddenly, *pop it in the oven.* 4. to come or go quickly or suddenly or unexpectedly, *popped out for coffee.* □**pop fly,** (in baseball) a high fly ball that does not travel far. **pop off,** *(slang)* to speak loudly or indiscreetly; to die. **pop out,** (in baseball) to be out by hitting a pop fly that is caught. **pop the question,** *(informal)* to propose marriage.

pop² *n. (informal)* father.

pop³ *adj.* in a popular modern style. **pop** *n.* pop music; *top of the pops,* most popular of current recordings; *pop group,* performing pop music; *pop festival,* at which pop music is performed. □**pop art,** a style of art that relies on images in posters and comic strips.

pop. *abbr.* 1. popular. 2. population.

pop·corn (pop-korn) *n.* 1. a kind of corn with hard kernels that burst outward when heated. 2. this corn when popped, used as a snack food. □**popcorn ball,** a ball of popcorn held together by a candy syrup.

pope (pohp) *n.* (often **Pope**) the bishop of Rome, head of the Roman Catholic Church.

pop·eyed (pop-id) *adj.* with bulging eyes.

pop·gun (pop-gun) *n.* a child's toy gun that shoots a cork etc. with a popping sound.

pop·in·jay (pop-in-jay) *n.* a vain talkative person.

pop·ish (poh-pish) *adj. (contemptuous)* of Roman Catholicism or the papal system.

pop·lar (pop-lăr) *n.* a kind of tall slender tree often with leaves that quiver easily.

pop·lin (pop-lin) *n.* a plain woven fabric usually of cotton.

pop·o·ver (pop-oh-věr) *n.* a light puffy muffin with a hollow center.

pop·pa (pop-ă) *n. (informal)* father.

pop·per (pop-ěr) *n.* a utensil for popping corn.

pop·pet (pop-it) *n.* (also **poppet valve**) a type of valve operated by a rising and falling stem.

pop·py (pop-ee) *n. (pl.* **-pies**) a plant with showy flowers and milky juice. □**poppy seed,** the seed of the poppy.

pop·py·cock (pop-ee-kok) *n. (slang)* nonsense.

pop·u·lace (pop-yŭ-lis) *n.* the general public.

pop·u·lar (pop-yŭ-lăr) *adj.* 1. liked or enjoyed by many people. 2. of or for the general public. 3. (of a belief etc.) held by many people, *popular superstitions.* **pop'u·lar·ly** *adv.* **pop·u·lar·i·ty** (pop-yŭ-lar-i-tee) *n.* □**popular front,** a political party representing left-wing groups.

pop·u·lar·ize (pop-yŭ-lă-riz) *v.* (**pop·u·lar·ized, pop·u·lar·iz·ing**) 1. to make generally liked. 2. to make generally known, to present (a subject etc.) so that it can be understood by ordinary people. **pop'u·lar·iz·er** *n.* **pop·u·lar·i·za·tion** (pop-yŭ-lă-ri-zay-shŏn) *n.*

pop·u·late (pop-yŭ-layt) *v.* (**pop·u·lat·ed, pop·u·lat·ing**) to supply with a population, to form the population of, *densely populated.*

pop·u·la·tion (pop-yŭ-lay-shŏn) *n.* the inhabitants of a place or district or country, the total number of these. □**population explosion,** a rapid or sudden increase in population.

pop·u·list (pop-yŭ-list) *adj.* of a political party or movement claiming to represent the whole of the people. **populist** *n.* **pop'u·lism** *n.*

pop·u·lous (pop-yŭ-lŭs) *adj.* thickly populated.

pop-up (pop-up) *n.* a pop fly.

p.o.r. *abbr.* pay on return.

por·ce·lain (pohr-sĕ-lin) *n.* 1. a fine kind of usually translucent pottery with a transparent glaze. 2. objects made of this.

por·ce·lain·ize (pohr-sĕ-li-nız) *v.* (**por·ce·**

lain·ized, por·ce·lain·iz·ing) to coat with a porcelain glaze.

porch (pohrch) *n.* 1. an open or enclosed room at the side of a house. 2. a roofed shelter forming the approach to the entrance of a house.

por·cine (por-sin) *adj.* of or like pigs.

por·cu·pine (por-kyŭ-pin) *n.* a rodent with a body and tail covered with protective spines.

pore¹ (pohr) *n.* one of the tiny openings on an animal's skin or on a leaf, through which moisture may be emitted (for example as sweat) or taken in.

pore² *v.* (**pored, por·ing**) **pore over** or **through,** to study (a thing) with close attention.

por·gy (por-gee) *n. (pl.* **-gies, -gy**) a perchlike sea fish.

pork (pohrk) *n.* unsalted pig flesh as food. □**pork barrel,** *(slang)* government funds used as a source of political benefit.

pork·er (pohr-kěr) *n.* a pig raised for food, a young fattened pig.

pork·pie (pohrk-pı) *n.* a pie filled with chopped pork. □**porkpie hat,** a hat with a flat rimmed crown and a brim turned up all around.

porn (porn) *n. (slang)* pornography.

por·nog·ra·phy (por-nog-ră-fee) *n.* writings or pictures or films etc. that are intended to stimulate erotic feelings by description or portrayal of sexual activity. **por·nog'ra·pher** *n.* **por·no·graph·ic** (por-nŏ-graf-ik) *adj.*

po·rous (pohr-ŭs) *adj.* 1. containing pores. 2. able to be permeated by liquid or air. **po·ros·i·ty** (pŏ-ros-i-tee) *n.*

por·phy·ry (por-fi-ree) *n. (pl.* **-ries**) a kind of rock containing crystals of minerals.

por·poise (por-pŏs) *n. (pl.* **-pois·es, -poise**) a sea animal resembling a dolphin or small whale, with a blunt rounded snout.

por·ridge (por-ij) *n.* (chiefly *British*) a food made by boiling oatmeal or other meal or cereal to a thick paste in water or milk.

por·rin·ger (por-in-jěr) *n. (old use)* a low cup or dish from which soup or porridge is eaten, especially by children.

port¹ (pohrt) *n.* 1. a harbor, a town with a harbor, especially one where goods are imported or exported by ship. 2. an airport where goods pass in and out of a country and where customs officers are stationed to supervise this. □**Port Louis,** the capital of Mauritius. **Port Moresby,** the capital of Papua New Guinea. **port of call,** a place where a ship stops during a journey. **port of entry,** a place where goods may be cleared through a customhouse; a place where aliens may enter a country.

port² *n.* 1. an opening in a ship's side for entrance, loading, etc. 2. a porthole.

port³ *n.* the left-hand side (when facing forward) of a ship or aircraft. **port** *v.* to turn this way, *port your helm.*

port⁴ *n.* a strong sweet usually dark red wine of Portugal.

Port. *abbr.* 1. Portugal. 2. Portuguese.

port·a·ble (pohr-tă-bĕl) *adj.* able to be carried, *portable typewriters.* **portable** *n.* a portable kind of typewriter, television set, etc. **port·a·bil·i·ty** (pohr-tă-bil-i-tee) *n.*

por·tage (pohr-tij) *n.* the carrying of boats or goods overland between two rivers etc., the route for this. **portage** *v.* (**por·taged, por·tag·ing**) to carry over a portage.

por·tal (pohr-tăl) *n.* a doorway or gateway, especially an imposing one. □**portal-to-portal pay,** wages that include allowances for the time a workman spends in going from the entrance of his factory, mine, etc. to his work station and back to the exit at the close of the work day.

Port-au-Prince (pohrt-oh-**prins**) the capital of Haiti.

port·cul·lis (pohrt-**kul**-is) *n.* a strong heavy vertical grating that can be lowered in grooves to block the gateway to a castle etc.

porte-co·chere (pohrt-koh-**shair**) *n.* a structure extending from the entrance of a building over the place where vehicles stop to discharge passengers.

por·tend (pohr-tend) *v.* to foreshadow.

por·tent (pohr-tent) *n.* an omen, a significant sign of something to come. **por·ten·tous** (pohr-ten-tŭs) *adj.*

por·ter (pohr-tĕr) *n.* 1. a person employed to carry luggage or other burdens. 2. an attendant on a railroad sleeping car. 3. *(old use)* a dark ale.

por·ter·house (pohr-tĕr-hows) *n.* (also **porterhouse steak**) a choice cut of beef.

port·fo·li·o (pohrt-foh-li-oh) *n.* (*pl.* **-li·os**) 1. a case for holding loose sheets of paper or drawings etc. 2. a set of investments held by one investor. 3. (in some countries) the position of a cabinet officer; *held the Treasury portfolio,* was in charge of the Treasury Department. □**minister without portfolio,** (in some countries) a cabinet officer who is not in charge of any government department.

port·hole (pohrt-hohl) *n.* a window-like structure in the side of a ship or aircraft.

por·ti·co (pohr-tĭ-koh) *n.* (*pl.* **-coes**) a structure consisting of a roof supported on columns, usually forming a porch to a building.

por·tiere (pohr-tyair) *n.* a curtain hung over a doorway.

por·tion (pohr-shŏn) *n.* 1. a part or share of something. 2. the amount of food allotted to one person. 3. one's destiny or lot. 4. a dowry. **portion** *v.* to divide into portions, to distribute in portions, *portion it out.*

por·tion·less (pohr-shŏn-lis) *adj.* without an inheritance or dowry.

Port·land (pohrt-lănd) **cement** a kind of cement colored like *Portland stone* from the Isle of Portland, in Dorset, England.

port·ly (pohrt-lee) *adj.* (**port·li·er, port·li·est**) (of a man) stout, corpulent. **port'li·ness** *n.*

port·man·teau (pohrt-man-toh) *n.* (*pl.* **-teaus, -teaux,** *pr.* -tohz) (chiefly *British*) a trunk for clothes etc. that opens into two equal parts. □**portmanteau word,** an invented word combining the sounds and meanings of two others, as *motel* (from *motor* and *hotel*), *moped* (from *motor* and *pedal*).

Port-of-Spain (pohrt-ŏv-spayn) the capital of Trinidad and Tobago.

Por·to No·vo (pohr-toh noh-voh) the capital of Benin.

por·trait (pohr-trit) *n.* 1. a picture or drawing or photograph of a person or animal. 2. a description in words. **por'trait·ist** *n.*

por·trai·ture (pohr-tri-chŭr) *n.* 1. the making of portraits. 2. a portrait.

por·tray (pohr-tray) *v.* 1. to make a picture of. 2. to describe in words or represent in a play

etc., *she is portrayed as a pathetic character.* **por·tray'al** *n.*

Port-Sal·ut (pohr-să-loo) *n.* a pale mild type of French cheese.

Por·tu·gal (pohr-chŭ-găl) a country in southwest Europe.

Por·tu·guese (pohr-chŭ-geez) *adj.* of Portugal or its people or language. **Portuguese** *n.* (*pl.* **-guese**) 1. a native of Portugal. 2. the language of Portugal. □**Portuguese man-of-war,** a sea animal with tentacles that have a poisonous sting.

por·tu·lac·a (pohr-chŭ-lak-ă) *n.* an annual plant with bright flowers.

pos. *abbr.* 1. position. 2. positive.

pose (pohz) *v.* (**posed, pos·ing**) 1. to put into or take a desired position for a portrait or photograph etc. 2. to take a particular attitude for effect. 3. to pretend to be, *posed as an expert.* 4. to put forward, to present, *pose a question* or *a problem.* **pose** *n.* 1. an attitude in which a person etc. is posed. 2. an affectation, a pretense.

pos·er[1] (poh-zĕr) *n.* a puzzling question or problem.

poser[2] *n.* a person who poses.

po·seur (poh-zur) *n.* a person who poses for effect or behaves affectedly.

posh (posh) *adj.* *(slang)* very smart, luxurious. ▷This word is sometimes said to have derived from the initials of *Port out, starboard home,* referring to the more expensive side for accommodation on ships formerly traveling between England and India. This suggestion lacks foundation. The origin of *posh* is uncertain.

pos·it (poz-it) *v.* to present or assume as fact.

po·si·tion (pŏ-zish-ŏn) *n.* 1. the place occupied by a person or thing. 2. the proper place for something, *in* or *out of position.* 3. an advantageous location, *maneuvering for position.* 4. the way in which a thing or its parts are placed or arranged. 5. a situation in relation to other people or things, *this puts me in a difficult position.* 6. a point of view, *what is their position on tax reform?* 7. rank or status, high social standing, *people of position.* 8. paid employment, a job. **position** *v.* to place in a certain position. □**position paper,** a document that presents one's position as a basis for negotiation or discussion.

pos·i·tive (poz-i-tiv) *adj.* 1. stated formally or explicitly, *positive rules.* 2. definite, leaving no room for doubt, *we have positive proof.* 3. holding an opinion confidently. 4. *(informal)* clear, out-and-out, *it's a positive miracle.* 5. constructive and helpful, *made some positive suggestions.* 6. having specific or definite qualities or characteristics; *the result of the test was positive,* indicated that a specific substance etc. was present. 7. (of a quantity) greater than zero. 8. containing or producing the kind of electrical charge produced by rubbing glass with silk; *positive terminal of a battery,* the one through which electric current enters the battery. 9. (of a photograph) having the lights and shades or colors as in the actual object or scene photographed, not as in a negative. **positive** *n.* a positive quality or quantity or photograph etc.

pos'i·tive·ly *adv.* **pos'i·tive·ness** *n.* □**positive pole,** the north-seeking pole of a magnet.

pos·i·tron (poz-i-tron) *n.* an elementary particle with the mass of an electron and a charge of the same amount as the electron's but positive.

poss. *abbr.* possessive.

pos·se (pos-ee) *n.* a body of men legally empowered to assist a sheriff etc. in arresting criminals etc.

pos·sess (pŏ-zes) *v.* 1. to hold belonging to oneself, to have or own. 2. to occupy or dominate the mind of, *be possessed by a devil or with an idea; fought like one possessed,* as if strengthened by an evil spirit or a powerful emotion. □**possessed of,** having, owning.

pos·ses·sion (pŏ-zesh-ŏn) *n.* 1. possessing, being possessed. 2. a thing possessed. □**take possession of,** to become the owner or possessor of.

pos·ses·sive (pŏ-zes-iv) *adj.* 1. of or indicating possession; *the possessive form of a word,* such as *your, John's, the baker's.* 2. showing a desire to possess or to retain what one possesses, *a possessive attitude toward her books.* 3. showing a desire to control or dominate (a person), *a possessive husband.* **pos·ses'sive·ly** *adv.* **pos·ses'sive·ness** *n.* □**possessive pronoun,** *see* **pronoun.**

pos·si·bil·i·ty (pos-ĭ-bil-i-tee) *n.* (*pl.* **-ties**) 1. the fact or condition of being possible. 2. something that may exist or happen, *rain is a possibility today.* 3. capability of being used or of producing good results, *the plan has distinct possibilities.*

pos·si·ble (pos-ĭ-běl) *adj.* capable of existing or happening or being done or used etc. **possible** *n.* a candidate who may be successful, one who may become a member of a team.

pos·si·bly (pos-ĭ-blee) *adv.* 1. in accordance with possibility, *can't possibly do it.* 2. perhaps, in spite of all one knows to the contrary.

pos·sum (pos-ŭm) *n.* an opossum □**play possum,** to pretend to be unaware of something. ▷From the opossum's habit of feigning death when in danger.

post¹ (pohst) *n.* 1. a piece of timber or metal set upright in the ground etc. to support something or to mark a position. 2. the starting post or winning post in a race; *left at the post,* outdistanced from the start. **post** *v.* to announce by putting up a notice or placard etc.; *post no bills,* a warning that notices must not be pasted up; *the ship was posted as missing,* was announced to be missing. □**post time,** the time at which all horses running in a race are required to be at the starting post.

post² *n.* 1. the place where a soldier is on watch, *a place of duty, the sentries are at their posts.* 2. a place occupied by soldiers, especially a frontier fort, the soldiers there. 3. a place occupied for purposes of trade, especially in a region that is not yet fully settled, *trading posts.* 4. a position of paid employment, *got a post with a textile firm.* **post** *v.* 1. to place or station, *we posted sentries.* 2. to appoint to a post or command. □**post exchange,** a store on government base for military personnel and their families.

post³ *n.* mail (*see* **mail¹**). **post** *v.* 1. to mail. 2. (in bookkeeping) to carry (an entry) from an auxiliary book to a more formal one. □**keep a person posted,** to keep him informed. **post chaise,** (*old use*) a closed horse-drawn carriage for two or four persons. **post office,** a building or room where postal business is carried on. **Post Office,** a public department or corporation responsible for postal service.

post- *prefix* after, as in *postwar.*

post·age (poh-stij) *n.* the charge for sending something by mail. □**postage meter,** a machine that marks the postage and postmark on mail and records the cost of postage incurred. **postage stamp,** a small adhesive stamp for sticking on

things to be mailed, showing the amount paid. **post·al** (poh-stăl) *adj.* of the post. □**postal card,** a postcard. **postal permit,** a printed marking on mail indicating that postage has been paid. **postal service,** a government agency or department that handles the transmission of mail.

post·card (pohst-kahrd) *n.* a card for conveyance by mail without an envelope, or a similar card for various purposes.

post·date (pohst-dayt) *v.* (**post·dat·ed, post·dat·ing**) to put a date on (a document or check etc.) that is later than the actual one.

post·doc·tor·al (pohst-dok-tŏ-răl) *adj.* of academic study beyond a doctoral degree.

post·er (poh-stĕr) *n.* a large sheet of paper announcing or advertising something, for display in a public place. □**poster paint,** a gummy opaque paint.

pos·te·ri·or (po-steer-i-ŏr) *adj.* situated behind or at the back. **posterior** *n.* the buttocks.

pos·ter·i·ty (po-ster-i-tee) *n.* 1. future generations. 2. a person's descendants.

pos·tern (poh-stĕrn) *n.* a small entrance at the back or side of a fortress etc.

post·grad·u·ate (pohst-graj-oo-it) *adj.* engaged in or involving study after taking a bachelor's degree or (in a high school) after graduation. **postgraduate** *n.* a student engaged in such studies.

post·haste (pohst-hayst) *adv.* with great speed or haste.

post·hu·mous (pos-chŭ-mŭs) *adj.* 1. (of a child) born after its father's death. 2. coming or happening after a person's death, *a posthumous award; a posthumous novel,* published after the author's death. **post'hu·mous·ly** *adv.*

post·hyp·not·ic (pohst-hip-not-ik) *adj.* of or relating to the period following a hypnotic trance.

pos·til·ion, pos·til·lion (poh-stil-yŏn) *n.* the rider on the near horse drawing a coach etc. without a coachman.

post-im·pres·sion·ist (pohst-im-presh-ŏ-nist) *n.* one of the painters in the last two decades of the 19th century employing a style directed to expressing the artist's conception of the objects represented rather than the conception of the ordinary observer. **post-im·pres'sion·ism** *n.*

post·lude (pohst-lood) *n.* a concluding musical piece or movement.

post·man (pohst-măn) *n.* (*pl.* **-men,** *pr.* -měn) a person who collects letters etc., a mailman.

post·mark (pohst-mahrk) *n.* an official mark stamped on something sent by mail, giving the place and date of marking. **postmark** *v.* to mark with a postmark.

post·mas·ter (pohst-mas-tĕr) *n.* a man in charge of a post office. □**postmaster general,** the official at the head of a country's postal service.

post me·ri·di·em (pohst mĕ-rid-i-ĕm) between noon and midnight. ▷Latin.

post·mis·tress (pohst-mis-tris) *n.* a woman in charge of a post office.

post·mor·tem (pohst-mor-tĕm) *adj. & adv.* after death. **postmortem** *n.* 1. an examination made after death to determine its cause. 2. *(informal)* a detailed discussion of something that is over.

post·na·sal (pohst-nay-zăl) *adj.* at the back of the nose. □**postnasal drip,** a trickling of mucus onto the pharynx from the postnasal area, caused by an allergy or cold etc.

post·na·tal (pohst-nay-tăl) *adj.* occurring or exist-

ing immediately after birth or after giving birth.
post·of·fice (pohst-aw-fis) **box** a rented numbered compartment in a post office where letters etc. are kept for the renter until called for.
post·op·er·a·tive (pohst-op-ĕ-ră-tiv) *adj.* existing or occurring after an operation.
post·or·bit·al (pohst-or-bi-tăl) *adj.* situated behind the socket (orbit) of the eye.
post·paid (pohst-payd) *adv.* with the postage paid by the sender.
post·par·tum (pohst-pahr-tŭm) *adj. & adv.* existing or occurring after childbirth, *postpartum depression.*
post·pone (pohst-pohn) *v.* (**post·poned, post·pon·ing**) to keep (an event) from occurring until a later time, *postpone the meeting.* **post·pone'ment** *n.*
post·pran·di·al (pohst-pran-di-ăl) *adj.* after a meal, especially dinner.
post·script (pohst-skript) *n.* a paragraph added at the end of something (especially in a letter, after the signature).
pos·tu·lant (pos-chŭ-lănt) *n.* a candidate for admission to a religious order.
pos·tu·late (pos-chŭ-layt) *v.* (**pos·tu·lat·ed, pos·tu·lat·ing**) to assume (a thing) to be true, especially as a basis for reasoning. **postulate** (pos-chŭ-lit) *n.* something postulated. **pos·tu·la·tion** (pos-chŭ-lay-shŏn) *n.*
pos·ture (pos-chŭr) *n.* an attitude of the body, the way a person etc. stands or sits or walks. **posture** *v.* (**pos·tured, pos·tur·ing**) to assume a posture, especially for effect. **pos'tur·al** *adj.* **pos'tur·er** *n.*
post·war (pohst-wor) *adj.* existing or occurring after a war.
po·sy (poh-zee) *n.* (*pl.* **-sies**) a small bunch of flowers.
pot (pot) *n.* 1. a rounded vessel of earthenware or metal or glass etc. used for holding liquids or solids, or for cooking in. 2. the contents of a pot. 3. *(informal)* the total amount bet in a gambling game. 4. *(slang)* a potbelly. 5. *(slang)* marijuana. **pot** *v.* (**pot·ted, pot·ting**) 1. to plant, preserve, or cook in a pot. 2. to shoot, to kill by a potshot. □**go to pot,** *(slang)* to deteriorate, to become ruined. **pot cheese,** cottage cheese. **pot liquor,** the broth remaining in a pot after food has been cooked in it. **pot roast,** a piece of meat cooked slowly in a covered pot.
pot. *abbr.* potential.
po·ta·ble (poh-tă-bĕl) *adj.* drinkable.
po·tage (poh-tahzh) *n.* a thick soup. ▷French.
pot·ash (pot-ash) *n.* any of various salts of potassium.
po·tas·si·um (pŏ-tas-i-ŭm) *n.* a soft silvery-white metallic element.
po·ta·to (pŏ-tay-toh) *n.* (*pl.* **-toes**) 1. a plant with starchy tubers that are used as food. 2. one of these tubers. □**potato beetle,** a striped beetle that feeds on potato leaves. **potato bug,** a potato beetle. **potato chip,** a thin crisp fried slice of potato, usually salted.
pot·bel·ly (pot-bel-ee) *n.* (*pl.* **-lies**) 1. a protuberant belly. 2. a person with this. **pot'bel·lied** *adj.* □**potbelly stove,** a stove shaped like a protuberant belly.
pot·boil·er (pot-boi-lĕr) *n.* a work of literature or art done merely to make a living.

po·teen (poh-teen) *n.* whiskey (especially Irish) that has been distilled illegally.
po·tent (poh-tĕnt) *adj.* having great natural power or influence, able to have a strong effect, *potent drugs.* **po·ten·cy** (poh-tĕn-see) *n.*
po·ten·tate (poh-tĕn-tayt) *n.* a monarch or ruler.
po·ten·tial (pŏ-ten-shăl) *adj.* capable of coming into being or of being developed or used etc., *a potential source of energy.* **potential** *n.* 1. ability or capacity available for use or development, *her potential for greatness.* 2. a measure of the voltage between two points. **po·ten'tial·ly** *adv.* **po·ten·ti·al·i·ty** (pŏ-ten-shi-al-i-tee) *n.* □**potential energy,** (in physics) the energy a body possesses because of its position or shape.
po·ten·ti·ate (pŏ-ten-shi-ayt) *v.* (**po·ten·ti·at·ed, po·ten·ti·at·ing**) 1. to make (especially a drug) more powerful. 2. to make possible. **po·ten·ti·a·tion** (pŏ-ten-shi-ay-shŏn) *n.*
pot·head (pot-hed) *n. (slang)* a person who uses marijuana frequently.
poth·er (po*th*-ĕr) *n.* 1. a verbal commotion, a fuss. 2. a cloud of dust or choking smoke.
pot·herb (pot-urb) *n.* a herb prepared and used as food or as seasoning for food.
pot·hole (pot-hohl) *n.* 1. a hole in the surface of a road. 2. a deep cylindrical hole formed in rock by the action of water, an underground cave.
pot·hook (pot-huuk) *n.* 1. a hook used for hanging pots or kettles over an open fire. 2. a curved stroke in writing.
po·tion (poh-shŏn) *n.* a liquid for drinking as a medicine or drug etc.
pot·luck (pot-luk) *n.* whatever food is available for a meal etc., *take potluck with us.*
pot·pie (pot-pɪ) *n.* 1. a deep-dish pie with meat, chicken, etc. 2. a stew with meat, chicken, etc. and dumplings.
pot·pour·ri (poh-puu-ree) *n.* 1. a scented mixture of dried petals and spices. 2. a literary or musical medley.
pot·sherd (pot-shurd) *n.* a broken piece of earthenware, especially in archaeology.
pot·shot (pot-shot) *n.* 1. a casual shot. 2. a shot aimed at an animal etc. within easy reach. 3. a critical remark made casually.
pot·tage (pot-ij) *n.* a thick soup or stew. □**sell one's soul for a mess of pottage,** to sacrifice one's principles for material comfort.
pot·ted (pot-id) *v.* see **pot. potted** *adj.* 1. (of plants) grown in a flower pot. 2. *(slang)* (of a person) drunk. 3. (of food) cooked or preserved in a pot.
pot·ter[1] (pot-ĕr) *n.* a person who makes earthenware dishes or ornaments etc. □**potter's wheel,** a rotating disk on which clay is shaped by a potter.
potter[2] = **putter**[3].
pot·ter's (pot-ĕrz) **field** a burial place for paupers, strangers, etc. ▷From the mention in Matthew 27:7 of the purchase of a field for this purpose.
pot·ter·y (pot-ĕ-ree) *n.* 1. vessels and other objects made of baked clay. 2. a potter's work or workshop.
pot·ty[1] (pot-ee) *adj.* (**pot·ti·er, pot·ti·est**) 1. *(slang)* tipsy. 2. (chiefly *British slang*) crazy.
potty[2] *n.* (*pl.* **-ties**) *(informal)* a pot for a child to use as a toilet. □**potty chair,** a small chair with an opening over a removable pot for toilet training a child. **potty seat,** a small seat fitting over a toilet seat for use by a child.
pouch (powch) *n.* a small bag or baglike formation,

tobacco pouch; the kangaroo's pouch. **pouch** v. **(pouched, pouch·ing)** to put into a pouch, to pocket.

poult (pohlt) n. the young of domestic fowl, turkey, pheasant, etc.

poul·ter·er (pohl-tĕ-rĕr) n. (old use) a dealer in poultry and game.

poul·tice (pohl-tis) n. a soft heated mass of bread or kaolin etc. applied to an inflamed or sore area of skin. **poultice** v. (poul·ticed, poul·tic·ing) to apply a poultice to.

poul·try (pohl-tree) n. domestic fowl, ducks, geese, turkeys, etc., especially as a source of food.

pounce (powns) v. **(pounced, pounc·ing)** to spring or swoop down on and grasp, as for prey; pounce on a mistake, to spot it quickly. **pounce** n. a pouncing movement.

pound¹ (pownd) n. 1. a measure of weight, 16 ounces avoirdupois (0.4536 kg) or 12 ounces troy (0.3732 kg). 2. the unit of money of Britain and certain other countries. □**pound cake,** a rich cake made with eggs, butter, sugar, and flour.

pound note, a British paper bill worth one pound.

pound² n. a place where stray animals, or motor vehicles left in unauthorized places, are taken and kept until claimed.

pound³ v. 1. to crush or beat with heavy repeated strokes. 2. to deliver heavy blows or repeated gunfire etc. 3. to make one's way heavily, pounding along. 4. (of the heart) to beat heavily, to thump.

pound·age (pown-dij) n. 1. pounds, weight in pounds. 2. a charge based on weight in pounds.

pound-fool·ish (pownd-foo-lish) adj. foolish about large sums of money etc. ▷From the phrase penny-wise and pound-foolish (see **penny**).

pour (pohr) v. 1. to flow or cause to flow in a stream or shower. 2. to pour tea etc. into cups, to serve by pouring. 3. to rain heavily. 4. to come or go or send out in large amounts or numbers, refugees poured out of the country; letters poured in. 5. to send (words or music etc.) out freely, he poured out his story. **pour'er** n. □**pour cold water on,** see **cold.**

pour·boire (poor-bwahr) n. a gratuity or tip. ▷French.

pour·par·ler (poor-pahr-lay) n. an informal discussion preliminary to negotiation. ▷French.

pousse-ca·fé (poos-ka-fay) n. (pl. -ca·fés, pr. -ka-fayz) a drink of one or more liqueurs taken especially with coffee after dinner. ▷French.

pout (powt) v. to push out one's lips, (of lips) to be pushed out, especially as a sign of annoyance or sulking. **pout** n. a pouting expression or attitude.

pov·er·ty (pov-ĕr-tee) n. 1. being poor, great lack of money or resources; monks who took a vow of poverty, who renounced the right to individual ownership of property. 2. scarcity, lack. 3. inferiority, poorness. □**poverty line** or **level,** the minimum income level needed to obtain the necessities of life.

pov·er·ty-strick·en (pov-ĕr-tee-strik-ĕn) adj. affected by poverty.

P.O.W. abbr. prisoner of war.

pow·der (pow-dĕr) n. 1. a mass of fine dry particles. 2. a medicine or cosmetic in this form. 3. gunpowder. **powder** v. to apply powder to, to cover with powder. □**powder blue,** pale blue.

powder flask, a small container formerly used for carrying gunpowder. **powder keg,** a barrel for gunpowder; a very dangerous situation. **powder puff,** a soft or fluffy pad for applying powder to the skin. **powder room,** a women's rest room; a lavatory. **powder snow,** loose dry snow.

pow·dered (pow-dĕrd) adj. made into powder, powdered milk.

pow·der·y (pow-dĕ-ree) adj. like powder.

pow·er (pow-ĕr) n. 1. the ability to do something. 2. vigor, energy, strength. 3. a property, great heating power. 4. control, influence, the party in power. 5. authority, their powers are defined by law. 6. an influential person or country or organization etc. 7. (informal) a large amount, did me a power of good. 8. (in mathematics) the product of a number multiplied by itself a given number of times, the third power of $2 = 2 \times 2 \times 2 = 8$. 9. mechanical or electrical energy as opposed to hand labor; power tools, tools using such energy. 10. the electrical supply, a power failure. 11. capacity for exerting mechanical force, horsepower. 12. the magnifying capacity of a lens. **power** v. to supply (vehicles etc.) with mechanical or electrical energy. □**power brakes,** brakes applied by compressed air or another power source and requiring little pressure on the pedal. **power broker,** (informal) a person who exerts influence (in government etc.) behind the scenes. **power dive,** an aircraft's dive made without shutting off engine power. **power of attorney,** the legal authority to act for another person. **power plant** or **station,** a building where electric power is generated for distribution. **power play,** (in sports) an offensive play in a team game directed by one team against a particular weakness of the other. **power politics,** political action based on threats to use force. **the powers that be,** the people in authority.

pow·er·boat (pow-ĕr-boht) n. a motorboat.

pow·ered (pow-ĕrd) adj. equipped with mechanical or electrical power.

pow·er·ful (pow-ĕr-fŭl) adj. having great power or strength or influence. **pow'er·ful·ly** adv.

pow·er·house (pow-ĕr-hows) n. (pl. -houses, pr. -how-ziz) 1. a power station. 2. an individual or group with great energy or force.

pow·er·less (pow-ĕr-lis) adj. without power to take action, wholly unable.

pow·wow (pow-wow) n. (informal) a meeting for discussion.

pox (poks) n. 1. a virus disease characterized by pocks. 2. (informal) syphilis. 3. a plant disease causing pocklike spots.

PP abbr. 1. parcel post. 2. past participle.

pp. abbr. 1. pages. 2. pianissimo.

ppd. abbr. 1. prepaid. 2. postpaid.

P.P.S. abbr. post-postscript, = an additional post-script.

ppt. abbr. precipitate.

P.Q. abbr. Province of Quebec.

Pr symbol praseodymium.

PR abbr. 1. payroll. 2. public relations. 3. Puerto Rico.

pr. abbr. 1. pair(s). 2. present. 3. price. 4. pronoun.

prac·ti·ca·ble (prak-ti-kă-bĕl) adj. able to be done. **prac·ti·ca·bil·i·ty** (prak-ti-kă-bil-i-tee) n. ▷Do not confuse practicable with practical.

prac·ti·cal (prak-ti-kăl) adj. 1. involving activity as distinct from study or theory, has had practical experience. 2. suitable for use, an ingenious but not very practical invention. 3. (of people) clever at doing and making things, *a practical handyman.* **4.** virtual, *he has practical control of the firm.* **practical** *n.* a practical examination, practical study. **prac·ti·cal·i·ty** (prak-ti-kal-i-tee) *n.* (*pl.* **-ties**) ☐**practical joke,** a humorous trick played on a person by a **practical joker. practical nurse,** a nurse who is trained in routine nursing but without the training of a registered nurse. ▷Do not confuse *practical* with *practicable.*

prac·ti·cal·ly (prak-tik-lee) *adv.* **1.** in a practical way. **2.** virtually, almost.

prac·tice (prak-tis) *n.* **1.** action as opposed to theory, *it works well in practice.* **2.** a habitual action, custom, *it is our practice to supply good material.* **3.** repeated exercise to improve one's skill, a spell of this, *target practice.* **4.** professional work, the business carried on by a doctor or lawyer, the patients or clients regularly consulting these, *has a large practice.* **practice** *v.* (**prac·ticed, prac·tic·ing**) **1.** to do something repeatedly in order to become skillful. **2.** to carry out in action, to do something habitually, *practice what you preach.* **3.** to do something actively, *a practicing Catholic.* **4.** (of a doctor or lawyer etc.) to be actively engaged in professional work. ☐**out of practice,** no longer possessing a former skill.

prac·ticed (prak-tist) *adj.* experienced, expert.

prac·ti·tion·er (prak-**tish**-ŏ-něr) *n.* a professional or practical worker, especially in medicine.

prag·mat·ic (prag-mat-ik) *adj.* treating things from a practical point of view, *a pragmatic approach to the problem.* **prag·mat′i·cal·ly** *adv.*

prag·ma·tism (prag-mă-tiz-ĕm) *n.* **1.** the matter-of-fact treatment of things. **2.** the theory that the truth or falsity of an idea can be judged only by the practical effects that arise from it.

Prague (prahg) the capital of Czechoslovakia.

Prai·a (prı̆-ă) the capital of Cape Verde Islands.

prai·rie (prair-ee) *n.* a broad, largely flat tract of grassland, especially in central North America. ☐**prairie dog,** a small burrowing North American rodent with a bark like a dog's. **prairie schooner,** a covered wagon used by pioneers in crossing the prairies.

praise (prayz) *v.* (**praised, prais·ing**) **1.** to express approval or admiration of. **2.** to honor (God) in words. **praise** *n.* praising, approval expressed in words.

praise·wor·thy (prayz-wur-*thee*) *adj.* deserving praise.

pra·line (prah-leen, pray-) *n.* a candy made by browning nuts in boiling sugar.

pram (pram) *n.* (chiefly *British*) a perambulator.

prance (prans) *v.* (**pranced, pranc·ing**) to move springily in eagerness, *prancing horses.* **pranc′er** *n.*

prank (prangk) *n.* mischief, a practical joke. **prank′ster** *n.*

pra·se·o·dym·i·um (pray-zi-oh-dim-i-ŭm) *n.* a metallic element.

prat (prat) *n.* (*slang*) the buttocks.

prate (prayt) *v.* (**prat·ed, prat·ing**) to chatter, to talk too much.

prat·fall (prat-fawl) *n.* (*informal*) **1.** a fall on the buttocks. **2.** a humiliating failure.

pra·tique (pra-teek) *n.* a license to have dealings with a port, granted to a ship after quarantine.

prat·tle (prat-ĕl) *v.* (**prat·tled, prat·tling**) to chatter in a childish way. **prattle** *n.* childish chatter.

prawn (prawn) *n.* an edible shellfish like a large shrimp.

pray (pray) *v.* **1.** to say prayers. **2.** to entreat. **3.** = please, *pray be seated.* ☐**praying mantis,** see **mantis.**

prayer (prair) *n.* **1.** a solemn request or thanksgiving to God or to an object of worship. **2.** a set form of words used in this, *the Lord's Prayer.* **3.** a religious service, *morning prayer.* **4.** the act of praying. **5.** entreaty to a person. ☐**prayer book,** a book of set prayers. **prayer mat,** a small carpet on which Muslims kneel to pray.

prayer·ful (prair-fŭl) *adj.* devout, expressing prayer. **prayer′ful·ly** *adv.*

pre- *prefix* before, beforehand, as in *prearm.*

preach (preech) *v.* **1.** to deliver (a sermon or religious address), to speak in public in support of a religion; *preach the gospel,* make it known by preaching. **2.** to advocate, to urge people to a certain quality or practice or action, *they preached economy.* **3.** to give moral advice in an obtrusive way. **preach′er** *n.* **preach′ment** *n.*

preach·y (pree-chee) *adj.* (**preach·i·er, preach·i·est**) (*informal*) fond of preaching or moralizing or holding forth.

pre·ad·o·les·cence (pree-ad-ŏ-les-ĕns) *n.* the stage of growth just before adolescence. **pre·ad·o·les′cent** *adj.* & *n.*

pre·am·ble (pree-am-bĕl) *n.* a preliminary statement, the introductory part of a document or law etc.

pre·amp (pree-amp) *n.* (*informal*) preamplifier.

pre·am·pli·fi·er (pree-am-pli-fı̆-ĕr) *n.* a device that amplifies weak electronic signals before feeding them to other amplifier circuits.

pre·arm (pree-ahrm) *v.* to arm in advance.

pre·ar·range (pree-ă-raynj) *v.* (**pre·ar·ranged, pre·ar·rang·ing**) to arrange beforehand. **pre·ar·range′ment** *n.*

pre·as·cer·tain (pree-as-ĕr-tayn) *v.* to learn beforehand.

pre·as·sem·ble (pree-ă-sem-bĕl) *v.* (**pre·as·sem·bled, pre·as·sem·bling**) to assemble beforehand.

pre·as·sign (pree-ă-sın) *v.* to assign in advance.

preb·end (preb-ĕnd) *n.* **1.** the part of the revenue of a cathedral or collegiate church granted to a canon or a member of the chapter as a stipend. **2.** the portion of land or tithe from which this stipend is drawn.

preb·en·dar·y (preb-ĕn-der-ee) *n.* (*pl.* **-dar·ies**) **1.** a clergyman receiving a stipend from a cathedral revenue. **2.** an honorary canon (not receiving such a stipend).

prec. *abbr.* **1.** preceded. **2.** preceding.

Pre·cam·bri·an (pree-kam-bri-ăn) *adj.* of the earliest geologic era, marked by the formation of Earth's crust and the earliest appearance of life. **Precambrian** *n.* the Precambrian era.

pre·can·cel (pree-kan-sĕl) *v.* to cancel before using, as a postage stamp. **pre·can·cel·la·tion** (pree-kan-sĕ-lay-shŏn) *n.*

pre·can·cer·ous (pree-kan-sĕ-rŭs) *adj.* likely to turn into cancer.

pre·car·i·ous (pri-kair-i-ŭs) *adj.* unsafe, not secure. **pre·car′i·ous·ly** *adv.* **pre·car′i·ous·ness** *n.*

pre·cast (pree-kast) *adj.* (of concrete) cast in blocks before use.

pre·cau·tion (pri-kaw-shŏn) *n.* something done in advance to avoid a risk; *take precautions,* do things as a precaution. **pre·cau′tion·ar·y** *adj.*

pre·cede (pri-seed) *v.* (**pre·ced·ed, pre·ced·**

ing) to come or go or place before in time or order etc.

prec·e·dence (pres-ĕ-dĕns) *n.* priority in time or order. ☐**take precedence,** to have priority.

prec·e·dent (pres-ĕ-dĕnt) *n.* a previous case that is taken as an example to be followed. **precedent** (pri-seed-ĕnt) *adj.* preceding in time, order, rank, etc.

pre·ced·ing (pri-see-ding) *adj.* previous, coming or going before; *the preceding page,* the page before this one.

pre·cen·tor (pri-sen-tŏr) *n.* a member of the clergy of a church or cathedral who is in general charge of music there.

pre·cept (pree-sept) *n.* a command, a rule of conduct.

pre·cep·tor (pri-sep-tŏr) *n.* a teacher, an instructor. **pre·cep·tress** (pri-sep-tris) *n. fem.*

pre·ces·sion (pri-sesh-ŏn) *n.* 1. the slow movement of an axis of a spinning body, such as a gyroscope etc., around another axis. 2. an act of preceding. **pre·ces·sion·al** (pri-sesh-ŏ-năl) *adj.*

pre-Chris·tian (pree-kris-chăn) *adj.* of the time before Christianity, *pre-Christian era.*

pre·cinct (pree-singkt) *n.* 1. a subdivision of a county or city or ward for election and police purposes. 2. a limited area. 3. an enclosed area, a boundary. 4. *precincts,* the area surrounding a place, *in the precincts of the forest.*

pre·ci·os·i·ty (presh-i-os-i-tee) *n.* (*pl.* -ties) an affectation, especially in language or style.

pre·cious (presh-ŭs) *adj.* 1. of great value or worth. 2. beloved. 3. affectedly refined. 4. (*informal,* used ironically) considerable, *did him a precious lot of good.* **precious** *adv. (informal)* very, *there's precious little money left.* **pre′cious·ly** *adv.* **pre′cious·ness** *n.* ☐**precious metals,** gold, silver, and platinum. **precious stone,** a piece of mineral having great value, especially as used in jewelry.

prec·i·pice (pres-ĭ-pis) *n.* a very steep or vertical face of a cliff or rock etc.

pre·cip·i·tan·cy (pri-sip-ĭ-tăn-see) *n.* (*pl.* -cies) being precipitate in action, a rash action.

pre·cip·i·tate (pri-sip-i-tayt) *v.* (**pre·cip·i·tat·ed, pre·cip·i·tat·ing**) 1. to throw down headlong. 2. to send rapidly into a certain state or condition, *precipitated the country into war.* 3. to cause to happen suddenly or soon, *this action precipitated a crisis.* 4. to cause (a substance) to be deposited in solid form from a solution in which it is present. 5. to condense (vapor) into drops that fall as rain or dew etc. **precipitate** (pri-sip-i-tit, -tayt) *n.* a substance precipitated from a solution, moisture condensed from vapor and deposited (rain, snow, hail, or dew). **precipitate** (pri-sip-i-tit, -tayt) *adj.* 1. headlong, violently hurried, *a precipitate departure.* 2. (of a person or action) hasty, rash. (▷Do not confuse *precipitate* with *precipitous.*) **pre·cip·i·tate·ly** (pri-sip-i-tit-lee) *adv.* **pre·cip·i·tate·ness** (pri-sip-i-tit-nis) *n.*

pre·cip·i·ta·tion (pri-sip-i-tay-shŏn) *n.* 1. precipitating or being precipitated. 2. (a quantity of) rain, snow, hail, etc. falling to the ground.

pre·cip·i·tous (pri-sip-i-tŭs) *adj.* like a precipice, steep. **pre·cip′i·tous·ly** *adv.* ▷Do not confuse *precipitous* with *precipitate (adj.).*

pré·cis (pray-see) *n.* a summary. **précis** *v.* (**pré·cised,** *pr.* -seed; **pré·cis·ing,** *pr.* -see-ing) to make a précis of.

pre·cise (pri-sɪs) *adj.* 1. exact, correctly and

clearly stated. 2. taking care to be exact, *she is very precise.* **pre·cise′ness** *n.*

pre·cise·ly (pri-sɪs-lee) *adv.* 1. in a precise manner, exactly. 2. (said in agreement) quite so, as you say.

pre·ci·sion (pri-sizh-ŏn) *n.* accuracy; *precision tools,* tools designed for very accurate work.

pre·clude (pree-klood) *v.* (**pre·clud·ed, pre·clud·ing**) to exclude the possibility of, to prevent.

pre·co·cious (pri-koh-shŭs) *adj.* 1. (of a child) having developed certain abilities earlier than is usual. 2. (of abilities or knowledge) showing such development. **pre·co′cious·ly** *adv.* **pre·coc·i·ty** (pri-kos-i-tee) *n.*

pre·con·ceived (pree-kŏn-seevd) *adj.* (of an idea or opinion) formed beforehand, formed before full knowledge or evidence is available.

pre·con·cep·tion (pree-kŏn-sep-shŏn) *n.* a preconceived idea.

pre·con·cert·ed (pree-kŏn-sur-tid) *adj.* agreed on or planned in advance.

pre·con·di·tion (pree-kŏn-dish-ŏn) *n.* a condition that must be fulfilled before something else can happen.

pre·cook (pree-kuuk) *v.* to cook (food) in advance of final cooking or so as to prepare it for later reheating.

pre·cur·sor (pri-kur-sŏr) *n.* 1. a person or thing that precedes another, a forerunner. 2. a thing that precedes a later and more developed form, *rocket bombs were the precursors of space probes.*

pred. *abbr.* predicate.

pre·da·ceous, pre·da·cious (pri-day-shŭs) *adj.* predatory, preying on others.

pre·date (pree-dayt) *v.* (**pre·dat·ed, pre·dat·ing**) to date (a check etc.) with a date earlier than the actual one.

pre·da·tion (pri-day-shŏn) *n.* 1. the process of preying. 2. a mode of survival in which food is obtained by capturing and feeding on animals.

pred·a·tor (pred-ă-tŏr) *n.* a predatory animal.

pred·a·to·ry (pred-ă-tohr-ee) *adj.* 1. (of animals) preying upon others. 2. plundering or exploiting others.

pre·dawn (pree-dawn) *n.* the period just before the first appearance of daylight in the morning.

pre·de·cease (pree-di-sees) *v.* (**pre·de·ceased, pre·de·ceas·ing**) to die earlier than (another person).

pred·e·ces·sor (pred-ĕ-ses-ŏr) *n.* 1. the former holder of an office or position. 2. an ancestor. 3. a thing to which another has succeeded, *it will share the fate of its predecessor.*

pre·des·ig·nate (pree-dez-ig-nayt) *v.* (**pre·des·ig·nat·ed, pre·des·ig·nat·ing**) to mark or point out beforehand.

pre·des·ti·na·tion (pree-des-ti-nay-shŏn) *n.* 1. the doctrine that God has foreordained all that happens, or that certain souls are destined for salvation and eternal life and others are not. 2. destiny, fate.

pre·des·tine (pree-des-tin) *v.* (**pre·des·tined, pre·des·tin·ing**) to destine beforehand, to appoint as if by fate.

pre·de·ter·mine (pree-di-tur-min) *v.* (**pre·de·ter·mined, pre·de·ter·min·ing**) to decide in advance, to predestine.

pred·i·ca·ble (pred-i-kă-běl) *adj.* that may be predicated or affirmed.

pre·dic·a·ment (pri-dik-ă-mĕnt) *n.* a difficult or unpleasant situation.

pred·i·cate (pred-ĭ-kit) *n.* the part of a sentence

that says something about the grammatical subject, as "is short" in *life is short*. **predicate** (pred-ĭ-kayt) *v.* (**pred·i·cat·ed, pred·i·cat·ing**) 1. to assert or affirm as true or existent. 2. to found or base (a statement or idea etc.) on something. 3. to assert (a thing) about a subject. **pred·i·ca·tion** (pred-ĭ-kay-shŏn) *n.*

pred·i·ca·tive (pred-ĭ-kay-tiv) *adj.* forming part or the whole of the predicate, as "old" in *the dog is old* (but not in *the old dog*). **pred'i·ca·tive·ly** *adv.*

pre·dict (pri-dikt) *v.* to forecast, to prophesy. **pre·dic'tor** *n.* **pre·dic·tion** (pri-dik-shŏn) *n.*

pre·dict·a·ble (pri-dik-tă-běl) *adj.* able to be predicted. **pre·dict'a·bly** *adj.* **pre·dict·a·bil·i·ty** (pri-dik-tă-bil-i-tee) *n.*

pre·di·ges·tion (pree-di-jes-chŏn) *n.* the artificial partial digestion of food, used especially to facilitate digestion for those who are ill. **pre·di·gest** (pree-di-jest) *v.*

pre·di·lec·tion (pred-ĭ-lek-shŏn) *n.* a special liking, a preference.

pre·dis·pose (pree-di-spohz) *v.* (**pre·dis·posed, pre·dis·pos·ing**) 1. to influence in advance, *circumstances predispose us to be lenient; we are predisposed in his favor*, inclined to favor him. 2. to make liable, as to a disease.

pre·dis·po·si·tion (pree-dis-pŏ-zish-ŏn) *n.* a state of mind or body that renders a person liable to act or behave in a certain way or to be subject to certain diseases, *a predisposition to bronchitis*.

pre·dom·i·nant (pri-dom-ĭ-nănt) *adj.* predominating. **pre·dom'i·nant·ly** *adv.* **pre·dom'i·nance** *n.*

pre·dom·i·nate (pri-dom-ĭ-nayt) *v.* (**pre·dom·i·nat·ed, pre·dom·i·nat·ing**) 1. to be greater than others in number or intensity etc., to be the main element. 2. to have or exert control.

pree·mie (pree-mee) *n.* (*informal*) a premature baby.

pre·em·i·nent (pree-em-ĭ-nĕnt) *adj.* excelling others, outstanding. **pre·em'i·nent·ly** *adv.* **pre·em'i·nence** *n.*

pre·empt (pree-empt) *v.* to take possession of (a thing) before anyone else can do so. **pre·emp·tion** (pree-emp-shŏn) *n.*

pre·emp·tive (pree-emp-tiv) *adj.* preempting; *a preemptive attack*, one intended to disable an enemy and so prevent him from attacking.

preen (preen) *v.* (of a bird) to smooth (its feathers) with its beak. □**preen oneself**, to groom oneself; to congratulate oneself, to show self-satisfaction.

pre·es·tab·lish (pree-e-stab-lish) *v.* to establish beforehand.

pre·ex·ist (pree-ig-zist) *v.* 1. to exist before. 2. to have a previous existence. **pre·ex·ist'ence** *n.* **pre·ex·ist'ent** *adj.*

pref. *abbr.* 1. preface. 2. preference. 3. preferred. 4. prefix.

pre·fab (pree-fab) *n.* (*informal*) a prefabricated building.

pre·fab·ri·cate (pree-fab-ri-kayt) *v.* (**pre·fab·ri·cat·ed, pre·fab·ri·cat·ing**) to manufacture in sections that are ready for assembly on a site. **pre·fab·ri·ca·tion** (pree-fab-ri-kay-shŏn) *n.*

pref·ace (pref-is) *n.* an introductory statement at the beginning of a book or speech. **preface** *v.* (**pref·aced, pref·ac·ing**) 1. to provide or introduce with a preface. 2. to lead up to (an event), *the music that prefaced the ceremony*.

pref·a·to·ry (pref-ă-tohr-ee) *adj.* serving as a preface, preliminary, *prefatory remarks*.

pre·fect (pree-fekt) *n.* the chief administrative official in certain departments in France, Japan, and other countries.

pre·fer (pri-fur) *v.* (**pre·ferred, pre·fer·ring**) 1. to choose as more desirable, to like better. 2. to put forward (an accusation etc.) for consideration by an authority, *they preferred charges of forgery against him*. 3. to promote (a person). □**preferred stock**, a type of company's stock on which the dividend is paid before any is paid on common stock and which has a superior claim on assets if the company enters into liquidation.

pref·er·a·ble (pref-ĕ-ră-běl) *adj.* more desirable. **pref'er·a·bly** *adv.*

pref·er·ence (pref-ĕ-rĕns) *n.* 1. preferring, being preferred, *do this in preference to that*. 2. a thing preferred. 3. a prior right to something. 4. the favoring of one person or country etc. rather than another.

pref·er·en·tial (pref-ĕ-ren-shăl) *adj.* giving or receiving preference, *preferential treatment*.

pre·fer·ment (pri-fur-mĕnt) *n.* promotion.

pre·fight (pree-frt) *adj.* occurring before the fight, *the prefight ceremonies lasted half an hour*.

pre·fig·ure (pree-fig-yŭr) *v.* (**pre·fig·ured, pre·fig·ur·ing**) 1. to represent beforehand by a person or thing of similar type. 2. to picture to oneself beforehand.

pre·fix (pree-fiks) *n.* (*pl.* **-fix·es**) 1. a word or syllable (such as *co-, ex-, non-, out-, pre-*) placed in front of a word to add to or change its meaning. 2. a title (such as *Mr.*) placed before a name. **prefix** (pree-fiks, pree-fiks) *v.* 1. to put as a prefix. 2. to put as an introduction.

pre·flight (pree-frt) *adj.* preliminary to airplane flight.

pre·form (pree-form) *v.* to form beforehand.

pre·gla·cial (pree-glay-shăl) *adj.* before the glacial era.

preg·na·ble (preg-nă-běl) *adj.* able to be captured etc., not impregnable. **preg·na·bil·i·ty** (preg-nă-bil-i-tee) *n.*

preg·nant (preg-nănt) *adj.* 1. (of a woman or female animal) having a child or young developing in the womb. 2. full of meaning, significant, *there was a pregnant pause*. 3. full of, *the situation was pregnant with danger*. **preg·nan·cy** (preg-năn-see) *n.* (*pl.* **-cies**).

pre·hard·en (pree-hahr-dĕn) *v.* to harden before treating.

pre·heat (pree-heet) *v.* to heat before treating or using.

pre·hen·sile (pri-hen-sil) *adj.* (of an animal's foot or tail etc.) able to grasp things.

pre·his·tor·ic (pree-hi-stor-ik) *adj.* 1. of the ancient period before written records of events were made. 2. (*informal*) completely out of date. **pre·his·tor'i·cal** *adj.*

pre·his·to·ry (pree-his-tŏ-ree) *n.* prehistoric events or times, the study of these.

pre·hu·man (pree-hyoo-măn) *adj.* coming before the appearance of human beings.

pre·ig·ni·tion (pree-ig-nish-ŏn) *n.* the premature firing of an explosive mixture in an internal combustion engine.

pre·in·dus·tri·al (pree-in-dus-tri-ăl) *adj.* coming before the industrial era.

pre·judge (pree-juj) *v.* (**pre·judged, pre·judg·ing**) to form a judgment on (a person or action etc.) before a proper inquiry is held or before full information is available.

prej·u·dice (prej-ŭ-dis) *n.* 1. an unreasoning opinion or like or dislike of something; *racial prejudice,* prejudice against people of other races. 2. harm to someone's rights etc. **prejudice** *v.* **(prej·u·diced, prej·u·dic·ing)** 1. to cause (a person) to have a prejudice. 2. to cause harm to, *it may prejudice our rights.* ☐**without prejudice,** (of an offer made for the purpose of settling a dispute) which must not be interpreted as an admission of liability, or used in evidence.

prej·u·diced (prej-ŭ-dist) *adj.* having a prejudice.

prej·u·di·cial (prej-ŭ-dish-ăl) *adj.* harmful to someone's rights or claims etc.

prel·ate (prel-it) *n.* a clergyman of high rank. **prel·a·cy** (prel-ă-see) *n.*

pre·launch (pree-lawnch) *adj.* preliminary to launching, *prelaunch procedures.*

pre·lim (pri-lim) *n. (informal)* 1. a preliminary. 2. a preliminary boxing match. **prelim.** *abbr.* preliminary.

pre·lim·i·nar·y (pri-lim-ĭ-ner-ee) *adj.* coming before a main action or event etc. and preparing for it, *some preliminary negotiations.* **preliminary** *n. (pl.* **-nar·ies)** a preliminary action or event or examination etc.

pre·lit·er·ate (pree-lit-ĕ-rit) *adj.* of a culture or society that does not have a written language.

prel·ude (prel-yood) *n.* 1. an action or event that precedes another and leads up to it. 2. the introductory part of a poem etc. 3. (in music) an introductory movement preceding a fugue or forming the first piece of a suite, a short piece of music of similar type.

prem. *abbr.* premium.

pre·mar·i·tal (pree-mar-i-tăl) *adj.* of the time before marriage.

pre·ma·ture (pree-mă-toor, -choor) *adj.* occurring or done before the usual or proper time, too early; *premature baby,* one born between three and twelve weeks before the expected time. **pre·ma·ture'ly** *adv.*

pre·med (pree-med) *adj. (informal)* premedical. **premed** *n. (informal)* a premedical student.

pre·med·i·cal (pree-med-i-kăl) *adj.* of or relating to preparatory study for medical school.

pre·med·i·tate (pri-med-i-tayt) *v.* **(pre·med·i·tat·ed, pre·med·i·tat·ing)** to plan beforehand, *a premeditated crime.* **pre·med·i·ta·tion** (pri-med-i-tay-shŏn) *n.*

pre·men·stru·al (pree-men-stroo-ăl) *adj.* of the time immediately before each menstruation.

pre·mier (pri-meer) *adj.* first in importance or order or time. **premier** *n.* a prime minister. **pre·mier'ship** *n.*

pre·miere (pri-myair) *n.* the first public performance or showing of a play or film. **premiere** (pri-meer) *v.* **(pre·miered, pre·mier·ing)** 1. to give a first public performance of. 2. to have a first public performance.

prem·ise (prem-is) *n. (pl.* **-is·es)** a statement on which reasoning is based.

prem·is·es (prem-i-siz) *n.* a house or other building with its grounds and outbuildings etc.; *on the premises,* in the buildings or grounds concerned.

pre·mi·um (pree-mi-ŭm) *n.* 1. an amount or installment to be paid for an insurance policy. 2. an addition to ordinary wages or charges etc., a bonus. 3. a gift provided with a purchase. ☐**at a premium,** above the nominal or usual price; highly valued or esteemed. **put a premium on,** to provide an incentive to (a certain action etc.).

pre·mix (pree-miks) *v.* to mix in advance of use.

pre·mo·lar (pree-moh-lăr) *adj.* in front of the true molar teeth.

pre·mo·ni·tion (pree-mŏ-nish-ŏn, prem-ŏ-) *n.* a presentiment. **pre·mon·i·to·ry** (pri-mon-i-tohr-ee) *adj.*

pre·na·tal (pree-nay-tăl) *adj.* occurring or existing before birth or before giving birth.

pre·nup·tial (pree-nup-shăl) *adj.* before marriage or before a wedding ceremony.

pre·oc·cu·pa·tion (pree-ok-yŭ-pay-shŏn) *n.* 1. the state of being preoccupied. 2. a thing that fills one's thoughts.

pre·oc·cu·pied (pree-ok-yŭ-pɪd) *adj.* having one's thoughts deeply engaged in something, inattentive in manner because of this.

pre·oc·cu·py (pree-ok-yŭ-pɪ) *v.* **(pre·oc·cu·pied, pre·oc·cu·py·ing)** 1. to occupy beforehand. 2. to occupy fully by absorbing the attention.

pre·op·er·a·tive (pree-op-ĕ-ră-tiv) *adj.* taking place before a surgical operation.

pre·or·dain (pree-or-dayn) *v.* to ordain beforehand. **pre·or·di·na·tion** (pree-or-di-nay-shŏn) *n.*

prep (prep) *v.* **(prepped, prep·ping)** *(informal)* to prepare, especially to make ready (a patient) for an operation. ☐**prep school,** a preparatory school.

prep. *abbr.* 1. preparation. 2. preparatory. 3. preposition.

pre·pack·age (pree-pak-ij) *v.* **(pre·pack·aged, pre·pack·ag·ing)** to pack (goods) ready for sale before distributing them.

pre·paid (pree-payd) *see* **prepay.**

prep·a·ra·tion (prep-ă-ray-shŏn) *n.* 1. preparing, being prepared. 2. a thing done to make ready for something; *make preparations for,* prepare for. 3. a substance or mixture (such as food or medicine) prepared for use, *a preparation of bismuth.*

pre·par·a·to·ry (pri-par-ă-tohr-ee, prep-ă-ră-) *adj.* preparing for something, *preparatory training.* **preparatory** *adv.* in a preparatory way. ☐**preparatory school,** a school where pupils are prepared for college.

pre·pare (pri-pair) *v.* **(pre·pared, pre·par·ing)** 1. to make or get ready. 2. to make (food or other substances) ready for use. ☐**be pre·pared to,** to be ready and willing to (do something).

pre·par·ed·ness (pri-pair-id-nis) *n.* readiness, especially military readiness for war.

pre·pay (pree-pay) *v.* **(pre·paid, pre·pay·ing)** to pay (a charge) beforehand, to pay the postage of (a letter etc.) beforehand, as by buying and affixing a postage stamp. **pre·pay'ment** *n.*

pre·plan (pree-plan) *v.* **(pre·planned, pre·plan·ning)** to arrange or plan beforehand.

pre·pon·der·ant (pri-pon-dĕ-rănt) *adj.* preponderating. **pre·pon'der·ant·ly** *adv.* **pre·pon'der·ance** *n.*

pre·pon·der·ate (pri-pon-dĕ-rayt) *v.* **(pre·pon·der·at·ed, pre·pon·der·at·ing)** to be greater than others in number or intensity etc.

prep·o·si·tion (prep-ŏ-zish-ŏn) *n.* a word used with a noun or pronoun to show place or position or time or means, such as *at* home, in the hall, on Sunday, by train. **prep·o·si'tion·al** *adj.*

pre·pos·sess (pree-pŏ-zes) *v.* 1. to imbue or inspire (a person) with a feeling etc. 2. to take possession of. 3. to prejudice, usually favorably and at first sight.

pre·pos·sess·ing (pree-pŏ-zes-ing) *adj.* attractive, making a good impression, *not very prepossessing.*

pre·pos·ter·ous (pri-pos-tĕ-rŭs) *adj.* utterly absurd, outrageous.

pre·puce (pree-pyoos) *n.* 1. the foreskin. 2. a similar structure at the tip of the clitoris.

Pre-Raph·a·el·ite (pree-raf-i-ĕ-lɪt) *n.* one of a group of 19th-century artists who aimed at producing work in the style of the Italian artists of before the time of Raphael.

pre·re·cord (pree-ri-kord) *v.* to record (a television or radio show) before actually broadcasting it.

pre-Ref·or·ma·tion (pree-ref-ŏr-may-shŏn) *adj.* before the Reformation.

pre·reg·is·ter (pree-rej-i-stĕr) *v.* to register beforehand. **pre·reg·is·tra·tion** (pree-rej-i-stray-shŏn) *n.*

pre-Ren·ais·sance (pree-ren-ă-sahns) *adj.* before the Renaissance.

pre·req·ui·site (pri-rek-wi-zit) *adj.* required as a condition or in preparation for something else. **prerequisite** *n.* a prerequisite thing. ▷Do not confuse *prerequisite* with *perquisite.*

pre·rog·a·tive (pri-rog-ă-tiv) *n.* a right or privilege belonging to a particular person or group.

pres. *abbr.* 1. present. 2. presidency. 3. president.

Pres. *abbr.* President.

pres·age (pres-ij) *n.* an omen, portent, or foreboding. **presage** (pres-ij, pri-sayj) *v.* (**pres·aged, pres·ag·ing**) to portend, to foreshadow.

pres·by·o·pi·a (prez-bi-oh-pi-ă) *n.* a form of farsightedness that comes with old age. **pres·by·op·ic** (prez-bi-op-ik) *adj.*

pres·by·ter (prez-bi-tĕr) *n.* 1. (in the Episcopal Church) a priest. 2. (in the Presbyterian Church) an elder.

Pres·by·te·ri·an (prez-bi-teer-i-ăn) *adj.* of a Presbyterian Church, which is governed by elders who are all of equal rank. **Presbyterian** *n.* a member of the Presbyterian Church. **Pres·by·te'ri·an·ism** *n.*

pre·school (pree-skool) *adj.* of the time before a child is old enough to attend school. **pre'school'er** *n.*

pre·sci·ence (pree-shi-ĕns, presh-i-) *n.* foreknowledge. **pre'sci·ent** *adj.*

pre·scribe (pri-skrɪb) *v.* (**pre·scribed, pre·scrib·ing**) 1. to advise the use of (a medicine etc.). 2. to lay down as a course or rule to be followed.

pre·script (pree-skript) *n.* a law or rule or command.

pre·scrip·tion (pri-skrip-shŏn) *n.* 1. a doctor's written instruction for the composition and use of a medicine. 2. the medicine prescribed in this way. 3. prescribing.

pre·scrip·tive (pri-skrip-tiv) *adj.* 1. prescribing. 2. laying down rules; *a prescriptive dictionary,* one that makes recommendations about usage etc.

pres·ence (prez-ens) *n.* 1. being present in a place, *your presence is required.* 2. a person's bearing, impressiveness of bearing, *has a fine presence.* 3. a person or thing that is or seems to be present in a place, *felt a presence in the room.* □**presence of mind,** ability to act quickly and in a practical way in an emergency.

pres·ent¹ (prez-ĕnt) *adj.* 1. being in the place in question, *no one else was present.* 2. being dealt with or discussed, *in the present case.* 3. existing or occurring now, *the present mayor.* **present** *n.* 1. present time, the time now passing. 2. the present tense. □**at present,** now. **for the present,** for now, temporarily. **present participle,** *see* **participle. present perfect, present tense,** *see* **tense¹.**

present² *n.* something given or received as a gift.

present (pri-zent) *v.* 1. to give as a gift or award, to offer for acceptance; *the check has not been presented,* has not been handed in for payment. 2. to introduce (a person) to another or others. 3. to bring (a play or new product etc.) to the public. 4. to show, to reveal, *presented a brave front to the world.* 5. to level or aim (a weapon). **pre·sent'er** *n.* □**present arms,** to hold a rifle etc. vertically in front of the body as a salute. **present oneself,** to appear or attend, as for an examination.

pre·sent·a·ble (pri-zen-tă-bĕl) *adj.* fit to be presented to someone, of good appearance. **pre·sent'a·bly** *adv.*

pres·en·ta·tion (prez-ĕn-tay-shŏn) *n.* 1. presenting, being presented. 2. something that is presented.

pres·ent-day (prez-ĕnt-day) *adj.* of present times, modern.

pre·sen·ti·ment (pri-zen-tĭ-mĕnt) *n.* a feeling that something is about to happen, a foreboding.

pres·ent·ly (prez-ĕnt-lee) *adv.* 1. soon, after a short time. 2. *(informal)* now. ▷Careful writers avoid use of *presently* in its second sense. Write *I am studying French now* not *presently studying French.*

pres·er·va·tion (prez-ĕr-vay-shŏn) *n.* preserving, being preserved.

pre·serv·a·tive (pri-zur-vă-tiv) *adj.* preserving things. **preservative** *n.* a substance that preserves perishable foods.

pre·serve (pri-zurv) *v.* (**pre·served, pre·serv·ing**) 1. to keep safe, to keep in an unchanged condition. 2. to keep from decay, to treat (food, such as fruit or meat) so that it can be kept for future use. 3. to keep (game, or a river etc.) undisturbed, for private use. **preserve** *n.* 1. (also **preserves**) preserved fruit, jam. 2. an area where game or fish are preserved. 3. activities or interests etc. regarded as belonging to a particular person. **pre·serv'er** *n.*

pre·set (pree-set) *v.* (**pre·set, pre·set·ting**) to set beforehand.

pre·shrunk (pree-shrungk) *adj.* (of fabric) subjected to a shrinking process before being used or sold, so that it will not shrink further when laundered.

pre·side (pri-zɪd) *v.* (**pre·sid·ed, pre·sid·ing**) to be president or chairman, to have the position of authority or control.

pres·i·dent (prez-i-dĕnt) *n.* 1. a person who is the head of a club or society or corporation etc. 2. (often *President*) the elected or appointed head of a republic. **pres·i·den·tial** (prez-i-den-shăl) *adj.* **pres·i·den·cy** (prez-i-dĕn-see) *n.*

pre·sid·i·o (pri-sid-i-oh) *n.* (*pl.* **-os**) (in Spain and South America) a fort or garrison town.

pre·sid·i·um (pri-sid-i-ŭm) *n.* (*pl.* **-sid·i·a**, *pr.* -sid-i-ă, **-sid·i·ums**) the standing committee in a Communist organization, especially that of the Supreme Soviet of the U.S.S.R.

pre·soak (pree-sohk) *v.* 1. a substance in which laundry may be soaked before washing. 2. the process of presoaking. **presoak** *v.* to soak before-hand.

pres. part. *abbr.* present participle.

press[1] (pres) *v.* 1. to apply weight or force steadily to (a thing). 2. to squeeze juice etc. from. 3. to make by pressing. 4. to flatten or smooth, to iron (clothes etc.). 5. to exert pressure on (an enemy etc.), to oppress. 6. to urge or entreat, to demand insistently, *press for a 35-hour week.* 7. to force the acceptance of, *they pressed candy upon us.* 8. to insist upon, *don't press that point.* 9. to throng closely. 10. to push one's way. **press** *n.* 1. pressing, *give it a slight press.* 2. crowding, a throng of people. 3. hurry, pressure of affairs, *the press of modern life.* 4. an instrument or machinery for compressing or flattening or shaping something. 5. a printing press, a printing or publishing firm. 6. newspapers and periodicals, the people involved in writing or producing these, *a press photographer.* □**be pressed for,** to have barely enough of, *we are pressed for time.* **press agent,** a person employed to take care of publicity. **press box,** a reporters' enclosure, especially at a sports event. **press clipping,** a cutting from a newspaper. **press conference,** an interview given to journalists by a person who wishes to make an announcement or answer questions. **press gallery,** a gallery for reporters, especially in a legislative assembly. **press release,** a news release, written information given to the press for publication.

press[2] *v.* *(old use)* to force to serve in the army or navy. □**press into service,** to bring into use as a makeshift.

press·ing (pres-ing) *adj.* 1. urgent, *a pressing need.* 2. urging something strongly, *a pressing invitation.* **pressing** *n.* a thing made by pressing, a phonograph record or series of these made at one time.

press·man (pres-măn) *n.* (*pl.* **-men,** *pr.* -měn) the operator of a printing press.

press·room (pres-room) *n.* 1. the room in a printing factory where the presses are kept. 2. a room set aside for reporters and journalists.

pres·sure (presh-ŭr) *n.* 1. the exertion of continuous force upon something. 2. the force exerted, that of the atmosphere, *pressure is high in eastern areas.* 3. a compelling or oppressive influence, *is under pressure to vote against it; the pressures of business life.* **pressure** *v.* (**pres·sured, pres·sur·ing**) to try to compel (a person) into some action. □**pressure center,** (in meteorology) a condition of the atmosphere with pressure above or below average. **pressure cooker,** a pot in which things can be cooked quickly by steam under high pressure. **pressure gauge,** a device for showing the pressure of air, steam, etc. **pressure group,** an organized group seeking to influence policy by concerted action and intensive propaganda. **pressure point,** a sensitive point on the skin; a part of the body which when pressed arrests the flow of blood through an artery lying close to the surface. **pressure suit,** a pressurized suit.

pres·sur·ize (presh-ŭ-rɪz) *v.* (**pres·sur·ized, pres·sur·iz·ing**) to keep (a closed compartment, such as an aircraft cabin) at a constant atmospheric pressure. **pres·sur·i·za·tion** (presh-ŭ-ri-zay-shŏn) *n.* □**pressurized cabin,** an aircraft cabin in which normal atmospheric pressure is maintained. **pressurized suit,** an inflatable suit designed to protect the body from

low pressure when flying at a high altitude.

pres·ti·dig·i·ta·tion (pres-ti-dij-i-tay-shŏn) *n.* sleight of hand. **pres·ti·dig·i·ta·tor** (pres-ti-dij-i-tay-tŏr) *n.*

pres·tige (pre-steezh, -steej) *n.* respect for a person resulting from his good reputation, past achievements, etc.

pres·ti·gious (pre-stij-ŭs) *adj.* having or bringing prestige. **pres·ti′gious·ly** *n.*

pres·to (pres-toh) *adv.* (especially in music) quickly. **presto!** *interj.* a conjurer's word used at a moment of sudden change.

pre·stressed (pree-strest) *adj.* (of concrete) strengthened by means of stretched wires within it.

pre·sum·a·ble (pri-zoo-mă-běl) *adj.* able to be presumed. **pre·sum′a·bly** *adv.*

pre·sume (pri-zoom) *v.* (**pre·sumed, pre·sum·ing**) 1. to take for granted, to suppose to be true. 2. to take the liberty of doing something, to venture, *may we presume to advise you?* 3. to be presumptuous. □**presume on,** to take unwarranted liberties because of, *they are presuming on her good nature.* ▷See the note under **assume.**

pre·sump·tion (pri-zump-shŏn) *n.* 1. presuming a thing to be true, something presumed. 2. presumptuous behavior.

pre·sump·tive (pri-zump-tiv) *adj.* giving grounds for presumption. □**heir presumptive,** *see* **heir.** ▷Do not confuse *presumptive* with *presumptuous.*

pre·sump·tu·ous (pri-zump-choo-ŭs) *adj.* behaving with impudent boldness, acting without authority. **pre·sump′tu·ous·ly** *adv.* **pre·sump′tu·ous·ness** *n.* ▷Do not confuse *presumptuous* with *presumptive.*

pre·sup·pose (pree-sŭ-pohz) *v.* (**pre·sup·posed, pre·sup·pos·ing**) 1. to take for granted. 2. to require as a prior condition, *effects presuppose causes.* **pre·sup·po·si·tion** (pree-sup-ŏ-zish-ŏn) *n.*

pre·tax (pree-taks) *adj.* existing before taxes are deducted, *pretax earnings.*

pre·teen (pree-teen) *n.* a child who has not yet become a teenager. **preteen** *adj.*

pre·tend (pri-tend) *v.* 1. to create a false appearance of something, either in play or so as to deceive others. 2. to claim falsely that one has or is something. 3. to lay claim, *he pretended to the title; pretended to exact knowledge,* claimed to have this. **pre·tend′ed·ly** *adv.*

pre·tend·er (pri-ten-děr) *n.* 1. a person who pretends. 2. a person who claims a throne or title etc.

pre·tense (pree-tens, pri-tens) *n.* 1. pretending, make-believe. 2. claim to merit or knowledge etc. 3. pretentiousness.

pre·ten·sion (pri-ten-shŏn) *n.* 1. the assertion of a claim to something. 2. pretentiousness.

pre·ten·tious (pri-ten-shŭs) *adj.* showy, pompous. **pre·ten′tious·ly** *adv.* **pre·ten′tious·ness** *n.*

pre·ter·mi·nal (pree-tur-mi-năl) *adj.* happening before death.

pre·ter·nat·u·ral (pree-těr-nach-ŭ-răl) *adj.* outside the ordinary course of nature, unusual. **pre·ter·nat′u·ral·ly** *adv.*

pre·test (pree-test) *n.* a preliminary test.

pre·text (pree-tekst) *n.* a reason put forward to conceal one's true reason.

Pre·to·ri·a (pri-tohr-i-ă) the administrative capital of the Republic of South Africa.

pret·ti·fy (prit-i-fɪ) *v.* (**pret·ti·fied, pret·ti·fy·**

ing) to make (a thing) look superficially pretty or pleasing. **pret·ti·fi·ca·tion** (prit-i-fi-kay-shŏn) *n.*

pret·ty (prit-ee) *adj.* (**pret·ti·er, pret·ti·est**) 1. attractive in a delicate way. 2. considerable; *cost me a pretty penny,* a lot of money. **pretty** *adv.* fairly, moderately, *it looks pretty good.* **pret'ti·ly** *adv.* **pret'ti·ness** *n.* □**pretty much** *or* **nearly** *or* **well,** almost.

pret·ty-pret·ty (prit-ee-prit-ee) *adj.* with the prettiness overdone.

pret·zel (pret-sĕl) *n.* a crisp biscuit baked in the shape of a loose knot or a stick and salted on the outside.

prev. *abbr.* 1. previous. 2. previously.

pre·vail (pri-vayl) *v.* 1. to be victorious, to gain the mastery. 2. to be more usual or frequent than others, to exist or occur generally, *a prevailing wind.* **pre·vail'ing·ly** *adv.* □**prevail on,** to persuade.

prev·a·lent (prev-ă-lĕnt) *adj.* existing or occurring generally, widespread. **prev'a·lent·ly** *adv.* **prev'a·lence** *n.*

pre·var·i·cate (pri-var-ĭ-kayt) *v.* (**pre·var·i·cat·ed, pre·var·i·cat·ing**) to tell lies, to speak evasively. **pre·var'i·ca·tor** *n.* **pre·var·i·ca·tion** (pri-var-ĭ-kay-shŏn) *n.*

pre·vent (pri-vent) *v.* 1. to keep (a thing) from happening, to make impossible. 2. to keep (a person) from doing something. **pre·ven·tion** (pri-ven-shŏn) *n.*

pre·vent·a·ble (pri-ven-tă-bĕl) *adj.* able to be prevented.

pre·ven·ta·tive (pri-ven-tă-tiv) *adj.* preventive. **preventative** *n.* a preventive. ▷See the note under **preventive.**

pre·ven·tive (pri-ven-tiv) *adj.* preventing something. **preventive** *n.* a thing that prevents something. □**preventive dentistry,** dentistry that is intended to prevent decay or malformations of the teeth. **preventive detention,** (in British law) imprisonment of a person who is thought likely to commit a crime. **preventive medicine,** the branch of medicine concerned with the prevention of disease. ▷Careful writers use *preventive* rather than *preventative.*

pre·ver·bal (pree-vur-băl) *adj.* not yet having acquired the ability to speak.

pre·view (pree-vyoo) *n.* an advance showing or viewing of a film or play etc. before it is shown to the general public. **preview** *v.* to view in advance of public presentation.

pre·vi·ous (pree-vi-ŭs) *adj.* 1. coming before in time or order. 2. done or acting prematurely, *you have been a little too previous.* **pre'vi·ous·ly** *adv.* □**previous engagement,** an appointment that prevents one from accepting another engagement. **previous to,** before.

pre·vi·sion (pree-vizh-ŏn) *n.* foreseeing, prescience.

pre·war (pree-wor) *adj.* existing or occurring before a certain war, especially before World War I or World War II.

prex·y (prek-see) *n.* (*pl.* **prex·ies**) (*slang*) president of a college or university.

prey (pray) *n.* 1. an animal that is hunted or killed by another for food. 2. a person or thing that falls victim to an enemy or fear or disease etc. **prey** *v.* (**preyed, prey·ing**) **prey on,** to seek or take as prey; to have a harmful influence on, *the problem preyed on his mind.* □**bird** *or* **beast of prey,** one that kills and eats other animals.

prf. *abbr.* proof.

pri·a·pic (pri-ap-ik) *adj.* phallic.

price (pris) *n.* 1. the amount of money for which a thing is bought or sold. 2. what must be given or done etc. in order to achieve something, *peace at any price.* **price** *v.* (**priced, pric·ing**) to fix or find or estimate the price of. □**a price on someone's head** *or* **life,** a reward offered for his capture or killing. **at a price,** at a high cost. **price-earnings ratio,** the market price of a share of stock divided by the earnings per share. **price oneself out of the market,** to charge such a high price for one's goods or services that no one will buy them. **price support,** maintenance of the price of a product, usually by the government. **price war,** a time of keen competition among retailers, when prices are continually cut.

price·less (pris-lis) *adj.* 1. invaluable. 2. (*slang*) very amusing or absurd. **price'less·ly** *adv.*

prick (prik) *v.* 1. to pierce slightly, to make a tiny hole in; *prick the bubble,* to show that something that has seemed important is nothing. 2. to goad by causing mental awareness, *my conscience is pricking me.* 3. to feel a pricking sensation. 4. to mark (a pattern etc.) with pricks or dots. **prick** *n.* 1. pricking, a mark or puncture made by this. 2. the sensation caused by a mark or puncture. 3. a thing that pricks. □**prick up one's ears,** (of a dog) to raise the ears erect when on the alert; (of a person) to become suddenly attentive.

prick·er (prik-ĕr) *n.* 1. a thorn or briar. 2. a pricking instrument.

prick·le (prik-ĕl) *n.* 1. a small thorn. 2. a pricking sensation. **prickle** *v.* (**prick·led, prick·ling**) to feel or cause a sensation of pricking.

prick·ly (prik-lee) *adj.* (**-li·er, -li·est**) 1. having prickles. 2. (of a person) irritable, touchy. **prick'li·ness** *n.* □**prickly heat,** an inflammation of the skin near the sweat glands with itching and a prickly sensation. **prickly pear,** a kind of cactus with pear-shaped edible fruit; its fruit.

pride (prid) *n.* 1. a feeling of pleasure or satisfaction in one's actions or qualities or possessions etc. 2. a person or thing that is a source of pride. 3. a proper sense of what is fitting for one's position or character, self-respect. 4. unduly high opinion of one's own qualities or merits. 5. a company (of lions). **pride** *v.* (**prid·ed, prid·ing**) **pride oneself on,** to be proud of. □**pride of place,** the most prominent position, awareness of this, arrogance.

prie-dieu (pree-dyuu) *n.* (*pl.* **-dieus, -dieux,** *pr.* dyuuz) a kneeling desk, especially for prayer.

priest (preest) *n.* 1. a clergyman. 2. a person who is appointed to perform religious rites in non-Christian religions. **priest'ess** *n. fem.* **priest'hood** *n.*

priest·ly (preest-lee) *adj.* of or like or suitable for a priest. **priest'li·ness** *n.*

prig (prig) *n.* a self-righteous person, one who displays or demands exaggerated correctness, especially in behavior. **prig'gish** *adj.* **prig'gish·ness** *n.*

prim (prim) *adj.* (**prim·mer, prim·mest**) stiffly formal and precise in manner or appearance or behavior, disliking what is rough or improper. **prim'ly** *adv.* **prim'ness** *n.*

prim. *abbr.* 1. primary. 2. primitive.

pri·ma (pree-mă) *adj.* **prima ballerina,** the chief female dancer in a ballet. **prima donna,** the chief female singer in an opera; *(informal)* a temperamental person.

pri·ma·cy (prɪ-mă-see) *n.* 1. preeminence. 2. the office of a primate of the church.

pri·ma fa·cie (prɪ-mă fay-shă) based on the first impression; *made out a prima facie case against him,* one that seemed, at first sight, to be valid; *prima facie evidence,* evidence that is immediately apparent.

pri·mal (prɪ-măl) *adj.* 1. primitive, primeval. 2. chief, fundamental. □**primal scream,** a primitive infantile scream, used in one kind of treatment of mental disorders.

pri·ma·ry (prɪ-me-ree, -mĕ-ree) *adj.* 1. earliest in time or order, first in a series, *the primary meaning of a word.* 2. of the first importance, chief. 3. not derived, *a primary source.* **primary** *n.* (*pl.* -ries) 1. a thing that is first in order, time, importance, etc. 2. a primary election. □**primary accent,** the most important stress of a word. **primary cell,** a battery that generates electricity by irreversible chemical reaction. **primary colors,** those colors from which all others can be made by mixing, (of paint) red and yellow and blue, (of light) red and green and violet. **primary education** *or* **school,** that in which the rudiments of knowledge are taught, the first three or four years of elementary school. **primary election,** a political election for selecting convention delegates or party nominees.

pri·mate (prɪ-mayt, for definition 1 also **prɪ-mit**) *n.* 1. an archbishop or bishop who ranks first among other bishops in a certain province or country. 2. a member of the highly developed order of animals that includes man, apes, and monkeys. **pri·ma·tial** (prɪ-may-shăl) *adj.*

prime[1] (prɪm) *adj.* 1. chief, most important, *the prime cause.* 2. first rate, excellent, *prime beef.* 3. basic, fundamental. □**prime meridian,** the zero meridian passing through Greenwich, England, from which longitude is reckoned east and west. **prime minister,** the chief minister in a government. **prime mover,** the initial source (natural or mechanical) of motive power. **prime number,** a number (as 2, 3, 5, 7, 11) that can be divided exactly only by itself and 1. **prime rate,** the lowest rate at which money can be borrowed commercially. **prime time,** the time at which the highest rates are charged, especially to advertisers on television.

prime[2] *n.* 1. the state of greatest perfection, the best part, *in the prime of life.* 2. the symbol ' added to a letter etc. as a distinguishing mark, or to a number as a symbol for minutes or feet.

prime[3] *v.* (**primed, prim·ing**) 1. to prepare (a thing) for use or action; *prime a pump,* cause liquid to flow into it to start it working. 2. to prepare (a surface) for painting by coating it with a substance that prevents the first coat of paint from being absorbed. 3. to equip (a person) with information. 4. to give (a person) plenty of food or drink in preparation for something.

prim·er[1] (prɪ-mĕr) *n.* 1. a substance used to prime a surface for painting. 2. a detonator for explosives.

prim·er[2] (prim-ĕr) *n.* an elementary textbook.

pri·me·val (prɪ-mee-văl) *adj.* of the earliest times of the world, ancient.

prim·i·tive (prim-i-tiv) *adj.* 1. of or at an early stage of civilization, *primitive tribes.* 2. simple or crude, using unsophisticated techniques, *primitive*

tools. **primitive** *n.* 1. an untutored painter with a naive style. 2. a picture by such a painter. **prim′i·tive·ly** *adv.*

prim·i·tiv·ism (prim-i-ti-viz-ĕm) *n.* 1. primitive behavior. 2. belief in the superiority of what is primitive. 3. the style of a primitive painter.

pri·mo·gen·i·tor (prɪ-mŏ-jen-i-tŏr) *n.* the earliest ancestor.

pri·mo·gen·i·ture (prɪ-mŏ-jen-i-chŭr) *n.* 1. the fact of being a firstborn child. 2. the system by which an eldest son inherits all his parents' property.

pri·mor·di·al (prɪ-mor-di-ăl), *adj.* primeval. **pri·mor′di·al·ly** *adv.*

primp (primp) *v.* 1. to use great care in making one's appearance tidy. 2. to groom (hair, clothes, etc.).

prim·rose (prim-rohz) *n.* 1. (also **primula**) a perennial plant bearing pale yellow flowers in the spring *(English primrose)* or variously colored flowers. 2. its flower. 3. pale yellow. □**primrose path,** a way of life devoted to ease and pleasure.

prim·u·la (prim-yuu-lă) *see* primrose.

prin. *abbr.* 1. principal. 2. principle.

prince (prins) *n.* 1. a male member of a royal family, (in Britain) a son or grandson of the sovereign. 2. a ruler, especially of a small state, *Prince Rainier of Monaco.* 3. a nobleman of various countries. 4. a man with outstanding qualities. □**prince consort,** a title conferred on the husband (who is himself a prince) of a reigning queen. **Prince Edward Island,** a province of Canada. **Prince of Darkness,** the Devil or Satan. **Prince of Peace,** Jesus Christ. **Prince of Wales,** a title usually conferred on the heir apparent to the British throne.

prince·ly (prins-lee) *adj.* 1. of a prince, worthy of a prince. 2. splendid, generous. **prince′li·ness** *n.*

prin·cess (prin-sis, -ses) *n.* 1. the wife of a prince. 2. a female member of a royal family, (in Britain) a daughter or granddaughter of the sovereign. **princess** *adj.* (of a woman's garment) made in panels extending from shoulder to hem and with a flared skirt, *princess style.* □**princess royal,** a title that may be conferred on the eldest daughter of the British sovereign.

prin·ci·pal (prin-sĭ-păl) *adj.* first in rank or importance, chief. **principal** *n.* 1. the person with highest authority in an organization etc., the head of certain schools. 2. a person who takes a leading part in an activity or in a play etc. 3. a person for whom another acts as agent, *I must consult my principal.* 4. a capital sum as distinguished from the interest or income on it. □**principal parts,** the forms of a verb from which all other forms can be deduced. ▷ Do not confuse *principal* with *principle.* *Principle* is never used correctly of a person.

prin·ci·pal·i·ty (prin-sĭ-pal-i-tee) *n.* (*pl.* -ties) a country ruled by a prince.

prin·ci·pal·ly (prin-sĭ-plee) *adv.* for the most part, chiefly.

prin·ci·ple (prin-sĭ-pĕl) *n.* 1. a basic truth or a general law or doctrine that is used as a basis of reasoning or a guide to action or behavior. 2. a personal code of right conduct, *a man of principle; has no principles.* 3. a general or scientific law shown in the way something works or used as the basis for the construction of a machine etc. □**in principle,** as regards the main elements but not necessarily the details. **on principle,** because of the principles of conduct one accepts, *we refused on principle.* ▷See the note under **principal.**

prink (pringk) *v.* to dress up, to primp.

print (print) *v.* 1. to press (a mark or design etc.) on a surface, to impress or stamp (a surface or fabric etc.) in this way. 2. to produce (lettering on a book or newspaper etc.) by applying inked type to paper, to publish in this way. 3. to write with unjoined letters like those used in printing books etc. 4. to produce a positive picture from (a photographic negative or transparency) by transmission of light. **print** *n.* 1. a mark or indentation left where something has pressed on a surface. 2. printed lettering or writing, words in printed form. 3. a printed picture or photograph or design. 4. printed fabric. □**in print,** (of a book) available from a publisher. **out of print,** (of a book) not available from a publisher. **printed circuit,** an electric circuit with thin strips of conducting material on a flat insulating sheet (instead of wires). **printed matter,** material that is printed and is eligible for special postal rates.

print·a·ble (prin-tă-bĕl) *adj.* 1. capable of being printed. 2. worthy of publication.

print·er (prin-tĕr) *n.* 1. a person whose job or business is the printing of books, newspapers, etc. 2. a printing instrument. □**printer's devil,** a printer's assistant.

print·ing (prin-ting) *n.* 1. the act, process, or business of producing printed material. 2. all of the copies printed at one time, *the book is in its second printing.* 3. written letters that resemble printed ones. □**printing press,** a machine for printing on paper etc. from type or plates.

print·out (print-owt) *n.* material produced in printed form from a computer or teleprinter.

pri·or[1] (prI-ŏr) *adj.* earlier, coming before another or others in time or order or importance. **prior** *adv.* □**prior to,** before, *prior to that date.*

prior[2] *n.* the monk who is head of a religious house or order or (in an abbey) ranking next below an abbot. **pri·or·ess** (prI-ŏ-ris) *n. fem.*

pri·or·i·ty (prI-or-i-tee) *n.* (*pl.* **-ties**) 1. being earlier or more important, precedence in rank etc., the right to be first. 2. something that is more important than other items or considerations, *has got his priorities wrong.*

pri·o·ry (prI-ŏ-ree) *n.* (*pl.* **-ries**) a monastery governed by a prior, a nunnery governed by a prioress.

prism (priz-ĕm) *n.* 1. a solid geometric shape with ends that are similar, equal, and parallel. 2. a transparent body of this form, usually triangular and made of glass, that breaks up light into the colors of the rainbow.

pris·mat·ic (priz-mat-ik) *adj.* 1. of or like a prism. 2. (of colors) formed or distributed as if by a prism, rainbowlike. **pris·mat'i·cal·ly** *adv.*

pris·on (priz-ŏn) *n.* 1. a building used to confine people who are convicted or (in certain cases) accused of crimes. 2. any place of custody or confinement. 3. imprisonment as a punishment. □**prison camp,** a camp serving as a prison for prisoners of war etc.

pris·on·er (priz-ŏ-nĕr) *n.* 1. a person kept in prison. 2. a person who is in custody and on trial for a criminal offense. 3. a captive. 4. a person or thing kept in confinement or held in another's grasp etc. □**prisoner of war,** an enemy captured in a war.

pris·sy (pris-ee) *adj.* (**-si·er, -si·est**) prim. **pris'si·ness** *n.*

pris·tine (pris-teen) *adj.* in its original and unspoiled condition, fresh as if new.

prith·ee (prith-ee) *interj.* (old use) pray, please.

pri·va·cy (prI-vă-see) *n.* being private, seclusion.

pri·vate (prI-vit) *adj.* 1. of or belonging to a particular person or persons, not public, *private property.* 2. not holding public office, *speaking as a private citizen; in private life,* as a private person, not as an official or public performer etc. 3. not to be made known publicly, confidential. 4. (of a place) secluded. 5. of or belonging to a profession practiced on one's own financial account and not as an employee, *in private practice.* **private** *n.* a soldier or marine of the lowest rank. **pri'vate·ly** *adv.* **pri'vate·ness** *n.* □**in private,** in the presence only of the person(s) directly concerned, not in public. **private detective,** one who undertakes investigations etc. for a fee, not as a member of a police force. **private enterprise,** management of business by private individuals or companies (contrasted with state ownership or control); an individual's initiative. **private eye,** (*informal*) a private detective. **private first class,** a soldier ranking above a private and below a corporal. **private means,** an income available from investments etc., not as an earned wage or salary. **private parts,** the genitals. **private school,** a school supported wholly by pupils' fees or endowments.

pri·va·teer (prI-vă-teer) *n.* 1. an armed vessel owned and commanded by private persons holding a commission from the government and authorized to use it against a hostile nation, especially to capture merchant shipping. 2. the commander or a member of the crew of this. **pri·va·teer'ing** *n.*

pri·va·tion (prI-vay-shŏn) *n.* loss or lack of something, especially of the necessaries of life.

priv·et (priv-it) *n.* a bushy shrub with small leaves, much used for hedges.

priv·i·lege (priv-ĭ-lij) *n.* a special right or advantage granted to one person or group. **privilege** *v.* (**priv·i·leged, priv·i·leg·ing**) to grant a privilege to.

priv·i·leged (priv-ĭ-lijd) *adj.* having privileges; *privileged information,* information that need not be disclosed in a court of law, etc.

priv·y (priv-ee) *adj.* 1. (old use) hidden, secret. 2. sharing secret knowledge. 3. private. **privy** *n.* (*pl.* **priv·ies**) a toilet, especially one in an outhouse. **priv'i·ly** *adv.* □**be privy to,** to be sharing in the secret of (a person's plans etc.). **privy council,** a body of distinguished advisers, as those advising the British sovereign on matters of state.

prix fixe (pree fiks) (*pl.* **prix fixes,** *pr.* pree fiks) a set price charged for any meal chosen from the menu listings.

prize[1] (prIz) *n.* 1. an award given as a symbol of victory or superiority. 2. something striven for or worth striving for. 3. something that can be won in a lottery etc. **prize** *v.* (**prized, priz·ing**) to value highly. **prize** *adj.* winning or likely to win a prize, excellent of its kind. □**prize ring,** an enclosed area for prizefighting; the practice of prizefighting.

prize[2] *n.* a ship or property captured at sea during a war.

prize[3] *v.* (**prized, priz·ing**) to force out or open by leverage.

prize·fight (prīz-fīt) *n.* a boxing match, usually for pay. **prize'fight·er** *n.*

prize·win·ner (prīz-win-ĕr) *n.* the winner of a prize.

pro¹ (proh) *n.* (*pl.* **pros**) (*informal*) a professional.

pro² *adv.* in favor of. **pro** *n.* (*pl.* **pros**) 1. a person favoring one side of an issue or argument. 2. an argument in favor of something. □**pro and con**, for and against.

pro- *prefix* favoring or siding with, as in *pro-American;* forward, downward, onward, as in *proclaim, proceed;* substituting for, as in *pronoun.*

pro·a·bor·tion (proh-ă-bor-shŏn) *adj.* favoring the right to choose to undergo or to perform an abortion.

pro·ad·min·is·tra·tion (proh-ad-min-i-stray-shŏn) *adj.* on the side of the administration.

prob. *abbr.* 1. probable. 2. probably. 3. problem.

prob·a·bil·i·ty (prob-ă-bil-i-tee) *n.* (*pl.* **-ties**) 1. being probable. 2. something that is probable, *the most probable event.* 3. a ratio expressing the chances that a certain event will occur. □**in all probability**, most probably.

prob·a·ble (prob-ă-bĕl) *adj.* likely to happen or be true. **prob'a·bly** *adv.*

pro·bate (proh-bayt) *n.* 1. the official process of proving that a will is valid. 2. a copy of a will with a certificate that it is valid, handed to executors. **probate** *v.* (**pro·bat·ed, pro·bat·ing**) to prove (a will) authentic or valid. □**probate court**, a court that oversees the administration of estates of deceased persons.

pro·ba·tion (proh-bay-shŏn) *n.* 1. the testing of a person's behavior or abilities etc. 2. a system whereby certain offenders are supervised by an official (*probation officer*) as an alternative to imprisonment. **pro·ba'tion·al** *adj.* **pro·ba·tion·ar·y** (proh-bay-shŏ-ne-ree) *adj.*

pro·ba·tion·er (proh-bay-shŏ-nĕr) *n.* a person who is undergoing a probationary period of testing.

pro·ba·tive (proh-bă-tiv) *adj.* 1. providing proof. 2. designed to test or try something.

probe (prohb) *n.* 1. a device for exploring an otherwise inaccessible place or object etc., a blunt-ended surgical instrument for exploring a wound; *space probe,* an unmanned exploratory spacecraft transmitting information about its environment etc. 2. a penetrating investigation, *ordered a probe into their expense accounts.* **probe** *v.* (**probed, prob·ing**) 1. to explore with a probe. 2. to penetrate with something sharp. 3. to make a penetrating investigation of.

pro·bi·ty (proh-bi-tee) *n.* honesty, integrity.

prob·lem (prob-lĕm) *n.* 1. something difficult to deal with or understand. 2. something difficult that has to be accomplished or answered or dealt with. 3. an exercise in a textbook or examination.

prob·lem·at·ic (prob-lĕ-mat-ik), **prob·lem·at·i·cal** (prob-lĕ-mat-i-kăl) *adj.* 1. difficult to deal with or understand. 2. questionable, doubtful. **prob·lem·at'i·cal·ly** *adv.*

pro·bos·cis (proh-bos-is) *n.* (*pl.* **-bos·cis·es, -bos·ci·des**, *pr.* -bos-i-deez) 1. a long flexible snout, an elephant's trunk. 2. an elongated mouth-part in certain insects, used for sucking things.

pro·busi·ness (proh-biz-nis) *adj.* favoring the interests of business over those of labor.

proc. *abbr.* 1. procedure. 2. proceedings. 3. process.

pro·caine (proh-kayn) *n.* a chemical compound used as a local anesthetic.

pro·cap·i·tal·ist (proh-kap-i-tă-list) *adj.* favoring capitalism or capitalist interests.

pro·ca·the·dral (proh-kă-thee-drăl) *n.* a church used as a cathedral temporarily.

pro·ce·dure (prŏ-see-jŭr) *n.* a series of actions done or appointed to be done in order to accomplish something, a way of conducting business, *parliamentary procedure.* **pro·ce'dur·al** *adj.*

pro·ceed (prŏ-seed) *v.* 1. to go forward or onward, to make one's way. 2. to continue, to carry on an activity, *please proceed with your work.* 3. to start a lawsuit, *he proceeded against the newspaper for libel.* 4. to come forth, to originate, *the evils that proceed from war.*

pro·ceed·ings (prŏ-see-dingz) *n. pl.* 1. a lawsuit, *start proceedings for divorce.* 2. what takes place at a formal meeting of a society etc. 3. a published report of a discussion or conference etc., *Proceedings of the Modern Language Association.*

pro·ceeds (proh-seedz) *n. pl.* the amount of money produced by a sale or performance etc.

proc·ess (pros-es, proh-ses) *n.* 1. a series of actions or operations used in making or manufacturing or achieving something. 2. a series of changes, a natural operation, *the digestive process.* 3. a course of events or time. 4. a lawsuit, a summons or writ. 5. a natural projection on the body or one of its parts. **process** *v.* to put through a manufacturing or other process or course of treatment; *your application is being processed,* is being dealt with. **proc'ess·or, proc'ess·er** *n.* □**data processing**, *see* **data. process cheese,** cheese treated to avoid further ripening or deterioration during storage. **process printing,** a way of printing colors by combining separate color plates. **process server,** a person who serves legal documents such as writs or warrants. **process shot,** (in film) a shot in which certain images are made to appear by artificial means.

pro·ces·sion (prŏ-sesh-ŏn) *n.* a number of people or vehicles or boats etc. going along in an orderly line.

pro·ces·sion·al (prŏ-sesh-ŏ-năl) *adj.* of or for a procession. **pro·ces'sion·al** *n.* a processional hymn, religious music for a procession.

pro·claim (proh-klaym) *v.* 1. to announce officially or publicly, to declare. 2. to make known unmistakably as being, *his accent proclaimed him a Scot.* **pro·cla·ma·tion** (prok-lă-may-shŏn) *n.*

pro·cliv·i·ty (proh-kliv-i-tee) *n.* (*pl.* **-ties**) a tendency.

pro·com·mu·nist (proh-kom-yŭ-nist) *adj.* favoring communist principles or ideas.

pro·con·sul (proh-kon-sŭl) *n.* (in Roman history) the governor of a province. **pro·con'su·lar** *adj.* **pro·con·su·late** (proh-kon-sŭ-lit) *n.*

pro·cras·ti·nate (prŏ-kras-tĭ-nayt) *v.* (**pro·cras·ti·nat·ed, pro·cras·ti·nat·ing**) to postpone action, to be dilatory. **pro·cras'ti·na·tor** *n.* **pro·cras·ti·na·tion** (prŏ-kras-ti-nay-shŏn) *n.*

pro·cre·ate (proh-kree-ayt) *v.* (**pro·cre·at·ed, pro·cre·at·ing**) to bring (a living thing) into existence by the natural process of reproduction, to generate. **pro'cre·a·tor** *n.* **pro'cre·a·tive** *adj.* **pro·cre·a·tion** (proh-kree-ay-shŏn) *n.*

Pro·crus·te·an, pro·crus·te·an (proh-krus-tee-ăn) *adj.* seeking to enforce conformity with a theory etc. by violent methods (as by cutting all that contradicts it). ▷Named after Procrustes, a robber in Greek legend, who fitted victims to his bed by stretching them or lopping bits off.

proc·tol·o·gist (prok-tol-ŏ-jist) *n.* an expert in proctology.

proc·tol·o·gy (prok-tol-ŏ-jee) *n.* a branch of medicine dealing with the structure and diseases of the rectum and anus. **proc·to·log·ic** (prok-tŏ-loj-ik) *adj.* **proc·to·log'i·cal** *adj.*

proc·tor (prok-tŏr) *n.* an official or a teacher who supervises an examination. **proctor** *v.* to perform this function. **proc·tor·i·al** (prok-tohr-ee-ăl) *adj.*

pro·cur·a·ble (prŏ-kyoor-ă-bĕl) *adj.* able to be procured.

proc·u·ra·tor (prok-yŭ-ray-tŏr) *n.* 1. the treasury officer in an imperial province of ancient Rome. 2. an agent or proxy.

pro·cure (prŏ-kyoor) *v.* (**pro·cured, pro·cur·ing**) to obtain by care or effort, to acquire. **pro·cure'ment** *n.*

pro·cur·er (prŏ-kyoor-ĕr) *n.* 1. one who procures something. 2. a pimp.

pro·cur·ess (prŏ-kyoor-is) *n.* a female pimp.

prod (prod) *v.* (**prod·ded, prod·ding**) 1. to poke. 2. to urge or stimulate into action. **prod** *n.* 1. a poke. 2. a stimulus to action. 3. a pointed instrument for prodding things.

prod. *abbr.* 1. produce. 2. produced. 3. producer. 4. product. 5. production.

prod·i·gal (prod-ĭ-găl) *adj.* 1. recklessly wasteful or extravagant. 2. lavish. **prodigal** *n.* a recklessly extravagant person. **prod'i·gal·ly** *adv.* **prod·i·gal·i·ty** (prod-ĭ-gal-i-tee) *n.*

pro·di·gious (prŏ-dij-ŭs) *adj.* 1. marvelous, amazing, *a prodigious achievement.* 2. enormous, *spent a prodigious amount.* **pro·di'gious·ly** *adv.*

prod·i·gy (prod-i-jee) *n.* (*pl.* -**gies**) 1. a person with exceptional qualities or abilities, a child with abilities very much beyond those appropriate to his age. 2. a marvelous thing, a wonderful example of something.

pro·duce (prŏ-doos) *v.* (**pro·duced, pro·duc·ing**) 1. to bring forward for inspection or consideration or use, *will produce evidence.* 2. to bring (a play or performance etc.) before the public. 3. to bring into existence, to cause (a reaction or sensation etc.), to bear or yield (offspring or products). 4. to manufacture. 5. to extend (a line). **produce** (prod-oos, proh-doos) *n.* 1. an amount or thing produced. 2. agricultural and natural products, *dairy produce.*

pro·duc·er (prŏ-doo-sĕr) *n.* 1. a person producing articles or agricultural products etc. (contrasted with a *consumer*). 2. a person generally responsible for the production of a film or play (apart from direction of the acting).

prod·uct (prod-ukt) *n.* 1. something produced by a natural process or by agriculture or manufacture or as a result. 2. (in mathematics) the result obtained by multiplying two quantities together.

pro·duc·tion (prŏ-duk-shŏn) *n.* 1. producing, being produced; *go into production,* begin being manufactured. 2. a thing produced, especially a play or film. 3. the amount produced.

pro·duc·tive (prŏ-duk-tiv) *adj.* tending or able to produce things, especially in large quantities. **pro·duc'tive·ly** *adv.* **pro·duc'tive·ness** *n.*

pro·duc·tiv·i·ty (proh-duk-tiv-i-tee) *n.* productiveness, efficiency in industrial production.

pro·em (proh-ĕm) *n.* 1. a preface or preamble to a book or speech. 2. a beginning or prelude.

prof (prof) *n.* (*informal*) professor.

Prof. (prŏ-fes-or) *n.* the title prefixed to a professor's name.

pro·fane (proh-fayn) *adj.* 1. secular, not sacred, *sacred and profane music.* 2. irreverent, blasphemous. **profane** *v.* (**pro·faned, pro·fan·ing**) to treat (a thing) with irreverence or lack of due respect. **pro·fane'ly** *adv.* **pro·fane'ness** *n.*

pro·fan·i·ty (proh-fan-i-tee) *n.* 1. irreverent language. 2. being profane, a profane thing.

pro·fas·cist (proh-fash-ist) *adj.* favoring fascistic principles or ideas.

pro·fem·i·nist (proh-fem-ĭ-nist) *adj.* favoring feminist principles or ideas.

pro·fess (prŏ-fes) *v.* 1. to state that one has (a quality or feeling etc.), to pretend, *she professed ignorance* or *to be ignorant of this law.* 2. to affirm one's faith in (a religion).

pro·fessed (prŏ-fest) *adj.* 1. avowed, openly acknowledged by oneself, *a professed Christian.* 2. falsely claiming to be something, *a professed friend.* 3. having taken the vows of a religious order, *a professed nun.* **pro·fess·ed·ly** (prŏ-fes-id-lee) *adv.*

pro·fes·sion (prŏ-fesh-ŏn) *n.* 1. an occupation, especially one that involves knowledge and training in a branch of advanced learning, *the dental profession.* 2. the people engaged in an occupation of this kind. 3. a declaration or avowal, *made professions of loyalty.*

pro·fes·sion·al (prŏ-fesh-ŏ-năl) *adj.* 1. of or belonging to a profession or its members. 2. having or showing the skill of a professional. 3. doing a certain kind of work as a full-time occupation or to make a living or (of sportsmen, contrasted with *amateur*) for payment. **professional** *n.* 1. a person working or performing for payment. 2. someone highly skilled. **pro·fes'sion·al·ly** *adv.*

pro·fes·sion·al·ism (prŏ-fesh-ŏ-nă-liz-ĕm) *n.* the qualities or skills of a profession or professionals.

pro·fes·sion·al·ize, pro·fes·sion·al·iz·ing (prŏ-fesh-ŏ-nă-līz) *v.* (**pro·fes·sion·al·ized, pro·fes·sion·al·iz·ing**) to give a professional quality to.

pro·fes·sor (prŏ-fes-ŏr) *n.* a university teacher of the highest rank. **pro·fes'sor·ship** *n.* **pro·fes·so·ri·al** (proh-fe-sohr-i-ăl) *adj.*

prof·fer (prof-ĕr) *v.* to offer. **proffer** *n.* an offer.

pro·fi·cient (prŏ-fish-ĕnt) *adj.* doing something correctly and competently through training or practice, skilled. **pro·fi'cient·ly** *adv.* **pro·fi·cien·cy** (prŏ-fish-ĕn-see) *n.*

pro·file (proh-fīl) *n.* 1. a side view, especially of the human face. 2. a drawing or other representation of this. 3. a short account of a person's character or career. **profile** *v.* (**pro·filed, pro·fil·ing**) to represent in profile, either in drawing or in writing.

prof·it (prof-it) *n.* 1. an advantage or benefit obtained from doing something. 2. money gained in a business transaction, the excess of returns over outlay. **profit** *v.* (**prof·it·ed, prof·it·ing**) 1. to take advantage to. 2. to obtain an advantage or benefit. **prof'it·less** *adj.* □**profit and loss,** the gain and loss that result from business transactions, reflected in statements of accounts. **profit sharing,** the sharing of profits, especially between employer and employee.

prof·it·a·ble (prof-i-tă-bĕl) *adj.* bringing profit or benefits. **prof'it·a·bly** *adv.* **prof·it·a·bil·i·ty** (prof-i-tă-bil-i-tee) *n.*

prof·it·eer (prof-i-teer) *n.* a person who makes excessive profits, especially by taking advantage of times of difficulty or scarcity (as in war). **profiteer** v. to make profits in this way. **prof· it·eer'ing** n.

pro·fit·er·ole (prŏ-fĭt-ĕ-rohl) n. a small cake with a chocolate or other filling.

prof·li·gate (prof-lĭ-git) adj. 1. recklessly wasteful or extravagant. 2. dissolute. **profligate** n. a profligate person. **prof'li·gate·ly** adv. **prof·li· ga·cy** (prof-lĭ-gă-see) n.

pro for·ma (proh for-mă) as a matter of form.

pro·found (prŏ-fownd) adj. 1. deep, intense, takes a profound interest in it. 2. having or showing great knowledge of or insight into a subject. 3. thorough. 4. complete, total. **pro·found'ly** adv. **pro·fun·di·ty** (prŏ-fun-di-tee) n.

pro·fuse (prŏ-fyoos) adj. 1. lavish, extravagant, profuse gratitude. 2. plentiful, a profuse variety. **pro·fuse'ly** adv. **pro·fuse'ness** n.

pro·fu·sion (prŏ-fyoo-zhŏn) n. abundance, a plentiful supply, a profusion of roses.

pro·gen·i·tor (proh-jen-i-tŏr) n. an ancestor.

prog·e·ny (proj-ĕ-nee) n. offspring, descendants.

pro·ges·ter·one (prŏ-jes-tĕ-rohn) n. a hormone that prevents ovulation.

prog·na·thous (prog-nă-thŭs) adj. with projecting jaws.

prog·no·sis (prog-noh-sis) n. (pl. **-ses**, pr. -seez) an advance indication, a forecast of the course of a disease.

prog·nos·tic (prog-nos-tik) n. 1. an advance indication or omen. 2. a forecast. **prognostic** adj.

prog·nos·ti·cate (prog-nos-ti-kayt) v. (**prog· nos·ti·cat·ed, prog·nos·ti·cat·ing**) to forecast. **prog·nos'ti·ca·tor** n. **prog·nos·ti·ca· tion** (prog-nos-ti-kay-shŏn) n.

pro·gov·ern·ment (proh-guv-ĕrn-mĕnt) adj. favoring the party in power.

pro·gram (proh-gram) n. 1. a plan of intended procedure. 2. a descriptive notice or list of an organized series of events (as of a concert or a course of study). 3. these events. 4. a broadcast performance. 5. a series of coded instructions for a computer. **program** v. (**pro·gramed** or **pro· grammed, pro·gram·ing** or **pro·gram·ming**) 1. to make a program of, to enter in a program. 2. to cause an automatic response in (a person), as by indoctrination. 3. to prepare material for programmed instruction, to teach by this. 4. to instruct (a computer) by means of a program. **pro'gram·a·ble, pro'gram·ma·ble** adj. **pro· gram·ma·bil·i·ty** (proh-gram-ă-bil-i-tee) n. **pro·gram·ma·tic** (proh-gră-mat-ik) adj. ☐**programmed instruction** or **learning**, teaching or learning that advances after the student has made a correct response to each unit in a series of small units of material.

pro·gram·mer, pro·gram·er (proh-gram-ĕr) n. a person who prepares instructions for a computer.

pro·gram·ming (proh-gram-ing) n. 1. developing a program for a computer. 2. indoctrinating people to respond automatically in learned behavior patterns.

prog·ress (prog-res) n. 1. forward or onward movement. 2. an advance or development, especially to a better state. **progress** (prŏ-gres) v. 1. to move forward or onward. 2. to advance or develop, especially to a better state. ☐**in prog· ress**, taking place, in the course of occurring. **pro·gres·sion** (prŏ-gresh-ŏn) n. 1. a mode of progressing. 2. a succession or series. 3. passing from one musical note or chord to another.

pro·gres·sive (prŏ-gres-iv) adj. 1. making continuous forward movement. 2. proceeding steadily or in regular degrees, a progressive improvement. 3. (of a card game or dance etc.) with a periodic change of partners. 4. (of a disease) gradually increasing in its effect. 5. advancing in social conditions or efficiency etc., a progressive nation or firm. 6. favoring progress or reform, a progressive party or policy. **progressive** n. 1. a person who favors a progressive policy. 2. a progressive tense. **pro·gres'sive·ly** adv. **pro·gres'sive·ness** n. ☐**progressive jazz**, a type of jazz combining jazz and classical elements. **progressive tense**, any of various verb tenses expressing action in progress, as in I am writing, I was writing, etc.

pro·hib·it (proh-hib-it) v. (**pro·hib·it·ed, pro· hib·it·ing**) to forbid.

pro·hi·bi·tion (proh-ĭ-bish-ŏn) n. 1. forbidding, being forbidden. 2. an edict or order that forbids. 3. Prohibition, a period from 1920–1933 when the manufacture and sale of alcoholic drinks were forbidden by law in the U.S. **pro·hi·bi'tion· ist** n.

pro·hib·i·tive (proh-hib-i-tiv) adj. preventing or intended to prevent the use or abuse or purchase of something, prohibitive taxes. **pro·hib'i·tive· ly** adv. **pro·hib·i·to·ry** (proh-hib-i-tohr-ee) adj.

pro·in·dus·try (proh-in-dŭ-stree) adj. favoring the interests of industry rather than those of government etc.

pro·in·te·gra·tion (proh-in-tĕ-gray-shŏn) adj. favoring racial integration in schools, housing, etc.

pro·ject (prŏ-jekt) v. 1. to extend outward from a surface, a projecting balcony. 2. to cast or throw outward. 3. to cause (a picture or shadow) to fall on a surface. 4. to imagine (a thing or oneself) in another situation or another person's feelings or a future time. 5. to plan (a scheme or course of action). 6. to represent (a solid thing) systematically on a plane surface, as maps of Earth are made. **project** (proj-ekt) n. 1. a plan or scheme or undertaking. 2. a task set as an educational exercise, requiring students to do their own research and present the results.

pro·jec·tile (prŏ-jek-til) n. a missile (as a bullet or arrow or rocket) that can be projected forcefully.

pro·jec·tion (prŏ-jek-shŏn) n. 1. projecting, being projected. 2. something that projects from a surface. 3. a thing that is projected. 4. a representation of the surface of Earth on a plane surface. 5. an estimate of future situations or trends etc. based on a study of present ones. ☐**projection booth**, a room in a movie theater where the motion picture projectors and spotlights are kept.

pro·jec·tion·ist (prŏ-jek-shŏ-nist) n. a person whose job is to operate a projector.

pro·jec·tor (prŏ-jek-tŏr) n. an apparatus for projecting photographs or a motion picture etc. onto a screen.

pro·la·bor (proh-lay-bŏr) adj. favoring the interests of labor over those of business.

pro·lapse (proh-laps) v. (**pro·lapsed, pro· laps·ing**) (of an organ of the body) to slip forward or down out of its place. **prolapse** (proh-laps) n. the prolapsing of an organ of the body.

pro·le·gom·e·non (proh-lĕ-gom-ĕ-non) n. (pl. **-na**, pr. -nă) preliminary matter in a book, the introduction.

pro·le·tar·i·an (proh-lĕ-tair-i-ăn) adj. of the proletariat. **proletarian** n. a member of the proletariat.

535   **proletariat / proofread**

pro·le·tar·i·at (proh-lĕ-tair-i-ăt) *n.* the working
class (contrasted with the *bourgeoisie*).
pro·lif·er·ate (proh-lif-ĕ-rayt) *v.* (**pro·lif·er·
at·ed, pro·lif·er·at·ing**) to produce new
growth or offspring rapidly, to multiply. **pro·
lif·er·a·tion** (proh-lif-ĕ-ray-shŏn) *n.*
pro·lif·ic (proh-lif-ik) *adj.* producing much fruit
or many flowers or offspring; *a prolific writer,* one
who writes many works. **pro·lif'i·cal·ly** *adv.*
pro·lix (proh-liks) *adj.* lengthy, tediously wordy.
pro·logue, pro·log (proh-lawg) *n.* 1. an introduction to a poem or play etc. 2. an act or event
serving as an introduction to something.
pro·long (prŏ-lawng) *v.* to lengthen (a thing) in
extent or duration. **pro·lon·ga·tion** (proh-
lawng-gay-shŏn) *n.*
pro·longed (prŏ-lawngd) *adj.* continuing for a long
time.
prom (prom) *n.* *(informal)* a dance, usually formal,
given at a school or college.
prom·e·nade (prom-ĕ-nayd, -nahd) *n.* 1. a leisurely walk in a public place. 2. a paved public
walk (especially along a sea front), an esplanade.
promenade *v.* (**prom·e·nad·ed, prom·e·
nad·ing**) to go or take for a promenade, to parade. ☐**promenade deck,** an upper deck on a
passenger ship, where passengers may promenade.
pro·me·thi·um (prŏ-mee-thi-ŭm) *n.* a radioactive
metallic element.
pro·mil·i·tar·y (proh-mil-i-ter-ee) *adj.* favoring
policies promoted by the military.
prom·i·nence (prom-ĭ-nĕns) *n.* 1. the state of being prominent, a prominent thing. 2. a cloud of
incandescent gas jutting out from the sun.
prom·i·nent (prom-ĭ-nĕnt) *adj.* 1. jutting out, projecting. 2. conspicuous. 3. important, well-known,
prominent citizens. **prom'i·nent·ly** *adv.*
pro·mis·cu·ous (prŏ-mis-kyoo-ŭs) *adj.* 1. indiscriminate. 2. having sexual relations with many
people. **pro·mis'cu·ous·ly** *adv.* **pro·mis'cu·
ous·ness** *n.* **prom·is·cu·i·ty** (prom-is-kyoo-
i-tee) *n.*
prom·ise (prom-is) *n.* 1. a declaration that one
will give or do or not do a certain thing. 2. an
indication of something that may be expected to
come or occur. 3. an indication of future success
or good results, *his work shows promise.* **promise**
v. (**prom·ised, prom·is·ing**) 1. to make a
promise to, to declare that one will give or do
or not do something. 2. to make (a thing) seem
likely; *it promises well,* seems likely to give good
results. ☐**Promised Land,** Canaan, which was
promised by God to Abraham and his descendants; any place of expected happiness.
prom·is·ing (prom-i-sing) *adj.* likely to turn out
well or produce good results. **prom'is·ing·ly**
adv.
prom·is·so·ry (prom-i-sohr-ee) *adj.* conveying a
promise. ☐**promissory note,** a signed promise
to pay a sum of money.
pro·mon·ar·chist (proh-mon-ăr-kist) *adj.* favoring a monarch or monarchy.
prom·on·to·ry (prom-ŏn-tohr-ee) *n.* high land
jutting out into the sea or a lake.
pro·mote (prŏ-moht) *v.* (**pro·mot·ed, pro·
mot·ing**) 1. to raise (a person) to a higher rank
or office. 2. to initiate or help the progress of,
promote friendship between nations. 3. to publicize
(a product) in order to sell it.
pro·mot·er (prŏ-moh-tĕr) *n.* a person who publi-
cizes a product or event.
pro·mo·tion (prŏ-moh-shŏn) *n.* 1. promoting, be-

ing promoted. 2. the publicity and advertising for
a product. **pro·mo'tion·al** *adj.*
prompt (prompt) *adj.* 1. made or done or doing
something without delay. 2. punctual. **prompt**
adv. punctually. **prompt** *v.* 1. to incite or stimulate (a person) to action. 2. to cause (a feeling
or thought or action). 3. to assist by supplying
(an actor or speaker) with words that should
or could come next. **prompt'ly** *adv.* **prompt'
ness** *n.*
prompt·book (prompt-buuk) *n.* a copy of a play
for a prompter's use.
prompt·er (promp-tĕr) *n.* a person (placed out of
sight of the audience) who prompts actors on the
stage.
prom·ul·gate (prom-ŭl-gayt) *v.* (**pro·mul·gat·
ed, pro·mul·gat·ing**) to make known to the
public, to proclaim. **prom'ul·ga·tor** *n.* **prom·
ul·ga·tion** (prom-ŭl-gay-shŏn) *n.*
pron. *abbr.* 1. pronoun. 2. pronounced. 3. pronunciation.
pro·na·tion·al·ist (proh-nash-ŏ-nă-list) *adj.* favoring a nationalistic government or group.
prone (prohn) *adj.* 1. lying face downward (contrasted with *supine*). 2. likely to do or suffer something, *prone to jealousy.* **prone'ness** *n.*
prong (prong) *n.* one of the projecting pointed parts
of a fork.
pronged (prongd) *adj.* having a certain number
or kind of prongs, *two-pronged; a three-pronged
attack,* in three areas.
prong·horn (prong-horn) *n.* a deerlike animal of
western North America resembling an antelope.
pro·noun (proh-nown) *n.* a word used as a substitute for a noun; *demonstrative pronouns,* this, that,
these, those; *interrogative pronouns,* who? what?
which? etc.; *personal pronouns,* I, me, we, us, thou,
thee, you, ye, he, him, she, her, it, they, them;
possessive pronouns, mine, yours, his, hers, its,
ours, theirs; *reflexive pronouns,* myself, oneself,
etc.; *relative pronouns,* who, what, which, that.
pro·nom·i·nal (proh-nom-i-năl) *adj.*
pro·nounce (prŏ-nowns) *v.* (**pro·nounced,
pro·nounc·ing**) 1. to utter (a sound) distinctly
or correctly or in a certain way, *can't pronounce
the letter r.* 2. to declare formally, *I now pronounce
you man and wife.* 3. to declare as one's opinion,
the wine was pronounced excellent. **pro·
nounce'a·ble** *adj.*
pro·nounced (prŏ-nownst) *adj.* definite, noticeable, *walks with a pronounced limp.*
pro·nounce·ment (prŏ-nowns-mĕnt) *n.* a declaration.
pron·to (pron-toh) *adv.* *(slang)* immediately.
pro·nun·ci·a·men·to (proh-nun-si-ă-men-toh)
n. (*pl.* **-tos**) a proclamation, manifesto, or pro-
nouncement.
pro·nun·ci·a·tion (prŏ-nun-si-ay-shŏn) *n.* 1. the
way a word is pronounced. 2. the way a person
pronounces words.
proof (proof) *n.* 1. a fact or thing that shows or
helps to show that something is true or exists.
2. a demonstration of the truth of something, *in
proof of my statement.* 3. the process of testing
whether something is true or good or valid, *put
it to the proof.* 4. a standard of strength for distilled
alcoholic liquors, *86 proof.* 5. an impression of
printed matter, produced so that corrections can
be made. 6. a trial print of a photograph. **proof**
adj. able to resist or withstand penetration or damage, *bulletproof; proof against the severest weather.*
proof·read (proof-reed) *v.* (**proof·read,** *pr.* -red.

proof·read·ing, *pr.* -reed-) to read and correct proofs. **proof'read·er** *n.* **proof'read·ing** *n.*
prop¹ (prop) *n.* 1. a support used to keep something from falling or sagging. 2. a person or thing depended on for support or help. **prop** *v.* **(propped, prop·ping)** to support with or as if with a prop, to keep from falling or failing, *prop it up.*
prop² *n.* (*informal*) a stage property.
prop³ *n.* (*informal*) a propeller.
prop. *abbr.* 1. property. 2. proposition. 3. proprietary. 4. proprietor.
prop·a·gan·da (prop-ă-gan-dă) *n.* publicity intended to spread ideas or information that will persuade or convince people. **prop·a·gan' dist** *n.*
prop·a·gan·dize (prop-ă-gan-dɪz) *v.* **(prop·a·gan·dized, prop·a·gan·diz·ing)** 1. to spread propaganda, to spread (ideas) in this way. 2. to subject to propaganda.
prop·a·gate (prop-ă-gayt) *v.* **(prop·a·gat·ed, prop·a·gat·ing)** 1. to breed or reproduce from parent stock, *propagate these plants from seeds or cuttings.* 2. to spread (news or ideas etc.). 3. to transmit, *the vibrations are propagated through the rock.* **prop'a·ga·tor** *n.* **prop·a·ga·tion** (prop-ă-gay-shŏn) *n.*
pro·pane (proh-payn) *n.* a hydrocarbon gas used as a fuel.
pro·pel (prŏ-pel) *v.* **(pro·pelled, pro·pel·ling)** to drive or push forward, to give an onward movement to.
pro·pel·lant, pro·pel·lent (prŏ-pel-ănt) *n.* a propelling agent, such as an explosive that propels a bullet from a firearm, fuel that provides thrust for a rocket, compressed gas that forces out the contents of an aerosol container.
pro·pel·ler (prŏ-pel-ĕr) *n.* a revolving device with blades for propelling a ship or aircraft to which it is fitted.
pro·pen·si·ty (prŏ-pen-si-tee) *n.* (*pl.* **-ties**) a tendency or inclination, *a propensity to laziness.*
prop·er (prop-ĕr) *adj.* 1. suitable, appropriate, *not a proper time for singing.* 2. correct, according to rules, *the proper way to hold the bat.* 3. according to social conventions, respectable. 4. strictly so called, *we drove from the suburbs to the city proper.* **prop'er·ly** *adv.* **prop'er·ness** *n.* ☐**proper fraction,** one that is less than 1, with the numerator less than the denominator, as ¾.
proper name *or* **noun,** the name of an individual person or thing, as *Jane, Seattle.*
prop·er·tied (prop-ĕr-teed) *adj.* having property.
prop·er·ty (prop-ĕr-tee) *n.* (*pl.* **-ties**) 1. a thing or things owned. 2. real estate, someone's land, *their property borders on ours.* 3. a movable object (such as furniture) used on stage during a performance of a play etc. 4. a quality or characteristic, *it has the property of dissolving grease.*
proph·e·cy (prof-ĕ-see) *n.* (*pl.* **-cies**) 1. the power of prophesying, *the gift of prophecy.* 2. a statement that tells what will happen. ▷Do not confuse *prophecy* with *prophesy.*
proph·e·sy (prof-ĕ-sɪ) *v.* **(proph·e·sied, proph·e·sy·ing)** to declare beforehand (what will happen), to foretell things as if by divine inspiration. **proph'e·si·er** *n.* ▷Do not confuse *prophesy* with *prophecy.*
proph·et (prof-it) *n.* 1. a person who foretells the future. 2. a divinely inspired teacher, revealer, or interpreter of God's will. 3. *Prophets,* twelve prophetical writers whose writings form a group

of books of the Old Testament. **proph·et·ess** (prof-i-tis) *n.* *fem.* ☐**the Prophet,** Muhammad.
pro·phet·ic (prŏ-fet-ik) *adj.* prophesying the future. **pro·phet'i·cal** *adj.* **pro·phet'i·cal·ly** *adv.*
pro·phy·lac·tic (proh-fi-lak-tik) *adj.* tending to prevent a disease or misfortune, *prophylactic measures were taken against the spread of cholera.* **prophylactic** *n.* a prophylactic substance or procedure. **pro·phy·lac'ti·cal·ly** *adv.*
pro·phy·lax·is (proh-fi-lak-sis) *n.* preventive treatment against a disease etc.
pro·pin·qui·ty (proh-ping-kwi-tee) *n.* nearness.
pro·pi·ti·ate (prŏ-pish-i-ayt) *v.* **(pro·pi·ti·at·ed, pro·pi·ti·at·ing)** to win the favor or forgiveness of, to placate. **pro·pi·ti·a·to·ry** (prŏ-pish-i-ă-tohr-ee) *adj.* **pro·pi·ti·a·tion** (prŏ-pish-i-ay-shŏn) *n.*
pro·pi·tious (prŏ-pish-ŭs) *adj.* favorable, giving a good omen or a suitable opportunity. **pro· pi'tious·ly** *adv.*
prop·jet (prop-jet) *n.* 1. a turboprop engine. 2. an airplane propelled by a turboprop engine.
prop·man (prop-man) *n.* (*pl.* **-men,** *pr.* -men) a person responsible for theatrical stage properties.
pro·po·nent (prŏ-poh-nĕnt) *n.* a person who puts forward a motion, theory, or proposal.
pro·por·tion (prŏ-pohr-shŏn) *n.* 1. a fraction or share of a whole. 2. a ratio, *the proportion of skilled workers to unskilled.* 3. the correct relation in size or amount or degree between one thing and another or between parts of a thing. 4. *proportions,* size, dimensions, *a ship of majestic proportions.* **proportion** *v.* **(pro·por·tioned, pro·por·tion·ing)** to make proportionate.
pro·por·tion·al (prŏ-pohr-shŏ-năl) *adj.* in correct proportion, corresponding in size or amount or degree. **pro·por'tion·al·ly** *adv.* **pro·por·tion·al·i·ty** (prŏ-pohr-shŏ-nal-i-tee) *n.* ☐**proportional representation,** an electoral system in which each party has a number of seats in proportion to the number of votes for its candidates.
pro·por·tion·ate (prŏ-pohr-shŏ-nit) *adj.* in proportion, corresponding, *the cost is proportionate to the quality.* **pro·por'tion·ate·ly** *adv.*
pro·por·tioned (prŏ-pohr-shŏnd) *adj.* having certain proportions, *a well-proportioned room.*
pro·pos·al (prŏ-poh-zăl) *n.* 1. the proposing of something. 2. the thing proposed. 3. a request that a person should agree to be married to the person asking.
pro·pose (prŏ-pohz) *v.* **(pro·posed, pro·pos·ing)** 1. to put forward for consideration; *propose a toast,* ask people formally to drink a toast. 2. to have and declare as one's plan or intention, *we propose to wait.* 3. to nominate as a candidate. 4. to make a proposal of marriage. **pro· pos'er** *n.*
prop·o·si·tion (prop-ŏ-zish-ŏn) *n.* 1. a statement, an assertion. 2. a proposal, a scheme proposed, *a majority voted for Proposition 2.* 3. (*informal*) a problem or undertaking, something to be dealt with, *not a paying proposition.* 4. a formal statement of a mathematical theorem or problem, often including the demonstration. **proposition** *v.* (*informal*) to put a proposal to (a person). **prop· o·si'tion·al** *adj.*
pro·pound (prŏ-pownd) *v.* to put forward for consideration. **pro·pound'er** *n.*

pro·pri·e·tar·y (prŏ-prɪ-ĕ-ter-ee) adj. 1. manufactured and sold by one particular firm, usually under a patent, proprietary medicines. 2. of an owner or ownership.
pro·pri·e·tor (prŏ-prɪ-ĕ-tŏr) n. the owner of a business. **pro·pri'e·tor·ship** n. **pro·pri'e·tress** n. fem. **pro·pri·e·tor·i·al** (prŏ-prɪ-ĕ-tohr-i-ăl) adj.
pro·pri·e·ty (prŏ-prɪ-ĕ-tee) n. (pl. -ties) 1. being proper or suitable. 2. correctness of behavior or morals; the proprieties, the requirements of correct behavior in society.
pro·pul·sion (prŏ-pul-shŏn) n. 1. the process of propelling or being propelled. 2. a propelling force, the 747 uses jet propulsion.
pro ra·ta (proh ray-tă, rah-tă) proportional, proportionally, if costs increase, there will be a pro rata increase in prices or prices will increase pro rata. ▷Latin, = according to the rate.
pro·rate (proh-rayt) v. (**pro·rat·ed, pro·rat·ing**) to allocate or distribute pro rata.
pro·re·form (proh-ri-form) adj. favoring reform of a government etc.
pro·rev·o·lu·tion·ar·y (proh-rev-ŏ-loo-shŏ-ner-ee) adj. favoring a change of government, especially by force.
pro·rogue (proh-rohg) v. (**pro·rogued, pro·rogu·ing**) to discontinue meetings of (the British Parliament or a similar body) without dissolving it. **pro·ro·ga·tion** (proh-rŏ-gay-shŏn) n.
pros see pro.
pro·sa·ic (proh-zay-ik) adj. lacking poetic beauty or fantasy, unimaginative, plain and ordinary. **pro·sa'i·cal·ly** adv.
pro·sce·ni·um (proh-see-ni-ŭm) n. (pl. -ni·ums, -ni·a, pr. -ni-ă) the part of a theater stage in front of the curtain, with its enclosing arch.
pro·sciut·to (proh-shoo-toh) n. Italian spiced ham.
pro·scribe (proh-skrɪb) v. (**pro·scribed, pro·scrib·ing**) 1. to forbid by law. 2. to reject (a practice etc.) as dangerous. **pro·scrip·tion** (proh-skrip-shŏn) n.
prose (prohz) n. written or spoken language not in verse form.
pros·e·cute (pros-ĕ-kyoot) v. (**pros·e·cut·ed, pros·e·cut·ing**) 1. to take legal proceedings against (a person etc.) for a crime. 2. to carry on or conduct, prosecuting their business. **pros'e·cu·tor** n. ▷Do not confuse prosecute with persecute.
pros·e·cu·tion (pros-ĕ-kyoo-shŏn) n. 1. prosecuting, being prosecuted. 2. the party prosecuting another for a crime.
pros·e·lyte (pros-ĕ-lɪt) n. a convert to a religion or opinion etc. proselyte. v. (**pros·e·lyt·ed, pros·e·lyt·ing**) to proselytize.
pros·e·lyt·ize (pros-ĕ-li-tɪz) v. (**pros·e·ly·tized, pros·e·ly·tiz·ing**) to try to convert people to one's beliefs or opinions. **pros·e·lyt·ism** (pros-ĕ-li-tiz-ĕm) n.
pro·slav·er·y (proh-slay-vĕ-ree) adj. favoring the institution of slavery.
pros·o·dy (pros-ĕ-dee) n. the study of verse forms and poetic meters.
pros·pect (pros-pekt) n. 1. an extensive view of a landscape etc., a mental view of matters. 2. an expectation, a possibility, prospects of success. 3. a chance of success or advancement, a job with prospects. 4. a possible customer or client etc., a possible or likely candidate. **prospect** v. to ex-plore in search of something, prospecting for gold. **pros'pect·or** n.
pro·spec·tive (prŏ-spek-tiv) adj. expected to be or to occur, future, possible, prospective customers. **pro·spec'tive·ly** adv.
pro·spec·tus (prŏ-spek-tŭs) n. (pl. -tus·es) a printed document describing and advertising the chief features of an investment or business enterprise.
pros·per (pros-pĕr) v. to be successful, to thrive.
pros·per·i·ty (pro-sper-i-tee) n. being prosperous.
pros·per·ous (pros-pĕ-rŭs) adj. financially successful. **pros'per·ous·ly** adv.
pros·tate (pros-tayt) n. (also **prostate gland**) a gland around the neck of the bladder in males. **pros'tat·ic** (pro-stat-ik) adj.
pros·ta·ti·tis (pros-tă-tɪ-tis) n. inflammation of the prostate gland.
pros·the·sis (pros-thee-sŭs) n. (pl. -ses, pr. -seez) 1. the addition of a letter or syllable at the beginning of a word, as be- in beloved. 2. an artificial limb, tooth, or other part of the body. 3. the making up of deficiencies by supplying such devices. **pros·thet·ic** (pros-thet-ik) adj. **pros·thet'i·cal·ly** adv.
pros·thet·ics (pros-thet-iks) n. the branch of medicine concerned with the replacement of parts of the body with artificial devices.
pros·ti·tute (pros-ti-toot) n. a person who engages in promiscuous sexual intercourse for payment. **prostitute** v. (**pros·ti·tut·ed, pros·ti·tut·ing**) 1. to make a prostitute of, prostitute oneself. 2. to put to an unworthy use, prostituting their artistic abilities. **pros·ti·tu·tion** (pros-ti-too-shŏn) n.
pros·trate (pros-trayt) adj. 1. face downward. 2. lying horizontally. 3. overcome, exhausted, prostrate with grief. **prostrate** v. (**pros·trat·ed, pros·trat·ing**) to cause to be prostrate; prostrate oneself, to cast oneself face downward on the ground in humility or adoration. **pros·tra·tion** (pro-stray-shŏn) n.
pro·suf·frage (proh-suf-rij) adj. favoring voting rights for all citizens.
pros·y (proh-zee) adj. (**pros·i·er, pros·i·est**) prosaic, dull.
Prot. abbr. Protestant.
pro·tac·tin·i·um (proh-tak-tin-i-ŭm) n. a radioactive metallic element.
pro·tag·o·nist (prŏ-tag-ŏ-nist) n. 1. one of the chief contenders in a contest. 2. an advocate or champion of a cause etc. 3. the leading character in a literary work.
pro·te·an (proh-tee-ăn) adj. 1. taking many forms. 2. variable, versatile.
pro·tect (prŏ-tekt) v. to keep from harm or injury. **pro·tec'tor** n. **pro·tec'tress** n. fem.
pro·tec·tion (prŏ-tek-shŏn) n. 1. protecting, being protected. 2. a person or thing that protects. 3. (informal) bribe money paid to keep oneself or one's property from being harmed or damaged.
pro·tec·tion·ism (prŏ-tek-shŏ-niz-ĕm) n. the policy of protecting domestic industries by taxing imports in order to discourage foreign competition. **pro·tec'tion·ist** adj. & n.
pro·tec·tive (prŏ-tek-tiv) adj. protecting, giving protection. **pro·tec'tive·ly** adv. **pro·tec'tive·ness** n.
pro·tec·tor·ate (prŏ-tek-tŏ-rit) n. a weak or underdeveloped country that is under the official protection and partial control of a stronger one.

pro·té·gé (proh-tĕ-*zh*ay) *n.* someone who is being helped by a person taking an interest in his welfare or career.

pro·té·gée (proh-tĕ-*zh*ay) *n.* a female protégé.

pro·tein (proh-teen) *n.* an organic compound containing nitrogen, occurring in plant and animal tissue and forming an essential part of the food of animals.

pro·test (proh-test) *n.* a statement or action showing one's disapproval of something. **protest** (prŏ-test) *v.* 1. to express one's disapproval of something. 2. to declare firmly or solemnly, *protesting their innocence.* **pro·test′er, pro·test′or** *n.* ▢**under protest,** unwillingly and after making protests.

Prot·es·tant (prot-ĕ-stănt) *n.* a member of any of the Christian bodies that separated from the Catholic Church in the Reformation, or of their later branches. **Prot′es·tant·ism** *n.*

prot·es·ta·tion (prot-ĕ-stay-shŏn, proh-te-) *n.* a firm declaration, *protestations of loyalty.*

pro·tha·la·mi·on (proh-thă-lay-mi-on), **pro·tha·la·mi·um** (proh-thă-lay-mi-ŭm) *n.* (*pl.* -mi·a, *pr.* -mi-ă) a song to celebrate a forthcoming wedding.

pro·to·col (proh-tŏ-kawl) *n.* 1. etiquette with regard to people's rank or status. 2. the first or original draft of an agreement (especially between nations), signed by those making it, in preparation for a treaty.

pro·ton (proh-ton) *n.* a particle of matter with a positive electric charge.

pro·to·plasm (proh-tŏ-plaz-ĕm) *n.* a colorless jellylike substance that is the main constituent of all animal and vegetable cells and tissues. **pro·to·plas·mic** (proh-tŏ-plaz-mik) *adj.* **pro·to·plas′mal** *adj.* **pro·to·plas·mat·ic** (proh-tŏ-plaz-mat-ik) *adj.*

pro·to·type (proh-tŏ-tɪp) *n.* a first or original example of something from which others have been or will be developed, a trial model (as of an aircraft).

pro·to·zo·a (proh-tŏ-zoh-ă) *n.* the biological class made up of protozoans.

pro·to·zo·an (proh-tŏ-zoh-ăn) *n.* any of a group of one-celled usually microscopic animals.

pro·to·zo·ol·o·gy (proh-tŏ-zoh-ol-ŏ-jee) *n.* the branch of zoology that deals with protozoa.

pro·tract (proh-trakt) *v.* to prolong in duration. **pro·trac·tion** (proh-trak-shŏn) *n.*

pro·trac·tor (proh-trak-tŏr) *n.* an instrument for measuring angles, usually a semicircle marked off in degrees.

pro·trude (proh-trood) *v.* (**pro·trud·ed, pro·trud·ing**) to project from a surface. **pro·tru·sion** (proh-troo-zhŏn) *n.* **pro·tru·sive** (proh-troo-siv) *adj.*

pro·tu·ber·ance (proh-too-bĕ-răns) *n.* a bulging part.

pro·tu·ber·ant (proh-troo-bĕ-rănt) *adj.* bulging outward from a surface.

proud (prowd) *adj.* 1. feeling or showing justifiable pride. 2. marked by such feeling, *a proud day for us.* 3. full of self-respect and independence, *too proud to ask for help.* 4. having an unduly high opinion of one's own qualities or merits. **proud** *adv.* (*informal*) proudly; *they did us proud,* treated us lavishly or with great honor; *our children did us proud,* made us feel proud. **proud′ly** *adv.*

pro·un·ion (proh-yoon-yŏn) *adj.* favoring the in-

terests of labor unions over those of industry.
prov. *abbr.* 1. province. 2. provincial. 3. provisional. 4. provost.
Prov. *abbr.* 1. Provençal. 2. Proverbs (Old Testament). 3. Province.

prov·a·ble (proo-vă-bĕl) *adj.* able to be proved.

prove (proov) *v.* (**proved, proved** or **prov·en, prov·ing**) 1. to give or be proof of. 2. to establish the validity of (a will). 3. to be found to be, *it proved to be a good thing.* 4. to test or try out. ▢**prove oneself,** to show that one has the required character or abilities. **proving ground,** a place or context for trying something out. ▷The past participle *proved* is preferred by careful writers. *They have proved their assertion* not *have proven.*

prov·en (proo-vĕn) *adj.* proved, *a person of proven ability.*

prov·e·nance (prov-ĕ-năns) *n.* (of a work of art etc.) a place of origin.

Pro·ven·çal (proh-vĕn-sahl) *adj.* of Provence, a region of southern France.

prov·en·der (prov-ĕn-dĕr) *n.* 1. fodder. 2. (*humorous*) food.

pro·ve·ni·ence (prŏ-veen-yĕns) *n.* provenance.

prov·erb (prov-ĕrb) *n.* 1. a short well-known saying stating a general truth, as *many hands make light work.* 2. *Proverbs,* a book of the Old Testament, containing proverbs ascribed to Solomon and others.

pro·ver·bi·al (prŏ-vur-bi-ăl) *adj.* 1. of or like a proverb, mentioned in a proverb. 2. well-known, notorious, *his meanness is proverbial.* **pro·ver′bi·al·ly** *adv.*

pro·vide (prŏ-vɪd) *v.* (**pro·vid·ed, pro·vid·ing**) 1. to cause (a person) to have possession or use of something, to supply. 2. to give or supply the necessities of life, *has to provide for his family.* 3. to make suitable preparation for something, *try to provide against emergencies.* 4. to stipulate (that), *the law provides that controls will be imposed.* **pro·vid′er** *n.*

pro·vid·ed (prŏ-vɪ-did) *conj.* on the condition, *we will come provided that our expenses are paid.*

prov·i·dence (prov-i-dĕns) *n.* 1. being provident. 2. God's or nature's care and protection.

Prov·i·dence (prov-i-dĕns) *n.* 1. God. 2. the capital of Rhode Island.

prov·i·dent (prov-i-dĕnt) *adj.* showing wise forethought for future needs or events, thrifty. **prov′i·dent·ly** *adv.*

prov·i·den·tial (prov-i-den-shăl) *adj.* happening very luckily. **prov·i·den′tial·ly** *adv.*

pro·vid·ing (prŏ-vɪ-ding) *conj.* provided.

prov·ince (prov-ins) *n.* 1. one of the principal administrative divisions in certain countries. 2. a district consisting of a group of adjacent dioceses, under the charge of an archbishop. 3. a range of learning or knowledge or responsibility or concern, *estimates of expenditure are the treasurer's province.* ▢**the provinces,** the whole of a country outside its capital city or metropolitan areas.

pro·vin·cial (prŏ-vin-shăl) *adj.* 1. of a province or provinces, *provincial government.* 2. having only limited interests and narrow-minded views, *provincial attitudes.* **provincial** *n.* a native or inhabitant of a province or of the provinces. **pro·vin′cial·ism** *n.*

pro·vi·sion (prŏ-vizh-ŏn) *n.* 1. providing, preparation of resources etc. for future needs, *made provision for their old age.* 2. a statement or clause in a treaty or contract etc. stipulating something, *under the provisions of his will.* 3. *provisions,* a supply of food and drink. **provision** *v.* to supply with provisions of food etc.

pro·vi·sion·al (prŏ-vizh-ŏ-năl) *adj.* arranged or agreed upon temporarily but possibly to be altered later. **pro·vi′sion·al·ly** *adv.*

pro·vi·so (prŏ-vi-zoh) *n.* (*pl.* **-sos**) something that is insisted upon as a condition of an agreement.

prov·o·ca·tion (prov-ŏ-kay-shŏn) *n.* 1. provoking, being provoked. 2. something that provokes anger or retaliation.

pro·voc·a·tive (prŏ-vok-ă-tiv) *adj.* 1. arousing or likely to arouse anger or interest or sexual desire. 2. deliberately annoying. **pro·voc′a·tive·ly** *adv.*

pro·voke (prŏ-vohk) *v.* **(pro·voked, pro·vok·ing)** 1. to make angry. 2. to rouse or incite (a person) to action. 3. to produce as a reaction or effect, *the joke provoked laughter.*

pro·vok·ing (prŏ-voh-king) *adj.* annoying. **pro·vok′ing·ly** *adv.*

pro·vo·lo·ne (proh-vŏ-loh-nee) *n.* a mellow Italian cheese made from heated and kneaded curd, smoked after drying.

pro·vost (proh-vohst) *n.* 1. an official in charge. 2. the head or a high administrative officer of certain colleges and preparatory schools. 3. the head of the chapter in certain cathedrals. ☐**provost marshal,** the head of military police in an army command; the naval officer in charge of prisoners in a court-martial.

prow (prow) *n.* the projecting front part of a ship or boat.

pro·war (proh-wor) *adj.* in favor of waging or continuing to wage war.

prow·ess (prow-is) *n.* great ability or daring.

prowl (prowl) *v.* 1. to go about stealthily in search of prey or plunder. 2. to pace or wander restlessly. **prowl** *n.* prowling, *on the prowl.* **prowl′er** *n.* ☐**prowl car,** *(informal)* a police patrol car.

prox·i·mal (prok-sī-măl) *adj.* (in anatomy) toward the center of the body or toward the point of attachment, *a proximal bone.*

prox·i·mate (prok-sī-mit) *adj.* nearest, next before or after, *the proximate cause of war.*

prox·im·i·ty (prok-sim-i-tee) *n.* 1. nearness. 2. neighborhood, *in the proximity of the station.* ☐**proximity fuse,** a radio device causing a projectile to explode when near a target.

prox·y (prok-see) *n.* (*pl.* **prox·ies**) 1. a person authorized to represent or act for another, the use of such a person, *voted by proxy.* 2. a document authorizing this. ☐**proxy vote,** a vote made by one person on behalf of another.

prs. *abbr.* pairs.

prude (prood) *n.* a person of extreme or exaggerated propriety concerning behavior or speech, one who is easily shocked by sexual matters. **prud′er·y** *n.*

pru·dent (proo-dĕnt) *adj.* showing carefulness and foresight, avoiding rashness. **pru′dent·ly** *adv.* **pru′dence** *n.*

pru·den·tial (proo-den-shăl) *adj.* showing or involving prudence.

prud·ish (proo-dish) *adj.* like a prude, showing prudery. **prud′ish·ly** *adv.* **prud′ish·ness** *n.*

prune¹ (proon) *n.* a dried plum.

prune² *v.* **(pruned, prun·ing)** 1. to trim by cutting away dead or overgrown branches on shoots. 2.

to shorten and improve (a speech or book etc.) by removing unnecessary parts. 3. to reduce, *costs must be pruned.*

pru·ri·ent (proor-i-ĕnt) *adj.* having or arising from lewd thoughts. **pru′ri·ence** *n.*

pru·ri·tus (pruu-ri-tis) *n.* itching.

Prus·sian (prush-ăn) *adj.* of Prussia, a former country of north Europe. ☐**Prussian blue,** a deep blue color.

prus·sic (prus-ik) **acid** hydrocyanic acid.

pry¹ (prī) *v.* **(pried, pry·ing)** to inquire or investigate or peer impertinently (and often furtively).

pry² *v.* **(pried, pry·ing)** 1. to force out or open by leverage. 2. to get with difficulty, *I had to pry the truth out of him.*

Ps., Psa. *abbr.* Psalm(s).

P.S. *abbr.* 1. postscript. 2. public school.

psalm (sahm) *n.* 1. a sacred song, especially one of those in the Book of Psalms in the Old Testament. 2. *Psalms,* a book of the Old Testament consisting of psalms, popularly known as "Psalms of David."

psalm·ist (sah-mist) *n.* a writer of psalms.

psal·mo·dy (sah-mŏ-dee) *n.* (*pl.* **-dies**) 1. the practice or art of singing psalms, hymns, anthems, etc., especially in public worship. 2. an arrangement of psalms for singing.

psal·ter (sawl-tĕr) *n.* a copy of the Book of Psalms.

pseud. *abbr.* pseudonym.

pseu·do (soo-doh) *adj.* false, insincere.

pseudo- *prefix* false, as in *pseudonym.*

pseu·do·a·ris·to·crat·ic (soo-doh-ă-ris-tŏ-krat-ik) *adj.* having aristocratic pretensions.

pseu·do·ar·tis·tic (soo-doh-ahr-tis-tik) *adj.* pretending to be artistic.

pseu·do·bi·o·graph·i·cal (soo-doh-bi-ŏ-graf-i-kăl) *adj.* falsely biographical, pretending to be factual about someone's life.

pseu·do·in·tel·lec·tu·al (soo-doh-in-tĕ-lek-choo-ăl) *adj.* having intellectual pretensions.

pseu·do·nym (soo-dŏ-nim) *n.* a false name used by an author. **pseu·don·y·mous** (soo-don-ĭ-mŭs) *adj.*

pseu·do·sci·en·tif·ic (soo-doh-si-ĕn-tif-ik) *adj.* pretending to be scientific, falsely represented as being scientific.

psf *abbr.* pounds per square foot.

pshaw (shaw) *interj.* an expression of contempt or impatience.

psi (sī) *n.* (*pl.* **psis,** *pr.* **siz**) 1. the twenty-third letter of the Greek alphabet (Ψ ψ). 2. parapsychological factors or faculties collectively.

psi *abbr.* pounds per square inch.

psit·ta·co·sis (sit-ă-koh-sis) *n.* parrot fever, a contagious disease of birds that can be transmitted to human beings as a form of pneumonia.

pso·ri·a·sis (sŏ-ri-ă-sis) *n.* a skin disease causing red scaly patches.

psst (pst) *interj.* an exclamation to attract someone's attention furtively.

PST *abbr.* Pacific Standard Time.

psych (sīk) *v.* *(slang)* 1. to work out the intentions of (a person) or the solution of (a problem etc.) by use of psychology. 2. to intimidate (a person) by making him feel mentally uneasy. ☐**psych out,** *(slang)* to analyze (a situation or person) beforehand. **psych up,** *(slang)* to ready oneself emotionally, *he was psyched up for the concert.*

psych. *abbr.* 1. psychologist. 2. psychology.

psy·che (sī-kee) *n.* 1. the human soul or spirit. 2. the human mind.

psy·che·del·ic (sɪ-kĕ-del-ik) *adj.* of or producing hallucinations and similar experiences, full of vivid or luminous colors. **psy·che·del'i·cal·ly** *adj.*

psy·chi·a·trist (si-kɪ-ă-trist) *n.* an expert in psychiatry.

psy·chi·a·try (si-kɪ-ă-tree) *n.* the branch of medicine dealing with mental disorders. **psy·chi·at·ric** (si-ki-at-rik) *adj.*

psy·chic (sɪ-kik) *adj.* 1. of the soul or mind. 2. concerned with processes that seem to be outside physical or natural laws, having or involving extrasensory perception or occult powers. **psychic** *n.* a person apparently susceptible to psychic influence, a medium.

psy·chi·cal (si-ki-kăl) *adj.* psychic, *psychical research.* **psy'chi·cal·ly** *adv.*

psy·cho (si-koh) *adj. (slang)* psychotic. **psycho** *n.* (*pl.* **-chos**) *(slang)* a psychotic person.

psy·cho·ac·tive (si-koh-ak-tiv) *adj.* affecting the mind.

psy·cho·a·nal·y·sis (si-koh-ă-nal-i-sis) *n.* a method of examining or treating mental conditions by bringing to light certain things in a person's subconscious mind that may be influencing behavior and mental state. **psy·cho·an·a·lyt·ic** (si-koh-an-ă-lit-ik) *adj.* **psy·cho·an·a·lyt'i·cal** *adj.*

psy·cho·an·a·lyst (si-koh-an-ă-list) *n.* an expert in psychoanalysis.

psy·cho·an·a·lyze (si-koh-an-ă-lız) *v.* **(psy·cho·an·a·lyzed, psy·cho·an·a·lyz·ing)** to treat (a person) by psychoanalysis.

psy·cho·dra·ma (si-koh-drah-mă) *n.* a method of group psychotherapy in which participants improvise dramatizations of emotionally significant situations.

psy·cho·gen·ic (si-koh-jen-ik) *adj.* originating in the mind.

psy·cho·log·i·cal (si-kŏ-loj-i-kăl) *adj.* 1. of or affecting the mind and its workings. 2. of psychology. **psy·cho·log'i·cal·ly** *adv.* □at the psychological moment, *(informal)* at the most appropriate moment. **psychological warfare,** actions or propaganda etc. designed to weaken an enemy's morale.

psy·chol·o·gist (si-kol-ŏ-jist) *n.* an expert in psychology.

psy·chol·o·gy (si-kol-ŏ-jee) *n.* 1. the study of the mind and how it works. 2. mental characteristics, *can you understand his psychology?*

psy·cho·neu·ro·sis (si-koh-nuu-roh-sis) *n.* neurosis.

psy·cho·path (si-kŏ-path) *n.* a person suffering from a severe mental disorder, especially with aggressive antisocial behavior. **psy·cho·path·ic** (si-kŏ-path-ik) *adj.*

psy·cho·pa·thol·o·gy (si-koh-pă-thol-ŏ-jee) *n.* the pathology of the mind.

psy·cho·sex·u·al (si-koh-sek-shoo-ăl) *adj.* of the interaction of psychological and sexual factors.

psy·cho·sis (si-koh-sis) *n.* (*pl.* **-ses,** *pr.* -seez) a severe mental disorder involving a person's whole personality.

psy·cho·so·mat·ic (si-koh-sŏ-mat-ik) *adj.* of or involving both the mind and the body; *psychosomatic illness,* one that is caused or aggravated by mental stress. **psy·cho·so·mat'i·cal·ly** *adv.*

psy·cho·ther·a·pist (si-koh-ther-ă-pist) *n.* an expert in the use of psychotherapy.

psy·cho·ther·a·py (si-koh-ther-ă-pee) *n.* treatment of mental disorders by the use of psychological methods.

psy·chot·ic (si-kot-ik) *adj.* of or relating to a psychosis, *a psychotic episode.* **psychotic** *n.* a person suffering from a psychosis. **psy·chot'i·cal·ly** *adv.*

Pt *symbol* platinum.

pt. *abbr.* 1. part. 2. past tense. 3. payment. 4. pint. 5. point. 6. port.

P.T. *abbr.* 1. Pacific Time. 2. physical therapy. 3. physical training.

PTA *abbr.* parent-teacher association.

ptar·mi·gan (tahr-mĭ-găn) *n.* (*pl.* **-gans, -gan**) a bird of the grouse family with plumage that turns white in winter.

PT (pee-tee) **boat** a motor torpedo boat.

pter·o·dac·tyl (ter-ŏ-dak-til) *n.* an extinct reptile with wings.

ptg. *abbr.* printing.

pto·maine (toh-mayn) *n.* a chemical substance, often poisonous, formed by bacteria in decaying matter. □**ptomaine poisoning,** an intestinal disorder caused by eating contaminated food.

Pu *sumbol* plutonium.

pub (pub) *n. (informal)* a bar. ▷An abbreviation of public house *(British).*

pub. *abbr.* 1. public. 2. publication. 3. published. 4. publisher. 5. publishing.

pu·ber·ty (pyoo-běr-tee) *n.* the stage at which a person's reproductive organs are in the process of becoming mature and he or she becomes capable of producing offspring. **pu'ber·tal** *adj.*

pu·bes (pyoo-beez) *n.* (*pl.* **-bes**) the lower part of the abdomen, covered with hair at and after puberty.

pu·bes·cent (pyoo-bes-ĕnt) *adj.* arriving or having arrived at puberty. **pu·bes'cence** *n.*

pu·bic (pyoo-bik) *adj.* of the lower part of the abdomen, at the front of the pelvis, *pubic hair.*

pu·bis (pyoo-bis) *n.* (*pl.* **-bes,** *pr.* -beez) the bone forming the front of each half of the pelvis.

publ. *abbr.* 1. public. 2. publication. 3. published. 4. publisher.

pub·lic (pub-lik) *adj.* of or for or known to people in general, not private, *a public holiday; in the public interest; public parks.* **public** *n.* members of the community in general or a particular section of this, *the American public.* □**in the public domain,** belonging to the community as a whole, especially no longer protected by copyright.

public accountant, an accountant available to the public at large. **public address system,** a system of loudspeakers to make something audible over a wide area. **public defender,** a lawyer appointed at public expense to represent the needy in criminal cases. **public enemy,** a criminal whom special efforts are made to apprehend. **public house,** *(British)* a building (not a hotel) licensed to sell beer and other alcoholic drinks to the general public for consumption on the premises (and not only with meals). **public opinion,** the collective opinion of many individuals on a conflict or issue. **public opinion poll,** a poll taken to sample public opinion. **public relations,** the promotion of goodwill between an organization etc. and the general public; the goodwill resulting from such activity.

pub·li·can (pub-li-kăn) *n.* 1. *(British)* the keeper of a public house. 2. (in the Bible) a tax collector.

pub·li·ca·tion (pub-li-kay-shŏn) *n.* 1. publishing,

being published. 2. something published, such as a book or newspaper.

pub·li·cist (pub-li-sist) *n.* an individual in the publicity business, especially a press agent.

pub·lic·i·ty (pub-lis-i-tee) *n.* 1. public attention directed upon a person or thing. 2. the process of drawing public attention to a person or thing, the spoken or written or other material by which this is done.

pub·li·cize (pub-li-sɪz) *v.* (**pub·li·cized, pub· li·ciz·ing**) to bring to the attention of the public, to advertise.

pub·lic·ly (pub-lik-lee) *adv.* in public, openly.

pub·lic-spir·it·ed (pub-lik-spir-i-tid) *adj.* ready to do things for the benefit of people in general.

pub·lish (pub-lish) *v.* 1. to issue copies of (a book etc.) to the public. 2. to make generally known. 3. to announce formally, *publish the banns of marriage.*

pub·lish·er (pub-li-shěr) *n.* a person or firm that issues copies of a book or newspaper etc. to the public (distinguished from a *printer*, who prints books etc. but does not issue them).

puce (pyoos) *adj. & n.* brownish purple.

puck[1] (puk) *n.* a mischievous or *(old use)* evil sprite.

puck[2] *n.* the hard rubber disk used in ice hockey.

puck·er (puk-ěr) *v.* to come together in small wrinkles or bulges, to cause to do this. **pucker** *n.* a wrinkle or bulge made in this way.

puck·ish (puk-ish) *adj.* impish.

pud·ding (puud-ing) *n.* a dessert of a soft creamy or spongy consistency.

pud·ding·head (puud-ing-hed) *n. (slang)* a stupid person.

pud·dle (pud-ěl) *n.* a small pool, especially of water left after rain on a road or other surface. **pud'dly** *adj.*

pud·dling (pud-ling) *n.* the process of producing wrought iron by stirring molten pig iron so as to expel carbon.

pu·den·da (pyoo-den-dă) *n. pl.* the genitals, especially of a woman. **pu·den'dal** *adj.*

pudg·y (puj-ee) *adj.* (**pudg·i·er, pudg·i·est**) short and fat.

pueb·lo (pweb-loh) *n. (pl. -los)* 1. a communal village dwelling of flat-roofed stone or adobe built by Indians in Mexico and the southwest U.S. 2. *Pueblo,* a member of a tribe living in these.

pu·er·ile (pyoo-ě-rɪl) *adj.* showing immaturity, suitable only for children, *asking puerile questions.* **pu·er·il·i·ty** (pyoo-ě-ril-i-tee) *n.*

pu·er·per·al (pyoo-ur-pě-răl) *adj.* of or associated with childbirth. ☐**puerperal fever,** a fever that results from an infection of the womb following childbirth or abortion.

Puer·to Ri·co (pwer-tŏ ree-koh) an island in the West Indies. **Puer·to Ri'can** *adj. & n.*

puff (puf) *n.* 1. a short light blowing of breath or wind etc., smoke or vapor sent out by this. 2. a powder puff. 3. a pastry filled with cream etc., *cream puffs.* 4. a piece of extravagant praise in a review or advertisement for a book or play etc.

puff *v.* 1. to send out a puff or puffs, to blow (smoke etc.) in puffs, to smoke (a pipe etc.) in puffs. 2. to breathe hard, to pant. 3. to make or become inflated, to swell. ☐**puff adder,** a large poisonous African viper that inflates the upper part of its body when excited. **puff pastry,** very light flaky pastry. **puff** *or* **puffed sleeve,** a sleeve that is very full at the shoulder. **puff up,** to swell with pride.

puff·ball (puf-bawl) *n.* a fungus with a ball-shaped spore case that bursts open when ripe.

puf·fin (puf-in) *n.* a seabird with a short striped bill.

puf·fy (puf-ee) *adj.* (**puf·fi·er, puf·fi·est**) puffed out, swollen. **puf'fi·ness** *n.*

pug[1] (pug) *n.* a dog of a dwarf breed resembling the bulldog. ☐**pug nose,** a short flattish turned-up nose.

pug[2] *n. (slang)* a pugilist.

pu·gil·ist (pyoo-jĭ-list) *n.* a professional boxer. **pu'gil·ism** *n.* **pu·gil·is·tic** (pyoo-jĭ-lis-tik) *adj.*

pug·na·cious (pug-nay-shŭs) *adj.* eager to fight, aggressive. **pug·na'cious·ly** *adv.* **pug·nac· i·ty** (pug-nas-i-tee) *n.*

pu·is·sance (pyoo-i-săns) *n.* great power or strength. **pu'is·sant** *adj.*

puke (pyook) *v.* (**puked, puk·ing**) *(slang)* to vomit. **puke** *n. (slang)* vomit.

puk·ka (puk-ă) *adj. (informal)* real, genuine.

pul·chri·tude (pul-kri-tood) *n.* beauty. **pul· chri·tu·di·nous** (pul-kri-too-di-nŭs) *adj.*

pule (pyool) *v.* (**puled, pul·ing**) to cry weakly, to whimper or whine.

pull (puul) *v.* 1. to exert force upon (a thing) so as to move it toward oneself or toward the source of the force; *pull a muscle,* damage it by abnormal strain; *pull a gun,* draw it and prepare to use it; *pull a horse,* to check it so as to lose a race. 2. to remove by pulling, *pull the cork.* 3. to propel (a boat) by pulling on its oars. 4. to exert a pulling or driving force, *the engine is pulling well.* 5. to attract, *attractions that pull the crowds.* **pull** *n.* 1. the act of pulling, the force exerted by this. 2. *(slang)* a means of exerting influence. 3. a deep draft of a drink, a draw at a pipe etc. 4. a prolonged effort in walking etc., *the long pull up the hill.* **pull'er** *n.* ☐**pull a fast one,** *(slang)* to act unfairly in order to gain an advantage. **pull a person's leg,** to tease him. **pull back,** to retreat or withdraw, to cause to do this. **pull down,** to demolish a building. **pull in,** to obtain as wages or profit; (of a train) to enter and stop at a station; (of a vehicle) to move to the side of the road or off the road; *(informal)* to take into custody. **pull off,** to succeed in achieving or winning something, *pulled it off.* **pull oneself together,** to regain one's self-control. **pull one's punches,** to avoid using one's full force. **pull one's weight,** to do one's fair share of work. **pull out,** to withdraw or cause to withdraw; (of a train) to move out of a station; (of a vehicle) to move away from the side of a road, or from behind another vehicle to overtake it. **pull rank,** to make unfair use of one's senior rank in demanding obedience. **pull strings,** to use one's influence, often secretly. **pull through,** to come or bring successfully through an illness or difficulty. **pull together,** to cooperate. **pull up,** to stop or cause (a person or vehicle etc.) to stop; to reprimand.

pul·let (puul-it) *n.* a young domestic hen from the time of beginning to lay until the first molt.

pul·ley (puul-ee) *n. (pl. -leys)* a wheel over which a rope or chain or belt passes, used in lifting things or to drive or be driven by an endless belt.

Pull·man (puul-măn) *n. (trademark)* a type of railroad sleeping car or parlor car.

pull·out (puul-owt) *n.* 1. the act of pulling out. 2. a planned withdrawal or retreat. 3. a page in a book that folds out for easy reference.

pull·o·ver (puul-oh-věr) *n.* a kind of sweater (with

or without sleeves) with no fastenings, put on by being pulled over the head.

pul·mo·nar·y (puul-mŏ-ner-ee, pul-) *adj.* of or affecting the lungs.

Pul·mo·tor (puul-moh-tŏr) *n. (trademark)* a type of mechanical device to assist in breathing.

pulp (pulp) *n.* 1. the soft moist part of fruit. 2. the soft tissue inside a tooth. 3. any soft moist mass of material, especially of wood fiber as used for making paper. **pulp** *v.* to reduce to pulp, to become pulpy. □**pulp magazine,** a cheap popular magazine (originally of the kind printed on rough paper made from wood pulp).

pul·pit (puul-pit) *n.* a raised enclosed platform in a church, used for preaching from.

pulp·wood (pulp-wuud) *n.* timber suitable for making pulp.

pulp·y (pul-pee) *adj.* like pulp, containing much pulp.

pul·que (puul-kay) *n.* a Mexican alcoholic drink made from the sap of the agave.

pul·sar (pul-sahr) *n.* a cosmic source of regularly and rapidly pulsating radio signals.

pul·sate (pul-sayt) *v.* (**pul·sat·ed, pul·sat·ing**) to expand and contract rhythmically, to vibrate, to quiver. **pul·sa·tion** (pul-say-shŏn) *n.*

pulse[1] (puls) *n.* 1. the rhythmical throbbing of the arteries as blood is propelled along them, this as felt in the wrists or temples etc. 2. any steady throb. 3. a single beat or throb. **pulse** *v.* (**pulsed, puls·ing**) to pulsate.

pulse[2] *n.* the edible seed of peas, beans, lentils, etc.

pul·ver·ize (pul-vě-rīz) *v.* (**pul·ver·ized, pul·ver·iz·ing**) 1. to crush into powder. 2. to become powder. 3. to defeat thoroughly. **pul·ver·i·za·tion** (pul-vě-ri-zay-shŏn) *n.*

pu·ma (pyoo-mă) *n.* a large American animal of the cat family, a cougar.

pum·ice (pum-is) *n.* a light porous kind of lava used for rubbing stains from the skin or as powder for polishing things. □**pumice stone,** pumice; a piece of this.

pum·mel (pum-ěl) *v.* (**pum·meled, pum·mel·ing**) to strike repeatedly, especially with the fist(s).

pump[1] (pump) *n.* a machine or device for forcing liquid, air, or gas into or out of something. **pump** *v.* 1. to raise or move or inflate by means of a pump. 2. to use a pump. 3. to empty by using a pump, *pump the ship dry.* 4. to move vigorously up and down like a pump handle. 5. to pour or cause to pour forth as if by pumping. 6. to question (a person) persistently to obtain information. □**pump gun,** a rifle or shotgun with pump action. **pump priming,** stimulation of the economy by increasing public spending.

pump[2] *n.* a light shoe worn for dancing etc.

pump-ac·tion (pump-ak-shŏn) *adj.* of a rifle or shotgun that ejects a spent cartridge and loads a new cartridge by manual force.

pum·per·nick·el (pum-pěr-nik-ěl) *n.* a coarse, dark rye bread.

pump·kin (pump-kin) *n.* the large round orange-colored fruit of a trailing vine, used as a vegetable and as a filling for pies.

pun (pun) *n.* a humorous use of a word to suggest another that sounds the same. **pun** *v.* (**punned, pun·ning**) to make a pun. **pun'ster** *n.*

punch[1] (punch) *v.* 1. to strike with the fist. 2. to herd, *cow punching.* **punch** *n.* 1. a blow with the fist. 2. *(slang)* vigor, effective force, *a speech with plenty of punch in it.* **punch'er** *n.* □**punching bag,** a suspended ball or bag that can be punched, as a form of exercise. **punch line,** words that give the point of a joke or story.

punch[2] *n.* a device for making holes in metal or leather, or for stamping a design on material.

punch *v.* to perforate with a punch, to make (a hole etc.) with a punch. □**punch or punched card,** a perforated card used to feed information into a machine, such as a computer. **punch press,** a machine for cutting, drawing, or shaping material under pressure. **punch or punched tape,** perforated paper tape used to feed information into a machine, such as a computer.

punch[3] *n.* a drink made of wine or spirits mixed with fruit juices etc. □**punch bowl,** a bowl in which this is mixed.

punch-drunk (punch-drungk) *adj.* 1. stupefied through being severely or repeatedly punched. 2. *(informal)* dazed or bewildered.

pun·cheon (pun-chŏn) *n.* a large cask to hold liquids.

punch·y (pun-chee) *adj. (informal)* 1. punch-drunk. 2. (of writing style) forceful.

punc·til·i·o (pungk-til-i-oh) *n.* (*pl.* **-i·os**) 1. a delicate point of ceremony or honor. 2. care in observing etiquette.

punc·til·i·ous (pungk-til-i-ŭs) *adj.* very careful to carry out duties or details of ceremony etc. correctly, conscientious. **punc·til'i·ous·ly** *adv.* **punc·til'i·ous·ness** *n.*

punc·tu·al (pungk-choo-ăl) *adj.* arriving or doing things at the appointed time, neither early nor late. **punc'tu·al·ly** *adv.* **punc·tu·al·i·ty** (pungk-choo-al-i-tee) *n.*

punc·tu·ate (pungk-choo-ayt) *v.* (**punc·tu·at·ed, punc·tu·at·ing**) 1. to insert punctuation marks in. 2. to interrupt at intervals, *her speech was punctuated with cheers.* 3. to emphasize, *punctuated his remarks by pounding the desk.*

punc·tu·a·tion (pungk-choo-ay-shŏn) *n.* the art or practice of punctuating, the marks used for this. □**punctuation mark,** any of the marks (period, comma, question mark, etc.) used in written or printed material to separate sentences etc. and to make the meaning clear.

punc·ture (pungk-chŭr) *n.* a small hole made by something sharp, *my left rear tire has a puncture.* **puncture** *v.* (**punc·tured, punc·tur·ing**) 1. to make a puncture in, to suffer a puncture. 2. to reduce the pride or confidence of, *punctured his conceit.*

pun·dit (pun-dit) *n.* a person who is an authority on a subject.

pun·gent (pun-jěnt) *adj.* 1. having a strong sharp taste or smell. 2. (of remarks) penetrating, biting. **pun'gent·ly** *adv.* **pun·gen·cy** (pun-jěn-see) *n.*

pun·ish (pun-ish) *v.* 1. to cause (an offender) to suffer for his offense. 2. to inflict a punishment for, *vandalism should be severely punished.* 3. to treat roughly, to test severely, *the race was run at a punishing pace.*

pun·ish·a·ble (pun-i-shă-běl) *adj.* liable to be punished, especially by law, *punishable offenses.*

pun·ish·ment (pun-ish-měnt) *n.* 1. punishing, being punished. 2. that which an offender is made to suffer because of his wrongdoing, *let the punishment fit the crime.*

pu·ni·tive (pyoo-ni-tiv) *adj.* inflicting or intended to inflict punishment.

punk[1] (pungk) *n.* 1. *(slang)* a worthless person, a young ruffian. 2. *(slang)* an inexperienced or insignificant young person. 3. a devotee of punk rock. **punk** *adj.* 1. *(slang)* worthless. 2. of punk rock or its devotees. □**punk rock,** a type of pop music involving outrage and shock effects in music, behavior, and dress.

punk² *n.* 1. rotten wood used as tinder. 2. a stick-shaped substance that smolders when lit.

punt¹ (punt) *n.* a flat-bottomed boat propelled by thrusting a long pole against the bottom of a river. **punt** *v.* 1. to propel (a punt) with a pole in this way. 2. to carry or travel in a punt. **punt′er¹** *n.*

punt² *v.* to kick (a football) after it has dropped from the hands and before it touches the ground. **punt** *n.* a kick of this kind. **punt′er²** *n.*

pu·ny (pyoo-nee) *adj.* **(-ni·er, -ni·est)** undersized, feeble. **pu′ni·ly** *adv.* **pu′ni·ness** *n.*

pup (pup) *n.* 1. a young dog. 2. a young wolf, rat, or seal. **pup** *v.* **(pupped, pup·ping)** to give birth to a pup or pups. □**pup tent,** a small tent of simple design.

pu·pa (pyoo-pă) *n.* (*pl.* **-pae,** *pr.* -pee, -pas) a chrysalis. **pu′pal** *adj.*

pu·pil¹ (pyoo-pĭl) *n.* a person who is taught by another.

pupil² *n.* an opening in the center of the iris of the eye, through which light passes to the retina.

pup·pet (pup-it) *n.* 1. a kind of doll that can be made to move by various means as an entertainment. 2. a person or group whose actions are entirely controlled by another. □**puppet government,** a government that appears to be autonomous but is controlled by another group or power. **puppet show,** an entertainment using puppets.

pup·pet·eer (pup-i-teer) *n.* a person who handles puppets or marionettes.

pup·py (pup-ee) *n.* (*pl.* **-pies**) a young dog. □**puppy love,** immature romantic affection.

pur·blind (pur-blīnd) *adj.* 1. partly blind, dim-sighted. 2. mentally obtuse or slow.

pur·chase (pur-chăs) *v.* **(pur·chased, pur·chas·ing)** to buy. **purchase** *n.* 1. buying. 2. something bought. 3. a firm hold to pull or raise something or prevent it from slipping, leverage. **pur′chas·er** *n.*

pur·dah (pur-dă) *n.* 1. the system in Muslim or Hindu communities of keeping women from the sight of men or strangers. 2. (in India etc.) a veil or curtain, especially one used in this system.

pure (pyoor) *adj.* **(pur·er, pur·est)** 1. not mixed with any other substance, free from impurities. 2. mere, nothing but, *pure nonsense.* 3. free from evil or sin. 4. chaste. 5. dealing with theory only, not with practical applications, *pure mathematics.* **pure′ness** *n.*

pure-blood·ed (pyoor-blud-id) *adj.* purebred.

pure·bred (pyoor-bred) *adj.* (of an animal) of unmixed descent.

pu·rée, pu·ree (pyuu-ray) *n.* pulped fruit or vegetables etc. cooked, and passed through a sieve or otherwise reduced to a uniform mess. **purée** *v.* **(pu·réed, pu·rée·ing)** to make into purée.

pure·ly (pyoor-lee) *adv.* 1. in a pure way. 2. entirely, only, *came purely out of interest.*

pur·ga·tive (pur-gă-tiv) *n.* a strong laxative. **purgative** *adj.*

pur·ga·to·ry (pur-gă-tohr-ee) *n.* 1. (in Roman Catholic belief) a place or condition in which souls undergo purification by temporary punishment. 2. a place or condition of suffering. **pur·ga·to·ri·al** (pur-gă-tohr-i-ăl) *adj.*

purge (purj) *v.* **(purged, purg·ing)** 1. to cause emptying of the bowels of (a person) by means of a purgative. 2. to rid of people or things consid-

ered undesirable or harmful. 3. to atone for (an offense, especially contempt of court). **purge** *n.* purging, ridding of undesirable things etc. **pur·ga·tion** (pur-gay-shŏn) *n.*

pu·ri·fy (pyoor-ĭ-fı) *v.* **(pur·i·fied, pur·i·fy·ing)** to make pure, to cleanse of impurities. **pu′ri·fi·er** *n.* **pur·i·fi·ca·tion** (pyoor-i-fĭ-kay-shŏn) *n.* **pu·rif·i·ca·to·ry** (pyuu-rif-i-kă-tohr-ee) *adj.*

Pu·rim (poor-im) *n.* a Jewish festival commemorating the defeat of Haman's plot to destroy the Jews in ancient Persia.

pu·rine (pyoor-een) *n.* a white crystalline base forming uric acid on oxidation.

pur·ist (pyoor-ist) *n.* a stickler for correctness. **pur·ist′ic** *adj.* **pur′ism** *n.*

Pu·ri·tan (pyoor-i-tăn) *n.* 1. a member of the party of English Protestants in the 16th and 17th centuries who wanted simpler forms of church ceremony and strictness and gravity in behavior. 2. **puritan,** a person who is extremely strict in morals and who looks upon some kinds of fun and pleasure as sinful. **pu·ri·tan·i·cal** (pyoor-i-tan-i-kăl) *adj.*

pu·ri·ty (pyoor-i-tee) *n.* cleanness, freedom from physical or moral pollution, pureness.

purl¹ (purl) *n.* a knitting stitch that produces a ridge toward the knitter. **purl** *v.* to make this stitch.

purl² *v.* (of a brook etc.) to flow with a swirling motion and babbling sound. **purl** *n.* this motion or sound.

pur·lieu (pur-loo, purl-yoo) *n.* (*pl.* **-lieus**) a suburb, an outlying district.

pur·loin (pŭr-loin) *v.* (*formal* or *humorous use*) to steal.

pur·ple (pur-pĕl) *n.* a color obtained by mixing red and blue. **purple** *adj.* of this color. **purple** *v.* **(pur·pled, pur·pling)** to make or become purple. □**born to the purple,** (*old use*) born in a reigning family; born into an aristocratic or influential family. **Purple Heart,** a U.S. decoration for members of the armed forces wounded in action. **purple martin,** a large American swallow with blue-black feathers. **purple passage,** a passage of purple prose. **purple prose,** very ornate writing in a literary work.

pur·plish (pur-plish) *adj.* rather purple.

pur·port (pŭr-pohrt) *n.* the meaning or intention of something said or written. **purport** (pŭr-pohrt) *v.* to pretend, to be intended to seem, *this letter purports to come from you.* **pur·port′ed·ly** *adv.*

pur·pose (pur-pŏs) *n.* 1. an intended result, something for which effort is being made, *this will serve our purpose.* 2. intention to act, determination. **purpose** *v.* **(pur·posed, pur·pos·ing)** to intend. □**on purpose,** by intention in order to do something, not by chance. **to no purpose,** with no result.

pur·pose·ful (pur-pŏs-fŭl) *adj.* having or showing a particular purpose, with determination. **pur′pose·ful·ly** *adv.* **pur′pose·ful·ness** *n.*

pur·pose·less (pur-pŏs-lis) *adj.* without a purpose.

pur·pose·ly (pur-pŏs-lee) *adv.* on purpose, intentionally.

purr (pur) *v.* 1. (of a cat etc.) to make the low vibrant sound that a cat makes when pleased. 2. (of machinery etc.) to make a similar sound. **purr** *n.* a purring sound.

purse (purs) *n.* 1. a small pouch of leather etc. for carrying money. 2. a handbag. 3. money, funds. 4. a sum of money as a present or prize.

purse v. **(pursed, purs·ing)** to pucker, *pursing her lips.* ☐**hold the purse strings,** to have control of expenditure.

purs·er (pur-sĕr) n. a ship's officer in charge of accounts, especially on a passenger ship.

purs·lane (purs-layn) n. a low trailing succulent herb sometimes used in salads.

pur·su·ance (pŭr-soo-ăns) n. performance or carrying out of something, *in pursuance of my duties.*

pur·su·ant (pŭr-soo-ănt) adj. **pursuant to,** in accordance with, according to.

pur·sue (pŭr-soo) v. **(pur·sued, pur·su·ing)** 1. to chase in order to catch or kill. 2. to afflict continually, *was pursued by misfortunes.* 3. to continue, to proceed along, *we pursued our course.* 4. to engage in, *pursuing her hobby.* 5. to strive for. **pur·su'er** n.

pur·suit (pŭr-soot) n. 1. pursuing, *in pursuit of the fox.* 2. an activity, something at which one works or gives one's time, *stamp collecting and similar pursuits.*

pu·ru·lent (pyoor-ŭ-lĕnt) adj. containing or consisting of pus, discharging pus. **pu'ru·lence** n.

pur·vey (pŭr-vay) v. **(pur·veyed, pur·vey·ing)** to supply (articles of food) as a business. **pur·vey'or** n.

pur·view (pur-vyoo) n. 1. scope, intention, or range, especially of a particular law, document, scheme, etc. 2. range of physical or mental vision.

pus (pus) n. thick yellowish matter produced from inflamed or infected tissue.

push (puush) v. 1. to exert force upon (a thing) so as to move it away from oneself or from the source of the force; *push one's way,* go forward by pushing. 2. to thrust or cause to thrust outward. 3. to extend by effort, *the frontier was pushed farther north.* 4. to make a vigorous effort in order to succeed or to surpass others. 5. to press (a person) to do something, to put a strain on the abilities or tolerance of, *don't push him for payment; pushed to the wall,* brought to insolvency. 6. to urge the use or adoption of (goods or ideas etc.), as by advertisement. 7. *(slang)* to sell (drugs) illegally. **push** n. 1. the act of pushing, the force exerted by this. 2. a vigorous effort, a military attack made in order to advance. 3. enterprise, self-assertion, determination to get on. ☐**be pushed for,** to have barely enough of, *I'm pushed for time.* **push around,** to treat contemptuously and unfairly; to bully. **push broom,** a long-handled wide broom used for sweeping. **push button,** a button to be pushed to operate an electrical circuit etc. **push off,** *(slang)* to go away. **push one's luck,** to take undue risks.

push-but·ton (puush-but-ŏn) adj. operated automatically by pressing a button.

push·cart (puush-kahrt) n. a handcart pushed by a street vendor.

push·er (puush-ĕr) n. 1. a person or thing that pushes. 2. *(slang)* a seller of illegal drugs.

push·ing (puush-ing) adj. 1. self-assertive, determined to get on. 2. having nearly reached a certain age, *pushing forty.*

push·o·ver (puush-oh-vĕr) n. 1. an opponent or difficulty that is easily overcome. 2. a person who is easily persuaded, convinced, etc.

push·up (puush-up) n. an exercise in which a person lies face downward and presses down on his hands so that the shoulders and trunk are raised.

push·y (puush-ee) adj. **(push·i·er, push·i·**

est) unpleasantly presuming and self-assertive. **pu·sil·lan·i·mous** (pyoo-sĭ-lan-ĭ-mŭs) adj. timid, cowardly. **pu·sil·la·nim·i·ty** (pyoo-sĭ-lă-nim-i-tee) n.

puss¹ (puus) n. a cat.

puss² n. *(slang)* a face.

puss·y¹ (puus-ee) n. (*pl.* **-ies**) *(children's use)* a cat. ☐**pussy willow,** a willow with furry catkins.

pus·sy² (pus-ee) adj. **(-si·er, -si·est)** full of or like pus.

puss·y·cat (puus-ee-kat) adj. 1. a kitten or cat. 2. *(informal)* a sweet person.

puss·y·foot (puus-ee-fuut) v. 1. to move stealthily. 2. to act cautiously, to avoid committing oneself.

pus·tule (pus-chool) n. a pimple or blister, especially one containing pus.

put (puut) v. **(put, put·ting)** 1. to move (a thing) to a specified place, to cause to occupy a certain place or position. 2. to cause to be in a certain state or relationship, *put the machine out of action; put her at her ease.* 3. to subject, *put it to the test.* 4. to estimate, *I put the cost at $400.* 5. to express or state, *put it tactfully.* 6. to impose as a tax etc. 7. to stake (money) in a bet. 8. to place as an investment, *put his money into land.* 9. to lay (blame) on. 10. (of ships) to proceed, *put into harbor.* **put** n. 1. a throw of the shot or weight. 2. an option to sell a specified amount of stock at a fixed price within a given period of time. ☐**be hard put,** to have difficulty in doing or providing something. **put across,** to succeed in communicating (an idea etc.), to make seem acceptable. **put away,** *(informal)* to put into prison or into a mental home; to consume as food or drink. **put by,** to save for future use. **put down,** to suppress by force or authority; to snub; to enter (a person's name) as one who will subscribe; to reckon or consider, *put him down as a fool;* to attribute, *put it down to nervousness; (slang)* to humiliate or speak ill of. **put in,** to enter (a claim); to spend (time) working. **put in for,** to apply for. **put it on,** *(informal)* to pretend an emotion. **put off,** to postpone; to postpone an engagement with (a person); to make excuses and try to avoid; to dissuade, to repel, *the smell puts me off.* **put on,** to stage (a play etc.); to increase, *putting on weight;* to cause to operate; to mislead deliberately, to fool; *put someone on, (informal)* mislead him by pretending the truth of that which is really false; to pretend (an emotion etc.). **put one's feet up,** to take a rest. **put one's foot down,** to insist on something firmly. **put one's foot in it** *or* **in one's mouth,** to make a blunder. **put out,** to disconcert or annoy or inconvenience (a person); to extinguish (a light or fire); to dislocate (a joint); (in baseball) to cause (a base runner) to be out. **put over,** to put across; *put something over on a person,* to deceive him. **put pen to paper,** to start writing. **put the clock back,** to go back to a past age or an out-of-date practice. **put the shot** *or* **weight,** to hurl it as an athletic exercise. **put through,** to complete (a business transaction) successfully; to connect by telephone; to cause to undergo, *put it through severe tests.* **put two and two together,** to draw a conclusion from the facts one knows. **put up,** to construct or build; to raise the price of; to provide or contribute, *the firm will put up the money;* to offer for sale; to give or receive accommodation; to pack up into a parcel or receptacle; to attempt or offer, *they put up no resistance.* **put upon,** to impose on. **put up to,** to instigate (a person) in, *who put him up to it?* **put up with,** to endure, to tolerate.

pu·ta·tive (pyoo-tă-tiv) *adj.* reputed, supposed, *his putative father.*

put·down (puut-down) *n. (slang)* a snub.

put-on (puut-on) *n.* a spoof, a parody, something intended to mislead. **put-on** *adj.* pretended, deliberately misleading.

put·out (puut-owt) *n.* (in baseball) a play in which a base runner is caused to be out.

pu·tre·fy (pyoo-trĕ-fɪ) *v.* **(pu·tre·fied, pu·tre·fy·ing)** to rot, to decay or cause to decay. **pu·tre·fac·tion** (pyoo-trĕ-fak-shŏn) *n.* **pu·tre·fac·tive** (pyoo-trĕ-fak-tiv) *adj.*

pu·tres·cent (pyoo-tres-ĕnt) *adj.* decaying, rotting. **pu·tres'cence** *n.*

pu·trid (pyoo-trid) *adj.* 1. decomposed, rotting. 2. foul smelling. 3. *(slang)* very distasteful or unpleasant. **pu'trid·ness** *n.* **pu·trid·i·ty** (pyoo-trid-i-tee) *n.*

putsch (puuch) *n.* an attempt at a revolution. ▷Swiss German, = thrust, blow.

putt (put) *v.* to strike (a golf ball) lightly to make it roll along the ground. **putt** *n.* a stroke of this kind. □**putting green,** (in golf) a smooth area of grass around the hole.

put·tee (put-ee, pu-tee) *n.* 1. a strip of cloth wound spirally around the leg from ankle to knee for support or protection. 2. a leather legging.

put·ter[1] (puut-ĕr) *n.* a person who puts.

put·ter[2] (put-ĕr) *n.* 1. a golf club used for putting. 2. a person who putts in golf.

put·ter[3] (put-ĕr) *v.* to occupy oneself aimlessly, *to putter around the kitchen.*

put·ty (put-ee) *n.* (*pl.* **-ties**) a soft paste that sets hard, used for fixing glass in window frames, filling up holes, etc. **putty** *v.* **(put·tied, put·ty·ing)** to cover, fix, or fill with putty. □**putty knife,** a tool with a flexible blade, used for puttying.

put-up (puut-up) *adj.* arranged fraudulently or secretly beforehand, *a put-up job.*

puz·zle (puz-ĕl) *n.* 1. a question that is difficult to answer, a problem. 2. a problem or toy designed to test one's knowledge or ingenuity or patience. **puzzle** *v.* **(puzz·zled, puz·zling)** 1. to make hard thought necessary, *a puzzling problem.* 2. to use hard thought, *she puzzled over it; puzzle it out,* solve or understand it by patient thought or ingenuity.

puz·zle·ment (puz-ĕl-mĕnt) *n.* the state of being puzzled.

puz·zler (puz-lĕr) *n.* a puzzling problem.

PVC *abbr.* polyvinyl chloride.

Pvt. *abbr.* private.

PW *abbr.* 1. prisoner of war. 2. public works.

pwt. *abbr.* pennyweight.

PX *abbr.* post exchange.

pyg·my (pig-mee) *n.* (*pl.* **-mies**) 1. a person or thing of unusually small size. 2. *Pygmy,* a member of a dwarf negroid people of equatorial Africa. **pygmy** *adj.* very small.

py·lon (pɪ-lon) *n.* 1. a tall latticework structure used for carrying overhead electric cables or as a boundary. 2. a structure marking a path for aircraft.

py·lo·rus (pɪ-lohr-ŭs) *n.* (*pl.* **-lo·ri,** *pr.* -lohr-ɪ) the opening from the stomach into the duodenum.

Pyong·yang (pyung-yahng) the capital of North Korea.

py·or·rhea (pɪ-ŏ-ree-ă) *n.* a disease of the tooth sockets causing discharge of pus and loosening of the teeth.

pyr·a·mid (pir-ă-mid) *n.* a structure with a flat (usually square) base and with sloping sides that meet at the top, especially one built by the ancient Egyptians as a tomb or by the Aztecs and Mayas as a platform for a temple. **pyramid** *v.* 1. to arrange or build in the shape of a pyramid. 2. to increase quickly on a widening base. **py·ra·mi·dal** (pi-ram-i-dăl) *adj.*

pyre (pɪr) *n.* a pile of wood etc. for burning a corpse as part of a funeral rite.

Pyr·e·nees (pir-ĕ-neez) *n. pl.* a range of mountains between France and Spain. **Pyr·e·ne·an** (pir-ĕ-nee-ăn) *adj.*

py·re·thrum (pɪ-ree-thrŭm) *n.* 1. a kind of chrysanthemum with finely divided leaves. 2. an insecticide made from its dried flowers.

Py·rex (pɪ-reks) *n. (trademark)* heat-resistant glassware used for cooking.

py·rite (pɪ-rɪt) *n.* a mineral (iron disulfide) used in the manufacture of sulfuric acid.

py·ri·tes (pɪ-rɪ-teez) *n.* a mineral that is a sulphide of iron *(iron pyrites)* or copper and iron *(copper pyrites).*

py·rol·y·sis (pɪ-rol-i-sis) *n.* chemical decomposition by the action of heat.

py·ro·ma·ni·ac (pɪ-rŏ-may-ni-ak) *n.* a person with an uncontrollable impulse to set things on fire. **py·ro·ma'nia** *n.*

py·rom·e·ter (pɪ-rom-ĕ-tĕr) *n.* an instrument for measuring high temperatures. **py·rom'et·ry** *n.*

py·ro·tech·nic (pɪ-rŏ-tek-nik) *adj.* of or like fireworks.

py·ro·tech·nics (pɪ-rŏ-tek-niks) *n.* 1. a firework display. 2. a display of brilliant wit etc.

Pyr·rhic (pir-ik) **victory** a victory gained at too great a cost, like that of Pyrrhus (king of Epirus) over the Romans in 279 B.C.

Py·thag·o·re·an (pi-thag-ŏ-ree-ăn) *adj.* of Pythagoras (6th century B.C.), philosopher and mathematician of Samos. □**Pythagorean theorem,** the theorem stating that a square erected on the hypotenuse of a right triangle is equal to the sum of squares erected on the other two sides.

py·thon (pɪ-thon) *n.* a large snake that crushes its prey.

pyx (piks) *n.* a vessel in which bread consecrated for Holy Communion is kept.

Q, q (kyoo) (*pl.* **Qs, Q's, q's**) the seventeenth letter of the alphabet.
Q *abbr.* 1. quarto. 2. Quebec. 3. Queen. 4. question.
q. *abbr.* 1. quart(s). 2. quarto. 3. queen. 4. query. 5. question. 6. quire.
Qa·tar (gah-tahr) a country in the Middle East on the Arabian Gulf.
Qa·ta·ri (gah-tahr-ee) *n.* a native of Qatar.
Q.E.D. *abbr.* which was the thing that had to be proved. ▷ From the Latin *quod erat demonstrandum.*
Qi·a·na (ki-ah-nă, -an-ă) *n. (trademark)* a silky synthetic fiber or fabric.
QM *abbr.* Quartermaster.
QMC *abbr.* Quartermaster Corps.
QMG *abbr.* Quartermaster General.
qq. v. *abbr.* which (things) see. ▷ From the Latin *quae vide.*
qr. *abbr.* 1. quarter. 2. quire.
qt. *abbr.* quart(s).
q.t. (kyoo-tee) *n.* **on the q.t.,** *(slang)* on the quiet.
qto. *abbr.* quarto.
qty. *abbr.* quantity.
qu. *abbr.* question.
qua (kway, kwah) *adv.* in the capacity or character of, *putting his duty qua citizen above other loyalties; art qua art.*
quack[1] (kwak) *n.* the harsh cry of a duck. **quack** *v.* to utter this sound.
quack[2] *n.* a person who falsely claims to have medical skill or to have remedies that will cure diseases etc. **quack'er·y** *n.* **quack'ish** *adj.*
quad[1] (kwod) *n. (informal)* a quadrangle.
quad[2] *n. (informal)* one of a set of quadruplets.
quad[3] *adj. (informal)* quadraphonic.
quad. *abbr.* quadrant.
Quad·ra·ges·i·ma (kwod-ră-jes-i-mă) *n.* the first Sunday in Lent.
quad·ran·gle (kwod-rang-gĕl) *n.* 1. a geometric figure with four corners. 2. a four-sided court bordered by large buildings. **quad·ran·gu·lar** (kwod-rang-gyŭ-lăr) *adj.*
quad·rant (kwod-rănt) *n.* 1. a quarter of a circle or of its circumference. 2. an instrument with an arc of 90° marked off in degrees, for measuring angles. 3. any one of the four parts of an area divided by perpendicular lines.
quad·ra·phon·ic (kwo-dră-fon-ik) *adj.* (of sound reproduction) using four transmission channels. **quadraphonic** *n.* quadraphonic transmission. **quad·ra·phon'ic·al·ly** *adv.*
quad·rat·ic (kwo-drat-ik) *adj.* involving the second and no higher power of an unknown quantity or variable. □**quadratic equation,** an algebraic equation involving quantities or variables of the second and no higher power.

quad·rat·ics (kwo-drat-iks) *n.* the branch of algebra dealing with quadratic equations.
quad·ren·ni·al (kwo-dren-i-ăl) *adj.* 1. lasting for four years. 2. happening every fourth year.
quad·ren·ni·um (kwo-dren-i-ŭm) *n.* (*pl.* **quad·ren·ni·ums, quad·ren·ni·a,** *pr.* kwo-dren-i-ă) a period of four years.
quad·ri·cen·ten·ni·al (kwod-ri-sen-ten-i-ăl) *n.* a four-hundredth anniversary. **quadricentennial** *adj.*
quad·ri·lat·er·al (kwod-ri-lat-ĕ-răl) *n.* a geometric figure with four sides. **quadrilateral** *adj.* having four sides.
qua·drille (kwo-dril) *n.* a square dance for four couples, the music for this.
quad·ril·lion (kwo-dril-yŏn) *n.* a million billions.
quad·ri·par·tite (kwod-rĭ-pahr-tɪt) *adj.* 1. consisting of four parts. 2. shared by four participants, *a quadripartite agreement.*
quad·ri·ple·gi·a (kwod-rĭ-plee-ji-ă) *n.* paralysis of both arms and both legs. **quad·ri·pleg'ic** *adj.* & *n.*
quad·riv·i·um (kwo-driv-i-ŭm) *n.* a medieval university course of arithmetic, geometry, astronomy, and music.
quad·roon (kwo-droon) *n.* an offspring of a mulatto and a white.
quad·ru·ped (kwod-rŭ-ped) *n.* a four-footed animal. **quad·ru·pe·dal** (kwo-droo-pĕ-dăl) *adj.*
quad·ru·ple (kwo-droo-pĕl, -drup-ĕl) *adj.* 1. consisting of four parts, involving four people or groups, *a quadruple alliance.* 2. four times as much as, *shall need quadruple that number of lights.* **quadruple** *v.* (**qua·dru·pled, qua·dru·pling**) to multiply or become multiplied by four; *costs had quadrupled,* had increased to four times the original amount. **quadruple** *n.* a number or amount four times greater than another.
quad·ru·plet (kwod-roo-plit) *n.* one of four children born at a birth.
quad·ru·pli·cate (kwo-droo-plĭ-kit) *n.* **in quadruplicate,** in four exactly similar examples or copies. **quad·ru·pli·ca·tion** (kwo-droo-plĭ-kay-shŏn) *n.*
quaff (kwahf) *v.* to drink (a thing) in long drafts. **quaff** *n.* a long draft.
quag·mire (kwag-mɪr) *n.* a bog or marsh.
qua·hog, qua·haug (kway-hog) *n.* an edible round clam of the Atlantic coast.
quail[1] (kwayl) *n.* (*pl.* **quail, quails**) a bird related to the partridge, used as food.
quail[2] *v.* to flinch, to show fear.
quaint (kwaynt) *adj.* odd in a pleasing way, attractive through being unusual or old-fashioned. **quaint'ly** *adv.* **quaint'ness** *n.*
quake (kwayk) *v.* (**quaked, quak·ing**) to shake

or tremble from unsteadiness, to shake with fear. **quake** *n.* 1. a quaking movement. 2. *(informal)* an earthquake. □**quaking aspen,** a tree of northern North America having small shimmering leaves that flutter in the slightest breeze.

Quak·er (kway-kĕr) *n.* a member of the Society of Friends, a Christian sect opposed to war and formerly noted for simplicity of dress and of living. □**Quaker meeting,** a religious meeting of Friends, silent until a member is moved to speak.

qual·i·fi·ca·tion (kwol-ĭ-fĭ-**kay**-shŏn) *n.* 1. qualifying, being qualified. 2. a thing that qualifies a person to do something or to have a certain right etc. 3. something that limits or restricts a meaning, *this statement needs certain qualifications.*

qual·i·fy (kwol-ĭ-fɪ) *v.* (**qual·i·fied, qual·i·fy·ing**) 1. to make or become competent or eligible or legally entitled to do something. 2. to make (a statement etc.) less general or extreme, to limit its meaning, *"in all cases" needs to be qualified as "in all known cases"; gave it only qualified approval,* not complete approval. 3. to describe, to attribute some quality to, *they qualified him as ambitious; adjectives qualify nouns.* **qual'i·fi·er** *n.*

qual·i·ta·tive (kwol-ĭ-tay-tiv) *adj.* of or concerned with quality, *qualitative analysis.* **qual'i·ta·tive·ly** *adv.*

qual·i·ty (kwol-ĭ-tee) *n.* (*pl.* **-ties**) 1. a degree or level of excellence, *goods of high quality.* 2. general excellence, *it has quality.* 3. a characteristic, something that is special in a person or thing, *has the quality of inspiring confidence.* □**quality control,** a system that maintains a certain standard of quality in a process or product.

qualm (kwahm) *n.* 1. a misgiving, a pang of conscience. 2. a sudden feeling of sickness or faintness.

quan·da·ry (kwon-dă-ree) *n.* (*pl.* **-ries**) a state of perplexity, a difficult situation.

quan·ta *see* **quantum.**

quan·ti·fi·a·ble (kwon-tĭ-fɪ-ă-bĕl) *adj.* able to be quantified.

quan·ti·fy (kwon-tĭ-fɪ) *v.* (**quan·ti·fied, quan·ti·fy·ing**) to express as a quantity.

quan·ti·ta·tive (kwon-tĭ-tay-tiv) *adj.* of or concerned with quantity, *quantitative analysis.* **quan'ti·ta·tive·ly** *adv.*

quan·ti·ty (kwon-tĭ-tee) *n.* (*pl.* **-ties**) 1. an amount or number of things, a specified or considerable amount or number; *it is found in quantity or in quantities,* in large amounts. 2. ability to be measured through having size or weight or amount or number. 3. a thing that has this ability, a figure or symbol representing it.

quan·tize (kwon-tɪz) *v.* (**quan·tized, quan·tiz·ing**) 1. to form into quanta. 2. to apply quantum mechanics to. **quan·ti·za·tion** (kwon-tɪ-zay-shŏn) *n.*

quan·tum (kwon-tŭm) *n.* (*pl.* **-ta,** *pr.* -tă) 1. the amount required or desired. 2. (in physics) a unit quantity of energy proportional to frequency of radiation. □**quantum theory,** a theory of physics based on the assumption that energy exists in indivisible units.

quar·an·tine (kwor-ăn-teen) *n.* 1. isolation imposed on people or animals that may have been exposed to an infectious or contagious disease which they could spread to others. 2. the period of this isolation. **quarantine** *v.* (**quar·an·tined,**

quar·an·tin·ing) to put into quarantine.

quark (kwork) *n.* one of three components of elementary particles assumed to exist as the basic units of all matter.

quar·rel (kwor-ĕl) *n.* 1. a violent disagreement, breaking of friendly relations. 2. a cause for complaint against a person or his actions, *we have no quarrel with him.* **quarrel** *v.* (**quar·reled, quar·rel·ing**) 1. to engage in a quarrel, to break off friendly relations. 2. to disagree with or complain about, *we are not quarreling with this decision.* **quar'rel·er** *n.*

quar·rel·some (kwor-ĕl-sŏm) *adj.* liable to quarrel with people.

quar·ry[1] (kwor-ee) *n.* (*pl.* **-ries**) 1. an intended prey or victim being hunted. 2. something that is sought or pursued.

quarry[2] *n.* an open excavation from which stone or slate etc. is obtained. **quarry** *v.* (**quar·ried, quar·ry·ing**) to obtain (stone etc.) from a quarry.

quart (kwort) *n.* a measure of capacity for liquids, two pints or a quarter of a gallon.

quar·ter (kwor-tĕr) *n.* 1. one of the four equal parts into which a thing is divided. 2. a quarter of a dollar, twenty-five cents. 3. one of four parts of an animal's or bird's carcass, each including a leg (or wing). 4. a fourth part of a calendar year, three months. 5. a fourth part of a lunar month. 6. a point of time fifteen minutes before or after every hour. 7. a direction or point of the compass, a district, a division of a town. 8. a person or group, especially regarded as a possible source of help or information etc., *got no sympathy from that quarter.* 9. mercy toward an enemy or opponent, *gave no quarter.* 10. quarters, lodgings, accommodation; *married quarters,* accommodation for married people. **quarter** *v.* 1. to divide into quarters. 2. to put (soldiers etc.) into lodgings. 3. (of a dog etc.) to search (ground) in every direction. □**quarter binding,** a bookbinding with narrow leather along the back and none at the corners. **quarter horse,** a strong horse of a breed able to run a quarter mile at high speed. **quarter note,** a musical note lasting one-quarter of the time of a full note. **quarter rest,** a musical pause lasting as long as a quarter note. **quarter section,** a tract of land half a mile square, containing 160 acres or one quarter of a square mile.

quar·ter·back (kwor-tĕr-bak) *n.* the member of a football team who calls the signals. **quarterback** *v.* 1. to direct the offense of (a football team). 2. *(informal)* to lead or manage.

quar·ter·deck (kwor-tĕr-dek) *n.* the part of the upper deck of a ship nearest the stern, usually reserved for the ship's officers.

quar·ter·fi·nal (kwor-tĕr-fɪ-năl) *n.* one of the matches or rounds preceding a semifinal.

quar·ter·ly (kwor-tĕr-lee) *adj.* produced or occurring once in every quarter of a year, *a quarterly dividend.* **quarterly** *n.* (*pl.* **-lies**) a quarterly periodical.

quar·ter·mas·ter (kwor-tĕr-mas-tĕr) *n.* 1. a military officer in charge of stores and assigning quarters etc. 2. a naval petty officer in charge of steering and signals etc. □**Quartermaster Corps,** the branch of the U.S. Army that deals with supplies. **Quartermaster General,** the general who commands the Quartermaster Corps.

quar·ter·staff (kwor-tĕr-staf) *n.* a stout pole six to eight feet long formerly used as a weapon.

quar·tet (kwor-tet) *n.* 1. a group of four instruments or voices, a musical composition for these. 2. a set of four.

quar·to (kwor-toh) *n.* (*pl.* **-tos**) the size of a book or page or sheet of paper given by folding a sheet of standard size (about 9½ x 12 inches) twice to form four leaves.

quartz (kworts) *n.* a kind of hard mineral occurring in various forms. □**quartz crystal,** a thin section of quartz precisely ground to vibrate at a certain speed. **quartz glass,** silica glass, highly transparent to ultraviolet light. **quartz lamp,** a quartz tube containing mercury vapor and transmitting ultraviolet light.

quartz·ite (kworts-ıt) *n.* a compact granular quartz rock.

qua·sar (kway-zahr) *n.* a starlike object that is the source of intense electromagnetic radiation. ▷From *quas*(istell)*ar* radio source.

quash (kwosh) *v.* 1. to annul, to reject (by legal authority) as not valid, *quashed the conviction.* 2. to suppress or crush (a rebellion etc.). ▷Do not confuse *quash* with *squash.*

qua·si (kway-zı) *adj.* seeming to be, *a quasi science.* **quasi** *adv.* seemingly, *quasi serious.*

quasi- *prefix* seeming to be something but not really so, as in *a quasiscientific explanation.*

qua·ter·cen·te·nar·y (kwah-tĕr-sen-tĕ-ner-ee) *n.* a four-hundredth anniversary.

Qua·ter·nar·y (kwah-tĕr-ner-ee) *adj.* of the most recent geologic period. **Quaternary** *n.* the Quaternary period.

quat·rain (kwah-trayn) *n.* a stanza of four lines.

quat·re·foil (kat-ĕr-foil) *n.* 1. a representation of a flower having four petals. 2. an architectural ornament having four lobes.

qua·ver (kway-vĕr) *v.* 1. to tremble, to vibrate. 2. to speak in a trembling voice. **quaver** *n.* 1. a quavering sound. 2. a trill.

quay (kee, kay) *n.* a landing place, usually built of stone or steel, alongside which ships can be tied up for loading and unloading.

quay·side (kee-sıd, kay-) *n.* land forming or beside a quay.

Que. *abbr.* Quebec.

quea·sy (kwee-zee) *adj.* (**-si·er, -si·est**) 1. feeling slightly sick. 2. having a digestion that is easily upset. 3. (of food) causing a feeling of sickness. 4. squeamish. **quea'si·ly** *adv.* **quea'si·ness** *n.*

Que·bec (kwi-bek) a province of Canada.

Que·bec·ois (kay-be-kwah) *n.* (*pl.* **-ois**) a native or inhabitant of Quebec.

queen (kween) *n.* 1. a woman who is the supreme ruler of an independent country by right of succession to the throne. 2. a king's wife. 3. a woman or place or thing regarded as supreme in some way, *Venice, the queen of the Adriatic.* 4. a playing card bearing a picture of a queen. 5. a piece in chess. 6. a perfect fertile female of a bee or ant or similar insect. **queen** *v.* to convert (a pawn in chess) to a queen when it reaches the opponent's end of the board, to be converted in this way. □**Queen Anne's lace,** the wild carrot. **queen bee,** a fully developed fertile female bee. **queen consort,** a reigning king's wife. **queen mother,** a dowager queen who is the mother of a reigning king or queen. **queen's pawn, knight, bishop,** etc., the pieces in chess placed nearest the queen at the start.

queen·ly (kween-lee) *adj.* like a queen in appearance or manner. **queen'li·ness** *n.*

queen-size (kween-sız) *adj.* (also **queen-sized**) (of a bed etc.) having dimensions of about five feet by seven feet.

queer (kweer) *adj.* 1. strange, odd, eccentric. 2. causing one to feel suspicious, of questionable character. 3. slightly ill or faint, *felt queer.* **queer** *v.* to spoil. **queer'ly** *adv.* **queer'ness** *n.* □**queer as a three-dollar bill,** (*slang*) counterfeit; strange, odd.

quell (kwel) *v.* to suppress, to reduce to submission, *quelled the rebellion.*

quench (kwench) *v.* 1. to extinguish (a fire or flame). 2. to satisfy (one's thirst) by drinking something. 3. to cool (a heated thing) by water. **quench'er** *n.* **quench'a·ble** *adj.* **quench'less** *adj.*

quer·u·lous (kwer-ŭ-lŭs) *adj.* complaining peevishly. **quer'u·lous·ly** *adv.* **quer'u·lous·ness** *n.*

que·ry (kweer-ee) *n.* (*pl.* **-ries**) 1. a question. 2. a question mark. **query** *v.* (**que·ried, que·ry·ing**) to ask a question or express doubt about.

quest (kwest) *n.* the act of seeking something, a search.

ques·tion (kwes-chŏn) *n.* 1. a sentence requesting information or an answer. 2. something being discussed or for discussion, a problem requiring solution. 3. the raising of doubt, *whether we shall win is open to question.* **question** *v.* 1. to ask questions of (a person). 2. to express doubt about. **ques'tion·er** *n.* □**in question,** being referred to or discussed; being disputed, *his honesty is not in question,* **it is a question of,** this is what is required or involved; *it is only a question of time,* it will happen sooner or later. **no question of,** no possibility of. **out of the question,** completely impracticable. **question mark,** the punctuation mark ? placed after a question.

ques·tion·a·ble (kwes-chŏ-nă-bĕl) *adj.* open to doubt or suspicion, not certainly true or advisable or honest. **ques'tion·a·bly** *adv.* **ques'tion·a·ble·ness** *n.* **ques·tion·a·bil·i·ty** (kwes-chŏ-nă-bil-i-tee) *n.*

ques·tion·naire (kwes-chŏ-nair) *n.* a list of questions seeking information about people's opinions or customs etc., especially for use in a survey.

quet·zal (ket-sahl) *n.* (*pl.* **-zals, -za·les,** *pr.* **-sah**les) a tropical American bird, the male of which has long green tail feathers.

queue (kyoo) *n.* 1. a pigtail. 2. a line or series of people awaiting their turn for something. **queue** *v.* (**queued, queu·ing**) to wait in a queue, *queuing up.*

Que·zon (kay-zon) City the capital of the Philippines.

quib·ble (kwib-ĕl) *n.* a petty objection. **quibble** *v.* (**quib·bled, quib·bling**) to make petty objections. **quib'bler** *n.*

quiche (keesh) *n.* an open unsweetened pastry shell with a rich custard filling, often flavored with bacon, mushrooms, etc.

quick (kwik) *adj.* 1. taking only a short time to do something or to be done. 2. able to notice or learn or think quickly. 3. (of temper) easily aroused. 4. (*old use*) alive, *the quick and the dead.* **quick** *n.* the sensitive flesh below the nails; *cut to the quick,* to have one's feelings deeply hurt. **quick** *adv.* quickly, *quick-drying.* **quick'ly** *adv.* **quick'ness** *n.* □**quick bread,** any bread leavened with baking powder, soda, etc. that can be baked as soon as it is mixed. **quick time,** a military marching pace of 120 steps to the minute. **quick trick,** a sure bridge trick that can be taken in the first or second round of play.

quick·en (kwik-ĕn) *v.* 1. to make or become quicker. 2. to stimulate, to make or become livelier, *our interest quickened.* 3. to reach a stage in pregnancy *(the quickening)* when the fetus makes movements that can be felt by the mother.

quick-freeze (kwik-freez) *v.* (quick·**froze, quick·froz·en, quick·freez·ing)** to freeze (food) rapidly for storing, so that it keeps its natural qualities.

quick·ie (kwik-ee) *n. (informal)* something done or made quickly or hastily.

quick·lime (kwik-lım) = **lime¹.**

quick·sand (kwik-sand) *n.* an area of loose wet deep sand into which heavy objects will sink.

quick·sil·ver (kwik-sil-vĕr) *n.* mercury.

quick·step (kwik-step) *n.* a ballroom dance with quick steps, music for this.

quick-tem·pered (kwik-tem-pĕrd) *adj.* easily angered.

quick-wit·ted (kwik-wit-id) *adj.* quick at understanding a situation or making jokes.

quid (kwid) *n.* a lump of tobacco for chewing.

quid pro quo (kwid proh kwoh) a thing given in return for something. ▷Latin, = something for something.

qui·es·cent (kwi-es-ĕnt) *adj.* inactive, quiet. **qui·es·cence** (kwi-es-ĕns) *n.* **qui·es·cen·cy** (kwi-es-ĕn-see) *n.*

qui·et (kwı-it) *adj.* 1. with little or no sound, not loud or noisy. 2. with little or no movement. 3. free from disturbance or vigorous activity, peaceful. 4. silent, *be quiet!* 5. unobtrusive, done in a restrained manner, *had a quiet laugh about it.* 6. (of colors or dress etc.) subdued, not showy. **quiet** *n.* quietness. **quiet** *v.* to make or become quiet, to calm. **qui'et·ly** *adv.* **qui'et·ness** *n.*

qui·e·tude (kwı-ĕ-tood) *n.* quietness.

qui·e·tus (kwı-ee-tŭs) *n. (pl.* **-tus·es)** death.

quill (kwil) *n.* 1. one of the large feathers on a bird's wing or tail. 2. an old type of pen made from this, *a quill pen.* 3. one of a porcupine's spines. 4. the hollow stem of a feather, a plectrum or other device made of this.

quilt (kwilt) *n.* a padded bed cover. **quilt** *v.* to line with padding and fix with crosslines of stitching. ▢**quilting bee,** a social gathering at which women quilt.

quince (kwins) *n.* 1. a hard yellowish pear-shaped fruit used for making jam. 2. the tree bearing it.

quin·cen·te·nar·y (kwin-sen-tĕ-ner-ee) *n.* a five-hundredth anniversary. **quincentenary** *adj.*

qui·nine (kwı-nın) *n.* a bitter medicinal drug used to treat malaria and in tonics. ▢**quinine water,** a soft drink tasting of quinine, often mixed with gin or vodka.

Quin·qua·ges·i·ma (kwin-kwă-jes-ĭ-mă) *n.* the Sunday before Lent (fifty days before Easter).

quin·quen·ni·al (kwin-kwen-i-ăl) *adj.* 1. lasting for five years. 2. happening every fifth year.

quin·sy (kwin-zee) *n. (old use)* severe inflammation of the throat, often with an abscess on one of the tonsils.

quint (kwint) *n. (informal)* one of a set of quintuplets.

quin·tes·sence (kwin-tes-ĕns) *n.* 1. an essence of a substance. 2. the essence or essential part of a

theory or speech or condition etc. 3. a perfect example of a quality. **quin·tes·sen·tial** (kwinti-sen-shăl) *adj.*

quin·tet (kwin-tet) *n.* 1. a group of five instruments or voices, a musical composition for these. 2. a set of five.

quin·til·lion (kwin-til-yŏn) *n.* a billion billions.

quin·tu·ple (kwin-too-pĕl, -tup-ĕl) *adj.* 1. consisting of five parts, involving five people or groups. 2. five times as much. **quintuple** *v.* **(quin·tu·pled, quin·tu·pling)** to multiply or become multiplied by five.

quin·tu·plet (kwin-tup-lit, -too-plit) *n.* one of five children born at one birth.

quip (kwip) *n.* a witty or sarcastic remark. **quip** *v.* **(quipped, quip·ping)** to utter as a quip.

quire (kwır) *n.* twenty-four sheets of paper bound or collected as a unit.

quirk (kwurk) *n.* 1. a peculiarity of a person's behavior. 2. a trick of fate.

quirt (kwurt) *n.* a short-handled riding whip with a braided leather lash.

quis·ling (kwiz-ling) *n.* a traitor, especially one who collaborates with an enemy occupying his country. ▷Named after V. Quisling, a pro-Nazi Norwegian leader in World War II.

quit (kwit) *v.* **(quit** or **quit·ted, quit·ting)** 1. to give up or abandon (a task etc.), *quit her job.* 2. *(informal)* to cease, *quit grumbling.* 3. to go away from, to leave, *quit the premises.* **quit** *adj.* rid (of an obligation), *glad to be quit of it.*

quit·claim (kwit-klaym) *n.* the renunciation of a right, especially to land.

quite (kwıt) *adv.* 1. completely, entirely, *quite finished.* 2. to some extent, somewhat, *quite a long time.* 3. really, actually, *it's quite a change.* ▢**quite a few,** a considerable number. **quite something,** a remarkable thing.

Qui·to (kee-toh) the capital of Ecuador.

quits (kwits) *adj.* even with, on even terms as a result of retaliation or repayment. ▢**call it quits,** to acknowledge that things are now even, to agree to cease quarreling.

quit·ter (kwit-ĕr) *n. (informal)* a person who gives up too easily.

quiv·er¹ (kwiv-ĕr) *n.* a case for holding arrows.

quiver² *v.* to shake or vibrate with a slight rapid motion. **quiver** *n.* a quivering movement or sound.

qui vive (kee veev) **on the qui vive,** on the alert, watchful. ▷French.

quix·ot·ic (kwik-sot-ik) *adj.* chivalrous and unselfish to an exaggerated extent. **quix·ot'i·cal·ly** *adv.* ▷Named after Don Quixote, hero of a Spanish story.

quiz (kwiz) *n. (pl.* **quiz·zes)** 1. a short test given to students. 2. a series of questions testing people's general knowledge, especially as a form of entertainment. **quiz** *v.* **(quizzed, quiz·zing)** to examine by questioning. ▢**quiz show,** a radio or television program that tests the knowledge of participants.

quiz·mas·ter (kwiz-mas-tĕr) *n.* the person who asks the questions in a quiz show.

quiz·zi·cal (kwiz-ĭ-kăl) *adj.* 1. done in a questioning way. 2. gently amused. **quiz'zi·cal·ly** *adv.* **quiz'zi·cal·ness** *n.* **quiz·zi·cal·i·ty** (kwiz-ĭkal-i-tee) *n.*

quoin (koin, kwoin) *n.* 1. the external angle of a building. 2. the stone or brick forming this angle, the cornerstone. 3. a wedge for locking type, raising the level of a gun, keeping a barrel from rolling, etc.

quoit (kwoit) *n.* a ring of metal or rubber or rope thrown to encircle a peg in the game of **quoits.**

Quon·set (kwon-sit) **hut** *(trademark)* a prefabricated semicylindrical building made of corrugated metal.

quo·rum (kwohr-ŭm) *n.* the minimum number of people that must be present at a meeting before its proceedings are to be regarded as valid.

quot. *abbr.* quotation.

quo·ta (kwoh-tă) *n.* 1. a fixed share that must be done or contributed or received. 2. the maximum number or amount of people or things that may be admitted, as to a country or institution, *import quotas.*

quot·a·ble (kwoh-tă-běl) *adj.* worth quoting.

quo·ta·tion (kwoh-tay-shŏn) *n.* 1. quoting, being quoted. 2. a passage quoted. 3. an amount stated as the current price of stocks or commodities. 4. a contractor's estimate of the cost of a piece of work to be done. □**quotation marks,** marks of punctuation (either single ' ' or double " ") enclosing words quoted or used for other reasons of style.

quote (kwoht) *v.* **(quot·ed, quot·ing)** 1. to repeat or write out words from a book or speech, *quote the Bible* or *from the Bible.* 2. to mention in support of a statement, *can you quote a recent example?* 3. to state the price of (goods or services), to give a quotation or estimate. 4. (in dictation etc.) begin the quotation, open the quotation marks (*see* **unquote**). **quote** *n. (informal)* 1. a quotation. 2. *quotes,* quotation marks.

quoth (kwohth) *v. (old use)* said.

quo·tid·i·an (kwoh-tid-i-ăn) *adj.* 1. daily. 2. commonplace, trivial.

quo·tient (kwoh-shĕnt) *n.* the result obtained when one amount is divided by another, as 3 in "12 ÷ 4 = 3."

q.v. *abbr.* which see (used as an indication that the reader should look at the reference given). ▷ From the Latin *quod vide.*

qy. *abbr.* query.

R

R, r (ahr) (*pl.* **Rs, R's, r's**) the eighteenth letter of the alphabet.
r. *abbr.* 1. rare. 2. rod(s). 3. roentgen(s). 4. (in baseball) run(s).
R. *abbr.* 1. radius. 2. railroad. 3. railway. 4. Republican. 5. right. 6. river. 7. road.
Ra *symbol* radium.
RA *abbr.* Regular Army.
R.A. *abbr.* Royal Academy.
Ra·bat (rah-baht) one of the two capitals of Morocco.
rab·bet (rab-it) *n.* a groove cut along the edge, face, or projecting angle of wood etc. usually to receive the edge of another piece. **rabbet** *v.* (**rab·bet·ed, rab·bet·ing**) 1. to join or fix with a rabbet. 2. to make a rabbet in.
rab·bi (rab-ɪ) *n.* (*pl.* **-bis**) the religious leader of a Jewish congregation.
rab·bin·ate (rab-i-nit) *n.* 1. the office of a rabbi. 2. a group of rabbis.
rab·bin·i·cal (ră-bin-i-kăl), **rab·bin·ic** (ră-bin-ik) *adj.* of rabbis or Jewish doctrines or law.
rab·bit (rab-it) *n.* (*pl.* **-bits, -bit**) a burrowing animal with long ears and a short furry tail. **rab'bit·y** *adj.* □**rabbit ears**, *(informal)* a small indoor television antenna consisting of two rods forming a V. **rabbit punch**, a short chop with the edge of one's hand on the back of a person's neck. **Welsh rabbit**, a dish of melted or toasted cheese on toast.
rab·ble (rab-ĕl) *n.* 1. a disorderly crowd, a mob. 2. *the rabble*, the common people, the lowest social classes.
rab·ble-rous·er (rab-ĕl-row-zĕr) *n.* a person who stirs up people in agitation for social or political reasons.
rab·id (rab-id) *adj.* 1. furious, fanatical, *rabid hate; a rabid socialist.* 2. affected with rabies. **rab'id·ly** *adv.* **rab'id·ness** *n.* **rab·id·i·ty** (ra-bid-i-tee) *n.*
ra·bies (ray-beez) *n.* a contagious fatal virus disease affecting dogs and similar animals, transmitted to man usually by the bite of an infected animal.
rac·coon (ra-koon) *n.* (*pl.* **-coons, -coon**) a nocturnal animal of North America, with grayish-brown fur, a sharp snout, and a bushy tail.
race¹ (rays) *n.* 1. a contest of speed in reaching a certain point or in doing or achieving something; *a race against time*, an effort to get something done before a certain time. 2. a strong fast current of water. 3. a channel for the balls in a ball bearing. **rac'er** *n.* **race** *v.* (**raced, rac·ing**) 1. to compete in a race, to have a race with. 2. to engage in horse racing, *a racing man.* 3. to move or cause to move or operate at full speed, *raced his engine.* □**racing form**, an information sheet giving details about horse races. **the races**, a series of races for horses or dogs at fixed times on a regular course.
race² *n.* 1. one of the great divisions of mankind with certain inherited physical characteristics in common (such as color of skin and hair, shape of eyes and nose). 2. a number of people related by common descent. 3. a genus or species or breed or variety of animals or plants; *the race* or *the human race*, mankind. □**race relations**, relations between members of different races in the same country. **race riot**, an outbreak of violence arising from racial antagonism.
race·course (rays-kohrs) *n.* a racetrack.
race·horse (rays-hors) *n.* a horse bred or kept for racing.
ra·ceme (ray-seem) *n.* flowers evenly spaced along a central stem, with the ones at the base opening first (as in lupines, hyacinths, etc.).
rac·e·mose (ras-ĕ-mohs) *adj.* in the form of a raceme.
race·track (rays-trak) *n.* a track for horse or vehicle races.
race·way (rays-way) *n.* 1. a racetrack for harness racing. 2. a channel for water.
ra·chi·tis (ră-kı-tis) *n.* rickets. **ra·chit·ic** (ră-kit-ik) *adj.*
ra·cial (ray-shăl) *adj.* of or based on race. **ra'cial·ly** *adv.*
ra·cial·ism (ray-shă-liz-ĕm) *n.* racism. **ra'cial·ist** *n.*
rac·ism (ray-siz-ĕm) *n.* 1. belief in the superiority of a particular race. 2. antagonism between people of different races. 3. the theory that human abilities are determined by race. **rac'ist** *n.*
rack¹ (rak) *n.* 1. a framework, usually with bars or pegs, for holding things or for hanging things on. 2. a shelf or framework of bars for holding light luggage in a train or bus etc. 3. a bar or rail with teeth or cogs into which those of a wheel or gear etc. fit. 4. an instrument of torture on which people were tied and stretched. 5. a triangular structure for setting up balls in the game of pool. **rack** *v.* 1. to inflict great torment on, *was racked with pain.* 2. to stretch the joints of (a person) by force, especially with a rack. □**rack and pinion**, a mechanism producing motion by gearing or by matching teeth on a bar *(rack)* with teeth on a pinion. **rack one's brains**, to think hard about a problem. **rack up**, *(informal)* to score as in sports; to achieve.
rack² *n.* destruction, *to go to rack and ruin.*
rack·et¹, rac·quet (rak-it) *n.* a stringed bat used in tennis and similar games.
racket² *n.* 1. a din, a noisy fuss. 2. a business or other activity in which dishonest methods are used. **racket** *v.* to move about noisily, to engage in wild social activities, *racketing about.*

rack·et·eer (rak-i-teer) *n.* a person who runs or works in a racket or dishonest business. **rack·et·eer'ing** *n.*

rack·e·ty (rak-i-tee) *adj.* noisy.

rac·on·teur (rak-on-tur) *n.* a person who tells anecdotes, *a good raconteur.*

rac·quet *see* **racket**[1].

rac·y (ray-see) *adj.* **(rac·i·er, ra·ci·est)** 1. spirited and vigorous in style, *a racy description of his adventures.* 2. risqué. **rac'i·ly** *adv.* **rac'i·ness** *n.*

rad. *abbr.* 1. (in mathematics) radical. 2. radio. 3. radius.

ra·dar (ray-dahr) *n.* 1. a system for detecting the presence or position or movement etc. of objects by sending out short radio waves that they reflect. 2. apparatus used for this. □**radar trap,** an arrangement using radar to detect vehicles traveling faster than the speed limit.

ra·dar·scope (ray-dahr-skohp) *n.* the screen on which radio waves from a radar receiver are displayed.

ra·di·al (ray-di-ăl) *adj.* of rays or radii, having spikes or lines etc. that radiate from a central point. **radial** *n.* a radial tire. **ra'di·al·ly** *adv.* □**radial engine,** an internal combustion engine with cylinders arranged along radii. **radial tire,** a tire strengthened with cords nearly at right angles to the center line of the tread.

ra·di·ant (ray-di-ănt) *adj.* 1. giving out rays of light. 2. looking very bright and happy. 3. transmitting heat by radiation, (of heat) transmitted in this way. **ra'di·ant·ly** *adv.* **ra'di·ance** *n.* **ra·di·an·cy** (ray-di-ăn-see) *n.* □**radiant energy,** energy transmitted in the form of electromagnetic waves. **radiant heat,** heat transmitted by radiation, not by conduction or convection.

ra·di·ate (ray-di-ayt) *n.* **(ra·di·at·ed, ra·di·at·ing)** 1. to spread outward (especially in lines or rays) from a central point, to cause to do this. 2. to send out (light or heat etc.) in rays, to be sent out as radiation. 3. to give forth a feeling of, *she radiated confidence.*

ra·di·a·tion (ray-di-ay-shŏn) *n.* 1. radiating, being radiated. 2. sending out of the rays and atomic particles characteristic of radioactive substances, these rays and particles. □**radiation sickness,** illness caused by exposure to excessive radiation, with symptoms of nausea, vomiting, loss of hair and teeth, and damage to blood-forming tissue.

ra·di·a·tor (ray-di-ay-tŏr) *n.* 1. an apparatus that radiates heat, especially a metal case through which steam or hot water circulates. 2. an engine-cooling apparatus in a motor vehicle or an aircraft.

rad·i·cal (rad-i-kăl) *adj.* 1. going to the root or foundation of something, fundamental. 2. drastic, thorough, *radical changes* or *reforms.* 3. desiring radical reforms, holding extremist views. 4. (in mathematics) of the root of a number or quantity. **radical** *n.* 1. a person desiring radical reforms or holding extremist views. 2. an element or atom, or group of these, normally forming part of a compound and remaining unaltered during the compound's ordinary chemical changes. 3. (in mathematics) a quantity forming or expressed as the root of another. **rad'i·cal·ly** *adv.* **rad'i·cal·ness** *n.* **rad'i·cal·ism** *n.* □**radical sign,** (in mathematics) √ , ∛ , ∜ , etc. indicating that the square, cube, fourth, etc. root of the number following is to be taken.

rad·i·cal·ize (rad-i-kă-lɪz) *v.* **(rad·i·cal·ized,**

rad·i·cal·iz·ing) to make radical, especially in politics. **rad·i·cal·i·za·tion** (rad-i-kă-li-zay-shŏn) *n.*

rad·i·cle (rad-i-kĕl) *n.* an embryo root (as of a pea or bean).

ra·di·i *see* **radius.**

ra·di·o (ray-di-oh) *n.* (*pl.* **-di·os**) 1. the process of sending and receiving messages etc. by electromagnetic waves without a connecting wire. 2. an apparatus for sending or receiving messages etc. in this way, a transmitter or receiver. 3. sound broadcasting, a sound-broadcasting station, *National Public Radio.* **radio** *adj.* of or using radio. **radio** *v.* **(ra·di·oed, ra·di·o·ing)** to send or signal or communicate with by radio. □**radio astronomy,** the study of radio waves received or reflected from stars or other celestial bodies. **radio beacon,** a radio station that continually transmits a signal used by ships and planes for navigational purposes. **radio car,** a car equipped with radio for communication. **radio frequency,** the frequency of radio waves, between 10 kilohertz and 300,000 megahertz, used in radio and television transmission. **radio station,** a broadcasting station; an organization involved in commercial broadcasting on assigned frequency; a station for transmitting and receiving radio signals.

ra·di·o·ac·tive (ray-di-oh-ak-tiv) *adj.* of or showing radioactivity. **ra·di·o·ac'tive·ly** *adv.*

ra·di·o·ac·tiv·i·ty (ray-di-oh-ak-tiv-i-tee) *n.* the property of having atoms that break up spontaneously and send out radiation capable of penetrating opaque bodies and producing electrical and chemical effects.

ra·di·o·car·bon (ray-di-oh-kahr-bŏn) *n.* a radioactive form of carbon that is present in organic materials. □**radiocarbon dating,** a method of deciding the age of prehistoric objects by measuring the decay of radiocarbon in them.

ra·di·o·gen·ic (ray-di-oh-jen-ik) *adj.* produced by radioactivity.

ra·di·o·gram (ray-di-oh-gram) *n.* 1. a radiograph. 2. a message transmitted by radiotelegraphy.

ra·di·o·graph (ray-di-oh-graf) *n.* a picture obtained by x-rays, gamma rays, etc. **radiograph** *v.* to make a radiograph of. **ra·di·o·graph·ic** (ray-di-oh-graf-ik) *adj.* **ra·di·o·graph'i·cal·ly** *adv.* **ra·di·og·ra·phy** (ray-di-og-ră-fee) *n.*

ra·di·o·i·so·tope (ray-di-oh-ɪ-sŏ-tohp) *n.* a radioactive isotope.

ra·di·ol·o·gist (ray-di-ol-ŏ-jist) *n.* an expert in radiology.

ra·di·ol·o·gy (ray-di-ol-ŏ-jee) *n.* the scientific study of x-rays and similar radiation, especially as used in medicine.

ra·di·o·man (ray-di-oh-man) *n.* (*pl.* **-men,** *pr.* -men) a person who operates a radio or maintains and repairs radio equipment.

ra·di·om·e·ter (ray-di-om-ĕ-tĕr) *n.* an instrument for measuring the intensity of radiant energy. **ra·di·om'e·try** *n.* **ra·di·o·met·ric** (ray-di-oh-met-rik) *adj.* **ra·di·o·met'ri·cal·ly** *adv.*

ra·di·o·phone (ray-di-oh-fohn) *n.* a radiotelephone.

ra·di·os·co·py (ray-di-os-kŏ-pee) *n.* the examination by x-rays etc. of objects opaque to light. **ra·di·o·scop·ic** (ray-di-oh-skop-ik) *adj.*

ra·di·o·sonde (ray-di-oh-sond) *n.* a miniature radio transmitter carried up in a balloon to broadcast information about pressure, temperature, etc. at various levels.

ra·di·o·tel·e·graph (ray-di-oh-tel-ĕ-graf) *n.* a telegraph utilizing radio waves in the transmission of a signal or message. **ra·di·o·tel·e·graph·ic** (ray-di-oh-tel-ĕ-graf-ik) *adj.* **ra·di·o·te·leg·ra·phy** (ray-di-oh-tĕ-leg-ră-fee) *n.*

ra·di·o·tel·e·phone (ray-di-oh-tel-ĕ-fohn) *n.* a telephone utilizing radio waves to transmit sound. **ra·di·o·tel·e·phon·ic** (ray-di-oh-tel-ĕ-fon-ik) *adj.* **ra·di·o·te·leph·o·ny** (ray-di-oh-tĕ-lef-ŏ-nee) *n.*

ra·di·o·ther·a·py (ray-di-oh-ther-ă-pee) *n.* the treatment of disease by x-rays or other forms of radiation. **ra·di·o·ther'a·pist** *n.*

rad·ish (rad-ish) *n.* 1. a plant with a crisp hot-tasting root that is eaten raw. 2. its root.

ra·di·um (ray-di-ŭm) *n.* a radioactive metallic element obtained from pitchblende. ☐**radium therapy,** treatment of disease by the use of radium.

ra·di·us (ray-di-ŭs) *n.* (*pl.* **-di·i,** *pr.* -di-ī, **-di·us·es**) 1. a straight line extending from the center of a circle or sphere to its circumference. 2. the length of this line, the distance from a center, *all schools within a radius of 20 miles.* 3. the thicker of the two long bones in the human forearm, the corresponding bone in animals.

RAdm *abbr.* Rear Admiral.

ra·dome (ray-dohm) *n.* a dome covering or protecting radar equipment, especially on the outer surface of aircraft.

ra·don (ray-don) *n.* a gaseous radioactive inert element arising from the disintegration of radium.

RAF, R.A.F. *abbr.* Royal Air Force.

raf·fi·a (raf-i-ă) *n.* soft fiber from the leaves of a kind of palm tree, used for tying up plants and for making mats etc.

raff·ish (raf-ish) *adj.* looking vulgarly flashy or disreputable or rakish. **raff'ish·ly** *adv.* **raff'ish·ness** *n.*

raf·fle (raf-ĕl) *n.* a lottery with an object as the prize, especially as a method of raising money for a charity. **raffle** *v.* (**raf·fled, raf·fling**) to offer (a thing) as the prize in a raffle.

raft[1] (raft) *n.* a flat floating structure made of timber or other materials, used especially as a substitute for a boat. **raft** *v.* 1. to transport as or on a raft. 2. to form into a raft.

raft[2] *n.* (*informal*) a large collection of things.

raft·er (raf-tĕr) *n.* one of the sloping beams forming the framework of a roof.

rag[1] (rag) *n.* 1. a torn or frayed or worn piece of woven material. 2. rags used as material for stuffing things or making paper etc. 3. (*contemptuous*) a newspaper. ☐**rag doll,** a stuffed cloth doll. **rag paper,** a quality paper made from linen or cotton pulp.

rag[2] *v.* (**ragged, rag·ging**) (*informal*) to tease, to play practical jokes on (a person).

rag[3] *n.* a piece of ragtime music.

ra·ga (rah-gă) *n.* (in Indian music) 1. notes used as a basis for improvisation. 2. a piece of music using a particular raga.

rag·a·muf·fin (rag-ă-muf-in) *n.* a person in ragged dirty clothes.

rag·bag (rag-bag) *n.* a bag in which scraps of fabric etc. are kept for future use.

rage (rayj) *n.* 1. violent anger, a fit of this. 2. a craze; *be all the rage,* to be temporarily very popular or fashionable. **rage** *v.* (**raged, rag·ing**) 1. to show violent anger. 2. (of a storm or battle etc.) to be violent, to continue furiously.

rag·ged (rag-id) *adj.* 1. torn, frayed, 2. wearing

torn clothes. 3. jagged. 4. faulty, lacking finish or smoothness or uniformity, *that crew's rowing is a bit ragged.* **rag'ged·ly** *adv.* **rag'ged·ness** *n.* ☐**ragged robin,** a deep pink or white wildflower with ragged petals.

rag·lan (rag-lăn) *n.* 1. (also **raglan sleeve**) a type of sleeve that continues to the neck and is joined to the body of the garment by sloping seams. 2. a loose overcoat or other garment having such sleeves.

ra·gout (ra-goo) *n.* a stew of meat and vegetables.

rag·pick·er (rag-pik-ĕr) *n.* a collector and seller of rags.

rag·time (rag-tim) *n.* a form of music with much syncopation in the melody and a steadily accented bass.

rag·weed (rag-weed) *n.* a plant with allergenic pollen.

rag·wort (rag-wurt) *n.* a wild plant with yellow flowers and ragged leaves.

rah (rah) *interj.* hurrah.

raid (rayd) *n.* 1. a sudden attack and withdrawal made by a military party or by ships or aircraft. 2. an attack made in order to steal. 3. a surprise visit by police etc. to arrest suspected people or seize illicit goods. **raid** *v.* to make a raid on (a place etc.); *raid the icebox,* to take food from a refrigerator. **raid'er** *n.*

rail[1] (rayl) *n.* 1. a horizontal or sloping bar forming part of a fence or the top of banisters or a protection against contact or falling over etc., or for hanging things on. 2. one of the lines of metal bars on which trains or other wheeled vehicles run. 3. railroads as a means of transport, *send it by rail.* **rail** *v.* to fit or protect with a rail, *rail it off.* ☐**go off the rails,** (*informal*) to become disorganized or out of control or insane.

rail[2] *n.* a kind of small wading bird.

rail[3] *v.* to complain or protest or reproach strongly, *railing at him.*

rail·head (rayl-hed) *n.* 1. the farthest point reached by a railroad under construction. 2. the point on a railroad at which road transport of goods begins.

rail·ing (ray-ling) *n.* a fence of rails supported on upright metal bars.

rail·ler·y (ray-lĕ-ree) *n.* (*pl.* **-ler·ies**) good-humored joking or teasing.

rail·road (rayl-rohd) *n.* 1. a system of transport using rails on which trains run. 2. the organization, equipment, and people required for its working. **railroad** *v.* 1. to rush, to force into hasty action, *railroaded him into accepting.* 2. to send by railroad. 3. to rush (a bill) through the legislature. 4. (*informal*) to convict and sentence in great haste. **rail'road·er** *n.* **rail'road·ing** *n.* ☐**railroad flat,** an apartment arranged like a railroad car with all the rooms in a row and no hallway.

rail·way (rayl-way) *n.* 1. a track for wheeled equipment. 2. (*British*) a railroad.

rai·ment (ray-mĕnt) *n.* (*old use*) clothing.

rain (rayn) *n.* 1. condensed moisture of the atmosphere falling in separate drops. 2. a fall or spell of this; *the rains,* the rainy season in tropical countries. 3. a shower of things. **rain** *v.* to send down or fall as or like rain; *it rains* or *is raining,* rain falls; *it rains in,* rain penetrates the house etc. ☐**be rained out,** (of a program held outdoors) to be prevented by rain from taking place. **rain check,** a ticket given for later use when a sports event etc. is rained out; (*informal*) a promise that an offer will be maintained though deferred. **rain date,** the date on which an event will take place if the original date is canceled because of rain. **rain forest,** a thick forest where there is heavy rainfall. **rain hat,** a waterproof or water-resistant hat or head covering.

rain·bow (rayn-boh) *n.* an arch of colors formed in rain or spray by the sun's rays. □**rainbow trout,** a large trout of Pacific coastal waters and streams of North America, colored red, pink, and lavender with a side stripe.

rain·coat (rayn-koht) *n.* a waterproof or water-resistant coat.

rain·drop (rayn-drop) *n.* a single drop of rain.

rain·fall (rayn-fawl) *n.* the total amount of rain falling within a given area in a given time.

rain·mak·ing (rayn-may-king) *n.* an attempt to increase rainfall by artificial means. **rain′mak·er** *n.*

rain·spout (rayn-spowt) *n.* a duct for draining a roof gutter.

rain·storm (rayn-storm) *n.* a storm with heavy rainfall.

rain·wa·ter (rayn-waw-tĕr) *n.* water that has fallen as rain, not obtained from wells etc.

rain·y (ray-nee) *adj.* (**rain·i·er, rain·i·est**) in or on which much rains falls. □**save for a rainy day,** to save money etc. for a time when one may need it.

raise (rayz) *v.* (**raised, rais·ing**) 1. to bring to or toward a higher or upright position. 2. to increase the amount or heighten the level of, *raise prices.* 3. to cause, to rouse, *raise doubts; raise a laugh,* cause people to laugh. 4. to breed or grow, *raise sheep* or *corn.* 5. to bring up, to rear, *raise a family.* 6. to collect, to manage to obtain, *raise an army; raise a loan.* 7. to put forward, *raise objections.* 8. to cause to come or appear, *raise the ghost.* **raise** *n.* 1. an increase in wages or salary. 2. an act or instance of raising. **rais′er** *n.* □**raise Cain** *or* **hell** etc., *(informal)* to make an uproar; to show great anger. **raise from the dead,** to restore to life. **raise one's eyebrows,** to show disdain or suspicion. **raise one's glass to,** to drink a toast to. **raise one's voice,** to speak; to speak more loudly. **raise the alarm,** to give a warning of imminent danger. **raise the siege,** to end it by withdrawing the besieging forces or compelling them to withdraw.

▷Do not confuse *raise* with *rise. Stores raise their prices. Prices rise. Stores raised their prices. Prices rose.*

rai·sin (ray-zin) *n.* a partially dried grape.

rai·son d'ê·tre (ray-zohn det-rĕ) the reason for or purpose of a thing's existence. ▷French, = reason for being.

ra·jah, ra·ja (rah-jă) *n.* (in former times) an Indian king or prince.

rake¹ (rayk) *n.* 1. a long-handled tool with prongs used for drawing together hay or fallen leaves etc. or for smoothing loose soil or gravel. 2. any similar implement, such as that used by a croupier for drawing in money at a gambling table or by a person digging clams. **rake** *v.* (**raked, rak·ing**) 1. to gather or smooth with a rake. 2. to search, *have been raking among old records.* 3. to direct gunfire along (a line) from end to end, to use one's eyes or a camera in this way. □**rake up,** *(informal)* to revive the memory of (a quarrel or other unpleasant incident).

rake² *n.* a backward slope (as of a ship's mast or

funnel, or of a driver's seat). **rake** *v.* (**raked, rak·ing**) to set at a sloping angle.

rake³ *n.* a man who lives an irresponsible and immoral life.

rake-off (rayk-awf) *n.* *(informal)* an illicit commission or share of profits.

rak·ish¹ (ray-kish) *adj.* 1. (of a ship) smart and fast looking. 2. (of a person) debonair and jaunty in appearance or manner.

rakish² *adj.* immoral or debauched. **rak′ish·ly** *adv.* **rak′ish·ness** *n.*

Ra·leigh (raw-lee) the capital of North Carolina.

ral·ly¹ (ral-ee) *v.* (**ral·lied, ral·ly·ing**) 1. to bring or come together for a united effort. 2. to reassemble for effort after defeat. 3. to rouse or revive, *rally one's courage.* 4. to recover one's strength after illness. 5. (of stock exchange prices etc.) to increase after falling. **rally** *n.* (*pl.* **-lies**) 1. an act of rallying, a recovery of energy or spirits etc. 2. (in tennis etc.) a series of strokes before a point is scored. 3. a mass meeting of people with a common interest. 4. a driving competition for cars or motorcycles over public roads.

rally² *v.* (**ral·lied, ral·ly·ing**) to ridicule, to tease.

ram (ram) *n.* 1. an uncastrated male sheep. 2. *the Ram,* a sign of the zodiac, Aries. 3. a battering ram or similar device. 4. a striking or plunging device in various machines. **ram** *v.* (**rammed, ram·ming**) 1. to force or drive into place by pressure. 2. to strike and push heavily, to crash against.

Ram·a·dan (ram-ă-dahn) *n.* the ninth month of the Muslim year, when Muslims fast between sunrise and sunset.

ram·ble (ram-bĕl) *v.* (**ram·bled, ram·bling**) 1. to take a ramble. 2. to take or write disconnectedly, to wander from the subject. **ramble** *n.* a walk taken for pleasure, with or without a definite route.

ram·bler (ram-blĕr) *n.* 1. a person who rambles, one who goes for a ramble. 2. a climbing rose.

ram·bling (ram-bling) *adj.* 1. wandering. 2. speaking or spoken or written disconnectedly, wandering from one subject to another. 3. (of a plant) straggling, climbing. 4. (of a house or street or village etc.) extending in various directions irregularly.

ram·bunc·tious (ram-bungk-shŭs) *adj.* 1. unruly. 2. uncontrollably exuberant. **ram·bunc′tious·ness** *n.*

ram·e·kin (ram-ĕ-kin) *n.* 1. a small mold for baking and serving an individual portion of food. 2. something baked and served in this, *cheese ramekins.*

ram·ie (ram-ee) *n.* 1. a tall East Asian plant. 2. its fiber, woven into durable material.

ram·i·fi·ca·tion (ram-ĭ-fĭ-kay-shŏn) *n.* 1. an arrangement of branching parts. 2. a part of a complex structure, something arising from it, *the ramifications of the plot.*

ram·i·fy (ram-ĭ-fī) *v.* (**ram·i·fied, ram·i·fy·ing**) to branch out or cause to branch out, to arrange into subdivisions or branches.

ram·jet (ram-jet) *n.* a type of jet engine in which air is drawn in and compressed by the forward movement of the aircraft.

ramp (ramp) *n.* 1. a slope joining two levels of floor or road etc. 2. a movable set of stairs put beside an aircraft so that people may enter or leave.

ram·page (ram-payj) *v.* (**ram·paged, ram·**

pag·ing) to behave violently, to race about wildly or destructively. **rampage** (ram-payj) n. violent behavior. **ram·pag·er** (ram-pay-jĕr) n. **ram·pa·geous** (ram-pay-jŭs) adj. □**on the rampage,** rampaging.

ram·pant (ram-pănt) adj. unrestrained, flourishing excessively, disease was rampant in the poorer districts. **ram'pant·ly** adv.

ram·part (ram-pahrt) n. a broad bank of earth built as a fortification, usually topped with a parapet and wide enough for troops etc. to walk on.

ram·rod (ram-rod) n. 1. an iron rod formerly used for ramming a charge into muzzle-loading guns; like a ramrod, stiff and straight. 2. a cleaning rod for small guns.

ram·shack·le (ram-shak-ĕl) adj. tumbledown, rickety.

ran (ran) see **run.**

ranch (ranch) n. 1. a cattle breeding establishment. 2. a farm where certain other animals are bred, a mink ranch. **ranch** v. to farm on a ranch. **ranch'er** n. **ranch·man** (ranch-măn) n. (pl. -**men,** pr. mĕn) □**ranch house,** a house with all the rooms on the same level and a low-pitched roof.

ran·cho (ran-choh) n. (pl. -**chos**) a ranch.

ran·cid (ran-sid) adj. smelling or tasting unpleasant like stale fat. **ran'cid·ness** n. **ran·cid·i·ty** (ran-sid-i-tee) n.

ran·cor (rang-kŏr) n. bitter feeling or ill will. **ran'cor·ous** adj. **ran'cor·ous·ly** adv.

rand (rand) n. (pl. **rand**) the unit of money in South Africa and in certain other countries.

R & B abbr. rhythm and blues.

R & D abbr. research and development.

ran·dom (ran-dŏm) adj. done or made or taken etc. at random, a random choice. **ran'dom·ly** adv. **ran'dom·ness** n. □**at random,** without a particular aim or purpose or principle. **random access,** access to computer data in any order the user desires.

R and R abbr. 1. rest and recreation. 2. rest and recuperation.

rand·y (ran-dee) adj. (**rand·i·er, rand·i·est**) lustful, eager for sexual gratification. **ran'di·ness** n.

ra·nee = rani.

rang (rang) see **ring².**

range (raynj) n. 1. a line or tier or series of things, a range of mountains. 2. an extent, the limits between which something operates or varies. 3. the distance over which one can see or hear, or to which a sound or signal or missile can travel, the distance that a ship or aircraft etc. can travel without refueling. 4. the distance to a thing being aimed at or looked at, at close range. 5. a large open stretch of grazing or hunting ground. 6. a place with targets for shooting practice. 7. an electric or gas stove with burners and an oven. **range** v. (**ranged, rang·ing**) 1. to arrange in a row or ranks or in a specified way. 2. to extend, to reach. 3. to vary between limits. 4. to wander or go about a place. □**range finder,** a device for calculating the distance of an object to be shot at or photographed.

range·land (raynj-land) n. land suitable for grazing livestock.

rang·er (rayn-jĕr) n. 1. a forest warden. 2. a member of a body of troops policing a thinly populated area. 3. a person who ranges. 4. a specially trained assault soldier.

Ran·goon (rang-goon) the capital of Burma.

rang·y (rayn-jee) adj. (**rang·i·er, rang·i·est**) tall and thin.

ra·ni (rah-nee) n. 1. the wife of a rajah. 2. a Hindu female ruler.

rank¹ (rangk) n. 1. a line of people or things; the ranks, ordinary soldiers (not officers). 2. a place in a scale of quality or value etc., a position or grade, of Cabinet rank. 3. high social position, people of rank. **rank** v. 1. to arrange in a rank. 2. to assign a rank to. 3. to have a certain rank or place, he ranks among the great statesmen. □**close ranks,** to maintain solidarity. **the rank and file,** the ordinary undistinguished people of an organization.

rank² adj. 1. growing too thickly and coarsely. 2. (of land) full of weeds. 3. foul-smelling. 4. unmistakably bad, out-and-out, rank poison; rank injustice. **rank'ly** adv. **rank'ness** n.

rank·ing (rang-king) adj. senior in position, foremost, highly regarded.

ran·kle (rang-kĕl) v. (**ran·kled, ran·kling**) to cause lasting and bitter annoyance or resentment.

ran·sack (ran-sak) v. 1. to search thoroughly or roughly. 2. to rob or pillage (a place). **ran'sack·er** n.

ran·som (ran-sŏm) n. the release of a captive in return for money or other payment demanded by his captors, the payment itself. **ransom** v. to obtain the release of (a captive) in return for payment. □**hold for ransom,** to hold (a captive) and demand ransom for his release; to demand concessions from (a person etc.) by threatening some damaging action.

rant (rant) v. to make a speech loudly and violently and theatrically. **rant'er** n. **rant'ing·ly** adv.

ra·nun·cu·lus (ră-nung-kyŭ-lŭs) n. (pl. -**lus·es, -li,** pr. -lı) a plant of the buttercup family.

rap¹ (rap) n. 1. a quick sharp blow. 2. a knock, a tapping sound. 3.(slang) blame, punishment. 4. (slang) a conversation. **rap** v. (**rapped, rap·ping**) 1. to strike quickly and sharply. 2. to make a knocking or tapping sound. 3. to reprimand. 4. (slang) to talk. □**rap out,** to say suddenly or sharply. **take the rap,** (slang) to take the blame, to suffer the punishment.

rap² n. (informal) the least bit. □**not care** or **give a rap,** not care at all.

ra·pa·cious (ră-pay-shŭs) adj. greedy and grasping (especially for money), plundering and robbing others. **ra·pa'cious·ly** adv. **ra·pa'cious·ness** n. **ra·pac·i·ty** (ră-pas-i-tee) n.

rape¹ (rayp) n. the act or crime of having sexual intercourse by using force, especially with a woman. **rape** v. (**raped, rap·ing**) to commit rape on. **rap'er** n. **rap'ist** n.

rape² n. a European plant of the mustard family grown as food for sheep and for its seed, from which oil is obtained.

rap·id (rap-id) adj. quick, swift. **rap'id·ly** adv. **rap'id·ness** n. **ra·pid·i·ty** (ră-pid-i-tee) n. **rapid** n. (usually rapids) a swift current in a river, usually over obstructions. □**rapid eye movement,** rapid movement of the eyes during sleep, especially during dreaming, associated with changes in electrical activity of the brain. **rapid transit,** high-speed urban transport of passengers.

ra·pi·er (ray-pi-ĕr) n. a thin light double-edged sword, used for thrusting.

rap·ine (rap-in) n. plundering, robbery.

rap·pel (ră-pel) n. the descent of a steep cliff by

using a double rope fixed at a higher point. **rap·pel** *v.* **(rap·pelled, rap·pel·ling)** to make such a descent.

rap·port (ra-pohr) *n.* a harmonious and understanding relationship between people.

rap·proche·ment (ra-prohsh-mahn) *n.* the recommencement of harmonious relations. ▷French.

rap·scal·lion (rap-skal-yŏn) *n.* a rascal.

rapt (rapt) *adj.* very intent and absorbed, enraptured. **rapt′ly** *adv.* **rapt′ness** *n.*

rap·ture (rap-chŭr) *n.* intense delight. **rap′tur·ous** *adj.* **rap′tur·ous·ly** *adv.* □in raptures, feeling or expressing rapture. **raptures of the deep,** caisson disease.

ra·ra a·vis (rair-ă ay-vis) a person or thing rarely encountered, a rarity. ▷Latin.

rare¹ (rair) *adj.* **(rar·er, rar·est)** 1. seldom found or occurring, very uncommon. 2. *(informal)* exceptionally good, *had a rare time.* 3. of low density, thin, *the rare atmosphere in the Himalayas.* **rare′ly** *adv.* **rare′ness** *n.* □**rare earth,** any of a group of metallic elements with similar chemical properties.

rare² *adj.* **(rar·er, rar·est)** (of meat) undercooked. **rare′ness** *n.*

rare·bit (rair-bit) *n.* **Welsh rarebit,** Welsh rabbit *(see rabbit).*

rar·e·fy (rair-ĕ-fī) *v.* **(rar·e·fied, rar·e·fy·ing)** (of air etc.) to make or become less dense than is normal. **rar·e·fac·tion** (rair-ĕ-fak-shŏn) *n.*

rar·ing (rair-ing) *adj.* *(informal)* enthusiastic, *raring to go.*

rar·i·ty (rair-i-tee) *n.* 1. rareness. 2. something uncommon, a thing valued because it is rare.

ras·cal (ras-kăl) *n.* 1. a dishonest person. 2. a mischievous person. **ras′cal·ly** *adj. & adv.* **ras·cal·i·ty** (ras-kal-i-tee) *n.*

rash¹ (rash) *n.* 1. an eruption of spots or patches on the skin. 2. a sudden outbreak of unpleasant events, *a rash of robberies.*

rash² *adj.* acting or done without due consideration of the possible consequences or risks. **rash′ly** *adv.* **rash′ness** *n.*

rash·er (rash-ĕr) *n.* 1. a slice of bacon or ham. 2. a serving of bacon or ham.

rasp (rasp) *n.* 1. a coarse file with raised sharp points on its surface. 2. a rough grating sound. **rasp** *v.* 1. to scrape with a rasp. 2. to make a rough grating sound, *a rasping voice.* 3. to utter gratingly, *he rasped out orders.* 4. to have a grating effect upon (a person's feelings).

rasp·ber·ry (raz-ber-ee) *n.* (*pl.* **-ries**) 1. an edible sweet red conical berry. 2. the bramble that bears it. 3. *(slang)* a vulgar sound or expression of disapproval or rejection.

Ras·ta·far·i·an (ras-tă-fair-i-ăn) *n.* a member of a Jamaican sect regarding blacks as a people chosen by God for salvation and having their true homeland in Africa.

ras·ter (ras-tĕr) *n.* the area on which the image is produced on a picture tube in a television set.

rat (rat) *n.* 1. a rodent resembling a mouse but larger. 2. *(slang)* a scoundrel, a treacherous person. **rat** *v.* **(rat·ted, rat·ting)** 1. to hunt or kill rats. 2. *(slang)* to withdraw treacherously from an undertaking, to break a promise; *he ratted on us,* he informed the authorities of our actions. □**rat cheese,** cheddar cheese. **rat race,** *(informal)* a fiercely competitive struggle to main-

tain one's position in work or life. **rat snake,** a common snake that eats rodents. **rat-tail file,** a long narrow round file used to enlarge holes etc. **rat terrier,** a terrier dog bred for catching rats. **smell a rat,** to have suspicions of foul play etc.

rat·a·fi·a (rat-ă-fee-ă) *n.* a liqueur flavored with fruit kernels.

ratch·et (rach-it) *n.* 1. a series of notches on a bar or wheel *(ratchet wheel)* in which a pawl engages to prevent backward movement. 2. the bar or wheel bearing these.

rate¹ (rayt) *n.* 1. a standard of reckoning, obtained by expressing the quantity or amount of one thing with respect to another, *walked at a rate of four miles an hour.* 2. a measure of value or charge or cost, *postal rates.* 3. speed, *drove at a great rate.* **rate** *v.* **(rat·ed, rat·ing)** 1. to estimate the worth or value of. 2. to assign a value to. 3. to consider, to regard as, *we rate him among our benefactors.* 4. to rank or be regarded in a certain way, *he rates as a benefactor.* 5. to deserve, *that joke didn't rate a laugh.* **rat′er** *n.* □**at any rate,** in any possible case, no matter what happens; at least. **at this** *or* **that rate,** *(informal)* if this is true or a typical specimen.

rate² *v.* **(rat·ed, rat·ing)** to scold angrily. **rat′er** *n.*

rath·er (rath-ĕr) *adv.* 1. slightly, more so than not, *rather dark.* 2. more exactly, *he is lazy rather than incompetent.* 3. more willingly, by preference, *would rather not go.*

raths·kel·ler (raht-skel-ĕr) *n.* a beer hall or a restaurant in a basement in the German style.

rat·i·fy (rat-ĭ-fī) *v.* **(rat·i·fied, rat·i·fy·ing)** to confirm or assent formally and make (an agreement etc.) officially valid. **rat′i·fi·er** *n.* **rat·i·fi·ca·tion** (rat-ĭ-fĭ-kay-shŏn) *n.*

rat·ing (ray-ting) *n.* the classification assigned to a person or thing in respect of rank, position, quality, popularity, etc., as in *a credit rating* or *the rating of a television or radio program.*

ra·tio (ray-shoh) *n.* (*pl.* **-ti·os**) 1. the relationship between two amounts reckoned as the number of times one contains the other. 2. a proportion.

ra·ti·oc·i·na·tion (rash-i-os-ĭ-nay-shŏn) *n.* the use of logical processes and formal reasoning. **ra·ti·oc·i·nate** (rash-i-os-ĭ-nayt) *v.* **(ra·ti·oc·i·nat·ed, ra·ti·oc·i·nat·ing)** **ra·ti·oc·i·na·tive** (rash-i-os-ĭ-nay-tiv) *adj.* **ra·ti·oc·i·na·tor** *n.*

ra·tion (rash-ŏn, ray-shŏn) *n.* a fixed quantity (especially of food) allowed to one person. **ration** *v.* to limit (food etc.) to a fixed ration, to allow (a person) only a certain amount.

ra·tion·al (rash-ŏ-năl) *adj.* 1. able to reason. 2. sane. 3. based on reasoning, not unreasonable. **ra′tion·al·ly** *adv.* **ra·tion·al·i·ty** (rash-ŏ-nal-i-tee) *n.* □**rational number,** a number that can be expressed without radical signs or by the ratio of two integers. ▷Do not confuse *rational* with *rationale.*

ra·tion·ale (rash-ŏ-nal) *n.* a fundamental reason, the logical basis of something. ▷Do not confuse *rationale* with *rational.*

ra·tion·al·ism (rash-ŏ-nă-liz-ĕm) *n.* the theory that reason is the foundation of certainty in knowledge. **ra′tion·al·ist** *n.* **ra·tion·al·is·tic** (rash-ŏ-nă-lis-tik) *adj.* **ra·tion·al·is′ti·cal·ly** *adv.*

ra·tion·al·ize (rash-ŏ-nă-līz) v. (**ra·tion·al·ized, ra·tion·al·iz·ing**) 1. to make logical and consistent, *tried to rationalize English spelling.* 2. to invent a rational explanation of, *tried to rationalize their fears.* 3. to find false reasons for (irrational or unworthy behavior). **ra′tion·al·iz·er** n. **ra·tion·al·i·za·tion** (rash-ŏ-nă-li-zay-shŏn) n.

rat·line, rat·lin (rat-lin) n. a small line fastened across a ship's shrouds like the rungs of a ladder.

rats (rats) *interj.* (slang) an expression of disgust, disappointment, etc.

rats·bane (rats-bayn) n. rat poison.

rat·tan (ra-**tan**) n. 1. an East Indian climbing palm with long thin pliable stems. 2. a piece of rattan stem used as cane, wickerwork, etc.

rat·ter (rat-ĕr) n. a dog or cat as a hunter of rats.

rat·tle (rat-ĕl) v. (**rat·tled, rat·tling**) 1. to make or cause to make a rapid series of short sharp hard sounds, to cause such sounds by shaking something. 2. to move or travel with a rattling noise. 3. to utter rapidly, *rattled off the oath.* 4. *(slang)* to agitate or fluster, to make nervous. **rattle** n. 1. a rattling sound. 2. a device or toy for making a rattling sound. 3. noise, an uproar. **rat′tly** adv.

rat·tle·brain (rat-ĕl-brayn) n. (informal) a foolish or frivolous person. **rat′tle·brained′** adj.

rat·tler (rat-lĕr) n. 1. a rattlesnake. 2. a person or thing that rattles.

rat·tle·snake (rat-ĕl-snayk) n. a poisonous American snake with a rattling structure in its tail.

rat·tle·trap (rat-ĕl-trap) n. a rickety object, especially an old car.

rat·tling (rat-ling) adj. (informal) vigorous, brisk, *a rattling pace.* **rattling** adv. (informal) very, *a rattling good story.*

rat·trap (rat-trap) n. 1. a trap for catching rats. 2. a filthy dilapidated building, place, etc.

rat·ty (rat-ee) adj. (**-ti·er, -ti·est**) 1. of or relating to rats. 2. infested with rats. 3. (slang) shabby.

rau·cous (raw-kŭs) adj. loud and harsh sounding. **rau′cous·ly** adv. **rau′cous·ness** n.

raun·chy (rawn-chee) adj. (**-chi·er, -chi·est**) *(slang)* 1. slovenly, disreputable. 2. coarsely outspoken, earthy. **raun′chi·ness** n. (slang).

rau·wol·fi·a (raw-wuul-fi-ă) n. 1. an extract from the root of an Indian tree, with medicinal properties. 2. this tree.

rav·age (rav-ij) v. (**rav·aged, rav·ag·ing**) to do great damage to, to devastate. **rav′ag·er** n. ▷Do not confuse *ravage* with *ravish.*

rav·ag·es (rav-i-jiz) n. pl. damage, devastation.

rave (rayv) v. (**raved, rav·ing**) 1. to talk wildly or furiously, to talk nonsensically in delirium; *raving mad,* completely mad. 2. (of the wind or sea) to howl, to roar. 3. to speak with rapturous admiration. **rave** n. 1. an act or instance of raving. 2. (informal) a very enthusiastic review of a book or play etc. □**raving beauty,** a notably beautiful person.

rav·el (rav-ĕl) v. (**rav·eled, rav·el·ing**) 1. to separate or untwist the threads or fibers of (cloth). 2. to tangle, to become tangled. **ravel** n. a tangle.

ra·ven (ray-vĕn) n. a large bird with glossy black feathers and a hoarse cry. **raven** adj. (especially of hair) glossy black.

rav·en·ing (rav-ĕ-ning) adj. hungrily seeking prey.

rav·en·ous (rav-e-nŭs) adj. very hungry.

rav′en·ous·ly adv. **rav′en·ous·ness** n.

ra·vine (ră-veen) n. a deep narrow gorge or cleft between mountains.

ra·vi·o·li (rav-i-oh-lee) n. an Italian dish consisting of small pasta cases containing meat.

rav·ish (rav-ish) v. 1. to rape (a woman or girl). 2. to fill with delight, to enrapture. **rav′ish·er** n. **rav′ish·ment** n. ▷Do not confuse *ravish* with *ravage.*

rav·ish·ing (rav-i-shing) adj. very beautiful, filling people with delight.

raw (raw) adj. 1. not cooked. 2. in its natural state, not yet or not fully processed or manufactured, *raw hides.* 3. (of alcohol) undiluted. 4. crude in artistic quality, lacking finish. 5. inexperienced, untrained, fresh to something, *raw recruits.* 6. stripped of skin and with the underlying flesh exposed, sensitive because of this. 7. (of an edge of cloth) not a selvage and not hemmed. 8. (of weather) damp and chilly. **raw′ly** adv. **raw′ness** n. □**in the raw,** in a raw state; crude, without a softening or refining influence, *life in the raw;* (slang) naked. **raw deal,** unfair treatment. **raw material,** any material or product that is processed to make another; that from which something is made; people who are to be trained.

raw·boned (raw-bohnd) adj. gaunt.

raw·hide (raw-hīd) n. 1. untanned leather. 2. a rope or whip made of this.

ray¹ (ray) n. 1. a single line or narrow beam of light or other radiation. 2. a trace of something good, *a ray of hope.* 3. one of a set of radiating lines or parts of things.

ray² n. any of several large sea fishes related to the shark and used as food, especially the skate.

ray·on (ray-on) n. a synthetic fiber or fabric made from cellulose.

raze (rayz) v. (**razed, raz·ing**) to destroy completely, to tear down to the ground. ▷Do not confuse *raze* with *raise.*

ra·zor (ray-zŏr) n. an instrument with a sharp blade or cutters, used in cutting hair especially in shaving. □**razor clam,** a bivalve mollusk with a shell like the long thin blade of a razor.

ra·zor·back (ray-zŏr-bak) adj. having a back that is narrow and sharp. **razorback** n. a hog with a sharp back, common in the southern U.S. **ra′zor-backed′** adj.

razz (raz) v. (slang) to ridicule, to tease. **razz** n. (slang) a raspberry (definition 3).

raz·zle-daz·zle (raz-ĕl-daz-ĕl) n. (informal) excitement, a stir with some confusion.

razz·ma·tazz (raz-mă-taz) n. (informal) razzle-dazzle.

Rb symbol rubidium.

RBI, R.B.I. abbr. (in baseball) run(s) batted in.

R.C. abbr. 1. Red Cross. 2. Roman Catholic.

RCAF abbr. Royal Canadian Air Force.

R.C.Ch. abbr. Roman Catholic Church.

RCMP abbr. Royal Canadian Mounted Police.

rcpt. abbr. receipt.

rct. abbr. recruit.

rd. abbr. 1. road. 2. rod(s). 3. round.

R.D. abbr. 1. refer to drawer (written on a check by a bank when the account has insufficient money to pay it). 2. rural delivery.

re (ree) prep. in the matter of, about, concerning.

re (ray) n. a name for the second note of a scale in music.

Re symbol rhenium.

re- *prefix* again, as in *rebuild;* back again, as in *recurve.* ▷The number of words with this prefix is almost unlimited, and many of those whose meanings are obvious are not listed below.

REA *abbr.* Rural Electrification Administration.

reach (reech) *v.* 1. to stretch out or extend. 2. to go as far as, to arrive at. 3. to stretch out one's hand in order to touch or grasp or take something, *reached for his gun.* 4. to establish communication with, *you can reach me by phone.* 5. to achieve, to attain, *reached a speed of 100 mph; reached a conclusion.* **reach** *n.* 1. an act of reaching. 2. the distance over which a person or thing can reach, the extent covered by one's mental powers or abilities. 3. a continuous extent, especially of water.

reach·a·ble (ree-chă-bĕl) *adj.* able to be reached.

re·act (ree-akt) *v.* to cause or undergo a reaction.

re·ac·tance (ree-ak-tăns) *n.* a component of impedance of an alternating current circuit etc. due to capacitance or inductance or both.

re·ac·tant (ree-ak-tănt) *n.* a substance undergoing a chemical reaction.

re·ac·tion (ree-ak-shŏn) *n.* 1. a response to a stimulus or act or situation etc. 2. a chemical change produced by two or more substances acting upon each other. 3. the occurrence of one condition after a period of the opposite, as of depression after excitement. ☐**reaction engine,** an engine that promotes propulsion by the emission of a jet of particles etc. in the opposite direction to that of desired motion. **reaction time,** the length of time between occurrence of an external stimulus and the start of a response.

re·ac·tion·ar·y (ree-ak-shŏ-ner-ee) *adj.* (*pl.* **-ar·ies**) opposed to progress or reform. **reactionary** *n.* a person who favors reactionary policies.

re·ac·ti·vate (ree-ak-tĭ-vayt) *v.* (**re·ac·ti·vat·ed, re·ac·ti·vat·ing**) to make active once again.

re·ac·tive (ree-ak-tiv) *adj.* having the ability to react. **re·ac'tive·ly** *adv.* **re·ac·tiv·i·ty** (ree-ak-tiv-i-tee) *n.*

re·ac·tor (ree-ak-tŏr) *n.* an apparatus for the controlled production of nuclear energy.

read (reed) *v.* (**read,** *pr.* red, **read·ing**) 1. to be able to understand the meaning of (written or printed words or symbols). 2. to speak (written or printed words etc.) aloud, *read to the children; read them a story.* 3. to study or discover by reading, *we read about the accident.* 4. *(British)* to carry out a course of study; *he is reading for the bar,* is studying to become a lawyer. 5. to interpret mentally, to find implications, *don't read too much into it.* 6. to have a certain wording, *the sign reads "Keep Left."* 7. (of a measuring instrument) to indicate or register, *the thermometer reads 20°.* **read** *n.* a session of reading, *had a nice quiet read.* ☐**read a person's hand,** to interpret the markings on it as a fortune teller does. **read between the lines,** to discover a hidden or implicit meaning in something. **read out of the ranks,**

to expel from a political party etc., as if by reading a dismissal form. **read proofs,** to read and mark corrections on a printer's proofs. **read up on,** to make a special study of (a subject) by reading. **well read,** (of a person) having knowledge of a subject or good general acquaintance with literature through reading.

read·a·ble (ree-dă-bĕl) *adj.* 1. pleasant and interesting to read. 2. legible. **read'a·bly** *adv.* **read·a·ble·ness** (ree-dă-bĕl-nis) *n.* **read·a·bil·i·ty** (ree-dă-bil-i-tee) *n.*

re·ad·dress (ree-ă-dres) *v.* to alter the address on (a letter etc.).

read·er (ree-dĕr) *n.* 1. a person who reads. 2. a book containing passages for practice in reading by students of a language.

read·er·ship (ree-dĕr-ship) *n.* the readers of a newspaper etc., the number of these.

read·i·ly (red-i-lee) *adv.* 1. without reluctance, willingly. 2. without difficulty.

read·i·ness (red-i-nis) *n.* being ready.

read·ing (ree-ding) *n.* 1. the act of one who reads. 2. being read, the way something is read, an occasion when something is read. 3. books etc. intended to be read. 4. an interpretation or rendering, *his reading of the leading role in the play.* 5. the form of a specific passage in a text. 6. the amount that is indicated or registered by a measuring instrument. ☐**reading desk,** a desk or lectern for a speaker's notes or for a book while it is being read. **reading glasses,** eyeglasses used for reading or other close work. **reading lamp,** a lamp for giving light by which a person can read. **reading room,** a room (in a club or library etc.) set aside for people who wish to read.

re·ad·just (ree-ă-just) *v.* 1. to adjust (a thing) again. 2. to adapt oneself again. **re·ad·just'ment** *n.*

read·out (reed-owt) *n.* the information produced by a computer, this information displayed in understandable form.

read·y (red-ee) *adj.* (**read·i·er, read·i·est**) 1. in a fit state for immediate action or use. 2. willing, *always ready to help a friend.* 3. about or inclined to do something, *looked ready to collapse.* 4. quick, *a ready wit.* 5. easily available, *found a ready market.* **ready** *adv.* beforehand, *ready cooked.* **ready** *v.* (**read·ied, read·y·ing**) to make ready, to prepare. ☐**at the ready,** ready for action. **ready money,** actual coin or bills; payment on the spot, not credit. **ready room,** a room for airplane pilots to await orders and to be briefed.

read·y-made (red-ee-mayd) *adj.* 1. (of clothes) made for selling in standard shapes and sizes, not to individual customers' orders. 2. (of opinions or excuses etc.) of a standard type, not original.

read·y-to-wear (red-ee-tŏ-wair) *adj.* (of clothes) ready-made.

re·a·gent (ree-ay-jĕnt) *n.* a substance used to produce a chemical reaction.

re·al (ree-ăl) *adj.* 1. existing as a thing or occurring as a fact, not imaginary. 2. genuine, natural, not imitation, *real pearls.* 3. true, complete, worthy

of the name, *there's no real cure; now you're in real trouble,* in great trouble. 4. (of income or value etc.) with regard to its purchasing power. 5. consisting of immovable property such as land or houses, *real property; real estate.* **real** *adv. (informal)* really, very. **re′al·ness** *n.* □**for real,** *(slang)* real, actual; in reality. **real estate,** immovable property such as land or houses. **real number,** a number that does not have imaginary parts, a rational number. **real time,** actual time elapsed, as during a computer's solving of a problem. **real wages,** wages gauged by their purchasing power, allowing for changes in the value of money.
▷Careful writers use *really* in such phrases as *really happy* and *really excited.* They do not write *real happy* or *real excited.*

re·al·ism (ree-ă-liz-ĕm) *n.* 1. (in art and literature) being true to nature, representing things as they are in reality. 2. the attitude of a realist.

re·al·ist (ree-ă-list) *n.* a person who faces facts, one whose ideas and practices are based on facts not on ideals or illusions.

re·al·is·tic (ree-ă-lis-tik) *adj.* 1. true to nature, closely resembling what is imitated or portrayed. 2. facing facts, based on facts not on ideals or illusions. **re·al·is′ti·cal·ly** *adv.*

re·al·i·ty (ree-al-i-tee) *n.* (*pl.* **-ties**) 1. the quality of being real, resemblance to an original. 2. all that is real, the real world as distinct from imagination or fantasy, *lost his grip on reality.* 3. something that exists or that is real, *the realities of the situation.*

re·al·ize (ree-ă-lız) *v.* (**re·al·ized, re·al·iz·ing**) 1. to be fully aware of, to accept as a fact, *realized his mistake.* 2. to convert (a hope or plan) into a fact, *our hopes were realized.* 3. to convert (securities or property) into money by selling. 4. to obtain or bring in as profit, (of goods) to fetch as a price. **re′al·iz·er** *n.* **re·al·i·za·tion** (ree-ă-li-**zay**-shŏn) *n.*

re·al·ly (ree-ă-lee) *adv.* 1. in fact. 2. positively, indeed, *a really nice girl.* **really** *interj.* an expression of interest or surprise or mild protest. ▷See the note under **real.**

realm (relm) *n.* 1. a kingdom, *peers of the realm.* 2. a field of activity or interest, *the realms of science.*

re·al·po·li·tik (ray-ahl-poh-li-teek) *n.* politics based on realities and material needs, rather than on morals or ideals.

Re·al·tor (ree-ăl-tŏr) *n. (trademark)* a person who deals in real estate, a member of the National Association of Realtors.

re·al·ty (ree-ăl-tee) *n.* real estate.

ream¹ (reem) *n.* 1. a quantity of paper (about five hundred sheets) of the same size. 2. reams, *(informal)* a great quantity of written matter.

ream² *v.* 1. to widen or shape with a reamer. 2. to extract or clean with a reamer.

ream·er (ree-mĕr) *n.* a tool with sharp edges, used to enlarge or finish a hole.

reap (reep) *v.* 1. to cut (grain or a similar crop) as harvest. 2. to receive as the consequence of actions, *reaped great benefit from their training.* **reap′er** *n.* □**the Grim Reaper,** death.

re·ap·pear (ree-ă-peer) *v.* to appear again. **re·ap·pear′ance** *n.*

re·ap·prais·al (ree-ă-pray-zăl) *n.* a new appraisal.

rear¹ (reer) *n.* the back part of something. **rear** *adj.* situated at or in the rear. □**bring up the rear,** *see* **bring. rear admiral,** *see* **admiral. rear end,** *(informal)* the buttocks. **rear guard,** the body of troops detached to protect the rear, especially in retreats. **rear-view mirror,** a mirror placed so that the driver of a vehicle can see traffic etc. behind reflected in it.

rear² *v.* 1. to bring up and educate (children), to breed and look after (animals), to cultivate (plants). 2. to build or set up (a monument etc.). 3. (of a horse etc.) to raise itself on its hind legs. 4. (of a building etc.) to extend to a great height.

re·arm (ree-ahrm) *v.* to arm again. **re·ar·ma·ment** (ree-ahr-mă-mĕnt) *n.*

rear·most (reer-mohst) *adj.* farthest back.

re·ar·range (ree-ă-raynj) *v.* (**re·ar·ranged, re·ar·rang·ing**) to arrange in a different way or order. **re·ar·range′ment** *n.*

rear·ward (reer-wărd) *adj.* at or toward the rear. **rear·ward, rear·wards** *adv.* toward the rear.

rea·son (ree-zŏn) *n.* 1. a motive or cause or justification of something, a fact put forward as this. 2. the ability to think and understand and draw conclusions. 3. sanity, *lost his reason.* 4. good sense or judgment, what is right or practical or possible; *will do anything within reason,* anything that seems reasonable. **reason** *v.* 1. to use one's ability to think and draw conclusions, to state as a step in this, *reasoning that the burglar was familiar with the house.* 2. to try to persuade someone by argument, *reasoned with the militants.* **rea′son·er** *n.* **rea′son·ing** *n.* □**by reason of,** through logical thinking. **stand to reason,** it can be logically proved that, it would be generally admitted. **within reason,** within the bounds of moderation.

rea·son·a·ble (ree-zŏ-nă-bĕl) *adj.* 1. ready to use or listen to reason, sensible, *a reasonable person.* 2. in accordance with reason, not absurd, logical. 3. moderate, not expensive or extortionate, *reasonable prices.* **rea′son·a·bly** *adv.* **rea′son·a·ble·ness** *n.* **rea·son·a·bil·i·ty** (ree-zŏ-nă-bil-i-tee) *n.*

re·as·sure (ree-ă-shoor) *v.* (**re·as·sured, re·as·sur·ing**) to restore confidence to, to remove the fears or doubts of. **re·as·sur′ance** *n.* **re·as·sur′ing·ly** *adv.*

re·bate (ree-bayt) *n.* a reduction in the amount to be paid, a partial refund. **rebate** *v.* (**re·bat·**

---

re·a·lign′ *v.*
re·a·lign′ment *n.*
re·al′lo·cate *v.* (-cat·ed, -cat·ing)
re·al·lo·ca′tion *n.*
re·ap·pli·ca′tion *n.*
re·ap·ply′ *v.* (-plied, -ply·ing)
re·ap·point′ *v.*
re·ap·point′ment *n.*

re·ap·por′tion *v.*
re·ap·por′tion·ment *n.*
re·ap·praise′ *v.* (-praised, -prais·ing)
re·ar·rest′ *v.*
re·as·sem′ble *v.* (-bled, -bling)
re·as·sem′bly *n.* (*pl.* -blies)
re·as·sert′ *v.*
re·as·ser′tion *n.*

re·as·sess′ *v.*
re·as·sess′ment *n.*
re·as·sign′ *v.*
re·as·sign′ment *n.*
re·a·wake′ *v.* (-woke *or* -waked, -wak·ing)
re·a·wak′en *v.*
re·bap′tism *n.*
re·bap′tize *v.* (-tized, -tiz·ing)

ed, **re·bat·ing**) to deduct or refund (money) from a bill or payment.

reb·el (ri-bel) *v.* (**re·belled, re·bel·ling**) 1. to refuse to continue allegiance to an established government, to take up arms against it. 2. to resist authority or control, to refuse to obey, to protest strongly. **rebel** (reb-ĕl) *n.* a person who rebels. **rebel** (reb-ĕl) *adj.* rebellious, in rebellion.

re·bel·lion (ri-bel-yŏn) *n.* open resistance to authority, especially organized armed resistance to an established government.

re·bel·lious (ri-bel-yŭs) *adj.* rebelling, insubordinate. **re·bel'lious·ly** *adv.* **re·bel'lious·ness** *n.*

re·birth (ree-burth) *n.* a return to life or activity, a revival.

re·born (ree-born) *adj.* 1. born again. 2. spiritually regenerated.

re·bound (ri-bownd) *v.* 1. to spring back after an impact with something. 2. to have an adverse effect upon the originator. 3. (in basketball) to take possession of the ball rebounding from the basket. **re·bound** (ree-bownd) *n.* 1. an act or instance of rebounding. 2. a basketball as it bounces off the basket rim or backboard. □**on the rebound,** (of a hit or catch) made to a ball that is rebounding; (of an action etc.) done while still reacting to depression or disappointment.

re·bo·zo (ri-boh-zoh) *n.* (*pl.* **-zos**) a long scarf worn over the head and shoulders by women of Spain and some Latin American countries.

re·buff (ri-buf) *n.* an unkind or contemptuous refusal, a snub. **rebuff** *v.* to give a rebuff to.

re·build (ree-bild) *v.* (**re·built, re·build·ing**) to build again after destruction or demolition.

re·buke (ri-byook) *v.* (**re·buked, re·buk·ing**) to reprove sharply or severely. **rebuke** *n.* a sharp or severe reproof.

re·bus (ree-bŭs) *n.* (*pl.* **-bus·es**) a riddle in which pictures represent words or phrases.

re·but (ri-but) *v.* (**re·but·ted, re·but·ting**) to refute or disprove (evidence or an accusation). **re·but'tal** *n.* **re·but'ter** *n.*

rec. *abbr.* 1. receipt. 2. record. 3. recording. 4. recreation.

re·cal·ci·trant (ri-kal-si-trănt) *adj.* disobedient, resisting authority or discipline. **re·cal'ci·trance** *n.* **re·cal·ci·tran·cy** (ri-kal-si-trăn-see) *n.*

re·call (ri-kawl) *v.* 1. to summon (a person) to return from a place. 2. to bring back into the mind, to remember or cause to remember. 3. to revoke, to annul. 4. to call back a defective product. **recall** (ri-kawl, ree-kawl) *n.* 1. recalling, being recalled. 2. a summons to come back. 3. the suspension of a public official from office by popular vote. 4. the act of remembering. 5. the act of annulling.

re·cant (ri-kant) *v.* to withdraw one's former statement or belief etc. formally, rejecting it as wrong or heretical. **re·can·ta·tion** (ree-kan-tay-shŏn) *n.*

re·cap¹ (ree-kap, ree-kap) *v.* (**re·capped, re·cap·ping**) (*informal*) to recapitulate. **recap** (ree-kap) *n.* (*informal*) a recapitulation.

recap² (ree-kap) *v.* (**re·capped, re·cap·ping**) to retread (a worn tire). **recap** (ree-kap) *n.* (*informal*) a recapped tire.

re·ca·pit·u·late (ree-kă-pich-ŭ-layt) *v.* (**re·ca·pit·u·lat·ed, re·ca·pit·u·lat·ing**) to state

again the main points of what has been said or discussed. **re·ca·pit·u·la·tion** (ree-kă-pich-ŭ-lay-shŏn) *n.* **re·ca·pit·u·la·tive** (ree-kă-pich-ŭ-lay-tiv) *adj.*

re·cap·ture (ree-kap-chŭr) *v.* (**re·cap·tured, re·cap·tur·ing**) 1. to capture (a person or thing that has escaped or been lost to an enemy). 2. to succeed in experiencing (a former state or emotion) again. **recapture** *n.* recapturing.

re·cast (ree-kast) *v.* (**re·cast, re·cast·ing**) to cast again, to put into a different form, *recast the question in different words.*

recd., rec'd. *abbr.* received.

re·cede (ri-seed) *v.* (**re·ced·ed, re·ced·ing**) 1. to go or shrink back from a certain point, to seem to go away from the observer, *the floods receded; the shore receded as we sailed away.* 2. to slope backward, *a receding chin.*

re·ceipt (ri-seet) *n.* 1. receiving, being received, *on receipt of your letter.* 2. a written acknowledgment that something has been received or that money has been paid. 3. (*old use*) a recipe. 4. *receipts,* the amount of money received. **receipt** *v.* to mark (a bill) as having been paid.

re·ceiv·a·ble (ri-see-vă-bĕl) *adj.* 1. capable of being received. 2. subject to payment, **accounts receivable.** **re·ceiv·a·bil·i·ty** (ri-see-vă-bil-i-tee) *n.*

re·ceive (ri-seev) *v.* (**re·ceived, re·ceiv·ing**) 1. to acquire or accept or take in (something offered or sent or given). 2. to experience, to be treated with, *it received close attention.* 3. to take the force or weight or impact of. 4. to serve as a receptacle for. 5. to allow to enter as a member or guest. 6. to greet on arrival. □**be on the receiving end,** to be the one who has to submit to something unpleasant. **receiving line,** a line formed by the host, hostess, and guests of honor to greet the guests.

re·ceiv·er (ri-see-vĕr) *n.* 1. a person or thing that receives something. 2. one who accepts stolen goods while knowing them to be stolen. 3. a person appointed by a court to be custodian of a business or property or funds of parties involved in a lawsuit. 4. a radio or television apparatus that receives broadcast signals and converts them into sound or a picture. 5. the part of a telephone that receives the incoming sound and is held to the ear.

re·ceiv·er·ship (ri-see-vĕr-ship) *n.* the position or function of an official receiver. □**in receivership,** under the jurisdiction of a court-appointed receiver.

re·cent (ree-sĕnt) *adj.* 1. not long past, happening or begun in a time shortly before the present. 2. *Recent,* of the most recent geologic epoch, including the present time. **Recent** *n.* the Recent epoch. **re'cent·ly** *adv.* **re'cent·ness** *n.* **re·cen·cy** (ree-sĕn-see) *n.*

re·cep·ta·cle (ri-sep-tă-kĕl) *n.* 1. something for holding or containing what is put into it. 2. an electrical outlet.

re·cep·tion (ri-sep-shŏn) *n.* 1. receiving, being received. 2. the way something is received, *the speech got a cool reception.* 3. an assembly held to receive guests, *wedding reception.* 4. the receiving of broadcast signals, the efficiency of this, *reception was poor.* □**reception room,** a room where visitors are received.

re·bill' *v.*
re·boil' *v.*

re·broad'cast *v.* (**-cast** *or* **-cast·ed, -cast·ing**)

re·budg'et *v.* (**-et·ed, -et·ing**)

re·cep·tion·ist (ri-sep-shŏ-nist) *n.* a person employed to receive and direct callers or clients or patients.

re·cep·tive (ri-sep-tiv) *adj.* able or quick or willing to receive knowledge or ideas or suggestions etc. **re·cep'tive·ly** *adv.* **re·cep'tive·ness** *n.* **re·cep·tiv·i·ty** (ree-sep-tiv-i-tee) *n.*

re·cep·tor (ri-sep-tŏr) *n.* an organ able to respond to light, heat, drugs, etc. and transmit a signal to a sensory nerve.

re·cess (ri-ses, ree-ses) *n.* 1. a part or space set back from the line of a wall etc., a small hollow place inside something. 2. temporary cessation from business, a time of this, *while Congress is in recess.* **recess** *v.* to make a recess in or of (a wall etc.), to set back.

re·ces·sion (ri-sesh-ŏn) *n.* 1. receding from a point or level. 2. a temporary decline in economic activity or prosperity. **re·ces'sion·ar·y** *adj.*

re·ces·sion·al (ri-sesh-ŏ-năl) *n.* a hymn sung while clergy and choir withdraw after a church service.

re·ces·sive (ri-ses-iv) *adj.* 1. tending to recede. 2. (of inherited characteristics) remaining latent when a dominant characteristic is present.

re·charge (ree-chahrj) *v.* **(re·charged, re·charg·ing)** to charge (a battery or gun etc.) again. ☐**recharge one's batteries,** to have a period of rest and recovery.

re·charge·a·ble (ree-chahr-jă-běl) *adj.* able to be recharged.

re·cher·ché (rě-shair-shay) *adj.* 1. devised or selected with care. 2. farfetched.

re·cid·i·vist (ri-sid-ĭ-vist) *n.* a person who constantly commits crimes and seems unable to be cured of criminal tendencies, a persistent offender. **re·cid'i·vism** *n.* **re·cid·i·vis·tic** (ri-sid-ĭ-vis-tik) *adj.*

recip. *abbr.* 1. reciprocal. 2. reciprocity.

rec·i·pe (res-ĭ-pee) *n.* 1. directions for preparing a dish etc. in cookery. 2. a way of achieving something, *a recipe for success.*

re·cip·i·ent (ri-sip-i-ěnt) *n.* a person who receives something.

re·cip·ro·cal (ri-sip-rŏ-kăl) *adj.* 1. given or received in return, *reciprocal help.* 2. given or felt by each toward the other, mutual, *reciprocal affection.* 3. corresponding but the other way around, *I thought he was a waiter, while he made the reciprocal mistake and thought that I was.* **reciprocal** *n.* a mathematical expression related to another in the way that 2/3 is related to 3/2. **re·cip'ro·cal·ly** *adv.*

re·cip·ro·cate (ri-sip-rŏ-kayt) *v.* **(re·cip·ro·cat·ed, re·cip·ro·cat·ing)** 1. to give and receive, to make a return for something done or given or felt. 2. (of a machine part) to move backward and forward alternately. **re·cip·ro·ca·tive** (ri-sip-rŏ-kay-tiv) *adj.* **re·cip·ro·ca·tion** (ri-sip-rŏ-kay-shŏn) *n.* ☐**reciprocating engine,** one in which the backward and forward motion of pistons produces rotary movement of the crankshaft.

rec·i·proc·i·ty (res-ĭ-pros-i-tee) *n.* a reciprocal condition or action, the giving of privileges in return for similar privileges, especially a foreign trade exchange or agreement.

re·cit·al (ri-sɪ-tăl) *n.* 1. reciting. 2. a long account of a series of events. 3. a musical entertainment given by one performer or group, a similar entertainment of any kind (as by a dancer). **re·cit'al·ist** *n.*

rec·i·ta·tion (res-i-tay-shŏn) *n.* 1. reciting. 2. a thing recited.

rec·i·ta·tive (res-i-tă-teev) *n.* a narrative or conversational part of an opera or oratorio, sung in a rhythm imitating that of ordinary speech.

re·cite (ri-sɪt) *v.* **(re·cit·ed, re·cit·ing)** 1. to repeat (a passage) aloud from memory, especially before an audience. 2. to state (facts) in order. **re·cit'er** *n.*

reck·less (rek-lis) *adj.* wildly impulsive, rash. **reck'less·ly** *adv.* **reck'less·ness** *n.*

reck·on (rek-ŏn) *v.* 1. to count up. 2. to include in a total or as a member of a particular class. 3. to have as one's opinion, to feel confident, *I reckon we shall win.* 4. to rely or base one's plans, *we reckoned on your support.* **reck'on·er** *n.* ☐**reckon with,** to take into account; *a person* or *thing to be reckoned with,* one that must be considered as important.

reck·on·ing (rek-ŏ-ning) *n.* 1. a time of reckoning. 2. a settling of accounts. 3. a calculation or expectation. ☐**day of reckoning,** the time when one must atone for one's actions or be punished.

re·claim (ree-klaym) *v.* 1. to take action so as to recover possession of. 2. to make (flooded or waste land) usable, as by draining or irrigating it. 3. to reform (a person). **re·claim'a·ble** *adj.* **rec·la·ma·tion** (rek-lă-may-shŏn) *n.*

re·cline (ri-klɪn) *v.* **(re·clined, re·clin·ing)** to have or put one's body in a more or less horizontal or leaning position.

re·clin·er (ri-klɪ-něr) *n.* 1. a person who reclines. 2. a chair with an adjustable sloping back.

rec·luse (rek-loos, ri-kloos) *n.* a person who lives alone and avoids mixing with people.

rec·og·ni·tion (rek-ŏg-nish-ŏn) *n.* recognizing, being recognized; *a presentation in recognition of his services,* as a token of appreciation.

rec·og·niz·a·ble (rek-ŏg-nɪ-ză-běl) *adj.* able to be recognized. **rec'og·niz·a·bly** *adv.*

re·cog·ni·zance (ri-kog-ni-zăns) *n.* a pledge made to a law court or magistrate that a person will observe some condition (such as to keep the peace) or appear when summoned, a sum of money pledged as surety for this.

rec·og·nize (rek-ŏg-nɪz) *v.* **(rec·og·nized, rec·og·niz·ing)** 1. to know again, to identify from one's previous knowledge or experience. 2. to realize or admit the nature of, *recognized the hopelessness of the situation.* 3. to acknowledge or accept formally as genuine or valid, *France has recognized the island's new government.* 4. to show appreciation of (ability or service etc.) by giving an honor or reward. 5. (of a chairman in a formal debate) to allow (a particular person) the right to speak next.

re·coil (ri-koil) *v.* 1. to move or spring back suddenly, to rebound. 2. to draw oneself back in fear or disgust. 3. to have an adverse effect upon the originator. **recoil** (ree-koil) *n.* the act or sensation of recoiling. **re·coil'less** *adj.*

---

re·chart' *v.*
re·check' *v.*
re·chris'ten *v.*

re·clas'si·fy *v.* **(-fied, -fy·ing)**
re·clean' *v.*

re·clothe' *v.* **(-clothed** *or* **-clad, -cloth·ing)**
re·coat' *v.*

rec·ol·lect (rek-ŏ-lekt) v. to remember. **rec· ol·lec·tion** (rek-ŏ-lek-shŏn) n.

re·com·bi·nant (ree-kom-bi-nănt) adj. of or relating to new combinations of genetic material.

re·com·mence (ree-kŏ-mens) v. **(re·com· menced, re·com·menc·ing)** to begin again. **re·com·mence'ment** n.

rec·om·mend (rek-ŏ-mend) v. 1. to advise (a course of action or a treatment etc.). 2. to praise as worthy of employment or favor or trial etc. 3. (of qualities or conduct) to make acceptable or desirable, this plan has much to recommend it. **rec·om·mend'a·ble** adj. **rec·om· mend'er** n. **rec·om·mend·a·to·ry** (rek-ŏ-men-dă-tohr-ee) adj. **rec·om·men·da·tion** (rek-ŏ-men-day-shŏn) n.

rec·om·pense (rek-ŏm-pens) v. **rec·om· pensed, rec·om·pen·sing)** to repay or reward, to compensate. **recompense** n. payment or reward etc. in return for something.

rec·on·cile (rek-ŏn-sıl) v. **(rec·on·ciled, rec· on·cil·ing)** 1. to restore friendship between (people) after an estrangement or quarrel. 2. to induce (a person or oneself) to accept an unwelcome fact or situation, is now reconciled to living far from home. 3. to bring (facts or statements etc.) into harmony or compatibility when they appear to conflict. **rec'on·cil·a·ble** adj. **rec'on·cil·a· bly** adv. **rec'on·ciler** n. **rec'on·cile·ment** n. **rec·on·cil·i·a·tion** (rek-ŏn-sil-i-ay-shŏn) n.

rec·on·dite (rek-ŏn-dıt, ri-kon-dıt) adj. (of a subject) obscure, (of an author) writing about an obscure subject. **rec'on·dite·ly** adv. **rec'on· dite·ness** n.

re·con·di·tion (ree-kŏn-dish-ŏn) v. to overhaul and make any necessary repairs to.

re·con·nais·sance (ri-kon-ă-săns) n. an exploration or examination of an area in order to obtain information about it (especially for military purposes), a preliminary survey.

re·con·noi·ter (ree-kŏ-noi-tĕr) v. to make a reconnaissance of (an area), to make a preliminary survey.

re·con·sid·er (ree-kŏn-sid-ĕr) v. to consider again, especially with the possibility of changing one's former decision. **re·con·sid·er·a·tion** (ree-kŏn-sid-ĕ-ray-shŏn) n.

re·con·sti·tute (ree-kon-sti-toot) v. **(re·con· sti·tut·ed, re·con·sti·tut·ing)** to reconstruct, to reorganize. **re·con·sti·tu·tion** (ree-kon-sti-too-shŏn) n.

re·con·struct (ree-kŏn-strukt) v. 1. to construct or build again. 2. to create or enact (past events) again, as in investigating the circumstances of a crime. **re·con·struc'tive** adj. **re·con·struc· tion** n. (ree-kŏn-struk-shŏn) □**Reconstruction,** the reincorporation of the seceded states into the U.S. (1865–77) after the Civil War.

re·cord (rek-ŏrd) n. 1. information preserved in a permanent form, especially in writing. 2. a document etc. bearing this. 3. a disk bearing recorded

sound. 4. facts known about a person's past, has a good record of service; have a record or a police record, to have past criminal convictions that are on record. 5. the best performance or most remarkable event etc. of its kind that is known; hold the record, to be the one who achieved this. **record** adj. best or highest or most extreme hitherto recorded, a record crop. **record** (ri-kord) v. 1. to set down in writing or other permanent form. 2. to preserve (sound) on a disk or magnetic tape for later reproduction. 3. to register on a measuring instrument. □**for the record,** so that facts may be recorded. **off the record,** stated unofficially or not for publication. **on record,** preserved in written records. **record changer,** that part of a record player that moves the records into playing position or removes them after playing. **record player,** an apparatus for reproducing sound from disks on which it is recorded.

re·cord-break·ing (rek-ŏrd-bray-king) adj. surpassing all previous records.

re·cord·er (ri-kor-dĕr) n. 1. a person that records something. 2. a judge in certain law courts. 3. a kind of flute held forward and downward from the mouth as it is played. 4. a machine or device that records sound.

re·cord·ing (ri-kor-ding) n. sound recorded on a disk or magnetic tape etc.

re·count[1] (ri-kownt) v. to narrate, to tell in detail, recounted his adventures.

re·count[2] (ree-kownt) v. to count again. **recount** (ree-kownt) n. a second counting, especially of election votes to check the totals.

re·coup (ri-koop) v. 1. to recover what one has lost or its equivalent, recoup oneself or recoup one's losses. 2. to reimburse or compensate, recoup a person for his losses.

re·course (ree-kohrs) n. a source of help. □**have recourse to,** to turn to (a person or thing) for help.

re·cov·er (ri-kuv-ĕr) v. 1. to regain possession or use or control of. 2. to obtain as compensation, sought to recover damages from the company. 3. to return to a normal condition after illness or unconsciousness. **re·cov'er·a·ble** adj. **re· cov'er·y** n. □**recover oneself,** to regain consciousness or calmness, or one's balance.

re·cov·er (ree-kuv-ĕr) v. to cover again, as a couch.

rec·re·ant (rek-ri-ănt) n. a coward, a traitor. **recreant** adj. craven, cowardly. **rec're·ant· ly** adv. **rec're·ance** n. **rec·re·an·cy** (rek-ri-ăn-see) n.

rec·re·ate (rek-ri-ayt) v. **(rec·re·at·ed, rec· re·at·ing)** to give new life or freshness to. **rec· re·a·tive** (rek-ri-ay-tiv) adj.

re·cre·ate (ree-kri-ayt) v. **(re·cre·at·ed, re· cre·at·ing)** to create over again.

rec·re·a·tion (rek-ri-ay-shŏn) n. the process or means of refreshing or entertaining oneself after work by some pleasurable activity. **rec·re· a'tion·al** adj. **rec·re·a·tive** (rek-ri-ay-tiv) adj.

re·com·bine' v. (-bined, -bin·ing)
re·com·mis'sion v.
re·con'cen·trate v. (-trat·ed, -trat·ing)
re·con·cen·tra'tion n.
re·con·den·sa'tion n.
re·con·dense' v. (-densed, -dens·ing)

re·con·firm' v.
re·con·fir·ma'tion n.
re·con·nect' v.
re·con'quer v.
re·con'quest n.
re·con'se·crate v. (-crat·ed, -crat·ing)
re·con·se·cra'tion n.
re·con·sign' v.

re·con·sign'ment n.
re·con·sol'i·date v. (-dat·ed, -dat·ing)
re·con·vene' v. (-vened, -ven·ing)
re·con·vert' v.
re·cook' v.
re·cop'y v. (-cop·ied, -cop·y·ing)

☐**recreation ground,** a public playground for children.
re·cre·a·tion (ree-kri-ay-shŏn) *n.* a rebirth.
re·crim·i·nate (ri-krim-ĭ-nayt) *v.* (**re·crim·i·nat·ed, re·crim·i·nat·ing**) 1. to indulge in counter charges. 2. to retort with an accusation. **re·crim·i·na·tive** (ri-krim-ĭ-nay-tiv) *adj.* **re·crim·i·na·tory** (ri-krim-ĭ-nă-tohr-ee) *adj.*
re·crim·i·na·tion (ri-krim-ĭ-nay-shŏn) *n.* an angry retort or accusation made in retaliation.
re·cru·desce (ree-kroo-des) *v.* (**re·cru·desced, re·cru·desc·ing**) (of a disease or sore or discontent) to break out again. **re·cru·des·cence** *n.* **re·cru·des·cent** *adj.*
re·cruit (ri-kroot) *n.* 1. a person who has just joined the armed forces and is not yet trained. 2. a new member of a society or other group. **recruit** *v.* 1. to form (an army or other group) by enlisting recruits. 2. to enlist (a person) as a recruit. 3. to refresh, *recruit one's strength.* **re·cruit'er** *n.* **re·cruit'ment** *n.*
rect. *abbr.* 1. receipt. 2. rectangle. 3. rectangular. 4. rectified. 5. rector. 6. rectory.
rect·al (rek-tăl) *adj.* of the rectum. **rec'tal·ly** *adv.*
rec·tan·gle (rek-tang-gĕl) *n.* a four-sided geometric figure with four right angles, especially one with adjacent sides unequal in length. **rec·tan·gu·lar** (rek-tang-gyŭ-lăr) *adj.*
rec·ti·fi·a·ble (rek-tĭ-fĭ-ă-bĕl) *adj.* able to be rectified.
rec·ti·fi·er (rek-tĭ-fĭ-ĕr) *n.* 1. an object that converts alternating current to direct current. 2. a person that makes things right or adjusts or corrects things.
rec·ti·fy (rek-tĭ-fī) *v.* (**rec·ti·fied, rec·ti·fy·ing**) 1. to put right, to correct, *rectify the error.* 2. to purify or refine, especially by distillation. 3. to convert (alternating current) to direct current. **rec·ti·fi·ca·tion** (rek-tĭ-fĭ-kay-shŏn) *n.*
rec·ti·lin·e·ar (rek-tĭ-lin-i-ăr) *adj.* bounded by straight lines, *a rectilinear figure.*
rec·ti·tude (rek-ti-tood) *n.* moral goodness, correctness of behavior or procedure.
rec·to (rek-toh) *n.* (*pl.* **-tos**) the right-hand page of an open book.
rec·tor (rek-tŏr) *n.* 1. a clergyman in charge of a parish. 2. the head of certain universities, colleges, schools, and religious institutions. **rec·tor·ate** (rek-tŏ-rit) *n.*
rec·to·ry (rek-tŏ-ree) *n.* (*pl.* **-ries**) the house of a rector.
rec·tum (rek-tŭm) *n.* (*pl.* **-tums, -ta,** *pr.* **-tă**) the last section of the large intestine, between colon and anus.
re·cum·bent (ri-kum-bĕnt) *adj.* lying down, reclining.
re·cu·per·ate (ri-koo-pĕ-rayt) *v.* (**re·cu·per·at·ed, re·cu·per·at·ing**) 1. to recover, to regain (one's health or strength) after illness or exhaustion. 2. to recover (losses). **re·cu·per·a·tion** (ri-koo-pĕ-ray-shŏn) *n.*
re·cu·per·a·tive (ri-koo-pĕ-ray-tiv) *adj.* of recuperation, *great recuperative powers.*
re·cur (ri-kur) *v.* (**re·curred, re·cur·ring**) to happen again, to keep occurring. ☐**recurring decimal,** a decimal fraction in which the same figures are repeated indefinitely, such as 3.999. . . or 4.014014. . . .

re·crit'i·cize *v.* (**-cized, -ciz·ing**)
re·cross' *v.*
re·crown' *v.*

re·cur·rent (ri-kur-ĕnt) *adj.* recurring, *a recurrent problem.* **re·cur'rent·ly** *adv.* **re·cur'rence** *n.*
re·curve (ree-kurv) *v.* (**re·curved, re·curv·ing**) to bend or be bent backward, *a flower with recurved petals.*
re·cy·cle (ree-sı-kĕl) *v.* (**re·cy·cled, re·cy·cling**) to convert (waste material) into a form in which it can be reused. **re·cy·cla·ble** (ree-sı-klă-bĕl) *adj.* **re·cy·cla·bil·i·ty** (ree-sı-klă-bil-i-tee) *n.*
red (red) *adj.* (**red·der, red·dest**) 1. of the color of blood or a color approaching this. 2. (of the face) flushed with anger or shame, (of the eyes) bloodshot or reddened with weeping. 3. Communist, favoring Communism, *Red China.* 4. anarchist. **red** *n.* 1. red color. 2. a red subtance or material, *red clothes.* 3. a red light. 4. the debit side of an account; *in the red,* having a debit balance, in debt. 5. a Communist. 6. an anarchist. **red'ly** *adv.* **red'ness** *n.* ☐**red alert,** a most urgent alert of imminent enemy attack. **red alga,** an alga containing red pigment. **Red Army,** the army of the U.S.S.R. **red blood cell,** a cell containing hemoglobin, carrying oxygen throughout the body, a red blood corpuscle. **red carpet,** privileged treatment given to an important visitor. **red cedar,** an American juniper tree; the wood of this tree. **red cent,** the smallest possible coin; *not worth a red cent,* of no value at all. **red clover,** a red-flowered clover, used as forage. **Red Cross,** an international organization for the treatment of the sick and wounded in war and the help of those afflicted by large-scale natural disasters. **red deer,** a European and Asian deer with a red-brown coat. **red flag,** one used as a warning of danger; the symbol of a left-wing revolutionary group. **red fox,** a fox with red-brown fur. **red giant,** a star in evolution with reddish hue, low surface temperature, and great volume. **red herring,** a misleading clue; something that draws attention away from the matter under consideration. **red lead,** red oxide of lead, used as a pigment. **red-letter day,** a day that is memorable because of some joyful occurrence. **red light,** a signal to stop on a road or railroad; a danger signal. **red-light district,** one containing many brothels. **red oak,** a common North American oak tree with spiny-tipped leaves; its wood. **red pepper,** a pepper with yellow or red pods that are used as a condiment; cayenne pepper. **red salmon,** a food fish of the North Pacific (also *sockeye salmon*). **Red Sea,** a narrow extension of the Indian Ocean between Africa and Arabia, connected to the Mediterranean by the Suez Canal. **red shift,** a displacement of spectral lines to longer wavelengths in radiation from distant galaxies etc. **red snapper,** a food fish of the Gulf of Mexico. **red spider,** a mite infesting hothouse plants, especially vines. **red squirrel,** a common squirrel with a reddish upper body. **red-tailed hawk,** a hawk common to North America, with a short red tail. **red tape,** excessive formalities in official transactions. **red tide,** a red discoloration of seawater, fatal to fish and other marine organisms.
re·dact (ri-dakt) *v.* to put into literary form, to arrange for publication, to edit. **re·dac'tor** *n.* **re·dac·tion** (ri-dak-shŏn) *n.* **re·dac'tion·al** *adj.*

re·crys'tal·lize *v.* (**-lized, -liz·ing**)

red-blood·ed (red-blud-id) *adj.* full of vigor. **red′-blood′ed·ness** *n.*

red·breast (red-brest) *n.* a robin.

red·brick (red-brik) *adj.* *(British)* of English universities founded in the 19th century or later, as distinct from Oxford and Cambridge *(Oxbridge).*

red·cap (red-kap) *n.* a railroad porter.

red·coat (red-koht) *n.* a British soldier in the American Revolution.

red·den (red-ĕn) *v.* to make or become red.

red·dish (red-ish) *adj.* rather red. **red′dish·ness** *n.*

red-dog (red-dawg) *v.* **(red-dogged, red-dog·ging)** (in football) to pursue (the opposing quarterback) doggedly while he is trying to throw a forward pass.

re·dec·o·rate (ree-dek-ŏ-rayt) *v.* **(re·dec·o·rat·ed, re·dec·o·rat·ing)** to decorate freshly. **re·dec·o·ra·tion** (ree-dek-ŏ-ray-shŏn) *n.*

re·deem (ri-deem) *v.* 1. to buy back, to recover (a thing) by payment or by doing something. 2. to clear (a debt etc.) by paying it off, *redeem the mortgage.* 3. to convert (bonds or tokens) into cash or merchandise. 4. to purchase the freedom of (a person) by payment. 5. to save from damnation or from the consequences of sin. 6. to make up for faults or deficiencies, *it has one redeeming feature.* □**redeem oneself,** to make up for one's former fault(s).

re·deem·a·ble (ri-dee-mă-bĕl) *adj.* able to be redeemed.

re·deem·er (ri-dee-mĕr) *n.* a person who redeems something. □**the Redeemer,** Christ as the redeemer of mankind.

re·demp·tion (ri-demp-shŏn) *n.* redeeming, being redeemed. **re·demp′tive** *adj.* **re·demp·to·ry** (ri-demp-tŏ-ree) *adj.*

re·de·ploy (ree-di-ploi) *v.* to send (troops or workers etc.) to a new place or task. **re·de·ploy′ment** *n.*

re·de·vel·op (ree-di-vel-op) *v.* 1. to remodel or to reconstruct (buildings). 2. to convert to a new use (land already developed). **re·de·vel′op·er** *n.* **re·de·vel′op·ment** *n.*

red-hand·ed (red-han-did) *adj.* in the act of crime, *was caught red-handed.*

red·head (red-hed) *n.* a person with reddish hair. **red′head·ed** *adj.*

red-hot (red-hot) *adj.* 1. so hot that it glows red. 2. highly excited or angry. 3. (of news) *(informal)* fresh, completely new.

re·di·rect (ree-di-rekt, -dɪ-) *v.* to direct or send to another place, to readdress, **re·di·rec·tion** (ree-di-rek-shŏn, -dɪ-) *n.*

re·dis·trict (ree-dis-trikt) *v.* to alter the boundaries of the districts of (an area), especially to change their political representation.

red·lin·ing (red-lɪ-ning) *n.* a practice by banks of arbitrarily denying mortgages in certain urban areas. **red′line** *v.* **(red·lined, red·lin·ing)** to treat in this way.

red·neck (red-nek) *n.* *(contemptuous)* a member of the white rural working class of the southern U.S.

re·do (ree-doo) *v.* **(re·did, re·done, re·do·ing)** 1. to do again. 2. to redecorate.

red·o·lent (red-ŏ-lĕnt) *adj.* 1. smelling strongly, *redolent of onions.* (▷Do not write *redolent of the smell of onions.*) 2. full of memories, *a town redolent of age and romance.* **red′o·lent·ly** *adv.* **red′o·lence** *n.* **red·o·len·cy** (red-ŏ-lĕn-see) *n.*

re·dou·ble (ree-dub-ĕl) *v.* **(re·dou·bled, re·dou·bling)** 1. to double again. 2. to make or become more intense, *redoubled their efforts.* 3. (in bridge) to double again a bid already doubled by an opponent. **redouble** *n.* (in bridge) the redoubling of a bid.

re·doubt (ri-dowt) *n.* a small fortification without flanking defenses.

re·doubt·a·ble (ri-dow-tă-bĕl) *adj.* formidable, especially as an opponent.

re·dound (ri-downd) *v.* to come back as an advantage or disadvantage, to accrue, *this will redound to our credit.*

re·dress (ri-dres) *v.* to set right, to rectify, *redress the balance.* **redress** *n.* reparation, amends for a wrong done, *has no chance of redress for this damage.*

red·skin (red-skin) *n.* *(contemptuous)* a North American Indian.

red·start (red-stahrt) *n.* a kind of songbird with black feathers marked with orange on the wings and tail.

re·duce (ri-doos) *v.* **(re·duced, re·duc·ing)** 1. to make or become less. 2. to make lower in rank or status. 3. to slim. 4. to subdue, to bring by force or necessity into a specified state or condition, *was reduced to despair or to borrowing.* 5. to convert into a simpler or more general form, *reduce the fraction to its lowest terms; the problem may be reduced to two main elements.* 6. to restore (a fractured or dislocated bone) to its proper position. **re·duc′er** *n.* **re·duc·tive** (ri-duk-tiv) *adj.* □**reduced circumstances,** poverty after a period of prosperity. **reducing agent,** a substance that removes oxygen or adds hydrogen or electrons, especially one that converts an oxide to metal.

re·duc·i·ble (ri-doo-si-bĕl) *adj.* able to be reduced. **re·duc′i·bly** *adv.*

re·duc·ti·o ad ab·sur·dum (ri-duk-shi-oh ad ab-sur-dŭm) 1. proof of falsity by showing an absurd logical consequence. 2. proof of truth by demonstrating the falsity of alternatives. 3. the carrying of a principle to impractical lengths. ▷Latin.

re·duc·tion (ri-duk-shŏn) *n.* 1. reducing, being reduced. 2. the amount by which something is reduced, especially in price. 3. anything made by reducing.

re·dun·dant (ri-dun-dănt) *adj.* 1. superfluous. 2. no longer needed. **re·dun′dant·ly** *adv.* **re·dun·dan·cy** (ri-dun-dăn-see) *n.*

re·du·pli·cate (ree-doo-plĭ-kayt) *v.* **(re·du·pli·**

---

re·ded′i·cate *v.* **(-cat·ed, -cat·ing)**
re·ded·i·ca′tion *n.*
re·de·fine′ *v.* **(-fined, -fin·ing)**
re·def·i·ni′tion *n.*
re·de·pos′it *v.*
re·de·sign′ *v.*

re·di·gest′ *v.*
re·dis·cov′er *v.*
re·dis·cov′er·y *n.* (*pl.* **-er·ies**)
re·dis·solve′ *v.* **(-solved, -solv·ing)**
re·dis·till′ *v.*
re·dis·trib′ute *v.* **(-ut·ed,**

-ut·ing)
re·dis·tri·bu′tion *n.*
re·di·vert′ *v.*
re·di·vide′ *v.* **(-vid·ed, -vid·ing)**
re·draft′ *n.* & *v.*
re·draw′ *v.* **(-drew, -drawn, -draw·ing)**

cat·ed, re·du·pli·cat·ing) to double (a letter or syllable) such as *bye-bye, goody-goody, super-duper.* **re·du·pli·ca·tion** (ree-doo-plĭ-kay-shŏn) *n.*

red·wing (red-wing) **blackbird** a North American blackbird with a red and yellow patch on the wings.

red·wood (red-wuud) *n.* 1. a very tall evergreen coniferous tree of California. 2. its reddish wood.

re·ech·o (ree-ek-oh) *v.* **(re·ech·oed, re·ech·o·ing)** to echo, to echo repeatedly, to resound.

reed (reed) *n.* 1. a water or marsh plant with tall straight hollow stems. 2. its stem. 3. a vibrating part that produces the sound in certain wind instruments.

reed·y (ree-dee) *adj.* 1. full of reeds. 2. like a reed in slenderness or (of grass) thickness. 3. (of the voice) having the thin high tone of a reed instrument. **reed′i·ness** *n.*

reef[1] (reef) *n.* a ridge of rock or coral or sand that reaches to or close to the surface of water.

reef[2] *n.* one of several strips at the top or bottom of a sail that can be drawn in so as to reduce the area of sail exposed to the wind. **reef** *v.* to shorten (a sail) by drawing in a reef or reefs.

reef·er[1] (ree-fĕr) *n.* a thick double-breasted jacket.

reefer[2] *n. (slang)* a marijuana cigarette.

reef (reef) **knot** a symmetrical double knot that is very secure.

reek (reek) *n.* a foul or stale smell. **reek** *v.* to smell strongly or unpleasantly, *reeking of tobacco.*

reel[1] (reel) *n.* 1. a cylinder or similar device on which something is wound. 2. this and what is wound on it, the amount held by a reel. **reel** *v.* 1. to wind on or off a reel. 2. to pull (a thing) in by using a reel. □**reel off,** to rattle off (a story etc.).

reel[2] *v.* to stagger, to have a violent swinging or spinning motion. **reel** *n.* a reeling motion.

reel[3] *n.* 1. a lively dance of Scottish origin. 2. the music for this dance.

re·e·lect (ree-i-lekt) *v.* to elect again. **re·e·lec·tion** (ree-i-lek-shŏn) *n.*

re·en·ter (ree-en-tĕr) *v.* to enter again.

re·en·try (ree-en-tree) *n.* the act of entering again, especially (of a spacecraft or missile etc.) reentering Earth's atmosphere.

re·es·tab·lish (ree-e-stab-lish) *v.* to establish again. **re·es·tab′lish·ment** *n.*

re·ex·am·ine (ree-ig-zam-in) *v.* **(re·ex·am·ined, re·ex·am·in·ing)** to examine again. **re·ex·am·i·na·tion** (ree-ig-zam-i-nay-shŏn) *n.*

ref (ref) *n. (informal)* a referee. **ref** *v.* **(reffed, ref·fing)** *(informal)* to referee.

ref. *abbr.* 1. referee. 2. reference. 3. reformation. 4. reformed. 5. refund.

re·fec·to·ry (ri-fek-tŏ-ree) *n.* (*pl.* **-ries**) the dining room of a monastery or college or similar establishment. □**refectory table,** a long narrow table with a broad supporting upright at each end, joined by a bar.

re·fer (ri-fur) *v.* **(re·ferred, re·fer·ring)** 1. to make an allusion, to direct people's attention by words, *I wasn't referring to you.* 2. to send on or direct (a person) to some authority or specialist or source of information. 3. to turn to (a thing) for information, *referred to the list of rules.* 4. to ascribe. **re·fer′rer** *n.*

ref·er·a·ble (ref-ĕ-ră-bĕl) *adj.* able to be referred.

ref·er·ee (ref-ĕ-ree) *n.* 1. an umpire in certain games or sports. 2. a person to whom disputes are referred for decision, an arbitrator. **referee** *v.* **(ref·er·eed, ref·er·ee·ing)** to act as referee in (a football game etc.).

ref·er·ence (ref-ĕ-rĕns) *n.* 1. the act of referring. 2. something that can be referred to as an authority or standard. 3. a statement referring to or mentioning something, *made no reference to recent events.* 4. a direction to a book or page or file etc. where information can be found, the book or passage etc. cited in this way. 5. a testimonial. 6. a person willing to testify to a person's character or ability or financial circumstances. □**in** *or* **with reference to,** in connection with, about. **reference book,** a book providing information for reference but not designed to be read straight through. **reference library** *or* **room,** one containing books that can be consulted but not taken away.

ref·er·en·dum (ref-ĕ-ren-dŭm) *n.* (*pl.* **-dums, -da,** *pr.* -dä) the referring of a question to the people of a country etc. for direct decision by a general vote, a vote taken in this way. ▷The Latin word *referendum* (= referring) has no plural in Latin, so careful writers prefer to use *referendums* as the plural in English.

ref·er·ent (ref-ĕ-rĕnt) *n.* what is symbolized by a word etc.

re·fer·ral (ri-fur-ăl) *n.* 1. referring, being referred. 2. a person referred or suggested to someone.

re·fill (ree-fil) *n.* 1. a second or later filling. 2. the material used for this, a thing that replaces something used up. **refill** (ree-fil) *v.* to fill again. **re·fill′a·ble** *adj.*

re·fine (ri-frn) *v.* **(re·fined, re·fin·ing)** 1. to remove impurities or defects from. 2. to make elegant or cultured. **re·fined′** *adj.*

re·fine·ment (ri-frn-mĕnt) *n.* 1. refining, being refined. 2. elegance of behavior or manners etc. 3. an improvement added to something, *the oven has automatic cleaning and other refinements.* 4. a piece of subtle reasoning, a fine distinction.

re·fin·er (ri-fr-nĕr) *n.* a person or organization

---

re·dye′ *v.* (-dyed, -dye·ing)

re·ed′it *v.*

re·ed′u·cate *v.* (-cat·ed, -cat·ing)

re·em·bark′ *v.*

re·em·bod′y *v.* (-bod·ied, -bod·y·ing)

re·e·merge′ *v.* (-merged, -merg·ing)

re·e·mer′gence *n.*

re·em′pha·size *v.* (-sized, -siz·ing)

re·em·ploy′ *v.*

re·em·ploy′ment *n.*

re·en·act′ *v.*

re·en·act′ment *n.*

re·en·gage′ *v.* (-gaged, -gag·ing)

re·en·list′ *v.*

re·en·list′ment *n.*

re·en·slave′ *v.* (-slaved, -slav·ing)

re·e·quip′ *v.* (-quipped, -quip·ping)

re·e·rect′ *v.*

re·es′ti·mate *v.*

re·es·ti·ma′tion *n.*

re·e·val′u·ate *v.* (-at·ed, -at·ing)

re·e·val·u·a′tion *n.*

re·ex·pe′ri·ence *v.* (-enced, -enc·ing)

re·ex·port′ *v.*

re·fash′ion *v.*

re·fas′ten *v.*

re·film′ *v.*

re·fil′ter *v.*

re·fi·nance′ *v.* (-nanced, -nanc·ing)

whose business is to refine crude oil or metal or sugar etc.

re·fin·er·y (ri-fī-nĕ-ree) *n.* (*pl.* **-er·ies**) a plant where crude substances are refined.

re·fit (ree-fit) *v.* (**re·fit·ted, re·fit·ting**) to renew or repair the fittings of. **refit** *n.* refitting.

refl. *abbr.* 1. reflex. 2. reflexive.

re·flect (ri-flekt) *v.* 1. to throw back (light or heat or sound). 2. to be thrown back in this way. 3. (of a mirror etc.) to show an image of. 4. to correspond to (a thing) because of its influence, *improved methods of agriculture were soon reflected in larger crops.* 5. to bring (credit or discredit). 6. to bring discredit, *this failure reflects upon the whole industry.* 7. to think deeply, to consider, to remind oneself of past events. **re·flec'tive·ly** *adv.* □**reflecting telescope,** a telescope provided with a curved mirror for gathering light.

re·flec·tion (ri-flek-shŏn) *n.* 1. reflecting, being reflected. 2. reflected light or heat etc., a reflected image. 3. discredit, a thing that brings this. 4. deep thought, an idea or statement produced by this.

re·flec·tive (ri-flek-tiv) *adj.* 1. reflecting. 2. thoughtful, *in a reflective mood.* **re·flec'tive·ly** *adv.*

re·flec·tor (ri-flek-tŏr) *n.* 1. a thing that reflects light or heat or images. 2. a reflecting telescope.

re·flex (ree-fleks) *n.* 1. a reflex action. 2. a reflex camera. **reflex** *adj.* 1. of or caused by a reflex. 2. bent back. **reflex** (ree-fleks) *v.* to flex again. □**reflex action,** an involuntary or instinctive movement in response to a stimulus. **reflex angle,** an angle of more than 180°. **reflex camera,** one in which the image given by the lens is reflected to the viewfinder.

re·flex·ive (ri-flek-siv) *adj.* (of a word or form) referring back to the subject of the verb, in which the action of the verb is performed on its subject, as in *he washed himself.* **reflexive** *n.* a reflexive word or form. **re·flex'ive·ly** *adv.* **re·flex'ive·ness** *n.* □**reflexive pronoun,** *see* **pronoun.**

re·flux (ri-fluks) *v.* to boil so that a vapor is liquefied and returned to the boiler. **reflux** (ree-fluks) *n.* 1. this method of boiling. 2. a backward flow.

re·for·est (ree-for-ist) *v.* to plant new trees in (an area formerly forested). **re·for·est·a·tion** (ree-for-i-stay-shŏn) *n.*

re·form (ri-form) *v.* to make or become better by removal or abandonment of imperfections or faults. **reform** *n.* reforming, being reformed. **re·formed'** *adj.* **re·form'a·ble** *adj.* **re·form'a·tive** *adj.* **re·form'er** *n.* □**Reformed Church,** one that accepted the principles of the Reformation, especially the Calvinist Church. **reformed spelling,** any of several suggested systems for simplifying the spelling of English words, especially by leaving out unpronounced letters.

re-form (ree-form) *v.* to form again. **re·for·ma·tion** (ree-for-may-shŏn) *n.*

ref·or·ma·tion (ref-ŏr-may-shŏn) *n.* reforming, being reformed, a great change for the better in public affairs. □**the Reformation,** the 16th-cen-

tury religious movement for reform of certain doctrines and practices of the Roman Catholic Church, resulting in the establishment of Reformed or Protestant Churches.

re·form·a·to·ry (ri-for-mă-tohr-ee) *n.* (*pl.* **-ries**) an institution where young offenders against the law are sent to be reformed.

re·fract (ri-frakt) *v.* to subject to refraction. **re·frac'tive** *adj.* **re·frac'tive·ness** *n.* **re·frac·tiv·i·ty** (ree-frak-tiv-i-tee) *n.*

re·frac·tion (ri-frak-shŏn) *n.* the bending of a ray of light or heat or sound at the boundary between two mediums of dissimilar nature.

re·frac·tor (ri-frak-tŏr) *n.* a telescope using a lens to produce an image.

re·frac·to·ry (ri-frak-tŏ-ree) *adj.* 1. resisting control or discipline, stubborn, *a refractory child.* 2. (of a disease etc.) not yielding to treatment. 3. (of a substance) resistant to heat, hard to fuse or work. **re·frac'to·ri·ly** *adv.* **re·frac'to·ri·ness** *n.*

re·frain[1] (ri-frayn) *n.* 1. the lines of a song that are repeated at the end of each verse. 2. the main part of a song, after the verse. 3. the music for either of these.

refrain[2] *v.* to keep oneself from doing something, *please refrain from talking.* **re·frain'ment** *n.*

re·fresh (ri-fresh) *v.* 1. to restore the strength and vigor of (a person etc.) by food or drink or rest. 2. to make cool again. □**refresh a person's memory,** to stimulate his memory by reminding him.

re·fresh·er (ri-fresh-ĕr) *n.* (*informal*) a drink. □**refresher course,** a course of instruction enabling a qualified person to keep abreast of recent developments in his subject.

re·fresh·ing (ri-fresh-ing) *adj.* 1. restoring strength and vigor. 2. welcome and interesting because of its novelty. **re·fresh'ing·ly** *adv.*

re·fresh·ment (ri-fresh-mĕnt) *n.* 1. refreshing, being refreshed. 2. something that refreshes, especially food and drink. 3. *refreshments,* food and drink that does not constitute a meal.

refrig. *abbr.* 1. refrigerating. 2. refrigeration.

re·frig·er·ant (ri-frij-ĕ-rănt) *n.* a substance used for cooling things or for keeping things cold.

re·frig·er·ate (ri-frij-ĕ-rayt) *v.* (**re·frig·er·at·ed, re·frig·er·at·ing**) to make extremely cold, especially in order to preserve and store food. **re·frig·er·a·tion** (ri-frij-ĕ-ray-shŏn) *n.*

re·frig·er·a·tor (ri-frij-ĕ-ray-tŏr) *n.* a cabinet or room in which food is stored at a very low temperature.

re·fu·el (ree-fyoo-ĕl) *v.* (**re·fu·eled, re·fu·el·ing**) to replenish the fuel supply of.

ref·uge (ref-yooj) *n.* shelter from pursuit or danger or trouble, a place giving this; *took refuge in silence,* became silent in order to avoid difficulty.

ref·u·gee (ref-yŭ-jee, ref-yŭ-jee) *n.* a person who has left his home and seeks refuge elsewhere, as from war or persecution or some natural disaster.

re·ful·gence (ri-ful-jĕns) *n.* a shining and gloriously bright state. **re·ful'gent** *adj.*

re·fund (ri-fund) *v.* to pay back (money received,

---

re·fin'ish *v.*

re·float' *v.*

re·flow'er *v.*

re·fo'cus *v.* (**-cused, -cus·ing**)

re·fold' *v.*

re·forge' *v.* (**-forged, -forg·ing**)

re·for'mu·late *v.* (**-lat·ed, -lat·ing**)

re·for·mu·la'tion *n.*

re·for'ti·fy *v.* (**-fied, -fy·ing**)

re·frac'ture *v.* (**-tured, -tur·ing**)

re·frame' *v.* (**-framed, -fram·ing**)

re·freeze' *v.* (**-froze, -fro·zen, -freez·ing**)

or expenses that a person has incurred). **refund** (ree-fund) *n.* money refunded, repayment. **re·fund'a·ble** *adj.* **re·fund'er** *n.*

re·fur·bish (ree-fur-bish) *v.* to make clean or bright again, to redecorate.

re·fus·al (ri-fyoo-zăl) *n.* refusing, being refused. ☐**first refusal,** the right to accept or refuse something before the choice is offered to others.

re·fuse[1] (ri-fyooz) *v.* (**re·fused, re·fus·ing**) to say or to show that one is unwilling to accept or give or do something, *refused to go; refused him permission to go; refused my request; car refused to start,* would not start.

ref·use[2] (ref-yoos) *n.* what is rejected as worthless, waste material.

re·fut·a·ble (ri-fyoo-tă-běl) *adj.* able to be refuted.

re·fute (ri-fyoot) *v.* (**re·fut·ed, re·fut·ing**) to prove that (a statement or opinion or person) is wrong. (▷It is incorrect to use *refute* to mean "to deny" or "to repudiate.") **re·fut'er** *n.* **ref·u·ta·tion** (ref-yŭ-tay-shŏn) *n.*

reg. *abbr.* 1. regiment. 2. region. 3. register. 4. registered. 5. regular. 6. regulation.

re·gain (ri-gayn) *v.* 1. to obtain possession or use or control of (a thing) again after loss. 2. to reach again, *regained the shore.* **re·gain'er** *n.*

re·gal (ree-găl) *adj.* like or fit for a king. **re'gal·ly** *adv.*

re·gale (ri-gayl) *v.* (**re·galed, re·gal·ing**) to feed or entertain well, *regaled themselves on caviar; regaled them with stories of the campaign.* **re·gale'ment** *n.*

re·ga·li·a (ri-gay-li-ă) *n. pl.* 1. the emblems of royalty used at coronations, *the regalia include crown, scepter, and orb.* 2. the emblems or costumes of an order (such as the Order of the Garter) or of a certain rank or office; *the mayoral regalia,* the mayor's chain of office etc. 3. elaborate dress.

re·gal·i·ty (ri-gal-i-tee) *n.* the attribute of kingly power.

re·gard (ri-gahrd) *v.* 1. to look steadily at. 2. to consider to be, *we regard the matter as serious.* 3. to concern or have a connection with, *he is innocent as regards the first charge.* **regard** *n.* 1. a steady gaze. 2. heed, consideration, *acted without regard to the safety of others.* 3. respect, *we have a great regard for him as our chairman.* 4. *regards,* greetings conveyed in a message, *give him my regards.* **re·gard'ful** *adj.*

re·gard·ing (ri-gahr-ding) *prep.* concerning, with reference to, *laws regarding picketing.*

re·gard·less (ri-gahrd-lis) *adv.* heedlessly, paying no attention to something, *regardless of expense.* ▷The word *irregardless* is incorrect.

re·gat·ta (ri-gat-ă) *n.* a number of boat or yacht races organized as a sporting event.

regd. *abbr.* registered.

re·gen·cy (ree-jĕn-see) *n.* (*pl.* **-cies**) 1. being a regent, a regent's period of office. 2. a group of people acting as regent. 3. *the Regency,* the period 1810–20 in England, when George, Prince of Wales, acted as regent.

re·gen·er·ate (ri-jen-ĕ-rayt) *v.* (**re·gen·er·at·ed, re·gen·er·at·ing**) 1. to give new life or vigor to. 2. to reform spiritually or morally. 3. to form afresh, to renew, or to restore by growing new tissue. **re·gen'er·a·tor** *n.* **re·gen·**

er·a·cy (ri-jen-ĕ-ră-see) *n.* **re·gen·er·a·tion** (ri-jen-ĕ-ray-shŏn) *n.*

re·gen·er·a·tive (ri-jen-ĕ-ră-tiv) *adj.* able to generate again, able to bring into renewed existence.

re·gent (ree-jĕnt) *n.* 1. a person appointed to rule a country while the monarch is too young or unable to rule, or is absent. 2. a member of the governing board of an educational institution. **regent** *adj.* acting as regent, *Prince Regent.*

reg·gae (rej-ee) *n.* a West Indian style of music with a strongly accented subsidiary beat.

reg·i·cide (rej-i-sıd) *n.* 1. a person who kills or participates in the killing of a king. 2. the crime itself. **reg·i·cid·al** (rej-i-sı-dăl) *adj.*

re·gime (rĕ-zheem) *n.* a method or system of government or administration.

reg·i·men (rej-ı-mĕn) *n.* 1. a prescribed course of exercise or way of life, especially a diet. 2. a government.

reg·i·ment (rej-ı-mĕnt) *n.* a military unit of ground forces organized into two or more battalions. **regiment** (rej-ı-ment) *v.* to organize (people or work or data etc.) rigidly into groups or into a pattern. **reg·i·men·ta·tion** (rej-ı-men-tay-shŏn) *n.*

reg·i·men·tal (rej-ı-men-tăl) *adj.* of an army regiment.

Re·gi·na (rĕ-jı-nă) the capital of the province of Saskatchewan, Canada.

re·gion (ree-jŏn) *n.* a continuous part of a surface or space or body, with or without definite boundaries or with certain characteristics.

re·gion·al (ree-jŏ-năl) *adj.* of, relating to, or typical of a large geographical region or of a particular bodily region. **re'gion·al·ly** *adv.*

re·gion·al·ism (ree-jŏ-nă-liz-ĕm) *n.* 1. a characteristic of an area. 2. a word or expression belonging to a particular area.

reg·is·ter (rej-i-stĕr) *n.* 1. an official list of names or items or attendances etc. 2. the book or other document(s) in which this is kept. 3. a mechanical device for indicating or recording speed, force, numbers, etc. automatically, *cash register.* 4. an adjustable device for widening or narrowing an opening, as for regulating the flow of hot air in a heating system. 5. the range of a human voice or of a musical instrument. **register** *v.* 1. to enter or cause to be entered in a register. 2. to set down formally in writing, to present for consideration. 3. to notice and remember. 4. (of an instrument) to indicate or record something automatically. 5. to make an impression on a person's mind, *his name did not register with me.* 6. to express (an emotion) on one's face or by gesture. **reg·is·trant** (rej-i-stránt) *n.* ☐**registered letter,** a letter sent by mail with special precautions for its safety. **registered nurse,** a graduate nurse who has been licensed by a state authority after passing a qualifying examination.

reg·is·trar (rej-i-strahr) *n.* an official with responsibility for keeping written records or registers especially at a school or university.

reg·is·tra·tion (rej-i-stray-shŏn) *n.* 1. registering, being registered. 2. documentation showing that someone or something has been registered. ☐**registration number,** a combination of letters and figures identifying a motor vehicle etc.

reg·is·try (rej-is-tree) *n.* (*pl.* **-tries**) 1. registration.

---

re·fur'nish *v.*

re·gath'er *v.*

re·ger'mi·nate *v.* (**-nat·ed, -nat·ing**)

re·ger·mi·na'tion *n.*

re·gild' *v.*

2. a place where written records or registers are kept.

reg·nal (reg-năl) *adj.* of or relating to a sovereign's reign.

reg·nant (reg-nănt) *adj.* 1. reigning. 2. predominant. 3. prevalent.

reg·o·lith (reg-ŏ-lith) *n.* the layer of rock fragments immediately above the solid rock of Earth's crust.

re·gress (ri-gres) *v.* to go back to an earlier or more primitive form or state. **regress** *n.* regressing. **re·gres′sor** *n.*

re·gres·sion (ri-gresh-ŏn) *n.* 1. a backward movement, a retreat. 2. a return to an earlier stage of development.

re·gres·sive (ri-gres-iv) *adj.* tending to regress.

re·gret (ri-gret) *n.* a feeling of sorrow for the loss of a person or thing, or of annoyance or disappointment or repentance; *send one's regrets,* to send polite expressions of regret or apology. **regret** *v.* (**re·gret·ted, re·gret·ting**) to feel regret about. **re·gret′ter** *n.*

re·gret·ful (ri-gret-fŭl) *adj.* feeling regret. **re·gret′ful·ly** *adv.*

re·gret·ta·ble (ri-gret-ă-bĕl) *adj.* that is to be regretted, *a regrettable incident.* **re·gret′ta·bly** *adv.*

regt. *abbr.* regiment.

reg·u·lar (reg-yŭ-lăr) *adj.* 1. acting or recurring or done in a uniform manner, or constantly at a fixed time or interval, *regular customers; his pulse is regular; keep regular hours,* to get up and go to bed at about the same times always. 2. conforming to a principle or to a standard of procedure. 3. even, symmetrical; *a regular pentagon,* with sides of equal length. 4. usual, normal, habitual, *has no regular occupation.* 5. belonging to the permanent armed forces of a country, *regular soldiers; the regular navy.* 6. (of a verb or noun etc.) having inflections that are of a normal type. 7. *(informal)* complete, out-and-out, *it's a regular mess.* **regular** *n.* 1. a member of the permanent armed forces of a country. 2. *(informal)* a regular customer or client etc. **reg′u·lar·ly** *adv.* **reg·u·lar·i·ty** (reg-yŭ-lar-i-tee) *n.*

reg·u·lar·ize (reg-yŭ-lă-rız) *v.* (**reg·u·lar·ized, reg·u·lar·iz·ing**) 1. to make regular. 2. to make lawful or correct, *regularize the position or situation.* **reg·u·lar·i·za·tion** (reg-yŭ-lă-ri-zay-shŏn) *n.*

reg·u·late (reg-yŭ-layt) *v.* (**reg·u·lat·ed, reg·u·lat·ing**) 1. to control or direct by means of rules and restrictions. 2. to adjust or control (a thing) so that it works correctly or according to one's requirements. **reg·u·la·tive** (reg-yŭ-lay-tiv) *adj.* **reg·u·la·to·ry** (reg-yŭ-lă-tohr-ee) *adj.* **reg·u·la·tor** (reg-yŭ-lay-tŏr) *n.*

reg·u·la·tion (reg-yŭ-lay-shŏn) *n.* 1. regulating, being regulated. 2. a rule or restriction; *regulation dress or size or speed* etc., that required by regulations.

re·gur·gi·tate (ri-gur-ji-tayt) *v.* (**re·gur·gi·ta·ted, re·gur·gi·tat·ing**) 1. to bring (swallowed food) up again to the mouth. 2. to cast or pour out again. **re·gur·gi·ta·tion** (ri-gur-ji-tay-shŏn) *n.*

re·ha·bil·i·tate (ree-ha-bil-i-tayt) *v.* (**re·ha·bil·i·tat·ed, re·ha·bil·i·tat·ing**) 1. to restore (a person) to a normal life by training, after a period of illness or imprisonment. 2. to reinstate. 3. to restore (a building etc.) to a good condition or for a new purpose. **re·ha·bil·i·ta·tive** (ree-hă-bil-i-tay-tiv) *adj.* **re·ha·bil·i·ta·tion** (ree-hă-bil-i-tay-shŏn) *n.*

re·hash (ree-hash) *v.* to put (old material) into a new form with no great change or improvement. **rehash** (ree-hash) *n.* 1. rehashing. 2. something made of rehashed material, *the program was a rehash of some old newsreels.*

re·hear (ree-heer) *v.* (**re·heard,** *pr.* ree-hurd, **re·hear·ing**) (in law) to consider (a case) anew or for a second time. **re·hear′ing** *n.*

re·hears·al (ri-hur-săl) *n.* 1. rehearsing. 2. a practice or trial performance.

re·hearse (ri-hurs) *v.* (**re·hearsed, re·hears·ing**) 1. to practice before performing in public. 2. to train (a person) by doing this. 3. to say over, to give an account of, *rehearsing his grievances.* **re·hears′er** *n.*

Reich (rɪk) *n.* the former German state; *the Third Reich,* Germany under the Nazi regime (1933–45).

reign (rayn) *n.* 1. a sovereign's rule, the period of this. 2. the controlling or dominating effect of a person or thing, *the reign of terror.* **reign** *v.* 1. to rule as king or queen. 2. to be supreme, to dominate; *silence reigned,* there was silence; *the reigning champion,* the one who is champion at present.

re·im·burse (ree-im-burs) *v.* (**re·im·bursed, re·im·burs·ing**) to repay, to refund. **re·im·burs′a·ble** *adj.* **re·im·burse′ment** *n.*

rein (rayn) *n.* 1. a long narrow strap fastened to the bit of a bridle and used to guide or check a horse being ridden or driven. 2. a means of control, *hold the reins of government.* **rein** *v.* to check or control with reins; *rein in,* to pull in or restrain with reins. □**give free rein to,** to allow freedom to, *give one's imagination free rein.* **keep a tight rein on,** to allow little freedom to.

re·in·car·nate (ree-in-kahr-nayt) *v.* (**re·in·car·nat·ed, re·in·car·nat·ing**) to bring back (a soul after death) into another body. **reincarnate** (ree-in-kahr-nit) *adj.* reincarnated. **re·in·car·na·tion** (ree-in-kahr-nay-shŏn) *n.*

rein·deer (rayn-deer) *n.* (*pl.* **-deer**) a kind of deer with large antlers, living in arctic regions. □**reindeer moss,** a lichen eaten by reindeer.

re·in·force (ree-in-fohrs) *v.* (**re·in·forced, re·in·forc·ing**) to strengthen or support by additional men or material or quantity. **re·in·forc′er** *n.* **re·in·force′ment** *n.* □**reinforced concrete,** concrete with metal bars or wire embedded in it to increase its strength.

re·in·force·ments (ree-in-fohrs-mĕnts) *n. pl.*

---

re·glue′ *v.* (-glued, -glu·ing)

re·grow′ *v.* (-grew, -grown, -grow·ing)

re·growth′ *n.*

re·hard′en *v.*

re·heat′ *v.*

re·hire′ *v.* (-hired, -hir·ing)

re·ig·nite′ *v.* (-nit·ed, -nit·ing)

re·im·pris′on *v.*

re·in·cor′po·rate *v.* (-rat·ed, -rat·ing)

re·in·cur′ *v.* (-curred, -cur·ring)

re·in·duct′ *v.*

re·in·duc′tion *n.*

re·in·fect′ *v.*

re·in·fec′tion *n.*

re·in·fest′ *v.*

additional men or ships etc. sent to reinforce armed forces.

re·in·state (ree-in-stayt) v. (**re·in·stat·ed, re·in·stat·ing**) to restore to a previous position. **re·in·state'ment** n.

re·in·sure (ree-in-shoor) v. (**re·in·sured, re·in·sur·ing**) to insure again, especially when the original insurer transfers some or all of the risk to a second insurer. **re·in·sur'ance** n.

re·is·sue (ree-ish-oo) v. (**re·is·sued, re·is·su·ing**) to issue (a thing) again. **reissue** n. something reissued.

REIT (reet, rɪt) abbr. Real-Estate Investment Trust.

re·it·er·ate (ree-it-ĕ-rayt) v. (**re·it·er·at·ed, re·it·er·at·ing**) to say or do again or repeatedly. **re·it·er·a·tive** (ree-it-ĕ-ray-tiv) adj. **re·it·er·a·tion** (ree-it-ĕ-ray-shŏn) n.

re·ject (ri-jekt) v. 1. to refuse to accept, to put aside or send back as not to be chosen or used or done etc. 2. to react against, the body may reject the transplanted tissue. 3. to fail to give due affection to, the child was rejected by both his parents. **reject** (ree-jekt) n. a person or thing that is rejected, especially as being below standard. **re·jec·tion** (ri-jek-shŏn) n. **re·ject'er** n.

re·joice (ri-jois) v. (**re·joiced, re·joic·ing**) 1. to feel or show great joy. 2. to make glad, this will rejoice your heart. **re·joic'er** n. **re·joic'ing** n.

re·join[1] (ree-join) v. to join again.

re·join[2] (ri-join) v. to say in answer, to retort.

re·join·der (ri-join-dĕr) n. something said in answer or retort.

re·ju·ve·nate (ri-joo-vĕ-nayt) v. (**re·ju·ve·nat·ed, re·ju·ve·nat·ing**) to restore youthful appearance or vigor to. **re·ju·ve·na·tion** (ri-joo-vĕ-nay-shŏn) n.

rel. abbr. 1. relating. 2. relative. 3. religion. 4. religious.

re·lapse (ri-laps) v. (**re·lapsed, re·laps·ing**) to fall back into a previous condition, or into a worse state after improvement. **relapse** n. relapsing, especially after partial recovery from illness.

re·late (ri-layt) v. (**re·lat·ed, re·lat·ing**) 1. to narrate, to tell in detail. 2. to bring into relation, to establish a relation between, trying to relate these effects to a possible cause. 3. to have reference to or connection with, he notices nothing but what relates to himself. 4. to establish a sympathetic or successful relationship with a person or thing, learning to relate to children. **re·lat'a·ble** adj. **re·lat'er** n.

re·lat·ed (ri-lay-tid) adj. having a common descent or origin. **re·lat'ed·ness** n.

re·la·tion (ri-lay-shŏn) n. 1. the way in which one thing is related to another, a similarity or correspondence or contrast between people or things or events. 2. being related. 3. a person who is a relative. 4. narrating, being narrated. 5. relations,

dealings with others, the country's foreign relations; sexual intercourse, had relations with him. **re·la'tion·ship** n.

rel·a·tive (rel-ă-tiv) adj. 1. considered in relation or proportion to something else, the relative merits of the two plans; lived in relative comfort. 2. having a connection with, facts relative to the matter in hand. 3. (in grammar) referring or attached to an earlier noun or clause or sentence; relative pronoun, see pronoun. **relative** n. 1. a person who is related to another by parentage or descent or marriage. 2. (in grammar) a relative pronoun or adjective or adverb. **rel'a·tive·ly** adv. **rel'a·tive·ness** n. □**relative clause**, a clause attached to an antecedent by a relative word.

relative humidity, the amount of water vapor in the air at a given temperature as compared with the greatest amount of water vapor that air can hold at that temperature.

rel·a·tiv·i·ty (rel-ă-tiv-i-tee) n. 1. relativeness. 2. Einstein's theory of the universe, showing that all motion is relative and treating time as a fourth dimension related to space.

re·lax (ri-laks) v. 1. to become or cause to become less tight or tense. 2. to make or become less strict, relax the rules. 3. to make or become less anxious or formal, to cease work or effort and indulge in recreation. **re·lax'er** n. **re·lax·a·tion** (ree-lak-say-shŏn) n.

re·lax·ant (ri-lak-sănt) adj. causing relaxation. **relaxant** n. a substance, especially a drug, that causes relaxation.

re·lay (ree-lay) n. 1. a fresh set of people or animals taking the place of others who have completed a spell of work, operating in relays. 2. a relay race, or any part of it. 3. a device that receives and sends on a telegraph message or broadcast etc. 4. a device activating changes in a circuit etc. in response to other changes affecting itself. **relay** (ree-lay) v. to receive and pass on (a message or broadcast etc.). □**relay race**, a race between teams in which each person in turn covers a part of the total distance.

re·lease (ri-lees) v. (**re·leased, re·leas·ing**) 1. to set free. 2. to remove from a fixed position, to allow to fall or fly etc.; released an arrow. 3. to issue (a film) for general exhibition, to make (information or a recording etc.) available to the public. 4. (in law) to remit (a debt), to surrender (a right), to make over (property) to another. **release** n. 1. releasing, being released; a happy release, death as a merciful release from suffering. 2. a handle or catch etc. that unfastens a device or machine part. 3. information or a film or recording etc. that is released to the public, a press release. 4. (in law) the conveyance of a right or estate to another, a document embodying this. **re·leas'er** n.

rel·e·gate (rel-ĕ-gayt) v. (**rel·e·gat·ed, rel·**

---

re·in·fuse' v. (**-fused, -fus·ing**)
re·in·fu'sion n.
re·in·oc'u·late v. (**-lat·ed, -lat·ing**)
re·in·oc·u·la'tion n.
re·in·sert' v.
re·in·ser'tion n.
re·in·spect' v.
re·in·stal·la'tion n.
re·in·stall'ment n.

re·in'te·grate v. (**-grat·ed, -grat·ing**)
re·in·te·gra'tion n.
re·in·ter'pret v.
re·in·ter·pre·ta'tion n.
re·in·tro·duce' v. (**-duced, -duc·ing**)
re·in·tro·duc'tion n.
re·in·vent' v.
re·in·vest' v.
re·in·vest'ment n.

re·in·vig'or·ate v. (**-at·ed, -at·ing**)
re·in·volve' v. (**-volved, -volv·ing**)
re·in·volve'ment n.
re·kin'dle v. (**-dled, -dling**)
re·la'bel v. (**-beled, -bel·ing**)
re·laun'der v.
re·lead' v.
re·learn' v. (**-learned, -learn·ing**)

e·gat·ing) 1. to send or consign to a less important place or condition. 2. to transfer (a matter, task, etc.) for discussion or execution. 3. to assign to a particular class or category. **rel·e·ga·tion** (rel-ĕ-gay-shŏn) n.

re·lent (ri-lent) v. to become less stern, to abandon one's harsh intentions and be more lenient. **re·lent·less** (ri-lent-lis) adj. 1. not relenting. 2. unceasing in its severity, the relentless pressure of business life. **re·lent′less·ly** adv. **re·lent′less·ness** n.

rel·e·vant (rel-ĕ-vănt) adj. related to the matter in hand. **rel′e·vant·ly** adv. **rel′e·vance** n. **rel·e·van·cy** (rel-ĕ-văn-see) n.

re·li·a·ble (ri-lɪ-ă-bĕl) adj. 1. able to be relied on. 2. consistently good in quality or performance. **re·li′a·bly** adv. **re·li′a·ble·ness** n. **re·li·a·bil·i·ty** (ri-lɪ-ă-bil-i-tee) n.

re·li·ance (ri-lɪ-ăns) n. 1. relying. 2. trust or confidence felt about something. **re·li′ant** adj.

rel·ic (rel-ik) n. 1. something that survives from an earlier age. 2. a surviving trace of a custom or practice. 3. part of a holy person's body or belongings kept after his death as an object of reverence. 4. relics, remnants, residue.

rel·ict (rel-ikt) n. 1. (old use) a widow. 2. a plant or animal that has survived in primitive form.

re·lief[1] (ri-leef) n. 1. ease given by reduction or removal of pain or anxiety or a burden etc. 2. something that relaxes tension or breaks up monotony, a humorous scene serving as comic relief. 3. assistance given to people in special need, a relief fund for the earthquake victims. 4. a person taking over another's turn of duty or the release from such duty. 5. the raising of the siege of a besieged town, the relief of Mafeking. □**relief pitcher,** a baseball pitcher who replaces another pitcher in a game.

relief[2] n. 1. a method of carving or molding in which the design projects from the surface. 2. a piece of carving etc. done in this way. 3. a similar effect achieved by the use of color or shading. □**relief map,** a map showing hills and valleys either by shading or by their being molded in relief.

re·lieve (ri-leev) v. (**re·lieved, re·liev·ing**) 1. to give relief to, to bring or be a relief to. 2. to introduce variation into, to make less monotonous. 3. to take a thing from (a person), the thief had relieved him of his watch. 4. to raise the siege of (a town). 5. to release (a person) from a duty or task by taking his place or providing a substitute. **re·liev′er** n. □**relieve oneself,** to urinate or defecate. **relieve one's feelings,** to use strong language or vigorous behavior when annoyed.

relig. abbr. religion.

re·li·gion (ri-lij-ŏn) n. 1. belief in the existence of a superhuman controlling power, especially of God or gods, usually expressed in worship. 2. a particular system of faith and worship, the Christian religion. 3. something compared to religious faith as a controlling influence on a person's life, football is his religion. **re·li′gion·ist** n.

re·lig·i·os·i·ty (ri-lij-i-os-i-tee) n. the state of being religious.

re·li·gious (ri-lij-ŭs) adj. 1. of religion, a religious service. 2. believing firmly in a religion and paying great attention to its practices. 3. of a monastic order; a religious house, a monastery or convent. 4. very conscientious, with religious attention to detail. **religious** n. a person bound by monastic vows. **re·li′gious·ly** adv. **re·li′gious·ness** n.

re·lin·quish (ri-ling-kwish) v. 1. to give up or cease from (a plan or habit or belief etc.). 2. to surrender possession of. 3. to cease to hold, relinquished the reins. **re·lin′quish·er** n. **re·lin′quish·ment** n.

rel·i·quar·y (rel-i-kwer-ee) n. (pl. -quar·ies) a receptacle for a relic or relics of a holy person.

rel·ish (rel-ish) n. 1. great enjoyment of food or other things. 2. an appetizing flavor or attractive quality. 3. a strong-tasting substance or food eaten with plainer food to add flavor. **relish** v. to enjoy greatly. **rel′ish·a·ble** adj.

re·live (ree-liv) v. (**re·lived, re·liv·ing**) to live (a period or experience) over again, especially in the imagination.

re·load (ree-lohd) v. to load again.

re·lo·cate (ree-loh-kayt) v. (**re·lo·cat·ed, re·lo·cat·ing**) to move (a person or thing) to a different place. **re·lo·ca·tion** (ree-loh-kay-shŏn) n.

re·luc·tant (ri-luk-tănt) adj. unwilling, grudging one's consent. **re·luc′tant·ly** adv. **re·luc′tance** n. **re·luc·tan·cy** (ri-luk-tăn-see) n.

re·ly (ri-lɪ) v. (**re·lied, re·ly·ing**) rely on, to trust confidently, to depend on for help etc.

rem (rem) n. a unit of ionizing radiation in human tissue, equivalent to one roentgen of x-rays.

REM (rem) n. rapid eye movement (see **rapid**).

re·main (ri-mayn) v. 1. to be there after other parts have been removed or used or dealt with. 2. to be in the same place or condition during further time, to continue to be, remained in Memphis until Easter; remained loyal.

re·main·der (ri-mayn-dĕr) n. 1. the remaining people or things or part. 2. the quantity left after subtraction or division. **remainder** v. to dispose of unsold copies of (a book) at a reduced price.

re·mains (ri-maynz) n. pl. 1. what remains after other parts or things have been removed or used. 2. ancient buildings or objects that have survived when others are destroyed, relics. 3. a dead body, his mortal remains.

re·make (ree-mayk) v. (**re·made, re·mak·ing**) to make again. **re·make** (ree-mayk) n. something remade, especially a movie film.

re·mand (ri-mand) v. to send back (a prisoner) into custody while further evidence is sought. **remand** n. remanding, being remanded. **re·mand′ment** n. □**on remand,** held in custody after being remanded.

re·mark (ri-mahrk) n. a written or spoken comment, anything that is said. **remark** v. 1. to make a remark, to say. 2. to notice.

re·mark·a·ble (ri-mahr-kă-bĕl) adj. worth noticing, exceptional, unusual. **re·mark′a·bly** adv. **re·mark′a·ble·ness** n.

re·me·di·a·ble (ri-mee-di-ă-bĕl) adj. capable of being remedied.

re·me·di·al (ri-mee-di-ăl) adj. providing a remedy

---

re·let′ter v.
re·li′cense v. (**-censed, -cens·ing**)
re·light′ v. (**-light·ed** or **-lit, -light·ing**)

re·line′ v. (**-lined, -lin·ing**)
re·man·u·fac′ture v. (**-tured, -tur·ing**)
re·mar′riage n.
re·mar′ry v. (**-ried, -ry·ing**)

re·match′ v.
re′match n.
re·meas′ure v. (**-ured, -ur·ing**)
re·meas′ure·ment n.

for a disease or deficiency, *remedial exercises.* **re·me′di·al·ly** *adv.*

rem·e·dy (rem-ĕ-dee) *n.* (*pl.* **-dies**) something that cures or relieves a disease or that puts right a matter. **remedy** *v.* (**rem·e·died, rem·e·dy·ing**) to be a remedy for, to put right.

re·mem·ber (ri-mem-bĕr) *v.* 1. to keep in one's mind. 2. to recall knowledge or experience to one's mind, to be able to do this. 3. to make a present to, *remembered me in his will.* 4. to mention as sending greetings, *remember me to your mother.* **re·mem′ber·a·ble** *adj.* **re·mem′ber·er** *n.* □**remember oneself,** to remember one's intentions or to behave with suitable dignity after a lapse.

re·mem·brance (ri-mem-brăns) *n.* 1. remembering, being remembered, memory. 2. something that reminds people, a memento or memorial. 3. the length of time over which a person's memory extends. 4. *remembrances,* greetings conveyed in a message.

re·mind (ri-mind) *v.* to cause to remember or think of something.

re·mind·er (ri-mɪn-dĕr) *n.* a thing that reminds someone, a letter sent to remind someone.

rem·i·nisce (rem-ĭ-nis) *v.* (**rem·i·nisced, rem·i·nisc·ing**) to think or talk about past events and experiences.

rem·i·nis·cence (rem-ĭ-nis-ĕns) *n.* 1. thinking or talking about past events. 2. a remembered impression. 3. (often *reminiscences*) a spoken or written account of what one remembers.

rem·i·nis·cent (rem-ĭ-nis-ĕnt) *adj.* 1. inclined to reminisce, *she was in a reminiscent mood.* 2. having characteristics that recall something to one's mind, *his style is reminiscent of Picasso's.* **rem·i·nis′cent·ly** *adv.*

re·miss (ri-mis) *adj.* negligent, *you have been remiss in your duties or very remiss.* **re·miss′ly** *adv.* **re·miss′ness** *n.*

re·mis·sion (ri-mish-ŏn) *n.* 1. God's pardon or forgiveness of sins. 2. the remitting of a debt or penalty, shortening of a convict's prison sentence on account of his good behavior. 3. reduction of the force or intensity of something, *slight remission of the pain.*

re·mit (ri-mit) *v.* (**re·mit·ted, re·mit·ting**) 1. (of God) to forgive (sins). 2. to cancel (a debt), to refrain from inflicting (a punishment). 3. to make or become less intense, *we must not remit our efforts.* 4. to send (money etc.) to a person or place, *please remit the interest to my home address.* 5. to send (a matter for decision) to some authority. 6. to postpone.

re·mit·tance (ri-mit-ăns) *n.* the sending of money to a person, the money sent.

rem·nant (rem-nănt) *n.* 1. a small remaining quantity or part or number of people or things. 2. a surviving trace of something. 3. a small piece of cloth left when the rest of the bolt has been used or sold.

re·mod·el (ree-mod-ĕl) *v.* (**re·mod·eled, re·mod·el·ing**) to model again or differently, to reconstruct or reorganize. **re·mod′el·er** *n.*

re·mon·strance (ri-mon-străns) *n.* remonstrating, a protest. **re·mon′strant** *adj.* **re·mon′strant·ly** *adv.*

re·mon·strate (ri-mon-strayt) *v.* (**re·mon·strat·ed, re·mon·strat·ing**) to make a protest, *remonstrated with him about his behavior.* **re·mon·stra·tive** (ri-mon-stră-tiv) *adj.* **re·mon′stra·tor** *n.* **re·mon·stra·tion** (ree-mon-stray-shŏn) *n.*

rem·o·ra (rem-ŏ-ră) *n.* a fish that attaches itself to ships, sharks, etc.

re·morse (ri-mors) *n.* deep regret for one's wrongdoing. **re·morse′ful** *adj.* **re·morse′ful·ly** *adv.* **re·morse·less** (ri-mors-lis) *adj.* relentless. **re·morse′less·ly** *adv.*

re·mote (ri-moht) *adj.* (**-mot·er, -mot·est**) 1. far apart, far away in place or time, *the remote past.* 2. far from civilization, *a remote village.* 3. not close in relationship or connection, *a remote ancestor; remote causes.* 4. slight, *I haven't the remotest idea.* **re·mote′ly** *adv.* **re·mote′ness** *n.* □**remote control,** control of apparatus etc. from a distance, usually by means of an electrically operated device, radio, etc.

re·mount (ree-mownt) *v.* to mount again. **remount** (ree-mownt) *n.* a fresh horse for a rider.

re·mov·a·ble (ri-moo-vă-bĕl) *adj.* able to be removed.

re·mov·al (ri-moo-văl) *n.* 1. removing, being removed. 2. transfer of furniture etc. to a different house etc.

re·move (ri-moov) *v.* (**re·moved, re·mov·ing**) 1. to take off or away from the place occupied. 2. to take off (clothing). 3. to dismiss from office. 4. to get rid of, *this removes the last of my doubts.* **remove** *n.* 1. the act of removing. 2. a stage or degree, a degree of difference, *this is several removes from the truth.* **re·mov′er** *n.* **re·moved** (ri-moovd) *adj.* distant, remote, *an accent not far removed from ours; a cousin once removed,* a cousin's child or parent; *twice removed,* a cousin's grandchild or grandparent.

re·mu·ner·ate (ri-myoo-nĕ-rayt) *v.* (**re·mu·ner·at·ed, re·mu·ner·at·ing**) to pay or reward (a person) for services rendered. **re·mu′ner·a·tor** *n.* **re·mu·ner·a·tion** (ri-myoo-nĕ-ray-shŏn) *n.* **re·mu·ner·a·to·ry** (ri-myoo-nĕ-ră-tohr-ee) *adj.*

re·mu·ner·a·tive (ri-myoo-nĕ-ră-tiv) *adj.* giving good remuneration, profitable. **re·mu′ner·a·tive·ly** *adv.* **re·mu′ner·a·tive·ness** *n.*

Ren·ais·sance (ren-ă-sahns) *n.* 1. the revival of art and literature in Europe (influenced by classical forms) in the 14th-16th centuries, the period of this. 2. *renaissance,* any similar revival.

re·nal (ree-năl) *adj.* of the kidneys.

re·name (ree-naym) *v.* (**re·named, re·nam·ing**) to give a fresh name to.

re·nas·cence (ri-nas-ĕns, -nay-sĕns) *n.* 1. a rebirth, a renewal. 2. = Renaissance. **re·nas′cent** *adj.*

rend (rend) *v.* (**rent, rend·ing**) *v.* to tear. **rend′er** [1] *v.*

ren·der [2] (ren-dĕr) *v.* 1. to give, especially in return or exchange or as something due, *a reward for services rendered.* 2. to present or send in; *account rendered,* a bill previously sent in and not yet paid. 3. to cause to become, *rendered him helpless.* 4. to portray (a scene or figure etc.), to give a performance of (a play or character). 5. to trans-

---

re·melt′ *v.*
re·men′tion *v.*
re·mil·i·ta·ri·za′tion *n.*

re·mil′i·ta·rize *v.* (**-rized, -riz·ing**)
re·mint *v.*

re·mold′ *v.*
re·mort′gage *v.* (**-gaged, -gag·ing**)

late, *rendered into English.* 6. to melt down (fat).
ren'der·er *n.*
ren·der·ing (ren-dĕ-ring) *n.* 1. the act of one who
renders. 2. a translation. 3. a drawing of a building
etc. done in perspective.
ren·dez·vous (rahn-dĕ-voo) *n.* (*pl.* **-vous,** *pr.*
-vooz) 1. a prearranged meeting. 2. a prearranged
or regular meeting place. **rendezvous** *v.* (**ren·
dez·voused,** *pr.* -vood, **ren·dez·vous·ing,** *pr.*
-voo-ing) to meet at a rendezvous.
ren·di·tion (ren-dish-ŏn) *n.* the way a dramatic
role or musical piece etc. is rendered or performed.
ren·e·gade (ren-ĕ-gayd) *n.* someone who deserts
from a group or cause or faith etc.
re·nege (ri-neg, -nig) *v.* (**re·neged, re·neg·
ing**) to fail to keep a promise etc., *reneged on
their agreement.* **re·neg'er** *n.*
re·ne·go·ti·ate (ree-ni-goh-shi-ayt) *v.* (**re·ne·
go·ti·at·ed, re·ne·go·ti·at·ing**) to negotiate
once again, as a contract. **re·ne·go·ti·a·tion**
(ree-ni-goh-shi-ay-shŏn) *n.*
re·new (ri-noo) *v.* 1. to restore to its original state.
2. to replace with a fresh supply, *baking supplies
need renewing.* 3. to get or make or give again,
renewed their acquaintance or *requests.* 4. to arrange for a continuation or continued validity of,
renew one's subscription or *lease* or *license.* **re·
new'al** *n.* **re·new'er** *n.*
re·new·a·ble (ri-noo-ă-bĕl) *adj.* able to be renewed.
ren·net (ren-it) *n.* a substance used to curdle milk
in making cheese or junket.
ren·nin (ren-in) *n.* a stomach enzyme used in the
processing of cheese.
re·nounce (ri-nowns) *v.* (**re·nounced, re·
nounc·ing**) 1. to give up (a claim or right etc.)
formally, *renounced his title.* 2. to reject, to refuse to abide by (an agreement etc.) **re·nounce'
ment** *n.*
ren·o·vate (ren-ŏ-vayt) *v.* (**ren·o·vat·ed, ren·
o·vat·ing**) to repair, to renew. **ren'o·va·tor**
n. **ren·o·va·tion** (ren-ŏ-vay-shŏn) *n.*
re·nown (ri-nown) *n.* fame.
re·nowned (ri-nownd) *adj.* famous, celebrated.
rent[1] (rent) *v. see* **rend. rent** *n.* a torn place in a
garment etc., a split.
rent[2] *n.* payment made periodically for the use of
land or living quarters or machinery etc. **rent**
v. 1. to pay rent for temporary use of. 2. to allow
to be used in return for payment of rent. □**for
rent,** available to be rented.
rent·a·ble (ren-tă-bĕl) *adj.* able to be rented.
rent·al (ren-tăl) *n.* 1. the amount paid or received
as rent. 2. renting. 3. a rented house etc.
rent-free (rent-free) *adj. & adv.* with exemption
from payment of rent.
re·nun·ci·a·tion (ri-nun-si-ay-shŏn) *n.* renounc-
ing, giving something up.
re·o·pen (ree-oh-pĕn) *v.* to open again.
re·or·der (ree-or-dĕr) *v.* 1. to order again, to order
further supplies of. 2. to put into a different order. **reorder** *n.* 1. a repeated order of products
from the same source. 2. the products thus supplied.

re·nom'i·nate *v.* (**-nat·ed,**
-nat·ing)
re·nom·i·na'tion *n.*
re·num'ber *v.*
re·ob·ject' *v.*
re·oc'cu·py *v.* (**-pied,**

-py·ing)
re·oc·cur' *v.* (**-curred,**
-cur·ring)
re·oc·cur'rence *n.*
re·or'i·ent *v.*
re·or·i·en·ta'tion *n.*

re·or·gan·ize (ree-or-gă-nɪz) *v.* (**re·or·gan·
ized, re·or·gan·iz·ing**) to organize in a new
way. **re·or·gan·i·za·tion** (ree-or-gă-ni-zay-
shŏn) *n.*
rep[1] (rep) *n.* a textile fabric with a corded effect,
used for curtains and upholstery.
rep[2] *n.* (*informal*) 1. repertory. 2. a representative.
3. reputation.
rep. *abbr.* 1. report. 2. reporter. 3. representative.
4. republic.
Rep. *abbr.* 1. Representative. 2. Republican.
re·pair[1] (ri-pair) *v.* 1. to put into good or sound
condition after damage or the effects of wear and
tear. 2. to put right, to make amends for; *repaired
the omission,* did what had been omitted. **repair**
n. 1. the act or process or instance of repairing
something. 2. condition as regards being repaired,
keep it in good repair. **re·pair'er** *n.*
repair[2] *v.* (*old use*) to go, *repaired to the music
room.*
re·pair·a·ble (ri-pair-ă-bĕl) *adj.* able to be repaired.
re·pair·man (ri-pair-man) *n.* (*pl.* **-men,** *pr.* -men)
a person whose job is to repair things.
re·par·a·tion (rep-ă-ray-shŏn) *n.* 1. making
amends. 2. *reparations,* compensation for war
damages, demanded by the victor from a defeated
enemy.
rep·ar·tee (rep-är-tee) *n.* a witty reply, ability to
make witty replies.
re·past (ri-past) *n.* (*formal*) a meal.
re·pa·tri·ate (ree-pay-tri-ayt) *v.* (**re·pa·tri·
at·ed, re·pa·tri·at·ing**) to send or bring back
(a person) to his own country. **re·pa·tri·ate** (ree-
pay-tri-it) *n.* a person who has been repatriated.
re·pa·tri·a·tion (ree-pay-tri-ay-shŏn) *n.*
re·pay (ri-pay) *v.* (**re·paid, re·pay·ing**) 1. to pay
back (money). 2. to do or make or give in return,
repaid kindness with kindness. **re·pay'ment** *n.*
re·pay·a·ble (ri-pay-ă-bĕl) *adj.* able or needing to
be repaid.
re·peal (ri-peel) *v.* to withdraw (a law) officially.
repeal *n.* the repealing of a law. **re·peal'er** *n.*
re·peat (ri-peet) *v.* 1. to say or do or occur again.
2. to say aloud (something heard or learned by
heart, *repeat the oath after me.* 3. to tell another
person (something told to oneself). **repeat** *n.* 1.
repeating. 2. something that is repeated, such as
a television or radio broadcast or a passage of
music. **re·peat'able** *adj.* □**repeating decimal,**
a recurring decimal. **repeating rifle,** a firearm
that fires several shots without reloading. **repeat
itself,** to recur in the same form. **repeat oneself,**
to say or do the same thing again.
re·peat·ed (ri-pee-tid) *adj.* recurring or done again
and again. **re·peat'ed·ly** *adj.*
re·peat·er (ri-pee-tĕr) *n.* 1. a device that repeats
a signal. 2. a repeating rifle or other firearm.
re·pel (ri-pel) *v.* (**re·pelled, re·pel·ling**) 1. to
drive away, *repelled the attackers.* 2. to refuse
to accept, *repelled all offers of help.* 3. to be impossible for (a substance) to penetrate, *the surface
repels moisture.* 4. to push away from itself by
an unseen force (the opposite of *attract*), *one north*

re·pack' *v.*
re·pack'age *v.* (**-aged,**
-ag·ing)
re·paint' *v.*
re·pave' *v.* (**-paved,**
-pav·ing)

magnetic pole repels another. 5. to be repulsive or distasteful to.

re·pel·lent, re·pel·lant (ri-pel-ĕnt) *adj.* 1. repelling, arousing distaste. 2. not penetrable by a specified substance, *the fabric is water-repellent.* **repellent, repellant** *n.* a substance that repels something, *insect repellents.* **re·pel'lent·ly** *adv.* **re·pel'lant·ly** *adv.*

re·pent (ri-pent) *v.* to feel regret about (what one has done or failed to do). **re·pent'er** *n.* **re·pent'ant** *adj.* **re·pent'ance** *n.*

re·per·cus·sion (ree-pĕr-kush-ŏn) *n.* 1. the recoil of something after impact. 2. an echo. 3. an indirect effect or reaction. **re·per·cus·sive** (ree-pĕr-kus-iv) *adj.*

rep·er·toire (rep-ĕr-twahr) *n.* a stock of songs or plays or acts etc. that a person or company knows and is prepared to perform.

rep·er·to·ry (rep-ĕr-tohr-ee) *n.* (*pl.* **-ries**) 1. a repertoire. 2. theatrical performances of various plays for short periods (not for indefinite runs as in Broadway theaters). □**repertory company** *or* **theater,** one giving such performances.

rep·e·ti·tion (rep-ĕ-tish-ŏn) *n.* repeating, being repeated, an instance of this.

rep·e·ti·tious (rep-ĕ-tish-ŭs) *adj.* repetitive. **rep·e·ti'tious·ly** *adv.* **rep·e·ti'tious·ness** *n.*

re·pet·i·tive (ri-pet-ĭ-tiv) *adj.* characterized by repetition. **re·pet'i·tive·ly** *adv.* **re·pet'i·tive·ness** *n.*

re·pine (ri-pɪn) *v.* **(re·pined, re·pin·ing)** to fret, to be discontented. **re·pin'er** *n.*

repl. *abbr.* 1. replace. 2. replacement.

re·place (ri-plays) *v.* **(re·placed, re·plac·ing)** 1. to put back in place. 2. to take the place of. 3. to find or provide a substitute for. **re·plac'er** *n.* **re·place'ment** *n.*

re·place·a·ble (ri-play-să-bĕl) *adj.* able to be replaced.

re·play (ree-play) *v.* to play (a match or recording etc.) again. **replay** (ree-play) *n.* replaying of a match or of a recorded incident in a game etc.

re·plen·ish (ri-plen-ish) *v.* to fill (a thing) again, to renew (a supply etc.). **re·plen'ish·er** *n.* **re·plen'ish·ment** *n.*

re·plete (ri-pleet) *adj.* 1. well-stocked or supplied. 2. full, gorged. **re·plete'ness** *n.* **re·ple·tion** (ri-plee-shŏn) *n.*

re·plev·in (ri-plev-in) *n.* 1. the restoration or recovery of sold merchandise for submission to trial and judgment. 2. the writ granting replevin. 3. the lawsuit arising out of replevin.

rep·li·ca (rep-lĭ-kă) *n.* an exact copy or reproduction of something.

rep·li·cate (rep-lĭ-kayt) *v.* **(rep·li·cat·ed, rep·li·cat·ing)** 1. to repeat. 2. to make a replica of. 3. to fold back on itself. **replicate** *n.* an identical or repeated procedure or experiment. **rep·li·ca·tion** (rep-lĭ-kay-shŏn) *n.*

re·ply (ri-plɪr) *v.* **(re·plied, re·ply·ing)** to make an answer, to say in answer. **reply** *n.* (*pl.* **-plies**) 1. replying. 2. what is replied, an answer.

re·port (ri-pohrt) *v.* 1. to give an account of (something seen or done or studied), to tell as news; *report progress,* to state what has been done so far. 2. to write or give a description of (an event etc.) for publication or broadcasting. 3. to make

a formal accusation about (an offense or offender). 4. to present oneself as arrived or returned, *report to me on Monday.* 5. to be responsible to a certain person as one's superior or supervisor. **report** *n.* 1. a spoken or written account of something seen or done or studied. 2. a description for publication or broadcasting. 3. a periodical statement about a pupil's or employee's work and conduct. 4. rumor, a piece of gossip. 5. an explosive sound like that made by a gun. **re·port'a·ble** *adj.* □**report card,** a record of a student's academic achievement.

re·port·age (ri-pohr-tij, rep-ŏr-tah*zh*) *n.* the reporting of news for the press etc., a typical style of doing this.

re·port·ed·ly (ri-pohr-tid-lee) *adv.* according to reports.

re·port·er (ri-pohr-tĕr) *n.* a person employed to report news etc. for publication or broadcasting.

rep·or·to·ri·al (rep-ŏr-tohr-i-ăl) *adj.*

re·pose¹ (ri-pohz) *n.* 1. rest, sleep. 2. a peaceful state or effect, tranquility. **repose** *v.* **(re·posed, re·pos·ing)** to rest, to lie. **re·pos'er** *n.* **re·pose'ful** *adj.* □**in repose,** (of a dead person) awaiting burial.

re·pose² *v.* **(re·posed, re·pos·ing)** to place (trust etc.) in.

re·pos·i·tor·y (ri-poz-i-tohr-ee) *n.* (*pl.* **-tor·ies**) a place where things are stored.

re·pos·sess (ree-pŏ-zes) *v.* to regain possession of (goods on which payments have not been kept up). **re·pos·ses·sion** (ree-pŏ-zesh-ŏn) *n.*

rep·re·hend (rep-ri-hend) *v.* to rebuke. **rep·re·hen·sion** (rep-ri-hen-shŏn) *n.*

rep·re·hen·si·ble (rep-ri-hen-sĭ-bĕl) *adj.* deserving rebuke. **rep·re·hen'si·bly** *adv.*

rep·re·sent (rep-ri-zent) *v.* 1. to show (a person or thing or scene) in a picture or play etc. 2. to describe or declare to be, *representing himself as an expert.* 3. to state in polite protest or remonstrance, *we must represent to them the risks involved.* 4. to symbolize, *in Roman numerals C represents 100.* 5. to be an example or embodiment of, *the election results represent the views of the electorate.* 6. to act as a deputy or agent or spokesman for, *the President was represented by his wife.*

rep·re·sen·ta·tion (rep-ri-zen-tay-shŏn) *n.* 1. the act of representing or being represented. 2. the group of elected representatives serving a constituency. 3. a statement made by way of allegation or to convey opinion. 4. a picture or image that represents something else. **rep·re·sen·ta'tion·al** *adj.*

rep·re·sent·a·tive (rep-ri-zen-tă-tiv) *adj.* 1. typical of a group or class. 2. containing examples of a number of types, *a representative selection.* 3. consisting of elected representatives, based on representation by these, *representative government.* **representative** *n.* 1. a sample or specimen of something. 2. a person's or firm's agent. 3. a person chosen to represent another or others, or to take part in a legislative assembly on their behalf. 4. a member of the House of Representatives. **rep·re·sent'a·tive·ly** *adv.* **rep·re·sent'a·tive·ness** *n.* □**House of Representatives,** the lower house of Congress in the U.S.

re·press (ri-pres) *v.* to keep down, to suppress,

---

re·peo'ple *v.* (-pled, -pling)
re·phrase' *v.* (-phrased, -phras·ing)

re·plan' *v.* (-planned, -plan·ning)
re·plant' *v.*

re·pol'ish *v.*
re·pop'u·late *v.* (-lat·ed, -lat·ing)

to keep (emotions etc.) from finding an outlet.
re·pres·sion (ri-presh-ŏn) *n.*
re·pressed (ri-prest) *adj.* suffering from repression of the emotions.
re·pres·sive (ri-pres-iv) *adj.* serving or intended to repress a person or thing. **re·pres'sive·ly** *adv.*
re·prieve (ri-preev) *n.* 1. postponement or cancellation of a punishment, especially of the death sentence. 2. temporary relief from danger, postponement of trouble. **reprieve** *v.* (**re·prieved, re·priev·ing**) to give a reprieve to.
rep·ri·mand (rep-ri-mand) *n.* a rebuke, especially a formal or official one. **reprimand** (rep-ri-**mand**) *v.* to give a reprimand to.
re·print (ree-print) *v.* to print again in the same or a new form. **reprint** (ree-print) *n.* the reprinting of a book, a book reprinted.
re·pris·al (ri-prɪ-zăl) *n.* an act of retaliation; *take reprisals,* retaliate.
re·prise (ri-preez) *n.* a repeated action, especially a repeated passage in music.
re·pro (ree-proh) *n.* (*pl.* **-pros**) *(informal)* a reproduction. ☐**repro proof,** *(informal)* a reproduction proof.
re·proach (ri-prohch) *v.* to express disapproval to (a person) for a fault or offense. **reproach** *n.* 1. reproaching, an instance of this. 2. a thing that brings disgrace or discredit. **re·proach'a·ble** *adj.* **re·proach'ing·ly** *adv.* ☐**above** *or* **beyond reproach,** deserving no blame, perfect.
re·proach·ful (ri-prohch-fŭl) *adj.* expressing reproach. **re·proach'ful·ly** *adv.* **re·proach'ful·ness** *n.*
rep·ro·bate (rep-rŏ-bayt) *n.* an immoral or unprincipled person. **reprobate** *adj.* immoral or unprincipled.
rep·ro·ba·tion (rep-rŏ-**bay**-shŏn) *n.* strong condemnation.
re·proc·ess (ree-pros-es, -proh-ses) *v.* to process again.
re·pro·duce (ree-prŏ-doos) *v.* (**re·pro·duced, re·pro·duc·ing**) 1. to produce a copy of (a picture etc.). 2. to cause to be seen or heard again or to occur again. 3. to have a specified quality when reproduced, *some colors don't reproduce well.* 4. to produce further members of the same species by natural means, to produce (offspring). **re·pro·duc'er** *n.*
re·pro·duc·i·ble (ree-prŏ-**doo**-si-bĕl) *adj.* able to be reproduced.
re·pro·duc·tion (ree-prŏ-**duk**-shŏn) *n.* 1. reproducing, being reproduced. 2. a copy of a painting etc.; *reproduction furniture,* made in imitation of an earlier style. ☐**reproduction proof,** a proof suitable for making a photographic plate.
re·pro·duc·tive (ree-prŏ-**duk**-tiv) *adj.* of or belonging to reproduction, *the reproductive system.*
re·prog·ra·phy (ri-prog-ră-fee) *n.* the science and practice of copying documents by photography, xerography.
re·proof (ri-proof) *n.* an expression of condemnation for a fault or offense.
re·prove (ri-proov) *v.* (**re·proved, re·prov·ing**) to give a reproof to. **re·prov'er** *n.* **re·prov·ing·ly** *adv.*
rept. *abbr.* report.
rep·tile (rep-til, -tɪl) *n.* a member of the class of cold-blooded animals with a backbone and relatively short legs or no legs at all, such as turtles, snakes, lizards, crocodiles. **rep·til·i·an** (rep-til-i-ăn) *adj.*
Repub. *abbr.* 1. Republic. 2. Republican.
re·pub·lic (ri-pub-lik) *n.* a country in which the supreme power is held by the people or their elected representatives, or by an elected or nominated president. ☐**Republic of China,** (also **Taiwan**) a country off the southeast coast of China.
re·pub·li·can (ri-pub-li-kăn) *adj.* of or like or advocating a republic. **republican** *n.* 1. a person advocating republican government. 2. *Republican,* a member of the *Republican Party,* one of the two main political parties in the U.S. **re·pub'li·can·ism** *n.*
re·pu·di·ate (ri-pyoo-di-ayt) *v.* (**re·pu·di·at·ed, re·pu·di·at·ing**) to reject or disown utterly, to deny, *repudiate the accusation; repudiate the agreement,* to refuse to abide by it. **re·pu'di·a·tor** *n.* **re·pu·di·a·tion** (ri-pyoo-di-ay-shŏn) *n.*
re·pug·nant (ri-pug-nănt) *adj.* distasteful, objectionable. **re·pug'nant·ly** *adv.* **re·pug'nance** *n.*
re·pulse (ri-puls) *v.* (**re·pulsed, re·puls·ing**) 1. to drive back (an attacking force). 2. to reject (an offer or help etc.) firmly, to rebuff. **repulse** *n.* 1. the act of repulsing or being repulsed. 2. a rebuff.
re·pul·sion (ri-pul-shŏn) *n.* 1. repelling, being repelled. 2. a feeling of strong distaste, revulsion. 3. (in physics) the tendency of bodies to repel each other.
re·pul·sive (ri-pul-siv) *adj.* arousing disgust. **re·pul'sive·ly** *adv.* **re·pul'sive·ness** *n.*
rep·u·ta·ble (rep-yŭ-tă-bĕl) *adj.* having a good reputation, respected. **rep'u·ta·bly** *adv.* **rep·u·ta·bil·i·ty** (rep-yŭ-tă-bil-i-tee) *n.*
rep·u·ta·tion (rep-yŭ-tay-shŏn) *n.* 1. what is generally said or believed about a person or thing, *a reputation for honesty.* 2. public recognition for one's abilities or achievements, *built up a reputation.*
re·pute (ri-pyoot) *n.* reputation, *I know him by repute.* **repute** *v.* (**re·put·ed, re·put·ing**) to consider, to reckon, *he is reputed to be the best.*
re·put·ed (ri-pyoo-tid) *adj.* said or thought to be; *his reputed father,* the man thought to be his father. **re·put'ed·ly** *adv.*
req. *abbr.* 1. require. 2. required. 3. requisition.
re·quest (ri-kwest) *n.* asking or being asked for a thing or to do something, a thing asked for; *a request program,* one consisting of items asked for by the public. **request** *v.* to make a request for. **re·quest'er** *n.* ☐**by** *or* **on request,** in response to a request.
Re·qui·em (rek-wee-ĕm) *n.* 1. a special Mass for the repose of the soul of the dead. 2. (also *requiem*) a musical setting for this.
re·quire (ri-kwɪr) *v.* (**re·quired, re·quir·ing**) 1. to need, to depend on for success or fulfillment etc., *cars require regular servicing.* 2. to order or oblige, *witnesses are required to take an oath before testifying.*
re·quire·ment (ri-kwɪr-mĕnt) *n.* a need.
req·ui·site (rek-wi-zit) *adj.* required by circum-

---

re·price' *v.* (**-priced, -pric·ing**)

re·pub·li·ca'tion *n.*
re·pub'lish *v.*

re·pur'chase *v.* (**-chased, -chas·ing**)

stances, necessary to success. **requisite** *n.* a thing needed for some purpose. **req'ui·site·ly** *adv.*

req·ui·si·tion (rek-wi-zish-ŏn) *n.* a formal written demand for something that is needed, an official order laying claim to the use of property or materials. **requisition** *v.* to demand or order by a requisition. **req·ui·si'tion·er** *n.*

re·quite (ri-kwɪt) *v.* (**re·quit·ed, re·quit·ing**) 1. to make a return for, to reward or avenge. 2. to give in return. 3. to make a return to, to repay. **re·quit'er** *n.* **re·quit'al** *n.*

rere·dos (reer-dos) *n.* an ornamental screen covering the wall above the back of an altar.

re·run (ree-run) *v.* (**re·ran, re·run, re·run·ning**) to run (a race or film etc.) again. **rerun** (ree-run) *n.* 1. the act of rerunning. 2. a repeated running of a film or television program etc.

res. *abbr.* 1. research. 2. reserve. 3. residence. 4. resolution.

re·sale (ree-sayl) *n.* sale to another person of something one has bought. **re·sal'a·ble** *adj.*

re·scind (ri-sind) *v.* to repeal or cancel (a law or rule etc.). **re·scind'a·ble** *adj.* **re·scind'er** *n.* **re·scis·sion** (ri-sizh-ŏn) *n.*

re·script (ree-skript) *n.* an official edict or announcement.

res·cue (res-kyoo) *v.* (**res·cued, res·cu·ing**) to save or bring away from attack or capture or danger etc. **rescue** *n.* rescuing, being rescued. **res'cu·er** *n.*

re·search (ri-surch, ree-surch) *n.* careful study and investigation, especially in order to discover new facts or information. **research** *v.* to do research into, *the subject has been fully researched.* **re·search'er** *n.*

re·sec·tion (ri-sek-shŏn) *n.* the surgical removal of tissue or part of an organ or bone.

re·sell (ree-sel) *v.* (**re·sold, re·sell·ing**) to sell (what one has bought) to another person.

re·sem·ble (ri-zem-bĕl) *v.* (**re·sem·bled, re·sem·bling**) to be like (another person or thing). **re·sem·blance** (ri-zem-blăns) *n.*

re·sent (ri-zent) *v.* to feel displeased and indignant about, to feel insulted by (something said or done). **re·sent'ment** *n.*

re·sent·ful (ri-zent-fūl) *adj.* feeling resentment. **re·sent'ful·ly** *adv.*

res·er·pine (ri-sur-pin, res-ĕr-) *n.* a drug used as a tranquilizer and in the treatment of hypertension.

res·er·va·tion (rez-ĕr-vay-shŏn) *n.* 1. reserving, being reserved. 2. a reserved seat or accommodation etc., a record of this, *our hotel reservations.* 3. a limitation on one's agreement or acceptance of an idea etc., *we accept the plan in principle but have certain reservations; without reservation,* completely, wholeheartedly. 4. an area of land reserved for occupation by an Indian tribe.

re·serve (ri-zurv) *v.* (**re·served, re·serv·ing**) 1. to put aside for a later occasion or for special use. 2. to retain, *the company reserves the right to offer a substitute.* 3. to order or set aside (seats or accommodation etc.) for a particular person to use at a future date. 4. to postpone, *reserve judgment.* **reserve** *n.* 1. something reserved for future use, an extra amount or stock kept available for use when needed. 2. (also *reserves*) forces outside the regular armed services and liable to be called out in an emergency, a member of these. 3. an area of land reserved for some special purpose, *a nature reserve.* 4. a limitation on one's agreement or acceptance of an idea etc. 5. a reserve price. 6. a tendency to avoid showing one's feelings and to lack cordiality toward other people. **reserve** *adj.* 1. being a reserve. 2. kept in reserve, *reserve funds.* □**in reserve,** in a state of being unused but available. **reserve price,** the lowest price that will be accepted for something sold at public auction.

re·served (ri-zurvd) *adj.* (of a person) showing reserve of manner. **re·serv·ed·ly** (ri-zur-vid-lee) *adv.* **re·serv'ed·ness** *n.*

re·serv·ist (ri-zur-vist) *n.* a member of a country's reserve forces.

res·er·voir (rez-ĕr-vwahr) *n.* 1. a natural or artificial lake that is a source or store of water for a town etc. 2. a container for a supply of fuel or other liquid. 3. any large extra or reserve supply.

re·shuf·fle (ree-shuf-ĕl) *v.* (**re·shuf·fled, re·shuf·fling**) 1. to shuffle (cards) again. 2. to interchange the posts or responsibilities of (a group of people). **reshuffle** *n.* reshuffling; *a Cabinet reshuffle,* redistribution of Cabinet posts among the same people.

re·side (ri-zɪd) *v.* (**re·sid·ed, re·sid·ing**) 1. to have one's home (in a certain place), to dwell permanently. 2. to be present or vested in a person, *supreme authority resides in the President.*

res·i·dence (rez-i-dĕns) *n.* 1. a place where one resides. 2. the act or period of residing in a particular place; *take up one's residence,* to begin to dwell. □**in residence,** living in a specified place for the performance of one's work or duties.

res·i·den·cy (rez-i-dĕn-see) *n.* (*pl.* **-cies**) 1. residence (definition 2). 2. a period of specialized medical training.

res·i·dent (rez-i-dĕnt) *adj.* residing, *in residence.* **resident** *n.* 1. a permanent inhabitant of a place, not a visitor. 2. a physician undergoing specialized medical training at a hospital.

res·i·den·tial (rez-i-den-shăl) *adj.* 1. containing or suitable for private houses, *a residential area.* 2. connected with or based on residence, *residential qualifications for voters.* **res·i·den'tial·ly** *adv.*

re·sid·u·al (ri-zij-oo-ăl) *adj.* left over as a residue. **residuals** *n.* payments (to an actor or writer) for each rerun of a television program or film. **re·sid'u·al·ly** *adv.*

re·sid·u·ar·y (ri-zij-oo-er-ee) *adj.* 1. residual. 2. of the residue of an estate; *residuary legatee,* the one who inherits the remainder of an estate after specific items have been allotted to others.

res·i·due (rez-i-doo) *n.* 1. the remainder, what is left over. 2. the substance left after combustion or evaporation.

re·sid·u·um (ri-zij-oo-ŭm) *n.* (*pl.* **-sid·u·a,** *pr.* -zij-oo-ă) residue.

re·sign (ri-zɪn) *v.* to give up or surrender (one's

---

re·ra'di·ate *v.* (-at·ed, -at·ing)
re·read' *v.* (-read, -read·ing)
re·screen' *v.*

re·seal' *v.*
re·seal'a·ble *adj.*
re·seed' *v.*
re'set *n.*
re·set' *v.* (-set, -set·ting)

re·set'tle *v.* (-tled, -tling)
re·set'tle·ment *n.*
re·shape' *v.* (-shaped, -shap·ing)
re·sharp'en *v.*

job or property or claim etc.). □**resign oneself to,** to be ready to accept and endure, to accept as inevitable.

res·ig·na·tion (rez-ig-nay-shŏn) *n.* 1. resigning. 2. a document or statement conveying that one wishes to resign. 3. a resigned attitude or expression.

re·signed (ri-zɪnd) *adj.* having or showing patient acceptance of an unwelcome task or situation. **re·sign'ed·ly** *adv.* □**be resigned to,** to resign oneself to.

re·sil·ient (ri-zil-yĕnt) *adj.* 1. springing back to its original form after being bent or stretched, springy. 2. (of a person) readily recovering from shock or depression etc. **re·sil'ient·ly** *adv.* **re·sil'ience** *n.* **re·sil·ien·cy** (ri-zil-yĕn-see) *n.*

res·in (rez-in) *n.* 1. a sticky substance that oozes from fir and pine trees and from many other plants, used in making varnish etc. 2. a similar substance made synthetically, used as a plastic or in making plastics. **res'in·ous** *adj.*

re·sist (ri-zist) *v.* 1. to oppose, to use force in order to prevent something from happening or being successful. 2. to regard (a plan or idea) unfavorably. 3. to be undamaged or unaffected by, to prevent from penetrating, *pans that resist heat.* 4. to refrain from accepting or yielding to, *can't resist chocolates* or *temptation.* **re·sist'er** *n.* **re·sist'i·ble** *adj.* **re·sist'less** *adj.*

re·sist·ance (ri-zis-tăns) *n.* 1. resisting, the power to resist something. 2. an influence that hinders or stops something. 3. the property of not conducting heat or electricity, the measure of this. 4. a secret organization resisting the authorities, especially in a conquered or enemy-occupied country. □**the line of least resistance,** the easiest method or course.

re·sist·ant (ri-zis-tănt) *adj.* offering resistance, capable of resisting, *heat-resistant plastics.*

re·sis·tiv·i·ty (ree-zis-tiv-i-tee) *n.* the power of a specified material to resist the passage of electric current.

re·sis·tor (ri-zis-tŏr) *n.* a device having resistance to the passage of electric current.

re·sole (ree-sohl) *v.* (**re·soled, re·sol·ing**) to put a new sole on (a shoe).

res·o·lute (rez-ŏ-loot) *adj.* showing great determination. **res'o·lute·ly** *adv.* **res'o·lute·ness** *n.*

res·o·lu·tion (rez-ŏ-loo-shŏn) *n.* 1. the quality of being resolute, great determination. 2. a mental pledge, something one intends to do, *New Year resolutions.* 3. a formal statement of opinion agreed on by a committee or assembly. 4. the solving of a problem or question. 5. the process of separating something or being separated into constituent parts.

re·solve (ri-zolv) *v.* (**re·solved, re·solv·ing**) 1. to decide firmly. 2. (of a committee or assembly) to pass a resolution. 3. to solve or settle (a problem or doubts etc.). 4. to separate into constituent parts; *the resolving power of a lens,* its ability to magnify things distinctly. **resolve** *n.* 1. something one has decided to do, a resolution, *and she kept her resolve.* 2. great determination. **re·solv'er** *n.* **re·solv'a·ble** *adj.*

re·solved (ri-zolvd) *adj.* (of a person) resolute.

res·o·nance (rez-ŏ-năns) *n.* 1. the state of being resonant. 2. a prolonged response or increase of

sound in one body reacting to sound waves from another body that is vibrating.

res·o·nant (rez-ŏ-nănt) *adj.* resounding, echoing. **res'o·nant·ly** *adv.*

res·o·nate (rez-ŏ-nayt) *v.* (**res·o·nat·ed, res·o·nat·ing**) to produce or to show resonance, to resound. **res'o·na·tor** *n.*

re·sorp·tion (ri-sorp-shŏn) *n.* the act of absorbing again or being absorbed, especially absorption of tissue within the body.

re·sort (ri-zort) *v.* 1. to turn for help, to adopt as an expedient, *resorted to violence.* 2. to go, especially as a frequent or customary practice, *police watched the bars to which he was known to resort.* **resort** *n.* 1. an expedient, resorting to this, *compulsion is our only resort; without resort to violence.* 2. a place resorted to, a popular holiday place. **re·sort'er** *n.* □**in the last resort,** when everything else has failed.

re·sound (ri-zownd) *v.* 1. (of a voice or sound etc.) to fill a place with sound, to produce echoes. 2. (of a place) to be filled with sound, to echo.

re·sound·ing (ri-zown-ding) *adj.* (of an event etc.) notable, *a resounding victory.* **re·sound'ing·ly** *adv.*

re·source (ree-sohrs, ri-sohrs) *n.* 1. something to which one can turn for help or support or to achieve one's purpose. 2. a means of relaxation or amusement. 3. ingenuity, quick wit. 4. *resources,* available assets, *we pooled our resources; a source of wealth to a country, *natural resources such as minerals.*

re·source·ful (ri-sohrs-fŭl) *adj.* clever at finding ways of doing things. **re·source'ful·ly** *adv.* **re·source'ful·ness** *n.*

resp. *abbr.* 1. respective. 2. respectively.

re·spect (ri-spekt) *n.* 1. admiration felt toward a person or thing that has good qualities or achievements, politeness arising from this. 2. attention, consideration, *showing respect for people's feelings.* 3. relation, reference, *this is true with respect to English but not to French.* 4. a particular detail or aspect, *in this one respect.* 5. *respects,* polite greetings; *pay one's respects,* make a polite visit; *pay one's last respects,* attend a person's funeral or wake etc. **respect** *v.* to feel or show respect for. **re·spect'er** *n.* □**be no respecter of persons,** to treat everyone in the same way without being influenced by their importance.

re·spect·a·ble (ri-spek-tă-bĕl) *adj.* 1. of moderately good social standing, honest and decent, proper in appearance or behavior. 2. of a moderately good standard or size etc., not bringing disgrace or embarrassment, *a respectable score.* **re·spect'a·bly** *adv.* **re·spect·a·bil·i·ty** (ri-spek-tă-bil-i-tee) *n.*

re·spect·ful (ri-spekt-fŭl) *adj.* showing respect. **re·spect'ful·ly** *adv.* **re·spect'ful·ness** *n.*

re·spect·ing (ri-spek-ting) *prep.* concerning, with respect to.

re·spec·tive (ri-spek-tiv) *adj.* belonging to each as an individual, *were given places according to their respective ranks.*

re·spec·tive·ly (ri-spek-tiv-lee) *adv.* for each separately, in the order mentioned.

res·pi·ra·tion (res-pi-ray-shŏn) *n.* 1. breathing. 2. a plant's absorption of oxygen and emission of carbon dioxide.

re·sol'der *v.*
re·so·lic'it *v.*
re·so·lic·i·ta'tion *n.*
re·sow' *v.* (-sowed, -sown or
-sowed, -sow·ing)
re·spell' *v.*

res·pi·ra·tor (res-pǐ-ray-tŏr) *n.* 1. a device worn over the nose and mouth to filter or purify the air before it is inhaled. 2. an apparatus for giving artificial respiration.

res·pi·ra·to·ry (res-pǐ-ră-tohr-ee) *adj.* of or involving respiration.

re·spire (ri-spɪr) *v.* (**re·spired, re·spir·ing**) to breathe, (of plants) to perform the process of respiration. **re·spir'a·ble** *adj.* **re·spir·a·bil·i·ty** (ri-spɪr-ă-bil-i-tee) *n.*

res·pite (res-pit) *n.* 1. an interval of rest or relief. 2. delay permitted before an obligation must be fulfilled or a penalty suffered.

re·splend·ent (ri-splen-dĕnt) *adj.* brilliant with color or decorations. **re·splend'ent·ly** *adv.* **re·splend'ence** *n.*

re·spond (ri-spond) *v.* to make an answer. **re·spond'er** *n.* ☐**respond to,** to act or behave in answer to or because of, *the horse responds to the bridle; the vehicle responds to its controls; the disease did not respond to treatment,* was not cured or relieved by it; *she responds to kindness,* behaves better if treated kindly.

re·spond·ent (ri-spon-dĕnt) *n.* a person who responds, especially a defendant in various legal proceedings. **respondent** *adj.* making answer.

re·sponse (ri-spons) *n.* 1. an answer. 2. any part of the liturgy said or sung in answer to the priest. 3. an act or feeling or movement produced by a stimulus or by another's action.

re·spon·si·bil·i·ty (ri-spon-sĭ-bil-i-tee) *n.* (*pl.* -ties) 1. being responsible. 2. something for which one is responsible.

re·spon·si·ble (ri-spon-sĭ-bĕl) *adj.* 1. legally or morally obliged to take care of something or to carry out a duty, liable to be blamed for loss or failure etc. 2. having to account for one's actions, *you will be responsible to the president himself.* 3. capable of rational conduct. 4. trustworthy, *a responsible person.* 5. involving important duties, *a responsible position.* 6. being the cause of something, *the plague was responsible for many deaths.* **re·spon'si·bly** *adv.* **re·spon'si·ble·ness** *n.*

re·spon·sive (ri-spon-siv) *adj.* responding warmly and favorably to an influence. **re·spon'sive·ly** *adv.* **re·spon'sive·ness** *n.*

rest[1] (rest) *v.* 1. to be still, to cease from movement or action or working, especially in order to regain one's energy. 2. to cause or allow to do this, *sit down and rest your feet.* 3. (of a matter under discussion) to be left without further investigation. 4. to place or be placed for support, *rested the parcel on the table.* 5. to rely, *the case rests on evidence of identification.* 6. (of a look) to alight, to be directed, *his gaze rested on his son.* **rest** *n.* 1. inactivity or sleep as a way of regaining one's energy, a period of this. 2. a prop or support for an object. 3. an interval of silence between notes in music, a sign indicating this. **rest'er** *n.* ☐**at rest,** not moving; (of the dead) free from trouble or anxiety; *set your mind at rest,* stop being anxious. **come to rest,** to cease movement. **lay**

to rest, *see* **lay**[3]. **rest cure,** a prolonged period of rest, usually in bed, as medical treatment. **rest home,** a place where old or frail people can be cared for. **rest room,** a public toilet.

rest[2] *v.* 1. to be left in the hands or charge of, *it rests with you to suggest terms.* 2. to remain in a specified state, *rest assured, it will be a success.* **rest** *n.* the rest, the remaining part, the others.

res·tau·rant (res-tă-rănt) *n.* a place where meals can be bought and eaten.

res·tau·ra·teur (res-tă-ră-tur) *n.* the proprietor of a restaurant.

rest·ful (rest-fŭl) *adj.* giving rest or a feeling of rest. **rest'ful·ly** *adv.* **rest'ful·ness** *n.*

res·ti·tu·tion (res-ti-too-shŏn) *n.* 1. restoration of a thing to its proper owner or its original state. 2. reparation for injury or damage.

res·tive (res-tiv) *adj.* restless, resisting control because made impatient by delay or restraint. **res'tive·ly** *adv.* **res'tive·ness** *n.*

rest·less (rest-lis) *adj.* 1. unable to rest or to be still. 2. without rest or sleep, *a restless night.* **rest'less·ly** *adv.* **rest'less·ness** *n.*

res·to·ra·tion (res-tŏ-ray-shŏn) *n.* 1. restoring, being restored. 2. an object restored to its original state, as a painting, an old building, etc. ☐**the Restoration,** the reestablishment of the monarchy in England in 1660 when Charles II became king.

re·stor·a·tive (ri-stohr-ă-tiv) *adj.* tending to restore health or strength. **restorative** *n.* a restorative food or medicine or treatment.

re·store (ri-stohr) *v.* (**re·stored, re·stor·ing**) 1. to bring back to its original state by repairing or rebuilding etc. 2. to bring back to good health or vigor. 3. to put back in its former position, to reinstate. **re·stor'er** *n.* **re·stor'a·ble** *adj.*

re·strain (ri-strayn) *v.* to hold back (a person or thing) from movement or action, to keep under control. **re·strain'er** *n.* **re·strain'a·ble** *adj.*

re·strained (ri-straynd) *adj.* showing restraint. **re·strain·ed·ly** (ri-stray-nid-lee) *adv.*

re·straint (ri-straynt) *n.* 1. restraining, being restrained. 2. something that restrains, a limiting influence. 3. avoidance of exaggeration in literary or artistic work. ☐**restraint of trade,** an action seeking to interfere with free-market conditions.

re·strict (ri-strikt) *v.* to put a limit on, to subject to limitations. **re·stric·tion** (ri-strik-shŏn) *n.* **re·strict'ed** *adj.* **re·strict'ed·ly** *adv.*

re·stric·tive (ri-strik-tiv) *adj.* restricting. **re·stric'tive·ly** *adv.* **re·stric'tive·ness** *n.* ☐**restrictive clause,** a clause that limits the meaning of a word or phrase, as "that she carried" in *the bag that she carried was heavy.* **restrictive practices,** agreements to limit competition or output in industry.

re·sult (ri-zult) *n.* 1. that which is produced by an activity or operation, an effect. 2. a statement of the score or marks or the name of the winner in a sporting event or competition or examination. 3. an answer or formula etc. obtained by calcula-

re·staff' *v.*
re·stage' *v.* (-staged, -stag·ing)
re·start' *v.*
re·state' *v.* (-stat·ed, -stat·ing)
re·stock' *v.*
re·straight'en *v.*

re·strength'en *v.*
re·string' *v.* (-strung, -string·ing)
re·struc'ture *v.* (-tured, -tur·ing)
re·stud'y *v.* (-stud·ied, -stud·y·ing)
re·stuff' *v.*

re·style' *v.* (-styled, -sty·ling)
re·sub·mis'sion *n.*
re·sub·mit' *v.* (-mit·ted, -mit·ting)
re·sub·scribe' *v.* (-scribed, -scrib·ing)
re·sub·scrip'tion *n.*

tion. **result** v. 1. to occur as a result, *the troubles that resulted from the merger.* 2. to have a specified result, *the match resulted in a draw.* □**get results,** to achieve a significant and satisfactory result.

re·sult·ant (ri-zul-tănt) *adj.* occurring as a result, *the resultant profit.* **resultant** *n.* a force etc. equivalent to two or more of these acting in different directions at the same point.

re·sume (ri-zoom) v. **(re·sumed, re·sum·ing)** 1. to get or take or occupy again; *resume one's seat,* to sit down again. 2. to begin again, to begin to speak or work or use again. **re·sump·tion** (ri-zump-shŏn) *n.*

ré·su·mé, re·su·me (rez-uu-may) *n.* 1. a summary. 2. a brief account of one's qualifications and experience, prepared for use in applying for a job.

re·sup·ply (ree-sŭ-plɪ) v. **(re·sup·plied, re·sup·ply·ing)** to supply again.

re·sur·face (ree-sur-fis) v. **(re·sur·faced, re·sur·fac·ing)** 1. to put a new surface on (a road etc.). 2. to come to the surface again; *the problem resurfaced,* reappeared.

re·sur·gence (ri-sur-jĕns) *n.* a rise or revival after defeat or destruction or disappearance etc. **re·sur′gent** *adj.*

res·ur·rect (rez-ŭ-rekt) v. to bring back into use, *resurrect an old custom.*

res·ur·rec·tion (rez-ŭ-rek-shŏn) *n.* 1. rising from the dead. 2. revival after disuse. □**the Resurrection,** Christ's rising from the dead.

re·sus·ci·tate (ri-sus-i-tayt) v. **(re·sus·ci·tat·ed, re·sus·ci·tat·ing)** 1. to bring back or come back from unconsciousness. 2. to revive (a custom or institution etc.). **re·sus·ci·ta·tion** (ri-sus-i-tay-shŏn) *n.*

re·sus·ci·ta·tor (ri-sus-i-tay-tŏr) *n.* 1. a person or thing that resuscitates. 2. a respiratory machine that provides oxygen or a mixture of oxygen and carbon dioxide to a person's lungs to restore respiration.

ret. *abbr.* 1. retain. 2. retired. 3. return.

re·tail (ree-tayl) *n.* the selling of goods to the general public (not for resale). **retail** *adj. & adv.* in the retail trade. **retail** v. 1. to sell or be sold in the retail trade. 2. to recount, to relate details of. **re′tail·er** *n.*

re·tain (ri-tayn) v. 1. to keep in one's possession or use. 2. to continue to have, not lose, *the fire had retained its heat.* 3. to keep in one's memory, *she retained a clear impression of the building.* 4. to hold in place; *a retaining wall,* one supporting and confining a mass of earth. 5. to hire by paying a retainer. **re·tain′ment** *n.*

re·tain·er (ri-tay-nĕr) *n.* 1. a fee paid to retain certain services. 2. *(old use)* an attendant of a person of rank. □**old retainer,** *(humorous use)* a faithful old servant.

re·take (ree-tayk) v. **(re·took, re·tak·en, re·tak·ing)** 1. to take again. 2. to recapture, as on film. **retake** (ree-tayk) *n.* 1. the act of retaking. 2. the second or subsequent filming of a scene.

re·tal·i·ate (ri-tal-i-ayt) v. **(re·tal·i·at·ed, re·tal·i·at·ing)** to repay an injury or insult etc.

with a similar one, to make a counterattack. **re·tal·i·a·tion** (ri-tal-i-ay-shŏn) *n.* **re·tal·i·a·to·ry** (ri-tal-i-ă-tohr-ee) *adj.*

re·tard (ri-tahrd) v. to cause delay to, to slow the progress of. **retard** *n.* a delay. **re·tard′er** *n.* **re·tar·da·tion** (ree-tahr-day-shŏn) *n.*

re·tard·ant (ri-tahr-dănt) *n.* something that retards, especially a substance that reduces the speed of a specific reaction. **retardant** *adj.* capable of retarding.

re·tard·ate (ri-tahr-dayt) *n.* a mentally retarded person.

re·tard·ed (ri-tahr-did) *adj.* backward in mental or physical development.

retch (rech) v. to strain one's throat as if vomiting.

retd. *abbr.* 1. retained. 2. retired. 3. returned.

re·tell (ree-tel) v. **(re·told, re·tell·ing)** to tell (a story etc.) again.

re·ten·tion (ri-ten-shŏn) *n.* retaining.

re·ten·tive (ri-ten-tiv) *adj.* able to retain things, *a retentive memory.* **re·ten′tive·ness** *n.*

re·think (ree-think) v. **(re·thought, re·think·ing)** to think about again, to plan again and differently.

ret·i·cent (ret-i-sĕnt) *adj.* not revealing one's thoughts and feelings readily, discreet. **ret′i·cent·ly** *adv.* **ret′i·cence** *n.*

ret·i·cle (ret-i-kĕl) *n.* the network of fine threads or lines in the focal plane of optical instruments to help accurate observation.

ret·i·na (ret-ĭ-nă) *n.* (*pl.* **-nas, -nae,** *pr.* -nee) a layer of membrane at the back of the eyeball, sensitive to light. **ret′i·nal** *adj.*

ret·i·nue (ret-ĭ-noo) *n.* a number of attendants accompanying an important person. **ret′i·nued** *adj.*

re·tire (ri-tɪr) v. **(re·tired, re·tir·ing)** 1. to give up one's regular work because of advancing age, to cause (an employee) to do this. 2. to withdraw, to retreat. 3. to go to bed or to one's private room. 4. to remove from circulation, as currency bills or bonds. 5. (in baseball) to cause (a batter) to be out. **re·tired′** *adj.* **re·tire′ment** *n.*

re·tir·ee (re-tɪ-ree) *n.* a person who has retired from his work.

re·tir·ing (ri-tɪr-ing) *adj.* shy, avoiding society. **re·tir′ing·ly** *adv.*

re·tort[1] (ri-tort) v. to make a quick or witty or angry reply. **retort** *n.* retorting, a reply of this kind.

retort[2] *n.* a vessel (usually of glass) with a long downward-bent neck, used in distilling liquids.

re·touch (ree-tuch) v. to improve or alter (a picture or photograph) by making minor alterations or removing flaws etc. **re·touch′er** *n.* **re·touch′a·ble** *adj.*

re·trace (ri-trays) v. **(re·traced, re·trac·ing)** to trace back to the source or beginning; *retrace one's steps,* go back the way one came. **re·trace′a·ble** *adj.*

re·tract (ri-trakt) v. 1. to pull (a thing) back or in, *the snail retracts its horns.* 2. to withdraw (a statement), to refuse to keep to (an agreement). **re·trac·tion** (ri-trak-shŏn) *n.*

---

re·sum′mon v.
re·sum′mon·a·ble *adj.*
re·sup·press′ v.
re·sup·pres′sion *n.*
re·sur·vey′ v.

re·swear′ v. **(-swore, -swear·ing)**
re·teach′ v. **(-taught, -teach·ing)**
re·test′ v.

re·thread′ v.
re·tie′ v. **(-tied, -ty·ing)**
re·ti′tle v. **(-tled, -tling)**

re·tract·a·ble (ri-trak-tă-běl) *adj.* able to be retracted.

re·trac·tile (ri-trak-til) *adj.* retractable.

re·trac·tor (ri-trak-tŏr) *n.* a device or muscle for retraction.

re·tread (ree-tred) *v.* to put a new tread on (a worn auto tire). **retread** (ree-tred) *n.* a retreaded tire or the tread itself.

re·treat (ri-treet) *v.* to withdraw after being defeated or when faced with danger or difficulty, to go away to a place of shelter. **retreat** *n.* 1. retreating, the military signal for this. 2. a military bugle call at sunset. 3. withdrawal into privacy or seclusion, a place for this. 4. a period of withdrawal from worldly activities for prayer and meditation.

re·trench (ri-trench) *v.* 1. to reduce the amount of, *retrench one's operations.* 2. to reduce one's expenditure or operations, *we shall have to retrench.* **re·trench′ment** *n.*

re·tri·al (ree-trɪ-ăl) *n.* the trying of a lawsuit again.

ret·ri·bu·tion (ret-rĭ-byoo-shŏn) *n.* a deserved punishment. **re·trib·u·to·ry** (ri-trib-yŭ-tohr-ee) *adj.*

re·trib·u·tive (ri-trib-yŭ-tiv) *adj.* happening or inflicted as retribution.

re·triev·a·ble (ri-tree-vă-běl) *adj.* able to be retrieved.

re·triev·al (ri-tree-văl) *n.* retrieving, being retrieved.

re·trieve (ri-treev) *v.* (**re·trieved, re·triev·ing**) 1. to regain possession of. 2. to find again (stored information etc.). 3. (of a dog) to find and bring in (killed or wounded game). 4. to rescue, to restore to a flourishing state, *retrieve one's fortunes.* 5. to set right (a loss or error or bad situation). **retrieve** *n.* possibility of recovery, *beyond retrieve.*

re·triev·er (ri-tree-věr) *n.* a dog of a breed that is often trained to retrieve game.

ret·ro·ac·tive (ret-roh-ak-tiv) *adj.* effective as from a past date; *a retroactive pay increase,* one that is backdated. **ret·ro·ac′tive·ly** *adv.*

ret·ro·fire (ret-roh-fir) *v.* (**ret·ro·fired, ret·ro·fir·ing**) to ignite (a retrorocket), to become ignited thus.

ret·ro·fit (ret-roh-fit) *v.* (**ret·ro·fit·ted, ret·ro·fit·ting**) to fit with new equipment, as an aircraft.

ret·ro·grade (ret-rŏ-grayd) *adj.* 1. going backward, *retrograde motion.* 2. reverting to an inferior state. **retrograde** *v.* (**ret·ro·grad·ed, ret·ro·grad·ing**) 1. to move backward, to recede, to retreat. 2. to deteriorate.

ret·ro·gress (ret-rŏ-gres) *v.* 1. to move backward, to deteriorate. 2. to revert. **ret·ro·gres·sion** (ret-rŏ-gresh-ŏn) *n.* **ret·ro·gres′sive** *adj.*

ret·ro·rock·et (ret-roh-rok-it) *n.* an auxiliary rocket discharging its exhaust in the opposite direction to the main rockets, used for slowing a spacecraft.

ret·ro·spect (ret-rŏ-spekt) *n.* a survey of past time or events. **ret·ro·spec·tion** (ret-rŏ-spek-shŏn) *n.* □**in retrospect,** when one looks back on a past event or situation.

ret·ro·spec·tive (ret-rŏ-spek-tiv) *adj.* 1. looking back on the past. 2. applying to the past as well as the future, *the law could not be made retrospective.* **retrospective** *n.* an exhibition of the work done by an artist at different stages of his career. **ret·ro·spec′tive·ly** *adv.*

ret·rous·sé (re-troo-say) *adj.* (of the nose) turned up at the tip.

re·try (ree-trɪ) *v.* (**re·tried, re·try·ing**) to try (a lawsuit or a defendant) again.

ret·si·na (ret-sĭ-nă) *n.* a resin-flavored Greek wine.

re·turn (ri-turn) *v.* 1. to come or go back. 2. to bring or give or put or send back. 3. to say in reply. 4. to state or describe officially, especially in answer to a formal demand for information. 5. to elect as a member of Congress or other legislative body. **return** *n.* 1. coming or going back. 2. bringing or giving or putting or sending or paying back. 3. the proceeds or profits of a transaction, *brings a good return on one's investment.* 4. a reply. 5. a return ticket. 6. a formal report, as of a set of transactions, *income tax return.* 7. (usually *returns*) a report of votes in an election. **re·turn′er** *n.* □**return match** *or* **game,** a second match or game between the same opponents. **return ticket,** a ticket for a journey to a place and back to one's starting point.

re·turn·a·ble (ri-tur-nă-běl) *adj.* that can be or must be returned.

re·turn·ee (ri-tur-nee) *n.* a person who returns, especially one returning from military service abroad.

re·type (ree-tɪp) *v.* (**re·typed, re·typ·ing**) to type again.

re·un·ion (ree-yoon-yŏn) *n.* 1. reuniting, being reunited. 2. a social gathering of people after being apart.

re·u·nite (ree-yoo-nɪt) *v.* (**re·u·nit·ed, re·u·nit·ing**) to unite again after separation.

re·us·a·ble (ree-yoo-ză-běl) *adj.* able to be reused. **re·us·a·bil·i·ty** (ree-yoo-ză-bil-i-tee) *n.*

re·use (ree-yoos) *n.* using or being used again. **reuse** (ree-yooz) *v.* (**re·used, re·us·ing**) to use again.

rev (rev) *n.* a revolution of an engine. **rev** *v.* (**revved, rev·ving**) 1. (of an engine) to revolve. 2. to cause (an engine) to run quickly, especially when starting.

rev. *abbr.* 1. revenue. 2. reverse. 3. review. 4. revised. 5. revision. 6. revolution.

Rev. *abbr.* 1. Revelation. 2. Reverend, *the Rev. John Smith* or *the Rev. J. Smith* or *the Rev. Mr. Smith.* (▷not *the Rev. Smith*).

re·val·ue (ree-val-yoo) *v.* (**re·val·ued, re·val·u·ing**) to reassess the value of.

re·vamp (ree-vamp) *v.* to renovate, to give a new appearance to.

re·vanch·ism (ri-vahn-chiz-ěm) *n.* the policy of seeking to recover lost territory etc.

re·veal (ri-veel) *v.* to make known, to uncover and allow to be seen. **re·veal′ment** *n.* **re·veal′ing·ly** *adv.*

rev·eil·le (rev-ě-lee) *n.* a morning bugle call to awaken military personnel.

rev·el (rev-ěl) *v.* (**rev·eled, rev·el·ing**) 1. to take

---

re·train′ *v.*

re·trans·late′ *v.* (**-lat·ed, -lat·ing**)

re·trans·mit′ *v.* (**-mit·ted, -mit·ting**)

re·u·ni·fi·ca′tion *n.*

re·u′ni·fy *v.* (**-fied, -fy·ing**)

re·up·hol′ster *v.*

re·u·ti·li·za′tion *n.*

re·u′ti·lize *v.* (**-lized, -liz·ing**)

re·ut′ter *v.*

re·val′u·ate *v.* (**-at·ed, -at·ing**)

re·val·u·a′tion *n.*

re·var′nish *v.*

great delight, *some people revel in gossip.* 2. to hold revels. **revel** *n.* 1. reveling. 2. *revels,* an occasion of boisterous merrymaking. **rev'el•er** *n.*
rev•e•la•tion (rev-ĕ-lay-shŏn) *n.* 1. revealing, making known something that was secret or hidden. 2. something revealed, especially something surprising. 3. *Revelation,* the last book of the New Testament (*see* **Apocalypse**). (▷This book is often referred to incorrectly as *Revelations.*) **rev•e•la'tion•al** *adj.* **re•vel•a•to•ry** (ri-vel-ă-tohr-ee, rev-ĕ-lă-) *adj.*
rev•el•ry (rev-ĕl-ree) *n.* reveling, revels.
re•venge (ri-venj) *n.* 1. punishment or injury inflicted in return for what one has suffered. 2. a desire to inflict this. 3. opportunity to defeat in a return game an opponent who won the first game. **revenge** *v.* **(re•venged, re•veng•ing)** to avenge; *be revenged* or *revenge oneself,* to get satisfaction by inflicting vengeance. **re•veng'er** *n.* **re•venge'ful** *adj.*
rev•e•nue (rev-ĕ-noo, -nyoo) *n.* a country's annual income from taxes, duties, etc., used for paying public expenses. ☐**revenue cutter,** a small armed government ship used to prevent smuggling. **revenue officer,** a government agent concerned with the enforcement of revenue laws and the prevention of smuggling. **revenue stamp,** a stamp that indicates a tax has been paid.
re•verb (ri-vurb, ree-vurb) *n. (informal)* 1. reverberation. 2. an echo produced electronically in recorded music. 3. a device for producing this.
re•ver•ber•ate (ri-vur-bĕ-rayt) *v.* **(re•ver•ber•at•ed, re•ver•ber•at•ing)** to echo, to resound. **re•ver'ber•a•tor** *n.* **re•ver•ber•a•tion** (ri-vur-bĕ-ray-shŏn) *n.*
re•vere (ri-veer) *v.* **(re•vered, re•ver•ing)** to feel deep respect or religious veneration for.
rev•er•ence (rev-ĕ-rĕns) *n.* 1. a feeling of awe and respect or veneration. 2. (*old use* or *humorous*) a title used in speaking to or about a clergyman, *your* or *his reverence.* **reverence** *v.* **(rev•er•enced, rev•er•enc•ing)** to feel or show reverence toward.
rev•er•end (rev-ĕ-rĕnd) *adj.* 1. deserving to be treated with respect. 2. *the Reverend,* the title of a clergyman (▷see the note under **Rev.**). **reverend** *n. (informal)* a clergyman.
rev•er•ent (rev-ĕ-rĕnt) *adj.* feeling or showing reverence. **rev'er•ent•ly** *adv.*
rev•er•en•tial (rev-ĕ-ren-shăl) *adj.* reverent.
rev•er•ie, rev•er•y (rev-ĕ-ree) *n.* (*pl.* -**er•ies**) a daydream, a state of daydreaming.
re•ver•sal (ri-vur-săl) *n.* reversing, being reversed.
re•verse (ri-vurs) *adj.* facing or moving in the opposite direction, opposite in character or order, upside down. **reverse** *v.* **(re•versed, re•vers•ing)** 1. to turn the other way around or up or inside out. 2. to convert to the opposite kind or effect, *reversed the tendency; reverse the charges,* make the recipient (not the caller) pay for a telephone call. 3. to annul (a decree or decision etc.). 4. to move in the opposite direction, (of a vehicle) to travel backward. 5. to make (an engine or machine) work in the opposite direction, to cause (a vehicle) to travel backward. **reverse** *n.* 1. the reverse side or effect. 2. the opposite of the usual manner, *the name was printed in reverse.* 3. a piece of misfortune, *suffered several reverses.* 4. reverse gear. **re•vers'er** *n.* **re•verse'ly** *adv.* ☐**reverse**

gear, a gear used to make a vehicle etc. travel backward.
re•vers•i•ble (ri-vur-si-bĕl) *adj.* able to be reversed, (of a garment) able to be worn with either side turned outward. **reversible** *n.* a reversible garment. **re•vers'i•bly** *adv.* **re•vers•i•bil•i•ty** (ri-vur-sĭ-bil-i-tee) *n.* **re•vers'i•ble•ness** *n.*
re•ver•sion (ri-vur-zhŏn) *n.* 1. reverting. 2. the legal right to possess something when its present holder relinquishes it, the returning of a right or property in this way. **re•ver•sion•ar•y** (ri-vur-zhŏ-ner-ee) *adj.* ▷Note that *reversion* does not mean *reversal.*
re•vert (ri-vurt) *v.* 1. to return to a former condition or habit or type. 2. to return to a subject in talk or thought. 3. (of property etc.) to return or pass to another owner by reversion. **re•vert'i•ble** *adj.*
re•view (ri-vyoo) *n.* 1. a general survey of past events or of a subject. 2. a reexamination or reconsideration; *the salary scale is under review,* is being reconsidered. 3. a ceremonial inspection of troops or a fleet etc. 4. a published report assessing the merits of a book or play etc. **review** *v.* 1. to survey. 2. to reexamine or reconsider. 3. to inspect (troops or a fleet etc.) ceremonially. 4. to write a review of (a book or play etc.). **re•view•er** (ri-vyoo-ĕr) *n.* ▷Do not confuse *review* with *revue.*
re•vile (ri-vɪl) *v.* **(re•viled, re•vil•ing)** to criticize angrily in abusive language. **re•vil'er** *n.* **re•vile'ment** *n.*
re•vise (ri-vɪz) *v.* **(re•vised, re•vis•ing)** 1. to reexamine and alter or correct. 2. to go over (work already learned) in preparation for an examination. **re•vis'er** *n.* **re•vi'sor** *n.* **re•vis'a•ble** *adj.*
re•vi•sion (ri-vizh-ŏn) *n.* ☐**Revised Version,** the revision (1870–84) of the Authorized Version of the Bible. **Revised Standard Version,** the revision (1937–52) of the American Standard Version of the Bible.
re•vi•sion•ist (ri-vizh-ŏ-nist) *n.* a Communist who insists on modifying the Marxist theories or practices that are considered authoritative. **re•vi'sion•ism** *n.*
re•vi•tal•ize (ree-vɪ-tă-lɪz) *v.* **(re•vi•tal•ized, re•vi•tal•iz•ing)** to bring back vitality to. **re•vi•tal•i•za•tion** (ree-vɪ-tă-li-zay-shŏn) *n.*
re•viv•al (ri-vɪ-văl) *n.* 1. reviving, being revived. 2. something brought back into use or fashion. 3. a reawakening of interest in religion, a special effort with meetings etc. to promote this.
re•viv•al•ist (ri-vɪ-vă-list) *n.* a person who organizes or conducts meetings to promote a religious revival.
re•vive (ri-vɪv) *v.* **(re•vived, re•viv•ing)** 1. to come or bring back to life or consciousness or strength. 2. to come or bring back into use or activity or fashion etc. **re•viv'er** *n.*
re•viv•i•fy (ri-viv-ĭ-fɪ) *v.* **(re•viv•i•fied, re•viv•i•fy•ing)** to give new life to. **re•viv•i•fi•ca•tion** (ri-viv-ĭ-fɪ-kay-shŏn) *n.*
re•vo•ca•ble (rev-ŏ-kă-bĕl) *adj.* able to be repealed, withdrawn, or rescinded.
re•voke (ri-vohk) *v.* **(re•voked, re•vok•ing)** 1. to withdraw or cancel (a decree or license etc.). 2. to fail to follow suit in a card game when able to do so. **re•vok'er** *n.* **rev•o•ca•tion** (rev-ŏ-kay-shŏn) *n.*
re•volt (ri-vohlt) *v.* 1. to take part in a rebellion. 2. to be in a mood of protest or defiance. 3. to

re•ver•i•fi•ca'tion *n.*   **re•ver'i•fy** *v.* (-fied, -fy•ing)   **re•vis'it** *v.*

feel strong disgust. 4. to cause a feeling of strong disgust in (a person). **revolt** n. 1. an act or state of rebelling or defying authority. 2. a sense of disgust. **re·volt'er** n.

re·volt·ing (ri-vohl-ting) adj. causing disgust. **re·volt'ing·ly** adv.

rev·o·lu·tion (rev-ŏ-loo-shŏn) n. 1. substitution of a new system of government, especially by force. 2. any complete change of method or conditions etc., a revolution in the treatment of burns. 3. revolving, rotation, a single complete orbit or movement of this kind.

rev·o·lu·tion·ar·y (rev-ŏ-loo-shŏ-ner-ee) adj. 1. of political revolution. 2. involving a great change, revolutionary new ideas. **revolutionary** n. (pl. -ar·ies) a person who begins or supports a political revolution. □**Revolutionary War,** see **American Revolution.**

rev·o·lu·tion·ist (rev-ŏ-loo-shŏ-nist) n. a person who takes part in a revolution or supports revolution.

rev·o·lu·tion·ize (rev-ŏ-loo-shŏ-nɪz) v. (**rev·o·lu·tion·ized, rev·o·lu·tion·iz·ing**) to alter (a thing) completely, the discovery will revolutionize our lives. **rev·o·lu'tion·iz·er** n.

re·volve (ri-volv) v. (**re·volved, re·volv·ing**) 1. to turn or cause to turn around, to rotate. 2. to move in a circular orbit. 3. to turn over (a problem etc.) in one's mind. **re·volv'a·ble** adj. □**revolving door,** a door with several partitions turning around a central axis. **revolving fund,** a fund from which loans are made by using money repaid on earlier loans.

re·volv·er (ri-vol-věr) n. a pistol with a revolving mechanism that makes it possible to fire it a number of times without reloading.

re·vue (ri-vyoo) n. a theatrical entertainment consisting of a series of unrelated skits and musical episodes, often satirizing current events. **re·vu'ist** n. ▷ Do not confuse revue with review.

re·vul·sion (ri-vul-shŏn) n. 1. a feeling of strong disgust. 2. a sudden violent change of feeling, a revulsion of public feeling in favor of the accused woman.

re·ward (ri-word) n. 1. something given or received in return for what is done or for a service or merit. 2. a sum of money offered for the detection of a criminal, return of lost property, etc. **reward** v. to give a reward to.

re·ward·ing (ri-wor-ding) adj. (of an occupation) well worth doing.

re·wire (ree-wɪr) v. (**re·wired, re·wir·ing**) to renew the electrical wiring of.

re·word (ree-wurd) v. to change the wording of.

re·work (ree-wurk) v. (**re·worked, re·work·ing**) 1. to do (something) again in order to bring about another result. 2. to think (a problem) through again in order to find the correct or best solution.

re·write (ree-rɪt) v. (**re·wrote, re·writ·ten, re·writ·ing**) to write (a thing) again in a different form or style. **re·writ'er** n.

Rey·kja·vik (ray-kyă-veek) the capital of Iceland.

re·zone (ree-zohn) v. (**re·zoned, re·zon·ing**) to change the zoning of.

RF abbr. radio frequency.

RFD abbr. rural free delivery.

Rh abbr. Rhesus. □**Rh factor,** a substance present in the blood of most people and some animals, causing a blood disorder in a newborn baby whose blood is Rh positive (= containing this substance) while its mother's blood is Rh negative (= not containing it).

Rh symbol rhodium.

r.h. abbr. right hand.

rhap·so·dize (rap-sŏ-dɪz) v. (**rhap·so·dized, rhap·so·diz·ing**) to talk or write about something in an ecstatic way.

rhap·so·dy (rap-sŏ-dee) n. (pl. -dies) 1. an ecstatic written or spoken statement. 2. a romantic musical composition in an irregular form. **rhap'so·dist** n. **rhap·sod·ic** (rap-sod-ik) adj. **rhap·sod'i·cal** adj. **rhap·sod'i·cal·ly** adv.

rhe·a (ree-ă) n. a South American flightless bird like an ostrich.

rhe·ni·um (ree-ni-ŭm) n. a rare metallic element of the manganese group.

rhe·ol·o·gy (ree-ol-ŏ-jee) n. the science dealing with the flow and the deformation of matter. **rhe·o·log·ic** (ree-ŏ-loj-ik) adj. **rhe·o·log'i·cal** adj. **rhe·ol'o·gist** n.

rhe·om·e·ter (ree-om-ĕ-tĕr) n. a meter that measures the flow of liquid matter.

rhe·o·stat (ree-ŏ-stat) n. an electrical instrument used to control current by varying resistance. **rhe·o·stat·ic** (ree-ŏ-stat-ik) adj.

rhe·sus (ree-sŭs) n. a small monkey common in northern India, used in biological experiments. □**Rhesus factor** = Rh factor.

rhet. abbr. 1. rhetoric. 2. rhetorical.

rhet·o·ric (ret-ŏ-rik) n. 1. the art of using words impressively, especially in public speaking. 2. language used for its impressive sound, affected or exaggerated expressions. **rhet·o·ri·cian** (ret-ŏ-rish-ăn) n. an expert in the effective use of language.

rhe·tor·i·cal (ri-tor-i-kăl) adj. expressed in a way that is designed to be impressive. **rhe·tor'i·cal·ly** adv. □**rhetorical question,** something phrased as a question only for dramatic effect and not to seek an answer, such as who cares? (= nobody cares).

rheu·mat·ic (roo-mat-ik) adj. of or affected with rheumatism. **rheu·mat'i·cal·ly** adv. □**rheumatic fever,** a serious form of rheumatism with fever, chiefly in children.

rheu·ma·tism (roo-mă-tiz-ĕm) n. any of several diseases causing pain in the joints or muscles or fibrous tissue, especially rheumatoid arthritis.

rheu·ma·toid (roo-mă-toid) adj. of rheumatism. □**rheumatoid arthritis,** a disease causing inflammation and stiffening of the joints.

Rhine·land (rɪn-land) the region of Germany lying west of the river Rhine.

rhine·stone (rɪn-stohn) n. an imitation diamond.

Rhine (rɪn) wine wine from the Rhine vineyards, usually white wine.

rhi·ni·tis (rɪ-nɪ-tis) n. inflammation of the mucous membrane of the nose.

rhi·no (rɪ-noh) n. (pl. -nos, -no) (slang) a rhinoceros.

rhi·noc·er·os (rɪ-nos-ĕ-rŏs) n. (pl. -er·os·es,

---

re·warm' v.	**-weav·ing)**	**re·weld'** v.
re·wash' v.	**re·wed'** v. (-wed·ded, wed·	**re·wid'en** v.
re·weave' v. (-wove or	ded or wed, -wed·ding)	**re·wind'** v. (-wound,
-weaved, -wo·ven,	**re·weigh'** v.	-wind·ing)

-er·os) a large thick-skinned animal of Africa and south Asia, with a horn or two horns on its nose.

rhi·zome (rı-zohm) *n.* a rootlike stem growing along or under the ground and sending out both roots and shoots. **rhi·zom·a·tous** (rı-zom-ă-tŭs) *adj.*

rho (roh) *n.* (*pl.* **rhos**) the seventeenth letter of the Greek alphabet (Ρ ρ).

Rhode (rohd) **Island** a state of the U.S.

Rho·de·sia (roh-dee-zhă) *see* **Zimbabwe**.

rho·di·um (roh-di-ŭm) *n.* a hard white metallic element of the platinum group.

rho·do·den·dron (roh-dŏ-den-drŏn) *n.* an evergreen shrub with large clusters of trumpet-shaped flowers.

rhomb·boid (rom-boid) *n.* a parallelogram with oblique angles and unequal adjacent sides.

rhom·bus (rom-bŭs) *n.* (*pl.* **-bus·es**, **-bi**, *pr.* -bı) a geometric figure shaped like the diamond on playing cards.

rhu·barb (roo-bahrb) *n.* 1. a garden plant with fleshy reddish leafstalks that are used like fruit. 2. *(slang)* a quarrel.

rhumb (rum) **line** a line cutting all meridians at the same angle, a line followed by a ship sailing in a fixed direction.

rhyme (rım) *n.* 1. identity of sound between words or syllables or the endings of lines of verse (such as *line/mine/pine, visit/is it*). 2. a poem with rhymes. 3. a word providing a rhyme to another. **rhyme** *v.* (**rhymed, rhym·ing**) to form a rhyme, to have rhymes. **rhym'er** *n.* **rhyme'ster** *n.* ☐**rhyming slang**, slang in which words are replaced by words that rhyme with them, such as *apples and pears* = stairs. **without rhyme or reason**, with no sensible or logical reason.

rhy·o·lite (rı-ŏ-lıt) *n.* a fine-grained volcanic rock.

rhythm (rith-ĕm) *n.* 1. the pattern produced by emphasis and duration of notes in music or by long and short syllables in words. 2. a movement with a regular succession of strong and weak elements, *the rhythm of the heart beating*. 3. a constantly recurring sequence of events. **rhyth·mic** (rith-mik) *adj.* **rhyth'mi·cal** *adj.* **rhyth'mi·cal·ly** *adv.* ☐**rhythm and blues**, popular music with blues themes and strong rhythm. **rhythm method**, contraception by avoiding sexual intercourse near the time of probable ovulation.

RI, R.I. *abbr.* Rhode Island.

ri·al (ree-awl) *n.* the unit of money in Iran and certain other countries.

rib (rib) *n.* 1. one of the curved bones around the chest. 2. a cut of meat from this part of an animal. 3. a curved structural part resembling a rib, such as a raised molding on a ceiling. 4. one of the hinged rods forming the framework of an umbrella. 5. a raised pattern of lines in knitting. 6. *ribs*, spareribs, especially barbecued ones. **rib** *v.* (**ribbed, rib·bing**) 1. to support (a structure) with ribs. 2. to knit as rib, *the cuffs are ribbed*. 3. *(informal)* to tease. **rib'ber** *n.*

rib·ald (rib-ăld) *adj.* humorous in a cheerful but vulgar or disrespectful way. **rib'ald·ly** *adv.* **rib'ald·ry** *n.*

rib·and (rib-ănd) *n.* (*old use*) a ribbon.

ribbed (ribd) *adj.* 1. with raised ridges. 2. knitted in rib.

rib·bon (rib-ŏn) *n.* 1. a narrow band of fine ornamental material used for decoration or for tying something. 2. a ribbon of special color or pattern worn to indicate the award of a medal or order etc. 3. a long narrow strip of material, such as an inked strip used in a typewriter; *in ribbons* or *torn to ribbons*, torn into ragged strips.

ri·bo·fla·vin (rı-boh-flay-vin) *n.* the chief growth-promoting factor in the vitamin B complex, occurring in eggs, liver, milk, leafy vegetables, etc.

ri·bo·nu·cle·ic (rı-boh-noo-klee-ik) **acid** a nucleic acid controlling the synthesis of proteins.

ri·bose (rı-bohs) *n.* a sugar found in nucleic acids.

ri·bo·some (rı-bŏ-sohm) *n.* a minute particle containing ribonucleic acid and proteins. **ri·bo·so·mal** (rı-boh-soh-măl) *adj.*

rice (rıs) *n.* 1. a kind of grass grown in marshes in hot countries, producing seeds that are used as food. 2. these seeds. **rice** *v.* (**riced, ric·ing**) to pass (cooked potatoes etc.) through a device to form thin strings. **ric'er** *n.*

rich (rich) *adj.* 1. having much wealth. 2. having a large supply of something, *the country is rich in natural resources*. 3. splendid, made of costly materials, elaborate, *rich furniture*. 4. producing or produced abundantly, *rich soil; a rich harvest*. 5. (of food) containing a large proportion of fat, butter, eggs, or spices etc. 6. (of a mixture in an internal combustion engine) containing more than the normal proportion of fuel. 7. (of a color or sound or smell) pleasantly deep or strong. 8. *(informal)* highly amusing. **rich'ness** *n.* ☐**the rich**, people having great wealth.

rich·es (rich-iz) *n. pl.* a great quantity of money or property or valuable possessions.

rich·ly (rich-lee) *adv.* 1. in a rich way. 2. thoroughly, *the book richly deserves its success*.

Rich·mond (rich-mŏnd) the capital of Virginia.

Rich·ter (rik-tĕr) **scale** a scale ranging from 0 to 10 for measuring the magnitude of earthquakes.

rick (rik) *n.* a built stack of hay etc.

rick·ets (rik-its) *n.* a children's disease caused by deficiency of vitamin D, resulting in softening and deformity of the bones.

rick·ett·si·a (ri-ket-si-ă) *n.* (*pl.* **-as**) a parasitic microorganism causing typhus.

rick·et·y (rik-i-tee) *adj.* shaky, insecure.

rick·ey (rik-ee) *n.* a drink usually containing lime juice and gin.

rick·rack (rik-rak) *n.* zigzag braid used for trimming.

rick·shaw, rick·sha (rik-shaw) *n.* a light two-wheeled hooded vehicle drawn by one or more persons.

ric·o·chet (rik-ŏ-shay, rik-ŏ-shay) *v.* (**ric·o·cheted, ric·o·chet·ing**, or **ric·o·chet·ted, ric·o·chet·ting**) to rebound from a surface as a missile does when it strikes with a glancing blow. **ricochet** *n.* a rebound of this kind, a hit made by it.

ri·cot·ta (ri-kot-ă) *n.* an Italian cottage cheese.

rid (rid) *v.* (**rid** or **rid·ded, rid·ding**) to free from something unpleasant or unwanted, *rid the house of mice; was glad to be rid of him*. **rid'der** *n.* ☐**get rid of**, to cause to go away; *(informal)* to succeed in selling.

rid·dance (rid-ăns) *n.* ridding. ☐**good riddance**, a welcome freedom from a person or thing one is rid of.

rid·den (rid-ĕn) *adj.* full of or dominated by, *rat-ridden cellars; drug-ridden*.

rid·dle[1] (rid-ĕl) *n.* 1. a question or statement designed to test ingenuity or give amusement in finding its answer or meaning. 2. something or some-one puzzling or mysterious.

riddle² *v.* (**rid·dled, rid·dling**) 1. to pierce with many holes, *riddled the car with bullets.* 2. to permeate thoroughly, *riddled with disease.*

ride (rɪd) *v.* (**rode, rid·den, rid·ing**) 1. to sit on and be carried by (a horse etc.). 2. to go on horse-back or bicycle or train or other conveyance. 3. to sit on and manage a horse. 4. to be supported on, to float or seem to float, *the ship rode the waves* or *rode at anchor; the moon was riding high.* 5. to yield to (a blow) so as to reduce its impact. 6. *(informal)* to try to annoy or to tease. **ride** *n.* 1. a spell of riding. 2. a journey in a vehicle, *only a short ride into town.* 3. the feel of a ride, *the car gives a smooth ride.* 4. a thing to ride for fun, such as a merry-go-round or roller coaster. □**let it ride,** to take no further action. **ride down,** to overtake or trample deliberately while riding on horseback. **ride for a fall,** to act riskily. **ride high,** to be successful. **ride out the storm,** to survive a storm or difficulty suc-cessfully. **ride up,** (of a garment) to work upward when worn. **take for a ride,** *(slang)* to take away by car and murder (a person); to deceive or swin-dle.

rid·er (rɪ-děr) *n.* 1. a person who rides a horse or bicycle etc. 2. an additional clause supplement-ing a statement etc., an expression of opinion added to a verdict.

rid·er·less (rɪ-děr-lis) *adj.* without a rider.

rid·er·ship (rɪ-děr-ship) *n.* the people who travel by a particular form of public transportation dur-ing a specified period of time.

ridge (rij) *n.* 1. a narrow raised strip, a line where two upward-sloping surfaces meet. 2. an elongated region of high barometric pressure. **ridge** *v.* (**ridged, ridg·ing**) 1. to break up into ridges. 2. to mark with ridges. 3. to plant in ridges. **ridg'y** *adj.* (**ridg·i·er, ridg·i·est**) □**ridge line,** a line marking the top of the ridge.

ridged (rijd) *adj.* formed into ridges.

ridge·pole (rij-pohl) *n.* the horizontal pole of a long tent.

rid·i·cule (rid-ĭ-kyool) *n.* the process of making a person or thing appear ridiculous. **ridicule** *v.* (**rid·i·culed, rid·i·cul·ing**) to subject to ridi-cule, to make fun of.

ri·dic·u·lous (ri-dik-yŭ-lŭs) *adj.* 1. deserving to be laughed at, especially in a malicious or scornful way. 2. not worth serious consideration, prepos-terous. **ri·dic'u·lous·ly** *adv.* **ri·dic'u·lous·ness** *n.*

Ries·ling (reez-ling) *n.* a kind of dry white wine.

rife (rɪf) *adj.* 1. occurring frequently, widespread, *crime was rife in the city.* 2. well provided, full, *the country was rife with rumors of war.* **rife'ly** *adv.* **rife'ness** *n.*

riff (rif) *n.* a short repeated phrase in jazz and simi-lar music.

rif·fle (rif-ěl) *v.* (**rif·fled, rif·fling**) 1. to turn (pages) in quick succession, to leaf through quickly, *riffled through the book.* 2. to shuffle (playing cards) rapidly by flexing and combining two halves of the pack.

riff·raff (rif-raf) *n.* the rabble, disreputable people.

ri·fle¹ (rɪ-fěl) *n.* 1. a gun with a long barrel cut with spiral grooves to make the bullet spin and so travel more accurately when fired. 2. *rifles,* troops equipped with rifles. **ri'fier** *n.*

rifle² *v.* (**ri·fled, ri·fling**) 1. to search and to rob,

rifled the safe. 2. to cut spiral grooves in (a gun barrel).

ri·fle·man (rɪ-fěl-măn) *n.* (*pl.* **-men,** *pr.* -měn) 1. a person using a rifle. 2. a soldier, especially in the infantry, armed with a rifle.

ri·fling (rɪ-fling) *n.* 1. the process of cutting spiral grooves (in a gun barrel). 2. these grooves.

rift (rift) *n.* 1. a cleft in earth or rock. 2. a crack or split in an object, a break in a cloud. 3. a breach in friendly relations between people or in the unity of a group. □**rift valley,** a steep-sided valley formed by subsidence of the earth's crust.

rig¹ (rig) *v.* (**rigged, rig·ging**) 1. to provide with clothes or equipment, *rigged them out.* 2. to fit (a ship) with spars, ropes, sails, etc. 3. to set up (a structure) quickly or with makeshift materials. **rig** *n.* 1. the way a ship's masts and sails etc. are arranged. 2. the equipment for a special pur-pose, as for drilling an oil well, *a test rig; an oil rig.* 3. *(informal)* an outfit of clothes. **rig'ger** *n.*

rig² *v.* (**rigged, rig·ging**) to manage or control fraudulently, *the election was rigged; rig the mar-ket,* to cause an artificial rise or fall in stock prices.

rig·a·ma·role (rig-ă-mă-rohl) = **rigmarole.**

rig·ging (rig-ing) *n.* the ropes etc. used to support masts and set or work the sails on a ship.

right (rɪt) *adj.* 1. (of conduct or actions etc.) morally good, in accordance with justice. 2. proper, cor-rect, true, *the right answer; right side,* (of fabric) the side meant to show. 3. in a good or normal condition, *all's right with the world; in his right mind,* sane. 4. *(informal)* real, properly so called, *made a right old mess of it.* 5. of the right-hand side. **right** *n.* 1. what is just, a fair claim or treat-ment, something one is entitled to. 2. the right-hand part or region. 3. the right hand, a blow with this. 4. the right foot in marching. 5. *the Right,* the right wing of a political party or other group. **right** *v.* 1. to restore to a proper or correct or upright position, *managed to right the boat.* 2. to set right, to make amends or take vengeance for, *to right the wrong.* 3. to correct, *the fault will right itself.* **right** *adv.* 1. on or toward the right-hand side, *turn right.* 2. straight, *go right on.* 3. *(informal)* immediately, *I'll be right back.* 4. all the way, completely, *went right around it.* 5. exactly, *right in the middle.* 6. very, fully, *dined right royally.* 7. rightly, *you did right to come.* 8. all right, that is correct, I agree. □**by right** *or* **rights,** if right were done. **in the right,** having justice or truth on one's side. **on the right side of,** in the favor of or liked by (a person); *on the right side of forty,* not yet 40 years old. **right about face,** a right turn continued to face rear; a reversal of policy; a retreat. **right angle,** an angle of 90°; *at right angles,* placed at or turning through a right angle. **right away,** immediately. **right circular cone,** a cone resulting from the rotation of a triangle on one of its legs. **right face,** a right turn. **right field,** the part of the baseball field to the catcher's right and beyond first base. **right of way,** the right to pass over another's land; a path that is subject to such a right; the right to proceed while another vehicle must wait. **right on!,** *(slang)* an exclamation of agreement or encouragement, especially to a speaker. **right wing,** those who support more con-servative or traditional policies than others in their group.

right-an·gled (rɪt-ang-gěld) *adj.* having a right an-gle.

right·eous (rɪ-chŭs) *adj.* 1. doing what is morally right, making a show of this. 2. morally justifiable, *full of righteous indignation.* **right′eous·ly** *adv.* **right′eous·ness** *n.*

right·ful (rɪt-fŭl) *adj.* in accordance with what is just or proper or legal. **right′ful·ly** *adv.* **right′ful·ness** *n.*

right-hand (rɪt-hand) *adj.* of or toward this side of a person or the corresponding side of a thing. □**right-hand man,** a person's indispensable or chief assistant.

right-hand·ed (rɪt-han-dĭd) *adj.* 1. using the right hand, usually by preference. 2. made with or operated by the right hand, as a blow or tool. 3. to be turned toward the right, as a screw. **right′-hand′ed·ly** *adv.* **right′-hand′ed·ness** *n.*

right-hand·er (rɪt-han-dĕr) *n.* a right-handed person or blow.

right·ist (rɪ-tist) *n.* a member of the right wing of a political party. **rightist** *adj.* of the right wing in politics etc. **right′ism** *n.*

right·ly (rɪt-lee) *adv.* justly, correctly, properly, justifiably.

right-mind·ed (rɪt-mɪn-dĭd) *adj.* having proper or honest principles.

right·ness (rɪt-nĭs) *n.* being just or correct or proper or justifiable.

right-to-work (rɪt-tŏ-wurk) *adj.* of or relating to laws banning the union shop.

right·y (rɪ-tee) *n.* (*pl.* **right·ies**) *(informal)* a right-handed person, especially a right-handed baseball pitcher.

rig·id (rij-id) *adj.* 1. stiff, not bending or yielding. 2. strict, inflexible, *rigid rules.* **rig′id·ly** *adv.* **rig′id·ness** *n.* **ri·gid·i·ty** (rĭ-jid-i-tee) *n.*

rig·ma·role (rig-mă-rohl) *n.* 1. a long rambling statement. 2. a complicated formal procedure.

rig·or (rig-ŏr) *n.* 1. severity, strictness. 2. harshness of weather or conditions, *the rigors of famine.* □**rigor mortis,** the stiffening of the body after death.

rig·or·ous (rig-ŏ-rŭs) *adj.* 1. strict, severe, *rigorous discipline.* 2. strictly accurate or detailed, *a rigorous search.* 3. harsh, unpleasant, *a rigorous climate.* **rig′or·ous·ly** *adv.*

rile (rɪl) *v.* (**riled, ril·ing**) *(informal)* to annoy, to irritate.

rill¹ (ril) *n.* a small stream.

rill² *n.* a long valley on the moon.

rim (rim) *n.* 1. the edge or border of something more or less circular. 2. the outer edge of a wheel, on which a tire is fitted. **rim** *v.* (**rimmed, rim·ming**) 1. to furnish with or to serve as a rim. 2. to edge, to border.

rime¹ (rɪm) *n.* frost. **rim′y** *adj.*

rime² = **rhyme.**

rimed (rɪmd) *adj.* coated with frost.

rim·fire (rim-fɪr) *adj.* 1. designed for the use of a cartridge that has the primer around the rim of the base, as a gun. 2. having the properties of such a cartridge.

rim·less (rim-lĭs) *adj.* (of eyeglasses) made without frames.

rind (rɪnd) *n.* a tough outer layer or skin on fruit, cheese, bacon, etc.

ring¹ (ring) *n.* 1. the outline of a circle. 2. something shaped like this, a circular band. 3. a small circular band of precious metal worn on the finger. 4. a circular or other enclosure for a circus or sports event or cattle show etc., a square area in which a boxing match or wrestling match is held. 5. *the ring,* prizefighting. 6. a combination of people acting together for control of operations or policy etc. **ring** *v.* 1. to enclose with a ring, to encircle. 2. to put a ring on (a bird etc.) to identify it. 3. to cut a ring in the bark of (a tree), especially to retard its growth and improve fruit production. □**ring finger,** the third finger, especially of the left hand, on which a wedding ring is worn. **ring-necked pheasant,** a pheasant, the male having a ring of white feathers around the neck. **ring-necked snake,** a common grass snake with rings of color around the neck. **run rings around,** to do things much better than (another person).

ring² *v.* (**rang, rung, ring·ing**) 1. to give out a loud clear resonant sound, like that of a bell when struck. 2. to cause (a bell) to do this. 3. to sound a bell as a summons, to signal by ringing, *bells rang out the old year.* 4. to be filled with sound, *the stadium rang with cheers.* 5. (of ears) to be filled with a ringing or humming sound. 6. to telephone. **ring** *n.* 1. the act of ringing a bell. 2. a ringing sound or tone. 3. a tone or feeling of a particular kind; *it has the ring of truth,* sounds true. 4. *(informal)* a telephone call. □**ring a bell,** *(informal)* to arouse a vague memory; to sound faintly familiar. **ring the curtain up** *or* **down,** to signal that the curtain on a theater stage should be raised or lowered; to mark the beginning or end of an enterprise etc. **ring up,** to record (an amount) on a cash register.

ring·er¹ (ring-ĕr) *n.* 1. a person, a thing that encircles. 2. a horseshoe or a quoit that is thrown over a peg.

ringer² *n.* 1. a person who rings bells. 2. *(slang)* a racehorse etc. fraudulently substituted for another. 3. *(slang)* a person's double.

ring·lead·er (ring-lee-dĕr) *n.* a person who leads others in mischief or wrongdoing or opposition to authority.

ring·let (ring-lĭt) *n.* a small curly lock of hair.

ring·mas·ter (ring-mas-tĕr) *n.* the person in charge of a circus performance.

ring·side (ring-sɪd) *n.* the area immediately beside a boxing ring. □**ringside seat,** a position from which one has a clear view of the scene of action.

ring·tailed (ring-tayld) *adj.* 1. with the tail ringed in alternate colors. 2. with the tail curled at the end.

ring·worm (ring-wurm) *n.* a skin disease producing round scaly patches on the skin, caused by a fungus.

rink (ringk) *n.* a skating rink (*see* **skate²**).

rink·y-dink (ring-kee-dingk) *adj.* *(slang)* small-time, shabby, unsophisticated. **rinky-dink** *n.* *(slang)* a person or thing of this kind.

rinse (rins) *v.* (**rinsed, rins·ing**) 1. to wash lightly with water. 2. to wash out soap or impurities from. **rinse** *n.* 1. rinsing. 2. a solution washed through hair to tint or condition it.

ri·ot (rɪ-ŏt) *n.* 1. a wild disturbance by a crowd of people. 2. a profuse display of something, *a riot of color.* 3. *(informal)* a very amusing thing or person. **riot** *v.* to take part in a riot or in disorderly revelry. **ri′ot·er** *n.* □**read the riot act,** to insist that disobedience etc. must cease. **riot gun,** a gun for use in dealing with riots. **riot squad,** a special squad of police trained in dealing with riots. **run riot,** to behave in an unruly way; (of plants) to grow or spread in an uncontrolled way.

ri·ot·ous (rī-ŏ-tŭs) *adj.* 1. disorderly, unruly. 2. boisterous, unrestrained, *riotous laughter*. **ri′ot·ous·ly** *adv.* **ri′ot·ous·ness** *n.*

rip¹ (rip) *v.* **(ripped, rip·ping)** 1. to tear apart, to remove by pulling roughly. 2. to become torn. 3. to rush along. **rip** *n.* a ripping, a torn place. **rip′per** *n.* □**let rip,** *(informal)* to refrain from checking the speed of (a thing) or from interfering; to speak or utter violently. **rip cord,** a cord for pulling to release a parachute from its pack. **rip into,** to criticize or scold severely. **rip off,** *(slang)* to defraud; to steal.

rip² *n.* a stretch of turbulent water in a sea or river.

R.I.P. *abbr.* rest in peace. ▷From the Latin *requiescat* (or *requiescant*) *in pace.*

ri·par·i·an (ri-pair-i-ăn) *adj.* of or on a riverbank, *a riparian proprietor; riparian rights.*

ripe (rīp) *adj.* **(rip·er, rip·est)** 1. (of fruit or grain etc.) ready to be gathered and used. 2. matured and ready to be eaten or drunk, *ripe cheese.* 3. (of a person's age) advanced, *lived to a ripe old age.* 4. ready, prepared or able to undergo something; *the time is ripe for revolution; the land is ripe for development.* **ripe′ly** *adv.* **ripe′ness** *n.*

rip·en (rī-pĕn) *v.* to make or become ripe.

rip·off (rip-awf) *n.* *(slang)* a fraudulent thing or act.

ri·poste (ri-pohst) *n.* a quick counterstroke, a quick retort. **riposte** *v.* **(ri·post·ed, ri·post·ing)** to deliver a riposte.

rip·ple (rip-ĕl) *n.* 1. a small wave or series of waves. 2. something resembling this in appearance or movement. 3. a gentle sound that rises and falls, *a ripple of laughter.* **ripple** *v.* **(rip·pled, rip·pling)** to cause or to form ripples. **rip′ply** *adj.* □**ripple effect,** a set of related consequences started by one event.

rip·roar·ing (rip-rohr-ing) *adj.* *(informal)* wildly noisy.

rip·saw (rip-saw) *n.* a coarse saw used for cutting wood in the direction of the grain.

rip·snort·er (rip-snor-tĕr) *n.* *(informal)* an energetic person or thing. **rip′snort′ing** *adj.*

rip·tide (rip-tīd) *n.* a tide running against another or others, creating turbulent waters.

rise (rīz) *v.* **(rose, ris·en, ris·ing)** 1. to come or go or grow or extend upward. 2. to get up from lying or sitting or kneeling, to get out of bed. 3. (of a meeting) to cease to sit for business. 4. to become upright or erect. 5. to come to life again after death, *Christ is risen.* 6. to rebel, *rise in revolt.* 7. (of the wind) to begin to blow or to blow more strongly. 8. (of the sun etc.) to become visible above the horizon. 9. to increase in amount or number or intensity, *prices are rising; her spirits rose,* she began to feel more cheerful. 10. to achieve a higher position or status, *rose to the rank of colonel; rise to the occasion,* to prove oneself able to deal with an unexpected situation. 11. (of bread or cake etc.) to swell by the action of yeast or other raising agent. 12. to have its origin, to begin or begin to flow, *the Mississippi rises in Minnesota.* **rise** *n.* 1. rising, an upward movement. 2. an upward slope, a small hill. 3. an increase in amount or number or intensity, an increase in wages. 4. an upward movement in rank or status. □**get a rise out of,** to draw (a person) into a display of annoyance or into making a retort. **give rise to,** to cause. **rise and shine,** get out of bed etc., get up from sleep. **rise up,** to come back to life; to revolt. **rising**

generation, young people, those who are growing up. ▷See the note under **raise.**

ris·er (rī-zĕr) *n.* 1. a person or thing that rises, *an early riser.* 2. a vertical piece between treads of a staircase.

ris·i·ble (riz-ī-bĕl) *adj.* 1. of or relating to laughter. 2. ludicrous, laughable. **ris·i·bil·i·ty** (riz-ī-bil-i-tee) *n.*

risk (risk) *n.* 1. the possibility of meeting danger or suffering harm or loss, exposure to this. 2. a person or thing insured or similarly representing a source of risk, *not a good risk.* **risk** *v.* to expose to the chance of injury or loss, to accept the risk of.

risk·y (ris-kee) *adj.* **(risk·i·er, risk·i·est)** full of risk. **risk′i·ly** *adv.* **risk′i·ness** *n.*

ri·sot·to (ri-sot-oh) *n.* (*pl.* **-tos**) an Italian dish of rice containing chopped meat or cheese and vegetables.

ris·qué (ri-skay) *adj.* (of a story) slightly indecent.

rite (rīt) *n.* a religious or other solemn ritual. □**rite of passage,** a ritual used when a person reaches a new status in life, as adolescence, marriage, etc.

rit·u·al (rich-oo-ăl) *n.* 1. the series of actions used in a religious or other ceremony, a particular form of this. 2. a procedure regularly followed. **ritual** *adj.* of or done as a ritual. **rit′u·al·ly** *adv.* **rit′u·al·ist** *n.* **rit′u·al·ism** *n.* **rit·u·al·is·tic** (rich-oo-ă-lis-tik) *adj.* **rit·u·al·is′ti·cal·ly** *adv.*

ritz·y (rit-see) *adj.* **(ritz·i·er, ritz·i·est)** *(informal)* high class, luxurious. **ritz′i·ly** *adv.* **ritz′i·ness** *n.* ▷Ritz was the name of luxurious hotels owned by César Ritz of Switzerland.

riv. *abbr.* river.

ri·val (rī-văl) *n.* 1. a person or thing competing with another. 2. a person or thing that can equal another in quality. **rival** *adj.* being a rival, competing. **rival** *v.* **(ri·valed, ri·val·ing)** 1. to be comparable to, to seem or be as good as. 2. to try to be as good as or outdo. **ri′val·ry** *n.* (*pl.* **-ries**)

rive (rīv) *v.* **(rived, rived** or **riv·en, riv·ing)** 1. to tear open or apart. 2. to split, as wood.

riv·en (riv-ĕn) *adj.* split, torn violently.

riv·er (riv-ĕr) *n.* 1. a large natural stream of water flowing in a channel. 2. a great flow, *rivers of blood.*

riv·er·bank (riv-ĕr-bangk) *n.* the land along the side of the river.

riv·er·bed (riv-ĕr-bed) *n.* the channel in which a river flows.

riv·er·boat (riv-ĕr-boht) *n.* a boat used on a river.

riv·er·side (riv-ĕr-sīd) *n.* the ground along the side of the river. **riverside** *adj.* on or near the riverside.

riv·et (riv-it) *n.* a nail or bolt for holding two pieces of metal together, its headless end being beaten or pressed down to form a head when it is in place. **rivet** *v.* **(riv·et·ed, riv·et·ing)** 1. to fasten with a rivet. 2. to flatten (the end of a bolt) when it is in place. 3. to fix, to make immovable, *she stood riveted to the spot.* 4. to attract and hold the attention of. **riv′et·er** *n.*

Riv·i·er·a (riv-i-air-ă) the region along the Mediterranean coast of southeast France, Monaco, and northwest Italy, famous for its natural beauty and containing many holiday resorts.

riv·u·let (riv-yŭ-lit) *n.* a small stream.

Ri·yadh (ree-yahd) the royal capital of Saudi Arabia.

ri·yal (ree-yawl) *n.* the unit of money in Saudi Arabia and the Yemen Arab Republic.

rm. *abbr.* 1. ream. 2. room.

Rn *symbol* radon.

R.N. *abbr.* registered nurse.

RNA *abbr.* ribonucleic acid.

rnd. *abbr.* round.

ro. *abbr.* rood(s).

roach[1] (rohch) *n.* 1. a cockroach. 2. *(slang)* a marijuana cigarette butt.

roach[2] *n.* (*pl.* **roach·es, roach**) a small European freshwater fish related to the carp.

road (rohd) *n.* 1. a way by which people or animals or vehicles may pass between places, especially one with a prepared surface. 2. a way of reaching or achieving something, *the road to success; you're in the road,* in the way, as an obstruction. 3. (often *roads*) an area of water near the shore where ships can ride at anchor. □**on the road,** traveling, especially as a salesman or performer or beggar. **road company,** a touring theatrical group. **road hog,** a reckless or inconsiderate and especially obstructive driver. **road map,** a map showing the roads of an area or country. **road sense,** ability to behave safely on roads, especially in traffic. **road show,** a theatrical performance by a company on tour. **road test,** a test of a vehicle by using it on a road.

road·a·bil·i·ty (roh-dă-bil-i-tee) *n.* the desirable qualities of an automobile on the road.

road·bed (rohd-bed) *n.* 1. the foundation structure of a railroad. 2. the whole material laid down for a road.

road·block (rohd-blok) *n.* 1. a barricade set up by the police or army to stop traffic for inspection or search etc. 2. anything that interferes with progress.

road·house (rohd-hows) *n.* (*pl.* **-hous·es,** *pr.* -how-ziz) an inn or club or restaurant on a country road.

road·run·ner (rohd-run-ĕr) *n.* a long-tailed bird of southwestern North America, able to run quickly.

road·side (rohd-sid) *n.* the border of a road. **roadside** *adj.* at or close to the roadside..

road·ster (rohd-stĕr) *n.* an open car without rear seats.

road·way (rohd-way) *n.* a road, this as distinct from a footpath beside it.

road·work (rohd-wurk) *n.* running long distances when training for athletic contests.

roam (rohm) *v.* to wander. **roam** *n.* a wander.

roan (rohn) *adj.* (of an animal) having a coat that is thickly sprinkled with white or gray hairs; *strawberry roan,* red mixed with white or gray. **roan** *n.* a roan horse or other animal.

roar (rohr) *n.* 1. a long deep loud sound, like that made by a lion. 2. loud laughter. **roar** *v.* 1. to give a roar. 2. to express in this way, *the crowd roared its approval.* 3. to be full of din. **roar′er** *n.*

roar·ing (rohr-ing) *adj.* 1. noisy. 2. briskly active, *did a roaring trade.* **roaring** *adv.* noisily, *roaring drunk.* **roaring** *n.* 1. the act of a person or animal that roars. 2. the loud deep noise made by an animal that roars.

roast (rohst) *v.* 1. to cook (meat etc.) in an oven or by exposure to heat. 2. to expose to great heat. 3. to undergo roasting. 4. to criticize, to honor with insulting remarks. **roast** *adj.* roasted, *roast beef.* **roast** *n.* 1. roast meat, a joint of meat for roasting. 2. an event in which the guest of honor is humorously subjected to severe criticism.

roast·er (roh-stĕr) *n.* 1. a dish for roasting food in. 2. a chicken, pig, etc. fit for roasting.

roast·ing (roh-sting) *adj.* very hot.

rob (rob) *v.* (**robbed, rob·bing**) 1. to steal from, to take unlawfully. 2. to deprive of what is due or normal, *robbing us of our sleep.* **rob′ber** *n.*

rob′ber·y *n.* (*pl.* **-ber·ies**) □**robber fly,** a predatory fly. **rob Peter to pay Paul,** to pay one debt by borrowing what one needs and so incurring another.

robe (rohb) *n.* a long loose garment, especially a ceremonial one or one worn as an indication of rank etc. **robe** *v.* (**robed, rob·ing**) to dress in a robe.

rob·in (rob-in) *n.* a small brown red-breasted bird. □**robin redbreast,** = robin. **rob·in's-egg** (rob-inz-eg) **blue,** the soft sky blue of a robin's egg.

ro·bot (roh-bot) *n.* 1. a machine resembling a person, able to perform simple manual tasks when directed. 2. a piece of apparatus operated by remote control. 3. a person who seems to act like a machine. □**robot bomb,** a rocket-propelled and gyroscopically guided bomb.

Rob Roy (rob-roi) a cocktail with Scotch, sweet vermouth, and bitters.

ro·bust (roh-bust, roh-bust) *adj.* strong, vigorous. **ro·bust′ly** *adv.* **ro·bust′ness** *n.*

rock[1] (rok) *n.* 1. the hard part of the earth's crust, underlying the soil. 2. a mass of this, a large stone or boulder. 3. something like a rock in solidity or firmness. □**on the rocks,** *(informal)* short of money; ruined, broken down; (of a drink) served undiluted, with ice cubes. **rock bass,** a freshwater game fish like a sunfish. **rock candy,** a hard sweet candy. **rock crystal,** a transparent colorless quartz usually in hexagonal prisms. **rock garden,** a garden with plants arranged among rocks. **rock hound,** *(informal)* a person who collects rocks; a geologist. **rock salt,** common salt as a solid mineral. **rock wool,** mineral wool made from limestone etc. and used as insulation.

rock[2] *v.* 1. to move or be moved gently to and fro while supported on something. 2. to shake violently. 3. to disturb greatly by shock, *the scandal rocked the country.* **rock** *n.* 1. rocking, a rocking movement. 2. a kind of popular modern music usually with a strong beat, rock-'n'-roll. □**rocking chair,** a chair mounted on rockers or with springs so that it can be rocked by the sitter. **rocking horse,** a wooden or plastic horse mounted on rockers or springs so that it can be rocked by a child sitting on it. **rock the boat,** *(informal)* to do something that upsets the plans or progress of one's group.

rock·bot·tom (rok-bot-ŏm) *adj.* *(informal)* of prices etc.) very low.

rock·bound (rok-bownd) *adj.* (of a coast) full of rocks.

rock·er (rok-ĕr) *n.* 1. a thing that rocks something or is rocked. 2. one of the curved bars on which a rocking chair etc. is mounted. 3. a rocking chair. 4. a switch that pivots between the "on" and "off" positions. □**off one's rocker,** *(slang)* crazy.

rock·et (rok-it) *n.* 1. a firework or similar device that rises into the air when ignited and then explodes. 2. a structure that flies by expelling gases produced by combustion, used to propel a warhead or spacecraft. 3. an engine producing thrust by means of fuel and oxidant carried within it. 4. a bomb or shell propelled by this. **rocket** *v.* to move rapidly upward or away. □**rocket gun,**

a weapon using a rocket as a projectile. **rocket ship,** a rocket-propelled spaceship.

rock·et·ry (rok-i-tree) *n.* the science or practice of using rockets for propelling missiles or spacecraft.

Rock·ies (rok-eez) *n. pl. (informal)* the Rocky Mountains.

rock-'n'-roll, rock-and-roll (rok-ĕn-rohl) *n.* a kind of popular music with a strong beat, containing elements of blues.

rock-ribbed (rok-ribd) *adj.* 1. rockbound. 2. firm and uncompromising in one's views, *a rock-ribbed monetarist.*

rock·y¹ (rok-ee) *adj.* (**rock·i·er, rock·i·est**) 1. of or like rock. 2. full of rocks. □**Rocky Mountains,** a mountain range in western North America.

rocky² *adj.* (**rock·i·er, rock·i·est**) unsteady. **rock'i·ness** *n.*

ro·co·co (rŏ-koh-koh) *n.* an ornate style of decoration common in Europe in the 18th century. **rococo** *adj.* of this style.

rod (rod) *n.* 1. a slender straight round stick or metal bar. 2. a cane or birch twig used for flogging people; *the rod,* the use of this. 3. a fishing rod. 4. a measure of length (especially of land) = 5½ yards. 5. *(slang)* a pistol or revolver.

rode (rohd) *see* **ride.**

ro·dent (roh-dĕnt) *n.* an animal (as a rat, mouse, squirrel) with strong front teeth used for gnawing things.

ro·de·o (roh-di-oh, roh-day-oh) *n.* (*pl.* **-os**) 1. a roundup of cattle on a ranch, for branding etc. 2. an exhibition of cowboys' skill in handling animals.

rod·o·mon·tade (rod-ŏ-mon-tayd) *v.* (**rod· o·mon·tad·ed, rod·o·mon·tad·ing**) to boast. **rodomontade** *n.* boastful talk. **rodomontade** *adj.* boastful.

roe¹ (roh) *n.* a mass of eggs in a female fish's ovary, a male fish's milt.

roe² *n.* (*pl.* **roes, roe**) a kind of small deer.

roe·buck (roh-buk) *n.* a male roe deer.

roent·gen·ol·o·gy (rent-gĕ-nol-ŏ-jee) *n.* the science of using x-rays in the diagnosis and treatment of disease. **roent·gen·ol'o·gist** *n.* **roent·gen· o·log·ic** (rent-gĕ-nŏ-loj-ik) *adj.* **roent·gen· o·log'i·cal** *adj.*

roent·gen (rent-gĕn) **ray** x-ray.

rog·er (roj-ĕr) *interj.* (in signaling) your message has been received and understood.

rogue (rohg) *n.* 1. a dishonest or unprincipled person. 2. a mischievous person. 3. a wild animal driven away from the herd or living apart from it, *rogue elephant.* **ro'guer·y** *n.* □**rogues' gallery,** a collection of photographs of criminals. **ro·guish** (roh-gish) *adj.* mischievous, affectedly playful. **ro'guish·ly** *adv.* **ro'guish·ness** *n.*

roil (roil) *v.* 1. to make (water etc.) turbid by stirring. 2. to annoy, to vex.

rois·ter·ing (roi-stĕ-ring) *adj. & n.* merrymaking noisily. **roist'er·er** *n.*

role, rôle (rohl) *n.* 1. an actor's part. 2. a person's or thing's function.

roll (rohl) *v.* 1. to move or cause to move along in contact with a surface, either on wheels or by turning over and over. 2. to turn on an axis or over and over, to cause to revolve. 3. to form into a cylindrical or spherical shape; *rolled into one,* combined in one person or thing. 4. to wind in or as a covering. 5. to flatten by means of a

roller, *roll out the pastry.* 6. to rock from side to side, as in walking. 7. to move or pass steadily, *the years rolled on.* 8. to undulate, *rolling hills.* 9. to make a long continuous vibrating sound, *the thunder rolled.* 10. *(slang)* to attack and rob (a person). **roll** *n.* 1. a cylinder formed by turning flexible material over and over upon itself without creasing it. 2. something having this shape, an undulation, *rolls of fat.* 3. a small individual portion of bread baked in a rounded shape 4. an official list or register; *strike off the rolls,* to debar (a person) from practicing his profession, as after dishonesty. 5. a rolling movement. 6. a long steady vibrating sound. □**roll back,** to cause to retreat or decrease. **roll bar,** an overhead metal bar to protect the occupants of a motor vehicle in the event of its overturning. **roll call,** the calling of a list of names, to check that all are present. **rolled gold,** a thin coating of gold applied to another metal. **roll in,** to arrive in great numbers or quantities; *(informal)* to arrive casually. **rolling mill,** a machine or factory for rolling metal into various shapes. **rolling pin,** a cylindrical device rolled over dough to flatten this. **rolling stock,** railroad cars and locomotives etc. **rolling stone,** a person who does not settle and live or work in one place. **roll of honor,** a list of people whose achievements are honored. **roll up,** *(informal)* to arrive in a vehicle, to arrive casually.

roll·back (rohl-bak) *n.* the act of rolling back, especially prices.

roll·er (roh-lĕr) *n.* 1. a cylinder used for flattening or spreading things, or on which something is wound. 2. a long swelling wave. □**roller bearing,** a bearing like a ball bearing but with small cylinders instead of balls. **roller coaster,** an amusement park ride with a series of alternate steep descents and ascents. **Roller Derby,** *(trademark)* a roller-skating contest between two teams skating on an oval track. **roller skate,** one of a pair of sets of four wheels attached to the soles of boots or shoes so that the wearer can glide over a hard surface. **roller towel,** a towel with its ends joined so that it is continuous, hung over a roller.

roll·er-skate (roh-lĕr-skayt) *v.* (**-skat·ed, -skat· ing**) to move on roller skates. **roll'er skat·er** *n.*

rol·lick·ing (rol-i-king) *adj.* full of boisterous high spirits.

roll·mop (rohl-mop) *n.* a rolled pickled herring fillet.

roll-on (rohl-on) *adj.* applied by means of a ball that rotates in the neck of a container, as a cosmetic etc.

roll·o·ver (rohl-oh-vĕr) *n.* 1. rolling over. 2. a bank deposit or loan etc. that may be renewed.

roll-top (rohl-top) **desk** a desk with a flexible cover that slides in curved grooves.

ro·ly-po·ly (roh-lee-poh-lee) *adj.* plump, pudgy.

rom. *abbr.* roman type.

Rom. *abbr.* 1. Roman. 2. Romania. 3. Romans.

ro·maine (roh-mayn) *n.* a lettuce with long leaves.

Ro·man (roh-măn) *adj.* 1. of ancient or modern Rome. 2. of the ancient Roman republic or empire. 3. of the Christian Church of Rome, *Roman Catholic.* **Roman** *n.* 1. a member of the ancient Roman republic or empire. 2. a native or inhabitant of Rome. 3. *roman,* plain upright type (not italic), like that used for the definitions in this dictionary. 4. *Romans,* a book of the New Testament, the epistle of St. Paul to the Church at Rome. □**Roman candle,** a tubular firework that sends out colored balls. **Roman Catholic,** of the church that acknowledges the Pope as its head; a member of this church. **Roman Catholicism,** the faith of the Roman Catholic Church. **Roman Empire,** the empire established by Augustus in 27 B.C. and lasting until 395 A.D. **Roman nose,** a nose with a high bridge. **Roman numerals,** letters representing numbers (I = 1, V = 5, X = 10, L = 50, C = 100, D = 500, M = 1000). **ro·man à clef** (roh-mahn ah klay) (*pl.* **ro·mans à clef,** *pr.* roh-mahnz ah klay) a novel presenting real events and people disguised as fiction. ▷French, = novel with a key.

ro·mance (roh-mans) *n.* 1. an imaginative story, literature of this kind, *medieval romances.* 2. a romantic situation or event or atmosphere. 3. a love story, a love affair resembling this. 4. a picturesque exaggeration or falsehood. **romance** *v.* (**ro·manced, ro·manc·ing**) 1. to exaggerate or distort the truth in an imaginative way. 2. to engage in romantic activities or courtship. **ro·manc'er** *n.* □**Romance languages,** those descended from Latin (French, Italian, Spanish, etc.).

Ro·man·esque (roh-mă-nesk) *n.* a style of art and architecture in Europe in about 1050–1200, with massive vaulting and round arches.

Ro·ma·ni·a (roh-may-ni-ă) = **Rumania.**

Ro·ma·no (roh-mah-noh) *n.* an Italian cheese.

Ro·mansh (roh-mahnsh) *n.* Alpine dialects derived from Latin, especially spoken in East Switzerland.

ro·man·tic (roh-man-tik) *adj.* 1. appealing to the emotions by its imaginative or heroic or picturesque quality. 2. involving a love affair. 3. enjoying romantic situations etc. 4. (of music or literature) richly imaginative, not conforming to classical conventions. **romantic** *n.* a person who enjoys romantic situations etc. **ro·man'ti·cal·ly** *adv.*

ro·man·ti·cism (roh-man-ti-siz-ĕm) *n.* a literary or artistic style characterized by grandeur or picturesqueness or passion rather than careful finish and proportion.

ro·man·ti·cize (roh-man-ti-siz) *v.* (**ro·man·ti·cized, ro·man·ti·ciz·ing**) 1. to make romantic. 2. to have romantic ideas.

Rom·a·ny (rom-ă-nee, roh-mă-) *n.* (*pl.* **-nies**) 1. a Gypsy. 2. the language of Gypsies. **Romany** *adj.* of Romanies or their language.

Rome (rohm) 1. the capital of Italy. 2. the ancient Roman republic or empire.

romp (romp) *v.* 1. to play about together in a lively way, as children do. 2. (*informal*) to get along easily; *romped home,* came in as an easy winner. **romp** *n.* a spell of romping. **romp'er** *n.*

romp·ers (rom-pĕrz) *n. pl.* a young child's one-piece garment, usually covering the trunk only.

ron·do (ron-doh) *n.* (*pl.* **-dos**) a piece of music with a theme that recurs several times.

rood (rood) *n.* 1. a crucifix. 2. a quarter of an acre. □**Holy Rood,** (*old use*) the Cross of Christ.

roof (roof) *n.* 1. a structure covering the top of a house or building. 2. the top of a car or tent etc.; *roof of the mouth,* a structure forming the upper part of the mouth cavity. **roof** *v.* to cover with a roof, to be the roof of. □**have a roof over one's head,** to have somewhere to live. **hit** *or* **raise the roof,** (*informal*) to become very angry. **roof garden,** a garden on the flat roof of a building.

roof·er (roo-fĕr) *n.* a maker or mender of roofs.

roof·ing (roo-fing) *n.* roof material.

roof·less (roof-lis) *adj.* without a roof.

roof·top (roof-top) *n.* the outer surface of the roof.

roof·tree (roof-tree) *n.* the ridge piece of a roof.

rook[1] (ruuk) *n.* a black crow that nests in colonies. **rook** *v.* to swindle, to charge (a person) an extortionate price.

rook[2] *n.* a chess piece with a top shaped like battlements.

rook·er·y (ruuk-ĕ-ree) *n.* (*pl.* **-er·ies**) 1. a colony of rooks, a place where these nest. 2. a colony or breeding place of penguins or seals.

rook·ie (ruuk-ee) *n.* 1. a new member of a team. 2. a new recruit in the army or on a police force.

room (room) *n.* 1. space that is or could be occupied by something; *make room for,* to clear a space or position etc. for a person or thing. 2. part of a building enclosed by walls or partitions, *the apartment has three rooms.* 3. opportunity or scope or ability to allow something, *no room for dispute.* 4. *rooms,* a set of rooms occupied by a person or family. **room** *v.* to live in a room or rooms, *my son rooms with my neighbor's son.* □**room and board,** lodging and food. **room clerk,** a hotel desk clerk. **room divider,** a piece of furniture used to divide a room into sections. **rooming house,** a house with furnished rooms for rent. **room service,** service of food etc. to a hotel guest in his room.

room·er (roo-mĕr) *n.* a person who rents a room in another's house and lives there.

room·ette (roo-met) *n.* a small private sleeping room on a train.

room·ful (room-fuul) *n.* (*pl.* **-fuls**) the amount that a room will hold.

room·mate (room-mayt) *n.* a person sharing a room with another.

room·y (roo-mee) *adj.* (**room·i·er, room·i·est**) having plenty of room to contain things. **room'i·ly** *adv.* **room'i·ness** *n.*

Roo·se·velt (roh-zĕ-velt), **Frank·lin Del·a·no** (del-ă-noh) (1882–1945) the thirty-second president of the U.S. 1933–45.

Roosevelt, The·o·dore (1858–1919) the twenty-sixth president of the U.S. 1901–09.

roost (roost) *n.* a place where birds perch or where they settle for sleep. **roost** *v.* (of birds) to perch, to settle for sleep. □**come home to roost,** (of an action) to react unfavorably on the doer.

roost·er (roo-stĕr) *n.* a male domestic fowl.

root[1] (root) *n.* 1. the part of a plant that attaches it to the earth and absorbs water and nourishment from the soil; *a person's roots,* what attaches him emotionally to a place where he or his ancestors lived for a long time. 2. a similar part attaching ivy etc. to its support, a rhizome. 3. a small plant with root attached, for transplanting. 4. an edible root, a plant with this (as carrot, turnip), *root crops.* 5. the part of a bodily organ or structure that is embedded in tissue, *the root of a tooth.* 6. a source or basis, *the root of all evil; get to the root of the matter,* discover its source and tackle it there. 7. a number in relation to a given number that it produces when multiplied by itself once (= *square root*) or a specified number of times, *2 is the cube root of 8 (2 × 2 × 2 = 8).* **root** *v.* 1. to take root, to cause to do this. 2. to cause to stand fixed and unmoving, *was rooted to the spot by fear.* 3. to establish firmly, *the feeling is deeply rooted.* □**root beer,** an effervescent soft drink made from an extract of roots etc. **root out** *or* **up,** to drag or dig up by

the roots; to get rid of. **take root,** to send down roots; (of an idea etc.) to become established.
root² v. 1. (of an animal) to turn up ground with its snout or beak in search of food. 2. to rummage, to find or extract by doing this, *root out some facts and figures.*
root³ v. *(slang)* to support actively by applause etc., *rooting for their team.*
root·less (root-lis) *adj.* 1. having no root or roots. 2. (of a person) having no roots in a community.
root·let (root-lit) *n.* a small root.
root·stock (root-stok) *n.* a rhizome.
rope (rohp) *n.* 1. strong thick cord, a length of this. 2. a quantity of similar things strung together, *a rope of pearls.* **rope** v. **(roped, rop·ing)** 1. to fasten or secure or catch with rope. 2. to fence off with rope(s). □**give a person enough rope,** to allow him freedom of action in the hope that he will bring about his own downfall. **know** *or* **learn the ropes,** to know or learn the procedure for doing something. **rope in,** to persuade (a person) to take part in an activity.
rope ladder, a ladder made of two long ropes connected by short crosspieces.
Roque·fort (rohk-fört) *n.* a kind of blue cheese, originally made from ewes' milk.
Ror·shach (rohr-shahk) **test** a psychological test in which standard ink blots are presented to a person for a statement of what they suggest to him.
ro·sa·ceous (roh-zay-shŭs) *adj.* of a rose.
ro·sa·ry (roh-ză-ree) *n.* (*pl.* **-ries**) 1. a set series of prayers used in the Roman Catholic Church, a book containing this. 2. a string of 55 or 165 beads for keeping count of this.
rose¹ (rohz) *n.* 1. a bush or shrub bearing ornamental usually fragrant flowers. 2. its flower. 3. deep pink color; *roses in her cheeks,* a rosy complexion. **rose** *adj.* deep pink. □**rose fever,** hay fever caused by rose pollen. **rose window,** a circular window in a church, with a pattern of tracery.
rose² *see* **rise.**
ro·sé (roh-zay) *n.* a light pink wine.
ro·se·ate (roh-zi-it) *adj.* deep pink, rosy.
rose·bud (rohz-bud) *n.* the bud of a rose.
rose·bush (rohz-buush) *n.* a rose plant.
rose-col·ored (rohz-kul-ŏrd) *adj.* 1. optimistic, sanguine, cheerful. 2. rosy. □**see things through rose-colored glasses,** to take an unduly cheerful view of things.
rose·mar·y (rohz-mair-ee) *n.* (*pl.* **-mar·ies**) a fragrant evergreen shrub with leaves that are used for flavoring.
ro·sette (roh-zet) *n.* 1. a rose-shaped badge or ornament made of ribbon etc. 2. a rose-shaped carving.
rose·wat·er (rohz-waw-tĕr) *n.* a fragrant liquid perfumed with roses.
rose·wood (rohz-wuud) *n.* any of several fragrant close-grained woods used for making furniture.
Rosh Ha·sha·nah, Rosh Ha·sha·na (rohsh hă-shah-nă) the Jewish New Year.
ros·in (roz-in) *n.* a kind of resin.
ros·ter (ros-tĕr) *n.* 1. a list showing people's turns of duty etc. 2. a list of persons.
ros·trum (ros-trŭm) *n.* (*pl.* **-trums, -tra,** *pr.* -tră) a platform for public speaking.
ros·y (roh-zee) *adj.* **(ros·i·er, ros·i·est)** 1. rose-colored, deep pink. 2. promising, hopeful, *a rosy future.* **ros′i·ly** *adv.* **ros′i·ness** *n.*
rot (rot) *v.* **(rot·ted, rot·ting)** 1. (of animal or

vegetable matter) to lose its original form by chemical action caused by bacteria or fungi etc. 2. to perish or become weak through lack of use or activity. **rot** *n.* 1. rotting, rottenness. 2. *(slang)* nonsense, an absurd statement or argument.
Ro·tar·i·an (roh-tair-i-ăn) *n.* a member of a Rotary Club.
ro·ta·ry (roh-tă-ree) *adj.* rotating, acting by rotating, *a rotary drill.* **rotary** *n.* (*pl.* **-ries**) 1. a rotary machine. 2. a traffic circle. □**Rotary Club,** a local branch of an international association formed by businessmen for the purpose of rendering service to the community.
ro·tate (roh-tayt, roh-tayt) *v.* **(ro·tat·ed, ro·tat·ing)** 1. to revolve or cause to revolve. 2. to arrange or deal with in a recurrent series. **ro′ta·tor** *n.* **ro·ta·tion** (roh-tay-shŏn) *n.* **ro·ta′tion·al** *adj.*
ro·ta·to·ry (roh-tă-tohr-ee) *adj.* rotating.
ROTC *abbr.* Reserve Officers' Training Corps.
rote (roht) *n.* **by rote,** by memory without thought of the meaning, *knew it only by rote;* by a fixed procedure, *working by rote.*
rot·gut (rot-gut) *n.* *(slang)* a liquor of poor quality.
ro·tis·ser·ie (roh-tis-ĕ-ree) *n.* a cooking device for roasting food on a revolving spit.
ro·to (roh-toh) *n.* (*pl.* **-tos**) rotogravure.
ro·to·gra·vure (roh-toh-gră-vyoor) *n.* a photogravure printed on a rotary machine.
ro·tor (roh-tŏr) *n.* a rotating part of a machine, *a helicopter rotor.*
rot·ten (rot-ĕn) *adj.* 1. rotting, rotted, breaking easily or falling to pieces from age or use. 2. morally corrupt. 3. *(informal)* contemptible, worthless. 4. *(informal)* unpleasant, *rotten weather.* **rot′ten·ly** *adv.* **rot′ten·ness** *n.*
rot·ten·stone (rot-ĕn-stohn) *n.* decomposed limestone used as a polishing powder.
ro·tund (roh-tund) *adj.* rounded, plump. **ro·tund′ly** *adv.* **ro·tund′ness** *n.* **ro·tun′di·ty** *n.* ▷Do not confuse *rotund* with *orotund.*
ro·tun·da (roh-tun-dă) *n.* a circular domed building or hall.
rou·ble = **ruble.**
rou·é (roo-ay) *n.* a dissolute elderly man.
rouge (roozh) *n.* 1. a reddish cosmetic for coloring the cheeks. 2. a fine red powder used for polishing metal. **rouge** *v.* **(rouged, roug·ing)** to color with rouge.
rough (ruf) *adj.* 1. having an uneven or irregular surface, coarse in texture, not level or smooth. 2. not gentle or restrained or careful, violent; *rough weather,* stormy. 3. lacking finish or delicacy, not perfected or detailed; *a rough estimate,* approximate; *rough accommodations,* lacking ordinary comfort or convenience. 4. *(informal)* unpleasant or disagreeable, *had a rough time.* **rough** *n.* 1. something rough, rough ground. 2. hardship, *take the rough with the smooth.* 3. an unfinished state. 4. a rough drawing or design etc. 5. (in golf) the rough ground off the fairway between the tee and the green. **rough** v. 1. to make rough. 2. to shape or plan or sketch roughly, *roughed out a scheme.* **rough** *adv.* in a rough manner. **rough′ly** *adv.* **rough′ness** *n.* □**in the rough,** in a rough, incomplete, or crude state. **rough it,** to do without ordinary comforts. **rough stuff,** *(slang)* violent behavior. **rough up,** *(slang)* to treat (a person) violently.
rough·age (ruf-ij) *n.* indigestible material in plants that are used as food (such as bran, green vegeta-

bles, and certain fruits), which stimulates the action of the intestines.

rough-and-read·y (ruf-ăn-red-ee) *adj.* 1. full of rough vigor and not refined. 2. rough or crude but effective.

rough-and-tum·ble (ruf-ăn-tum-běl) *n.* a haphazard fight or struggle. **rough-and-tumble** *adj.* disorderly, irregular.

rough·cast (ruf-kast) *n.* plaster of lime and gravel, used for covering the outsides of buildings. **roughcast** *v.* (**rough·cast, rough·cast·ing**) to coat with this.

rough-cut (ruff-kut) *adj.* cut in small uneven pieces.

rough·en (ruf-ĕn) *v.* to make or become rough.

rough·hew (ruf-hyoo) *v.* (**rough·hewed, rough·hewn, rough·hew·ing**) to shape roughly.

rough·hewn (ruf-hyoon) *adj.* uncouth.

rough·house (ruf-hows) *n.* (*pl.* **-hous·es,** *pr.* -how-ziz) (*slang*) a disturbance with violent behavior or fighting. **roughhouse** *v.* (**rough·housed,** *pr.* ruf-howst, -howzd, **rough·hous·ing,** *pr.* ruf-how-sing, -how-zing) to make such a disturbance, to handle (a person) roughly.

rough·neck (ruf-nek) *n.* 1. a rowdy. 2. a skilled worker on an oil rig.

rough·shod (ruf-shod) *adj.* (of a horse) having shoes with the nail heads left projecting to prevent slipping. □**ride roughshod over,** to treat inconsiderately or arrogantly.

rou·lade (roo-lahd) *n.* 1. a florid passage of runs in solo vocal music, usually sung to one syllable. 2. a dish of thin-sliced meat rolled around a filling and cooked.

rou·lette (roo-let) *n.* a gambling game in which a small ball falls at random into one of the compartments on a revolving wheel.

Rou·ma·ni·a (roo-may-ni-ă) = **Rumania.**

round (rownd) *adj.* 1. having a curved shape or outline, shaped like a circle or sphere or cylinder. 2. full, complete, *a round dozen.* **round** *n.* 1. a round object. 2. a circular or recurring course or series; *the daily round,* ordinary occupations of the day; *a round of drinks,* one for each person in a group. 3. a round on which things are to be inspected or delivered, *make* or *go on one's rounds; a round of golf;* playing all holes on a course once. 4. a musical composition for two or more voices in which each sings the same melody but starts at a different time. 5. a single shot or volley of shots from one or more firearms, ammunition for this. 6. one stage in a competition or struggle, one section of a boxing match. 7. a cut of beef between the rump and the leg. **round** *adv. & prep.* around. **round** *v.* 1. to make or become round. 2. to make into a round figure or number; *round it off,* increase or decrease it in order to make it the nearest multiple of ten (as making $1.96 into $2.00). 3. to travel around (something), *the car rounded the corner.* □**in the round,** (of sculpture) with all sides shown, not attached to a background; (of a theater) with seats on all sides of the stage. **round and round,** turning or going around several times. **round dance,** one in which dancers form a ring; a dance performed by couples progressing around a room. **round figure** *or* **number,** a whole number, usually a multiple of ten. **round lot,** the standard unit in which stock exchange commodities or securities are bought and sold, 100 shares in active stock, 10 shares in inactive stock. **round robin,**

a tournament in which each competitor plays against every other. **round table,** a conference where people meet around a table to discuss something. **round trip,** a trip to one or more places and back again. **round up,** to gather (animals or people or things) into one place.

round·a·bout (rownd-ă-bowt) *adj.* indirect, not using the shortest or most direct route, *heard the news in a roundabout way.*

roun·de·lay (rown-dĕ-lay) *n.* a short simple song with a refrain.

round·house (rownd-hows) *n.* (*pl.* **-hous·es,** *pr.* -how-ziz) 1. a blow given with a wide swing of the arm. 2. a locomotive repair shed. 3. a cabin or set of cabins on the after part of the quarterdeck, especially on a sailing ship.

round·ish (rown-dish) *adj.* approximately round in shape.

round·ly (rownd-lee) *adv.* 1. thoroughly, severely, *was roundly scolded.* 2. in a rounded way.

round·shoul·dered (rownd-shohl-dĕrd) *adj.* bent forward so that the back is convex.

round·up (rownd-up) *n.* the gathering up of animals or people or things into one place; *roundup of the news,* a summary of events.

round·worm (rownd-wurm) *n.* a worm with a rounded body.

rouse (rowz) *v.* (**roused, rous·ing**) 1. to cause (a person) to wake. 2. to cause to become active or excited. 3. (of a person etc.) to wake. **rous'er** *n.*

rous·ing (row-zing) *adj.* vigorous, stirring, *three rousing cheers.*

roust·a·bout (rows-tă-bowt) *n.* an unskilled worker in an oil field or on the docks or in a circus.

rout[1] (rowt) *n.* utter defeat, a disorderly retreat of defeated troops. **rout** *v.* to defeat completely, to put to flight.

rout[2] *v.* 1. to fetch or force out, *routed him out of bed.* 2. to rummage.

route (root) *n.* the course or way taken to get from starting point to destination. **route** *v.* (**rout·ed, rout·ing**) to send by a certain route.

rou·tine (roo-teen) *n.* 1. a standard course of procedure, a series of acts performed regularly in the same way. 2. a set sequence of movements in a dance or other performance. **routine** *adj.* in accordance with routine. **rou·tine'ly** *adv.* **rou·tin·ize** (roo-tee-nɪz) *v.* (**rou·tin·ized, rou·tin·iz·ing**).

roux (roo) *n.* a mixture of heated fat and flour used as a basis for a sauce.

rove[1] (rohv) *v.* (**roved, rov·ing**) to roam. **rov'er** *n.* □**roving eye,** a tendency to flirt.

row[1] (roh) *n.* 1. a number of people or things in a more or less straight line. 2. a line of seats across a theater etc. □**row house,** a house in a row of nearly identical houses joined one to the next by shared walls.

row[2] *v.* 1. to propel (a boat) by using oars. 2. to carry in a boat that one rows. 3. to row a race with. **row** *n.* a spell of rowing, an excursion in a rowboat. **row'er** *n.* □**rowing machine,** a machine for exercising the muscles that are used in rowing.

row[3] (row) *n.* (*informal*) 1. a loud noise. 2. a quarrel, a heated argument. 3. the process or condition of being reprimanded, *got into a row for being late.* **row** *v.* (*informal*) 1. to quarrel or argue heatedly. 2. to reprimand.

row·an (roh-ăn) *n.* the European mountain ash.

row·boat (roh-boht) *n.* a boat for rowing.
row·dy (row-dee) *adj.* (**-di·er, -di·est**) noisy and disorderly. **rowdy** *n.* a rowdy person. **row′di·ly** *adv.* **row′di·ness** *n.* **row′dy·ism** *n.* **row′dy·ish** *adj.*
row·el (row-ĕl) *n.* a spiked revolving disk at the end of a spur on a riding boot. **rowel** *v.* to use a rowel.
roy·al (roi-ăl) *adj.* 1. of or suitable or worthy of a king or queen. 2. belonging to the family of a king or queen, in the service or under the patronage of royalty; *Royal Air Force, Royal Marines, Royal Navy,* the British air force etc. **roy′al·ly** *adv.* □**Royal Academy,** *(British)* the Royal Academy of Arts. **royal blue,** deep pure vivid blue. **royal colony,** a colony administered and governed by the crown through an appointed representative or council. **royal flush,** *see* **flush²**. **royal jelly,** a substance secreted by the honeybee workers and fed to the future queen bees. **royal palm,** a tall feather palm tree. **royal road,** a way of attaining something without trouble.
roy·al·ist (roi-ă-list) *n.* 1. a person who favors monarchy. 2. a diehard conservative, *economic royalist.*
roy·al·ty (roi-ăl-tee) *n.* (*pl.* **-ties**) 1. being royal. 2. a royal person or persons, *in the presence of royalty.* 3. payment by a mining or oil company to the owner of the land, *oil royalties.* 4. payment to an author etc. for each copy of his book sold or for each public performance of his work, payment to a patentee for the use of his patent.
rpm, RPM *abbr.* revolutions per minute.
R.P.O *abbr.* railway post office.
rps *abbr.* revolutions per second.
rpt. *abbr.* 1. repeat. 2. report.
R.R. *abbr.* 1. railroad. 2. rural route.
RSFSR *abbr.* Russian Soviet Federated Socialist Republic.
RSV *abbr.* Revised Standard Version.
R.S.V.P. *abbr.* (in an invitation) please reply. ▷From the French, *répondez s'il vous plaît.*
rt. *abbr.* right.
rte. *abbr.* route.
Ru *symbol* ruthenium.
rub (rub) *v.* (**rubbed, rub·bing**) 1. to press something against (a surface) and slide it to and fro, to apply in this way. 2. to polish or clean by rubbing, to make or become dry or smooth or sore etc. in this way; *rub brasses,* to take an impression of brass memorial tablets by rubbing colored wax or chalk etc. over paper laid upon them. **rub** *n.* 1. the act or process of rubbing. 2. a difficulty or impediment, *there's the rub.* □**rub a person's nose in it,** *see* nose. **rub down,** to dry or smooth or reduce the level of (a thing) by rubbing. **rub it in,** to emphasize or remind a person constantly of an unpleasant fact. **rub off,** to be removed or transferred by or as if by rubbing. **rub out,** to remove (marks etc.) by using an eraser; *(slang)* to murder. **rub shoulders with,** to associate with (certain people). **rub the wrong way,** to irritate or repel (a person) by one's action.
rub·ber¹ (rub-ĕr) *n.* 1. a tough elastic substance made from the coagulated juice of certain tropical plants or synthetically. 2. an eraser. 3. a person who rubs something, a device for rubbing things. □**rubber band,** a loop of rubber to hold papers etc. together. **rubber cement,** a kind of glue. **rubber check,** a check that bounces (*see* bounce). **rubber plant,** a plant yielding rubber.

rubber stamp, a device for imprinting a mark on to a surface; one who mechanically gives approval to the actions of another person or group.
rubber tree, a tree yielding rubber.
rubber² *n.* a match of two or three successive games at bridge etc.
rub·ber·ize (rub-ĕ-rɪz) *v.* (**rub·ber·ized, rub·ber·iz·ing**) to treat or coat with rubber.
rub·ber·neck (rub-ĕr-nek) *n.* *(slang)* a gaping sightseer, an inquisitive person. **rubberneck** *v.* to behave as a rubberneck.
rub·ber·stamp (rub-ĕr-stamp) *v.* *(informal)* to approve automatically without due consideration.
rub·ber·y (rub-ĕ-ree) *adj.* like rubber.
rub·bish (rub-ish) *n.* 1. waste or worthless material. 2. nonsense. **rub′bish·y** *adj.*
rub·ble (rub-ĕl) *n.* waste or rough fragments of stone or brick etc.
rub·down (rub-down) *n.* a massage.
rube (roob) *n.* *(slang)* a country bumpkin.
ru·bel·la (roo-bel-ă) *n.* German measles.
Ru·bi·con (roo-bĭ-kon) *n.* **cross the Rubicon,** to take a decisive step that commits one to an enterprise. ▷The river Rubicon was the ancient boundary between Gaul and Italy; by crossing it into Italy Julius Caesar committed himself to war with Pompey.
ru·bi·cund (roo-bĭ-kund) *adj.* (of the complexion) red, ruddy.
ru·bid·i·um (roo-bid-i-ŭm) *n.* a soft silvery element.
ru·ble (roo-bĕl) *n.* the unit of money in Russia.
ru·bric (roo-brik) *n.* words put as a heading or a note of explanation or a direction of how something must be done.
ru·by (roo-bee) *n.* (*pl.* **-bies**) 1. a red gem. 2. deep red color. **ruby** *adj.* deep red. □**ruby wedding,** the 40th anniversary of a wedding.
ru·by-throat·ed (roo-bee-throh-tid) **hummingbird** a hummingbird with a ruby red throat.
ruche (roosh) *n.* a gathered trimming. **ruche** *v.* (**ruched, ruch·ing**) to gather (fabric) ornamentally.
ruck·sack (ruk-sak, ruuk-) *n.* a bag worn slung by straps from both shoulders and resting on the back, used by walkers and climbers for carrying their possessions.
ruck·us (ruk-ŭs) *n.* a rumpus.
ruc·tion (ruk-shŏn) *n.* *(informal)* a rumpus.
rud·der (rud-ĕr) *n.* a vertical piece of metal or wood hinged to the stern of a boat or rear of an airplane and used for steering. **rud′der·less** *adj.*
rud·dy (rud-ee) *adj.* (**-di·er, -di·est**) reddish, (of a person's face) having a fresh healthy reddish color. **rud′di·ly** *adv.* **rud′di·ness** *n.*
rude (rood) *adj.* (**rud·er, rud·est**) 1. impolite, showing no respect or consideration. 2. primitive, roughly made, *rude stone implements.* 3. violent, startling, *a rude awakening.* **rude′ly** *adv.* **rude′ness** *n.*
ru·di·ment (roo-dĭ-měnt) *n.* 1. a part or organ that is incompletely developed. 2. *rudiments,* basic or elementary principles, *learning the rudiments of chemistry.* **ru·di·men·ta·ry** (roo-dĭ-men-tĕ-ree) *adj.*
rue¹ (roo) *n.* a shrub with bitter leaves formerly used in medicine. □**rue anemone,** a small delicate spring plant having pinkish or white flowers.
rue² *v.* (**rued, ru·ing**) to repent or regret; *he'll live to rue it,* will some day regret it.
rue·ful (roo-fŭl) *adj.* showing or feeling good-hu-

mored regret. **rue'ful·ly** adv. **rue'ful·ness** n.

ruff (ruf) n. 1. a deep starched pleated frill worn around the neck in the 16th century. 2. a projecting or colored ring of feathers or fur around the neck of a bird or animal. **ruffed** adj. **ruff'like** adj. □**ruffed grouse**, a North American game bird with black feathers on each side of the neck.

ruf·fi·an (ruf-i-ăn) n. a violent lawless person.

ruf·fle (ruf-ĕl) v. (**ruf·fled, ruf·fling**) 1. to disturb the smoothness or evenness of. 2. to upset the calmness or even temper of (a person). 3. to become ruffled. **ruffle** n. a gathered ornamental frill.

rug (rug) n. 1. a thick floor mat. 2. a lap robe. 3. (slang) a toupee. **rug'like** adj. □**pull the rug from under**, to remove the support of (a theory etc.).

rug·by (rug-bee) n. (also **Rugby**) the game of **Rugby football**, a kind of football played with an oval ball that may be kicked or carried. ▷Named after Rugby School in Warwickshire, England, where it was first played.

rug·ged (rug-id) adj. 1. having an uneven surface or an irregular outline, craggy. 2. rough and unyielding, a rugged individualist. **rug'ged·ly** adv. **rug'ged·ness** n.

ru·in (roo-in) n. 1. severe damage or destruction. 2. complete loss of one's fortune or resources or prospects. 3. the remains of something decayed or destroyed, the house was a ruin; the ruins of Pompeii. 4. a cause of ruin. **ruin** v. to damage (a thing) so severely that it is useless, to bring into a ruined condition. **ru·in·a·tion** (roo-i-nay-shŏn) n.

ru·in·ous (roo-i-nŭs) adj. 1. bringing or likely to bring ruin. 2. in ruins, ruined, the house is in a ruinous condition. **ru'in·ous·ly** adv. **ru'in·ous·ness** n.

rule (rool) n. 1. a statement of what can or must or should be done in a certain set of circumstances or in playing a game. 2. the customary or normal state of things or course of action, seaside holidays became the rule. 3. exercise of authority, control, governing, countries that were under French rule. 4. a straight often jointed measuring device used by carpenters etc. **rule** v. (**ruled, rul·ing**) 1. to have authoritative control over people or a country, to govern. 2. to keep (a person or feeling etc.) under control, to dominate. 3. to give a decision as judge or other authority, the chairman ruled that the question was out of order. 4. to draw (a line) using a ruler or other straight edge, to mark parallel lines on (writing paper etc.). □**as a rule**, usually, more often than not. **rule of the road**, the rules regulating the movements of vehicles or riders or ships with respect to each other. **rule of thumb**, a rough practical method or procedure. **rule out**, to exclude as irrelevant or ineligible. **rule the roost**, to be the dominant person.

rul·er (roo-lĕr) n. 1. a person who rules by authority. 2. a straight strip of wood or metal etc. used for measuring or for drawing straight lines.

rum (rum) n. alcoholic spirit distilled from sugar cane residues or molasses.

Rum. abbr. 1. Rumania. 2. Rumanian.

Ru·ma·ni·a (roo-may-ni-ă) a country in southeastern Europe. **Ru·ma'ni·an** adj. & n.

rum·ba (rum-bă) n. a ballroom dance of Cuban origin, music for this.

rum·ble (rum-bĕl) v. (**rum·bled, rum·bling**) 1. to make a deep heavy continuous sound, like thunder. 2. to utter in a deep voice. **rumble** n. 1. a

rumbling sound. 2. (slang) a street gang fight. **rum'bler** n. **rum'bly** adj. **rum'bling·ly** adv.

rumb·ling (rum-bling) n. 1. a rumbling sound. 2. (often rumblings) signs of unrest.

ru·mi·nant (roo-mĭ-nănt) n. an animal that chews the cud.

ru·mi·nate (roo-mĭ-nayt) v. (**ru·mi·nat·ed, ru·mi·nat·ing**) 1. to chew the cud. 2. to meditate, to ponder. **ru'mi·nat·ing·ly** adv. **ru·mi·na·tive** (roo-mĭ-nay-tiv) adj. **ru·mi·na·tion** (roo-mĭ-nay-shŏn) n.

rum·mage (rum-ij) v. (**rum·maged, rum·mag·ing**) to make a search by turning things over or disarranging them. **rummage** n. a search of this kind. □**rummage sale**, a sale of miscellaneous second-hand goods to raise money for a charity.

rum·my¹ (rum-ee) n. a card game in which players try to form sets or sequences of cards.

rummy² n. (pl. **-mies**) (slang) a drunkard.

ru·mor (roo-mŏr) n. information spread by word of mouth but not certainly true. □**be rumored**, to be spread as a rumor.

rump (rump) n. 1. the buttocks, the corresponding part of an animal or bird. 2. a cut of meat from an animal's hindquarters.

rum·ple (rum-pĕl) v. (**rum·pled, rum·pling**) to make or become crumpled, to make (something smooth) untidy. **rum'ply** adj.

rum·pus (rum-pŭs) n. (informal) an uproar, an angry dispute. □**rumpus room**, a room, usually in the basement of a house, for games, hobbies, etc.

rum·run·ner (rum-run-ĕr) n. a smuggler of rum or other liquor. **rum'run·ning** adj. & n.

run (run) v. (**ran, run, run·ning**) 1. to move with quick steps, never having both or all feet on the ground at once. 2. to go or travel smoothly or swiftly, (of salmon) to go up river in large numbers from the sea. 3. to compete in a race or contest, to seek election, ran for president. 4. to spread rapidly or beyond the intended limit, the dye has run. 5. to flow or cause to flow, to exude liquid, run some water into it; smoke makes my eyes run; run dry, to become dry. 6. to function, to be in action, left the engine running. 7. to travel or convey from point to point, the bus runs every hour; we'll run you home; run the blockade, to continue to pass through it; run contraband goods, smuggle them in. 8. to extend, a fence runs around the estate; the show runs almost two hours, lasts that long. 9. to be current or operative or valid, the lease runs for 20 years; musical ability runs in the family. 10. to be in a specified condition, feeling ran high; run a temperature, to be feverish. 11. to cause to run or go or extend or function. 12. to manage, to organize, who runs the country? 13. to own and use (a vehicle etc.). 14. (of a newspaper) to print as an item. 15. to sew (fabric) loosely or quickly. 16. to be expressed in a specific manner; his statement ran as follows, was expressed in these words. **run** n. 1. an act or spell or course of running. 2. a point scored in baseball. 3. a vertical flaw in a stocking etc. caused by a stitch or stitches becoming undone through several rows. 4. a continuous stretch or sequence or spell, a production run; a run in hearts, a numerical sequence in this suit of cards. 5. a general demand for goods etc., there's been a run on canned meat; a run on the bank, a sudden withdrawal of deposits by many customers. 6. a large number of salmon going up river from the sea.

7. a general type or class of things. 8. an enclosure where domestic animals can range. 9. a track for some purpose, *ski run.* 10. permission to make unrestricted use of something, *he has the run of the house.* **run′less** *adj.* □**in the long run,** over a period of time. **on the run,** fleeing from pursuit or capture; hurrying about. **run across,** to happen to meet or find. **run afoul of,** to run into trouble with. **run after,** to seek the company or attentions of. **run around with,** to keep company with. **run away,** to leave quickly or secretly. **run away with,** to elope with (a person); to win (a prize etc.) easily; to accept (an idea) too hastily; to carry off (stolen property). **run down,** to stop because not rewound; to reduce the numbers of; to knock down with a moving vehicle or ship; to discover after searching; to speak of in a slighting way; *be run down,* to be dilapidated or weak or exhausted. **run for it,** to try to escape by running. **run in,** *(informal)* to arrest and take into custody. **run into,** to collide with; to happen to meet. **run off,** to run away; to produce (copies) on a machine. **run on,** to talk continually. **run out,** (of time or a stock of something) to become used up, (of a person) to have used up one's stock; to escape from a container. **run over,** to knock down or crush with a vehicle; to study or repeat quickly. **run risks,** to take risks. **run through,** to study or repeat quickly. **run up,** to raise (a flag) on a mast; to allow (a bill) to mount; to add up (a column of figures); to make quickly by sewing, *run up some curtains.*

run·a·bout (run-ă-bowt) *n.* a light automobile or motorboat.

run·a·round (run-ă-rownd) *n.* an evasive response.

run·a·way (run-ă-way) *n.* a person who has run away. **runaway** *adj.* 1. having run away or being out of control. 2. won easily, *a runaway victory.*

run·down (run-down) *n.* a detailed analysis.

run-down (run-down) *adj.* 1. in a state of neglect. 2. weakened, as from overwork, poor nutrition, etc.

rune (roon) *n.* any of the letters in an alphabet used by early Germanic peoples. **run′ic** *adj.*

rung[1] (rung) *n.* one of the crosspieces of a ladder etc. **rung′less** *adj.*

rung[2] *see* **ring**[2].

run-in (run-in) *n.* a direct confrontation, a quarrel.

run·let (run-lit) *n.* a small stream.

run·nel (run-ĕl) *n.* a brook.

run·ner (run-ĕr) *n.* 1. a person or animal that runs, one taking part in a race. 2. a messenger. 3. a creeping stem that issues from the main stem and takes root. 4. a groove or rod or roller for a thing to move on, one of the long strips on which a sledge etc. slides. 5. a long narrow strip of carpet, or of ornamental cloth for a table etc.

run·ner-up (run-ĕr-up) *n.* a person or team finishing second in a competition.

run·ning (run-ing) *see* **run.** **running** *adj.* 1. performed while running, *a running jump* or *kick.* 2. following each other without interval, *for four days running.* 3. continuous, *a running battle; running commentary,* one on an event as it happens. **running** *n.* the act of running. □**in** *or* **out of the running,** with a good or with no chance of winning. **running board,** a ledge formerly under the doors of a car to assist passengers in getting in and out of the car. **running gear,** the working mechanisms of a vehicle, those not used for power. **running lights,** the lights on boats and aircraft

at night. **running mate,** a candidate for a secondary position in an election. **running stitch,** a line of evenly spaced stitches made by a straight thread passing in and out of the material.

run·ny (run-ee) *adj.* (-ni·er, -ni·est) 1. semiliquid. 2. tending to flow or exude fluid.

run·off (run-awf) *n.* 1. liquid that drains off, as water after a rain. 2. a deciding race after a tie.

run-of-the-mill (run-ŏv-*th*ĕ-mil) *adj.* ordinary, not special.

run-on (run-on) *n.* 1. printing that continues on the same line as that which precedes. 2. a line of poetry to be read as continuing the sense of the preceding line. **run-on** *adj.*

runt (runt) *n.* an undersized person or animal; *the runt of a litter,* the smallest animal in a litter. **runt′y** *adj.* (runt·i·er, runt·i·est) **runt′i·ness** *n.*

run·way (run-way) *n.* a prepared surface on an airfield, on which aircraft take off and land.

ru·pee (roo-pee, roo-pee) *n.* the unit of money in India, Pakistan, and certain other countries.

rup·ture (rup-chŭr) *n.* 1. breaking, breach. 2. an abdominal hernia. **rupture** *v.* (rup·tured, rup·tur·ing) 1. to burst or break (tissue etc.), to become burst or broken. 2. to affect with hernia.

ru·ral (roor-ăl) *adj.* of or in or like the countryside. **ru′ral·ly** *adv.* **ru′ral·ism** *n.* □**rural free delivery,** free postal delivery service in country areas.

ruse (rooz) *n.* a deception or trick.

rush[1] (rush) *n.* a marsh plant with a slender pithy stem used for making mats, chair seats, baskets, etc.

rush[2] *v.* 1. to go or come or convey with great speed. 2. to act hastily, to force into hasty action. 3. to attack or capture with a sudden assault. **rush** *n.* 1. rushing, an instance of this. 2. a period of great activity. 3. a sudden great demand for goods etc. 4. *(informal)* the first print of a motion picture before it is cut and edited. **rush** *adj.* done with haste or with minimum delay, *a rush job.* **rush′er** *n.* **rush′ing·ly** *adv.* □**rush hour,** the time each day when traffic is busiest.

rusk (rusk) *n.* a kind of dry toasted bread, especially used for feeding babies.

Russ. *abbr.* 1. Russia. 2. Russian.

rus·set (rus-it) *adj.* soft reddish brown. **russet** *n.* 1. russet color. 2. an apple with a rough skin of this color.

Rus·sia (rush-ă) a country extending from eastern Europe to the Pacific, the U.S.S.R.

Rus·sian (rush-ăn) *adj.* of Russia or its people or language. **Russian** *n.* 1. a native or inhabitant of Russia. 2. the language of Russia. □**Russian dressing,** a salad dressing with mayonnaise, chopped pickles and pimentos, chili sauce, etc. **Russian Orthodox Church,** the church that was once the established church of Russia. **Russian roulette,** an act of bravado in which a person holds to his head a revolver of which one (unknown) chamber contains a bullet, and pulls the trigger. **Russian wolfhound,** a borzoi.

rust (rust) *n.* 1. a reddish-brown or yellowish-brown coating formed on iron or other metal by the effect of moisture, and gradually corroding it. 2. reddish brown. 3. a plant disease with rust-colored spots, the fungus causing this. **rust** *v.* 1. to affect or be affected with rust. 2. to lose quality or efficiency by lack of use. **rust′less** *adj.*

rus·tic (rus-tik) *adj.* 1. having the qualities ascribed

to country people or peasants, simple and unsophisticated, rough and unrefined. 2. made of rough timber or untrimmed branches, *rustic seat* or *bridge*. **rustic** *n.* a countryman, a peasant. **rus′ti·cal·ly** *adv.* **rus·tic·i·ty** (rus-tis-i-tee) *n.*
rus·ti·cate (rus-ti-kayt) *v.* (**rus·ti·cat·ed, rus·ti·cat·ing**) to settle in the country and live a rural life. **rus′ti·ca·tor** *n.* **rus·ti·ca·tion** (rus-ti-kay-shŏn) *n.*
rus·tle (rus-ĕl) *v.* (**rus·tled, rus·tling**) 1. to make a sound like that of paper being crumpled, to cause to do this. 2. *(informal)* to steal (horses or cattle), *cattle rustling*. **rustle** *n.* a rustling sound. **rus′tler** *n.* **rus′tling·ly** *adv.* □**rustle up,** *(informal)* to prepare or produce, *try and rustle up a meal.*
rust·proof (rust-proof) *adj.* not liable to rust.
rust·y (rus-tee) *adj.* (**rust·i·er, rust·i·est**) 1. affected with rust. 2. rust colored. 3. having lost quality or efficiency by lack of use. **rust′i·ness** *n.*
rut[1] (rut) *n.* 1. a deep track made by wheels in soft ground. 2. a habitual usually dull course of

life, *getting into a rut.* **rut′ted** *adj.* **rut′ty** *adj.* **rut′ti·ness** *n.*
rut[2] *n.* the periodic sexual excitement of a male deer or goat or ram etc. **rut** *v.* (**rut·ted, rut·ting**) to be affected with this. **rut′tish** *adj.*
ru·ta·ba·ga (roo-tă-bay-gă) *n.* a Swedish turnip.
Ruth (rooth) *n.* a book of the Old Testament.
ru·the·ni·um (roo-thee-ni-ŭm) *n.* a rare hard white metallic element.
ruth·er·ford·i·um (ru*th*-ĕr-for-di-ŭm) *n.* the proposed name of a synthetic element.
ruth·less (rooth-lis) *adj.* having no pity or compassion. **ruth′less·ly** *adv.* **ruth′less·ness** *n.*
Rwan·da (ruu-wahn-dă) a country in East Africa. **Rwan′dan** *adj.* & *n.*
rwy. *abbr.* railway.
Rx *abbr.* a medical prescription.
ry. *abbr.* railway.
ry·a (ree-ă) *n.* a hand-woven shag rug.
rye (rī) *n.* 1. a kind of cereal grain used for making flour or as food for cattle. 2. a kind of whiskey made from rye. 3. a bread made from rye.

S

S, s (es) (*pl.* **Ss, S's, s's**) the nineteenth letter of the alphabet.

s *suffix* used to form the plural of nouns, abbreviations, numbers, letters, and symbols; used to form adverbs, as in *evenings, always, besides;* used to form third person singular present indicative of verbs, as in *eats, says.*

S *symbol* sulfur.

s. *abbr.* 1. saint. 2. second. 3. section. 4. series. 5. shilling(s). 6. sign. 7. singular. 8. small. 9. son. 10. south. 11. stere(s). 12. substantive.

's 1. contraction of *is,* as in *he's here.* 2. contraction of *has,* as in *he's gone.* 3. contraction of *does,* as in *what's he do?* 4. contraction of *us,* as in *let's go.* 5. possessive form of singular and plural nouns not ending in *s,* as in *man's, people's, men's.*

S. *abbr.* 1. Saint. 2. Saturday. 3. school. 4. Sea. 5. Senate. 6. September. 7. south. 8. southern. 9. Sunday.

S.A. *abbr.* 1. Salvation Army. 2. seaman apprentice. 3. South Africa.

Sab·bath (sab-ăth) *n.* 1. a rest day appointed for Jews on the last day of the week (Saturday). 2. Sunday as a Christian day of abstinence from work and play.

sab·bat·i·cal (să-bat-i-kăl) *adj.* of or like the Sabbath. □**sabbatical leave,** leave granted at (often seven-year) intervals to a university professor etc. for study and travel.

sa·ber (say-běr) *n.* a cavalry sword with a curved blade. □**saber rattling,** a display of military strength. **saber saw,** a lightweight electric saw.

Sa·bin (say-bin) **vaccine** a polio vaccine, taken orally. ▷Named after Albert B. Sabin (1906–), the American physician who developed it.

sa·ble (say-běl) *n.* 1. a small weasel-like animal of arctic and adjacent regions, valued for its dark brown fur. 2. its fur. 3. the color black. **sable** *adj.* 1. of the sable's fur, *a sable coat.* 2. black.

sab·ot (sab-oh) *n.* (*pl.* **-ots**) a shoe hollowed out from one piece of wood, or with a wooden sole.

sab·o·tage (sab-ŏ-tahzh) *n.* willful damaging of machinery or materials, or disruption of work, by dissatisfied workmen or hostile agents. **sabotage** *v.* (**sab·o·taged, sab·o·tag·ing**) 1. to commit sabotage on. 2. to destroy or render useless, *sabotaged my plans.*

sab·o·teur (sab-ŏ-tur) *n.* a person who commits sabotage.

sa·bra (sah-bră) *n.* a native-born Israeli.

sa·bre = **saber.**

sac (sak) *n.* a bag-like part in an animal or plant.

SAC *abbr.* Strategic Air Command.

sac·cha·rin (sak-ă-rin) *n.* a very sweet substance used as a substitute for sugar.

sac·cha·rine (sak-ă-rin) *adj.* intensely and unpleasantly sweet, *saccharine sentiments.*

sac·er·do·tal (sas-ĕr-doh-tăl, sak-) *adj.* of priests or the priesthood, priestly. **sac·er·do'tal·ly** *adv.* **sac·er·do'tal·ism** *n.*

sa·chem (say-chěm) *n.* the supreme chief of some American Indian tribes.

sa·chet (sa-shay) *n.* a small bag filled with a sweet-smelling substance for laying among clothes etc. to scent them.

sack¹ (sak) *n.* 1. a large bag of strong coarse fabric etc. for storing and carrying goods. 2. this with its contents, the amount it contains. 3. *the sack, (informal)* dismissal from one's employment or position, *got the sack.* 4. *(informal)* a bed; *hit the sack,* go to bed. **sack** *v.* 1. to put into a sack or sacks. 2. *(informal)* to dismiss from a job. **sack'ful** *n.* (*pl.* **-fuls,** *pr.* -fülz) □**sack race,** a race in which each competitor is tied in a sack up to his waist or neck and moves by jumping.

sack² *v.* to plunder (a captured town etc.) in a violent destructive way. **sack** *n.* the act or process of sacking a place.

sack³ *n.* a dry Spanish wine.

sack·cloth (sak-klawth) *n.* a coarse fabric for making sacks; *sackcloth and ashes,* a symbol of regret and repentance. ▷From the ancient custom of wearing sackcloth and sprinkling ashes on one's head in penitence or mourning.

sack·ing (sak-ing) *n.* material for making sacks.

sac·ra·ment (sak-ră-měnt) *n.* 1. a formal symbolic religious rite, especially the Christian ceremonies of baptism and the Eucharist. 2. (often *Sacrament*) the consecrated elements in the Eucharist, especially the bread, *receive the Sacrament.* **sac·ra·men·tal** (sak-ră-men-tăl) *adj.* **sac·ra·men'tal·ly** *adv.*

Sac·ra·men·to (sak-ră-men-toh) the capital of California.

sa·cred (say-krid) *adj.* 1. associated with or dedicated to God or a god, or regarded with reverence because of this. 2. dedicated to some person or purpose, *sacred to the memory of those who fell in battle.* 3. connected with religion, not secular, *sacred music.* 4. sacrosanct. **sa'cred·ly** *adv.* **sa'cred·ness** *n.* □**sacred cow,** an idea or institution that its supporters will not allow to be criticized. ▷The phrase refers to the Hindus' respect for the cow as a sacred animal.

sac·ri·fice (sak-rĭ-fɪs) *n.* 1. the slaughter of a victim or the presenting of a gift or doing of an act in order to win the favor of a god. 2. the giving up of a valued thing for the sake of another that is more important or more worthy. 3. the thing offered or given up. 4. the sale of something at much less than its real value. 5. (in baseball) a fly ball or a bunt hit by a batter for the purpose of advancing a base runner. **sacrifice** *v.* (**sac·ri·ficed, sac·ri·fic·ing**) 1. to offer or give up as a sacrifice. 2. to give up (a thing) in order to achieve something else. *her description of events sacrificed accuracy to vividness.* 3. to sell (a thing) at much less than its real value. **sac·ri·fi·cial** (sak-rī-fish-ăl) *adj.* **sac·ri·fi'cial·ly** *adv.*

sac·ri·lege (sak-krī-lij) *n.* disrespect or damage to something regarded as sacred. **sac·ri·le·gious** (sak-rī-leej-ŭs) *adj.* **sac·ri·le'gious·ly** *adv.*

sac·ris·tan (sak-ri-stăn) *n.* the person in charge of the contents of a church, especially the sacred vessels etc. used in worship.

sac·ris·ty (sak-ri-stee) *n.* (*pl.* **-ties**) the place in a church where sacred vessels etc. are kept.

sac·ro·il·i·ac (sak-roh-il-i-ak) *n.* the joint between the bone of the hip and the five fused vertebrae close to the base of the spine.

sac·ro·sanct (sak-rŏ-sangkt) *adj.* reverenced or respected and therefore secure from violation or damage.

sac·rum (sak-rŭm, say-krŭm) *n.* (*pl.* **sac·ra,** *pr.* sak-ră, say-kră) the composite triangular bone of fused vertebrae forming the back of the pelvis.

sad (sad) *adj.* (**sad·der, sad·dest**) 1. showing or causing sorrow, unhappy. 2. regrettable. **sad'ly** *adv.* **sad'ness** *n.* □**sad sack,** (*slang*) a very incompetent person.

sad·den (sad-ĕn) *v.* to make sad.

sad·dle (sad-ĕl) *n.* 1. a seat for a rider, placed on a horse or other animal or forming part of a bicycle etc. 2. a saddle-shaped thing, a ridge of high land between two peaks. 3. a cut of meat consisting of the two loins. **saddle** *v.* (**sad·dled, sad·dling**) 1. to put a saddle on (an animal). 2. to burden (a person) with a task. □**in the saddle,** in a controlling position. **saddle blanket,** a blanket or pad laid on a horse's back under the saddle to prevent irritation. **saddle horse,** a horse for riding. **saddle shoe,** a shoe with a contrasting band of color across the instep. **saddle soap,** a soap used for cleaning and preserving leather. **saddle sore,** an irritation or sore on a horse's back caused by a badly fitted saddle; a sore or irritation on a person caused by horseback riding. **saddle stitching,** a long running stitch made with thick thread, used decoratively.

sad·dle·backed (sad-ĕl-bakt) *adj.* with the upper outline concave.

sad·dle·bag (sad-ĕl-bag) *n.* a strong bag fixed behind a saddle or one of a pair slung over a horse etc.

sad·dle·bow (sad-ĕl-boh) *n.* the arched front of a saddle.

sad·dle·cloth (sad-ĕl-klawth) *n.* (*pl.* **-cloths**) the pad placed under a racehorse saddle, showing the horse's number.

sad·dler (sad-lĕr) *n.* a person who makes or deals in saddles and harness.

sad·dler·y (sad-lĕ-ree) *n.* a saddler's goods or business.

Sad·du·cee (saj-ŭ-see) *n.* a member of the Jewish sect or party of the time of Christ that denied the resurrection of the dead, the existence of spirits, and the obligation of the traditional oral law. **Sad'du·cee·ism** *n.* **Sad·du·ce·an** (saj-ŭ-see-ăn) *adj.*

sad·ism (sad-iz-ĕm, say-diz-) *n.* enjoyment of inflicting or watching cruelty, this as a form of sexual perversion. **sad'ist** *adj.* & *n.* **sa·dis·tic** (să-dis-tik) *adj.* **sa·dis'ti·cal·ly** *adv.*

sad·o·mas·o·chism (sad-oh-mas-ŏ-kiz-ĕm, say-

doh-) *n.* the combination of sadism and masochism in one person. **sad·o·mas'o·chist** *n.* **sad·o·mas·o·chis·tic** (sad-oh-mas-ŏ-kis-tik, say-doh-) *adj.*

sa·fa·ri (să-fahr-ee) *n.* 1. a hunting or exploratory expedition, especially in East Africa. 2. a similar expedition organized as a vacation tour. □**safari jacket,** a belted jacket in linen or similar fabric. **safari park,** an amusement park where exotic wild animals are kept in the open for visitors to see.

safe (sayf) *adj.* (**saf·er, saf·est**) 1. free from risk or danger, not dangerous. 2. providing security or protection. **safe** *adv.* safely; *play safe,* not take risks. **safe** *n.* a strong locked cupboard or cabinet for valuables. **safe'ly** *adv.* **safe'ness** *n.* □**on the safe side,** allowing a margin of security against risks. **safe conduct,** the right to pass through a district on a particular occasion without risk of arrest or harm (as in time of war). **safe period,** (in birth control) the time in a woman's menstrual cycle when sexual intercourse is least likely to result in conception.

safe-crack·er (sayf-krak-ĕr) *n.* a criminal who breaks safes open.

safe-de·pos·it (sayf-dĕ-poz-it) **box** a box in a bank vault that is rented out for the keeping of a person's valuables.

safe·guard (sayf-gahrd) *n.* a means of protection. **safeguard** *v.* to protect.

safe·keep·ing (sayf-kee-ping) *n.* preservation in a safe place.

safe·ty (sayf-tee) *n.* (*pl.* **-ties**) 1. being safe, freedom from risk or danger. 2. (in football) a position in the defensive backfield, a player who plays this position. □**safety catch,** a device that prevents a mechanism from being operated accidentally or dangerously; a locking device on a gun trigger. **safety glass,** glass that will not splinter when broken. **safety lamp,** a miner's lamp with the flame protected so that it will not ignite gases. **safety match,** a match that ignites only on a specially prepared surface. **safety net,** a net placed to catch an acrobat etc. in case he falls from a height. **safety pin,** a pin with a guard protecting the point to prevent it from pricking the user or coming out. **safety razor,** a razor with a guard to prevent the blade from cutting the skin deeply. **safety valve,** a valve that opens automatically to relieve excessive pressure in a steam boiler; an outlet for releasing feelings of anger or excitement etc. harmlessly.

saf·flow·er (saf-low-ĕr) *n.* a thistlelike plant yielding a red dye used in rouge etc. and seeds rich in oil. □**safflower oil,** its edible oil.

saf·fron (saf-rŏn) *n.* 1. the orange-colored stigmas of a kind of crocus, used for coloring and flavoring food. 2. the color of these.

S. Afr. *abbr.* South Africa.

sag (sag) *v.* (**sagged, sag·ging**) 1. to sink or curve down in the middle under weight or pressure. 2. to hang loosely and unevenly, to droop. **sag** *n.* sagging.

sa·ga (sah-gă) *n.* a long story with many episodes.

sa·ga·cious (să-gay-shŭs) *adj.* showing wisdom in one's understanding and judgment of things. **sa·ga'cious·ly** *adv.* **sa·gac·i·ty** (să-gas-i-tee) *n.*

sage[1] (sayj) *n.* 1. an herb with fragrant grayish-green leaves used to flavor food. 2. sagebrush.

sage[2] *adj.* (**sag·er, sag·est**) profoundly wise, having wisdom gained from experience. **sage**

n. a profoundly wise man. **sage'ly** *adv.* **sage' ness** *n.*

sage·brush (sayj-brush) *n.* a growth of plants native to the dry plains of the western U.S.

Sag·it·ta·ri·us (saj-i-tair-i-ŭs) *n.* a sign of the zodiac, the Archer. **Sag·it·ta'ri·an** *adj.* & *n.*

sa·go (say-goh) *n.* a starchy food in the form of hard white grains, used in puddings, obtained from the pith of a kind of palm tree (the *sago palm*).

sa·gua·ro (să-wahr-oh) *n.* (*pl.* **-ros**) a giant cactus of the southwestern U.S. and Mexico.

sa·hib (sah-ib) *n.* a former title of address to European men in India.

said (sed) *see* **say.**

sail (sayl) *n.* 1. a piece of canvas or other fabric spread on rigging to catch the wind and drive a ship or boat along. 2. these sails collectively. 3. a journey by ship or boat, *Haifa is three days' sail from Naples.* 4. something resembling a sail in function, *the sails of a windmill.* **sail** *v.* 1. to travel on water by use of sails or engine power. 2. to start on a voyage, *we sail next week.* 3. to travel on or over (water) in a ship or boat, *sailed the seas.* 4. to control the navigation of (a ship), to set (a toy boat) afloat. 5. to move swiftly and smoothly, to walk in a stately manner, *she sailed into the room.* □**sailing ship,** a ship driven by sails. **sail into,** (*slang*) to attack physically or verbally, *sailed into him;* to begin to work vigorously on, *sailed into my work.* **set sail,** to begin a sea voyage.

sail·boat (sayl-boht) *n.* a boat propelled by sail.

sail·cloth (sayl-klawth) *n.* 1. canvas for sails. 2. a strong canvaslike dress material.

sail·fish (sayl-fish) *n.* a large marine fish with a sail-like dorsal fin.

sail·or (say-lŏr) *n.* 1. a man who works as a member of a ship's crew, a member of a country's navy, especially one below the rank of officer. 2. a traveler considered as liable or not liable to seasickness, *a bad* or *good sailor.* □**sailor hat,** a straw hat with a flat top and straight brim.

sail·plane (sayl-playn) *n.* a glider designed for soaring.

saint (saynt) *n.* 1. a holy person, one declared (in the Roman Catholic or Orthodox Church) to have won a high place in heaven and to be worthy of veneration. 2. *Saint,* the title of such a person or of one receiving veneration. 3. one of the souls of the dead in paradise. 4. a member of the Christian Church or (in certain religious bodies) of one's own branch of it. 5. a very good or patient or unselfish person. **saint'ed** *adj.* **saint'dom** *n.* **saint'hood** *n.* □**St. Andrew's Cross,** an X-shaped cross. **St. Bernard,** a very large dog originally kept by the monks of Hospice on Great St. Bernard Pass in the Alps for the rescue of travelers. **St. Lucia** (loo-shă) an island country in the West Indies. **St. Patrick's Day,** March 17, in honor of St. Patrick, the patron saint of Ireland. **St. Paul,** the capital of Minnesota. **St. Valentine's Day,** February 14, in honor of St. Valentine, involving the exchange of valentines. **St. Vitus' dance,** a children's disease in which the limbs twitch uncontrollably.

saint·ly (saynt-lee) *adj.* (**-li·er, -li·est**) like a saint. **saint'li·ness** *n.*

sake[1] (sayk) *n.* **for the sake of,** in order to please or honor (a person) or get or keep (a thing).

sa·ke[2], **sa·ki** (sah-kee) *n.* a Japanese rice wine.

sa·laam (să-lahm) *n.* an Oriental salutation, a low bow. **salaam** *v.* to make a salaam to.

sa·la·cious (să-lay-shŭs) *adj.* lewd, erotic. **sa·la'cious·ly** *adv.* **sa·la'cious·ness** *n.* **sa·lac· i·ty** (să-las-i-tee) *n.*

sal·ad (sal-ăd) *n.* a cold dish consisting of one or more vegetables (usually raw), often chopped or sliced and seasoned. □**salad days,** the time when one was youthful and inexperienced. **salad dressing,** a sauce used with salad.

sal·a·man·der (sal-ă-man-děr) *n.* 1. a lizard-like animal related to the newts. 2. (in mythology) a lizard-like animal living in fire.

sa·la·mi (să-lah-mee) *n.* a strongly flavored sausage, originally Italian.

sal·a·ried (sal-ă-reed) *adj.* receiving a salary.

sal·a·ry (sal-ă-ree) *n.* (*pl.* **-ries**) a fixed payment made by an employer at regular intervals to a person, usually calculated on an annual or monthly basis.

sale (sayl) *n.* 1. selling, being sold. 2. an instance of this, the amount sold, *made a sale; our sales were enormous.* 3. an event at which goods are sold, especially by public auction or for charity. 4. disposal of a shop's stock at reduced prices, as at the end of a season. **sal'a·ble** *adj.* □**for** *or* **on sale,** offered for purchase. **sales department,** the department concerned with selling its firm's products. **sales promotion,** the techniques used for increasing sales of a product. **sales resistance,** the opposition or apathy of a prospective customer etc. to be overcome by salesmanship. **sales talk,** persuasive talk designed to make people buy goods or accept an idea. **sales tax,** the tax on receipts from sales.

Sa·lem (say-lěm) the capital of Oregon.

sales·clerk (saylz-klurk) *n.* a salesman or saleswoman.

sales·girl (saylz-gurl) *n.* a saleswoman.

sales·man (saylz-măn) *n.* (*pl.* **-men,** *pr.* -měn) a man employed to sell goods or services.

sales·man·ship (saylz-măn-ship) *n.* 1. the principles and techniques of selling, *no understanding of salesmanship.* 2. skill in selling, *admiration for his salesmanship.*

sales·per·son (saylz-pur-sŏn) *n.* a salesman or saleswoman.

sales·wom·an (saylz-wuum-ăn) *n.* (*pl.* **-wom· en,** *pr.* -wim-in) a woman employed to sell goods or services.

sal·i·cyl·ic (sal-ĭ-sil-ik) **acid** a benzene derivative used in the manufacture of aspirin etc.

sa·li·ent (say-li-ěnt) *adj.* projecting, prominent, most noticeable, *the salient features of the plan.* **salient** *n.* a projecting part, especially of a battle line. **sa'li·ent·ly** *adv.* **sa'li·ence** *n.* **sa·li·en· cy** (say-li-ĕn-see) *n.*

sa·line (say-leen) *adj.* salty, containing salt or salts. **sa·lin·i·ty** (să-lin-i-tee) *n.*

Salis·bur·y (sawlz-ber-ee, -bŭ-ree) the capital of Zimbabwe, formerly Rhodesia.

Salisbury steak a ground beef steak fried or broiled and often served with a sauce. ▷Named after J. H. Salisbury, a 19th century English dietitian.

sa·li·va (să-lı-vă) *n.* the colorless liquid discharged into the mouth by various glands, assisting in chewing and digestion.

sal·i·var·y (sal-ĭ-ver-ee) *adj.* of or producing saliva, *salivary glands.*

sal·i·vate (sal-ĭ-vayt) *v.* (**sal·i·vat·ed, sal·**

i·vat·ing) to produce saliva. **sal·i·va·tion** (sal-ĭ-vay-shŏn) *n.*

Salk (sawk) **vaccine** the first vaccine developed against polio. ▷Named after J. E. Salk (1914–), the microbiologist who developed it.

sal·low¹ (sal-oh) *adj.* (of a person's skin or complexion) yellowish. **sal'low·ness** *n.*

sallow² *n.* an Old World willow tree, especially of a low-growing or shrubby kind.

sal·ly (sal-ee) *n.* (*pl.* **-lies**) 1. a sudden rush forward in attack, a sortie. 2. an excursion. 3. a lively or witty remark. **sally** *v.* (**sal·lied, sal·ly·ing**) **sally forth** *or* **out**, to make a sally (in attack) or an excursion.

sal·ma·gun·di (sal-mă-gun-dee) *n.* 1. a dish of chopped meat, anchovies, eggs, onions, etc. and seasoning. 2. a general mixture, a miscellaneous collection of articles, subjects, qualities, etc.

salm·on (sam-ŏn) *n.* (*pl.* **-on, -ons**) 1. a large fish with pinkish flesh, much valued for food and sport. 2. salmon pink. ☐**salmon pink**, orange-pink like the flesh of salmon. **salmon trout**, a European trout resembling salmon.

sal·mo·nel·la (sal-mŏ-nel-ă) *n.* a pathogenic bacterium, especially of a type causing food poisoning.

sa·lon (să-lon, sal-on) *n.* 1. an elegant room in a large house, used for receiving guests. 2. a gathering in such a room. 3. a room or establishment where a hairdresser, beauty specialist, couturier, etc. receives clients.

sa·loon (să-loon) *n.* 1. a place where alcoholic drinks may be bought and drunk. 2. a public room, as on a ship.

sal·sa (sal-să) *n.* a type of Latin American dance music.

sal (sal) **soda** sodium carbonate, washing soda.

salt (sawlt) *n.* 1. sodium chloride, a substance obtained from mines or by evaporation of seawater (in which it is present), used to flavor and preserve food. 2. a chemical compound of a metal and an acid. **salt** *adj.* tasting of salt, impregnated with or preserved in salt. **salt** *v.* 1. to season with salt. 2. to preserve in salt. 3. to put aside for the future, *salt it away.* 4. to make (a mine) appear rich by fraudulently inserting previously mined metal into it before it is viewed. ☐**old salt**, an experienced sailor. **salt lake**, a lake of salt water. **Salt Lake City**, the capital of Utah. **salt lick**, a place where animals go to lick rock or earth impregnated with salt. **salt marsh**, a marsh that is flooded by the sea at high tide. **salt of the earth**, people with a wholesome influence upon society. **salt pan**, a natural or artificial hollow by the sea where salt is obtained from seawater by evaporation. **salt pork**, pork cured with salt. **salt shaker**, a container of salt for sprinkling on food. **take it with a grain** *or* **pinch of salt**, not believe it wholly. **worth one's salt**, competent, deserving one's position.

SALT (sawlt) *n.* Strategic Arms Limitation Talks.

salt·cel·lar (sawlt-sel-ăr) *n.* a dish or perforated pot holding salt for use at meals.

sal·tine (sawl-teen) *n.* a thin crisp salted cracker.

salt·pe·ter (sawlt-pee-tĕr) *n.* a salty white powder (potassium nitrate) used in making gunpowder and preserving meat, and medicinally.

salt·wa·ter (sawlt-waw-tĕr) *adj.* of or living in salt water. ☐**saltwater taffy**, a chewy sugar and molasses candy, traditionally sold at the seashore.

salt·y (sawl-tee) *adj.* (**salt·i·er, salt·i·est**) 1. containing or tasting of salt. 2. (of speech) indecent, spicy. **salt'i·ness** *n.*

sa·lu·bri·ous (să-loo-bri-ŭs) *adj.* health-giving. **sa·lu'bri·ous·ly** *adv.* **sa·lu'bri·ous·ness** *n.* **sa·lu·bri·ty** (să-loo-bri-tee) *n.*

Sa·lu·ki (să-loo-kee) *n.* (*pl.* **-kis**) (also **saluki**) a tall swift slender silky-coated dog.

sal·u·tar·y (sal-yŭ-ter-ee) *adj.* producing a beneficial or wholesome effect.

sal·u·ta·tion (sal-yŭ-tay-shŏn) *n.* 1. a word or words or gesture of greeting, an expression of respect. 2. a formal word or phrase (as "Dear Sir") at the head of a letter.

sa·lu·ta·to·ri·an (să-loo-tă-tohr-i-ăn) *n.* a student in some schools and colleges who gives the welcoming address at commencement exercises.

sa·lute (să-loot) *n.* 1. a gesture of respect or greeting or polite recognition. 2. a formal military movement or position of the body, or a discharge of guns or use of flags, as a sign of respect. **salute** *v.* (**sa·lut·ed, sa·lut·ing**) 1. to greet with a polite gesture. 2. to perform a formal military salute, to greet with this. 3. to express respect or admiration for.

Sal·va·do·ran (sal-vă-dor-ăn) *adj.* of El Salvador. **Sal·va·do·re·an** (sal-vă-dohr-i-ăn) *n.* a native of El Salvador.

sal·vage (sal-vij) *n.* 1. rescue of a wrecked or damaged ship or its cargo, rescue of property from fire or other disaster. 2. the goods or property saved. 3. the saving and use of waste paper, scrap metal, etc. 4. the items saved. **salvage** *v.* (**sal·vaged, sal·vag·ing**) to save from loss or for use as salvage. **sal'vage·a·ble** *adj.*

sal·va·tion (sal-vay-shŏn) *n.* 1. saving of the soul from sin and its consequences, the state of being saved. 2. preservation from loss or calamity, a thing that preserves from these, *the loan was our salvation.* **sal·va'tion·al** *adj.* ☐**Salvation Army**, an international Christian organization founded on military lines to do charitable work and spread Christianity.

salve (sav) *n.* 1. a soothing ointment. 2. something that soothes conscience or wounded feelings. **salve** *v.* (**salved, salv·ing**) to soothe (conscience etc.).

sal·ver (sal-vĕr) *n.* a tray (usually of metal) on which letters or cards or refreshments are placed for handing to people.

sal·vi·a (sal-vi-ă) *n.* a plant with spikes of red or blue flowers.

sal·vo (sal-voh) *n.* (*pl.* **-vos, -voes**) 1. the firing of a number of guns simultaneously, especially as a salute. 2. a volley of applause.

SAM (sam) *n.* surface-to-air missile.

Sam. *abbr.* Samuel.

S. Am., S. Amer. *abbr.* 1. South America. 2. South American.

Sa·mar·i·tan (să-mar-i-tăn) *n.* a native of Samaria, a district of ancient Palestine. ☐**good Samaritan**, someone who readily gives help to a person in distress who has no claim on him. ▷Named after the parable of the Good Samaritan, in Luke.

sa·mar·i·um (să-mair-i-ŭm) *n.* a rare-earth metallic element.

sam·ba (sahm-bă) *n.* (*pl.* **-bas**) 1. a Brazilian dance of African origin, a ballroom dance imitative of this. 2. the music for this dance. **samba** *v.* (**-baed, -ba·ing**) to dance the samba.

same (saym) *adj.* 1. being of one kind, not changed or changing or different. 2. previously mentioned.

3. *the same,* the same thing, *would do the same again;* in the same manner, *we still feel the same about it.* **same** *adv.* & *pronoun (informal)* = the same (definition 3 above), *same for me, please; we feel the same as you do.* **same'ness** *n.* being the same, lack of variety. □**same here,** *(informal)* the same applies to me; I agree.

sam·iz·dat (sam-iz-dat) *n.* a system of clandestine publication of banned literature in the U.S.S.R.

Sa·mo·a (să-moh-ă) a group of islands in the Pacific Ocean, of which the eastern part *(American Samoa)* is a territory of the U.S., and the western part *(Western Samoa)* is an independent country. **Sa·mo'an** *adj.* & *n.*

sam·o·var (sam-ŏ-vahr) *n.* a metal urn with an interior heating tube to keep water at boiling point for making tea, used in Russia and elsewhere.

Sam·o·yed (sam-ŏ-yed) *n.* 1. a member of a people of Siberian Mongols. 2. the language of these people. 3. a dog of white arctic breed.

sam·pan (sam-pan) *n.* a small flat-bottomed boat used along coasts and rivers of China.

sam·ple (sam-pĕl) *n.* a small separated part showing the quality of the whole, a specimen. **sample** *v.* **(sam·pled, sam·pling)** to test by taking a sample or getting an experience of.

sam·pler (sam-plĕr) *n.* 1. a person who samples. 2. a piece of embroidery worked in various stitches to display skill in needlework.

Sam·u·el (sam-yoo-ĕl) *n.* 1. a Hebrew prophet. 2. either of two books of the Old Testament telling the story of his times.

sam·u·rai (sam-ŭ-rı) *n.* (*pl.* **-rai**) 1. a Japanese army officer. 2. a member of the former military caste in Japan.

Sa·n'a (sah-nah) the capital of the Yemen Arab Republic.

san·a·to·ri·um (san-ă-tohr-i-ŭm) *n.* (*pl.* **-to·ri·ums, -to·ri·a,** *pr.* -tohr-i-ă) 1. a sanitarium. 2. a health resort.

sanc·ti·fy (sangk-tĭ-fı) *v.* **(sanc·ti·fied, sanc·ti·fy·ing)** to make holy or sacred. **sanc'ti·fi·er** *n.* **sanc·ti·fi·ca·tion** (sangk-tĭ-fĭ-kay-shŏn) *n.*

sanc·ti·mo·ni·ous (sangk-tĭ-moh-ni-ŭs) *adj.* making a show of righteousness or piety. **sanc·ti·mo'ni·ous·ly** *adv.* **sanc·ti·mo'ni·ous·ness** *n.*

sanc·ti·mo·ny (sangk-tĭ-moh-nee) *n.* hypocritical righteousness or piety.

sanc·tion (sangk-shŏn) *n.* 1. permission or approval for an action or behavior etc. 2. action taken by a country to penalize or coerce a country or organization that is considered to have violated a law or code of practice or basic human rights. **sanction** *v.* to give sanction or approval to, to authorize. **sanc'tion·er** *n.*

sanc·ti·ty (sangk-tĭ-tee) *n.* (*pl.* **-ties**) sacredness, holiness.

sanc·tu·ar·y (sangk-choo-ar-ee) *n.* (*pl.* **-ar·ies**) 1. a sacred place, the holiest part of a temple, the part of a chancel containing the altar. 2. an area where birds or wild animals are protected and encouraged to breed. 3. refuge, a place of refuge, *seek sanctuary.*

sanc·tum (sangk-tŭm) *n.* (*pl.* **-tums, -ta,** *pr.* -tă) 1. a holy place. 2. a person's private room.

sand (sand) *n.* 1. very fine loose fragments resulting from the wearing down of rock, found in deserts, seashores, riverbeds, etc.; *the sands are running out,* the time allowed is nearly at an end (▷from

the use of sand in an hourglass). 2. an expanse of sand, a sandbank, *White Sands.* 3. light brown color like that of sand. **sand** *v.* 1. to sprinkle or cover with sand. 2. to smooth or polish with sand or sandpaper. **sand'er** *n.* □**sand castle,** a structure of sand made for recreation on the seashore. **sand dollar,** a round flat sea urchin. **sand dune,** loose sand formed into a mound by wind. **sand painting,** an American Indian ceremonial design made with colored sands. **sand shark,** a shark found in the shallow coastal water of the Atlantic. **sand trap,** (in golf) a hazard, usually near the putting green, consisting of a shallow sandy pit.

san·dal (san-dăl) *n.* a light shoe consisting of a sole with straps or thongs over the foot.

san·daled (san-dăld) *adj.* wearing sandals.

san·dal·wood (san-dăl-wuud) *n.* a kind of scented wood from a tropical tree.

sand·bag (sand-bag) *n.* a bag filled with sand, used to protect a wall or building (as in war, or as a defense against rising floodwater), or as a weapon. **sandbag** *v.* **(sand·bagged, sand·bag·ging)** 1. to protect with sandbags. 2. to hit with a sandbag. **sand'bag·ger** *n.*

sand·bank (sand-bangk) *n.* a deposit of sand under water, causing a river etc. to be shallow at that point.

sand·bar (sand-bahr) *n.* a sandbank at the mouth of a harbor or river.

sand·blast (sand-blast) *v.* to clean or treat with a jet of sand driven by compressed air or steam. **sand'blast·er** *n.*

sand·box (sand-boks) *n.* a box containing sand for children to play in.

sand·hog (sand-hog) *n.* 1. a person who works in sand. 2. a person employed in digging underwater tunnels.

S&L *abbr.* savings and loan.

sand·lot (sand-lot) *n.* an unoccupied sandy lot used for games, usually by children. □**sandlot baseball,** a baseball game played in a sandlot.

sand·lot·ter (sand-lot-ĕr) *n.* a person who plays sandlot baseball.

sand·man (sand-man) *n.* (*pl.* **-men,** *pr.* -men) the personification of tiredness causing children's eyes to close toward bedtime.

sand·pa·per (sand-pay-pĕr) *n.* paper with a coating of sand or other abrasive substance, used for smoothing or polishing surfaces. **sandpaper** *v.* to smooth or polish with sandpaper.

sand·pi·per (sand-pı-pĕr) *n.* any of several birds with long pointed bills, living in open wet sandy places.

sand·stone (sand-stohn) *n.* a rock formed of compressed sand.

sand·storm (sand-stohrm) *n.* a desert storm of wind with clouds of sand.

sand·wich (sand-wich) *n.* 1. two or more slices of bread with a layer of filling between. 2. something resembling this in arrangement. **sandwich** *v.* to insert (a thing) between two others. □**sandwich coin,** a U.S. coin with a layer of one metal between layers of another metal. **sandwich man,** a man walking in the street and carrying advertising signs, which hang before and behind.

sand·y (san-dee) *adj.* **(sand·i·er, sand·i·est)** 1. like sand, covered with sand. 2. (of hair) yellowish red, (of a person) having hair of this color. **sand'i·ness** *n.*

sane (sayn) *adj.* (**san·er, san·est**) 1. having a sound mind, not mad. 2. showing good judgment, sensible and practical. **sane′ly** *adv.* **sane′ness** *n.*

San·for·ized (san-fŏ-rīzd) *adj.* *(trademark)* (of fabric) treated to resist shrinking.

sang (sang) *see* **sing.**

sang·froid (sahn-frwah) *n.* calmness in danger or difficulty.

san·gri·a (sang-gree-ă) *n.* a Spanish drink of red wine with lemonade etc.

san·gui·nar·y (sang-gwĭ-ner-ee) *adj.* 1. full of bloodshed. 2. bloodthirsty. **san′gui·nar·i·ly** *adv.*

san·guine (sang-gwin) *adj.* hopeful, optimistic, *they are not very sanguine about their chances of winning.*

sanit. *abbr.* 1. sanitary. 2. sanitation.

san·i·tar·i·um (san-i-tair-i-ŭm) *n.* (*pl.* **-tar·i·ums, -tar·i·a,** *pr.* -tair-i-ă) an establishment for treating chronic diseases (such as tuberculosis) or for convalescents.

san·i·tar·y (san-i-ter-ee) *adj.* 1. of hygiene, hygienic. 2. of sanitation. □**sanitary napkin,** an absorbent pad worn during menstruation.

san·i·ta·tion (san-i-tay-shŏn) *n.* arrangements to protect public health, especially by drainage and the efficient disposal of sewage.

san·i·tize (san-i-tīz) *v.* (**san·i·tized, san·i·tiz·ing**) to make hygienic.

san·i·ty (san-i-tee) *n.* being sane.

San Jo·sé (san hoh-zay) the capital of Costa Rica.

San Juan (san wahn) the capital of Puerto Rico.

sank (sangk) *see* **sink.**

San Ma·ri·no (san mă-ree-noh) 1. a small independent republic in northeast Italy. 2. its capital.

sans (sanz) *prep.* without. □**sans serif,** a form of type without serifs.

Sans., Sansk. *abbr.* Sanskrit.

San·skrit (san-skrit) *n.* the ancient language of the Hindus in India, one of the oldest known Indo-European languages.

San·ta Claus (san-tă klawz) a person said to fill children's stockings with presents on the night before Christmas. ▷From the Dutch name *Sante Klaas* = St. Nicholas.

San·ta Fe (san-ta fay) the capital of New Mexico.

San·ti·a·go (san-ti-ah-goh) the capital of Chile.

São To·mé (sown tuu-may) the capital of **São Tomé and Prín·ci·pe** (preen-si-pay), a country consisting of two islands off the west coast of Africa.

sap¹ (sap) *n.* the vital liquid that circulates in plants, carrying food to all parts. **sap** *v.* (**sapped, sap·ping**) to exhaust (strength etc.) gradually. **sap′per** *n.*

sap² *n.* a trench or tunnel made in order to get closer to an enemy. **sap** *v.* (**sapped, sap·ping**) 1. to dig a sap. 2. to undermine, to make insecure by removing foundations, to destroy insidiously. **sap′per** *n.*

sap³ *n.* *(slang)* a foolish person.

sa·pi·ent (say-pi-ĕnt) *adj.* pretending to be full of wisdom. **sa′pi·ent·ly** *adv.* **sa′pi·ence** *n.*

sap·ling (sap-ling) *n.* a young tree.

sa·pon·i·fy (să-pon-ĭ-fī) *v.* (**sa·pon·i·fied, sa·pon·i·fy·ing**) 1. to turn (fat or oil) into soap by decomposition with an alkali. 2. to convert (an ester) to acid and alcohol.

sap·phire (saf-ır) *n.* 1. a transparent blue precious stone. 2. its color. **sapphire** *adj.* bright blue.

sap·py (sap-ee) *adj.* (**-pi·er, -pi·est**) *adj.* 1. full of sap. 2. *(slang)* silly. **sap′pi·ness** *n.*

sap·ro·phyte (sap-rŏ-fīt) *n.* a fungus or similar plant living on decayed organic matter. **sap·ro·phyt·ic** (sap-rŏ-fit-ik) *adj.*

sap·suck·er (sap-suk-ĕr) *n.* an American woodpecker that drills holes in trees in order to drink sap from them.

sap·wood (sap-wuud) *n.* the soft outer layers of recently formed wood between the heartwood and the bark.

Sar·a·cen (sar-ă-sĕn) *n.* an Arab or Muslim at the time of the Crusades. **Sar·a·cen·ic** (sar-ă-sen-ik) *adj.*

sar·casm (sahr-kaz-ĕm) *n.* 1. an ironical remark or taunt. 2. the use of such taunts.

sar·cas·tic (sahr-kas-tik) *adj.* using or showing sarcasm. **sar·cas′ti·cal·ly** *adv.*

sar·co·ma (sahr-koh-mă) *n.* (*pl.* **-mas, -ma·ta,** *pr.* -mă-tă) a malignant tumor on connective tissue.

sar·coph·a·gus (sahr-kof-ă-gŭs) *n.* (*pl.* **-gi,** *pr.* -jī, -gī, **-gus·es**) a stone coffin, often decorated with carvings.

sar·dine (sahr-deen) *n.* a young herring or similar small fish, often canned as food tightly packed in oil.

sar·don·ic (sahr-don-ik) *adj.* humorous in a grim or sarcastic way. **sar·don′i·cal·ly** *adv.*

sarge (sahrj) *n.* *(slang)* sergeant.

sa·ri, sa·ree (sahr-ee) *n.* (*pl.* **-ris, -rees**) a length of cotton or silk cloth draped around the body, worn as the main garment by Hindu women.

sa·rong (să-rawng) *n.* a Malay and Javanese garment worn by both sexes, consisting of a strip of cloth worn tucked around the waist or under the armpits.

sar·sa·pa·ril·la (sahr-să-pă-ril-ă) *n.* 1. a tropical American plant with trailing roots. 2. the roots. 3. (*pr.* sas-pă-ril-ă) soda water made from the dried roots, as root beer etc.

sar·to·ri·al (sahr-tohr-i-ăl) *n.* of tailoring, of men's clothing, *sartorial elegance.* **sar·to′ri·al·ly** *adv.*

sash¹ (sash) *n.* a long strip of cloth worn around the waist or over one shoulder and across the body for ornament or as part of a uniform.

sash² *n.* either of a pair of frames holding the glass panes of a window and sliding up and down in grooves. □**sash cord,** strong cord used for attaching a weight to each end of a sash so that it can be balanced at any height.

sa·shay (sa-shay) *v.* to walk or move ostentatiously, casually, or diagonally.

Sask. *abbr.* Saskatchewan.

Sas·katch·e·wan (sas-kach-ĕ-wăn) a province of Canada.

sass (sas) *n.* *(slang)* impudence, impertinent speech, *don't give me any of your sass.*

sas·sa·fras (sas-ă-fras) *n.* 1. a North American tree with a bark used medicinally or in perfumery. 2. its bark.

sas·sy (sas-ee) *adj.* (**-si·er, -si·est**) *(informal)* saucy.

sat *see* **sit.**

SAT *abbr.* Scholastic Aptitude Test.

sat. *abbr.* 1. saturate. 2. saturated. 3. saturation.

Sat. *abbr.* 1. Saturday. 2. Saturn.

Sa·tan (say-tăn) the Devil.

Sa·tan·ic (say-tan-ik) *adj.* 1. of Satan. 2. *satanic, devilish, hellish.* **sa·tan′i·cal** *adj.* **sa·tan′i·cal·ly** *adv.*

Sa·tan·ism (say-tă-niz-ĕm) *n.* worship of Satan, often using distorted forms of Christian worship.

satch·el (sach-ĕl) *n.* a small bag for carrying light articles, sometimes hung over the shoulder or carried on the back.

sate (sayt) *v.* (**sat·ed, sat·ing**) to satiate.

sa·teen (sa-teen) *n.* a closely woven cotton fabric resembling satin.

sat·el·lite (sat-ĕ-lit) *n.* 1. a heavenly body revolving around a planet, an artificial body placed in orbit to revolve similarly. 2. a person's follower or hanger-on. 3. a country that is subservient to another and follows its lead.

sa·ti·a·ble (say-shă-bĕl) *adj.* able to be satiated. **sa'ti·a·bly** *adv.*

sa·ti·ate (say-shi-ayt) *v.* (**sa·ti·at·ed, sa·ti·at·ing**) to satisfy an appetite fully, to glut or cloy with an excess of something. **sa·ti·a·tion** (say-shi-ay-shŏn) *n.*

sa·ti·e·ty (să-ti-ĕ-tee) *n.* the condition or feeling of being satiated.

sat·in (sat-in) *n.* a silky material woven in such a way that it is glossy on one side only. **satin** *adj.* smooth as satin. **sat'in·y** *adj.*

sat·in·wood (sat-in-wuud) *n.* 1. the smooth hard wood of various tropical trees, used for making furniture. 2. a tree yielding this.

sat·ire (sat-ir) *n.* 1. the use of ridicule or irony or sarcasm in speech or writing. 2. a novel or play or film etc. that ridicules people's hypocrisy or foolishness in this way, often by parody.

sa·tir·ic (să-tir-ik), **sa·tir·i·cal** (să-tir-i-kăl) *adj.* using satire, criticizing in a humorous or sarcastic way. **sa·tir'i·cal·ly** *adv.*

sat·i·rist (sat-ĭ-rist) *n.* a person who writes satires or uses satire.

sat·i·rize (sat-ĭ-riz) *v.* (**sat·i·rized, sat·i·riz·ing**) to attack with satire, to describe satirically. **sat'i·riz·er** *n.*

sat·is·fac·tion (sat-is-fak-shŏn) *n.* 1. satisfying, being satisfied. 2. something that satisfies a desire or gratifies a feeling. 3. compensation for injury or loss, *demand satisfaction.*

sat·is·fac·to·ry (sat-is-fak-tŏ-ree) *adj.* satisfying expectations or needs, adequate. **sat·is·fac'to·ri·ly** *adv.*

sat·is·fy (sat-is-fi) *v.* (**sat·is·fied, sat·is·fy·ing**) 1. to give (a person) what he wants or demands or needs, to make pleased or contented; *be satisfied with something* or *to do something,* to demand no more than this, to consider that this is enough. 2. to put an end to (a demand or craving) by giving what is required, *satisfy one's hunger.* 3. to provide with sufficient proof, to convince; *the police are satisfied that his death was accidental,* they feel certain of this. 4. to pay (a creditor). **sat'is·fi·er** *n.* **sat'is·fy·ing·ly** *adv.*

sa·to·ri (să-tohr-ee) *n.* (in Zen Buddhism) sudden enlightenment.

sa·trap (say-trap) *n.* 1. the governor of a province in the ancient Persian empire. 2. a subordinate ruler, a colonial governor, etc.

sat·u·rate (sach-ŭ-rayt) *v.* (**sat·u·rat·ed, sat·u·rat·ing**) 1. to make thoroughly wet, to soak. 2. to cause to absorb or accept as much as possible; *the market for used cars is saturated,* can take no more. **sat·u·ra·tion** (sach-ŭ-ray-shŏn) *n.* **sat·ur·a·ble** (sach-ŭ-ră-bĕl) *adj.* □**saturation point,** the stage beyond which no more can be absorbed or accepted.

Sat·ur·day (sat-ŭr-day) *n.* the day of the week

following Friday. □**Saturday night special,** *(slang)* a small inexpensive pistol.

Sat·urn (sat-ŭrn) *n.* 1. the Roman god of agriculture. 2. a planet in the solar system.

sat·ur·na·li·a (sat-ŭr-nay-li-ă) *n.* (*pl.* **-a, -as**) wild revelry. **sat·ur·na'li·an** *adj.*

sat·ur·nine (sat-ŭr-nin) *adj.* (of a person or his looks) having a gloomy forbidding appearance.

sat·ur·nin·i·ty (sat-ŭr-nin-i-tee) *n.*

sa·tyr (say-tir) *n.* 1. one of a class of woodland gods in ancient Greek and Roman mythology, in human form but having a goat's ears, tail, and legs. 2. a grossly lustful man.

sa·ty·ri·a·sis (say-ti-ri-ă-sis) *n.* excessive uncontrollable sexual desire in males.

sauce (saws) *n.* 1. a liquid or semiliquid preparation served with food to add flavor or richness. 2. (*informal*) impudence. 3. *(slang)* whiskey.

sauce·pan (saws-pan) *n.* a metal cooking pot with a long handle at the side, used for boiling things over heat.

sau·cer (saw-sĕr) *n.* 1. a small shallow curved dish on which a cup stands. 2. something shaped like this.

sau·cy (saw-see) *adj.* (**-ci·er, -ci·est**) 1. impudent. 2. jaunty. **sau'ci·ly** *adv.* **sau'ci·ness** *n.*

Sa·u·di A·ra·bi·a (sah-oo-dee ă-ray-bi-ă) a country in the Middle East. **Saudi** *n.* (*pl.* **-dis**) a native or inhabitant of Saudi Arabia.

sau·er·bra·ten (sow-ĕr-brah-tĕn) *n.* a German pot roast marinated in vinegar, sugar, and seasonings.

sau·er·kraut (sow-ĕr-krowt) *n.* a German dish of shredded pickled cabbage.

sau·na (saw-nă) *n.* a Finnish-style steam bath, a building or room for this.

saun·ter (sawn-tĕr) *v.* to walk in a leisurely way. **saunter** *n.* a leisurely walk or walking pace. **saun'ter·er** *n.*

sau·ri·an (sor-i-ăn) *adj.* of or like a lizard. **saurian** *n.* an animal of the lizard family.

sau·sage (saw-sij) *n.* chopped seasoned meat enclosed in a cylindrical case made from animal entrails or synthetic material. □**sausage meat,** meat prepared for this or as a stuffing etc.

sau·té (saw-tay) *v.* (**sau·téed, sau·té·ing**) to fry quickly in a small amount of fat. **sauté** *n.* a dish prepared in this way.

sau·terne (soh-turn) *n.* a light sweet white French wine.

sav·age (sav-ij) *adj.* 1. in a primitive or uncivilized state, *savage tribes.* 2. wild and fierce, *savage animals.* 3. cruel and hostile, *savage criticism.* 4. (*informal*) very angry. **savage** *n.* a member of a savage tribe. **savage** *v.* (**sav·aged, sav·ag·ing**) to attack savagely, to maul. **sav'age·ly** *adv.* **sav'age·ness, sav'age·ry** *n.*

sa·van·na, sa·van·nah (să-van-ă) *n.* a grassy plain in hot regions, with few or no trees.

sa·vant (sa-vahnt) *n.* a learned person.

sa·vate (să-vat) *n.* a form of boxing in which the feet as well as the fists are used.

save (sayv) *v.* (**saved, sav·ing**) 1. to rescue, to keep from danger or harm or capture. 2. to keep from the power of sin or its spiritual consequences. 3. to avoid wasting, *save fuel.* 4. to keep for future use or enjoyment, to put aside (money) for future use. 5. to make unnecessary, *did it to save a trip.* 6. in sports, to prevent an opponent from scoring. **save** *n.* the act of saving in soccer etc. **save** *prep.* except, *in all cases save one.* **sav'er** *n.* **sav'a·ble** *adj.* □**save one's breath,** to keep silent because it would be useless to speak. **saving grace,** a good quality that redeems a person whose other qualities are not good.

sav·ing (say-ving) *prep.* except.

sav·ings (say-vingz) *n. pl.* money put aside for future use. □**savings account,** a deposit account on which interest is paid. **savings bank,** a bank that primarily receives savings accounts.

sav·ior (sayv-yŏr) *n.* a person who rescues or delivers people from harm or danger; *the* or *our Savior,* Christ as the savior of mankind.

sa·voir faire (sav-wahr fair) knowledge of how to behave in any situation that may arise, social tact. ▷French.

sa·vor (say-vŏr) *n.* 1. the taste or smell of something. 2. the power to arouse enjoyment, *felt that life had lost its savor.* **savor** *v.* 1. to have a certain taste or smell. 2. to taste or smell (a thing) with enjoyment. 3. to give a certain impression, *the reply savors of impertinence.*

sa·vor·y[1] (say-vŏ-ree) *n.* a low-growing herb with a spicy smell and flavor, used in cooking.

savory[2] *adj.* 1. having an appetizing taste or smell. 2. having a salt or piquant and not sweet flavor. **sa·vor·i·ness** *n.*

sa·voy (să-voi) *n.* a hardy cabbage with wrinkled leaves.

sav·vy (sav-ee) *n. (slang)* common sense, understanding. **savvy** *v.* **(sav·vied, sav·vy·ing)** *(slang)* to understand.

saw[1] (saw) *see* **see**[1].

saw[2] *n.* a tool with a zigzag edge for cutting wood etc. **saw** *v.* **(sawed, sawed** or **sawn, saw·ing)** 1. to cut with a saw. 2. to make a to-and-fro movement like that of sawing. □**saw grass,** a plant with leaves having toothed edges like a saw.

saw[3] *n.* a proverbial saying, an old maxim.

saw·bones (saw-bohnz) *n. (slang)* a surgeon.

saw·buck (saw-buk) *n. (slang)* a ten-dollar bill.

saw·dust (saw-dust) *n.* powdery fragments of wood produced when timber is sawed.

saw·fish (saw-fish) *n.* (*pl.* **-fish, -fish·es)** a large fish having a blade-like snout with jagged edges that it uses as a weapon.

saw·fly (saw-flɪ) *n.* (*pl.* **-flies)** an insect that is destructive to plants, which it pierces with a jagged organ in order to lay its eggs.

saw·horse (saw-hors) *n.* a rack supporting wood for sawing.

saw·mill (saw-mil) *n.* a mill with power-operated saws where timber is cut into planks etc.

sawn (sawn) *see* **saw**[2].

saw-toothed (saw-tootht) *adj.* shaped like the teeth of a saw.

saw·yer (saw-yĕr) *n.* a workman who saws timber.

sax (saks) *n. (informal)* a saxophone.

sax·i·frage (sak-si-frij) *n.* a rock plant with clusters of small white, yellow, or red flowers.

Sax·on (sak-sŏn) *n.* 1. a member of a Germanic people who occupied parts of England in the 5th to 6th centuries. 2. their language. **Saxon** *adj.* of the Saxons or their language.

sax·o·phone (sak-sŏ-fohn) *n.* a wind instrument with a reed in the mouthpiece, and with keys operated by the player's fingers. **sax'o·phon·ist** *n.*

say (say) *v.* **(said, say·ing)** 1. to utter or recite in a speaking voice. 2. to state, to express in words, to have a specified wording, *the notice says "keep out."* 3. to give as an argument or excuse, *there's much to be said on both sides.* 4. to give as one's

opinion or decision, *it's hard to say which one of them is taller.* 5. to suppose as a possibility, to take (a specified amount) as being near enough, *let's allow, say, an hour for the meeting.* **say** *n.* the power to decide, *has no say in the matter.* **say** *interj. (informal)* used to gain attention or show approval, *say, can we get some service over here?;* say, that's a good idea. □**have one's say,** to say all one wishes to say. **I'll say,** *(informal)* yes indeed.

say·ing (say-ing) *n.* a well-known phrase or proverb or other statement.

say-so (say-soh) *n.* 1. the power to decide something. 2. a command. 3. a mere assertion without proof.

Sb *symbol* antimony.

Sc *symbol* scandium.

SC *abbr.* South Carolina.

sc. *abbr.* 1. scale. 2. scene. 3. science. 4. scientific.

Sc. *abbr.* 1. Scotch. 2. Scotland. 3. Scots. 4. Scottish.

S.C. *abbr.* 1. Security Council. 2. Signal Corps. 3. South Carolina. 4. Supreme Court.

scab (skab) *n.* 1. a crust forming over a sore as it heals. 2. a skin disease or plant disease that causes scablike roughness. 3. *(informal, contemptuous)* a person who refuses to join a strike or labor union or takes a striker's place or breaks the rules of his trade or group. **scab** *v.* **(scabbed, scab·bing)** 1. (of sores) to form a scab, to heal over. 2. *(informal,* of persons) to act as a scab. **scab'by** *adj.* **scab'bi·ly** *adv.* **scab'bi·ness** *n.*

scab·bard (skab-ărd) *n.* the sheath of a sword or dagger or bayonet.

sca·bies (skay-beez) *n.* a contagious skin disease causing itching.

sca·bi·ous (skay-bi-ŭs) *n.* a wild or cultivated annual herbaceous plant with thickly clustered blue, pink, or white flowers.

scab·rous (skab-rŭs) *adj.* 1. (of persons or plants etc.) having a rough skin or surface, scurfy. 2. (of a subject or situation etc.) requiring tactful treatment, hard to handle with decency. 3. indecent, salacious. 4. behaving indecently or immorally.

scads (skadz) *n. (slang)* large quantities, *scads of money.*

scaf·fold (skaf-ŏld) *n.* 1. a temporary structure of poles and planks etc. providing workmen with a platform on which to stand while constructing or repairing or cleaning a house etc. 3. a wooden platform for the execution of criminals; *the scaffold,* death by execution. **scaffold** *v.* to fit scaffolding to (a building).

scaf·fold·ing (skaf-ŏl-ding) *n.* 1. a scaffold or a group of scaffolds. 2. the poles etc. from which scaffolds are made.

scal·a·ble (skay-lă-bĕl) *adj.* able to be scaled.

scal·a·wag (skal-ă-wag) *n.* 1. *(informal)* a rascal, a good-for-nothing person. 2. a white Southerner who supported Republican Party policy during the Reconstruction period after the Civil War.

scald (skawld) *v.* 1. to injure or pain with hot liquid or steam. 2. to heat (milk) to near boiling point. 3. to cleanse (pans etc.) with boiling water. **scald** *n.* an injury to the skin by scalding.

scale[1] (skayl) *n.* 1. one of the thin overlapping plates of horny membrane or hard substance that protect the skin of many fishes and reptiles. 2. something resembling this (as on a plant), a flake of skin. 3. an incrustation inside a boiler or kettle etc. in which hard water is regularly used, a similar incrustation on teeth. **scale** v. (**scaled, scal·ing**) 1. to remove scales or scale from. 2. to come off in scales or flakes. **scaled** adj. **scale'less** adj. □**scale insect**, a small insect that attaches itself to the food plant and is covered by a waxy tough scale.

scale² n. 1. the pan of a balance. 2. (often *scales*) an instrument for weighing things; *the Scales,* a sign of the zodiac, Libra. □**tip** or **turn the scale(s)**, to be the decisive factor in a situation. **tip the scales at**, to weigh, *tipped the scales at two hundred pounds.*

scale³ n. 1. an ordered series of units or degrees or qualities etc. for purposes of measurement or classification. 2. an arrangement of notes in a system of music, ascending or descending by fixed intervals. 3. the ratio of the actual measurements of something and those of a drawing or map or model of it, a line with marks showing this, *the scale is one inch to the mile; a scale model,* one with measurements in uniform proportion to those of the original. 4. the relative size or extent of something, *war on a grand scale.* **scale** v. (**scaled, scal·ing**) 1. to climb, *scaled the cliff.* 2. to represent in measurements or extent in proportion to the size of the original; *scale it up* or *down,* make it larger or smaller in proportion.

sca·lene (skay-leen, skay-leen) adj. having unequal sides, *scalene triangle.*

scal·lion (skal-yŏn) n. 1. a long-necked onion without a normal bulb. 2. a shallot.

scal·lop (skal-ŏp) n. 1. a shellfish with two hinged fan-shaped shells. 2. the edible muscle of this. 3. one shell of this, used as a container in which food is cooked and served. 4. one of a series of semicircular curves used as an ornamental edging. **scallop** v. (**scal·loped, scal·lop·ing**) 1. to ornament with scallops. 2. in cooking, to escallop. **scal'lop·er** n.

scal·ly·wag = **scalawag**.

scalp (skalp) n. 1. the skin of the head excluding the face. 2. this with the hair, formerly cut from an enemy's head as a trophy by American Indians. **scalp** v. to take the scalp of.

scal·pel (skal-pĕl) n. a surgeon's small light straight knife.

scal·y (skay-lee) adj. (**scal·i·er, scal·i·est**) covered with scales or scale (*see* **scale¹**).

scam (skam) n. (*slang*) a fraudulent scheme, especially for making money quickly.

scamp (skamp) n. a rascal. **scamp** v. to do (work) hastily and inadequately.

scamp·er (skam-pĕr) v. to run hastily, to run about playfully as a child does. **scamper** n. a scampering run.

scam·pi (skam-pee) n. pl. large prawns or shrimps, these used as food especially fried in oil and garlic.

scan (skan) v. (**scanned, scan·ning**) 1. to look at all parts of (a thing) intently. 2. to glance at quickly and not thoroughly. 3. to sweep a radar or electronic beam over (an area) in search of something. 4. to resolve (a picture) into elements of light and shade for television transmission. 5. to analyze the rhythm of (a line of verse). 6. (of verse) to be correct in rhythm. **scan** n. the act or process of scanning. **scan'ner** n.

Scand. abbr. 1. Scandinavia. 2. Scandinavian.

scan·dal (skan-dăl) n. 1. something shameful or disgraceful. 2. gossip about other people's faults and wrongdoing. □**scandal sheet**, a newspaper etc. giving prominence to gossip and scandal.

scan·dal·ize (skan-dă-lız) v. (**scan·dal·ized, scan·dal·iz·ing**) to shock by something shameful or disgraceful. **scan'dal·iz·er** n.

scan·dal·mon·ger (skan-dăl-mong-gĕr) n. a person who invents or spreads scandal.

scan·dal·ous (skan-dă-lŭs) adj. 1. shameful, disgraceful. 2. containing scandal, *scandalous reports.* **scan'dal·ous·ly** adv.

Scan·di·na·vi·a (skan-di-nay-vi-ă) Norway, Sweden, Denmark, and Iceland considered as a unit. **Scan·di·na'vi·an** adj. & n.

scan·di·um (skan-di-ŭm) n. a rare metallic element.

scan·sion (skan-shŏn) n. the scanning of lines of verse, the way verse scans.

scant (skant) adj. scanty, insufficient, *was treated with scant courtesy.* **scant** v. to skimp, to stint, to provide grudgingly.

scan·ties (skan-teez) n. pl. women's short panties.

scant·y (skan-tee) adj. (**scant·i·er, scant·i·est**) 1. of small amount or extent, *scanty vegetation.* 2. barely enough. **scant'i·ly** adv. **scant'i·ness** n.

scape·goat (skayp-goht) n. a person who is made to bear blame or punishment that should rightly fall on others. ▷Named after the goat which, in ancient Jewish religious custom, was allowed to escape into the wilderness after the high priest had symbolically laid the sins of the people upon it.

scape·grace (skayp-grays) n. a rascal, a rogue, a person who is constantly getting into trouble.

scap·u·la (skap-yŭ-lă) n. (pl. **-lae**, pr. **-lee, -las**) the shoulder blade. **scap'u·lar** adj.

scap·u·lar (skap-yŭ-lăr) n. 1. a monk's short cloak covering the shoulders. 2. a badge of affiliation with an ecclesiastical order, consisting of two strips of cloth hanging down the breast and back and joined across the shoulders.

scar (skahr) n. 1. a mark left where a wound or injury or sore has healed, or on a plant from which a leaf has fallen. 2. a mark left by damage. 3. a lasting effect produced by grief etc. **scar** v. (**scarred, scar·ring**) to mark with a scar, to form a scar or scars. **scar'less** adj.

scar·ab (skar-ăb) n. 1. a sacred beetle of ancient Egypt. 2. a carving of this, engraved with symbols on the flat side and used in ancient Egypt as a charm.

scarce (skairs) adj. (**scarc·er, scarc·est**) not enough to supply a demand or need, rare. □**make oneself scarce**, (*informal*) to go away, to depart quietly.

scarce·ly (skairs-lee) adv. 1. only just, almost not, *she is scarcely seventeen years old; I scarcely know him.* 2. not, surely not, *you can scarcely expect me to believe that.*

scar·ci·ty (skair-si-tee) n. being scarce, a shortage.

scare (skair) v. (**scared, scar·ing**) to frighten or become frightened suddenly. **scare** n. a sudden fright, alarm caused by a rumor, *a bomb scare.*

scare·crow (skair-kroh) n. 1. a figure of a man dressed in old clothes, set up in a field to scare birds away from crops. 2. a badly-dressed or grotesque person.

scared·y-cat (skair-dee-kat) n. (*informal*) a timid person.

scare·mon·ger (skair-mong-gĕr) n. a person who raises unnecessary or excessive alarm. **scare'mon·ger·ing** n.

scarf (skahrf) n. (pl. **scarfs, scarves,** pr. skahrvz)

1. a long narrow strip of material worn for warmth or ornament around the neck. 2. a square of material worn around the neck or tied over a woman's hair.

scar·i·fy (skar-ĭ-fī) *v.* (**scar·i·fied, scar·i·fy·ing**) 1. to make slight cuts in (skin or tissue) surgically. 2. to pain (a person) by severe criticism etc. 3. to loosen the surface of (soil etc.). **scar·i·fi·ca·tion** (skar-ĭ-fī-kay-shŏn) *n.* ▷This word does not mean *scare*.

scar·la·ti·na (skahr-lă-tee-nă) *n.* scarlet fever.

scar·let (skahr-lit) *adj.* of brilliant red color. **scarlet** *n.* 1. scarlet color. 2. a scarlet substance or material, scarlet clothes. □**scarlet fever,** an infectious fever caused by bacteria, producing a scarlet rash. **scarlet letter,** a scarlet letter **A** formerly worn by a person convicted of adultery. **scarlet pimpernel,** a variety of the pimpernel plant with scarlet flowers. **scarlet runner,** a climbing bean with scarlet flowers. **scarlet tanager,** an American bird, the male of which has bright red plumage with black wings and tail during the mating season. **scarlet woman,** *(old use)* a notorious prostitute.

scarp (skahrp) *n.* a steep slope on a hillside.

scar·y (skair-ee) *adj.* (**scar·i·er, scar·i·est**) 1. frightening. 2. easily frightened. **scar'i·ness** *n.*

scat (skat) *v.* (**scat·ted, scat·ting**) *(informal)* to depart quickly.

scath·ing (skay-*th*ing) *adj.* (of criticism) very severe. **scath'ing·ly** *adv.*

sca·tol·o·gy (skă-tol-ŏ-gee) *n.* 1. preoccupation with excrement. 2. preoccupation with obscene literature. 3. the study of fossil excrement. **scat·o·log·i·cal** (skat-ŏ-loj-i-kăl) *adj.*

scat·ter (skat-ĕr) *v.* 1. to throw or put here and there, to cover in this way, *scatter gravel on the road* or *scatter the road with gravel; there were some scattered villages,* situated far apart. 2. to go or send in different directions. **scatter** *n.* scattering, the extent over which something is scattered. □**scatter pin,** a small ornamental pin, usually worn with others on a dress etc. **scatter rug,** a small rug, one of several to be placed here and there in a room.

scat·ter·brain (skat-ĕr-brayn) *n.* a person who is unable to concentrate or do things in a systematic way. **scat'ter·brained** *adj.*

scaup (skawp) *n.* a kind of diving duck of northern coasts.

scav·enge (skav-inj) *v.* (**scav·enged, scav·eng·ing**) 1. (of an animal) to search for decaying flesh as food. 2. to search for usable objects or material among rubbish or discarded things. **scav'en·ger** *n.*

sce·nar·i·o (si-nair-i-oh) *n.* (*pl.* **-os**) 1. the outline or script of a film, with details of the scenes. 2. a detailed summary of the action of a play, with notes on scenery and special effects. 3. an imagined sequence of future events. **sce·nar'ist** *n.*

scene (seen) *n.* 1. the place of an actual or fictional event; *the scene of the crime,* where it happened. 2. a piece of continuous action in a play or film, a subdivision of an act. 3. an incident thought of as resembling this. 4. a dramatic outburst of temper or emotion, a stormy interview, *made a scene.* 5. a stage set. 6. a landscape or view as seen by a spectator, *the rural scene before us.* 7. *(slang)* an area of action, a way of life, *the drug scene; not my scene,* not what I like or want to take part in. □**be on the scene,** to be present. **make the scene,** *(slang)* to participate in a par-

ticular activity, to be in a particular place.

scen·er·y (see-nĕ-ree) *n.* 1. the general appearance of a landscape. 2. picturesque features of a landscape. 3. structures used on a theater stage to represent features in the scene of the action.

sce·nic (see-nik) *adj.* having fine natural scenery, *the scenic road along the coast.* **sce'ni·cal·ly** *adv.* □**scenic railway,** a miniature railway running through artificial picturesque scenery as an amusement at a fair etc.

scent (sent) *n.* 1. the characteristic smell of something. 2. a sweet-smelling liquid made from essence of flowers or aromatic chemicals. 3. the trail left by an animal and perceptible to hounds' sense of smell, indications that can be followed similarly, *followed* or *lost the scent; on the scent of talent.* 4. an animal's sense of smell, *dogs hunt by scent.* **scent** *v.* 1. to discover by sense of smell, *the dog scented a rat.* 2. to begin to suspect the presence or existence of, *she scented trouble.* 3. to put scent on (a thing), to make fragrant. **scent'ed** *adj.* **scent'less** *adj.*

scep·ter (sep-tĕr) *n.* a staff carried by a king or queen as a symbol of sovereignty.

sch. *abbr.* school.

sched·ule (skej-ool) *n.* a program or timetable of planned events or of work. **schedule** *v.* (**sched·uled, sched·ul·ing**) to include in a schedule, to appoint for a certain time, *the train is scheduled to stop at Norwalk.* **sched'u·lar** *adj.* □**on schedule,** punctual according to the timetable.

sche·mat·ic (ski-mat-ik) *adj.* in the form of a diagram or chart. **schematic** *n.* a schematic diagram. **sche·mat'i·cal·ly** *adv.*

scheme (skeem) *n.* 1. a plan of work or action. 2. a secret or underhand plan, *a scheme to defraud people.* 3. an orderly planned arrangement, *a color scheme.* **scheme** *v.* (**schemed, schem·ing**) to make plans, to plan in a secret or underhanded way. **schem'er** *n.* **schem'ing** *adj.*

scher·zo (sker-tsoh) *n.* (*pl.* **-zos, -zi,** *pr.* -tsee) a lively vigorous musical composition or independent passage in a longer work.

Schick (shik) **test** a test to determine immunity to diphtheria. ▷Named after B. Schick (1877–1967), the pediatrician who developed it.

schil·ling (shil-ing) *n.* the unit of money in Austria.

schism (siz-ĕm) *n.* division into opposing groups because of a difference in belief or opinion, especially in a religious body.

schis·mat·ic (siz-mat-ik) *adj.* of or involving schism. **schismatic** *n.* a person who takes part in a schism.

schist (shist) *n.* a rock with layers of different minerals that splits into thin irregular plates. **schis·tose** (shis-tohs) *adj.* **schis·tous** (shis-tŭs) *adj.*

schiz·o (skit-soh, skid-zoh) *adj. & n.* (*pl.* **-os**) *(informal)* schizophrenic.

schiz·oid (skit-zoid) *adj.* resembling or suffering from schizophrenia. **schizoid** *n.* a schizoid person.

schiz·o·phre·ni·a (skit-sŏ-free-ni-ă) *n.* a severe mental disorder in which a person becomes unable to act or reason in a rational way, often with delusions and withdrawal from social relationships.

schiz·o·phren·ic (skit-sŏ-fren-ik) *adj.* of or suffering from schizophrenia. **schizophrenic** *n.* a schizophrenic person.

schle·miel (shlĕ-meel) *n.* *(slang)* a bungling or unlucky person.

schlepp, schlep (shlep) v. (slang) to carry.
schlepp n. (slang) a clumsy stupid person.
schlock (shlok) adj. (slang) of poor quality, second-hand, trashy. **schlock** n. (slang) a thing or things of this kind.
schmaltz (shmahlts) n. sugary sentimentality, especially in music or literature. **schmaltz'y** adj.
schmo (shmoh) n. (pl. **schmoes**) (slang) a foolish or stupid person.
schmooze (shmooz) v. (**schmoozed, schmooz·ing**) (slang) to gossip, to chat. **schmooze** n. (slang) such talk.
schnapps (shnahps) n. a kind of strong liquor.
schnau·zer (shnow-zĕr) n. a house dog of a German breed with a close wiry coat.
schnit·zel (shnit-sĕl) n. a fried veal cutlet.
schnook (shnuuk) n. a stupid or easily deceived person.
schol·ar (skol-ăr) n. 1. a person with great learning in a particular subject. 2. a person who is skilled in academic work. 3. a person who holds a scholarship. **schol'ar·ly** adj. **schol'ar·li·ness** n.
schol·ar·ship (skol-ăr-ship) n. 1. a grant of money toward a person's education. 2. great learning in a particular subject. 3. the methods and achievements characteristic of scholars and academic work.
scho·las·tic (skŏ-las-tik) adj. of schools or education, academic. **scho·las'ti·cal·ly** adv.
scho·las·ti·cism (skŏ-las-tĭ-siz-ĕm) n. the theology and philosophy of the Middle Ages under the influence of Aristotle and the early Christian writers.
school[1] (skool) n. a great number of fish or whales etc. swimming together.
school[2] n. 1. an institution for educating children or for giving instruction. 2. its buildings. 3. its pupils. 4. the time during which teaching is done there, school ends at 4:30 p.m. 5. the process of being educated in a school, always hated school. 6. experience that gives discipline or instruction, learned his tactics in a hard school. 7. a group or succession of philosophers, artists, etc. following the same teachings or principles. **school** v. to train or discipline. □**of the old school**, according to old standards, a gentleman of the old school. **school age**, the age range in which children normally attend school. **school board**, the local body in charge of public education. **school of thought**, either of two ways of looking at a problem; the holder of one of these. **school year**, the months of the year in which children are required to attend school.
school·bag (skool-bag) n. a bag for carrying books etc. to and from school.
school·book (skool-buuk) n. a book for use in schools.
school·boy (skool-boi) n. a boy at school.
school·child (skool-chĭld) n. (pl. **-chil·dren,** pr. -chil-drin) a child at school.
school·girl (skool-gurl) n. a girl at school.
school·house (skool-hows) n. (pl. **-hous·es,** pr. -how-ziz) a building used as a school.
school·ing (skoo-ling) n. education in a school.
school·marm (skool-mahrm) n. a woman teacher, especially a prim and fussy one who is devoted to her work.
school·mas·ter (skool-mas-tĕr) n. a male schoolteacher.
school·mate (skool-mayt) n. a classmate.
school·mis·tress (skool-mis-tris) n. a female schoolteacher.

school·room (skool-room) n. a room used for lessons in a school or private house.
school·teach·er (skool-tee-chĕr) n. a teacher in a school.
schoon·er (skoo-nĕr) n. 1. a kind of sailing ship with two or more masts. 2. (informal) a very tall glass for beer etc.
schot·tische (shot-ish) n. 1. a kind of slow polka. 2. music for this dance.
schuss (shuus) n. a straight downhill run on skis. **schuss** v. to execute a schuss.
schuss·boom·er (shuus-boo-mĕr) n. a skier who executes a schuss, especially with skill.
schwa (shwah) n. an indistinct vowel sound, as in the second syllable of common or comma.
sci. abbr. 1. science. 2. scientific.
sci·at·ic (sı-at-ik) adj. of the hip or the **sciatic nerve,** the largest nerve in the human body, running from pelvis to thigh.
sci·at·i·ca (sı-at-i-kă) n. neuralgia of the hip and thigh, pain in the sciatic nerve.
sci·ence (sı-ĕns) n. 1. a branch of knowledge requiring systematic study and method, especially one of those dealing with substances, animal and vegetable life, and natural laws; natural sciences, biology, geology, etc.; physical sciences, physics, chemistry, etc. 2. an expert's skillful technique, with skill and science. □**science fiction,** stories based on imaginary future scientific discoveries or changes of the environment or space travel and life on other planets.
sci·en·tif·ic (sı-ĕn-tif-ik) adj. 1. of or used in a science, scientific apparatus. 2. using careful and systematic study, observations, and tests of conclusions etc. **sci·en·tif'i·cal·ly** adv.
sci·en·tist (sı-ĕn-tist) n. an expert in one or more of the natural or physical sciences.
sci-fi (sı-fı) n. (informal) science fiction.
scil·la (sil-ă) n. a plant with small blue hanging flowers, growing from a bulb.
scim·i·tar (sim-i-tăr) n. a short curved Oriental sword.
scin·til·la (sin-til-ă) n. a trace, not a scintilla of evidence.
scin·til·late (sin-tĭ-layt) v. (**scin·til·lat·ed, scin·til·lat·ing**) 1. to sparkle, to give off sparks. 2. to be brilliant, a scintillating discussion. **scin'til·lat·ing·ly** adv. **scin·til·la·tion** (sin-tĭ-lay-shŏn) n.
sci·on (sı-ŏn) n. a descendant of a family, especially a noble one.
scis·sors (siz-ŏrz) n. pl. a cutting instrument made of two blades with handles for the thumb and finger(s) of one hand, pivoted so that the cutting edges can be closed on what is to be cut. **scissor** v. to cut with scissors. □**scissor kick** or **scissors kick,** a movement of the legs in swimming, resembling the action of scissors.
scle·ro·sis (skli-roh-sis) n. (pl. **-ses,** pr. -seez) a diseased condition in which soft tissue (as of the arteries) hardens or thickens. **scle·rot·ic** (skli-rot-ik) adj.
scoff (skof) v. to jeer, to speak contemptuously. **scof'fer** n. **scoff'ing·ly** adv.
scoff·law (skof-law) n. a person who habitually flouts the law, especially one who does not pay traffic fines etc.
scold (skohld) v. to rebuke (a child or servant). **scold** n. a constantly nagging person.
scold·ing (skohl-ding) n. a lengthy rebuke to a child or servant.
sconce (skons) n. an ornamental bracket fixed to

a wall for holding a candle or electric light etc.
scone (skohn, skon) *n.* a soft flat cake of barley meal or oatmeal or flour, baked quickly and eaten buttered.

scoop (skoop) *n.* 1. a deep shovel-like tool for taking up and moving grain, sugar, coal, etc. 2. a ladle, a device with a small round bowl and a handle used for serving ice cream etc. 3. a scooping movement. 4. a piece of news discovered and published by one newspaper in advance of its rivals. **scoop** *v.* 1. to lift or hollow with or as if with a scoop. 2. to forestall (a rival newspaper) with a news scoop.

scoot (skoot) *v.* to run or dart, to go away hastily.

scoot·er (skoo-tĕr) *n.* 1. a child's toy vehicle with a footboard on wheels and a long steering handle. 2. a kind of lightweight motorcycle.

scope[1] (skohp) *n.* 1. the range of something, *the subject is outside the scope of this inquiry.* 2. opportunity, outlet, *a kind of work that gives scope for her abilities.*

scope[2] *n. (informal)* a viewing instrument, as a microscope, periscope, telescope, etc.

sco·pol·a·mine (skŏ-pol-ă-meen) *n.* a water-soluble alkaloid used as a sedative and for other medicinal purposes.

scor·bu·tic (skor-byoo-tik) *adj.* of or like or affected by scurvy.

scorch (skorch) *v.* 1. to burn or become burned on the surface, to make or become discolored in this way. 2. *(slang)* to drive or ride at a very high speed. **scorch** *n.* a mark made by scorching. **scorch'ing·ly** *adv.* □**scorched earth policy,** the deliberate burning of crops etc. and removing or destroying anything that might be of use to an enemy occupying the country.

scorch·er (skor-chĕr) *n. (informal)* a very hot day.

scorch·ing (skor-ching) *adj. (informal)* extremely hot.

score (skohr) *n.* 1. the number of points made by each player or side in a game, or gained in a competition etc. 2. a record of this, a tally. 3. a reason or motive, *was rejected on the score of being old-fashioned; on that score,* so far as that matter is concerned. 4. a set of twenty; *scores of things,* very many. 5. a line or mark cut into something. 6. a copy of a musical composition showing the notes on sets of staves. 7. the music for an opera or musical comedy etc. **score** *v.* **(scored, scor·ing)** 1. to gain (a point or points) in a game etc., to make a score. 2. to keep a record of the score. 3. to be worth as points in a game, *a goal scores 6 points.* 4. to achieve, *scored a great success.* 5. to have an advantage, *he scores by knowing the language well.* 6. to make a clever retort that puts an opponent at a disadvantage. 7. to cut a line or mark(s) into (a thing); *score it out,* cancel it by drawing a line through the words etc. 8. to write out as a musical score, to arrange (a piece of music) for instruments. **scor'er** *n.* **score'less** *adj.* □**know the score,** *(informal)* to be aware of the essential facts. **settle old scores,** to get even with a person for past wrongdoing.

score·board (skohr-bohrd) *n.* a board where the score of a game is displayed.

score·card (skohr-kahrd) *n.* a card for entering scores.

sco·ri·a (skohr-i-ă) *n.* (*pl.* **sco·ri·ae,** *pr.* skohr-i-ee) 1. cellular lava or fragments of it. 2. the slag or dross left after melting metal.

scorn (skorn) *n.* strong contempt; *laughed it to*

scorn, ridiculed it. **scorn** *v.* 1. to feel or show strong contempt for. 2. to reject or refuse scornfully, *would scorn to ask for favors.* **scorn'er** *n.*

scorn·ful (skorn-fŭl) *adj.* feeling or showing scorn. **scorn'ful·ly** *adv.* **scorn'ful·ness** *n.*

Scor·pi·o (skor-pi-oh) *n.* a sign of the zodiac, the Scorpion. **Scor'pi·an** *adj. & n.*

scor·pi·on (skor-pi-ŏn) *n.* 1. a small animal of the spider group with lobster-like claws and a sting in its long jointed tail. 2. *the Scorpion,* Scorpio.

Scot (skot) *n.* a native of Scotland.

Scot. *abbr.* 1. Scotland. 2. Scottish.

scotch (skoch) *v.* to put an end to, *scotched the rumor.*

Scotch (skoch) *adj.* of Scotland or Scottish people or their form of English.(▷Modern Scots prefer to use the words *Scots* and *Scottish,* not *Scotch,* except when the word is applied to whisky and in the compounds listed below.) **Scotch** *n.* 1. the Scottish dialect. 2. Scotch whisky, the kind distilled in Scotland especially from malted barley. □**Scotch broth,** soup or stew containing pearl barley and vegetables. **Scotch pine,** a Eurasian pine. **Scotch tape,** *(trademark)* an adhesive tape, usually transparent or semitransparent. **Scotch terrier,** a small terrier with rough hair and short legs. **Scotch woodcock,** scrambled eggs on toast, garnished with anchovies.

scot-free (skot-free) *adj.* 1. unharmed, not punished. 2. free of obligation.

Scot·land (skot-lănd) the country forming the northern part of Great Britain.

Scotland Yard 1. the headquarters of the London Metropolitan Police. 2. its Criminal Investigation Department.

Scots (skots) *adj.* Scottish. **Scots** *n.* the Scottish dialect. **Scots·man** (skots-măn) *n.* (*pl.* **-men,** *pr.* -měn) **Scots·wom·an** (skots-wuum-ăn) *n. fem.* (*pl.* **-wom·en,** *pr.* -wim-in).

Scot·ti·cism (skot-i-siz-ěm) *n.* a Scottish word or phrase.

Scot·tish (skot-ish) *adj.* of Scotland or its people or their form of the English language.

scoun·drel (skown-drěl) *n.* a dishonest or unprincipled person.

scour[1] (skowr) *v.* 1. to cleanse or brighten by rubbing. 2. to clear out (a channel or pipe etc.) by the force of water flowing through or over it. 3. to purge drastically. **scour** *n.* scouring, the action of water on a channel etc., *the scour of the tide.* **scour'er** *n.*

scour[2] *v.* to travel over (an area) in search of something, to search thoroughly.

scourge (skurj) *n.* 1. a whip for flogging people. 2. a person or thing regarded as a great affliction, *the scourge of war.* **scourge** *v.* **(scourged, scourg·ing)** 1. to flog with a whip. 2. to afflict greatly.

scout (skowt) *n.* 1. a person sent out to gather information, as about an enemy's movements or strength. 2. a ship or aircraft designed for reconnoitering. 3. *Scout,* a member of the Boy Scouts or Girl Scouts of America. **scout** *v.* to act as scout, to make a search.

scout·mas·ter (skowt-mas-tĕr) *n.* 1. an officer in charge of scouts. 2. the adult leader of a group of Boy Scouts.

scow (skow) *n.* a flat-bottomed boat used as a lighter etc.

scowl (skowl) *n.* a sullen or angry frown. **scowl**

v. to make a scowl. **scowl'er** *n.* **scowl'ing·ly** *adv.*

SCPO *abbr.* senior chief petty officer.

scrab·ble (skrab-ĕl) *v.* **(scrab·bled, scrab·bling)** 1. to make a scratching movement or sound with the hands or feet. 2. to grope busily or struggle to find or obtain something. **scrab'bler** *n.*

Scrab·ble (skrab-ĕl) *n. (trademark)* a game played on a board in which words are built up from letters printed on small square counters.

scrag·gly (skrag-lee) *adj.* **(-gli·er, -gli·est)** 1. shaggy, unkempt. 2. jagged, uneven.

scrag·gy (skrag-ee) *adj.* **(-gi·er, -gi·est)** scrawny. **scrag'gi·ness** *n.*

scram[1] (skram) *v.* **(scrammed, scram·ming)** *(slang)* to go away.

scram[2] *v.* **(scrammed, scram·ming)** 1. to stop the reaction in (an atomic reactor) by inserting the control rods. 2. (of a reactor) to stop in this way.

scram·ble (skram-bĕl) *v.* **(scram·bled, scram·bling)** 1. to move as best one can over rough ground, to move hastily and awkwardly. 2. to struggle eagerly to do or obtain something. 3. (of aircraft or their crew) to hurry and take off quickly, as to attack an invading enemy. 4. to mix together indiscriminately. 5. to cook (egg) by mixing its contents and heating the mixture in a pan until it thickens. 6. to make (a telephone conversation etc.) unintelligible except to a person with a special receiver, by altering the frequencies on which it is transmitted. **scramble** *n.* 1. a climb or walk over rough ground. 2. an eager struggle to do or obtain something.

scram·bler (skram-blĕr) *n.* 1. one who scrambles. 2. an electronic device for scrambling a transmitted telephone conversation or unscrambling it at the receiving end.

scrap[1] (skrap) *n.* 1. a small detached piece of something, a fragment, a remnant. 2. rubbish, waste material, discarded metal suitable for being reprocessed. **scrap** *v.* **(scrapped, scrap·ping)** to discard as useless. ☐**scrap heap,** a heap of waste material. **scrap metal,** metal collected for reworking.

scrap[2] *n. (informal)* a fight or quarrel. **scrap** *v.* **(scrapped, scrap·ping)** *(informal)* to fight, to quarrel. **scrap'per** *n.*

scrap·book (skrap-buuk) *n.* a book in which newspaper clippings and similar souvenirs are mounted.

scrape (skrayp) *v.* **(scraped, scrap·ing)** 1. to make (a thing) clean or smooth or level by passing the hard edge of something across it. 2. to pass (an edge) across in this way. 3. to remove by doing this, *scrape mud off shoes.* 4. to excavate by scraping, *scrape a hole.* 5. to damage by scraping. 6. to make the sound of scraping. 7. to pass along or through something with difficulty, with or without touching it. 8. to obtain or amass with difficulty or by careful saving, *scrape a living; scrape something together* or *up.* 9. to be very economical. **scrape** *n.* 1. a scraping movement or sound. 2. a scraped mark or injury. 3. an awkward situation resulting from an escapade. ☐**scrape through,** to get through a situation or pass an examination by only a very narrow margin. **scraping the barrel,** driven to using one's last and inferior resources because the better ones are finished.

scrap·er (skray-pĕr) *n.* a device used for scraping things.

scrap·ings (skray-pingz) *n. pl.* fragments produced by scraping.

scrap·ple (skrap-ĕl) *n.* a cornmeal mush loaf made with pork, onion, spices, etc.

scrap·py[1] (skrap-ee) *adj.* **(-pi·er, -pi·est)** made up of scraps or odds and ends or disconnected elements.

scrappy[2] *adj.* **(-pi·er, -pi·est)** pugnacious, aggressive.

scratch (skrach) *v.* 1. to make a shallow mark or wound on (a surface) with something sharp. 2. to form by scratching. 3. to scrape with the fingernails in order to relieve itching; *scratch my back and I'll scratch yours,* promote my interests and I will promote yours. 4. to make a thin scraping sound. 5. to obtain with difficulty, *scratch a living.* 6. to cancel by drawing a line through, *scratch it out.* 7. to withdraw from a race or competition, *was obliged to scratch; scratched his horse.* **scratch** *n.* 1. a mark or wound made by scratching. 2. a spell of scratching. 3. a line from which competitors start in a race when they receive no handicap; *a scratch player,* one who receives no handicap in a game. **scratch** *adj.* collected from whatever is available, *a scratch team.* ☐**scratch pad,** a pad of paper for jotting or scribbling. **scratch paper,** paper for jotting or scribbling. **scratch sheet,** a publication that provides information on the horses and betting odds during a racing day. **scratch test,** a test for allergy in which the skin is scratched and various allergens are applied to the scratch. **start from scratch,** to begin at the very beginning; to begin with no advantage or preparation. **up to scratch,** up to the required standard.

scratch·y (skrach-ee) *adj.* **(scratch·i·er, scratch·i·est)** 1. (of a pen) tending to make a scratching sound or catch in paper. 2. (of cloth etc.) tending to cause itching. 3. (of a drawing) looking like a series of scratches. 4. (of a record) producing noise caused by scratches on its surface. **scratch'i·ly** *adv.* **scratch'i·ness** *n.*

scrawl (skrawl) *n.* bad handwriting, something written in this. **scrawl** *v.* to write in a scrawl. **scrawl'y** *adj.*

scrawn·y (skraw-nee) *adj.* **(scrawn·i·er, scrawn·i·est)** lean and bony.

scream (skreem) *v.* 1. to make a long piercing cry of pain or terror or annoyance or excitement. 2. to utter in a screaming tone. 3. (of the wind or a machine etc.) to make a loud piercing sound. 4. to laugh uncontrollably. **scream** *n.* 1. a screaming cry or sound. 2. *(slang)* an extremely amusing person or thing.

scream·ing·ly (skree-ming-lee) *adv.* so as to cause screams of laughter, *screamingly funny.*

scree (skree) *n.* a mass of loose stones on a mountain side, sliding when trodden on.

screech (skreech) *n.* a harsh high-pitched scream or sound. **screech** *v.* to make a screech, to utter with a screech. **screech'y** *adj.* **(screech·i·er, screech·i·est)** ☐**screech owl,** an owl that makes a screeching cry (not a hoot).

screed (skreed) *n.* a tiresomely long list or letter or other document.

screen (skreen) *n.* 1. an upright structure used to conceal or protect or divide something. 2. anything serving a similar purpose, *under the screen of night.* 3. a fine mesh used on windows and

doors etc. to keep insects out. **4.** a blank surface on which photographic slides, movies, television transmissions, etc. are projected. **5.** a large sieve, especially one used for sorting grain or coal etc. into sizes. **screen** *v.* **1.** to shelter or conceal or protect. **2.** to protect (a person) from discovery or deserved blame by diverting suspicion from him. **3.** to show (slides, movies, etc.) on a screen. **4.** to pass (grain or coal etc.) through a screen. **5.** to examine systematically in order to discover something, such as the presence or absence of a substance or disease. **screen'er** *n.* □**screen pass,** a football play in which a pass receiver is protected from tacklers by a screen of blockers. **screen test,** a test of a person's suitability for taking part in a film.
screen·ing (skree-ning) *n.* **1.** fine mesh used for making screens for windows, doors, etc. **2.** the showing of a film.
screen·play (skreen-play) *n.* the script of a film.
screen·writ·er (skreen-rɪ-těr) *n.* a writer of film scripts.
screw (skroo) *n.* **1.** a metal pin with a spiral ridge (the *thread*) around its length, used for holding things together by being twisted in under pressure, or secured by a nut. **2.** a thing turned like a screw and used for tightening something or exerting pressure. **3.** a propeller, especially of a ship or motorboat. **4.** the act of screwing. **5.** *(slang)* a prison guard. **screw** *v.* **1.** to fasten or tighten with a screw or screws. **2.** to turn (a screw), to twist or become twisted; *screw up one's face,* to twist it out of the natural expression, as in disgust. **3.** to oppress, to extort, *screwed a promise out of her.* **4.** *(vulgar slang)* to cheat, to trick, *how much did they screw you out of?* □**have a screw loose,** *(informal)* to be slightly mad. **have one's head screwed on the right way,** to have sound common sense. **put the screws on,** *(informal)* to put pressure on, as to intimidate or extort money. **screw up,** *(slang)* to bungle (a task etc.). **screw up one's courage,** to muster courage.
screw·ball (skroo-bawl) *n.* *(slang)* **1.** a crazy person. **2.** (in baseball) a pitch that curves to the right when thrown by a right-handed pitcher and to the left when thrown by a left-handed pitcher.
screw·driv·er (skroo-drɪ-věr) *n.* **1.** a tool with a narrow flattened end for turning screws that have a slotted head into which this fits. **2.** a cocktail made of vodka and orange juice.
screw·y (skroo-ee) *adj.* (**screw·i·er, screw·i·est**) *(slang)* crazy, eccentric.
scrib·ble (skrib-ĕl) *v.* (**scrib·bled, scrib·bling**) **1.** to write hurriedly or carelessly. **2.** to make meaningless marks; *scribble it out,* obliterate it by scribbling on it. **scribble** *n.* something scribbled, hurried or careless writing, *scribbled meaningless marks.* **scrib'bler** *n.*
scribe (skrɪb) *n.* **1.** a person who (before the invention of printing) made copies of writings. **2.** (in New Testament times) a professional religious scholar.
scrim (skrim) *n.* a loosely woven cotton fabric.
scrim·mage (skrim-ij) *n.* **1.** a confused struggle, a skirmish. **2.** (in football) the sequence of play beginning with the snapping of the ball and ending when the ball is declared out of play. **3.** a football practice session. **scrimmage** *v.* (**scrim·maged, scrim·mag·ing**) to engage in a football scrimmage, especially during a practice session.

scrimp (skrimp) *v.* to supply or use rather less than what is needed, to skimp.
scrim·shaw (skrim-shaw) *n.* **1.** the art of carving shells, walrus tusks, etc. **2.** an example of this work.
scrip (skrip) *n.* **1.** a certificate showing that the holder is entitled to a payment or other benefit. **2.** paper certificates used in place of money (as by an employee in a company store) or as legal currency in an emergency. ▷Do not confuse *scrip* with *script.*
script (skript) *n.* **1.** handwriting. **2.** a style of printed or typewritten characters resembling this. **3.** the text of a play or film or broadcast etc. **script** *v.* to write a script for (a film etc.). ▷Do not confuse *script* with *scrip.*
Script. *abbr.* **1.** Scriptural. **2.** Scripture.
script·ure (skrip-chŭr) *n.* **1.** any sacred writings. **2.** *Scripture* or *the Scriptures,* the sacred writings of the Christians (the Old and New Testaments) or the Jews (the Old Testament). **scrip'tur·al** *adj.* **scrip'tur·al·ly** *adv.*
scrive·ner (skriv-něr) *n.* *(old use)* **1.** a copyist, a drafter of documents. **2.** a notary.
scrod (skrod) *n.* a young cod or haddock.
scrof·u·la (skrof-yŭ-lă) *n.* a disease causing glandular swellings.
scroll (skrohl) *n.* **1.** a roll of paper or parchment. **2.** an ornamental design resembling a scroll or in spiral form.
Scrooge (skrooj) *n.* a miser. ▷Named after a character in Dickens' novel *A Christmas Carol.*
scro·tum (skroh-tŭm) *n.* (*pl.* **-ta,** *pr.* -tă, **-tums**) the pouch of skin that encloses the testicles in most mammals, behind the penis.
scrounge (skrownj) *v.* (**scrounged, scroung·ing**) *(slang)* **1.** to ask for as a gift, to go about begging. **2.** to collect by foraging. **scroung'er** *n.* *(slang).*
scrub[1] (skrub) *n.* vegetation consisting of stunted trees or shrubs, land covered with this. □**scrub oak,** a dwarf oak.
scrub[2] *v.* (**scrubbed, scrub·bing**) **1.** to rub hard with something coarse or bristly. **2.** *(slang)* to cancel, to scrap, *we'll have to scrub our plans.* **scrub** *n.* scrubbing, being scrubbed, *give it a scrub.* □**scrub nurse,** a nurse trained to assist surgeons during surgery. **scrub up,** (of a surgeon etc.) to clean the hands and arms by scrubbing, before an operation.
scrub·ber (skrub-ĕr) *n.* an apparatus for purifying gases emitted from a furnace.
scrub·by (skrub-ee) *adj.* (**-bi·er, -bi·est**) small and mean or shabby.
scruff (skruf) *n.* the back of the neck as used to grasp or lift or drag a person or animal.
scruff·y (skruf-ee) *adj.* (**scruff·i·er, scruff·i·est**) shabby and untidy. **scruff'i·ly** *adv.* **scruff'i·ness** *n.*
scrump·tious (skrump-shŭs) *adj.* *(informal)* delicious, delightful. **scrump'tious·ly** *adv.* **scrump'tious·ness** *n.*
scrunch (skrunch) *v.* to crunch.
scru·ple (skroo-pĕl) *n.* a feeling of doubt or hesitation about doing or allowing an action, produced by one's conscience or principles. **scruple** *v.* (**scru·pled, scru·pling**) to hesitate because of scruples.
scru·pu·lous (skroo-pyŭ-lŭs) *adj.* **1.** very conscientious even in small matters, painstakingly care-

ful and thorough. 2. strictly honest or honorable, *they are not very scrupulous in their business dealings.* **scru'pu·lous·ly** *adv.* **scru'pu·lous·ness** *n.* **scru·pu·los·i·ty** (skroo-pyŭ-los-i-tee) *n.*

scru·ti·nize (skroo-tĭ-nīz) *v.* **(scru·ti·nized, scru·ti·niz·ing)** to look at or examine carefully. **scru'ti·niz·er** *n.*

scru·ti·ny (skroo-tĭ-nee) *n.* (*pl.* **-nies**) a careful look at or examination of something.

scu·ba (skoo-bă) *n.* a self-contained underwater breathing apparatus.

scud (skud) *v.* **(scud·ded, scud·ding)** to move along straight and fast and smoothly, *clouds were scudding across the sky.* **scud** *n.* clouds or spray driven by the wind.

scuff (skuf) *v.* 1. to scrape or drag (one's feet) in walking. 2. to mark or wear away by doing this. 3. to scrape (a thing) with one's foot or feet. **scuff** *n.* 1. the act of scuffing, the sound or mark produced by this. 2. a backless slipper.

scuf·fle (skuf-ĕl) *n.* a confused struggle or disorderly fight at close quarters. **scuffle** *v.* **(scuf·fled, scuf·fling)** to engage in a scuffle.

scull (skul) *n.* 1. one of a pair of small oars used by a single rower. 2. an oar that rests on the stern of a boat, worked with a screwlike movement. 3. a light racing boat. **scull** *v.* to row with sculls.

scul·ler·y (skul-ĕ-ree) *n.* (*pl.* **-ler·ies**) a room where dishes etc. are washed up.

scul·lion (skul-yŏn) *n.* a cook's assistant, a washer of dishes and pots.

sculpt (skulpt) *v.* to sculpture.

sculp·tor (skulp-tŏr) *n.* a person who makes sculptures. **sculp·tress** (skulp-tris) *n. fem.*

sculp·tur·al (skulp-chŭ-răl) *adj.* of sculpture.

sculp·ture (skulp-chŭr) *n.* 1. the art of carving in wood or stone or producing shapes in cast or welded metal etc. 2. a work made in this way. **sculpture** *v.* **(sculp·tured, sculp·tur·ing)** to represent in sculpture, to decorate with sculptures, to be a sculptor.

scum (skum) *n.* 1. impurities that rise to the surface of a liquid, a film of material floating on the surface of a stretch of water. 2. people regarded as the most worthless part of the population. **scum'my** *adj.*

scup·per (skup-ĕr) *n.* an opening in a ship's side to carry off water from the deck.

scurf (skurf) *n.* 1. flakes of dry skin, especially from the scalp. 2. any dry scaly matter on a surface. **scurf'y** *adv.*

scur·ril·ous (skur-ĭ-lŭs) *adj.* 1. abusive and insulting, *a scurrilous attack on his character.* 2. coarsely humorous. **scur'ril·ous·ly** *adv.* **scur·ril·i·ty** (skŭ-ril-i-tee) *n.*

scur·ry (skur-ee) *v.* **(scur·ried, scur·ry·ing)** to run or move hurriedly, especially with quick short steps, to hurry. **scurry** *n.* (*pl.* **-ries**) scurrying, a rush.

scur·vy (skur-vee) *n.* a disease caused by lack of vitamin C in the diet. **scurvy** *adj.* **(scur·vi·er, scur·vi·est)** contemptible, *a scurvy fellow.*

scut (skut) *n.* a short tail, especially that of a hare or rabbit or deer.

scutch·eon (skuch-ŏn) *n.* an escutcheon.

scut·tle[1] (skut-ĕl) *n.* a bucket or portable boxlike container for holding a supply of coal in a room.

scuttle[2] *n.* a small opening with a lid, on a ship's

deck or side or in a roof or wall. **scuttle** *v.* **(scut·tled, scut·tling)** to let water into (a ship) in order to sink her.

scuttle[3] *v.* **(scut·tled, scut·tling)** to scurry, to hurry away. **scuttle** *n.* a scurrying movement.

scut·tle·butt (skut-ĕl-but) *n.* 1. a water cask usually on a ship's deck with a hole in the top for dipping. 2. (*informal*) rumor, gossip.

scythe (sɪth) *n.* an implement with a slightly curved blade at an angle to the handle, used for cutting long grass or grain. **scythe** *v.* **(scythed, scyth·ing)** to cut with a scythe.

SD *abbr.* standard deviation.

s.d. *abbr.* without naming a date. ▷Latin *sine die* without a day.

S.D. *abbr.* 1. Doctor of Science. 2. South Dakota. 3. standard deviation.

Se *symbol* selenium.

SE *abbr.* southeast.

sea (see) *n.* 1. the expanse of salt water that covers most of Earth's surface and surrounds the continents. 2. any part of this as opposed to dry land or fresh water, a named section of it partly enclosed by land, *the Mediterranean Sea.* 3. a large inland lake of either salt or fresh water, *the Sea of Galilee.* 4. the waves of the sea, the movement or state of these; *a heavy sea,* with great waves. 5. a vast expanse of something, *a sea of faces.* □**at sea,** in a ship on the sea; perplexed, not knowing how to proceed. **by sea,** carried or conveyed in a ship. **on the sea,** in a ship on the sea; situated on a coast. **sea anchor,** a baglike contrivance to retard drifting and maintain the direction of a ship or seaplane. **sea anemone,** a tube-shaped sea animal with petallike tentacles around its mouth. **sea bass,** a seafish like a bass. **sea bird,** a bird that frequents the sea or the land near the sea. **sea biscuit,** hardtack. **sea breeze,** a gentle wind blowing landward from the sea. **sea calf,** a common seal. **sea change,** a transformation. **sea chest,** a sailor's storage chest. **sea cow,** a walrus, a manatee. **sea cucumber,** a sea animal with a long body and tentacles at one end. **sea dog,** a common seal; an old experienced sailor. **sea fan,** a fanlike polyp. **sea green,** bluish green. **sea holly,** an evergreen plant with spiny leaves and blue flowers. **sea horse,** a small fish with a horselike head at right angles to its body, and a tail that can be wrapped around a support. **Sea Island cotton,** a fine quality of cotton originally grown on the islands off Georgia and South Carolina. **sea lane,** a lane for ships (*see* lane, definition 5). **sea legs,** ability to walk steadily on the deck of a moving ship, *hasn't got his sea legs yet.* **sea level,** the level corresponding to that of the surface of the sea halfway between high and low water. **sea lion,** a kind of large seal of the Pacific Ocean. **sea power,** the ability to control and make successful use of the sea, especially in war; a country having this. **sea room,** a clear space at sea allowing a ship to turn etc. **sea rover,** a pirate ship. **sea salt,** salt obtained from seawater by evaporation. **sea serpent,** a huge serpentine monster reported as seen in the sea. **sea shell,** the shell of any mollusk living in salt water. **sea snake,** a poisonous marine snake with a finlike tail. **sea urchin,** a sea animal with a round shell covered in sharp spikes. **sea wolf,** a sea elephant; a bass or wolffish; a pirate.

sea·bed (see-bed) *n.* the ocean floor.
Sea·bee (see-bee) *n.* **1.** a U.S. naval construction battalion. **2.** a member of this.
sea·board (see-bohrd) *n.* the coast or its outline.
sea·borne (see-bohrn) *adj.* conveyed by sea.
sea·coast (see-kohst) *n.* the land adjacent to the sea.
sea·far·er (see-fair-ĕr) *n.* a seafaring person.
sea·far·ing (see-fair-ing) *adj. & n.* working or traveling on the sea, especially as one's regular occupation.
sea·food (see-food) *n.* fish or shellfish from the sea eaten as food.
sea·front (see-frunt) *n.* the part of a town facing the sea.
sea·go·ing (see-goh-ing) *adj.* **1.** (of ships) oceangoing. **2.** (of people) seafaring.
sea gull a gull.
seal[1] (seel) *n.* an amphibious sea animal with short limbs that serve chiefly for swimming, and thick fur or bristles. **seal** *v.* to hunt seals, *they went sealing.*
seal[2] *n.* (*pl.* **seals, seal**) **1.** a substance or fitting used to close an opening etc. and prevent air or liquid etc. from passing through it. **2.** a gem or piece of metal etc. with an engraved design that is pressed on wax or other soft material to leave an impression; *seals of office,* those held by a person while he holds a certain position. **3.** this impression or a piece of wax bearing it, attached to a document as a guarantee of authenticity, or to an envelope or box or room etc. to show that (while the seal is unbroken) the contents have not been tampered with since it was affixed. **4.** a mark or event or action etc. serving to confirm or guarantee something, *gave it their seal of approval.* **5.** a small decorative paper sticker resembling a postage stamp. **seal** *v.* **1.** to close securely so as to prevent penetration, to coat or surface with a protective material or sealant, to stick down (an envelope etc.); *it's a sealed book to me,* it is a subject of which I have no understanding. **2.** to affix a seal to. **3.** to stamp or certify as authentic in this way. **4.** to settle or decide, *his fate was sealed.* □**sealed orders,** orders for a procedure, not to be examined before a specified time. **sealing wax,** a substance that is soft when heated but hardens when cooled, used for sealing letters or for impressing with an engraved design.
seal off, to prevent access to (an area).
seal·ant (see-lănt) *n.* a substance used for coating a surface to make it watertight or airtight.
seal·er (see-lĕr) *n.* **1.** a ship or person engaged in seal hunting. **2.** an inspector of weights and measures. **3.** a sealant.
seal·skin (seel-skin) *n.* the skin or prepared fur of a seal used as a clothing material.
Seal·y·ham (see-li-hăm) *n.* a terrier of a breed that has short legs and wiry hair.
seam (seem) *n.* **1.** the line or groove where two edges join, especially of cloth or leather etc. or wood. **2.** a surface line, such as a wrinkle or scar. **3.** a layer of coal etc. in the ground. **seam** *v.* **1.** to join by means of a seam. **2.** to mark with a wrinkle or scar etc. **seam'less** *adj.*
sea·man (see-măn) *n.* (*pl.* **-men,** *pr.* -mĕn) **1.** a sailor, especially one below the rank of officer. **2.** a person who is skilled in seafaring. **sea'man·ship** *n.* □**seaman apprentice,** an enlisted navy man or woman one rank below a seaman. **sea-**

man recruit, the lowest ranking navy man or woman.
sea·mount (see-mownt) *n.* an underwater mountain.
seam·stress (seem-stris) *n.* a woman whose job is sewing things.
seam·y (see-mee) *adj.* (**seam·i·er, seam·i·est**) **1.** unpleasant, unattractive, *a seamy neighborhood.* **2.** showing seams. □**the seamy side,** the less presentable or less attractive aspect of life.
sé·ance (say-ahns) *n.* a spiritualist meeting.
sea·plane (see-playn) *n.* an airplane designed to land on and take off from a stretch of water.
sea·port (see-pohrt) *n.* a port on the coast.
sear (seer) *v.* to scorch or burn the surface of; *a searing pain,* a burning pain.
search (surch) *v.* **1.** to look or go over (a place etc.) in order to find something. **2.** to examine the clothes and body of (a person) to see if something is concealed there. **3.** to examine thoroughly, *search your conscience.* **search** *n.* the act or process of searching. **search'er** *n.* □**search party,** a group of people organized to look for a lost person or thing. **search warrant,** a warrant allowing officials to enter the premises of a person thought to be concealing stolen property etc.
search·ing (sur-ching) *adj.* (of an investigation or scrutiny) thorough.
search·light (surch-lit) *n.* **1.** an outdoor electric lamp with a reflector producing a powerful beam that can be turned in any direction, used for discovering hostile aircraft etc. **2.** its beam.
sea·scape (see-skayp) *n.* a picture or view of the sea.
sea·shore (see-shohr) *n.* land close to the sea.
sea·sick (see-sik) *adj.* made sick or queasy by the motion of a ship. **sea'sick·ness** *n.*
sea·side (see-sid) *n.* the seacoast, especially as a place for vacations.
sea·son (see-zŏn) *n.* **1.** a section of the year with distinct characteristics of temperature and rainfall. **2.** the time of year when something is common or plentiful, or when an activity takes place, *the hunting season; the baseball season.* **season** *v.* **1.** to give extra flavor to (food) by adding salt or pepper or other sharp-tasting substances. **2.** to bring into a fit condition for use by drying or treating or allowing to mature, to become seasoned in this way. **3.** to make (people) experienced by training and practice, *seasoned soldiers.* **sea'son·er** *n.* □**in season,** (of food) available plentifully and in good condition for eating; (of an animal) in heat; (of advice) given when likely to be heeded. **out of season,** (of food) not in season. **season ticket,** a ticket that allows a person to attend performances, games, etc. for a specified period.
sea·son·a·ble (see-zŏ-nă-bĕl) *adj.* **1.** suitable for the season, *frost is seasonable in winter.* **2.** timely, opportune. **sea'son·a·bly** *adv.* ▷Do not confuse *seasonable* with *seasonal.*
sea·son·al (see-zŏ-năl) *adj.* of a season or seasons, varying according to these; *he found only seasonal work,* he worked only during certain seasons. **sea'son·al·ly** *adv.* ▷Do not confuse *seasonal* with *seasonable.*
sea·son·ing (see-zŏ-ning) *n.* a substance used to season food.
seat (seet) *n.* **1.** a thing made or used for sitting

on. **2.** a place where one sits, a place for one person to sit in a theater or vehicle etc. **3.** the right to sit as a member of a council or committee or legislative body etc. **4.** the horizontal part of a chair etc. on which a sitter's body rests. **5.** the part supporting another part in a machine. **6.** the buttocks, the part of a skirt or trousers covering these. **7.** the place where something is based or located, *the seat of government; a seat of learning.* **seat** *v.* **1.** to cause to sit; *seat oneself or be seated,* to sit down. **2.** to provide sitting accommodation for, *the hall seats five hundred.* **3.** to put a seat on (a chair). □**by the seat of one's** *or* **the pants,** by instinct rather than rule. **seat belt,** a strap securing a person to his seat in a vehicle or aircraft, for safety.

seat·ed (see-tid) *adj.* sitting.

seat·ing (see-ting) *n.* **1.** the act of providing with or escorting to a seat. **2.** the seats in a theater etc., considered collectively, *seating for five hundred.* **3.** the upholstery for a chair etc.

sea·wall (see-wawl) *n.* a wall or embankment made to check the encroachment of the sea.

sea·ward (see-wărd) *adj. & adv.* toward the sea.

sea·wards (see-wărdz) *adv.* seaward.

sea·wa·ter (see-waw-těr) *n.* the salt water of a sea or an ocean.

sea·way (see-way) *n.* **1.** an inland waterway open to seagoing ships. **2.** a ship's progress.

sea·weed (see-weed) *n.* any plant that grows in the sea or on rocks washed by the sea.

sea·wor·thy (see-wur-*thee*) *adj.* (of a ship) in a fit state for a sea voyage. **sea′wor·thi·ness** *n.*

se·ba·ceous (si-bay-shŭs) *adj.* secreting an oily or greasy substance, *sebaceous glands.*

SEC *abbr.* Securities and Exchange Commission.

sec. *abbr.* **1.** second. **2.** secondary. **3.** secretary. **4.** section.

se·cant (see-kant) *n.* **1.** an intersecting line, especially the radius of a circle produced through one end of an arc to meet tangent to the other end. **2.** the ratio of this line to the radius.

se·cede (si-seed) *v.* (**se·ced·ed, se·ced·ing**) to withdraw oneself from membership of an organization. **se·ced′er** *n.*

se·ces·sion (si-sesh-ŏn) *n.* **1.** seceding. **2.** *Secession,* the withdrawal from the Union (1860–61) of eleven U.S. southern states.

se·ces·sion·ist (si-sesh-ŏ-nist) *n.* a person or group supporting the right of secession. **se·cessionist** *adj.*

se·clude (si-klood) *v.* (**se·clud·ed, se·clud·ing**) to keep (a person) apart from others.

se·clud·ed (si-kloo-did) *adj.* (of a place) screened or sheltered from view.

se·clu·sion (si-kloo-zhŏn) *n.* secluding, being secluded, privacy.

se·clu·sive (si-kloo-siv) *adj.* secluding, tending to seclude oneself.

sec·ond (sek-ŏnd) *adj.* **1.** next after first. **2.** another after the first, *a second chance.* **3.** of a secondary kind, subordinate, inferior, *second quality; the second team.* **second** *n.* **1.** something that is second, the second day of a month. **2.** second gear. **3.** an attendant of a person taking part in a duel or boxing match. **4.** a sixtieth part of a minute of time or angular measurement. **5.** (*informal*) a short time, *wait a second.* **6.** an item of inferior quality. **second** *adv.* in second place or rank or position. **second** *v.* **1.** to assist. **2.** to state for-

mally that one supports a motion that has been put forward by another person, in order to show that the proposer is not isolated or as a means of bringing it to be voted on. **sec′ond·er** *n.* □**at second hand,** obtained indirectly, not from the original source. **second base,** (in baseball) the second in order of bases from home plate; the portion of the field near this base. **second baseman,** the baseball player stationed at second base. **second best,** of second or inferior quality; *come off second best,* to be the loser in a contest or dispute. **second childhood,** childishness caused by mental weakness in old age. **second class,** the second best quality; the second best accommodation in a boat etc. **second coming,** the return of Christ, especially as preliminary to his expected personal reign on Earth. **second cousin,** *see* **cousin. second fiddle,** a subsidiary or secondary role, *had to play second fiddle to his brother.* **second gear,** the second lowest gear in a motor vehicle. **second growth,** the plant growth coming after a virgin forest is destroyed. **second in command,** the person next in rank to the commanding or chief officer or official. **second lieutenant,** *see* **lieutenant. second mate,** an officer immediately below first mate on a merchant ship. **second name,** a surname. **second nature,** a habit or characteristic that has become automatic, *secrecy is second nature to him.* **second officer,** a second mate. **second person,** *see* **person. second sight,** the supposed power to foresee future events. **second string,** (*informal*) (in sports) the players of a team less proficient than first string. **second teeth,** adults' permanent teeth, appearing after the milk teeth have fallen out. **second thoughts,** a change of mind after reconsideration. **second wind,** recovery of one's ease of breathing during exercise, after having become out of breath; renewed energy for effort.

sec·ond·ar·y (sek-ŏn-der-ee) *adj.* **1.** coming after what is primary. **2.** of lesser importance or rank etc. than the first. **3.** derived from what is primary or original, *secondary sources.* **secondary** *n.* (in football) the players in the defensive backfield. **sec′ond·ar·i·ly** *adv.* □**secondary accent,** (in a word) a stress accent not as strong as a primary accent. **secondary boycott,** a boycott against a firm by a labor union that is not directly involved in its dispute with another firm. **secondary colors,** colors obtained by mixing two primary colors. **secondary education** *or* **school,** that for people who have received primary education but have not yet proceeded to a university or an occupation. **secondary sex characteristic,** a characteristic that is distinctive of one sex but not directly related to reproduction.

sec·ond-class (sek-ŏnd-klas) *adj. & adv.* **1.** of second or inferior quality. **2.** in or traveling by less good accommodation than first-class. **3.** (of mail) to be given lower priority than first-class mail. □**second-class citizen,** (*informal*) a person treated badly by society.

sec·ond-de·gree (sek-ŏnd-dĕ-gree) **burn** a burn with blistering.

sec·ond-guess (sek-ŏnd-ges) *v.* (*informal*) to criticize (a person etc.) or explain (a situation) from hindsight.

sec·ond·hand (sek-ŏnd-hand) *adj. & adv.* **1.** bought after use by a previous owner. **2.** dealing in used goods, *a secondhand shop.* **3.** (of informa-

tion) taken on another's authority and not obtained by original observation or research.
sec·ond·ly (sek-önd-lee) *adv.* second, as a second consideration.
sec·ond-rate (sek-önd-rayt) *adj.* inferior in quality.
sec·onds (sek-öndz) *n. pl.* 1. goods of second quality, having some flaw(s). 2. a second helping of food.
sec·ond-sto·ry (sek-önd-stohr-ee) **man** *(informal)* a cat burglar.
se·cre·cy (see-krĕ-see) *n.* (*pl.* **-cies**) 1. being kept secret. 2. keeping things secret, *was pledged to secrecy.*
se·cret (see-krit) *adj.* 1. kept or intended to be kept from the knowledge or view of others, to be known only by specified people. 2. working or operating secretly. **secret** *n.* 1. something kept or intended to be kept secret. 2. a mystery, a thing no one properly understands, *the secrets of nature.* 3. a method (not known to everyone) for attaining something, *the secret of good health.* **se'cret·ly** *adv.* □in secret, secretly. **secret agent,** a spy acting for a country. **secret ballot,** one in which individual voters' choices are not made public. **secret police,** a police force operating in secret for political purposes. **Secret Service,** an agency of the U.S. government chiefly concerned with arresting counterfeiters and with protecting the lives of the president, presidential candidates, their immediate families, etc. **secret society,** a society whose members are sworn to secrecy about it.
sec·re·tar·i·al (sek-rĕ-ter-i-ăl) *adj.* of the work of a secretary.
sec·re·tar·i·at (sek-rĕ-ter-i-ăt) *n.* 1. the members of a government administrative office collectively. 2. the buildings or rooms occupied by a secretariat.
sec·re·tar·y (sek-rĕ-ter-ee) *n.* (*pl.* **-tar·ies**) 1. a person employed to help deal with correspondence, typing, filing, and similar routine work. 2. an official in charge of the correspondence and records of an organization. 3. an official in charge of a particular government department, *Secretary of Labor.* 4. a writing desk with drawers. □**secretary bird,** a long-legged African bird with a crest likened to quill pens placed behind a writer's ear.
sec·re·tar·y-gen·er·al *n.* (sek-rĕ-ter-ee-jen-ĕ-räl) the principal administrator of certain large organizations.
se·crete[1] (si-kreet) *v.* (**se·cret·ed, se·cret·ing**) to put (an object) into a place of concealment.
secrete[2] *v.* (**se·cret·ed, se·cret·ing**) to form and send out (a substance) into the body, either for excretion *(kidneys secrete urine)* or for use within the body *(the liver secretes bile).*
se·cre·tion (si-kree-shŏn) *n.* 1. secreting, being secreted. 2. a substance secreted by an organ or cell of the body. **se·cre·to·ry** (si-kree-tŏ-ree) *adj.*
se·cre·tive (see-krĕ-tiv, si-kree-) *adj.* making a secret of things unnecessarily, uncommunicative. **se'cre·tive·ly** *adv.* **se'cre·tive·ness** *n.*
sect (sekt) *n.* a group of people with religious or other beliefs that differ from those more generally accepted.
sect. *abbr.* section.
sec·tar·i·an (sek-tair-i-ăn) *adj.* 1. of or belonging to a sect or sects. 2. narrow-mindedly putting

the beliefs or interests of one's sect before more general interests. **sectarian** *n.* a person adhering to a sect, especially in a bigoted fashion. **sec·tar'i·an·ism** *n.*
sec·tion (sek-shŏn) *n.* 1. a distinct part or portion of something. 2. a cross section. 3. the process of cutting or separating something surgically. **section** *v.* to divide into sections. □**section gang,** a group of railroad workers who maintain a section of track.
sec·tion·al (sek-shŏ-năl) *adj.* 1. of a section or sections. 2. of one section of a group or community as distinct from others or from the whole. 3. made in sections, *sectional fishing rod.* **sec'tion·al·ism** *n.* **sec'tion·al·iy** *adv.*
sec·tor (sek-tŏr) 1. one of the parts into which a battle area is divided for the purpose of controlling operations. 2. a similar division of an activity, *the private sector of the economy.* 3. a section of a circular area between two lines drawn from its center to its circumference.
sec·u·lar (sek-yŭ-lär) *adj.* 1. concerned with worldly affairs rather than spiritual ones. 2. not involving or belonging to religion, *secular music; secular clergy,* clergy who are not members of a monastic community. **sec'u·lar·ly** *adv.*
sec·u·lar·ism (sek-yŭ-lă-riz-ĕm) *n.* a secular system of belief, an opposition to or rejection of religion. **sec'u·lar·ist** *adj.* & *n.* **sec·u·lar·is·tic** (sek-yŭ-lă-ris-tik) *adj.*
sec·u·lar·ize (sek-yŭ-lă-rız) *v.* (**sec·u·lar·ized, sec·u·lar·iz·ing**) 1. to make secular. 2. to separate from sacred or religious connections. **sec'u·lar·iz·er** *n.* **sec·u·lar·i·za·tion** (sek-yŭ-lă-ri-zay-shŏn) *n.*
se·cure (si-kyoor) *adj.* safe (especially against attack), certain not to slip or fail, reliable. **secure** *v.* (**se·cured, se·cur·ing**) 1. to make secure. 2. to fasten securely. 3. to obtain. 4. to guarantee by pledging something as security, *the loan is secured on their business.* **se·cure'ly** *adv.* **se·cure'ness** *n.* **se·cur'er** *n.*
se·cu·ri·ty (si-kyoor-i-tee) *n.* (*pl.* **-ties**) 1. a state or feeling of being secure, something that gives this. 2. the safety of a country or organization against espionage or theft or other danger. 3. a thing that serves as a guarantee or pledge, *offered the deed of his house as security for the loan.* 4. a certificate showing ownership of financial stocks or bonds. □**security blanket,** something that gives a person a sense of security.
secy. *abbr.* secretary.
se·dan (si-dan) *n.* 1. an enclosed car for four or more persons including the driver. 2. (also **sedan chair**) an enclosed chair for one person (used in the 17th and 18th centuries), mounted on two poles and carried by two bearers.
se·date (si-dayt) *adj.* calm and dignified, not lively. **sedate** *v.* (**se·dat·ed, se·dat·ing**) to treat (a person) with sedatives. **se·date'ly** *adv.* **se·date'ness** *n.* **se·da·tion** (si-day-shŏn) *n.*
sed·a·tive (sed-ă-tiv) *adj.* having a calming or soothing effect. **sedative** *n.* a sedative medicine or influence.
sed·en·tar·y (sed-ĕn-ter-ee) *adj.* 1. spending much time seated, *sedentary workers.* 2. requiring much sitting, *sedentary work.* **sed'en·tar·i·ness** *n.*
Se·der (say-dĕr) *n.* the ritual for the first night or first two nights of Passover.
sedge (sej) *n.* a grasslike plant growing in marshes or near water, a bed of this. **sedg'y** *adj.*

sed·i·ment (sed-i-měnt) *n.* 1. very fine particles of solid matter suspended in a liquid or settling to the bottom of it. 2. solid matter (such as sand, gravel) that is carried by water or wind and settles on the surface of land. **sed·i·men·ta·tion** (sed-i-měn-tay-shŏn) *n.*

sed·i·men·ta·ry (sed-i-men-tă-ree) *adj.* of or like sediment; *sedimentary rocks,* those formed from sediment carried by water or wind.

se·di·tion (si-dish-ŏn) *n.* words or actions that make people rebel against the authority of the government. **se·di'tion·ist** *n.* **se·di'tious** *adj.*

se·duce (se-doos) *v.* (**se·duced, se·duc·ing**) 1. to persuade (especially into wrongdoing) by offering temptations, *was seduced into betraying his country.* 2. to tempt (a person) into sexual intercourse. **se·duc'er** *n.*

se·duc·tion (si-duk-shŏn) *n.* 1. seducing, being seduced. 2. a tempting and attractive feature, *the seductions of country life.*

se·duc·tive (si-duk-tiv) *adj.* tending to seduce, alluring. **se·duc'tive·ly** *adv.* **se·duc'tive·ness** *n.*

sed·u·lous (sej-ŭ-lŭs) *adj.* diligent and persevering. **sed'u·lous·ly** *adv.* **sed'u·lous·ness** *n.*

se·dum (see-dŭm) *n.* a kind of plant with fleshy leaves, often with pink or white or yellow flowers.

see[1] (see) *v.* (**saw, seen, see·ing**) 1. to perceive with the eyes, to have or use the power of doing this. 2. to perceive with the mind, to understand, *I can't see why not; do you see?* do you understand? 3. to have a certain opinion about; *as I see it,* in my opinion. 4. to consider, to take time to do this, *must see what can be done; let me see, how can we fix it?* 5. to watch, to be a spectator of, *went to see a movie.* 6. to look at for information, *see page 310.* 7. to meet, to be near and recognize, *saw her in church.* 8. to discover, *see who is at the door.* 9. to experience, to undergo, *saw service during the war; won't see fifty again,* is over this age. 10. to grant or obtain an interview with, to consult, *the manager will see you now; must see the doctor about my wrist.* 11. to escort, to conduct, *see her to the door.* 12. to make sure, *see that this letter goes today.* □**see about,** to attend to. **see off,** to accompany (a person) to his point of departure for a journey and take leave of him when he sets out. **see red,** *(informal)* to be suddenly filled with fury. **see stars,** to see dancing lights before one's eyes as the result of a blow on the head. **see the light,** *(informal)* to understand after failing to do so, to realize one's mistakes. **see things,** to have hallucinations. **see through,** to understand the true nature of, not be deceived by; *see a thing through,* not abandon it before it is completed. **see to,** to attend to.

see[2] *n.* the position or district of a bishop or archbishop, *the see of Canterbury.* □**the Holy See** *or* **the See of Rome,** the papacy.

seed (seed) *n.* (*pl.* **seeds** *or* **seed**) 1. a fertilized ovule of a plant, capable of developing into a plant like its parent. 2. seeds as collected for sowing, *to be kept for seed.* 3. semen, milt. 4. *(old use)* offspring, descendants, *Abraham and his seed.* 5. something from which a tendency or feeling etc. can develop, *sowing the seeds of doubt in their minds.* 6. *(informal)* a seeded player, as in a golf or tennis tournament. **seed** *v.* 1. to plant seeds in, to sprinkle with seeds. 2. to place particles in (a cloud) to cause condensation and produce rain. 3. to remove seeds from (fruit). 4. to name (a strong player) as not to be matched against another named in this way in the early rounds of an elimination tournament, so as to increase the interest of later rounds. **seed'er** *n.* □**go** *or* **run to seed,** to cease flowering as seed develops; to become shabby and careless of appearance; to deteriorate in ability or efficiency. **seed bed,** a bed of fine soil in which seeds are sown. **seed money,** money to initiate a project. **seed pearl,** a very small pearl.

seed·less (seed-lis) *adj.* not containing seeds.

seed·ling (seed-ling) *n.* a very young plant growing from a seed.

seed·y (see-dee) *adj.* (**seed·i·er, seed·i·est**) 1. full of seeds. 2. shabby and disreputable. **seed'i·ly** *adv.* **seed'i·ness** *n.*

see·ing (see-ing) *see* **see**[1]. □**Seeing Eye dog,** a dog trained to guide a blind person. **seeing that,** in view of the fact that, because.

seek (seek) *v.* (**sought, seek·ing**) to make a search or inquiry for, to try to find or obtain or do. **seek'er** *n.* □**seek out,** to seek specially, to make a special effort to meet and address (a person).

seem (seem) *v.* to appear to be or exist or be true.

seem·ing (see-ming) *adj.* having an appearance of being something but not necessarily being this in fact. **seem'ing·ly** *adv.* **seem'ing·ness** *n.*

seem·ly (seem-lee) *adj.* (**-li·er, -li·est**) proper, suitable, in accordance with accepted standards of good taste. **seem'li·ness** *n.*

seen (seen) *see* **see**[1].

seep (seep) *v.* to ooze slowly out or through.

seep·age (see-pij) *n.* seeping, the amount that seeps out.

se·er (see-ěr) *n.* a prophet, a person who sees visions. **seer·ess** (seer-is) *n. fem.*

seer·suck·er (seer-suk-ěr) *n.* fabric having a puckered surface and often a striped pattern.

see·saw (see-saw) *n.* 1. a children's amusement consisting of a long board balanced on a central support so that when a child sits on either end the two of them can make each end go up and the other down alternately. 2. an up-and-down change that is constantly repeated. **seesaw** *v.* to ride on a seesaw, to make this movement.

seethe (see*th*) *v.* (**seethed, seeth·ing**) 1. to bubble or surge as in boiling. 2. to be very agitated or excited. **seeth'ing·ly** *adv.*

see-through (see-throo) *adj.* *(informal)* transparent.

seg·ment (seg-měnt) *n.* a part cut off or separable or marked off as though separable from the other parts of a thing. **segment** (seg-ment) *v.* to cut or separate into segments. **seg·men·tal** (seg-men-tăl) *adj.* **seg·men·ta·tion** (seg-měn-tay-shŏn) *n.*

seg·ment·ed (seg-men-tid) *adj.* divided into segments.

seg·re·gate (seg-rě-gayt) *v.* (**seg·re·gat·ed, seg·re·gat·ing**) 1. to put apart from the rest, to isolate. 2. to separate (people) according to their race. **seg·re·ga·tion** (seg-rě-gay-shŏn) *n.*

seg·re·ga·tion·ist (seg-rě-gay-shŏ-nist) *n.* a person who is in favor of racial segregation.

sei·gneur (say-nyur) *n.* a feudal lord, a lord of the manor. **sei·gneur·y** (sayn-yŭ-ree) *n.*

seign·ior (sayn-yŏr, seen) *n.* a feudal lord, a gentleman. **seign'ior·age** *n.* **sei·gnio·ri·al** (saynyohr-i-ăl, see-) *adj.*

seine (sayn) *n.* a large fishing net that hangs vertically with floats at the top and weights at the bottom, the ends being drawn together to enclose fish as it is hauled ashore. **seine** v. **(seined, sein·ing)** to fish or catch with a seine. **sein′er** n.

seism (sɪ-zĕm) n. an earthquake.

seis·mic (sɪz-mik) adj. of an earthquake or earthquakes. **seis′mi·cal·ly** adv. **seis·mic·i·ty** (sɪz-mis-i-tee) n.

seis·mo·gram (sɪz-mŏ-gram) n. a record given by a seismograph.

seis·mo·graph (sɪz-mŏ-graf) n. an instrument for detecting, recording, and measuring earthquakes. **seis·mog·ra·phy** (sɪz-mog-ră-fee) n. **seis·mo·graph·ic** (sɪz-mŏ-graf-ik) adj.

seis·mog·ra·pher (sɪz-mog-ră-fĕr) n. an expert in the use of seismographs.

seis·mol·o·gist (sɪz-mol-ŏ-jist) n. an expert in seismology.

seis·mol·o·gy (sɪz-mol-ŏ-jee) n. the study of earthquakes and their phenomena. **seis·mo·log·i·cal** (sɪz-mŏ-loj-i-kăl) adj.

seis·mom·e·ter (sɪz-mom-ĕ-tĕr) n. an instrument showing the force, direction, etc. of an earthquake by measuring the actual movement of the ground. **seis·mo·met·ric** (sɪz-mŏ-met-rik) adj.

seize (seez) v. **(seized, seiz·ing)** 1. to take hold of (a thing) forcibly or suddenly or eagerly. 2. to take possession of (a thing) forcibly or by legal right, seize smuggled goods. 3. to have a sudden overwhelming effect on, panic seized us; the swimmer was seized by a cramp. □**seize on**, to make use of (an excuse etc.) eagerly.

sei·zure (see-zhŭr) n. 1. seizing, being seized. 2. a sudden attack of epilepsy or apoplexy etc.

sel. abbr. 1. select. 2. selected. 3. selection.

sel·dom (sel-dŏm) adv. rarely, not often.

se·lect (si-lekt) v. to pick out as best or most suitable. **select** adj. 1. chosen for excellence. 2. (of a society) exclusive, admitting only certain people as members. **se·lect′ness** n. **se·lec′tor** n. □**select committee**, a small committee appointed to make a special investigation.

se·lect·ee (si-lek-tee) n. a conscript.

se·lec·tion (si-lek-shŏn) n. 1. selecting, being selected. 2. the people or things selected. 3. a collection of things from which a choice can be made, they stock a large selection of goods.

se·lec·tive (si-lek-tiv) adj. chosen or choosing carefully. **se·lec′tive·ly** adv. **se·lec·tiv·i·ty** (si-lek-tiv-i-tee) n. □**selective service**, a U.S. government system for selecting personnel for compulsory military service.

se·lect·man (si-lekt-măn) n. (pl. -men, pr. -mĕn) an elected officer in a New England town.

sel·e·nite (sel-ĕ-nɪt) n. a gypsum occurring as transparent crystals or thin plates.

se·le·ni·um (si-lee-ni-ŭm) n. a nonmetallic element of the sulfur group that varies in its electrical resistivity with the intensity of its illumination.

sel·e·nog·ra·phy (sel-ĕ-nog-ră-fee) n. the study of or mapping of the moon. **sel·e·nog′ra·pher** n.

sel·e·nol·o·gy (sel-ĕ-nol-ŏ-jee) n. the scientific study of the moon.

self (self) n. (pl. **selves**, pr. selvz) 1. a person as an individual, one's own self. 2. a person's special nature; she is her old self again, has regained her former personality. 3. one's own interests or advantage or pleasure, always puts self first. **self** adj. of the same color or material as that used for the whole, a dress with self belt.

self- prefix meaning of or to or done by oneself or itself, as in self-accuser, self-explanatory, self-inflicted.

self-ab·ne·ga·tion (self-ab-nĕ-gay-shŏn) n. self-denial.

self-act·ing (self-ak-ting) adj. automatic.

self-ad·dressed (self-ă-drest) adj. (of an envelope for containing a reply) addressed to oneself.

self-ag·gran·dize·ment (self-ă-gran-diz-mĕnt) n. an increase of one's power, rank, wealth, etc. **self′-ag·gran′diz·ing** adj.

self-as·ser·tive (self-ă-sur-tiv) adj. asserting oneself confidently. **self-as·ser′tive·ness** n.

self-as·sured (self-ă-shoord) adj. self-confident.

self-cen·tered (self-sen-tĕrd) adj. thinking chiefly of oneself or one's own affairs, selfish. **self′-cen′tered·ly** adv. **self′-cen′tered·ness** n.

self-com·mand (self-kŏ-mand) n. self-control.

self-con·fessed (self-kŏn-fest) adj. openly admitting oneself to be, a self-confessed glutton.

self-con·fi·dent (self-kon-fi-dĕnt) adj. having confidence in one's own abilities. **self′-con′fi·dence** n.

self-con·grat·u·la·tion (self-kŏn-grach-ŭ-lay-shŏn) n. an expression or feeling of satisfaction with oneself. **self-con·grat·u·la·to·ry** (self-kŏn-grach-ŭ-lă-tohr-ee) adj.

self-con·scious (self-kon-shŭs) adj. embarrassed or unnatural in manner from knowing that one is being observed by others. **self′-con′scious·ly** adv. **self′-con′scious·ness** n.

self-con·tained (self-kŏn-taynd) adj. 1. complete in itself. 2. (of a person) able to do without the company of others, reserved.

self-con·trol (self-kŏn-trohl) n. ability to control one's behavior and not act emotionally. **self′-con·trolled′** adj.

self-cor·rect·ing (self-kŏ-rek-ting) adj. automatically adjusting to correct mistakes.

self-crit·i·cism (self-krit-i-siz-ĕm) n. criticizing oneself.

self-de·cep·tion (self-dĕ-sep-shŏn) n. deceiving oneself.

self-de·feat·ing (self-di-fee-ting) adj. serving to defeat one's own purpose.

self-de·fense (self-di-fens) n. defense of oneself, or of one's rights or good reputation etc., against attack.

self-de·ni·al (self-di-nɪ-ăl) n. deliberately going without the things one would like to have.

self-de·struct (self-di-strukt) v. (informal) to destroy itself at a designated time. **self′-de·struc′tive** adj.

self-de·struc·tion (self-di-struk-shŏn) n. destruction of oneself.

self-de·ter·mi·na·tion (self-di-tur-mĭ-nay-shŏn) n. the ability to decide one's purpose, direction, etc.

self-de·vo·tion (self-di-voh-shŏn) *n.* devotion of oneself to a person or cause.

self-dis·ci·pline (self-dis-ĭ-plin) *n.* training oneself to produce self-control or a particular skill etc.

self-doubt (self-dowt) *n.* a feeling of uncertainty about one's own motives, abilities, etc.

self-ed·u·cat·ed (self-ej-ŭ-kay-tid) *adj.* lacking formal education, educated by one's own efforts.

self-ef·fac·ing (self-i-fay-sing) *adj.* tending to avoid the notice of others, humble. **self'-ef·face'ment** *n.*

self-em·ployed (self-em-ploid) *adj.* working independently and not for an employer. **self'-em·ploy'ment** *n.*

self-es·teem (self-e-steem) *n.* a favorable opinion of oneself, self-respect.

self-ev·i·dent (self-ev-i-dĕnt) *adj.* clear without proof or explanation or further evidence.

self-ex·am·i·na·tion (self-ig-zam-ĭ-nay-shŏn) *n.* examination of one's motives, actions etc.

self-ex·plan·a·to·ry (self-ik-splan-ă-tohr-ee) *adj.* explaining itself, requiring no further explanation.

self-ex·pres·sion (self-ik-spresh-ŏn) *n.* expression of one's own thoughts or feelings through painting, literature, etc.

self-fer·ti·li·za·tion (self-fur-tĭ-lĭ-zay-shŏn) *n.* the fertilization of a plant by a gamete from the same plant.

self-ful·fill·ing (self-fuul-fil-ing) *adj.* 1. of or relating to the fulfillment of one's ambitions etc. 2. (of prophecy) turning out to be correct because actions taken by the person making the prophecy have a direct influence on the events. **self'-ful·fill'ment** *n.*

self-gov·ern·ing (self-guv-ĕr-ning) *adj.* (of a country) governing itself. **self'-gov'ern·ment** *n.*

self-help (self-help) *n.* use of one's own powers to achieve things, without dependence on aid from others. **self-help** *adj.* (of books etc.) intended to aid in self-help.

self-im·por·tant (self-im-por-tănt) *adj.* having a high opinion of one's own importance, pompous. **self'-im·por'tant·ly** *adv.* **self'-im·por'tance** *n.*

self-im·posed (self-im-pohzd) *adj.* imposed by oneself on oneself.

self-im·prove·ment (self-im-proov-mĕnt) *n.* bettering one's mind or character etc. by one's own efforts.

self-in·duced (self-in-doost) *adj.* produced or caused by oneself or itself.

self-in·dul·gent (self-in-dul-jĕnt) *adj.* readily yielding to temptations of ease or pleasure etc. **self'-in·dul'gence** *n.*

self-in·flict·ed (self-in-flik-tid) *adj.* inflicted by oneself on oneself.

self-in·ter·est (self-in-tĕ-rist, -in-trist) *n.* one's own personal advantage. **self'-in'ter·est·ed** *adj.*

self·ish (sel-fish) *adj.* acting or done according to one's own interests and needs without regard for those of others, keeping good things for oneself and not sharing. **self'ish·ly** *adv.* **self'ish·ness** *n.*

self-knowl·edge (self-nol-ij) *n.* understanding or knowledge of one's motives, abilities, etc.

self-less (self-lis) *adj.* unselfish. **self'less·ly** *adv.* **self'less·ness** *n.*

self-made (self-mayd) *adj.* having risen from poverty or obscurity and achieved success by one's own efforts, *a self-made man.*

self-mas·ter·y (self-mas-tĕ-ree) *n.* self-control.

self-op·er·at·ing (self-op-ĕ-ray-ting) *adj.* automatic.

self-pit·y (self-pit-ee) *n.* pity for oneself.

self-pol·li·na·tion (self-pol-ĭ-nay-shŏn) *n.* the transfer of pollen from the anther to the stigma of the same flower.

self-por·trait (self-pohr-trit) *n.* a portrait of himself by an artist, an account of himself by a writer.

self-pos·sessed (self-pŏ-zest) *adj.* calm and dignified. **self-pos·ses·sion** (self-pŏ-zesh-ŏn) *n.*

self-pres·er·va·tion (self-prez-ĕr-vay-shŏn) *n.* protection of oneself from harm or injury, the instinct to ensure one's own survival.

self-pro·pelled (self-prŏ-peld) *adj.* (of a vehicle etc.) having its own means of propulsion. **self'-pro·pel'ling** *adj.* **self-pro·pul·sion** (self-prŏ-pul-shŏn) *n.*

self-pro·tec·tion (self-prŏ-tek-shŏn) *n.* protection of oneself or itself.

self-re·al·i·za·tion (self-ree-ă-li-zay-shŏn) *n.* the fulfillment or realization of one's potential etc.

self-reg·u·lat·ing (self-reg-yŭ-lay-ting) *adj.* 1. (of a group or system) directing or controlling itself without outside influence. 2. (of a machine) functioning automatically.

self-re·li·ant (self-ri-lx-ănt) *adj.* independent, relying on one's own abilities and resources. **self'-re·li'ance** *n.*

self-re·proach (self-ri-prohch) *n.* disapproval of oneself for a fault or offense.

self-re·spect (self-ri-spekt) *n.* proper regard for oneself and one's own dignity and principles etc. **self'-re·spect'ing** *adj.*

self-re·straint (self-ri-straynt) *n.* self-control.

self-right·eous (self-rx-chŭs) *adj.* smugly sure of one's own righteousness. **self'-right'eous·ly** *adv.* **self'-right'eous·ness** *n.*

self-ris·ing (self-rx-zing) *adj.* (of flour) rising without the addition of a leavening agent.

self-rule (self-rool) *n.* self-government.

self-sac·ri·fice (self-sak-rĭ-fis) *n.* sacrifice of one's own interests and desires so that others may benefit. **self'-sac'ri·fic·ing** *adj.*

self-same (self-saym) *adj.* the very same, *died in the selfsame house where he was born.*

self-sat·is·fied (self-sat-is-fid) *adj.* pleased with oneself and one's own achievements, conceited. **self-sat·is·fac·tion** (self-sat-is-fak-shŏn) *n.*

self-seal·ing (self-see-ling) *adj.* (of an automobile tire etc.) capable of sealing itself.

self-seek·ing (self-see-king) *adj.* & *n.* seeking to promote one's own interests rather than those of others. **self'-seek'er** *n.*

self-serv·ice (self-sur-vis) *adj.* (of a restaurant or shop or filling station) at which customers help themselves and pay a cashier for what they have taken.

self-serv·ing (self-sur-ving) *adj.* placing one's own interests before those of others.

self-start·er (self-stahr-tĕr) *n.* 1. a device for start-

---

self'-dis·cov'er·y *n.*
self'-en·closed' *adj.*
self'-en·joy'ment *n.*
self'-en·rich'ment *n.*

self'-glo·ri·fi·ca'tion *n.*
self'-hate' *n.*
self'-hyp·no'sis *n.*
self'-i·den·ti·fi·ca'tion *n.*

self'-kind'ness *n.*
self'-lu'bri·cat'ed *adj.*
self'-per·pet'u·at·ing *adj.*
self'-pro·claimed' *adj.*

ing the engine of a motor vehicle without the use of a crank. 2. a person who has initiative. **self'-start'ing** *adj.*

self-styled (self-stɪld) *adj.* using a name or description one has adopted for oneself, usually without right, *one of these self-styled fast safe drivers.*

self-suf·fi·cient (self-sŭ-fish-ĕnt) *adj.* able to provide what one needs without outside help. **self-suf·fi·cien·cy** (self-sŭ-fish-ĕn-see) *n.*

self-sup·port·ing (self-sŭ-pohr-ting) *adj.* able to support oneself or itself without help.

self-sus·tain·ing (self-sŭ-stay-ning) *adj.* self-supporting.

self-taught (self-tawt) *adj.* having taught oneself without formal teaching from another person.

self-willed (self-wild) *adj.* obstinately doing what one wishes, stubborn.

self-wind·ing (self-wɪn-ding) *adj.* (of a watch or clock) having a mechanism that winds it automatically.

sell (sel) *v.* (**sold, sell·ing**) 1. to transfer the ownership of (goods etc.) in exchange for money. 2. to keep a stock of (goods) for sale, to be a dealer in, *do you sell tobacco?* 3. to promote sales of, *the author's name alone will sell many copies.* 4. (of goods) to find buyers, *the book is selling well.* 5. to be on sale at a certain price, *it sells for $1.50.* 6. to persuade a person into accepting (a thing) by convincing him of its merits, *tried to sell him the idea of merging the two departments.* **sell** *n.* 1. the manner of selling something; *hard sell*, aggressive salesmanship. 2. *(informal)* a deception, a disappointment. ☐**sell down the river**, *(informal)* to betray or defraud. **sell off**, to dispose of by selling, especially at a reduced price. **sell out**, to dispose of (all one's stock etc.) by selling; *(slang)* to betray.

sell·er (sel-ĕr) *n.* 1. a person who sells something. 2. a thing that sells well or badly, *those sandals were good sellers.* ☐**seller's market**, a state of affairs when goods are scarce and prices are high.

sell·out (sel-owt) *n.* 1. the selling of all tickets for a show etc., a great commercial success. 2. a betrayal.

Selt·zer (selt-sĕr) *n.* 1. a medicinal mineral water, originally from Nieder-Selters, in Germany. 2. *seltzer*, an artificial substitute for this, soda water.

sel·vage (sel-vij) *n.* an edge of cloth so woven that it does not unravel. **sel'vaged** *adj.*

selves *see* **self.**

sem. *abbr.* seminary.

se·man·tic (si-man-tik) *adj.* 1. relating to meaning in language. 2. relating to the connotation of words. **se·man'ti·cal·ly** *adv.*

se·man·tics (si-man-tiks) *n.* 1. the branch of philology dealing with meanings. 2. meaning, connotation. 3. the interpretation of symbols other than words (such as road signs). **se·man·ti·cist** (si-man-ti-sist) *n.*

sem·a·phore (sem-ă-fohr) *n.* 1. a system of signaling by holding the arms in certain positions to indicate letters of the alphabet. 2. a device with mechanically moved arms, used for signaling on railroads. **semaphore** *v.* (**sem·a·phored, sem·a·phor·ing**) to signal by semaphore.

sem·blance (sem-blăns) *n.* 1. an outward appearance (either real or pretended), a show, *spoke with a semblance of friendship.* 2. a resemblance or likeness to something.

se·men (see-mĕn) *n.* the whitish sperm-bearing fluid produced by male animals.

se·mes·ter (si-mes-tĕr) *n.* a half-year course or term in a school or university. **se·mes·tral** (si-mes-trăl) *adj.* **se·mes·tri·al** (si-mes-tri-ăl) *adj.*

sem·i (sem-ɪ) *n.* (*pl.* **sem·is**) *(informal)* a semi-trailer truck.

semi- *prefix* meaning half, partly, as in *semicircle, semidetached.*

sem·i·an·nu·al (sem-i-an-yoo-ăl) *adj.* occurring or published etc. twice a year. **sem·i·an'nu·al·ly** *adv.*

sem·i·ar·id (sem-i-ar-id) *adj.* (of a region, land, etc.) having little rainfall.

sem·i·au·to·mat·ic (sem-i-aw-tŏ-mat-ik) *adj.* 1. partially automatic. 2. (of a rifle) having automatic cartridge action but requiring manual pressure on the trigger for each shot. **sem·i·au·to·mat'i·cal·ly** *adv.*

sem·i·cir·cle (sem-i-sur-kĕl) *n.* half of a circle, something arranged in this shape. **sem·i·cir·cu·lar** (sem-i-sur-kyŭ-lăr) *adj.*

sem·i·co·lon (sem-i-koh-lŏn) *n.* the punctuation mark ; used to separate parts of a sentence where there is a more distinct break than that represented by a comma.

sem·i·con·duc·tor (sem-i-kŏn-duk-tŏr) *n.* a substance that (in certain conditions) conducts electricity but not as well as most metals do. **sem·i·con·duct'ing** *adj.*

sem·i·con·scious (sem-i-kon-shŭs) *adj.* not fully conscious. **sem·i·con'scious·ness** *n.*

sem·i·de·tached (sem-i-di-tacht) *adj.* (of a house) being one of a pair of houses that have one wall in common with each other but are detached from other houses.

sem·i·fi·nal (sem-i-fɪ-năl) *n.* the match or round preceding the final. **semifinal** *adj.*

sem·i·fi·nal·ist (sem-i-fɪ-nă-list) *n.* one who takes part in a semifinal.

sem·i·fit·ted (sem-i-fit-id) *adj.* (of a garment) shaped to the body but not closely fitted.

sem·i·flu·id (sem-i-floo-id) *adj.* of a consistency between solid and fluid.

sem·i·month·ly (sem-i-munth-lee) *adj.* occurring or published etc. twice a month.

sem·i·nal (sem-ɪ-năl) *adj.* 1. of seed or semen. 2. giving rise to new developments, *seminal ideas.* **sem'i·nal·ly** *adv.*

sem·i·nar (sem-ɪ-nahr) *n.* a small class for advanced discussion and research.

sem·i·nar·y (sem-ɪ-ner-ee) *n.* (*pl.* **-nar·ies**) a school for training priests or ministers or rabbis. **sem·i·nar·i·an** (sem-ɪ-ner-i-ăn) *n.*

Sem·i·nole (sem-ɪ-nohl) *n.* (*pl.* **-noles, -nole**) 1. a member of an American Indian tribe of Florida. 2. the language of this tribe.

sem·i·per·me·a·ble (sem-i-pur-mi-ă-bĕl) *adj.* permeable to some substances but not to others. **sem·i·per·me·a·bil·i·ty** (sem-i-pur-mi-ă-bil-i-tee) *n.*

sem·i·pre·cious (sem-i-presh-ŭs) *adj.* (of a gemstone) less valuable than those called precious.

sem·i·pri·vate (sem-i-prɪ-vit) *adj.* having some privacy but not fully private.

sem·i·pro (sem-i-proh) *n.* (*pl.* **-pros**) *(informal)* a semiprofessional baseball player etc.

sem·i·pro·fes·sion·al (sem-i-prŏ-fesh-ŏ-năl) *adj.* 1. engaged on a part-time basis in a sport

self'-tor'ment *n.*   **self'-trained'** *adj.*   **self'-trou'bled** *adj.*

etc. for pay. **2.** of or involving a person or work that does not have or require the skill and knowledge of a profession. **semiprofessional** *n.* **sem·i·pro·fes′sion·al·ly** *adv.*

sem·i·skilled (sem-i-skild) *adj.* having or requiring some training but less than that needed for skilled work.

sem·i·soft (sem-i-sawft) *adj.* having a consistency that is neither hard nor soft but somewhere in between.

sem·i·sweet (sem-i-sweet) *adj.* (of chocolate or cookies) slightly sweetened.

Sem·ite (sem-ıt) *n.* a member of the group of races that includes the Jews and Arabs and formerly the Phoenicians and Assyrians.

Se·mit·ic (sı-mit-ik) *adj.* of the Semites or their language. **Semitic** *n.* a family of languages including Hebrew and Arabic.

sem·i·tone (sem-i-tohn) *n.* (in music) a half step or half tone, an interval midway between two whole tones.

sem·i·trail·er (sem-i-tray-lĕr) *n.* a trailer having wheels at the back but supported by a towing vehicle in the front, used for hauling freight.

sem·i·trans·par·ent (sem-i-trans-par-ĕnt) *adj.* not quite transparent.

sem·i·vow·el (sem-i-vow-ĕl) *n.* a sound, or a letter (such as *y* and *w*) representing a sound, intermediate between a vowel and a consonant.

sem·i·week·ly (sem-i-week-lee) *adj.* occurring or published etc. twice a week.

sem·o·li·na (sem-ŏ-lee-nă) *n.* hard round grains left when wheat has been ground and sifted, used to make puddings and pasta.

sem·per fi·de·lis (sem-pĕr fi-day-lis) always faithful, the motto of the U.S. Marine Corps. ▷Latin.

Sen., sen. *abbr.* **1.** senate. **2.** senator. **3.** senior.

sen·ate (sen-it) *n.* **1.** a legislative council. **2.** *Senate,* the upper house of the legislatures of the U.S. and many of its state governments, and of Canada, France, and certain other countries. **3.** the governing body in the ancient Roman republic.

sen·a·tor (sen-ă-tŏr) *n.* a member of a senate. **sen·a·to·ri·al** (sen-ă-tohr-i-ăl) *adj.*

send (send) *v.* (**sent, send·ing**) **1.** to order or cause or enable to go to a certain destination, to have (a thing) conveyed. **2.** to send a message or letter, *she sent to say she was coming.* **3.** to cause to move or go; *sent him flying,* knocked him headlong; *sent his temperature up; the lecture sent us to sleep.* **send′er** *n.* □**send away for,** to order (goods etc.) by mail. **send for,** to order (a person) to come to one's presence; to cause (a thing) to be brought or delivered from elsewhere. **send up,** *(slang)* to sentence to prison, *he was sent up for twenty years.* (▷From *send up the river to Sing Sing,* a prison 35 miles north of New York City on the Hudson River.) **send word,** to send information.

send·off (send-awf) *n.* a friendly demonstration at a person's departure.

Sen·e·ca (sen-ĕ-kă) *n.* (*pl.* **-cas, -ca**) **1.** a member of a tribe of the Iroquois Confederacy of North American Indians. **2.** the language of this tribe.

Sen·e·gal (sen-ĕ-gawl) a country in West Africa. **Sen·e·ga·lese** (sen-ĕ-gă-leez) *adj. & n.* (*pl.* **-lese**).

se·nes·cence (si-nes-ĕns) *n.* the state or process of growing old. **se·nes′cent** *adj.*

se·nile (see-nıl) *adj.* **1.** suffering from bodily or

mental weakness because of old age. **2.** (of illness etc.) characteristic of elderly people, *senile diabetes.* **se·nil·i·ty** (si-nil-i-tee) *n.*

sen·ior (seen-yŏr) *adj.* **1.** older in age; *Tom Brown senior,* the older person of that name. **2.** higher in rank or authority. **3.** for older children, *senior school.* **senior** *n.* a senior person, a student in his last year of high school or college; *he is my senior,* is older than I am. □**senior chief petty officer,** (in the U.S. Navy) the petty officer ranking below master chief petty officer. **senior citizen,** an elderly person, one who has retired and is living on a pension. **senior high school,** one that offers only the last two or three years of ordinary high school study. **senior master sergeant,** a noncommissioned officer ranking below chief master sergeant.

sen·ior·i·ty (seen-yor-i-tee) *n.* (*pl.* **-ties**) **1.** the state of being senior. **2.** precedence by reason of length of service, as in a profession, union, etc.

sen·na (sen-ă) *n.* the dried pods or leaves of a tropical tree, used as a laxative.

se·ñor (sen-yohr) *n.* (*pl.* **se·ñors, se·ño·res,** *pr.* sen-yohr-es) the title of a Spanish-speaking man, = Mr. or sir.

se·ño·ra (sen-yohr-ă) *n.* the title of a Spanish-speaking woman, = Mrs. or madam.

se·ño·ri·ta (sen-yŏ-ree-tă) *n.* the title of a Spanish-speaking girl or unmarried woman, = Miss.

sen·sa·tion (sen-say-shŏn) *n.* **1.** an awareness or feeling produced by stimulation of a sense organ or of the mind. **2.** ability to feel such stimulation, *loss of sensation in the fingers.* **3.** a condition of eager interest or excitement or admiration aroused in a number of people, a person or thing arousing this.

sen·sa·tion·al (sen-say-shŏ-năl) *adj.* **1.** producing eager interest or excitement or admiration in many people. **2.** *(informal)* extraordinary. **sen·sa′tion·al·ly** *adv.*

sen·sa·tion·al·ism (sen-say-shŏ-nă-liz-ĕm) *n.* use of subject matter or words or style etc. (in a book, newspaper, film etc.) in order to produce excessive emotional excitement in people. **sen·sa′tion·al·ist** *n.*

sense (sens) *n.* **1.** any of the special powers by which a living thing becomes aware of things; *the five senses,* the faculties of sight, hearing, smell, taste, and touch, by which the external world is perceived. **2.** ability to perceive or feel or be conscious of a thing, awareness or recognition of something, *has no sense of shame; sense of humor,* ability to appreciate humor. **3.** the power of making a good judgment about something, practical wisdom, *had the sense to get out of the way.* **4.** the way in which a word or phrase or passage etc. is to be understood, its meaning or one of its meanings. **5.** possession of a meaning or of reasonableness. **sense** *v.* (**sensed, sens·ing**) **1.** to perceive by one of the senses. **2.** to become aware of (a thing) by getting a mental impression, *sensed that he was unwelcome.* **3.** (of a machine) to detect. □**come to one's senses,** to regain consciousness; to become sensible after behaving stupidly. **in a sense** *or* **in one sense,** if the statement is understood in a particular way, *what you say is true in a sense.* **make sense,** to have a meaning; to be sensible and practicable idea. **make sense of,** to find a meaning in.

sense·less (sens-lis) *adj.* **1.** not showing good sense, foolish. **2.** meaningless, purposeless,

senseless violence. 3. unconscious. **sense′less·
ly** *adv.* **sense′less·ness** *n.*
sense organ any of the organs (such as the eye
or ear) by which the body becomes aware of stimuli from the external world.
sen·si·bil·i·ty (sen-sĭ-bil-i-tee) *n.* (*pl.*
-ties) the
ability to feel things mentally, sensitiveness, delicacy of feeling. ▷This word does not mean "possession of good sense."
sen·si·ble (sen-sĭ-bĕl) *adj.* 1. having or showing
good sense. 2. aware, *we are sensible of the honor
you have done us.* 3. (of clothing etc.) practical
rather than fashionable, *sensible shoes.* **sen′si·
bly** *adv.* **sen′si·ble·ness** *n.*
sen·si·tive (sen-sĭ-tiv) *adj.* 1. affected by something, responsive to stimuli, *plants are sensitive
to light.* 2. receiving impressions quickly and easily, *sensitive fingers.* 3. alert and considerate about
other people's feelings. 4. easily hurt or offended.
5. (of an instrument etc.) readily responding to
or recording slight changes of condition. 6. (of
a subject) requiring tactful treatment. **sen′si·
tive·ly** *adv.* **sen′si·tive·ness** *n.* **sen·si·tiv·
i·ty** (sen-sĭ-tiv-i-tee) *n.* (*pl.* -ties) □**sensitive
plant,** a mimosa or other plant with leaves that
fold or droop when touched. **sensitivity training,** training conducted in group sessions to increase the social and occupational effectiveness
of the group members.
sen·si·tize (sen-sĭ-tīz) *v.* (**sen·si·tized, sen·
si·tiz·ing**) to make sensitive or abnormally sensitive. **sen·si·ti·za·tion** (sen-sĭ-tĭ-zay-shŏn) *n.*
sen·si·tom·e·ter (sen-sĭ-tom-ĕ-tĕr) *n.* a device for
measuring the sensitivity of photographic film.
sen·si·to·met·ric (sen-sĭ-tŏ-met-rik) *adj.*
sen·sor (sen-sŏr) *n.* a device (such as a photoelectric cell) that reacts to a certain stimulus.
sen·so·ry (sen-sŏ-ree) *adj.* of the senses, receiving
or transmitting sensations, *sensory nerves.*
sen·su·al (sen-shoo-ăl) *adj.* 1. physical, gratifying
to the body, *sensual pleasures.* 2. indulging oneself
with physical pleasures, showing that one does
this, *a sensual face.* **sen′su·al·ly** *adv.* **sen′su·
al·ness** *n.* **sen′su·al·ist** *n.* **sen·su·al·i·ty**
(sen-shoo-al-i-tee) *n.* **sen·su·al·ism** (sen-shoo-
ăl-izm) *n.*
sen·su·ous (sen-shoo-ŭs) *adj.* affecting or appealing to the senses, especially by beauty or delicacy.
sen′su·ous·ly *adv.* **sen′su·ous·ness** *n.*
▷This word does not have the implication of undesirable behavior that *sensual* can have.
sent (sent) *see* **send.**
sent. *abbr.* sentence.
sen·tence (sen-tĕns) *n.* 1. a set of words containing
a verb (either expressed or understood) that is
complete in itself as an expression of thought.
2. the punishment awarded by a law court to a
person convicted in a criminal trial, declaration
of this. **sentence** *v.* (**sen·tenced, sen·tenc·
ing**) to pass sentence upon (a person), to condemn
(to punishment).
sen·ten·tious (sen-ten-shŭs) *adj.* putting on an
air of wisdom, dull and moralizing. **sen·
ten′tious·ly** *adv.* **sen·ten′tious·ness** *n.*
sen·tient (sen-shĕnt) *adj.* capable of perceiving and
feeling things, *sentient beings.* **sen′tient·ly** *adv.*
sen·ti·ment (sen-tĭ-mĕnt) *n.* 1. a mental attitude
produced by one's feeling about something, an
opinion. 2. emotion as opposed to reason, sentimentality.
sen·ti·men·tal (sen-tĭ-men-tăl) *adj.* 1. showing or

influenced by romantic or nostalgic feeling. 2.
characterized by emotions as opposed to reason.
sen·ti·men′tal·ly *adv.* **sen·ti·men′tal·ism** *n.*
sen·ti·men′tal·ist *n.* **sen·ti·men·tal·i·ty**
(sen-tĭ-men-tal-i-tee) *n.*
sen·ti·men·tal·ize (sen-tĭ-men-tă-lız) *v.* (**sen·
ti·men·tal·ized, sen·ti·men·tal·iz·ing**) 1. to
be sentimental. 2. to have sentimental feelings toward (a person or thing). **sen·ti·men·ta·li·
za·tion** (sen-tĭ-men-tă-li-zay-shŏn) *n.*
sen·ti·nel (sen-tĭ-nĕl) *n.* a sentry.
sen·try (sen-tree) *n.* (*pl.* -tries) a soldier posted
to keep watch and guard something. □**sentry
box,** a wooden structure large enough to shelter
a standing sentry.
Seoul (sohl) the capital of South Korea.
sep. *abbr.* 1. separate. 2. separated.
se·pal (see-păl) *n.* one of the leaflike parts forming
the calyx of a flower.
sep·a·ra·ble (sep-ă-ră-bĕl) *adj.* able to be separated. **sep′a·ra·bly** *adv.*
sep·a·rate (sep-ă-rayt) *v.* (**sep·a·rat·ed, sep·
a·rat·ing**) 1. to divide, to keep apart; *separate
the cream,* extract it from the milk. 2. to be between, *the Mississippi separates Iowa from Illinois.*
3. to become separate, to go different ways, to
withdraw oneself from a union, to cease to live
together as a married couple. **separate** (sep-ă-
rit, sep-rit) *adj.* forming a unit by itself, not joined
or united with others. **sep′a·rate·ly** *adv.*
sep′a·rate·ness *n.*
sep·a·rates (sep-ă-rits, sep-rits) *n. pl.* individual
items of clothing for wearing together in various
combinations.
sep·a·ra·tion (sep-ă-ray-shŏn) 1. separating, being separated. 2. a legal arrangement by which
a married couple live apart but without ending
the marriage. □**separation center,** a place for
processing military personnel for return to civilian
life.
sep·a·ra·tist (sep-ă-ră-tist) *n.* a person who favors
separation from a larger unit, as to achieve political independence. **sep′a·ra·tism** *n.*
sep·a·ra·tive (sep-ă-ray-tiv) *adj.* 1. tending to
cause separation. 2. tending toward separation.
3. expressing separation.
sep·a·ra·tor (sep-ă-ray-tŏr) *n.* a machine that separates things (such as cream from milk).
Se·phar·dic (si-fahr-dik) **Jew** a Jew of Spanish
or Portuguese descent.
se·pi·a (see-pi-ă) *n.* 1. brown coloring matter used
in inks and watercolors. 2. dark or yellowish
brown color. **sepia** *adj.* of sepia color.
se·poy (see-poi) *n.* (*in former times*) an Indian
soldier under European, especially British, discipline.
sep·sis (sep-sis) *n.* a septic condition.
Sept. *abbr.* September.
Sep·tem·ber (sep-tem-bĕr) *n.* the ninth month of
the year.
sep·tet (sep-tet) *n.* a group of seven instruments
or voices, a musical composition for these.
sep·tic (sep-tik) *adj.* infected with harmful microorganisms that cause pus to form. □**septic
tank,** a tank into which sewage is conveyed and
in which it is disintegrated through bacterial
activity.
sep·ti·ce·mi·a (sep-ti-see-mi-ă) *n.* blood poisoning.
sep·tu·a·ge·nar·i·an (sep-choo-ă-jĕ-**nair**-i-ăn)
n. a person in his or her seventies.

Sep·tu·a·ges·i·ma (sep-too-ă-jes-ĭ-mă) *n.* the third Sunday before the beginning of Lent.

Sep·tu·a·gint (sep-too-ă-jint) *n.* the earliest Greek version of the Old Testament.

sep·tum (sep-tŭm) *n.* (*pl.* **-ta**, *pr.* **-tă**) a partition between two cavities, such as that in the nose between the nostrils.

sep·tu·ple (sep-tŭ-pĕl) *adj.* sevenfold. **septuple** *v.* (**sep·tu·pled**, **sep·tu·pling**) to make or become seven times greater.

sep·ul·cher (sep-ŭl-kĕr) *n.* a tomb.

se·pul·chral (si-pul-krăl) *adj.* 1. of a tomb, *sepulchral monument.* 2. looking or sounding dismal, funereal; *a sepulchral voice,* deep and hollow-sounding. **se·pul'chral·ly** *adv.*

sep·ul·ture (sep-ŭl-chŭr) *n.* burying, putting in the grave.

seq. *abbr.* the following (item). ▷Latin *sequens.*

seqq. *abbr.* the following (items). ▷Latin *sequentia.*

se·quel (see-kwĕl) *n.* 1. what follows or arises out of an earlier event. 2. a novel or film etc. that continues the story of an earlier one.

se·quence (see-kwĕns) *n.* 1. the following of one thing after another in an orderly or continuous way. 2. a series without gaps, a set of things that belong next to each other in a particular order; *in sequence,* in this order; *out of sequence,* not in it. 3. a section dealing with one scene or topic in a film.

se·quent (see-kwĕnt) *adj.* following as a sequence or consequence, consecutive.

se·quen·tial (si-kwen-shăl) *adj.* 1. forming a sequence, following in succession. 2. occurring as a result. **se·quen'tial·ly** *adv.* **se·quen·ti·al·i·ty** (si-kwen-shi-al-i-tee) *n.*

se·ques·ter (si-kwes-tĕr) *v.* 1. to seclude. 2. to confiscate.

se·ques·trate (si-kwes-trayt) *v.* (**se·ques·trat·ed, se·ques·trat·ing**) to sequester. **se·ques·tra·tion** (si-kwes-tray-shŏn) *n.*

se·quin (see-kwin) *n.* a circular spangle ornamenting clothing or other material. **se'quined** *adj.*

se·quoi·a (si-kwoi-ă) *n.* a coniferous tree of California, growing to a great height.

ser. *abbr.* 1. serial. 2. series.

se·ra *see* **serum.**

se·ragl·io (si-ral-yoh) *n.* (*pl.* **-ragl·ios**) the harem of a Muslim palace.

se·ra·pe (sĕ-rah-pee) *n.* a shawl or blanket worn as a cloak by Spanish Americans.

ser·aph (ser-ăf) *n.* (*pl.* **-aphs, -a·phim,** *pr.* **-ă-** fim) a member of the highest order of angels in ancient Christian belief. **se·raph·ic** (sĕ-raf-ik) *adj.* **se·raph'i·cal·ly** *adv.*

Serb (surb), **Ser·bi·an** (sur-bi-ăn) *n.* 1. a native or inhabitant of Serbia. 2. the language of Serbia.

Ser·bi·a (sur-bi-ă) the southeast portion of Yugoslavia.

Ser·bo-Cro·a·tian (sur-boh-kroh-ay-shŏn) *n.* the Slavonic language of the Serbs and Croats.

sere (seer) *adj.* withered, dried up now.

ser·e·nade (ser-ĕ-nayd) *n.* a song or tune played by a lover to his lady, or suitable for this. **serenade** *v.* (**ser·e·nad·ed, ser·e·nad·ing**) to sing or play a serenade to. **ser·e·nad'er** *n.*

ser·en·dip·i·ty (ser-ĕn-dip-ĭ-tee) *n.* the making of pleasant discoveries by accident, the knack of doing this. **ser·en·dip'i·tous** *adj.*

se·rene (sĕ-reen) *adj.* 1. calm and cheerful. 2. the title used in speaking of or to members of certain European royal families, *His* or *Her* or *Your* Se-

rene Highness. **se·rene'ly** *adv.* **se·rene'ness** *n.* **se·ren·i·ty** (sĕ-ren-i-tee) *n.*

serf (surf) *n.* 1. a farm laborer who was forced to work for his landowner in the Middle Ages. 2. an oppressed laborer. **serf'dom** *n.*

Serg., Sergt. *abbr.* Sergeant.

serge (surj) *n.* a strong twilled worsted fabric used for making clothes.

ser·geant (sahr-jănt) *n.* 1. a noncommissioned army officer ranking above corporal. 2. a police officer ranking below captain or lieutenant. □**sergeant at arms,** an officer of a group or organization in charge of preserving the rules and regulations and in maintaining order. **sergeant first class,** a noncommissioned officer above a staff sergeant. **sergeant major,** the highest noncommissioned rank in the U.S. Army and Marine Corps.

se·ri·al (seer-i-ăl) *n.* a story presented in a series of installments. **serial** *adj.* of or forming a series. **se'ri·al·ly** *adv.* **se'ri·al·ist** *n.* □**serial number,** a number that identifies one item in a series of things.

se·ri·al·ize (seer-i-ă-lız) *v.* (**se·ri·al·ized, se·ri·al·iz·ing**) to present as a serial. **se·ri·al·i·za·tion** (seer-i-ă-li-zay-shŏn) *n.*

se·ri·a·tim (seer-i-ay-tim) *adv.* point by point, taking one subject etc. after another in an orderly sequence.

se·ries (seer-eez) *n.* (*pl.* **-ries**) 1. a number of things of the same kind, or related to each other in a similar way, occurring or arranged or produced in order. 2. a set of stamps or coins etc. issued at one time or in one country.

ser·if (ser-if) *n.* a small line finishing off the strokes of a letter, as in T.

ser·i·graph (ser-ĭ-graf) *n.* a print made by means of a silk screen. **se·rig·ra·pher** (si-rig-ră-fĕr) *n.* **se·rig'ra·phy** *n.*

se·ri·o·com·ic (seer-i-oh-kom-ik) *adj.* partly serious and partly comic.

se·ri·ous (seer-i-ŭs) *adj.* 1. solemn and thoughtful, not smiling. 2. sincere, in earnest, not casual or lighthearted, *made a serious attempt.* 3. important, *this is a serious decision.* 4. causing great concern, not slight, *serious illness.* **se'ri·ous·ly** *adv.* **se'ri·ous·ness** *n.*

ser·mon (sur-mŏn) *n.* 1. a talk on a religious or moral subject, especially one delivered by a clergyman during a religious service. 2. a long moralizing talk.

ser·mon·ize (sur-mŏ-nız) *v.* (**ser·mon·ized, ser·mon·iz·ing**) to give a long moralizing talk.

se·rol·o·gy (si-rol-ŏ-jee) *n.* the scientific study of sera and their effects. **se·ro·log·ic** (seer-ŏ-loj-ik) *adj.* **se·ro·log'i·cal** *adj.*

se·rous (seer-ŭs) *adj.* of or resembling serum.

ser·pent (sur-pĕnt) *n.* a snake, especially a large one.

ser·pen·tine (sur-pĕn-teen) *adj.* twisting and curving like a snake, *a serpentine road.* **serpentine** *n.* a soft mineral rock usually dark green, used as decorative material.

ser·rate (ser-it, -ayt), **ser·rat·ed** (ser-ay-tid, si-ray-) *adj.* having a series of small projections like the teeth of a saw. **ser·ra·tion** (si-ray-shŏn) *n.*

ser·ried (ser-eed) *adj.* (of rows of people or things) arranged in a close series.

se·rum (seer-ŭm) *n.* (*pl.* **se·ra,** *pr.* seer-ă, **se·rums**) 1. the thin yellowish fluid that remains from blood when the rest has clotted. 2. this taken from an immunized animal and used for inoculations. 3. any watery fluid from animal tissue (as in a blister).

serv. *abbr.* service.

ser·val (sur-văl) *n.* a tawny black-spotted long-legged African tiger cat.

serv·ant (sur-vănt) *n.* 1. a person employed to do domestic work in a household or as a personal attendant. 2. an employee considered as performing services for his employer, *a faithful servant of the company.*

serve (surv) *v.* (**served, serv·ing**) 1. to perform services for (a person or community etc.), to work for, *served his country; served the national interest,* helped it. 2. to be employed or performing a spell of duty, to be a member of the armed forces, *served in the Navy.* 3. to be suitable for, to do what is required, *it will serve our purpose; it will serve.* 4. to provide a facility for, *the area is served by a number of buses.* 5. to spend time in, to undergo, *served his apprenticeship; served a prison sentence.* 6. (of a male animal) to copulate with. 7. to set out or present (food etc.) for others to consume, to attend to (customers in a shop). 8. (of a quantity of food) to be enough for, *this recipe serves six persons.* 9. to set the ball in play at tennis etc. 10. to assist in a religious service. 11. to deliver (a legal writ etc.) to the person named, *served him with the writ* or *served the writ on him.* 12. to treat in a certain way, *she was most unjustly served.* **serve** *n.* a service in tennis etc., a person's turn for this, the ball served. **serv′er** *n.* □*it* **serves him right,** an expression of satisfaction at seeing a person get something unpleasant that he deserved. **serve up,** to offer for acceptance, *served up the same old entertainments again.*

serv·ice (sur-vis) *n.* 1. *(old use)* being a servant, a servant's status, *be in service.* 2. the occupation or process of working for an employer or of assisting another person or persons. 3. an agency of a government, *the Foreign Service; state employment service.* 4. a system or arrangement that performs work for customers or supplies public needs, *laundry services are available; the bus service; essential services,* public supply of water, electricity, etc. 5. a branch of the armed forces; *the services,* the navy, army, marines, and air force. 6. use, assistance, a helpful or beneficial act, *did me a service; be of service,* to be useful, to help. 7. a meeting of a congregation for worship of God, a religious ceremony. 8. the serving of a legal writ. 9. the serving of food or goods, provision of help for customers or clients, *quick service.* 10. a set of dishes, plates, etc. for serving a meal, *a dinner service.* 11. the act or manner or turn of serving in tennis etc., the game in which one serves, *lost his service.* 12. maintenance and repair of a car or of machinery or appliances at intervals. 13. the serving of a mare etc. by a male animal. **service** *v.* (**serv·iced, serv·ic·ing**) 1. to maintain or repair (a piece of machinery etc.). 2. to supply with service(s). 3. to pay the interest on, *the amount needed to service this loan.* 4. to serve (definition 6). □**at the service of,** ready to obey orders or be used. **be of service,** to be useful or helpful. **service area,** an area beside a freeway or expressway where gasoline and refreshments etc. are available. **service charge,** an additional charge for service. **service module,** that part of a spacecraft containing the main engine and power supplies. **service station,** a place where

gasoline and automobile repair etc. are available. **service stripe,** a military stripe indicating time on active duty, worn on an enlisted man's sleeve.

serv·ice·a·ble (sur-vi-să-běl) *adj.* 1. usable. 2. suitable for ordinary use or wear, hard-wearing. **serv′ice·a·bly** *adv.* **serv′ice·a·ble·ness** *n.* **serv·ice·a·bil·i·ty** (sur-vi-să-bil-i-tee) *n.*

serv·ice·man (sur-vis-man) *n.* (*pl.* -**men,** *pr.* -men) 1. a man who is a member of the armed services. 2. a man whose job is to repair or maintain equipment.

serv·ice·wom·an (sur-vis-wuum-ăn) *n.* (*pl.* -**wom·en,** *pr.* -wim-in) a woman who is a member of the armed services.

ser·vile (sur-vɪl) *adj.* 1. suitable for a servant, menial, *servile tasks.* 2. excessively submissive, lacking independence, *servile flattery* or *imitation.* **ser′vile·ly** *adv.* **ser·vil·i·ty** (sur-vil-i-tee) *n.*

ser·ving (sur-ving) *n.* a helping.

ser·vi·tor (sur-vi-tŏr) *n.* an attendant, a servant.

ser·vi·tude (sur-vi-tood) *n.* the condition of being forced to work for others and having no freedom.

ser·vo (sur-voh) *n.* (*pl.* -**vos**) *(informal)* a servomechanism.

ser·vo·mech·an·ism (sur-voh-mek-ă-niz-ĕm) *n.* a controlling mechanism that is activated electronically by a radio etc. signal.

ser·vo·mo·tor (sur-voh-moh-tŏr) *n.* the motor part of a servomechanism.

ses·a·me (ses-ă-mee) *n.* 1. a plant of tropical Asia with seeds (**sesame seeds**) that are used as food or as a source of oil. 2. its seeds. □**open sesame,** a special way of obtaining access to something that is usually inaccessible. ▷These words were used, in one of the Arabian Nights stories, to cause a door to open.

ses·qui·cen·ten·ni·al (ses-kwi-sen-ten-i-ăl) *adj.* of the one hundred and fiftieth anniversary.

ses·qui·pe·da·li·an (ses-kwi-pi-day-li-ăn) *adj.* 1. having many syllables. 2. tending to use long words.

ses·sile (ses-il) *adj.* 1. (of a flower, leaf, etc.) attached directly by the base without the stalk or peduncle. 2. fixed in one position, immobile.

ses·sion (sesh-ŏn) *n.* 1. a meeting or series of meetings for discussing or deciding something. 2. a period spent continuously in an activity, *an all-night session of poker.* 3. the academic year or term in certain universities. 4. the governing body of a Presbyterian church.

set (set) *v.* (**set, set·ting**) 1. to put or place, to cause to stand in position. 2. to put in contact with; *set fire to,* to cause to burn. 3. to fix in position, to adjust the hands of (a clock) or the mechanism of (a trap etc.); *set the table,* lay it for a meal. 4. to represent as happening in a certain place, or at a certain time, *the story is set in Egypt in 2000 B.C.* 5. to provide a tune for, *set it to music.* 6. to make or become hard or firm or established; *they are set against change,* have this as a permanent attitude. 7. (of fabric etc.) to fall or hang in a certain way, *the collar sets well.* 8. to fix or decide or appoint, *set a date for the wedding.* 9. to arrange and protect (a broken bone) so that it will heal. 10. to fix (hair) while it is damp so that it will dry in the desired style. 11. to place (a jewel) in a surrounding framework, to decorate with jewels, *the bracelet is set with emeralds.* 12. to establish, *set a new record for the high jump.* 13. to offer or assign as something to be done, *set them a task.* 14. to put into a specified state, *set them free; set it swinging.* 15. to have a certain movement, *the current sets strongly eastward.* 16. to be brought toward or below the horizon by Earth's movement, *the sun sets.* 17. (in certain dances) to face another dancer and make certain steps, *set to your partners.* 18. (in bridge) to defeat an opposing partnership's contract. 19. to arrange or compose type. **set** *n.* 1. a number of people or things that are grouped together as similar or forming a unit. 2. a group of games forming a unit or part of a match in tennis etc. 3. (in mathematics) a collection of things having a common property. 4. a radio or television receiver. 5. the way something sets or is set or placed or arranged, *the set of his shoulders.* 6. the process or style of setting hair. 7. the scenery in use for a play or film, the stage etc. where this is being performed, *be on the set by 7 a.m.* **set** *adj.* 1. fixed, predetermined, *a set time; set menu.* 2. firm, hard, established, *he was set in his opinions.* 3. ready, prepared, *are you set for the trip?* □**be set on,** to be determined about. **set about,** to begin (a task). **set apart,** to save for a special purpose; to distinguish from others in a group, *his sense of humor set him apart.* **set aside,** to save or reserve (a thing). **set back,** to halt or slow the progress of, to cause a change for the worse; *(slang)* to cost, *it set me back $50.* **set eyes on,** to catch sight of. **set forth,** to set out. **set in,** to become established, *depression had set in.* **set off,** to begin a journey; to cause to begin, *set off a chain reaction;* to ignite or cause to explode; to improve the appearance of (a thing) by providing a contrast. **set one's hand to,** to begin (a task); to sign (a document). **set one's teeth,** to clench them. **set out,** to declare or make known, *set out the terms of the agreement;* to begin a journey; **set out to do something,** make a start with a particular intention. **set sail,** to hoist sail(s); to begin a voyage. **set theory,** the study of sets in mathematics, without regard to the nature of their individual constituents. **set to,** to begin doing something vigorously; to begin fighting or arguing. **set up,** to place in view; to arrange; to begin or create (a business etc.); to establish in some capacity; to begin making (a sound); to cause; *set up housekeeping,* to establish a household. **set upon,** to attack. ▷Do not confuse *set* with *sit.* It is incorrect to write *that idea sets well with me* or *I set in my chair all evening.* Write *idea sits well* and *sat in my chair.*

set·back (set-bak) *n.* 1. something that sets back progress. 2. (in architecture) the placement of an upper story of a building back from the edge of the lower part, such a story.

set·tee (se-tee) *n.* a long seat with a back and usually with arms, for two or more people.

set·ter (set-ĕr) *n.* 1. a person or thing that sets something, *typesetter.* 2. a dog of a long-haired breed that is trained to stand rigid when it scents game.

set·ting (set-ing) *n.* 1. the way or place in which something is set. 2. music for the words of a song etc. 3. a set of dishes or silverware for one person.

set·tle[1] (set-ĕl) *n.* a wooden seat for two or more people, with a high back and arms.

settle[2] *v.* (**set·tled, set·tling**) 1. to place (a thing etc.) so that it stays in position. 2. to establish or become established more or less permanently. 3. to make one's home, to occupy as settlers,

settled in Canada; *colonists settled the coast.* 4. to sink or come to rest, to cause to do this, to become compact in this way, *dust settled on the shelves.* 5. to arrange as desired, to end or arrange conclusively, to deal with, *settled the dispute.* 6. to make or become calm or orderly, to stop being restless. 7. to pay (a debt or bill or claim etc.). 8. to bestow legally, *settled all his property on his wife.* □**settle down,** to become settled after wandering or movement or restlessness or disturbance etc. **settle up,** to pay what is owing.

set·tle·ment (set-ĕl-mĕnt) *n.* 1. settling, being settled. 2. a legal or financial arrangement. 3. an amount or property settled legally on a person. 4. a place occupied by settlers or colonists etc.

set·tler (set-lĕr) *n.* a person who goes to live permanently in a previously unoccupied land.

set-to (set-too) *n.* (*pl.* **-tos**) *(informal)* a fight or argument.

set-up (set-up) *n.* 1. *(informal)* the structure of an organization. 2. *(slang)* a situation contrived to cheat a person or fix blame on him. 3. *(informal)* the things needed (other than whiskey) for serving alcoholic drinks.

sev·en (sev-ĕn) *adj. & n.* one more than six (7, VII). □**the seven seas,** the waters of the world that can be navigated by ships.

sev·en·fold (sev-ĕn-fohld) *adj. & adv.* seven times as much or as many.

sev·en·teen (sev-ĕn-teen) *adj. & n.* one more than sixteen (17, XVII). **sev′en·teenth′** *adj. & n.*

seventeen-year locust a cicada of the eastern U.S. that emerges in its adult form from the soil approximately every seventeen years.

sev·enth (sev-ĕnth) *adj. & n.* 1. next after sixth. 2. one of seven equal parts of a thing. **sev′enth·ly** *adv.* □**seventh heaven,** a state of intense delight.

sev·en·ties (sev-ĕn-teez) *n. pl.* the numbers or years or degrees of temperatures from seventy to seventy-nine.

sev·en·ty (sev-ĕn-tee) *adj. & n.* (*pl.* **-ties**) seven times ten (70, LXX). **sev·en·ti·eth** (sev-ĕn-ti-ith) *adj. & n.*

sev·en·ty-eight (sev-ĕn-ti-ayt) *n. (informal)* a phonograph record designed to be played at a speed of 78 revolutions per minute.

sev·er (sev-ĕr) *v.* to cut or break off from a whole, to separate; *sever a contract,* to end it.

sev·er·al (sev-ĕ-răl) *adj.* 1. a few, more than two but not many. 2. separate, individual, *we all went our several ways.* **several** *pronoun* several people or things.

sev·er·al·ly (sev-ĕ-ră-lee) *adv.* separately.

sev·er·ance (sev-ĕ-răns) *n.* severing, being severed. □**severance pay,** an amount of money paid to an employee on termination of his contract.

se·vere (sĕ-veer) *adj.* (**-ver·er, -ver·est**) 1. strict, without sympathy, imposing harsh rules on others. 2. intense, forceful, *severe gales.* 3. making great demands on endurance or energy or ability etc., *the pace was severe.* 4. plain and without decoration, *a severe style of dress.* **se·vere′ly** *adv.* **se·vere′ness** *n.* **se·ver·i·ty** (sĕ-ver-i-tee) *n.*

Se·ville (sĕ-vil) *n.* (also **Seville orange**) a bitter orange used for making marmalade. ▷Named after Seville in Spain.

Sè·vres (sev-rĕ) *n.* fine porcelain made at Sèvres in France.

sew (soh) *v.* (**sewed, sewn** or **sewed, sew·**

ing) 1. to fasten by passing thread again and again through material, using a threaded needle or an awl etc. or a sewing machine. 2. to make or attach or fasten by sewing. 3. to work with needle and thread or with a sewing machine. □**sewing ma-chine,** a machine for sewing or stitching things.
sew·age (soo-ij) *n.* liquid waste matter drained away from houses, towns, factories, etc. for disposal.
sew·er[1] (soh-ĕr) *n.* a person or thing that sews.
sew·er[2] (soo-ĕr) *n.* a drain for carrying away sewage.
sew·er·age (soo-ĕ-rij) *n.* a system of sewers, drainage by this.
sew·ing (soh-ing) *n.* 1. the work or activity of one who sews. 2. work in the process of being sewn.
sewn (sohn) *see* **sew.** □**have a thing sewn up,** *(informal)* to have it all arranged or won.
sex (seks) *n.* 1. either of the two main groups (*male* and *female*) into which living things are placed according to their reproductive functions, the fact of belonging to one of these. 2. sexual feelings or impulses, attraction between members of the two sexes. 3. *(informal)* sexual intercourse, *have sex with someone.* **sex** *v.* to judge the sex of, *to sex chickens.* □**sex act,** sexual intercourse. **sex appeal,** sexual attractiveness. **sex change,** a change of sex, usually by surgical means. **sex chromosome,** a chromosome concerned in determining the sex of an organism.
sex·a·ge·nar·i·an (sek-să-jĕ-nair-i-ăn) *n.* a person in his or her sixties.
Sex·a·ges·i·ma (sek-să-jes-i-mă) *n.* the second Sunday before Lent.
sexed (sekst) *adj.* having sexual characteristics or impulses, *highly sexed.*
sex·ist (sek-sist) *adj.* 1. discriminating in favor of members of one sex. 2. assuming that a person's abilities and social functions are determined by his or her sex. **sexist** *n.* a person who does this. **sex′ism** *n.*
sex·less (seks-lis) *adj.* 1. lacking sex, neuter. 2. not involving sexual feelings. **sex′less·ly** *adv.* **sex′less·ness** *n.*
sex·ol·o·gist (sek-sol-ŏ-jist) *n.* an expert in sexology.
sex·ol·o·gy (sek-sol-ŏ-jee) *n.* the study of human sexual relationships. **sex·o·log·i·cal** (sek-sŏ-loj-i-kăl) *adj.*
sex·pot (seks-pot) *n. (slang)* a sexy person.
sex-starved (seks-stahrvd) *adj. (informal)* lacking sexual gratification.
sex·tant (seks-tănt) *n.* an instrument used in navigating and surveying, for finding one's position by measuring the altitude of the sun etc.
sex·tet, sex·tette (seks-tet) *n.* a group of six instruments or voices, a musical composition for these.
sex·tile (seks-til) *adj.* (of stars) in the position of being 60° distant from each other.
sex·ton (seks-tŏn) *n.* an official whose job is to take care of a church and church property.
sex·tu·ple (seks-too-pĕl) *adj.* sixfold.
sex·tu·plet (seks-tup-lit) *n.* one of six children born at one birth.
sex·u·al (sek-shoo-ăl) *adj.* 1. of sex or the sexes or the relationship or feelings etc. between them. 2. (of reproduction) occurring by fusion of male and female cells. **sex′u·al·ly** *adv.* □**sexual intercourse,** copulation.
sex·u·al·i·ty (sek-shoo-al-i-tee) *n.* 1. the fact of

belonging to one of the sexes. 2. sexual characteristics or impulses.
sex·y (sek-see) *adj.* (**sex·i·er, sex·i·est**) sexually attractive or stimulating. **sex′i·ly** *adv.* **sex′i·ness** *n.*
Sey·chelles (say-shelz) a country on a group of islands in the Indian Ocean.
SF *abbr.* 1. (in baseball) sacrifice fly. 2. science fiction.
SFC *abbr.* sergeant first class.
SG *abbr.* 1. senior grade. 2. sergeant. 3. solicitor general. 4. surgeon general.
Sgt. *abbr.* sergeant.
Sgt. Maj. *abbr.* sergeant major.
sh (sh) *interj.* hush.
sh. *abbr.* share.
shab·by (shab-ee) *adj.* (**-bi·er, -bi·est**) 1. worn and threadbare, not kept in good condition, (of a person) poorly dressed. 2. unfair, dishonorable, *a shabby trick.* **shab′bi·ly** *adv.* **shab′bi·ness** *n.*
shack (shak) *n.* a roughly built hut or shed.
shack·le (shak-ĕl) *n.* one of a pair of iron rings joined by a chain, for fastening a prisoner's wrists or ankles. **shackle** *v.* (**shack·led, shack·ling**) 1. to put shackles on. 2. to impede or restrict, *shackled by tradition.*
shad (shad) *n.* (*pl.* **shad, shads**) a deep-bodied fish that goes upriver to spawn, used as food. □**shad roe,** the eggs of the female shad, used as food.
shade (shayd) *n.* 1. comparative darkness or coolness found where something blocks rays of light or heat. 2. shelter from the sun's light and heat, a place sheltered from these. 3. the darker part of a picture. 4. a color, a degree or depth of color, *in shades of blue.* 5. a differing variety, *all shades of opinion.* 6. a small amount, *she's a shade better today.* 7. a ghost. 8. a screen used to block or moderate light or heat, a translucent cover for making a lamp less glaringly bright or for directing its beam, *an eye shield.* 9. a window blind. **shade** *v.* (**shad·ed, shad·ing**) 1. to block the rays of. 2. to give shade to, to make dark. 3. to darken (parts of a drawing etc.) so as to give effects of light and shade or gradations of color. 4. to pass gradually into another color or variety, *the blue here shades into green; where socialism shaded into communism.* □**put in the shade,** to cause to appear inferior by contrast, to outshine.
shades (shaydz) *n. pl.* 1. the darkness of night or evening. 2. *(slang)* sunglasses. 3. reminders of some person or time or thing, *shades of the 1930s.*
shad·ing (shay-ding) *n.* (in art) gradation of color produced by darkening parts of a drawing, especially with parallel pencil lines.
shad·ow (shad-oh) *n.* 1. shade. 2. a patch of this with the shape of the body that is blocking the rays. 3. a person's inseparable attendant or companion. 4. a slight trace, *no shadow of doubt.* 5. a shaded part of a picture. 6. gloom, *the news cast a shadow over the proceedings.* 7. something weak or unsubstantial, a ghost, *worn to a shadow.* **shadow** *v.* 1. to cast shadow over. 2. to follow and watch secretly. **shad′ow·er** *n.* **shad′ow·y** *adj.* **shad′ow·i·ness** *n.* □**Shadow Cabinet,** *(British)* members of an opposition party who act as spokesmen on matters for which Cabinet ministers hold responsibility.
shad·ow·box·ing (shad-oh-bok-sing) *n.* boxing

against an imaginary opponent as a form of training.

shad·y (shay-dee) *adj.* **(shad·i·er, shad·i·est)** 1. giving shade. 2. situated in the shade, *a shady corner.* 3. disreputable, not completely honest, *shady dealings.* **shad'i·ly** *adv.* **shad'i·ness** *n.*

shaft (shaft) *n.* 1. a spear or arrow or similar device, its long slender stem. 2. a remark aimed or striking like an arrow, *shafts of wit.* 3. a ray (of light), a bolt (of lightning). 4. any long narrow straight part of something, as of a supporting column or a golf club. 5. a large axle. 6. one of a pair of long bars between which a horse is harnessed to draw a vehicle. 7. a vertical or sloping passage giving access to a mine, or containing an elevator, or giving an outlet for air or smoke etc. 8. *(slang)* inconsiderate or unjust treatment, *gave him the shaft.* **shaft** *v.* 1. to propel with a pole. 2. *(slang)* to treat inconsiderately or unjustly.

shag (shag) *n.* 1. a rough mass of hair or fiber. 2. a long-napped rough cloth. 3. a strong coarse kind of cut tobacco.

shag·gy (shag-ee) *adj.* **(-gi·er, -gi·est)** 1. having long rough hair or fiber. 2. rough and thick and untidy, *shaggy hair.* **shag'gi·ly** *adv.* **shag'gi·ness** *n.* ☐**shaggy dog story,** a lengthy anecdote with a peculiar twist of humor at the end.

Shah (shah) *n.* the title of the former king of Iran.

shake (shayk) *v.* **(shook, shak·en, shak·ing)** 1. to move quickly and often jerkily up and down or back and forth. 2. to dislodge by doing this, *shook snow off his hat.* 3. to make uneasy, to shock or disturb, to upset the calmness of. 4. to make less firm. 5. (of a voice) to tremble, to become weak or faltering. 6. to shake hands, *let's shake on it.* **shake** *n.* 1. shaking, being shaken. 2. a shaking movement. 3. a jolt or shock. 4. a milk shake. 5. a moment, *be there in two shakes.* **shak'able** *adj.* ☐**no great shakes,** *(slang)* not very good. **shake down,** to become harmoniously adjusted to new conditions etc.; *(slang)* to extort money from. **shake hands,** to clasp right hands in greeting or parting or agreement. **shake in one's shoes,** to tremble with fear. **shake off,** to get rid of, as dust etc., illness, a bad habit, an undesirable companion. **shake one's fist,** to make this threatening gesture at a person. **shake one's head,** to turn it from side to side in refusal or denial or disapproval. **shake up,** to mix by shaking; to restore to shape by shaking; to rouse from a stagnant or lethargic or convention-ridden state. **the shakes,** a fit of trembling or shivering. **two shakes of a lamb's tail,** a very short time.

shake·down (shayk-down) *(slang) n.* 1. a thorough search. 2. an extortion scheme. **shakedown** *adj.* as or for a period of adjustment etc., *the ship's shakedown cruise.*

shak·er (shay-kĕr) *n.* 1. a person or thing that shakes something. 2. a container in which ingredients for cocktails etc. are mixed by being shaken. 3. *Shaker,* a member of an American religious sect with a simple life in celibate mixed communities.

Shake·spear·e·an (shayk-speer-i-an) *adj.* of Shakespeare.

shake·up (shayk-up) *n.* an upheaval, a reorganization.

shak·o (shak-oh, shay-koh) *n.* (*pl.* **-os, -oes**) a form of military hat, more or less cylindrical with a peak and an upright plume or tuft.

shak·y (shay-kee) *adj.* **(shak·i·er, shak·i·est)** 1. shaking, unsteady, trembling. 2. unreliable, wavering. **shak'i·ly** *adv.* **shak'i·ness** *n.*

shale (shayl) *n.* stone that splits easily into fine pieces, rather like slate. ☐**shale oil,** oil obtained from bituminous shale.

shall (shal) *auxiliary verb* (**shalt** is used with *thou*) 1. used with *I* and *we* to express the future tense in statements and questions (but *will* is used with other words, *I shall arrive tomorrow* (but *they will arrive); shall I open the window?* 2. used with words other than *I* and *we* in promises or statements of intention or obligation, *you shall have it* (but *I will have it =* I intend to have it); *thou shalt not kill.* 3. sometimes *shall* is used in questions with words other than *I* and *we* because *will* would look like a request, as in *shall you take the children?* (See **tense**[1].)

shal·lop (shal-ŏp) *n.* a light open boat for shallow water.

shal·lot (shă-lot, shal-ŏt) *n.* an onionlike plant that forms clusters of bulbs as it grows.

shal·low (shal-oh) *adj.* 1. not deep, *a shallow stream.* 2. not thinking or thought out deeply, not capable of deep feelings, *a shallow person or book.* **shallow** *n.* (often *shallows*) a shallow place. **shal'low·ly** *adv.* **shal'low·ness** *n.*

sha·lom (shă-lohm) *n.* a salutation at meeting or parting, used among Jews. ▷Hebrew, = peace.

shalt (shalt) *see* **shall.**

sham (sham) *n.* 1. a pretense, a thing or feeling that is not genuine. 2. a person who shams. **sham** *adj.* pretended, not genuine. **sham** *v.* (**shammed, sham·ming**) to pretend or pretend to be, *to sham illness.* **sham'mer** *n.*

sha·man (shah-măn, shay-) *n.* a priest or witch doctor among certain peoples, claiming to have sole contact with the gods etc.

sha·man·ism (shah-mă-niz-ĕm, shay-) *n.* a primitive Asiatic religion believing in the power of the shaman.

sham·ble (sham-bĕl) *v.* (**sham·bled, sham·bling**) to walk or run in an awkward or lazy way. **shamble** *n.* a shambling movement.

sham·bles (sham-bĕlz) *n.* a scene or condition of great bloodshed or disorder.

shame (shaym) *n.* 1. a painful mental feeling aroused by a sense of having done something wrong or dishonorable or improper or ridiculous. 2. ability to feel this, *he has no shame.* 3. a person or thing that causes shame. 4. something regrettable, a pity, *it's a shame you can't come.* **shame** *v.* (**shamed, sham·ing**) to bring shame on, to make ashamed, to compel by arousing feelings of shame, *was shamed into contributing more.*

shame·faced (shaym-fayst) *adj.* 1. looking ashamed. 2. bashful, shy. **shame·fac·ed·ly** (shaym-fay-sid-lee) *adv.* **shame'fac'ed·ness** *n.*

shame·ful (shaym-fŭl) *adj.* causing shame, disgraceful. **shame'ful·ly** *adv.* **shame'ful·ness** *n.*

shame·less (shaym-lis) *adj.* having or showing no feeling of shame, impudent. **shame'less·ly** *adv.* **shame'less·ness** *n.*

sham·my (sham-ee) *n.* (*pl.* **-mies**) chamois leather.

sham·poo (sham-poo) *n.* 1. a liquid used to lather and wash the hair; *dry shampoo,* a powder brushed into hair to clean without wetting it. 2. a liquid or chemical for cleaning the surface of a carpet or upholstery, or for washing a car. 3. shampooing, *had a shampoo and set.* **shampoo** *v.* (**sham·pooed, sham·poo·ing**) to wash or clean with a shampoo. **sham·poo'er** *n.*

sham·rock (sham-rok) *n.* a cloverlike plant with three leaves on each stem, the national emblem of Ireland.

sha·mus (shah-mŭs, shay-) *n.* (*pl.* -mus·es) (*slang*) a police detective or private detective.

shang·hai (shang-hɪ, shang-hɪ) *v.* (**shang-haied, shang·hai·ing**) to take (a person) by force or trickery and compel him to do something.

Shan-gri-la (shang-gri-lah) *n.* an imaginary paradise on Earth. ▷ From the name of a hidden valley in James Hilton's novel *Lost Horizon.*

shank (shangk) *n.* 1. the leg, *long shanks.* 2. the leg from knee to ankle, the corresponding part of an animal's leg (especially as a cut of meat). 3. a long narrow part of something, a shaft. □**shanks' mare,** one's own legs used for walking; *ride shanks' mare,* to walk.

shan't (shant) = shall not.

shan·tung (shan-tung) *n.* a kind of soft Chinese silk, fabric resembling this.

shan·ty¹ (shan-tee) *n.* (*pl.* -ties) a shack.

shanty² *n.* (*pl.* -ties) = **chantey.**

shan·ty·town (shan-tee-town) *n.* a town consisting of shanties.

shape (shayp) *n.* 1. an area or form with a definite outline, the appearance produced by this. 2. the form or condition in which something appears, *a monster in human shape.* 3. the proper form or condition of something, *get it into shape.* 4. a pattern or mold. **shape** *v.* (**shaped, shap·ing**) 1. to give a certain shape to. 2. to develop into a certain shape or condition; *it is shaping up well,* looks promising. 3. to adapt or modify (one's plans or ideas etc.). **shap'er** *n.* □**shape up,** (*informal*) to get into better physical condition; to improve in performance of a job etc. **take shape,** to take a specified form.

SHAPE (shayp) *n. S*upreme *H*eadquarters *A*llied *P*owers, *E*urope.

shape·less (shayp-lis) *adj.* 1. having no definite shape. 2. not shapely. **shape'less·ly** *adv.* **shape'less·ness** *n.*

shape·ly (shayp-lee) *adj.* (-li·er, -li·est) having a pleasing shape, well formed or proportioned. **shape'li·ness** *n.*

shard (shahrd) *n.* 1. a potsherd. 2. the wing case of a beetle.

share¹ (shair) *n.* 1. a part given to an individual out of a larger amount that is being divided or of a burden or achievement, the part one is entitled to have or do. 2. one of the equal parts forming a business company's capital and entitling the holder to a proportion of the profits. **share** *v.* (**shared, shar·ing**) 1. to give portions of (a thing) to two or more people, *share equally.* 2. to give away part of, *would share his last crust.* 3. to have a share of, to use or possess or benefit from (a thing) jointly with others, *share a room; we share the credit.* **shar'er** *n.*

share² *n.* a plowshare.

share·crop·per (shair-krop-ĕr) *n.* a tenant farmer who pays part of his crop as rent to the owner. **share'crop·ping** *n.*

share·hold·er (shair-hohl-dĕr) *n.* a person who owns a share in a business company.

shark (shahrk) *n.* 1. a seafish with a triangular fin on its back, some kinds of which are large and dangerous to people. 2. a person who ruthlessly extorts money from another or others, a swindler.

shark·skin (shahrk-skin) *n.* a dull-surfaced smooth usually heavy fabric.

sharp (shahrp) *adj.* 1. having a fine edge or point that is capable of cutting or piercing, not blunt. 2. narrowing to a point or edge, *a sharp ridge.* 3. steep, angular, not gradual, *a sharp slope; a sharp turn.* 4. well-defined, distinct, *in sharp focus.* 5. intense, forceful, loud and shrill, (of temper) irritable; *she has a sharp tongue,* often speaks harshly and angrily. 6. (of tastes and smells) producing a smarting sensation. 7. quick to see or hear or notice things, intelligent. 8. quick to seize an advantage; *be too sharp for someone,* to outwit him. 9. unscrupulous. 10. vigorous, brisk, *a sharp walk.* 11. (of clothes) flashy. 12. (in music) above the correct pitch; *C sharp, F sharp,* etc., a semitone higher than the corresponding note or key of natural pitch. **sharp** *adv.* 1. punctually, *at six o'clock sharp.* 2. suddenly, *stopped sharp.* 3. at a sharp angle, *turn sharp right at the junction.* 4. above the correct pitch in music, *was singing sharp.* **sharp** *n.* 1. (in music) a note that is a semitone higher than the corresponding one of natural pitch, the sign ♯ indicating this. 2. (*informal*) a swindler. **sharp'ly** *adv.* **sharp'ness** *n.* □**sharp practice,** business dealings that are dishonest or barely honest.

sharp·en (shahr-pĕn) *v.* to make or become sharp. **sharp'en·er** *n.*

sharp·er (shahr-pĕr) *n.* a swindler, especially at cards.

sharp-eyed (shahrp-ɪd) *adj.* quick at noticing things.

sharp·ie (shahr-pee) *n.* (*slang*) 1. a clever alert person. 2. a sharper. 3. a man who dresses in flashy clothes.

sharp·shoot·er (shahrp-shoo-tĕr) *n.* a skilled marksman. **sharp'shoot·ing** *n.*

shat·ter (shat-ĕr) *v.* 1. to break or become broken violently into small pieces. 2. to destroy utterly, *shattered our hopes.* 3. to disturb or upset the calmness of, *we were shattered by the news.* **shat'ter·ing·ly** *adv.* **shat·ter·proof** (shat-ĕr-proof) *adj.*

shave (shayv) *v.* (**shaved, shaved** or **shav·en, shav·ing**) 1. to scrape (growing hair) off the skin with a razor, to remove hair from the chin etc. 2. to cut or scrape thin slices from the surface of (wood etc.). 3. to graze gently in passing. 4. to reduce or remove, *shave production costs; shave ten percent off our estimates.* **shave** *n.* the shaving of hair from the face, *needs a shave.* **shav'a·ble** *adj.* □**close shave,** see **close¹.** **shaving brush,** a brush for lathering the chin etc. before shaving. **shaving cream,** cream for applying to the chin etc. to assist shaving.

shav·er (shay-vĕr) *n.* 1. a person or thing that shaves. 2. an electric razor. 3. (*informal*) a youngster.

shave·tail (shayv-tayl) *n.* (*slang*) 1. a newly commissioned officer, a second lieutenant. 2. a newly broken-in mule.

shav·ings (shay-vingz) *n. pl.* thin strips of wood etc. shaved off the surface of a piece.

shawl (shawl) *n.* a large piece of fabric worn around the shoulders or head, or wrapped around a baby, as a covering. □**shawl collar,** a rolled collar extended downward to meet or cross at the waist.

Shaw·nee (shaw-nee) *n.* (*pl.* -nees, -nee) a member of an Algonquin-speaking tribe of Indians in Oklahoma.

she (shee) *pronoun* the female person or animal mentioned, a thing (such as a vehicle or ship or aircraft) personified as female. **she** *n.* a female animal; *she-wolf,* a female wolf.

sheaf (sheef) *n.* (*pl.* **sheaves**, *pr.* sheevz) 1. a bundle of stalks of corn etc. tied together after reaping. 2. a bundle of arrows or papers or other things laid lengthwise together.

shear (sheer) *v.* (**sheared, shorn** or **sheared, shear·ing**) 1. to cut or trim with shears or another sharp device, to remove (a sheep's wool) in this way. 2. to strip bare, to deprive, *shorn of his glory.* 3. to break because of strain, with lateral shift of layers. **shear** *n.* the strain produced by pressure in the structure of a substance, its successive layers being shifted laterally over each other.

shears (sheerz) *n. pl.* a clipping or cutting instrument working like scissors but much larger and usually operated with both hands.

shear·wa·ter (sheer-waw-těr) *n.* a seabird with long wings, skimming close to the water as it flies.

sheath (sheeth) *n.* (*pl.* **sheaths**, *pr.* sheethz) 1. a close-fitting covering, a cover for a blade or tool. 2. a woman's close-fitting dress. □**sheath knife,** a daggerlike knife carried in a sheath.

sheathe (sheethe) *v.* (**sheathed, sheath·ing**) 1. to put into a sheath. 2. to encase in a covering.

sheath·ing (shee-thing) *n.* 1. a covering or casing that sheathes something. 2. the act of putting something in a sheath.

sheave (shiv, sheev) *n.* a pulley with a grooved wheel for a rope to run on.

she·bang (shi-bang) *n.* (informal) an affair, an organization, *the whole shebang.*

shed[1] (shed) *n.* a small building, usually one-storied, for storing things or sheltering livestock etc. or for use as a workshop.

shed[2] *v.* (**shed, shed·ding**) 1. to lose (a thing) by a natural falling off, *trees shed their leaves.* 2. to take off, *shed one's clothes.* 3. to allow to pour forth, *shed tears; shed one's blood,* to be wounded or killed for one's country etc. 4. to send forth, *shed light.*

she'd (sheed) = she had, she would.

sheen (sheen) *n.* gloss, luster. **sheen'y** *adj.*

sheep (sheep) *n.* (*pl.* **sheep**) a grass-eating animal with a thick fleecy coat, kept in flocks for its fleece and for its flesh as meat. □**like sheep,** (of people) easily led or influenced. **make sheep's eyes at,** to gaze at amorously. **separate the sheep from the goats,** to separate the good from the wicked. **sheep farmer,** one who breeds sheep.

sheep-dip (sheep-dip) *n.* a liquid for cleansing sheep of vermin or preserving their wool.

sheep·dog (sheep-dawg) *n.* a dog of a breed trained to guard and herd sheep.

sheep·ish (shee-pish) *adj.* bashful, embarrassed through shame. **sheep'ish·ly** *adv.* **sheep'ish·ness** *n.*

sheep·shank (sheep-shangk) *n.* a knot used to shorten a rope without cutting it.

sheeps·head (sheeps-hed) *n.* a large edible seafish with a sheeplike head.

sheep·skin (sheep-skin) *n.* 1. a garment or rug made of sheep's skin with the fleece on. 2. leather made from sheep's skin. 3. (informal) a diploma.

sheer[1] (sheer) *adj.* 1. pure, not mixed or qualified, *sheer luck.* 2. (of a rock or waterfall etc.) having a vertical or almost vertical surface, with no slope. 3. (of fabric) very thin, transparent. **sheer** *adv.* directly, straight up or down, *the cliff rises sheer from the sea.* **sheer'ly** *adv.* **sheer'ness** *n.*

sheer[2] *v.* to swerve from a course.

sheet[1] (sheet) *n.* 1. a large rectangular piece of cotton or similar fabric, used in pairs as inner bedclothes between which a person sleeps. 2. a large thin piece of any material (such as paper, glass, metal). 3. a piece of paper for writing or printing on, a complete and uncut piece (of the size in which it is made). 4. a wide expanse of water or snow or flame etc. □**sheet lightning,** lightning that looks like a sheet of light across the sky. **sheet music,** music published on loose sheets of paper and not bound into a book.

sheet[2] *n.* a rope or chain attached to the lower corner of a sail, to secure or adjust it.

sheik, sheikh (sheek, shayk) *n.* the leader of an Arab tribe or village.

sheik·dom, sheikh·dom (sheek-dŏm, shayk-) *n.* the territory of a sheik.

shek·el (shek-ĕl) *n.* 1. an ancient Hebrew etc. weight and silver coin. 2. *shekels, (slang)* money, riches. 3. the unit of money in Israel.

shel·drake (shel-drayk) *n.* (*pl.* **-drakes, -drake**) a wild duck with bright plumage.

shel·duck (shel-duk) *n.* (*pl.* **-ducks, -duck**) a female sheldrake.

shelf (shelf) *n.* (*pl.* **shelves**, *pr.* shelvz) 1. a flat rectangular piece of wood or metal or glass etc. fastened horizontally to a wall or in a cupboard or bookcase for things to be placed on. 2. something resembling this, a ledge or steplike projection. □**on the shelf,** (of a person) made to be inactive as no longer of use. **shelf life,** the time for which a stored thing remains usable.

shell (shel) *n.* 1. the hard outer covering of eggs, nuts, and of animals such as snails and crabs and tortoises. 2. the walls of an unfinished or burned-out building or ship. 3. any structure that forms a firm framework or covering. 4. the metal framework of the body of a vehicle. 5. a light boat for rowing races. 6. a metal case filled with explosive, to be fired from a large gun. **shell** *v.* 1. to remove the shell of, *shell peas.* 2. to fire explosive shells at. **shelled** *adj.* **shell'er** *n.* □**come out of one's shell,** to become more sociable and less shy. **shell bean,** a bean with seeds that are removed before cooking, and used as food. **shell game,** a swindling sleight-of-hand game using shells; *(slang)* any fraud or deceit. **shell out,** *(slang)* to pay out (money, or a required amount).

shell shock, *(informal)* nervous breakdown resulting from exposure to battle conditions.

she'll (sheel) = she will.

shel·lac (shě-lak) *n.* thin flakes of a resinous substance used in making varnish. **shellac** *v.* (**shel·lacked, shel·lack·ing**) 1. to varnish with shellac. 2. *(slang)* to defeat or thrash soundly. **shel·lack'er** *n.*

shell·back (shel-bak) *n.* an old sailor.

shell·fire (shel-fīr) *n.* the firing or shooting of explosive shells.

shell·fish (shel-fish) *n.* (*pl.* **-fish, -fish·es**) a water animal that has a shell, especially one of edible kinds such as oysters, crabs, and shrimps.

shel·ter (shel-těr) *n.* 1. something that serves as a shield or barrier against attack, danger, heat, wind, etc. 2. a structure built to keep rain etc. off people, *a bus shelter.* 3. refuge, a shielded condition, *sought shelter from the rain.* **shelter** *v.* 1. to provide with shelter. 2. to protect from blame or trouble or competition. 3. to find or take shelter.

shelve (shelv) *v.* (**shelved, shelv·ing**) 1. to ar-

range on a shelf or shelves. 2. to fit (a wall or cupboard etc.) with shelves. 3. to put aside for later consideration, to reject (a plan etc.) temporarily or permanently. 4. to slope, *the river bottom shelves here.* **shelv′er** *n.*
shelv·ing (shel-ving) *n.* shelves, material for making these.
she·nan·i·gans (shĕ-nan-ĭ-gănz) *n. pl. (slang)* 1. high-spirited behavior. 2. trickery.
shep·herd (shep-ĕrd) *n.* a man who tends a flock of sheep while they are at pasture. **shepherd** *v.* to guide or direct (people). **shep·herd·ess** (shep-ĕr-dis) *n. fem.*
Sher·a·ton (sher-ă-tŏn) *n.* a late 18th-century style of English furniture, named after Thomas Sheraton (1751–1806), its designer.
sher·bet (shur-bit) *n.* a frozen dessert usually flavored with fruit.
sher·iff (sher-if) *n.* 1. the chief law-enforcing officer of a county or similar subdivision of a state. 2. a county official in England.
Sher·pa (shur-pă) *n.* (*pl.* -pas, -pa) a member of a Himalayan people living on the borders of Nepal and Tibet.
sher·ry (sher-ee) *n.* (*pl.* -ries) a fortified wine (either sweet or dry), originally from southern Spain.
she's (sheez) = she is, she has.
Shet·land (shet-lănd) *n.* an island area of Scotland. **Shetland** *adj.* of the Shetlands or Shetland Islands, an island area of Scotland. ☐**Shetland pony,** a pony of a very small rough-coated breed. **Shetland sheepdog,** a dog of a breed resembling a small collie. **Shetland wool,** fine loosely twisted wool from Shetland sheep.
Shet·land·er (shet-lăn-dĕr) *n.* a native or inhabitant of the Shetlands.
Shi·ah (shee-ă) *n.* a Muslim sect, especially in Iran, that regards Ali as the first successor of Muhammad and rejects the first three Sunnite caliphs.
shib·bo·leth (shib-ŏ-lith) *n.* 1. a test word or principle or behavior or opinion, the use of or inability to use which reveals one's party, nationality, orthodoxy, etc. 2. an old slogan or principle that is still considered essential by some members of a party, *outworn shibboleths.* ▷From the story in the Bible, in which "shibboleth" was a kind of password.
shield (sheeld) *n.* 1. a piece of armor carried on the arm to protect the body against missiles or thrusts. 2. a trophy in the form of this. 3. an object or structure or layer of material that protects something. **shield** *v.* to protect or screen, to protect from discovery. **shield′er** *n.*
shift (shift) *v.* 1. to change or move from one position to another. 2. to change form or character. 3. to change (gears) in a motor vehicle. 4. to transfer (blame or responsibility etc.). 5. to manage to do something; *shifted for himself,* managed without help. **shift** *n.* 1. a change of place or form or character etc. 2. a set of workers who start work as another set finishes, the time for which they work, *the night shift.* 3. a gear shift. 4. a piece of evasion. 5. a scheme for achieving something. 6. a woman's straight-cut dress. ☐**shift one's ground,** to change the basis of one's argument.
shift·less (shift-lis) *adj.* lazy and inefficient, lacking resourcefulness. **shift′less·ly** *adv.* **shift′less·ness** *n.*
shift·y (shif-tee) *adj.* (**shift·i·er, shift·i·est**) evasive, not straightforward in manner or character,

untrustworthy. **shift′i·ly** *adv.* **shift′i·ness** *n.*
Shi·ite (shee-ɪt) *n.* a member of the Shiah sect, one of the two branches of Islam.
shill (shil) *n. (slang)* a person employed to decoy or entice others. **shill** *v. (slang)* to decoy, to entice.
shil·le·lagh, shil·la·lah (shĭ-lay-lă, -lay-lee) *n.* an Irish cudgel of blackthorn or oak.
shil·ling (shil-ing) *n.* a former British coin.
shil·ly-shal·ly (shil-ee-shal-ee) *v.* (**shil·ly-shal·lied, shil·ly-shal·ly·ing**) to be unable to make up one's mind firmly. **shil′ly-shal′li·er** *n.*
shim (shim) *n.* a thin slip or wedge used in machinery etc. to make parts fit.
shim·mer (shim-ĕr) *v.* to shine with a soft light that appears to quiver. **shimmer** *n.* a shimmering effect. **shim′mer·y** *adj.* **shim′mer·ing·ly** *adv.*
shim·my (shim-ee) *n.* (*pl.* -mies) 1. a ragtime dance characterized by rapid shaking of the body. 2. an abnormal vibration of the front wheels of a motor vehicle. **shimmy** *v.* (**shim·mied, shim·my·ing**) 1. to dance the shimmy. 2. to vibrate abnormally.
shin (shin) *n.* 1. the front of the leg below the knee. 2. the lower part of the foreleg in cattle, especially as a cut of beef. **shin** *v.* (**shinned, shin·ning**) to climb up by using arms and legs (not on a ladder).
shin·bone (shin-bohn) *n.* the inner and usually larger of the two bones from knee to ankle.
shin·dig (shin-dig) *n. (informal)* a festive gathering, especially a boisterous one.
shine (shɪn) *v.* (**shone** or **shined, shin·ing**) 1. to give out or reflect light, to be bright, to glow. 2. to cause to shine, *shine your flashlight on it.* 3. (of the sun etc.) to be visible and not obscured by clouds. 4. to excel in some way, *does not shine in math; shining example,* an excellent one. 5. to polish. **shine** *n.* 1. brightness. 2. a high polish. ☐**take a shine to,** *(informal)* to take a liking to.
shin·er (shɪ-nĕr) *n. (slang)* a black eye.
shin·gle[1] (shing-gĕl) *n.* a rectangular slip of wood used in rows for covering roofs. **shingle** *v.* (**shin·gled, shin·gling**) 1. to roof with shingles. 2. to cut (a woman's hair) in a short tapering style at the back, with all ends exposed. **shin′gler** *n.*
shin·gle[2] *n.* small rounded pebbles, a stretch of these on a shore. **shin′gly** *adj.*
shin·gles (shing-gĕlz) *n.* a painful disease caused by the chicken pox virus, with blisters forming along the path of a nerve or nerves.
shin·ny (shin-ee) *v.* (**shin·nied, shin·ny·ing**) to shin up a tree etc.
Shin·to (shin-toh) *n.* a Japanese religion revering ancestors and nature spirits. **Shin′to·ism** *n.* **Shin′to·ist** *adj. & n.* **Shin·to·is·tic** (shin-toh-is-tik) *adj.*
shin·y (shɪ-nee) *adj.* (**shin·i·er, shin·i·est**) shining, rubbed until glossy. **shin′i·ly** *adv.* **shin′i·ness** *n.*
ship (ship) *n.* a large seagoing vessel. **ship** *v.* (**shipped, ship·ping**) 1. to put or take on board a ship for conveyance to a destination. 2. to transport. ☐**ship biscuit,** a hard coarse biscuit formerly used on board ship. **ship of state,** a nation, compared to a ship at sail. **ship of the line,** a heavily armed warship. **ship one's oars,** to take them from the oarlocks and lay them in the boat. **ship out,** to put out to sea as a sailor. **ship's boy,** a steward, a cabin boy. **ship's papers,** documents establishing the ownership, nationality, nature of the cargo, etc. of a ship.

-ship *suffix* used to form abstract nouns from adjectives, as in *hardship*, or nouns meaning status, honor, office, skill, etc., as in *friendship, statesmanship.*

ship·board (ship-bohrd) *adj.* happening on board a ship, *a shipboard encounter.* **shipboard** *n.* □on **shipboard,** on board a ship.

ship·build·er (ship-bil-dĕr) *n.* a person engaged in shipbuilding.

ship·build·ing (ship-bil-ding) *n.* the business of constructing ships.

ship·fit·ter (ship-fit-ĕr) *n.* a person who forms plates etc. for use in shipbuilding.

ship·load (ship-lohd) *n.* as much as a ship will hold.

ship·mate (ship-mayt) *n.* a person traveling or working on the same ship as another.

ship·ment (ship-mĕnt) *n.* 1. the putting of goods on a ship etc. 2. the amount shipped, a consignment.

ship·own·er (ship-oh-nĕr) *n.* a person who owns a ship or holds shares in a shipping company.

ship·per (ship-ĕr) *n.* a person or firm whose business is transporting goods by ship.

ship·ping (ship-ing) *n.* 1. ships, especially those of a country or port. 2. transporting goods by ship.

ship·shape (ship-shayp) *adj. & adv.* in good order, tidy.

ship·side (ship-sɪd) *n.* the area alongside a ship.

shipt. *abbr.* shipment.

ship·worm (ship-wurm) *n.* a worm-shaped mollusk boring into ship timbers.

ship·wreck (ship-rek) *n.* destruction of a ship by storm or striking rock etc.

ship·wrecked (ship-rekt) *adj.* having suffered a shipwreck.

ship·wright (ship-rɪt) *n.* a shipbuilder.

ship·yard (ship-yahrd) *n.* a shipbuilding establishment.

shire (shɪr) *n.* a county in Great Britain.

shirk (shurk) *v.* to avoid (a duty or work etc.) selfishly or unfairly. **shirk′er** *n.*

shirr (shur) *v.* 1. to gather (cloth) with parallel threads run through it. 2. to bake (eggs without their shells) in a small dish or casserole.

shirr·ing (shur-ing) *n.* shirred material.

shirt (shurt) *n.* a loose-fitting garment of cotton or silk etc. for the upper part of the body. **shirt′less** *adj.* □in one's shirt sleeves, with no jacket over one's shirt; ready to go to work. **keep one's shirt on,** *(slang)* to keep one's temper. **lose one's shirt,** *(slang)* to lose all one's money by betting it (on a horse etc.). **shirt dress,** a woman's dress with the bodice shaped like a shirt.

shirt·ing (shur-ting) *n.* material for making shirts.

shirt·waist (shurt-wayst) *n.* a woman's blouse resembling a man's shirt.

shish ke·bab (shish kĕ-bob) a dish of Middle Eastern origin, consisting of pieces of marinated meat and vegetables cooked on skewers.

shiv (shiv) *n. (slang)* a knife, a switchblade.

Shi·va (shee-vă) *n.* a Hindu god held supreme by his special votaries, and held by others to be the principle of destruction, associated with Brahma and Vishnu in a triad.

shiv·a·ree (shiv-ă-ree) *n.* a serenade played for a newly married couple, using pots and pans and horns etc. **shivaree** *v.* **(shiv·a·reed, shiv·a·ree·ing)** to serenade in this way.

shiv·er¹ (shiv-ĕr) *v.* to tremble slightly especially with cold or fear. **shiver** *n.* a shivering movement; *it gives me the shivers,* makes me shiver with fear or horror. **shiv′er·y** *adj.* **shiv′er·ing·ly** *adv.* **shiv′er·er** *n.*

shiver² *v.* to shatter.

shiv·ers (shiv-ĕrz) *n. pl.* shattered fragments.

shoal *n.* 1. a shallow place, an underwater sandbank. 2. *shoals,* hidden dangers or difficulties. **shoal′y** *adj.*

shoat (shoht) *n.* a young pig.

shock¹ (shok) *n.* a bushy untidy mass of hair.

shock² *n.* 1. the effect of a violent impact or shake. 2. a violent shake of the earth's crust in an earthquake. 3. a sudden violent effect upon a person's mind or emotions (as by news of a disaster), *his death was a great shock to her.* 4. an acute state of physical collapse caused by physical injury or pain or by mental shock, *went into shock.* 5. an electric shock *(see* **electric**). **shock** *v.* 1. to affect with great indignation or horror or disgust, to seem highly improper or scandalous or outrageous to (a person). 2. to give an electric shock to. 3. to cause an acute sense of weakness in (a person or animal). □**shock absorber,** a device for absorbing vibration in a vehicle. **shock tactics,** sudden violent action taken to achieve one's purpose. **shock therapy,** treatment of psychiatric patients by means of an electric shock *(electroshock)* or a drug causing a similar effect. **shock treatment,** shock therapy; *(slang)* harsh treatment designed to change a person's attitude (as toward work etc.). **shock troops,** troops specially trained for violent assaults. **shock wave,** a sharp wave of increased atmospheric pressure, caused by an explosion or by a body moving faster than sound.

shock³ *n.* a group of sheaves of corn etc. bundled together and standing upright in a field.

shock⁴ *n. (informal)* a shock absorber.

shock·er (shok-ĕr) *n. (informal)* a shocking person or thing, a very bad specimen of something.

shock·ing (shok-ing) *adj.* causing great astonishment or indignation or disgust, scandalous. **shock′ing·ly** *adv.*

shod (shod) *see* **shoe.**

shod·dy (shod-ee) *n.* (*pl.* **-dies**) 1. fiber made from old cloth shredded. 2. cloth made partly from this. **shoddy** *adj.* **(-di·er, -di·est)** of poor quality or workmanship. **shod′di·ly** *adv.* **shod′di·ness** *n.*

shoe (shoo) *n.* 1. an outer covering for a person's foot, with a fairly stiff sole. 2. a horseshoe. 3. an object like a shoe in appearance or use. 4. the part of a brake that presses against the wheel or its drum in a vehicle. **shoe** *v.* **(shod** or **shoed, shoe·ing)** to fit with a shoe or shoes. □**be in a person's shoes,** to be in his situation or plight.

shoe·bill (shoo-bil) *n.* a large African bird resembling a stork, with a bill shaped somewhat like a shoe.

shoe·horn (shoo-horn) *n.* a curved piece of metal or other stiff material for easing one's heel into the back of a shoe.

shoe·lace (shoo-lays) *n.* a cord for fastening together the edges of a shoe's uppers.

shoe·mak·er (shoo-may-kĕr) *n.* a person whose trade is making or repairing boots and shoes.

shoe·shine (shoo-shɪn) *n.* the polishing of shoes.

shoe·string (shoo-string) *n.* a shoelace. □**on a shoestring,** with only a small amount of capital and resources, as in running a business. **shoe-string catch**, (in baseball) a catch of a ball made by an outfielder at his shoestrings. **shoestring potato**, a long thin fried potato. **shoestring tackle**, (in football) a tackle made at or near the ball-carrier's ankles.

shoe·tree (shoo-tree) *n*. a shaped block for keeping a shoe in shape.

sho·gun (shoh-gŭn) *n*. a Japanese hereditary commander in chief and virtual ruler before 1868.

shone (shohn) *see* **shine**.

shoo (shoo) *interj*. a sound uttered to frighten animals away. **shoo** *v*. **(shooed, shoo·ing)** to drive away by this.

shoo-in (shoo-in) *n*. *(informal)* something easy or certain to succeed.

shook (shuuk) *see* **shake**. □**shook up**, *(slang)* emotionally unsettled.

shoot (shoot) *v*. **(shot, shoot·ing)** 1. to fire (a gun or other weapon, or a missile), to use a gun etc., *can't shoot straight*. 2. to kill or wound with a missile from a gun etc. 3. to hunt with a gun for sport, to go over (an area) in shooting game. 4. to send out swiftly or violently, *the fountain shot water high into the air*. 5. to move swiftly, *the car shot past me*. 6. (of a plant) to put forth buds or shoots. 7. to slide (the bolt of a door) into or out of its fastening. 8. to have one's boat move swiftly over (rapids etc.). 9. to take a shot at the goal in basketball, hockey, etc. 10. to photograph or film. 11. *shoot!*, *(slang)* say what you have to say. **shoot** *n*. 1. a young branch or new growth of a plant. 2. an expedition for shooting game. **shoot'er** *n*. □**have shot one's bolt**, to have made one's last possible effort. **shoot at** or **for**, to try for; to strive toward. **shoot dice**, to play at dice. **shoot down**, to cause (a flying aircraft) to fall to the ground by shooting; *(informal)* to argue effectively against (a proposal etc.). **shooting gallery**, a place for shooting at targets with rifles etc. **shooting iron**, a firearm. **shooting star**, a small meteor appearing like a star, moving rapidly and then disappearing. **shooting stick**, a walking stick with a small folding seat at the handle end. **shoot it out**, *(slang)* to engage in a decisive gun battle. **shoot one's mouth off**, *(slang)* to talk too freely. **shoot the works**, *(slang)* to use all one's effort or resources. **shoot up**, to rise suddenly; (of a person) to grow rapidly; to terrorize (a town etc.) with indiscriminate gunfire; *(slang)* to inject oneself with a drug.

shop (shop) *n*. 1. a building or room where goods or services are on sale to the public, a store. 2. a workshop. 3. one's own work or profession as a subject of conversation, *is always talking shop*. **shop** *v*. **(shopped, shop·ping)** to go to a shop or shops to buy things. □**shop around**, to look for the best bargain. **shop steward**, a labor union official elected by fellow workers as their spokesman.

shop·keep·er (shop-kee-pĕr) *n*. a person who owns or manages a shop.

shop·lift·er (shop-lif-tĕr) *n*. a person who steals goods that are on display in a store, after entering as a customer. **shop'lift·ing** *n*.

shoppe (shop) *n*. (usually in a name) a small shop.

shop·per (shop-ĕr) *n*. a person who shops.

shop·ping (shop-ing) *n*. 1. buying goods. 2. the goods bought. □**shopping bag**, a bag for holding goods bought. **shopping center**, a group of stores built as a unit and sharing parking facilities.

shop·talk (shop-tawk) *n*. discussion about one's work or profession.

shop·worn (shop-wohrn) *adj*. (of goods) soiled or faded from being on display.

shor·an (shohr-ăn) *n*. a system of aircraft navigation using the return of two radar signals by two ground stations. ▷From *short range* navigation.

shore[1] (shohr) *n*. the land along the edge of the sea or of a large body of water. **shore'less** *adj*. □**shore leave**, (in the Navy etc.) permission to go ashore. **shore patrol**, U.S. Navy police.

shore[2] *v*. **(shored, shor·ing)** to prop or support with a length of timber set at a slant. **shore** *n*. a support of this kind.

shore·bird (shohr-burd) *n*. a bird normally found at the seashore.

shore·line (shohr-lɪn) *n*. the line formed at the meeting place of shore and water.

shore·ward (shohr-wărd) *adj*. & *adv*. toward the shore. **shore·wards** (shohr-wărdz) *adv*.

shor·ing (shohr-ing) *n*. a number of timbers etc. supporting something.

shorn (shohrn) *see* **shear**.

short (short) *adj*. 1. measuring little from end to end in space or time. 2. seeming to be shorter than it really is, *for one short hour*. 3. not lasting, not going far into the past or future, *a short memory*. 4. insufficient, having an insufficient supply, *water is short; we are short of water; short-staffed*. 5. *(informal)* having little of a certain quality, *he's short on tact*. 6. concise, brief. 7. curt. 8. (of vowel sounds) relatively brief or light (*see* **long**, definition 7). 9. (of an alcoholic drink) small, *a short beer*. 10. (of temper) easily lost. 11. (of pastry) rich and flaky through containing much shortening. 12. (of a sale of stocks etc.) made without the seller's actually owning what he sells. **short** *adv*. suddenly, abruptly, *stopped short*. **short** *n*. *(informal)* 1. a short drink. 2. a short circuit. 3. *shorts*, trousers that do not reach to the knee; *athletic shorts*, those worn in sports; men's underpants. **short** *v*. *(informal)* to short-circuit. **short'ness** *adj*. □**cut short**, to bring abruptly to a halt. **for short**, as an abbreviation, *Raymond is called Ray for short*. **get** or **have by the short hairs**, *(slang)* to have at one's mercy. **in short**, in brief, in summary. **in short supply**, scarce. **make short work of**, to deal with (a thing) rapidly. **sell short**, to disparage; to sell (stocks etc.) when one does not own them. **short circuit**, a connection (usually a fault) in an electrical circuit in which current, finding a path of lesser resistance, flows by a shorter route than the normal one. **short division**, the process of dividing one number by another without writing down one's calculations. **short for**, an abbreviation of, *"Ray" is short for "Raymond."* **short odds**, nearly even odds in betting. **short of**, without going the length of, *will do anything for her short of inviting her to stay*. **short rations**, very small rations. **short shrift**, curt treatment. **short story**, a story with a fully developed theme but shorter than a novel. **short ton**, *see* **ton**.

short·age (shor-tij) *n*. a lack of something that is needed, insufficiency.

short·bread (short-bred) *n*. a rich sweet cookie.

short·cake (short-kayk) *n*. a cake of short pastry usually served with strawberries or other fruit.

short·change (short-chaynj) *v*. **(short·changed,**

short·chang·ing) 1. to rob by giving insufficient change. 2. to cheat (a person).

short-cir·cuit (short-sur-kit) *v.* 1. to cause a short circuit in. 2. to bypass.

short·com·ing (short-kum-ing) *n.* failure to reach a required standard, a fault.

short·cut (short-kut) *n.* a route or method that is quicker than the usual one.

short·en (shor-těn) *v.* to make or become shorter. **short'en·er** *n.*

short·en·ing (shor-tě-ning) *n.* fat used to make pastry etc. rich and crumbly.

short·fall (short-fawl) *n.* a deficit.

short·hand (short-hand) *n.* a method of writing very rapidly, using quickly made symbols.

short·hand·ed (short-han-did) *adj.* having an insufficient number of workmen or helpers.

short·horn (short-horn) *n.* one of a breed of cattle with short horns.

short-lived (short-lıvd, -livd) *adj.* having a short life, not lasting long.

short·ly (short-lee) *adv.* 1. in a short time, not long, soon, *coming shortly; shortly afterward.* 2. in a few words. 3. curtly.

short-or·der (short-or-děr) **cook** a cook who prepares fast foods.

short-range (short-raynj) *adj.* having a short range, relating to a short period of future time, *a short-range plan.*

short·sight·ed (short-sı-tid) *adj.* 1. able to see clearly only what is close. 2. lacking foresight. **short'sight'ed·ly** *adv.* **short'sight'ed·ness** *n.*

short-sleeved (short-sleevd) *adj.* with sleeves not reaching below the elbow.

short·stop (short-stop) *n.* (in baseball) 1. the position between second and third base. 2. the player at this position.

short-tem·pered (short-tem-pěrd) *adj.* easily becoming angry.

short-term (short-turm) *adj.* of or for a short period.

short·wave (short-wayv) *n.* a radio wave of about sixty meters wavelength.

short-wind·ed (short-win-did) *adj.* 1. having easily-exhausted breathing power, short of breath. 2. unable or unwilling to speak or perform at length.

Sho·sho·ne, Sho·sho·ni (shŏ-shoh-nee) *n.* (*pl.* **-nes, -ne, -nis, -ni**) 1. a member of a group of Indian tribes of the southwestern U.S., speaking a common language. 2. this language.

shot (shot) *see* **shoot. shot** *n.* (*pl.* **shots, shot**) 1. the firing of a gun etc., the sound of this. 2. a person with regard to his skill in shooting, *he's a good shot.* 3. (*pl.* **shot**) a single missile for a cannon or gun, a nonexplosive projectile, as a BB. 4. lead pellets for firing from small guns. 5. a heavy ball thrown as a sport. 6. *(informal)* the launching of a rocket or spacecraft. 7. a stroke in tennis or billiards etc. 8. an attempt to hit something or reach a target. 9. an attempt to do something, *have a shot at this crossword.* 10. an injection. 11. a small measure (often one ounce) of straight liquor. 12. a photograph, the scene photographed, a single continuous photographed scene in a film. **shot** *adj. (slang)* exhausted. □**call the shots,** *(slang)* to control or direct; to make the decisions. **like a shot,** without hesitation, willingly. **shot glass,** a small glass for measuring or serving a shot of liquor. **shot in the arm,** a

stimulus or encouragement. **shot in the dark,** a mere guess. **shot put,** the sport of putting the shot.

shot·gun (shot-gun) *n.* a gun for firing small shot at close range. □**shotgun wedding,** one that is enforced, especially because the bride is pregnant.

should (shuud) *auxiliary verb,* used to express 1. duty or obligation, *you should have told me.* 2. an expected future event, *they should be here by ten.* 3. a possible event, *if you should happen to see him.* 4. with *I* and *we* to form a polite statement or a conditional or indefinite clause, *I should like to come; if their forecast had been right, they would have won and we should* (▷not *would*) *have lost.*

shoul·der (shohl-děr) *n.* 1. the part of the body at which the arm or foreleg or wing is attached, the part of the human body between this and the neck. 2. the part of a garment covering the shoulder. 3. the upper foreleg and adjacent parts of an animal as a cut of meat. 4. a projection compared to the human shoulder, *the shoulder of a bottle.* **shoulder** *v.* 1. to push with one's shoulder. 2. to take (a burden) upon one's shoulders. 3. to take (blame or responsibility) upon oneself. □**cry on someone's shoulder,** to tell another person one's problems in order to get sympathy. **put one's shoulder to the wheel,** to make an effort. **shoulder arms,** to hold a rifle with the barrel against one's shoulder. **shoulder bag,** a handbag hung on a strap over the shoulder. **shoulder belt,** a bandolier or other band passing over one shoulder and under the opposite arm. **shoulder blade,** either of the two large flat bones at the top of the back. **shoulder patch,** an identification patch worn on or near the shoulder of a uniform. **shoulder strap,** a strap that passes over the shoulder, especially to support something. **shoulder to shoulder,** side by side and close together.

shoul·der-high (shohl-děr-hı) *adj.* up to or as high as the shoulders.

should·n't (shuud-ěnt) = should not.

shout (showt) *n.* a loud cry or utterance of words calling attention or expressing joy or excitement or disapproval. **shout** *v.* to utter a shout, to utter or call loudly. **shout'er** *n.* □**shout down,** to silence (a person) by shouting.

shove (shuv) *n.* a rough push. **shove** *v.* (**shoved, shov·ing**) 1. to push roughly. 2. *(informal)* to put, *shove it in the drawer.* □**shove off,** to push a boat so that it moves from the shore; *(informal)* to go away.

shov·el (shuv-ěl) *n.* 1. a tool for scooping up earth or snow etc. 2. a large mechanically operated device used for the same purpose. **shovel** *v.* (**shov·eled, shov·el·ing**) 1. to shift or clear with or as if with a shovel. 2. to scoop or thrust roughly, *shoveling food into his mouth.* **shov'el·ful** *n.* (*pl.* **-fuls**).

shov·el·er (shuv-ě-lěr) *n.* a duck with a broad shovel-like beak.

show (shoh) *v.* (**showed, shown** or **showed, show·ing**) 1. to allow or cause to be seen, to offer for inspection or viewing. 2. to demonstrate, to point out, to prove, to cause (a person) to understand, *show us how it works; showed them the door,* dismissed them. 3. to conduct, *show them in* or *out.* 4. to present an image of, *this picture shows the hotel.* 5. to exhibit in a show. 6. to treat in a certain way, *showed us much kindness.*

7. to be able to be seen, *the lining is showing.* 8. *(informal)* to prove one's ability or worth to, *we'll show them!* **show** *n.* 1. showing, being shown. 2. a display, a public exhibition for competition or entertainment or advertisement etc., a pageant, *a dog show; a puppet show; the boat show.* 3. any public performance or broadcast. 4. *(informal)* any business or undertaking, *he runs the whole show.* 5. an outward appearance, an insincere display, *under a show of friendship.* 6. a pompous display. □**give the show away,** *(informal)* to reveal things that were intended to be secret. **nothing to show for it,** no visible result of one's efforts. **run the show,** *(informal)* to control or manage a business etc. **show bill,** an advertising poster. **show biz** *(slang)* = **show business,** the entertainment or theatrical profession. **show girl,** a female dancer in the chorus line of a nightclub etc. **show jumping,** the sport of riding horses to jump over obstacles, in competition. **show off,** to display well or proudly or ostentatiously; to try to impress people. **show of hands,** raising of hands to vote for or against something. **show oneself,** to be seen in public. **show one's face,** to let oneself be seen. **show up,** to be clearly visible; to reveal (a fault or inferiority etc.); *(informal)* to appear, to be present. **show window,** a store window for displaying goods. **steal the show,** to outshine other performers etc. unexpectedly; to receive credit or applause due to others, *she does all the hard work but he steals the show.* **stop the show,** to perform so well as to cause a temporary halt in performance because of prolonged applause.

show·boat (shoh-boht) *n.* a river steamboat in which theatrical performances are given. **showboat** *v. (informal)* to perform in a manner designed to attract attention.

show·case (shoh-kays) *n.* a glass-covered case in which things are exhibited.

show·down (shoh-down) *n.* a final test, disclosure of intentions or conditions etc.

show·er (show-ĕr) *n.* 1. a brief fall of rain or snow etc., or of bullets, dust, or stones etc. 2. a sudden influx of letters or gifts etc. 3. a device or stall in which water is sprayed on a person's body to wash him, a wash in this. 4. a party for giving presents to a person, especially to a bride-to-be. **shower** *v.* 1. to pour down or come in a shower. 2. to send or give (many letters or gifts etc.) to. 3. to wash oneself in sprayed water. □**shower bath,** a bath in which water is sprayed from above; the apparatus or premises for this.

show·er·proof (show-ĕr-proof) *adj.* (of fabric) able to keep out slight rain. **showerproof** *v.* to make showerproof.

show·er·y (show-ĕ-ree) *adj.* (of weather) with many showers.

show·ing (shoh-ing) *n.* the evidence or quality that a person shows, *on today's showing, he will fail.*

show·man (shoh-măn) *n.* (*pl.* -men, *pr.* -mĕn) 1. an organizer of theatrical events, circuses, or similar entertainment. 2. a person who is good at showmanship.

show·man·ship (shoh-măn-ship) *n.* skill in presenting an entertainment or goods or one's abilities to the best advantage.

shown (shohn) *see* **show.**

show·off (shoh-awf) *n.* a person who tries to impress others.

show·piece (shoh-pees) *n.* an excellent specimen used for exhibition.

show·place (shoh-plays) *n.* a place that tourists etc. go to see.

show·room (shoh-room) *n.* a room in which goods are displayed for inspection and purchase.

show·stop·per (shoh-stop-ĕr) *n.* a performer or performance or part of a performance receiving prolonged applause.

show·y (shoh-ee) *adj.* (**show·i·er, show·i·est**) 1. making a good display. 2. brilliant, gaudy. **show'i·ly** *adv.* **show'i·ness** *n.*

shpt. *abbr.* shipment.

shrank (shrangk) *see* **shrink.**

shrap·nel (shrap-nĕl) *n.* 1. an artillery shell containing bullets or pieces of metal that it scatters as it explodes. 2. the pieces it scatters.

shred (shred) *n.* 1. a small piece torn or cut from something. 2. a small amount, *not a shred of evidence.* **shred** *v.* (**shred·ded, shred·ding**) to tear or cut into shreds. **shred'der** *n.*

shrew (shroo) *n.* 1. a small mouselike animal. 2. a sharp-tempered scolding woman.

shrewd (shrood) *adj.* having or showing sound judgment and common sense, clever. **shrewd'ly** *adv.* **shrewd'ness** *n.*

shrew·ish (shroo-ish) *adj.* sharp-tempered and scolding. **shrew'ish·ness** *n.*

shriek (shreek) *n.* a shrill cry or scream. **shriek** *v.* to make a shriek, to utter with a shriek.

shrift (shrift) *n.* **short shrift,** *see* **short.**

shrike (shrɪk) *n.* a bird with a strong hooked beak that impales its prey (small birds and insects) on thorns.

shrill (shril) *adj.* piercing and high-pitched in sound. **shrill** *v.* to sound or utter shrilly. **shril'ly** *adv.* **shrill'ness** *n.*

shrimp (shrimp) *n.* (*pl.* **shrimps, shrimp**) 1. a small shellfish often used as food, pink when boiled. 2. *(slang)* a very small person.

shrimp·ing (shrim-ping) *n.* fishing for shrimp.

shrine (shrɪn) *n.* an altar or chapel or other place that is hallowed because of its special associations.

shrink (shringk) *v.* (**shrank** or **shrunk, shrunk** or **shrunk·en, shrink·ing**) 1. to make or become smaller, especially by the action of moisture or heat or cold, *it shrank; it has shrunk.* 2. to draw back so as to avoid something, to withdraw, to be unwilling to do something (as because of shame or dislike). **shrink** *n. (slang)* a psychiatrist or other psychotherapist (▷short for *head shrinker*). **shrink'a·ble** *adj.* □**shrinking violet,** a shy modest person.

shrink·age (shring-kij) *n.* the process of shrinking, the amount by which something has shrunk.

shrink-wrap (shringk-rap) *v.* to wrap (an article) in material that shrinks tightly around it.

shrive (shrɪv) *v.* (**shrove** or **shrived, shriv·en** or **shrived, shriv·ing**) *(old use)* 1. to hear the confession of, to assign penance to and absolve. 2. to confess one's sins to a priest for this purpose.

shriv·el (shriv-ĕl) *v.* (**shriv·eled, shriv·el·ing**) 1. to shrink and wrinkle from great heat or cold or lack of moisture. 2. to cause to shrivel.

shroud (shrowd) *n.* 1. a sheet in which a dead body is wrapped for burial, a garment for the dead. 2. something that conceals, *wrapped in a shroud of secrecy.* 3. one of a set of ropes supporting the mast of a ship. **shroud** *v.* 1. to wrap in a shroud. 2. to protect or conceal in wrappings. 3. to conceal, *his past life is shrouded in mystery.*

Shrove (shrohv) **Tuesday** the day before Ash Wednesday.

shrub (shrub) *n.* a woody plant smaller than a tree and usually divided into separate stems from near the ground. **shrub′by** *adj.*

shrub·ber·y (shrub-ĕ-ree) *n.* (*pl.* -ber·ies) 1. an area planted with shrubs. 2. shrubs collectively.

shrug (shrug) *v.* **(shrugged, shrug·ging)** to raise (the shoulders) as a gesture of indifference or doubt or helplessness. **shrug** *n.* this movement. □**shrug off,** to dismiss (a thing) as unimportant.

shrunk (shrungk), **shrunk·en** (shrung-kĕn) *see* **shrink.**

sht. *abbr.* sheet.

shtg. *abbr.* shortage.

shtick (shtik) *n.* *(slang)* a short comic routine or other short performance.

shuck (shuk) *n.* 1. a husk, a pod. 2. the shell of an oyster or clam. **shuck** *v.* to remove the shucks of, to shell.

shucks (shuks) *interj.* a mild expression of distaste or disappointment.

shud·der (shud-ĕr) *v.* 1. to shiver violently with horror or fear or cold. 2. to make a strong shaking movement. **shudder** *n.* a shuddering movement. **shud′der·ing·ly** *adv.*

shuf·fle (shuf-ĕl) *v.* **(shuf·fled, shuf·fling)** 1. to walk without lifting the feet clear of the ground, to move (one's feet) in this way. 2. to slide (cards) over one another so as to change their order. 3. to rearrange, to jumble. 4. to keep shifting one's position. 5. to get rid of (a burden etc.), *shuffled off the responsibility on to others; shuffled out of it.* **shuffle** *n.* 1. a shuffling movement or walk. 2. shuffling of cards etc. 3. a rearrangement, *the latest Cabinet shuffle.* **shuf′fler** *n.*

shuf·fle·board (shuf-ĕl-bohrd) *n.* a game in which disks are driven over a marked surface.

shun (shun) *v.* **(shunned, shun·ning)** to avoid, to keep away from. **shun′ner** *n.*

shunt (shunt) *v.* 1. to divert into an alternative course. 2. to move (a train) on to a side track. **shunt** *n.* shunting, being shunted. **shunt′er** *n.*

shush (shush) *(informal)* = **hush.**

shut (shut) *v.* **(shut, shut·ting)** 1. to move (a door or lid or window etc.) into position so that it blocks an opening. 2. to move or be moved into such a position, *the lid shuts automatically.* 3. to prevent access to (a place or receptacle etc.) by shutting a door etc.; *shut one's eyes* or *ears* or *mind to a thing,* to refuse to take notice of it or hear it. 4. to bring or fold the parts of (a thing) together, *shut the book.* 5. to keep in or out by shutting a door etc., *shut out the noise.* 6. to trap (a finger or dress etc.) by shutting something on it. □**shut a person's mouth,** *(slang)* to prevent him from revealing something. **shut down,** to cease working or business, either for the day or permanently; to cause to do this. **shut off,** to stop the flow of (water or gas etc.) by shutting a valve. **shut out,** to exclude (a landscape etc.) from view; to keep someone or something out; to prevent (an opponent) from scoring. **shut up,** to shut securely; to shut all the doors and windows of (a house); to put away in a box etc.; *(informal)* to stop talking or making a noise, to cause to do this, to silence. **shut your mouth,** *(slang)* be silent.

shut·down (shut-down) *n.* the process or an instance of ceasing working or business, either for the day or permanently.

shut·eye (shut-ı) *n.* *(slang)* sleep.

shut-in (shut-in) *n.* a person forced to remain indoors (as in a hospital) by disease etc.

shut·out (shut-owt) *n.* (in baseball etc.) a game in which one side fails to score.

shut·ter (shut-ĕr) *n.* 1. a panel or screen that can be closed over a window. 2. a device that opens and closes the aperture of a camera lens to allow light to fall on the film.

shut·ter·bug (shut-ĕr-bug) *n.* *(informal)* a devoted amateur photographer.

shut·tered (shut-ĕrd) *adj.* 1. fitted with shutters. 2. with the shutters closed.

shut·tle (shut-ĕl) *n.* 1. a holder carrying the weft thread to and fro across the loom in weaving. 2. a holder carrying the lower thread in a sewing machine. 3. a bus, plane, train, etc. used in a shuttle service. **shuttle** *v.* **(shut·tled, shut·tling)** to move or travel or send back and forth. □**shuttle service,** a transport service in which a vehicle etc. goes to and fro over a relatively short distance.

shut·tle·cock (shut-ĕl-kok) *n.* 1. a small rounded piece of cork with a ring of feathers, or of other material made in this shape, struck back and forth in badminton. 2. something that is passed repeatedly back and forth.

shy[1] (shı) *adj.* **(shy·er, shy·est)** 1. (of a person) timid and lacking self-confidence in the presence of others, avoiding company, reserved. 2. (of behavior) showing shyness, *a shy smile.* 3. (of an animal) timid and avoiding observation. **shy** *v.* **(shied, shy·ing)** to jump or move suddenly in alarm, *the horse shied at the noise.* **shy′ly** *adv.* **shy′ness** *n.*

shy[2] *v.* **(shied, shy·ing)** to fling or throw (a stone etc.).

shy·lock (shı-lok) *n.* a hard-hearted moneylender. ▷From Shylock, a moneylender in Shakespeare's *The Merchant of Venice* (1600).

shy·ster (shı-stĕr) *n.* *(informal)* a person who is unscrupulous in professional matters, especially a tricky lawyer.

Si *symbol* silicon.

SI *abbr.* Système International. ▷French, = International System of Units.

Si·a·mese (sı-ă-meez) *adj.* of Siam (now called Thailand) or its people or language. **Siamese** *n.* (*pl.* -mese) 1. a native of Siam. 2. the language of Siam. 3. a Siamese cat. □**Siamese cat,** a cat of a breed that has short pale fur with darker face, ears, tail, and feet. **Siamese twins,** twins whose bodies are joined in some way at birth. ▷Named for two Siamese males, born joined at the waist, who were exhibited in America by P. T. Barnum (1811–1874).

Si·be·ri·an (sı-beer-i-ăn) *adj.* of Siberia, a northern region of the U.S.S.R.

sib·i·lant (sib-ı-lănt) *adj.* having a hissing sound. **sibilant,** *n.* one of the speech sounds that sound like hissing, such as *s, sh.* **sib′i·lant·ly** *adv.* **sib′i·lance** *n.* **sib·i·late** (sib-ı-layt) *v.* **(sib·i·lat·ed, sib·i·lat·ing).**

sib·ling (sib-ling) *n.* a child in relation to another or others of the same parent, a brother or sister.

sib·yl (sib-il) *n.* 1. one of the women who in ancient times acted in various places as a reputed mouthpiece of a god, uttering oracles and prophecies. 2. a fortuneteller. 3. a witch. **sib·yl·line** (sib-ı-lın) *adj.*

sic[1] (sik) *adv.* used or spelled in that way. (Latin, = thus). ▷This word is placed in brackets after a word that seems odd or is wrongly spelled, to show that one is quoting it exactly as it was given. Write it thus [*sic*].

sic² *v.* **(sicked, sick·ing)** to urge or command (a dog) to attack.

Si·cil·ian (si-sil-yăn) *adj.* of Sicily, an Italian island in the Mediterranean. **Sicilian** *n.* a native or inhabitant of Sicily.

sick (sik) *adj.* 1. physically or mentally unwell. 2. likely to vomit, *feel sick.* 3. distressed or disgusted, *sick at heart; their ignorance makes me sick.* 4. bored with something through having already had or done too much of it, *I'm sick of cabbage.* 5. finding amusement in misfortune or in morbid subjects, *sick jokes.* **sick'ish** *adj.* □**be sick,** to vomit. **sick bay,** a room or rooms for sick people in a ship. **sick headache,** a migraine. **sick leave,** leave of absence because of illness. **sick list,** a list of people who are ill, especially in a military unit; *on the sick list,* ill. **sick pay,** pay given to an employee who is absent through illness.

sick·bed (sik-bed) *n.* the bed of a sick person.

sick·en (sik-ĕn) *v.* 1. to begin to be ill. 2. to make or become distressed or disgusted, *the sight of blood sickened him.*

sick·en·ing (sik-ĕ-ning) *adj.* annoying, disgusting. **sick'en·ing·ly** *adv.*

sick·le (sik-ĕl) *n.* 1. a tool with a curved blade and a short handle, used for cutting grain etc. 2. something shaped like this, such as the crescent moon. □**sickle cell anemia,** a severe hereditary anemia characterized by fragile sickle-shaped red blood cells.

sick·ly (sik-lee) *adj.* **(-li·er, -li·est)** 1. often ill, *a sickly child.* 2. unhealthy looking. 3. causing ill health, *a sickly climate.* 4. causing sickness or distaste, *sickly smell; sickly sentimentality.* 5. weak, *sickly smile.*

sick·ness (sik-nis) *n.* 1. illness. 2. a disease. 3. vomiting.

sick·out (sik-owt) *n.* a stoppage of work by workers who cannot legally strike but stay away from their jobs claiming illness.

sick·room (sik-room) *n.* a room occupied by a sick person, or kept ready for the sick.

side (sīd) *n.* 1. one of the more or less flat inner or outer surfaces of an object, especially as distinct from the top and bottom, front and back, or ends. 2. either surface of a flat object (such as a piece of paper). 3. any of the bounding lines of a plane figure such as a triangle or square. 4. either of the two halves into which an object or body can be divided by a line down its center. 5. the part near the edge and away from the center of something; *take* or *put to one side,* put aside. 6. a slope of a hill or ridge. 7. the region next to a person or thing, *stood at my side.* 8. one aspect or view of something, *study all sides of the problem; she is on the fat side,* rather fat. 9. one of two opposing groups or teams etc. 10. the line of descent through father or mother, *his mother's side of the family.* **side** *adj.* to the side, *side door.* **side** *v.* **(sid·ed, sid·ing)** to take the side of a person in a dispute, *sided with his son.* □**on the side,** *(informal)* as a sideline; as a surreptitious or illicit activity; (in ordering food in a restaurant) as a side dish, *salad on the side.* **side arm,** a weapon, as a pistol or bayonet etc., carried at the side or waist. **side by side,** standing close together. **side dish,** extra food subsidiary to the main dish. **side effect,** a secondary (usually less desirable) effect. **side issue,** an issue that is not the main one. **side road,** a road leading off a main road; a minor road. **side street,** a street lying aside from

main ones. **side table,** a table at the side of a room or apart from the main table. **side view,** a view of something sideways. **side whiskers,** whiskers on the cheek. **side wind,** a wind from one side (not front or back).

side·arm (sīd-ahrm) *adj. & adv.* with a throwing motion that sweeps the arm forward at approximately shoulder height and parallel to the ground.

side·board (sīd-bohrd) *n.* a table or flat-topped piece of dining room furniture with drawers and cupboards for china etc.

side·burns (sīd-burnz) *n. pl.* short side whiskers.

side·car (sīd-kahr) *n.* 1. a small vehicle attached to the side of a motorcycle, to seat a passenger. 2. a cocktail of orange liqueur, lemon juice, and brandy.

side·kick (sīd-kik) *n. (informal)* a close associate.

side·light (sīd-līt) *n.* 1. light from one side (not front or back). 2. minor or casual light shed on a subject etc. 3. a light at either side of a ship under way.

side·line (sīd-līn) *n.* 1. something done in addition to one's main work or activity. 2. *sidelines,* lines bounding a football field etc. at its sides, the space just outside these, a place for spectators as distinct from participants. **sideline** *v.* **(side·lined, side·lin·ing)** to remove (an athlete) from a game or from regular participation in a sport. □**on the sidelines,** not participating, acting as a spectator.

side·long (sīd-lawng) *adj. & adv.* to one side, sideways, *a sidelong glance.*

side·man (sīd-man) *n.* (*pl.* **-men,** *pr.* **-men**) an instrumentalist in an orchestra or band, especially one who supports a soloist.

side·piece (sīd-pees) *n.* a piece in or on or forming the side of something.

si·de·re·al (sī-deer-i-ăl) *adj.* of or measured by the stars.

side·sad·dle (sīd-sad-ĕl) *n.* a saddle for a woman rider to sit on with both feet on the same side of the horse. **sidesaddle** *adv.* sitting in this way.

side·show (sīd-shoh) *n.* 1. a minor show attached to a principal one, as at a circus. 2. a minor incident or affair.

side·slip (sīd-slip) *v.* **(side·slipped, side·slip·ping)** to skid, to move sideways instead of forward.

side·split·ting (sīd-split-ing) *adj.* causing violent laughter.

side·step (sīd-step) *v.* **(side·stepped, side·step·ping)** 1. to avoid by stepping sideways. 2. to evade (a question or responsibility etc.).

side·stroke (sīd-strohk) *n.* 1. a stroke toward or from a side. 2. a swimming stroke in which the swimmer lies on his side.

side·swipe (sīd-swip) *n.* a glancing blow along the side. **sideswipe** *v.* **(side·swiped, side·swip·ing)** to hit (a person or thing) in this way.

side·track (sīd-trak) *v.* 1. to turn into a siding, to shunt. 2. to divert (a person) from the main issue. 3. to postpone or evade action or decision upon (a matter).

side·walk (sīd-wawk) *n.* a path, usually paved, at the side of a street, for use by pedestrians.

side·wall (sīd-wawl) *n.* the side of a tire between its tread and the rim of the wheel.

side·ways (sīd-wayz) *adj. & adv.* 1. to or from one side (not forward or back). 2. with one side facing forward, *sat sideways in the bus.*

side·wheel·er (sīd-hwee-lĕr) *n.* a steamer with a paddle wheel on each side.

side·wind·er (sīd-win-dĕr) *n.* 1. a sideways blow.

2. a small rattlesnake that moves forward diagonally.

sid·ing (sɪ-ding) *n.* 1. a short stretch of track by the side of a railroad track and opening into it at one end or both for shunting purposes. 2. material for covering the outside walls of a frame house, *aluminum siding.*

si·dle (sɪ-dĕl) *v.* **(si·dled, si·dling)** to advance in a timid or furtive or cringing manner, to edge.

siege (seej) *n.* the surrounding and blockading of a town or fortress by armed forces, in order to capture it. ☐**lay siege to,** to begin besieging. **raise the siege,** *see* **raise. siege gun,** a gun used in sieges, too heavy for field use.

si·en·na (si-en-ă) *n.* a kind of clay used as coloring matter. ☐**burnt sienna,** reddish brown. **raw sienna,** brownish yellow.

si·er·ra (si-er-ă) *n.* a long chain of mountains with sharp slopes and an irregular outline, in Spain or the Americas.

Si·er·ra Le·o·ne (si-er-ă li-oh-nee) a country in West Africa. **Si·er'ra Le·o'ne·an** *adj. & n.*

si·es·ta (si-es-tă) *n.* an afternoon nap or rest, especially in hot countries.

sieve (siv) *n.* a utensil consisting of a frame with wire mesh, used for sorting solid or coarse matter (which is retained in it) from liquid or fine matter (which passes through), or for reducing a soft mixture squeezed through it to a uniform pulp. **sieve** *v.* **(sieved, siev·ing)** to put through a sieve.

sift (sift) *v.* 1. to sieve. 2. to sprinkle lightly from a perforated container. 3. to examine carefully and select or analyze. 4. (of snow or light) to fall as if from a sieve. **sift'er** *n.*

sig. *abbr.* 1. signal. 2. signature.

sigh (sɪ) *n.* a long deep breath given out audibly, expressing sadness, tiredness, relief etc. **sigh** *v.* 1. to give a sigh, to express with a sigh. 2. (of wind etc.) to make a similar sound. 3. to yearn. **sigh'er** *n.*

sight (sɪt) *n.* 1. the faculty of seeing, ability to see. 2. seeing or being seen, *lost sight of it.* 3. the range over which a person can see or an object can be seen, *within sight of the castle.* 4. a thing seen or visible or worth seeing, a display, *our tulips are a wonderful sight this year; see the sights of New York,* its noteworthy places. 5. *(informal)* something regarded as unsightly or looking ridiculous, *she looks a sight in those clothes.* 6. *(informal)* a great quantity, *it cost a sight of money; a darned sight better.* 7. a device looked through to help aim or observe with a gun or telescope etc., aim or observation using this; *set one's sights on,* strive for, aim at. **sight** *v.* 1. to get a sight of, to observe the presence of, *we sighted land.* 2. to aim or observe by using the sight in a gun or telescope etc. ☐**at** *or* **on first sight,** on first glimpse or impression. **catch sight of,** to glimpse, *caught sight of the church steeple in the distance.* **in sight,** visible, clearly near at hand, *victory was in sight.* **know by sight,** to recognize (a person or thing) seen before. **lower one's sights,** to adopt a less ambitious policy. **not by a long sight,** definitely not. **out of sight,** not visible; *(informal)* marvelous. **sight draft,** a bank draft to be paid upon presentation. **sight for sore eyes,** *(informal)* a person or thing one is glad to see. **sight line,** the line from a person's eye to what is seen. **sight unseen,** without previous inspection.

sight·ed (sɪ-tid) *adj.* having sight, not blind.

sight·less (sɪt-lis) *adj.* blind.

sight·ly (sɪt-lee) *adj.* **(-li·er, -li·est)** attractive to the sight, not unsightly. **sight'li·ness** *n.*

sight·read (sɪt-reed) *v.* **(sight·read, sight·read·ing)** to read or perform (music etc.) at first sight, without preparation. **sight'read·er** *n.* **sight'read·ing** *n.*

sight·see·ing (sɪt-see-ing) *n.* visiting places of interest in a town etc.

sight·se·er (sɪt-see-ĕr) *n.* one who goes sightseeing.

sig·ma (sig-mă) *n.* the eighteenth letter of the Greek alphabet (Σ σ).

sign (sɪn) *n.* 1. something perceived that suggests the existence of a fact or quality or condition, either past or present or future, *it shows signs of decay* or *of being a success.* 2. a mark or device with a special meaning, a symbol. 3. a signboard, road sign, or billboard, the device on these, a notice. 4. an action or gesture conveying information or a command etc. 5. any of the twelve divisions of the zodiac (*see* **zodiac**), a symbol representing one of these. **sign** *v.* 1. to make a sign, *signed to me to come.* 2. to write (one's name) on a document etc. to guarantee that it is genuine or has one's authority or consent etc., *signed his name; signed the letter; sign here.* 3. to convey by signing a document, *signed away her right to the house.* 4. to engage or be engaged as an employee by signing a contract of employment. 5. to communicate in sign language. **sign'er** *n.* ☐**sign in,** to sign something as an indication that one has arrived or is present. **sign language,** the gestures used for communication with deaf people. **sign off,** (in broadcasting) to announce the end of one's program or transmission. **sign on** *or* **up,** to sign a contract of employment; to enlist in a military service; to register oneself for a program, benefit, etc. **sign out,** to sign something as an indication that one is departing.

sig·nal (sig-năl) *n.* 1. a sign or gesture giving information or a command, a message made up of such signs. 2. an act or event that immediately produces a general reaction, *his arrival was the signal for an outburst of cheering.* 3. an object placed to give notice or warning, *traffic signals; railroad signals.* 4. a sequence of electrical impulses or radio waves transmitted or received. **signal** *v.* **(sig·naled, sig·nal·ing)** to make a signal or signals, to direct or communicate with or announce in this way. **signal** *adj.* remarkably good or bad, *a signal success.* **sig'nal·ly** *adv.* **sig'nal·er** *n.* ☐**Signal Corps,** a U.S. Army corps responsible for military communications etc.

sig·nal·ize (sig-nă-lɪz) *v.* **(sig·nal·ized, sig·nal·iz·ing)** to make noteworthy. **sig·nal·i·za·tion** (sig-nă-li-zay-shŏn) *n.*

sig·nal·man (sig-năl-măn) *n.* (*pl.* **-men,** *pr.* -mĕn) one who is responsible for displaying naval signals or operating railroad signals.

sig·na·to·ry (sig-nă-tohr-ee) *n.* (*pl.* **-ries**) any of the parties who sign a treaty or other agreement.

sig·na·ture (sig-nă-chŭr) *n.* 1. a person's name or initials written by himself in signing something. 2. a key signature or time signature in music. 3. a section of a book made from one sheet folded and cut, often marked with a letter or figure as a guide to the binder. ☐**key signature,** the sharps or flats after the clef in a musical score, showing its key. **time signature,** a fraction (such as ¾) printed at the beginning of a piece of music, showing the number of beats in the bar and their rhythm.

sign·board (sɪn-bohrd) *n.* a board bearing a sign or advertisement.

sig·net (sig-nit) *n.* a person's seal used with or instead of a signature. ☐**signet ring,** a finger ring with an engraved design, formerly used as a seal.

sig·nif·i·cance (sig-nif-ĭ-kăns) *n.* 1. what is meant by something, *what is the significance of this symbol?* 2. being significant, importance, *the event is of no significance.*

sig·nif·i·cant (sig-nif-ĭ-kănt) *adj.* 1. having a meaning. 2. full of meaning, *a significant glance.* 3. important, noteworthy, *significant developments.* **sig·nif'i·cant·ly** *adv.*

sig·ni·fi·ca·tion (sig-nif-ĭ-kay-shŏn) *n.* meaning.

sig·ni·fy (sig-nĭ-fɪ) *v.* **(sig·ni·fied, sig·ni·fy·ing)** 1. to be a sign or symbol of. 2. to have as a meaning. 3. to make known, *signified her approval.* 4. to be of importance, to matter, *it doesn't signify.*

si·gnor (seen-yohr) *n.* (*pl.* **si·gnors, si·gno·ri,** *pr.* seen-yohr-ee) the title of an Italian man, = Mr. or sir.

si·gno·ra (seen-yohr-ä) *n.* (*pl.* **si·gnor·as, si·gno·re,** *pr.* seen-yohr-ay) the title of an Italian woman, = Mrs. or madam.

si·gno·ri·na (seen-yŏ-ree-nä) *n.* (*pl.* **-nas, -ne,** *pr.* -nay) the title of an Italian unmarried woman or girl, = Miss.

sign·post (sɪn-pohst) *n.* 1. a post to which a sign is attached. 2. an indication.

Sikh (seek) *n.* a member of a certain Hindu religious sect. **Sikh'ism** *n.*

si·lage (sɪ-lij) *n.* green fodder stored and fermented in a silo.

si·lence (sɪ-lĕns) *n.* 1. absence of sound. 2. avoidance or absence of speaking or of making a sound. 3. the fact of not mentioning something or of refusing to betray a secret, *a vow of silence.* **silence** *v.* **(si·lenced, si·lenc·ing)** to make silent. ☐**in silence,** without speaking or making a sound.

si·lenc·er (sɪ-lĕn-sĕr) *n.* a device for reducing the sound made by a gun.

si·lent (sɪ-lĕnt) *adj.* 1. not speaking, not making or accompanied by a sound. 2. saying little. **si'lent·ly** *adv.* **si'lent·ness** *n.* ☐**silent majority,** people of moderate opinions who rarely make themselves heard. **silent partner,** an inactive partner, one not sharing in the actual work of the firm.

sil·hou·ette (sil-oo-et) *n.* 1. a dark shadow or outline seen against a light background. 2. a profile portrait in solid black. **silhouette** *v.* **(sil·hou·et·ted, sil·hou·et·ting)** to show as a silhouette, *was silhouetted against the screen.*

sil·i·ca (sil-i-kă) *n.* a compound of silicon occurring as quartz or flint and in sandstone and other rocks. ☐**silica gel,** a gelatinous form of silica used chiefly to dehumidify and dehydrate the air in containers etc.

sil·i·cate (sil-i-kit, -kayt) *n.* any of the insoluble compounds of silica.

si·li·ceous, (si-lish-ŭs) *adj.* of or like silica.

sil·i·con (sil-ĭ-kon) *n.* a chemical found widely in the earth in its compound forms. ☐**silicon chip,** a microchip. ▷Do not confuse *silicon* with *silicone.*

sil·i·cone (sil-ĭ-kohn) *n.* any of the organic compounds of silicon, widely used in paints, varnish, and lubricants. ▷Do not confuse *silicone* with *silicon.*

sil·i·co·sis (sil-ĭ-koh-sis) *n.* an abnormal condition of the lungs caused by inhaling dust that contains silica.

silk (silk) *n.* 1. the fine strong soft fiber produced by a silkworm in making its cocoon, or by certain other insects or spiders. 2. thread or cloth made from it, fabric resembling this. 3. clothing made from silk. 4. fine soft strands like threads of silk. 5. *silks,* a jockey's cap and jacket in the horse owner's colors. ☐**silk hat,** a tall cylindrical hat covered with silk plush.

silk·en (sil-kĕn) *adj.* like silk.

silk·screen (silk-skreen) *n.* 1. a print-making process using a screen of silk or other fine fabric as a stencil, with one or more inks being pressed through the fabric and on to the paper etc. below. 2. a print made by this process.

silk-stock·ing (silk-stok-ing) *adj.* (*informal*) wealthy, aristocratic, *they lived in a silk-stocking district.*

silk·worm (silk-wurm) *n.* a caterpillar (of a kind of moth) that feeds on mulberry leaves and spins its cocoon of silk.

silk·y (sil-kee) *adj.* **(silk·i·er, silk·i·est)** as soft or fine or smooth as silk. **silk'i·ly** *adv.* **silk'i·ness** *n.*

sill (sil) *n.* a strip of stone or wood or metal at the base of a window or door.

sil·ly (sil-ee) *adj.* **(-li·er, -li·est)** 1. lacking good sense, foolish, unwise. 2. feebleminded. 3. (*informal*) dazed, *knocked him silly.* **sill'li·ness** *n.*

si·lo (sɪ-loh) *n.* (*pl.* **-los**) 1. a pit or airtight structure in which green crops are pressed and undergo fermentation for use as fodder. 2. a pit or tower for storing grain or cement or radioactive waste. 3. an underground place where a missile is kept ready for firing.

silt (silt) *n.* sediment deposited by water in a channel or harbor etc. **silt** *v.* to block or clog or become blocked with silt, *the harbor is or has silted up.* **silt'y** *adj.* **sil·ta·tion** (sil-tay-shŏn) *n.*

silt·stone (silt-stohn) *n.* rock of hardened silt.

Si·lu·ri·an (si-luur-i-ăn) *adj.* of the geologic period of the Paleozoic era before the Devonian and after the Ordovician. **Silurian** *n.* the Silurian period.

sil·ver (sil-vĕr) *n.* 1. a shiny white precious metal. 2. coins made of this or of an alloy resembling it. 3. silver dishes or ornaments, metal eating utensils. 4. a silver medal (awarded as second prize). 5. the color of silver. **silver** *adj.* made of silver, colored like silver. **silver** *v.* 1. to coat or plate with silver. 2. to give a silvery appearance to, to become silvery, (of hair) to turn gray or white. ☐**born with a silver spoon in one's mouth,** born or destined to be wealthy. **silver anniversary,** the 25th anniversary, especially of a wedding. **silver birch,** = yellow birch. **silver bromide,** a light-sensitive compound used in photographic emulsions. **silver lining,** a consolation or hopeful prospect in the midst of misfortune, *every cloud has a silver lining.* **silver maple,** a maple with light green and silvery white leaves. **silver nitrate,** a water-soluble poisonous compound used in photography, optics, and as an antiseptic etc. **silver plate,** vessels, spoons, etc. of silver or of copper plated with silver. **silver screen,** motion pictures collectively; a superior type of screen on which to project motion pictures. **Silver Star,** a medal awarded to a soldier for gallantry in action.

sil·ver·fish (sil-vĕr-fish) *n.* (*pl.* **-fish, -fish·es**) 1. a silver-colored fish, especially a colorless goldfish. 2. a small insect with a fishlike body, found in books and damp places.

sil·ver-plate (sil-věr-playt) v. **(sil·ver-plat·ed, sil·ver-plat·ing)** to plate with silver.

sil·ver·smith (sil-věr-smith) n. a person whose trade is making articles in silver.

sil·ver-tongued (sil-věr-tungd) adj. eloquent, persuasive.

sil·ver·ware (sil-věr-wair) n. 1. articles made of silver. 2. eating utensils made of silver, silverplate, stainless steel, etc.

sil·ver·y (sil-vě-ree) adj. 1. like silver in color or appearance. 2. having a clear gentle ringing sound.

sim·i·an (sim-i-ăn) adj. monkeylike. **simian** n. an ape or monkey.

sim·i·lar (sim-ĭ-lăr) adj. 1. like, alike, resembling something but not the same. 2. of the same kind or nature or amount. **sim′i·lar·ly** adv. **sim·i·lar·i·ty** (sim-ĭ-lar-i-tee) n. (pl. -ties).

sim·i·le (sim-ĭ-lee) n. a figure of speech using as or like in which two unlike things are compared, such as he's fit as a fiddle; went through it like a hot knife through butter.

si·mil·i·tude (si-mil-ĭ-tood) n. similarity.

sim·mer (sim-ěr) v. 1. to keep (a pan or its contents) almost at boiling point, to be kept like this, to boil very gently. 2. to be in a state of excitement or anger or laughter that is only just kept under control. **simmer** n. a simmering state. □**simmer down,** to become less excited or agitated.

Si·mon·iz (sɪ-mŏ-nɪz) n. (trademark) a kind of wax for polishing automobiles.

si·mon·ize (sɪ-mŏ-nɪz)v. **(si·mon·ized, si·mon·iz·ing)** to polish (an automobile etc.) with Simoniz or other wax.

Si·mon Le·gree (sɪ-mŏn lě-gree) a cruel master. ▷From the brutal slave owner in Harriet Beecher Stowe's novel Uncle Tom's Cabin (1852).

si·mon-pure (sɪ-mŏn-pyoor) adj. real, genuine. ▷From a character in S. Centlivre's play A Bold Stroke for a Wife (1718).

si·mo·ny (sim-ŏn-ee) n. the buying or selling of positions in the Church.

sim·pa·ti·co (sim-pah-ti-koh) adj. (informal) likable, congenial.

sim·per (sim-pěr) v. to smile in an affected way. **simper** n. an affected smile. **sim′per·ing·ly** adv. **sim′per·er** n.

sim·ple (sim-pěl) adj. **(-pler, -plest)** 1. of one element or kind, not compound or complex. 2. not complicated or elaborate, not showy or luxurious. 3. foolish, inexperienced. 4. feebleminded. 5. of humble rank, simple ordinary people. **sim′ply** adv. **sim′ple·ness** n. □**simple fraction,** a fraction both of whose parts are whole numbers. **simple fracture,** a fracture of the bone only, with the bone not piercing the skin. **simple interest,** interest paid only on the original capital, not on the interest added to it. **simple sentence,** a sentence with no coordinate or subordinate clauses. **simple time,** (in music) two or three beats in a bar. ▷Do not confuse simple with simplistic.

sim·ple-heart·ed (sim-pěl-hahr-tid) adj. sincere, free of deceit.

sim·ple-mind·ed (sim-pěl-mɪn-did) adj. 1. unsophisticated. 2. without cunning. 3. feebleminded. **sim′ple-mind′ed·ly** adv. **sim′ple-mind′ed·ness** n.

sim·ple·ton (sim-pěl-tŏn) n. a foolish or easily deceived person, a half-wit.

sim·plic·i·ty (sim-plis-i-tee) n. (pl. -ties) being simple. □**be simplicity itself,** to be very easy.

sim·pli·fy (sim-plĭ-fɪ) v. **(sim·pli·fied, sim·pli·fy·ing)** to make simple, to make easy to do or understand. **sim·pli·fi·ca·tion** (sim-plĭ-fɪ-kay-shŏn) n.

sim·plis·tic (sim-plis-tik) adj. tending to simplify something unjustifiably, a simplistic solution. **sim·plis′ti·cal·ly** adv. ▷Do not confuse simplistic with simple.

sim·u·late (sim-yŭ-layt) v. **(sim·u·lat·ed, sim·u·lat·ing)** 1. to reproduce the conditions of (a situation), as by means of a model, for study or testing or training etc. 2. to pretend to have or feel, they simulated indignation. 3. to imitate the form or condition of. **sim′u·la·tive** adj. **sim′u·la·tor** n. **sim·u·la·tion** (sim-yŭ-lay-shŏn) n. **sim·u·lat·ed** (sim-yŭ-lay-tid) adj. (of furs or pearls etc.) manufactured to look like natural products.

si·mul·cast (sɪ-mŭl-kast) v. **(si·mul·cast, si·mul·cast·ing)** to broadcast the same program on radio and television at the same time. **simulcast** n. a program broadcast this way.

si·mul·ta·ne·ous (sɪ-mŭl-tay-ni-ŭs) adj. occurring or operating at the same time. **si·mul·ta′ne·ous·ly** adv. **si·mul·ta′ne·ous·ness** n. **si·mul·ta·ne·i·ty** (sɪ-mŭl-tă-nee-i-tee) n.

sin (sin) n. 1. the breaking of a religious or moral law, an act that does this. 2. a serious fault or offense. 3. something contrary to common sense, it's a sin to stay indoors on this fine day. **sin** v. **(sinned, sin·ning)** to commit a sin. □**for my sins,** (humorous) as a penalty for something or other that I have done. **live in sin,** (informal) to cohabit without marrying.

since (sins) adv., conj., & prep. 1. after (a certain event or past time), between then and now. 2. ago, before now, it happened long since. 3. for the reason that, because, since we have no money, we can't buy it.

sin·cere (sin-seer) adj. **(-cer·er, -cer·est)** free from pretense or deceit in feeling or manner or actions. **sin·cere′ly** adv. **sin·cer·i·ty** (sin-seri-tee) n.

sine (sɪn) n. (in a right-angled triangle) the ratio of the length of a side opposite one of the acute angles to the length of the hypotenuse.

si·ne·cure (sɪ-ně-kyoor) n. an official position that gives the holder profit or honor with no work attached.

si·ne di·e (sɪ-nee dɪ-ee) indefinitely, with no appointed date, the business was adjourned sine die. ▷Latin, = without a day.

si·ne qua non (sɪ-nee kway non) an indispensable condition or qualification. ▷Latin, = without which not.

sin·ew (sin-yoo) n. 1. tough fibrous tissue uniting muscle to bone. 2. a tendon. 3. sinews, muscles, strength.

sin·ew·y (sin-yoo-ee) adj. like sinew, muscular.

sin·ful (sin-fŭl) adj. full of sin, wicked. **sin′ful·ly** adv. **sin′ful·ness** n.

sing (sing) v. **(sang, sung, sing·ing)** 1. to make musical sounds with the voice, especially in a set tune. 2. to perform (a song). 3. to make a humming or buzzing or whistling sound, the kettle sings. 4. (slang) to turn informer. □**sing a person's praises,** to praise him greatly. **sing out,** to call out loudly.

sing. abbr. singular.

Sin·ga·pore (sing-ă-pohr) 1. a country consisting of a group of islands south of the Malay peninsula. 2. its capital city.

singe (sinj) v. **(singed, singe·ing)** to burn slightly, to burn the ends or edges of. **singe** n. a slight burn.

sing·er (sing-ĕr) n. a person who sings, especially as a professional.

Sin·gha·lese (sing-gă-leez) = **Sinhalese.**

sin·gle (sing-gĕl) adj. 1. one only, not double or multiple. 2. designed for one person or thing, *single beds.* 3. taken separately, *every single thing.* 4. unmarried. 5. (of a flower) having only one circle of petals. **single** n. 1. one person or thing, a single one. 2. a room etc. for one person. 3. a single ticket. 4. a pop record with one piece of music on each side. 5. (in baseball) a hit that enables the batter to advance to first base. 6. *(informal)* a one-dollar bill. 7. *(informal)* an unmarried person, *a singles party.* 8. *singles,* a game with one player on each side, as in tennis, *a singles match.* **single** v. **(sin·gled, sin·gling)** 1. to choose or distinguish from others, *singled him out.* 2. to hit a single in baseball. **sing'ly** adv. **sin'gle·ness** n. ☐**single bond,** one covalent bond linking two atoms of a molecule. **single combat,** a duel. **single cut,** (of a file) with grooves cut in one direction only. **single decker,** a bus with only one deck. **single file,** *see* **file².**

single standard, a single set of rules or criteria applying to everyone.

sin·gle-ac·tion (sing-gĕl-ak-shŏn) adj. (of a gun) needing to be cocked by hand before every shot.

sin·gle-breast·ed (sing-gĕl-bres-tid) adj. (of a coat) fastening but not overlapping widely across the breast.

sin·gle-hand·ed (sing-gĕl-han-did) adj. without help from other persons.

sin·gle-mind·ed (sing-gĕl-mɪn-did) adj. with one's mind set on a single purpose.

sin·gle-space (sing-gĕl-spays) v. **(-spaced, -spac·ing)** to type (copy) leaving no blank spaces between lines.

sin·gle·ton (sing-gĕl-tŏn) n. something occurring singly, not as one of a group.

sin·gle·tree (sing-gĕl-tree) n. a whiffletree.

sing·song (sing-sawng) adj. with a monotonous rise and fall of the voice in speaking. **singsong** n. a singsong manner of speaking.

sin·gu·lar (sing-gyŭ-lăr) n. the form of a noun or verb used with reference to one person or thing, *the singular is "man," the plural is "men."* **singular** adj. 1. of this form. 2. uncommon, extraordinary, *spoke with singular shrewdness.* **sin'gu·lar·ly** adv. **sin·gu·lar·i·ty** (sing-gyŭ-lar-i-tee) n.

Sin·ha·lese (sin-hă-leez) adj. of Sri Lanka or its people or language. **Sinhalese** n. (pl. **Sinhalese**) 1. a native of Sri Lanka. 2. the Sinhalese language.

sin·is·ter (sin-i-stĕr) adj. 1. suggestive of evil. 2. involving wickedness, criminal, *sinister motives.* **sin'is·ter·ly** adv.

sink (singk) v. **(sank** or **sunk, sunk** or **sunk·en, sink·ing)** 1. to fall slowly downward, to come gradually to a lower level or pitch. 2. to become wholly or partly submerged in water etc., (of a ship) to go to the bottom of the sea. 3. to pass into a less active condition, *she sank into sleep.* 4. to lose value or strength etc. gradually. 5. to cause or allow to sink. 6. to dig (a well) or bore (a shaft). 7. to send (a ball) into a pocket or hole in billiards, golf, etc. 8. to invest (money). **sink** n. 1. a fixed basin with a drainage pipe and usually with a water supply, in a kitchen etc. 2. a cesspool;

a sink of iniquity, a place where evil people or practices tend to collect. 3. a marsh or pool in which water (as from a river) disappears by evaporation or percolation. 4. a sinkhole. **sink'a·ble** adj. ☐**sink in,** to penetrate; to become understood. **sinking feeling,** a feeling caused by hunger or fear. **sinking fund,** a fund set aside for the purpose of wiping out a country's or business company's debt gradually.

sink·er (sink-kĕr) n. 1. a weight used to sink a fishing line or a line used in taking soundings. 2. *(slang)* a doughnut. 3. (in baseball) a pitch that dips sharply as it reaches home plate.

sink·hole (singk-hohl) n. 1. low land where drainage collects. 2. a cavity formed in rock by water.

sin·less (sin-lis) adj. free from sin.

sin·ner (sin-ĕr) n. a person who sins.

Sinn Fein (shin fayn) a nationalist political party in Ireland.

Si·nol·o·gy (sɪ-nol-ŏ-jee) n. the study of the Chinese language, history, culture, etc. **Si·nol'o·gist** n.

sin·u·ous (sin-yoo-ŭs) adj. with many curves, undulating. **sin'u·ous·ly** adv. **sin·u·os·i·ty** (sin-yoo-os-i-tee) n.

si·nus (sɪ-nŭs) n. (pl. **-nus·es**) a cavity in bone or tissue, especially that in the skull connecting with the nostrils.

si·nus·i·tis (sɪ-nŭ-sɪ-tis) n. inflammation of one or more sinuses in the skull.

Sioux (soo) n. (pl. **Sioux**) a member of a group of Indian tribes formerly living in the western U.S.

sip (sip) v. **(sipped, sip·ping)** to take a sip of, to drink in small mouthfuls. **sip** n. 1. the act of sipping. 2. a small mouthful of liquid.

si·phon (sɪ-fŏn) n. 1. a pipe or tube in the form of an upside-down **U,** used for forcing liquid to flow from one container to another by utilizing atmospheric pressure. 2. a bottle from which aerated water is forced out through a tube by pressure of gas. 3. the sucking tube of some insects or small animals. **siphon** v. 1. to flow or draw out through a siphon. 2. to take from a source, *funds were siphoned off for this purpose.* **si'phon·al** adj. **si·phon·ic** (sɪ-fon-ik) adj.

sir (sur) n. 1. a polite form of address to a man. 2. *Sir,* a title prefixed to the name of a knight or baronet, *Sir John Moore, Sir J. Moore, Sir John.*

sire (sɪr) n. 1. *(old use)* a father or male ancestor. 2. *(old use)* a title of respect, used to a king. 3. the male parent of an animal. **sire** v. **(sired, sir·ing)** (of an animal) to be the sire of, to beget.

si·ren (sɪr-ĕn) n. 1. a device that makes a loud prolonged sound as a signal. 2. a dangerously fascinating woman. ▷Named after the Sirens in Greek legend, women who lived on an island and by their singing lured seafarers to destruction on the rocks surrounding it.

Sir·i·us (sir-i-ŭs) n. the brightest star in the sky, part of the Canis Major constellation.

sir·loin (sur-loin) n. the upper (best) part of loin of beef.

si·roc·co (si-rok-oh) n. (pl. **-cos**) a hot wind that reaches Italy from Africa.

si·sal (sɪ-săl, sis-ăl) n. 1. rope fiber made from the leaves of a tropical plant. 2. the plant itself.

sis·kin (sis-kin) n. a greenish songbird of Europe, related to the goldfinch.

sis·sy (sis-ee) *n.* (*pl.* **-sies**) an effeminate boy or man, a cowardly person. **sis·si·fied** (sis-ĭ-frd) *adj.*

sis·ter (sis-tĕr) *n.* 1. a daughter of the same parents as another person. 2. a fellow woman, one who is a fellow member of a group or sect. 3. a nun; *Sister,* the title of a nun. □**sister ship,** a ship built in the same design as another.

sis·ter·hood (sis-tĕr-huud) *n.* 1. the relationship of sisters. 2. an order of nuns, a society of women doing religious or charitable work.

sis·ter-in-law (sis-tĕr-in-law) *n.* (*pl.* **sis·ters-in-law**) the sister of one's husband or wife, the wife of one's brother.

sit (sit) *v.* (**sat, sit·ting**) 1. to take or be in a position in which the body rests more or less upright on the buttocks, *we were sitting gossiping; sit one's horse,* to sit or keep one's seat on it. 2. to cause to sit, to place in a sitting position, *sat him down.* 3. to pose for a portrait. 4. (of birds) to perch, (of certain animals) to rest with legs bent and body along the ground. 5. (of birds) to remain on the nest to hatch eggs. 6. to be situated, to lie. 7. to baby-sit. 8. to occupy a seat as a member of a committee etc. 9. (of a legislative body or a law court or a committee) to be in session. 10. (of clothes) to fit in a certain way, *the coat sits badly on the shoulders.* □**be sitting pretty,** *(informal)* to be in an advantageous situation. **sit at a person's feet,** to be his pupil or disciple. **sit back,** to relax one's efforts. **sit down,** to take a seat after standing. **sit in judgment,** to make judgments about other people. **sit in on,** to be present as an observer at (a meeting etc.). **sit on,** *(informal)* to delay action concerning, *the Government has been sitting on the report; (slang)* to repress or snub, *someone should sit on him.* **sit on the fence,** *see* **fence. sit out,** to take no part in (a dance etc.); to stay until the end of, *had to sit the concert out.* **sit tight,** *(informal)* to remain firmly where one is, to take no action and not yield. **sit up,** to rise to a sitting posture from lying down; to sit upright and not slouch; to remain out of bed, *sat up late; make a person sit up,* to cause him surprise or alarm, to arouse his interest. ▷See the note under *set.*

si·tar (si-**tahr**) *n.* an Indian musical instrument resembling a guitar.

sit·com (sit-kom) *n.* *(informal)* a situation comedy.

sit-down (sit-down) *adj.* (of a meal) taken seated. □**sit-down strike,** a strike in which strikers refuse to leave their place of work.

site (srt) *n.* 1. the ground on which a town or building stood or stands or is to stand. 2. the place where some activity or event takes place or took place, *camping site; the site of the battle.* **site** *v.* (**sit·ed, sit·ing**) to locate, to provide with a site. ▷Do not confuse *site* with *cite.*

sit-in (sit-in) *n.* occupation of a building etc. as a form of protest.

sit·ter (sit-ĕr) *n.* 1. a person who is seated. 2. one who is sitting for a portrait. 3. a sitting hen. 4. a baby-sitter.

sit·ting (sit-ing) *see* **sit. sitting** *adj.* (of an animal) not running, (of a game bird) not flying, *shot a sitting pheasant.* **sitting** *n.* 1. the time during which a person or assembly etc. sits continuously, *lunch is served in two sittings.* 2. a clutch of eggs. □**sitting duck** *or* **target,** *(slang)* a person or thing that is a helpless victim of attack. **sitting room,** a room used for sitting in, not a bedroom.

sit·u·ate (sich-oo-ayt) *v.* (**sit·u·at·ed, sit·u·at·ing**) to place or put in a certain position. □**be situated,** to be in a certain position.

sit·u·a·tion (sich-oo-ay-shŏn) *n.* 1. a place (with its surroundings) that is occupied by something. 2. a set of circumstances. (▷It is incorrect to use this word in phrases such as "when you're in a strike situation" instead of "when there is a strike.") 3. a position of employment, *situations wanted.* **sit·u·a′tion·al** *adj.* □**situation comedy,** a comedy in which humor derives from characters' misunderstandings and embarrassments.

sit-up (sit-up) *n.* an exercise in which a person lying supine sits up without bending his legs.

si·tus (sɪ-tŭs) *n.* (*pl.* **-tus**) 1. the proper or primary position of an organ of the body. 2. location.

sitz (sits, zits) **bath** 1. a bathtub in which one sits immersed to the hips. 2. a bath taken in such a bathtub.

six (siks) *adj. & n.* one more than five (6, VI). □**at sixes and sevens,** in disorder.

six·fold (siks-fohld) *adj.* six times as much or as many.

six·foot·er (siks-fuut-ĕr) *n.* *(informal)* a person or thing six feet tall.

six-gun (siks-gun) *n.* a six-chambered revolver.

six-pack (siks-pak) *n.* six bottles or cans of soda or beer etc. packaged and sold as one unit.

six·pence (siks-pĕns) *n.* *(British)* 1. the sum of 6p (6 pennies). 2. *(old use)* the sum of 6d (6 old pennies), a coin worth this.

six-shoot·er (siks-shoo-tĕr) *n.* a six-gun.

six·teen (siks-teen) *adj. & n.* one more than fifteen (16, XVI). **six′teenth′** *adj. & n.*

sixth (siksth) *adj. & n.* 1. next after fifth. 2. one of six equal parts of a thing. **sixth′ly** *adv.* □**sixth sense,** a supposed extra power of perception other than the five physical ones, intuition.

six·ties (siks-teez) *n. pl.* the numbers or years or degrees of temperature from sixty to sixty-nine.

six·ty (siks-tee) *adj. & n.* (*pl.* **-ties**) six times ten (60, LX). **six·ti·eth** (siks-tee-ith) *adj. & n.* □**like sixty,** *(informal)* very easily or fast. **sixty-four (thousand) dollar question,** the most difficult question of all.

siz·a·ble (sɪ-ză-bĕl) *adj.* of large or fairly large size. **siz′a·bly** *adv.*

size[1] (sɪz) *n.* 1. the measurements or extent of something. 2. any of the series of standard measurements in which things of the same kind are made and sold. **size** *v.* (**sized, siz·ing**) to group or sort according to size. □**size up,** to estimate the size of; *(informal)* to form a judgment of (a person or situation etc.). **the size of it,** *(informal)* the way it is, the facts about it.

size[2] *n.* a gluey solution used to glaze paper or stiffen textiles etc. **size** *v.* (**sized, siz·ing**) to treat with size.

siz·ing (siz-ing) *n.* size[2].

siz·zle (siz-ĕl) *v.* (**siz·zled, siz·zling**) 1. to make a hissing sound like that of frying. *(informal)* to be very hot, to be angry or resentful. **sizzle** *n.* 1. a sizzling sound. 2. a state of great heat or excitement.

S.J. *abbr.* Society of Jesus.

S.J.D. *abbr.* Doctor of Juridical Science. ▷Latin *Scientiae Juridicae Doctor.*

skate[1] (skayt) *n.* (*pl.* **skate, skates**) a large flatfish used as food.

skate[2] *n.* 1. a roller skate. 2. an ice skate. **skate** *v.* (**skat·ed, skat·ing**) to move on skates, to per-

form (a specified figure) in this way. **skat′er** n.
□**skating rink,** a stretch of natural or artificial
ice used for skating; a smooth floor used for roller
skating.

skate·board (skayt-bohrd) n. a small board with
wheels like those of roller skates, for riding on
(as a sport) while standing. **skateboard** v. to
use a skateboard. **skate′board·er** n. **skate′**
board·ing n.

ske·dad·dle (ski-dad-ĕl) v. **(ske·dad·dled,**
ske·dad·dling) (slang) to go away quickly.

skeet (skeet) n. (also **skeet shooting**) a shooting
sport in which a clay target is thrown from a
trap to simulate the flight of a bird.

skein (skayn) n. 1. a loosely coiled bundle of yarn
or thread. 2. a number of wild geese etc. in flight.

skel·e·tal (skel-ĕ-tăl) adj. of or like a skeleton.
skel′e·tal·ly adv.

skel·e·ton (skel-ĕ-tŏn) n. 1. the supporting structure of an animal body, consisting of bones. 2.
the shell or other hard structure covering or supporting an invertebrate animal. 3. a very lean person or animal. 4. any supporting structure or
framework, as of a building. 5. an outline of a
literary work etc. □**skeleton crew,** a permanent
nucleus ready for supplementing. **skeleton in
the closet,** a discreditable secret. **skeleton key,**
a key made so as to fit many locks. **skeleton
staff,** the minimum needed to do the essential
things in work that normally requires more staff.

skep·tic (skep-tik) n. a skeptical person, one who
doubts the truth of religious doctrines. **skep·**
ti·cism (skep-ti-siz-ĕm) n.

skep·ti·cal (skep-ti-kăl) adj. inclined to disbelieve
things, doubting or questioning the truth of claims
or statements etc. **skep′ti·cal·ly** adv.

sketch (skech) n. 1. a rough drawing or painting.
2. a brief account of something. 3. a short usually
comic play. **sketch** v. to make a sketch or
sketches, to make a sketch of. **sketch′er** n.

sketch·book (skech-buuk) n. a pad of drawing
paper for sketching on.

sketch·y (skech-ee) adj. **(sketch·i·er, sketch·**
i·est) rough and not detailed or careful or substantial. **sketch′i·ly** adv. **sketch′i·ness** n.

skew (skyoo) adj. slanting, askew. **skew** v. to make
skew, to turn or twist around.

skew·er (skyoo-ĕr) n. a pin thrust through meat
to hold it compactly together while it is cooked.
skewer v. to pierce or hold in place with a skewer
or other pointed object.

ski (skee) n. (pl. **skis**) one of a pair of long narrow
strips of wood etc. fixed under the feet for traveling over snow. **ski** v. **(skied, ski·ing)** to travel
on skis. **ski′er** n. □**ski boot,** a boot to wear
while skiing. **ski jump,** a steep slope leveling off
before a sharp drop to allow a skier to leap
through the air. **ski lift** or **ski tow,** a device for
carrying skiers up a slope, usually on seats slung
from an overhead cable. **ski mask,** a mask worn
to protect the face while skiing. **ski run,** a slope
suitable for skiing down, **ski suit,** a protective
suit worn while skiing.

skid (skid) v. **(skid·ded, skid·ding)** (of a vehicle
or its wheels) to slide uncontrollably on slippery
ground. **skid** n. 1. a skidding movement. 2. a
log or plank etc. used to make a track over which
heavy objects may be dragged or rolled. 3. a runner on certain aircraft, for use when landing. 4.
a wedge or a wooden or metal shoe that acts as
a braking device on the wheel of a cart. **skid′dy**

adj. □**on the skids,** (slang) on the way to ruin.
put the skids under, (slang) to cause to hurry;
to hasten the downfall of. **skid row,** a slum area
where vagrants live.

skiff (skif)n. a small light boat for rowing or scull-
ing.

skill (skil) n. ability to do something well.

skilled (skild) adj. 1. skillful. 2. (of work) needing
great skill, (of a worker) highly trained or experienced in such work.

skil·let (skil-it) n. a frying pan.

skill·ful (skil-fŭl) adj. having or showing great skill.
skill′ful·ly adv. **skill′ful·ness** n.

skim (skim) v. **(skimmed, skim·ming)** 1. to take
(floating matter) from the surface of a liquid, to
clear (a liquid) in this way. 2. to move lightly
and quickly over a surface, to glide through air.
3. to read quickly, noting only the chief points,
skim through a newspaper or skim it. 4. (slang)
to hide (profits) illegally in order to avoid tax
payments. □**skim milk,** milk from which cream
has been removed. **skim the cream off,**
(informal) to take the best part.

skim·mer (skim-ĕr) n. 1. a ladle etc. for skimming
things. 2. a stiff flat straw hat. 3. a long-winged
sea bird that feeds by skimming over the water
with its lower mandible immersed.

ski·mo·bile (skee-mŏ-beel) n. a snowmobile.

skimp (skimp) v. to scrimp.

skimp·y (skim-pee) adj. **(skimp·i·er, skimp·**
i·est) scanty, especially through being skimped.
skimp′i·ly adv. **skimp′i·ness** n.

skin (skin) n. 1. the flexible continuous covering
of the human or other animal body. 2. an animal's
skin removed from its body, with or without the
hair still attached. 3. material made from this.
4. a vessel for water or wine, made from an animal's whole skin. 5. a person's complexion. 6.
an outer layer or covering, as the rind of fruit
or the plating on an aircraft etc. 7. the skinlike
film that forms on the surface of certain liquids.
skin v. **(skinned, skin·ning)** 1. to strip or scrape
the skin from. 2. to cover or become covered with
new skin, the wound had skinned over. **skin′less**
adj. □**be nothing but skin and bone,** to be
very thin. **by the skin of one's teeth,** only
just, barely. **get under a person's skin,**
(informal) to interest or annoy him greatly. **save
one's skin,** to avoid injury or loss. **skin flick,**
(slang) a pornographic film. **skin game,** (slang)
a swindling game. **skin graft,** a piece of skin
cut from another part or person and surgically
substituted for a damaged part.

skin-deep (skin-deep) adj. superficial, not deep or
lasting.

skin-dive (skin-dɪv) v. **(skin-dived, skin-div·**
ing) to swim deep under water with flippers and
breathing apparatus.

skin div·ing (skin dɪv-ing) underwater swimming.
skin div′er n.

skin·flint (skin-flint) n. a miserly person.

skin·ny (skin-ee) adj. **(-ni·er, -ni·est)** (of a person
or animal) very thin.

skin·ny-dip (skin-ee-dip) v. **(skin·ny-dipped,**
skin·ny-dip·ping) (informal) to swim in the
nude. **skin′ny-dip·per** n.

skin·tight (skin-tɪt) adj. (of clothing etc.) very
close-fitting.

skip (skip) v. **(skipped, skip·ping)** 1. to move
along lightly, especially by taking two steps with
each foot in turn. 2. to cause this to happen to

(a thing), *skip stones across the pond.* **3.** to pass quickly from one subject or point to another. **4.** to omit in reading or dealing with a thing. **5.** *(slang)* to go away hastily or secretly. **skip** *n.* a skipping movement. ☐**skip bail,** to jump bail *(see* **jump***).* **skip it!,** *(slang)* leave that subject.

ski·plane (skee-playn) *n.* an airplane that has skis for landing on and taking off from snow.

skip·per¹ (skip-ĕr) *n.* **1.** one who skips. **2.** a small dark thick-bodied butterfly.

skipper² *n.* a captain. **skipper** *v.* to captain.

skirl (skurl) *n.* the shrill shound characteristic of bagpipes. **skirl** *v.* to make this sound.

skir·mish (skur-mish) *n.* a minor fight or conflict. **skirmish** *v.* to take part in a skirmish. **skir′mish·er** *n.*

skirt (skurt) *n.* a woman's garment hanging from the waist, this part of a garment. **skirt** *v.* **1.** to go or be situated along the edge of. **2.** to avoid dealing directly with (a question or controversial topic etc.).

skit (skit) *n.* a short play or piece of writing that is a humorous imitation of a serious one, a piece of humorous mimicry.

skit·ter (skit-ĕr) *v.* **1.** to skip or glide quickly. **2.** to hurry about, to dart off.

skit·tish (skit-ish) *adj.* frisky. **skit′tish·ly** *adv.* **skit′tish·ness** *n.*

skiv·vy (skiv-ee) *n.* (*pl.* **-vies**) *(slang)* **1.** cotton T-shirt. **2.** underwear consisting of shorts and a T-shirt.

skoal (skohl) *interj.* (used as a toast) to your health! **Skt.** *abbr.* Sanskrit.

sku·a (skyoo-ă) *n.* a kind of large sea gull.

skul·dug·ger·y (skul-dug-ĕ-ree) *n.* *(informal)* trickery.

skulk (skulk) *v.* to loiter or move or conceal oneself stealthily. **skulk′er** *n.*

skull (skul) *n.* **1.** the bony framework of the head, the part of this protecting the brain. **2.** a representation of this; *skull and crossbones,* this with two bones crossed below it as an emblem of death or piracy or as a warning label on bottles etc. of poison.

skull·cap (skul-kap) *n.* a small close-fitting cap with no brim, worn on top of the head.

skunk (skungk) *n.* (*pl.* **skunks, skunk**) **1.** a black and white bushy-tailed North American mammal about the size of a cat, able to spray an evil smelling liquid from glands near its tail. **2.** *(slang)* a contemptible person. **skunk** *v.* *(slang)* to defeat decisively. ☐**skunk cabbage,** a broad-leaved plant with an unpleasant smell.

skunk·weed (skungk-weed) *n.* **1.** an unpleasant-smelling perennial herb. **2.** skunk cabbage.

sky (skī) *n.* (*pl.* **skies**) **1.** the region of the clouds or upper air. **2.** climate or weather shown by this, *the sunny skies of Italy.* ☐**sky marshal,** an armed federal security guard assigned to ride in an airplane to prevent skyjacking. **sky pilot,** *(slang)* a chaplain or clergyman.

sky-blue (skī-bloo) *adj.* & *n.* bright clear blue.

sky·cap (skī-kap) *n.* a baggage porter at an airport.

sky·dive (skī-dīv) *v.* (**sky·dived, sky·div·ing**) to engage in skydiving. **sky′div·er** *n.*

sky·div·ing (skī-dī-ving) *n.* the sport of jumping from an airplane and performing acrobatics before opening the parachute at a low altitude.

Skye (skī) **terrier** a variety of Scotch terrier with long hair and a long body.

sky-high (skī-hī) *adj.* & *adv.* very high.

sky·jack (skī-jak) *v.* to hijack (an aircraft). **sky′jack·er** *n.* **sky′jack·ing** *n.*

sky·lark (skī-lahrk) *n.* a lark that soars while singing. **skylark** *v.* to play about lightheartedly. **sky′lark·er** *n.*

sky·light (skī-līt) *n.* a window set in the line of a roof or ceiling.

sky·line (skī-līn) *n.* the outline of hills, buildings, etc., defined against the sky, the visible horizon.

sky·rock·et (skī-rok-it) *n.* a rocket that rises high into the air before exploding. **skyrocket** *v.* to rise sharply.

sky·scrap·er (skī-skray-pĕr) *n.* a very tall building with many stories.

sky·ward (skī-wărd) *adv.* toward the sky.

sky·writ·ing (skī-rī-ting) *n.* legible smoke trails made by an airplane, especially for advertising. **sky′writ·er** *n.*

slab (slab) *n.* a flat broad fairly thick piece of something solid.

slack¹ (slak) *adj.* **1.** loose, not tight or tense. **2.** slow, sluggish, negligent. **3.** (of trade or business) with little happening, not busy. **slack** *n.* **1.** the slack part of a rope etc., *haul in the slack.* **2.** *slacks,* trousers for informal or sports wear. **slack** *v.* **1.** to slacken. **2.** to be idle or lazy about work. **slack′ly** *adv.* **slack′er** *n.* **slack′ness** *n.* ☐**slack suit,** casual clothes of slacks and a jacket or shirt. ▷Do not confuse *slack* with *slake.*

slack·en (slak-ĕn) *v.* to make or become slack.

slack-jawed (slak-jawd) *adj.* having one's mouth open, *slack-jawed with astonishment.*

slag (slag) *n.* **1.** solid nonmetallic waste matter left when metal has been separated from ore by smelting. **2.** lava fragments similar to this.

slain (slayn) *see* **slay.**

slake (slayk) *v.* (**slaked, slak·ing**) **1.** to satisfy or make less strong, *slake one's thirst.* **2.** to combine (lime) chemically with water. ▷Do not confuse *slake* with *slack.*

sla·lom (slah-lŏm) *n.* a ski race down a zigzag course.

slam (slam) *v.* (**slammed, slam·ming**) **1.** to shut forcefully with a loud noise. **2.** to put or knock or hit forcefully. **3.** *(slang)* to criticize severely. **slam** *n.* **1.** a slamming noise. **2.** the winning of twelve or thirteen tricks in the game of bridge. ☐**grand slam,** *see* **grand. little** *or* **small slam,** the winning of twelve tricks in the game of bridge.

slam-bang (slam-bang) *adv.* *(informal)* **1.** noisily, violently. **2.** recklessly, slapdash.

slan·der (slan-dĕr) *n.* **1.** a false statement uttered maliciously that damages a person's reputation. **2.** the crime of uttering this. **slander** *v.* to utter a slander about. **slan′der·er** *n.* **slan′der·ous** *adj.* **slan′der·ous·ly** *adv.*

slang (slang) *n.* words, phrases, or particular meaning of these, that are used very informally for vividness or novelty or to avoid being conventional. **slang′y** *adj.* **slang′i·ness** *n.* ▷In this dictionary, words and definitions marked *slang* are not acceptable when speaking or writing formally.

slant (slant) *v.* **1.** to slope. **2.** to present (news etc.) from a particular point of view. **slant** *n.* **1.** a slope. **2.** the way something is presented, an attitude or bias. **slant′ing·ly** *adv.*

slant-wise (slant-wīz) *adv.* in a slanting position.

slap (slap) *v.* (**slapped, slap·ping**) **1.** to strike with the open hand or with something flat. **2.** to put forcefully down, *slapped the money on the*

counter. **3.** to put hastily or carelessly, *slapped paint on the walls.* **slap** *n.* a blow with the open hand or with something flat. **slap** *adv.* with a slap, directly, *ran slap into him.* **slap'per** *n.* □**slap a person down,** *(informal)* to snub or reprimand him. **slap in the face,** an insult.
slap·dash (slap-dash) *adj.* hasty and careless. **slapdash** *adv.* in a slapdash way.
slap·hap·py (slap-hap-ee) *adj. (informal)* **1.** punch-drunk. **2.** cheerfully casual.
slap·stick (slap-stik) *n.* comedy with boisterous action.
slash (slash) *v.* **1.** to make a sweeping stroke or strokes with a sword or knife or whip etc., to strike in this way. **2.** to make an ornamental slit in (a garment), especially to show underlying fabric. **3.** to reduce drastically, *prices were slashed.* **4.** to criticize vigorously. **slash** *n.* **1.** a slashing cut, a wound made by this. **2.** the debris resulting from the felling or destruction of trees. **3.** (in printing) a virgule. **slash'er** *n.*
slat (slat) *n.* one of the thin narrow strips of wood or metal or plastic arranged so as to overlap and form a screen, as in a Venetian blind.
slate (slayt) *n.* **1.** a kind of rock that is easily split into flat smooth plates. **2.** a piece of this used as roofing material or (formerly) for writing on. **3.** a list of nominees for office etc. **slate** *v.* **(slat· ed, slat·ing) 1.** to cover or roof with slates. **2.** to nominate, to propose (for office etc.). **3.** to make arrangements for (an event etc.). **slat'y** *adj.* □**a clean slate,** a record of good conduct with nothing discreditable; *wipe the slate clean,* to forgive and forget past offenses.
slate-blue (slayt-bloo) *adj. & n.* grayish-blue.
slate-gray (slayt-gray) *adj. & n.* bluish-gray.
slath·er (slath-ĕr) *v.* **1.** to spread thickly. **2.** to squander.
slat·tern (slat-ĕrn) *n.* a slovenly woman. **slat'tern·ly** *adj. & adv.*
slaugh·ter (slaw-tĕr) *n.* **1.** the killing of animals for food. **2.** the ruthless killing of a great number of people or animals, a massacre. **slaughter** *v.* **1.** to kill (animals) for food. **2.** to kill ruthlessly or in great numbers. **3.** *(informal)* to defeat utterly. **slaugh'ter·er** *n.*
slaugh·ter·house (slaw-tĕr-hows) *n.* (*pl.* **-hous· es,** *pr.* -how-ziz) a place where animals are killed for food.
Slav (slahv) *n.* a member of any of the peoples of East and Central Europe who speak a Slavic language.
Slav. *abbr.* Slavic.
slave (slayv) *n.* **1.** a person who is the property of another and obliged to work for him. **2.** one who is dominated by another person or by an influence, *a slave to duty.* **3.** a person compelled to work very hard for someone else, a drudge. **4.** a mechanism controlled by another mechanism and repeating its actions. **slave** *v.* **(slaved, slav· ing)** to work very hard. □**slave bracelet,** a bracelet or thin chain worn around the ankle. **slave driver,** an overseer of slaves at work; a person who makes others work very hard. **slave labor,** work done by slaves; persons (such as political prisoners) forced to perform labor; any forced or poorly paid labor. **slave ship,** a ship used in transporting slaves. **Slave State,** any of the southern states in the U.S. where slavery was legal before the Civil War.

slav·er (slav-ĕr) *v.* to have saliva flowing from the mouth.
slav·er·y (slay-vĕ-ree) *n.* **1.** the condition of a slave. **2.** the existence of slaves, *to abolish slavery.* **3.** very hard work, drudgery.
Slav·ic (slah-vik) *adj.* of the Slavs or their languages.
slav·ish (slay-vish) *adj.* **1.** like a slave, excessively submissive. **2.** showing no independence or originality. **slav'ish·ly** *adv.* **slav'ish·ness** *n.*
Sla·von·ic (slă-von-ik) *adj.* Slavic.
slaw (slaw) *n. (informal)* coleslaw.
slay (slay) *v.* **(slew,** *pr.* sloo, **slain, slay·ing)** to kill.
slea·zy (slee-zee) *adj.* **(-zi·er, -zi·est)** *(informal)* dirty and slovenly. **slea'zi·ly** *adv.* **slea'zi· ness** *n.*
sld. *abbr.* **1.** sailed. **2.** sealed.
sled (sled) *n.* a narrow cart with runners instead of wheels, used for traveling on snow or bare ground or in sport for traveling downhill at speed.
sledge¹ (slej) *n.* a strong heavy sled used especially for carrying freight across snow or ice.
sledge² *n.* a sledgehammer.
sledge·ham·mer (slej-ham-ĕr) *n.* a large heavy hammer used with both hands.
sleek (sleek) *adj.* **1.** smooth and glossy, *sleek hair.* **2.** looking well-fed and thriving. **sleek** *v.* to make sleek by smoothing. **sleek'ly** *adv.* **sleek' ness** *n.*
sleep (sleep) *n.* **1.** the natural recurring condition of rest in animals, in which there is unconsciousness with the nervous system inactive and muscles relaxed. **2.** a spell of this, *a long sleep.* **3.** the inert condition of hibernating animals. **sleep** *v.* **(slept, sleep·ing) 1.** to be in a state of sleep. **2.** to spend (time) in sleeping; *sleep it off,* get rid of a hangover etc. by sleeping. **3.** to stay for a night's sleep. **4.** to provide with sleeping accommodation, *the cottage sleeps four.* □**sleeping bag,** a lined bag in which a person may sleep, especially while camping. **sleeping car,** a railroad car fitted with berths or beds for passengers. **sleeping pill,** a pill to help a person to sleep. **sleeping sickness,** a disease with symptoms that include extreme sleepiness, spread by the bite of the tsetse fly. **sleep like a top,** to sleep soundly. **sleep on it,** to delay deciding about something until the next day.
sleep·er (slee-pĕr) *n.* **1.** one who sleeps. **2.** a sleeping car, a berth in this. **3.** *(informal)* an unexpected success, such as a book or a political candidate.
sleep-in (sleep-in) *adj.* sleeping by night at one's place of work, *a sleep-in maid.*
sleep·less (sleep-lis) *adj.* unable to sleep, without sleep. **sleep'less·ly** *adv.* **sleep'less·ness** *n.*
sleep·walk·er (sleep-waw-kĕr) *n.* a person who walks while asleep. **sleep'walk·ing** *n.*
sleep·y (slee-pee) *adj.* **(sleep·i·er, sleep·i· est) 1.** feeling or showing a desire to sleep. **2.** inactive, without stir or bustle, *a sleepy little town.* **sleep'i·ly** *adv.* **sleep'i·ness** *n.*
sleep·y·head (slee-pee-hed) *n.* a sleepy person.
sleet (sleet) *n.* snow and rain falling at the same time, hail or snow that melts while falling. **sleet** *v.* to fall as sleet in a shower, *it is sleeting.* **sleet'y** *adj.*
sleeve (sleev) *n.* **1.** the part of a garment covering the arm or part of it. **2.** a tube enclosing a rod

or another tube. 3. a windsock, a drogue towed by an aircraft. 4. the cover of a phonograph record. **sleeved** *adj.* □**up one's sleeve,** concealed but available for use, in reserve; *laugh up one's sleeve,* to laugh secretly or be secretly pleased with oneself.

sleeve·less (sleev-lis) *adj.* without sleeves.

sleigh (slay) *n.* a sled, especially one used as a passenger vehicle drawn by horses. **sleigh** *v.* to ride in a sleigh. **sleigh′ing** *n.*

sleight (slɪt) *n.* **sleight of hand,** great skill in using the hands to perform conjuring tricks etc.

slen·der (slen-dĕr) *adj.* 1. slim and graceful. 2. small in amount, scanty, *slender means.* **slen′der·ly** *adv.* **slen′der·ness** *n.*

slen·der·ize (slen-dĕ-rız) *v.* (**slen·der·ized, slen·der·iz·ing**) to make or become slender.

slept (slept) *see* **sleep.**

sleuth (slooth) *n.* (*informal*) a detective.

sleuth·ing *n.* (sloo-thing) searching for information as a detective does.

slew[1] (sloo) = **slue.**

slew[2] *see* **slay.**

slew[3] *n.* (*informal*) a large number.

slew[4] *n.* a slough (= swamp).

slice (slıs) *n.* 1. a thin broad piece (or a wedge) cut from something. 2. a portion or share. 3. an implement with a thin broad blade for lifting or serving fish etc. 4. a slicing stroke in golf. **slice** *v.* (**sliced, slic·ing**) 1. to cut into slices. 2. to cut from a larger piece. 3. to cut cleanly or easily. 4. to strike (a ball, in golf) badly so that it spins away from the direction intended, going to the right of a right-handed player. **slice′a·ble** *adj.* **slic′er** *n.* □**slice of life,** a realistic representation of everyday experience.

slick (slik) *adj.* 1. done or doing things smoothly and cleverly but perhaps with some trickery. 2. smooth in manner or speech. 3. smooth and slippery, *the roads were slick with oil.* **slick** *n.* a slippery place, a thick patch of oil floating on the sea. **slick** *v.* to make sleek. **slick′ly** *adv.* **slick′ness** *n.*

slick·er (slik-ĕr) *n.* 1. a raincoat of oilskin or other smooth material. 2. (*informal*) a stylish person with a smooth but deceptive manner, *a city slicker.* **slick′ered** *adj.*

slide (slıd) *v.* (**slid, slid·ing**) 1. to move or cause to move along a smooth surface with the same area in continuous contact with this. 2. to glide more or less erect over ice or another smooth surface without skates. 3. to move or cause to move quietly or unobtrusively, *slid a coin into his hand.* 4. to pass gradually into a condition or habit. 5. (in baseball, of a base runner) to drop to the ground and skid rapidly toward a base in order to reach it without being tagged out. **slide** *n.* 1. the act of sliding. 2. a smooth surface for sliding on. 3. an inclined plane for goods etc. or for children to play on. 4. a sliding part of a machine or instrument. 5. a small glass plate on which things are placed for examination under a microscope. 6. a mounted picture or transparency for showing on a blank surface by means of a projector. 7. a landslide or avalanche. **slid′a·ble** *adj.* □**let a thing slide,** to fail to give it proper attention, to make no effort to control it. **slide fastener,** a zipper. **slide rule,** a ruler with a sliding central strip, marked with logarithmic scales and used for making calcula-

tions rapidly. **slide trombone,** a trombone with a slide for controlling pitch. **sliding door,** a door that slides across an opening, not turning on hinges. **sliding scale,** a scale of fees or taxes or wages etc. that varies in accordance with the variation of some standard.

slid·er (slı-dĕr) *n.* 1. a person or thing that slides. 2. (in baseball) a fast pitch that curves away from the batter as it reaches him.

slight (slıt) *adj.* 1. not much or great or thorough; *paid not the slightest attention,* paid none at all. 2. slender, not heavily built. **slight** *v.* to treat or speak of (a person etc.) as not worth one's attention, to insult by lack of respect or courtesy. **slight** *n.* an insult given in this way. **slight′ly** *adv.* **slight′ness** *n.*

slim (slim) *adj.* (**slim·mer, slim·mest**) 1. of small girth or thickness, not heavily built. 2. small, insufficient, *only a slim chance of success.* **slim** *v.* (**slimmed, slim·ming**) to make oneself slimmer by dieting, exercise, etc. **slim′ly** *adv.* **slim′ness** *n.*

slime (slım) *n.* an unpleasant slippery thick liquid substance.

slim·y (slı-mee) *adj.* (**slim·i·er, slim·i·est**) 1. like slime, covered or smeared with slime. 2. disgustingly dishonest or meek or flattering. **slim′i·ly** *adv.* **slim′i·ness** *n.*

sling[1] (sling) *n.* 1. a belt or strap or chain etc. looped around an object to support or lift it. 2. a bandage looped around the neck to form a support for an injured arm. 3. a looped strap used to throw a stone or other missile. **sling** *v.* (**slung, sling·ing**) 1. to suspend or lift with a sling. 2. to hurl (a stone) with a sling. 3. (*informal*) to throw.

sling[2] *n.* a sweetened cocktail of gin etc. and water.

sling·shot (sling-shot) *n.* a device (often Y-shaped) with elastic for shooting small stones.

slink (slingk) *v.* (**slunk, slink·ing**) to move in a stealthy or guilty or shamefaced way.

slink·y (sling-kee) *adj.* 1. moving in a slinking way. 2. smooth and sinuous. 3. (*informal*) (of women's clothes) close-fitting and flowing.

slip[1] (slip) *v.* (**slipped, slip·ping**) 1. to slide accidentally, to lose one's balance in this way. 2. to go or put or be put with a smooth movement. 3. to escape hold or capture by being slippery or not grasped firmly. 4. to make one's way quietly or unobserved. 5. to detach or release; *slip a stitch,* (in knitting) to transfer it to the other needle without looping the yarn through it. 6. to escape, to become detached from, *the ship slipped her moorings; it slipped my memory.* 7. to make a careless mistake. 8. to fall below the normal standard, to lapse, to deteriorate. **slip** *n.* 1. the act of slipping. 2. an accidental or casual mistake. 3. a petticoat, a pillowcase. 4. a slipway. □**give a person the slip,** to escape from him or avoid him skillfully. **let slip,** to release accidentally or deliberately; to miss (an opportunity); to reveal news etc. unintentionally or thoughtlessly. **slip of the pen** *or* **tongue,** a small mistake in which one thing is written or said accidentally instead of another. **slip out of,** to take off easily, as a garment. **slipped disk,** *see* **disk. slip something over on,** to trick. **slip stitch,** a loose hemming stitch in sewing, a slipped stitch in knitting. **slip up,** (*informal*) to make an accidental or casual mistake.

slip[2] *n.* 1. a long narrow strip of thin wood or paper etc. 2. a cutting taken from a plant for grafting or planting. 3. a thin liquid containing fine clay, for coating pottery. □**a slip of a girl**, a small girl.

slip·cov·er (slip-kuv-ĕr) *n.* 1. a removable cloth cover for furniture. 2. a book jacket.

slip·knot (slip-not) *n.* a knot that can slide easily along the rope etc. on which it is tied, or one that can be undone by pulling.

slip-on (slip-on) *adj.* (of clothes) easily slipped on and off. **slip-on** *n.* a slip-on garment.

slip·o·ver (slip-oh-vĕr) *n.* a shoe, garment, etc. that can be easily slipped on or off, especially a sweater.

slip·page (slip-ij) *n.* 1. an amount or extent of slipping. 2. an act or instance of slipping.

slip·per (slip-ĕr) *n.* a light loose comfortable shoe for indoor wear.

slip·per·y (slip-ĕ-ree) *adj.* **(-per·i·er, -per·i·est)** 1. smooth and difficult to hold, causing slipping by its wetness or smoothness. 2. (of a person) not to be trusted to keep an agreement etc., *a slippery customer.* **slip′per·i·ness** *n.* □**slippery elm,** a North American red elm with an inner bark that is used in medicine.

slip·shod (slip-shod) *adj.* not doing things carefully, not done or arranged carefully.

slip·stream (slip-streem) *n.* a current of air driven backward as something is propelled forward.

slip·way (slip-way) *n.* a sloping structure used as a landing stage or on which ships are built or repaired.

slit (slit) *n.* a narrow straight cut or opening. **slit** *v.* **(slit, slit·ting)** 1. to cut a slit in. 2. to cut into strips. □**slit trench,** a narrow trench for a soldier or weapon.

slith·er (sli*th*-ĕr) *v.* to slide unsteadily, to move with an irregular slipping movement. **slith′er·y** *adj.*

sliv·er (sliv-ĕr) *n.* a thin strip cut or split from wood or glass etc.

sliv·o·vitz (sliv-ŏ-vits) *n.* a Balkan plum brandy.

slob (slob) *n.* *(slang, contemptuous)* a stupid or clumsy person.

slob·ber (slob-ĕr) *v.* to slaver or dribble; *slobber over a person,* to behave with repulsively excessive affection to him. **slobber** *n.* spittle running from the mouth, slaver. **slob′ber·y** *adj.* **slob′ber·er** *n.*

sloe (sloh) *n.* blackthorn, its small bluish-black plumlike fruit. □**sloe gin,** a gin in which sloes have been steeped.

sloe-eyed (sloh-ɪd) *adj.* with eyes of bluish-black color.

slog (slog) *v.* **(slogged, slog·ging)** 1. to hit hard. 2. to work or walk hard and steadily. **slog** *n.* 1. a hard hit. 2. a spell of hard steady work or walking. **slog′ger** *n.*

slo·gan (sloh-găn) *n.* a word or phrase adopted as a motto, a short catchy phrase used in advertising. **slo·gan·eer** (sloh-gă-neer) *n.*

sloop (sloop) *n.* a small one-masted fore-and-aft-rigged vessel with a mainsail and jib.

slop[1] (slop) *v.* **(slopped, slop·ping)** 1. to spill over or cause to spill, to splash liquid on. 2. to plod clumsily, especially through mud or puddles etc. 3. to feed (a pig) with slops. **slop** *n.* 1. weak unappetizing drink or liquid food. 2. (often *slops*) a quantity of slopped liquid; (often *slops*) swill fed to pigs.

slop[2] *n.* 1. a loose outer garment worn by a work-

man. 2. clothes and bedding supplied to seamen. □**slop chest,** a store of clothing and personal goods for sale to seamen on a voyage.

slope (slohp) *v.* **(sloped, slop·ing)** 1. to lie or turn at an angle from the horizontal or vertical. 2. to place in this position. **slope** *n.* 1. a sloping surface or direction, a stretch of rising or falling ground. 2. the amount by which something slopes.

slop·py (slop-ee) *adj.* **(-pi·er, -pi·est)** 1. having a liquid consistency that splashes easily, excessively liquid, *sloppy oatmeal.* 2. slipshod. 3. weakly sentimental. **slop′pi·ly** *adv.* **slop′pi·ness** *n.*

slosh (slosh) *v.* 1. to pour (liquid) clumsily. 2. to splash, to move with a splashing sound. **slosh** *n.* a splashing sound. **slosh′y** *adj.*

sloshed (slosht) *adj.* *(slang)* drunk.

slot (slot) *n.* 1. a narrow opening through which something is to be put. 2. a groove or channel or slit into which something fits. 3. a position in a series or scheme; *the program has its regular slot,* its regular time for transmission. **slot** *v.* **(slot·ted, slot·ting)** 1. to make a slot or slots in. 2. to put into a slot. □**slot car,** an electric racing car that runs on a track. **slot machine,** a machine operated by a coin put in a slot, as to dispense small articles or for gambling.

sloth (slawth) *n.* 1. laziness. 2. an animal of tropical America that lives in trees and is capable of only very slow movement.

sloth·ful (slawth-fŭl) *adj.* lazy. **sloth′ful·ly** *adv.* **sloth′ful·ness** *n.*

slouch (slowch) *v.* to stand or sit or move in a lazy awkward way, not with an upright posture. **slouch** *n.* 1. a slouching movement or posture. 2. an awkward, or lazy or incompetent person. **slouch′y** *adj.* **slouch′ing·ly** *adv.* □**slouch hat,** a man's hat with a wide flexible brim.

slough[1] (slow) *n.* 1. a swamp or marshy place. 2. (*pr.* sloo) a state of hopeless depression.

slough[2] (sluf) *v.* to shed, *a snake sloughs its skin periodically.* **slough** *n.* a snake's cast skin, dead tissue that drops away.

Slo·vak (sloh-vak) *n.* 1. a member of the Slavic people inhabiting Slovakia etc. 2. the language of these people. **Slovak** *adj.*

slov·en·ly (sluv-ĕn-lee) *adj.* **(-en·li·er, -en·li·est)** careless and untidy in appearance, not methodical in work. **slov′en·li·ness** *n.*

slow (sloh) *adj.* 1. not quick or fast, acting or moving or done without haste or rapidity. 2. (of a clock) showing a time earlier than the correct one. 3. mentally dull, stupid. 4. lacking liveliness, sluggish, *business is slow today.* 5. (of photographic film) not very sensitive to light, (of a lens) having only a small aperture. 6. tending to cause slowness. **slow** *adv.* slowly, *go slow.* **slow** *v.* to reduce the speed of, to go more slowly, *slow down* or *up.* **slow′ly** *adv.* **slow′ness** *n.* □**slow motion,** the operation of a motion picture that makes movements appear to be performed more slowly than in real life. ▷Do not confuse the adjective *slow* with the adverb *slow.* The adjective *slow* is used correctly in many expressions: *work is slow, his slow pace, my slow mind.* The adverb *slow* is used mainly by highway police, who order us to *go slow.* Careful writers prefer to use the adverb *slowly: work is going slowly, he returned slowly to his seat, I think too slowly.*

slow·down (sloh-down) *n.* 1. an act or instance

of slowing down. 2. a deliberately slow pace of work as an organized protest by employees.
slow·poke (sloh-pohk) *n.* a person who is slow in his actions or work.
slow-up (sloh-up) *n.* an act or instance of slowing up.
slow-wit·ted (sloh-wit-id) *adj.* mentally slow, having below-average intelligence or understanding.
SLR *abbr.* single-lens reflex.
slub (slub) *n.* 1. a thick place or lump in yarn or thread. 2. wool etc. slightly twisted in preparation for spinning. **slub** *v.* **(slubbed, slub·bing)** to twist (wool etc.) in preparation for spinning.
sludge (sluj) *n.* thick greasy mud, something resembling this. **sludg'y** *adj.*
slue (sloo) *v.* **(slued, slu·ing)** to turn or swing around.
slug[1] (slug) *n.* 1. a small slimy animal like a snail without a shell. 2. a roundish lump of metal, a bullet of irregular shape, a pellet for firing from an air gun.
slug[2] *v.* **(slugged, slug·ging)** *(informal)* to strike with a hard heavy blow. **slug** *n.* *(informal)* a blow of this kind.
slug·gard (slug-ărd) *n.* a slow or lazy person.
slug·gish (slug-ish) *adj.* slow-moving, not alert or lively. **slug'gish·ly** *adv.* **slug'gish·ness** *n.*
sluice (sloos) *n.* 1. an artificial channel for conducting water in a stream etc. 2. the water controlled by this. 3. a channel carrying off water. 4. a place where objects are rinsed. 5. the act of rinsing. **sluice** *v.* **(sluiced, sluic·ing)** 1. to let out (water) by means of a sluice. 2. to flood or scour or rinse with a flow of water. □**sluice gate**, a sliding gate or other contrivance for controlling the volume or flow of water in a sluice.
sluice·way (sloos-way) *n.* 1. an artificial water channel, especially for washing ore. 2. a water channel controlled by a sluice gate.
slum (slum) *n.* a dirty overcrowded district inhabited by very poor people. **slum** *v.* **(slummed, slum·ming)** to visit a slum, especially out of curiosity or for charitable purposes.
slum·ber (slum-běr) *n.* sleep. **slumber** *v.* to sleep. **slum'ber·er** *n.* □**slumber party**, a pajama party.
slum·ber·ous (slum-bě-rŭs), **slum·brous** (slum-brŭs) *adj.* 1. of or relating to slumber. 2. sluggish, drowsy. 3. causing sleep.
slum·lord (slum-lord) *n.* a landlord (especially absentee) of slum buildings who charges high rents and refuses to make repairs, improvements, etc.
slump (slump) *n.* a sudden or great fall in prices or values or in the demand for goods etc. **slump** *v.* 1. to undergo a slump. 2. to sit or flop down heavily and slackly.
slung (slung) *see* **sling.**
slunk (slungk) *see* **slink.**
slur (slur) *v.* **(slurred, slur·ring)** 1. to write or pronounce indistinctly with each letter or sound running into the next. 2. to mark (notes) with a slur in music, to perform in the way indicated by this. 3. to pass lightly over (a fact etc.), *slurred over it.* 4. to speak ill of. **slur** *n.* 1. a slurred letter or sound. 2. a curved line placed over notes in music to show that they are to be sung to one syllable or played smoothly without a break. 3. discredit, *there is no slur on his reputation.*
slurp (slurp) *v.* *(slang)* to make a noisy sucking sound in eating or drinking. **slurp** *n.* *(slang)* this sound.

slur·ry (slur-ee) *n.* (*pl.* **-ries**) thin mud, thin liquid cement.
slush (slush) *n.* 1. partly melted snow on the ground. 2. silly sentimental talk or writing. **slush'y** *adj.* **slush'i·ness** *n.* □**slush fund**, a fund of money for illegal purposes such as bribing officials.
slut (slut) *n.* 1. a slovenly woman. 2. an immoral woman, a prostitute. **slut'tish** *adj.* **slut'tish·ness** *n.*
sly (slī) *adj.* **(sly·er, sly·est)** 1. done or doing things in an unpleasantly cunning and secret way. 2. mischievous and knowing, *with a sly smile.* **sly'ly** *adv.* **sly'ness** *n.* □**on the sly**, slyly, secretly.
Sm *symbol* samarium.
SM *abbr.* 1. Master of Science. 2. Sergeant Major.
sm. *abbr.* small.
smack[1] (smak) *n.* 1. a slap. 2. a hard hit. 3. a loud kiss. **smack** *v.* to slap, to hit hard; *smack one's lips,* to close and then part them noisily in enjoyment. **smack** *adv.* *(informal)* with a smack, directly, *went smack through the window.*
smack[2] *n.* a slight flavor or trace of something. **smack** *v.* to have a slight flavor or trace of something, *his manner smacks of conceit.*
smack[3] *n.* a boat with a single mast used for coasting or fishing.
smack[4] *n.* *(slang)* heroin.
smack·er (smak-ěr) *n.* *(slang)* a dollar.
small (smawl) *adj.* 1. not large or big. 2. not great in size or importance or number etc. 3. of the smaller kind, *the small intestine.* 4. doing things on a small scale, *a small farmer.* 5. petty. **small** *n.* the most slender part of something; *small of the back,* the part of the back at the waist. **small** *adv.* in a small size or way, into small pieces, *chop it small.* **small'ish** *adj.* **small'ness** *n.* □**look** *or* **feel small**, to be humiliated. **no small thing**, something considerable; *no small excitement,* great excitement. **small arms**, low-caliber firearms. **small capital**, a letter shaped like a capital but only about as high as a lower-case letter. **small change**, coins of little value; something trivial. **small fry**, *see* **fry**[2]. **small game**, the smaller animals (birds etc.) hunted for sport. **small potatoes**, *(informal)* a person or thing of small significance or value. **small print**, matter printed in small type; limitations (in a contract etc.) stated inconspicuously in this way. **small slam**, *see* **slam**. **small talk**, social conversation on unimportant subjects.
small-mind·ed (smawl-mın-did) *adj.* narrow or selfish in outlook.
small·pox (smawl-poks) *n.* a contagious disease caused by a virus, with pustules that often leave disfiguring scars.
small-scale (smawl-skayl) *adj.* 1. drawn to a small scale so that few details are shown. 2. not extensive, involving only small quantities etc.
small-time (smawl-tırm) *adj.* of an unimportant level, *small-time crooks.* **small'-tim'er** *n.*
smart (smahrt) *adj.* 1. forceful, brisk, *a smart pace.* 2. clever, ingenious. 3. neat and elegant, *a smart dresser.* **smart** *v.* to feel a stinging pain (bodily or mental). **smart** *n.* a stinging pain. **smart'ly** *adv.* **smart'ing·ly** *adv.* **smart'ness** *n.* □**smart aleck**, *(informal)* a know-it-all. **smart bomb**, *(slang)* a bomb guided to its target by a laser beam or television etc. **smart money**, money paid or exacted as a penalty or compensation;

money wagered or invested by persons with acumen in financial matters etc., *the smart money was on the gray.* **smart set,** the class of wealthy fashionable elegant persons, *clothing for the smart set only.*

smart·en (smahr-tĕn) *v.* (also **smarten up**) to make or become smarter.

smart·y (smahr-tee) *n.* (*pl.* **smart·ies**) *(slang)* a smart aleck. **smarty** *adj.* ☐**smarty pants,** *(slang)* a would-be clever person.

smash (smash) *v.* 1. to break or become broken suddenly and noisily into pieces. 2. to strike or move with great force. 3. to strike (a ball) forcefully downward in tennis etc. 4. to crash (a vehicle), to have a crash. 5. to overthrow or destroy, *police smashed the drug ring.* 6. to ruin or become ruined financially. **smash** *n.* 1. the act or sound of smashing. 2. a collision. 3. a disaster, financial ruin. ☐**smash hit,** *(slang)* an extremely successful thing.

smashed (smasht) *adj. (slang)* drunk.

smash·er (smash-ĕr) *n.* an excellent person or thing.

smash·ing (smash-ing) *adj. (informal)* excellent.

smash-up (smash-up) *n.* a complete smash, a violent collision of motor vehicles.

smat·ter·ing (smat-ĕ-ring) *n.* a slight superficial knowledge of a language or subject.

smear (smeer) *v.* 1. to spread with a greasy or sticky or dirty substance. 2. to try to damage the reputation of. **smear** *n.* 1. something smeared on a surface, a mark made by this. 2. a specimen of material smeared on a microscope slide for examination. 3. an attempt to damage a reputation, *a smear campaign.* **smear'er** *n.*

smear·y (smeer-ee) *adj.* 1. smeared. 2. tending to smear things.

smell (smel) *n.* 1. the faculty of perceiving things by their action on the sense organs of the nose. 2. the quality that is perceived in this way. 3. an unpleasant quality of this kind. 4. an act of smelling something. **smell** *v.* (**smelled, smell·ing**) 1. to perceive the smell of, to detect or test by one's sense of smell. 2. to give off a smell. 3. to give off an unpleasant smell. ☐**smelling salts,** a solid preparation of ammonia used for smelling as a stimulant to relieve faintness etc.

smell·er (smel-ĕr) *n. (slang)* the nose.

smell·y (smel-ee) *adj.* having a strong or unpleasant smell. **smell'i·ness** *n.*

smelt[1] (smelt) *v.* to heat and melt (ore) so as to obtain the metal it contains, to obtain (metal) in this way. **smelt'er** *n.* an apparatus or person that smelts.

smelt[2] *n.* a small fish related to salmon.

smid·gen, smid·gin (smij-ĕn) *n. (informal)* a small bit or amount.

smi·lax (smɪ-laks) *n.* 1. a kind of climbing shrub. 2. a kind of climbing asparagus cultivated for its decorative leaves.

smile (smɪl) *n.* a facial expression indicating pleasure or amusement, with the lips stretched and turning upward at their ends. **smile** *v.* (**smiled, smil·ing**) 1. to give a smile, to express by smiling, *smiled her thanks.* 2. to look bright or favorable; *fortune smiled on us,* favored us. **smil'er** *n.* **smil'ing·ly** *adv.*

smirch (smurch) *v.* 1. to smear or soil. 2. to bring discredit upon (a reputation). **smirch** *n.* a smear, discredit.

smirk (smurk) *n.* a self-satisfied smile. **smirk** *v.* to

give a smirk. **smirk'er** *n.* **smirk'ing·ly** *adv.*

smite (smɪt) *v.* (**smote, smit·ten** or **smote, smit·ing**) 1. to hit hard. 2. to have a sudden effect on, *his conscience smote him.* **smit'er** *n.*

smith (smith) *n.* 1. a person who makes things in metal. 2. a blacksmith.

smith·er·eens (smith-ĕ-reenz) *n. pl. (informal)* small fragments.

smith·y (smith-ee, smith-ee) *n.* (*pl.* **smith·ies**) 1. a blacksmith. 2. his workshop.

smit·ten (smit-ĕn) *see* **smite.** ☐**smitten with,** affected by (a disease or desire or fascination etc.).

smock (smok) *n.* an outer garment shaped like a long loose shirt. **smock** *v.* to ornament with smocking.

smock·ing (smok-ing) *n.* a decoration of close gathers stitched into a honeycomb pattern.

smog (smog) *n.* fog polluted by smoke. **smog'gy** *adj.* (**-gi·er, -gi·est**).

smoke (smohk) *n.* 1. the visible vapor given off by a burning substance. 2. an act or spell of smoking tobacco, *wanted a smoke.* 3. *(informal)* a cigarette or cigar. **smoke** *v.* (**smoked, smok·ing**) 1. to give out smoke or steam or other visible vapor. 2. (of a fireplace) to send smoke into a room instead of up the chimney. 3. to darken with smoke, *smoked glass.* 4. to preserve by treating with smoke, *smoked salmon.* 5. to draw into the mouth the smoke from a cigarette or cigar or tobacco pipe, to use (a cigarette etc.) in this way, to do this as a habit. ☐**smoke bomb,** a bomb that gives out dense smoke when it explodes. **smoke out,** to drive out by means of smoke; *(informal)* to expose. **smoke screen,** a mass of smoke used to conceal the movements of troops; something intended to conceal or disguise one's activities. **smoking car,** a railroad car designated for those who smoke. **smoking jacket,** a man's loose jacket worn for lounging, especially at home.

smoke-eat·er (smohk-ee-tĕr) *n. (slang)* a fireman.

smoke·house (smohk-hows) *n.* (*pl.* **-hous·es,** *pr.* -how-ziz) a building used for smoking meat, fish, etc.

smoke·jump·er (smohk-jum-pĕr) *n.* a fire fighter who parachutes to forest fires not reachable by those on the ground.

smoke·less (smohk-lis) *adj.* 1. free from smoke. 2. producing little or no smoke, *smokeless fuel.*

smok·er (smoh-kĕr) *n.* 1. a person who smokes tobacco as a habit. 2. *(informal)* a smoking car.

smoke·stack (smohk-stak) *n.* a pipe carrying off gases and smoke from buildings, locomotives, etc.

smok·ey (smoh-kee) *n.* (in CB radio) a state policeman, a highway patrolman.

smok·y (smoh-kee) *adj.* (**smok·i·er, smok·i·est**) 1. giving off much smoke. 2. covered or filled with smoke. 3. grayish, *smoky blue.* **smok'i·ness** *n.*

smol·der (smohl-dĕr) *v.* 1. to burn slowly with smoke but no flame. 2. to burn inwardly with concealed anger or jealousy etc. 3. (of feelings etc.) to exist in a suppressed state, *discontent smoldered.*

smooch (smooch) *v. (informal)* to engage in kissing and caressing. **smooch** *n.* a caress or kiss.

smooth (smooth) *adj.* 1. having an even surface with no projections, free from roughness. 2. not harsh in sound or taste. 3. moving evenly without jolts or bumping. 4. pleasantly polite but perhaps insincere. **smooth** *adv.* smoothly, *the course of* *true love never did run smooth.* **smooth** *v.* 1. to make or become smooth. 2. to remove problems or dangers from, *smooth a person's path.* **smooth** *n.* a smooth surface. **smooth'ly** *adv.* **smooth'ness** *n.* **smooth'er** *n.* □smooth **muscle,** a muscle without striations, usually in a thin sheet and performing an involuntary function.

smooth·bore (smooth-bohr) *adj.* (of a firearm) having an unrifled barrel. **smooth'bore** *n.* a smoothbore firearm.

smooth·ie (smoo-*thee*) *n. (informal)* a smooth person.

smooth-tongued (smooth-tungd) *adj.* pleasantly polite or convincing but insincere.

smor·gas·bord (smor-găs-bohrd) *n.* Swedish hors d'œuvres, a buffet meal with a variety of dishes.

smote (smoht) *see* **smite.**

smoth·er (smuth-ĕr) *v.* 1. to suffocate or stifle, to be suffocated. 2. to put out or keep down (a fire) by heaping ash on it. 3. to cover thickly. 4. to restrain or suppress, *smothered a smile.* **smother** *n.* a dense cloud of dust or smoke etc. **smoth'er·y** *adj.*

SMSgt *abbr.* Senior Master Sergeant.

smudge (smuj) *n.* 1. a dirty or blurred mark. 2. dense smoke that protects crops against frost, insect attack, etc. **smudge** *v.* (smudged, smudg·ing) 1. to make a smudge on or with. 2. to become smudged or blurred. **smudg'y** *adj.* □smudge **pot,** a container with burning material that produces smudge.

smug (smug) *adj.* (smug·ger, smug·gest) self-satisfied. **smug'ly** *adv.* **smug'ness** *n.*

smug·gle (smug-ĕl) *v.* (smug·gled, smug·gling) 1. to convey secretly. 2. to bring (goods) into or out of a country illegally, especially without paying customs duties. **smug'gler** *n.*

smut (smut) *n.* 1. a small flake of soot, a small black mark made by this or otherwise. 2. indecent talk or pictures or stories.

smutch (smuch) *n.* a smudge.

smut·ty (smut-ee) *adj.* (-ti·er, -ti·est) 1. marked with smuts. 2. (of talk or pictures or stories) indecent. **smut'ti·ness** *n.*

Sn *symbol* tin.

snack (snak) *n.* a small or casual or hurried meal. **snack** *v.* to have a snack. **snack'er** *n.* □snack **bar,** a place where snacks are sold.

snaf·fle (snaf-ĕl) *n.* a horse's bit without a curb.

sna·fu (sna-foo) *n. (slang)* a state of utter confusion. **snafu** *adj.* in this state. ▷From *situation normal, all fouled up.*

snag (snag) *n.* 1. a jagged projection. 2. a tear in fabric that has caught on a snag. 3. an unexpected difficulty. **snag** *v.* (snagged, snag·ging) to catch or tear or be caught on a snag. **snag'gy** *adj.*

snail (snayl) *n.* a soft-bodied animal with a shell that can enclose its whole body. **snail'like** *adj.* □snail's **pace,** a very slow pace.

snake (snayk) *n.* 1. a reptile with a long narrow body and no legs. 2. a treacherous person. 3. a plumbing device used to dislodge obstructions in pipes. 4. a steel wire used to assist in threading electrical wires. **snake** *v.* (snaked, snak·ing) to move, twist, etc. like a snake. **snake'like** *adj.* **snak'y** *adj.* **snak'i·ly** *adv.* □snake **charmer,** an entertainer who seems to make snakes move to music. **snake in the grass,** an enemy who pretends to be a friend.

snake·bird (snayk-burd) *n.* a fish-eating bird with a long slender neck.

snake·skin (snayk-skin) *n.* leather made from snakes' skins.

snap (snap) *v.* (snapped, snap·ping) 1. to make or cause to make a sharp cracking sound. 2. to break suddenly or with a cracking sound, *the rope snapped.* 3. to bite or try to bite with a snatching movement, *the dog snapped at her ankles.* 4. to take or accept eagerly, *snapping up bargains.* 5. to speak with sudden irritation. 6. to move smartly, *snapped to attention.* 7. to take a snapshot of. 8. (in football) to put the ball into play on the ground by a quick backward movement. **snap** *n.* 1. the act or sound of snapping. 2. a fastener that closes with a snap. 3. a small crisp brittle cookie, *ginger snaps.* 4. a sudden brief spell, especially of cold weather. 5. a snapshot. 6. *Snap,* a card game in which players call "Snap" when two similar cards are exposed. 7. the act of snapping the ball in football. 8. *(informal)* an easy task, *it's a snap.* **snap** *adv.* with a snapping sound. **snap** *adj.* sudden, done or arranged at short notice, *a snap decision.* □snap **at,** to try to bite; to speak irritably to; to accept (an offer etc.) eagerly. **snap bean,** a bean eaten as young pods snapped into pieces. **snap fastener,** a small device fastened by pressing to engage two parts. **snap one's fingers,** to make a crackling noise by flipping the thumb against a finger, usually in order to draw attention; *snap one's fingers at,* to defy. **snap out of it,** *(slang)* to make oneself recover quickly from an illness or mood etc. **snapping turtle,** a large American freshwater tortoise that seizes prey by snapping its jaws. **snap up,** to pick up or buy or take quickly, *snapped up the bargains.*

snap·drag·on (snap-drag-ŏn) *n.* a garden plant with flowers that have a mouthlike opening.

snap·per (snap-ĕr) *n.* 1. a person or thing that snaps. 2. any of several seafish used as food.

snap·pish (snap-ish) *adj.* bad-tempered and inclined to snap at people. **snap'pish·ly** *adv.*

snap·py (snap-ee) *adj.* (-pi·er, -pi·est) *(informal)* 1. brisk, vigorous, *a snappy pace.* 2. neat and elegant, *a snappy dresser.* **snap'pi·ly** *adv.* □make **it snappy,** *(informal)* be quick about it.

snap·shot (snap-shot) *n.* a photograph taken informally or casually.

snare (snair) *n.* 1. a trap for catching birds or animals, usually with a noose. 2. something liable to entangle a person or expose him to danger or failure etc. 3. one of the strings of gut or hide stretched across the lower head of a snare drum to produce a rattling effect. 4. a snare drum. **snare** *v.* (snared, snar·ing) to trap in a snare. □snare **drum,** a drum with snares.

snark (snahrk) *n.* an imaginary animal of ill-defined characteristics and potential. ▷From Lewis Carroll's poem "The Hunting of the Snark" (1876).

snarl[1] (snahrl) *v.* 1. to growl angrily with the teeth bared. 2. to speak or utter in a bad-tempered way. **snarl** *n.* the act or sound of snarling. **snarl'er** *n.* **snarl'y** *adj.* **snarl'ing·ly** *adv.*

snarl[2] *v.* to tangle, to become entangled. **snarl** *n.* a tangle. **snarl'y** *adj.* □snarl **up,** to make or become jammed or tangled, *traffic was snarled up.*

snatch (snach) *v.* 1. to seize quickly or eagerly. 2. to take quickly or when a chance occurs, *snatched a few hours' sleep.* **snatch** *n.* 1. the act of snatching. 2. a short or brief part, *snatches of song; works in snatches,* in short spells.

snaz·zy (snaz-ee) *adj.* **(-zi·er, -zi·est)** *(slang)* smart, stylish. **snaz'zi·ness** *n.*

sneak (sneek) *v.* **(sneaked, sneak·ing)** to go or take or convey furtively. **sneak** *adj.* acting or done without warning, *sneak attack.* **sneak** *n.* a sneaking or underhand person. **sneak'ing·ly** *adv.* **sneak'y** *adj.* **sneak'i·ness** *n.* □**sneak preview,** a preview of a motion picture presented so that the producers etc. can observe the audience's reaction. **sneak thief,** a burglar who enters by sneaking or reaching through an open door or window. ▷The past form *snuck* is acceptable only when the writer is attempting to portray regional dialect.

sneak·er (snee-kĕr) *n.* a soft-soled shoe.

sneak·ing (snee-king) *adj.* persistent but not openly acknowledged, *had a sneaking affection for him.*

sneer (sneer) *n.* a scornful expression or remark. **sneer** *v.* to show contempt by a sneer. **sneer'er** *n.* **sneer'ful** *adj.* **sneer'ing·ly** *adv.*

sneeze (sneez) *n.* a sudden audible involuntary expulsion of air through the nose and mouth, to expel an irritant substance from the nostrils. **sneeze** *v.* **(sneezed, sneez·ing)** to give a sneeze. **sneez'er** *n.* **sneez'y** *adj.* □**not to be sneezed at,** *(slang)* not to be despised, worth having.

snick·er (snik-ĕr) *v.* to give a sly giggle. **snicker** *n.* this giggle. **snick'er·ing·ly** *adv.*

snide (snıd) *adj.* 1. (of a trick etc.) dishonorable, spiteful. 2. sneering or derogatory in a sly way.

sniff (snif) *v.* 1. to draw up air audibly through the nose. 2. to draw in through the nose as one breathes, to try the smell of. **sniff** *n.* the act or sound of sniffing. **sniff'er** *n.* **sniff'ing·ly** *adv.* □**sniff at,** *(informal)* to show contempt for. **sniff out,** *(slang)* to perceive, to discover, as by smelling.

snif·fle (snif-ĕl) *v.* **(snif·fled, snif·fling)** to sniff slightly or repeatedly. **sniffle** *n.* the act or sound of sniffling. **snif'fler** *n.* □**the sniffles,** *(informal)* a slight cold.

snif·fy (snif-ee) *adj.* **(-fi·er, -fi·est)** *(informal)* contemptuous. **sniff'i·ly** *adv.* **sniff'i·ness** *n.*

snif·ter (snif-tĕr) *n.* 1. a pear-shaped glass for brandy, liqueur, etc. 2. *(slang)* a small drink of liquor.

snig·ger (snig-ĕr) = **snicker.**

snip (snip) *v.* **(snipped, snip·ping)** to cut with scissors or shears in small quick strokes. **snip** *n.* 1. the act or sound of snipping. 2. a piece snipped off. 3. *(informal)* a small or unimportant person.

snipe (snıp) *n.* *(pl.* **snipes, snipe)** a wading bird with a long straight bill, frequenting marshes. **snipe** *v.* 1. to fire shots from a hiding place. 2. to make sly critical remarks attacking a person or thing.

snip·er (snı-pĕr) *n.* 1. a person who fires shots from a hiding place, usually at long range. 2. a person who kills by sniping.

snip·pet (snip-it) *n.* 1. a small piece cut off. 2. a fragment of information or news, a brief extract.

snip·py (snip-ee) *adj.* **(-pi·er, -pi·est)** 1. *(informal)* short, curt, *a snippy reply.* 2. scrappy, in snips. **snip'pi·ly** *adv.* **snip'pi·ness** *n.*

snips (snips) *n. pl.* hand shears for cutting metal.

snit (snit) *n.* an agitated state, *in a snit.*

snitch (snich) *v.* *(slang)* 1. to steal. 2. to act as an informer. **snitch** *n.* *(slang)* an informer.

sniv·el (sniv-ĕl) *v.* **(sniv·eled, sniv·el·ing)** to cry or complain in a miserable whining way. **snivel** *n.*

snob (snob) *n.* a person who has an exaggerated respect for social position or wealth or for certain attainments or tastes, and who despises people whom he considers inferior; *snob appeal* or *value,* qualities that appeal to people's snobbish feelings. **snob'ber·y** *n.*

snob·bish (snob-ish) *adj.* of or like a snob. **snob'bish·ly** *adv.* **snob'bish·ness** *n.*

snood (snood) *n.* a loose baglike ornamental net in which a woman's hair is held at the back.

snook·er (snuuk-ĕr) *n.* a game played on a billiard table with fifteen red and six other colored balls.

snook·ered (snuuk-ĕrd) *adj.* 1. in a position in snooker where a direct shot would lose points. 2. *(slang)* thwarted or defeated.

snoop (snoop) *v.* *(informal)* to pry inquisitively. **snoop** *n.* **snoop'er** *n.* **snoop'y** *adj.*

snoot (snoot) *n.* 1. *(slang)* the nose. 2. *(informal)* a snob.

snoot·y (snoo-tee) *adj.* **(snoot·i·er, snoot·i·est)** *(informal)* haughty and contemptuous. **snoot'i·ly** *adv.* **snoot'i·ness** *n.*

snooze (snooz) *n.* *(informal)* a nap. **snooze** *v.* **(snoozed, snooz·ing)** *(informal)* to take a snooze. **snooz'er** *n.*

snore (snohr) *n.* a snorting or grunting sound made during sleep. **snore** *v.* **(snored, snor·ing)** to make such sounds. **snor'er** *n.*

snor·kel (snor-kĕl) *n.* 1. a breathing tube to enable a person to swim under water. 2. a device by which a submerged submarine can take in and expel air. **snorkel** *v.* to swim with the aid of a snorkel.

snort (snort) *n.* 1. a rough sound made by forcing breath suddenly through the nose, usually expressing annoyance or disgust. 2. *(slang)* a small drink of liquor, usually drunk quickly. **snort** *v.* to utter a snort. **snort'er** *n.*

snot (snot) *n.* *(vulgar)* 1. mucous discharge from the nose. 2. a contemptible person. **snot'ty** *adj.*

snout (snowt) *n.* 1. an animal's long projecting nose or nose and jaws. 2. the projecting front part of something.

snow (snoh) *n.* 1. crystals of ice that form from atmospheric vapor and fall in light white flakes. 2. a fall or layer of snow. 3. something resembling snow. 4. *(slang)* cocaine. **snow** *v.* 1. (of snow) to fall, *it is snowing.* 2. to scatter or fall like snow. 3. *(slang)* to attempt to deceive by glib talk. □**snow bird,** a white or partly white bird, especially the snow bunting. **snowed in,** snowbound. **snowed under,** covered with snow; overwhelmed with a mass of letters or work etc. **snow fence,** a barrier against drifting snow. **snow goose,** a wild white goose of North America. **snow job,** *(slang)* an attempt at deception by overwhelming with details. **snow line,** the level above which an area is covered permanently with snow. **snow tire,** a tire with a deep tread used for gaining greater traction in the snow.

snow·ball (snoh-bawl) *n.* 1. snow pressed into a small compact mass for throwing in play. 2. a shrub with round white flowers. 3. crushed ice flavored with colored syrup and served in a cone-shaped paper cup. **snowball** *v.* 1. to throw snowballs at, to play in this way. 2. to grow quickly in size or intensity, as a snowball does when rolled in more snow, *opposition to the war snowballed.*

snow·bank (snoh-bangk) *n.* a snowdrift, an accumulation of snow created by a snowplow or shoveling.

snow·bell (snoh-bel) *n.* a small tree with white flowers.

snow·ber·ry (snoh-ber-ee) *n.* (*pl.* **-ries**) a garden shrub with white berries.

snow-blind (snoh-blɪnd) *adj.* unable to see owing to the effects on the eye of the reflection of light off snow. **snow'blind·ness** *n.*

snow·bound (snoh-bownd) *adj.* 1. prevented by snow from going out or traveling. 2. blocked by snow.

snow-capped (snoh-kapt) *adj.* (of a mountain) covered at the top with snow.

snow·drift (snoh-drift) *n.* a bank of snow heaped up by wind.

snow·drop (snoh-drop) *n.* 1. a small flower growing from a bulb, with hanging white flowers blooming in early spring.

snow·fall (snoh-fawl) *n.* a fall of snow, the amount that falls.

snow·field (snoh-feeld) *n.* a permanent wide expanse of snow.

snow·flake (snoh-flayk) *n.* a flake of snow.

snow·man (snoh-man) *n.* (*pl.* **-men,** *pr.* -men) a figure made in snow roughly in the shape of a man.

snow·mo·bile (snoh-mŏ-beel) *n.* a motor vehicle used to travel over the snow, especially with skis and a caterpillar track. **snow'mo·bil·er** *n.* **snow'mo·bil·ing** *n.*

snow·plow (snoh-plow) *n.* a machine for clearing snow from a road or railroad track etc.

snow·shoe (snoh-shoo) *n.* a racket head, usually strung with rawhide, attached to the foot and enabling the wearer to walk on the snow without sinking in. **snowshoe** *v.* **(snow·shoed, snow·shoe·ing)** to travel on snowshoes.

snow·storm (snoh-storm) *n.* a storm in which snow falls.

snow·suit (snoh-soot) *n.* a child's outer garment designed for wear in cold weather.

snow-white (snoh-hwɪt) *adj.* pure white.

snow·y (snoh-ee) *adj.* **(snow·i·er, snow·i·est)** 1. with snow falling, *snowy weather.* 2. covered with snow. 3. as white as snow. □**snowy egret,** a white egret. **snowy owl,** a large white owl.

snub (snub) *v.* **(snubbed, snub·bing)** to reject or humiliate (a person) by treating him scornfully or in an unfriendly way. **snub** *n.* treatment of this kind.

snub-nosed (snub-nohzd) *adj.* having a short and stumpy nose.

snuck (snuk) *see* the note under **sneak.**

snuff[1] (snuf) *n.* powdered tobacco for sniffing into the nostrils. **snuff** *v.* to draw in through the nose.

snuff[2] *v.* to put out (a candle) by covering or pinching the flame. **snuf'fer** *n.*

snuff·box (snuf-boks) *n.* a container for holding snuff.

snuff-col·ored (snuf-kul-ŏrd) *adj.* dark yellowish brown.

snuf·fle (snuf-ĕl) *v.* **(snuf·fled, snuf·fling)** to sniff in a noisy way, to breathe noisily through a partly blocked nose. **snuffle** *n.* a snuffling sound. **snuf'fly** *adj.*

snug (snug) *adj.* **(snug·ger, snug·gest)** cozy, (of a garment) close-fitting. **snug'ly** *adv.* **snug' ness** *n.*

snug·gies (snug-eez) *n. (informal)* long knitted underwear for women and children.

snug·gle (snug-ĕl) *v.* **(snug·gled, snug·gling)** to nestle, to cuddle.

so[1] (soh) *adv. & conj.* 1. to the extent or in the manner or with the result indicated, *it was so dark that we could not see.* 2. very, *we are so pleased to see you.* 3. for that reason, *so they ran away.* 4. also, *if you go, so shall I.* **so** pronoun that, the same thing, *do you think so?; and so say all of us.* □**and so on,** and others of the same kind. **or so,** or about that number or amount, *two hundred or so.* **so as to,** in order to. **so far, so good,** progress has been satisfactory up to this point. **so long!,** *(informal)* goodby till we meet again. **so long as,** provided that, on condition that. **so many,** as if they or it were, *cried like so many babies.* **so much,** as if it were, *melted like so much snow; so much for that idea,* no more need be said of it. **so that,** in order that. **so what?,** *(informal)* that fact has no importance.

so[2] *n.* sol[1].

so., So. *abbr.* 1. south. 2. southern.

s.o. *abbr.* strikeout.

soak (sohk) *v.* 1. to place or lie in a liquid so as to become thoroughly wet. 2. (of liquid) to penetrate gradually, (of rain etc.) to drench. 3. to absorb, *soak it up with a sponge; soak up knowledge.* 4. *(slang)* to extract much money from (a person) by charging or taxing him very heavily. **soak** *n.* 1. the act or process of soaking. 2. *(slang)* a heavy drinker. **soak'er** *n.*

so-and-so (soh-ăn-soh) *n.* (*pl.* **so-and-sos**) 1. a person or thing that need not be named. 2. *(informal,* to avoid using a vulgar word) a disliked person, *he is a so-and-so!*

soap (sohp) *n.* a substance used for washing and cleaning things, made of fat or oil combined with an alkali. **soap** *v.* to apply soap to. □**no soap,** *(slang)* nothing doing. **soap bubble,** a globe of air enclosed in an iridescent film of soapy water, made especially by blowing through a pipe or ring dipped in soapsuds. **soap flakes,** soap prepared in small flakes for washing clothes etc. **soap opera,** a sentimental broadcast serial with a domestic setting. **soap powder,** powder of soap with additives.

soap·box (sohp-boks) *n.* a makeshift stand for a street orator.

soap·stone (sohp-stohn) *n.* steatite.

soap·suds (sohp-sudz) *n. pl.* froth of soapy water.

soap·y (soh-pee) *adj.* **(soap·i·er, soap·i·est)** 1. like soap. 2. covered or impregnated with soap. 3. *(informal)* trying to win favor by flattery or excessive politeness. **soap'i·ly** *adv.* **soap'i· ness** *n.*

soar (sohr) *v.* 1. to rise high in flight. 2. to rise very high, *prices soared.* **soar'er** *n.*

sob (sob) *n.* uneven drawing of breath in weeping or when out of breath. **sob** *v.* **(sobbed, sob· bing)** to weep or breathe or utter with sobs. **sob'ber** *n.* **sob'bing·ly** *adv.* □**sob sister,** a journalist who writes or edits sob stories. **sob story,** a story intended to arouse sympathy.

so·ber (soh-bĕr) *adj.* 1. not intoxicated. 2. serious and self-controlled, not frivolous. 3. (of color) not bright or conspicuous. **sober** *v.* to make or become sober, *sober up* or *down.* **so'ber·ly** *adv.* **so'ber·ness** *n.*

so·bri·e·ty (sŏ-brī-ĕ-tee) *n.* being sober.
so·bri·quet (soh-brī-kay) *n.* a nickname.
soc. *abbr.* 1. social. 2. society.
so-called (soh-kawld) *adj.* called by that name or description but perhaps not deserving it, *a so-called expert.*
soc·cer (sok-ĕr) *n.* a game played by two teams of eleven players in which the ball may not be handled during play except by the goalkeeper.
so·cia·ble (soh-shă-bĕl) *adj.* fond of company, characterized by friendly companionship. **so′cia·bly** *adv.* **so·cia·bil·i·ty** (soh-shă-bil-i-tee) *n.*
so·cial (soh-shăl) *adj.* 1. living in an organized community, not solitary. 2. of society or its organization, of the mutual relationships of people or classes living in an organized community, *social problems.* 3. of or designed for companionship and sociability, *a social club.* 4. sociable. **social** *n.* a social gathering, especially one organized by a club, congregation etc. **so′cial·ly** *adv.* □**social climber,** a person seeking to gain a higher rank in society. **social science,** the scientific study of human society and social relationships. **social security,** government assistance for those who lack economic security through being unemployed or aged or ill or disabled etc. **social studies,** a course of study including civics, geography, history, etc. **social work,** organized work directed toward helping people with problems of health, housing, education, etc. **social worker,** a person trained in social work.
so·cial·ism (soh-shă-liz-ĕm) *n.* a political and economic theory advocating that land, transport, natural resources, and the chief industries should be owned and managed by the government. **so′cial·ist** *n. & adj.* **so·cial·is·tic** (soh-shă-lis-tik) *adj.*
so·cial·ite (soh-shă-līt) *n.* a person who is prominent in fashionable society.
so·cial·ize (soh-shă-līz) *v.* (**so·cial·ized, so·cial·iz·ing**) 1. to organize in a socialistic manner. 2. to behave sociably, to take part in social activities. **so·cial·i·za·tion** (soh-shă-li-zay-shŏn) *n.* **so′cial·iz·er** *n.* □**socialized medicine,** the provision of medical services for all from public funds.
so·ci·e·ty (sŏ-sī-e-tee) *n.* (*pl.* **-ties**) 1. an organized community, the system of living in this. 2. people of the higher social classes. 3. company, companionship, *always enjoy his society; he is at his best in society.* 4. a group of people organized for some common purpose. **so·ci·e·tal** (sŏ-sī-ĕ-tăl) *adj.* □**Society of Friends,** Quakers. **Society of Jesus,** Jesuits.
sociol. *abbr.* 1. sociological. 2. sociology.
so·ci·ol·o·gist (soh-si-ol-ŏ-jist, -shi-) *n.* an expert in sociology.
so·ci·ol·o·gy (soh-si-ol-ŏ-jee, -shi-) *n.* the scientific study of human society and its development and institutions, or of social problems. **so·ci·o·log·i·cal** (soh-si-ŏ-loj-i-kăl, -shi-) *adj.* **so·ci·o·log′i·cal·ly** *adv.*
so·ci·o·path (soh-si-ŏ-path, -shi-) *n.* a psychopath with strongly antisocial tendencies.
sock¹ (sok) *n.* 1. (*pl.* **socks** or **sox**) a short stocking not reaching the knee. 2. an ancient comic actor's light shoe. 3. comic drama. 4. a windsock. □**socked in,** (*informal*) (of an airplane) unable to fly because of bad weather conditions.
sock² *v.* (*slang*) to hit forcefully. **sock** *n.* (*slang*) a forceful blow. □**sock it to a person,** (*slang*) to attack him forcefully.

sock·et (sok-it) *n.* 1. a hollow into which something fits, *a tooth socket.* 2. a device for receiving an electric light bulb in order to make a connection. □**socket wrench,** a wrench with a socket attachment at the end.
sock·eye (sok-ī) **salmon** a blue-back salmon found in northern Pacific coastal waters.
So·crat·ic (sŏ-krat-ik) *adj.* of the Greek philosopher and teacher Socrates (of the 5th century B.C.) or his theories. □**Socratic irony,** a pose of ignorance assumed in order to confute others by enticing them into a display of supposed knowledge. **Socratic method,** dialectic, procedure by question and answer.
sod (sod) *n.* turf, a piece of this. **sod** *v.* (**sodded, sod·ding**) to cover (ground) with sods.
so·da (soh-dă) *n.* 1. a compound of sodium in common use, especially sodium carbonate *(washing soda),* bicarbonate *(baking soda),* and hydroxide *(caustic soda).* 2. soda water, *Scotch and soda.* □**soda bread,** bread made with baking soda (not yeast). **soda cracker,** a thin cracker leavened with baking soda. **soda fountain,** a store or section of a store that serves soda, ice cream, etc. **soda jerk,** (*informal*) an attendant at a soda fountain. **soda pop,** a carbonated drink with artificial flavoring. **soda water,** water mady fizzy by being charged with carbon dioxide under pressure.
sod·den (sod-ĕn) *adj.* made very wet. **sod′den·ly** *adv.* **sod′den·ness** *n.*
so·di·um (soh-di-ŭm) *n.* a soft silver-white metal. □**sodium bicarb,** sodium bicarbonate. **sodium bicarbonate,** (also called *baking soda*) a white water-soluble powder used in baking powder, fire extinguishers, as an antacid, etc. **socium chloride,** common salt. **sodium lamp,** a lamp using an electrical discharge in sodium vapor and giving a yellow light, often used in street lighting. **sodium nitrate,** a water-soluble crystalline compound used in fertilizers, explosives, curing meat, etc. **Sodium Pentothal,** (*trademark*) a sodium salt of Pentothal used in psychiatry and in surgery as an anesthetic. **sodium phosphate,** a water-soluble compound used in dyeing, electroplating, manufacturing of cheese, ceramic glazes, fertilizers, detergents, etc.
sod·om·y (sod-ŏ-mee) *n.* a copulation-like act between male persons or between a person and an animal.
so·fa (soh-fă) *n.* a long upholstered seat with a back and raised ends or arms.
So·fi·a (soh-fee-ă) the capital of Bulgaria.
soft (sawft) *adj.* 1. not hard or firm. 2. smooth, not rough or stiff. 3. not loud. 4. gentle, soothing; *a soft answer,* a good-tempered one. 5. not physically robust, feeble. 6. easily influenced, tenderhearted. 7. (*slang*) easy, comfortable, *a soft job; soft living.* 8. (of currency) likely to drop suddenly in value. 9. (of drinks) nonalcoholic. 10. (of water) free from mineral salts that prevent soap from lathering. 11. (of color or light) not bright or dazzling, (of an outline) not sharp. 12. (of consonants) not hard (*see* **hard** definition 11). **soft** *adv.* softly; *fall soft,* on a soft surface. **soft′ly** *adv.* **soft′ness** *n.* □**be soft on,** (*informal*) to feel affection for; to treat mildly. **soft coal,** bituminous coal. **soft drugs,** drugs that are not likely to cause addiction. **soft goods,** textiles. **soft in the head,** soft-headed. **soft landing,** a landing in which a spacecraft etc. reaches ground without being destroyed. **soft lens,** a kind of contact lens of flexible plastic. **soft line,** (in politics etc.) a

conciliatory position. **soft palate,** the rear part of the palate. **soft pedal,** (in a piano) a pedal for reducing volume. **soft rock,** a sedimentary rock. **soft sell,** quietly persuasive salesmanship. **soft shoulder,** the unpaved side of a road. **soft soap,** semiliquid soap; (informal) persuasive talk, flattery. **soft spot,** a feeling of affection toward a person or thing. **soft touch,** a person who is easily duped or who readily gives money when asked; a person or team that is easily defeated; an activity that is easily accomplished.

soft·ball (sawft-bawl) n. 1. a modified form of baseball using a ball like a baseball but softer and larger. 2. this ball.

soft-boiled (sawft-boild) adj. (of eggs) boiled but without allowing yolk and white to become set.

soft·bound (sawft-bownd) adj. paperback.

soft-core (sawft-kohr) adj. (of pornography) not describing or showing sexual acts explicitly.

soft·cov·er (sawft-kuv-ĕr) adj. paperback. **softcover** n. a paperback book.

soft·en (saw-fĕn) v. to make or become soft or softer. **soft'en·er** n. □**soften up,** to make weaker by attacking repeatedly; to make less able to resist (salesmanship etc.) by making preliminary approaches.

soft-head·ed (sawft-hed-id) adj. idiotic, foolish.

soft-heart·ed (sawft-hahr-tid) adj. compassionate.

soft·ie (sawf-tee) n. (informal) a person who is physically weak or not hardy, or who is softhearted.

soft-ped·al (sawft-ped-ăl) v. (-aled, -al·ing) (informal) to refrain from emphasizing, soft-pedaled his criticism.

soft-shell (sawft-shel) clam a North American edible clam that has a thin white shell.

soft-shell crab a crab that has a soft shell after a recent molt.

soft-spok·en (sawft-spoh-kĕn) adj. having a soft voice.

soft·ware (sawft-wair) n. computer programs or the tapes containing these (as distinct from hardware).

soft·wood (sawft-wuud) n. the soft light wood obtained from coniferous trees, such as pine.

sog·gy (sog-ee) adj. (-gi·er, -gi·est) 1. sodden. 2. moist and heavy in texture, soggy bread. **sog'gi·ly** adv. **sog'gi·ness** n.

soi·gné (swahn-yay) adj. (of a woman, **soignée**) well-groomed and sophisticated. ▷French.

soil¹ (soil) n. 1. the loose upper layer of earth in which plants grow. 2. ground as territory, on American soil.

soil² v. to make or become dirty.

soi·ree, soi·rée (swah-ray) n. a social gathering in the evening, as for music.

so·journ (soh-jurn) n. a temporary stay. **sojourn (soh-jurn, soh-jurn)** v. to stay at a place temporarily. **so'journ·er** n.

sol¹ (sohl) n. a name for the fifth note of a scale in music.

sol² (sol) n. a liquid solution or suspension of a colloid.

Sol (sol) n. the sun.

sol. abbr. 1. soluble. 2. solution.

Sol. abbr. Solomon.

sol·ace (sol-is) n. comfort in distress, something that gives this. **solace** v. **(sol·aced, sol·ac·ing)** to give solace to. **sol'ac·er** n.

so·lar (soh-lăr) adj. 1. of or derived from the sun, solar energy. 2. reckoned by the sun, solar time.

□**solar battery,** a device to convert solar radiation into electricity. **solar eclipse,** an eclipse of the sun. **solar flare,** a small outburst of gases from the sun's surface. **solar heating,** heating derived from solar energy. **solar home,** a home heated by or otherwise equipped to use solar energy. **solar month,** one-twelfth of a solar year. **solar plexus,** the network of nerves at the pit of the stomach; this area. **solar system,** the sun with the heavenly bodies that revolve around it. **solar wind,** a continuous flow of charged particles from the sun. **solar year,** the time between one vernal equinox and another.

so·lar·i·um (sŏ-lair-i-ŭm) n. a room or balcony, often enclosed with glass, where sunlight can be enjoyed for medical purposes or for pleasure.

sold (sohld) see **sell.** □**sold on,** (slang) enthusiastic about.

sol·der (sod-ĕr) n. a soft alloy used to cement metal parts together. **solder** v. to join with solder. **sol'der·er** n. □**soldering iron,** a tool used hot for applying solder.

sol·dier (sohl-jĕr) n. a member of an army, especially a private or N.C.O. **soldier** v. 1. to serve as a soldier. 2. to shirk one's work, he soldiers on the job. □**soldier of fortune,** an adventurous person ready to serve any country or person that will hire him.

sol·dier·ly (sohl-jĕr-lee) adj. like a soldier.

sol·dier·y (sohl-jĕ-ree) n. soldiers collectively or as a class.

sole¹ (sohl) n. 1. the undersurface of a foot. 2. the part of a shoe or stocking etc. that covers this (often excluding the heel). **sole** v. **(soled, sol·ing)** to put a sole on (a shoe).

sole² n. (pl. **sole, soles)** a kind of flatfish used as food.

sole³ adj. 1. one and only, our sole objection is this. 2. belonging exclusively to one person or group, we have the sole right to sell these cars. **sole'ly** adv.

sol·e·cism (sol-ĕ-siz-ĕm) n. a mistake in the use of language, an offense against good manners or etiquette. ▷Do not confuse solecism with solipsism.

sol·emn (sol-ĕm) adj. 1. not smiling or cheerful. 2. dignified and impressive, a solemn occasion. 3. formal, accompanied with a religious or other ceremony. **sol'emn·ly** adv. **sol'emn·ness** n. **so·lem·ni·ty (sŏ-lem-ni-tee)** n. (pl. **-ties)**

sol·em·nize (sol-ĕm-nız) v. **(sol·em·nized, sol·em·niz·ing)** 1. to celebrate (a festival etc.). 2. to perform (a marriage ceremony) with formal rites. **sol·em·ni·za·tion (sol-ĕm-ni-zay-shŏn)** n.

so·le·noid (soh-lĕ-noid) n. a coil of wire that becomes magnetic when an electrical current is passed through it. **so·le·noi·dal (soh-lĕ-noi-dăl)** adj.

sol·fa (sohl-fah) n. the system of syllables doh, ray, me, fah, sol, la, te, used to represent notes of a musical scale.

so·lic·it (sŏ-lis-it) v. 1. to seek to obtain, to ask for earnestly, solicit votes or for votes. 2. (of a prostitute) to make an immoral sexual offer, especially in a public place. **so·lic·i·ta·tion (sŏ-lis-i-tay-shŏn)** n.

so·lic·i·tor (sŏ-lis-i-tŏr) n. 1. one who solicits. 2. a law officer of a city or town etc. 3. (British) a lawyer who advises clients on legal matters and prepares legal documents for them but who does not represent them as an advocate except in certain lower courts. □**solicitor general,** the law officer below attorney general.

so·lic·i·tous (sŏ-lis-i-tŭs) *adj.* anxious and concerned about a person's welfare or comfort. **so·lic′i·tous·ly** *adv.* **so·lic′i·tous·ness** *n.*

so·lic·i·tude (sŏ-lis-i-tood) *n.* solicitous concern.

sol·id (sol-id) *adj.* 1. keeping its shape, firm, not liquid or gas. 2. not hollow. 3. of the same substance throughout, *solid silver.* 4. continuous, without a break, *for two solid hours.* 5. strongly constructed, not flimsy. 6. having three dimensions, concerned with solids, *solid geometry.* 7. sound and reliable, *there are solid arguments against it.* 8. unanimous, *the miners are solid on this issue.* **solid** *n.* 1. a solid substance or body or food. 2. a body or shape with three dimensions. **sol′id·ly** *adv.* **sol′id·ness** *n.* **so·lid·i·ty** (sŏ-lid-i-tee) *n.* □**solid geometry,** the geometry dealing with bodies or surfaces having three dimensions. **Solid South,** the bloc of southern states that formerly supported the Democratic Party in elections. ▷Do not confuse *solid* with *stolid.*

sol·i·dar·i·ty (sol-i-dar-i-tee) *n.* unity resulting from common interests or feelings or sympathies.

so·lid·i·fy (sŏ-lid-ĭ-fī) *v.* (**so·lid·i·fied, so·lid·i·fy·ing**) to make or become solid. **so·lid·i·fi·ca·tion** (sŏ-lid-ĭ-fĭ-**kay**-shŏn) *n.*

sol·id-state (sol-id-stayt) *adj.* using transistors (which make use of the electronic properties of solids) instead of electron tubes.

so·lil·o·quize (sŏ-lil-ŏ-kwIz) *v.* (**so·lil·o·quized, so·lil·o·quiz·ing**) to utter a soliloquy.

so·lil·o·quy (sŏ-lil-ŏ-kwee) *n.* (*pl.* **-quies**) a speech (especially in a play) in which a person expresses his thoughts aloud without addressing any person.

sol·ip·sism (sol-ip-siz-ĕm) *n.* the philosophical theory that the self is the only knowable, or the only existent, thing. **sol′ip·sist** *adj.* & *n.* **sol·ip·sis·tic** (sol-ip-sis-tik) *adj.* ▷Do not confuse *solipsism* with *solecism.*

sol·i·taire (sol-i-tair) *n.* 1. a diamond or other gem set by itself. 2. a card game for one person in which cards have to be brought into a particular arrangement.

sol·i·tar·y (sol-i-ter-ee) *adj.* 1. alone, without companions. 2. single, *a solitary example.* 3. not frequented, lonely, *a solitary valley.* **solitary** *n.* (*pl.* **-tar·ies**) 1. a recluse. 2. (*slang*) solitary confinement. **sol′i·tar·i·ly** *adv.* □**solitary confinement,** isolation in a separate cell as a punishment.

sol·i·tude (sol-i-tood) *n.* being solitary.

so·lo (soh-loh) *n.* (*pl.* **-los**) 1. a musical composition or passage for a single voice or instrument with or without subordinate accompaniment. 2. any performance by one person alone. 3. a pilot's flight in an aircraft without an instructor or companion. **solo** *adj.* & *adv.* unaccompanied, alone, *for solo flute; flying solo.*

so·lo·ist (soh-loh-ist) *n.* a person who performs a solo.

so·lon (soh-lŏn) *n.* a wise legislator. ▷From Solon (6th century B.C.), an Athenian statesman.

sol·stice (sol-stis) *n.* either of the times in the year when the sun is farthest from the equator, the point reached by the sun at these times; *summer solstice,* about June 22; *winter solstice,* about December 22. **sol·sti·tial** (sol-stish-ăl) *adj.*

sol·u·ble (sol-yŭ-bĕl) *adj.* 1. able to be dissolved

in liquid. 2. able to be solved, *a soluble problem.* **sol·u·bil·i·ty** (sol-yŭ-bil-i-tee) *n.*

sol·ute (sol-yoot) *n.* a dissolved substance.

so·lu·tion (sŏ-loo-shŏn) *n.* 1. a liquid in which something is dissolved. 2. dissolving or being dissolved into liquid form. 3. the process of solving a problem etc., the answer found.

solv·a·ble (sol-vă-bĕl) *adj.* able to be solved.

solve (solv) *v.* (**solved, solv·ing**) to find the answer to (a problem or puzzle) or the way out of (a difficulty). **solv′er** *n.*

sol·vent (sol-vĕnt) *adj.* 1. having enough money to pay one's debts and liabilities. 2. able to dissolve another substance. **solvent** *n.* a liquid used for dissolving something. **sol·ven·cy** (sol-vĕn-see) *n.*

So·ma·li·a (sŏ-mah-li-ă) a country in East Africa. **So·ma·li** (sŏ-mah-lee) *n.* (*pl.* **-lis, -li**) **So·ma′li·an** *adj.* & *n.*

so·ma·tic (soh-mat-ik) *adj.* of the body, corporeal, physical. **so·mat′i·cal·ly** *adv.* □**somatic cell,** a cell of the body organs and tissues, as opposed to a germ cell.

som·ber (som-bĕr) *adj.* dark, gloomy, dismal. **som′ber·ly** *adv.*

som·bre·ro (som-brair-oh) *n.* (*pl.* **-ros**) a felt or straw hat with a very wide brim, worn especially in Latin American countries.

some (sum) *adj.* & *pronoun* 1. an unspecified quantity, *buy some apples.* 2. an amount that is less than the whole, *some of them were late.* 3. an unspecified person or thing, *some fool locked the door.* 4. a considerable quantity, *that was some years ago.* 5. approximately, *waited some twenty minutes.* 6. (*slang*) remarkable, *that was some storm!* **some** *adv.* (*informal*) 1. to some degree or extent, *we talked some.* 2. to a great degree or extent, *that's going some.* □**some time,** unspecified time in the future, *let's meet some time* (▷not *sometime*).

-some[1] *suffix* used to form adjectives meaning action, quality, state, as in *quarrelsome, burdensome.*

-some[2] *suffix* used to form nouns from numbers meaning group of, as in *foursome.*

some·bod·y (sum-bod-ee) *n.* & *pronoun* 1. an unspecified person. 2. a person of importance.

some·day (sum-day) *adv.* in the future.

some·how (sum-how) *adv.* 1. in some unspecified or unexplained manner, *I never liked her, somehow.* 2. by one means or another, *must get it finished somehow.*

some·one (sum-wun) *n.* & *pronoun* somebody.

some·place (sum-plays) *adv.* somewhere.

som·er·sault (sum-ĕr-sawlt) *n.* an acrobatic movement in which a person rolls his body head over heels on the ground or in the air. **somersault** *v.* to turn a somersault.

some·thing (sum-thing) *n.* & *pronoun* 1. an unspecified thing; *see something of a person,* meet him occasionally or for a short time; *he is something of an expert,* to some extent. 2. an important or praiseworthy thing; □**make something of oneself,** to make oneself important, to improve one's station in life. **something like,** approximately, *it cost something like ten dollars;* rather like, *it's something like a rabbit; (informal)* impressive, *that's something like it!*

some·time (sum-tIm) *adj.* former, *her sometime friend.* **sometime** *adv.* at an unstated or indefinite time.

some·times (sum-tımz) *adv.* at some times but not all the time.

some·way (sum-way) *adv. (informal)* (also **some·ways**) somehow, in some manner.

some·what (sum-hwot) *adv.* to some extent, *it's somewhat difficult.* □**more than somewhat,** *(informal)* very.

some·where (sum-hwair) *adv.* at or in or to an unspecified place or position. □**get somewhere,** *(informal)* to achieve some success.

som·me·lier (sum-ĕl-yay) *n.* (*pl.* **-liers**) a waiter in charge of wine in a restaurant.

som·nam·bu·lism (som-nam-byŭ-liz-ĕm) *n.* sleepwalking. **som·nam'bu·list** *n.*

som·no·lent (som-nŏ-lĕnt) *adj.* sleepy, asleep. **som'no·lence** *n.*

son (sun) *n.* 1. a male child in relation to his parents. 2. a male descendant. 3. a form of address to a boy or young man. 4. *the Son,* the second person of the Trinity, incarnate in Christ. □**son of a gun,** *(humorous)* a person.

so·nar (soh-nahr) *n.* a device for detecting objects under water by reflection of sound waves. ▷From *sound na*vigation (and) *r*anging.

so·na·ta (sŏ-nah-tă) *n.* a musical composition for one instrument or two, usually with three or four movements. □**sonata form,** a type of composition in which two themes are successively set forth, developed, and restated.

son·a·ti·na (son-ă-tee-nă) *n.* a simple or short sonata.

sonde (sond) *n.* a device sent up to obtain information about atmospheric conditions.

song (sawng) *n.* 1. singing. 2. a musical composition for singing. □**for a song,** very cheaply. **make a song and dance,** *(informal)* to make a great fuss. **song cycle,** a series of songs composed around a central event or idea. **Song of Solomon** *or* **Song of Songs,** a poetic book of the Old Testament, traditionally attributed to Solomon.

song·bird (sawng-burd) *n.* a bird with a musical cry.

song·fest (sawng-fest) *n.* an informal gathering at which songs are sung.

song·ster (sawng-stĕr) *n.* 1. a singer. 2. a songbird.

song·stress (sawng-stris) *n.* a female singer.

son·ic (son-ik) *adj.* of or involving sound waves. □**sonic barrier,** the sound barrier. **sonic boom,** a loud noise heard when the shock wave caused by an aircraft traveling at supersonic speed reaches the hearer.

son-in-law (sun-in-law) *n.* (*pl.* **sons-in-law**) a daughter's husband.

son·net (son-it) *n.* a poem of fourteen lines with lengths and rhymes in accordance with one of several patterns. **son·net·eer** (son-i-teer) *n.* □**sonnet sequence,** a set of sonnets on one theme.

son·ny (sun-ee) *n.* (*pl.* **-nies**) *(informal)* a form of address to a boy.

so·no·rous (sŏ-nohr-ŭs) *adj.* resonant, giving a deep powerful sound. **so·no'rous·ly** *adv.* **so·nor·i·ty** (sŏ-nor-i-tee) *n.* (*pl.* **-ties**).

soon (soon) *adv.* 1. in a short time, not long after the present or a specified time. 2. early, quickly, *spoke too soon.* 3. willingly, *I'd as soon stay at home.* □**sooner or later,** at some time, eventually.

soot (suut) *n.* the black powdery substance that rises in the smoke of coal or wood etc.

sooth (sooth) *n. (old use)* truth, fact, *in sooth.*

soothe (sooth) *v.* (**soothed, sooth·ing**) to calm, to ease (pain etc.). **sooth'er** *n.* **sooth'ing** *adj.* **sooth'ing·ly** *adv.*

sooth·say·er (sooth-say-ĕr) *n.* a person who foretells the future. **sooth'say·ing** *n.*

soot·y (suut-ee) *adj.* (**soot·i·er, soot·i·est**) 1. full of soot, covered with soot. 2. like soot, black.

sop (sop) *n.* 1. a piece of bread dipped in liquid before being eaten or cooked. 2. a concession that is made in order to pacify or bribe a troublesome person. **sop** *v.* (**sopped, sop·ping**) 1. to dip (a thing) in liquid. 2. to soak up (liquid) with something absorbent.

SOP *abbr.* Standard Operating Procedure.

soph (sof) *n. (informal)* a sophomore.

soph·ism (sof-iz-ĕm) *n.* a false argument, especially one intended to deceive.

soph·ist (sof-ist) *n.* 1. a person who uses sophistry, a quibbler. 2. *Sophist,* (in ancient Greece) a paid teacher of philosophy and rhetoric.

so·phis·ti·cate (sŏ-fis-ti-kayt) *v.* (**so·phis·ti·cat·ed, so·phis·ti·cat·ing**) to make sophisticated. **sophisticate** (sŏ-fis-ti-kit) *n.* a sophisticated person.

so·phis·ti·cat·ed (sŏ-fis-ti-kay-tid) *adj.* 1. characteristic of fashionable life and its ways, experienced in this and lacking natural simplicity. 2. complicated, elaborate, *sophisticated electronic devices.* **so·phis·ti·ca·tion** (sŏ-fis-ti-kay-shŏn) *n.*

soph·ist·ry (sof-i-stree) *n.* (*pl.* **-ries**) clever and subtle but perhaps misleading reasoning.

soph·o·more (sof-ŏ-mohr) *n.* a second-year university or high school student.

soph·o·mor·ic (sof-ŏ-mor-ik) *adj.* 1. of or like a sophomore. 2. intellectually pretentious and overconfident like the traditional sophomore.

sop·o·rif·ic (sop-ŏ-rif-ik) *adj.* tending to cause sleep. **soporific** *n.* a medicinal substance that causes sleep. **sop·o·rif'i·cal·ly** *adv.*

sop·ping (sop-ing) *adj.* very wet, drenched.

sop·py (sop-ee) *adj.* (**-pi·er, -pi·est**) 1. very wet. 2. *(informal)* sentimental in a sickly way. **sop'pi·ness** *n.*

so·pran·o (sŏ-prah-noh) *n.* (*pl.* **-pran·os**) 1. the highest female or boy's singing voice. 2. a singer with such a voice, a part written for it.

sor·cer·er (sor-sĕ-rĕr) *n.* a magician, especially one supposedly aided by evil spirits. **sor'cer·ess** *n. fem.*

sor·cer·y (sor-sĕ-ree) *n.* (*pl.* **-cer·ies**) a sorcerer's art or practices.

sor·did (sor-did) *adj.* 1. dirty, squalid. 2. (of motives or actions) lacking dignity, not honorable, mercenary. **sor'did·ly** *adv.* **sor'did·ness** *n.*

sore (sohr) *adj.* (**sor·er, sor·est**) 1. causing pain from injury or disease. 2. suffering pain, *felt sore all over.* 3. causing mental pain or annoyance, *a sore subject.* 4. *(old use)* serious, *in sore need.* 5. distressed, vexed. **sore** *n.* 1. a sore place, especially where the skin is raw. 2. a source of distress or annoyance. **sore'ly** *adv.* **sore'ness** *n.* □**sore throat,** a throat that is painful or sensitive because of inflammation.

sore·head (sohr-hed) *n. (informal)* a grumpy person.

sor·ghum (sor-gŭm) *n.* a tropical cereal grass.

so·ror·i·ty (sŏ-ror-i-tee) *n.* (*pl.* **-ties**) a women's society in a college or university. □**sorority house,** a building providing living accommodations for the members of a sorority.

sorp·tion (sorp-shŏn) *n.* absorption and adsorption considered jointly. **sorp·tive** (sorp-tiv) *adj.*

sor·rel[1] (sor-ĕl) *n.* a plant with sharp-tasting leaves used in salads, etc.

sorrel[2] *adj. & n.* light reddish brown, a horse of this color.

sor·row (sahr-oh) *n.* 1. mental suffering caused by loss or disappointment etc. 2. something that causes this. **sorrow** *v.* to feel sorrow, to grieve.

sor·row·ful (sahr-ŏ-fŭl) *adj.* feeling or showing sorrow. **sor'row·ful·ly** *adv.* **sor'row·ful·ness** *n.*

sor·ry (sahr-ee) *adj.* (**-ri·er, -ri·est**) 1. feeling pity or regret or sympathy; *sorry!* I am sorry, I beg your pardon. 2. wretched, *in a sorry plight.* **sor'ri·ly** *adv.* **sor'ri·ness** *n.*

sort (sort) *n.* 1. a particular kind or variety. 2. *(informal)* a person with regard to his character, *quite a good sort.* **sort** *v.* to arrange according to sort or size or destination etc. **sort'er** *n.* □of **a sort** *or* **of sorts,** not fully deserving the name given. **out of sorts,** slightly unwell or depressed. **sort of,** *(informal)* somewhat, rather, *I sort of expected it.* (▷Careful writers use *somewhat* or *rather* in such sentences.) **sort out,** to disentangle; to select from others; *sort out the men from the boys,* show which people are truly competent etc.

sor·tie (sor-tee) *n.* 1. an attack by troops coming out from a besieged place. 2. a flight of an aircraft on a military operation.

SOS the international code signal of extreme distress. **SOS** (es-oh-es) *n.* an urgent appeal for help or response.

so-so (soh-soh) *adj. & adv. (informal)* only moderately good or well.

sot (sot) *n.* a drunkard. **sot'tish** *adj.* **sot'tish·ly** *adv.*

sot·to vo·ce (sot-oh voh-chee) in an undertone. ▷Italian.

sou (soo) *n.* a former French coin of various values. □**not worth a sou,** worth no money at all.

sou·brette (soo-bret) *n.* 1. a maidservant or similar character (especially with the implication of pertness or coquetry) in a comedy. 2. a person playing such a role. 3. a lively or pert woman.

souf·flé (soo-flay) *n.* a light spongy dish made with beaten egg white.

sough (sow) *n.* a moaning, whistling, or rushing sound as of wind in the trees etc. **sough** *v.* to make this sound.

sought (sawt) *see* **seek.**

sought-af·ter (sawt-af-tĕr) *adj.* much sought for purchase or use etc.

soul (sohl) *n.* 1. the spiritual or immortal element in a person. 2. a person's mental or moral or emotional nature, *his whole soul revolted from it; cannot call his soul his own,* is completely under the control of another person. 3. a personification or pattern; *she is the soul of honor,* incapable of dishonorable conduct. 4. a person, *there's not a soul about.* □**soul brother,** a fellow black male. **soul food,** the traditional food of American blacks. **soul mates,** people ideally suited to each other. **soul sister,** a fellow black woman.

soul·ful (sohl-fŭl) *adj.* 1. having or showing deep feeling. 2. emotional. **soul'ful·ly** *adv.* **soul'ful·ness** *n.*

soul·less (sohl-lis) *adj.* 1. lacking sensitivity or noble qualities. 2. dull, uninteresting. **soul'less·ness** *n.*

soul-search·ing (sohl-sur-ching) *n.* examination of one's own conscience.

sound[1] (sownd) *n.* 1. vibrations that travel through the air and are detectable (at certain frequencies) by the ear. 2. the sensation produced by these vibrations, a particular kind of it, *the sound of music.* 3. any articulate utterance made in speech. 4. sound reproduced in a film etc. 5. the mental impression produced by a statement or description etc., *we don't like the sound of the new scheme.* **sound** *v.* 1. to produce or cause to produce sound, *sound the trumpet.* 2. to utter, to pronounce, *the "h" in "hour" is not sounded.* 3. to give an impression when heard, *it sounds like an owl; the news sounds good,* seems to be good. 4. to give an audible signal for, *sound the retreat.* 5. to test by noting the sound produced, *the doctor sounds a patient's lungs with a stethoscope.* **sound'er**[1] *n.* **sound'less** *adj.* □**sound barrier,** the high resistance of air to objects moving at speeds near that of sound. **sound booth,** a soundproof booth for testing hearing etc. **sound effects,** sounds (other than speech or music) made artificially for use in a play or film etc. **sounding board,** a board to reflect sound or increase resonance. **sound off,** *(informal)* to express one's opinions loudly and freely. **sound truck,** a truck equipped with a loudspeaker for making announcements, speeches, etc.

sound[2] *adj.* 1. healthy, not diseased or damaged. 2. correct, logical, well-founded, *sound reasoning.* 3. financially secure, *a sound investment.* 4. thorough, *a sound thrashing; sound sleep,* deep and unbroken. **sound** *adv.* soundly, *is sound asleep.* **sound'ly** *adv.* **sound'ness** *n.*

sound[3] *v.* 1. to test the depth or quality of the bottom of (the sea or a river etc.) especially by a weighted line *(sounding line),* to measure depth etc. in this way. 2. to examine with a probe. 3. (of a whale or fish) to drive to the bottom. **sound** *n.* a surgeon's probe. **sound'er**[2] *n.* □**sound out,** to question (a person), especially in a cautious or reserved manner, about his opinions or inclinations, *sound him out about cooperating with us.*

sound[4] *n.* 1. a strait. 2. an arm of the sea.

sound·ing (sown-ding) *n.* measurement of the depth of water (*see* **sound**[3]).

sound·ing *adj.* resounding.

sound·proof (sownd-proof) *adj.* not able to be penetrated by sound. **soundproof** *v.* to make soundproof.

sound·track (sownd-trak) *n.* 1. a narrow strip at the side of motion picture film for carrying recorded sound. 2. the sound itself.

soup (soop) *n.* liquid food made of stock from stewed meat or fish or vegetables etc. □**in the soup,** *(slang)* in difficulties. **soup and fish,** *(slang)* evening dress for a man. **soup kitchen,** a place where soup and other food is supplied free to the needy in times of distress. **soup up,** *(informal)* to increase the power of (an engine); to enliven.

soup·çon (soop-son, soop-son) *n.* a very small quantity, a trace, *add a soupçon of garlic.* ▷French.

soup·y (soo-pee) *adj.* (**soup·i·er, soup·i·est**) 1. like soup. 2. foggy, cloudy. 3. *(slang)* over-sentimental.

sour (sowr) *adj.* 1. tasting sharp like unripe fruit. 2. not fresh, tasting or smelling sharp or unpleasant from fermentation or staleness. 3. (of soil) excessively acid, deficient in lime. 4. bad-tempered, disagreeable in manner, *gave me a sour look.* **sour** *n.* an acid drink; *a whiskey sour,* whiskey with lemon juice or lime juice. **sour** *v.* to make or become sour, *was soured by misfortune.* **sour′ly** *adv.* **sour′ness** *n.* ☐**sour cream,** cream deliberately fermented by the action of bacteria. **sour grapes,** said when a person pretends to despise something he cannot have. (▷From the fable of the fox who wanted some grapes but found that they were out of reach and so pretended that they were sour and undesirable anyway.) **sour mash,** a brewed or distilled mash made acid to promote fermentation. **sour salt,** a citric acid crystal used in flavoring foods etc. **sour·ball (sowr-bawl)** *n.* a hard round candy with tart or acid flavor.

source (sohrs) *n.* 1. the place from which something comes or is obtained. 2. the starting point of a river. 3. a person or book etc. supplying information. ☐**at the source,** at the point of origin.

sour·dough (sowr-doh) *n.* 1. a fermented bread dough. 2. *(slang)* a pioneer, an old-timer, especially in Alaska. ☐**sourdough bread,** a bread leavened with sourdough.

sour·puss (sowr-puus) *n.* *(slang)* a sour-tempered person.

souse (sows) *v.* **(soused, sous·ing)** 1. to steep in pickling brine, *soused herrings.* 2. to plunge or soak in liquid, to drench, to throw (liquid) over a thing. 3. *(slang)* to make drunk. **souse** *n.* 1. a dip or plunge or drenching in water. 2. food steeped in pickle, especially a pig's head, ears, and feet. 3. *(slang)* a drunkard. **soused (sowst)** *adj.* *(slang)* drunk.

south (sowth) *n.* 1. the point or direction opposite north. 2. the southern part of something. **south** *adj. & adv.* toward or in the south; *a south wind,* blowing from the south. ☐**South African,** of southern Africa or of the Republic of South Africa; a native or inhabitant of the Republic of South Africa. **South America,** a continent in the southern Western Hemisphere. **South American,** of South America or its inhabitants. **South Carolina,** a state of the U.S. **South Carolinian,** a native or inhabitant of South Carolina. **South China Sea,** part of the Western Pacific between southeast Asia and the Philippines. **South Dakota,** a state of the U.S. **South Dakotan,** a native or inhabitant of South Dakota. **south pole,** (of a magnet) the pole that is attracted to the south. **South Pole,** the southernmost pole of Earth. **South Sea,** the southern Pacific Ocean. **South Sea Islands,** islands in the South Sea. **the Republic of South Africa,** a country in the south of Africa. **the South,** the area of the U.S. south of Pennsylvania and east of the Mississippi River; those states in that geographical region that were part of the Confederacy.

south·bound (sowth-bownd) *adj.* traveling southwards.

south·east (sowth-eest) *n.* 1. the point or direction midway between south and east. 2. *Southeast,* the southeast region of the U.S. **southeast** *adj. & adv.* toward or in the southeast. **south·east′er·ly** *adj. & adv.* **south·east·ward (sowth-eest-wărd)** *adj. & adv.* **south·east′wards** *adv.*

south·er·ly (suth-ĕr-lee) *adj. & adv.* in or toward the south; *a southerly wind,* blowing from the south (approximately). **southerly** *n.* (*pl.* -lies) a southerly wind.

south·ern (suth-ĕrn) *adj.* of or in the south. ☐**Southern Hemisphere,** the half of Earth between the South Pole and the equator. **southern lights,** the aurora australis.

south·ern·er (suth-ĕr-nĕr) *n.* 1. a native or inhabitant of the south. 2. a native or inhabitant of the southern U.S.

south·ern·most (suth-ĕrn-mohst) *adj.* farthest south.

south·land (sowth-land) *n.* a southern part of a country etc.

south·paw (sowth-paw) *n.* *(informal)* a left-handed person, especially in sports.

south·ward (sowth-wărd) *adj.* toward the south, in the south. **southward, southwards (sowth-wardz)** *adv.* toward the south. **south′ward·ly** *adj. & adv.*

south·west (sowth-west) *n.* 1. the point or direction midway between south and west. 2. *Southwest,* the southwest region of the U.S. **southwest** *adj. & adv.* toward or in the southwest. **south·west′ern** *adj.* **south·west′er·ly** *adj. & adv.* **south·west·ward (sowth-west-wărd)** *adj. & adv.* **south·west′wards** *adv.*

south·west·er (sowth-wes-tĕr) *n.* (also **sou·west·er,** *pr.* sow-wes-tĕr) a waterproof hat with a broad flap at the back. 2. a strong wind or storm from the southwest.

sou·ve·nir (soo-vĕ-neer) *n.* something bought or given or kept as a reminder of an incident or a place visited.

sov·er·eign (sov-ĕ-rin, sov-rin) *n.* 1. a king or queen who is the supreme ruler of a country. 2. a British gold coin, nominally worth one pound. **sovereign** *adj.* 1. supreme, *sovereign power.* 2. possessing sovereign power, independent, *sovereign states.* 3. very effective, *a sovereign remedy.* **sov′er·eign·ty** *n.* (*pl.* -ties).

so·vi·et (soh-vi-et) *n.* an elected council in the U.S.S.R. **Soviet** *adj.* of the Soviet Union. **so′vi·et·ism** *n.* **so′vi·et·ize** *v.* **(so·vi·et·ized, so·vi·et·iz·ing)** to bring under Soviet control or into a Soviet type of government. ☐**Soviet Union,** the U.S.S.R. **Supreme Soviet,** the governing council of the U.S.S.R. or of one of its constituent republics.

so·vi·et·ol·o·gist (soh-vi-ĕ-tol-ŏ-jist) *n.* a person who makes a special study of the Soviet Union.

sow¹ (soh) *v.* **(sowed, sown** or **sowed, sow·ing)** 1. to plant or scatter (seed) for growth, to plant seed in (a field etc.). 2. to implant or spread (feelings or ideas), *they sowed hatred among the people.* **sow′er** *n.*

sow² (sow) *n.* a fully grown female pig.

sox (soks) *n.* see **sock¹.**

soy (soi) *n.* the soybean. ☐**soy sauce,** a sauce made by fermenting soybeans in brine.

soy·bean (soi-been) *n.* a kind of bean (originally from southeast Asia) from which an edible oil and flour are obtained.

SP *abbr.* Shore Patrol.

sp. *abbr.* 1. special. 2. species. 3. specimen. 4. spelling. 5. spirit.

Sp. *abbr.* 1. Spain. 2. Spaniard. 3. Spanish.

spa (spah) *n.* a curative mineral spring, a place with such a spring.

space (spays) *n.* 1. the boundless expanse in which all objects exist and move. 2. a portion of this, an area or volume for a particular purpose, *the box takes too much space; parking spaces.* 3. an interval between points or objects, *an empty area, separated by a space of ten feet; there's a space for your signature.* 4. the area of paper used in writing or printing something, *would take too* *much space to explain in detail.* **5.** a large area, *the wide open spaces.* **6.** outer space (*see* **outer**). **7.** an interval of time, *within the space of an hour.* **space** *v.* (**spaced, spac·ing**) to arrange with spaces between, *space them out.* □**space bar,** a bar in a typewriter for making a space between words etc. **space heater,** a self-contained device for heating the room etc. in which it is placed. **space out,** to put more or wider spaces or intervals between. **space probe,** an unmanned rocket with instruments to detect conditions in outer space. **space shuttle,** a spacecraft for repeated use, as between Earth and a space station. **space station,** an artificial satellite used as a base for operations in space. **space travel,** travel in outer space. **space walk,** physical activity by an astronaut in space outside his spacecraft.

space·craft (spays-kraft) *n.* (*pl.* **-craft**) a vehicle for traveling in outer space.

spaced-out (spayst-owt) *adj. (slang)* under the influence of drugs or alcohol.

space·flight (spays-flīt) *n.* **1.** a flight into space. **2.** space travel.

space·man (spays-man) *n.* (*pl.* **-men,** *pr.* -men) an astronaut.

space·ship (spays-ship) *n.* a spacecraft, especially one manned by a crew.

space·suit (spays-soot) *n.* a sealed pressurized suit allowing the wearer to leave a spacecraft and move about independently in outer space.

space-time (spays-tīm) **continuum** fusion of the concepts of space and time, with time as a fourth dimension.

spa·cious (spay-shŭs) *adj.* providing much space, roomy. **spa′cious·ly** *adv.* **spa′cious·ness** *n.*

spade[1] (spayd) *n.* **1.** a tool for digging ground, with a broad metal blade and a wooden handle. **2.** a tool of similar shape for other purposes. **spade** *v.* (**spad·ed, spad·ing**) to dig with a spade. **spade·ful** (spayd-fuul) *n.* (*pl.* **-fuls**). □**call a spade a spade,** to call a thing by its proper name, to speak plainly or bluntly.

spade[2] *n.* a playing card of the suit (*spades*) marked with black figures shaped like an inverted heart with a short stem.

spade·work (spayd-wurk) *n.* hard work done in preparation for something.

spa·dix (spay-diks) *n.* (*pl.* **-dix·es, -di·ces,** *pr.* -di-seez) a spike of flowers closely arranged around a fleshy axis and usually enclosed in a spathe.

spa·ghet·ti (spă-get-ee) *n.* pasta made in solid sticks, between macaroni and vermicelli in thickness.

Spain (spayn) a country in southwest Europe.

spake (spayk) *see* **speak.**

Spam (rhymes with *ham*) *n.* (*trademark*) a canned luncheon meat.

span (span) *n.* **1.** the distance (about nine inches or twenty-three centimeters) between the tips of a person's thumb and little finger when these are stretched apart. **2.** the distance or part between the uprights supporting an arch or bridge. **3.** length across something, as an airplane's or bird's wings. **4.** length in time from beginning to end, *the span of life.* **5.** a matched pair of horses, mules, etc. **span** *v.* (**spanned, span·ing**) **1.** to extend across, to bridge. **2.** to stretch one's hand across in one span, *span an octave on the piano.*

Span. *abbr.* Spanish.

span·gle (spang-gĕl) *n.* a small thin piece of glitter-

ing material, especially one of many ornamenting a dress etc. **spangle** *v.* (**span·gled, span·gling**) to cover with spangles or sparkling objects. **span·gly** *adv.*

Span·iard (span-yărd) *n.* a native of Spain.

span·iel (span-yĕl) *n.* a kind of dog with long drooping ears and a silky coat.

Span·ish (span-ish) *adj.* of Spain or its people or language. **Spanish** *n.* the language of Spain and of most countries in Central and South America. □**Spanish America,** the Spanish-speaking countries of Central America and South America. **Spanish-American** *adj.* of these Spanish-speaking countries. **Spanish fly,** a bright green beetle dried and powdered, used as an aphrodisiac, irritant, etc. **Spanish moss,** a moss of the southern U.S. that hangs from the branches of trees. **Spanish omelet,** an omelet with chopped vegetables.

spank (spangk) *v.* to slap on the buttocks. **spank** *n.* such a slap.

spank·ing (spang-king) *adj. (informal)* brisk, lively, *a spanking pace.* **spanking** *adv. (informal)* excellently, strikingly, *a spanking fine horse.*

span·ner (span-ĕr) *n.* a type of wrench.

spar[1] (spahr) *n.* a strong pole used for a mast or yard or boom on a ship.

spar[2] *n.* any of several kinds of nonmetallic minerals that split easily.

spar[3] *v.* (**sparred, spar·ring**) **1.** to box, especially for practice. **2.** to quarrel or argue. □**sparring partner,** a boxer employed to give another boxer practice; a person with whom one enjoys frequent arguments.

Spar (spahr) *n.* an enlisted woman in the U.S. Coast Guard women's reserve.

spare (spair) *v.* (**spared, spar·ing**) **1.** to be merciful toward, to refrain from hurting or harming; *spare me this ordeal,* do not inflict it on me; *if I am spared,* if I live so long. **2.** to use with great restraint; *does not spare himself,* works very hard. **3.** to part with, to be able to afford to give, *we can't spare him until next week; can you spare me a moment?; enough and plenty to spare,* more than is needed. **spare** *adj.* (**spar·er, spar·est**) **1.** additional to what is usually needed or used, in reserve for use when needed, *a spare wheel; spare time,* time not needed for work or other purposes. **2.** thin, lean. **3.** small in quantity, *on a spare diet.* **spare** *n.* a spare part or thing kept in reserve for use when needed. **spare′ly** *adv.* **spare′ness** *n.* □**spare tire,** (*informal*) a roll of fat around the waist.

spare·rib (spair-rib) *n.* a cut of pork from the lower ribs.

spar·ing (spair-ing) *adj.* economical, not generous or wasteful. **spar′ing·ly** *adv.*

spark[1] (spahrk) *n.* **1.** a fiery particle, as one thrown off by a burning substance or caused by friction. **2.** a flash of light produced by an electrical discharge. **3.** a particle of a quality or of energy or genius, *hasn't a spark of generosity in him.* **spark** *v.* to give off a spark or sparks. □**spark off,** to trigger off. **spark plug,** a device producing an electrical spark to fire the mixture in an internal combustion engine.

spark[2] *n.* a lively young man, a dandy. **spark** *v. (informal)* to court.

spar·kle (spahr-kĕl) *v.* (**spar·kled, spar·kling**) **1.** to shine brightly with flashes of light. **2.** to show brilliant wit or liveliness. **sparkle** *n.* a sparkling light or brightness. □**sparkling wine,** wine that is effervescent.

spar·kler (spahr-klĕr) *n.* 1. a sparking firework. 2. *sparklers, (slang)* diamonds.

spar·row (spar-oh) *n.* a small brownish-gray bird. □**sparrow hawk,** a small American falcon or European hawk that preys on small birds.

sparse (spahrs) *adj.* (**spars·er, spars·est**) thinly scattered, not dense. **sparse·ly** *adv.* **sparse′ness** *n.* **spar·si·ty** (spahr-si-tee) *n.*

Spar·tan (spahr-tăn) *adj.* (of conditions) simple and sometimes harsh, without comfort or luxuries. ▷Named after the citizens of Sparta, a city in ancient Greece, who were renowned for hardiness.

spasm (spaz-ĕm) *n.* 1. a strong involuntary contraction of a muscle. 2. a sudden brief spell of activity or emotion, *a spasm of coughing.*

spas·mod·ic (spaz-mod-ik) *adj.* 1. occurring at irregular intervals. 2. of or like a spasm, characterized by spasms. **spas·mod′i·cal·ly** *adv.*

spas·tic (spas-tik) *adj.* physically disabled because of cerebral palsy, a condition in which there are faulty links between the brain and the motor nerves, causing jerky or involuntary movements through difficulty in controlling the muscles. **spastic** *n.* a person suffering from this condition. **spas′ti·cal·ly** *adv.* **spas·tic·i·ty** (spas-tis-i-tee) *n.*

spat[1] (spat) *see* **spit**[1].

spat[2] *n.* a short gaiter covering the instep and ankle.

spat[3] *n.* (*informal*) a slight quarrel. **spat** *v.* (**spat·ted, spat·ting**) (*informal*) to bicker.

spat[4] *n.* the spawn of a bivalve shellfish, especially an oyster.

spate (spayt) *n.* a sudden flood or rush, *a spate of orders.*

spathe (spayth) *n.* a large petal-like part of a flower, surrounding a central spike.

spa·tial (spay-shăl) *adj.* of or relating to space, existing in space. **spa′tial·ly** *adv.*

spat·ter (spat-ĕr) *v.* 1. to scatter or fall in small drops. 2. to splash with drops, *spattered her dress with mud.* **spatter** *n.* a splash or splashes, the sound of spattering.

spat·u·la (spach-ŭ-lă) *n.* a tool like a knife with a broad blunt flexible blade. **spat′u·lar** *adj.*

spat·u·late (spach-ŭ-lit, -layt) *adj.* shaped like a spatula, with a broad rounded end.

spav·in (spav-in) *n.* a disease of a horse's hock with a hard bony tumor or swelling. **spa′vined** *adj.*

spawn (spawn) *n.* 1. the eggs of fish or frogs or shellfish. 2. (*contemptuous*) offspring. 3. the threadlike matter from which fungi grow, *mushroom spawn.* **spawn** *v.* 1. to deposit spawn, to produce from spawn. 2. to generate, especially in large numbers, *the reports spawned by that committee.* **spawn′er** *n.*

spay (spay) *v.* to sterilize (a female animal) by removing the ovaries.

SPCA *abbr.* Society for the Prevention of Cruelty to Animals.

SPCC *abbr.* Society for the Prevention of Cruelty to Children.

speak (speek) *v.* (**spoke** or (*old use*) **spake, spo·ken, speak·ing**) 1. to utter words in an ordinary voice (not singing), to hold a conversation, to make a speech, *spoke for an hour.* 2. to utter (words), to express or make known, *spoke the truth.* 3. to use or be able to use (a certain language) in speaking, *we speak French.* 4. to

make a polite or friendly remark, *she always speaks when we meet; they haven't spoken for years,* avoid conversing through not being on friendly terms. 5. to be evidence of something; *it speaks volumes for his patience,* is good or favorable evidence of it; *the facts speak for themselves,* need no supporting evidence. **speak′a·ble** *adj.* □**be on speaking terms,** to be on friendly terms with each other. **not** *or* **nothing to speak of,** very little, only very slightly. **so to speak,** if I may express it this way. **speak for oneself,** to give one's own opinion. **speaking in tongues,** glossolalia. **speaking tube,** a tube for conveying a voice from one room etc. to another. **speak one's mind,** to give one's opinion frankly. **speak one's piece,** to speak bluntly and frankly. **speak out,** to speak loudly or freely; to speak one's mind. **speak up,** to speak more loudly, to speak out.

speak·eas·y (speek-ee-zee) *n.* (*pl.* **-eas·ies**) a place selling liquor illegally during the period of Prohibition.

speak·er (spee-kĕr) *n.* 1. a person who speaks, one who makes a speech. 2. a loudspeaker. 3. *the Speaker,* the presiding officer in a legislative assembly, with responsibility for keeping order etc., *Speaker of the House.*

spear (speer) *n.* 1. a weapon for hurling, with a long shaft and a pointed tip. 2. a pointed stem, as of asparagus. **spear** *v.* to pierce with or as if with a spear. **spear′er** *n.* □**spear gun,** a device used to propel a spear in underwater fishing.

spear·fish[1] (speer-fish) *v.* to use a spear gun in underwater fishing.

spearfish[2] *n.* (*pl.* **-fish, -fish·es**) a large sea fish with a spearlike upper jaw.

spear·head (speer-hed) *n.* the foremost part of an attacking or advancing force. **spearhead** *v.* to be the spearhead of.

spear·mint (speer-mint) *n.* a common garden mint used in cooking and to flavor chewing gum.

spec[1] (spek) *n.* specification. □**spec sheet,** (*informal*) a sheet enumerating the specifications of an appliance, machinery, etc.

spec[2] *n.* **on spec,** (*slang*) as a speculation, without being certain of achieving what one wants.

spec. *abbr.* 1. special. 2. specially. 3. specification.

spe·cial (spesh-ăl) *adj.* 1. of a particular kind, for a particular purpose, not general, *a special key; special training.* 2. exceptional in amount or quality or intensity, *take special care of it.* **special** *n.* a special thing, a special train or edition etc. **spe′cial·ly** *adv.* □**special delivery,** mail delivered in advance of regular mail. **Special Forces,** a branch of the U.S. army consisting of soldiers who are trained in guerrilla warfare.

spe·cial·ist (spesh-ă-list) *n.* a person who is an expert in a special branch of a subject, especially of medicine.

spe·cial·ize (spesh-ă-lɪz) *v.* (**spe·cial·ized, spe·cial·iz·ing**) 1. to become a specialist. 2. to have a product etc. to which one devotes special attention, *the shop specializes in sports goods.* 3. to adapt for a particular purpose, *specialized organs such as the ear.* **spe·cial·i·za·tion** (spesh-ă-li-zay-shŏn) *n.*

spe·cial·ty (spesh-ăl-tee) *n.* (*pl.* **-ties**) a special quality or characteristic or product, an activity in which a person specializes.

spe·cie (spee-shee) *n.* coin as opposed to paper money.

spe·cies (spee-sheez) *n.* (*pl.* **-cies**) 1. a group of animals or plants within a genus, differing only in minor details from the others. 2. a distinct kind or sort, *a species of athlete.*

specif. *abbr.* 1. specific. 2. specifically.

spe·cif·ic (spi-sif-ik) *adj.* 1. particular, clearly distinguished from others, *the money was given for a specific purpose.* 2. expressing oneself in exact terms, not vague, *please be specific about your requirements.* **specific** *n.* a specific aspect or influence, a remedy for a specific disease or condition. **spe·cif'i·cal·ly** *adv.* **spec·i·fic·i·ty** (spes-ĭ-fis-i-tee) *n.* □**specific gravity,** the ratio between the weight of a substance and that of the same volume of a standard substance (usually water for liquids and solids, air for gases).

spec·i·fi·ca·tion (spes-ĭ-fĭ-kay-shŏn) *n.* 1. specifying, being specified. 2. the details describing something to be done or made.

spec·i·fy (spes-ĭ-fī) *v.* **(spec·i·fied, spec·i·fy·ing)** to mention (details, ingredients, etc.) clearly and definitely, to include in a list of specifications.

spec·i·men (spes-ĭ-měn) *n.* 1. a part or individual taken as an example of a whole or of a class, especially for investigation or scientific examination. 2. a quantity of a person's urine etc. taken for testing. 3. *(informal)* a person of a specified sort, *he seems a peculiar specimen.*

spe·cious (spee-shŭs) *adj.* seeming good or sound at first sight but lacking real merit, *specious reasoning.* **spe'cious·ly** *adv.* **spe'cious·ness** *n.*

speck (spek) *n.* a small spot or particle. **speck** *v.* to mark with specks.

speck·le (spek-ĕl) *n.* a small spot, a speck, especially as a natural marking. **speckle** *v.* **(speck·led, speck·ling)** to mark with speckles.

speck·led (spek-ĕld) *adj.* marked with speckles. □**speckled trout,** a brook trout.

specs (speks) *n. pl. (informal)* 1. spectacles. 2. specifications.

spec·ta·cle (spek-tă-kĕl) *n.* 1. a striking or impressive sight, *a magnificent spectacle.* 2. a lavish public show or pageant. 3. a ridiculous sight, *made a spectacle of himself.* 4. spectacles, eyeglasses.

spec·tac·u·lar (spek-tak-yŭ-lăr) *adj.* striking, impressive, amazing. **spectacular** *n.* 1. a spectacular performance. 2. a lavishly produced film etc. **spec·tac'u·lar·ly** *adv.*

spec·ta·tor (spek-tay-tŏr) *n.* a person who watches a show or game or incident etc. □**spectator sports,** sports that attract many spectators.

spec·ter (spek-tĕr) *n.* 1. a ghost. 2. a haunting fear of future trouble, *the specter of defeat loomed over them.*

spec·tral (spek-trăl) *adj.* 1. of or like a specter. 2. of the spectrum.

spec·tro·gram (spek-trŏ-gram) *n.* a record obtained with a spectrograph.

spec·tro·graph (spek-trŏ-graf) *n.* an apparatus for photographing spectra of substances. **spec·tro·graph·ic** (spek-trŏ-graf-ik) *adj.* **spec·tro·graph'i·cal·ly** *adv.*

spec·trom·e·ter (spek-trom-ĕ-tĕr) *n.* a spectroscope that can be used for the measurement of observed spectra. **spec·tro·met·ric** (spek-trŏ-met-rik) *adj.*

spec·tro·scope (spek-trŏ-skohp) *n.* an instrument for producing and examining spectra. **spec·tro·scop·ic** (spek-trŏ-skop-ik) *adj.* **spec·tro·scop'i·cal** *adj.* **spec·tro·scop'i·cal·ly** *adv.* **spec·tros·co·pist** (spek-tros-kŏ-pist) *n.* **spec·tros'co·py** *n.*

spec·trum (spek-trŭm) *n.* (*pl.* **-tra,** *pr.* -tră, **-trums**) 1. the bands of color as seen in a rainbow, forming a series according to their wavelengths. 2. a similar series of bands of sound. 3. an entire range of related qualities or ideas etc., *the whole spectrum of science.*

spec·u·late (spek-yŭ-layt) *v.* **(spec·u·lat·ed, spec·u·lat·ing)** 1. to form opinions about something without having definite knowledge or evidence. 2. to buy or sell goods or stocks and shares etc. in the hope of making a profit but with risk of loss, to do this rashly. **spec'u·la·tor** *n.* **spec·u·la·tion** (spek-yŭ-lay-shŏn) *n.*

spec·u·la·tive (spek-yŭ-lay-tiv) *adj.* 1. of or based on speculation, *speculative reasoning.* 2. involving financial speculation and risk of loss, *a speculative investment.* **spec'u·la·tive·ly** *adv.*

spec·u·lum (spek-yŭ-lŭm) *n.* (*pl.* **-la,** *pr.* -lă, **-lums**) a medical instrument for dilating cavities of the body in order to look inside.

sped (sped) *see* **speed.**

speech (speech) *n.* 1. the act or power or manner of speaking; *have speech with a person,* talk with him. 2. words spoken, a spoken communication to an audience. 3. language or dialect. □**speech clinic,** a clinic at which speech therapy is provided by specialists. **speech therapy,** treatment to improve a stammer or other defect of speech.

speech·i·fy·ing (spee-chi-fī-ing) *n. (informal)* making a speech or speeches, talking as if doing this.

speech·less (speech-lis) *adj.* silent, unable to speak because of great emotion etc. **speech'less·ly** *adv.*

speed (speed) *n.* 1. the rate of time at which something moves or operates. 2. rapidity of movement. 3. the sensitivity of photographic film to light, the power of a lens to admit light. 4. *(slang)* an amphetamine drug. **speed** *v.* **(sped** or **speed·ed, speed·ing)** 1. to move or pass quickly, *the years sped by.* 2. to send quickly, *to speed you on your way.* 3. to travel at an illegal or dangerous speed. **speed'er** *n.* **speed'ing** *adj. & n.* **speed'y** *adj.* **speed'i·ly** *adv.* **speed'ster** *n.* □**at full** or **top speed,** as rapidly as possible. **speed limit,** the maximum permitted speed of a vehicle on a road etc. **speed trap,** a radar trap or other arrangement to detect vehicles that are traveling faster than the speed limit. **speed up,** to move or work or cause to work at greater speed.

speed·boat (speed-boht) *n.* a fast motorboat.

speed·om·e·ter (spi-dom-ĕ-tĕr) *n.* a device in a motor vehicle, showing its speed.

speed·way (speed-way) *n.* 1. a course for automobile or motorcycle racing. 2. a road or track reserved for fast traffic.

speed·well (speed-wel) *n.* a wild plant with small blue flowers.

speed·y (spee-dee) *adj.* **(speed·i·er, speed·i·est)** 1. moving quickly. 2. done or coming without delay. **speed'i·ly** *adv.* **speed'i·ness** *n.*

spe·le·ol·o·gist (spee-li-ol-ŏ-jist) *n.* an expert in speleology.

spe·le·ol·o·gy (spee-li-ol-ŏ-jee) *n.* the exploration and scientific study of caves. **spe·le·o·log·i·cal** (spee-li-ŏ-loj-i-kăl) *adj.*

spell¹ (spel) *n.* 1. words supposed to have magic power. 2. the state of being influenced by this, *laid them under a spell.* 3. fascination, attraction, *the spell of eastern countries.*

spell² *v.* **(spelled** or **spelt, spell·ing)** 1. to write or name in their correct sequence the letters that form (a word or words). 2. (of letters) to form as a word, *c a t* spells *"cat."* 3. to have as a necessary result, *these changes spell ruin to the farmer.* ☐**spelling bee,** a competition in spelling. **spelling book,** a book for teaching spelling. **spell out,** to spell aloud; to make out (words) laboriously letter by letter; to state explicitly, to explain in detail.

spell³ *n.* 1. a period of time. 2. a period of a certain type of weather, *during the cold spell.* 3. a period of a certain activity, *did a spell of driving.* **spell** *v.* (**spelled, spell·ing**) to relieve (a person) in work etc. by taking one's turn.

spell·bind·er (spel-bın-děr) *n.* a speaker, especially a politician, who can hold audiences spellbound. **spell'bind·ing** *adj.*

spell·bound (spel-bownd) *adj.* with the attention held as if by a spell, entranced.

spell·down (spel-down) *n.* a spelling competition in which each contestant who makes a spelling error sits down.

spell·er (spel-ěr) *n.* 1. a person with regard to his spelling ability, *a bad speller.* 2. a spelling book.

spelt¹ (spelt) *see* **spell².**

spelt² *n.* a kind of wheat.

spe·lunk·ing (spi-lung-king) *n.* the sport of exploring caves. **spe·lun'ker** *n.*

spend (spend) *v.* (**spent, spend·ing**) 1. to pay out (money) in buying something. 2. to use for a certain purpose, to use up, *don't spend too much time on it.* 3. to pass, *spent a holiday in Greece.* **spend'er** *n.*

spend·thrift (spend-thrift) *n.* a person who spends money extravagantly and wastefully.

spent (spent) *v. see* **spend. spent** *adj.* used up, having lost its force or strength; *a spent match,* one that has been struck and extinguished and is now useless.

sperm (spurm) *n.* (*pl.* **sperm, sperms**) 1. a male reproductive cell, capable of fertilizing an ovum. 2. semen. ☐**sperm whale,** a large whale from which a waxy oil is obtained.

sper·ma·cet·i (spur-mă-set-ee, -see-tee) *n.* a white waxy substance contained in the head of a sperm whale etc., used for candles and ointments.

sper·mat·ic (spur-mat-ik) *adj.* of sperm; *spermatic cord,* that supporting the testicle within the scrotum.

sper·ma·to·zo·on (spur-mă-tŏ-zoh-ŏn, -mat-ŏ-) *n.* (*pl.* **-zo·a,** *pr.* **-zoh-ă**) the male fertilizing element contained in the semen of animals.

sper·mi·cide (spur-mĭ-sıd) *n.* a substance that kills sperm. **sper·mi·ci·dal** (spur-mĭ-sı-dăl) *adj.*

spew (spyoo) *v.* 1. to vomit. 2. to cast out in a stream.

sp. *abbr.* specific gravity.

sphag·num (sfag-nŭm) *n.* a kind of moss that grows in bogs.

sphere (sfeer) *n.* 1. a perfectly round solid geometric figure. 2. something shaped like this. 3. a field of action or influence or existence, a person's place in society, *took him out of his sphere.* **sphe·ric·i·ty** (sfi-ris-i-tee) *n.*

spher·i·cal (sfer-i-kăl) *adj.* shaped like a sphere. **spher'i·cal·ly** *adv.*

sphe·roid (sfeer-oid) *n.* a spherelike but not perfectly spherical body. **sphe·roi·dal** (sfi-roi-dăl) *adj.*

sphinc·ter (sfingk-těr) *n.* a ring of muscle surrounding an opening in the body and able to close it by contracting.

sphinx (sfingks) *n.* (*pl.* **sphinx·es, sphin·ges,** *pr.* **sfin-jeez**) 1. *the Sphinx,* (in Greek mythology) a winged monster at Thebes that killed all who could not answer the riddle it put to them. 2. any of the ancient stone statues in Egypt with a recumbent lion's body and a human or animal's head, especially the large one near the pyramids at Giza. 3. a statue resembling these. 4. a person who does not reveal his thoughts and feelings.

sphyg·mo·ma·nom·e·ter (sfig-moh-mă-nom-ĕ-těr) *n.* an instrument for measuring blood pressure.

spice (spıs) *n.* 1. a substance (obtained from plants) with a strong taste or smell, used for flavoring food. 2. such substances collectively, *the spice market.* 3. a thing that adds zest or excitement, *variety is the spice of life.* **spice** *v.* (**spiced, spic·ing**) to flavor with spice. ☐**Spice Islands,** the Molucca Islands.

spice·bush (spıs-buush) *n.* a fragrant North American shrub, also called *Benjamin bush.*

spick-and-span (spik-ăn-span) *adj.* neat and clean, new looking.

spic·ule (spik-yool) *n.* a small sharp pointed part. **spic·u·lar** (spik-yū-lăr) *adj.*

spic·y (spı-see) *adj.* (**spic·i·er, spic·i·est**) 1. like spice, flavored with spice. 2. (of stories) slightly scandalous or improper. **spic'i·ly** *adv.* **spic'i·ness** *n.*

spi·der (spı-děr) *n.* an animal (not an insect) with a segmented body and eight jointed legs, spinning webs to trap insects that are its prey. ☐**spider plant,** a grasslike plant with arching stems carrying young plants.

spi·der·y (spı-dĕ-ree) *adj.* 1. having thin angular lines like a spider's legs. 2. like a cobweb. 3. full of spiders.

spied (spıd) *see* **spy.**

spiel (speel, shpeel) *n.* (*slang*) a glib or lengthy speech, usually intended to persuade. **spiel** *v.* (**spiel·ed, spiel·ing**) (*slang*) to talk glibly or lengthily. **spiel'er** *n.*

spiff·y (spif-ee) *adj.* (**spiff·i·er, spiff·i·est**) (*slang*) smart, handsome. **spiff'i·ly** *adv.* **spiff'i·ness** *n.*

spig·ot (spig-ŏt) *n.* a peg or plug used to stop the vent of a cask or to control the flow of a tap.

spike¹ (spık) *n.* 1. a sharp projecting point, a pointed piece of metal. 2. *spikes,* shoes (worn by runners, baseball players, etc.) fitted with spikes. **spike** *v.* (**spiked, spik·ing**) 1. to put spikes on, *spiked running shoes.* 2. to pierce or fasten with a spike. 3. (*informal*) to add alcohol to (a drink). 4. (in volleyball, football, etc.) to hit or throw (the ball) almost straight down. **spik'y** *adj.* (**spik·i·er, spik·i·est**). ☐**spike a person's guns,** to thwart him.

spike² *n.* 1. an ear of corn. 2. a long cluster of flowers with short stalks or no stalks on a central stem.

spill¹ (spil) *n.* a thin strip of wood or of twisted paper used to transfer flame, as for lighting a pipe.

spill² *v.* (**spilled** or **spilt, spill·ing**) 1. to cause or allow (a liquid etc.) to run over the edge of its container. 2. (of liquid etc.) to become spilled. 3. to throw from a horse or vehicle. 4. (*slang*) to make known, *spilled the news.* **spill** *n.* spilling, being spilled, a fall. **spill'a·ble** *adj.* ☐**spill blood,** to shed blood in killing or wounding. **spill over,** to overflow from something that is full. **spill the beans,** (*slang*) to let out information indiscreetly.

spill·age (spil-ij) *n.* spilling, the amount spilled.

spill·way (spil-way) *n.* a passage for surplus water from a dam.

spilt (spilt) *see* **spill**[2].

spin (spin) *v.* (**spun, spin·ning**) 1. to turn or cause to turn rapidly on its axis; *spin a coin,* toss it; *my head is spinning,* I feel dizzy. 2. to draw out and twist (raw cotton or wood etc.) into threads, to make (yarn) in this way. 3. (of a spider or silkworm) to make from a fine threadlike material emitted from the body, *spinning its web.* **spin** *n.* 1. a spinning movement. 2. a short drive in a vehicle. □**spin a yarn,** to tell an invented story, especially in order to deceive someone. **spin cast,** to cast a fishing line on a stationary spool. **spinning jenny,** an early machine for spinning with more than one spindle at a time. **spinning wheel,** a household implement for spinning yarn or thread with a spindle driven by a wheel-driven crank or treadle. **spin off,** to throw off by centrifugal force in spinning; to create as a spinoff. **spin out,** to cause to last a long time.

spin·ach (spin-ich) *n.* a vegetable with dark green leaves.

spi·nal (spy-năl) *adj.* of the spine. □**spinal anesthesia,** anesthesia produced by the injection of an anesthetic into the spinal column providing an insensibility to pain without loss of consciousness. **spinal column,** the spine. **spinal cord,** the rope-like mass of nerve fibers enclosed within the spinal column. **spinal tap,** the removal of spinal fluid by needle, usually for diagnostic tests.

spin·dle (spin-děl) *n.* 1. a slender rod on which thread is twisted or wound in spinning. 2. a pin or axis that revolves or on which something revolves. 3. a spindle tree. **spin′dling** *adj.* □**spindle tree,** a European shrub or small tree with pink or red berries (**spindle berry**) and hard wood formerly used for spindles.

spin·dly (spind-lee) *adj.* (**-dli·er, -dli·est**) long or tall and thin.

spin·drift (spin-drift) *n.* spray blown along the surface of the sea.

spin-dry (spin-dry) *v.* (**spin-dried, spin-dry·ing**) to dry in a machine with a rapidly rotating drum in which moisture is removed from washed articles by centrifugal force.

spine (spyn) *n.* 1. the backbone. 2. one of the sharp needlelike projections on certain plants (such as cacti) and animals (such as hedgehogs). 3. the part of a book where the pages are hinged, this section of the jacket or cover.

spine-chill·ing (spyn-chil-ing) *adj.* (of a book or film etc.) causing a thrill of terror.

spi·nel (spi-nel) *n.* a hard crystalline mineral of various colors consisting chiefly of magnesia and alumina.

spine·less (spyn-lis) *adj.* 1. having no backbone. 2. lacking determination or strength of character. **spine′less·ness** *n.*

spin·et (spin-it, spi-net) *n.* a kind of small piano or harpsichord.

spin·na·ker (spin-ă-kěr) *n.* a large triangular extra sail on a racing yacht.

spin·ner (spin-ěr) *n.* a person or thing that spins.

spin·ner·et (spin-ě-ret) *n.* 1. the spinning organ of a spider, silkworm, etc. 2. a device for forming filaments of synthetic fiber.

spin·off (spin-awf) *n.* a benefit or product produced incidentally from a larger product or process or while developing this.

spin·ster (spin-stěr) *n.* a woman who has not married. **spin·ster·hood** (spin-stěr-huud) *n.*

spin·y (spy-nee) *adj.* (**spin·i·er, spin·i·est**) full of spines, prickly. □**spiny lobster,** a lobster-like creature with a spiny shell and no claws.

spi·ra·cle (spyr-ă-kěl) *n.* 1. a small opening in an insect's body, used for breathing. 2. the blow hole of a whale etc.

spi·ral (spyr-ăl) *adj.* advancing or ascending in a continuous curve that winds around a central point or axis. **spiral** *n.* 1. a spiral line, a thing of spiral form. 2. a continuous increase or decrease in two or more quantities alternately because of their dependence on each other, *the spiral of rising wages and prices.* **spiral** *v.* (**spi·raled, spi·raling**) to move in a spiral course. **spi′ral·ly** *adv.*

spire (spyr) *n.* a pointed structure in the form of a tall cone or pyramid, especially on a church tower. **spir′y** *adj.*

spi·re·a (spy-ree-ă) *n.* a shrub or plant with small white or pink flowers.

spir·it (spir-it) *n.* 1. a person's mind or feelings or animating principle as distinct from his body, *shall be with you in spirit.* 2. soul. 3. a disembodied soul, a ghost. 4. life and consciousness not associated with a body, *God is pure spirit; the Spirit,* the Holy Spirit (*see* **holy**). 5. a person's nature. 6. a person with certain mental or moral qualities, *a few brave spirits went swimming.* 7. the characteristic quality or mood of something, *the spirit of the times; the spirit of the law,* its real purpose as distinct from a strict interpretation of its words. 8. liveliness, readiness to assert oneself, *answered with spirit.* 9. *spirits,* a person's feeling of cheerfulness or depression, *raised their spirits.* 10. a distilled extract. 11. strong distilled alcoholic drink, such as whiskey or gin. **spirit** *v.* to carry off swiftly and secretly, *spirited him away.* □**spirit gum,** a quick-drying solution of gum used especially for attaching false hair. **spirit lamp,** a lamp that burns methylated spirit or a similar fluid. **spirit level,** a glass tube nearly filled with liquid and containing an air bubble, used to test whether something is horizontal by means of the position of this bubble.

spir·it·ed (spir-i-tid) *adj.* 1. full of spirit, lively, ready to assert oneself. 2. having mental spirit or spirits of a certain kind, *a poor-spirited creature.* **spir′it·ed·ly** *adv.*

spir·it·less (spir-it-lis) *adj.* not spirited. **spir′it·less·ly** *adv.*

spir·it·u·al (spir-i-choo-ăl) *adj.* 1. of the human spirit or soul, not physical or worldly. 2. of a church or religion. **spiritual** *n.* a religious folk song of American blacks or one resembling this. **spir′it·u·al·ly** *adv.* **spir·it·u·al·i·ty** (spir-i-choo-al-i-tee) *n.* ▷Do not confuse *spiritual* with *spirituous.*

spir·it·u·al·ism (spir-i-choo-ă-liz-ěm) *n.* the belief that spirits of the dead can and do communicate with the living, practices based on this. **spir′it·u·al·ist** *n.* **spir·it·u·al·is·tic** (spir-i-choo-ă-lis-tik) *adj.*

spir·it·u·al·ize (spir-i-choo-ă-lyz) *v.* (**spir·it·u·al·ized, spir·it·u·al·iz·ing**) to make spiritual.

spir·it·u·ous (spir-i-choo-ŭs) *adj.* containing much alcohol; *spirituous liquors,* those that are distilled and not only fermented. ▷Do not confuse *spirituous* with *spiritual.*

spi·ro·chete (spyr-ŏ-keet) *n.* a spiral-shaped bacterium.

spit[1] (spit) v. **(spit** or **spat, spit·ting)** 1. to eject from the mouth, to eject saliva. 2. to make a noise like spitting as a cat does when angry or hostile, (of a person) to show anger, *spitting with fury.* 3. to utter violently, *spat curses at me.* **spit** n. 1. spittle. 2. the act of spitting. **spit'ter** n. □**spit and polish,** cleaning and polishing of equipment etc., especially by soldiers. **spit curl,** a curl of hair pressed tight against the cheek or forehead. **spit it out,** *(slang)* say what you wish without delay. **spitting image** or **spit and image,** *(informal)* an exact likeness.

spit[2] n. 1. a long thin metal spike thrust through meat to hold it while it is roasted. 2. a long narrow strip of land projecting into the sea. **spit** v. **(spit·ted, spit·ting)** to pierce with or as if with a spit.

spit·ball (spit-bawl) n. 1. a ball of chewed paper used as a missile. 2. (in baseball) an illegal pitch in which the pitcher moistens the ball with saliva to impart spin.

spite (spit) n. malicious desire to hurt or annoy or humiliate another person. **spite** v. **(spit·ed, spit·ing)** to hurt or annoy etc. from spite, *did it just to spite him.* □**in spite of,** not being prevented by, *enjoyed ourselves in spite of the weather.*

spite·ful (spit-fŭl) adj. full of spite, showing or caused by spite. **spite'ful·ly** adv. **spite'ful·ness** n.

spit·fire (spit-fɪr) n. a fiery-tempered person.

spit·tle (spit-ĕl) n. saliva, especially that ejected from the mouth.

spit·toon (spi-toon) n. a receptacle for spitting into.

spitz (spits) n. a small dog with a pointed muzzle, especially a Pomeranian.

splash (splash) v. 1. to cause (liquid) to fly about in drops, to wet with such drops. 2. (of liquid) to be splashed. 3. to move or fall with splashing, *we splashed through the puddles.* 4. to decorate with irregular patches of color etc. 5. to display in large print, *the news was splashed across the Sunday papers.* 6. to spend (money) freely and ostentatiously. **splash** n. 1. splashing, a sound or mark made by this. 2. a quantity of liquid splashed. 3. *(informal)* a small quantity of soda water or other liquid in a drink. 4. a patch of color or light. 5. a striking or ostentatious display or effect. **splash'y** adj. **(splash·i·er, splash·i·est) splash'i·ly** adv. **splash'i·ness** n. □**splash down,** (of a spacecraft) to alight in the sea.

splash·board (splash-bohrd) n. a guard in front of a vehicle or over or beside the wheel of a vehicle to keep mud etc. off the occupants.

splash·down (splash-down) n. the alighting of a spacecraft on the sea.

splat·ter (splat-ĕr) v. to splash noisily. **splatter** n. a noisy splashing sound.

splay (splay) v. to spread apart, to slant (the sides of an opening) so that the inside is wider than the outside or vice versa; *splayed his feet,* placed them with the toes turned outward not forward. **splay** adj. splayed. **splay** n. a splayed position or side etc.

splay·foot (splay-fuut) n. a broad flat foot turned outward. **splay'foot·ed** adj.

spleen (spleen) n. an organ of the body situated at the left of the stomach and involved in maintaining the proper condition of the blood.

splen·did (splen-did) adj. 1. magnificent, display-

ing splendor. 2. excellent, *a splendid achievement.* **splen'did·ly** adv.

splen·dor (splen-dŏr) n. brilliance, magnificent display or appearance, grandeur. **splen'dor·ous** adj. **splen'drous** adj.

sple·net·ic (spli-net-ik) adj. 1. (of a person) ill-tempered, peevish. 2. of the spleen.

splen·ic (splen-ik) adj. of or in the spleen.

splice (splɪs) v. **(spliced, splic·ing)** 1. to join (two ends of rope) by untwisting and interweaving the strands of each. 2. to join (pieces of film or timber etc.) by overlapping the ends. **splice** n. a joint made by splicing. **splic'er** n.

splint (splint) n. a strip of rigid material bound to an injured part of the body to prevent movement, as while a broken bone heals. **splint** v. to secure with a splint.

splin·ter (splin-tĕr) n. a thin sharp piece of wood or stone etc. broken off from a larger piece. **splinter** v. to break or become broken into splinters. **splin'ter·y** adj. □**splinter group,** a small group that has broken away from a larger one, as in a political party.

split (split) v. **(split, split·ting)** 1. to break or become broken into parts, especially lengthwise or along the grain of wood etc. 2. to divide into parts, to divide and share. 3. to come apart, to tear, *this coat has split at the seams.* 4. to divide or become divided into disagreeing or hostile groups. 5. *(slang)* to depart, to quit one another's company; *the couple split,* were separated. **split** n. 1. splitting, being split. 2. the place where something has split or torn. 3. something split or divided. 4. a sweet dish of split fruit with cream or ice cream etc., *banana split.* 5. an acrobatic position in which the legs are stretched along the floor in opposite directions and at right angles to the trunk. □**split decision,** (in boxing, law cases, etc.) a decision in which the judges or jurors are not unanimous. **split hairs,** *see* hair. **split infinitive,** an infinitive with a word placed between *to* and the verb, as in *to thoroughly understand.* (▷Many people dislike this construction and it can usually be avoided, as by writing *to understand thoroughly.*) **split one's sides,** to laugh very heartily. **split second,** a very brief moment. **split shift,** a shift in which there are two or more periods of duty. **split the difference,** to take an amount halfway between two proposed amounts. **split ticket,** a ballot cast for candidates of more than one party.

split-lev·el (split-lev-ĕl) adj. (of a building) having adjoining rooms at levels midway between stories in other parts.

split-sec·ond (split-sek-ŏnd) adj. 1. very rapid. 2. accurate to a very small fraction of time, *split-second timing.*

split·ting (split-ing) adj. (of a headache) very severe, feeling as if it will split one's head.

split-up (split-up) n. a splitting or separation.

splotch (sploch) n. a splash or blotch on material etc. **splotch** v. to mark with splotches. **splotch'y** adj.

splurge (splurj) n. an ostentatious display, especially of wealth. **splurge** v. **(splurged, splurg·ing)** to spend money freely.

splut·ter (splut-ĕr) v. 1. to make a rapid series of spitting sounds. 2. to speak or utter rapidly or indistinctly (as in rage). **splutter** n. a spluttering sound. **splut'ter·er** n.

spoil (spoil) v. **(spoiled** or **spoilt, spoil·ing)** 1.

to damage, to make useless or unsatisfactory. 2. to become unfit for use. 3. to harm the character of (a person) by lack of discipline or excessive generosity or pampering. **spoils** *n.* 1. plunder. 2. benefits gained by a victor, profitable advantages of an official position. □**spoils system,** the practice of giving public offices to supporters of the successful party. **spoil·age** (spoi-lij) *n.* □**be spoiling for,** to desire eagerly, *he is spoiling for a fight.*

spoil·er (spoi-lĕr) *n.* 1. a person or thing that spoils. 2. a device on an aircraft or vehicle to reduce its speed by interrupting air flow.

spoil·sport (spoil-spohrt) *n.* a person who spoils the enjoyment of others.

spoke[1] (spohk) *n.* one of the bars or wire rods that connect the center or hub of a wheel to its rim. □**put a spoke in a person's wheel,** to thwart his intentions.

spoke[2] (spohk), **spo·ken** (spoh-kĕn) *see* **speak.**

spoke·shave (spohk-shayv) *n.* a tool for planing something curved.

spokes·man (spohks-măn) *n.* (*pl.* **-men,** *pr.* -měn) a person who speaks on behalf of a group. **spokes·wom·an** (spohks-wuum-ăn) *n. fem.* (*pl.* **-wom·en,** *pr.* -wim-in). **spokes'per·son** *n.* either of these.

spo·li·a·tion (spoh-li-ay-shŏn) *n.* pillaging. **spo·li·a·tor** (spoh-li-ay-tŏr) *n.*

spon·dee (spon-dee) *n.* a metrical foot consisting of two long syllables.

sponge (spunj) *n.* 1. a kind of water animal with a porous structure. 2. the skeleton of this, or a substance of similar texture, used for washing, cleaning, or padding. 3. a thing of light open texture, something absorbent. 4. sponging, washing with a sponge. **sponge** *v.* **(sponged, spong·ing)** 1. to wipe or wash with a sponge. 2. to live off the generosity of others, to scrounge, *to sponge on people.* □**sponge cake,** a cake with a light open texture. **sponge rubber,** rubber made with many small spaces like a sponge. **throw in the sponge,** *see* **throw.**

spong·er (spun-jĕr) *n.* a person who sponges on others.

spon·gy (spun-jee) *adj.* **(-gi·er, -gi·est)** like a sponge in texture, soft and springy. **spon'gi·ly** *adv.* **spon'gi·ness** *n.*

spon·sor (spon-sŏr) *n.* 1. a person who makes himself responsible for another who is undergoing training etc. 2. a godparent. 3. a person who puts forward a proposal, as for a new law. 4. a person or firm that provides funds for a broadcast or for a musical, artistic, or sporting event. 5. a person who subscribes to charity in return for a specified activity by another person. **sponsor** *v.* to act as sponsor for. **spon'sor·ship** *n.*

spon·ta·ne·ous (spon-tay-ni-ŭs) *adj.* resulting from natural impulse, not caused or suggested from outside, not forced. **spon·ta'ne·ous·ly** *adv.* **spon·ta'ne·ous·ness** *n.* **spon·ta·ne·i·ty** (spon-tă-nee-i-tee, -nay-) *n.* □**spontaneous combustion,** the bursting into flame of a substance (as a mass of oily rags) because of heat produced by its own rapid oxidation and not by flame etc. from an external source.

spoof (spoof) *n.* *(slang)* a hoax, a humorous imitation. **spoof** *v.* *(slang)* to hoax, to imitate humorously.

spook (spook) *n.* 1. *(informal)* a ghost. 2. *(slang)*

a spy. **spook** *v.* 1. to haunt as a ghost. 2. *(slang)* to frighten.

spook·y (spoo-kee) *adj.* **(spook·i·er, spook·i·est)** *(informal)* ghostly, eerie.

spool (spool) *n.* a reel on which something is wound, such as yarn or photographic film.

spoon (spoon) *n.* 1. a utensil consisting of an oval or round bowl and a handle, used for conveying food to the mouth or for stirring or measuring. 2. the amount it contains. **spoon** *v.* to take or lift with a spoon. **spoon·ful** (spoon-fuul) *n.* (*pl.* **-fuls).** □**spoon bread,** a soft corn meal bread.

spoon·bill (spoon-bil) *n.* a wading bird with a very broad flat tip to its bill.

spoon·er·ism (spoo-nĕ-riz-ĕm) *n.* interchange of the initial letters of two words, usually as a slip of the tongue, such as *boiled sprats* (= spoiled brats). ▷Named after the Reverend W. A. Spooner (1884–1930), said to have made such errors in speaking.

spoon-feed (spoon-feed) *v.* **(spoon-fed, spoon-feed·ing)** 1. to feed with liquid food from a spoon. 2. to give excessive help to (a person etc.) so that the recipient does not need to make any effort.

spoor (spoor) *n.* the track or scent left by an animal.

spo·rad·ic (spŏ-rad-ik) *adj.* occurring here and there, scattered. **spo·rad'i·cal·ly** *adv.*

spo·ran·gi·um (spŏ-ran-ji-ŭm) *n.* (*pl.* **-gi·a,** *pr.* -ji-ă) a receptacle in which spores are formed in certain plants.

spore (spohr) *n.* one of the tiny reproductive cells of plants such as fungi and ferns.

sport (spohrt) *n.* 1. an athletic (especially outdoor) activity. 2. any game or pastime, an outdoor pastime such as hunting or fishing. 3. such activities or pastimes collectively, the world of sport. 4. amusement, fun, *said it in sport.* 5. *(slang)* a sportsmanlike person. 6. an animal or plant that is strikingly differently from its parent(s). 7. *(informal)* a person who spends money freely. **sport** *v.* 1. to play, to amuse oneself, 2. to wear or display, *sported a gold tie pin.* □**make sport of,** to make fun of. **sport fish,** a game fish. **sports car,** an open low-built fast car. **sports coat** *or* **jacket,** a man's jacket for informal wear (not part of a suit). **sport shirt,** a man's casual long- or short-sleeved shirt usually worn without a tie.

sport·ing (spohr-ting) *adj.* 1. interested in sport, concerned with sport, *a sporting man.* 2. sportsmanlike. □**a sporting chance,** a reasonable chance of success. **sporting house,** *(old use)* a brothel.

spor·tive (spohr-tiv) *adj.* playful. **spor'tive·ly** *adv.*

sports·cast (spohrts-kast) *n.* a broadcast of sporting news or a sporting event. **sports'cast·er** *n.*

sports·man (spohrts-măn) *n.* (*pl.* **-men,** *pr.* -měn) 1. a man who takes part in sports. 2. a sportsmanlike person.

sports·man·like (spohrts-măn-lık) *adj.* behaving fairly and generously.

sports·man·ship (spohrts-măn-ship) *n.* 1. the ability and attitude of a sportsman. 2. sportsmanlike behavior.

sports·wear (spohrts-wair) *n.* clothing worn for sports, any clothing resembling this.

sports·wom·an (spohrts-wuum-ăn) *n.* (*pl.* **-wom·en,** *pr.* -wim-in) a woman who takes part in sports.

sports·writ·er (spohrts-rı-tĕr) *n.* a person who writes (especially as a journalist) about sports.
sports′writ·ing *n.*
sport·y (spohr-tee) *adj.* (**sport·i·er, sport·i·est**) *(informal)* 1. fond of sport. 2. dashing.
spot (spot) *n.* 1. a roundish area different in color from the rest of a surface. 2. a roundish mark or stain. 3. a particular place or locality. 4. *(informal)* a brief advertisement on radio or television. 5. a drop, *a few spots of rain.* 6. a spotlight.
spot *v.* (**spot·ted, spot·ting**) 1. to mark with a spot or spots. 2. *(informal)* to catch sight of, to detect or recognize, *spotted him at once as an Englishman.* 3. to watch for and take note of, *train-spotting.* **spot′ted** *adj.* □**hit the spot,** to be very satisfying, as of thirst or hunger etc. **in a spot,** *(slang)* in difficulties. **on the spot,** without delay or change of place; at the scene of action; (of a person) alert, equal to dealing with a situation; *put a person on the spot,* to put him in a difficult position, to compel him to take action or justify himself. **spot cash,** cash down. **spot check,** a check made suddenly on something chosen at random. **spotted fever,** any of various fevers, such as typhus, in which spots appear on the skin. **spotted hyena,** an African hyena with a yellow-gray coat and brown or black spots. **spotted sandpiper,** a North American sandpiper with spotted plumage in the summer. **spot welding,** welding of small areas that are in contact.
spot·less (spot-lıs) *adj.* free from stain or blemish, perfectly clean. **spot′less·ly** *adv.*
spot·light (spot-lıt) *n.* 1. a beam of light directed on a small area, a lamp giving this. 2. public attention; *in the spotlight,* receiving full attention or publicity. **spotlight** *v.* 1. to direct a spotlight on. 2. to draw attention to, to make conspicuous.
spot·ter (spot-ĕr) *n.* 1. (in wartime etc.) a civilian who watches for approaching enemy aircraft. 2. a person employed in a drycleaning establishment to clean spots off clothing.
spot·ty (spot-ee) *adj.* (**-ti·er, -ti·est**) 1. marked with spots. 2. inconsistent, uneven. **spot′ti·ly** *adv.* **spot′ti·ness** *n.*
spouse (spows) *n.* a person's husband or wife.
spout (spowt) *n.* 1. a projecting tube through which liquid is poured or conveyed. 2. a jet of liquid. **spout** *v.* 1. to come or send out forcefully as a jet of liquid, *water spouted from the pump; the wound was spouting blood.* 2. to utter or speak lengthily.
spp. *abbr.* species *(pl.).*
sprain (sprayn) *v.* to injure (a joint or its muscles or ligaments) by wrenching it violently. **sprain** *n.* an injury caused in this way.
sprang (sprang) *see* **spring.**
sprat (sprat) *n.* a small herringlike European fish.
sprawl (sprawl) *v.* 1. to sit or lie or fall with the arms and legs spread out loosely. 2. to spread out in an irregular or straggling way. **sprawl** *n.* a sprawling attitude or movement or arrangement. **sprawl′er** *n.*
spray[1] (spray) *n.* 1. a single shoot or branch with its leaves and twigs and flowers. 2. a bunch of cut flowers etc. arranged decoratively. 3. an ornament in similar form.
spray[2] *n.* 1. water or other liquid dispersed in very small drops. 2. a liquid preparation for spraying. 3. a device for spraying liquid. **spray** *v.* to send

out (liquid) or be sent out in very small drops, to wet with liquid in this way. **spray′er** *n.*
□**spray gun,** a gunlike device for spraying liquid.
spread (spred) *v.* (**spread, spread·ing**) 1. to open out, to unroll or unfold, *the peacock spreads its tail; spread the map out.* 2. to become longer or wider, *the stain began to spread.* 3. to cover the surface of, to apply as a layer, *spread the bread with jam; spread the paint evenly.* 4. to be able to be spread, *it spreads like butter.* 5. to make or become more widely known or felt or suffered, *spread the news; panic spread.* 6. to distribute or become distributed, *settlers spread inland.* 7. to distribute over a period, *spread the payments over twelve months.* **spread** *n.* 1. spreading, being spread. 2. the extent or expanse or breadth of something. 3. expansion; *middle-aged spread,* increased bodily girth in middle age. 4. a bedspread. 5. *(informal)* a lavish meal. 6. the range of something. 7. any food, as jam, butter, etc., for spreading on bread etc. **spread′er** *n.* **spread′a·ble** *adj.* □**spread eagle,** the figure of an eagle with legs and wings extended, as an emblem. **spread oneself thin,** to undertake so many responsibilities at one time that none can be met satisfactorily.
spread-ea·gle (spred-ee-gĕl) *v.* (**-ea·gled, -ea·gling**) to spread out (a person's body) with arms and legs extended.
spree (spree) *n.* *(informal)* 1. a lively outing, some fun; *a shopping* or *spending spree,* an outing or period in which one shops or spends freely. 2. a drinking bout.
sprig (sprig) *n.* 1. a small branch, a shoot. 2. an ornament or decoration in this form.
spright·ly (sprıt-lee) *adj.* (**-li·er, -li·est**) lively, full of energy. **spright′li·ness** *n.*
spring (spring) *v.* (**sprang** or **sprung, sprung, spring·ing**) 1. to jump, to move rapidly or suddenly, especially in a single movement. 2. to grow or issue, to arise, *weeds sprang up; their discontent springs from distrust of their leaders.* 3. to become warped or split. 4. to rouse (game) from cover or from a hole; *spring a prisoner from jail,* to arrange his escape. 5. to cause to operate suddenly, *sprang the trap.* 6. to produce or develop suddenly or unexpectedly, *sprang a surprise on us.* **spring** *n.* 1. the act of springing, a jump. 2. a device (usually of bent or coiled metal) that reverts to its original position after being compressed or tightened or stretched, used to drive clockwork (in groups) to make a seat etc. more comfortable. 3. elasticity. 4. a place where water comes up naturally from the ground, the flow of this. 5. the season in which vegetation begins to appear, from March to May in the northern hemisphere. □**spring a leak,** to develop a leak. **spring balance,** a device that measures weight by tension of a spring. **spring chicken,** a young fowl for eating; *(slang)* a young person. **spring fever,** a lazy restless feeling often associated with the coming of spring. **spring mattress,** one containing springs. **spring tide,** the tide when there is the largest rise and fall of water, occurring shortly after the new and full moon. **spring train·ing,** the training program undertaken by baseball teams in preparation for the regular season.
spring·board (spring-bohrd) *n.* a flexible board for giving impetus to a person who jumps on it, used in gymnastics and in diving.

spring·bok (spring-bok) *n.* (*pl.* **-boks, -bok**) a South African gazelle that can spring high into the air.

spring-clean·ing (spring-klee-ning) *n.* cleaning one's home thoroughly, especially in the spring.

Spring·field (spring-feeld) the capital of Illinois.

spring-load·ed (spring-loh-did) *adj.* (of a device) kept in the ready position by a spring.

spring·time (spring-tɪm) *n.* the season of spring.

spring·y (spring-ee) *adj.* (**spring·i·er, spring·i·est**) able to spring back easily after being squeezed or stretched. **spring′i·ness** *n.*

sprin·kle (spring-kĕl) *v.* (**sprin·kled, sprin·kling**) to scatter or fall in small drops or particles, to scatter small drops etc. on (a surface). **sprinkle** *n.* a sprinkling.

sprink·ler (spring-klĕr) *n.* a device for sprinkling water.

sprin·kling (spring-kling) *n.* 1. something sprinkled. 2. a few here and there. □**sprinkling can,** a watering can.

sprint (sprint) *v.* to run at full speed, especially over a short distance. **sprint** *n.* a run of this kind, a similar spell of maximum effort in swimming, cycling, etc. **sprint′er** *n.*

sprit (sprit) *n.* a small spar reaching diagonally from a mast to the upper outer corner of a sail.

sprite (sprɪt) *n.* an elf or fairy or goblin.

sprit·sail (sprit-sayl) *n.* a sail extended by a sprit.

sprock·et (sprok-it) *n.* one of a series of teeth on a wheel (*sprocket wheel*) engaging with links on a chain.

sprout (sprowt) *v.* 1. to begin to grow or appear, to put forth shoots. 2. to cause to spring up as a growth, *has sprouted horns.* **sprout** *n.* the shoot of a plant.

spruce[1] (sproos) *adj.* (**spruc·er, spruc·est**) neat and trim in appearance, smart. **spruce** *v.* (**spruced, spruc·ing**) to smarten, *spruce oneself up.* **spruce′ly** *adv.* **spruce′ness** *n.*

spruce[2] *n.* 1. a kind of fir with dense foliage. 2. the wood of this tree.

sprung (sprung) *see* **spring.**

spry (sprɪ) *adj.* (**spry·er** or **spri·er, spry·est** or **spri·est**) active, nimble, lively. **spry′ly** *adv.* **spry′ness** *n.*

spud (spud) *n.* 1. a small narrow spade for digging up weeds or cutting their roots. 2. (*slang*) a potato.

spume (spyoom) *n.* froth, foam.

spu·mo·ni, spu·mo·ne (spŭ-moh-nee) *n.* an Italian ice cream usually containing chopped fruit and nuts.

spun (spun) *see* **spin.** □**spun glass,** fiberglass. **spun silk,** yarn or fabric made from waste silk. **spun sugar,** a fluffy mass made from boiled sugar drawn into long threads.

spunk (spungk) *n.* (*slang*) courage. **spunk′y** *adj.* (**spunk·i·er, spunk·i·est**) **spunk′i·ness** *n.*

spur (spur) *n.* 1. a pricking device with a projecting point or toothed wheel, worn on a horseman's heel. 2. a stimulus or incentive. 3. something shaped like a spur, a hard projection on a cock's leg, a slender hollow projection on a flower. 4. a ridge projecting from a mountain. 5. a branch road or railroad. **spur** *v.* (**spurred, spur·ring**) 1. to urge (one's horse) on by pricking it with spurs. 2. to urge on, to incite, *spurred the men to greater effort.* 3. to stimulate, *spurred their interest.* □**on the spur of the moment,** on an impulse, without previous planning. **win one's spurs,** to prove one's ability, to win distinction.

spurge (spurj) *n.* a kind of plant or bush with a bitter milky juice.

spu·ri·ous (spyoor-i-ŭs) *adj.* not genuine or authentic. **spu′ri·ous·ly** *adv.* **spu′ri·ous·ness** *n.*

spurn (spurn) *v.* to reject scornfully.

spurred (spurd) *adj.* having spurs, fitted with spurs.

spurt (spurt) *v.* 1. to gush, to send out (a liquid) suddenly. 2. to increase one's speed suddenly. **spurt** *n.* 1. a sudden gush. 2. a short burst of activity, a sudden increase in speed.

sput·nik (sput-nik) *n.* a Russian artificial satellite orbiting Earth.

sput·ter (sput-ĕr) *v.* to splutter, to make a series of quick explosive sounds, *sausages sputtered in the pan.* **sputter** *n.* a sputtering sound. **sput′ter·er** *n.*

spu·tum (spyoo-tŭm) *n.* (*pl.* **-ta,** *pr.* -tă) spittle, matter that is spat out.

spy (spɪ) *n.* (*pl.* **spies**) a person who secretly watches or gathers information about the activities of others and reports the result, one employed by a government to do this in another country. **spy** *v.* (**spied, spy·ing**) 1. to see, to catch sight of. 2. to be a spy, to keep watch secretly, *he was spying on them; spy out the land,* investigate its features etc. secretly.

spy·glass (spɪ-glas) *n.* a small telescope.

sq. *abbr.* 1. squadron. 2. square. 3. the one following (▷Latin *sequens*).

sqq. *abbr.* the ones following (▷Latin *sequentia*).

squab (skwob) *n.* (*pl.* **squabs, squab**) a young pigeon.

squab·ble (skwob-ĕl) *v.* (**squab·bled, squab·bling**) to quarrel in a petty or noisy way, as children do. **squabble** *n.* a quarrel of this kind.

squad (skwod) *n.* a small group of people working or being trained together, especially in the armed forces. □**squad car,** a police car having a radio link with headquarters.

squad·ron (skwod-rŏn) *n.* a military or naval unit varying in size and nature.

squal·id (skwol-id) *adj.* 1. dirty and unpleasant, especially because of neglect or poverty. 2. morally degrading. **squal′id·ly** *adv.* **squal′id·ness** *n.* **squal′or** *n.*

squall[1] (skwawl) *n.* a sudden storm of wind, especially with rain or snow or sleet. **squall′y** *adj.*

squall[2] *n.* a harsh cry or scream, especially of a baby. **squall** *v.* to utter a squall.

squan·der (skwon-dĕr) *v.* to spend wastefully.

square (skwair) *n.* 1. a geometric figure with four equal sides and four right angles. 2. an area or object shaped like this. 3. a four-sided area surrounded by buildings, *Washington Square.* 4. (in astrology) the aspect of two planets 90° apart, regarded as having an unfavorable influence. 5. an L-shaped or T-shaped instrument for obtaining or testing right angles. 6. the product obtained when a number is multiplied by itself, *nine is the square of three* (9 = 3 x 3). 7. (*slang*) a person considered old-fashioned or conventional, one who does not know or does not like the current trends. **square** *adj.* (**squar·er, squar·est**) 1. of square shape. 2. right-angled, *the desk has square corners.* 3. of or using units that express the measure of an area; *one square mile,* a unit equal to the area of a square with sides one mile long. 4. of comparatively broad sturdy shape, *a man of square frame.* 5. equal, with no balance of advantage or debt etc. on either side, *the golfers* *were all square at the fourth hole.* **6.** straightforward, uncompromising, *got a square refusal.* **7.** substantial, *a square meal.* **8.** fair, honest, *a square deal.* **9.** *(slang)* old-fashioned, conventional. **square** *adv.* squarely, directly, *hit him square on the jaw.* **square** *v.* **(squared, squaring)** **1.** to make right-angled, *square the corners.* **2.** to mark with squares, *squared paper.* **3.** to place evenly or squarely, *squared his shoulders.* **4.** to multiply (a number) by itself, *three squared is nine* ($3^2 = 9$), $3 \times 3 = 9$. **5.** to settle or pay, *that squares the account.* **6.** to be or make consistent, *his story doesn't square with yours; try and square the two stories.* **square′ly** *adv.* **square′ness** *n.* □**a square deal,** fair treatment, a fair bargain. **back to square one,** back to the starting point in an enterprise etc., with no progress made. **on the square,** *(informal)* honest, honestly. **square dance,** a dance in which four couples face inward from four sides. **squared away,** tidied up. **square knot,** a knot with the free ends paralleling the fixed ends. **square measure,** measure expressed in square feet etc. **square off,** to get ready to fight, to assume the attitude of a boxer. **square peg in a round hole,** a person who is not fitted for his job. **square root,** a number of which the given number is the square (*see n.* definition 6), *three is the square root of nine.* **square sail,** a four-sided sail extended on a yard slung to the mast by the middle. **square shooter,** an honest person. **square up,** to pay or settle an account etc. **square with,** to be consistent with.

square-rigged (skwair-rigd) *adj.* with the principal sails at right angles to the length of the ship. **square′-rig·ger** *n.* a ship with square-rigged sail.

square-shoul·dered (skwair-shohl-dĕrd) *adj.* having broad and not sloping shoulders.

squar·ish (skwair-ish) *adj.* approximately square.

squash[1] (skwosh) *v.* **1.** to crush, to squeeze or become squeezed flat or into pulp. **2.** to pack tightly, to crowd, to squeeze into a small space. **3.** to suppress, *squashed the rebellion.* **4.** to silence with a crushing reply. **squash** *n.* **1.** a crowd of people squashed together. **2.** the sound of something being squashed. **3.** the game of squash racquets. **squash′y** *adj.* **(squash·i·er squash·i·est)** □**squash racquets,** a game played with rackets and a small ball in a closed court. ▷ Do not confuse *squash* with *quash.*

squash[2] *n.* (*pl.* **squash·es, squash**) a kind of gourd used as a vegetable, the plant that bears it.

squat (skwot) *v.* **(squat·ted, squat·ting)** **1.** to sit on one's heels or crouch with knees drawn up closely. **2.** (of an animal) to crouch close to the ground. **3.** *(informal)* to sit. **4.** to be a squatter, to occupy as a squatter. **squat** *n.* **1.** a squatting posture. **2.** the act of squatting. **squat** *adj.* short and thick, dumpy. **squat′ness** *n.*

squat·ter (skwot-ĕr) *n.* **1.** one who sits in a squatting posture. **2.** a person who settles on unoccupied land in order to acquire a legal right to it. **3.** a person who takes temporary possession of unoccupied buildings for living in, without authority. □**squatter's right,** the right of squatters to claim land as their own after a prescribed period of continuous occupancy.

squaw (skwaw) *n.* a North American Indian woman or wife.

squawk (skwawk) *n.* a loud harsh cry. **squawk**

v. **1.** to utter a squawk. **2.** *(slang)* to complain. **squawk′er** *n.* □**squawk box,** *(informal)* a loudspeaker.

squaw (skwaw) **man** a non-Indian man, especially a white man, married to a squaw.

squeak (skweek) *n.* a short high-pitched cry or sound. **squeak** *v.* to utter or make a squeak. **squeak′er** *n.* □**a narrow squeak,** a narrow escape from danger or failure.

squeak·y (skwee-kee) *adj.* **(squeak·i·er, squeak·i·est)** making a squeaking sound.

squeal (skweel) *n.* a long shrill cry or sound. **squeal** *v.* to utter a squeal, to make this sound. **2.** *(slang)* to protest sharply. **3.** *(slang)* to become an informer. **squeal′er** *n.*

squeam·ish (skwee-mish) *adj.* **1.** easily sickened or disgusted or shocked. **2.** excessively scrupulous about principles. **squeam′ish·ly** *adv.* **squeam·ish·ness** *n.*

squee·gee (skwee-jee) *n.* a tool with a rubber blade on a handle, used for sweeping or squeezing away water or moisture. **squeegee** *v.* **(squee·geed, squee·gee·ing)** to treat with a squeegee.

squeeze (skweez) *v.* **(squeezed, squeez·ing)** **1.** to exert pressure on from opposite or all sides. **2.** to treat in this way so as to extract moisture or juice, to extract (moisture etc.) by squeezing. **3.** to force into or through, to force one's way, to crowd, *we squeezed six people into the car; she squeezed through the gap.* **4.** to produce by pressure or effort. **5.** to obtain by compulsion or strong urging, *squeezed a promise from them.* **6.** to extort money etc. from, to harass in this way, *heavy taxation is squeezing small firms.* **squeeze** *n.* **1.** squeezing, being squeezed. **2.** an affectionate clasp or hug. **3.** a small amount of liquid produced by squeezing, *a squeeze of lemon juice.* **4.** a crowd or crush, the pressure of this, *we all got in, but it was a tight squeeze.* **5.** hardship or difficulty caused by shortage of money or time etc. **6.** restrictions on borrowing etc. during a financial crisis, *a credit squeeze.* □**squeeze bottle,** a flexible container whose contents are extracted by squeezing it. **squeeze play,** (in baseball) a play in which the ball is bunted to enable a runner on third base to break for home plate as soon as the ball is pitched.

squeez·er (skwee-zĕr) *n.* a device for squeezing juice from fruit by pressure.

squelch (skwelch) *v.* **1.** to stamp on, to crush flat. **2.** to suppress, to quell. **3.** to silence, as with a crushing reply. **4.** to make a sound like someone treading on thick mud. **squelch** *n.* the act or sound of squelching. **squelch′er** *n.*

squib (skwib) *n.* **1.** a small firework that makes a hissing sound and then explodes. **2.** a short satirical composition, a lampoon.

squid (skwid) *n.* (*pl.* **squid, squids**) a sea creature related to the cuttlefish, with ten arms around the mouth.

squig·gle (skwig-ĕl) *n.* a short curly line, especially in handwriting. **squiggle** *v.* **(squig·gled, squig·gling)** to make such a line, to draw as a squiggle. **squig′gly** *adj.*

squint (skwint) *v.* **1.** to look at (a thing) with the eyes turned sideways or half shut, or through a narrow opening. **2.** to be cross-eyed. **squint** *n.* **1.** a squinting position of the eyelids or eyeballs. **2.** a stealthy or sideways glance. **3.** *(informal)* a look, *have a squint at this.* **squint′er** *n.* **squint′y** *adj.*

squint-eyed (skwint-ɪd) *adj.* 1. cross-eyed. 2. looking spiteful or malicious.

squire (skwɪr) *n.* 1. a country gentleman in England, especially the chief landowner in a district. 2. *(old use)* an attendant on a knight. 3. a woman's escort. 4. (as a title of respect) a magistrate or lawyer. **squire** *v.* (**squired, squir·ing**) to escort.

squirm (skwurm) *v.* 1. to wriggle or writhe. 2. to feel embarrassment or uneasiness. **squirm** *n.* a squirming movement. **squirm'er** *n.* **squirm'y** *adj.*

squir·rel (skwur-ĕl) *n.* (*pl.* **-rels, -rel**) 1. a small tree-climbing animal with a bushy tail and usually red or gray fur. 2. its fur. ☐**squirrel away,** to hoard (a thing).

squir·rel·ly (skwur-ĕ-lee) *adj.* *(slang)* eccentric, odd.

squirt (skwurt) *v.* to send out (liquid) or be sent out from or as if from a syringe, to wet in this way. **squirt** *n.* 1. a syringe. 2. a jet of liquid. 3. *(informal)* a small or unimportant but annoying person.

Sr *symbol* strontium.

Sr. *abbr.* 1. Senior. 2. Señor. 3. Sir. 4. Sister.

Sri Lan·ka (sree lang-kä) a country (formerly called Ceylon) in the Indian Ocean. **Sri Lan'kan** *adj.* & *n.*

SRO *abbr.* standing room only.

SS *abbr.* 1. Schutzstaffel (the Nazi special police force). 2. steamship. 3. Sunday school. 4. sworn statement.

ss. *abbr.* 1. sections. 2. shortstop.

SSA *abbr.* Social Security Administration.

SSE *abbr.* south-southeast.

SSgt *abbr.* staff sergeant.

SSR *abbr.* Soviet Socialist Republic.

SSS *abbr.* Selective Service System.

SST *abbr.* supersonic transport.

SSW *abbr.* south-southwest.

ST *abbr.* Standard Time.

st. *abbr.* 1. stanza. 2. state. 3. stitch. 4. stone (weight).

St. *abbr.* 1. Saint. 2. statute(s). 3. Strait. 4. Street.

s.t. *abbr.* short ton.

sta. *abbr.* 1. station. 2. stationary.

stab (stab) *v.* (**stabbed, stab·bing**) 1. to pierce or wound with a pointed tool or weapon. 2. to aim a blow with or as if with a pointed weapon. 3. to cause a sensation of being stabbed, *a stabbing pain.* **stab** *n.* 1. the act of stabbing, a blow or thrust wound made by stabbing. 2. a sensation of being stabbed, *felt a stab of fear.* 3. *(informal)* an attempt; *make* or *take* or *have a stab at it,* try to do it. ☐**a stab in the back,** a treacherous attack.

sta·bile (stay-beel) *n.* an abstract sculpture or structure of sheet metal, etc.

sta·bil·i·ty (stă-bil-i-tee) *n.* being stable.

sta·bi·lize (stay-bĭ-lɪz) *v.* (**sta·bi·lized, sta·bi·liz·ing**) to make or become stable. **sta·bi·li·za·tion** (stay-bĭ-lĭ-zay-shŏn) *n.*

sta·bi·liz·er (stay-bĭ-lɪ-zĕr) *n.* a device to prevent a ship from rolling or to keep an airplane steady during flight.

sta·ble[1] (stay-bĕl) *adj.* firmly fixed or established, not readily changing or fluctuating, not easily destroyed or decomposed. **sta'bly** *adv.*

stable[2] *n.* 1. a building in which horses are kept. 2. an establishment for training racehorses, the horses from a particular establishment. **stable** *v.* (**sta·bled, sta·bling**) to put or keep in a stable.

sta·ble·boy (stay-bĕl-boi) *n.* a person (of either sex) who works in a stable.

stac·ca·to (stă-kah-toh) *adj.* & *adv.* (especially in music) in a sharp disconnected manner, not running on smoothly.

stack (stak) *n.* 1. a circular or rectangular pile of hay etc., usually with a pointed top. 2. an orderly pile or heap. 3. *(informal)* a large quantity, *have stacks* or *a whole stack of work to get through.* 4. a smokestack. 5. *stacks,* the section of a library where most of the books are kept. **stack** *v.* 1. to pile in a stack or stacks. 2. to arrange (cards) secretly for cheating; *the cards were stacked against him,* circumstances put him at a disadvantage. 3. to instruct (aircraft) to fly around the same point at different altitudes while waiting to land. ☐**blow one's stack,** *(slang)* to show great anger. **stack up,** *(informal)* to compare, *how do these results stack up against the earlier ones?*

sta·di·um (stay-di-ŭm) *n.* (*pl.* **-di·ums, -di·a,** *pr.* -di-ă) an enclosed athletic or sportsground with tiers of seats for spectators.

staff (staf) *n.* (*pl.* **staffs** for definitions 2, 3 & 4, also **staves,** *pr.* stayvz, for 1 & 5) 1. (*pl. staves* or *staffs*) a stick or pole used as a weapon or support or measuring stick, or as a symbol of authority. 2. a body of officers assisting a commanding officer and concerned with an army or regiment or fleet etc. as a whole. 3. a group of assistants by whom a business is carried on, those responsible to a manager or person of authority. 4. people in authority within an organization (as distinct from pupils etc.), or those doing administrative work as distinct from manual work. 5. (*pl. staves* or *staffs*) one of the sets of five horizontal lines on which music is written. **staff** *v.* to provide with a staff of employees or assistants. **staff'er** *n.* ☐**staff officer,** a member of a military staff (*see* definition 2). **staff of life,** bread.

staff sergeant, a noncommissioned officer ranking (in the U.S. Army) below a sergeant first class and above a sergeant, (in the Air Force) below a technical sergeant and above a sergeant, (in the Marine Corps) below a gunnery sergeant and above a sergeant.

stag (stag) *n.* a fully grown male deer. **stag** *adj.* of or for men only. **stag** *adv.* not accompanied by a woman. ☐**stag beetle,** a beetle with branched projecting mouth parts that resemble a stag's antlers. **stag party,** a party of or for men only.

stage (stayj) *n.* 1. a platform on which plays etc. are performed before an audience. 2. *the stage,* theatrical work, the profession of actors and actresses. 3. a raised floor or platform, as on scaffolding. 4. a point or period in the course or development of something, *the talks have reached a critical stage.* 5. a stopping place on a route, the distance between two of these; *we traveled by easy stages,* a short distance at a time. 6. a section of a space rocket with a separate engine, jettisoned when its fuel is exhausted. **stage** *v.* (**staged, stag·ing**) 1. to present (a play etc.) on the stage. 2. to arrange and carry out, *decided to stage a sit-in.* ☐**go on the stage,** to become an actor or actress. **stage door,** the actors' and crew's etc. entrance from the street to the backstage area of a theater. **stage fright,** nervousness on facing an audience. **stage left,** the part of the stage that is on an actor's left as he faces the audience. **stage-manage,** to organize things as or like a stage manager. **stage manager,** the person responsible for the scenery and other practical arrangements in the production of a play. **stage right,** the part of the stage that is on an actor's right as he faces the audience. **stage whisper,** a whisper that is meant to be overheard.

stage·coach (stayj-kohch) *n.* a large closed horse-drawn coach formerly running regularly by stages between places.

stage·craft (stayj-kraft) *n.* skill or experience in writing or staging plays.

stage-door (stayj-dohr) **John·ny** *(informal)* a man who spends time at a theater courting an actress or chorus girl.

stage·hand (stayj-hand) *n.* a person handling scenery etc. during a performance on the stage.

stage·struck (stayj-struk) *adj.* having an obsessive desire to become an actor or actress.

stag·fla·tion (stag-flay-shŏn) *n.* a period in which inflation occurs without a corresponding increase in production. ▷A combination of the words *stagnation* and *inflation.*

stag·ger (stag-ĕr) *v.* 1. to move or go unsteadily, as if about to fall. 2. to shock deeply, to cause astonishment or worry or confusion to, *we were staggered by the news.* 3. to place in a zigzag or alternating arrangement. 4. to arrange (people's holidays or hours of work etc.) so that their times do not coincide exactly. **stagger** *n.* an unsteady staggering movement. **stag'ger·ing·ly** *adv.*

stag·ger·ing (stag-ĕ-ring) *adj.* bewildering, astonishing, *the total cost is staggering.*

stag·ing (stay-jing) *n.* 1. scaffolding, a temporary platform or support. 2. the presentation of a production on the stage. □**staging area,** an intermediate assembly point for troops in transit. **staging post,** a regular stopping place on a long route.

stag·nant (stag-nănt) *adj.* 1. (of water) not flowing, still and stale. 2. showing no activity, *business was stagnant.*

stag·nate (stag-nayt) *v.* **(stag·nat·ed, stag·nat·ing)** 1. to be stagnant. 2. (of a person) to become dull through inactivity and lack of variety or opportunity. **stag·na·tion** (stag-nay-shŏn) *n.*

stag·y (stay-jee) *adj.* theatrical in style or manner.

staid (stayd) *adj.* steady and serious in manner, tastes etc., sedate. **staid'ly** *adv.*

stain (stayn) *v.* 1. to discolor or become discolored by a substance. 2. to blemish, *it stained his good reputation.* 3. to color with a pigment that penetrates. **stain** *n.* 1. a mark caused by staining. 2. a blemish, *without a stain on his character.* 3. a liquid used for staining things. **stain'er** *n.* □**stained glass,** glass colored with transparent coloring.

stain·less (stayn-lis) *adj.* free from stains or blemishes. □**stainless steel,** steel containing chromium and not liable to rust or tarnish under ordinary conditions.

stair (stair) *n.* 1. one of a flight of fixed steps. 2. *stairs,* a flight of steps. □**stair rod,** a rod for securing a stair carpet in the angle between two stairs.

stair·case (stair-kays) *n.* a flight of stairs (often with banisters) and its supporting structure.

stair·way (stair-way) *n.* a staircase.

stair·well (stair-wel) *n.* (in a building) the vertical area in which the stairs are located.

stake (stayk) *n.* 1. a stick or post sharpened at one end for driving into the ground as a support or marker etc. 2. the post to which a person was bound for execution by being burned alive; *the stake,* this method of execution. 3. money etc. wagered on the result of a race or other event; *stakes,* (in names of horse races) money offered as a prize, the race itself, *the Belmont Stakes.* 4. something invested in an enterprise and giving a share or interest in it. **stake** *v.* **(staked, stak·ing)** 1. to fasten or support with stakes. 2. to mark (an area) with stakes. 3. to wager or risk (money etc.) on an event. 4. *(informal)* to give financial or other support to. □**at stake,** being risked, depending on the outcome of an event. **pull up stakes,** to depart, to go to live elsewhere. **stake a claim,** to claim or obtain a right to something. **stake out,** to mark (an area) with stakes; *(informal)* to place (an area etc.) under surveillance, to assign (a person) to such a task. **stake race,** a horse race for which the owners of the horses put up part of the prize money.

stake·out (stayk-owt) *n.* surveillance of a building etc., as by police.

sta·lac·tite (stă-lak-tīt) *n.* a deposit of calcium carbonate hanging like an icicle from the roof of a cave etc.

sta·lag·mite (stă-lag-mīt) *n.* a deposit like a stalactite but standing like a pillar on the floor of a cave etc.

stale (stayl) *adj.* **(stal·er, stal·est)** 1. lacking freshness, dry or musty or unpleasant because not fresh. 2. uninteresting because not new or because heard often before, *stale news or jokes.* 3. having one's ability to perform spoiled by too much practice. **stale** *v.* **(staled, stal·ing)** to make or become stale. **stale'ly** *adv.* **stale'ness** *n.*

stale·mate (stayl-mayt) *n.* 1. a drawn position in chess, in which a player can make no move without putting his king in check. 2. a deadlock, a drawn contest. **stalemate** *v.* **(stale·mat·ed, stale·mat·ing)** to bring to a position of stalemate or deadlock.

Sta·lin·ism (stah-li-niz-ĕm) *n.* the policy of Joseph Stalin (1879–1953) in government of the U.S.S.R. **Sta'lin·ist** *adj. & n.*

stalk[1] (stawk) *n.* 1. the main stem of a plant. 2. a stem attaching a leaf or flower or fruit to another stem or to a twig. 3. a similar support of a part or organ in animals or of a device. **stalked** *adj.*

stalk[2] *v.* 1. to walk in a stately or imposing manner. 2. to track or pursue (game etc.) stealthily. **stalk'er** *n.* □**stalking horse,** a person or thing used to conceal one's real intentions.

stall (stawl) *n.* 1. a stable or cow barn, a compartment for one animal in this. 2. a compartment for one person. 3. a seat with its back and sides more or less enclosed, in a church etc. 4. a booth or stand or table where goods are displayed for sale. 5. stalling of an engine or aircraft. **stall** *v.* 1. to place or keep (an animal) in a stall, especially for fattening. 2. (of an engine) to stop suddenly because of an overload or insufficient fuel. 3. (of an aircraft) to begin to drop because the speed is too low for the plane to answer to its controls. 4. to cause (an engine or aircraft) to stall. 5. to use delaying tactics in order to gain time, to turn aside (a person or request) in this way.

stal·lion (stal-yŏn) *n.* an uncastrated male horse, especially one kept for breeding.

stal·wart (stawl-wărt) *adj.* 1. sturdy. 2. strong and faithful, *stalwart supporters.* **stalwart** *n.* a stalwart person.

sta·men (stay-mĕn) *n.* (*pl.* **sta·mens**) the male

fertilizing organ of flowering plants, bearing pollen.

stam·i·na (stam-ĭ-nă) *n.* staying power, ability to withstand prolonged physical or mental strain.

stam·i·nate (stam-ĭ-nit, -nayt) *adj.* 1. having stamens but no pistils. 2. having stamens.

stam·mer (stam-ĕr) *v.* to speak or utter with involuntary pauses or rapid repetitions of the same syllable. **stammer** *n.* stammering speech, a tendency to stammer. **stam′mer·er** *n.* **stam′mer·ing·ly** *adv.*

stamp (stamp) *v.* 1. to bring one's foot down heavily on the ground, *stamped hard* or *stamped his foot.* 2. to walk with loud heavy steps. 3. to strike or press with a device that leaves a mark or pattern etc., to cut or shape in this way. 4. to fix a postage or other stamp to. 5. to give a certain character to, *this achievement stamps him as a genius.* **stamp** *n.* 1. the act or sound of stamping. 2. an instrument for stamping a pattern or mark, the mark itself. 3. a piece of paper bearing an official design, for affixing to an envelope or document to indicate that postage or duty or other fee has been paid. 4. a distinguishing mark, a clear indication, *the story bears the stamp of truth.* ☐**stamp collecting,** the collecting of postage stamps as objects of interest or value. **stamping ground,** *(informal)* a person's or animal's usual haunt or place of action. **stamp on,** to crush by stamping; to quell. **stamp out,** to extinguish by stamping, *stamped out the fire;* to suppress (a rebellion etc.) by force.

stam·pede (stam-peed) *n.* 1. a sudden rush of a herd of frightened animals. 2. a rush of people under a sudden common impulse, *stampede to buy gold.* **stampede** *v.* (stam·ped·ed, stam·ped·ing) to take part or cause to take part in a stampede, to cause to act hurriedly.

stance (stans) *n.* 1. the position in which a person or animal stands. 2. an attitude, usually toward a specific issue etc., *a positive stance on civil liberties.*

stanch¹ (stawnch) *v.* to restrain the flow of (blood etc.) or from (a wound).

stanch² = **staunch¹.**

stan·chion (stan-chŏn) *n.* an upright bar or post forming a support.

stand (stand) *v.* (stood, stand·ing) 1. to have or take or keep a stationary upright position, *we were standing talking about the weather.* 2. to be of a specified height, *stands six feet two inches.* 3. to be situated. 4. to place, to set upright, *stand the vase on the table.* 5. to remain firm or valid or in a specified condition, *the offer still stands; the thermometer stood at 90°.* 6. to remain stationary or unused. 7. to offer oneself for election, *she stood for Congress.* 8. to undergo, *he stood trial for murder.* 9. to steer a specified course in sailing. 10. to put up with, to endure, *can't stand that noise.* 11. to provide at one's own expense, *stood him a drink.* **stand** *n.* 1. a stationary condition. 2. a position taken up, *took his stand near the door.* 3. resistance to attack, the period of this, *make a stand.* 4. a halt to give a performance, *the band did a one-night stand.* 5. a rack or pedestal etc. on which something may be placed, *umbrella stand.* 6. *stands,* a raised structure with seats at a sports ground etc. 7. a small often temporary structure for displaying goods, *newspaper stand.* 8. a standing place for vehicles, *taxi stand.* 9. a witness box. ☐**as it stands,** in the present

state of affairs; in its present condition, unaltered, *leave it as it stands.* **it stands to reason,** it is obvious or logical. **stand a chance,** to have a chance of success. **stand alone,** to be unequaled. **stand by,** to look on without interfering; to support or side with (a person) in difficulty or dispute; to stand ready for action; to keep to (a promise or agreement). **stand for,** to represent, *a policeman's badge stands for law and order;* "*U.S.*" *stands for* "*United States*"; *(informal)* to tolerate. **stand off,** to remain at a distance. **stand on,** to insist on formal observance of, *stand on ceremony.* **stand on end,** (of hair) to become erect from fear or horror. **stand one's ground,** not yield. **stand on one's own feet,** to be independent. **stand out,** to be conspicuous. **stand over,** to supervise (a person or thing) closely; to be postponed. **stand treat,** *(informal)* to pay for another person's drink or entertainment etc. **stand up,** to come to or place in a standing position; to be valid, to endure, *that argument won't stand up; stand a person up,* fail to keep an appointment with him. **stand up for,** to defend or support (a person or opinion). **stand up to,** to resist courageously; to remain durable in (hard use or wear).

stand·ard (stan-dărd) *n.* 1. a thing or quality or specification by which something may be tested or measured. 2. the required level of quality, *was rejected as being below standard.* 3. the average quality, *the standard of her work is high.* 4. a specified level of proficiency. 5. the prescribed proportion of the weight of fine metal to be used in coins. 6. the basis to which the value of a monetary system is related, *the gold standard.* 7. a distinctive flag, *the royal standard.* 8. an upright support. **standard** *adj.* 1. serving as or conforming to a standard, *standard measures of length.* 2. of average or usual quality, not of special design etc., *the standard model of this car.* 3. of recognized merit or authority, *the standard book on spiders.* 4. widely used and regarded as the usual form, *standard car battery.* ☐**standard English,** the form of English speech used, with local variations, by the majority of educated English-speaking people. **standard gauge,** the standard width of a railroad track, four feet, eight and one-half inches between the rails. **standard of living,** the level of material comfort enjoyed by a person or group. **standard time,** the uniform time for places in approximately the same longitude, and established in a country or region by law or custom.

stand·ard·bear·er (stan-dărd-bair-ĕr) *n.* a prominent leader in a political party or a cause.

stand·ard·bred (stan-dărd-bred) *n.* a horse of a breed used chiefly for harness racing.

stand·ard·ize, stand·ard·iz·ing (stan-dăr-dīz) *v.* (stand·ard·ized, stand·ard·iz·ing) to cause to conform to a standard. **stand·ard·i·za·tion** (stan-dăr-di-zay-shŏn) *n.*

stand·by (stand-bī) *n.* (*pl.* -bys) a person or thing available as a substitute or in an emergency. **standby** *adj.* ready for use or action as a substitute etc.

stand·ee (stan-dee) *n.* *(informal)* a person who stands in a bus or theater etc. because all seats are occupied.

stand·in (stand-in) *n.* 1. a person who takes the place of an actor while lighting etc. is arranged. 2. *(informal)* a person who deputizes for another.

stand·ing (stan-ding) *adj.* 1. upright; *standing corn,* not yet harvested. 2. (of a jump) performed without a run. 3. permanent, remaining effective or valid, *a standing invitation*. **standing** *n*. 1. status, *people of high standing*. 2. past duration, *a friendship of long standing*. □**standing army**, a permanently maintained army. **standing committee**, a permanent committee. **standing room**, space for people to stand in.

stand·off (stand-awf) *n*. *(informal)* a draw or tie in a game.

stand·off·ish (stand-aw-fish) *adj*. *(informal)* aloof in manner.

stand·out (stand-owt) *n*. a remarkable person or thing.

stand·pipe (stand-pɪp) *n*. a vertical pipe for fluid to rise in, as to provide a water supply outside or at a distance from buildings.

stand·point (stand-point) *n*. a point of view.

stand·still (stand-stil) *n*. a stoppage, an inability to proceed.

stand-up (stand-up) *adj*. 1. (of a collar) upright, not turned down. 2. (of a meal) eaten while standing. 3. (of a comedian) performing (often while standing) alone on stage.

stank (stangk) *see* **stink**.

stan·za (stan-zǎ) *n*. a group of lines, often rhymed, forming a subdivision of a poem.

sta·pes (stay-peez) *n*. (*pl*. **-pes**) a small stirrup-shaped bone in the ear of a mammal.

staph (staf) *n*. *(informal)* staphylococcus.

staph·y·lo·coc·cus (staf-ĭ-lŏ-kok-ŭs) *n*. (*pl*. **-coc·ci**, *pr*. -kok-sɪ) a kind of microorganism that causes pus to form. **staph·y·lo·coc′cal** *adj*. **staph·y·lo·coc·cic** (staf-ĭ-lŏ-kok-sik) *adj*.

sta·ple[1] (stay-pĕl) *n*. 1. a U-shaped piece of metal or wire for holding something in place. 2. a piece of metal or wire driven into papers etc. and clenched to fasten them. **staple** *v*. (**sta·pled, sta·pling**) to secure with a staple or staples. **sta′pler** *n*.

staple[2] *adj*. principal, standard, *rice is their staple food*. **staple** *n*. a staple food or product etc.

star (stahr) *n*. 1. a celestial body appearing as a point of light in the night sky. 2. (in astronomy) any large light-emitting gaseous ball, such as the sun. 3. a heavenly body regarded as influencing a person's fortunes, *thank your lucky stars*. 4. a figure or object or ornament with rays or radiating points, an asterisk, a star-shaped mark indicating a category of excellence. 5. a brilliant person, a famous actor or actress or other performer. **star** *v*. (**starred, star′ring**) 1. to put an asterisk or star symbol beside (a name or item in a list etc.). 2. to present or perform as a star actor. **star′less** *adj*. **star′like** *adj*. □**Star Chamber**, an English civil and criminal court noted for arbitrary procedure and severe treatment, abolished in 1604; any arbitrary oppressive tribunal. **star cut**, a gem cut having one large hexagonal surface surrounded by six smaller facets in the shape of equilateral triangles. **star dust**, a multitude of stars looking like dust; a romantic sensation. **star of Bethlehem**, a plant having white starlike flowers striped with green. **Star of David**, the six-pointed star used as a Jewish and Israeli symbol. **star route**, a postal delivery route served by private contractors. **Stars and Bars**, the flag of the Confederate States of America. **Stars and Stripes**, the national flag of the U.S. **star sapphire**, a sapphire, polished but not faceted, that reflects light in the shape of a six-rayed star. **star shell**, a military

shell designed to burst in air and light up the enemy's position.

star·board (stahr-bŏrd) *n*. the right-hand side (when facing forward) of a ship or aircraft. **starboard** *adj*.

starch (stahrch) *n*. 1. a white carbohydrate that is an important element in human food. 2. a preparation of this or other substances for stiffening fabrics. 3. stiffness of manner. **starch** *v*. to stiffen with starch.

starch·y (stahr-chee) *adj*. (**starch·i·er, starch·i·est**) 1. of or like starch. 2. containing much starch. 3. stiff and formal in manner. **starch′i·ness** *n*.

star-crossed (stahr-krawst) *adj*. *(old use)* ill-fated.

star·dom (stahr-dŏm) *n*. being a star actor or performer.

stare (stair) *v*. (**stared, star·ing**) 1. to gaze fixedly with the eyes wide open, especially in astonishment. 2. (of the eyes) to be wide open with fixed gaze. **stare** *n*. a staring gaze. □**stare a person in the face**, to be glaringly obvious or clearly imminent, *ruin stared him in the face*.

star·fish (stahr-fish) *n*. a star-shaped sea creature.

star·gaze (stahr-gayz) *v*. (**star·gazed, star·gaz·ing**) 1. *(humorous)* to study the stars as an astronomer or astrologer. 2. to daydream. **star′gaz·er** *n*.

stark (stahrk) *adj*. 1. stiff in death. 2. desolate, cheerless, *stark prison conditions*. 3. sharply evident, *in stark contrast*. 4. downright, complete, *stark madness*. **stark** *adv*. completely; wholly, *stark raving mad*. **stark′ly** *adv*. **stark′ness** *n*.

star·let (stahr-lit) *n*. a young film actress who shows promise of becoming a star.

star·light (stahr-lɪt) *n*. light from the stars.

star·ling (stahr-ling) *n*. a noisy bird with glossy blackish speckled feathers that forms large flocks.

star·lit (stahr-lit) *adj*. lit by starlight.

star·ry (stahr-ee) *adj*. (**-ri·er, -ri·est**) 1. set with stars. 2. shining like stars.

star·ry-eyed (stahr-ee-ɪd) *adj*. 1. romantically enthusiastic. 2. enthusiastic but impractical.

Star-Span·gled (stahr-spang-gĕld) **Banner, The** the national anthem of the U.S.

star-stud·ded (stahr-stud-id) *adj*. containing many stars, *the show has a star-studded cast*.

start (stahrt) *v*. 1. to begin or cause to begin a process or course of action, (of an engine) to begin running. 2. to cause or enable to begin, to establish or found, *the parents started a play group; start a baby*, to conceive. 3. to begin a journey. 4. to make a sudden movement from pain or surprise etc., *started at the sound of gunfire*. 5. to spring suddenly, *started from his seat*. 6. to rouse (game etc.) from its lair or covert. **start** *n*. 1. the beginning of a journey or activity or race, the place where a race starts. 2. an opportunity for or assistance in starting. 3. an advantage gained or allowed in starting, the amount of this, *had ten seconds* or *ten yards start*. 4. a sudden movement of surprise or pain etc. □**for a start**, as a thing to start with. **start in**, *(informal)* to begin. **starting gate**, a removable barrier behind which horses are lined up at the start of a race. **starting point**, the point from which something begins. **start off**, to begin, to begin to move. **start out**, to begin, to begin a journey; to intend when starting, *started out to write a novel*. **start up**, to start; to set in motion, to start an activity etc.

start·er (stahr-tĕr) *n*. 1. a person or thing that

starts something. 2. one who gives the signal for a race to start. 3. a horse or competitor at the start of a race, *list of probable starters.* □**for starters,** *(slang)* to start with.

star·tle (stahr-těl) *v.* (**star·tled, star·tling**) to cause to make a sudden movement from surprise or alarm, to take by surprise.

star·tling (stahrt-ling) *adj.* surprising, astonishing.

starve (stahrv) *v.* (**starved, starv·ing**) 1. to die or suffer acutely from lack of food, to cause to do this. 2. to suffer or cause to suffer for lack of something needed, *was starved for affection.* 3. *(informal)* to feel very hungry or very cold. 4. to force by starvation, *starved them into surrender.* **star·va·tion** (stahr-vay-shŏn) *n.* □**starvation diet,** not enough food to support life adequately.

starve·ling (stahrv-ling) *n.* a starving or ill-fed person or animal.

stash (stash) *v.* *(slang)* to stow. **stash** *n.* *(slang)* 1. a hiding place for something. 2. the thing hidden.

stat. *abbr.* 1. statuary. 2. statue. 3. statute(s).

state (stayt) *n.* 1. the quality of a person's or thing's characteristics or circumstances. 2. an excited or agitated condition of the mind, *she got into a state.* 3. a grand imposing style, *arrived in state.* 4. (often *State*) an organized community under one government *(the State of Israel)* or forming part of a federal republic *(the state of Vermont).* 5. civil government, *matters of state.* **state** *adj.* 1. of or for or concerned with the state. 2. involving ceremony, used or done on ceremonial occasions, *state occasions.* **state** *v.* (**stat·ed, stat·ing**) 1. to express in spoken or written words. 2. to fix or specify, *must be inspected at stated intervals.* □**lie in state,** to be laid out for viewing before burial. **State Department,** the department of foreign affairs in the U.S. government. **state of the art,** the current state of development or knowledge of a subject. **state's evidence,** evidence given for or by the state in a criminal case, especially by the accused's accomplice who becomes a voluntary witness. **state trooper,** a member of the police force of a state of the U.S. **the States,** the U.S.

state·craft (stayt-kraft) *n.* the art of conducting affairs of state.

state·hood (stayt-huud) *n.* the condition or status of being a state, *Alaska achieved statehood in 1959.*

state·house (stayt-hows) *n.* (*pl.* **-hous·es,** *pr.* -how-ziz) the building where a state legislature meets.

state·less (stayt-lis) *adj.* (of a person) not a citizen or subject of any country.

state·ly (stayt-lee) *adj.* (**-li·er, -li·est**) dignified, imposing, grand. **state'li·ness** *n.*

state·ment (stayt-měnt) *n.* 1. stating. 2. something stated. 3. a formal account of facts, a written report of a financial account.

state·room (stayt-room) *n.* a passenger's private compartment on a ship or train.

state·side (stayt-sıd) *adj.* of, in, or toward the U.S., as viewed from outside the country. **stateside** *adv.* in or toward the U.S.

states·man (stayts-măn) *n.* (*pl.* **-men,** *pr.* -měn) a person who is skilled or prominent in the management of state affairs. **states'man·like** *adj.* **states'man·ship** *n.* **states·wom·an** (stayts-wuum-ăn) *n. fem.* (*pl.* **-wom·en,** *pr.* -wim-in).

stat·ic (stat-ik) *adj.* 1. of force acting by weight without motion (as opposed to *dynamic*). 2. not

moving, stationary. 3. not changing. **static** *n.* 1. atmospherics. 2. static electricity. 3. radio interference caused by atmospheric electricity, the noise of this. 4. *(slang)* criticism. 5. *statics,* a branch of physics that deals with bodies at rest or forces in equilibrium. □**static electricity,** electricity present in a body and not flowing as current.

sta·tion (stay-shŏn) *n.* 1. a place where a person or thing stands or is stationed. 2. an establishment or building where a public service is based or which is equipped for certain activities, *the fire station; an agricultural research station.* 3. a broadcasting establishment with its own frequency. 4. a stopping place on a railroad or bus route with buildings for passengers or goods or both. 5. postition in life, status, *she had ideas above her station.* **station** *v.* to put at or in a certain place for a purpose, *the regiment was stationed in Germany.* □**station break,** a pause between or during broadcast programs for identification of the station transmitting them. **stations of the cross,** a series of fourteen images or pictures representing events in Christ's Passion before which prayers are said in certain churches. **station wagon,** an automobile having as its trunk area an extension of the seating area, and with folding or removable rear seats.

sta·tion·ar·y (stay-shŏ-ner-ee) *adj.* 1. not moving, not movable. 2. not changing in condition or quantity etc. ▷Do not confuse *stationary* with *stationery.*

sta·tion·er (stay-shŏ-něr) *n.* a person who sells writing materials (paper, pens, ink, etc.).

sta·tion·er·y (stay-shŏ-ner-ee) *n.* writing paper, envelopes, and other articles sold by a stationer. ▷Do not confuse *stationery* with *stationary.*

sta·tion·mas·ter (stay-shŏn-mas-těr) *n.* the official in charge of a railroad station.

sta·tis·tic (stă-tis-tik) *n.* an item of information expressed in numbers, *there is no reliable statistic* or *there are no reliable statistics on this problem.* ▷See the note under **statistics.**

stat·is·ti·cian (stat-i-stish-an) *n.* an expert in statistics.

sta·tis·tics (stă-tis-tiks) *n.* the science of collecting, classifying, and interpreting information based on the numbers of things. **sta·tis'ti·cal** *adj.* **sta·tis'ti·cal·ly** *adv.* ▷Note that *statistics* in this meaning is singular, *statistics is my favorite subject.*

stat·u·ar·y (stach-oo-er-ee) *n.* statues.

stat·ue (stach-oo) *n.* a sculptured or cast or molded figure of a person or animal, usually of life size or larger. ▷Do not confuse *statue* with *statute.*

stat·u·esque (stach-oo-esk) *adj.* like a statue in size or dignity or stillness.

stat·u·ette (stach-oo-et) *n.* a small statue.

stat·ure (stach-ŭr) *n.* 1. the natural height of the body. 2. greatness gained by ability or achievement.

sta·tus (stay-tŭs, stat-ŭs) *n.* (*pl.* **-tus·es**) 1. a person's position or rank in relation to others, a person's or thing's legal position. 2. high rank or prestige. □**status symbol,** a possession or activity etc. regarded as evidence of a person's high status.

sta·tus quo (stay-tŭs kwoh, stat-ŭs) the state of affairs as it is or as it was before a recent change, *maintain the status quo.* ▷Latin, = the state in which.

sta·tute (stach-oot) *n.* 1. a law passed by a legisla-

tive body. **2.** one of the rules of an institution, *the university statutes.* ☐**statute mile,** *see* **mile.**
statute of limitations, a statute specifying the period of time beyond which legal action may not be taken. ▷Do not confuse *statute* with *statue.*
stat·u·to·ry (stach-ŭ-tohr-ee) *adj.* fixed or done or required by statute. **stat′u·to·ri·ly** *adv.* ☐**statutory law,** statutes collectively, as opposed to case law or common law.
staunch[1] (stawnch) *adj.* firm in attitude or opinion or loyalty. **staunch′ly** *adv.* **staunch′ness** *n.*
staunch[2] = **stanch**[1].
stave (stayv) *n.* **1.** one of the curved strips of wood forming the side of a barrel or tub. **2.** a staff in music (*see* **staff** definition 5). **stave** *v.* **(staved** or **stove, stav·ing)** to dent or break a hole, *stove or staved it in.* ☐**stave off,** to ward off permanently or temporarily, *we staved off disaster* (▷not *stove* in this sense).
stay[1] (stay) *n.* **1.** a rope or wire supporting or bracing a mast, spar, pole, etc. **2.** any prop or support, *he was the prop and stay of his parents in their old age.*
stay[2] *v.* **(stayed, stay·ing) 1.** to continue to be in the same place or state, *stay here; stay awake; stay away from the meeting,* not go to it. **2.** to remain or dwell temporarily, especially as a guest or visitor. **3.** to satisfy temporarily, *we stayed our hunger with a sandwich.* **4.** to postpone, *stay judgment.* **5.** to pause in movement or action or speech. **6.** to show endurance, as in a race or task; *stay the course,* be able to reach the end of a race etc. **stay** *n.* **1.** a period of temporary dwelling or visiting, *made a short stay in Athens.* **2.** a postponement, as of carrying out a judgment, *was granted a stay of execution.* ☐**staying power,** endurance.
stay-at-home (stay-ăt-hohm) *adj.* remaining at home habitually. **stay-at-home** *n.* a person who does this.
stay·er (stay-ĕr) *n.* a person with great staying power.
stbd. *abbr.* starboard.
std. *abbr.* standard.
Ste. *abbr.* Saint (female). ▷French *sainte.*
stead (sted) *n.* **in a person's** *or* **thing's stead,** instead of him or it. **stand a person in good stead,** to be of great advantage or service to him.
stead·fast (sted-fast) *adj.* firm and not changing or yielding, *a steadfast refusal.* **stead′fast·ly** *adv.* **stead′fast·ness** *n.*
stead·y (sted-ee) *adj.* **(stead·i·er, stead·i·est) 1.** firmly supported or balanced, not shaking or rocking or tottering. **2.** done or operating or happening in a uniform and regular manner, *a steady pace.* **3.** behaving in a serious and dependable manner, not frivolous or excitable. **steady** *n.* *(informal)* a regular boyfriend or girlfriend. **steady** *adv.* steadily. **steady** *v.* **(stead·ied, stead·y·ing)** to make or become steady. **stead′i·ly** *adv.* **stead′i·ness** *n.* ☐**go steady,** *(informal)* to go about regularly with a member of the opposite sex though not yet engaged to be married to him or her. **steady state theory,** the theory holding that the universe was not created by any past event and that it is limitless and ever expanding.
steak (stayk) *n.* a thick slice of meat (especially beef) or fish, cut for grilling or frying etc. ☐**steak knife,** a sharp table knife, usually with a serrated edge, for cutting steak etc.
steak·house (stayk-hows) *n.* (*pl.* **-hous·es,** *pr.*

-how-ziz) a restaurant that specializes in serving steaks.
steal (steel) *v.* **(stole, sto·len, steal·ing) 1.** to take another person's property without right or permission, to take dishonestly. **2.** to obtain by surprise or a trick or surreptitiously, *stole a kiss; stole a look at her.* **3.** to move secretly or without being noticed, *stole out of the room.* **4.** (in baseball) to gain (a base) without the aid of a hit or an error, by deceiving the fielders. **steal** *n.* **1.** stealing, theft. **2.** *(slang)* an easy task, a good bargain. ☐**steal a march on,** to gain an advantage over (a person) secretly or slyly or by acting in advance of him. **steal the show,** to outshine other performers unexpectedly.
stealth (stelth) *n.* stealthiness.
stealth·y (stel-thee) *adj.* **(stealth·i·er, stealth·i·est)** acting or done in a quiet or secret way so as to avoid being noticed. **stealth′i·ly** *adv.* **stealth′i·ness** *n.*
steam (steem) *n.* **1.** invisible gas into which water is changed by boiling, used as motive power. **2.** the mist that forms when steam condenses in the air. **3.** energy or power; *run out of steam,* to become exhausted before something is finished. **steam** *v.* **1.** to give out steam or vapor. **2.** to cook or treat by steam. **3.** to move by the power of steam, *the ship steamed down the river.* **4.** to cover or become covered with condensed steam, *the windows were steamed up.* ☐**let off steam,** *see* **let. steam bath,** a bath in which the bather or the substance to be heated is immersed in steam. **steamed up,** *(slang)* excited or angry. **steam engine,** an engine or locomotive driven by steam. **steam fitter,** a person whose work is installing or repairing steam pipes etc. **steam heat,** heat given out by steam from radiators etc. **steam iron,** an electric iron that can emit jets of steam from its flat surface. **steam room,** a room equipped as a steam bath. **steam shovel,** a large machine for excavating worked by steam. **steam table,** a counter (in restaurants etc.) fitted with containers for food that is heated from below by steam or hot water. **steam up,** to cover or become covered with condensed water vapor; *(slang)* to make or become excited or angry.
steam·boat (steem-boht) *n.* a steam-driven boat, especially a relatively small one used in inland waters.
steam·er (stee-mĕr) *n.* **1.** a steam-driven ship. **2.** a container in which things are cooked or treated by steam. **3.** a soft-shelled clam. ☐**steamer rug,** a heavy blanket of the kind used on deck chairs on passenger ships. **steamer trunk,** a large low trunk.
steam·roll·er (steem-roh-lĕr) *n.* a heavy slow-moving engine with a large roller, used in road-making. **steamroller** *v.* to crush or defeat by weighty influence.
steam·ship (steem-ship) *n.* a steam-driven ship.
steam·y (stee-mee) *adj.* **(steam·i·er, steam·i·est)** like steam, full of steam. **steam′i·ly** *adv.* **steam′i·ness** *n.*
stear·ic (steer-ik) **acid** a white fatty acid obtained from animal or vegetable fats.
ste·a·tite (stee-ă-tı̄t) *n.* a grayish talc that feels smooth and soapy, soapstone.
steed (steed) *n.* *(poetical)* a horse.
steel (steel) *n.* **1.** a very strong alloy of iron and carbon much used for making vehicles, tools, weapons, etc.; *nerves of steel,* very strong nerves. **2.** a tapered usually roughened steel rod for sharp-

ening knives. **steel** *v.* to make hard or resolute, *steel oneself* or *steel one's heart.* ☐**steel band,** a band of West Indian musicians with instruments made from oil drums. **steel blue,** a metallic gray-blue. **steel engraving,** an engraving on or an impression taken from a steel plate. **steel gray,** a dark gray. **steel mill,** a steelworks. **steel wool,** fine shavings of steel massed together for use as an abrasive.

steel·work (steel-wurk) *n.* 1. articles made of steel. 2. *steelworks,* a place where steel is manufactured.

steel·work·er (steel-wur-kĕr) *n.* a person who works in a steelworks.

steel·y (stee-lee) *adj.* (**steel·i·er, steel·i·est**) like steel in color or hardness. **steel·i·ness** *n.*

steel·yard (steel-yahrd) *n.* a kind of balance with a short arm to take the thing being weighed and a long graduated arm along which a weight is moved until it balances this.

steep¹ (steep) *v.* 1. to soak or be soaked in liquid. 2. to permeate thoroughly, *the story is steeped in mystery.*

steep² *adj.* 1. sloping sharply not gradually. 2. (*informal*, of a price) unreasonably high. **steep'ly** *adv.* **steep'ness** *n.*

steep·en (stee-pĕn) *v.* to make or become steeper.

stee·ple (stee-pĕl) *n.* a tall tower with a spire on top, rising above the roof of a church. **stee'pled** *adj.*

stee·ple·chase (stee-pĕl-chays) *n.* 1. a horse race across country or on a course with hedges and ditches to jump. 2. a cross-country race for runners.

stee·ple·jack (stee-pĕl-jak) *n.* a man who climbs tall chimneys or steeples to do repairs.

steer¹ (steer) *n.* a young male of domestic cattle, castrated and raised for beef.

steer² *v.* 1. to direct the course of, to guide (a vehicle or boat etc.) by its mechanism. 2. to be able to be steered, *the car steers well.* **steer'er** *n.* **steer'a·ble** *adj.* ☐**steer clear of,** to take care to avoid. **steering committee,** a committee deciding the order of dealing with business, or priorities and the general course of operations. **steering wheel,** a wheel for controlling the steering mechanism of a vehicle or boat etc.

steer·age (steer-ij) *n.* 1. steering. 2. (*old use*) the cheapest section of accommodation for passengers in a ship, situated below decks.

steers·man (steerz-măn) *n.* (*pl.* **-men,** *pr.* -mĕn) a person who steers a ship.

stein (stīn) *n.* a large earthenware mug especially for beer.

ste·la (stee-lă) *n.* (*pl.* **ste·lae,** *pr.* stee-lee) an upright slab or pillar, usually with an inscription and sculpture, especially one used as a gravestone.

ste·le (stee-lee) *n.* (*pl.* **ste·les**) 1. the central tube in the stem or root of a vascular plant. 2. a stela.

stel·lar (stel-ăr) *adj.* of a star or stars.

stem¹ (stem) *n.* 1. the main central part (usually above the ground) of a tree or shrub or plant. 2. a slender part supporting a fruit or flower or leaf. 3. any slender upright part, as that of a wineglass between bowl and foot. 4. the winding shaft of a type of watch. 5. the main part of a noun or verb, from which other parts or words are made, as by altering the endings. 6. the curved timber or metal piece at the fore end of a ship, a ship's bows. **stem** *v.* (**stemmed, stem·ming**) to remove the stem from. ☐**from stem to stern,** from end to end of a ship. **stem from,** to arise from, to have as its source.

stem² *v.* (**stemmed, stem·ming**) 1. to check the flow of, to dam up. 2. (in skiing) to slow one's movement by forcing the heel of one or both skis outward. ☐**stem turn,** a turn made by stemming with one ski.

stem·ware (stem-wair) *n.* glasses with stems.

stem-wind·er (stem-wın-dĕr) *n.* a watch wound by turning a knob on the end of the stem.

stench (stench) *n.* a foul smell.

sten·cil (sten-sıl) *n.* 1. a sheet of metal or card etc. with a design cut out, painted or inked over to produce a corresponding design on the surface below. 2. a waxed sheet from which a stencil is made by a typewriter. 3. the decoration or lettering etc. produced by a stencil. **stencil** *v.* (**stenciled, sten·cil·ing**) to produce or ornament by means of a stencil.

sten·o (sten-oh) *n.* (*pl.* **-os**) (*informal*) 1. a stenographer. 2. stenography.

steno., stenog. *abbr.* 1. stenographer. 2. stenography.

ste·nog·ra·pher (stĕ-nog-ră-fĕr) *n.* a person who can write shorthand, one employed to do this.

ste·nog·ra·phy (stĕ-nog-ră-fee) *n.* shorthand.

sten·o·graph·ic (sten-ŏ-graf-ik) *adj.* **sten·o·graph'i·cal·ly** *adv.*

sten·o·type (sten-ŏ-tıp) *n.* 1. a letter or letters representing syllables or units of sound 2. **Stenotype,** (*trademark*) a machine like a typewriter used for typing these.

sten·to·ri·an (sten-tohr-i-ăn) *adj.* (of a voice) extremely loud.

step (step) *v.* (**stepped, step·ping**) 1. to lift and set down the foot or alternate feet as in walking. 2. to move a short distance in this way, *step aside; step into a job,* to acquire it without effort. **step** *n.* 1. a complete movement of one foot and leg in stepping. 2. the distance covered by this. 3. a short distance, *it's only a step to the bus stop.* 4. a series of steps forming a particular pattern in dancing. 5. the sound of a step, a manner of stepping as seen or heard, *I recognized your step.* 6. a rhythm of stepping, as in marching. 7. one of a series of things done in some process or course of action, *discussed the next step.* 8. a level surface for placing the foot on in climbing up or down. 9. a stage in a scale of promotion or precedence. ☐**in step,** stepping in time with other people in marching or dancing; conforming to what others are doing. **out of step,** not in step. **step by step,** one step at a time; proceeding steadily from one stage to the next. **step down,** to decrease, *step down the voltage;* to resign, *stepped down from the board.* **step in,** to intervene. **step on it,** (*slang*) to hurry. **step out,** to walk briskly, to stride; to take part in lively social activities. **step up,** to increase, *step up the voltage.* **take steps,** to begin to do what is necessary for a certain purpose. **watch your step,** (*informal*) be careful.

step- *prefix* meaning related by remarriage of one parent. **step'child** (*pl.* **-child·ren**), **step'daugh·ter, step'son** *n.* the child of one's wife or husband, by an earlier marriage. **step'broth·er, step'sis·ter** *n.* the child of one's stepfather or stepmother. **step'fa·ther, step'moth·er, step'par·ent** *n.* the husband or wife of one's parent, by a later marriage.

steph·a·no·tis (stef-ă-noh-tis) *n.* a tropical climbing plant with fragrant white waxy flowers.

step-in (step-in) *adj.* (of a garment) put on by being stepped into, without fastenings.

step·lad·der (step-lad-ĕr) *n.* a short ladder with

flat steps (not rungs) and a framework that supports it.

steppe (step) *n.* a level grassy plain with few trees, especially in southeast Europe and Siberia.

step·ping·stone (step-ing-stohn) *n.* 1. a raised stone providing a place to step on in crossing a stream etc. 2. a means or stage of progress toward achieving something.

ster. *abbr.* sterling.

stere (steer) *n.* a unit of volume equal to one cubic meter.

ster·e·o (ster-i-oh) *n.* (*pl.* **-os**) 1. stereophonic sound or recording. 2. a stereophonic record player or radio set. **stereo** *adj.* stereophonic.

ster·e·o·phon·ic (ster-i-ŏ-fon-ik) *adj.* (of sound reproduction) using two transmission channels in order to give the effect of naturally distributed sound. **ster·e·o·phon'i·cal·ly** *adv.*

ster·e·o·scope (ster-i-ŏ-skohp) *n.* a device for viewing a pair of photographs taken at slightly different angles, looking at each with one eye, the combined images giving an impression of depth and solidity.

ster·e·o·scop·ic (ster-i-ŏ-skop-ik) *adj.* giving a three-dimensional effect. **ster·e·o·scop'i·cal·ly** *adv.*

ster·e·o·tape (ster-i-ŏ-tayp) *n.* magnetic tape on which stereophonic sound is recorded and played back.

ster·e·o·type (ster-i-ŏ-tɪp) *n.* 1. a printing plate cast from a mold of type. 2. an idea or character etc. that is standardized in a conventional form without individuality. **stereotype** *v.* (**ster·e·o·typed, ster·e·o·typ·ing**) to make stereotypes of. **ster'e·o·typ·er** *n.*

ster·e·o·typed (ster-i-ŏ-tɪ-pĕr) *adj.* standardized and hackneyed, *stereotyped phrases such as "it takes all sorts to make a world."*

ster·ile (ster-il) *adj.* 1. barren. 2. free from living microorganisms. 3. unproductive, *a sterile discussion.* **ste·ril·i·ty** (stĕ-ril-i-tee) *n.*

ster·i·lize (ster-i-lɪz) *v.* (**ster·i·lized, ster·i·liz·ing**) 1. to make sterile or free from microorganisms. 2. to make unable to produce offspring, especially by removal or obstruction of reproductive organs. **ster'i·liz·er** *n.* **ster·i·li·za·tion** (ster-i-li-zay-shŏn) *n.*

ster·ling (stur-ling) *n.* 1. British money. 2. tableware made of sterling silver. **sterling** *adj.* 1. (of precious metal) genuine, of standard purity. 2. excellent, of solid worth, *her sterling qualities.* □**sterling silver,** silver of 92½ percent purity; objects made of this.

stern¹ (sturn) *adj.* strict and severe, not lenient or cheerful or kindly. **stern'ly** *adv.* **stern'ness** *n.*

stern² *n.* the rear end of a boat or ship.

ster·num (stur-nŭm) *n.* (*pl.* **-nums, -na,** *pr.* **-nă**) the breastbone. **ster'nal** *adj.*

stern·wheel·er (sturn-hwee-lĕr) *n.* a steamboat propelled by one large paddle wheel at the stern.

ster·oid (ster-oid) *n.* any of a group of organic compounds that includes certain hormones and other bodily secretions.

ster·ol (ster-awl) *n.* one of a group of complex solid alcohols, such as cholesterol.

ster·to·rous (stur-tŏ-rŭs) *adj.* making a snoring or rasping sound. **ster'to·rous·ly** *adv.*

stet (stet) *v.* (**stet·ted, stet·ting**) 1. (placed beside a word that has been crossed out by mistake) let it stand as written or printed. 2. to write "stet," to cancel a correction. ▷Latin, = let it stand.

steth·o·scope (steth-ŏ-skohp) *n.* an instrument

for listening to sounds within the body, such as breathing and heartbeats. **steth·o·scop·ic** (steth-ŏ-skop-ik) *adj.* **ste·thos·co·py** (ste-thos-kŏ-pee) *n.*

Stet·son (stet-sŏn) *n.* a slouch hat with a very wide brim and a high crown.

ste·ve·dore (stee-vĕ-dohr) *n.* a man employed in loading and unloading ships.

stew¹ (stoo) *v.* 1. to cook or be cooked by simmering for a long time in a closed vessel. 2. (*informal*) to be worried or anxious. **stew** *n.* a dish (especially of meat) made by stewing. □**in a stew,** (*informal*) in a state of great anxiety or agitation. **stew in one's own juice,** to be obliged to suffer the consequences of one's own actions.

stew·ard (stoo-ărd) *n.* 1. a person employed to manage another's property, especially a large estate. 2. one whose job is to arrange for the supply of food to a ship or club etc. 3. a passengers' attendant and waiter on a ship or airplane or train. 4. one of the officials managing a horse race or show etc. **stew'ard·ship** *n.*

stew·ard·ess (stoo-ăr-dis) *n.* a woman attendant and waitress on a ship or aircraft.

stewed (stood) *adj.* (*slang*) drunk.

stg. *abbr.* sterling.

stick¹ (stik) *n.* 1. a short relatively slender piece of wood for use as a support or weapon or as firewood; *only a few sticks of furniture,* items of furniture. 2. a cane. 3. the implement used to propel the ball in hockey, polo, etc. 4. a slender often cylindrical piece of a substance, as sealing wax, chewing gum, dynamite. 5. a number of bombs released in succession to fall in a row. 6. (*informal*) a stupid or uninteresting person. □**stick insect,** an insect with a twiglike body. **stick shift,** a manually operated gearshift in an automobile. **the sticks,** (*slang*) rural areas.

stick² *v.* (**stuck, stick·ing**) 1. to thrust (a thing or its point) into something, to stab. 2. to fix by means of a pointed object. 3. (*informal*) to put, *stick the parcel on the table.* 4. to fix or be fixed by glue or suction etc. or as if by these. 5. to fix or be fixed in one place and unable to move, *the boat stuck on a sandbank; I was stuck on the last question,* found it too difficult to do. 6. (*informal*) to remain in the same place, *they stuck indoors all day.* 7. (*informal,* of an accusation) to be established as valid, *we couldn't make the charges stick.* 8. (*slang*) to endure, to tolerate. 9. (*informal*) to impose a difficult or unpleasant task upon, *we were stuck with the job of clearing up.* 10. to provide (a plant) with a stick as a support. □**stick around,** to linger, remain near the same place. **stick at it,** (*informal*) to continue one's efforts. **sticking plaster,** a strip of fabric with an adhesive on one side, used for covering small cuts etc. **stick in one's throat,** to be against one's principles. **stick it out,** to endure to the end in spite of difficulty or unpleasantness. **stick one's neck out,** to expose oneself deliberately to danger or argument. **stick out,** to stand above the surrounding surface; to be conspicuous. **stick to,** to remain faithful to (a friend or promise etc.); to abide by and not alter, *he stuck to his story; stick to it,* = stick at it. **stick to one's guns,** to hold one's position against attack or argument. **stick to the ribs,** (of food) to keep one from soon becoming hungry. **stick up,** (*slang*) to rob by threatening with a gun. **stick up for,** (*informal*) = stand up for. **stick with,** to remain with or faithful to.

stick·ball (stik-bawl) n. a game similar to baseball played on city streets using a rubber ball and a broom handle.

stick·er (stik-ĕr) n. 1. an adhesive label or sign. 2. a person who persists in his efforts.

stick-in-the-mud (stik-in-thĕ-mud) n. a person who will not adopt new ideas etc.

stick·le·back (stik-ĕl-bak) n. a small fish with sharp spines on its back.

stick·ier (stik-lĕr) n. a person who insists on something, *a stickler for punctuality.*

stick-to-it·ive·ness (stik-too-ĭt-iv-nis) n. *(informal)* persistence.

stick·up (stik-up) n. *(slang)* a robbery at gunpoint.

stick·y (stik-ee) adj. **(stick·i·er, stick·i·est)** 1. sticking or tending to stick to what is touched. 2. (of weather) hot and humid, causing perspiration. 3. *(informal)* making objections, *he was very sticky about giving me leave.* 4. *(slang)* very unpleasant, *sticky situation.* **stick′i·ly** adv. **stick′i·ness** n.

stick·y-fin·gered (stik-ee-fing-gĕrd) adj. liable to steal things.

stiff (stif) adj. 1. not bending or moving or changing its shape easily. 2. not fluid, thick and hard to stir, *a stiff dough.* 3. difficult, *a stiff examination.* 4. formal in manner, not pleasantly sociable or friendly. 5. (of a price or penalty) high, severe. 6. (of a breeze) blowing briskly. 7. (of a drink or dose) strong. 8. *(informal)* to an extreme degree, *bored stiff.* **stiff** n. *(slang)* 1. a corpse. 2. a hopeless person; *big stiff,* complete fool. **stiff′ly** adv. **stiff′ness** n. ☐**stiff upper lip,** fortitude in enduring grief etc.

stiff·en (stif-ĕn) v. to make or become stiff. **stiff′en·er** n.

stiff-necked (stif-nekt) adj. 1. obstinate. 2. haughty.

sti·fle (stɪ-fĕl) v. **(sti·fled, sti·fling)** 1. to suffocate, to feel or cause to feel unable to breathe for lack of air. 2. to restrain or suppress, *stifled a yawn.* **sti′fling** adj. **sti′fling·ly** adv.

stig·ma (stig-mă) n. (*pl.* **stig·mas, stig·ma·ta,** *pr.* stig-mah-tă, stig-mă-tă) 1. a mark of shame, a strain on a person's good reputation. 2. the part of a pistil that receives the pollen in pollination. 3. *stigmata,* marks corresponding to those left on Christ's body by the nails and spear at his crucifixion. **stig·mat·ic** (stig-mat-ik) adj.

stig·ma·tize (stig-mă-tɪz) v. **(stig·ma·tized, stig·ma·tiz·ing)** to brand as something disgraceful, *he was stigmatized as a coward.*

stile (stɪl) n. an arrangement of steps or bars for people to climb in order to get over or through a fence etc. but preventing the passage of sheep or cattle.

sti·let·to (sti-let-oh) n. (*pl.* **-tos, -toes**) 1. a dagger with a narrow blade. 2. a pointed device for making eyelet holes etc. ☐**stiletto heel,** a high pointed heel on a shoe.

still[1] (stil) adj. 1. without or almost without motion or sound. 2. (of wine etc.) not sparkling or fizzy. **still** n. 1. silence and calm, *in the still of the night.* 2. a photograph as distinct from a motion picture, a single photograph taken from a motion picture film. **still** v. to make or become still, *to still the waves.* **still** adv. 1. motionlessly, *stand still.* 2. then or now or for the future as before, *the Pyramids are still standing.* 3. nevertheless. 4. in a greater amount or degree, *that would be still better* or *better still.* **still′ness** n. ☐**still life,** a

painting of lifeless things such as cut flowers or fruit.

still[2] n. a distilling apparatus, especially for making whiskey.

still·birth (stil-burth) n. a birth of a dead child.

still·born (stil-born) adj. 1. born dead. 2. (of an idea or plan) not developing.

stilt (stilt) n. 1. one of a pair of poles with a rest for the foot some way up it, enabling the user to walk with feet at a distance above the ground. 2. one of a set of piles or posts supporting a building etc. 3. a long-legged marsh bird.

stilt·ed (stil-tid) adj. stiffly or artificially formal, *written in stilted language.*

Stil·ton (stil-tŏn) n. a rich blue-veined cheese.

stim·u·lant (stim-yŭ-lănt) adj. stimulating. **stimulant** n. a stimulant drug or drink, a stimulating event etc. ▷Do not confuse *stimulant* with *stimulus.*

stim·u·late (stim-yŭ-layt) v. **(stim·u·lat·ed, stim·u·lat·ing)** 1. to make more vigorous or active. 2. to apply a stimulus to. **stim′u·la·tor** n. **stim·u·la·tion** (stim-yŭ-lay-shŏn) n. **stim′u·lat·ing·ly** adv.

stim·u·la·tive (stim-yŭ-lay-tiv) adj. stimulating.

stim·u·lus (stim-yŭ-lŭs) n. (*pl.* **-li,** *pr.* **-lɪ**) something that rouses a person or thing to activity or energy or that produces a reaction in an organ or tissue of the body. ▷Do not confuse *stimulus* with *stimulant.*

sting (sting) n. 1. a sharp-pointed part or organ of an insect etc., used for wounding and often injecting poison. 2. a stiff sharp-pointed hair on certain plants, causing inflammation if touched. 3. infliction of a wound by a sting, the wound itself. 4. any sharp bodily or mental pain, a wounding effect, *the sting of remorse.* 5. *(slang)* a swindle. **sting** v. **(stung, sting·ing)** 1. to wound or affect with a sting, to be able to do this. 2. to feel or cause to feel sharp bodily or mental pain. 3. to stimulate sharply as if by a sting, *was stung into answering rudely.* 4. *(slang)* to cheat (a person) by overcharging, to extort money from. **sting′ing·ly** adv.

sting·er (sting-ĕr) n. 1. the stinging part of an insect etc. 2. a cocktail made from brandy and crème de menthe. 3. *(slang)* a swindle.

sting·ray (sting-ray) n. a tropical fish with sharp spines that can cause severe wounds.

stin·gy (stin-jee) adj. **(-gi·er, -gi·est)** spending or giving or given grudgingly or in small amounts. **stin′gi·ly** adv. **stin′gi·ness** n.

stink (stingk) n. 1. an offensive smell. 2. *(informal)* an offensive fuss, *made a stink about it.* **stink** v. **(stank** or **stunk, stunk, stink·ing)** 1. to give off an offensive smell. 2. to seem very unpleasant or unsavory or dishonest, *the whole business stinks.* ☐**stink bomb,** a small bomb emitting an offensive smell when exploded.

stink·bug (stingk-bug) n. any insect having an unpleasant odor.

stink·er (sting-kĕr) n. 1. a person or thing that stinks. 2. *(slang)* something offensive or severe or difficult to do.

stink·horn (stingk-horn) n. a fungus with an offensive smell.

stink·ing (sting-king) adj. *(slang)* very bad. **stinking** adv. *(slang)* extremely, *stinking rich.*

stink·pot (stingk-pot) n. 1. a missile containing explosives etc. that give offensive vapors, formerly used in naval warfare. 2. an objectionable person or thing. 3. any receptacle containing something that stinks.

stink·weed (stingk-weed) *n.* any of several plants with an offensive smell.

stint (stint) *v.* to restrict to a small allowance, to be niggardly, *don't stint on food.* **stint** *n.* 1. a limitation of supply or effort, *gave help without stint.* 2. a fixed or allotted amount of work, *did her stint of filing.* **stint'er** *n.* **stint'ing** *adj.* **stint'ing·ly** *adv.*

sti·pend (stī-pend) *n.* a salary, a fixed money allowance at regular intervals. **sti'pend·less** *adj.*

stip·ple (stip-ĕl) *v.* (**stip·pled, stip·pling**) 1. to paint or draw or engrave in small dots (not in lines or strokes). 2. to roughen the surface of (cement etc.). **stipple** *n.*

stip·u·late (stip-yŭ-layt) *v.* (**stip·u·lat·ed, stip·u·lat·ing**) to demand or insist upon as part of an agreement.

stip·u·la·tion (stip-yŭ-lay-shŏn) *n.* 1. stipulating. 2. something stipulated.

stir[1] (stur) *v.* (**stirred, stir·ring**) 1. to move or cause to move, *not a leaf stirred; wind stirred the sand.* 2. to mix or move (a substance) by moving a spoon etc. around in it. 3. to arouse or excite or stimulate, *the story stirred their interest; stir up trouble.* **stir** *n.* 1. the act or process of stirring, *give the soup a stir.* 2. a commotion or disturbance, excitement, *the news caused a stir.* **stir'rer** *n.*

stir[2] *n.* (*slang*) prison, *in stir.*

stir·cra·zy (stur-kray-zee) *adj.* mentally abnormal from being imprisoned or otherwise confined.

stir·ring (stur-ing) *adj.* exciting, stimulating. **stir'ring·ly** *adv.*

stir·rup (stur-ŭp, stir-) *n.* a metal or leather support for a rider's foot, hanging from the saddle. ☐**stirrup cup,** a drink handed to a rider on horseback at a meet. **stirrup pump,** a small portable pump with a stirrup-shaped footrest, used for extinguishing small fires.

stitch (stich) *n.* 1. a single movement of a threaded needle in and out of fabric in sewing or tissue in surgery. 2. a single complete movement of a needle or hook in knitting or crochet. 3. the loop of thread made in this way. 4. a particular method of arranging the thread, *cross-stitch; purl stitch.* 5. the least bit of clothing, *without a stitch on.* 6. a sudden sharp pain in the muscles at the side of the body. **stitch** *v.* to sew, to join or close with stitches. ☐**in stitches,** (*informal*) laughing uncontrollably.

stk. *abbr.* stock.

stoat (stoht) *n.* the ermine, especially when its fur is brown.

stock (stok) *n.* 1. an amount of something available for use, *has a stock of jokes.* 2. the total of goods kept by a trader or shopkeeper. 3. livestock. 4. a line of ancestry, *a woman of Irish stock.* 5. raw material used in manufacturing something. 6. the capital of a business company, represented by shares. 7. a person's standing in the opinion of others; *his stock is high,* he is well thought of. 8. liquid made by stewing bones or meat or fish or vegetables, used as a basis for making soup, sauce, etc. 9. a garden plant with fragrant single or double flowers. 10. the lower and thicker part of a tree trunk. 11. a growing plant into which a graft is inserted. 12. a part serving as the base, holder, or handle for the working parts of an implement or machine; *the stock of a rifle,* the wooden or metal part to which the barrel is at-

tached. 13. *stocks,* a wooden framework with holes for the legs of a seated person, used like the pillory; the framework on which a ship rests during construction; *on the stocks,* being constructed or repaired. **stock** *adj.* 1. kept in stock and regularly available, *one of our stock items.* 2. commonly used, *a stock argument.* **stock** *v.* 1. to keep (goods) in stock. 2. to provide with goods or livestock or a supply of something, *stocked his farm with Jersey cows; a well-stocked library.* ☐**in stock,** available in a shop etc. without needing to be obtained specially. **out of stock,** sold out. **stock car,** an ordinary car strengthened for use in racing; a railroad boxcar for transporting livestock. **stock company,** a group of actors who appear regularly at a particular theater; a company or corporation that issues shares to represent its capital. **stock exchange,** a place where stocks and other securities are publicly bought and sold; an association of dealers conducting such business according to fixed rules. **stock market,** the stock exchange or transactions there. **stock size,** one of the standard sizes in which ready-made garments are made. **stock up,** to assemble a stock of goods etc. **take stock of,** to make an inventory of; to observe with a view to estimating character etc.

stock·ade (sto-kayd) *n.* a protective fence of upright stakes.

stock·breed·er (stok-bree-dĕr) *n.* a farmer who raises livestock. **stock'breed·ing** *n.*

stock·brok·er (stok-broh-kĕr) *n.* a person who buys and sells securities on behalf of customers.

stock·hold·er (stok-hohl-dĕr) *n.* a person who holds stock in a company.

Stock·holm (stok-hohm) the capital of Sweden.

stock·ing (stok-ing) *n.* a close-fitting covering for the foot and part or all of the leg. ☐**in one's stocking feet,** wearing stockings but not shoes. **stocking cap,** a knitted usually conical cap. **stocking mask,** a stocking worn over the head as a criminal's disguise.

stock-in-trade (stok-in-trayd) *n.* all the stock and other requisites for carrying on a trade or business.

stock·man (stok-man) *n.* (*pl.* **-men,** *pr.* -men) 1. a man owning or raising livestock. 2. a person in charge of a stock of goods in a warehouse etc.

stock·pile (stok-pīl) *n.* an accumulated stock of goods or materials etc. kept in reserve. **stockpile** *v.* (**stock·piled, stock·pil·ing**) to accumulate a stockpile of.

stock·pot (stok-pot) *n.* (in cooking) a pot for making or keeping stock (definition 8).

stock·room (stok-room) *n.* a room where goods are kept in stock are stored.

stock·still (stok-stil) *adj.* motionless.

stock·tak·ing (stok-tay-king) *n.* 1. making an inventory of the stock in a shop etc. 2. a review of one's position and resources.

stock·y (stok-ee) *adj.* (**stock·i·er, stock·i·est**) short and solidly built. **stock'i·ly** *adv.* **stock'i·ness** *n.*

stock·yard (stok-yahrd) *n.* an enclosure with pens etc. for the sorting or temporary keeping of livestock.

stodg·y (stoj-ee) *adj.* (**stodg·i·er, stodg·i·est**) 1. (of food) heavy and filling, indigestible. 2. (of a book etc.) written in a heavy uninteresting way. 3. (of a person) uninteresting, not lively. **stodg'i·ly** *adv.* **stodg'i·ness** *n.*

sto·ic (stoh-ik) *n.* a stoical person.

sto·i·cal (stoh-i-kăl) *adj.* calm and not excitable, bearing difficulties or discomfort without complaining. **sto′i·cal·ly** *adv.*

sto·i·cism (stoh-i-siz-ĕm) *n.* being stoical.

stoke (stohk) *v.* (**stoked, stok·ing**) to tend and put fuel on (a furnace or fire etc.). ☐**stoke up**, to stoke and add fuel; *(informal)* to eat large quantities of food.

stok·er (stoh-kĕr) *n.* 1. a person who stokes a furnace etc., especially on a ship. 2. a mechanical device for doing this.

STOL (stohl) *n.* short *t*akeoff and *l*anding.

stole[1] (stohl) *n.* 1. a woman's wide scarflike garment worn around the shoulders. 2. a clergyman's vestment consisting of a long strip of silk or other material worn around the neck with the ends hanging down in front.

stole[2], **sto·len** (stoh-lĕn) *see* **steal.**

stol·id (stol-id) *adj.* not feeling or showing emotion, not excitable. **stol′id·ly** *adv.* **sto·lid·i·ty** (stŏ-lid-i-tee) *n.* ▷Do not confuse *stolid* with *solid*.

sto·ma (stoh-mă) *n.* (*pl.* **-ma·ta,** *pr.* -mă-tă, **-mas**) 1. a small mouthlike opening of lower animals. 2. a minute opening in the epidermis of a leaf etc.

stom·ach (stum-ăk) *n.* 1. the internal organ in which the first part of digestion occurs. 2. the abdomen. 3. appetite for food. 4. appetite or spirit for danger or an undertaking etc., *had no stomach for the fight.* **stomach** *v.* to endure or tolerate, *can't stomach all that violence.* ☐**stomach pump,** a suction pump for emptying the stomach.

stom·ach·ache (stum-ăk-ayk) *n.* pain in the belly or bowels.

stom·ach·er (stum-ă-kĕr) *n.* an ornamented front piece of a woman's dress (originally worn also by men) covering the breast and stomach, especially in the 15th–17th centuries.

sto·mach·ic (stŏ-mak-ik) *adj.* 1. of the stomach. 2. aiding stomach action, promoting digestion or appetite.

stomp (stomp) *v.* 1. to tread heavily. 2. to stamp one's feet. **stomp** *n.* 1. a stamping of the foot. 2. a lively jazz dance with heavy stamping. **stomp′er** *n.*

stone (stohn) *n.* 1. a piece of rock, usually detached from the earth's crust and of fairly small size. 2. stones or rock as a substance or material, as for building. 3. a piece of stone shaped for a particular purpose, as for a tombstone or millstone. 4. a precious stone (*see* **precious**). 5. a small piece of hard substance formed in the bladder or kidney or gallbladder. 6. the hard case around the kernel of certain fruits, the seed of grapes. 7. *(pl.* **stone**) a British unit of weight, = fourteen pounds. **stone** *adj.* made of stone, *stone floors.* **stone** *v.* (**stoned, ston·ing**) 1. to pelt with stones. 2. to remove the stones from (fruit). ☐**leave no stone unturned,** to try every possible means. **Stone Age,** the very early period of civilization when weapons and tools were made of stone not metal. **stone marten,** a whitebreasted marten found in southern Europe and Asia. **stone's throw,** a short distance.

stone-blind (stohn-blind) *adj.* completely blind.

stone-broke (stohn-brohk) *adj.* entirely without money.

stone·chat (stohn-chat) *n.* a small Old World black-and-white songbird with a rattling cry.

stone·crop (stohn-krop) *n.* a kind of sedum with yellow flowers, often growing on rocks and walls.

stoned (stohnd) *adj. (slang)* drunk or under the influence of a drug.

stone-dead (stohn-ded) *adj. (slang)* completely dead.

stone-deaf (stohn-def) *adj. (informal)* completely deaf.

stone·ma·son (stohn-may-sŏn) *n.* a person who cuts and dresses stone or builds in stone.

stone·wall (stohn-wawl) *v. (informal)* to obstruct by stonewalling.

stone·wall·ing (stohn-waw-ling) *n. (informal)* obstructing a discussion etc. by noncommittal replies.

stone·ware (stohn-wair) *n.* very hard pottery made from clay containing much silica or from a composition of clay and flint.

stone·work (stohn-wurk) *n.* masonry.

ston·y (stoh-nee) *adj.* (**ston·i·er, ston·i·est**) 1. full of stones. 2. hard as stone, unfeeling. 3. not responsive, *a stony gaze.* **ston′i·ly** *adv.* **ston′i·ness** *n.*

stood (stuud) *see* **stand.**

stooge (stooj) *n. (slang)* 1. a comedian's assistant, used as a target for jokes. 2. a subordinate who does routine work. 3. a person whose actions are entirely controlled by another. **stooge** *v.* (**stooged, stoog·ing**) *(slang)* to act as a stooge.

stool (stool) *n.* 1. a movable seat without arms or back. 2. a footstool. 3. feces. ☐**stool pigeon,** a person acting as a decoy, especially to trap a criminal; an informer.

stoop[1] (stoop) *v.* 1. to bend forward and down. 2. to condescend, to lower oneself morally, *he wouldn't stoop to cheating.* **stoop** *n.* a posture of the body with shoulders bent forward, *he walks with a stoop.* **stoop′ing·ly** *adv.*

stoop[2] *n.* a small porch at a door to a house.

stop (stop) *v.* (**stopped, stop·ping**) 1. to put an end to (movement or progress or operation etc.), to cause to halt or pause. 2. to refrain from continuing, to cease motion or working. 3. *(slang)* to receive in one's body, *stopped a bullet.* 4. *(informal)* to stay, *we stopped for lunch.* 5. to close by plugging or obstructing, *stop the holes* or *stop them up.* 6. to keep back, to refuse to give or allow; *stop a check,* order the bank not to honor it when it is presented for payment. 7. to press down a string or block a hole in a musical instrument in order to obtain the desired pitch. **stop** *n.* 1. stopping, being stopped, a pause or check, *ran without a stop; put a stop to it,* cause it to cease. 2. a place where a train or bus etc. stops regularly. 3. *(chiefly British)* a punctuation mark, especially a period. 4. an obstruction or device that stops or regulates movement or operation. 5. a row of organ pipes providing tones of one quality, the knob or lever controlling these; *pull out all the stops,* make all possible efforts. 6. a key or lever regulating pitch in a wind instrument. 7. one of the standard sizes of aperture in an adjustable lens. ☐**stop at nothing,** to be completely ruthless or unscrupulous. **stop by** *or* **in,** to call or visit briefly, often on the way to or from another place. **stop down,** to reduce the aperture of a lens in photography. **stop off** *or* **over,** to break one's journey. **stop order,** an order to a stockbroker to sell a stock when it falls to a specified price. **stop up,** to clog, to obstruct.

stop·cock (stop-kok) *n.* an externally operated

valve inserted in a pipe to regulate passage of its contents.

stop·gap (stop-gap) *n.* a temporary substitute.

stop·light (stop-lɪt) *n.* 1. a red light in traffic signals. 2. one of a pair of red lights on the rear of a motor vehicle, showing when the brakes are applied.

stop·o·ver (stop-oh-vĕr) *n.* a break in one's journey, especially for a night.

stop·page (stop-ij) *n.* 1. stopping, being stopped. 2. an obstruction.

stop·per (stop-ĕr) *n.* a plug for closing a bottle etc. **stopper** *v.* to close with a stopper.

stop·ple (stop-ĕl) *n.* the stopper of a bottle or other vessel. **stopple** *v.* (stop′pled, stop′pling) to close with a stopple.

stop·watch (stop-woch) *n.* a watch with a mechanism for starting and stopping it at will, used in timing races etc.

stor·age (stohr-ij) *n.* 1. storing of goods etc. 2. space available for this. 3. the charge for it. □**storage battery,** a rechargeable battery that stores electrical energy in a chemical form.

store (stohr) *n.* 1. a stock or supply of something available for use. 2. a retail establishment selling goods of many kinds. 3. **stores,** articles of a particular kind or for a special purpose accumulated for use, a supply of things needed, *naval stores.* 4. a device in a computer for storing and retrieving information. **store** *v.* (**stored, stor·ing**) 1. to collect and keep for future use. 2. to put (furniture etc.) into a warehouse for temporary keeping. 3. to stock with something useful, *a mind well stored with information.* □**in store,** being stored; kept available for use; destined to happen, imminent, *there's a surprise in store for you.* **set store by,** to value greatly.

store·front (stohr-frunt) *n.* the wall and windows etc. of a store on the side facing the street.

store·house (stohr-hows) *n.* (*pl.* **-hous·es,** *pr.* -how-ziz) a building where things are stored; *a storehouse of information,* a book or person etc. containing much information.

store·keep·er (stohr-kee-pĕr) *n.* a person who owns or manages a store.

store·room (stohr-room) *n.* a room used for storing things.

sto·rey = **story²**.

sto·ried (stohr-eed) *adj.* celebrated in legend, associated with stories or legends or history.

stork (stork) *n.* a large long-legged wading bird with a long straight bill, sometimes nesting on buildings and humorously pretended to be the bringer of babies.

storm (storm) *n.* 1. a violent disturbance of the atmosphere with strong winds and usually rain or snow or thunder etc. 2. a violent shower of missiles or blows. 3. a great outbreak of applause or anger or criticism etc. 4. a violent military attack on a place. **storm** *v.* 1. (of wind or rain) to rage, to be violent. 2. to move or behave violently or very angrily, to rage, *stormed out of the room; stormed at us for being late.* 3. to attack or capture by storm, *they stormed the citadel.* □**storm cellar,** a cellar or other underground shelter providing refuge during cyclones etc. **storm center,** the area at the center of a storm; the center of a disturbance or trouble. **storm door,** an additional outer door for protection in bad weather or winter. **storm lantern,** a hurricane lamp. **storm sewer,** a sewer designed to

carry away rainfall. **storm trooper,** a member of the Nazi political militia. **storm warning** or **signal,** a warning that a storm is approaching; any sign that trouble is approaching. **storm window,** an additional window outside another for extra protection against cold weather. **take by storm,** to capture by a violent attack; to captivate rapidly.

storm·y (stor-mee) *adj.* (**storm·i·er, storm·i·est**) 1. full of storms, affected by storms, *a stormy night; stormy coasts.* 2. (of wind etc.) violent as in a storm. 3. full of violent anger or outbursts, *a stormy interview.* **storm′i·ly** *adv.* **storm′i·ness** *n.* □**stormy petrel,** a kind of petrel said to be active before storms; a person whose presence seems to foretell or attract trouble.

sto·ry¹ (stohr-ee) *n.* (*pl.* **-ries**) 1. an account of an incident or of a series of incidents, either true or invented. 2. a report of an item of news, material for this. 3. *(informal)* a lie.

story² *n.* (*pl.* **-ries**) one horizontal section of a building, all the rooms at the same level, *a two-story house.* **stor′ied** *adj.* *a two-storied house.*

sto·ry·board (stohr-ee-bohrd) *n.* 1. a series of sketches showing the significant changes of scene etc. in a film etc. 2. a careful plan with sketches for a projected work.

sto·ry·book (stohr-ee-buuk) *n.* a book of fictional stories. □**storybook ending,** a very happy ending.

sto·ry·tell·er (stohr-ee-tel-ĕr) *n.* 1. a person who narrates stories. 2. *(informal)* a liar. **sto′ry·tell·ing** *n.*

stoup (stoop) *n.* a stone basin for holy water, especially in the wall of a church.

stout (stowt) *adj.* 1. of considerable thickness or strength, *a stout stick.* 2. (of a person) solidly built and rather fat. 3. brave and resolute, *a stout heart.* **stout** *n.* a strong dark beer brewed with roasted malt or barley. **stout′ly** *adv.* **stout′ness** *n.*

stout·heart·ed (stowt-hahr-tid) *adj.* courageous.

stove¹ (stohv) *n.* an appliance in which heat is produced by combustion of fuel or electrically for use in cooking or in warming rooms etc.

stove² *see* **stave.**

stove·pipe (stohv-pɪp) *n.* a metal pipe conducting smoke and gases from a stove to a chimney. □**stovepipe hat,** a tall silk hat.

stow (stoh) *v.* to place in a receptacle for storage. □**stow away,** to put away in storage or in reserve; to conceal oneself as a stowaway.

stow·age (stoh-ij) *n.* 1. stowing, being stowed. 2. space available for this. 3. the charge for it.

stow·a·way (stoh-ă-way) *n.* a person who conceals himself on a ship or airplane etc. so as to travel without charge or unseen.

S.T.P. *abbr.* standard temperature and pressure.

stra·bis·mus (stră-biz-mŭs) *n.* a squint, cross-eye.

strad·dle (strad-ĕl) *v.* (**strad·dled, strad·dling**) 1. to sit or stand across (a thing) with the legs wide apart. 2. to stand with the legs wide apart. 3. to extend across. 4. to waver between two policies etc. regarding (an issue). **straddle** *n.* the position or act of straddling. **strad′dler** *n.*

Strad·i·var·i·us (strad-i-vair-i-ŭs) *n.* a violin or other stringed instrument made by the Italian violin-maker Antonio Stradivari (*c.*1644–1737) or his followers.

strafe (strayf) *v.* (**strafed, straf·ing**) to attack

(ground troops etc.) with machine guns from a low-flying airplane.

strag·gle (strag-ĕl) v. (**strag·gled, strag·gling**) 1. to grow or spread in an irregular or untidy manner, not remaining compact. 2. to go or wander separately not in a group, to drop behind others. **strag′gler** n.

strag·gly (strag-lee) adj. straggling.

straight (strayt) adj. (▷Do not confuse straight with strait.) 1. extending or moving continuously in one direction, not curved or bent. 2. correctly arranged, in proper order, tidy. 3. in unbroken succession, ten straight wins. 4. candid, not evasive, honest. 5. (slang) heterosexual. 6. not modified or elaborate, without additions, (of alcoholic drinks) not diluted. **straight** adv. 1. in a straight line; he shoots straight, with good aim. 2. direct, without delay, went straight home. 3. straightforwardly, told him straight. **straight** n. 1. the straight part of something, as the last section of a racetrack. 2. (slang) a heterosexual person. 3. (in poker) a sequence of five cards. **straight′ly** adv. **straight′ness** n. □**go straight,** to live an honest life after being a criminal. **straight and narrow,** the way of virtuous conduct . **straight angle,** an angle of 180°. **straight away** or **straight off,** without delay. **straight face,** without a smile even though amused. **straight flush,** see **flush²**. **straight from the shoulder,** honestly and directly. **straight man,** a person who says things so that a comedian can make jokes about them. **straight off,** without hesitation or deliberation etc., can't tell you straight off. **straight razor,** a razor with a long blade that folds into its handle for storage. **straight shooter,** an honest person. **straight ticket,** a candidate list of one party as voted for without exception, vote a straight ticket. **straight time,** the established hours of work in a business or industry; the scale of payment for this. **straight whiskey,** pure unblended whiskey.

straight-arm (strayt-ahrm) v. to push away (a person) with one's arm outstretched.

straight·a·way (strayt-ă-way) n. the straight part of a racecourse etc.

straight·edge (strayt-ej) n. a bar with one edge accurately straight, used for testing straightness.

straight·en (strayt-těn) v. to make or become straight. **straight′en·er** n. ▷Do not confuse straightened with straitened.

straight·for·ward (strayt-for-wărd, strayt-for-) adj. 1. honest, frank. 2. (of a task etc.) without complications. **straight·for′ward·ly** adv. **straight·for′ward·ness** n.

straight·way (strayt-way) adv. at once, immediately.

strain¹ (strayn) v. 1. to stretch tightly. to make taut. 2. to injure or weaken by excessive stretching or by overexertion, strain one's heart. 3. to hold in a tight embrace. 4. to make an intense effort; strain one's ears, try hard to hear. 5. to apply (a meaning or rule etc.) beyond its true application. 6. to pass through a sieve or similar device in order to separate solids from the liquid containing them, (of liquid) to filter. **strain** n. 1. straining, being strained, the force exerted. 2. an injury caused by straining a muscle etc. 3. a severe demand on one's mental or physical strength or on one's resources, exhaustion caused by this. 4. a passage from a tune. 5. the tone or style of something written or spoken, continued in a more

cheerful strain. □**strain every nerve,** to make all possible efforts.

strain² n. 1. a line of descent of animals or plants or microorganisms, a variety or breed of these, a new strain of flu virus. 2. a slight or inherited tendency in a character, there's a strain of insanity in the family.

strained (straynd) adj. (of behavior or manner) produced by effort, not arising from genuine feeling; strained relations, unpleasant tension between people.

strain·er (stray-něr) n. 1. a device for keeping something taut. 2. a utensil for straining liquids.

strait (strayt) adj. (old use) narrow, restricted. **strait** n. 1. a narrow stretch of water connecting two seas, the Strait of Gibraltar. 2. straits, a strait, a difficult state of affairs, in dire straits. ▷Do not confuse strait with straight.

strait·ened (stray-těnd) adj. made narrow, not spacious enough. □**straitened circumstances,** barely sufficient money to live on. ▷Do not confuse straitened with straightened.

strait·jack·et (strayt-jak-it) n. a strong jacketlike garment put around a violent person to restrain his arms. **straitjacket,** v. 1. to restrain by a straitjacket. 2. to restrict severely.

strait·laced (strayt-layst) adj. very prim and proper.

strake (strayk) n. a continuous line of planking or metal plates from stem to stern of a ship.

strand¹ (stand) n. 1. one of the threads or wires etc. twisted together to form a rope, yarn, or cable. 2. a single thread or strip of fiber. 3. a lock of hair.

strand² n. a shore. **strand** v. to run or cause to run aground.

strand·ed (stran-did) adj. left in difficulties, as without funds or means of transport.

strange (straynj) adj. (**strang·er, strang·est**) 1. not familiar or well known, not one's own, alien, in a strange land. 2. unusual, surprising, it's strange that you haven't heard. 3. fresh, unaccustomed, she is strange to the work. **strange′ly** adv. **strange′ness** n.

stran·ger (strayn-jěr) n. 1. a person in a place or company etc. that he does not belong to, a person one does not know. 2. one who is unaccustomed to a certain feeling or experience or task, a stranger to poverty.

stran·gle (strang-gěl) v. (**stran·gled, stran·gling**) 1. to kill or be killed by squeezing the throat. 2. to restrict or prevent the proper growth or operation or utterance of. **stran′gler** n.

stran·gle·hold (strang-gěl-hohld) n. a strangling grip.

stran·gu·late (strang-gyŭ-layt) v. (**stran·gu·lat·ed, stran·gu·lat·ing**) to compress (a vein or intestine etc.) so that nothing can pass through it.

stran·gu·la·tion (strang-gyŭ-lay-shŏn) n. 1. strangling, being strangled. 2. strangulating, being strangulated.

strap (strap) n. 1. a strip of leather or other flexible material, often with a buckle, for holding things together or in place. 2. a shoulder strap. 3. a loop for grasping to steady oneself in a moving vehicle. **strap** v. (**strapped, strap·ping**) 1. to secure with a strap or straps. 2. to bind (an injury), strap it up. 3. to beat with a strap.

strap·hang·er (strap-hang-ěr) n. a subway, bus,

or train passenger who has to stand and hold a strap for lack of sitting space.

strap·less (strap-lis) *adj.* without shoulder straps.

strapped (strapt) *adj. (slang)* short of something, *strapped for cash.*

strap·ping (strap-ing) *adj.* tall and healthy looking.

strapping *n.* straps, material for making these.

stra·ta *see* **stratum.**

strat·a·gem (strat-ă-jĕm) *n.* a cunning method of achieving something, a piece of trickery.

stra·te·gic (stră-tee-jik) *adj.* 1. of strategy. 2. giving an advantage, *a strategic position.* □**strategic materials,** those essential for war. **strategic weapons,** missiles etc. that can reach an enemy's home territory (as distinct from *tactical weapons* which are for use in a battle or at close quarters). **stra·te'gi·cal·ly** *adv.*

strat·e·gist (strat-ĕ-jist) *n.* an expert in strategy.

strat·e·gy (strat-ĕ-jee) *n.* (*pl.* **-gies**) 1. the planning and directing of the whole operation of a campaign or war. 2. a plan or policy of this kind or to achieve something, *our economic strategy.*

strath·spey (strath-spay) *n.* a kind of Scottish dance, music for this.

strat·i·fy (strat-ĭ-fı) *v.* (**strat·i·fied, strat·i·fy·ing**) to arrange in strata. **strat·i·fi·ca·tion** (strat-ĭ-fĭ-kay-shŏn) *n.*

stra·to·cu·mu·lus (stray-toh-**kyoo**-myŭ-lŭs, strat-oh-) *n.* (*pl.* **-li,** *pr.* lı) clouds combining features of stratus and cirrus or cumulus.

strat·o·sphere (strat-ŏ-sfeer) *n.* a layer of Earth's atmosphere between about six and fifteen miles (ten and sixty kilometers) above Earth's surface. **strat·o·spher·ic** (strat-ŏ-sfer-ik) *adj.*

stra·tum (stray-tŭm, strat-ŭm) *n.* (*pl.* **stra·ta,** *pr.* stray-tă, strat-ă) 1. one of a series of layers, especially of rock in the earth's crust. 2. a social level or class, *the various strata of society.* ▷ It is incorrect to use *strata* as a singular.

stra·tus (stray-tŭs, strat-ŭs) *n.* (*pl.* **stra·ti,** *pr.* stray-tı, strat-ı) a continuous horizontal sheet of cloud.

straw (straw) *n.* 1. dry cut stalks of grain used as material for bedding, thatching, fodder, etc. 2. a single stalk or piece of this. 3. a narrow strawlike tube of paper or plastic etc. for sucking up liquid in drinking. 4. an insignificant amount, *don't care a straw.* □**a straw in the wind,** a slight indication of how things may develop. **straw boss,** an assistant foreman, someone with little authority. **straw man,** a stuffed effigy; an imaginary person set up as an opponent etc.; a sham argument set up for demolition. **straw poll** or **straw vote,** an unofficial poll as a test of general feeling.

straw·ber·ry (straw-ber-ee) *n.* (*pl.* **-ries**) a soft juicy edible red fruit with yellow seeds on the surface, the plant that bears it. □**strawberry blond,** reddish blond. **strawberry mark,** a reddish birthmark.

stray (stray) *v.* 1. to leave one's group or proper place with no settled destination or purpose, to roam. 2. to deviate from a direct course or from a subject. **stray** *adj.* 1. having strayed. 2. isolated, occurring here and there but not as one of a group, *a stray taxi.* **stray** *n.* a person or domestic animal that has strayed, a stray thing. **stray'er** *n.*

streak (streek) *n.* 1. a thin line or band of a different color or substance from its surroundings; *a streak of lightning,* a flash. 2. an element in a person's character, *has a jealous streak.* 3. a spell or series, *had a long winning streak.* **streak** *v.* 1. to mark

with streaks. 2. to move very rapidly. 3. to run naked through a public place as a humorous or defiant act. **streak'er** *n.*

streak·y (stree-kee) *adj.* full of streaks, (of bacon etc.) with alternate layers or streaks of fat and lean. **streak'i'ness** *n.*

stream (streem) *n.* 1. a body of water flowing in its bed, a brook or river. 2. a flow of any liquid or of a mass of things or people. 3. the current or direction of something flowing or moving, *against the stream.* **stream** *v.* 1. to flow or move as a stream. 2. to emit a stream of, to run with liquid, *the wound streamed blood; with streaming eyes.* 3. to float or wave at full length. **stream'y** *adj.* □**on stream,** in active operation or production. **stream of consciousness,** a style of writing depicting the continuous flow of a person's thoughts.

stream·bed (streem-bed) *n.* the channel or former channel of a stream.

stream·er (stree-mĕr) *n.* 1. a long narrow flag. 2. a long narrow ribbon or strip of paper attached at one or both ends.

stream·let (streem-lit) *n.* a small stream.

stream·line (streem-lın) *v.* (**stream·lined, stream·lin·ing**) 1. to give a streamlined form to. 2. to make more efficient by simplifying, removing superfluities, etc.

stream·lined (streem-lınd) *adj.* having a smooth even shape that offers the least resistance to movement through air or water.

stream·lin·er (streem-lı-nĕr) *n.* a fast streamlined passenger train.

street (street) *n.* a public road in a town or village with houses on one or both sides. □**street Arab,** a homeless child who makes a living by stealing or begging. **street cleaner,** a person employed to clean streets and sidewalks.

street·car (street-kahr) *n.* a public passenger vehicle running on rails laid in the street.

street·walk·er (street-waw-kĕr) *n.* a prostitute seeking customers in the street.

strength (strengkth, strength) *n.* 1. the quality of being strong, the intensity of this. 2. a source of strength, the particular respect in which a person or thing is strong, *his strength is in his mathematical ability.* 3. the number of people present or available, the full complement, *the department is below strength.* □**in strength,** in large numbers, *supporters were present in strength.* **on the strength of,** on the basis of, using (a fact etc.) as one's support.

strength·en (strengk-thĕn, streng-) *v.* to make or become stronger. **strength'en·er** *n.*

stren·u·ous (stren-yoo-ŭs) *adj.* 1. energetic, making great efforts. 2. requiring great effort, *a strenuous task.* **stren'u·ous·ly** *adv.* **stren'u·ous·ness** *n.*

strep (strep) *n. (informal)* streptococcus. □**strep throat,** a streptococcal infection of the throat, accompanied by soreness, fever, etc.

strep·to·coc·cus (strep-tŏ-kok-ŭs) *n.* (*pl.* **-coc·ci,** *pr.* -kok-sı) any of a group of bacteria that cause serious infections. **strep·to·coc'cal** *adj.*

strep·to·my·cin (strep-tŏ-mı-sin) *n.* a kind of antibiotic drug.

stress (stres) *n.* 1. emphasis, *don't lay too much stress on last year's results.* 2. the extra force used in speaking a particular syllable or word, or on a sound in music. 3. pressure, tension, strain. **stress** *v.* to lay stress on.

stretch (strech) *v.* 1. to pull out tightly or into a greater length or extent or size. 2. to be able to be stretched without breaking, to tend to become stretched, *knitted fabrics stretch.* 3. to be continuous from a point or between points, *the wall stretches right around the estate.* 4. to thrust out one's limbs and tighten the muscles after being relaxed. 5. to make great demands on the abilities of (a person). 6. to strain to the utmost or beyond a reasonable limit; *stretch the truth,* to exaggerate or lie. **stretch** *n.* 1. stretching, being stretched. 2. the ability to be stretched, *this elastic has lost its stretch.* 3. a continuous expanse or tract, a continuous period of time. 4. *(slang)* a period of service or imprisonment. **stretch** *adj.* able to be stretched, *stretch fabrics.* **stretch′a·ble** *adj.* ☐**at a stretch,** without interruption. **stretch a point,** to agree to something beyond the limit of what is normally allowed. **stretch one's legs,** to go walking as a relief from sitting or lying. **stretch out,** to extend (a hand or foot) by straightening the arm or leg.

stretch·er (strech-ĕr) *n.* 1. a framework of poles, canvas etc. for carrying a sick or injured person in a lying position. 2. any of various devices for stretching things or holding things taut or braced. ☐**stretcher bearer,** a person who helps to carry a stretcher.

stretch·y (strech-ee) *adj.* (**stretch·i·er, stretch·i·est**) *(informal)* able to be stretched, liable to become stretched.

strew (stroo) *v.* (**strewed, strewed** or **strewn, strew·ing**) to scatter over a surface, to cover with scattered things.

stri·a (strɪ-ă) *n.* (*pl.* **stri·ae,** *pr.* strɪ-ee) a linear mark on a surface, a slight ridge or furrow.

stri·at·ed (strɪ-ay-tid) *adj.* marked with striations.

stri·a·tion (strɪ-ay-shŏn) *n.* one of a series of ridges or furrows or linear marks.

strick·en (strik-ĕn) *adj.* 1. affected or overcome by an illness or shock or grief, *stricken with flu; grief-stricken.* 2. deleted.

strict (strikt) *adj.* 1. precisely limited or defined, without exception or deviation. 2. requiring or giving complete obedience or exact performance, not lenient or indulgent. **strict′ly** *adv.* **strict′ness** *n.* ☐**strictly speaking,** if one uses words in their exact sense.

stric·ture (strik-chŭr) *n.* 1. severe criticism or condemnation. 2. abnormal constriction of a tubelike part of the body.

stride (strɪd) *v.* (**strode, strid·den, strid·ing**) 1. to walk with long steps. 2. to stand astride. **stride** *n.* 1. a single long step, the length of this. 2. a person's manner of striding. 3. progress, *has made great strides toward independence.* **strid′er** *n.* ☐**get into one's stride,** to settle into a fast and steady pace of work. **take it in one's stride,** to do it without needing a special effort.

stri·dent (strɪ-dĕnt) *adj.* loud and harsh. **stri′dent·ly** *adv.* **stri·den·cy** (strɪ-dĕn-see) *n.*

strife (strɪf) *n.* quarreling, conflict.

strike (strɪk) *v.* (**struck, struck** or **strick·en, strik·ing**) 1. to bring or come into sudden hard contact with, to inflict (a blow), to knock with a blow or stroke. 2. to attack suddenly, (of a disease) to afflict. 3. (of lightning) to descend upon and blast. 4. to produce (sparks or a sound etc.) by striking something, to produce (a musical note) by pressing a key, to make (a coin or medal) by stamping metal etc.; *strike a match,* ignite it by friction; *strike a bargain,* make one. 5. to bring into a specified state by or as if by striking, *he was struck blind.* 6. to indicate (the hour) or be indicated by a sound, *clock struck two; two o'clock struck.* 7. (of plant cuttings) to put down roots. 8. to reach (gold or oil etc.) by digging or drilling. 9. to occur to the mind of, to produce a mental impression on, *an idea struck me; she strikes me as being efficient.* 10. to lower or take down (a flag or tent etc.). 11. to stop work in protest about a grievance. 12. to penetrate or cause to penetrate, to fill with sudden fear etc. 13. to proceed in a certain direction, *strike northwest through the forest.* 14. to arrive at (an average or balance) by balancing or equalizing the items. 15. to assume (an attitude) suddenly and dramatically. **strike** *n.* 1. an act or instance of striking. 2. an attack. 3. a workers' refusal to work, in protest about a grievance. 4. a sudden discovery of gold or oil etc. 5. (in baseball) a batter's unsuccessful attempt to hit a pitched ball, or any other event counting similarly against him. ☐**on strike,** (of workers) striking. **strike home,** to get a blow right to the target; to have the desired effect, *the message struck home.* **strike it rich,** to find a source of prosperity. **strike off,** to cross off; to remove (a person) from a professional register because of misconduct. **strike oil,** to find oil by drilling etc.; to find a source of prosperity. **strike out,** to cross out; to fail; (in baseball) to retire or be retired by a strikeout; to begin a trip etc. vigorously. **strike pay,** an allowance made by a trade union to members on strike. **strike up,** to begin playing or singing; to start (a friendship etc.) rapidly or casually. **strike while the iron is hot,** to take action promptly at a good opportunity. **strike zone,** (in baseball) the space directly above home plate and between the batter's shoulders and knees.

strike·bound (strɪk-bownd) *adj.* immobilized by a workers' strike.

strike·break·er (strɪk-bray-kĕr) *n.* a person who is employed in place of strikers. **strike′break·ing** *n.*

strike·out (strɪk-owt) *n.* (in baseball) an out resulting from three strikes.

strik·er (strɪ-kĕr) *n.* 1. a person or thing that strikes. 2. a worker who is on strike.

strik·ing (strɪ-king) *adj.* sure to be noticed, attractive and impressive. **strik′ing·ly** *adv.*

string (string) *n.* 1. narrow cord. 2. a length of this or some other material used to fasten or lace or pull something, or interwoven in a frame to form the head of a racket. 3. a piece of catgut or cord or wire stretched and caused to vibrate so as to produce tones in a musical instrument. 4. a strip of tough fiber on a bean etc. 5. a set of objects strung together or of people or events coming after one another. 6. the racehorses trained at one stable. 7. something ranked as one's first or second etc. resource; *have two strings to one's bow,* not be obliged to rely on only one resource. 8. a condition that is insisted upon, *the offer has too many strings attached.* 9. *strings,* stringed instruments, or their players. **string** *v.* (**strung, string·ing**) 1. to fit or fasten with string(s). 2. to thread (beads etc.) on a string. 3. to trim the tough fiber from (beans). ☐**pull strings,** *see* **pull. string along,** *(informal)* to deceive. **string along with,** *(informal)* to accompany; to have faith in. **string bean,** a green bean having a long pod and eaten as a vegetable. **string out,** to spread out in a line. **string quartet,** a quartet for stringed instruments. **string tie,** a very narrow necktie, usually tied in a bow. **string up,** to kill by hanging.

string·course (string-kohrs) *n.* a raised horizontal line of bricks etc. around a building.

stringed (stringd) *adj.* (of instruments) having strings that are played by touching or with a bow or plectrum.

strin·gent (strin-jĕnt) *adj.* 1. (of a rule) strict. 2. (of financial conditions) tight. **strin'gent·ly** *adv.* **strin·gen·cy** (strin-jĕn-see) *n.*

string·er (string-ĕr) *n.* 1. a long horizontal structural member, especially a piece of timber, that supports two upright pieces in a framework. 2. a news correspondent working as a free lance.

string·y (string-ee) *adj.* (**string·i·er, string·i·est**) 1. like string. 2. (of beans etc.) having a strip of tough fiber. **string'i·ness** *n.*

strip¹ (strip) *v.* (**stripped, strip·ping**) 1. to take off (clothes or coverings or parts etc.); *strip a machine down,* take it apart to inspect or adjust it. 2. to undress oneself. 3. to deprive, as of property or titles. 4. to tear away; *stripped the gearwheel,* tore off its cogs. □**strip joint,** *(slang)* a club at which striptease performances are given. **strip mine,** a mine worked by removing the surface material that overlies the ore etc. **strip poker,** a poker game in which the losers of a hand are required to remove an article of clothing.

strip² *n.* a long narrow piece or area. □**strip cropping** *or* **farming,** the planting of ground with alternating strips of different crops to prevent erosion of the soil. **strip lighting,** lighting by long tubular fluorescent lamps. **strip map,** a long narrow map charting only the immediate area around a particular route.

stripe (strip) *n.* 1. a long narrow band on a surface, differing in color or texture from its surroundings. 2. a chevron on a sleeve, indicating the wearer's rank. 3. a type of character, opinion, etc., *a man of that stripe.* **stripe** *v.* (**striped, strip·ing**) to mark with stripes. □**striped bass,** a game fish of North America with black-striped sides.

strip·er (strip-ĕr) *n.* a striped bass.

strip·ling (strip-ling) *n.* a youth.

strip·tease (strip-teez) *n.* an entertainment in which a woman (or occasionally a man) gradually undresses before an audience. **strip'teas·er** *n.*

strive (striv) *v.* (**strove, striv·en** *or* **strived, striv·ing**) 1. to make great efforts. 2. to carry on a conflict. **striv'er** *n.*

strobe (strohb) *n.* (*informal*) a stroboscope. **strobe** *adj.* (*informal*) stroboscopic.

stro·bo·scope (stroh-bŏ-skohp) *n.* 1. a lamp made to flash intermittently. 2. a device using this to determine speeds of rotation, etc. 3. an electronic flash that fires repeatedly with hundreds or thousands of flashes per second, used especially to produce photographs of movement at successive stages. **stro·bo·scop·ic** (stroh-bŏ-skop-ic) *adj.*

strode (strohd) *see* **stride.**

stroke¹ (strohk) *n.* 1. an act of striking something. 2. a single movement or action or effort, a successful or skillful effort, *hasn't done a stroke of work; a stroke of genius; a stroke of luck,* a sudden fortunate occurrence. 3. one of a series of repeated movements, a particular sequence of these (as in swimming). 4. one hit at the ball in various games, (in golf) this used as a unit of scoring. 5. the

oarsman nearest the stern of a racing boat, setting the time of the stroke. 6. a mark made by a movement of a pen or paintbrush etc. 7. the sound made by a clock striking; *on the stroke of ten,* exactly at ten o'clock. 8. an attack of apoplexy or paralysis. **stroke** *v.* (**stroked, strok·ing**) to act as stroke to (a boat or crew).

stroke² *v.* (**stroked, strok·ing**) to pass the hand gently along the surface of. **stroke** *n.* an act or spell of stroking.

stroll (strohl) *v.* to walk in a leisurely way. **stroll** *v.* a leisurely walk.

stroll·er (stroh-lĕr) *n.* 1. a person who is strolling. 2. a folding chair on wheels, in which a child can be pushed along.

strong (strawng) *adj.* (**strong·er, strong·est**) 1. having power of resistance to being broken or damaged or captured etc. 2. capable of exerting great power, physically powerful, powerful through numbers or resources or quality; *a strong candidate,* one likely to win; *strong acids,* those with a powerful chemical effect. 3. concentrated, having a large proportion of a flavoring or coloring element, (of a drink) containing much alcohol. 4. having a considerable effect on one of the senses, *a strong smell.* 5. having a certain number of members, *an army five thousand strong.* 6. (of verbs) changing the vowel in the past tense (as *ring/rang, strike/struck*), not adding a suffix (as *float/floated*). **strong** *adv.* strongly, vigorously, *going strong.* **strong'ly** *adv.* □**strong language,** forcible language, oaths or swearing. **strong point,** a thing at which one excels. **strong suit,** a suit (in a hand of cards) in which one can take tricks; a thing at which one excels.

strong-arm (strawng-ahrm) *adj.* using force or sheer strength, *strong-arm tactics.* **strong-arm** *v.*

strong·box (strawng-boks) *n.* a strongly made small chest for valuables.

strong·hold (strawng-hohld) *n.* 1. a fortified place. 2. a center of support for a cause etc.

strong·man (strawng-man) *n.* (*pl.* **-men,** *pr.* -men) 1. a muscular person, especially one performing feats of strength etc. in a circus. 2. a masterful or capable person, as in a business. 3. a dictator.

strong·mind·ed (strawng-min-did) *adj.* having a determined mind.

strong·point (strawng-point) *n.* a specially fortified position in a system of defenses.

strong·room (strawng-room) *n.* (chiefly *British*) a room designed for storage and protection of valuables against fire or theft.

stron·ti·um (stron-chi-ŭm) *n.* a soft silver-white metal, having a radioactive isotope (**strontium 90**) that concentrates in bones when taken into an animal's body.

strop (strop) *n.* a strip of leather on which a razor is sharpened, an implement or machine serving the same purpose. **strop** *v.* (**stropped, strop·ping**) to sharpen on or with a strop.

strove (strohv) *see* **strive.**

struck (struk) *see* **strike.**

struc·tur·al (stuk-chŭ-răl) *adj.* 1. of a structure or framework. 2. used in construction of buildings etc., *structural steel.* **struc'tur·al·ly** *adv.*

struc·ture (struk-chŭr) *n.* 1. the way in which something is constructed or organized. 2. a supporting framework or the essential parts of a thing. 3. a constructed thing, a complex whole, a building. **structure** *v.* (**struc·tured, struc·tur·ing**) to give structure to, to organize.

stru·del (stroo-dĕl, shtroo-) *n.* a pastry usually made of thin dough rolled around a filling of fruit or cheese etc.

strug·gle (strug-ĕl) *v.* **(strug·gled, strug·gling)** 1. to move one's limbs or body in a vigorous effort to get free. 2. to make a vigorous effort under difficulties, to make one's way or a living etc. with difficulty. 3. to try to overcome an opponent or problem etc. **struggle** *n.* a spell of struggling, a vigorous effort, a hard contest. **strug′ gler** *n.*

strum (strum) *v.* **(strummed, strum·ming)** to play (a stringed instrument) with a light sweeping motion across the strings. **strum** *n.* the act or sound made by strumming.

strum·pet (strum-pit) *n. (old use)* a prostitute.

strung (strung) *see* **string.**

strut (strut) *n.* 1. a bar of wood or metal inserted into a framework to strengthen and brace it. 2. a strutting walk. **strut** *v.* **(strut·ted, strut·ting)** to walk in a pompous self-satisfied way.

strych·nine (strik-nɪn) *n.* a bitter highly poisonous substance, used in very small doses as a stimulant.

stub (stub) *n.* 1. a short stump. 2. a detachable section of a check or ticket etc. kept as a record after the rest has been torn off. **stub** *v.* **(stubbed, stub·bing)** to strike against a hard object, *stub one's toe; stub out a cigarette,* extinguish it by pressing it against something hard.

stub·ble (stub-ĕl) *n.* 1. the lower ends of the stalks of grain left in the ground after the harvest is cut. 2. a short stiff growth of hair or beard, especially that growing after shaving. **stub′bly** *adj.*

stub·born (stub-ŏrn) *adj.* obstinate, not docile, not easy to control or deal with. **stub′born·ly** *adv.* **stub′born·ness** *n.*

stub·by (stub-ee) *adj.* **(-bi·er, -bi·est)** like a stub, short and heavy or thick. **stub′bi·ness** *n.*

stuc·co (stuk-oh) *n. (pl.* **-coes, -cos)** plaster or cement used for coating surfaces of walls or molding to form architectural decorations. **stucco** *v.* **(stuc·coed, stuc·co·ing)** to coat with stucco.

stuck (stuk) *see* **stick².** **stuck** *adj.* 1. unable to move or make progress, *I'm stuck!* 2. (of an animal) that has been stabbed or had its throat cut. □**stuck on,** *(slang)* infatuated with (a person or thing). **stuck with,** *(informal)* unable to get rid of.

stuck-up (stuk-up) *adj. (informal)* conceited, snobbish.

stud¹ (stud) *n.* 1. a short large-headed nail, a rivet, a small knob projecting from a surface. 2. a device like a button on a shank, as used to fasten a detachable shirt collar. 3. the upright beam used in a wall to form a frame for plaster etc. **stud** *v.* **(stud·ded, stud·ding)** to decorate with studs or precious stones set into a surface, to strengthen with studs.

stud² *n.* 1. a male horse or other animal kept for breeding. 2. the place where these are kept. □**at stud,** (of a male horse) available for breeding on payment of a fee. **stud farm,** a place where horses are bred. **stud poker,** a form of poker with betting after the dealing of successive rounds of cards face up.

stud. *abbr.* student.

stud·book (stud-buuk) *n.* a book containing the pedigrees of horses.

stud·ding (stud-ing) *n.* studs (nails, beams, etc.), material for these.

stu·dent (stoo-dĕnt) *n.* a person who is engaged in studying something, a pupil at a university or other place of higher education or technical training, *medical students.*

stud·ied (stud-eed) *adj.* carefully and intentionally contrived, *answered with studied indifference.* **stud′ied·ly** *adv.*

stu·di·o (stoo-di-oh) *n. (pl.* **-os)** 1. the working room of a painter, sculptor, photographer, etc. 2. a room or premises where motion pictures are made. 3. a room from which radio or television programs are regularly broadcast or in which recordings are made. □**studio apartment,** a one-room apartment with a kitchen and bathroom. **studio couch,** a divanlike couch that can be converted into a bed.

stu·di·ous (stoo-di-ŭs) *adj.* 1. involving study, habitually spending much time in studying. 2. deliberate, painstaking, *studious politeness.* **stu′di·ous·ly** *adv.* **stu′di·ous·ness** *n.*

stud·y (stud-ee) *n. (pl.* **stud·ies)** 1. the process of studying, the pursuit of some branch of knowledge. 2. its subject, a thing that is investigated; *the proper study of mankind is man.* 3. a work presenting the result of investigations into a particular subject, *the program is a study of race relations in the South.* 4. a musical composition designed to develop a player's skill. 5. a preliminary drawing, *a study for the Mona Lisa.* 6. a room used by a person for work that involves studying. **study** *v.* **(stud·ied, stud·y·ing)** 1. to give one's attention to acquiring knowledge of (a subject). 2. to examine attentively, *we studied the map.* 3. to give care and consideration to, *she studies the convenience of others.* **stud′i·er** *n.*

stuff (stuf) *n.* 1. material. 2. *(slang)* unnamed things, belongings, subject matter, activities, etc., *leave your stuff; Westerns are kid stuff; he knows his stuff,* is an expert in his subject or trade; *do your stuff,* your task or performance; *that's the stuff!,* that is good or what is required. 3. *(slang)* valueless matter, trash, *stuff and nonsense!* **stuff** *v.* 1. to pack or cram, to fill tightly, to stop up. 2. to fill the empty carcass of (a bird or animal) with material to restore its original shape, as for exhibition in a museum. 3. to fill with padding. 4. to fill with seasoned stuffing. 5. to fill (a person or oneself) with food, to eat greedily. □**stuffed shirt,** *(informal)* a pompous person. **stuff up,** to plug, to stop up.

stuff·ing (stuf-ing) *n.* 1. padding used to stuff cushions etc. 2. a seasoned mixture of bread crumbs etc. put as a filling into poultry, rolled meat, vegetables, etc. before cooking. □**knock the stuffing out of,** *(informal)* to make feeble or weak, to defeat utterly. **stuffing box,** (in a machine) a boxlike structure around a moving shaft where this enters an enclosed space, packed with grease etc. to prevent leakage of gas or liquid at this point.

stuff·y (stuf-ee) *adj.* **(stuff·i·er, stuff·i·est)** 1. lacking fresh air or sufficient ventilation. 2. dull, uninteresting. 3. (of the nose) blocked with secretions so that breathing is difficult. 4. *(informal)* old-fashioned and narrow-minded. 5. *(informal)* showing annoyance. **stuff′i·ly** *adv.* **stuff′i·ness** *n.*

stul·ti·fy (stul-tĭ-fɪ) *v.* **(stul·ti·fied, stul·ti·fy·ing)** to impair or make ineffective, *their uncooperative approach has stultified the discussions.* **stul·ti·fi·ca·tion** (stul-tĭ-fɪ-kay-shŏn) *n.*

stum·ble (stum-bĕl) v. **(stum·bled, stum·bling)** 1. to strike one's foot on something and lose one's balance. 2. to walk with frequent stumbles. 3. to make a blunder or frequent blunders in speaking or playing music etc., *stumbled through the recitation.* **stumble** n. an act of stumbling. **stum'bler** n. **stum'bling·ly** adv. □**stumble across** or **on,** to discover accidentally. **stumbling block,** an obstacle, something that causes difficulty or hesitation.

stum·ble·bum (stum-bĕl-bum) n. *(slang)* an incompetent clumsy person, especially a third-rate boxer.

stump (stump) n. 1. the base of a tree remaining in the ground when the rest has fallen or been cut down. 2. a corresponding remnant of broken tooth or amputated limb or of something worn down. 3. a place used by an orator, especially a politician, for speechmaking. **stump** v. 1. to walk stiffly or noisily. 2. (in politics) to travel through a district making speeches in different places. 3. *(informal)* to be too difficult for, to baffle, *the question stumped him.*

stump·y (stum-pee) adj. **(stump·i·er, stump·i·est)** short and thick. **stump'i·ly** adv. **stump'i·ness** n.

stun (stun) v. **(stunned, stun·ning)** 1. to knock senseless. 2. to daze or shock by the impact of strong emotion.

stung (stung) see **sting.**

stunk (stungk) see **stink.**

stun·ning (stun-ing) adj. *(informal)* extremely attractive. **stun'ning·ly** adv.

stunt[1] (stunt) v. to hinder the growth or development of. **stunt'ed·ness** n.

stunt[2] n. *(informal)* something unusual or difficult done as a performance or to attract attention, *a publicity stunt.* □**stunt man,** a person employed to take an actor's place in performing dangerous stunts.

stu·pe·fy (stoo-pĕ-fı) v. **(stu·pe·fied, stu·pe·fy·ing)** 1. to dull the wits or senses of. 2. to stun with astonishment. **stu·pe·fa·cient** (stoo-pĕ-fay-shĕnt) adj. **stu·pe·fac·tion** (stoo-pĕ-fak-shŏn) n.

stu·pen·dous (stoo-pen-dŭs) adj. amazing, exceedingly great, *they took stupendous risks.* **stu·pen'dous·ly** adv.

stu·pid (stoo-pid) adj. 1. not intelligent or clever, slow at learning or understanding things. 2. in a state of stupor, *he was knocked stupid.* **stu'pid·ly** adv. **stu·pid·i·ty** (stoo-pid-i-tee) n.

stu·por (stoo-pŏr) n. a dazed or almost unconscious condition brought on by shock, drugs, drink, etc. **stu'por·ous** adj.

stur·dy (stur-dee) adj. **(-di·er, -di·est)** strongly built, hardy, vigorous. **stur'di·ly** adv. **stur'di·ness** n.

stur·geon (stur-jŏn) n. (pl. **-geon, -geons**) a large sharklike fish with flesh that is valued as food and roe that is made into caviar.

stut·ter (stut-ĕr) v. to stammer, especially by repeating the first consonants of words. **stutter** n. stuttering speech, a tendency to stutter. **stut'ter·er** n. **stut'ter·ing·ly** adv.

St. Vi·tus' (saynt vı-tŭs) **dance** see **saint.**

sty[1] (stı) n. (pl. **sties**) a pigsty.

sty[2], **stye** n. an inflamed swelling on the edge of the eyelid.

Styg·i·an (stij-i-ăn) adj. 1. of the river Styx. 2. murky, gloomy.

style (stıl) n. 1. the manner of writing or speaking or doing something (contrasted with the subject matter or the thing done). 2. shape or design, *a new style of coat.* 3. elegance, distinction. 4. a narrow extension of the ovary in a plant, supporting the stigma. **style** v. **(styled, styl·ing)** to design or shape or arrange, especially in a fashionable style. **styl'ing** n. □**in style,** elegantly, luxuriously.

styl·ish (stı-lish) adj. in fashionable style, elegant. **styl'ish·ly** adv. **styl'ish·ness** n.

styl·ist (stı-list) n. 1. a person who achieves or aims at a good style in what he does. 2. a person who styles things.

sty·lis·tic (stı-lis-tik) adj. of literary or artistic style. **sty·lis'ti·cal·ly** adv.

sty·lis·tics (stı-lis-tiks) n. the study of literary style.

styl·ize (stı-lız) v. **(styl·ized, styl·iz·ing)** to make (an artistic representation etc.) conform to a conventional style. **styl'ized** adj.

sty·lus (stı-lŭs) n. (pl. **-lus·es**) 1. a pen or other pointed tool used for writing on wax or engraving or cutting stencils etc. 2. a needlelike device used to cut grooves in records or to follow such grooves in reproducing sound from records.

sty·mie (stı-mee) n. 1. (in golf) a situation on the putting green when one ball lies between another ball and the hole, formerly a possible obstruction to the play of the farther ball. 2. something that blocks or thwarts one's activities, *lay someone a stymie.* **stymie** v. **(sty·mied, sty·mie·ing)** to block or thwart the activities of.

styp·tic (stip-tik) adj. checking the flow of blood by causing blood vessels to contract. □**styptic pencil,** a stick of a styptic material used to dry up small cuts or sores.

sty·rene (stır-een) n. a liquid hydrocarbon easily polymerized and used in making plastic.

Sty·ro·foam (stır-ŏ-fohm) n. *(trademark)* a lightweight polystyrene foam used as insulation, packing material, etc.

Styx (stiks) n. (in Greek mythology) the river over which the souls of the dead had to pass to reach Hades.

sua·sion (sway-zhŏn) n. persuasion. □**moral suasion,** a strong recommendation that is not an order.

suave (swahv) adj. smooth-mannered. **suave'ly** adv. **sauve'ness** n. **sauv·i·ty** (swah-vi-tee) n.

sub (sub) n. *(informal)* 1. a submarine. 2. a substitute. **sub** v. **(subbed, sub·bing)** to substitute.

sub- prefix meaning under, as in *submarine;* subordinate, as in *subservient.*

sub·a·cute (sub-ă-kyoot) adj. (in medicine) between acute and chronic.

sub·al·pine (sub-al-pın) adj. of the higher slopes of mountains just below the timberline.

sub·a·que·ous (sub-ay-kwi-ŭs) adj. underwater.

sub·arc·tic (sub-ahrk-tik) adj. of or like regions somewhat south of the Arctic Circle.

sub·as·sem·bly (sub-ă-sem-blee) n. (pl. **-blies**) an assembly within an assembly.

sub·a·tom·ic (sub-ă-tom-ik) adj. occurring in or smaller than an atom.

sub·base·ment (sub-bays-mĕnt) n. a story below the basement.

sub·cat·e·go·ry (sub-kat-ĕ-gohr-ee) n. (pl. **-ries**) a division of a category.

sub·class (sub-klass) n. a division of a class.

sub·com·mit·tee (sub-kŏ-mit-ee) n. a committee

formed for a special purpose from some members of the main committee.

sub·com·pact (sub-kom-pakt) *n.* a very small automobile, smaller than a compact.

sub·con·scious (sub-kon-shŭs) *adj.* of our own mental activities of which we are not aware. **subconscious** *n.* the part of the mind in which these activities take place. **sub·con'scious·ly** *adv.* **sub·con'scious·ness** *n.* ▷Do not confuse *subconscious* with *unconscious.*

sub·con·ti·nent (sub-kon-tĭ-nĕnt) *n.* a large land mass that forms part of a continent. **sub·con·ti·nen·tal** (sub-kon-tĭ-nen-tăl) *adj.*

sub·con·tract (sub-kŏn-trakt) *v.* to give or accept a contract to carry out all or part of another contract. **subcontract** (sub-kon-trakt) *n.* **sub·con'trac·tor** *n.*

sub·cul·ture (sub-kul-chŭr) *n.* a social culture within a larger culture.

sub·cu·ta·ne·ous (sub-kyoo-tay-ni-ŭs) *adj.* under the skin, *subcutaneous injection; subcutaneous tissue.* **sub·cu·ta'ne·ous·ly** *adj.*

sub·deb (sub-deb), **sub·deb·u·tante** (sub-deb-yŭ-tahnt) *n.* a girl who is about to become a debutante, or one of corresponding age.

sub·dis·ci·pline (sub-dis-ĭ-plin) *n.* a division within a branch of learning.

sub·di·vide (sub-di-vīd) *v.* **(sub·di·vid·ed, sub·di·vid·ing)** to divide into smaller parts after a first divison. **sub·di·vi·sion** (sub-di-vĭzh-ŏn) *n.*

sub·due (sub-doo) *v.* **(sub·dued, sub·du·ing)** 1. to overcome, to bring under control. 2. to make quieter or less intense; *subdued lighting,* not strong or intense.

sub·ed·i·tor (sub-ed-i-tŏr) *n.* an assistant editor.

sub·floor (sub-flohr) *n.* a foundation for a floor in a building.

sub·freez·ing (sub-free-zing) *adj.* below freezing.

sub·group (sub-groop) *n.* a division of a group.

sub·head (sub-hed) *n.* *(informal)* a subheading.

sub·head·ing (sub-hed-ing) *n.* a subordinate heading.

sub·hu·man (sub-hyoo-măn) *adj.* less than human, not fully human.

subj. *abbr.* 1. subject(s). 2. subjective. 3. subjunctive.

sub·ject (sub-jikt) *adj.* 1. not politically independent, *subject peoples.* 2. owing obedience to, under the authority of, *we are all subject to the laws of the land.* **subject** *n.* 1. a person subject to a particular political rule, any member of a state except the supreme ruler, *British subjects.* 2. the person or thing that is being discussed or described or represented or studied. 3. the word or words in a sentence that name who or what does the action or undergoes what is stated by the verb, as *"the book"* in *the book fell off the table.* 4. the theme or chief phrase in a sonata etc. **subject** (sub-jekt) *v.* 1. to bring (a country) under one's control. 2. to cause to undergo or experience, *subjecting the metal to severe tests.* **sub·jec·tion** (sub-jek-shŏn) *n.* ☐**subject matter,** the matter treated in a book or speech etc. **subject to,** liable to, *trains are subject to delay during fog;* depending upon as a condition, *subject to your approval; subject to contract,* provided that a contract is made.

sub·jec·tive (sub-jek-tiv) *adj.* 1. existing in a person's mind and not produced by things outside it, not objective. 2. depending on personal taste or views etc. **sub·jec'tive·ly** *adv.* **sub·**

jec'tive·ness *n.* **sub·jec·tiv·i·ty** (sub-jek-tiv-i-tee) *n.*

sub·join (sub-join) *v.* to add at the end.

sub ju·di·ce (sub joo-di-see) under judicial consideration, not yet decided. ▷Latin, = under a judge.

sub·ju·gate (sub-jŭ-gayt) *v.* **(sub·ju·gat·ed, sub·ju·gat·ing)** to subdue or bring (a country etc.) into subjection. **sub·ju·ga·tion** (sub-jŭ-gay-shŏn) *n.*

sub·junc·tive (sub-jungk-tiv) *adj.* of the form of a verb used in expressing what is imagined or wished or possible, such as *"were"* in *if I were you.* **subjunctive** *n.* a subjunctive form.

sub·lease (sub-lees) *v.* **(sub·leased, sub·leas·ing)** to sublet. **sublease** (sub-lees) *n.* a lease granted by subletting.

sub·let (sub-let) *v.* **(sub·let, sub·let·ting)** to let (accommodation etc. that one holds by lease) to a subtenant, to obtain a lease of as a subtenant. **sub·le·thal** (sub-lee-thăl) *adj.* not quite lethal.

sub·li·mate (sub-lĭ-mayt) *v.* **(sub·li·mat·ed, sub·li·mat·ing)** 1. to divert the energy of (an emotion or impulse arising from a primitive instinct) into a culturally higher activity. 2. to sublime. **sub·li·ma·tion** (sub-lĭ-may-shŏn) *n.*

sub·lime (sŭ-blım) *adj.* 1. of the most exalted or noble or impressive kind. 2. extreme, lofty, like that of a person who does not fear the consequences, *with sublime indifference.* **sublime** *v.* **(sub·limed, sub·lim·ing)** to convert (a substance) from its solid state directly to its vapor by heat (and usually to allow it to solidify again). **sub·lime'ly** *adv.* **sub·lime'ness** *n.* **sub·lim·i·ty** (sŭ-blim-i-tee) *n.*

sub·lim·i·nal (sub-lim-ĭ-năl) *adj.* below the threshold of consciousness; *subliminal advertising,* advertising presented by a very brief television picture etc. that influences the viewer without his consciously perceiving it. **sub·lim'i·nal·ly** *adv.*

sub·lu·nar (sub-loo-năr), **sub·lu·nar·y** (sub-loo-nă-ree) *adj.* 1. beneath the moon. 2. of this world, earthly.

sub·ma·chine (sub-mă-sheen) **gun** a lightweight machine gun held in the hand for firing.

sub·mar·gin·al (sub-mahr-jĭ-năl) *adj.* below a specified minimum; *submarginal farmland,* land that is not profitable to farm.

sub·ma·rine (sub-mă-reen) *adj.* under the surface of the sea, *submarine cables.* **submarine** (sub-mă-reen) *n.* 1. a ship that can operate under water. 2. a hero sandwich. **sub·ma·rin'er** *n.* ☐**submarine chaser,** a small patrol boat equipped for military operations against submarines.

sub·max·il·la (sub-mak-sĭ-lă) *n.* (*pl.* **-lae,** *pr.* **-lee)** the lower jaw. **sub·max·il·lar·y** (sub-mak-sĭ-ler-ee) *adj.*

sub·merge (sub-murj) *v.* **(sub·merged, sub·merg·ing)** 1. to place below water or other liquid, to flood. 2. (of a submarine) to dive, to go below the surface. **sub·mer'gence** *n.* **sub·mer'gi·ble** *adj.* **sub·mer·gi·bil·i·ty** (sŭb-mur-jĭ-bil-i-tee) *n.*

sub·merse (sub-murs) *v.* **(sub·mersed, sub·mers·ing)** to submerge. *n.* **sub·mer·sion** (sŭb-mur-zhŏn) *n.*

sub·mers·i·ble (sŭb-mur-sĭ-bĕl) *adj.* capable of being submerged. **submersible** *n.* a ship capable of submerging. **sub·mers·i·bil·i·ty** (sŭb-mur-sĭ-bil-i-tee) *n.*

sub·mi·cro·scop·ic (sub-mɪ-krŏ-skop-ik) *adj.* too small to be seen by an ordinary microscope.

sub·min·i·a·ture (sub-min-i-ă-chŭr) *adj.* 1. of greatly reduced size. 2. (of a camera) using extremely narrow film (especially 16 millimeter).

sub·min·i·a·tur·ize (sub-min-i-ă-chŭ-rɪz) *v.* **(sub·min·i·a·tur·ized, sub·min·i·a·tur·iz·ing)** to make or design (especially electronic components) very small. **sub·min·i·a·tur·i·za·tion** (sub-min-i-ă-chŭ-ri-zay-shŏn) *n.*

sub·mis·sion (sŭb-mish-ŏn) *n.* 1. submitting, being submitted. 2. something submitted, a theory etc. submitted by counsel to a judge or jury. 3. being submissive, obedience.

sub·mis·sive (sŭb-mis-iv) *adj.* submitting to power or authority, willing to obey. **sub·mis′sive·ly** *adv.* **sub·mis′sive·ness** *n.*

sub·mit (sŭb-mit) *v.* **(sub·mit·ted, sub·mit·ting)** 1. to yield (oneself) to the authority or control of another, to surrender. 2. to subject (a person or thing) to a process. 3. to present for consideration or decision.

sub·mo·lec·u·lar (sub-mŏ-lek-yŭ-lăr) *adj.* smaller than a molecule.

sub·mul·ti·ple (sub-mul-ti-pĕl) *n.* a number that will divide exactly another specified number.

sub·nor·mal (sub-nor-măl) *adj.* 1. less than normal. 2. below the normal standard of intelligence. **sub·nor·mal·i·ty** (sub-nor-mal-i-tee) *n.*

sub·or·bi·tal (sub-or-bi-tăl) *adj.* not completing a full orbit around Earth etc.

sub·or·der (sub-or-dĕr) *n.* a division of an order.

sub·or·di·nate (sŭ-bor-dĭ-nit) *adj.* 1. of lesser importance or rank. 2. working under the control or authority of another person. **subordinate** *n.* a person in a subordinate position. **subordinate** (sŭ-bor-dĭ-nayt) *v.* **(sub·or·di·nat·ed, sub·or·di·nat·ing)** to make subordinate, to treat as of lesser importance than something else. **sub·or′di·nate·ly** *adv.* **sub·or·di·na·tion** (sŭ-bor-dĭ-nay-shŏn) *n.* ☐ **subordinate clause,** a clause that modifies the principal clause in a sentence, as *"since winter arrived"* in *It has been cold since winter arrived.*

sub·orn (sŭ-born) *v.* to induce (a person) by bribery or other means to commit perjury or some other unlawful act. **sub·or·na·tion** (sub-or-nay-shŏn) *n.*

sub·phy·lum (sub-fɪ-lŭm) *n.* a category of plants and animals between phylum and class.

sub·plot (sub-plot) *n.* a subordinate plot in a play etc.

sub·poe·na (sŭ-pee-nă) *n.* a writ commanding a person to appear in a law court. **subpoena** *v.* **(sub·poe·naed, sub·poe·na·ing)** to summon with a subpoena.

sub·ro·gate (sub-rŏ-gayt) *v.* **(sub·ro·gat·ed, sub·ro·gat·ing)** to substitute one person (or party in a legal proceeding) for another, especially a creditor. **sub·ro·ga·tion** (sub-rŏ-gay-shŏn) *n.*

sub ro·sa (sub roh-ză) in confidence, in secrecy. ▷ Latin, = under the rose, which was an emblem of secrecy.

sub·scribe (sŭb-skrɪb) *v.* **(sub·scribed, sub·scrib·ing)** 1. to contribute (a sum of money); *subscribe to a periodical,* pay in advance for a series of issues. 2. to sign, *subscribe one's name; subscribe a document.* 3. to express one's agreement, *we cannot subscribe to this theory.*

sub·scrib·er (sŭb-skrɪ-bĕr) *n.* a person who subscribes.

sub·script (sub-skript) *adj.* written or printed below (and sometimes to the right of) another symbol. **subscript** *n.* a subscript symbol.

sub·scrip·tion (sŭb-skrip-shŏn) *n.* 1. subscribing. 2. money subscribed. 3. the right to receive a periodical for a certain period of time upon payment of a fee.

sub·sec·tion (sub-sek-shŏn) *n.* a division of a section.

sub·se·quent (sub-sĕ-kwĕnt) *adj.* following in time or order or succession, coming after. **sub′se·quent·ly** *adv.*

sub·ser·vi·ent (sŭb-sur-vi-ĕnt) *adj.* 1. subordinate. 2. servile, obsequious. **sub·ser′vi·ent·ly** *adv.* **sub·ser′vi·ence** *n.* **sub·ser·vi·en·cy** (sŭb-sur-vi-ĕn-see) *n.*

sub·set (sub-set) *n.* (in mathematics) a set made up of parts of a larger set.

sub·side (sŭb-sɪd) *v.* **(sub·sid·ed, sub·sid·ing)** 1. to sink to a lower or to the normal level. 2. (of land) to sink because of mining operations etc. underneath. 3. to become less active or intense, *the excitement subsided.* 4. (of a person) to sink into a chair etc. **sub·sid′ence** *n.*

sub·sid·i·ar·y (sŭb-sid-i-er-ee) *adj.* 1. of secondary importance. 2. (of a business company) controlled by another. **subsidiary** *n.* (*pl.* **-ar·ies**) a subsidiary thing.

sub·si·dize (sub-si-dɪz) *v.* **(sub·si·dized, sub·si·diz·ing)** to pay a subsidy to, to support by subsidies.

sub·si·dy (sub-si-dee) *n.* (*pl.* **-dies**) a grant of money paid to an industry or other cause needing help, or to keep down the price at which commodities etc. are sold to the public.

sub·sist (sŭb-sist) *v.* to exist or continue to exist, to keep oneself alive, *managed to subsist on a diet of vegetables.*

sub·sist·ence (sŭb-sis-tĕns) *n.* subsisting, a means of doing this. ☐ **subsistence allowance,** an allowance or advance of pay granted for maintenance. **subsistence level,** merely enough to supply the bare necessities of life.

sub·soil (sub-soil) *n.* soil lying immediately beneath the surface layer.

sub·son·ic (sub-son-ik) *adj.* (of speed) less than the speed of sound, (of aircraft) flying at subsonic speeds, not supersonic.

sub·spe·cies (sub-spee-sheez) *n.* (*pl.* **-cies**) a division of a species. **sub·spe·cif·ic** (sub-spi-sif-ik) *adj.* **sub·spe·cif′i·cal·ly** *adv.*

subst. *abbr.* 1. substantive. 2. substantively. 3. substitute.

sub·stance (sub-stăns) *n.* 1. matter with more or less uniform properties, a particular kind of this. 2. the essence of something spoken or written, *we agree with the substance of this argument.* 3. reality, solidity. 4. (*old use*) wealth and possessions, *waste one's substance.*

sub·stand·ard (sub-stan-dărd) *adj.* below the usual or required standard.

sub·stan·tial (sŭb-stan-shăl) *adj.* 1. of solid material or structure. 2. of considerable amount or intensity or validity, *a substantial fee; substantial reasons.* 3. possessing much property or wealth, *substantial farmers.* 4. in essentials, virtual, *we are in substantial agreement.* **sub·stan′tial·ly** *adv.*

sub·stan·ti·ate (sŭb-stan-shi-ayt) *v.* **(sub·stan·ti·at·ed, sub·stan·ti·at·ing)** to support (a statement or claim etc.) with evidence, to prove.

sub·stan·ti·a·tion (sŭb-stan-shi-ay-shŏn) *n.*
sub·stan·tive (sub-stăn-tiv) *n.* a noun. **substantive** *adj.* real, substantial. **sub′stan·tive·ly** *adv.* **sub·stan·ti·val** (sub-stăn-tɪ-văl) *adj.*
sub·sta·tion (sub-stay-shŏn) *n.* a subordinate station, as for the distribution of electric current.
sub·sti·tute (sub-sti-toot) *n.* a person or thing that acts or serves in place of another. **substitute** *v.* **(sub·sti·tut·ed, sub·sti·tut·ing)** 1. to put or use as a substitute. 2. to serve as a substitute. **substitute** *adj.* acting or serving in place of another. **sub·sti·tut·a·bil·i·ty** (sub-sti-too-tă-bil-i-tee) *n.* **sub·sti·tu·tion** (sub-sti-too-shŏn) *n.*
sub·stra·tum (sub-stray-tŭm) *n.* (*pl.* **-ta**, *pr.* -tă, **-tums**) an underlying layer or substance.
sub·struc·ture (sub-struk-chŭr) *n.* an underlying or supporting structure.
sub·sume (sŭb-soom) *v.* **(sub·sumed, sub·sum·ing)** to bring or include under a particular rule or classification etc. **sub·sum′a·ble** *adj.*
sub·sys·tem (sub-sis-tĕm) *n.* a subordinate system.
sub·teen (sub-teen) *n.* a young person approaching his or her teens.
sub·ten·ant (sub-ten-ănt) *n.* a person who rents accommodation etc. from one who holds it by lease. **sub·ten·an·cy** (sub-ten-ăn-see) *n.*
sub·tend (sŭb-tend) *v.* 1. (in geometry) to be opposite to, to extend under. 2. (in botany) to enclose in an axil.
sub·ter·fuge (sub-tĕr-fyooj) *n.* a trick or excuse used in order to avoid blame or defeat, trickery.
sub·ter·ra·ne·an (sub-tĕ-ray-ni-ăn), **sub·ter·ra·ne·ous** (sub-tĕ-ray-ni-ŭs) *adj.* underground.
sub·ti·tle (sub-tɪ-tĕl) *n.* 1. a subordinate title. 2. a caption on a movie screen, showing the dialogue etc. of a silent film or translating that of a foreign one. **subtitle** *v.* **(sub·ti·tled, sub·ti·tling)** to provide with a subtitle.
sub·tle (sut-ĕl) *adj.* 1. slight and difficult to detect or analyze. 2. making or able to make fine distinctions, having acute perception, *a subtle mind.* 3. ingenious, crafty. **sub′tle·ty** *n.* **sub′tle·ness** *n.* **sub′tly** (sut-lee) *adv.*
sub·to·tal (sub-toh-tăl) *n.* the total of part of a group of figures. **subtotal** (sub-toh-tăl) *v.* **(sub·to·taled, sub·to·tal·ing)** to add up part of (a group of figures).
sub·tract (sŭb-trakt) *v.* to deduct, to remove (a part or quantity or number) from a greater one. **sub·trac·tion** (sŭb-trak-shŏn) *n.*
sub·tra·hend (sub-tră-hend) *n.* a quantity or number to be subtracted.
sub·trop·i·cal (sub-trop-i-kăl) *adj.* of regions bordering on the tropics.
sub·urb (sub-urb) *n.* a residential community lying outside the central part of a town.
sub·ur·ban (sŭ-bur-băn) *adj.* of a suburb or suburbs.
sub·ur·ban·ite (sŭ-bur-băn-ɪt) *n.* a person who lives in a suburb.
sub·ur·bi·a (sŭ-bur-bi-ă) *n.* suburbs and their inhabitants.
sub·ven·tion (sŭb-ven-shŏn) *n.* a subsidy.
sub·ver·sion (sŭb-vur-zhŏn) *n.* subverting.
sub·ver·sive (sŭb-vur-siv) *adj.* tending to subvert. **subversive** *n.* **sub·ver′sive·ly** *adv.*
sub·vert (sŭb-vurt) *v.* to overthrow the authority of (a religion or government etc.) by weakening people's trust or belief. **sub·vert′er** *n.*
sub·way (sub-way) *n.* an underground railroad.

sub·ze·ro (sub-zeer-oh) *adj.* (of temperatures) below zero.
suc·ceed (sŭk-seed) *v.* 1. to be successful. 2. to come next to in time or order, to follow, to take the place previously filled by, *Hoover succeeded Coolidge.* **suc·ceed′er** *n.*
suc·cess (sŭk-ses) *n.* 1. a favorable outcome, doing what was desired or attempted, the attainment of wealth or fame or position. 2. a person or thing that is successful.
suc·cess·ful (sŭk-ses-fŭl) *adj.* having success. **suc·cess′ful·ly** *adv.*
suc·ces·sion (sŭk-sesh-ŏn) *n.* 1. following in order, a series of people or things following each other. 2. succeeding to the presidency or to an inheritance or position, the right of doing this, the sequence of people with this right. **suc·ces′sion·al** *adj.* □**in succession,** one after another.
suc·ces·sive (sŭk-ses-iv) *adj.* following one after another, in an unbroken series. **suc·ces′sive·ly** *adv.*
suc·ces·sor (sŭk-ses-ŏr) *n.* a person or thing that succeeds another.
suc·cinct (sŭk-singkt) *adj.* concise, expressed briefly and clearly. **suc·cinct′ly** *adv.* **suc·cinct′ness** *n.*
suc·cor (suk-ŏr) *n.* help given in time of need. **succor** *v.* to give such help.
suc·co·tash (suk-ŏ-tash) *n.* a dish of beans and kernels of corn boiled together.
Suc·coth = Sukkoth.
suc·cu·lent (suk-yŭ-lĕnt) *adj.* 1. (of food) juicy. 2. (of plants) having thick fleshy leaves or stems. **succulent** *n.* a succulent plant. **suc′cu·lent·ly** *adv.* **suc′cu·lence** *n.* **suc·cu·len·cy** (suk-yŭ-lĕn-see) *n.*
suc·cumb (sŭ-kum) *v.* to give way to something overpowering. **suc·cumb′er** *n.*
such (such) *adj.* 1. of the same kind or degree, *people such as these.* 2. of the kind or degree described, *there's no such person.* 3. so great or intense, *it gave her such a fright.* **such** pronoun that, the action or thing referred to, *such being the case, we can do nothing.* □**as such,** as what has been specified, in itself, *interested in getting a good photograph, not in the castle as such.*
such-and-such (such-ăn-such) *adj.* particular but not specified, *says he will arrive at such-and-such a time but is always late.*
such·like (such-lɪk) *adj.* (*informal*) of the same kind. □**and suchlike,** and things of this kind.
suck (suk) *v.* 1. to draw (liquid or air etc.) into the mouth by using the lip muscles, to draw liquid etc. from (a thing) in this way. 2. to squeeze in the mouth by using the tongue, *sucking a candy.* 3. to draw in, *plants suck moisture from the soil; the canoe was sucked into the whirlpool.* **suck** *n.* the act or process of sucking. □**suck up to,** (*slang*) to toady to.
suck·er (suk-ĕr) *n.* 1. a person or thing that sucks. 2. an organ of certain animals, or a device of rubber etc., that can adhere to a surface by suction. 3. a shoot coming up from the roots or underground stem of a tree or shrub. 4. (*slang*) a person who is easily deceived. 5. a lollipop. 6. a freshwater fish of North America that has a mouth shaped as if for sucking together. □**be a sucker for,** (*slang*) to be always unable to resist the attractions of. **sucker bet,** a bet that the taker has no chance of winning.

suck·le (suk-ĕl) *v.* (**suck·led, suck·ling**) 1. to feed (young) at the breast or udder. 2. (of young) to take milk in this way.

suck·ling (suk-ling) *n.* a child or animal that is not yet weaned.

Su·cre (soo-krĕ) the capital of Bolivia.

su·crose (soo-krohs) *n.* sugar obtained from plants such as sugar cane or sugar beet.

suc·tion (suk-shŏn) *n.* 1. sucking. 2. production of a partial or complete vacuum so that external atmospheric pressure forces fluid or other substance into the vacant space or causes adhesion of surfaces, *vacuum cleaners work by suction.* **suc'tioned** *adj.* ☐**suction pump,** a pump that draws liquid through a pipe into a chamber from which the air is drawn by a piston.

Su·dan (soo-dan) a country in northeast Africa. **Su·da·nese** (soo-dă-neez) *adj.* & *n.* (*pl.* **-nese**).

sud·den (sud-ĕn) *adj.* happening or done quickly or unexpectedly or without warning. **sud'den·ly** *adv.* **sud'den·ness** *n.* ☐**all of a sudden,** suddenly. **sudden death,** *(informal)* the decision of a tied contest by the next game, the next score made, etc.

suds (sudz) *n. pl.* 1. soapsuds. 2. *(slang)* beer. **suds'y** *adj.* (**suds·i·er, suds·i·est**).

sue (soo) *v.* (**sued, su·ing**) 1. to bring legal proceedings against. 2. to make an application, *sue for peace.* **su'er** *n.*

suede (swayd) *n.* leather with the flesh side rubbed so that it has a velvety nap. ☐**suede cloth,** woven cloth imitating this.

su·et (soo-it) *n.* hard fat from around the kidneys of cattle and sheep, used in cooking.

suff. *abbr.* 1. sufficient. 2. suffix.

suf·fer (suf-ĕr) *v.* 1. to undergo or be subjected to (pain, loss, grief, damage, etc.), *suffers from neuralgia.* 2. to feel pain or grief, to be subjected to damage or a disadvantage. 3. to permit. 4. to tolerate; *she does not suffer fools gladly,* behaves intolerantly toward incompetent people. **suf'fer·er** *n.* **suf'fer·a·ble** *adj.*

suf·fer·ance (suf-ĕ-răns) *n.* **on sufferance,** tolerated but only grudgingly or because there is no positive objection.

suf·fice (sŭ-fis) *v.* (**suf·ficed, suf·fic·ing**) to be enough, to meet the needs of.

suf·fi·cient (sŭ-fish-ĕnt) *adj.* enough. **suf·fi'cient·ly** *adv.* **suf·fi·cien·cy** (sŭ-fish-ĕn-see) *n.*

suf·fix (suf-iks) *n.* (*pl.* **-fix·es**) a letter or combination of letters added at the end of a word to make another word (such as *y* added to *rust* to make *rusty*) or as an inflection (such as *ing* added to *suck* to make *sucking*). **suffix** *v.* to add at the end, especially as a suffix. **suf·fix·ion** (sŭ-fik-shŏn) *n.*

suf·fo·cate (suf-ŏ-kayt) *v.* (**suf·fo·cat·ed, suf·fo·cat·ing**) 1. to kill by stopping the breathing. 2. to cause discomfort to (a person) by making breathing difficult. 3. to be suffocated. **suf'fo·cat·ing·ly** *adv.* **suf·fo·ca·tion** (suf-ŏ-kay-shŏn) *n.*

suf·fra·gan (suf-ră-găn) *n.* 1. a **suffragan bishop,** a bishop consecrated to help the bishop of a diocese with administration. 2. a bishop in relation to an archbishop.

suf·frage (suf-rij) *n.* the right to vote in political elections. **suf'fra·gist** *n.*

suf·fra·gette (suf-ră-jet) *n.* a woman who, in the early 20th century, agitated for women to have the right to vote in political elections.

suf·fuse (sŭ-fyooz) *v.* (**suf·fused, suf·fus·ing**) (of color or moisture) to spread throughout or over. **suf·fu·sion** (sŭ-fyoo-zhŏn) *n.*

Su·fi (soo-fee) *n.* (*pl.* **-fis**) a member of an ascetic and mystical Muslim sect. **Su·fism** (soo-fiz-ĕm) *n.* **Su·fi·ism** (soo-fi-iz-ĕm) *n.* **Su·fis·tic** (soo-fis-tik) *adj.*

sug·ar (shuug-ăr) *n.* a sweet crystalline substance obtained from the juices of various plants. **sugar** *v.* to sweeten with sugar, to coat with sugar. **sug'ar·less** *adj.* ☐**sugar beet,** the kind of beet from which sugar is extracted. **sugar cane,** a tropical grass with tall jointed stems from which sugar is obtained. **sugar daddy,** *(informal)* an elderly man who lavishes gifts on a young woman. **sugar loaf,** a solid cone-shaped mass of sugar, as sold in former times. **sugar maple,** a tree of eastern North America from the sap of which syrup or sugar can be made.

sug·ar·coat (shuug-ăr-koht) *v.* 1. to enclose (food) in sugar. 2. to make superficially attractive or less unpleasant.

sug·ar·plum (shuug-ăr-plum) *n.* a candy, especially a small ball of boiled sugar.

sug·ar·y (shuug-ă-ree) *adj.* 1. containing or resembling sugar. 2. sweet, excessively sweet in style or manner. **sug'ar·i·ness** *n.*

sug·gest (sŭg-jest) *v.* 1. to cause (an idea or possibility) to be present in the mind. 2. to propose (a plan or theory) for acceptance or rejection.

sug·gest·i·ble (sŭg-jes-ti-bĕl) *adj.* 1. easily influenced by people's suggestions. 2. that may be suggested. **sug·gest·i·bil·i·ty** (sŭg-jes-tĭ-bil-i-tee) *n.*

sug·ges·tion (sŭg-jes-chŏn) *n.* 1. suggesting, being suggested. 2. something suggested. 3. a slight trace, *he speaks with a suggestion of a French accent.*

sug·ges·tive (sŭg-jes-tiv) *adj.* 1. conveying a suggestion. 2. tending to convey an indecent or improper meaning. **sug·ges'tive·ly** *adv.* **sug·ges'tive·ness** *n.*

su·i·cid·al (soo-i-sī-dăl) *adj.* 1. of suicide. 2. (of a person) liable to commit suicide. 3. destructive to one's own interests.

su·i·cide (soo-i-sīd) *n.* 1. the intentional killing of oneself, an instance of this. 2. a person who commits suicide. 3. an act that is destructive to one's own interests; *political suicide,* ruination of one's own or one's party's political prospects. ☐**commit suicide,** to kill oneself intentionally. **suicide pact,** an agreement between people to commit suicide together.

su·i ge·ne·ris (soo-ee jen-ĕ-ris) of its own kind, unique. ▷Latin.

suit (soot) *n.* 1. a set of clothing to be worn together, especially a jacket and trousers or skirt. 2. clothing for use in a particular activity, *a business suit.* 3. a set of armor. 4. any of the four sets (spades, hearts, diamonds, clubs) into which a pack of cards is divided. 5. a lawsuit. 6. *(formal)* a request or appeal; *press one's suit,* to request persistently. **suit** *v.* 1. to satisfy, to meet the demands or needs of. 2. to be convenient or right for. 3. to give a pleasing appearance or effect upon, *red doesn't suit her.* 4. to adapt, to make suitable, *suit your style to your audience; suit action to the word,* do at once the action just promised. ☐**suit yourself,** do as you please; find something that satisfies you. ▷Do not confuse *suit* with *suite.*

suit·a·ble (soo-tă-bĕl) *adj.* right for the purpose

or occasion. **suit'a·bly** *adv.* **suit'a·ble·ness** *n.* **suit·a·bil·i·ty** (soo-tǎ-bil-i-tee) *n.*

suit·case (soot-kays) *n.* a rectangular case for carrying clothes, usually with a hinged lid and a handle.

suite (sweet) *n.* 1. a set of rooms or furniture. 2. a set of attendants, a retinue. 3. a set of musical pieces or extracts. ▷Do not confuse *suite* with *suit.*

suit·ing (soo-ting) *n.* material for making suits.

suit·or (soo-tŏr) *n.* 1. a man who is courting a woman. 2. a person bringing a lawsuit.

su·ki·ya·ki (soo-ki-yah-kee) *n.* a Japanese dish of sliced meat fried with vegetables and soy sauce.

Suk·koth (suuk-ŏs, soo-kot) *n.* a Jewish thanksgiving festival celebrated in autumn to commemorate the sheltering of the Jews in tents in the wilderness after the exodus from Egypt.

sul·fa (sul-fǎ) *n.* **sulfa drug,** any of a group of chemical compounds with antibacterial properties, related to sulfanilamide.

sul·fa·nil·a·mide (sul-fǎ-nil-ǎ-mid) *n.* a synthetic organic chemical compound with antibacterial properties.

sul·fate (sul-fayt) *n.* a salt of sulfuric acid.

sul·fide (sul-fid) *n.* a compound of sulfur with another element or radical.

sul·fite (sul-fit) *n.* a salt of sulfurous acid.

sul·fur (sul-fŭr) *n.* a pale yellow substance that burns with a blue flame and a stifling smell, used in industry and in medicine. **sul·fu·re·ous** (sul-fyoor-i-ŭs) *adj.* ☐**sulfur dioxide,** a poisonous gas formed in the burning of sulfur, used in industry.

sul·fu·ric (sul-fyoor-ik) *adj.* containing a proportion of sulfur. ☐**sulfuric acid,** a strong corrosive acid.

sul·fur·ous (sul-fŭ-rŭs) *adj.* 1. of or like sulfur. 2. containing a proportion of sulfur. ☐**sulfurous acid,** a weak unstable acid.

sulk (sulk) *v.* to be sulky. **sulk** *n.* (also **sulks**) a fit of sulkiness.

sulk·y (sul-kee) *adj.* (**sulk·i·er, sulk·i·est**) sullen, silent or aloof because of resentment or bad temper. **sulky** *n.* a light two-wheeled carriage for one person, especially as used in harness racing. **sulk'i·ly** *adv.* **sulk'i·ness** *n.*

sul·len (sul-ĕn) *adj.* 1. gloomy and unresponsive from resentment or bad temper. 2. dark and dismal, *sullen skies.* **sul'len·ly** *adv.* **sul'len·ness** *n.*

sul·ly (sul-ee) *v.* (**sul·lied, sul·ly·ing**) to stain or blemish, to spoil the purity or splendor of, *sullied his reputation.*

sul·tan (sul-tăn) *n.* the ruler of certain Muslim countries.

sul·tan·a (sul-tan-ă) *n.* 1. a seedless raisin; *sultana grape,* the small yellow grape from which it is produced. 2. the wife, mother, or daughter of a sultan.

sul·tan·ate (sul-tă-nayt) *n.* the territory of a sultan.

sul·try (sul-tree) *adj.* (**-tri·er, -tri·est**) 1. hot and humid. 2. (of a woman) of dark mysterious beauty. **sul'tri·ness** *n.*

sum (sum) *n.* 1. a total. 2. a particular amount of money, *for the sum of $5.* 3. a problem in arithmetic, *good at sums.* **sum** *v.* (**summed, sum·ming**) to find the sum of. ☐**sum total,** a total. **sum up,** to give the total of; to summarize; (of a judge) to summarize the evidence or argument; to form an opinion of, *sum a person up.*

su·mac (soo-mak) *n.* a shrub or small tree with feathery leaves and clusters of usually red berries.

Su·me·ri·an (soo-meer-i-ăn) *adj.* of the ancient civilization of Sumer, a region in southern Mesopotamia. **Sumerian** *n.* 1. the Sumerian language. 2. a Sumerian person.

sum·ma cum lau·de (sum-ă kum law-dee) with greatest academic distinction. ▷Latin, = with highest praise.

sum·ma·rize (sum-ă-riz) *v.* (**sum·ma·rized, sum·ma·riz·ing**) to make or be a summary of. **sum·ma·ri·za·tion** (sum-ă-rī-zay-shŏn) *n.*

sum·ma·ry (sum-ă-ree) *n.* (*pl.* **-ries**) a statement giving the main points of something briefly. **summary** *adj.* 1. brief, giving the main points only, *a summary account.* 2. done or given without delay or attention to detail or formal procedure. **sum·mar·i·ly** (su-mer-ĭ-lee) *adv.*

sum·ma·tion (su-may-shŏn) *n.* finding of a total or sum, summing up.

sum·mer (sum-ĕr) *n.* the warmest season of the year, from June to August in the northern hemisphere. ☐**summer camp,** a camp providing sporting facilities etc. for children during their summer vacation. **summer school,** a course of lectures etc. held during the summer vacation. **summer solstice,** *see* **solstice. summer squash,** a squash that is eaten before it fully ripens, such as zucchini. **summer stock,** the production of plays by a company of actors during the summer. **summer time,** daylight saving time (*see* **daylight**).

sum·mer·house (sum-ĕr-hows) *n.* (*pl.* **-hous·es,** *pr.* -how-ziz) a light building in a garden or park, providing shade in summer.

sum·mer·time (sum-ĕr-tim) *n.* the season of summer.

sum·mer·y (sum-ĕ-ree) *adj.* like summer, suitable for summer.

sum·mit (sum-it) *n.* the highest point of something, the top of a mountain. ☐**summit conference,** a meeting between heads of two or more governments.

sum·mon (sum-ŏn) *v.* 1. to send for (a person), to order to appear in a law court. 2. to call together, to order to assemble, *summon a meeting.* 3. to gather together (one's strength or courage) in order to do something. 4. to call upon (a person etc.) to do something, *summon the fort to surrender.* **sum'mon·er** *n.*

sum·mons (sum-ŏnz) *n.* (*pl.* **-mons·es**) 1. a command to do something or appear somewhere. 2. an order to appear in a law court, a document containing this. **summons** *v.* to serve with a summons. ▷It is equally correct to use *summon* as a verb with this meaning.

su·mo (soo-moh) *n.* a Japanese form of wrestling in which defeat follows touching the ground except with the feet, or failure to keep within a marked area.

sump (sump) *n.* a hole or low area into which waste liquid drains.

sump·tu·ous (sump-choo-ŭs) *adj.* splendid and costly looking. **sump'tu·ous·ly** *adv.* **sump'tu·ous·ness** *n.*

sun (sun) *n.* 1. the star around which Earth travels and from which it receives light and warmth. 2. this light or warmth, *let the sun in.* 3. any fixed star with or without planets. **sun** *v.* (**sunned, sun·ning**) to expose to the sun; *sun oneself,* to bask in sunshine. ☐**sun dance,** a dance of North American Indians in honor of the sun. **sun deck,**

a flat roof or raised open platform exposed to the sun. **sun god,** the sun worshipped as a god.
sun hat, sun helmet, a hat or helmet worn to protect the head from sun. **sun lamp,** a lamp producing ultraviolet rays, with effects like those of the sun. **sun visor,** *see* **visor.**

Sun. *abbr.* Sunday.

sun·bath (sun-bath) *n.* exposure of one's body to the sun.

sun·bathe (sun-bay*th*) *v.* (**sun·bathed, sun·bath·ing**) to expose one's body to the sun. **sun′bath·er** *n.*

sun·beam (sun-beem) *n.* a ray of sun.

Sun·belt (sun-belt) *n.* *(informal)* the southwestern U.S.

sun·bon·net (sun-bon-it) *n.* a bonnet shaped so as to shade the face and neck.

sun·burn (sun-burn) *n.* tanning or inflammation of the skin caused by exposure to sun. **sunburn** *v.* to undergo or cause to undergo this.

sun·burst (sun-burst) *n.* 1. a burst of sunlight, as through parted clouds. 2. a firework or ornament or piece of jewelry imitating the sun and its rays.

sun·dae (sun-day) *n.* a dish of ice cream and crushed fruit, nuts, syrup, etc.

Sun·day (sun-day) *n.* the first day of the week, observed by Christians as a day of rest and worship. □**Sunday best,** best clothes, kept for Sunday use. **Sunday painter,** an amateur painter, one who paints solely for pleasure. **Sunday punch,** *(slang)* a boxer's most powerful punch; anything capable of maximum effectiveness against an opponent. **Sunday school,** a school for religious instruction of children, held on Sundays.

sun·der (sun-děr) *v.* to break or tear apart, to sever.

sun·dew (sun-doo) *n.* a small bog plant with hairs secreting moisture that traps insects.

sun·di·al (sun-di-ăl) *n.* a device that shows the time by means of the shadow of a rod or plate on a scaled dial.

sun·down (sun-down) *n.* sunset.

sun·dress (sun-dres) *n.* a dress allowing arms, shoulders, and back to be exposed to sun.

sun·dries (sun-dreez) *n. pl.* various small items not named individually.

sun·dry (sun-dree) *adj.* various, several.

sun·fish (sun-fish) *n.* (*pl.* **-fish, -fish·es**) 1. a large ocean fish with an almost spherical body. 2. a small flat-bodied freshwater fish of North America.

sun·flow·er (sun-flow-ěr) *n.* a tall garden plant bearing large flowers with golden petals around a dark center, producing seeds that yield an edible oil.

sung (sung) *see* **sing.**

sun·glasses (sun-glas-iz) *n.* eyeglasses with tinted lenses to protect the eyes from sunlight or glare.

sunk (sungk), **sunk·en** (sung-kěn) *see* **sink. sunk, sunken** *adj.* 1. submerged. 2. lying below the level of the surrounding area. 3. depressed or hollow, *sunken cheeks.*

sun·less (sun-lis) *adj.* without sunshine.

sun·light (sun-lɪt) *n.* light from the sun.

sun·lit (sun-lit) *adj.* lit by sunlight.

Sun·na (suun-ă) *n.* the traditional portion of Muslim law based on Muhammad's words or acts but not written by him.

Sun·nite (suun-ɪt) *n.* a member of the Muslim religious sect that opposes the Shiite sect in accepting the first four caliphs as legitimate successors of Muhammad and viewing Sunna as a basis for law.

sun·ny (sun-ee) *adj.* (**-ni·er, -ni·est**) 1. bright with sunlight, full of sunshine. 2. (of a person or mood) cheerful. **sun′ni·ly** *adv.* **sun′ni·ness** *n.* □**sunny side,** the more cheerful aspect of circumstances. **sunny side up,** (of a fried egg) not turned over during cooking.

sun·rise (sun-rɪz) *n.* the rising of the sun, the time of this.

sun·roof (sun-roof) *n.* a sliding panel in the roof of an automobile.

sun·seek·er (sun-see-kěr) *n.* a person who travels to a warmer climate to enjoy the sunshine.

sun·set (sun-set) *n.* 1. the setting of the sun, the time of this. 2. the western sky full of color at sunset. □**sunset law,** a law requiring periodic evaluation of government agencies and programs, to justify their continuing existence.

sun·shade (sun-shayd) *n.* 1. a parasol. 2. an awning.

sun·shine (sun-shɪn) *n.* direct sunlight uninterrupted by clouds. □**sunshine law,** a law making official meetings and records of most government agencies accessible to the public.

sun·spot (sun-spot) *n.* one of the dark patches sometimes observed on the sun's surface.

sun·stroke (sun-strohk) *n.* illness caused by too much exposure to sun.

sun·tan (sun-tan) *n.* a tan produced by exposure to the sun. **sun′tanned** *adj.*

sun·up (sun-up) *n.* sunrise.

sup (sup) *v.* (**supped, sup·ping**) to eat supper.

sup. *abbr.* 1. superior. 2. superlative. 3. supplement. 4. supplementary. 5. supply. 6. supra.

su·per (soo-pěr) *n.* *(informal)* 1. a superintendent. 2. a supernumerary. **super** *adj.* *(informal)* excellent, superb.

super- *prefix* meaning over, beyond, exceeding, as in *superhuman, supernatural.*

su·per·a·bun·dant (soo-pěr-ă-bun-dănt) *adj.* very abundant, more than enough. **su·per·a·bun′dant·ly** *adv.* **su·per·a·bun′dance** *n.*

su·per·an·nu·ate (soo-pěr-an-yoo-ayt) *v.* (**su·per·an·nu·at·ed, su·per·an·nu·at·ing**) 1. to discharge (an employee) into retirement with a pension. 2. to discard as too old for use. **su·per·an′nu·at·ed** *adj.*

su·perb (soo-purb) *adj.* of the most impressive or splendid kind, excellent. **su·perb′ly** *adv.*

su·per·bomb (soo-pěr-bom) *n.* an extremely destructive bomb.

su·per·car·go (soo-pěr-kahr-goh) *n.* (*pl.* **-goes, -gos**) the person on a merchant ship who is in charge of the cargo.

su·per·charge (soo-pěr-chahrj) *v.* (**su·per·charged, su·per·charg·ing**) to increase the power of (an engine) by using a device that supplies air or fuel at above the normal pressure. **su′per·charg·er** *n.*

su·per·cil·i·ous (soo-pěr-sil-i-ŭs) *adj.* with an air of superiority, haughty and scornful. **su·per·cil′i·ous·ly** *adv.* **su·per·cil′i·ous·ness** *n.*

su·per·con·duc·tiv·i·ty (soo-pěr-kon-duk-tiv-i-tee) *n.* the property of zero electrical resistance in some substances at temperatures near absolute zero. **su·per·con·duc·tive** (soo-pěr-kŏn-duk-tiv) *adj.* **su·per·con·duc′tor** *n.*

su·per·cool (soo-pěr-kool) *v.* to cool (a liquid) below its freezing point without its becoming solid or crystalline.

su·per·du·per (soo-pĕr-doo-pĕr) *adj. (informal)* excellent, superb.

su·per·e·go (soo-pĕr-ee-goh) *n.* (*pl.* **-gos**) a person's ideals for himself, acting like a conscience in directing his behavior.

su·per·er·o·ga·tion (soo-pĕr-er-ŏ-gay-shŏn) *n.* the doing of more than is required by duty, *works of supererogation.* **su·per·e·rog·a·to·ry** (soo-pĕr-ĕ-rohg-ĕ-tohr-ee) *adj.*

su·per·fi·cial (soo-pĕr-fish-ăl) *adj.* 1. of or on the surface, not deep or penetrating, *a superficial wound; superficial knowledge,* not thorough or penetrating. 2. (of a person) having no depth of character or feeling. **su·per·fi'cial·ly** *adv.* **su·per·fi'cial·ness** *n.* **su·per·fi·ci·al·i·ty** (soo-pĕr-fish-i-al-i-tee) *n.*

su·per·fine (soo-pĕr-frn) *adj.* of extra-high quality, *superfine sugar.*

su·per·flu·i·ty (soo-pĕr-floo-i-tee) *n.* (*pl.* **-ties**) a superfluous amount.

su·per·flu·ous (soo-pur-floo-ŭs) *adj.* more than is required. **su·per'flu·ous·ly** *adv.* **su·per' flu·ous·ness** *n.*

su·per·gal·ax·y (soo-pĕr-gal-ăk-see) *n.* (*pl.* **-ax·ies**) a galaxy composed of other galaxies. **su·per·ga·lac·tic** (soo-pĕr-gă-lak-tik) *adj.*

su·per·heat (soo-pĕr-heet) *v.* to heat (liquid) above its boiling point without allowing it to vaporize, to heat (vapor) above boiling point.

su·per·het·er·o·dyne (soo-pĕr-het-ĕ-rŏ-dın) *adj.* of a system of radio reception using ultrasonic frequency to secure great selectivity.

su·per·high·way (soo-pĕr-hı-way) *n.* a broad main highway for fast traffic.

su·per·hu·man (soo-pĕr-hyoo-măn) *adj.* 1. beyond ordinary human capacity or power. 2. higher than humanity, divine. **su·per·hu'man·ly** *adv.*

su·per·im·pose (soo-pĕr-im-pohz) *v.* (**su·per·im·posed, su·per·im·pos·ing**) to lay or place (a thing) on top of something else. **su·per·im·po·si·tion** (soo-pĕr-im-pŏ-zish-ŏn) *n.*

su·per·in·tend (soo-pĕr-in-tend) *v.* to supervise. **su·per·in·tend'ence** *n.* **su·per·in·tend·en·cy** (soo-pĕr-in-ten-dĕn-see) *n.*

su·per·in·ten·dent (soo-pĕr-in-ten-dĕnt) *n.* 1. a person who superintends. 2. a person in charge of the upkeep of a building, especially an apartment house.

su·pe·ri·or (soo-peer-i-ŏr) *adj.* 1. higher in position or rank. 2. better or greater in some way, of high or higher quality. 3. showing that one feels oneself to be better or wiser etc. than others, conceited, supercilious. 4. not influenced by, not giving way to, *she is superior to flattery.* **superior** *n.* 1. a person or thing of higher rank or ability or quality. 2. the head of a monastery or other religious community. **su·pe'ri·or·ly** *adv.* **su·pe·ri·or·i·ty** (soo-peer-i-or-i-tee) *n.*

su·per·jet (soo-pĕr-jet) *n.* a jet airplane capable of traveling at supersonic speed.

superl. *abbr.* superlative.

su·per·la·tive (soo-pur-lă-tiv) *adj.* 1. of the highest degree or quality, *a man of superlative wisdom.* 2. of a grammatical form that expresses the highest or a very high degree of a quality, such as *dearest, shyest, best.* **superlative** *n.* a superlative form of a word. **su·per'la·tive·ly** *adv.* **su·per'la·tive·ness** *n.*

su·per·lin·er (soo-pĕr-lı-nĕr) *n.* a very large or very fast ocean liner.

su·per·man (soo-pĕr-man) *n.* (*pl.* **-men**, *pr.* -men) a man of superhuman powers.

su·per·mar·ket (soo-pĕr-mahr-kit) *n.* a large self-service store selling groceries and household goods.

su·per·nal (suu-pur-năl) *adj.* 1. heavenly, divine. 2. of the sky. 3. lofty.

su·per·nat·u·ral (soo-pĕr-nach-ŭ-răl) *adj.* of or caused by power above the forces of nature. **su·per·nat'u·ral·ly** *adv.* **su·per·nat'u·ral·ness** *n.* **su·per·nat'u·ral·ism** *n.*

su·per·no·va (soo-pĕr-noh-vă) *n.* a star that suddenly increases very greatly in brightness because of an explosion ejecting most of its mass.

su·per·nu·mer·ar·y (soo-pĕr-noo-mĕ-rer-ee) *adj.* in excess of the normal number, extra. **supernumerary** *n.* (*pl.* **-ar·ies**) 1. a supernumerary person or thing. 2. an actor who appears on stage but does not speak.

su·per·phos·phate (soo-pĕr-fos-fayt) *n.* a fertilizer containing soluble phosphates.

su·per·pose (soo-pĕr-pohz) *v.* (**su·per·posed, su·per·pos·ing**) 1. to place on or above something else. 2. to bring into the same position so as to coincide. **su·per·pos'a·ble** *adj.* **su·per·po·si·tion** (soo-pĕr-pŏ-zish-ŏn) *n.*

su·per·pow·er (soo-pĕr-pow-ĕr) *n.* one of the most powerful nations of the world.

su·per·sales·man (soo-pĕr-saylz-măn) *n.* (*pl.* **-men**, *pr.* -mĕn) an extremely skilled and persuasive salesman.

su·per·sat·u·rate (soo-pĕr-sach-ŭ-rayt) *v.* (**su·per·sat·u·rated, su·per·sat·u·rat·ing**) to add to (especially a solution) beyond the saturation point. **su·per·sat·u·ra·tion** (soo-pĕr-sach-ŭ-ray-shŏn) *n.*

su·per·scribe (soo-pĕr-skrıb) *v.* (**su·per·scribed, su·per·scrib·ing**) to write at the top of or on the outside of (a document etc.).

su·per·script (soo-pĕr-skript) *adj.* written or printed above and to the right of another symbol. **superscript** *n.* a superscript symbol.

su·per·scrip·tion (soo-pĕr-skrip-shŏn) *n.* a word or words written at the top or on the outside of a letter etc.

su·per·sede (soo-pĕr-seed) *v.* (**su·per·sed·ed, su·per·sed·ing**) 1. to take the place of, *cars have superseded horse-drawn carriages.* 2. to put or use in place of (another person or thing).

su·per·son·ic (soo-pĕr-son-ik) *adj.* of or having a speed greater than that of sound. **su·per·son'i·cal·ly** *adv.*

su·per·son·ics (soo-pĕr-son-iks) *n.* the science that studies supersonic phenomena.

su·per·star (soo-pĕr-stahr) *n.* a great star in entertainment etc.

su·per·sti·tion (soo-pĕr-stish-ŏn) *n.* 1. belief that events can be influenced by certain acts or circumstances that have no demonstrable connection with them, an idea or practice based on this. 2. a belief that is held by a number of people but without foundation.

su·per·sti·tious (soo-pĕr-stish-ŭs) *adj.* based on or influenced by superstition. **su·per·sti'tious·ly** *adv.*

su·per·struc·ture (soo-pĕr-struk-chŭr) *n.* a structure that rests upon something else, a building as distinct from its foundations.

su·per·tank·er (soo-pĕr-tang-kĕr) *n.* a very large tanker.

su·per·vene (soo-pĕr-veen) v. (**su·per·vened, su·per·ven·ing**) to occur as an interruption or a change from some condition or process. **su·per·ven·tion** (soo-pĕr-ven-shŏn) n.

su·per·vise (soo-pĕr-vɪz) v. (**su·per·vised, su·per·vis·ing**) to direct and inspect (work or workers or the operation of an organization). **su'per·vi·sor** n. **su·per·vi·sion** (soo-pĕr-vɪzh-ŏn) n.

su·per·vi·so·ry (soo-pĕr-vɪ-zŏ-ree) adj. supervising, supervisory duties.

su·per·wom·an (soo-pĕr-wuum-ăn) n. (pl. **-wom·en**, pr. -wim-in) a woman of superhuman powers.

su·pine (soo-pɪn) adj. 1. lying face upward (contrasted with prone). 2. not inclined to take action, indolent. **su·pine'ly** adv. **su·pine'ness** n.

supp., suppl. abbr. 1. supplement. 2. supplementary.

sup·per (sup-ĕr) n. an evening meal, the last meal of the day. □**supper club**, a nightclub.

sup·per·less (sup-ĕr-lis) adj. without supper.

sup·per·time (sup-ĕr-tɪm) n. the time when supper is served.

sup·plant (sŭ-plant) v. to oust and take the place of. **sup·plant'er** n. **sup·plan·ta·tion** (sup-lan-tay-shŏn) n.

sup·ple (sup-ĕl) adj. (**sup·pler, sup·plest**) bending easily, flexible, not stiff. **sup'ple·ly** adv. **sup'ple·ness** n.

sup·ple·ment (sup-lĕ-mĕnt) n. 1. a thing added as an extra or to make up for a deficiency. 2. a part added to a book etc. to give further information or to treat a particular subject, a set of special pages issued with a newspaper. **supplement** (sup-lĕ-ment) v. to provide or be a supplement to. **sup·ple·men·tal** (sup-lĕ-men-tăl) adj.

sup·ple·men·ta·ry (sup-lĕ-men-tă-ree) adj. serving as a supplement.

sup·pli·ant (sup-li-ănt) n. a person asking humbly for something. **suppliant** adj.

sup·pli·cant (sup-li-kănt) n. a suppliant. **supplicant** adj.

sup·pli·cate (sup-li-kayt) v. (**sup·pli·cat·ed, sup·pli·cat·ing**) to ask humbly for, to beseech. **sup·pli·ca·tion** (sup-li-kay-shŏn) n.

sup·ply (sŭ-plɪ) v. (**sup·plied, sup·ply·ing**) 1. to give or provide with (something needed or useful), to make available for use. 2. to make up for, to satisfy, supply a need. **supply** n. (pl. **-plies**) 1. providing of what is needed. 2. a stock or store, an amount of something provided or available, the water supply; an inexhaustible supply of fish. 3. supplies, provisions kept in storage and distributed when needed. 4. the quantity of commodities or services available in the market, especially at a specific price. **sup·pli'er** n.

sup·port (sŭ-pohrt) v. 1. to keep from falling or sinking, to hold in position, to bear the weight of. 2. to give strength to, to enable to last or continue, too little food to support life. 3. to supply with necessaries, he has a family to support. 4. to assist by one's approval or presence or by subscription to funds, to be a fan of (a particular sports team); support a resolution, speak or vote in favor of it. 5. to take a secondary part, the play has a strong supporting cast. 6. to corroborate, to bring facts to confirm (a statement etc.). 7. to endure or tolerate, we cannot support such insolence. **support** n. 1. supporting, being supported, we need your support. 2. a person or thing that

supports. **sup·port'er** n. **sup·port'ive** adj. **sup·port'a·ble** adj.

sup·pose (sŭ-pohz) v. (**sup·posed, sup·pos·ing**) 1. to be inclined to think, to accept as true or probable, I don't suppose they will come. 2. to assume as true for the purpose of argument, suppose the world were flat. 3. to consider as a proposal, suppose we try another. 4. to require as a condition, to presuppose, that supposes a mechanism without flaws. □**be supposed to,** to be expected or intended to, to have as a duty.

sup·posed (sŭ-pohzd) adj. believed to exist or to have a certain character or identity, his supposed brother.

sup·pos·ed·ly (sŭ-poh-zid-lee) adv. according to supposition.

sup·po·si·tion (sup-ŏ-zish-ŏn) n. supposing, what is supposed, the article is based on supposition not on fact.

sup·po·si·tious (sup-ŏ-zish-ŭs) adj. hypothetical, based on supposition.

sup·pos·i·ti·tious (sŭ-poz-ĭ-tish-ŭs) adj. substituted for the real person or thing, spurious.

sup·pos·i·to·ry (sŭ-poz-ĭ-tohr-ee) n. (pl. **-ries**) a solid piece of medicinal substance placed in the rectum or vagina or urethra and left to melt.

sup·press (sŭ-pres) v. 1. to put an end to the activity or existence of, especially by force or authority, suppress the rebellion. 2. to keep from being known or seen, suppress the truth; suppress a newspaper, prevent its publication. **sup·pres'sive** adj. **sup·pres·sion** (sŭ-presh-ŏn) n.

sup·press·i·ble (sŭ-pres-i-bĕl) adj. able to be suppressed.

sup·pres·sor (sŭ-pres-ŏr) n. a person or thing that suppresses, a device to suppress electrical interference.

sup·pu·rate (sup-yŭ-rayt) v. (**sup·pu·rat·ed, sup·pu·rat·ing**) to form pus, to fester. **sup·pu·ra·tive** (sup-yŭ-ray-tiv) adj. **sup·pu·ra·tion** (sup-yŭ-ray-shŏn) n.

su·pra (soo-prǎ) adv. above or before (in a book or writing). ▷Latin, = above.

su·pra·na·tion·al (soo-prǎ-nash-ŏ-nǎl) adj. transcending national limits.

su·prem·a·cist (soo-prem-ă-sist) n. an advocate of some group's (especially a racial group's) supremacy.

su·prem·a·cy (soo-prem-ă-see) n. being supreme, the position of supreme authority or power.

su·preme (soo-preem) adj. 1. highest in authority or rank, the supreme commander. 2. highest in importance or intensity or quality, most outstanding, supreme courage; the supreme sacrifice, involving one's death (as in war). 3. (of food) served in rich cream sauce, chicken supreme. **su·preme'ly** adv. **su·preme'ness** n. □**Supreme Being,** God. **supreme commander,** military commander of all allied forces. **Supreme Court,** the highest of the U.S. and of most states.

supt. abbr. superintendent.

supvr. abbr. supervisor.

sur·charge (sur-chahrj) n. 1. payment demanded in addition to the usual charge. 2. an additional or excessive load. 3. a mark printed over a postage stamp, changing its value. **surcharge** (sur-chahrj) v. (**sur·charged, sur·charg·ing**) 1. to make a surcharge on, to charge extra. 2. to overload. 3. to print a surcharge on (a stamp). **sur·charg'er** n.

sur·cin·gle (sur-sing-gĕl) n. a band around a

horse's body to keep a pack etc. in place.

sur·coat (sur-koht) *n.* *(old use)* a loose robe worn over armor.

surd (surd) *adj.* 1. a mathematical quantity (especially a root) that cannot be expressed in finite terms of whole numbers or quantities. 2. a sound uttered with the breath and not the voice, as *f* or *s.*

sure (shoor) *adj.* (**sur·er, sur·est**) 1. having or seeming to have sufficient reason for one's beliefs, free from doubts; *be sure of a person,* able to rely on him. 2. certain to do something or to happen, *the book is sure to be a success.* 3. undoubtedly true, *one thing is sure.* 4. reliable, secure, unfailing, *there's only one sure way; be sure to write,* do not fail to write. **sure** *adv.* *(informal)* certainly, *it sure was cold.* (▷Careful writers use *surely* in this sentence.) **sure′ness** *n.* □**as sure as,** as certainly as. **for sure,** *(informal)* for certain. **make sure,** to act so as to be certain; to feel confident (perhaps mistakenly), *confound that man! I made sure he would be here in time.* **sure enough,** certainly, in fact. **sure thing,** a certainty. **to be sure,** it is admitted, certainly, *she's not perfect, to be sure.*

sure·fire (shoor-fir) *adj.* certain to succeed.

sure·foot·ed (shoor-fuut-id) *adj.* never slipping or stumbling. **sure′foot′ed·ness** *n.*

sure·ly (shoor-lee) *adv.* 1. in a sure manner, without doubt, securely. 2. used for emphasis, *surely you won't desert us?* 3. (as an answer) certainly, *"Will you help?" "Surely."*

sure·ty (shoor-ĕ-tee) *n.* (*pl.* **-ties**) 1. a guarantee. 2. a person who makes himself responsible for another person's payment of a debt or performance of an undertaking.

surf (surf) *n.* the white foam of waves breaking on a rock or shore. **surf** *v.* to go surfing. □**surf casting,** fishing from the shore into the sea.

sur·face (sur-fis) *n.* 1. the outside of an object. 2. any of the sides of an object. 3. the uppermost area, the top of a table or desk etc., *a working surface.* 4. the top of a body of water. 5. the outward appearance of something, the qualities etc. perceived by casual observation (as distinct from deeper or hidden ones). **surface** *adj.* of or on the surface only, of the surface of land or sea (as distinct from in the air or underground, or under water). **surface** *v.* (**sur·faced, sur·fac·ing**) 1. to put a specified surface on. 2. to come or bring to the surface. □**surface mail,** mail carried by sea not by air. **surface tension,** the tension of the surface film of a liquid, tending to minimize its surface area.

sur·face-to-air (sur-fis-tŏ-air) *adj.* of a missile, message, etc. that can be sent from a point on land or sea to a target in the air.

sur·face-to-sur·face (sur-fis-tŏ-sur-fis) *adj.* of a missile, message, etc. that can be sent from a point on land or sea to a target elsewhere on land or sea.

sur·face-to-un·der·wa·ter (sur-fis-too-un-dĕr-waw-tĕr) *adj.* of a missile, message, etc. that can be sent from a point on land or sea to an underwater target.

surf·board (surf-bohrd) *n.* a long narrow board used in surfing.

sur·feit (sur-fit) *n.* too much of something (especially food and drink), a feeling of discomfort arising from this. **surfeit** *v.* to cause to take too much of something, to satiate, to cloy.

surf·er (sur-fĕr) *n.* a person who goes surfing.

surf·ing (sur-fing) *n.* the sport of balancing oneself on a board while being carried on waves to the shore.

surg. *abbr.* 1. surgeon. 2. surgery. 3. surgical.

surge (surj) *v.* (**surged, surg·ing**) to move forward in or like waves, to increase in volume or intensity. **surge** *n.* a wave, a surging movement or increase, an onrush.

sur·geon (sur-jŏn) *n.* a medical practitioner who performs surgical operations, a specialist in surgery. □**surgeon general,** the head of a public health service or of the medical service in a branch of the armed forces.

sur·ger·y (sur-jĕ-ree) *n.* (*pl.* **-ger·ies**) 1. the treatment of injuries and disorders and disease by cutting or manipulation of the affected parts. 2. an operating room.

sur·gi·cal (sur-ji-kăl) *adj.* of surgery or surgeons, used in surgery. **sur′gi·cal·ly** *adv.*

Su·ri·nam (soor-ĭ-nahm) a country on the north coast of South America. **Su·ri·nam′er** *n.*

sur·ly (sur-lee) *adj.* (**-li·er, -li·est**) bad-tempered and unfriendly. **sur′li·ly** *adv.* **sur′li·ness** *n.*

sur·mise (sŭr-mɪz) *n.* a conjecture. **surmise** *v.* (**sur·mised, sur·mis·ing**) to conjecture.

sur·mount (sŭr-mownt) *v.* to overcome (a difficulty), to get over (an obstacle). □**be surmounted by,** to have on or over the top, *the spire is surmounted by a weather vane.*

sur·mount·a·ble (sŭr-mown-tă-bĕl) *adj.* able to be overcome.

sur·name (sur-naym) *n.* the name held by all members of a family. **surname** *v.* (**sur·named, sur·nam·ing**) to give as a surname.

sur·pass (sŭr-pas) *v.* to do or be better than, to excel. **sur·pass′a·ble** *adj.*

sur·pass·ing (sŭr-pas-ing) *adj.* greatly excelling or exceeding others. **sur·pass′ing·ly** *adv.*

sur·plice (sur-plis) *n.* a loose white vestment with full sleeves, worn over the cassock by clergy and choir at a religious service.

sur·plus (sur-plus) *n.* an amount left over after what is required has been used, especially an excess of public revenue over expenditure during a budgetary year. **surplus** *adj.* being a surplus. □**surplus value,** the difference between the value of work done and wages paid.

sur·prise (sŭr-prɪz) *n.* 1. the emotion aroused by something sudden or unexpected. 2. an event or thing that arouses this emotion. 3. the process of catching a person etc. unprepared; *a surprise attack* or *visit,* one made unexpectedly. **surprise** *v.* (**sur·prised, sur·pris·ing**) 1. to cause to feel surprise. 2. to come upon or attack suddenly and without warning, to capture in this way. 3. to startle (a person) into action by catching him unprepared. 4. to discover (a secret etc.) by unexpected action. **sur·pris′er** *n.* □**surprised at,** scandalized by, *we are surprised at your behavior.* **surprise party,** a party given for a person who has not been told in advance, and which is intended to surprise him.

sur·prised (sŭr-prɪzd) *adj.* experiencing surprise.

sur·pris·ing (sŭr-prɪ-zing) *adj.* causing surprise. **sur·pris′ing·ly** *adv.*

sur·re·al·ism (sŭ-ree-ă-liz-ĕm) *n.* a 20th-century movement in art and literature that seeks to express what is in the subconscious mind by depicting objects and events as seen in dreams etc. **sur·re·al** (sŭ-ree-ăl) *adj.* **sur·re′al·ist** *adj.* & *n.* **sur·**

re·al·is·tic (sŭ-ree-ă-lis-tik) adj. sur·re·al·is'ti·cal·ly adv.

sur·ren·der (sŭ-ren-dĕr) v. 1. to hand over, to give into another person's power or control, especially on demand or under compulsion. 2. to give oneself up, to accept an enemy's demand for submission. 3. to give way to an emotion, surrendered herself to grief. 4. to give up one's rights under (an insurance policy) in return for a smaller sum payable immediately. surrender n. surrendering, being surrendered.

sur·rep·ti·tious (sur-ĕp-tish-ŭs) adj. acting or done stealthily. sur·rep·ti'tious·ly adv. sur·rep·ti'tious·ness n.

sur·rey (sur-ee) n. (pl. -reys) a light four-wheeled carriage with two seats facing forward.

sur·ro·gate (sur-ŏ-git) n. 1. a deputy. 2. a substitute.

sur·round (sŭ-rownd) v. 1. to come or lie or be all around. 2. to place all around, to encircle with enemy forces. surround n. a border or edging. □be surrounded by or with, to have on all sides.

sur·round·ings (sŭ-rown-dingz) n. pl. the things or conditions around and liable to affect a person or place.

sur·tax (sur-taks) n. an additional tax imposed on income or goods already taxed.

sur·tout (sŭr-too) n. (old use) an overcoat or frock coat.

surv. abbr. 1. survey. 2. surveying. 3. surveyor.

sur·veil·lance (sŭr-vay-läns) n. supervision or close observation, especially of a suspected person.

sur·vey (sŭr-vay) v. 1. to look at and take a general view of. 2. to make or present a survey of, the report surveys progress made in the past year. 3. to examine the condition of (a building etc.). 4. to measure and map out the size, shape, position, and elevation etc. of (an area of land). survey (sur-vay) n. (pl. -veys) 1. a general look at something. 2. a general examination of a situation or subject, an account of this. 3. the surveying of land etc., a map or plan produced by this. □surveyor's chain, a distance of sixty-six feet, a basic unit in surveying. surveyor's measure, a system of measuring used in surveying.

sur·vey·ing (sŭr-vay-ing) n. the work of a surveyor.

sur·vey·or (sur-vay-ŏr) n. a person whose job is to survey land or buildings.

sur·viv·al (sŭr-vɪ-văl) n. 1. surviving. 2. something that has survived from an earlier time. □survival of the fittest, the process or result of natural selection (see natural).

sur·vive (sŭr-vɪv) v. (sur·vived, sur·viv·ing) 1. to continue to live or exist. 2. to live or exist longer than, to remain alive or in existence after, few flowers survived the frost.

sur·vi·vor (sŭr-vɪ-vŏr) n. one who survives, one who survives another.

sus·cep·ti·bil·i·ty (sŭ-sep-tĭ-bil-i-tee) n. 1. being susceptible. 2. susceptibilities, a person's feelings that may be hurt or offended.

sus·cep·ti·ble (sŭ-sep-tĭ-bĕl) adj. 1. liable to be affected by something; susceptible to colds, catching colds easily. 2. impressionable, falling in love easily. 3. able to undergo something; susceptible of proof, able to be proved. sus·cep'ti·bly adv.

sus·cep·tive (sŭ-sep-tiv) adj. susceptible.

sus·pect (sŭ-spekt) v. 1. to have an impression of the existence or presence of, we suspected a trap. 2. to have suspicions or doubts about, to mistrust, we suspect their motives. 3. to feel that (a person) is guilty but have little or no proof. suspect (sus-pekt) n. a person who is suspected of a crime etc. suspect (sus-pekt, sŭ-spekt) adj. suspected, open to suspicion.

sus·pend (sŭ-spend) v. 1. to hang up. 2. to keep from falling or sinking in air or liquid etc., particles are suspended in the fluid. 3. to postpone, suspend judgment. 4. to put a temporary stop to, suspend play. 5. to deprive temporarily of a position or a right. □suspended animation, a state of cessation of vital functions without death. suspended sentence, a sentence of imprisonment that is not enforced subject to good behavior.

sus·pend·er (sŭ-spen-dĕr) n. (usually suspenders) straps used to keep trousers up, fastened to the waistband and passing over the shoulders.

sus·pense (sŭ-spens) n. a state or feeling of anxious uncertainty while awaiting news or an event etc. sus·pense'ful adj.

sus·pen·sion (sŭ-spen-shŏn) n. 1. suspending, being suspended. 2. the means by which a vehicle is supported on its axles. □suspension bridge, a bridge suspended from cables that pass over supports at each end.

sus·pen·so·ry (sŭ-spen-sŏ-ree) adj. (of a ligament, muscle, bandage, etc.) holding an organ etc. suspended.

sus·pi·cion (sŭ-spish-ŏn) n. 1. suspecting, being suspected. 2. a partial or unconfirmed belief. 3. a slight trace.

sus·pi·cious (sŭ-spish-ŭs) adj. feeling or causing suspicion. sus·pi'cious·ly adv. sus·pi'cious·ness n.

sus·tain (sŭ-stayn) v. 1. to support. 2. to keep alive; sustaining food, food that keeps up one's strength. 3. to keep (a sound or effort etc.) going continuously. 4. to undergo, to suffer, sustained a defeat. 5. to endure without giving way, sustained the attack. 6. (of a court or other authority) to confirm or uphold the validity of, the objection was sustained. sus·tain'a·ble adj.

sus·te·nance (sus-tĕ-năns) n. 1. the process of sustaining life by food. 2. the food itself, nourishment.

su·tra (soo-trä) n. 1. a saying or set of sayings in Hindu literature. 2. the narrative part of Buddhist literature.

sut·tee (su-tee) n. 1. the Hindu custom formerly requiring a widow to throw herself on her husband's funeral pyre. 2. a widow who did this.

su·ture (soo-chŭr) n. surgical stitching of a wound, a stitch or thread etc. used in this. suture v. (su·tured, su·tur·ing) to stitch (a wound).

Su·va (soo-vah) the capital of Fiji.

su·ze·rain (soo-zĕ-rin) n. 1. a country or ruler that has some authority over another country that is self-governing in its internal affairs. 2. an overlord in feudal times. su'ze·rain·ty n.

s.v. abbr. under the word, for "span" see s.v. "spick." ▷Latin sub voce or sub verbo.

svc., svce. abbr. service.

svelte (svelt) adj. (svelt·er, svelt·est) (of a person) slender and graceful.

svgs. abbr. savings.

SW, S.W. abbr. 1. southwest. 2. southwestern.

Sw. abbr. Swedish.

swab (swob) n. 1. a mop or absorbent pad for cleansing or drying or absorbing things. 2. a specimen of a secretion taken with this. 3. *(slang)* a sailor. **swab** *v.* **(swabbed, swab·bing)** to cleanse or wipe with a swab.

swad·dle (swod-ĕl) *v.* **(swad·dled, swad·dling)** to swathe in wraps or clothes or warm garments. □**swaddling clothes,** strips of cloth formerly wrapped around a newborn baby to restrain its movements.

swag (swag) *n.* loot.

swag·ger (swag-ĕr) *v.* to walk or behave in a self-important manner, to strut. **swagger** *n.* a swaggering walk or way of behaving. **swag′ger·er** *n.* □**swagger stick,** a short cane sometimes carried by army officers or soldiers.

Swa·hi·li (swah-hee-lee) *n.* a Bantu language widely used in East Africa. **Swa·hi′li·an** *adj.*

swain (swayn) *n.* *(old use)* 1. a lover or suitor. 2. a young rustic.

swal·low[1] (swol-oh) *v.* 1. to cause or allow (food etc.) to go down one's throat, to work the muscles of the throat as when doing this. 2. to take in so as to engulf or absorb, *she was swallowed up in the crowd.* 3. to accept; *swallow a story,* believe it too easily; *swallow an insult,* accept it meekly. 4. to repress (a sound or emotion etc.), *swallowed his pride.* **swallow** *n.* the act of swallowing, the amount swallowed in one movement.

swallow[2] *n.* a small migratory insect-eating bird with a forked tail and long pointed wings.

swal-low-tailed (swol-oh-tayld) *adj.* having a deeply forked tail.

swam (swam) *see* **swim.**

swa·mi (swah-mee) *n.* (*pl.* **-mis**) a Hindu religious teacher.

swamp (swomp) *n.* a marsh. **swamp** *v.* 1. to flood, to drench or submerge in water. 2. to overwhelm with a great mass or number of things. **swamp′y** *adj.* **swamp′i·ness** *n.* □**swamp fever,** malaria.

swamp·land (swomp-land) *n.* a swamp.

swan (swon) *n.* a large usually white water bird with a long slender neck. □**swan dive,** a dive executed with arms outspread until close to the water.

swank (swangk) *n.* *(informal)* 1. elegance or smartness. 2. boastful behavior, ostentation. **swank** *adj.* *(informal)* swanky.

swank·y (swang-kee) *adj.* **(swank·i·er, swank·i·est)** *(informal)* 1. elegant or smart. 2. boastful, ostentatious.

swans·down (swonz-down) *n.* 1. a swan's fine soft down, used for trimmings and especially in powder puffs. 2. a kind of thick cotton cloth with a soft nap on one side.

swap (swop) *v.* **(swapped, swap·ping)** *(informal)* to exchange. **swap** *n.* *(informal)* 1. an exchange. 2. a thing suitable for swapping.

sward (sword) *n.* an expanse covered with short grass, lawnlike ground.

swarm[1] (sworm) *n.* 1. a large number of insects or birds or small animals or people flying or moving about in a cluster. 2. a cluster of honeybees leaving the hive with a queen bee to establish a new home. **swarm** *v.* 1. to move in a swarm, to come together in large numbers. 2. (of bees) to cluster in a swarm. 3. (of a place) to be crowded or overrun, *swarming with tourists.*

swarm[2] *v.* **swarm up,** to climb by gripping with arms and legs.

swarth·y (swor-*thee*) *adj.* **(swarth·i·er, swarth·i·est)** having a dark complexion. **swarth′i·ness** *n.*

swash·buck·ling (swosh-buk-ling) *adj.* swaggering aggressively. **swash′buck·ler** *n.*

swas·ti·ka (swos-ti-kă) *n.* a symbol formed by a cross with the ends bent at right angles, used as a Nazi emblem.

swat (swot) *v.* **(swat·ted, swat·ting)** to hit hard with something flat, to crush (a fly etc.) in this way. **swat′ter** *n.*

swatch (swoch) *n.* a sample, especially of cloth or fabric.

swath (swoth) *n.* 1. the space that a scythe or mowing machine cuts in one sweep or passage. 2. a line of grass or wheat etc. lying after being cut. 3. a broad strip.

swathe (swo*th*, sway*th*) *v.* **(swathed, swath·ing)** to wrap in layers of bandage or wrappings or warm garments.

sway (sway) *v.* 1. to swing or cause to swing gently, to lean from side to side or to one side. 2. to influence the opinions or sympathy or actions of, *his speech swayed many voters.* 3. to waver in one's opinion or attitude. **sway** *n.* 1. a swaying movement. 2. influence, power, *hold sway.*

sway·back (sway-bak) *n.* an abnormal inward curvature of the spine, especially in horses. **sway′backed** *adj.*

Swa·zi·land (swah-zi-land) a country in southeast Africa. **Swa·zi** (swah-zee) *n.* (*pl.* **-zis, -zi**) & *adj.*

swear (swair) *v.* **(swore, sworn, swear·ing)** 1. to state or promise on oath, *swear it* or *swear to it.* 2. *(informal)* to state emphatically, *swore he hadn't touched it.* 3. to cause to take an oath, *swore him to secrecy; the jury had been sworn.* 4. to use curses or profane language in anger or surprise etc. **swear′er** *n.* □**swear by,** *(informal)* to have great confidence in. **swear in,** to admit (a person) to office etc. by causing him to take an oath. **swear off,** to swear to abstain from.

swear·word (swair-wurd) *n.* a profane word used in anger etc.

sweat (swet) *n.* 1. moisture that is given off by the body through the pores of the skin. 2. a state of sweating or being covered by sweat. 3. *(informal)* a state of great anxiety. 4. *(informal)* a laborious task. 5. moisture forming in drops on a surface, as by condensation. **sweat** *v.* **(sweat** or **sweat·ed, sweat·ing)** 1. to give out sweat, to cause to do this. 2. *(informal)* to be in a state of great anxiety. 3. *(informal)* to work long and hard. □**no sweat,** *(informal)* there is no need to worry. **sweat blood,** *(slang)* to work very hard at something; to be in a state of great anxiety. **sweat gland,** a spiral tubular gland secreting sweat below the skin. **sweat it out,** *(informal)* to endure it to the end. **sweat off,** to get rid of by sweating. **sweat pants,** loose trousers with tight-fitting cuffs, worn especially by athletes. **sweat shirt,** a sleeved sweater worn especially by athletes. **sweat socks,** heavy socks worn by athletes to absorb perspiration. **sweat suit,** sweat pants and a sweat shirt worn together.

sweat·band (swet-band) *n.* a band of absorbent material for absorbing or wiping away sweat.

sweat·er (swet-ĕr) *n.* a pullover or knitted jacket.

sweat·shop (swet-shop) *n.* a business, especially a factory, that employs workers at low wages for long hours under poor conditions.

sweat·y (swet-ee) *adj.* **(sweat·i·er, sweat·i·est)** damp with sweat. **sweat′i·ly** *adv.* **sweat′i·ness** *n.*

Swed. *abbr.* 1. Sweden. 2. Swedish.

Swede (sweed) *n.* a native of Sweden.
Swe·den (swee-děn) a country in northern Europe.
Swed·ish (swee-dish) *adj.* of Sweden or its people or language. **Swedish** *n.* the language of Sweden.
sweep (sweep) *v.* **(swept, sweep·ing)** 1. to clear away with or as if with a broom or brush. 2. to clean or clear (a surface or area) by doing this. 3. to move or remove by pushing, *the floods swept away fences.* 4. to go smoothly and swiftly or majestically, *she swept out of the room.* 5. to extend in a continuous line or slope, *the mountains sweep down to the sea.* 6. to pass quickly over or along, *winds sweep the hillside; a new fashion is sweeping America.* 7. to touch lightly. 8. to win all possible games, prizes, etc. **sweep** *n.* 1. a sweeping movement. 2. a sweeping line or slope. 3. the act of sweeping with a broom etc., *give it a good sweep.* 4. a chimney sweep. 5. the winning of all the prizes, nearly all of the votes, etc. □**make a clean sweep,** to get rid of everything or of all staff etc.; to win all the prizes. **sweep all before one,** to be very successful. **sweep the board,** to win all the prizes.
sweep·er (swee-pĕr) *n.* 1. a person who sweeps a place. 2. a thing that sweeps, a carpet sweeper.
sweep·ing (swee-ping) *adj.* 1. of great scope, comprehensive, *sweeping changes.* 2. (of a statement) making no exceptions or limitations, *sweeping generalizations.* **sweeping** *n.* the act of sweeping. **sweepings** *n. pl.* dust or scraps etc. collected by sweeping.
sweep·stakes (sweep-stayks), **sweep·stake** (sweep-stayk) *n.* 1. a form of gambling on horse races etc. in which the money staked is divided among those who have drawn numbered tickets for the winners. 2. a race etc. with betting of this kind. 3. a lottery.
sweet (sweet) *adj.* 1. tasting as if containing sugar, not bitter. 2. fragrant. 3. melodious. 4. fresh, (of food) not stale, (of water) not salt. 5. pleasant, gratifying, *(informal)* pretty or charming. 6. having a pleasant nature, lovable. **sweet** *n.* a candy or other sweet food. **sweet'ly** *adv.* **sweet'ness** *n.* □**at one's own sweet will or in one's own sweet time,** just as or when one pleases. **sweet basil,** basil. **sweet cider,** *see* **cider. sweet clover,** any of various plants grown as fodder or to improve the soil. **sweet corn,** a kind of corn with sweet grains and eaten while young, **sweet gum,** an American tree having hard wood and yielding sap used commercially in making medicines and perfumes. **sweet marjoram,** an herb used in cooking. **sweet on,** *(informal),* fond of or in love with. **sweet pea,** a climbing garden plant with fragrant flowers in many colors. **sweet pepper,** *see* **pepper. sweet potato,** a climbing plant with sweet tuberous roots used for food. **sweet talk,** flattery. **sweet tooth,** a liking for sweet things. **sweet William,** a garden plant with clustered fragrant flowers.
sweet-and-sour (sweet-ăn-sowr) *adj.* cooked in sauce containing sugar and either vinegar or lemon.
sweet·bread (sweet-bred) *n.* an animal's thymus gland or pancreas used as food.
sweet·bri·er (sweet-brı-ĕr) *n.* a small fragrant wild rose of Europe and central Asia.
sweet·en (swee-těn) *v.* to make or become sweet or sweeter.
sweet·en·er (swee-tě-něr), **sweet·en·ing** (swee-

tě-ning) *n.* a substance used to sweeten food or drink.
sweet·heart (sweet-hahrt) *n.* a person's beloved, one of a pair of people who are in love with each other. □**sweetheart contract,** *(slang)* a labor contract dishonestly made and unduly favorable to management.
sweet·ie (swee-tee) *n. (informal)* a sweetheart.
sweet·ish (swee-tish) *adj.* rather sweet.
sweet·meat (sweet-meet) *n.* any very sweet food, especially candy or preserved fruit.
sweet-talk (sweet-tawk) *v. (informal)* to flatter, to coax.
swell (swel) *v.* **(swelled, swelled** or **swol·len, swell·ing)** 1. to make or become larger because of pressure from within, to curve outward. 2. to make or become larger in amount or volume or numbers or intensity. **swell** *n.* 1. the act or state of swelling. 2. the heaving of the sea with waves that do not break. 3. a gradual increase of loudness in music, a mechanism in an organ for obtaining this. 4. *(slang)* a person of high social position. **swell** *adj. (informal)* smart, excellent. □**swelled head,** *(slang)* conceit.
swell·ing (swel-ing) *n.* an abnormally swollen place on the body.
swel·ter (swel-tĕr) *v.* to be uncomfortably hot, to suffer from the heat.
swept (swept) *see* **sweep.**
swept-wing (swept-wing) *adj.* (of an aircraft) with wings slanting markedly backward from the direction of flight.
swerve (swurv) *v.* **(swerved, swerv·ing)** to turn or cause to turn aside from a straight course. **swerve** *n.* a swerving movement or direction.
swift (swift) *adj.* quick, rapid. **swift** *n.* a swiftly flying insect-eating bird with long narrow wings. **swift'ly** *adv.* **swift'ness** *n.*
swig (swig) *v.* **(swigged, swig·ging)** *(informal)* to take a drink or drinks of, *swigging beer.* **swig** *n. (informal)* a drink or swallow.
swill (swil) *v.* 1. to feed to animals, *swill the pigs.* 2. (of water) to pour. 3. to drink in large quantities. **swill** *n.* 1. a sloppy mixture of waste food fed to pigs. 2. garbage. **swill'er** *n.*
swim (swim) *v.* **(swam, swum, swim·ming)** 1. to propel the body through water by movements of the limbs or fins or tail etc. 2. to cross by swimming, *swim the English Channel.* 3. to cause to swim, *swim your horse across the stream.* 4. to float. 5. to be covered or flooded with liquid, *eyes swimming in tears.* 6. to seem to be whirling or waving, to have a dizzy sensation, *everything swam before her eyes; my head is swimming.* **swim** *n.* 1. a period of swimming. 2. the main current of affairs. **swim'mer** *n.* □**in the swim,** active in or knowing what is going on. **swim bladder,** a fish's air bladder. **swimming pool,** an artificial pool for swimming in.
swim·ming·ly (swim-ing-lee) *adv.* with easy unobstructed progress.
swim·suit (swim-soot) *n.* a garment worn for swimming.
swim·wear (swim-wair) *n.* clothing for swimming.
swin·dle (swin-děl) *v.* **(swin·dled, swin·dling)** to cheat (a person) in a business transaction, to obtain by fraud. **swindle** *n.* a piece of swindling, a fraudulent person or thing. **swin'dler** *n.*
swine (swin) *n. (pl.* **swine)** 1. a pig. 2. *(informal)* a hated person or thing.

swine·herd (swɪn-hurd) *n. (old use)* a person taking care of a number of pigs.

swing (swing) *v.* **(swung, swing·ing)** 1. to move to and fro while hanging or supported, to cause to do this. 2. to hang by its ends, *swung a hammock between the two trees.* 3. to turn (a wheel etc.) smoothly, to turn to one side or in a curve, *the car swung into the drive.* 4. to walk or run with an easy rhythmical movement. 5. to lift with a swinging movement. 6. to change from one opinion or mood etc. to another. 7. to influence (voting etc.) decisively; *swing the deal, (informal)* to succeed in arranging it. 8. *(slang)* to be executed by hanging. 9. to play (music) with a swing rhythm. 10. *(slang)* to be lively or up-to-date. **swing** *n.* 1. a swinging movement or action or rhythm. 2. a seat slung by ropes or chains for swinging in, a spell of swinging in this. 3. the extent to which a thing swings, the amount by which votes or opinions or points scored etc. change from one side to the other. 4. a kind of jazz with the time of the melody varied while the accompaniment is in strict time. **swing'y** *adj.* **swing'er** *n.* □**in full swing,** with activity at its greatest. **swing bridge,** a bridge that can be swung aside to allow ships to pass. **swinging door,** a door that opens in either direction and closes itself when released. **swing shift,** a late work shift, usually from 4 P.M. until midnight.

swing·ing (swing-ing) *adj. (slang)* lively and up-to-date.

swin·ish (swɪ-nish) *adj.* like a swine, beastly.

swipe (swɪp) *v.* **(swiped, swip·ing)** *(informal)* 1. to hit with a swinging blow. 2. to steal, especially by snatching. **swipe** *n. (informal)* a swinging blow.

swirl (swurl) *v.* to move or flow or carry along with a whirling movement. **swirl** *n.* a swirling movement. **swirl'y** *adj.*

swish (swish) *v.* to strike or move or cause to move with a hissing sound. **swish** *n.* a swishing sound.

Swiss (swis) *adj.* of Switzerland or its people. **Swiss** *n. (pl.* **Swiss)** a native of Switzerland. □**Swiss chard,** *see* **chard. Swiss cheese,** a hard pale cheese with internal holes. **Swiss Guards,** a body of soldiers at the Vatican, serving the pope. **Swiss steak,** steak with flour pounded in, and cooked with vegetables.

switch (swich) *n.* 1. a device that is operated to complete or break an electric circuit. 2. a device at the junction of railroad tracks for diverting trains from one track to another. 3. a flexible shoot cut from a tree, a tapering rod or whip resembling this. 4. a tress of real or false hair tied at one end. 5. a shift or change in opinion or methods or policy etc. **switch** *v.* 1. to turn (an electrical or other appliance) on or off by means of a switch. 2. to transfer (a train) to another track. 3. to divert (thoughts or talk) to another subject. 4. to change or exchange (positions or methods or policy etc.). 5. to whip with a switch. 6. to swing around quickly, to snatch suddenly, *the cow switches her tail; switched it out of my hand.* □**switched on,** *(slang)* alert to what is going on, up-to-date. **switch hitter,** (in baseball) a player who can bat equally well right-handed or left-handed.

switch·back (swich-bak) *n.* a zigzag road for ascending or descending steep slopes.

switch·blade (swich-blayd) *n.* a pocketknife with a blade released by a spring.

switch·board (swich-bohrd) *n.* a panel with a set of switches for making telephone connections or operating electric circuits.

switch·man (swich-măn) *n. (pl.* **-men,** *pr.* -měn) a person in charge of railroad switches.

Switz. *abbr.* Switzerland.

Swit·zer·land (swit-sĕr-lănd) a country in central Europe.

swiv·el (swiv-ĕl) *n.* a link or pivot between two parts enabling one of them to revolve without turning the other. **swivel** *v.* **(swiv·eled, swiv·el·ing)** to turn on or as if on a swivel. □**swivel chair,** a chair with a seat that can turn horizontally on a pivot.

swiz·zle (swiz-ĕl) *n.* a frothy mixed drink of rum, lime juice, and sugar. □**swizzle stick,** a stick used for stirring a drink to make it frothy or flat.

swol·len (swoh-lĕn) *see* **swell.**

swoon (swoon) *v.* to faint. **swoon** *n.* a faint. **swoon'ing·ly** *adv.*

swoop (swoop) *v.* to come down with a rushing movement like a bird upon its prey, to make a sudden attack. **swoop** *n.* a swooping movement or attack. □**at one fell swoop,** *see* **fell.**

swop (swop) = **swap.**

sword (sohrd) *n.* a weapon with a long blade and a hilt. □**at swords' points,** (of two or more persons) ready to fight, showing hostility toward each other. **sword dance,** a dance in which swords are brandished or a performer treads about swords placed on the ground.

sword·fish (sohrd-fish) *n. (pl.* **-fish, -fish·es)** a sea fish with a long swordlike upper jaw.

sword·play (sohrd-play) *n.* 1. the act or the art of using a sword. 2. fencing.

swords·man (sohrdz-măn) *n. (pl.* **-men,** *pr.* -měn) a person having skill in the use of a sword. **swords'man·ship** *n.*

sword·tail (sohrd-tayl) *n.* a brightly colored tropical fish with a tail resembling a sword.

swore (swohr), **sworn** (swohrn) *see* **swear. sworn** *adj.* open and determined in devotion or enmity, *sworn friends, sworn foes.*

swum (swum) *see* **swim.**

swung (swung) *see* **swing.**

syb·a·rite (sib-ă-rɪt) *n.* a person who is excessively fond of comfort and luxury. **syb·a·rit·ic** (sib-ă-rit-ik) *adj.*

syc·a·more (sik-ă-mohr) *n.* a large eastern North American plane tree.

syc·o·phant (sik-ŏ-fănt) *n.* a person who tries to win people's favor by flattering them. **syc·o·phan·tic** (sik-ŏ-fan-tik) *adj.* **syc·o·phan'ti·cal·ly** *adv.* **syc·o·phan·cy** (sik-ŏ-făn-see) *n.*

syl., syll. *abbr.* 1. syllable. 2. syllabus.

syl·la·bar·y (sil-ă-ber-ee) *n. (pl.* **-bar·ies)** 1. a list of syllables. 2. a list of characters representing syllables and serving the purpose, in some languages or stages of writing, of an alphabet.

syl·lab·ic (si-lab-ik) *adj.* of or in syllables. **syl·lab'i·cal·ly** *adv.*

syl·lab·i·cate (si-lab-ĭ-kayt) *v.* **(syl·lab·i·cat·ed, syl·lab·i·cat·ing)** to syllabify. **syl·lab·i·ca·tion** (si-lab-ĭ-kay-shŏn) *n.*

syl·lab·i·fy (si-lab-ĭ-fɪ) *v.* **(syl·lab·i·fied, syl·lab·i·fy·ing)** to divide into or articulate by syllables. **syl·lab·i·fi·ca·tion** (si-lab-ĭ-fɪ-kay-shŏn) *n.*

syl·la·ble (sil-ă-bĕl) *n.* one of the units of sound into which a word can be divided, *there are two syllables in "unit," three in "divided," and one* in "can." □in words of one syllable, expressed very simply or bluntly.

syl·la·bus (sil-ă-bŭs) n. (pl. -bus·es, -bi, pr, -bɪ) an outline of the subjects that are included in a course of study.

syl·lo·gism (sil-ŏ-jiz-ĕm) n. a form of reasoning in which a conclusion is reached from two statements, as in "All men must die; I am a man; therefore, I must die." syl·lo·gis·tic (sil-ŏ-jis-tik) adj. syl·lo·gis'ti·cal·ly adv.

sylph (silf) n. a slender girl or woman.

syl·van (sil-văn) adj. of the woods, having woods.

sym. abbr. 1. symbol. 2. symmetrical. 3. symphony. 4. symptom.

sym·bi·o·sis (sim-bɪ-oh-sis, -bi-) n. (pl. -ses) the association of two different organisms living attached to each other or one within the other to their mutual advantage. sym·bi·ot·ic (sim-bɪ-ot-ik, -bi-) adj.

sym·bol (sim-bŏl) n. 1. a thing regarded as suggesting something or embodying certain characteristics, the cross is the symbol of Christianity; the lion is the symbol of courage. 2. a mark or sign with a special meaning, such as mathematical signs (as + and − for addition and subtraction), punctuation marks, written or printed forms of notes in music.

sym·bol·ic (sim-bol-ik), sym·bol·i·cal (sim-bol-i-kăl) adj. of or using or used as a symbol. sym·bol'i·cal·ly adv.

sym·bol·ism (sim-bŏ-liz-ĕm) n. use of symbols to express things.

sym·bol·ize (sim-bŏ-lɪz) v. (sym·bol·ized, sym·bol·iz·ing) 1. to be a symbol of. 2. to represent by means of a symbol. sym·bol·i·za·tion (sim-bŏ-li-zay-shŏn) n.

sym·met·ri·cal (si-met-ri-kăl) adj. able to be divided into parts that are the same in size and shape and similar in position on either side of a dividing line or around a center. sym·met'ri·cal·ly adv.

sym·me·try (sim-ĕ-tree) n. (pl. -tries) 1. being symmetrical. 2. pleasing proportion between parts of a whole.

sym·pa·thet·ic (sim-pă-thet-ik) adj. 1. feeling or expressing or resulting from sympathy. 2. likable, he's not a sympathetic character. 3. showing approval or support, he is sympathetic to our plan. sym·pa·thet'i·cal·ly adv. □sympathetic nervous system, a system of nerves uniting the interior organs and the blood vessels and passing along the spinal column.

sym·pa·thize (sim-pă-thɪz) v. (sym·pa·thized, sym·pa·thiz·ing) to feel or express sympathy. sym'pa·thiz·er n.

sym·pa·thy (sim-pă-thee) n. (pl. -thies) 1. sharing or the ability to share another person's emotions or sensations. 2. a feeling of pity or tenderness toward one suffering pain or grief or trouble. 3. liking for each other produced in people who have similar opinions or tastes. 4. approval of an opinion or desire. □be in sympathy with, to feel approval of (an opinion or desire). sympathy strike, a strike by workers in support of other strikers.

sym·pho·ny (sim-fŏ-nee) n. (pl. -nies) a long elaborate musical composition (usually in several parts) for a full orchestra. sym·phon·ic (sim-fon-ik) adj. □symphony orchestra, a large orchestra playing symphonies etc.

sym·po·si·um (sim-poh-zi-ŭm) n. (pl. -po·

si·ums, -po·si·a, pr. -poh-zi-ă) a meeting for discussion of a particular subject.

symp·tom (simp-tŏm) n. a sign of the existence of a condition, especially a perceptible change from what is normal in the body or its functioning, indicating disease or injury.

symp·to·mat·ic (simp-tŏ-mat-ik) adj. serving as a symptom.

syn. abbr. 1. synonym. 2. synonymous. 3. synonymy.

syn·a·gogue (sin-ă-gog) n. a building for public Jewish worship.

syn·apse (sin-aps) n. a place where nerve cells join.

sync, synch (singk) n. (informal) synchronization.

syn·chron·ic (sing-kron-ik) adj. describing a subject (especially a language) as it exists at a particular time.

syn·chro·nize (sing-krŏ-nɪz) v. (syn·chro·nized, syn·chro·niz·ing) 1. to occur or exist at the same time. 2. to operate at the same rate and simultaneously. 3. to cause to occur or operate at the same time, to cause (clocks etc.) to show the same time. syn'chro·niz·er n. syn·chro·ni·za·tion (sing-krŏ-ni-zay-shŏn) n.

syn·chro·nous (sing-krŏ-nŭs) adj. 1. existing or occurring at the same time. 2. operating at the same rate and simultaneously. syn'chro·nous·ly adv.

syn·co·pate (sing-kŏ-payt) v. (syn·co·pat·ed, syn·co·pat·ing) v. to change the beats or accents in (a passage of music) by putting a strong stress instead of a weak one (and vice versa). syn·co·pa·tion (sing-kŏ-pay-shŏn) n.

syn·co·pe (sing-kŏ-pee) n. 1. a faint, fainting. 2. the shortening of a word by dropping sounds or letters from within the word.

syn·cret·ic (sin-kret-ik) adj. combining different beliefs or principles.

synd. abbr. 1. syndicate. 2. syndicated.

syn·di·cate (sin-dĭ-kit) n. an association of people or firms combining to carry out a business or commercial undertaking. syndicate (sin-dĭ-kayt) v. (syn·di·cat·ed, syn·di·cat·ing) 1. to combine into a syndicate. 2. to publish through an association that acquires stories, articles, cartoons, etc. for simultaneous publication in numerous newspapers and periodicals. syn·di·ca·tion (sin-dĭ-kay-shŏn) n.

syn·drome (sin-drohm) n. 1. a set of signs and symptoms that together indicate the presence of a disease or abnormal condition. 2. a combination of opinions, behavior, etc. that are characteristic of a particular condition.

syn·ec·do·che (si-nek-dŏ-kee) n. a figure of speech in which a part is named but the whole is understood (as fifty strings for fifty stringed instruments) or vice versa (as the United States beat Russia at hockey).

syn·er·gism (sin-ĕr-jiz-ĕm) n. the combined effect of drugs etc. that exceeds that of their individual effects. syn'er·gist n. syn·er·gis·tic (sin-ĕr-jis-tik) adj. syn·er·gis'ti·cal·ly adv.

syn·od (sin-ŏd) n. a council attended by senior clergy or church officials to discuss questions of policy, teaching, etc. syn'od·al adj. syn·od·ic (si-nod-ik) syn·od'i·cal adj.

syn·o·nym (sin-ŏ-nim) n. a word or phrase with a meaning similar to that of another in the same language.

syn·on·y·mous (si-non-ĭ-mŭs) adj. equivalent in

meaning. **syn·on·y·my** (si-non-ĭ-mee) *n.*

syn·op·sis (si-nop-sis) *n.* (*pl.* **-ses,** *pr.* -seez) a summary, a brief general survey.

syn·op·tic (si-nop-tik) *adj.* 1. of or forming a synopsis. 2. of the **synoptic Gospels,** those of Matthew, Mark, and Luke, which have many similarities (whereas that of John differs greatly). **syn·op'ti·cal** *adj.*

syn·tax (sin-taks) *n.* the way in which words are arranged to form phrases and sentences. **syn·tac·tic** (sin-tak-tik) *adj.* **syn·tac'ti·cal** *adj.* **syn·tac'ti·cal·ly** *adv.*

syn·the·sis (sin-thĕ-sis) *n.* (*pl.* **-ses,** *pr.* -seez) 1. the combining of separate parts or elements to form a complex whole. 2. the combining of substances to form a compound, artificial production of a substance that occurs naturally in plants or animals.

syn·the·size (sin-thĕ-sɪz) *v.* (**syn·the·sized, syn·the·siz·ing**) to make by synthesis. **syn'the·siz·er** *n.*

syn·thet·ic (sin-thet-ik) *adj.* 1. made by synthesis, manufactured as opposed to produced naturally, *synthetic rubber.* 2. (*informal*) artificial, affected, *decorated in synthetic Tudor style.* **synthetic** *n.* a synthetic substance or fabric (as nylon). **syn·thet'i·cal·ly** *adv.*

syph·i·lis (sif-ĭ-lis) *n.* a venereal disease transmitted by contact or contracted by an unborn child from its mother's blood. **syph·i·lit·ic** (sif-ĭ-lit-ik) *adj. & n.*

Syr·i·a (seer-i-ă) a country in the Middle East. **Syr'i·an** *adj. & n.*

sy·rin·ga (sĭ-ring-gă) *n.* 1. the botanical name for lilac. 2. (*old use*) the mock orange.

sy·ringe (sĭ-rinj) *n.* 1. a device for drawing in liquid and forcing it out again in a fine stream. 2. a hypodermic syringe (*see* **hypodermic**). **syringe** *v.* (**sy·ringed, sy·ring·ing**) to wash out or spray with a syringe.

syr·inx (sir-ingks) *n.* (*pl.* **sy·rin·ges,** *pr.* sĭ-rin-jeez, **syr·inx·es**) the part of a bird's throat where its song is produced.

syr·up (sir-ŭp) *n.* 1. a thick sweet liquid, water in which sugar is dissolved, often with added flavoring or medication. 2. the boiled-down juice of a plant or fruit, *maple syrup.* **syr'up·y** *adj.*

syst. *abbr.* system.

sys·tem (sis-tĕm) *n.* 1. a set of connected things or parts that form a whole or work together, *a railroad system; the nervous system,* (*see* **nervous**); *the solar system,* (*see* **solar**). 2. an animal body as a whole, *too much alcohol poisons the system.* 3. a set of rules or principles or practices forming a particular philosophy or form of government etc. 4. a method of classification or notation or measurement etc., *the metric system.* 5. orderliness, being systematic, *she works without system.* □**get a thing out of one's system,** to be rid of its effects. **systems analysis,** analysis of an operation in order to decide how a computer may be used to perform it. **systems analyst,** an expert in systems analysis.

sys·tem·at·ic (sis-tĕ-mat-ik) *adj.* methodical, according to a plan and not casually or at random. **sys·tem·at'i·cal** *adj.* **sys·tem·at'i·cal·ly** *adv.*

sys·tem·a·tize (sis-tĕ-mă-tɪz) *v.* (**sys·tem·a·tized, sys·tem·a·tiz·ing**) to arrange according to a system. **sys·tem·a·ti·za·tion** (sis-tĕ-mă-ti-zay-shŏn) *n.*

sys·tem·ic (si-stem-ik) *adj.* 1. of or affecting the body as a whole. 2. (of a fungicide etc.) entering a plant by way of the roots or shoots and passing into the tissues. **sys·tem'i·cal·ly** *adv.*

sys·to·le (sis-tŏ-lee) *n.* the contraction of the heart, alternating with the diastole. **sys·tol·ic** (si-stol-ik) *adj.*

Sze·chwan (se-chwahn) a province in central China.

T

T, t (tee) (*pl.* **Ts, T's, t's**) the twentieth letter of the alphabet. □**to a T,** perfectly, *fits her to a T.*
t. *abbr.* 1. teaspoon(s). 2. temperature. 3. (in grammar) tense. 4. time. 5. ton(s). 6. transit. 7. transitive. 8. troy.
T. *abbr.* 1. tablespoon(s). 2. Territory. 3. Testament. 4. true. 5. Tuesday.
't (t) it (in shortened form); *'tis,* it is.
Ta *symbol* tantalum.
tab (tab) *n.* a small projecting flap or strip, especially one by which something can be grasped or hung or fastened or identified. **tab** *v.* **(tabbed, tab·bing)** 1. to provide with tabs. 2. *(informal)* to designate, to choose. □**keep a tab** *or* **tabs on,** *(informal)* to keep account of, to keep under observation. **pick up the tab,** *(informal)* to be the one who pays the bill. **tab key,** *(informal)* the tabulator key on a typewriter.
tab·ard (tab-ărd) *n.* a short tunic-like garment open at the sides, worn by a herald, emblazoned with the arms of the sovereign.
Ta·bas·co (tă-bas-koh) *n.* *(trademark)* a very hot peppery sauce used for seasoning.
tab·by (tab-ee) *n.* (*pl.* **-bies**) (also **tabby cat**) a cat with gray or brownish fur and dark stripes.
tab·er·nac·le (tab-ĕr-nak-ĕl) *n.* 1. (often *Tabernacle*) the portable shrine used by the Israelites during their wanderings in the wilderness. 2. a receptacle containing consecrated elements of the Eucharist. 3. a meeting place for worship.
ta·ble (tay-bĕl) *n.* 1. a piece of furniture consisting of a flat top supported on one or more legs. 2. food served on a table; *she sets a good table,* provides good meals. 3. a group of people seated at a table. 4. a list of facts or figures systematically arranged, especially in columns; *learn one's tables,* to learn the multiplication tables etc. in mathematics. **table** *v.* **(ta·bled, ta·bling)** 1. (in parliamentary procedure) to set aside (a motion, bill, etc.) indefinitely. 2. *(British)* to submit for discussion. □**at table,** (chiefly *British*) while taking a meal at a table. **on the table,** (of a motion, bill, etc.) postponed. **table linen,** tablecloths, napkins, etc. **table manners,** ability to behave properly while eating at a table. **table salt,** salt powdered for use in a saltcellar. **table tennis,** a game like tennis played on a table with a net across it.
tab·leau (tab-loh) *n.* (*pl.* **-leaux, -leaus,** *pr.* -lohz) 1. a silent and motionless group of people etc. arranged to represent a scene. 2. a dramatic or picturesque scene.
ta·ble·cloth (tay-bĕl-klawth) *n.* a cloth for covering a table, especially at meals.
ta·ble d'hôte (tab-ĕl doht) (*pl.* **ta·bles d'hôte,** *pr.* **tab**-ĕlz doht) (of a restaurant meal) served at a fixed inclusive price. ▷French, = host's table.

ta·ble·hop (tay-bĕl-hop) *v.* **(ta·ble·hopped, ta·ble·hop·ping)** *(informal)* to move from one table to another, talking to those seated at each. **ta'ble·hop·per** *n.* *(informal).*
ta·ble·land (tay-bĕl-land) *n.* a plateau of land.
ta·ble·spoon (tay-bĕl-spoon) *n.* 1. a large spoon for serving food at the table. 2. a measurement used in cooking, = one tablespoonful. **ta'ble·spoon·ful** *n.* (*pl.* **-fuls**) ½ fluid ounce.
tab·let (tab-lit) *n.* 1. a slab or panel bearing an inscription or picture, especially one fixed to a wall as a memorial. 2. sheets of paper glued together along one edge. 3. a small measured amount of a drug compressed into a solid form.
ta·ble·ware (tay-bĕl-wair) *n.* dishes, silver, etc. for use at the dining table.
tab·loid (tab-loid) *n.* 1. a newspaper (usually containing numerous pictures) printed on sheets that are half the size of larger newspapers. 2. such a newspaper containing sensational news.
ta·boo, ta·bu (ta-boo) *n.* (*pl.* **-boos, -bus**) a ban or prohibition on something that is regarded by religion or custom as not to be done or touched or used etc. **taboo** *adj.* prohibited by a taboo, *taboo words.* **taboo** *v.* **(ta·booed, ta·boo·ing)** to place under a taboo.
ta·bor (tay-bŏr) *n.* a small drum, especially one formerly used to accompany a pipe or fife.
tab·u·lar (tab-yŭ-lăr) *adj.* arranged or displayed in a table or list. **tab'u·lar·ly** *adv.*
tab·u·late (tab-yŭ-layt) *v.* **(tab·u·lat·ed, tab·u·lat·ing)** to arrange (facts or figures) in the form of a table or list. **tab·u·la·tion** (tab-yŭ-lay-shŏn) *n.*
tab·u·la·tor (tab-yŭ-lay-tŏr) *n.* 1. a person or thing that tabulates facts or figures. 2. a device on a typewriter for advancing to a series of set positions in tabular work, operated by a *tabular key.*
TAC *abbr.* Tactical Air Command.
tach (tak) *n.* *(informal)* a tachometer.
ta·chom·e·ter (ta-kom-ĕ-tĕr) *n.* an instrument for measuring speed of rotation.
tach·y·car·di·a (tak-ĭ-kahr-di-ă) *n.* abnormally rapid heartbeat.
tac·it (tas-it) *adj.* implied or understood without being put into words. **tac'it·ly** *adv.* **tac'it·ness** *n.*
tac·i·turn (tas-i-turn) *adj.* habitually saying very little, uncommunicative. **tac'i·turn·ly** *adv.* **tac·i·tur·ni·ty** (tas-i-tur-ni-tee) *n.*
tack (tak) *n.* 1. a small nail with a broad head. 2. a long stitch used to hold fabric in position lightly or temporarily, or *(tailor's tacks)* to mark the place for a tuck etc. 3. the direction of a ship's course as determined by the position of its sails, a temporary oblique course to take advantage of a wind; *port tack,* with the wind on the port side. 4. a

697

course of action or policy, *he's on the wrong tack.* 5. riding harness, saddles, etc. **tack** *v.* 1. to nail with a tack or tacks. 2. to stitch with tacks. 3. to add as an extra thing, *a service charge was tacked onto the bill.* 4. to sail a zigzag course in order to take advantage of a wind, to make a tack or tacks. **tack′er** *n.* □**tack hammer,** a light hammer for driving tacks. **tack room,** the room where tack for riding is kept.

tack·le (tak-ĕl) *n.* 1. a set of ropes and pulleys for lifting weights or working a ship's sails. 2. equipment for a task or sport, *fishing tackle.* 3. the act of tackling in football. 4. either of two linemen on a football team, positioned between a guard and an end. **tackle** *v.* (**tack·led, tack·ling**) 1. to grapple with, to try to deal with or overcome (an awkward thing or an opponent or problem); *tackle a person about something,* to initiate a discussion with him about an awkward matter. 2. (in football) to seize and stop by forcing to the ground (an opponent running with the ball). **tack′ler** *n.*

tack·y[1] (tak-ee) *adj.* (**tack·i·er, tack·i·est**) (of paint or varnish etc.) slightly sticky, not quite dry. **tack′i·ness** *n.*

tacky[2] *adj.* (**tack·i·er, tack·i·est**) (*informal*) shabby, cheap. **tack′i·ness** *n.*

ta·co (tah-koh) *n.* (*pl.* **-cos**) a tortilla folded up and filled, usually with a spicy meat sauce.

tac·o·nite (tak-ŏ-nɪt) *n.* an iron ore of low grade.

tact (takt) *n.* skill in avoiding giving offense or in winning goodwill by saying or doing the right thing.

tact·ful (takt-fŭl) *adj.* having or showing tact. **tact′ful·ly** *adv.*

tac·tic (tak-tik) *n.* 1. a means of accomplishing a goal. 2. *tactics,* the art of placing or maneuvering forces skillfully in a battle (distinguished from *strategy*); 3. any maneuvering, a procedure adopted in order to achieve something.

tac·ti·cal (tak-ti-kăl) *adj.* 1. of tactics (distinguished from *strategic*). 2. planning or planned skillfully. **tac′ti·cal·ly** *adv.* □**tactical weapons,** *see* **strategic weapons.**

tac·ti·cian (tak-tish-ăn) *n.* an expert in tactics.

tac·tile (tak-til) *adj.* of or using the sense of touch, *tactile organs.*

tact·less (takt-lis) *adj.* lacking in tact. **tact′less·ly** *adv.* **tact′less·ness** *n.*

tad (tad) *n.* (*informal*) a little child.

ta·da (tah-dah) *interj.* (*informal*) listen, an introduction or announcement is about to be made.

tad·pole (tad-pohl) *n.* the larva of a frog or toad etc. at the stage when it lives in water and has gills and a tail.

Ta·dzhik·i·stan (tă-jik-i-stan) a republic of the U.S.S.R. bordering on China and Afghanistan.

taf·fe·ta (taf-i-tă) *n.* a crisp shiny silklike dress fabric.

taff·rail (taf-rayl) *n.* a rail around the stern of a vessel.

taf·fy (taf-ee) *n.* a chewy candy made by boiling sugar or molasses and pulling it until it reaches the desired color and consistency. □**taffy pull,** a social gathering at which taffy is made.

Taft (taft), **Wil·liam How·ard** (1857–1930) the twenty-seventh president of the U.S. 1909–13.

tag[1] (tag) *n.* 1. a metal or plastic point at the end of a shoelace etc. 2. a label tied or stuck into something to identify it or show its price etc. 3. any loose or ragged end or projection. 4. a stock phrase or much-used quotation. 5. a descriptive word or phrase. **tag** *v.* (**tagged, tag·ging**) 1. to label with a tag. 2. to attach, to add as an extra thing, *a postscript was tagged on to her letter.* 3. (*informal*) to follow, to trail behind. □**tag along,** (*informal*) to go along with another or others. **tag line,** the last line of a story, speech, etc.; a term or phrase that becomes associated with a person, product, etc. **tag sale,** a sale of used household articles held in a private home.

tag[2] *n.* a children's game in which one chases the rest until he touches another. **tag** *v.* (**tagged, tag·ging**) to catch up with and touch, as in the game of tag. □**tag out,** to tag (a person) who is then out of the game; (in baseball) to touch (a base runner) with the ball held in the hand or glove before he reaches base.

TAG *abbr.* 1. talented and gifted. 2. The Adjutant General.

Ta·ga·log (tah-gah-log) *n.* (*pl.* **-logs, -log**) 1. a member of a Malayan people of the Philippine Islands. 2. the principal language of these islands.

Ta·hi·ti (tă-hee-tee) an island in the south Pacific. **Ta·hi·tian** (tă-hee-shăn) *adj. & n.*

tai chi (tɪ jee) (also **t'ai chi ch'uan,** *pr.* **chwahn**) a stylized form of warlike movements, developed as exercises by the Chinese.

tai·ga (tɪ-gă) *n.* the evergreen forests of the far northern regions, especially of Canada and Russia.

tail (tayl) *n.* 1. the hindmost part of an animal, especially when extending beyond the rest of the body; *with his tail between his legs,* (of an animal or person) looking defeated or dejected. 2. something resembling this in its shape or position, the rear part, an inferior part, a part that hangs down or behind. 3. (*informal*) a person following or shadowing another. **tail** *v.* (*slang*) to follow closely, to shadow. □**on a person's tail,** following him closely. **tail end,** the hindmost or very last part. **tail wind,** a following wind.

tail·back (tayl-bak) *n.* (in football) in certain offensive formations the back farthest from the line of scrimmage.

tail·coat (tayl-koht) *n.* a man's coat with the skirt tapering and divided at the back, worn as part of formal evening dress or morning dress.

tail·gate (tayl-gayt) *n.* a door or gate, often downward hinged, at the rear of a motor vehicle. **tailgate** *v.* (**tail·gat·ed, tail·gat·ing**) to follow dangerously close behind another motor vehicle.

tail·ing (tay-ling) *n.* 1. the part of a projecting stone or brick that is cemented into a wall. 2. *tailings,* leftover or inferior parts of ore, grain, etc.

tail·less (tayl-lis) *adj.* having no tail.

tail·light (tayl-lɪt) *n.* a light, usually red, at the back of a vehicle.

tail·or (tay-lŏr) *n.* a maker of men's clothes, especially to order. **tailor** *v.* 1. to make (clothes) as a tailor, to make in a simple smooth-fitting design. 2. to make or adapt for a special purpose, *the new factory is tailored to our needs.*

tai·lor-made (tay-lŏr-mayd) *adj.* 1. made by a tailor. 2. made in a simple smooth-fitting design. 3. perfectly suited for the purpose.

tail·piece (tayl-pees) *n.* a decoration printed in the blank space at the end of a chapter or book.

tail·pipe (tayl-pɪp) *n.* the exhaust pipe of a motor vehicle.

tails (taylz) *n. pl.* 1. an evening suit with a tailcoat. 2. the reverse of a coin, turned upward after being tossed.

tail·spin (tayl-spin) *n.* 1. an aircraft's spiral dive

with the tail making wider circles than the front. 2. *(informal)* a state of panic or depression etc.
tail·stock (tayl-stok) *n.* the adjustable part of a lathe, holding a spindle that does not rotate.
taint (taynt) *n.* a trace of some bad quality or decay or infection. **taint** *v.* to affect with a taint; *tainted meat,* slightly decayed.
Tai·pei (tɪ-pay) the capital of the Republic of China.
Tai·wan (tɪ-wahn) an island off the southeast coast of China. *See* **Republic of China.**
Tai·wan·ese (tɪ-wah-neez) *adj. & n.* 1. of or relating to Taiwan. 2. a native or inhabitant of Taiwan.
take (tayk) *v.* **(took,** *pr.* tuuk, **tak·en, tak·ing)** 1. to get into one's hands etc. 2. to get possession of, to capture, to win, *took many prisoners; took first prize.* 3. to be successful or effective, *the inoculation did not take.* 4. to remove from its place, *someone has taken my bicycle.* 5. to subtract. 6. to make use of, to indulge in, *take this opportunity; take a holiday; take the first turn on the left,* go into it. 7. to occupy (a position), especially as one's right; *take a chair,* sit down on one; *take the chair,* act as chairman. 8. to obtain after fulfilling necessary conditions *(take a degree),* to obtain the use of by payment *(take an apartment),* to buy (a certain newspaper etc.) regularly. 9. to use as a means of transport, *take the train.* 10. to consume, *we'll take tea now.* 11. to require, *it takes a strong man to lift that; these things take time,* require much time; *it takes some doing,* is hard to do; *do you take sugar?,* do you use it in tea etc.? 12. to cause to come or go with one, to carry or remove, *take the letters to the post office.* 13. to be affected by, to catch, *the child took sick.* 14. to experience or exert (a feeling or effort), *took pity on him; take care.* 15. to find out and record, *take his name; we'll take your measurements.* 16. to interpret in a certain way, *we take it that you are satisfied; I take your point,* accept that it is valid. 17. to adopt a specified attitude toward, *take things coolly; take it well,* not be upset or resentful. 18. to accept, to endure, *take risks; he can't take a joke,* resents being laughed at. 19. to perform, to deal with, to move around or over, *take a decision; took the corner too fast; take an examination,* sit for it; *take a subject at school,* study it. 20. to make by photography, to photograph (a person or thing). **take** *n.* 1. the amount of game or fish etc. taken or caught. 2. an instance of photographing a scene for a motion picture. 3. *(slang)* money taken in business, receipts. □**be taken by** or **with,** to find attractive. **be taken ill,** to become ill. **for the taking,** available, *yours for the taking.* **on the take,** *(slang)* seeking profit or advantage selfishly; willing to obtain money dishonestly, especially by taking bribes. **take advantage of,** to seize (an opportunity); to use (another person) unfairly. **take after,** to resemble (a parent etc.). **take away,** to remove or carry away; to subtract. **take back,** to withdraw (a statement); to carry (a person) back in thought to a past time. **take care,** to be careful. **take care of,** to look after, to be responsible for. **take down,** to write down (spoken words); to humiliate; to remove (a building or structure) by taking it to pieces. **take exception,** to disagree. **take for,** to regard as; to mistake for. **take in,** to accept into one's house etc.; to include; to make (a garment etc.) smaller; to understand; to deceive or cheat (a person); *(informal)* to visit (a place) en route. **take it,** to

suppose; *(slang)* to withstand hardship, criticism, etc. **take it into one's head,** to decide suddenly. **take it on the chin,** to suffer a severe blow from an event etc. **take it out of,** to exhaust the strength of. **take it out on,** to work off one's frustration by attacking or maltreating (a person etc.). **take it upon oneself,** to undertake, to assume a responsibility. **take life,** to kill. **take off,** to take (clothing etc.) from the body; to mimic humorously; to leave the ground and become airborne; *take oneself off,* depart; *I take off my hat to him,* applaud him as admirable. **take on,** to acquire; to undertake (work or responsibility); to engage (an employee); to agree to play against (a person in a game); *(informal)* to show great emotion, to make a fuss. **take one's time,** to loiter, not to hurry in doing something. **take out,** to escort on an outing; to obtain or get (an insurance policy etc.) issued; *(slang)* to destroy, to kill; *take a person out of himself,* make him forget his troubles. **take over,** to take control of (a business etc.). **take part,** to share in an activity. **take sides,** to support one side or another. **take stock,** to make an inventory of the stock in a shop etc.; to examine one's position and resources. **take to,** to adopt as a habit or custom or course; to go to as a refuge; to develop a liking or ability for. **take up,** to take as a hobby or business; to make a protégé of (a person); to occupy (time or space); to begin (residence etc.); to resume at the point where something was left; to absorb (a liquid); to investigate (a matter) further; to shorten (a garment); to accept (an offer etc.); *take a person up on his offer,* accept it. **take-up spool,** the spool on to which film or tape etc. is wound after use. **take up with,** to begin to associate with. ▷See the note under **bring.**
take·off (tayk-awf) *n.* 1. a piece of humorous mimicry. 2. the process of taking off in flying.
take-out (tayk-owt) *adj.* 1. (of food) bought at a restaurant for eating elsewhere. 2. (of a restaurant) selling such food.
take·o·ver (tayk-oh-věr) *n.* assumption of control, especially of a business.
tak·er (tay-kěr) *n.* a person who takes something (especially a bet), *there were no takers.*
tak·ing (tay-king) *adj.* attractive, captivating.
talc (talk) *n.* 1. a soft smooth mineral that is powdered for use as a lubricant. 2. talcum powder.
tal·cum (tal-kŭm) *n.* = talc. □**talcum powder,** talc powdered and usually perfumed, applied to the skin to make it feel smooth and dry.
tale (tayl) *n.* 1. a narrative or story. 2. a report spread by gossip. 3. a lie or falsehood.
tale·bear·er (tayl-bair-ěr) *n.* a person who tells tales *(see* **tell).**
tal·ent (tal-ěnt) *n.* 1. special or very great ability, people who have this. 2. a unit of money used in certain ancient countries. □**talent scout,** a person whose job is to find talented performers for the entertainment industry.
tal·ent·ed (tal-ěn-tid) *adj.* having talent.
ta·ler (tah-lěr) *n.* any of numerous large coins formerly used in German states.
tales·man (taylz-măn) *n.* (*pl.* **-men,** *pr.* -měn) a person summoned to jury duty.
tal·is·man (tal-is-măn) *n.* (*pl.* **-mans**) an object supposed to bring good luck.
talk (tawk) *v.* 1. to convey or exchange ideas by spoken words. 2. to have the power of speech, *child is learning to talk.* 3. to express or utter or discuss in words, *you are talking nonsense; talk*

scandal. **4.** to use (a particular language), *talk French.* **5.** to affect or influence by talking, *talked him into going to Spain.* **6.** to give away information, *we have ways of making you talk.* **talk** *n.* **1.** talking, conversation, discussion. **2.** a style of speech, *baby talk.* **3.** an informal lecture. **4.** rumor, gossip, its theme, *there is talk of a general election; it's the talk of the town.* **5.** talking or promises etc. without action or results. **talk′er** *n.* □**money talks**, it has influence. **now you're talking**, *(slang)* I welcome that offer or suggestion. **talk away**, to consume (time) in talking, *talk away the hours.* **talk back to**, to reply defiantly to. **talk down**, to silence (a person) by talking loudly or persistently; to bring (a pilot or aircraft) to a landing by radio instructions from the ground. **talk down to**, to speak to in condescendingly simple language. **talk into**, to persuade. **talk of**, to discuss; to express some intention of. **talk out of**, to prevent by use of discouraging arguments. **talk over**, to discuss. **talk show**, a radio or television program featuring conversation of an interviewer and guests. **talk through one's hat**, *see* **hat. talk to**, *(informal)* to reprove.

talk·a·tive (taw-kă-tiv) *adj.* talking very much. **talk′a·tive·ly** *adv.* **talk′a·tive·ness** *n.*

talk·ing-to (taw-king-too) *n. (informal)* a reproof, *give him a good talking-to.*

tall (tawl) *adj.* **1.** of more than average height. **2.** having a certain height, *six feet tall.* **tall′ness** *n.* □**tall drink**, one that is large in quantity or is served in a tall glass. **tall order**, *(informal)* a difficult task. **tall story** *or* **tale**, *(informal)* one that is difficult to believe.

Tal·la·has·see (tal-ă-has-ee) the capital of Florida.

tall·boy (tawl-boi) *n. (British)* a tall chest of drawers, a highboy.

tall·ish (taw-lish) *adj.* rather tall.

tal·lith (tah-lis) *n. (pl.* **ta·li·thim**, *pr.* tah-lee-sim) a shawl worn by Jews while praying.

tal·low (tal-oh) *n.* animal fat used to make candles, soap, lubricants, etc. **tal′low·y** *adj.*

tal·ly (tal-ee) *n. (pl.* **-lies**) the reckoning of a debt or score. **tally** *v.* **(tal·lied, tal·ly·ing)** to correspond, *see that the goods tally with what we ordered; the two witnesses' stories tallied.* **tal′li·er** *n.*

tal·ly·ho (tal-ee-hoh) *interj.* a huntsman's cry to the hounds on sighting the fox.

tal·ly·man (tal-ee-măn) *n. (pl.* **-men**, *pr.* -měn) a person who keeps a tally of goods.

Tal·mud (tahl-muud) *n.* a collection of ancient writings on Jewish civil and ceremonial law and legend. **Tal·mud·ic** (tahl-moo-dik) *adj.*

tal·on (tal-ŏn) *n.* a claw, especially of a bird of prey.

ta·lus (tay-lŭs) *n. (pl.* **-lus·es**) a sloping mass of rock fragments at the foot of a cliff.

tam (tam) *n.* a tam-o'-shanter.

tam·a·ble (tay-mă-bĕl) *adj.* able to be tamed.

ta·ma·le (tă-mah-lee) *n.* a Mexican dish of seasoned meat and cornmeal steamed or baked in corn husks.

tam·a·rack (tam-ă-rak) *n.* **1.** an American larch. **2.** its wood.

tam·a·rind (tam-ă-rind) *n.* **1.** a tropical tree bearing fruit with acid pulp. **2.** its fruit.

tam·a·risk (tam-ă-risk) *n.* an evergreen shrub with feathery branches and spikes of pink or white flowers.

tam·bou·rine (tam-bŏ-reen) *n.* a percussion instrument consisting of a small hoop with parchment stretched over one side, and jingling metal disks in slots around the hoop.

tame (taym) *adj.* **(tam·er, tam·est)** **1.** (of animals) gentle and not afraid of human beings, not wild or fierce. **2.** docile. **3.** not exciting or interesting. **tame** *v.* **(tamed, tam·ing)** to make tame or manageable. **tame′ly** *adv.* **tame′ness** *n.*

tam·er (tay-měr) *n.* a person who tames and trains wild animals, *lion tamer.*

Tam·il (tam-il) *n.* **1.** a member of a people of southern India and Sri Lanka. **2.** their language.

tam-o'-shan·ter (tam-ŏ-shan-tĕr) *n.* a beret with a soft full top.

tamp (tamp) *n.* to pack or ram down tightly.

tam·per (tam-pĕr) *v.* **tamper with**, to meddle or interfere with, to alter without authority, *someone has tampered with the switches;* to influence illegally, to bribe, *tamper with a jury.* **tam′per·er** *n.*

tam·pon (tam-pon) *n.* a plug of absorbent material inserted into the body to stop bleeding or absorb natural secretions.

tan[1] (tan) *v.* **(tanned, tan·ning)** **1.** to convert (animal hide) into leather by treating it with tannic acid or mineral salts etc. **2.** to make or become brown by exposure to sun. **3.** *(slang)* to thrash. **tan** *n.* **1.** yellowish brown. **2.** brown color in skin exposed to the sun. **3.** tree bark used in tanning hides. **tan** *adj.* **(tan·ner, tan·nest)** yellowish brown.

tan[2] *abbr.* tangent.

tan·a·ger (tan-ă-jĕr) *n.* an American songbird, the male usually having brilliant plumage.

Ta·na·na·rive (ta-na-na-reev) the capital of the Malagasy Republic.

tan·bark (tan-bahrk) *n.* the bark of certain trees used in tanning.

T & E *abbr.* travel and entertainment.

tan·dem (tan-děm) *n.* **1.** a bicycle with seats and pedals for two or more people one behind another. **2.** an arrangement of people or things one behind another. **tandem** *adv.* one behind another. **tandem** *adj.* with parts or things placed one behind the other. □**in tandem**, arranged in this way; working together.

tang (tang) *n.* **1.** a strong taste or flavor or smell. **2.** a projection on the blade of a knife or chisel etc. by which it is held firm in its handle.

tan·ge·lo (tan-jĕ-loh) *n. (pl.* **-los**) **1.** a hybrid between a tangerine and a grapefruit. **2.** its fruit.

tan·gent (tan-jĕnt) *n.* a straight line that touches the outside of a curve but does not intersect it. **tangent** *adj.* touching. **tan·gen·tial** (tan-jen-shăl) *adj.* **tan·gen′tial·ly** *adv.* **tan·gen·ti·al·i·ty** (tan-jen-shi-al-i-tee) *n.* □**go off on** *or* **at a tangent**, to diverge suddenly from a line of thought etc. or from the matter in hand.

tan·ge·rine (tan-jĕ-reen) *n.* **1.** a kind of small flattened orange, a variety of mandarin. **2.** its deep orange-yellow color.

tan·gi·ble (tan-jĭ-bĕl) *adj.* **1.** able to be perceived by touch. **2.** clear and definite, real, *tangible advantages.* **tan′gi·bly** *adv.* **tan′gi·ble·ness** *n.* **tan·gi·bil·i·ty** (tan-jĭ-bil-i-tee) *n.*

tan·gle (tang-gĕl) *v.* **(tan·gled, tan·gling)** **1.** to twist or become twisted into a confused mass. **2.** to entangle. **3.** to become involved in conflict with. **tangle** *n.* a tangled mass or condition. □**tangle with**, to argue or fight with.

tan·go (tang-goh) *n.* (*pl.* **-gos**) a ballroom dance with gliding steps, music for this. **tango** *v.* (**-goed, go·ing**) to dance the tango.

tang·y (tang-ee) *adj.* (**tang·i·er, tang·i·iest**) having a strong taste or flavor or smell.

tank (tangk) *n.* 1. a large container for holding liquid or gas. 2. a heavily armored fighting vehicle carrying guns and moving on caterpillar tracks. **tank** *v.* **tank up,** to fill the tank of a vehicle etc.; *(slang)* to drink heavily. **tank'ful** *n.* (*pl.* **-fuls**) □**tank farm,** an area where petroleum is stored in tanks. **tank suit,** a simple bathing suit. **tank town,** a small town, especially one where trains obtain water.

tank·ard (tang-kărd) *n.* a large one-handled drinking vessel, usually of silver or pewter and often with a lid.

tank·er (tang-kĕr) *n.* a ship or aircraft or vehicle for carrying oil or other liquid in bulk.

tan·ner (tan-ĕr) *n.* a person who tans hides into leather.

tan·ner·y (tan-ĕ-ree) *n.* (*pl.* **-ner·ies**) a place where hides are tanned into leather.

tan·nic (tan-ik) *adj.* of tannin. □**tannic acid,** tannin.

tan·nin (tan-in) *n.* any of several compounds obtained from oak galls and various tree barks (also found in tea), used chiefly in tanning and dyeing.

tan·sy (tan-zee) *n.* (*pl.* **-sies**) a plant with yellow flowers in clusters and feathery leaves.

tan·ta·lize (tan-ta-lız) *v.* (**tan·ta·lized, tan·ta·liz·ing**) to tease or torment by the sight of something that is desired but kept out of reach or withheld. (▷In Greek mythology, Tantalus was condemned to stand in Hades surrounded by water and fruit that receded when he tried to reach them.) **tan'ta·liz·ing·ly** *adv.* **tan'ta·liz·er** *n.* **tan·ta·li·za·tion** (tan-tă-li-zay-shŏn) *n.*

tan·ta·lum (tan-tă-lŭm) *n.* a rare hard white metallic element highly resistant to heat and to the action of acids.

tan·ta·mount (tan-tă-mownt) *adj.* equivalent, *the Queen's request was tantamount to a command.*

tan·trum (tan-trŭm) *n.* an outburst of bad temper, especially in a child.

Tan·za·ni·a (tan-ză-nee-ă) a country in East Africa. **Tan·za·ni'an** *adj. & n.*

Tao·ism (dow-iz-ĕm) *n.* a religious doctrine originally based on writings attributed to the Chinese philosopher Lao-tse, who lived around 500 B.C. **Tao'ist** *adj. & n.*

tap[1] (tap) *n.* 1. a device for drawing liquid from a cask or for allowing liquid or gas to come from a pipe in a controllable flow. 2. a device for cutting a screw thread inside a cavity. 3. a connection for tapping a telephone. **tap** *v.* (**tapped, tap·ping**) 1. to fit a tap into (a cask) in order to draw out its contents. 2. to draw off (liquid) by means of a tap or through an incision. 3. to extract or obtain supplies or information from. 4. to cut a screw thread inside (a cavity). 5. to make a connection in (a circuit etc.) so as to divert electricity or fit a listening device for overhearing telephone communications. **tap'per** *n.* □**on tap,** (of liquid or gas) ready to be drawn off by a tap; *(informal)* available. **tap water,** water supplied through pipes to taps in a building.

tap[2] *v.* (**tapped, tap·ping**) 1. to strike with a quick light blow, to knock gently on (a door etc.). 2. to strike (an object) lightly against something.

tap *n.* a quick light blow, the sound of this. **tap'per** *n.* □**tap dance,** a dance in which an elaborate rhythm is tapped with the feet.

tape (tayp) *n.* 1. a narrow strip of woven cotton etc. used for tying or fastening or labeling things, a piece of this stretched across a racetrack at the finish line. 2. a narrow continuous strip of paper or other flexible material (as that on which a teleprinter prints a message), adhesive tape, insulating tape, magnetic tape. 3. a tape measure. 4. a tape recording. **tape** *v.* (**taped, tap·ing**) 1. to tie or fasten with tape. 2. to record on magnetic tape. □**tape cartridge,** a cassette containing recording tape. **tape deck,** *see* **deck**[1]. **tape measure,** a strip of tape or flexible metal marked in inches or centimeters etc. for measuring length. **tape player,** a machine that plays back tape recordings. **tape recorder,** an apparatus for recording sounds on magnetic tape and playing back the recording. **tape recording,** a recording made on magnetic tape.

ta·per (tay-pĕr) *n.* a wick coated thinly with wax, burned to give a light or to light candles etc. **taper** *v.* to make or become gradually narrower. □**taper off,** to become less in amount etc. or cease gradually.

tape-re·cord (tayp-ri-kord) *v.* to record on a tape recorder.

tap·es·try (tap-i-stree) *n.* (*pl.* **-tries**) a piece of strong fabric with a pictorial or ornamental design woven into it or embroidered on it, used for hanging on walls or as an upholstery material.

tape·worm (tayp-wurm) *n.* a tapelike worm that can live as a parasite in the intestines of man and other animals.

tap·i·o·ca (tap-ee-oh-kă) *n.* a starchy substance in hard white grains obtained from cassava and used for making puddings.

ta·pir (tay-pĭr) *n.* (*pl.* **-pirs, -pir**) a small piglike animal with a long flexible snout.

tap·pet (tap-it) *n.* a projection in a piece of machinery that causes a certain movement by tapping against something, as used to open and close a valve.

tap·room (tap-room) *n.* a room where alcoholic drinks are on tap, a bar.

tap·root (tap-root) *n.* the chief root of a plant, growing straight downward.

taps (taps) *n. pl.* a signal given by a bugle for lights to be put out in soldiers' quarters, a similar signal at a military funeral or a memorial service.

tar[1] (tahr) *n.* 1. a thick dark inflammable liquid obtained by distilling wood or coal or peat etc. 2. a similar substance formed by burning tobacco. **tar** *v.* (**tarred, tar·ring**) to coat with tar. □**be tarred with the same brush,** to have the same faults as someone else. **tar and feather,** to punish (a person) by smearing with tar and then covering with feathers.

tar[2] *n.* *(informal)* a sailor.

tar·an·tel·la (tar-ăn-tel-ă) *n.* a rapid whirling dance of southern Italy.

ta·ran·tu·la (tă-ran-chŭ-lă) *n.* (*pl.* **-las, -lae**) 1. a large black spider of southern Europe. 2. a hairy American spider.

tar·boosh (tahr-boosh) *n.* a cap like a fez, worn alone or as part of a turban.

tar·dy (tahr-dee) *adj.* (**tar·di·er, tar·di·est**) *adj.* 1. slow to act or move or happen. 2. behind time. **tar'di·ly** *adv.* **tar'di·ness** *n.*

tare[1] (tair) *n.* a kind of vetch.

tare² *n.* an allowance made to the purchaser for the weight of the container in which goods are packed, or for the vehicle transporting them, in instances where the goods are weighed together with their container or vehicle.

tar·get (tahr-git) *n.* 1. the object or mark that a person tries to hit in shooting etc., a disk painted with concentric circles for this purpose in archery. 2. a person or thing against which criticism or scorn etc. is directed. 3. an objective, a minimum result aimed at, *export targets.* **target** *v.* to make a target of. □**target date,** the date aimed for in planning something.

tar·iff (ta-rif) *n.* 1. a list of fixed charges, especially for rooms and meals etc. at a hotel. 2. duty to be paid on imports or exports.

Tar·mac (tahr-mak) *n.* 1. *(trademark)* material for surfacing roads etc., consisting of broken stone or slag mixed with tar. 2. *tarmac,* an area surfaced with this, especially on an airfield.

tarn (tahrn) *n.* a small mountain lake.

tar·na·tion (tahr-**nay**-shŏn) *interj.* damnation, hell.

tarnation *n.* damnation.

tar·nish (tahr-nish) *v.* 1. to lose or cause (metal) to lose its luster by exposure to air or damp. 2. to stain or blemish (a reputation etc.). **tarnish** *n.* loss of luster, a stain or blemish.

ta·ro (tahr-oh) *n.* (*pl.* **-ros**) 1. a tropical plant with a tuberous root. 2. this root used as food especially in Polynesian islands.

ta·rot (ta-roh) *n.* 1. a deck of twenty-two cards with special pictures, used in fortunetelling. 2. a game played with a pack of seventy-eight cards that are used also for fortunetelling.

tar·pa·per (tahr-pay-pěr) *n.* thick paper impregnated or coated with tar and used as a building material, especially to waterproof roofs.

tar·pau·lin (tahr-paw-lin, tahr-pŭ-) *n.* 1. canvas made waterproof, especially by being tarred. 2. a sheet of this used as a covering.

tar·pon (tahr-pŏn) *n.* (*pl.* **-pons, -pon**) a large silvery game fish common in the Gulf of Mexico.

tar·ra·gon (tar-ă-gon) *n.* a plant with leaves that are used for flavoring salads and in making a vinegar.

tar·ry¹ (tahr-ee) *adj.* (**-ri·er, -ri·est**) of or like tar. **tar'ri·ness** *n.*

tar·ry² (tar-ee) *v.* (**tar·ried, tar·ry·ing**) to delay in coming or going.

tar·sal (tahr-săl) *adj.* of the tarsus. **tarsal** *n.* one of the tarsal bones.

tar·si·er (tahr-si-ĕr) *n.* a small monkeylike animal of the East Indies, with large eyes and a long tail.

tar·sus (tahr-sŭs) *n.* (*pl.* **-si**, *pr.* **-si**) the seven small bones that make up the ankle.

tart¹ (tahrt) *adj.* 1. sharp-tasting, acid. 2. sharp in manner, biting, *a tart reply.* **tart'ly** *adv.* **tart'ness** *n.*

tart² *n.* 1. a pie containing fruit or sweet filling. 2. a piece of pastry with jam etc. on top. 3. *(slang)* a girl or woman of immoral character, a prostitute.

tar·tan (tahr-tăn) *n.* 1. the distinctive pattern of a Highland clan, with colored stripes crossing at right angles. 2. a similar pattern. 3. fabric woven in such a pattern.

tar·tar (tahr-tăr) *n.* 1. a hard chalky deposit that forms on the teeth. 2. a reddish deposit that forms on the side of a cask in which wine is fermented. □**cream of tartar,** *see* **cream.**

Tar·tar (tahr-tăr) *n.* 1. a member of a group of Central Asian peoples including Mongols and Turks. 2. (often *tartar*) a person who is violent-tempered or difficult to deal with.

tar·tar·ic (tahr-tar-ik) *adj.* of or derived from tartar, *tartaric acid.*

tar·tar (tahr-tăr) **sauce, sauce tartare** (tahr-tahr) a sauce of mayonnaise containing chopped pickles etc.

tar·tar (tahr-tăr) **steak** raw ground beefsteak, blended with raw egg, chopped onion, salt, and pepper.

task (task) *n.* a piece of work to be done. **task** *v.* to make great demands upon (a person's powers). □**take a person to task,** to rebuke him. **task force,** a group and resources specially organized for a particular task.

task·mas·ter (task-mas-tĕr) *n.* a person considered with regard to the way in which he imposes tasks, *a hard taskmaster.*

Tas·ma·ni·a (taz-**may**-ni-ă) an island off the southeast coast of Australia. **Tas·ma'ni·an** *adj.* & *n.*

Tass (tahs) *n.* the official news agency of the Soviet Union.

tas·sel (tas-ĕl) *n.* 1. a bunch of threads tied at one end and hanging loosely, used as an ornament. 2. the tassel-like head of certain plants (as corn).

tas·seled (tas-ĕld) *adj.* ornamented with a tassel or tassels.

taste (tayst) *n.* 1. the sensation caused in the tongue by things placed upon it. 2. the faculty of perceiving this sensation. 3. a small quantity of food or drink taken as a sample, a slight experience of something, *a taste of fame.* 4. a liking, *she has always had a taste for foreign travel; add sugar to taste,* in the amount that is liked. 5. ability to perceive and enjoy what is beautiful or harmonious or to know what is fitting for an occasion etc., choice made according to this; *the remark was in bad taste,* was unsuitable or offensive. **taste** *v.* (**tast·ed, tast·ing**) 1. to discover or test the flavor of (a thing) by taking it into the mouth. 2. to be able to perceive flavors. 3. to have a certain flavor, *it tastes sour.* 4. to experience, *taste the joys of freedom.* **tast'er** *n.* □**taste bud,** one of the small projections on the tongue by which flavors are perceived. **to one's taste,** pleasing.

taste·ful (tayst-fŭl) *adj.* showing good taste. **taste'ful·ly** *adv.* **taste'ful·ness** *n.*

taste·less (tayst-lis) *adj.* 1. having no flavor. 2. showing poor taste, *tasteless decorations.* **taste'less·ly** *adv.* **taste'less·ness** *n.*

tast·y (tay-stee) *adj.* (**tast·i·er, tast·i·est**) having a strong flavor, appetizing. **tast'i·ly** *adv.* **tast'i·ness** *n.*

tat¹ (tat) *v.* (**tat·ted, tat·ting**) to do tatting, to make by tatting.

tat² *see* **tit².**

ta·ta·mi (tă-tah-mee) *n.* (*pl.* **-mi, -mis**) a Japanese floor mat made of rice straw.

tat·ter (tat-ĕr) *n.* an irregularly torn piece, especially of cloth, left hanging. **tatter** *v.* to tear to tatters, to become ragged.

tat·ter·de·mal·ion (tat-ĕr-di-mayl-yŏn) *n.* a ragamuffin.

tat·tered (tat-ĕrd) *adj.* ragged, torn into tatters.

tat·ters (tat-ĕrz) *n. pl.* rags, irregularly torn pieces. □**in tatters,** in rags; ripped apart.

tat·ter·sall (tat-ĕr-sawl) *n.* a pattern of colored lines forming squares like a tartan. ▷From R.

Tattersall, an English horseman who died in 1795.

tat·ting (tat-ing) *n.* 1. a kind of lace made by hand with a small shuttle. 2. the process of making this.

tat·tle (tat-ĕl) *v.* (**tat·tled, tat·tling**) to chatter or gossip idly, to reveal information in this way. **tattle** *n.* idle chatter or gossip. **tat'tler** *n.*

tat·tle·tale (tat-ĕl-tayl) *n.* a tattler, especially a child who informs against another.

tat·too[1] (ta-too) *n.* (*pl.* **-toos**) 1. an evening drum or bugle signal calling soldiers back to their quarters. 2. an elaboration of this with music and marching, as an entertainment. 3. a drumming or tapping sound.

tattoo[2] *v.* (**tat·tooed, tat·too·ing**) to mark (skin) with indelible patterns by puncturing it and inserting a dye, to make (a pattern) in this way. **tattoo** *n.* a tattooed pattern. **tat·too'er** *n.* **tat·too'ist** *n.*

tau (taw) *n.* the nineteenth letter of the Greek alphabet (Tτ).

taught *see* **teach.**

taunt (tawnt) *v.* to jeer at, to try to provoke with scornful remarks or criticism. **taunt** *n.* a taunting remark. **taunt'ing·ly** *adv.* **taunt'er** *n.*

taupe (tohp) *n.* a dark gray color with a brownish tinge.

Tau·rus (tor-ŭs) *n.* a sign of the zodiac, the Bull. **Tau·re·an** (tor-i-ăn) *adj.* & *n.*

taut (tawt) *adj.* stretched firmly, not slack. **taut'ly** *adv.* **taut'ness** *n.*

tau·tol·o·gy (taw-tol-ŏ-jee) *n.* (*pl.* **-gies**) saying of the same thing twice over in different words, especially as a fault of style, such as *they arrived one after the other in succession.* **tau·tol'o·gous** *adj.* **tau·to·log·i·cal** (taw-tŏ-loj-i-kăl) *adj.* **tau·to·log'i·cal·ly** *adv.*

tav·ern (tav-ĕrn) *n.* 1. a bar. 2. (*old use*) an inn.

taw (taw). *n.* 1. a large marble for shooting in the game of marbles. 2. the line from which the players shoot.

taw·dry (taw-dree) *adj.* (**-dri·er, -dri·est**) showy or gaudy but without real value. **taw'dri·ly** *adv.* **taw'dri·ness** *n.*

taw·ny (taw-nee) *adj.* (**-ni·er, -ni·est**) brownish yellow, brownish orange. **taw'ni·ness** *n.*

tax (taks) *n.* 1. a sum of money to be paid by people or business firms to a government, to be used for public purposes, *a tax on one's strength.* **tax** *v.* 1. to impose a tax on, to require (a person) to pay tax. 2. to make heavy demands on. 3. to accuse in a challenging or reproving way, *taxed him with having left the door unlocked.* **tax'er** *n.* **tax·a·tion** (tak-say-shŏn) *n.* □**tax deduction**, an expense that can be deducted from income before computing the tax; a person whose support is considered to be such an expense. **tax evasion**, the crime of avoiding payment of some or all the tax that is due. **tax loss**, a net capital loss established at year's end and used as a tax deduction. **tax rate**, the percentage of value or income etc. required to be paid in taxes. **tax return**, the printed form that is filled in and sent with a tax payment. **tax shelter**, a financial operation for the purpose of acquiring expenses or depreciation allowances etc. that will reduce income tax due. **tax stamp**, a stamp placed on certain products, papers, etc. to indicate that taxes have been paid.

tax·a·ble (tak-să-bĕl) *adj.* able or liable to be taxed.

tax·de·duct·i·ble (taks-di-duk-ti-bĕl) *adj.* allowed

to be deducted from income before computing the tax.

tax-ex·empt (taks-ig-zempt) *adj.* not taxable.

tax·i (tak-see) *n.* (*pl.* **tax·is, tax·ies**) a taxicab. **taxi** *v.* (**tax·ied, tax·i·ing** *or* **tax·y·ing**) 1. to go or convey in a taxi. 2. (of aircraft) to move along ground or water under its own power, especially before or after flying. □**taxi dancer**, a dancing partner who is paid for each dance.

tax·i·cab (tak-see-kab) *n.* a car that carries paying passengers, usually with a meter to record the fare payable.

tax·i·der·my (tak-si-dur-mee) *n.* the art of preparing and mounting the skins of animals in lifelike form. **tax'i·der·mist** *n.*

tax·i·me·ter (tak-see-mee-tĕr) *n.* an automatic device fitted to a taxicab and indicating the fare due for the distance traveled.

tax·on·o·my (tak-son-ŏ-mee) *n.* the principles or science of classification, especially in biology. **tax·on'o·mist** *n.* **tax·o·nom·ic** (tak-sŏ-nom-ik) *adj.* **tax·o·nom'i·cal·ly** *adv.*

tax·pay·er (taks-pay-ĕr) *n.* a person who pays tax (especially income tax). **tax'pay·ing** *adj.*

Tay·lor (tay-lŏr), **Zach·a·ry** (1784–1850) the twelfth president of the U.S. 1849–50.

Tb *symbol* terbium.

tb. *abbr.* tablespoon.

T.B. *abbr.* tuberculosis.

T-bar (tee-bahr) **lift** a ski lift with T-shaped bars against which skiers may lean as they are carried uphill while wearing their skis.

T-bone (tee-bohn) **steak** steak from the thin end of the loin, containing a T-shaped bone.

tbs., tbsp. *abbr.* tablespoon(s).

Tc *symbol* technetium.

TC *abbr.* teachers college.

TCBM *abbr.* transcontinental ballistic missile.

TD *abbr.* 1. touchdown. 2. Treasury Department.

TDY *abbr.* temporary duty.

Te *symbol* tellurium.

tea (tee) *n.* 1. the dried leaves of the tea plant. 2. the hot drink that is made by steeping these in boiling water. 3. a drink made by steeping the leaves of other plants in water, *camomile tea; herb tea.* 4. a late afternoon social gathering or reception at which tea and coffee are served. □**tea bag**, a small porous bag holding about a teaspoonful of tea for steeping. **tea biscuit**, a kind of small soft sweetened biscuit. **tea cozy**, a cover placed over a teapot to keep the tea hot. **tea dance**, an afternoon tea with dancing. **tea leaf**, a leaf of tea, especially after steeping. **tea party**, a party at which tea is served. **tea plant**, an evergreen shrub grown in China, India, etc. **tea rose**, a kind of delicately scented rose. **tea service**, a teapot with matching containers for sugar and cream and sometimes other pieces. **tea set**, a set of cups and plates etc. for serving tea. **tea table**, a small table for serving tea. **tea wagon**, a small table with wheels, used for serving tea.

tea·cake (tee-kayk) *n.* a small sweet cake.

tea·cart (tee-kahrt) *n.* a tea wagon.

teach (teech) *v.* (**taught,** *pr.* tawt, **teach·ing**) 1. to impart information or skill to (a person) or about (a subject etc.). 2. to do this for a living. 3. to put forward as a fact or principle; *Christ taught forgiveness,* taught that we must forgive our enemies. 4. to cause to adopt (a practice etc.) by example or experience, *(informal)* to deter by punishment etc., *that will teach you not to meddle.*

teach·a·ble (tee-chă-bĕl) *adj.* 1. able to learn by being taught. 2. (of a subject) able to be taught.

teach·er (tee-chĕr) *n.* a person who teaches others, especially in a school. □**teacher's aide,** a classroom assistant to a schoolteacher. **teachers college,** a college where the students are trained to be teachers in primary or secondary schools.

teach·in (teech-in) *n.* a program of lecture and discussion on a subject of topical interest, conducted as a protest against the policies of a government, institution, etc.

teach·ing (tee-ching) *n.* what is taught, *the teachings of the church.* □**teaching aid,** something used by a teacher to help to instruct pupils or to arouse their interest. **teaching assistant** *or* **fellow,** a graduate student who receives a grant for which some time must be spent teaching or assisting a teacher. **teaching fellowship,** a graduate scholarship that requires the recipient to teach while pursuing his studies. **teaching hospital,** a hospital where medical students are taught. **teaching machine,** a mechanical or electronic device for giving instruction.

tea·cup (tee-kup) *n.* a cup from which tea is drunk.

tea·house (tee-hows) *n.* (*pl.* **-hous·es,** *pr.* -howziz) a restaurant in the Far East in which tea and other refreshments are served.

teak (teek) *n.* 1. (also **teakwood**) the strong heavy wood of a tall evergreen Asian tree, used for making furniture and in shipbuilding. 2. the tree itself.

tea·ket·tle (tee-ket-ĕl) *n.* a kettle with a handle and a spout, used to boil water.

teal (teel) *n.* (*pl.* **teals, teal**) a kind of small freshwater duck. □**teal blue,** a deep greenish blue.

team (teem) *n.* 1. a set of players forming one side in certain games and sports. 2. a set of people working together. 3. two or more animals harnessed together to draw a vehicle or farm implement. **team** *v.* to combine into a team or set or for a common purpose. □**team spirit,** willingness to act for the good of one's group rather than oneself.

team·mate (teem-mayt) *n.* a fellow member of a team.

team·ster (teem-stĕr) *n.* 1. a truck driver, especially a member of the Teamsters Union. 2. (*old use*) the driver of a team of horses.

team·work (teem-wurk) *n.* organized cooperation.

tea·pot (tee-pot) *n.* a vessel with a lid and spout in which tea is made and from which it is poured.

tear[1] (tair) *v.* (**tore,** *pr.* tohr, **torn,** *pr.* tohrn, **tear·ing**) 1. to pull forcibly apart or away or to pieces. 2. to make (a hole or a split) in this way. 3. to become torn, to be able to be torn, *paper tears easily.* 4. to subject (a person etc.) to conflicting desires or demands, *torn between love and duty.* 5. to run, walk, or travel hurriedly. **tear** *n.* a hole or split caused by tearing. □**tear oneself away,** to leave in spite of a strong desire to stay. **tear one's hair,** to pull it in anger or perplexity or despair.

tear[2] (teer) *n.* a drop of the salty water that appears in or flows from the eye as the result of grief or other emotion, or irritation by fumes etc. **tear·y** *adj.* (**tear·i·er, tear·i·est**) □**in tears,** shedding tears. **tear gas,** a gas that causes severe irritation of the eyes.

tear·drop (teer-drop) *n.* a single tear.

tear·ful (teer-fŭl) *adj.* shedding or ready to shed tears, sad. **tear'ful·ly** *adv.*

tear·jerk·er (teer-jur-kĕr) *n.* (*informal*) a story or

motion picture etc. calculated to produce tears of sadness or sympathy.

tea·room (tee-room) *n.* a restaurant serving tea or coffee etc. and light meals, favored by women customers.

tease (teez) *v.* (**teased, teas·ing**) 1. to try to provoke in a playful or unkind way by jokes or questions or petty annoyances. 2. to beg or urge persistently. 3. to pick (wool etc.) into separate strands. 4. to fluff (hair) by holding the ends and combing toward the scalp. 5. to brush up the nap on (cloth). **tease** *n.* a person who is fond of teasing others. **teas'ing·ly** *adv.*

teas·er (tee-zĕr) *n.* (*informal*) 1. one who teases. 2. a problem that is difficult to solve.

tea·spoon (tee-spoon) *n.* 1. a small spoon for stirring tea. 2. a measurement used in cooking, = one teaspoonful. **tea'spoon·ful** *n.* (*pl.* **-fuls**) ⅙ fluid ounce.

teat (teet, tit) *n.* a nipple on an animal's milk-secreting organ.

tea·time (tee-tɪm) *n.* the time at which tea is served, usually in the late afternoon.

tech. *abbr.* 1. technical. 2. technician. 3. technological. 4. technology.

tech·ne·ti·um (tek-nee-shi-ŭm) *n.* an artificially produced radioactive metallic element.

tech·nic (tek-nik) *n.* technique.

tech·ni·cal (tek-ni-kăl) *adj.* 1. of the mechanical arts and applied sciences, *a technical education* or *school.* 2. of a particular subject or craft etc. or its techniques, *the technical terms of chemistry; technical skill.* 3. (of a book etc.) requiring specialized knowledge, using technical terms. 4. in a strict legal sense, *technical assault.* **tech'ni·cal·ly** *adv.* **tech'ni·cal·ness** *n.* □**technical knockout,** (in boxing) a referee's ending of a match because one of the boxers is unable to continue, his opponent being declared the winner. **technical school,** a school that teaches applied science or vocational subjects. **technical sergeant,** a noncommissioned officer in the U.S. Air Force ranking next above a staff sergeant.

tech·ni·cal·i·ty (tek-ni-kal-i-tee) *n.* (*pl.* **-ties**) 1. being technical. 2. a technical word or phrase or point, *was acquitted on a technicality.*

tech·ni·cian (tek-nish-ăn) *n.* an expert in the techniques of a particular subject or craft.

Tech·ni·col·or (tek-ni-kul-ŏr) *n.* (*trademark*) a process for making motion pictures in color.

tech·nique (tek-neek) *n.* the method of doing or performing something (especially in an art or science), skill in this.

tech·noc·ra·cy (tek-nok-ră-see) *n.* (*pl.* **-cies**) government by technical experts, as scientists, engineers, etc. **tech·no·crat** (tek-nŏ-krat) *n.* **tech·no·crat·ic** (tek-nŏ-krat-ik) *adj.*

tech·nol·o·gist (tek-nol-ŏ-jist) *n.* an expert in technology.

tech·nol·o·gy (tek-nol-ŏ-jee) *n.* 1. the scientific study of mechanical arts and applied sciences (as engineering). 2. these subjects, their practical application in industry etc. **tech·no·log·i·cal** (tek-nŏ-loj-i-kăl) *adj.* **tech·no·log'i·cal·ly** *adv.*

tec·ton·ics (tek-ton-iks) *n.* 1. the study of geological structural features. 2. the whole art of producing beautiful and useful buildings. **tec·ton'ic** *adj.*

ted·dy (ted-ee) **bear** a soft furry toy bear.

Te De·um (tay day-ŭm) a Latin hymn beginning "Te Deum laudamus" (= we praise thee O God).

te·di·ous (tee-di-ŭs) *adj.* tiresome because of its

length or slowness or dullness, boring. **te′di·ous·ly** adv. **te′di·ous·ness** n.

te·di·um (tee-di-ŭm) n. tediousness.

tee (tee) n. 1. the cleared space from which a player strikes the ball in golf at the beginning of play for each hole. 2. a small peg on which the ball is placed for being struck. **tee** v. **(teed, tee·ing)** to place (a ball) on a tee in golf. □**tee off,** to play the ball from the tee; (slang) to make angry. **tee up,** to tee.

teem[1] (teem) v. 1. to be full of, the river was teeming with fish. 2. to be present in large numbers, fish teem in that river.

teem[2] v. (of water or rain etc.) to pour.

teen·age (teen-ayj) adj. of teenagers.

teen·aged (teen-ayjd) adj. in one's teens.

teen·ag·er (teen-ay-jĕr) n. a person in his or her teens.

teens (teenz) n. pl. the years of a person's age from 13 to 19.

teen·sy-ween·sy (teen-see-ween-see) adj. (informal) tiny.

tee·ny (tee-nee) adj. **(-ni·er, -ni·est)** (informal) tiny.

tee·ny·bop·per (tee-nee-bop-ĕr) n. (informal) a teenage girl who follows the latest fashions in clothes and pop music etc.

tee·ny-wee·ny (tee-nee-wee-nee) adj. (informal) tiny.

tee·pee = **tepee.**

tee shirt = **T-shirt.**

tee·ter (tee-tĕr) v. to stand or move unsteadily.

tee·ter-tot·ter (tee-tĕr-tot-ĕr) n. a seesaw. **teeter-totter** v. to seesaw.

teeth see **tooth.**

teethe (tee*th*) v. **(teethed, teeth·ing)** (of a baby) to have its first teeth beginning to grow through the gums. □**teething ring,** a small ring for a baby to bite on while teething.

tee·to·tal (tee-toh-tăl) adj. abstaining completely from alcoholic drinks. **tee·to′tal·er** n. **tee·to′tal·ism** n.

Tef·lon (tef-lon) n. (trademark) a plastic used to line pans etc. to prevent sticking.

Te·gu·ci·gal·pa (te-goo-see-gahl-pah) the capital of Honduras.

Te·he·ran, Te·hran (te-rahn) the capital of Iran.

tek·tite (tek-tīt) n. a small roundish glassy body thought to originate in outer space. **tek·tit·ic** (tek-tit-ik) adj.

tel. abbr. 1. telegram. 2. telegraph. 3. telephone.

tel·e·cast (tel-ĕ-kast) v. **(tel·e·cast** or **tel·e·cast·ed, tel·e·cast·ing)** to broadcast by television. **telecast** n. a television broadcast. **tel′e·cast·er** n.

tel·e·com·mu·ni·ca·tions (tel-ĕ-kŏ-myoo-ni-kay-shŏnz) n. the means of communication over long distances, as by cable or telegraph or telephone or radio or television.

teleg. abbr. telegraphy.

tel·e·gen·ic (tel-ĕ-jen-ik) adj. (of a person) appearing attractive on television.

tel·e·gram (tel-ĕ-gram) n. a message sent by telegraph.

tel·e·graph (tel-ĕ-graf) n. a system or apparatus for sending messages over a distance, especially by transmission of electrical impulses along wires. **telegraph** v. to send (a message) or communicate with (a person) by telegraph.

te·leg·ra·pher (tĕ-leg-ră-fĕr) n. a person whose job is to send and receive messages by telegraph.

te·leg·ra·phy (tĕ-leg-ră-fee) n. the process of communication by telegraph. **tel·e·graph·ic** (tel-ĕ-graf-ik) adj. **tel·e·graph′i·cal·ly** adv. □**telegraphic address,** an abbreviated or other registered address for use in telegrams.

tel·e·ki·ne·sis (tel-ĕ-ki-nee-sis) n. the process of moving things without touching them and without using ordinary physical means.

te·lem·e·ter (tĕ-lem-ĕ-tĕr) n. an apparatus for recording the readings of an instrument that is at a distance, usually by means of radio. **telemeter** v. to record readings thus, to transmit (readings) to a telemeter. **te·lem′e·try** n. **tel·e·met·ric** (tel-ĕ-met-rik) adj.

tel·e·path·ic (tel-ĕ-path-ik) adj. of or using telepathy, able to communicate by telepathy. **tel·e·path′i·cal·ly** adv.

te·lep·a·thy (tĕ-lep-ĕ-thee) n. communication from one mind to another without the use of speech or writing or gestures etc.

tel·e·phone (tel-ĕ-fohn) n. 1. a system of transmitting sound (especially speech) over a distance by wire or cord or radio. 2. an instrument used in this, with a receiver and mouthpiece and a bell to indicate an incoming call. **telephone** v. **(tel·e·phoned, tel·e·phon·ing)** to send (a message) or speak to (a person) by telephone. **tel′e·phon·er** n. **tel·e·phon·ic** (tel-ĕ-fon-ik) adj. □**telephone book** or **directory,** a book listing the names and telephone numbers of people who have a telephone. **telephone booth,** a booth containing a telephone for public use. **telephone number,** a number assigned to a particular instrument and used in making connection. **telephone pole,** a pole that supports wires.

te·leph·o·ny (tĕ-lef-ŏ-nee) n. the process of transmitting sound by telephone.

tel·e·pho·to (tel-ĕ-foh-toh) adj. telephoto. □**telephoto lens,** a lens producing a large image of a distant object that is photographed.

tel·e·pho·to·graph (tel-ĕ-foh-tŏ-graf) n. a photograph of a distant object taken by a camera of a telescopic and an ordinary lens combined, giving a large image. **tel·e·pho·tog·ra·phy** (tel-ĕ-foh-tŏ-graf-ik) adj. **telephotography** (tel-ĕ-foh-tŏg-ră-fee) n.

tel·e·play (tel-ĕ-play) n. a play written for television.

Tel·e·promp·ter (tel-ĕ-prŏmp-tĕr) n. (trademark) a device by which a person reading a script before a television camera can read a script while appearing to look at the camera.

tel·e·scope (tel-ĕ-skohp) n. an optical instrument using lenses or mirrors to make distant objects appear larger when viewed through it. **telescope** v. **(tel·e·scoped, tel·e·scop·ing)** 1. to make or become shorter by sliding overlapping sections one into another. 2. to compress or become compressed forcibly. 3. to condense so as to occupy less space or time. □**radio telescope,** an apparatus for collecting radio waves emitted by celestial objects and recording their intensity. **tel·e·scop·ic** (tel-ĕ-skop-ik) adj. 1. of a telescope, emitted by a telescope. 2. visible only through a telescope. 3. capable of being magnified. □**telescopic stars,** stars visible only through a telescope. **telescopic antenna,** an antenna fitted with sections that slide into each other. **telescopic sight,** a telescope fitted to a gun for magnifying the image of the target. **tel·e·scop′i·cal·ly** adv.

tel·e·thon (tel-ĕ-thon) n. a televised fund-raising program of long duration.

tele·pr…

Tel·e·type (tel-ĕ-tɪp) *n.* *(trademark)* a teletype-writer.

tel·e·type·writ·er (tel-ĕ-tɪp-rɪ-tĕr) *n.* a telegraph instrument for transmitting messages by typing. **tel′e·typ·ist** *n.*

tel·e·view (tel-ĕ-vyoo) *v.* to watch by means of television. **tel′e·view·er** *n.*

tel·e·vise (tel-ĕ-vɪz) *v.* **(tel·e·vised, tel·e·vis·ing)** to transmit by television.

tel·e·vi·sion (tel-ĕ-vizh-ŏn) *n.* 1. a system for re-producing on a screen a view of scenes or events or plays etc. by radio transmission. 2. (also *television set*) an apparatus with a screen for re-ceiving pictures transmitted in this way. 3. televised programs, television as a medium of communication.

Tel·ex (tel-eks) *n.* 1. *(trademark)* a system for send-ing or receiving messages on a teletypewriter using public telecommunication lines. 2. *telex,* a mes-sage sent by this. **telex** *v.* to send (a message), to communicate with (a person) thus.

tell (tel) *v.* **(told, tell·ing)** 1. to make known, espe-cially in spoken or written words. 2. to give in-formation to. 3. to utter, *tell the truth.* 4. to reveal a secret, *promise you won't tell.* 5. to decide or ̄ ̄mine, *how do you tell which button to press?* ̄ ̄tinguish, *I can't tell him from his brother.* ̄ ̄ce a noticeable effect, *the strain began* ̄ ̄im. 8. to direct or order, *tell them to* ̄ ̄**ble** *adj.* □**tell fortunes,** see ̄ ̄**l off,** *(informal)* to reprimand or ̄ ̄, *(informal)* to reveal the activities ̄ ̄ telling others. **tell tales,** to report ̄ ̄te ̄be secret. **tell the time,** to read ̄ ̄clock. **you're telling me,** *(slang)* ̄ ̄to ̄of that.

̄ ̄**tell·i** ̄ a person who tells or gives ̄ ̄strik ̄ething. 2. a person appointed ̄ ̄**tell·tal** ̄bank cashier. **tell′er·ship** *n.* ̄ ̄2. a me ̄having a noticeable effect, ̄ ̄**telltale** ̄ument. **tell′ing·ly** *adv.* ̄ ̄a telltale ̄ a person who tells tales. ̄ ̄**tel·lu·ri·an** ̄that serves as an indicator. ̄ ̄**tel·lu·ri·um** (̄or indicating something, ̄ ̄silver-white e ̄*adj.* of the earth. ̄ ̄**tel·ly** (tel-ee) ̄ ̄sion set. ̄ ̄*n.* ̄. a rare brittle lustrous ̄ ̄**tem·blor** (tem-blŏr) ̄) television, a televi- ̄ ̄confuse ̄*temblor* w ̄ ̄**te·mer·i·ty** (tĕ-mer-ı̆-thquake. ▷Do not ̄ ̄**temp** (temp) *n.* (inform ̄ ̄**temp.** *abbr.* 1. temperat ̄dacity, rashness. ̄ ̄**tem·per** (tem-pĕr) *n.* 1. ̄orary employee. ̄ ̄regards calmness or ang ̄of the mind as ̄ ̄a fit of anger, *in a temp* ̄ood temper. 2. ̄ ̄provocation, *keep or lose o* ̄lmness under ̄ ̄dency to have fits of anger, ̄per. 4. a ten- ̄ ̄the condition of a tempered me ̄ temper. 5. ̄ ̄ness and elasticity. **temper** *v.* ̄gards hard- ̄ ̄or be brought to the required de ̄ing (metal) ̄ ̄and elasticity by heating and the ̄ hardness ̄ ̄bring (clay etc.) to the required c ̄ng. 2. to ̄ ̄moistening and mixing. 3. to moder ̄ency by ̄ ̄the effects of; *temper justice with merc* ̄ soften ̄ ̄ful in awarding punishment. ̄ ̄merci- ̄ ̄**tem·per·a** (tem-pĕ-rä) *n.* 1. a method of ̄ ̄using colors mixed with egg. 2. a paintin ̄nting ̄ ̄in this way. ̄done

tem·per·a·ment (tem-pĕ-ră-mĕnt) *n.* 1. a person's nature as it controls the way he behaves and feels and thinks, *a nervous temperament.* 2. a nature that is liable to produce temperamental behavior.

tem·per·a·men·tal (tem-pĕ-ră-men-tăl) *adj.* 1. of or in a person's temperament. 2. not having a calm temperament, having fits of excitable or moody behavior. **tem·per·a·men′tal·ly** *adv.*

tem·per·ance (tem-pĕ-răns) *n.* 1. self-restraint in one's behavior or in eating and drinking. 2. total abstinence from alcoholic drinks.

tem·per·ate (tem-pĕ-rit) *adj.* 1. self-restrained in one's behavior, moderate. 2. (of climate) having a mild temperature without extremes of heat and cold. **tem′per·ate·ly** *adv.* **tem′per·ate·ness** *n.* □**Temperate Zone,** the area of Earth's sur-face between the Arctic Circle and the tropic of Cancer or between the Antarctic Circle and the tropic of Capricorn, with a temperate climate.

tem·per·a·ture (tem-pĕ-ră-chŭr) *n.* 1. the inten-sity of heat or cold in a body or room or country etc. 2. a measure of this shown by a thermometer. 3. an abnormally high temperature of the body, *have a temperature.* □**take a person's tem-perature,** to measure it in order to ascertain any variation from normal.

tem·pest (tem-pist) *n.* a violent storm. □**tempest in a teapot,** great excitement over a trivial mat-ter.

tem·pes·tu·ous (tem-pes-choo-ŭs) *adj.* stormy, full of commotion. **tem·pes′tu·ous·ly** *adv.* **tem·pes′tu·ous·ness** *n.*

Tem·plar (tem-plăr) *n.* a member of a medieval religious and military order *(Knights Templars)* for protection of pilgrims to the Holy Land.

tem·plate (tem-plit) *n.* 1. a pattern or gauge, usu-ally of thin board or metal, used as a guide for cutting metal or stone or wood etc. 2. a timber or metal plate used to distribute weight in a wall or under a beam.

tem·ple[1] (tem-pĕl) *n.* a building dedicated to the presence or service of a god or gods.

temple[2] *n.* the flat part at each side of the head between forehead and ear.

tem·po (tem-poh) *n.* (*pl.* **-pos, -pi,** *pr.* -pee) 1. the time or speed or rhythm of a piece of music, *in waltz tempo.* 2. the pace of any movement or activity, *the tempo of the war is quickening.*

tem·po·ral[1] (tem-pŏ-răl) *adj.* 1. secular, of worldly affairs as opposed to spiritual. 2. of or denoting time.

temporal[2] *adj.* of the temple(s) of the head, *the temporal artery.*

tem·po·rar·y (tem-pŏ-rer-ee) *adj.* lasting or meant to last for a limited time only, not permanent. **temporary** *n.* (*pl.* **-rar·ies**) a person employed temporarily. **tem′po·rar·i·ness** *n.* **tem·po·rar·i·ly** (tem-pŏ-rer-ĭ-lee) *adv.*

tem·po·rize (tem-pŏ-rɪz) *v.* **(tem·po·rized, tem·po·riz·ing)** to compromise temporarily, or avoid giving a definite answer or decision, in order to gain time. **tem′po·riz·er** *n.* **tem·po·ri·za·tion** (tem-pŏ-ri-zay-shŏn) *n.*

tempt (tempt) *v.* 1. to persuade or try to persuade (especially into doing something wrong or unwise) by the prospect of pleasure or advantage. 2. to arouse a desire in, to attract; *I'm tempted to ques-tion this,* feel inclined to do so. 3. to risk provoking (fate or Providence) by deliberate rashness. **tempt′er** *n.* **tempt·ress** (temp-tris) *n. fem.*

temp·ta·tion (temp-tay-shŏn) *n.* 1. tempting, be-

ing tempted. 2. something that tempts or attracts.
tempt·ing (temp-ting) *adj.* attractive, inviting, *a tempting offer.* **tempt'ing·ly** *adv.*

tem·pu·ra (tem-poo-rah) *n.* a Japanese dish of fish or shellfish, deep-fried in a batter.

ten (ten) *adj. & n.* one more than nine (10, X). □**ten-cent store,** a store selling a variety of inexpensive items. **Ten Commandments,** the laws given to Moses by God, the foundation of Judeo-Christian morality. **ten-gallon hat,** a cowboy's large broad-brimmed hat.

ten·a·ble (ten-ă-běl) *adj.* able to be defended against attack or objection, *a tenable position* or *theory.* **ten'a·bly** *adv.* **ten'a·ble·ness** *n.* **ten·a·bil·i·ty** (ten-ă-bil-i-tee) *n.*

te·na·cious (tě-nay-shŭs) *adj.* 1. holding or clinging firmly to something, such as rights or principles. 2. (of memory) retentive. 3. sticking firmly together or to an object or surface. **te·na'cious·ly** *adv.* **te·nac·i·ty** (tě-nas-i-tee) *n.*

ten·an·cy (ten-ăn-see) *n.* (*pl.* **-cies**) 1. the use of land or buildings as a tenant. 2. the period of this.

ten·ant (ten-ănt) *n.* 1. a person who rents land or buildings from a landlord. 2. (in law) an occupant or owner of land or a building. **ten'ant·less** *adj.* □**tenant farmer,** a farmer who farms someone else's land and pays rent in cash or a share of the produce.

ten·ant·ry (ten-ăn-tree) *n.* the tenants of land or buildings on one estate.

tend[1] (tend) *v.* to take care of or look after (a person or thing).

tend[2] *v.* 1. to be likely to behave in a certain way or to have a certain characteristic. 2. to have a certain influence, *recent laws tend to increase customers' rights.* 3. to take a certain direction, *the track tends upward.*

ten·den·cy (ten-děn-see) *n.* (*pl.* **-cies**) 1. the way a person or thing tends to be or behave, *a tendency to fat* or *toward fatness; homicidal tendencies.* 2. the direction in which something moves or changes, a trend, *an upward tendency.*

ten·den·tious (ten-den-shŭs) *adj.* (of a speech or piece of writing etc.) aimed at helping a cause, not impartial. **ten·den'tious·ly** *adv.* **ten·den'tious·ness** *n.*

ten·der[1] (ten-děr) *adj.* 1. not tough or hard, easy to chew, *tender meat.* 2. easily damaged, delicate, *tender plants; of tender age,* young and vulnerable. 3. sensitive, painful when touched. 4. easily moved to pity or sympathy, *a tender heart.* 5. loving, gentle. **ten'der·ly** *adv.* **ten'der·ness** *n.*

tender[2] *v.* 1. to offer formally, *tender one's resignation.* 2. to make a tender (for goods or work). **tender** *n.* a formal offer to supply goods or carry out work or buy at a stated price; *put work out to tender,* ask for such offers. **ten'der·a·ble** *adj.* **ten'der·er** *n.* □**legal tender,** currency that must, by law, be accepted in payment.

tender[3] *n.* 1. a person who tends or looks after something. 2. a vessel or vehicle traveling to and from a larger one to convey stores or passengers etc. 3. a car attached to a steam locomotive, carrying fuel and water etc.

ten·der·foot (ten-děr-fuut) *n.* (*pl.* **-foots, -feet**) a newcomer who is unused to hardships, an inexperienced person.

ten·der·heart·ed (ten-děr-hahr-tid) *adj.* having a tender heart, easily moved by pity. **ten'der·heart·ed·ness** *n.*

ten·der·ize (ten-dě-rīz) *v.* (**ten·der·ized, ten·der·iz·ing**) to make more tender. **ten'der·iz·er** *n.*

ten·der·loin (ten-děr-loin) *n.* 1. the middle part of a beef or pork loin. 2. *(informal)* the district of a city known for its corruption and high crime rate.

ten·don (ten-dŏn) *n.* a strong band or cord of tissue connecting a muscle to some other part. **ten·di·nous** (ten-dĭ-nŭs) *adj.*

ten·dril (ten-dril) *n.* 1. a threadlike part by which a climbing plant clings to a support. 2. a slender curl of hair etc.

ten·e·brous (ten-ě-brŭs), **te·neb·ri·ous** (tě-neb-ri-ŭs) *adj. (old use)* dark, gloomy.

ten·e·ment (ten-ě-měnt) *n.* 1. a badly maintained apartment house, generally in a crowded urban area. 2. any house with apartments for rent. 3. (in law) land or other permanent property held by a tenant, *lands and tenements.*

ten·et (ten-it) *n.* a firm belief or principle or doctrine of a person or group.

ten·fold (ten-fohld) *adj. & adv.* ten times as much or as many.

10–4 (ten-fohr) *n.* (in CB radio) a term meaning "OK," or "yes" etc.

Tenn. *abbr.* Tennessee.

Ten·nes·see (ten-ě-see) a state of the U.S. **Ten·nes·see'an** *adj. & n.*

ten·nis (ten-is) *n.* a game for two or four persons played by striking a ball with rackets over a low net. □**tennis ball,** a fuzzy-coated rubber ball used for playing tennis. **tennis elbow,** a sprained elbow caused by playing tennis. **tennis shoe,** a very flexible shoe with a soft rubber sole, worn for playing tennis.

ten·on (ten-ŏn) *n.* a projection shaped to fit into a mortise.

ten·or (ten-ŏr) *n.* 1. the general routine or course of something, *disrupting the even tenor of his life.* 2. the general meaning or drift, *the tenor of his lecture.* 3. the highest normal adult male singing voice, a singer with this, a part written for it. 4. a musical instrument with approximately the range of a tenor voice, *tenor saxophone.*

ten·pen·ny (ten-pen-ee) *adj.* costing ten pennies. □**tenpenny nail,** a three-inch-long nail.

ten·pin (ten-pin) *n.* 1. a bowling pin. 2. *tenpins,* the game of bowling with ten bowling pins.

tense[1] (tens) *n.* any of the forms of a verb that indicate the time of action etc. as past or present or future. □**present tense,** I come, you come, he comes. **past tense,** I came. **future tense,** I shall come, you will come, he will come, we shall come, they will come. **present perfect tense,** I have come, you have come, he has come, we have come. **past perfect tense,** I had come. **future perfect tense,** I shall have come, you will have come, we shall have come, they will have come.

tense[2] *adj.* (**tens·er, tens·est**) 1. stretched tightly. 2. with muscles tight in attentiveness for what may happen. 3). unable to relax, edgy. 4. causing tenseness, *a tense moment.* **tense** *v.* (**tensed, tens·ing**) to make or become tense. **tense'ly** *adv.* **tense'ness** *n.*

ten·sile (ten-sĭl) *adj.* 1. of tension; *tensile strength,* resistance to breaking under tension. 2. capable of being stretched.

ten·sion (ten-shŏn) *n.* 1. stretching, being stretched. 2. tenseness, the condition when feelings are tense. 3. the effect produced by forces pulling against each other. 4. electromotive force, voltage, *high-tension wires*. **ten′sion·al** *adj.*

tent (tent) *n.* a portable shelter or dwelling made of canvas etc. **tent** *v.* 1. to camp in a tent. 2. to cover (as) with a tent. □**tent caterpillar,** a caterpillar that lives in groups in large webs spun on trees. **tent show,** a show presented in a tent, as a circus.

ten·ta·cle (ten-tă-kĕl) *n.* a slender flexible part extending from the body of certain animals (as snails, octopuses), used for feeling or grasping things or moving. **ten′ta·cled** *adj.* **ten·tac·u·lar** (ten-tak-yū-lăr) *adj.*

ten·ta·tive (ten-tă-tiv) *adj.* hesitant, not definite, done as a trial, *a tentative suggestion.* **ten′ta·tive·ly** *adv.* **ten′ta·tive·ness** *n.*

ten·ter·hook (ten-tĕr-huuk) *n.* each of the hooks that hold cloth stretched for drying during its manufacture. □**on tenterhooks,** in a state of suspense or strain because of uncertainty.

tenth (tenth) *adj. & n.* 1. next after ninth. 2. one of ten equal parts of a thing. **tenth′ly** *adv.*

10–13 (ten-thur-teen) *n.* (in CB radio) weather and road conditions.

ten·u·ous (ten-yoo-ŭs) *adj.* 1. very thin in form or consistency, *tenuous threads.* 2. having little substance or validity, very slight, *tenuous distinctions.* **ten′u·ous·ly** *adv.* **ten′u·ous·ness** *n.* **ten·u·i·ty** (tĕ-noo-i-tee) *n.*

ten·ure (ten-yŭr) *n.* 1. the holding of office or of land or other permanent property or accommodation etc., the period or manner of this, *freehold tenure.* 2. a permanent appointment as a teacher etc.

ten·ured (ten-yŭrd) *adj.* having tenure.

te·o·sin·te (tay-oh-sin-tee) *n.* a tall grass of Mexico and Central America resembling corn and used as fodder.

te·pee (tee-pee) *n.* a conical tent of the American Indians, made of skins, cloth, or canvas.

tep·id (tep-id) *adj.* slightly warm, lukewarm. **tep′id·ly** *adv.* **tep′id·ness** *n.* **te·pid·i·ty** (te-pid-i-tee) *n.*

te·qui·la (tĕ-kee-lă) *n.* a Mexican liquor distilled from mescal.

ter. *abbr.* 1. terrace. 2. territorial. 3. territory.

ter·bi·um (tur-bi-ŭm) *n.* a metallic element of the lanthanide series.

ter·cen·te·nar·y (tur-sen-tĕ-ner-ee) *n.* (*pl.* **-nar·ies**) a 300th anniversary. **ter·cen·ten·ni·al** (tur-sen-ten-i-ăl) *n. & adj.*

term (turm) *n.* 1. the time for which something lasts, a fixed or limited time, *during his term of office; a term of imprisonment.* 2. completion of this, *a pregnancy approaching term.* 3. one of the periods, each lasting for a number of weeks, during which instruction is given in a school, college, or university or in which a law court holds sessions, alternating with holidays or vacations. 4. each of the quantities or expressions in a mathematical series or ratio etc. 5. a word or phrase considered as the name or symbol of something, *"the clink" is a slang term for "prison."* 6. language or the manner of its use, *protested in strong terms.* 7. stipulations made, conditions offered or accepted, *peace terms.* 8. payment offered or asked, *buy on easy terms.* 9. a relation between people, *on friendly terms.* **term** *v.* to call by a certain term or expression, *this music is termed plainsong.* □**bring to terms,** to compel agree-

ment to conditions. **come to terms,** to reach an agreement; to reconcile oneself to a difficulty etc., *came to terms with his handicap.* **in terms of,** expressed with regard to, *what will you need in terms of equipment?* **term insurance,** life insurance bought for a specific number of years and expiring completely at the end of the specified time.

ter·ma·gant (tur-mă-gănt) *n.* a shrewish bullying woman.

ter·mi·na·ble (tur-mĭ-nă-bĕl) *adj.* able to be terminated. ▷Do not confuse *terminable* with *terminal.*

ter·mi·nal (tur-mĭ-năl) *adj.* 1. of or forming or situated at the end or boundary of something. 2. forming or undergoing the last stage of a fatal disease, *terminal cancer.* **terminal** *n.* 1. a terminating point or part. 2. a terminus for railroad trains or long-distance buses, a building (at an airport or in a town) where air passengers arrive and depart. 3. a point of connection in an electric circuit or device. **ter′mi·nal·ly** *adv.* ▷Do not confuse *terminal* with *terminable.*

ter·mi·nate (tur-mĭ-nayt) *v.* (**ter·mi·nat·ed, ter·mi·nat·ing**) to end. **ter′mi·na·tor** *n.* **ter·mi·na·tive** (tur-mĭ-nay-tiv) *adj.* **ter·mi·na·tion** (tur-mĭ-nay-shŏn) *n.*

ter·mi·nol·o·gy (tur-mĭ-nol-ŏ-jee) *n.* (*pl.* **-gies**) 1. the technical terms of a particular subject. 2. proper use of words as names or symbols. **ter·mi·no·log·i·cal** (tur-mĭ-nŏ-loj-i-kăl) *adj.* **ter·mi·no·log′i·cal·ly** *adv.*

ter·mi·nus (tur-mi-nŭs) *n.* (*pl.* **-ni,** *pr.* -nɪ, **-nus·es**) the end of something, the last station at the end of a railroad or bus route.

ter·mite (tur-mɪt) *n.* a small insect that is very destructive to timber, especially in tropical areas (also called *white ant,* but not of the ant family).

tern (turn) *n.* a seabird with long pointed wings and a forked tail.

ter·na·ry (tur-nă-ree) *adj.* 1. composed of three parts. 2. using three as a base, as in mathematics. 3. third.

terp·si·cho·re·an (turp-sĭ-kŏ-ree-ăn) *adj.* having to do with dancing.

terr. *abbr.* 1. terrace. 2. territorial. 3. territory.

ter·race (ter-ăs) *n.* 1. a raised level place, one of a series of these into which a hillside is shaped for cultivation. 2. a nearly flat strip of land with an abrupt or sloping descent along the edges. 3. a paved area beside a house. 4. a small outside balcony. 5. the flat roof of a house, especially in the Far East. **terrace** *v.* (**ter·raced, ter·rac·ing**) to form into a terrace or terraces.

ter·ra cot·ta (ter-ă kot-ă) 1. a kind of brownish-red unglazed pottery. 2. its color.

ter·ra fir·ma (ter-ă fur-mă) dry land, the ground.

ter·rain (tĕ-rayn) *n.* a stretch of land, with regard to its natural features.

ter·ra in·cog·ni·ta (ter-ă in-kog-ni-tă) unknown or unexplored regions. ▷Latin.

Ter·ra·my·cin (ter-ă-mɪ-sin) *n.* (*trademark*) an antibiotic.

ter·ra·pin (ter-ă-pin) *n.* an edible North American freshwater turtle.

ter·rar·i·um (tĕ-rair-ee-ŭm) *n.* (*pl.* **-rar·i·ums, -rar·i·a,** *pr.* -rair-ee-ă) 1. a sealed transparent globe etc. containing growing plants. 2. a place where land animals are kept in nearly their natural state for observation.

ter·raz·zo (tĕ-raz-oh) *n.* a flooring material of

stone chips set in concrete and given a smooth surface.

ter·res·tri·al (tĕ-res-tri-ăl) *adj.* 1. of the earth. 2. of or living on land. **ter·res′tri·al·ly** *adv.*

ter·ri·ble (ter-ĭ-bĕl) *adj.* 1. appalling, distressing. 2. extreme, hard to bear, *the heat was terrible.* 3. *(informal)* very bad, *I'm terrible at tennis.* **ter′ri·bly** *adv.* **ter′ri·ble·ness** *n.*

ter·ri·er (ter-ee-ĕr) *n.* a kind of small hardy active dog.

ter·rif·ic (tĕ-rif-ik) *adj. (informal)* of great size or intensity, *a terrific storm.* 2. excellent, *did a terrific job.* **ter·rif′i·cal·ly** *adv.*

ter·ri·fied (ter-ĭ-fīd) *adj.* feeling terror.

ter·ri·fy (ter-ĭ-fī) *v.* **(ter·ri·fied, ter·ri·fy·ing)** to fill with terror. **ter′ri·fy·ing·ly** *adv.* **ter′ri·fi·er** *n.*

ter·ri·to·ri·al (ter-ĭ-tohr-i-ăl) *adj.* 1. of territory or land. 2. limited to a district. □**territorial waters,** the sea within a certain distance of a country's coast and subject to its control.

ter·ri·to·ry (ter-ĭ-tohr-ee) *n.* (*pl.* **-ries**) 1. land under the control of a ruler or state or city etc. 2. *Territory,* a country or area forming part of the U.S. or Australia or Canada but not ranking as a state or province. 3. an area for which a person has responsibility or over which a salesman etc. operates. 4. a sphere of action or thought, a province. 5. an area claimed or dominated by one person or group or animal and defended against others.

ter·ror (ter-ŏr) *n.* 1. extreme fear. 2. a terrifying person or thing. 3. *(informal)* a formidable person, a troublesome person or thing.

ter·ror·ism (ter-ŏ-riz-ĕm) *n.* use of violence and intimidation, especially for political purposes. **ter′ror·ist** *n.* & *adj.*

ter·ror·ize (ter-ŏ-rīz) *v.* **(ter·ror·ized, ter·ror·iz·ing)** to fill with terror, to coerce by terrorism. **ter′ror·iz·er** *n.* **ter·ror·i·za·tion** (ter-ŏ-ri-zay-shŏn) *n.*

ter·ror-strick·en (ter-ŏr-strik-ĕn) *adj.* stricken with terror.

ter·ry (ter-ee) *n.* (*pl.* **-ries**) (also **terry cloth**) a cotton fabric used for towels etc., with raised loops left uncut.

terse (turs) *adj.* **(ters·er, ters·est)** concise, curt. **terse′ly** *adv.* **terse′ness** *n.*

ter·ti·ar·y (tur-shi-er-ee) *adj.* 1. coming after secondary, of the third rank or stage etc. 2. *Tertiary,* of the first geologic period of the Cenozoic era. **Tertiary** *n.* the Tertiary period.

tes·sel·late (tes-ĕ-layt) *v.* **(tes·sel·lat·ed, tes·sel·lat·ing)** to make or lay out in a mosaic pattern of small square blocks, *tesselated pavement.* **tes·sel·la·tion** (tes-ĕ-lay-shŏn) *n.*

test (test) *n.* 1. a critical examination or evaluation of the qualities or abilities etc. of a person or thing. 2. a means or procedure for making this. 3. an examination (especially in a school) on a limited subject. **test** *v.* to subject to a test. □**put to the test,** to cause to undergo a test. **stand the test,** to undergo it successfully. **test ban,** a ban on tests, especially tests of nuclear bombs. **test case,** a lawsuit providing a decision that is taken as applying to similar cases in the future. **test drive,** a drive taken in order to judge the performance of a car before buying it. **test pattern,** a pattern on a television screen, used for adjusting reception. **test pilot,** a pilot employed to fly new airplanes in order to test their perfor-

mance. **test tube,** a tube of thin glass with one end closed, used in laboratories. **test-tube baby,** *(informal)* a baby conceived by artificial insemination, or developing elsewhere than in a mother's body.

test. *abbr.* 1. testator. 2. testatrix. 3. testimony.

Test. *abbr.* Testament.

tes·ta·ment (tes-tă-mĕnt) *n.* 1. a will. 2. a written statement of one's beliefs. □**Old Testament,** the books of the Bible telling of the history of the Jews and their beliefs. **New Testament,** the books of the Bible telling of the life and teaching of Christ and his earliest followers.

tes·ta·men·ta·ry (tes-tă-men-tă-ree) *adj.* of or given in a person's will.

tes·tate (tes-tayt) *adj.* having left a valid will at death.

tes·ta·tor (tes-tay-tŏr) *n.* a person who has made a will.

tes·ta·trix (tes-tă-triks) *n.* a woman testator.

test·er[1] (tes-tĕr) *n.* a person or thing that tests.

tester[2] *n.* a canopy, especially over a four-poster bed.

tes·tes *see* **testis.**

tes·ti·cle (tes-ti-kĕl) *n.* a male reproductive organ in which sperm-bearing fluid is produced, (in man) each of the two enclosed in the scrotum.

tes·ti·fy (tes-tĭ-fī) *v.* **(tes·ti·fied, tes·ti·fy·ing)** 1. to bear witness to (a fact etc.), to give evidence. 2. to be evidence of. **tes′ti·fi·er** *n.*

tes·ti·mo·ni·al (tes-tĭ-moh-ni-ăl) *n.* 1. a formal statement testifying to a person's character or abilities or qualifications. 2. something given to a person to show appreciation of his services or achievements. **testimonial** *adj.* of or comprising a testimonial.

tes·ti·mo·ny (tes-tĭ-moh-nee) *n.* (*pl.* **-nies**) 1. a declaration or statement (especially one made under oath). 2. evidence in support of something.

tes·tis (tes-tis) *n.* (*pl.* **-tes,** *pr.* teez) a testicle.

tes·tos·ter·one (tes-tos-tĕ-rohn) *n.* a male sex hormone formed in the testicles.

tes·ty (tes-tee) *adj.* **(-ti·er, -ti·est)** easily annoyed, irritable. **tes′ti·ly** *adv.* **tes′ti·ness** *n.*

tet·a·nus (tet-ă-nŭs) *n.* a disease in which the muscles contract and stiffen (as in lockjaw), caused by bacteria that enter the body. **tet′a·nal** *adj.*

tête-à-tête (tayt-ă-tayt) *n.* a private conversation, especially between two people. **tête-à-tête** *adj.* & *adv.* together in private.

teth·er (te*th*-ĕr) *n.* a rope or chain by which an animal is fastened while grazing. **tether** *v.* to fasten (an animal) with a tether. □**at the end of one's tether,** having reached the limit of one's endurance.

tet·ra·eth·yl (tet-ră-eth-ĭl) **lead** a liquid added to gasoline as an antiknock agent.

tet·ra·he·dron (tet-ră-hee-drŏn) *n.* (*pl.* **-drons, -dra,** *pr.* -dră) a solid with four sides, a pyramid with three triangular sides and a triangular base. **tet·ra·he′dral** *adj.*

te·tram·e·ter (te-tram-ĕ-tĕr) *n.* a line of verse with four metrical feet.

te·trarch (tee-trahrk) *n.* 1. one of four joint rulers. 2. (in Roman history) the governor of the fourth part of a country or province.

tet·ra·va·lent (tet-ră-vay-lĕnt) *adj.* having a valence of four.

te·trox·ide (te-trok-sɪd) *n.* an oxide having four oxygen atoms in each molecule.

Teut. *abbr.* Teutonic

Teu·ton·ic (too-ton-ik) *adj.* 1. of the Germanic peoples or their languages. 2. German. **Teu·ton** (too-tŏn) *n.*

Tex. *abbr.* Texas.

Tex·as (tek-săs) a state of the U.S. **Tex'an** *adj. & n.* □**Texas leaguer,** (in baseball) a fly ball that falls to the ground between the infield and the outfield and results in a base hit.

text (tekst) *n.* 1. the wording of something written or printed. 2. the main body of a book or page etc. as distinct from illustrations or notes. 3. a sentence from Scripture used as the subject of a sermon or discussion. 4. a book or play etc. prescribed for study.

text·book (tekst-buuk) *n.* a book of information for use in studying a subject.

tex·tile (teks-til) *n.* woven or machine-knitted fabric. **textile** *adj.* of textiles.

tex·tu·al (teks-choo-ăl) *adj.* of or in a text. **tex'tu·al·ly** *adv.*

tex·ture (teks-chŭr) *n.* the way a fabric or other substance feels to the touch, its thickness or firmness or solidity. **tex'tur·al** *adj.*

tex·tured (teks-chŭrd) *adj.* 1. having a certain texture, *coarse-textured.* 2. (of yarn or fabric) crimped or curled or looped.

T (tee) **formation** (in football) an offensive formation in which the quarterback stands directly behind the center, the fullback behind the quarterback, and the halfbacks on either side, forming a **T.**

T-group (tee-groop) *n.* a group involved in sensitivity training.

Th *symbol* thorium.

Th. *abbr.* Thursday.

-th[1] *suffix* used to form nouns from verbs, as in *growth*, and from adjectives, as in *length.*

-th[2] *suffix* used to form ordinal and fractional numbers with all simple numbers from four onward, as in *fourth, twentieth.*

-th[3] *suffix (old use)* used to form the third person present singular of verbs, as in *doth, saith.*

Thai·land (tɪ-land) a country in southeast Asia. **Thai** *adj. & n.*

thal·a·mus (thal-ă-mŭs) *n.* (*pl.* **-mi,** *pr.* -mɪ) the interior region of the brain where sensory nerves originate. **tha·lam·ic** (thă-lam-ik) *adj.*

tha·lid·o·mide (thă-lid-ŏ-mɪd) *n.* a sedative drug found (in 1961) to have caused malformation of the limbs of babies whose mothers took it during pregnancy.

thal·li·um (thal-i-ŭm) *n.* a soft white poisonous metallic substance.

than (*th*an) *conj.* used to introduce the second element in a comparison, *his brother is taller than he is; his brother is taller than he; she likes you more than me;* or in a statement of difference, *the only person other than himself; not known elsewhere than in New York.* ▷You will understand why it is correct to write *his brother is taller than he* if you recognize that the statement means "his brother is taller than he *is.*" You will understand why it is correct to write *she likes you more than me* if you recognize that the statement means "she likes you more than *she likes* me."

than·a·tol·o·gy (than-ă-tol-ŏ-jee) *n.* the scientific study of phenomena accompanying death. **than·a·tol'o·gist** *n.*

than·a·top·sis (than-ă-top-sis) *n.* a meditation on or view of death.

thane (thayn) *n.* 1. (in English history) one holding land from a king by military service, ranking between ordinary freemen and hereditary nobles. 2. (in Scottish history) the chief of a clan.

thank (thangk) *v.* to express gratitude to; *he has only himself to thank,* it is his own fault. **thank'er** *n.* □**thank God** *or* **thank goodness,** an exclamation of relief. **thank you,** a polite expression of thanks.

thank·ful (thangk-fŭl) *adj.* feeling or expressing gratitude. **thank'ful·ness** *n.*

thank·ful·ly (thangk-fŭ-lee) *adv.* 1. in a thankful way. 2. we are thankful, *thankfully, it has stopped raining.* ▷This second use is similar to that of *hopefully,* which many people regard as unacceptable.

thank·less (thangk-lis) *adj.* not likely to win thanks, *a thankless task.* **thank'less·ly** *adv.*

thanks (thangks) *n. pl.* an expression of gratitude, *(informal)* thank you. □**thanks to,** on account of, as the result of.

thanks·giv·ing (thangks-giv-ing) *n.* 1. an expression of gratitude, especially to God. 2. *Thanksgiving* (also *Thanksgiving Day*), a holiday for giving thanks to God, in the U.S. on the fourth Thursday in November, in Canada on the second Monday in October.

thank-you (thangk-yoo) *n.* an expression of gratitude.

that (*th*at) *adj. & pronoun* (*pl.* **those,** *pr.* thohz) the person or thing referred to or pointed to or understood, the farther or less obvious one of two.

that *adv.* so, to such an extent, *I'll go that far.*

that *relative pronoun* used to introduce a clause that is essential in order to define or identify something, *the book that I sent you; the man that she married.* **that** *conj.* introducing a dependent clause, *we hope that all will go well.* □**at that,** *see* **at. that's that,** the thing is settled or completed. ▷Some writers have difficulty in choosing between the relative pronouns *which* and *that.* Besides studying their definitions and the note under **which,** you may be helped by remembering that the relative pronoun *that* can often be omitted without changing the meaning of the clause that follows: *the book* that *I sent you; the man* that *she married.* The relative pronoun *which* introduces a clause that can be left out entirely without changing the meaning of the sentence: *this typewriter,* which *I bought for $50, breaks down often; her automobile,* which *always needs care, takes up too much of her time.*

thatch (thach) *n.* 1. a roof or roof covering made of straw or reeds or palm leaves. 2. *(informal)* a thick growth of hair on the head. **thatch** *v.* to roof or cover with thatch, to make (a roof) of thatch. **thatch'er** *n.*

thaw (thaw) *v.* 1. to pass into a liquid or unfrozen state after being frozen. 2. to become warm enough to melt ice etc. or to lose numbness. 3. to become less cool or less formal in manner. 4. to cause to thaw. **thaw** *n.* thawing, weather that thaws ice etc.

THC *abbr.* *tetra*hydro*c*annabinol, the chemical ingredient in marijuana that causes intoxication.

Th.D. *abbr.* Doctor of Theology.

the (*th*ĕ, *th*i before a vowel sound) *adj.* (called the *definite article*) 1. applied to a noun standing for a specific person or thing *(the president; the man in gray),* or one or all of a kind *(diseases of the eye; the rich),* or an occupation or pursuit etc. *(too fond of the bottle).* 2. (*pr.* thee) used to emphasize excellence or importance; *he's the Sir Law-rence*, the one who is so famous. 3. *(informal)* my, our, your, etc., *the wife*. 4. (of prices) per, *shoes at $55 the pair*. **the** *adv*. in that degree, by that amount, *all the better; the more the merrier*.

theat. *abbr*. 1. theater. 2. theatrical.

the·a·ter (thee-ă-tĕr) *n*. 1. a building or outdoor structure for the performance of plays and similar entertainments. 2. a room or hall for lectures etc. with seats in tiers. 3. an operating theater. 4. a scene of important events, *Belgium was the theater of war*. 5. the writing, acting, and producing of plays. □**theater of the absurd**, drama that uses seemingly pointless or ridiculous episodes and language in an effort to depict futility, loneliness, and anxiety in 20th-century life. **theater weapons**, those that are intermediate between tactical and strategic.

the·a·ter·go·er (thee-ă-tĕr-goh-ĕr) *n*. a person who attends plays.

the·a·ter-in-the-round (thee-ă-tĕr-in-thĕ-rownd) *n*. a dramatic performance on a stage surrounded by spectators.

the·a·tre = theater.

the·at·ri·cal (thi-at-ri-kăl) *adj*. 1. of or for the theater. 2. (of behavior) exaggerated and designed to make a showy effect. **the·at'ri·cal·ly** *adv*. **the·at·ri·cal·i·ty** (thi-at-ri-kal-i-tee) *n*.

the·at·ri·cals (thi-at-ri-kălz) *n*. *pl*. theatrical performances, *amateur theatricals*.

the·at·rics (thi-at-riks) *n*. 1. the staging of plays. 2. theatrical mannerisms or behavior.

thee (*thee*) *pronoun* the objective case of *thou*[1].

theft (theft) *n*. stealing.

their (*thair*) *adj*. of or belonging to them. ▷Do not confuse *their* with *there* or *they're*.

theirs (*thairz*) *possessive pronoun* of or belonging to them, the thing(s) belonging to them. ▷It is incorrect to write *their's* (see the note under **its**).

the·ism (thee-iz-ĕm) *n*. belief in the existence of gods or a god. **the'ist** *adj*. & *n*. **the·is·tic** (thee-is-tik) *adj*. **the·is'ti·cal·ly** *adv*.

them (*them*) *pronoun* 1. the objective case of **they**, *we saw them*. 2. *(informal)* = they, *it's them all right*.

theme (theem) *n*. 1. the subject about which a person speaks or writes or thinks. 2. a melody that is repeated or on which variations are constructed. 3. a school composition or essay on a given subject. **the·mat·ic** (thi-mat-ik) *adj*. **the·mat'i·cal·ly** *adv*. □**theme park**, an amusement or recreational park that features a particular subject or subjects. **theme song**, the recurrent melody in a musical play or film; the signature tune of a performer or show.

them·selves (*them-selvz*) *pronoun pl*. corresponding to *they* and *them*, used in the same ways as **himself**.

then (*then*) *adv*. 1. at that time. 2. next, after that, and also. 3. in that case, therefore, *if that's yours, then this must be mine*. **then** *adj*. of that time, *the then president*. **then** *n*. that time, *from then on*.

thence (*thens*) *adv*. from that place or source.

thence·forth (*thens*-fohrth), **thence·for·ward** (*thens*-for-wărd), **thence·for·wards** (*thens*-for-wărdz) *adv*. from then on.

the·oc·ra·cy (thi-ok-ră-see) *n*. (*pl*. **-cies**) 1. a form of government by God or a god directly or through a priestly order. 2. a state having this

form of government. **the·o·crat·ic** (thee-ŏ-krat-ik) *adj*. **the·o·crat'i·cal·ly** *adv*.

the·od·o·lite (thi-od-ŏ-līt) *n*. a surveying instrument with a rotating telescope, used for measuring horizontal and vertical angles.

theol. *abbr*. 1. theological. 2. theology.

the·o·lo·gian (thee-ŏ-loh-jăn) *n*. an expert in theology.

the·ol·o·gy (thi-ol-ŏ-jee) *n*. (*pl*. **-gies**) the study of religion, a system of religion. **the·o·log·i·cal** (thee-ŏ-loj-i-kăl) *adj*. **the·o·log'i·cal·ly** *adv*.

the·o·rem (thee-ŏ-rĕm) *n*. 1. a mathematical statement to be proved by a chain of reasoning. 2. a rule in algebra etc., especially one expressed as a formula.

the·o·ret·i·cal (thee-ŏ-ret-i-kăl), **the·o·ret·ic** (thee-ŏ-ret-ik) *adj*. based on theory not on practice or experience. **the·o·ret'i·cal·ly** *adv*. **the·o·re·ti·cian** (thee-ŏ-rĕ-tish-ăn) *n*.

the·o·rist (thee-ŏ-rist) *n*. a person who theorizes.

the·o·rize (thee-ŏ-rīz) *v*. **(the·o·rized, the·o·riz·ing)** to form a theory or theories. **the'o·riz·er** *n*.

the·o·ry (thee-ŏ-ree) *n*. (*pl*. **-ries**) 1. a set of ideas formulated (by reasoning from known facts) to explain something, *Darwin's theory of evolution*. 2. an opinion or supposition. 3. ideas or suppositions in general (contrasted with *practice*). 4. a statement of the principles on which a subject is based, *theory of music*.

the·os·o·phy (thi-os-ŏ-fee) *n*. (*pl*. **-phies**) any of several systems of philosophy that aim at a direct knowledge of God by means of spiritual ecstasy and contemplation. **the·os'o·phist** *n*. **the·o·soph·ic** (thee-ŏ-sof-ik) *adj*. **the·o·soph'i·cal** *adj*. **the·o·soph'i·cal·ly** *adv*.

ther·a·peu·tic (ther-ă-pyoo-tik) *adj*. of the healing of disease, curative. **ther·a·peu'ti·cal·ly** *adv*.

ther·a·peu·tics (ther-ă-pyoo-tiks) *n*. medical treatment of disease.

ther·a·pist (ther-ă-pist) *n*. a specialist in a certain kind of therapy.

ther·a·py (ther-ă-pee) *n*. (*pl*. **-pies**) 1. any treatment designed to relieve or cure an illness or disability. 2. physiotherapy, psychotherapy.

there (*thair*) *adv*. 1. in or at or to that place. 2. at that point in a process or series of events. 3. in that matter, *I can't agree with you there*. 4. used for emphasis in calling attention, *hey, you there!* 5. used to introduce a sentence where the verb comes before its subject, *there was plenty to eat*. **there** *n*. that place, *we live near there*. **there** *interj*. an exclamation of satisfaction or dismay *(there! what did I tell you!)* or used to soothe a child etc. *(there, there!)*. ▷Do not confuse *there* with *their* or *they're*.

there·a·bouts (*thair*-ă-bowts), **there·a·bout** (*thair*-ă-bowt) *adv*. 1. somewhere near there. 2. somewhere near that number or quantity or time etc.

there·af·ter (*thair*-af-tĕr) *adv*. after that.

there·at (*thair*-at) *adv*. 1. at that place. 2. on that account. 3. after that.

there·by (*thair*-bī, *thair*-bī) *adv*. by that means; *thereby hangs a tale*, there is something that could be told about that.

there·for (*thair*-for) *adv*. in return for.

there·fore (*thair*-fohr) *adv*. for that reason.

there·from (*thair*-frum) *adv*. *(old use)* from that or it.

there·in (*th*air-in) *adv.* *(formal)* in that place, in that respect.

there·in·af·ter (*th*air-in-af-tĕr) *adv.* *(formal)* later in the same document.

there·of (*th*air-uv) *adv.* *(formal)* of that, of it.

there·on (*th*air-on) *adv.* 1. on that or it. 2. *(old use)* thereupon.

there·to (*th*air-too) *adv.* *(formal)* to that, to it.

there·to·fore (*th*air-tŏ-fohr) *adv.* *(formal)* before that time.

there·up·on (*th*air-ŭ-pon) *adv.* in consequence of that, immediately after that.

there·with (*th*air-with, -with) *adv.* 1. *(formal)* with that. 2. *(old use)* thereupon.

therm. *abbr.* thermometer.

ther·mal (thur-măl) *adj.* 1. of heat, using or operated by heat. 2. warm or hot, *thermal springs.* 3. designed to provide insulation and help retain heat, *thermal underwear; thermal windows.* **thermal** *n.* a rising current of hot air. **ther'mal·ly** *adv.* □**thermal barrier,** the limit imposed on the speed of a rocket or airplane etc. by the high temperature resulting from friction between such objects and Earth's atmosphere when traveling at supersonic speeds. **thermal pollution,** pollution caused by discharging heated water into a river or lake etc. to the detriment of plant and animal life. **thermal spring,** a spring producing water that is relatively warm. **thermal unit,** a unit for measuring heat.

ther·mic (thur-mik) *adj.* thermal.

therm·i·on·ic (thurm-i-on-ik) **tube** a vacuum tube in which a flow of electrons is emitted by heated electrodes, used in radio etc.

ther·mis·tor (thĕr-mis-tŏr) *n.* an electrical resistor whose resistance is greatly reduced by heating.

ther·mo·cline (thur-mŏ-klīn) *n.* a layer of water in a large body of water that separates warmer water above from colder water below. **ther·mo·clin·al** (thur-mŏ-klɪ-năl) *adj.*

ther·mo·cou·ple (thur-mŏ-kup-ĕl) *n.* a device for measuring temperatures by means of the thermoelectric voltage developing between two pieces of wire of different metals joined to each other at each end.

ther·mo·dy·nam·ics (thur-moh-dɪ-nam-iks) *n.* a branch of physics dealing with the relation between heat and other forms of energy. **ther·mo·dy·nam'ic** *adj.* **ther·mo·dy·nam'i·cal·ly** *adv.*

ther·mo·e·lec·tric (thur-moh-i-lek-trik) *adj.* producing electricity by difference of temperature. **ther·mo·e·lec'tri·cal** *adj.* **ther·mo·e·lec' tri·cal·ly** *adv.*

ther·mom·e·ter (thĕr-mom-ĕ-tĕr) *n.* an instrument for measuring temperature, especially a graduated glass tube containing mercury or alcohol that expands when heated. **ther·mom'e·try** *n.* **ther·mo·met·ric** (ther-mŏ-met-rik) *adj.* **ther·mo·met'ri·cal** *adj.* **ther·mo·met'ri·cal·ly** *adv.*

ther·mo·nu·cle·ar (thur-moh-noo-klee-ăr) *adj.* of nuclear reactions that occur at very high temperatures. □**thermonuclear bomb,** a bomb that uses such reactions.

ther·mo·plas·tic (thur-mŏ-plas-tik) *adj.* becoming soft and plastic when heated and hardening when cooled. **thermoplastic** *n.* a thermoplastic substance. **ther·mo·plas·tic·i·ty** (thur-moh-plas-tis-i-tee) *n.*

ther·mo·reg·u·la·tor (thur-moh-reg-yŭ-lay-tŏr) *n.* a device that regulates temperature.

ther·mos (thur-mŏs) *n.* a kind of vacuum bottle.

ther·mo·set·ting (thur-moh-set-ing) *adj.* (of plastics) setting permanently when heated.

ther·mo·sphere (thur-mŏ-sfeer) *n.* the upper region of Earth's atmosphere that extends from the mesosphere to outer space and in which the temperature increases with distance away from Earth. **ther·mo·spher·ic** (thur-mŏ-sfer-ik) *adj.*

ther·mo·stat (thur-mo-stat) *n.* a device that automatically regulates temperature by cutting off and restoring the supply of heat to a piece of equipment or a room etc. **ther·mo·stat·ic** (thur-mŏ-stat-ik) *adj.* **ther·mo·stat'i·cal·ly** *adv.*

ther·mo·stat·ics (thur-mŏ-stat-iks) *n.* the branch of physics that deals with the equilibrium of heat.

the·sau·rus (thi-sor-ŭs) *n.* (*pl.* **-sau·rus·es,** **-sau·ri,** *pr.* -sor-ɪ) 1. a dictionary or encyclopedia, *a thesaurus of slang.* 2. a book containing sets of words grouped according to their meanings.

these *see* **this.**

the·sis (thee-sis) *n.* (*pl.* **-ses,** *pr.* -seez) 1. a statement or theory put forward and supported by arguments. 2. a lengthy written essay submitted by a candidate for a university degree.

Thes·pi·an (thes-pi-ăn) *adj.* (also **thespian**) of drama and the theater. **thespian** *n.* an actor or actress.

Thes·sa·lo·ni·ans (thes-ă-loh-nee-ănz) *n.* either of two books of the New Testament, written by St. Paul to the Church at Thessalonica.

the·ta (thay-tă) *n.* the eighth letter of the Greek alphabet (Θ θ).

they (*th*ay) *pronoun* 1. the people or things mentioned. 2. people in general, *they say the play is a success.* 3. those in authority, *they are putting a tax on margarine.* 4. used informally instead of "he or she," *I am never angry with anyone unless they deserve it.*

they'd (*th*ayd) = they had, they would.

they'll (*th*ayl) = they will.

they're (*th*air) = they are. ▷Do not confuse *they're* with *their* or *there.*

they've (*th*ayv) = they have.

thi·a·mine (thɪ-ă-min) *n.* (also **thiamin**) vitamin B, essential to nerve function.

thick (thik) *adj.* 1. of great or specified distance between opposite surfaces. 2. (of a line etc.) broad not fine. 3. made of thick material, *a thick coat.* 4. having units that are crowded or numerous, dense, *a thick forest; thick fog; thick darkness,* difficult to see through. 5. densely covered or filled, *her roses were thick with aphids.* 6. (of a liquid or paste) relatively stiff in consistency, not flowing easily; *thick soup,* thickened. 7. (of the voice) not sounding clear. 8. (of an accent) very noticeable, *a thick brogue.* 9. stupid. 10. *(informal)* on terms of close association or friendliness, *her parents are very thick with mine.* **thick** *adv.* thickly, *blows came thick and fast.* **thick** *n.* the busiest part of a crowd or fight or activity, *in the thick of it.* **thick'ly** *adv.* □**a bit thick,** *(slang)* beyond what is reasonable or endurable. **thick head,** stupidity; a feeling of confusion. **through thick and thin,** in spite of all the difficulties.

thick·en (thik-ĕn) *v.* to make or become thicker or of a stiffer consistency; *the plot thickens,* becomes more complicated. **thick'en·er** *n.* **thick'en·ing** *n.*

thick·et (thik-it) *n.* a number of shrubs and small trees etc. growing close together.

thick-head·ed (thik-hed-id) *adj.* stupid.

thick·ish (thik-ish) *adj.* rather thick.

thick·ness (thik-nis) *n.* 1. the quality of being thick, the extent to which something is thick. 2. a layer, *use three thicknesses of cardboard.* 3. the part between opposite surfaces, *steps cut in the thickness of the wall.*

thick·set (thik-set) *adj.* 1. with parts set or growing close together, *a thickset hedge.* 2. having a stocky or burly body.

thick-skinned (thik-skind) *adj.* not very sensitive to criticism or snubs.

thick·wit·ted (thik-wit-id) *adj.* stupid.

thief (theef) *n.* (*pl.* **thieves,** *pr.* theevz) one who steals, especially stealthily and without violence. **thiev·ish** (thee-vish) *adj.*

thieve (theev) *v.* (**thieved, thiev·ing**) to be a thief, to steal.

thiev·er·y (thee-vĕ-ree) *n.* (*pl.* **-er·ies**) stealing, the practice of this.

thigh (thı) *n.* the part of the human leg between hip and knee, the corresponding part in other animals.

thigh·bone (thı-bohn) *n.* the femur.

thim·ble (thim-bĕl) *n.* a small metal or plastic cap worn on the end of the finger to protect it and push the needle in sewing.

thim·ble·ful (thim-bĕl-fuul) *n.* (*pl.* **-fuls**) a very small quantity of liquid to drink.

Thim·bu (tim-boo) the capital of Bhutan.

thin (thin) *adj.* (**thin·ner, thin·nest**) 1. of small thickness or diameter. 2. (of a line etc.) narrow, not broad. 3. made of thin material, *a thin dress.* 4. lean, not plump. 5. not dense or plentiful. 6. having units that are not crowded or numerous. 7. (of a liquid or paste) flowing easily, not thick. 8. lacking strength or substance or an important ingredient, feeble, *a thin excuse.* **thin** *adv.* thinly, *cut the bread thin.* **thin** *v.* (**thinned, thin·ning**) to make or become thinner. **thin'ly** *adv.* **thin'ness** *n.* □**thin out,** to make or become fewer or less crowded; *thin out seedlings,* remove a few to improve the growth of the rest.

thine (thın) *adj.* (*old use*) of or belonging to thee. **thine** *possessive pronoun* (*old use*) the thing(s) belonging to thee.

thing (thing) *n.* 1. whatever is or may be an object of perception or knowledge or thought. 2. an unnamed object or item, *there are six things on my list.* 3. an inanimate object as distinct from a living creature. 4. (in pity or contempt) a creature, *poor thing!* 5. an act or fact or idea or task etc., *a difficult thing to do; she takes things too seriously.* 6. a specimen or type of something, *the latest thing in hats.* 7. *things,* personal belongings, clothing, *pack your things;* implements or utensils, *my painting things;* circumstances or conditions, *things began to improve.* □**do one's own thing,** *(informal)* to follow one's own interests or urges. **have a thing about,** *(informal)* to have an obsession or prejudice about. **make a thing of it,** to get excited about it; to insist that it is important. **the thing,** what is conventionally proper or is fashionable; what is important or suitable, *that bowl is just the thing for roses.*

thing·a·ma·jig (thing-ă-mă-jig), **thing·u·ma·bob** (thing-ŭ-mă-bob) *n.* *(informal)* what-d'you-call-it.

think (thingk) *v.* (**thought, think·ing**) 1. to exercise the mind in an active way, to form connected ideas. 2. to have as an idea or opinion, *we think we shall win.* 3. to form as an intention or plan, *can't think what to do next; she's thinking of emi-* grating; *I couldn't think of doing that,* I regard that course as unacceptable. 4. to take into consideration, *think how nice it would be.* 5. to call to mind, to remember, *can't think where I put it.* 6. to be of the opinion, to judge, *it is thought to be a fake.* **think** *n.* *(informal)* an act of thinking, *must have a think about that.* **think'a·ble** *adj.* **think'a·bly** *adv.* □**put on one's thinking cap,** *(informal)* to try to find a solution to a problem by thought. **think again,** to reconsider and change one's mind. **think aloud,** to utter one's thoughts as they occur. **think better of it,** to change one's mind after reconsideration. **think nothing of,** to consider unremarkable. **think out,** to analyze or produce by thought. **think over,** to reach a decision about by thinking. **think tank,** *(informal)* a research organization that analyzes political or social or economic etc. problems for the government or for business firms. **think twice,** to consider very carefully before doing something. **think up,** *(informal)* to invent or produce by thought.

think·er (thing-kĕr) *n.* a person who thinks deeply or in a specified way, *an original thinker.*

think·ing (thing-king) *adj.* using thought or rational judgment about things, *all thinking men.*

thin·ner (thin-ĕr) *n.* a substance for thinning paint.

thin·nish (thin-ish) *adj.* rather thin.

thin-skinned (thin-skind) *adj.* 1. having a thin skin. 2. oversensitive to criticism or snubs.

third (thurd) *adj.* next after second. **third** *n.* 1. something that is third. 2. third gear. 3. one of three equal parts of a thing. **third** *adv.* in the third place. **third'ly** *adv.* □**third base,** (in baseball) the third in order of bases from home plate; the portion of the field near this base. **third baseman,** the player stationed at third base. **third class,** a low class in accommodations etc., a class of mail for printed circulars etc. **third degree,** *(slang)* long and severe questioning by police to get information or a confession. **third dimension,** depth, the quality that makes an object solid; that which adds to reality or significance. **third party,** another person etc. besides the two principal ones involved. **third-party insurance,** that in which the insurer gives protection to the insured against liability for damage or injury to any other person. **third person,** *see* **person.** **third rail,** the rail of an electric railroad that carries the electric current. **Third World** (often **third world**), the developing countries of Asia, Africa, and Latin America not politically aligned with Communist or Western nations.

third-rate (thurd-rayt) *adj.* very inferior in quality.

thirst (thurst) *n.* 1. the feeling caused by a desire or need to drink. 2. a strong desire, *a thirst for adventure.* **thirst** *v.* to feel a thirst.

thirst·y (thur-stee) *adj.* (**thirst·i·er, thirst·i·est**) 1. feeling thirst. 2. (of land) in need of water. 3. *(informal)* causing thirst, *thirsty work.* **thirst'i·ly** *adv.* **thirst'i·ness** *n.*

thir·teen (thur-teen) *adj. & n.* one more than twelve (13, XIII). **thir'teenth'** *adj. & n.*

thir·ties (thur-teez) *n. pl.* the numbers or years or degrees of temperature from 30 to 39.

thir·ty (thur-tee) *adj. & n.* (*pl.* **-ties**) three times ten (30, XXX). **thir'ti·eth** *adj. & n.*

this (this) *adj. & pronoun* (*pl.* **these,** *pr.* theez) 1. the person or thing close at hand or touched or just mentioned or about to be mentioned, the nearer or more obvious one of two. 2. the present day or time, *she ought to have been here by this.*

this adv. (informal) to such an extent, we're surprised he got this far. □**this and that,** various things. **this world,** see **world** (definition 5).

this·tle (this-ĕl) n. a prickly plant with purple, white, or yellow flowers. **this'tly** adj.

this·tle·down (this-ĕl-down) n. the very light fluff on thistle seeds by which they are carried by the wind.

thith·er (thith-ĕr) adv. (also **thith·er·ward,** pr. thith-ĕr-wărd) to or toward that place. **thither** adj. on the more distant side.

tho, tho' (informal) = **though.**

thole (thohl) n. (also **thole·pin**) a peg set in the gunwale of a boat to serve as an oarlock.

thong (thong) n. a narrow strip of hide or leather used as a fastening or lash etc.

tho·rax (thohr-aks) n. (pl. **tho·rax·es, tho·ra·ces,** pr. thohr-ă-seez) the part of the body between head or neck and the abdomen. **tho·rac·ic** (thŏ-ras-ik) adj.

tho·ri·um (thohr-i-ŭm) n. a radioactive metallic substance.

thorn (thorn) n. 1. a sharp pointed projection on a plant. 2. a thorny tree or shrub. **thorn'less** adj. **thorn'proof'** adj. □**a thorn in one's flesh,** a constant source of annoyance. **thorn apple,** a prickly poisonous fruit, especially of jimson weed; the fruit of the hawthorn.

thorn·y (thor-nee) adj. (**thorn·i·er, thorn·i·est**) 1. having many thorns. 2. like a thorn. 3. troublesome, difficult to deal with, a thorny problem. **thorn'i·ly** adv. **thorn'i·ness** n.

tho·ron (thohr-on) n. a radioactive isotope of radon resulting from the decomposition of thorium.

thor·ough (thur-oh) adj. complete in every way, not merely superficial, doing things or done with great attention to detail. **thor'ough·ly** adv. **thor'ough·ness** n.

thor·ough·bred (thur-oh-bred) adj. (especially of a horse) bred of pure or pedigree stock. **thoroughbred** n. a thoroughbred animal.

thor·ough·fare (thur-oh-fair) n. a public way open at both ends.

thor·ough·go·ing (thur-oh-goh-ing) adj. thorough.

those see **that.**

thou[1] (thow) pronoun (old use) you.

thou[2] (thow) n. (pl. **thous, thou**) (slang) a thousand, especially a thousand dollars.

though (thoh) conj. in spite of the fact that, even supposing, it's true, though hard to believe. **though** adv. (informal) however, she's right, though.

thought[1] (thawt) see **think.**

thought[2] n. 1. the process or power of thinking. 2. a way of thinking that is characteristic of a particular class or nation or period, in modern thought. 3. meditation, deep in thought. 4. an idea or chain of reasoning produced by thinking. 5. an intention, we had no thought of giving offense. 6. consideration, □**thought control,** use of propaganda and force to control political opinion and public attitudes.

thought·ful (thawt-fŭl) adj. 1. thinking deeply, often absorbed in thought. 2. (of a book or writer or remark etc.) showing signs of careful thought. 3. showing thought for the needs of others, considerate. **thought'ful·ly** adv. **thought'ful·ness** n.

thought·less (thawt-lis) adj. 1. not alert to possible effects or consequences. 2. inconsiderate. **thought'less·ly** adv. **thought'less·ness** n.

thought-pro·vok·ing (thawt-prŏ-voh-king) adj. giving rise to serious thought.

thou·sand (thow-zănd) adj. & n. (pl. **-sands, -sand**) ten hundred (1000, M). **thou'sandth** adj. & n.

thou·sand·fold (thow-zănd-fohld) adj. & adv. one thousand times as much or as many.

thrall (thrawl) n. 1. a slave of or to a person or thing. 2. bondage, in thrall.

thrall·dom (thrawl-dŏm) n. bondage.

thrash (thrash) v. 1. to beat with a stick or whip. 2. to defeat thoroughly in a contest. 3. to thresh. 4. to hit with repeated blows like a flail, to make violent movements. **thrash'er** n. □**thrash out,** to discuss thoroughly.

thrash·er (thrash-ĕr) n. a long-tailed thrushlike bird of North America.

thread (thred) n. 1. a thin length of any substance. 2. a length of spun cotton or wool etc. used in making cloth or in sewing or knitting. 3. something compared to this; lose the thread of an argument, lose the chain of thought connecting it; pick up the threads, proceed with something after an interruption. 4. the spiral ridge of a screw. **thread** v. 1. to pass a thread through the eye of (a needle). 2. to pass (a strip of film etc.) through or around something into the proper position for use. 3. to put (beads) on a thread. 4. to cut a thread on (a screw). **thread'er** n. □**thread one's way,** to make one's way through (a crowd or streets etc.).

thread·bare (thred-bair) adj. 1. (of cloth) with the nap worn off and threads visible. 2. (of a person) wearing threadbare or shabby clothes.

threat (thret) n. 1. an expression of one's intention to punish or hurt or harm a person or thing. 2. an indication of something undesirable, there's a threat of rain. 3. a person or thing regarded as liable to bring danger or catastrophe, machinery was seen as a threat to people's jobs.

threat·en (thret-ĕn) v. 1. to make a threat or threats against (a person etc.), to try to influence by threats. 2. to be a warning of, the clouds threatened rain. 3. to seem likely to be or do something undesirable, the scheme threatens to be expensive. 4. to be a threat to, the dangers that threaten us. **threat'en·er** n. **threat'en·ing·ly** adv.

three (three) adj. & n. one more than two (3, III). □**three base hit,** (in baseball) a hit that allows the batter to advance to third base. **three-four time,** three-quarter time. **three-point landing,** a perfect landing of an airplane on the two main wheels and the tail wheel or skid simultaneously. **three-ring circus,** a circus having performances in three rings at the same time; (informal) a scene of complete confusion, an extravagant performance.

three-bag·ger (three-bag-ĕr) n. (informal) a three base hit.

three-cor·nered (three-kor-nĕrd) adj. 1. triangular. 2. (of a contest) between three parties.

three-di·men·sion·al (three-di-men-shŏ-năl) adj. (also **3-D**) having three dimensions (length, breadth, depth), or appearing to have depth as well as length and breadth.

three·fold (three-fohld) adj. & adv. 1. three times as much or as many. 2. consisting of three parts.

three-hand·ed (three-han-did) adj. (of a card game) played by three people.

three-lane (three-layn) adj. marked out for three lanes of traffic.

three-leg·ged (three-leg-id) *adj.* having three legs; *three-legged race,* a race between pairs of runners with the right leg of one tied to the left leg of the other.

three-ply (three-plɪ) *adj.* made of three strands or layers.

three-quar·ter (three-kwor-tĕr) *adj.* consisting of three quarters of a whole. □**three-quarter time,** (in music) three beats in a bar, with a time signature of ¾, waltz time.

three·score (three-skohr) *n.* *(old use)* sixty; *threescore years and ten,* the age of 70 as a normal limit of life.

three·some (three-sŏm) *n.* three people together, a trio.

three-wheel·er (three-hwee-lĕr) *n.* a vehicle with three wheels, as a tricycle.

thren·o·dy (thren-ŏ-dee) *n.* (*pl.* **-dies**) a song of lamentation, especially on a person's death.

thresh (thresh) *v.* 1. to beat out or separate (grain) from husks of corn. 2. to make violent movements, *threshing about.* **thresh′er** *n.*

thresh·old (thresh-ohld, -hohld) *n.* 1. a piece of wood or stone forming the bottom of a doorway. 2. the entrance of a house etc. 3. the point of entry or beginning of something, *on the threshold of a new era.* 4. the lowest limit at which a stimulus becomes perceptible. 5. the highest limit at which pain etc. is bearable.

threw *see* **throw.**

thrice (thrɪs) *adv.* *(old use)* three times.

thrift (thrift) *n.* economical management of money or resources. **thrift′less** *adj.* □**thrift shop,** a shop selling used articles, especially for charity.

thrift·y (thrif-tee) *adj.* (**thrift·i·er, thrift·i·est**) practicing thrift, economical. **thrift′i·ly** *adv.* **thrift′i·ness** *n.*

thrill (thril) *n.* a nervous tremor caused by emotion or sensation, a wave of feeling or excitement. **thrill** *v.* to feel or cause to feel a thrill. **thrill′ing·ly** *adv.*

thrill·er (thril-ĕr) *n.* an exciting story or play or film, especially one involving crime.

thrips (thrips) *n.* (*pl.* **thrips**) an insect that is harmful to plants. ▷Note that *a thrips* is the correct singular form, not *a thrip.*

thrive (thrɪv) *v.* (**throve** or **thrived, thrived** or **thriv·en, thriv·ing**) 1. to grow or develop well and vigorously. 2. to prosper, to be successful, *a thriving industry.*

throat (throht) *n.* 1. the front of the neck. 2. the passage in the neck through which food passes to the esophagus and air passes to the lungs. 3. a narrow passage or funnel.

throat·y (throh-tee) *adj.* (**throat·i·er, throat·i·est**) 1. uttered deep in the throat. 2. hoarse. **throat′i·ly** *adv.* **throat′i·ness** *n.*

throb (throb) *v.* (**throbbed, throb·bing**) 1. (of the heart or pulse etc.) to beat with more than usual force or rapidity. 2. to vibrate or sound with a persistent rhythm; *a throbbing wound,* giving pain in a steady rhythm. **throb** *n.* throbbing.

throe (throh) *n.* (*pl.* **throes**) a severe pang of pain. □**in the throes of,** *(informal)* struggling with the task of, *in the throes of spring-cleaning.*

throm·bo·sis (throm-boh-sis) *n.* (*pl.* **-ses,** *pr.* -seez) formation of a clot of blood in a blood vessel or organ of the body. **throm·bot·ic** (throm-bot-ik) *adj.*

throm·bus (throm-bŭs) *n.* (*pl.* **-bi,** *pr.* -bɪ) a clot formed in thrombosis.

throne (throhn) *n.* 1. the special chair or seat used by a king, queen, or bishop etc. on ceremonial occasions. 2. sovereign power, *came to the throne.*

throng (throng) *n.* a crowded mass of people. **throng** *v.* 1. to come or go or press in a throng. 2. to fill (a place) with a throng.

throt·tle (throt-ĕl) *n.* a valve controlling the flow of fuel or steam etc. to an engine, the lever or pedal operating this. **throttle** *v.* (**throt·tled, throt·tling**) 1. to strangle. 2. to suppress. **throt′tler** *n.* □**throttle back** *or* **down,** to obstruct the flow of fuel or steam and reduce the speed of (an engine).

through (throo) *prep.* 1. from end to end or side to side of, entering at one side and coming out at the other. 2. between or among, *scuffling through fallen leaves.* 3. from beginning to end of, so as to have finished or completed; *he is through his exam,* has passed it. 4. up to and including, *Friday through Tuesday.* 5. by reason of, by the agency or means or fault of, *lost it through carelessness.* **through** *adv.* 1. through something. 2. with a connection made to a desired telephone etc., *you're through to Chicago.* 3. finished, *wait till I'm through with these papers.* 4. having no further dealings, *I'm through with that monster!* **through** *adj.* going through something, (of traffic) passing through a place without stopping, (of travel or passengers etc.) going to the end of a journey without a change of line or vehicle etc. □**through and through,** through again and again; thoroughly, completely. **through street,** a street where traffic has the right of way at intersections.

through·out (throo-owt) *prep.* right through, from beginning to end of (a place or course or period).

throughout *adv.* in every part, in all respects, *timber was rotten throughout.*

through·way = **thruway.**

throve (throhv) *see* **thrive.**

throw (throh) *v.* (**threw,** *pr.* throo, **thrown, throw·ing**) 1. to send with some force through the air or in a certain direction; *throw a shadow,* cause there to be one. 2. to use as a missile, *throw stones.* 3. to hurl to the ground, *the horse threw its rider.* 4. *(informal)* to disconcert, *the question threw me.* 5. to put (clothes etc.) on or off hastily or casually. 6. to cause (dice) to fall to the table, to obtain (a number) by this. 7. to shape (rounded pottery) on a potter's wheel. 8. to turn or direct or move (a part of the body) quickly, *threw his head back.* 9. to cause to be in a certain state, *they were thrown out of work; thrown into confusion.* 10. to cause to extend, *threw a bridge across the river.* 11. to move (a switch or lever) so as to operate it. 12. to have (a fit or tantrum). **throw** *n.* 1. the act of throwing. 2. the distance something is or may be thrown. 3. a light shawl or blanket. **throw′er** *n.* □**throw a party,** *(slang)* to hold a party. **throw away,** to part with as useless or unwanted; to fail to make use of, *throw away an opportunity.* **throw in,** to include (a thing) with what one is selling, without additional charge; to put in (a remark) casually or as an addition. **throw in the towel** *or* **sponge,** to admit defeat or failure and abandon a contest or effort. (▷From the practice of admitting defeat in a boxing match by throwing into the ring the towel or sponge used between rounds.) **throw off,** to manage to get rid of or become free from, *throw off a cold* or *one's pursuers;* to confuse or distract (a person); to compose easily as if without effort, *threw off a few lines of verse.* **throw oneself into,** to engage vigorously in. **throw oneself on,** to entrust oneself entirely to (a person's mercy etc.). **throw out,** to put out suddenly or forcibly; to expel (a troublemaker etc.); to throw away; to reject (a proposed plan etc.). **throw over,** to desert or abandon. **throw rug,** a small carpet that is easily moved about. **throw the book at,** *(informal)* to make all possible charges against (a person). **throw together,** to bring (people) casually into association. **throw up,** to vomit; to raise quickly or suddenly; to resign from, *throw up one's job.* **throw weight,** the weight of a missile payload that can be lifted by the launcher.

throw·a·way (throh-ă-way) *n.* 1. a manufactured item to be thrown away after one use. 2. a handbill or circular. **throwaway** *adj.* designed to be thrown away after being used once.

throw·back (throh-bak) *n.* an animal etc. showing characteristics of an ancestor that is earlier than its parents.

thrum (thrum) *v.* **(thrummed, thrum·ming)** to strum, to sound monotonously. **thrum** *n.* a thrumming sound.

thrush (thrush) *n.* any of several songbirds, especially one with a brownish back and speckled breast.

thru (throo) *adj., adv., & prep. (informal)* through.

thrust (thrust) *v.* **(thrust, thrust·ing)** 1. to push forcibly. 2. to make a forward stroke with a sword etc. 3. to put forcibly into a position or condition, to force the acceptance of, *some have greatness thrust upon them.* **thrust** *n.* 1. a thrusting movement or force. 2. a hostile remark aimed at a person. **thrust'er** *n.*

thru·way (throo-way) *n.* an expressway.

thud (thud) *n.* a low dull sound like that of a blow or something that does not resound. **thud** *v.* **(thud·ded, thud·ding)** to make a thud, to fall with a thud. **thud'ding·ly** *adv.*

thug (thug) *n.* a vicious or brutal ruffian. **thug'gish** *adj.* **thug'ger·y** *n.*

Thu·le (too-lee) *n.* the ancient name for the world's northernmost region.

thu·li·um (thoo-li-ŭm) *n.* a metallic element in the rare-earth group.

thumb (thum) *n.* 1. the short thick finger set apart from the other four. 2. the part of a mitten or glove covering this. **thumb** *v.* to wear or soil or turn pages etc. with the thumbs; *a well-thumbed book,* one that shows signs of much use. □**be all thumbs,** to be very clumsy at handling things. **thumb a ride,** to get a ride by signaling with one's thumb; to hitchhike. **thumb index,** a set of notches in the edges of a book's leaves, marked with letters etc. to enable the user to open the book directly at a particular section. **thumb one's nose,** to place one's thumb to the nose with fingers spread out as a gesture of contempt or defiance. **thumbs down,** a gesture of rejection. **thumbs up,** a gesture of satisfaction. **under a person's thumb,** completely under his influence.

thumb·nail (thum-nayl) *n.* the nail of the thumb. □**thumbnail sketch,** a brief description of something.

thumb·screw (thum-skroo) *n.* 1. an instrument of torture for squeezing the thumb. 2. a screw with a flattened head for the thumb to turn.

thumb·tack (thum-tak) *n.* a tack with a wide flat head permitting it to be pressed into soft wood etc. with the thumb.

thump (thump) *v.* to beat or strike or knock heavily (especially with the fist), to thud. **thump** *n.* a heavy blow, a dull sound made by this.

thump·ing (thum-ping) *adj. (informal)* large, *a thumping lie.*

thun·der (thun-dĕr) *n.* 1. the loud noise accompanying lightning. 2. any similar noise, *thunders of applause.* **thunder** *v.* 1. to sound with thunder, *it thundered.* 2. to make a noise like thunder, to sound loudly, *the train thundered past.* 3. to utter loudly, to make a forceful attack in words, *reformers thundered against gambling.* **thun'der·y** *adj.* **thun'der·er** *n.* □**steal a person's thunder,** to forestall him by using his ideas or words etc. before he can do so himself. ▷From the remark of a dramatist when the stage thunder intended for his play was taken and used for another.

thun·der·a·tion (thun-dĕ-ray-shŏn) *interj.* an exclamation of anger or surprise.

thun·der·bird (thun-dĕr-burd) *n.* (in the mythology of some American Indian tribes) a large bird thought to bring thunder, lightning, and rain.

thun·der·bolt (thun-dĕr-bohlt) *n.* 1. an imaginary destructive missile thought of as sent to Earth with a lightning flash. 2. a very startling and formidable event or statement.

thun·der·clap (thun-dĕr-klap) *n.* a clap of thunder.

thun·der·cloud (thun-dĕr-klowd) *n.* a storm cloud charged with electricity and producing thunder and lightning.

thun·der·head (thun-dĕr-hed) *n.* a rounded cumulus cloud projecting upward and heralding thunder.

thun·der·ous (thun-dĕ-rŭs) *adj.* like thunder. **thun'der·ous·ly** *adv.*

thun·der·show·er (thun-dĕr-show-ĕr) *n.* a rain shower accompanied by thunder and lightning.

thun·der·storm (thun-dĕr-storm) *n.* a storm accompanied by thunder and lightning.

thun·der·struck (thun-dĕr-struk) *adj.* amazed.

Thur., Thurs. *abbr.* Thursday.

Thurs·day (thurz-day) *n.* the day of the week following Wednesday.

thus (*th*us) *adv.* 1. in this way, like this, *hold the wheel thus.* 2. as a result of this, *he was the eldest son and thus heir to the title.* 3. to this extent, *thus far.* ▷The word *thusly* as a substitute for *thus* is always incorrect.

thwack (thwak) *v.* to strike with a heavy blow. **thwack** *n.* a heavy blow, the sound of this. **thwack'er** *n.*

thwart (thwort) *v.* to prevent (a person) from doing what he intends, to prevent (a plan etc.) from being accomplished. **thwart** *n.* an oarsman's bench across a boat. **thwart** *adj.* lying across (a ship). **thwart** *adv.* (on a ship) crosswise.

thy (*th*ī) *adj. (old use)* of or belonging to thee.

thyme (tīm) *n.* any of several herbs with fragrant leaves.

thy·mine (thī-meen) *n.* a crystalline base found as a constituent of DNA or derived from the thymus gland.

thy·mus (thī-mŭs) *n.* (also **thymus gland**) a ductless gland near the base of the neck (in man, it becomes much smaller at the end of childhood).

thy·roid (thī-roid) *n.* (also **thyroid gland**) a large ductless gland at the front of the neck, secreting a hormone that regulates the body's growth and development. **thyroid** *adj.* of or relating to the thyroid gland.

thy·rox·ine (thɪ-rok-seen) *n.* a white crystalline amino acid, the active constituent of the thyroid gland's secretions.

thy·self (thɪ-self) *pronoun* corresponding to *thee* and *thou*, used in the same ways as **himself**.

ti (tee) *n.* a name for the seventh note of a scale in music.

Ti *symbol* titanium.

ti·ar·a (ti-ar-ă) *n.* 1. a woman's ornamental crescent-shaped headdress, worn on ceremonial occasions. 2. the pope's diadem, pointed at the top and surrounded by three crowns.

Ti·bet (ti-bet) a former country north of India, now part of China. **Ti·bet′an** *adj.* & *n.*

tib·i·a (tib-i-ă) *n.* (*pl.* **tib·i·ae**, *pr.* tib-i-ee, **tib·i·as**) the shinbone. **tib′i·al** *adj.*

tic (tik) *n.* an involuntary spasmodic twitching of the muscles, especially of the face.

tick[1] (tik) *n.* 1. a regularly repeated clicking sound, especially that of a watch or clock. 2. a mark (often √) placed against an item in a list etc. to show that it has been checked or is correct. **tick** *v.* 1. (of a clock etc.) to make a series of ticks. 2. to put a tick beside (an item). □**tick off**, to mark with a tick; *(slang)* to anger or annoy. **what makes a person tick**, what makes him behave as he does.

tick[2] *n.* any of several bloodsucking mites or parasitic insects.

tick[3] *n.* the case of a mattress or pillow or bolster, holding the filling.

tick·er (tik-ĕr) *n.* 1. a telegraphic device that receives and prints stock prices on paper tape *(ticker tape).* 2. *(slang)* the heart. □**ticker-tape parade**, a parade in which tape from stock tickers and shredded paper are thrown from windows to greet a celebrity.

tick·et (tik-it) *n.* 1. a written or printed piece of card or paper that entitles the holder to a certain right (as to travel by train or bus etc., or to occupy a seat in a theater etc.) or serves as a receipt. 2. a certificate of qualification as a ship's master or pilot etc. 3. a label attached to a thing and giving its price or other particulars. 4. an official notification of a traffic offense, *parking ticket.* 5. a list of the candidates put forward by one party in an election. **ticket** *v.* (**tick·et·ed, tick·et·ing**) to put a ticket on (an article for sale etc.). □**that's the ticket**, *(slang)* that is the correct or desirable thing.

tick·ing (tik-ing) *n.* strong fabric for making ticks for mattresses or pillows etc.

tick·le (tik-ĕl) *v.* (**tick·led, tick·ling**) 1. to touch or stroke lightly so as to cause a slight tingling sensation, usually with involuntary movement and laughter. 2. to feel this sensation, *my foot tickles.* 3. to amuse, to please (a person's vanity or sense of humor etc.). **tickle** *n.* the act or sensation of tickling. **tick′ler** *n.* □**tickled pink** *or* **to death**, *(informal)* extremely amused or pleased. **tickle one's memory**, to jog one's memory. **tickler file**, a memorandum book or card file etc. to jog one's memory.

tick·lish (tik-lish) *adj.* 1. sensitive to tickling. 2. (of a problem) requiring careful handling. **tick′lish·ly** *adv.* **tick′lish·ness** *n.*

tick-tack-toe, tic-tac-toe (tik-tak-toh) *n.* a game of alternating turns in which each player tries to fill in a straight line of O's or X's in a nine-square figure before his opponent does so.

tick·tock (tik-tok) *n.* the ticking sound of a clock.

tid·al (tɪ-dăl) *adj.* of or affected by a tide or tides. **tid′al·ly** *adv.* □**tidal basin**, an artificially made body of water that is subject to the rise and fall of the tide. **tidal flat**, flat marshy tideland. **tidal wave**, a great ocean wave, such as one caused by an earthquake; a great wave of enthusiasm or indignation etc.

tid·bit (tid-bit) *n.* a choice bit of something, as of food or gossip or information.

tid·dly·wink (tid-lee-wingk) *n.* one of the small counters flicked into a cup in the game of **tiddlywinks**.

tide (tɪd) *n.* 1. the regular rise and fall in the level of the sea, caused by the attraction of the moon and the sun. 2. water as moved by this. 3. a trend of opinion or fortune or events, *the rising tide of discontent.* 4. *(old use)* a season, *yuletide.* **tide** *v.* (**tid·ed, tid·ing**) to float with the tide. **tide′less** *adj.* □**tide a person over**, to help him through a difficult period by providing what he needs.

tide·land (tɪd-land) *n.* land that is submerged at high tide.

tide·mark (tɪd-mahrk) *n.* a mark made by the tide at high water.

tide·wa·ter (tɪd-waw-tĕr) *n.* 1. water that is carried in by the tide or affected by the tide. 2. low-lying coastland drained by tidal streams.

tide·way (tɪd-way) *n.* the channel where a tide runs, the tidal part of a river.

ti·dings (tɪ-dingz) *n. pl.* news.

ti·dy (tɪ-dee) *adj.* (**-di·er, -di·est**) 1. neat and orderly in arrangement or in one's ways. 2. *(informal)* fairly large, considerable, *left a tidy fortune when he died.* **tidy** *n.* (*pl.* **-dies**) a decorative covering used to prevent soiling and wear on the arms and back of an upholstered chair. **tidy** *v.* (**ti·died, ti·dy·ing**) to make tidy. **ti′di·ly** *adv.* **ti′di·ness** *n.*

tie (tɪ) *v.* (**tied, ty·ing**) 1. to attach or fasten or bind with a cord or something similar. 2. to arrange (string or ribbon or a necktie etc.) to form a knot or bow, to form (a knot or bow) in this way. 3. to unite (notes in music) with a tie. 4. to make the same score as another competitor, *they tied for second place.* 5. to restrict or limit to certain conditions or to an occupation or place etc. **tie** *n.* 1. a cord etc. used for fastening or by which something is tied. 2. a necktie. 3. something that unites things or people, a bond. 4. something that restricts a person's freedom of action. 5. a curved line (in a musical score) over two notes of the same pitch, indicating that the second is not sounded separately. 6. equality of score between two or more competitors. 7. one of the parallel crossbeams used to support the rails of a railroad track. □**fit to be tied**, *(slang)* very angry. **tie beam**, a horizontal beam connecting rafters. **tie breaker**, a means of deciding the winner when competitors have tied. **tie clasp** *or* **clip**, an ornamental clip for holding a necktie in place. **tie down**, to restrict or bind; *the children tie her down*, prevent her from pursuing other interests. **tie in**, to link or (of information or facts) to agree or be connected with something else. **tie rod**, a connecting rod, especially that between the wheels of a vehicle, controlling its steering. **tie up**, to fasten with a cord etc.; to restrict movement or passage, *the accident tied up traffic for miles;* to invest or reserve (capital etc.) so that it is not readily available for use; to make restrictive conditions about (a bequest etc.); to occupy (a person) so that he has no time for other things; (of a boxer) to make (an opponent) unable to strike effective blows.

tie·back (tɪ-bak) *n.* a strip of cloth or cord fastening a curtain back from a window.

tie-dye (tɪ-dɪ) *v.* **(tie-dyed, tie-dy·ing)** to produce dyed patterns by tying parts of a fabric so that they are protected from the dye. **tie′-dy·ing** *n.*

tie-in (tɪ-ɪn) *n.* 1. a close association or connection. 2. a marketing arrangement for related products.

tie·pin (tɪ-pin) *n.* an ornamental pin for holding a necktie in place.

tier (teer) *n.* any of a series of rows or ranks or units of a structure placed one above the other. **tiered** (teerd) *adj.* arranged in tiers.

tie-up (tɪ-up) *n.* 1. a connection, a link. 2. a temporary obstruction or stoppage, as of traffic or work etc.

tiff (tif) *n.* a petty quarrel.

ti·ger (tɪ-gĕr) *n.* a large Asian animal of the cat family, with yellowish and black stripes. **ti′ger·ish** *adj.* **ti·gress** (tɪ-gris) *n. fem.* □**tiger cat,** a domestic cat with dark stripes. **tiger lily,** a tall garden lily with dark-spotted orange flowers. **tiger moth,** a moth with wings that are streaked like a tiger's skin. **tiger shark,** a voracious warmwater shark.

ti·ger's-eye (tɪ-gĕrz-ɪ) *n.* 1. a yellow-brown gem of brilliant luster. 2. a pottery glaze of similar appearance.

tight (tɪt) *adj.* 1. fixed or fastened or drawn together firmly and hard to move or undo. 2. fitting closely, made so that a specified thing cannot penetrate, *a tight joint; watertight; tight controls,* strictly imposed. 3. with things or people arranged closely together, *a tight little group; a tight schedule,* leaving no time to spare. 4. tense, stretched so as to leave no slack. 5. *(informal)* drunk. 6. (of money or materials) not easily obtainable, (of the money market) in which money and credit are severely restricted. 7. stingy, *tight with his money.* **tight** *adv.* tightly, *hold tight.* **tight′ly** *adv.* **tight′ness** *n.* □**in a tight corner** *or* **spot,** in a difficult situation.

tight·en (tɪ-tĕn) *v.* to make or become tighter. □**tighten one's belt,** to content oneself with less food etc. when money or supplies are scarce.

tight·fist·ed (tɪt-fis-tid) *adj.* stingy.

tight-knit (tɪt-nit) *adj.* well organized, *a tight-knit group.*

tight·lipped (tɪt-lipt) *adj.* 1. keeping the lips compressed firmly together to restrain one's emotion or comments. 2. grim-looking.

tight·rope (tɪt-rohp) *n.* a rope stretched tightly high above the ground, on which acrobats perform. □**tightrope walker,** an acrobat who walks on a tightrope.

tights (tɪts) *n. pl.* 1. a close-fitting garment covering the legs and lower part of the body, worn by acrobats, dancers, etc. 2. panty hose.

tight·wad (tɪt-wod) *n. (slang)* a stingy person.

ti·glon (tɪ-glŏn) *n.* the offspring of a tiger and a lioness.

til·de (til-dĕ) *n.* a mark **ũ** put over a letter, as the *n* in Spanish when pronounced *ny,* as in *señor,* or the *a* or *o* in Portuguese when nasalized as in *São Paulo.*

tile (tɪl) *n.* 1. a thin slab of baked clay or other material used in rows for covering roofs or walls or floors; *carpet tiles,* carpet made in small squares for laying in rows. 2. a length of earthenware or concrete pipe, used for land drainage, in sewers, etc. 3. one of the small flat pieces used in mah jongg. **tile** *v.* **(tiled, til·ing)** to cover with tiles. **til′er** *n.*

til·ing (tɪ-ling) *n.* a surface made of tiles.

till¹ (til) *v.* to prepare and use (land) for growing crops. **till′er¹** *n.* **till′a·ble** *adj.*

till² *conj. & prep.* until.

till³ *n.* a drawer for money behind the counter in a shop or bank etc.

till·age (til-ij) *n.* 1. tilling land. 2. land that has been tilled.

till·er² (til-ĕr) *n.* a horizontal bar by which the rudder of a small boat is turned in steering.

tilt (tilt) *v.* 1. to move or cause to move into a sloping position. 2. to run or thrust with a lance in jousting. **tilt** *n.* tilting, a sloping position. □**at full tilt,** at full speed, with full force. **tilt at windmills,** to battle with enemies who are only imaginary. ▷From the story of Don Quixote who attacked windmills, thinking they were giants.

tim·bale (tim-băl) *n.* a dish of minced meat, fish, or vegetables in a small drum-shaped pastry shell.

tim·ber (tim-bĕr) *n.* 1. wood prepared for use in building or carpentry. 2. growing trees suitable for this. 3. a piece of wood or a wooden beam used in constructing a house or ship. **timber** *v.* to build, support, or cover with timber. **timber!** *interj.* a shouted warning that a tree is about to fall. □**timber rattlesnake,** a rattlesnake found in the eastern U.S. **timber wolf,** a large gray wolf of North America.

tim·bered (tim-bĕrd) *adj.* 1. (of a building) constructed of timber or with a timber framework. 2. (of land) wooded.

tim·ber·ing (tim-bĕ-ring) *n.* timbers, work made of timber.

tim·ber·line (tim-bĕr-lɪn) *n.* (also **timber line**) tree line.

tim·bre (tam-bĕr) *n.* the characteristic quality of the sound produced by a particular voice or instrument.

tim·brel (tim-brĕl) *n. (old use)* a tambourine or similar instrument.

Tim·buk·tu (tim-buk-too) a very remote place. ▷From *Timbuktu* in Mali.

time (tɪm) *n.* 1. all the years of the past, present, and future. 2. the passing of these taken as a whole, *time will show who is right.* 3. a portion of time associated with certain events or conditions or experiences, *in the time of the Tudors; in Tudor times; in times of hardship; have a good time,* enjoy oneself. 4. a portion of time between two points, the point or period allotted or available or suitable for something, *the time it takes to do this; now is the time to buy; lunchtime.* 5. the point of time when something must occur or end. 6. an occasion or instance, *the first time we saw him; I told you three times; four times three,* three taken four times. 7. a point of time stated in hours and minutes of the day, *the time is exactly two o'clock.* 8. any of the standard systems by which time is reckoned, *Mountain Standard Time.* 9. measured time spent in work etc., *on short time; paid time and a half,* paid at one and a half times the usual rate. 10. tempo in music, rhythm depending on the number and accentuation of beats in a bar. **time** *v.* **(timed, tim‑ing)** 1. to choose the time or moment for, to arrange the time of. 2. to measure the time taken by (a race or runner or process etc.). □**against time,** with the utmost speed so as to reach a goal by a specified time, *racing against time.* **ahead of the times,** having ideas too enlightened to be accepted by one's contemporaries. **ahead of time,** earlier than expected or promised. **at the same time,** in spite of this, however. **at times,** sometimes. **behind the times,** *see* **behind. behind time,** late. **do time,** *(slang)* to serve a prison sentence. **for the time being,** until some other arrangement is made. **from time to time,** at in‑tervals. **half the time,** *(informal)* as often as not. **have a time,** to have a very bad (or very good) time. **have no time for,** to be unable or unwilling to spend time on, to despise. **in good time** or **all in good time,** *see* **good. in no time,** in an instant, very rapidly. **in one's time,** at a previous period in one's life. **in time,** not late; eventually, sooner or later. **keep time,** to walk, dance, sing, etc. in tempo; *keep good time,* (of a clock) to work accurately. **on one's own time,** outside working hours. **on time,** punctually. **take one's time,** *see* **take. the time of one's life,** a period of exceptional enjoyment. **time after time,** on many occasions, in many instances. **time and again** or **time and time again,** time after time. **time and motion study,** a means of measuring the efficiency of industrial or other operations. **time bomb,** a bomb that can be set to explode after a certain interval. **time capsule,** a container filled with objects typical of the present time, buried in the foundation of a new building etc. for discov‑ery in the future. **time clock,** a clock with a device for recording workmen's hours of work. **time deposit,** a bank deposit not repayable be‑fore a set date or without advance notice. **time exposure,** a photographic exposure in which the shutter is left open for more than a second or two and not operated at an automatically con‑trolled speed. **time limit,** a limit of time within which something must be done. **time lock,** a lock that cannot be opened before a set time, as that of a bank vault. **time machine,** (in science fiction) a machine that would enable people to move back‑ward or forward in time. **time of day,** the hour by the clock. **time sharing,** the use of a computer by several subscribers. **time sheet,** a record of hours worked. **time signal,** an audible indication of the exact time of day. **time zone,** a region (between two parallels of longitude) where a com‑mon standard time is used.

time‑card (tɪm‑kahrd) *n.* a card for recording a workman's hours of work.

time‑con‑sum‑ing (tɪm‑kŏn‑soo‑ming) *adj.* occu‑pying much time.

time‑hon‑ored (tɪm‑on‑ŏrd) *adj.* honored because of long tradition or custom.

time‑keep‑er (tɪm‑kee‑pĕr) *n.* a person who re‑cords time, especially of workmen or in a game.

time‑lag (tɪm‑lag) *n.* an interval of time between two connected events.

time‑lapse (tɪm‑laps) *adj.* (of motion‑picture pho‑tography) containing frames taken at long inter‑vals but shown at a normal pace to accelerate the viewing of events, as the opening of a bud into a flower.

time‑less (tɪm‑lis) *adj.* 1. not to be thought of as having duration. 2. not affected by the passage

of time. **time′less‑ly** *adv.* **time′less‑ness** *n.*

time‑ly (tɪm‑lee) *adj.* occurring at just the right time, *a timely warning.* **time′li‑ness** *n.*

time‑out (tɪm‑owt) *n.* a brief intermission, espe‑cially in a game.

time‑piece (tɪm‑pees) *n.* a clock or watch.

tim‑er (tɪ‑mĕr) *n.* 1. a person who times something. 2. a timing device.

time‑sav‑ing (tɪm‑say‑ving) *adj.* reducing the time it takes to do something, *a timesaving device.*

time‑serv‑er (tɪm‑sur‑vĕr) *n.* a person who, espe‑cially for selfish ends, adapts himself to opinions of the times or of persons in power.

time‑ta‑ble (tɪm‑tay‑bĕl) *n.* a list showing the times of arrival and departure of buses, railroad trains, etc.

time‑worn (tɪm‑wohrn) *adj.* 1. worn by long use. 2. trite, hackneyed.

tim‑id (tim‑id) *adj.* easily alarmed, not bold, shy. **tim′id‑ly** *adv.* **tim′id‑ness** *n.* **ti‑mid‑i‑ty** (ti‑mid‑i‑tee) *n.*

tim‑ing (tɪ‑ming) *n.* the way something is timed.

tim‑or‑ous (tim‑ŏ‑rŭs) *adj.* timid. **tim′or‑ous‑ly** *adv.* **tim′or‑ous‑ness** *n.*

tim‑o‑thy (tim‑ŏ‑thee) *n.* a kind of grass grown as fodder for cattle.

Tim‑o‑thy (tim‑ŏ‑thee) *n.* (in the New Testament) either of two epistles of St. Paul addressed to Timothy, his convert and assistant.

tim‑pa‑ni (tim‑pă‑nee) *n. pl.* kettledrums, used es‑pecially in a symphony orchestra.

tim‑pan‑ist (tim‑pă‑nist) *n.* a person who plays the drums in a symphony orchestra.

tin (tin) *n.* 1. a silvery‑white metal. 2. tin plate. **tin** *v.* **(tinned, tin‑ning)** 1. to coat with tin. □**tin ear,** *(informal)* tone deafness. **tin god,** a person who is unjustifiably given great veneration. **tin lizzie,** a small cheap automobile. **Tin Pan Alley,** the world of the composers and publishers etc. of popular music. **tin plate,** sheet iron or sheet steel coated thinly with tin. **tin soldier,** a toy soldier made of tin or lead.

tinct. *abbr.* tincture.

tinc‑ture (tingk‑chŭr) *n.* 1. a solution consisting of a medicinal substance dissolved in alcohol. 2. a slight tinge or trace of some element or quality. **tincture** *v.* **(tinc‑tured, tinc‑tur‑ing)** to tinge.

tin‑der (tin‑dĕr) *n.* any dry substance that catches fire easily.

tin‑der‑box (tin‑dĕr‑boks) *n.* a metal box formerly used in kindling a fire, containing dry material that caught fire from a spark produced by flint and steel.

tine (tɪn) *n.* any of the points or prongs of a fork or harrow or antler.

tin‑foil (tin‑foil) *n.* a thin sheet of tin or tin alloy, used for wrapping and packing things.

ting (ting) *n.* a sharp ringing sound. **ting** *v.* to make a ting.

ting‑a‑ling (ting‑ă‑ling) *n.* the sound of a small bell.

tinge (tinj) *v.* **(tinged, tinge‑ing)** 1. to color slightly, *tinged with pink.* 2. to give a slight trace of some element or quality to, *their admiration was tinged with envy.* **tinge** *n.* a slight coloring or trace.

tin‑gle (ting‑gĕl) *v.* **(tin‑gled, tin‑gling)** to have a slight pricking or stinging sensation. **tingle** *n.* this sensation. **tin′gler** *n.* **tin′gly** *adj.*

tin‑horn (tin‑horn) *n.* *(slang)* a pretentious but un‑impressive person. **tinhorn** *adj.* *(slang)* cheap, un‑important, *a tinhorn gambler.*

tink·er (ting-kĕr) *n.* *(old use)* a traveling mender of pots and pans. **tinker** *v.* to work at something casually, trying to repair or improve it. **tink'er·er** *n.* □**tinker's dam** *or* **damn,** something without value; *don't care a tinker's dam,* do not care at all.

tin·kle (ting-kĕl) *n.* a series of short light ringing sounds. **tinkle** *v.* **(tin·kled, tin·kling)** to make or cause to make a tinkle.

tin·ny (tin-ee) *adj.* **(-ni·er, -ni·est)** 1. of or like tin, (of metal objects) not looking strong or solid. 2. having a metallic taste or a thin metallic sound. **tin'ni·ly** *adv.* **tin'ni·ness** *n.*

tin·plat·ed (tin-play-tid) *adj.* coated with tin.

tin·sel (tin-sĕl) *n.* a glittering metallic substance used in strips or threads to give an inexpensive sparkling effect. **tin'seled** *adj.*

tin·smith (tin-smith) *n.* a worker in tin and tin plate.

tint (tint) *n.* 1. a variety of a particular color. 2. a slight trace of a different color, *red with a bluish tint.* **tint** *v.* to apply or give a tint to, to color slightly. **tint'er** *n.*

tin·tin·nab·u·la·tion (tin-ti-nab-yŭ-lay-shŏn) *n.* the sound of bells ringing.

tin·type (tin-tɪp) *n.* an old kind of positive photograph made from the exposure of a sensitized plate of enameled iron or tin.

tin·ware (tin-wair) *n.* pots or pans etc. made of tin or tin plate.

tin·works (tin-wurks) *n.* (*pl.* **-works**) a place where tin is mined or processed or made into articles.

ti·ny (tɪ-nee) *adj.* **(-ni·er, -ni·est)** very small. **ti'ni·ness** *n.*

tip[1] (tip) *n.* 1. the very end of a thing, especially of something small or tapering. 2. a small part or piece fitted to the end of something, *cigarettes with filter tips.* **tip** *v.* **(tipped, tip·ping)** to provide with a tip, *filter-tipped.* □**on the tip of one's tongue,** just about to be spoken or remembered. **tip of the iceberg,** *see* **iceberg.**

tip[2] *v.* **(tipped, tip·ping)** to tilt or topple, to cause to do this. **tip** *n.* a slight tilt or push. □**tip the balance** *or* **scale,** to be just enough to cause one scale pan to go lower than the other; to be the deciding factor for or against something.

tip[3] *v.* **(tipped, tip·ping)** to strike or touch lightly. **tip** *n.* a light stroke or touch.

tip[4] *v.* **(tipped, tip·ping)** 1. to make a small gift of money to (a person), especially in acknowledgment of his services. 2. to name as a likely winner of a contest etc. **tip** *n.* 1. a small gift of money. 2. private or special information (as about horse races or the stock market) likely to profit the receiver if he acts upon it. 3. a small but useful piece of advice on how to do something. □**tip off,** to give an advance warning or hint or inside information to (a person).

tip-in (tip-in) *n.* 1. a special page in a book or magazine pasted at the inside edge of a regular page. 2. (in basketball) a goal made by tipping the ball into the basket at close range.

tip·off (tip-awf) *n.* advance or inside information.

tip·per (tip-ĕr) *n.* a person who leaves a gratuity.

tip·pet (tip-it) *n.* a small cape or collar of fur etc. with ends hanging down in front.

tip·ple (tip-ĕl) *v.* **(tip·pled, tip·pling)** to drink (wine or whiskey etc.), to be in the habit of drinking. **tip'pler** *n.*

tip·ster (tip-stĕr) *n.* *(informal)* a person who gives tips about horse races etc.

tip·sy (tip-see) *adj.* **(-si·er, -si·est)** slightly drunk, showing or caused by slight intoxication, *a tipsy lurch.* **tip'si·ly** *adv.* **tip'si·ness** *n.*

tip·toe (tip-toh) *v.* **(tip·toed, tip·toe·ing)** to walk very quietly or carefully, with heels not touching the ground. **tiptoe** *n.* the tip of toe. **tiptoe** *adv.* on tiptoe. □**on tiptoe,** walking or standing on one's toes.

tip·top (tip-top) *n.* the highest point. **tiptop** *adj.* excellent, very best, *tiptop quality.*

ti·rade (tɪ-rayd) *n.* a long angry or violent piece of criticism or denunciation.

Ti·ra·na (ti-rah-nä) the capital of Albania.

tire[1] (tɪr) *v.* **(tired, tir·ing)** to make or become tired.

tire[2] *n.* a covering fitted around the rim of a wheel to absorb shocks, usually of reinforced rubber filled with air or covering a pneumatic inner tube.

tired (tɪrd) *adj.* feeling that one would like to sleep or rest. □**tired of,** having had enough of (a thing or activity) and feeling impatient or bored.

tire·less (tɪr-lis) *adj.* not tiring easily, having inexhaustible energy. **tire'less·ly** *adv.* **tire'less·ness** *n.*

tire·some (tɪr-sŏm) *adj.* annoying. **tire'some·ly** *adv.* **tire'some·ness** *n.*

'tis (tiz) *(old use)* = it is.

tis·sue (tish-oo) *n.* 1. the substance forming an animal or plant body, a particular kind of this, *muscular tissue.* 2. tissue paper. 3. a disposable piece of soft absorbent paper used as a handkerchief etc. 4. fine gauzy fabric. 5. something thought of as an interwoven series, *a tissue of lies.* □**tissue paper,** very thin soft paper used for wrapping and packing things.

tit[1] (tit) *n.* any of several small birds, especially the titmouse.

tit[2] *n.* **tit for tat,** an equivalent given in retaliation for an injury etc.

tit[3] *n.* *(slang)* 1. a nipple or teat. 2. either of a woman's breasts.

ti·tan (tɪ-tăn) *n.* a person of great size or strength or importance. ▷ The Titans were a race of giants in Greek mythology.

ti·tan·ic (tɪ-tan-ik) *adj.* gigantic, immense.

ti·ta·ni·um (tɪ-tay-ni-ŭm) *n.* a gray metallic element occurring in many clays and used to clean and harden molten steel.

tithe (tɪtth) *n.* one-tenth of the annual produce of agriculture etc., formerly paid as tax to support clergy and church. **tithe** *v.* **(tithed, tith·ing)** to contribute one-tenth of one's income to one's church. **tith'er** *n.*

ti·tian (tish-ăn) *n.* bright golden auburn as a color of hair. ▷ Named after Tiziano Vecelli (Titian) an Italian painter of the 15th–16th centuries.

tit·il·late (tit-ĭ-layt) *v.* **(tit·il·lat·ed, tit·il·lat·ing)** to excite or stimulate pleasantly. **tit·il·lat·ing·ly** *adv.* **tit·il·la·tion** (tit-ĭ-lay-shŏn) *n.*

tit·i·vate (tit-ĭ-vayt) *v.* **(tit·i·vat·ed, tit·i·vat·ing)** *(informal)* to smarten up, to put the finishing touches to. **tit·i·va·tion** (tit-ĭ-vay-shŏn) *n.*

ti·tle (tɪ-tĕl) *n.* 1. the name of a book or poem or picture etc. 2. a word used to show a person's rank or office (as *king, mayor, captain*) or used in speaking of or to him or her (as *Lord, Mrs., Doctor*). 3. the legal right to ownership of property, a document conferring this. 4. a champion-

ship in sport, *the world heavyweight title.* **title** v.
(ti·tled, ti·tling) to give a title to (a book etc.).
☐**title deed,** a legal document proving a person's
title to a property. **title page,** a page at the beginning of a book giving the title, author's name,
and other particulars. **title role,** the part in a
play etc. from which the title is taken, as the
part of Hamlet in the play of that name.

ti·tled (tı-tĕld) *adj.* having a title of nobility, *titled
ladies.*

tit·mouse (tit-mows) *n.* (*pl.* **-mice,** *pr.* -mıs) any
of a number of small songbirds usually having
soft dull plumage.

tit·ter (tit-ĕr) *n.* a high-pitched giggle. **titter** v. to
give a titter. **tit′ter·ing·ly** *adv.*

tit·tle (tit-ĕl) *n.* a very small piece.

tit·tle-tat·tle (tit-ĕl-tat-ĕl) **(tit·tle-tat·tled, tit·
tle-tat·tling)** v. to tattle. **tittle-tattle** *n.* a tattle.

tit·u·lar (tich-ü-lär) *adj.* 1. of or belonging to a
title. 2. having the title of ruler etc. but without
real authority, *the titular head of the state.*

Ti·tus (tı-tŭs) *n.* (in the New Testament) the epistle
of St. Paul addressed to Titus, his convert and
assistant.

tiz·zy (tiz-ee) *n.* (*pl.* **-zies**) *(slang)* a state of nervous
agitation or confusion, *in a tizzy.*

tk. *abbr.* 1. tank. 2. truck.

TKO *abbr.* technical knockout.

tkt. *abbr.* ticket.

Tl *symbol* thallium.

TLC *abbr.* tender loving care.

Tm *symbol* thulium.

TM *abbr.* 1. trademark. 2. transcendental meditation.

T-man (tee-man) *n.* (*pl.* **T-men,** *pr.* tee-men)
(informal) an agent of the U.S. Treasury Department.

TN *abbr.* Tennessee.

tn. *abbr.* 1. ton(s). 2. town.

tng. *abbr.* training.

tnpk. *abbr.* turnpike.

TNT *abbr.* trinitrotoluene, a powerful explosive.

to (too) *prep.* 1. in the direction of, so as to approach
or reach or be in (a place or position or state
etc.), *walked to the station; rose to power; was sent
to prison; back to back.* 2. as far as, not falling
short of, *patriotic to the core; from noon to two
o'clock; goods to the value of $100; cooked to per-
fection.* 3. as compared with, in respect of, *won
by three goals to two; made to measure; his remarks
were not to the point.* 4. for (a person or thing)
to hold or possess or be affected etc. by, *give it
to me; spoke to her; kind to animals; accustomed
to it; drank a toast to the bride.* **to** (with a verb)
1. forming an infinitive, or expressing purpose
or consequence etc., *he wants to go; does it to
annoy.* 2. used alone when the verb is understood,
meant to call but forgot to. **to** *adv.* 1. to or in
the normal or required position, to a closed or
almost closed position, *push the door to.* 2. into
a state of consciousness, *when she came to.* 3.
into a state of activity, *set to.* ☐**to and fro,** backward and forward. **to wit,** *see* **wit².** ▷Do not
confuse *to* with *too* or *two.*

toad (tohd) *n.* a froglike animal living chiefly on
land and having a clumsy and usually warty body.

toad·stool (tohd-stool) *n.* a fungus (especially a
poisonous one) with a round top and a slender
stalk.

toad·y (toh-dee) *n.* (*pl.* **toad·ies**) a person who

flatters and behaves obsequiously to another in
the hope of gain or advantage for himself. **toady**
v. **(toad·ied, toad·y·ing)** to behave as a toady.

toast (tohst) *n.* 1. a slice of toasted bread. 2. the
person or thing in whose honor a company is
requested to drink, the call to drink or an instance
of drinking in this way. **toast** v. 1. to brown
the surface of (bread etc.) by placing before a
fire or other source of heat. 2. to warm (one's
feet etc.) in this way. 3. to honor or pledge good
wishes to by drinking.

toast·er (toh-stĕr) *n.* an electrical device for toast-
ing bread.

toast·mas·ter (tohst-mas-tĕr) *n.* a person who announces the toasts at a public dinner etc. **toast·
mis·tress** (tohst-mis-tris) *n. fem.*

to·bac·co (tŏ-bak-oh) *n.* (*pl.* **-cos, -coes**) 1. a
plant grown for its leaves, which are used for
smoking or for making snuff. 2. its leaves, especially as prepared for smoking.

to·bac·co·nist (tŏ-bak-ŏ-nist) *n.* a shopkeeper
who sells cigarettes, cigars, and pipe tobacco.

To·ba·go (tŏ-bay-goh) an island in the West Indies
(*see* **Trinidad**).

to-be (tŏ-bee) *adj.* future, soon to become, *the bride-
to-be.*

to·bog·gan (tŏ-bog-än) *n.* a long light narrow sled
curved upward at the front, used for sliding downhill. **toboggan** v. to ride on a toboggan.
to·bog′gan·ist *n.*

toc·ca·ta (tŏ-kah-tä) *n.* a musical composition for
a piano or organ etc.

toc·sin (tok-sin) *n.* 1. a bell rung as an alarm. 2.
a signal of disaster.

to·day (tŏ-day) *n.* this present day or age. **today**
adv. 1. on this present day. 2. at the present time.

tod·dle (tod-ĕl) v. **(tod·dled, tod·dling)** 1. (of
a young child) to walk with short unsteady steps.
2. *(informal)* to walk.

tod·dler (tod-lĕr) *n.* a child who has only recently
learned to walk.

tod·dy (tod-ee) *n.* (*pl.* **-dies**) a sweetened drink
of liquor and hot water.

to-do (tŏ-doo) *n.* a fuss or commotion.

toe (toh) *n.* 1. one of the divisions (five in man)
of the front part of the foot. 2. the part of a
shoe or stocking that covers the toes. 3. anything
similar to a toe in form or position. **toe** v. **(toed,
toe·ing)** to touch or reach with the toes. ☐**be
on one's toes,** to be alert or eager. **toe dance,**
a dance performed on the tips of the toes. **toe
in,** (of vehicle wheels) to be set so that the front
part points slightly inward. **toe out,** (of vehicle
wheels) to be set so that the back part points
slightly inward. **toe the line,** to conform (especially under compulsion) to the requirements of
one's group or party.

toe·cap (toh-kap) *n.* the outer covering of the toe
of a boot or shoe.

toe·hold (toh-hohld) *n.* a slight foothold.

toe·nail (toh-nayl) *n.* the nail of a human toe.

toe·shoe (toh-shoo) *n.* a ballet slipper worn for
dancing on the tips of the toes.

tof·fee (taw-fee) *n.* (*pl.* **-fees**) 1. a candy similar
to taffy but more brittle in texture. 2. (chiefly
British) taffy.

to·fu (toh-foo) *n.* bean curd.

tog (tog) v. **(togged, tog·ging)** *(informal)* **tog
up** *or* **out,** to dress.

to·ga (toh-gä) *n.* (*pl.* **-gas**) a loose flowing outer garment worn by men in ancient Rome. **to·gaed** (toh-găd) *adj.*

to·geth·er (tŏ-*geth*-ĕr) *adv.* 1. in or into company or conjunction, toward each other, so as to unite. 2. one with another, *compare them together.* 3. simultaneously, *both together exclaimed.* 4. in an unbroken succession, *he is away for weeks together.* **to·geth'er·ness** *n.* □**get it (all *or* one's act) together,** *(informal)* to organize or control oneself; to work productively. **together with,** as well as, and also.

tog·ger·y (tog-ĕ-ree) *n.* *(informal)* clothing.

tog·gle (tog-ĕl) *n.* a fastening device consisting of a short piece of wood or metal etc. secured by its centers and passed through a loop or hole etc. **toggle** *v.* **(tog·gled, tog·gling)** to furnish or fasten with a toggle. □**toggle bolt,** a screwlike device that spreads out to hold in a hollow wall. **toggle switch,** a switch operated by a projecting lever.

To·go (toh-goh) a country in West Africa. **To·go·lese** (toh-gŏ-leez) *adj. & n.* (*pl.* -lese).

togs (togz) *n. pl.* *(informal)* clothes.

toil (toil) *v.* 1. to work long or laboriously. 2. to move laboriously, *we toiled up the hill.* **toil** *n.* hard or laborious work. **toil'er** *n.*

toil·et (toi-lit) *n.* 1. a bowl-shaped structure used for defecation and urination, usually a fixture and with a drainage pipe and flushing apparatus. 2. a room with this. 3. the process of dressing and grooming oneself. □**toilet paper,** thin soft tissue for cleaning oneself after using the toilet. **toilet soap,** soap for washing oneself. **toilet training,** the process of training a child to control urination and defecation and use a toilet. **toilet water,** scented water for use on the skin.

toi·let·ries (toi-li-treez) *n. pl.* (in shops) articles or preparations used in washing and grooming oneself.

toi·lette (twah-let) *n.* 1. toilet (sense 3). 2. style of dress.

toil·worn (toil-wohrn) *adj.* worn by toil, showing marks of this.

To·kay (toh-kay) *n.* 1. a sweet aromatic dessert wine made in Hungary. 2. a similar California wine.

toke (tohk) *v.* **(toked, tok·ing)** *(slang)* to smoke marijuana. **toke** *n.* *(slang)* a puff of a marijuana cigarette.

to·ken (toh-kĕn) *n.* 1. a sign or symbol or evidence of something, *a token of our esteem.* 2. a keepsake or memorial of friendship etc. 3. a device like a coin bought for use with machines etc. or for making certain payments, *bus tokens.* **token** *adj.* serving as a token or pledge but often on a small scale, *token resistance.* □**by the same token,** similarly, moreover.

to·ken·ism (toh-kĕ-niz-ĕm) *n.* a policy of making only a token effort or of doing no more than is nominally necessary.

To·ky·o (toh-ki-oh) the capital of Japan.

tol·bu·ta·mide (tol-byoo-tă-mıd) *n.* a drug for mild cases of diabetes, taken orally.

told (tohld) *see* **tell.** □**all told,** counting everything or everyone, *we were sixteen all told.*

tole (tohl) *n.* a kind of lacquered or enameled metalware, used for trays, lamp shades, etc.

tol·er·able (tol-ĕ-ră-bĕl) *adj.* 1. able to be tolerated, endurable. 2. fairly good, passable. **tol'er·a·bly** *adv.*

tol·er·ance (tol-ĕ-răns) *n.* 1. willingness or ability to tolerate a person or thing. 2. the permitted variation in the measurement or weight etc. of an object.

tol·er·ant (tol-ĕ-rănt) *adj.* having or showing tolerance. **tol'er·ant·ly** *adv.*

tol·er·ate (tol-ĕ-rayt) *v.* **(tol·er·at·ed, tol·er·at·ing)** 1. to permit without protest or interference. 2. to bear (pain etc.), to be able to take (a medicine) or undergo (radiation etc.) without harm. **tol'er·a·tor** *n.* **tol·er·a·tive** (tol-ĕ-ray-tive) *adj.* **tol·er·a·tion** (tol-ĕ-ray-shŏn) *n.*

toll¹ (tohl) *n.* 1. a tax or duty paid for the use of a public road or harbor etc. or for service rendered. 2. the loss or damage caused by a disaster or incurred in achieving something; *the death toll in the earthquake,* the number of deaths it caused. □**take its toll,** to be accompanied by loss or injury etc. **toll bridge,** a bridge at which a toll is charged. **toll call,** a telephone call for which the charge is higher than for local calls. **toll road,** a highway on which a toll is charged.

toll² *v.* 1. to ring (a bell) with slow strokes, especially for a death or funeral. 2. (of a bell) to sound in this way, to indicate by tolling. **toll** *n.* the stroke of a tolling bell.

toll·booth (tohl-booth) *n.* a booth where a toll is paid, as on entering a toll road.

toll·gate (tohl-gayt) *n.* a bar or gate across a road to prevent the passage of persons or vehicles etc. until the toll is paid.

toll·house (tohl-hows) *n.* a house occupied by the collector of tolls on a road etc. □**tollhouse cookie,** a cookie containing chocolate chips.

tol·u·ene (tol-yoo-een) *n.* a colorless aromatic liquid hydrocarbon derivative of benzene.

tom (tom) *n.* 1. a male animal, especially a male cat. 2. a male turkey.

Tom (tom) *n.* **Tom Collins,** a tall iced drink made with gin, soda water, lemon or lime juice, and sugar. **Tom, Dick, and Harry,** *(contemptuous)* ordinary people, people taken at random.

tom·a·hawk (tom-ă-hawk) *n.* a light ax used as a tool or weapon by North American Indians. **tomahawk** *v.* to strike or cut or kill with a tomahawk.

to·ma·to (tŏ-may-toh, -mah-) *n.* (*pl.* -toes) 1. a plant bearing a glossy red or yellow fruit eaten as a vegetable, the fruit itself. 2. *(slang)* a pretty girl.

tomb (toom) *n.* 1. a grave or other place of burial. 2. a vault or stone monument in which one or more people are buried.

tom·boy (tom-boi) *n.* a girl who is boisterous and boyish.

tomb·stone (toom-stohn) *n.* a memorial stone set up over a grave.

tom·cat (tom-kat) *n.* a male cat.

tome (tohm) *n.* a book or volume, especially a large heavy one.

tom·fool (tom-fool) *adj.* extremely foolish. **tomfool** *n.* an extremely foolish person. **tom·fool'er·y** *n.*

tom·my (tom-ee) **gun** a submachine gun.

tom·my·rot (tom-ee-rot) *n.* *(slang)* nonsense, an absurd statement or argument.

to·mor·row (tŏ-mor-oh) *n.* 1. the day after today. 2. the near future. **tomorrow** *adv.* on the day after today, at some future date.

tom-tom (tom-tom) *n.* 1. an African or Asian drum beaten with the hands. 2. a tall drum used in jazz bands.

ton (tun) *n.* 1. a measure of weight, either 2240 lbs. or 1016.06 kg. *(long ton)* or 2000 lbs. or 907.20 kg. *(short ton).* 2. a measure of capacity for various materials, 40 cubic feet of timber. 3. a unit of cargo-carrying capacity for ships, usually estimated at 40 cubic feet. 4. *(informal)* a large amount, *tons of money.*

ton·al (toh-năl) *adj.* 1. of a tone or tones. 2. of tonality. **ton'al·ly** *adv.*

to·nal·i·ty (toh-nal-i-tee) *n.* (*pl.* **-ties**) 1. the character of a melody, depending on the scale or key in which it is composed. 2. the color scheme of a picture.

tone (tohn) *n.* 1. a musical or vocal sound, especially with reference to its pitch and quality and strength. 2. the manner of expression in speaking or writing, *an apologetic tone.* 3. any one of the five intervals between one note and the next which, together with two semitones, make up an octave. 4. proper firmness of the organs and tissues of the body, *muscle tone.* 5. a tint or shade of a color, the general effect of color or of light and shade in a picture. 6. the general spirit or character prevailing, *set the tone with a dignified speech.* **tone** *v.* **(toned, ton·ing)** 1. to give a particular tone of sound or color to. 2. to give proper firmness to (muscles or organs or skin etc.). **ton'er** *n.* □**tone arm,** the tubular arm containing the pickup of a record player. **tone down,** to make or become softer in tone of sound or color; to make (a statement) less strong or harsh. **tone poem,** an orchestral composition illustrating a poetic idea. **tone up,** to make or become brighter or more vigorous or intense.

tone-deaf (tohn-def) *adj.* unable to perceive accurately differences of musical pitch. **tone'-deaf'ness** *n.*

tone·less (tohn-lis) *adj.* without positive tone, not expressive. **tone'less·ly** *adv.*

tong (tawng) *n.* a Chinese guild, association, or secret society in the U.S.

Ton·ga (tong-gă) (also **Friendly Islands**) a country consisting of a group of islands in the Pacific. **Ton'gan** *adj.* & *n.*

tongs (tawngz) *n. pl.* an instrument with two arms joined at one end, used for grasping and holding things.

tongue (tung) *n.* 1. the fleshy muscular organ in the mouth, used in tasting, licking, swallowing, and (in man) speaking. 2. the tongue of an ox etc. as food. 3. the ability to speak or manner of speaking, *a persuasive tongue; have lost one's tongue,* be too bashful or surprised to speak. 4. a language, *his native tongue is German.* 5. a projecting strip or flap. 6. a tapering jet of flame. **tongue** *v.* **(tongued, tongu·ing)** to produce staccato or other effects in a wind instrument by use of the tongue. □**tongue depressor,** a flat thin wooden stick used to hold down the tongue while the throat is being examined. **tongue twister,** a sequence of words that is difficult to pronounce quickly and correctly, as *she sells sea shells.* **with one's tongue hanging out,** thirsty; eagerly expectant. **with tongue in cheek,** speaking with sly sarcasm.

tongued (tungd) *adj.* 1. having a tongue. 2. having a certain manner of speaking, *sharp-tongued.*

tongue-lash·ing (tung-lash-ing) *n.* a severe rebuke.

tongue-tied (tung-trd) *adj.* 1. silent because of shyness or embarrassment. 2. unable to speak normally because the ligament connecting the tongue

to the base of the mouth is abnormally short.

ton·ic (ton-ik) *n.* 1. a medicine with an invigorating effect, taken after illness or weakness. 2. anything that restores people's energy or good spirits. 3. a keynote in music. 4. tonic water. **tonic** *adj.* having the effect of a tonic, toning up the muscles etc. □**tonic water,** mineral water, especially if slightly flavored with quinine.

to·night (tŏ-nrt) *n.* 1. the present evening or night. 2. the evening or night of today. **tonight** *adv.* on the present evening or night or that of today.

ton·nage (tun-ij) *n.* 1. the carrying capacity of a ship or ships, expressed in tons. 2. the charge per ton for carrying cargo or freight.

ton·neau (tu-noh) *n.* (*pl.* **-neaus, -neaux,** *pr.* **-nohz**) the section for back seats in an early automobile.

ton·sil (ton-sĭl) *n.* either of two small organs at the sides of the throat near the root of the tongue.

ton·sil·lec·to·my (ton-sĭ-lek-tŏ-mee) *n.* (*pl.* **-mies**) surgical removal of tonsils.

ton·sil·li·tis (ton-sĭ-lr-tis) *n.* inflammation of the tonsils.

ton·so·ri·al (ton-sohr-i-ăl) *adj. (humorous)* of a barber or his work; *tonsorial parlor,* a barbershop.

ton·sure (ton-shŭr) *n.* 1. shaving the top or all of the head of a person entering certain priesthoods or monastic orders. 2. the part of the head shaven in this way. **ton'sured** *adj.*

ton·y (toh-nee) *adj.* **(ton·i·er, ton·i·est)** *(slang)* high-class, stylish.

too (too) *adv.* 1. to a greater extent than is desirable. 2. *(informal)* very, *he's not too well today.* 3. also, *take the others too.* □**too bad,** *(informal)* regrettable, a pity. **too much for,** easily able to defeat (an opponent etc.); more than can be endured by (a person). ▷Do not confuse *too* with *to* or *two.*

took *see* **take.**

tool (tool) *n.* 1. a thing (usually something held in the hand) for working on something. 2. a simple machine, as a lathe. 3. anything used in an occupation or pursuit, *a dictionary is a useful tool.* 4. a person used as a mere instrument by another. **tool** *v.* 1. to shape or ornament by using a tool. 2. to provide oneself or equip (a factory etc.) with necessary tools, *tool up.* 3. *(slang)* to drive or ride in a casual or leisurely way, *tooling along.* □**tool up,** to equip with tools.

toot¹ (toot) *n.* a short sound produced by a horn or whistle etc. **toot** *v.* to make or cause to make a toot. **toot'er** *n.*

toot² *n.* a drinking bout. □**go on a toot,** to get drunk.

tooth (tooth) *n.* (*pl.* **teeth,** *pr.* teeth) 1. each of the hard white bony structures rooted in the gums, used for biting and chewing things. 2. a similar structure in the mouth or alimentary canal of certain invertebrate animals. 3. a toothlike part or projection, as on a gear, saw, comb, or rake. 4. a liking for a particular type of food, *he has a sweet tooth.* □**cut one's teeth on,** to use or learn about when young or inexperienced. **get one's teeth into,** to begin serious work on. **in the teeth of,** in spite of; in opposition to; directly against (the wind). **put teeth into,** to make (a law or regulation) able to be applied effectively. **tooth and nail,** fiercely; with all one's might. **tooth powder,** powder for cleaning the teeth.

tooth·ache (tooth-ayk) *n.* an ache in a tooth or teeth.

tooth·brush (tooth-brush) *n.* a brush for cleaning the teeth.

toothed (tootht) *adj.* having teeth or teeth of a certain kind, *sharp-toothed.*

tooth·less (tooth-lis) *adj.* having no teeth.

tooth·paste (tooth-payst) *n.* paste for cleaning the teeth.

tooth·pick (tooth-pik) *n.* a small pointed piece of wood etc. for removing bits of food from between the teeth.

tooth·some (tooth-sŏm) *adj.* 1. pleasant to eat. 2. attractive, *a toothsome blonde.* **tooth′some·ness** *n.*

tooth·y (too-thee) *adj.* (**tooth·i·er, tooth·i·est**) having many or large teeth. **tooth′i·ly** *adv.*

toots (tuuts) *n.* *(slang)* a term of endearment, now somewhat disrespectful.

toot·sy (tuut-see) *n.* (*pl.* **-sies**) *(slang)* 1. a foot. 2. a girlfriend, *she's his tootsy.*

top[1] (top) *n.* 1. the highest point or part of something, the upper surface. 2. the highest rank or degree, the highest or most honorable position, *he is at the top of his profession.* 3. the utmost degree or intensity, *shouted at the top of his voice.* 4. a thing forming the upper part of something, the creamy part of milk, a garment covering the upper part of the body. 5. the covering or stopper of a bottle or tube. **top** *adj.* highest in position or rank or place or degree, *at top speed; top prices.* **top** *v.* (**topped, top·ping**) 1. to provide or be a top for. 2. to reach the top of. 3. to be higher than, to surpass; *top the list,* to be at the top of it. 4. to add as a final thing or finishing touch. 5. to remove the top of (a plant or fruit). 6. (in golf) to strike the (ball) above its center. □**at the top,** in the highest rank in a profession etc. **blow one's top,** *see* **blow**[1]. **on top,** above; in a superior position; in addition. **on top of,** in addition to; having mastered (a thing) thoroughly; *be on top of the world,* very happy. **the tops,** the very best. **top banana,** *(slang)* the first or leading comedian in a show; a person who excels or leads in a particular field. **top brass,** *see* **brass,** definition 6. **top dog,** *(slang)* the master or victor. **top drawer,** *(informal)* the highest social position or quality, *out of the top drawer.* **top hat,** a man's tall stiff black or gray hat worn with formal dress. **top kick,** *(slang)* a first sergeant. **top off,** to put a finishing touch to; to fill an almost full automobile gas tank. **top out,** (of plants) to grow tops, tassels, etc.; to reach a peak or level off; (of business activity or the stock market) to reach a peak before going down. **top secret,** one of the highest categories of secrecy. **top sergeant,** *(slang)* a first sergeant.

top[2] *n.* a toy that spins on its point when set in motion by hand or by a string or spring etc.

to·paz (toh-paz) *n.* 1. a semiprecious stone of various colors, especially yellow. 2. the yellow color of a topaz.

top·coat (top-koht) *n.* a lightweight overcoat.

top·dress (top-dres) *v.* to apply manure etc. on the top of (soil) without plowing it in.

top·dress·ing (top-dres-ing) *n.* 1. the process of top-dressing soil. 2. the substance used for this.

tope[1] (tohp) *v.* (**toped, top·ing**) to drink intoxicating liquor to excess, especially habitually. **top′er** *n.*

tope[2] *n.* a dome-shaped Buddhist monument for religious relics.

To·pe·ka (tŏ-pee-kă) the capital of Kansas.

top·flight (top-flīt) *adj.* in the highest rank of achievement.

top-heav·y (top-hev-ee) *adj.* over-weighted at the top and therefore in danger of falling over. **top′-heav·i·ness** *n.*

to·pi (toh-pee) *n.* a light pith sun helmet.

to·pi·ar·y (toh-pi-er-ee) *n.* 1. the art of clipping shrubs etc. into ornamental shapes. 2. (*pl.* **-aries**) an example of this. **topiary** *adj.* of or involving this art.

top·ic (top-ik) *n.* the subject of a discussion or written work.

top·i·cal (top-i-kăl) *adj.* having reference to current events. **top′i·cal·ly** *adv.* **top·i·cal·i·ty** (top-i-kal-i-tee) *n.*

top·knot (top-not) *n.* a tuft or crest or knot of ribbon etc. on top of the head.

top·less (top-lis) *adj.* 1. (of a woman's garment) leaving the breasts bare. 2. (of a woman) wearing such a garment. **top′less·ness** *n.* □**topless bar,** a bar featuring bare-breasted waitresses or dancers.

top-lev·el (top-lev-ĕl) *adj.* of the highest level, *top-level diplomatic meeting.*

top·mast (top-mast, -măst) *n.* the mast of a sailing ship next above the lower mast.

top·most (top-mohst) *adj.* highest.

top·notch (top-noch) *adj.* *(informal)* first-rate.

topog. *abbr.* 1. topographic(al). 2. topography.

to·pog·ra·phy (tŏ-pog-ra-fee) *n.* (*pl.* **-phies**) the features of a place or district, the position of its rivers, mountains, roads, buildings, etc. **to·pog′ra·pher** *n.* **top·o·graph·ic** (top-ŏ-graf-ik) *adj.* **top·o·graph′i·cal** *adj.* **top·o·graph′i·cal·ly** *adv.*

top·ping (top-ing) *n.* something forming a top, especially a sauce on top of a dessert.

top·ple (top-ĕl) *v.* (**top·pled, top·pling**) 1. to fall headlong or as if top-heavy, to totter and fall. 2. to cause to do this. 3. to overthrow, to cause to fall from authority, *the crisis toppled the government in England.*

top-rank·ing (top-rang-king) *adj.* of the highest rank.

top·sail (top-sayl, -săl) *n.* the square sail next above the lowest on a square-rigged sailing ship.

top·side (top-sīd) *adv.* 1. on deck. 2. to or on the surface or top.

top·sides (top-sīdz) *n. pl.* the sides of a ship above the waterline.

top·soil (top-soil) *n.* the top layer of soil as distinct from the subsoil.

top·sy-tur·vy (top-see-tur-vee) *adj. & adv.* in or into a state of great disorder.

toque (tohk) *n.* a woman's close-fitting brimless hat with a high crown.

tor (tor) *n.* a hill or rocky peak.

To·rah (toh-ră) *n.* 1. the Pentateuch or a scroll containing this. 2. *torah,* all of the sacred Jewish religious writings and law.

torch (torch) *n.* 1. a burning stick of resinous wood, or of combustible material fixed on a stick and ignited, used as a light for carrying in the hand. 2. any of several devices that direct a very hot flame on a selected spot. □**carry a torch for,** to be filled with unreturned love for (a person). **torch song,** a sentimental song of unrequited love.

torch·bear·er (torch-bair-ĕr) *n.* 1. a person who carries a torch. 2. a person who leads or inspires etc., *the party's torchbearer.*

torch·light (torch-lıt) *n.* the light of a torch or torches; *a torchlight procession,* one in which burning torches are used.

tore *see* **tear**[1].

tor·e·a·dor (tor-i-ă-dor) *n.* a bullfighter, especially on horseback.

to·re·ro (tŏ-rair-oh) *n.* a bullfighter.

tor·ment (tor-ment) *n.* 1. severe physical or mental suffering. 2. something causing this. **torment** (tor-ment) *v.* 1. to subject to torment. 2. to tease or try to provoke by annoyances etc. **tor·men'tor** *n.* **tor·ment'ed·ly** *adv.* **tor·ment' ing·ly** *adv.*

torn *see* **tear**[1].

tor·na·do (tor-nay-doh) *n.* (*pl.* **-does, -dos**) a violent and destructive whirlwind advancing in a narrow path.

tor·pe·do (tor-pee-doh) *n.* (*pl.* **-does**) 1. a cigar-shaped explosive underwater missile, launched against a ship from a submarine or surface ship or aircraft. 2. *(slang)* a hired assassin. **torpedo** *v.* (**tor·pe·doed, tor·pe·do·ing**) 1. to destroy or attack with a torpedo. 2. to ruin or wreck (a policy or conference etc.) suddenly. □**torpedo boat,** a small fast lightly armed warship for carrying or discharging torpedoes. **torpedo tube,** the tube from which torpedoes are discharged.

tor·pid (tor-pid) *adj.* sluggish and inactive. **tor'pid·ly** *adv.* **tor·pid·i·ty** (tor-pid-i-tee) *n.* **tor·por** (tor-pŏr) *n.* a torpid condition.

torque (tork) *n.* a force causing rotation or torsion in machinery. □**torque converter,** a device to transmit the correct torque from engine to axle in a motor vehicle.

torr (tor) *n.* a unit of pressure in measuring a partial vacuum, = 1/760 of standard atmosphere.

tor·rent (tor-ĕnt) *n.* 1. a rushing stream of water or lava. 2. a downpour of rain. 3. a violent flow, *a torrent of words.*

tor·ren·tial (taw-ren-shăl) *adj.* like a torrent.

tor·rid (tor-id) *adj.* 1. (of climate or land) very hot and dry. 2. intense, passionate, *torrid love scenes.* **tor'rid·ly** *adv.* **tor'rid·ness** *n.* **tor·rid·i·ty** (tor-rid-i-tee) *n.* □**Torrid Zone,** the tropics.

tor·sion (tor-shŏn) *n.* 1. twisting, especially of one end of a thing while the other is held fixed. 2. the state of being spirally twisted. **tor'sion·al** *adj.* **tor'sion·al·ly** *adv.*

tor·so (tor-soh) *n.* (*pl.* **-sos**) 1. the trunk of the human body. 2. a statue lacking head and limbs.

tort (tort) *n.* (in law) any private or civil wrong (other than breach of contract) for which the wronged person may claim damages.

torte (tort) *n.* (*pl.* **tortes**) a kind of rich round layer cake.

tor·til·la (tor-tee-yă) *n.* a flat round bread made of cornmeal.

tor·toise (tor-tŏs) *n.* a land turtle of warm climates. □**tortoise shell,** the semitransparent mottled yellowish-brown shell of certain turtles, used for making combs etc.; a cat or butterfly with mottled coloring resembling this.

tor·toise-shell (tor-tŏs-shel) *adj.* having coloring and markings like a tortoise shell.

tor·to·ni (tor-toh-nee) *n.* a rich frozen dessert made of heavy cream, eggs, sugar, and often chopped cherries or almonds or macaroon crumbs.

tor·tu·ous (tor-choo-ŭs) *adj.* 1. full of twists and turns. 2. (of policy etc.) devious, not straightforward. **tor'tu·ous·ly** *adv.* **tor'tu·ous·ness** *n.*

tor·ture (tor-chŭr) *n.* 1. the infliction of severe pain

as a punishment or means of coercion. 2. a method of torturing. 3. severe physical or mental pain. **torture** *v.* (**tor·tured, tor·tur·ing**) 1. to inflict torture upon, to subject to great pain or anxiety. 2. to force out of its natural position or shape. **tor'tur·er** *n.* **tor·tured·ly** (tor-chŭrd-lee) *adv.*

To·ry (tohr-ee) *n.* (*pl.* **-ries**) 1. (in Great Britain) a member of the Conservative Party. 2. a colonist loyal to England during the American Revolution. 3. (in England during the 18th century) the party that supported George III and the established order in Church and State. 4. (often *tory*) a person of conservative opinions. **Tory, tory** *adj.* conservative.

toss (taws) *v.* 1. to throw lightly or carelessly or easily; *toss one's head,* to throw it back in contempt or impatience. 2. to send (a coin) spinning in the air to decide something according to the way it lies after falling. 3. to throw or roll about from side to side restlessly or with an uneven motion. 4. to coat (food) by gently shaking it in dressing etc. **toss** *n.* 1. a tossing action or movement. 2. the result obtained by tossing a coin. □**toss off,** to drink off rapidly; to finish or compose rapidly or without much thought or effort.

toss·pot (taws-pot) *n.* a heavy drinker.

toss·up (taws-up) *n.* 1. the tossing of a coin. 2. an even chance.

tot[1] (tot) *n.* 1. a small child. 2. (chiefly *British informal*) a small quantity of alcoholic drink.

tot[2] *v.* (**tot·ted, tot·ting**) **tot up,** (*informal*) to add up, *tot this up; it tots up to $20.*

tot. *abbr.* total.

to·tal (toh-tăl) *adj.* 1. including everything or everyone, comprising the whole, *the total number of persons; a total eclipse,* in which the whole disk of the moon etc. is obscured. 2. utter, complete, *in total darkness.* **total** *n.* the total number or amount, a count of all the items. **total** *v.* (**to· taled, to·tal·ing**) 1. to reckon the total of. 2. to amount to. 3. *(slang)* to demolish (an automobile) totally. **to'tal·ly** *adv.* □**total recall,** the ability to remember everything in complete detail.

to·tal·i·tar·i·an (toh-tal-i-tair-i-ăn) *adj.* of a form of government in which no rival parties or loyalties are permitted, usually demanding total submission of the individual to the requirements of the state. **to·tal·i·tar'i·an·ism** *n.*

to·tal·i·ty (toh-tal-i-tee) *n.* (*pl.* **-ties**) 1. the quality of being total. 2. a total number or amount.

to·tal·i·za·tor (toh-tă-li-zay-tŏr) *n.* a device automatically registering the number and amount of bets staked, with a view to dividing the total amount among those betting on the winner.

to·tal·ize (toh-tă-lız) *v.* (**to·tal·ized, to·tal· iz·ing**) to find the total of. **to'tal·iz·er** *n.*

tote[1] (toht) *v.* (**tot·ed, tot·ing**) (*informal*) to total. **tote** *n.* (*informal*) a totalizator. □**tote board,** (*informal*) a totalizator.

tote[2] *v.* (**tot·ed, tot·ing**) (*informal*) to carry. □**tote bag,** a large bag for carrying books or other items.

to·tem (toh-tĕm) *n.* 1. a natural object, especially an animal, adopted among North American Indians as the emblem of a clan or family. 2. an image of this. □**totem pole,** a pole carved or painted with a series of totems.

t'oth·er (tu*th*-ĕr) = the other.

tot·ter (tot-er) *v.* 1. to walk unsteadily. 2. to rock or shake as if about to collapse. **totter** *n.* an unsteady or shaky walk or movement. **tot′ter·y** *adj.* **tot′ter·er** *n.*

tou·can (too-kan) *n.* a tropical American bird with an immense beak.

touch (tuch) *v.* 1. to be or come together so that there is no space between, to meet (another object) in this way. 2. to put one's hand etc. on (a thing) lightly. 3. to press or strike lightly. 4. to draw or paint with light strokes, *touch in the details*. 5. to move or meddle with, to harm, *leave your things here, no one will touch them*. 6. to have to do with the slightest degree, to attempt, *the firm doesn't touch business of that kind*. 7. to eat or drink even a little of, *she hasn't touched her breakfast*. 8. to reach, *the speedometer touched 120*. 9. to equal in excellence, *no other cloth can touch it for quality*. 10. to affect slightly. 11. to rouse sympathy or other emotion in. 12. *(slang)* to persuade to give (money) as a loan or gift, *touched him for a dollar.* **touch** *n.* 1. the act or fact of touching. 2. the faculty of perceiving things or their qualities through touching them. 3. small things done in producing a piece of work, *add the finishing touches*. 4. a performer's way of touching the keys or strings of a musical instrument etc. 5. a manner or style of workmanship, a person's special skill, *he hasn't lost his touch*. 6. a relationship of communication or knowledge, *we've lost touch with her*. 7. a slight trace, *there's a touch of frost in the air; a touch of flu*. 8. *(slang)* the act of obtaining money from a person. **touch′er** *n.* □**in touch with,** in communication with; having interest in or information about. **out of touch,** no longer in touch (with a person or subject etc.). **soft touch,** *see* **soft. touch bottom,** to reach the worst point of misfortune etc. **touch down,** (of an aircraft) to land. **touch football,** football in which touching is used instead of tackling. **touch off,** to cause to explode; to cause to start, *his arrest touched off a riot.* **touch on,** to deal with or mention (a subject) briefly. **touch up,** to improve (a thing) by making small alterations or additions. **touch wood,** to touch something made of wood in superstitious or humorous hope that this will avert ill luck.

touch·a·ble (tuch-ă-běl) *adj.* able to be touched.

touch-and-go (tuch-ăn-goh) *adj.* uncertain as regards result.

touch·back (tuch-bak) *n.* a football play in which the ball is kicked into or beyond the end zone, or is intercepted or recovered there by the defending team.

touch·down (tuch-down) *n.* 1. (in football) a play scoring six points made by carrying or catching the ball beyond the opponent's goal line. 2. (of an aircraft or spacecraft) the moment of landing.

tou·ché (too-shay) *interj.* an acknowledgement that one's opponent has made a hit in fencing or a valid accusation or criticism in a discussion.

touch·ing (tuch-ing) *adj.* rousing kindly feelings or sympathy or pity. **touching** *prep.* concerning. **touch′ing·ly** *adv.*

touch·stone (tuch-stohn) *n.* a standard or criterion by which something is judged. ▷Alloys of gold and silver were formerly tested by being rubbed against a fine-grained stone.

Touch-Tone (tuch-tohn) *n.* *(trademark)* a telephone that is dialed by touching buttons that produce tones to activate the mechanism.

touch-type (tuch-tɪp) *v.* **(touch-typed, touch-**

typ·ing) to use a typewriter without looking at the keys. **touch′-typ·ist** *n.*

touch·wood (tuch-wuud) *n.* wood in a soft rotten state and easily inflammable, used as tinder.

touch·y (tuch-ee) *adj.* **(touch·i·er, touch·i·est)** easily offended. **touch′i·ly** *adv.* **touch′i·ness** *n.*

tough (tuf) *adj.* 1. difficult to break or cut or chew. 2. able to endure hardship, not easily hurt or damaged or injured. 3. unyielding, stubborn, resolute; *get tough with a person,* to adopt a firm attitude in dealing with him. 4. difficult, *a tough job.* 5. (of luck etc.) hard, unpleasant. 6. vicious, rough and violent. **tough** *n.* a rough and violent person, *young toughs.* **tough′ly** *adv.* **tough′ness** *n.*

tough·en (tuf-ĕn) *v.* to make or become tough. **tough′en·er** *n.*

tough-mind·ed (tuf-mɪn-did) *adj.* realistic and not sentimental.

tou·pee (too-pay) *n.* a wig, an artificial patch of hair worn to cover a bald spot.

tour (toor) *n.* a journey through a country or town or building etc. visiting various places or things of interest, or giving performances. **tour** *v.* to make a tour of. □**on tour,** touring. **touring car,** an early style of large open automobile with room for at least five passengers and luggage. **tour of duty,** a period of duty on military or diplomatic service, the time to be spent at a station.

tour de force (toor dĕ fohrs) (*pl.* **tours de force,** *pr.* toor dĕ **fohrs**) an outstandingly skillful performance or achievement. ▷French.

tour·ism (toor-iz-ĕm) *n.* 1. visiting places as a tourist. 2. the business of providing accommodation and services etc. for tourists.

tour·ist (toor-ist) *n.* a person who is traveling or visiting a place for recreation. □**tourist class,** a class of passenger accommodation in a ship or airplane etc., lower than first class. **tourist court,** a motel. **tourist home,** a private home accepting tourists as paying guests. **tourist trap,** a business that exploits tourists.

tour·ist·y (toor-i-stee) *adj.* designed to attract tourists.

tour·ma·line (toor-mă-lin) *n.* a mineral of various colors, possessing unusual electric properties and used as a gem.

tour·na·ment (toor-nă-mĕnt, tur-) *n.* a contest of skill among a number of competitors, involving a series of matches.

tour·ne·dos (toor-nă-dohs) *n.* (*pl.* **-dos**) a small piece of fillet of beef cooked with a strip of fat wrapped around it.

tour·ney (toor-nee, tur-) *n.* (*pl.* **-neys**) a tournament.

tour·ni·quet (tur-nĭ-kit) *n.* a device or a strip of material drawn tightly around a limb to stop the flow of blood from an artery by compressing it.

tou·sle (tow-zĕl) *v.* **(tou·sled, tou·sling)** to make (hair etc.) untidy by ruffling it.

tout (towt) *v.* *(informal)* 1. to offer racing tips for a share of the resulting gains. 2. to recommend or praise highly. **tout** *n.* a person who touts things, a tipster touting information about racehorses etc.

tow[1] (toh) *n.* short coarse fibers of flax or hemp, used for making yarn etc.

tow[2] *v.* to pull along behind one. **tow** *n.* towing, being towed. □**in tow,** being towed; *(informal)* following behind, under one's charge, *he arrived with his family in tow.* **tow truck,** a truck equipped for towing automobiles.

tow·age (toh-ij) *n.* the charge for being towed.

to·ward (tohrd) *prep.* 1. in the direction of, *walked or faced toward the sea.* 2. in relation to, regarding, *the way he behaved toward his children.* 3. for the purpose of achieving or promoting, *efforts toward peace.* 4. as a contribution to, *put the money toward a new bicycle.* 5. near, approaching, *toward four o'clock.*

to·wards (tohrdz) = **toward.**

tow·a·way (toh-ă-way) **zone** a zone in which illegally parked cars may be towed away and held by the police.

tow·boat (toh-boht) *n.* a boat that pulls or pushes loaded barges.

tow·el (tow-ĕl) *n.* a piece of absorbent cloth or paper for drying oneself or wiping things dry. **towel** *v.* **(tow·eled, tow·el·ing)** to wipe or dry with a towel.

tow·el·ing (tow-ĕ-ling) *n.* a fabric for making towels.

tow·er (tow-ĕr) *n.* a tall usually square or circular structure, either standing alone (as a fort) or forming part of a church or castle or other large building. **tower** *v.* to be of great height, to be taller or more eminent than others, *he towered above everyone.* ☐**tower of strength,** a person who gives strong and reliable support.

tow·er·ing (tow-ĕ-ring) *adj.* 1. very tall, lofty. 2. (of rage etc.) extreme, intense. **tow'er·ing·ly** *adv.*

tow·head·ed (toh-hed-id) *adj.* having very light-colored hair. **tow'head** *n.*

tow·hee (tow-hee) *n.* a North American finch with a long tail.

town (town) *n.* 1. a collection of dwellings and other buildings, larger than a village, especially one not created a city. 2. its inhabitants. 3. a town or city as distinct from country. 4. the central business and shopping area of a neighborhood. 5. a geographical and political unit in New England and some other states where the town meeting has sovereign power. ☐**go to town,** *(slang)* to do something lavishly or with great enthusiasm; to succeed. **on the town,** *(slang)* on a spree in town. **town clerk,** an officer of a town, in charge of records etc. **town crier,** an officer who formerly shouted public announcements in a town. **town hall,** a building containing local government offices and usually a hall for public events. **town meeting,** a meeting of voters of the town for the transaction of public business.

town·house (town-hows) *n.* (*pl.* **-hous·es,** *pr.* -how-ziz) 1. a residence in town as distinct from country. 2. a house in a row of connected houses or a house in a compact planned group in a town.

towns·folk (townz-fohk) *n.* townspeople.

town·ship (town-ship) *n.* 1. a division of a county. 2. a district six miles square.

towns·man (townz-măn) *n.* (*pl.* **-men,** *pr.* mĕn) a man who lives in a town.

towns·peo·ple (townz-pee-pĕl) *n. pl.* the people of a town.

towns·wom·an (townz-wuum-ăn) *n.* (*pl.* **-wom·en,** *pr.* -wim-in) a woman who lives in a town.

tow·path (toh-path) *n.* a path along a canal or river for use in towing boats.

tow·rope (toh-rohp) *n.* a rope used in towing boats.

tox·e·mi·a (tok-see-mi-ă) *n.* 1. blood poisoning. 2. a condition in pregnancy in which blood pressure is abnormally high. **tox·e'mic** *adj.*

tox·ic (tok-sik) *adj.* 1. of or caused by poison. 2.

poisonous. **tox'i·cal·ly** *adv.* **tox·ic·i·ty** (tok-sis-i-tee) *n.*

tox·i·col·o·gist (tok-si-kol-ŏ-jist) *n.* a specialist in toxicology.

tox·i·col·o·gy (tok-si-kol-ŏ-jee) *n.* the scientific study of poisons. **tox·i·co·log·ic** (tok-si-kŏ-loj-ik) *adj.* **tox·i·co·log'i·cal** *adj.* **tox·i·co·log'i·cal·ly** *adv.*

tox·in (tok-sin) *n.* a poisonous substance of animal or vegetable origin, especially one formed in the body by microorganisms.

toy (toi) *n.* 1. a thing to play with, especially for a child. 2. a thing intended for amusement rather than for serious use. **toy** *adj.* 1. serving as a toy. 2. (of a dog) of a diminutive breed or variety, kept as a pet. **toy** *v.* **toy with,** to handle or finger idly; to deal with or consider without seriousness, *toyed with the idea of going to Spain.*

tp. *abbr.* township.

t.p. *abbr.* title page.

tpk., tpke. *abbr.* turnpike.

tr. *abbr.* 1. transitive. 2. translated. 3. translation. 4. translator. 5. transpose. 6. treasurer. 7. troop.

trace[1] (trays) *n.* 1. a track or mark left behind. 2. a visible or other sign of what has existed or happened. 3. a very small quantity, *contains traces of soda.* **trace** *v.* **(traced, trac·ing)** 1. to follow or discover by observing marks, tracks, pieces of evidence, etc. 2. to mark out, to sketch the outline of, to form (letters etc.) laboriously, *traced his signature shakily; the policy he traced out was never followed.* 3. to copy (a map or drawing etc.) on transparent paper placed over it or by using carbon paper below. ☐**trace element,** a substance occurring or required, especially in soil, only in minute amounts.

trace[2] *n.* each of the two side straps or chains or ropes by which a horse draws a vehicle. ☐**kick over the traces,** (of a person) to become insubordinate or reckless.

trace·a·ble (tray-să-bĕl) *adj.* able to be traced.

trac·er (tray-sĕr) *n.* 1. a person or thing that traces. 2. (also **tracer bullet**) a bullet that leaves a trail of smoke etc. by which its course can be observed. 3. a radioactive substance that can be traced in its course through the human body or a series of reactions etc. by the radiation it produces.

trac·er·y (tray-sĕ-ree) *n.* (*pl.* **-er·ies**) 1. an openwork pattern in stone (as in a church window). 2. a decorative pattern of lines resembling this.

tra·che·a (tray-ki-ă) *n.* (*pl.* **-che·ae,** *pr.* -ki-ee) the windpipe. **tra'che·al** *adj.*

tra·che·ost·o·my (tray-ki-ost-ŏ-mee) *n.* (*pl.* **-mies**) an opening made surgically into the trachea from the outside of the neck.

tra·cho·ma (tră-koh-mă) *n.* a contagious disease of the eye causing inflammation of the inner surface of the eyelids.

trac·ing (tray-sing) *n.* a copy of a map or drawing etc. made by tracing it. ☐**tracing paper,** transparent paper for making tracings.

track (trak) *n.* 1. a mark or series of marks left by a moving person or animal or thing. 2. a course taken. 3. a course of action or procedure; *you're on the right track,* following the right line of procedure or inquiry etc. 4. a path or rough road, especially one made by people or animals or carts etc. passing. 5. a prepared course for racing etc. 6. a section of a phonograph record with a recorded sequence, one channel of a recording tape. 7. a continuous line of a railroad; *single track,* only one pair of rails. 8. the continuous band around the wheels of a tank or tractor etc. **track** *v.* 1. to follow the track of, to find or observe by doing this. 2. (of wheels) to run so that the hind wheel is exactly in the forward wheel's track. 3. (of a stylus) to follow a groove. 4. (of a motion-picture camera) to move along a set path while taking a picture. □**in one's tracks**, *(slang)* where one stands, instantly. **keep** *or* **lose track of**, to keep or fail to keep oneself informed about. **make tracks**, *(slang)* to go away. **make tracks for**, *(slang)* to go to or toward. **off the track**, away from the subject at hand. **on the right** *or* **wrong track**, following the right or wrong line of inquiry etc. **on** *or* **from the wrong side of the tracks**, in or from the socially inferior part of town. **track and field**, a variety of running and throwing events, as pole vaulting, broad jumping, shot-putting, etc. engaged in on an oval track and the field it surrounds. **track down**, to reach or capture by tracking. **track events**, (in sports) races as distinct from field events (*see* **field**). **tracking station**, a radar or radio station that monitors and maintains communication with a satellite or rocket. **track meet**, a sports contest with a variety of running and jumping events. **track record**, *(informal)* a person's past achievements. **track shoes**, spiked shoes worn by a runner. **track suit**, a warm loose-fitting suit worn by an athlete etc. during practice.

track·age (trak-ij) *n.* the total amount of track owned by a railroad.

track·er (trak-ĕr) *n.* a person or thing that tracks.

track·less (trak-lis) *adj.* 1. showing no tracks. 2. not on tracks.

track·walk·er (trak-waw-kĕr) *n.* a person employed to walk along railroad track and inspect it.

tract[1] (trakt) *n.* 1. a large stretch of land. 2. a system of connected parts in an animal body along which something passes, *the digestive tract.*

tract[2] *n.* a pamphlet containing a short essay, especially on a religious subject.

trac·ta·ble (trak-tă-bĕl) *adj.* easy to manage or deal with, docile. **trac′ta·bly** *adv.* **trac·ta·bil·i·ty** (trak-tă-bil-i-tee) *n.*

trac·tate (trak-tayt) *n.* a treatise.

trac·tion (trak-shŏn) *n.* 1. pulling or drawing a load along a surface. 2. the grip of a tire on the road or a wheel on a rail etc. 3. continuous pull on a limb etc. in medical treatment. **trac′tion·al** *adj.* **trac·tive** (trak-tiv) *adj.* □**traction engine**, a steam or diesel engine for drawing a heavy load along a road or across a field etc.

trac·tor (trak-tŏr) *n.* a powerful motor vehicle for pulling farm machinery or other heavy equipment. □**tractor trailer**, a truck with a tractor unit and a trailer unit.

trade (trayd) *n.* 1. exchange of goods for money or other goods. 2. business of a particular kind, *the tourist trade.* 3. business carried on to earn one's living or for profit (distinguished from a *profession*), a skilled handicraft, *he's a butcher by trade; learn a trade.* 4. the people engaged in a particular trade, *we sell furniture to the trade, not to private buyers.* 5. a trade wind. **trade** *v.* **(trad·ed, trad·ing)** 1. to engage in trade, to buy and sell. 2. to exchange (goods etc.) in trading. **trad′er** *n.* □**trade book**, a book sold to the general public in stores, as distinguished from a textbook etc. **trade in**, to give (a used article)

as partial payment for another article. **trade name**, a name given by a manufacturer to a proprietary article or material; the name by which a thing is known in the trade; the name under which a person or firm trades. **trade on**, to make great use of for one's own advantage, *trading on his brother's reputation.* **trade paperback**, a large softbound book sold in bookstores. **trade route**, a route usually taken by traders, caravans, merchant vessels, etc. **trade school**, a high school emphasizing the skilled trades. **trade secret**, a technique used in the trade, especially by one company, but kept from being generally known. **trade union**, (*pl.* **trade unions**) a labor union. **trade wind**, one of the winds blowing continually toward the equator over most of the tropics, from the northeast in the northern hemisphere and southeast in the southern hemisphere.

trade·in (trayd-in) *n.* an article given as partial payment for a newly purchased one.

trade·mark (trayd-mahrk) *n.* a manufacturer's or trader's registered emblem or name etc. used to identify his goods.

trade·off (trayd-awf) *n.* an exchange, especially by way of compromise.

trad·er (tray-dĕr) *n.* a person engaged in trading.

trad·ing (tray-ding) **post** 1. a store established in an undeveloped area, for exchanging goods. 2. a station of the floor of a stock exchange for the trading of a particular stock or bond.

trading stamp a stamp given by a shopkeeper to a customer, quantities of which are exchangeable for various articles or for cash.

tra·di·tion (tră-dish-ŏn) *n.* 1. the handing down of beliefs or customs from one generation to another, especially without writing. 2. a belief or custom handed down in this way, a long-established custom or method of procedure. **tra·di·tion·al** *adj.* **tra·di·tion·al·ly** *adv.* **tra·di·tion·less** *adj.*

tra·di·tion·al·ist (tră-dish-ŏ-nă-list) *n.* a person who follows or upholds traditional beliefs etc.

tra·duce (tră-doos) *v.* (**tra·duced, tra·duc·ing**) to misrepresent, to slander. **tra·duc′er** *n.* **tra·duce′ment** *n.*

traf·fic (traf-ik) *n.* 1. pedestrians or vehicles or ships or aircraft moving along a route. 2. trading, especially when illegal or morally wrong, *drug traffic.* **traffic** *v.* (**traf·ficked, traf·fick·ing**) to trade. **traf′fick·er** *n.* □**traffic circle**, a circular roadway at the intersection of two or more roads for enabling easy movement of cars. **traffic jam**, a condition in which road traffic cannot proceed freely and comes to a standstill. **traffic light**, an automatic signal controlling traffic at junctions etc. by means of colored lights. **traffic manager**, a person who manages the transportation or routing of goods or items of business. **traffic pattern**, a pattern above an airfield for planes to use in preparing to land.

tra·ge·di·an (tră-jee-di-ăn) *n.* 1. a writer of tragedies. 2. an actor in tragedy.

tra·ge·di·enne (tră-jee-di-en) *n.* an actress in tragedy.

trag·e·dy (traj-ĕ-dee) *n.* (*pl.* **-dies**) 1. a serious play with unhappy events or a sad ending. 2. the branch of drama that consists of such plays. 3. an event that causes great sadness, a calamity.

trag·ic (traj-ik) *adj.* 1. of or in the style of tragedy, *he was a great tragic actor.* 2. sorrowful. 3. causing great sadness, calamitous. □**tragic flaw**, the flaw in a tragic hero's character that brings about his downfall.

trag·i·cal (traj-i-kăl) *adj*. 1. sorrowful. 2. causing great sadness. **trag'i·cal·ly** *adv*.

trag·i·com·e·dy (traj-i-kom-ĕ-dee) *n*. (*pl*. **-dies**) a play with both tragic and comic elements. **trag·i·com·ic** (traj-i-kom-ik) *adj*.

trail (trayl) *v*. 1. to drag or be dragged along behind, especially on the ground. 2. to hang or float loosely, (of a plant) to grow lengthily downward or along the ground. 3. to move wearily, to lag or straggle. 4. to be losing in a game or other contest. 5. to diminish or become fainter, *her voice trailed away*. 6. to follow the trail of, to track. **trail** *n*. 1. something that trails or hangs trailing. 2. a line of people or things following behind something. 3. a mark left where something has passed, a trace, *vandals left a trail of wreckage; a snail's slimy trail*. 4. a track or scent followed in hunting. 5. a beaten path, especially through a wild region. □**trail bike**, a lightweight motorcycle with large heavy-tread balloon tires for riding on dirt trails. **trailing arbutus**, a North American creeping herb with fragrant white or pink flowers.

trail·blaz·er (trayl-blay-zĕr) *n*. 1. a person who beats a path through a wild and unsettled region. 2. a person who pioneers new approaches or new fields of endeavor. **trail'blaz·ing** *adj. & n*.

trail·er (tray-lĕr) *n*. 1. a truck or other container designed to be hauled by a vehicle. 2. a vehicle used as a home or office and drawn from place to place by another vehicle. 3. a short extract from a film, shown in advance to advertise it. 4. a person or thing that trails. □**trailer camp** *or* **trailer park**, a place for trailers or mobile homes to park, providing electrical outlets and water.

train (trayn) *n*. 1. a locomotive with a series of linked railroad cars. 2. a number of people or animals moving in a line, *a camel train*. 3. a body of followers, a retinue. 4. a sequence of things, *a train of events; a train of thought; certain consequences followed in its train*, after it, as a result. 5. a set of parts in machinery, actuating one another in a series. 6. a part of a long dress or robe that trails on the ground behind the wearer. **train** *v*. 1. to bring to a desired standard of efficiency or condition or behavior etc. by instruction and practice. 2. to undergo such a process, *she trained as a secretary*. 3. to make or become physically fit for a sport by exercise or diet. 4. to teach and accustom (a person or animal) to do something. 5. to aim (a gun or camera etc.), *trained his gun on the doorway*. 6. to cause (a plant) to grow in the required shape. **trained** *adj*. **train'ing** *n*. □**in training**, undergoing training for a sport; physically fit as a result of this. **out of training**, not fit in this way. **training pants**, heavy absorbent underpants worn by a child who is not completely toilet trained. **training ship**, a ship for training sailors in seamanship.

train·a·ble (tray-nă-bĕl) *adj*. able to be trained.

train·ee (tray-nee) *n*. a person being trained for an occupation etc.

train·er (tray-nĕr) *n*. 1. a person who trains, one who trains racehorses or athletes etc. 2. an aircraft or device simulating it used to train pilots.

train·load (trayn-lohd) *n*. the full capacity of a train, freight or passengers.

train·man (trayn-măn) *n*. (*pl*. **-men**, *pr*. -mĕn) a

person who works on a railroad train, as a brakeman, a conductor, etc.

train·sick (trayn-sik) *adj*. made sick or queasy by the motion of a train. **train'sick·ness** *n*.

traipse (trayps) *v*. **(traipsed, traips·ing)** (*informal*) to trudge.

trait (trayt) *n*. a characteristic.

trai·tor (tray-tŏr) *n*. a person who behaves disloyally, one who betrays his country. **trai'tor·ous** *adj*.

trai·tress (tray-tris) *n*. a woman who acts as a traitor.

tra·jec·to·ry (tră-jek-tŏ-ree) *n*. (*pl*. **-ries**) the path of a bullet or rocket etc. or of a body moving under certain forces.

tram (tram) *n*. 1. (chiefly *British*) a streetcar. 2. an open car or wagon run on rails to carry loads in a mine.

tram·mel (tram-ĕl) *n*. 1. a kind of dragnet for catching fish. 2. *trammels*, things that hamper one's activities. **trammel** *v*. **(tram·meled, tram·mel·ing)** to hamper.

tramp (tramp) *v*. 1. to walk with heavy steps. 2. to travel on foot across (an area), *tramping the hills*. 3. to trample, *tramp it down*. **tramp** *n*. 1. the sound of heavy footsteps. 2. a long walk, *went for a tramp*. 3. a person who goes from place to place as a vagrant. 4. (*slang*) a sexually immoral woman. 5. (also **tramp streamer**) a freighter that does not travel on a regular route. **tramp'er** *n*.

tram·po·line (tram-pŏ-leen) *n*. a sheet of strong canvas attached by springs to a horizontal frame, used for jumping on in acrobatic leaps. **tram·po·lin'er** *n*. **tram·po·lin'ist** *n*.

tram·way (tram-way) *n*. 1. the rails for a tram. 2. an aerial passenger or freight car suspended from a cable.

trance (trans) *n*. 1. a sleeplike state, as that induced by hypnosis. 2. a dreamy state in which a person is absorbed with his thoughts.

tran·quil (trang-kwil) *adj*. calm and undisturbed, not agitated. **tran'quil·ly** *adv*. **tran·quil·i·ty** (trang-kwil-i-tee) *n*.

tran·quil·ize (trang-kwi-lɪz) *v*. **(tran·quil·ized, tran·quil·iz·ing)** to make tranquil, to calm.

tran·quil·iz·er (trang-kwi-lɪ-zĕr) *n*. a drug used to relieve anxiety and make a person feel calm.

trans. *abbr*. 1. transaction. 2. transitive. 3. translated. 4. translation. 5. translator. 6. transportation. 7. transverse.

trans- *prefix* across or beyond, as in *transcontinental;* on or to the other side of, as in *transoceanic;* through, as in *transmit;* into another state or place, as in *transform*.

trans·act (tran-sakt, -zakt) *v*. to perform or carry out (business). **trans·ac'tor** *n*.

trans·ac·tion (tran-sak-shŏn, -zak-) *n*. 1. transacting. 2. business transacted. 3. *transactions*, a record of its proceedings published by a learned society. **trans·ac'tion·al** *adj*.

trans·al·pine (trans-al-pɪn) *adj*. beyond the Alps (usually as viewed from Italy).

trans-A·mer·i·can (trans-ă-mer-i-kăn) *adj*. across or beyond America.

trans·at·lan·tic (trans-ăt-lan-tik) *adj*. 1. on or from the other side of the Atlantic. 2. crossing the Atlantic, *a transatlantic flight*.

trans·ceiv·er (tran-see-vĕr) *n*. a combined radio transmitter and receiver.

tran·scend (tran-send) *v*. 1. to go or be beyond

the range of (human experience or belief or powers of description etc.). 2. to surpass.

tran·scend·ent (tran-sen-děnt) *adj.* going beyond the limits of ordinary experience, surpassing.

tran·scen·den·tal (tran-sen-den-tăl) *adj.* 1. transcendent. 2. abstract, obscure, visionary. **tran·scen·den'tal·ly** *adv.* □**transcendental meditation,** a process seeking to induce detachment from problems and relief from anxiety etc. by a system of meditation.

tran·scen·den·tal·ism (tran-sen-den-tă-liz-ĕm) *n.* the philosophy that reality cannot be known and that the divine is the guiding principle in man. **tran·scen·den'tal·ist** *n.* & *adj.*

tran·con·ti·nen·tal (trans-kon-ti-nen-tăl) *adj.* extending or traveling across a continent.

tran·scribe (tran-skrıb) *v.* (**tran·scribed, tran·scrib·ing**) 1. to copy in writing, to write out (shorthand etc.) in ordinary characters. 2. to record (sound) for later reproduction or broadcasting. 3. to arrange (music) for a different instrument etc. **tran·scrib'er** *n.* **tran·scrip·tion** (tran-skrip-shŏn) *n.*

tran·script (tran-skript) *n.* a written or recorded copy.

trans·duc·er (trans-doo-sĕr) *n.* a device that converts waves etc. from one system and conveys related waves to another (as a radio receiver, which receives electromagnetic waves and sends out sound waves).

tran·sept (tran-sept) *n.* the part that is at right angles to the nave in a cross-shaped church, either arm of this, *the north and south transepts.*

trans·fer (trans-fur) *v.* (**trans·ferred, trans·fer·ring**) 1. to convey or move or hand over (a thing) from one place or person or group etc. to another. 2. to convey (a drawing or pattern etc.) from one surface to another. 3. to change from one station or route or conveyance to another during a journey. 4. to change to another group or occupation etc., *she has transferred to the sales department.* **transfer** (trans-fĕr) *n.* 1. transferring, being transferred. 2. a document that transfers property or a right from one person to another. 3. a design that is or can be transferred from one surface to another, a paper bearing such a design. **trans·fer·al** (trans-fur-ăl) *n.* **trans·fer·rer** (trans-fur-ĕr) *n.*

trans·fer·a·ble (trans-fĕ-ră-bĕl) *adj.* able to be transferred. **trans·fer·a·bil·i·ty** (trans-fĕ-ră-bil-i-tee) *n.*

trans·fer·ence (trans-fur-ĕns) *n.* transferring, being transferred.

trans·fig·ure (trans-fig-yŭr) *v.* (**trans·fig·ured, trans·fig·ur·ing**) to make a great change in the appearance of, especially to something nobler or more beautiful, *her face was transfigured by happiness.* **trans·fig·u·ra·tion** (trans-fig-yŭ-ray-shŏn) *n.* □**the Transfiguration,** the Christian festival (August 6) commemorating Christ's transfiguration on the mountain.

trans·fix (trans-fiks) *v.* (**trans·fixed, trans·fix·ing**) 1. to pierce with or impale on something sharp pointed. 2. to make (a person) motionless with fear or astonishment etc.

trans·form (trans-form) *v.* 1. to make a great change in the appearance or character of, *the caterpillar is transformed into a butterfly.* 2. to change the voltage of (electric current). 3. to become transformed. **trans·for·ma·tion** (trans-fŏr-may-shŏn) *n.*

trans·form·er (trans-for-mĕr) *n.* an apparatus for reducing or increasing the voltage of alternating current.

trans·fuse (trans-fyooz) *v.* (**trans·fused, trans·fus·ing**) to give a transfusion of (a fluid) or to (a person or animal). **trans·fus'a·ble** *adj.* **trans·fus'er** *n.*

trans·fus·ion (trans-fyoo-zhŏn) *n.* an injection of blood or other fluid into a blood vessel of a person or animal.

trans·gress (trans-gres) *v.* 1. to break (a rule or law etc.), to go beyond (a limitation). 2. to sin. **trans·gres'sor** *n.* **trans·gres·sion** (trans-gresh-ŏn) *n.*

tran·ship (tran-ship) *v.* (**tran·shipped, tran·ship·ping**) to transship.

tran·sient (tran-shĕnt, -zhĕnt) *adj.* passing away quickly, not lasting or permanent. **transient** *n.* a temporary visitor or worker etc. **tran'sient·ly** *adv.* **tran'sience** *n.* **tran·sien·cy** (tran-shĕn-see, -zhĕn-) *n.*

tran·sis·tor (tran-zis-tŏr) *n.* 1. a semiconductor device with three electrodes, performing the same functions as an electron tube but smaller and using less power. 2. (*informal*) a portable radio equipped with transistors.

tran·sis·tor·ize (tran-zis-tŏ-rız) *v.* (**tran·sis·tor·ized, tran·sis·tor·iz·ing**) to equip with transistors.

trans·it (tran-sit, -zit) *n.* 1. the process of going or conveying or being conveyed across or over or through, *the goods were delayed in transit.* 2. the apparent passage of a heavenly body across the disk of the sun or a planet or across the meridian of a place, *to observe the transit of Venus.* 3. a surveyor's instrument for measuring horizontal angles. **transit** *v.* (**trans·it·ed, trans·it·ing**) to make a transit across. □**transit visa,** a visa allowing the holder to pass through a country but not to stay there.

tran·si·tion (tran-zish-ŏn) *n.* the process of changing from one state or style etc. to another, *the transition from childhood to adult life.* **tran·si'tion·al** *adj.* **tran·si'tion·al·ly** *adv.*

tran·si·tive (tran-si-tiv, -zi-) *adj.* (of a verb) used with a direct object either expressed or understood, as *pick* in *pick peas* or *pick until you are tired* (but not in *he picked at the hole to make it bigger*). **tran'si·tive·ly** *adv.* **tran'si·tive·ness** *n.* **tran·si·tiv·i·ty** (tran-si-tiv-i-tee) *n.*

tran·si·to·ry (tran-si-tohr-ee, -zi-) *adj.* existing for a time but not lasting. **tran'si·to·ri·ness** *n.*

Trans·kei (trans-kay) a country in Africa.

transl. *abbr.* 1. translated. 2. translation.

trans·lat·a·ble (trans-lay-tă-bĕl) *adj.* able to be translated.

trans·late (trans-layt) *v.* (**trans·lat·ed, trans·lat·ing**) 1. to express in another language or in simpler words. 2. to be able to be translated, *the poems don't translate well.* 3. to interpret, *we translated his silence as disapproval.* **trans·la'tor** *n.* **trans·la·tion** (trans-lay-shŏn) *n.* ▷Do not confuse *translate* with *transliterate.*

trans·lit·er·ate (trans-lit-ĕ-rayt) *v.* (**trans·lit·er·at·ed, trans·lit·er·at·ing**) to represent (letters or words) in the letters of a different alphabet. **trans·lit·er·a·tion** (trans-lit-ĕ-ray-shŏn) *n.* ▷Do not confuse *transliterate* with *translate.*

trans·lu·cent (trans-loo-sĕnt) *adj.* allowing light to pass through but not transparent. **trans·lu'cent·ly** *adv.* **trans·lu'cence** *n.* **trans·lu·cen·cy** (trans-loo-sĕn-see) *n.*

trans·mi·grate (trans-mı-grayt) *v.* (**trans·mi·**

grat·ed, trans·mi·grat·ing) 1. to pass into, to become incarnate in a different body, as the soul. 2. to migrate. **trans·mi′gra·tor** n. **trans·mi·gra·to·ry** (trans-mɪ-grǎ-tohr-ee) adj.

trans·mi·gra·tion (trans-mɪ-gray-shŏn) n. migration. ☐**transmigration of the soul,** the passing of a person's soul into another body after his death.

trans·mis·si·ble see transmit.

trans·mis·sion (trans-mish-ŏn) n. 1. transmitting, being transmitted. 2. a broadcast. 3. the gear by which power is transmitted from engine to axle in a motor vehicle.

trans·mit (trans-mit) v. **(trans·mit·ted, trans·mit·ting)** 1. to send or pass on from one person or place or thing to another, transmit the message; the disease is transmitted by mosquitoes. 2. to allow to pass through or along, to be a medium for, iron transmits heat. 3. to send out (a signal or program etc.) by telegraph wire or radio waves. **trans·mit′ta·ble** adj. **trans·mit′tal** n. **trans·mit′tance** n. **trans·mis·si·ble** (trans-mis-ĭ-bĕl) adj.

trans·mit·ter (trans-mit-ĕr) n. a person or thing that transmits, a device or equipment for transmitting electric or radio signals.

trans·mog·ri·fy (trans-mog-rĭ-fɪ) v. **(trans·mog·ri·fied, trans·mog·ri·fy·ing)** (humorous) to transform, especially in a magical or surprising way. **trans·mog·ri·fi·ca·tion** (trans-mog-rĭ-fĭ-kay-shŏn) n.

trans·mute (trans-myoot) v. **(trans·mut·ed, trans·mut·ing)** to cause (a thing) to change in form or nature or substance. **trans·mut′a·ble** adj. **trans·mu·ta·tion** (trans-myoo-tay-shŏn) n.

trans·na·tion·al (trans-nash-ŏ-năl) adj. extending beyond national boundaries.

trans·o·ce·an·ic (trans-oh-shi-an-ik) adj. 1. on or from the other side of the ocean. 2. crossing the ocean.

tran·som (tran-sŏm) n. 1. a horizontal bar of wood or stone across the top of a door or window. 2. a window above the transom of a door or larger window.

tran·son·ic (tran-son-ik) adj. relating to speeds close to that of sound.

transp. abbr. transportation.

trans·pa·cif·ic (trans-pă-sif-ik) adj. 1. beyond the Pacific. 2. crossing the Pacific.

trans·par·en·cy (trans-par-ĕn-see) n. (pl. -cies) 1. being transparent. 2. a photographic slide, especially on film as distinct from glass.

trans·par·ent (trans-par-ĕnt) adj. 1. allowing light to pass through so that objects behind can be seen clearly. 2. easily understood, (of an excuse or motive etc.) of such a kind that the truth behind it is easily perceived. 3. clear and unmistakable, a man of transparent honesty. **trans·par′ent·ly** adv.

tran·spire (tran-spɪr) v. **(tran·spired, tran·spir·ing)** 1. (of information etc.) to leak out, to become known, no details of the contract were allowed to transpire. 2. (informal) to happen, we'll see what transpires. 3. (of plants) to give off watery vapor from the surface of leaves etc. **tran·spi·ra·tion** (tran-spi-ray-shŏn) n. ▷Careful writers do not use transpire in its second definition; events occur, not transpire.

trans·plant (trans-plant) v. 1. to remove and replant or establish elsewhere. 2. to transfer (living tissue or an organ) from one part of the body or one person or animal to another. 3. to be able

to be transplanted, some organs transplant easily. **transplant** (trans-plant) n. 1. the transplanting of tissue or an organ. 2. the thing transplanted. **trans·plan·ta·tion** (trans-plan-tay-shŏn) n.

trans·po·lar (trans-poh-lăr) adj. across the north or south poles.

tran·spon·der (tran-spon-dĕr) n. a device for receiving a radio signal and automatically transmitting a different signal.

trans·port (trans-pohrt) v. 1. to convey from one place to another. 2. (old use) to deport to a penal settlement, as a criminal. **transport** (trans-pohrt) n. 1. the act or process of transporting something. 2. means of conveyance, have you got transport? 3. a ship or airplane for carrying troops or supplies. 4. the condition of being carried away by strong emotion, in transports of rage. **trans·port′er** n. **trans·por·ta·tion** (trans-pŏr-tay-shŏn) n.

trans·port·ed (trans-pohr-tid) adj. carried away by strong emotion, she was transported with joy.

trans·pose (trans-pohz) v. **(trans·posed, trans·pos·ing)** 1. to cause (two or more things) to change places, to change the position of (a thing) in a series. 2. to put (a piece of music) into a different key. **trans·po·si·tion** (trans-pŏ-zish-ŏn) n.

trans·sex·u·al (trans-sek-shoo-ăl) n. 1. a person who emotionally feels himself or herself to be a member of the opposite sex. 2. a person who has had surgery and hormone treatment to change sex. **trans·sex′u·al·ism** n.

trans·ship (trans-ship) v. **(trans·shipped, trans·ship·ping)** to transfer (cargo) from one ship or conveyance to another. **trans·ship′ment** n.

trans·Si·be·ri·an (trans-sɪ-beer-i-ăn) adj. across or beyond Siberia

trans·son·ic = transonic.

tran·sub·stan·ti·a·tion (tran-sŭb-stan-shi-ay-shŏn) n. the doctrine that the bread and wine in the Eucharist are converted by consecration into the body and blood of Christ, though their appearance remains the same.

trans·u·ran·ic (trans-yuu-ran-ik) adj. belonging to a group of radioactive elements whose atoms are heavier than those of uranium.

trans·verse (trans-vurs, trans-vurs) adj. lying or acting in a crosswise direction. **transverse** n. something transverse. **trans·verse′ly** adv.

trans·ves·tism (trans-ves-tiz-ĕm) n. dressing in clothing of the opposite sex, as a form of psychological abnormality. **trans·ves·tite** (trans-ves-tɪt) n.

trap[1] (trap) n. 1. a device for catching and holding animals. 2. an arrangement for capturing or detecting a person unawares or making him betray himself, anything deceptive. 3. a golf bunker. 4. a device for sending something into the air to be shot at. 5. a device for preventing the passage of water or steam or silt etc., a U-shaped or S-shaped section of a pipe that holds liquid and so prevents foul gases coming up from a drain. 6. a two-wheeled carriage drawn by a horse. 7. (slang) the mouth, shut your trap. 8. traps, percussion instruments in a jazz band. **trap** v. **(trapped, trap·ping)** to catch or hold in a trap.

trap[2] n. a dark colored igneous rock.

trap·door (trap-dohr) n. a door in a floor or ceiling or roof.

tra·peze (tra-peez) n. a horizontal bar hung by ropes as a swing for acrobatics.

tra·pe·zi·um (tra-pee-zi-ŭm) *n.* (*pl.* **-zi·ums, -zi·a,** *pr.* -zi-ă) a four-sided figure no two sides of which are parallel.

trap·e·zoid (trap-ĕ-zoid) *n.* a four-sided figure having two sides parallel, two sides not.

trap·per (trap-ĕr) *n.* a person who traps animals, especially for furs.

trap·pings (trap-ingz) *n. pl.* ornamental accessories or adjuncts, *he had all the trappings of high office but very little power.*

Trap·pist (trap-ist) *n.* a member of an order of monks and nuns founded at La Trappe in France, noted for silence and other austerities.

trap·rock (trap-rok) *n.* = **trap².**

trap·shoot·ing (trap-shoo-ting) *n.* the sport of shooting at objects released from a trap.

trash (trash) *n.* 1. worthless stuff, rubbish. 2. *(informal)* worthless people. **trash'y** *adj.*

trau·ma (trow-mă) *n.* (*pl.* **-mas, -ma·ta,** *pr.* -mă-tă) 1. a wound or injury. 2. emotional shock producing a lasting effect upon a person. **trau·ma·tize** (trow-mă-tız) *v.* (**trau·ma·tized, trau·ma·tiz·ing**).

trau·mat·ic (trow-mat-ik) *adj.* 1. of or causing trauma. 2. *(informal,* of an experience) very unpleasant. **trau·mat'i·cal·ly** *adv.*

tra·vail (tră-vayl) *n.* 1. a painful or laborious effort. 2. *(old use)* the pangs of childbirth. **travail** *v.* 1. to make a painful effort. 2. *(old use)* to suffer the pangs of childbirth.

trav·el (trav-ĕl) *v.* (**trav·eled, trav·el·ing**) 1. to go from one place or point to another, to make a journey. 2. to journey along or through, to cover (a distance) in traveling. 3. to go from place to place as a salesman. 4. to move or proceed in a specified manner or at a specified rate, *light travels faster than sound.* 5. *(informal)* to associate or to be in company with, *he travels with a rough crowd.* 6. *(informal)* to withstand a long journey, *some wines travel badly.* 7. (in basketball) to take too many steps while in possession of the ball. 8. *(informal)* to move at high speed along a road etc., *the car was certainly traveling.* **travel** *n.* 1. traveling, especially in foreign countries. 2. the range or rate or method of movement of a machine part. 3. *travels,* a series of journeys or wanderings. ☐**travel agent,** one making arrangements for travelers. **travel alarm,** a small alarm clock in a case. **traveling bag,** a small bag carried in the hand, usually for a traveler's clothes. **traveling salesman,** a salesman who travels in a specified area for the purpose of soliciting business for his company.

trav·eled (trav-ĕld) *adj.* having traveled widely.

trav·el·er (trav-ĕ-lĕr) *n.* 1. a person who travels or is traveling. 2. a traveling salesman. ☐**traveler's check,** a check for a fixed amount, sold by a bank etc. and usually able to be cashed in various countries.

trav·e·logue, trav·e·log (trav-ĕ-lawg) *n.* a film or illustrated lecture about travel.

trav·erse (trav-ĕrs) *n.* 1. a thing (especially part of a structure) that lies across another. 2. a zigzag course or road, each leg of this. 3. a lateral movement across something. 4. a steep slope that has to be crossed from side to side in mountaineering. **traverse** (tră-vurs) *v.* (**trav·ersed, trav·ers·ing**) to travel or lie or extend across. **tra·vers·al** (tră-vur-săl) *n.* ☐**traverse** (trav-ĕrs) **rod,** a rod for draperies that allows them to be opened or closed at the pull of a cord.

trav·es·ty (trav-i-stee) *n.* (*pl.* **-ties**) an absurd or inferior imitation, *his trial was a travesty of justice.* **travesty** *v.* (**trav·es·tied, trav·es·ty·ing**) to make or be a travesty of.

tra·vois (tră-voi) *n.* (*pl.* **-vois**) a North American Indian vehicle of two joined poles pulled by a horse etc. and carrying a burden.

trawl (trawl) *n.* a large wide-mouthed fishing net dragged along the bottom of the sea etc. by a boat. **trawl** *v.* 1. to fish with a trawl or seine. 2. to catch by trawling.

trawl·er (traw-lĕr) *n.* a boat used in trawling.

tray (tray) *n.* 1. a flat utensil, usually with a raised edge, on which small articles are placed for display or carrying. 2. a tray of food, *have a tray in one's room.* 3. an open receptacle for holding a person's correspondence in an office. 4. a traylike (often removable) receptacle forming a compartment in a trunk or cabinet or other container.

treach·er·ous (trech-ĕ-rŭs) *adj.* 1. behaving with or showing treachery. 2. not to be relied on, deceptive, not giving a firm support, *the roads were icy and treacherous.* **treach'er·ous·ly** *adv.* **treach'er·ous·ness** *n.*

treach·er·y (trech-ĕ-ree) *n.* (*pl.* **-er·ies**) betrayal of a person or cause, an act of disloyalty.

trea·cle (tree-kĕl) *n.* 1. *(British)* molasses. 2. cloying flattery.

tread (tred) *v.* (**trod, trod·den** or **trod, tread·ing**) 1. to set one's foot down, to walk or step, (of a foot) to be set down. 2. to walk on, to press or crush with the feet, to make (a path or trail or mark etc.) by walking. 3. (of a male bird) to copulate with (a female bird). **tread** *n.* 1. the manner or sound of walking, *a heavy tread.* 2. the top surface of a stair. 3. the part of a wheel or tire etc. that touches the ground. ☐**tread on a person's toes,** *(informal)* to offend or vex him. **tread water,** to keep oneself upright in water by making treading movements with the legs.

trea·dle (tred-ĕl) *n.* a lever worked by the foot to drive a wheel, as in a lathe or sewing machine. **treadle** *v.* (**trea·dled, trea·dling**) to work a treadle.

tread·mill (tred-mil) *n.* 1. a wide mill wheel turned by the weight of people treading on steps fixed around its edge, formerly worked by prisoners as a punishment. 2. tiring monotonous routine work.

treas. *abbr.* 1. treasure. 2. treasury.

trea·son (tree-zŏn) *n.* treachery toward one's country or its ruler. **trea'son·ous** *adj.*

trea·son·a·ble (tree-zŏ-nă-bĕl) *adj.* involving the crime of treason.

treas·ure (trezh-ŭr) *n.* 1. precious metals or gems, a hoard of these, *buried treasure.* 2. a highly valued object, *art treasures.* 3. a beloved or highly valued person. **treasure** *v.* (**treas·ured, treas·ur·ing**) to value highly, to keep or store as precious, *a treasured possession; treasure it.* **treas'ur·a·ble** *adj.* ☐**treasure house,** a place in which treasure is stored or where things of great value or interest are to be found. **treasure hunt,** a search for treasure; a game in which players try to find a hidden object. **treasure trove,** gold or silver coins or plate or bullion found hidden and of unknown ownership; something very useful or desirable that a person finds.

treas·ur·er (trezh-ŭ-rĕr) *n.* a person in charge of the funds of an institution or club etc.

treas·ur·y (trezh-ŭ-ree) *n.* (*pl.* **-ur·ies**) 1. a treasure house, something regarded as containing things of great value or interest, *the book is a treasury of useful information.* 2. *the Treasury,* the department managing the public revenue of a country. ☐**treasury bill,** a U.S. government certificate of obligation maturing in about 90 days and bearing no interest but sold in the open market at a discount. **treasury bond,** an interest-bearing U.S. Treasury Department bond. **treasury certificate,** a U.S. government certificate of obligation maturing in one year or less with interest payable upon the submission of coupons.

treat (treet) *v.* 1. to act or behave toward or deal with (a person or thing) in a certain way, *treated him roughly; treat it as a joke.* 2. to present or deal with (a subject), *recent events are treated in detail.* 3. to give medical or surgical treatment to, *treated him for sunstroke; how would you treat a sprained ankle?* 4. to subject (a substance or thing) to a chemical or other process. 5. to supply (a person) with food or entertainment etc. at one's own expense in order to give pleasure, to buy or give or allow to have as a treat, *treated myself to a taxi.* 6. to negotiate terms, *treating with their enemies to secure a cease-fire.* **treat** *n.* 1. something that gives great pleasure, especially something not always available or that comes unexpectedly. 2. an entertainment etc. designed to do this. 3. the treating of others to something at one's own expense; *it's my treat,* I will pay. **treat′er** *n.*

trea·tise (tree-tis) *n.* a written work dealing systematically with one subject.

treat·ment (treet-měnt) *n.* 1. the process or manner of dealing with a person or thing. 2. something done in order to relieve or cure an illness or abnormality etc.

trea·ty (tree-tee) *n.* (*pl.* **-ties**) a formal agreement between two or more countries.

tre·ble (treb-ĕl) *adj.* 1. three times as much or as many. 2. (of a voice etc.) high-pitched, soprano. **treble** *n.* 1. a treble quantity or thing. 2. a high-pitched or soprano voice etc., a person or musical instrument with this. **treble** *v.* (**tre·bled, tre·bling**) to make or become three times as much or as many, *costs had trebled.* **tre′bly** *adv.* ☐**treble clef,** a musical sign that places G above middle C on the second lowest line of the staff.

tree (tree) *n.* 1. a perennial plant with a single stem or trunk that is usually without branches for some distance above the ground. 2. a framework of wood for various purposes, as in *shoetree.* 3. a family tree (*see* **family**). **tree** *v.* (**treed, tree·ing**) to force (a person or animal) to take refuge up a tree. ☐**cannot see the forest for the trees,** cannot get a clear view of the whole because of too many details. **tree farm,** an area of trees grown for commercial purposes, employing a system of reforestation to produce timber continuously. **tree fern,** a large fern with an upright woody stem. **tree frog,** a frog that lives in trees. **tree house,** a structure built in a tree, for children to play in. **tree line,** the line above which no trees grow. **tree of heaven,** an ornamental Asian tree with ill-scented flowers. **tree surgeon,** a person who treats damaged or diseased trees in order to preserve them. **up a tree,** (*slang*) in great difficulties.

tree·less (tree-lis) *adj.* without trees.

tree·top (tree-top) *n.* the topmost branches of a tree.

tre·foil (tree-foil) *n.* 1. a plant with three leaflets, as clover. 2. an ornament or design shaped like this.

trek (trek) *n.* a long arduous journey. **trek** *v.* (**trekked, trek·king**) to make a trek. **trek′ker** *n.*

trel·lis (trel-is) *n.* a light framework of crossing wooden or metal bars, used to support climbing plants. **trellis** *v.* to furnish or to support a vine with a trellis.

trem·a·tode (trem-ă-tohd) *n.* a parasitic flatworm, as a fluke (*see* **fluke**[3]).

trem·ble (trem-bĕl) *v.* (**trem·bled, trem·bling**) 1. to shake involuntarily from fear or cold etc., to quiver. 2. to be in a state of great anxiety or agitation, *I tremble to think what has become of him.* **tremble** *n.* a trembling or quivering movement, a tremor. **trem′bling·ly** *adv.* **trem′bler** *n.* ▷Do not confuse *trembler* with *temblor.*

trem·bly (trem-blee) *adj.* (**-bli·er, -bli·est**) (*informal*) trembling.

tre·men·dous (tri-men-dŭs) *adj.* 1. immense, *a tremendous quantity of coal.* 2. (*informal*) excellent, *gave a tremendous performance.* **tre·men′dous·ly** *adv.* **tre·men′dous·ness** *n.* ▷Careful writers do not use *tremendous* in its second definition.

trem·o·lo (trem-ŏ-loh) *n.* (*pl.* **-los**) a trembling or vibrating effect in music or in singing.

trem·or (trem-ŏr, tree-mŏr) *n.* 1. a slight shaking or trembling movement, a vibration; *an earth tremor,* a slight earthquake. 2. a thrill of fear or other emotion.

trem·u·lous (trem-yŭ-lŭs) *adj.* 1. trembling from nervousness or weakness. 2. easily made to quiver. **trem′u·lous·ly** *adv.* **trem′u·lous·ness** *n.*

trench (trench) *n.* a deep ditch dug in the ground, as for drainage or to give troops shelter from enemy fire. **trench** *v.* to dig trenches in (ground). ☐**trench coat,** a belted coat or raincoat with pockets and flaps like those of a military uniform coat. **trench foot,** a disease of the feet caused by excessive moisture and cold. **trench knife,** a short knife used in hand-to-hand combat. **trench mouth,** Vincent's angina, a disease with ulcerations of the mucous membranes in the mouth and throat. **trench warfare,** hostilities carried on from more or less permanent trenches.

trench·ant (tren-chănt) *adj.* (of comments or policies etc.) penetrating, strong and effective, *made some trenchant criticisms* or *reforms.* **trench′ant·ly** *adv.* **trench′an·cy** *n.*

trench·er (tren-chěr) *n.* 1. a digger of trenches. 2. (*old use*) a wooden platter for serving food.

trench·er·man (tren-chěr-măn) *n.* (*pl.* **-men,** *pr.* -měn) a person who eats heartily.

trend (trend) *n.* the general direction that something takes, a continuing tendency, *the trend of prices is upward.* **trend** *v.* 1. to have specified a general direction, to bend or to turn away in a specified direction. 2. to be chiefly directed, to have a general and continued tendency. **trend′i·ly** *adv.* **trend′i·ness** *n.*

trend-set·ter (trend-set-ěr) *n.* a person who leads the way in fashion etc.

trend·y (tren-dee) *adj* (**trend·i·er, trend·i·est**) (*informal*) up-to-date, following the latest trends of fashion. **trend′i·ly** *adv.* **trend′i·ness** *n.*

Tren·ton (tren-tŏn) the capital of New Jersey.
tre·pan (tri-pan) *n.* a trephine. **trepan** *v.* **(tre·panned, tre·pan·ning)** to trephine. **trep·a·na·tion** (trep-ă-nay-shŏn) *n.*
tre·phine (tri-fɪn) *n.* a surgeon's cylindrical saw for removing a section of the skull. **trephine** *v.* **(tre·phined, tre·phin·ing)** to cut with a trephine. **treph·i·na·tion** (tref-ĭ-nay-shŏn) *n.*
trep·i·da·tion (trep-i-day-shŏn) *n.* a state of fear and anxiety, nervous agitation.
tres·pass (tres-păs) *v.* 1. to enter a person's land or property unlawfully. 2. to intrude or make use of unreasonably, *trespass on someone's time* or *hospitality.* 3. to sin or do wrong, *as we forgive them that trespass against us.* **trespass** *n.* 1. the act of trespassing. 2. sin, wrongdoing, *forgive us our trespasses.* **tres'pass·er** *n.*
tress (tres) *n.* 1. a lock of hair. 2. *tresses,* the hair of the head.
tres·tle (tres-ĕl) *n.* 1. one of a pair or set of supports on which a board is rested to form a table. 2. an open braced framework for supporting a bridge.
trey (tray) *n.* the three on dice or cards.
tri- *prefix* three, triple, as in *tripod, triad.*
tri·a·ble (trī-ă-bĕl) *adj.* able to be tried.
tri·ad (trī-ad) *n.* a group or set of three. **tri·ad·ic** (trī-ad-ik) *adj.*
tri·age (tree-ahzh) *n.* 1. a sorting according to quality. 2. the assignment of degrees of urgency to decide the order of treatment of people injured in a battle or disaster etc.
tri·al (trī-ăl) *n.* 1. the formal hearing and judging of the facts in a civil or criminal case by a court of law in order to decide the charges or claims at issue. 2. the process of testing qualities or performance by use and experience. 3. an effort or an attempt. 4. a person or thing that tries one's patience or endurance, a hardship. **trial** *adj.* of or used in a trial or trials. □**on trial,** undergoing a trial; on approval. **trial and error,** the process of succeeding in an attempt by trying repeatedly and learning from one's failures. **trial balloon,** an experiment to see how a planned policy or program etc. will be received by the public. **trial lawyer,** a lawyer specializing in cases that require court trial. **trial marriage,** a relationship in which a man and woman live together with an expectation of marriage. **trial run,** an initial test of operation or effectiveness.
tri·an·gle (trī-ang-gĕl) *n.* 1. a geometric figure with three sides and three angles. 2. something shaped like this, a percussion instrument consisting of a steel rod bent into this shape and struck with another steel rod.
tri·an·gu·lar (trī-ang-gyŭ-lăr) *adj.* 1. shaped like a triangle. 2. involving three people, *a triangular contest.* **tri·an'gu·lar·ly** *adv.*
tri·an·gu·late (trī-ang-gyŭ-layt) *v.* **(tri·an·gu·lat·ed, tri·an·gu·lat·ing)** 1. to divide into triangles. 2. to measure or map out (an area) in surveying by means of calculations based on a network of triangles measured from a base line. **tri·an·gu·la·tion** (trī-ang-gyŭ-lay-shŏn) *n.*
Tri·as·sic (trī-as-ik) *adj.* of the first geologic period of the Mesozoic era. **Triassic** *n.* the Triassic period.
trib. *abbr.* tributary.
trib·al (trī-băl) *adj.* of a tribe or tribes.
tribe (trīb) *n.* 1. a racial group (especially in a primitive or nomadic culture) living as a community

under one or more chiefs. 2. a set or class of people, a flock, *he despises the whole tribe of politicians.*
tribes·man (trībz-măn) *n.* (*pl.* **-men,** *pr.* -měn) a member of a racial tribe. **tribes·wom·an** (trībz-wuum-ăn) *n. fem.* (*pl.* **-wom·en,** *pr.* -wim-in).
trib·u·la·tion (trib-yŭ-lay-shŏn) *n.* great affliction, a cause of this.
tri·bu·nal (trī-byoo-năl) *n.* 1. a court of justice. 2. a board of officials appointed to make a judgment or act as arbitrators on a particular problem or on problems of a certain kind.
trib·une (trib-yoon, tri-byoon) *n.* 1. an officer chosen by the Roman people to protect their liberties from being infringed by the senate and magistrates. 2. a person who protects the rights of people.
trib·u·tar·y (trib-yŭ-ter-ee) *n.* (*pl.* **-tar·ies**) a river or stream that flows into a larger one or a lake. **tributary** *adj.* flowing in this way.
trib·ute (trib-yoot) *n.* 1. something said or done or given as a mark of respect or admiration etc. 2. an indication of the effectiveness of, *his recovery is a tribute to the doctors' skill.* 3. payment that one country or ruler was formerly obliged to pay to a more powerful one. □**pay tribute to,** to express respect or admiration for.
trice (trīs) *n.* **in a trice,** in an instant.
tri·ceps (trī-seps) *n.* (*pl.* **-ceps·es, -ceps**) the large muscle at the back of the upper arm.
tri·cer·a·tops (trī-ser-ă-tops) *n.* a dinosaur with a bony crest on the neck, two long horns from the forehead, and one short bone from the nose.
tri·chi·na (tri-kɪ-nă) *n.* (*pl.* **-nae,** *pr.* -nee) a hairlike worm parasitic in the body of man and carnivores.
trich·i·no·sis (trik-ĭ-noh-sis) *n.* the disease caused by eating undercooked pork containing trichinae.
tri·chol·o·gy (tri-kol-ŏ-jee) *n.* the scientific study of hair and its diseases. **tri·chol'o·gist** *n.*
trick (trik) *n.* 1. something done in order to deceive or outwit someone. 2. a deception or illusion, *a trick of the light.* 3. a particular technique, the exact or best way of doing something. 4. a feat of skill done for entertainment, *conjuring tricks.* 5. a mannerism, *he has a trick of repeating himself.* 6. a mischievous or foolish or discreditable act, a practical joke. 7. the cards played in one round of a card game, the round itself, a point gained as a result of this. 8. a person's turn of duty at the helm of a ship, usually for two hours. **trick** *v.* 1. to deceive or persuade by a trick, to mislead. 2. to deck or decorate, *tricked out in all her finery.* **trick'er** *n.* □**do the trick,** *(informal)* to achieve what is required. **how's tricks?,** *(slang)* how are things? **not miss a trick,** *(slang)* to be alert to everything. **trick knee,** *(informal)* a condition in which the knee suddenly stiffens or gives way. **trick or treat,** a Halloween tradition among children who call at houses and threaten to play pranks if candy and gifts are not given to them. **trick out** *or* **up,** to dress, to decorate.
trick·er·y (trik-ĕ-ree) *n.* (*pl.* **-er·ies**) use of tricks, deception.
trick·le (trik-ĕl) *v.* **(trick·led, trick·ling)** 1. to flow or cause to flow in a thin stream. 2. to come or go slowly or gradually, *people trickled into the hall.* **trickle** *n.* a trickling flow, a small amount coming or going slowly, *a trickle of information.*
tricks·ter (trik-stĕr) *n.* a person who tricks or cheats people.

trick·y (trik-ee) *adj.* (**trick·i·er, trick·i·est**) 1. crafty, deceitful. 2. requiring skillful handling, *a tricky task.* **trick′i·ly** *adv.* **trick′i·ness** *n.*

tri·col·or (trɪ-kul-ŏr) *n.* a flag with three colors in stripes, especially that of France. **tricolor** *adj.* having three colors.

tri·cot (tree-koh) *n.* fine jersey fabric.

tri·cy·cle (trɪ-si-kĕl) *n.* a three-wheeled pedal-driven vehicle.

tri·dent (trɪ-dĕnt) *n.* a three-pronged fishing spear, carried by Neptune and Britannia as a symbol of power over the sea.

tried (trɪd) *see* **try**. **tried and true,** tested and proven worthy or good.

tri·en·ni·al (trɪ-en-i-ăl) *adj.* 1. lasting for three years. 2. happening every third year. **tri·en′ni·al·ly** *adv.*

tri·er (trɪ-ĕr) *n.* a person who tries hard, one who always does his best.

tri·fle (trɪ-fĕl) *n.* 1. something of only slight value or importance. 2. a very small amount, especially of money, *it cost a mere trifle; he seems a trifle angry,* slightly angry. **trifle** *v.* (**tri·fled, tri·fling**) to behave or talk frivolously. **tri′fler** *n.* □**trifle with,** to toy with; to treat casually or without due seriousness.

tri·fling (trɪ-fling) *adj.* trivial. **tri′fling·ly** *adv.*

tri·fo·cals (trɪ-foh-kălz) *n.* a pair of eyeglasses with three lenses, for near and intermediate and far distances.

tri·fo·li·ate (trɪ-foh-li-it) *adj.* 1. of a compound leaf with three leaflets. 2. of a plant having such leaves.

trig. *abbr.* trigonometry.

trig·ger (trig-ĕr) *n.* a lever or catch for releasing a spring, especially so as to fire a gun. **trigger** *v.* to set in action, to be the immediate cause of. □**quick on the trigger,** quick to respond. **trigger finger,** the finger that pulls the trigger of a gun. **trigger off,** to trigger.

trig·ger-hap·py (trig-ĕr-hap-ee) *adj.* apt to shoot on slight provocation.

trig·ger·man (trig-ĕr-man) *n.* (*pl.* **-men,** *pr.* -men) *(slang)* 1. a man employed to kill with a gun. 2. a gangster's bodyguard.

tri·glyc·er·ide (trɪ-glis-ĕ-rɪd) *n.* an ester of glycerol.

trig·o·nom·e·try (trig-ŏ-nom-ĕ-tree) *n.* the branch of mathematics dealing with the relationship of sides and angles of triangles etc. **trig·o·no·met·ric** (trig-ŏ-nŏ-met-rik) *adj.* **trig·o·no·met′ri·cal** *adj.* **trig·o·no·met′ri·cal·ly** *adv.*

tri·lat·er·al (trɪ-lat-ĕ-răl) *adj.* having three sides or three participants.

tri·lin·gual (trɪ-ling-gwăl) *adj.* speaking or using three languages.

trill (tril) *n.* 1. a vibrating sound made by the voice or in bird song. 2. quick alteration of two notes in music that are a tone or semitone apart. **trill** *v.* to sound or sing with a trill.

tril·lion (tril-yŏn) *n.* a million millions. **tril′lionth** *adj.* & *n.*

tril·li·um (tril-i-ŭm) *n.* an herb having a circular arrangement of three leaves with a single flower.

tril·o·gy (tril-ŏ-jee) *n.* (*pl.* **-gies**) a group of three related literary or operatic works.

trim (trim) *adj.* (**trim·mer, trim·mest**) neat and orderly, having a smooth outline or compact structure. **trim** *v.* (**trimmed, trim·ming**) 1. to make neat or smooth by cutting away irregular parts. 2. to remove or reduce by cutting. 3. to ornament. 4. to make (a boat or airplane) evenly balanced by arranging the position of its cargo or passengers etc. 5. to arrange (sails) to suit the wind. 6. *(informal)* to punish or beat etc. 7. *(informal)* to cheat. **trim** *n.* 1. condition as regards readiness or fitness, *in good trim.* 2. trimming on a dress or furniture etc., the color or type of upholstery and other fittings in a car. 3. the trimming of hair etc. **trim′ly** *adv.* **trim′ness** *n.* **trim′mer** *n.*

tri·ma·ran (trɪ-mă-ran) *n.* a vessel like a catamaran, with three hulls side by side.

tri·mes·ter (trɪ-mes-tĕr, trɪ-mes-) *n.* a period of three months.

trim·e·ter (trim-ĕ-tĕr) *n.* a verse of three measures.

trim·ming (trim-ing) *n.* 1. something added as an ornament or decoration on a dress or furniture etc. 2. *(informal)* a punishment or beating. 3. *(informal)* a cheating. 4. *trimmings,* pieces cut off when something is trimmed; the usual accompaniments of something, extras, *roast turkey with all the trimmings.*

tri·month·ly (trɪ-munth-lee) *adj.* occurring every three months.

trine (trɪn) *n.* 1. a set of three. 2. (in astrology) the aspect of two planets one-third of the zodiac (= 120°) apart, regarded as having a favorable influence. **trine** *adj.* of or having this aspect.

Trin·i·dad (trin-i-dad) an island in the West Indies, forming part of the country of *Trinidad and Tobago.* **Trin·i·dad·i·an** (trin-i-**dad**-i-ăn) *adj.* & *n.*

Trin·i·tar·i·an (trin-i-tair-i-ăn) *n.* a person who believes in the doctrine of the Trinity. **Trin·i·tar′i·an·ism** *n.*

trin·i·ty (trin-i-tee) *n.* (*pl.* **-ties**) a group of three. □**the Trinity,** the three persons of the Godhead (Father, Son, Holy Spirit) as constituting one God. **Trinity Sunday,** the Sunday after Whitsunday, celebrated in honor of the Holy Trinity.

trin·ket (tring-kit) *n.* a small fancy article or piece of jewelry.

tri·no·mi·al (trɪ-noh-mi-ăl) *adj.* consisting of or relating to three terms. **trinomial** *n.* an algebraic expression or scientific name consisting of three terms.

tri·o (tree-oh) *n.* (*pl.* **-os**) 1. a group or set of three. 2. a group of three singers or players, a musical composition for these.

tri·ode (trɪ-ohd) *n.* a vacuum tube having three electrodes.

tri·o·let (trɪ-ŏ-lit) *n.* a poem with eight lines and two rhymes, of which the first, fourth, and seventh lines are the same and the eighth line is the same as the second.

tri·ox·ide (trɪ-ok-sɪd) *n.* an oxide containing three oxygen atoms.

trip (trip) *v.* (**tripped, trip·ping**) 1. to walk or run or dance with quick light steps, (of rhythm) to run lightly. 2. *(informal)* to have a long visionary experience caused by a hallucinogenic drug. 3. to stumble, to catch one's foot on something and fall, to cause to do this. 4. to make a slip or blunder, to cause to do this. 5. to release (a switch or catch) so as to operate a mechanism. **trip** *n.* 1. a journey or excursion, especially for pleasure. 2. *(informal)* a long visionary experience caused by a hallucinogenic drug. 3. a stumble. 4. a device for tripping a mechanism. □**trip hammer,** a large hammer operated by a tripping mechanism. **trip up,** to stumble or cause to stumble; to make a slip or blunder, to cause (a person) to do this so as to detect him in an error or inconsistency.

tri·par·tite (trɪ-**pahr**-tɪt) *adj.* consisting of three parts.

tripe (trɪp) *n.* 1. the stomach of an ox etc. as food. 2. *(slang)* nonsense, something worthless.

triph·thong (trif-thawng) *n.* three vowel characters representing a sound of a single vowel, as in *beau.*

tri·plane (trɪ-playn) *n.* an airplane with three sets of wings.

tri·ple (**trip**-ĕl) *adj.* 1. consisting of three parts, involving three people or groups. 2. three times as much or as many. **triple** *n.* 1. a set of three. 2. a number or amount three times greater than another. 3. a three base hit. **triple** *v.* (**tri·pled, tri·pling**) 1. to make or become three times as much or as many. 2. (in baseball) to hit a triple. □**triple crown,** the winning by the same horse of the Kentucky Derby, the Preakness, and the Belmont Stakes in one season; any comparable feat in other sports. **triple threat,** a person skilled in three fields or in three areas within the same field, as in football with running, punting, and passing.

tri·plet (**trip**-lit) *n.* 1. one of three children or animals born at one birth. 2. a set of three things.

tri·plex (**trip**-leks) *adj.* triple, threefold. **triplex** *n.* an apartment with rooms on three floors.

trip·li·cate (**trip**-lĭ-kit) *n.* one of three things that are exactly alike. **triplicate** *adj.* threefold, being a triplicate. **triplicate** (**trip**-lĭ-kayt) *v.* (**trip·li·cat·ed, trip·li·cat·ing**) to make or be three identical copies of. **trip·li·ca·tion** (trip-lĭ-kay-shŏn) *n.*

tri·ply (**trip**-lee) *adv.* in a triple manner.

tri·pod (**trɪ**-pod) *n.* a three-legged stand for a camera or surveying instrument etc. **trip·o·dal** (**trip**-ŏ-dăl) *adj.*

Trip·o·li (**trip**-ŏ-lee) the capital of Libya.

trip·tych (**trip**-tik) *n.* a picture or carving on three panels fixed or hinged side by side, especially as an altarpiece.

tri·reme (**trɪ**-reem) *n.* an ancient warship with three banks of oars, especially a Greek one.

tri·sect (trɪ-**sekt**) *v.* to divide into three equal parts. **tri·sec·tion** (trɪ-**sek**-shŏn) *n.*

trite (trɪt) *adj.* (**trit·er, trit·est**) (of a phrase or opinion) commonplace, hackneyed. **trite′ness** *n.*

trit·i·um (**trit**-i-ŭm) *n.* a heavy radioactive isotope of hydrogen with a mass about three times that of ordinary hydrogen.

tri·ton (**trɪ**-tŏn) *n.* a nucleus of a tritium atom, consisting of a proton and two neutrons.

trit·u·rate (**trich**-ŭ-rayt) *v.* (**trit·u·rat·ed, trit·u·rat·ing**) 1. to grind to a fine powder. 2. to masticate thoroughly. **trit′u·ra·tor** *n.* **trit·u·ra·ble** (trich-ŭ-ră-bĕl) *adj.* **trit·u·ra·tion** (trich-ŭ-ray-shŏn) *n.*

tri·umph (**trɪ**-ŭmf) *n.* 1. the fact of being successful or victorious, joy at this. 2. a great success or achievement. **triumph** *v.* to be successful or victorious, to rejoice at one's success etc.; *triumph over difficulties,* overcome them.

tri·um·phal (trɪ-um-făl) *adj.* of or celebrating a triumph. □**triumphal arch,** one built to commemorate a victory.

tri·um·phant (trɪ-um-fănt) *adj.* 1. victorious, successful. 2. rejoicing at success etc. **tri·um′phant·ly** *adv.*

tri·um·vir (trɪ-**um**-vĭr) *n.* (*pl.* **-virs, -vi·ri,** *pr.* -vĭ-rɪ) a person united with two others in office, a member of a triumvirate.

tri·um·vi·rate (trɪ-**um**-vĭ-rit) *n.* 1. the office of a triumvir. 2. a set of triumvirs or of any three persons, especially in authority.

tri·une (**trɪ**-yoon) *adj.* three in one, *a triune Godhead.*

tri·va·lent (trɪ-**vay**-lĕnt) *adj.* having a valence of three.

triv·et (**triv**-it) *n.* 1. a short-legged metal plate upon which hot dishes are placed. 2. an iron stand, especially a tripod, for a kettle or pot etc. placed over a fire.

triv·i·a (**triv**-i-ă) *n. pl.* unimportant matters or things.

triv·i·al (**triv**-i-ăl) *adj.* of only small value or importance. **triv′i·al·ly** *adv.* **triv·i·al·i·ty** (triv-i-al-i-tee) *n.*

triv·i·um (**triv**-i-ŭm) *n.* (*pl.* **triv·i·a**) a medieval university course of grammar, rhetoric, and logic.

tri·week·ly (trɪ-**week**-lee) *adj.* produced or occurring three times in a week or every three weeks.

tro·che (**troh**-kee) *n.* a small medicated tablet or lozenge.

tro·chee (**troh**-kee) *n.* a foot in prose consisting of one long followed by one short syllable.

trod (trod), **trod·den** (trod-ĕn) *see* **tread.**

trog·lo·dyte (**trog**-lŏ-dɪt) *n.* a cave dweller in ancient times.

troi·ka (**troi**-kă) *n.* 1. a Russian vehicle with a team of three horses abreast. 2. a group of three persons, especially as an administrative council.

Tro·jan (**troh**-jăn) *adj.* of Troy (an ancient city in Asia Minor) or its people. **Trojan** *n.* a native or inhabitant of Troy. □**work like a Trojan,** to work with great energy and endurance.

troll¹ (trohl) *v.* 1. to sing in a carefree jovial way. 2. to fish by drawing bait along in the water. **troll** *n.* 1. a fishing lure. 2. the act of trolling. **troll′er** *n.*

troll² *n.* a giant or a friendly but mischievous dwarf in Scandinavian mythology.

trol·ley (**trol**-ee) *n.* (*pl.* **-leys**) 1. a wheeled vehicle or basket operated on an overhead track. 2. an apparatus that collects electric current from an overhead wire and transmits it to the motor of a streetcar or other electric vehicle. 3. a trolley car. □**trolley bus,** a bus powered by electricity from an overhead wire to which it is linked by a pole and contact wheel. **trolley car,** an electric streetcar powered in the same way.

trol·lop (**trol**-ŏp) *n.* *(old use)* a slatternly woman, a prostitute.

trom·bone (trom-**bohn**) *n.* a large brass wind instrument with a sliding tube.

trom·bon·ist (trom-**boh**-nist) *n.* a person who plays a trombone.

tromp (tromp) *v.* *(informal)* to tramp.

trompe l'oeil (tromp **lay**) a style of painting designed to make the viewer think the objects represented are real. ▷French, = deceives the eye.

troop (troop) *n.* 1. a company of people or animals. 2. *troops,* soldiers, armed forces. **troop** *v.* to assemble or go as a troop or in great numbers. □**troop carrier,** a large aircraft or armored vehicle for transporting troops. **trooping the color,** the ceremony of carrying the regimental flag along ranks of soldiers.

troop·er (**troo**-pĕr) *n.* 1. a soldier in a cavalry or armored unit. 2. a member of a state police force.

3. a police officer on horseback. ☐**swear like a trooper,** to swear forcibly. ▷Do not confuse *trooper* with *trouper*.

troop·ship (troop-ship) *n.* a ship for transporting troops.

trop. *abbr.* 1. tropic. 2. tropical.

trope (trohp) *n.* the use of a word in other than its literal sense.

tro·phy (troh-fee) *n.* (*pl.* **-phies**) 1. something taken in war or hunting etc. as a souvenir of success. 2. an object awarded as a prize or token of victory.

trop·ic (trop-ik) *n.* 1. a line of latitude 23°27′ north of the equator *(tropic of Cancer)* or the same latitude south of it *(tropic of Capricorn).* 2. **tropics,** the region between these, with a hot climate. **tropic** *adj.* of or relating to the tropics.

trop·i·cal (trop-i-kăl) *adj.* of or found in or like the tropics. **trop′i·cal·ly** *adv.*

tro·pism (troh-piz-ĕm) *n.* a turning of an organism in a particular direction in response to an external stimulus.

trop·o·sphere (trop-ŏ-sfeer) *n.* the layer of atmospheric air extending about seven miles upward from Earth's surface. **trop·o·spher·ic** (trop-ŏ-sfer-ik) *adj.*

trot (trot) *n.* 1. the running action of a horse etc. with legs moving as in a walk. 2. a slowish run. **trot** *v.* (**trot·ted, trot·ting**) 1. to go or cause to go at a trot. 2. *(informal)* to walk or go, *trot around to the drugstore.* ☐**trot out,** *(informal)* to produce, to bring out for inspection or approval etc., *trotted out the same old excuse.* **trotting race,** a race in which horses pull small vehicles at a trot.

troth (trawth) *n.* *(old use)* 1. truth. 2. faith, loyalty.

Trot·sky·ism (trot-ski-iz-ĕm) *n.* the political or economic principles of Leon Trotsky (1879–1940), a Russian leader and revolutionary urging worldwide socialist revolution. **Trot′sky·ist** *adj. & n.* **Trot·sky·ite** (trot-ski-ıt) *n.*

trot·ter (trot-ĕr) *n.* a horse of a special breed trained for trotting races.

trou·ba·dour (troo-bă-dohr) *n.* 1. a lyric poet in southern France in the 11th-13th centuries. 2. a wandering musician.

trou·ble (trub-ĕl) *n.* 1. difficulty, inconvenience, distress, vexation, misfortune. 2. a cause of any of these. 3. conflict, public unrest. 4. unpleasantness involving punishment or rebuke. 5. faulty functioning of mechanism or of the body or mind, *engine trouble; stomach trouble.* **trouble** *v.* (**trou·bled, trou·bling**) 1. to cause trouble or distress or pain or inconvenience to. 2. to be disturbed or worried, to be subjected to inconvenience or unpleasant exertion, *don't trouble about it.* 3. to cause to move irregularly, *wind troubled the waters.* ☐**be no trouble,** to cause no inconvenience or difficulty. **go to some trouble,** = take trouble. **in trouble,** involved in something liable to bring punishment or rebuke; *(informal)* pregnant while unmarried. **make trouble,** to stir up disagreement or disturbance or unpleasantness. **take trouble,** to use much care and effort in doing something; *take the trouble to do something,* exert oneself to do it. **trouble spot,** a place where trouble frequently occurs.

trou·ble·mak·er (trub-ĕl-may-kĕr) *n.* a person who habitually stirs up trouble.

trou·ble·shoot (trub-ĕl-shoot) *v.* (**trou·ble·**

shoot·ed or **trou·ble·shot, trou·ble·shoot·ing**) to be a troubleshooter, to deal with by doing this.

trou·ble·shoot·er (trub-ĕl-shoo-tĕr) *n.* a person employed to trace and correct faults in machinery etc. or to act as a mediator in disputes.

trou·ble·some (trub-ĕl-sŏm) *adj.* giving trouble, causing annoyance. **trou′ble·some·ly** *adv.*

trough (trawf) *n.* 1. a long narrow open receptacle, especially for holding water or food for animals. 2. a channel for conveying liquid. 3. a depression between two waves or ridges. 4. an elongated region of low atmospheric pressure.

trounce (trowns) *v.* (**trounced, trounc·ing**) 1. to thrash. 2. to defeat heavily. **trounc′er** *n.*

troupe (troop) *n.* a company of actors or acrobats etc.

troup·er (troo-pĕr) *n.* 1. a member of a theatrical troupe. 2. a staunch colleague, *a good trouper.* ▷Do not confuse *trouper* with *trooper.*

trou·sers (trow-zĕrz) *n. pl.* a two-legged outer garment reaching from the waist usually to the ankles.

trous·seau (troo-soh) *n.* (*pl.* **-seaux, -seaus,** *pr.* -sohz) a bride's collection of clothing etc. to begin married life.

trout (trowt) *n.* (*pl.* **trout, trouts**) any of several chiefly freshwater fish valued as food and game.

trow·el (trow-ĕl) *n.* 1. a small tool with a flat blade for spreading mortar etc. 2. a small garden tool with a curved blade for lifting plants or scooping things.

troy (troi) *adj.* expressed or measured in troy weight. ☐**troy weight,** a system of weights used for precious metals and gems, in which 1 pound = 12 ounces or 5760 grains.

tru·ant (troo-ănt) *n.* 1. a child who stays away from school without leave. 2. a person who absents himself from work or duty. **truant** *v.* to play truant. **truant** *adj.* as or like a truant. **tru·an·cy** (troo-ăn-see) *n.* ☐**play truant,** to stay away as a truant. **truant officer,** an officer of a public school who investigates absences of pupils.

truce (troos) *n.* an agreement to cease hostilities temporarily.

truck[1] (truk) *n.* 1. a large automotive vehicle designed to carry heavy loads. 2. an open container on wheels for transporting loads, a hand cart. 3. a swiveling frame with one or more pairs of wheels under each end of a railroad or subway car etc. **truck** *v.* 1. to convey on or in a truck. 2. to drive a truck. **truck′er** *n.*

truck[2] *v.* to exchange, to barter. **truck** *n.* 1. garden produce grown for the market. 2. *(informal)* dealings; *have no truck with,* to have no dealings with. ☐**truck farm,** a farm raising produce for the market.

truck·age (truk-ij) *n.* 1. transportation by truck. 2. the charge for this transport.

truck·ing (truk-ing) *n.* the business or act of transporting goods by truck.

truck·le (truk-ĕl) *v.* (**truck·led, truck·ling**) to submit obsequiously, *refusing to truckle to bullies.* **truck′ler** *n.* ☐**truckle bed,** a trundle bed.

truck·load (truk-lohd) *n.* the full load of a truck.

truc·u·lent (truk-yŭ-lĕnt) *adj.* defiant and aggressive. **truc′u·lent·ly** *adv.* **truc′u·lence** *n.* **truc·u·len·cy** (truk-yŭ-lĕn-see) *n.*

trudge (truj) *v.* (**trudged, trudg·ing**) to walk laboriously. **trudge** *n.* a trudging walk.

true (troo) *adj.* **(tru·er, tru·est)** 1. in accordance with fact. 2. in accordance with correct principles or an accepted standard, rightly so called, genuine and not false, *he was the true heir; the true north,* according to Earth's axis, not the magnetic north. 3. exact, accurate, (of the voice etc.) in good tune. 4. accurately placed or balanced or shaped. 5. loyal, faithful. **true** *adv.* truly, accurately. **true** *n.* exact position or adjustment; *out of true,* misaligned. **true** *v.* (trued, tru·ing or true·ing) to make true. **true'ness** *n.* □**true bill,** a bill of indictment endorsed by the grand jury as being sustained by evidence.

true-blue (troo-bloo) *adj.* completely true to one's principles, firmly loyal.

true·heart·ed (troo-hahr-tid) *adj.* faithful, loyal.

truf·fle (truf-ĕl) *n.* 1. a rich-flavored fungus that grows underground and is valued as a delicacy. 2. a soft candy made of a chocolate mixture.

tru·ism (troo-iz-ĕm) *n.* 1. a statement that is obviously true, especially one that is hackneyed, as *nothing lasts forever.* 2. a statement that merely repeats an idea already implied in one of its words, as *there's no need to be unnecessarily careful.* ▷Do not confuse *truism* with *truth.*

tru·ly (troo-lee) *adv.* 1. truthfully. 2. sincerely, genuinely, *we are truly grateful.* 3. faithfully, loyally. □**yours truly,** see **yours.**

Tru·man (troo-măn), **Har·ry S.** (1884–1972) the thirty-third president of the U.S. 1945–53.

trump (trump) *n.* 1. a playing card of a suit (*trump* or *trumps,* both treated as singular) temporarily ranking above others. 2. *(informal)* a person who behaves in a helpful or useful way. **trump** *v.* to take (a card or trick) with a trump, to play a trump. □**trump card,** a card of the trump suit; a valuable resource, a means of gaining what one wants. **trump up,** to invent (an excuse or accusation etc.) fraudulently.

trump·er·y (trum-pĕ-ree) *n.* (*pl.* **-er·ies**) 1. worthless finery. 2. rubbish, nonsense. **trumpery** *adj.* showy but worthless.

trum·pet (trum-pit) *n.* 1. a metal wind instrument with a bright ringing tone, consisting of a narrow straight or curved tube flared at the end. 2. something shaped like this. **trumpet** *v.* (**trum·pet·ed, trum·pet·ing**) 1. to blow a trumpet, to proclaim by or as if by the sound of a trumpet. 2. (of an elephant) to make a loud resounding sound with its trunk.

trum·pet·er (trum-pĕ-tĕr) *n.* a person who plays or sounds a trumpet. □**trumpeter swan,** a large North American wild swan having a loud cry.

trun·cate (trung-kayt) *v.* (**trun·cat·ed, trun·cat·ing**) to shorten by cutting off the top or end. **truncate** *adj.* truncated. **trun·ca·tion** (trung-kay-shŏn) *n.*

trun·cheon (trun-chŏn) *n.* *(British)* a policeman's nightstick.

trun·dle (trun-dĕl) *v.* (**trun·dled, trun·dling**) to roll along, to move along heavily on a wheel or wheels, *trundling a wheelbarrow; a bus trundled up.* **trun'dler** *n.* □**trundle bed,** a low bed on wheels that may be pushed under another.

trunk (trungk) *n.* 1. the main stem of a tree. 2. the body apart from head and limbs. 3. a large box with a hinged lid for transporting or storing clothes etc. 4. the compartment of an automobile for carrying luggage. 5. the long flexible nose of an elephant. 6. *trunks,* men's shorts for swimming, boxing, and other athletics. □**trunk line,** a main

long-distance railroad line or truck route; a main telephone line.

truss (trus) *n.* 1. a framework of beams or bars supporting a roof or bridge etc. 2. a padded belt or other device worn to support a hernia. **truss** *v.* 1. to tie or bind securely, *truss him up; truss a chicken,* fasten its legs and wings securely before cooking. 2. to support (a roof or bridge etc.) with trusses. **truss'er** *n.*

trust (trust) *n.* 1. firm belief in the reliability or truth or strength etc. of a person or thing. 2. confident expectation. 3. responsibility arising from trust placed in the person given authority, *a position of trust.* 4. property legally entrusted to a person with instructions to use it for another's benefit or for a specified purpose. 5. an association of business firms, formed to reduce or defeat competition; *antitrust legislation,* laws to combat this. **trust** *v.* 1. to have or place trust in, to treat as reliable. 2. to entrust. 3. to hope earnestly, *I trust he is not hurt.* **trust'er** *n.* □**in trust,** held as a trust (definition 4). **on trust,** accepted without investigation, *don't take the statement on trust;* on credit, *they bought goods on trust.* **trust account,** an account holding property in trust for distribution during the life or after the death of the grantor. **trust company,** a company formed to act as trustee or to deal with trusts. **trust fund,** money etc. held in trust. **trust territory,** a territory under trusteeship of a country designated by the U.N. **trust to,** to place reliance on, *trusting to luck.*

trus·tee (trus-tee) *n.* 1. a person who holds and administers property in trust for another. 2. a member of a group of people managing the business affairs of an institution.

trus·tee·ship (trus-tee-ship) *n.* 1. the function of a trustee. 2. the management of a territory by a country as granted by the U.N.

trust·ful (trust-fūl) *adj.* full of trust, not feeling or showing suspicion. **trust'ful·ly** *adv.* **trust'ful·ness** *n.*

trust·wor·thy (trust-wur-*th*ee) *adj.* worthy of trust, reliable. **trust'wor·thi·ness** *n.*

trust·y (trus-tee) *adj.* (**trust·i·er, trust·i·est**) *(old use)* trustworthy, *his trusty sword.* **trusty** *n.* (*pl.* **-ies**) a prisoner who is granted special privileges or given responsibilities because of continuous good behavior.

truth (trooth) *n.* 1. the quality of being true. 2. something that is true. □**truth serum,** a substance administered on the supposition that it will make a person tell the truth. ▷Do not confuse *truth* with *truism.*

truth·ful (trooth-fūl) *adj.* 1. habitually telling the truth. 2. true, *a truthful account of what happened.* **truth'ful·ly** *adv.* **truth'ful·ness** *n.*

try (trī) *v.* (**tried, try·ing**) 1. to attempt, to make an effort to do something. 2. to test, to use or do or test the possibilities of something in order to discover whether it is satisfactory or useful for a purpose, *try your strength; try soap and water; try the public library; try shaking it.* 3. to try to open (a door or window) in order to discover whether it is locked. 4. to be a strain on, *small print tries the eyes; you are trying my patience.* 5. to examine and decide (a case or issue) in a law court, to hold a trial of (a person), *he was tried for murder.* **try** *n.* (*pl.* **tries**) an attempt; *the old college try,* a wholehearted attempt. □**try for,** to attempt to reach or attain or obtain; to compete for. **try it on,** *(informal)* to do something experimentally in order to discover whether it will be tolerated. **try on,** to put (a garment etc.) on to see whether it fits and looks well. **try one's hand,** to attempt something for the first time. **try one's luck,** to attempt something to see if one can be successful. **try out,** to test by use. **try out for,** to compete for (a role in a play, membership in a team, etc.).

try·ing (trī-ing) *adj.* putting a strain on one's temper or patience, annoying. **try'ing·ly** *adv.*

try·out (trī-owt) *n.* a test of effectiveness, popularity, etc.

tryst (trist) *n.* *(old use)* an appointed meeting, an appointment, especially one made by lovers. **tryst** *v.* *(old use)* to meet for a tryst.

tsar = **czar.**

tset·se (tset-see, tsee-tsee) **fly** a tropical African fly that carries and transmits disease (especially sleeping sickness) by its bite.

T.Sgt. *abbr.* technical sergeant.

T-shirt (tee-shurt) *n.* a short-sleeved shirt having the shape of a T when spread out flat.

tsp. *abbr.* 1. teaspoon(s). 2. teaspoonful(s).

T (tee) **square** a T-shaped instrument for measuring or constructing right angles.

tsu·na·mi (tsoo-nah-mee) *n.* a series of huge sea waves caused by disturbance of the ocean floor or by seismic movement. **tsu·na'mic** *adj.*

tub (tub) *n.* 1. an open flat-bottomed usually round container used for washing or for holding liquids or soil for plants etc. 2. a bathtub.

tu·ba (too-bă) *n.* a large low-pitched brass wind instrument.

tub·by (tub-ee) *adj.* (**-bi·er, -bi·est**) short and fat. **tub'bi·ness** *n.*

tube (toob) *n.* 1. a long hollow cylinder, especially for holding or conveying liquids etc. 2. anything shaped like this. 3. a cylinder of flexible material with a screw cap, holding pastes etc. ready for use. **tube'less** *adj.* **tube'like** *adj.* □**down the tube,** *(informal)* wasted, ruined. **the tube,** *(informal)* television.

tu·ber (too-bĕr) *n.* a short thick rounded root (as of a dahlia) or underground stem (as of a potato), producing buds from which new plants will grow.

tu·ber·cle (too-bĕr-kĕl) *n.* a small rounded projection or swelling.

tu·ber·cu·lar (tuu-bur-kyŭ-lăr) *adj.* of or affected with tuberculosis.

tu·ber·cu·lin (tuu-bur-kyŭ-lin) *n.* the sterile liquid from cultures of tubercle bacillus, used in diagnosis and treatment of tuberculosis.

tu·ber·cu·lo·sis (tuu-bur-kyŭ-loh-sis) *n.* 1. an infectious wasting disease affecting various parts of the body, in which tubercles appear on body tissue. 2. tuberculosis of the lungs. **tu·ber·cu·lous** (tuu-bur-kyŭ-lŭs) *adj.*

tube·rose (toob-rohz) *n.* a tropical plant with fragrant white funnel-shaped flowers.

tu·ber·ous (too-bĕ-rŭs) *adj.* of or like a tuber, bearing tubers.

tub·ing (too-bing) *n.* tubes, a length of tube.

tu·bu·lar (too-byŭ-lăr) *adj.* tube-shaped, (of furniture) made of tube-shaped pieces. **tu'bu·lar·ly** *adv.*

tu·bule (too-byool) *n.* a small tube or tube-shaped part.

tuck (tuk) *n.* a flat fold stitched in a garment etc. to make it smaller or as an ornament. **tuck** *v.* 1. to put a tuck or tucks in (a garment etc.). 2.

to turn (ends or edges etc.) or fold (a part) in or into or under something so as to be concealed or held in place. 3. to cover snugly and compactly, *tucked him in bed.* 4. to put away compactly, *tucked it in a drawer.* □**tuck in,** *(slang)* to eat (food) heartily.

tuck·er (tuk-ĕr) *v.* *(informal)* to tire, to weary. □**tuckered out,** *(informal)* tired, exhausted.

Tu·dor (too-dŏr) *adj.* of or belonging to the period of time in England from Henry VII to Elizabeth I, as a style of houses etc.

Tues., Tue. *abbr.* Tuesday.

Tues·day (tooz-day) *n.* the day of the week following Monday.

tu·fa (too-fă) *n.* a porous rock formed around mineral springs. **tu·fa·ceous** (too-fay-shŭs) *adj.*

tuft (tuft) *n.* a bunch of threads or grass or feathers or hair etc. held or growing together at the base. **tuft** *v.* to make depressions in (a mattress or cushion) by stitching tightly through it at a number of points, so as to hold the stuffing in place.

tuft·ed (tuf-tid) *adj.* having a tuft or tufts, (of a bird) having a tuft of projecting feathers on its head.

tug (tug) *v.* (**tugged, tug·ging**) 1. to pull vigorously or with great effort. 2. to tow by means of a tug. **tug** *n.* 1. a vigorous pull. 2. a tugboat. **tug'ger** *n.* □**tug of war,** a contest in which two teams hold a rope at opposite ends and pull until one hauls the other over a central point.

tug·boat (tug-boht) *n.* a small powerful boat for towing others.

tu·i·tion (too-ish-ŏn) *n.* 1. the process of teaching, instruction. 2. a fee for instruction.

tu·la·re·mi·a (too-lă-ree-mi-ă) *n.* a severe infectious bacterial disease of man and domestic animals, transmitted by contact or by insect bites.

tu·lip (too-lip) *n.* a garden plant growing from a bulb, with a large cup-shaped flower on a tall stem.

tulip tree 1. a kind of magnolia. 2. a North American tree with large greenish tuliplike flowers.

tulle (tool) *n.* a kind of fine silky net used for veils and dresses.

tum·ble (tum-bĕl) *v.* (**tum·bled, tum·bling**) 1. to fall helplessly or headlong, to cause to do this (as by pushing). 2. to fall in value or amount. 3. to roll over and over or in a disorderly way. 4. to move or rush in a hasty careless way, *tumbled into bed.* 5. to throw or push carelessly in a confused mass. 6. to rumple or disarrange. **tumble** *n.* 1. a tumbling fall. 2. an untidy state, *things were all in a tumble.* □**tumble to,** *(informal)* to realize or grasp (the meaning of something).

tum·ble·down (tum-bĕl-down) *adj.* falling or fallen into ruin, dilapidated.

tum·bler (tum-blĕr) *n.* 1. a person who turns somersaults etc., an acrobat. 2. a drinking glass with no handle or stem. 3. a pivoted piece in a lock that holds the bolt until lifted by a key. 4. any of several kinds of pivoted or swiveling parts in a mechanism.

tum·ble·weed (tum-bĕl-weed) *n.* a plant, especially of the prairies, forming a globular bush that breaks off in late summer and is rolled about by the wind.

tum·brel (tum-brĕl) *n.* *(old use)* an open cart, especially the kind used to carry condemned people to the guillotine during the French Revolution.

tu·mes·cent (too-mes-ĕnt) *adj.* becoming tumid, swelling. **tu·mes'cence** *n.*

tu·mid (too-mid) *adj.* 1. (of parts of the body) swollen, inflated. 2. bombastic. **tu·mid·i·ty** (too-mid-i-tee) *n.*

tum·my (tum-ee) *n.* (*pl.* **-mies**) *(informal)* the stomach.

tu·mor (too-mŏr) *n.* an abnormal mass of new tissue growing on or in the body. **tu'mor·ous** *adj.*

tu·mult (too-mŭlt) *n.* 1. an uproar. 2. a state of confusion and agitation, *her mind was in a tumult.*

tu·mul·tu·ous (too-mul-choo-ŭs) *adj.* making a tumult, *tumultuous applause.*

tun (tun) *n.* a large cask for wine or beer etc.

tu·na (too-nă) *n.* (*pl.* **-na, -nas**) 1. a large seafish used as food. 2. (also **tuna fish**) its flesh (usually tinned) as food.

tun·dra (tun-dră) *n.* the vast level treeless arctic regions where the subsoil is frozen.

tune (toon) *n.* a melody, especially a well-marked one. **tune** *v.* **(tuned, tun·ing)** 1. to put (a musical instrument) in tune. 2. to tune in (a radio receiver etc.). 3. to adjust (an engine) to run smoothly. **tun'a·ble** *adj.* **tun'a·bly** *adv.* **tun·a·bil·i·ty** (too-nă-bil-i-tee) *n.* □**in tune**, playing or singing at the correct musical pitch; *in tune with one's company*, in harmonious adjustment to it. **out of tune**, not in tune. **to the tune of,** the considerable sum or amount of, *received compensation to the tune of $5000.* **tune in,** to set a radio receiver to the right wavelength to receive a certain transmitted signal; *(slang)* to listen carefully, to be enthusiastic. **tune out,** to cut out radio signals etc. by tuning; *(slang)* to stop listening. **tune up,** (of an orchestra) to bring instruments to the correct or uniform pitch. **tuning fork,** a steel device like a two-pronged fork, which produces a note of fixed pitch, usually middle C, when struck.

tune·ful (toon-fŭl) *adj.* melodious, having a pleasing tune. **tune'ful·ly** *adv.* **tune'ful·ness** *n.*

tune·less (toon-lis) *adj.* not melodious, without a tune. **tune'less·ly** *adv.*

tun·er (too-nĕr) *n.* 1. a person or thing that tunes. 2. the part of a radio receiver that selects wavelengths.

tune·up (toon-up) *n.* the adjustment of a car engine etc. to bring it to its most efficient condition.

tung·sten (tung-stĕn) *n.* a heavy gray metallic substance used for the filaments of electric lamps and in making a kind of steel **(tungsten steel)**. **tung·sten·ic** (tung-sten-ik) *adj.*

tu·nic (too-nik) *n.* 1. a close-fitting jacket worn as part of a uniform. 2. a woman's light hiplength garment, often worn over trousers or a skirt.

Tu·nis (too-nis) the capital of Tunisia.

Tu·ni·sia (too-nee-zhă) a country in North Africa. **Tu·ni'sian** *adj. & n.*

tun·nel (tun-ĕl) *n.* an underground passage, a passage for a highway or railroad through a hill or under a river etc., a passage made by a burrowing animal. **tunnel** *v.* **(tun·neled, tun·nel·ing)** to dig a tunnel, to make a tunnel through. **tun'nel·er** *n.* □**tunnel vision,** defective vision in which a person can see only straight ahead in a very narrow field; narrow-mindedness, especially in solving problems.

Tu·pi (too-pee) *n.* (*pl.* **-pis, -pi**) 1. a South American Indian tribe. 2. the language of this tribe.

tuque (took) *n.* a stocking cap worn in Canada.

tur·ban (tur-băn) *n.* 1. a man's headdress consisting of a scarf wound around a cap, worn especially by Muslims and Sikhs. 2. a woman's hat resembling this.

tur·bid (tur-bid) *adj.* 1. (of liquids) muddy, not clear. 2. confused, disordered, *a turbid imagination.* **tur'bid·ly** *adv.* **tur'bid·ness** *n.* **tur·bid·i·ty** (tur-bid-i-tee) *n.* ▷Do not confuse *turbid* with *turgid.*

tur·bine (tur-bin) *n.* a machine or motor driven by a wheel that is turned by the pressure of air, steam, water, or gas, *gas turbine.*

tur·bo·e·lec·tric (tur-boh-i-lek-trik) *adj.* of or using a generator driven by a turbine.

tur·bo·fan (tur-boh-fan) *n.* a jet engine using air in the combustion of fuel.

tur·bo·jet (tur-boh-jet) *n.* 1. a turbine engine that delivers its power in the form of a jet of hot gases. 2. an aircraft driven by this instead of by propellers.

tur·bo·prop (tur-boh-prop) *n.* 1. a jet engine in which a turbine is used as a turbojet and also to drive a propeller. 2. an aircraft driven by this.

tur·bot (tur-bŏt) *n.* (*pl.* **-bot, -bots**) a large flat sea fish of European waters valued as food.

tur·bu·lent (tur-byŭ-lĕnt) *adj.* 1. in a state of commotion or unrest, (of air or water) moving violently and unevenly. 2. unruly. **tur'bu·lent·ly** *adv.* **tur'bu·lence** *n.*

tu·reen (tuu-reen) *n.* a deep covered dish from which soup is served at the table.

turf (turf) *n.* (*pl.* **turfs**) 1. short grass and the surface layer of earth bound together by its roots. 2. a piece of this cut from the ground. 3. a slab of peat for fuel. 4. *the turf*, the racecourse, horse racing. 5. *(slang)* one's own neighborhood or territory. **turf** *v.* to lay (ground) with turf.

tur·gid (tur-jid) *adj.* 1. swollen or distended and not flexible. 2. (of language or style) pompous, not flowing easily. **tur'gid·ly** *adv.* **tur·gid·i·ty** (tur-jid-i-tee) *n.* ▷Do not confuse *turgid* with *turbid.*

Turk (turk) *n.* a native or inhabitant of Turkey. □**Young Turk,** a member of a Turkish reformist party of 1908; *(young Turk),* a political reformist.

Turk. *abbr.* 1. Turkey. 2. Turkish.

tur·key (tur-kee) *n.* (*pl.* **-keys, -key**) 1. a large bird reared for its flesh. 2. its flesh as food. □**cold turkey,** *see* **cold. talk turkey,** *(informal)* to talk in a frank and businesslike way. **turkey buzzard,** an American carrion vulture. **turkey cock,** the male turkey; a pompous or self-important person. **turkey vulture,** turkey buzzard.

Tur·key (tur-kee) a country in Asia Minor and southeast Europe.

Turk·ish (tur-kish) *adj.* of Turkey or its people or language. **Turkish** *n.* the language of Turkey. □**Turkish bath,** exposure of the whole body to hot air or steam to induce sweating, followed by washing. **Turkish coffee,** strong usually sweet black coffee made from very finely ground beans. **Turkish delight,** a candy consisting of lumps of flavored gelatine coated with powdered sugar. **Turkish towel,** a towel made of terry cloth.

Turk·me·ni·stan (turk-me-ni-stan) a republic of the U.S.S.R. bordering on Iran and the Caspian Sea. **Tur·ko·man** (tur-kŏ-măn) *n.* a native or inhabitant of Turkmenistan.

tur·mer·ic (tur-mĕ-rik) *n.* 1. a plant of the ginger family. 2. its root powdered for use as a dye or stimulant or flavoring, especially in curry powder.

tur·moil (tur-moil) *n.* a state of great disturbance or confusion.

turn (turn) *v.* 1. to move or cause to move around a point or axis; *turn somersaults,* perform them by turning one's body; *it would make him turn in his grave,* would disturb a dead person's eternal rest if he knew about it. 2. to change or cause to change in position so that a different side becomes uppermost or nearest to a certain point. 3. to give a new direction to, to take a new direction, to aim or become aimed in a certain way, *the river turns north at this point; turn the hose on them; our thoughts turned to Christmas presents.* 4. to go or move or travel around, to go to the other side of; *turn the enemy's flank,* pass around it so as to attack him from the side or rear. 5. to pass (a certain hour or age), *it's turned midnight.* 6. to cause to go, to send or put, *turn the horse into the field.* 7. to change or become changed in nature or form or appearance etc., *the caterpillar turned into a chrysalis; he turned Communist; the leaves turned* or *turned brown.* 8. to make or become sour, *the milk has turned.* 9. to make or become nauseated, *it turns my stomach.* 10. to shape in a lathe. 11. to give an elegant form to, *turned phrases that delighted us.* 12. to make (a profit), *turned an honest penny.* **turn** *n.* 1. turning, being turned, *a turning movement.* 2. a change of direction or condition etc., the point at which this occurs. 3. an angle, a bend or corner in a road. 4. character or tendency, *he's of a mechanical turn of mind.* 5. service of a specified kind, *did me a good turn; it served its turn,* served a useful purpose. 6. an opportunity or obligation etc. that comes to each of a number of people or things in succession, *wait your turn.* 7. a short performance in an entertainment. 8. *(informal)* an attack of illness, a momentary nervous shock, *gave me a turn.* □**at every turn,** in every place; continually. **in turn,** in succession; *in one's turn,* when one's turn comes. **not know which way to turn,** not know how to proceed or where to seek help. **not turn a hair,** to show no agitation. **out of turn,** before or after one's turn; *speak out of turn,* to speak in an indiscreet or presumptuous way. **to a turn,** so as to be cooked perfectly. **turn against,** to make or become hostile to. **turn away,** to send away, to reject. **turn down,** to fold down; to reduce the volume or flow of (sound or gas or heat etc.) by turning a knob or tap; to reject. **turn in,** to hand in; to deliver as a score etc.; *(informal)* to go to bed. **turn loose,** to let (a person or thing) go; to put into operation; to give (a person) freedom to take action. **turn off,** to enter a side road; to stop the flow or operation of by turning a tap or switch; *(slang)* to cause to lose interest. **turn on,** to depend on; to start the flow or operation of by turning a tap or switch; *(slang)* to excite (a person) sexually or with drugs etc.; turn upon (*see* below). **turn one's back on,** to abandon. **turn out,** to expel; to turn off (an electric light etc.); to equip or dress, *well turned out;* to produce by work; to empty, *turn out the attic; (informal)* to come out; to call (a military guard) from the guardroom; to prove to be, to be eventually, *we'll see how things turn out.* **turn over,** to hand over; to transfer; to consider carefully, *turn it over in your mind.* **turn over a new leaf,** to abandon one's previous bad ways. **turn tail,** to run away. **turn the corner,** to pass a critical point safely, as in an illness. **turn the**

tables, to reverse a situation and put oneself in a superior position. **turn to,** to set about one's work. **turn turtle,** to capsize. **turn up,** to discover or reveal; to be found; to make one's appearance; to happen or present itself; to increase the volume or flow of (sound or gas or heat etc.) by turning a knob or tap. **turn upon,** to become suddenly hostile to, *turned upon me for no reason.*

turn·a·bout (turn-ă-bowt) *n.* a change or reversal of loyalty, opinion, belief, etc.

turn·a·round (turn-ă-rownd) *n.* 1. a place to turn a vehicle around. 2. a turnabout. 3. the process of unloading and reloading of a ship etc., making it ready to leave.

turn·buck·le (turn-buk-ĕl) *n.* a device for tightly connecting parts of a metal rod or wire.

turn·coat (turn-koht) *n.* a person who changes his principles.

turn·down (turn-down) *adj.* folding downward, as a collar. **turndown** *n. (informal)* a rejection.

turn·er (tur-nĕr) *n.* 1. a person who works with a lathe. 2. a device for turning things, as a *pancake turner.*

turn·ing (tur-ning) *n.* 1. the action or course of a person or thing that turns. 2. the point at which a thing changes direction. □**turning point,** a point at which a decisive change takes place.

tur·nip (tur-nip) *n.* 1. a plant with a round white root used as a vegetable and for feeding cattle etc. 2. its root.

turn·key (turn-kee) *n.* (*pl.* **-keys**) a person in charge of prison keys.

turn·off (turn-awf) *n.* a side road or ramp branching off a main road.

turn·out (turn-owt) *n.* 1. the process of turning out an attic etc. 2. the number of people who come to a public or social function. 3. something arrayed, an outfit.

turn·o·ver (turn-oh-vĕr) *n.* 1. turning over. 2. a small pie in which a piece of pastry is folded over so as to enclose filling. 3. the amount of money turned over in a business. 4. the rate at which goods are sold. 5. the rate at which workers leave and are replaced, *a rapid turnover of staff.*

turn·pike (turn-pık) *n.* 1. *(old use)* a tollgate. 2. a high-speed expressway on which users pay tolls.

turn·spit (turn-spit) *n.* 1. a rotating spit. 2. a person or device that turns a spit.

turn·stile (turn-stıl) *n.* a device for admitting people to a building etc. one at a time, with barriers (often of horizontal bars) that revolve around a central post as each person passes through.

turn·ta·ble (turn-tay-bĕl) *n.* a circular revolving platform or support, as for the record in a record player.

tur·pen·tine (tur-pĕn-tın) *n.* an oil distilled from the resin of certain trees, used for thinning paint and as a solvent.

tur·pi·tude (tur-pi-tood) *n.* wickedness.

turps (turps) *n. (informal)* turpentine.

tur·quoise (tur-kwoiz, -koiz) *n.* 1. a sky-blue precious stone. 2. sky-blue or greenish-blue color. **turquoise** *adj.* of this color.

tur·ret (tur-it) *n.* 1. a small towerlike projection on a building or defensive wall. 2. a low usually revolving structure protecting a gun and gunners in a ship or airplane or fort or tank. 3. a rotating holder for various dies and cutting tools in a lathe or drill etc. **tur'ret·ed** *adj.*

tur·tle (tur-tĕl) *n.* (*pl.* **-tles, -tle**) 1. a slow-moving four-footed reptile with its body enclosed in a

hard shell, living on land or in fresh or salt water.
2. its flesh, used for making soup.

tur·tle·dove (tur-tĕl-duv) n. a wild European dove noted for its soft cooing and for its affection toward its mate and young.

tur·tle·neck (tur-tĕl-nek) n. a shirt or sweater with a high round close-fitting neck.

tusk (tusk) n. one of the pair of long pointed teeth that project outside the mouth in the elephant, walrus, etc. **tusked** adj.

tusk·er (tus-kĕr) n. an elephant or wild boar with developed tusks.

tus·sie (tus-e) n. a struggle, a conflict. **tussle** v. **(tus·sled, tus·sling)** to take part in a tussle.

tus·sock (tus-ŏk) n. a tuft or clump of grass. **tus'sock·y** adj. □**tussock moth,** a moth with tufted larvae.

tu·te·lage (too-tĕ-lij) n. 1. guardianship. 2. instruction.

tu·te·lar·y (too-tĕ-ler-ee) adj. serving as guardian, protective.

tu·tor (too-tŏr) n. 1. a private teacher. 2. (in some universities) a teacher below professorial rank. **tutor** v. to act as tutor to, to teach.

tu·to·ri·al (too-tohr-i-ăl) adj. of or relating to a tutor. **tutorial** n. a type of college course.

tut·ti·frut·ti (too-tee-froo-tee) n. ice cream containing or flavored with mixed fruits.

tu·tu (too-too) n. a ballet dancer's short skirt made of layers of stiffened frills.

tux (tuks) n. (informal) a tuxedo.

tux·e·do (tuk-see-doh) n. (pl. **-dos**) a dinner jacket, evening dress including this.

TV (tee-vee) n. television. □**TV dinner,** a cooked meal for one person, packed and frozen in a foil tray and ready for heating.

TVA abbr. Tennessee Valley Authority.

twad·dle (twod-ĕl) n. nonsense, **twaddle** v. **(twad·dled, twad·dling)** to talk nonsense **twad'dler** n.

twain (twayn) adj. & n. (old use) two.

twang (twang) n. 1. a sharp ringing sound like that made by a tense wire when plucked. 2. a nasal intonation in speech. **twang** v. to make or cause to make a twang, to play (a guitar etc.) by plucking the strings. **twang'y** adj.

'twas (twuz) (old use) = it was.

tweak (tweek) v. to pinch and twist sharply, to pull with a sharp jerk. **tweak** n. a sharp pinch or twist or pull.

tweed (tweed) n. 1. a twilled usually woolen material, often woven of mixed colors. 2. tweeds, clothing made of tweed. **tweed'y** adj. **(tweed·i·er, tweed·i·est).**

'tween (tween) prep. (old use) between.

tweet (tweet) n. the chirp of a small bird. **tweet** v. to make a tweet.

tweet·er (twee-tĕr) n. a small loudspeaker for accurately reproducing high-frequency signals.

tweeze (tweez) v. **(tweezed, tweez·ing)** to pull out with tweezers, as hair, thorns, etc.

tweez·ers (twee-zĕrz) n. pl. small pincers for picking up or pulling very small things.

twelfth (twelfth) adj. & n. 1. next after eleventh. 2. one of twelve equal parts of a thing.

twelve (twelv) adj. & n. one more than eleven (12, XII). □**twelve-tone scale,** a musical scale using twelve chromatic notes of an octave arranged in chosen order without a conventional key.

twen·ties (twen-teez) n. pl. the numbers or years or degrees of temperature from 20 to 29.

twen·ty (twen-tee) adj. & n. (pl. **-ties**) twice ten (20, XX). **twen'ti·eth** adj. & n. □**twentytwenty vision** or **20/20 vision,** normal standard of vision.

twen·ty-one (twen-tee-wun) n. a card game (also called blackjack) in which the players try to get cards totaling as close as possible to twenty-one points but without exceeding that amount.

'twere (twur) = it were.

twerp (twurp) n. (slang) a stupid or insignificant person.

twice (twɪs) adv. 1. two times, on two occasions. 2. in double amount or degree, twice as strong.

twid·dle (twid-ĕl) v. **(twid·dled, twid·dling)** to twirl or handle aimlessly, to twist (a thing) quickly to and fro. **twiddle** n. 1. a slight twirl. 2. a twirled mark or sign. □**twiddle one's thumbs,** to twist them around each other idly for lack of occupation. **twid'dler** n.

twig (twig) n. a small shoot issuing from a branch or stem. **twig'gy** adj.

twi·light (twɪ-lɪt) n. light from the sky when the sun is below the horizon (especially after sunset), the period of this. □**twilight sleep,** a partial narcosis, especially as a means of making childbirth less painful.

twill (twil) n. textile fabric woven so that parallel diagonal lines are produced.

twilled (twild) adj. woven so that parallel diagonal lines are produced.

twin (twin) n. 1. one of two children or animals born at one birth. 2. one of two people or things that are exactly alike. 3. the Twins, a sign of the zodiac, Gemini. **twin** adj. being a twin or twins, twin sister. **twin** v. **(twinned, twin·ning)** to combine as a pair. □**twin beds,** a pair of single beds. **twin-engine plane,** an aircraft with two engines.

twine (twɪn) n. strong thread or string made of two or more strands twisted together. **twine** v. **(twined, twin·ing)** to twist, to wind or coil.

twinge (twinj) n. a slight or brief pang. **twinge** v. **(twinged, twing·ing)** 1. to give the mind or body a sudden pain. 2. to have a twinge.

twin·kle (twing-kĕl) v. **(twin·kled, twin·kling)** 1. to shine with a light that flickers rapidly, to sparkle. 2. (of the eyes) to be bright or sparkling with amusement. 3. (of the feet in dancing etc.) to move with short rapid movements. **twinkle** n. a twinkling light or look or movement. **twin'kler** n.

twin·kling (twing-kling) n. 1. an instant. 2. the act of shining brightly intermittently. □**in the twinkling of an eye,** in an instant.

twirl (twurl) v. to twist lightly or rapidly. **twirl** n. 1. a twirling movement. 2. a twirled mark or sign. **twirl'er** n.

twist (twist) v. 1. to wind (strands etc.) around each other so as to form a single cord, to interweave. 2. to make by doing this. 3. to pass or coil around something. 4. to give a spiral form to, as by turning the ends in opposite directions. 5. to take a spiral or winding form or course, to turn or bend around, the road twisted and turned; he twisted around in his seat. 6. to rotate or revolve, to cause to do this; twist slowly in the wind, stand helpless as though subject to every turn of fate. 7. to wrench out of its normal shape; a twisted mind, one that works in a perverted way. 8. to distort the meaning of, tried to twist his words into an admission of guilt. **twist** n. 1. twisting, being twisted. 2. something formed by twisting, a turn in a twisting course. **3.** a peculiar tendency of mind or character. **4.** a dance with twisting gyrations of the body and arms. **5.** *(informal)* a sliver of lemon peel etc., for adding to a drink. **twist′·a·ble** *adj.* □**twist a person's arm,** *(informal)* to coerce him or her.

twist·er (twis-tĕr) *n.* **1.** a person or thing that twists. **2.** (in baseball) a batted or pitched ball that moves with a spin. **3.** *(informal)* a tornado or whirlwind.

twit[1] (twit) *v.* **(twit·ted, twit·ting)** to taunt. **twit** *n.* a taunting remark.

twit[2] *n.* *(slang)* a foolish or insignificant person.

twitch (twich) *v.* **1.** to pull with a light jerk. **2.** to quiver or contract spasmodically. **twitch** *n.* a twitching movement. **twitch′ing·ly** *adv.*

twit·ter (twit-ĕr) *v.* **1.** to make a series of light chirping sounds. **2.** to talk rapidly in an anxious or nervous way. **twitter** *n.* twittering.

'twixt (twikst) *prep. (old use)* betwixt.

two (too) *adj. & n.* one more than one (2, II). □**be of** *or* **in two minds,** to be undecided. **two bits,** *(slang)* twenty-five cents. ▷Do not confuse *two* with *to* or *too.*

two-bag·ger (too-bag-ĕr) *n.* *(informal)* a double in baseball.

two-bit (too-bit) *adj. (slang)* **1.** cheap. **2.** small-time, insignificant.

two-by-four (too-bɪ-fohr) *adj.* **1.** two units thick and four units wide. **2.** *(slang)* very small, as a *two-by-four room.* **two-by-four** *n.* a long piece of wood measuring two inches thick and four inches wide.

two-di·men·sion·al (too-di-men-shŏ-năl) *adj.* having two dimensions, as length and breadth.

two-edged (too-ejd) *adj.* **1.** having two cutting edges. **2.** cutting both ways.

two-faced (too-fayst) *adj.* insincere, deceitful.

two·fer (too-fĕr) *n.* *(informal)* a ticket allowing a person to buy two theater tickets for the regular price of one.

two-fist·ed (too-fis-tid) *adj. (informal)* vigorous.

two·fold (too-fohld) *adj. & adv.* **1.** twice as much or as many. **2.** consisting of two parts.

2,4-D a white crystalline powder, used as a weed killer.

2,4,5-T a solid compound, used for brush and weed control.

two-hand·ed (too-han-did) *adj.* **1.** having two hands. **2.** requiring to be used with both hands. **3.** able to be worked, played, etc. by two persons.

two-ply (too-plɪ) *adj.* made of two strands or layers.

two·seat·er (too-see-tĕr) *n.* a vehicle, an aircraft, etc. having two seats.

two·sid·ed (too-sɪ-did) *adj.* having two sides or aspects etc.

two·some (too-sŏm) *n.* two people together, a couple or pair.

two-step (too-step) *n.* a dance with a sliding step in march or polka time.

two-time (too-tɪm) *v.* **(two·timed, two·tim·ing)** *(slang)* to doublecross. **two′tim·er** *n.*

two-tone (too-tohn) *adj.* having two colors or sounds.

'twould (twuud) = it would.

two-way (too-way) *adj.* involving two ways or participants; *two-way switch,* a switch that allows electric current to be turned on or off from either of two points; *two-way traffic,* lanes of traffic traveling in opposite directions.

two-wheel·er (too-hwee-lĕr) *n.* *(informal)* a vehicle with two wheels.

twp. *abbr.* township.

TWX *abbr.* teletypewriter exchange.

TX *abbr.* Texas.

-ty *suffix* used to form nouns meaning quality or condition, as in *priority, subtlety.*

ty·coon (tɪ-koon) *n.* a wealthy and influential businessman or industrialist, a magnate.

ty·ing (tɪ-ing) *see* **tie.**

tyke (tik) *n. (informal)* a small child.

Ty·ler (tɪ-lĕr), **John** (1790–1862) the tenth president of the U.S. 1841–45.

tym·pan (tim-păn) *n.* a printing apparatus to equalize pressure between the platen etc. and the printing sheet.

tym·pan·ic (tim-pan-ik) *adj.* relating to the tympanum of the ear. □**tympanic membrane,** the eardrum, which separates the middle ear from the external ear passage.

tym·pa·num (tim-pă-năm) *n.* (*pl.* **-nums, -na,** *pr.* -nă) **1.** the middle ear. **2.** the eardrum. **3.** a drumhead.

typ. *abbr.* **1.** typographer. **2.** typographic. **3.** typographical. **4.** typography.

type (tɪp) *n.* **1.** a class of people or things that have characteristics in common, a kind, *men of this type; another type of climate.* **2.** a typical example or instance. **3.** *(informal)* a person of specified character, *brainy types.* **4.** a small block with a raised letter or figure etc. used in printing, a set or supply or kind or size of these, *printed in large type.* **type** *v.* **(typed, typ·ing) 1.** to classify according to type. **2.** to write with a typewriter. □**type found·er,** a person who designs and makes metal type for printing. ▷It is incorrect to omit *of* in such expressions as *another type of climate, that type of bread.*

type·cast (tɪp-kast) *v.* **(type·cast, type·cast·ing)** to cast (an actor) in the kind of part that he has the reputation of playing successfully or which seems to fit his personality.

type·face (tɪp-fays) *n.* **1.** the design or style of printing type. **2.** a set of types in one design.

type·script (tɪp-skript) *n.* a typewritten document.

type·set (tɪp-set) *v.* **(type·set, type·set·ting)** to set type in proper order for printing. **type′set·ter** *n.* **type′set·ting** *adj. & n.*

type·write (tɪp-rit) *v.* **(type·wrote, type·writ·ten, type·writ·ing)** to write with a typewriter. **type′writ·ing** *n.*

type·writ·er (tɪp-rɪ-tĕr) *n.* a machine for producing characters similar to those of print by pressing keys that cause raised metal letters etc. to strike the paper, usually through inked ribbon.

type·writ·ten (tɪp-rit-ĕn) *adj.* written with a typewriter.

ty·phoid (tɪ-foid) *n.* (also **typhoid fever**) a serious infectious feverish disease that attacks the intestines, caused by bacteria taken into the body in food or drink.

ty·phoon (tɪ-foon) *n.* a violent hurricane in the western Pacific.

ty·phus (tɪ-fŭs) *n.* an infectious disease with fever, great weakness, and purple spots on the body. **ty′phous** *adj.*

typ·i·cal (tip-i-kăl) *adj.* **1.** having the distinctive qualities of a particular type of person or thing, serving as a representative specimen, *a typical Kansan.* **2.** characteristic, *he answered with typical curtness.* **typ′i·cal·ly** *adv.* **typ′i·cal·ness** *n.*

typ·i·fy (tip-ĭ-fī) *v.* (**typ·i·fied, typ·i·fy·ing**) to be a representative specimen of.

typ·ist (tī-pist) *n.* a person who types, especially one employed to do so.

ty·po (tī-poh) *n.* (*pl.* **-pos**) *(informal)* a typographical error.

ty·pog·ra·phy (tī-pog-ră-fee) *n.* 1. the art or practice of printing. 2. the style or appearance of printed matter. **ty·pog′ra·pher** *n.* **ty·po·graph·ic** (tī-pŏ-graf-ik) *adj.* **ty·po·graph′i·cal** *adj.* **ty·po·graph′i·cal·ly** *adv.* □**typographical error,** a printing or typing error made by pressing the wrong key on a keyboard.

ty·ran·nic (ti-ran-ik), **ty·ran·ni·cal** (ti-ran-i-kăl) *adj.* as or like a tyrant, obtaining obedience from everyone by force or threats. **ty·ran′ni·cal·ly** *adv.* **ty·ran′ni·cal·ness** *n.*

tyr·an·nize (tir-ă-nīz) *v.* (**tyr·an·nized, tyr·an·niz·ing**) to rule as or like a tyrant. **tyr′an·niz·er** *n.*

ty·ran·no·saur (ti-ran-ŏ-sor) *n.* (also **ty·ran·no·saur·us**) a kind of dinosaur, the largest known carnivore.

tyr·an·nous (tir-ă-nŭs) *adj.* tyrannical.

tyr·an·ny (tir-ă-nee) *n.* (*pl.* **-nies**) 1. government by a tyrannical ruler. 2. oppressive or tyrannical use of power.

ty·rant (tī-rănt) *n.* a ruler or other person who uses his power in a harsh or oppressive way, one who insists on absolute obedience.

ty·ro (tī-roh) *n.* (*pl.* **-ros**) a beginner, a novice.

Tyr·ol (ti-rohl) *n.* an Alpine district of Austria and Italy. **Tyr·o·lese** (tir-ŏ-leez) *adj. & n.* (*pl.* **-lese**) **Ty·ro·le·an** (ti-roh-li-ăn) *adj. & n.*

tzar = **czar.**

tza·ri·na = **czarina.**

U

U, u (yoo) (*pl.* **Us, U's, u's**) the twenty-first letter of the alphabet.
U *symbol* uranium.
U. *abbr.* 1. unit. 2. university.
Ua·boe the capital of Nauru. ▷The pronunciation of Uaboe has not been determined.
u·biq·ui·tous (yoo-bik-wi-tŭs) *adj.* being everywhere at the same time. **u·biq'ui·tous·ly** *adv.* **u·biq'ui·ty** *n.*
U-boat (yoo-boht) *n.* a German submarine, especially in World War II.
u.c. *abbr.* upper case.
ud·der (ud-ĕr) *n.* a bag-like milk-secreting organ of a cow or ewe or female goat etc., with two or more teats.
UFO *abbr.* unidentified flying object.
U·gan·da (yoo-gan-dă) a country in East Africa. **U·gan'dan** *adj & n.*
ugh (ug) *interj.* an exclamation of disgust or horror.
ug·li (ug-lee) *n.* (*pl.* **-lis, -lies**) (also **ugli fruit**) a mottled green and yellow citrus fruit, a hybrid of a grapefruit and a tangerine.
ug·ly (ug-lee) *adj.* (**-li·er, -li·est**) 1. unpleasant to look at or to hear. 2. unpleasant in any way, hostile and threatening, *the crowd was in an ugly mood.* **ug'li·ness** *n.* ▢**ugly customer,** an unpleasantly formidable person. **ugly duckling,** a person who at first seems unpromising but later becomes much admired or very able (▷like the cygnet in the brood of ducks in Hans Christian Andersen's story).
uh (u) *interj.* an exclamation indicating a pause.
UHF *abbr.* ultrahigh frequency.
U.K. *abbr.* United Kingdom.
u·kase (yoo-kays) *n.* 1. an edict of the czarist Russian government. 2. an arbitrary order.
U·kraine (yoo-krayn) a republic of the U.S.S.R., north of the Black Sea. **U·krain·i·an** (yoo-kray-ni-ăn) *n.* 1. a native of the Ukraine. 2. the language of the Ukraine.
u·ku·le·le (yoo-kŭ-lay-lee) *n.* a small four-stringed guitar.
UL *abbr.* Underwriters' Laboratories.
U·lan Ba·tor (oo-lahn bah-tor) the capital of the Mongolian People's Republic.
ul·cer (ul-sĕr) *n.* an open sore on the surface of the body or one of its organs. **ul'cer·ous** *adj.*
ul·cer·ate (ul-sĕ-rayt) *v.* (**ul·cer·at·ed, ul·cer·at·ing**) to cause an ulcer in or on, to become affected with an ulcer. **ul·cer·a·tive** (ul-sĕ-ray-tiv) *adj.* **ul·cer·a·tion** (ul-sĕ-ray-shŏn) *n.*
ul·lage (ul-ij) *n.* the amount by which a cask etc. falls short of being full, the loss by evaporation or leakage.
ul·na (ul-nă) *n.* (*pl.* **-nae,** *pr.* **-nee, -nas**) the thinner of the two long bones in the forearm, the corresponding bone in an animal. **ul'nar** *adj.*

Ul·ster (ul-stĕr) 1. a former province of Ireland comprising the present Northern Ireland and the counties of Cavan, Donegal, and Monaghan (which are now in the Republic of Ireland). 2. (used loosely) = Northern Ireland. 3. *ulster,* a long loose overcoat of rough cloth, often with a belt.
ult. *abbr.* ultimate.
ul·te·ri·or (ul-teer-i-ŏr) *adj.* beyond what is obvious or admitted, *ulterior motives.* **ul·te'ri·or·ly** *adv.*
ul·ti·mate (ul-tĭ-mit) *adj.* 1. last, final; *the ultimate deterrent,* threatened use of nuclear weapons. 2. basic, fundamental, *the ultimate cause.* **ul'ti·mate·ly** *adv.*
ul·ti·ma·tum (ul-tĭ-may-tŭm, -mah-) *n.* (*pl.* **-tums, -ta,** *pr.* -tă) a final demand or statement of terms, rejection of which may lead to the ending of friendly relations or a declaration of war.
ul·tra (ul-tră) *adj.* extreme, beyond the usual. **ultra** *n.* a person favoring extreme views or measures, especially in religion or politics.
ultra- *prefix* beyond, extremely, excessively, as in *ultraconservative, ultramodern.*
ul·tra·cen·tri·fuge (ul-tră-sen-trĭ-fyooj) *n.* a high-speed centrifuge used to determine the size of small particles and large molecules by their rate of sedimentation. **ul·tra·cen·trif·u·gal** (ul-tră-sen-trif-yŭ-găl) *adj.* **ul·tra·cen·trif·u·ga·tion** (ul-tră-sen-trif-yŭ-gay-shŏn) *n.*
ul·tra·con·ser·va·tive (ul-tră-kŏn-sur-vă-tiv) *adj.* extremely conservative.
ul·tra·fash·ion·a·ble (ul-tră-fash-ŏ-nă-bĕl) *adj.* excessively fashionable.
ul·tra·fiche (ul-tră-feesh) *n.* an extremely reduced microfiche.
ul·tra·high (ul-tră-hɪ) *adj.* (of frequency) in the range of 300 to 3000 megahertz.
ul·tra·ma·rine (ul-tră-mă-reen) *adj. & n.* bright deep blue.
ul·tra·mi·cro·scope (ul-tră-mɪ-krŏ-skohp) *n.* an instrument revealing, by scattered light, objects too small to be seen with an ordinary microscope.
ul·tra·mi·cro·scop·ic (ul-tră-mɪ-krŏ-skop-ik) *adj.* too small to be seen with an ordinary microscope. **ul·tra·mi·cro·scop'i·cal·ly** *adv.*
ul·tra·min·i·a·ture (ul-tră-min-i-ă-chŭr) *adj.* extremely small. **ul·tra·min·i·a·tur·i·za·tion** (ul-tră-min-i-ă-chŭ-ri-zay-shŏn) *n.*
ul·tra·mod·ern (ul-tră-mod-ĕrn) *adj.* extremely modern, as a design, idea, etc.
ul·tra·mon·tane (ul-tră-mon-tayn) *adj.* 1. situated south of the Alps. 2. favorable to the absolute authority of the pope in matters of faith and discipline. **ul·tra·mon·tan·ism** (ul-tră-mon-tă-niz-ĕm) *n.*

ul·tra·pure (ul-tră-pyoor) *adj.* extremely pure.
ul·tra·pure'ly *adv.*
ul·tra·short (ul-tră-short) *adj.* extremely short.
ul·tra·son·ic (ul-tră-son-ik) *adj.* (of sound waves) with a pitch that is above the upper limit of normal human hearing. **ul·tra·son'i·cal·ly** *adv.*
ul·tra·son·ics (ul-tră-son-iks) *n.* the scientific study of ultrasonic waves and their use.
ul·tra·sound (ul-tră-sownd) *n.* sound having ultrasonic frequency, ultrasonic waves.
ul·tra·vi·o·let (ul-tră-vɪ-ŏ-lit) *adj.* 1. (of radiation) having a wavelength that is slightly shorter than that of visible light rays at the violet end of the spectrum. 2. of or using this radiation, *an ultraviolet lamp.* **ultraviolet** *n.*
ul·tra vi·res (ul-tră vɪ-reez) beyond one's legal power or authority. ▷Latin.
ul·u·late (yool-yŭ-layt) *v.* (**ul·u·lat·ed, ul·u·lat·ing**) 1. to howl, to wail. 2. to hoot. **ul·u·la·tion** (yool-yŭ-lay-shŏn) *n.*
um·bel (um-běl) *n.* a flower cluster in which the flowers are on stalks of nearly equal length springing from the same point on the main stem. **um·bel·late** (um-bě-layt) *adj.*
um·ber (um-běr) *n.* a natural coloring matter like ocher but darker and browner. **umber** *adj.* of the color umber. ☐**burnt umber,** reddish brown.
um·bil·i·cal (um-bil-i-kăl) *adj.* of the navel. ☐**umbilical cord,** the flexible tubular structure of tissue connecting the placenta to the navel of the fetus and carrying nourishment to the fetus while it is in the womb.
um·bil·i·cus (um-bil-ĭ-kŭs) *n.* (*pl.* **-ci,** *pr.* **-kɪ, -sɪ, -cus·es**) the navel.
um·bra (um-bră) *n.* (*pl.* **-bras, -brae,** *pr.* -bree) 1. the total shadow cast by Earth or the moon in an eclipse. 2. the dark central part of a sunspot. **um'bral** *adj.*
um·brage (um-brij) *n.* a feeling of being offended. ☐**take umbrage,** to take offense.
um·brel·la (um-brel-ă) *n.* 1. a portable protection against rain, consisting of a circular piece of fabric mounted on a foldable frame of spokes attached to a central stick that serves as a handle. 2. any kind of general protecting force or influence; *the contract included an umbrella clause,* one providing protection against unspecified conditions. ☐**umbrella stand,** a stand for holding closed umbrellas, usually with a pan at the bottom to catch drippings. **umbrella tree,** a small magnolia with leaves in an umbrella-like whorl at the end of each branch.
u·mi·ak (oo-mi-ak) *n.* an Eskimo skin-and-wood open boat propelled by paddle.
um·laut (uum-lowt) *n.* 1. a vowel change in Germanic languages by which the vowel is influenced by a vowel or semivowel in the following syllable. 2. the mark ̈ used to show this in German and other languages, as in *führer.*
ump (ump) *n. & v. (informal)* umpire.
um·pire (um-pɪr) *n.* a person appointed to see that the rules of a game or contest are observed and to settle disputes (as in a game of baseball etc.), or to give a decision on any disputed question. **umpire** *v.* (**um·pired, um·pir·ing**) to act as umpire in (a game).
ump·teen (ump-teen) *adj. (slang)* very many. **ump'teenth'** *adj.*
UMT *abbr.* universal military training.
Um·ta·ta (uum-tah-tă) the capital of Transkei.
UMW *abbr.* United Mine Workers.
UN *abbr.* United Nations.

un- *prefix* 1. not, as in *uncertain, uncertainty.* 2. reversing the action indicated by the simple verb, as in *unlock* = release from being locked. ▷The number of words with this prefix is almost unlimited, and many of those whose meanings are obvious are not listed below.

---

un·a·ble (un-ay-běl) *adj.* not able.
un·a·bridged (un-ă-brijd) *adj.* not abridged.
un·ac·com·pa·nied (un-ă-kum-pă-need) *adj.* 1. not accompanied. 2. without musical accompaniment.
un·ac·count·a·ble (un-ă-kown-tă-běl) *adj.* 1. unable to be explained or accounted for. 2. not accountable for one's actions etc. **un·ac·count'a·bly** *adv.*
un·ac·count·ed (un-ă-kown-tid) *adj.* of which no account is given. ☐**unaccounted for,** unexplained, not included in an account.
un·ac·cus·tomed (un-ă-kus-tŏmd) *adj.* not accustomed.
un·a·dul·ter·at·ed (un-ă-dul-tě-ray-tid) *adj.* 1. not altered by the addition of another substance, pure. 2. complete, *unadulterated nonsense.*
un·ad·vised (un-ad-vɪzd) *adj.* 1. indiscreet, rash. 2. not having had advice. **un·ad·vis·ed·ly** (un-ad-vɪ-zid-lee) *adv.*
un·af·fect·ed (un-ă-fek-tid) *adj.* 1. not affected by. 2. free from affectation, genuine, sincere. **un·af·fect'ed·ly** *adv.*
un·aid·ed (un-ay-did) *adj.* not aided.
un·al·ien·a·ble (un-ayl-yě-nă-běl) *adj. (old use)* inalienable.
un·a·ligned (un-ă-lɪnd) *adj.* not aligned.
un·al·loyed (un-ă-loid) *adj.* not alloyed, pure, *unalloyed joy.*
un-A·mer·i·can (un-ă-mer-ĭ-kăn) *adj.* 1. not in accordance with American characteristics. 2. contrary to the interests of the U.S.

---

un·a·bashed' *adj.*	**un·ac·cred·it·ed** *adj.*	**un·a·larmed'** *adj.*
un·a·bash'ed·ly *adv.*	**un·ac·knowl'edged** *adj.*	**un·a·like'** *adj. & adv.*
un·a·bat'ed *adj.*	**un·ac·quaint'ed** *adj.*	**un·al·layed'** *adj.*
un·ab·solved' *adj.*	**un·a·dapt'ed** *adj.*	**un·al·le'vi·at·ed** *adj.*
un·ab·sorbed' *adj.*	**un·ad·dressed'** *adj.*	**un·al·lied'** *adj.*
un·ac'cent·ed *adj.*	**un·ad·just'ed** *adj.*	**un·al'pha·bet·ized** *adj.*
un·ac·cen'tu·at·ed *adj.*	**un·a·dorned'** *adj.*	**un·al'ter·a·ble** *adj.*
un·ac·cep'ta·ble *adj.*	**un·ad'ver·tised** *adj.*	**un·al'ter·a·bly** *adv.*
un·ac·cep'ta·bly *adv.*	**un·ad·vis'a·ble** *adj.*	**un·al'tered** *adj.*
un·ac·claimed' *adj.*	**un·af·fil'i·at·ed** *adj.*	**un·am·big'u·ous** *adj.*
un·ac'cli·mat·ed *adj.*	**un·a·fraid'** *adj.*	**un·am·big'u·ous·ly** *adv.*
un·ac·com'mo·dat·ing *adj.*	**un·aged'** *adj.*	**un·am·bi'tious** *adj.*
un·ac·com'plished *adj.*	**un·ag'ing** *adj.*	**un·a·me'na·ble** *adj.*

u·nan·i·mous (yoo-nan-ĭ-mŭs) *adj.* all agreeing in an opinion or decision, (of an opinion or decision etc.) held or given by everyone. **u·nan'i·mous·ly** *adv.* **u·na·nim·i·ty** (yoo-nă-nim-i-tee) *n.*

un·an·swer·a·ble (un-an-sĕ-ră-bĕl) *adj.* unable to be answered or refuted by a good argument to the contrary.

un·an·swered (un-an-sĕrd) *adj.* not answered.

un·ap·pe·tiz·ing (un-ap-ĕ-tĭ-zing) *adj.* not appealing or appetizing.

un·armed (un-ahrmd) *adj.* not armed, without weapons.

un·asked (un-askt) *adj.* not asked, without being requested.

un·as·sail·a·ble (un-ă-say-lă-bĕl) *adj.* not open to attack or question. **un·as·sail'a·bly** *adv.*

un·as·sum·ing (un-ă-soo-ming) *adj.* not arrogant, unpretentious. **un·as·sum'ing·ly** *adv.*

un·at·tached (un-ă-tacht) *adj.* 1. not attached. 2. not married or engaged to be married.

un·at·tend·ed (un-ă-ten-did) *adj.* 1. not accompanied or waited upon. 2. (of a vehicle etc.) having no person in charge of it. 3. not attended, as by a consequence. □**unattended to,** not attended to.

un·a·vail·ing (un-ă-vay-ling) *adj.* achieving nothing, ineffectual. **un·a·vail'ing·ly** *adv.*

un·a·void·a·ble (un-ă-voi-dă-bĕl) *adj.* unable to be avoided. **un·a·void'a·bly** *adv.* **un·a·void·a·bil·i·ty** (un-ă-voi-dă-bil-i-tee) *n.*

un·a·ware (un-ă-wair) *adj.* & *adv.* not aware. **un·a·ware'ness** *n.*

un·a·wares (un-ă-wairz) *adv.* unexpectedly, without noticing.

un·bal·anced (un-bal-ănst) *adj.* 1. not balanced. 2. mentally unsound.

un·bar (un-bahr) *v.* (**un·barred, un·bar·ring**) 1. to remove the bar from (a gate etc.). 2. to unlock, to open.

un·bear·a·ble (un-bair-ă-bĕl) *adj.* not bearable, unable to be endured. **un·bear'a·bly** *adv.*

un·beat·a·ble (un-bee-tă-bĕl) *adj.* impossible to defeat or surpass.

un·beat·en (un-bee-tĕn) *adj.* not defeated, (of a record etc.) not surpassed.

un·be·com·ing (un-bi-kum-ing) *adj.* 1. not suitable, *behavior unbecoming to a gentleman.* 2. not suited to the wearer, *an unbecoming hat.* **un·be·com'ing·ly** *adv.*

un·be·known (un-bi-nohn), **un·be·knownst** (un-bi-nohnst) *adj.* unknown; *they did it unbeknown to us,* without our being aware of it.

un·be·lief (un-bi-leef) *n.* 1. incredulity. 2. disbelief, especially in divine revelation or in a particular religion. **un·be·liev'ing** *adj.*

un·be·liev·a·ble (un-bi-lee-vă-bĕl) *adj.* not believable. **un·be·liev'a·bly** *adv.*

un·be·liev·er (un-bi-lee-vĕr) *n.* a person who does not believe, especially one who does not accept a religious belief.

un·bend (un-bend) *v.* (**un·bent, un·bend·ing**) 1. to change or become changed from a bent position. 2. to become relaxed or affable.

un·bend·ing (un-ben-ding) *adj.* inflexible, refusing to alter one's demands.

un·bi·ased (un-br-ăst) *adj.* not biased or prejudiced, impartial. **un·bi'ased·ly** *adv.*

un·bid·den (un-bid-ĕn) *adj.* not commanded or invited.

un·bind (un-brnd) *v.* (**un·bound, un·bind·ing**) to release from bonds or binding.

un·blessed, un·blest (un-blest) *adj.* not blessed. **un·bless·ed·ness** (un-bles-id-nis) *n.*

un·blink·ing (un-bling-king) *adj.* 1. not blinking. 2. without reaction, as to fear, sorrow, etc. 3. not wavering.

un·block (un-blok) *v.* to remove an obstruction from.

un·blush·ing (un-blush-ing) *adj.* 1. not blushing. 2. without shame. **un·blush'ing·ly** *adv.*

un·bolt (un-bohlt) *v.* to release (a door etc.) by drawing back the bolt(s). **un·bolt'ed** *adj.*

un·born (un-born) *adj.* not yet born.

un·bos·om (un-buuz-ŏm) *v.* **unbosom oneself,** to reveal one's thoughts or feelings.

un·bound·ed (un-bown-did) *adj.* boundless, without limits. **un·bound'ed·ly** *adv.*

un·bowed (un-bowd) *adj.* 1. not bowed. 2. not yielding or surrendering.

un·break·a·ble (un-bray-kă-bĕl) *adj.* not breakable.

un·bri·dled (un-bri-dĕld) *adj.* unrestrained,

---

un·am·or'tized *adj.*
un·am'pli·fied *adj.*
un·a·mused' *adj.*
un·a·mus'ing *adj.*
un·an'chored *adj.*
un·an'i·mat·ed *adj.*
un·an·nounced' *adj.*
un·an·tic'i·pat·ed *adj.*
un·a·pol·o·get'ic *adj.*
un·ap·par'ent *adj.*
un·ap·peal'ing *adj.*
un·ap·peal'ing·ly *adv.*
un·ap·peas'a·ble *adj.*
un·ap·peased' *adj.*
un·ap'pli·ca·ble *adj.*
un·ap·plied' *adj.*
un·ap·point'ed *adj.*
un·ap·por'tioned *adj.*
un·ap·pre'ci·at·ed *adj.*
un·ap·pre'ci·a·tive *adj.*
un·ap·pre·hen'sive *adj.*
un·ap·proach'a·ble *adj.*
un·ap·pro'pri·at·ed *adj.*
un·ap·proved' *adj.*

un·ap·prov'ing *adj.*
un·ap·prov'ing·ly *adv.*
un·ar·gu·a·ble *adj.*
un·ar'mored *adj.*
un·art'ful *adj.*
un·ar·tic'u·late *adj.*
un·ar·tic'u·lat·ed *adj.*
un·ar·tic'u·late·ly *adv.*
un·ar·tis'tic *adj.*
un·a·shamed' *adj.*
un·a·sham'ed·ly *adv.*
un·as'pi·rat·ed *adj.*
un·a·spir'ing *adj.*
un·as·ser'tive *adj.*
un·as·ser'tive·ly *adv.*
un·as·sessed' *adj.*
un·as·signed' *adj.*
un·as·sim'i·lat·ed *adj.*
un·as·sist'ed *adj.*
un·at·tain'a·ble *adj.*
un·at·tempt'ed *adj.*
un·at·test'ed *adj.*
un·at·tract'ed *adj.*
un·at·trac'tive *adj.*

un·at·trac'tive·ly *adv.*
un·at·trac'tive·ness *n.*
un·aus·pi'cious *adj.*
un·aus·pi'cious·ly *adv.*
un·au·then'ti·cat·ed *adj.*
un·au'thor·ized *adj.*
un·a·vail·a·bil'i·ty *n.*
un·a·vail'a·ble *adj.*
un·a·venged' *adj.*
un·a·vowed' *adj.*
un·a·wak'ened *adj.*
un·awed' *adj.*
un·baked' *adj.*
un·bap'tized *adj.*
un·be·fit'ting *adj.*
un·be·fit'ting·ly *adv.*
un·be·hold'en *adj.*
un·be·loved' *adj.*
un·blamed' *adj.*
un·bleached' *adj.*
un·blem'ished *adj.*
un·bound' *adj.*
un·brand'ed *adj.*
un·brib'a·ble *adj.*

their unbridled insolence. **un·bri′dled·ly** *adv.*

un·bro·ken (un-broh-kĕn) *adj.* not broken, not interrupted; *an unbroken record,* one not surpassed.

un·buck·le (un-buk-ĕl) *v.* (**un·buck·led, un·buck·ling**) to release the buckle of (a shoe, strap, etc.).

un·bur·den (un-bur-dĕn) *v.* to relieve of a burden; *unburdened herself to me,* relieved her conscience by confessing to me.

un·but·ton (un-but-ŏn) *v.* to open (a coat etc.) by taking buttons out of buttonholes.

un·called-for (un-kawld-for) *adj.* offered or intruded impertinently or unjustifiably.

un·can·ny (un-kan-ee) *adj.* 1. strange and rather frightening. 2. extraordinary, beyond what is normal, *they predicted the results with uncanny accuracy.* **un·can′ni·ly** *adv.*

un·cap (un-kap) *v.* (**un·capped, un·cap·ping**) to remove a cover or cap from.

un·cared-for (un-kaird-for) *adj.* neglected.

un·ceas·ing (un-see-sing) *adj.* not ceasing. **un·ceas′ing·ly** *adv.*

un·cer·e·mo·ni·ous (un-ser-ĕ-moh-ni-ŭs) *adj.* without proper formality or dignity. **un·cer·e·mo′ni·ous·ly** *adv.* **un·cer·e·mo′ni·ous·ness** *n.*

un·cer·tain (un-sur-tin) *adj.* 1. not known certainly. 2. not knowing certainly. 3. not to be depended on, *his aim is uncertain.* 4. changeable, *an uncertain temper.* **un·cer′tain·ly** *adv.* **un·cer′tain·ty** *n.* (*pl.* **-ties**) □in no uncertain terms, clearly and forcefully.

un·chain (un-chayn) *v.* to remove from chains.

un·char·i·ta·ble (un-char-i-tă-bĕl) *adj.* not charitable or kind, severe in judgment. **un·char′i·ta·bly** *adv.* **un·char′i·ta·ble·ness** *n.*

un·chart·ed (un-chahr-tid) *adj.* not mapped, unknown.

un·chaste (un-chayst) *adj.* not chaste. **un·chaste′ly** *adv.* **un·chaste′ness** *n.* **un·chas·ti·ty** (un-chas-ti-tee) *n.*

un·chris·tian (un-kris-chăn) *adj.* contrary to Christian principles, uncharitable.

un·ci·al (un-shi-ăl, -shăl) *adj.* of or written with large rounded unjoined letters used in manuscripts of the 4th–8th centuries, from which modern capital letters are largely derived. **uncial** *n.* an uncial letter or style or manuscript.

un·civ·il (un-siv-il) *adj.* ill-mannered, impolite.

un·civ·i·lized (un-siv-i-lIzd) *adj.* 1. not civilized, barbarous. 2. not enlightened.

un·clad (un-klad) *adj.* not dressed, naked.

un·clasp (un-klasp) *v.* 1. to loosen the clasp of. 2. to release the grip of, as a hand etc. 3. to become unclasped.

un·clas·si·fied (un-klas-ĭ-fId) 1. not restricted for reasons of military security. 2. not categorized or classified.

un·cle (ung-kĕl) *n.* 1. a brother or brother-in-law of one's father or mother. 2. *(children's informal)* prefixed to the given name of an unrelated man friend. □say uncle, *(slang)* to give up in defeat.

Uncle Sam, *(informal)* the personification of the U.S. **Uncle Tom,** *(contemptuous)* a black subservient to whites. ▷From Harriet Beecher Stowe's *Uncle Tom's Cabin* (1852).

un·clean (un-kleen) *adj.* 1. not clean. 2. unchaste, sinful. 3. unfit to be eaten, ceremonially impure. **un·clean′ly** *adv.* **un·clean′ness** *n.*

un·clean·ly (un-klen-lee) *adj.* not cleanly. **un·clean′li·ness** *n.*

un·clench (un-klench) *v.* to open or to be opened after being clenched.

un·cloak (un-klohk) *v.* 1. to remove a cloak from, to take off a cloak. 2. to expose.

un·clog (un-klog) *v.* (**un·clogged, un·clog·ging**) to remove a blockage from.

un·clothe (un-kloh*th*) *v.* (**un·clothed** or **un·clad, un·cloth·ing**) to strip the clothing from, to make bare.

un·coil (un-koil) *v.* to release from a coiled condition.

un·come·ly (un-kum-lee) *adj.* 1. improper; unseemly. 2. not pleasant in appearance.

un·com·fort·a·ble (un-kumf-tă-bĕl, -kum-fŏr-tă-bĕl) *adj.* 1. causing discomfort. 2. not comfortable, uneasy. **un·com′fort·a·bly** *adv.* **un·com′fort·a·ble·ness** *n.*

un·com·mit·ted (un-kŏ-mit-id) *adj.* not committed, especially to a specific course of action.

un·com·mon (un-kom-ŏn) *adj.* not common, unusual. **un·com′mon·ly** *adv.* **un·com′mon·ness** *n.*

un·com·mu·ni·ca·tive (un-kŏ-myoo-ni-kay-tiv) *adj.* not inclined to give information or an opinion etc., silent. **un·com·mu′ni·ca·tive·ness** *n.*

un·com·pro·mis·ing (un-kom-prŏ-mI-zing) *adj.* not allowing or seeking compromise, inflexible. **un·com′pro·mis·ing·ly** *adv.*

un·bruised′ *adj.*	**un·change′a·ble** *adj.*	**un·clear′ly** *adv.*
un·brushed′ *adj.*	**un·changed′** *adj.*	**un·cloud′ed** *adj.*
un·budg′et·ed *adj.*	**un·chang′ing** *adj.*	**un·clut′tered** *adj.*
un·budg′ing *adj.*	**un·chap′er·oned** *adj.*	**un·coat′ed** *adj.*
un·bur′ied *adj.*	**un·char·ac·ter·is′tic** *adj.*	**un·col·lect′ed** *adj.*
un·burned′ *adj.*	**un·chas′tened** *adj.*	**un·col′ored** *adj.*
un·bur′nished *adj.*	**un·chas′tised** *adj.*	**un·combed′** *adj.*
un·burnt′ *adj.*	**un·checked′** *adj.*	**un·com·bined′** *adj.*
un·can′celed *adj.*	**un·cheer′ful** *adj.*	**un·com′fort·ed** *adj.*
un·car′ing *adj.*	**un·cheer′ful·ly** *adv.*	**un·com′fort·ing** *adj.*
un·car′ing·ly *adv.*	**un·chilled′** *adj.*	**un·com·mend′a·ble** *adj.*
un·car′pet·ed *adj.*	**un·cho′sen** *adj.*	**un·com·pen·sat·ed** *adj.*
un·cashed′ *adj.*	**un·chris′tened** *adj.*	**un·com·plain′ing** *adj.*
un·cat′a·logued *adj.*	**un·cir′cum·cised** *adj.*	**un·com·plet′ed** *adj.*
un·caught′ *adj.*	**un·claimed′** *adj.*	**un·com·pli·cat·ed** *adj.*
un·cel′e·brat·ed *adj.*	**un·clar′i·fied** *adj.*	**un·com·pli·men′ta·ry** *adj.*
un·cen′sored *adj.*	**un·clas·si·fi·a·ble** *adj.*	**un·com·pound′ed** *adj.*
un·cen′sured *adj.*	**un·cleaned′** *adj.*	**un·com·pre·hend′ing** *adj.*
un·cer′ti·fied *adj.*	**un·clear′** *adj.*	**un·com·pre·hend′ing·ly** *adv.*
un·chal′lenged *adj.*	**un·cleared′** *adj.*	**un·con·cealed′** *adj.*

un·con·cern (un-kŏn-surn) *n.* 1. freedom from anxiety. 2. indifference, apathy.

un·con·cerned (un-kŏn-surnd) *adj.* not feeling or showing concern, free from anxiety. **un·con·cern·ed·ly** (un-kŏn-sur-nid-lee) *adv.*

un·con·di·tion·al (un-kŏn-**dish**-ŏ-năl) *adj.* not subject to conditions or limitations, *unconditional surrender.* **un·con·di'tion·al·ly** *adv.*

un·con·di·tioned (un-kŏn-**dish**-ŏnd) *adj.* 1. not subject to conditions. 2. not determined by previous conditions.

un·con·gen·ial (un-kŏn-**jeen**-yăl) *adj.* not congenial.

un·con·quer·a·ble (un-kong-kĕ-ră-bĕl) *adj.* not able to be conquered.

un·con·scion·a·ble (un-kon-shŏ-nă-bĕl) *adj.* 1. unscrupulous. 2. contrary to what one's conscience feels is right, outrageous. **un·con'scion·a·bly** *adv.*

un·con·scious (un-kon-shŭs) *adj.* 1. not conscious, not aware. 2. done or spoken etc. without conscious intention, *unconscious humor.* 3. *the unconscious,* the part of the mind containing thoughts not normally accessible to consciousness but found to affect behavior. (▷Do not confuse *unconscious* with *subconscious.*) **un·con'scious·ly** *adv.* **un·con'scious·ness** *n.*

un·con·sti·tu·tion·al (un-kon-sti-**too**-shŏ-năl) *adj.* not in accordance with a political constitution or with procedural rules. **un·con·sti·tu'tion·al·ly** *adv.* **un·con·sti·tu·tion·al·i·ty** (un-kon-sti-too-shŏ-**nal**-i-tee) *n.*

un·con·trol·la·ble (un-kŏn-troh-lă-bĕl) *adj.* not able to be controlled. **un·con·trol'la·bly** *adv.*

un·con·ven·tion·al (un-kŏn-ven-shŏ-năl) *adj.* 1. not bound by convention or custom. 2. unusual. **un·con·ven'tion·al·ly** *adv.* **un·con·ven·tion·al·i·ty** (un-kŏn-ven-shŏ-**nal**-i-tee) *n.*

un·co·op·er·a·tive (un-koh-op-ĕ-ră-tiv) *adj.* not cooperative.

un·cork (un-kork) *v.* to draw a cork from; *uncork one's feelings,* give vent to them.

un·count·ed (un-kown-tid) *adj.* 1. not counted. 2. beyond counting, innumerable.

un·cou·ple (un-kup-ĕl) *v.* **(un·cou·pled, un·cou·pling)** to disconnect (railroad cars etc.) from being connected by a coupling.

un·couth (un-kooth) *adj.* awkward or clumsy in manner, boorish. **un·couth'ness** *n.*

un·cov·er (un-kuv-ĕr) *v.* 1. to remove the covering from. 2. to reveal or expose, *their deceit was uncovered.*

un·crit·i·cal (un-krit-i-kăl) *adj.* 1. not critical, disinclined or not competent to criticize. 2. not in accordance with principles of criticism. **un·crit'i·cal·ly** *adv.*

un·cross (un-kraws) *v.* to remove from a crossed position, as legs, arms, knives, etc.

unc·tion (ungk-shŏn) *n.* 1. anointing with oil, especially as a religious rite. 2. pretended earnestness, excessive politeness. ▷Do not confuse *unction* with *unctuousness.*

unc·tu·ous (ungk-choo-ŭs) *adj.* having an oily manner, smugly earnest or virtuous. **unc'tu·ous·ly** *adv.* **unc'tu·ous·ness** *n.* ▷Do not confuse *unctuousness* with *unction.*

un·curl (un-kurl) *v.* to remove from a curled position, to straighten.

un·cut (un-kut) *adj.* not cut, (of a gem) not shaped by cutting, (of a book, play, or motion picture) not shortened, (of fabric) with the loops of the pile not cut.

un·daunt·ed (un-dawn-tid) *adj.* 1. not discouraged. 2. not giving in to fear. **un·daunt'ed·ly** *adv.*

un·de·ceive (un-di-seev) *v.* **(un·de·ceived, un·de·ceiv·ing)** to disillusion (a person).

un·de·cid·ed (un-di-sɪ-did) *adj.* 1. not yet settled or certain, *the point is still undecided.* 2. not having made up one's mind.

un·de·mon·stra·tive (un-dĕ-**mon**-stră-tiv) *adj.* not given to or making outward expression of one's feelings.

un·de·ni·a·ble (un-di-nɪ-ă-bĕl) *adj.* impossible to deny, undoubtedly true. **un·de·ni'a·bly** *adv.*

un·der (un-dĕr) *prep.* 1. in or to a position lower than, below. 2. less than, *it's under a mile from here.* 3. inferior to, of lower rank than, *no one under a bishop.* 4. governed or controlled by, *the country prospered under his rule.* 5. undergoing, *the road is under repair.* 6. subject to an obligation imposed by, *he is under contract to our firm.* 7. in accordance with, *it is permissible under our agreement.* 8. designated or indicated by, *writes under an assumed name.* 9. in the category of, *file it under "Estimates."* 10. (of land) planted with, *500 acres under wheat.* 11. propelled by, *under sail; under one's own steam,* moving without external aid. 12. attested by, *under my hand* (= signature) *and seal.* **under** *adv.* 1. in or to a lower position or subordinate condition. 2. in or into a state of unconsciousness. 3. below a certain quantity or rank or age etc., *children of five and under.* **under** *adj.* lower, situated underneath, *the*

---

un·con·clud'ed *adj.*
un·con·fined' *adj.*
un·con·firmed' *adj.*
un·con·gealed' *adj.*
un·con·nec'ted *adj.*
un·con'quered *adj.*
un·con'se·crat·ed *adj.*
un·con·sid'ered *adj.*
un·con·soled' *adj.*
un·con·sol'i·dat·ed *adj.*
un·con·strained' *adj.*
un·con·strict'ed *adj.*
un·con·sumed' *adj.*
un·con·sum·mat·ed *adj.*
un·con·tam'i·nat·ed *adj.*
un·con·test'ed *adj.*
un·con·tra·dict'ed *adj.*
un·con·trolled' *adj.*

un·con·vert'ed *adj.*
un·con·vict'ed *adj.*
un·con·vinced' *adj.*
un·con·vinc'ing *adj.*
un·con·vinc'ing·ly *adv.*
un·cooked' *adj.*
un·co·or'di·nat·ed *adj.*
un·cor·rect'ed *adj.*
un·cor·rob'o·rat·ed *adj.*
un·cor·rupt'ed *adj.*
un·count'a·ble *adj.*
un·cred'it·ed *adj.*
un·crowd'ed *adj.*
un·crowned' *adj.*
un·cul'ti·vat·ed *adj.*
un·cul'tured *adj.*
un·curbed' *adj.*
un·cured' *adj.*

un·cus'tom·ar·y *adj.*
un·dam'aged *adj.*
un·damped' *adj.*
un·dat'ed *adj.*
un·de·ci'pher·a·ble *adj.*
un·de·clared' *adj.*
un·dec'o·rat·ed *adj.*
un·de·feat'ed *adj.*
un·de·fend'ed *adj.*
un·de·filed' *adj.*
un·de·fin'a·ble *adj.*
un·de·fin'a·bly *adv.*
un·de·fined' *adj.*
un·de·mand'ing *adj.*
un·dem·o·crat'ic *adj.*
un·dem·o·crat'i·cal·ly *adv.*
un·de·nied' *adj.*
un·de·pend'a·ble *adj.*

under layers. □**under the sun,** anywhere in the world, existing. **under way,** moving on water; in progress. ▷Sometimes incorrectly written as *under weigh,* through confusion with *weigh anchor.*

under- *prefix* below, beneath, as in *undercoat;* lower, subordinate, as in *undersecretary;* insufficiently, incompletely, as in *undercooked.*

un·der·a·chieve (un-děr-ă-cheev) *v.* (**un·der·a·chieved, un·der·a·chiev·ing**) to do less well than was expected, especially in school. **un·der·a·chiev′er** *n.* **un·der·a·chieve′ment** *n.*

un·der·act (un-děr-akt) *v.* to act a part with insufficient force.

un·der·age (un-děr-ayj) *adj.* 1. not old enough, especially for some legal right. 2. not yet of adult status.

un·der·arm (un-děr-ahrm) *adj.* 1. under the armpit. 2. underhand (definition 2).

un·der·bel·ly (un-děr-bel-ee) *n.* (*pl.* **-lies**) the undersurface of an animal or thing, especially as an area vulnerable to attack, *the soft underbelly of Europe.*

un·der·bid (un-děr-bid) *v.* (**un·der·bid, un·der·bid·ding**) 1. to make a lower bid than (another person). 2. to bid less than is justified in the game of bridge. **un′der·bid·der** *n.*

un·der·bod·y (un-děr-bod-ee) *n.* (*pl.* **-bod·ies**) the undersurface of the body of an animal, vehicle, etc.

un·der·bred (un-děr-bred) *adj.* 1. ill-bred, vulgar. 2. not of pure breeding.

un·der·brush (un-děr-brush) *n.* the undergrowth in a forest.

un·der·car·riage (un-děr-kar-ij) *n.* 1. the supporting frame of a vehicle. 2. an airplane's landing wheels and their supports.

un·der·charge (un-děr-chahrj) *v.* (**un·der·charged, un·der·charg·ing**) 1. to charge too low a price. 2. to give less than a proper charge to (a battery etc.). **un′der·charge** *n.*

un·der·class·man (un-děr-klas-măn) *n.* (*pl.* **-men,** *pr.* -měn) a freshman or sophomore in a high school or college.

un·der·clothes (un-děr-klohz, -kloh*th*z) *n. pl.* underwear.

un·der·cloth·ing (un-děr-kloh-*th*ing) *n.* underwear.

un·der·coat (un-děr-koht) *n.* 1. a layer of paint under a finishing coat, the paint used for this. 2. the short hair under a growth of longer hair on some animals.

un·der·coat·ing (un-děr-koh-ting) *n.* a rustproof coating on the undersurface of a vehicle.

un·der·cook (un-děr-kuuk) *v.* to cook insufficiently.

un·der·cov·er (un-děr-kuv-ĕr) *adj.* 1. doing things secretly, done secretly. 2. engaged in spying by working among those to be spied on, *undercover agents.*

un·der·cur·rent (un-děr-kur-ĕnt) *n.* 1. a current that is below a surface or below another current. 2. an underlying feeling or influence or trend.

un·der·cut (un-děr-kut) *v.* (**un·der·cut, un·der·cut·ting**) 1. to cut away the part below. 2. to sell or work for a lower price than (another person). 3. to strike (a ball) with a downward motion of the club or racket etc. in order to cause it to rise or to give it backspin.

un·der·de·vel·oped (un-děr-di-vel-ŏpt) *adj.* not fully developed, (of a film) not developed enough to give a satisfactory image, (of a country) not having reached its potential level in economic development.

un·der·dog (un-děr-dawg) *n.* a person or country etc. in an inferior or subordinate position.

un·der·done (un-děr-dun) *adj.* not thoroughly done, (of meat) not completely cooked throughout.

un·der·draw·ers (un-děr-drorz) *n. pl.* underpants.

un·der·ed·u·cat·ed (un-der-ej-ŭ-kay-tid) *adj.* inadequately educated.

un·der·em·pha·size (un-děr-em-fă-sɪz) *v.* (**un·der·em·pha·sized, un·der·em·pha·siz·ing**) to give an insufficient degree of emphasis to. **un·der·em′pha·sis** *n.*

un·der·em·ployed (un-děr-em-ploid) *adj.* not fully employed.

un·der·es·ti·mate (un-děr-es-tǐ-mayt) *v.* (**un·der·es·ti·mat·ed, un·der·es·ti·mat·ing**) to make too low an estimate of. **underestimate** (un-děr-es-tǐ-mit) *n.* an estimate that is too low. **un·der·es·ti·ma·tion** (un-děr-es-tǐ-may-shŏn) *n.*

un·der·ex·pose (un-děr-ik-spohz) *v.* (**un·der·ex·posed, un·der·ex·pos·ing**) to expose for too short a time. **un·der·ex·po·sure** (un-děr-ik-spoh-zhŭr) *n.*

un·der·feed (un-děr-feed) *v.* (**un·der·fed, un·der·feed·ing**) 1. to feed inadequately. 2. to feed with fuel etc. from beneath.

un·der·fi·nanced (un-děr-fi-nanst) *adj.* not adequately financed.

un·der·floor (un-děr-flohr) *adj.* situated beneath the floor.

un·der·foot (un-děr-fuut) *adv.* on the ground, under one's feet.

un·der·gar·ment (un-děr-gahr-měnt) *n.* an article of underwear.

un·der·gird (un-děr-gurd) *v.* (**un·der·gird·ed, un·der·gird·ing**) to make secure underneath; *undergirded their argument with numerous facts,* gave support to it.

un·der·go (un-děr-goh) *v.* (**un·der·went, un·der·gone, un·der·go·ing**) to experience, to endure, to be subjected to, *the new aircraft underwent intensive trials.*

un·der·grad (un-děr-grad) *n.* *(informal)* undergraduate.

un·der·grad·u·ate (un-děr-graj-oo-it) *n.* a student at a college or university who has not yet taken a degree. **undergraduate** *adj.*

un·der·ground (un-děr-grownd) *adj.* 1. under the surface of the ground. 2. secret, of a secret political organization or one for resisting enemy forces controlling a country. **underground** *adv.* 1. under the surface of the ground. 2. in secret, in hiding. **underground** (un-děr-grownd) *n.* 1. an underground organization. 2. (chiefly *British*) a subway. □**underground press,** *(informal)* unconventional and experimental publications. **underground railroad** or **railway,** a railroad system in underground tunnels; the system by which those opposed to slavery assisted slaves in escaping to places of safety.

un·der·growth (un-děr-grohth) *n.* shrubs and bushes etc. growing closely, especially when beneath trees.

un·der·hand (un-děr-hand) *adj.* 1. done or doing things in a sly or secret way. 2. (in softball) pitching or pitched with the hand brought forward and upward and not raised above shoulder level.

underhand *adv.* in an underhand manner.
un·der·hand·ed (un-dĕr-han-did) *adj.* underhand. **un·der·hand′ed·ly** *adv.* **un·der·hand′ed·ness** *n.*
un·der·lay (un-dĕr-lay) *v.* (**un·der·laid, un·der·lay·ing**) to lay something under (a thing) as a support or in order to raise it. **underlay** (un-dĕr-lay) *n.* a layer of material (as felt, rubber, etc.) laid under another as a protection or support. ▷ Do not confuse the verb *underlay* with the verb *underlie.*
un·der·lie (un-dĕr-lɪ) *v.* (**un·der·lay, un·der·lain, un·der·ly·ing**) 1. to lie or exist beneath. 2. to be the basis of (a theory etc.), to be the facts that account for, *good reasons underlie her behavior.* ▷ Do not confuse the verb *underlie* with the verb *underlay.*
un·der·line (un-dĕr-lɪn, un-dĕr-lɪn) *v.* (**un·der·lined, un·der·lin·ing**) 1. to draw a line under. 2. to emphasize. **underline** *n.* a line drawn under a word etc.
un·der·ling (un-dĕr-ling) *n.* a subordinate.
un·der·lip (un-dĕr-lip) *n.* the lower lip.
un·der·ly·ing (un-dĕr-lɪ-ing) *see* **underlie.**
un·der·manned (un-dĕr-mand) *adj.* (of a ship etc.) having too few people to operate it properly, understaffed.
un·der·men·tioned (un-dĕr-men-shŏnd) *adj.* mentioned below.
un·der·mine (un-dĕr-mɪn) *v.* (**un·der·mined, un·der·min·ing**) 1. to make a mine or tunnel beneath, especially one causing weakness at the base. 2. to weaken gradually, *his health or confidence was undermined.*
un·der·most (un-dĕr-mohst) *adj. & adv.* lowest in rank or position etc.
un·der·neath (un-dĕr-neeth) *prep.* beneath or below or on the inside of (a thing). **underneath** *adv.* at or in or to a position underneath something.
un·der·nour·ished (un-dĕr-nur-isht) *adj.* inadequately nourished for normal development. **un·der·nour′ish·ment** *n.*
un·der·paid (un-dĕr-payd) *adj.* paid too little.
un·der·pants (un-dĕr-pants) *n. pl.* an undergarment covering the lower part of the body.
un·der·part (un-dĕr-pahrt) *n.* the part underneath.
un·der·pass (un-dĕr-pas) *n.* a road that passes under another, a crossing of this kind.
un·der·pay (un-dĕr-pay) *v.* (**un·der·paid, un·der·pay·ing**) to pay less money than is deserved.
un·der·pin (un-dĕr-pin) *v.* (**un·der·pinned, un·der·pin·ning**) to support, to strengthen from beneath.
un·der·pin·ning (un-dĕr-pin-ing) *n.* a support system of masonry etc. under a wall or foundation; *underpinnings of the theory,* the facts supporting it.
un·der·play (un-dĕr-play, un-dĕr-play) *v.* 1. to underact. 2. to understate.
un·der·pop·u·lat·ed (un-dĕr-pop-yŭ-lay-tid) *adj.* lightly populated.
un·der·pow·ered (un-dĕr-pow-ĕrd) *adj.* not adequately powered, as an engine.
un·der·priced (un-dĕr-prɪst) *adj.* priced below the standard price.
un·der·priv·i·leged (un-dĕr-priv-i-lijd) *adj.* less privileged than others, not enjoying the normal standard of living or rights in a community.
un·der·pro·duce (un-dĕr-prŏ-doos) *v.* (**un·der·pro·duced, un·der·pro·duc·ing**) to produce

less than is usual or required. **un·der·pro·duc·tion** (un-dĕr-prŏ-duk-shŏn) *n.*
un·der·rate (un-dĕr-rayt) *v.* (**un·der·rat·ed, un·der·rat·ing**) to underestimate.
un·der·rep·re·sent·ed (un-dĕr-rep-ri-zen-tid) *adj.* inadequately represented.
un·der·score (un-dĕr-skohr) *v.* (**un·der·scored, un·der·scor·ing**) to underline. **underscore** (un-dĕr-skohr) *n.* an underline.
un·der·sea (un-dĕr-see) *adj. & adv.* below the surface of the sea. **un·der·seas** (un-dĕr-seez) *adv.*
un·der·sec·re·tar·y (un-dĕr-sek-rĕ-ter-ee) *n.* (*pl.* **-tar·ies**) a person who is directly subordinate to an official who has the title of "secretary."
un·der·sell (un-dĕr-sel) *v.* (**un·der·sold, un·der·sel·ling**) to sell at a lower price than (another person). ☐ **undersell oneself,** to understate one's own merits.
un·der·sexed (un-dĕr-sekst) *adj.* having less than the normal degree of sexual desires.
un·der·shirt (un-dĕr-shurt) *n.* an undergarment worn under a shirt, especially by men and children.
un·der·shoot (un-dĕr-shoot) *v.* (**un·der·shot, un·der·shoot·ing**) (of an airplane) to land short of, *the plane undershot the runway.*
un·der·shorts (un-dĕr-shorts) *n. pl.* short underpants.
un·der·shot (un-dĕr-shot) *adj.* 1. (of a water wheel) turned by water flowing under it. 2. (of the lower jaw) projecting beyond the upper jaw.
un·der·side (un-dĕr-sɪd) *n.* the side or surface underneath.
un·der·signed (un-dĕr-sɪnd) *adj.* who has or have signed at the bottom of this document, *we, the undersigned.*
un·der·sized (un-dĕr-sɪzd), **un·der·size** (un-dĕr-sɪz) *adj.* of less than the usual size.
un·der·skirt (un-dĕr-skurt) *n.* a skirt for wearing beneath another, a petticoat.
un·der·slung (un-dĕr-slung) *adj.* 1. supported from above. 2. (of a vehicle chassis) hanging lower than the axles.
un·der·staffed (un-dĕr-staft) *adj.* having less than the necessary number of staff.
un·der·stand (un-dĕr-stand) *v.* (**un·der·stood, un·der·stand·ing**) 1. to perceive the meaning or importance or nature of; *we understand each other,* we know each other's views or are in agreement. 2. to know the ways or workings of, to know how to deal with, *he understands machinery.* 3. to know the explanation and not be offended, *we shall understand if you can't come.* 4. to become aware from information received, to draw as a conclusion, *I understand she is in Paris.* 5. to take for granted, *your expenses will be paid, that's understood.* 6. to supply (a word or words) mentally, *before "coming?" the words "are you" are understood.*
un·der·stand·a·ble (un-dĕr-stan-dă-bĕl) *adj.* able to be understood. **un·der·stand′a·bly** *adv.*
un·der·stand·ing (un-dĕr-stan-ding) *adj.* having or showing insight or good judgment, or sympathy toward others' feelings and points of view. **understanding** *n.* 1. the power of thought, intelligence. 2. ability to understand. 3. ability to show insight or feel sympathy, kindly tolerance. 4. harmony in opinion or feeling, *a better understanding among nations.* 5. an informal or preliminary agreement, *reached an understanding.* **un·der·stand′ing·ly** *adv.*

un·der·state (un-děr-stayt) *v.* **(un·der·stat·ed, un·der·stat·ing)** to state (a thing) in very restrained terms, to represent as being less than it really is. **un·der·state′ment** *n.*

un·der·steer (un-děr-steer) *v.* (of a car etc.) to have a tendency to turn less sharply than was intended.

un·der·stood (un-děr-stuud) *adj.* 1. implied without being put into words. 2. agreed upon.

un·der·stud·y (un-děr-stud-ee) *n.* (*pl.* **-stud·ies**) a person who studies the part in a play or the duties etc. of another in order to be able to take his place at short notice if necessary. **understudy** *v.* **(un·der·stud·ied, un·der·stud·y·ing)** to act as understudy to, to learn (a part etc.) as understudy.

un·der·sur·face (un-děr-sur-fis) *n.* a lower or under surface.

un·der·take (un-děr-tayk) *v.* **(un·der·took, un·der·tak·en, un·der·tak·ing)** 1. to agree or promise to do something, to make oneself responsible for, *undertook the cooking* or *undertook to do the cooking.* 2. to guarantee, *we cannot undertake that you will make a profit.*

un·der·tak·er (un-děr-tay-kěr) *n.* a person whose business is to prepare the dead for burial or cremation and make arrangements for funerals.

un·der·tak·ing (un-děr-tay-king) *n.* 1. work etc. undertaken. 2. a promise or guarantee. 3. the business of an undertaker.

un·der-the-coun·ter (un-děr-*thě*-kown-těr) *adj.* under-the-table.

un·der-the-ta·ble (un-děr-*thě*-tay-běl) *adj.* transacted in an underhand or illegal way.

un·der·things (un-děr-thingz) *n. pl.* women's underwear.

un·der·tone (un-děr-tohn) *n.* 1. a low or subdued tone; *they spoke in undertones,* spoke quietly. 2. a color that modifies another, *pink with mauve undertones.* 3. an underlying quality or implication, an undercurrent of feeling, *a threatening undertone.*

un·der·tow (un-děr-toh) *n.* a current below the surface of the sea, moving in an opposite direction to the surface current.

un·der·trick (un-děr-trik) *n.* a trick not taken and by which players fall short of a contract made in the game of bridge.

un·der·val·ue (un-děr-val-yoo) *v.* **(un·der·val·ued, un·der·val·u·ing)** to put too low a value on.

un·der·wa·ter (un-děr-waw-těr) *adj.* situated or used or done beneath the surface of water. **underwater** *adv.* beneath the surface of water.

un·der·wear (un-děr-wair) *n.* garments worn under indoor clothing.

un·der·weight (un-děr-wayt) *adj.* weighing less than is normal or required or permissible.

un·der·went (un-děr-went) *see* **undergo.**

un·der·world (un-děr-wurld) *n.* 1. (in mythology) the abode of spirits of the dead, under the earth. 2. the part of society habitually engaged in crime.

un·der·write (un-děr-rrt, un-děr-rrt) *v.* **(un·der·wrote, un·der·writ·ten, un·der·writ·ing)** 1. to sign and accept liability under (an insurance policy), thus guaranteeing payment in the event of loss or damage. 2. to undertake to finance (an enterprise). 3. to undertake to buy all the stock in (a company etc.) that is not bought by the public. **un′der·writ·er** *n.*

un·de·served (un-di-zurvd) *adj.* not deserved as reward or punishment. **un·de·serv·ed·ly** (un-di-zur-vid-lee) *adv.*

un·de·signed (un-di-zınd) *adj.* unintentional. **un·de·sign·ed·ly** (un-di-zı-nid-lee) *adv.*

un·de·sir·a·ble (un-di-zır-ă-běl) *adj.* not desirable, objectionable. **undesirable** *n.* a person who is undesirable to a community.

un·de·vel·oped (un-di-vel-ŏpt) *adj.* not developed.

un·de·vi·at·ing (un-dee-vi-ay-ting) *adj.* keeping a definite course. **un·de′vi·at·ing·ly** *adv.*

un·dies (un-deez) *n. pl.* (*informal*) women's underwear.

un·dig·ni·fied (un-dig-nĭ-fıd) *adj.* not dignified.

un·dis·tort·ed (un-dis-tor-tid) *adj.* not distorted.

un·do (un-doo) *v.* **(un·did, un·done, un·do·ing)** 1. to unfasten, to untie, to unwrap. 2. to annul, to cancel the effect of, *cannot undo the past.*

un·do·ing (un-doo-ing) *n.* bringing or being brought to ruin, a cause of this, *drink was his undoing.*

un·done (un-dun) *adj.* 1. unfastened. 2. not done, *left the work undone.* 3. (*old use*) brought to ruin or destruction, *we are undone!*

un·doubt·ed (un-dow-tid) *adj.* not regarded as doubtful, not disputed. **un·doubt′ed·ly** *adv.*

un·dreamed (un-dreemd), **un·dreamt** (un-dremt) *adj.* **undreamed-of, undreamt-of,** not imagined, not thought to be possible.

un·dress (un-dres) *v.* to take off one's clothes or the clothes of (another person). **undress** *n.* 1. the state of being not clothed or not fully clothed. 2. clothes or a uniform for nonceremonial occasions.

un·due (un-doo) *adj.* excessive, disproportionate.

---

un·de·scrib′a·ble *adj.*
un·de·scrib′a·bly *adv.*
un·de·serv′ing *adj.*
un·de·sired′ *adj.*
un·de·stroyed′ *adj.*
un·de·tect′ed *adj.*
un·de·ter′mi·na·ble *adj.*
un·de·ter′mi·na·bly *adv.*
un·de·ter′mined *adj.*
un·de·terred′ *adj.*
un·di·ag′nosed′ *adj.*
un·dif·fer·en′ti·at·ed *adj.*
un·di·gest′ed *adj.*
un·di·lut′ed *adj.*
un·di·min′ished *adj.*
un·dimmed′ *adj.*

un·dip·lo·mat′ic *adj.*
un·dip·lo·mat′i·cal·ly *adv.*
un·di·rect′ed *adj.*
un·dis·cern′i·ble *adj.*
un·dis·cern′i·bly *adv.*
un·dis·cern′ing *adj.*
un·dis′ci·plined *adj.*
un·dis·closed′ *adj.*
un·dis·cour′aged *adj.*
un·dis·cov′ered *adj.*
un·dis·crim′i·nat·ing *adj.*
un·dis·crim′i·nat·ing·ly *adv.*
un·dis·guised′ *adj.*
un·dis·mayed′ *adj.*
un·dis·put′a·ble *adj.*

un·dis·put′a·bly *adv.*
un·dis·put′ed *adj.*
un·dis·solved′ *adj.*
un·dis·tin′guish·a·ble *adj.*
un·dis·tin′guished *adj.*
un·dis·trib′ut·ed *adj.*
un·dis·turbed′ *adj.*
un·di·vid′ed *adj.*
un·di·vulged′ *adj.*
un·doc′u·ment·ed *adj.*
un·dog·mat′ic *adj.*
un·dog·mat′i·cal·ly *adv.*
un·do·mes′ti·cat·ed *adj.*
un·draped′ *adj.*
un·drink′a·ble *adj.*
un·drink′a·bly *adv.*

un·du·lant (un-jŭ-lănt) *adj.* moving like waves. **un′du·lance** *n.*

un·du·late (un-jŭ-layt) *v.* (**un·du·lat·ed, un·du·lat·ing**) to have or cause to have a wavy movement or appearance. **un·du·la·tion** (un-jŭ-lay-shŏn) *n.*

un·du·ly (un-doo-lee) *adv.* excessively, disproportionately.

un·dy·ing (un-dɪ-ing) *adj.* everlasting, never-ending, *undying fame.* **un·dy′ing·ly** *adv.*

un·earned (un-urnd) *adj.* not earned. □**unearned income,** income from interest on investments and similar sources, not wages or salary or fees. **unearned run,** (in baseball) a run scored as the result of an error or a walk etc.

un·earth (un-urth) *v.* 1. to uncover or obtain from the ground by digging. 2. to bring to light, to find by searching.

un·earth·ly (un-urth-lee) *adj.* 1. not earthly. 2. supernatural, mysterious and frightening. 3. *(informal)* absurdly early or inconvenient, *getting up at this unearthly hour.*

un·eas·y (un-ee-zee) *adj.* (**-eas·i·er, -eas·i·est**) 1. not comfortable, *passed an uneasy night.* 2. not confident, worried. 3. worrying, *they had an uneasy suspicion that all was not well.* **un·eas′i·ly** *adv.* **un·eas′i·ness** *n.*

un·eat·a·ble (un-ee-tă-bĕl) *adj.* not fit to be eaten (because of its condition).

un·e·co·nom·ic (un-ee-kŏ-nom-ik, -ek-ŏ-) *adj.* not profitable, not likely to be profitable.

un·e·co·nom·i·cal (un-ee-kŏ-nom-i-kăl, -ek-ŏ-) *adj.* not economical. **un·e·co·nom′i·cal·ly** *adv.*

un·ed·u·cat·ed (un-ej-ŭ-kay-tid) *adj.* not educated, ignorant.

un·em·ploy·a·ble (un-em-ploi-ă-bĕl) *adj.* unfit for paid employment because of character, lack of abilities, etc.

un·em·ployed (un-em-ploid) *adj.* 1. having no employment, temporarily without a paid job. 2. not in use. **un·em·ploy′ment** *n.*

un·end·ing (un-en-ding) *adj.* endless. **un·end′ing·ly** *adv.*

un·e·qual (un-ee-kwăl) *adj.* 1. not equal. 2. (of work or achievements etc.) not of the same quality throughout. 3. not with equal advantage to both sides, not well matched, *unequal bargain or contest.* **un·e′qual·ly** *adv.* □**be unequal to,** (of a person) to be not strong enough or not clever enough etc. for, *was unequal to the task.*

un·e·qualed (un-ee-kwăld) *adj.* without an equal.

un·e·quiv·o·cal (un-i-kwiv-ŏ-kăl) *adj.* clear and unmistakable, not ambiguous. **un·e·quiv′o·cal·ly** *adv.*

un·err·ing (un-ur-ing) *adj.* making no mistake, *with unerring accuracy.* **un·err′ing·ly** *adv.*

un·es·cap·a·ble (un-e-skay-pă-bĕl) *adj.* unavoidable, unable to be escaped. **un·es·cap′a·bly** *adv.*

UNESCO (yoo-nes-koh) *n.* United Nations Educational, Scientific, and Cultural Organization.

un·eth·i·cal (un-eth-i-kăl) *adj.* not ethical, unscrupulous in business or professional conduct. **un·eth′i·cal·ly** *adv.*

un·e·ven (un-ee-vĕn) *adj.* 1. not level or smooth. 2. varying, not uniform. 3. unequal. **un·e′ven·ly** *adv.* **un·e′ven·ness** *n.*

un·e·vent·ful (un-i-vent-fŭl) *adj.* not eventful. **un·e·vent′ful·ly** *adv.*

un·ex·am·pled (un-ig-zam-pĕld) *adj.* having no precedent or nothing else that can be compared with it, *an unexampled opportunity.*

un·ex·cep·tion·a·ble (un-ik-sep-shŏ-nă-bĕl) *adj.* with which no fault can be found. **un·ex·cep′tion·a·bly** *adv.* ▷Do not confuse *unexceptionable* with *unexceptional.*

un·ex·cep·tion·al (un-ik-sep-shŏ-năl) *adj.* not exceptional, quite ordinary. ▷Do not confuse *unexceptional* with *unexceptionable.*

un·ex·pect·ed (un-ik-spek-tid) *adj.* not expected, surprising. **un·ex·pect′ed·ly** *adv.* **un·ex·pect′ed·ness** *n.*

un·fail·ing (un-fay-ling) *adj.* never ending, constant, reliable, *his unfailing good humor.* **un·fail′ing·ly** *adv.* **un·fail′ing·ness** *n.*

un·fair (un-fair) *adj.* not impartial, not in accordance with justice. **un·fair′ly** *adv.* **un·fair′ness** *n.*

un·faith·ful (un-fayth-fŭl) *adj.* 1. not loyal, not keeping to one's promise. 2. having committed adultery. **un·faith′ful·ly** *adv.* **un·faith′ful·ness** *n.*

un·fal·ter·ing (un-fawl-tĕ-ring) *adj.* not faltering. **un·fal′ter·ing·ly** *adv.*

un·fa·mil·iar (un-fă-mil-yăr) *adj.* not familiar. **un·fa·mil′iar·ly** *adv.* **un·fa·mil·i·ar·i·ty** (un-fă-mil-i-ar-i-tee) *n.*

un·fas·ten (un-fas-ĕn) *v.* to make loose, to open the fastening(s) of.

un·fa·vor·a·ble (un-fay-vŏ-ră-bĕl) *adj.* not favorable. **un·fa′vor·a·bly** *adv.*

---

un·dyed′ *adj.*	**un·en′vi·a·ble** *adj.*	**un·ex·pe′ri·enced** *adj.*
un·eat′en *adj.*	**un·en′vi·a·bly** *adv.*	**un·ex·pired′** *adj.*
un·ed′i·fy·ing *adj.*	**un·e·quat′ed** *adj.*	**un·ex·plain′a·ble** *adj.*
un·ed′u·ca·ble *adj.*	**un·e·quipped′** *adj.*	**un·ex·plain′a·bly** *adv.*
un·e·man′ci·pat·ed *adj.*	**un·es·cort′ed** *adj.*	**un·ex·plained′** *adj.*
un·em·bar′rassed *adj.*	**un·es·sen′tial** *adj.*	**un·ex·plod′ed** *adj.*
un·em·bel′lished *adj.*	**un·es·sen′tials** *n.*	**un·ex·ploit′ed** *adj.*
un·e·mo′tion·al *adj.*	**un·es·tab′lished** *adj.*	**un·ex·plored′** *adj.*
un·em·phat′ic *adj.*	**un·ex·ag′ger·at·ed** *adj.*	**un·ex·posed′** *adj.*
un·en·closed′ *adj.*	**un·ex·ca′va·ted** *adj.*	**un·ex·pressed′** *adj.*
un·en·cum′bered *adj.*	**un·ex·celled′** *adj.*	**un·ex′pur·gat·ed** *adj.*
un·en·force′a·ble *adj.*	**un·ex·cit′ed** *adj.*	**un·ex·tend′ed** *adj.*
un·en·forced′ *adj.*	**un·ex·cit′ing** *adj.*	**un·ex·tin′guished** *adj.*
un·en·light′ened *adj.*	**un·ex·cus′a·ble** *adj.*	**un·fad′ing** *adj.*
un·en·rolled′ *adj.*	**un·ex·cus′a·bly** *adv.*	**un·fash′ion·a·ble** *adj.*
un·en′tered *adj.*	**un·ex·cused′** *adj.*	**un·fash′ion·a·bly** *adv.*
un·en′ter·pris·ing *adj.*	**un·ex′e·cut·ed** *adj.*	**un·fath′om·a·ble** *adj.*
un·en·thu·si·as′tic *adj.*	**un·ex′er·cised** *adj.*	**un·fath′om·a·bly** *adv.*
un·en·thu·si·as′ti·cal·ly *adv.*	**un·ex·pend′ed** *adj.*	**un·fath′omed** *adj.*

un·fazed (un-**fayzd**) *adj.* not fazed, not disconcerted.

un·feel·ing (un-**fee**-ling) *adj.* 1. lacking the power of sensation or sensitivity. 2. unsympathetic, not caring about others' feelings. **un·feel'ing·ly** *adv.* **un·feel'ing·ness** *n.*

un·feigned (un-**faynd**) *adj.* not feigned, genuine.

un·fet·ter (un-**fet**-ĕr) *v.* 1. to remove from fetters. 2. to liberate.

un·fil·i·al (un-**fil**-i-ăl) *adj.* not befitting the obligation of a son or daughter to a parent.

un·fin·ished (un-**fin**-isht) *adj.* not finished.

un·fit (un-**fit**) *adj.* 1. unsuitable. 2. not in perfect health or physical condition. **unfit** *v.* (**un·fit·ted, un·fit·ting**) to make unsuitable. **un·fit'ting·ly** *adv.*

un·flag·ging (un-**flag**-ing) *adj.* not lagging, not losing vigor, *unflagging support.*

un·flap·pa·ble (un-**flap**-ă-bĕl) *adj.* *(informal)* remaining calm in a crisis, not getting into a flap. **un·flap'pa·bly** *adv.* **un·flap·pa·bil·i·ty** (un-flap-ă-bil-i-tee) *n.*

un·fledged (un-**flejd**) *adj.* 1. (of a bird) not yet fledged. 2. (of a person) inexperienced.

un·flinch·ing (un-**flin**-ching) *adj.* not flinching. **un·flinch'ing·ly** *adv.*

un·fold (un-**fohld**) *v.* 1. to open, to spread (a thing) or become spread out. 2. to become visible or known, *as the story unfolds.*

un·for·get·ta·ble (un-fŏr-get-ă-bĕl) *adj.* not able to be forgotten. **un·for·get'ta·bly** *adv.*

un·formed (un-**fohrmd**) *adj.* 1. not formed, not developed. 2. shapeless.

un·for·tu·nate (un-for-chŭ-nit) *adj.* 1. having bad luck. 2. unsuitable, regrettable, *a most unfortunate choice of words.* **unfortunate** *n.* an unfortunate person. **un·for'tu·nate·ly** *adv.* **un·for'tu·nate·ness** *n.*

un·found·ed (un-**fown**-did) *adj.* 1. not established. 2. not based in reality or on fact.

un·freeze (un-**freez**) *v.* (**un·froze, un·fro·zen, un·freez·ing**) to thaw, to cause to thaw.

un·fre·quent·ed (un-free-kwĕn-tid) *adj.* not frequented by people.

un·friend·ly (un-**frend**-lee) *adj.* not friendly. **un·friend'li·ness** *n.*

un·frock (un-**frok**) *v.* to deprive (a priest) of his priesthood.

un·fruit·ful (un-**froot**-fŭl) *adj.* 1. not fruitful, barren or infertile. 2. not producing good results. **un·fruit'ful·ness** *n.*

un·furl (un-**furl**) *v.* to unroll, to spread out.

un·fur·nished (un-fur-nisht) *adj.* without furni-

ture. □**unfurnished with,** not provided with.

un·gain·ly (un-**gayn**-lee) *adj.* awkward looking, clumsy, ungraceful. **un·gain'li·ness** *n.*

un·gen·er·ous (un-jen-ĕ-rŭs) *adj.* not generous.

un·gird (un-**gurd**) *v.* *(old use)* to remove a belt or girdle or sword from.

un·god·ly (un-**god**-lee) *adj.* 1. not giving reverence to God, not religious, wicked. 2. *(informal)* outrageous, very inconvenient, *phoning at this ungodly hour.* **un·god'li·ness** *n.*

un·gov·ern·a·ble (un-guv-ĕr-nă-bĕl) *adj.* uncontrollable, *an ungovernable temper.*

un·grace·ful (un-**grays**-fŭl) *adj.* not graceful. **un·grace'ful·ly** *adv.*

un·gra·cious (un-**gray**-shŭs) *adj.* not kindly or courteous or attractive. **un·gra'cious·ly** *adv.* **un·gra'cious·ness** *n.*

un·grate·ful (un-**grayt**-fŭl) *adj.* not grateful. **un·grate'ful·ly** *adv.* **un·grate'ful·ness** *n.*

un·ground·ed (un-**grown**-did) *adj.* 1. not founded in fact. 2. not instructed.

un·grudg·ing (un-gruj-ing) *adj.* not grudging. **un·grudg'ing·ly** *adv.*

un·guard·ed (un-gahr-did) *adj.* 1. not guarded. 2. thoughtless, incautious, *in an unguarded moment.*

un·guent (ung-gwĕnt) *n.* an ointment or lubricant.

un·gu·late (ung-gyŭ-lit) *adj.* 1. having hoofs. 2. characteristic of hoofs. **ungulate** *n.* an animal with hoofs.

un·hal·lowed (un-hal-ohd) *adj.* 1. not hallowed. 2. unholy, wicked.

un·hand (un-**hand**) *v.* 1. to take one's hands off. 2. to release from one's grasp.

un·hand·some (un-han-sŏm) *adj.* not handsome.

un·hand·y (un-han-dee) *adj.* not handy.

un·hap·py (un-hap-ee) *adj.* (**-pi·er, -pi·est**) 1. not happy, sad. 2. unfortunate. 3. unsuitable. **un·hap'pi·ly** *adv.* **un·hap'pi·ness** *n.*

un·har·ness (un-hahr-nis) *v.* 1. to remove a harness from. 2. to release, to liberate.

un·health·y (un-hel-thee) *adj.* (**-health·i·er, -health·i·est**) 1. not having or not showing good health. 2. harmful to health or morals. 3. *(informal)* unwise, dangerous. **un·health'i·ness** *n.*

un·heard (un-hurd) *adj.* not heard. □**unheard-of,** not previously known of or done.

un·hinge (un-**hinj**) *v.* (**un·hinged, un·hing·ing**) 1. to take (a door etc.) off its hinges. 2. to cause to become mentally unbalanced, *the shock unhinged his mind.*

un·ho·ly (un-hoh-lee) *adj.* (**-ho·li·er, -ho·li·est**) 1. wicked, irreverent. 2. *(informal)* very

un·fear'ing *adj.*	**un·for·giv'a·bly** *adv.*	**un·ham'pered** *adj.*
un·fea'si·ble *adj.*	**un·for·giv'en** *adj.*	**un·hard'ened** *adj.*
un·fed' *adj.*	**un·for·giv'ing** *adj.*	**un·harmed'** *adj.*
un·felt' *adj.*	**un·for'mu·lat·ed** *adj.*	**un·harm'ful** *adj.*
un·fem'i·nine *adj.*	**un·for·sak'en** *adj.*	**un·har·mo'ni·ous** *adj.*
un·fenced' *adj.*	**un·for'ti·fied** *adj.*	**un·har'vest·ed** *adj.*
un·fer·ment'ed *adj.*	**un·framed'** *adj.*	**un·hatched'** *adj.*
un·fer'ti·lized *adj.*	**un·ful·filled'** *adj.*	**un·head'ed** *adj.*
un·filled' *adj.*	**un·fun'ny** *adj.*	**un·healed'** *adj.*
un·fil'tered *adj.*	**un·gen'tle·man·ly** *adj.*	**un·health'ful** *adj.*
un·flat'ter·ing *adj.*	**un·glazed'** *adj.*	**un·heed'ed** *adj.*
un·fla'vored *adj.*	**un·glued'** *adj.*	**un·heed'ful** *adj.*
un·fo'cused *adj.*	**un·grad'ed** *adj.*	**un·help'ful** *adj.*
un·fore·see'a·ble *adj.*	**un·gram·mat'i·cal** *adj.*	**un·her'ald·ed** *adj.*
un·fore·see'a·bly *adv.*	**un·gram·mat'i·cal·ly** *adv.*	**un·hes'i·tat·ing** *adj.*
un·fore·seen' *adj.*	**un·grat'i·fy·ing** *adj.*	**un·hes'i·tat·ing·ly** *adv.*
un·for·giv'a·ble *adj.*	**un·guid'ed** *adj.*	**un·hin'dered** *adj.*

great, outrageous, *making an unholy row.* **un·ho′li·ness** *n.*

un·hook (un-huuk) *v.* 1. to detach from a hook or hooks. 2. to unfasten by releasing the hook(s).

un·hoped-for (un-hohpt-for) *adj.* not hoped for or expected.

un·horse (un-hors) *v.* (**un·horsed, un·hors·ing**) to throw or drag (a rider) from a horse.

uni- *prefix* one or only one, as in *unicellular.*

u·ni·ax·i·al (yoo-ni-ak-si-ăl) *adj.* having a single axis.

u·ni·cam·er·al (yoo-ni-kam-ĕ-răl) *adj.* of only one legislative chamber, *a unicameral legislature.*

UNICEF (yoo-ni-sef) *n.* United Nations Children's Fund. ▷From its original name, *United Nations International Children's Emergency Fund.*

u·ni·cel·lu·lar (yoo-ni-sel-yŭ-lăr) *adj.* one-celled.

u·ni·corn (yoo-nĭ-korn) *n.* a mythical animal resembling a horse with a single horn projecting from its forehead.

u·ni·cy·cle (yoo-ni-sı-kĕl) *n.* a single-wheeled vehicle, especially as used by acrobats.

un·i·den·ti·fied (un-ı-den-tĭ-frd) *adj.* not identified. □**unidentified flying object,** a high-speed flying object, supposedly seen in the sky and said to come from outer space.

u·ni·di·rec·tion·al (yoo-ni-di-rek-shŏ-năl) *adj.* having only one direction of motion or operation etc.

u·ni·form (yoo-nĭ-form) *n.* distinctive clothing intended to identify the wearer as a member of a certain organization or group. **uniform** *v.* to outfit with a uniform. **uniform** *adj.* always the same, not varying, *planks of uniform thickness.* **u′ni·form·ly** *adv.* **u′ni·form·ness** *n.* **u·ni·form·i·ty** (yoo-nĭ-for-mi-tee) *n.* □**Uniform Code of Military Justice,** the laws governing members of the armed forces.

u·ni·formed (yoo-nĭ-formd) *adj.* wearing a uniform.

u·ni·fy (yoo-nĭ-fı) *v.* (**u·ni·fied, u·ni·fy·ing**) to form into a single unit, to unite. **u′ni·fi·er** *n.* **u·ni·fi·ca·tion** (yoo-nĭ-fĭ-kay-shŏn) *n.*

u·ni·lat·er·al (yoo-nĭ-lat-ĕ-răl) *adj.* one-sided, done by or affecting one person or group or country etc. and not another. **u·ni·lat′er·al·ly** *adv.*

u·ni·lin·gual (yoo-nĭ-ling-gwăl) *adj.* of only one language.

un·im·peach·a·ble (un-im-pee-chă-bĕl) *adj.* completely trustworthy, not open to doubt or question, *unimpeachable honesty.* **un·im·peach′a·bly** *adv.*

un·im·proved (un-im-proovd) *adj.* 1. not made

better. 2. not made use of. 3. (of land) not used for agriculture or building.

un·in·hib·it·ed (un-in-hib-i-tid) *adj.* not inhibited. **un·in·hib′it·ed·ly** *adv.*

un·in·spired (un-in-sprrd) *adj.* not inspired, (of oratory etc.) commonplace.

un·in·tel·li·gent (un-in-tel-i-jĕnt) *adj.* not intelligent. **un·in·tel′li·gent·ly** *adv.* ▷Do not confuse *unintelligent* with *unintelligible.*

un·in·tel·li·gi·ble (un-in-tel-i-jĭ-bĕl) *adj.* not intelligible, impossible to understand. **un·in·tel′li·gi·bly** *adv.* ▷Do not confuse *unintelligible* with *unintelligent.*

un·in·ten·tion·al (un-in-ten-shŏ-năl) *adj.* not intentional, accidental. **un·in·ten′tion·al·ly** *adv.*

un·in·ter·est·ed (un-in-tĕ-ris-tid, -tris-tid) *adj.* not interested, showing or feeling no concern. **un·in′ter·est·ed·ly** *adv.* ▷See the note under **disinterested.**

un·in·ter·rupt·ed (un-in-tĕ-rup-tid) *adj.* not interrupted. **un·in·ter·rupt′ed·ly** *adv.*

un·ion (yoon-yŏn) *n.* 1. uniting, being united. 2. a whole formed by uniting parts, an association formed by the uniting of people or groups. 3. a labor union. 4. a coupling for pipes or rods. 5. *Union,* the United States, especially the northern states (which favored federal union) during the Civil War. □**union catalog,** a catalog showing the combined holdings of several libraries. **Union Jack,** the national flag of the United Kingdom. **Union of Soviet Socialist Republics,** a country (= Russia) extending from eastern Europe to the Pacific, consisting of 15 republics. **union shop,** a factory etc. that employs only members of a labor union. **union suit,** a single undergarment for body and legs.

un·ion·ism (yoon-yŏ-niz-ĕm) *n.* 1. the principle of union; *trade unionism,* belief in and support for labor unions. 2. adherence to the policy of maintaining the federal union during the Civil War.

un·ion·ist (yoon-yŏ-nist) *n.* 1. a member of a labor union, a supporter of labor unions. 2. one who favors union.

un·ion·ize (yoon-yŏ-nız) *v.* (**un·ion·ized, un·ion·iz·ing**) to organize into or to join a labor union. **un·ion·i·za·tion** (yoon-yŏ-ni-zay-shŏn) *n.*

u·nique (yoo-neek) *adj.* 1. being the only one of its kind, *this vase is unique.* 2. unusual, remarkable, *this makes it even more unique.* (▷Many people regard the use in definition 2 as illogical and incorrect.) **u·nique′ly** *adv.* **u·nique′ness** *n.*

---

un·hon′ored *adj.*
un·hur′ried *adj.*
un·hur′ried·ly *adv.*
un·hurt′ *adj.*
un·hy′phen·at·ed *adj.*
un·i·den′ti·fi·a·ble *adj.*
un·id·i·o·mat′ic *adj.*
un·id·i·o·mat′i·cal·ly *adv.*
un·il′lus·trat·ed *adj.*
un·im·ag′i·na·ble *adj.*
un·im·ag′i·na·bly *adv.*
un·im·ag′i·na·tive *adj.*
un·im·paired′ *adj.*
un·im·pas′sioned *adj.*
un·im·ped′ed *adj.*
un·im·por′tant *adj.*

un·im·pos′ing *adj.*
un·im·pov′er·ished *adj.*
un·im·pressed′ *adj.*
un·im·pres′sive *adj.*
un·im·pres′sive·ly *adv.*
un·in·closed′ *adj.*
un·in·cor′po·rat·ed *adj.*
un·in·cum′bered *adj.*
un·in·dem′ni·fied *adj.*
un·in·dorsed′ *adj.*
un·in·fect′ed *adj.*
un·in′flu·enced *adj.*
un·in·form′a·tive *adj.*
un·in·formed′ *adj.*
un·in·hab′it·a·ble *adj.*
un·in·hab′it·ed *adj.*

un·in·i′ti·at·ed *adj.*
un·in′jured *adj.*
un·in′no·va·tive *adj.*
un·in·spir′ing *adj.*
un·in·spir′ing·ly *adv.*
un·in·sur′a·ble *adj.*
un·in·sured′ *adj.*
un·in·tend′ed *adj.*
un·in′ter·est·ing *adj.*
un·in′ter·est·ing·ly *adv.*
un·in·vest′ed *adj.*
un·in·vit′ed *adj.*
un·in·vit′ing *adj.*
un·in·vit′ing·ly *adv.*
un·in·volved′ *adj.*
un·i′roned *adj.*

u·ni·sex (yoo-ni-seks) *n.* the tendency of the human sexes to become indistinguishable in dress etc. **unisex** *adj.* designed in a style suitable for people of either sex.

u·ni·son (yoo-ni-sŏn) *n.* **in unison, 1.** sounding or singing together at the same pitch or a corresponding one. **2.** in agreement or concord, *all the firms acted in unison.*

u·nit (yoo-nit) *n.* **1.** an individual thing or person or group regarded for purposes of calculation etc. as single and complete, or as part of a complex whole, *the family as the unit of society.* **2.** a quantity chosen as a standard in terms of which other quantities may be expressed, or for which a stated charge is made. **3.** a part or group with a specified function within a complex machine or organization. **4.** a piece of furniture for fitting with other like it or made of complementary parts. ▢**unit pricing,** pricing of articles according to a standard unit or unit price (as per pound or quart). **unit rule,** (at political conventions) the practice of recording the votes of a delegation as unanimously cast in favor of the candidate selected by the majority of the delegation, overlooking the wishes of the minority.

U·ni·tar·i·an (yoo-ni-tair-i-ăn) *n.* a member of a Christian religious denomination maintaining that God is one person, not a Trinity. **U·ni·tar′i·an·ism** *n.*

u·ni·tar·y (yoo-ni-ter-ee) *adj.* of a unit or units.

u·nite (yoo-nɪt) *v.* (**u·nit·ed, u·nit·ing**) **1.** to join together, to make or become one. **2.** to agree or combine or cooperate, *they all united in condemning the action.* **u·nit′ed** *adj.* ▢**United Arab Emirates,** a country consisting of a federation of seven emirates on or near the Persian Gulf. **united front,** a coalition formed to thwart a common menace. **United Kingdom,** Great Britain and Northern Ireland. **United Nations,** an international peace-seeking organization of about 150 countries. **United States Air Force,** a branch of the U.S. armed forces providing military air services. **United States Army,** the permanent military forces of the U.S. armed services. **United States Marine Corps,** the ground combat branch of the U.S. Navy. **United States Navy,** the permanent naval forces of the U.S. armed services, including the Navy, Marine Corps, and at times the U.S. Coast Guard. **United States of America** *or* **United States,** a country in North America consisting of 50 states and the District of Columbia. **United States Postal Service,** the U.S. governmental service responsible for the transportation of mail.

u·ni·tize (yoo-ni-tɪz) *v.* (**u·ni·tized, u·ni·tiz·ing**) **1.** to make into a unit. **2.** to make into units.

u·ni·ty (yoo-ni-tee) *n.* (*pl.* **-ties**) **1.** the state of being one or a unit. **2.** a thing forming a complex whole. **3.** the number one in mathematics. **4.** harmony, agreement in feelings or ideas or aims etc., *dwell together in unity.*

univ. *abbr.* **1.** universal. **2.** university.

Univ. *abbr.* University.

u·ni·va·lent (yoo-ni-vay-lĕnt) *adj.* having a valence of one.

u·ni·valve (yoo-ni-valv) *adj.* having one valve. **univalve** *n.* a univalve mollusk.

u·ni·ver·sal (yoo-ni-vur-săl) *adj.* of or for or done by all. **u·ni·ver′sal·ly** *adv.* **u·ni·ver·sal·i·ty** (yoo-ni-vĕr-sal-i-tee) *n.* ▢**universal joint,** a joint that connects two shafts in such a way that they can be at any angle to each other. **universal product code,** a code of short black lines on a product, for use by an electronic cash register.

U·ni·ver·sal·ist (yoo-ni-vur-să-list) *n.* a member of a denomination of Christians, now combined with the Unitarians, who hold that all mankind will eventually be saved.

u·ni·verse (yoo-ni-vurs) *n.* all existing things, including Earth and its creatures and all the heavenly bodies.

u·ni·ver·si·ty (yoo-ni-vur-si-tee) *n.* (*pl.* **-ties**) an educational institution, composed of one or more colleges and graduate schools, that provides instruction and facilities for research in many branches of advanced learning, and awards degrees.

un·just (un-just) *adj.* not just or fair. **un·just′ly** *adv.* **un·just′ness** *n.*

un·jus·ti·fi·a·ble (un-jus-tĭ-fɪ-ă-bĕl) *adj.* not able to be justified.

un·kempt (un-kempt) *adj.* looking untidy or neglected.

un·kind (un-kɪnd) *adj.* not kind, harsh. **un·kind′ly** *adj. & adv.* **un·kind′ness** *n.*

un·know·ing (un-noh-ing) *adj.* not knowing, unaware. **un·know′ing·ly** *adv.*

un·known (un-nohn) *adj.* not known, not identified. **unknown** *n.* an unknown person or thing. **unknown** *adv.* ▢**unknown to,** without the knowledge of.

un·lace (un-lays) *v.* (**un·laced, un·lac·ing**) **1.** to undo the laces of. **2.** to unfasten or loosen in this manner.

un·latch (un-lach) *v.* to unfasten by lifting a latch.

un·law·ful (un-law-fŭl) *adj.* **1.** not according to the law, illegal. **2.** born of parents not married to each other. **un·law′ful·ly** *adv.* **un·law′ful·ness** *n.*

un·lead·ed (un-led-id) *adj.* not containing lead, *unleaded gasoline.*

un·learn (un-lurn) *v.* to cause (a thing) to be no longer in one's knowledge or memory.

un·leash (un-leesh) *v.* **1.** to set free from a leash or restraint. **2.** to set (a thing) free so that it can attack or pursue something.

un·leav·ened (un-lev-ĕnd) *adj.* not leavened, (of bread) made without yeast or other leavening agent.

un·less (un-les) *conj.* if . . . not, except when, *we shall not move unless we are obliged to.*

un·let·tered (un-let-ĕrd) *adj.* **1.** uneducated. **2.** illiterate.

un·li·censed (un-lɪ-sĕnst) *adj.* **1.** not licensed. **2.** unrestrained.

un·like (un-lɪk) *adj.* **1.** not like, different from. **2.** not characteristic of, *such behavior is quite unlike him.* **unlike** *prep.* differently from, *unlike her mother, she enjoys riding.* **un·like′ness** *n.*

un·like·ly (un-lɪk-lee) *adj.* **1.** not likely to happen or be true, *an unlikely tale.* **2.** not likely to be successful, *the most unlikely candidate.* **un·like′li·hood** *n.* **un·like′li·ness** *n.*

---

un·jus′ti·fi·a·bly *adv.*
un·jus′ti·fied *adj.*
un·kept′ *adj.*

un·know′a·ble *adj.*
un·la′beled *adj.*
un·la·ment′ed *adj.*

un·lam′i·nat·ed *adj.*
un·light′ed *adj.*
un·lik′a·ble *adj.*

un·lim·ber (un-lim-běr) *v.* to make (a gun etc.) ready for action.

un·lim·it·ed (un-lim-i-tid) *adj.* not limited, very great in number or quantity.

un·lined (un-lınd) *adj.* 1. without a lining. 2. not marked with lines or wrinkles.

un·list·ed (un-lis-tid) *adj.* not included in a list, not in a published list of telephone numbers or stock exchange prices.

un·load (un-lohd) *v.* 1. to remove a load from (a ship etc.), to remove cargo. 2. to get rid of. 3. to remove the charge from (a gun etc.).

un·lock (un-lok) *v.* 1. to release the lock of (a door etc.). 2. to release by or as if by unlocking.

un·looked-for (un-luukt-for) *adj.* unexpected.

un·loose (un-loos) *v.* (**un·loosed, un·loos·ing**) 1. to release. 2. to untie or loosen.

un·loos·en (un-loo-sĕn) *v.* to loosen.

un·luck·y (un-luk-ee) *adj.* (**-luck·i·er, -luck·i·est**) not lucky, wretched, having or bringing bad luck. **un·luck'i·ly** *adv.*

un·man (un-man) *v.* (**un·manned, un·man·ning**) to weaken the self-control or courage of (a man).

un·man·ly (un-man-lee) *adj.* 1. not manly. 2. lacking courage. **un·man'li·ness** *n.*

un·manned (un-mand) *adj.* operated without a crew, *unmanned spaceflights.*

un·man·ner·ly (un-man-ĕr-lee) *adj.* 1. without good manners. 2. showing a lack of good manners. **un·man'ner·li·ness** *n.*

un·mar·ried (un-mar-eed) *adj.* not married.

un·mask (un-mask) *v.* 1. to remove the mask from, to remove one's mask. 2. to expose the true character of.

un·matched (un-macht) *adj.* not matched in abilities or characteristics etc.

un·mean·ing (un-mee-ning) *adj.* having no significance, meaningless.

un·meet (un-meet) *adj.* not suitable.

un·men·tion·a·ble (un-men-shŏ-nă-bĕl) *adj.* so bad or embarrassing or shocking that it may not be spoken of. **unmentionables** *n. pl.* unmentionable things or people; *her unmentionables,* her underwear.

un·mer·ci·ful (un-mur-si-fŭl) *adj.* 1. merciless, cruel. 2. extreme, excessive, *unmerciful jollity.* **un·mer'ci·ful·ly** *adv.*

un·mind·ful (un-mınd-fŭl) *adj.* not mindful, neglectful.

un·mis·tak·a·ble (un-mi-stay-kă-bĕl) *adj.* clear and obvious, not able to be mistaken for another. **un·mis·tak'a·bly** *adv.*

un·mit·i·gat·ed (un-mit-i-gay-tid) *adj.* not modified, absolute, *an unmitigated scoundrel.*

un·moor (un-moor) *v.* 1. to release the moorings of, to pull up all but one anchor of (a vessel). 2. to become unmoored.

un·mor·al (un-mor-ăl) *adj.* not concerned with morality. **un·mo·ral·i·ty** (un-mŏ-ral-i-tee) *n.*

un·moved (un-moovd) *adj.* not moved, not changed in one's purpose, not affected by emotion.

un·muz·zle (un-muz-ĕl) *v.* (**un·muz·zled, un·muz·zling**) 1. to remove a muzzle from. 2. to relieve of an obligation to remain silent.

un·nat·u·ral (un-nach-ŭ-răl) *adj.* 1. not natural or normal. 2. lacking natural feelings of affection. 3. artificial. **un·nat'u·ral·ly** *adv.* **un·nat'u·ral·ness** *n.*

un·nec·es·sar·y (un-nes-ĕ-ser-ee) *adj.* 1. not necessary. 2. more than is necessary, *with unnecessary care.* **un·nec'es·sar·i·ness** *n.* **un·nec·es·sar·i·ly** (un-nes-ĕ-ser-ĭ-lee) *adv.*

un·nerve (un-nurv) *v.* (**un·nerved, un·nerv·ing**) to cause to lose courage or determination.

un·num·bered (un-num-bĕrd) *adj.* 1. not marked with a number. 2. countless.

un·ob·tru·sive (un-ŏb-troo-siv) *adj.* not obtrusive, not making oneself or itself noticed. **un·ob·tru'sive·ly** *adv.*

un·oc·cu·pied (un-ok-yŭ-pıd) *adj.* 1. without occupants or inhabitants. 2. (of a person) doing no work, not active.

un·of·fend·ing (un-ŏ-fen-ding) *adj.* not offending, harmless, innocent.

un·or·gan·ized (un-or-gă-nızd) *adj.* 1. not organized, without orderly structure. 2. (of employees) not belonging to a labor union.

un·pack (un-pak) *v.* to open and remove the contents of (luggage etc.), to take out from its packaging or from a suitcase etc.

un·paid (un-payd) *adj.* 1. (of a debt) not yet paid. 2. not receiving payment for work etc.

un·par·al·leled (un-par-ă-leld) *adj.* not paralleled, never yet equaled, *unparalleled enthusiasm.*

---

un·lit' *adj.*
un·liv'a·ble *adj.*
un·lo'cat·ed *adj.*
un·lov'a·ble *adj.*
un·loved' *adj.*
un·lov'ing *adj.*
un·made' *adj.*
un·man'age·a·ble *adj.*
un·mapped' *adj.*
un·marked' *adj.*
un·marred' *adj.*
un·mas'tered *adj.*
un·meas'ured *adj.*
un·med'i·ta·ted *adj.*
un·me·lo'di·ous *adj.*
un·mend'ed *adj.*
un·men'tioned *adj.*
un·mer'it·ed *adj.*
un·me·thod'i·cal *adj.*
un·me·thod'i·cal·ly *adv.*
un·mil'i·tar·y *adj.*
un·mis·tak'en *adj.*

un·mis·tak'en·ly *adv.*
un·mixed' *adj.*
un·mold'ed *adj.*
un·mo·lest'ed *adj.*
un·mol'li·fied *adj.*
un·mo'ti·vat·ed *adj.*
un·mount'ed *adj.*
un·mourned' *adj.*
un·mown' *adj.*
un·muf'fle *v.* (**un·muf·fled, un·muf·fling**)
un·mu'si·cal *adj.*
un·named' *adj.*
un·nat'u·ral·ized *adj.*
un·nav'i·ga·ble *adj.*
un·need'ed *adj.*
un·ne·go'ti·a·ble *adj.*
un·neigh'bor·ly *adj.*
un·no'tice·a·ble *adj.*
un·no'tice·a·bly *adv.*
un·no'ticed *adj.*
un·ob·jec'tion·a·ble *adj.*

un·ob·liged' *adj.*
un·ob·lig'ing *adj.*
un·ob·scured' *adj.*
un·ob·serv'ant *adj.*
un·ob·served' *adj.*
un·ob·serv'ing *adj.*
un·ob·struct'ed *adj.*
un·ob·tain'a·ble *adj.*
un·of·fen'sive *adj.*
un·of·fen'sive·ly *adv.*
un·of'fered *adj.*
un·o'pened *adj.*
un·op·posed' *adj.*
un·or·dained' *adj.*
un·o·rig'i·nal *adj.*
un·or'tho·dox *adj.*
un·os·ten·ta'tious *adj.*
un·os·ten·ta'tious·ly *adv.*
un·owned' *adj.*
un·pac'i·fied *adj.*
un·paint'ed *adj.*
un·pal'at·a·ble *adj.*

un·par·lia·men·ta·ry (un-pahr-lă-men-tă-ree) *adj.* contrary to parliamentary custom.

un·per·son (un-pur-sŏn) *n.* a person whose name or existence is ignored or denied.

un·pile (un-pɪl) *v.* (un·piled, un·pil·ing) to remove from a piled condition.

un·pin (un-pin) *v.* (un·pinned, un·pin·ning) to unfasten or detach by removing pins.

un·pleas·ant (un-plez-ănt) *adj.* not pleasant. un·pleas′ant·ly *adv.* un·pleas′ant·ness *n.*

un·plug (un-plug) *v.* (un·plugged, un·plug·ging) 1. to remove a plug from. 2. to disconnect electrically by removing a plug from an outlet.

un·plumbed (un-plumd) *adj.* 1. not tested or measured with a plumb line. 2. not explored thoroughly, *unplumbed meanings.*

un·pop·u·lar (un-pop-yŭ-lăr) *adj.* not popular, not liked or enjoyed by people in general. un·pop′u·lar·ly *adv.* un·pop·u·lar·i·ty (un-pop-yŭ-lar-i-tee) *n.*

un·prec·e·dent·ed (un-pres-ĕ-den-tid) *adj.* for which there is no precedent, unparalleled.

un·pre·dict·a·ble (un-pri-dik-tă-bĕl) *adj.* impossible to predict. un·pre·dict′a·bly *adv.* un·pre·dict·a·bil·i·ty (un-pri-dik-tă-bil-i-tee) *n.*

un·prej·u·diced (un-prej-ŭ-dist) *adj.* not prejudiced.

un·pre·med·i·tat·ed (un-pri-med-i-tay-tid) *adj.* not planned beforehand.

un·pre·pared (un-pri-paird) *adj.* not prepared beforehand, not ready or equipped to do something.

un·pre·pos·sess·ing (un-pree-pŏ-zes-ing) *adj.* unattractive, not making a good impression.

un·pre·ten·tious (un-pri-ten-shŭs) *adj.* not pretentious, not showy or pompous. un·pre·ten′tious·ly *adv.* un·pre·ten′tious·ness *n.*

un·prin·ci·pled (un-prin-sĭ-pĕld) *adj.* without good moral principles, unscrupulous.

un·print·a·ble (un-prin-tă-bĕl) *adj.* too rude or indecent to be printed.

un·pro·fes·sion·al (un-prŏ-fesh-ŏ-năl) *adj.* contrary to professional standards of behavior.

un·prof·it·a·ble (un-prof-i-tă-bĕl) *adj.* 1. not producing a profit. 2. serving no useful purpose, *quarreling is unprofitable.* un·prof′it·a·bly *adv.*

un·qual·i·fied (un-kwol-ĭ-frd) *adj.* 1. (of a person) not legally or officially qualified to do something. 2. not restricted or modified, *gave it our unqualified approval.* un·qual′i·fied·ly *adv.*

un·ques·tion·a·ble (un-kwes-chŏ-nă-bĕl) *adj.* not questionable, too clear to be doubted. un·ques′tion·a·bly *adv.*

un·ques·tioned (un-kwes-chŏnd) *adj.* not disputed or doubted.

un·ques·tion·ing (un-kwes-chŏ-ning) *adj.* 1. asking no questions. 2. done etc. without asking questions. un·ques′tion·ing·ly *adv.*

un·qui·et (un-kwɪ-it) *adj.* 1. restless, agitated, *spent an unquiet hour waiting.* 2. perturbed, anxious, *the surgeon seemed unquiet.* un·qui′et·ly *adv.* un·qui′et·ness *n.*

un·quote (un-kwoht) *v.* (un·quot·ed, un·quot·ing) (in dictation etc.) end the quotation, insert the closing quotation marks, *Lincoln said (quote) "The ballot is stronger than the bullet" (unquote).*

un·rav·el (un-rav-ĕl) *v.* (un·rav·eled, un·rav·el·ing) 1. to disentangle. 2. to undo (knitted fabric). 3. to become unraveled.

un·read (un-red) *adj.* 1. not read. 2. (of a person) not well read.

un·re·al (un-ree-ăl) *adj.* not real, existing in the imagination only. un·re·al·i·ty (un-ree-al-i-tee) *n.*

un·rea·son·a·ble (un-ree-zŏ-nă-bĕl) *adj.* 1. not reasonable in one's attitude etc. 2. excessive, going beyond the limits of what is reasonable or just. un·rea′son·a·bly *adv.* un·rea′son·a·ble·ness *n.*

un·rea·soned (un-ree-zŏnd) *adj.* not thought out rationally or realistically.

un·rea·son·ing (un-ree-zŏ-ning) *adj.* not reasoning, irrational.

un·re·con·struct·ed (un-ree-kŏn-struk-tid) *adj.* obstinately unwilling to give up one's earlier beliefs.

---

un·par′don·a·ble *adj.*
un·par′don·a·bly *adv.*
un·pat′ent·ed *adj.*
un·pa·tri·ot′ic *adj.*
un·pa·tri·ot′i·cal·ly *adv.*
un·paved′ *adj.*
un·pen′e·trat·ed *adj.*
un·per·ceived′ *adj.*
un·per·cep′ti·ble *adj.*
un·per·cep′ti·bly *adv.*
un·per·cep′tive *adj.*
un·per·cep′tive·ly *adv.*
un·per·fect′ed *adj.*
un·per·formed′ *adj.*
un·per·suad′ed *adj.*
un·per·sua′sive *adj.*
un·per·sua′sive·ly *adv.*
un·per·turb′a·ble *adj.*
un·per·turb′a·bly *adv.*
un·picked′ *adj.*
un·planned′ *adj.*
un·plant′ed *adj.*
un·play′a·ble *adj.*
un·pleased′ *adj.*
un·pleas′ing *adj.*
un·pleas′ing·ly *adv.*
un·plowed′ *adj.*
un·po·et′ic *adj.*

un·po·et′i·cal *adj.*
un·poised′ *adj.*
un·pol′ished *adj.*
un·pol′lut′ed *adj.*
un·pop′u·lat·ed *adj.*
un·posed′ *adj.*
un·pos·ses′sive *adj.*
un·prac′ticed *adj.*
un·pre·dict′ed *adj.*
un·pre·par′ed·ness *n.*
un·pre·sent′a·ble *adj.*
un·pre·sent′a·bly *adv.*
un·pre·served′ *adj.*
un·pressed′ *adj.*
un·pre·vent′a·ble *adj.*
un·proc′essed *adj.*
un·pro·claimed′ *adj.*
un·pro·cur′a·ble *adj.*
un·pro·duc′tive *adj.*
un·pro·duc′tive·ly *adv.*
un·prom′is·ing *adj.*
un·prompt′ed *adj.*
un·pro·nounce′a·ble *adj.*
un·pro·nounced′ *adj.*
un·pro·pi′tious *adj.*
un·pro·pi′tious·ly *adv.*
un·pro·tect′ed *adj.*
un·pro·tec′tive *adj.*

un·pro·test′ing *adj.*
un·prov′a·ble *adj.*
un·proved′ *adj.*
un·prov′en *adj.*
un·pro·vid′ed *adj.*
un·pro·voked′ *adj.*
un·pub′lished *adj.*
un·pun′ish·a·ble *adj.*
un·pun′ished *adj.*
un·quench′a·ble *adj.*
un·quenched′ *adj.*
un·rat′i·fied *adj.*
un·read′a·ble *adj.*
un·re·al·is′tic *adj.*
un·re·al·is′ti·cal·ly *adv.*
un·re′al·ized *adj.*
un·re·cep′tive *adj.*
un·reck′oned *adj.*
un·re·claimed′ *adj.*
un·rec′og·niz·a·ble *adj.*
un·rec′og·nized *adj.*
un·rec·om·mend′ed *adj.*
un·rec·on·cil′a·ble *adj.*
un·rec·on·cil′a·bly *adv.*
un·rec′on·ciled *adj.*
un·re·cord′ed *adj.*
un·rec′ti·fied *adj.*
un·re·deem′a·ble *adj.*

un·reel (un-reel) *v.* to unwind from a reel.

un·re·gen·er·ate (un-ri-jen-ĕ-rit) *adj.* 1. persisting in opposition to new ideas etc. 2. not reformed or converted to a new way of life or religion etc.

un·re·lent·ing (un-ri-len-ting) *adj.* not becoming less in intensity or severity. **un·re·lent'ing·ly** *adv.*

un·re·lieved (un-ri-leevd) *adj.* not relieved, without anything to give variation, *unrelieved gloom; a plain black dress unrelieved by any touches of color.*

un·re·mit·ting (un-ri-mit-ing) *adj.* not relaxing or ceasing, persistent. **un·re·mit'ting·ly** *adv.*

un·re·quit·ed (un-ri-kwɪ-tid) *adj.* (of love) not returned or rewarded.

un·re·served (un-ri-zurvd) *adj.* without reservation or restriction, complete. **un·re·serv·ed·ly** (un-ri-zur-vid-lee) *adv.*

un·rest (un-rest) *n.* restlessness, agitation.

un·re·strained (un-ri-straynd) *adj.* not restrained. **un·re·strain·ed·ly** (un-ri-stray-nid-lee) *adv.*

un·right·eous (un-rī-chŭs) *adj.* not righteous, unjust, wicked. **un·right'eous·ly** *adv.* **un·right'eous·ness** *n.*

un·ripe (un-rɪp) *adj.* not yet ripe.

un·ri·valed (un-rɪ-văld) *adj.* having no equal, incomparable.

un·robe (un-rohb) *v.* (**un·robed, un·rob·ing**) to undress.

un·roll (un-rohl) *v.* to open or become opened after being rolled.

un·roof (un-roof) *v.* to remove the roof of.

un·ruf·fled (un-ruf-ĕld) *adj.* 1. not upset, calm. 2. not ruffled, smooth, *unruffled feathers.*

un·ru·ly (un-roo-lee) *adj.* (**-li·er, -li·est**) not easy to control or discipline, disorderly. **un·ru'li·ness** *n.*

un·sad·dle (un-sad-ĕl) *v.* (**un·sad·dled, un·sad·dling**) to remove the saddle from (a horse).

un·said (un-sed) *see* **unsay. unsaid** *adj.* not spoken or expressed, *many things were left unsaid.*

un·salt·ed (un-sawl-tid) *adj.* not seasoned with salt.

un·san·i·tar·y (un-san-i-ter-ee) *adj.* unclean, likely to be harmful to health.

un·sat·u·rat·ed (un-sach-ŭ-ray-tid) *adj.* 1. not saturated. 2. able to combine with another substance.

un·saved (un-sayvd) *adj.* not saved, lacking spiritual salvation.

un·sa·vor·y (un-say-vŏ-ree) *adj.* 1. disagreeable to the taste or smell. 2. morally unpleasant or disgusting, *has an unsavory reputation.* **un·sav'or·i·ness** *n.*

un·say (un-say) *v.* (**un·said, un·say·ing**) to take back or retract, *what's said can't be unsaid.*

un·scarred (un-skahrd) *adj.* not scarred.

un·scathed (un-skaythd) *adj.* without suffering any injury.

un·schooled (un-skoold) *adj.* untrained, uneducated.

un·sci·en·tif·ic (un-sɪ-ĕn-tif-ik) *adj.* 1. not familiar with science, *an unscientific person.* 2. not in accordance with scientific principles, *an unscientific assertion.* **un·sci·en·tif'i·cal·ly** *adv.*

un·scram·ble (un-skram-bĕl) *v.* to sort out from a scrambled state, to make (a scrambled transmission) intelligible.

un·scratched (un-skracht) *adj.* 1. not scratched. 2. unharmed, *came through the war unscratched.*

un·screw (un-skroo) *v.* to loosen (a screw or nut etc.) by turning it, to unfasten by removing screws.

un·script·ed (un-skrip-tid) *adj.* without a prepared script.

un·scru·pu·lous (un-skroo-pyŭ-lŭs) *adj.* without moral scruples, not prevented from doing wrong by scruples of conscience. **un·scru'pu·lous·ly** *adv.* **un·scru'pu·lous·ness** *n.*

un·seal (un-seel) *v.* to break the seal of, to open.

un·sea·son·a·ble (un-see-zŏ-nă-bĕl) *adj.* 1. not suitable for the season. 2. untimely, inopportune. **un·sea'son·a·bly** *adv.* **un·sea'son·a·ble·ness** *n.*

un·sea·soned (un-see-zŏnd) *adj.* 1. without food seasoning. 2. inexperienced. 3. not dried or aged etc., *unseasoned wood.*

un·seat (un-seet) *v.* 1. to dislodge (a rider) from horseback or from a bicycle etc. 2. to remove from a political office, *was unseated at the last election.*

un·seed·ed (un-see-did) *adj.* not seeded in a tournament, especially in tennis.

un·seem·ly (un-seem-lee) *adj.* not seemly, improper.

un·seen (un-seen) *adj.* not seen, invisible.

un·seg·re·gat·ed (un-seg-rĕ-gay-tid) *adj.* not segregated.

un·self·ish (un-sel-fish) *adj.* not selfish, considering the needs of others before one's own. **un·self'ish·ly** *adv.* **un·self'ish·ness** *n.*

un·set·tle (un-set-ĕl) *v.* (**un·set·tled, un·set·**

---

un·re·fined' *adj.*	**un·rep·re·sent'a·tive** *adj.*	**un·safe'** *adj.*
un·re·flect'ing *adj.*	**un·rep·re·sent'ed** *adj.*	**un·sal'a·ble** *adj.*
un·re·flec'tive *adj.*	**un·re·pressed'** *adj.*	**un·sal'vage·a·ble** *adj.*
un·re·formed' *adj.*	**un·re·sent'ful** *adj.*	**un·sanc'ti·fied** *adj.*
un·reg'i·ment·ed *adj.*	**un·re·sist'ing** *adj.*	**un·sanc'tioned** *adj.*
un·reg'is·tered *adj.*	**un·re·solved'** *adj.*	**un·sat·is·fac'to·ry** *adj.*
un·reg'u·lat·ed *adj.*	**un·re·spon'sive** *adj.*	**un·sat'is·fied** *adj.*
un·re·hearsed' *adj.*	**un·re·spon'sive·ly** *adv.*	**un·scent'ed** *adj.*
un·re·lat'ed *adj.*	**un·rest'ful** *adj.*	**un·sched'uled** *adj.*
un·re·li'a·ble *adj.*	**un·re·strict'ed** *adj.*	**un·schol'ar·ly** *adj.*
un·re·mem'bered *adj.*	**un·re·strict'ed·ly** *adv.*	**un·sea'wor·thy** *adj.*
un·re·morse'ful *adj.*	**un·re·turned'** *adj.*	**un·se·clud'ed** *adj.*
un·re·morse'ful·ly *adv.*	**un·re·vealed'** *adj.*	**un·see'ing** *adj.*
un·re·mu'ner·at·ed *adj.*	**un·re·ward'ed** *adj.*	**un·se·lec'tive** *adj.*
un·re·mu'ner·a·tive *adj.*	**un·re·ward'ing** *adj.*	**un·se·lec'tive·ly** *adv.*
un·rent'ed *adj.*	**un·rhymed'** *adj.*	**un·self-con'scious** *adj.*
un·re·paid' *adj.*	**un·ri'pened** *adj.*	**un·self-con'scious·ly** *adv.*
un·re·pent'ant *adj.*	**un·ro·man'tic** *adj.*	**un·sen'si·tive** *adj.*
un·re·placed' *adj.*	**un·ro·man'ti·cal·ly** *adv.*	**un·sen·ti·men'tal** *adj.*
un·re·port'ed *adj.*	**un·ruled'** *adj.*	**un·serv'ice·a·ble** *adj.*

tling) to make uneasy, to disturb the settled calm or stability of. **un·set·tle·ment** (un-set-ĕl-mĕnt) *n.*

un·set·tled (un-set-ĕld) *adj.* not settled, liable to change.

un·shack·le (un-shak-ĕl) *v.* **(un·shack·led, un·shack·ling)** to free from shackles or from restraint.

un·shak·a·ble (un-shay-kă-bĕl) *adj.* not shakable, firm.

un·shaped (un-shaypt) *adj.* not shaped or formed.

un·sheathe (un-shee*th*) *v.* **(un·sheathed, un·sheath·ing)** to draw from a sheath.

un·ship (un-ship) *v.* **(un·shipped, un·ship·ping)** 1. to remove or discharge (cargo or passengers) from a ship. 2. to remove (a mast, oar, etc.) from a fixed position.

un·shod (un-shod) *adj.* without shoes.

un·shrink·a·ble (un-shring-kă-bĕl) *adj.* not liable to become shrunk.

un·sight·ly (un-srt-lee) *adj.* not pleasant to look at, ugly. **un·sight'li·ness** *n.*

un·signed (un-srnd) *adj.* not signed.

un·skilled (un-skild) *adj.* not needing or not having skill or special training, *unskilled work and unskilled workers.*

un·skill·ful (un-skil-fŭl) *adj.* 1. not skillful. 2. clumsy. **un·skill'ful·ly** *adv.*

un·snap (un-snap) *v.* **(un·snapped, un·snap·ping)** to undo by opening a snap fastener.

un·snarl (un-snahrl) *v.* to free from tangles.

un·so·cia·ble (un-soh-shă-bĕl) *adj.* not sociable, withdrawing oneself from others.

un·so·cial (un-soh-shăl) *adj.* 1. unsociable. 2. not suitable for society. **un·so'cial·ly** *adv.*

un·so·lic·it·ed (un-sŏ-lis-i-tid) *adj.* not asked for, given or done voluntarily.

un·so·phis·ti·cat·ed (un-sŏ-fis-tĭ-kay-tid) *adj.* not sophisticated, simple and natural or naïve.

un·sought (un-sawt) *adj.* not sought.

un·sound (un-sownd) *adj.* not sound or strong, not free from defects or mistakes. **un·sound'ly** *adv.* **un·sound'ness** *n.* □of unsound mind, insane.

un·spar·ing (un-spair-ing) *adj.* giving freely and lavishly, *unsparing in one's efforts.* **un·spar'ing·ly** *adv.* **un·spar'ing·ness** *n.*

un·speak·a·ble (un-spee-kă-bĕl) *adj.* too great or too bad to be described in words, very objectionable. **un·speak'a·bly** *adv.*

un·spec·i·fied (un-spes-ĭ-fɪd) *adj.* not specified.

un·spot·ted (un-spot-id) *adj.* 1. not marked with spots. 2. morally pure. 3. unnoticed.

un·sta·ble (un-stay-bĕl) *adj.* 1. not stable, tending to change suddenly. 2. mentally or emotionally unbalanced. **un·sta'bly** *adv.* **un·sta'ble·ness** *n.*

un·stead·y (un-sted-ee) *adj.* not steady. **un·stead'i·ly** *adv.* **un·stead'i·ness** *n.*

un·stint·ed (un-stin-tid) *adj.* given freely and lavishly.

un·stop (un-stop) *v.* 1. to free from obstruction. 2. to remove a stopper from. **un·stop'pa·ble** *adj.*

un·strap (un-strap) *v.* **(un·strapped, un·strap·ping)** to remove a strap from.

un·stressed (un-strest) *adj.* 1. not subjected to stress. 2. not pronounced with stress.

un·strung (un-strung) *adj.* 1. having the strings of (a bow, harp, etc.) removed or loosened. 2. unnerved, nervously agitated.

un·stuck (un-stuk) *adj.* detached after being stuck on or together. □**come unstuck,** *(informal)* to suffer disaster, to fail.

un·stud·ied (un-stud-eed) *adj.* natural in manner, not affected, *with unstudied elegance.*

un·sub·stan·tial (un-sŭb-stan-shăl) *adj.* not substantial, flimsy, having little or no factual basis. **un·sub·stan'tial·ly** *adv.*

un·suc·cess·ful (un-sŭk-ses-fŭl) *adj.* not achieving success. **un·suc·cess'ful·ly** *adv.*

un·suit·a·ble (un-soo-tă-bĕl) *adj.* not suitable. **un·suit'a·bly** *adv.* **un·suit·a·bil·i·ty** (un-soo-tă-bil-i-tee) *n.*

un·sul·lied (un-sul-eed) *adj.* not sullied, pure.

un·sung (un-sung) *adj.* 1. not sung. 2. not celebrated; *unsung heroes,* those whose heroism has not been honored or acclaimed.

un·sus·pect·ing (un-sŭs-pekt-ing) *adj.* feeling no suspicion.

un·swerv·ing (un-swur-ving) *adj.* not turning aside, unchanging, *unswerving loyalty.*

un·tan·gle (un-tang-gĕl) *v.* to free from tangles or confusion.

---

un·shad'ed *adj.*
un·sha'ken *adj.*
un·shamed' *adj.*
un·shared' *adj.*
un·shaved' *adj.*
un·shav'en *adj.*
un·shelled' *adj.*
un·shield'ed *adj.*
un·shorn' *adj.*
un·sift'ed *adj.*
un·si'lenced *adj.*
un·sink'a·ble *adj.*
un·slaked' *adj.*
un·smil'ing *adj.*
un·smil'ing·ly *adv.*
un·soiled' *adj.*
un·sold' *adj.*
un·sol'dier·ly *adj.*
un·so·lic'i·tous *adj.*
un·solv'a·ble *adj.*
un·solved' *adj.*
un·sort'ed *adj.*
un·spe'cial·ized *adj.*

un·spe·cif'ic *adj.*
un·spe·cif'i·cal·ly *adv.*
un·spell'a·ble *adj.*
un·spent' *adj.*
un·spoiled' *adj.*
un·sports'man·like *adj.*
un·stained' *adj.*
un·stamped' *adj.*
un·stand'ard·ized *adj.*
un·sta'pled *adj.*
un·starched' *adj.*
un·stat'ed *adj.*
un·ster'i·lized *adj.*
un·stint'ing *adj.*
un·stint'ing·ly *adv.*
un·strained' *adj.*
un·struc'tured *adj.*
un·sub·mis'sive *adj.*
un·sub·stan'ti·at·ed *adj.*
un·suit'ed *adj.*
un·su'per·vised *adj.*
un·sup·port'ed *adj.*
un·sup·pressed' *adj.*

un·sup·press'i·ble *adj.*
un·sure' *adj.*
un·sure'ly *adv.*
un·sure'ness *n.*
un·sur·pass'a·ble *adj.*
un·sur·passed' *adj.*
un·sus·cep'ti·ble *adj.*
un·sus·pect'ed *adj.*
un·sus·pi'cious *adj.*
un·sus·tained' *adj.*
un·swayed' *adj.*
un·sweet'ened *adj.*
un·swept' *adj.*
un·sym·met'ri·cal *adj.*
un·sym·met'ri·cal·ly *adv.*
un·sym·pa·thet'ic *adj.*
un·sym·pa·thet'i·cal·ly *adv.*
un·sys·tem·at'ic *adj.*
un·tact'ful *adj.*
un·taint'ed *adj.*
un·tal'ent·ed *adj.*
un·tamed' *adj.*
un·tanned' *adj.*

un·tapped (un-tapt) *adj.* not tapped, not yet made use of, *the country's untapped resources.*

un·taught (un-tawt) *adj.* 1. not taught, not instructed by teaching, ignorant. 2. not acquired by teaching, natural, spontaneous.

un·ten·a·ble (un-ten-ă-bĕl) *adj.* (of a theory) not tenable, not able to be held, because strong arguments can be produced against it.

un·think·a·ble (un-thing-kă-bĕl) *adj.* incredible, too unlikely or undesirable to be considered.

un·think·ing (un-thing-king) *adj.* thoughtless, done or said etc. without consideration. **un·think′ing·ly** *adv.*

un·thought (un-thawt) *adj.* not thought of.

un·thought·ful (un-thawt-fŭl) *adj.* not thoughtful.

un·ti·dy (un-tɪ-dee) *adj.* (-di·er, -di·est) not tidy. **un·ti′di·ly** *adv.* **un·ti′di·ness** *n.*

un·tie (un-tɪ) *v.* (un·tied, un·ty·ing) to unfasten, to release from being tied up.

un·til (un-til) *prep. & conj.* up to (a specified time), up to the time when, *wait until evening, ring until someone answers.* ▷Use *until* rather than *till,* especially when it stands first, as in *until last year, we had never been abroad,* and in formal use, as in *he lived there until his death.*

un·time·ly (un-tɪm-lee) *adj.* 1. happening at an unsuitable time. 2. happening too soon or sooner than is normal, *his untimely death.* **untimely** *adv.* **un·time′li·ness** *n.*

un·tir·ing (un-tɪr-ing) *adj.* not tiring. **un·tir′ing·ly** *adv.*

un·told (un-tohld) *adj.* 1. not told. 2. not counted, too much or too many to be counted, *untold wealth* or *wealth untold.*

un·touch·a·ble (un-tuch-ă-bĕl) *adj.* not able to be touched, not allowed to be touched. **un·touchable** *n.* a member of the lowest Hindu caste in India, held to defile members of a higher caste on contact. **un·touch′a·bly** *adv.*

un·to·ward (un-tohrd) *adj.* inconvenient, awkward, *if nothing untoward happens.*

un·trace·a·ble (un-tray-să-bĕl) *adj.* unable to be traced.

un·tried (un-trɪd) *adj.* not yet tried or tested.

un·true (un-troo) *adj.* 1. not true, contrary to facts. 2. not faithful or loyal.

un·truth (un-trooth) *n.* 1. an untrue statement, a lie. 2. lack of truth. **un·truth′ful** *adj.* **un·truth′ful·ly** *adv.* **un·truth′ful·ness** *n.*

un·tu·tored (un-too-tŏrd) *adj.* (of a person) not taught.

un·twist (un-twist) *v.* to remove from a twisted position.

un·used (un-yoozd) *adj.* not yet used.

un·u·su·al (un-yoo-zhoo-ăl) *adj.* not usual, exceptional, remarkable. **un·u′su·al·ly** *adv.* **un·u′su·al·ness** *n.*

un·ut·ter·a·ble (un-ut-ĕ-ră-bĕl) *adj.* too great or too intense to be expressed in words, *unutterable joy.* **un·ut′ter·a·bly** *adv.*

un·var·nished (un-vahr-nisht) *adj.* 1. not varnished. 2. (of a statement etc.) plain and straightforward, *the unvarnished truth.*

un·veil (un-vayl) *v.* 1. to remove a veil from, to remove one's veil. 2. to remove concealing drapery from, as part of a ceremony, *unveiled the portrait.* 3. to disclose, to make publicly known.

un·versed (un-vurst) *adj.* not experienced in something, *he was unversed in the ways of polite society.*

un·voiced (un-voist) *adj.* not spoken, not voiced.

un·want·ed (un-won-tid) *adj.* not wanted. ▷Do not confuse *unwanted* with *unwonted.*

un·war·rant·a·ble (un-wor-ăn-tă-bĕl) *adj.* unjustifiable. **un·war′rant·a·bly** *adv.*

un·war·rant·ed (un-wor-ăn-tid) *adj.* unauthorized, unjustified.

un·wa·ry (un-wair-ee) *adj.* not cautious. **un·war′i·ly** *adv.* **un·war′i·ness** *n.*

un·washed (un-wosht) *adj.* not washed, not usually washed or clean. □**the great unwashed,** *(contemptuous)* the uninformed masses.

un·well (un-wel) *adj.* not in good health.

un·whole·some (un-hohl-sŏm) *adj.* 1. harmful to health or to moral well-being. 2. unhealthy looking. **un·whole′some·ly** *adv.* **un·whole′some·ness** *n.*

un·wield·y (un-weel-dee) *adj.* awkward to move or control because of its size or shape or weight. **un·wield′i·ness** *n.*

un·will·ing (un-wil-ing) *adj.* not willing, reluctant, hesitating to do something. **un·will′ing·ly** *adv.* **un·will′ing·ness** *n.*

un·wind (un-wɪnd) *v.* (un·wound, un·wind·ing) 1. to draw out or become drawn out from being wound. 2. *(informal)* to relax after a period of work or tension.

un·wise (un-wɪz) *adj.* not wise, foolish. **un·wise′ly** *adv.*

un·wished (un-wisht) *adj.* not wished.

un·wit·ting (un-wit-ing) *adj.* 1. unaware. 2. unintentional. **un·wit′ting·ly** *adv.*

un·wont·ed (un-wohn-tid) *adj.* not customary or usual, *spoke with unwonted rudeness.* **un·wont′ed·ly** *adv.* ▷Do not confuse *unwonted* with *unwanted.*

un·world·ly (un-wurld-lee) *adv.* not worldly, spiritually minded. **un·world′li·ness** *n.*

un·worn (un-wohrn) *adj.* not yet worn.

un·tar′nished *adj.*	**un·trav′eled** *adj.*	**un·ven′ti·lat·ed** *adj.*
un·tast′ed *adj.*	**un·treat′ed** *adj.*	**un·ver′i·fi·a·ble** *adj.*
un·taxed′ *adj.*	**un·trimmed′** *adj.*	**un·ver′i·fied** *adj.*
un·teach′a·ble *adj.*	**un·trod′den** *adj.*	**un·watched′** *adj.*
un·tempt′ed *adj.*	**un·trou′bled** *adj.*	**un·wa′ver·ing** *adj.*
un·tempt′ing *adj.*	**un·trust′ful** *adj.*	**un·waxed′** *adj.*
un·tend′ed *adj.*	**un·trust′worth·i·ness** *n.*	**un·weak′ened** *adj.*
un·test′ed *adj.*	**un·trust′wor·thy** *adj.*	**un·wea′ry·ing** *adj.*
un·thank′ful *adj.*	**un·typ′i·cal** *adj.*	**un·wed′** *adj.*
un·tilled′ *adj.*	**un·typ′i·cal·ly** *adv.*	**un·wel′come** *adj.*
un·tit′led *adj.*	**un·us′a·ble** *adj.*	**un·wel′comed** *adj.*
un·touched′ *adj.*	**un·u′ti·lized** *adj.*	**un·wit′nessed** *adj.*
un·trained′ *adj.*	**un·ut′tered** *adj.*	**un·wom′an·ly** *adj.*
un·tram′meled *adj.*	**un·vac′ci·nat·ed** *adj.*	**un·won′** *adj.*
un·trans·lat′a·ble *adj.*	**un·var′ied** *adj.*	**un·work′a·ble** *adj.*
un·trans·lat′ed *adj.*	**un·var′y·ing** *adj.*	**un·wor′ried** *adj.*

un·wor·thy (un-wur-*thee*) *adj.* 1. not worthy, lacking worth or excellence. 2. not deserving, *he is unworthy of this honor.* 3. unsuitable to the character of a person or thing, *such conduct is unworthy of a president.* **un·wor'thi·ly** *adv.* **un·wor'thi·ness** *n.*

un·wrap (un-rap) *v.* **(un·wrapped, un·wrap·ping)** to open or become opened from being wrapped.

un·writ·ten (un-rit-ĕn) *adj.* not written. ☐**unwritten law,** one that rests on custom or tradition not on a statute.

un·yield·ing (un-yeel-ding) *adj.* firm, not yielding to pressure or influence. **un·yield'ing·ly** *adv.*

un·yoke (un-yohk) *v.* **(un·yoked, un·yok·ing)** to free from a yoke.

un·zip (un-zip) *v.* **(un·zipped, un·zip·ping)** to open or become opened by the undoing of a zipper.

un·zipped (un-zipt) *adj.* 1. (of a zipper) open. 2. *(informal)* bearing no zip code, *unzipped mail.*

up (up) *adv.* 1. to an erect or vertical position, *stand up.* 2. to or in or at a higher place or level or value or condition, to a larger size, farther north; *they are two goals up,* are winning by this amount; *he's up in years,* he is old; *the sun is up,* has risen. 3. so as to be inflated, *pump up the tires.* 4. to the place or time or amount etc. in question, *up till now; can take up to four passengers.* 5. out of bed, (of a stage curtain) raised at the start of a performance, (of a jockey) in the saddle. 6. into a condition of activity or efficiency, *getting up steam; stirred up trouble; house is up for sale; the team is up for the game, (informal)* at its best. 7. apart, into pieces, *tore it up.* 8. apiece; *the score was 13 up,* tied at 13 points for each side. 9. into a compact state, securely, *pack it up; tie it up.* 10. to be finished, *your time is up.* 11. happening (especially of something unusual or undesirable), *something is up.* 12. (in baseball) at bat. **up** *prep.* 1. upward along or through or into, from bottom to top of. 2. at a higher part of, *build it farther up the slope.* **up** *adj.* directed upward, *the up escalator.* **up** *v.* **(upped, up·ping)** *(informal)* 1. to begin to do something suddenly or unexpectedly, *he upped and demanded an inquiry.* 2. to increase, *they promptly upped the price.* ☐**on the up and up,** *(informal)* honest, honestly. **up against,** close to; in or into contact with; *(informal)* faced with, as an opponent or problem; *up against it,* in great difficulties. **up and around** *or* **about,** recovered from an illness. **up in** *or* **on,** *(informal)* knowledgeable about, *not up in mathematics.* **ups and downs,** alternate good and bad fortune. **up to,** occupied with, doing, *what is he up to?;* required as a duty or obligation from, *it's up to us to help her;* capable of, *don't feel up to a long walk.* **up to date,** in current fashion; in accordance with what is now known or required, *bring the files up to date.*

up-and-com·ing (up-ăn-kum-ing) *adj.* *(informal)* enterprising and likely to be successful.

u·pas (yoo-păs) *n.* a Javanese tree yielding a poisonous sap.

up·beat (up-beet) *n.* (in music) the unaccented beat before a downbeat, the upward swing of a conductor's hand to indicate this. **upbeat** *adj.* optimistic, cheerful.

up·braid (up-brayd) *v.* to reproach. **up·braid'er** *n.*

up·bring·ing (up-bring-ing) *n.* training and education during childhood.

UPC *abbr.* universal product code.

up·chuck (up-chuk) *v.* *(slang)* to vomit.

up·com·ing (up-kum-ing) *adj.* about to take place.

up·coun·try (up-kun-tree) *adj. & adv.* toward the interior of a country.

up·date (up-dayt) *v.* **(up·dat·ed, up·dat·ing)** to bring up to date. **update** (up-dayt) *n.* updated news or information. **up·dat'a·ble** *adj.*

up·draft (up-draft) *n.* an upward current of air or gases.

up·end (up-end) *v.* to set or rise up on end.

up·grade (up-grayd) *v.* **(up·grad·ed, up·grad·ing)** to raise to a higher grade or rank. **upgrade** (up-grayd) *n.* an upward incline or slope. ☐**on the upgrade,** going up, rising in quality or rank.

up·growth (up-grohth) *n.* the process or result of growing upward.

up·heav·al (up-hee-văl) *n.* 1. a sudden heaving upward. 2. a violent change or disturbance.

up·heave (up-heev) *v.* **(up·heaved, up·heav·ing)** to lift forcibly.

up·hill (up-hil) *adv.* in an upward direction, on an upward slope. **uphill** *adj.* 1. going or sloping upward. 2. difficult, *it was uphill work.*

up·hold (up-hohld) *v.* **(up·held, up·hold·ing)** 1. to support, to keep from falling. 2. to support a decision or statement or belief. **up·hold'er** *n.*

up·hol·ster (up-hohl-stĕr) *v.* to put a fabric covering, padding, springs, etc. on (furniture). **up·hol'ster·er** *n.*

up·hol·ster·y (up-hohl-stĕ-ree) *n.* (*pl.* **-ster·ies**) 1. the work of upholstering furniture. 2. the material used for this.

UPI *abbr.* United Press International.

up·keep (up-keep) *n.* keeping something in good condition and repair, the cost of this.

up·land (up-lănd) *n.* the higher or inland parts of a country. **upland** *adj.* of or in uplands.

up·lift (up-lift) *n.* 1. being raised. 2. a mentally or morally elevating influence. **uplift** (up-lift) *v.* to raise. **up·lift'ment** *n.*

up·most (up-mohst) *adj.* uppermost.

up·on (ŭ-pon) *prep.* on, *Stratford upon Avon; Christmas is almost upon us; row upon row of seats.* ☐**once upon a time,** *see* **once.**

up·per (up-ĕr) *adj.* 1. higher in place or position. 2. situated on higher ground or to the north; *Upper Egypt,* the part farthest from the Nile delta. 3. ranking above others; *the upper class,* people of the highest social class. **upper** *n.* 1. the part of a boot or shoe above the sole; *on one's uppers,* very short of money. 2. *(slang)* a stimulant drug. 3. an upper berth. ☐**upper case,** capital letters for printing type. **upper crust,** *(informal)* the highest social group. **upper hand,** mastery, dominance, *gained the upper hand.* **upper house,** one, generally smaller, branch of a bicameral legislature, as the U.S. Senate. **Upper Volta,** a country in West Africa.

up·per-class (up-ĕr-klas) *adj.* relating to the highest class in society.

up·per·class·man (up-ĕr-klas-măn) *n.* (*pl.* **-men,** *pr.* -mĕn) a junior or senior in high school or college.

up·per·cut (up-ĕr-kut) *n.* a blow in boxing, delivered upward with the arm bent.

up·per·most (up-ĕr-mohst) *adj.* highest in place

---

un·wov'en *adj.*   **un·wrin'kled** *adj.*   **un·yield'ing·ness** *n.*

or rank. **uppermost** *adv.* on or to the top or most prominent position.

up·pish (up-ish) *adj. (informal)* pert, arrogant.

up·pi·ty (up-i-tee) *adj. (informal)* arrogant, snobbish.

up·raise (up-rayz) *v.* (**up·raised, up·rais·ing**) to raise up.

up·right (up-rīt) *adj.* 1. in a vertical position. 2. (of a piano) with the strings mounted vertically. 3. strictly honest or honorable. **upright** *n.* 1. a post or rod placed upright, especially as a support. 2. an upright piano. **up′right·ly** *adv.* **up′right·ness** *n.* □**upright piano,** a piano with vertical strings.

up·ris·ing (up-rī-zing) *n.* a rebellion, a revolt against the authorities.

up·riv·er (up-riv-ĕr) *adj. & adv.* toward the starting point of a river.

up·roar (up-rohr) *n.* an outburst of noise and excitement or anger.

up·roar·i·ous (up-rohr-i-ŭs) *adj.* very noisy, with loud laughter. **up·roar′i·ous·ly** *adv.* **up·roar′i·ous·ness** *n.*

up·root (up-root) *v.* 1. to pull out of the ground together with its roots. 2. to force to leave a native or established place, *we don't want to uproot ourselves and live abroad.*

UPS *abbr.* United Parcel Service.

up·set (up-set) *v.* (**up·set, up·set·ting**) 1. to overturn, to become overturned. 2. to disrupt, *fog upset the timetable.* 3. to distress the mind or feelings of, to disturb the temper or digestion of. 4. to defeat unexpectedly (a formidable opponent), especially in politics or sports. **upset** (up-set) *n.* 1. upsetting, being upset, *a stomach upset.* 2. the defeat of a person or group expected to win. □**upset price,** the lowest acceptable selling price in an auction. **upset the applecart,** to spoil a situation or someone's plans.

up·shift (up-shift) *v.* to shift into a higher gear as a vehicle increases speed. **upshift** *n.*

up·shot (up-shot) *n.* outcome.

up·side-down (up-sīd-down) *adj. & adv.* 1. with the upper part underneath instead of on top. 2. in great disorder. □**upside-down cake,** a cake baked with fruit on the bottom, turned over and served with the fruit on top.

up·si·lon (yoop-si-lon) *n.* the twentieth letter of the Greek alphabet (Υ υ).

up·stage (up-stayj) *adj. & adv.* 1. nearer the back of a theater stage. 2. snobbish, snobbishly. **upstage** *v.* (**up·staged, up·stag·ing**) 1. to move upstage from (an actor) and make him face away from the audience. 2. to divert attention from or outshine (a person).

up·stairs (up-stairz) *adv.* up the stairs, to or on an upper floor. **upstairs** *adj.* situated upstairs. **upstairs** *n.* the upper floor of a house.

up·stand·ing (up-stan-ding) *adj.* well set up, honest.

up·start (up-stahrt) *n.* a person who has risen suddenly to a high position, especially one who behaves arrogantly. **upstart** *adj.* of or like an upstart.

up·state (up-stayt) *adj. & adv.* in or toward the northern part of a state, especially the part that is north of a major city; *upstate New York,* the part of New York State remote from New York City. **upstate** *n.* this part of a state.

up·stream (up-streem) *adj. & adv.* in the direction from which a stream flows.

up·stroke (up-strohk) *n.* an upward stroke.

up·surge (up-surj) *n.* an upward surge, a rise.

up·swept (up-swept) *adj.* 1. combed up and arranged on top of the head, as hair. 2. curved or sloped upward.

up·swing (up-swing) *n.* an upward movement or trend.

up·take (up-tayk) *n.* 1. *(informal)* ability to understand what is meant, *quick in* or *on the uptake.* 2. a ventilating duct rising from below.

up·thrust (up-thrust) *n.* 1. an upward thrust. 2. an upward displacement of part of Earth's crust.

up·tight (up-tīt) *adj. (informal)* 1. nervously tense. 2. angry. **up′tight′ness** *n.*

up-to-date (up-tŏ-dayt) *adj.* 1. in current fashion, *up-to-date clothes.* 2. extending to the present time, including the latest information.

up·town (up-town) *adj. & adv.* in or toward the upper part of a city. **uptown** *n.* this part of a city.

up·turn (up-turn) *v.* to turn upward, to turn upside down, to turn up (ground, in plowing etc.). **upturn** (up-turn) *n.* 1. an upheaval. 2. an upward trend in business or fortune etc., an improvement.

up·ward (up-wărd) *adj. & adv.* moving or leading or pointing toward what is higher or more important or earlier. **upwards** *adv.* toward what is higher etc. **up′ward·ly** *adv.* **up′ward·ness** *n.* □**upward mobility,** movement to a higher economic or social status. **upward of,** more than.

up·wind (up-wind) *adj. & adv.* in the direction from which the wind is blowing.

u·ra·cil (yoor-ă-sil) *n.* a crystalline compound formed by the hydrolysis of RNA.

u·ran·ic (yuu-ran-ik) *adj.* of or containing uranium.

u·ra·ni·um (yuu-ray-ni-ŭm) *n.* a heavy gray metallic element used as a source of nuclear energy.

U·ra·nus (yoor-ă-nŭs, yuu-ray-) *n.* 1. a planet in the solar system. 2. the ruler of the heavens in Greek mythology. **U·ra·ni·an** (yuu-ray-ni-ăn) *adj.*

ur·ban (ur-băn) *adj.* of or situated in a city or town. □**urban guerrilla,** a terrorist operating in an urban area. **urban renewal,** slum clearance. **urban sprawl,** uncontrolled expansion of urban areas.

ur·bane (ur-bayn) *adj.* having manners that are smooth and polite. **ur·bane′ly** *adv.* **ur·ban·i·ty** (ur-ban-i-tee) *n.*

ur·ban·ite (ur-bă-nīt) *n.* a dweller in a city or town.

ur·ban·ize (ur-bă-nīz) *v.* (**ur·ban·ized, ur·ban·iz·ing**) to change (a place) into a town-like area. **ur·ban·i·za·tion** (ur-bă-ni-zay-shŏn) *n.*

ur·chin (ur-chin) *n.* 1. a mischievous or needy boy. 2. a sea urchin.

Ur·du (oor-doo) *n.* a language related to Hindi, one of the official languages of Pakistan.

u·re·a (yuu-ree-ă) *n.* a soluble colorless crystalline compound contained especially in the urine of mammals.

u·re·mi·a (yuu-ree-mi-ă) *n.* a toxic condition resulting from retention in the blood of wastes normally excreted in the urine.

u·re·ter (yuu-ree-tĕr) *n.* either of the two ducts by which urine passes from the kidneys to the bladder.

u·re·thra (yuu-ree-thră) *n.* (*pl.* -**thras, -thrae,** *pr.* -three) the duct by which urine is discharged from the body. **u·re′thral** *adj.*

urge (urj) *v.* (**urged, urg·ing**) 1. to drive onward, to encourage to proceed, *urging them on.* 2. to try hard or persistently to persuade, *urged him to accept the job.* 3. to recommend strongly with reasoning or entreaty, *urged on them the importance of keeping to the schedule.* **urge** *n.* a feeling or desire that urges a person to do something.

ur·gent (ur-jĕnt) *adj.* 1. needing immediate attention or action or decision. 2. showing that something is urgent, *spoke in an urgent whisper.* **ur'gent·ly** *adv.* **ur·gen·cy** (ur-jĕn-see) *n.*

u·ric (yoor-ik) *adj.* of urine. ☐**uric acid,** a compound found in small quantities in the healthy urine of mammals, the chief constituent in the urine of birds and reptiles.

u·ri·nal (yoor-ĭ-năl) *n.* 1. a receptacle for urine, for use by a bedridden male person. 2. a structure to receive urine in a men's lavatory, a room or building containing this.

u·ri·nal·y·sis (yoor-ĭ-nal-i-sis) *n.* the chemical analysis of urine, especially for diagnostic purposes.

u·ri·nar·y (yoor-ĭ-ner-ee) *adj.* of urine or its excretion, *urinary organs.*

u·ri·nate (yoor-ĭ-nayt) *v.* (**u·ri·nat·ed, u·ri·nat·ing**) to discharge urine from the body. **u·ri·na·tion** (yoor-ĭ-nay-shŏn) *n.*

u·rine (yoor-in) *n.* waste liquid that collects in the bladder and is discharged from the body.

urn (urn) *n.* 1. a vase, usually with a stem and base, especially one used for holding the ashes of a cremated person. 2. a large metal container with a tap in which tea or coffee is made or from which it is served.

u·ro·gen·i·tal (yoor-oh-jen-i-tăl) *adj.* of or pertaining to urinary and genital organs.

u·rol·o·gist (yuu-rol-ŏ-jist) *n.* a specialist in urology.

u·rol·o·gy (yuu-rol-ŏ-jee) *n.* the branch of medicine that deals with the urinary system. **u·ro·log·ic** (yoor-ŏ-loj-ik) *adj.* **u·ro·log'i·cal** *adj.*

ur·sine (ur-sɪn) *adj.* of or like a bear.

ur·ti·car·i·a (ur-tĭ-kair-i-ă) *n.* a skin eruption, hives.

U·ru·guay (yoor-ŭ-gway) *n.* a country in South America. **U·ru·guay·an** (yoor-ŭ-gway-ăn) *adj. & n.*

us (us) *pronoun* 1. the objective case of **we.** 2. (*informal*) = we, *it's us.* 3. (*informal*) me, *give us your hand.*

U.S., U.S.A. *abbr.* United States of America.

us·a·ble (yoo-ză-bĕl) *adj.* able to be used, fit for use. **us'a·ble·ness** *n.* **us·a·bil·i·ty** (yoo-ză-bil-i-tee) *n.*

USAF, U.S.A.F. *abbr.* United States Air Force.

us·age (yoo-sij) *n.* 1. the manner of using or treating something, *it was damaged by rough usage.* 2. a habitual or customary practice, especially in the way words are used, *modern English usage.*

USCG *abbr.* United States Coast Guard.

USDA *abbr.* United States Department of Agriculture.

use (yooz) *v.* (**used, us·ing**) 1. to cause to act or serve for a purpose or as an instrument or as material for consumption. 2. to cause oneself to be known or addressed by (a name or title). 3. to treat in a specified way, to behave toward, *they used her shamefully.* 4. to exploit selfishly. **use** (yoos) *n.* 1. using, being used. 2. the right or power of using something, *lost the use of his arm.* 3. the purpose for which something is used, work that a person or thing is able to do. **us'er** *n.*

☐**have no use for,** to have no purpose for which a thing can be used; to refuse to tolerate, to dislike. **make use of,** to use, to exploit. **used to,** was or were accustomed in the past, *we used to go by train; they used not to do this;* having become familiar with (a thing) by practice or habit, *is used to getting up early.* **use up,** to use the whole of (material etc.); to find a use for (remaining material or time); to exhaust or tire out.

used (yoozd) *adj.* (of clothes or vehicles etc.) secondhand.

use·ful (yoos-fŭl) *adj.* able to produce good results, able to be used for some practical purpose. **use'ful·ly** *adv.* **use'ful·ness** *n.* ☐**make oneself useful,** to perform some practical or beneficial service.

use·less (yoos-lis) *adj.* serving no useful purpose, not able to produce good results. **use'less·ly** *adv.* **use'less·ness** *n.*

USES *abbr.* United States Employment Service.

ush·er (ush-ĕr) *n.* 1. a person who shows people to their seats in a public hall etc. or into someone's presence. 2. an official acting as doorkeeper. 3. a member of the groom's wedding party, who assists the guests to their seats in the church etc. **usher** *v.* to lead in or out, to escort as usher.

ush·er·ette (ush-ĕ-ret) *n.* a woman who ushers people to their seats in a theater.

USIA *abbr.* United States Information Agency.

USMC *abbr.* United States Marine Corps.

USN *abbr.* United States Navy.

USO *abbr.* United Service Organization.

U.S.P. *abbr.* United States Pharmacopeia.

U.S.S. *abbr.* United States Ship.

U.S.S.R., USSR *abbr.* Union of Soviet Socialist Republics.

usu. *abbr.* 1. usual. 2. usually.

u·su·al (yoo-zhoo-ăl) *adj.* such as happens or is done or used etc. in many or most instances; *the usual* or *my usual,* what I usually have, my usual drink etc. **u'su·al·ly** *adv.* **u'su·al·ness** *n.*

u·su·fruct (yoo-zŭ-frukt) *n.* the right of enjoying the use and advantages of another's property short of destruction or waste of its substance. **u·su·fruc·tu·ar·y** (yoo-zŭ-fruk-choo-er-ee) *n.* (*pl.* -ar·ies).

u·su·rer (yoo-zhŭ-rĕr) *n.* a person who lends money at excessively high interest.

u·surp (yoo-surp, -zurp) *v.* to take (power or a position or right) wrongfully or by force. **u·surp'er** *n.* **u·sur·pa·tion** (yoo-sŭr-pay-shŏn) *n.*

u·su·ry (yoo-zhŭ-ree) *n.* (*pl.* -ries) 1. the lending of money at excessively high interest. 2. an excessively high rate of interest. **u·su·ri·ous** (yoo-zhoor-i-ŭs) *adj.*

UT, Ut. *abbr.* Utah.

U·tah (yoo-taw) a state of the U.S.

Ute (yoot) *n.* (*pl.* **Utes**) a member of an Indian tribe of Utah and Colorado.

u·ten·sil (yoo-ten-sĭl) *n.* an instrument or container, especially for domestic use.

u·ter·ine (yoo-tĕ-rin) *adj.* of the uterus.

u·ter·us (yoo-tĕ-rŭs) *n.* (*pl.* -ter·i, *pr.* -tĕ-rɪ, -us·es) the hollow organ (in woman and other female mammals) in which a child or the young is conceived and nourished while developing before birth, the womb.

u·til·i·tar·i·an (yoo-til-i-tair-i-ăn) *adj.* 1. designed to be useful rather than decorative or luxurious, severely practical. 2. of utilitarianism.

u·til·i·tar·i·an·ism (yoo-til-i-tair-i-ă-niz-ĕm) *n.* 1.

the doctrine that actions are right because they are useful. 2. the doctrine that the greatest happiness of the greatest number should be the guiding principle of conduct.

u·til·i·ty (yoo-til-i-tee) *n.* (*pl.* **-ties**) 1. usefulness. 2. a useful thing; *public utilities,* public services such as the supply of water or gas or electricity etc. **utility** *adj.* severely practical. ☐**utility infielder, utility outfielder,** (in baseball) a player who can play well in a variety of positions on the field. **utility room,** a room containing one or more large fixed domestic appliances (as a washing machine). **utility vehicle,** a vehicle serving various purposes.

u·ti·lize (yoo-ti-lɪz) *v.* (**u·ti·lized, u·ti·liz·ing**) to use, to find a use for. **u′ti·liz·a·ble** *adj.* **u′ti·liz·er** *n.* **u·ti·li·za·tion** (yoo-ti-li-zay-shŏn) *n.*

ut·most (ut-mohst) *adj.* furthest, greatest, extreme, *with the utmost care.* **utmost** *n.* the furthest point or degree etc. ☐**do one's utmost,** to do as much as possible.

U·to·pi·a, u·to·pi·a (yoo-toh-pi-ă) *n.* 1. an imaginary place or state of things where everything is perfect. 2. an impractical scheme for achieving such a state. **U·to·pi·an, u·to·pi·an** (yoo-toh-pi-ăn) *adj.* & *n.*

ut·ter[1] (ut-ĕr) *adj.* complete, absolute, *utter bliss.* **ut′ter·ly** *adv.*

utter[2] *v.* to make (a sound or words) with the mouth or voice, *uttered a sigh.* **ut′ter·er** *n.* **ut′ter·ance** *n.*

ut·ter·most (ut-ĕr-mohst) *adj.* & *n.* utmost.

U-turn (yoo-turn) *n.* 1. the driving of a vehicle in a U-shaped course so as to proceed in an opposite direction. 2. *(informal)* a reversal of policy.

UV *abbr.* ultraviolet.

u·vu·la (yoo-vyŭ-lă) *n.* (*pl.* **-las, lae,** *pr.* -lee) the small fleshy projection hanging from the back of the roof of the mouth above the throat. **u′vu·lar** *adj.*

ux. *abbr.* wife. ▷ Latin *uxor.*

ux·o·ri·ous (uk-sohr-i-ŭs) *adj.* obsessively fond of one's wife. **ux·o′ri·ous·ly** *adv.* **ux·o′ri·ous·ness** *n.*

Uz·bek·i·stan (uuz-bek-i-stan) a republic of the U.S.S.R. bordering on Afghanistan. **Uz′bek** n. 1. a native or inhabitant of Uzbekistan. 2. a language of this region.

V

V, v (vee) (*pl.* **Vs, V's, v's**) 1. the twenty-second letter of the alphabet. 2. the Roman numeral symbol for 5.

V *abbr.* 1. vector. 2. velocity. 3. Vice. 4. victory. 5. Village. 6. volts.

V *symbol* vanadium.

v. *abbr.* 1. velocity. 2. verb. 3. verse. 4. version. 5. versus. 6. voice. 7. voltage. 8. volts. 9. volume.

VA *abbr.* 1. Veterans Administration. 2. vice admiral. 3. Virginia.

Va. *abbr.* Virginia.

va·can·cy (vay-kăn-see) *n.* (*pl.* **-cies**) 1. the condition of being vacant, emptiness. 2. an unoccupied position of employment, *we have a vacancy for a typist.* 3. unoccupied accommodation, *this hotel has no vacancies.*

va·cant (vay-kănt) *adj.* 1. empty, not filled or occupied, *a vacant seat; applied for a vacant position.* 2. showing no sign of thought or intelligence, having a blank expression. **va'cant·ly** *adv.*

va·cate (vay-kayt) *v.* (**va·cat·ed, va·cat·ing**) to cease to occupy (a place or position).

va·ca·tion (vay-kay-shŏn) *n.* a time of rest and recreation away from one's work or school, a holiday. **vacation** *v.* to spend a holiday. **va·ca'tion·er, va·ca'tion·ist** *n.*

vac·ci·nate (vak-sĭ-nayt) *v.* (**vac·ci·nat·ed, vac·ci·nat·ing**) to inoculate with a vaccine, especially against smallpox. **vac·ci·na·tion** (vak-sĭ-nay-shŏn) *n.*

vac·cine (vak-seen) *n.* 1. a preparation of cowpox virus introduced into a person's bloodstream to immunize him against smallpox. 2. any preparation used similarly to give immunity against an infection.

vac·il·late (vas-ĭ-layt) *v.* 1. to waver, to keep changing one's mind. 2. to swing or sway unsteadily. **vac'il·la·tor** *n.* **vac·il·la·tion** (vas-ĭ-lay-shŏn) *n.*

va·cu·i·ty (va-kyoo-i-tee) *n.* (*pl.* **-ties**) 1. emptiness. 2. vacuousness.

vac·u·ole (vak-yoo-ohl) *n.* a minute cavity in an organ or cell, containing air, fluid, etc. **vac·u·o·lar** (vak-yoo-oh-lăr) *adj.*

vac·u·ous (vak-yoo-ŭs) *adj.* empty-headed, inane, expressionless, *a vacuous stare.* **vac'u·ous·ly** *adv.* **vac'u·ous·ness** *n.*

vac·u·um (vak-yoo-ŭm) *n.* (*pl.* **-u·ums, -u·a**, *pr.* -yoo-ă) 1. space completely empty of matter, space in a container from which the air has been pumped out. 2. absence of normal or previous contents. **vacuum** *v.* (*informal*) to clean with a vacuum cleaner. ▢ **vacuum cleaner**, an electrical appliance that takes up dust, dirt, etc. by suction. **vacuum flask** *or* **bottle**, a flask with a double wall that encloses a vacuum, used for keeping liquids hot or cold. **vacuum pump**, a pump for

producing a vacuum. **vacuum tube**, a sealed tube with an almost perfect vacuum, allowing free passage of electric current.

vac·u·um-packed (vak-yoo-ŭm-pakt, -yoom-) *adj.* sealed in a pack from which most of the air has been removed.

va·de me·cum (vay-dee mee-kŭm) (*pl.* **va·de me·cums**) a handbook or other small useful work of reference. ▷ Latin.

VADM *abbr.* Vice-Admiral.

Va·duz (fah-doots) the capital of Liechtenstein.

vag·a·bond (vag-ă-bond) *n.* a wanderer, a vagrant, especially an idle or dishonest one. **vagabond** *adj.* of or like a vagabond. **vag·a·bond·age** (vag-ă-bon-dij) *n.*

va·gar·y (vă-gair-ee, vay-gă-ree) *n.* (*pl.* **-gar·ies**) a capricious act or idea or fluctuation, *vagaries of fashion.*

va·gi·na (vă-jı-nă) *n.* (*pl.* **-nas, -nae**, *pr.* -nee) the passage leading from the vulva to the womb in women and female animals. **vag·i·nal** (vaj-ĭ-năl) *adj.*

vag·i·ni·tis (vaj-ĭ-nı-tis) *n.* inflammation of the vagina.

va·grant (vay-grănt) *n.* a person without a settled home or regular work. **vagrant** *adj.* 1. wandering, from place to place, itinerant. 2. of vagrants. **va'grant·ly** *adv.* **va·gran·cy** (vay-grăn-see) *n.*

vague (vayg) *adj.* (**vagu·er, vagu·est**) 1. not clearly expressed or perceived or identified. 2. not expressing one's thoughts clearly or precisely. **vague'ly** *adv.* **vague'ness** *n.*

vain (vayn) *adj.* 1. conceited, especially about one's appearance. 2. having no value or significance, *vain triumphs.* 3. useless, futile, *in the vain hope of persuading him.* **vain'ly** *adv.* **vain'ness** *n.* ▢ **in vain**, with no result, uselessly, *we tried, but in vain.* **take God's name in vain**, to use it irreverently.

vain·glo·ry (vayn-glohr-ee) *n.* extreme vanity, boastfulness. **vain·glo·ri·ous** (vayn-glohr-i-ŭs) *adj.*

val. *abbr.* 1. value. 2. valued.

val·ance (val-ans, vay-lăns) *n.* a short curtain around the frame or canopy of a bedstead, or above a window or under a shelf. ▷ Do not confuse *valance* with *valence.*

vale (vayl) *n.* a valley. ▢ **vale of tears**, the world as the scene of life, trouble, etc.

val·e·dic·tion (val-ĕ-dik-shŏn) *n.* saying farewell, the words used in this.

val·e·dic·to·ri·an (val-ĕ-dik-tohr-i-ăn) *n.* the highest ranking member of a graduating class, giving the valedictory oration at commencement exercises.

val·e·dic·to·ry (val-ĕ-dik-tŏ-ree) *adj.* saying farewell, *valedictory remarks.* **valedictory** *n.* (*pl.*

-ries) a valedictory oration, especially in college, usually given by the valedictorian.

va·lence (vay-lĕns) *n.* the capacity of an atom to combine with another or others, as compared with that of the hydrogen atom, *carbon has a valence of four.* ▷Do not confuse *valence* with *valance.*

Va·len·ci·ennes (vă-len-si-enz) *n.* a rich lace. ▷Named for the city in northeastern France where it was made in the 17th–18th centuries.

va·len·cy (vay-lĕn-see) *n.* (*pl.* **-cies**) valence.

val·en·tine (val-ĕn-tɪn) *n.* 1. a sweetheart chosen on St. Valentine's Day (February 14, on which birds were supposed to pair). 2. a card or gift or picture etc. sent on this day (often anonymously) to one's valentine.

va·le·ri·an (vă-leer-i-ăn) *n.* a strong-smelling herb with pink or white flowers.

val·et (val-it, va-lay) *n.* 1. a man's personal attendant who takes care of clothes etc. 2. a hotel employee with similar duties. **valet** *v.* (**val·et·ed, val·et·ing**) to act as valet to. □**valet parking,** (at restaurants etc.) parking service in which an attendant parks patrons' automobiles.

val·e·tu·di·nar·i·an (val-ĕ-too-dĭ-nair-i-ăn) *n.* a person who pays excessive attention to preserving his health. **val·e·tu·di·nar·i·an·ism** *n.*

Val·hal·la (val-hal-ă) *n.* (in Norse mythology) the hall in which the souls of slain heroes feasted.

val·iant (val-yănt) *adj.* brave, courageous. **val'iant·ly** *adv.* **val'ian·cy** *n.*

val·id (val-id) *adj.* 1. having legal force, legally acceptable or usable, *a valid passport.* 2. (of reasoning etc.) sound and to the point, logical. **val'id·ly** *adv.* **val'id·ness** *n.* **va·lid·i·ty** (vă-lid-i-tee) *n.*

val·i·date (val-i-dayt) *v.* (**val·i·dat·ed, val·i·dat·ing**) to make valid, to confirm. **val·i·da·tion** (val-i-day-shŏn) *n.*

va·lise (vă-lees) *n.* a small suitcase.

Va·li·um (val-i-ŭm) *n.* (*trademark*) a tranquilizer.

Val·kyr·ie (val-keer-ee) *n.* (in Norse mythology) one of the war maidens who selected heroes who were to die in battle.

Val·let·ta (vah-let-ă) the capital of Malta.

val·ley (val-ee) *n.* (*pl.* **-leys**) 1. a long low area between hills. 2. a region drained by a river, *the Nile Valley.*

val·or (val-ŏr) *n.* bravery, especially in fighting. **val'or·ous** *adj.* **val'or·ous·ly** *adv.*

val·or·ize (val-ŏ-rɪz) *v.* (**val·or·ized, val·or·iz·ing**) to raise or fix the price of a commodity by artificial means, especially by government action. **val·or·i·za·tion** (val-ŏ-ri-zay-shŏn) *n.*

valse (vahls) *n.* = waltz.

val·u·a·ble (val-yoo-ă-bĕl) *adj.* of great value or price or worth. **valuables** *n. pl.* valuable things, especially small personal possessions. ▷Do not confuse *valuable* with *invaluable.*

val·u·ate (val-yoo-ayt) *v.* (**val·u·at·ed, val·u·at·ing**) to make a valuation of. **val'u·a·tor** *n.*

val·u·a·tion (val-yoo-ay-shŏn) *n.* estimation of a thing's value (especially by a professional appraiser) or of a person's merit, the value decided upon.

val·ue (val-yoo) *n.* 1. the amount of money or other commodity or service etc. considered to be equivalent to something else or for which a thing can be exchanged. 2. desirability, usefulness, importance, *he learned the value of regular exercise.* 3. the ability of a thing to serve a purpose or

cause an effect, *the food value of milk; news value.* 4. the amount or quantity denoted by a figure etc., the duration of a musical sound indicated by a note, the relative importance of each playing card etc. in a game; *tone values in a painting,* the relative lightness and darkness of its parts. 5. *values,* standards or principles considered valuable or important in life, *lack of moral values.* **value** *v.* (**val·ued, val·u·ing**) 1. to estimate the value of. 2. to consider to be of great worth or importance. **val'u·er** *n.*

val·ue-add·ed (val-yoo-ad-id) **tax** tax on the amount by which the value of an article has been increased at each stage of its production.

val·ued (val-yood) *adj.* highly regarded, *a valued friend.*

val·ue·less (val-yoo-lis) *adj.* having no value. ▷Do not confuse *valueless* with *invaluable.*

valve (valv) *n.* 1. a device for controlling the flow of gas or liquid through a pipe. 2. a structure in the heart or in a blood vessel allowing blood to flow in one direction only. 3. a device for varying the length of the tube in a brass wind instrument. 4. each half of the hinged shell of mollusks such as oysters. **valved** *adj.* **valve'less** *adj.*

val·vu·lar (val-vyŭ-lăr) *adj.* of the valves of the heart or blood vessels.

va·moose (va-moos) *v.* (**va·moosed, va·moos·ing**) (*slang*) to go away hurriedly.

vamp[1] (vamp) *n.* 1. the upper front part of a boot or shoe. 2. (in music) a brief accompaniment. **vamp** *v.* 1. to make from odds and ends, *we'll vamp something up.* 2. to improvise a musical accompaniment to a song or dance.

vamp[2] *n.* a seductive woman who uses her attraction to exploit men, an unscrupulous flirt. **vamp** *v.* to exploit or flirt with (a man) unscrupulously.

vam·pire (vam-pɪr) *n.* 1. a ghost or reanimated body supposed to leave a grave at night and suck the blood of living people. 2. a person who preys on others. □**vampire bat,** a tropical bloodsucking bat.

van[1] (van) *n.* 1. a covered vehicle for transporting goods or horses etc. or prisoners, *moving van; police van.* 2. a similar vehicle equipped for camping, recreation, etc.

van[2] *n.* the vanguard, the forefront.

va·na·di·um (vă-nay-di-ŭm) *n.* a hard gray metallic element, used for strengthening some steels.

Van Al·len (van al-ĕn) **belt** one of two regions partly surrounding Earth at heights of several thousand miles, containing intense radiation and many high-energy charged particles.

Van Bu·ren (van byoor-ĕn), **Mar·tin** (1782–1862) the eighth president of the U.S. 1837–41.

van·dal (van-dăl) *n.* 1. a person who willfully or maliciously damages public or private property or the beauties of nature. 2. *Vandal,* a member of a Germanic people who, in the 4th–5th centuries, ravaged Gaul, Spain, North Africa, and Rome, destroying many books and works of art. **van'dal·ism** *n.*

van·dal·ize (van-dăl-ɪz) *v.* (**van·dal·ized, van·dal·iz·ing**) to damage willfully or maliciously, *vandalized the synagogue.*

Van·dyke (van-dɪk) (also **vandyke**) *n.* a neat pointed beard like those in portraits by Van Dyck, a 17th-century portrait painter.

vane (vayn) *n.* 1. a weather vane. 2. the blade of a propeller, sail of a windmill, or similar device acting on or moved by wind or water.

van·guard (van-gahrd) n. 1. the foremost part of an army or fleet advancing or ready to do so. 2. the leaders of a movement or fashion etc.

va·nil·la (vă-nil-ă) n. 1. a flavoring obtained from the pods of a tropical climbing orchid, or made synthetically. 2. this orchid.

van·ish (van-ish) v. to disappear completely. **van′ish·er** n. □**vanishing act,** an unannounced or unauthorized departure; a magician's illusion causing his assistant to appear to vanish. **vanishing point,** the point at which parallel lines viewed in perspective appear to meet.

van·i·ty (van-i-tee) n. (pl. **-ties**) 1. conceit, especially about one's appearance. 2. futility, worthlessness, something vain, *the pomp and vanity of this world.* □**vanity case,** a small bag or case used by a woman for carrying cosmetics etc. **vanity plate,** (informal) an automobile license plate bearing the owner's name or distinctive letters or numbers. **vanity press,** a publisher who will publish anyone's work for a fee.

van·quish (vang-kwish) v. to conquer. **van′quish·er** n.

van·tage (van-tij) n. a superior position or opportunity, *she spoke from the vantage of great experience.* □**vantage point,** a place from which one has a good view of something. ▷ Do not confuse *vantage* with *advantage.*

vap·id (vap-id) adj. insipid, uninteresting. **vap′id·ly** adv. **vap′id·ness** n. **va·pid·i·ty** (va-pid-i-tee) n.

va·por (vay-pŏr) n. 1. moisture or other substance diffused or suspended in air. 2. the airlike substance into which certain liquid or solid substances can be converted by heating (*see* **gas**). **va′por·ish** adj. **va′por·ish·ness** n. □**vapor lock,** a stoppage in the flow of a pump or pipe, caused by an air bubble. **vapor trail,** (of an aircraft or spacecraft in flight) a condensation trail.

va·por·ize (vay-pŏ-rɪz) v. (**va·por·ized, va·por·iz·ing**) to convert or be converted into vapor. **va′por·iz·er** n. **va·por·i·za·tion** (vay-pŏ-ri-zay-shŏn) n.

va·por·ous (vay-pŏ-rŭs), **va·por·y** (vay-pŏ-ree) adj. 1. having the characteristics of a vapor. 2. producing vapor. 3. full of vapor. **va′por·ous·ly** adv. **va′por·ous·ness** n.

va·que·ro (vah-kair-oh) n. (pl. **-ros**) (in South America) a herdsman.

var. abbr. 1. variable. 2. variant. 3. variation. 4. variety. 5. various.

var·i·a·ble (vair-i-ă-běl) adj. varying, changeable, (of a star) periodically varying in brightness. **variable** n. something that varies or can vary, a variable quantity. **var′i·a·bly** adv. **var′i·a·ble·ness** n. **var·i·a·bil·i·ty** (vair-i-ă-bil-i-tee) n.

var·i·ance (vair-i-ăns) n. **at variance,** disagreeing, conflicting, (of people) in a state of discord or enmity.

var·i·ant (vair-i-ănt) adj. differing from something or from a standard, *"gipsy" is a variant spelling of "gypsy."* **variant** n. a variant form or spelling etc.

var·i·a·tion (vair-i-ay-shŏn) n. 1. varying, the extent to which something varies. 2. a variant, a repetition of a melody in a different (usually more elaborate) form.

var·i·col·ored (vair-i-kul-ŏrd) adj. 1. variegated in color. 2. of various or different colors.

var·i·cose (var-ĭ-kohs) adj. (of a vein) permanently swollen or enlarged. **var·i·cos·i·ty** (var-ĭ-kos-i-tee) n.

var·ied (vair-eed) *see* **vary.** **varied** adj. of different sorts, full of variety.

var·i·e·gat·ed (vair-i-ĕ-gay-tid) adj. marked with irregular patches of different colors. **var·i·e·ga·tion** (vair-i-ĕ-gay-shŏn) n.

va·ri·e·tal (vă-rɪ-ĕ-tăl) adj. of or relating to a variety. **va·ri′e·tal·ly** adv.

va·ri·e·ty (vă-rɪ-ĕ-tee) n. (pl. **-ties**) 1. the quality of not being the same or of not being the same at all times. 2. a quantity or range of different things, *for a variety of reasons.* 3. a class of things that differ from others in the same general group, a member of such a class, *several varieties of spaniel.* 4. an entertainment (also **variety show**) consisting of a series of short performances of different kinds (such as singing, dancing, acrobatics). □**variety meats,** the edible parts of animals other than the flesh. **variety store,** a store selling many kinds of small items.

var·i·form (vair-ĭ-form) adj. having various forms.

va·ri·o·la (vă-rɪ-ŏ-lă) n. smallpox.

var·i·o·rum (vair-i-ohr-ŭm) adj. with notes of various editors or commentators or with various versions of a text, *a variorum edition of Horace.* **variorum** n. a variorum edition.

var·i·ous (vair-i-ŭs) adj. 1. of several kinds, unlike one another. 2. more than one, individual and separate, *we met various people.* **var′i·ous·ly** adv. **var′i·ous·ness** n.

var·let (vahr-lit) n. (old use) 1. a knight's attendant. 2. a menial, a low fellow, a rascal.

var·mint (vahr-mint) n. (informal) 1. a mischievous or discreditable person. 2. an objectionable animal or bird or insect.

var·nish (vahr-nish) n. a liquid that dries to form a hard shiny transparent coating, used on wood or metal etc. **varnish** v. to coat with varnish.

var·si·ty (vahr-si-tee) n. (pl. **-ties**) the team representing a school, college, etc. in a sport, *the football varsity.* **varsity** adj. of such a team, *varsity football.*

va·ry (vair-ee) v. (**var·ied, var·y·ing**) 1. to make or become different, *you can vary the pressure; his temper varies from day to day.* 2. to be different or of different kinds, *opinions vary on this point.* **var′y·ing·ly** adv.

vas·cu·lar (vas-kyū-lăr) adj. consisting of vessels or ducts for conveying blood or sap within an organism, *vascular system.*

vase (vays, vayz, vahz) n. an open usually tall vessel of glass, pottery, etc. used for holding cut flowers or as an ornament.

vas·ec·to·my (va-sek-tŏ-mee) n. (pl. **-mies**) surgical removal of part of each of the ducts through which semen passes from the testicles, especially as a method of birth control.

Vas·e·line (vas-ĕ-leen) n. (trademark) petroleum jelly used as an ointment or lubricant.

vas·o·mo·tor (vas-oh-moh-tŏr) adj. causing constriction or dilation of the blood vessels.

vas·sal (vas-ăl) n. (in feudal times) a humble servant or subordinate.

vas·sal·age (vas-ă-lij) n. 1. the condition or service of a vassal. 2. land held by a vassal.

vast (vast) adj. 1. immense, very great in area or size, *a vast expanse of water.* 2. (informal) very great, *it makes a vast difference.* **vast′ly** adv. **vast′ness** n.

vat (vat) n. a tank or other great vessel for holding liquids.

VAT, V.A.T. abbr. value-added tax.

Vat·i·can (vat-i-kăn) n. 1. the pope's official residence in Rome. 2. the papal government. ☐**Vatican City,** an independent papal state in Rome, including the Vatican and St. Peter's Church.

vaude·ville (vawd-vil) *n.* variety entertainment.

vaude·vil·lian (vawd-vil-yăn) *n.* a performer of vaudeville.

vault[1] **(vawlt)** *n.* 1. an arched roof. 2. a vaultlike covering; *the vault of heaven,* the sky. 3. a cellar or underground room used as a place of storage. 4. a burial chamber, *the family vault.* **vault** *v.* to form into or cover with a vault.

vault[2] *v.* to jump or leap, especially while resting on the hand(s) or with the help of a pole, *vaulted the gate* or *over the gate.* **vault** *n.* a leap performed in this way. **vault'er** *n.*

vault·ed (vawl-tid) *adj.* 1. covered with a vault. 2. made in the form of a vault.

vault·ing (vawl-ting) *n.* the structure forming a vault.

vaunt (vawnt) *v.* to boast. **vaunt** *n.* a boast. **vaunt'ed** *adj.*

vb. *abbr.* verb.

VC *abbr.* Vietcong.

VD *abbr.* venereal disease.

V-Day (vee-day) *n.* a day of victory.

veal (veel) *n.* calf's flesh as food.

vec·tor (vek-tŏr) *n.* 1. something (such as velocity) that has both magnitude and direction. 2. the carrier of a disease or infection. **vec·to·ri·al** (vek-tohr-i-ăl) *adj.*

Ve·da (vay-dă) *n.* the ancient Hindu scriptures, especially the Rig-Veda, Sama-Veda, Yajur-Veda, and Artharva-Veda. **Ve'dic** *adj.*

V-E (vee-ee) **Day** May 8, 1945, the day of victory in Europe for the Allies in World War II.

veep (veep) *n.* *(informal)* vice president.

veer (veer) *v.* to change direction or course, (of wind) to change gradually in a clockwise direction. **veer** *n.* a change in direction. **veer'ing·ly** *adv.*

veer·y (veer-ee) *n.* (*pl.* **veer·ies**) a thrush of the eastern U.S.

Ve·ga (vay-gă) *n.* a first magnitude star in the constellation Lyra.

veg·an (vej-an) *n.* a strict vegetarian who eats no animal products (such as eggs) at all. **veg'an·ism** *n.*

veg·e·ta·ble (vej-tă-bĕl, vej-ĕ-) *n.* 1. a plant of which some part is used (raw or cooked) as food, especially as an accompaniment to meat. 2. a person leading a dull monotonous life, one who is physically alive but mentally inert owing to injury or illness or abnormality. **vegetable** *adj.* of or from or relating to plant life.

veg·e·tal (vej-ĕ-tăl) *adj.* 1. of the nature of plants. 2. vegetative.

veg·e·tar·i·an (vej-ĕ-**tair**-i-ăn) *n.* a person who eats no meat. **veg·e·tar'i·an·ism** *n.*

veg·e·tate (vej-ĕ-tayt) *v.* (**veg·e·tat·ed, veg·e·tat·ing**) to live an uneventful or monotonous life.

veg·e·ta·tion (vej-ĕ-**tay**-shŏn) *n.* 1. plants collectively. 2. vegetating. **veg·e·ta'tion·al** *adj.*

veg·e·ta·tive (vej-ĕ-tay-tiv) *adj.* 1. of vegetation. 2. concerned with growth and development, as opposed to sexual reproduction. 3. living an uneventful or monotonous life.

ve·he·ment (vee-ĕ-mĕnt) *adj.* showing strong feeling, intense, *a vehement denial.* **ve'he·ment·ly** *adv.* **ve'he·mence** *n.* **ve·he·men·cy** (vee-ĕ-mĕn-see) *n.*

ve·hi·cle (vee-i-kĕl) *n.* 1. a conveyance for transporting passengers or goods on land or in space. 2. a means by which something is expressed or displayed, *art can be a vehicle for propaganda; the play was an excellent vehicle for this actress's talents.*

ve·hic·u·lar (vee-**hik**-yŭ-lăr) *adj.* of vehicles, *vehicular traffic.*

V-eight, V-8 (vee-ayt) an internal combustion engine with four cylinders on each side of the block, arranged in the form of a V.

veil (vayl) *n.* a piece of fine net or other fabric worn as part of a headdress or to protect or conceal the face. **veil** *v.* to cover with or as if with a veil; *a veiled threat,* partially concealed. ☐**beyond the veil,** in the unknown state of life after death. **draw a veil over,** to avoid discussing or calling attention to. **take the veil,** to become a nun.

veil·ing (vay-ling) *n.* thin material for making veils.

vein (vayn) *n.* 1. one of the tubes carrying blood from all parts of the body to the heart. 2. one of the threadlike structures forming the framework of a leaf or of an insect's wing. 3. a narrow strip or streak of a different color, as in marble. 4. a long continuous or branching deposit of mineral or ore, especially in a fissure. 5. a mood or manner, *she spoke in a humorous vein.* **vein'ing** *n.*

veined (vaynd) *adj.* filled or marked with veins.

vel. *abbr.* 1. vellum. 2. velocity.

ve·lar (vee-lăr) *adj.* 1. of a veil or vellum. 2. (of sound) pronounced with the back of the tongue near the soft palate.

Vel·cro (vel-kroh) *n.* *(trademark)* a nylon tape with tiny fibers that adhere easily to other surfaces, used to fasten clothing etc.

veld, veldt (velt, felt) *n.* open grassland in South Africa.

vel·le·i·ty (vĕ-lee-i-tee) *n.* (*pl.* **-ties**) 1. a low degree of volition not prompting to action. 2. a slight wish or inclination.

vel·lum (vel-ŭm) *n.* 1. a kind of fine parchment. 2. smooth writing paper.

ve·loc·i·pede (vĕ-los-ĭ-peed) *n.* a light vehicle propelled by a rider, especially a child's tricycle.

ve·loc·i·ty (vĕ-los-i-tee) *n.* (*pl.* **-ties**) speed, especially in a given direction.

ve·lour (vĕ-loor) *n.* a plushlike fabric.

ve·lum (vee-lŭm) *n.* (*pl.* **-la,** *pr.* **-lă**) a membrane or membranous covering, especially the soft palate.

vel·vet (vel-vit) *n.* 1. a woven fabric (especially of silk or nylon) with thick short pile on one side. 2. a furry skin covering a growing antler. **vel'vet·y** *adj.* ☐**all velvet,** all profit. **in** *or* **on velvet,** in an advantageous or prosperous position. **velvet glove,** outward gentleness of treatment cloaking inflexibility.

vel·vet·een (vel-vĕ-teen) *n.* cotton velvet.

ven. *abbr.* venerable.

ve·nal (vee-năl) *adj.* 1. able to be bribed. 2. (of conduct) influenced by bribery. **ve'nal·ly** *adv.* **ve·nal·i·ty** (vee-nal-i-tee) *n.* ▷Do not confuse *venal* with *venial.*

vend (vend) *v.* to sell or offer for sale. **vend'i·ble** *adj.* ☐**vending machine,** a slot machine where small articles can be obtained.

ven·det·ta (ven-det-ă) *n.* a feud.

ven·dor (ven-dŏr) *n.* 1. a person who sells something. 2. a vending machine.

ve·neer (vĕ-neer) *n.* 1. a thin layer of finer wood

covering the surface of cheaper wood in furniture etc. 2. a superficial show of some good quality, *a veneer of politeness.* **veneer** *v.* to cover with a veneer.

ven·er·a·ble (ven-ĕ-ră-bĕl) *adj.* 1. worthy of deep respect because of age or associations etc., *these venerable ruins.* 2. the title of an archdeacon in the Church of England. **ven′er·a·bly** *adv.* **ven·er·a·bil·i·ty** (ven-ĕ-ră-bil-i-tee) *n.*

ven·er·ate (ven-ĕ-rayt) *v.* **(ven·er·at·ed, ven·er·at·ing)** to regard with deep respect, to honor as hallowed or sacred. **ven·er·a·tion** (ven-ĕ-ray-shŏn) *n.*

ve·ne·re·al (vĕ-neer-i-ăl) *adj.* (of disease or infection) contracted by sexual intercourse with a person who is already infected.

Ve·ne·tian (vĕ-nee-shăn) *adj.* of Venice. □**Venetian blind,** a window blind consisting of horizontal slats that can be adjusted to let in or exclude light.

Ven·e·zue·la (ven-ĕ-zway-lă) a country in South America. **Ven·e·zue′lan** *adj. & n.*

venge·ance (ven-jăns) *n.* retaliation for hurt or harm done to oneself or to a person etc. whom one supports. □**take vengeance,** to inflict harm in retaliation. **with a vengeance,** in an extreme degree.

venge·ful (venj-fŭl) *adj.* seeking vengeance. **venge′ful·ly** *adv.* **venge′ful·ness** *n.*

V-en·gine (vee-en-jin) *n.* an internal combustion engine in which the two cylinder blocks are arranged in the form of a V.

ve·ni·al (vee-ni-ăl) *adj.* (of a sin or fault) pardonable, not serious. **ve′ni·al·ly** *adv.* ▷Do not confuse *venial* with *venal.*

ven·i·punc·ture (ven-i-pungk-chŭr) *n.* the puncture of a vein, especially with a hypodermic needle, to withdraw blood or for intravenous injection.

ve·ni·re (vi-nɪ-ree) *n.* 1. (also **venire fa·ci·as,** *pr.* fay-shi-ăs) a writ directing a sheriff to summon people for a jury. 2. a panel of people thus summoned.

ve·ni·re·man (vi-nɪ-ri-măn) *n.* (*pl.* **-men,** *pr.* -mĕn) a person summoned under a writ of venire.

ven·i·son (ven-i-sŏn) *n.* deer's flesh as food.

ven·om (ven-ŏm) *n.* 1. poisonous fluid secreted by certain snakes, scorpions, etc. and injected into a victim by a bite or sting. 2. strong bitter feeling or language, hatred.

ven·om·ous (ven-ŏ-mŭs) *adj.* 1. secreting venom, *venomous snakes.* 2. full of bitter feeling or hatred, *venomous words.* **ven′om·ous·ly** *adv.*

vent¹ (vent) *n.* a slit in a garment (especially a coat or jacket) at the bottom of a back or side seam.

vent² *n.* an opening allowing air or gas or liquid to pass out of or into a confined space, *a smoke vent.* **vent** *v.* 1. to make a vent in. 2. to give vent to, *vented his anger on the office boy.* □**give vent to,** to give an outlet to (feelings etc.), to express freely, *gave vent to his anger.*

ven·ti·late (ven-tĭ-layt) *v.* **(ven·ti·lat·ed, ven·ti·lat·ing)** 1. to cause air to enter or circulate freely in (a room etc.). 2. to express (an opinion etc.) publicly so that others may consider and discuss it. **ven·ti·la·tion** (ven-tĭ-lay-shŏn) *n.*

ven·ti·la·tor (ven-tĭ-lay-tŏr) *n.* a device for ventilating a room etc.

ven·tral (ven-trăl) *adj.* of or on the abdomen, *this fish has a ventral fin.* **ven′tral·ly** *adv.*

ven·tri·cle (ven-tri-kĕl) *n.* a cavity or chamber in

an organ of the body, especially one of the two in the heart that pump blood into the arteries by contracting. **ven·tric·u·lar** (ven-trik-yŭ-lăr) *adj.*

ven·tril·o·quist (ven-tril-ŏ-kwist) *n.* an entertainer who produces voice sounds so that they seem to come from a source other than himself. **ven·tril′o·quism** *n.* **ven·tril·o·quy** (ven-tril-ŏ-kwee) *n.*

ven·ture (ven-chŭr) *n.* an undertaking that involves risk. **venture** *v.* **(ven·tured, ven·tur·ing)** 1. to dare, *did not venture to stop him.* 2. to dare to go or do or utter, *did not venture forth; ventured an opinion.* **ven′tur·er** *n.* □**venture capital,** money invested in an enterprise, especially a new one.

ven·ture·some (ven-chŭr-sŏm) *adj.* ready to take risks, daring. **ven′ture·some·ly** *adv.* **ven′ture·some·ness** *n.*

ven·tur·ous (ven-chŭ-rŭs) *adj.* venturesome. **ven′tur·ous·ly** *adv.* **ven′tur·ous·ness** *n.*

ven·ue (ven-yoo) *n.* 1. an appointed place of meeting. 2. (in law) the county etc. within which a jury must be gathered and a case tried (originally the area in which the crime etc. occurred).

Ve·nus (vee-nŭs) *n.* 1. the goddess of love in Roman mythology. 2. a planet in the solar system. **Ve·nu·si·an** (vĕ-noo-si-ăn) *adj. & n.* □**Venus** or **Venus's flytrap,** an herb with leaves that close on insects etc.

ver. *abbr.* 1. verse. 2. version.

ve·ra·cious (vĕ-ray-shŭs) *adj.* 1. truthful. 2. true. **ve·ra′cious·ly** *adv.* **ve·ra′cious·ness** *n.* **ve·rac·i·ty** (vĕ-ras-i-tee) *n.* (*pl.* **-ties**).

ve·ran·da (vĕ-ran-dă) *n.* a roofed porch along the side of a house.

verb (vurb) *n.* a word or words indicating action or occurrence or being, as *bring, came, exist, are fighting, have sat.* **verb′less** *adj.*

ver·bal (vur-băl) *adj.* 1. of or in words, *verbal accuracy.* 2. spoken, not written, *a verbal statement.* (▷Careful writers do not use *verbal* in this sense. *We gave them oral instructions because they were illiterate* makes clear the distinction between *verbal* and *oral.*) 3. of a verb, *verbal inflections.* **verbal** *n.* a verbal noun. **ver′bal·ly** *adv.* □**verbal noun,** a noun (such as *singing, drinking*) derived from a verb.

ver·bal·ize (vur-bă-lɪz) *v.* **(ver·bal·ized, ver·bal·iz·ing)** to put into words. **ver·bal·i·za·tion** (vur-bă-li-zay-shŏn) *n.*

ver·ba·tim (vĕr-bay-tim) *adv. & adj.* in exactly the same words, word for word, *copied it verbatim; a verbatim account.*

ver·be·na (vĕr-bee-nă) *n.* a plant having clusters of brightly colored flowers. □**lemon verbena,** a similar plant with lemon-scented leaves.

ver·bi·age (vur-bee-ij) *n.* an excessive number of words used to express an idea.

ver·bose (vĕr-bohs) *adj.* using more words than are needed. **ver·bose′ly** *adv.* **ver·bose′ness** *n.* **ver·bos·i·ty** (vĕr-bos-i-tee) *n.*

ver·bo·ten (vĕr-boh-tĕn) *adj.* forbidden, especially by authority. ▷German.

ver·dant (vur-dănt) *adj.* (of grass or fields) green. **ver′dant·ly** *adv.*

ver·dict (vur-dikt) *n.* 1. the decision reached by a jury. 2. a decision or opinion given after examining or testing or experiencing something.

ver·di·gris (vur-dĭ-grees, -gris) *n.* green rust on copper or brass or bronze.

ver·dure (vur-jŭr) *n.* green vegetation, its greenness.

verge (vurj) *n.* 1. the extreme edge or brink of something. 2. the point beyond which something new begins or occurs, *on the verge of ruin.* **verge** *v.* **(verged, verg·ing) verge on,** to border on, to approach closely.

ver·ger (vur-jĕr) *n.* 1. (chiefly *British*) a sexton. 2. an official who carries the mace etc. before a bishop or other dignitary.

ver·i·fy (ver-ĭ-fɪ) *v.* **(ver·i·fied, ver·i·fy·ing)** to check the truth or correctness of, *please verify these figures.* **ver'i·fi·a·ble** *adj.* **ver'i·fi·er** *n.*

ver·i·fi·ca·tion (ver-ĭ-fĭ-kay-shŏn) *n.*

ver·i·ly (ver-ĭ-lee) *adv. (old use)* in truth.

ver·i·si·mil·i·tude (ver-i-si-mil-i-tood) *n.* an appearance of being true.

ver·i·ta·ble (ver-i-tă-bĕl) *adj.* real, rightly named, *a veritable villain.* **ver'i·ta·bly** *adv.*

ver·i·ty (ver-i-tee) *n.* (*pl.* **-ties**) *(old use)* the truth of something, *the old verities.*

ver·meil (vur-mil) *n.* 1. silver gilt. 2. an orange-red garnet. 3. vermilion red.

ver·mi·cel·li (vur-mi-chel-ee) *n.* pasta made in long slender threads.

ver·mic·u·lite (vĕr-mik-yŭ-lɪt) *n.* a mineral usually resulting from the alteration of mica under heat.

ver·mi·form (vur-mĭ-form) *adj.* wormlike in shape, *the vermiform appendix.*

ver·mi·fuge (vur-mĭ-fyooj) *n.* a drug that expels intestinal worms.

ver·mil·ion (vĕr-mil-yŏn) *n. & adj.* bright red.

ver·min (vur-min) *n. pl.* 1. small annoying and often harmful animals or insects, such as cockroaches, rats, mice, or lice. 2. people who are unpleasant or harmful to society.

ver·min·ous (vur-mĭ-nŭs) *adj.* infested with vermin.

Ver·mont (vĕr-mont) a state of the U.S. **Ver·mont'er** *n.*

ver·mouth (vĕr-mooth) *n.* white wine flavored with fragrant herbs.

ver·nac·u·lar (vĕr-nak-yŭ-lăr) *n.* 1. the language of a country or district. 2. everyday speech. **vernacular** *adj.* **ver·nac'u·lar·ly** *adv.*

ver·nal (vur-năl) *adj.* of or occurring in the season of spring. **ver'nal·ly** *adv.* □**vernal equinox,** *see* **equinox.**

ver·nal·ize (vur-nă-lɪz) *v.* **(ver·nal·ized, ver·nal·iz·ing)** to cool (seeds) before planting in order to accelerate flowering. **ver·nal·i·za·tion** (vur-nă-li-zay-shŏn) *n.*

ver·ni·er (vur-ni-ĕr) *n.* a small movable graduated scale for obtaining fractional parts of the subdivisions on a fixed scale of a barometer, sextant, etc.

ve·ron·i·ca (vĕ-ron-ĭ-kă) *n.* an herb often with blue flowers, speedwell.

ver·ru·ca (vĕ-roo-kă) *n.* (*pl.* **-cae,** *pr.* -see) a wart.

ver·sa·tile (vur-să-til) *adj.* able to do, or be used for, many different things. **ver'sa·tile·ly** *adv.* **ver·sa·til·i·ty** (vur-să-til-i-tee) *n.*

verse (vurs) *n.* 1. a metrical form of composition, as distinct from prose. 2. a metrical composition. 3. an author's metrical or poetical works. 4. a group of lines forming a unit in a poem or hymn. 5. each of the short numbered divisions of a chapter of the Bible.

versed (vurst) *adj.* **versed in,** experienced or skilled in, having a knowledge of.

ver·si·cle (vur-si-kĕl) *n.* each of the short sentences in the liturgy, said or sung by the clergyman and alternating with the "responses" of the congregation.

ver·si·fy (vur-sĭ-fɪ) *v.* **(ver·si·fied, ver·si·fy·ing)** 1. to turn prose into verse. 2. to express in verse. 3. to compose verses. **ver'si·fi·er** *n.*

ver·si·fi·ca·tion (vur-sĭ-fĭ-kay-shŏn) *n.*

ver·sion (vur-zhŏn) *n.* 1. a particular person's account of a matter. 2. a translation into another language, *the Revised Version of the Bible.* 3. a special or variant form of a thing, *the deluxe version of this car.* **ver'sion·al** *adj.*

vers li·bre (vair lee-brĕ) verse with no regular metrical pattern. ▷French, = free verse.

ver·so (vur-soh) *n.* (*pl.* **-sos**) the left-hand page of an open book.

ver·sus (vur-sŭs) *prep.* against, *Notre Dame versus Purdue.*

vert. *abbr.* vertical.

ver·te·bra (vur-tĕ-bră) *n.* (*pl.* **-brae,** *pr.* -bree, **-bras**) any of the individual bones or segments that form the backbone. **ver'te·bral** *adj.* □**vertebral column,** a spinal column.

ver·te·brate (vur-tĕ-brayt, -brit) *n.* an animal that has a backbone. **vertebrate** *adj.* of such an animal.

ver·tex (vur-teks) *n.* (*pl.* **-tex·es, -ti·ces,** *pr.* -ti-seez) the highest point of a hill or structure, the apex of a cone or triangle. ▷Do not confuse *vertex* with *vortex.*

ver·ti·cal (vur-ti-kĕl) *adj.* 1. perpendicular to the horizontal, moving or placed in this way, upright. 2. in the direction from top to bottom of a picture etc. **vertical** *n.* a vertical line or part or position. **ver'ti·cal·ly** *adv.* **ver'ti·cal·ness** *n.* **ver·ti·cal·i·ty** (vur-ti-kal-i-tee) *n.*

ver·ti·gi·nous (vĕr-tij-ĭ-nŭs) *adj.* 1. causing vertigo. 2. whirling. 3. affected with vertigo. **ver·tig'i·nous·ly** *adv.*

ver·ti·go (vur-tĭ-goh) *n.* (*pl.* **ver·ti·goes**) a sensation of dizziness and a feeling of losing one's balance.

ver·vain (vur-vayn) *n.* a tall wild plant with hairy leaves and small white or blue or purple flowers.

verve (vurv) *n.* enthusiasm, liveliness, vigor.

ver·y (ver-ee) *adv.* 1. in a high degree, extremely, *very good.* 2. in the fullest sense, *drink it to the very last drop.* 3. exactly, *sat in the very same seat.* **very** *adj.* 1. itself or himself etc. and no other, actual, truly such, *it's the very thing we need!* 2. extreme, utter, *at the very end.* □**very high frequency,** a frequency in the range of 30 to 300 megahertz. **very low frequency,** a frequency between 10 and 30 kilohertz. **very well,** an expression of consent.

ves·i·cant (ves-i-kănt) *adj.* producing blisters. **vesicant** *n.* a substance that acts in this way.

ves·i·cle (ves-i-kĕl) *n.* 1. a small hollow structure in a plant or animal body. 2. a blister. **ve·sic·u·lar** (vĕ-sik-yŭ-lăr) *adj.* **ve·sic·u·late** (vĕ-sik-yŭ-lit) *adj.*

ves·per (ves-pĕr) *adj.* of evening, of vespers.

ves·pers (ves-pĕrz) *n. pl.* (also **Vespers**) a church service held in the evening, evensong.

ves·per·tine (ves-pĕr-tin) *adj.* of or occurring in or active in the evening.

ves·sel (ves-ĕl) *n.* 1. a structure designed to travel on water and carry people or goods, a ship or boat. 2. a hollow receptacle, especially for liquid. 3. a tubelike structure in the body of an animal or plant, conveying or holding blood or other fluid.

vest (vest) *n.* 1. a man's close-fitting waist-length sleeveless collarless garment buttoned down the front, usually worn over a shirt and under a jacket. 2. a woman's similar garment. **vest** *v.* 1. to confer as a firm or legal right, *the power of making laws is vested in the legislature; the legislature is vested with this power.* 2. to clothe, especially with ecclesiastical vestments. ☐**vested interest,** an advantageous right that is securely held by a person or group.

ves·tal (ves-tăl) *adj.* 1. of the Roman goddess Vesta or of the vestal virgins. 2. chaste. **vestal** *n.* a chaste woman. **ves'tal·ly** *adv.* ☐**vestal virgin,** (in ancient Rome) one of the virgins consecrated to the goddess Vesta and tending the sacred fire kept burning in her temple.

ves·ti·bule (ves-tĭ-byool) *n.* 1. an entrance hall or lobby of a building. 2. a church porch. 3. a cavity forming an entrance to another in the body. **ves·tib·u·lar** (ves-tib-yŭ-lăr) *adj.*

ves·tige (ves-tij) *n.* 1. a trace, a small remaining bit of what once existed, *not a vestige of the abbey remains.* 2. a very small amount, *not a vestige of truth in it.*

ves·tig·i·al (ves-tij-i-ăl) *adj.* remaining as a vestige of what once existed. **ves·tig'i·al·ly** *adv.*

vest·ing (ves-ting) *n.* 1. a heavy or medium weight cloth with ridges, used for garments. 2. the granting to an employee of rights to pension benefits without regard to future employment status.

vest·ment (vest-měnt) *n.* a ceremonial robe or other garment, especially one worn by clergy or choir at a religious service.

vest-pock·et (vest-pok-ět) *adj.* 1. suitable for carrying in the vest pocket, *a vest-pocket notebook.* 2. very small, *a vest-pocket park.*

ves·try (ves-tree) *n.* (*pl.* **-tries**) 1. a room or building attached to a church, where vestments are kept and where clergy and choir robe themselves. 2. a chapel or meeting room in some churches. 3. (in the Protestant Episcopal Church) a committee responsible for the temporal affairs of a parish.

vet[1] (vet) *n.* *(informal)* a veterinarian. **vet** *v.* (**vet·ted, vet·ting**) to examine carefully and critically for faults or errors etc, *vetted the manuscript.*

vet[2] *n.* *(informal)* a veteran.

vet. *abbr.* 1. veteran. 2. veterinarian. 3. veterinary.

vetch (vech) *n.* a plant of the pea family, used as fodder for cattle.

vet·er·an (vet-ĕ-răn) *n.* 1. a person with long experience. 2. a person who has served in the armed forces. **veteran** *adj.* ☐**Veterans Day,** November 11, a U.S. holiday in honor of all veterans of the armed services. **Veterans of Foreign Wars of the United States,** a society for veterans who served overseas in wartime.

vet·er·i·nar·i·an (vet-ĕr-ĭ-nair-i-ăn) *n.* a veterinary surgeon or physician.

vet·er·i·nar·y (vet-ĕr-ĭ-ner-ee) *adj.* of or for the treatment of diseases and disorders of farm and domestic animals, *veterinary medicine.*

ve·to (vee-toh) *n.* (*pl.* **-toes**) 1. an authoritative rejection or prohibition of something that is proposed. 2. the right to make such a rejection or prohibition. **veto** *v.* (**ve·toed, ve·to·ing**) to reject or prohibit authoritatively. **ve'to·er** *n.*

vex (veks) *v.* to annoy, to irritate, to cause worry to (a person).

vex·a·tion (vek-say-shŏn) *n.* 1. vexing, being vexed, a state of irritation or worry. 2. something that causes this.

vex·a·tious (vek-say-shŭs) *adj.* causing vexation, annoying. **vex·a'tious·ly** *adv.* **vex·a'tious·ness** *n.*

VF *abbr.* voice frequency.

VFD *abbr.* volunteer fire department.

VFW *abbr.* Veterans of Foreign Wars.

VHF *abbr.* very high frequency.

VI, V.I. *abbr.* Virgin Islands.

v.i. *abbr.* verb intransitive.

vi·a (vi-ă, vee-ă) *prep.* by way of, through, *from Des Moines to Cheyenne via Omaha.*

vi·a·ble (vi-ă-bĕl) *adj.* 1. (of a fetus) sufficiently developed to be able to survive after birth. 2. (of plants) able to live or grow. 3. practicable, able to exist successfully, *a viable plan; is the newly created state viable?* **vi'a·bly** *adv.* **vi·a·bil·i·ty** (vi-ă-bil-i-tee) *n.*

vi·a·duct (vi-ă-dukt) *n.* a long bridgelike structure (usually with a series of arches) for carrying a road or railroad over a valley or dip in the ground.

vi·al (vi-ăl) *n.* a small bottle, especially for liquid medicine.

vi·and (vi-ănd) *n.* (usually **viands**) an article of food, *delectable viands were provided.*

vi·at·i·cum (vi-at-ĭ-kŭm) *n.* (*pl.* **-ca,** *pr.* **-kă, -cums**) 1. the Eucharist as given to a person in danger of dying. 2. provisions or an official allowance of money for a journey.

vibes (vibz) *n. pl.* 1. *(informal)* a vibraharp. 2. *(slang)* mental or emotional vibrations; *bad vibes,* an impression of bad feelings or presentiments.

vi·bra·harp (vi-bră-hahrp) *n.* a musical instrument with metal bars played with mallets, also having an electronic resonator.

vi·brant (vi-brănt) *adj.* vibrating, resonant, thrilling with energy or activity. **vi'brant·ly** *adv.* **vi·bran·cy** (vi-brăn-see) *n.*

vi·bra·phone (vi-bră-fohn) *n.* a vibraharp.

vi·brate (vi-brayt) *v.* (**vi·brat·ed, vi·brat·ing**) 1. to move rapidly and continuously to and fro. 2. to resound, to sound with a rapid slight variation of pitch.

vi·bra·tion (vi-bray-shŏn) *n.* 1. a vibrating movement or sensation or sound. 2. *vibrations,* mental stimuli thought to be given out by a person or place etc., the emotional sensations these produce. **vi·bra'tion·al** *adj.*

vi·bra·to (vi-brah-toh) *n.* (*pl.* **-tos**) a vibrating effect in music, with rapid slight variation of pitch.

vi·bra·tor (vi-bray-tŏr) *n.* a device that vibrates or causes vibration.

vi·bra·to·ry (vi-bră-tohr-ee) *adj.* causing vibration.

vi·bur·num (vi-bur-nŭm) *n.* a kind of shrub, usually with white flowers.

vic. *abbr.* vicinity.

vic·ar (vik-ăr) *n.* 1. (in the Church of England) a clergyman in charge of a parish. 2. (in the Protestant Episcopal Church) a minister in charge of a chapel in a parish. 3. (in the Roman Catholic Church) a church official who is a deputy for a bishop or the pope. ☐**Vicar of Christ,** the pope.

vic·ar·age (vik-ă-rij) *n.* the house of a vicar.

vi·car·i·ous (vi-kair-i-ŭs) *adj.* (of feelings or emotions) felt through sharing imaginatively in the feelings or activities etc. of another person, *vicarious pleasure.* **vi·car'i·ous·ly** *adv.* **vi·car'i·ous·ness** *n.*

vice¹ (vis) *n.* 1. evil or grossly immoral conduct, great wickedness. 2. a particular form of this, a fault or bad habit, *smoking isn't one of my vices.* 3. criminal and immoral practices such as prostitution. □**vice squad,** a division of police enforcing laws against prostitution etc.

vice² *prep.* in place of, *Mr. Smith has been appointed as chief accountant vice Mr. Brown, who has retired.*

vice- *prefix* (usually written without the hyphen) acting as substitute or deputy for, as in *viceroy;* next in rank to, as in *vice-consul.*

vice ad·mi·ral (vis ad-mĭ-răl) a naval officer next in rank below an admiral.

vice-con·sul (vis-kon-sŭl) *n.* a consular officer next in rank below the consul.

vi·cen·ni·al (vi-sen-i-ăl) *adj.* lasting, or occurring every, twenty years.

vice pres·i·dent (vis prez-i-děnt) the official next in rank to the president. **vice pres·i·den·cy** (vis prez-i-děn-see) **vice pres·i·den·tial** (vis prez-i-den-shăl).

vice·re·gal (vis-ree-găl) *adj.* of a viceroy. **vice·re'gal·ly** *adv.*

vice·roy (vis-roi) *n.* a person governing a colony or province etc. as the sovereign's representative. **vice·roy·al·ty** (vis-roi-ăl-tee) *n.*

vice ver·sa (vis vur-să) the other way around, *we gossip about them and vice versa* (= and they gossip about us).

vi·chy·ssoise (vish-ee-swahz) *n.* a creamy soup of leeks and potatoes, served chilled.

Vi·chy (vish-ee) **water** 1. fizzy mineral water from Vichy in central France. 2. any water like this.

vi·cin·i·ty (vi-sin-i-tee) *n.* (*pl.* **-ties**) the surrounding district; *there is no good school in the vicinity, near by.*

vi·cious (vish-ŭs) *adj.* 1. acting or done with evil intentions, brutal, strongly spiteful. 2. (of animals) savage and dangerous, bad-tempered. 3. severe, *a vicious wind.* **vi'cious·ly** *adv.* **vi'cious·ness** *n.* □**vicious circle,** a state of affairs in which a cause produces an effect that itself produces or intensifies the original cause. **vicious spiral,** a similar continual interaction, as one causing a steady increase of prices and wages, hostility between nations, etc.

vi·cis·si·tude (vi-sis-i-tood) *n.* a change of circumstances affecting one's life.

vic·tim (vik-tim) *n.* 1. a person who is injured or killed by another or as the result of an occurrence, *victims of the earthquake.* 2. a person who suffers because of a trick. 3. a living creature killed and offered as a religious sacrifice.

vic·tim·ize (vik-tĭ-miz) *v.* (**vic·tim·ized, vic·tim·iz·ing**) to make a victim of, to single out (a person) to suffer ill treatment. **vic'tim·iz·er** *n.* **vic·tim·i·za·tion** (vik-tĭ-mi-zay-shŏn) *n.*

vic·tim·less (vik-tim-lis) *adj.* without a victim. □**victimless crime,** a crime not involving injury to a person.

vic·tor (vik-tŏr) *n.* the winner in a battle or contest.

vic·to·ri·a (vik-tohr-i-ă) *n.* a low light four-wheeled carriage with a seat for two, a raised driver's seat, and a collapsible top.

Vic·to·ri·an (vik-tohr-i-ăn) *adj.* 1. belonging to or characteristic of the reign of Queen Victoria (1837–1901) in England. 2. prudish. **Victorian** *n.* a person living at this time. **Vic·to'ri·an·ism** *n.*

vic·to·ri·ous (vik-tohr-i-ŭs) *adj.* having gained the victory. **vic·to'ri·ous·ly** *adv.* **vic·to'ri·ous·ness** *n.*

vic·to·ry (vik-tŏ-ree) *n.* (*pl.* **-ries**) success in a battle or contest or game etc. achieved by gaining mastery over one's opponent(s) or achieving the highest score. □**Victory Medal,** a bronze medal given to all those who served in the U.S. armed forces in the World Wars.

vict·ual·er (vit-ă-lěr) *n.* a person who supplies victuals.

vict·uals (vit-ălz) *n. pl.* food, provisions.

vi·cu·ña, vi·cu·na (vi-koo-nă) *n.* 1. a South American animal related to the llama, with fine silky wool. 2. cloth made from its wool, an imitation of this.

vid·e·o (vid-ee-oh) *n.* television, especially television pictures as distinct from sound, *we have lost video but are still receiving audio.*

vid·e·o cas·sette (vid-ee-oh kă-set) a cartridge containing videotape.

vid·e·o·disc (vid-ee-oh-disk) *n.* a disk suitable for recording television pictures and sound.

vid·e·o·tape (vid-i-oh-tayp) *n.* magnetic tape suitable for recording television pictures and sound. **videotape** *v.* (**vid·e·o·taped, vid·e·o·tap·ing**) to record on videotape.

vie (vi) *v.* (**vied, vy·ing**) to carry on a rivalry, to compete, *vying with each other for the title.* **vi'er** *n.*

Vi·en·na (vi-en-ă) the capital of Austria. **Vi·en·nese** (vee-ě-neez) *adj.* & *n.* (*pl.* **-nese**).

Vien·tiane (vyen-tyahn) the capital of Laos.

Vi·et·cong (vee-et-kong) *n.* (*pl.* **-cong**) 1. the army and guerrilla force supported by the government of North Vietnam in its war against South Vietnam. 2. a member of this force.

Vi·et·minh (vee-et-min) *n.* (*pl.* **-minh**) 1. the Vietnamese army that fought against the Japanese and French in Indochina in 1941–1951. 2. a member of this army.

Vi·et·nam (vee-et-nahm) a country in southeast Asia. **Vi·et·nam·ese** (vee-et-nă-meez) *adj.* & *n.* (*pl.* **-ese**).

view (vyoo) *n.* 1. what can be seen from a specified point, fine natural scenery, *the view from the summit.* 2. range of vision, *the ship sailed into view.* 3. visual inspection of something, *we had a private view of the exhibition before it was opened.* 4. a mental survey of a subject etc. 5. a mental attitude, an opinion, *they have strong views about tax reform.* **view** *v.* 1. to survey with the eyes or mind. 2. to inspect, to look over (a house etc.) with the idea of buying it. 3. to watch television. 4. to regard or consider, *we view the matter seriously.* □**in view of,** having regard to, considering, *in view of the excellence of the work, we do not mind the cost.* **on view,** displayed for inspection. **with a view to,** with the hope or intention of.

view·er (vyoo-ěr) *n.* 1. a person who views something. 2. a person watching a television program. 3. a device used in inspecting photographic slides etc.

view·find·er (vyoo-fin-děr) *n.* a device on a camera enabling the user to see the area that will be photographed through the lens.

view·point (vyoo-point) *n.* a point of view, a standpoint.

vi·ges·i·mal (vi-jes-ĭ-măl) *adj.* 1. of twentieths or twenty. 2. reckoning or reckoned by twenties.

vig·il (vij-ĭl) *n.* 1. staying awake to keep watch or to pray, a period of this, *keep vigil; a long vigil.* 2. the eve of a religious festival.

vig·i·lant (vij-ĭ-lănt) *adj.* watchful, on the lookout for possible danger etc. **vig'i·lant·ly** *adv.* **vig'i·lance** *n.*

vig·i·lan·te (vij-ĭ-lan-tee) *n.* a member of a self-appointed group of people who try to prevent crime and disorder in a community where law enforcement is imperfect or has broken down.

vi·gnette (vin-yet) *n.* 1. a photograph or portrait with the edges of the background gradually shaded off. 2. a short description or character sketch. **vignette** *v.* (vi·gnet·ted, vi·gnet·ting) to shade off in the style of a vignette.

vig·or (vig-ŏr) *n.* 1. active physical or mental strength, energy, flourishing physical condition. 2. forcefulness of language or composition etc. **vig·or·ous** (vig-ŏ-rŭs) *adj.* full of vigor. **vig'or·ous·ly** *adv.* **vig'or·ous·ness** *n.*

Vi·king (vi-king) *n.* a Scandinavian trader and pirate of the 8th–10th centuries.

vil. *abbr.* village.

vile (vil) *adj.* (**vil·er, vil·est**) 1. extremely disgusting, *a vile smell.* 2. despicable on moral grounds. 3. *(informal)* bad, *this vile weather.* **vile'ly** *adv.* **vile'ness** *n.*

vil·i·fy (vil-ĭ-fī) *n.* (**vil·i·fied, vil·i·fy·ing**) to say evil things about. **vil'i·fi·er** *n.* **vil·i·fi·ca·tion** (vil-ĭ-fĭ-kay-shŏn) *n.*

vil·la (vil-ă) *n.* a large and luxurious estate in the country.

vil·lage (vil-ij) *n.* 1. a small community in the country. 2. the residents of such a community. □**village green,** a small open park in the center of a village.

vil·lag·er (vil-i-jĕr) *n.* an inhabitant of a village.

vil·lain (vil-ĭn) *n.* 1. a person who is guilty or capable of great wickedness, a wrongdoer. 2. a character in a story or play whose evil actions or motives are important in the plot. **vil'lain·y** *n.* (*pl.* **-lain·ies**) **vil·lain·ess** (vil-ĭ-nis) *n. fem.*

vil·lain·ous (vil-ĭ-nŭs) *adj.* 1. wicked, worthy of a villain. 2. *(informal)* abominably bad, *villainous handwriting.* **vil'lain·ous·ly** *adv.* **vil'lain·ous·ness** *n.*

vil·lein (vil-ĕn) *n.* a feudal serf, a tenant entirely subject to a lord or attached to a manor.

vil·lus (vil-ŭs) *n.* (*pl.* **vil·li,** *pr.* vil-ī) 1. each of the short hairlike processes on some membranes, especially on the mucous membrane of the small intestine. 2. *villi,* the long soft hair covering parts of certain plants.

vim (vim) *n.* *(informal)* vigor, energy.

vin·ai·grette (vin-ă-gret) *n.* a small ornamental bottle for holding smelling salts. □**vinaigrette sauce,** salad dressing made of oil and vinegar.

vin·ci·ble (vin-sĭ-bĕl) *adj.* that can be overcome or conquered.

vin·di·cate (vin-dĭ-kayt) *v.* (**vin·di·cat·ed, vin·di·cat·ing**) 1. to clear of blame or suspicion. 2. to justify by evidence or results, to prove (a thing) to be valid, *our policy has been vindicated by this success; he vindicated his claim to the title.* **vin'di·ca·tor** *n.* **vin·di·ca·tion** (vin-dĭ-kay-shŏn) *n.*

vin·dic·tive (vin-dik-tiv) *adj.* having or showing a desire for revenge. **vin·dic'tive·ly** *adv.* **vin·dic'tive·ness** *n.*

vine (vin) *n.* a climbing or trailing woody-stemmed plant.

vin·e·gar (vin-ĕ-găr) *n.* a sour liquid made from wine, cider, malt, etc. by fermentation, used in flavoring food and for pickling.

vin·e·gar·y (vin-ĕ-gă-ree) *adj.* 1. like vinegar. 2. sour-tempered.

vine·yard (vin-yărd) *n.* a plantation of vines producing grapes for wine making.

vin·tage (vin-tij) *n.* 1. the gathering of grapes for wine making, the season of this. 2. wine made from a particular season's grapes, the date of this as an indication of the wine's quality, *a vintage year; a good vintage.* 3. the date or period when something was produced or existed. **vintage** *adj.* of high quality, especially from a past period. □**vintage wine,** wine of high quality from vintage years. **vintage year,** a year in which the wine is of high quality.

vi·nyl (vi-nil) *n.* a kind of plastic, especially polyvinyl chloride.

vi·ol (vi-ŏl) *n.* a stringed musical instrument similar to a violin but held vertically.

vi·o·la¹ (vee-oh-lă) *n.* a stringed musical instrument slightly larger than a violin and of lower pitch. **vi·ol'ist** *n.*

vi·o·la² (vi-ŏ-lă) *n.* a plant of the genus to which pansies and violets belong, especially a hybrid cultivated variety.

vi·o·late (vi-ŏ-layt) *v.* (**vi·o·lat·ed, vi·o·lat·ing**) 1. to break or act contrary to (an oath or treaty etc.). 2. to treat (a sacred place) with irreverence or disrespect. 3. to disturb (a person's privacy). 4. to rape. **vi'o·la·tor** *n.* **vi·o·la·tive** (vi-ŏ-lay-tiv) *adj.* **vi·o·la·tion** (vi-ŏ-lay-shŏn) *n.*

vi·o·lence (vi-ŏ-lĕns) *n.* being violent, violent acts or conduct etc. □**do violence to,** to act contrary to, to be a breach of.

vi·o·lent (vi-ŏ-lĕnt) *adj.* involving great force or strength or intensity; *a violent death,* caused by physical violence, not natural. **vi'o·lent·ly** *adv.*

vi·o·let (vi-ŏ-lit) *n.* 1. a small wild or garden plant, often with purple flowers. 2. the color at the opposite end of the spectrum from red, bluish purple. **violet** *adj.* bluish purple.

vi·o·lin (vi-ŏ-lin) *n.* a musical instrument with four strings of treble pitch, played with a bow.

vi·o·lin·ist (vi-ŏ-lin-ist) *n.* a person who plays the violin.

vi·o·lon·cel·lo (vee-ŏ-lŏn-chel-oh) *n.* (*pl.* **-los**) a cello.

VIP *abbr.* *(informal)* very important person.

vi·per (vi-pĕr) *n.* a small poisonous snake; *a viper in the bosom,* a person who betrays those who have helped him. **vi'per·ous** *adj.* **vi·per·ine** (vi-pĕ-rin) *adj.*

vi·ra·go (vi-rah-goh) *n.* (*pl.* **-goes**) a shrewish bullying woman.

vi·ral (vi-răl) *adj.* of or relating to or caused by a virus.

vir·e·o (veer-i-oh) *n.* (*pl.* **-os**) a small greenish American songbird.

vir·gin (vur-jin) *n.* 1. a person (especially a woman) who has never had sexual intercourse. 2. *the Virgin,* the Virgin Mary, mother of Christ. 3. *the Virgin,* a sign of the zodiac, Virgo. **virgin** *adj.* 1. virginal. 2. spotless, undefiled. 3. untouched, in its original state, not yet used; *virgin soil,* not yet dug or used for crops; *virgin wood,* hereto wool. **vir·gin·i·ty** (vir-jin-i-tee) *n.* □**virgin birth,** (in Christian teaching) the birth of Christ without a human father. **Virgin Islands,** either of two groups of islands in the West Indies, one group belonging to the U.S. and the other to Great Britain.

vir·gin·al (vur-jǐ-nǎl) *adj.* of or being or suitable for a virgin. **virginal** *n.* (often **virginals**) a keyboard instrument of the 16th–17th centuries, the earliest form of harpsichord. **vir′gin·al·ly** *adv.*

Vir·gin·ia (vǐr-jin-yǎ) a state of the U.S. **Vir·gin′ian** *adj.* & *n.* □**Virginia creeper**, an ornamental climbing plant with leaves that turn red in autumn. **Virginia ham,** a ham from a hog cured in hickory smoke. **Virginia reel,** a country dance.

Vir·go (vur-goh) *n.* a sign of the zodiac, the Virgin.

vir·gule (vur-gyool) *n.* a slanting line / to mark the division of words or lines.

vir·i·des·cent (vir-i-des-ĕnt) *adj.* greenish, tending to become green.

vir·ile (vǐr-ǐl) *adj.* having masculine strength or vigor, having procreative power. **vi·ril·i·ty** (vǐ-ril-i-tee) *n.*

vi·rol·o·gy (vɪ-rol-ŏ-jee) *n.* the scientific study of viruses. **vi·rol′o·gist** *n.* **vi·ro·log·i·cal** (vɪ-rŏ-loj-i-kǎl) *adj.*

vir·tu·al (vur-choo-ǎl) *adj.* being so in effect though not in name or according to strict definition, *he is the virtual head of the firm; gave what was a virtual promise.* **vir′tu·al·ly** *adv.*

vir·tue (vur-choo) *n.* 1. moral excellence, goodness, a particular form of this, *patience is a virtue.* 2. chastity, especially of a woman. 3. a good quality, an advantage, *the seat has the virtue of being adjustable.* □**by** or **in virtue of,** by reason of, because of, *he is entitled to a pension by virtue of his long service.* **make a virtue of necessity,** to do with a good grace what one must do anyway.

vir·tu·o·so (vur-choo-oh-soh) *n.* (*pl.* **-sos, -si,** *pr.* -see) a person who excels in the technique of doing something, especially singing or playing music. **vir·tu·os·i·ty** (vur-choo-os-i-tee) *n.* (*pl.* **-ties**).

vir·tu·ous (vur-choo-ŭs) *adj.* having or showing moral virtue. **vir′tu·ous·ly** *adv.* **vir′tu·ous· ness** *n.*

vir·u·lent (vir-yŭ-lĕnt) *adj.* 1. (of poison or disease) extremely strong or violent. 2. strongly and bitterly hostile, *virulent abuse.* **vir′u·lent·ly** *adv.* **vir′u·lence, vir′u·len·cy** *n.*

vi·rus (vɪ-rŭs) *n.* (*pl.* **-rus·es**) a very simple organism (smaller than bacteria) capable of causing disease.

vis. *abbr.* 1. visibility. 2. visual.

vi·sa (vee-zǎ) *n.* an official stamp or mark put on a passport by officials of a foreign country to show that the holder may enter their country. **visa** *v.* (**vi·saed, vi·sa·ing**) to put a visa on (a passport).

vi·saed (vee-zǎd) *adj.* marked with a visa.

vis·age (viz-ij) *n.* a person's face.

vis-à-vis (vee-zǎ-vee) *adv.* & *prep.* 1. in a position facing one another, opposite to. 2. in relation to, as compared with.

vis·cer·a (vis-ĕ-rǎ) *n. pl.* the internal organs of the body, especially the intestines.

vis·cer·al (vis-ĕ-rǎl) *adj.* 1. relating to the viscera. 2. relating to inward feelings. **vis′cer·al·ly** *adv.*

vis·cid (vis-id) *adj.* (of liquid) thick and gluey. **vis′cid·ly** *adv.* **vis·cid·i·ty** (vi-sid-i-tee) *n.*

vis·cose (vis-kohs) *n.* 1. cellulose in a viscous state, used in the manufacture of rayon etc. 2. fabric made of this.

vis·cos·i·ty (vis-kos-i-tee) *n.* (*pl.* **-ties**) the quality or degree of being viscous.

vis·count (vɪ-kownt) *n.* 1. a nobleman ranking between earl and baron, *Viscount Samuel.* 2. the courtesy title of an earl's eldest son, *Viscount Linley.* **vis·count·ess** (vɪ-kown-tis) *n. fem.*

vis·cous (vis-kŭs) *adj.* thick and gluey, not pouring easily. **vis′cous·ly** *adv.* **vis′cous·ness** *n.*

vise (vɪs) *n.* an instrument with two jaws that grip a thing securely so as to leave the hands free for working on it, used especially in carpentry and metal working.

Vish·nu (vish-noo) *n.* a Hindu god regarded by his worshipers as the supreme deity and savior.

vis·i·bil·i·ty (viz-ĭ-bil-i-tee) *n.* 1. being visible. 2. the range or possibility of vision as determined by conditions of light and atmosphere, *the airplane turned back because of poor visibility.*

vis·i·ble (viz-i-bĕl) *adj.* able to be seen or noticed. **vis′i·bly** *adv.* ▷Do not confuse *visible* with *visual.*

Vis·i·goth (viz-ǐ-goth) *n.* a West Goth, a member of a branch of Goths who settled in France and Spain in the 5th–8th centuries. **Vis·i·goth·ic** (viz-ǐ-goth-ik) *adj.*

vi·sion (vizh-ŏn) *n.* 1. the faculty of seeing, sight. 2. something seen in the imagination or in a dream etc. 3. imaginative insight into a subject or problem etc., foresight and wisdom in planning, *a statesman with vision.* 4. a person or sight of unusual beauty. **vision** *v.* to see, to envision.

vi·sion·ar·y (vizh-ŏ-ner-ee) *adj.* 1. existing only in the imagination, fanciful, not practical, *visionary schemes.* 2. indulging in fanciful ideas or theories. **visionary** *n.* (*pl.* **-ar·ies**) a person with visionary ideas.

vis·it (viz-it) *v.* 1. to go or come to see (a person or place etc.) either socially or on business or for some other purpose. 2. to stay temporarily with (a person) or at (a place). 3. (in the Bible) to inflict punishment for, *visiting the sins of the fathers upon the children.* **visit** *n.* an act of visiting, a temporary stay. □**visiting fireman,** *(informal)* a person given especially cordial treatment while visiting an organization, city, etc.; a tourist who is expected to spend money freely. **visiting nurse,** a registered nurse employed by an agency to treat the sick in their homes or to take part in other types of public health programs. **visiting professor,** a professor spending a semester or more at a university other than his own.

vis·i·tant (viz-i-tǎnt) *n.* 1. a visitor, especially a supernatural one. 2. a migratory bird that is a visitor to an area.

vis·it·a·tion (viz-i-tay-shŏn) *n.* 1. an official visit, especially of inspection. 2. trouble or disaster looked upon as punishment from God. **vis·it· a′tion·al** *adj.* □**visitation rights,** a parent's right to visit his or her children when they are in the custody of the other parent.

vis·i·tor (viz-i-tŏr) *n.* 1. one who visits a person or place. 2. a migratory bird that lives in an area temporarily or at a certain season.

vi·sor (vɪ-zŏr) *n.* 1. the movable front part of a helmet, covering the face. 2. the projecting front part of a cap. **vi′sor·less** *adj.* □**sun visor,** a fixed or movable flap at the top of a vehicle's windshield, protecting the eyes from bright sunshine etc.

vi·sored (vɪ-zŏrd) *adj.* covered by a visor.

vis·ta (vis-tǎ) *n.* 1. a view, especially one seen through a long narrow opening such as an avenue of trees. 2. a mental view of an extensive period or series of past or future events.

VISTA (vis-tă) *n*. *V*olunteers *i*n *S*ervice *t*o *A*merica.

vis·u·al (viz*h*-oo-ăl) *adj*. of or used in seeing, received through sight; *a good visual memory*, ability to remember what one sees. **vis'u·al·ly** *adv*. □**visual aid**, a picture or filmstrip etc. as an aid to teaching. **visual arts**, the arts appreciated through the sense of sight, as painting, sculpture, etc. ▷Do not confuse *visual* with *visible*.

vis·u·al·ize (viz*h*-oo-ă-līz) *v*. (**vis·u·al·ized, vis·u·al·iz·ing**) to form a mental picture of. **vis'u·al·iz·er** *n*. **vis·u·al·i·za·tion** (viz*h*-oo-ă-li-zay-shŏn) *n*.

vi·tal (vī-tăl) *adj*. 1. connected with life, essential to life, *vital functions*. 2. essential to the existence or success or operation of something, extremely important. 3. full of vitality, *she's a vital sort of person*. **vi'tal·ly** *adv*. □**vital parts**, the parts of the body (such as heart, lungs, brain) that are essential to the maintenance of life. **vital signs**, the measurable signs of bodily function, such as blood pressure, pulse, and respiration. **vital statistics**, statistics relating to population figures or births and deaths; *(informal)* the measurements of a woman's bust, waist, and hips.

vi·tal·i·ty (vī-tal-i-tee) *n*. (*pl*. **-ties**) liveliness, vigor, persistent energy.

vi·tal·ize (vī-tă-līz) *v*. (**vi·tal·ized, vi·tal·iz·ing**) to put life or vitality into. **vi'tal·iz·er** *n*. **vi·tal·i·za·tion** (vī-tă-li-zay-shŏn) *n*.

vi·tals (vī-tălz) *n*. *pl*. the vital parts of the body.

vi·ta·min (vī-tă-min) *n*. any of a number of organic substances present in many foods and essential to the nutrition of man and other animals. □**vitamin A**, the vitamin found in green and yellow vegetables, egg yolks, etc., essential for growth and the prevention of night blindness etc. **vitamin B**, a vitamin within the vitamin B complex. **vitamin B₁**, thiamine. **vitamin B₂**, riboflavin. **vitamin B₆**, pyridoxine. **vitamin B₁₂**, a vitamin found in liver, milk, eggs, fish, etc., used in the treatment of pernicious anemia. **vitamin B complex**, a group of vitamins containing vitamin B₁, vitamin B₂, etc. **vitamin C**, ascorbic acid. **vitamin D**, a vitamin found in milk, fish liver oils, etc., which helps prevent rickets. **vitamin E**, a vitamin found in wheat-germ oil that is said to contribute to the health of the nervous system. **vitamin K**, the vitamin found in leafy vegetables, rice, bran, etc. that promotes blood clotting.

vi·ti·ate (vish-i-ayt) *v*. (**vi·ti·at·ed, vi·ti·at·ing**) 1. to make imperfect, to spoil. 2. to weaken the force of, to make ineffective, *this admission vitiates your claim*. **vi'ti·a·tor** *n*. **vi·ti·a·tion** (vish-i-ay-shŏn) *n*.

vit·i·cul·ture (vit-ī-kul-chŭr) *n*. 1. the cultivation of grapevines. 2. the study of grapes. **vit·i·cul·tur·al** (vit-ī-kul-chŭ-răl) *adj*. **vit·i·cul'tur·ist** *n*.

vit·re·ous (vit-ri-ŭs) *adj*. having a glasslike texture or finish, *vitreous enamel*. □**vitreous humor**, the transparent jellylike tissue filling the eyeball behind the lens.

vit·ri·fy (vit-rī-fī) *v*. (**vit·ri·fied, vit·ri·fy·ing**) to convert or be converted into glass or a glasslike substance, especially by heat. **vit·ri·fac·tion** (vit-rī-fak-shŏn) *n*. **vit·ri·fi·ca·tion** (vit-rī-fī-kay-shŏn) *n*.

vit·ri·ol (vit-ri-ŏl) *n*. 1. sulfuric acid or one of its salts. 2. savagely hostile comments or criticism. **vit·ri·ol·ic** (vit-ri-ol-ik) *adj*.

vit·tles (vit-ĕlz) *n*. *(informal)* victuals.

vi·tu·per·ate (vī-too-pĕ-rayt) *v*. (**vi·tu·per·at·ed, vi·tu·per·at·ing**) to use abusive language. **vi·tu·per·a·tive** (vī-too-pĕ-ray-tiv) *adj*. **vi·tu'per·a·tive·ly** *adv*. **vi·tu·per·a·tion** (vī-too-pĕ-ray-shŏn) *n*.

vi·va (vee-vă) *interj*. a cry used as a salute etc., "long live." ▷Italian.

vi·va·ce (vi-vah-chay) *adj*. & *adv*. (of music) in a lively brisk manner. ▷Italian.

vi·va·cious (vi-vay-shŭs) *adj*. lively, high-spirited. **vi·va'cious·ly** *adv*. **vi·va'cious·ness** *n*. **vi·vac·i·ty** (vi-vas-i-tee) *n*.

vi·var·i·um (vī-vair-i-ŭm) *n*. (*pl*. **-var·i·ums**, **-var·i·a**, *pr*. **-vair**-i-ă) a place artificially prepared for keeping animals in nearly their natural state.

vi·va vo·ce (vī-vă voh-see) (of an examination in universities) 1. spoken not written, conducted orally. 2. a spoken examination.

viv·id (viv-id) *adj*. 1. (of light or color) bright and strong, intense. 2. producing strong and clear mental pictures, *a vivid description*. 3. (of the imagination) creating ideas etc. in an active and lively way. **viv'id·ly** *adv*. **viv'id·ness** *n*.

viv·i·fy (viv-ī-fī) *v*. (**viv·i·fied, viv·i·fy·ing**) to give life to, to enliven, to animate. **viv'i·fi·er** *n*. **viv·i·fi·ca·tion** (viv-ī-fī-kay-shŏn) *n*.

vi·vip·ar·ous (vi-vip-ă-rŭs) *adj*. 1. bringing forth young alive, not hatching by means of an egg. 2. producing bulbs or seeds that germinate while still attached to the parent plant. **vi·vip'ar·ous·ly** *adv*. **viv·i·par·i·ty** (viv-ī-par-i-tee) *n*.

viv·i·sec·tion (viv-i-sek-shŏn) *n*. performance of surgical experiments on living animals. **viv·i·sec'tion·ist** *n*. **viv·i·sect** (viv-i-sekt) *v*. to perform a vivisection on.

vix·en (vik-sĕn) *n*. 1. a female fox. 2. a quarrelsome woman. **vix'en·ish** *adj*. **vix'en·ish·ly** *adv*.

viz. *adv*. namely, *the case is made in three sizes, viz. large, medium, and small*. ▷In reading aloud, the word "namely" is usually spoken where "viz." (short for Latin *videlicet*) is written.

vi·zier (vi-zeer) *n*. an official of high rank in certain Muslim countries.

V-J (vee-jay) **Day** August 15, 1945, when Japan surrendered to the Allies in World War II.

VLF *abbr*. very low frequency.

V.M.D. *abbr*. Doctor of Veterinary Medicine.

V neck (vee nek) a V-shaped neckline on a sweater etc.

VOA *abbr*. 1. Voice of America. 2. Volunteers of America.

vocab. *abbr*. vocabulary.

vo·ca·ble (voh-kă-bĕl) *n*. a word, especially with reference to its form rather than its meaning.

vo·cab·u·lar·y (voh-kab-yŭ-ler-ee) *n*. (*pl*. **-lar·ies**) 1. a list of words with their meanings, especially one given in a reading book etc. of a foreign language. 2. the words known to a person or used in a particular book or subject etc.

vo·cal (voh-kăl) *adj*. 1. of or for or uttered by the voice. 2. expressing one's feelings freely in speech, *he was vocal about his rights*. **vocal** *n*. a piece of sung music. **vo'cal·ly** *adv*. □**vocal cords**, the folds of lining membrane of the larynx that produce the voice.

vo·cal·ic (voh-kal-ik) *adj*. of or consisting of vowels.

vo·cal·ist (voh-kă-list) *n*. a singer, especially in a pop group.

vo·cal·ize (voh-kă-līz) *v*. (**vo·cal·ized, vo·**

cal·iz·ing) 1. to utter. 2. *(informal)* to use the voice, as in speech or song. **vo′cal·iz·er** *n.* **vo·cal·i·za·tion** (voh-kă-li-zay-shŏn) *n.*
vo·ca·tion (voh-kay-shŏn) *n.* 1. a feeling that one is called by God to a certain career or occupation. 2. a natural liking for a certain type of work. 3. a person's trade or profession. **vo·ca′tion·al** *adj.* □**vocational guidance**, advice about suitable careers. **vocational school**, a school that provides practical training in a trade.
vo·cif·er·ate (voh-sif-ĕ-rayt) *v.* **(vo·cif·er·at·ed, vo·cif·er·at·ing)** to speak or say loudly or noisily, to shout. **vo·cif·er·a·tion** (voh-sif-ĕ-ray-shŏn) *n.*
vo·cif·er·ous (voh-sif-ĕ-rŭs) *adj.* making a great outcry, expressing one's views forcibly and insistently. **vo·cif′er·ous·ly** *adv.* **vo·cif′er·ous·ness** *n.*
vod·ka (vod-kă) *n.* alcoholic liquor distilled chiefly from rye, especially in Russia.
vogue (vohg) *n.* 1. current fashion, *large hats are the vogue.* 2. popular favor or acceptance, *his novels had a great vogue ten years ago.* **vogu′ish** *adj.* □**in vogue**, in fashion. **out of vogue**, out of fashion.
voice (vois) *n.* 1. sounds formed in the larynx and uttered by the mouth, especially human utterance in speaking, singing, etc. 2. ability to produce such sounds, *she has a cold and has lost her voice; she is in good voice,* singing or speaking well. 3. expression of one's opinion etc. in spoken or written words, the opinion itself, the right to express opinion, *gave voice to his indignation; I have no voice in the matter.* 4. any of the sets of forms of a verb that show the relation of the subject to the action, *active voice; passive voice* (see **active** and **passive**). **voice** *v.* **(voiced, voic·ing)** 1. to put into words, to express, *she voiced her opinion.* 2. to utter with resonance of the vocal cords (as *z*), not only with the breath (as *s*). □**voice box**, the larynx. **voice vote**, a vote taken by noting the relative strength of calls of *aye* and *no.* **with one voice**, unanimously.
voice·less (vois-lis) *adj.* 1. having no voice. 2. not voiced. **voice′less·ly** *adv.* **voice′less·ness** *n.*
voice-o·ver (vois-oh-věr) *n.* (in a film, television program, etc.) narration by a voice not accompanied by a picture of the speaker.
voice·print (vois-print) *n.* a visual record of speech, analyzed with respect to frequency, duration, and amplitude.
void (void) *adj.* 1. empty, vacant. 2. not legally valid. **void** *n.* empty space, emptiness. **void** *v.* 1. to make legally void, *the contract was voided by his death.* 2. to excrete (urine or feces). **void′a·ble** *adj.* **void′er** *n.*
voile (voil) *n.* a very thin light dress material.
vol. *abbr.* 1. volume. 2. volunteer.
vol·a·tile (vol-ă-til) *adj.* 1. (of a liquid) evaporating rapidly. 2. (of a person) lively, changing quickly or easily from one mood or interest to another. **vol·a·til·i·ty** (vol-ă-til-i-tee) *n.*
vol·a·til·ize (vol-ă-til-iz) *v.* **(vol·a·til·ized, vol·a·til·iz·ing)** to evaporate, to cause to evaporate.
vol·can·ic (vol-kan-ik) *adj.* of, like, or produced by a volcano. **vol·can′i·cal·ly** *adv.* □**volcanic glass**, the natural glass produced by quick cooling of molten lava.
vol·can·ism (vol-kă-niz-ĕm) *n.* volcanic power and activity.

vol·ca·no (vol-kay-noh) *n.* (*pl.* **-noes, -nos**) a mountain or hill with openings through which lava, cinders, gases, etc. from below Earth's crust are or have been expelled.
vol·can·ol·o·gy (vol-kă-nol-ŏ-jee) *n.* the scientific study of volcanoes and their phenomena. **vol·can·ol′o·gist** *n.* **vol·can·o·log·i·cal** (vol-kă-nŏ-loj-i-kăl) *adj.*
vole (vohl) *n.* any of several small animals resembling rats or mice.
vo·li·tion (vŏ-lish-ŏn) *n.* use of one's own will in choosing or making a decision etc.; *she did it of her own volition,* voluntarily. **vo·li′tion·al** *adj.* **vo·li′tion·al·ly** *adv.*
vol·ley (vol-ee) *n.* (*pl.* **-leys**) 1. simultaneous discharge of a number of missiles, the missiles themselves. 2. a number of questions or curses etc. directed in quick succession at someone. 3. return of the ball in tennis etc. before it touches the ground. **volley** *v.* **(vol·leyed, vol·ley·ing)** 1. to discharge or fly or sound in a volley. 2. to return (a ball) by a volley. **vol′ley·er** *n.*
vol·ley·ball (vol-ee-bawl) *n.* a game for two teams of six players volleying a large ball by hand over a net.
vol·plane (vol-playn) *v.* **(vol·planed, vol·plan·ing)** to glide in an airplane.
volt (vohlt) *n.* a unit of electromotive force, force sufficient to carry one ampere of current against one ohm resistance.
vol·tage (vohl-tij) *n.* electromotive force expressed in volts.
vol·ta·ic (vol-tay-ik) *adj.* of electricity from a primary battery, galvanic.
volte-face (volt-fahs) *n.* (*pl.* **volte-face**) a complete change of one's attitude toward something. ▷French.
volt·me·ter (vohlt-mee-těr) *n.* an instrument measuring electric potential in volts.
vol·u·ble (vol-yŭ-běl) *adj.* talking very much, speaking or spoken with great fluency. **vol′u·bly** *adv.* **vol·u·bil·i·ty** (vol-yŭ-bil-i-tee) *n.*
vol·ume (vol-yŭm) *n.* 1. a book, especially one of a set. 2. the amount of space (often expressed in cubic units) that a three-dimensional thing occupies or contains. 3. the size or amount of something, a quantity, *the great volume of water pouring over the dam; the volume of business has increased.* 4. the strength or power of sound, *the noise had doubled in volume.*
vol·u·met·ric (vol-yŭ-met-rik) *adj.* of measurement by volume. **vol·u·met′ri·cal·ly** *adv.*
vo·lu·mi·nous (vŏ-loo-mĭ-nŭs) *adj.* 1. having great volume, bulky; *voluminous skirts,* large and full. 2. (of writings) great in quantity. **vo·lu′mi·nous·ly** *adv.* **vo·lu′mi·nous·ness** *n.* **vo·lu·mi·nos·i·ty** (vŏ-loo-mĭ-nos-i-tee) *n.*
vol·un·tar·y (vol-ŭn-ter-ee) *adj.* 1. acting or done or given etc. of one's own free will and not under compulsion. 2. working or done without payment, *voluntary workers* or *work.* 3. (of an organization) maintained by voluntary contributions or voluntary workers. 4. (of bodily movements) controlled by the will. **voluntary** *n.* an organ solo played before, during, or after a church service. **vol′un·tar·i·ly** *adv.*
vol·un·teer (vol-ŭn-teer) *n.* 1. a person who offers to do something. 2. a person who enrolls for military or other service voluntarily, not as a conscript. **volunteer** *v.* to undertake or offer volun-

tarily, to be a volunteer. □**volunteer army,** an army consisting of volunteers.

vo·lup·tu·ar·y (vŏ-lup-choo-er-ee) *n.* (*pl.* **-ar·ies**) a person whose life is devoted to indulgence in luxury and sensual pleasure.

vo·lup·tu·ous (vŏ-lup-choo-ŭs) *adj.* 1. fond of luxury or sumptuous living. 2. giving a sensation of luxury and pleasure. 3. (of a woman) having a full and attractive figure. **vo·lup′tu·ous·ly** *adv.* **vo·lup′tu·ous·ness** *n.*

vom·it (vom-it) *v.* (**vom·it·ed, vom·it·ing**) to eject (matter) from the stomach through the mouth, to be sick. **vomit** *n.* matter vomited from the stomach.

voo·doo (voo-doo) *n.* (*pl.* **-doos**) a form of religion based on belief in witchcraft and magical rites, practiced by some people in the West Indies and America. **voo′doo·ism** *n.*

vo·ra·cious (voh-ray-shŭs) *adj.* 1. greedy in eating, ravenous. 2. desiring much; *a voracious reader,* one who reads much and eagerly. **vo·ra′cious·ly** *adv.* **vo·ra′cious·ness** *n.* **vo·rac·i·ty** (voh-ras-i-tee) *n.*

vor·tex (vor-teks) *n.* (*pl.* **-tex·es, -ti·ces,** *pr.* -ti-seez) a whirling mass of water or air, a whirlpool or whirlwind. **vor·ti·cal** (vor-ti-kăl) *adj.* ▷ Do not confuse *vortex* with *vertex.*

vo·ta·ry (voh-tă-ree) *n.* (*pl.* **-ries**) 1. a person vowed to the service of God etc., as a priest or nun. 2. an ardent follower, a devoted adherent or advocate of a person, system, religion, occupation, etc.

vote (voht) *n.* 1. a formal expression of one's opinion or choice on a matter under discussion, as by ballot or show of hands. 2. an opinion or choice expressed in this way, *the vote went against accepting the plan.* 3. the total number of votes given by a certain group, *that policy will lose us the labor vote.* 4. the right to vote, *Swiss women now have the vote.* **vote** *v.* (**vot·ed, vot·ing**) 1. to express an opinion or choice by a vote. 2. to decide by a majority of votes. 3. (*informal*) to declare by general consent, *the meal was voted excellent.* 4. (*informal*) to suggest, *I vote that we avoid him in the future.* **vote′less** *adj.* **vot′er** *n.* □**vote down,** to reject (a proposal etc.) by votes. **vote in,** to elect by votes. **voting machine,** a machine automatically registering votes.

vo·tive (voh-tiv) *adj.* given in fulfillment of a vow, *votive offerings at the shrine.*

vouch (vowch) *v.* **vouch for,** to guarantee the certainty or accuracy or reliability etc. of, *I will vouch for his honesty.*

vouch·er (vow-chĕr) *n.* 1. a document establishing that money has been paid or goods etc. delivered. 2. a document (issued in token of payment made or promised) that can be exchanged for certain goods or services.

vouch·safe (vowch-sayf) *v.* (**vouch·safed, vouch·saf·ing**) to give or grant in a gracious or condescending manner, *they did not vouchsafe a reply or to reply.*

vow (vow) *n.* a solemn promise or undertaking, especially in the form of an oath to God or a god or a saint. **vow** *v.* to promise solemnly, *they vowed vengeance against their oppressor.* **vow′er** *n.*

vow·el (vow-ĕl) *n.* 1. a speech sound made without audible stopping of the breath (opposed to a *conso-*

nant). 2. a letter or letters representing such a sound, as a, e, i, o, u, ee.

vox po·pu·li (voks pop-yŭ-lı) public opinion. ▷ Latin, = the people's voice.

voy·age (voi-ij) *n.* a journey by water (especially a long one) or in space. **voyage** *v.* (**voy·aged, voy·ag·ing**) to make a voyage. **voy′ag·er** *n.*

vo·ya·geur (vwah-yah-zhur) *n.* 1. a man employed in the transportation of goods and passengers between trading posts. 2. a Canadian boatman.

vo·yeur (vwah-yur, voi-) *n.* a person who obtains sexual gratification from looking at the sexual actions or organs of others. **vo·yeur′ism** *n.* **vo·yeur·is·tic** (vwah-yŭ-ris-tik, voi-) *adj.*

V.P. *abbr.* vice president.

vs. *abbr.* 1. verse. 2. versus.

V sign (vee sın) a gesture of victory, made by the raised hand with first and second fingers spread in the form of a V.

vss. *abbr.* 1. verses. 2. versions.

V/STOL (vee-stohl) *adj.* (of aircraft) vertical short takeoff and landing.

VT, Vt. *abbr.* Vermont.

v.t. *abbr.* verb transitive.

VTOL *abbr.* vertical takeoff and landing.

vul·can·ite (vul-kă-nıt) *n.* a hard black vulcanized rubber, ebonite.

vul·can·ize (vul-kă-nız) *v.* (**vul·can·ized, vul·can·iz·ing**) to treat (rubber or similar material) with sulfur etc. in order to increase its elasticity and strength. **vul′can·iz·er** *n.* **vul·can·i·za·tion** (vul-kă-ni-zay-shŏn) *n.*

Vulg. *abbr.* Vulgate.

vul·gar (vul-găr) *adj.* 1. lacking in refinement or good taste, coarse. 2. commonly used and incorrect (but not coarse; see **vulgarism,** definition 1). **vul′gar·ly** *adv.* **vul′gar·ness** *n.* **vul·gar·i·ty** (vul-gar-i-tee) *n.* (*pl.* **-ties**). □**Vulgar Latin,** the informal Latin used in classical times.

vul·gar·i·an (vul-gair-i-ăn) *n.* a vulgar person, especially a rich one.

vul·gar·ism (vul-gă-riz-ĕm) *n.* 1. a word or phrase used mainly by people who are ignorant of standard usage, *"he is learning her to drive"* is a *vulgar usage* or is a *vulgarism* for *"he is teaching her to drive."* 2. a coarse word or phrase.

vul·gar·ize (vul-gă-rız) *v.* (**vul·gar·ized, vul·gar·iz·ing**) 1. to cause (a person or his manners etc.) to become vulgar. 2. to reduce to the level of being usual or ordinary, to spoil by making ordinary or too well known. **vul′gar·iz·er** *n.* **vul·gar·i·za·tion** (vul-gă-ri-zay-shŏn) *n.*

Vul·gate (vul-gayt) *n.* the 4th-century Latin version of the Bible.

vul·ner·a·ble (vul-nĕ-ră-bĕl) *adj.* 1. able to be hurt or wounded or injured. 2. unprotected, exposed to danger or attack. **vul′ner·a·bly** *adv.* **vul·ner·a·bil·i·ty** (vul-nĕ-ră-bil-i-tee) *n.*

vul·pine (vul-pın) *adj.* 1. of or like a fox. 2. crafty, cunning.

vul·ture (vul-chŭr) *n.* 1. a large bird of prey that lives on the flesh of dead animals. 2. a greedy person seeking to profit from the misfortunes of others.

vul·va (vul-vă) *n.* (*pl.* **-vae,** *pr.* **-vee, -vas**) the external parts of the female genital organs.

vv. *abbr.* verses.

vy·ing (vı-ing) *see* **vie.**

W

W, w (dub-ĕl-yoo) (*pl.* **Ws, W's, w's**) the twenty-third letter of the alphabet.
W *symbol* tungsten.
w. *abbr.* 1. water. 2. watt(s). 3. week(s). 4. weight. 5. west. 6. western. 7. wide. 8. width. 9. wife. 10. with. 11. won.
W., W *abbr.* 1. Wales. 2. warden. 3. warehouse. 4. Washington. 5. watt(s). 6. Wednesday. 7. weight. 8. Welsh. 9. West. 10. Western. 11. width.
w/ *abbr.* with.
WA *abbr.* Washington.
Wac (wak) *n.* a member of the Women's Army Corps.
WAC *abbr.* Women's Army Corps.
wack·y (wak-ee) *adj.* (**wack·i·er, wack·i·est**) *(slang)* crazy. **wack′i·ness** *n.*
wad (wod) *n.* 1. a lump or bundle of soft material used to keep things apart or in place, stop up a hole, etc. 2. *(informal)* a collection of documents or banknotes placed together. 3. *(slang)* a large quantity, especially of money. **wad** *v.* (**wad·ded, wad·ding**) to line or stuff or protect with wadding.
wad·ding (wod-ing) *n.* soft fibrous material used for padding or packing or lining things.
wad·dle (wod-ĕl) *v.* (**wad·dled, wad·dling**) to walk with short steps and a swaying movement. **waddle** *n.* a waddling walk. **wad′dler** *n.*
wade (wayd) *v.* (**wad·ed, wad·ing**) 1. to walk through water or mud or anything that prevents the feet from moving freely, to walk across (a stream etc.) in this way. 2. to make one's way slowly and with difficulty; *wade through a book*, read through it in spite of its dullness or difficulty or length etc. **wad′a·ble** *adj.* □**wade in,** *(informal)* to intervene, to make a vigorous attack. **wade into,** *(informal)* to attack (a person or task) vigorously. **wading bird,** any long-legged water bird that wades in shallow water.
wad·er (wayd-ĕr) *n.* 1. a person who wades. 2. a wading bird. 3. *waders,* high waterproof boots worn for fishing etc.
wa·di (wah-dee) *n.* a rocky watercourse that is dry except in the rainy season, in North Africa and the Middle East.
Waf (waf) *n.* a member of the women's branch of the Air Force.
WAF *abbr.* Women in the Air Force.
wa·fer (way-fĕr) *n.* 1. a kind of thin light cracker or biscuit. 2. a thin disk of unleavened bread used in the Eucharist.
waf·fle[1] (wof-ĕl) *n.* *(informal)* vague wordy talk or writing showing indecision or evasiveness. **waffle** *v.* (**waf·fled, waf·fling**) *(informal)* to talk or write waffle, *the diplomat waffled on the question of arms control.*
waffle[2] *n.* a small cake made of batter and eaten hot, cooked in a **waffle iron** which has two metal pans hinged together, marked with a projecting pattern that presses into the batter when the pans are closed upon it.
waft (wahft) *v.* to carry or travel lightly and easily through the air or over water. **waft** *n.* 1. a wafted odor. 2. a movement of air.
wag (wag) *v.* (**wagged, wag·ging**) to shake or move briskly to and fro; *tongues are wagging,* talk or gossip is going on. **wag** *n.* 1. a single wagging movement. 2. a person who is fond of making jokes or playing practical jokes.
wage (wayj) *v.* (**waged, wag·ing**) to engage in, *wage war.* **wage** *n.* (often *wages*) regular payment to an employee in return for his work or services, *he earns a good wage* or *good wages.*
wage-price (wayj-prīs) **guideline** a ceiling standard set by the federal government for increases in salaries, benefits, and prices.
wa·ger (way-jĕr) *n.* a bet. **wager** *v.* to bet. **wa′ger·er** *n.*
wag·ger·y (wag-ĕ-ree) *n.* (*pl.* **-ger·ies**) 1. the actions or humor of a wag. 2. a jest.
wag·gish (wag-ish) *adj.* of or like a wag, said or done in a joking way. **wag′gish·ly** *adv.* **wag′gish·ness** *n.*
wag·gle (wag-ĕl) *v.* (**wag·gled, wag·gling**) to wag. **waggle** *n.* a waggling movement.
wag·on (wag-ŏn) *n.* 1. a four-wheeled vehicle for carrying goods. 2. *(informal)* a station wagon. 3. *(informal)* a patrol wagon. □**on the wagon** or **water wagon,** *(slang)* abstaining from alcohol. **wagon train,** a group of wagons and horses carrying supplies and settlers.
wag·on·er (wag-ŏ-nĕr) *n.* the driver of a wagon.
wa·gon-lit (va-gon-lee) *n.* (*pl.* **wa·gons-lits,** *pr.* va-gon-lee) a sleeping car on a European railroad. ▷French.
wag·tail (wag-tayl) *n.* any of several small birds with a long tail that moves up and down constantly when the bird is standing.
wa·hoo (wah-hoo) *n.* (*pl.* **-hoos**) a North American shrub or tree, so named by the Indians.
waif (wayf) *n.* a homeless and helpless person, an unowned or abandoned child.
wail (wayl) *v.* 1. to utter a long sad cry, to lament or complain persistently. 2. (of wind etc.) to make a sound like a person wailing. **wail** *n.* a wailing cry or sound or utterance.
wain (wayn) *n.* *(old use)* a farm wagon.
wain·scot (wayn-skŏt) *n.* wooden paneling on the wall of a room, especially a dado of wood. **wainscot** *v.* (**wain·scot·ed, wain·scot·ing**) to panel with wainscot.
wain·scot·ing (wayn-skoh-ting) *n.* wainscot, material for this.
wain·wright (wayn-rīt) *n.* *(old use)* a wagon builder.
waist (wayst) *n.* 1. the part of the human body

779

below the ribs and above the bones of the pelvis, normally narrower than the rest of the body. 2. the part of a garment covering this. 3. a narrow part in the middle of a long object. 4. a blouse or bodice.

waist·band (wayst-band) n. a band (as at the top of a skirt) that fits around the waist.

waist·coat (wes-kŏt) n. (chiefly *British*) a vest.

waist·line (wayst-lın) n. 1. the circumference of the body at the waist. 2. the narrowest part of a garment, fitting at or just above or below the waist.

wait (wayt) v. 1. to postpone an action or departure for a specified time or until some expected event occurs, *we waited until evening; wait your turn,* wait until it is your turn; *we'll wait dinner for you,* will postpone it until you are present. 2. to be postponed, *this question will have to wait until our next meeting.* 3. to wait on people at a meal. **wait** n. an act or period of waiting, *we had a long wait for the train.* □**waiting game,** deliberate delay in taking action so as to act more effectively later. **waiting list,** a list of people waiting for a chance to obtain something when it becomes available. **waiting room,** a room provided for people to wait in, as at a railroad station or a doctor's or dentist's office. **wait on,** to hand food and drink to (a person or persons) at a meal; to fetch and carry for (a person) as a servant or attendant. ▷It is considered incorrect to use *wait on* in the sense of "to wait for," *sorry we have no peas, we're waiting on them.*

wait·er (way-tĕr) n. a man employed to serve food and drink to customers at tables in a hotel or restaurant etc. **wait·ress** (way-tris) n. *fem.*

waive (wayv) v. (**waived, waiv·ing**) to refrain from using or insisting upon (one's right or claim or privilege etc.), to forgo or dispense with. ▷Do not confuse *waive* with *wave.*

waiv·er (way-vĕr) n. the waiving of a legal right, a document recording this. ▷Do not confuse *waiver* with *waver.*

wake[1] (wayk) v. (**woke** or **waked, waked** or **wok·en, wak·ing**) 1. = wake up *(see below).* 2. to disturb by noise, to cause to reecho, *the shout woke echoes in the valley.* **wake** n. the watch near a corpse before burial, lamentations and merrymaking in connection with this. □**wake up,** to cease to sleep, to cause to cease sleeping; to become alert, to realize, *he woke up to the fact that she meant it;* to cease or cause to cease from inactivity or inattention etc., *he needs something to wake him up.*

wake[2] n. 1. the track left on water's surface by a ship etc. 2. air currents left behind an aircraft etc. moving through air. □**in the wake of,** behind; following after.

wake·ful (wayk-fŭl) adj. 1. (of a person) unable to sleep. 2. (of a night etc.) with little sleep. **wake·ful·ness** n.

wak·en (way-kĕn) v. to wake.

wake-rob·in (wayk-rob-in) n. a trillium.

wak·ing (way-king) adj. being awake, *in his waking hours.*

Wal·dorf (wawl-dorf) **salad** a salad of chopped apples, celery, and nuts mixed with mayonnaise. ▷Named for the Waldorf-Astoria Hotel in New York City.

wale (wayl) n. 1. a lengthwise ridge on woven or knitted fabric, especially on corduroy. 2. the weave or texture of a fabric. 3. a welt (definition 2). **wale** v. (**waled, wal·ing**) to provide or to mark with wales.

Wales (waylz) the country forming the western part of Great Britain.

walk (wawk) v. 1. to progress by lifting and setting down each foot in turn so that one foot is on the ground while the other is being lifted, (of quadrupeds) to go with the slowest gait, always having at least two feet on the ground. 2. to travel or go on foot, to take exercise in this way. 3. to go over on foot, *walked the fields in search of wild flowers.* 4. to cause to walk with one, to accompany in walking. 5. to ride or lead (a horse or dog etc.) at a walking pace. 6. (in baseball) to give (a batter) a base on balls, to reach first base in this way. **walk** n. 1. a journey on foot, especially for pleasure or exercise, *went for a walk.* 2. the manner or style of walking, a walking pace. 3. a place for walking, a route followed or distance covered in walking, *a five-minute walk from here.* □**walk away with,** (informal) to win easily. **walking stick,** a cane carried or used as a support when walking; a plant-eating insect with a twiglike body. **walk off with,** (informal) to win easily, *walked off with the first prize;* to steal, *walked off with merchandise under his coat.* **walk of life,** social rank, profession, or occupation. **walk on air,** to walk buoyantly because of happiness. **walk out,** to depart suddenly and angrily; to go on strike suddenly. **walk out on,** to desert; to leave in the lurch. **walk over,** (informal) to defeat easily; to treat badly, *walked all over him.* **walk tall,** to feel justifiable pride.

walk·a·way (wawk-ă-way) n. an easy victory or achievement.

walk·er (waw-kĕr) n. 1. a person who walks. 2. a framework for a person (as a baby or a crippled person) who is unable to walk without support.

walk·ie-talk·ie (waw-kee-taw-kee) n. a small radio transmitter and receiver that a person can carry with him as he walks about.

walk-in (wawk-in) adj. large enough to be walked into, *a walk-in closet.* **walk-in** n. (informal) 1. an easy victory, especially in an election. 2. a customer or client who walks in from the street without an appointment.

walk-on (wawk-on) n. (informal) a part in a play in which the actor or actress appears on stage but does not speak.

walk·out (wawk-owt) n. a sudden angry departure, especially as a protest or strike.

walk·o·ver (wawk-oh-vĕr) n. a walkaway.

walk·up (wawk-up) n. (informal) 1. an apartment above the ground floor in a building with access to the upper floors only by stairs. 2. a building of this kind, with no elevator.

walk·way (wawk-way) n. a passage for walking along (especially one connecting different sections of a building), a wide path in a garden etc.

wall (wawl) n. 1. a continuous upright structure forming one of the sides of a building or room, or serving to enclose or protect or divide an area. 2. something thought of as resembling this in form or function, the outermost part of a hollow structure, tissue surrounding an organ of the body etc. **wall** v. to surround or enclose with a wall, *a walled garden; wall up a fireplace,* block it with bricks etc. built as a wall. **walled** adj. □**drive** or **send a person up the wall,** (informal) to make him crazy or furious. **go to the wall,** to suffer defeat or failure or ruin; *the business finally went to the* *wall,* went bankrupt. **off the wall,** *(slang)* bizarre, eccentric.

wal·la·by (wol-ă-bee) *n.* (*pl.* **-bies, -by**) a kind of small kangaroo.

wall·board (wawl-bohrd) *n.* a large sheet of a manufactured building material used to make walls and ceilings.

wal·let (wol-it) *n.* a small flat folding case for paper money or small documents etc.

wall·eye (wawl-ı) *n.* 1. an eye showing an abnormal amount of white, or turned outward. 2. an American pike with large prominent eyes. **wall·eyed** (wawl-ıd) *adj.*

wall·flow·er (wawl-flow-ĕr) *n.* 1. a European garden plant blooming in spring, with clusters of fragrant flowers. 2. *(informal)* a woman sitting out dances for lack of partners.

Wal·loon (wo-loon) *n.* 1. a member of a people in southern Belgium and neighboring parts of France. 2. a French dialect of southern Belgium.

wal·lop (wol-ŏp) *v.* (**wal·loped, wal·lop·ing**) *(informal)* to thrash, to hit hard, to beat. **wallop** *n.* *(informal)* 1. a heavy resounding blow or the power to strike such a blow. 2. an overwhelming emotional effect, *the movie's ending delivers a real wallop.*

wal·lop·ing (wol-ŏ-ping) *adj.* *(informal)* big, thumping, *a walloping lie.* **walloping** *n.* *(informal)* a beating, a defeat.

wal·low (wol-oh) *v.* 1. to roll about in water or mud or sand etc. 2. to indulge oneself or take unrestrained pleasure in something, *wallowing in luxury.* **wallow** *n.* the act of wallowing.

wall·pa·per (wawl-pay-pĕr) *n.* paper for pasting on the interior walls of rooms. **wallpaper** *v.* to paste such paper on.

Wall Street the U.S. money market. ▷The name of a street in New York City, in or near which the chief financial institutions are concentrated.

wall-to-wall (wawl-tŏ-wawl) *adj.* 1. (of a carpet) covering the whole floor of a room. 2. *(slang)* crowded, *wall-to-wall people.*

wal·nut (wawl-nut) *n.* 1. a nut containing an edible kernel with a wrinkled surface. 2. the tree that bears it. 3. the wood of this tree, used (especially as a veneer) in making furniture.

wal·rus (wawl-rŭs) *n.* (*pl.* **-rus·es, -rus**) a large amphibious animal of arctic regions, related to the seal and sea lion and having a pair of long tusks. □**walrus mustache,** a long thick mustache that hangs down at the sides.

waltz (wawlts) *n.* 1. a ballroom dance for couples, with a graceful flowing melody in triple time. 2. music for this. **waltz** *v.* 1. to dance a waltz. 2. to move (a person) in or as if in a waltz. 3. *(informal)* to move gaily or casually, *came waltzing in.* **waltz'er** *n.*

wam·pum (wom-pŭm) *n.* 1. beads made from shells and strung for money or decoration by North American Indians. 2. *(slang)* money.

wan (won) *adj.* (**wan·ner, wan·nest**) pallid, especially from illness or exhaustion; *a wan smile,* a faint smile from a person who is ill or tired or unhappy. **wan'ly** *adv.* **wan'ness** *n.*

wand (wond) *n.* a slender rod for carrying in the hand, especially one associated with the working of magic.

wan·der (won-dĕr) *v.* 1. to go from place to place without a settled route or destination or special purpose. 2. (of a road or river) to wind, to mean-

der. 3. to leave the right path or direction, to stray from one's group or from a place. 4. to digress from a subject; *his mind is wandering,* he is inattentive or speaking disconnectedly through illness or weakness. **wan'der·er** *n.* □**wandering Jew,** a kind of trailing plant. ▷Named for a legendary person said to have been condemned to wander the earth until Christ's second coming, as a punishment for striking Christ on the day of the Crucifixion.

wan·der·lust (won-dĕr-lust) *n.* strong desire to travel.

wane (wayn) *v.* (**waned, wan·ing**) 1. (of the moon) to show a gradually decreasing area of brightness after being full. 2. to decrease in vigor or strength or importance, *his influence was waning.* **wane** *n.* the process of waning. □**on the wane,** waning.

wan·gle (wang-gĕl) *v.* (**wan·gled, wan·gling**) *(informal)* to obtain or arrange by using trickery or improper influence or persuasion etc. **wan'gler** *n.*

Wan·kel (vahn-kĕl, wahn-) **engine** a rotary internal-combustion engine with a continuously rotated and eccentrically pivoted nearly triangular shaft. ▷Named for its inventor, F. Wankel, German engineer (1902–　　).

want (wont) *v.* 1. to desire, to wish for. 2. to require or need; *your hair wants cutting; that wants some doing,* is hard to do; *you want to be more careful,* ought to be more careful. 3. *(informal)* to desire to come or go or get, *the cat wants out.* 4. to lack, to have an insufficient supply of. 5. to be without the necessaries of life, *waste not, want not; want for nothing,* not be needy. 6. *(old use)* to fall short of, *it still wanted two hours till midnight.* **want** *n.* 1. a desire for something, a requirement, *a man of few wants.* 2. lack or need of something, deficiency, *the plants died from want of water.* 3. lack of the necessaries of life, *living in great want.* □**want ad,** *(informal)* a newspaper or magazine advertisement by a person or firm seeking something.

want·ed (won-tid) *adj.* (of a suspected criminal) being sought by the police for questioning or arrest.

want·ing (won-ting) *adj.* lacking, deficient, not equal to requirements. **wanting** *prep.* 1. without, *a pot wanting a lid.* 2. minus, *a year wanting a few days.*

wan·ton (won-tŏn) *adj.* irresponsible, lacking proper restraint or motives. **wanton** *n.* an immoral person, especially a woman. **wan'ton·ly** *adv.* **wan'ton·ness** *n.*

wap·i·ti (wop-i-tee) *n.* (*pl.* **-ties, -ti**) the North American elk, resembling a deer but larger.

war (wor) *n.* 1. strife (especially between countries) involving military or naval or air attacks. 2. open hostility between people. 3. a strong effort to combat crime or disease or poverty etc. **war** *v.* (**warred, war·ring**) to make war, *the two nations warred continually; she warred against discrimination,* fought vigorously against it. **war'less** *adj.* free from war. □**at war,** engaged in a war. **have been in the wars,** *(humorous)* to show signs of injury or rough usage. **War Between the States,** the American Civil War. **war bonnet,** an American Indian headdress with long trailing feathers. **war chest,** *(informal)* funds for war or for a campaign. **war clouds,** a state of international affairs that threatens war. **war corre-**

spondent, a reporter assigned to send reports from the scene of a war. **war crime,** an action, committed during a war, violating the laws of war or constituting a crime against humanity. **war cry,** a word or cry shouted in attacking or in rallying one's side; *(informal)* the slogan of a political or other party. **war dance,** a dance performed by certain primitive peoples before battle or after a victory. **war game,** a game in which models representing troops etc. are moved about on maps; a training exercise in which sets of armed forces participate in mock opposition to each other. **war horse,** a powerful horse used in war; *(informal)* a veteran soldier or politician. **war memorial,** a memorial erected to those who died in a war. **War of Independence,** the American Revolution. **war of nerves,** an effort to wear down one's opponent by gradually destroying his morale. **war paint,** paint put on the body by certain primitive peoples before battle; *(informal)* ceremonial dress, makeup applied to the skin etc. **war widow,** a woman whose husband has been killed in a war. **war zone,** a combat area during war in which all, including neutrals, are subject to attack.

war·ble¹ (wor-bĕl) *v.* (**war·bled, war·bling**) to sing, especially with a gentle trilling note as certain birds do. **warble** *n.* a warbling sound.

warble² *n.* 1. a lump or swelling on a horse's skin caused by excessive rubbing of a saddle. 2. a tumor on cattle, containing warble fly larvae. **war′bled** *adj.* □**warble fly,** an insect whose larvae burrow under the skin of cattle etc.

war·bler (wor-blĕr) *n.* any of several small birds (not necessarily one noted for its song).

ward (word) *n.* 1. a room with beds for a particular group of patients in a hospital. 2. an administrative division of a city or town, especially for elections. 3. a person, especially a child, under the care of a guardian or the protection of a court. **ward** *v.* **ward off,** to keep at a distance (a person or thing that threatens danger), to fend off. □**ward heeler,** *(contemptuous)* a local worker for a professional politician.

-ward *suffix* used to form adjectives and adverbs meaning to or in the direction of, as in *eastward, downward.*

war·den (wor-dĕn) *n.* 1. the chief officer administering a prison. 2. an official responsible for enforcing certain laws or regulations, as an air-raid warden or game warden. 3. a churchwarden.

ward·robe (word-rohb) *n.* 1. a large cupboard where clothes are stored, usually with pegs or rails etc. from which they hang. 2. a stock of clothes. 3. a theatrical company's stock of costumes.

ward·room (word-room) *n.* (on a warship) the living quarters used by commissioned officers, especially their dining room.

ware (wair) *n.* 1. manufactured goods (especially pottery) of the kind specified, *Delft ware.* 2. **wares,** articles offered for sale, *traders displayed their wares.*

ware·house (wair-hows) *n.* (*pl.* **-hous·es,** *pr.* -how-ziz) a building for storing goods or for storing furniture on behalf of its owners. **warehouse** *v.* (**ware·housed, ware·hous·ing**) to store in a warehouse. **ware′house·man** (wair-hows-măn) *n.* (*pl.* **-men,** *pr.* -měn) **ware′hous·er** *n.*

war·fare (wor-fair) *n.* making war, fighting, a particular form of this, *guerrilla warfare.*

war·head (wor-hed) *n.* the explosive head of a missile or torpedo or similar weapon.

war·like (wor-lık) *adj.* 1. fond of making war, aggressive, *a warlike people.* 2. of or for war, *warlike preparations.*

war·lock (wor-lok) *n.* a sorcerer, a male witch.

war·lord (wor-lord) *n.* a military commander-in-chief, especially one who has seized power over a section of a country.

warm (worm) *adj.* 1. moderately hot, not cold or cool. 2. (of clothes etc.) keeping the body warm. 3. enthusiastic, hearty, *a warm supporter; the speaker got a warm reception,* a vigorous response (either favorable or unfavorable). 4. kindly and affectionate, *she has a warm heart.* 5. (of colors) suggesting warmth, containing reddish shades. 6. (of the scent in hunting) still fairly fresh and strong. 7. *(informal)* (of the seeker in children's games etc.) near the object sought, on the verge of finding it. **warm** *v.* to make or become warm or warmer. **warm′ly** *adv.* **warm′ness** *n.* **warm′er** *n.* □**keep a place warm,** to occupy it temporarily so that it can be available for a certain person at a later date. **warming pan,** a covered metal pan with a long handle, formerly filled with hot coals and used for warming beds. **warm to,** to become cordial or well-disposed to (a person); to become more animated about (a task). **warm up,** to make or become warm; to reheat (food etc.); to prepare for athletic exercise by practice beforehand; to make or become more lively.

warm-blood·ed (worm-blud-id) *adj.* having blood that remains warm (ranging from 36° to 42° C, 96° to 108° F) despite changes in surrounding temperature.

warmed-o·ver (wormd-oh-vĕr) *adj.* 1. reheated, *warmed-over food.* 2. repeated, stale, *a warmed-over idea.*

warm·heart·ed (worm-hahr-tid) *adj.* having a kindly and affectionate disposition. **warm′heart′ed·ly** *adv.* **warm′heart′ed·ness** *n.*

warm·ish (wor-mish) *adj.* rather warm.

war·mong·er (wor-mung-gĕr) *n.* a person who seeks to bring about war. **war′mon·ger·ing** *adj.* & *n.*

warmth (wormth) *n.* warmness, the state of being warm.

warm-up (worm-up) *n.* an athlete's exercise or practice period immediately prior to a contest.

warn (worn) *v.* to inform (a person) about a present or future danger or about something that must be reckoned with, to advise about action in such circumstances, *we warned them to take waterproof clothing.* □**warn off,** to tell (a person) to keep away or to avoid (a thing).

warn·ing (wor-ning) *n.* something that serves to warn. **warning** *adj.* serving to warn. **warn′ing·ly** *adv.* □**warning track,** (in baseball) a dirt track around the perimeter of the grass field, warning fielders chasing batted balls that they are dangerously near walls or fences.

warp (worp) *v.* 1. to cause (timber etc.) to become bent by uneven shrinkage or expansion, to become bent in this way. 2. to distort (a person's judgment or principles). 3. to haul (a ship) in some direction by means of a rope attached to a fixed point. **warp** *n.* 1. a warped condition. 2. threads stretched lengthwise in a loom, to be crossed by the weft. **warp′er** *n.*

war·path (wor-path) *n.* the route taken on a warlike

expedition of North American Indians. □**on the warpath**, seeking hostile confrontation or revenge.

war·plane (wor-playn) *n.* a military aircraft.

war·rant (wor-änt) *n.* 1. written authorization to do something, *the police have a warrant for his arrest.* 2. authorization to purchase stock in a company under specified conditions. 3. a justification or authorization for an action etc., *he had no warrant for saying this.* 4. a proof or guarantee. **warrant** *v.* 1. to serve as a warrant for, to justify, *nothing can warrant such rudeness.* 2. to prove or guarantee; *he'll be back, I'll warrant you,* I assure you. □**warrant officer,** a member of the armed services ranking between commissioned and noncommissioned officers.

war·ran·tee (wor-än-tee) *n.* a person to whom a warranty is made.

war·ran·tor (wor-än-tor) *n.* a person who makes a warranty.

war·ran·ty (wor-än-tee) *n.* (*pl.* **-ties**) 1. a guarantee, especially one given to the buyer of an article and involving a promise to repair defects that become apparent in it within a specified period. 2. authority or justification for doing something.

war·ren (wor-ën) *n.* 1. a piece of ground in which there are many burrows in which rabbits live and breed. 2. a building or district with many narrow winding passages.

war·ring (wor-ing) *adj.* engaged in war, *warring factions.*

war·ri·or (wor-i-ör) *n.* a person who fights in battle, a member of any of the armed services.

War·saw (wor-saw) the capital of Poland.

war·ship (wor-ship) *n.* a ship for use in war.

wart (wort) *n.* 1. a small hard roundish abnormal growth on the skin, caused by a virus. 2. a similar growth on a plant. **wart'y** *adj.* □**warts and all,** without concealment of blemishes or defects or unattractive features.

wart·hog (wort-hog) *n.* a kind of African pig with two large tusks and wartlike growths on its face.

war·time (wor-tım) *n.* the period when a war is being waged.

war·y (wair-ee) *adj.* (**war·i·er, war·i·est**) cautious, in the habit of looking out for possible danger or difficulty. **war'i·ly** *adv.* **war'i·ness** *n.*

was (wuz) *see* **be.**

wash (wosh) *v.* 1. to cleanse with water or other liquid; *wash the stain away* or *out,* remove it by washing. 2. to wash oneself, to wash clothes etc. 3. to be washable, *cotton washes well.* 4. to flow past or against, to go splashing or flowing, *the sea washes the base of the cliffs; waves washed over the deck.* 5. (of moving liquid) to carry in a specified direction, *a wave washed him overboard; the meal was washed down with beer,* beer was drunk with or after it. 6. to sift (ore) by the action of water. 7. to coat with a wash of paint or metal etc. 8. to erode or be carried away by water. 9. (*informal,* of reasoning) to be valid, *that argument won't wash.* **wash** *n.* 1. washing, being washed, *give it a good wash.* 2. *the wash,* the process of laundering. 3. a quantity of clothes etc. that are being washed or to be washed or have just been washed. 4. disturbed water or air behind a moving ship or aircraft etc. 5. the lapping or surging of ocean waves or water in motion, or the sound of this. 6. a liquid for spreading over a surface to cleanse or heal or color something, *colors her hair with a wash.* 7. a thin coating

of color painted over a surface. 8. the erosion of earth by moving water. 9. (in western U.S.) a dry stream bed. 10. liquid food or swill for pigs etc. **wash** *adj.* washable, *wash pants.* □**come out in the wash,** (of difficulties) to be eliminated during the progress of work etc.; to become evident. **wash dirty linen in public,** to discuss one's family scandals or quarrels publicly. **wash drawing,** a drawing that is made with washes of color, especially black or gray watercolors. **wash one's hands of,** to refuse to take responsibility for. **wash out,** to wash (clothes etc.); to make (a game or horse race etc.) impossible by heavy rainfall; (*informal*) to cancel; (*slang*) to fail, *he washed out of flight training.* **wash up,** to wash (dishes etc.) after use; to wash oneself; to cast up on the shore; *be washed up,* (*slang*) to have failed, to be ruined.

Wash. *abbr.* Washington.

wash·a·ble (wosh-ä-bël) *adj.* able to be washed without suffering damage. **washables** *n.* (*informal*) items of clothing that are washable. **wash·a·bil·i·ty** (wosh-ä-bil-i-tee) *n.*

wash-and-wear (wosh-än-wair) *adj.* easily washed and needing little or no ironing.

wash·ba·sin (wosh-bay-sin) *n.* a washbowl.

wash·board (wosh-bohrd) *n.* a corrugated board for use when scrubbing clothes.

wash·bowl (wosh-bohl) *n.* a bowl or basin (usually fixed to a wall) for washing one's hands in.

wash·cloth (wosh-klawth) *n.* a small cloth for washing the face or body.

washed-out (wosht-owt) *adj.* 1. faded by washing. 2. (*informal*) utterly exhausted.

wash·er (wosh-ër) *n.* 1. a machine for washing things. 2. a ring of rubber or metal etc. placed between two surfaces (as under a nut or at a joint) to give tightness or prevent leakage.

wash·er·wom·an (wosh-ër-wuum-än) *n.* (*pl.* **-wom·en,** *pr.* -wim-in) a woman whose occupation is washing clothes etc.

wash·house (wosh-hows) *n.* an outbuilding where washing is done.

wash·ing (wosh-ing) *n.* clothes etc. that are being washed or to be washed or have just been washed. □**washing machine,** a machine for washing clothes etc. **washing soda,** sodium carbonate, used (dissolved in water) for washing and cleaning things. **washing up,** the process of washing dishes etc. after use, or washing oneself.

Wash·ing·ton (wosh-ing-tön) 1. a state of the U.S. 2. the administrative capital of the U.S., covering the same area as the District of Columbia. □**Washington's Birthday,** a legal holiday in February celebrating George Washington's birthday.

Wash·ing·ton (wosh-ing-tön), **George** (1732–99) the first President of the U.S. 1789–97.

wash·out (wosh-owt) *n.* (*slang*) a complete failure.

wash·rag (wosh-rag) *n.* a washcloth.

wash·room (wosh-room) *n.* a lavatory.

wash·stand (wosh-stand) *n.* a piece of furniture to hold a basin and jug of water etc. for washing.

wash·tub (wosh-tub) *n.* a tub for washing clothes.

wash·y (wosh-ee) *adj.* (**wash·i·er, wash·i·est**) 1. (of liquids) thin, watery. 2. (of colors) washed-out. **wash'i·ness** *n.*

was·n't (wuz-ënt) = was not.

wasp (wosp) *n.* a winged insect with a slender body, a very slender waist, and a formidable sting.

wasp'y adj. □**wasp waist,** a very slender waist, especially a woman's.

WASP, Wasp (wosp) n. (contemptuous) a white Anglo-Saxon Protestant.

wasp·ish (wos-pish) adj. irritable, sharp in retort. **wasp'ish·ly** adv. **wasp'ish·ness** n.

was·sail (wos-ĭl) n. 1. a festive occasion with much drinking. 2. (old use) a salutation of good health, a toast to a person. 3. a drink consumed on such occasions, as spiced ale etc. **wassail** v. to make merry, to drink a wassail. **was'sail·er** n.

Was·ser·mann (wos-ĕr-măn) **test** (also **Wasserman**) a test for syphilis using a blood sample. ▷Named for A. von Wasserman, German pathologist (1866–1925).

wast (wost) (old use) the past tense of **be**, used with thou.

wast·age (ways-tij) n. loss by waste, use, deterioration etc.

waste (wayst) v. (**wast·ed, wast·ing**) 1. to use extravagantly or needlessly or without an adequate result; he is wasted as a schoolmaster, the job does not use his abilities fully; advice is wasted on him, has no effect when given. 2. to fail to use (an opportunity). 3. to make or become gradually weaker, wasting away for lack of food; a wasting disease. 4. (slang) to kill. **waste** adj. 1. left over or thrown away because not wanted; waste products, useless byproducts of manufacture or of a bodily process. 2. (of land) not used or cultivated or built up on, unfit for use. **waste** n. 1. an act of wasting or using something ineffectively, a waste of time. 2. waste material or food, waste products; wastes, excrement. 3. a stretch of waste land. **wast'er** n. □**waste breath** or **words,** to talk uselessly. **waste pipe,** a pipe that carries off water etc. that has been used or is not required.

waste·bas·ket (wayst-bas-kit) n. an open container in which wastepaper is placed for removal.

waste·ful (wayst-fŭl) adj. using more than is needed, showing waste. **waste'ful·ly** adv. **waste'ful·ness** n.

waste·land (wayst-lănd) n. an expanse of waste land.

waste·pa·per (wayst-pay-pĕr) n. paper regarded as spoiled or valueless and thrown away. □**wastepaper basket,** a wastebasket.

wast·rel (ways-trĕl) n. a wasteful person, especially one who wastes money.

watch (woch) v. 1. to look at, to keep one's eyes fixed on, to keep under observation. 2. to be on the alert, to take heed, watch for an opportunity; watch your chance, wait alertly for the right moment. 3. to be careful about. 4. to safeguard, to exercise protective care, he employed an accountant to watch his interests or watch over them. **watch** n. 1. the act of watching, especially to see that all is well, constant observation or attention, keep watch. 2. a period (usually four hours) for which a division of a ship's company remains on duty, a turn of duty, the part (usually half) of a ship's company on duty during a watch. 3. a small portable device indicating the time, usually worn on the wrist or carried in the pocket. **watch'er** n. □**on the watch,** alert for something. **watch chain,** a metal chain guard for a pocket watch. **watch night,** a religious service on the last night of the year. **watch oneself,** to be careful or discreet. **watch one's step,** to be careful not to stumble or fall or do something wrong. **watch out,** to be on one's guard. **watch**

pocket, a small pocket for holding a pocket watch, as in a vest or trousers.

watch·band (woch-band) n. the strap or band holding a wristwatch on the wrist.

watch·case (woch-kays) n. the outer metal case enclosing the works of a watch.

watch·dog (woch-dawg) n. 1. a dog kept to guard property etc. 2. a person who acts as guardian of people's rights etc.

watch·ful (woch-fŭl) adj. watching or observing closely. **watch'ful·ly** adv. **watch'ful·ness** n.

watch·mak·er (woch-may-kĕr) n. a person who makes or repairs watches. **watch'mak·ing** n.

watch·man (woch-măn) n. (pl. -men, pr. -měn) a man employed to look after an empty building etc., especially at night. **watch·wom·an** (woch-wuum-ăn) n. fem. (pl. -wom·en, pr. -wim-in).

watch·tow·er (woch-tow-ĕr) n. a tower from which observation can be kept.

watch·word (woch-wurd) n. a word or phrase expressing briefly the principles of a party or group.

wa·ter (waw-tĕr) n. 1. a colorless odorless tasteless liquid that is a compound of oxygen and hydrogen. 2. a sheet or body of water, such as a lake or sea. 3. water as supplied for domestic use. 4. a watery secretion (such as sweat or saliva), urine. 5. a watery solution or other preparation, lavender water; soda water. 6. the level of the tide, at high water. 7. the transparency and luster of a gem; a diamond of the first water, of the finest quality. **water** v. 1. to sprinkle with water. 2. to supply with water, to give drinking water to (an animal). 3. to dilute with water. 4. (of a ship etc.) to take in a supply of water. 5. to secrete tears or saliva; make one's mouth water, arouse desire. □**by water,** (of travel) in a boat or ship or barge etc. **water ballet,** a synchronized swimming performance accompanied by music. **water bird,** a bird that swims on or wades in water. **water biscuit,** an unsweetened biscuit made from flour and water. **water buffalo,** the common domestic buffalo of India and Indonesia etc. **water bug,** an aquatic insect. **water chestnut,** a Chinese plant with an edible tuber; its tuber. **water closet,** (British) a toilet that is flushed by water; the room containing this. **water cooler,** a device providing cooled drinking water. **water down,** to dilute; to make less forceful or vivid. **water gap,** a crosswise cut in a mountain ridge, through which water flows. **water gas,** a gas, mainly hydrogen and carbon monoxide, made by decomposing steam with red hot coke. **water gate,** a floodgate. **water glass,** a drinking glass; a thick liquid used for coating eggs in order to preserve them. **water hole,** a shallow depression or cavity in which water collects, especially in the bed of a river otherwise dry; a watering place in the desert; a pond. **watering can,** a container with a long tubular spout, holding water for watering plants. **watering hole,** (slang) a bar or nightclub. **watering place,** a pool etc. where animals go to drink water; a spa or seaside resort. **water jump,** a place where a horse in a steeplechase etc. must jump over water. **water level,** the surface of water in a reservoir etc., the height of this; = water table (see below). **water lily,** a plant that grows in water, with broad floating leaves and white, yellow, blue, or red flowers. **water main,** a main pipe in a water-supply system. **water mill,** a mill worked by a waterwheel. **water moccasin,** a cottonmouth; a harmless water

snake resembling the poisonous cottonmouth.
water ouzel, a water bird with thick oily plumage, having a jerking motion when walking or perching. **water pipe,** a pipe conveying water; a hookah. **water pistol,** a toy pistol that shoots a jet of water. **water polo,** a game played by teams of swimmers with an inflated ball. **water rat,** a ratlike animal that lives beside a lake or stream; a muskrat; *(slang)* a person who is excessively fond of swimming. **water ski,** either of a pair of flat boards on which a person stands for **water-skiing,** the sport of skimming over the surface of water while holding a tow line from a motor boat. **water snake,** a harmless snake living in or near water. **water softener,** a substance or apparatus for softening hard water. **water spaniel,** a large spaniel of a variety sometimes used for retrieving waterfowl. **water strider,** an insect with hairy feet that enable it to move rapidly about on the surface of the water. **water table,** the level below which the ground is saturated with water. **water tower,** a tower that holds a water tank at a height to secure pressure for distributing water. **water wings,** floats worn by a person learning to swim.
wa·ter·bed (waw-tĕr-bed) *n.* a bed having a mattress filled with water.
wa·ter·borne (waw-tĕr-bohrn) *adj.* 1. (of goods) conveyed by water. 2. (of disease) communicated or propagated by use of contaminated drinking water.
wa·ter·col·or (waw-tĕr-kul-ŏr) *n.* 1. artists' paint in which the pigment is diluted with water (not oil). 2. a picture painted with paints of this kind. **wa'ter·col·or·ist** *n.*
wa·ter·course (waw-tĕr-kohrs) *n.* a stream or brook or artificial waterway, its channel.
wa·ter·craft (waw-tĕr-kraft) *n.* a vessel traveling on water, all such vessels collectively.
wa·ter·cress (waw-tĕr-kres) *n.* a kind of cress that grows in streams or ponds, with strong-tasting leaves, used in salad.
wa·tered (waw-tĕrd) *adj.* (of silk fabric) having an irregular wavy marking.
wa·ter·fall (waw-tĕr-fawl) *n.* a stream that falls from a height.
wa·ter·fowl (waw-tĕr-fowl) *n.* (*pl.* **-fowl**) water birds, especially game birds that swim.
wa·ter·front (waw-tĕr-frunt) *n.* the part of a town that borders on a river or lake or sea.
Wa·ter·gate (waw-tĕr-gayt) *n.* a political scandal that involves government officials abusing their powers of office by committing illegal acts, *we don't want a new Watergate.* ▷From the name of the building in Washington, D.C., that housed the headquarters of the Democratic National Committee, which was broken into by people connected with the Republican presidential campaign of 1972.
wa·ter·less (waw-tĕr-lis) *adj.* without water.
wa·ter·line (waw-tĕr-lin) *n.* the line along which the surface of water touches a ship's side.
wa·ter·logged (waw-tĕr-lawgd) *adj.* 1. (of timber or a ship) saturated or filled with water so that it will barely float. 2. (of ground) so saturated with water that it is useless or unable to be worked.
Wa·ter·loo (waw-tĕr-loo) *n.* a decisive defeat. □**meet one's Waterloo,** to lose a decisive contest. ▷From the name of the village in Belgium where Napoleon was defeated in 1815.

wa·ter·mark (waw-tĕr-mahrk) *n.* 1. a mark showing how high a river or tide rises or how low it falls. 2. a manufacturer's design in some kinds of paper, visible when the paper is held against light. **watermark** *v.* to impress such a mark on (paper) in making.
wa·ter·mel·on (waw-tĕr-mel-ŏn) *n.* a melon with a smooth green skin, red pulp, and sweet juice.
wa·ter·pow·er (waw-tĕr-pow-ĕr) *n.* the power obtained from flowing or falling water, used to drive machinery or turbines that generate electric current.
wa·ter·proof (waw-tĕr-proof) *adj.* unable to be penetrated by water. **waterproof** *v.* to make waterproof. **wa'ter·proof·ing** *n.*
wa·ter·re·pel·lent (waw-tĕr-ri-pel-ĕnt) *adj.* not easily penetrated by water.
wa·ter·re·sist·ant (waw-tĕr-ri-zis-tănt) *adj.* resisting but not completely repelling water.
wa·ter·shed (waw-tĕr-shed) *n.* 1. a line of high land where streams on one side flow into one river or sea and streams on the other side flow into another. 2. a turning point in the course of events. 3. a region drained by a river or river system.
wa·ter·side (waw-tĕr-sıd) *n.* the edge of a river or lake or sea.
wa·ter·spout (waw-tĕr-spowt) *n.* a funnel-shaped column of water between sea and cloud, formed when a whirlwind draws up a whirling mass of water.
wa·ter·tight (waw-tĕr-tıt) *adj.* 1. made or fastened so that water cannot get in or out. 2. (of an excuse or alibi) impossible to set aside or disprove, (of an agreement) leaving no possibility of escape from its provisions.
wa·ter·way (waw-tĕr-way) *n.* a route for travel by water, a navigable channel.
wa·ter·wheel (waw-tĕr-hweel) *n.* a wheel turned by a flow of water, used to work machinery.
wa·ter·works (waw-tĕr-wurks) *n. pl.* an establishment with pumping machinery etc. for supplying water to a district.
wa·ter·y (waw-tĕ-ree) *adj.* 1. of or like water. 2. made weak or thin by too much water. 3. full of water or moisture, *watery eyes.* 4. (of colors) pale; *a watery moon* or *sky,* looking as if rain will come. □**watery grave,** death by drowning.
WATS (wots) *n.* Wide Area Telephone Service. □**WATS line,** a telephone line permitting unlimited long-distance calls for a monthly charge.
watt (wot) *n.* a unit of electric power.
watt·age (wot-ij) *n.* an amount of electric power, expressed in watts.
wat·tle (wot-ĕl) *n.* 1. a structure of interwoven sticks and twigs used as material for fences, walls, etc. 2. a red fleshy fold of skin hanging from the head or throat of certain birds, as the turkey.
wave (wayv) *n.* 1. a ridge of water moving along the surface of the sea etc. or arching and breaking on the shore. 2. something compared to this, such as an advancing group of attackers, a temporary increase of an influence or condition *(a wave of anger),* a spell of hot or cold weather *(a heat wave).* 3. a wavelike curve or arrangement of curves, as in a line or in hair. 4. an act of waving. 5. the wavelike motion by which heat, light, sound, or electricity etc. is spread or carried, a single curve in the course of this. **wave** *v.* **(waved, wav·ing)** 1. to move loosely to and fro or up and down. 2. to move (one's arm or hand or something held) to and fro as a signal

or greeting. 3. to signal or express in this way, *waved him away; waved goodby.* 4. to give a wavy course or appearance to. 5. to be wavy. □**wave aside,** to dismiss (an objection etc.) as unimportant or irrelevant. **wave band,** a range of wavelengths between certain limits. **wave down,** to signal (a vehicle or its driver) to stop, by waving one's hand. **wave front,** (in physics) the surface containing points affected in the same way by a wave at a given time. ▷Do not confuse *wave* with *waive.*

Wave (wayv) *n.* a woman serving in the U.S. Navy. ▷From *WAVES,* women accepted for volunteer emergency service.

wave·length (wayv-lengkth) *n.* the distance between corresponding points in a sound wave or an electromagnetic wave.

wave·let (wayv-lit) *n.* a small wave.

wa·ver (way-věr) *n.* 1. to be or become unsteady, to begin to give way, *the line of troops wavered and then broke; his courage wavered.* 2. (of light) to flicker. 3. to show hesitation or uncertainty, *he wavered between two opinions.* **wa′ver·ing·ly** *adv.* **wa′ver·er** *n.* ▷Do not confuse *waver* with *waiver.*

wav·y (way-vee) *adj.* (**wav·i·er, wav·i·est**) full of waves or wavelike curves. **wav′i·ness** *n.*

wax[1] (waks) *n.* 1. beeswax. 2. any of various soft sticky substances that melt easily (especially those obtained from petroleum), used for various purposes such as making candles or polishes. 3. a yellow waxlike substance secreted in the ears. **wax** *v.* to coat or polish or treat with wax. **wax′er** *n.* □**wax bean,** a yellowish string bean with a waxy pod. **wax myrtle,** a small tree with berries that have a coating of wax, used in candle making; a bayberry (definition 1). **wax paper,** paper waterproofed with a layer of wax.

wax[2] *v.* 1. (of the moon) to show a bright area that is becoming gradually larger until it becomes full. 2. to increase in vigor or strength or importance, *kingdoms waxed and waned.* 3. (old use) to become, *they waxed fat.*

wax·en (wak-sĕn) *adj.* made of wax, like wax in its paleness or smoothness.

wax·wing (waks-wing) *n.* any of several small birds with small red tips (like sealing wax) on some of its wing feathers.

wax·work (waks-wurk) *n.* 1. an object modeled in wax, especially a model of a person with the face etc. made in wax, clothed to look lifelike and to be exhibited. 2. *waxworks,* a museum of wax figures.

wax·y (wak-see) *adj.* (**wax·i·er, wax·i·est**) like wax. **wax′i·ly** *adv.* **wax′i·ness** *n.*

way (way) *n.* 1. a line of communication between places, such as a path or road. 2. the best route, the route taken or intended, *asked the way to Boston.* 3. a method or style, a person's chosen or desired course of action, *do it my way; have one's way,* cause people to do as one wishes. 4. traveling distance, *it's a long way to Tokyo.* 5. the amount of difference between two states or conditions, *his work is a long way from being perfect.* 6. space free of obstacles so that people can pass; *make way,* allow room for others to proceed. 7. the route over which a person or thing is moving or would naturally move, *don't get in the way of the trucks.* 8. a specified direction, *which way is she looking?* 9. a manner, *she spoke in a kindly way.* 10. a habitual manner or course of action

or events, *you'll soon get used to our ways.* 11. a talent or skill, *she has a way with flowers.* 12. advance in some direction, progress, *we made our way to the front; he started as office boy and worked his way up.* 13. a respect, a particular aspect of something, *it's a good plan in some ways.* 14. a condition or state, *things are in a bad way.* **way** *adv.* (informal) far, *the shot was way off the target.* □**by the way,** by the roadside during a journey; incidentally, as a more or less irrelevant comment. **by way of,** as a substitute for or a form of, *smiled by way of greeting.* **come one's way,** to fall to one's lot; to become available. **give way,** *see* **give. in a way,** to a limited extent; in some respects. **in no way,** not at all. **in the way,** forming an obstacle or hindrance. **look the other way,** to ignore a person or thing deliberately. **make way,** *see* **make. on one's way,** in the process of traveling or approaching. **on the way,** on one's way; (of a baby) conceived but not yet born. **out of the way,** *see* **out. under way,** *see* **under. way back,** (informal) a long way back. **ways and means,** methods of achieving something, especially means of providing money for government. **way station,** a minor station on a railroad.

way·bill (way-bil) *n.* a list of the goods carried by a freight transport vehicle.

way·far·er (way-fair-ĕr) *n.* a traveler, especially on foot. **way′far·ing** *adj. & n.*

way·lay (way-lay) *v.* (**way·laid, way·lay·ing**) to lie in wait for, especially so as to talk to or rob. **way·lay′er** *n.*

way-out (way-owt) *adj.* (informal) unusual in style, exotic.

-ways *suffix* used to form adverbs meaning direction or manner, as in *lengthways, sideways.*

way·side (way-sid) *n.* the side of a road or path, land bordering this.

way·ward (way-wărd) *adj.* childishly self-willed, not obedient or easily controlled. **way′ward·ness** *n.*

way·worn (way-wohrn) *adj.* tired with travel.

W.B.C. *abbr.* white blood cells.

W.C. *abbr.* water closet.

W.C.T.U. *abbr.* Women's Christian Temperance Union.

we (wee) *pronoun* 1. used by a person referring to himself and another or others, or speaking on behalf of a nation or group or firm etc. 2. used instead of "I" by a royal person in formal proclamations and by the writer of an editorial article in a newspaper etc. 3. (humorous, identifying oneself with the person addressed) you, *and how are we today?*

weak (week) *adj.* 1. lacking strength or power or number, easily broken or bent or defeated, *a weak barrier; a weak team.* 2. lacking vigor, not acting strongly, *weak eyes; a weak stomach,* easily upset. 3. not convincing or forceful, *the evidence is weak.* 4. dilute, having little of a certain substance in proportion to the amount of water, *weak tea; a weak solution of salt and water.* 5. (of verbs) forming the past tense etc. by adding a suffix (as in *walk/walked, waste/wasted*) not by changing the vowel (*see* **strong,** definition 6.) □**weak sister,** (slang) an ineffective person.

weak·en (wee-kĕn) *v.* to make or become weaker. **weak′en·er** *n.*

weak·fish (week-fish) *n.* (*pl.* **-fish, -fish·es**) an ocean fish found along the East coast of the U.S., used for food.

weak-kneed (week-need) *adj.* giving way weakly, especially when intimidated.

weak·ling (week-ling) *n.* a feeble person or animal.

weak·ly (week-lee) *adv.* in a weak manner. **weakly** *adj.* (-li·er, -li·est) sickly, not robust.

weak-mind·ed (week-mɪn-did) *adj.* lacking determination.

weak·ness (week-nis) *n.* 1. the state of being weak. 2. a weak point, a defect or fault. 3. inability to resist something, a particular fondness, *she has a weakness for coffee creams.*

weal[1] (weel) *n.* a welt (definition 2).

weal[2] *n.* *(old use)* prosperity, well-being.

wealth (welth) *n.* 1. riches, possession of these. 2. a great quantity, *a book with a wealth of illustrations.*

wealth·y (wel-thee) *adj.* (wealth·i·er, wealth·i·est) having wealth, rich. **wealth'i·ness** *n.*

wean (ween) *v.* 1. to accustom (a baby) to take food other than milk. 2. to cause (a person) to give up a habit or interest etc. gradually.

wean·ling (ween-ling) *n.* a newly weaned child or animal.

weap·on (wep-ŏn) *n.* 1. a thing designed or used as a means of inflicting bodily harm, such as a gun or bomb or stick, or a horn or claw. 2. an action or procedure used as a means of getting the better of someone in a conflict, *use the weapon of a general strike.* **weap'on·less** *adj.*

weap·on·ry (wep-ŏn-ree) *n.* weapons collectively.

wear (wair) *v.* (wore, worn, wear·ing) 1. to have on the body, as clothing or ornaments or makeup; *she wears her hair long,* keeps it that way. 2. to have (a certain look) on one's face, *wearing a frown.* 3. to injure the surface of or become injured by rubbing or stress or use, to make (a hole etc.) in this way. 4. to exhaust or overcome by persistence, *wore down the opposition.* 5. to endure continued use, *this fabric wears well.* 6. (of time) to pass gradually, *the night wore on.* **wear** *n.* 1. wearing or being worn as clothing, *choose cotton for summer wear.* 2. clothing, *men's wear is on the ground floor.* 3. damage resulting from ordinary use. 4. capacity to endure being used, *there's a lot of wear left in that coat.* **wear'er** *n.* □**wear and tear,** damage sustained as a result of ordinary use. **wear down,** to impair by wearing for a long period of time; to overcome by constant pressure, *wore down his opponent.* **wear off,** to disappear slowly or gradually. **wear one's heart on one's sleeve,** *see* heart. **wear out,** to use or be used until no longer usable. **wear the pants in one's family,** *(slang)* (of a wife) to dominate her husband.

wear·a·ble (wair-ă-bĕl) *adj.* able to be worn.

wea·ri·some (weer-i-sŏm) *adj.* causing weariness. **wea'ri·some·ly** *adv.* **wea'ri·some·ness** *n.*

wea·ry (weer-ee) *adj.* (-ri·er, -ri·est) 1. very tired, especially from exertion or endurance. 2. tired of something, *weary of war.* 3. tiring, tedious. **weary** *v.* (wea·ried, wea·ry·ing) to make or become weary. **wea'ri·ly** *adv.* **wea'ri·ness** *n.*

wea·sel (wee-zĕl) *n.* a small fierce animal with a long slender body and brown fur, living on small animals, birds' eggs, etc. **weasel** *v.* to quibble. **wea'sel·ly** *adj.* □**weasel out,** to get out of (an obligation etc.). **weasel words,** words used to remove any real force from the expression containing them.

weath·er (weth-ĕr) *n.* the condition of the atmosphere at a certain place and time, with reference to the presence or absence of sunshine, rain, wind, etc. **weather** *adj.* windward, *on the weather side.* **weather** *v.* 1. to dry or season by exposure to the action of the weather. 2. to become dried or discolored or worn etc. in this way. 3. to sail to windward of, *the ship weathered the Cape.* 4. to come safely through, *weathered the storm.* □**keep a weather eye open** *or* **out,** to be watchful. **under the weather,** feeling unwell or depressed. **weather vane,** a revolving pointer mounted in a high place and turning easily in the wind to show the wind's direction.

weath·er-beat·en (weth-ĕr-bee-tĕn) *adj.* bronzed or damaged or worn by exposure to weather.

weath·er·board (weth-ĕr-bohrd) *n.* clapboard. **weath'er·board·ing** *n.*

weath·er·bound (weth-ĕr-bownd) *adj.* unable to proceed owing to bad weather.

weath·er·cock (weth-ĕr-kok) *n.* 1. a weather vane in the shape of a cock. 2. a changeable person.

weath·er·glass (weth-ĕr-glas) *n.* a barometer.

weath·er·ing (weth-ĕ-ring) *n.* the action or effect of weather conditions on exposed wood, rock, etc.

weath·er·man (weth-ĕr-man) *n.* (*pl.* -men, *pr.* -men) a meteorologist, especially one who broadcasts a weather forecast.

weath·er·proof (weth-ĕr-proof) *adj.* unable to be penetrated or damaged by rain, wind, cold, etc. **weatherproof** *v.* to make weatherproof.

weath·er·strip·ping (weth-ĕr-strip-ing) *n.* strips of material used to make doors or windows weatherproof. **weath'er·strip** *v.* (weath·er·stripped, weath·er·strip·ping) to apply such material to.

weath·er·worn (weth-ĕr-wohrn) *adj.* damaged by storms etc.

weave (weev) *v.* (wove, wo·ven, weav·ing) 1. to make (fabric etc.) by passing crosswise threads or strips under and over lengthwise ones. 2. to form (thread etc.) into fabric in this way. 3. (of a spider etc.) to spin or form (a cobweb). 4. to put together into a connected whole, to compose (a story etc.). 5. to move from side to side in an intricate course, *weaving his way through the crowd.* **weave** *n.* a style or pattern of weaving, *a loose weave.* **weav'er** *n.*

weav·er·bird (wee-vĕr-burd) *n.* a tropical bird that builds a nest of elaborately interwoven twigs etc.

web (web) *n.* 1. the network of fine strands made by a spider etc. 2. a network, *a web of deceit.* 3. skin filling the spaces between the toes of birds such as ducks and animals such as frogs. **webbed** *adj.*

web·bing (web-ing) *n.* strong bands of woven fabric used in upholstery, belts, etc.

web-foot·ed (web-fuut-id) *adj.* having the toes joined by web.

wed (wed) *v.* (wed·ded *or* wed, wed·ding) 1. to marry. 2. to unite, *if we can wed efficiency to economy.* □**wedded to,** devoted to and unable to abandon (an occupation or opinion etc.).

Wed. *abbr.* Wednesday.

we'd (weed) = we had, we should.

wed·ding (wed-ing) *n.* 1. a marriage ceremony and festivities. 2. the anniversary of a wedding, *our silver wedding.* 3. a uniting or blending together. □**wedding cake,** a rich iced cake cut and eaten at a wedding. **wedding day,** the day or anniversary of a wedding. **wedding ring,** a ring placed on the bride's finger and usually worn permanently afterward; one worn similarly by a married man.

wedge (wej) *n.* 1. a piece of wood or metal etc. thick at one end and tapered to a thin edge at the other, thrust between things to force them apart or prevent free movement etc. 2. a wedge-shaped thing, *a wedge of cake.* 3. *(informal)* a hero sandwich. **wedge** *v.* **(wedged, wedg·ing)** 1. to force apart or fix firmly by using a wedge. 2. to thrust or pack tightly between other things or people or in a limited space, to be immovable because of this.

Wedg·wood (wej-wuud) *n.* 1. a kind of fine pottery named after Josiah Wedgwood, its original 18th century manufacturer. 2. the blue color characteristic of this.

wed·lock (wed-lok) *n.* the married state; *born out of wedlock,* illegitimate.

Wednes·day (wenz-day) *n.* the day of the week following Tuesday.

wee (wee) *adj.* **(we·er, we·est)** 1. *(Scottish)* little, *wee Georgie.* 2. *(informal)* tiny, *it's a wee bit too long.* □**wee hours,** the hours soon after midnight.

weed (weed) *n.* a wild plant growing where it is not wanted. **weed** *v.* to remove weeds from, to uproot weeds. **weed'er** *n.* □**weed out,** to remove as inferior or undesirable.

weed-kill·er (weed-kil-ĕr) *n.* a substance used to destroy weeds.

weeds (weedz) *n. pl.* deep mourning formerly worn by widows.

weed·y (wee-dee) *adj.* **(weed·i·er, weed·i·est)** 1. full of weeds. 2. thin and weak looking. **weed'i·ly** *adv.* **weed'i·ness** *n.*

week (week) *n.* 1. a period of seven successive days, especially one reckoned from midnight at the end of Saturday. 2. the six days other than Sunday, the five days other than Saturday and Sunday, *never go there during the week.* 3. the period for which one regularly works during the week, *a forty-hour week.*

week·day (week-day) *n.* a day other than Sunday, or other than Saturday and Sunday.

week·end (week-end) *n.* the period of time between Friday night and Monday morning. **weekend** *v.* to spend a weekend.

week·end·er (week-en-dĕr) *n.* 1. a person spending a weekend holiday. 2. a small suitcase suitable for a weekend.

week·ly (week-lee) *adj.* happening or published or payable etc. once a week. **weekly** *adv.* once a week. **weekly** *n.* (*pl.* **-lies**) a weekly newspaper or magazine.

ween (ween) *v.* *(old use)* to be of an opinion.

wee·ny (wee-nee) *adj.* *(informal)* tiny.

weep (weep) *v.* **(wept, weep·ing)** 1. to shed tears. 2. to shed or ooze moisture in drops. **weep** *n.* a spell of weeping. **weep'er** *n.*

weep·ing (wee-ping) *adj.* (of a tree) having drooping branches, *weeping willow.*

weep·y (wee-pee) *adj.* **(weep·i·er, weep·i·est)** *(informal)* inclined to weep, tearful.

wee·vil (wee-vil) *n.* a kind of small beetle that feeds on farm crops. **wee'vil·y** *adj.*

wee-wee (wee-wee) *v.* **(wee·weed, wee·wee·ing)** *(children's use)* to urinate. **weewee** *n.* *(children's use)* urine, urination.

weft (weft) *n.* (also **woof**) crosswise threads woven under and over the warp to make fabric.

weigh (way) *v.* 1. to measure the weight of, espe-

cially by means of scales or a similar instrument. 2. to have a certain weight. 3. to consider carefully the relative importance or value of, *weigh the pros and cons.* 4. to have importance or influence, *this evidence weighed with the jury.* 5. to be burdensome, *the responsibility weighed heavily upon him.* **weigh'er** *n.* □**under weigh,** *(incorrect use) see* **under. weigh anchor,** to raise the anchor and start a voyage. **weigh down,** to bring or keep down by its weight; to depress or make troubled, *weighed down with cares.* **weigh in,** to be weighed, (of a boxer) before a contest, (of a jockey) after a race. **weigh in with,** *(informal)* to contribute (a comment) to a discussion. **weigh one's words,** to select carefully those that convey exactly what one means.

weight (wayt) *n.* 1. an object's mass numerically expressed according to a recognized scale of units. 2. the property of heaviness. 3. a unit or system of units by which weight is measured, *tables of weights and measures; troy weight.* 4. a piece of metal of known weight used in scales for weighing things. 5. a heavy object, especially one used to bring or keep something down, *the clock is worked by weights.* 6. a load to be supported, *the pillars carry a great weight.* 7. a heavy burden of responsibility or worry. 8. importance, influence, a convincing effect, *the weight of the evidence is against you.* **weight** *v.* 1. to attach a weight to, to hold down with a weight or weights. 2. to burden with a load. 3. to bias or arrange the balance of, *the test was weighted in favor of candidates with scientific knowledge.* □**carry weight,** *see* **carry. throw one's weight around,** *(informal)* to use one's influence aggressively. **weight lifter,** a person who engages in **weight lifting,** the athletic sport of lifting heavy weights.

weight·less (wayt-lis) *adj.* having no weight, or with no weight relative to its surroundings (as in a spacecraft that is outside the action of gravity). **weight'less·ly** *adv.* **weight'less·ness** *n.*

weight·y (way-tee) *adj.* **(weight·i·er, weight·i·est)** 1. having great weight, heavy. 2. burdensome. 3. showing or deserving earnest thought. 4. important, influential. **weight'i·ly** *adv.* **weight'i·ness** *n.*

Wei·mar·an·er (wɪ-mă-rah-nĕr) *n.* a hunting dog with pale eyes and a smooth short usually gray coat.

weir (weer) *n.* 1. a small dam built across a river or canal so that water flows over it, serving to regulate the flow or to raise the level of water upstream. 2. a fence, as of brushwood or stakes with nets, built in a stream or channel to catch fish.

weird (weerd) *adj.* strange and uncanny or bizarre. **weird'ly** *adv.* **weird'ness** *n.*

weird·ie (weer-dee), **weird·o** (weer-doh) *n.* *(slang)* an eccentric person.

Welch (welch) *adj. & n.* = **Welsh.**

wel·come (wel-kŏm) *adj.* 1. received with pleasure, *a welcome guest or gift; make a person welcome,* cause him to feel welcome. 2. ungrudgingly permitted, *anyone is welcome to try it; you're welcome,* a polite phrase replying to thanks for something. **welcome** *interj.* a greeting expressing pleasure at a person's coming. **welcome** *v.* **(wel·comed, wel·com·ing)** 1. to greet with pleasure or ceremony. 2. to be glad to receive, *we welcome this opportunity.* **welcome** *n.* a greeting or reception, especially a glad and kindly one.

weld (weld) *v.* 1. to unite or fuse (pieces of metal) by hammering or pressure, usually after softening by heat. 2. to make by welding. 3. to be able to be welded. 4. to unite into a whole. **weld** *n.* a joint or union made by welding. **weld′er** *n.*

wel·fare (wel-fair) *n.* 1. well-being. 2. welfare work. 3. government financial assistance to needy persons. □**on welfare,** *(informal)* receiving financial assistance from the government because of need. **welfare state,** a country seeking to ensure the welfare of all its citizens by providing extensive social services. **welfare work,** organized efforts to secure the welfare of the poor or disabled etc.

wel·kin (wel-kin) *n.* *(poetical)* the sky, *let the welkin ring.*

well¹ (wel) *n.* 1. a shaft dug in the ground to obtain water or oil etc. from below the earth's surface. 2. a spring serving as a source of water. 3. an enclosed space resembling the shaft of a well, a deep enclosed space containing a staircase or elevator in a building. 4. a source, especially of emotions, information, etc. **well** *v.* to rise or spring, *tears welled up in her eyes.*

well² *adv.* **(better, best)** 1. in a good manner or style, satisfactorily, rightly. 2. thoroughly, carefully, *polish it well.* 3. by a considerable margin, *she is well over forty.* 4. favorably, kindly, *they think well of him.* 5. with good reason, easily, probably, *you may well ask; it may well be our last chance.* **well** *adj.* 1. in good health. (▷See the note under **good.**) 2. in satisfactory state or position, *all's well.* **well** *interj.* expressing surprise or relief or resignation etc., or used to introduce a remark when one is hesitating. □**as well, as well as,** *see* **as. be well away,** to have started and made considerable progress. **let well enough alone,** to leave things as they are and not meddle unnecessarily.

we'll (weel) = we shall, we will.

well-ac·quaint·ed (wel-ă-kwain-tid) *adj.* thoroughly acquainted.

well-ad·vised (wel-ăd-vɪzd) *adj.* showing good sense.

well-ap·point·ed (wel-ă-poin-tid) *adj.* having the necessary equipment or furniture for efficiency and comfort, *a well-appointed kitchen.*

well-at·tend·ed (wel-ă-ten-did) *adj.* having many people in attendance.

well-bal·anced (wel-bal-ănst) *adj.* 1. sane, sensible. 2. equally matched.

well-be·haved (wel-bi-hayvd) *adj.* having good manners or conduct.

well-be·ing (wel-bee-ing) *n.* good health, happiness, and prosperity.

well-born (wel-born) *adj.* born of a good family.

well-bred (wel-bred) *adj.* 1. showing good breeding, well-mannered. 2. (of a horse etc.) of good breed or stock.

well-built (wel-bilt) *adj.* 1. built correctly. 2. *(informal)* sturdy, shapely.

well-con·nect·ed (wel-kŏ-nek-tid) *adj.* related to good families.

well-de·fined (wel-di-frnd) *adj.* thoroughly de-

fined, accurately outlined, clearly determined or indicated.

well-de·vel·oped (wel-di-vel-ŏpt) *adj.* *(informal)* sturdy, shapely.

well-dis·posed (wel-di-spohzd) *adj.* having kindly or favorable feelings (toward a person or plan etc.).

well-done (wel-dun) *adj.* 1. done efficiently and with skill. 2. (of meat) cooked thoroughly.

well-dressed (wel-drest) *adj.* dressed attractively and appropriately.

well-earned (wel-urnd) *adj.* fully deserved.

well-fa·vored (wel-fay-vŏrd) *adj.* good-looking.

well-fed (wel-fed) *adj.* plump.

well-fixed (wel-fikst) *adj.* *(informal)* wealthy.

well-found·ed (wel-fown-did) *adj.* (of a suspicion or other belief or sentiment) having foundation in fact or reason.

well-groomed (wel-groomd) *adj.* carefully tended, neat and clean in one's personal appearance.

well-ground·ed (wel-grown-did) *adj.* 1. thoroughly trained in the rudiments. 2. well-founded.

well-head (wel-hed) *n.* 1. a source, especially of a spring. 2. a shelter built over a well.

well-heeled (wel-heeld) *adj.* *(informal)* wealthy.

well-in·formed (wel-in-formd) *adj.* having good knowledge or information.

wel·ling·ton (wel-ing-tŏn) *n.* a tall leather boot with the front covering the knee.

Wel·ling·ton (wel-ing-tŏn) the capital of New Zealand.

well-in·ten·tioned (wel-in-ten-shŏnd) *adj.* having or showing good intentions.

well-judged (wel-jujd) *adj.* (of an action) showing good judgment or tact or aim.

well-kept (wel-kept) *adj.* (of a person) well-groomed, (of a room etc.) tidy; *a well-kept secret,* one not divulged.

well-knit (wel-nit) *adj.* having a compact body, not ungainly.

well-known (wel-nohn) *adj.* 1. fully known. 2. familiar. 3. widely known.

well-made (wel-mayd) *adj.* made with care and skill.

well-man·nered (wel-man-ĕrd) *adj.* having or showing good manners.

well-mean·ing (wel-mee-ning) *adj.* (also **well-meant,** *pr.* wel-ment) acting or done with good intentions but not having a good effect.

well-nigh (wel-nɪ) *adv.* almost.

well-off (wel-awf) *adj.* 1. in a satisfactory or good situation. 2. fairly rich.

well-oiled (wel-oild) *adj.* *(slang)* drunk.

well-or·dered (wel-or-dĕrd) *adj.* arranged in an orderly manner.

well-pre·served (wel-pri-zurvd) *adj.* showing little sign of age.

well-read (wel-red) *adj.* having read much literature.

well-rea·soned (wel-ree-zŏnd) *adj.* based on fact and clear reasoning.

well-round·ed (wel-rown-did) *adj.* 1. varied and complete. 2. (of a person) having developed many

well′-ac·cept′ed *adj.*
well′-ad·just′ed *adj.*
well′-armed′ *adj.*
well′-cho′sen *adj.*
well′-de·served′ *adj.*

well′-formed′ *adj.*
well′-hid′den *adj.*
well′-liked′ *adj.*
well′-loved′ *adj.*
well′-paid′ *adj.*

well′-planned′ *adj.*
well′-po·si′tioned *adj.*
well′-qual′i·fied *adj.*
well′-rec′og·nized *adj.*
well′-rep·re·sent′ed *adj.*

abilities. 3. complete and symmetrical. 4. complete and well-expressed, as a sentence.

well-sea·soned (wel-see-zŏnd) *adj.* 1. thoroughly flavored with condiments etc. 2. sufficiently aged. 3. highly experienced.

well-spo·ken (wel-spoh-kĕn) *adj.* speaking in a polite and correct way.

well·spring (wel-spring) *n.* 1. the source of a stream. 2. an inexhaustible supply.

well-thought-of (wel-thawt-uv) *adj.* greatly esteemed.

well-timed (wel-trmd) *adj.* opportune, timely.

well-to-do (wel-tŏ-doo) *adj.* fairly rich.

well-trav·eled (wel-trav-ĕld) *adj.* widely traveled.

well-turned (wel-turnd) *adj.* 1. neatly expressed, as a compliment, phrase, or verse. 2. shaped well.

well-used (wel-yoozd) *adj.* much used.

well-wish·er (wel-wish-ĕr) *n.* a person who wishes another well.

well-worn (wel-wohrn) *adj.* 1. much worn by use. 2. (of a phrase) much used, hackneyed.

welsh (welsh) *v.* 1. to fail to pay one's gambling debts, *they welshed on us.* 2. to break an agreement, *they welshed on the agreement.* **welsh'er** *n.*

Welsh (welsh) *adj.* of Wales or its people or language. **Welsh** *n.* 1. the Welsh language. 2. *the Welsh,* Welsh people. **Welsh·man** (welsh-măn) *n.* (*pl.* **-men,** *pr.* -mĕn) **Welsh·wom·an** (welsh-wuum-ăn) *n. fem.* (*pl.* **-wom·en,** *pr.* -wim-in) ☐**Welsh corgi,** *see* **corgi. Welsh rabbit** *or* **rarebit,** *see* **rabbit.**

welt (welt) *n.* 1. a strip of leather etc. sewn around the edge of the upper of a boot or shoe for attaching it to the sole. 2. a ridge raised on the flesh by a heavy blow, especially by the stroke of a whip or stick. 3. a ribbed or strengthened border of a knitted garment, as at the waist.

wel·ter (wel-tĕr) *v.* 1. to roll, to wallow; *weltering in their own blood,* prostrate and soaked in it. 2. (of a ship etc.) to be tossed to and fro on the waves. **welter** *n.* a state of turmoil, a disorderly mixture.

wel·ter·weight (wel-tĕr-wayt) *n.* a boxer between lightweight and middleweight weighing up to 147 pounds.

wen (wen) *n.* a more or less permanent benign tumor on the skin, especially on the head.

wench (wench) *n.* (*old use*) a girl or young woman.

wend (wend) *v.* **wend one's way,** to go.

went (went) *see* **go**[1].

wept (wept) *see* **weep.**

were (wur) *see* **be.**

were·n't (wur-ĕnt) = were not.

were·wolf (weer-wuulf, wur-, wair-) *n.* (*pl.* **-wolves,** *pr.* -wuulvz) (in myths) a person who at times turns into a wolf.

west (west) *n.* 1. the point on the horizon where the sun sets, the direction in which the point lies. 2. the western part of something. 3. *the West,* Europe and America in contrast to Oriental countries; the noncommunist countries of Europe and America; the part of the U.S. lying west of the originally settled areas or of the Mississippi. **west** *adj. & adv.* toward or in the west; *a west wind,* blowing from the west. ☐**West Berlin,** the western division of the city of Berlin, the portion of

Berlin incorporated into West Germany. **West Germany,** the republic created in 1949 from the U.S., British, and French occupied zones in Germany. **West Indian,** of or from the **West Indies,** islands off the coast of Central America; a person of West Indian birth or descent. **West Point,** the U.S. Military Academy. **West Virginia,** a state of the U.S.

west·bound (west-bownd) *adj.* traveling westward.

west·er·ing (wes-tĕ-ring) *adj.* (of the sun) moving toward the west.

wes·ter·ly (wes-tĕr-lee) *adj.* in or toward the west; *a westerly wind,* blowing from the west (approximately). **westerly** *n.* (*pl.* **-lies**) a westerly wind.

west·ern (wes-tĕrn) *adj.* (also **Western**) of or in the west. **western** *n.* (often *Western*) a film or story dealing with life in the western U.S. during the wars with the Indians, or with cowboys etc. **West'ern·er** *n.* ☐**Western Hemisphere,** the western part of the globe including North and South America with surrounding islands and waters. **western omelet,** an omelet filled with diced green peppers, ham, and onions. **Western saddle,** a heavy saddle with a high pommel and a pommel horn, the kind used by cowboys. **Western Samoa,** an independent state consisting of the western part of Samoa. **western sandwich,** a sandwich with a western omelet filling.

west·ern·ize (wes-tĕr-nɪz) *v.* (**west·ern·ized, west·ern·iz·ing**) to make (an Oriental person or country) more like the West in ideas and institutions etc. **west·ern·i·za·tion** (wes-tĕr-ni-zay-shŏn) *n.*

west·ern·most (wes-tĕrn-mohst) *adj.* farthest west.

west·ward (west-wărd) *adj.* toward the west, in the west. **westward, westwards** (west-wardz) *adv.* toward the west.

wet (wet) *adj.* (**wet·ter, wet·test**) 1. soaked or covered or moistened with water or other liquid. 2. rainy, *wet weather.* 3. (of paint or ink etc.) recently applied and not yet dry. 4. allowing the sale of alcohol. **wet** *v.* (**wet·ted, wet·ting**) 1. to make or become wet. 2. to urinate. **wet** *n.* 1. moisture, liquid that wets something. 2. wet weather. 3. a person who favors the sale of alcohol. **wet'ly** *adv.* **wet'ness** *n.* **wet'ter** *n.* ☐**all wet,** (*slang*) wrong, in error. **wet behind the ears,** immature, inexperienced. **wet blanket,** a gloomy person who prevents others from enjoying themselves. **wet cell,** a cell with a liquid electrolyte. **wet nurse,** a woman employed to suckle another's child. **wet one's whistle,** (*informal*) to take a drink. **wet suit,** a rubber garment worn by a skin diver for warmth in cold water. **wetting agent,** a mixture added to a liquid to increase its ability to spread over a surface.

wet·back (wet-bak) *n.* (*slang*) an illegal immigrant from Mexico to the U.S.

weth·er (weth-ĕr) *n.* a castrated ram.

wet·lands (wet-lăndz) *n.* swamps and other damp areas of land.

wet-nurse (wet-nurs) *v.* 1. to suckle another's child, to act as a wet nurse. 2. (*informal*) to look after or coddle as if helpless.

we've (weev) = we have.

---

well'-sat·is·fied *adj.*
well'-spent' *adj.*

well'-sup·plied' *adj.*
well'-sup·port'ed *adj.*

well'-treat'ed *adj.*
well'-trod' *adj.*

whack (hwak) *n.* 1. a heavy resounding blow or the sound of such a blow. 2. *(informal)* an attempt, *have a whack at it.* 3. *(slang)* a share, *a whack of it.* **whack** *v.* to strike or beat vigorously; *whack out a solution to the problem,* produce one by vigorous thought. **whack'er** *n.* □**out of whack,** *(slang)* not in good condition.

whale (hwayl) *n.* (*pl.* **whales, whale**) any of several very large sea animals some of which are hunted for their oil and flesh. **whale** *v.* (**whaled, whal·ing**) *(informal)* to beat or thrash. □**a whale of a,** *(informal)* an exceedingly great or good, *had a whale of a time.*

whale·boat (hwayl-boht) *n.* a long narrow boat of a type formerly used in whaling, with a bow at each end for ease in maneuvering.

whale·bone (hwayl-bohn) *n.* a horny springy substance from the upper jaw of some kinds of whales, formerly used as stiffening.

whal·er (hway-lĕr) *n.* a person or ship engaged in whaling.

whal·ing (hway-ling) *n.* fishing for whales.

wham (hwam) *interj.* & *n.* the sound of a forcible impact. **wham** *v.* (**whammed, wham·ming**) to hit with such a sound.

wham·my (hwam-ee) *n.* (*pl.* **-mies**) *(slang)* a supernatural power, especially one bringing bad luck, a jinx, *she put a double whammy on him.*

whang (hwang) *v.* to strike heavily and loudly. **whang** *n.* a whanging sound or blow.

wharf (hworf) *n.* (*pl.* **wharves,** *pr.* hworvz, **wharfs**) a landing place where ships may moor for loading and unloading.

wharf·age (hwor-fij) *n.* 1. the use of a wharf. 2. the charge for this.

wharf·in·ger (hwor-fin-jĕr) *n.* the owner or supervisor of a wharf.

what (hwut) *adj.* 1. asking for a statement of amount or number or kind, *what stores have we got?* 2. which, *what languages does he speak?* 3. how great or strange or remarkable, *what a fool you are!* 4. the or any that, *lend me what money you can spare.* **what** *pronoun* 1. what thing or things, *what did you say?; this is what I mean.* 2. a request for something to be repeated because one has not heard or understood. **what** *adv.* to what extent or degree, *what does it matter?* **what** *interj.* an exclamation of surprise. □**what about,** what is the news about (a subject); what do you think of, how would you deal with; shall we do or have, *what about some tea?* **what-d'you-call it, what's-his** (*or* **her** *or* **its)-name,** substitutes for a name that one cannot remember. **what for?,** for what reason or purpose?; *give a person what for,* *(slang)* to punish or scold him. **what have you,** other similar things. **what is more,** as an additional point, moreover. **what not,** other similar things. **what's what,** what things are useful or important etc., *she knows what's what.* **what with,** on account of (various causes), *what with overwork and undernourishment he fell ill.*

what·ev·er (hwut-ev-ĕr) *adj.* 1. of any kind or number, *take whatever books you need.* 2. of any kind at all, *there is no doubt whatever.* **whatever** *pronoun* anything or everything that, no matter what, *do whatever you like; keep calm, whatever happens.* □**or whatever,** or anything similar.

what'll (hwut-ĕl) = what shall, what will.

what·not (hwut-not) *n.* 1. something trivial or indefinite. 2. a stand with shelves for small objects.

what's (hwuts) = what is, what has, what does.

what·so·ev·er (hwut-soh-ev-ĕr) *adj.* & *pronoun* = **whatever.**

wheal (hweel) *n.* 1. a raised itching spot on the skin, as from an insect bite. 2. = **weal.**

wheat (hweet) *n.* grain from which flour is made, the plant that produces this. □**wheat germ,** the nucleus of the seed of wheat, used as a source of vitamins.

wheat·en (hwee-tĕn) *adj.* made from wheat flour.

whee·dle (hwee-dĕl) *v.* (**whee·dled, whee·dling**) to coax, to persuade or obtain by coaxing. **whee'dler** *n.*

wheel (hweel) *n.* 1. a disk or circular frame arranged to revolve on a shaft that passes through its center. 2. something resembling this. 3. a machine etc. of which a wheel is an essential part. 4. motion like that of a wheel, or of a line of men that pivots on one end. 5. *wheels,* *(slang)* a car. **wheel** *v.* 1. to push or pull (a bicycle or cart etc. with wheels) along. 2. to turn or cause to turn like a wheel, to change direction and face another way, *he wheeled around in astonishment.* 3. to move in circles or curves. **wheeled** *adj.* **wheel'less** *adj.* □**at the wheel,** driving a vehicle or directing a ship's course; in control of affairs. **wheeling and dealing,** *(slang)* scheming so as to exert influence. **wheels within wheels,** secret or indirect motives and influences interacting with one another.

wheel·bar·row (hweel-bar-oh) *n.* an open container for moving small loads, with a wheel or ball beneath one end, and two straight handles (by which it is pushed) and legs at the other.

wheel·base (hweel-bays) *n.* the distance between the front and rear axles of a vehicle.

wheel·chair (hweel-chair) *n.* an invalid's chair on wheels.

wheel·er (hwee-lĕr) *n.* 1. a person or thing that wheels. 2. a wheelwright.

wheel·er-deal·er (hwee-lĕr-dee-lĕr) *n.* *(slang)* a person who seeks profit or power by scheming to exert influence.

wheel·horse (hweel-hors) *n.* 1. a horse harnessed next to the wheels and behind another. 2. a steady worker.

wheel·wright (hweel-rīt) *n.* *(old use)* a person who makes and repairs wheels.

wheeze (hweez) *v.* (**wheezed, wheez·ing**) to breathe with an audible hoarse whistling sound. **wheeze** *n.* 1. the sound of wheezing. 2. *(slang)* an old overused saying or joke. **wheez'y** *adj.* (**wheez·i·er, wheez·i·est**).

whelk (hwelk) *n.* any of several spiral-shelled sea mollusks, especially one used as food in Europe.

whelm (hwelm) *v.* *(literary)* to engulf, to submerge, to overwhelm.

whelp (hwelp) *n.* a young dog, a pup. **whelp** *v.* to give birth to (a whelp or whelps).

when (hwen) *adv.* 1. at what time? on what occasion? 2. at which time, *there are times when joking is out of place.* **when** *conj.* 1. at the time that, on the occasion that, whenever, as soon as. 2. although, considering that, since, *why risk it when you know it's dangerous?* **when** *pronoun* what or which time, *from when does the agreement date?* **when** *n.* the time, *told me the when and the how of it.*

whence (hwens) *adv.* & *conj.* from where, from what place or source, from which. ▷ It is incorrect to write *from whence.* Omit *from.* *I know not whence he came.*

when·ev·er (hwen-ev-ĕr) *adv. & conj.* at whatever time, on whatever occasion, every time that.

where (hwair) *adv. & conj.* 1. at or in what or which place or position or circumstances. 2. in what respect, from what place or source or origin. 3. to what place. 4. in or at or to the place in which, *leave it where it is.* **where** *pronoun* what place, *where does she come from?* **where** *n.* a place, the scene of something, *have they fixed the where and when?* ▷It is incorrect to use *where* to mean *when* or *that.* Do not write *Lincoln's birthday is a day where there is no school* or *I can tell by her expression where she is unhappy.* Write *when there is no school* and *that she is unhappy.*

where·a·bouts (hwair-ă-bowts) *adv.* in or near what place. **whereabouts** *n.* a person's or thing's approximate location, *his whereabouts are* or *is uncertain.*

where·as (hwair-az) *conj.* 1. since it is the fact that. 2. but in contrast, *he is English, whereas his wife is French.*

where·by (hwair-br) *conj.* by which.

where·fore (hwair-fohr) *adv. & conj. (old use)* for what reason, for this reason. **wherefore** *n.* the reason.

where·in (hwair-in) *adv. & conj.* in what, in which.

where·of (hwair-uv) *adv. & conj.* of which, of what.

where·on (hwair-on) *adv. & conj.* on which, on what.

where·to (hwair-too) *adv. & conj.* to what, to which.

where·up·on (hwair-ŭ-pon) *adv. & conj.* after which, and then.

wher·ev·er (hwair-ev-ĕr) *adv. & conj.* in or to whatever place, in every place that.

where·with·al (hwair-with-awl) *n. (informal)* the things (especially money) needed for a purpose.

whet (hwet) *v.* (**whet·ted, whet·ting**) 1. to sharpen by rubbing against a stone etc. 2. to stimulate, *whet one's appetite* or *interest.* **whet′ ter** *n.*

wheth·er (hweth-ĕr) *conj.* introducing an alternative possibility, *we don't know whether she will come or not.*

whet·stone (hwet-stohn) *n.* a shaped stone used for sharpening tools.

whew (hwyoo) *interj.* an exclamation of astonishment or dismay or relief.

whey (hway) *n.* watery liquid left when milk forms curds, as in cheese making.

whf. *abbr.* wharf.

which (hwich) *adj. & pronoun* 1. what particular one or ones of a set of things or people, *which Bob do you mean?* 2. and that, *we invited him to come, which he did very willingly.* **which** *relative pronoun,* the thing or animal referred to, *the house, which is large, is left to his son.* ▷Used especially of an incidental description rather than one that defines or identifies something. (See the note under **that.**)

which·ev·er (hwich-ev-ĕr) *adj. & pronoun* any which, that or those which, *take whichever* or *whichever one you like.*

whiff (hwif) *n.* a puff of air or smoke or odor. **whiff** *v.* 1. to blow or puff lightly. 2. to smell.

whif·fle·tree (hwif-ĕl-tree) *n.* a crossbar, pivoted in the middle, to the ends of which traces are attached for pulling a horsedrawn carriage, cart, etc.

Whig (hwig) *n.* 1. a supporter of the American Rev-

olution. 2. a member of the political party (1834–56) succeeded by the Republicans, in opposition to the Democratic Party.

while (hwɪl) *n.* a period of time, the time spent in doing something, *a long while ago; we've waited all this while; worth one's while, see* **worth. while** *conj.* 1. during the time that, as long as, *make hay while the sun shines.* 2. although, *while I admit that he is sincere, I think he is mistaken.* 3. on the other hand, *she is dark, while her sister is fair.* **while** *v.* (**whiled, whil·ing**) **while away,** to pass (time) in a leisurely or interesting manner.

whim (hwim) *n.* a sudden fancy, a sudden unreasoning desire or impulse.

whim·per (hwim-pĕr) *v.* to whine softly, to make feeble frightened or complaining sounds. **whimper** *n.* a whimpering sound. **whim′per· ing·ly** *adv.* **whim′per·er** *n.*

whim·si·cal (hwim-zi-kăl) *adj.* 1. impulsive and playful. 2. fanciful, quaint. **whim′si·cal·ly** *adv.* **whim·si·cal·i·ty** (hwim-zi-kal-i-tee) *n.*

whim·sy (hwim-zee) *n.* (*pl.* **-sies**) a whim.

whine (hwɪn) *v.* (**whined, whin·ing**) 1. to make a long high complaining cry like that of a child or dog. 2. to make a long high shrill sound resembling this. 3. to complain in a petty or feeble way, to utter complainingly. **whine** *n.* a whining cry or sound or complaint. **whin′er** *n.* **whin′y** *adj.* **whin′ing·ly** *adv.*

whin·ny (hwin-ee) *n.* a gentle or joyful neigh. **whinny** *v.* (**whin·nied, whin·ny·ing**) to utter a whinny.

whip (hwip) *n.* 1. a cord or strip of leather fastened to a handle, used for urging animals on or for striking a person or animal in punishment. 2. a blow struck by or as by this, a whipping motion. 3. an official of a political party in a legislative body with authority to maintain discipline among members of his party, especially in voting along party lines. 4. a dessert made by whipping a mixture of cream etc. with fruit or flavoring. **whip** *v.* (**whipped, whip·ping**) 1. to strike or urge on with a whip. 2. to beat (cream or eggs etc.) into a froth. 3. to move or take suddenly, *whipped out a knife.* 4. (in sewing) to overcast (an edge). 5. *(informal)* to defeat, to outdo. 6. to thrash or flap about. **whip′per** *n.* □**have the whip hand,** to be in a controlling position. **whip into shape,** *(informal)* to bring into line. **whip up,** to incite, to stir up, *whip up support for the proposal.*

whip·cord (hwip-kord) *n.* 1. cord made of tightly twisted strands. 2. a kind of twilled fabric with prominent ridges.

whip·lash (hwip-lash) *n.* the lash of a whip; *whiplash injury,* injury to the neck caused by a sudden jerk of the head (as when traveling in a vehicle that collides with something).

whip·per·snap·per (hwip-ĕr-snap-ĕr) *n.* a young and insignificant person who behaves in a presumptuous way.

whip·pet (hwip-it) *n.* a small dog resembling a greyhound, used for racing.

whip·ping (hwip-ing) **boy** a person who is regularly made to bear the blame and punishment when someone is at fault. ▷Formerly, in some countries, a boy was educated with a young prince and whipped in his stead for the prince's faults.

whip·poor·will (hwip-ŏr-wil) *n.* a North American bird with a call that resembles the sound of its name.

whip·saw (hwip-saw) *n.* 1. a narrow saw blade

with ends held by a frame. 2. a keyhole saw.
whipsaw v. to cheat or be cheated in two ways at the same time.
whir (hwur) v. **(whirred, whir·ring)** to move with or to make a continuous buzzing sound. **whir** n. a buzzing or vibrating sound like that of a wheel turning rapidly.
whirl (hwurl) v. 1. to swing or spin around and around, to cause to have this motion. 2. to travel swiftly in a curved course. 3. to convey or go rapidly in a vehicle, *the car whirled them away.* **whirl** n. 1. a whirling movement. 2. a confused state, *her thoughts were in a whirl.* 3. a bustling activity, *the social whirl.* 4. *(slang)* a try, *give it a whirl.* **whirl'er** n.
whirl·pool (hwurl-pool) n. a current of water whirling in a circle, often drawing floating objects toward its center.
whirl·wind (hwurl-wind) n. a mass of air whirling rapidly about a central point; *a whirlwind courtship,* a very rapid one.
whirl·y·bird (hwur-li-burd) n. *(informal)* a helicopter.
whish (hwish) v. to move with a swish. **whish** n. a whishing sound.
whisk (hwisk) v. 1. to move with a quick light sweeping movement. 2. to convey or go rapidly, *he was whisked off to the airport.* 3. to brush or sweep lightly from a surface, *whisked away the crumbs.* 4. to beat (eggs etc.) into a froth. **whisk** v. 1. a whisking movement. 2. an instrument for beating eggs etc. 3. a bunch of strips of straw etc. tied to a handle, used for flicking flies away etc. □**whisk broom,** a short-handled broom for brushing clothes.
whisk·er (hwis-kĕr) n. 1. one of the long hairlike bristles growing near the mouth of a cat and certain other animals. 2. *(informal)* a very small distance, *within a whisker of it.* 3. whiskers, hair growing on a man's face, especially on the cheek.
whisk·ered (hwis-kĕrd) adj. having whiskers.
whis·key, whis·ky (hwis-kee) n. (pl. **-keys, -kies**) 1. an alcoholic liquor distilled from a fermented mash of corn, barley, or other grains. 2. a drink of this. ▷The spelling *whiskey* is used for American and Irish products, *whisky* for Scotch and Canadian.
whis·per (hwis-pĕr) v. 1. to speak or utter softly, using the breath but not the vocal cords. 2. to converse privately or secretly, to plot or spread (a tale) as a rumor in this way. 3. (of leaves or fabrics etc.) to rustle. **whisper** n. 1. a whispering sound or remark, whispering speech, *spoke in a whisper.* 2. a rumor, *heard a whisper that the firm was closing down.* **whis'per·er** n. □**whispering gallery,** a gallery or dome in which the slightest sound made at a particular point can be heard at another far off.
whist (hwist) n. a card game usually for two pairs of players.
whis·tle (hwis-ĕl) n. 1. a shrill sound made by forcing breath through the lips with these contracted to a narrow opening. 2. a similar sound made by a bird or by something thrown, or produced by a pipe etc. 3. an instrument that produces a shrill sound when air or steam is forced through it against a sharp edge or into a bell. **whistle** v. **(whis·tled, whis·tling)** to make this sound, to summon or signal or produce a tune in this way. **whis'tler** n. □**whistle for,** *(informal)* to expect in vain, to wish for but have to go without. **whis-**

tle stop, a small unimportant town on a railroad line; a brief stop (during a tour made by a politician etc.), as for purposes of electioneering.
whit (hwit) n. the least possible amount, *not a whit better.*
white (hwit) adj. **(whit·er, whit·est)** 1. of the very lightest color, like snow or common salt. 2. having a pale skin. 3. pale in the face from illness or fear or other emotion. **white** n. 1. white color. 2. a white substance or material, white clothes. 3. a white person. 4. the white part of something (as of the eyeball, around the iris). 5. the transparent substance around the yolk of an egg, turning white when cooked. 6. the white men in chess etc., the player using these. **white'ly** adv. **white'ness** n. □**white ant,** a termite. **white birch,** a European birch. **white blood cell,** a white or colorless corpuscle. **white bread,** bread made from very finely ground flour. **white Christmas,** one with snow. **white dwarf,** a small very dense faint star. **white elephant,** a useless possession. **white feather,** a symbol of cowardice. **white flag,** a symbol of surrender. **White Friars,** Carmelites. **white gold,** a pale alloy of gold with nickel etc. **white goods,** household linens, as towels, sheets, tablecloths, etc.; household appliances, as refrigerators, stoves, etc. **white heat,** the temperature at which heated metal looks white. **White House,** the official residence in Washington, D.C., of the President of the U.S.; *(informal)* the executive branch of the government of the U.S. **white lie,** a harmless lie (as one told for the sake of politeness). **white matter,** the fibrous part of the brain and spinal cord. **white meat,** poultry, veal, rabbit, pork; the breast of chicken or turkey. **white paper,** a report issued by the government to give information about its policy on a particular matter. **white pepper,** a condiment made from the ripe or husked dried berries of the pepper plant. **white pine,** a pine tree of eastern North America. **white rat,** an albino rat used in experiments. **white room,** *see* **clean room. white sale,** a sale of household linen. **white sauce,** a sauce made from butter, flour, seasonings, and milk or stock. **white slave,** a woman who is tricked and forced into prostitution. **white slavery,** this practice or state. **white supremacy,** a doctrine based on belief in the supposed natural superiority of white men over blacks and other nonwhite races, used to justify subordination of nonwhites. **white tie,** a man's white bow tie worn with full evening dress; men's full evening dress. **white water,** shallow or foamy water. **white wine,** amber or golden or pale yellow wine, not red or rosé.
white·bait (hwit-bayt) n. (pl. **-bait**) a small silvery-white fish.
white·cap (hwit-kap) n. white-crested waves at sea.
white·col·lar (hwit-kol-ăr) adj. of workers who are not engaged in manual labor, such as office workers. □**white-collar crime,** pilfering, embezzling, etc. carried out in the course of white-collar work.
white-faced (hwit-fayst) adj. 1. pale from illness or fright or actors' makeup etc. 2. (of horses, cattle, etc.) having a white or partially white face.
white·fish (hwit-fish) n. (pl. **-fish, -fish·es**) a freshwater fish of the Northern hemisphere, used as food.
white·fly (hwit-fli) n. (pl. **-flies**) a small insect that attacks shrubs etc.
white·head (hwit-hed) n. a white-topped pimple.

white-hot (hwɪt-hot) *adj.* 1. at white heat, hotter than red-hot, *white-hot steel.* 2. extremely intense, *white-hot anger.*

whit·en (hwɪ-tĕn) *n.* to make or become white or whiter. **whit′en·er** *n.* **whit′en·ing** *n.*

white-tailed (hwɪt-tayld) **deer** a North American deer with a white tail.

white·wall (hwɪt-wawl) *n.* a tire with a white side-wall.

white·wash (hwɪt-wosh) *n.* 1. a liquid containing quicklime or powdered chalk used for painting walls, ceilings, etc. 2. a means of glossing over mistakes or faults so as to clear someone's reputation. 3. *(informal)* a defeat in a sports contest in which the loser scores no points. **whitewash** *v.* 1. to paint with whitewash. 2. to clear the reputation of (a person etc.) by glossing over mistakes and faults. 3. *(informal)* to hold scoreless in a sports contest.

white·wood (hwɪt-wuud) *n.* a light-colored wood, a tree having such wood.

whith·er (hwith-ĕr) *adv. (old use)* to what place.

whit·ing[1] (hwɪ-ting) *n.* (*pl.* **-ing, ings**) a small sea fish with white flesh, used as food.

whiting[2] *n.* a chalk prepared by drying, grinding, etc. for use in whitewashing or making putty.

whit·ish (hwɪ-tish) *adj.* rather white.

whit·low (hwit-loh) *n.* a small abscess under or near a fingernail or toenail.

Whit·sun (hwit-sŭn) *n.* Whitsunday.

Whit·sun·day (hwit-sun-day) *n.* the seventh Sunday after Easter, commemorating the descent of the Holy Spirit upon the Apostles at Pentecost.

whit·tle (hwit-ĕl) *v.* (**whit·tled, whit·tling**) 1. to trim or shape (wood) by cutting thin slices from the surface. 2. to reduce by removing various amounts, *whittled down the cost by cutting out all but the essential items.* **whit′tler** *n.*

whiz (hwiz) *v.* (**whizzed, whiz·zing**) 1. to make a sound like that of something moving at great speed through air. 2. to move very quickly. **whiz** *n.* (*pl.* **whiz·zes**) 1. a whizzing sound. 2. *(slang)* a remarkably skillful person, *a whiz at math.* □**whiz kid**, *(informal)* an exceptionally brilliant or successful young person.

who (hoo) *pronoun* 1. what or which person or persons. 2. the particular person or persons, *this is the man who wanted to see you.*

WHO *abbr.* World Health Organization.

whoa (hwoh) *interj.* a command to a horse etc. to stop or stand still.

who'd (hood) = who had, who would.

who·dun·it (hoo-dun-it) *n.* *(informal)* a detective or mystery story or play etc. ▷Humorous representation of the incorrect phrase "who done it?"

who·ev·er (hoo-ev-ĕr) *pronoun* any or every person who, no matter who.

whole (hohl) *adj.* 1. with no part removed or left out, *told them the whole story; whole-wheat.* 2. not injured or broken, *there's not a plate left whole.* **whole** *n.* 1. the full or complete amount, all the parts or members. 2. a complete system made up of parts, *the universe is a whole and Earth is part of this.* **whole′ness** *n.* □**on the whole**, considering everything; in respect of the whole though some details form exceptions. **whole hog**, see **hog. whole milk**, milk with all its constituents. **whole number**, a number containing no fractions. **whole step**, (in music) a whole tone.

whole·heart·ed (hohl-hahr-tid) *adj.* without

doubts or reservations, *wholehearted approval.* **whole′heart′ed·ly** *adv.* **whole′heart′ed·ness** *n.*

whole·sale (hohl-sayl) *n.* the selling of goods in large quantities to be retailed by others. **wholesale** *adj. & adv.* 1. in the wholesale trade. 2. on a large scale, *wholesale destruction.* **wholesale** *v.* (**whole·saled, whole·sal·ing**) to sell in the wholesale trade. **whole′sal·er** *n.*

whole·some (hohl-sŏm) *adj.* good for physical or mental health or moral condition, showing a healthy condition. **whole′some·ly** *adv.* **whole′some·ness** *n.*

whole-wheat (hohl-hweet) *adj.* containing all the parts of the wheat kernel.

who'll (hool) = who will.

whol·ly (hohl-lee) *adv.* entirely, with nothing excepted or removed.

whom (hoom) *pronoun* the objective case of **who.**

whom·ev·er (hoom-ev-ĕr) *pronoun* the objective case of **whoever.**

whom·so·ev·er (hoom-soh-ev-ĕr) *pronoun* the objective case of **whosoever.**

whoop (hoop, hwoop) *v.* to utter a loud cry of excitement. **whoop** *n.* this cry. **whoop′er** *n.* □**whooping cough**, an infectious disease especially of children, with a cough that is followed by a long rasping indrawn breath. **whooping crane**, a crane that makes a whooping or whistling sound. **whoop it up**, *(slang)* to engage in noisy revelry.

whoop-de-do (hwoop-di-doo) *n.* *(informal)* 1. a noisy celebration. 2. great general excitement.

whoop·ee (hwuup-ee, wuup-ee) *interj.* an exclamation of exuberant joy. □**make whoopee**, *(slang)* to engage in noisy revelry.

whoops (hwuups, wuups) *interj. (informal)* an exclamation of surprise or apology.

whoosh (hwuush) *v.* to make or move or be moved with a sound like that of rushing air or water. **whoosh** *n.* this sound.

whop·per (hwop-er) *n.* *(informal)* 1. something very large. 2. a lie.

whop·ping (hwop-ing) *adj. (informal)* very large or remarkable, *a whopping lie.*

whore (hohr) *n.* a prostitute, a sexually immoral woman. **whor′ish** *adj.*

whorl (hworl) *n.* 1. a coiled form, one turn of a spiral. 2. a complete circle formed by ridges in a fingerprint. 3. a ring of leaves or petals around a stem or central point. **whorled** *adj.*

whor·tle·ber·ry (hwur-tĕl-ber-ee) *n.* (*pl.* **-ries**) a North European shrub or its blue berry.

who's (hooz) = who is, who has. ▷Do not confuse *who's* with *whose.*

whose (hooz) *pronoun & adj.* of whom, of which, *whose is this?; the people whose house we admired; the house whose owner takes pride in it.* ▷Do not confuse *whose* with *who's.*

who·so·ev·er (hoo-soh-ev-ĕr) *pronoun* any or every person who, no matter who.

whs., whse. *abbr.* warehouse.

whsle. *abbr.* wholesale.

why (hwɪ) *adv.* 1. for what reason or purpose? 2. on account of which, *the reasons why it happened are not clear.* **why** *interj.* an exclamation of surprised discovery or recognition. **why** *conj.* for what reason, *this is why I am leaving.* **why** *n.* a reason, an explanation. □**whys and wherefores**, reasons.

WI *abbr.* Wisconsin.

W.I. *abbr.* West Indies.

wick (wik) *n.* a length of thread in the center of a candle or oil lamp or cigarette lighter etc. by which the flame is kept supplied with melted grease or fuel.

wick·ed (wik-id) *adj.* 1. morally bad, offending against what is right. 2. very bad or formidable, severe. 3. malicious, mischievous, *a wicked grin*. **wick'ed·ly** *adv.* **wick'ed·ness** *n.*

wick·er (wik-ĕr) *n.* thin canes or reeds woven together as material for making furniture or baskets etc. **wicker** *adj.* made of wicker. **wick·er·work** (wik-ĕr-wurk) *n.*

wick·et (wik-it) *n.* 1. a small door or gate usually beside or within a larger one for use when this is not open. 2. a small opening in a door or wall, as in a theater's ticket booth. 3. (in croquet) one of the hoops through which the ball must be driven.

wick·i·up (wik-i-up) *n.* an American Indian hut of frame covered with grass etc.

wid. *abbr.* 1. widow. 2. widower.

wide (wɪd) *adj.* (**wid·er, wid·est**) 1. measuring much from side to side, not narrow, *a wide river.* 2. in width, *one meter wide.* 3. extending far, having great range, *a wide knowledge of art.* 4. open to the full extent, *staring with wide eyes.* 5. at a considerable distance from the point or mark aimed at; *his guess was wide of the mark,* quite incorrect. **wide** *adv.* widely, to the full extent, far from the target. **wide'ly** *adv.* **wide'ness** *n.* □**give a wide berth to,** *see* **berth. wide world,** the whole world, great as it is.

wide-an·gle (wɪd-ang-gĕl) *adj.* (of a lens) able to include a wider field of vision than a standard lens does.

wide-a·wake (wɪd-ă-wayk) *adj.* 1. completely awake. 2. fully alert.

wide-eyed (wɪd-ɪd) *adj.* with eyes opened widely in amazement or innocent surprise.

wide·mouthed (wɪd-mow*th*d, -mowtht) *adj.* 1. having a wide mouth, as a person, a river, a jar, etc. 2. having the mouth opened wide because of surprise or fear.

wid·en (wɪ-dĕn) *v.* to make or become wider. **wid'en·er** *n.*

wide-o·pen (wɪd-oh-pĕn) *adj.* 1. exposed to attack. 2. (of a contest) with no contestant who can be predicted as a certain winner. 3. without laws or law enforcement on gambling, prostitution, etc.

wide-rang·ing (wɪd-rayn-jing) *adj.* covering an extensive range.

wide·spread (wɪd-spred) *adj.* found or distributed over a wide area.

widg·eon (wij-ŏn) *n.* any of several kinds of wild duck.

wid·ow (wid-oh) *n.* a woman whose husband has died and who has not married again. **widow** *v.* to make into a widow. **wid'ow·hood** *n.* □**widow's peak,** a V-shaped growth of hair toward the center of the forehead.

wid·owed (wid-ohd) *adj.* made a widow or widower.

wid·ow·er (wid-oh-ĕr) *n.* a man whose wife has died and who has not married again. **wid'ow·er·hood** *n.*

width (width) *n.* 1. wideness. 2. distance or measurement from side to side. 3. a piece of material of full width as woven, *use two widths to make this curtain.*

wield (weeld) *v.* 1. to hold and use (a weapon or tool etc.) with the hands. 2. to have and use (power). **wield'er** *n.*

wie·ner (wee-nĕr) *n.* *(slang)* a frankfurter. □**wiener roast,** a party involving the roasting of frankfurters. **Wiener schnitzel** (shnit-sĕl), a breaded, fried, and garnished veal cutlet.

wife (wɪf) *n.* (*pl.* **wives,** *pr.* wɪvz) a married woman in relation to her husband. **wife'less** *adj.* **wife'ly** *adj.* **wife'hood** *n.*

wig (wig) *n.* a covering made of real or artificial hair, worn on the head. **wig** *v.* (**wigged, wig·ging**) to cover with a wig.

wig·gle (wig-ĕl) *v.* (**wig·gled, wig·gling**) to move or cause to move repeatedly from side to side, to wriggle. **wiggle** *n.* a wiggling movement. **wig'gler** *n.* **wig'gly** *adj.* □**get a wiggle on,** make haste.

wig·let (wig-lit) *n.* a small wig.

wig·wag (wig-wag) *v.* (**wig·wagged, wig·wag·ging**) 1. to move to and fro. 2. to wave flags thus in signaling. **wigwag** *n.* 1. a message so signaled. 2. the process of sending a message in this manner.

wig·wam (wig-wom) *n.* a hut or tent made by fastening skins or mats over a framework of poles, as formerly used by American Indians.

wil·co (wil-koh) *interj.* = "will comply," used in signaling etc. to indicate that directions received will be carried out.

wild (wɪld) *adj.* 1. living or growing in its original natural state, not domesticated or tame or cultivated. 2. not civilized, barbarous, *wild tribes.* 3. (of scenery) looking very desolate, not cultivated. 4. lacking restraint or discipline or control, disorderly. 5. tempestuous, stormy, *a wild night.* 6. full of strong unrestrained feeling, very eager or excited or enthusiastic or angry etc. 7. extremely foolish or unreasonable, *these wild ideas.* 8. random, *a wild guess.* 9. (of a playing card) having its value determined by the players. **wild** *n.* (usually **wilds**) 1. a desert or wilderness. 2. *the wilds,* districts far from civilization. **wild** *adv.* in a wild manner, *shooting wild.* **wild'ly** *adv.* **wild'ness** *n.* □**run wild,** to grow or live without being checked or disciplined or restrained. **sow one's wild oats,** *see* **oat. wild and woolly,** *(informal)* lacking refinement(s), barbarous. **wild flower,** a flower or flowering plant that grows without cultivation. **wild man,** a savage. **wild rice,** a tall grass yielding edible grains. **wild rose,** a rose with a flower having only one circle of petals. **Wild West,** the western states of the U.S. during the period when they were lawless frontier districts. **Wild West show,** a show demonstrating feats from the Wild West, such as horseback riding, shooting, rope twirling, etc.

wild·cat (wɪld-kat) *adj.* *(informal)* 1. reckless or impractical especially in business and finance, *wildcat schemes.* 2. (of strikes) sudden and unofficial. 3. of or relating to oil prospecting by an independent prospector. **wildcat** *v.* (**wild·cat·ted, wild·cat·ting**) *(informal)* to drill for oil etc. as an independent prospector. **wildcat** *n.* 1. a medium-sized undomesticated cat, especially a bobcat or lynx. 2. *(informal)* a hot-tempered or violent person.

wild·cat·ter (wɪld-kat-ĕr) *n.* *(informal)* an independent oil prospector.

wil·de·beest (wil-dĕ-beest) *n.* (*pl.* **-beests, -beest**) a gnu.

wil·der·ness (wil-dĕr-nis) *n.* a wild uncultivated area of land.

wild-eyed (wīld-īd) *adj.* 1. having an insane or extremely agitated look in the eyes. 2. irrational.

wild·fire (wīld-fīr) *n.* **spread like wildfire,** (of rumors etc.) to spread very fast.

wild·fowl (wīld-fowl) *n.* birds that are hunted as game, especially ducks and geese.

wild-goose (wīld-goos) **chase** a useless search, a hopeless quest.

wild·life (wīld-līf) *n.* wild animals collectively.

wild·wood (wīld-wuud) *n.* an uncultivated or unfrequented woodland.

wile (wīl) *n.* 1. a piece of trickery intended to deceive or attract someone. 2. *wiles,* beguiling or flirtatious behavior. **wile** *v.* **(wiled, wil·ing) wile away,** = while away (*see* **while**).

will[1] (wil) *auxiliary verb* (**wilt** is used with *thou*), *see* **shall.**

will[2] *n.* 1. the mental faculty by which a person decides upon and controls his own actions or those of others. 2. willpower. 3. determination; *they set to work with a will,* in a determined and energetic way. 4. that which is desired or determined, *may God's will be done.* 5. a person's attitude in wishing good or bad to others; *with the best will in the world,* however good one's intentions are. 6. written directions made by a person for the disposal of his property after his death. **will** *v.* 1. to exercise one's willpower, to influence or compel by doing this. 2. to intend unconditionally, *God has willed it.* 3. to bequeath by a will, *she willed her money to a hospital.* **willed** *adj.* □**at will,** whenever one pleases, *he comes and goes at will.* **have one's will,** to get what one desires.

will·ful (wil-fŭl) *adj.* 1. done with deliberate intention and not as an accident, *willful murder.* 2. self-willed, obstinate, *a willful child.* **will′ful·ly** *adv.* **will′ful·ness** *n.*

wil·lies (wil-eez) *n. pl.* **the willies,** *(slang)* nervous discomfort.

will·ing (wil-ing) *adj.* 1. doing readily what is required, having no objection. 2. given or performed willingly, *we received willing help.* **will′ing·ly** *adv.* **will′ing·ness** *n.*

wil·li·waw (wil-ĭ-waw) *n.* a sudden cold windstorm of mountainous coasts.

will-o'-the-wisp (wil-ŏ-*th*ĕ-wisp) *n.* a hope or aim that lures a person on but can never be fulfilled.

wil·low (wil-oh) *n.* 1. any of several trees or shrubs with very flexible branches, usually growing near water. 2. its wood. □**willow pattern,** a conventional Chinese design including a willow tree and a river, done in blue on a white background, especially on china.

wil·low·ware (wil-oh-wair) *n.* dinnerware with a willow pattern.

wil·low·y (wil-oh-ee) *adj.* 1. full of willow trees. 2. slender and supple.

will·pow·er (wil-pow-ĕr) *n.* the control exercised by one's will, especially over one's own actions and impulses.

wil·ly-nil·ly (wil-ee-nil-ee) *adv.* whether one desires it or not.

Wil·son (wil-sŏn), **(Thom·as) Wood·row** (1856–1924) the twenty-eighth president of the U.S. 1913–21.

wilt[1] (wilt) *see* **will**[1].

wilt[2] *v.* 1. (of plants or flowers) to lose freshness and droop. 2. to cause to do this. 3. (of a person) to become limp from exhaustion. **wilt** *n.* a plant disease that causes wilting.

Wil·ton (wil-tŏn) *n.* (also **Wilton carpet**) a kind of carpet with loops cut into thick pile, first made at Wilton in England.

wil·y (wī-lee) *adj.* **(wil·i·er, wil·i·est)** full of wiles, crafty, cunning. **wil′i·ness** *n.*

wim·ble (wim-bĕl) *n.* an instrument for boring holes.

wim·ple (wim-pĕl) *n.* a medieval headdress of linen or silk folded around the head and neck, covering all but the front of the face.

win (win) *v.* **(won, win·ning)** 1. to be victorious in (a battle or game or race etc.), to gain a victory. 2. to obtain or achieve as the result of a battle or contest or bet etc. 3. to obtain as a result of effort or perseverance, *he won their confidence.* 4. to gain the favor or support of, *soon won his audience over.* **win** *n.* victory in a game or contest. □**win through,** to achieve success eventually. **you can't win,** *(informal)* there is no way of achieving success or of pleasing people.

wince (wins) *v.* **(winced, winc·ing)** to make a slight involuntary movement from pain or distress or embarrassment etc. **wince** *n.* a wincing movement. **winc′er** *n.*

winch (winch) *n.* a machine for hoisting or pulling things by means of a cable that winds around a revolving drum or wheel. **winch** *v.* to hoist or pull with a winch.

wind[1] (wind) *n.* 1. a current of air either occurring naturally in the atmosphere or put in motion by the movement of something through the air or produced artificially by bellows etc. 2. smell carried by the wind, *the deer we were stalking had got our wind.* 3. gas forming in the stomach or intestines and causing discomfort. 4. breath as needed in exertion or speech or for sounding a musical instrument. 5. useless or boastful talk. 6. *winds,* the wind instruments of an orchestra. **wind** *v.* 1. to detect by the presence of a smell, *the hounds had winded the fox.* 2. to cause to be out of breath, *we were quite winded by the climb.* □**get wind of,** to hear a hint or rumor of. **in the wind,** happening or about to happen. **like the wind,** very swiftly. **take the wind out of a person's sails,** to take away his advantage suddenly, to frustrate him by anticipating his arguments etc. **wind chill factor,** an index of the combined effects of wind and low temperature on a person. **wind instrument,** a musical instrument in which sound is produced by a current of air, especially by the player's breath (as a trumpet or flute). **wind tunnel,** a tunnellike apparatus for producing an air stream of known velocity past a model of an aircraft etc. to investigate the flow or effect of wind pressure on the structure.

wind[2] (wind) *v.* **(wound,** *pr.* wownd, **wind·ing)** 1. to go or cause to go in a curving or spiral or twisting course, *the road winds its way* or *winds through the hills.* 2. to twist or wrap closely around and around upon itself so as to form a ball. 3. to wrap, to encircle, *wound a bandage around his finger.* 4. to haul or hoist or move by turning a handle or windlass etc., *wind the car window down.* 5. to wind up (a clock etc.). **wind** *n.* a single turn in winding a clock or string etc. **wind′er** *n.* □**winding sheet,** a sheet in which a corpse is wrapped for burial. **wind up,** to set or keep (a clock etc.) going by tightening its spring or adjusting its weights; to bring or come to an end; to settle and finally close the business and financial transactions of (a company going into liquidation); (of a baseball pitcher) to prepare to deliver a pitch; *(informal)* to come to a place, *he'll wind up in jail.*

wind·age (win-dij) *n.* 1. the influence of wind in changing the course of a missile. 2. the amount by which the course is changed.

wind·bag (wind-bag) *n. (informal)* a person who talks lengthily.

wind·blown (wind-blohn) *adj.* 1. blown by the wind, as hair. 2. having growth shaped by the prevailing winds, as trees.

wind·break (wind-brayk) *n.* a screen or row of trees etc. shielding something from the full force of the wind.

wind·bro·ken (wind-broh-kĕn) *adj.* (of horses) affected by impaired breathing.

wind·burn (wind-burn) *n.* a reddening of the skin caused by excessive exposure to the wind.

wind·fall (wind-fawl) *n.* 1. an apple or pear etc. blown off a tree by the wind. 2. a piece of unexpected good fortune, especially a sum of money acquired. □**windfall profits tax,** *(informal)* a tax levied on sudden and excessive profits made by a business.

Wind·hoek (vint-huuk) the capital of Namibia.

wind·jam·mer (wind-jam-ĕr) *n.* a merchant sailing ship.

wind·lass (wind-lăs) *n.* a device for pulling or hoisting things (such as a bucket of water from a well) by means of a rope or chain that winds around an axle.

wind·less (wind-lis) *adj.* without wind. **wind′less·ly** *adv.* **wind′less·ness** *n.*

wind·mill (wind-mil) *n.* a mill worked by the action of wind on projecting parts that radiate from a central shaft.

win·dow (win-doh) *n.* 1. an opening in the wall or roof of a building or in a car etc. to admit light and often air, usually filled with glass in a fixed or hinged or sliding frame. 2. this glass, with or without its frame, *broke the window.* 3. a space for the display of goods behind the window of a shop etc. 4. an opening resembling a window. **win′dow·less** *adj.* □**window box,** a trough fixed outside a window, for growing plants and flowers. **window dressing,** the displaying of goods attractively in a shop window; presentation of facts so as to create a favorable impression. **window on the world,** a means of observing and learning about people of other countries. **window seat,** a seat fixed under a window that is in a recess or bay of a room. **window sill,** the sill or ledge under a window.

win·dow·pane (win-doh-payn) *n.* a sheet of glass in a window.

win·dow-shop (win-doh-shop) *v.* (**win·dow-shopped, win·dow-shop·ping**) to look at goods displayed in shop windows etc. without necessarily intending to buy. **win′dow shop·per** *n.*

wind·pipe (wind-pıp) *n.* the principal passage by which air reaches the lungs, leading from the throat to the bronchial tubes.

wind·proof (wind-proof) *adj.* wind resistant, as a jacket, coat, etc.

wind·row (wind-roh) *n.* a line of raked hay or grain etc. made to permit drying by the wind.

wind·shield (wind-sheeld) *n.* the glass in the window at the front of a motor vehicle.

wind·sock (wind-sok) *n.* a tube-shaped piece of canvas open at both ends, flown at an airfield to show the direction of the wind.

wind·storm (wind-storm) *n.* a storm with very strong winds and little or no rain.

wind·surf·ing (wind-surf-ing) *n.* the sport of surfing on a board to which a sail is fixed.

wind·swept (wind-swept) *adj.* exposed to strong winds.

wind·up (wınd-up) *n.* 1. *(informal)* a conclusion, a finish. 2. the winding movements made by a baseball pitcher preparing to pitch.

wind·ward (wind-wărd) *adj.* situated in the direction from which the wind blows. **windward** *adv.* toward the wind. **windward** *n.* the windward side or region. □**Windward Islands,** a group of islands in the southeast West Indies.

wind·y (win-dee) *adj.* (**wind·i·er, wind·i·est**) 1. with much wind, *a windy night.* 2. exposed to high winds. 3. wordy, full of useless talk, *a windy speaker.* **wind′i·ly** *adv.* **wind′i·ness** *n.*

wine (wın) *n.* 1. fermented grape juice as an alcoholic drink. 2. a fermented drink made from other fruits or plants, *dandelion wine.* 3. dark purplish red. **wine** *v.* (**wined, win·ing**) to drink wine, to entertain with wine; *they wined and dined us,* entertained us to a meal with wine. □**wine cellar,** a cellar in which wine is stored; a store of wine.

wine·glass (wın-glas) *n.* a glass for drinking wine from.

wine·grow·er (wın-groh-ĕr) *n.* a person who grows grapes for wine.

wine·press (wın-pres) *n.* a press in which grapes are squeezed.

win·er·y (wı-nĕ-ree) *n.* (*pl.* **-er·ies**) an establishment for making wine.

wine·skin (wın-skin) *n.* the whole skin of a goat etc. sewn up and used to hold wine.

wing (wing) *n.* 1. one of a pair of projecting parts by which a bird or bat or insect etc. is able to fly. 2. a corresponding part in a nonflying bird or insect. 3. one of the parts projecting widely from the sides of an airplane and acting upon the air so that the airplane is supported in flight. 4. something resembling a wing in appearance or position (such as a thin projection on maple and sycamore seeds). 5. a projecting part extending from one end of a building, *the north wing was added in the 17th century.* 6. either end of an army or fleet lined up for battle. 7. either of the players (*left wing, right wing*) in hockey etc. whose place is at the extreme end of the forward line. 8. an air force unit of several squadrons. 9. a section of a political party or other group, with more extreme views than those of the majority. 10. *wings,* the sides of a theater stage out of sight of the audience; *waiting in the wings,* waiting in readiness. 11. *wings,* a pilot's badge. **wing** *v.* 1. to fly, to travel by means of wings, *a bird winging its way home.* 2. to wound slightly in the wing or arm. □**on the wing,** flying. **take wing,** to fly away. **under one's wing,** under one's protection. **wing bolt,** a bolt with a head resembling a wing nut. **wing chair,** an armchair with projecting sidepieces at the top of a high back. **wing collar,** a man's high stiff collar with the upper corners turned down. **wing it,** *(slang)* to throw it; to do something impromptu. **wing nut,** a nut with projections so that it can be turned by thumb and finger on a screw. **wing shot,** a shot taken at a bird in flight; an expert in shooting birds in flight. **wing tip,** the outer end of the wing of a bird or the wing of an aircraft; a style of shoe with a perforated pattern on the toecap and along the sides.

wing·ding (wing-ding) *n. (slang)* a wild party.

winged (wingd, *poetic* wing-id) *adj.* having wings.

wing·less (wing-lis) *adj.* without wings.

wing·span (wing-span) *n.* 1. the measurement between the tips of an airplane's wings. 2. a bird's wingspread.

wing·spread (wing-spred) *n.* 1. (of a bird) the measurement across the wings when extended. 2. an airplane's wingspan.

wink (wingk) *v.* 1. to close and open one eye deliberately, especially as a private signal to someone. 2. (of a light or star etc.) to shine with a light that flashes quickly on and off or twinkles. **wink** *n.* 1. an act of winking. 2. a brief period of sleep, *didn't sleep a wink.* **wink'er** *n.* ☐**wink at,** to pretend not to notice something that should be stopped or condemned.

win·ner (win-ĕr) *n.* 1. a person who wins. 2. something successful, *her latest novel is a winner.*

win·ning (win-ing) *see* **win. winning** *adj.* charming, persuasive, *a winning smile.* **win'ning·ly** *adv.*

win·nings (win-ingz) *n. pl.* money won in betting or at cards etc.

win·now (win-oh) *v.* 1. to expose (grain) to a current of air by tossing or fanning it so that the loose dry outer part is blown away, to separate (chaff) in this way. 2. to sift or separate from worthless or inferior elements, *winnow out the truth from the falsehoods.*

win·o (wi-noh) *n.* (*pl.* **-os**) *(slang)* an alcoholic, especially one who is reduced to drinking cheap wine.

win·some (win-sŏm) *adj.* having an engagingly attractive appearance or manner. **win'some·ly** *adv.* **win'some·ness** *n.*

win·ter (win-tĕr) *n.* the coldest season of the year, generally from December to March in the northern hemisphere. **winter** *v.* 1. to spend the winter, *decided to winter in Arizona.* 2. to keep or feed (plants or animals) during the winter. **winter** *adj.* 1. characteristic of or used in or lasting for the winter. 2. (of fruit or vegetables) ripening late or keeping until or during winter. 3. sown in autumn and reaped in spring, *winter wheat.* ☐**winter sports,** open-air sports on snow or ice, as skiing, skating.

win·ter·green (win-tĕr-green) *n.* 1. a shrub with aromatic leaves yielding an oil. 2. the flavor of this oil.

win·ter·ize (win-tĕ-riz) *v.* (**win·ter·ized, win·ter·iz·ing**) to adapt for operation or for use in cold weather.

win·ter·kill (win-tĕr-kil) *v.* to die or kill by overexposure to the winter cold, as a crop or a plant.

win·ter·time (win-tĕr-tim) *n.* the season of winter.

win·try (win-tree) *adj.* (**-tri·er, -tri·est**) 1. of or like winter, cold, *wintry weather.* 2. (of a smile etc.) chilly, lacking warmth or vivacity.

win·y (wi-nee) *adj.* (**win·i·er, win·i·est**) like wine, *a winy taste.*

wipe (wip) *v.* (**wiped, wip·ing**) 1. to clean or dry the surface of by rubbing something over it. 2. to remove by wiping, *wipe your tears away.* 3. to spread (a substance) thinly over a surface. **wipe** *n.* the act of wiping, *give this plate a wipe.* ☐**wipe out,** to cancel; to destroy completely, *the whole army was wiped out.*

wip·er (wi-pĕr) *n.* 1. something that wipes or is used for wiping. 2. (also **windshield wiper**) a rubber strip mechanically moved to and fro across a windshield to remove rain etc.

wire (wir) *n.* 1. a strand or slender usually flexible rod of metal. 2. a cable used to carry telephone or telegraph messages. 3. a piece of wire used to carry electric current. 4. (in horse racing) the finish line. 5. *(informal)* a telegram. **wire** *v.* **(wired, wir·ing)** 1. to provide or fasten or strengthen with wire(s). 2. to install wiring in (a house). 3. *(informal)* to send a telegram. 4. *(slang)* to arrange the outcome of (a sports event) beforehand, *the race was wired.* ☐**get one's wires crossed,** to become confused and misunderstand. **under the wire,** barely in time. **wire cutter,** a tool for cutting wire. **wire recorder,** an instrument recording sound on a steel wire by an electromagnetic process. **wire service,** a news-gathering organization that sends news by wire or electronic means to subscribers. **wire wheel,** a vehicle wheel with wire spokes.

wire·draw (wir-draw) *v.* **(wire·drew, wire·drawn, wire·draw·ing)** 1. to draw metal out into wire. 2. to protract unduly. 3. to refine or apply or press an argument, point, etc. with idle or excessive subtlety.

wire·hair (wir-hair) *n.* a fox terrier with wiry hair.

wire·haired (wir-haird) *adj.* (of a dog) having stiff wiry hair.

wire·less (wir-lis) *adj.* 1. without wires. 2. of or relating to radio communications. **wireless** *n.* (chiefly *British*) a radio.

Wire·pho·to (wir-foh-toh) *n. (trademark)* a device for sending photographs by wire. **wirephoto** *v.* to send in this way.

wire·tap (wir-tap) *v.* **(wire·tapped, wire·tap·ping)** to eavesdrop on a telephone conversation by tapping the wire (*see* **tap** definition 5). **wiretap** *n.* an instrument used in wiretapping. **wire'tap·per** *n.*

wire·worm (wir-wurm) *n.* the destructive wormlike larva of a kind of beetle.

wir·ing (wir-ing) *n.* a system of wires for conducting electricity in a building.

wir·y (wir-ee) *adj.* **(wir·i·er, wir·i·est)** 1. like wire. 2. (of a person) lean but strong. **wir'i·ness** *n.*

Wis., Wisc. *abbr.* Wisconsin.

Wis·con·sin (wis-kon-sin) a state of the U.S.

wis·dom (wiz-dŏm) *n.* 1. being wise, soundness of judgment. 2. wise sayings; *the Wisdom of Solomon,* a book of the Apocrypha. ☐**wisdom tooth,** the third and hindmost molar tooth on each side of the upper and lower jaws, usually cut (if at all) after the age of twenty.

wise[1] (wiz) *adj.* **(wis·er, wis·est)** 1. having or showing soundness of judgment. 2. having knowledge, *where ignorance is bliss, 'tis folly to be wise.* 3. *(slang)* aware, informed, *be* or *get wise to something; put him wise to it,* tell him about it. **wise** *v.* **(wised, wis·ing)** *(slang)* to inform, *wise him up about it.* **wise'ly** *adv.* ☐**be none the wiser,** to know no more than before; to be unaware of what has happened. **wise guy,** *(informal)* a know-it-all.

wise[2] *n.* *(old use)* way, manner, *in no wise.*

-wise *suffix* used to form adjectives and adverbs of manner, direction, etc., as in *clockwise, lengthwise.* ▷The ill-advised practice of attaching -wise to a growing number of words has led to some awkward expressions. *Moneywise I am not in good condition* means *I am nearly out of money*. *Militarywise we have never been weaker* means *our military forces need strengthening*.

wise·a·cre (wɪz-ay-kĕr) *n.* a person who pretends to have great wisdom, a know-it-all.

wise·crack (wɪz-krak) *n. (informal)* a witty or clever remark. **wisecrack** *v. (informal)* to make a wisecrack.

wish (wish) *n.* 1. a desire or mental aim. 2. an expression of desire about another person's welfare, *with best wishes*. **wish** *v.* 1. to have or express as a wish. 2. to formulate a wish, *wish when you see a shooting star.* 3. to hope or express hope about another person's welfare, *wish me luck; wish someone well*, hope that he prospers; *wish him "good day,"* greet him in this way. 4. *(informal)* to foist, *the dog was wished on us while its owners were on vacation.* **wish′er** *n.* □**wish for**, to desire to have, to express a wish that one may have (a thing).

wish·bone (wish-bohn) *n.* a forked bone between the neck and breast of a bird (pulled in two between two persons, the one who gets the longer part having the supposed right to magic fulfillment of any wish).

wish·ful (wish-fŭl) *adj.* desiring. **wish′ful·ly** *adv.* **wish′ful·ness** *n.* □**wishful thinking**, a belief that is founded on what one wishes to be true rather than on fact.

wish·y-wash·y (wish-ee-wosh-ee) *adj.* weak or feeble in color, character, etc., lacking strong or positive qualities. **wish′y-wash·i·ness** *n.*

wisp (wisp) *n.* 1. a small separate bunch or bundle of something, *wisps of hair.* 2. a small streak of smoke or cloud etc. 3. a small thin person. **wisp′y** *adj.* (**wisp·i·er, wisp·i·est**).

wis·te·ri·a (wi-steer-i-ă) *n.* a climbing plant with hanging clusters of blue, purple, or white flowers.

wist·ful (wist-fŭl) *adj.* full of sad or vague longing. **wist′ful·ly** *adv.* **wist′ful·ness** *n.*

wit[1] (wit) *n.* 1. the ability to combine words or ideas etc. ingeniously so as to produce a kind of clever humor that appeals to the intellect. 2. a witty person. 3. intelligence, understanding, *hadn't the wit to see what was needed; use your wits.* □**at one's wits' end**, at the end of one's mental resources, not knowing what to do. **have** *or* **keep one's wits about one**, to be or remain mentally alert and intelligent or ready to act. **scared out of one's wits**, crazy with fear.

wit[2] *v.* **to wit**, that is to say, namely.

witch (wich) *n.* 1. a person (especially a woman) who practices witchcraft. 2. a bewitching woman; *old witch*, an ugly woman. **witch** *v.* to bewitch. **witch′ing** *adj. & n.* □**witch doctor**, the tribal magician of a primitive people. **witch hazel**, a North American shrub with yellow flowers; an astringent lotion prepared from its leaves and bark. **witch hunt**, a search to find and destroy or persecute people thought to be witches, or others suspected of holding unorthodox or unpopular views. **witching hour**, the time when witches are active, midnight.

witch·craft (wich-kraft) *n.* the practice of magic.

witch·er·y (wich-ĕ-ree) *n.* (*pl.* **-ies**) 1. witchcraft. 2. the bewitching power of something.

with (wɪth) *prep.* 1. in the company of, among. 2. having, characterized by, *a man with a sinister expression.* 3. using as an instrument or means, *hit it with a hammer.* 4. on the side of, of the same opinion as, *we're all with you on this matter.* 5. in the care or charge of, *leave a message with the receptionist.* 6. in the employment etc. of, *he is with Shell.* 7. at the same time as, in the same way or direction or degree as, *rise with the sun; swimming with the tide; he became more tolerant with age.* 8. because of, *shaking with laughter.* 9. feeling or showing, *heard it with calmness.* 10. under the conditions of, *sleeps with the window open; he won with ease*, easily; *with your permission*, if you will allow it. 11. by addition or possession of, *fill it with water; laden with baggage.* 12. in regard to, toward, *lost my temper with him.* 13. in opposition to, *he argued with me.* 14. in spite of, *with all his roughness, he's very good-natured.* 15. so as to be separated from, *we parted with our luggage reluctantly.* □**I'm not with you**, *(informal)* I cannot follow your meaning. **with it**, *(informal)* up-to-the-minute, capable of understanding and appreciating current fashions and ideas.

with·al (wɪth-awl) *adv. (old use)* 1. in addition. 2. nevertheless. 3. at the same time.

with·draw (wɪth-draw, with-) *v.* (**with·drew, with·drawn, with·draw·ing**) 1. to take back or away, *withdrew troops from the frontier.* 2. to remove (money deposited) from a bank etc. 3. to cancel (a promise or statement etc.). 4. to go away from company or from a place; *withdraw into oneself*, become unresponsive or unsociable.

with·draw·al (wɪth-draw-ăl, with-) *n.* 1. withdrawing. 2. the process of ceasing to take drugs to which one is addicted, often with unpleasant reactions, *withdrawal symptoms.*

with·drawn (wɪth-drawn, with-) *adj.* (of a person) unresponsive, unsociable. **with·drawn′ness** *n.*

with·er (wɪth-ĕr) *v.* 1. to make or become shriveled, to lose or cause to lose freshness and vitality. 2. to subdue or overwhelm by scorn, *withered him with a glance.*

with·ers (wɪth-ĕrz) *n. pl.* the ridge between a horse's shoulder blades.

with·hold (with-hohld) *v.* (**with·held, with·hold·ing**) 1. to refuse to give or grant or allow, *withhold permission.* 2. to hold back, to restrain, *we could not withhold our laughter.* **with·hold′er** *n.* □**withholding tax**, a tax deducted from income at the source.

with·in (wɪth-in) *prep.* 1. inside, enclosed by. 2. not beyond the limit or scope of, *success was within our grasp; he acted within his rights.* 3. in a time no longer than, *we shall finish within an hour.* **within** *adv.* inside, *seen from within.* **within** *n.* the inner part of a place.

with·out (wɪth-owt) *prep.* 1. not having or feeling or showing, free from, *without food; they are without fear.* 2. in the absence of, *no smoke without fire.* 3. with no action of, *we can't leave without thanking them.* 4. *(old use)* outside, *without a city wall.* **without** *adv.* 1. outside, *the house as seen from without.* 2. not having (something understood), *we'll have to do without.* □**without prejudice**, *see* **prejudice.**

with·stand (with-stand, wɪth-) *v.* (**with·stood, with·stand·ing**) to endure successfully.

wit·less (wit-lis) *adj.* foolish, unintelligent. **wit′less·ly** *adv.* **wit′less·ness** *n.*

wit·ness (wit-nis) *n.* (*pl.* **-ness·es**) 1. a person who sees or hears something, *there were no witnesses to their quarrel.* 2. a person who gives evidence in court. 3. a person who is present at an event in order to testify to the fact that it took place, one who confirms that a signature is genuine by adding his own signature. 4. something that serves as evidence, *his tattered clothes were witness to his poverty.* **witness** *v.* to be a witness at or of, to sign (a document) as a witness. **wit′ness•er** *n.* ☐**bear witness,** *see* **bear²**. **witness stand,** an enclosure from which witnesses give evidence in court.

wit•ted (wit-id) *adj.* having wits of a certain kind, *quick-witted.*

wit•ti•cism (wit-i-siz-ĕm) *n.* a witty remark.

wit•ting (wit-ing) *adj.* aware, intentional.

wit•ting•ly (wit-ing-lee) *adv.* knowing what one does, intentionally.

wit•ty (wit-ee) *adj.* (-ti•er, -ti•est) full of wit. **wit′ti•ly** *adv.* **wit′ti•ness** *n.*

wive (wiv) *v.* (wived, wiv•ing) *(old use)* to provide with a wife, to take a wife.

wives *see* **wife.**

wiz•ard (wiz-ărd) *n.* 1. a male witch, a magician. 2. a person with amazing abilities, *a financial wizard.* **wiz′ard•ry** *n.*

wiz•ened (wiz-ĕnd) *adj.* full of wrinkles, shriveled with age, *a wizened face.*

wk. *abbr.* 1. week. 2. work.

wkly. *abbr.* weekly.

WL *abbr.* wavelength.

WNW *abbr.* west-northwest.

WO *abbr.* warrant officer.

w/o *abbr.* without.

woad (wohd) *n.* 1. a kind of blue dye formerly obtained from a European plant of the mustard family. 2. this plant.

wob•ble (wob-ĕl) *v.* (wob•bled, wob•bling) 1. to stand or move unsteadily, to rock from side to side. 2. (of a voice) to quiver. **wobble** *n.* a wobbling movement, a quiver. **wob′bly** *adj.* **wob′bli•ness** *n.*

Wo•den (woh-dĕn) *n.* the chief god of the Anglo-Saxon pagans.

woe (woh) *n.* 1. sorrow, distress. 2. trouble causing this, misfortune. **woe** *interj.* an exclamation of sorrow or distress.

woe•be•gone (woh-bi-gawn) *adj.* looking unhappy.

woe•ful (woh-fŭl) *adj.* 1. full of woe, sad. 2. deplorable, *woeful ignorance.* **woe′ful•ly** *adv.* **woe′ful•ness** *n.*

wok (wok) *n.* a bowl-shaped pot used in cooking Chinese food.

woke (wohk), **wok•en** (woh-kĕn) *see* **wake¹**.

wold (wohld) *n.* an area of open upland country.

wolf (wuulf) *n.* (*pl.* **wolves,** *pr.* wuulvz) 1. a fierce wild animal of the dog family, feeding on the flesh of other animals and often hunting in packs. 2. a greedy or grasping person. 3. *(slang)* a man who aggressively seeks to attract women for sexual purposes. **wolf** *v.* to eat (food) quickly and greedily. ☐**keep the wolf from the door,** to ward off hunger or starvation. **wolf in sheep's clothing,** a person who appears friendly or harmless but is really an enemy. **wolf whistle,** a whistle uttered by a man in admiration of a woman's appearance.

wolf•hound (wuulf-hownd) *n.* any of several large dogs (such as a borzoi) of a kind originally used for hunting wolves.

wolf•ram (wuul-frăm) *n.* 1. tungsten. 2. wolframite.

wolf•ram•ite (wuul-fră-mɪt) *n.* an ore yielding tungsten.

wolfs•bane (wuulfs-bayn) *n.* a plant with yellow flowers.

wol•ver•ine (wuul-vĕ-reen) *n.* a North American animal of the weasel family.

wolves *see* **wolf.**

wom•an (wuum-ăn) *n.* (*pl.* **wom•en,** *pr.* wim-in) 1. an adult female person. 2. women in general. 3. *(informal)* a female servant. ☐**woman of the streets,** a prostitute. **woman of the world,** *see* **world. women's liberation** *or* **women's lib,** a movement urging the liberation of women from domestic duties and from a subordinate role in society and business etc. **women's rights,** the right of women to have a position of legal and social equality with men.

wom•an•hood (wuum-ăn-huud) *n.* the state of being a woman.

wom•an•ish (wuum-ă-nish) *adj.* like a woman, suitable for women but not for men.

wom•an•ize (wuum-ă-nɪz) *v.* (**wom•an•ized, wom•an•iz•ing**) (of a man) to seek the company of women for sexual purposes. **wom′an•iz•er** *n.*

wom•an•kind (wuum-ăn-kɪnd) *n.* women in general.

wom•an•like (wuum-ăn-lɪk) *adj.* like a woman.

wom•an•ly (wuum-ăn-lee) *adj.* having or showing qualities that are characteristic of or suitable for a woman. **wom′an•li•ness** *n.*

womb (woom) *n.* the uterus. **wombed** *adj.*

wom•bat (wom-bat) *n.* an Australian animal resembling a small bear.

wom•en *see* **woman.**

wom•en•folk (wim-in-fohk) *n. pl.* (also **wom•enfolks**) women in general, the women of one's family.

won (wun) *see* **win.**

won•der (wun-dĕr) *n.* 1. a feeling of surprise mingled with admiration or curiosity or bewilderment. 2. something that arouses this, a marvel, a remarkable thing or event. **wonder** *v.* 1. to feel wonder or surprise, *I wonder that he wasn't killed.* 2. to feel curiosity about, to desire to know, to try to form an opinion or decision about, *we're still wondering what to do next.* **won′der•er** *n.* ☐**do** *or* **work wonders,** to produce remarkably successful results. **I shouldn't wonder,** *(informal)* I should not be surprised. **no wonder,** it is not surprising. **wonder drug,** a new drug with amazing curative effect.

won•der•ful (wun-dĕr-fŭl) *adj.* marvelous, surprisingly fine or excellent. **won′der•ful•ly** *adv.* **won′der•ful•ness** *n.*

won•der•land (wun-dĕr-land) *n.* a land or place full of marvels or wonderful things.

won•der•ment (wun-dĕr-mĕnt) *n.* a feeling of wonder, surprise.

won•drous (wun-drŭs) *adj.* wonderful. **won′drous•ly** *adv.* **won′drous•ness** *n.*

wont (wohnt) *adj. (old use)* accustomed, *he was wont to go to bed early.* **wont** *n.* a habit or custom, *went to bed early, as was his wont.* ▷Do not confuse *wont* with *won't.*

won't (wohnt) = will not. ▷Do not confuse *won't* with *wont.*

wont•ed (wohn-tid) *adj.* customary, *he listened with his wonted courtesy.*

woo (woo) *v.* (**wooed, woo•ing**) 1. to try to win the affection of, especially in order to marry. 2. to try to achieve or obtain, *woo fame or success.* 3. to seek the favor of, to try to coax or persuade, *wooing customers into the shop.* **woo′er** *n.*

wood (wuud) *n.* 1. the tough fibrous substance of a tree and its branches, enclosed by the bark. 2. this cut for use as timber or fuel etc. 3. (also *woods*) trees growing fairly densely over an area of ground. 4. a golf club with a wooden head. **wood** *adj.* made of, used for, or dwelling in wood or woods. **wood** *v.* 1. to plant with trees. 2. to take in or supply with wood. ▷**out of the woods**, clear of danger or difficulty. **wood alcohol**, methyl alcohol. **wood ibis**, an American wading bird frequenting wooded swamps. **wood louse**, a small wingless creature with seven pairs of legs, living in decaying wood, damp soil, etc. **wood pulp**, wood fiber reduced chemically or mechanically to pulp as material for paper. **wood screw**, a screw that has a sharp point allowing it to be screwed into wood. **wood thrush**, a thrush of eastern North America.

wood·bine (wuud-bın) *n.* any of several climbing vines, including the Virginia creeper and honeysuckle.

wood·block (wuud-blok) *n.* 1. a woodcut. 2. a block of wood.

wood·bor·er (wuud-bohr-ĕr) *n.* 1. a tool for boring wood. 2. an insect that bores into wood.

wood·carv·er (wuud-kahr-vĕr) *n.* a person who carves wood.

wood·carv·ing (wuud-kahr-ving) *n.* 1. the art of carving objects from pieces of wood. 2. an object carved from wood.

wood·chop·per (wuud-chop-ĕr) *n.* a person who chops wood.

wood·chuck (wuud-chuk) *n.* a North American burrowing marmot.

wood·cock (wuud-kok) *n.* (*pl.* **-cocks, -cock**) a kind of game bird related to the snipe.

wood·craft (wuud-kraft) *n.* 1. knowledge of woodland conditions, especially that used in hunting. 2. woodworking. **wood·crafts·man** (wuud-krafts-măn) *n.* (*pl.* **-men**, *pr.* **-mĕn**).

wood·cut (wuud-kut) *n.* 1. an engraving made on wood. 2. a print made from this, especially as an illustration in a book.

wood·cut·ter (wuud-kut-ĕr) *n.* 1. a person who cuts wood. 2. a maker of woodcuts.

wood·ed (wuud-id) *adj.* covered with growing trees.

wood·en (wuud-ĕn) *adj.* 1. made of wood. 2. stiff and unnatural in manner, showing no expression or animation. **wood′en·ly** *adv.* **wood′en·ness** *n.* ▢**wooden Indian**, a wooden statue of an Indian, formerly used as an advertisement in front of a cigar store; *(informal)* a person showing no emotion.

wood·en·head·ed (wuud-ĕn-hed-id) *adj.* stupid.

wood·land (wuud-lănd) *n.* wooded country.

wood·lot (wuud-lot) *n.* an area on a farm set aside for trees.

wood·man (wuud-măn) *n.* (*pl.* **-men**, *pr.* **-men**) 1. a timber cutter, *woodman spare that tree.* 2. a woodsman.

wood·note (wuud-noht) *n.* a musical tone occurring in nature or the wild, as that of a bird.

wood·peck·er (wuud-pek-ĕr) *n.* a bird that clings to tree trunks and taps them with its beak to discover insects.

wood·pile (wuud-pıl) *n.* a stack of wood, especially for fuel.

wood·ruff (wuud-rŭf) *n.* a white-flowered plant grown especially for its fragrant whorled leaves.

wood·shed (wuud-shed) *n.* a shed where wood is stored, especially wood for fuel.

woods·man (wuudz-măn) *n.* (*pl.* **-men**, *pr.* **-měn**) a dweller in or frequenter of woods, a person skilled in woodcraft.

wood·wind (wuud-wind) *n.* 1. any of the wind instruments of an orchestra that are (or were originally) made of wood, such as the clarinet and oboe. 2. these collectively.

wood·work (wuud-wurk) *n.* things made from wood, especially the wooden fittings of a house.

wood·work·ing (wuud-wur-king) *n.* the art or practice of making things from wood. **woodworking** *adj.*

wood·worm (wuud-wurm) *n.* the larva of a kind of beetle that bores into wooden furniture and fittings.

wood·y (wuud-ee) *adj.* (**wood·i·er, wood·i·est**) 1. like wood, consisting of wood, *the woody parts of a plant.* 2. full of woods, *a woody area.* **wood′i·ness** *n.*

woof (wuuf) *n.* a weft.

woof·er (wuuf-ĕr) *n.* a loudspeaker for accurately reproducing low-frequency sounds.

wool (wuul) *n.* 1. the fine soft hair that forms the fleece of sheep and goats etc. 2. yarn made from this, fabric made from this yarn. 3. something resembling sheep's wool in texture. ▢**pull the wool over someone's eyes**, to deceive him. **wool·en** (wuul-ĕn) *adj.* made of wool.

wool·ens (wuul-ĕnz) *n. pl.* woolen cloth or clothing.

wool·gath·er·ing (wuul-gath-ĕ-ring) *n.* being in a dreamy or absent-minded state.

wool·grow·er (wuul-groh-ĕr) *n.* a person who raises sheep for wool.

wool·ly (wuul-ee) *adj.* (**-li·er, -li·est**) 1. covered with wool or wool-like hair. 2. like wool, woolen, *a woolly hat.* 3. not thinking clearly, not clearly expressed or thought out, vague. **woolly** *n.* (*pl.* **-lies**) (often *woollies*) *(informal)* a knitted woolen garment, especially long underwear. **wool′li·ness** *n.* ▢**wild and woolly**, *see* **wild. woolly aphid**, a plant louse covered with tiny white strands. **woolly bear**, a large hairy caterpillar.

wooz·y (woo-zee) *adj.* (**wooz·i·er, wooz·i·est**) *(informal)* dizzy, dazed. **wooz′i·ly** *adv.* **wooz′i·ness** *n.*

Worces·ter·shire (wuus-tĕr-sheer) **sauce** a pungent seasoning sauce first made in Worcester, England.

word (wurd) *n.* 1. a sound or sounds expressing a meaning independently and forming one of the basic elements of speech. 2. this represented by letters or symbols. 3. something said, a remark or statement, *he didn't utter a word; too funny for words,* extremely funny. 4. a message, information, *we sent word of our safe arrival.* 5. a promise or assurance; *take my word for it,* accept my assurance that it is true. 6. a command or spoken signal, *don't fire till I give you the word.* **word.** *v.* to phrase, to select words to express, *word it tactfully.* ▢**by word of mouth**, in spoken (not written) words. **have a word**, to converse briefly. **have words**, to quarrel. **in a word**, briefly, to sum up. **in so many words**, explicitly or bluntly. **man of his word**, one who keeps his promises. **take someone at his word**, to act on the assumption that he means what he says. **the Word** or **Word of God**, the Bible, especially the Gospel; (in the Gospel of St. John) the Second Person of the Trinity. **word for word,** in exactly the same words; *translate it word for word,* literally. **word of honor,** a promise made upon one's honor (*see* **honor**). **word order,** the arrangement of words in a sentence etc. **word processing,** an electronic system that rapidly processes the text of letters, reports, etc. **word square,** a set of words of equal length so chosen that when they are written under each other the letters read downward in columns give the same words.

word·age (wur-dij) *n.* 1. words, wording. 2. a count of words, the number of words used. 3. verbiage.

word·book (wurd-buuk) *n.* a book with lists of words, a vocabulary book.

word·ing (wur-ding) *n.* the way something is worded.

word·less (wurd-lis) *adj.* without words, not expressed in words, *wordless sympathy.*

word·play (wurd-play) *n.* a joke using features of words, a pun, etc.

word·y (wur-dee) *adj.* (**word·i·er, word·i·est**) using too many words. **word′i·ly** *adv.* **word′i·ness** *n.*

wore (wohr) *see* **wear.**

work (wurk) *n.* 1. use of bodily or mental power in order to do or make something, especially as contrasted with play or recreation. 2. something to be undertaken, the materials for this. 3. a thing done or produced by work, the result of action. 4. a piece of literary or musical composition, *one of Mozart's later works.* 5. what a person does to earn a living, employment. 6. doings or experiences of a certain kind, *nice work!* 7. ornamentation of a certain kind, articles having this, things or parts made of certain materials or with certain tools, *fine filigree work.* 8. *works,* operations in building etc.; the operative parts of a machine; a place where industrial or manufacturing processes are carried on. **work** *v.* 1. to perform work, to be engaged in bodily or mental activity. 2. to make efforts, *work for peace.* 3. to be employed, to have a job, *she works in a bank.* 4. to operate, to do this effectively, *it works by electricity; a can opener that really works; that method won't work.* 5. to operate (a thing) so as to obtain material or benefit from it, *the mine is still being worked; my partner works the Dallas area,* covers it in his work. 6. to purchase with one's labor, *work one's passage.* 7. to cause to work or function, *he works his staff very hard; can you work the elevator?* 8. to bring about, to accomplish, *work miracles.* 9. to shape or knead or hammer etc. into a desired form or consistency, *work the mixture into a paste.* 10. to do or make by needlework or fretwork etc., *work your initials on it.* 11. to excite progressively, *worked them into a frenzy; the candidate worked the crowd,* sought enthusiastic support for himself. 12. to make (a way) or pass or cause to pass slowly or by effort, *the grub works its way into timber; work the stick into the hole.* 13. to become through repeated stress or pressure, *the screw had worked loose.* 14. to be in motion, *his face worked violently.* 15. to ferment, *the yeast began to work.* 16. to solve by calculation, *work the problem.* □**at work,** working; at one's place of employment; operating, having an effect, *there are secret influences at work.* **give him the works,** *(slang)* give or tell him everything; give him cruel or drastic treatment. **out of work,** unemployed, without

a job. **work camp,** a labor camp for prisoners etc. **work clothes,** sturdy clothes worn for work by a laborer. **worked up,** excited. **work ethic,** a belief in the moral and sociological importance of work. **work farm,** a farm for juvenile offenders. **work force,** the total number of workers engaged or available. **work in,** to find a place for, to insert. **work of art,** a fine picture or building or composition etc. **work off,** to get rid of by activity, *worked off his annoyance on his secretary.* **work on,** to use one's influence on (a person). **work out,** to find or solve by calculation; to be calculated, *it works out to $24.50 each;* to plan the details etc. of, *work out a plan;* to have a specified result, *it worked out very well;* to exercise, to practice for a sports contest. **work over,** to examine thoroughly; to treat with violence. **work sheet,** a paper on which work done is recorded. **work study,** study of people's work and methods, with a view to making them more efficient. **work train,** a train transporting railroad maintenance workers. **work up,** to bring gradually to a more developed state; to excite progressively; to advance in one's job.

work·a·ble (wur-kă-bĕl) *adj.* able to be worked or used or acted upon successfully. **work′a·ble·ness** *n.*

work·a·day (wur-kă-day) *adj.* ordinary, everyday.

work·a·hol·ic (wur-kă-haw-lik) *n. (informal)* a person obsessed with work. **work·a·hol·ism** (wur-kă-haw-liz-ĕm) *n.*

work·bag (wurk-bag) *n.* a bag holding materials and implements for work.

work·bas·ket (wurk-bas-kit) *n.* a basket holding sewing materials.

work·bench (wurk-bench) *n.* a bench for mechanical work, especially carpentry.

work·book (wurk-buuk) *n.* 1. an operating manual for equipment. 2. an instructional practice book. 3. a book for recording work completed.

work·box (wurk-boks) *n.* a box for holding implements and materials for work.

work·day (wurk-day) *n.* a working day.

work·er (wur-kĕr) *n.* 1. a person who works, one who works well or in a certain way, *a slow worker.* 2. a neuter or undeveloped female bee or ant etc. that does the work of the hive or colony but cannot reproduce. 3. a member of the working class.

work·horse (wurk-hors) *n.* 1. a horse that performs heavy labor. 2. a person who works extremely hard and accepts extra labor.

work·house (wurk-hows) *n.* (*pl.* **-hous·es,** *pr.* -how-ziz) a former public institution where people unable to support themselves were housed and (if able-bodied) made to work.

work·ing (wur-king) *adj.* 1. engaged in work, especially manual labor, working-class, *a working man.* 2. of or for work. 3. adequate or satisfactory for use, *a working knowledge of Arabic.* **working** *n.* 1. the way a thing works or the result of its working. 2. (usually *workings*) a mine or quarry etc., a part of this in which work is or has been carried on, *disused mine workings.* □**working capital,** capital used in the carrying on of business, not invested in its buildings and equipment etc. **working class,** the class of people who are employed for wages, especially in manual or industrial work. **working day,** a day on which work is regularly done; the portion of the day spent in working. **working hours,** the hours regularly spent in work. **working knowledge,**

knowledge adequate for dealing with something. **working model,** a model of a machine etc. able to operate though on a reduced scale. **working order,** a condition in which a machine etc. works satisfactorily. **working papers,** legal papers required for minors etc. for employment.

work·ing-class (wur-king-klas) *adj.* of the working class.

work·ing·man (wur-king-man) *n.* (*pl.* **-men,** *pr.* -men) a man who works, especially one who works at manual labor. **work·ing·wom·an** (wur-king-wuum-ăn) *n. fem.* (*pl.* **-wom·en,** *pr.* -wim-in).

work·load (wurk-lohd) *n.* the amount of work to be done by a particular employee etc.

work·man (wurk-măn) *n.* (*pl.* **-men,** *pr.* -měn) 1. a man hired to do manual labor. 2. a person who works in a certain way, *a conscientious workman.* **work·wom·an** (wurk-wuum-ăn) *n. fem.* (*pl.* **-wom·en,** *pr.* -wim-in) □**workmen's compensation insurance,** insurance that an employer is required to carry for employees who may be injured on the job.

work·man·like (wurk-măn-lık) *adj.* characteristic of a good workman, practical.

work·man·ship (wurk-măn-ship) *n.* a person's skill in working, the quality of this as seen in something produced.

work·out (wurk-owt) *n.* 1. a practice or test, especially in athletics. 2. physical exercise.

work·room (wurk-room) *n.* a room in which work is done.

work·shop (wurk-shop) *n.* 1. a room or building in which manual work or manufacture is carried on. 2. a meeting of trained personnel to engage in discussion, exchange of ideas, etc. for mutual benefit.

work·ta·ble (wurk-tay-běl) *n.* a table for work, usually with drawers for materials etc.

work·week (wurk-week) *n.* the total number of working days or hours in a week.

world (wurld) *n.* 1. the universe, all that exists. 2. Earth with all its countries and peoples. 3. a heavenly body like it. 4. a section of Earth, *the western world.* 5. a time or state or scene of human existence; *this world,* this mortal life. 6. the people or things belonging to a certain class or sphere of activity, *the sporting world; the insect world.* 7. everything, all people, *felt that the world was against him.* 8. material things and occupations (contrasted with spiritual), *renounced the world and became a nun.* 9. a very great amount, *it will do him a world of good; she is worlds better today.* □**for all the world like,** precisely like. **how** *or* **why in the world,** an emphatic form of *how, why,* etc. **man** *or* **woman of the world,** a person who is experienced in the ways of human society. **not for the world** *or* **not for all the world,** not for anything no matter how great. **not of** *or* **for this world,** supernatural. **out of this world,** *(informal)* incredibly good etc., indescribable. **think the world of,** to have the highest possible opinion of. **World Bank,** the International Bank for Reconstruction and Development. **World Court,** the Permanent Court of International Justice. **world power,** a country with influence in international politics. **World Series,** the series of games that determines the champion major league baseball team in the U.S. **world's fair,** an international exposition of arts, science, industry, and agriculture. **world war,** a war involving many important countries; *First World War* or *World War I,* that of 1914–18; *Second World War,* or *World War II,* 1939–45. **World War III,** a hypothetical atomic world war of the future.

world·beat·er (wurld-bee-těr) *n.* a person or thing surpassing all others.

world-fa·mous (wurld-fay-mŭs) *adj.* famous throughout the world.

world·ly (wurld-lee) *adj.* (**-li·er, -li·est**) 1. of or belonging to life on Earth, not spiritual. 2. devoted to the pursuit of pleasure or material gains or advantages. **world'li·ness** *n.* □**worldly wisdom,** wisdom and shrewdness in dealing with worldly affairs.

world·ly-wise (wurld-lee-wız) *adj.* having worldly wisdom.

world-wea·ry (wurld-wee-ree) *adj.* bored with human affairs.

world·wide (wurld-wıd) *adj.* extending through the whole world.

worm (wurm) *n.* 1. any of several types of animal with a soft rounded or flattened body and no backbone or limbs. 2. the wormlike larva of certain insects. 3. *worms,* parasitic worms in the intestinal tract or other tissues, any disease caused by these. 4. an insignificant or contemptible person. **worm** *v.* 1. to move with a twisting movement like a worm; *worm one's way* or *oneself,* make one's way by wriggling or with slow or patient progress. 2. to obtain by crafty persistence, *wormed the secret out of him.* 3. to rid of parasitic worms. □**worm gear,** an arrangement of a toothed wheel worked by a revolving spiral. **worm wheel,** the wheel of a worm gear.

worm-eat·en (wurm-ee-těn) *adj.* full of holes made by insect larvae.

worm·wood (wurm-wuud) *n.* 1. a woody plant with a bitter flavor. 2. bitter mortification.

worm·y (wur-mee) *adj.* (**worm·i·er, worm·i·est**) full of worms, worm-eaten. **worm'i·ness** *n.*

worn (wohrn) *see* **wear. worn** *adj.* 1. damaged by use or wear. 2. looking tired and exhausted.

worn-out (wohrn-owt) *adj.* 1. used until no longer usable. 2. exhausted.

wor·ried (wur-eed) *adj.* feeling or showing worry.

wor·ri·some (wur-i-sŏm) *adj.* causing worry. **wor'ri·some·ly** *adv.*

wor·ry (wur-ee) *v.* (**wor·ried, wor·ry·ing**) 1. to be troublesome to, to disturb the peace of mind of. 2. to give way to anxiety. 3. to seize with the teeth and shake or pull about, *the dog was worrying a rat.* **worry** *n.* (*pl.* **-ries**) 1. a state of worrying, mental uneasiness. 2. something that causes this. **wor'ri·er** *n.* □**worry beads,** a string of beads for fiddling with to occupy or calm oneself. **worry through,** to obtain (a solution to a problem etc.) by persistent effort.

wor·ry·wart (wur-ee-wort) *n.* a person who habitually worries needlessly.

worse (wurs) *adj. & adv.* 1. more bad, more badly, more evil or ill. 2. less good, in or into less good health or condition or circumstances. **worse** *n.* something worse, *there's worse to come.* □**the worse for wear,** damaged by use; injured or exhausted. **worse luck!** such is my bad fortune.

wors·en (wur-sĕn) *v.* to make or become worse.

wor·ship (wur-ship) *n.* 1. reverence and respect paid to God or a god. 2. acts or ceremonies displaying this. 3. adoration of or devotion to a person or thing. 4. *(British)* a title of respect used to or of a mayor or certain magistrates, *his worship; your worship; their worships.* **worship** *v.*

(wor·shiped, wor·ship·ing) 1. to honor as a deity, to pay worship to. 2. to take part in an act of worship. 3. to idolize, to treat with adoration. **wor′ship·er** *n.*

wor·ship·ful (wur-ship-fŭl) *adj.* feeling or showing devotion or reverence. **wor′ship·ful·ly** *adv.*

worst (wurst) *adj. & adv.* most bad, most badly, most evil or ill, least good. **worst** *n.* the worst part or feature or state or event etc., *we are prepared for the worst.* **worst** *v.* to get the better of, to defeat or outdo. □**at worst,** in the worst possible case. **get the worst of,** to be defeated in. **if the worst comes to the worst,** if the worst happens. **in the worst way,** *(informal)* very much, *he needs money in the worst way.*

wor·sted (wuus-tid, wur-stid) *n.* fine smooth yarn spun from long strands of wool, fabric made from this.

wort (wurt) *n.* *(old use* except in names of plants) plant, herb, *liverwort.*

worth (wurth) *adj.* 1. having a specified value, *a book worth $15.95.* 2. giving or likely to give a satisfactory or rewarding return for, deserving, *the book is worth reading; the scheme is worth a trial.* 3. possessing as wealth, having property to the value of, *he was worth a million dollars when he died.* **worth** *n.* 1. value, merit, usefulness, *people of great worth to the community.* 2. the amount of something that a specified sum will buy, *give me a dollar's worth of stamps.* □**for all one is worth,** *(informal)* with all one's energy, making every effort. **for what it's worth,** without any guarantee or promise of its truth or usefulness etc. **worth one's while,** worth the time or effort needed, *the gain isn't worth your while.*

worth·less (wurth-lis) *adj.* having no value or usefulness. **worth′less·ness** *n.*

worth·while (wurth-hwil) *adj.* worth giving time, interest, etc. to, *a worthwhile undertaking.*

wor·thy (wur-*thee*) *adj.* **(-thi·er, -thi·est)** 1. having great merit, deserving respect or support, *a worthy cause; worthy citizens.* 2. having sufficient worth or merit, *the cause is worthy of support.* **worthy** *n.* (*pl.* **-thies**) a worthy person. **wor′thi·ly** *adv.* **wor′thi·ness** *n.*

would (wuud) *auxiliary verb* used 1. in senses corresponding to **will**[1] in the past tense *(we said we would do it),* conditional statements *(you could do it if you would try),* questions *(would they like it?)* and polite requests and statements *(would you come in please?; I would say it's about right).* 2. expressing something to be expected *(that's just what he would do!)* or something that happens from time to time *(occasionally the machine would go wrong).* 3. expressing probability, *she would be about sixty when she died.* 4. in an incorrect use with *I* and *we* (*see* **should** definition 4).

would-be (wuud-bee) *adj.* desiring or pretending to be, *a would-be humorist.*

would·n't (wuud-ĕnt) = would not. □**I wouldn't know,** *(informal)* I do not know and cannot be expected to know.

wound[1] (woond) *n.* 1. injury done to animal or vegetable tissue by a cut, stab, blow, or tear. 2. injury to a person's reputation or feelings etc. **wound** *v.* to inflict a wound or wounds upon. **wound′ing·ly** *adv.*

wound[2] *see* **wind**[2].

wove (wohv) *see* **weave.** **wove** *adj.* (of paper) made on a frame of closely woven wire.

wo·ven (woh-vĕn) *see* **weave.**

wow[1] (wow) *interj.* an exclamation of astonishment or admiration. **wow** *n.* *(slang)* a sensational success. **wow** *v.* *(slang)* to impress or excite greatly.

wow[2] *n.* (in sound reproduction) a slow fluctuation of sound, perceptible in long notes.

WP *abbr.* word processing.

wpm *abbr.* words per minute.

wpn. *abbr.* weapon.

wrack[1] (rak) *n.* *(old use)* ruin, a destroyed remnant.

wrack[2] *n.* seaweed thrown up on the shore or growing there, used for manure.

wraith (rayth) *n.* a ghost, a spectral apparition of a living person supposed to be a sign that he will die soon.

wran·gle (rang-gĕl) *v.* **(wran·gled, wran·gling)** 1. to have a noisy angry argument or quarrel. 2. to tend or herd (cattle or horses) in the western U.S. **wrangle** *n.* an argument or quarrel of this kind. **wran′gler** *n.*

wrap (rap) *v.* **(wrapped, wrap·ping)** 1. to enclose in soft or flexible material used as a covering. 2. to arrange (a flexible covering or a garment etc.) around a person or thing, *wrap a scarf around your neck.* **wrap** *n.* a shawl or coat or cloak etc. worn for warmth. □**under wraps,** in concealment or secrecy. **wrapped up in,** with one's attention deeply occupied by, *she is completely wrapped up in her children;* deeply involved in, *the country's prosperity is wrapped up in its mineral trade.* **wrap up,** to enclose in wrappings; to put on warm clothing; *(slang)* to finish, to cease talking.

wrap·a·round (rap-ă-rownd) *n.* an object that extends around a thing, especially a garment that wraps around a person.

wrap·per (rap-ĕr) *n.* 1. a cover of paper etc. wrapped around something. 2. a loose dressing gown.

wrap·ping (rap-ing) *n.* material used to wrap something. □**wrapping paper,** paper used for wrapping packages.

wrasse (ras) *n.* a brightly-colored sea fish with thick lips and strong teeth.

wrath (rath) *n.* anger, indignation.

wrath·ful (rath-fŭl) *adj.* full of anger or indignation. **wrath′ful·ly** *adv.* **wrath′ful·ness** *n.*

wreak (reek) *v.* to inflict, to cause, *wreak vengeance on a person; fog wreaked havoc with traffic.*

wreath (reeth) *n.* (*pl.* **wreaths,** *pr.* reethz) 1. flowers or leaves etc. fastened into a ring and used as a decoration or placed on a grave etc. as a mark of respect. 2. a curving line of mist or smoke.

wreathe (reeth) *v.* **(wreathed, wreath·ing)** 1. to encircle or decorate with or as if with a wreath. 2. to twist into a wreath; *their faces were wreathed in smiles,* wrinkled with smiling. 3. to wind, *the snake wreathed itself around the branch.* 4. to move in a curving line, *smoke wreathed upward.*

wreck (rek) *n.* 1. the disabling or destruction of something, especially of a ship by storms or accidental damage. 2. a ship that has suffered wreck. 3. the remains of a greatly damaged building or vehicle or thing. 4. a person whose physical or mental health has been damaged or destroyed, *a nervous wreck.* **wreck** *v.* to cause the wreck of; *wrecked the old building,* tore it down; *a mistake that wrecked his career,* ruined it; *overwork wrecked her,* destroyed her health.

wreck·age (rek-ij) *n.* 1. the remains of something wrecked. 2. wrecking.

wreck·er (rek-ĕr) *n.* 1. a person who wrecks something. 2. a person employed in demolition work. 3. a tow truck.

wren (ren) *n.* a very small usually brown songbird.

wrench (rench) *v.* to twist or pull violently around, to damage or pull by twisting, *wrenched it off.* **wrench** *n.* 1. a violent twist or twisting pull. 2. pain caused by parting, *leaving home was a great wrench.* 3. an adjustable tool for gripping and turning nuts, bolts, etc.

wrest (rest) *v.* 1. to wrench away, *wrested his sword from him.* 2. to obtain by effort or with difficulty, *wrested a confession from him.* 3. to twist or distort. **wrest′er** *n.*

wres·tle (res-ĕl) *v.* (**wres·tled, wres·tling**) 1. to fight (especially as a sport) by grappling with a person and trying to throw him to the ground. 2. to fight with (a person) in this way, *police wrestled him to the ground.* 3. to struggle to deal with or overcome, *wrestled with the problem.* **wrestle** *n.* a wrestling match, a hard struggle. **wres′tler** *n.*

wres·tling (res-ling) *n.* a sport in which two opponents grapple with each other in an attempt to press the adversary's shoulders to the mat.

wretch (rech) *n.* 1. a very unfortunate or miserable person. 2. a despicable person.

wretch·ed (rech-id) *adj.* 1. miserable, unhappy. 2. of poor quality, unsatisfactory. 3. causing discomfort or nuisance, confounded, *this wretched car won't start.* **wretch′ed·ly** *adv.* **wretch′ed·ness** *n.*

wrig·gle (rig-ĕl) *v.* (**wrig·gled, wrig·gling**) to move with short twisting movements; *wriggle out of a difficulty,* escape from it cunningly. **wriggle** *n.* a wriggling movement. **wrig′gly** *adj.* **wrig′gler** *n.*

wring (ring) *v.* (**wrung, wring·ing**) 1. to twist and squeeze in order to remove liquid. 2. to remove (liquid) in this way. 3. to squeeze firmly or forcibly; *they wrung his hand,* squeezed it warmly or emotionally; *wring one's hands,* squeeze them together emotionally; *wring the bird's neck,* kill it by twisting its neck. 4. to extract or obtain with effort or difficulty, *wrung a promise from him.* **wring** *n.* a wringing movement, a squeeze or twist. □**wringing wet,** so wet that moisture can be wrung from it.

wring·er (ring-ĕr) *n.* a device with a pair of rollers between which washed clothes etc. are passed so that water is squeezed out.

wrin·kle (ring-kĕl) *n.* 1. a small crease, a small furrow or ridge in the skin (especially the kind produced by age). 2. *(informal)* a clever idea or device. 3. *(informal)* a slight problem, *wrinkles to be ironed out.* **wrinkle** *v.* (**wrin·kled, wrin·kling**) to make wrinkles in, to form wrinkles.

wrist (rist) *n.* 1. the joint connecting hand and forearm. 2. the part of a garment covering this. □**slap on the wrist,** a correction, a warning.

wrist·band (rist-band) *n.* the band forming or concealing the end of the shirt sleeve, the cuff.

wrist·let (rist-lit) *n.* a band or bracelet etc. worn around the wrist.

wrist·watch (rist-woch) *n.* a watch worn on a strap or band etc. around the wrist.

writ[1] (rit) *n.* a formal written command issued by a court or ruling authority directing a person to act or refrain from acting in a certain way.

writ[2] *adj. (old use)* written. □**writ large,** in an emphasized form, clearly recognizable.

write (rīt) *v.* (**wrote, writ·ten, writ·ing**) 1. to make letters or other symbols on a surface, especially with a pen or pencil on paper. 2. to form (letters or words or a message etc.) in this way; *write a check,* write the appropriate figures and words and signature etc. to make it valid. 3. to compose in written form for publication, to be an author, *write books* or *music; he makes a living by writing.* 4. to write and send a letter, *write to me often.* 5. to write to, *I will write you soon.* 6. to indicate clearly, *guilt was written all over her.* □**write down,** to put into writing. **write in,** to insert (a name not listed on a ballot etc.) instead of voting for one that is on it. **write off,** to cancel; to recognize as lost. **write out,** to write (a thing) in full or in a finished form. **write up,** to write (a report etc.) of, to record (a sale) etc.

write-in (rīt-in) *n.* 1. a candidate not listed on a ballot, but written in by a voter. 2. a vote for such a candidate. **write-in** *adj.*

write·off (rīt-awf) *n.* something written off as lost, such as a vehicle too badly damaged to be worth repairing.

writ·er (rī-tĕr) *n.* 1. a person who writes or has written something, one who writes in a certain way. 2. a person who writes books etc., an author. □**writer's cramp,** cramp in the muscles of the hand.

write-up (rīt-up) *n.* a published account of something, a review.

writhe (rīth) *v.* (**writhed, writh·ing**) 1. to twist one's body about, as in pain. 2. to wriggle, *writhing snakes.* 3. to suffer because of great shame or embarrassment, *writhing under the insult.*

writ·ing (rī-ting) *n.* 1. handwriting. 2. literary work, a piece of this, *in the writings of Charles Dickens.* □**in writing,** in written form. **the writing on the wall,** an event signifying that something is doomed (▷after the Biblical story of the writing that appeared on the wall of Belshazzar's palace, foretelling his doom). **writing desk,** a desk for writing, especially one with compartments for papers etc. **writing paper,** paper for writing on, especially for writing letters.

writ·ten (rit-ĕn) *see* **write.**

wrong (rawng) *adj.* 1. (of conduct or actions) morally bad, contrary to justice or to what is right. 2. incorrect, not true. 3. not what is required or suitable or most desirable, *backed the wrong horse; get hold of the wrong end of the stick,* misunderstand a statement or situation; *wrong side,* (of fabric) the side that is not meant to show. 4. not in a normal condition, not functioning normally, *there's something wrong with the gearbox.* **wrong** *adv.* in a wrong manner or direction, mistakenly, *you guessed wrong.* **wrong** *n.* 1. what is morally wrong, a wrong action. 2. injustice, an unjust action or treatment, *they did us a great wrong.* **wrong** *v.* 1. to do wrong to, to treat unjustly, *a wronged wife.* 2. to attribute bad motives to (a person) mistakenly. **wrong′ly** *adv.* **wrong′ness** *n.* □**get a person wrong,** to misunderstand him. **in the wrong,** not having justice or truth on one's side. **on the wrong side of,** in disfavor with or not liked by (a person); *on the wrong side of forty,* over forty years old.

wrong·do·ing (rawng-doo-ing) *n.* action contrary to law or to moral standards. **wrong'do·er** *n.*

wrong·ful (rawng-fŭl) *adj.* contrary to what is fair or just or legal. **wrong'ful·ly** *adv.* **wrong'ful·ness** *n.*

wrong·head·ed (rawng-hed-id) *adj.* perverse and obstinate. **wrong'head·ed·ly** *adv.* **wrong'head·ed·ness** *n.*

wrote (roht) *see* **write.**

wroth (rawth) *adj. (old use)* angry.

wrought (rawt) *(old use)* = worked. **wrought** *adj.* (of metals) beaten out or shaped by hammering. ☐**wrought iron,** iron made by forging or rolling, not cast.

wrought-up (rawt-up) *adj.* very excited or perturbed.

wrung (rung) *see* **wring.**

wry (rı) *adj.* **(wri·er, wri·est)** 1. twisted or bent out of shape. 2. twisted into an expression of disgust or disappointment or mockery, *a wry face.* 3. (of humor) dry and mocking. **wry'ly** *adv.* **wry'ness** *n.*

WSW *abbr.* west-southwest.

wt. *abbr.* weight.

wurst (wurst, woorst) *n. (informal)* sausage.

WV *abbr.* West Virginia.

W. Va. *abbr.* West Virginia.

WW I *abbr.* World War I.

WW II *abbr.* World War II.

WY *abbr.* Wyoming.

Wyo. *abbr.* Wyoming.

Wy·o·ming (wı-oh-ming) a state of the U.S.

X

X, x (eks) (*pl.* **Xs, X's, x's**) 1. the twenty-fourth letter of the alphabet. 2. the Roman numeral symbol for 10.

x *symbol* 1. an unknown quantity. 2. times (indicating multiplication), $2 \times 2 = 4$. 3. power of magnification. 4. by (indicating dimension), *a 3×5 card.* 5. x-rated.

x (eks) *v.* (**x-ed** or **x'd, x-ing** or **x'ing**) *(informal)* to cancel by writing a series of x's over, *x out your mistakes.*

X *abbr.* experimental.

X *symbol* 1. Christ (*see* the note under **Xmas**). 2. a signature by a person unable to write his name.

x-ax·is (eks-ak-sis) *n.* (*pl.* **-ax·es**, *pr.* -ak-seez) the horizontal axis in a plane coordinate system, along which the abscissa is measured.

X chromosome a chromosome in which the number of cells of one sex (in humans, the female) is twice that of the other sex.

Xe *symbol* xenon.

xe·bec (zee-bek) *n.* a small three-masted Mediterranean vessel.

xen·o·lith (zen-ŏ-lith) *n.* a stone or rock occurring in a rock system to which it does not belong. **xen·o·lith·ic** (zen-ŏ-lith-ik) *adj.*

xe·non (zee-non) *n.* a heavy inert gaseous element.

xen·o·pho·bi·a (zen-ŏ-foh-bi-ă) *n.* strong dislike or distrust of foreigners. **xen·o·pho'bic** *adj.* **xen·o·phobe** (zen-ŏ-fohb) *n.*

xe·rog·ra·phy (zi-rog-ră-fee) *n.* a dry copying process in which dark powder adheres to parts of a sheet of paper etc. that become electrically charged as a result of exposure to light from the bright parts of an image that is to be copied. **xe·ro·graph·ic** (zeer-ŏ-graf-ik) *adj.*

xe·ro·phyte (zeer-ŏ-fīt) *n.* a plant able to grow in very dry conditions, as in a desert. **xe'ro·phyt·ism** *n.* **xe·ro·phyt·ic** (zeer-ŏ-fit-ik) *adj.* **xe·ro·phyt'i·cal·ly** *adv.*

Xer·ox (zeer-oks) *n.* *(trademark)* 1. a process for producing xerographic copies without the use of wet materials. 2. a copy made in this way. **xer·ox** *v.* to copy or be copied by a process of this kind.

xi (zī, sī) *n.* (*pl.* **xis**) the fourteenth letter of the Greek alphabet (Ξ ξ).

XL *abbr.* extra large.

Xmas (kris-măs) *n.* = **Christmas.** ▷The *X* represents the Greek letter chi (= ch), the first letter of *Christos* (the Greek word for *Christ*).

Xn. *abbr.* Christian.

Xnty. *abbr.* Christianity.

x-rat·ed (eks-ray-tid) *adj.* (of films) not to be seen by persons under seventeen years old. **x-rat·ing** *n.*

x-ray (eks-ray) *n.* (also **x ray, X-ray**) a photograph or examination made by means of a kind of electromagnetic radiation (**x-rays**) that can penetrate solids and make it possible to see into or through them. **x-ray** *v.* to photograph or examine or treat by this radiation. □**x-ray astronomy,** the study of the emission of x-rays by stars, observable only from satellites in outer space. **x-ray star,** a star emitting a high proportion of x-rays.

xy·lem (zī-lĕm) *n.* the woody tissue of a plant.

xy·lo·phone (zī-lŏ-fohn) *n.* a musical instrument consisting of flat wooden bars, graduated in length, which produce different notes when struck with small hammers. **xy'lo·phon·ist** *n.* **xy·lo·phon·ic** (zī-lŏ-fon-ik) *adj.*

Y

Y, y (wı) (*pl.* **Ys, Y's, y's**) the twenty-fifth letter of the alphabet.

-y[1] *suffix* used to form adjectives with these meanings: full of, as in *messy;* having the quality of, as in *slangy;* like, as in *gluey;* addicted to, as in *horsy;* inclined to, as in *preachy;* apt to, as in *runny;* somewhat, as in *nippy;* having marked or superficial characteristics, as in *catty.*

-y[2] *suffix* (*pl.* **-ies**) used to form nouns meaning state or condition or quality, as in *glory;* action or its result, as in *remedy;* business or goods, as in *bindery;* an entire object formed, as in *company, library.*

-y[3] *suffix* (*pl.* **-ies**) used to form diminutive nouns and pet names, as in *granny, Sally.*

Y *symbol* yttrium.

y. *abbr.* 1. year(s). 2. yard(s).

Y. *abbr.* 1. YMCA. 2. YMHA. 3. YWCA. 4. YWHA.

yacht (yaht) *n.* 1. a light sailing vessel for racing. 2. a similar vessel for travel on sand or ice. 3. a power or sailing vessel used for private pleasure excursions. **yacht** *v.* to race or cruise in a yacht.

yacht·ing (yah-ting) *n.* racing or cruising in a yacht.

yachts·man (yahts-măn) *n.* (*pl.* **-men,** *pr.* -měn) a person who owns or sails a yacht. **yachts′man·ship** *n.* **yachts·wom·an** (yahts-wuum-ăn) *n. fem.* (*pl.* **-wom·en,** *pr.* -wim-in).

yack = **yak**[2].

yack·e·ty-yak (yak-ĕ-tee-yak) *n.* (*slang)* persistent chatter. **yack·e·ty-yak** *v.* (**yack·e·ty-yakked, yack·e·ty-yak·king**) *(slang)* to chatter persistently.

yah (yah) *interj.* an exclamation of scorn or defiance.

ya·hoo (yah-hoo) *n.* a coarse or brutish person. ▷The name of an imaginary race of brutish men in Swift's *Gulliver's Travels* (1726).

Yah·weh (yah-we) *n.* the ancient Hebrew name for God, corresponding to Jehovah.

yak[1] (yak) *n.* a long-haired ox of central Asia.

yak[2] *v.* (**yakked, yak·king**) *(slang)* to chatter persistently. **yak** *n. (slang)* persistent chatter.

yam (yam) *n.* 1. the edible starchy tuber of a tropical climbing plant, the plant itself. 2. the sweet potato (*see* **sweet**).

yam·mer (yam-ĕr) *v. (slang)* 1. to wail or grumble. 2. to persist in talking loudly. **yam′mer·er** *n.*

yank (yangk) *v. (informal)* to pull with a sudden sharp tug. **yank** *n. (informal)* a sudden sharp tug.

Yank (yangk) *n. (informal)* Yankee (definition 1).

Yan·kee (yang-kee) *n.* 1. an American. 2. an inhabitant of the northern states of the U.S., especially New England. **Yankee** *adj.*

Ya·oun·de (ya-oon-day) the capital of Cameroon.

yap (yap) *n.* 1. a shrill bark. 2. *(slang)* a mouth, *shut your yap.* **yap** *v.* (**yapped, yap·ing**) 1. to

bark shrilly. 2. *(slang)* to chatter, to complain.

yard[1] (yahrd) *n.* 1. a measure of length, = 3 feet or 0.9144 meter. 2. a long polelike piece of wood stretched horizontally or crosswise from a mast to support a sail. □**yard goods,** fabrics sold by the yard.

yard[2] *n.* 1. the grounds around a house or other building. 2. a piece of enclosed ground, especially one attached to a building or surrounded by buildings or used for a particular kind of work etc., *a lumber yard.* 3. an area of railroad tracks and switches where trains are assembled.

yard·age (yahr-dij) *n.* a length measured in yards.

yard·arm (yahrd-ahrm) *n.* either end of a yard supporting a sail.

yard·bird (yahrd-burd) *n. (slang)* a convict or prisoner.

yard·man (yahrd-man) *n.* (*pl.* **-men,** *pr.* -men) a gardener, a man who does various outdoor jobs.

yard·mas·ter (yahrd-mas-tĕr) *n.* the manager of a railroad yard.

yard·stick (yahrd-stik) *n.* a standard of comparison.

yar·mul·ke (yahr-mŭl-kĕ) *n.* a skullcap worn by Jewish men, especially in a synagogue.

yarn (yahrn) *n.* 1. any spun thread, especially of the kinds prepared for knitting or weaving or ropemaking. 2. *(informal)* a tale, especially one that is exaggerated or invented. **yarn** *v. (informal)* to tell yarns.

yar·row (yar-oh) *n.* a plant with feathery leaves and strong-smelling white or pinkish flowers.

yaw (yaw) *v.* (of a ship or aircraft etc.) to fail to hold a straight course, to turn from side to side. **yaw** *n.* a yawing movement or course.

yawl (yawl) *n.* a kind of sailing boat with two masts.

yawn (yawn) *v.* 1. to open the mouth wide and draw in breath (often involuntarily), as when sleepy or bored. 2. to have a wide opening, to form a chasm. **yawn** *n.* the act of yawning. **yawn′er** *n.*

yaws (yawz) *n.* a tropical skin disease causing raspberry-like swellings.

y-ax·is (wı-ak-sis) *n.* the vertical axis in a plane coordinate system, along which the ordinate is measured.

Yb *symbol* ytterbium.

Y chromosome a chromosome occurring in the cells of only one sex (in humans, the male), whose presence or absence in the zygote determines the sex of the new individual formed in reproduction.

y·clept (ee-klept) *adj.* (also **y·cleped**) *(old use)* called (by the name of).

yd. *abbr.* yard.

yds. *abbr.* yards.

YDT, Y.D.T. *abbr.* Yukon Daylight Time.

ye[1] (yee) *pronoun (old use)* you.

ye² *adj. (supposed old use)* the, *ye olde teashoppe.*

yea (yay) *adv. & n. (old use)* yes.

yeah (yair) *adv. (informal)* yes. □**oh yeah?,** an expression of incredulity.

year (yeer) *n.* 1. the time taken by Earth to make one complete orbit of the sun, about 365¼ days. 2. the period from January 1 to December 31 inclusive. 3. any period of twelve consecutive months. 4. *years,* age in years, *he looks younger than his years;* a very long time, *we've been waiting for years.*

year·book (yeer-buuk) *n.* an annual publication containing current information about a particular subject.

year-end (yeer-end) *n.* the end of a year. **year-end** *adj.* occurring at the end of a year.

year·ling (yeer-ling) *n.* an animal between one and two years old.

year·long (yeer-lawng) *adj.* lasting a year.

year·ly (yeer-lee) *adj.* happening or published or payable etc. once a year, annual. **yearly** *adv.* annually.

yearn (yurn) *v.* to be filled with great longing.

year-round (yeer-rownd) *adj.* existing or operating throughout the year.

yeast (yeest) *n.* a kind of fungus that causes alcohol and carbon dioxide to be produced while it is developing, used to cause fermentation in making beer and wines and as a leavening agent in baking.

yeast·y (yees-tee) *adj.* (**yeast·i·er, yeast·i·est**) 1. frothy like yeast when it is developing. 2. tasting of yeast. 3. very enthusiastic or joyful. **yeast'i·ly** *adv.* **yeast'i·ness** *n.*

yegg (yeg) *n. (slang)* 1. a safecracker. 2. a thug.

yell (yel) *v.* to give a loud cry, to shout. **yell** *n.* 1. a loud cry. 2. an organized cry used by students to encourage an athletic team, *the college yell.* **yell'er** *n.*

yel·low (yel-oh) *adj.* 1. of the color of buttercups and ripe lemons, or a color approaching this. 2. *(informal)* cowardly. **yellow** *n.* 1. yellow color. 2. a yellow substance or material, especially the yolk of an egg. **yellow** *v.* to make or become yellow. **yel'low·ly** *adv.* **yel'low·ness** *n.* □**yellow birch,** an American tree with silvery or yellowish bark. **yellow fever,** a tropical disease with fever and jaundice. **yellow jack,** yellow fever; a flag raised to show that a ship is in quarantine. **yellow jacket,** a wasp with black and yellow bands around its body. **yellow pages,** the section of a telephone directory (printed on yellow paper) that lists business subscribers according to the goods or services they offer. **yellow peril,** the supposed danger that the yellow races may overwhelm the white or overrun the world. **yellow streak,** *(informal)* cowardice in a person's character.

yel·low·bel·lied (yel-oh-bel-eed) *adj.* cowardly. □**yellowbellied sapsucker** *or* **woodpecker,** a bird of eastern America with straw-yellow feathers on its belly.

yel·low-dog (yel-oh-dawg) **contract** an employment contract that prevents workers from joining a labor union.

yel·low·ham·mer (yel-oh-ham-ĕr) *n.* a kind of European bunting, the male of which has a yellow head, neck, and breast.

yel·low·ish (yel-oh-ish) *adj.* rather yellow.

yelp (yelp) *n.* a sharp shrill cry or bark. **yelp** *v.* to utter a yelp.

Yem·en (yem-ĕn) the name of two countries in the Arabian peninsula, *the Yemen Arab Republic* and *the People's Democratic Republic of Yemen.*

Yem'en·ite *adj. & n.* **Yem·e·ni** (yem-ĕ-nee) *adj. & n.*

yen¹ (yen) *n.* (*pl.* **yen**) the unit of money in Japan.

yen² *n. (informal)* a longing, a yearning.

yeo·man (yoh-măn) *n.* (*pl.* **-men,** *pr.* -mĕn) 1. a petty officer of the U.S. Navy whose duties are chiefly clerical. 2. *(British)* a man who owns and works a small farm. □**yeoman service,** long and useful service.

yeo·man·ry (yoh-măn-ree) *n.* a body of yeomen (definition 2).

yes (yes) *adv.* 1. it is so, the statement is correct. 2. what you request or command will be done. 3. (as a question) what do you want? 4. (in answer to a summons etc.) I am here. **yes** *n.* (*pl.* **yes·es**) the word or answer "yes." □**yes man,** a man who always agrees with his superior in a weak or sycophantic way.

ye·shi·va (yĕ-shee-vă) *n.* (*pl.* **-vas**) 1. a Jewish elementary school. 2. a seminary for rabbinical students.

yes·ter·day (yes-tĕr-day) *adv.* 1. the day before today. 2. the recent past. **yesterday** *adv.* on the day before today, in the recent past.

yes·ter·year (yes-tĕr-yeer) *n.* last year or recent years.

yet (yet) *adv.* 1. up to this or that time and continuing, still, *there's life in the old dog yet.* 2. by this or that time, so far, *it hasn't happened yet.* 3. besides, in addition, *heard it yet again.* 4. before the matter is done with, eventually, *I'll get even with you yet.* 5. even, *she became yet more excited.* 6. nevertheless, *strange yet true.* **yet** *conj.* nevertheless, but in spite of that, *he worked hard, yet he failed.* □**as yet,** *see* **as.**

yet·i (yet-ee) *n.* (*pl.* **yet·is**) the native (Sherpa) name for the "Abominable Snowman" (*see* **abominable**).

yew (yoo) *n.* 1. an evergreen tree with dark green needlelike leaves and red berries. 2. its wood.

Yid·dish (yid-ish) *n.* a language used by Jews in or from central and eastern Europe, based on a German dialect and with words from Hebrew and various modern languages.

yield (yeeld) *v.* 1. to give or return as fruit or gain or result, *the land yields good crops; the investment yields 15%.* 2. to surrender, to do what is requested or ordered, *the town yielded; he yielded to persuasion.* 3. to be inferior or confess inferiority, *I yield to none in appreciation of his merits.* 4. (of traffic) to allow other traffic to have the right of way. 5. to be able to be forced out of the natural or usual shape, as when under pressure. 6. to allow another the right to speak in a debate etc. **yield** *n.* the amount yielded or produced, the quantity obtained.

yin and yang (yin ăn yang) (in Chinese philosophy) the passive female *(yin)* and the active male *(yang)* principles of the universe.

yip (yip) *v.* (**yipped, yip·ping**) to yelp. **yip** *n.* a yelp.

yip·pee (yip-ee) *interj.* an exclamation of excitement.

YMCA *abbr.* Young Men's Christian Association.

YMHA *abbr.* Young Men's Hebrew Association.

y.o. *abbr.* year(s) old.

y.o.b. *abbr.* year of birth.

yo·del (yoh-dĕl) *v.* (**yo·deled, yo·del·ing**) to sing, or utter a musical call, so that the voice alternates continually between falsetto and its normal pitch. **yodel** n. a yodeling cry. **yo'del·er** n.

yo·ga (yoh-gă) n. 1. a Hindu system of meditation and self-control designed to produce mystical experience and spiritual insight. 2. a system of physical exercises and breathing control.

yo·ghurt, yo·gurt (yoh-gŭrt) n. a food prepared from milk that has been thickened by the action of certain bacteria.

yo·gi (yoh-gee) n. (pl. **-gis**) a devotee of yoga.

yoke (yohk) n. (pl. **yokes**) 1. a wooden crosspiece fastened over the necks of two oxen or other animals pulling a cart or plow etc. 2. a piece of timber shaped to fit a person's shoulders and to hold a pail or other load slung from each end. 3. a part of a garment fitting around the shoulders or hips and from which the rest hangs. 4. oppression, burdensome restraint, *throw off the yoke of servitude.* **yoke** v. (**yoked, yok·ing**) 1. to put a yoke upon, to harness by means of a yoke, *yoke oxen to the plow.* 2. to unite, *yoked to an unwilling partner.* ▷Do not confuse *yoke* with *yolk.*

yo·kel (yoh-kĕl) n. a simple country fellow, a country bumpkin.

yolk (yohk) n. the round yellow internal part of an egg. ▷Do not confuse *yolk* with *yoke.*

Yom Kip·pur (yom kip-ŭr) the Day of Atonement, the most solemn day of the Jewish year, eight days after Rosh Hashanah, observed with fasting and prayers of repentance.

yon (yon) adj. & adv. (old use) yonder.

yon·der (yon-dĕr) adv. over there. **yonder** adj. situated or able to be seen over there.

yore (yohr) n. **of yore,** of long ago, *in days of yore.*

York·shire (york-shĭr) a former county of England. ☐**Yorkshire pudding,** a baked batter pudding eaten with roast beef. **Yorkshire terrier,** a terrier of a small long-haired toy breed.

you (yoo) pronoun 1. the person(s) addressed. 2. one, anyone, everyone, *you never can tell.*

you-all (yoo-awl) pronoun (Southern U.S. informal) you (pl.).

you'd (yood) = you had, you would.

you'll (yool) = you will.

young (yung) adj. 1. having lived or existed for only a short time; *the young,* young people. 2. not far advanced in time, *the night is young.* 3. youthful, having little experience. 4. used in speaking of or to a young person, *young Smith.* **young** n. the offspring of animals, before or soon after birth. ☐**with young,** (of animals) pregnant. **young blood,** (informal) young people; new ideas. **young lady,** a genteel young woman; a man's sweetheart or girl friend. **young man,** a woman's sweetheart or boy friend.

young·ish (yung-ish) adj. fairly young.

young·ling (yung-ling) n. a young person, animal, or plant. **youngling** adj.

young·ster (yung-stĕr) n. a young person, a child.

your (yoor) adj. of or belonging to you.

you're (yoor) = you are.

yours (yoorz) possessive pronoun 1. belonging to you, the thing(s) belonging to you, *she especially liked yours.* 2. used in phrases for ending letters: **yours,** used casually to friends. **sincerely yours,** used in letters to acquaintances and to friends (other than close friends), and often also in business letters addressing a person by name (as beginning "Dear Mr. Brown"), where it is now more frequently used than *yours truly.* **very truly yours,** a form of *yours truly* (now seldom used). **yours truly,** used to slight acquaintances and in business letters; *(informal)* = me, *the awkward jobs are always left for yours truly.* ▷It is incorrect to write *your's* (see the note under **its**).

your·self (yoor-self) pronoun (pl. **-selves,** pr. **-selvz**) corresponding to *you,* used in the same ways as *himself.*

youth (yooth) n. (pl. **youths,** pr. yoothz) 1. being young. 2. the period between childhood and maturity, the vigor or lack of experience etc. characteristic of this. 3. a young man, *a youth of sixteen.* 4. young people collectively, *the youth of the country.* ☐**youth hostel,** a hostel providing cheap accommodation where young people who are hiking or on tour etc. may stay overnight.

youth·ful (yooth-fŭl) adj. 1. young, looking or seeming young. 2. characteristic of young people, *youthful impatience.* **youth'ful·ly** adv. **youth'ful·ness** n.

you've (yoov) = you have.

yowl (yowl) n. a loud wailing cry, a howl. **yowl** v. to utter a yowl.

yo-yo (yoh-yoh) n. (pl. **-yos**) 1. a toy consisting of two circular parts with a deep groove between, which can be made to rise and fall on a string (attached to it) when this is jerked by a finger. 2. (slang) a stupid person.

yr. abbr. 1. year. 2. younger. 3. your.

yrbk. abbr. yearbook.

yrs. abbr. 1. years. 2. yours.

YST abbr. Yukon Standard Time.

yt·ter·bi·um (i-tur-bi-ŭm) n. a metallic element.

yt·tri·um (ee-tri-ŭm) n. a metallic element.

yu·an (yoo-ahn) n. (pl. **yu·an**) the unit of money in China.

yuc·ca (yuk-ă) n. a tall plant with white bell-like flowers and stiff spiky leaves.

Yu·go·sla·vi·a (yoo-goh-slah-vi-ă) a country in the Balkans, bordering on the Adriatic Sea. **Yu·go·slav** (yoo-goh-slahv) adj. & n. **Yu·go·sla'vi·an** adj. & n.

Yu·kon (yoo-kon) a territory of northwest Canada.

yule (yool) n. (also **Yule, yuletide, Yuletide**) (old use) the Christmas festival. ☐**yule log,** a large log traditionally burned in the fireplace on Christmas Eve.

yum·my (yum-ee) adj. (**-mi·er, -mi·est**) (informal) tasty, delicious.

yurt (yoort) n. a circular skin- or felt-covered tent with a collapsible frame, originally used by Mongolian nomads.

YWCA abbr. Young Women's Christian Association.

YWHA abbr. Young Women's Hebrew Association.

Z

Z, z (zee) (*pl.* **Zs, Z's, z's**) the twenty-sixth letter
of the alphabet.
Z *symbol* atomic number.
z. *abbr.* 1. zero. 2. zone.
Za·ire (zah-eer) a country in Central Africa. **Za·**
ir′i·an *adj. & n.*
Zam·bi·a (zam-bi-ă) a country in Central Africa.
Zam′bi·an *adj. & n.*
za·ny (zay-nee) *n.* (*pl.* **-nies**) a comical or eccentric
person. **zany** *adj.* (**-ni·er, -ni·est**) crazily funny.
za′ni·ly *adv.* **za′ni·ness** *n.*
zap (zap) *v.* (**zapped, zap·ping**) *(slang)* to hit,
attack, knock out, or kill.
zeal (zeel) *n.* enthusiasm, hearty and persistent effort.
zeal·ot (zel-ŏt) *n.* a zealous person, a fanatic.
zeal·ous (zel-ŭs) *adj.* full of zeal. **zeal′ous·ly**
adv. **zeal′ous·ness** *n.* ▷Do not confuse *zealous*
with *jealous.*
ze·bra (zee-bră) *n.* (*pl.* **-bras, -bra**) an African
animal of the horse family with a body entirely
covered by black and white stripes.
ze·bu (zee-byoo) *n.* (*pl.* **-bus, -bu**) a humped ox
found in India, East Asia, and Africa.
zed (zed) *n.* *(British)* the letter *z.*
Zeit·geist (tsɪt-gɪst) *n.* the trend of thought and
feeling in a period. ▷German, = time spirit.
Zen (zen) *n.* a form of Buddhism emphasizing the
value of meditation and intuition.
ze·na·na (ze-nah-nă) *n.* that part of a house in
which women of high-caste families were formerly
secluded in India.
ze·nith (zee-nith) *n.* 1. the part of the sky that is
directly above an observer. 2. the highest point,
his power was at its zenith. **ze·nith·al** (zee-ni-
thăl) *adj.*
ze·o·lite (zee-ŏ-lɪt) *n.* one of a number of minerals
consisting mainly of hydrous silicates of calcium,
sodium, and aluminum, and used to soften water.
ze·o·lith·ic (zee-ŏ-lith-ik) *adj.*
zeph·yr (zef-ĭr) *n.* a soft gentle wind.
Zep·pe·lin, zep·pe·lin (zep-ĕ-lin) *n.* a large cylindrical airship having a rigid covered frame containing gas cells, built originally for military use
in Germany in the early 20th century. ▷Named
for Count F. von Zeppelin (1838–1917), who constructed the original.
ze·ro (zeer-oh) *n.* (*pl.* **-ros, -roes**) 1. naught, the
figure 0. 2. nothing, nil. 3. the point marked 0
on a graduated scale, especially on a thermometer.
4. the temperature corresponding to zero. **zero**
v. (**ze·roed, ze·ro·ing**) to adjust (an instrument
etc.) to zero. **zero** *adj.* without quantity, value,
or magnitude. □**zero hour,** the hour at which
something is timed to begin. **zero in on,** to focus
one's aim on, to go purposefully toward. **zero**

population growth, replacement of the existing
population without increasing it.
zest (zest) *n.* 1. keen enjoyment or interest. 2. a
pleasantly stimulating quality, *the risk added zest
to the adventure.* **zest′ful** *adj.* **zest′ful·ly** *adv.*
zest′ful·ness *n.*
ze·ta (zay-tă) *n.* the sixth letter of the Greek alphabet (Z ζ).
Zeus (zoos) *n.* the supreme deity in Greek mythology.
zig·zag (zig-zag) *n.* a line or course that turns right
and left alternately at sharp angles. **zigzag** *adj.*
& *adv.* forming or in a zigzag. **zigzag** *v.* (**zig·**
zagged, zig·zag·ging) to move in a zigzag
course.
zilch (zilch) *n.* *(slang)* nothing, zero.
zil·lion (zil-yŏn) *n.* *(informal)* an indefinite large
number.
Zim·bab·we (zim-bahb-we) a country in central
Africa. **Zim·bab′we·an** *adj. & n.*
zinc (zingk) *n.* a hard bluish-white metallic element.
zinc *v.* (**zincked, zinck·ing**) to coat or treat
with zinc. □**zinc ointment,** an ointment containing 20% zinc oxide. **zinc oxide,** a powder used
as a pigment, in treating certain skin conditions,
and in many other ways.
zing (zing) *n.* 1. a high-pitched humming sound.
2. *(informal)* vigor, energy. **zing** *v.* 1. to move
swiftly or with a zing. 2. *(slang)* to criticize
harshly.
zin·ni·a (zin-i-ă) *n.* a daisy-like garden plant with
brightly-colored flowers.
Zi·on (zɪ-ŏn) *n.* 1. the holy hill of ancient Jerusalem,
Mount Zion. 2. the Jewish people. 3. the Jewish
homeland as a symbol of Judaism. 4. the kingdom
of heaven.
Zi·on·ism (zɪ-ŏ-niz-ĕm) *n.* a movement founded
in 1897 that has sought and achieved the founding
and development of a Jewish homeland (now Israel) in Palestine. **Zi′on·ist** *adj. & n.*
zip[1] (zip) *n.* 1. a short sharp sound like that of a
bullet going through the air. 2. energy, vigor, liveliness. **zip** *v.* (**zipped, zip·ping**) 1. to open or
close with a zipper. 2. to move with the sound
of "zip" or at high speed. □**zip gun,** a homemade
gun consisting of a tube attached to a piece of
wood etc. and firing real bullets.
zip[2] *n.* *(slang)* zero, nothing, especially as a score
in a sports event.
zip[3] *v.* (**zipped, zip·ping**) *(informal)* to put a zip
code on.
zip code (also **ZIP code**) a system of five-figure
numbers used to identify postal delivery areas.
▷From *zone improvement plan.*
zip·per (zip-ĕr) *n.* a fastening device consisting of
two flexible strips of material with projections

that interlock when brought together by a sliding tab. **zipper** v. *(informal)* to fasten with a zipper. **zip′pered** *adj.*

zip·py (zip-ee) *adj.* **(-pi·er, -pi·est)** *(informal)* lively and vigorous.

zir·con (zur-kon) *n.* a bluish-white gem cut from a translucent mineral.

zir·co·ni·um (zĭr-koh-ni-ŭm) *n.* a gray metallic element used in various industrial applications.

zith·er (zith-ĕr) *n.* a musical instrument with many strings stretched over a shallow boxlike body, played by plucking with the fingers of both hands. **zith′er·ist** *n.*

Zn *symbol* zinc.

zo·di·ac (zoh-di-ak) *n.* (in astrology) 1. a band of the sky containing the paths of the sun, moon, and principal planets, divided into twelve equal parts (called *signs of the zodiac*) each named from a constellation that was formerly situated in it. 2. a diagram of these signs. **zo·di·a·cal** (zoh-dĭ-ă-kăl) *adj.*

Zom·ba (zom-bă) the capital of Malawi.

zom·bie (zom-bee) *n.* 1. (in voodoo) a corpse said to have been revived by witchcraft. 2. *(informal)* a person thought to resemble this, one who seems to have no mind or will.

zone (zohn) *n.* an area that has particular characteristics or a particular purpose or use. **zone** v. **(zoned, zon·ing)** 1. to divide into zones. 2. to designate (an area) for a specific use, to arrange or distribute by zones, to assign to a particular area. **zon′al** *adj.* **zoned** *adj.* **zo·na·tion** (zoh-nay-shŏn) *n.* □**zone defense**, a system of defense in basketball or football etc. in which each defensive player has an assigned zone in which to play.

zonked (zongkt) *adj.* *(slang)* intoxicated by alcohol or stupefied by a drug.

zoo (zoo) *n.* (*pl.* **zoos**) a place where wild animals are kept for exhibition and study.

zo·o·ge·og·ra·phy (zoh-ŏ-ji-og-ră-fee) *n.* the scientific study of the local distribution of animals. **zo·o·ge·o·graph′ic** (zoh-ŏ-jee-ŏ-graf-ik) *adj.* **zo·o·ge·o·graph′i·cal** *adj.*

zool. *abbr.* 1. zoological. 2. zoology.

zo·ol·o·gist (zoh-ol-ŏ-jist) *n.* an expert in zoology.

zo·ol·o·gy (zoh-ol-ŏ-jee) *n.* the scientific study of animals. **zo·o·log·i·cal** (zoh-ŏ-loj-i-kăl) *adj.* □**zoological garden**, a zoo.

zoom (zoom) v. 1. to move quickly, especially with a buzzing sound. 2. to rise quickly, *prices had zoomed.* 3. (in photography) to alter the size of the image by means of a zoom lens. **zoom** *n.* an act of zooming. □**zoom lens**, a camera lens

that can be adjusted from a long shot to a close-up (and vice versa), giving an effect of going steadily closer to (or farther from) the subject.

zo·o·mor·phism (zoh-ŏ-mor-fiz-ĕm) *n.* 1. belief in gods of animal form. 2. the representation of animal forms in art.

zo·o·phyte (zoh-ŏ-fīt) *n.* a plantlike animal, especially coral, sponge, sea anemone, and jellyfish.

zo·o·plank·ton (zoh-ŏ-plangk-tŏn) *n.* plankton consisting of animals.

zo·o·spore (zoh-ŏ-spohr) *n.* an asexual spore capable of motion.

zoot (zoot) **suit** *(informal)* a man's suit with a long loose jacket and high-waisted loose tapering trousers. **zoot′suit′er** *n.* *(informal)* a person who wears such clothing.

Zo·ro·as·tri·an·ism (zohr-oh-as-tri-ă-niz-ĕm) *n.* the religion of the Magi and of ancient Persia, founded by Zoroaster. **Zo·ro·as′tri·an** *adj.* & *n.*

Zou·ave (zoo-ahv) *n.* 1. a member of a French infantry corps originally formed of Algerians and retaining their Oriental uniform. 2. a member of any military group wearing such a uniform, especially certain volunteers in the U.S. Civil War.

zow·ie (zow-ee) *interj.* *(informal)* an expression of excitement and approval.

zoy·si·a (zoi-si-ă) *n.* a thick creeping perennial grass, sometimes used in lawns.

ZPG *abbr.* zero population growth.

Zr *symbol* zirconium.

zuc·chet·to (zoo-ket-oh) *n.* (*pl.* **-toes**) (in the Roman Catholic Church) an ecclesiastical skullcap, black for a priest, purple for a bishop, red for a cardinal, and white for the pope.

zuc·chi·ni (zoo-kee-nee) *n.* (*pl.* **-ni, -nis**) a greenskinned summer squash.

Zu·lu (zoo-loo) *n.* (*pl.* **-lus, -lu**) 1. a member of a Bantu people of South Africa. 2. their language. **Zulu** *adj.* of Zulus or their language.

Zu·ñi (zoo-nyee) *n.* (*pl.* **-ñis, -ñi**) 1. a member of an Indian tribe of North America living in western New Mexico. 2. their language. **Zu′ñi·an** *adj.* & *n.*

zwie·back (zwī-bak, swī-, zwee-, swee-) *n.* a kind of bread thickly sliced and toasted until it is very dry.

zy·gote (zī-goht) *n.* the cell formed by the union of two gametes, the first cell of a new individual. **zy·got·ic** (zī-got-ik) *adj.*

zy·mur·gy (zī-mur-jee) *n.* the branch of applied chemistry dealing with the use of fermentation in brewing etc.

Index to Entries
with Usage Notes

device
devise
different
dint
diphtheria
diphthong
disassemble
disburse
discomfit
discomfort
discreet
discrete
disguise
disinterested
disperse
disremember
dissect
dissemble
distinct
distinctive
distract
dive
dog
dogged
douse
dowse
drag
drink
drought
drown
drunk
drunken
dual
due
duel
dumb
dyslexia
each
earthly
earthy
ecology
economic
economical
effect
effective
effectual
effeminate
either
elder[1]
elegy
elicit
elusive
emend
emigrate
eminent
empathy
endemic
energize
enervate
enormity
sure
se
ology

enviable
envious
epic
epidemic
epitaph
epithet
epitome
epoch
equable
equitable
erupt
espresso
essay
et al.
etc.
etymology
eulogy
eve
evening
every
everyone
exaltation
exceed
except
excess
exercise
exhaustive
exorcise
expedient
expeditious
extant
extent
extrinsic
exult
facility
factious
faculty
fake
fakir
farther
farthest
faun
fawn
feel
ferment
few
fiction
fictitious
figurative
finalize
financial
fish
flaccid
flair
flammable
flare
flaunt
fleshly
fleshy
flout
fly[2]
foment
foot

former
formidable
fortuitous
fortunate
fractious
fruition
fulsome
fungus
further
furthest
gamble
gambol
gibe
gire
good
gourmand
gourmet
graduate
graffito
grill
grille
guise
hail[2]
hale[1]
hardly
headquarters
her
hers
historic
historical
hopefully
host[2]
if
illicit
illusion
illusive
immanent
immigrate
imminent
impedance
impediment
impel
imply
incredible
incredulous
indeterminable
indeterminate
indict
indite
individual
infer
inflammable
informal
ingenious
ingenuous
inherit
inhuman
inhumane
insidious
intense
intensive
interment
internment

intrinsic
invaluable
invidious
irrupt
it
its
it's
jealous
jetsam
jibe
jive
kind[1]
kudos
last[2]
latter
laudable
laudatory
lay[3]
leading[1]
learn
leave[1]
lend
less
lesser
lessor
let[2]
lie[2]
like[1]
like[2]
likely
linage
lineage
literal
loan
loath
loathe
loop
loupe
luxuriant
luxurious
magnate
magnet
majority
marital
martial
may
me
media
mediocre
medium
metal
mettle
might[2]
mil
militate
mill
mine[1]
minister
mischievous
mitigate
monetary
money
moot

moral
morale
most
mucous
mucus
mute
nauseous
naval
navel
negligence
negligible
Negro
neither
noisome
non-
none
nonflammable
nowhere
nuclear
number
odious
odorous
of
off
official
officious
old
onto
oral
ordinance
ordnance
orientate
orotund
ours
pained
painful
pair
palate
palette
pallet[1]
pallet[2]
parameter
paratroops
parlay
parley
pedal
peddle
pence
penny
per
permit
perquisite
persecute
personal
personnel
perspicacious
perverse
pervert

phosphorus
pi[1]
pibroch
plenitude
plurality
poet
poorly
practicable
practical
precipitate
precipitous
prerequisite
presently
presume
presumptive
presumptuous
preventative
preventive
principal
principle
prophecy
prophesy
prosecute
prove
quash
raise
rational
rationale
ravage
ravish
raze
real
redolent
referendums
refute
regardless
Rev.
revelation
reverend
reversion
review
revue
rise
rotund
scarify
Scotch
scrip
script
seasonable
seasonal
sensibility
sensuous
set
should
sic
silicon
silicone
simple

simplistic
sit
site
situation
slack
slake
slang
slow
sneak
solecism
solid
solipsism
some
sort
species
spiritual
spirituous
split
squash
stationary
stationery
statistic
statistics
statue
statute
stave
stimulant
stimulus
stolid
straight
straighten
strait
straitened
stratum
subconscious
suit
suite
summons
sure
take
temblor
terminable
terminal
than
thankfully
that
their
theirs
there
they're
thrips
thus
to
too
translate
transliterate
transpire
tremble

tremendous
trooper
trouper
truism
truth
turbid
turgid
two
type
unconscious
unction
unctuousness
under
underlay
underlie
unexceptionable
unexceptional
unintelligent
unintelligible
uninterested
unique
until
unwanted
unwonted
uxorious
valance
valence
valuable
valueless
vantage
venal
venial
verbal
vertex
visible
visual
viz.
vortex
wait
waive
waiver
wave
waver
well[2]
whence
where
which
whiskey, whisky
who's
whose
-wise
wont
won't
yoke
yolk
yours
zealous

The Metric System
of Weights and Measures

Linear Measure

1 millimeter	= 0.039 inch
1 centimeter = 10 millimeters	= 0.394 inch
1 decimeter = 10 centimeters	= 3.94 inches
1 meter = 10 decimeters	= 1.094 yards
1 dekameter = 10 meters	= 10.94 yards
1 hectometer = 100 meters	= 109.4 yards
1 kilometer = 1,000 meters	= 0.6214 mile

Square Measure

1 square centimeter	= 0.155 square inch
1 square meter	= 1.196 square yards
1 are = 100 square meters	= 119.6 square yards
1 hectare = 100 ares	= 2.471 acres
1 square kilometer	= 0.386 square mile

Cubic Measure

1 cubic centimeter	= 0.061 cubic inch
1 cubic meter	= 1.308 cubic yards

Capacity Measure

1 milliliter	= 0.002 pint
1 centiliter = 10 milliliters	= 0.021 pint
1 deciliter = 10 centiliters	= 0.211 pint
1 liter = 10 deciliters	= 2.057 quarts
1 dekaliter = 10 liters	= 2.642 gallons
1 hectoliter = 100 liters	= 26.42 gallons
1 kiloliter = 1,000 liters	= 264.25 gallons

Weight

1 milligram	= 0.015 grain
1 centigram = 10 milligrams	= 0.154 grain
1 decigram = 10 centigrams	= 1.543 grains
1 gram = 10 decigrams	= 0.0353 ounce
1 dekagram = 10 grams	= 0.353 ounce
1 hectogram = 100 grams	= 0.22 pound
1 kilogram = 1,000 grams	= 2.205 pounds
1 metric ton = 1,000 kilograms	= 2205 pounds